MW00770900

Presented To:

By:

On:

NASB 2020 Large Print Personal Size Reference Bible
Copyright © 2022 by Holman Bible Publishers
Brentwood, Tennessee

New American Standard Bible – NASB 2020
Copyright © 1960, 1962, 1963, 1968, 1971, 1972, 1973, 1975,
1977, 1995, 2020 by The Lockman Foundation
A Corporation Not for Profit, La Habra, California
All Rights Reserved

The "NASB," "NAS," "New American Standard Bible," "New American
Standard," and lighthouse logo are trademarks registered in the United States
Patent and Trademark Office by The Lockman Foundation. Use of these
trademarks requires the permission of The Lockman Foundation.

Requests for quotations, reprints, or other permission requests, must be
directed to and approved in writing by The Lockman Foundation.

The interior of the *New American Standard Large Print Personal Size Reference
Bible* was designed and typeset by 2K/DENMARK, Højbjerg, Denmark. Proofreading
was provided by Peachtree Publishing Service, Peachtree City, Georgia.

Binding	*ISBN*
Black Genuine Leather	978-1-0877-5628-8
Black Genuine Leather (Indexed)	978-1-0877-5766-7
Burnt Sienna LeatherTouch	978-1-0877-5627-1
Burnt Sienna LeatherTouch (Indexed)	978-1-0877-5765-0
Olive LeatherTouch	978-1-0877-5626-4
Olive LeatherTouch (Indexed)	978-1-0877-5767-4
Teal LeatherTouch	978-1-0877-5781-0
Teal LeatherTouch (Indexed)	978-1-0877-5782-7
Charcoal LeatherTouch	979-8-3845-0946-2
Charcoal LeatherTouch (Indexed)	979-8-3845-0947-9
Sage SuedeSoft LeatherTouch	979-8-3845-0948-6
Sage SuedeSoft LeatherTouch(Indexed)	979-8-3845-0949-3

Printed in China
6 7 8 9 — 27 26 25 24

RRD

THE
HOLY BIBLE

New American Standard Bible

NASB | HOLMAN®
BIBLES

TABLE OF CONTENTS

Foreword..IV
Preface to the New American Standard Bible.........................V
Explanation of General Format....................................IX
Abbreviations and Special Markings................................X

THE OLD TESTAMENT

Genesis	1	Haggai	1283
Exodus	73	Zechariah	1286
Leviticus	134	Malachi	1299
Numbers	178		
Deuteronomy	239	**THE NEW TESTAMENT**	
Joshua	292	Matthew	1305
Judges	327	Mark	1354
Ruth	362	Luke	1384
1 Samuel	367	John	1435
2 Samuel	414	Acts	1473
1 Kings	454	Romans	1523
2 Kings	500	1 Corinthians	1543
1 Chronicles	544	2 Corinthians	1562
2 Chronicles	583	Galatians	1575
Ezra	633	Ephesians	1582
Nehemiah	647	Philippians	1589
Esther	668	Colossians	1594
Job	679	1 Thessalonians	1599
Psalms	729	2 Thessalonians	1603
Proverbs	859	1 Timothy	1606
Ecclesiastes	903	2 Timothy	1612
Song of Solomon	914	Titus	1616
Isaiah	923	Philemon	1619
Jeremiah	1019	Hebrews	1621
Lamentations	1114	James	1637
Ezekiel	1124	1 Peter	1642
Daniel	1199	2 Peter	1648
Hosea	1223	1 John	1652
Joel	1238	2 John	1657
Amos	1244	3 John	1658
Obadiah	1255	Jude	1659
Jonah	1257	Revelation	1661
Micah	1260		
Nahum	1269		
Habakkuk	1273		
Zephaniah	1278	Topical Index	1685

FOREWORD

SCRIPTURAL PROMISE

*"The grass withers, the
flower fades,
but the word of our God stands
forever."*
Isaiah 40:8

The New American Standard Bible has been produced with the conviction that the words of Scripture as originally penned in the Hebrew, Aramaic, and Greek were inspired by God. Since they are the eternal Word of God, the Holy Scriptures speak with fresh power to each generation, to give wisdom that leads to salvation, that people may serve Christ to the glory of God.

The NASB strives to adhere as closely as possible to the original languages of the Holy Scriptures and to make the translation in a fluent and readable style according to current English usage.

THE FOURFOLD AIM OF THE LOCKMAN FOUNDATION

1. These publications shall be true to the original Hebrew, Aramaic, and Greek.
2. They shall be grammatically correct.
3. They shall be understandable.
4. They shall give the Lord Jesus Christ His proper place, the place which the Word gives Him; therefore, no work will ever be personalized.

PREFACE TO THE NEW AMERICAN STANDARD BIBLE

In the history of English Bible translations, the King James Version is the most prestigious. This time-honored version of 1611, itself a revision of the Bishops' Bible of 1568, became the basis for the English Revised Version appearing in 1881 (New Testament) and 1885 (Old Testament). The American counterpart of this last work was published in 1901 as the American Standard Version. The ASV, a product of both British and American scholarship, has been highly regarded for its scholarship and accuracy. Recognizing the values of the American Standard Version, The Lockman Foundation felt an urgency to preserve these and other lasting values of the ASV by incorporating recent discoveries of Hebrew and Greek textual sources and by rendering it into current English. Therefore, in 1959 a new and original translation project was launched, based on the time-honored principles of translation used for the ASV and KJV to produce an accurate and readable English text. The result is the New American Standard Bible.

This edition of the NASB represents updates according to modern English usage and refinements recommended over the last several years as well as updates based on current research of the ancient manuscripts.

PRINCIPLES OF TRANSLATION

Modern English Usage: The goal is to render the grammar and terminology in contemporary English. When it was felt that the word-for-word literalness was unacceptable to the modern reader, a change was made in the direction of a more current English idiom. In editions that include the full set of translator's notes, in the instances where this has been done, a more literal rendering is indicated by "Lit" notes when necessary. These notes provide the "literal" meaning of the word or phrase in question, or as more technically known, its formal equivalent in the immediate context. Almost all words have a range of meanings, and a "Lit" note supplies the literal or formal meaning for that particular context. There are a few exceptions to this procedure. Punctuation is a relatively modern invention, and ancient writers often linked most of their sentences with "and" or other connectives, which are sometimes omitted at the beginning of sentences for better English. Also, the Hebrew idiom "answered and said" is sometimes reduced to "answered" or "said" as demanded by the context. For current English the idiom "it came about that" has not been translated in the New Testament except when a major transition is needed.

Gender Accuracy: In past editions it was common practice to translate the Greek word *anthropoi* as "men" and the Hebrew *adam* when used as a plural as "men," as well as all pluralistic uses of *ish* and similar words. The same was true for singulars, as masculine. This was never intended to be gender-exclusive when the context indicated that women were included;

it was assumed at that time that readers inferred the inclusion of women. Gender accuracy is important, however, so in this edition Greek and Hebrew words that are not actually exclusive in gender as they are used in a given context are rendered by inclusive terms, such as "people." Just as important, when the words in the original languages are in fact referring only to males or females, the distinction is maintained in English.

The Word Brethren: This word was used in past editions of the NASB as the plural of the Greek "brothers" (*adelphoi*) because it can still be used in a formal setting to address members of a profession, society, or church, regardless of gender. However, most people today would seldom use "brethren" informally and not often in most churches. This created the challenge of choosing a replacement that would have the same meaning that led to the original usage of "brethren," and only "brothers" was deemed adequate. To be gender-accurate, when it is clear that the author or speaker is referring to women as well as men, *"and sisters"* is added in italic for accuracy and clarity. The italic is necessary to indicate that the addition is implied in the meaning of *adelphoi* for the context, and the addition is not in the Greek text itself.

Let's for Action: In most places the phrase "let us" has been replaced with "let's" when a proposal is being made by one or more persons within a group to engage in an action. Such a proposal is common not only in English, but also in the ancient languages of the Bible; however, it is expressed in the ancient languages grammatically rather than by using an auxiliary, "helping" verb such as "let." It is common today for readers to understand "let us" to mean "allow us," so in effect, "let us" has become unintentionally misleading to most readers. Therefore, the simple contraction "let's" has emerged as the clearest expression because this form reflects the nuance of meaning in the original languages—that is, a proposal to do something. However, in some situations "Let Us" is retained for intimate discourse within the Godhead, as in Gen 1:26. "Let us" is also kept when there is a request for permission, and in some other select cases.

Alternative Readings: In addition to the more literal renderings explained under MODERN ENGLISH USAGE, notations have been made to include alternate translations, readings of variant manuscripts, and explanatory equivalents of the text. Only such notations have been used as have been felt justified in assisting the reader's comprehension of the terms used by the original author.

Hebrew Text: In the present translation BIBLIA HEBRAICA STUTTGARTENSIA and, where available, BIBLIA HEBRAICA QUINTA have been employed, together with the LXX, the Dead Sea Scrolls, ancient versions, and the most recent scholarship from lexicography.

Hebrew Tenses: The timing of tenses in Hebrew can be a challenging element of translation and

careful attention has been given to the requirements of accurate translation, the sequence of tenses, and the immediate and broad contexts.

The Proper Name of God in the Old Testament: In the Scriptures, the name of God is most significant. It is inconceivable to think of spiritual matters without a proper designation for the Supreme Deity. The most common name for the Deity is "God," a translation of the original *Elohim*. One of the titles for God is "Lord," a translation of *Adonai*. There is another name which is understood as God's special or proper name, that is, the four Hebrew letters equivalent to the English letters YHWH (Exodus 3:14 and Isaiah 42:8). This name has not been pronounced by the Jewish people because of reverence for the great sacredness of the divine name. This edition consistently translates this name as "Lord." The only exception to this translation of "YHWH" is when it occurs in immediate proximity to the word "Lord," that is, *Adonai*. In that case it is regularly translated "God" in order to avoid confusion.

For many years YHWH has been transliterated as Yahweh, however there is no complete certainty about this pronunciation. While "Yah" can be verified separately, the rest of the name cannot.

Names in the New Testament: The Greek versions of Hebrew names found in the New Testament, such as "Zacharias," are usually given in their original Hebrew forms, as in "Zechariah" for "Zacharias." Exceptions occur when the person is very commonly known by another name in English versions of the Bible. One of the most notable of such names is "James." An accurate translation would render this name "Jacob." Unfortunately, many would find it confusing to suddenly change the name "James" to "Jacob." There are other special cases where we do not follow the pattern outlined above, and these are often noted. The name "Jesus" itself is a special case, based on the Greek, from an abbreviated form of "Joshua." In fact, in two cases in the New Testament the Greek name refers instead to the famous Joshua of the Old Testament (Acts 7:45; Heb 4:8).

Greek Text: Consideration was given to the latest available manuscripts with a view to determining the best Greek text. In most instances the 28th edition of the Nestle-Aland Novum Testamentum Graece was followed. For Acts and the General Epistles, the Editio Critica Maior (ECM) was followed in most instances. However, the apparatuses provided by both editions are intended to enable scholars to make informed decisions about readings, and sometimes alternate readings with better support to those chosen by the editors were preferred.

Greek Tenses: A careful distinction has been made in the treatment of the Greek aorist tense (usually translated as the English past, "He did") and the Greek imperfect tense (normally rendered either as English past progressive, "He was doing"; or, if inceptive, as "He began to do" or "He started to do"; or else if

customary past, as "He used to do"). "Began" is italicized if it is added to translate an imperfect tense, in order to distinguish it from the Greek verb for "begin." In some contexts the difference between the Greek imperfect and the English past is conveyed better by the choice of vocabulary or by other words in the context, and in such cases the Greek imperfect may be rendered as a simple past tense (e.g., "had an illness for many years" would be preferable to "was having an illness for many years" and the first option would be common in English).

Not all aorist tenses have been rendered as English pasts ("He did"), because some of them are clearly to be rendered as English perfects ("He has done"), or even as past perfects ("He had done"), judging from the context in which they occur. Such aorists have been rendered as perfects or past perfects in this translation.

As for the distinction between aorist and present imperatives, these have usually been rendered as imperatives in the customary way, rather than attempting any fine distinction such as "Begin to do!" (for the aorist imperative), or, "Continually do!" (for the present imperative).

As for the sequence of tenses, care was taken to follow English rules rather than Greek in translating Greek presents, imperfects, and aorists. For example where English says, "We knew that he was doing," Greek puts it, "We knew that he does"; similarly, "We knew that he had done" is the English for "We knew that he did." Likewise, the English, "When he had come, they met him," is represented in Greek by, "When he came, they met him." In all cases a consistent transition has been made from the Greek tense in the subordinate clause to the appropriate tense in English.

In the rendering of negative questions introduced by the Greek particle *mē* (which always expects the answer "No") the wording has been altered from a mere, "Will he not do this?" to a more accurate, "He will not do this, will he?"

EXPLANATION OF GENERAL FORMAT

Notes and Cross References are placed adjoining the text and listed under verse numbers to which they refer. Superior numbers refer to literal renderings, alternate translations, or explanations. Superior letters refer to cross references. Cross references in italics are parallel passages.

Quotation Marks are used in the text in accordance with modern English usage.

Capitalized Words are used to provide helpful information. Personal pronouns are capitalized when pertaining to Deity. The word "Law" is capitalized when pertaining to Mosaic Law.

Italics are used in the text to indicate words that are not found in the original Hebrew, Aramaic, or Greek but are implied by it, or are sometimes necessary for correct English. Italics are used in the marginal notes to signify alternate readings for the text. Roman text in these marginal alternate readings is the same as italics in the Bible text. There are also special cases of italics referring to words that actually are in the original text. Italic "began" mentioned in GREEK TENSES is one example, where "began" communicates the grammatical tense of a verb. Another is italic possessive pronouns for Greek articles ("the" in Greek) used as possessive pronouns, a common feature in the Greek language. "*His* good pleasure," literally: "the good pleasure" in Phil 2:13 is an example. The purpose of the italic in this case is to inform the reader that the expected Greek word (the Greek possessive pronoun) is not found in the original text, but is represented by another word (the article) in the original text.

Small Caps in the New Testament are used in the text to indicate Old Testament quotations or references to Old Testament texts. Variations of Old Testament wording are found in New Testament citations depending on whether the New Testament writer translated from a Hebrew text, used existing Greek or Aramaic translations, or paraphrased the material. It should be noted that modern rules for the indication of direct quotation were not used in biblical times, and the ancient writer would use exact quotations or references to quotation without any specific indication of them.

Asterisks are used to mark verbs that are historical presents in the Greek grammar and have been translated with an English past tense in order to conform to modern usage. The translators recognized that in some contexts the present tense seems more unexpected and unjustified to the English reader than a past tense would have been. But Greek authors frequently used the present tense for the sake of heightened vividness, thereby transporting their readers in imagination to the actual scene at the time of occurrence. However, the translators felt that it would be wise to change these historical presents to English past tenses.

ABBREVIATIONS AND SPECIAL MARKINGS

Aram	=	Aramaic
DSS	=	Dead Sea Scrolls
Gr	=	Greek
Heb	=	Hebrew
Lat	=	Latin
LXX	=	Greek translation of O.T. (Septuagint)
MT	=	Masoretic Text
Lit	=	A literal translation (formal equivalent)
Or	=	An alternate translation justified by the original language
Ancient versions	=	O.T. manuscripts that are not Hebrew

[[ ]]	=	In text, double brackets indicate words very likely not in the original manuscripts
[ ]	=	In text, brackets indicate words probably not in the original manuscripts
[ ]	=	In notes, brackets indicate references to a name, place, or thing similar to, but not identical with that in the text
cf.	=	compare
ff	=	following verses
mg	=	Refers to a marginal reading on another verse
ms, mss	=	manuscript(s)
v, vv	=	verse(s)

THE OLD TESTAMENT

GENESIS

THE CREATION

1 ^AIn the beginning God ^Bcreated the heavens and the earth. ²And the earth was a ^{1,A}formless and desolate emptiness, and ^Bdarkness was over the surface of the deep, and the Spirit of God was hovering over the surface of the waters. ³Then ^AGod said, "¹Let there be light"; and there was light. ⁴God saw that the light was good; and God ^Aseparated the light from the darkness. ^{5A}God called the light "day," and the darkness He called "night." And there was evening and there was morning, one day.

⁶Then God said, "Let there be an ^Aexpanse in the midst of the waters, and let it separate the waters from the waters." ⁷God made the ¹expanse, and separated the waters that were below the expanse from the waters ^Athat were above the expanse; and it was so. ⁸God called the expanse "heaven." And there was evening and there was morning, a second day.

⁹Then God said, "^ALet the waters below the heavens be gathered into one place, and let ^Bthe dry land appear"; and it was so. ¹⁰And God called the dry land "earth," and the ^Agathering of the waters He called "seas"; and God saw that it was good. ¹¹Then God said, "Let the earth sprout ^Avegetation, plants yielding seed, *and* fruit trees on the earth bearing fruit according to their kind with seed in them"; and it was so. ¹²The earth produced vegetation, plants yielding seed according to their kind, and trees bearing fruit with seed in them, according to their kind; and God saw that it was good. ¹³And there was evening and there was morning, a third day.

¹⁴Then God said, "Let there be ^Alights in the expanse of the heavens to separate the day from the night, and they shall serve as ^Bsigns and for seasons, and for days and years; ¹⁵and they shall serve as lights in the expanse of the heavens to give light on the earth"; and it was so. ¹⁶God made the two great lights, the ^Agreater light to govern the day, and the lesser light to govern the night; *He made* the stars also. ^{17A}God placed them in the expanse of the heavens to give light on the earth, ¹⁸and to ^Agovern the day and the night, and to separate the light from the darkness; and God saw that it was good. ¹⁹And there was evening and there was morning, a fourth day.

²⁰Then God said, "Let the waters teem with swarms of living creatures, and let birds fly above the earth in the open expanse of the heavens." ²¹And God created ^Athe great sea creatures and every living creature that moves, with which the waters swarmed, according to

---

1:1^APs 102:25　^BJob 38:4　1:2^AJer 4:23　^BJob 38:9
1:3^APs 33:6, 9; 2 Cor 4:6　1:4^AIs 45:7　1:5^APs 74:16
1:6^AIs 40:22; 2 Pet 3:5　1:7^APs 148:4　1:9^APs 104:6-9
^BPs 24:1, 2　1:10^APs 33:7; 95:5　1:11^APs 65:9-13;
Heb 6:7　1:14^APs 74:16　^BJer 10:2　1:16^APs 136:8, 9
1:17^AJer 33:20, 25　1:18^AJer 31:35　1:21^APs 104:25-28

1:2¹Or *waste*　1:3¹I.e., a command, not a request; and so throughout the ch　1:7¹Or *firmament*

their kind, and every winged bird according to its kind; and God saw that it was good. ²²God blessed them, saying, "Be fruitful and multiply, and fill the waters in the seas, and let birds multiply on the earth." ²³And there was evening and there was morning, a fifth day.

²⁴^AThen God said, "Let the earth produce living creatures according to their kind: livestock and crawling things and animals of the earth according to their kind"; and it was so. ²⁵God made the ^Aanimals of the earth according to their kind, and the livestock according to their kind, and everything that crawls on the ground according to its kind; and God saw that it was good.

²⁶Then God said, "¹Let ^AUs make mankind in Our image, according to Our likeness; and ²let them ^Brule over the fish of the sea and over the birds of the sky and over the livestock and over all the earth, and over every crawling thing that crawls on the earth." ²⁷So God created man ^Ain His own image, in the image of God He created him; male and female He created them. ²⁸God blessed them; and God said to them, "^ABe fruitful and multiply, and fill the earth, and subdue it; and rule over the fish of the sea and over the birds of the sky and over every living thing that moves on the earth." ²⁹Then God said, "Behold, ^AI have given you every plant yielding seed that is on the surface of all the earth, and every tree which has fruit yielding seed; it shall be food for you; ³⁰and ^Ato every animal of the earth and to every bird of the sky and to everything that moves on the earth which has life, *I have given* every green plant for food"; and it was so. ³¹And God saw

all that He had made, and behold, it was very ^Agood. And there was evening and there was morning, the sixth day.

2 And so the heavens and the earth were completed, and all ^Atheir heavenly ¹lights. ²By ^Athe seventh day God completed His work which He had done, and He rested on the seventh day from all His work which He had done. ³Then God blessed the seventh day and sanctified it, because on it He rested from all His work which God had created and made.

THE CREATION OF MAN AND WOMAN

⁴^AThis is the account of the heavens and the earth when they were created, in the day that the LORD God made earth and heaven. ⁵^ANow no shrub of the field was yet on the earth, and no plant of the field had yet sprouted, for the LORD God had not sent rain upon the earth, and there was no man to cultivate the ground. ⁶But a mist used to rise from the earth and water the whole surface of the ground. ⁷Then the LORD God formed the man of ^Adust from the ground, and breathed into his nostrils the breath of life; and the ^Bman became a living ¹person. ⁸The LORD God planted a ^Agarden toward the east, in Eden; and there He placed the man whom He had formed. ⁹Out of the ground the LORD God caused every tree to

1:24^AGen 2:19; 6:20   1:25^AGen 7:21, 22; Jer 27:5
1:26^AGen 3:22   ^BPs 8:6-8   1:27^AGen 5:1f; 1 Cor 11:7
1:28^AGen 9:1, 7; Lev 26:9   1:29^APs 104:14; 136:25
1:30^APs 145:15, 16; 147:9   1:31^APs 104:24, 28; 119:68
2:1^ADeut 4:19; 17:3   2:2^AEx 20:8-11; 31:17
2:4^AJob 38:4-11   2:5^AGen 1:11   2:7^AGen 3:19
^B1 Cor 15:45   2:8^AGen 13:10; Is 51:3

1:26 ¹I.e., indicating united action, not a request
²I.e., have them rule   2:1 ¹Lit *host* i.e., sun, stars, etc.
2:7 ¹Or *soul*

grow that is pleasing to the sight and good for food; ^the tree of life *was* also in the midst of the garden, and the tree of the knowledge of good and evil.

¹⁰ Now a ^river flowed out of Eden to water the garden; and from there it divided and became four rivers. ¹¹The name of the first is Pishon; it flows around the whole land of ^Havilah, where there is gold. ¹²The gold of that land is good; the bdellium and the onyx stone are there *as well.* ¹³The name of the second river is Gihon; it flows around the whole land of Cush. ¹⁴The name of the third river is ^Tigris; it flows east of Assyria. And the fourth river is the ᴮEuphrates.

¹⁵Then the Lᴏʀᴅ God took the man and put him in the Garden of Eden to cultivate it and tend it. ¹⁶The Lᴏʀᴅ God ^commanded the man, saying, "From any tree of the garden you may freely eat; ¹⁷but from the tree of the knowledge of good and evil you shall not eat, for on the day that you eat from it ^you will certainly die."

¹⁸Then the Lᴏʀᴅ God said, "It is not good for the man to be alone; ^I will make him a helper suitable for him." ¹⁹^And out of the ground the Lᴏʀᴅ God formed every animal of the field and every bird of the sky, and brought *them* to the man to see what he would call them; and whatever the man called a living creature, that was its name. ²⁰The man gave names to all the livestock, and to the birds of the sky, and to every animal of the field, but for ¹Adam there was not found ^a helper suitable for him. ²¹So the Lᴏʀᴅ God caused a ^deep sleep to fall upon the man, and he slept; then He took one of his ribs and closed up the

flesh at that place. ²²And the Lᴏʀᴅ God ¹fashioned into a woman ^the rib which He had taken from the man, and brought her to the man. ²³Then the man said,

"^At last this is bone of my
   bones,
And flesh of my flesh;
She shall be called 'woman,'
Because she was taken out of
   man."

²⁴^For this reason a man shall leave his father and his mother, and be joined to his wife; and they shall become one flesh. ²⁵^And the man and his wife were both naked, but they were not ashamed.

THE FALL OF MANKIND

3 Now ^the serpent was more cunning than any animal of the field which the Lᴏʀᴅ God had made. And he said to the woman, "Has God really said, 'You shall not eat from any tree of the garden'?" ²The woman said to the serpent, "^From the fruit of the trees of the garden we may eat; ³but from the fruit of the tree which is in the middle of the garden, God has said, 'You shall not eat from it or touch it, or you will die.'" ⁴^The serpent said to the woman, "You certainly will not die! ⁵For God knows that on the day you eat from it your eyes will be opened, and ^you will become like God, knowing good and evil." ⁶^When the woman saw that the tree was good for food, and

2:9 ^Gen 3:22; Rev 2:7   2:10 ^Ps 46:4   2:11 ^Gen 25:18
2:14 ^Dan 10:4   ᴮGen 15:18   2:16 ^Gen 3:2, 3
2:17 ^Deut 30:15, 19, 20; Rom 6:23   2:18 ^1 Cor 11:9
2:19 ^Gen 1:24   2:20 ^Gen 2:18   2:21 ^Gen 15:12
2:22 ^1 Cor 11:8, 9   2:23 ^Gen 29:14; Eph 5:28, 29
2:24 ^Matt 19:5; Mark 10:7, 8   2:25 ^Gen 3:7, 10, 11
3:1 ^2 Cor 11:3; Rev 12:9   3:2 ^Gen 2:16, 17
3:4 ^John 8:44; 2 Cor 11:3   3:5 ^Is 14:14; Ezek 28:2, 12-17
3:6 ^Rom 5:12-19; 1 Tim 2:14

2:20 ¹Or *man*   2:22 ¹Lit *built*

that it was a delight to the eyes, and that the tree was desirable to make *one* wise, she took some of its fruit and ate; and she also gave *some* to her husband with her, and he ate. [7] Then the eyes of both of them were opened, and they ^knew that they were naked; and they sewed fig leaves together and made themselves waist coverings.

[8] Now they heard the sound of ^the Lord God walking in the garden in the cool of the day, and the man and his wife hid themselves from the presence of the Lord God among the trees of the garden. [9] Then the Lord God called to the man, and said to him, "^Where are you?" [10] He said, "^I heard the sound of You in the garden, and I was afraid because I was naked; so I hid myself." [11] And He said, "Who told you that you were naked? Have you eaten from the tree from which I commanded you not to eat?" [12] ^The man said, "The woman whom You gave *to be* with me, she gave me some of *the fruit of* the tree, and I ate." [13] Then the Lord God said to the woman, "What is this *that* you have done?" And the woman said, "^The serpent deceived me, and I ate." [14] Then the Lord God said to the serpent,

"Because you have done this,
    Cursed are you more than all
        the livestock,
    And more than any animal of
        the field;
    On your belly you shall go,
    And ^dust you shall eat
    All the days of your life;
[15]   And I will ^make enemies
    Of you and the woman,
    And of your ¹offspring and her
        ²Descendant;

He shall bruise you on the
        head,
    And you shall bruise Him on
        the heel."
[16] To the woman He said,
    "I will greatly multiply
    Your pain in childbirth,
    In pain you shall ^deliver
        children;
    Yet your desire will be for your
        husband,
    And he shall rule over you."
[17] Then to Adam He said, "Because you have listened to the voice of your wife, and have eaten from the tree about which I commanded you, saying, 'You shall not eat from it';
    ^Cursed is the ground because
        of you;
    With hard labor you shall eat
    from it
    All the days of your life.
[18]   "Both thorns and thistles it
        shall grow for you;
    Yet you shall eat the plants of
        the field;
[19]   By the sweat of your face
    You shall eat bread,
    Until you ^return to the
        ground,
    Because from it you were
        taken;
    For you are dust,
    And to dust you shall return."
[20] Now the man named his wife ¹,^Eve, because she was the mother of all *the* living. [21] And the Lord God made garments of skin for Adam and his wife, and clothed them.

3:7 ^Is 47:3; Lam 1:8   3:8 ^Lev 26:12; Deut 23:14
3:9 ^Gen 4:9; 18:9   3:10 ^Ex 20:18, 19; Deut 5:25
3:12 ^Job 33:33; Prov 28:13   3:13 ^2 Cor 11:3; 1 Tim 2:14
3:14 ^Is 65:25; Mic 7:17   3:15 ^Rev 12:17
3:16 ^John 16:21; 1 Tim 2:15   3:17 ^Gen 5:29;
Rom 8:20-22   3:19 ^Ps 90:3; 104:29
3:20 ^2 Cor 11:3; 1 Tim 2:13

3:15 ¹Lit *seed*   ²Lit *Seed;* i.e., a prophetic reference to Christ   3:20 ¹I.e., living; or life

²²Then the LORD God said, "Behold, the man has become like one of Us, knowing good and evil; and now, he might reach out with his hand, and take *fruit* also from ᴬthe tree of life, and eat, and live forever"— ²³therefore the LORD God sent him out of the Garden of Eden, to cultivate the ground from which he was taken. ²⁴So He drove the man out; and at the east of the Garden of Eden He stationed the ᴬcherubim and the flaming sword which turned every direction to guard the way to the tree of life.

CAIN AND ABEL

4 Now the man had relations with his wife Eve, and she conceived and gave birth to Cain, and she said, "I have obtained a male *child* with *the help of* the LORD." ²And again, she gave birth to his brother Abel. Now ᴬAbel was a keeper of flocks, but Cain was a cultivator of the ground. ³So it came about in the course of time that Cain brought an offering to the LORD from the fruit of the ground. ⁴ᴬAbel, on his part also brought *an offering,* from the firstborn of his flock and from their fat portions. And the LORD had regard for Abel and his offering; ⁵but ᴬfor Cain and his offering He had no regard. So Cain became very angry and his face was gloomy. ⁶Then the LORD said to Cain, "ᴬWhy are you angry? And why is your face gloomy? ⁷If you do well, will *your face* not be cheerful? ᴬAnd if you do not do well, sin is lurking at the door; and its desire is for you, ᴮbut you must master it." ⁸Cain talked to his brother Abel; and it happened that when they were in the field Cain rose up against his brother Abel and ᴬkilled him.

⁹Then the LORD said to Cain, "ᴬWhere is Abel your brother?" And he said, "I do not know. Am I my brother's keeper?" ¹⁰Then He said, "What have you done? ᴬThe voice of your brother's blood is crying out to Me from the ground. ¹¹Now ᴬyou are cursed from the ground, which has opened its mouth to receive your brother's blood from your hand. ¹²ᴬWhen you cultivate the ground, it will no longer yield its strength to you; you will be a wanderer and a drifter on the earth." ¹³Cain said to the LORD, "My punishment is too great to endure! ¹⁴Behold, You have driven me this day from the face of the ground; and I will be hidden from Your face, and ᴬI will be a wanderer and a drifter on the earth, and ᴮwhoever finds me will kill me." ¹⁵So the LORD said to him, "Therefore whoever kills Cain, vengeance will be taken on him ᴬseven times *as much.*" And the LORD placed a mark on Cain, so that no one finding him would kill him.

¹⁶Then Cain left the presence ᴬof the LORD, and settled in the land of Nod, east of Eden.

¹⁷Cain had relations with his wife and she conceived, and gave birth to Enoch; and *Cain* built a city, and named the city Enoch, after the name of his son. ¹⁸Now to Enoch was born Irad, and Irad fathered Mehujael, and Mehujael fathered Methushael, and Methushael fathered Lamech. ¹⁹Lamech took

3:22ᴬGen 2:9; Rev 22:14 3:24ᴬEx 25:18-22; Ezek 10:1-20 4:2ᴬLuke 11:50, 51 4:4ᴬHeb 11:4 4:5ᴬ1 Sam 16:7 4:6ᴬJohn 4:4 4:7ᴬNum 32:23 ᴮJob 11:14, 15 4:8ᴬMatt 23:35; Luke 11:51 4:9ᴬGen 3:9 4:10ᴬNum 35:33; Deut 21:1-9 4:11ᴬGen 3:14; Deut 28:15-20 4:12ᴬDeut 28:15-24; Joel 1:10-20 4:14ᴬDeut 28:64-67 ᴮNum 35:19 4:15ᴬGen 4:24 4:16ᴬ2 Kin 24:20; Jer 23:39

^two wives for himself: the name of the one was Adah, and the name of the other, Zillah. ²⁰Adah gave birth to Jabal; he was the father of those who live in tents and *have* livestock. ²¹His brother's name was Jubal; he was the father of all those who play the lyre and flute. ²²As for Zillah, she also gave birth to Tubal-cain, the forger of all implements of bronze and iron; and the sister of Tubal-cain was Naamah.

²³Lamech said to his wives,

"Adah and Zillah,
Listen to my voice,
You wives of Lamech,
Pay attention to my words,
^For I have killed a man for
   wounding me;
And a boy for striking me!
²⁴ "If Cain is avenged ^seven
   times,
Then Lamech seventy-seven
   times!"

²⁵Adam had relations with his wife again; and she gave birth to a son, and named him Seth, for, *she said,* "God has appointed me another child in place of Abel, ^because Cain killed him." ²⁶To Seth also ^a son was born; and he named him Enosh. Then *people* began to call upon the name of the LORD.

DESCENDANTS OF ADAM

5 This is the book of the generations of Adam. On the day when God created man, He made him ^in the likeness of God. ²He created them ^male and female, and He blessed them and named them "mankind" on the day when they were created. ³When Adam had lived 130 years, he fathered *a son* in his own likeness, according to his image, and named him Seth. ⁴Then the days of Adam after he fathered Seth were eight hundred years, and he fathered *other* sons and daughters. ⁵So all the days that Adam lived were 930 years, and he died.

⁶Now Seth lived 105 years, and fathered Enosh. ⁷Then Seth lived 807 years after he fathered Enosh, and he fathered *other* sons and daughters. ⁸So all the days of Seth were 912 years, and he died.

⁹Now Enosh lived ninety years, and fathered Kenan. ¹⁰Then Enosh lived 815 years after he fathered Kenan, and he fathered *other* sons and daughters. ¹¹So all the days of Enosh were 905 years, and he died.

¹²Now Kenan lived seventy years, and fathered Mahalalel. ¹³Then Kenan lived 840 years after he fathered Mahalalel, and he fathered *other* sons and daughters. ¹⁴So all the days of Kenan were 910 years, and he died.

¹⁵Now Mahalalel lived sixty-five years, and fathered Jared. ¹⁶Then Mahalalel lived 830 years after he fathered Jared, and he fathered *other* sons and daughters. ¹⁷So all the days of Mahalalel were 895 years, and he died.

¹⁸Now Jared lived 162 years, and fathered Enoch. ¹⁹Then Jared lived eight hundred years after he fathered Enoch, and he fathered *other* sons and daughters. ²⁰So all the days of Jared were 962 years, and he died.

²¹Now Enoch lived sixty-five years, and fathered Methuselah. ²²Then Enoch ^walked with God three hundred years after he fathered Methuselah, and he

4:19^Gen 2:24   4:23^Ex 20:13; Lev 19:18
4:24^Gen 4:15   4:25^Gen 4:8   4:26^Luke 3:38
5:1^Gen 1:26, 27; Col 3:10   5:2^Matt 19:4; Mark 10:6
5:22^Mic 6:8; Mal 2:6

fathered *other* sons and daughters. ²³So all the days of Enoch were 365 years. ²⁴Enoch walked with God; and he was ¹not, for God ^took him.

²⁵Now Methuselah lived 187 years, and fathered Lamech. ²⁶Then Methuselah lived 782 years after he fathered Lamech, and he fathered *other* sons and daughters. ²⁷So all the days of Methuselah were 969 years, and he died.

²⁸Now Lamech lived 182 years, and fathered a son. ²⁹And he named him Noah, saying, "This one will give us comfort from our work and from the hard labor of our hands *caused* by ^the ground which the Lord has cursed." ³⁰Then Lamech lived 595 years after he fathered Noah, and he fathered *other* sons and daughters. ³¹So all the days of Lamech were 777 years, and he died.

³²Now after Noah was ^five hundred years old, Noah fathered Shem, Ham, and Japheth.

THE CORRUPTION OF MANKIND

6 Now it came about, when mankind began to multiply on the face of the land, and daughters were born to them, ²that the sons of God saw that the daughters of mankind were beautiful; and they took wives for themselves, whomever they chose. ³Then the Lord said, "^My Spirit will not remain with man forever, because he is also *flesh; nevertheless his days shall be* 120 years." ⁴The ¹·^Nephilim were on the earth in those days, and also afterward, when the sons of God came in to the daughters of mankind, and they bore children to them. Those were the mighty men who *were* of old, men of renown.

⁵Then the Lord saw that the wickedness of mankind was great

on the earth, and that ^every intent of the thoughts of their hearts was only evil continually. ⁶So ^the Lord was sorry that He had made mankind on the earth, and He was ᴮgrieved in His heart. ⁷Then the Lord said, "^I will wipe out mankind whom I have created from the face of the land; mankind, and animals as well, and crawling things, and the birds of the sky. For I am sorry that I have made them." ⁸But Noah ^found favor in the eyes of the Lord.

⁹These are *the records of* the generations of Noah. Noah was a ^righteous man, ᴮblameless in his generation. Noah walked with God. ¹⁰And Noah fathered three sons: Shem, Ham, and Japheth.

¹¹Now the earth was ^corrupt in the sight of God, and the earth was ᴮfilled with violence. ¹²And God looked on the earth, and behold, it was corrupt; for ^humanity had corrupted its way upon the earth.

¹³Then God said to Noah, "^The end of humanity has come before Me; for the earth is filled with violence because of people; and behold, I am about to destroy them with the earth. ¹⁴Make for yourself an ark of gopher wood; you shall make the ark with compartments, and cover it inside and out with pitch. ¹⁵This is how you shall make it: the length of the ark *shall be* ¹three hundred cubits, its width fifty cubits, and its height thirty

5:24 ^2 Kin 2:10; Ps 49:15   5:29 ^Gen 3:17-19; 4:11
5:32 ^Gen 7:6   6:3 ^Gal 5:16, 17; 1 Pet 3:20
6:4 ^Num 13:33   6:5 ^Gen 8:21; Ps 14:1-3
6:6 ^Jer 18:7-10   ᴮIs 63:10   6:7 ^Deut 28:63; 29:20
6:8 ^Gen 19:19; Ex 33:17   6:9 ^2 Pet 2:5   ᴮGen 17:1
6:11 ^Deut 31:29   ᴮEzek 8:17   6:12 ^Ps 14:1-3
6:13 ^Is 34:1-4; Ezek 7:2, 3

5:24 ¹LXX *not found*   6:4 ¹Lit *fallen ones;* LXX *giants*
6:15 ¹About 450 ft. long, 75 ft. wide, and 45 ft. high
or 135 m, 23 m, and 14 m

cubits. ¹⁶You shall make a window for the ark, and finish it to a ¹cubit from the top; and put the door of the ark on the side; you shall make it with lower, second, and third decks. ¹⁷Now behold, ^I Myself am bringing the flood of water upon the earth, to destroy all flesh in which there is the breath of life, from under heaven; everything that is on the earth shall perish. ¹⁸But I will establish ^My covenant with you; and you shall enter the ark—you, your sons, your wife, and your sons' wives with you. ¹⁹^And of every living thing of all flesh, you shall bring two of every *kind* into the ark, to keep *them* alive with you; they shall be male and female. ²⁰^Of the birds according to their kind, and of the animals according to their kind, of every crawling thing of the ground according to its kind, two of every *kind* will come to you to keep *them* alive. ²¹As for you, take for yourself some of every ^food that is edible, and gather *it* to yourself; and it shall be food for you and them." ²²^So Noah did *these things;* according to everything that God had commanded him, so he did.

THE FLOOD

7 Then the Lord said to Noah, "Enter the ark, you and all your household, for you *alone* I have seen *to be* ^righteous before Me in this generation. ²You shall take with you seven pairs of every ^clean animal, a male and his female; and two of the animals that are not clean, a male and his female; ³also of the birds of the sky, seven pairs, male and female, to keep *their* offspring alive on the face of all the earth. ⁴For after seven more days,

I will send rain on the earth for forty days and forty nights; and I will wipe out from the face of the land ^every living thing that I have made." ⁵So ^Noah acted in accordance with everything that the Lord had commanded him.

⁶Now Noah was ^six hundred years old when the flood of water came upon the earth. ⁷Then ^Noah and his sons, his wife, and his sons' wives with him entered the ark because of the waters of the flood. ⁸^Of clean animals and animals that are not clean and birds and everything that crawls on the ground, ⁹they *all* went into the ark to Noah by twos, male and female, as God had commanded Noah. ¹⁰Now it came about after ^the seven days, that the waters of the flood came upon the earth. ¹¹In the six hundredth year of Noah's life, in the second month, on the seventeenth day of the month, on that day all ^the fountains of the great deep burst open, and the floodgates of the sky were opened. ¹²^The rain fell upon the earth for forty days and forty nights.

¹³On this very same day ^Noah, Shem, Ham, and Japheth, the sons of Noah, and Noah's wife and the three wives of his sons with them, entered the ark, ¹⁴they and every animal according to its kind, and all the livestock according to their kind, and every crawling thing that crawls on the earth according to its kind, and every bird according to

6:17^2 Pet 2:5   6:18^Gen 9:9-16; 17:7
6:19^Gen 7:2, 14, 15   6:20^Gen 7:3   6:21^Gen 1:29, 30
6:22^Gen 7:5; Heb 11:7   7:1^Gen 6:9   7:2^Lev 11:1-31;
Deut 14:3-20   7:4^Gen 6:7, 13   7:5^Gen 6:22
7:6^Gen 5:32   7:7^Gen 6:18; 7:13   7:8^Gen 6:19, 20;
7:2, 3   7:10^Gen 7:4   7:11^Gen 8:2   7:12^Gen 7:4, 17
7:13^Gen 6:18; 7:7

6:16 ¹One cubit is about 18 in. or 45 cm

its kind, all sorts of birds. ¹⁵So they went into the ark to Noah, ^by twos of all flesh in which there was the breath of life. ¹⁶Those that entered, male and female of all flesh, entered as God had commanded him; and the LORD closed *the door* behind him.

¹⁷Then the flood came upon the earth for ^forty days, and the water increased and lifted up the ark, so that it rose above the earth. ¹⁸The water prevailed and increased greatly upon the earth, and the ark floated on the surface of the water. ¹⁹And the water prevailed more and more upon the earth, so that all the high mountains everywhere under the heavens were covered. ²⁰The water prevailed ¹fifteen cubits higher, ^and the mountains were covered. ²¹So ^all creatures that moved on the earth perished: birds, livestock, animals, and every swarming thing that swarms upon the earth, and all mankind; ²²of all that was on the dry land, all ^in whose nostrils was the breath of the spirit of life, died. ²³So He wiped out every living thing that was upon the face of the land, from mankind to animals, to crawling things, and the birds of the sky, and they were wiped out from the earth; and only ^Noah was left, together with those that were with him in the ark. ²⁴^The water prevailed upon the earth for 150 days.

THE FLOOD SUBSIDES

8 But God remembered Noah and all the animals and all the livestock that were with him in the ark; and ^God caused a wind to pass over the earth, and the water subsided. ²Also ^the fountains of the deep and the floodgates of the sky were closed, and ^the rain from the sky was restrained; ³and the water receded steadily from the earth, and at the end ^of 150 days the water decreased. ⁴Then in the seventh month, on the seventeenth day of the month, ^the ark rested upon the mountains of Ararat. ⁵And the water decreased steadily until the tenth month; in the tenth month, on the first day of the month, the tops of the mountains became visible.

⁶Then it came about at the end of forty days, that Noah opened the ^window of the ark which he had made; ⁷and he sent out a raven, and it flew here and there until the water was dried up from the earth. ⁸Then he sent out a dove, to see if the water was low on the surface of the land; ⁹but the dove found no resting place for the sole of its foot, so it returned to him in the ark, for the water was on the surface of all the earth. Then he put out his hand and took it, and brought it into the ark to himself. ¹⁰So he waited another seven days longer; and again he sent out the dove from the ark. ¹¹And the dove came to him in the evening, and behold, in its beak was a fresh olive leaf. So Noah knew that the water was low on the earth. ¹²Then he waited another seven days longer, and sent out ^the dove; but it did not return to him again.

¹³Now it came about in the ^six hundred and first year, in the first *month,* on the first of the month,

7:15 ^Gen 6:19; 7:9   7:17 ^Gen 7:4   7:20 ^Gen 8:4
7:21 ^Gen 6:7, 13, 17; 7:4   7:22 ^Gen 2:7
7:23 ^Matt 24:38, 39; Luke 17:26, 27   7:24 ^Gen 8:3
8:1 ^Ex 14:21; 15:10; Job 12:15   8:2 ^Gen 7:11
^Gen 7:4, 12   8:3 ^Gen 7:24   8:4 ^Gen 7:20
8:6 ^Gen 6:16   8:12 ^Jer 48:28   8:13 ^Gen 7:6

7:20 ¹About 23 ft. or 6.7 m

that the water was dried up from the earth. Then Noah removed the covering of the ark, and looked, and behold, the surface of the ground had dried up. ¹⁴And in the second month, on the twenty-seventh day of the month, the earth was dry. ¹⁵Then God spoke to Noah, saying, ¹⁶"Go out of the ark, you and your wife and your sons and your sons' wives with you. ¹⁷Bring out with you every living thing of all flesh that is with you, birds and animals and every crawling thing that crawls on the earth, that they may ᴬbreed abundantly on the earth, and ᴬbe fruitful and multiply on the earth." ¹⁸So Noah went out, and his sons and his wife, and his sons' wives with him. ¹⁹Every animal, every crawling thing, and every bird, everything that moves on the earth, went out by their families from the ark.

²⁰Then Noah built an altar to the Lord, and took some of every *kind of* ᴬclean animal and some of every clean bird and offered burnt offerings on the altar. ²¹The Lord smelled the soothing aroma, and the Lord said to Himself, "I will never again ᴬcurse the ground on account of man, for ᴮthe intent of man's heart is evil from his youth; and I will never again destroy every living thing, as I have done.

²² "While the earth remains,
　Seedtime and harvest,
　Cold and heat,
　ᴬSummer and winter,
　And day and night
　Shall not cease."

COVENANT OF THE RAINBOW

9 Then God blessed Noah and his sons, and said to them, "ᴬBe fruitful and multiply, and fill the earth. ²The fear of you and the terror of you will be on every animal of the earth and on every bird of the sky; on everything that crawls on the ground, and on all the fish of the sea. They are handed over to you. ³Every moving thing that is alive shall be food for you; I have given everything to you, ᴬas *I gave* the green plant. ⁴But you shall not eat flesh with its life, *that is,* ᴬits blood. ⁵I certainly will require your lifeblood; ᴬfrom every animal I will require it. And from *every* person, from every man *as* his brother I will require the life of a person.

⁶ "ᴬWhoever sheds human blood,
　By man his blood shall be
　　shed,
　For in the image of God
　He made mankind.

⁷ "As for you, ᴬbe fruitful and
　　multiply;
　Populate the earth abundantly
　　and multiply in it."

⁸Then God spoke to Noah and to his sons with him, saying, ⁹"Now behold, ᴬI Myself am establishing My covenant with you, and with your descendants after you; ¹⁰and with every living creature that is with you: the birds, the livestock, and every animal of the earth with you; of all that comes out of the ark, every animal of the earth. ¹¹I establish My covenant with you; and all flesh shall ᴬnever again be eliminated by the waters of a flood, ᴮnor shall there again be a flood to destroy the earth." ¹²God said, "This is ᴬthe sign of the covenant which I am making between Me

8:17 ᴬGen 1:22, 28　8:20 ᴬGen 7:2; Lev 11:1-47
8:21 ᴬIs 54:9　ᴮGen 6:5　8:22 ᴬPs 74:17
9:1 ᴬGen 1:28; 9:7　9:3 ᴬGen 1:29　9:4 ᴬLev 7:26f;
17:10-16　9:5 ᴬEx 21:28, 29　9:6 ᴬEx 21:12-14;
Lev 24:17　9:7 ᴬGen 9:1　9:9 ᴬGen 6:18
9:11 ᴬGen 8:21　ᴮIs 54:9　9:12 ᴬGen 9:13, 17; 17:11

and you and every living creature that is with you, for all future generations; [13]I have set My ^rainbow in the cloud, and it shall serve as a sign of a covenant between Me and the earth. [14]It shall come about, when I make a cloud appear over the earth, that the rainbow will be seen in the cloud, [15]and ^I will remember My covenant, which is between Me and you and every living creature of all flesh; and never again shall the water become a flood to destroy all flesh. [16]When the rainbow is in the cloud, then I will look at it, to remember the ^everlasting covenant between God and every living creature of all flesh that is on the earth." [17]And God said to Noah, "This is the sign of the covenant which I have established between Me and all flesh that is on the earth."

[18]Now the sons of Noah who came out of the ark were Shem, Ham, and Japheth; and ^Ham was the father of Canaan. [19]These three were the sons of Noah, and ^from these the whole earth was populated.

[20]Then Noah began farming and planted a vineyard. [21]He drank some of the wine and ^became drunk, and uncovered himself inside his tent. [22]Ham, the father of Canaan, ^saw the nakedness of his father, and told his two brothers outside. [23]But Shem and Japheth took a garment and laid it on both their shoulders and walked backward and covered the nakedness of their father; and their faces were turned away, so that they did not see their father's nakedness. [24]When Noah awoke from his wine, he knew what his youngest son had done to him. [25]So he said,

"^Cursed be Canaan;
[1,B]A servant of servants
  He shall be to his brothers."
[26]He also said,

"^Blessed be the LORD,
  The God of Shem;
  And may Canaan be his
  servant.
[27] "^May God enlarge Japheth,
  And may he live in the tents of
  Shem;
  And may Canaan be his
  servant."

[28]Noah lived 350 years after the flood. [29]So all the days of Noah were 950 years, and he died.

DESCENDANTS OF NOAH

10 Now these are *the records of* the generations of the sons of Noah: Shem, Ham, and Japheth; and sons were born to them after the flood.

[2]^The sons of Japheth were ^BGomer, Magog, Madai, Javan, Tubal, Meshech, and Tiras. [3]The sons of Gomer were ^Ashkenaz, Riphath, and Togarmah. [4]The sons of Javan were Elishah, ^Tarshish, Kittim, and Dodanim. [5]From these *the people of* the coastlands of the nations were separated into their lands, every one according to his language, according to their families, into their nations.

[6]^The sons of Ham were Cush, Mizraim, Put, and Canaan. [7]The sons of Cush were ^Seba, Havilah, Sabtah, ^BRaamah, and Sabteca; and the sons of Raamah were ^BSheba

---

9:13^Ezek 1:28   9:15^Lev 26:42, 45; Deut 7:9
9:16^Gen 17:13, 19; 2 Sam 23:5   9:18^Gen 9:25-27;
10:6   9:19^Gen 9:1, 7; 10:32   9:21^Prov 20:1
9:22^Hab 2:15   9:25^Deut 27:16   ^BJosh 9:23
9:26^Gen 14:20; 24:27   9:27^Gen 10:2-5; Is 66:19
10:2^1 Chr 1:5-7   ^BEzek 38:2, 6   ^AJer 51:27
10:4^Ezek 27:12, 25   10:6^1 Chr 1:8-10
10:7^Is 43:3   ^BEzek 27:22

9:25 [1]I.e., The lowest of servants

and Dedan. ⁸Now Cush fathered Nimrod; he became a mighty one on the earth. ⁹He was a mighty hunter before the Lᴏʀᴅ; therefore it is said, "Like Nimrod a mighty hunter before the Lᴏʀᴅ." ¹⁰And the beginning of his kingdom was ¹ˑᴬBabel, Erech, Accad, and Calneh, in the land of Shinar. ¹¹From that land he went ᴬto Assyria, and built Nineveh, Rehoboth-Ir, Calah, ¹²and Resen between Nineveh and Calah; that is the great city. ¹³Mizraim fathered ᴬLudim, Anamim, Lehabim, Naphtuhim, ¹⁴ᴬPathrusim, Casluhim (from whom came the Philistines), and Caphtorim.

¹⁵Canaan fathered Sidon, his firstborn, and ᴬHeth, ¹⁶ᴬthe Jebusite, the Amorite, the Girgashite, ¹⁷the Hivite, the Arkite, the Sinite, ¹⁸the Arvadite, the Zemarite, and the Hamathite; and afterward the families of the Canaanite were spread abroad. ¹⁹ᴬThe territory of the Canaanite extended from Sidon going toward Gerar, as far as Gaza; *and* going toward Sodom and Gomorrah, Admah, and Zeboiim, as far as Lasha. ²⁰These are the sons of Ham, according to their families, according to their languages, by their lands, *and* by their nations.

²¹Also to Shem, the father of all the children of Eber, *and* the older brother of Japheth, *children* were born. ²²The sons of Shem *were* ᴬElam, Asshur, ᴮArpachshad, Lud, and Aram. ²³The sons of Aram *were* ᴬUz, Hul, Gether, and Mash. ²⁴Arpachshad fathered ᴬShelah; and Shelah fathered Eber. ²⁵ᴬTwo sons were born to Eber; the name of the one *was* Peleg, for in his days the earth was divided; and his brother's name *was* Joktan. ²⁶Joktan fathered Almodad,

Sheleph, Hazarmaveth, Jerah, ²⁷Hadoram, Uzal, Diklah, ²⁸Obal, Abimael, Sheba, ²⁹Ophir, Havilah, and Jobab; all of these were the sons of Joktan. ³⁰Now their settlement extended from Mesha going toward Sephar, the hill country of the east. ³¹These are the sons of Shem, according to their families, according to their languages, by their lands, *and* according to their nations.

³²These are the families of the sons of Noah, according to their descendants, by their nations; and ᴬout of these the nations were separated on the earth after the flood.

THE TOWER OF BABEL

11 Now all the earth used the same language and the same words. ²And it came about, as they journeyed east, that they found a plain in the land ᴬof Shinar and settled there. ³Then they said to one another, "Come, let's make bricks and ¹fire *them* thoroughly." And they used brick for stone, and they used ᴬtar for mortar. ⁴And they said, "Come, let's build ourselves a city, and a tower whose top *will reach* into heaven, and let's make ᴬa name for ourselves; otherwise we ᴮwill be scattered abroad over the face of all the earth." ⁵Now ᴬthe Lᴏʀᴅ came down to see the city and the tower which the men had built. ⁶And the Lᴏʀᴅ said, "Behold, they are one people, and they all have ᴬthe same

10:10ᴬGen 11:9   10:11ᴬMic 5:6   10:13ᴬJer 46:9
10:14ᴬ1 Chr 1:12   10:15ᴬGen 23:3   10:16ᴬGen
15:19-21   10:19ᴬNum 34:2-12   10:22ᴬGen 14:1, 9
ᴮGen 11:10   10:23ᴬJob 1:1; Jer 25:20
10:24ᴬGen 11:12; Luke 3:35   10:25ᴬ1 Chr 1:19
10:32ᴬGen 9:19   11:2ᴬGen 10:10; 14:1
11:3ᴬGen 14:10   11:4ᴬGen 6:4   ᴮDeut 4:27
11:5ᴬGen 18:21; Ex 3:8   11:6ᴬGen 11:1

10:10¹Or *Babylon*   11:3¹I.e., in a kiln to harden them

language. And this is what they have started to do, and now nothing which they plan to do will be impossible for them. [7]Come, [1,A]let Us go down and there [B]confuse their language, so that they will not understand one another's speech." [8]So the LORD [A]scattered them abroad from there over the face of all the earth; and they stopped building the city. [9]Therefore it was named [1,A]Babel, because there the LORD confused the language of all the earth; and from there the LORD scattered them abroad over the face of all the earth.

DESCENDANTS OF SHEM

[10,A]These are *the records of* the generations of Shem. Shem was a hundred years old when he fathered Arpachshad, two years after the flood; [11]and Shem lived five hundred years after he fathered Arpachshad, and he fathered *other* sons and daughters.

[12]Arpachshad lived thirty-five years, and fathered Shelah; [13]and Arpachshad lived 403 years after he fathered Shelah, and he fathered *other* sons and daughters.

[14]Shelah lived thirty years, and fathered Eber; [15]and Shelah lived 403 years after he fathered Eber, and he fathered *other* sons and daughters.

[16]Eber lived thirty-four years, and fathered Peleg; [17]and Eber lived 430 years after he fathered Peleg, and he fathered *other* sons and daughters.

[18]Peleg lived thirty years, and fathered Reu; [19]and Peleg lived 209 years after he fathered Reu, and he fathered *other* sons and daughters.

[20]Reu lived thirty-two years, and fathered Serug; [21]and Reu lived 207 years after he fathered Serug, and he fathered *other* sons and daughters.

[22]Serug lived thirty years, and fathered Nahor; [23]and Serug lived two hundred years after he fathered Nahor, and he fathered *other* sons and daughters.

[24]Nahor lived twenty-nine years, and fathered [A]Terah; [25]and Nahor lived 119 years after he fathered Terah, and he fathered *other* sons and daughters.

[26]Terah lived seventy years, and [A]fathered Abram, Nahor, and Haran.

[27]Now these are *the records of* the generations of Terah. Terah fathered Abram, Nahor, and Haran; and Haran fathered [A]Lot. [28]Haran died during the lifetime of his father Terah in the land of his birth, in [A]Ur of the Chaldeans. [29]Abram and [A]Nahor took wives for themselves. The name of Abram's wife was [B]Sarai, and the name of Nahor's wife was Milcah, the daughter of Haran, the father of Milcah and Iscah. [30,A]Sarai was unable to conceive; she did not have a child.

[31]Now Terah took his son Abram, and Lot the son of Haran, his grandson, and his daughter-in-law Sarai, his son Abram's wife, and they departed together from [A]Ur of the Chaldeans to go to the land of Canaan; and they went as far as Haran and settled there. [32]The days of Terah were 205 years; and Terah died in Haran.

11:7[A]Gen 1:26   [B]Deut 28:49   11:8[A]Gen 11:4; Ps 92:9
11:9[A]Gen 10:10   11:10[A]Gen 10:22-25
11:24[A]Josh 24:2   11:26[A]Josh 24:2   11:27[A]Gen 13:10;
14:12   11:28[A]Gen 11:31   11:29[A]Gen 24:10
[B]Gen 17:15   11:30[A]Gen 16:1   11:31[A]Gen 15:7; Neh 9:7

11:7[1]I.e., indicating united action, not a request
11:9[1]Or *Babylon;* cf. Heb *balal,* confuse

ABRAM JOURNEYS TO EGYPT

12 Now ^the Lord said to Abram, "Go from your country,
And from your relatives
And from your father's house,
To the land which I will show you;

2 And ^I will make you into a great nation,
And I will bless you,
And make your name great;
And *you shall* ^be a blessing;

3 And I will bless those who bless you,
And the one who curses you I will curse.
^And in you all the families of the earth will be blessed."

4 So Abram went *away* as the Lord had spoken to him; and ^Lot went with him. Now Abram was seventy-five years old when he departed from Haran. 5 Abram took his wife Sarai and his nephew Lot, and all their ^possessions which they had accumulated, and the people which they had acquired in Haran, and they set out for the land of Canaan; so they came to the land of Canaan. 6 Abram passed through the land as far as the site of ^Shechem, to the oak of Moreh. Now the Canaanites *were* in the land at that time. 7 And the Lord ^appeared to Abram and said, "^To your descendants I will give this land." So he built an altar there to the Lord who had appeared to him. 8 Then he proceeded from there to the mountain on the east of Bethel, and pitched his tent with ^Bethel on the west and Ai on the east; and there he built an altar to the Lord and called upon the name of the Lord. 9 Then Abram journeyed on, continuing toward ^the 1Negev.

10 Now there was ^a famine in the land; so Abram went down to Egypt to live there for a time, because the famine was ^severe in the land. 11 It came about, when he was approaching Egypt, that he said to his wife Sarai, "See now, I know that you are a ^beautiful woman; 12 ^and when the Egyptians see you, they will say, 'This is his wife'; and they will kill me, but they will let you live. 13 Please say that you are ^my sister so that it may go well for me because of you, and that I may live on account of you." 14 Now it came about, when Abram entered Egypt, that the Egyptians saw that the woman was very beautiful. 15 Pharaoh's officials saw her and praised her to Pharaoh; and ^the woman was taken into Pharaoh's house. 16 Therefore he treated Abram well for her sake; and ^he gave him sheep, oxen, male donkeys, male servants and female servants, female donkeys, and camels.

17 But the Lord ^struck Pharaoh and his house with great plagues because of Sarai, Abram's wife. 18 Then Pharaoh called Abram and said, "^What is this *that* you have done to me? Why did you not tell me that she was your wife? 19 Why did you say, 'She is my sister,' so that I took her for myself as a wife? Now then, here is your wife, take her and go!" 20 And Pharaoh commanded *his* men concerning him; and they escorted him away, with his wife and all that belonged to him.

12:1 ^Gen 15:7; Acts 7:3   12:2 ^Deut 26:5   ^Zech 8:13
12:3 ^Gen 22:18; Acts 3:25   12:4 ^Gen 11:27, 31
12:5 ^Gen 13:6   12:6 ^Gen 35:4; Deut 11:30
12:7 ^Gen 17:1   ^Gen 13:15   12:8 ^Josh 8:9, 12
12:9 ^Gen 13:1, 3   12:10 ^Gen 26:1   ^Gen 43:1
12:11 ^Gen 26:7; 29:17   12:12 ^Gen 20:11
12:13 ^Gen 20:2, 5, 12; 26:7   12:15 ^Gen 20:2
12:16 ^Gen 13:2   12:17 ^Gen 20:18; 1 Chr 16:21
12:18 ^Gen 20:9, 10; 26:10

12:9 1I.e., South country

ABRAM AND LOT

13 So Abram went up from Egypt to ^the ¹Negev, he and his wife and all that belonged to him, and Lot with him.

²Now Abram was ^very rich in livestock, silver, and gold. ³And he went on his journeys from the ¹Negev as far as Bethel, to the place where his tent had been at the beginning, ^between Bethel and Ai, ⁴to the place of the ^altar which he had made there previously; and there Abram called on the name of the LORD. ⁵Now ^Lot, who went with Abram, also had flocks, herds, and tents. ⁶And ^the land could not support *both of* them while living together, for their possessions were so great that they were not able to remain together. ⁷^And there was strife between the herdsmen of Abram's livestock and the herdsmen of Lot's livestock. Now the Canaanites and the Perizzites were living in the land at that time.

⁸^So Abram said to Lot, "Please let there be no strife between you and me, nor between my herdsmen and your herdsmen, for we are relatives! ⁹Is the entire land not before you? Please separate from me; if *you choose* the left, then I will go to the right; or if *you choose* the right, then I will go to the left." ¹⁰Lot raised his eyes and saw all the vicinity of the ^Jordan, that it was well watered everywhere—*this was* before the LORD ᴮdestroyed Sodom and Gomorrah—like the garden of the LORD, like the land of Egypt going toward Zoar. ¹¹So Lot chose for himself all the vicinity of the Jordan, and Lot journeyed eastward. So they separated from each other. ¹²Abram settled in the land of Canaan, while Lot settled in ^the cities of the vicinity of the *Jordan,* and moved his tents as far as Sodom. ¹³Now ^the men of Sodom were exceedingly wicked sinners against the LORD.

¹⁴The LORD said to Abram, after Lot had separated from him, "Now raise your eyes and look from the place where you are, ^northward and southward, and eastward and westward; ¹⁵^for all the land which you see I will give to you and to your descendants forever. ¹⁶I will make your descendants ^as *plentiful as* the dust of the earth, so that if anyone can count the dust of the earth, then your descendants could also be counted. ¹⁷Arise, ^walk about in the land through its length and width; for I will give it to you." ¹⁸Then Abram moved his tent and came and lived by the ^oaks of Mamre, which are in Hebron; and there he built an altar to the LORD.

WAR OF THE KINGS

14 And it came about in the days of Amraphel king of ^Shinar, Arioch king of Ellasar, Chedorlaomer king of Elam, and Tidal king of Goiim, ²*that* they made war with Bera king of Sodom, and with Birsha king of Gomorrah, Shinab king of ^Admah, and Shemeber king of ᴮZeboiim, and the king of Bela (that is, Zoar). ³All these *kings* came as allies to the Valley of Siddim (that is, ^the Salt Sea). ⁴For twelve years they had served Chedorlaomer, but

13:1^Gen 12:9   13:2^Gen 24:35   13:3^Gen 12:8
13:4^Gen 12:7, 8   13:5^Gen 12:5   13:6^Gen 36:7
13:7^Gen 26:20   13:8^Prov 15:18; 20:3
13:10^Deut 34:3   ᴮGen 19:24   13:12^Gen 14:2;
19:24, 25, 29   13:13^Gen 18:20;
Ezek 16:49   13:14^Gen 28:14   13:15^Gen 12:7
13:16^Gen 16:10; 28:14   13:17^Num 13:17-24
13:18^Gen 14:13   14:1^Gen 10:10; 11:2
14:2^Gen 10:19   ᴮDeut 29:23
14:3^Num 34:12; Deut 3:17

13:1 ¹I.e., South country   13:3 ¹I.e., South country

in the thirteenth year they rebelled. ⁵And in the fourteenth year Chedorlaomer and the kings who were with him came and defeated the ^Rephaim in Ashteroth-karnaim, and the Zuzim in Ham, and the Emim in Shaveh-kiriathaim, ⁶and the ^Horites on their Mount Seir, as far as El-paran, which is by the wilderness. ⁷Then they turned back and came to En-mishpat (that is, ^Kadesh), and conquered all the country of the Amalekites, and also the Amorites, who lived in ^BHazazon-tamar. ⁸And the king of Sodom and the king of Gomorrah, the king of Admah and the king of Zeboiim, and the king of Bela (that is, Zoar) came out; and they lined up for battle against them in ^the Valley of Siddim, ⁹against Chedorlaomer king of Elam, Tidal king of Goiim, Amraphel king of Shinar, and Arioch king of Ellasar— four kings against five. ¹⁰Now the Valley of Siddim was full of tar pits; and ^the kings of Sodom and Gomorrah fled, and they fell into them. But those who survived fled to the hill country. ¹¹Then they took all the possessions of Sodom and Gomorrah and all their food supply, and departed. ¹²They also took Lot, Abram's nephew, and his possessions and departed, ^for he was living in Sodom.

¹³Then a survivor came and told Abram the Hebrew. Now he was residing by the oaks of Mamre the Amorite, brother of Eshcol and brother of Aner, and they were ^allies with Abram. ¹⁴When Abram heard that ^his relative had been taken captive, he led out his trained men, ^Bborn in his house, *numbering* 318, and went in pursuit as far as Dan. ¹⁵Then ^he divided his forces against them by night, he and his servants, and defeated them, and pursued them as far as Hobah, which is north of Damascus. ¹⁶He ^brought back all the possessions, and also brought back his relative Lot with his possessions, and also the women, and the *other* people.

GOD'S PROMISE TO ABRAM

¹⁷Then after his return from the defeat of Chedorlaomer and the kings who were with him, the king of Sodom went out to meet him at the Valley of Shaveh (that is, ^the King's Valley). ¹⁸And ^Melchizedek the king of Salem brought out bread and wine; now he was a priest of God Most High. ¹⁹And he blessed him and said,

"Blessed be Abram of God Most
  High,
  ^Possessor of heaven and
  earth;
²⁰ And blessed be God Most
  High,
  Who has handed over your
  enemies to you."

And ^he gave him a tenth of everything. ²¹Then the king of Sodom said to Abram, "Give the people to me and take the possessions for yourself." ²²But Abram said to the king of Sodom, "I have sworn to the LORD God Most High, ^Possessor of heaven and earth, ²³that ^I will not take a thread or a sandal strap or anything that is yours, so that you do not say, 'I have made Abram rich.' ²⁴I will take nothing except what the young men have eaten, and the share of the men who

14:5^Deut 3:11, 13   **14:6**^Gen 36:20; Deut 2:12, 22
14:7^Num 13:26   ^B 2 Chr 20:2   **14:8**^Gen 14:3
14:10^Gen 14:17, 21, 22   **14:12**^Gen 13:12
14:13^Gen 21:27, 32   **14:14**^Gen 14:12   ^B Gen 12:5
14:15^Judg 7:16   **14:16**^1 Sam 30:8, 18, 19
14:17^2 Sam 18:18   **14:18**^Heb 7:1-10   **14:19**^Gen 14:22
14:20^Heb 7:4   **14:22**^Ps 24:1   **14:23**^2 Kin 5:16

went with me, ^Aner, Eshcol, and Mamre; let them take their share."

ABRAM PROMISED A SON

15 After these things the word of the LORD came to Abram in a vision, saying,

"^Do not fear, Abram,
I am ^a shield to you;
Your reward shall be very
    great."

² But Abram said, "Lord GOD, what will You give me, since I am childless, and the heir of my house is Eliezer of Damascus?" ³ Abram also said, "Since You have given me no son, one who has been ^born in my house is my heir." ⁴ Then behold, the word of the LORD came to him, saying, "This man will not be your heir; ^but one who will come from your own body shall be your heir." ⁵ And He took him outside and said, "Now look toward the heavens and ^count the stars, if you are able to count them." And He said to him, "So shall your descendants be." ⁶^Then he believed in the LORD; and He credited it to him as righteousness. ⁷ And He said to him, "I am the LORD who brought you out of ^Ur of the Chaldeans, to ^give you this land to possess it." ⁸ But he said, "Lord GOD, ^how may I know that I will possess it?" ⁹ So He said to him, "Bring Me a three-year-old heifer, a three-year-old female goat, a three-year-old ram, a turtledove, and a young pigeon." ¹⁰ Then he brought all these to Him and cut them in two, and laid each half opposite the other; but he ^did not cut the birds. ¹¹ And birds of prey came down upon the carcasses, and Abram drove them away.

¹² Now when the sun was going down, ^a deep sleep fell upon Abram; and behold, terror *and* great darkness fell upon him. ¹³ Then *God* said to Abram, "Know for certain that ^your descendants will be strangers in a land that is not theirs, where ^they will be enslaved and oppressed for four hundred years. ¹⁴ But I will also judge the nation whom they will serve, and afterward they will come out ^with many possessions. ¹⁵ As for you, ^you shall go to your fathers in peace; you will be buried at a good old age. ¹⁶ Then in the fourth generation they will return here, for ^the wrongdoing of the Amorite is not yet complete."

¹⁷ Now it came about, when the sun had set, that it was very dark, and behold, a smoking oven and a flaming torch *appeared* which ^passed between these pieces. ¹⁸ On that day the LORD made a covenant with Abram, saying,

"To your descendants I have
    given this land,
From ^the river of Egypt as far
    as the great river, the river
    Euphrates:
¹⁹^the *land of the* Kenite, the Kenizzite, the Kadmonite, ²⁰ the Hittite, the Perizzite, the Rephaim, ²¹ the Amorite, the Canaanite, the Girgashite, and the Jebusite."

SARAI AND HAGAR

16 Now ^Sarai, Abram's wife, had not borne him a child, but she had ^an Egyptian slave woman whose name was Hagar. ² So Sarai said to Abram, "See now, the LORD

14:24 ^Gen 14:13   15:1 ^Gen 21:17   ^Deut 33:29
15:3 ^Gen 14:14   15:4 ^Gal 4:28   15:5 ^Gen 22:17;
Deut 1:10   15:6 ^Rom 4:3, 20-22; Gal 3:6
15:7 ^Gen 11:31   ^Gen 13:15, 17   15:8 ^Judg 6:36-40;
Luke 1:18   15:10 ^Lev 1:17   15:12 ^Gen 2:21; 28:11
15:13 ^Acts 7:6   ^Ex 1:11   15:14 ^Ex 12:32-38
15:15 ^Gen 25:8; 47:30   15:16 ^Lev 18:24-28
15:17 ^Jer 34:18, 19   15:18 ^Num 34:1-15
15:19 ^Ex 3:17; 23:28   16:1 ^Gen 11:30   ^Gen 12:16

has prevented me from bearing *children*. ^Please have relations with my slave woman; perhaps I will obtain children through her." And Abram listened to the voice of Sarai. ³And *so* after Abram had lived ^ten years in the land of Canaan, Abram's wife Sarai took Hagar the Egyptian, her slave woman, and gave her to her husband Abram as his wife. ⁴Then he had relations with Hagar, and she conceived; and when *Hagar* became aware that she had conceived, her mistress was insignificant in her sight. ⁵So Sarai said to Abram, "^May the wrong done to me be upon you! I put my slave woman into your arms, but when she saw that she had conceived, I was insignificant in her sight. May the LORD judge between you and me." ⁶But Abram said to Sarai, "Look, your slave woman is in your power; do to her what is good in your sight." So Sarai treated her harshly, and ^she fled from her presence.

⁷Now ^the angel of the LORD found her by a spring of water in the wilderness, by the spring on the way to Shur. ⁸He said, "Hagar, Sarai's slave woman, ^from where have you come, and where are you going?" And she said, "I am fleeing from the presence of my mistress Sarai." ⁹So the angel of the LORD said to her, "Return to your mistress, and submit to her authority." ¹⁰The ^angel of the LORD also said to her, "^I will greatly multiply your descendants so that they will be too many to count." ¹¹The angel of the LORD said to her further,

"Behold, you are pregnant,
    And you will give birth to a
        son;
    And you shall name him
        ¹Ishmael,

Because ^the LORD has heard
    your affliction.
¹² "But he will be a wild donkey of
        a man;
    His hand *will be* against
        everyone,
    And everyone's hand *will be*
        against him;
    And he will live ^in defiance of
        all his brothers."

¹³Then she called the name of the LORD who spoke to her, "You are a God who sees me"; for she said, "^Have I even seen *Him* here *and lived* after He saw me?" ¹⁴Therefore the well was called ¹Beer-lahai-roi; behold, it is between ^Kadesh and Bered.

¹⁵So Hagar bore a son to Abram; and Abram named his son, to whom Hagar gave birth, Ishmael. ¹⁶Abram was ^eighty-six years old when Hagar bore Ishmael to him.

ABRAHAM AND THE COVENANT OF CIRCUMCISION

17 Now when Abram was ninety-nine years old, the LORD appeared to Abram and said to him,

"I am God ^Almighty;
    Walk before Me, and be
        ^blameless.
² "I will make My ^covenant
        between Me and you,
    And I will multiply you
        exceedingly."

³Abram ^fell on his face, and God talked with him, saying,

16:2 ^Gen 30:3, 4, 9, 10   16:3 ^Gen 12:4
16:5 ^Jer 51:35   16:6 ^Gen 16:9   16:7 ^Gen 21:17, 18;
22:11, 15   16:8 ^Gen 3:9; 1 Kin 19:9, 13
16:10 ^Gen 22:15-18   ᴮGen 17:20   16:11 ^Ex 2:23, 24;
3:7, 9   16:12 ^Gen 25:18   16:13 ^Gen 32:30; Ps
139:1-12   16:14 ^Gen 14:7   16:16 ^Gen 12:4; 16:3
17:1 ^Gen 28:3   ᴮGen 6:9   17:2 ^Gen 15:18
17:3 ^Gen 17:17; 18:2

16:11 ¹I.e., God hears   16:14 ¹I.e., the well of the living one who sees me

⁴ "As for Me, behold, My
    covenant is with you,
And you will be the father of a
    ^multitude of nations.
⁵ "No longer shall you be named
    ¹Abram,
But your name shall be
    ²Abraham;
For ^I have made you the father
    of a multitude of nations.
⁶I will make you exceedingly fruitful, and I will make nations of you, and ^kings will come from you. ⁷I will establish My covenant between Me and you and your descendants after you throughout their generations as an ^everlasting covenant, ^Bto be God to you and to your descendants after you. ⁸And ^I will give to you and to your descendants after you the land where you live as a stranger, all the land of Canaan, as an everlasting possession; and I will be their God."

⁹God said further to Abraham, "Now as for you, ^you shall keep My covenant, you and your descendants after you throughout their generations. ¹⁰^This is My covenant, which you shall keep, between Me and you and your descendants after you: every male among you shall be circumcised. ¹¹And ^you shall be circumcised in the flesh of your foreskin, and it shall be the sign of the covenant between Me and you. ¹²And every male among you who is ^eight days old shall be circumcised throughout your generations, *including* a slave who is born in the house or who is bought with money from any foreigner, who is not of your descendants. ¹³A slave who is born in your house or ^who is bought with your money shall certainly be circumcised; so My covenant shall

be in your flesh as an everlasting covenant. ¹⁴But *as for* an uncircumcised male, one who is not circumcised in the flesh of his foreskin, that person shall be ^cut off from his people; he has broken My covenant."

¹⁵Then God said to Abraham, "As for your wife Sarai, you shall not call her *by* the name ¹Sarai, but ²Sarah *shall be* her name. ¹⁶I will bless her, and indeed I will give you ^a son by her. Then I will bless her, and she shall be *a mother of* nations; kings of peoples will come from her." ¹⁷Then Abraham fell on his face and laughed, and said in his heart, "Will a child be born to a man a hundred years old? And ^will Sarah, who is ninety years old, give birth *to a child?*" ¹⁸And Abraham said to God, "Oh that Ishmael might live before You!" ¹⁹But God said, "No, but your wife Sarah will bear you a son, and you shall name him ¹Isaac; and ^I will establish My covenant with him as an everlasting covenant for his descendants after him. ²⁰As for Ishmael, I have heard you; behold, I will bless him, and ^make him fruitful and multiply him exceedingly. ^BHe shall father twelve princes, and I will make him into a great nation. ²¹But I will establish My covenant with Isaac, whom ^Sarah will bear to you at this season next year." ²²When He finished talking with him, ^God went up from Abraham.

17:4^Gen 35:11; 48:19   17:5^Rom 4:17   17:6^Gen 17:16; 35:11   17:7^Gen 17:13, 19   ^BGen 26:24   17:8^Gen 12:7; 13:15, 17   17:9^Ex 19:5   17:10^John 7:22; Acts 7:8
17:11^Ex 12:48; Deut 10:16   17:12^Lev 12:3
17:13^Ex 12:44   17:14^Ex 4:24-26   17:16^Gen 18:10
17:17^Gen 21:7   17:19^Gen 26:2-5   17:20^Gen 16:10
^BGen 25:12-16   17:21^Gen 21:2   17:22^Gen 18:33; 35:13

17:5 ¹I.e., exalted father   ²I.e., father of a multitude
17:15 ¹I.e., princess   ²I.e., princess (in another dialect)   17:19 ¹I.e., he laughs

²³Then Abraham took his son Ishmael, and all *the slaves* who were ^born in his house and all who were bought with his money, every male among the men of Abraham's household, and circumcised the flesh of their foreskin on this very same day, ᴮas God had said to him. ²⁴Now Abraham was ninety-nine years old when ^he was circumcised in the flesh of his foreskin. ²⁵And his son ^Ishmael was thirteen years old when he was circumcised in the flesh of his foreskin. ²⁶On this very same day Abraham was circumcised, as well as his son Ishmael. ²⁷And all the men of his household, those who were ^born in the house or bought with money from a foreigner, were circumcised with him.

BIRTH OF ISAAC PROMISED

18 Now the Lᴏʀᴅ appeared to Abraham by the ^oaks of Mamre, while he was sitting at the tent door in the heat of the day. ²When he raised his eyes and looked, behold, three ^men were standing opposite him; and when he saw *them*, he ran from the tent door to meet them and bowed down to the ground, ³and said, "My Lord, if now I have found favor in Your sight, please do not pass Your servant by. ⁴Please let a little water be brought and ^wash ¹your feet, and make yourselves comfortable under the tree; ⁵and I will ^bring a piece of bread, so that you may refresh yourselves; after that you may go on, since you have visited your servant." And they said, "So do as you have said." ⁶So Abraham hurried into the tent to Sarah, and said, "Quickly, prepare three measures of fine flour, knead *it*, and

make bread cakes." ⁷Abraham also ran to the herd, and took a tender and choice calf and gave *it* to the servant, and he hurried to prepare it. ⁸He took curds and milk and the calf which he had prepared, and set *it* before them; and he was standing by them under the tree as they ate.

⁹Then they said to him, "Where is your wife Sarah?" And he said, "There, in the tent." ¹⁰He said, "^I will certainly return to you at this time next year; and behold, your wife Sarah will have a son." And Sarah was listening at the tent door, which was behind him. ¹¹Now ^Abraham and Sarah were old, advanced in age; Sarah was past childbearing. ¹²So Sarah laughed to herself, saying, "^After I have become old, am I to have pleasure, my lord being old also?" ¹³But the Lᴏʀᴅ said to Abraham, "Why did Sarah laugh, saying, 'Shall I actually give birth *to a child*, when I am *so* old?' ¹⁴^Is anything too difficult for the Lᴏʀᴅ? At the appointed time I will return to you, at this time next year, and Sarah will have a son." ¹⁵Sarah denied *it*, however, saying, "I did not laugh"; for she was afraid. And He said, "No, but you did laugh."

¹⁶Then ^the men rose up from there, and looked down toward Sodom; and Abraham was walking with them to send them off. ¹⁷The Lᴏʀᴅ said, "Shall I hide from Abraham ^what I am about to do, ¹⁸since Abraham will certainly become a

17:23 ^Gen 14:14　ᴮGen 17:9-11　17:24 ^Rom 4:11
17:25 ^Gen 16:16　17:27 ^Gen 14:14　18:1 ^Gen 13:18;
14:13　18:2 ^Gen 18:16, 22; 32:24　18:4 ^Gen 19:2;
24:32　18:5 ^Judg 6:18, 19; 13:15, 16　18:10 ^Gen 21:2;
Rom 9:9　18:11 ^Gen 17:17; Rom 4:19　18:12 ^Luke 1:18
18:14 ^Jer 32:17, 27; Zech 8:6　18:16 ^Gen 18:2, 22; 19:1
18:17 ^Gen 18:21; 19:24
―――――――――――――――――
18:4 ¹ I.e., referring to the three visitors

great and mighty nation, and in him ^all the nations of the earth will be blessed? ¹⁹For I have ^chosen him, so that he may command his children and his household after him to keep the way of the LORD by doing righteousness and justice, so that the LORD may bring upon Abraham what He has spoken about him." ²⁰And the LORD said, "^The outcry of Sodom and Gomorrah is indeed great, and their sin is exceedingly grave. ²¹I will ^go down now and see whether they have done entirely as the outcry, which has come to Me *indicates;* and if not, I will know."

ABRAHAM APPEALS FOR SODOM

²²Then ^the men turned away from there and went toward Sodom, while Abraham was still standing before the LORD. ²³Abraham approached and said, "^Will You indeed sweep away the righteous with the wicked? ²⁴Suppose there are fifty righteous people within the city; will You indeed sweep *it* away and not spare the place for the sake of the fifty righteous who are in it? ²⁵Far be it from You to do such a thing, to kill the righteous with the wicked, so that the righteous and the wicked are *treated* alike. Far be it from You! Shall not ^the Judge of all the earth deal justly?" ²⁶So the LORD said, "^If I find in Sodom fifty righteous within the city, then I will spare the entire place on their account." ²⁷And Abraham replied, "Now behold, I have ventured to speak to the Lord, although I am *only*^dust and ashes. ²⁸Suppose the fifty righteous are lacking five, will You destroy the entire city because of five?" And He said, "I will not destroy *it* if I find forty-five there." ²⁹And he spoke to

Him yet again and said, "Suppose forty are found there?" And He said, "I will not do *it* on account of the forty." ³⁰Then he said, "Oh may the Lord not be angry, and I shall speak; suppose thirty are found there?" And He said, "I will not do *it* if I find thirty there." ³¹And he said, "Now behold, I have ventured to speak to the Lord; suppose twenty are found there?" And He said, "I will not destroy *it* on account of the twenty." ³²Then he said, "^Oh may the Lord not be angry, and I shall speak only this once: suppose ten are found there?" And He said, "I will not destroy *it* on account of the ten." ³³As soon as He had finished speaking to Abraham ^the LORD departed, and Abraham returned to his place.

THE DOOM OF SODOM

19 Now the ^two angels came to Sodom in the evening as Lot was sitting at the gate of Sodom. When ^BLot saw *them,* he stood up to meet them and bowed down *with his* face to the ground. ²And he said, "Now behold, my lords, please turn aside into your servant's house, and spend the night, and wash your feet; then you may rise early and go on your way." They said, "No, but we shall spend the night in the public square." ³Yet he strongly urged them, so they turned aside to him and entered his house; ^and he prepared a feast for them and baked unleavened bread, and they ate. ⁴Before they lay down, ^the men

18:18^Gen 12:3; Acts 3:25   **18:19**^Neh 9:7
18:20^Gen 19:13; Ezek 16:49, 50   **18:21**^Gen 11:5;
Ex 3:8   **18:22**^Gen 18:16; 19:1   **18:23**^Ex 23:7;
Num 16:22   **18:25**^Deut 1:16, 17; 32:4   **18:26**^Jer 5:1
18:27^Gen 3:19; Job 30:19   **18:32**^Judg 6:39
18:33^Gen 17:22; 35:13   **19:1**^Gen 18:2, 22
^BGen 18:2-5   **19:3**^Gen 18:6-8   **19:4**^Gen 13:13; 18:20

of the city—the men of Sodom—surrounded the house, both young and old, all the people from every quarter; [5]and they called to Lot and said to him, "[A]Where are the men who came to you tonight? Bring them out to us that we may [1]have relations with them." [6]But Lot went out to them at the doorway, and shut the door behind him, [7]and said, "Please, my brothers, do not act wickedly. [8]Now look, [A]I have two daughters who have not had relations with *any* man; please let me bring them out to you, and do to them whatever you like; only do not do anything to these men, because they have come under the shelter of my roof." [9]But they said, "Get out of the way!" They also said, "This one came in as a foreigner, and already [A]he is acting like a judge; now we will treat you worse than them!" So they pressed hard against Lot and moved forward to break the door. [10]But [A]the men reached out their hands and brought Lot into the house with them, and shut the door. [11]Then [A]they struck the men who were at the doorway of the house with blindness, from the small to the great, so that they became weary of *trying* to find the doorway.

[12]Then the *two* men said to Lot, "Whom else do you have here? A son-in-law and your sons and daughters, and whomever you have in the city, bring *them* out of the place; [13]for we are about to destroy this place, because [A]their outcry has become so great before the LORD that the LORD has sent us to destroy it." [14]So Lot went out and spoke to his sons-in-law, who were to marry his daughters, and said, "Up, [A]get out of this place, for the LORD is destroying the city." But he appeared to his sons-in-law to be joking.

[15]When morning dawned, the angels urged Lot, saying, "Up, take your wife and your two daughters who are here, or you will be swept away in the punishment of the city." [16]But he hesitated. So the men [A]grasped his hand and the hand of his wife and the hands of his two daughters, because the compassion of the LORD *was* upon him; and they brought him out and put him outside the city. [17]When they had brought them outside, one said, "[A]Escape for your life! Do not look behind you, and do not stay anywhere in the surrounding area; escape to [B]the mountains, or you will be swept away." [18]But Lot said to them, "Oh no, my lords! [19]Now behold, your servant has found favor in your sight, and you have magnified your compassion, which you have shown me by saving my life; but I cannot escape to the mountains, for the disaster will overtake me and I will die; [20]now behold, this town is near *enough* to flee to, and it is small. Please, let me escape there (is it not small?) so that my life may be saved." [21]And he said to him, "Behold, I grant you this request also, not to overthrow the town of which you have spoken. [22]Hurry, escape there, for I cannot do anything until you arrive there." Therefore the town was named [1,A]Zoar.

[23]The sun had risen over the earth when Lot came to Zoar.

19:5 [A]Lev 18:22; Judg 19:22　19:8 [A]Judg 19:24
19:9 [A]Ex 2:14　19:10 [A]Gen 19:1　19:11 [A]Deut 28:28, 29;
2 Kin 6:18　19:13 [A]Gen 18:20　19:14 [A]Num 16:21, 45;
Rev 18:4　19:16 [A]Deut 5:15; 6:21　19:17 [A]Jer 48:6
[B]Gen 14:10　19:22 [A]Gen 13:10; 14:2

19:5 [1] Lit *know them*; i.e., have intercourse
19:22 [1] I.e., small

²⁴Then the LORD ᴬrained brimstone and fire on Sodom and Gomorrah from the LORD out of heaven, ²⁵and ᴬHe overthrew those cities, and all the surrounding area, and all the inhabitants of the cities, and what grew on the ground. ²⁶But Lot's wife, from behind him, ᴬlooked *back,* and she became a pillar of salt.

²⁷Now Abraham got up early in the morning *and went* to ᴬthe place where he had stood before the LORD; ²⁸and he looked down toward Sodom and Gomorrah, and toward all the land of the surrounding area; and behold, he saw ᴬthe smoke of the land ascended like the smoke of a furnace.

²⁹So it came about, when God destroyed the cities of the surrounding area, that God remembered Abraham, and ᴬsent Lot out of the midst of the destruction, when He overthrew the cities in which Lot had lived.

LOT AND HIS DAUGHTERS

³⁰Now Lot went up from Zoar with his two daughters and ᴬstayed in the mountains, because he was afraid to stay in Zoar; and he stayed in a cave, he and his two daughters. ³¹Then the firstborn said to the younger, "Our father is old, and there is not a man on earth to ᴬhave relations with us according to the custom of all the earth. ³²Come, ᴬlet's make our father drink wine, and let's sleep with him so that we may keep our family alive through our father." ³³So they made their father drink wine that night, and the firstborn went in and slept with her father; and he did not know when she lay down or got up. ³⁴On the following day, the firstborn said

to the younger, "Look, I slept last night with my father; let's make him drink wine tonight too, then you go in and sleep with him, so that we may keep our family alive through our father." ³⁵So they had their father drink wine that night too, and the younger got up and slept with him; and he did not know when she lay down or got up. ³⁶And *so* both of the daughters of Lot conceived by their father. ³⁷The firstborn gave birth to a son, and named him ᴬMoab; he is the father of the Moabites to this day. ³⁸As for the younger, she also gave birth to a son, and named him Ben-ammi; he is the father of the sons of ᴬAmmon to this day.

ABRAHAM'S TREACHERY

20 Now Abraham journeyed from ᴬthere toward the land of the ¹Negev, and settled between Kadesh and Shur; then he lived for a time in ᴮGerar. ²And Abraham said of his wife Sarah, "ᴬShe is my sister." So Abimelech king of Gerar sent *men* and took Sarah. ³But God came to Abimelech in a dream of the night, and said to him, "Behold, ᴬyou are a dead man because of the woman whom you have taken, for she is married." ⁴Now Abimelech had not come near her; and he said, "Lord, ᴬwill You kill a nation, even *though* blameless? ⁵Did he himself not say to me, 'She is my sister'? And she ᴬherself said, 'He

19:24ᴬDeut 29:23; Ps 11:6   **19:25**ᴬDeut 29:23; Ps 107:34   **19:26**ᴬGen 19:17; Luke 17:32
19:27ᴬGen 18:22   **19:28**ᴬRev 9:2; 18:9
19:29ᴬ2 Pet 2:7   **19:30**ᴬGen 19:17, 19
19:31ᴬGen 16:2, 4; 38:8   **19:32**ᴬLuke 21:34
19:37ᴬDeut 2:9   **19:38**ᴬDeut 2:19   **20:1**ᴬGen 18:1
ᴮGen 26:1, 6   **20:2**ᴬGen 12:11-13; 20:12
20:3ᴬGen 20:7   **20:4**ᴬGen 18:23-25   **20:5**ᴬGen 20:13

20:1¹I.e., South country

is my brother.' In the integrity of my heart and the innocence of my hands I have done this." ⁶Then God said to him in the dream, "Yes, I know that in the integrity of your heart you have done this, and I also ᴬkept you from sinning against Me; therefore I did not let you touch her. ⁷Now then, return the man's wife, for ᴬhe is a prophet, and he will pray for you and you will live. But if you do not return *her,* know that you will certainly die, you and all who are yours."

⁸So Abimelech got up early in the morning and called all his servants, and told all these things in their presence; and the people were greatly frightened. ⁹ᴬThen Abimelech called Abraham and said to him, "What have you done to us? And how have I sinned against you, that you have brought on me and on my kingdom a great sin? You have done to me things that ought not to be done." ¹⁰And Abimelech said to Abraham, "What have you encountered, that you have done this thing?" ¹¹Abraham said, "Because I thought, surely there is no ᴬfear of God in this place, and ᴮthey will kill me because of my wife. ¹²Besides, she actually is my sister, the daughter of my father, but not the daughter of my mother; and she became my wife; ¹³and it came about, when ᴬGod caused me to wander from my father's house, that I said to her, 'This is the kindness which you will show to me: everywhere we go, say of me, "He is my brother."'" ¹⁴ᴬAbimelech then took sheep and oxen and male and female servants, and gave them to Abraham, and returned his wife Sarah to him. ¹⁵Abimelech said, "ᴬBehold, my land is before you;

settle wherever you please." ¹⁶To Sarah he said, "Look, I have given your ᴬbrother a thousand pieces of silver. It is your vindication before all who are with you, and before everyone you are cleared." ¹⁷Then ᴬAbraham prayed to God, and God healed Abimelech and his wife and his female slaves, so that they gave birth *to children.* ¹⁸ᴬFor the LORD had completely closed all the wombs of the household of Abimelech because of Sarah, Abraham's wife.

ISAAC IS BORN

21 ᴬThen the LORD took note of Sarah as He had said, and the LORD did for Sarah as He had promised. ²ᴬSo Sarah conceived and bore a son to Abraham in his old age, at the appointed time of which God had spoken to him. ³Abraham named his son who was born to him, the son whom Sarah bore to him, ᴬIsaac. ⁴Then Abraham circumcised his son Isaac when he was ᴬeight days old, as God had commanded him. ⁵Now Abraham was ᴬa hundred years old when his son Isaac was born to him. ⁶Sarah said, "God has made ᴬlaughter for me; everyone who hears will laugh with me." ⁷And she said, "ᴬWho would have said to Abraham that Sarah would nurse children? Yet I have given birth to a son in his old age."

⁸And the child grew and was weaned, and Abraham held a great feast on the day that Isaac was weaned.

20:6ᴬ1 Sam 25:26, 34   **20:7**ᴬ1 Sam 7:5; 2 Kin 5:11
20:9ᴬGen 12:18   **20:11**ᴬNeh 5:15   ᴮGen 12:12
20:13ᴬGen 12:1–9   **20:14**ᴬGen 12:16   **20:15**ᴬGen 13:9;
34:10   **20:16**ᴬGen 20:5   **20:17**ᴬNum 12:13;
James 5:16   **20:18**ᴬGen 12:17   **21:1**ᴬGen 17:16, 21;
18:10, 14   **21:2**ᴬActs 7:8; Gal 4:22   **21:3**ᴬGen 17:19, 21
21:4ᴬGen 17:12; Acts 7:8   **21:5**ᴬGen 17:17
21:6ᴬGen 18:13; Ps 126:2   **21:7**ᴬGen 18:11, 13

SARAH TURNS AGAINST HAGAR

⁹Now Sarah saw ᴬthe son of Hagar the Egyptian, whom she had borne to Abraham, ᴮmocking *Isaac.* ¹⁰Therefore she said to Abraham, "ᴬDrive out this slave woman and her son, for the son of this slave woman shall not be an heir with my son Isaac!" ¹¹ᴬThe matter distressed Abraham greatly because of his son *Ishmael.* ¹²But God said to Abraham, "Do not be distressed because of the boy and your slave woman; whatever Sarah tells you, listen to her, for ᴬthrough Isaac your descendants shall be named. ¹³And of ᴬthe son of the slave woman I will make a nation also, because he is your descendant." ¹⁴So Abraham got up early in the morning and took bread and a skin of water, and gave *them* to Hagar, putting *them* on her shoulder, and *gave her* the boy, and sent her away. And she departed and wandered about in the wilderness of Beersheba.

¹⁵When the water in the skin was used up, she left the boy under one of the bushes. ¹⁶Then she went and sat down opposite him, about a bowshot away, for she said, "May I not see the boy die!" And she sat opposite him, and ᴬraised her voice and wept. ¹⁷God ᴬheard the boy crying; and the angel of God called to Hagar from heaven and said to her, "What is the matter with you, Hagar? Do not fear, for God has heard the voice of the boy where he is. ¹⁸Get up, lift up the boy, and hold him by the hand, ᴬfor I will make a great nation of him." ¹⁹Then God ᴬopened her eyes, and she saw a well of water; and she went and filled the skin with water and gave the boy a drink.

²⁰And ᴬGod was with the boy, and he grew; and he lived in the wilderness and became an archer. ²¹ᴬHe lived in the wilderness of Paran, and his mother took a wife for him from the land of Egypt.

COVENANT WITH ABIMELECH

²²Now it came about at that time that Abimelech and Phicol, the commander of his army, spoke to Abraham, saying, "ᴬGod is with you in all that you do; ²³so now, ᴬswear to me here by God that you will not deal falsely with me or with my offspring or with my descendants, but according to the kindness that I have shown to you, you shall show to me and to the land in which you have resided." ²⁴Abraham said, "I swear it." ²⁵But Abraham complained to Abimelech because of the well of water which the servants of Abimelech ᴬhad seized. ²⁶And Abimelech said, "I do not know who has done this thing; you did not tell me, nor did I hear of it until today."

²⁷So Abraham took sheep and oxen and gave them to Abimelech, and ᴬthe two of them made a covenant. ²⁸But Abraham set seven ewe lambs of the flock by themselves. ²⁹Then Abimelech said to Abraham, "What do these seven ewe lambs mean, which you have set by themselves?" ³⁰He said, "You shall take these seven ewe lambs from my hand so that it may be a ᴬwitness for me, that I dug this well." ³¹Therefore he called that place ᴬBeersheba,

21:9 ᴬGen 16:1, 4, 15   ᴮGal 4:29   21:10 ᴬGal 4:30
21:11 ᴬGen 17:18   21:12 ᴬRom 9:7; Heb 11:18
21:13 ᴬGen 16:10; 21:18   21:16 ᴬJer 6:26; Amos 8:10
21:17 ᴬEx 3:7; Deut 26:7   21:18 ᴬGen 16:10; 21:13
21:19 ᴬNum 22:31; 2 Kin 6:17   21:20 ᴬGen 28:15;
39:2, 3, 21   21:21 ᴬGen 25:18   21:22 ᴬGen 26:28;
Is 8:10   21:23 ᴬJosh 2:12; 1 Sam 24:21
21:25 ᴬGen 26:15, 18, 20–22   21:27 ᴬGen 26:31
21:30 ᴬGen 31:48   21:31 ᴬGen 21:14; 26:33

because there the two of them took an oath. ³²So they made a covenant at Beersheba; and Abimelech and Phicol, the commander of his army, got up and returned to the land of the Philistines. ³³ *Abraham* planted a tamarisk tree at Beersheba, and there ^Ahe called on the name of the LORD, the Everlasting God. ³⁴And Abraham resided ^Ain the land of the Philistines for many days.

THE OFFERING OF ISAAC

22 Now it came about after these things, that ^AGod tested Abraham, and said to him, "Abraham!" And he said, "Here I am." ²Then He said, "Take now ^Ayour son, your only son, whom you love, Isaac, and go to the land of ^BMoriah, and offer him there as a burnt offering on one of the mountains of which I will tell you." ³So Abraham got up early in the morning and saddled his donkey, and took two of his young men with him and his son Isaac; and he split wood for the burnt offering, and set out and went to the place of which God had told him. ⁴On the third day Abraham raised his eyes and saw the place from a distance. ⁵Then Abraham said to his young men, "Stay here with the donkey, and I and the boy will go over there; and we will worship and return to you." ⁶And Abraham took the wood for the burnt offering and ^Alaid it on his son Isaac, and he took in his hand the fire and the knife. So the two of them walked on together. ⁷Isaac spoke to his father Abraham and said, "My father!" And he said, "Here I am, my son." And he said, "Look, the fire and the wood, but where is the ^Alamb for the burnt offering?" ⁸Abraham said, "God will

provide for Himself the lamb for the burnt offering, my son." So the two of them walked on together.

⁹Then they came to ^Athe place of which God had told him; and Abraham built the altar there and arranged the wood, and bound his son Isaac and ^Blaid him on the altar, on top of the wood. ¹⁰And Abraham reached out with his hand and took the knife to slaughter his son. ¹¹But ^Athe angel of the LORD called to him from heaven and said, "Abraham, Abraham!" And he said, "Here I am." ¹²He said, "Do not reach out your hand against the boy, and do not do anything to him; for now I know that you fear God, since you have not withheld ^Ayour son, your only son, from Me." ¹³Then Abraham raised his eyes and looked, and behold, behind *him was* a ram caught in the thicket by its horns; and Abraham went and took the ram and offered it up as a burnt offering in the place of his son. ¹⁴And Abraham named that place The LORD Will Provide, as it is said to this day, "On the mountain of the LORD ^Ait will be provided."

¹⁵Then the angel of the LORD called to Abraham a second time from heaven, ¹⁶and said, "^ABy Myself I have sworn, declares the LORD, because you have done this thing and have not withheld your son, your only son, ¹⁷indeed I will greatly bless you, and I will greatly ^Amultiply your ¹seed as the stars of the heavens and as the sand, which is on the seashore; and your

21:33 ^AGen 12:8   21:34 ^AGen 22:19   22:1 ^ADeut 8:2, 16; Heb 11:17   22:2 ^AGen 22:12, 16   ^B2 Chr 3:1
22:6 ^AJohn 19:17   22:7 ^AEx 29:38-42; John 1:29, 36
22:9 ^AGen 22:2   ^BHeb 11:17-19   22:11 ^AGen 16:7-11; 21:17, 18   22:12 ^AGen 22:2, 16   22:14 ^AGen 22:8
22:16 ^APs 105:9; Luke 1:73   22:17 ^AJer 33:22; Heb 11:12

22:17 ¹Or *descendants*

¹seed shall possess the gate of their enemies. ¹⁸And ^in your ¹seed all the nations of the earth shall be blessed, because you have ᴮobeyed My voice." ¹⁹^So Abraham returned to his young men, and they got up and went together to Beersheba; and Abraham lived in Beersheba.

²⁰Now it came about after these things, that Abraham was told, saying, "Behold, ^Milcah also has borne children to your brother Nahor: ²¹Uz his firstborn, Buz his brother, Kemuel (the father of Aram), ²²Chesed, Hazo, Pildash, Jidlaph, and Bethuel"— ²³and *it was* Bethuel *who* fathered ^Rebekah. These eight Milcah bore to Nahor, Abraham's brother. ²⁴His concubine, whose name was Reumah, also gave birth to Tebah, Gaham, Tahash, and Maacah.

DEATH AND BURIAL OF SARAH

23 Now Sarah lived 127 years; *these were* the years of the life of Sarah. ²Sarah died in ^Kiriath-arba (that is, Hebron) in the land of Canaan; and Abraham came in to mourn for Sarah and to weep for her. ³Then Abraham arose from *mourning* before his dead, and spoke to the ^sons of Heth, saying, ⁴"I am a stranger and a foreign resident among you; ^give me a ᴮburial site among you so that I may bury my dead out of my sight." ⁵The sons of Heth answered Abraham, saying to him, ⁶"Hear us, my lord: you are a ^mighty prince among us; bury your dead in the choicest of our graves; none of us will refuse you his grave for burying your dead." ⁷So Abraham stood up and bowed to the people of the land, the sons of Heth. ⁸And he spoke with them, saying, "If you are willing to *let me*

bury my dead out of my sight, listen to me, and plead with ^Ephron the son of Zohar for me, ⁹that he may give me the cave of Machpelah which he owns, which is at the end of his field; for the full price let him give it to me in your presence for a burial site." ¹⁰Now Ephron was sitting among the sons of Heth; and Ephron the Hittite answered Abraham so that the sons of Heth heard, ^that is, all who entered the gate of his city, saying, ¹¹"No, my lord, listen to me; ^I give you the field, and I give you the cave that is in it. In the presence of the sons of my people I give it to you; bury your dead." ¹²And Abraham bowed before the people of the land. ¹³But he spoke to Ephron so that the people of the land heard, saying, "If you will only please listen to me; I will give the price of the field, accept *it* from me so that I may bury my dead there." ¹⁴Then Ephron answered Abraham, saying to him, ¹⁵"My lord, listen to me: *a plot of* land worth ¹four hundred ^shekels of silver—what is that between me and you? So bury your dead." ¹⁶Abraham listened to Ephron; and Abraham ^weighed out for Ephron the silver which he had named in the presence of the sons of Heth, four hundred shekels of silver, *currency* acceptable to a merchant.

¹⁷So ^Ephron's field, which was in Machpelah, which faced Mamre, the field and the cave which was in it, and all the trees which were in the

22:18^Gen 12:3   ᴮGen 18:19   22:19^Gen 22:5
22:20^Gen 11:29   22:23^Gen 24:15   23:2^Josh 14:15;
15:13   23:3^Gen 10:15; 15:20   23:4^Acts 7:16
ᴮGen 49:30   23:6^Gen 14:14; 20:7   23:8^Gen 25:9
23:10^Gen 23:18; Ruth 4:1, 11   23:11^2 Sam 24:21-24
23:15^Ex 30:13; Ezek 45:12   23:16^2 Sam 14:26;
Jer 32:9, 10   23:17^Gen 25:9; 49:29, 30

22:18 ¹Or *descendants*   23:15 ¹About 12.5 lb. or 5.7 kg

field, that were within all the confines of its border, were deeded over [18]to Abraham as a possession ^in the presence of the sons of Heth, before all who entered the gate of his city. [19]After this, Abraham buried his wife Sarah in the cave of the field of Machpelah facing Mamre (that is, Hebron), in the land of Canaan. [20]So the field and the cave that was in it were ^deeded over to Abraham for a burial site by the sons of Heth.

A BRIDE FOR ISAAC

24 Now ^Abraham was old, advanced in age; and the LORD had blessed Abraham in every way. [2]Abraham said to his servant, the oldest of his household who was in ^charge of all that he owned, "[B]Please place your hand under my thigh, [3]and I will make you swear by the LORD, the God of heaven and the God of earth, that you ^shall not take a wife for my son from the daughters of [B]the Canaanites, among whom I live; [4]but you will go to ^my country and to my relatives, and take a wife for my son Isaac." [5]The servant said to him, "Suppose the woman is not willing to follow me to this land; should I take your son back to the land from where you came?" [6]Then Abraham said to him, "^Beware that you do not take my son back there! [7]The LORD, the God of heaven, who took me from my father's house and from the land of my birth, and who spoke to me and who swore to me, saying, 'To your descendants I will give this land'—He will send ^His angel ahead of you, and you will take a wife for my son from there. [8]But if the woman is not willing to follow you, then you will ^be free of this oath of mine; [B]only do not take

my son back there." [9]So the servant ^placed his hand under the thigh of his master Abraham, and swore to him concerning this matter.

[10]Then the servant took ten camels from the camels of his master, and went out with a variety of ^good things of his master's in his hand; so he set out and went to Mesopotamia, to [B]the city of Nahor. [11]He made the camels kneel down outside the city by ^the well of water when it was evening, the time when women go out to draw water. [12]And he said, "^LORD, God of my master Abraham, please grant me success today, and show kindness to my master Abraham. [13]Behold, ^I am standing by the spring, and the daughters of the men of the city are coming out to draw water; [14]now may it be that the young woman to whom I say, 'Please let down your jar so that I may drink,' and who answers, 'Drink, and I will water your camels also'— *may* she *be the one* whom You have appointed for Your servant Isaac; and by this I will know that You have shown kindness to my master."

REBEKAH IS CHOSEN

[15]And it came about, before he had finished speaking, that behold, ^Rebekah, who was born to Bethuel the son of [B]Milcah, the wife of Abraham's brother Nahor, came out with her jar on her shoulder. [16]The young woman was ^very beautiful, a virgin; no man had had relations with her. She went down to

23:18^Gen 23:10   23:20^Jer 32:10-14
24:1^Gen 18:11   24:2^Gen 39:4-6   [B]Gen 24:9
24:3^Deut 7:3   [B]Gen 10:15-19   24:4^Gen 12:1;
Heb 11:15   24:6^Gen 24:8   24:7^Ex 23:20, 23
24:8^Josh 2:17-20   [B]Gen 24:6   24:9^Gen 24:2
24:10^Gen 24:22, 53   [B]Gen 11:31, 32
24:11^Gen 24:42   24:12^Gen 24:27, 42, 48; 26:24
24:13^Gen 24:43   24:15^Gen 22:20, 23   [B]Gen 11:29
24:16^Gen 12:11; 26:7

the spring, filled her jar, and came up. [17]Then the servant ran to meet her, and said, "[A]Please let me drink a little water from your jar." [18]And [A]she said, "Drink, my lord"; then she quickly lowered her jar to her hand, and gave him a drink. [19]Now when she had finished giving him a drink, [A]she said, "I will also draw *water* for your camels until they have finished drinking." [20]So she quickly emptied her jar into the trough, and ran back to the well to draw, and she drew for all his camels. [21][A]Meanwhile, the man was taking a close look at her in silence, to find out whether the LORD had made his journey successful or not.

[22]When the camels had finished drinking, the man took a [A]gold ring weighing a [1]half-shekel, and two bracelets for her wrists weighing ten shekels in gold, [23]and he said, "Whose daughter are you? Please tell me, is there room for us to stay overnight at your father's house?" [24]She said to him, "[A]I am the daughter of Bethuel, Milcah's son, whom she bore to Nahor." [25]Again she said to him, "We have plenty of both straw and feed, and room to stay overnight." [26]Then the man [A]bowed low and worshiped the LORD. [27]And he said, "Blessed be the LORD, the God of my master Abraham, who has not abandoned [A]His kindness and His trustworthiness toward my master; as for me, the LORD has guided me in the way to the house of my master's brothers."

[28]Then [A]the young woman ran and told her mother's household about these things. [29]Now Rebekah had a brother whose name was [A]Laban; and Laban ran outside to the man at the spring. [30]When he saw the ring and the bracelets on his sister's wrists, and when he heard the words of his sister Rebekah, saying, "This is what the man said to me," he went to the man; and behold, he was standing by the camels at the spring. [31]And he said, "[A]Come in, blessed of the LORD! Why do you stand outside, since I have prepared the house, and a place for the camels?" [32]So the man entered the house. Then [A]Laban unloaded the camels, and he gave straw and feed to the camels, and water to wash his feet and the feet of the men who were with him. [33]But when *food* was set before him to eat, he said, "I will not eat until I have stated my business." And he said, "Speak on." [34]So he said, "I am [A]Abraham's servant. [35]The LORD has greatly [A]blessed my master, so that he has become rich; and He has given him [B]flocks and herds, and silver and gold, and servants and slave women, and camels and donkeys. [36]Now [A]my master's wife Sarah bore a son to my master in her old age, and he has given him all that he has. [37][A]My master made me swear, saying, 'You shall not take a wife for my son from the daughters of the Canaanites, in whose land I live; [38]but you shall go to my father's house and to my relatives, and take a wife for my son.' [39]Then [A]I said to my master, 'Suppose the woman does not follow me.' [40]And he said to me, '[A]The LORD, before

24:17[A]John 4:7   24:18[A]Gen 24:14, 46
24:19[A]Gen 24:14   24:21[A]Gen 24:12-14, 27, 52
24:22[A]Gen 24:47; Ex 32:2, 3   24:24[A]Gen 24:15
24:26[A]Gen 24:48, 52; Ex 4:31   24:27[A]Gen 32:10;
Ps 98:3   24:28[A]Gen 29:12   24:29[A]Gen 29:5, 13
24:31[A]Gen 29:13   24:32[A]Gen 43:24; Judg 19:21
24:34[A]Gen 24:2   24:35[A]Gen 24:1   [B]Gen 13:2
24:36[A]Gen 21:1-7   24:37[A]Gen 24:2-4
24:39[A]Gen 24:5   24:40[A]Gen 24:7

24:22 [1]A shekel was about 0.4 oz. or 11 gm

whom I have walked, will send His angel with you to make your journey successful, and you will take a wife for my son from my relatives and from my father's house; ⁴¹ᴬthen you will be free from my oath, when you come to my relatives; and if they do not give her to you, you will be free from my oath.'

⁴² "So ᴬI came today to the spring, and said, 'Lᴏʀᴅ, God of my master Abraham, if now You will make my journey on which I have been going successful; ⁴³behold, ᴬI am standing by the spring, and may it be that the young unmarried woman who comes out to draw *water,* and to whom I say, "Please let me drink a little water from your jar"; ⁴⁴and she says to me, "You drink, and I will draw for your camels also"— let her be the woman whom the Lᴏʀᴅ has appointed for my master's son.'

⁴⁵ "Before I had finished ᴬspeaking in my heart, behold, Rebekah came out with her jar on her shoulder, and went down to the spring and drew *water,* and I said to her, 'Please let me drink.' ⁴⁶She quickly lowered her jar from her *shoulder,* and said, 'ᴬDrink, and I will water your camels also'; so I drank, and she watered the camels also. ⁴⁷ᴬThen I asked her, and said, 'Whose daughter are you?' And she said, 'The daughter of Bethuel, Nahor's son, whom Milcah bore to him'; and I put the ring on her nose, and the bracelets on her wrists. ⁴⁸And I bowed low and worshiped the Lᴏʀᴅ, and blessed the Lᴏʀᴅ, the God of my master Abraham, ᴬwho had guided me in the right way to take the daughter of my master's brother for his son. ⁴⁹So now if you are going to

ᴬdeal kindly and truthfully with my master, tell me; and if not, tell me now, so that I may turn to the right or the left."

⁵⁰Then Laban and Bethuel replied, "The matter has come from the Lᴏʀᴅ; ᴬ*so* we cannot speak to you bad or good. ⁵¹Here is Rebekah before you, take *her* and go, and let her be the wife of your master's son, as the Lᴏʀᴅ has spoken."

⁵²When Abraham's servant heard their words, he ᴬbowed himself to the ground before the Lᴏʀᴅ. ⁵³And the servant brought out ᴬarticles of silver and articles of gold, and garments, and gave them to Rebekah; he also gave precious things to her brother and to her mother. ⁵⁴Then he and the men who were with him ate and drank and spent the night. When they got up in the morning, he said, "ᴬSend me away to my master." ⁵⁵But her brother and her mother said, "ᴬLet the young woman stay with us *a few* days, say ten; afterward she may go." ⁵⁶However, he said to them, "Do not delay me, since ᴬthe Lᴏʀᴅ has prospered my way. Send me away so that I may go to my master." ⁵⁷And they said, "We will call the young woman and ask her." ⁵⁸Then they called Rebekah and said to her, "Will you go with this man?" And she said, "I will go." ⁵⁹So they sent away their sister Rebekah and ᴬher nurse with Abraham's servant and his men. ⁶⁰And they blessed Rebekah and said to her,

"May you, our sister,

24:41 ᴬGen 24:8   24:42 ᴬGen 24:11, 12
24:43 ᴬGen 24:13   24:45 ᴬ1 Sam 1:13
24:46 ᴬGen 24:18, 19   24:47 ᴬGen 24:23, 24
24:48 ᴬGen 24:27; Ps 32:8   24:49 ᴬGen 47:29; Josh 2:14
24:50 ᴬGen 31:24, 29   24:52 ᴬGen 24:26, 48
24:53 ᴬGen 24:10, 22; Ex 3:22   24:54 ᴬGen 24:56, 59;
30:25   24:55 ᴬJudg 19:4   24:56 ᴬGen 24:40
24:59 ᴬGen 35:8

^Become thousands of ten
thousands,
And may ^B^your descendants
possess
The gate of those who hate
them."

61 Then Rebekah got up with her female attendants, and they mounted the camels and followed the man. So the servant took Rebekah and departed.

ISAAC MARRIES REBEKAH

62 Now Isaac had come *back* from a journey to ^Beer-lahai-roi; for he was living in the Negev. 63 Isaac went out ^to meditate in the field toward evening; and ^B^he raised his eyes and looked, and behold, camels were coming. 64 Rebekah raised her eyes, and when she saw Isaac, she dismounted from the camel. 65 She said to the servant, "Who is that man walking in the field to meet us?" And the servant said, "He is my master." Then she took her veil and covered herself. 66 The servant told Isaac all the things that he had done. 67 Then Isaac brought her into his mother Sarah's tent, and he took Rebekah, and she became his wife, and ^he loved her; so Isaac was comforted after ^B^his mother's death.

ABRAHAM'S DEATH

25 Now Abraham took another wife, whose name was Keturah. 2 ^She bore to him Zimran, Jokshan, Medan, Midian, Ishbak, and Shuah. 3 Jokshan fathered Sheba and Dedan. And the sons of Dedan were Asshurim, Letushim, and Leummim. 4 The sons of Midian *were* Ephah, Epher, Hanoch, Abida, and Eldaah. All of these *were* the sons of Keturah. 5 ^Now

Abraham gave all that he had to Isaac; 6 but to the sons of his concubines, Abraham gave gifts while he was still living, and ^sent them away from his son Isaac eastward, to the land of the east.

7 These are all the years of Abraham's life that he lived, ^175 years. 8 Abraham breathed his last and died at a good old age, an old man and satisfied *with life;* and he was ^gathered to his people. 9 Then his sons Isaac and Ishmael buried him in ^the cave of Machpelah, in the field of Ephron the son of Zohar the Hittite, facing Mamre, 10 ^the field which Abraham purchased from the sons of Heth; there Abraham was buried with his wife Sarah. 11 It came about after the death of Abraham, that ^God blessed his son Isaac; and Isaac lived by Beer-lahai-roi.

DESCENDANTS OF ISHMAEL

12 Now these are *the records of* the generations of ^Ishmael, Abraham's son, whom Hagar the Egyptian, Sarah's slave woman, bore to Abraham; 13 and these are the names of ^the sons of Ishmael, by their names, in the order of their birth: Nebaioth, the firstborn of Ishmael, Kedar, Adbeel, Mibsam, 14 Mishma, Dumah, Massa, 15 Hadad, Tema, Jetur, Naphish, and Kedemah. 16 These are the sons of Ishmael and these are their names, by their villages, and by their camps; ^twelve princes according to their tribes. 17 These

24:60 ^Num 10:36   ^B^Gen 22:17   **24:62** ^Gen 16:14;
25:11   **24:63** ^Josh 1:8   ^B^Gen 18:2   **24:67** ^Gen 29:18
^B^Gen 23:1, 2   **25:2** ^1 Chr 1:32, 33   **25:5** ^Gen 24:35, 36
25:6 ^Gen 21:14   **25:7** ^Gen 12:4   **25:8** ^Gen 25:17;
35:29   **25:9** ^Gen 23:17, 18; 49:29, 30
25:10 ^Gen 23:3-16   **25:11** ^Gen 26:3   **25:12** ^Gen 16:15
25:13 ^1 Chr 1:29-31   **25:16** ^Gen 17:20

are the years of the life of Ishmael, ^137 years; and he breathed his last and died, and was gathered to his people. ^18They settled from ^Havilah to Shur which is east of Egypt going toward Assyria; he settled in defiance of all his relatives.

ISAAC'S SONS

^19Now these are *the records of* ^the generations of Isaac, Abraham's son: Abraham fathered Isaac; ^20and Isaac was forty years old when he took Rebekah, the ^daughter of Bethuel the Aramean of Paddan-aram, the ^Bsister of Laban the Aramean, to be his wife. ^21Isaac prayed to the LORD on behalf of his wife, because she was unable to have children; and the LORD answered him, and his wife Rebekah ^conceived. ^22But the children struggled together within her; and she said, "If it is so, why am I *in* this *condition?*" So she went to ^inquire of the LORD. ^23And the LORD said to her,

"^ATwo nations are in your
    womb;
And two peoples will be
    separated from your body;
And one people will be
    stronger than the other;
And the older will serve the
    younger."

^24When her days *leading* to the delivery were at an end, behold, there were twins in her womb. ^25Now the first came out red, ^all over like a hairy garment; and they named him Esau. ^26Afterward his brother came out with ^his hand holding on to Esau's heel, so ^Bhe was named ^IJacob; and Isaac was sixty years old when she gave birth to them.

^27When the boys grew up, Esau became a skillful hunter, a man of the field; but Jacob was a civilized man, ^living in tents. ^28Now Isaac loved Esau because he had ^a taste for game; but Rebekah loved Jacob. ^29When Jacob had cooked a ^stew *one day,* Esau came in from the field and he was exhausted; ^30and Esau said to Jacob, "Please let me have a mouthful of that red stuff there, for I am exhausted." Therefore he was called ^IEdom *by* name. ^31But Jacob said, "First sell me your ^birthright." ^32Esau said, "Look, I am about to die; so of what *use* then is the birthright to me?" ^33And Jacob said, "First swear to me"; so he swore *an oath* to him, and ^sold his birthright to Jacob. ^34Then Jacob gave Esau bread and lentil stew; and he ate and drank, and got up and went on his way. So Esau despised his birthright.

ISAAC SETTLES IN GERAR

26 Now there was ^a famine in the land, besides the previous famine that had occurred in the days of Abraham. So Isaac went to Gerar, to ^BAbimelech king of the Philistines. ^2And the LORD ^appeared to him and said, "Do not go down to Egypt; stay in the land of which I shall tell you. ^3Live for a time in this land and I will be with you and bless you, for to you and to your descendants I will give all these lands, and I will establish ^the

25:17 ^Gen 16:16   25:18 ^1 Sam 15:7   25:19 ^Matt 1:2
25:20 ^Gen 22:23   ^BGen 24:29   25:21 ^Rom 9:10
25:22 ^1 Sam 9:9; 10:22   25:23 ^Gen 17:4-6, 16;
Num 20:14   25:25 ^Gen 27:11   25:26 ^Hos 12:3
^BGen 27:36   25:27 ^Heb 11:9   25:28 ^Gen 27:19
25:29 ^2 Kin 4:38   25:31 ^Deut 21:16, 17; 1 Chr 5:1, 2
25:33 ^Heb 12:16   26:1 ^Gen 12:10   26:2 ^Gen 20:1, 2
26:2 ^Gen 12:7; 17:1   26:3 ^Gen 22:16-18; Ps 105:9

25:26 ^1 I.e., one who takes by the heel or supplants
25:30 ^1 I.e., red

oath which I swore to your father Abraham. 4^I will multiply your descendants as the stars of heaven, and will give your descendants all these lands; and ^by your descendants all the nations of the earth shall be blessed, 5because Abraham ^obeyed Me and fulfilled *his* duty to Me, *and kept* My commandments, My statutes, and My laws."

6So Isaac lived in Gerar. 7When the men of the place asked about his wife, he said, "^She is my sister," for he was afraid to say, "my wife," *thinking,* "the men of the place might kill me on account of Rebekah, since she is beautiful." 8Now it came about, when he had been there a long time, that Abimelech king of the Philistines looked down through a window, and saw *them,* and behold, Isaac was caressing his wife Rebekah. 9Then Abimelech called Isaac and said, "Behold, she certainly is your wife! So how *is it that* you said, 'She is my sister'?" And Isaac said to him, "Because I thought, 'otherwise I might be killed on account of her.'" 10And ^Abimelech said, "What is this *that* you have done to us? One of the people might easily have slept with your wife, and you would have brought guilt upon us." 11So Abimelech commanded all the people, saying, "He who ^touches this man or his wife will certainly be put to death."

12Now Isaac sowed in that land and reaped in the same year a hundred times *as much.* And ^the LORD blessed him, 13and the man ^became rich, and continued to grow richer until he became very wealthy; 14for ^he had possessions of flocks and herds, and a great

household, so that the Philistines envied him. 15Now ^all the wells which his father's servants had dug in the days of his father Abraham, the Philistines stopped up by filling them with dirt. 16Then Abimelech said to Isaac, "Go away from us, for you are ^too powerful for us." 17So Isaac departed from there and camped in the Valley of Gerar, and settled there.

ARGUMENT OVER THE WELLS

18Then Isaac dug again the wells of water which had been dug in the days of his father Abraham, for the Philistines had stopped them up after the death of Abraham; and he gave them the same names which his father had given them. 19But when Isaac's servants dug in the valley and found there a well of flowing water, 20the herdsmen of Gerar ^quarreled with the herdsmen of Isaac, saying, "The water is ours!" So he named the well Esek, because they argued with him. 21Then they dug another well, and they quarreled over it too, so he named it Sitnah. 22Then he moved away from there and dug another well, and they did not quarrel over it; so he named it Rehoboth, for he said, "At last the LORD has made room for us, and we will be ^fruitful in the land."

23And he went up from there to ^Beersheba. 24And the LORD ^appeared to him the same night and said,

26:4^Gen 15:5   ^BGen 22:18   26:5^Gen 22:16
26:7^Gen 12:13; 20:2, 12   26:10^Gen 20:9
26:11^Ps 105:15   26:12^Gen 24:1; 26:3
26:13^Prov 10:22   26:14^Gen 24:35; 25:5
26:15^Gen 21:25, 30   26:16^Ex 1:9
26:20^Gen 21:25   26:22^Gen 17:6; Ex 1:7
26:23^Gen 22:19   26:24^Gen 26:2

"I am the God of your father
   Abraham;
Do not fear, for I am with you.
I ᴮwill bless you and multiply
   your descendants,
For the sake of My servant
   Abraham."

²⁵So he built an ^altar there and
called upon the name of the LORD,
and pitched his tent there; and
there Isaac's servants dug a well.

COVENANT WITH ABIMELECH

²⁶Then ^Abimelech came to him
from Gerar with his adviser Ahuz-
zath, and Phicol the commander
of his army. ²⁷Isaac said to them,
"^Why have you come to me, since
you hate me and have sent me away
from you?" ²⁸They said, "We have
seen plainly ^that the LORD has been
with you; so we said, 'An oath must
now be *taken* by us,' *that is,* by you
and us. So let us make a covenant
with you, ²⁹that you will do us no
harm, just as we have not touched
you and have done to you nothing
but good, and have sent you away
in peace. You are now the ^blessed
of the LORD." ³⁰Then ^he made them
a feast, and they ate and drank. ³¹In
the morning they got up early and
^exchanged oaths; then Isaac sent
them away, and they left him in
peace. ³²Now it came about on the
same day, that Isaac's servants came
in and told him about the well which
they had dug, and said to him, "We
have found water." ³³So he called it
¹Shibah; therefore the name of the
city is ^Beersheba to this day.

³⁴When Esau was forty years old
^he married Judith the daughter of
Beeri the Hittite, and Basemath the
daughter of Elon the Hittite; ³⁵and
^they brought grief to Isaac and
Rebekah.

JACOB'S DECEPTION

27 Now it came about, when
Isaac was old and ^his eyes
were too dim to see, that he called
his older son Esau and said to him,
"My son." And he said to him, "Here
I am." ²Then ^Isaac said, "Behold
now, I am old *and* I do not know the
day of my death. ³Now then, please
take your gear, your quiver and
your bow, and go out to the field
and ^hunt game for me; ⁴and prepare a delicious meal for me such as
I love, and bring it to me that I may
eat, so that ^my soul may bless you
before I die."

⁵Now Rebekah was listening
while Isaac spoke to his son Esau.
So when Esau went to the field
to hunt for game to bring *home,*
⁶^Rebekah said to her son Jacob,
"Behold, I heard your father speak
to your brother Esau, saying, ⁷'Bring
me *some* game and prepare a delicious meal for me, so that I may eat,
and bless you in the presence of the
LORD before my death.' ⁸So now, my
son, ^listen to me as I command
you. ⁹Go now to the flock and
bring me two choice young goats
from there, so that I may prepare
them *as* a delicious meal for your
father, such as he loves. ¹⁰Then you
shall bring *it* to your father, that he
may eat, so that he may bless you
before his death." ¹¹But Jacob said
to his mother Rebekah, "Behold,
my brother Esau is a ^hairy man
and I am a smooth man. ¹²^Perhaps

26:24 ᴮGen 22:17   26:25 ^Gen 12:7, 8; 13:4, 18
26:26 ^Gen 21:22   26:27 ^Judg 11:7
26:28 ^Gen 21:22, 23   26:29 ^Gen 24:31; Ps 115:15
26:30 ^Gen 19:3   26:31 ^Gen 21:31   26:33 ^Gen 21:31
26:34 ^Gen 28:8; 36:2   26:35 ^Gen 27:46
27:1 ^Gen 48:10; 1 Sam 3:2   27:2 ^Gen 47:29
27:3 ^Gen 25:28   27:4 ^Gen 27:19, 25, 31; 48:9, 15, 16
27:6 ^Gen 25:28   27:8 ^Gen 27:13, 43
27:11 ^Gen 25:25   27:12 ^Gen 27:21, 22

26:33 ¹Meaning uncertain, perhaps *oath*

my father will touch me, then I will be like a deceiver in his sight, and I will bring upon myself a curse and not a blessing." ¹³But his mother said to him, "Your curse be on me, my son; only ^Aobey my voice, and go, get *the goats* for me." ¹⁴So he went and got *them,* and brought *them* to his mother; and his mother made a delicious meal such as his father loved. ¹⁵Then Rebekah took the best ^Agarments of her elder son Esau, which were with her in the house, and put them on her younger son Jacob. ¹⁶And she put the skins of the young goats on his hands and on the smooth part of his neck. ¹⁷She also gave the delicious meal and the bread which she had made to her son Jacob.

¹⁸Then he came to his father and said, "My father." And he said, "Here I am. Who are you, my son?" ¹⁹Jacob said to his father, "I am Esau your firstborn; I have done as you told me. ^ACome now, sit and eat of my game, so that ^Byou may bless me." ²⁰Isaac said to his son, "How is it that you have *it* so quickly, my son?" And he said, "^ABecause the LORD your God made *it* come to me." ²¹Then Isaac said to Jacob, "Please come close, so that ^AI may feel you, my son, whether you are really my son Esau or not." ²²So Jacob came close to his father Isaac, and he touched him and said, "The voice is the voice of Jacob, but the hands are the hands of Esau." ²³And he did not recognize him, because his hands were ^Ahairy like his brother Esau's hands; so he blessed him. ²⁴And he said, "Are you really my son Esau?" And he said, "I am." ²⁵So he said, "Bring *it* to me, and I will eat of my son's game, that ^AI may bless you." And

he brought *it* to him, and he ate; he also brought him wine and he drank. ²⁶Then his father Isaac said to him, "Please come close and kiss me, my son." ²⁷So he came close and kissed him; and when he smelled the smell of his garments, he ^Ablessed him and said,

"See, the smell of my son
Is like the smell of a field
     ^Bwhich the LORD has blessed;
28   Now may ^AGod give you of the
          dew of heaven,
     And of the fatness of the earth,
     And an abundance of grain
          and new wine;
29   May peoples serve you,
     And nations bow down to you;
     Be master of your brothers,
     And may your mother's sons
          bow down to you.
     ^ACursed be those who curse
          you,
     And blessed be those who
          bless you."

THE STOLEN BLESSING

³⁰Now it came about, as soon as Isaac had finished blessing Jacob, and Jacob had hardly gone out from the presence of his father Isaac, that his brother Esau came in from his hunting. ³¹Then he also made a delicious meal, and brought it to his father; and he said to his father, "^ALet my father arise and eat of his son's game, that you may bless me." ³²His father Isaac said to him, "^AWho are you?" And he said, "I am your son, your firstborn, Esau." ³³Then Isaac trembled violently, and said, "Who then was he

27:13^AGen 27:8   27:15^AGen 27:27   27:19^AGen 27:31
^BGen 27:4   27:20^AGen 24:12   27:21^AGen 27:12
27:23^AGen 27:16   27:25^AGen 27:4   27:27^AHeb 11:20
^BPs 65:10   27:28^AGen 27:39; Deut 33:13, 28
27:29^AGen 12:3; Num 24:9   27:31^AGen 27:19
27:32^AGen 27:18

who hunted game and brought *it* to me, so that I ate from all *of it* before you came, and blessed him? ᴬYes, *and* he shall be blessed." ³⁴When Esau heard the words of his father, ᴬhe cried out with an exceedingly great and bitter cry, and said to his father, "Bless me, me as well, my father!" ³⁵And he said, "ᴬYour brother came deceitfully and has taken away your blessing." ³⁶Then *Esau* said, "Is he not rightly named ᴬJacob, for he has betrayed me these two times? He took away my birthright, and behold, now he has taken away my blessing." And he said, "Have you not reserved a blessing for me?" ³⁷But Isaac replied to Esau, "Behold, I have made him ᴬyour master, and I have given to him all his relatives as servants; and with grain and new wine I have sustained him. What then can I do for you, my son?" ³⁸Esau said to his father, "Do you have only one blessing, my father? Bless me, me as well, my father." So Esau raised his voice and ᴬwept.

³⁹Then ᴬhis father Isaac answered and said to him,

"Behold, away from the fertility
  of the earth shall be your
  dwelling,
And away from the dew of
  heaven from above.
⁴⁰ "And by your sword you shall
  live,
And ᴬyou shall serve your
  brother;
But it shall come about ᴮwhen
  you become restless,
That you will break his yoke
  from your neck."

⁴¹So Esau ᴬheld a grudge against Jacob because of the blessing with which his father had blessed him; and Esau said to himself, "The days of mourning for my father are near; then I will kill my brother Jacob." ⁴²Now when the words of her elder son Esau were reported to Rebekah, she sent *word* and called her younger son Jacob, and said to him, "Behold your brother Esau is consoling himself concerning you *by planning* to kill you. ⁴³Now then, my son, obey my voice, and arise, flee to ᴬHaran, to my brother ᴮLaban! ⁴⁴Stay with him ᴬa few days, until your brother's fury subsides, ⁴⁵until your brother's anger against you subsides and he forgets ᴬwhat you did to him. Then I will send *word* and get you from there. Why should I lose you both in one day?"

⁴⁶And Rebekah said to Isaac, "I am tired of living because of ᴬthe daughters of Heth; if Jacob takes a wife from the daughters of Heth like these from the daughters of the land, what good will my life be to me?"

JACOB IS SENT AWAY

28 So Isaac called Jacob and blessed him and commanded him, saying to him, "ᴬYou shall not take a wife from the daughters of Canaan. ²Arise, go to Paddan-aram, to the house of ᴬBethuel your mother's father; and from there take to yourself a wife from the daughters of Laban, your mother's brother. ³May God Almighty bless you and make you fruitful and multiply you, so that you may become a ᴬmultitude of peoples. ⁴May He also give you the

27:33ᴬGen 28:3, 4   27:34ᴬHeb 12:17   27:35ᴬGen 27:19
27:36ᴬGen 25:26, 32-34   27:37ᴬGen 27:28, 29
27:38ᴬHeb 12:17   27:39ᴬHeb 11:20   27:40ᴬGen 25:23
ᴮ2 Kin 8:20-22   27:41ᴬGen 32:3-11; 37:4, 8
27:43ᴬGen 11:31   ᴮGen 24:29   27:44ᴬGen 31:41
27:45ᴬGen 27:12, 19, 35   27:46ᴬGen 26:34, 35; 28:8
28:1ᴬGen 24:3, 4   28:2ᴬGen 25:20
28:3ᴬGen 35:11; 48:4

^Ablessing of Abraham, to you and to your descendants with you, so that you may possess the land where you live as a stranger, which God gave to Abraham." ⁵Then ^AIsaac sent Jacob away, and he went to Paddan-aram to Laban, son of Bethuel the Aramean, the brother of Rebekah, the mother of Jacob and Esau.

⁶Now Esau saw that Isaac had blessed Jacob and sent him away to Paddan-aram to take to himself a wife from there, *and that* when he blessed him he commanded him, saying, "^AYou shall not take a wife from the daughters of Canaan," ⁷and that Jacob had obeyed his father and his mother and had gone to Paddan-aram. ⁸So Esau saw that ^Athe daughters of Canaan displeased his father Isaac; ⁹and Esau went to Ishmael, and married, ^Abesides the wives that he had, Mahalath the daughter of Ishmael, Abraham's son, the sister of Nebaioth.

JACOB'S DREAM

¹⁰Then Jacob departed from ^ABeersheba and went toward ^BHaran. ¹¹And he happened upon a ^Aparticular place and spent the night there, because the sun had set; and he took one of the stones of the place and made it a support for his head, and lay down in that place. ¹²And he had a dream, and behold, a ladder was set up on the earth with its top reaching to heaven; and behold, ^Athe angels of God were ascending and descending on it. ¹³Then behold, the LORD was standing above it and said, "I am the LORD, ^Athe God of your father Abraham and the God of Isaac; the land on which you lie I will give

to you and to ^Byour descendants. ¹⁴Your descendants will also be like the dust of the earth, and you will spread out ^Ato the west and to the east, and to the north and to the south; and in you and in your descendants shall all the families of the earth be blessed. ¹⁵Behold, I am with you and will keep you wherever you go, and ^Awill bring you back to this land; for I will not leave you until I have done what I have promised you." ¹⁶Then Jacob ^Aawoke from his sleep and said, "The LORD is certainly in this place, and I did not know it!" ¹⁷And he was afraid and said, "^AHow awesome is this place! This is none other than the house of God, and this is the gate of heaven!"

¹⁸So Jacob got up early in the morning, and took ^Athe stone that he had placed as a support for his head, and set it up as a memorial stone, and poured oil on its top. ¹⁹Then he named that place ¹,^ABethel; but previously the name of the city had been ^BLuz. ²⁰Jacob also made a vow, saying, "^AIf God will be with me and will keep me on this journey that I take, and give me ^Bfood to eat and garments to wear, ²¹and I return to my father's house in safety, ^Athen the LORD will be my God. ²²And this stone, which I have set up as a memorial stone, will be God's house, and ^Aof everything that You give me I will assuredly give a tenth to You."

28:4 ^AGen 12:2; 22:17   28:5 ^AGen 27:43   28:6 ^AGen 28:1
28:8 ^AGen 24:3; 26:34, 35   28:9 ^AGen 26:34; 36:2
28:10 ^AGen 26:23   ^BGen 12:4, 5   28:11 ^AGen 28:19
28:12 ^AJohn 1:51   28:13 ^AGen 26:3, 24   ^BGen 12:7
28:14 ^AGen 13:14, 15   28:15 ^AGen 48:21; Deut 30:3
28:16 ^A1 Kin 3:15; Jer 31:26   28:17 ^APs 68:35
28:18 ^AGen 28:11; 35:14   28:19 ^AJudg 1:23   ^BGen 35:6
28:20 ^AGen 28:15   ^B1 Tim 6:8   28:21 ^ADeut 26:17
28:22 ^ALev 27:30; Deut 14:22

28:19 ¹I.e., the house of God

JACOB MEETS RACHEL

29 Then Jacob set out on his journey, and went to the land of ^the people of the east. ²He looked, and saw ^a well in the field, and behold, three flocks of sheep were lying there beside it, because they watered the flocks from that well. Now the stone on the mouth of the well was large. ³When all the flocks were gathered there, they would roll the stone from the mouth of the well and water the sheep. Then they would put the stone back in its place on the mouth of the well.

⁴Jacob said to them, "My brothers, where are you from?" And they said, "We are from ^Haran." ⁵So he said to them, "Do you know Laban the ^son of Nahor?" And they said, "We know *him*." ⁶And he said to them, "Is it well with him?" And they said, "It is well, and here is his daughter ^Rachel coming with the sheep." ⁷Then he said, "Look, it is still high day; it is not time for the livestock to be gathered. Water the sheep, and go, pasture them." ⁸But they said, "We cannot, until all the flocks are gathered, and they roll the stone from the mouth of the well; then we water the sheep."

⁹While he was still speaking with them, Rachel came with her father's sheep, for she was a shepherdess. ¹⁰When Jacob saw Rachel the daughter of his mother's brother Laban, and the sheep of his mother's brother Laban, Jacob went up and rolled the stone from the mouth of the well, and watered the flock of his mother's brother Laban. ¹¹Then Jacob ^kissed Rachel, and raised his voice and wept. ¹²Jacob told Rachel that he was a ^relative of her father and that he was Rebekah's son, and she ran and told her father.

¹³So when ^Laban heard the news about Jacob, his sister's son, he ran to meet him, and ^Bembraced him and kissed him, and brought him to his house. Then he told Laban all these things. ¹⁴And Laban said to him, "You certainly are ^my bone and my flesh." And he stayed with him a month.

¹⁵Then Laban said to Jacob, "Because you are my relative, should you therefore serve me for nothing? Tell me, what shall ^your wages be?" ¹⁶Now Laban had two daughters; the name of the older was Leah, and the name of the younger was Rachel. ¹⁷And Leah's eyes were weak, but Rachel was ^beautiful in figure and appearance. ¹⁸Now Jacob ^loved Rachel, so he said, "^BI will serve you seven years for your younger daughter Rachel." ¹⁹Laban said, "It is better that I give her to you than to give her to another man; stay with me." ²⁰So Jacob served seven years for Rachel, and they seemed to him like *only* a few days ^because of his love for her.

LABAN'S TREACHERY

²¹Then Jacob said to Laban, "Give *me* my wife, for my time is completed, that I may ^have relations with her." ²²So Laban gathered all the people of the place and held a feast. ²³Now in the evening he took his daughter Leah and brought her to him; and *Jacob* had relations with her. ²⁴Laban also gave his female slave Zilpah to

29:1 ^Judg 6:3, 33   **29:2** ^Gen 24:10, 11; Ex 2:15, 16
29:4 ^Gen 28:10   **29:5** ^Gen 24:24, 29   **29:6** ^Ex 2:16
29:11 ^Gen 33:4   **29:12** ^Gen 28:5   **29:13** ^Gen
24:29-31   ^BGen 33:4   **29:14** ^Gen 2:23; Judg 9:2
29:15 ^Gen 31:41   **29:17** ^Gen 12:11, 14; 26:7
29:18 ^Gen 24:67   ^BHos 12:12   **29:20** ^Song 8:7
29:21 ^Judg 15:1

his daughter Leah as a slave. ²⁵So it came about in the morning that, behold, it was Leah! And he said to Laban, "ᴬWhat is this *that* you have done to me? Was it not for Rachel that I served with you? Why then have you deceived me?" ²⁶But Laban said, "It is not the practice in our place to marry off the younger before the firstborn. ²⁷Complete the week of this one, and we will give you the other also for the service which ᴬyou shall serve with me, for another seven years." ²⁸Jacob did so and completed her week, and he gave him his daughter Rachel as his wife. ²⁹Laban also gave his female slave Bilhah to his daughter Rachel as her slave. ³⁰So *Jacob* had relations with Rachel also, and indeed ᴬhe loved Rachel more than Leah, and he served with Laban for another seven years.

³¹Now the Lᴏʀᴅ saw that Leah was unloved, and He opened her womb, but Rachel was unable to have children. ³²Leah conceived and gave birth to a son, and named him Reuben, for she said, "Because the Lᴏʀᴅ has ᴬseen my affliction; surely now my husband will love me." ³³Then she conceived again and gave birth to a son, and said, "ᴬBecause the Lᴏʀᴅ has heard that I am unloved, He has therefore given me this *son* also." So she named him Simeon. ³⁴And she conceived again and gave birth to a son, and said, "Now this time my husband will become attached to me, because I have borne him three sons." Therefore he was named ᴬLevi. ³⁵And she conceived again and gave birth to a son, and said, "This time I will praise the Lᴏʀᴅ." Therefore she named him ᴬJudah. Then she stopped having children.

THE SONS OF JACOB

30 Now when Rachel saw that ᴬshe had not borne Jacob *any* children, she became jealous of her sister; and she said to Jacob, "Give me children, or else I am going to die." ²Then Jacob's anger burned against Rachel, and he said, "Am I in the place of God, who has ᴬwithheld from you the fruit of the womb?" ³Then she said, "ᴬHere is my female slave Bilhah: have relations with her that she may give birth ¹on my knees, so that ᴬby her I too may obtain a child." ⁴So ᴬshe gave him her slave Bilhah as a wife, and Jacob had relations with her. ⁵Bilhah conceived and bore Jacob a son. ⁶Then Rachel said, "God has ᴬvindicated me, and has indeed heard my voice and has given me a son." Therefore she named him Dan. ⁷And Rachel's slave Bilhah conceived again and bore Jacob a second son. ⁸So Rachel said, "*With* mighty wrestling I have wrestled with my sister, *and* I have indeed prevailed." And she named him Naphtali.

⁹When Leah saw that she had stopped having children, she took her slave Zilpah and gave her to Jacob as a wife. ¹⁰And Leah's slave Zilpah bore Jacob a son. ¹¹Then Leah said, "How fortunate!" So she named him Gad. ¹²And Leah's slave Zilpah bore Jacob a second son. ¹³Then Leah said, "Happy am I! For women ᴬwill call me happy." So she named him Asher.

¹⁴Now in the days of wheat harvest Reuben went and found

29:25ᴬGen 12:18; 20:9   29:27ᴬGen 31:41
29:30ᴬGen 29:17, 18   29:32ᴬGen 16:11; 31:42
29:33ᴬDeut 21:15   29:34ᴬGen 49:5   29:35ᴬGen 49:8;
Matt 1:2   30:1ᴬGen 29:31   30:2ᴬGen 20:18; 29:31
30:3ᴬGen 16:2   30:4ᴬGen 16:3, 4   30:6ᴬPs 35:24;
Lam 3:59   30:13ᴬLuke 1:48

30:3 ¹I.e., prob. referring to a ritual of adoption

ᴬmandrake fruits in the field, and brought them to his mother Leah. Then Rachel said to Leah, "Please give me some of your son's mandrakes." ¹⁵But she said to her, "Is it a small matter for you to take my husband? And would you take my son's mandrakes also?" So Rachel said, "Therefore he may sleep with you tonight in return for your son's mandrakes." ¹⁶When Jacob came in from the field in the evening, Leah went out to meet him and said, "You must have relations with me, for I have indeed hired you with my son's mandrakes." So he slept with her that night. ¹⁷God listened to Leah, and she conceived and bore Jacob a fifth son. ¹⁸Then Leah said, "God has given me my reward, because I gave my slave to my husband." So she named him Issachar. ¹⁹And Leah conceived again and bore a sixth son to Jacob. ²⁰Then Leah said, "God has endowed me with a good gift; finally my husband will acknowledge me *as his wife,* because I have borne him six sons." So she named him Zebulun. ²¹Afterward she gave birth to a daughter, and named her Dinah.

²²Then ᴬGod remembered Rachel, and God listened to her and ᴮopened her womb. ²³So she conceived and gave birth to a son, and said, "God has ᴬtaken away my disgrace." ²⁴And she named him Joseph, saying, "ᴬMay the LORD give me another son."

JACOB PROSPERS

²⁵Now it came about, when Rachel had given birth to Joseph, that Jacob said to Laban, "ᴬSend me away, so that I may go to my own place and to my own country. ²⁶Give *me* my wives and my

children ᴬfor whom I have served you, and let me go; for you yourself know my service which I have rendered you." ²⁷But Laban said to him, "If it pleases you at all, *stay with me;* I have determined by divination ᴬthat the LORD has blessed me on your account." ²⁸He continued, "ᴬName me your wages, and I will give them." ²⁹But *Jacob* said to him, "ᴬYou yourself know how I have served you and how your livestock have fared with me. ³⁰For you had little before I came, and it has increased to a multitude, and the LORD has blessed you wherever I turned. But now, when shall I provide for my own household also?" ³¹So he said, "What shall I give you?" And Jacob said, "You shall not give me anything. If you will do this *one* thing for me, I will again pasture *and* keep your flock: ³²let me pass through your entire flock today, removing from there every ᴬspeckled or spotted sheep and every black sheep among the lambs, and the spotted or speckled among the goats; and *those* shall be my wages. ³³So my honesty will answer for me later, when you come concerning my wages. Every one that is not speckled or spotted among the goats, or black among the lambs, *if found* with me, will be considered stolen." ³⁴Laban said, "Good, let it be according to your word." ³⁵So he removed on that day the striped or spotted male goats, and all the speckled or spotted female goats, every one with white on it, and all the black ones

30:14ᴬSong 7:13   30:22ᴬ1 Sam 1:19, 20   ᴮGen 29:31
30:23ᴬIs 4:1; Luke 1:25   30:24ᴬGen 35:17
30:25ᴬGen 24:54, 56   30:26ᴬGen 29:18, 20, 27;
Hos 12:12   30:27ᴬGen 26:24; Is 61:9
30:28ᴬGen 29:15; 31:7, 41   30:29ᴬGen 31:6
30:32ᴬGen 31:8

among the sheep, and put them in the care of his sons. ³⁶And he put *a distance of* three days' journey between himself and Jacob, and Jacob fed the rest of Laban's flocks.

³⁷Then Jacob took fresh rods of poplar, almond, and plane trees, and peeled white stripes in them, exposing the white that *was* in the rods. ³⁸He set the rods which he had peeled in front of the flocks in the drinking troughs, *that is,* in the watering channels where the flocks came to drink; and they mated when they came to drink. ³⁹So the flocks mated by the rods, and the flocks delivered striped, speckled, and spotted *offspring.* ⁴⁰Then Jacob separated the lambs, and made the flocks face toward the striped and all the black in the flock of Laban; and he put his own herds apart, and did not put them with Laban's flock. ⁴¹Moreover, whenever the stronger of the flock were mating, Jacob would place the rods in the sight of the flock in the drinking troughs, so that they would mate by the rods; ⁴²but when the flock was sickly, he did not put *them* in; so the sickly were Laban's, and the stronger *were* Jacob's. ⁴³So ᴬthe man became exceedingly prosperous, and had large flocks, and female and male servants, and camels and donkeys.

JACOB LEAVES SECRETLY FOR CANAAN

31 Now Jacob heard the words of Laban's sons, saying, "Jacob has taken away all that was our father's, and from what belonged to our father he has made all this wealth." ²And Jacob saw the ¹attitude of Laban, and behold, it was not *friendly* toward him as *it had been* before. ³Then the LORD said

to Jacob, "Return to the land of your fathers and to your relatives, and ᴬI will be with you." ⁴So Jacob sent *word* and called Rachel and Leah to his flock in the field, ⁵and said to them, "I see your father's attitude, that it is not *friendly* toward me as *it was* before, but ᴬthe God of my father has been with me. ⁶ᴬYou know that I have served your father with all my strength. ⁷Yet your father has ᴬcheated me and ᴮchanged my wages ten times; however, God did not allow him to do me harm. ⁸If ᴬhe said this: 'The speckled shall be your wages,' then all the flock delivered speckled; and if he said this: 'The striped shall be your wages,' then all the flock delivered striped. ⁹So God has ᴬtaken away your father's livestock and given *them* to me. ¹⁰And it came about at the time when the flock was breeding that I raised my eyes and saw in a dream—and behold—the male goats that were mating *were* striped, speckled, or mottled. ¹¹Then ᴬthe angel of God said to me in the dream, 'Jacob'; and I said, 'Here I am.' ¹²He said, 'Now raise your eyes and see *that* all the male goats that are mating are striped, speckled, or mottled; for ᴬI have seen everything that Laban has been doing to you. ¹³I am ᴬthe God *of* Bethel, where you ᴮanointed a memorial stone, where you made a vow to Me; now arise, leave this land, and return to the land of your birth.' " ¹⁴Rachel and Leah said to him, "Do we still have any share or

---

30:43 ᴬGen 12:16; 13:2   31:3 ᴬGen 28:15
31:5 ᴬGen 21:22; 28:13, 15   31:6 ᴬGen 30:29
31:7 ᴬGen 29:25   ᴮGen 31:41   31:8 ᴬGen 30:32
31:9 ᴬGen 31:1, 16   31:11 ᴬGen 16:7–11; 22:11, 15
31:12 ᴬEx 3:7   31:13 ᴬGen 28:13, 19   ᴮGen 28:18, 20

31:2 ¹Lit *face*

inheritance in our father's house? ¹⁵Are we not regarded by him as foreigners? For ^he has sold us, and has also entirely consumed our purchase price. ¹⁶Surely all the wealth which God has taken away from our father belongs to us and our children; now then, do whatever God has told you."

¹⁷Then Jacob stood up and put his children and his wives on camels; ¹⁸and he drove away all his livestock and all his property which he had acquired, the livestock he possessed which he had acquired in Paddan-aram, ^to go to the land of Canaan to his father Isaac. ¹⁹Laban had gone to shear his flock, and Rachel stole the ^household idols that were her father's. ²⁰And Jacob deceived Laban the Aramean by not telling him that he was fleeing. ²¹So he fled with all that he had; and he got up and crossed the *Euphrates* River, and set out for the hill country of ^Gilead.

LABAN PURSUES JACOB

²²When Laban was informed on the third day that Jacob had fled, ²³he took his kinsmen with him and pursued him *a distance of* seven days' journey, and he overtook him in the hill country of Gilead. ²⁴However, ^God came to Laban the Aramean in a ^Bdream of the night and said to him, "Be careful that you do not speak to Jacob either good or bad."

²⁵And Laban caught up with Jacob. Now Jacob had pitched his tent in the hill country, and Laban with his kinsmen camped in the hill country of Gilead. ²⁶Then Laban said to Jacob, "What have you done by deceiving me and carrying away my daughters like captives of the sword? ²⁷Why did you flee secretly and deceive me, and did not tell me, so that I might have sent you away with joy and with songs, with ^tambourine and with lyre; ²⁸and did not allow me ^to kiss my ¹grandchildren and my daughters? Now you have done foolishly. ²⁹It is in my power to do you harm, but ^the God of your father spoke to me last night, saying, 'Be careful not to speak either good or bad to Jacob.' ³⁰Now you have indeed gone away because you longed greatly for your father's house; *but* why did you steal ^my gods?" ³¹Then Jacob replied to Laban, "Because I was afraid, for I thought that you would take your daughters from me by force. ³²^The one with whom you find your gods shall not live; in the presence of our relatives point out what is yours among my belongings and take *it* for yourself." Now Jacob did not know that Rachel had stolen them.

³³So Laban went into Jacob's tent, and into Leah's tent, and into the tent of the two slave women, but he did not find *them*. Then he went out of Leah's tent and entered Rachel's tent. ³⁴Now Rachel had taken the household idols and put them in the camel's saddlebag, and she sat on them. So Laban searched through all the tent, but did not find *them*. ³⁵And she said to her father, "May my lord not be angry that I cannot ^stand in your presence, because the ¹way of women is upon me." So he searched but did not find the ^Bhousehold idols.

31:15^Gen 29:20, 23, 27   31:18^Gen 35:27
31:19^Gen 31:30, 34; 35:2   31:21^Gen 37:25
31:24^Gen 20:3   ^BGen 31:11   31:27^Ex 15:20
31:28^Gen 31:55   31:29^Gen 31:5, 24, 42, 53
31:30^Gen 31:19; Josh 24:2   31:32^Gen 44:9
31:35^Lev 19:32   ^BGen 31:19

31:28¹Lit *sons*   31:35¹I.e., menstruation

36Then Jacob became angry and argued with Laban; and Jacob said to Laban, "What is my offense? What is my sin that you have hotly pursued me? 37Though you have searched through all my property, what have you found of all your household property? Set *it* here in front of my relatives and your relatives, so that they may decide between the two of us. 38For these twenty years I *have been* with you; your ewes and your female goats have not miscarried, nor have I eaten the rams of your flocks. 39I did not *even* bring to you that which was torn *by wild animals;* I took the loss myself. You demanded it of my hand *whether* stolen by day or stolen by night. 40*This is how* I was: by day the heat consumed me and the frost by night, and my sleep fled from my eyes. 41For these twenty years I have been in your house; ^AI served you fourteen years for your two daughters, and six years for your flock, and you changed my wages ten times. 42If the God of my father, the God of Abraham and the fear of Isaac, had not been for me, surely now you would have sent me away emptyhanded. ^AGod has seen my affliction and the labor of my hands, so He ^Brendered judgment last night."

THE COVENANT OF MIZPAH

43Then Laban replied to Jacob, "The daughters are my daughters, the ¹children are my ¹grandchildren, ^Athe flocks are my flocks, and everything that you see is mine. But what can I do this day to these daughters of mine or to their children to whom they have given birth? 44So now come, let's ^Amake a covenant, you and I, and it shall be a witness between you

and me." 45Then Jacob took ^Aa stone and set it up *as* a memorial stone. 46Jacob said to his relatives, "Gather stones." So they took stones and made a heap, and they ate there by the heap. 47Now Laban ^Acalled it ¹Jegar-sahadutha, but Jacob called it ²Galeed. 48Laban said, "^AThis heap is a witness between you and me this day." Therefore it was named Galeed, 49and ¹,^AMizpah, for he said, "May the LORD keep watch between you and me when we are absent one from the other. 50If you mistreat my daughters, or if you take wives besides my daughters, *although* no one is with us, see, ^AGod is witness between you and me." 51Laban also said to Jacob, "Behold this heap and behold the memorial stone which I have set between you and me. 52This heap is a witness, and the memorial stone is a witness, that I will not pass by this heap to you for harm, and you will not pass by this heap and this memorial stone to me, for harm. 53The God of Abraham and the God of Nahor, the God of their father, ^Ajudge between us." So Jacob swore by ^Bthe fear of his father Isaac. 54Then Jacob ^Aoffered a sacrifice on the mountain, and called his relatives to the meal; and they ate the meal and spent the night on the mountain. 55Then early in the morning Laban got up, and ^Akissed his ¹grandchildren and his daughters and blessed them. Then Laban departed and returned to his place.

31:41^AGen 29:27, 30 31:42^AEx 3:7 ^BGen 31:24, 29
31:43^AGen 31:1 31:44^AGen 21:27, 32; 26:28
31:45^AGen 28:18; Josh 24:26, 27 31:47^AJosh 22:34
31:48^AJosh 24:27 31:49^AJudg 11:29; 1 Sam 7:5, 6
31:50^AJer 29:23; 42:5 31:53^AGen 16:5 ^BGen 31:42
31:54^AEx 18:12 31:55^AGen 31:28, 43

31:43 ¹Lit *sons* 31:47 ¹I.e., the heap of witness, in Aram ²I.e., the heap of witness, in Heb 31:49 ¹Lit *the Mizpah;* i.e., the watchtower 31:55 ¹Lit *sons*

JACOB'S FEAR OF ESAU

32 Now as Jacob went on his way, ᴬthe angels of God met him. ²And when he saw them, Jacob said, "This is God's camp." So he named that place ¹·ᴬMahanaim.

³Then Jacob sent messengers ahead of himself to his brother Esau in the land of ᴬSeir, the country of ᴮEdom. ⁴He commanded them, saying, "This is what you shall say to my lord Esau: 'Your servant Jacob says the following: "I have resided with Laban, and ᴬstayed until now; ⁵and ᴬI have oxen, donkeys, flocks, and male and female servants; and I have sent *messengers* to tell my lord, ᴮso that I may find favor in your sight."'"

⁶And the messengers returned to Jacob, saying, "We came to your brother Esau, and furthermore ᴬhe is coming to meet you, and four hundred men are with him." ⁷Then Jacob was ᴬgreatly afraid and distressed; and he divided the people who were with him, and the flocks, the herds, and the camels, into two companies; ⁸for he said, "If Esau comes to the one company and attacks it, then the company which is left will escape."

⁹Then Jacob said, "God of my father Abraham and God of my father Isaac, Lᴏʀᴅ, who said to me, 'ᴬReturn to your country and to your relatives, and I will make you prosper,' ¹⁰I am unworthy ᴬof all the favor and of all the faithfulness, which You have shown to Your servant; for with *only* my staff I crossed this Jordan, and now I have become two companies. ¹¹ᴬSave me, please, ᴮfrom the hand of my brother, from the hand of Esau; for I fear him, that he will come and attack me *and* the mothers with the children. ¹²For

You said, 'ᴬI will assuredly make you prosper and make your descendants as the sand of the sea, which is too great to be counted.'"

¹³So he spent the night there. Then he selected from what he had with him a ᴬgift for his brother Esau: ¹⁴two hundred female goats and twenty male goats, two hundred ewes and twenty rams, ¹⁵thirty milking camels and their colts, forty cows and ten bulls, *and* twenty female donkeys and ten male donkeys. ¹⁶Then he placed *them* in the care of his servants, every flock by itself, and said to his servants, "Pass on ahead of me, and put a space between flocks." ¹⁷And he commanded the one in front, saying, "When my brother Esau meets you and asks you, saying, 'To whom do you belong, and where are you going, and to whom do these *animals* in front of you belong?' ¹⁸then you shall say, '*These* belong to your servant Jacob; it is a gift sent to my lord Esau. And behold, he also is behind us.'" ¹⁹Then he commanded also the second and the third, and all those who followed the flocks, saying, "In this way you shall speak to Esau when you find him; ²⁰and you shall say, 'Behold, your servant Jacob also is behind us.'" For he said, "I will appease him with the gift that goes ahead of me. Then afterward I will see his face; perhaps he will accept me." ²¹So the gift passed on ahead of him, while he himself spent that night in the camp.

32:1ᴬ2 Kin 6:16, 17; Ps 34:7   **32:2**ᴬJosh 21:38; 2 Sam 2:8   **32:3**ᴬGen 14:6   ᴮGen 25:30   **32:4**ᴬGen 31:41   **32:5**ᴬGen 30:43   ᴮGen 33:8   **32:6**ᴬGen 33:1   **32:7**ᴬGen 32:11   **32:9**ᴬGen 28:15; 31:3, 13   **32:10**ᴬGen 24:27   **32:11**ᴬPs 59:1, 2   ᴮGen 27:41, 42   **32:12**ᴬGen 28:14   **32:13**ᴬGen 43:11

32:2¹I.e., Two Camps, or Two Companies

²²Now he got up that same night and took his two wives, his two female slaves, and his eleven children, and crossed the shallow place of the ^Jabbok. ²³He took them and sent them across the stream. And he sent across whatever he had.

JACOB WRESTLES

²⁴Then Jacob was left alone, and a man ^wrestled with him until daybreak. ²⁵When *the man* saw that he had not prevailed against him, he touched the socket of Jacob's hip; and the socket of Jacob's hip was dislocated while he wrestled with him. ²⁶Then he said, "Let me go, for the dawn is breaking." But he said, "^I will not let you go unless you bless me." ²⁷So he said to him, "What is your name?" And he said, "Jacob." ²⁸Then ^he said, "Your name shall no longer be Jacob, but ¹Israel; for you have contended with God and with men, and have prevailed." ²⁹And ^Jacob asked him and said, "Please tell me your name." But he said, "Why is it that you ask my name?" And he blessed him there. ³⁰So Jacob named the place ¹Peniel, for *he said,* "^I have seen God face to face, yet my life has been spared." ³¹Now the sun rose upon him just as he crossed over ^Penuel, and he was limping on his hip. ³²Therefore, to this day the sons of Israel do not eat the tendon of the hip which is on the socket of the hip, because he touched the socket of Jacob's hip in the tendon of the hip.

JACOB MEETS ESAU

33 Then Jacob raised his eyes and looked, and behold, ^Esau was coming, and four hundred men with him. So he divided the children among Leah and Rachel, and the two slave women. ²He put the slave women and their children in front, and Leah and her children next, and Rachel and Joseph last. ³But he himself passed on ahead of them and ^bowed down to the ground seven times, until he came near to his brother. ⁴Then Esau ran to meet him and embraced him, and ^fell on his neck and kissed him, and they wept. ⁵He raised his eyes and saw the women and the children, and said, "Who are these with you?" So he said, "^The children whom God has graciously given your servant." ⁶Then the slave women came forward with their children, and they bowed down. ⁷And Leah likewise came forward with her children, and they bowed down; and afterward Joseph came forward with Rachel, and they bowed down. ⁸And he said, "What do you mean by all this company which I have met?" And he said, "^To find favor in the sight of my lord." ⁹But Esau said, "^I have plenty, my brother; let what you have be your own." ¹⁰Jacob said, "No, please, if now I have found favor in your sight, then accept my gift from my hand, for I see your face as one sees the face of God, and you have received me favorably. ¹¹Please accept my gift which has been brought to you, ^because God has dealt graciously with me and because I have plenty." So he urged him, and he accepted *it.*

32:22 ^Deut 3:16; Josh 12:2   32:24 ^Hos 12:3, 4
32:26 ^Hos 12:4   32:28 ^Gen 35:10; 1 Kin 18:31
32:29 ^Judg 13:17, 18   32:30 ^Gen 16:13; Ex 24:10, 11
32:31 ^Judg 8:8   33:1 ^Gen 32:6   33:3 ^Gen 42:6; 43:26
33:4 ^Gen 45:14, 15   33:5 ^Gen 48:9; Ps 127:3
33:8 ^Gen 32:5   33:9 ^Gen 27:39, 40   33:11 ^Gen 30:43

32:28 ¹I.e., he who contends with God; or God contends   32:30 ¹I.e., the face of God

¹²Then Esau said, "Let's journey on and go, and I will go ahead of you." ¹³But he said to him, "My lord knows that the children are frail and that the flocks and herds that are nursing are a matter of concern to me. And if they are driven hard *just* one day, all the flocks will die. ¹⁴Please let my lord pass on ahead of his servant, and I will proceed at my leisure, at the pace of the cattle that are ahead of me and at the pace of the children, until I come to my lord at ᴬSeir."

¹⁵Then Esau said, "Please let me leave with you some of the people who are with me." But he said, "What need is there? ᴬLet me find favor in the sight of my lord." ¹⁶So Esau returned that day on his way to Seir. ¹⁷But Jacob journeyed to ¹·ᴬSuccoth, and built for himself a house and made booths for his livestock; therefore the place is named Succoth.

JACOB SETTLES IN SHECHEM

¹⁸Now Jacob came safely to the city of ᴬShechem, which is in the land of Canaan, when he came from ᴮPaddan-aram, and camped before the city. ¹⁹ᴬHe bought the plot of land where he had pitched his tent from the hand of the sons of Hamor, Shechem's father, for a hundred pieces of money. ²⁰Then he erected there an altar and called it ¹El-Elohe-Israel.

THE TREACHERY OF JACOB'S SONS

34 Now ᴬDinah the daughter of Leah, whom she had borne to Jacob, went out to visit the daughters of the land. ²When Shechem the son of Hamor ᴬthe Hivite, the prince of the land, saw her, he took her and lay with her

and raped her. ³But he was deeply attracted to Dinah the daughter of Jacob, and he loved the girl and spoke tenderly to her. ⁴So Shechem ᴬspoke to his father Hamor, saying, "Get me this young woman as a wife." ⁵Now Jacob heard that he had defiled his daughter Dinah; but his sons were with his livestock in the field, so Jacob said nothing until they came in. ⁶Then Hamor the father of Shechem went out to Jacob to speak with him. ⁷Now the sons of Jacob came in from the field when they heard *about it;* and the men were grieved, and they were very angry because he had done a ᴬdisgraceful thing in Israel by ¹sleeping with Jacob's daughter, for such a thing ought not to be done.

⁸But Hamor spoke with them, saying, "The soul of my son Shechem longs for your daughter; please give her to him in marriage. ⁹And intermarry with us; give your daughters to us and take our daughters for yourselves. ¹⁰So you will live with us, and ᴬthe land shall be open to you; live and trade in it and acquire property in it." ¹¹Shechem also said to her father and to her brothers, "Let me find favor in your sight, and I will give whatever you tell me. ¹²Demand of me ever so much bridal payment and gift, and I will give whatever you tell me; but give me the girl in marriage."

¹³But Jacob's sons answered Shechem and his father Hamor with deceit, because he had defiled

33:14ᴬGen 32:3   33:15ᴬRuth 2:13   33:17ᴬJosh 13:27; Judg 8:5, 14   33:18ᴬJosh 24:1   ᴮGen 28:2
33:19ᴬJosh 24:32; John 4:5   34:1ᴬGen 30:21
34:2ᴬGen 34:30   34:4ᴬJudg 14:2   34:7ᴬDeut 22:20-30; Judg 20:6   34:10ᴬGen 13:9; 20:15

33:17¹I.e., booths   33:20¹I.e., God, the God of Israel
34:7¹I.e., violating her

their sister Dinah. ¹⁴They said to them, "We cannot do this thing, *that is,* give our sister to a ᴬman who is uncircumcised, for that would be a disgrace to us. ¹⁵Only on this *condition* will we consent to you: if you will become like us, in that every male of you will be circumcised, ¹⁶then we will give our daughters to you, and we will take your daughters for ourselves, and we will live with you and become one people. ¹⁷But if you do not listen to us to be circumcised, then we will take our daughter and go."

¹⁸Now their words seemed reasonable to Hamor and Shechem, Hamor's son. ¹⁹The young man did not delay to do this, because he was delighted with Jacob's daughter. Now he was more respected than all the household of his father. ²⁰So Hamor and his son Shechem came to the ᴬgate of their city and spoke to the people of their city, saying, ²¹"These men are friendly to us; therefore let them live in the land and trade in it, for behold, the land is large enough for them. We will take their daughters in marriage, and give our daughters to them. ²²Only on this *condition* will the men consent to us to live with us, to become one people: that every male among us be circumcised just as they are circumcised. ²³Will their livestock and their property and all their animals not be ours? Let's just consent to them, and they will live with us." ²⁴ᴬAll who went out of the gate of his city listened to Hamor and to his son Shechem, and every male was circumcised, all who went out of the gate of his city.

²⁵Now it came about on the third day, when they were in pain, that two of Jacob's sons—ᴬSimeon and Levi, Dinah's brothers—each took his sword and came upon the city undetected, and killed every male. ²⁶They killed Hamor and his son Shechem with the edge of the sword, and took Dinah from Shechem's house, and left. ²⁷Jacob's sons came upon those killed and looted the city, because they had defiled their sister. ²⁸They took their flocks, their herds, and their donkeys, and that which was in the city and that which was in the field; ²⁹and they captured and looted all their wealth and all their little ones and their wives, even everything that *was* in the houses. ³⁰Then Jacob said to Simeon and Levi, "You have ᴬbrought trouble on me by ᴮmaking me repulsive among the inhabitants of the land, among the Canaanites and the Perizzites; and since my men are few in number, they will band together against me and attack me, and I will be destroyed, I and my household!" ³¹But they said, "Should he treat our sister like a prostitute?"

JACOB MOVES TO BETHEL

35 Then God said to Jacob, "Arise, go up to ᴬBethel and live there, and make an altar there to God, who appeared to you ᴮwhen you fled from your brother Esau." ²So Jacob said to his household and to all who were with him, "Remove ᴬthe foreign gods which are among you, and purify yourselves and change your garments; ³and let's arise and go up to Bethel, and I will make an altar there to God, ᴬwho answered me on the

34:14 ᴬGen 17:14   34:20 ᴬRuth 4:1; 2 Sam 15:2
34:24 ᴬGen 23:10   34:25 ᴬGen 49:5-7
34:30 ᴬJosh 7:25   ᴮEx 5:21   35:1 ᴬGen 28:19
ᴮGen 27:43   35:2 ᴬGen 31:19, 30, 34   35:3 ᴬPs 107:6

day of my distress and [B]has been with me wherever I have gone." [4]So they gave Jacob all the foreign gods which they had and the rings which were in their ears, and Jacob hid them under the oak which was near Shechem.

[5]As they journeyed, there was [A]a great terror upon the cities which were around them, and they did not pursue the sons of Jacob. [6]So Jacob came to [A]Luz (that is, Bethel), which is in the land of Canaan, he and all the people who were with him. [7]Then [A]he built an altar there, and called the place El-bethel, because there God had revealed Himself to him when he fled from his brother. [8]Now [A]Deborah, Rebekah's nurse, died, and she was buried below Bethel under the oak; and it was named [1]Allon-bacuth.

JACOB IS NAMED ISRAEL

[9]Then God appeared to Jacob again when he came from Paddan-aram, and He [A]blessed him. [10][A]God said to him,

"Your name is Jacob;
    You shall no longer be called
        Jacob,
    But Israel shall be your name."
So He called him Israel. [11]God also said to him,
"I am God Almighty;
    [A]Be fruitful and multiply;
    A nation and a [B]multitude of
        nations shall come from you,
    And kings shall come from
        you.
[12] "And [A]the land which I gave to
        Abraham and Isaac,
    I will give to you,
    And I will give the land to your
        descendants after you."
[13]Then [A]God went up from him at the place where He had spoken with

him. [14]So Jacob set up [A]a memorial stone in the place where He had spoken with him, a memorial of stone, and he poured out a drink offering on it; he also poured oil on it. [15]And Jacob named the place where God had spoken with him, [1][A]Bethel.

[16]Then they journeyed on from Bethel; but when there was still some distance to go to [A]Ephrath, Rachel began to give birth and she suffered severe difficulties in her labor. [17]And when she was suffering severe difficulties in her labor, the midwife said to her, "Do not fear, for [A]you have another son!" [18]And it came about, as her soul was departing (for she died), that she named him [1]Ben-oni; but his father called him [2]Benjamin. [19]So [A]Rachel died and was buried on the way to Ephrath (that is, Bethlehem). [20]And Jacob set up a memorial stone over her grave; that is the [A]memorial stone of Rachel's grave to this day. [21]Then Israel journeyed on and pitched his tent beyond the [A]tower of Eder.

THE SONS OF ISRAEL

[22]And it came about, while Israel was living in that land, that [A]Reuben went and slept with his father's concubine Bilhah, and Israel heard *about it.*

Now there were twelve sons of Jacob— [23][A]the sons of Leah *were*

35:3 [B]Gen 28:15   **35:5** [A]Ex 15:16; 23:27
35:6 [A]Gen 28:19; 48:3   **35:7** [A]Gen 35:3
35:8 [A]Gen 24:59   **35:9** [A]Gen 32:29   **35:10** [A]Gen 17:5;
32:28   **35:11** [A]Gen 9:1, 7   [B]Gen 48:4   **35:12** [A]Gen 12:7;
13:15   **35:13** [A]Gen 17:22; 18:33   **35:14** [A]Gen 28:18, 19;
31:45   **35:15** [A]Gen 28:19   **35:16** [A]Gen 35:19; Ruth 4:11
35:17 [A]Gen 30:24   **35:19** [A]Gen 48:7   **35:20** [A]1 Sam 10:2
35:21 [A]Mic 4:8   **35:22** [A]Gen 49:4; 1 Chr 5:1
35:23 [A]Gen 29:31-35; 30:18-20

35:8 [1]I.e., oak of weeping   **35:15** [1]I.e., house of God
35:18 [1]I.e., the son of my sorrow   [2]I.e., the son of the
right hand

Reuben, Jacob's firstborn, then Simeon, Levi, Judah, Issachar, and Zebulun; [24]ᴬthe sons of Rachel *were* Joseph and Benjamin; [25]and ᴬthe sons of Bilhah, Rachel's female slave, *were* Dan and Naphtali; [26]and ᴬthe sons of Zilpah, Leah's female slave, *were* Gad and Asher. These *were* the sons of Jacob who were born to him in Paddan-aram.

[27]Jacob came to his father Isaac at ᴬMamre of ᴮKiriath-arba (that is, Hebron), where Abraham and Isaac had resided.

[28]Now the days of Isaac were ᴬ180 years. [29]Then Isaac breathed his last and died, and was ᴬgathered to his people, an old man of ripe age; and his sons Esau and Jacob buried him.

ESAU MOVES

36 Now these are *the records of* the generations of ᴬEsau (that is, Edom).

[2]Esau ᴬtook his wives from the daughters of Canaan: Adah the daughter of Elon the Hittite, and ᴮOholibamah the daughter of Anah, the granddaughter of Zibeon the Hivite; [3]also Basemath, Ishmael's daughter, the sister of Nebaioth. [4]Adah bore ᴬEliphaz to Esau, and Basemath gave birth to Reuel, [5]and Oholibamah gave birth to Jeush, Jalam, and Korah. These are the sons of Esau who were born to him in the land of Canaan.

[6]ᴬThen Esau took his wives, his sons, his daughters, and all his household, and his livestock and all his cattle, and all his property which he had acquired in the land of Canaan, and went to *another* land away from his brother Jacob. [7]ᴬFor their possessions had become too great for them to live together,

and the ᴮland where they resided could not support them because of their livestock. [8]So Esau lived in the hill country of ᴬSeir; Esau is Edom.

DESCENDANTS OF ESAU

[9]These then are *the records of* the generations of Esau the father of the Edomites in the hill country of Seir. [10]These are the names of Esau's sons: Eliphaz the son of Esau's wife Adah, *and* Reuel the son of Esau's wife Basemath. [11]The sons of Eliphaz were Teman, Omar, Zepho, Gatam, and Kenaz. [12]Timna was a concubine of Esau's son Eliphaz, and she bore ᴬAmalek to Eliphaz. These are the sons of Esau's wife Adah. [13]And these are the sons of Reuel: Nahath, Zerah, Shammah, and Mizzah. These were the sons of Esau's wife Basemath. [14]And these were the sons of Esau's wife Oholibamah, the daughter of Anah, the granddaughter of Zibeon: she bore to Esau Jeush, Jalam, and Korah.

[15]These are the chiefs of the sons of Esau. The sons of Eliphaz, the firstborn of Esau, are chief Teman, chief Omar, chief Zepho, chief Kenaz, [16]chief Korah, chief Gatam, *and* chief Amalek. These are the chiefs descended from Eliphaz in the land of Edom; these are the sons of Adah. [17]And these are the sons of Reuel, Esau's son: chief Nahath, chief Zerah, chief Shammah, *and* chief Mizzah. These are the chiefs descended from Reuel in the land of Edom; these are the sons of Esau's wife Basemath. [18]And these

35:24 ᴬGen 30:22-24; 35:18 35:25 ᴬGen 30:5-8
35:26 ᴬGen 30:10-13 35:27 ᴬGen 13:18 ᴮJosh 14:15
35:28 ᴬGen 25:26 35:29 ᴬGen 25:8; 49:33
36:1 ᴬGen 25:30 36:2 ᴬGen 28:9 ᴮGen 36:25
36:4 ᴬ1 Chr 1:35 36:6 ᴬGen 12:5 36:7 ᴬGen 13:6
ᴮHeb 11:9 36:8 ᴬGen 32:3
36:12 ᴬEx 17:8-16; Num 24:20

are the sons of Esau's wife Oholi-bamah: chief Jeush, chief Jalam, *and* chief Korah. These are the chiefs descended from Esau's wife Oholibamah, the daughter of Anah. ¹⁹These are the sons of Esau (that is, Edom), and these are their chiefs.

²⁰These are the sons of Seir ᴬthe Horite, the inhabitants of the land: Lotan, Shobal, Zibeon, Anah, ²¹Dishon, Ezer, and Dishan. These are the chiefs descended from the Horites, the sons of Seir in the land of Edom. ²²And the sons of Lotan were Hori and Hemam; and Lotan's sister was Timna. ²³And these are the sons of Shobal: Alvan, Mana-hath, Ebal, Shepho, and Onam. ²⁴And these are the sons of Zibeon: Aiah and Anah—he is the Anah who found the hot springs in the wilderness when he was pasturing the donkeys of his father Zibeon. ²⁵And these are the children of Anah: Dishon, and Oholibamah, the daughter of Anah. ²⁶And these are the sons of ᴬDishon: Hem-dan, Eshban, Ithran, and Cheran. ²⁷These are the sons of Ezer: Bil-han, Zaavan, and Akan. ²⁸These are the sons of Dishan: Uz and Aran. ²⁹These are the chiefs descended from the Horites: chief Lotan, chief Shobal, chief Zibeon, chief Anah, ³⁰chief Dishon, chief Ezer, *and* chief Dishan. These are the chiefs descended from the Horites, according to their *various* chiefs in the land of Seir.

³¹Now these are the kings who reigned in the land of Edom before any ᴬking reigned over the sons of Israel. ³²ᴬBela the son of Beor reigned in Edom, and the name of his city was Dinhabah. ³³Then Bela died, and Jobab the son of Zerah of Bozrah became king in his place.

³⁴Then Jobab died, and Husham of the land of the Temanites became king in his place. ³⁵Then Husham died, and Hadad the son of Bedad, who defeated Midian in the field of Moab, became king in his place; and the name of his city was Avith. ³⁶Then Hadad died, and Samlah of Masrekah became king in his place. ³⁷Then Samlah died, and Shaul of Rehoboth on the *Euphrates* River became king in his place. ³⁸Then Shaul died, and Baal-hanan the son of Achbor became king in his place. ³⁹Then Baal-hanan the son of Ach-bor died, and Hadar became king in his place; and the name of his city was Pau; and his wife's name was Mehetabel, the daughter of Matred, daughter of Mezahab.

⁴⁰Now these are the names of the chiefs descended from Esau, according to their families *and* their localities, by their names: chief Timna, chief Alvah, chief Jetheth, ⁴¹chief Oholibamah, chief Elah, chief Pinon, ⁴²chief Kenaz, chief Teman, chief Mibzar, ⁴³chief Magdiel, *and* chief Iram. These are the chiefs of Edom (that is, Esau, the father of the Edomites), accord-ing to their settlements in the land of their possession.

JOSEPH'S DREAMS

37 Now Jacob lived in ᴬthe land where his father had lived as a stranger, in the land of Canaan. ²These are *the records of* the gen-erations of Jacob.

Joseph, *when he was* seventeen years of age, was pasturing the flock with his brothers, while he was *still* a youth, along with ᴬthe sons of

36:20 ᴬGen 14:6; Deut 2:12, 22   36:26 ᴬ1 Chr 1:41
36:31 ᴬGen 17:6, 16; 35:11   36:32 ᴬ1 Chr 1:43
37:1 ᴬGen 17:8; 28:4   37:2 ᴬGen 35:25, 26

Bilhah and the sons of Zilpah, his father's wives. And Joseph brought back a ᴮbad report about them to their father. ³Now Israel loved Joseph more than all his *other* sons, because he was ᴬthe son of his old age; and he made him a ᴮmulticolored tunic. ⁴And his brothers saw that their father loved him more than all his brothers; and *so* they ᴬhated him and could not speak to him on friendly terms.

⁵Then Joseph ᴬhad a dream, and when he told it to his brothers, they hated him even more. ⁶He said to them, "Please listen to this dream which I have had; ⁷for behold, we were binding sheaves in the field, and behold, my sheaf stood up and also remained standing; and behold, your sheaves gathered around and ᴬbowed down to my sheaf." ⁸Then his brothers said to him, "ᴬAre you actually going to reign over us? Or are you really going to rule over us?" So they hated him even more for his dreams and for his words.

⁹Then he had yet another dream, and informed his brothers of it, and said, "Behold, I have had yet *another* dream; and behold, the sun and the moon, and eleven stars were bowing down to me." ¹⁰He also told *it* to his father as well as to his brothers; and his father rebuked him and said to him, "What is this dream that you have had? Am I and your mother and ᴬyour brothers actually going to come to bow down to the ground before you?" ¹¹And ᴬhis brothers were jealous of him, but his father ᴮkept the matter *in mind*.

¹²Then his brothers went to pasture their father's flock in Shechem. ¹³And Israel said to Joseph, "Are your brothers not pasturing *the flock* in ᴬShechem? Come, and I will send you to them." And he said to him, "I will go." ¹⁴Then he said to him, "Go now and see about the welfare of your brothers and the welfare of the flock, and bring word back to me." So he sent him from the Valley of ᴬHebron, and he came to Shechem.

¹⁵A man found him, and behold, he was wandering in the field; and the man asked him, "What are you looking for?" ¹⁶He said, "I am looking for my brothers; please tell me where they are pasturing *the flock*." ¹⁷Then the man said, "They have moved from here; for I heard *them* say, 'Let's go to ᴬDothan.'" So Joseph went after his brothers and found them at Dothan.

THE PLOT AGAINST JOSEPH

¹⁸When they saw him from a distance, and before he came closer to them, they ᴬplotted against him to put him to death. ¹⁹They said to one another, "Here comes this dreamer! ²⁰Now then, come and let's kill him, and throw him into one of the pits; and ᴬwe will say, 'A vicious animal devoured him.' Then we will see what will become of his dreams!" ²¹But ᴬReuben heard *this* and rescued him out of their hands by saying, "Let's not take his life." ²²Then Reuben said to them, "Shed no blood. Throw him into this pit that is in the wilderness, but do not lay a hand on him"—so that *later* he might rescue him out

37:2 ᴮ1 Sam 2:22-24　37:3 ᴬGen 44:20
ᴮGen 37:23, 32　37:4 ᴬGen 27:41; 1 Sam 17:28
37:5 ᴬGen 28:12; 31:10, 11, 24　37:7 ᴬGen 42:6, 9; 43:26
37:8 ᴬGen 49:26; Deut 33:16　37:10 ᴬGen 27:29
37:11 ᴬActs 7:9　ᴮDan 7:28　37:13 ᴬGen 33:18-20
37:14 ᴬGen 13:18; 23:2, 19　37:17 ᴬ2 Kin 6:13
37:18 ᴬPs 31:13; 37:12, 32　37:20 ᴬGen 37:32, 33
37:21 ᴬGen 42:22

of their hands, to return him to his father. ²³So it came about, when Joseph reached his brothers, that they stripped Joseph of his tunic, the multicolored tunic that was on him; ²⁴and they took him and threw him into the pit. Now the pit was empty, without any water in it.

²⁵Then they sat down to eat a meal. But as they raised their eyes and looked, behold, a caravan of Ishmaelites was coming from Gilead, with their camels carrying ᴬlabdanum resin, ᴮbalsam, and myrrh, on their way to bring *them* down to Egypt. ²⁶And Judah said to his brothers, "What profit is it for us to kill our brother and ᴬcover up his blood? ²⁷ᴬCome, and let's sell him to the Ishmaelites and not lay our hands on him, for he is our brother, our *own* flesh." And his brothers listened *to him.* ²⁸Then some Midianite traders passed by, so they pulled *him* out and lifted Joseph out of the pit, and ᴬsold him to the Ishmaelites for ¹twenty *shekels* of silver. So ᴮthey brought Joseph into Egypt.

²⁹Now Reuben returned to the pit, and behold, Joseph was not in the pit; so he ᴬtore his garments. ³⁰He returned to his brothers and said, "ᴬThe boy is not *there;* as for me, where am I to go?" ³¹So ᴬthey took Joseph's tunic, and slaughtered a male goat, and dipped the tunic in the blood; ³²and they sent the multicolored tunic and brought it to their father and said, "We found this; please examine *it to see whether* it is your son's tunic or not." ³³Then he examined it and said, "*It is* my son's tunic. ᴬA vicious animal has devoured him; ᴮJoseph has surely been torn to pieces!" ³⁴So Jacob ᴬtore his clothes, and put on a sackcloth *undergarment* over his waist,

and mourned for his son many days. ³⁵Then all his sons and all his daughters got up to comfort him, but he refused to be comforted. And he said, "Surely I will ᴬgo down to Sheol in mourning for my son." So his father wept for him. ³⁶Meanwhile, the Midianites ᴬsold him in Egypt to Potiphar, Pharaoh's officer, the captain of the bodyguard.

JUDAH AND TAMAR

38 And it came about at that time, that Judah departed from his brothers and visited a certain ᴬAdullamite, whose name was Hirah. ²Judah saw there a daughter of a certain Canaanite whose name was ᴬShua; and he took her *as a wife* and had relations with her. ³And she conceived and gave birth to a son, and he named him ᴬEr. ⁴Then she conceived again and gave birth to a son, and she named him ᴬOnan. ⁵She gave birth to yet another son and named him ᴬShelah; and it was at Chezib that she gave birth to him.

⁶Now Judah took a wife for Er his firstborn, and her name *was* Tamar. ⁷But ᴬEr, Judah's firstborn, was evil in the sight of the Lᴏʀᴅ, so the Lᴏʀᴅ took his life. ⁸Then Judah said to Onan, "ᴬHave relations with your brother's wife and perform your duty as a brother-in-law to her, and raise up a child for your brother." ⁹Now Onan knew that the ᴬchild

37:25 ᴬGen 43:11   ᴮJer 8:22   37:26 ᴬGen 37:20
37:27 ᴬGen 42:21   37:28 ᴬGen 45:4, 5   ᴮGen 39:1
37:29 ᴬGen 37:34; 44:13   37:30 ᴬGen 42:13, 36
37:31 ᴬGen 37:3, 23   37:33 ᴬGen 37:20   Gen 44:28
37:34 ᴬGen 37:29   37:35 ᴬGen 25:8; 35:29
37:36 ᴬGen 39:1   38:1 ᴬJosh 15:35; 1 Sam 22:1
38:2 ᴬ1 Chr 2:3   38:3 ᴬGen 46:12; Num 26:19
38:4 ᴬGen 46:12   38:5 ᴬNum 26:20   38:7 ᴬGen 46:12;
Num 26:19   38:8 ᴬDeut 25:5, 6; Matt 22:24
38:9 ᴬDeut 25:6

37:28 ¹About 10 oz. or 280 gm

would not be his; so when he had relations with his brother's wife, he wasted his seed on the ground so that he would not give a child to his brother. [10] But what he did was displeasing in the sight of the LORD; so He ^took his life also. [11] Then Judah said to his daughter-in-law Tamar, "^Remain a widow in your father's house until my son Shelah grows up"; for he thought, "*I am afraid* that he too may die like his brothers." So Tamar went and lived in her father's house.

[12] Now after a considerable time Shua's daughter, the wife of Judah, died; and when the time of mourning was ended, Judah went up to his sheepshearers at ^Timnah, he and his friend Hirah the Adullamite. [13] And Tamar was told, "Behold, your father-in-law is going up to ^Timnah to shear his sheep." [14] So she removed her widow's garments and ^covered *herself* with a veil, and wrapped herself, and sat in the gateway of Enaim, which is on the road to Timnah; for she saw that Shelah had grown up, and ^Bshe had not been given to him as a wife. [15] When Judah saw her, he assumed she *was* a prostitute, for she had covered her face. [16] So he turned aside to her by the road, and said, "Here now, let me have relations with you"; for he did not know that she was his daughter-in-law. And she said, "What will you give me, that you may have relations with me?" [17] He said, therefore, "I will send you a young goat from the flock." She then said, "Will you give a pledge until you send *it?*" [18] He said, "What pledge shall I give you?" And she said, "^Your seal and your cord, and your staff that is in your hand." So he gave *them* to her and

had relations with her, and she conceived by him. [19] Then she got up and departed, and removed her veil and put on her widow's garments.

[20] When Judah sent the young goat by his friend the Adullamite, to receive the pledge from the woman's hand, he did not find her. [21] He asked the people of her place, saying, "Where is the temple prostitute who was by the road at Enaim?" But they said, "There has been no temple prostitute here." [22] So he returned to Judah, and said, "I did not find her; and furthermore, the people of the place said, 'There has been no temple prostitute here.'" [23] Then Judah said, "Let her keep them, otherwise we will become a laughingstock. After all, I sent this young goat, but you did not find her."

[24] Now it was about three months later that Judah was informed, "Your daughter-in-law Tamar has prostituted herself, and behold, she is also pregnant by prostitution." Then Judah said, "Bring her out and ^have her burned!" [25] It was while she was being brought out that she sent *word* to her father-in-law, saying, "I am pregnant by the man to whom these things belong." She also said, "^Please examine and see, whose signet ring and cords and staff are these?" [26] And Judah recognized *them*, and said, "^She is more righteous than I, since ^BI did not give her to my son Shelah." And he did not have relations with her again.

[27] It came about at the time she was giving birth, that behold, there were ^twins in her womb.

38:10 ^Gen 46:12; Num 26:19   **38:11** ^Ruth 1:12, 13   **38:12** ^Josh 15:10, 57   **38:13** ^Josh 15:10, 57; Judg 14:1   **38:14** ^Gen 24:65   ^BGen 38:11, 26   **38:18** ^Gen 38:25; 41:42   **38:24** ^Lev 21:9   **38:25** ^Gen 37:32   **38:26** ^1 Sam 24:17   ^BGen 38:14   **38:27** ^Gen 25:24-26

²⁸Moreover, it took place while she was giving birth, that one *baby* put out a hand, and the midwife took and tied a scarlet *thread* on his hand, saying, "This one came out first." ²⁹But it came about as he drew back his hand that behold, his brother came out. Then she said, "What a breach you have made for yourself!" So he was named ^{1,A}Perez. ³⁰Afterward his brother came out who had the scarlet *thread* on his hand; and he was named ^{1,A}Zerah.

JOSEPH'S SUCCESS IN EGYPT

39 Now Joseph had been taken down to Egypt; and Potiphar, an Egyptian officer of Pharaoh, the captain of the bodyguard, bought him from the ^AIshmaelites, who had taken him down there. ²And ^Athe Lord was with Joseph, so he became a successful man. And he was in the house of his master, the Egyptian. ³Now his master ^Asaw that the Lord was with him and *that* the Lord ^Bmade all that he did prosper in his hand. ⁴So Joseph ^Afound favor in his sight and became his personal servant; and he made him overseer over his house, and put him in charge of ^Ball that he owned. ⁵It came about that from the time he made him overseer in his house and over all that he owned, the Lord ^Ablessed the Egyptian's house on account of Joseph; so the Lord's blessing was upon all that he owned, in the house and in the field. ⁶So he left Joseph in charge of everything that he owned; and with him *there* he did not concern himself with anything except the food which he ate.

Now Joseph was ^Ahandsome in form and appearance. ⁷And it came about after these events that his master's wife had her eyes on Joseph, and she said, "^ASleep with me." ⁸But ^Ahe refused and said to his master's wife, "Look, with me *here,* my master does not concern himself with anything in the house, and he has put me in charge of all that he owns. ^{9A}There is no one greater in this house than I, and he has withheld nothing from me except you, because you are his wife. How then could I do this great evil, and sin against God?" ¹⁰Though she spoke to Joseph day after day, he did not listen to her to lie beside her *or* be with her. ¹¹Now it happened one day that he went into the house to do his work, and none of the people of the household was there inside. ¹²So she grabbed him by his garment, saying, "Sleep with me!" But he left his garment in her hand and fled, and went outside. ¹³When she saw that he had left his garment in her hand and had fled outside, ¹⁴she called to the men of her household and said to them, "See, he has brought in a Hebrew to us to make fun of us; he came in to me to sleep with me, and I screamed. ¹⁵When he heard that I raised my voice and screamed, he left his garment beside me and fled and went outside." ¹⁶So she left his garment beside her until his master came home. ¹⁷Then she ^Aspoke to him with these words: "The Hebrew slave, whom you brought to us, came in to me to make fun of me; ¹⁸but when I raised my voice

38:29^AGen 46:12; Ruth 4:12   38:30^A1 Chr 2:4
39:1^AGen 37:25, 28, 36; Ps 105:17   39:2^AGen 39:3, 21, 23;
Acts 7:9   39:3^AGen 21:22   ^BPs 1:3   39:4^AGen 18:3
^BGen 24:2   39:5^AGen 30:27   39:6^AGen 29:17;
1 Sam 16:12   39:7^A2 Sam 13:11   39:8^AProv 6:23, 24
39:9^AGen 41:40   39:17^AEx 23:1; Prov 26:28

38:29¹I.e., a breach   38:30¹I.e., a dawning or brightness

and screamed, he left his garment beside me and fled outside."

JOSEPH IMPRISONED

¹⁹ Now when his master heard the words of his wife which she spoke to him, saying, "This is what your slave did to me," ^his anger burned. ²⁰ So Joseph's master took him and ^put him into the prison, the place where the king's prisoners were confined; and he was there in the prison. ²¹ But the LORD was with Joseph and extended kindness to him, and ^gave him favor in the sight of the warden of the prison. ²² And the warden of the prison ^put Joseph in charge of all the prisoners who were in the prison; so that whatever was done there, he was responsible *for it*. ²³ The warden of the prison did not supervise anything under Joseph's authority, because ^the LORD was with him; and, the LORD made whatever he did prosper.

JOSEPH INTERPRETS DREAMS

40 Then it came about after these things, *that* ^the cupbearer and the baker for the king of Egypt offended their lord, the king of Egypt. ² And Pharaoh was ^furious with his two officials, the chief cupbearer and the chief baker. ³ So he put them in confinement in the house of the ^captain of the bodyguard, in the prison, the *same* place where Joseph was imprisoned. ⁴ And the captain of the bodyguard put Joseph in charge of them, and he took care of them; and they were in confinement for some time. ⁵ Then the cupbearer and the baker for the king of Egypt, who were confined in the prison, both had a dream the same night, each

man with his *own* dream *and* each dream with its *own* interpretation. ⁶ When Joseph came to them in the morning and saw them, behold, they were dejected. ⁷ So he asked Pharaoh's officials who were with him in confinement in his master's house, "^Why are your faces so sad today?" ⁸ And they said to him, "^We have had a dream, and there is no one to interpret it." Then Joseph said to them, "^Do interpretations not belong to God? Tell *it* to me, please."

⁹ So the chief cupbearer told his dream to Joseph, saying to him, "In my dream, behold, *there was* a vine in front of me; ¹⁰ and on the vine *were* three branches. And as it was budding, its blossoms came out, *and* its clusters produced ripe grapes. ¹¹ Now Pharaoh's cup was in my hand; so I took the grapes and squeezed them into Pharaoh's cup, and I put the cup into Pharaoh's hand." ¹² Then Joseph said to him, "This is the ^interpretation of it: the three branches are three days; ¹³ within three more days Pharaoh will ¹lift up your head and restore you to your office; and you will put Pharaoh's cup into his hand as in your former practice when you were his cupbearer. ¹⁴ Only keep me in mind when it goes well for you, and please ^do me a kindness by mentioning me to Pharaoh, and get me out of this prison. ¹⁵ For ^I was in fact kidnapped from the land of the Hebrews, and even here I have

---

39:19 ^Prov 6:34   39:20 ^Gen 40:3; Ps 105:18
39:21 ^Ex 3:21; 11:3   39:22 ^Gen 39:4; 40:3, 4
39:23 ^Gen 39:2, 3   40:1 ^Gen 40:11, 13; Neh 1:11
40:2 ^Prov 16:14   40:3 ^Gen 39:1, 20   40:7 ^Neh 2:2
40:8 ^Gen 41:15   ᴮDan 2:27, 28   40:12 ^Dan 2:36;
4:18, 19   40:14 ^Josh 2:12; 1 Sam 20:14
40:15 ^Gen 37:26-28

40:13 ¹ I.e., a royal gesture of forgiveness

done nothing that they should have put me into the dungeon."

[16] When the chief baker saw that he had interpreted favorably, he said to Joseph, "I also *saw* in my dream, and behold, *there were* three baskets of white bread on my head; [17] and in the top basket *there were* some of all kinds of baked food for Pharaoh, and the birds were eating them out of the basket on my head." [18] Then Joseph answered and said, "This is its interpretation: the three baskets are three days; [19] within three more days Pharaoh will lift up your head from you and will hang you on a wooden *post,* and the birds will eat your flesh off you."

[20] So it came about on the third day, *which was* [A] Pharaoh's birthday, that he held a feast for all his servants; [B] and he lifted up the head of the chief cupbearer and the head of the chief baker among his servants. [21] He restored the chief cupbearer to his office, and [A] he put the cup into Pharaoh's hand; [22] but [A] he hanged the chief baker, just as Joseph had interpreted to them. [23] Yet the chief cupbearer did not remember Joseph, but [A] forgot him.

PHARAOH'S DREAM

41 Now it happened at the end of two full years that Pharaoh had a dream, and behold, he was standing by the Nile. [2] And behold, from the Nile seven cows came up, fine-looking and fat; and they grazed in the [A] marsh grass. [3] Then behold, seven other cows came up after them from the Nile, ugly and thin, and they stood by the *other* cows on the bank of the Nile. [4] Then the ugly and thin cows ate the seven fine-looking and fat cows. Then Pharaoh awoke. [5] But he fell asleep and dreamed a second time; and behold, seven ears of grain came up on a single stalk, plump and good. [6] Then behold, seven ears, thin and scorched by the east wind, sprouted up after them. [7] And the thin ears swallowed the seven plump and full ears. Then Pharaoh awoke, and behold, *it was* a dream. [8] Now in the morning [A] his spirit was troubled, so he sent *messengers* and called for all the soothsayer priests of Egypt, and all its wise men. And Pharaoh told them his dreams, but [B] there was no one who could interpret them for Pharaoh.

[9] Then the chief cupbearer spoke to Pharaoh, saying, "I would make mention today of [A] my *own* offenses. [10] Pharaoh was [A] furious with his servants, and he put me in confinement in the house of the captain of the bodyguard, *both* me and the chief baker. [11] Then [A] we had a dream one night, he and I; each of us dreamed according to the interpretation of his *own* dream. [12] Now a Hebrew youth *was* there with us, a [A] servant of the captain of the bodyguard, and we told him *the dreams,* and [B] he interpreted our dreams for us. For each man he interpreted according to his *own* dream. [13] And just [A] as he interpreted for us, so it happened; *Pharaoh* restored me in my office, but he hanged the chief baker."

JOSEPH INTERPRETS

[14] Then Pharaoh sent *word* and [A] called for Joseph, and they [B] hurriedly brought him out of the

40:20 [A] Matt 14:6   [B] 2 Kin 25:27   40:21 [A] Gen 40:13
40:22 [A] Gen 40:19; Esth 7:10   40:23 [A] Job 19:14;
Ps 31:12   41:2 [A] Job 8:11; Is 19:6, 7   41:8 [A] Dan 2:1, 3
[B] Dan 4:7   41:9 [A] Gen 40:14, 23   41:10 [A] Gen 40:2, 3
41:11 [A] Gen 40:5   41:12 [A] Gen 37:36   [B] Gen 40:12
41:13 [A] Gen 40:21, 22   41:14 [A] Ps 105:20   [B] Dan 2:25

dungeon; and when he had shaved himself and changed his clothes, he came to Pharaoh. [15]Pharaoh said to Joseph, "I have had a dream, ^but no one can interpret it; and I have heard it said about you, that when you hear a dream you can interpret it." [16]Joseph then answered Pharaoh, saying, "It has nothing to do with me; ^God will give Pharaoh an answer for his own good." [17]So Pharaoh said to Joseph, "In my dream, there I was, standing on the bank of the Nile; [18]and behold, seven cows, fat and fine-looking came up out of the Nile, and they grazed in the marsh grass. [19]Then behold, seven other cows came up after them, poor and very ugly and thin, such as I had never seen for ugliness in all the land of Egypt; [20]and the thin and ugly cows ate the first seven fat cows. [21]Yet when they had devoured them, it could not be detected that they had devoured them, for they were just as ugly as before. Then I awoke. [22]I saw also in my dream, and behold, seven ears of grain, full and good, came up on a single stalk; [23]and behold, seven ears, withered, thin, *and* scorched by the east wind sprouted up after them; [24]and the thin ears swallowed the seven good ears. Then ^I told it to the soothsayer priests, but there was no one who could explain it to me."

[25]And Joseph said to Pharaoh, "Pharaoh's dreams are one *and the same;* ^God has told to Pharaoh what He is about to do. [26]The seven good cows are seven years; and the seven good ears are seven years; the dreams are one *and the same.* [27]The seven thin and ugly cows that came up after them are seven years, and the seven thin ears scorched by the east wind ^will be seven years of famine. [28]It is as I have spoken to Pharaoh: ^God has shown Pharaoh what He is about to do. [29]Behold, ^seven years of great abundance are coming in all the land of Egypt; [30]and after them ^seven years of famine will come, and all the abundance will be forgotten in the land of Egypt, and the famine will ravage the land. [31]So the abundance will be unknown in the land because of that subsequent famine; for it *will be* very severe. [32]Now as for the repeating of the dream to Pharaoh twice, *it means* that ^the matter is confirmed by God, and God will quickly bring it about. [33]So now let Pharaoh look for a man ^discerning and wise, and appoint him over the land of Egypt. [34]Let Pharaoh take action to appoint overseers in charge of the land, and let him take a fifth *of the produce* of the land of Egypt *as a tax* in the seven years of abundance. [35]Then have them ^collect all the food of these good years that are coming, and store up the grain for food in the cities under Pharaoh's authority, and have them guard *it.* [36]Let the food be *used* as a reserve for the land for the seven years of famine which will occur in the land of Egypt, so that the land will not perish during the famine."

[37]Now the proposal seemed good to Pharaoh and to all his servants.

JOSEPH IS MADE A RULER OF EGYPT

[38]Then Pharaoh said to his servants, "Can we find a man like this, ^in whom there is a divine spirit?"

41:15 ^Gen 41:8   41:16 ^Gen 40:8; Deut 29:29
41:24 ^Is 8:19; Dan 4:7   41:25 ^Gen 41:28, 32;
Dan 2:28, 29, 45   41:27 ^2 Kin 8:1   41:28 ^Gen 41:25, 32
41:29 ^Gen 41:47   41:30 ^Gen 41:54, 56; Ps 105:16
41:32 ^Gen 41:25, 28   41:33 ^Gen 41:39
41:35 ^Gen 41:48   41:38 ^Job 32:8; Dan 4:8, 9, 18

³⁹So Pharaoh said to Joseph, "Since God has informed you of all this, there is no one as ᴬdiscerning and wise as you are. ⁴⁰ᴬYou shall be in charge of my house, and all my people shall be obedient to you; only *regarding* the throne will I be greater than you." ⁴¹Pharaoh also said to Joseph, "See, I have placed you ᴬover all the land of Egypt." ⁴²Then Pharaoh ᴬtook off his signet ring from his hand and put it on Joseph's hand, and clothed him in garments of fine linen, and put the gold necklace around his neck. ⁴³And he had him ride in his second chariot; and they proclaimed ahead of him, "Bow the knee!" And he placed him over all the land of Egypt. ⁴⁴Moreover, Pharaoh said to Joseph, "*Though* I am Pharaoh, yet ᴬwithout your permission no one shall raise his hand or foot in all the land of Egypt." ⁴⁵Then Pharaoh named Joseph ¹Zaphenath-paneah; and he gave him Asenath, the daughter of Potiphera priest of ᴬOn, to *be his* wife. And Joseph went out over the land of Egypt.

⁴⁶Now Joseph was ᴬthirty years old when he stood in the presence of Pharaoh, king of Egypt. And Joseph went out from the presence of Pharaoh and went through all the land of Egypt. ⁴⁷During the seven years of plenty the land produced abundantly. ⁴⁸So he collected all the food of *these* seven years which occurred in the land of Egypt and put the food in the cities; he put in every city the food from its own surrounding fields. ⁴⁹Joseph stored up grain in great abundance like the sand of the sea, until he stopped measuring *it,* for it was beyond measure.

THE SONS OF JOSEPH

⁵⁰Now before the year of famine came, ᴬtwo sons were born to Joseph, whom Asenath, the daughter of Potiphera, priest of On, bore to him. ⁵¹Joseph named the firstborn ¹Manasseh; "For," *he said,* "God has made me forget all my trouble and all of my father's household." ⁵²And he named the second ¹Ephraim; "For," *he said,* "ᴬGod has made me fruitful in the land of my affliction."

⁵³When the seven years of plenty which had taken place in the land of Egypt came to an end, ⁵⁴and ᴬthe seven years of famine began to come, just as Joseph had said, then there was famine in all the lands; but in all the land of Egypt there was bread. ⁵⁵So when all the land of Egypt suffered famine, the people cried out to Pharaoh for bread; and Pharaoh said to all the Egyptians, "Go to Joseph; ᴬwhatever he says to you, you shall do." ⁵⁶When the famine was *spread* over the entire face of the earth, then Joseph opened all the storehouses and sold grain to the Egyptians; and the famine was severe in the land of Egypt. ⁵⁷Then *the people of* all the earth came to Egypt to buy grain from Joseph, because ᴬthe famine was severe in all the earth.

JOSEPH'S BROTHERS SENT TO EGYPT

42 Now ᴬJacob saw that there was grain in Egypt, and Jacob said to his sons, "Why are you staring at one another?" ²Then he

41:39ᴬGen 41:33   **41:40**ᴬPs 105:21; Acts 7:10
41:41ᴬGen 42:6; Ps 105:21   **41:42**ᴬEsth 3:10; 8:2
41:44ᴬPs 105:22   **41:45**ᴬJer 43:13; Ezek 30:17
41:46ᴬGen 37:2   **41:50**ᴬGen 48:5   **41:52**ᴬGen 17:6;
28:3   **41:54**ᴬPs 105:16; Acts 7:11   **41:55**ᴬJohn 2:5
41:57ᴬGen 12:10   **42:1**ᴬActs 7:12

41:45¹Prob. Egyptian for "God speaks; he lives"
41:51¹I.e., making to forget   **41:52**¹I.e., fruitfulness

said, "Look, I have heard that there is grain in Egypt; go down there and buy *some* for us from that place, ^so that we may live and not die." ³So ten of Joseph's brothers went down to buy grain from Egypt. ⁴But Jacob did not send Joseph's brother ^Benjamin with his brothers, for he said, "I am afraid that harm may happen to him." ⁵So the sons of Israel came to buy grain among those who were coming, ^because the famine was *also* in the land of Canaan.

⁶Now ^Joseph was the ruler over the land; he was the one who sold grain to all the people of the land. And Joseph's brothers came and ᴮbowed down to him *with their* faces to the ground. ⁷When Joseph saw his brothers, he recognized them, but he disguised himself to them and ^spoke to them harshly. He said to them, "Where have you come from?" And they said, "From the land of Canaan, to buy food."

⁸But Joseph had recognized his brothers, although ^they did not recognize him. ⁹And Joseph ^remembered the dreams which he had about them, and he said to them, "You are spies; you have come to look at the undefended parts of our land." ¹⁰And they said to him, "No, ^my lord, but your servants have come to buy food. ¹¹We are all sons of one man; we are ^honest men, your servants are not spies." ¹²Yet he said to them, "No, but you have come to look at the undefended parts of our land!" ¹³But they said, "Your servants are twelve brothers *in all,* the sons of one man in the land of Canaan; and behold, the youngest is with our father today, and ^one is no longer alive." ¹⁴Yet Joseph said to them, "It is as I said to you, you are spies; ¹⁵by

this you will be tested: ^by the life of Pharaoh, you shall not leave this place unless your youngest brother comes here! ¹⁶Send one of you and have him get your brother, while you remain confined, so that your words may be tested, whether there is ^truth in you. But if not, by the life of Pharaoh, you are certainly spies!" ¹⁷So he put them all together in ^prison for three days.

¹⁸Now Joseph said to them on the third day, "Do this and live, for ^I fear God: ¹⁹if you are honest men, let one of your brothers be confined in your prison; but as for *the rest of* you, go, carry grain for the famine of your households, ²⁰and ^bring your youngest brother to me, so that your words may be verified, and you will not die." And they did so. ²¹Then they said to one another, "^Truly we are guilty concerning our brother, because we saw the distress of his soul when he pleaded with us, yet we would not listen; for that reason this distress has happened to us." ²²Reuben answered them, saying, "^Did I not tell you, 'Do not sin against the boy'; and you would not listen? Now *justice for* his blood is required." ²³They did not know, however, that Joseph understood, for there was an interpreter between them. ²⁴Then he turned away from them and ^wept. But when he returned to them and spoke to them, he took Simeon from them and bound him before their eyes. ²⁵^Then Joseph

42:2 ^Gen 43:8; Ps 33:18, 19 42:4 ^Gen 35:18, 24
42:5 ^Gen 12:10; Acts 7:11 42:6 ^Gen 41:41, 55
ᴮIs 60:14 42:7 ^Gen 42:30 42:8 ^Gen 37:2; 41:46
42:9 ^Gen 37:6-9 42:10 ^Gen 37:8 42:11 ^Gen 42:16,
19, 31, 34 42:13 ^Gen 37:33; 42:32 42:15 ^1 Sam 17:55
42:16 ^Gen 42:11 42:17 ^Gen 40:4, 7 42:18 ^Gen 39:9;
Lev 25:43 42:20 ^Gen 42:34; 43:5 42:21 ^Gen
37:26-28; Hos 5:15 42:22 ^Gen 37:21, 22
42:24 ^Gen 43:30; 45:14, 15 42:25 ^Rom 12:17, 20, 21;
1 Pet 3:9

gave orders to fill their bags with grain, but *also* to return every man's money in his sack, and to give them provisions for the journey. And that is what was done for them.

26 So they loaded their donkeys with their grain and departed from there. 27 But when one *of them* opened his sack to give his donkey feed at the overnight campsite, he saw his ^money; and behold, it was in the opening of his sack! 28 So he said to his brothers, "My money has been returned, and look, it is right in my sack!" Then their hearts sank, and they *turned* trembling to one another, saying, "^What is this that God has done to us?"

SIMEON IS HELD HOSTAGE

29 When they came to their father Jacob in the land of Canaan, they told him everything that had happened to them, saying, 30 "The man, the lord of the land, ^spoke harshly with us, and took us for spies of the country. 31 But we said to him, 'We are ^honest men; we are not spies. 32 We are twelve brothers, sons of our father; one is no longer alive, and the youngest is with our father today in the land of Canaan.' 33 But the man, the lord of the land, said to us, '^By this I will know that you are honest men: leave one of your brothers with me and take *grain for* the famine of your households, and go. 34 But bring your youngest brother to me so that I may know that you are not spies, but honest men. I will give your brother to you, and you may ^trade in the land.'"

35 Now it came about, as they were emptying their sacks, that behold, ^every man's bag of money *was* in his sack; and when they and their father saw their bags of money,

they were afraid. 36 And their father Jacob said to them, "You have ^deprived me of my sons: Joseph is gone, and Simeon is gone, and *now* you would take Benjamin; all these things are against me." 37 Then Reuben spoke to his father, saying, "You may put my two sons to death if I do not bring him *back* to you; put him in my care, and I will return him to you." 38 But Jacob said, "My son shall not go down with you; for his ^brother is dead, and he alone is left. ^BIf harm should happen to him on the journey you are taking, then you will bring my gray hair down to Sheol in sorrow."

THE RETURN TO EGYPT

43
^ANow the famine was severe in the land. 2 So it came about, when they had finished eating the grain which they had brought from Egypt, that their father said to them, "Go back, buy us a little food." 3 Judah spoke to him, however, saying, "^AThe man sternly warned us, 'You shall not see my face unless your brother is with you.' 4 If you send our brother with us, we will go down and buy you food. 5 But if you do not send *him,* we will not go down; for the man said to us, 'You will not see my face unless your brother is with you.'" 6 Then Israel said, "Why did you treat me so badly, by telling the man whether you still had *another* brother?" 7 But they said, "The man specifically asked about us and our relatives, saying, '^AIs your father still alive? Have you *another*

42:27 ^Gen 43:21, 22   42:28 ^Gen 43:23
42:30 ^Gen 42:7   42:31 ^Gen 42:11
42:33 ^Gen 42:19, 20   42:34 ^Gen 34:10
42:35 ^Gen 43:12, 15, 21   42:36 ^Gen 43:14
42:38 ^Gen 37:33, 34   ^BGen 42:4   43:1 ^Gen 12:10;
26:1   43:3 ^Gen 43:5; 44:23   43:7 ^Gen 42:13; 43:27

brother?' So we answered his questions. Could we possibly know that he would say, 'Bring your brother down'?" 8 So Judah said to his father Israel, "Send the boy with me and we will arise and go, ^so that we may live and not die, we as well as you and our little ones. 9 ^I myself will take responsibility for him! You may demand him back from me. If I do not bring him *back* to you and present him to you, then you can let me take the blame forever. 10 For if we had not delayed, surely by now we could have returned twice."

11 Then their father Israel said to them, "If *it must be* so, then do this: take some of the best products of the land in your bags, and carry down to the man as a gift, a little ^balsam and a little honey, labdanum resin and myrrh, pistachio nuts and almonds. 12 And take double *the* money in your hand, and take back in your hand ^the money that was returned in the opening of your sacks; perhaps it was a mistake. 13 Take your brother also, and arise, return to the man; 14 and may God Almighty grant you compassion in the sight of the man, so that he will release to you ^your other brother and Benjamin. And as for me, ^B if I am bereaved of my sons, I am bereaved!" 15 So the men took ^this gift, and they took double *the* money in their hand, and Benjamin; then they set out and went down to Egypt, and stood before Joseph.

JOSEPH SEES BENJAMIN

16 When Joseph saw Benjamin with them, he said to his ^house steward, "Bring the men into the house, and slaughter an animal and make preparations; for the men are to dine with me at noon." 17 So the man

did as Joseph said, and brought the men to Joseph's house. 18 Now the men were afraid, because they were brought to Joseph's house; and they said, "*It is* because of the money that was returned in our sacks the first time that we are being brought in, so that he may attack us and overpower us, and take us as slaves with our donkeys." 19 So they approached Joseph's house steward, and spoke to him at the entrance of the house, 20 and said, "Oh, my lord, we indeed came down the first time to buy food, 21 and it happened when we came to the campsite, that we opened our sacks, and behold, ^each man's money was in the opening of his sack, our money in full. So we have brought it back in our hand. 22 We have also brought down other money in our hand to buy food; we do not know who put our money in our sacks." 23 But he said, "Peace be to you, do not be afraid. Your God and the God of your father has given you treasure in your sacks; your money was in my possession." Then ^he brought Simeon out to them. 24 Then the man brought the men into Joseph's house and ^gave them water, and they washed their feet; and he gave their donkeys feed. 25 So they prepared ^the gift for Joseph's arrival at noon; for they had heard that they were to eat a meal there.

26 When Joseph came home, they brought into the house to him the gift which was in their hand, and they ^bowed down to the ground before him. 27 Then he asked them

43:8 ^Gen 42:2   43:9 ^Gen 42:37; Philem 18, 19
43:11 ^Gen 37:25; Jer 8:22   43:12 ^Gen 42:25, 35; 43:21, 22
43:14 ^Gen 42:24   ^B Gen 42:36   43:15 ^Gen 43:11
43:16 ^Gen 44:1   43:21 ^Gen 42:27, 35
43:23 ^Gen 42:24   43:24 ^Gen 18:4; 19:2
43:25 ^Gen 43:11, 15   43:26 ^Gen 37:7, 10

about their welfare, and said, "^Is your old father well, of whom you spoke? Is he still alive?" 28 And they said, "Your servant our father is well; he is still alive." Then ^they bowed down *again* 'in homage. 29 And as he raised his eyes and saw his brother Benjamin, his mother's son, he said, "Is this ^your youngest brother, of whom you spoke to me?" Then he said, "May God be gracious to you, my son." 30 Joseph then hurried *out*, for ^he was deeply stirred over his brother, and he looked *for a place* to weep; so he entered his chamber and wept there. 31 Then he washed his face and came out; and he ^controlled himself and said, "Serve the meal." 32 Then they served him by himself, and Joseph's brothers by themselves, and the Egyptians who ate with him by themselves; because the Egyptians could not eat bread with the Hebrews, for that is an ^abomination to the Egyptians. 33 Now they were seated before him, from ^the firstborn according to his birthright to the youngest according to his youth, and the men looked at one another in astonishment. 34 Then he took portions to them from his own table, ^but Benjamin's portion was five times as much as any of theirs. So they drank freely with him.

THE BROTHERS ARE BROUGHT BACK

44 ^Then he commanded his house steward, saying, "Fill the men's sacks with food, as much as they can carry, and put each man's money in the opening of his sack. 2 And put my cup, the silver cup, in the opening of the sack of the youngest, and his money for the grain." And he did as

Joseph had told *him*. 3 As soon as it was light, the men were sent away, they with their donkeys. 4 They had *just* left ^the city, *and* were not far away, when Joseph said to his house steward, "Up, follow the men; and when you overtake them, say to them, 'Why have you repaid evil for good? 5 Is this not *that* from which my lord drinks, and which he indeed uses for ^divination? You have done wrong in doing this!'"

6 So 'he overtook them and spoke these words to them. 7 And they said to him, "Why does my lord say such words as these? Far be it from your servants to do such a thing! 8 Behold, ^the money which we found in the opening of our sacks we have brought back to you from the land of Canaan. How then could we steal silver or gold from your lord's house? 9 ^With whomever of your servants it is found, he shall die, and we also shall be my lord's ^B slaves." 10 So he said, "Now let it indeed be according to your words; he with whom it is found shall be my slave, but *the rest of* you shall be *considered* innocent." 11 Then they hurried, each man lowered his sack to the ground, and each man opened his sack. 12 And he searched, beginning with the oldest and ending with the youngest; and ^the cup was found in Benjamin's sack. 13 Then they tore their clothes *in grief*, and when each man had loaded his donkey, they returned to ^the city.

43:27 ^Gen 43:7; 45:3   43:28 ^Gen 37:7, 10
43:29 ^Gen 42:13   43:30 ^1 Kin 3:26   43:31 ^Gen 45:1
43:32 ^Gen 46:34; Ex 8:26   43:33 ^Gen 42:7
43:34 ^Gen 35:24; 45:22   44:1 ^Gen 42:25
44:4 ^Gen 44:13   44:5 ^Lev 19:26; Deut 18:10-14
44:8 ^Gen 43:21   44:9 ^Gen 31:32   ^B Gen 44:16
44:12 ^Gen 44:2   44:13 ^Gen 44:4

43:28 'I.e., great respect and honor to a superior
44:6 'I.e., the steward

¹⁴When Judah and his brothers came to Joseph's house, he was still there, and ᴬthey fell down to the ground before him. ¹⁵Joseph said to them, "What is this thing that you have done? Do you not know that a man who is like me can indeed practice ᴬdivination?" ¹⁶So Judah said, "What can we say to my lord? What *words* can we speak? And how can we justify ourselves? God has found out the guilt of your servants; behold, we are my lord's ᴬslaves, both we and the one in whose possession the cup has been found." ¹⁷But he said, "Far be it from me to do this. The man in whose possession the cup has been found, he shall be my slave; but as for you, go up in peace to your father."

¹⁸Then Judah approached him and said, "Oh my lord, may your servant please speak a word in my lord's ears, and do not be angry with your servant; for ᴬyou are equal to Pharaoh. ¹⁹ᴬMy lord asked his servants, saying, 'Have you a father or a brother?' ²⁰And we said to my lord, 'We have an old father and ᴬa little boy *born in our father's* old age. Now ᴮhis brother is dead, so he alone is left of his mother, and his father loves him.' ²¹Then you said to your servants, 'ᴬBring him down to me so that I may set my eyes on him.' ²²But we said to my lord, 'The boy cannot leave his father, for if he should leave his father, his father would die.' ²³You said to your servants, however, 'ᴬUnless your youngest brother comes down with you, you will not see my face again.' ²⁴So it came about when we went up to your servant my father, we told him the words of my lord. ²⁵And ᴬour father said, 'Go back, buy us a little food.' ²⁶But we said, 'We

cannot go down. If our youngest brother is with us, then we will go down; for we cannot see the man's face unless our youngest brother is with us.' ²⁷Then your servant my father said to us, 'You know that ᴬmy wife bore me two sons; ²⁸and the one left me, and ᴬI said, "Surely he is torn to pieces," and I have not seen him since. ²⁹If you also take this one from me, and harm happens to him, you will ᴬbring my gray hair down to Sheol in sorrow.' ³⁰So now, when I come to your servant, my father, and the boy is not with us— since ᴬour father's life is so attached to the boy's life— ³¹when he sees that the boy is not *with us,* he will die. So your servants will ᴬbring the gray hair of your servant, our father, down to Sheol in sorrow. ³²For your servant ᴬaccepted responsibility for the boy from my father, saying, 'If I do not bring him *back* to you, then my father can let me take the blame forever.' ³³So now, please let your servant remain as a slave to my lord instead of the boy, and let the boy go up with his brothers. ³⁴For how shall I go up to my father if the boy is not with me? *I fear* that I may see the evil that would overtake my father."

JOSEPH DEALS KINDLY WITH HIS BROTHERS

45 Then Joseph could not control himself in front of everyone standing before him, and he shouted, "Have everyone leave me!" So there was no one with him

44:14ᴬGen 37:7, 10　**44:15**ᴬGen 44:5　**44:16**ᴬGen 44:9
44:18ᴬGen 37:7, 8; 41:40-44　**44:19**ᴬGen 43:7
44:20ᴬGen 37:3　ᴮGen 37:33　**44:21**ᴬGen 42:15, 20
44:23ᴬGen 43:3, 5　**44:25**ᴬGen 43:2
44:27ᴬGen 46:19　**44:28**ᴬGen 37:31-35
44:29ᴬGen 42:38; 44:31　**44:30**ᴬ1 Sam 18:1
44:31ᴬGen 44:29　**44:32**ᴬGen 43:9

^when Joseph made himself known to his brothers. ²Then ^he wept so loudly that the Egyptians heard *it,* and the household of Pharaoh heard *about it.* ³And Joseph said to his brothers, "^I am Joseph! ᴮIs my father still alive?" But his brothers could not answer him, for they were terrified in his presence.

⁴Then Joseph said to his brothers, "Please come closer to me." And they came closer. And he said, "I am your brother Joseph, whom you ^sold to Egypt. ⁵Now do not be grieved or angry with yourselves because you sold me here, for ^God sent me ahead of you to save lives. ⁶For the famine *has been* in the land ^these two years, and there are still five years in which there will be neither plowing nor harvesting. ⁷So ^God sent me ahead of you to ensure for you a remnant on the earth, and to keep you alive by a great deliverance. ⁸Now, therefore, it was not you who sent me here, but God; and He has made me a ^father to Pharaoh and lord of all his household, and ruler over all the land of Egypt. ⁹Hurry and go up to my father, and ^say to him, 'This is what your son Joseph says: "God has made me lord of all Egypt; come down to me, do not delay. ¹⁰For you shall live in the land of ^Goshen, and you shall be near me, you and your children and your grandchildren, and your flocks and your herds and all that you have. ¹¹There I will also ^provide for you, for there are still five years of famine *to come,* and you and your household and all that you have would be impoverished."' ¹²Behold, your eyes see, and the eyes of my brother Benjamin *see,* that it is my mouth which is speaking to you.

¹³Now you must tell my father of all my splendor in Egypt, and all that you have seen; and you must hurry and ^bring my father down here." ¹⁴Then he fell on his brother Benjamin's neck and ^wept, and Benjamin wept on his neck. ¹⁵And he kissed all his brothers and wept on them, and afterward his brothers talked with him.

¹⁶Now when ^the news was heard in Pharaoh's house that Joseph's brothers had come, it pleased Pharaoh and his servants. ¹⁷Then Pharaoh said to Joseph, "Say to your brothers, 'Do this: load your livestock and go to the land of Canaan, ¹⁸and take your father and your households and come to me; and ^I will give you the best of the land of Egypt, and you will eat the fat of the land.' ¹⁹Now you are ordered, 'Do this: take ^wagons from the land of Egypt for your little ones and for your wives, and bring your father and come. ²⁰And do not concern yourselves with your property, for the best of all the land of Egypt is yours.'"

²¹Then the sons of Israel did so; and Joseph gave them ^wagons according to the command of Pharaoh, and gave them provisions for the journey. ²²To each of them he gave ^changes of garments, but to Benjamin he gave three hundred *pieces of* silver and ᴮfive changes of garments. ²³And to his father he sent the following: ten male donkeys loaded with the best things of Egypt, ten female donkeys loaded

45:1 ^Acts 7:13   45:2 ^Gen 45:14, 15; 46:29
45:3 ^Acts 7:13   ᴮGen 43:27   45:4 ^Gen 37:28
45:5 ^Gen 45:7, 8; Ps 105:17   45:6 ^Gen 37:2; 41:46, 53
45:7 ^Gen 45:5   45:8 ^Judg 17:10   45:9 ^Acts 7:14
45:10 ^Gen 46:28, 34; 47:1   45:11 ^Gen 47:12
45:13 ^Acts 7:14   45:14 ^Gen 45:2   45:16 ^Acts 7:13
45:18 ^Gen 27:28   45:19 ^Gen 45:21, 27; Num 7:3–8
45:21 ^Gen 45:19   45:22 ^2 Kin 5:5   ᴮGen 43:34

with grain, bread, and sustenance for his father on the journey. ²⁴So he sent his brothers away, and as they departed, he said to them, "Do not quarrel on the journey." ²⁵Then they went up from Egypt, and came to the land of Canaan, to their father Jacob. ²⁶And they told him, saying, "Joseph is still alive, and indeed he is ruler over all the land of Egypt." But he was stunned, for ᴬhe did not believe them. ²⁷When they told him all the words of Joseph that he had spoken to them, and when he saw the ᴬwagons that Joseph had sent to carry him, then the spirit of their father Jacob revived. ²⁸Then Israel said, "It is enough; my son Joseph is still alive. I will go and see him before I die."

JACOB MOVES TO EGYPT

46 So Israel set out with all that he had, and came to ᴬBeersheba, and offered sacrifices to the God of his father Isaac. ²And God spoke to Israel in visions of the night and said, "ᴬJacob, Jacob." And he said, "Here I am." ³Then He said, "I am God, the God of your father; do not be afraid to go down to Egypt, for I will ᴬmake you into a great nation there. ⁴ᴬI will go down with you to Egypt, and I will also assuredly bring you up again; and Joseph will close your eyes."

⁵Then Jacob left Beersheba, and the sons of Israel carried their father Jacob and their little ones and their wives in the ᴬwagons which Pharaoh had sent to carry him. ⁶They also took their livestock and their possessions, which they had acquired in the land of Canaan, and ᴬcame to Egypt, Jacob and all his descendants with him:

⁷his sons and his grandsons with him, his daughters and his granddaughters, and all his descendants he brought with him to Egypt.

THOSE WHO CAME TO EGYPT

⁸Now these are the ᴬnames of the sons of Israel who went to Egypt, Jacob and his sons: Reuben, Jacob's firstborn. ⁹And the sons of Reuben: Hanoch, Pallu, Hezron, and Carmi. ¹⁰And the ᴬsons of Simeon: Jemuel, Jamin, Ohad, Jachin, Zohar, and Shaul the son of a Canaanite woman. ¹¹And the sons of Levi: Gershon, Kohath, and Merari. ¹²And the sons of Judah: Er, Onan, Shelah, Perez, and Zerah (but Er and Onan died in the land of Canaan). And the ᴬsons of Perez were Hezron and Hamul. ¹³And the sons of Issachar: Tola, Puvvah, Iob, and Shimron. ¹⁴And the sons of Zebulun: Sered, Elon, and Jahleel. ¹⁵These are the sons of Leah, whom she bore to Jacob in Paddan-aram, with his daughter Dinah; all his sons and his daughters *numbered* thirty-three. ¹⁶And the ᴬsons of Gad: Ziphion, Haggi, Shuni, Ezbon, Eri, Arodi, and Areli. ¹⁷And the ᴬsons of Asher: Imnah, Ishvah, Ishvi, Beriah, and their sister Serah. And the sons of Beriah: Heber and Malchiel. ¹⁸These are the sons of Zilpah, whom Laban gave to his daughter Leah; and she bore to Jacob these sixteen persons. ¹⁹The sons of Jacob's wife Rachel: Joseph and Benjamin. ²⁰ᴬNow to Joseph in the land of Egypt were born Manasseh and Ephraim,

45:26 ᴬGen 37:31-35   45:27 ᴬGen 45:19
46:1 ᴬGen 21:31; 28:10   46:2 ᴬGen 22:11; 31:11
46:3 ᴬEx 1:9; Deut 26:5   46:4 ᴬGen 28:15; 48:21
46:5 ᴬGen 45:21   46:6 ᴬDeut 26:5; Ps 105:23
46:8 ᴬEx 1:1-4; 1 Chr 2:1ff   46:10 ᴬEx 6:15
46:12 ᴬ1 Chr 2:5   46:16 ᴬNum 26:15-18
46:17 ᴬ1 Chr 7:30   46:20 ᴬGen 41:50-52

whom Asenath, the daughter of Potiphera, priest of On, bore to him. [21]And the ^sons of Benjamin: Bela, Becher, Ashbel, Gera, Naaman, Ehi, Rosh, Muppim, Huppim, and Ard. [22]These are the sons of Rachel, who were born to Jacob; *there were* fourteen persons in all. [23]And the sons of Dan: Hushim. [24]And the sons of Naphtali: Jahzeel, Guni, Jezer, and Shillem. [25]These are the ^sons of Bilhah, whom ^BLaban gave to his daughter Rachel, and she bore these to Jacob; *there were* seven persons in all. [26]^AAll the people belonging to Jacob, who came to Egypt, his direct descendants, not including the wives of Jacob's sons, *were* sixty-six persons in all, [27]and the sons of Joseph, who were born to him in Egypt, were two; ^all the people of the house of Jacob, who came to Egypt, *were* seventy.

[28]Now *Jacob* sent Judah ahead of him to Joseph, to guide him to ^AGoshen; and they came into the land of Goshen. [29]And Joseph prepared his chariot and went up to Goshen to meet his father Israel; as soon as he appeared to him, *Joseph* threw himself on his neck and ^wept on his neck a long time. [30]Then Israel said to Joseph, "Now let me die, since I have seen your face, that you are still alive." [31]But Joseph said to his brothers and to his father's household, "^AI will go up and tell Pharaoh, and will say to him, 'My brothers and my father's household, who *were* in the land of Canaan, have come to me; [32]and the men are shepherds, for they have been keepers of livestock; and they have brought their flocks and their herds and all that they have.' [33]When Pharaoh calls for you and says, '^AWhat is your occupation?'

[34]you shall say, 'Your servants have been ^keepers of livestock since our youth even until now, both we and our fathers,' so that you may live in the land of ^BGoshen; for every shepherd is an abomination to the Egyptians."

JACOB'S FAMILY SETTLES IN GOSHEN

47 Then ^AJoseph went in and told Pharaoh, and said, "My father and my brothers and their flocks and their herds and all that they have, have come out of the land of Canaan; and behold, they are in the land of ^BGoshen." [2]And he took five men from among his brothers and ^presented them to Pharaoh. [3]Then Pharaoh said to his brothers, "^AWhat is your occupation?" So they said to Pharaoh, "Your servants are shepherds, both we and our fathers." [4]They also said to Pharaoh, "We have come to reside in the land, for there is no pasture for your servants' flocks, for ^the famine is severe in the land of Canaan. Now, therefore, please let your servants live in the land of Goshen." [5]Then Pharaoh said to Joseph, "Your father and your brothers have come to you. [6]The land of Egypt is at your disposal; settle your father and your brothers in ^the best of the land, let them live in the land of Goshen; and if you know any capable men among them, then put them in charge of my livestock."

[7]Then Joseph brought his father Jacob and presented him to Pharaoh;

46:21^1 Chr 7:6   46:25^AGen 30:5, 7   ^BGen 29:29
46:26^AEx 1:5   46:27^ADeut 10:22; Acts 7:14
46:28^AGen 45:10   46:29^AGen 45:14, 15
46:31^AGen 47:1   46:33^AGen 47:2, 3   46:34^AGen 13:7, 8
^BGen 45:10, 18   47:1^AGen 46:31   ^BGen 45:10
47:2^AActs 7:13   47:3^AGen 46:33   47:4^AGen 43:1;
Acts 7:11   47:6^AGen 45:10, 18; 47:11

and Jacob ^blessed Pharaoh. ⁸And Pharaoh said to Jacob, "How many years have you lived?" ⁹So Jacob said to Pharaoh, "The years of my living abroad are 130; few and unpleasant have been the years of my life, nor have they attained ^the years that my fathers lived during the days of their living abroad." ¹⁰So Jacob ^blessed Pharaoh, and went out from his presence. ¹¹Now Joseph settled his father and his brothers and gave them property in the land of Egypt, in the best of the land, in the land of ^Rameses, as Pharaoh had ordered. ¹²Joseph also ^provided his father and his brothers and all his father's household with food, according to the number of their little ones.

¹³Now there was no food in all the land, because the famine was very severe, so that ^the land of Egypt and the land of Canaan languished because of the famine. ¹⁴And ^Joseph collected all the money that was found in the land of Egypt and in the land of Canaan *in payment* for the grain which they bought, and Joseph brought the money into Pharaoh's house. ¹⁵When the money was all spent in the land of Egypt and in the land of Canaan, all the Egyptians came to Joseph saying, "Give us food, for ^why should we die in your presence? For *our* money is gone." ¹⁶Then Joseph said, "Give up your livestock, and I will give you *food* for your livestock, since *your* money is gone." ¹⁷So they brought their livestock to Joseph, and Joseph gave them food in exchange for the horses and the flocks and the herds and the donkeys; and he fed them with food in exchange for all their livestock that year. ¹⁸But when that year ended,

they came to him the next year and said to him, "We will not hide from my lord the fact that our money is all spent, and the livestock are my lord's. There is nothing left for my lord except our bodies and our lands. ¹⁹Why should we die before your eyes, both we and our land? Buy us and our land for food, and we and our land will be slaves to Pharaoh. So give us seed, so that we may live and not die, and that the land may not be desolate."

RESULT OF THE FAMINE

²⁰So Joseph bought all the land of Egypt for Pharaoh, for every Egyptian sold his field, because the famine was severe upon them. So the land became Pharaoh's. ²¹As for the people, he relocated them to the cities from one end of Egypt's border to the other. ²²Only the land of the priests he did not buy, because the priests had an allotment from Pharaoh, and they lived off the allotment which Pharaoh gave them. Therefore, they did not sell their land. ²³Then Joseph said to the people, "Behold, today I have purchased you and your land for Pharaoh; now, *here is* seed for you, and you may sow the land. ²⁴At the harvest you shall give a ^fifth to Pharaoh, and four-fifths shall be your own for seed of the field and for your food, and for those of your households and as food for your little ones." ²⁵So they said, "You have saved our lives! Let us find favor in the sight of my lord, and we will be Pharaoh's slaves." ²⁶Joseph made it a statute concerning the land of Egypt, *valid*

47:7^2 Sam 14:22; 1 Kin 8:66   47:9^Gen 25:7; 35:28
47:10^Gen 47:7   47:11^Ex 1:11; 12:37
47:12^Gen 45:11   47:13^Gen 41:30; Acts 7:11
47:14^Gen 41:56   47:15^Gen 47:19
47:24^Gen 41:34

to this day, that Pharaoh was to have the fifth; ^only the land of the priests did not become Pharaoh's.

²⁷ Now Israel lived in the land of Egypt, in Goshen, and they acquired property in it and ^were fruitful and became very numerous. ²⁸ And Jacob lived in the land of Egypt for ^seventeen years; so the length of Jacob's life was 147 years.

²⁹ When the time for Israel to die drew near, he called his son Joseph and said to him, "Please, if I have found favor in your sight, ^place your hand under my thigh now and ᴮdeal with me in kindness and faithfulness: please do not bury me in Egypt, ³⁰but when I ¹lie down with my fathers, you shall carry me out of Egypt and bury me in ^their burial place." And he said, "I will do as you have said." ³¹And he said, "Swear to me." So he swore to him. Then ^Israel bowed *in worship* at the head of the bed.

ISRAEL'S LAST DAYS

48 Now it came about after these things that Joseph was told, "Behold, your father is sick." So he took his two sons ^Manasseh and Ephraim with him. ²When it was told to Jacob, "Behold, your son Joseph has come to you," Israel collected his strength and sat up in the bed. ³Then Jacob said to Joseph, "God Almighty appeared to me at ^Luz in the land of Canaan and blessed me, ⁴and He said to me, 'Behold, I will make you fruitful and numerous, and I will make you a multitude of peoples, and will give this land to your descendants after you as ^an everlasting possession.' ⁵Now your two sons, who were born to you in the land of Egypt before I came to you in Egypt,

are mine; ^Ephraim and Manasseh shall be mine, as ᴮReuben and Simeon are. ⁶But your children that you have fathered after them shall be yours; they shall be called by the names of their brothers in their inheritance. ⁷Now as for me, when I came from Paddan, ^Rachel died, to my sorrow, in the land of Canaan on the journey, when there was still some distance to go to Ephrath. I buried her there on the way to Ephrath (that is, Bethlehem)."

⁸When Israel ^saw Joseph's sons, he said, "Who are these?" ⁹And Joseph said to his father, "^They are my sons, whom God has given me here." So he said, "Bring them to me, please, so that I may bless them." ¹⁰Now ^the eyes of Israel were *so* dim from age *that* he could not see. And Joseph brought them close to him, and he ᴮkissed them and embraced them. ¹¹And Israel said to Joseph, "I never expected to see your face, and behold, God has let me see your children as well!" ¹²Then Joseph took them from his knees, and ^bowed with his face to the ground. ¹³And Joseph took them both, Ephraim with his right hand toward Israel's left, and Manasseh with his left hand toward Israel's right, and brought them close to him. ¹⁴But Israel reached out his right hand and placed it on the head of Ephraim, who was the younger, and his left hand on Manasseh's head, crossing

47:26^Gen 47:22   47:27^Deut 26:5; Acts 7:17
47:28^Gen 47:9   47:29^Gen 24:2   ᴮGen 24:49
47:30^Gen 23:17-20; Acts 7:15, 16   47:31^1 Kin 1:47
48:1^Gen 41:51, 52; Josh 14:4   48:3^Gen 28:19; 35:6
48:4^Gen 17:8   48:5^Gen 41:50-52   ᴮ1 Chr 5:1, 2
48:7^Gen 35:19, 20   48:8^Gen 48:10
48:9^Gen 33:5   48:10^Gen 27:1   ᴮGen 27:27
48:12^Gen 42:6

47:30 ¹I.e., die

his hands, although ^Manasseh was the firstborn. ¹⁵And he blessed Joseph, and said,

"The God before whom my fathers Abraham and Isaac walked,
^The God who has been my shepherd all my life to this day,
¹⁶ ^The angel who has redeemed me from all evil,
Bless the boys;
And may my name live on in them,
And the names of my fathers Abraham and Isaac;
And may they grow into a multitude in the midst of the earth."

¹⁷When Joseph saw that his father ^placed his right hand on Ephraim's head, it displeased him; and he grasped his father's hand to move it from Ephraim's head to Manasseh's head. ¹⁸And Joseph said to his father, "Not so, my father, for this one is the firstborn. Place your right hand on his head." ¹⁹But his father refused and said, "I know, my son, I know; he also will become a people and he also will be great. However, his younger brother shall be greater than he, and ^his descendants shall become a multitude of nations." ²⁰So ^he blessed them that day, saying,

"By you Israel will pronounce blessing, saying,
'May God make you like Ephraim and Manasseh!'"

And *so* he put Ephraim before Manasseh. ²¹Then Israel said to Joseph, "Behold, I am about to die, but God will be with you, and ^bring you back to the land of your fathers. ²²And I give you one portion more than your brothers, ^which I took

from the hand of the Amorite with my sword and my bow."

JACOB'S PROPHECY CONCERNING HIS SONS

49 Then Jacob summoned his sons and said, "Assemble yourselves, so that I may tell you what will happen to you ^in the days to come.
² "Gather together and listen, sons of Jacob;
Yes, ^listen to Israel your father.

³ "Reuben, you are my firstborn,
My might and ^the beginning of my strength,
Preeminent in dignity and preeminent in power.
⁴ "Uncontrollable as water, you shall not have preeminence,
^Because you went up to your father's bed;
Then you defiled *it*—he went up to my couch.

⁵ "^Simeon and Levi are brothers;
Their ¹swords are implements of violence.
⁶ "^May my soul not enter into their council;
May my glory not be united with their assembly;
For in their anger they killed men,
And in their self-will they lamed oxen.
⁷ "Cursed be their anger, for it is fierce;

48:14 ^Gen 41:51, 52   48:15 ^Gen 49:24
48:16 ^Gen 22:11, 15–18; 31:11   48:17 ^Gen 48:14
48:19 ^Gen 28:14; 46:3   48:20 ^Heb 11:21
48:21 ^Gen 28:15; 46:4   48:22 ^Josh 24:32; John 4:5
49:1 ^Num 24:14   49:2 ^Ps 34:11   49:3 ^Deut 21:17;
Ps 78:51   49:4 ^Gen 35:22; Deut 27:20
49:5 ^Gen 34:25-30   49:6 ^Ps 64:2

49:5 ¹Or *plans;* meaning uncertain

And their wrath, for it is
cruel.
^AI will scatter them in Jacob,
And disperse them among
Israel.

8 "As for you, Judah, your
brothers shall praise you;
Your hand shall be on the neck
of your enemies;
^AYour father's sons shall bow
down to you.
9 "Judah is a ^Alion's cub;
From the prey, my son, you
have gone up.
He crouches, he lies down as
a lion,
And as a lion, who dares to stir
him up?
10 "^AThe scepter will not depart
from Judah,
Nor the ruler's staff from
between his feet,
Until Shiloh comes,
And ^Bto him *shall be* the
obedience of the peoples.
11 "He ties *his* foal to the vine,
And his donkey's colt to the
choice vine;
^AHe washes his garments in
wine,
And his robes in the blood of
grapes.
12 "His eyes are dull from wine,
And his teeth white from
milk.
13 "^AZebulun will reside at the
seashore;
And he *shall be* a harbor for
ships,
And his flank *shall be* toward
Sidon.
14 "Issachar is a strong donkey,
^ALying down between the
sheepfolds.

15 "When he saw that a resting
place was good
And that the land was
pleasant,
He bowed his shoulder to
carry *burdens,*
And became a slave at forced
labor.
16 "^ADan shall judge his people,
As one of the tribes of Israel.
17 "Dan shall be a serpent in the
way,
A horned viper in the path,
That bites the horse's heels,
So that its rider falls backward.
18 "^AFor Your salvation I wait, LORD.
19 "^AAs for Gad, a band of raiders
shall attack him,
But he will attack *at* their
heels.
20 "^AAs for Asher, his food shall be
rich,
And he will yield royal
delicacies.
21 "^ANaphtali is a doe let loose;
He utters beautiful words.
22 "^AJoseph is a fruitful branch,
A fruitful branch by a spring;
Its branches hang over a wall.
23 "The archers provoked him,
And shot *at him* and were
hostile toward him;
24 But his bow remained firm,
And his arms were agile,
From the hands of the Mighty
One of Jacob

49:7 ^AJosh 19:1, 9; 21:1-42   49:8 ^AGen 27:29; 1 Chr 5:2
49:9 ^AEzek 19:5-7; Mic 5:8   49:10 ^ANum 24:17
^BPs 72:8-11   49:11 ^AIs 63:2   49:13 ^ADeut 33:18, 19
49:14 ^AJudg 5:16; Ps 68:13   49:16 ^ADeut 33:22;
Judg 18:26, 27   49:18 ^AEx 15:2; Ps 25:5
49:19 ^ADeut 33:20   49:20 ^ADeut 33:24, 25
49:21 ^ADeut 33:23   49:22 ^ADeut 33:13-17

(From there is ^the Shepherd,
^B^the Stone of Israel),
25 From the God of your father
    who helps you,
    And by the Almighty who
    blesses you
    With ^blessings of heaven
    above,
    Blessings of the deep that lies
    beneath,
    Blessings of the breasts and of
    the womb.
26 "The blessings of your father
    Have surpassed the blessings
    of my ancestors
    Up to the furthest boundary of
    ^the everlasting hills;
    May they be on the head of
    Joseph,
    And on the top of the head
    of the one distinguished
    among his brothers.
27 "Benjamin is a ravenous wolf;
    In the morning he devours the
    prey,
    And in the evening he divides
    the spoils."
28 All these are the twelve tribes of
Israel, and this is what their father
said to them when he blessed them.
He blessed them, every one with
the blessing appropriate to him.

JACOB DIES
29 Then he commanded them and
said to them, "I am about to be
gathered to my people; ^bury me
with my fathers in the cave that is
in ^B^the field of Ephron the Hittite,
30 in the ^cave that is in the field
of Machpelah, which is opposite
Mamre, in the land of Canaan,
which Abraham bought along with
the field from Ephron the Hittite
as a burial site. 31 There they buried ^Abraham and his wife ^B^Sarah,

there they buried Isaac and his wife
Rebekah, and there I buried Leah—
32 the field and the cave that is in it,
purchased from the sons of Heth."
33 When Jacob finished commanding his sons, he drew his feet into
the bed and ^breathed his last, and
was ^B^gathered to his people.

JACOB IS BURIED
50 Then Joseph fell on his
father's face, and wept
over him and kissed him. 2 Joseph
commanded his servants the physicians to embalm his father. So
the physicians ^embalmed Israel.
3 Now forty days were required for
it, for such is the period required
for embalming. And the Egyptians
^wept for him seventy days.

4 When the days of mourning
for him were past, Joseph spoke to
the household of Pharaoh, saying,
"If now I have found favor in your
sight, please speak to Pharaoh, saying, 5 '^My father made me swear,
saying, "Behold, I am about to die;
in my grave which I dug for myself
in the land of Canaan, there you
shall bury me." Now then, please
let me go up and bury my father;
then I will return.'" 6 Pharaoh said,
"Go up and bury your father, as he
made you swear."

7 So Joseph went up to bury his
father, and with him went up all
the servants of Pharaoh, the elders
of his household and all the elders
of the land of Egypt, 8 and all the
household of Joseph and his brothers and his father's household; they
left only their little ones and their

49:24 ^Ps 23:1   ^B^Is 28:16   49:25 ^Gen 27:28
49:26 ^Deut 33:15, 16   49:29 ^Gen 47:30
^B^Gen 23:16-20   49:30 ^Gen 23:3-20
49:31 ^Gen 25:9   ^B^Gen 23:19   49:33 ^Acts 7:15
^B^Gen 49:29   50:2 ^Matt 26:12; Mark 16:1
50:3 ^Num 20:29; Deut 34:8   50:5 ^Gen 47:29-31

flocks and their herds in the land of Goshen. 9Chariots with teams of horses also went up with him; and it was a very great company. 10When they came to the threshing floor of Atad, which is beyond the Jordan, they ^mourned there with a very great and sorrowful lamentation; and he observed seven days of mourning for his father. 11Now when the inhabitants of the land, the Canaanites, saw the mourning at the threshing floor of Atad, they said, "This is a grievous mourning for the Egyptians." Therefore it was named Abel-mizraim, which is beyond the Jordan.

BURIAL AT MACHPELAH

12And so his sons did for him as he had commanded them; 13for his sons carried him to the land of Canaan and buried him in ^the cave of the field of Machpelah opposite Mamre, which Abraham had bought along with the field as a burial site from Ephron the Hittite. 14And after he had buried his father, Joseph returned to Egypt, he and his brothers, and all who had gone up with him to bury his father.

15When Joseph's brothers had seen that their father was dead, they said, "^What if Joseph holds a grudge against us and pays us back in full for all the wrong which we did to him!" 16So they sent instructions to Joseph, saying, "Your father commanded us before he died, saying, 17'This is what you shall say to Joseph: "Please forgive, I beg you, the offense of your brothers and their sin, for they did you wrong."'

And now, please forgive the offense of the servants of the God of your father." And Joseph wept when they spoke to him. 18Then his brothers also came and ^fell down before him and said, "Behold, we are your servants." 19But Joseph said to them, "Do not be afraid, for am I in God's place? 20As for you, ^you meant evil against me, but God meant it for good in order to bring about this present result, to keep many people alive. 21So therefore, do not be afraid; ^I will provide for you and your little ones." So he comforted them and spoke kindly to them.

DEATH OF JOSEPH

22Now Joseph stayed in Egypt, he and his father's household, and Joseph lived 110 years. 23Joseph saw the third generation of Ephraim's sons; also the sons of Machir, the son of Manasseh, were ^born on Joseph's knees. 24Joseph said to his brothers, "^I am about to die, but God will assuredly take care of you and bring you up from this land to the land which He promised on oath to Abraham, to Isaac, and to Jacob." 25Then Joseph made the sons of Israel swear, saying, "God will assuredly take care of you, and ^you shall carry my bones up from here." 26So Joseph died at the age of 110 years; and they ^embalmed him and placed him in a coffin in Egypt.

50:10^Acts 8:2   50:13^Gen 23:16-20; Acts 7:16
50:15^Gen 37:28; 42:21, 22   50:18^Gen 37:8-10;
41:43   50:20^Gen 37:26, 27; 45:5, 7
50:21^Gen 45:11; 47:12   50:23^Gen 30:3
50:24^Ex 3:16, 17; Heb 11:22   50:25^Ex 13:19;
Heb 11:22   50:26^Gen 50:2

EXODUS

ISRAEL MULTIPLIES IN EGYPT

1 Now these are the ^names of the sons of Israel who came to Egypt with Jacob; they came, each one with his household: ²Reuben, Simeon, Levi, and Judah; ³Issachar, Zebulun, and Benjamin; ⁴Dan and Naphtali, Gad and Asher. ⁵All the people who descended from Jacob were ^seventy people, but Joseph was *already* in Egypt. ⁶And ^Joseph died, and all his brothers and all that generation. ⁷But the sons of Israel ^were fruitful and increased greatly, and multiplied, and became exceedingly mighty, so that the land was filled with them.

⁸Now a new ^king arose over Egypt, who did not know Joseph. ⁹And ^he said to his people, "Behold, the people of the sons of Israel are too many and too mighty for us. ¹⁰Come, let us ^deal shrewdly with them, otherwise they will multiply, and in the event of war, they will also join those who hate us, and fight against us and depart from the land." ¹¹So they appointed ^taskmasters over them to oppress them with hard labor. And they built for Pharaoh ᴮstorage cities, Pithom and Raamses. ¹²But the more they oppressed them, ^the more they multiplied and the more they spread out, so that they dreaded the sons of Israel. ¹³The Egyptians used violence to compel the sons of Israel ^to labor; ¹⁴and they made ^their lives bitter with hard labor in mortar and bricks and at all *kinds of* labor in the field, all their labors which they violently had them perform as slaves.

¹⁵Then the king of Egypt spoke to the Hebrew midwives, one of whom was named Shiphrah, and the other was named Puah; ¹⁶and he said, "When you are helping the Hebrew women to give birth and see *them* upon the birthstool, ^if it is a son, then you shall put him to death; but if it is a daughter, then she shall live." ¹⁷But the midwives ^feared God, and did not do as the king of Egypt had commanded them, but let the boys live. ¹⁸So the king of Egypt called for the midwives and said to them, "Why have you done this thing, and let the boys live?" ¹⁹The midwives said to Pharaoh, "Because the Hebrew women are not like the Egyptian women; for they are vigorous and give birth before the midwife can get to them." ²⁰So ^God was good to the midwives, and the people multiplied, and became very mighty. ²¹And because the midwives feared God, He ^established households for them. ²²Then Pharaoh commanded all his people, saying, "^Every son who is born, ¹you are to throw into the Nile, but every daughter, you are to keep alive."

1:1^Gen 46:8-27   1:5^Gen 46:26, 27; Deut 10:22
1:6^Gen 50:26   1:7^Deut 26:5; Ps 105:24
1:8^Acts 7:18, 19   1:9^Ps 105:24, 25   1:10^Acts 7:19
1:11^Gen 15:13   ᴮ1 Kin 9:19   1:12^Ex 1:7
1:13^Gen 15:13; Deut 4:20   1:14^Ex 2:23; 6:9
1:16^Acts 7:19   1:17^Ex 1:21; Prov 16:6
1:20^Prov 11:18; Eccl 8:12   1:21^1 Sam 2:35;
2 Sam 7:11, 27   1:22^Acts 7:19

1:22¹Some ancient versions insert *to the Hebrews*

THE BIRTH OF MOSES

2 Now a man from ^the house of Levi went and married a daughter of Levi. ²And the woman conceived and gave birth to a son; and when she saw that he was ^beautiful, she hid him for three months. ³But when she could no longer hide him, she got him a papyrus basket and covered it with tar and pitch. Then she put the child in it and set *it* among the ^reeds by the bank of the Nile. ⁴And his sister stood at a distance to find out what would happen to him.

⁵Now the daughter of Pharaoh came down ^to bathe at the Nile, with her female attendants walking alongside the Nile; and she saw the basket among the reeds and sent her slave woman, and she brought it *to her*. ⁶When she opened *it*, she saw the child, and behold, *the* boy was crying. And she had pity on him and said, "This is one of the Hebrews' children." ⁷Then his sister said to Pharaoh's daughter, "Shall I go and call a woman for you who is nursing from the Hebrew women, so that she may nurse the child for you?" ⁸Pharaoh's daughter said to her, "Go *ahead*." So the girl went and called the child's mother. ⁹Then Pharaoh's daughter said to her, "Take this child away and nurse him for me, and I will give *you* your wages." So the woman took the child and nursed him. ¹⁰And the child grew, and she brought him to Pharaoh's daughter and ^he became her son. And she named him Moses, and said, "Because I drew him out of the water."

¹¹Now it came about in those days, ^when Moses had grown up, that he went out to his fellow Hebrews and looked at their hard labors; and he saw an Egyptian beating a Hebrew, one of his fellow Hebrews. ¹²So he looked this way and that, and when he saw that there was no one *around*, he ^struck and killed the Egyptian, and hid his body in the sand. ¹³Now he went out ^the next day, and behold, two Hebrews were fighting with each other; and he said to the offender, "Why are you striking your companion?" ¹⁴But he said, "^Who made you a ruler and a judge over us? Do you intend to kill me as you killed the Egyptian?" Then Moses was afraid and said, "Surely the matter has become known!"

MOSES ESCAPES TO MIDIAN

¹⁵When Pharaoh heard about this matter, he tried to kill Moses. But ^Moses fled from the presence of Pharaoh and settled in the land of Midian, and he sat down by a well.

¹⁶Now ^the priest of Midian had seven daughters; and they came to draw water and filled the troughs to water their father's flock. ¹⁷Then the shepherds came and drove them away, but ^Moses stood up and helped them and watered their flock. ¹⁸When they came to their father ^Reuel, he said, "Why have you come *back* so soon today?" ¹⁹They said, "An Egyptian saved us from the shepherds, and what is more, he even drew water for us and watered the flock." ²⁰So he said to his daughters, "Where is he then? Why is it that you have left

2:1 ^Ex 6:16, 18, 20   2:2 ^Acts 7:20; Heb 11:23
2:3 ^Is 19:6   2:4 ^Ex 15:20; Num 26:59   2:5 ^Ex 7:15;
8:20   2:10 ^Acts 7:21   2:11 ^Acts 7:23; Heb 11:24-26
2:12 ^Acts 7:24, 25   2:13 ^Acts 7:26-28
2:14 ^Gen 19:9; Acts 7:27, 28   2:15 ^Acts 7:29;
Heb 11:27   2:16 ^Ex 3:1; 18:12   2:17 ^Gen 29:3, 10
2:18 ^Ex 3:1; Num 10:29

the man behind? Invite him to have something to eat." ²¹And Moses was willing to live with the man. And he gave his daughter ^Zipporah to Moses. ²²Then she gave birth to ^a son, and he named him Gershom, for he said, "I have been a stranger in a foreign land."

²³Now it came about in *the course of* those many days that the king of Egypt died. And the sons of Israel groaned because of the bondage, and they cried out; and ^their cry for help because of *their* bondage ascended to God. ²⁴So ^God heard their groaning; and God remembered His covenant with Abraham, Isaac, and Jacob. ²⁵And ^God saw the sons of Israel, and God took notice *of them.*

THE BURNING BUSH

3 Now Moses was pasturing the flock of his father-in-law Jethro, the priest of Midian; and he led the flock to the west side of the wilderness and came to ^Horeb, the mountain of God. ²Then ^the angel of the LORD appeared to him in a blazing fire from the midst of a bush; and he looked, and behold, the bush was burning with fire, yet the bush was not being consumed. ³So Moses said, "^I must turn aside and see this marvelous sight, why the bush is not burning up!" ⁴When the LORD saw that he turned aside to look, ^God called to him from the midst of the bush and said, "Moses, Moses!" And he said, "Here I am." ⁵Then He said, "Do not come near here; ^remove your sandals from your feet, for the place on which you are standing is holy ground." ⁶And He said, "^I am the God of your father—the God of Abraham, the God of Isaac, and the God of

Jacob." Then Moses hid his face, for he was afraid to look at God.

⁷And the LORD said, "I have certainly ^seen the oppression of My people who are in Egypt, and have heard their outcry because of their taskmasters, for I am aware of their sufferings. ⁸So I have come down ^to rescue them from the power of the Egyptians, and to bring them up from that land to a good and spacious land, to a land flowing with milk and honey, to the place of the Canaanite, the Hittite, the Amorite, the Perizzite, the Hivite, and the Jebusite. ⁹And now, behold, ^the cry of the sons of Israel has come to Me; furthermore, I have seen the oppression with which the Egyptians are oppressing them.

THE MISSION OF MOSES

¹⁰And now come, and I will send you to Pharaoh, ^so that you may bring My people, the sons of Israel, out of Egypt." ¹¹But Moses said to God, "^Who am I, that I should go to Pharaoh, and that I should bring the sons of Israel out of Egypt?" ¹²And He said, "Assuredly I will be with you, and this shall be the sign to you that it is I who have sent you: when you have brought the people out of Egypt, ^you shall worship God at this mountain."

¹³Then Moses said to God, "Behold, I am going to the sons of Israel, and I will say to them, 'The God of your fathers has sent me to you.' Now they may say to me, 'What is His name?' What shall I

2:21^Ex 4:25; 18:2   2:22^Ex 4:20; 18:3, 4
2:23^Deut 26:7; James 5:4   2:24^Ex 6:5; Acts 7:34
2:25^Ex 3:7; Acts 7:34   3:1^Ex 33:6; 1 Kin 19:8
3:2^Ex 3:4-11, 16; Acts 7:30   3:3^Acts 7:31   3:4^Ex 4:5
3:5^Josh 5:15; Acts 7:33   3:6^Gen 28:13; Ex 3:16
3:7^Ex 2:25; Neh 9:9   3:8^Gen 15:13-16; Ex 6:6-8
3:9^Ex 2:23   3:10^Mic 6:4; Acts 7:6, 7   3:11^Ex 4:10;
1 Sam 18:18   3:12^Ex 19:2, 3; Acts 7:7

say to them?" [14] And God said to Moses, "[1,A]I AM WHO I AM"; and He said, "This is what you shall say to the sons of Israel: 'I AM has sent me to you.'" [15] God furthermore said to Moses, "This is what you shall say to the sons of Israel: 'The LORD, the God of your fathers, the God of Abraham, the God of Isaac, and the God of Jacob, has sent me to you.' This is My name forever, and this is the [1,A]name for all generations *to use* to call upon Me. [16] Go and gather the elders of Israel together and say to them, 'The LORD, the God of your fathers, the God of Abraham, Isaac, and Jacob has appeared to me, saying, "[A]I am indeed concerned about you and what has been done to you in Egypt. [17] So I said, I will bring you up out of the oppression of Egypt to the land of [A]the Canaanite, the Hittite, the Amorite, the Perizzite, the Hivite, and the Jebusite, to a land [B]flowing with milk and honey."' [18] Then they will pay attention to what you say; and you with the elders of Israel will come to the king of Egypt, and you will say to him, 'The LORD, the God of the Hebrews, has met with us. So now, please let us go a [A]three days' journey into the wilderness, so that we may sacrifice to the LORD our God.' [19] But I know that the king of Egypt will not permit you to go, [A]except under compulsion. [20] So I will reach out with My hand and strike Egypt with all My [A]miracles which I shall do in the midst of it; and after that he will let you go. [21] I will grant this people [A]favor in the sight of the Egyptians; and it shall be that when you go, you will not go empty-handed. [22] But every woman [A]shall ask her neighbor and the woman who lives in her house

for articles of silver and articles of gold, and clothing; and you will put them on your sons and daughters. So you will plunder the Egyptians."

MOSES GIVEN SIGNS

4 Then Moses said, "What if they will not believe me or [A]listen to what I say? For they may say, 'The LORD has not appeared to you.'" [2] The LORD said to him, "What is that in your hand?" And he said, "[A]A staff." [3] Then He said, "Throw it on the ground." So he threw it on the ground, and [A]it turned into a serpent; and Moses fled from it. [4] But the LORD said to Moses, "Reach out with your hand and grasp *it* by its tail"—so he reached out with his hand and caught it, and it turned into a staff in his hand— [5] "so that [A]they may believe that the LORD, the God of their fathers, the God of Abraham, the God of Isaac, and the God of Jacob, has appeared to you."

[6] The LORD furthermore said to him, "Now put your hand inside the fold of your robe." So he put his hand inside the fold, and when he took it out, behold, his hand was [A]leprous like snow. [7] Then He said, "Put your hand inside the fold of your robe again." So he put his hand into the fold again, and when he took it out of the fold, behold, [A]it was restored like *the rest of* his flesh. [8] "So if they will not believe you nor pay attention to the evidence of the first sign, they may

3:14 [A] Ex 6:3; John 8:24, 28, 58   3:15 [A] Ps 30:4; Hos 12:5
3:16 [A] Ex 4:31; Ps 33:18f   3:17 [A] Josh 24:11   [B] Ex 3:8
3:18 [A] Ex 5:3; 8:27   3:19 [A] Ex 6:1   3:20 [A] Ex 7:3; 15:11
3:21 [A] Ex 11:3; 12:36   3:22 [A] Gen 15:14; Ex 11:2
4:1 [A] Ex 3:18; 6:30   4:2 [A] Ex 4:17, 20   4:3 [A] Ex 7:10-12
4:5 [A] Ex 4:31; 19:9   4:6 [A] Num 12:10; 2 Kin 5:27
4:7 [A] Num 12:13-15; Deut 32:39

3:14 [1] Related to the name of God, *YHWH*, rendered LORD, which is derived from the verb *HAYAH*, *to be*
3:15 [1] I.e., name used in prayer, vows, and ceremony

believe the evidence of the last sign. [9]But if they will not believe even these two signs nor pay attention to what you say, then you shall take some water from the Nile and pour it on the dry ground; and the water which you take from the Nile [A]will turn into blood on the dry ground."

[10]Then Moses said to the LORD, "Please, Lord, [A]I have never been eloquent, neither recently nor in time past, nor since You have spoken to Your servant; for I am slow of speech and slow of tongue." [11]But the LORD said to him, "Who has made the human mouth? Or [A]who makes *anyone* unable to speak or deaf, or able to see or blind? Is it not I, the LORD? [12]Now then go, and I Myself will be with your mouth, and [A]instruct you in what you are to say." [13]But he said, "Please, Lord, now send *the message* by whomever You will."

AARON TO BE MOSES' MOUTHPIECE

[14]Then the anger of the LORD burned against Moses, and He said, "Is there not your brother Aaron the Levite? I know that he speaks fluently. And moreover, behold, [A]he is coming out to meet you; when he sees you, he will be overjoyed. [15]So you are to speak to him and [A]put the words in his mouth; and I Myself will be with your mouth and his mouth, and I will instruct you in what you are to do. [16][A]He shall speak for you to the people; and he will be as a mouth for you and you will be as God to him. [17]And you shall take in your hand this staff, [A]with which you shall perform the signs."

[18]Then Moses departed and returned to [A]his father-in-law Jethro, and said to him, "Please,

let me go, that I may return to my brothers who are in Egypt, and see if they are still alive." And Jethro said to Moses, "Go in peace." [19]Now the LORD said to Moses in Midian, "Go back to Egypt, for [A]all the men who were seeking your life are dead." [20]So Moses took his wife and his [A]sons and mounted them on a donkey, and returned to the land of Egypt. Moses also took the staff of God in his hand.

[21]And the LORD said to Moses, "When you go back to Egypt, see that you perform before Pharaoh all [A]the wonders which I have put in your power; but I will harden his heart so that he will not let the people go. [22]Then you shall say to Pharaoh, 'This is what the LORD says: "[A]Israel is My son, My firstborn. [23]So I said to you, 'Let My son go so that he may serve Me'; but you have refused to let him go. Behold, [A]I am going to kill your son, your firstborn.""

[24]But it came about at the overnight encampment on the way, that the LORD met Moses, and [A]sought to put him to death. [25]So Zipporah took [A]a flint and cut off her son's foreskin and threw it at Moses' feet; and she said, "You are indeed a groom of blood to me!" [26]So He left him alone. At that time she said, "*You are* a groom of blood"— because of the circumcision.

[27][A]Now the LORD said to Aaron, "Go to meet Moses in the wilderness." So he went and met him at the mountain of God and kissed

4:9 [A]Ex 7:19, 20   4:10 [A]Ex 3:11; Jer 1:6   4:11 [A]Ps 94:9; Luke 1:20, 64   4:12 [A]Matt 10:19, 20; Mark 13:11
4:14 [A]Ex 4:27   4:15 [A]Ex 4:12, 30; 7:1f   4:16 [A]Ex 7:1, 2
4:17 [A]Ex 7:9-20; 14:16   4:18 [A]Ex 2:21; 3:1
4:19 [A]Ex 2:15, 23   4:20 [A]Ex 18:3, 4; Acts 7:29
4:21 [A]Ex 3:20; 11:9, 10   4:22 [A]Is 63:16; 64:8
4:23 [A]Ex 11:5; 12:29   4:24 [A]Num 22:22
4:25 [A]Gen 17:14; Josh 5:2, 3   4:27 [A]Ex 4:14

him. [28]ᴬMoses told Aaron all the words of the LORD with which He had sent him, and ᴮall the signs that He had commanded him *to do*. [29]Then Moses and Aaron went and ᴬassembled all the elders of the sons of Israel; [30]and Aaron spoke all the words which the LORD had spoken to Moses. He then performed the ᴬsigns in the sight of the people. [31]So ᴬthe people believed; and when they heard that the LORD was concerned about the sons of Israel and that He had seen their affliction, they bowed low and worshiped.

ISRAEL'S LABOR INCREASED

5 And afterward Moses and Aaron came and said to Pharaoh, "This is what the LORD, the God of Israel says: 'ᴬLet My people go so that they may celebrate a feast to Me in the wilderness.'" [2]But Pharaoh said, "ᴬWho is the LORD that I should obey His voice to let Israel go? I do not know the LORD, and besides, ᴮI will not let Israel go." [3]Then they said, "ᴬThe God of the Hebrews has met with us. Please, let us go a three days' journey into the wilderness so that we may sacrifice to the LORD our God, otherwise He will strike us with plague or with the sword." [4]But the king of Egypt said to them, "Moses and Aaron, why do you let the people neglect their work? Get *back* to your ᴬlabors!" [5]Again Pharaoh said, "Look, ᴬthe people of the land are now many, and you would have them cease from their labors!" [6]So the same day Pharaoh commanded ᴬthe taskmasters over the people and their foremen, saying, [7]"You are no longer to give the people straw to make bricks as previously; have them go and gather straw for themselves. [8]But you shall impose on them the quota of bricks which they were making before; you are not to reduce any of it. Because they are ᴬlazy, for that reason they cry out, 'Let us go and sacrifice to our God.' [9]Let the labor be heavier on the men, and have them work at it so that they will pay no attention to false words."

[10]So ᴬthe taskmasters of the people and their foremen went out and spoke to the people, saying, "This is what Pharaoh says: 'I am not going to give you *any* straw. [11]You go, get straw for yourselves wherever you can find *it*; but none of your labor will be reduced.'" [12]So the people scattered through all the land of Egypt to gather stubble for straw. [13]And the taskmasters pressed them, saying, "Complete your work quota, *your* daily amount, just as when you had straw." [14]Moreover, the foremen of the sons of Israel, whom Pharaoh's taskmasters had set over them, ᴬwere beaten and asked, "Why have you not completed your required task of making bricks either yesterday or today, as before?"

[15]Then the foremen of the sons of Israel came and cried out to Pharaoh, saying, "Why do you deal this way with your servants? [16]There is no straw given to your servants, yet they keep saying to us, 'Make bricks!' And behold, your servants are being beaten; but it is the fault of your *own* people." [17]But he said, "You are ᴬlazy, *very* lazy; for that reason you say, 'Let us go *and* sacrifice to the LORD.' [18]So go now *and* work; for you will be given no straw,

4:28ᴬEx 4:15f   ᴮEx 4:8f   4:29ᴬEx 3:16   4:30ᴬEx 4:1-9   4:31ᴬEx 3:18; 19:9   5:1ᴬEx 4:23; 7:16 5:2ᴬ2 Kin 18:35   ᴮEx 3:19   5:3ᴬEx 3:18   5:4ᴬEx 1:11; 6:5-7   5:5ᴬEx 1:7, 9   5:6ᴬEx 1:11; 3:7   5:8ᴬEx 5:17 5:10ᴬEx 1:11; 3:7   5:14ᴬIs 10:24   5:17ᴬEx 5:8

but you must deliver the quota of bricks." [19]The foremen of the sons of Israel saw that they were in trouble, since they were told, "You must not reduce your daily amount of bricks." [20]When they left Pharaoh's presence, they met Moses and Aaron as they were waiting for them. [21]And they said to them, "[A]May the LORD look upon you and judge *you*, because you have [B]made us repulsive in Pharaoh's sight and in the sight of his servants, to put a sword in their hand to kill us!"

[22]Then Moses returned to the LORD and said, "[A]Lord, why have You brought harm to this people? Why did You ever send me? [23]Ever since I came to Pharaoh to speak in Your name, he has done harm to this people, [A]and You have not rescued Your people at all."

GOD PROMISES ACTION

6 Then the LORD said to Moses, "Now you shall see what I will do to Pharaoh; for [A]under compulsion he will let them go, and under compulsion he will drive them out of his land."

[2]God spoke further to Moses and said to him, "I am [A]the LORD; [3]and I appeared to Abraham, Isaac, and Jacob as [A]God Almighty, but *by* [B]My name, [1]LORD, I did not make Myself known to them. [4]I also established [A]My covenant with them, to give them the land of Canaan, the land in which they lived as strangers. [5]Furthermore I have [A]heard the groaning of the sons of Israel, because the Egyptians are holding them in bondage, and I have remembered My covenant. [6]Say, therefore, to the sons of Israel, 'I am the LORD, and [A]I will bring you out from under the labors of the Egyptians, and I will rescue you from their bondage. I will also redeem you with an outstretched arm, and with great judgments. [7]Then I will take you [A]as My people, and I will be your God; and you shall know that I am the LORD your God, who brought you out from under the labors of the Egyptians. [8]I will bring you to the land which [A]I swore to give to Abraham, Isaac, and Jacob, and I will give it to you *as* a possession; I am the LORD.'" [9]So Moses said this to the sons of Israel, but they did not listen to Moses on [A]account of *their* [1]despondency and cruel bondage.

[10]Now the LORD spoke to Moses, saying, [11]"[A]Go, tell Pharaoh king of Egypt to let the sons of Israel go out of his land." [12]But Moses spoke before the LORD, saying, "Behold, the sons of Israel have not listened to me; how then will Pharaoh listen to me, as I am [A]unskilled in speech?" [13]Nevertheless, the LORD spoke to Moses and to Aaron and gave them a command concerning the sons of Israel and Pharaoh king of Egypt, to bring the sons of Israel out of the land of Egypt.

THE HEADS OF ISRAEL

[14]These are the heads of their fathers' households. [A]The sons of Reuben, Israel's firstborn: Hanoch and Pallu, Hezron and Carmi; these are the families of Reuben. [15]And the [A]sons of Simeon: Jemuel, Jamin, Ohad, Jachin, Zohar, and Shaul the

---

5:21[A]Gen 16:5   [B]Gen 34:30   5:22[A]Num 11:11; Jer 4:10
5:23[A]Ex 3:8   6:1[A]Ex 3:19, 20; 7:4, 5   6:2[A]Ex 3:14, 15
6:3[A]Gen 17:1   [B]Ps 68:4   6:4[A]Gen 12:7; 15:18
6:5[A]Ex 2:24   6:6[A]Ex 3:17; 7:4   6:7[A]Ex 19:5; Deut 4:20
6:8[A]Ex 15:18; 26:3   6:9[A]Ex 2:23   6:11[A]Ex 4:22, 23
6:12[A]Jer 1:6   6:14[A]Gen 46:9; Num 26:5-11
6:15[A]Gen 46:10; 1 Chr 4:24

6:3 [1]Heb YHWH, usually rendered LORD
6:9 [1]Or *impatience*

son of a Canaanite woman; these are the families of Simeon. [16]And these are the names of ^the sons of Levi according to their generations: Gershon, Kohath, and Merari; and the length of Levi's life was 137 years. [17]^The sons of Gershon: Libni and Shimei, according to their families. [18]And ^the sons of Kohath: Amram, Izhar, Hebron, and Uzziel; and the length of Kohath's life was 133 years. [19]And ^the sons of Merari: Mahli and Mushi. These are the families of the Levites according to their generations. [20]Now ^Amram married his father's sister Jochebed, and she bore him Aaron and Moses; and the length of Amram's life was 137 years. [21]And ^the sons of Izhar: Korah, Nepheg, and Zichri. [22]And ^the sons of Uzziel: Mishael, Elzaphan, and Sithri. [23]Aaron married Elisheba, the daughter of ^Amminadab, the sister of Nahshon, and she bore him Nadab and Abihu, Eleazar and Ithamar. [24]And the ^sons of Korah: Assir, Elkanah, and Abiasaph; these are the families of the Korahites. [25]Now Aaron's son Eleazar married one of the daughters of Putiel, and she bore him ^Phinehas. These are the heads of the fathers' *households* of the Levites according to their families. [26]It was *the same* Aaron and Moses to whom the LORD said, "^Bring out the sons of Israel from the land of Egypt according to their multitudes." [27]They were the ones ^who spoke to Pharaoh king of Egypt about bringing out the sons of Israel from Egypt; it was *the same* Moses and Aaron.

[28]Now it came about on the day when the LORD spoke to Moses in the land of Egypt, [29]that the LORD spoke to Moses, saying, "I am the LORD; ^say to Pharaoh king of Egypt all that I say to you." [30]But Moses said before the LORD, "Behold, I am ^unskilled in speech; how then will Pharaoh listen to me?"

I WILL EXTEND MY HAND

7 Then the LORD said to Moses, "^See, I have made you *as* God to Pharaoh, and your brother Aaron shall be your prophet. [2]As for you, you shall speak all that I command you, and your brother ^Aaron shall speak to Pharaoh that he let the sons of Israel go out of his land. [3]But ^I will harden Pharaoh's heart, so that I may ^Bmultiply My signs and My wonders in the land of Egypt. [4]When ^Pharaoh does not listen to you, I will lay My hand on Egypt and bring out My armies, My people the sons of Israel, from the land of Egypt by great judgments. [5]Then the Egyptians shall know that I am the LORD, when I ^extend My hand over Egypt and bring out the sons of Israel from their midst." [6]So Moses and Aaron did *this;* ^as the LORD commanded them, so they did. [7]And Moses was ^eighty years old and Aaron eighty-three, when they spoke to Pharaoh.

AARON'S STAFF TURNS INTO A SERPENT

[8]Now the LORD spoke to Moses and Aaron, saying, [9]"When Pharaoh speaks to you, saying, 'Work a miracle,' then you shall say to Aaron,

6:16 ^Gen 46:11; Num 3:17   6:17 ^Num 3:18-20; 1 Chr 6:17-19   6:18 ^Num 3:19; 1 Chr 6:2, 18
6:19 ^Num 3:20; 1 Chr 6:19   6:20 ^Ex 2:1, 2; Num 26:59   6:21 ^Num 16:1; 1 Chr 6:37, 38
6:22 ^Lev 10:4; Num 3:30   6:23 ^Ruth 4:19, 20; 1 Chr 2:10   6:24 ^Num 26:11; 1 Chr 6:22, 23, 37
6:25 ^Num 25:7-13; Ps 106:30   6:26 ^Ex 3:10; 6:13
6:27 ^Ex 5:1   6:29 ^Ex 6:11; 7:2   6:30 ^Ex 4:10; Jer 1:6
7:1 ^Ex 4:16   7:2 ^Ex 4:15   7:3 ^Ex 4:21   ^BActs 7:36
7:4 ^Ex 3:19, 20; 7:13, 16, 22   7:5 ^Ex 3:20
7:6 ^Gen 6:22; Ex 7:2   7:7 ^Deut 29:5; Acts 7:23, 30

^A"Take your staff and throw *it* down before Pharaoh, *so that* it may turn into a serpent.'" ¹⁰So Moses and Aaron came to Pharaoh, and so they did, just as the Lord had commanded; and Aaron threw his staff down before Pharaoh and his servants, and it ^Aturned into a serpent. ¹¹Then Pharaoh also called for *the* wise men and *the* sorcerers, and they too, *the* ^Asoothsayer priests of Egypt, did the same with their secret arts. ¹²For each one threw down his staff, and they turned into serpents. But Aaron's staff swallowed their staffs. ¹³Yet ^APharaoh's heart was hardened, and he did not listen to them, just as the Lord had said.

WATER TURNED INTO BLOOD

¹⁴Then the Lord said to Moses, "Pharaoh's heart is stubborn; he refuses to let the people go. ¹⁵Go to Pharaoh in the morning just as ^Ahe is going out to the water, and position yourself to meet him on the bank of the Nile; and you shall take in your hand the staff that was turned into a serpent. ¹⁶And you shall say to him, 'The Lord, the God of the Hebrews, sent me to you, saying, "^ALet My people go, so that they may serve Me in the wilderness. But behold, you have not listened up to now." ¹⁷This is what the Lord says: "By this you shall know that I am the Lord: behold, I am going to strike the water that is in the Nile with the staff that is in my hand, and ^Ait will be turned into blood. ¹⁸Then ^Athe fish that are in the Nile will die, the Nile will stink, and the Egyptians will ᴮno longer be able to drink water from the Nile."'" ¹⁹Then the Lord said to Moses, "Say to Aaron, 'Take your

staff and ^Aextend your hand over the waters of Egypt, over their rivers, over their streams, over their pools, and over all their reservoirs of water, so that they may become blood; and there will be blood through all the land of Egypt, both in *containers of* wood and in *containers of* stone.'"

²⁰So Moses and Aaron did just as the Lord had commanded. And he lifted up the staff and struck the water that *was* in the Nile in the sight of Pharaoh and in the sight of his servants; and ^Aall the water that *was* in the Nile was turned into blood. ²¹Then the fish that *were* in the Nile died, and the Nile stank, so that the Egyptians could not drink water from the Nile. And the blood was through all the land of Egypt. ²²^ABut the soothsayer priests of Egypt did the same with their secret arts; and Pharaoh's heart was hardened, and he did not listen to them, just as the Lord had said. ²³Then Pharaoh turned and went into his house with no concern even for this. ²⁴So all the Egyptians dug around the Nile for water to drink, because they could not drink from the water of the Nile. ²⁵Seven days passed after the Lord had struck the Nile.

FROGS OVER THE LAND

8 Then the Lord said to Moses, "Go to Pharaoh and say to him, 'This is what the Lord says: "^ALet My people go, so that they may serve Me. ²But if you refuse to let *them* go, behold, I am going

7:9^Ex 4:2, 17   7:10^Ex 4:3; 7:9   7:11^Dan 2:2; 2 Tim 3:8   7:13^Ex 4:21; 7:3, 22   7:15^Ex 2:5; 8:20   7:16^Ex 4:23; 5:1, 3   7:17^Ex 4:9; Rev 11:6   7:18^Ex 7:21   ᴮEx 7:24   7:19^Ex 8:5, 6, 16; 9:22   7:20^Ps 78:44; 105:29   7:22^Ex 7:11; 8:7   8:1^Ex 3:18; 4:23

to strike your entire territory with frogs. ³The Nile will ^swarm with frogs, which will come up and go into your house, and into your bedroom and on your bed, and into the houses of your servants, and on your people, and into your ovens and kneading bowls. ⁴So the frogs will come up on you, your people, and on all your servants."'" ⁵Then the LORD said to Moses, "Say to Aaron, '^Extend your hand with your staff over the rivers, over the streams, and over the pools, and make frogs come up on the land of Egypt.'" ⁶So Aaron extended his hand over the waters of Egypt, and the ^frogs came up and covered the land of Egypt. ⁷However, ^the soothsayer priests did the same with their secret arts, making frogs come up on the land of Egypt.

⁸Then Pharaoh called for Moses and Aaron and said, "^Plead with the LORD to remove the frogs from me and from my people; and I will let the people go, so that they may sacrifice to the LORD." ⁹And Moses said to Pharaoh, "The honor is yours to tell me: when shall I plead for you and your servants and your people, that the frogs be destroyed from you and your houses, *that* they be left only in the Nile?"

¹⁰Then he said, "Tomorrow." So he said, "*May it be* according to your word, so that you may know that there is ^no one like the LORD our God. ¹¹The ^frogs will depart from you and your houses, and from your servants and your people; they will be left only in the Nile." ¹²Then Moses and Aaron went out from Pharaoh, and ^Moses cried out to the LORD concerning the frogs which He had inflicted upon Pharaoh. ¹³The LORD did according to the word of Moses, and the frogs died out of the houses, the courtyards, and the fields. ¹⁴So they piled them in heaps, and the land stank. ¹⁵But when Pharaoh saw that there was relief, he hardened his heart and ^did not listen to them, just as the LORD had said.

THE PLAGUE OF INSECTS

¹⁶Then the LORD said to Moses, "Say to Aaron, 'Extend your staff and strike the dust of the earth, so that it may turn into gnats through all the land of Egypt.'" ¹⁷They did so; and Aaron extended his hand with his staff and struck the dust of the earth, and there were gnats on *every* ¹person and animal. All the dust of the earth turned into ^gnats through all the land of Egypt. ¹⁸The soothsayer priests tried with their secret arts to produce gnats, but ^they could not; so there were gnats on *every* person and animal. ¹⁹Then the soothsayer priests said to Pharaoh, "^This is the finger of God." But Pharaoh's heart was hardened, and he did not listen to them, just as the LORD had said.

²⁰Then the LORD said to Moses, "^Rise early in the morning and present yourself before Pharaoh, as he comes out to the water; and say to him, 'This is what the LORD says: "Let My people go, so that they may serve Me. ²¹For if you are not going to let My people go, behold, I will send swarms of

8:3 ^Ps 105:30   8:5 ^Ex 7:19   8:6 ^Ps 78:45; 105:30
8:7 ^Ex 7:11, 22   8:8 ^Ex 8:28; 9:28   8:10 ^Ex 9:14;
Deut 4:35, 39   8:11 ^Ex 8:13   8:12 ^Ex 8:30; 9:33
8:15 ^Ex 7:4   8:17 ^Ps 105:31   8:18 ^Ex 7:11, 12; 8:7
8:19 ^Ps 8:3; Luke 11:20   8:20 ^Ex 7:15; 9:13

8:17 ¹I.e., Egyptians and their livestock

flies on you and on your servants and on your people, and into your houses; and the houses of the Egyptians will be full of swarms of flies, and also the ground on which they *live.* ²²ᴬBut on that day I will set apart the land of Goshen, where My people are living, so that no swarms of flies will be there, in order that you may know that I, the LORD, am in the midst of the land. ²³I will put a division between My people and your people. Tomorrow this sign will occur.”’” ²⁴Then the LORD did so. And thick swarms of flies entered the house of Pharaoh and the houses of his servants, and the land was ᴬlaid waste because of the swarms of flies in all the land of Egypt.

²⁵Then Pharaoh called for Moses and Aaron and said, “ᴬGo, sacrifice to your God within the land.” ²⁶But Moses said, “It is not permissible *for us* to do so, because we will sacrifice to the LORD our God that which is ᴬan abomination to the Egyptians. If we sacrifice that which is an abomination to the Egyptians before their eyes, will they not stone us? ²⁷We must go a ᴬthree days’ journey into the wilderness and sacrifice to the LORD our God, just as He commands us.” ²⁸Pharaoh said, “I will let you go, so that you may sacrifice to the LORD your God in the wilderness; only you shall not go very far away. ᴬPlead for me.” ²⁹Then Moses said, “Behold, I am going to leave you, and I will plead with the LORD that the swarms of flies may depart from Pharaoh, from his servants, and from his people tomorrow; only do not let Pharaoh ᴬdeal deceitfully again in not

letting the people go to sacrifice to the LORD.”

³⁰So ᴬMoses left Pharaoh and pleaded with the LORD. ³¹The LORD did as Moses asked, and removed the swarms of flies from Pharaoh, from his servants, and from his people; not one remained. ³²But Pharaoh hardened his heart this time also, and ᴬhe did not let the people go.

EGYPTIAN LIVESTOCK DIE

9 Then the LORD said to Moses, “Go to Pharaoh and speak to him, ‘This is what the LORD, the God of the Hebrews says: “ᴬLet My people go, so that they may serve Me. ²For ᴬif you refuse to let *them* go and continue to hold them, ³behold, ᴬthe hand of the LORD will come *with* a very severe plague on your livestock which are in the field, on the horses, on the donkeys, on the camels, on the herds, and on the flocks. ⁴ᴬBut the LORD will make a distinction between the livestock of Israel and the livestock of Egypt, so that nothing will die of all that belongs to the sons of Israel.”’” ⁵And the LORD set a definite time, saying, “Tomorrow the LORD will do this thing in the land.” ⁶So the LORD did this thing on the next day, and ᴬall the livestock of Egypt died; but not one of the livestock of the sons of Israel died. ⁷And Pharaoh sent *men,* and *they learned that,* behold, not even one of the livestock of Israel was dead. But ᴬthe

8:22ᴬEx 9:4, 6, 24; 10:23   8:24ᴬPs 78:45; 105:31
8:25ᴬEx 9:28; 10:8, 24   8:26ᴬGen 43:32; Deut 7:25f
8:27ᴬEx 3:18; 5:3   8:28ᴬEx 8:8; 1 Kin 13:6
8:29ᴬEx 8:8, 15   8:30ᴬEx 8:12   8:32ᴬEx 4:21; 8:8, 15
9:1ᴬEx 4:23; 8:1   9:2ᴬEx 8:2   9:3ᴬEx 7:4; 1 Sam 5:6
9:4ᴬEx 8:22   9:6ᴬEx 9:19, 20, 25; Ps 78:48
9:7ᴬEx 7:14; 8:32

heart of Pharaoh was hardened, and he did not let the people go.

THE PLAGUE OF BOILS

⁸Then the LORD said to Moses and Aaron, "Take for yourselves handfuls of soot from a kiln, and Moses shall toss it toward the sky in the sight of Pharaoh. ⁹Then it will become fine dust over all the land of Egypt, and will turn into ᴬboils breaking out with sores on *every* person and animal through all the land of Egypt." ¹⁰So they took soot from a kiln, and stood before Pharaoh; and Moses tossed it toward the sky, and it became boils breaking out with sores on *every* person and animal. ¹¹ᴬThe soothsayer priests could not stand before Moses because of the boils, for the boils were on the soothsayer priests as well as on all the Egyptians. ¹²But ᴬthe LORD hardened Pharaoh's heart, and he did not listen to them, just as the LORD had spoken to Moses.

¹³Then the LORD said to Moses, "ᴬRise up early in the morning and stand before Pharaoh and say to him, 'This is what the LORD, the God of the Hebrews says: "Let My people go, so that they may serve Me. ¹⁴For this time I am going to send all My plagues on you and your servants and your people, so that ᴬyou may know that there is no one like Me in all the earth. ¹⁵For had I now put out My hand and struck you and your people with plague, you would then have been eliminated from the earth. ¹⁶But indeed, ᴬfor this reason I have allowed you to remain, in order to show you My power and in order to proclaim My name throughout the earth. ¹⁷Still you exalt yourself against My people by not letting them go.

THE PLAGUE OF HAIL

¹⁸Behold, about this time tomorrow, ᴬI will send a very heavy hail, such as has not been *seen* in Egypt from the day it was founded until now. ¹⁹So now, send *word,* bring ᴬyour livestock and whatever you have in the field to safety. ᴮEvery person and animal that is found in the field and is not brought home, when the hail comes down on them, will die."'" ²⁰ᴬ*Everyone* among the servants of Pharaoh who feared the word of the LORD hurried to bring his servants and his livestock into the houses; ²¹but *everyone* who did not pay regard to the word of the LORD left his servants and his livestock in the field.

²²Now the LORD said to Moses, "Reach out with your hand toward the sky, so that ᴬhail may fall on all the land of Egypt, on *every* person and animal, and on every plant of the field, throughout the land of Egypt." ²³So Moses reached out with his staff toward the sky, and the LORD sent thunder and ᴬhail, and fire ran *down* to the earth. And the LORD rained hail on the land of Egypt. ²⁴So there was hail, and fire flashing intermittently in the midst of the hail, *which was* very heavy, such as had not occurred in all the land of Egypt since it became a nation. ²⁵ᴬThe hail struck everything that was in the field through all the land of Egypt, from people to animals; the hail also struck every plant of the field, and shattered every tree of the field. ²⁶ᴬOnly in the land of

9:9 ᴬDeut 28:27; Rev 16:2   9:11 ᴬEx 8:18   9:12 ᴬEx 4:21; 10:1, 20   9:13 ᴬEx 8:20   9:14 ᴬEx 8:10; Deut 3:24   9:16 ᴬProv 16:4; Rom 9:17   9:18 ᴬEx 9:23, 24   9:19 ᴬEx 9:6   ᴮEx 9:25   9:20 ᴬProv 13:13   9:22 ᴬRev 16:21   9:23 ᴬGen 19:24; Josh 10:11   9:25 ᴬEx 9:19; Ps 78:47, 48   9:26 ᴬEx 8:22; 9:4, 6

Goshen, where the sons of Israel *were,* was there no hail.

²⁷Then Pharaoh sent for Moses and Aaron, and said to them, "ᴬI have sinned this time; the Lᴏʀᴅ is the righteous one, and I and my people are the wicked ones. ²⁸ᴬPlead with the Lᴏʀᴅ, for there has been enough of God's thunder and hail; and I will let you go, and you shall stay no longer." ²⁹Moses said to him, "As soon as I go out of the city, I will spread out my hands to the Lᴏʀᴅ; the thunder will cease and there will no longer be hail, so that you may know that ᴬthe earth is the Lᴏʀᴅ's. ³⁰But as for you and your servants, I know that ᴬyou do not yet fear the Lᴏʀᴅ God." ³¹(Now the flax and the ᴬbarley were ruined, for the barley was in the ear and the flax was in bud. ³²But the wheat and the spelt were not ruined, for they *ripen* late.) ³³ᴬSo Moses left the city from *his meeting* with Pharaoh, and spread out his hands to the Lᴏʀᴅ; and the thunder and the hail stopped, and rain no longer poured on the earth. ³⁴But when Pharaoh saw that the rain and the hail and the thunder had stopped, he sinned again and hardened his heart, he and his servants. ³⁵So Pharaoh's heart was hardened, and he did not let the sons of Israel go, just as the ᴬLᴏʀᴅ had spoken through Moses.

THE PLAGUE OF LOCUSTS

10 Then the Lᴏʀᴅ said to Moses, "Go to Pharaoh, for ᴬI have hardened his heart and the heart of his servants, so that I may perform these signs of Mine among them, ²and ᴬthat you may tell in the presence of your son, and of your grandson, how I made a mockery of

the Egyptians and how I performed My signs among them, so that you may know that I am the Lᴏʀᴅ."

³So Moses and Aaron went to Pharaoh and said to him, "This is what the Lᴏʀᴅ, the God of the Hebrews says: 'How long will you refuse to ᴬhumble yourself before Me? Let My people go, so that they may serve Me. ⁴For if you refuse to let My people go, behold, tomorrow I will bring locusts into your territory. ⁵And they will cover the surface of the land, so that no one will be able to see the land. ᴬThey will also eat the rest of what has survived—what is left to you from the hail—and they will eat every tree of yours which grows in the field. ⁶Then ᴬyour houses will be filled *with them,* together with the houses of all your servants and the houses of all the Egyptians, *something* which neither your fathers nor your grandfathers have seen, from the day that they came upon the earth until this day.'" And he turned and left Pharaoh. ⁷Then Pharaoh's servants said to him, "How long shall this man be ᴬa snare to us? Let the people go, so that they may serve the Lᴏʀᴅ their God. Do you not yet realize that Egypt is destroyed?" ⁸So Moses and Aaron ᴬwere brought back to Pharaoh, and he said to them, "ᴮGo, serve the Lᴏʀᴅ your God! Who specifically are the ones who are going?" ⁹Moses said, "ᴬWe shall go with our young and our old; with our sons and our daughters, with

9:27ᴬEx 10:16, 17; Lam 1:18   9:28ᴬEx 8:8, 28; 10:17
9:29ᴬEx 19:5; Ps 24:1   9:30ᴬIs 26:10   9:31ᴬRuth 1:22;
2:23   9:33ᴬEx 8:12; 9:29   9:35ᴬEx 4:21
10:1ᴬEx 4:21; John 12:40   10:2ᴬEx 12:26, 27; Deut 4:9
10:3ᴬ1 Kin 21:29; 2 Chr 34:27   10:5ᴬJoel 1:4; 2:25
10:6ᴬEx 8:3, 21   10:7ᴬEx 23:33; Josh 23:13
10:8ᴬEx 8:8   ᴮEx 8:25   10:9ᴬEx 12:37, 38

our flocks and our herds we shall go, for we must hold a feast to the LORD." ¹⁰Then he said to them, "So may the LORD be with you, when I let you and your little ones go! Watch out, for evil is on your mind! ¹¹Not so! Go now, *but only* the men *among you,* and serve the LORD, since that is what you desire." So ^they were driven out from Pharaoh's presence.

¹²Then the LORD said to Moses, "^Reach out with your hand over the land of Egypt for the locusts, so that they may come up on the land of Egypt and ᴮeat every plant of the land, everything that the hail has left." ¹³So Moses reached out with his staff over the land of Egypt, and the LORD directed an east wind on the land all that day and all that night; and when it was morning, the east wind brought the ^locusts. ¹⁴^The locusts came up over all the land of Egypt and settled in all the territory of Egypt; *they were* very numerous. There had never been so *many* locusts, nor would there be so *many* again. ¹⁵For they covered the surface of the whole land, so that the land was darkened; and they ^ate every plant of the land and all the fruit of the trees that the hail had left. Therefore nothing green was left on tree or plant of the field throughout the land of Egypt. ¹⁶Then Pharaoh hurriedly called for Moses and Aaron, and he said, "^I have sinned against the LORD your God and against you. ¹⁷So now, please forgive my sin only this once, and ^plead with the LORD your God, that He would only remove this death from me." ¹⁸Then ^he left Pharaoh and pleaded with the LORD. ¹⁹So the LORD shifted *the wind* to a very strong west wind, which picked up the locusts and drove them into the Red Sea; not one locust was left in all the territory of Egypt. ²⁰But ^the LORD hardened Pharaoh's heart, and he did not let the sons of Israel go.

DARKNESS OVER THE LAND

²¹Then the LORD said to Moses, "^Reach out with your hand toward the sky, so that there may be darkness over the land of Egypt, even a darkness which may be felt." ²²So Moses reached out with his hand toward the sky, and there was ^thick darkness in all the land of Egypt for three days. ²³They did not see one another, nor did anyone rise from his place for three days, ^but all the sons of Israel had light in their dwellings. ²⁴Then Pharaoh called for Moses, and said, "Go, serve the LORD; only let your flocks and your herds be left behind. Even ^your little ones may go with you." ²⁵But Moses said, "You must also let us have sacrifices and burnt offerings, so that we may sacrifice *them* to the LORD our God. ²⁶^Therefore, our livestock too shall go with us; not a hoof shall be left behind, for we shall take some of them to serve the LORD our God. And until we arrive there, we ourselves do not know with what we shall serve the LORD." ²⁷But ^the LORD hardened Pharaoh's heart, and he was not willing to let them go. ²⁸Then Pharaoh said to him, "^Get away from me! Be careful, do not see my face again, for on the day you see my face, you shall die!" ²⁹Moses said,

10:11 ^Ex 10:28   10:12 ^Ex 7:19   ᴮEx 10:5, 15
10:13 ^Ps 78:46; 105:34   10:14 ^Deut 28:38; Ps 78:46
10:15 ^Ex 10:5; Ps 105:34f   10:16 ^Ex 9:27
10:17 ^Ex 8:8, 28; 1 Kin 13:6   10:18 ^Ex 8:30
10:20 ^Ex 4:21; 11:10   10:21 ^Ex 9:22
10:22 ^Ps 105:28; Rev 16:10   10:23 ^Ex 8:22
10:24 ^Ex 10:10   10:26 ^Ex 10:9   10:27 ^Ex 4:21;
14:4, 8   10:28 ^Ex 10:11

"You have spoken correctly; ^AI shall never see your face again!"

THE LAST PLAGUE

11 Now the LORD said to Moses, "One more plague I will bring on Pharaoh and on Egypt; ^Aafter that he will let you go from here. When he lets you go, he will assuredly drive you out from here completely. ²Speak now so that the people hear, that ^Aeach man is to ask of his neighbor, and each woman of her neighbor, articles of silver and articles of gold." ³And the LORD gave the people favor in the sight of the Egyptians. ^AFurthermore, the man Moses *himself* was greatly esteemed in the land of Egypt, *both* in the sight of Pharaoh's servants and in the sight of the people.

⁴Then Moses said, "This is what the LORD says: 'About ^Amidnight I am going out into the midst of Egypt, ⁵and ^Aall the firstborn in the land of Egypt shall die, from the firstborn of the Pharaoh who sits on his throne, to the firstborn of the slave girl who is behind the millstones; all the firstborn of the cattle as well. ⁶So there shall be ^Aa great cry in all the land of Egypt, such as there has not been *before* and such as shall never be again. ⁷^ABut not *even* a dog will threaten any of the sons of Israel, *nor anything* from person to animal, so that you may learn how the LORD distinguishes between Egypt and Israel.' ⁸And ^Aall these servants of yours will come down to me and bow themselves before me, saying, 'Go out, you and all the people who follow you,' and after that I will go out." And he left Pharaoh in the heat of anger.

⁹Then the LORD said to Moses, "Pharaoh will not listen to you, so ^Athat My wonders will be multiplied in the land of Egypt." ¹⁰So ^AMoses and Aaron performed all these wonders before Pharaoh; yet ^Bthe LORD hardened Pharaoh's heart, and he did not let the sons of Israel go out of his land.

THE PASSOVER LAMB

12 Now the LORD said to Moses and Aaron in the land of Egypt, ²^A"This month shall be the beginning of months for you; it is to be the first month of the year for you. ³Speak to all the congregation of Israel, saying, 'On the tenth of this month they are, each one, to take a lamb for themselves, according to the fathers' households, a lamb for each household. ⁴Now if the household is too small for a lamb, then he and his neighbor nearest to his house are to take one according to the number of persons *in them;* in proportion to what each one should eat, you are to divide the lamb. ⁵Your lamb shall be ^Aan unblemished male a year old; you may take it from the sheep or from the goats. ⁶You shall keep it until the ^Afourteenth day of the same month, then the whole assembly of the congregation of Israel is to slaughter it at twilight. ⁷^AMoreover, they shall take some of the blood and put it on the two doorposts and on the lintel of the houses in which they eat it. ⁸They shall eat the flesh ^Athat *same* night, roasted with fire, and they shall eat it with ^Bunleavened bread and

10:29 ^A Ex 11:8; Heb 11:27   11:1 ^A Ex 12:31, 33, 39
11:2 ^A Ex 3:22; 12:35, 36   11:3 ^A Deut 34:10-12
11:4 ^A Ex 12:29   11:5 ^A Ex 12:12, 29; Ps 78:51
11:6 ^A Ex 12:30   11:7 ^A Ex 8:22; Josh 10:21
11:8 ^A Ex 12:31-33   11:9 ^A Ex 7:3   11:10 ^A Ex 4:21
^B Ex 9:12   12:2 ^A Ex 13:4; Deut 16:1   12:5 ^A Lev 22:18-21;
Heb 9:14   12:6 ^A Ex 12:14, 17; Lev 23:5   12:7 ^A Ex 12:22
12:8 ^A Ex 34:25   ^B Deut 16:3, 4

bitter herbs. [9]Do not eat any of it raw or boiled at all with water, but rather roasted with fire, *both* its head and its legs along with [A]its entrails. [10A]And you shall not leave any of it over until morning, but whatever is left of it until morning, you shall completely burn with fire. [11]Now you shall eat it in this way: *with your garment* belted around your waist, your sandals on your feet, and your staff in your hand; and you shall eat it in a hurry—it is [A]the LORD's Passover. [12]For [A]I will go through the land of Egypt on that night, and fatally strike all the firstborn in the land of Egypt, from the human *firstborn* to animals; and against all the gods of Egypt I will execute judgments—I am the LORD. [13A]The blood shall be a sign for you on the houses where you live; and when I see the blood I will pass over you, and no plague will come upon you to destroy *you* when I strike the land of Egypt.

FEAST OF UNLEAVENED BREAD

[14]'Now [A]this day shall be a memorial to you, and you shall celebrate it *as* a feast to the LORD; throughout your generations you are to celebrate it *as* a permanent ordinance. [15]For [A]seven days you shall eat unleavened bread, but on the first day you shall remove dough with yeast from your houses; for whoever eats anything with yeast from the first day until the seventh day, that person shall be cut off from Israel. [16]And [A]on the first day you shall have a holy assembly, and *another* holy assembly on the seventh day; no work at all shall be done on them, except for what must be eaten by every person— that alone may be prepared by

you. [17]You shall also keep [A]the *Feast of* Unleavened Bread, for on this [B]very day I brought your multitudes out of the land of Egypt; therefore you shall keep this day throughout your generations as a permanent ordinance. [18A]In the first *month,* on the fourteenth day of the month at evening, you shall eat unleavened bread, until the twenty-first day of the month at evening. [19]For seven days there shall be no dough with yeast found in your houses; for whoever eats anything with yeast, that [A]person shall be cut off from the congregation of Israel, whether *he is* a stranger or a native of the land. [20]You shall not eat anything with yeast; in all your dwellings you shall eat unleavened bread.'"

[21]Then [A]Moses called for all the elders of Israel and said to them, "Go and [B]take for yourselves lambs according to your families, and slaughter the Passover *lamb.* [22]And [A]you shall take a bunch of hyssop and dip it in the blood which is in the basin, and apply some of the blood that is in the basin to the lintel and the two doorposts; and none of you shall go outside the door of his house until morning.

A MEMORIAL OF REDEMPTION

[23]For the LORD will pass through to strike the Egyptians; but when He sees the blood on the lintel and on the two doorposts, the LORD will pass over the door and will not allow the [A]destroyer to come in to

12:9 [A]Ex 29:13, 17, 22   12:10 [A]Ex 16:19; 23:18
12:11 [A]Ex 12:13, 21, 43   12:12 [A]Ex 11:4, 5
12:13 [A]Heb 11:28   12:14 [A]Ex 12:6; Lev 23:4, 5
12:15 [A]Ex 13:6, 7; 23:15   12:16 [A]Lev 23:7, 8;
Num 28:18, 25   12:17 [A]Deut 16:3-8   [B]Ex 12:41
12:18 [A]Ex 12:2; Lev 23:5-8   12:19 [A]Num 9:13
12:21 [A]Heb 11:28   [B]Ex 12:3   12:22 [A]Ex 12:7
12:23 [A]1 Cor 10:10; Heb 11:28

your houses to strike *you*. 24 And
^you shall keep this event as an
ordinance for you and your children forever. 25 When you enter the
land which the Lord will give you,
as He has promised, you shall keep
this rite. 26^And when your children say to you, 'What does this
rite mean to you?' 27 then you shall
say, 'It is a Passover sacrifice to
^the Lord because He passed over
the houses of the sons of Israel in
Egypt when He struck the Egyptians, but spared our homes.'"
^And the people bowed low and
worshiped.

28 Then the sons of Israel went
and did *so*; just as the Lord had
commanded Moses and Aaron, so
they did.

29 Now it came about at ^midnight
that ^the Lord struck all the firstborn in the land of Egypt, from the
firstborn of Pharaoh who sat on his
throne to the firstborn of the captive who was in the dungeon, and
all the firstborn of cattle. 30 And
Pharaoh got up in the night, he and
all his servants and all the Egyptians, and there was ^a great cry
in Egypt, for there was no home
where there was not someone
dead. 31 Then he called for Moses
and Aaron at night and said, "Rise
up, ^get out from among my people,
both you and the sons of Israel; and
go, worship the Lord, as you have
said. 32 Take ^both your flocks and
your herds, as you have said, and
go, and bless me also."

EXODUS OF ISRAEL

33 ^The Egyptians urged the people,
to send them out of the land in a
hurry, for they said, "We will all be
dead." 34 So the people took ^their
dough before it was leavened, *with*
their kneading bowls bound up in
the clothes on their shoulders.

35 ^Now the sons of Israel had
done according to the word of
Moses, for they had requested from
the Egyptians articles of silver and
articles of gold, and clothing; 36 and
the Lord had given the people
favor in the sight of the Egyptians,
so that they let them have their
request. Therefore they ^plundered
the Egyptians.

37 Now the ^sons of Israel journeyed from ^Rameses to Succoth,
about six hundred thousand men
on foot, aside from children. 38 A
mixed multitude also went up with
them, along with flocks and herds,
a ^very large number of livestock.
39 And they baked the dough which
they had brought out of Egypt into
cakes of unleavened bread. For
it had no yeast, since they were
^driven out of Egypt and could not
delay, nor had they prepared any
provisions for themselves.

40 Now the time that the sons of
Israel had lived in Egypt was ^430
years. 41 And at the end of 430 years,
on ^this very day, all the multitudes
of the Lord departed from the land
of Egypt.

ORDINANCE OF THE PASSOVER

42 ^It is a night to be observed for
the Lord, for having brought them
out of the land of Egypt; this night
is for the Lord, to be observed by
all the sons of Israel throughout
their generations.

12:24^Ex 12:14, 17; 13:5, 10   12:26^Ex 10:2; Deut 32:7
12:27^Ex 12:11   ^Ex 4:31   12:29^Ex 11:4, 5   ^Num 8:17
12:30^Ex 11:6   12:31^Ex 8:25   12:32^Ex 10:9, 26
12:33^Ex 10:7; Ps 105:38   12:34^Ex 12:39
12:35^Ex 3:21, 22; Ps 105:37   12:36^Ex 3:22
12:37^Num 33:3, 5   ^Gen 47:11   12:38^Ex 17:3;
Deut 3:19   12:39^Ex 6:1; 11:1   12:40^Gen 15:13, 16;
Acts 7:6   12:41^Ex 12:17   12:42^Ex 13:10; Deut 16:1

⁴³And the LORD said to Moses and Aaron, "This is the ordinance of ^the Passover: no ᴮforeigner is to eat it; ⁴⁴but *as for* every ^slave that someone has purchased with money, after you have circumcised him, then he may eat it. ⁴⁵^A stranger or a hired worker shall not eat it. ⁴⁶It is to be eaten in a single house; you are not to bring any of the meat outside of the house, ^nor are you to break any bone of it. ⁴⁷^All the congregation of Israel are to celebrate this. ⁴⁸But ^if a stranger resides with you and celebrates the Passover to the LORD, all of his males are to be circumcised, and then he shall come near to celebrate it; and he shall be like a native of the land. But no uncircumcised male may eat it. ⁴⁹^The same law shall apply to the native as to the stranger who resides among you."

⁵⁰Then all the sons of Israel did *so;* they did just as the LORD had commanded Moses and Aaron. ⁵¹And on that very day the LORD brought the sons of Israel out of the land of Egypt ^according to their multitudes.

13 Then the LORD spoke to Moses, saying, ²"^Sanctify to Me every firstborn, the firstborn of every womb among the sons of Israel, among people and animals *alike;* it belongs to Me."

³And Moses said to the people, "^Remember this day in which you departed from Egypt, from the house of slavery; for by a powerful hand the LORD brought you out from this place. And nothing with yeast shall be eaten. ⁴On this day in the ^month of Abib, you are about to go out *from here.* ⁵And it shall be when the LORD brings you to the land of the Canaanite, the Hittite, the Amorite, the Hivite, and the Jebusite, which ^He swore to your fathers to give you, a land flowing with milk and honey, ᴮthat you shall perform this rite in this month. ⁶For ^seven days you shall eat unleavened bread, and on the seventh day there shall be a feast to the LORD. ⁷Unleavened bread shall be eaten throughout the seven days; and ^nothing with yeast shall be seen among you, nor shall any dough with yeast be seen among you in all your borders. ⁸And ^you shall tell your son on that day, saying, '*It is* because of what the LORD did for me when I came out of Egypt.' ⁹And ^it shall serve as a sign to you on your hand, and as a reminder on your forehead, that the law of the LORD may be in your mouth; for with a powerful hand the LORD brought you out of Egypt. ¹⁰Therefore, you shall ^keep this ordinance at its appointed time from year to year.

¹¹"Now when the LORD brings you to the land of the Canaanite, as ^He swore to you and to your fathers, and gives it to you, ¹²^you shall devote to the LORD every firstborn of a womb, and every firstborn offspring of an animal that you own; the males belong to the LORD. ¹³But every firstborn of a donkey you shall redeem with a lamb, but if you do not redeem *it,* then you shall break its neck; and ^every firstborn among

12:43 ^Num 9:14   ᴮEx 12:48   12:44 ^Gen 17:12, 13; Lev 22:11   12:45 ^Lev 22:10   12:46 ^Num 9:12; Ps 34:20   12:47 ^Ex 12:6; Num 9:13, 14   12:48 ^Num 9:14   12:49 ^Lev 24:22; Num 15:15, 16, 29   12:51 ^Ex 6:26   13:2 ^Ex 13:12, 13, 15; 22:29   13:3 ^Ex 12:42; Deut 16:3   13:4 ^Ex 12:2; Deut 16:1   13:5 ^Ex 6:8   ᴮEx 12:25   13:6 ^Ex 12:15-20   13:7 ^Ex 12:19   13:8 ^Ex 10:2; Ps 44:1   13:9 ^Ex 12:14; Deut 6:8   13:10 ^Ex 12:24, 25; 13:5   13:11 ^Gen 15:18; Ps 105:42-45   13:12 ^Ex 13:1, 2; Lev 27:26   13:13 ^Num 3:46

your sons you shall redeem. ¹⁴ And it shall be when your son asks you in time to come, saying, 'What is this?' then you shall say to him, "With a powerful hand the LORD brought us out of Egypt, from the house of slavery. ¹⁵ And it came about, when Pharaoh was stubborn about letting us go, that the ᴬLORD put to death every firstborn in the land of Egypt, from human firstborns to animal firstborns. Therefore, I sacrifice to the LORD the males, every firstborn of a womb, but every firstborn of my sons I redeem.' ¹⁶ So ᴬit shall serve as a sign on your hand and as phylacteries on your forehead, for with a powerful hand the LORD brought us out of Egypt."

GOD LEADS THE PEOPLE

¹⁷ Now when Pharaoh had let the people go, God did not lead them by the way of the land of the Philistines, even though it was near; for God said, "ᴬThe people might change their minds when they see war, and return to Egypt." ¹⁸ Therefore God led the people around by way of the wilderness to the Red Sea; and the sons of Israel went up ᴬin battle formation from the land of Egypt. ¹⁹ And Moses took ᴬthe bones of Joseph with him, for he had made the sons of Israel solemnly swear, saying, "God will certainly take care of you, and you shall carry my bones from here with you." ²⁰ Then they set out from ᴬSuccoth and camped in Etham, on the edge of the wilderness. ²¹ And ᴬthe LORD was going before them in a pillar of cloud by day to lead them on the way, and in a pillar of fire by night to give them light, so that they might travel by day and by night. ²² He ᴬdid not take away the pillar of cloud by day, nor the pillar of fire by night, from the presence of the people.

PHARAOH IN PURSUIT

14 Now the LORD spoke to Moses, saying, ² "Tell the sons of Israel to turn back and camp in front of ᴬPi-hahiroth, between ᴮMigdol and the sea; you shall camp in front of Baal-zephon, opposite it, by the sea. ³ For Pharaoh will say of the sons of Israel, 'They are wandering aimlessly in the land; the wilderness has shut them in.' ⁴ And I will harden Pharaoh's heart, and ᴬhe will chase after them; and I will be honored through Pharaoh and all his army, and ᴮthe Egyptians will know that I am the LORD." And they did so.

⁵ When the king of Egypt was told that the people had fled, Pharaoh and his servants had a change of heart toward the people, and they said, "What is this *that* we have done, that we have let Israel go from serving us?" ⁶ So he had *horses* harnessed *to* his chariot and took his people with him; ⁷ and he took six hundred select chariots, and all the *other* chariots of Egypt with officers over all of them. ⁸ So ᴬthe LORD hardened the heart of Pharaoh, king of Egypt, and he chased after the sons of Israel as the sons of Israel were going out boldly. ⁹ Then the Egyptians chased after them *with* all the horses *and* chariots of Pharaoh, his horsemen and his army, and they overtook them camping by the sea,

13:14 ᴬEx 13:3, 9; 13:15 ᴬEx 12:29 13:16 ᴬEx 13:9;
Deut 6:8 13:17 ᴬEx 14:11, 12; Deut 17:16
13:18 ᴬJosh 1:14; 4:12, 13 13:19 ᴬGen 50:24, 25;
Acts 7:15, 16 13:20 ᴬEx 12:37; Num 33:6
13:21 ᴬEx 14:19, 24; 33:9, 10 13:22 ᴬNeh 9:19
14:2 ᴬNum 33:7 ᴮJer 44:1 14:4 ᴬEx 14:23
ᴮEx 7:5 14:8 ᴬEx 14:4

^beside Pi-hahiroth, in front of Baal-zephon.

¹⁰ As Pharaoh approached, the sons of Israel looked, and behold, the Egyptians were coming after them, and they became very frightened; ^so the sons of Israel cried out to the Lord. ¹¹ Then ^they said to Moses, "Is it because there were no graves in Egypt that you have taken us away to die in the wilderness? Why have you dealt with us in this way, bringing us out of Egypt? ¹²^Is this not the word that we spoke to you in Egypt, saying, 'Leave us alone so that we may serve the Egyptians'? For it would have been better for us to serve the Egyptians than to die in the wilderness!"

THE SEA IS DIVIDED

¹³ But Moses said to the people, "Do not fear! Stand by and see ^the salvation of the Lord, which He will perform for you today; for the Egyptians whom you have seen today, you will never see them again, ever. ¹⁴ The Lord will fight for you, while ^you keep silent."

¹⁵ Then the Lord said to Moses, "Why are you crying out to Me? Tell the sons of Israel to go forward. ¹⁶ As for you, lift up ^your staff and reach out with your hand over the sea and divide it, and the sons of Israel shall go through the midst of the sea on dry land. ¹⁷ And as for Me, behold, ^I will harden the hearts of the Egyptians so that they will go in after them; and I will be honored through Pharaoh and all his army, through his chariots and his horsemen. ¹⁸^Then the Egyptians will know that I am the Lord, when I am honored through Pharaoh, through his chariots, and through his horsemen."

¹⁹ Then ^the angel of God, who had been going before the camp of Israel, moved and went behind them; and the pillar of cloud moved from before them and stood behind them. ²⁰ So it came between the camp of Egypt and the camp of Israel; and there was the cloud along with the darkness, yet it gave light at night. Therefore the one did not approach the other all night.

²¹ Then Moses reached out with his hand over the sea; and the Lord swept the sea *back* by a strong east wind all night, and turned the sea into dry land, and ^the waters were divided. ²² So the sons of Israel went through the midst of the sea on the dry land, and ^the waters *were like* a wall to them on their right and on their left. ²³ Then ^the Egyptians took up the pursuit, and all Pharaoh's horses, his chariots, and his horsemen went in after them into the midst of the sea. ²⁴ But at the morning watch, ^the Lord looked down on the army of the Egyptians through the pillar of fire and cloud, and brought the army of the Egyptians into confusion. ²⁵ He caused their chariot wheels to swerve, and He made them drive with difficulty; so the Egyptians *each* said, "Let me flee from Israel, ^for the Lord is fighting for them against the Egyptians."

²⁶ Then the Lord said to Moses, "^Reach out with your hand over the sea so that the waters may come back over the Egyptians, over their chariots and their horsemen." ²⁷ So

14:9 ^Ex 14:2   14:10 ^Josh 24:7; Neh 9:9   14:11 ^Ex 5:21;
Ps 106:7, 8   14:12 ^Ex 6:9   14:13 ^Ex 14:30; 15:2
14:14 ^Is 30:15   14:16 ^Ex 4:17, 20; Is 10:26
14:17 ^Ex 14:4, 8   14:18 ^Ex 14:25   14:19 ^Ex 13:21, 22
14:21 ^Ex 15:8; Josh 3:16   14:22 ^Ex 14:29; 15:8
14:23 ^Ex 14:4, 17   14:24 ^Ex 13:21
14:25 ^Ex 14:4, 14, 18   14:26 ^Ex 14:16

Moses reached out with his hand over the sea, and ^the sea returned to its normal state at daybreak, while the Egyptians were fleeing right into it; then the Lord overthrew the Egyptians in the midst of the sea. 28 The waters returned and covered the chariots and the horsemen, Pharaoh's entire army that had gone into the sea after them; ^not even one of them remained. 29 But the sons of Israel walked on ^dry land through the midst of the sea, and the waters *were like* a wall to them on their right and on their left.

30 So the Lord saved Israel that day from the hand of the Egyptians, and Israel ^saw the Egyptians dead on the seashore. 31 When Israel saw the great power which the Lord had used against the Egyptians, the people feared the Lord, and ^they believed in the Lord and in His servant Moses.

THE SONG OF MOSES AND ISRAEL

15 ^Then Moses and the sons of Israel sang this song to the Lord, saying:

"I will sing to the Lord, for He is highly exalted;
The horse and its rider He has hurled into the sea.
2 "^The Lord is my strength and song,
And He has become my salvation;
This is my God, and I will praise Him;
My father's God, and I will ^exalt Him.
3 "^The Lord is a warrior;
^The Lord is His name.
4 "^Pharaoh's chariots and his army He has thrown into the sea;
And the choicest of his officers are drowned in the Red Sea.

5 "The waters cover them;
^They went down into the depths like a stone.
6 "Your right hand, Lord, is majestic in power;
^Your right hand, Lord, destroys the enemy.
7 "And in the greatness of Your excellence You ^overthrow those who rise up against You;
You send out Your burning anger, *and* it consumes them like chaff.
8 "At the blast of Your nostrils the waters were piled up,
^The flowing waters stood up like a heap;
The depths were congealed in the heart of the sea.
9 "^The enemy said, 'I will pursue, I will overtake, I will divide the spoils;
I shall be satisfied against them;
I will draw my sword, my hand will destroy them.'
10 "You blew with Your wind, the sea covered them;
^They sank like lead in the mighty waters.
11 "Who is like You among the gods, Lord?
Who is like You, majestic in holiness,
Awesome in praises, ^working wonders?
12 "^You reached out with Your right hand,
The earth swallowed them.
13 "In Your faithfulness You have ^led the people whom You have ^redeemed;

14:27 ^Josh 4:18   14:28 ^Ps 78:53; 106:11
14:29 ^Ex 14:22; Ps 66:6   14:30 ^Ps 58:10; 59:10
14:31 ^Ps 106:12; John 2:11   15:1 ^Ps 106:12; Rev 15:3
15:2 ^Hab 3:18f   ^B Is 25:1   15:3 ^Rev 19:11   ^B Ex 3:15
15:4 ^Ex 14:6, 7, 17, 28   15:5 ^Ex 15:10; Neh 9:11
15:6 ^Ps 118:15, 16   15:7 ^Ex 14:27   15:8 ^Ps 78:13
15:9 ^Ex 14:5, 8, 9   15:10 ^Ex 15:5   15:11 ^Ps 72:18;
136:4   15:12 ^Ex 15:6   15:13 ^Ps 77:20   ^B Ex 15:16

In Your strength You have guided *them* to Your holy habitation.

14 "ᴬThe peoples have heard, they tremble;
Anguish has gripped the inhabitants of Philistia.

15 "Then the chiefs of Edom were terrified;
ᴬThe leaders of Moab, trembling grips them;
ᴮAll the inhabitants of Canaan have despaired.

16 "Terror and dread fall upon them;
ᴬBy the greatness of Your arm they are motionless as stone,
Until Your people pass over, Lᴏʀᴅ,
Until the people pass over whom You ᴮhave purchased.

17 "You will bring them and plant them in ᴬthe mountain of Your inheritance,
The place, Lᴏʀᴅ, which You have made as Your dwelling,
ᴮThe sanctuary, Lord, which Your hands have established.

18 "ᴬThe Lᴏʀᴅ shall reign forever and ever."

19 For the horses of Pharaoh with his chariots and his horsemen went into the sea, and the Lᴏʀᴅ brought back the waters of the sea on them, but the sons of Israel walked on ᴬdry land through the midst of the sea.

20 ᴬMiriam the prophetess, Aaron's sister, took the tambourine in her hand, and all the women went out after her with tambourines and with dancing. 21 And Miriam answered them,

"ᴬSing to the Lᴏʀᴅ, for He is highly exalted;
The horse and his rider He has hurled into the sea."

THE Lᴏʀᴅ PROVIDES WATER

22 Then Moses led Israel from the Red Sea, and they went out into ᴬthe wilderness of ᴮShur; and they went three days in the wilderness and found no water. 23 When they came to ᴬMarah, they could not drink the waters of Marah, because they were bitter; for that reason it was named ¹Marah. 24 So the people ᴬgrumbled at Moses, saying, "What are we to drink?" 25 Then he cried out to the Lᴏʀᴅ, and the Lᴏʀᴅ showed him a tree; and he threw *it* into the waters, and the waters became sweet.

There He ᴬmade for them a statute and regulation, and there He ᴮtested them. 26 And He said, "ᴬIf you will listen carefully to the voice of the Lᴏʀᴅ your God, and do what is right in His sight, and listen ᴮto His commandments, and keep all His statutes, I will put none of the diseases on you which I have put on the Egyptians; for I, the Lᴏʀᴅ, am your healer."

27 Then they came to ᴬElim where there *were* twelve springs of water and seventy date palms, and they camped there beside the waters.

THE Lᴏʀᴅ PROVIDES MANNA

16 Then they set out from Elim, and all the congregation of the sons of Israel came to the wilderness of ᴬSin, which is between Elim and Sinai, on the fifteenth day of the second month after their departure from the land of Egypt. 2 But the whole congregation of the

15:14ᴬDeut 2:25; Hab 3:7   15:15ᴬNum 22:3, 4
ᴮJosh 2:9, 11, 24   15:16ᴬEx 15:5, 6   ᴮPs 74:2
15:17ᴬPs 2:6   ᴮPs 78:69   15:18ᴬPs 10:16;
Is 57:15   15:19ᴬEx 14:22, 29   15:20ᴬEx 2:4; Mic 6:4
15:21ᴬEx 15:1   15:22ᴬNum 33:8   ᴮGen 16:7
15:23ᴬNum 33:8; Ruth 1:20   15:24ᴬEx 14:11; Ps 106:13
15:25ᴬJosh 24:25   ᴮEx 16:4   15:26ᴬDeut 7:12
ᴮEx 20:2-17   15:27ᴬNum 33:9   16:1ᴬNum 33:10, 11;
Ezek 30:15

15:23¹I.e., bitterness

sons of Israel ^grumbled against Moses and Aaron in the wilderness. ³The sons of Israel said to them, "If only we had died by the Lord's hand in the land of Egypt, ^when we sat by the pots of meat, when we ate bread until *we were* full; for you have brought us out into this wilderness to kill this entire assembly with hunger!"

⁴Then the Lord said to Moses, "Behold, I will rain bread from heaven for you; and the people shall go out and gather a day's portion every day, so that I may ^test them, whether or not they will walk in My ¹instruction. ⁵^On the sixth day, when they prepare what they bring in, it will be twice as much as they gather daily." ⁶So Moses and Aaron said to all the sons of Israel, "At evening ^you will know that the Lord has brought you out of the land of Egypt; ⁷and in the morning you will see ^the glory of the Lord, for He hears your grumblings against the Lord; and what are we, that you grumble against us?"

THE LORD PROVIDES MEAT

⁸And Moses said, "*This will happen* when the Lord gives you meat to eat in the evening, and bread to the full in the morning; for the Lord hears your grumblings which you grumble against Him. And what are we? Your grumblings are ^not against us but against the Lord."

⁹Then Moses said to Aaron, "Say to all the congregation of the sons of Israel, '^Come forward before the Lord, for He has heard your grumblings.'" ¹⁰And it came about, as Aaron spoke to the entire congregation of the sons of Israel, that they looked toward the wilderness, and behold, ^the glory of the Lord

appeared in the cloud. ¹¹And the Lord spoke to Moses, saying, ¹²"I have heard the grumblings of the sons of Israel; speak to them, saying, 'At twilight you shall eat meat, and in the morning you shall be filled with bread; and ^you shall know that I am the Lord your God.'"

¹³So it came about at evening that ^the quails came up and covered the camp, and in the morning there was a layer of dew around the camp. ¹⁴^When the layer of dew evaporated, behold, on the surface of the wilderness there was a fine flake-like thing, fine as the frost on the ground. ¹⁵When the sons of Israel saw *it,* they said to one another, "What is it?" For they did not know what it was. And Moses said to them, "^It is the bread which the Lord has given you to eat. ¹⁶This is what the Lord has commanded: 'Everyone gather as much as he will eat; you shall take ¹,^an omer apiece according to the number of people each of you has in his tent.'" ¹⁷The sons of Israel did so, and *some* gathered much and *some* little. ¹⁸When they measured it by the ¹omer, ^the one who had gathered much did not have too much, and the one who had gathered little did not have too little; everyone gathered as much as he would eat. ¹⁹Moses said to them, "^No one is to leave any of it until morning." ²⁰But they did not listen to Moses, and

16:2^Ps 106:25; 1 Cor 10:10   16:3^Num 11:4, 5
16:4^Ex 15:25; Deut 8:2, 16   16:5^Ex 16:22
16:6^Ex 6:7   16:7^Is 35:2; John 11:4, 40
16:8^1 Sam 8:7; Luke 10:16   16:9^Num 16:16
16:10^Ex 13:21; 1 Kin 8:10f   16:12^Ex 6:7; Joel 3:17
16:13^Ps 78:27-29; 105:40   16:14^Num 11:7-9
16:15^John 6:31; 1 Cor 10:3   16:16^Ex 16:32, 36
16:18^2 Cor 8:15   16:19^Ex 12:10; 16:23

16:4¹Or *law*   16:16¹Lit *an omer for a head;* about 3 qt. or 2.8 liters   16:18¹About 3 qt. or 2.8 liters

some left part of it until morning, and it bred worms and stank; and Moses was angry with them. [21] They gathered it morning by morning, everyone as much as he would eat; but when the sun became hot, it would melt.

THE SABBATH

[22] ^Now on the sixth day they gathered twice as much bread, 'two omers for each one. When all the leaders of the congregation came and told Moses, [23] then he said to them, "This is what the LORD meant: ^Tomorrow is a Sabbath observance, a holy Sabbath to the LORD. Bake what you will bake and boil what you will boil, and all that is left over put aside to be kept until morning." [24] So they put it aside until morning, as Moses had ordered, and ^it did not stink nor was there a maggot in it. [25] Then Moses said, "Eat it today, for today is a Sabbath to the LORD; today you will not find it in the field. [26] ^Six days you shall gather it, but on the seventh day, the Sabbath, there will be none."

[27] Yet it came about on the seventh day that some of the people went out to gather, but they found none. [28] Then the LORD said to Moses, "^How long do you refuse to keep My commandments and My 'instructions? [29] See, the LORD has given you the Sabbath; for that reason He gives you bread for two days on the sixth day. Remain, everyone, in his place; no one is to leave his place on the seventh day." [30] So the people rested on the seventh day.

[31] And the house of ^Israel named the bread manna, and it was like coriander seed, white, and its taste was like wafers with honey. [32] Then Moses said, "This is what the LORD has commanded: 'A 'full omer of it is to be kept safe throughout your generations, so that they may see the bread that I fed you in the wilderness, when I brought you out of the land of Egypt.'" [33] And Moses said to Aaron, "^Take a jar and put a 'full omer of manna in it, and place it before the LORD to be kept safe throughout your generations." [34] As the LORD commanded Moses, so Aaron placed it before ^the Testimony, to be kept. [35] And ^the sons of Israel ate the manna for forty years, until they came to an inhabited land; they ate the manna until they came to the border of the land of Canaan. [36] (Now ^an 'omer is a tenth of an ephah.)

WATER IN THE ROCK

17 Then all the congregation of the sons of Israel journeyed by stages from the wilderness of ^Sin, according to the command of the LORD, and camped at ^BRephidim, and there was no water for the people to drink. [2] So the people quarreled with Moses and said, "Give us water so that we may drink!" And Moses said to them, "Why do you quarrel with me? ^Why do you test the LORD?" [3] But the people were thirsty for water there; and they ^grumbled against Moses and said, "Why is it that you have brought us up from Egypt, to kill us and our children and ^Bour livestock with

16:22 ^Ex 16:5   16:23 ^Gen 2:3; Lev 23:3
16:24 ^Ex 16:20   16:26 ^Ex 20:9, 10
16:28 ^2 Kin 17:14; Ps 106:13   16:31 ^Num 11:7–9;
Deut 8:3, 16   16:33 ^Heb 9:4; Rev 2:17
16:34 ^Ex 25:16, 21; Num 17:10   16:35 ^Deut 8:2f;
Josh 5:12   16:36 ^Ex 16:16   17:1 ^Num 33:12   ^BEx 19:2
17:2 ^Deut 6:16; Matt 4:7   17:3 ^Ex 16:2, 3   ^BEx 12:38

16:22 'About 6 qt. or 5.6 liters   16:28 'Or laws
16:32 'About 3 qt. or 2.8 liters   16:33 'About 3 qt. or
2.8 liters   16:36 'About 3 qt. or 2.8 liters

thirst?" [4] So Moses cried out to the LORD, saying, "What am I to do with this people? A ^little more and they will stone me!" [5] Then the LORD said to Moses, "Pass before the people and take with you some of ^the elders of Israel; and take in your hand your staff with which ^Byou struck the Nile, and go. [6] Behold, I will stand before you there on the rock at ^Horeb; and ^Byou shall strike the rock, and water will come out of it, so that the people may drink." And Moses did so in the sight of the elders of Israel. [7] Then he named the place [1]Massah and [2]Meribah because of the quarrel of the sons of Israel, and because they ^tested the LORD, saying, "Is the LORD among us, or not?"

MIRACULOUS BATTLE
AGAINST AMALEK

[8] Then ^Amalek came and fought against Israel at Rephidim. [9] So Moses said to ^Joshua, "Choose men for us and go out, fight against Amalek. Tomorrow I will station myself on the top of the hill with ^Bthe staff of God in my hand." [10] Joshua did just as Moses told him, and fought against Amalek; and Moses, Aaron, and ^Hur went up to the top of the hill. [11] So it came about, when Moses held his hand up, that Israel prevailed; but when he let his hand down, Amalek prevailed. [12] And Moses' hands were heavy. So they took a stone and put it under him, and he sat on it; and Aaron and Hur ^supported his hands, one on one side and one on the other. So his hands were steady until the sun set. [13] And Joshua defeated Amalek and his people with the edge of the sword.

[14] Then the LORD said to Moses, "^Write this in a book as a memorial and recite it to Joshua, that I will utterly wipe out the memory of Amalek from under heaven." [15] And Moses built an ^altar and named it The LORD is My Banner; [16] and he said, "^Because the LORD has sworn, the LORD will have war against Amalek from generation to generation."

JETHRO, MOSES' FATHER-IN-LAW

18 Now ^Jethro, the priest of Midian, Moses' father-in-law, heard about everything that God had done for Moses and for Israel His people, how the LORD had brought Israel out of Egypt. [2] And Jethro, Moses' father-in-law, took *in* Moses' wife ^Zipporah, after he had sent her away, [3] and her ^two sons, one of whom was named Gershom, for Moses said, "I have been a stranger in a foreign land." [4] And the other was named ^Eliezer, for *he said,* "^BThe God of my father was my help, and saved me from the sword of Pharaoh."

[5] Then Jethro, Moses' father-in-law, came with his sons and his wife to Moses in the wilderness where he was camped, at ^the mountain of God. [6] And he sent word to Moses: "I, your father-in-law Jethro, am coming to you with your wife and her two sons with her." [7] Then Moses went out to meet his father-in-law, and he bowed down and kissed him; and they ^asked each other about their welfare, and went into the tent. [8] Moses told

17:4 ^Num 14:10; 1 Sam 30:6   **17:5** ^Ex 3:16, 18
^BEx 7:20   **17:6** ^Ex 3:1   ^BNum 20:10, 11
17:7 ^Num 14:22; Deut 33:8   **17:8** ^Gen 36:12;
Deut 25:17–19   **17:9** ^Ex 24:13   ^BEx 4:20
17:10 ^Ex 24:14; 31:2   **17:12** ^Is 35:3   **17:14** ^Ex 24:4;
Num 33:2   **17:15** ^Ex 24:4   **17:16** ^Gen 22:16
18:1 ^Ex 2:16, 18; 3:1   **18:2** ^Ex 2:21; 4:25   **18:3** ^Ex 2:22;
Acts 7:29   **18:4** ^1 Chr 23:15, 17   ^BGen 49:25
18:5 ^Ex 3:1, 12; 24:13   **18:7** ^Gen 43:27; 2 Sam 11:7

17:7 [1] I.e., test   [2] I.e., quarrel

his father-in-law everything that the LORD had done to Pharaoh and to the Egyptians for Israel's sake, all the hardship that had confronted them on the journey, and *how* ᴬthe LORD had rescued them. 9 And Jethro rejoiced over all ᴬthe goodness which the LORD had done for Israel, in rescuing them from the hand of the Egyptians. 10 So Jethro said, "ᴬBlessed be the LORD who rescued you from the hand of the Egyptians and from the hand of Pharaoh, *and* who rescued the people from under the hand of the Egyptians. 11 Now I know that ᴬthe LORD is greater than all the gods; indeed, it was proven when they acted insolently against the people." 12 ᴬThen Jethro, Moses' father-in-law, took a burnt offering and sacrifices for God, and Aaron came with all the elders of Israel to eat a meal with Moses' father-in-law before God.

JETHRO COUNSELS MOSES

13 And it came about the next day, that Moses sat to judge the people, and the people stood before Moses from the morning until the evening. 14 Now when Moses' father-in-law saw all that he was doing for the people, he said, "What is this thing that you are doing for the people? Why do you alone sit *as judge* and all the people stand before you from morning until evening?" 15 Moses said to his father-in-law, "Because the people come to me ᴬto inquire of God. 16 When they have a ᴬdispute, it comes to me, and I judge between someone and his neighbor and make known the statutes of God and His laws." 17 Moses' father-in-law then said to him, "The thing that you are doing is not good. 18 ᴬYou will surely wear

out, both yourself and these people who are with you, because the task is too heavy for you; ᴮyou cannot do it alone. 19 Now listen to me: I will give you counsel, and God be with you. You be the people's representative before God, and you ᴬbring the disputes to God, 20 ᴬthen admonish them about the statutes and the laws, and make known to them ᴮthe way in which they are to walk and the work they are to do. 21 Furthermore, you shall select out of all the people ᴬable men ᴮwho fear God, men of truth, those who hate dishonest gain; and you shall place *these* over them *as* leaders of thousands, of hundreds, of fifties, and of tens. 22 Let them judge the people at all times; and let it be that they will bring to you every major matter, but they will judge every minor matter themselves. So it will be easier for you, and ᴬthey will carry *the burden* with you. 23 If you do this thing and God *so* commands you, then you will be able to endure, and all these people also will go to their places in peace."

24 So Moses listened to his father-in-law and did everything that he had said. 25 Moses chose ᴬable men out of all Israel and made them heads over the people, leaders of thousands, of hundreds, of fifties, and of tens. 26 Then they judged the people at all times; ᴬthey would bring the difficult matter to Moses, but they would judge every minor matter themselves. 27 Then Moses ᴬsaid

18:8 ᴬEx 15:6, 16 18:9 ᴬIs 63:7-14 18:10 ᴬGen 14:20; 2 Sam 18:28 18:11 ᴬPs 95:3; 97:9
18:12 ᴬGen 31:54; Ex 24:5 18:15 ᴬNum 9:6, 8; Deut 17:8-13 18:16 ᴬEx 24:14 18:18 ᴬNum 11:14, 17
ᴮDeut 1:9 18:19 ᴬNum 27:5 18:20 ᴬDeut 1:18
ᴮPs 143:8 18:21 ᴬActs 6:3 ᴮGen 42:18
18:22 ᴬNum 11:17 18:25 ᴬEx 18:21; Deut 1:15
18:26 ᴬEx 18:22 18:27 ᴬNum 10:29, 30

goodbye to his father-in-law, and Jethro went his way to his own land.

MOSES ON SINAI

19 In the third month after the sons of Israel had gone out of the land of Egypt, on that very day they came into the wilderness of ^Sinai. ²When they set out from ^Rephidim, they came to the wilderness of Sinai and camped in the wilderness; and there Israel camped in front of the mountain. ³And Moses went up to God, and ^the LORD called to him from the mountain, saying, "This is what you shall say to the house of Jacob and tell the sons of Israel: ⁴'You yourselves have seen what I did to the Egyptians, and *how* I carried you on ^eagles' wings, and brought you to Myself. ⁵Now then, ^if you will indeed obey My voice and ᴮkeep My covenant, then you shall be My own possession among all the peoples, for all the earth is Mine; ⁶and you shall be to Me ^a kingdom of priests and ᴮa holy nation.' These are the words that you shall speak to the sons of Israel."

⁷^So Moses came and called the elders of the people, and set before them all these words which the LORD had commanded him. ⁸Then ^all the people answered together and said, "All that the LORD has spoken we will do!" And Moses brought back the words of the people to the LORD. ⁹Then the LORD said to Moses, "Behold, I will come to you in a thick cloud, so that the ^people may hear when I speak with you and may also trust in you forever." Then Moses told the words of the people to the LORD.

¹⁰The LORD also said to Moses, "Go to the people and ^consecrate them today and tomorrow, and have them wash their garments; ¹¹and have them ready for the third day, for on ^the third day the LORD will come down on Mount Sinai in the sight of all the people. ¹²But you shall set boundaries for the people all around, saying, 'Beware that you do not go up on the mountain or touch the border of it; ^whoever touches the mountain shall certainly be put to death. ¹³No hand shall touch him, but ^he shall certainly be stoned or ¹shot through; whether animal or person, *the violator* shall not live.' When the ram's horn sounds a long blast, they shall come up to the mountain." ¹⁴So Moses went down from the mountain to the people and consecrated the people, and they washed their garments. ¹⁵He also said to the people, "Be ready for the third day; do not go near a woman."

¹⁶^So it came about on the third day, when it was morning, that there were thunder and lightning flashes and a thick cloud over the mountain and a very loud trumpet sound, so that all the people who *were* in the camp trembled. ¹⁷And Moses brought the people out of the camp to meet God, and they stood at the foot of the mountain.

THE LORD VISITS SINAI

¹⁸^Now Mount Sinai *was* all in smoke because the LORD descended upon it in fire; and its smoke ascended like the smoke of a furnace, and

19:1^Deut 1:6; 4:10, 15   **19:2**^Ex 17:1; Num 33:15
19:3^Ex 3:4   **19:4**^Deut 32:11; Rev 12:14   **19:5**^Deut 5:2f
ᴮPs 78:10   **19:6**^Rev 1:6   ᴮIs 62:12   **19:7**^Ex 4:29, 30
19:8^Ex 4:31; 24:3, 7   **19:9**^Deut 4:12, 36
19:10^Lev 11:44, 45   **19:11**^Ex 19:16   **19:12**^Heb 12:20
19:13^Heb 12:20   **19:16**^Heb 12:18, 19, 21
19:18^Deut 4:11; Ps 104:32
19:13 ¹I.e., with arrows

the entire mountain quaked violently. ¹⁹When the sound of the trumpet grew louder and louder, Moses spoke, and ᴬGod answered him with thunder. ²⁰Then ᴬthe LORD came down on Mount Sinai, to the top of the mountain; and the LORD called Moses to the top of the mountain, and Moses went up. ²¹Then the LORD spoke to Moses: "Go down, warn the people, so that ᴬthey do not break through to the LORD to stare, and many of them perish. ²²Also have the ᴬpriests who approach the LORD consecrate themselves, or else the LORD will break out against them." ²³And Moses said to the LORD, "The people cannot come up to Mount Sinai, for You warned us, saying, 'ᴬSet boundaries around the mountain and consecrate it.'" ²⁴Then the LORD said to him, "Go down and come up *again,* ᴬyou and Aaron with you; but do not let the ᴮpriests and the people break through to come up to the LORD, or He will break out against them." ²⁵So Moses went down to the people and told them.

THE TEN COMMANDMENTS

20 Then God spoke all these words, saying,

²"I am the LORD your God, ᴬwho brought you out of the land of Egypt, out of the house of slavery.

³"You shall have no other ᴬgods before Me.

⁴"ᴬYou shall not make for yourself an idol, or any likeness of what is in heaven above or on the earth beneath, or in the water under the earth. ⁵ᴬYou shall not worship them nor serve them; for I, the LORD your God, am a ᴮjealous God, inflicting the ʲpunishment of

the fathers on the children, on the third and the fourth generations of those who hate Me, ⁶but showing favor to ᴬthousands, to those who love Me and keep My commandments.

⁷"ᴬYou shall not take the name of the LORD your God in vain, for the LORD will not leave him unpunished who takes His name in vain.

⁸"Remember ᴬthe Sabbath day, to keep it holy. ⁹ᴬFor six days you shall labor and do all your work, ¹⁰but the seventh day is a Sabbath of the LORD your God; *on it* ᴬyou shall not do any work, you, or your son, or your daughter, your male slave or your female slave, or your cattle, or your resident who stays with you. ¹¹ᴬFor in six days the LORD made the heavens and the earth, the sea and everything that is in them, and He rested on the seventh day; for that reason the LORD blessed the Sabbath day and made it holy.

¹²"ᴬHonor your father and your mother, so that your ᴮdays may be prolonged on the land which the LORD your God gives you.

¹³"ᴬYou shall not murder.

¹⁴"ᴬYou shall not commit adultery.

¹⁵"ᴬYou shall not steal.

¹⁶"ᴬYou shall not give false testimony against your neighbor.

19:19 ᴬPs 81:7   19:20 ᴬNeh 9:13
19:21 ᴬEx 3:5; 1 Sam 6:19   19:22 ᴬLev 10:3; 21:6-8
19:23 ᴬEx 19:12   19:24 ᴬEx 24:1, 9, 12   ᴮEx 19:22
20:2 ᴬEx 13:3; Deut 7:8   20:3 ᴬEx 15:11; 20:23
20:4 ᴬLev 19:4; Deut 4:15-19   20:5 ᴬEx 23:24   ᴮNah 1:2
20:6 ᴬDeut 7:9   20:7 ᴬLev 19:12; Deut 6:13
20:8 ᴬLev 26:2; Deut 5:12   20:9 ᴬDeut 5:13; Luke 13:14
20:10 ᴬNeh 13:16-19   20:11 ᴬGen 2:2, 3; Ex 31:17
20:12 ᴬLev 19:3   ᴮJer 35:7   20:13 ᴬLuke 18:20; Rom 13:9
20:14 ᴬLev 20:10; Deut 5:18   20:15 ᴬEx 21:16;
Lev 19:11, 13   20:16 ᴬDeut 5:20; Matt 19:18

20:5 ʲI.e., punishment for the wrongdoing

¹⁷"You shall not covet your neighbor's house; ^you shall not covet your neighbor's wife, or his male slave, or his female slave, or his ox, or his donkey, or anything that belongs to your neighbor."

¹⁸And ^all the people were watching *and hearing* the thunder and the lightning flashes, and the sound of the trumpet, and the mountain smoking; and when the people saw *it all,* they trembled and stood at a distance. ¹⁹^Then they said to Moses, "Speak to us yourself and we will listen; but do not have God speak to us, or we will die!" ²⁰However, Moses said to the people, "Do not be afraid; for God has come in order ^to test you, and in order that ᴮthe fear of Him may remain with you, so that you will not sin." ²¹So the people stood at a distance, while Moses approached ^the thick darkness where God *was.*

²²Then the Lᴏʀᴅ said to Moses, "This is what you shall say to the sons of Israel: 'You yourselves have seen that ^I have spoken to you from heaven. ²³You shall not make *other gods* besides Me; ^gods of silver or gods of gold, you shall not make for yourselves. ²⁴You shall make ^an altar of earth for Me, and you shall sacrifice on it your burnt offerings and your peace offerings, your sheep and your oxen; in every place where I cause My name to be remembered, I will come to you and bless you. ²⁵And if you make an altar of stone for Me, ^you shall not build it of cut stones, for if you wield your chisel on it, you will profane it. ²⁶And you shall not go up by steps to My altar, so that ^your nakedness will not be exposed on it.'

ORDINANCES FOR THE PEOPLE

21 "Now these are the ^ordinances which you are to set before them:

²"If you buy ^a Hebrew slave, he shall serve for six years; but on the seventh he shall leave as a free man without a payment *to you.* ³If he comes alone, he shall leave alone; if he is the husband of a wife, then his wife shall leave with him. ⁴If his master gives him a wife, and she bears him sons or daughters, the wife and her children shall belong to her master, and he shall leave alone. ⁵But ^if the slave plainly says, 'I love my master, my wife, and my children; I will not leave as a free man,' ⁶then his master shall bring him to God, then he shall bring him to the door or the doorpost. And his master shall pierce his ear with an ¹awl; and he shall serve him permanently.

⁷"Now ^if a man sells his daughter as a female slave, she is not to go free ᴮas the male slaves do. ⁸If she is displeasing in the eyes of her master who designated her for himself, then he shall let her be redeemed. He does not have authority to sell her to a foreign people, because of his unfairness to her. ⁹And if he designates her for his son, he shall deal with her according to the custom of daughters. ¹⁰If he takes to himself another woman, he may not reduce her food, her clothing, or ^her conjugal rights. ¹¹But if he will not do these three *things* for

20:17^Prov 6:29; Matt 5:28   **20:18**^Ex 19:16, 18; Heb 12:18, 19   **20:19**^Gal 3:19; Heb 12:19
20:20^Deut 13:3   ᴮIs 8:13   **20:21**^Ex 19:16; Deut 5:22
20:22^Deut 4:36; Neh 9:13   **20:23**^Ex 32:1, 2, 4;
Deut 29:17   **20:24**^Ex 20:25; 27:1-8
20:25^Deut 27:5, 6; Josh 8:31   **20:26**^Ex 28:42, 43
21:1^Ex 24:3, 4; Deut 4:14   **21:2**^Lev 25:39-43;
Deut 15:12-18   **21:5**^Deut 15:16, 17   **21:7**^Neh 5:5
ᴮEx 21:2, 3   **21:10**^1 Cor 7:3, 5

21:6¹I.e., a pointed tool

her, then she shall go free for nothing, without *payment of* money.

PERSONAL INJURIES

¹²ᴬ"He who strikes someone so that he dies shall certainly be put to death. ¹³ᴬYet if he did not lie in wait *for him,* but God caused *him* to fall into his hand, then I will appoint you a place to which he may flee. ¹⁴ᴬIf, however, someone is enraged against his neighbor, so as to kill him in a cunning way, you are to take him *even* from My altar, to be put to death.

¹⁵"And one who strikes his father or his mother shall certainly be put to death.

¹⁶"Now ᴬone who kidnaps someone, whether he sells him or he is found in his possession, shall certainly be put to death.

¹⁷"And ᴬone who curses his father or his mother shall certainly be put to death.

¹⁸"Now if people have a quarrel and one strikes the other with a stone or with a fist, and he does not die but is confined to bed, ¹⁹if he gets up and walks around outside on his staff, then he who struck him shall go unpunished; he shall only pay for his loss of time, and shall pay for his care until he is completely healed.

²⁰"And if someone strikes his male or female slave with a rod and *the slave* dies at his hand, he shall be punished. ²¹If, however, *the slave* survives a day or two, no vengeance shall be taken; ᴬfor *the slave* is his property.

²²"Now if people struggle with each other and strike a pregnant woman so that she gives birth prematurely, but there is no injury, *the guilty person* shall certainly be fined as the woman's husband may demand of him, and he shall ᴬpay as the judges *decide.* ²³But if there is *any further* injury, ᴬthen you shall appoint *as a penalty* life for life, ²⁴ᴬeye for eye, tooth for tooth, hand for hand, foot for foot, ²⁵burn for burn, wound for wound, bruise for bruise.

²⁶"And if someone strikes the eye of his male or female slave and destroys it, he shall let the slave go free on account of the eye. ²⁷And if he knocks out a tooth of his male or female slave, he shall let the slave go free on account of the tooth.

²⁸"Now if an ox gores a man or a woman to death, ᴬthe ox shall certainly be stoned and its flesh shall not be eaten; but the owner of the ox shall go unpunished. ²⁹If, however, an ox was previously in the habit of goring and its owner has been warned, yet he does not confine it and it kills a man or a woman, the ox shall be stoned and its owner also shall be put to death. ³⁰If a ransom is demanded of him, then he shall give for the redemption of his life whatever is demanded of him. ³¹Whether it gores a son or a daughter, it shall be done to him according to the same rule. ³²If the ox gores a male or female slave, the owner shall give his *or her* master ¹,ᴬthirty shekels of silver, and the ox shall be stoned.

PROPERTY RIGHTS

³³"Now if someone opens a pit, or digs a pit and does not cover it, and

21:12ᴬLev 24:17; Matt 26:52   21:13ᴬNum 35:10–34;
Deut 19:1–13   21:14ᴬDeut 19:11, 12; 1 Kin 2:28–34
21:16ᴬDeut 24:7   21:17ᴬLev 20:9; Matt 15:4
21:21ᴬLev 25:44–46   21:22ᴬEx 21:30;
Deut 22:18, 19   21:23ᴬLev 24:19; Deut 19:21
21:24ᴬLev 24:20; Deut 19:21   21:28ᴬGen 9:5;
Ex 21:32   21:32ᴬZech 11:12; Matt 26:15

21:32¹About 15 oz. or 425 gm

an ox or a donkey falls into it, ³⁴the owner of the pit shall make restitution; he shall give money to its owner, and the dead *animal* shall become his.

³⁵"And if someone's ox injures another's ox so that it dies, then they shall sell the live ox and divide its proceeds equally; and they shall also divide the dead *ox.* ³⁶Or *if* it is known that the ox was previously in the habit of goring, yet its owner has not confined it, he must make restitution of ox for ox, and the dead *animal* shall become his.

PROPERTY RIGHTS

22 "If someone steals an ox or a sheep and slaughters it or sells it, he shall pay five oxen for the ox and ^four sheep for the sheep— ²If the ^thief is caught while breaking in and is struck so that he dies, there will be no guilt for bloodshed on his account. ³If the sun has risen on him, *there will be* guilt for bloodshed on his account—*A thief* shall certainly make restitution; if he owns nothing, then he shall be ^sold for his theft. ⁴If what he stole is actually found alive in his possession, whether an ox or a donkey or a sheep, ^he shall pay double.

⁵"If someone lets a field or vineyard be grazed *bare* and lets his animal loose so that it grazes in another person's field, he shall make restitution from the best of his own field and the best of his own vineyard.

⁶"If a fire breaks out and spreads to thorn bushes, and stacked grain or the standing grain or the field *itself* is consumed, the one who started the fire must make restitution.

⁷"^If someone gives his neighbor money or goods to keep *for him* and it is stolen from the neighbor's house, if the thief is caught, *then the thief* shall pay double. ⁸If the thief is not caught, then the owner of the house shall appear before ^the judges, *to determine* whether he laid his hands on his neighbor's property. ⁹For every breach of trust, *whether it is* for ox, for donkey, for sheep, for clothing, *or* for any lost thing about which one says, 'This is it,' the case of both parties shall come before ^the judges; he whom the judges condemn shall pay double to his neighbor.

¹⁰"If someone gives his neighbor a donkey, an ox, a sheep, or any animal to keep *for him,* and it dies or is injured or is driven away while no one is looking, ¹¹an ^oath before the LORD shall be taken by the two of them that he has not laid a hand on his neighbor's property; and its owner shall accept *it,* and he shall not *be compelled to* make restitution. ¹²But if it is actually stolen from him, he shall make restitution to its owner. ¹³If it is all torn to pieces, have him bring it as evidence; he shall not *be compelled to* make restitution for what has been torn to pieces.

¹⁴"And if someone borrows *an animal* from his neighbor, and it is injured or dies while its owner is not with it, he shall make full restitution. ¹⁵If its owner is with it, *the borrower* shall not *be compelled to* make restitution. If it is hired, it came by its hire.

22:1^2 Sam 12:6; Luke 19:8   22:2^Matt 6:19; 1 Pet 4:15   22:3^Matt 18:25   22:4^Ex 22:7   22:7^Lev 6:1-7   22:8^Ex 22:9; Deut 17:8, 9   22:9^Ex 22:8, 28; Deut 25:1   22:11^Heb 6:16

VARIOUS LAWS

¹⁶ "'If a man seduces a virgin who is not ¹betrothed and sleeps with her, he must pay a dowry for her *to be* his wife. ¹⁷If her father absolutely refuses to give her to him, he shall pay money equal to the ^dowry for virgins.

¹⁸ "You shall not allow a ^sorceress to live.

¹⁹ "^Whoever has sexual intercourse with an animal must be put to death.

²⁰ "^He who sacrifices to any god, other than to the LORD alone, shall be utterly destroyed.

²¹ "^You shall not oppress a stranger nor torment him, for you were strangers in the land of Egypt. ²²^You shall not oppress any widow or orphan. ²³If you oppress him at all, *and* if he does cry out to Me, ^I will assuredly hear his cry; ²⁴and My anger will be kindled, and I will kill you with the sword, ^and your wives shall become widows and your children fatherless.

²⁵ "If you lend money to My people, to the poor among you, you are not to act as a creditor to him; you shall not charge him ^interest. ²⁶If you ever seize your neighbor's cloak^as a pledge, you are to return it to him before the sun sets, ²⁷for that is his only covering; it is his cloak for his body. What else is he to sleep in? And it will come about that when he cries out to Me, I will listen *to him,* for ^I am gracious.

²⁸ "You shall not curse God, ^nor curse a ruler of your people.

²⁹ "You shall not hold back *the offering from* your entire harvest and your wine. ^The firstborn of your sons you shall give to Me. ³⁰^You shall do the same with your oxen *and* with your sheep. It shall be with its mother for seven days; on the eighth day you shall give it to Me.

³¹ "^You shall be holy people to Me, therefore you shall not eat *any* flesh torn to pieces in the field; you shall throw it to the dogs.

VARIOUS LAWS

23

"^You shall not give a false report; do not join your hand with a wicked person to be a malicious witness. ²You shall not follow the crowd in doing evil, nor shall you testify in a dispute so as to join together with a crowd in order to ^pervert *justice;* ³^nor shall you show favor to a poor person in his dispute.

⁴ "^If you encounter your enemy's ox or his donkey wandering away, you must return it to him. ⁵^If you see the donkey of one who hates you lying *helpless* under its load, you shall not leave it *helpless* for its owner; you must arrange *the load* with him.

⁶ "^You shall not pervert the justice *due* to your needy *brother* in his dispute. ⁷^Keep far from a false charge, and ⁸do not kill the innocent or the righteous, for I will not acquit the guilty.

⁸ "^You shall not take a bribe, for a bribe blinds the clear-sighted and subverts the cause of the just.

22:16^Deut 22:28, 29   22:17^Gen 34:12; 1 Sam 18:25
22:18^Lev 19:31; 20:6, 27   22:19^Lev 18:23; Deut 27:21
22:20^Ex 32:8; 34:15   22:21^Deut 27:19; Zech 7:10
22:22^Deut 24:17, 18; Jer 7:6, 7   22:23^Job 34:28;
James 5:4   22:24^Ps 109:2, 9   22:25^Neh 5:7;
Ezek 18:8   22:26^Prov 20:16; Amos 2:8
22:27^Ex 34:6   22:28^Eccl 10:20; Acts 23:5
22:29^Ex 13:2, 12   22:30^Deut 15:19; Lev 22:27
22:31^Ex 19:6; Lev 11:44   23:1^Ex 20:16; Lev 19:11f
23:2^Deut 16:19; 24:17   23:3^Ex 23:6; Lev 19:15
23:4^Deut 22:1–4   23:5^Deut 22:4   23:6^Ex 23:2, 3;
Lev 19:15   23:7^Eph 4:25   ᴮEx 20:13;
23:8^Prov 15:27; Is 5:22, 23

22:16 ¹A betrothed couple was considered legally married, but did not yet live together

⁹ "ᴬYou shall not oppress a stranger, since you yourselves know the feelings of a stranger, for you *also* were strangers in the land of Egypt.

THE SABBATH AND THE LAND

¹⁰ "Now ᴬyou shall sow your land for six years and gather in its yield, ¹¹but *in* the seventh year you shall let it rest and lie uncultivated, so that the needy of your people may eat; and whatever they leave the animal of the field may eat. You are to do the same with your vineyard *and* your olive grove.

¹² "ᴬFor six days you are to do your work, but on the seventh day you shall cease *from labor* so that your ox and your donkey may rest, and the son of your female slave, as well as the stranger *residing with you, may* refresh themselves. ¹³Now ᴬconcerning everything which I have said to you, be careful; and do not mention the name of other gods, nor let *them* be heard from your mouth.

THREE NATIONAL FEASTS

¹⁴ "ᴬThree times a year you shall celebrate a feast to Me. ¹⁵You shall keep ᴬthe Feast of Unleavened Bread; for seven days you are to eat unleavened bread, as I commanded you, at the appointed time in the month of Abib, for in that month you came out of Egypt. And no one is to appear before Me empty-handed. ¹⁶Also *you shall keep* ᴬthe Feast of the Harvest *of* the first fruits of your labors *from* what you sow in the field; also the Feast of the Ingathering at the end of the year when you gather in *the fruit of* your labors from the field. ¹⁷ᴬThree times a year all your males shall appear before the Lord Goᴅ.

¹⁸ "ᴬYou shall not offer the blood of My sacrifice with leavened bread; nor is the fat of My feast to remain overnight until morning. ¹⁹ "You shall bring the choice first fruits of your soil into the house of the Lᴏʀᴅ your God.

"ᴬYou are not to boil a young goat in the milk of its mother.

CONQUEST OF THE LAND

²⁰ "Behold, I am going to send an angel before you to guard you along the way and ᴬto bring you into the place which I have prepared. ²¹Be attentive to him and obey his voice; ᴬdo not be rebellious toward him, for he will not pardon your rebellion, since My name is in him. ²²But if you truly obey his voice and do all that I say, then ᴬI will be an enemy to your enemies and an adversary to your adversaries. ²³ᴬFor My angel will go before you and bring you into *the land of* the Amorites, the Hittites, the Perizzites, the Canaanites, the Hivites, and the Jebusites; and I will completely destroy them. ²⁴ᴬYou shall not worship their gods, nor serve them, nor do according to their deeds; but you shall utterly overthrow them and break their memorial stones in pieces. ²⁵And you shall serve the Lᴏʀᴅ your God, and He will bless your bread and your water; and ᴬI will remove sickness from your midst. ²⁶There will be no one miscarrying or ᴬunable to have children in your land; I will

23:9 ᴬLev 19:33f; Deut 24:17f   **23:10** ᴬLev 25:1-7
23:12 ᴬEx 20:8-11; 31:15   **23:13** ᴬDeut 4:9, 23;
1 Tim 4:16   **23:14** ᴬEx 23:17; Deut 16:16
23:15 ᴬEx 12:14-20; Lev 23:6-8   **23:16** ᴬLev 23:16;
Num 28:26   **23:17** ᴬEx 23:14; Deut 16:16
23:18 ᴬEx 34:25; Lev 2:11   **23:19** ᴬDeut 14:21
23:20 ᴬEx 15:16, 17   **23:21** ᴬDeut 9:7; Ps 78:40, 56
Josh 24:8, 11   **23:24** ᴬEx 20:5; Deut 12:30f
23:25 ᴬEx 15:26; Deut 7:15   **23:26** ᴬDeut 7:14

fulfill the number of your days. ²⁷I will ^send My terror ahead of you, and throw into confusion all the people among whom you come, and I will make all your enemies turn *their* backs to you. ²⁸And I will send hornets ahead of you so that they will ^drive out the Hivites, the Canaanites, and the Hittites from you. ²⁹^I will not drive them out from you in a single year, so that the land will not become desolate and the animals of the field become too numerous for you. ³⁰I will drive them out from you ^little by little, until you become fruitful and take possession of the land. ³¹^I will set your boundary from the Red Sea to the sea of the Philistines, and from the wilderness to the *Euphrates* River; ^Bfor I will hand over the inhabitants of the land to you, and you will drive them out from you. ³²^You shall make no covenant with them or with their gods. ³³^They shall not live in your land, otherwise they will make you sin against Me; for *if* you serve their gods, ^Bit is certain to be a snare to you."

PEOPLE AFFIRM THEIR COVENANT WITH GOD

24 Then He said to Moses, "^Come up to the Lord, you and Aaron, Nadab and Abihu, and seventy of the elders of Israel, and you shall worship at a distance. ²Moses alone, however, shall approach the Lord, but they shall not approach, nor shall the people come up with him."

³Then Moses came and reported to the people all the words of the Lord and all the ordinances; and all the people answered with one voice and said, "^All the words which the Lord has spoken we will do!" ⁴And

^Moses wrote down all the words of the Lord. Then he got up early in the morning, and built an altar at the foot of the mountain with twelve memorial stones for the twelve tribes of Israel. ⁵And he sent young men of the sons of Israel, ^and they offered burnt offerings and sacrificed bulls as peace offerings to the Lord. ⁶^Moses took half of the blood and put *it* in basins, and the *other* half of the blood he sprinkled on the altar. ⁷Then he took ^the Book of the Covenant and read *it* as the people listened; and they said, "All that the Lord has spoken we will do, and we will be obedient!" ⁸So ^Moses took the blood and sprinkled *it* on the people, and said, "Behold the blood of the covenant, which the Lord has made with you in accordance with all these words."

⁹Then Moses went up with Aaron, ^Nadab and Abihu, and seventy of the elders of Israel, ¹⁰and ^they saw the God of Israel; and under His feet there appeared to be a pavement of sapphire, as clear as the sky itself. ¹¹Yet He did not reach out with His hand against the nobles of the sons of Israel; and ^they saw God, and they ate and drank.

¹²Now the Lord said to Moses, "Come up to Me on the mountain and stay there, and ^I will give you the stone tablets with the Law and the commandments which I have written for their instruction." ¹³So Moses got up along with ^Joshua

23:27^Gen 35:5; Ex 15:16   23:28^Ex 33:2; 34:11
23:29^Deut 7:22   23:30^Deut 7:22   23:31^Gen 15:18
^BDeut 2:36   23:32^Ex 34:12; Deut 7:2
23:33^Deut 7:1-5, 16   ^BJudg 2:3   24:1^Ex 19:24
24:3^Ex 19:8; Deut 5:27   24:4^Ex 17:14; Deut 31:9
24:5^Ex 18:12   24:6^Heb 9:18   24:7^Ex 24:4;
Heb 9:19   24:8^Heb 9:19, 20   24:9^Ex 24:1
24:10^Ex 24:11; Num 12:8   24:11^Gen 16:13; 32:30
24:12^Ex 31:18; 32:15   24:13^Ex 17:9-14

his servant, and Moses went up to ⁸the mountain of God. ¹⁴But to the elders he said, "Wait here for us until we return to you. And behold, ^Aaron and Hur are with you; whoever has a legal matter, have him approach them." ¹⁵Then Moses went up to the mountain, and ^the cloud covered the mountain. ¹⁶^The glory of the LORD settled on Mount Sinai, and the cloud covered it for six days; and on the seventh day He called to Moses from the midst of the cloud. ¹⁷And to the eyes of the sons of Israel, the appearance of the glory of the LORD was like a ^consuming fire on the mountain top. ¹⁸Then Moses entered the midst of the cloud as he went up to the mountain; and Moses was on the mountain for ^forty days and forty nights.

OFFERINGS FOR THE SANCTUARY

25 Then the LORD spoke to Moses, saying, ²"^Tell the sons of Israel to take a contribution for Me; from everyone whose heart moves him you shall take My contribution. ³This is the contribution which you are to take from them: gold, silver, and bronze, ⁴¹,^violet, purple, and scarlet *material,* fine linen, goat *hair,* ⁵rams' skins dyed red, ¹fine leather, acacia wood, ⁶oil for lighting, ^balsam oil for the anointing oil and for the fragrant incense, ⁷onyx stones and setting stones for the ^ephod and for the breastpiece. ⁸Have them ^construct a sanctuary for Me, so that I may dwell among them. ⁹^According to all that I am going to show you *as* the pattern of the tabernacle and the pattern of all its furniture, so you shall construct *it.*

ARK OF THE COVENANT

¹⁰"Now ^they shall construct an ¹ark of acacia wood ²two and a half cubits long, one and a half cubits wide, and one and a half cubits high. ¹¹You shall ^overlay it with pure gold, inside and out you shall overlay it, and you shall make a gold molding around it. ¹²You shall also cast four gold rings for it and fasten them on its four feet; two rings shall be on one side of it, and two rings on the other side of it. ¹³And you shall make poles of acacia wood and overlay them with gold. ¹⁴You shall put the poles into the rings on the sides of the ark, to carry the ark with them. ¹⁵The ^poles shall remain in the rings of the ark; they shall not be removed from it. ¹⁶You shall ^put into the ark the testimony which I shall give you.

¹⁷"And you shall ^make ¹an atoning cover of pure gold, ²two and a half cubits long and one and a half cubits wide. ¹⁸You shall make two cherubim of gold; make them of hammered work at the two ends of the atoning cover. ¹⁹Make one cherub at one end and one cherub at the other end; you shall make the cherubim *of one piece* with the atoning cover at its two ends. ²⁰And ^the cherubim shall have *their*

24:13 ⁸Ex 3:1   24:14^Ex 17:10, 12   24:15^Ex 19:9
24:16^Ex 16:10; Num 14:10   24:17^Deut 4:24;
Heb 12:29   24:18^Ex 34:28; Deut 9:9   25:2^Ex 35:4-9
25:4^Ex 28:5, 6, 8   25:6^Ex 30:23f   25:7^Ex 28:4,
6-14   25:8^Ex 36:1-5   25:9^Acts 7:44; Heb 8:2, 5
25:10^Deut 10:3; Heb 9:4   25:11^Heb 9:4
25:15^1 Kin 8:8   25:16^1 Kin 8:9; Heb 9:4
25:17^Ex 37:6   25:20^1 Chr 28:18; Heb 9:5

25:4 ¹Or *bluish;* LXX *hyacinth* in color   25:5 ¹Meaning of the Heb uncertain   25:10 ¹I.e., chest   ²About 3.7 ft. long and 2.2 ft. wide and high or 1.1 m and 68 cm   25:17 ¹Also called *a mercy seat,* and so throughout the ch; i.e., where blood was sprinkled on the Day of Atonement   ²About 3.7 ft. long and 2.2 ft. wide or 1.1 m and 68 cm

wings spread upward, covering the atoning cover with their wings and facing one another; the faces of the cherubim are to be *turned* toward the atoning cover. [21]Then ^you shall put the atoning cover on top of the ark, and in the ark you shall put the testimony which I will give to you. [22]There I will meet with you; and from above the atoning cover, from ^between the two cherubim which are upon the ark of the testimony, I will speak to you about every commandment that I will give you for the sons of Israel.

BREAD OF THE PRESENCE

[23]"^You shall also make a table of acacia wood, 'two cubits long and one cubit wide, and one and a half cubits high. [24]You shall overlay it with pure gold and make a gold ^border around it. [25]And you shall make for it a rim of a 'hand width around *it;* and you shall make a gold border for the rim around it. [26]You shall also make four gold rings for it and put rings on the four corners which are on its four legs. [27]The rings shall be close to the rim, as holders for the poles to carry the table. [28]And you shall make the poles of acacia wood and overlay them with gold, so that with them the table may be carried. [29]You shall also make its ^dishes, its pans, its jars, and its libation bowls with which to pour drink offerings; you shall make them of pure gold. [30]And you shall set ^the bread of the Presence on the table before Me continually.

THE GOLDEN LAMPSTAND

[31]"^Then you shall make a lampstand of pure gold. The lampstand, its base and its shaft, are to be made of hammered work; its cups, its bulbs, and its flowers shall be *of one piece* with it. [32]^Six branches shall go out from its sides; three branches of the lampstand from its one side and three branches of the lampstand from its other side. [33]Three cups *shall be* shaped like almond blossoms on the one branch, a bulb and a flower, and three cups shaped like almond blossoms on the other branch, a bulb and a flower—the same for six branches going out from the lampstand; [34]and ^on the lampstand four cups shaped like almond blossoms, its bulbs and its flowers. [35]^A bulb shall be under the *first* pair of branches *coming* out of it, and a bulb under the *second* pair of branches *coming* out of it, and a bulb under the *third* pair of branches *coming* out of it, for the six branches coming out of the lampstand. [36]^Their bulbs and their branches shall be *of one piece* with it; all of it *shall be* one piece of hammered work of pure gold. [37]Then you shall make its lamps seven *in number;* and ^they shall mount its lamps so as to shed light on the space in front of it. [38]Its tongs and its trays *shall be* of pure gold. [39]It shall be made from a 'talent of pure gold, with all these utensils. [40]^See that you make *them* by the pattern for them, which was shown to you on the mountain.

25:21^Ex 26:34; 40:20   25:22^Ps 80:1; Is 37:16
25:23^Ex 37:10-16   25:24^Ex 25:11   25:29^Ex 37:16;
Num 4:7   25:30^Ex 39:36; Lev 24:5-9
25:31^Ex 37:17-24; Zech 4:2   25:32^Ex 37:18
25:33^Ex 37:19   25:34^Ex 37:20   25:35^Ex 37:21
25:36^Ex 37:22   25:37^Num 8:2   25:40^Heb 8:5

25:23'About 3 ft. long, 1.5 ft. wide, 2.25 ft. high or 90
cm, 45 cm, and 68 cm   25:25'About 3 in. or 7.5 cm
25:39'About 75 lb. or 34 kg

CURTAINS OF LINEN

26 "ᴬMoreover, you shall make the tabernacle with ten curtains of fine twisted linen and ¹violet, purple, and scarlet *material;* you shall make them with cherubim, the work of a skilled embroiderer. ²The length of each curtain shall be ¹twenty-eight cubits, and the width of each curtain four cubits; all the curtains shall have the same measurements. ³Five curtains shall be joined to one another, and *the other* five curtains *shall be* joined to one another. ⁴You shall make loops of violet on the edge of the outermost curtain in the *first* set, and likewise you shall make *them* on the edge of the curtain that is outermost in the second set. ⁵You shall make fifty loops in the one curtain, and you shall make fifty loops on the edge of the curtain that is in the second set; the loops shall be opposite each other. ⁶You shall also make fifty clasps of gold, and join the curtains to one another with the clasps so that the ¹tabernacle will be a unit.

CURTAINS OF GOATS' HAIR

⁷"Then ᴬyou shall make curtains of goats' *hair* as a tent over the tabernacle; you shall make eleven curtains in all. ⁸The length of each curtain *shall be* ¹thirty cubits, and the width of each curtain four cubits; the eleven curtains shall have the same measurements. ⁹You shall join five curtains by themselves and the *other* six curtains by themselves, and you shall double over the sixth curtain at the front of the tent. ¹⁰You shall make fifty loops on the edge of the curtain that is outermost in the *first* set, and fifty loops on the edge of the curtain *that is outermost in* the second set.

¹¹"You shall also make fifty clasps of bronze, and you shall put the clasps into the loops and join the tent together so that it will be a unit. ¹²The overhanging part that is left over in the curtains of the tent, the half curtain that is left over, shall hang over the back of the tabernacle. ¹³The ¹cubit on one side and the cubit on the other, of what is left over in the length of the curtains of the tent, shall hang over the sides of the tabernacle on one side and on the other, to cover it. ¹⁴And ᴬyou shall make a covering for the tent of rams' skins dyed red and a covering of ¹fine leather above.

BOARDS AND BASES

¹⁵"Then you shall make ᴬthe boards for the tabernacle of acacia wood, standing upright. ¹⁶¹Ten cubits *shall be* the length of each board and one and a half cubits the width of each board. ¹⁷*There shall be* two tenons for each board, fitted to one another; that is what you shall do for all the boards of the tabernacle. ¹⁸You shall make the boards for the tabernacle: twenty boards for the south side. ¹⁹You shall make forty ᴬbases of silver under the twenty boards, two bases under one board for its two tenons and two bases under another board for its two tenons; ²⁰and for the second side of

26:1 ᴬEx 36:8-19   26:7 ᴬEx 36:14   26:14 ᴬEx 36:19   26:15 ᴬEx 36:20-34   26:19 ᴬEx 38:27

26:1 ¹Or *bluish;* LXX *hyacinth* in color, and so throughout the ch   26:2 ¹About 42 ft. long and 6 ft. wide or 13 m and 1.8 m   26:6 ¹Or *dwelling place,* and so throughout the ch   26:8 ¹About 45 ft. long and 6 ft. wide or 13.5 m and 1.8 m   26:13 ¹About 18 in. or about 45 cm   26:14 ¹Meaning of the Heb uncertain   26:16 ¹About 15 ft. long and 2.2 ft. wide or 4.6 m and 68 cm

the tabernacle, on the north side, twenty boards, [21]and their forty bases of silver; two bases under one board and two bases under another board. [22]For the back of the tabernacle, to the west, you shall make six boards. [23]You shall make two boards for the corners of the tabernacle at the back. [24]They shall be double beneath, and together they shall be complete to its top to the first ring; this is how it shall be with both of them: they shall form the two corners. [25]And there shall be eight boards with their bases of silver, sixteen bases; two bases under one board and two bases under another board.

[26]"Then you shall make ^bars of acacia wood, five for the boards of one side of the tabernacle, [27]and five bars for the boards of the other side of the tabernacle, and five bars for the boards of the side of the tabernacle for the back *side* to the west. [28]The middle bar in the center of the boards shall pass through from end to end. [29]And you shall overlay the boards with gold, and make their rings of gold *as* holders for the bars; and you shall overlay the bars with gold. [30]Then you shall erect the tabernacle ^according to its plan which you have been shown on the mountain.

THE VEIL AND CURTAIN

[31]"You shall also make ^a veil of violet, purple, and scarlet *material,* and fine twisted linen; it shall be made with cherubim, the work of a skilled embroiderer. [32]Then you shall hang it on four pillars of acacia overlaid with gold, their hooks *also of* gold, on four bases of silver. [33]You shall hang up the veil under the clasps, and bring in the ark of the testimony there within the veil; and the veil shall serve as a partition for you ^between the Holy Place and the Most Holy Place. [34]^You shall put the 'atoning cover on the ark of the testimony in the Most Holy Place. [35]And ^you shall set the table outside the veil, and the lampstand opposite the table on the side of the tabernacle toward the south; and you shall put the table on the north side.

[36]"^You shall also make a curtain for the doorway of the tent of violet, purple, and scarlet *material* and fine twisted linen, the work of a weaver. [37]And ^you shall make five pillars of acacia for the curtain and overlay them with gold, their hooks *also of* gold; and you shall cast five bases of bronze for them.

THE BRONZE ALTAR

27 "Now you shall make ^the altar of acacia wood, 'five cubits long and five cubits wide; the altar shall be square, and its height shall be [2]three cubits. [2]You shall make ^its horns on its four corners; its horns shall be of one piece with it, and you shall overlay it with bronze. [3]And you shall make its pails for removing its ashes, and its shovels, its basins, its forks, and its firepans; you shall make all its utensils of bronze. [4]You shall also make for it a grating, a netting of bronze, and on the netting you shall make four bronze rings at its four corners. [5]And you shall put it

26:26^Ex 36:31   26:30^Acts 7:44; Heb 8:5
26:31^Matt 27:51; Heb 9:3   26:33^Heb 9:2f
26:34^Ex 40:20; Lev 16:2   26:35^Ex 40:22
26:36^Ex 36:37   26:37^Ex 36:38
27:1^Ex 38:1-7   27:2^Ps 118:27

26:34[1]Also called *mercy seat;* i.e., where blood was sprinkled on the Day of Atonement   27:1[1]About 7.5 ft. or 2.3 m   [2]About 4.5 ft. or 1.4 m

under the ledge of the altar, so that the netting will reach halfway up the altar. ⁶You shall also make carrying poles for the altar, poles of acacia wood and overlay them with bronze. ⁷Its poles shall be inserted into the rings, so that the poles will be on the two sides of the altar ᴬwhen it is carried. ⁸You shall make it hollow with planks; ᴬas it was shown to you on the mountain, so they shall make *it.*

COURTYARD OF THE TABERNACLE

⁹"Now you shall make ᴬthe courtyard of the tabernacle. On the south side *there shall be* hangings for the courtyard of fine twisted linen, a 'hundred cubits long for one side; ¹⁰and its pillars *shall be* twenty, with their twenty bases of bronze; the hooks of the pillars and their bands *shall be* of silver. ¹¹Likewise for the north side in length *there shall be* hangings a 'hundred *cubits* long, and its twenty pillars with their twenty bases of bronze; the hooks of the pillars and their bands *shall be* of silver. ¹²*For* the width of the courtyard on the west side *shall be* hangings of 'fifty cubits, *with* their ten pillars and their ten bases. ¹³The width of the courtyard on the east side *shall be* fifty cubits. ¹⁴The hangings for the *one* side *of the gate shall be* 'fifteen cubits, *with* their three pillars and their three bases. ¹⁵And for the other side *there shall be* hangings of fifteen cubits, *with* their three pillars and their three bases. ¹⁶And for the gate of the courtyard *there shall be* a curtain of 'twenty cubits, of ²violet, purple, and scarlet *material* and fine twisted linen, the work of a weaver, *with* their four pillars and their four bases.

¹⁷All the pillars around the courtyard shall be joined together *with* silver, *with* their hooks of silver and their bases of bronze. ¹⁸The length of the courtyard *shall be* a 'hundred cubits, and the width fifty throughout, and the height five cubits of fine twisted linen, and their bases of bronze. ¹⁹All the utensils of the tabernacle *used* in all its service, and all its pegs, and all the pegs of the courtyard, *shall be* of bronze.

²⁰"And you shall command the sons of Israel that they bring you ᴬclear oil of beaten olives for the light, to make a lamp burn continually. ²¹In the ᴬtent of meeting, outside ᴮthe veil which is before the testimony, Aaron and his sons shall keep it in order from evening to morning before the Lᴏʀᴅ; *it shall be* a permanent statute throughout their generations for the sons of Israel.

GARMENTS OF THE PRIESTS

28 "Then bring forward to yourself your brother Aaron, and his sons with him, from among the sons of Israel, to serve as priest to Me—Aaron, ᴬNadab and Abihu, Eleazar and Ithamar, Aaron's sons. ²And you shall make ᴬholy garments for Aaron your brother, for glory and for beauty. ³You shall speak to all the skillful people ᴬwhom I have endowed with the spirit of wisdom, that they make

27:7ᴬNum 4:15   27:8ᴬActs 7:44; Heb 8:5
27:9ᴬEx 38:9-20   27:20ᴬEx 35:8, 28; Lev 24:1-4
27:21ᴬEx 25:22   ᴮEx 26:31, 33   28:1ᴬEx 24:1, 9
28:2ᴬEx 39:1-31; Lev 8:7-9, 30
28:3ᴬ1 Cor 12:7-11; Eph 1:17

27:9 'About 150 ft. or 46 m   27:11 'About 150 ft. or 46 m   27:12 'About 75 ft. or 23 m   27:14 'About 23 ft. or 6.8 m   27:16 'About 30 ft. or 9 m   ²Or *bluish;* LXX *hyacinth* in color   27:18 'About 150 ft. long, 75 ft. wide, and 7.5 ft. high or about 46 m, 23 m, and 2.3 m

Aaron's garments to consecrate him, that he may serve as priest to Me. ⁴And these are the garments which they shall make: a ᴬbreastpiece, an ephod, a robe, a tunic of checkered work, a turban, and a sash. They shall make holy garments for your brother Aaron and his sons, so that he may serve as priest to Me. ⁵They shall take ᴬthe gold, the ¹violet, the purple, the scarlet *material,* and the fine linen.

⁶"They shall also make ᴬthe ephod of gold, of violet, purple, *and* scarlet *material,* and fine twisted linen, the work of the skilled embroiderer. ⁷It shall have two shoulder pieces joined to its two ends, so that it may be joined. ⁸The skillfully woven band of its overlay, which is on it, shall be like its workmanship, of the same material: of gold, of violet and purple and scarlet *material* and fine twisted linen. ⁹And you shall take two onyx stones and engrave on them the names of the sons of Israel, ¹⁰six of their names on the one stone and the names of the remaining six on the other stone, according to their birth. ¹¹As a jeweler engraves a signet, you shall engrave the two stones according to the names of the sons of Israel; you shall set them in filigree settings of gold. ¹²And you shall put the two stones on the shoulder pieces of the ephod, *as* stones of memorial for the sons of Israel, and Aaron shall ᴬcarry their names before the Lᴏʀᴅ on his two shoulders as a memorial. ¹³And ᴬyou shall make filigree settings of gold, ¹⁴and two chains of pure gold; you shall make them of twisted cord work, and you shall put the corded chains on the filigree settings.

¹⁵"ᴬYou shall make a breastpiece of judgment, the work of a skilled embroiderer; like the work of the ephod you shall make it: of gold, of violet, purple, and scarlet *material,* and fine twisted linen you shall make it. ¹⁶It shall be square *and* folded double, a ¹span in length and a span in width. ¹⁷And you shall mount on it four rows of stones; the first row *shall be* a row of ruby, topaz, and emerald; ¹⁸and the second row a turquoise, a sapphire, and a diamond; ¹⁹and the third row a jacinth, an agate, and an amethyst; ²⁰and the fourth row a beryl, and an onyx, and a jasper; they shall be set in gold filigree. ²¹The stones shall be *engraved* according to the names of the sons of Israel: twelve, according to their names; they shall be *like* the engravings of a signet, each ᴬaccording to his name for the twelve tribes. ²²You shall also make on the breastpiece twisted chains of cord work in pure gold. ²³And you shall make on the breastpiece two rings of gold, and shall put the two rings on the two ends of the breastpiece. ²⁴And you shall put the two cords of gold on the two rings at the ends of the breastpiece. ²⁵You shall put the *other* two ends of the two cords on the two filigree *settings,* and put them on the shoulder pieces of the ephod, at the front of it. ²⁶And you shall make two rings of gold and place them on the two ends of the breastpiece, on the edge of it, which is toward the inner side of the ephod. ²⁷And you shall make two rings of gold

---

28:4 ᴬEx 28:15-43   28:5 ᴬEx 25:3   28:6 ᴬEx 39:2-7;
Lev 8:7   28:12 ᴬEx 28:29; 39:6f   28:13 ᴬEx 39:16-18
28:15 ᴬEx 39:8-21   28:21 ᴬRev 7:4-8; 21:12

28:5 ¹Or *bluish;* LXX *hyacinth* in color, and so
throughout the ch   28:16 ¹About 9 in. or 23 cm

and put them on the bottom of the two shoulder pieces of the ephod, on the front of it close to the place where it is joined, above the skillfully woven band of the ephod. ²⁸And they shall bind the breastpiece by its rings to the rings of the ephod with a violet cord, so that it will be on the skillfully woven band of the ephod, and that the breastpiece will not come loose from the ephod. ²⁹So Aaron shall carry the names of the sons of Israel in the breastpiece of judgment over his heart when he enters the Holy Place, as a memorial before the LORD continually. ³⁰And ᴬyou shall put in the breastpiece of judgment the ^{1,ᴮ}Urim and the Thummim, and they shall be over Aaron's heart when he goes in before the LORD; and Aaron shall carry the judgment of the sons of Israel over his heart before the LORD continually.

³¹"ᴬYou shall make the robe of the ephod all of violet. ³²There shall be an opening at its top in the middle of it; around its opening there shall be a binding of woven work, like the opening of a coat of mail, so that it will not be torn. ³³You shall make on its hem pomegranates of violet, purple, and scarlet *material* all around on its hem, and bells of gold between them all around: ³⁴a golden bell and a pomegranate, a golden bell and a pomegranate, all around on the hem of the robe. ³⁵It shall be on Aaron when he ministers; and its sound shall be heard when he enters and leaves the Holy Place before the LORD, so that he will not die.

³⁶"You shall also make ᴬa plate of pure gold and engrave on it, like the engravings of a signet, 'ᴮHoly to the LORD.' ³⁷You shall fasten it on a violet cord, and it shall be on the turban; it shall be at the front of the turban. ³⁸It shall be on Aaron's forehead, and Aaron shall take away the guilt of the holy things which the sons of Israel consecrate, regarding all their holy gifts; and it shall always be on his forehead, so that ᴬthey may be accepted before the LORD.

³⁹"And you shall weave ᴬthe tunic of checkered work of fine linen, and shall make a turban of fine linen, and you shall make a sash, the work of a weaver.

⁴⁰"For Aaron's sons you shall also make ᴬtunics; you shall also make sashes for them, and you shall make caps for them, for glory and for beauty. ⁴¹Then you shall put them on Aaron your brother and on his sons with him; and you shall ᴬanoint them and ordain them and consecrate them, so that they may serve Me as priests. ⁴²You shall make for them ᴬlinen undergarments to cover *their* bare flesh; they shall reach from the waist even to the thighs. ⁴³And they shall be on Aaron and on his sons when they enter the tent of meeting, or ᴬwhen they approach the altar to minister in the Holy Place, so that they do not incur guilt and die. ᴮIt *shall be* a statute forever to him and to his descendants after him.

CONSECRATION OF THE PRIESTS

29 "ᴬNow this is what you shall do to them to consecrate them to serve as priests to Me: take one bull and two rams without

---

28:30 ᴬLev 8:8   ᴮDeut 33:8   28:31 ᴬEx 39:22-26
28:36 ᴬEx 39:30, 31   ᴮZech 14:20   28:38 ᴬLev 22:27;
Is 56:7   28:39 ᴬEx 39:27-29   28:40 ᴬEx 28:4; 39:27, 41
28:41 ᴬEx 29:7, 9; Lev 8:1-36   28:42 ᴬLev 6:10;
Ezek 44:18   28:43 ᴬEx 20:26   ᴮEx 27:21
29:1 ᴬLev 8:1-34

28:30 ¹I.e., lights and perfections

blemish, ²and ^unleavened bread and unleavened cakes mixed with oil, and unleavened wafers spread with oil; you shall make them of fine wheat flour. ³And you shall put them in one basket, and present them in the basket along with the bull and the two rams. ⁴Then ^you shall bring Aaron and his sons to the doorway of the tent of meeting and wash them with water. ⁵And you shall take the garments, and put on Aaron the ^tunic and the robe of the ephod, and the ephod and the breastpiece, and wrap his waist with the skillfully woven band of the ephod; ⁶and you shall set the turban on his head and put ^the holy crown on the turban. ⁷Then you shall take ^the anointing oil and pour it on his head, and anoint him. ⁸You shall also bring his sons and put ^tunics on them. ⁹And you shall wrap their waists with sashes, Aaron and his sons, and fit caps on them, and they shall have ^the priesthood by a permanent statute. So you shall ordain Aaron and his sons.

THE SACRIFICES

¹⁰"Then you shall bring the bull in front of the tent of meeting, and Aaron and his sons shall ^lay their hands on the head of the bull. ¹¹And you shall slaughter the bull before the LORD at the doorway of the tent of meeting. ¹²Then you shall ^take some of the blood of the bull and put *it* on the horns of the altar with your finger; and you shall pour out all *the rest of* the blood at the base of the altar. ¹³And you shall ^take all the fat that covers the entrails, and the lobe of the liver, and the two kidneys and the fat that is on them, and offer them up in smoke on the altar. ¹⁴But ^the flesh of the

bull and its hide and its refuse, you shall burn with fire outside the camp; it is a sin offering.

¹⁵"^You shall also take the one ram, and Aaron and his sons shall lay their hands on the head of the ram; ¹⁶and you shall slaughter the ram and take its blood and sprinkle it around on the altar. ¹⁷Then you shall cut the ram into its pieces, and wash its entrails and its legs, and put *them* with its pieces and its head. ¹⁸And you shall offer up in smoke the whole ram on the altar; it is a burnt offering to the LORD: ^it is a soothing aroma, an offering by fire to the LORD.

¹⁹"Then ^you shall take the other ram, and Aaron and his sons shall lay their hands on the head of the ram. ²⁰And you shall slaughter the ram, and take some of its blood and put *it* on the lobe of Aaron's right ear and on the lobes of his sons' right ears, and on the thumbs of their right hands, and on the big toes of their right feet, and sprinkle the *rest of the* blood around on the altar. ²¹Then you shall take some of the blood that is on the altar and some of the ^anointing oil, and sprinkle *it* on Aaron and on his garments, and on his sons and on his sons' garments with him; so he and his garments shall be consecrated, as well as his sons and his sons' garments with him.

²²"You shall also take the fat from the ram and the fat tail, and the fat that covers the entrails and the lobe of the liver, and the two kidneys

29:2 ^Lev 2:4; 6:19-23   29:4 ^Ex 40:12; Lev 8:6   29:5 ^Ex 28:39; Lev 8:7   29:6 ^Ex 28:36, 37; Lev 8:9   29:7 ^Num 35:25; Ps 133:2   29:8 ^Ex 28:39, 40; Lev 8:13   29:9 ^Ex 40:15; Deut 18:5   29:10 ^Lev 1:4; 8:14   29:12 ^Lev 8:15   29:13 ^Lev 3:3, 4   29:14 ^Lev 4:11, 12, 21; Heb 13:11   29:15 ^Lev 8:18   29:18 ^Gen 8:21; Ex 29:25   29:19 ^Lev 8:22f   29:21 ^Ex 30:25, 31; Lev 8:30

and the fat that is on them, and the right thigh (for it is a ram of ordination), ²³and one loaf of bread, and ^one cake of bread *mixed with* oil, and one wafer from the basket of unleavened bread which is *set* before the LORD; ²⁴and you shall put all these in the hands of Aaron and in the hands of his sons, and shall wave them as a wave offering before the LORD. ²⁵Then ^you shall take them from their hands, and offer them up in smoke on the altar on the burnt offering for a soothing aroma before the LORD; it is an offering by fire to the LORD.

²⁶"Then you shall take ^the breast of Aaron's ram of ordination, and wave it as a wave offering before the LORD; and it shall be your portion. ²⁷You shall consecrate the breast of the wave offering and the thigh of the contribution which was waved and which was offered from the ram of ordination, from the one which was for Aaron and from the one which was for his sons. ²⁸It shall be for Aaron and his sons as *their* portion forever from the sons of Israel, for it is a contribution; and it shall be a contribution from the sons of Israel from the sacrifices of their peace offerings, their contribution to the LORD.

²⁹"^The holy garments of Aaron shall be for his sons after him, so that they may be anointed and ordained in them. ³⁰For seven days the one of his sons who is priest in his place shall put them on when he enters the tent of meeting to minister in the Holy Place.

FOOD OF THE PRIESTS

³¹"Now you shall take the ram of ordination and ^boil its flesh in a holy place. ³²Then Aaron and his

sons shall eat the flesh of the ram and the bread that is in the basket, at the doorway of the tent of meeting. ³³So ^they shall eat those things by which atonement was made at their ordination *and* consecration; but a layman shall not eat *them*, because they are holy. ³⁴And ^if any of the flesh of ordination or any of the bread remains until morning, then you shall burn the remainder with fire; it shall not be eaten, because it is holy.

³⁵"So you shall do for Aaron and for his sons, according to all that I have commanded you; you shall ordain them for ^seven days. ³⁶^Each day you shall offer a bull as a sin offering for atonement, and you shall purify the altar when you make atonement for it, and you shall anoint it to consecrate it. ³⁷For seven days you shall make atonement for the altar and consecrate it; then ^the altar shall be most holy, *and* whatever touches the altar shall be holy.

³⁸"Now ^this is what you shall offer on the altar: two one-year-old lambs each day, continuously. ³⁹The ^one lamb you shall offer in the morning, and the other lamb you shall offer at twilight; ⁴⁰and there *shall be* a ¹tenth *of an ephah* of fine flour mixed with a ²fourth of a hin of beaten oil, and a fourth of a hin of wine for a drink offering with one lamb. ⁴¹The other lamb you shall offer at twilight, and shall offer with it the same grain offering

29:23^Lev 8:26   29:25^Lev 8:28
29:26^Lev 7:31, 34; 8:29   29:29^Num 20:26, 28
29:31^Lev 8:31   29:33^Lev 10:14   29:34^Ex 34:25;
Lev 8:32   29:35^Lev 8:33   29:36^Heb 10:11
29:37^Ex 30:28f   29:38^Num 28:3-31; 29:6-38
29:39^Ezek 46:13-15

29:40¹About 3 qt. or 2.8 liters
²About 0.95 qt. or 0.9 liter

and the same drink offering as in the morning, for a soothing aroma, an offering by fire to the Lord. ⁴²It shall be a continual burnt offering throughout your generations at the doorway of the tent of meeting before the Lord, ^where I will meet with you, to speak to you there. ⁴³I will meet there with the sons of Israel, and it shall be consecrated by My glory. ⁴⁴I will consecrate the tent of meeting and the altar; I will also consecrate Aaron and his sons to serve as priests to Me. ⁴⁵And ^I will dwell among the sons of Israel and will be their God. ⁴⁶And they shall know that ^I am the Lord their God who brought them out of the land of Egypt, so that I might dwell among them; I am the Lord their God.

THE ALTAR OF INCENSE

30 "Now you shall make ^an altar as a place for burning incense; you shall make it of acacia wood. ²Its length *shall be* ¹a cubit, and its width a cubit; it shall be square, and its height *shall be* two cubits; its horns *shall be* of one piece with it. ³You shall overlay it with pure gold, its top and its sides all around, and its horns; and you shall make a gold molding all around for it. ⁴You shall also make two gold rings for it under its molding; you shall make *them* on its two sides—on opposite sides—and they shall be holders for poles with which to carry it. ⁵And you shall make the poles of acacia wood and overlay them with gold. ⁶You shall put this altar in front of the veil that is near the ark of the testimony, in front of the ¹,^atoning cover that is over *the ark of* the testimony, where I will meet with you. ⁷Aaron shall

burn fragrant incense on it; he shall burn it every morning when he trims the lamps. ⁸And when Aaron sets up the lamps at twilight, he shall burn incense. *There shall be* perpetual incense before the Lord throughout your generations. ⁹You shall not offer any strange incense on this altar, or burnt offering, or meal offering; and you shall not pour out a drink offering on it. ¹⁰However, Aaron shall ^make atonement on its horns once a year; he shall make atonement on it with the blood of the sin offering of atonement once a year throughout your generations. It is most holy to the Lord."

¹¹The Lord also spoke to Moses, saying, ¹²"When you take ^a census of the sons of Israel to count them, then each one *of them* shall give a ransom for himself to the Lord, when you count them, so that there will be no plague among them when you count them. ¹³This *is what* everyone who is counted shall give: half a ¹shekel according to the shekel of the sanctuary (^the shekel is twenty gerahs), half a shekel as a contribution to the Lord. ¹⁴Everyone who is counted, from twenty years old and over, shall give the contribution to the Lord. ¹⁵The rich shall not pay more, and the poor shall not pay less, than the half shekel, when you give the contribution to the Lord to make atonement for yourselves. ¹⁶And you shall take the

---

29:42 ^Ex 25:22; Num 17:4   29:45 ^Zech 2:10;
2 Cor 6:16   29:46 ^Ex 20:2   30:1 ^Ex 37:25-29
30:6 ^Ex 25:21f   30:10 ^Lev 16:18   30:12 ^Ex 38:25, 26;
Num 1:2   30:13 ^Num 3:47; Ezek 45:12

30:2 ¹About 1.5 ft. long and wide and 3 ft. high or 45 cm and 90 cm   30:6 ¹Also called *mercy seat;* i.e., where blood was sprinkled on the Day of Atonement
30:13 ¹A shekel was about 0.4 oz. or 11 gm

atonement money from the sons of Israel and give it for the service of the tent of meeting, so that it may be a memorial for the sons of Israel before the Lord, to make atonement for yourselves."

¹⁷Then the Lord spoke to Moses, saying, ¹⁸"You shall also make ᴬa basin of bronze, with its base of bronze, for washing; and you shall ᴮput it between the tent of meeting and the altar, and you shall put water in it. ¹⁹Aaron and his sons shall ᴬwash their hands and their feet from it; ²⁰when they enter the tent of meeting, they shall wash with water, so that they do not die; or when they approach the altar to minister, by offering up in smoke a fire *sacrifice* to the Lord. ²¹So they shall wash their hands and their feet, so that they do not die; and ᴬit shall be a permanent statute for them, for Aaron and his descendants throughout their generations."

THE ANOINTING OIL

²²Moreover, the Lord spoke to Moses, saying, ²³"Take also for yourself the finest of spices: of liquid myrrh ¹five hundred *shekels,* and of fragrant cinnamon half as much, 250, and of fragrant cane 250, ²⁴and of cassia 500, according to the shekel of the sanctuary, and of olive oil a ¹hin. ²⁵You shall make from these a holy anointing oil, a fragrant mixture of ointments, the work of a perfumer; it shall be ᴬa holy anointing oil. ²⁶And ᴬyou shall anoint the tent of meeting with it, and the ark of the testimony, ²⁷and the table and all its utensils, and the lampstand and its utensils, and the altar of incense, ²⁸and the altar of burnt offering

and all its utensils, and the basin and its stand. ²⁹You shall also consecrate them, so that they may be most holy; whatever touches them shall be holy. ³⁰And ᴬyou shall anoint Aaron and his sons, and consecrate them, so that they may serve as priests to Me. ³¹Furthermore, you shall speak to the sons of Israel, saying, 'This shall be a holy anointing oil to Me throughout your generations. ³²It shall not be poured on anyone's body, nor shall you make *any* like it in the same proportions; ᴬit is holy, *and* it shall be holy to you. ³³ᴬWhoever mixes *any* like it or whoever puts any of it on a layman shall be cut off from his people.'"

THE INCENSE

³⁴Then the Lord said to Moses, "Take for yourself spices—stacte, onycha, and galbanum, spices and pure frankincense; there shall be an equal part of each. ³⁵You shall make incense from it *all,* a skillful mixture, the work of a perfumer, salted, pure, *and* holy. ³⁶And you shall crush some of it very fine, and put part of it in front of the testimony in the tent of meeting ᴬwhere I will meet with you; it shall be most holy to you. ³⁷And the incense which you shall make, ᴬyou shall not make in the same proportions for yourselves; it shall be holy to you for the Lord. ³⁸ᴬWhoever makes *any* like it, to use as perfume, shall be cut off from his people."

30:18 ᴬEx 38:8　ᴮEx 40:30　**30:19**ᴬEx 40:31f; Is 52:11
30:21ᴬEx 28:43　**30:25**ᴬEx 37:29; Lev 8:10
30:26ᴬEx 40:9; Lev 8:10　**30:30**ᴬEx 29:7; Lev 8:12
30:32ᴬEx 30:25, 37　**30:33**ᴬEx 30:38　**30:36**ᴬEx 29:42
30:37ᴬEx 30:32　**30:38**ᴬEx 30:33

30:23¹About 15.5 and 7.75 lb. or 7 and 3.5 kg
30:24¹About 1 gallon or 3.8 liters

THE SKILLED CRAFTSMEN

31 ^A Now the LORD spoke to Moses, saying, ² "See, I have called by name Bezalel, the ^A son of Uri, the son of Hur, of the tribe of Judah. ³ And I have ^A filled him with the Spirit of God in wisdom, in understanding, in knowledge, and in all *kinds of* craftsmanship, ⁴ to create artistic designs for work in gold, in silver, and in bronze, ⁵ and in the cutting of stones for settings, and in the carving of wood, so that he may work in all *kinds of* craftsmanship. ⁶ And behold, I Myself have appointed with him ^A Oholiab, the son of Ahisamach, of the tribe of Dan; and in the hearts of all who are skillful I have put skill, so that they may make everything that I have commanded you: ⁷ ^A the tent of meeting, ^B the ark of testimony, the ¹ atoning cover that is on it, and all the furniture of the tent, ⁸ ^A the table and its utensils, the ^B pure *gold* lampstand with all its utensils, and the altar of incense, ⁹ ^A the altar of burnt offering with all its utensils, and the basin and its stand, ¹⁰ the ^A woven garments as well: the holy garments for Aaron the priest and the garments of his sons, *with which* to carry out their priesthood; ¹¹ ^A the anointing oil also, and the fragrant incense for the Holy Place, they are to make *them* according to everything that I have commanded you."

THE SIGN OF THE SABBATH

¹² Now the LORD spoke to Moses, saying, ¹³ "Now as for you, speak to the sons of Israel, saying, '^A You must keep My Sabbaths; for *this* is a sign between Me and you throughout your generations, so that you may know that I am the LORD who sanctifies you. ¹⁴ Therefore you are to keep the Sabbath, for it is holy to you. ^A Everyone who profanes it must be put to death; for whoever does *any* work on it, that person shall be cut off from among his people. ¹⁵ ^A For six days work may be done, but on the seventh day there is a Sabbath of complete rest, holy to the LORD; ^B whoever does *any* work on the Sabbath day must be put to death. ¹⁶ So the sons of Israel shall keep the Sabbath, to celebrate the Sabbath throughout their generations as a permanent covenant.' ¹⁷ It is a sign between Me and the sons of Israel forever; ^A for in six days the LORD made heaven and earth, but on the seventh day He ceased *from labor,* and was refreshed."

¹⁸ When He had finished speaking with him on Mount Sinai, He gave Moses ^A the two tablets of the testimony, tablets of stone, written by the finger of God.

THE GOLDEN CALF

32 Now when the people saw that Moses delayed to come down from the mountain, the people assembled around Aaron and said to him, "Come, ^A make us a god who will go before us; for ^B this Moses, the man who brought us up from the land of Egypt—we do not know what happened to him." ² Aaron said to them, "^A Tear off the gold rings which are in the ears of your wives, your sons, and your

31:1 ^A Ex 35:30-36:1   **31:2** ^A 1 Chr 2:20   **31:3** ^A 1 Kin 7:14; 1 Cor 12:4-8   **31:6** ^A Ex 35:34   **31:7** ^A Ex 36:8-38   ^B Ex 37:1-5   **31:8** ^A Ex 37:10-16   ^B Lev 24:4   **31:9** ^A Ex 38:1-7   **31:10** ^A Ex 39:1   **31:11** ^A Ex 30:23-32   **31:13** ^A Ex 20:8   **31:14** ^A Ex 31:15; John 7:23   **31:15** ^A Deut 5:12-14   ^B Ex 31:14   **31:17** ^A Gen 1:31; Ex 20:11   **31:18** ^A Deut 4:13; 5:22   **32:1** ^A Acts 7:40   ^B Ex 14:11   **32:2** ^A Ex 35:22

31:7 ¹ Also called *mercy seat;* i.e., where blood was sprinkled on the Day of Atonement

daughters, and bring *them* to me." ³So all the people tore off the gold rings which were in their ears and brought *them* to Aaron. ⁴Then he took *the gold* from their hands, and fashioned it with an engraving tool and made it into a ᴬcast metal calf; and they said, "This is your god, Israel, who brought you up from the land of Egypt." ⁵Now when Aaron saw *this,* he built an altar in front of it; and Aaron made a proclamation and said, "Tomorrow *shall be* a feast to the Lᴏʀᴅ." ⁶So the next day they got up early and offered burnt offerings, and brought peace offerings; and ᴬthe people sat down to eat and to drink, and got up to engage in lewd behavior.

⁷Then the Lᴏʀᴅ spoke to Moses, "Go down at once, for your people, whom you brought up from the land of Egypt, have ᴬbehaved corruptly. ⁸They have quickly turned aside from the way which I commanded them. ᴬThey have made for themselves a cast metal calf, and have worshiped it and have sacrificed to it and said, 'ᴮThis is your god, Israel, who brought you up from the land of Egypt!'" ⁹Then the Lᴏʀᴅ said to Moses, "I have seen this people, and behold, they are ᴬan obstinate people. ¹⁰So now ᴬleave Me alone, that My anger may burn against them and that I may destroy them; and ᴮI will make of you a great nation."

MOSES' PLEA

¹¹Then ᴬMoses pleaded with the Lᴏʀᴅ his God, and said, "Lᴏʀᴅ, why does Your anger burn against Your people whom You have brought out from the land of Egypt with great power and with a mighty hand? ¹²Why should ᴬthe Egyptians

talk, saying, 'With evil *motives* He brought them out, to kill them on the mountains and to destroy them from the face ᴬof the earth'? Turn from Your burning anger and relent of *doing* harm to Your people. ¹³Remember Abraham, Isaac, and Israel, Your servants to whom You ᴬswore by Yourself, and said to them, 'I will ᴮmultiply your descendants as the stars of the heavens, and all this land of which I have spoken I will give to your descendants, and they shall inherit *it* forever.'" ¹⁴ᴬSo the Lᴏʀᴅ relented of the harm which He said He would do to His people.

¹⁵ᴬThen Moses turned and went down from the mountain with the two tablets of the testimony in his hand, ᴮtablets which were written on both sides; they were written on one *side* and the other. ¹⁶The tablets were God's work, and the writing was God's writing engraved on the tablets. ¹⁷Now when Joshua heard the sound of the people as they shouted, he said to Moses, "*There is* a sound of war in the camp." ¹⁸But he said,

"It is not the sound of the cry of
    victory,
Nor is it the sound of the cry of
    defeat;
But I hear the sound of
    singing."

MOSES' ANGER

¹⁹And it came about, as soon as Moses approached the camp, that ᴬhe saw the calf and *the people* dancing; and Moses' anger burned, and

32:4ᴬPs 106:19; Acts 7:41 32:6ᴬ1 Cor 10:7
32:7ᴬGen 6:11f 32:8ᴬEx 20:3, 4, 23 ᴮ1 Kin 12:28
32:9ᴬIs 48:4; Acts 7:51 32:10ᴬDeut 9:14
ᴮNum 14:12 32:11ᴬDeut 9:18, 26 32:12ᴬDeut 9:28;
Josh 7:9 32:13ᴬHeb 6:13 ᴮGen 26:4
32:14ᴬPs 106:45 32:15ᴬDeut 9:15 ᴮEx 31:18
32:19ᴬEx 32:6; Deut 9:16

he threw the tablets from his hands and shattered them to pieces at the foot of the mountain. ²⁰ Then ^Ahe took the calf which they had made and completely burned *it* with fire, and ground it to powder, and scattered it over the surface of the water and made the sons of Israel drink *it.*

²¹ Then Moses said to Aaron, "What did this people do to you, that you have brought *such* a great sin upon them?" ²² And Aaron said, "Do not let the anger of my lord burn; you know the people yourself, ^Athat they are prone to evil. ²³ For ^Athey said to me, 'Make a god for us who will go before us; for this Moses, the man who brought us up from the land of Egypt—we do not know what happened to him.' ²⁴ So I said to them, 'Whoever has any gold, let them tear it off.' Then they gave *it* to me, and ^AI threw it into the fire, and out came this calf."

²⁵ Now when Moses saw that the people were out of control—for Aaron had ^Alet them get out of control to *the point of being* an object of ridicule among their enemies— ²⁶ Moses then stood at the gate of the camp, and said, "Whoever is for the LORD, *come* to me!" And all the sons of Levi gathered together to him. ²⁷ And he said to them, "This is what the LORD, the God of Israel says: 'Every man *of you* put his sword on his thigh, and go back and forth from gate to gate in the camp, and kill every man his brother, and every man his friend, and every man his neighbor.'" ²⁸ So ^Athe sons of Levi did as Moses instructed, and about three thousand men of the people fell that day. ²⁹ Then Moses said, "Dedicate yourselves today to the LORD—for every man has been against his son and against his brother—in order that He may bestow a blessing upon you today."

³⁰ And on the next day Moses said to the people, "^AYou yourselves have committed a great sin; and now I am going up to the LORD; perhaps I can ^Bmake atonement for your sin." ³¹ Then Moses returned to the LORD and said, "Oh, this people has committed a great sin, and they have made a ^Agod of gold for themselves! ³² But now, if You will forgive their sin, *very well;* but if not, please wipe me out from Your ^Abook which You have written!" ³³ However, the LORD said to Moses, "Whoever has sinned against Me, ^AI will wipe him out of My book. ³⁴ But go now, lead the people ^Awhere I told you. Behold, ^BMy angel shall go before you; nevertheless on the day when I punish, I will punish them for their sin." ³⁵ ^AThen the LORD struck the people *with a plague,* because of what they did with the calf which Aaron had made.

THE JOURNEY RESUMED

33 Then the LORD spoke to Moses, "Depart, go up from here, you and the people whom you have brought up from the land of Egypt, to the land of which ^AI swore to Abraham, Isaac, and Jacob, saying, '^BTo your descendants I will give it.' ² And I will send an angel before you and ^AI will drive out the Canaanite, the Amorite, the Hittite, the Perizzite, the Hivite, and the Jebusite. ³ *Go up* to a land flowing with milk and honey; for I will

32:20 ^ADeut 9:21   32:22 ^ADeut 9:24   32:23 ^AEx 32:1-4   32:24 ^AEx 32:4   32:25 ^A1 Kin 12:28-30; 14:16   32:28 ^ANum 25:7-13; Deut 33:9   32:30 ^A1 Sam 12:20, 23   ^BNum 25:13   32:31 ^AEx 20:23   32:32 ^ADan 12:1; Mal 3:16, 17   32:33 ^APs 9:5; Rev 3:5   32:34 ^AEx 3:17   ^BEx 23:20   32:35 ^AEx 32:28   33:1 ^AEx 32:13   ^BGen 12:7   33:2 ^AEx 23:27-31; Josh 24:11

not go up in your midst, because you are ^an obstinate people, and I might destroy you on the way."

⁴When the people heard this sad word, ^they went into mourning, and none of them put on his jewelry. ⁵For the LORD had said to Moses, "Say to the sons of Israel, 'You are ^an obstinate people; *if* I were to go up in your midst for *just* one moment, I would destroy you. So now, take off your jewelry that I may know what I shall do to you.'" ⁶So the sons of Israel stripped themselves of their jewelry, from Mount Horeb *onward.*

⁷Now Moses used to take the tent and pitch it outside the camp, a good distance from the camp, and he called it the tent of meeting. And ^everyone who sought the LORD would go out to the tent of meeting which was outside the camp. ⁸And it came about, whenever Moses went out to the tent, that all the people would arise and stand, each at the entrance of his tent, and gaze after Moses until he entered the tent. ⁹Whenever Moses entered the tent, ^the pillar of cloud would descend and stand at the entrance of the tent; ᴮand the LORD would speak with Moses. ¹⁰When all the people saw the pillar of cloud standing at the entrance of the tent, all the people would stand and worship, each at the entrance of his tent. ¹¹So ^the LORD used to speak to Moses face to face, just as a man speaks to his friend. When Moses returned to the camp, his servant Joshua, the son of Nun, a young man, would not depart from the tent.

MOSES INTERCEDES

¹²Then Moses said to the LORD, "See, You say to me, '^Bring up this people!' But You Yourself have not let me know whom You will send with me. ᴮMoreover, You have said, 'I have known you by name, and you have also found favor in My sight.' ¹³Now then, if I have found favor in Your sight in any way, please ^let me know Your ways so that I may know You, in order that I may find favor in Your sight. Consider too, that this nation is Your people." ¹⁴And He said, "^My presence shall go *with you,* and I will give you rest." ¹⁵Then he said to Him, "^If Your presence does not go *with us,* do not lead us up from here. ¹⁶For how then can it be known that I have found favor in Your sight, I and Your people? Is it not by Your going with us, so that ^we, I and Your people, may be distinguished from all the *other* people who are on the face of the earth?"

¹⁷The LORD said to Moses, "I will also do this thing of which you have spoken; ^for you have found favor in My sight and I have known you by name." ¹⁸^Then *Moses* said, "Please, show me Your glory!" ¹⁹And He said, "^I Myself will make all My goodness pass before you, and will proclaim the name of the LORD before you; and ᴮI will be gracious to whom I will be gracious, and will show compassion to whom I will show compassion." ²⁰He further said, "You cannot see My face, ^for mankind shall not see Me and live!" ²¹Then the LORD said, "Behold, there is a place by

33:3 ^Ex 32:9; 33:5   33:4 ^Num 14:1, 39   33:5 ^Ex 33:3
33:7 ^Ex 29:42f   33:9 ^Ex 13:21   ᴮPs 99:7
33:11 ^Num 12:8; Deut 34:10   33:12 ^Ex 3:10
ᴮEx 33:17   33:13 ^Ps 25:4; 119:33   33:14 ^Deut 4:37;
Is 63:9   33:15 ^Ps 80:3, 7, 19   33:16 ^Lev 20:24, 26
33:17 ^Ex 33:12   33:18 ^Ex 33:20-23   33:19 ^Ex 34:6, 7
ᴮRom 9:15   33:20 ^Is 6:5; 1 Tim 6:16

Me, and ^you shall stand *there* on the rock; ²²and it will come about, while My glory is passing by, that I will put you in the cleft of the rock and ^cover you with My hand until I have passed by. ²³Then I will take My hand away and you shall see My back, but ^My face shall not be seen."

THE TWO TABLETS REPLACED

34 Now the LORD said to Moses, "Cut out for yourself two stone tablets like the former ones, and ^I will write on the tablets the words that were on the former tablets which you smashed. ²So be ready by morning, and come up in the morning to ^Mount Sinai, and present yourself there to Me on the top of the mountain. ³And ^no one is to come up with you, nor let anyone be seen anywhere on the mountain; even the flocks and the herds are not to graze in front of that mountain." ⁴So he cut out ^two stone tablets like the former ones, and Moses got up early in the morning and went up to Mount Sinai, as the LORD had commanded him, and he took *the* two stone tablets in his hand. ⁵And ^the LORD descended in the cloud and stood there with him as he called upon the name of the LORD. ⁶Then the LORD passed by in front of him and proclaimed, "The LORD, the LORD God, ^compassionate and merciful, slow to anger, and abounding in faithfulness and truth; ⁷who ^keeps faithfulness for thousands, who forgives wrongdoing, violation *of His Law,* and sin; yet He will by no means leave *the guilty* unpunished, inflicting the ¹punishment of fathers on the children and on the grandchildren to the third and fourth generations."

⁸And Moses hurried ^to bow low toward the ground and worship. ⁹Then he said, "If in any way I have found favor in Your sight, Lord, please may the Lord go along in our midst, even though the people are so obstinate, and ^pardon our wrongdoing and our sin, and ᴮtake us as Your own possession."

THE COVENANT RENEWED

¹⁰Then God said, "Behold, ^I am going to make a covenant. Before all your people ᴮI will perform miracles which have not been produced in all the earth nor among any of the nations; and all the people among whom you live will see the working of the LORD, for it is a fearful thing that I am going to perform with you.

¹¹"Be sure to comply with what I am commanding you this day: behold, ^I am going to drive out the Amorite from you, and the Canaanite, the Hittite, the Perizzite, the Hivite, and the Jebusite. ¹²^Be careful that you do not make a covenant with the inhabitants of the land into which you are going, or it will become a snare in your midst. ¹³^But *rather,* you are to tear down their altars and smash their memorial stones, and cut down their ¹Asherim ¹⁴—for ^you shall not worship any other god, because the LORD, whose name is Jealous, is a jealous God— ¹⁵otherwise you might make a covenant

33:21^Ps 18:2, 46; 62:7   33:22^Ps 91:1, 4; Is 49:2
33:23^Ex 33:20; John 1:18   34:1^Deut 10:2, 4
34:2^Ex 19:11, 18, 20   34:3^Ex 19:12, 13
34:4^Ex 34:1   34:5^Ex 19:9; 33:9   34:6^Joel 2:13;
Rom 2:4   34:7^Ps 103:3; 1 John 1:9   34:8^Ex 4:31
34:9^Ex 34:7   ᴮPs 33:12   34:10^Deut 5:2   ᴮPs 72:18
34:11^Ex 33:2   34:12^Ex 23:32, 33   34:13^Ex 23:24;
Deut 12:3   34:14^Ex 20:3, 5; Deut 4:24

34:7 ¹I.e., punishment for the wrongdoing   34:13 ¹I.e., wooden symbols of a female deity (Asherah)

with the inhabitants of the land, and they would prostitute themselves with their gods and ^sacrifice to their gods, and someone might invite you to eat of his sacrifice, [16]and ^you might take some of his daughters for your sons, and his daughters might prostitute themselves with their gods and cause your sons *also* to prostitute themselves with their gods. [17]^You shall not make for yourself *any* gods cast in metal.

[18]"You shall keep ^the Feast of Unleavened Bread. For seven days you are to eat unleavened bread, as I commanded you, at the appointed time in the month of Abib; for in the month of Abib you came out of Egypt.

[19]"^The firstborn from every womb belongs to Me, and all your male livestock, the firstborn from cattle and sheep. [20]You shall redeem with a lamb the firstborn from a donkey; and if you do not redeem *it,* then you shall break its neck. You shall redeem ^all the firstborn of your sons. None are to appear before Me empty-handed.

[21]"You shall work ^six days, but on the seventh day you shall rest; *even* during plowing time and harvest you shall rest. [22]And you shall celebrate ^the Feast of Weeks, *that is,* the first fruits of the wheat harvest, and the Feast of Ingathering at the turn of the year. [23]^Three times a year all your males are to appear before the Lord GOD, the God of Israel. [24]For I will ^drive out nations from you and enlarge your borders, and no one will covet your land when you go up three times a year to appear before the LORD your God.

[25]"^You shall not offer the blood of My sacrifice with leavened bread, [B]nor is the sacrifice of the Feast of the Passover to be left over until morning.

[26]"You shall bring ^the very first of the first fruits of your soil into the house of the LORD your God.

"You shall not boil a young goat in its mother's milk."

[27]Then the LORD said to Moses, "^Write down these words, for in accordance with these words I have made a covenant with you and with Israel." [28]So he was there with the LORD for forty days and forty nights; he did not eat bread or drink water. And [1,A]He wrote on the tablets the words of the covenant, [B]the Ten Commandments.

MOSES' FACE SHINES

[29]And it came about, when Moses was coming down from Mount Sinai (and the two tablets of the testimony *were* in Moses' hand as he was coming down from the mountain), that Moses did not know that ^the skin of his face shone because of his speaking with Him. [30]So when Aaron and all the sons of Israel saw Moses, behold, the skin of his face shone, and ^they were afraid to approach him. [31]Then Moses called to them, and Aaron and all the rulers in the congregation returned to him; and Moses spoke to them. [32]Afterward all the sons of Israel came near, and he commanded them *to do* everything that the LORD had

34:15 ^Ex 22:20; 32:8   34:16 ^Josh 23:12, 13; 1 Kin 11:1-4   34:17 ^Lev 19:4; Deut 5:8   34:18 ^Lev 23:6; Num 28:16f   34:19 ^Ex 13:2; 22:29f   34:20 ^Ex 13:15; Num 3:45   34:21 ^Lev 23:3; Deut 5:13f
34:22 ^Ex 23:16; Num 28:26   34:23 ^Ex 23:14-17
34:24 ^Ex 33:2; Ps 78:55   34:25 ^Ex 23:18   [B]Ex 12:10
34:26 ^Ex 23:19; Deut 26:2   34:27 ^Ex 17:14; 24:4
34:28 ^Ex 31:18   [B]Deut 4:13   34:29 ^Matt 17:2; 2 Cor 3:7   34:30 ^2 Cor 3:7
_____
34:28 [1]I.e., the LORD

spoken to him on Mount Sinai. [33] When Moses had finished speaking with them, [A]he put a veil over his face. [34] But whenever Moses went in before the LORD to speak with Him, [A]he would take off the veil until he came out; and whenever he came out and spoke to the sons of Israel what he had been commanded, [35][A]the sons of Israel would see the face of Moses, that the skin of Moses' face shone. So Moses would put the veil back over his face until he went in to speak with Him.

THE SABBATH EMPHASIZED

35 Then Moses assembled all the congregation of the sons of Israel, and said to them, "[A]These are the things that the LORD has commanded *you* to do:

[2] "For six days work may be done, but on the seventh day you shall have a holy *day*, [A]a Sabbath of complete rest to the LORD; [B]whoever does any work on it shall be put to death. [3][A]You shall not kindle a fire in any of your dwellings on the Sabbath day."

[4] Moses spoke to all the congregation of the sons of Israel, saying, "This is the thing which the LORD has commanded, saying, [5][A]Take from among you a contribution to the LORD; whoever is of a willing heart is to bring it as the LORD's contribution: gold, silver, and bronze, [6] and [1]violet, purple, and scarlet *material,* fine linen, goats' hair, [7] and rams' skins dyed red, and [1]fine leather, and acacia wood, [8] and oil for lighting, and spices for the anointing oil, and for the fragrant incense, [9] and onyx stones and setting stones for the ephod and for the breastpiece.

TABERNACLE ARTISANS

[10] "[A]Have every skillful person among you come and make all that the LORD has commanded: [11] the [A]tabernacle, its tent and its covering, its hooks and its boards, its bars, its pillars, and its bases; [12] the [A]ark and its poles, the [1]atoning cover, and the covering curtain; [13] the [A]table and its poles, and all its utensils, and the bread of the Presence; [14] the [A]lampstand also for the light and its utensils and its lamps, and the oil for the light; [15] and the [A]altar of incense and its poles, and the anointing oil and the [B]fragrant incense, and the curtain for the doorway at the entrance of the tabernacle; [16][A]the altar of burnt offering with its bronze grating, its poles, and all its utensils, the basin and its stand; [17][A]the hangings of the courtyard, its pillars and its bases, and the curtain for the gate of the courtyard; [18] the pegs of the tabernacle and the pegs of the courtyard and their ropes; [19] the [A]woven garments for ministering in the Holy Place, the holy garments for Aaron the priest and the garments of his sons, to serve as priests.'"

GIFTS RECEIVED

[20] Then all the congregation of the sons of Israel departed from Moses' presence. [21] And [A]everyone whose heart stirred him and

34:33 [A]2 Cor 3:13   34:34 [A]2 Cor 3:16   34:35 [A]2 Cor 3:13
35:1 [A]Ex 34:32   35:2 [A]Ex 16:23   [B]Num 15:32-36
35:3 [A]Ex 12:16; 16:23   35:5 [A]Ex 25:1-9   35:10 [A]Ex 31:6
35:11 [A]Ex 26:1-30   35:12 [A]Ex 25:10-22
35:13 [A]Ex 25:23-30   35:14 [A]Ex 25:31ff
35:15 [A]Ex 30:1-6   [B]Ex 30:34-38   35:16 [A]Ex 27:1-8
35:17 [A]Ex 27:9-18   35:19 [A]Ex 31:10; 39:1
35:21 [A]Ex 25:2; 36:2

35:6 [1]Or *bluish;* LXX *hyacinth* in color, and so throughout the ch   35:7 [1]Meaning of the Heb uncertain, and so throughout the ch   35:12 [1]Also called *mercy seat;* i.e., where blood was sprinkled on the Day of Atonement

everyone whose spirit moved him came *and* brought the Lord's contribution for the work of the tent of meeting and for all its service, and for the holy garments. [22]Then all whose hearts moved them, both men and women, came *and* brought brooches and earrings and signet rings and bracelets, all articles of gold; so *did* everyone who presented an offering of gold to the Lord. [23]Everyone who was in possession of violet, purple, or scarlet *material* or fine linen or goats' *hair,* or rams' skins dyed red or fine leather, brought them. [24]Everyone who could make a contribution of silver and bronze brought the Lord's contribution; and everyone who was in possession of acacia wood for any work of the service brought it. [25]And all the skilled women spun with their hands, and brought what they had spun, *in* violet, purple, *and* scarlet *material,* and *in* fine linen. [26]And all the women whose heart stirred with a skill spun the goats' *hair.* [27]The rulers, moreover, brought the onyx stones and the stones for setting for the ephod and for the breastpiece; [28]and ^the spice and the oil for the light and for the anointing oil, and for the fragrant incense. [29]The Israelites, all the men and women, whose heart moved them to bring *material* for all the work, which the Lord had commanded through Moses to be done, brought a ^voluntary offering to the Lord.

[30]^Then Moses said to the sons of Israel, "See, the Lord has called by name Bezalel the son of Uri, the son of Hur, of the tribe of Judah. [31]And He has filled him with the Spirit of God, in wisdom, in understanding, in knowledge, and in all craftsmanship; [32]to create designs for working in gold, in silver, and in bronze, [33]and in the cutting of stones for settings and in the carving of wood, so as to perform in every inventive work. [34]He also has put in his heart to teach, both he and ^Oholiab, the son of Ahisamach, of the tribe of Dan. [35]^He has filled them with skill to perform every work of an engraver, of a designer, and of an embroiderer, in violet, purple, *and* in scarlet *material,* and in fine linen, and of a weaver, as performers of every work and makers of designs.

THE TABERNACLE UNDERWRITTEN

36 "Now Bezalel, Oholiab, and every skillful person in whom the Lord has put skill and understanding to know how to perform all the work in the construction of the sanctuary, shall perform in accordance with everything that the Lord has commanded."

[2]Then Moses called Bezalel, Oholiab, and every skillful person in whom the Lord had put skill, ^everyone whose heart stirred him, to come to the work to perform it. [3]They received from Moses every contribution which the sons of Israel had brought to perform the work in the construction of the sanctuary. And they still *continued* bringing to him voluntary offerings every morning. [4]And all the skillful people who were performing all the work of the sanctuary came, each from the work which they were performing, [5]and they said to Moses, "^The people are bringing much more than enough for

35:28^Ex 30:23ff   35:29^Ex 35:21; 1 Chr 29:9
35:30^Ex 31:1-6   35:34^Ex 31:6   35:35^Ex 31:3, 6;
1 Kin 7:14   36:2^Ex 35:21, 26   36:5^2 Chr 24:14; 31:6-10

the construction work which the LORD commanded *us* to perform." ⁶So Moses issued a command, and circulated a proclamation throughout the camp, saying, "No man or woman is to perform work any longer for the contributions of the sanctuary." So the people were restrained from bringing *any more.* ⁷ᴬFor the material they had was sufficient and more than enough for all the work, to perform it.

CONSTRUCTION BEGINS

⁸ᴬAll the skillful people among those who were performing the work made the tabernacle with ten curtains; of fine twisted linen and ¹violet, purple, and scarlet *material,* with cherubim, the work of a skilled embroiderer, Bezalel made them. ⁹The length of each curtain was ¹twenty-eight cubits, and the width of each curtain four cubits; all the curtains had the same measurements. ¹⁰He joined five curtains to one another, and *the other* five curtains he joined to one another. ¹¹And he made loops of violet on the edge of the outermost curtain in the first set; he did likewise on the edge of the curtain that was outermost in the second set. ¹²He made ᴬfifty loops in the one curtain, and he made fifty loops on the edge of the curtain that was in the second set; the loops were opposite each other. ¹³He also made ᴬfifty clasps of gold, and joined the curtains to one another with the clasps, so that the tabernacle was a unit.

¹⁴Then ᴬhe made curtains of goats' *hair* for a tent over the tabernacle; he made eleven curtains *in all.* ¹⁵The length of each curtain *was* thirty cubits, and four cubits *was* the width of each curtain; the eleven curtains had the same measurements. ¹⁶He joined five curtains by themselves, and *the other* six curtains by themselves. ¹⁷Moreover, he made fifty loops on the edge of the curtain that was outermost in the *first* set, and he made fifty loops on the edge of the curtain *that was outermost in* the second set. ¹⁸He also made fifty clasps of bronze to join the tent together so that it would be a unit. ¹⁹And he made a covering for the tent of rams' skins dyed red, and a covering of ¹fine leather above.

²⁰ᴬThen he made the boards for the tabernacle of acacia wood, standing upright. ²¹Ten cubits *was* the length of each board, and one and a half cubits the width of each board. ²² *There were* two tenons for each board, fitted to one another; he did this to all the boards of the tabernacle. ²³So he made the boards for the tabernacle: twenty boards for the south side; ²⁴and he made forty bases of silver under the twenty boards; two bases under one board for its two tenons, and two bases under another board for its two tenons. ²⁵Then for the second side of the tabernacle, on the north side, he made twenty boards, ²⁶and their forty bases of silver; two bases under one board, and two bases under another board. ²⁷And for the back of the tabernacle, to the west, he made six boards. ²⁸He made two boards for the corners of the tabernacle at the back. ²⁹They

36:7ᴬ1 Kin 8:64   36:8ᴬEx 26:1-14   36:12ᴬEx 26:5
36:13ᴬEx 26:6   36:14ᴬEx 26:7-14   36:20ᴬEx 26:15-29

36:8 ¹Or *bluish;* LXX *hyacinth* in color, and so throughout the ch   36:9 ¹About 42 ft. long and 6 ft. wide or 13 m and 1.8 m   36:19 ¹Meaning of the Heb uncertain

were double beneath, and together they were complete to its top, to the first ring; he did this with both of them for the two corners. ³⁰There were eight boards with their bases of silver, sixteen bases, two bases under every board.

³¹Then he made ᴬbars of acacia wood, five for the boards of one side of the tabernacle, ³²and five bars for the boards of the other side of the tabernacle, and five bars for the boards of the tabernacle for the back *side* to the west. ³³And he made the middle bar to pass through in the center of the boards from end to end. ³⁴Then he overlaid the boards with gold, and made their rings of gold *as* holders for the bars, and overlaid the bars with gold.

³⁵ᴬMoreover, he made the veil of violet, purple, and scarlet *material,* and fine twisted linen; he made it with cherubim, the work of a skilled embroiderer. ³⁶And he made four pillars of acacia for it, and overlaid them with gold, with their hooks of gold; and he cast four bases of silver for them. ³⁷He also made a ᴬcurtain for the doorway of the tent, of violet, purple, and scarlet *material,* and fine twisted linen, the work of a weaver; ³⁸and *he made* its ᴬfive pillars with their hooks, and he overlaid their tops and their bands with gold; but their five bases were of bronze.

CONSTRUCTION CONTINUES

37 ᴬNow Bezalel made the ark of acacia wood; its length was two and a half cubits, its width one and a half cubits, and its height one and a half cubits; ²and he overlaid it with pure gold inside and out, and made a gold molding for it all around. ³He cast four rings of

gold for it on its four feet; two rings on one side of it, and two rings on the other side of it. ⁴And he made poles of acacia wood and overlaid them with gold. ⁵He put the poles into the rings on the sides of the ark, to carry it. ⁶He also made ¹an atoning cover of pure gold, two and a half cubits long and one and a half cubits wide. ⁷And he made two cherubim of gold; he made them of hammered work at the two ends of the atoning cover: ⁸one cherub at the one end and one cherub at the other end; he made the cherubim *of one piece* with the atoning cover at the two ends. ⁹And the cherubim had *their* wings spread upward, covering the atoning cover with their wings, with their faces toward each other; the faces of the cherubim were toward the atoning cover.

¹⁰ᴬThen he made the table of acacia wood, two cubits long, a cubit wide, and one and a half cubits high. ¹¹He overlaid it with pure gold, and made a gold molding for it all around. ¹²And he made a rim for it of a ¹hand width all around, and made a gold molding for its rim all around. ¹³He also cast four gold rings for it and put the rings on the four corners that were on its four legs. ¹⁴Close by the rim were the rings, the holders for the poles to carry the table. ¹⁵And he made the poles of acacia wood and overlaid them with gold, to carry the table. ¹⁶He also made the utensils which were on the table, its dishes,

36:31ᴬEx 26:26-29   36:35ᴬEx 26:31-37
36:37ᴬEx 26:36   36:38ᴬEx 26:37   37:1ᴬEx 25:10-20
37:10ᴬEx 25:23-29

37:6¹Also called *a mercy seat,* and so throughout the ch; i.e., where blood was sprinkled on the Day of Atonement   37:12¹About 3 in. or 7.5 cm

its pans, its libation bowls, and its jars, with which to pour out drink offerings, of pure gold.

17ᴬThen he made the lampstand of pure gold. He made the lampstand of hammered work, its base and its shaft; its cups, its bulbs, and its flowers were *of one piece* with it. 18There were six branches going out of its sides; three branches of the lampstand from the one side of it and three branches of the lampstand from the other side of it; 19three cups shaped like almond *blossoms,* a bulb and a flower on one branch, and three cups shaped like almond *blossoms,* a bulb and a flower on the other branch—so for the six branches going out of the lampstand. 20And on the lampstand *there were* four cups shaped like almond *blossoms,* its bulbs and its flowers; 21and a bulb was under the *first* pair of branches *coming* out of it, and a bulb under the *second* pair of branches *coming* out of it, and a bulb under the *third* pair of branches *coming* out of it, for the six branches coming out of the lampstand. 22Their bulbs and their branches were *of one piece* with it; the whole of it *was* a single hammered work of pure gold. 23And he made its seven lamps with its tongs and its trays of pure gold. 24He made it and all its utensils from a ¹talent of pure gold.

25ᴬThen he made the altar of incense of acacia wood: a cubit long and a cubit wide, square, and two cubits high; its horns were *of one piece* with it. 26And he overlaid it with pure gold, its top and its sides all around, and its horns; and he made a gold molding for it all around. 27He also made two golden rings for it under its molding, on its

two sides—on opposite sides—as holders for poles with which to carry it. 28And he made the poles of acacia wood and overlaid them with gold. 29ᴬThen he made the holy anointing oil and the pure, fragrant incense of spices, the work of a perfumer.

THE TABERNACLE COMPLETED

38 ᴬThen he made the altar of burnt offering of acacia wood, five cubits long, and five cubits wide, square, and three cubits high. 2And he made its horns on its four corners, its horns being *of one piece* with it, and he overlaid it with bronze. 3He also made all the utensils of the altar, the pails, the shovels, the basins, the meat-forks, and the firepans; he made all its utensils of bronze. 4And he made for the altar a grating of bronze netting beneath, under its ledge, reaching halfway up. 5He also cast four rings on the four ends of the bronze grating *as* holders for the poles. 6He made the poles of acacia wood and overlaid them with bronze. 7Then he inserted the poles into the rings on the sides of the altar, with which to carry it. He made it hollow with planks.

8ᴬMoreover, he made the basin of bronze with its base of bronze, from the mirrors of the serving women who served at the doorway of the tent of meeting.

9ᴬThen he made the courtyard: for the south side the hangings of the courtyard were of fine twisted linen, a hundred cubits; 10their twenty pillars, and their twenty

bases, *were made* of bronze; the hooks of the pillars and their bands *were* of silver. ¹¹For the north side *there were* a hundred cubits; their twenty pillars and their twenty bases *were* of bronze, the hooks of the pillars and their bands *were* of silver. ¹²For the west side *there were* hangings of fifty cubits *with* their ten pillars and their ten bases; the hooks of the pillars and their bands *were* of silver. ¹³For the east side, fifty cubits. ¹⁴The hangings for the *one* side *of the gate were* fifteen cubits, *with* their three pillars and their three bases, ¹⁵and so for the other side. On both sides of the gate of the courtyard *were* hangings of fifteen cubits, *with* their three pillars and their three bases. ¹⁶All the hangings of the courtyard all around *were* of fine twisted linen. ¹⁷And the bases for the pillars *were* of bronze, the hooks of the pillars and their bands, of silver; and the overlaying of their tops, of silver, and all the pillars of the courtyard were furnished with silver bands. ¹⁸Now the curtain of the gate of the courtyard was the work of the weaver, of ¹violet, purple, and scarlet *material* and fine twisted linen. And the length *was* twenty cubits and the height *was* five cubits, corresponding to the hangings of the courtyard. ¹⁹Their four pillars and their four bases *were* of bronze; their hooks *were* of silver, and the overlaying of their tops and their bands *were* of silver. ²⁰All the pegs of the tabernacle and of the courtyard all around *were* of bronze.

THE COST OF THE TABERNACLE

²¹This is the number of the things for the tabernacle, the tabernacle of the testimony, as they were counted according to the command of Moses, for the service of the Levites, by the hand of Ithamar the son of Aaron the priest. ²²Now ^Bezalel the son of Uri, the son of Hur, of the tribe of Judah, made everything that the Lᴏʀᴅ had commanded Moses. ²³With him *was* ^Oholiab the son of Ahisamach, of the tribe of Dan, an engraver and a skilled embroiderer, and a weaver in violet, in purple, and in scarlet *material,* and fine linen.

²⁴All the gold that was used for the work, in all the work of the sanctuary, which was the gold of the wave offering, was twenty-nine ¹talents and 730 ²shekels, according to ^the shekel of the sanctuary. ²⁵And ^the silver of those of the congregation who were counted was a hundred talents and 1,775 shekels, according to the shekel of the sanctuary; ²⁶^a beka a head (*that is,* half a shekel according to the shekel of the sanctuary), *assessed* to each one who passed over to those who were counted, from twenty years old and upward, for 603,550 men. ²⁷The hundred talents of silver were *used* for casting the bases of the sanctuary and the bases of the veil; a hundred bases for the hundred talents, a talent for a base. ²⁸And of the 1,775 *shekels,* he made hooks for the pillars, and overlaid their tops and made bands for them. ²⁹And the bronze of the wave offering was seventy talents and 2,400 shekels. ³⁰With it he made the bases to

38:22^Ex 31:2   **38:23**^Ex 31:6   **38:24**^Lev 27:25; Num 18:16   **38:25**^Ex 30:11-16   **38:26**^Ex 30:13, 15

38:18¹Or *bluish;* LXX *hyacinth* in color, and so throughout the ch   **38:24**¹A talent was about 75 lb. or 34 kg   ²A shekel was about 0.4 oz. or 11 gm

the doorway of the tent of meeting, and the bronze altar and its bronze grating, and all the utensils of the altar, ³¹and the bases of the courtyard all around and the bases of the gate of the courtyard, and all the pegs of the tabernacle and all the pegs of the courtyard all around.

THE PRIESTLY GARMENTS

39 Now from the ¹violet, purple, and scarlet *material* they made finely ^woven garments for ministering in the Holy Place, as well as the holy garments which were for Aaron, just as the Lord had commanded Moses.

²^He made the ephod of gold *and* of violet, purple, and scarlet *material,* and fine twisted linen. ³Then they hammered out gold sheets and cut *them* into threads to be woven in *with* the violet, the purple, and the scarlet *material,* and the fine linen, the work of a skilled embroiderer. ⁴They made attaching shoulder pieces for the ephod; it was attached at its two *upper* ends. ⁵And the skillfully woven band of its overlay which was on it was like its workmanship, of the same material: of gold *and* of violet, purple, and scarlet *material,* and fine twisted linen, just as the Lord had commanded Moses.

⁶^They also made the onyx stones, set in gold filigree *settings;* they were engraved *like* the engravings of a signet, according to the names of the sons of Israel. ⁷And ^he placed them on the shoulder pieces of the ephod *as* memorial stones for the sons of Israel, just as the Lord had commanded Moses.

⁸And ^he made the breastpiece, the work of a skilled embroiderer,

like the workmanship of the ephod: of gold *and* of violet, purple, and scarlet *material* and fine twisted linen. ⁹It was square; they made the breastpiece folded double, a ¹span long and a span wide when folded double. ¹⁰And they mounted four rows of stones on it. The first row *was* a row of ruby, topaz, and emerald; ¹¹and the second row, a turquoise, a sapphire, and a diamond; ¹²and the third row, a jacinth, an agate, and an amethyst; ¹³and the fourth row, a beryl, an onyx, and a jasper. They were set in gold filigree *settings* when they were mounted. ¹⁴The stones corresponded to the names of the sons of Israel; they were twelve, corresponding to their names, *engraved with* the engravings of a signet, each with its name for the twelve tribes. ¹⁵And they made for the breastpiece chains like cords, work of twisted cords of pure gold. ¹⁶They made two gold filigree *settings* and two gold rings, and put the two rings on the two ends of the breastpiece. ¹⁷Then they put the two gold cords in the two rings at the ends of the breastpiece. ¹⁸And they put the *other* two ends of the two cords on the two filigree *settings,* and put them on the shoulder pieces of the ephod at the front of it. ¹⁹They made two gold rings and placed *them* on the two ends of the breastpiece, on its inner edge which was next to the ephod. ²⁰Furthermore, they made two gold rings and placed them on the bottom of the two shoulder pieces of the ephod, on the front of it, close to the place where it

39:1^Ex 31:10; 35:19   39:2^Ex 28:6-12   39:6^Ex 28:9-11
39:7^Ex 28:12   39:8^Ex 28:15-28

39:1¹Or *bluish;* LXX *hyacinth* in color, and so throughout the ch   39:9¹About 9 in. or 23 cm

joined, above the woven band of the ephod. ²¹And they bound the breastpiece by its rings to the rings of the ephod with a violet cord, so that it would be on the woven band of the ephod, and that the breastpiece would not come loose from the ephod, just as the LORD had commanded Moses.

²²ᴬThen he made the robe of the ephod of woven work, all of violet; ²³ᴬand the opening of the robe was *at the top* in the center, as the opening of a coat of mail, with a binding all around its opening, so that it would not be torn. ²⁴And they made pomegranates of violet, purple, and scarlet *material and* twisted *linen* on the hem of the robe. ²⁵They also made bells of pure gold, and put the bells between the pomegranates all around on the hem of the robe, ²⁶alternating a bell and a pomegranate all around on the hem of the robe for the service, just as the LORD had commanded Moses.

²⁷ᴬThey also made the tunics of finely woven linen for Aaron and his sons, ²⁸and the turban of fine linen, and the decorated caps of fine linen, and the linen undergarments of fine twisted linen, ²⁹and the sash of fine twisted linen, and violet, purple, and scarlet *material,* the work of the weaver, just as the LORD had commanded Moses.

³⁰ᴬThey also made the plate of the holy crown of pure gold, and inscribed it like the engravings of a signet, "Holy to the LORD." ³¹Then they fastened a violet cord to it, to fasten it on the turban above, just as the LORD had commanded Moses.

³²So all the work of the tabernacle of the tent of meeting was completed; and the sons of Israel did according to all that the LORD had commanded Moses; so they did. ³³Then they brought the tabernacle to Moses, the tent and all its furnishings: its clasps, its boards, its bars, its pillars, and its bases; ³⁴and the covering of rams' skins dyed red, and the covering of ¹fine leather, and the covering curtain; ³⁵the ark of the testimony, its poles, and the ¹atoning cover; ³⁶the table, all its utensils, and the bread of the Presence; ³⁷the pure *gold* lampstand, with its arrangement of lamps and all its utensils, and the oil for the light; ³⁸and the gold altar, and the anointing oil and the fragrant incense, and the curtain for the doorway of the tent; ³⁹the bronze altar and its bronze grating, its poles and all its utensils, the basin and its stand; ⁴⁰the hangings for the courtyard, its pillars and its bases, and the curtain for the gate of the courtyard, its ropes and its pegs, and all the equipment for the service of the tabernacle, for the tent of meeting; ⁴¹the woven garments for ministering in the Holy Place, and the holy garments for Aaron the priest and the garments of his sons, to serve as priests. ⁴²So the sons of Israel did all the work according to everything that the LORD had commanded Moses. ⁴³And Moses examined all the work, and behold, they had done it; just as the LORD had commanded, this they had done. So Moses ᴬblessed them.

39:22ᴬEx 28:31, 34   39:23ᴬEx 28:32
39:27ᴬEx 28:39, 40, 42   39:30ᴬEx 28:36, 37
39:43ᴬLev 9:22, 23; Num 6:23-26

39:34¹Meaning of the Heb uncertain   39:35¹Also called *mercy seat;* i.e., where blood was sprinkled on the Day of Atonement

THE TABERNACLE ERECTED

40 Then the LORD spoke to Moses, saying, 2"^On the first day of the first month you shall set up the tabernacle of the tent of meeting. 3^You shall place the ark of the testimony there, and you shall screen off the ark with the veil. 4Then you shall ^bring in the table and arrange what belongs on it; and you shall bring in the lampstand and mount its lamps. 5You shall also ^set the gold altar of incense in front of the ark of the testimony, and set up the curtain for the doorway to the tabernacle. 6And you shall set the altar of burnt offering in front of the doorway of the tabernacle of the tent of meeting. 7Then you shall ^set the basin between the tent of meeting and the altar, and put water in it. 8You shall also set up the courtyard all around and hang up the curtain for the gate of the courtyard. 9Then you shall take the anointing oil and ^anoint the tabernacle and everything that is in it, and consecrate it and all its furnishings; and it shall be holy. 10You shall also anoint the altar of burnt offering and all its utensils, and consecrate the altar, and ^the altar shall be most holy. 11And you shall anoint the basin and its stand, and consecrate it. 12Then you shall ^bring Aaron and his sons to the doorway of the tent of meeting and wash them with water. 13And ^you shall put the holy garments on Aaron and anoint him and consecrate him, so that he may serve as a priest to Me. 14You shall also bring his sons and put tunics on them; 15and you shall anoint them just as you have anointed their father, so that they may serve as priests to

Me; and their anointing will qualify them for a ^permanent priesthood throughout their generations." 16So Moses did *these things;* according to all that the LORD had commanded him, so he did.

17Now ^in the first month of the second year, on the first *day* of the month, the tabernacle was erected. 18Moses erected the tabernacle and laid its bases, and set up its boards, and inserted its bars, and erected its pillars. 19And he spread the tent over the tabernacle and put the covering of the tent on top of it, just as the LORD had commanded Moses. 20Then he took ^the testimony and put *it* into the ark, and attached the poles to the ark, and put the 'atoning cover on top of the ark. 21He then brought the ark into the tabernacle, and ^set up a veil for the covering, and screened off the ark of the testimony, just as the LORD had commanded Moses. 22He also ^put the table in the tent of meeting on the north side of the tabernacle, outside the veil. 23And he set the arrangement of ^bread in order on it before the LORD, just as the LORD had commanded Moses. 24Then he placed the lampstand in the tent of meeting, opposite the table, on the south side of the tabernacle. 25And he ^lighted the lamps before the LORD, just as the LORD had commanded Moses. 26Then he ^placed the gold altar in the tent of meeting in front of the veil; 27and he

40:2^Ex 19:1; Num 1:1   40:3^Ex 26:33; Num 4:5
40:4^Ex 26:35; 40:22   40:5^Ex 40:26
40:7^Ex 30:18; 40:30   40:9^Ex 30:26; Lev 8:10
40:10^Ex 29:37   40:12^Lev 8:1-6   40:13^Ex 28:41;
Lev 8:13   40:15^Ex 29:9; Num 25:13   40:17^Ex 40:2
40:20^2 Chr 5:10; Heb 9:4   40:21^Ex 26:33
40:22^Ex 26:35   40:23^Ex 25:30; Lev 24:5, 6
40:25^Ex 25:37; 40:4   40:26^Ex 30:6; 40:5

40:20 ¹Also called *mercy seat;* i.e., where blood was sprinkled on the Day of Atonement

^Aburned fragrant incense on it, just as the LORD had commanded Moses. 28Then he set up the curtain for the doorway of the tabernacle. 29And he ^Aset the altar of burnt offering *in front of* the doorway of the tabernacle of the tent of meeting, and ^Boffered on it the burnt offering and the meal offering, just as the LORD had commanded Moses. 30He placed the basin between the tent of meeting and the altar, and put water in it for washing. 31AFrom it Moses and Aaron and his sons washed their hands and their feet. 32When they entered the tent of meeting, and when they approached the altar, they washed, just as the LORD had commanded Moses. 33And he ^Aerected the courtyard all around the tabernacle and the altar, and hung up the curtain for the gate of the courtyard. So Moses finished the work.

THE GLORY OF THE LORD

34AThen the cloud covered the tent of meeting, and the glory of the LORD filled the tabernacle. 35And Moses ^Awas not able to enter the tent of meeting because the cloud had settled on it, and the glory of the LORD filled the tabernacle. 36Throughout their journeys, ^Awhenever the cloud was taken up from over the tabernacle, the sons of Israel would set out; 37but ^Aif the cloud was not taken up, then they did not set out until the day when it was taken up. 38For throughout their journeys, ^Athe cloud of the LORD was on the tabernacle by day, and there was fire in it by night, in the sight of all the house of Israel.

40:27^AEx 30:7   40:29^AEx 40:6   ^BEx 29:38-42
40:31^AEx 30:19, 20   40:33^AEx 27:9-18; 40:8
40:34^ANum 9:15-23   40:35^A1 Kin 8:11; 2 Chr 5:13, 14
40:36^ANum 9:17; Neh 9:19   40:37^ANum 9:19-22
40:38^APs 78:14; Is 4:5

LEVITICUS

THE LAW OF BURNT OFFERINGS

1 Now ^the Lord called to Moses and spoke to him from the tent of meeting, saying, ²"Speak to the sons of Israel and say to them, 'When anyone of you brings an offering to the Lord, you shall bring your offering of livestock from ^the herd or the flock. ³If his offering is a ^burnt offering from the herd, he shall offer a male without defect; he shall offer it at the doorway of the tent of meeting, so that he may be accepted before the Lord. ⁴And ^he shall lay his hand on the head of the burnt offering, so that it may be accepted for him to make atonement on his behalf. ⁵Then he shall slaughter the bull before the Lord; and Aaron's sons the priests shall offer up ^the blood and ᴮsprinkle the blood around on the altar that is at the doorway of the tent of meeting. ⁶^He shall then skin the burnt offering and cut it into its pieces. ⁷And ^the sons of Aaron the priest shall put fire on the altar and arrange wood on the fire. ⁸Then Aaron's sons the priests shall arrange the pieces, *with* the head and the ^suet, on the wood which is on the fire that is on the altar. ⁹Its ^entrails, however, and its legs he shall wash with water. And ᴮthe priest shall offer all of it up in smoke on the altar as a burnt offering, an offering by fire as a soothing aroma to the Lord.

¹⁰'But if his offering is from the flock, *either* from the sheep or from the goats, as a burnt offering, he shall offer a ^male without defect. ¹¹And ^he shall slaughter it on the side of the altar northward before the Lord, and Aaron's sons the priests shall sprinkle its blood around on the altar. ¹²He shall then cut it into its pieces with its head and its ^suet, and the priest shall arrange them on the wood which is on the fire that is on the altar. ¹³The entrails, however, and the legs he shall wash with water. And ^the priest shall offer all of it, and offer it up in smoke on the altar; it is a burnt offering, an offering by fire of a soothing aroma to the Lord.

¹⁴'But if his offering to the Lord is a burnt offering of birds, then he shall bring his offering from the ^turtledoves or from young doves. ¹⁵The priest shall bring it to the altar, and pinch off its head, and offer it up in smoke on the altar; and its blood is to be drained out ^on the side of the altar. ¹⁶He shall also remove its craw with its feathers and throw it beside the altar eastward, to the place of the ^fatty ashes. ¹⁷Then he shall tear it by its wings, *but* ^shall not sever *it*. And the priest shall offer it up in smoke on the altar, on the wood which is on the fire; it is a burnt offering, an offering by fire of a soothing aroma to the Lord.

1:1^Ex 19:3; Num 7:89   1:2^Lev 22:18f   1:3^Lev 6:8-13   1:4^Ex 29:10, 15, 19; Lev 3:2, 8   1:5^Lev 17:11   ᴮHeb 12:24   1:6^Lev 7:8   1:7^Lev 6:8-13   1:8^Lev 3:3, 4; 8:20   1:9^Ex 12:9   ᴮNum 28:11-14   1:10^Ezek 43:22; 1 Pet 1:19   1:11^Ex 24:6; Lev 8:19   1:12^Lev 3:3, 4   1:13^Num 15:4-7; 28:11-14   1:14^Lev 5:7, 11; Luke 2:24   1:15^Lev 5:9   1:16^Lev 6:10   1:17^Gen 15:10; Lev 5:8

THE LAW OF GRAIN OFFERINGS

2 'Now when anyone presents a ^grain offering as an offering to the Lord, his offering shall be of fine flour, and he shall pour oil on it and put frankincense on it. ²He shall then bring it to Aaron's sons the priests; and he shall take from it ^his handful of its fine flour and of its oil, with all of its frankincense. And the priest shall offer *it* up in smoke *as* its memorial portion on the altar, an offering by fire of a soothing aroma to the Lord. ³^The remainder of the grain offering belongs to Aaron and his sons: a most holy part of the offerings to the Lord by fire.

⁴'Now when you bring an offering of a grain offering baked in an oven, *it shall be*^unleavened cakes of fine flour mixed with oil, or unleavened wafers spread with oil. ⁵And if your offering is a grain offering *made*^on the griddle, *it shall be* of fine flour, unleavened, mixed with oil; ⁶you shall break it into bits and pour oil on it; it is a grain offering. ⁷Now if your offering is a grain offering *made* ^in a pan, it shall be made of fine flour with oil. ⁸When you bring in the grain offering which is made of these things to the Lord, it shall be presented to the priest, and he shall bring it to the altar. ⁹The priest then shall take up from the grain offering ^its memorial portion, and shall offer *it* up in smoke on the altar *as* an offering by fire of a soothing aroma to the Lord. ¹⁰^The remainder of the grain offering belongs to Aaron and his sons: a most holy part of the offerings to the Lord by fire.

¹¹'^No grain offering, which you bring to the Lord, shall be made with leaven, for you shall not offer up in smoke any leaven or any honey as an offering by fire to the Lord. ¹²^As an offering of first fruits you shall bring them to the Lord, but they shall not ascend as a soothing aroma on the altar. ¹³Every grain offering of yours, moreover, you shall season with salt, so that ^the salt of the covenant of your God will not be lacking from your grain offering; with all your offerings you shall offer salt.

¹⁴'Also if you bring a grain offering of early ripened things to the Lord, you shall bring ^fresh heads of grain roasted in the fire, crushed grain of new growth, for the grain offering of your early ripened produce. ¹⁵You shall then put oil on it and place incense on it; it is a grain offering. ¹⁶Then the priest shall offer up in smoke ^its memorial portion, part of its crushed grain and its oil with all its incense as an offering by fire to the Lord.

THE LAW OF PEACE OFFERINGS

3 'Now if his offering is a sacrifice of peace offerings, if he is going to offer from the herd, whether male or female, he shall offer it ^without defect before the Lord. ²And ^he shall lay his hand on the head of his offering and ^slaughter it at the doorway of the tent of meeting, and Aaron's sons the priests shall sprinkle the blood around on the altar. ³From the sacrifice of the peace offerings he shall then present an offering by fire to the Lord, the fat that covers the

2:1^Lev 6:14-18; Num 15:4   2:2^Lev 5:12; 6:15   2:3^Lev 2:10; 6:16   2:4^Ex 29:2   2:5^Lev 6:21; 7:9   2:7^Lev 7:9   2:9^Lev 2:2, 16; 5:12   2:10^Lev 2:3; 6:16   2:11^Ex 34:25; Lev 6:16, 17   2:12^Ex 34:22; Lev 7:13   2:13^2 Chr 13:5; Ezek 43:24   2:14^Lev 23:14   2:16^Lev 2:2   3:1^Lev 1:3; 22:20-24   3:2^Lev 1:4   ^Ex 29:11, 16, 20

entrails and all the fat that is on the entrails, ⁴and the two kidneys with the fat that is on them, which is on the loins, and the lobe of the liver, which he shall remove with the kidneys. ⁵Then Aaron's sons shall offer it up in smoke on the altar ᴬon the burnt offering, which is on the wood that is on the fire; it is an offering by fire of a soothing aroma to the Lord. ⁶But if his offering for a sacrifice of peace offerings to the Lord is from the flock, he shall offer it, male or female, ᴬwithout defect. ⁷If he is going to offer a lamb for his offering, then he shall offer it ᴬbefore the Lord, ⁸and ᴬhe shall lay his hand on the head of his offering and ᴮslaughter it in front of the tent of meeting, and Aaron's sons shall sprinkle its blood around on the altar. ⁹From the ᴬsacrifice of peace offerings he shall then bring as an offering by fire to the Lord, its fat, the entire fat tail which he shall remove close to the backbone, the fat that covers the entrails, and all the fat that is on the entrails, ¹⁰and the two kidneys with the fat that is on them, which is on the loins, and the lobe of the liver, which he shall remove ᴬwith the kidneys. ¹¹Then the priest shall offer *it* up in smoke on the altar *as* ᴬfood, an offering by fire to the Lord.

¹²'Now if his offering is ᴬa goat, then he shall offer it before the Lord, ¹³and he shall lay his hand on its head and slaughter it in front of the tent of meeting, and the sons of Aaron shall sprinkle its blood around on the altar. ¹⁴From it he shall present his offering as an offering by fire to the Lord, the fat that covers the entrails and all the fat that is on the entrails, ¹⁵and the two kidneys with the fat that is

on them, which is on the loins, and the lobe of the liver, which he shall remove ᴬwith the kidneys. ¹⁶The priest shall offer them up in smoke on the altar *as* food, an offering by fire as a soothing aroma; ᴬall fat is the Lord's. ¹⁷It is a permanent statute throughout your generations in all your dwelling places: you shall not eat any fat ᴬor any blood.'"

THE LAW OF SIN OFFERINGS

4 Then the Lord spoke to Moses, saying, ²"Speak to the sons of Israel, saying, 'If a person sins ᴬunintentionally in any of the things which the Lord has commanded not to be done, and commits any of them, ³ᴬif the anointed priest sins so as to bring guilt on the people, then he is to offer to the Lord a bull without defect as a sin offering for his sin which he has committed. ⁴He shall bring the bull to the doorway of the tent of meeting before the Lord, and ᴬhe shall lay his hand on the head of the bull and slaughter the bull before the Lord. ⁵Then the ᴬanointed priest is to take some of the blood of the bull and bring it to the tent of meeting, ⁶and the priest shall dip his finger in the blood and sprinkle some of the blood seven times before the Lord, in front of ᴬthe veil of the sanctuary. ⁷The priest shall also put some of the blood on the horns of ᴬthe altar of fragrant incense which is before the Lord in the tent of meeting; and all *the rest of* the blood of the bull he shall pour out at the

3:5 ᴬEx 29:38-42; Num 28:3-10   3:6 ᴬLev 3:1; 22:20-24
3:7 ᴬLev 17:8, 9; 1 Kin 8:62   3:8 ᴬLev 1:4   ᴮLev 3:2
3:9 ᴬLev 17:5; Num 7:88   3:10 ᴬLev 3:4, 15
3:11 ᴬLev 3:16; 21:6, 8, 17, 22   3:12 ᴬNum 15:6-11
3:15 ᴬLev 3:4; 7:4   3:16 ᴬLev 7:23-25   3:17 ᴬLev 7:26;
17:10-16   4:2 ᴬLev 4:22, 27; 5:15-18
4:3 ᴬLev 4:14, 23, 28   4:4 ᴬLev 1:4; Num 8:12
4:5 ᴬLev 4:3, 17   4:6 ᴬEx 40:21, 26   4:7 ᴬLev 8:15; 16:18

base of the altar of burnt offering, which is at the doorway of the tent of meeting. 8 And ^he shall remove from it all the fat of the bull of the sin offering: the fat that covers the entrails, and all the fat which is on the entrails, 9 and the two kidneys with the fat that is on them, which is on the loins, and the lobe of the liver, which he shall remove ^with the kidneys 10 (just as it is removed from the ox of the sacrifice of peace offerings); and the priest is to offer them up in smoke on the altar of burnt offering. 11 But ^the hide of the bull and all its flesh, along with its head, its legs, its entrails, and its refuse, 12 that is, all *the rest of* the bull, he is to bring out to ^a clean place outside the camp where the fatty ashes are poured out, and burn it on wood with fire; where the fatty ashes are poured out it shall be burned.

13 '^Now if the entire congregation of Israel does wrong unintentionally and the matter escapes the notice of the assembly, and they commit any of the things which the Lord has commanded not to be done, and they become guilty; 14 when the sin which they have committed becomes known, then the assembly shall offer ^a bull of the herd as a sin offering and bring it in front of the tent of meeting. 15 Then ^the elders of the congregation shall lay their hands on the head of the bull before the Lord, and the bull shall be slaughtered before the Lord. 16 Then the anointed priest is to bring some of the blood of the bull to the tent of meeting; 17 and ^the priest shall dip his finger in the blood and sprinkle *it* seven times before the Lord, in front of the veil. 18 He shall then put some of the blood on the horns of ^the altar which is before the Lord in the tent of meeting; and all *the rest of* the blood he shall pour out at the base of the altar of burnt offering which is at the doorway of the tent of meeting. 19 And ^he shall remove all its fat from it and offer it up in smoke on the altar. 20 He shall also do with the bull just as he did with ^the bull of the sin offering; he shall do the same with it. So ^B the priest shall make atonement for them, and they will be forgiven. 21 Then he is to bring the bull out to *a place* outside the camp and burn it just as he burned the first bull; it is ^the sin offering for the assembly.

22 'When ^a leader sins and unintentionally does any of the things which the Lord his God has commanded not to be done, and he becomes guilty, 23 if his sin which he has committed is made known to him, he shall bring as his offering a ^goat, a male without defect. 24 And he shall lay his hand on the head of the male goat and slaughter it in the place where they slaughter the burnt offering before the Lord; it is a sin offering. 25 Then the priest is to take some of the blood of the sin offering with his finger and put it on ^the horns of the altar of burnt offering; and *the rest of* its blood he shall pour out at the base of the altar of burnt offering. 26 And he shall offer ^all its fat up in smoke on the altar as *in the case of* the fat of the sacrifice of peace offerings. So the priest shall make atonement

for him regarding his sin, and he will be forgiven.

27 'Now if anyone of the common people sins ^unintentionally by doing any of the things which the LORD has commanded not to be done, and becomes guilty, 28 if his sin which he has committed is made known to him, then he shall bring as his offering a ^goat, a female without defect, for his sin which he has committed. 29 And ^he shall lay his hand on the head of the sin offering and slaughter the sin offering at the place of the burnt offering. 30 The priest shall then take some of its blood with his finger and put it on the horns of ^the altar of burnt offering; and all *the rest of* its blood he shall pour out at the base of the altar. 31^Then he shall remove all its fat, just as the fat was removed from the sacrifice of peace offerings; and the priest shall offer it up in smoke on the altar as a soothing aroma to the LORD. So the priest shall make atonement for him, and he will be forgiven.

32 'But if he brings ^a lamb as his offering for a sin offering, he shall bring a female without defect. 33 And ^he shall lay his hand on the head of the sin offering and slaughter it as a sin offering ^in the place where they slaughter the burnt offering. 34 And the priest is to take some of the blood of the sin offering with his finger and put it on the horns of ^the altar of burnt offering, and all *the rest of* its blood he shall pour out at the base of the altar. 35 Then he shall remove all its fat, just as the fat of the lamb is removed from the sacrifice of the peace offerings, and the priest shall offer it up in smoke on the altar, on the offerings by fire to

the LORD. So ^the priest shall make atonement for him regarding his sin which he has committed, and he will be forgiven.

THE LAW OF GUILT OFFERINGS

5 'Now if a person sins after he hears a public ^order *to testify* when he is a witness, whether he has seen or *otherwise* known, if he does not tell *it,* then he will bear his punishment. 2 Or if a person touches ^any unclean thing, whether a carcass of an unclean animal, or the carcass of unclean cattle, or a carcass of unclean swarming things, though it is hidden from him and he is unclean, then he will be guilty. 3 Or if he touches human uncleanness, of whatever *sort* his uncleanness *may* be with which he becomes unclean, and it is hidden from him, and then he comes to know *it,* he will be guilty. 4 Or if a person ^swears thoughtlessly with his lips to do evil or to do good, in whatever *matter* people speak thoughtlessly with an oath, and it is hidden from him, and then he comes to know *it,* he will be guilty of one of these things. 5 So it shall be when he becomes guilty of one of these things, that he shall ^confess that in which he has sinned. 6 He shall also bring his guilt offering to the LORD for his sin which he has committed, ^a female from the flock, a lamb or a goat as a sin offering. So the priest shall make atonement on his behalf for his sin.

4:27^Lev 4:2; Num 15:27   4:28^Lev 4:3, 14, 23, 32   4:29^Lev 1:4; 4:4, 24   4:30^Lev 4:7, 18, 25, 34   4:31^Lev 4:8   4:32^Lev 4:28   4:33^Lev 1:4, 5   ^Lev 4:29   4:34^Lev 4:7, 18, 25, 30   4:35^Lev 4:20   5:1^Prov 29:24; Jer 23:10   5:2^Num 19:11-16; Deut 14:8   5:4^Num 30:6, 8; Ps 106:33   5:5^Lev 16:21; Prov 28:13   5:6^Lev 4:28, 32

⁷'But if he cannot afford a lamb, then he shall bring to the LORD his guilt offering for that in which he has sinned, two turtledoves or two young doves, ^one as a sin offering and the other as a burnt offering. ⁸He shall bring them to the priest, who shall first offer that which is for the sin offering, and shall pinch off its head at the front of its neck, but he ^shall not sever *it.* ⁹He shall also sprinkle some of the blood of the sin offering on the side of the altar, while the rest of the blood shall be drained out ^at the base of the altar: it is a sin offering. ¹⁰The second he shall then prepare as a burnt offering ^according to the ordinance. So the priest shall make atonement on his behalf for his sin which he has committed, and it will be forgiven him.

¹¹'But ^if his means are insufficient for two turtledoves or two young doves, then for his offering for that which he has sinned, he shall bring the tenth of an ¹ephah of fine flour as a sin offering; he shall not put oil on it or place incense on it, for it is a sin offering. ¹²He shall bring it to the priest, and the priest shall take his handful of it as its memorial portion and offer *it* up in smoke on the altar, with the offerings of the LORD by fire: it is a sin offering. ¹³So the priest shall make atonement for him concerning his sin which he has committed from ^one of these, and it will be forgiven him; then ᴮ*the rest* shall become the priest's, like the grain offering.'"

¹⁴Then the LORD spoke to Moses, saying, ¹⁵"If a person acts unfaithfully and sins unintentionally against the LORD's holy things, then he shall bring his ^guilt offering to the LORD: ᴮa ram without defect from the flock, according to your assessment in silver by shekels, in *terms of* the shekel of the sanctuary, as a guilt offering. ¹⁶And ^he shall make restitution for that which he has sinned against the holy thing, and shall add to it a fifth part of it and give it to the priest. The priest shall then make atonement for him with the ram of the guilt offering, and it will be forgiven him.

¹⁷"Now if a person sins and does any of the things which the LORD has commanded not to be done, ^though he was unaware, he is still guilty and shall bear his punishment. ¹⁸He is then to bring to the priest ^a ram without defect from the flock, according to your assessment, as a guilt offering. So the priest shall make atonement for him concerning his sin which he committed unintentionally and did not know *it,* and it will be forgiven him. ¹⁹It is a guilt offering; he was certainly guilty before the LORD."

GUILT OFFERING

6 Then the LORD spoke to Moses, saying, ²"^When a person sins and acts unfaithfully against the LORD, and disavows *the rightful claim of* his neighbor regarding a deposit or a security entrusted *to him,* or regarding robbery, or he has extorted from his neighbor, ³or ^has found what was lost and lied about it and sworn falsely, so that he sins regarding any of the things that people do; ⁴then it shall be, when he sins and becomes guilty, that he

5:7^Lev 12:6, 8; 14:22, 30, 31 5:8^Lev 1:17
5:9^Lev 4:7, 18 5:10^Lev 1:14-17 5:11^Lev 14:21-32;
27:8 5:13^Lev 5:4, 5 ᴮLev 2:3 5:15^Lev 7:1-10
ᴮLev 6:6 5:16^Lev 6:5; Num 5:7, 8 5:17^Lev 4:2;
5:19 5:18^Lev 5:15 6:2^Ex 22:7-15
6:3^Ex 23:4; Deut 22:1-4

5:11 ¹About 1 cubic foot or 0.03 cubic meters

shall ^restore what he took by robbery or acquired by extortion, or the deposit which was entrusted to him, or the lost property which he found, ⁵or anything about which he swore falsely; he shall make restitution for it in full and add to it a fifth more. ^He shall give it to the one to whom it belongs on the day *he presents* his guilt offering. ⁶Then he shall bring to the priest his guilt offering to the Lord, ^a ram without defect from the flock, according to your assessment, as a guilt offering, ⁷and ^the priest shall make atonement for him before the Lord, and he will be forgiven for any one of the things which he may have done to incur guilt."

THE PRIEST'S PART IN THE OFFERINGS

⁸Then the Lord spoke to Moses, saying, ⁹"Command Aaron and his sons, saying, 'This is ^the law for the burnt offering: the burnt offering itself *shall remain* on the hearth on the altar all night until the morning, and the fire on the altar is to be kept burning on it. ¹⁰The priest is to put on ^his linen robe, and he shall put on linen undergarments next to his body; and he shall take up the fatty ashes *to* which the fire reduces the burnt offering on the altar and place them beside the altar. ¹¹Then he shall take off his garments and put on other garments, and carry the fatty ashes outside the camp to a clean place. ¹²The fire on the altar shall be kept burning on it. It shall not go out, but the priest shall burn wood on it every morning; and he shall lay out the burnt offering on it, and offer up in smoke the fat portions of the peace offerings ^on it. ¹³Fire shall be kept burning

continually on the altar; it is not to go out.

¹⁴'Now this is the law of the grain offering: the sons of Aaron shall present it before the Lord in front of the altar. ¹⁵^Then one *of them* shall lift up from it a handful of the fine flour of the grain offering, with its oil and all the incense that is on the grain offering, and he shall offer *it* up in smoke on the altar, a soothing aroma, as its memorial offering to the Lord. ¹⁶And Aaron and his sons are to eat ^what is left of it. It shall be eaten as unleavened cakes in a holy place; they are to eat it in the courtyard of the tent of meeting. ¹⁷^It shall not be baked with leaven. I have given it as their share from My offerings by fire; it is most holy, like the sin offering and the guilt offering. ¹⁸^Every male among the sons of Aaron may eat it; it is a permanent ordinance throughout your generations, from the offerings by fire to the Lord. ᴮWhoever touches them will become consecrated.'"

¹⁹Then the Lord spoke to Moses, saying, ²⁰"This is the offering which Aaron and his sons are to present to the Lord on the day when he is anointed; the tenth of an ¹ephah of fine flour as ^a regular grain offering, half of it in the morning and half of it in the evening. ²¹It shall be prepared with oil on a ^griddle. When it is *well* stirred, you shall bring it. You shall present the grain offering in baked pieces as a soothing aroma to the

6:4^Lev 24:18, 21   6:5^Num 5:7-8   6:6^Lev 5:15
6:7^Lev 7:2-5   6:9^Ex 29:38-42; Num 28:3-10
6:10^Ex 28:39, 42; 39:27, 28   6:12^Lev 3:5
6:15^Lev 2:2, 9   6:16^Lev 10:12-14; Ezek 44:29
6:17^Lev 2:11   6:18^1 Cor 9:13   ᴮLev 6:27
6:20^Num 4:16   6:21^Lev 2:5

6:20¹About 1 cubic foot or 0.03 cubic meters

Lord. ²²The anointed priest who will be in his place among his sons shall offer it. By a permanent ordinance it shall be entirely offered up in smoke to the Lord. ²³So every grain offering of the priest shall be burned entirely. It shall not be eaten."

²⁴Then the Lord spoke to Moses, saying, ²⁵"Speak to Aaron and to his sons, saying, 'This is the law of the sin offering: ^in the place where the burnt offering is slaughtered, the sin offering shall be slaughtered before the Lord; it is most holy. ²⁶^The priest who offers it for sin shall eat it. It shall be eaten in a holy place, in the courtyard of the tent of meeting. ²⁷^Whoever touches its flesh will become consecrated; and when any of its blood spatters on a garment, you shall wash what spattered on it in a holy place. ²⁸Also ^the earthenware vessel in which it was boiled shall be broken; and if it was boiled in a bronze vessel, then it shall be scoured and rinsed in water. ²⁹Every male among the priests may eat it; ^it is most holy. ³⁰But no sin offering ^of which any of the blood is brought into the tent of meeting to make atonement in the Holy Place shall be eaten; it shall be burned with fire.

THE PRIEST'S PART IN THE OFFERINGS

7 'Now this is the law of the ^guilt offering; it is most holy. ²In ^the place where they slaughter the burnt offering they are to slaughter the guilt offering, and *the priest* shall sprinkle its blood around on the altar. ³Then he shall offer from it all its fat: the ^fat tail and the fat that covers the entrails, ⁴and the two kidneys with the fat that is on them, which is on the loins; and

he shall remove the lobe on the liver ^with the kidneys. ⁵The priest shall offer them up in smoke on the altar as an offering by fire to the Lord; it is a guilt offering. ⁶^Every male among the priests may eat it. It shall be eaten in a holy place; it is most holy. ⁷The guilt offering is like the sin offering: there is one law for them. The ^priest who makes atonement with it shall have it. ⁸Also the priest who presents anyone's burnt offering, that priest shall have for himself the hide of the burnt offering which he has presented. ⁹Likewise, every grain offering that is baked in the oven and everything prepared in a pan or on a ^griddle shall belong to the priest who presents it. ¹⁰Every grain offering, mixed with oil or dry, shall belong to all the sons of Aaron, to all alike.

¹¹'Now this is the law of the ^sacrifice of peace offerings which shall be presented to the Lord. ¹²If he offers it by way of thanksgiving, then along with the sacrifice of thanksgiving he shall offer ^unleavened cakes mixed with oil, and unleavened wafers spread with oil, and cakes *of well* stirred fine flour mixed with oil. ¹³With the sacrifice of his peace offerings for thanksgiving, he shall present his offering with cakes of ^leavened bread. ¹⁴Of this he shall present one of every offering as a contribution to the Lord; ^it shall belong to the priest who sprinkles the blood of the peace offerings.

6:25 ^Lev 1:11   6:26 ^Lev 6:29   6:27 ^Lev 7:19
6:28 ^Lev 11:33; 15:12   6:29 ^Lev 6:17, 25
6:30 ^Lev 4:1-21   7:1 ^Lev 5:14-6:7   7:2 ^Lev 1:11
7:3 ^Lev 3:9   7:4 ^Lev 3:4   7:6 ^Lev 6:18, 29;
Num 18:9   7:7 ^1 Cor 9:13; 10:18   7:9 ^Lev 2:5
7:11 ^Lev 3:1   7:12 ^Lev 2:4; Num 6:15
7:13 ^Lev 23:17, 18; Amos 4:5   7:14 ^Num 18:8, 11, 19

¹⁵ʼNow *as for* the flesh of the sacrifice of his thanksgiving peace offerings, it shall be eaten on the day of his offering; he shall not leave any of it over until morning. ¹⁶But if the sacrifice of his offering is a ^vow or a voluntary offering, it shall be eaten on the day that he offers his sacrifice, and on the next day what is left of it may be eaten; ¹⁷^but what is left over from the flesh of the sacrifice on the third day shall be burned with fire. ¹⁸So if any of the flesh of the sacrifice of his peace offerings is *ever* eaten on the third day, he who offers it will not be accepted, *and* it will not be credited to him. It will be an ^unclean thing, and the person who eats it shall bear his punishment.

¹⁹ʼAlso the flesh that touches anything unclean shall not be eaten; it shall be burned with fire. As for *other* flesh, anyone who is clean may eat *such* flesh. ²⁰^But the person who eats the flesh of the sacrifice of peace offerings which belong to the LORD, when he is unclean, that person ᴮshall be cut off from his people. ²¹^When anyone touches anything unclean, whether human uncleanness, or an unclean animal, or any unclean ¹detestable thing, and eats of the flesh of the sacrifice of peace offerings which belong to the LORD, that person shall be cut off from his people.'"

²²Then the LORD spoke to Moses, saying, ²³"Speak to the sons of Israel, saying, 'You shall not eat ^any fat *from* an ox, a sheep, or a goat. ²⁴Also the fat of *an animal* which dies and the fat of an animal ^torn *by animals* may be put to any *other* use, but you certainly are not to eat it. ²⁵For whoever eats the fat of the animal from which

an offering by fire is offered to the LORD, the person who eats *it* shall also be cut off from his people. ²⁶And ^you are not to eat any blood, either of bird or animal, in any of your dwellings. ²⁷Any person who eats any blood, that person shall also be cut off from his people.'"

²⁸Then the LORD spoke to Moses, saying, ²⁹"Speak to the sons of Israel, saying, 'He who offers ^the sacrifice of his peace offerings to the LORD shall bring his offering to the LORD from the sacrifice of his peace offerings. ³⁰His own hands are to bring offerings by fire to the LORD. He shall bring the fat with the breast, so that the ^breast may be presented as a wave offering before the LORD. ³¹And the priest shall offer up the fat in smoke on the altar, but ^the breast shall belong to Aaron and to his sons. ³²And you shall give ^the right thigh to the priest as a contribution from the sacrifices of your peace offerings. ³³The one among the sons of Aaron who offers the blood of the peace offerings and the fat, the right thigh shall be his as *his* portion. ³⁴For I have taken from the sons of Israel ^the breast of the wave offering and the thigh of the contribution from the sacrifices of their peace offerings, and have given them to Aaron the priest and to his sons as *their* allotted portion forever from the sons of Israel.

³⁵ʼThis is the ^allotment to Aaron and the allotment to his sons from

7:15 ^Lev 22:29, 30   7:16 ^Lev 19:5–8   7:17 ^Ex 12:10
7:18 ^Lev 19:7; Prov 15:8   7:20 ^Num 19:13   ᴮLev 7:25
7:21 ^Lev 5:2, 3   7:23 ^Lev 3:17   7:24 ^Ex 22:31;
Lev 17:15   7:26 ^1 Sam 14:33; Acts 15:20   7:29 ^Lev 3:1
7:30 ^Ex 29:26, 27; Lev 8:29   7:31 ^Num 18:11;
Deut 18:3   7:32 ^Ex 29:27; Lev 7:34   7:34 ^Ex 29:27;
Lev 10:14, 15   7:35 ^Num 18:8

7:21 ¹Some mss *swarming thing*

the offerings by fire to the Lord, on that day when he presented them to serve as priests to the Lord. [36] These the Lord had commanded to be given them from the sons of Israel on the day that He ^anointed them. It is *their* allotted portion forever throughout their generations.'"

[37] This is the law of the burnt offering, the grain offering, the sin offering and the guilt offering, and ^the ordination offering and the sacrifice of peace offerings, [38] ^which the Lord commanded Moses on Mount Sinai on the day that He commanded the sons of Israel to present their offerings to the Lord in the wilderness of Sinai.

THE CONSECRATION OF AARON AND HIS SONS

8 Then the Lord spoke to Moses, saying, [2] "^Take Aaron and his sons with him, and the garments and the anointing oil, and the bull of the sin offering, and the two rams and the basket of unleavened bread, [3] and assemble all the congregation at the doorway of the tent of meeting." [4] So Moses did just as the Lord commanded him. When the congregation was assembled at the doorway of the tent of meeting, [5] Moses said to the congregation, "This is the thing which the Lord has commanded *us* to do."

[6] Then ^Moses had Aaron and his sons come near, and he ^Bwashed them with water. [7] Then he ^put the tunic on Aaron and wrapped his waist with the sash, and clothed him with the robe and put the ephod on him; and he wrapped his waist with the artistic band of the ephod, with which he fitted *it* to him. [8] He then placed the breastpiece on him, and in the breastpiece

he put the [1,]^Urim and the Thummim. [9] He also placed the turban on his head, and on the turban, at its front, he placed ^the golden plate, the holy crown, just as the Lord had commanded Moses.

[10] Moses then took ^the anointing oil and anointed the tabernacle and everything that was in it, and consecrated them. [11] He also sprinkled some of it on the altar seven times and anointed the altar and all its utensils, and the basin and its stand, to ^consecrate them. [12] Then he poured some of the ^anointing oil on Aaron's head and anointed him, to consecrate him. [13] ^Next Moses had Aaron's sons come near, and he clothed them with tunics and wrapped their waists with sashes, and bound caps on them, just as the Lord had commanded Moses.

[14] Then he brought ^the bull of the sin offering, and Aaron and his sons laid their hands on the head of the bull of the sin offering. [15] Next Moses slaughtered *it* and took the blood and with his finger ^put *some of it* around on the horns of the altar, and purified the altar. Then he poured out *the rest of* the blood at the base of the altar and consecrated it, to make atonement for it. [16] He also ^took all the fat that was on the entrails and the lobe of the liver, and the two kidneys and their fat; and Moses offered it up in smoke on the altar. [17] ^But the bull and its hide, its flesh, and its refuse

7:36 ^Ex 40:13-15; Lev 8:12, 30   **7:37** ^Ex 29:22-34; Lev 8:22, 23   **7:38** ^Lev 26:46; Deut 4:5   **8:2** ^Ex 28:1
8:6 ^Ex 29:4-6   ^B 1 Cor 6:11   **8:7** ^Ex 28:4
8:8 ^Ezra 2:63; Neh 7:65   **8:9** ^Ex 28:36
8:10 ^Ex 30:26-29; Lev 8:2   **8:11** ^Ex 29:36, 37; 30:29
8:12 ^Lev 21:10, 12; Ps 133:2   **8:13** ^Ex 29:8, 9
8:14 ^Ps 66:15; Ezek 43:19   **8:15** ^Lev 4:7; Ezek 43:20
8:16 ^Ex 29:13   **8:17** ^Ex 29:14; Lev 4:11, 12

8:8 [1] Meanings of *Urim* and *Thummim* uncertain

he burned in the fire outside the camp, just as the LORD had commanded Moses.

18 Then he presented ^the ram of the burnt offering, and Aaron and his sons laid their hands on the head of the ram. 19 And Moses slaughtered *it* and sprinkled the blood around on the altar. 20 When he had cut the ram into its pieces, Moses ^offered up the head and the pieces and the suet in smoke. 21 After he had washed the entrails and the legs with water, Moses ^offered up the whole ram in smoke on the altar. It was a burnt offering for a soothing aroma; it was an offering by fire to the LORD, just as the LORD had commanded Moses.

22 Then he presented the second ram, ^the ram of ordination, and Aaron and his sons laid their hands on the head of the ram. 23 And Moses slaughtered *it* and took some of its blood and ^put it on the lobe of Aaron's right ear, and on the thumb of his right hand and on the big toe of his right foot. 24 He also had Aaron's sons come near; and Moses put some of the blood on the lobe of their right ear, and on the thumb of their right hand and on the big toe of their right foot. Moses then ^sprinkled *the rest of* the blood around on the altar. 25 He then took the fat, and the fat tail, and all the fat that was on the entrails, and the lobe of the liver, the two kidneys and their fat, and the right thigh. 26 And ^from the basket of unleavened bread that was before the LORD, he took one unleavened cake and one cake of bread *mixed with* oil and one wafer, and placed *them* on the portions of fat and on the right thigh. 27 He then ^put all *these* on the hands of Aaron

and on the hands of his sons, and presented them as a wave offering before the LORD. 28 Then Moses ^took them from their hands and offered them up in smoke on the altar with the burnt offering. They were an ordination offering for ^B a soothing aroma; it was an offering by fire to the LORD. 29 Moses also took ^the breast and presented it as a wave offering before the LORD; it was Moses' portion of the ram of ordination, just as the LORD had commanded Moses.

30 So Moses ^took some of the anointing oil and some of the blood which was on the altar, and sprinkled it on Aaron, on his garments, on his sons, and on the garments of his sons with him; and he consecrated Aaron, his garments, and his sons, and the garments of his sons with him.

31 Then Moses said to Aaron and to his sons, "^Boil the flesh at the doorway of the tent of meeting, and eat it there together with the bread which is in the basket of the ordination offering, just as I commanded, saying, 'Aaron and his sons shall eat it.' 32 And ^the remainder of the flesh and of the bread you shall burn in the fire. 33 And ^you shall not go outside the doorway of the tent of meeting for seven days, until the day that the period of your ordination is fulfilled; for he will ordain you through seven days. 34 The LORD has commanded *us* to do as has been done this day, to make atonement on your behalf. 35 At the doorway

8:18 ^Ex 29:15; Lev 8:2   8:20 ^Lev 1:8   8:21 ^Ex 29:18
8:22 ^Ex 29:31; Lev 8:2   8:23 ^Ex 29:20, 21
8:24 ^Heb 9:18-22   8:26 ^Ex 29:23   8:27 ^Ex 29:24
8:28 ^Ex 29:25   ^B Gen 8:21 ^Lev 7:31-34
8:30 ^Ex 29:21   8:31 ^Ex 29:31   8:32 ^Ex 29:34
8:33 ^Ex 29:35

of the tent of meeting, moreover, you shall remain day and night for seven days and ^fulfill *your* duty to the LORD, so that you will not die; for so I have been commanded." ³⁶Aaron and his sons did all the things which the LORD had commanded through Moses.

AARON OFFERS SACRIFICES

9 Now it came about ^on the eighth day that Moses called Aaron and his sons and the elders of Israel; ²and he said to Aaron, "^Take for yourself a calf, a bull, as a sin offering and a ram as a burnt offering, *both* without defect, and offer *them* before the LORD. ³Then you shall speak to the sons of Israel, saying, 'Take a male goat as a sin offering, and a calf and a lamb, both one year old, without defect, as a burnt offering, ⁴and an ox and a ram for peace offerings, to sacrifice before the LORD, and a grain offering mixed with oil; for today ^the LORD will appear to you.'" ⁵So they took what Moses had commanded to the front of the tent of meeting, and the whole congregation came near and stood before the LORD. ⁶And Moses said, "This is the thing which the LORD has commanded you to do, so that ^the glory of the LORD may appear to you." ⁷Moses then said to Aaron, "Come near to the altar and ^offer your sin offering and your burnt offering, so that you may make atonement for yourself and for the people; then make the offering for the people, so that you may make atonement for them, just as the LORD has commanded."

⁸^So Aaron came near to the altar and slaughtered the calf of the sin offering which was for himself. ⁹Aaron's sons then presented the blood to him; and he dipped his finger in the blood and ^put *some* on the horns of the altar, and poured out *the rest of* the blood at the base of the altar. ¹⁰The fat and the kidneys and the lobe of the liver of the sin offering he then offered up in smoke on the altar, just as the LORD had commanded Moses. ¹¹^The flesh and the hide, however, he burned with fire outside the camp.

¹²Then he slaughtered the burnt offering; and Aaron's sons brought the blood to him, and he sprinkled it around on the altar. ¹³They brought the burnt offering to him in pieces, with the head, and he offered *them* up in smoke on the altar. ¹⁴He also washed the entrails and the legs, and offered *them* up in smoke with the burnt offering on the altar.

¹⁵Then he presented the people's offering, and took the ^goat of the sin offering which was for the people, and slaughtered it and offered it for sin, like the first. ¹⁶He also presented the burnt offering, and offered it according to ^the ordinance. ¹⁷Next he presented ^the grain offering, and filled his hand with some of it and offered *it* up in smoke on the altar, besides the burnt offering of the morning.

¹⁸Then ^he slaughtered the ox and the ram, the sacrifice of peace offerings which was for the people; and Aaron's sons brought the blood to him, and he sprinkled it around on the altar. ¹⁹As for the portions of fat from the ox and from the ram, the fat tail, the *fat* ^covering, the

8:35^1 Kin 2:3; Ezek 48:11   9:1^Ezek 43:27
9:2^Ezek 29:1; Lev 4:3   9:4^Ex 29:43   9:6^Ex 24:16;
Lev 9:23   9:7^Heb 5:3; 7:27   9:8^Lev 4:1-12
9:9^Lev 4:7   9:11^Lev 4:11, 12; 8:17   9:15^Lev
4:27-31   9:16^Lev 1:1-13   9:17^Lev 2:1-3
9:18^Lev 3:1-11   9:19^Lev 3:9

kidneys, and the lobe of the liver, [20] they now placed the portions of fat on the breasts; and he offered them up in smoke on the altar. [21] But ^the breasts and the right thigh Aaron presented as a wave offering before the LORD, just as Moses had commanded.

[22] Then Aaron lifted up his hands toward the people and ^blessed them, and he stepped down after making the sin offering, the burnt offering, and the peace offerings. [23] And Moses and Aaron went into the tent of meeting. When they came out and blessed the people, ^the glory of the LORD appeared to all the people. [24] ^Then fire went out from the LORD and consumed the burnt offering and the portions of fat on the altar; and when all the people saw it, they shouted and fell face downward.

THE SIN OF NADAB AND ABIHU

10 Now Nadab and Abihu, the sons of Aaron, took their respective ^firepans, and after putting fire in them, placed incense on the fire and offered strange fire before the LORD, which He had not commanded them. [2] ^And fire came out from the presence of the LORD and consumed them, and they died before the LORD. [3] Then Moses said to Aaron, "It is what the LORD spoke, saying,

'By those who ^come near Me I
    will be treated as holy,
And before all the people I will
    be honored.'"

So Aaron, therefore, kept silent.

[4] Moses called also to ^Mishael and Elzaphan, the sons of Aaron's uncle Uzziel, and said to them, "Come forward, carry your relatives away from the front of the sanctuary to *an area* outside of the camp." [5] So they came forward and carried them, *still* in their ^tunics, to *an area* outside the camp, just as Moses had said. [6] Then Moses said to Aaron and to his sons Eleazar and Ithamar, "^Do not uncover your heads nor tear your clothes, so that you do not die and He does not become wrathful against all the congregation. But your kinsmen, the entire house of Israel, shall weep for the burning which the LORD has brought about. [7] You shall not even go out from the doorway of the tent of meeting, or you will die; for ^the LORD's anointing oil is upon you." So they did according to the word of Moses.

[8] The LORD then spoke to Aaron, saying, [9] "^Do not drink wine or strong drink, neither you nor your sons with you, when you come into the tent of meeting, so that you do not die—it is a permanent statute throughout your generations— [10] and ^to make a distinction between the holy and the profane, and between the unclean and the clean, [11] and ^so as to teach the sons of Israel all the statutes which the LORD has spoken to them through Moses."

[12] Then Moses spoke to Aaron, and to his surviving sons, Eleazar and Ithamar, "^Take the grain offering that is left over from the LORD's offerings by fire and eat it as unleavened bread beside the altar, for it is most holy. [13] You shall eat it in a holy place, because it

9:21 ^Ex 29:26, 27; Lev 7:30-34   9:22 ^Deut 21:5; Luke 24:50   9:23 ^Lev 9:6; Num 16:19
9:24 ^1 Kin 18:38, 39; 2 Chr 7:1   10:1 ^Lev 16:12
10:2 ^Num 16:35; 26:61   10:3 ^Ex 19:22; Lev 21:6
10:4 ^Ex 6:22   10:5 ^Ex 29:5; Lev 8:13   10:6 ^Lev 21:1-5, 10-12   10:7 ^Ex 28:41; Lev 21:12
10:9 ^1 Tim 3:3; Titus 1:7   10:10 ^Lev 11:47; Ezek 22:26
10:11 ^Deut 17:10, 11; 33:10   10:12 ^Lev 6:14-18

is your allotted portion and your sons' allotted portion from the LORD's offerings by fire; for so I have been commanded. 14 [A]The breast of the wave offering, however, and the thigh of the offering you may eat in a clean place, you and your sons and your daughters with you; for they have been given as your allotted portion and your sons' allotted portion from the sacrifices of the peace offerings of the sons of Israel. 15 They shall bring [A]the thigh offered by lifting up and the breast offered by waving, along with the offerings by fire of the portions of fat, to present as a wave offering before the LORD; so it shall be a thing perpetually due you and your sons with you, just as the LORD has commanded."

16 But Moses searched carefully for the [A]goat of the sin offering, and behold, it had been burned! So he was angry with Aaron's surviving sons Eleazar and Ithamar, saying, 17 "Why [A]did you not eat the sin offering at the holy place? For it is most holy, and He gave it to you to take away the guilt of the congregation, to make atonement for them before the LORD. 18 Behold, [A]since its blood had not been brought inside, into the sanctuary, you certainly should have [B]eaten it in the sanctuary, just as I commanded!" 19 But Aaron said to Moses, "Behold, this *very* day they [A]presented their sin offering and their burnt offering before the LORD. When things like these happened to me, if I had eaten a sin offering today, would it have been good in the sight of the LORD?" 20 When Moses heard *that,* it was good in his sight.

LAWS ABOUT ANIMALS FOR FOOD

11 The LORD spoke again to Moses and to Aaron, saying to them, 2 "Speak to the sons of Israel, saying, '[A]These are the creatures which you may eat from all the animals that are on the earth. 3 Whatever has a divided hoof, showing split hoofs, *and* chews the cud, among the animals, that you may eat. 4 Nevertheless, [A]you are not to eat of these, among those which chew the cud, or among those which have a divided hoof: the camel, for though it chews cud, it does not have a divided hoof; it is unclean to you. 5 Likewise, the rock hyrax, for though it chews cud, it does not have a divided hoof; it is unclean to you. 6 The rabbit also, for though it chews cud, it does not have a divided hoof; it is unclean to you. 7 And the pig, for though it has a divided hoof, and *so* it shows a split hoof, it does not chew cud; it is unclean to you. 8 You shall not eat *any* of their flesh nor touch their carcasses; they are unclean to you.

9 '[A]These you may eat, of whatever is in the water: everything that has fins and scales, in the water, in the seas, or in the rivers, you may eat. 10 [A]But whatever is in the seas and in the rivers that does not have fins and scales among all the teeming life of the water, and among all the living creatures that are in the water, they are detestable things to you, 11 and they shall be detestable to you; you may not eat *any* of their flesh, and you shall detest their carcasses. 12 Whatever in the

10:14 [A]Lev 7:30-34; Num 18:11 **10:15** [A]Lev 7:34
10:16 [A]Lev 9:3, 15 **10:17** [A]Lev 6:24-30
10:18 [A]Lev 6:30 [B]Lev 6:26 **10:19** [A]Lev 9:8, 12
11:2 [A]Deut 14:3-21 **11:4** [A]Acts 10:14 **11:9** [A]Deut 14:9
11:10 [A]Deut 14:10

water does not have fins and scales is detestable to you.

AVOID THE UNCLEAN

13 'Moreover, these ^you shall detest among the birds; they are detestable, not to be eaten: the eagle, the vulture, and the buzzard, 14 the red kite, the falcon in its kind, 15 every raven in its kind, 16 the ostrich, the owl, the seagull, and the hawk in its kind, 17 the little owl, the cormorant, and the great owl, 18 the white owl, the pelican, and the carrion vulture, 19 the stork, the heron in its kinds, the hoopoe, and the bat.

20 'All the winged insects that walk on *all* fours are detestable to you. 21 Yet these you may eat among all the winged insects that walk on *all* fours: those which have jointed legs above their feet with which to jump on the earth. 22 These of them you may eat: the locust in its kinds, the devastating locust in its kinds, the cricket in its kinds, and the grasshopper in its kinds. 23 But all *other* winged insects which are four-footed are detestable to you.

24 'By these, moreover, you will be made unclean; whoever touches their carcasses becomes unclean until evening, 25 and ^whoever picks up any of their carcasses shall wash his clothes and be unclean until evening. 26 As for all the animals which have a divided hoof but do not show a split *hoof,* or do not chew the cud, they are unclean to you; whoever touches them becomes unclean. 27 Also whatever walks on its paws, among all the creatures that walk on *all* fours, are unclean to you; whoever touches their carcasses becomes unclean until evening, 28 and the one who picks up their carcasses shall wash

his clothes and be unclean until evening; they are unclean to you.

29 'Now these are to you the unclean among the swarming things which swarm on the earth: the mole, the mouse, and the great lizard in its kinds, 30 the gecko, the crocodile, the lizard, the sand reptile, and the chameleon. 31 These are to you the unclean among all the swarming things; whoever touches them when they are dead becomes unclean until evening. 32 Also anything on which one of them may fall when they are dead becomes unclean, including any wooden article, or clothing, or a hide, or a sack—any article of which use is made—^it shall be put in the water and be unclean until evening, then it becomes clean. 33 As for any ^earthenware vessel into which one of them may fall, whatever is in it becomes unclean and you shall break the vessel. 34 Any of the food which may be eaten, on which water comes, shall become unclean, and any liquid which may be drunk in every vessel shall become unclean. 35 Moreover, everything on which part of their carcass may fall becomes unclean; an oven or a stove shall be smashed; they are unclean and shall continue as unclean to you. 36 Nevertheless, a spring or a cistern collecting water shall be clean, though the one who touches their carcass shall be unclean. 37 Now if a part of their carcass falls on any seed for sowing which is to be sown, it is clean. 38 But if water is put on the seed and a part of their carcass falls on it, it is unclean to you.

11:13 ^Deut 14:12-19   11:25 ^Lev 11:40
11:32 ^Lev 15:12   11:33 ^Lev 6:28; 15:12

[39] 'Also if one of the animals dies which you have for food, the one who touches its carcass becomes unclean until evening. [40] ^He, too, who eats some of its carcass shall wash his clothes and be unclean until evening, and the one who picks up its carcass shall wash his clothes and be unclean until evening.

[41] 'Now every swarming thing that swarms on the earth is detestable, not to be eaten. [42] Whatever crawls on its belly, and whatever walks on *all* fours, whatever has many feet, in regard to every swarming thing that swarms on the earth, you shall not eat them, because they are detestable. [43] ^Do not make yourselves detestable through any of the swarming things that swarm; and you shall not make yourselves unclean with them so that you become unclean. [44] For I am the LORD your God. Consecrate yourselves therefore, and ^be holy, because I am holy. And you shall not make yourselves unclean with any of the swarming things that swarm on the earth. [45] ^For I am the LORD who brought you up from the land of Egypt, to be your God; so you shall be holy, because I am holy.'"

[46] This is the law regarding the animal and the bird, and every living thing that moves in the waters and everything that swarms on the earth, [47] ^to make a distinction between the unclean and the clean, and between the edible creature and the creature which is not to be eaten.

LAWS OF MOTHERHOOD

12 Then the LORD spoke to Moses, saying, [2] "Speak to the sons of Israel, saying:

'When a woman gives birth and delivers a male *child,* then she shall be unclean for seven days; ^as *she is* in the days of her menstruation, she shall be unclean. [3] Then on ^the eighth day the flesh of his foreskin shall be circumcised. [4] And she shall stay *at home* in *her condition of* blood purification for thirty-three days; she shall not touch any consecrated thing, nor enter the sanctuary until the days of her purification are completed. [5] But if she gives birth to a female *child,* then she shall be unclean for two weeks, as in her menstruation; and she shall stay *at home* in *her condition of* blood purification for sixty-six days.

[6] 'When the days of her purification are completed, for a son or for a daughter, she shall bring to the priest at the doorway of the tent of meeting a one-year-old lamb as a burnt offering and a young pigeon or a turtledove as a sin offering. [7] Then he shall offer it before the LORD and make atonement for her, and she shall be cleansed from the flow of her blood. This is the law for her who gives birth to *a child, whether* a male or a female. [8] But if she cannot afford a lamb, then she shall take ^two turtledoves or two young doves, the one as a burnt offering and the other as a sin offering; and the ^priest shall make atonement for her, and she will be clean.'"

THE TEST FOR LEPROSY

13 Then the LORD spoke to Moses and to Aaron, saying, [2] "When someone has on the skin of his body a swelling, or a scab, or a bright spot, and it becomes an

---

11:40 ^Deut 14:21; Ezek 44:31   11:41 ^Lev 11:29
11:43 ^Lev 20:25   11:44 ^Lev 19:2; 1 Pet 1:16
11:45 ^Ex 20:2; Lev 22:33   11:47 ^Lev 10:10;
Ezek 44:23   12:2 ^Lev 15:19; 18:19   12:3 ^Gen 17:12;
Luke 1:59   12:6 ^Luke 2:22   12:8 ^Luke 2:22-24
^B Lev 4:26

infection of ¹leprosy on the skin of his body, ^then he shall be brought to Aaron the priest or to one of his sons the priests. ³The priest shall look at the infected area on the skin of the body, and if the hair in the infection has turned white and the infection appears to be deeper than the skin of his body, it is an infection of leprosy; when the priest has looked at him, he shall pronounce him unclean. ⁴But if the bright spot is white on the skin of his body, and it does not appear to be deeper than the skin, and the hair on it has not turned white, then the priest shall isolate *the person who has* the infection for seven days. ⁵Then the priest shall look at him on the seventh day, and if in his eyes the infection has not changed *and* the infection has not spread on the skin, then the priest shall isolate him for seven more days. ⁶The priest shall then look at him again on the seventh day, and if the infected area has faded and the infection has not spread on the skin, then the priest shall pronounce him clean; it is *only* a rash. And he shall ^wash his clothes and be clean.

⁷"But if the rash spreads farther on the skin after he has shown himself to the priest for his cleansing, he shall appear again to the priest. ⁸And the priest shall look, and if the rash has spread on the skin, then the priest shall pronounce him unclean; it is leprosy.

⁹"When the infection of leprosy is on someone, then he shall be brought to the priest. ¹⁰The priest shall then look, and if there is a ^white swelling on the skin, and it has turned the hair white, and there is new raw flesh in the swelling, ¹¹it is a chronic leprosy on the skin of his body, and the priest shall pronounce him unclean; he shall not isolate him, for he is unclean. ¹²If the leprosy breaks out farther on the skin, and the leprosy covers all the skin of *the person who has* the infection from his head even to his feet, as far as the priest can see, ¹³then the priest shall look, and behold, *if* the leprosy has covered his entire body, he shall pronounce *the one who has* the infection clean; it has all turned white *and* he is clean. ¹⁴But whenever raw flesh appears on him, he shall be unclean. ¹⁵The priest shall look at the raw flesh, and he shall pronounce him unclean; the raw flesh is unclean, it is leprosy. ¹⁶Or if the raw flesh turns back and is changed to white, then he shall ^come to the priest, ¹⁷and the priest shall look at him, and behold, *if* the infected area has turned white, then the priest shall pronounce *the one who has* the infection clean; he is clean.

¹⁸"Now when the body has a boil on its skin and it is healed, ¹⁹and in the place of the boil there is a white swelling or a reddish-white, bright spot, then it shall be shown to the priest; ²⁰and the priest shall look, and behold, *if* it appears to be deeper than the skin, and the hair on it has turned white, then the priest shall pronounce him unclean; it is the infection of leprosy, it has broken out in the boil. ²¹But if the priest looks at it, and behold, there are no white hairs in it and it is not deeper than the skin

13:2 ^Deut 24:8   13:6 ^Lev 11:25; 14:8
13:10 ^2 Kin 5:27; 2 Chr 26:19, 20   13:16 ^Luke 5:12-14

13:2 ¹ I.e., or a serious, unspecified disease, and so throughout the ch

and is faded, then the priest shall isolate him for seven days; 22 and if it spreads farther on the skin, then the priest shall pronounce him unclean; it is an infection. 23 But if the bright spot remains in its place and does not spread, it is *only* the scar of the boil; and the priest shall pronounce him clean.

24 "Or if the body sustains in its skin a burn by fire, and the raw *flesh* of the burn becomes a bright spot, reddish-white, or white, 25 then the priest shall look at it. And if the hair in the bright spot has ^turned white and it appears to be deeper than the skin, it is leprosy; it has broken out in the burn. Therefore, the priest shall pronounce him unclean; it is an infection of leprosy. 26 But if the priest looks at it, and indeed, there is no white hair in the bright spot and it is no deeper than the skin, but is dim, then the priest shall isolate him for seven days; 27 and the priest shall look at him on the seventh day. If it spreads farther in the skin, then the priest shall pronounce him unclean; it is an infection of leprosy. 28 But if the bright spot remains in its place and has not spread in the skin, but is dim, it is the swelling from the burn; and the priest shall pronounce him clean, for it is *only* the scar of the burn.

29 "Now if a man or woman has an infection on the head or on the beard, 30 then the priest shall look at the infection, and if it appears to be deeper than the skin and there is thin yellowish hair in it, then the priest shall pronounce him unclean; it is a scale, it is leprosy of the head or of the beard. 31 But if the priest looks at the infection of the scale, and indeed, it appears to be no deeper than the skin and there is no black hair in it, then the priest shall isolate *the person* with the scaly infection for seven days. 32 And on the seventh day the priest shall look at the infection, and if the scale has not spread and no yellowish hair has grown in it, and the appearance of the scale is no deeper than the skin, 33 then he shall shave himself, but he shall not shave the scale; and the priest shall isolate *the person* with the scale for seven more days. 34 Then on the seventh day the priest shall look at the scale, and if the scale has not spread in the skin and it appears to be no deeper than the skin, the priest shall pronounce him clean; and he shall wash his clothes and be clean. 35 But if the scale spreads farther in the skin after his cleansing, 36 then the priest shall look at him, and if the scale has spread on the skin, the priest need not look for the yellowish hair; he is unclean. 37 If in his sight the scale has remained, however, and black hair has grown in it, the scale has healed, *and* he is clean; and the priest shall pronounce him clean.

38 "When a man or a woman has bright spots on the skin of the body, white bright spots, 39 then the priest shall look, and if the bright spots on the skin of their bodies are a faint white, it is eczema that has broken out on the skin; he is clean.

40 "Now if a man loses the hair of his head, he is *only* ^bald; he is clean. 41 And if his head becomes bald at the front and sides, he is bald on the forehead; he is clean. 42 But if on the bald head or the bald forehead there occurs a reddish-white

13:25 ^Num 12:10; 2 Kin 5:27
13:40 ^Is 15:2; Amos 8:10

infection, it is leprosy breaking out on his bald head or on his bald forehead. ⁴³Then ᴬthe priest shall look at him; and if the swelling of the infection is reddish-white on his bald head or on his bald forehead, like the appearance of leprosy in the skin of the body, ⁴⁴he is a leprous man, he is unclean. The priest must pronounce him unclean; his infection is on his head.

⁴⁵"As for the person who has the leprous infection, his clothes shall be torn and *the hair of* his head shall be uncovered, and he shall ᴬcover his mustache and call out, 'Unclean! Unclean!' ⁴⁶He shall remain unclean all the days during which he has the infection; he is unclean. He shall live alone; he shall live ᴬoutside the camp.

⁴⁷"When a garment has a mark of leprosy in it, whether it is a wool garment or a linen garment, ⁴⁸whether in ¹warp or ²woof, of linen or of wool, whether in leather or in any article made of leather, ⁴⁹if the ¹mark is greenish or reddish in the garment or in the leather, whether in the warp or in the woof, or in any article of leather, it is a leprous mark and it shall be shown to the priest. ⁵⁰Then ᴬthe priest shall look at the mark and shall quarantine the article with the mark for seven days. ⁵¹He shall then look at the mark on the seventh day; if the mark has spread in the garment, whether in the ¹warp or in the woof, or in the leather, whatever the purpose for which the leather is used, the mark is a leprous malignancy, it is unclean. ⁵²So he shall burn the garment, whether *it is* the ¹warp or the woof, in wool or in linen, or any article of leather, in which the mark occurs;

for it is a leprous malignancy. It shall be burned in the fire.

⁵³"But if the priest looks, and indeed the mark has not spread in the garment, either in the ¹warp or in the woof, or in any article of leather, ⁵⁴then the priest shall order them to wash the thing in which the mark occurs, and he shall quarantine it for seven more days. ⁵⁵After the article with the mark has been washed, the priest shall again look, and if the mark has not changed its appearance, even *if* the mark has not spread, it is unclean; you shall burn it in the fire, whether an eating away has produced bareness on the back or on the front of it.

⁵⁶"But if the priest looks, and indeed the mark has faded after it has been washed, then he shall tear it out of the garment or out of the leather, whether from the ¹warp or from the woof; ⁵⁷yet if it appears again in the garment, whether in the warp or in the woof, or in any article of leather, it is an outbreak; the article with the mark shall be burned in the fire. ⁵⁸But the garment, whether the warp or the woof, or any article of leather from which the mark has disappeared when you washed it, shall then be washed a second time and will be clean."

⁵⁹This is the law for the mark of leprosy in a garment of wool or linen, whether in the warp or in the woof, or in any article of leather, for pronouncing it clean or unclean.

13:43 ᴬLev 10:10; Ezek 22:26   13:45 ᴬEzek 24:17, 22; Mic 3:7   13:46 ᴬNum 5:1-4; 12:14   13:50 ᴬEzek 44:23

13:48 ¹I.e., lengthwise material in weaving   ²I.e., material woven crosswise   13:49 ¹Lit *infestation;* possibly material already contaminated prior to weaving   13:51 ¹See notes v 48   13:52 ¹See notes v 48   13:53 ¹See notes v 48   13:56 ¹See notes v 48

LAW OF CLEANSING A PERSON
WITH LEPROSY

14 Then the LORD spoke to Moses, saying, ² "This shall be the law of the person with leprosy on the day of his cleansing. ᴬNow he shall be brought to the priest; ³ and the priest shall go ᴬout to *a place* outside of the camp. Then the priest shall look, and if the leprous infection has been healed in the person with leprosy, ⁴ then the priest shall give orders to take two live clean birds, ᴬcedar wood, a scarlet string, and hyssop for the one who is to be cleansed. ⁵ The priest shall also give orders to slaughter the one bird in an earthenware vessel over running water. ⁶ *As for* the live bird, he shall take it together with ᴬthe cedar wood, the scarlet string, and the hyssop, and shall dip them and the live bird in the blood of the bird that was slaughtered over the running water. ⁷ᴬHe shall then sprinkle seven times the one who is to be cleansed from the leprosy and shall pronounce him clean, and shall let the live bird go free over the open field. ⁸ The one to be cleansed shall then wash his clothes and shave off all his hair, and bathe in water and be clean. And afterward he may enter the camp, but he ᴬshall stay outside his tent for seven days. ⁹ Then it shall be on the seventh day that he shall shave off all his hair: he shall shave his head and his beard and his eyebrows, even all his hair. He shall then wash his clothes and bathe his body in water and ᴬbe clean.

¹⁰ "Now on the eighth day he is to take two male lambs without defect, and a yearling ewe lamb without defect, and three-tenths *of an* ¹ephah of fine flour mixed with oil as a grain offering, and one ²,ᴬlog of oil; ¹¹ and the priest who is going to pronounce *him* clean shall present the person to be cleansed and the offerings before the LORD at the doorway of the tent of meeting. ¹² Then the priest shall take the one male lamb and bring it as a ᴬguilt offering, with the ¹log of oil, and present them as a ᴮwave offering before the LORD. ¹³ Next he shall slaughter the male lamb in ᴬthe place where they slaughter the sin offering and the burnt offering, at the place of the sanctuary—for the guilt offering, like the sin offering, belongs to the priest; it is most holy. ¹⁴ The priest shall then take some of the blood of the guilt offering, and the priest shall put *it* on ᴬthe lobe of the right ear of the one to be cleansed, and on the thumb of his right hand, and on the big toe of his right foot. ¹⁵ The priest shall also take some of the ¹,ᴬlog of oil, and pour *it* into his left palm; ¹⁶ the priest shall then dip his right-hand finger into the oil that is in his left palm, and with his finger sprinkle some of the oil seven times before the LORD. ¹⁷ Of the remaining oil which is in his palm, the priest shall put some on the right ear lobe of the one to be cleansed, and on the thumb of his right hand, and on the big toe of his right foot, on the blood of the guilt offering; ¹⁸ as for the rest of the oil that is in the priest's palm, he shall put *it* on the

14:2 ᴬMatt 8:4; Luke 5:14   14:3 ᴬLev 13:46
14:4 ᴬLev 14:6, 49, 51, 52; Num 19:6   14:6 ᴬLev 14:4
14:7 ᴬEzek 36:25   14:8 ᴬNum 5:2, 3; 2 Chr 26:21
14:9 ᴬLev 14:8, 20   14:10 ᴬLev 14:12, 15, 21, 24
14:12 ᴬLev 5:6, 18   ᴮEx 29:22-24, 26   14:13 ᴬEx 29:11;
Lev 1:11   14:14 ᴬEx 29:20; Lev 8:23, 24   14:15 ᴬLev 14:10

14:10 ¹About 1 cubic foot or 0.03 cubic meters
²About 0.6 pt. or 0.3 liter   14:12 ¹About 0.6 pt. or
0.3 liter   14:15 ¹About 0.6 pt. or 0.3 liter

head of the one to be cleansed. So the priest shall make ^atonement on his behalf before the LORD. ¹⁹The priest shall next offer the ^sin offering and make atonement for the one to be cleansed from his uncleanness. Then afterward, he shall slaughter the burnt offering. ²⁰The priest shall offer up the burnt offering and the grain offering on the altar. So the priest shall make atonement for him, and ^he will be clean.

²¹ "^But if he is poor and his means are insufficient, then he is to take one male lamb for a guilt offering as a wave offering to make atonement for him, and a tenth *of an* ¹*ephah* of fine flour mixed with oil as a grain offering, and a ²log of oil, ²²and two turtledoves or two young doves, which are within his means. ^The one shall be a sin offering, and the other a burnt offering. ²³^Then on the eighth day he shall bring them for his cleansing to the priest, at the doorway of the tent of meeting, before the LORD. ²⁴The priest shall take the lamb of the guilt offering and ^the ¹log of oil, and the priest shall offer them as a wave offering before the LORD. ²⁵Next he shall slaughter the lamb of the guilt offering; and the priest is to take some of the blood of the guilt offering and put *it* on ^the lobe of the right ear of the one to be cleansed, and on the thumb of his right hand, and on the big toe of his right foot. ²⁶The priest shall also pour some of the oil into his left palm; ²⁷and with his right-hand finger the priest shall sprinkle some of the oil that is in his left palm seven times before the LORD. ²⁸The priest shall then put some of the oil that is in his palm on the lobe of the right

ear of the one to be cleansed, and on the thumb of his right hand, and on the big toe of his right foot, on the place of the blood of the guilt offering. ²⁹Moreover, the rest of the oil that is in the priest's palm, he shall put on the head of the one to be cleansed, to make atonement on his behalf before the LORD. ³⁰He shall then offer one of the turtle-doves or young doves, which are within his means. ³¹*He shall offer* what he can afford, ^the one as a sin offering and the other as a burnt offering, together with the grain offering. So the priest shall make atonement before the LORD on behalf of the one to be cleansed. ³²This is the law *for him* in whom there is an infection of leprosy, whose means are limited for his cleansing."

CLEANSING A LEPROUS HOUSE

³³The LORD further spoke to Moses and to Aaron, saying:

³⁴ "^When you enter the land of Canaan, which I am giving you as a possession, and I put a spot of leprosy on a house in the land of your possession, ³⁵then the one who owns the house shall come and tell the priest, saying, '*Something* like ^a spot *of leprosy* has become visible to me in the house.' ³⁶The priest shall then command that they empty the house before the priest goes in to look at the spot, so that everything in the house need not become unclean; and afterward the priest

14:18 ^Lev 4:26; Heb 2:17   14:19 ^Lev 14:12
14:20 ^Lev 14:8, 9   14:21 ^Lev 5:11; 12:8
14:22 ^Lev 5:7   14:23 ^Lev 14:10, 11   14:24 ^Lev 14:10
14:25 ^Lev 14:14   14:31 ^Lev 5:7   14:34 ^Deut 7:1;
32:49   14:35 ^Ps 91:10

14:21 ¹About 1 cubic foot or 0.03 cubic meters
²About 0.6 pt. or 0.3 liter   14:24 ¹About 0.6 pt. or
0.3 liter

shall go in to look at the house. [37]So he shall look at the spot, and if the spot on the walls of the house has greenish or reddish depressions and appears deeper than the surface, [38]the priest shall come out of the house, to the doorway, and quarantine the house for seven days. [39]Then the priest shall return on the seventh day and make an inspection. If the spot has indeed spread on the walls of the house, [40]the priest shall order them to pull out the stones with the spot on them and throw them away at an unclean place outside the city. [41]And he shall have the house scraped all around inside, and they shall dump the plaster that they scrape off at an unclean place outside the city. [42]Then they shall take other stones and replace the *discarded* stones, and he shall take other plaster and replaster the house.

[43]"If, however, the spot breaks out again in the house after he has pulled out the stones and scraped the house, and after it has been replastered, [44]then the priest shall come in and make an inspection. If he sees that the spot has indeed spread in the house, it is ^a malignant spot in the house; it is unclean. [45]*The owner* shall therefore tear down the house, its stones, its timbers, and all the plaster of the house, and he shall take *them* outside the city to an ^unclean place. [46]Moreover, whoever goes into the house during the time that he has quarantined it, becomes ^unclean until evening. [47]Likewise, whoever lies down in the house shall wash his clothes, and whoever eats in the house shall wash his clothes.

[48]"If, on the other hand, the priest comes in and makes an inspection and the spot has not indeed spread in the house after the house has been replastered, then the priest shall pronounce the house clean because the spot has not reappeared. [49]To cleanse the house then, he shall take ^two birds, cedar wood, a scarlet string, and hyssop, [50]and he shall slaughter the one bird in an earthenware vessel over running water. [51]Then he shall take the cedar wood, the ^hyssop, and the scarlet string, with the live bird, and dip them in the blood of the slaughtered bird as well as in the running water, and sprinkle the house seven times. [52]So he shall cleanse the house with the blood of the bird and with the running water, along with the live bird, the cedar wood, the hyssop, and the scarlet string. [53]However, he shall let the live bird go free outside the city into the open field. So he shall make atonement for the house, and it will be clean."

[54]This is the law for any spot of leprosy—even for a ^scale, [55]and for the ^leprous garment or house, [56]and ^for a swelling, for a scab, and for a bright spot— [57]to teach when they are unclean and when they are clean. This is the law of leprosy.

CLEANSING UNHEALTHINESS

15 The LORD also spoke to Moses and to Aaron, saying, [2]"Speak to the sons of Israel, and say to them, '^When any man has a discharge from his body, his discharge is unclean. [3]This, moreover, shall be his uncleanness in his discharge: it is his uncleanness

14:44^Lev 13:51   14:45^Lev 14:41
14:46^Num 19:7, 10, 21, 22   14:49^Lev 14:4
14:51^1 Kin 4:33; Ps 51:7   14:54^Lev 13:30
14:55^Lev 13:47-52   14:56^Lev 13:2
15:2^Num 5:2; 2 Sam 3:29

whether his body allows its discharge to flow or whether his body obstructs its discharge. ⁴Every bed on which the man with the discharge lies becomes unclean, and everything on which he sits becomes unclean. ⁵Anyone, moreover, who touches his bed shall wash his clothes and bathe in water and be unclean until evening; ⁶and whoever sits on the thing on which the man with the discharge has been sitting, shall wash his clothes and bathe in water and be unclean until evening. ⁷Also whoever touches the man with the discharge shall wash his clothes and bathe in water and be unclean until evening. ⁸Or if the man with the discharge spits on one who is clean, he too shall wash his clothes and bathe in water and be unclean until evening. ⁹Every saddle on which the man with the discharge rides becomes unclean. ¹⁰Whoever then touches any of the things which were under him shall be unclean until evening, and the one who carries them shall wash his clothes and bathe in water and be unclean until evening. ¹¹Likewise, whomever the man with the discharge touches without having rinsed his hands in water shall wash his clothes and bathe in water and be unclean until evening. ¹²However, an ^earthenware vessel which the man with the discharge touches shall be broken, and every wooden vessel·shall be rinsed in water.

¹³'Now when the man with the discharge becomes cleansed from his discharge, then he ^shall count off for himself seven days for his cleansing; he shall then wash his clothes and bathe his body in running water and will become clean.

¹⁴Then on the eighth day he shall take for himself ^two turtledoves or two young doves, and come before the Lord to the doorway of the tent of meeting and give them to the priest; ¹⁵and the priest shall offer them, one as a sin offering and the other as a burnt offering. So ^the priest shall make atonement on his behalf before the Lord because of his discharge.

¹⁶'^Now if a man has a seminal emission, he shall bathe all his body in water and be unclean until evening. ¹⁷As for any garment or any leather on which there is a seminal emission, it shall be washed with water and be unclean until evening. ¹⁸If a man sleeps with a woman *so that* there is a seminal emission, they shall both bathe in water and be ^unclean until evening.

¹⁹'^When a woman has a discharge, *if* her discharge in her body is blood, she shall continue in her menstrual impurity for seven days; and whoever touches her shall be unclean until evening. ²⁰Everything also on which she lies during her menstrual impurity shall be unclean, and everything on which she sits shall be unclean. ²¹Anyone who touches her bed shall wash his clothes and bathe in water and be unclean until evening. ²²Whoever touches any object on which she sits shall wash his clothes and bathe in water and be unclean until evening. ²³Whether it be on the bed or on the thing on which she is sitting, when he touches it, he shall be unclean until evening. ²⁴^If a man actually sleeps with her so that her

15:12 ^Lev 6:28; 11:33   15:13 ^Lev 8:33; 14:8
15:14 ^Lev 14:22, 23   15:15 ^Lev 14:19, 31
15:16 ^Lev 22:4; Deut 23:10, 11   15:18 ^1 Sam 21:4
15:19 ^Lev 12:2   15:24 ^Lev 18:19; 20:18

menstrual impurity is on him, he shall be unclean seven days, and every bed on which he lies shall be unclean.

25 ^Now if a woman has a discharge of her blood for many days, not at the period of her menstrual impurity, or if she has a discharge beyond that period, for all the days of her impure discharge she shall continue as though in her menstrual impurity; she is unclean. 26 Any bed on which she lies all the days of her discharge shall be to her like her bed at menstruation; and every object on which she sits shall be unclean, like her uncleanness at that time. 27 Likewise, whoever touches them shall be unclean, and shall wash his clothes and bathe in water and be unclean until evening. 28 When she becomes clean from her discharge, she shall count off for herself seven days; and afterward she will be clean. 29 Then on the eighth day she shall take for herself two turtledoves or two young doves, and bring them to the priest, to the doorway of the tent of meeting. 30 And the priest shall offer the ^one as a sin offering, and the other as a burnt offering. So the priest shall make atonement on her behalf before the Lord because of her impure discharge.'

31 "And so you shall keep the sons of Israel separated from their uncleanness, so that they will not die in their uncleanness by their ^defiling My tabernacle that is among them." 32 This is the law for the one with a discharge, and for the man who has a seminal emission so that he is unclean by it, 33 and for the woman who is ill because of menstrual impurity, and for the one who has a discharge,

whether a male or a female, or a man who sleeps with an unclean woman.

LAW OF ATONEMENT

16 Now the Lord spoke to Moses after ^the death of the two sons of Aaron, when they had approached the presence of the Lord and died. 2 The Lord said to Moses:

"Tell your brother Aaron that he shall not enter at any time into the Holy Place inside the veil, before the ^1atoning cover which is on the ark, or he will die; for ^I will appear in the cloud over the atoning cover. 3 Aaron shall enter the Holy Place with this: with a bull as a ^sin offering and a ram as a burnt offering. 4 He shall put on the ^holy linen tunic, and the linen undergarments shall be next to his body, and he shall be wrapped about the waist with the linen sash and the linen turban wound around *his forehead* (these are holy garments). He shall bathe his body in water and put them on. 5 And he shall take from the congregation of the sons of Israel ^two male goats as a sin offering, and one ram as a burnt offering. 6 Then ^Aaron shall offer the bull as the sin offering, which is for himself, so that he may make atonement for himself and for his household. 7 He shall then take the two goats and present them before the Lord at the doorway of the tent of meeting. 8 Aaron shall cast lots for

15:25 ^Matt 9:20; Luke 8:43   15:30 ^Lev 5:7
15:31 ^Ezek 5:11; 36:17   16:1 ^Lev 10:1, 2
16:2 ^Ex 25:21, 22; 1 Kin 8:10–12   16:3 ^Lev 4:1–12;
Heb 9:7   16:4 ^Ex 28:39, 42   16:5 ^2 Chr 29:21;
Ezek 45:22   16:6 ^Heb 5:3

16:2 ^1 Also called *mercy seat*, and so throughout the ch; i.e., where blood was sprinkled on the Day of Atonement

the two goats, one lot for the LORD and the other lot for the ¹scapegoat. ⁹Then Aaron shall offer the goat on which the lot for the LORD fell, and make it a sin offering. ¹⁰But the goat on which the lot for the scapegoat fell shall be presented alive before the LORD, to make ᴬatonement upon it, to send it into the wilderness as the scapegoat.

¹¹"Then Aaron shall offer the bull of the sin offering ᴬwhich is for himself and make atonement for himself and ᴮfor his household, and he shall slaughter the bull of the sin offering which is for himself. ¹²He shall take a ᴬfirepan full of coals of fire from upon the altar before the LORD and two handfuls of finely ground ᴮsweet incense, and bring *it* inside the veil. ¹³He shall put the incense on the fire before the LORD, so that the cloud of incense may cover the ᴬatoning cover that is on *the ark of* the testimony, otherwise he will die. ¹⁴Moreover, ᴬhe shall take some of the blood of the bull and sprinkle *it* ᴮwith his finger on the atoning cover on the east *side;* also in front of the atoning cover he shall sprinkle some of the blood with his finger seven times.

¹⁵"Then he shall slaughter the goat of the sin offering, ᴬwhich is for the people, and bring its blood inside the veil and do with its blood as he did with the blood of the bull, and sprinkle it on the atoning cover and in front of the atoning cover. ¹⁶ᴬHe shall make atonement for the Holy Place, because of the impurities of the sons of Israel and because of their unlawful acts regarding all their sins; and he shall do so for the tent of meeting which remains with them in the midst of their impurities. ¹⁷When he goes in to make atonement in the Holy Place, no one shall be in the tent of meeting until he comes out, so that he may make atonement for himself and for his household, and for all the assembly of Israel. ¹⁸Then he shall go out to the altar that is before the LORD and make atonement for it; he shall take some of the blood from the bull and *some* of the blood from the goat, and ᴬput it on the horns of the altar on all sides. ¹⁹ᴬWith his finger he shall sprinkle some of the blood on it seven times and cleanse it, and consecrate it from the impurities of the sons of Israel.

²⁰"When he finishes atoning for the Holy Place and the tent of meeting and the altar, he shall offer the live goat. ²¹Then Aaron shall lay both of his hands on the head of the live goat, and ᴬconfess over it all the wrongdoings of the sons of Israel and all their unlawful acts regarding all their sins; and he shall place them on the head of the goat and send *it* away into the wilderness by the hand of a man who *stands* ready. ²²Then the goat shall carry on itself all their wrongdoings to an isolated territory; he shall release the goat in the wilderness.

²³"Then Aaron shall come into the tent of meeting and take off ᴬthe linen garments which he put on when he went into the Holy Place, and shall leave them there. ²⁴And ᴬhe shall bathe his body with water in a holy place and put on ᴮhis

16:10 ᴬ Is 53:4-10; Rom 3:25   16:11 ᴬ Heb 7:27
ᴮ Lev 16:33   16:12 ᴬ Lev 10:1   ᴮ Ex 30:34-38
16:13 ᴬ Ex 25:21   16:14 ᴬ Heb 9:25   ᴮ Lev 4:6, 17
16:15 ᴬ Heb 7:27; 9:7, 12   16:16 ᴬ Ex 30:10; Heb 2:17
16:18 ᴬ Lev 4:25; Ezek 43:20, 22   16:19 ᴬ Lev 16:14;
Ezek 43:20   16:21 ᴬ Lev 5:5   16:23 ᴬ Lev 16:4;
Ezek 42:14   16:24 ᴬ Lev 16:4   ᴮ Ex 28:40, 41

16:8 ¹ I.e., the goat that leaves (escapes); or *goat of removal* of sins

clothes, and come out and offer his burnt offering and the burnt offering of the people, and make atonement for himself and for the people. 25 Then he shall offer up in smoke the fat of the sin offering on the altar. 26 The one who released the goat as the scapegoat ^shall wash his clothes and bathe his body with water; then afterward he shall come into the camp. 27 But the bull of the sin offering and the goat of the sin offering, ^whose blood was brought in to make atonement in the Holy Place, shall be taken outside the camp, and they shall burn their hides, their flesh, and their refuse in the fire. 28 Then the ^one who burns them shall wash his clothes and bathe his body with water; and afterward he shall come into the camp.

AN ANNUAL ATONEMENT

29 "This shall be a permanent statute for you: ^in the seventh month, on the tenth day of the month, you shall humble yourselves and not do any work, whether the native, or the stranger who resides among you; 30 for it is on this day that atonement shall be made for you to ^cleanse you; you will be clean from all your sins before the LORD. 31 It is to be a Sabbath of solemn rest for you, so that you may ^humble yourselves; it is a permanent statute. 32 So the priest who is anointed and ordained to serve as priest in his father's place shall make atonement: he shall put on ^the linen garments, the holy garments, 33 and make atonement for the holy sanctuary, and he shall make atonement for the tent of meeting and for the altar. He shall also make atonement for ^the priests and for all the people of the assembly. 34 Now you shall have this as a permanent statute, to ^make atonement for the sons of Israel for all their sins once every year." And just as the LORD had commanded Moses, so he did.

BLOOD FOR ATONEMENT

17 Then the LORD spoke to Moses, saying, 2 "Speak to Aaron and to his sons and to all the sons of Israel, and say to them, 'This is what the LORD has commanded, saying, 3 "Anyone from the house of Israel who slaughters an ox, a lamb, or a goat in the camp, or slaughters it outside the camp, 4 and ^has not brought it to the doorway of the tent of meeting to present it as an offering to the LORD in front of the tabernacle of the LORD, bloodshed is to be counted against that person. He has shed blood, and that person shall be cut off from among his people. 5 This shall be done so that the sons of Israel will bring their sacrifices which they were sacrificing in the open field—so that they will bring them to the LORD at the doorway of the tent of meeting to the priest, and sacrifice them as sacrifices of peace offerings to the LORD. 6 The priest shall sprinkle the blood on the altar of the LORD at the doorway of the tent of meeting, and ^offer up the fat in smoke as a soothing aroma to the LORD. 7 And ^they shall no longer offer their sacrifices to the goat demons with which they play the prostitute. This shall be a permanent statute to them throughout their generations."'

16:26 ^Lev 11:25, 40   16:27 ^Lev 6:30; Heb 13:11
16:28 ^Num 19:8   16:29 ^Lev 23:27; Num 29:7
16:30 ^Jer 33:8; Eph 5:26   16:31 ^Ezra 8:21; Is 58:3, 5
16:32 ^Lev 16:4   16:33 ^Lev 16:11   16:34 ^Heb 9:7
17:4 ^Deut 12:5-21   17:6 ^Num 18:17
17:7 ^Ex 22:20; 1 Cor 10:20

8"Then you shall say to them, 'Anyone from the house of Israel, or from the strangers who reside among them, who offers a burnt offering or sacrifice, 9and ^does not bring it to the doorway of the tent of meeting to offer it to the Lord, that person also shall be cut off from his people.

10'And anyone from the house of Israel, or from the strangers who reside among them, who eats any blood, ^I will set My face against that person who eats the blood, and will cut him off from among his people. 11For ^the life of the flesh is in the blood, and I have given it to you on the altar to make atonement for your souls; for it is the blood by reason of the life that makes atonement.' 12Therefore I said to the sons of Israel, 'No person among you may eat blood, nor may any stranger who resides among you eat blood.' 13So when anyone from the sons of Israel, or from the strangers who reside among them, while hunting catches an animal or a bird which may be eaten, ^he shall pour out its blood and cover it with dirt.

14"^For *as for the* life of all flesh, its blood is *identified* with its life. Therefore I said to the sons of Israel, 'You are not to eat the blood of any flesh, for the life of all flesh is its blood; whoever eats it shall be cut off.' 15And ^any person who eats an animal which dies or is torn *by animals,* whether he is a native or a stranger, shall wash his clothes and bathe in water, and remain unclean until evening; then he will become clean. 16But if he does not wash *his clothes* and bathe his body, then ^he shall bear *the responsibility for* his guilt."

LAWS ON IMMORAL RELATIONS

18 Then the Lord spoke to Moses, saying, 2"Speak to the sons of Israel and say to them, '^I am the Lord your God. 3You shall not do what is ^done in the land of Egypt where you lived, nor are you to do what is done in the land of Canaan where I am bringing you; you shall not walk in their statutes. 4You are to perform My judgments and keep My statutes, to live in accord with them; ^I am the Lord your God. 5So you shall keep My statutes and My judgments, ^which, *if* a person follows them, then he will live by them; I am the Lord.

6'None *of you* shall approach any blood relative of his to uncover nakedness; I am the Lord. 7^You shall not uncover the nakedness of your father, that is, the nakedness of your mother. She is your mother; you are not to uncover her nakedness. 8^You shall not uncover the nakedness of your father's wife; it is your father's nakedness. 9*As for* ^the nakedness of your sister, *either* your father's daughter or your mother's daughter, *whether* born in the household or born outside *the household,* you shall not uncover their nakedness. 10The nakedness of your son's daughter or your daughter's daughter, their nakedness you shall not uncover; for their nakedness is yours. 11The nakedness of your father's wife's daughter, born to your father, she is your sister; you shall not uncover her nakedness. 12^You shall not uncover the

17:9 ^Ex 20:24; Lev 17:4   17:10 ^Lev 20:3, 6; Jer 44:11
17:11 ^Gen 9:4; Lev 17:14   17:13 ^Deut 12:16
17:14 ^Gen 9:4; Lev 17:11   17:15 ^Ex 22:31; Lev 7:24
17:16 ^Num 19:20   18:2 ^Ex 6:7; Ezek 20:5
18:3 ^Ezek 20:7, 8   18:4 ^Lev 18:2   18:5 ^Rom 10:5;
Gal 3:12   18:7 ^Lev 20:11; Deut 27:20   18:8 ^Lev 20:11;
1 Cor 5:1   18:9 ^Lev 18:11; Deut 27:22   18:12 ^Lev 20:19

nakedness of your father's sister; she is your father's blood relative. [13] You shall not uncover the nakedness of your mother's sister, for she is your mother's blood relative. [14] ^You shall not uncover the nakedness of your father's brother. You shall not approach his wife; she is your aunt. [15] ^You shall not uncover the nakedness of your daughter-in-law. She is your son's wife; you shall not uncover her nakedness. [16] ^You shall not uncover the nakedness of your brother's wife; it is your brother's nakedness. [17] ^You shall not uncover the nakedness of a woman and of her daughter, nor shall you take her son's daughter or her daughter's daughter, to uncover her nakedness; they are blood relatives. It is an outrageous sin. [18] And you shall not marry a woman in addition to her sister as a second wife while she is alive, to uncover her nakedness.

[19] ^'Also you shall not approach a woman to uncover her nakedness during her menstrual impurity. [20] And ^you shall not have sexual intercourse with your neighbor's wife, to be defiled with her. [21] You shall not give any of your children ^to offer them to Molech, nor shall you profane the name of your God; I am the LORD. [22] ^You shall not sleep with a male as one sleeps with a female; it is an abomination. [23] ^Also you shall not have sexual intercourse with any animal to be defiled with it, nor shall any woman stand before an animal to mate with it; it is a perversion.

[24] 'Do not defile yourselves by any of these things; for by all these things ^the nations which I am driving out from you have become

defiled. [25] For the land has become defiled, ^therefore I have brought its punishment upon it, so the land has vomited out its inhabitants. [26] But as for you, you are to keep My statutes and My judgments, and you shall not do any of these abominations, *neither* the native, nor the stranger who resides among you [27] (for the people of the land who were *there* before you did all these abominations, and the land has become defiled), [28] so that the land will not vomit you out should you defile it, as it has vomited out the nation which was *there* before you. [29] For whoever does any of these abominations, those persons who do *so* shall be cut off from among their people. [30] So you are to keep ^your commitment to Me not to practice any of the abominable customs which have been practiced before you, so that you do not defile yourselves with them; I am the LORD your God.'"

IDOLATRY FORBIDDEN

19 Then the LORD spoke to Moses, saying:

[2] "Speak to all the congregation of the sons of Israel and say to them, '^You shall be holy, for I the LORD your God am holy. [3] Every one of you ^shall revere his mother and his father, and you shall keep ^BMy Sabbaths; I am the LORD your God. [4] Do not turn to ^idols or make for yourselves cast metal gods; I am the LORD your God.

18:14 ^Lev 20:20   18:15 ^Lev 20:12   18:16 ^Lev 20:21
18:17 ^Lev 20:14   18:19 ^Lev 15:24; 20:18
18:20 ^Lev 20:10; Heb 13:4   18:21 ^Lev 20:2-5;
Deut 12:31   18:22 ^Lev 20:13; Rom 1:27
18:23 ^Lev 20:15, 16; Deut 27:21   18:24 ^Lev 18:3;
Deut 18:12   18:25 ^Lev 20:23; Deut 9:5
18:30 ^Lev 22:9; Deut 11:1   19:2 ^Eph 1:4; 1 Pet 1:16
19:3 ^Deut 5:16   ^BEx 20:8   19:4 ^Lev 26:1; Ps 115:4-7

⁵'Now when you offer a sacrifice of peace offerings to the Lord, you shall offer it so that you may be accepted. ⁶It shall be eaten on the same day you offer *it,* and on the next day; but what remains until the third day shall be burned with fire. ⁷So if it is eaten at all on the third day, it is unclean; it will not be accepted. ⁸And everyone who eats it will bear *the consequences for* his guilt, because he has profaned the holy thing of the Lord; and that person shall be cut off from his people.

VARIOUS LAWS

⁹'ᴬNow when you reap the harvest of your land, you shall not reap to the very edges of your field, nor shall you gather the gleanings of your harvest. ¹⁰And you shall not glean your vineyard, nor shall you gather the fallen grapes of your vineyard; you shall leave them for the needy and for the stranger. I am the Lord your God.

¹¹'ᴬYou shall not steal, nor deal falsely, nor lie to one another. ¹²And you shall not swear falsely by My name, so as to ᴬprofane the name of your God; I am the Lord.

¹³'ᴬYou shall not oppress your neighbor, nor rob *him.* The wages of a hired worker are not to remain with you all night until morning. ¹⁴You shall not curse a person who is deaf, nor ᴬput a stumbling block before a person who is blind, but you shall revere your God; I am the Lord.

¹⁵'ᴬYou shall not do injustice in judgment; you shall not show partiality to the poor nor give preference to the great, but you are to judge your neighbor fairly. ¹⁶You shall not go about as ᴬa slanderer among your people; *and* you are not to jeopardize the life of your neighbor. I am the Lord.

¹⁷'You ᴬshall not hate your fellow countryman in your heart; you may certainly rebuke your neighbor, but you are not to incur sin because of him. ¹⁸You shall not take vengeance, nor hold any grudge against the sons of your people, but ᴬyou shall love your neighbor as yourself; I am the Lord.

¹⁹'You are to keep My statutes. You shall not cross-breed two kinds of your cattle; ᴬyou shall not sow your field with two kinds of seed, nor wear a garment of two kinds of material mixed together.

²⁰'ᴬNow if a man has sexual relations with a woman who is a slave acquired for *another* man, but who has in no way been redeemed nor given her freedom, there shall be punishment; they shall not, *however,* be put to death, because she was not free. ²¹He shall bring his guilt offering to the Lord to the doorway of the tent of meeting, ᴬa ram as a guilt offering. ²²The priest shall also make atonement for him with the ram of the guilt offering before the Lord for his sin which he has committed, and the sin which he has committed will be forgiven him.

²³'Now when you enter the land and plant all kinds of trees for food, then you shall count their fruit as forbidden. For three years it shall be forbidden to you; *it* shall not be eaten. ²⁴And in the fourth year all its fruit shall be holy, an offering of

19:9 ᴬLev 23:22; Deut 24:20-22   19:11 ᴬEx 20:15, 16
19:12 ᴬLev 18:21   19:13 ᴬEx 22:7-15, 21-27
19:14 ᴬDeut 27:18   19:15 ᴬEx 23:3, 6; Deut 16:19
19:16 ᴬJer 6:28; Ezek 22:9   19:17 ᴬ1 John 2:9, 11; 3:15
19:18 ᴬRom 13:9; Gal 5:14   19:19 ᴬDeut 22:9, 11
19:20 ᴬDeut 22:23-27   19:21 ᴬLev 6:1-7

praise to the LORD. ²⁵But in the fifth year you shall eat its fruit, so that its yield may increase for you; I am the LORD your God.

²⁶'You shall not eat *any meat* with the blood. You shall not practice ᴬdivination nor soothsaying. ²⁷ᴬYou shall not round off the hairline of your heads, nor trim the edges of your beard. ²⁸You shall not make any cuts in your body for the dead, nor make any tattoo marks on yourselves: I am the LORD.

²⁹ᴬDo not profane your daughter by making her a prostitute, so that the land does not fall into prostitution, and the land *does not* become full of outrageous sin. ³⁰You shall ᴬkeep My Sabbaths and ᴮrevere My sanctuary; I am the LORD.

³¹'Do not turn to ᴬmediums or spiritists; do not seek them out to be defiled by them. I am the LORD your God.

³²ᴬYou shall stand up in the presence of the grayheaded and honor elders, and you shall fear your God; I am the LORD.

³³ᴬWhen a stranger resides with you in your land, you shall not do him wrong. ³⁴The stranger who resides with you shall be to you as the native among you, and ᴬyou shall love him as yourself, for you were strangers in the land of Egypt; I am the LORD your God.

³⁵ᴬYou shall do no wrong in judgment, in measurement of weight, or volume. ³⁶You shall have ᴬaccurate balances, accurate weights, an accurate ¹ephah, and an accurate ²hin; I am the LORD your God, who brought you out from the land of Egypt. ³⁷So you shall keep all My statutes and all My ordinances, and do them; I am the LORD.'"

ON HUMAN SACRIFICE AND IMMORALITIES

20 Then the LORD spoke to Moses, saying, ²"You shall also say to the sons of Israel:

'Anyone from the sons of Israel or from the strangers residing in Israel ᴬwho gives any of his children to Molech, shall certainly be put to death; the people of the land shall stone him with stones. ³I will also set My face against that man and will cut him off from among his people, because he has given some of his children to Molech, ᴬso as to defile My sanctuary and ᴮto profane My holy name. ⁴If the people of the land, however, should ever disregard that man when he gives any of his children to Molech, so as not to put him to death, ⁵then I Myself will set My face against that man and against his family, and I will cut off from among their people both him and all those who play the prostitute with him, by playing the prostitute with Molech.

⁶'As for the person who turns to ᴬmediums and to spiritists, to play the prostitute with them, I will also set My face against that person and will cut him off from among his people. ⁷You shall consecrate yourselves therefore and ᴬbe holy, for I am the LORD your God. ⁸So ᴬyou shall keep My statutes and practice them; I am the LORD who sanctifies you.

19:26 ᴬDeut 18:10; 2 Kin 17:17
19:27 ᴬLev 21:5; Deut 14:1 **19:29** ᴬLev 21:9;
Deut 22:21 **19:30** ᴬLev 19:3 ᴮLev 26:2
19:31 ᴬLev 20:6, 27; Deut 18:11 **19:32** ᴬLam 5:12;
1 Tim 5:1 **19:33** ᴬEx 22:21; Deut 24:17, 18
19:34 ᴬLev 19:18 **19:35** ᴬDeut 25:13-16; Ezek 45:10
19:36 ᴬDeut 25:13-15; Prov 20:10 **20:2** ᴬLev 18:21
20:3 ᴬLev 15:31 ᴮLev 18:21 **20:6** ᴬLev 19:31
20:7 ᴬEph 1:4; 1 Pet 1:16 **20:8** ᴬEx 31:13

19:36 ¹I.e., a dry measure, about 1 cubic foot or 0.03 cubic meters ²I.e., a liquid measure, about 1 gallon or 3.8 liters

9 ᴬIf *there is* anyone who curses his father or his mother, he shall certainly be put to death. He has cursed his father or his mother, *and has brought* his own death upon himself.

10 ᴬIf *there is* a man who commits adultery with another man's wife, one who commits adultery with his friend's wife, the adulterer and the adulteress must be put to death. 11 ᴬIf *there is* a man who sleeps with his father's wife, he has uncovered his father's nakedness. Both of them must be put to death, *they have brought* their own deaths upon themselves. 12 ᴬIf *there is* a man who sleeps with his daughter-in-law, both of them must be put to death. They have committed incest, *and have brought* their own deaths upon themselves. 13 ᴬIf *there is* a man who sleeps with a male as those who sleep with a woman, both of them have committed a detestable act; they must be put to death. *They have brought* their own deaths upon themselves. 14 ᴬIf *there is* a man who marries a woman and her mother, it is an outrageous sin; both he and they shall be burned with fire, so that there will be no *such* outrageous sin in your midst. 15 ᴬIf *there is* a man who has sexual intercourse with an animal, he must be put to death; you shall also kill the animal. 16 If *there is* a woman who approaches any animal to mate with it, you shall kill the woman and the animal; they must be put to death. *They have brought* their own deaths upon themselves.

17 ᴬIf *there is* a man who takes his sister, his father's daughter or his mother's daughter, so that he sees her nakedness and she sees his nakedness, it is a disgrace; and they shall be cut off in the sight of the sons of their people. He has uncovered his sister's nakedness; he bears his guilt. 18 ᴬIf *there is* a man who sleeps with a menstruous woman and uncovers her nakedness, he has exposed her flow, and she has uncovered the flow of her blood; so both of them shall be cut off from among their people. 19 ᴬYou shall also not uncover the nakedness of your mother's sister or of your father's sister, for *such a one* has uncovered his blood relative; they will bear their guilt. 20 ᴬIf *there is* a man who sleeps with his uncle's wife, he has uncovered his uncle's nakedness; they will bear their sin. They will die childless. 21 ᴬIf *there is* a man who takes his brother's wife, it is detestable; he has uncovered his brother's nakedness. They will be childless.

22 'You are therefore to keep all My statutes and all My ordinances, and do them, so that the land to which I am bringing you to live will not ᴬvomit you out. 23 Furthermore, you shall not follow ᴬthe customs of the nation which I am going to drive out before you, because they did all these things; therefore I have felt disgust for them. 24 So I have said to you, "ᴬYou are to take possession of their land, and I Myself will give it to you to possess, a land flowing with milk and honey." I am the LORD your God, who has singled you out from the peoples. 25 ᴬYou are therefore to make a distinction

20:9 ᴬEx 21:17; Deut 27:16   20:10 ᴬLev 18:20; Deut 5:18
20:11 ᴬLev 18:7, 8; Deut 27:20   20:12 ᴬLev 18:15
20:13 ᴬLev 18:22   20:14 ᴬLev 18:17; Deut 27:23
20:15 ᴬLev 18:23; Deut 27:21   20:17 ᴬLev 18:9;
Deut 27:22   20:18 ᴬLev 15:24; 18:19
20:19 ᴬLev 18:12, 13   20:20 ᴬLev 18:14   20:21 ᴬLev 18:16
20:22 ᴬLev 18:28   20:23 ᴬLev 18:3   20:24 ᴬEx 13:5;
33:1-3   20:25 ᴬLev 11:1-47; Deut 14:3-21

between the clean animal and the unclean, and between the unclean bird and the clean; and you shall not make yourselves detestable by animal or by bird, or by anything that crawls on the ground, which I have distinguished for you as unclean. 26 So you are to be holy to Me, for I the LORD am holy; and I ^have singled you out from the peoples to be Mine.

27 'Now a man or a woman ^who is a medium or a spiritist must be put to death. They shall be stoned with stones; *they have brought* their own deaths upon themselves.'"

REGULATIONS CONCERNING PRIESTS

21 Then the LORD said to Moses, "Speak to the priests, the sons of Aaron, and say to them: ^"No one shall defile himself for a *dead* person among his people, 2 ^except for his relatives who are nearest to him, his mother, his father, his son, his daughter, and his brother, 3 also for his virgin sister who is near to him because she has not had a husband; for her, he may defile himself. 4 He shall not defile himself as a relative by marriage among his people, so as to profane himself. 5 ^They shall not shave any area on their heads bald, nor shave off the edges of their beards, nor make any cuts in their flesh. 6 They shall be holy to their God and ^not profane the name of their God, because they present the offerings by fire to the LORD, B the food of their God; so they shall be holy. 7 ^They shall not take a woman who is a prostitute and profaned, nor shall they take a woman divorced from her husband; for he is holy to his God. 8 You shall consecrate him, therefore, because he

offers ^the food of your God. He shall be holy to you; for I the LORD, who sanctifies you, am holy. 9 ^Also the daughter of any priest, if she profanes herself by prostitution, she profanes her father; she shall be burned with fire.

10 'The priest who is 1highest among his brothers, on whose head the anointing oil has been poured and who has been consecrated to wear the garments, ^shall not uncover his head nor tear his clothes; 11 ^nor shall he approach any dead person, nor defile himself *even* for his father or his mother; 12 ^nor shall he leave the sanctuary nor profane the sanctuary of his God, for the consecration of the anointing oil of his God is on him; I am the LORD. 13 He shall take a wife in her virginity. 14 ^A widow, or a divorced woman, or one who is profaned by prostitution, these he shall not take; but rather he is to marry a virgin of his own people, 15 so that he will not profane his children among his people; for I am the LORD who sanctifies him.'"

16 Then the LORD spoke to Moses, saying, 17 "Speak to Aaron, saying, 'None of your descendants throughout their generations who has an impairment shall approach to offer the ^food of his God. 18 ^For no one who has an impairment shall approach: a man who is blind, or one who limps, or one who has a ^slit nose, or one with *any* conspicuous feature, 19 or someone who

20:26 ^Lev 20:24　20:27 ^Lev 19:31　21:1 ^Lev 19:28;
Ezek 44:25　21:2 ^Lev 21:11　21:5 ^Deut 14:1;
Ezek 44:20　21:6 ^Lev 18:21　B Lev 3:11
21:7 ^Lev 21:13, 14　21:8 ^Lev 21:6　21:9 ^Gen 38:24;
Lev 19:29　21:10 ^Lev 10:6　21:11 ^Lev 19:28;
Num 19:14　21:12 ^Lev 10:7　21:14 ^Lev 21:7;
Ezek 44:22　21:17 ^Lev 21:6　21:18 ^Lev 22:19-25

21:10 1 I.e., the high priest

has a broken foot or broken hand, 20 or a contorted back, or *one who is* a dwarf, or *has* a spot in his eye, or a festering rash or scabs, or ^crushed testicles. 21 No man among the descendants of Aaron the priest who has an impairment is to come forward to offer the LORD's offerings by fire; *since* he has an impairment, he shall not come forward to offer ^the food of his God. 22 He may eat ^the food of his God, *both* of the most holy and of the holy, 23 only he shall not come up to the veil or approach the altar, since he has an impairment, so that he does not profane My sanctuaries. For I am the LORD who sanctifies them.'" 24 So Moses spoke to Aaron and to his sons and to all the sons of Israel.

VARIOUS RULES FOR PRIESTS

22 Then the LORD spoke to Moses, saying, 2 "Tell Aaron and his sons to be careful with the holy *gifts* of the sons of Israel, which they dedicate to Me, so as not to profane My holy name; I am the LORD. 3 Say to them, '^Any man among all your descendants throughout your generations who approaches the holy *gifts* which the sons of Israel consecrate to the LORD, while he has an uncleanness, that person shall be cut off from My presence; I am the LORD. 4 ^No man of the descendants of Aaron, who has leprosy or has a discharge, may eat of the holy *gifts* until he is clean. And one who touches anything made unclean by a corpse, or a man who has a seminal emission, 5 or ^a man who touches any swarming things by which he is made unclean, or *touches* any person by whom he is made unclean, whatever his uncleanness; 6 a person who touches any such thing shall

be unclean until evening, and shall not eat of the holy *gifts* unless he has bathed his body in water. 7 But when the sun sets, he will be clean, and afterward he may eat of the holy *gifts,* for ^it is his food. 8 He shall not eat ^*an animal* which dies or is torn *by animals,* becoming unclean by it; I am the LORD. 9 They shall therefore perform *their* ^duty to Me, so that they do not bear sin because of it and die by it because they profane it; I am the LORD who sanctifies them.

10 '^No 1layman, however, is to eat the holy *gift;* a foreign resident with the priest or a hired worker shall not eat the holy *gift.* 11 ^But if a priest buys a slave as *his* property with his money, that person may eat of it, and those who are born in his house may eat of his food. 12 If a priest's daughter is married to a layman, she shall not eat of the offering of the holy *gifts.* 13 But if a priest's daughter becomes a widow or divorced, and has no child and returns to her father's house as in her youth, she may eat of her father's food; ^but no layman shall eat of it. 14 ^If, however, someone eats a holy *food* unintentionally, then he shall add to it a fifth of it and shall give the holy *food* to the priest. 15 And ^they shall not profane the holy *gifts* of the sons of Israel, which they offer to the LORD, 16 and *thereby* ^bring upon them punishment for guilt by eating their holy *gifts;* for I am the LORD who sanctifies them.'"

21:20 ^Deut 23:1; Is 56:3-5   21:21 ^Lev 21:6
21:22 ^1 Cor 9:13   22:3 ^Lev 7:20, 21; Num 19:13
22:4 ^Lev 14:1-32   22:5 ^Lev 11:23-28   22:7 ^Num 18:11
22:8 ^Lev 7:24; 11:39, 40   22:9 ^Lev 18:30
22:10 ^Ex 29:33; Lev 22:13   22:11 ^Gen 17:13; Ex 12:44
22:13 ^Lev 22:10   22:14 ^Lev 5:15, 16
22:15 ^Num 18:32   22:16 ^Lev 10:17; 22:9

22:10 1 Or *unauthorized person*

FLAWLESS ANIMALS FOR SACRIFICE

¹⁷Then the LORD spoke to Moses, saying, ¹⁸"Speak to Aaron and to his sons, and to all the sons of Israel, and say to them, 'ᴬAnyone of the house of Israel or of the strangers in Israel who presents his offering, whether it is any of their vows or any of their voluntary offerings, which they present to the LORD as a burnt offering— ¹⁹ᴬfor you to be accepted—*it must be* a male without defect from the cattle, the sheep, or the goats. ²⁰ᴬWhatever has a defect, you shall not offer, for it will not be accepted for you. ²¹When someone offers a sacrifice of peace offerings to the LORD ᴬto fulfill a special vow or for a voluntary offering, of the herd or of the flock, it must be without defect to be accepted; there shall be no defect in it. ²²*Those that are* blind, fractured, maimed, or *have* a wart, a festering rash, or scabs, you shall not offer to the LORD, nor make of them an offering by fire on the altar to the LORD. ²³Now *as for* an ox or a lamb which has an overgrown or stunted *member,* you may present it as a voluntary offering, but for a vow it will not be accepted. ²⁴Also ᴬanything *with its testicles* squashed, crushed, torn off, or cut off, you shall not offer to the LORD, nor sacrifice in your land, ²⁵nor shall you offer any of these *animals taken* from the hand of a foreigner ᴬas the food of your God; for their deformity is in them, they have an impairment. They will not be accepted for you.'"

²⁶Then the LORD spoke to Moses, saying, ²⁷"When an ox or a sheep or a goat is born, it shall remain ᴬseven days with its mother, and from the eighth day on it will be considered acceptable as a sacrifice of an offering by fire to the LORD. ²⁸ᴬBut, *whether* it is an ox or a sheep, you shall not slaughter *both* it and its young in one day. ²⁹When you sacrifice ᴬa sacrifice of thanksgiving to the LORD, you shall sacrifice it so that you may be accepted. ³⁰It shall be eaten on the same day; you shall leave none of it until morning. I am the LORD. ³¹ᴬSo you shall keep My commandments, and do them; I am the LORD.

³²"And you shall not profane My holy name, but I will be sanctified among the sons of Israel; I am the LORD who sanctifies you, ³³ᴬwho brought you out from the land of Egypt, to be your God; I am the LORD."

LAWS OF HOLY DAYS

23 The LORD spoke again to Moses, saying, ²"Speak to the sons of Israel and say to them, 'The LORD's appointed times which you shall ᴬproclaim as holy convocations—My appointed times are these:

³'ᴬFor six days work may be done, but on the seventh day there is a Sabbath of complete rest, a holy convocation. You shall not do any work; it is a Sabbath to the LORD in all your dwellings.

⁴'These are the ᴬappointed times of the LORD, holy convocations which you shall proclaim at the times appointed for them. ⁵ᴬIn the first month, on the fourteenth day of the month at twilight is the LORD's Passover. ⁶Then on the fifteenth day of the same month there

22:18ᴬNum 15:14   22:19ᴬLev 21:18-21; Deut 15:21
22:20ᴬMal 1:8, 14; Heb 9:14   22:21ᴬNum 15:3, 8
22:24ᴬLev 21:20   22:25ᴬLev 21:22   22:27ᴬEx 22:30
22:28ᴬDeut 22:6, 7   22:29ᴬLev 7:12   22:31ᴬLev 19:37;
Num 15:40   22:33ᴬLev 11:45   23:2ᴬLev 23:21
23:3ᴬLev 19:3; Deut 5:13, 14   23:4ᴬEx 23:14;
Lev 23:2   23:5ᴬDeut 16:1; Josh 5:10

is the ^Feast of Unleavened Bread to the LORD; for seven days you shall eat unleavened bread. ⁷On the first day you shall have a holy convocation; you shall ^not do any laborious work. ⁸But for seven days you shall present an offering by fire to the LORD. On the seventh day is a holy convocation; you shall not do any laborious work.'"

⁹Then the LORD spoke to Moses, saying, ¹⁰"Speak to the sons of Israel and say to them, 'When you enter the land which I am going to give to you and you ^gather its harvest, then you shall bring in the sheaf of the first fruits of your harvest to the priest. ¹¹He shall wave the sheaf before the LORD for you to be accepted; on the day after the Sabbath the priest shall wave it. ¹²Now on the day when you wave the sheaf, you shall offer a male lamb one year old without defect as a burnt offering to the LORD. ¹³Its ^grain offering shall then be ¹two-tenths *of an ephah* of fine flour mixed with oil, an offering by fire to the LORD *for* a soothing aroma, with its drink offering, a ²fourth of a hin of wine. ¹⁴Until this very day, until you have brought in the offering of your God, ^you shall eat neither bread nor roasted grain nor new produce. It is to be a permanent statute throughout your generations in all your dwelling places.

¹⁵'^You shall also count for yourselves from the day after the Sabbath, from the day when you brought in the sheaf of the wave offering; there shall be seven complete Sabbaths. ¹⁶You shall count fifty days to the day after the seventh Sabbath; then you shall present a ^new grain offering to the

LORD. ¹⁷You shall bring in from your dwelling places two *loaves* of bread as a wave offering, *made of* ¹two-tenths *of an ephah;* they shall be of a fine flour, baked ^with leaven as first fruits to the LORD. ¹⁸Along with the bread you shall present seven one-year-old male lambs without defect, and a bull of the herd and two rams; they are to be a burnt offering to the LORD, with their grain offering and their drink offerings, an offering by fire of a soothing aroma to the LORD. ¹⁹You shall also offer ^one male goat as a sin offering, and two male lambs one year old as a sacrifice of peace offerings. ²⁰The priest shall then wave them with the bread of the first fruits as a wave offering with two lambs before the LORD; they are to be holy to the LORD for the priest. ²¹On this very day you shall make a proclamation as well; you are to have a holy convocation. You shall do no laborious ^work. It is to be a permanent statute in all your dwelling places throughout your generations.

²²'^When you reap the harvest of your land, moreover, you shall not reap to the very edges of your field nor gather the gleaning of your harvest; you are to leave them for the needy and the stranger. I am the LORD your God.'"

²³Again the LORD spoke to Moses, saying, ²⁴"Speak to the sons of Israel, saying, '^In the seventh

23:6 ^Ex 12:14-20; Deut 16:3-8
23:7 ^Lev 23:8, 21, 25, 35, 36   23:10 ^Ex 23:19; 34:26
23:13 ^Lev 6:20   23:14 ^Ex 34:26; Num 15:20, 21
23:15 ^Num 28:26-31; Deut 16:9-12   23:16 ^Num 28:26
23:17 ^Lev 2:12; 7:13   23:19 ^Lev 4:23; Num 28:30
23:21 ^Lev 23:7   23:22 ^Deut 24:19; Ruth 2:15f
23:24 ^Num 29:1

23:13 ¹About 0.13 cubic feet or 0.004 cubic meters
²About 0.25 gallon or 1 liter   23:17 ¹About 0.13 cubic
feet or 0.004 cubic meters

month on the first of the month you shall have a rest, a [B]reminder by blowing *of trumpets,* a holy convocation. [25]You shall [A]not do any laborious work, but you shall present an offering by fire to the LORD.'"

THE DAY OF ATONEMENT

[26]Then the LORD spoke to Moses, saying, [27]"On exactly the tenth day of this seventh month is [A]the Day of Atonement; it shall be a holy convocation for you, and you shall humble yourselves and present an offering by fire to the LORD. [28]You shall not do any work on this very day, for it is a Day of Atonement, [A]to make atonement on your behalf before the LORD your God. [29]If there is any person who does not humble himself on this very day, [A]he shall be cut off from his people. [30]As for any person who does any work on this very day, that person I will eliminate from among his people. [31]You shall not do any work. It is to be a permanent statute throughout your generations in all your dwelling places. [32]It *is to be* a Sabbath of complete rest for you, and you shall humble yourselves; on the ninth of the month at evening, from evening until evening, you shall keep your Sabbath."

[33]Again the LORD spoke to Moses, saying, [34]"Speak to the sons of Israel, saying, 'On [A]the fifteenth of this seventh month is the Feast of Booths for seven days to the LORD. [35]On the first day is a holy convocation; you shall [A]not do any laborious work. [36][A]For seven days you shall present an offering by fire to the LORD. On the eighth day you shall have a holy convocation and present an offering by fire to the

LORD; it is an assembly. You shall not do any laborious work.

[37]"These are the appointed times of the LORD which you shall proclaim as holy convocations, to present offerings by fire to the LORD—burnt offerings and grain offerings, sacrifices and drink offerings, [A]*each* day's matter on its own day— [38]besides *those of* the Sabbaths of the LORD, and besides your gifts and besides all your vowed and voluntary offerings, which you give to the LORD.

[39]'On exactly the fifteenth day of the seventh month, [A]when you have gathered in the crops of the land, you shall celebrate the feast of the LORD for seven days, with a rest on the first day and a rest on the eighth day. [40]Now on the first day you shall take for yourselves the foliage of beautiful trees, palm branches and branches of trees with thick branches and willows of the brook, and you shall rejoice before the LORD your God for seven days. [41]So you shall celebrate it *as* a feast to the LORD for seven days in the year. *It shall be* a permanent statute throughout your generations; you shall celebrate it in the seventh month. [42]You shall live [A]in booths for seven days; all the native-born in Israel shall live in booths, [43]so that [A]your generations may know that I had the sons of Israel live in booths when I brought them out from the land of Egypt. I am the LORD your God.'" [44]So Moses declared to the sons of Israel [A]the appointed times of the LORD.

23:24 [B]Num 10:9, 10 23:25 [A]Lev 23:21 23:27 [A]Ex 30:10; Lev 16:30 23:28 [A]Lev 16:34 23:29 [A]Gen 17:14; Lev 13:46 23:34 [A]Num 29:12 23:35 [A]Lev 23:25 23:36 [A]Num 29:12-34 23:37 [A]Num 28:1-29:38 23:39 [A]Ex 23:16 23:42 [A]Lev 23:34 23:43 [A]Deut 31:13; Ps 78:5f 23:44 [A]Lev 23:37

THE LAMP AND THE BREAD OF THE SANCTUARY

24 Then the LORD spoke to Moses, saying, 2"Command the sons of Israel that they bring to you ᴬclear oil from beaten olives for the light, to make a lamp burn continually. 3 Outside the veil of the testimony in the tent of meeting, Aaron shall keep it in order from evening to morning before the LORD continually; *it shall be* a permanent statute throughout your generations. 4 He shall keep the lamps in order on the ᴬpure *gold* lampstand before the LORD continually.

5"ᴬThen you shall take fine flour and bake twelve cakes with it; 'two-tenths *of an ephah* shall be *in* each cake. 6 And you shall set them *in* two rows, six *to* a row, on the ᴬpure *gold* table before the LORD. 7 You shall put pure frankincense on each row so that it may be ᴬa memorial portion for the bread, an offering by fire to the LORD. 8 Every Sabbath day he shall set it in order before the LORD ᴬcontinually; it is an everlasting covenant for the sons of Israel. 9 And ᴬit shall be for Aaron and his sons, and they shall eat it in a holy place; for it is most holy to him from the LORD's offerings by fire, *his* portion forever."

10 Now the son of an Israelite woman—his father was an Egyptian—went out among the sons of Israel; and the Israelite woman's son and an Israelite man had a fight within the camp. 11 And the son of the Israelite woman blasphemed the ᴬName and cursed. So they brought him to Moses. (Now his mother's name was Shelomith, the daughter of Dibri, of the tribe of Dan.) 12 Then they put him in custody, *waiting for Moses* to give them a clear decision in accordance with ᴬthe command of the LORD.

13 Then the LORD spoke to Moses, saying, 14"Bring the one who has cursed outside the camp, and have all who heard him ᴬlay their hands on his head; then have all the congregation stone him. 15 You shall also speak to the sons of Israel, saying, 'ᴬIf anyone curses his God, then he will bear *the responsibility for* his sin. 16 Moreover, the one who ᴬblasphemes the name of the LORD must be put to death; all the congregation shall certainly stone him. The stranger as well as the native, when he blasphemes the Name, shall be put to death.

AN EYE FOR AN EYE

17 'Now ᴬif someone takes any human life, he must be put to death. 18 But ᴬthe one who takes the life of an animal shall make restitution, life for life. 19 If someone injures his neighbor, just as he has done, so shall it be done to him: 20 fracture for fracture, ᴬeye for eye, tooth for tooth; just as he has injured a person, so shall it be inflicted on him. 21 So the one who kills an animal shall make restitution, but ᴬthe one who kills a person shall be put to death. 22 There shall be *only* ᴬone standard for you; it shall be for the stranger as well as the native, for I am the LORD your God.'" 23 Then Moses spoke to the sons of Israel, and they brought the one who

24:2 ᴬEx 27:20, 21   24:4 ᴬEx 25:31; 31:8
24:5 ᴬEx 25:30; 40:23   24:6 ᴬEx 25:24; 1 Kin 7:48
24:7 ᴬLev 2:2, 9, 16   24:8 ᴬEx 25:30; Num 4:7
24:9 ᴬMatt 12:4; Luke 6:4   24:11 ᴬJob 2:5, 9; Is 8:21
24:12 ᴬEx 18:15; Num 15:34   24:14 ᴬDeut 13:9; 17:7
24:15 ᴬEx 22:28   24:16 ᴬMatt 12:31; Mark 3:28f
24:17 ᴬNum 35:30, 31; Deut 27:24   24:18 ᴬLev 24:21
24:20 ᴬMatt 5:38   24:21 ᴬLev 24:17
24:22 ᴬEx 12:49; Num 15:15, 16, 29

24:5 ' About 0.13 cubic feet or 0.004 cubic meters

had cursed outside the camp, and stoned him with stones. So the sons of Israel did just as the LORD had commanded Moses.

THE SABBATICAL YEAR
AND YEAR OF JUBILEE

25 The LORD then spoke to Moses on Mount Sinai, saying, ²"Speak to the sons of Israel and say to them, 'When you come into the land which I am going to give you, then the land shall have a Sabbath to the LORD. ³For ^six years you shall sow your field, and for six years you shall prune your vineyard and gather in its produce, ⁴but during ^the seventh year the land shall have a Sabbath rest, a Sabbath to the LORD; you shall not sow your field nor prune your vineyard. ⁵You shall not reap your harvest's ¹after-growth, and you shall not gather your grapes of untrimmed vines; the land shall have a sabbatical year. ⁶^*All of* you shall have the Sabbath *produce* of the land as food; for yourself, your male and female slaves, and your hired worker and your foreign resident, those who live as strangers among you. ⁷Even your cattle and the animals that are in your land shall have all its produce to eat.

⁸'You are also to count off seven Sabbaths of years for yourself, seven times seven years, so that you have the time of the seven Sabbaths of years, *that is,* forty-nine years. ⁹You shall then sound a ram's horn abroad on ^the tenth day of the seventh month; on the Day of Atonement you shall sound a horn all through your land. ¹⁰So you shall consecrate the fiftieth year and ^proclaim ¹a release throughout the land to all its inhabitants. It

shall be a jubilee for you, and each of you shall return to his own property, and each of you shall return to his family. ¹¹You shall have the fiftieth year as a jubilee; you shall not sow, nor harvest its after-growth, nor gather grapes *from* its untrimmed vines. ¹²For it is a jubilee; it shall be holy to you. You shall eat its produce from the field.

¹³^'On this year of jubilee each of you shall return to his own property. ¹⁴Furthermore, if you make a sale to your friend, or buy from your friend's hand, ^you shall not wrong one another. ¹⁵Corresponding to the number of years after the jubilee, you shall buy from your friend; he is to sell to you according to the number of years of crops. ¹⁶^In proportion to a greater number of years you shall increase its price, and in proportion to fewer years you shall decrease its price, because *it is* the number of crops *that* he is selling to you. ¹⁷So ^you shall not wrong one another, but you shall fear your God; for I am the LORD your God.

¹⁸'You shall therefore follow My statutes and keep My judgments so as to carry them out, so that ^you may live securely on the land. ¹⁹Then the land will yield its produce, so that you can eat your fill and live securely on it. ²⁰But if you say, "^What are we going to eat in the seventh year if we do not sow nor gather in our produce?" ²¹then ^I will so order My blessing for you

25:3^Ex 23:10, 11   25:4^Lev 25:20
25:6^Lev 25:20, 21   25:9^Lev 23:27
25:10^Jer 34:8, 15, 17   25:13^Lev 25:10; 27:24
25:14^Lev 25:17   25:16^Lev 25:27, 51, 52
25:17^Jer 7:5, 6; 1 Thess 4:6   25:18^Lev 26:5;
Deut 12:10   25:20^Lev 25:4   25:21^Deut 28:8

25:5 ¹Lit *growth from spilled kernels*
25:10 ¹Or *freedom*

in the sixth year that it will bring forth the produce for three years. 22When you are sowing the eighth year, you can still eat ^old things from the produce, eating *the old* until the ninth year when its produce comes in.

THE LAW OF REDEMPTION

23'The land, moreover, shall not be sold permanently, because ^the land is Mine; for you are *only* strangers and residents with Me. 24So for every piece of your property, you are to provide for the redemption of the land.

25'^If a fellow countryman of yours becomes so poor that he sells part of his property, then his closest ¹redeemer is to come and buy back what his relative has sold. 26Or in case someone has no redeemer, but recovers to find sufficient means for its redemption, 27^then he shall calculate the years since its sale and refund the balance to the man to whom he sold it, and so return to his property. 28But if he has not found sufficient means to get it back for himself, then what he has sold shall remain in the hands of its purchaser until the year of jubilee; but at the jubilee it shall revert, so that ^he may return to his property. 29'Likewise, if a man sells a dwelling house in a walled city, then his redemption right remains *valid* until a full year after its sale; his right of redemption lasts a full year. 30But if it is not bought back for him within the space of a full year, then the house that is in the walled city passes permanently to its purchaser throughout his generations; it does not revert in the jubilee. 31The houses of the villages, however, which have no surrounding wall,

shall be regarded as open fields; they have redemption rights and revert in the jubilee. 32As for the ^cities of the Levites, the Levites have a permanent right of redemption for the houses of the cities which are their possession. 33What, therefore, belongs to the Levites may be redeemed, and a house sale in the city of this possession reverts in the jubilee, because the houses of the cities of the Levites are their possession among the sons of Israel. 34^But pasture fields of their cities shall not be sold, for that is their permanent possession.

OF POOR COUNTRYMEN

35'^Now in case a countryman of yours becomes poor and his means among you falter, then you are to sustain him, *like* a stranger or a resident, so that he may live with you. 36^Do not take *any kind of* interest from him, but fear your God, so that your countryman may live with you. 37You shall not give him your silver at interest, nor your food for profit. 38^I am the LORD your God, who brought you out of the land of Egypt to give you the land of Canaan, *and* ^Bto be your God.

39'Now ^if a countryman of yours becomes so poor with regard to you that he sells himself to you, you shall not subject him to a slave's service. 40He shall be with you as a hired worker, ^as *if he were* a foreign resident; he shall serve with you up to the year of jubilee. 41He shall then leave you, he and his

25:22^Lev 26:10   25:23^Ex 19:5   25:25^Ruth 2:20; 4:4, 6   25:27^Lev 25:16   25:28^Lev 25:10, 13 25:32^Num 35:1-8; Josh 21:2   25:34^Num 35:2-5 25:35^Deut 15:7-11; 24:14, 15   25:36^Ex 22:25; Deut 23:19, 20   25:38^Lev 11:45   ^BGen 17:7 25:39^Ex 21:2-6; Deut 15:12-18   25:40^Ex 21:2

25:25¹I.e., male relative to act in his behalf

sons with him, and shall go back to his family, so that he may return to the property of his forefathers. ⁴²For they are My servants whom I brought out from the land of Egypt; they are not to be sold *in* a slave sale. ⁴³ᴬYou shall not rule over him with severity, but are to revere your God. ⁴⁴As for your male and female slaves whom you may have—you may acquire male and female slaves from the *pagan* nations that are around you. ⁴⁵You may also acquire *them* from the sons of the foreign residents who reside among you, and from their families who are with you, whom they will have produced in your land; they also may become your possession. ⁴⁶You may also pass them on as an inheritance to your sons after you, to receive as a possession; you can use them as permanent slaves. ᴬBut in respect to your countrymen, the sons of Israel, you shall not rule with severity over one another.

OF REDEEMING A PERSON
WHO IS POOR

⁴⁷'Now if the means of a stranger or of a foreign resident with you becomes sufficient, and a countryman of yours becomes poor in relation to him and sells himself to a stranger who is residing with you, or to the descendants of a stranger's family, ⁴⁸then he shall have redemption right after he has been sold. One of his brothers may redeem him, ⁴⁹or his uncle, or his uncle's son may redeem him, or one of his blood relatives from his family may redeem him; or ᴬif he prospers, he may redeem himself. ⁵⁰He then, with his purchaser, shall calculate from the year when he sold himself to him up to the year of jubilee; and the price of his sale shall correspond to the number of years *calculated. It is* like the days of a hired worker *that* he will be with him. ⁵¹If there are still many years *remaining,* ᴬhe shall refund part of his purchase price in proportion to them for his own redemption; ⁵²but if few years remain until the year of jubilee, he shall so calculate with him. In proportion to his years he is to refund *the amount for* his redemption. ⁵³He shall be with him like a worker hired year by year; ᴬhe shall not rule over him with severity in your sight. ⁵⁴Even if he is not redeemed by these means, ᴬhe shall still leave in the year of jubilee, he and his sons with him. ⁵⁵For the sons of Israel are My servants; they are My servants whom I brought out from the land of Egypt. I am the LORD your God.

BLESSINGS OF OBEDIENCE

26 'You shall not make for yourselves idols, nor shall you set up for yourselves a carved image or ᴬa memorial stone, nor shall you place a ᴮfigured stone in your land to bow down to it; for I am the LORD your God. ²ᴬYou shall keep My Sabbaths and revere My sanctuary; I am the LORD. ³ᴬIf you walk in My statutes and keep My commandments so as to carry them out, ⁴thenᴬI shall give you rains in their season, so that the land will yield its produce and the trees of the field will bear their fruit. ⁵Indeed, *your* threshing season will last for you until grape gathering, and grape gathering will last until sowing time. So you will

25:43ᴬEzek 34:4; Col 4:1   25:46ᴬLev 25:43
25:49ᴬLev 25:26, 27   25:51ᴬLev 25:16
25:53ᴬLev 25:43   25:54ᴬLev 25:10, 13, 28
26:1ᴬEx 23:24   ᴮNum 33:52   26:2ᴬLev 19:30
26:3ᴬDeut 7:12-26; 28:1-14   26:4ᴬDeut 11:14

eat your food to the full and ^live securely in your land. 6^I shall also grant peace in the land, so that ^you may lie down, with no one to make *you* afraid. I shall also eliminate harmful animals from the land, and no sword will pass through your land. 7Instead, you will chase your enemies, and they will fall before you by the sword; 8^five of you will chase a hundred, and a hundred of you will chase ten thousand; and your enemies will fall before you by the sword. 9So I will turn toward you and make you fruitful and multiply you, and I will ^confirm My covenant with you. 10And ^you will eat the old supply, and clear out the old because of the new. 11^Moreover, I will make My dwelling among you, and My soul will not reject you. 12^I will also walk among you and be your God, and you shall be My people. 13^I am the Lord your God, who brought you out of the land of Egypt so that *you* would not be their slaves, and ^I broke your yoke and made you walk erect.

PENALTIES OF DISOBEDIENCE

14'^But if you do not obey Me and do not carry out all these commandments, 15if, instead, you ^reject My statutes, and if your soul loathes My ordinances so as not to carry out all My commandments, *but rather* to break My covenant, 16I, in turn, will do this to you: I will summon a ^sudden terror against you, consumption and fever that will make the eyes fail and the soul languish; also, you will sow your seed uselessly, for your enemies will eat it. 17And I will set My face against you so that you will be defeated before your enemies; and ^those who hate you will rule over you, and you will

flee when no one is pursuing you. 18If also after these things you do not obey Me, then I will punish you ^seven times more for your sins. 19I will also ^break down your pride of power; and I will make your sky like iron and your earth like bronze. 20^Your strength will be consumed uselessly, for your land will not yield its produce and the trees of the land will not yield their fruit.

21'Yet if you ^show hostility toward Me and are unwilling to obey Me, I will increase the plague on you seven times according to your sins. 22^I will also let loose among you the animals of the field, which will deprive you of your children and eliminate your cattle, and reduce your number so that ^your roads become deserted.

23'^And if by these things you do not learn your lesson regarding Me, but you show hostility toward Me, 24then I in turn will ^show hostility toward you; and I, even I, will strike you seven times for your sins. 25I will also bring upon you a sword which will execute vengeance for the covenant; and when you gather together into your cities, I will send a ^plague among you, so that you will be handed over to the enemy. 26When I break your staff of bread, ten women will bake your bread in one oven, and they will bring back your bread in rationed amounts, so that you will ^eat and not be satisfied.

26:5^Lev 25:18, 19; Ezek 34:25　26:6^Ps 29:11
^Zeph 3:13　26:8^Deut 32:30　26:9^Gen 17:7
26:10^Lev 25:22　26:11^Ex 25:8; Ezek 37:26
26:12^Deut 23:14; 2 Cor 6:16　26:13^Ex 20:2
^Ezek 34:27　26:14^Deut 28:15-68; Josh 23:15
26:15^Lev 26:11; 2 Kin 17:15　26:16^Deut 28:22;
Ps 78:33　26:17^Ps 106:41　26:18^Lev 26:21, 24, 28
26:19^Is 28:1-3; Ezek 24:21　26:20^Is 17:10, 11; Jer 12:13
26:21^Lev 26:23, 27, 40　26:22^2 Kin 17:25　^Judg 5:6
26:23^Lev 26:21; Jer 5:3　26:24^Lev 26:28, 41
26:25^Num 14:12　26:26^Mic 6:14

²⁷'Yet if in spite of this you do not obey Me, but act with hostility against Me, ²⁸then ᴬI will act with wrathful hostility against you, and I for My part will punish you seven times for your sins. ²⁹Further, ᴬyou will eat the flesh of your sons, and you will eat the flesh of your daughters. ³⁰I then ᴬwill destroy your high places, and cut down your incense altars, and pile your remains on the remains of your idols, for My soul will loathe you. ³¹I will turn your cities into ᴬruins as well and make your sanctuaries desolate, and I will not smell your soothing aromas. ³²And I will make ᴬthe land desolate so that your enemies who settle in it will be appalled at it. ³³You, however, I ᴬwill scatter among the nations, and I will draw out a sword after you, as your land becomes desolate and your cities become ruins.

³⁴'ᴬThen the land will restore its Sabbaths all the days of the desolation, while you are in your enemies' land; then the land will rest and restore its Sabbaths. ³⁵All the days of *its* desolation it will have the rest which it did not have on your Sabbaths, while you were living on it. ³⁶As for those among you who are left, I will also bring ᴬdespair into their hearts in the lands of their enemies. And the sound of a scattered leaf will chase them, and even when no one is pursuing they will flee as though from the sword, and they will fall. ³⁷ᴬThey will then stumble over each other as if *running* from the sword, although no one is pursuing; and you will have no strength to stand before your enemies. ³⁸Instead, ᴬyou will perish among the nations, and your enemies' land will consume you. ³⁹ᴬSo those of you who may be left will rot away because of their wrongdoing in the lands of your enemies; and also because of the wrongdoing of their forefathers they will rot away with them.

⁴⁰'But ᴬ*if* they confess their wrongdoing and the wrongdoing of their forefathers, in their unfaithfulness which they committed against Me, and also in their acting with hostility against Me— ⁴¹I also was acting with hostility against them, to bring them into the land of their enemies—or if their uncircumcised heart is humbled so that ᴬthey then make amends for their wrongdoing, ⁴²then I will remember ᴬMy covenant with Jacob, and I will remember also My covenant with Isaac, and My covenant with Abraham as well, and I will remember the land. ⁴³ᴬFor the land will be abandoned by them, and will restore its Sabbaths while it is made desolate without them. They, meanwhile, will be making amends for their wrongdoing, because they rejected My ordinances and their soul loathed My statutes. ⁴⁴Yet in spite of this, when they are in the land of their enemies, I will not reject them, nor will I so loathe them as ᴬto destroy them, breaking My covenant with them; for I am the Lᴏʀᴅ their God. ⁴⁵But I will remember for them the ᴬcovenant with their ancestors, whom I brought out of the land of Egypt in the sight of the nations, so that I might be their God. I am the Lᴏʀᴅ.'"

26:28ᴬLev 26:24, 41; Is 59:18   26:29ᴬ2 Kin 6:29
26:30ᴬEzek 6:3, 6; Amos 7:9   26:31ᴬNeh 2:3;
Jer 44:2, 6, 22   26:32ᴬJer 9:11; 25:11   26:33ᴬEzek 12:15;
Zech 7:14   26:34ᴬLev 26:43; 2 Chr 36:21
26:36ᴬIs 30:17; Lam 1:3, 6   26:37ᴬJer 6:21; Nah 3:3
26:38ᴬDeut 4:26   26:39ᴬEzek 4:17; 33:10
26:40ᴬJer 3:12-15; Hos 5:15   26:41ᴬEzek 20:43
26:42ᴬGen 28:13-15; 35:11, 12   26:43ᴬLev 26:34
26:44ᴬDeut 4:31; Jer 30:11   26:45ᴬEx 6:6-8

46ᴬThese are the statutes and ordinances and laws which the Lᴏʀᴅ established between Himself and the sons of Israel through Moses on Mount Sinai.

RULES CONCERNING ASSESSMENTS

27 Again, the Lᴏʀᴅ spoke to Moses, saying, 2"Speak to the sons of Israel and say to them, 'ᴬWhen someone makes an explicit vow, he *shall be valued* according to your assessment of persons belonging to the Lᴏʀᴅ. 3If your assessment is of a male from twenty years even to sixty years old, then your assessment shall be fifty shekels of silver, by ᴬthe shekel of the sanctuary. 4Or if the person is a female, then your assessment shall be thirty shekels. 5And if *the person* is from five years even to twenty years old, then your assessment for a male shall be twenty shekels, and for a female, ten shekels. 6But if *the person is* from a month even up to five years old, then your assessment shall be ᴬfive shekels of silver for a male, and for a female your assessment shall be three shekels of silver. 7If *the person is* from sixty years old and upward, if a male, then your assessment shall be fifteen shekels, and for a female, ten shekels. 8But if he is poorer than your assessment, then he shall be presented before the priest, and the priest shall assess him; ᴬaccording to the means of the one who vowed, the priest shall assess him.

9'Now if it is an animal of the kind that one can present as an offering to the Lᴏʀᴅ, any such *animal* that one gives to the Lᴏʀᴅ shall be holy. 10ᴬHe shall not replace it nor exchange it, a good for a bad, or a bad for a good; yet if he does exchange animal for animal, then both it and its substitute shall become holy. 11If, however, it is any unclean animal of the kind which one does not present as an offering to the Lᴏʀᴅ, then he shall place the animal before the priest. 12And the priest shall assess it as either good or bad; as you, the priest, assess it, so shall it be. 13But if he should ever *want to* redeem it, then he shall add a fifth of it to your assessment.

14'Now if someone consecrates his house as holy to the Lᴏʀᴅ, then the priest shall assess it as either good or bad; as the priest assesses it, so shall it stand. 15Yet if the one who consecrates *it* should *want to* redeem his house, then he shall add a fifth of your assessment price to it, so that it may be his.

16'Again, if someone consecrates to the Lᴏʀᴅ part of the field of his own property, then your assessment shall be proportionate to the seed needed for it: a ¹homer of barley seed at fifty shekels of silver. 17If he consecrates his field as of the year of jubilee, according to your assessment it shall stand. 18If he consecrates his field after the jubilee, however, then the priest shall calculate the price for him proportionate to the years that are left until the year of jubilee; and it shall be deducted from your assessment. 19If the one who consecrates it should ever *want to* redeem the field, then he shall add a fifth of your assessment price to it, so that it may belong to him. 20Yet if he does not redeem the field, but has sold the field to another person, it

26:46ᴬLev 7:38; 27:34   27:2ᴬNum 6:2; Deut 23:21-23
27:3ᴬEx 30:13; Lev 27:25   27:6ᴬNum 18:16
27:8ᴬLev 5:11; 14:21-24   27:10ᴬLev 27:33

27:16¹About 7.7 cubic feet or 0.22 cubic meters

may no longer be redeemed; ²¹and when it reverts in the jubilee, the field shall be holy to the Lord, like a field banned from secular use; ^it shall be for the priest as his property. ²²Or if he consecrates to the Lord a field which he has bought, which is not a part of the field of his own property, ²³then the priest shall calculate for him the amount of your assessment up to the year of jubilee; and he shall on that day give your assessment as holy to the Lord. ²⁴In the year of jubilee the field shall return to the one from whom he bought it, to whom the possession of the land belongs. ²⁵Every assessment of yours, moreover, shall be by ^the shekel of the sanctuary. The shekel shall be twenty gerahs.

²⁶'^However, a firstborn among animals, which as a firstborn belongs to the Lord, no one may consecrate; whether ox or sheep, it is the Lord's. ²⁷But if *it is* among the unclean animals, then he shall redeem it according to your assessment and add to it a fifth of it; and if it is not redeemed, then it shall be sold according to your assessment. ²⁸'Nevertheless, ^anything which someone sets apart to the Lord for

¹destruction out of all that he has, of man or animal or of the field of his own property, shall not be sold nor redeemed. Anything set apart for destruction is most holy to the Lord. ²⁹No one who may have been set apart among mankind shall be ransomed; he must be put to death.

³⁰'Now ^all the tithe of the land, of the seed of the land *or* of the fruit of the tree, is the Lord's; it is holy to the Lord. ³¹If, therefore, someone should ever *want to* redeem part of his tithe, he shall add to it a fifth of it. ³²For every tenth part of herd or flock, whatever ^passes under the rod, the tenth one shall be holy to the Lord. ³³^He is not to be concerned whether *it is* good or bad, nor shall he exchange it; yet if he does exchange it, then both it and its substitute shall become holy. It shall not be redeemed.'"

³⁴^These are the commandments which the Lord commanded Moses for the sons of Israel on Mount Sinai.

27:21 ^Num 18:14; Ezek 44:29
27:25 ^Ex 30:13; Lev 27:3   27:26 ^Ex 13:2
27:28 ^Num 18:14; Josh 6:17-19   27:30 ^Gen 28:22;
Neh 13:12   27:32 ^Jer 33:13; Ezek 20:37
27:33 ^Lev 27:10   27:34 ^Lev 26:46; Deut 4:5

27:28 ¹I.e., as an offering

NUMBERS

THE CENSUS OF ISRAEL'S WARRIORS

1 Now the LORD spoke to Moses in the wilderness of Sinai, in the tent of meeting, on ^the first *day* of the second month, in the second year after they had come out of the land of Egypt, saying, 2 "^Take a census of all the congregation of the sons of Israel, by their families, by their fathers' households, according to the number of names, every male, head by head 3 from ^twenty years old and upward, whoever *is able to* go to war in Israel. You and Aaron shall count them by their armies. 4 With you, moreover, there shall be a man of each tribe, ^each one head of his father's household. 5 These then are the names of the men who shall stand with you: ^of *the tribe of* Reuben, Elizur the son of Shedeur; 6 of *the tribe of* Simeon, Shelumiel the son of Zurishaddai; 7 of *the tribe of* Judah, ^Nahshon the son of Amminadab; 8 of Issachar, Nethanel the son of Zuar; 9 of Zebulun, Eliab the son of Helon; 10 of the sons of Joseph: of Ephraim, Elishama the son of Ammihud; of Manasseh, Gamaliel the son of Pedahzur; 11 of Benjamin, Abidan the son of Gideoni; 12 of Dan, Ahiezer the son of Ammishaddai; 13 of Asher, Pagiel the son of Ochran; 14 of Gad, Eliasaph the son of ^Deuel; 15 of Naphtali, Ahira the son of Enan. 16 These are *the men* who were ^called *from* the congregation, the leaders of their fathers' tribes; they were the heads of divisions of Israel."

17 So Moses and Aaron took these men who had been designated by name, 18 and they assembled all the congregation on the first *day* of the second month. Then they registered by ^ancestry in their families, by their fathers' households, according to the number of names, from twenty years old and upward, head by head, 19 just as ^the LORD had commanded Moses. So he counted them in the wilderness of Sinai.

20 ^Now the sons of Reuben, Israel's firstborn, their descendants by their families, by their fathers' households, according to the number of names, head by head, every male from twenty years old and upward, whoever *was able to* go to war, 21 their numbered men of the tribe of Reuben *were* 46,500.

22 ^Of the sons of Simeon, their descendants by their families, by their fathers' households, their numbered men, according to the number of names, head by head, every male from twenty years old and upward, whoever *was able to* go to war, 23 their numbered men of the tribe of Simeon *were* 59,300.

24 ^Of the sons of Gad, their descendants by their families, by their fathers' households, according to the number of names, from twenty years old and upward, whoever *was able to* go to war, 25 their

1:1 ^Ex 40:2, 17   1:2 ^Ex 12:37; 38:25, 26   1:3 ^Ex 30:14; 38:26   1:4 ^Ex 18:21, 25; Deut 1:15   1:5 ^Deut 33:6; Rev 7:5   1:7 ^Ruth 4:20; Luke 3:32   1:14 ^Num 2:14   1:16 ^Ex 18:21; Num 7:2   1:18 ^Ezra 2:59; Heb 7:3   1:19 ^2 Sam 24:1   1:20 ^Num 26:5-7   1:22 ^Num 26:12-14   1:24 ^Josh 4:12; Jer 49:1

numbered men of the tribe of Gad *were* 45,650.

26ᴬOf the sons of Judah, their descendants by their families, by their fathers' households, according to the number of names, from twenty years old and upward, whoever *was able to* go to war, **27**their numbered men of the tribe of Judah *were* 74,600.

28ᴬOf the sons of Issachar, their descendants by their families, by their fathers' households, according to the number of names, from twenty years old and upward, whoever *was able to* go to war, **29**their numbered men of the tribe of Issachar *were* 54,400.

30ᴬOf the sons of Zebulun, their descendants by their families, by their fathers' households, according to the number of names, from twenty years old and upward, whoever *was able to* go to war, **31**their numbered men of the tribe of Zebulun *were* 57,400.

32ᴬOf the sons of Joseph, *namely,* of the sons of Ephraim, their descendants by their families, by their fathers' households, according to the number of names, from twenty years old and upward, whoever *was able to* go to war, **33**their numbered men of the tribe of Ephraim *were* 40,500.

34ᴬOf the sons of Manasseh, their descendants by their families, by their fathers' households, according to the number of names, from twenty years old and upward, whoever *was able to* go to war, **35**their numbered men of the tribe of Manasseh *were* 32,200.

36ᴬOf the sons of Benjamin, their descendants by their families, by their fathers' households, according to the number of names, from twenty years old and upward, whoever *was able to* go to war, **37**their numbered men of the tribe of Benjamin *were* 35,400.

38ᴬOf the sons of Dan, their descendants by their families, by their fathers' households, according to the number of names, from twenty years old and upward, whoever *was able to* go to war, **39**their numbered men of the tribe of Dan *were* 62,700.

40ᴬOf the sons of Asher, their descendants by their families, by their fathers' households, according to the number of names, from twenty years old and upward, whoever *was able to* go to war, **41**their numbered men of the tribe of Asher *were* 41,500.

42ᴬOf the sons of Naphtali, their descendants by their families, by their fathers' households, according to the number of names, from twenty years old and upward, whoever *was able to* go to war, **43**their numbered men of the tribe of Naphtali *were* 53,400.

44These are the ones who were numbered, whom Moses and Aaron counted, with the leaders of Israel, twelve men, each of whom was of his father's household. **45**So all the numbered men of the sons of Israel by their fathers' households, from twenty years old and upward, whoever *was able to* go to war in Israel, **46**all the numbered men were ᴬ603,550.

LEVITES EXEMPTED

47ᴬThe Levites, however, were not counted among them by their

1:26ᴬPs 78:68; Matt 1:2   1:28ᴬNum 26:23-25
1:30ᴬNum 26:26, 27   1:32ᴬJer 7:15; Obad 19
1:34ᴬNum 26:28-34   1:36ᴬ2 Chr 17:17; Rev 7:8
1:38ᴬGen 30:6; 46:23   1:40ᴬNum 26:44-47
1:42ᴬNum 26:48-50   1:46ᴬNum 2:32; 26:51
1:47ᴬNum 2:33; 26:57-64

fathers' tribe. ⁴⁸For the Lᴏʀᴅ had spoken to Moses, saying, ⁴⁹"Only the tribe of Levi ^you shall not count, nor shall you take their census among the sons of Israel. ⁵⁰And you shall ^appoint the Levites over the ¹tabernacle of the testimony, and over all its furnishings and over everything that belongs to it. They shall carry the tabernacle and all its furnishings, and they shall take care of it; they shall also camp around the tabernacle. ⁵¹^So when the tabernacle is to move on, the Levites shall take it down; and when the tabernacle encamps, the Levites shall set it up. But the ¹layman who comes near *it* shall be put to death. ⁵²^So the sons of Israel shall camp, each man by his own camp, and each man by his own flag, according to their armies. ⁵³But the Levites shall camp around the tabernacle of the testimony, so that there will be no *divine* wrath against the congregation of the sons of Israel. ^So the Levites shall be responsible for service to the tabernacle of the testimony." ⁵⁴And the sons of Israel did *so;* in accordance with all that the Lᴏʀᴅ had commanded Moses, so they did.

ARRANGEMENT OF THE CAMPS

2 Now the Lᴏʀᴅ spoke to Moses and to Aaron, saying, ²"^The sons of Israel shall camp, each by his own flag, with the banners of their fathers' households; they shall camp around the tent of meeting at a distance. ³Now those who camp on the east side toward the sunrise *shall be* of the flag of the camp of Judah, by their armies; and the leader of the sons of Judah: ^Nahshon the son of Amminadab, ⁴and his army, their numbered

men: 74,600. ⁵Those who camp next to him *shall be* the tribe of Issachar; and the leader of the sons of Issachar: ^Nethanel the son of Zuar, ⁶and his army, their numbered men: 54,400. ⁷*Then follows* the tribe of Zebulun; and the leader of the sons of Zebulun: ^Eliab the son of Helon, ⁸and his army, his numbered men: 57,400. ⁹The total of the numbered men of the camp of Judah: 186,400, by their armies. ^They shall set out first.

¹⁰"On the south side *shall be* the flag of the camp of Reuben by their armies; and the leader of the sons of Reuben: ^Elizur the son of Shedeur, ¹¹and his army, their numbered men: 46,500. ¹²And those who camp next to him *shall be* the tribe of Simeon; and the leader of the sons of Simeon: ^Shelumiel the son of Zurishaddai, ¹³and his army, their numbered men: 59,300. ¹⁴Then *follows* the tribe of Gad; and the leader of the sons of Gad: ^Eliasaph the son of Deuel, ¹⁵and his army, their numbered men: 45,650. ¹⁶The total of the numbered men of the camp of Reuben: 151,450 by their armies. And ^they shall set out second.

¹⁷"^Then the tent of meeting shall set out *with* the camp of the Levites in the midst of the camps; just as they camp, so they shall set out, every man in his place by their flags. ¹⁸"On the west side *shall be* the flag of the camp of Ephraim by their

1:49 ^Num 26:62   1:50 ^Ex 38:21; Num 3:6-8, 25-37
1:51 ^Num 4:1-33   1:52 ^Num 2:2, 34
1:53 ^Num 8:24; 1 Chr 23:32   2:2 ^Num 1:52; 24:2
2:3 ^1 Chr 2:10; Luke 3:32, 33   2:5 ^Num 1:8; 7:18, 23
2:7 ^Num 1:9   2:9 ^Num 10:14   2:10 ^Num 1:5
2:12 ^Num 1:6   2:14 ^Num 1:14; 7:42
2:16 ^Num 10:18   2:17 ^Num 1:53

1:50 ¹Lit *dwelling place,* and so throughout the ch
1:51 ¹Lit *stranger*

armies; and the leader of the sons of Ephraim: ᴬElishama the son of Ammihud, ¹⁹and his army, their numbered men: 40,500. ²⁰Next to him *shall be* the tribe of Manasseh; and the leader of the sons of Manasseh: ᴬGamaliel the son of Pedahzur, ²¹and his army, their numbered men, 32,200. ²²Then *follows* the tribe of Benjamin; and the leader of the sons of Benjamin: ᴬAbidan the son of Gideoni, ²³and his army, their numbered men, 35,400. ²⁴The total of the numbered men of the camp of Ephraim: 108,100, by their armies. And ᴬthey shall set out third.

²⁵"On the north side *shall be* the flag of the camp of Dan by their armies; and the leader of the sons of Dan: ᴬAhiezer the son of Ammishaddai, ²⁶and his army, their numbered men: 62,700. ²⁷Those who camp next to him *shall be* the tribe of Asher; and the leader of the sons of Asher: ᴬPagiel the son of Ochran, ²⁸and his army, their numbered men: 41,500. ²⁹Then *follows* the tribe of Naphtali; and the leader of the sons of Naphtali: ᴬAhira the son of Enan, ³⁰and his army, their numbered men: 53,400. ³¹The total of the numbered men of the camp of Dan *was* 157,600. ᴬThey shall set out last by their flags."

³²These are the numbered men of the sons of Israel by their fathers' households; the total of the numbered men of the camps by their armies, ᴬ603,550. ³³ᴬThe Levites, however, were not counted among the sons of Israel, just as the LORD had commanded Moses. ³⁴So the sons of Israel did *all this;* according to all that the LORD commanded Moses, so they camped by their flags, and so they set out, everyone by his family according to his father's household.

LEVITE PRIESTHOOD ESTABLISHED

3 ᴬNow these are *the records of* the generations of Aaron and Moses at the time when the LORD spoke with Moses on Mount Sinai. ²ᴬThese then are the names of the sons of Aaron: Nadab the firstborn, and Abihu, Eleazar and Ithamar. ³These are the names of the sons of Aaron, the ᴬanointed priests, whom he ordained to serve as priests. ⁴ᴬBut Nadab and Abihu died in the presence of the LORD when they offered strange fire before the LORD in the wilderness of Sinai; and they had no children. So Eleazar and Ithamar served as priests in the lifetime of their father Aaron.

⁵Then the LORD spoke to Moses, saying, ⁶"ᴬBring the tribe of Levi forward and present them before Aaron the priest, that they may serve him. ⁷They shall perform the duties for him and for the whole congregation in front of the tent of meeting, to do the ᴬservice of the tabernacle. ⁸They shall also take care of all the furnishings of the tent of meeting, along with the duties of the sons of Israel, to do the service of the tabernacle. ⁹So you shall ᴬassign the Levites to Aaron and to his sons; they are exclusively assigned to him from the sons of Israel. ¹⁰So you shall appoint Aaron and his sons that ᴬthey may keep their priesthood, but ᴮthe layman who comes near shall be put to death."

¹¹Again the LORD spoke to Moses, saying, ¹²"Now, behold, I ᴬhave taken the Levites from among the

2:18ᴬNum 1:10   2:20ᴬNum 1:10   2:22ᴬNum 1:11
2:24ᴬNum 10:22   2:25ᴬNum 1:12   2:27ᴬNum 1:13
2:29ᴬNum 1:15   2:31ᴬNum 10:25   2:32ᴬEx 38:26;
Num 1:46   2:33ᴬNum 1:47; 26:57-62   3:1ᴬEx 6:20-27
3:2ᴬEx 6:23; Num 26:60   3:3ᴬEx 28:41
3:4ᴬLev 10:1, 2; Num 26:61   3:6ᴬNum 8:6-22;
Deut 10:8   3:7ᴬNum 1:50   3:9ᴬNum 18:6
3:10ᴬEx 29:9   ᴮNum 1:51   3:12ᴬNum 3:45

sons of Israel instead of every ᴮfirstborn, the firstborn of the womb among the sons of Israel. So the Levites shall be Mine. ¹³For ᴬall the firstborn are Mine; on the day that I fatally struck all the firstborn in the land of Egypt, I sanctified to Myself all the firstborn in Israel, from the human *firstborn* to animals. They shall be Mine; I am the Lᴏʀᴅ."

¹⁴Then the Lᴏʀᴅ spoke to Moses ᴬin the wilderness of Sinai, saying, ¹⁵"ᴬCount the sons of Levi by their fathers' households, by their families; every male from a month old and upward you shall count." ¹⁶So Moses counted them according to the word of the Lᴏʀᴅ, just as he had been commanded. ¹⁷ᴬThese, then, are the sons of Levi by their names: Gershon, Kohath, and Merari. ¹⁸And these are the names of the ᴬsons of Gershon by their families: Libni and Shimei; ¹⁹and the sons of Kohath by their families: Amram and Izhar, Hebron and Uzziel; ²⁰and the sons of Merari by their families: Mahli and Mushi. These are the families of the Levites according to their fathers' households.

²¹Of Gershon *was* the family of the Libnites and the family of the Shimeites; these *were* the families of the Gershonites. ²²Their numbered men, in the counting of every male from a month old and upward, their numbered men *were* 7,500. ²³The families of the Gershonites were to camp behind the tabernacle westward, ²⁴and the leader of the fathers' households of the Gershonites: Eliasaph the son of Lael.

DUTIES OF THE LEVITES

²⁵Now ᴬthe duties of the sons of Gershon in the tent of meeting *included* the tabernacle and the

tent, its covering, and the curtain for the entrance of the tent of meeting, ²⁶and ᴬthe curtains of the courtyard, the curtain for the entrance of the courtyard which is around the tabernacle and the altar, and its ropes, according to all the service concerning them.

²⁷Of Kohath *was* the family of the Amramites, the family of the Izharites, the family of the Hebronites, and the family of the Uzzielites; these were the families of the Kohathites. ²⁸In the counting of every male from a month old and upward, *there were* 8,600, performing the duties of the sanctuary. ²⁹The families of the sons of Kohath were to camp on the south side of the tabernacle, ³⁰and the leader of the fathers' households of the Kohathite families: Elizaphan the son of Uzziel. ³¹Now their duties *included* ᴬthe ark, the table, the lampstand, the altars, the utensils of the sanctuary with which they minister, the curtain, and all the service concerning them; ³²and Eleazar the son of Aaron the priest *was* the head of the leaders of Levi, *and he had* the supervision of those who performed the duties of the sanctuary.

³³Of Merari *was* the family of the Mahlites and the family of the Mushites; these *were* the families of Merari. ³⁴Their numbered men in the counting of every male from a month old and upward: 6,200. ³⁵And the leader of the fathers' households of the families of Merari *was* Zuriel the son of Abihail. They were to ᴬcamp on the northward

3:12 ᴮEx 13:2   3:13 ᴬEx 13:2; Lev 27:26   3:14 ᴬEx 19:1
3:15 ᴬNum 1:47   3:17 ᴬEx 6:16-22   3:18 ᴬEx 6:17
3:25 ᴬNum 4:24-26   3:26 ᴬEx 27:9, 12, 14, 15
3:31 ᴬEx 25:10-22   3:35 ᴬNum 1:53; 2:25

side of the tabernacle. ³⁶Now the appointment of duties of the sons of Merari *included* the framework of the tabernacle, its bars, its pillars, its bases, all its equipment, and all the service concerning them, ³⁷and the pillars around the courtyard with their bases, their pegs, and their ropes.

³⁸Now those who were to ᴬcamp in front of the tabernacle eastward, in front of the tent of meeting toward the sunrise, *were* Moses and Aaron and his sons, performing the duties of the sanctuary for the obligation of the sons of Israel; but the layman coming near was to be put to death. ³⁹All the numbered men of the Levites, whom Moses and Aaron counted at the command of the LORD by their families, every male from a month old and upward, *were* ᴬtwenty-two thousand.

FIRSTBORN REDEEMED

⁴⁰Then the LORD said to Moses, "ᴬCount every firstborn male of the sons of Israel from a month old and upward, and make a list of their names. ⁴¹And you ᴬshall take the Levites for Me—I am the LORD— instead of all the firstborn among the sons of Israel; and the cattle of the Levites in place of all the firstborn among the cattle of the sons of Israel." ⁴²So Moses counted all the firstborn among the sons of Israel, just as the LORD had commanded him; ⁴³and all the firstborn males, by the number of names from a month old and upward for their numbered men, were ᴬ22,273.

⁴⁴Then the LORD spoke to Moses, saying, ⁴⁵"ᴬTake the Levites in place of all the firstborn among the sons of Israel, and the cattle of the Levites in place of their cattle.

And the Levites shall be Mine; I am the LORD. ⁴⁶ᴬAnd as a redemption price for the 273 of the firstborn of the sons of Israel who are in excess of *the number of* the Levites, ⁴⁷you shall take ᴬfive shekels apiece, per head; you shall take *them* in terms of the shekel of the sanctuary (the shekel is twenty ¹gerahs), ⁴⁸and you shall give the money, the redemption price of those who are in excess among them, to Aaron and to his sons." ⁴⁹So Moses took the redemption money from those who were in excess of *the number of* those redeemed by the Levites; ⁵⁰from the firstborn of the sons of Israel he took the money in terms of the shekel of the sanctuary, 1,365. ⁵¹Then Moses gave the redemption money to Aaron and to his sons, at the command of the LORD, just as the LORD had commanded Moses.

DUTIES OF THE KOHATHITES

4 Then the LORD spoke to Moses and to Aaron, saying, ²"Take a census of the descendants of Kohath from among the sons of Levi, by their families, by their fathers' households, ³from ᴬthirty years old and upward, even to fifty years old, everyone who can enter the service *of ministry* to do work in the tent of meeting. ⁴This is the work of the descendants of Kohath in the tent of meeting, *concerning* the most holy things.

⁵"When the camp sets out, Aaron and his sons shall go in and take down the veil of the curtain, and

3:38 ᴬNum 1:53; 2:3   3:39 ᴬNum 3:43; 26:62
3:40 ᴬNum 3:15   3:41 ᴬNum 3:12, 45   3:43 ᴬNum 3:39
3:45 ᴬNum 3:12   3:46 ᴬEx 13:13, 15; Num 18:15, 16
3:47 ᴬLev 27:6; Num 18:16   4:3 ᴬ1 Chr 23:3, 24, 27;
Ezra 3:8

3:47 ¹A gerah is about 0.025 oz. or 0.7 gm

cover the ^ark of the testimony with it; ⁶and they shall place a ^covering of ¹fine leather on it, and spread over it a cloth of pure ²violet, and insert its carrying poles. ⁷Over the table of *the bread of* the Presence they shall also spread a cloth of violet and put on it the dishes, the pans, the sacrificial bowls, and the jugs for the drink offering; and ^the continual bread shall be on it. ⁸And they shall spread over them a cloth of scarlet *material,* and cover the same with a covering of fine leather, and they shall insert its carrying poles. ⁹Then they shall take a violet cloth and cover the ^lampstand for the light, along with its lamps, its tongs, its trays, and all its oil containers, by which they attend to it; ¹⁰and they shall put it and all its utensils in a covering of fine leather, and put it on the carrying bars. ¹¹Over the golden altar they shall spread a violet cloth, and cover it with a covering of fine leather, and they shall insert its carrying poles; ¹²and they shall take all the utensils of service, with which they serve in the sanctuary, and put *them* in a violet cloth and cover them with a covering of fine leather, and put them on the carrying bars. ¹³Then they shall clean away the ashes from the ^altar, and spread a purple cloth over it. ¹⁴They shall also put on it all its utensils by which they serve in connection with it: the firepans, the forks, shovels, and the basins, all the utensils of the altar; and they shall spread a cover of fine leather over it and insert its carrying poles. ¹⁵When Aaron and his sons have finished covering the holy *objects* and all the furnishings of the sanctuary,

when the camp is to set out, after that the sons of Kohath shall come to carry *them by the poles,* so that they will not touch the holy *objects* ^and die. These are the things in the tent of meeting that the sons of Kohath are to carry.

¹⁶"Now the responsibility of Eleazar the son of Aaron the priest is ^the oil for the light, the ᴮfragrant incense, the continual grain offering, and the anointing oil—the responsibility of all the tabernacle and everything that is in it, with the sanctuary and its furnishings."

¹⁷Then the LORD spoke to Moses and to Aaron, saying, ¹⁸"Do not let the tribe of the families of the Kohathites be eliminated from among the Levites. ¹⁹Rather, do this for them so that they will live and ^not die when they approach the most holy *objects:* Aaron and his sons shall go in and assign each of them to his work and to his load; ²⁰but ^they shall not come in to see the holy *objects* even for a moment, or they will die."

DUTIES OF THE GERSHONITES

²¹Then the LORD spoke to Moses, saying, ²²"Take a census of the sons of Gershon also, by their fathers' households, by their families; ²³from ^thirty years old and upward to fifty years old you shall count them: all who can enter to perform service, to do the work in the tent of meeting. ²⁴This is the service of the families of the Gershonites, in

4:5 ^Ex 25:10-16   4:6 ^Num 4:25   4:7 ^Ex 25:30; Lev 24:5-9   4:9 ^Ex 25:31   4:13 ^Ex 27:1-8 4:15 ^Num 1:51; 2 Sam 6:6, 7   4:16 ^Num 24:1-3 ᴮEx 30:34-38   4:19 ^Num 4:15   4:20 ^Ex 19:21; 1 Sam 6:19   4:23 ^Num 4:3; 1 Chr 23:3, 24, 27

4:6 ¹Meaning of the Heb uncertain, and so throughout the ch   ²Or *bluish;* LXX *hyacinth* in color, and so throughout the ch

serving and in carrying: ²⁵they shall carry ^the curtains of the tabernacle and the tent of meeting *with* its covering and the covering of fine leather that is on top of it, and the curtain for the entrance of the tent of meeting, ²⁶and ^the curtains of the courtyard, the curtain for the entrance of the gate of the courtyard that is around the tabernacle and the altar, and their ropes and all the equipment for their service; and everything that is to be done by them, they shall perform. ²⁷All the service of the sons of the Gershonites, that is, all their loads and all their work, shall be *performed* at the command of Aaron and his sons; and you shall assign to them as a duty all their loads. ²⁸This is the service of the families of the sons of the Gershonites in the tent of meeting; and their duties *shall be* under the direction of Ithamar the son of Aaron the priest.

DUTIES OF THE MERARITES

²⁹"*As for* the sons of Merari, you shall count them by their families, by their fathers' households; ³⁰from ^thirty years old and upward, even to fifty years old, you shall count them, everyone who can enter the service to do the work of the tent of meeting. ³¹Now this is the duty of their loads, for all their service in the tent of meeting: the boards of the tabernacle, its bars, its pillars, and its bases, ³²and the pillars around the courtyard and their bases, their pegs, and their ropes, with all their equipment and with all their service; and you shall assign by names *of the men* the items that each is to carry. ³³This is the service of the families of the sons of Merari, according to

all their service in the tent of meeting, under the direction of Ithamar the son of Aaron the priest."

³⁴So Moses, Aaron, and the leaders of the congregation counted the sons of the Kohathites by their families and by their fathers' households, ³⁵from ^thirty years old and upward even to fifty years old, everyone who could enter the service for work in the tent of meeting. ³⁶Their numbered men by their families were 2,750. ³⁷These were the numbered men of the Kohathite families, everyone who was serving in the tent of meeting, whom Moses and Aaron counted according to the commandment of the LORD through Moses.

³⁸And the numbered men of the sons of Gershon by their families and by their fathers' households, ³⁹from thirty years old and upward even to fifty years old, everyone who could enter the service for work in the tent of meeting— ⁴⁰their numbered men by their families, by their fathers' households, were 2,630. ⁴¹These were the numbered men of the families of the sons of Gershon, everyone who was serving in the tent of meeting, whom Moses and Aaron counted according to the commandment of the LORD.

⁴²And the numbered men of the families of the sons of Merari by their families, by their fathers' households, ⁴³from ^thirty years old and upward even to fifty years old, everyone who could enter the service for work in the tent of meeting— ⁴⁴their numbered men by their families were 3,200. ⁴⁵These were the numbered men of the families of the sons of Merari,

4:25 ^Ex 40:19   4:26 ^Ex 38:9   4:30 ^Num 4:3; 8:24-26   4:35 ^1 Chr 23:24   4:43 ^Num 8:24-26

whom Moses and Aaron counted according to the commandment of the LORD through Moses.

⁴⁶All the numbered men of the Levites, whom Moses, Aaron, and the leaders of Israel counted, by their families and by their fathers' households, ⁴⁷from thirty years old and upward even to fifty years old, everyone who could enter to do the work of service and the work of carrying in the tent of meeting— ⁴⁸their numbered men were ^8,580. ⁴⁹According to the commandment of the LORD through Moses, they ^were counted, everyone by his serving or carrying; so *these were* his numbered men, just as the LORD had commanded Moses.

ON DEFILEMENT

5 Then the LORD spoke to Moses, saying, ²"Command the sons of Israel that they ^send away from the camp everyone with leprosy, everyone having a discharge, and everyone who is unclean because of *contact with* a *dead* person. ³You shall send away both male and female; you shall send them outside the camp so that they do not defile their camp where I dwell ^in their midst." ⁴And the sons of Israel did so and sent them outside the camp; just as the LORD had spoken to Moses, that is what the sons of Israel did.

⁵Then the LORD spoke to Moses, saying, ⁶"Speak to the sons of Israel: '^When a man or woman commits any of the sins of mankind, acting unfaithfully against the LORD, and that person is guilty, ⁷then he shall confess his sin which he has committed, and he ^shall make restitution in full for his wrong and add to it a fifth of it, and give *it* to him whom he has wronged. ⁸But

if the person has no ¹redeemer to whom restitution may be made for the wrong, the restitution which is made for the wrong *must go* to the LORD for the priest, besides the ram of atonement, by which atonement is made for him. ⁹^Also every contribution pertaining to all the holy *gifts* of the sons of Israel, which they offer to the priest, shall be his. ¹⁰So every person's holy *gifts* shall be his; whatever anyone gives to the priest, it ^becomes his.'"

THE ADULTERY TEST

¹¹Then the LORD spoke to Moses, saying, ¹²"Speak to the sons of Israel and say to them, 'If any man's wife ^goes astray and is unfaithful to him, ¹³and a man has ^sexual relations with her and it is hidden from the eyes of her husband and she remains undiscovered, although she has defiled herself, and there is no witness against her and she has not been caught in the act, ¹⁴if an attitude of ^jealousy comes over him and he is jealous of his wife when she has defiled herself, or if an attitude of jealousy comes over him and he is jealous of his wife when she has not defiled herself, ¹⁵the man shall then bring his wife to the priest, and shall bring *as* an offering for her a tenth of an ¹ephah of barley meal; he shall not pour oil on it nor put frankincense on it, because it is a grain offering of jealousy, a grain offering of reminder, ^a reminder of wrongdoing.

4:48 ^Num 3:39 4:49 ^Num 1:47 5:2 ^Lev 13:8, 46; Num 12:10, 14, 15 5:3 ^Lev 26:12; Num 35:34 5:6 ^Lev 5:14-6:7 5:7 ^Lev 6:4, 5 5:9 ^Lev 7:32, 34; 10:14, 15 5:10 ^Lev 10:13 5:12 ^Num 5:19-21, 29 5:13 ^Lev 18:20; 20:10 5:14 ^Prov 6:34; Song 8:6 5:15 ^1 Kin 17:18; Ezek 29:16

5:8 ¹I.e., male relative to act in his behalf
5:15 ¹About 1 cubic foot or 0.03 cubic meters

16 'Then the priest shall bring her forward and have her stand before the LORD, 17 and the priest shall take holy water in an earthenware container; and he shall take some of the dust that is on the floor of the tabernacle and put *it* in the water. 18 The priest shall then have the woman stand before the LORD and let down *the hair of* the woman's head, and place the grain offering of reminder in her hands, that is, the grain offering of jealousy; and in the hand of the priest is to be the water of bitterness that brings a curse. 19 And the priest shall have her take an oath and shall say to the woman, "If no man has had sexual relations with you and if you have not ^gone astray into uncleanness, *as you are* under *the authority of* your husband, be immune to this water of bitterness that brings a curse; 20 if, however, you have ^gone astray, *though* under *the authority of* your husband, and if you have defiled yourself and a man other than your husband has had sexual intercourse with you" 21 (then the priest shall have the woman ^swear with the oath of the curse, and the priest shall say to the woman), "may the LORD make you a curse and an oath among your people by the LORD's making your thigh shriveled and your ¹belly swollen; 22 and this water that brings a curse shall go into your stomach, to make your belly swell up and your thigh shrivel." And the woman ^shall say, "Amen, Amen."

23 'The priest shall then write these curses on a scroll, and he shall wash them off into the water of bitterness. 24 Then he shall make the woman drink the water of bitterness that brings a curse, so that the water which brings a curse will go into her and cause bitterness. 25 And the priest shall take the grain offering of jealousy from the woman's hand, and he shall wave the grain offering before the LORD and bring it to the altar; 26 and ^the priest shall take a handful of the grain offering as its reminder offering and offer *it* up in smoke on the altar, and afterward he shall make the woman drink the water. 27 When he has made her drink the water, then it will come about, if she has defiled herself and has been unfaithful to her husband, that the water which brings a curse will go into her and cause bitterness, and her belly will swell up and her thigh will shrivel, and the woman will become ^a curse among her people. 28 But if the woman has not defiled herself and is clean, she will be immune and conceive children.

29 'This is the law of jealousy: when a wife, *who is* under *the authority of* her husband, ^goes astray and defiles herself, 30 or when an attitude of jealousy comes over a man and he is jealous of his wife, he shall then have the woman stand before the LORD, and the priest shall apply all of this law to her. 31 The man, moreover, will be free of guilt, but that woman shall ^bear *the consequences of* her guilt.'"

LAW OF THE NAZIRITES

6 Again the LORD spoke to Moses, saying, 2 "Speak to the sons of Israel and say to them, 'When a man or woman makes a special vow, *namely,* the vow of ^a ¹Nazirite, to

5:19 ^Num 5:12 5:20 ^Num 5:12 5:21 ^Josh 6:26;
Neh 10:29 5:22 ^Deut 27:15 5:26 ^Lev 2:2, 9
5:27 ^Jer 29:18; 44:12 5:29 ^Num 5:12
5:31 ^Lev 20:17 6:2 ^Judg 13:5; Amos 2:11, 12

5:21 ¹Possibly the womb, and so throughout the ch
6:2 ¹I.e., one consecrated to God

live as a Nazirite for the LORD, ³he shall ^abstain from wine and strong drink; he shall consume no vinegar, *whether made* from wine or strong drink, nor shall he drink any grape juice nor eat fresh or dried grapes. ⁴All the days of his consecration he shall not eat anything that is produced from the grape vine, from *the* seeds even to *the* skin.

⁵'All the days of his vow of consecration ^no razor shall pass over his head. He shall be holy until the days are fulfilled which he lives as a Nazirite for the LORD; he shall let the locks of hair on his head grow long.

⁶'^All the days of his life as a Nazirite for the LORD he shall not come up to a dead person. ⁷He ^shall not make himself unclean for his father or for his mother, for his brother or for his sister, when they die, because his consecration to God is on his head. ⁸All the days of his consecration he is holy to the LORD.

⁹'But if *someone* dies very suddenly beside him and he defiles his consecrated head *of hair*, then ^he shall shave his head on the day when he becomes clean; he shall shave it on the seventh day. ¹⁰Then on the eighth day he shall bring ^two turtledoves or two young doves to the priest, to the entrance of the tent of meeting. ¹¹And the priest shall offer ^one as a sin offering and *the* other as a burnt offering, and make atonement for him regarding his sin because of the *dead* person. And on that same day he shall consecrate his head, ¹²and shall live his days of consecration as a Nazirite for the LORD, and shall bring a male lamb a year old as a guilt offering; but the preceding days will not count, because his consecration was defiled.

¹³'Now this is the law of the Nazirite ^when the days of his consecration are fulfilled: he shall bring his offering to the entrance of the tent of meeting. ¹⁴And he shall present his offering to the LORD: one male lamb a year old without defect as a burnt offering, one ^ewe lamb a year old without defect as a sin offering, one ram without defect as a peace offering, ¹⁵and a basket of ^unleavened loaves of fine flour mixed with oil and unleavened wafers spread with oil, along with their grain offering and their drink offering. ¹⁶Then the priest shall present *them* before the LORD and offer his sin offering and his burnt offering. ¹⁷He shall also offer the ram as a sacrifice of peace offerings to the LORD, together with the basket of unleavened bread; the priest shall also offer its grain offering and its drink offering. ¹⁸^The Nazirite shall then shave his consecrated head *of hair* at the entrance of the tent of meeting, and take the consecrated hair of his head and put *it* on the fire which is under the sacrifice of peace offerings. ¹⁹^And the priest shall take the ram's shoulder *when it has been* boiled, and one unleavened loaf from the basket and one unleavened wafer, and shall put *them* on the hands of the Nazirite after he has shaved his consecrated *hair*. ²⁰Then the priest shall wave them as a wave offering before the LORD. It is holy for the priest, together with the breast *offered as a* wave offering, and the thigh *offered*

6:3 ^Luke 1:15   6:5 ^1 Sam 1:11   6:6 ^Lev 21:1-3; Num 19:11-22   6:7 ^Num 9:6   6:9 ^Lev 14:8, 9   6:10 ^Lev 5:7; 14:22   6:11 ^Lev 5:7   6:13 ^Acts 21:26   6:14 ^Lev 14:10; Num 15:27   6:15 ^Ex 29:2; Lev 2:4   6:18 ^Num 6:9; Acts 21:23, 24   6:19 ^Lev 7:28-34

as a contribution; and ^afterward the Nazirite may drink wine.'

²¹"This is the law of the Nazirite who vows his offering to the LORD according to his consecration, in addition to what *else* he can afford; corresponding to his vow which he makes, so he shall do according to the law of his consecration."

AARON'S BENEDICTION

²²Then the LORD spoke to Moses, saying, ²³"Speak to Aaron and to his sons, saying, 'In this way ^you shall bless the sons of Israel. You are to say to them:

24 The LORD ^bless you, and keep you;

25 The LORD ^cause His face to shine on you, And be gracious to you;

26 The LORD ^lift up His face to you, And ᴮgive you peace.'

²⁷So they shall ^invoke My name on the sons of Israel, and *then* I will bless them."

OFFERINGS OF THE LEADERS

7 Now on ^the day that Moses had finished setting up the tabernacle, he anointed it and consecrated it with all its furnishings, and the altar and all its utensils; he anointed them and consecrated them also. ²Then ^the leaders of Israel, the heads of their fathers' households, made an offering (they were the leaders of the tribes; they were the supervisors over the numbered men). ³When they brought their offering before the LORD, six ^covered carts and twelve oxen, a cart for *every* two of the leaders and an ox for each one, then they

presented them in front of the tabernacle. ⁴Then the LORD spoke to Moses, saying, ⁵"Accept *these things* from them, that they may be used in the service of the tent of meeting, and you shall give them to the Levites, *to* each man according to his service." ⁶So Moses took the carts and the oxen and gave them to the Levites. ⁷Two carts and four oxen he gave to the sons of Gershon, according to ^their service, ⁸and four carts and eight oxen he gave to the sons of Merari, according to ^their service, under the direction of Ithamar the son of Aaron the priest. ⁹But he did not give *any* to the sons of Kohath, because theirs *was* ^the service of the holy *objects, which* they carried on the shoulder.

¹⁰And the leaders offered the dedication *offering* for the altar when ^it was anointed, so the leaders offered their offering before the altar. ¹¹Then the LORD said to Moses, "They shall present their offering, one leader each day, for the dedication of the altar."

¹²Now the one who presented his offering on the first day was Nahshon the son of Amminadab, of the tribe of Judah; ¹³and his offering *was* one silver ^dish whose weight *was* 130 *shekels, and* one silver bowl of seventy shekels in ¹sanctuary shekels, both of them full of fine flour mixed with oil as a grain offering; ¹⁴one gold pan of ten *shekels,* full of incense; ¹⁵one bull, one ram, *and* one male lamb one year old, as a burnt offering; ¹⁶^one

6:20^Eccl 9:7   6:23^1 Chr 23:13   6:24^Deut 28:3-6; Ps 28:9   6:25^Ps 80:3, 7, 19   6:26^Ps 4:6   ᴮPs 29:11 6:27^2 Sam 7:23; 2 Chr 7:14   7:1^Ex 40:17 7:2^Num 1:5-16   7:3^Is 66:20   7:7^Num 4:24-26 7:8^Num 4:31, 32   7:9^Num 4:5-15   7:10^Num 7:1; 2 Chr 7:9   7:13^Ex 25:29; 37:16   7:16^Lev 4:23

7:13¹About 0.4 oz. or 11 gm, and so through v 86

male goat as a sin offering; [17]and for the sacrifice of peace offerings, two oxen, five rams, five male goats, *and* five male lambs one year old. This *was* the offering of ^Nahshon the son of Amminadab.

[18]On the second day Nethanel the son of Zuar, leader of Issachar, presented *an offering;* [19]he presented as his offering one silver dish whose weight *was* 130 *shekels, and* one silver bowl of seventy shekels in sanctuary shekels, both of them full of fine flour mixed with oil as a grain offering; [20]one gold pan of ten *shekels,* full of incense; [21]one bull, one ram, *and* one male lamb one year old, as a burnt offering; [22]one male goat as a sin offering; [23]and for the sacrifice of ^peace offerings, two oxen, five rams, five male goats, *and* five male lambs one year old. This *was* the offering of Nethanel the son of Zuar.

[24]On the third day *it was* Eliab the son of Helon, leader of the sons of Zebulun; [25]his offering *was also* one silver dish whose weight *was* 130 *shekels, and* one silver bowl of seventy shekels in sanctuary shekels, both of them full of fine flour mixed with oil as a grain offering; [26]one gold pan of ten *shekels,* full of incense; [27]one bull, one ram, *and* one ^male lamb one year old, as a burnt offering; [28]one male goat as a sin offering; [29]and for the sacrifice of peace offerings, two oxen, five rams, five male goats, *and* five male lambs one year old. This *was* the offering of Eliab the son of Helon.

[30]On the fourth day *it was* Elizur the son of Shedeur, leader of the sons of Reuben; [31]his offering *was also* one silver dish whose weight *was* 130 *shekels, and* one silver bowl of seventy shekels in sanctuary

shekels, both of them full of fine flour mixed with oil as a grain offering; [32]one gold pan of ten *shekels,* full of incense; [33]one bull, one ram, *and* one ^male lamb one year old, as a burnt offering; [34]one male goat as a sin offering; [35]and for the sacrifice of peace offerings, two oxen, five rams, five male goats, *and* five male lambs one year old. This *was* the offering of Elizur the son of Shedeur.

[36]On the fifth day *it was* Shelumiel the son of Zurishaddai, leader of the sons of Simeon; [37]his offering *was also* one silver dish whose weight *was* 130 *shekels, and* one silver bowl of seventy shekels in sanctuary shekels, both of them full of fine flour mixed with oil as a grain offering; [38]one gold pan of ten *shekels,* full of incense; [39]one bull, one ram, *and* one male lamb one year old, as a burnt offering; [40]one male goat as a sin offering; [41]and for the sacrifice of peace offerings, two oxen, five rams, five male goats, *and* five male lambs one year old. This *was* the offering of Shelumiel the son of Zurishaddai.

[42]On the sixth day *it was* ^Eliasaph the son of Deuel, leader of the sons of Gad; [43]his offering *was also* one silver dish whose weight *was* 130 *shekels, and* one silver bowl of seventy shekels in sanctuary shekels, both of them full of ^fine flour mixed with oil as a grain offering; [44]one gold pan of ten *shekels,* full of incense; [45]^one bull, one ram, *and* one male lamb one year old, as a burnt offering; [46]one male goat as a sin offering; [47]and for the sacrifice of peace offerings, two oxen, five rams, five male goats, *and* five male lambs

7:17^Luke 3:32, 33   **7:23**^Lev 7:11-13   **7:27**^Is 53:7;
John 1:29   **7:33**^Heb 9:28   **7:42**^Num 1:14; 10:20
7:43^Lev 2:5; 14:10   **7:45**^Ps 50:8-14; Is 1:11

one year old. This *was* the offering of Eliasaph the son of Deuel.

⁴⁸On the seventh day *it was* ^Elishama the son of Ammihud, leader of the sons of Ephraim; ⁴⁹his offering *was also* one silver dish whose weight *was* 130 *shekels, and* one silver bowl of seventy shekels in sanctuary shekels, both of them full of fine flour mixed with oil as a grain offering; ⁵⁰one gold pan of ten *shekels,* full of ^incense; ⁵¹^one bull, one ram, *and* one male lamb one year old, as a burnt offering; ⁵²one male goat as a sin offering; ⁵³and for the sacrifice of peace offerings, two oxen, five rams, five male goats, *and* five male lambs one year old. This *was* the offering of Elishama the son of Ammihud.

⁵⁴On the eighth day *it was* ^Gamaliel the son of Pedahzur, leader of the sons of Manasseh; ⁵⁵his offering *was also* one silver dish whose weight *was* 130 *shekels, and* one silver bowl of seventy shekels in sanctuary shekels, both of them full of fine flour mixed with oil as a grain offering; ⁵⁶one gold pan of ten *shekels,* full of ^incense; ⁵⁷one bull, one ram, *and* one ^male lamb one year old, as a burnt offering; ⁵⁸one male goat as a sin offering; ⁵⁹and for the ^sacrifice of peace offerings, two oxen, five rams, five male goats, *and* five male lambs one year old. This *was* the offering of Gamaliel the son of Pedahzur.

⁶⁰On the ninth day *it was* ^Abidan the son of Gideoni, leader of the sons of Benjamin; ⁶¹his offering *was also* one silver dish whose weight *was* 130 *shekels, and* one silver bowl of seventy shekels in sanctuary shekels, both of them full of fine flour mixed with oil as a grain offering; ⁶²one gold pan of ten

shekels, full of ^incense; ⁶³one bull, one ram, *and* one male lamb one year old, as a burnt offering; ⁶⁴one male goat as a ^sin offering; ⁶⁵and for the sacrifice of ^peace offerings, two oxen, five rams, five male goats, *and* five male lambs one year old. This *was* the offering of Abidan the son of Gideoni.

⁶⁶On the tenth day *it was* ^Ahiezer the son of Ammishaddai, leader of the sons of Dan; ⁶⁷his offering *was also* one silver dish whose weight *was* 130 *shekels, and* one silver bowl of seventy shekels in sanctuary ^shekels, both of them full of fine flour mixed with oil as a grain offering; ⁶⁸one gold pan of ten *shekels,* full of ^incense; ⁶⁹one bull, one ram, *and* one male lamb one year old, as a burnt offering; ⁷⁰one male goat as a sin offering; ⁷¹and for the sacrifice of peace offerings, two oxen, five rams, five male goats, *and* five male lambs one year old. This *was* the offering of Ahiezer the son of Ammishaddai.

⁷²On the eleventh day *it was* ^Pagiel the son of Ochran, leader of the sons of Asher; ⁷³his offering *was also* one silver dish whose weight *was* 130 *shekels, and* one silver bowl of seventy shekels in sanctuary shekels, both of them full of fine flour mixed with oil as a grain offering; ⁷⁴one gold pan of ten *shekels,* full of ^incense; ⁷⁵one bull, one ram, *and* one male lamb one year old, as a burnt offering; ⁷⁶one male goat as a sin offering; ⁷⁷and for the sacrifice of peace offerings, two

7:48 ^Num 1:10; 1 Chr 7:26   7:50 ^Ezek 8:11; Luke 1:10
7:51 ^Mic 6:6-8   7:54 ^Num 2:20   7:56 ^Ex 30:7
7:57 ^Acts 8:32; Rev 5:6   7:59 ^Lev 3:1-17
7:60 ^Num 1:11; 2:22   7:62 ^Rev 5:8; 8:3, 4
7:64 ^2 Cor 5:21   7:65 ^Col 1:20   7:66 ^Num 1:12;
2:25   7:67 ^Ex 30:13; Lev 27:25   7:68 ^Ps 141:2
7:72 ^Num 1:13; 2:27   7:74 ^Mal 1:11

oxen, five rams, five male goats, *and* five male lambs one year old. This *was* the offering of Pagiel the son of Ochran.

⁷⁸ On the twelfth day *it was* ᴬAhira the son of Enan, leader of the sons of Naphtali; ⁷⁹ his offering *was also* one ᴬsilver dish whose weight *was* 130 *shekels, and* one silver bowl of seventy shekels in sanctuary shekels, both of them full of fine flour mixed with oil as a grain offering; ⁸⁰ one gold pan of ten *shekels,* full of incense; ⁸¹ one bull, one ram, *and* one male lamb one year old, as a burnt offering; ⁸² one male goat as a sin offering; ⁸³ and for the sacrifice of peace offerings, two oxen, five rams, five male goats, *and* five male lambs one year old. This *was* the offering of Ahira the son of Enan.

⁸⁴ This *was* ᴬthe dedication *offering* for the altar from the leaders of Israel when ᴮit was anointed: twelve silver dishes, twelve silver bowls, *and* twelve gold pans, ⁸⁵ each silver dish *weighing* 130 *shekels* and each bowl seventy; all the silver of the utensils *totaled* 2,400 in sanctuary shekels; ⁸⁶ the twelve gold pans full of incense, *weighing* ten *shekels* apiece in sanctuary ᴬshekels, all the gold of the pans *totaled* 120 *shekels.* ⁸⁷ All the oxen for the burnt offering *totaled* twelve bulls, *all* the rams, twelve, the male lambs one year old with their grain offering, twelve, and the male goats as a sin offering, twelve; ⁸⁸ and all the oxen for the sacrifice of peace offerings *totaled* twenty-four bulls, *all* the rams, sixty, the male goats, sixty, *and* the male lambs one year old, sixty. ᴬThis *was* the dedication *offering* for the altar after it was anointed.

⁸⁹ Now when ᴬMoses entered the tent of meeting to speak with Him, he heard the voice speaking to him from above ᴮthe ¹atoning cover that was on the ark of the testimony, from between the two cherubim; so He spoke to him.

THE SEVEN LAMPS

8 Then the Lord spoke to Moses, saying, ² "Speak to Aaron and say to him, 'When you mount the lamps, the seven lamps will ᴬprovide light in the front of the lampstand.'" ³ Therefore Aaron did so; he mounted its lamps at the front of the lampstand, just as the Lord had commanded Moses. ⁴ Now this was the workmanship of the lampstand, hammered work of gold; from its base to its flower ornamentation it was hammered work; ᴬaccording to the pattern which the Lord had shown Moses, so he made the lampstand.

CLEANSING THE LEVITES

⁵ Again the Lord spoke to Moses, saying, ⁶ "Take the Levites from among the sons of Israel and ᴬcleanse them. ⁷ This is what you shall do to them, for their cleansing: sprinkle purifying ᴬwater on them, and have them ᴮuse a razor over their whole body, and they shall wash their clothes and cleanse themselves. ⁸ Then have them take a bull with ᴬits grain offering, fine flour mixed with oil; and you shall take a second bull as a

---

7:78 ᴬ Num 1:15; 2:29   7:79 ᴬ Ezra 1:9, 10; Dan 5:2
7:84 ᴬ Num 7:10   ᴮ Num 7:1   7:86 ᴬ Ex 30:13
7:88 ᴬ Num 7:1, 10   7:89 ᴬ Ex 40:34, 35   ᴮ Ex 25:21, 22
8:2 ᴬ Ex 25:37; Lev 24:2, 4   8:4 ᴬ Ex 25:9, 31-40;
37:17-24   8:6 ᴬ Is 52:11   8:7 ᴬ Num 19:9, 13, 20
ᴮ Lev 14:8, 9   8:8 ᴬ Lev 2:1; Num 15:8-10

7:89 ¹ Also called *mercy seat;* i.e., where blood was sprinkled on the Day of Atonement

sin offering. 9So ^you shall present the Levites in front of the tent of meeting. ^BYou shall also assemble the whole congregation of the sons of Israel, 10and present the Levites before the Lord; and the sons of Israel ^shall lay their hands on the Levites. 11Aaron then shall present the Levites before the Lord as a ^wave offering from the sons of Israel, so that they may qualify to perform the service of the Lord. 12Now ^the Levites shall lay their hands on the heads of the bulls; then you are to offer the one as a sin offering and the other as a burnt offering to the Lord, to make atonement for the Levites. 13And you shall have the Levites stand before Aaron and his sons so as to present them as a wave offering to the Lord.

14"So you shall single out the Levites from among the sons of Israel, and ^the Levites shall be Mine. 15Then after that the Levites may go in to serve the tent of meeting. But you shall cleanse them and ^present them as a wave offering; 16for they are exclusively given to Me from among the sons of Israel. I have taken them for Myself ^instead of the firstborn of every womb, the firstborn of all the sons of Israel. 17For ^every firstborn among the sons of Israel is Mine, among the people and among the animals; on the day that I fatally struck all the firstborn in the land of Egypt, I sanctified them for Myself. 18But I have taken the Levites instead of every firstborn among the sons of Israel. 19And ^I have given the Levites as a gift to Aaron and to his sons from among the sons of Israel, to perform the service of the sons of Israel at the tent of meeting and to make atonement on behalf of the sons of Israel, so that there will be no affliction among the sons of Israel due to their approaching the sanctuary."

20So *this is what* Moses, Aaron, and all the congregation of the sons of Israel did to the Levites; according to everything that the Lord had commanded Moses regarding the Levites, so the sons of Israel did to them. 21^The Levites, too, purified themselves from sin and washed their clothes; and Aaron presented them as a wave offering before the Lord. Aaron also made atonement for them to cleanse them. 22Then after that the Levites went in to perform their service in the tent of meeting before Aaron and his sons; just as the Lord had commanded Moses concerning the Levites, so they did to them.

RETIREMENT FOR THE LEVITES

23Now the Lord spoke to Moses, saying, 24"This is what *applies* to the Levites: from ^twenty-five years old and upward they shall enter to perform service in the work of the tent of meeting. 25But at the age of fifty years they shall retire from service in the work and not work anymore. 26They may, however, assist their brothers in the tent of meeting, ^to fulfill an obligation, but they *themselves* shall do no work. In this way you shall deal with the Levites in their obligations."

8:9 ^Ex 29:4   ^BLev 8:3   8:10 ^Lev 1:4
8:11 ^Lev 7:30, 34   8:12 ^Ex 29:10   8:14 ^Num 3:12;
16:9   8:15 ^Ex 29:24   8:16 ^Ex 13:2; Num 3:12, 45
8:17 ^Ex 13:2, 12, 13, 15; Luke 2:23   8:19 ^Num 3:9
8:21 ^Num 8:7   8:24 ^Num 4:3; 1 Chr 23:3, 24, 27
8:26 ^Num 1:53

THE PASSOVER

9 Now the LORD spoke to Moses in the wilderness of Sinai, in ^the first month of the second year after they had come out of the land of Egypt, saying, ²"Now the sons of Israel are to celebrate the Passover at ^its appointed time. ³On the fourteenth day of this month, at twilight, you shall celebrate it at its appointed time; you shall celebrate it in accordance with all its statutes and all its ordinances." ⁴So Moses told the sons of Israel to celebrate the Passover. ⁵And ^they celebrated the Passover in the first *month*, on the fourteenth day of the month, at twilight, in the wilderness of Sinai; in accordance with everything that the LORD had commanded Moses, so the sons of Israel did. ⁶But there were *some* men who were ^unclean because of *contact with a* dead person, so that they could not celebrate Passover on that day; and they came before Moses and Aaron on that day. ⁷Those men said to him, "*Though* we are unclean because of a dead person, why are we kept from presenting the offering of the LORD at its appointed time among the sons of Israel?" ⁸Moses then said to them, "^Wait, and I will listen to what the LORD will command concerning you."

⁹Then the LORD spoke to Moses, saying, ¹⁰"Speak to the sons of Israel, saying, 'If any one of you or of your generations becomes unclean because of a *dead* person, or is on a distant journey, he may, however, celebrate the Passover to the LORD. ¹¹In the second month on the ^fourteenth day at twilight, they shall celebrate it; they shall eat it with unleavened bread and bitter herbs. ¹²They ^shall not leave any of it until morning, ^nor break a bone of it; they shall celebrate it in accordance with the whole statute of the Passover. ¹³But the person who is clean and is not on a journey, yet refrains from celebrating the Passover, that person shall then be cut off from his people, because he did not present the offering of the LORD at its appointed time. That person ^will bear *the responsibility for* his sin. ¹⁴And if a stranger resides among you and celebrates the Passover to the LORD, according to the statute of the Passover and its ordinance, so he shall celebrate *it*; you shall have the ^same statute, both for the stranger and for the native of the land.'"

THE CLOUD ON THE TABERNACLE

¹⁵Now on ^the day that the tabernacle was erected, the cloud covered the tabernacle, the tent of the testimony, and in the evening it was like the appearance of fire over the tabernacle until morning. ¹⁶That is how it was continuously; ^the cloud would cover it *by day*, and the appearance of fire by night. ¹⁷^Whenever the cloud was lifted from over the tent, afterward the sons of Israel would set out; and in the place where the cloud settled down, there the sons of Israel would camp. ¹⁸At the command of the LORD the sons of Israel would set out, and at the command of the LORD they would camp; ^as long as the cloud settled over the tabernacle, they remained camped. ¹⁹Even

9:1^Ex 40:2, 17; Num 1:1   9:2^Ex 12:6; Deut 16:1, 2
9:5^Josh 5:10   9:6^Num 5:2; 19:11-22   9:8^Ex 18:15;
Ps 85:8   9:11^2 Chr 30:2, 15   9:12^Ex 12:10
^John 19:36   9:13^Num 5:31   9:14^Ex 12:49;
Lev 24:22   9:15^Ex 40:2, 17   9:16^Ex 40:34; Neh 9:12
9:17^Ex 40:36-38; Num 10:11, 12   9:18^1 Cor 10:1

when the cloud lingered over the tabernacle for many days, the sons of Israel would comply with the LORD's ordinance and not set out. ²⁰If sometimes the cloud remained a few days over the tabernacle, ^in accordance with the command of the LORD they remained camped. Then in accordance with the command of the LORD they set out. ²¹If sometimes the cloud remained from evening until morning, when the cloud was lifted in the morning they would set out; or *if it remained* in the daytime and at night, whenever the cloud was lifted, they would set out. ²²Whether it was two days, a month, or a year that the cloud lingered over the tabernacle, staying above it, the sons of Israel remained camped and did not set out; but ^when it was lifted, they did set out. ²³^At the command of the LORD they camped, and at the command of the LORD they set out; they did what the LORD required, in accordance with the command of the LORD through Moses.

THE SILVER TRUMPETS

10 The LORD spoke further to Moses, saying, ²"Make yourself two trumpets of silver, you shall make them of hammered work; and you shall use them for ^summoning the congregation and breaking camp. ³Now ^when both are blown, all the congregation shall meet you at the entrance of the tent of meeting. ⁴But if *only* one is blown, then the ^leaders, the heads of the divisions of Israel, shall meet you. ⁵And when you blow an alarm, the camps that are pitched ^on the east side shall set out. ⁶Then when you sound an alarm the second time, the camps

that are pitched on ^the south side shall set out; an alarm is to be sounded for them to break camp. ⁷When convening the assembly, however, you shall blow *the trumpets* without ^sounding an alarm. ⁸^The sons of Aaron, moreover, the priests, shall blow the trumpets; and *this* shall be a permanent statute for you throughout your generations. ⁹And when you go to war in your land against the enemy who attacks you, then you shall sound an alarm with the trumpets, so that you will be ^thought of by the LORD your God, and be saved from your enemies. ¹⁰Also on the day of your joy and at your appointed feasts, and on the first *days* of your months, ^you shall blow the trumpets over your burnt offerings, and over the sacrifices of your peace offerings; and they shall be as a reminder of you before your God. I am the LORD your God."

THE TRIBES LEAVE SINAI

¹¹Now in ^the second year, in the second month, on the twentieth of the month, the cloud was lifted from above the tabernacle of the testimony; ¹²and the sons of Israel set out on ^their journeys from the wilderness of Sinai. Then the cloud settled in the ^Bwilderness of Paran. ¹³^So they moved on for the first time in accordance with the command of the LORD through Moses. ¹⁴The flag of the camp of the sons of Judah, by their armies, ^set out first, with Nahshon the son of Amminadab,

9:20^Ps 48:14; Prov 3:5, 6   9:22^Ex 40:36, 37
9:23^Ps 73:24; Is 63:14   10:2^Is 1:13   10:3^Jer 4:5;
Joel 2:15   10:4^Ex 18:21; Num 1:16   10:5^Num 10:14
10:6^Num 10:18   10:7^Joel 2:1   10:8^Num 31:6;
Josh 6:4   10:9^Gen 8:1; Ps 106:4   10:10^Ps 81:3-5
10:11^Ex 40:17   10:12^Ex 40:36   ^B^Num 12:16
10:13^Deut 1:6   10:14^Num 2:3-9

over its army, 15and Nethanel the son of Zuar, over the tribal army of the sons of Issachar; 16and Eliab the son of Helon over the tribal army of the sons of Zebulun.

17ᴬThen the tabernacle was taken down; and the sons of Gershon and the sons of Merari, who were carrying the tabernacle, set out. 18Next ᴬthe flag of the camp of Reuben, by their armies, set out with Elizur the son of Shedeur, over its army, 19and Shelumiel the son of Zurishaddai over the tribal army of the sons of Simeon, 20and Eliasaph the son of Deuel was over the tribal army of the sons of Gad.

21ᴬThen the Kohathites set out, carrying the holy *objects;* and the tabernacle was set up before their arrival. 22ᴬNext the flag of the camp of the sons of Ephraim, by their armies, set out, with Elishama the son of Ammihud over its army, 23and Gamaliel the son of Pedahzur over the tribal army of the sons of Manasseh; 24and Abidan the son of Gideoni over the tribal army of the sons of Benjamin.

25ᴬThen the flag of the camp of the sons of Dan, by their armies, *which* formed the rear guard for all the camps, set out, with Ahiezer the son of Ammishaddai over its army, 26and Pagiel the son of Ochran over the tribal army of the sons of Asher; 27and Ahira the son of Enan over the tribal army of the sons of Naphtali. 28This was the order of marching for the sons of Israel by their armies as they set out.

29Then Moses said to Hobab the son of Reuel the Midianite, Moses' father-in-law, "We are setting out to the place of which the Lord said, 'ᴬI will give it to you.' Come with us and we will do you good, for the Lord

ᴮhas promised good concerning Israel." 30But he said to him, "ᴬI will not come, but rather will go to my *own* land and relatives." 31Then he said, "Please do not leave us, since you know where we should camp in the wilderness, and you ᴬwill be as eyes for us. 32So it will be, if you go with us, that whatever good the Lord does for us, ᴬwe will do for you."

33So they moved on from the mountain of the Lord three days' journey, with ᴬthe ark of the covenant of the Lord going on in front of them for the three days, to seek out ᴮa resting place for them. 34ᴬAnd the cloud of the Lord was over them by day when they set out from the camp.

35Then it came about when the ark set out that Moses said,
  "Rise up, Lord!
  And may Your enemies be
    scattered,
  And those ᴬwho hate You flee
    from Your presence."
36And when it came to rest, he said,
  "Return, Lord,
  To the myriad ᴬthousands of
    Israel."

THE PEOPLE COMPLAIN

11 Now the people became like ᴬthose who complain of adversity in the ears of the Lord; and the Lord heard *them* and His anger was kindled, and the fire of the Lord burned among them and consumed *some* at the outskirts of the camp. 2ᴬThe people then cried out to Moses; and Moses prayed to

10:17ᴬNum 4:21-32 10:18ᴬNum 2:10-16
10:21ᴬNum 4:4-20 10:22ᴬNum 2:18-24
10:25ᴬNum 2:25-31 10:29ᴬEx 6:4-8 ᴮDeut 4:40
10:30ᴬJudg 1:16; Matt 21:28, 29 10:31ᴬJob 29:15
10:32ᴬLev 19:34; Deut 10:18 10:33ᴬDeut 1:33
ᴮIs 11:10 10:34ᴬNum 9:15-23 10:35ᴬDeut 7:10; 32:41
10:36ᴬNum 1:10 11:1ᴬNum 14:2; 16:11
11:2ᴬNum 12:11, 13; 21:7

the LORD, and the fire died out. ³So that place was named ¹,ᴬTaberah, because the fire of the LORD burned among them.

⁴Now the ᴬrabble who were among them had greedy cravings; and the sons of Israel also wept again and said, "Who will give us meat to eat? ⁵ᴬWe remember the fish which we used to eat for free in Egypt, the cucumbers, the melons, the leeks, the onions, and the garlic; ⁶but now ᴬour appetite is gone. There is nothing at all to look at except this manna!"

⁷ᴬNow the manna was like coriander seed, and its appearance like that of ¹bdellium. ⁸The people would roam about and gather it and grind it between two millstones, or pound it in the mortar, and boil it in the pot and make loaves with it; and its taste was like the taste of cake baked with oil. ⁹ᴬWhen the dew came down on the camp at night, the manna would come down with it.

THE COMPLAINT OF MOSES

¹⁰Now Moses heard the people weeping throughout their families, each one at the entrance of his tent; and the anger of the LORD became very hot, and Moses was displeased. ¹¹ᴬSo Moses said to the LORD, "Why have You been so hard on Your servant? And why have I not found favor in Your sight, that You have put the burden of all this people on me? ¹²Was it I who conceived all this people? Or did I give birth to them, that You should say to me, 'Carry them in your arms, as a nurse carries a nursing infant, to the land which ᴬYou swore to their fathers'? ¹³Where am I to get meat to give to ᴬall this people? For they weep before me, saying, 'Give us meat so that we may eat!' ¹⁴ᴬI am not able to carry all this people by myself, because it is too burdensome for me. ¹⁵ᴬSo if You are going to deal with me this way, please kill me now, if I have found favor in Your sight, and do not let me see my misery."

SEVENTY ELDERS TO ASSIST MOSES

¹⁶The LORD therefore said to Moses, "Gather for Me ᴬseventy men from the elders of Israel, whom you know to be the elders of the people and their officers, and bring them to the tent of meeting, and have them take their stand there with you. ¹⁷Then I will come down and speak with you there, and I will take away some of ᴬthe Spirit who is upon you, and put Him upon them; and they shall bear the burden of the people with you, so that you will not bear it by yourself. ¹⁸And you shall say to the people, 'ᴬConsecrate yourselves for tomorrow, and you shall eat meat; for you have wept in the ears of the LORD, saying, "Oh that someone would give us meat to eat! For we were well-off in Egypt." Therefore the LORD will give you meat and you shall eat. ¹⁹You shall eat, not one day, nor two days, nor five days, nor ten days, nor twenty days, ²⁰but for a whole month, until it comes out of your nose and makes you nauseated; because ᴬyou have rejected the LORD who is among you and have

11:3ᴬDeut 9:22   11:4ᴬ1 Cor 10:6   11:5ᴬEx 16:3
11:6ᴬNum 21:5   11:7ᴬEx 16:31   11:9ᴬEx 16:13, 14
11:11ᴬEx 5:22; Deut 1:12   11:12ᴬGen 24:7; Ex 13:5, 11
11:13ᴬNum 11:21, 22; John 6:5-9   11:14ᴬEx 18:18;
Deut 1:12   11:15ᴬEx 32:32   11:16ᴬEx 24:1, 9
11:17ᴬ1 Sam 10:6; Joel 2:28   11:18ᴬEx 19:10, 22
11:20ᴬJosh 24:27; 1 Sam 10:19

11:3¹I.e., the place for burning   11:7¹I.e., a tree gum

wept before Him, saying, "Why did we ever leave Egypt?"'" [21]But Moses said, "The people, among whom I am *included*, are six hundred thousand on foot! Yet You have said, 'I will give them meat, so that they may eat for a whole month.' [22]Are flocks and herds to be slaughtered for them, so that it will be sufficient for them? Or are all the fish of the sea to be caught for them, so that it will be sufficient for them?" [23]Then the LORD said to Moses, "Is ᴬthe LORD's power too little? Now you shall see whether ᴮMy word will come true for you or not."

[24]So Moses went out and ᴬtold the people the words of the LORD. He also gathered seventy men of the elders of the people, and positioned them around the tent. [25]ᴬThen the LORD came down in the cloud and spoke to him; and He took away some of the Spirit who was upon him and placed *Him* upon the seventy elders. And when the Spirit rested upon them, they prophesied. Yet they did not do *it* again.

[26]But two men had remained in the camp; the name of the one was Eldad, and the name of the other, Medad. And ᴬthe Spirit rested upon them (and they were among those who had been registered, but had not gone out to the tent), and they prophesied in the camp. [27]So a young man ran and informed Moses, and said, "Eldad and Medad are prophesying in the camp." [28]Then ᴬJoshua the son of Nun, the personal servant of Moses from his youth, responded and said, "My lord Moses, restrain them!" [29]But Moses said to him, "Are you jealous for my sake? ᴬIf only all the LORD's people were prophets, that the LORD would put His Spirit upon them!" [30]Then

Moses returned to the camp, *both* he and the elders of Israel.

THE QUAIL AND THE PLAGUE

[31]ᴬNow a wind burst forth from the LORD and it brought quail from the sea, and dropped *them* beside the camp, about a day's journey on this *side* and a day's journey on the other *side* all around the camp, and about [1]two cubits *deep* on the surface of the ground. [32]And the people spent all that day, all night, and all the next day, and they gathered the quail (the one who gathered least gathered [1]ten ᴬhomers) and spread *them* out for themselves all around the camp. [33]ᴬWhile the meat was still between their teeth, before it was chewed, the anger of the LORD was kindled against the people, and the LORD struck the people with a very severe plague. [34]So that place was named [1],ᴬKibroth-hattaavah, because there they buried the people who had been greedy. [35]From Kibroth-hattaavah ᴬthe people set out for Hazeroth, and they remained at Hazeroth.

THE MURMURING OF MIRIAM AND AARON

12 Then Miriam and Aaron spoke against Moses because of the Cushite woman whom he had married (for he had married a ᴬCushite woman); [2]ᴬand they said, "Is it a fact that the LORD has spoken only through Moses? Has He

11:23 ᴬIs 50:2   ᴮEzek 12:25   11:24 ᴬNum 11:16
11:25 ᴬNum 11:17; 12:5   11:26 ᴬNum 24:2; 1 Sam 10:6
11:28 ᴬEx 33:11; Josh 1:1   11:29 ᴬ1 Cor 14:5
11:31 ᴬPs 78:26-28; 105:40   11:32 ᴬEzek 45:11
11:33 ᴬPs 78:29-31; 106:15   11:34 ᴬDeut 9:22
11:35 ᴬNum 33:17   12:1 ᴬEx 2:21   12:2 ᴬNum 16:3

11:31 [1]About 3 ft. or 90 cm   11:32 [1]About 77 cubic feet or 2.2 cubic meters   11:34 [1]I.e., the graves of greediness

not spoken through us as well?" And the LORD heard *this*. ³(Now the man Moses was ^very humble, more than any person who was on the face of the earth.) ⁴And the LORD suddenly said to Moses and to Aaron and Miriam, "You three go out to the tent of meeting." So the three of them went out. ⁵^Then the LORD came down in a pillar of cloud and stood at the entrance of the tent; and He called Aaron and Miriam. When they had both come forward, ⁶He said,

"Now hear My words:
If there is a prophet among
 you,
I, the LORD, will make Myself
 known to him in a ^vision.
I will speak with him in a
 ᴮdream.
⁷ "*It is* not this way *for* My
 servant Moses;
^He is faithful in all My
 household;
⁸ With him I speak mouth to
 mouth,
That is, openly, and not using
 mysterious language,
And he beholds ^the form of
 the LORD.
So why were you not afraid
To speak against My servant,
 against Moses?"

⁹And the anger of the LORD burned against them and ^He departed. ¹⁰But when the cloud had withdrawn from above the tent, behold, Miriam *was* leprous, as ^*white as* snow. As Aaron turned toward Miriam, behold, she *was* leprous. ¹¹Then Aaron said to Moses, "Oh, my lord, I beg you, ^do not hold us responsible for this sin by which we have turned out to be foolish, and by which we have sinned. ¹²Oh, do not let her be like a dead person, whose

flesh is half eaten away when he comes out of his mother's womb!" ¹³So Moses cried out to the LORD, saying, "God, ^heal her, please!" ¹⁴But the LORD said to Moses, "If her father had only spit in her face, would she not be put to shame for seven days? Have her shut ^outside the camp for seven days, and afterward she may be received again." ¹⁵So ^Miriam was shut outside the camp for seven days, and the people did not move on until Miriam was received again.

¹⁶Afterward, however, the people moved on from Hazeroth and camped in the wilderness of Paran.

SPIES VIEW THE LAND

13 Then ^the LORD spoke to Moses, saying, ²"^Send out men for yourself to spy out the land of Canaan, which I am going to give the sons of Israel; you shall send a man from each of their fathers' tribes, every one a leader among them." ³So Moses sent them from the wilderness of Paran at the command of the LORD, all of them men who were heads of the sons of Israel. ⁴These then *were* their names: from the tribe of Reuben, Shammua the son of Zaccur; ⁵from the tribe of Simeon, Shaphat the son of Hori; ⁶from the tribe of Judah, ^Caleb the son of Jephunneh; ⁷from the tribe of Issachar, Igal the son of Joseph; ⁸from the tribe of Ephraim, ^Hoshea the son of Nun; ⁹from the tribe of Benjamin, Palti the son of Raphu; ¹⁰from

12:3^Matt 11:29 12:5^Ex 19:9; 34:5 12:6^1 Sam 3:15
ᴮGen 31:11 12:7^Heb 3:2, 5 12:8^Ex 24:10, 11;
Deut 5:8 12:9^Gen 17:22; 18:33 12:10^Ex 4:6;
2 Kin 5:27 12:11^2 Sam 19:19; 24:10 12:13^Is 30:26;
Jer 17:14 12:14^Num 5:1-4 12:15^Deut 24:9
13:1^Deut 1:22, 23 13:2^Deut 1:22; 9:23
13:6^Num 14:6, 30; Josh 14:6 13:8^Num 13:16;
Deut 32:44

the tribe of Zebulun, Gaddiel the son of Sodi; [11]from the tribe of Joseph, from the tribe of Manasseh, Gaddi the son of Susi; [12]from the tribe of Dan, Ammiel the son of Gemalli; [13]from the tribe of Asher, Sethur the son of Michael; [14]from the tribe of Naphtali, Nahbi the son of Vophsi; [15] *and* from the tribe of Gad, Geuel the son of Machi. [16]These are the names of the men whom Moses sent to spy out the land; but Moses called ^Hoshea the son of Nun, Joshua.

[17]When Moses sent them to spy out the land of Canaan, he said to them, "Go up there into ^the [1]Negev; then go up into the hill country. [18]See what the land is *like,* and whether the people who live in it are strong or weak, whether they are few or many. [19]And how is the land in which they live, is it good or bad? And how are the cities in which they live, are *the people* in *open* camps or in fortifications? [20]And ^how is the land, is it productive or unproductive? Are there trees in it or not? And show yourselves courageous and get some of the fruit of the land." Now the time was the season of the first ripe grapes.

[21]So they went up and spied out the land from the wilderness of Zin as far as Rehob, ^at Lebo-hamath. [22]When they had gone up into the Negev, they came to Hebron where ^Ahiman, Sheshai, and Talmai, the descendants of Anak were. (Hebron was built seven years before Zoan in Egypt.) [23]Then they came to the Valley of [1,^]Eshcol, and from there they cut off a branch with a single cluster of grapes; and they carried it on a pole between two *men,* with some of the pomegranates and the figs. [24]That place was called the Valley of Eshcol, because of the cluster which the sons of Israel cut off from there.

THE SPIES' REPORTS

[25]When they returned from spying out the land, at the end of forty days, [26]they went on and came to Moses and Aaron and to all the congregation of the sons of Israel, in the wilderness of Paran at ^Kadesh; and they brought back word to them and to all the congregation, and showed them the fruit of the land. [27]So they reported to him and said, "We came into the land where you sent us, and it certainly does flow with milk and honey, and ^this is its fruit. [28]Nevertheless, the people who live in the land are strong, and the cities are fortified *and* very large. And indeed, we saw ^the descendants of Anak there! [29]Amalek is living in the land of the Negev, the Hittites, the Jebusites, and ^the Amorites are living in the hill country, and [B]the Canaanites are living by the sea and by the side of the Jordan."

[30]Then Caleb quieted the people before Moses and said, "We should by all means go up and take possession of it, for we will certainly prevail over it." [31]But the men who had gone up with him said, "^We are not able to go up against the people, because they are too strong for us." [32]So they brought a bad report of the land which they had spied out to the sons of Israel, saying, "The

13:16 ^Num 13:8; Deut 32:44   13:17 ^Gen 12:9; 13:1, 3
13:20 ^Deut 1:24, 25   13:21 ^Josh 13:5
13:22 ^Josh 15:14   13:23 ^Num 13:24; Deut 1:24
13:26 ^Num 20:1, 14; 32:8   13:27 ^Deut 1:25
13:28 ^Num 13:33   13:29 ^Josh 10:6   [B]Num 14:43, 45
13:31 ^Deut 1:28; 9:1-3

13:17 [1]I.e., South country, and so throughout the ch
13:23 [1]I.e., cluster (of grapes)

land through which we have gone to spy out is ^a a land that devours its inhabitants; and ^B all the people whom we saw in it are people of *great* stature. 33 We also saw the ^A Nephilim there (the sons of Anak are part of the Nephilim); and we were like grasshoppers in our own sight, and so we were in their sight."

THE PEOPLE REBEL

14 Then all the congregation raised their voices and cried out, and the people wept that night. 2 And all the sons of Israel grumbled against Moses and Aaron; and the entire congregation said to them, "^A If only we had died in the land of Egypt! Or *even* if we had died in this wilderness! 3 So why is the LORD bringing us into this land ^A to fall by the sword? ^B Our wives and our little ones will become plunder! Would it not be better for us to return to Egypt?" 4 So they said to one another, "^A Let's appoint a leader and return to Egypt!"

5 ^A Then Moses and Aaron fell on their faces in the presence of all the assembly of the congregation of the sons of Israel. 6 And Joshua the son of Nun and Caleb the son of Jephunneh, of those who had spied out the land, tore their clothes; 7 and they spoke to all the congregation of the sons of Israel, saying, "^A The land which we passed through to spy out is an exceedingly good land. 8 ^A If the LORD is pleased with us, then He will bring us into this land and give it to us—a land which flows with milk and honey. 9 Only ^A do not rebel against the LORD; and do not fear the people of the land, for they will be our prey. Their protection is gone from them, and the LORD is with us; do not fear them." 10 But

all the congregation said to stone them with stones. Then ^A the glory of the LORD appeared in the tent of meeting to all the sons of Israel.

MOSES PLEADS FOR THE PEOPLE

11 And the LORD said to Moses, "How long will this people be disrespectful to Me? And how long will ^A they not believe in Me, despite all the signs that I have performed in their midst? 12 I will strike them with plague and dispossess them, and I ^A will make you into a nation greater and mightier than they."

13 ^A But Moses said to the LORD, "Then the Egyptians will hear of it, for by Your strength You brought this people up from their midst, 14 and they will tell *it* to the inhabitants of this land. They have heard that You, LORD, are in the midst of this people, because ^A You, LORD, are seen eye to eye, while Your cloud stands over them; and You go before them in a pillar of cloud by day, and in a pillar of fire by night. 15 Now if You put this people to death all at once, ^A then the nations who have heard of Your fame will say, 16 'Since the LORD ^A could not bring this people into the land which He promised them by oath, He slaughtered them in the wilderness.' 17 So now, please, let the power of the Lord be great, just as You have declared, saying, 18 '^A The LORD is slow to anger and abundant in mercy, forgiving wrongdoing and violation *of His Law;* but He will by no means leave *the guilty*

13:32 ^A Ezek 36:13, 14   ^B Amos 2:9   13:33 ^A Gen 6:4
14:2 ^A Num 11:5; 20:3, 4   14:3 ^A Ex 5:21   ^B Num 14:31
14:4 ^A Neh 9:17   14:5 ^A Num 16:4   14:7 ^A Num 13:27;
Deut 1:25   14:8 ^A Deut 10:15   14:9 ^A Deut 1:26; 9:23, 24
14:10 ^A Ex 16:10; Lev 9:23   14:11 ^A Ps 106:24
14:12 ^A Ex 32:10   14:13 ^A Ex 32:11-14; Ps 106:23
14:14 ^A Ex 13:21; Deut 5:4   14:15 ^A Ex 32:12
14:16 ^A Josh 7:7   14:18 ^A Ps 145:8; John 4:2

unpunished, inflicting the 'punishment of the fathers on the children to the third and the fourth *generations*.' ¹⁹Please ^forgive the guilt of this people in accordance with the greatness of Your mercy, just as You also have forgiven this people, from Egypt even until now."

THE LORD PARDONS AND REBUKES

²⁰So the LORD said, "^I have forgiven *them* in accordance with your word; ²¹however, as I live, ^all the earth will be filled with the glory of the LORD. ²²Certainly ^all the people who have seen My glory and My signs which I performed in Egypt and in the wilderness, yet have put Me to the test these ten times and have not listened to My voice, ²³^shall by no means see the land which I swore to their fathers, nor shall any of those who were disrespectful to Me see it. ²⁴But as for My servant Caleb, ^because he has had a different spirit and has followed Me fully, ^ᴮI will bring him into the land which he entered, and his descendants shall take possession of it. ²⁵^Now the Amalekites and the Canaanites live in the valleys; turn tomorrow and set out for the wilderness by the way of the Red Sea."

²⁶The LORD spoke to Moses and Aaron again, saying, ²⁷"How long *shall I put up* with this evil congregation who are ^grumbling against Me? I have heard the complaints of the sons of Israel which they are voicing against Me. ²⁸Say to them, 'As I live,' declares the LORD, 'just as ^you have spoken in My hearing, so I will do to you; ²⁹^your dead bodies will fall in this wilderness, all ^ᴮyour numbered men according to your complete number from twenty years old and upward, who

have grumbled against Me. ³⁰By no means will you come into the land where I swore to settle you, ^except for Caleb the son of Jephunneh and Joshua the son of Nun. ³¹^Your children, however, whom you said would become plunder—I will bring them in, and they will know the land which you have rejected. ³²^But as for you, your dead bodies will fall in this wilderness. ³³Also, your sons will be shepherds in the wilderness for ^forty years, and they will suffer *for* your unfaithfulness, until your bodies perish in the wilderness. ³⁴In accordance with the ^number of days that you spied out the land, forty days, for every day you shall suffer the punishment for your guilt a year, *that is,* forty years, and you will know My opposition. ³⁵^I, the LORD, have spoken, I certainly will do this to all this evil congregation who are gathered together against Me. They shall be worn out in this wilderness, and there they shall die.'"

³⁶^As for the men whom Moses sent to spy out the land, and who returned and led all the congregation to grumble against him by bringing a bad report about the land, ³⁷those men who brought the bad report of the land also died by a ^plague in the presence of the LORD. ³⁸But Joshua the son of Nun and Caleb the son of Jephunneh remained alive out of those men who went to spy out the land.

14:19 ^Ex 32:32; 34:9   14:20 ^Mic 7:18-20
14:21 ^Is 6:3; Hab 2:14   14:22 ^1 Cor 10:5
14:23 ^Num 26:65; Heb 3:18   14:24 ^Num 14:6-9
ᴮJosh 14:6-15   14:25 ^Num 13:29   14:27 ^Num 11:1
14:28 ^Deut 2:14, 15; Heb 3:17   14:29 ^Heb 3:17
ᴮNum 1:45, 46   14:30 ^Num 14:24   14:31 ^Num 14:3
14:32 ^Num 26:64, 65; 1 Cor 10:5   14:33 ^Deut 2:7;
8:2, 4   14:34 ^Num 13:25   14:35 ^Num 23:19
14:36 ^Num 13:4-16, 32   14:37 ^Num 16:49

14:18 ¹I.e., punishment for the wrongdoing

ISRAEL REPULSED

39 Now when Moses spoke ^these words to all the sons of Israel, ^Bthe people mourned greatly. 40 In the morning, however, they got up early and went up to the ridge of the hill country, saying, "^Here we are; and we will go up to the place which the LORD has promised, for we have sinned." 41 But Moses said, "^Why then are you ^Bviolating the command of the LORD, when *doing so* will not succeed? 42 ^Do not go up, for the LORD is not among you, to prevent you from being defeated by your enemies. 43 For the Amalekites and the Canaanites will be there to confront you, and you will fall by the sword, since you have turned back from following the LORD. And the LORD will not be with you." 44 But they *foolishly* dared to go up to the ridge of the hill country; neither ^the ark of the covenant of the LORD nor Moses left the camp. 45 Then the Amalekites and the Canaanites who lived in that hill country came down, and struck them and scattered them as far as ^Hormah.

LAWS FOR CANAAN

15 Now the LORD spoke to Moses, saying, 2 "^Speak to the sons of Israel and say to them, 'When you enter the land where you are going to live, which I am giving you, 3 and you make an offering by fire to the LORD, a burnt offering or a sacrifice to ^fulfill a special vow, or as a voluntary offering or at your ^Bappointed times, to make a soothing aroma to the LORD from the herd or from the flock, 4 then ^the one who presents his offering shall present to the LORD a grain offering of a tenth *of an* ¹*ephah* of fine flour mixed with a fourth of a ²hin of oil, 5 and you shall

prepare wine for the drink offering, a fourth of a hin, with the burnt offering or for the sacrifice, for ^each lamb. 6 Or for a ram you shall prepare as a grain offering two-tenths *of an ephah* of fine flour mixed with a third of a hin of oil; 7 and for the drink offering you shall offer a third of a hin of wine as a soothing aroma to the LORD. 8 And when you prepare ^a bull as a burnt offering or a sacrifice, to fulfill a special vow, or for peace offerings to the LORD, 9 then you shall offer with the bull a grain offering of three-tenths *of an ephah* of fine flour mixed with half a hin of oil; 10 and you shall offer as the drink offering half a hin of wine as an offering by fire, as a soothing aroma to the LORD.

11 "This is how it shall be done for each ox, or for each ram, or for each of the male lambs, or of the goats. 12 According to the number that you prepare, so you shall do for each one according to their number. 13 Everyone who is a native shall do these things in this way, in presenting an offering by fire as a soothing aroma to the LORD.

LAW FOR THE STRANGER

14 Now if a stranger resides among you, or one who *may be* among you throughout your generations, and he *wants to* make an offering by fire, as a soothing aroma to the LORD, just as you do so shall he do. 15 *As for* the assembly, there shall be ^one statute for you and for the

14:39 ^Num 14:28-35   ᴮEx 33:4   14:40 ^Deut 1:41-44
14:41 ^2 Chr 24:20;   ᴮNum 14:25   14:42 ^Deut 1:42
14:44 ^Num 31:6   14:45 ^Num 21:3   15:2 ^Lev 23:10
15:3 ^Lev 22:21   ᴮLev 23:1-44   15:4 ^Num 28:1-29:40
15:5 ^Lev 1:10; Num 15:11   15:8 ^Lev 1:3; 3:1
15:15 ^Num 9:14; 15:29

15:4 ¹An ephah was about 7.4 gallons or 28 liters
² A hin also was about 1 gallon or 3.8 liters

stranger who resides *among you,* a permanent statute throughout your generations; as you are, so shall the stranger be before the Lord. [16]There is to be ^one law and one ordinance for you and for the stranger who resides with you.'"

[17]Then the Lord spoke to Moses, saying, [18]"Speak to the sons of Israel and say to them, 'When you enter the land where I am bringing you, [19]then it shall be, that when you eat from the ^food of the land, you shall lift up an offering to the Lord. [20]^Of the first of your dough you shall lift up a loaf as an offering; as an offering of the threshing floor, so you shall lift it up. [21]From the first of your dough you shall give to the Lord an offering throughout your generations.

[22]'But when you ^unintentionally do wrong and fail to comply with all these commandments which the Lord has spoken to Moses, [23]*that is,* all that the Lord has commanded you through Moses from the day that the Lord gave commandments and onward, throughout your generations, [24]then it shall be, if it is done ^unintentionally, without the knowledge of the congregation, that all the congregation shall offer one bull as a burnt offering, as a soothing aroma to the Lord, ^Bwith its grain offering and its drink offering, according to the ordinance, and one male goat as a sin offering. [25]Then ^the priest shall make atonement for all the congregation of the sons of Israel, and they will be forgiven; for it was an unintentional wrong, and they have brought their offering, an offering by fire to the Lord, and their sin offering before the Lord, for their unintentional wrong. [26]So all the congregation of the sons of Israel will be forgiven, as well as the stranger who resides among them, for *guilt was attributed* to all the people through an ^unintentional wrong.

[27]'Also, if one person sins ^unintentionally, then he shall offer a one-year-old female goat as a sin offering. [28]And ^the priest shall make atonement before the Lord for the person who goes astray by an unintentional sin, making atonement for him so that he may be forgiven. [29]You shall have one law for the native among the sons of Israel and for the stranger who resides among them, for one who does *anything wrong* unintentionally. [30]But the person who does *wrong*^defiantly, whether he is a native or a stranger, that one is blaspheming the Lord; and that person shall be cut off from among his people. [31]Since he has ^despised the word of the Lord and has broken His commandment, that person shall be completely cut off; his guilt *will be* on him.'"

SABBATH-BREAKING PUNISHED

[32]Now while the sons of Israel were in the wilderness, they found a man ^gathering wood on the Sabbath day. [33]And those who found him gathering wood brought him to Moses and Aaron, and to all the congregation; [34]and they placed him in custody, ^because it had not been decided what should be done to him. [35]Then the Lord said to Moses, "The man must be put to death; ^all the congregation shall

15:16^Lev 24:22   15:19^Josh 5:11, 12   15:20^Ex 34:26; Lev 23:14   15:22^Lev 4:2   15:24^Lev 4:2, 22, 27   ^BNum 15:8-10   15:25^Lev 4:20; Heb 2:17   15:26^Num 15:24   15:27^Lev 4:27-31; Luke 12:48   15:28^Lev 4:35   15:30^Num 14:40-44; Deut 17:12, 13   15:31^2 Sam 12:9; Prov 13:13   15:32^Lev 31:14, 15; 35:2, 3   15:34^Num 9:8   15:35^Lev 24:14-23; Deut 21:21

stone him with stones outside the camp." [36] So all the congregation brought him outside the camp and stoned him to death with stones, just as the LORD had commanded Moses.

[37] The LORD also spoke to Moses, saying, [38] "Speak to the sons of Israel and tell them that they shall make for themselves ^tassels on the corners of their garments throughout their generations, and that they shall put on the tassel of each corner a ¹violet thread. [39] It shall be a tassel for you to look at and ^remember all the commandments of the LORD, so that you will do them and not follow your own heart and your own eyes, which led you to prostitute yourselves, [40] so that you will remember and do all My commandments and ^be holy to your God. [41] I am the LORD your God who brought you out from the land of Egypt to be your God; I am the LORD your God."

KORAH'S REBELLION

16 Now ^Korah the son of Izhar, the son of Kohath, the son of Levi, with Dathan and Abiram, the sons of Eliab, and On the son of Peleth, sons of Reuben, took *men,* [2] and they stood before Moses, together with some of the sons of Israel, 250 leaders of the congregation ^chosen in the assembly, men of renown. [3] They assembled together ^against Moses and Aaron, and said to them, "You have gone far enough! For all the congregation are holy, every one of them, and ^the LORD is in their midst; so why do you exalt yourselves above the assembly of the LORD?"

[4] When Moses heard *this,* ^he fell on his face; [5] and he spoke to Korah and all his group, saying, "Tomorrow morning the LORD will make known who is His, and who is holy, and will bring *that one* near to Himself; indeed, ^the one whom He will choose, He will bring near to Himself. [6] Do this: take censers for yourselves, Korah and your whole group, [7] and put fire in them, and place incense upon them in the presence of the LORD tomorrow; and the man whom the LORD chooses *shall be* the one who is holy. ^You have gone far enough, you sons of Levi!"

[8] Then Moses said to Korah, "Hear now, you sons of Levi: [9] ^Is it too small *an honor* for you that the God of Israel has singled you out from the congregation of Israel, to bring you near to Himself, to perform the service of the tabernacle of the LORD, and to stand before the congregation to minister to them; [10] and that He has brought you near, *Korah,* and all your brothers, sons of Levi, with you? But are you ^seeking the priesthood as well? [11] Therefore you and your whole group are the ones gathered together ^against the LORD; but as for Aaron, who is he, that ^you grumble against him?"

[12] Then Moses sent a summons to Dathan and Abiram, the sons of Eliab; but they said, "We will not come up. [13] Is it not enough that you have brought us up out of a land flowing with milk and honey ^to have us die in the wilderness, but you would also appoint yourself as master over us? [14] Indeed, you have

15:38 ^Deut 22:12; Matt 23:5   15:39 ^Deut 4:23; 8:11, 14, 19   15:40 ^Lev 11:44, 45   16:1 ^Ex 6:21; Jude 11
16:2 ^Num 1:16; 26:9   16:3 ^Ps 106:16   ᴮNum 5:3
16:4 ^Num 14:5   16:5 ^Num 17:5, 8   16:7 ^Num 16:3
16:9 ^Is 7:13   16:10 ^Num 3:10; 18:1-7   16:11 ^Ex 16:7
ᴮ1 Cor 10:10   16:13 ^Num 14:2, 3

15:38 ¹Or *bluish;* LXX *hyacinth* in color, and so throughout the ch

not brought us into a land flowing with milk and honey, nor have you given us an inheritance of ^fields and vineyards. Would you ^gouge out the eyes of these men? We will not come up!"

¹⁵Then Moses became very angry and said to the Lᴏʀᴅ, "^Pay no attention to their offering! ^I have not taken a single donkey from them, nor have I done harm to any of them." ¹⁶Moses said to Korah, "You and all your group be present before the Lᴏʀᴅ tomorrow, you and they along with Aaron. ¹⁷And each *of you* take his censer and put incense on it, and each *of you* bring his censer before the Lᴏʀᴅ, 250 censers; also you and Aaron *shall* each *bring* his censer." ¹⁸So they took, each one his *own* censer, and put fire on it, and placed incense on it; and they stood at the entrance of the tent of meeting, with Moses and Aaron. ¹⁹So Korah assembled all the congregation against them at the entrance of the tent of meeting. And ^the glory of the Lᴏʀᴅ appeared to all the congregation.

²⁰Then the Lᴏʀᴅ spoke to Moses and Aaron, saying, ²¹"^Separate yourselves from among this congregation, ^so that I may consume them instantly." ²²But they fell on their faces and said, "God, ^the God of the spirits of humanity, when one person sins, will You be angry with the entire congregation?"

²³Then the Lᴏʀᴅ spoke to Moses, saying, ²⁴"Speak to the congregation, saying, '^Get away from *the areas* around the tents of Korah, Dathan, and Abiram.'"

²⁵Then Moses arose and went to Dathan and Abiram, with the elders of Israel following him, ²⁶and he spoke to the congregation,

saying, "^Get away now from the tents of these wicked men, and do not touch anything that belongs to them, ^or you will be swept away in all their sin!" ²⁷So they moved away from *the areas* around the tents of Korah, Dathan, and Abiram; and Dathan and Abiram came out *and* stood at the entrances of their tents, along with their wives, ^their sons, and their little ones. ²⁸Then Moses said, "By this you shall know that ^the Lᴏʀᴅ has sent me to do all these deeds; for it is not my doing. ²⁹If these men die the death of all mankind, or if they suffer the ^fate of all mankind, *then* the Lᴏʀᴅ has not sent me. ³⁰But if the Lᴏʀᴅ brings about an entirely new thing and the ground opens its mouth and swallows them with everything that is theirs, and they ^descend alive into ¹Sheol, then you will know that these men have been disrespectful to the Lᴏʀᴅ."

³¹And as he finished speaking all these words, the ground that was under them split open; ³²and ^the earth opened its mouth and swallowed them, their households, and all the people who belonged to Korah with all *their* possessions. ³³So they and all that belonged to them went down alive to Sheol; and the earth closed over them, and they perished from the midst of the assembly. ³⁴Then all Israel who *were* around them fled at their outcry, for they said, "The earth might swallow us!" ³⁵^Fire also came out from the

16:14 ^Ex 23:10, 11   ^1 Sam 11:2   16:15 ^Gen 4:4, 5
^1 Sam 12:3   16:19 ^Num 14:10; 20:6
16:21 ^Num 16:45   ^Ex 32:10, 12   16:22 ^Num 27:16
16:24 ^Num 16:45   16:26 ^Is 52:11   ^Gen 19:15, 17
16:27 ^Num 26:11   16:28 ^Ex 3:12-15; 4:12, 15
16:29 ^Eccl 3:19   16:30 ^Ps 55:15   16:32 ^Deut 11:6;
Ps 106:17   16:35 ^Num 11:1-3

16:30 ¹I.e., the netherworld

LORD and consumed the [B]250 men who were offering the incense.

[36] Then the LORD spoke to Moses, saying, [37] "Tell Eleazar, the son of Aaron the priest, that he shall pick up the censers from the midst of the burned area, because they are holy; and you are to scatter the burning coals farther away. [38] As for the censers of these men who have sinned at the cost of their own lives, have them made into hammered sheets as plating for the altar, since they did present them before the LORD and they are holy; and [A]they shall serve as a sign to the sons of Israel." [39] So the priest Eleazar took the bronze censers which the men who were burned had offered, and they hammered them out as plating for the altar, [40] as a reminder to the sons of Israel so that [A]no layman, *anyone* who was not of the descendants of Aaron, would approach to burn incense before the LORD; then he would not become like Korah and his group—just as the LORD had spoken to him through Moses.

MURMURING AND PLAGUE

[41] But on the next day all the congregation of the sons of Israel [A]grumbled against Moses and Aaron, saying, "You are the ones who have caused the death of the LORD's people!" [42] It came about, however, when the congregation had assembled against Moses and Aaron, that they turned toward the tent of meeting, and behold, the cloud covered it and [A]the glory of the LORD appeared. [43] Then Moses and Aaron came to the front of the tent of meeting, [44] and the LORD spoke to Moses, saying, [45] "[A]Get away from among this congregation so that I may consume them instantly." Then they fell on

their faces. [46] And Moses said to Aaron, "Take your censer and put fire in it from the altar, and place incense *on it;* then bring it quickly to the congregation and [A]make atonement for them, for [B]wrath has gone out from the LORD, the plague has begun!" [47] Then Aaron took *it* just as Moses had spoken, and he ran into the midst of the assembly; and behold, the plague had begun among the people. [A]So he put *on* the incense and made atonement for the people. [48] And he took his stand between the dead and the living, so that the plague was brought to a halt. [49][A]But those who died by the plague were 14,700 *in number,* besides those who died on account of Korah. [50] Then Aaron returned to Moses at the entrance of the tent of meeting, for the plague had been brought to a halt.

AARON'S STAFF BUDS

17 Then the LORD spoke to Moses, saying, [2] "Speak to the sons of Israel, and obtain from them a staff for each father's household: twelve staffs, from all their leaders for their fathers' households. You shall write each man's name on his staff, [3] and write Aaron's name on the staff of Levi; for *there is to be* one staff for the head *of each* of their fathers' households. [4] You shall then leave them in the tent of meeting in front of [A]the testimony, where I meet with you. [5] And it will come about that the staff of [A]the man whom I choose will sprout. So I will relieve Myself of the grumblings of the sons of

Israel, who are grumbling against you." [6]So Moses spoke to the sons of Israel, and all their leaders gave him a staff, one for each leader, for their fathers' households, twelve staffs *in all,* with the staff of Aaron among their staffs. [7]Then Moses left the staffs before the LORD in [A]the tent of the testimony.

[8]Now on the next day Moses went into the tent of the testimony; and behold, [A]Aaron's staff for the house of Levi had sprouted and produced buds and bloomed with blossoms, and it yielded ripe almonds. [9]Moses then brought out all the staffs from the presence of the LORD to all the sons of Israel; and they looked, and each man took his staff. [10]But the LORD said to Moses, "Put the staff of Aaron [A]back in front of the testimony to be kept as a sign against the [B]rebels, so that you may put an end to their grumblings against Me and they do not die." [11]Moses did *so;* just as the LORD had commanded him, so he did.

[12]Then the sons of Israel spoke to Moses, saying, "[A]Behold, we are passing away, we are perishing, we are all perishing! [13A]Everyone who comes near, who comes near to the tabernacle of the LORD, must die. Are we to perish completely?"

DUTIES OF LEVITES

18 So the LORD said to Aaron, "You, your sons, and your father's household with you shall [A]bear the guilt in connection with the sanctuary, and you and your sons with you shall bear the guilt in connection with your priesthood. [2]But also bring your brothers with you, the tribe of Levi, the tribe of your father, so that they may [A]join you and serve you, while you and

your sons with you are before the tent of the testimony. [3]And they shall perform duties for you and the duties of the whole tent, but [A]they shall not come near the furnishings of the sanctuary and the altar, or both they and you will die. [4]They shall join you and perform the duties of the tent of meeting, for all the service of the tent; but an unauthorized person shall not come near you. [5]So you shall perform the [A]duties of the sanctuary and the duties of the altar, so that there will no longer be wrath on the sons of Israel. [6]Behold, I Myself [A]have taken your fellow Levites from among the sons of Israel; *they are* [B]a gift to you, dedicated to the LORD, to perform the service for the tent of meeting. [7]But you and your sons with you shall [A]attend to your priesthood for everything that concerns the altar and inside the veil, and you are to perform service. I am giving you the priesthood as a service that is a gift, and the unauthorized person who comes near shall be put to death."

THE PRIESTS' PORTION

[8]Then the LORD spoke to Aaron, "Now behold, I Myself have put you in charge of My [A]offerings, all the holy gifts of the sons of Israel I have given to you as a portion and to your sons as a permanent allotment. [9]This shall be yours from the most holy *gifts reserved* from the fire; every offering of theirs, namely [A]every grain offering, every [B]sin offering, and every

17:7 [A]Num 1:50, 53; 9:15   17:8 [A]Ezek 17:24; Heb 9:4
17:10 [A]Num 17:4   [B]Deut 9:7, 24   17:12 [A]Is 6:5
17:13 [A]Num 1:51   18:1 [A]Ex 28:38; Lev 10:17
18:2 [A]Num 3:5-10   18:3 [A]Num 4:15-20   18:5 [A]Ex 27:21;
Lev 24:3   18:6 [A]Num 3:12, 45   [B]Num 3:9
18:7 [A]Ex 29:9   18:8 [A]Lev 6:16, 18; 7:28-34
18:9 [A]Lev 2:1-16   [B]Lev 6:30

guilt offering, with which they shall make restitution to Me, *shall be* most holy for you and for your sons. ¹⁰As the most holy *gifts* you shall eat it; every male shall eat it. It shall be holy to you. ¹¹This also is yours, the offering of their gift, that is, all the wave offerings of the sons of Israel; I have ^given them to you and to your sons and daughters with you as a permanent allotment. Everyone of your household who is clean may eat it. ¹²^All the best of the fresh oil and all the best of the fresh wine and of the grain, the first fruits of what they give to the LORD, I have given them to you. ¹³^The first ripe fruits of all that is in their land, which they bring to the LORD, shall be yours; everyone of your household who is clean may eat it. ¹⁴^Everything banned from secular use in Israel shall be yours. ¹⁵^Every firstborn of the womb of all flesh, whether human or animal, which they offer to the LORD, shall be yours; however you must redeem the human firstborn, and the firstborn of unclean animals you shall redeem. ¹⁶As to their redemption price, from a month old you shall redeem them, by your assessment, five ¹shekels in silver by the shekel of the sanctuary, which is twenty gerahs. ¹⁷But ^the firstborn of an ox, the firstborn of a sheep, or the firstborn of a goat, you shall not redeem; they are holy. ᴮYou shall sprinkle their blood on the altar and offer up their fat in smoke *as* an offering by fire, for a soothing aroma to the LORD. ¹⁸However, their meat shall be yours; it shall be yours like the ^breast of a wave offering and like the right thigh. ¹⁹All the offerings of the holy *gifts*, which the sons of Israel offer to the LORD, I have given to you and your sons and your daughters with you, as a permanent allotment. It is ^a permanent covenant of salt before the LORD to you and your descendants with you." ²⁰Then the LORD said to Aaron, "You shall have no inheritance in their land nor own any portion among them; ^I am your portion and your inheritance among the sons of Israel.

²¹"To the sons of Levi, behold, I have given all the ^tithe in Israel as an inheritance, in return for their service which they perform, the service of the tent of meeting. ²²And ^the sons of Israel shall not come near the tent of meeting again, or they will bring sin on themselves and die. ²³Only the Levites shall perform the service of the tent of meeting, and they shall ^bear their *own* guilt; *it shall be* a permanent statute throughout your generations, and among the sons of Israel they shall have no inheritance. ²⁴For the tithe of the sons of Israel, which they offer as an offering to the LORD, I have given to the Levites as an inheritance; therefore I have said concerning them, '^They shall have no inheritance among the sons of Israel.'"

²⁵Then the LORD spoke to Moses, saying, ²⁶"Moreover, you shall speak to the Levites and say to them, 'When you take from the sons of Israel the tithe which I have given you from them for your inheritance, then you shall present

18:11^Lev 22:1-16   18:12^Ps 81:16; 147:14
18:13^Ex 22:29; 34:26   18:14^Lev 27:1-33
18:15^Ex 13:13, 15; Num 3:46   18:17^Deut 15:19
ᴮLev 3:2   18:18^Lev 7:31   18:19^2 Chr 13:5
18:20^Josh 13:33; Ezek 44:28   18:21^Lev 27:30-33;
Deut 14:22-29   18:22^Num 1:51   18:23^Num 18:1
18:24^Deut 10:9

18:16 ¹A shekel is about 0.4 oz. or 11 gm

an offering from it to the LORD, a ^tithe of the tithe. ²⁷Your offering shall be credited to you like the grain from the threshing floor or the full produce from the wine vat. ²⁸So you shall also present an offering to the LORD from all your tithes, which you receive from the sons of Israel; and from it you shall give the LORD's offering to Aaron the priest. ²⁹Out of all your gifts you shall present every offering due to the LORD, from all the best of them, the sacred part from them.' ³⁰And you shall say to them, 'When you have offered from it the best of it, then *the rest* shall be credited to the Levites like the product of the threshing floor, and like the product of the wine vat. ³¹You may eat it anywhere, you and your households, for it is your compensation in return for your service in the tent of meeting. ³²And you will bring on yourselves no sin by reason of it when you have offered the best of it. But you shall not ^profane the sacred gifts of the sons of Israel, so that you do not die.'"

ORDINANCE OF THE RED HEIFER

19 Then the LORD spoke to Moses and Aaron, saying, ²"This is the statute of the law which the LORD has commanded, saying, 'Speak to the sons of Israel that they bring you an ^unblemished red heifer in which there is no defect *and* ^Bon which a yoke has never been mounted. ³And you shall give it to Eleazar the priest, and it shall ^be brought outside the camp and be slaughtered in his presence. ⁴And Eleazar the priest shall take some of its blood with his finger and ^sprinkle some of its blood toward the front of the tent of meeting

seven times. ⁵Then the heifer shall be burned in his sight; ^its hide, its flesh, and its blood, with its refuse, shall be burned. ⁶And the priest shall take ^cedar wood, hyssop, and scarlet *material,* and throw it into the midst of the burning heifer. ⁷The priest ^shall then wash his clothes and bathe his body in water, and afterward come into the camp; but the priest will be unclean until evening. ⁸The one who burns the heifer shall also wash his clothes in water and bathe his body in water, and will be unclean until evening. ⁹Now a man who is clean shall gather up the ashes of the heifer and put them outside the camp in a clean place, and the congregation of the sons of Israel shall keep them for ^water to remove impurity; it is purification from sin. ¹⁰And the one who gathers the ashes of the heifer ^shall wash his clothes and will be unclean until evening; and it shall be a permanent statute for the sons of Israel and for the stranger who resides among them.

¹¹'^The one who touches the dead body of any person will also be unclean for seven days. ¹²That one shall ^purify himself with the water on the third day and on the seventh day, *and then* he will be clean; but if he does not purify himself on the third day and on the seventh day, he will not be clean. ¹³^Anyone who touches a dead body, the body of a person who has died, and does not purify himself, defiles the tabernacle of the LORD; and that person

18:26 ^Neh 10:38 18:32 ^Lev 22:15, 16
19:2 ^Lev 22:20-25 ᴮDeut 21:3 19:3 ^Lev 4:11, 12, 21; Num 19:9 19:4 ^Lev 4:6, 17; 16:14 19:5 ^Ex 29:14; Lev 4:11, 12 19:6 ^Lev 14:4 19:7 ^Lev 16:26, 28; 22:6 19:9 ^Num 8:7; 31:23 19:10 ^Num 19:7 19:11 ^Lev 21:1, 11; Acts 21:26, 27 19:12 ^Num 19:19; 31:19 19:13 ^Lev 7:21; 22:3-7

shall be cut off from Israel. Since the water for impurity was not sprinkled on him, he will be unclean; his uncleanness is still on him.

¹⁴ 'This is the law when a person dies in a tent: everyone who comes into the tent and everyone who is in the tent will be unclean for seven days. ¹⁵ And every open container, which has no cover tied down on it, will be unclean. ¹⁶ᴬAlso, anyone who in the open field touches one who has been killed with a sword or one who has died *naturally,* or *touches* a human bone or a grave, will be unclean for seven days. ¹⁷ Then for the unclean *person* they shall take some of the ashes of the burnt ᴬpurification from sin and running water shall be added to them in a container. ¹⁸ And a clean person shall take hyssop and dip *it* in the water, and sprinkle *it* on the tent, on all the furnishings, on the persons who were there, and on the one who touched the bone or the one who was killed or the one who died *naturally,* or the grave. ¹⁹ Then the clean *person* ᴬshall sprinkle on the unclean on the third day and on the seventh day; and on the seventh day he shall purify him, and he shall wash his clothes and bathe *himself* in water and will be clean by evening.

²⁰ 'But the person who is unclean and does not purify himself, that person shall be cut off from the midst of the assembly, because he has ᴬdefiled the sanctuary of the Lᴏʀᴅ; the water for impurity has not been sprinkled on him, *so* he is unclean. ²¹ So it shall be a permanent statute for them. And the one ᴬwho sprinkles the water for impurity shall wash his clothes, and the one who touches the water for impurity will be unclean until evening. ²² ᴬFurthermore, anything that

the unclean *person* touches will be unclean; and the person who touches *it* will be unclean until evening.' "

DEATH OF MIRIAM

20 Then the sons of Israel, the whole congregation, came to the ᴬwilderness of Zin in the first month; and the people stayed at Kadesh. Now Miriam died there and was buried there.

² ᴬThere was no water for the congregation, ᴮand they assembled against Moses and Aaron. ³ Then the people argued with Moses and spoke, saying, " ᴬIf only we had perished ᴮwhen our brothers perished before the Lᴏʀᴅ! ⁴ ᴬWhy then have you brought the Lᴏʀᴅ's assembly into this wilderness, for us and our livestock to die here? ⁵ Why did you make us come up from Egypt, to bring us into this wretched place? ᴬIt is not a place of grain or figs or vines or pomegranates, nor is there water to drink!" ⁶ Then Moses and Aaron came in from the presence of the assembly to the entrance of the tent of meeting and ᴬfell on their faces. And the glory of the Lᴏʀᴅ appeared to them; ⁷ then the Lᴏʀᴅ spoke to Moses, saying,

THE WATERS OF MERIBAH

⁸ "Take ᴬthe staff; and you and your brother Aaron assemble the congregation and speak to the rock before their eyes, that it shall yield its water. So you shall bring water for them out of the rock, and have the congregation and their livestock drink."

19:16 ᴬNum 31:19   19:17 ᴬNum 19:9   19:19 ᴬEzek 36:25; Heb 10:22   19:20 ᴬNum 19:13   19:21 ᴬNum 19:7
19:22 ᴬLev 5:2, 3; 22:5, 6   20:1 ᴬNum 13:21; 33:36
20:2 ᴬEx 17:1   ᴮNum 16:19, 42   20:3 ᴬNum 14:2, 3
ᴮNum 16:31-35   20:4 ᴬEx 17:3   20:5 ᴬNum 16:14
20:6 ᴬNum 14:5   20:8 ᴬEx 4:17, 20; 17:5, 6

⁹So Moses took the staff ᴬfrom before the LORD, just as He had commanded him; ¹⁰and Moses and Aaron summoned the assembly in front of the rock. And he said to them, "ᴬListen now, you rebels; shall we bring water for you out of this rock?" ¹¹Then Moses raised his hand and struck the rock twice with his staff; and ᴬwater came out abundantly, and the congregation and their livestock drank. ¹²But the LORD said to Moses and Aaron, "ᴬSince you did not trust in Me, to treat Me as holy in the sight of the sons of Israel, for that reason you shall not bring this assembly into the land which I have given them." ¹³Those *were called* the waters of ¹,ᴬMeribah, because the sons of Israel argued with the LORD, and He proved Himself holy among them.

¹⁴From Kadesh Moses then sent messengers to ᴬthe king of Edom *to say,* "This is what your brother Israel has said: 'You ᴮknow all the hardship that has overtaken us; ¹⁵that our fathers went down to Egypt, and we stayed in Egypt a long time, and the Egyptians treated us and our fathers badly. ¹⁶But ᴬwhen we cried out to the LORD, He heard our voice and sent an angel, and brought us out from Egypt; now behold, we are at Kadesh, a town on the edge of your territory. ¹⁷Please ᴬlet us pass through your land. We will not pass through field or vineyard; we will not even drink water from a well. We will go along the king's road, not turning to the right or left, until we pass through your territory.'"

¹⁸ᴬEdom, however, said to him, "You shall not pass through us, or I will come out with the sword against you." ¹⁹Again, the sons of Israel said to him, "We will go up by the road, and if I and ᴬmy livestock do drink any of your water, ᴮthen I will pay its price. Let me only pass through on my feet, nothing *more.*" ²⁰But he said, "ᴬYou shall not pass through." And Edom came out against him with a heavy force and a strong hand. ²¹ᴬSo Edom refused to allow Israel to pass through his territory; ᴮthen Israel turned away from him.

²²Now when they set out from ᴬKadesh, the sons of Israel, the whole congregation, came to Mount Hor.

DEATH OF AARON

²³Then the LORD spoke to Moses and Aaron at ᴬMount Hor by the border of the land of Edom, saying, ²⁴"Aaron will be gathered to his people; for he shall not enter the land which I have given to the sons of Israel, because ᴬyou rebelled against My command at the waters of Meribah. ²⁵Take Aaron and his son ᴬEleazar, and bring them up to Mount Hor. ²⁶Then strip Aaron of his garments and put them on his son Eleazar. So Aaron will be ᴬgathered *to his people* and will die there." ²⁷So Moses did just as the LORD had commanded, and they went up to Mount Hor in the sight of all the congregation. ²⁸And after Moses stripped Aaron of his garments and ᴬput them on his son Eleazar, Aaron died there on the mountain top. Then Moses and Eleazar came down from the

20:9 ᴬNum 17:10   20:10 ᴬPs 106:33   20:11 ᴬPs 78:16; Is 48:21   20:12 ᴬNum 20:24; Deut 3:26, 27   20:13 ᴬEx 17:7; Ps 95:8   20:14 ᴬGen 36:31-39   ᴮJosh 9:9, 10, 24   20:16 ᴬEx 2:23; 3:7   20:17 ᴬNum 21:22   20:18 ᴬNum 24:18   20:19 ᴬEx 12:38   ᴮDeut 2:6, 28   20:20 ᴬJudg 11:17   20:21 ᴬJudg 11:17   ᴮDeut 2:8   20:22 ᴬNum 20:1, 14   20:23 ᴬNum 33:37   20:24 ᴬNum 20:5, 10   20:25 ᴬNum 3:4   20:26 ᴬNum 20:24   20:28 ᴬEx 29:29

20:13 ¹ I.e., contention

mountain. ²⁹When all the congregation saw that Aaron had died, the whole house of Israel wept for Aaron for thirty ᴬdays.

ARAD CONQUERED

21 When the Canaanite, the king of ᴬArad, who lived in the ¹Negev, heard that Israel was coming by the way of Atharim, he fought against Israel and took some of them captive. ²So ᴬIsrael made a vow to the Lᴏʀᴅ and said, "If You will indeed hand over this people to me, then I will utterly destroy their cities." ³The Lᴏʀᴅ heard the voice of Israel and turned over the Canaanites; then they utterly destroyed them and their cities. And the place was named ¹ᐟᴬHormah.

⁴Then they set out from Mount Hor by the way of the Red Sea, to ᴬgo around the land of Edom; and the people became impatient because of the journey. ⁵So the people spoke against God and Moses: "ᴬWhy have you brought us up from Egypt to die in the wilderness? For there is no food and no water, and ᴮwe are disgusted with this miserable food."

THE BRONZE SERPENT

⁶ᴬThen the Lᴏʀᴅ sent fiery serpents among the people and they bit the people, so that ᴮmany people of Israel died. ⁷So the people came to Moses and said, "We have sinned, because we have spoken against the Lᴏʀᴅ and against you; ᴬintercede with the Lᴏʀᴅ, that He will remove the serpents from us." And Moses interceded for the people. ⁸Then the Lᴏʀᴅ said to Moses, "Make a ᴬfiery *serpent,* and put it on a flag *pole;* and it shall come about, that everyone who is bitten, and looks

at it, will live." ⁹So Moses made a ᴬbronze serpent and put it on the flag *pole;* and it came about, that if a serpent bit someone, and he looked at the bronze serpent, he lived.

¹⁰ᴬNow the sons of Israel moved out and camped in Oboth. ¹¹Then they journeyed from Oboth and camped at Iye-abarim, in the wilderness which is opposite Moab, to the east. ¹²ᴬFrom there they set out and camped in ¹Wadi Zered. ¹³From there they journeyed and camped on the other side of the Arnon, which is in the wilderness that comes out of the border of the Amorites; ᴬfor the Arnon is the border of Moab, between Moab and the Amorites. ¹⁴For that reason it is said in the Book of the Wars of the Lᴏʀᴅ,

"Waheb in Suphah,
     And the ¹wadis of the Arnon,
15   And the slope of the wadis
     That extends to the site of ᴬAr,
     And leans to the border of
        Moab."

¹⁶ᴬFrom there *they continued* to Beer, that is the well where the Lᴏʀᴅ said to Moses, "Assemble the people, that I may give them water." ¹⁷ᴬThen Israel sang this song:
"Spring up, O well! Sing to it!
18   "The well, which the leaders dug,
     Which the nobles of the
        people hollowed out,
     With the scepter *and* with
        their staffs."

20:29 ᴬGen 50:3, 10; Deut 34:8   21:1 ᴬJosh 12:14;
Judg 1:16   21:2 ᴬGen 28:20; Judg 11:30
21:3 ᴬNum 14:45   21:4 ᴬDeut 2:8   21:5 ᴬNum 14:2, 3
ᴮNum 11:6   21:6 ᴬDeut 8:15   ᴮ1 Cor 10:9
21:7 ᴬ1 Sam 12:19; Acts 8:24   21:8 ᴬIs 14:29; John 3:14
21:9 ᴬ2 Kin 18:4; John 3:14, 15   21:10 ᴬNum 33:43, 44
21:12 ᴬNum 33:45   21:13 ᴬNum 22:36; Judg 11:18
21:15 ᴬNum 21:28; Deut 2:9, 18, 29   21:16 ᴬNum
33:46-49   21:17 ᴬEx 15:1; Ps 105:2

21:1 ¹I.e., South country   21:3 ¹I.e., a devoted thing;
or Destruction   21:12 ¹I.e., a dry stream bed, except
in the rainy season   21:14 ¹I.e., dry stream beds

And from the wilderness *they continued* to Mattanah, ¹⁹ and from Mattanah to Nahaliel, and from Nahaliel to Bamoth, ²⁰ and from Bamoth to the valley that is in the land of Moab, at the top of Pisgah, which overlooks the desert.

TWO VICTORIES

²¹ᴬThen Israel sent messengers to Sihon, king of the Amorites, saying, ²²"ᴬLet me pass through your land. We will not turn off into field or vineyard; we will not drink water from wells. We will go by the king's road until we have passed through your border." ²³ᴬBut Sihon would not permit Israel to pass through his border. Instead, Sihon gathered all his people and went out against Israel in the wilderness, and came to ᴮJahaz and fought against Israel. ²⁴Then ᴬIsrael struck him with the edge of the sword, and took possession of his land from the Arnon to the Jabbok, as far as the sons of Ammon; for the ᴮborder of the sons of Ammon *was* Jazer. ²⁵Israel took all these cities, and ᴬIsrael lived in all the cities of the Amorites, in Heshbon and in all her villages. ²⁶For Heshbon was the city of Sihon, king of the Amorites, who had fought against the former king of Moab and had taken all his land out of his hand, as far as the Arnon. ²⁷For that reason those who use proverbs say,

"Come to Heshbon! Let it be
built!
So let the city of Sihon be
established.
²⁸ "ᴬFor a fire spread from Heshbon,
A flame from the town of
Sihon;
It devoured ᴮAr of Moab,
The dominant heights of the
Arnon.

²⁹ "Woe to you, Moab!
You are destroyed, people of
Chemosh!
ᴬHe has given his sons as
fugitives,
ᴮAnd his daughters into
captivity,
To an Amorite king, Sihon.
³⁰ "But we have shot them down
with arrows,
Heshbon is destroyed as far as
ᴬDibon,
Then we have laid waste as far
as Nophah,
Which *reaches* to Medeba."

³¹So Israel lived in the land of the Amorites. ³²Now Moses sent *men* to spy out ᴬJazer, and they captured its villages and dispossessed the Amorites who *were* there.

³³ᴬThen they turned and went up by the way of Bashan, and Og the king of Bashan went out against them with all his people, for battle at ᴮEdrei. ³⁴But the LORD said to Moses, "ᴬDo not fear him, for I have handed him over to you, and all his people and his land; and you shall do to him as you did to Sihon, king of the Amorites, who lived in Heshbon." ³⁵So ᴬthey killed him and his sons and all his people, until there was no survivor left; and they took possession of his land.

BALAK SENDS FOR BALAAM

22 ᴬThen the sons of Israel journeyed on, and camped in the plains of Moab beyond the Jordan *opposite* Jericho.

21:21ᴬDeut 2:26-37; Judg 11:19   21:22ᴬNum 20:16, 17
21:23ᴬNum 20:21   ᴮDeut 2:32   21:24ᴬAmos 2:9
ᴮDeut 2:37   21:25ᴬAmos 2:10   21:28ᴬJer 48:45
ᴮNum 21:15   21:29ᴬIs 15:5   ᴮIs 16:2
21:30ᴬNum 32:3, 34; Jer 48:18, 22
21:32ᴬNum 32:1, 3, 35; Jer 48:32
21:33ᴬDeut 3:1-7   ᴮJosh 13:12   21:34ᴬDeut 3:2
21:35ᴬDeut 3:3, 4   22:1ᴬNum 33:48, 49

²Now ^Balak the son of Zippor saw all that Israel had done to the Amorites. ³^So Moab was in great fear because of the people, for they were numerous; and Moab was in dread of the sons of Israel. ⁴Moab said to the elders of ^Midian, "Now this horde will eat up all that is around us, as the ox eats up the grass of the field!" And Balak the son of Zippor was king of Moab at that time. ⁵So he sent messengers to ^Balaam the son of Beor, at ᴮPethor, which is near the *Euphrates* River, *in* the land of the sons of his people, to call for him, saying, "Behold, a people came out of Egypt; behold, they have covered the surface of the land, and they are living opposite me. ⁶^Now, therefore, please come, curse this people for me since they are too mighty for me; perhaps I will be able to defeat them and drive them out of the land. For I know that he whom you bless is blessed, and he whom you curse is cursed."

⁷So the elders of Moab and the elders of Midian left with the *fees for* ^divination in their hands; and they came to Balaam and repeated Balak's words to him. ⁸And he said to them, "Spend the night here, and I will bring word back to you just as the LORD may speak to me." And the leaders of Moab stayed with Balaam. ⁹Then ^God came to Balaam and said, "Who are these men with you?" ¹⁰Balaam said to God, "Balak the son of Zippor, king of Moab, sent *word* to me: ¹¹'Behold, there is a people who came out of Egypt, and they cover the surface of the land; now come, curse them for me; perhaps I will be able to fight against them and drive them out.'" ¹²But God said to Balaam, "Do not go with them; ^you shall not curse the people, for they

are blessed." ¹³So Balaam got up in the morning and said to Balak's representatives, "Go *back* to your land, for the LORD has refused to let me go with you." ¹⁴And the representatives from Moab got up and went to Balak, and said, "Balaam refused to come with us."

¹⁵Then Balak sent representatives once again, more numerous and more distinguished than the previous. ¹⁶They came to Balaam and said to him, "This is what Balak the son of Zippor says: 'I beg you, let nothing keep you from coming to me; ¹⁷for I will indeed honor you richly, and I will do whatever you tell me. ^Please come then, curse this people for me.'" ¹⁸But Balaam replied to the servants of Balak, "^*Even* if Balak were to give me his house full of silver and gold, I could not do *anything, either* small or great, contrary to the command of the LORD my God. ¹⁹Now please, you also stay here tonight, and I will find out what else the LORD will say to me." ²⁰And God came to Balaam at night and said to him, "If the men have come to call you, rise *and* go with them; but you shall do ^only the thing that I tell you."

²¹^So Balaam arose in the morning, saddled his donkey, and went with the leaders of Moab.

THE ANGEL AND BALAAM

²²But God was angry that he was going, ^and the angel of the LORD took his stand in the road as an adversary against him. Now he was

22:2 ^Judg 11:25   22:3 ^Ex 15:15   22:4 ^Num 25:15–18; 31:1–3   22:5 ^Jude 11   ᴮDeut 23:4   22:6 ^Num 22:17; 23:7, 8   22:7 ^Num 23:23; Josh 13:22   22:9 ^Gen 20:3 22:12 ^Num 23:8; 24:9   22:17 ^Num 22:6 22:18 ^1 Kin 22:14; 2 Chr 18:13   22:20 ^Num 22:35; 24:13   22:21 ^2 Pet 2:15   22:22 ^Ex 23:20

riding on his donkey, and his two servants were with him. ²³When the donkey saw the angel of the LORD standing in the road with his sword drawn in his hand, the donkey turned off from the road and went into the field; and Balaam struck the donkey to guide her back onto the road. ²⁴Then the angel of the LORD stood in a narrow path of the vineyards, *with* a stone wall on this side and on that side. ²⁵When the donkey saw the angel of the LORD, she pressed herself against the wall and pressed Balaam's foot against the wall, so he struck her again. ²⁶Then the angel of the LORD went farther, and stood in a narrow place where there was no way to turn to the right or to the left. ²⁷When the donkey saw the angel of the LORD, she lay down under Balaam; so ^Balaam was angry and struck the donkey with his staff. ²⁸Then ^the LORD opened the mouth of the donkey, and she said to Balaam, "What have I done to you, that you have struck me these three times?" ²⁹And Balaam said to the donkey, "*It is* because you have made a mockery of me! If only there had been a sword in my hand! For ^I would have killed you by now!" ³⁰But the donkey said to Balaam, "Am I not your donkey on which you have ridden all your life to this day? Have I ever been in the habit of doing such a thing to you?" And he said, "No."

³¹Then the LORD opened Balaam's eyes, and he saw ^the angel of the LORD standing in the way with his sword drawn in his hand; and he bowed all the way to the ground. ³²Then the angel of the LORD said to him, "Why have you struck your donkey these three times? Behold, I have come out as an adversary, because your way was ^reckless *and* contrary to me. ³³But the donkey saw me and turned away from me these three times. If she had not turned away from me, I certainly would have killed you just now, and let her live." ³⁴So Balaam said to the angel of the LORD, "^I have sinned, for I did not know that you were standing in the way against me. Now then, if it is displeasing to you, I will turn back." ³⁵But the angel of the LORD said to Balaam, "Go with the men, but ^you shall speak only the word that I tell you." So Balaam went along with the representatives of Balak.

³⁶When Balak heard that Balaam was coming, he went out to meet him at the city of Moab, which is on the Arnon border, at the extreme end of the border. ³⁷Then Balak said to Balaam, "Did I not urgently send *word* to you to call for you? Why did you not come to me? Am I really unable to honor you?" ³⁸So Balaam said to Balak, "Behold, I have come to you now! ^Am I really able to speak anything? The word that God puts in my mouth, that *only* shall I speak." ³⁹And Balaam went with Balak, and they came to Kiriath-huzoth. ⁴⁰Balak sacrificed oxen and sheep, and sent *some* to Balaam and the leaders who were with him.

⁴¹Then it came about in the morning that Balak took Balaam and brought him up to ^the high places of Baal, and he saw from there a ᴮportion of the people.

22:27^James 1:19   22:28^2 Pet 2:16
22:29^Prov 12:10; Matt 15:19   22:31^Josh 5:13-15
22:32^2 Pet 2:15   22:34^Num 14:40
22:35^Num 22:20   22:38^Num 22:18
22:41^Num 21:28   ᴮNum 23:13

THE PROPHECIES OF BALAAM

23

Then Balaam said to Balak, "Build seven altars for me here, and prepare seven bulls and seven rams for me here." ²Balak did just as Balaam had spoken, and Balak and Balaam offered up a bull and a ram on *each* altar. ³Then Balaam said to Balak, "Stand beside your burnt offering, and I will go; perhaps the LORD will come to meet me, and whatever He shows me I will tell you." So he went to a bare hill.

⁴Now God met with Balaam, and he said to Him, "I have set up the seven altars, and I have offered up a bull and a ram on *each* altar." ⁵Then the LORD ᴬput a word in Balaam's mouth and said, "Return to Balak, and this is what you shall speak." ⁶So he returned to him, and behold, he was standing beside his burnt offering, he and all the leaders of Moab. ⁷And he took up his discourse and said,

"From ᴬAram Balak has brought
    me,
  Moab's king from the
    mountains of the East,
  saying,
'Come, declare Jacob cursed for
    me,
  And come, curse Israel!'
8 "ᴬHow am I to put a curse on
    him upon whom God has not
    put a curse?
  And how am I to curse him
    whom the LORD has not
    cursed?
9 "For I see him from the top of
    the rocks,
  And I look at him from the
    hills;
  ᴬBehold, a people that lives in
    isolation,
  And does not consider itself *to
    be* among the nations.

10 "ᴬWho has counted the dust of
    Jacob,
  Or the number of the fourth
    part of Israel?
  May I die the death of the
    upright,
  And may my end be like his!"

¹¹Then Balak said to Balaam, "What have you done to me? ᴬI took you to put a curse on my enemies, but behold, you have actually blessed *them!*" ¹²He replied, "Must I not be careful to speak ᴬwhat the LORD puts in my mouth?"

¹³Then Balak said to him, "Please come with me to another place from where you may see them, *although* you will only see the extreme end of them and will not see all of them; and put a curse on them for me from there." ¹⁴So he took him to the field of Zophim, to the top of Pisgah, and he built seven altars and offered a bull and a ram on *each* altar. ¹⁵Then he said to Balak, "Stand here beside your burnt offering while I myself meet *the* LORD over there." ¹⁶Then the LORD met Balaam and ᴬput a word in his mouth, and said, "Return to Balak, and this is what you shall speak." ¹⁷So he came to him, and behold, he was standing beside his burnt offering, and the leaders of Moab with him. And Balak said to him, "What has the LORD spoken?" ¹⁸Then he took up his discourse and said,

"Arise, Balak, and hear;
  Listen to me, son of Zippor!
19 "ᴬGod is not a man, that He
    would lie,
  Nor a son of man, that He
    would change His mind;

23:5 ᴬDeut 18:18; Jer 1:9   23:7 ᴬNum 22:5; Deut 23:4
23:8 ᴬNum 22:12   23:9 ᴬDeut 32:8; 33:28
23:10 ᴬGen 13:16; 28:14   23:11 ᴬNeh 13:2
23:12 ᴬNum 22:20   23:16 ᴬNum 22:20
23:19 ᴬ1 Sam 15:29

Has He said, and will He not
    do it?
Or has He spoken, and will He
    not make it good?

20 "Behold, I have received *a
    command* to bless;
When He has blessed,
    ^AI cannot revoke it.

21 "He has not looked at
    misfortune in Jacob;
Nor has He seen trouble in
    Israel;
^AThe LORD his God is with him,
And the joyful shout of a king
    is among them.

22 "^AGod brings them out of Egypt,
He is for them like the horns of
    the wild ox.

23 "^AFor there is no magic curse
    against Jacob,
Nor is there any divination
    against Israel;
At the *proper* time it shall be
    said to Jacob
And to Israel, what God has
    done!

24 "^ABehold, a people rises like a
    lioness,
And like a lion it raises itself;
It will not lie down until it
    devours the prey,
And drinks the blood of those
    slain."

25 Then Balak said to Balaam, "Do not curse them at all nor bless them at all!" 26 But Balaam replied to Balak, "Did I not tell you, '^AWhatever the LORD speaks, I must do'?"

27 Then Balak said to Balaam, "Please come, I will take you to another place; perhaps it will be agreeable with God that you curse them for me from there." 28 So Balak took Balaam to the top of Peor, which overlooks the desert. 29 And Balaam said to Balak, "Build seven altars for me here and prepare seven bulls and seven rams for me here." 30 Balak did just as Balaam had said, and offered up a bull and a ram on *each* altar.

THE PROPHECY FROM PEOR

24 When Balaam saw that it pleased the LORD to bless Israel, he did not go as at other times to seek omens, rather he turned his attention toward the ^Awilderness. 2 And Balaam raised his eyes and saw Israel camping tribe by tribe; and ^Athe Spirit of God came upon him. 3 Then he took up his discourse and said,

"^AThe declaration of Balaam the
    son of Beor,
And the declaration of the
    man whose eye is opened;
4   The declaration of him who
    ^Ahears the words of God,
Who sees the vision of the
    Almighty,
Falling down, yet having his
    eyes uncovered,
5   How pleasant are your tents,
    Jacob,
Your dwelling places, Israel!
6   "Like valleys that stretch out,
Like gardens beside a river,
Like ^Aaloes planted by the
    LORD,
Like ^Bcedars beside the waters.
7   "Water will flow from his
    buckets,
And his seed *will be* by many
    waters,
And his king shall be higher
    than ^AAgag,
And his kingdom shall be
    exalted.

23:20 ^AIs 43:13   23:21 ^AEx 3:12; Deut 31:23
23:22 ^ANum 24:8   23:23 ^ANum 22:7; Josh 13:22
23:24 ^AGen 49:9; Nah 2:11, 12   23:26 ^ANum 22:18
24:1 ^ANum 23:28   24:2 ^A1 Sam 19:20; Rev 1:10
24:3 ^ANum 24:15, 16   24:4 ^ANum 22:20
24:6 ^APs 45:8   ^BPs 1:3   24:7 ^A1 Sam 15:8

8 "ᴬGod brings him out of Egypt,
   He is for him like the horns of
   the wild ox.
   He will devour the nations
   who are his adversaries,
   And will crush their bones,
   And smash *them* with his
   arrows.
9 "He crouches, he lies down like
   a lion,
   And like a lioness, who dares
   to rouse him?
   ᴬBlessed is *everyone* who
   blesses you,
   And cursed is *everyone* who
   curses you."

10 Then Balak's anger burned against Balaam, and he struck his hands together; and Balak said to Balaam, "I called you to curse my enemies, but behold, you have persisted in blessing them these three times! 11 So flee to your place now. I said I would honor you greatly, but behold, the Lᴏʀᴅ has held you back from honor." 12 And Balaam said to Balak, "ᴬDid I not in fact tell your messengers whom you had sent to me, saying, 13 'If Balak were to give me his house full of silver and gold, I could not do *anything* contrary to the command of the Lᴏʀᴅ, either good or bad, ᴬof my own accord. ᴮWhat the Lᴏʀᴅ speaks, I will speak'? 14 So now, behold, ᴬI am going to my people; come, *and* I will advise you of what this people will do to your people in the days to come."

15 Then he took up his discourse and said,
   "ᴬThe declaration of Balaam the
   son of Beor,
   And the declaration of the
   man whose eye is opened,
16 The declaration of him who
   hears the words of God,

And knows the knowledge of
   the Most High,
   Who sees the vision of the
   Almighty,
   Falling down, yet having his
   eyes uncovered:
17 I see him, but not now;
   I look at him, but not near;
   A star shall appear from Jacob,
   ᴬA scepter shall rise from Israel,
   And shall smash the forehead
   of Moab,
   And overcome all the sons of
   Sheth.
18 "ᴬAnd Edom shall be a
   possession,
   ᴮSeir, its enemies, also will be a
   possession,
   While Israel performs
   valiantly.
19 "One from Jacob shall rule,
   And will eliminate the
   survivors from the city."

20 And he looked at Amalek and took up his discourse and said,
   "Amalek was the first of the
   nations,
   ᴬBut his end *shall be*
   destruction."
21 And he looked at the ᴬKenite, and took up his discourse and said,
   "Your dwelling place is
   enduring,
   And your nest is set in the cliff.
22 "Nevertheless Kain will suffer
   devastation;
   How long will ᴬAsshur keep
   you captive?"
23 Then he took up his discourse and said,
   "Oh, who can live unless God
   has ordained it?

24:8 ᴬNum 23:22   24:9 ᴬGen 12:3; 27:29
24:12 ᴬNum 22:18   24:13 ᴬNum 16:28   ᴮNum 22:20
24:14 ᴬNum 31:8, 16; Josh 13:22   24:15 ᴬNum 24:3, 4
24:17 ᴬGen 49:10   24:18 ᴬAmos 9:11, 12   ᴮGen 32:3
24:20 ᴬNum 24:24   24:21 ᴬGen 15:19
24:22 ᴬGen 10:21, 22

²⁴ "But ships *shall come* from the
coat of ᴬKittim,
And they shall oppress Asshur
and oppress ᴮEber;
So they also *will come* to
destruction."

²⁵ Then Balaam arose, and he departed and returned to ᴬhis place, and Balak also went on his way.

THE SIN OF PEOR

25 While Israel remained at Shittim, the people began ᴬto commit infidelity with the daughters of Moab. ²For ᴬthey invited the people to the sacrifices of their gods, and the people ate and bowed down to their gods. ³So ᴬIsrael became followers of Baal of Peor, and the LORD was angry with Israel. ⁴And the LORD said to Moses, "Take all the leaders of the people and execute them in broad daylight before the LORD, ᴬso that the fierce anger of the LORD may turn away from Israel." ⁵So Moses said to the judges of Israel, "Each of you ᴬkill his men who have become followers of Baal of Peor."

⁶Then behold, one of the sons of Israel came and brought to his relatives a ᴬMidianite woman, in the sight of Moses and in the sight of the whole congregation of the sons of Israel, while they were weeping at the entrance of the tent of meeting. ⁷ᴬWhen Phinehas the son of Eleazar, the son of Aaron the priest, saw it, he rose up from the midst of the congregation and took a spear in his hand, ⁸and he went after the man of Israel into the inner room of the tent and pierced both of them, the man of Israel and the woman, through the abdomen. ᴬSo the plague on the sons of Israel was brought to a halt. ⁹ᴬBut those who died from the plague were twenty-four thousand *in number.*

THE ZEAL OF PHINEHAS

¹⁰Then the LORD spoke to Moses, saying, ¹¹"ᴬPhinehas the son of Eleazar, the son of Aaron the priest, has averted My wrath from the sons of Israel in that he was jealous with My jealousy among them, so that I did not destroy the sons of Israel ᴮin My jealousy. ¹²Therefore say, 'Behold, I am giving him My ᴬcovenant of peace; ¹³and it shall be for him and for his descendants after him, a covenant of a ᴬpermanent priesthood, because he was jealous for his God and ᴮmade atonement for the sons of Israel.'"

¹⁴Now the name of the dead man of Israel who was killed with the Midianite woman, was Zimri the son of Salu, a leader of a father's household among the Simeonites. ¹⁵And the name of the Midianite woman who was killed was Cozbi the daughter of ᴬZur, who was head of the people of a father's household in Midian.

¹⁶Then the LORD spoke to Moses, saying, ¹⁷"ᴬBe hostile to the Midianites and attack them; ¹⁸for they have been hostile to you with their tricks, with which they have deceived you in the matter of Peor and in the matter of Cozbi, the daughter of the leader of Midian, their sister who was killed on the day of the plague because of Peor."

24:24 ᴬEzek 27:6   ᴮGen 10:21   24:25 ᴬNum 24:14
25:1 ᴬ1 Cor 10:8; Rev 2:14   25:2 ᴬEx 34:15; Deut 32:38
25:3 ᴬPs 106:28, 29; Hos 9:10   25:4 ᴬDeut 13:17
25:5 ᴬEx 32:27   25:6 ᴬNum 22:4   25:7 ᴬPs 106:30
25:8 ᴬNum 16:46-48   25:9 ᴬNum 16:48-50; 31:16
25:11 ᴬPs 106:30   ᴮEx 20:5   25:12 ᴬIs 54:10;
Ezek 34:25   25:13 ᴬEx 29:9   ᴮNum 16:46
25:15 ᴬNum 31:8   25:17 ᴬNum 25:1; 31:1-3

CENSUS OF A NEW GENERATION

26 Then it came about after the ^plague, that the LORD spoke to Moses and to Eleazar the son of Aaron the priest, saying, 2 "^Take a census of all the congregation of the sons of Israel from twenty years old and upward, by their fathers' households, whoever is able to go to war in Israel." 3 So Moses and Eleazar the priest spoke with them ^in the plains of Moab by the Jordan at Jericho, saying, 4 "*Take a census of the people* from twenty years old and upward, as the LORD has commanded Moses."

Now the sons of Israel who came out of the land of Egypt *were as follows:*

5 Reuben, Israel's firstborn, the sons of Reuben: *of* Hanoch, the family of the Hanochites; of Pallu, the family of the Palluites; 6 of Hezron, the family of the Hezronites; of Carmi, the family of the Carmites. 7 These are the families of the Reubenites, and those who were counted of them were ^43,730. 8 The son of Pallu: Eliab. 9 The sons of Eliab: Nemuel, Dathan, and Abiram. These are the Dathan and Abiram who were ^called by the congregation, who fought against Moses and against Aaron in the group of Korah, when they fought against the LORD, 10 and ^the earth opened its mouth and swallowed them up along with Korah, when that group died, when the fire devoured 250 men, so that they became a warning sign. 11 ^The sons of Korah, however, did not die.

12 The sons of Simeon by their families: of Nemuel, the family of the Nemuelites; of Jamin, the family of the Jaminites; of Jachin, the family of the Jachinites; 13 of Zerah, the family of the Zerahites; of Shaul, the family of the Shaulites. 14 These are the families of the Simeonites, ^22,200 *in number.*

15 The sons of Gad by their families: of Zephon, the family of the Zephonites; of Haggi, the family of the Haggites; of Shuni, the family of the Shunites; 16 of Ozni, the family of the Oznites; of Eri, the family of the Erites; 17 of Arod, the family of the Arodites; of Areli, the family of the Arelites. 18 These are the families of the sons of Gad according to those who were numbered of them, ^40,500.

19 The ^sons of Judah *were* Er and Onan, but Er and Onan died in the land of Canaan. 20 The ^sons of Judah by their families were: of Shelah, the family of the Shelanites; of Perez, the family of the Perezites; of Zerah, the family of the Zerahites. 21 The sons of Perez were: of Hezron, the family of the Hezronites; of Hamul, the family of the Hamulites. 22 These are the families of Judah by those who were numbered of them, ^76,500.

23 The ^sons of Issachar by their families: *of* Tola, the family of the Tolaites; of Puvah, the family of the Punites; 24 of Jashub, the family of the Jashubites; of Shimron, the family of the Shimronites. 25 These are the families of Issachar by those who were numbered of them, ^64,300.

26 The ^sons of Zebulun by their families: of Sered, the family of the Seredites; of Elon, the family

26:1 ^Num 25:9 26:2 ^Ex 30:11-16; Num 1:2
26:3 ^Num 22:1; 35:1 26:7 ^Num 1:21 26:9 ^Num 1:16;
16:2 26:10 ^Num 16:32 26:11 ^Num 16:27, 33;
Deut 24:16 26:14 ^Num 1:23 26:18 ^Num 1:25
26:19 ^Gen 38:2; 46:12 26:20 ^1 Chr 2:3; Rev 7:5
26:22 ^Num 1:27 26:23 ^Gen 46:13; 1 Chr 7:1
26:25 ^Num 1:29 26:26 ^Gen 46:14

of the Elonites; of Jahleel, the family of the Jahleelites. ²⁷These are the families of the Zebulunites by those who were numbered of them, ^60,500.

²⁸The ^sons of Joseph by their families: Manasseh and Ephraim. ²⁹The sons of Manasseh: of Machir, the family of the Machirites; and ^Machir fathered Gilead: of Gilead, the family of the Gileadites. ³⁰These are the sons of Gilead: *of* Iezer, the family of the ^Iezerites; of Helek, the family of the Helekites; ³¹and *of* Asriel, the family of the Asrielites; and *of* Shechem, the family of the Shechemites; ³²and *of* Shemida, the family of the Shemidaites; and *of* Hepher, the family of the Hepherites. ³³Now Zelophehad the son of Hepher had no sons, only daughters; and ^the names of the daughters of Zelophehad were Mahlah, Noah, Hoglah, Milcah, and Tirzah. ³⁴These are the families of Manasseh; and those who were numbered of them were ^52,700.

³⁵These are the sons of Ephraim by their families: of Shuthelah, the family of the Shuthelahites; of Becher, the family of the Becherites; of Tahan, the family of the Tahanites. ³⁶These are the sons of Shuthelah: of Eran, the family of the Eranites. ³⁷These are the families of the sons of Ephraim by those who were numbered of them, ^32,500. These are the sons of Joseph by their families.

³⁸The sons of Benjamin by their families: of Bela, the family of the Belaites; of Ashbel, the family of the Ashbelites; of Ahiram, the family of the Ahiramites; ³⁹of Shephupham, the family of the Shuphamites; of Hupham, the family of the Huphamites. ⁴⁰The sons of Bela were Ard and Naaman: *of Ard,* the family of the Ardites; of Naaman, the family of the Naamites. ⁴¹These are the sons of Benjamin by their families; and those who were numbered of them were ^45,600.

⁴²These are the sons of Dan by their families: of Shuham, the family of the Shuhamites. These are the families of Dan by their families. ⁴³All the families of the Shuhamites, by those who were numbered of them, were ^64,400.

⁴⁴The ^sons of Asher by their families: of Imnah, the family of the Imnites; of Ishvi, the family of the Ishvites; of Beriah, the family of the Beriites. ⁴⁵Of the sons of Beriah: of Heber, the family of the Heberites; of Malchiel, the family of the Malchielites. ⁴⁶And the name of the daughter of Asher *was* Serah. ⁴⁷These are the families of the sons of Asher by those who were numbered of them, ^53,400.

⁴⁸The ^sons of Naphtali by their families: of Jahzeel, the family of the Jahzeelites; of Guni, the family of the Gunites; ⁴⁹of Jezer, the family of the Jezerites; of ^Shillem, the family of the Shillemites. ⁵⁰These are the families of Naphtali by their families; and those who were numbered of them were ^45,400.

⁵¹These are the ones who were numbered of the sons of Israel, ^601,730.

⁵²Then the Lᴏʀᴅ spoke to Moses, saying, ⁵³"Among these the land shall be divided as an inheritance according to the number of names.

26:27^Num 1:31   26:28^Gen 46:20; Deut 33:16f
26:29^Josh 17:1; 1 Chr 7:14f   26:30^Judg 6:11, 24, 34
26:33^Num 27:1   26:34^Num 1:35   26:37^Num 1:33
26:41^Num 1:37   26:43^Num 1:39   26:44^Gen 46:17;
1 Chr 7:30   26:47^Num 1:41   26:48^Gen 46:24;
1 Chr 7:13   26:49^1 Chr 7:13   26:50^Num 1:43
26:51^Ex 12:37; Num 1:46

⁵⁴ᴬTo a larger *group* you shall increase their inheritance, and to a smaller *group* you shall decrease their inheritance; each shall be given their inheritance corresponding to *the total of* those who were numbered of them. ⁵⁵But the land shall be ᴬdivided by lot. They shall receive their inheritance according to the names of the tribes of their fathers. ⁵⁶Corresponding to the selection by lot, their inheritance shall be divided between the larger and the smaller *groups*."

⁵⁷ᴬThese are those who were numbered of the Levites according to their families: of Gershon, the family of the Gershonites; of Kohath, the family of the Kohathites; of Merari, the family of the Merarites. ⁵⁸These are the families of Levi: the family of the Libnites, the family of the Hebronites, the family of the Mahlites, the family of the Mushites, *and* the family of the Korahites. ᴬKohath fathered Amram. ⁵⁹And the name of Amram's wife ᴬwas Jochebed, the daughter of Levi, who was born to Levi in Egypt; and she bore to Amram Aaron and Moses, and their sister Miriam. ⁶⁰ᴬAnd to Aaron were born Nadab and Abihu, Eleazar and Ithamar. ⁶¹ᴬBut Nadab and Abihu died when they offered strange fire before the Lord. ⁶²Those who were numbered of them were twenty-three thousand, every male from a month old and upward, for ᴬthey were not numbered among the sons of Israel since no inheritance was given to them among the sons of Israel.

⁶³These are the ones who were numbered by Moses and Eleazar the priest, who numbered the sons of Israel in the plains of Moab by the Jordan at Jericho. ⁶⁴ᴬBut among these there was not a man of those who were numbered by Moses and Aaron the priest, who numbered the sons of Israel in the wilderness of Sinai. ⁶⁵For the Lord had said of them, "ᴬThey shall certainly die in the wilderness." And not a man was left of them, except Caleb the son of Jephunneh and Joshua the son of Nun.

A LAW OF INHERITANCE

27 Then ᴬthe daughters of Zelophehad, the son of Hepher, the son of Gilead, the son of Machir, the son of Manasseh, of the families of Manasseh the son of Joseph, came forward; and these are the names of his daughters: Mahlah, Noah, Hoglah, Milcah, and Tirzah. ²They stood before Moses, before Eleazar the priest, before the leaders, and all the congregation at the entrance of the tent of meeting, saying, ³"Our father ᴬdied in the wilderness, yet he was not among the group of those who gathered together against the Lord, in the group of Korah; but he died in his own sin, and he had no sons. ⁴Why should the name of our father be withdrawn from among his family *simply* because he had no son? Give us property among our father's brothers." ⁵ᴬSo Moses brought their case before the Lord.

⁶Then the Lord said to Moses, ⁷"ᴬThe daughters of Zelophehad are right *about their* statements. You shall certainly give them

26:54ᴬNum 33:54   26:55ᴬNum 33:54; 34:13
26:57ᴬGen 46:11; 1 Chr 6:1, 16   26:58ᴬEx 6:20
26:59ᴬEx 2:1, 2; 6:20   26:60ᴬNum 3:2
26:61ᴬLev 10:1, 2; Num 3:4   26:62ᴬNum 1:47
26:64ᴬDeut 2:14-16; Heb 3:17   26:65ᴬNum 14:26-35;
Ps 90:3-10   27:1ᴬNum 26:33; 36:1
27:3ᴬNum 26:64, 65   27:5ᴬNum 9:8; 27:21
27:7ᴬNum 36:2; Josh 17:4

hereditary property among their father's brothers, and you shall transfer the inheritance of their father to them. ⁸Further, you shall speak to the sons of Israel, saying, 'If a man dies and has no son, then you shall transfer his inheritance to his daughter. ⁹And if he has no daughter, then you shall give his inheritance to his brothers. ¹⁰If he has no brothers, then you shall give his inheritance to his father's brothers. ¹¹And if his father has no brothers, then you shall give his inheritance to his nearest relative in his own family, and he shall take possession of it; and it shall be a ^statutory ordinance to the sons of Israel, just as the Lord has commanded Moses.'"

¹²Then the Lord said to Moses, "Go up to this ^mountain of Abarim, and see the land which I have given to the sons of Israel. ¹³When you have seen it, you too will be gathered to your people, ^just as Aaron your brother was; ¹⁴for in the wilderness of Zin, during the strife of the congregation, ^you rebelled against My command to treat Me as holy before their eyes at the water." (These are the waters of Meribah of Kadesh in the wilderness of Zin.)

JOSHUA TO SUCCEED MOSES

¹⁵Then Moses spoke to the Lord, saying, ¹⁶"^May the Lord, the God of the spirits of humanity, appoint a man over the congregation, ¹⁷who ^will go out and come in before them, and lead them out and bring them in, so that the congregation of the Lord will not be like sheep that have no shepherd." ¹⁸So the Lord said to Moses, "Take Joshua the son of Nun, a man ^in whom is the Spirit, and lay your hand on

him; ¹⁹and have him stand before Eleazar the priest and before all the congregation, and ^commission him in their sight. ²⁰And you shall put some of your authority on him, so that all the congregation of the sons of Israel will obey *him*. ²¹Moreover, he shall stand before Eleazar the priest, who shall inquire for him ^by the judgment of the Urim before the Lord. At his command they shall go out, and at his command they shall come in, *both* he and all the sons of Israel with him, all the congregation." ²²Then Moses did just as the Lord commanded him; he took Joshua and had him stand before Eleazar the priest and before all the congregation. ²³Then he laid his hands on him and ^commissioned him, just as the Lord had spoken through Moses.

LAWS FOR OFFERINGS

28 Then the Lord spoke to Moses, saying, ²"Command the sons of Israel and say to them, 'You shall be careful to present to Me My offering, My ^food for My offerings by fire, of a soothing aroma to Me, at their appointed time.' ³And you shall say to them, 'This is the offering by fire which you shall offer to the Lord: two male lambs one year old without defect *as* a continual burnt offering every day. ⁴You shall offer the one lamb in the morning, and the other lamb you shall offer at twilight; ⁵also a tenth of an ephah of fine flour as a ^grain offering, mixed

27:11 ^Num 35:29   27:12 ^Num 33:47, 48
27:13 ^Num 20:24, 28; Deut 10:6   27:14 ^Deut 32:51;
Ps 106:32   27:16 ^Num 16:22   27:17 ^Deut 31:2;
2 Chr 1:10   27:18 ^Num 11:25-29; Deut 34:9
27:19 ^Num 3:28; 31:3, 7, 8, 23   27:21 ^Ex 28:30;
1 Sam 28:6   27:23 ^Deut 31:23   28:2 ^Lev 3:11
28:3 ^Ex 29:38-42   28:5 ^Lev 2:1

with a fourth of a ¹hin of pure oil. ⁶It is a continual burnt offering which was ordained on Mount Sinai as a soothing aroma, an offering by fire to the LORD. ⁷Then the drink offering with it *shall be* a fourth of a hin for each lamb; ^in the Holy Place pour out a drink offering of strong drink to the LORD. ⁸The other lamb you shall offer at twilight; as the grain offering of the morning and as its drink offering, you shall offer it, an offering by fire, a soothing aroma to the LORD.

⁹'Then on the Sabbath day two male lambs one year old without defect, and two-tenths *of an ephah* of fine flour mixed with oil as a grain offering, and its drink offering: ¹⁰ *This is* the burnt offering of every Sabbath in addition to the ^continual burnt offering and its drink offering.

¹¹'Then ^at the beginning of *each of* your months you shall present a burnt offering to the LORD: two bulls and one ram, seven male lambs one year old without defect; ¹²^and three-tenths *of an ephah* of fine flour mixed with oil as a grain offering, for each bull; and two-tenths of fine flour mixed with oil as a grain offering, for the one ram; ¹³and a tenth *of an ephah* of fine flour mixed with oil as a grain offering for each lamb, as a burnt offering of a soothing aroma, an offering by fire to the LORD. ¹⁴Their drink offerings shall be half a hin of wine for a bull and a third of a hin for the ram and a fourth of a hin for a lamb; this is the burnt offering of each month throughout the months of the year. ¹⁵And one male goat as a sin offering to the LORD; it shall be offered with its drink offering in addition to the ^continual burnt offering.

¹⁶'^The LORD's Passover *shall be* on the fourteenth day of the first month. ¹⁷^On the fifteenth day of this month *there shall be* a feast; unleavened bread shall be eaten for seven days. ¹⁸On the ^first day *there shall be* a holy assembly; you shall do no laborious work. ¹⁹But you shall present an offering by fire, a burnt offering to the LORD: two bulls and one ram, and seven male lambs one year old, *that* you have ^without defect. ²⁰For their grain offering, you shall offer fine flour mixed with oil: three-tenths *of an ephah* for a bull, and two-tenths for the ram. ²¹A tenth *of an ephah* you shall offer for each of the seven lambs; ²²and one male goat as a ^sin offering to make atonement for you. ²³You shall present these besides ^the burnt offering of the morning, which is for a continual burnt offering. ²⁴In this way you shall present daily, for seven days, ^the food of the offering by fire, of a soothing aroma to the LORD; it shall be presented with its drink offering in addition to the continual burnt offering. ²⁵On the seventh day you shall have a holy assembly; ^you shall do no laborious work.

²⁶'Also on ^the day of the first fruits, when you present a new grain offering to the LORD in your *Feast of* Weeks, you shall have a holy assembly; you shall do no laborious work. ²⁷But you shall offer a burnt offering as a soothing aroma to the LORD: two bulls,

28:7 ^Ex 29:42   28:10 ^Num 28:3   28:11 ^Num 10:10; Ezek 46:6, 7   28:12 ^Num 15:4–12   28:15 ^Num 28:3   28:16 ^Lev 23:5–8; Deut 16:1–8   28:17 ^Lev 23:6   28:18 ^Lev 23:7   28:19 ^Deut 15:21   28:22 ^Rom 8:3; Gal 4:4f   28:23 ^Num 28:3   28:24 ^Lev 3:11   28:25 ^Num 28:18   28:26 ^Lev 23:15–21; Deut 16:9–12

28:5 ¹ About 1 gallon or 3.8 liters, and so throughout the ch

one ram, *and* seven male lambs one year old; [28] and *as* their grain offering, fine flour mixed with oil: three-tenths *of an ephah* for each bull, two-tenths for the one ram, [29] *and* a tenth for each of the seven lambs; [30] *also* one male goat to make atonement for you. [31] ^Besides the continual burnt offering and its grain offering, you shall present *them* with their drink offerings. They shall be without defect.

OFFERINGS OF THE SEVENTH MONTH

29 [1] ^"Now in the seventh month, on the first *day* of the month, you shall have a holy assembly; you shall do no laborious work. It will be to you a day for blowing trumpets. [2] And you shall offer a burnt offering as a soothing aroma to the LORD: one bull, one ram, *and* seven male lambs one year old without defect; [3] also their grain offering, fine flour mixed with oil: three-tenths *of an* ¹*ephah* for the bull, two-tenths for the ram, [4] and a tenth for each of the seven lambs, [5] and one male goat as a sin offering, to make atonement for you, [6] besides the burnt offering of the new moon and its grain offering, and the ^continual burnt offering and its grain offering, and their drink offerings, according to their ordinance, for a soothing aroma, an offering by fire to the LORD.

[7] "Then on ^the tenth *day* of this seventh month you shall have a holy assembly, and you shall humble yourselves; you shall not do any work. [8] You shall present a burnt offering to the LORD *as* a soothing aroma: one bull, one ram, *and* seven male lambs one year old, *that* you have ^without defect; [9] and their grain offering, fine flour

mixed with oil: three-tenths *of an ephah* for the bull, two-tenths for the one ram, [10] *and* a tenth for each of the seven lambs; [11] one male goat as a sin offering, besides ^the sin offering of atonement and ^the continual burnt offering, and its grain offering, and their drink offerings.

[12] "Then on ^the fifteenth day of the seventh month you shall have a holy assembly; you shall do no laborious work, and you shall celebrate *with* a feast to the LORD for seven days. [13] You shall present a burnt offering, an offering by fire as a soothing aroma to the LORD: thirteen bulls, two rams, *and* fourteen male lambs one year old, which are without defect; [14] and their grain offering, fine flour mixed with oil: three-tenths *of an ephah* for each of the thirteen bulls, two-tenths for each of the two rams, [15] and a tenth for each of the fourteen lambs; [16] and one male goat as a sin offering, ^besides the continual burnt offering, its grain offering, and its drink offering.

[17] "Then on ^the second day: twelve bulls, two rams, *and* fourteen male lambs one year old without defect; [18] and their grain offering and their drink offerings for the bulls, for the rams, and for the lambs, by their number ^according to the ordinance; [19] and one male goat as a sin offering, ^besides the continual burnt offering and its grain offering, and their drink offerings.

[20] "Then on the third day: eleven bulls, two rams, *and* fourteen male

28:31 ^Num 28:3   29:1 ^Ex 23:16; Lev 23:23-25
29:6 ^Num 28:3   29:7 ^Lev 16:29-34; 23:26-32
29:8 ^Deut 15:21; 17:1   29:11 ^Lev 16:3, 5   [8] Num 28:3
29:12 ^Lev 23:33-35; Deut 16:13-15   29:16 ^Num 28:3
29:17 ^Lev 23:36   29:18 ^Lev 2:1-16   29:19 ^Num 28:8

29:3 ¹About 1 cubic foot or 0.03 cubic meters, and so throughout the ch

lambs one year old without defect; ²¹and their grain offering and their drink offerings for the bulls, for the rams, and for the lambs, by their number according to the ordinance; ²²and one male goat as a sin offering, besides the continual burnt offering and its grain offering, and its drink offering.

²³'Then on the fourth day: ten bulls, two rams, *and* fourteen male lambs one year old without defect; ²⁴their grain offering and their drink offerings for the bulls, for the rams, and for the lambs, by their number according to the ordinance; ²⁵and one male goat as a sin offering, besides the continual burnt offering, its grain offering, and its drink offering.

²⁶'Then on the fifth day: nine bulls, two rams, *and* fourteen male lambs one year old ^without defect; ²⁷and their grain offering and their drink offerings for the bulls, for the rams, and for the lambs, by their number according to the ordinance; ²⁸and one male goat as a sin offering, besides the continual burnt offering and its grain offering, and its drink offering.

²⁹'Then on the sixth day: eight bulls, two rams, *and* fourteen male lambs one year old without defect; ³⁰and their grain offering and their drink offerings for the bulls, for the rams, and for the lambs, by their number according to the ordinance; ³¹and one male goat as a sin offering, besides the continual burnt offering, its grain offering, and its drink offerings.

³²'Then on the seventh day: seven bulls, two rams, *and* fourteen male lambs one year old without defect; ³³and their grain offering and their drink offerings for the bulls, for the

rams, and for the lambs, by their number according to the ordinance; ³⁴and one male goat as a sin offering, besides the continual burnt offering, its grain offering, and its drink offering.

³⁵'^On the eighth day you shall have a sacred assembly; you shall do no laborious work. ³⁶But you shall present a burnt offering, an offering by fire, as a soothing aroma to the LORD: one bull, one ram, *and* seven male lambs one year old without defect; ³⁷their grain offering and their drink offerings for the bull, for the ram, and for the lambs, by their number according to the ordinance; ³⁸and one male goat as a sin offering, besides the continual burnt offering and its grain offering, and its drink offering.

³⁹'You shall present these to the LORD at your ^appointed times, besides your vowed offerings and your voluntary offerings, for your burnt offerings, your grain offerings, your drink offerings, and for your peace offerings.'" ⁴⁰And Moses spoke to the sons of Israel in accordance with everything that the LORD had commanded Moses.

THE LAW OF VOWS

30 Then Moses spoke to ^the heads of the tribes of the sons of Israel, saying, "This is the word which the LORD has commanded: ²^If a man makes a vow to the LORD, or takes an oath to put himself under a binding obligation, he shall not break his word; he shall act in accordance with everything that comes out of his mouth.

29:26^Heb 7:26   **29:35**^Lev 23:36   **29:39**^Lev 23:2
30:1^Num 1:4, 16; 7:2   **30:2**^Deut 23:21-23;
Matt 5:33

³"And if a woman makes a vow to the LORD, and puts herself under a binding obligation in her father's house in her youth, ⁴and her father hears her vow and her obligation under which she has put herself, and her father says nothing to her, then all her vows shall remain valid and every binding obligation under which she has put herself shall remain valid. ⁵But if her father expresses disapproval to her on the day he hears *of it,* none of her vows or her obligations under which she has put herself shall remain valid; and the LORD will forgive her because her father has expressed disapproval to her.

⁶"However, if she happens to marry while under her vows or the impulsive statement of her lips by which she has obligated herself, ⁷and her husband hears of it and says nothing to her on the day he hears *it,* then her vows shall remain valid and her binding obligations under which she has put herself shall remain valid. ⁸But if on the day her husband hears *of it,* he expresses disapproval to her, then he will annul her vow which she is under and the impulsive statement of her lips by which she has obligated herself; and the LORD will forgive her.

⁹"But *as for* the vow of a widow or of a divorced woman, every binding obligation under which she has put herself, shall remain valid against her. ¹⁰However, if *a married woman* vowed *in* her husband's house, or put herself under a binding obligation with an oath, ¹¹and her husband heard *it,* but said nothing to her *and* did not express disapproval to her, then all her vows shall remain valid and every binding obligation under which she put herself shall remain valid. ¹²But if her husband actually annuls them on the day he hears *them,* then no utterance from her lips concerning her vows or the obligation *she put on* herself shall remain valid; her husband has annulled them, and the LORD will forgive her.

¹³"Every vow and every binding oath to humble herself, her husband may confirm it or her husband may annul it. ¹⁴But if her husband in fact says nothing to her from day to day, then he confirms all her vows or all her binding obligations which are on her; he has confirmed them, because he said nothing to her on the day he heard them. ¹⁵However, if he actually annuls them ¹after he has heard them, then he shall bear *the responsibility for* her guilt."

¹⁶These are the statutes which the LORD commanded Moses *concerning matters* between a man and his wife, *and* between a father and his daughter *while she is* in her youth *in* her father's house.

THE SLAUGHTER OF MIDIAN

31 Then the LORD spoke to Moses, saying, ²"ᴬTake vengeance on the Midianites for the sons of Israel; afterward you will be gathered to your people." ³So Moses spoke to the people, saying, "Arm men from among you for the war, so that they may go against Midian to execute ᴬthe LORD's vengeance on Midian. ⁴You shall send a thousand from each tribe of all the tribes of Israel to the war." ⁵So

31:2ᴬNum 25:1, 16, 17   31:3ᴬLev 26:25
30:15¹I.e., perhaps a long delay before he annuls them

there were selected from the thousands of Israel, a thousand from each tribe, twelve thousand armed for war. ⁶And Moses sent them, a thousand from each tribe, to the war, and Phinehas the son of Eleazar the priest, to the war with them, and the holy implements and ^the trumpets for the alarm in his hand. ⁷So they made war against Midian, just as the Lᴏʀᴅ had commanded Moses, and ^they killed every male. ⁸They killed the kings of Midian along with the *rest of* those killed: Evi, Rekem, ^Zur, Hur, and Reba, the five kings of Midian. They also killed ᴮBalaam the son of Beor with the sword. ⁹And the sons of Israel took captive the women of Midian and their little ones; and they plundered all their cattle, all their flocks, and all their property. ¹⁰Then they burned all their cities where they lived and all their encampments. ¹¹And ^they took all the plunder and all the spoils, both of people and of livestock. ¹²They brought the captives and the spoils and the plunder to Moses, to Eleazar the priest, and to the congregation of the sons of Israel, to the camp at the plains of Moab which are by the Jordan, *opposite* Jericho.

¹³And Moses, Eleazar the priest, and all the leaders of the congregation went out to meet them outside the camp. ¹⁴But Moses was angry with the officers of the army, the commanders of thousands and the commanders of hundreds, who had come from service in the war. ¹⁵And Moses said to them, "Have you spared ^all the women? ¹⁶Behold, they caused the sons of Israel, through the counsel of Balaam, to be unfaithful to the Lᴏʀᴅ in the matter of Peor, so that the plague

took place among the congregation of the Lᴏʀᴅ! ¹⁷^Now therefore, kill every male among the little ones, and kill every woman who has known a man intimately. ¹⁸However, all the girls who have not known a man intimately, keep alive for yourselves. ¹⁹^And *as for* you, camp outside the camp for seven days; whoever has killed a person and whoever has touched *anyone* killed, purify yourselves, you and your captives, on the third day and on the seventh day. ²⁰And you shall purify for yourselves every garment, every article of leather, every work of goats' *hair,* and every article of wood."

²¹Then Eleazar the priest said to the men of war who had gone to battle, "This is the statute of the Law which the Lᴏʀᴅ has commanded Moses: ²²only the gold and the silver, the bronze, the iron, the tin, and the lead, ²³everything that can withstand the fire, you shall pass through the fire, and it will be clean, only it shall be purified with ^water for impurity. But whatever cannot withstand the fire you shall pass through the water. ²⁴And you shall wash your clothes on the seventh day and you will be clean; and afterward you may enter the camp."

DIVISION OF THE PLUNDER

²⁵Then the Lᴏʀᴅ spoke to Moses, saying, ²⁶"You and Eleazar the priest and the heads of the fathers' *households* of the congregation take a count of the spoils that were captured, both of people and of

31:6 ^Num 10:8, 9   31:7 ^Deut 20:13; 1 Kin 11:15, 16
31:8 ^Num 25:15   ᴮJosh 13:22   31:11 ^Deut 20:14
31:15 ^Deut 20:14   31:16 ^Num 25:1-9
31:17 ^Deut 7:2; 20:16-18   31:19 ^Num 19:11-22
31:23 ^Num 19:9, 17

livestock; [27] and ^divide the spoils between the warriors who went to battle and all the congregation. [28] Also, ^collect a tribute tax for the LORD from the men of war who went to battle, one in five hundred of the persons, of the cattle, of the donkeys, and of the sheep; [29] take it from their half and give it to Eleazar the priest, as an offering to the LORD. [30] And from the sons of Israel's half, you shall take one drawn from every fifty of the persons, of the cattle, of the donkeys, and of the sheep, from all the animals; and give them to the Levites who ^perform the duty of the tabernacle of the LORD." [31] Moses and Eleazar the priest did just as the LORD had commanded Moses.

[32] Now the spoils that remained from the plunder which the men of war had plundered was 675,000 sheep, [33] seventy-two thousand cattle, [34] sixty-one thousand donkeys, [35] and of *captive* people, of the women who had not known a man intimately, in all were thirty-two thousand people.

[36] The half, the share of those who went to war, was *as follows:* the number of sheep was 337,500, [37] the LORD's tribute tax of the sheep was 675; [38] the cattle were thirty-six thousand, from which the LORD's tribute tax was seventy-two; [39] the donkeys were 30,500, from which the LORD's tribute tax was sixty-one; [40] and the *captive* people were sixteen thousand, from whom the LORD's tribute tax was thirty-two persons. [41] And Moses gave the tribute tax, *which was* the LORD's offering, to Eleazar the priest, just ^as the LORD had commanded Moses.

[42] As for the sons of Israel's half, which Moses separated from the men who had gone to war— [43] now the congregation's half was 337,500 sheep, [44] thirty-six thousand cattle, [45] 30,500 donkeys, [46] and the *captive* people were sixteen thousand— [47] from the sons of Israel's half Moses took one drawn from every fifty, both of people and of animals, and gave them to the Levites, who performed the duty of the tabernacle of the LORD, just as the LORD had commanded Moses.

[48] Then the officers who were over the thousands of the army, the commanders of thousands and the commanders of hundreds, approached Moses, [49] and they said to Moses, "Your servants have taken a census of the men of war who are under our authority, and no man of us is missing. [50] So we have brought as an offering to the LORD what each man found, articles of gold, armlets and bracelets, signet rings, earrings, and necklaces, ^to make atonement for ourselves before the LORD." [51] Moses and Eleazar the priest took the gold from them, all kinds of crafted articles. [52] All the gold of the offering which they offered up to the LORD, from the commanders of thousands and the commanders of hundreds, was 16,750 shekels. [53] ^The men of war had taken plunder, every man for himself. [54] So Moses and Eleazar the priest took the gold from the commanders of thousands and of hundreds, and brought it to the tent of meeting as ^a memorial for the sons of Israel before the LORD.

31:27 ^Josh 22:8　31:28 ^Num 18:21-30
31:30 ^Num 3:7, 8, 25, 26, 31, 36, 37; 18:3, 4
31:41 ^Num 5:9, 10; 18:19　31:50 ^Ex 30:12-16
31:53 ^Num 31:32; Deut 20:14　31:54 ^Ex 30:16

REUBEN AND GAD SETTLE IN GILEAD

32 Now the sons of Reuben and the sons of Gad had a ^very large number of livestock. So when they saw the land of ^BJazer and the land of Gilead, that it was indeed a place suitable for livestock, ²the sons of Gad and the sons of Reuben came and spoke to Moses, Eleazar the priest, and to the leaders of the congregation, saying, ³"^Ataroth, Dibon, Jazer, Nimrah, Heshbon, Elealeh, Sebam, Nebo, and Beon, ⁴the land ^which the LORD conquered before the congregation of Israel, is a land for livestock, and your servants have livestock." ⁵And they said, "If we have found favor in your sight, let this land be given to your servants as *our* property; do not take us across the Jordan."

⁶But Moses said to the sons of Gad and the sons of Reuben, "Should your brothers go to war while you remain here? ⁷^And why are you discouraging the sons of Israel from crossing over into the land which the LORD has given them? ⁸This is what your fathers did when I sent them from ^Kadesh-barnea to see the land. ⁹For when they went up to ^the Valley of Eshcol and saw the land, they discouraged the sons of Israel so that they did not go into the land which the LORD had given them. ¹⁰So ^the LORD's anger burned on that day, and He swore, saying, ¹¹"^None of the men who came up from Egypt, from twenty years old and upward, shall see the land which I swore to Abraham, to Isaac, and to Jacob; for they did not follow Me fully, ¹²except Caleb the son of Jephunneh the Kenizzite and Joshua the son of Nun; ^for they have followed the LORD fully.' ¹³^So the LORD's anger burned against

Israel, and He made them wander in the wilderness for forty years, until the entire generation of those who had done evil in the sight of the LORD came to an end. ¹⁴Now behold, you have risen up in your fathers' place, born of sinful men, to add still more to the burning ^anger of the LORD against Israel. ¹⁵For *if* you ^turn away from following Him, He will once more leave them in the wilderness, and you will destroy all these people."

¹⁶Then they approached him and said, "We will build sheepfolds for our livestock here and cities for our little ones; ¹⁷^but we ourselves will be armed, hurrying ahead of the sons of Israel, until we have brought them to their place, while our little ones live in the fortified cities because of the inhabitants of the land. ¹⁸^We will not return to our homes until every one of the sons of Israel has gained possession of his inheritance. ¹⁹But we will not have an inheritance with them on the other side of the Jordan and beyond, because our inheritance has come to us ^on this side of the Jordan toward the east."

²⁰^So Moses said to them, "If you will do this, if you will arm yourselves before the LORD for the war, ²¹and all of you armed men cross over the Jordan before the LORD until He has driven His enemies out from Him, ²²^and the land is subdued before the LORD, then afterward you may return and be free

32:1^Ex 12:38   ^BNum 21:32   **32:3**^Num 32:34-38
32:4^Num 21:34   **32:7**^Num 13:27-14:4
32:8^Num 13:3, 26; Deut 1:19-25   **32:9**^Num 13:24;
Deut 1:24   **32:10**^Num 14:11f; Deut 1:34
32:11^Num 14:28-30   **32:12**^Deut 1:36; Josh 14:8f
32:13^Num 14:33-35   **32:14**^Deut 1:34f
32:15^Deut 30:17, 18; 2 Chr 7:19, 20   **32:17**^Josh 4:12, 13
32:18^Josh 22:1-4   **32:19**^Josh 12:1; 13:8
32:20^Deut 3:18   **32:22**^Deut 3:20

of obligation toward the LORD and toward Israel, and this land shall be yours as property before the LORD. ²³But if you do not do so, behold, you have sinned against the LORD, and be sure that ^your sin will find you out. ²⁴Build yourselves cities for your little ones, and sheepfolds for your sheep, and ^do what you have promised."

²⁵Then the sons of Gad and the sons of Reuben spoke to Moses, saying, "Your servants will do just as my lord commands. ²⁶^Our little ones, our wives, our livestock, and all our cattle shall remain there in the cities of Gilead, ²⁷while your servants, *that is,* everyone who is armed for war, ^cross over in the presence of the LORD to battle, just as my lord says."

²⁸So Moses gave the command regarding them to Eleazar the priest, to Joshua the son of Nun, and to the heads of the fathers' *households* of the tribes of the sons of Israel. ²⁹And Moses said to them, "If the sons of Gad and the sons of Reuben, everyone who is armed for battle, cross with you over the Jordan in the presence of the LORD, and the land is subdued before you, then you shall give them the land of Gilead as *their* property; ³⁰but if they do not cross over with you armed, they shall instead be settled among you in the land of Canaan." ³¹And the sons of Gad and the sons of Reuben answered, saying, "As the LORD has said to your servants, so we will do. ³²We ourselves will cross over armed in the presence of the LORD into the land of Canaan, and the property of our inheritance *shall remain* with us across the Jordan."

³³^So Moses gave to them, to the sons of Gad, the sons of Reuben,

and to the half-tribe of Joseph's son Manasseh, the kingdom of Sihon, king of the Amorites and the kingdom of Og, the king of Bashan, the land with its cities with *their* territories, the cities of the surrounding land. ³⁴And the sons of Gad built Dibon, Ataroth, ^Aroer, ³⁵Atroth-shophan, Jazer, Jogbehah, ³⁶^Beth-nimrah, and Beth-haran as fortified cities, and sheepfolds for sheep. ³⁷The sons of Reuben built Heshbon, Elealeh, Kiriathaim, ³⁸^Nebo, and Baal-meon—*their* names being changed—and Sibmah, and they gave *other* names to the cities which they built. ³⁹The sons of ^Machir the son of Manasseh went to Gilead and took it, and dispossessed the Amorites who were in it. ⁴⁰So Moses gave ^Gilead to Machir the son of Manasseh, and he lived in it. ⁴¹Jair the son of Manasseh went and took its towns, and called them ^Havvoth-jair. ⁴²Nobah went and took Kenath and its villages, and named it Nobah, after ^his own name.

REVIEW OF THE JOURNEY FROM EGYPT TO JORDAN

33 These are the journeys of the sons of Israel, by which they came out of the land of Egypt by their armies, under ^the leadership of Moses and Aaron. ²Moses recorded their starting places according to their journeys by the command of the LORD, and these are their journeys according to their starting places. ³^Now they journeyed from Rameses in

32:23^Gen 4:7; Is 59:12   32:24^Num 30:2
32:26^Josh 1:14   32:27^Josh 4:12   32:33^Deut 3:8-17; Josh 12:1-6   32:34^Deut 2:36
32:36^Num 32:3   32:38^Is 46:1   32:39^Gen 50:23
32:40^Deut 3:12, 13, 15; Josh 17:1   32:41^Deut 3:14; Judg 10:4   32:42^2 Sam 18:18; Ps 49:11
33:1^Ps 105:26; Mic 6:4   33:3^Ex 12:37

the first month, on the fifteenth day of the first month; on the day after the Passover the sons of Israel ᴮstarted out boldly in the sight of all the Egyptians, ⁴while the Egyptians were burying all their firstborn whom the LORD had fatally struck among them. The LORD had also executed judgments ᴬagainst their gods.

⁵Then ᴬthe sons of Israel journeyed from Rameses and camped in Succoth. ⁶ᴬThey journeyed from Succoth and camped in Etham, which is on the edge of the wilderness. ⁷ᴬThen they journeyed from Etham and turned back to Pi-hahiroth, which faces Baal-zephon; and they camped before Migdol. ⁸ᴬThey journeyed from Pi-hahiroth and passed through the midst of the sea to the wilderness; and ᴮthey went three days' journey in the wilderness of Etham and camped at Marah. ⁹ᴬThey journeyed from Marah and came to Elim; and in Elim there were twelve springs of water and seventy palm trees, and they camped there. ¹⁰They journeyed from Elim and camped by the Red Sea. ¹¹And they journeyed from the Red Sea and camped in ᴬthe wilderness of Sin. ¹²They journeyed from the wilderness of Sin and camped at Dophkah. ¹³They journeyed from Dophkah and camped at Alush. ¹⁴And they journeyed from Alush and camped ᴬat Rephidim; now it was there that the people had no water to drink. ¹⁵And they journeyed from Rephidim and camped in ᴬthe wilderness of Sinai. ¹⁶They journeyed from the wilderness of Sinai, and camped at ᴬKibroth-hattaavah.

¹⁷They journeyed from Kibroth-hattaavah and camped at ᴬHazeroth.

¹⁸They journeyed from Hazeroth and camped at Rithmah. ¹⁹They journeyed from Rithmah and camped at Rimmon-perez. ²⁰They journeyed from Rimmon-perez and camped at ᴬLibnah. ²¹They journeyed from Libnah and camped at Rissah. ²²They journeyed from Rissah and camped in Kehelathah. ²³They journeyed from Kehelathah and camped at Mount Shepher. ²⁴They journeyed from Mount Shepher and camped at Haradah. ²⁵They journeyed from Haradah and camped at Makheloth. ²⁶They journeyed from Makheloth and camped at Tahath. ²⁷They journeyed from Tahath and camped at Terah. ²⁸They journeyed from Terah and camped at Mithkah. ²⁹They journeyed from Mithkah and camped at Hashmonah. ³⁰They journeyed from Hashmonah and camped at ᴬMoseroth. ³¹They journeyed from Moseroth and camped at Bene-jaakan. ³²They journeyed from ᴬBene-jaakan and camped at Hor-haggidgad. ³³They journeyed from Hor-haggidgad and camped at ᴬJotbathah. ³⁴They journeyed from Jotbathah and camped at Abronah. ³⁵They journeyed from Abronah and camped at ᴬEzion-geber. ³⁶They journeyed from Ezion-geber and camped in the wilderness of ᴬZin, that is, Kadesh. ³⁷They journeyed from Kadesh and camped at Mount Hor, ᴬat the edge of the land of Edom.

³⁸ᴬThen Aaron the priest went up to Mount Hor at the command of

33:3 ᴮEx 14:8   33:4 ᴬEx 12:12   33:5 ᴬEx 12:37
33:6 ᴬEx 13:20   33:7 ᴬEx 14:1, 2
33:8 ᴬEx 14:22   ᴮEx 15:22, 23   33:9 ᴬEx 15:27
33:11 ᴬEx 16:1   33:14 ᴬEx 17:1   33:15 ᴬEx 19:1
33:16 ᴬNum 11:34   33:17 ᴬNum 11:35   33:20 ᴬDeut 1:1
33:30 ᴬDeut 10:6   33:32 ᴬGen 36:27; 1 Chr 1:42
33:33 ᴬDeut 10:7   33:35 ᴬDeut 2:8   33:36 ᴬNum 20:1
33:37 ᴬNum 20:16   33:38 ᴬNum 20:28; Deut 10:6

the LORD, and died there in the fortieth year after the sons of Israel had come from the land of Egypt, on the first *day* in the fifth month. [39] Aaron was 123 years old when he died on Mount Hor.

[40] Now the Canaanite, the king of ^Arad who lived in the Negev in the land of Canaan, heard about the coming of the sons of Israel.

[41] Then they journeyed from Mount Hor and camped at Zalmonah. [42] They journeyed from Zalmonah and camped at Punon. [43] They journeyed from Punon and camped at ^Oboth. [44] They journeyed from Oboth and camped at Iye-abarim, at the border of Moab. [45] They journeyed from Iyim and camped at Dibon-gad. [46] They journeyed from Dibon-gad and camped at Almondiblathaim. [47] They journeyed from Almon-diblathaim and camped in the mountains of ^Abarim, before Nebo. [48] They journeyed from the mountains of Abarim and ^camped in the plains of Moab, by the Jordan *opposite* Jericho. [49] They camped by the Jordan, from Beth-jeshimoth as far as ^Abel-shittim, in the plains of Moab.

LAW FOR POSSESSING THE LAND

[50] Then the LORD spoke to Moses in the plains of Moab by the Jordan *opposite* Jericho, saying, [51] "Speak to the sons of Israel and say to them, '^When you cross the Jordan into the land of Canaan, [52] you shall drive out all the inhabitants of the land from you, and ^destroy all their *idolatrous* sculptures, destroy all their cast metal images, and eliminate all their high places; [53] ^and you shall take possession of the land and live in it, for I have given the land to you to possess it.

[54] ^You shall maintain the land as an inheritance by lot according to your families; to the larger you shall give more inheritance, and to the smaller you shall give less inheritance. Wherever the lot falls to anyone, that shall be his. You shall pass on *land* as an inheritance according to the tribes of your fathers. [55] But if you do not drive out the inhabitants of the land from you, then it will come about that those whom you let remain of them *will be* ^like thorns in your eyes and like pricks in your sides, and they will trouble you in the land in which you live. [56] And just as I plan to do to them, I will do to you.'"

INSTRUCTION FOR APPORTIONING CANAAN

34 Then the LORD spoke to Moses, saying, [2] "Command the sons of Israel and say to them, 'When you enter ^the land of Canaan, this is the land that shall fall to you as an inheritance, *that is, the* land of Canaan according to its borders. [3] ^Your southern region shall extend from the wilderness of Zin along the side of Edom, and your southern border shall extend from the end of the Salt Sea eastward. [4] Then your border shall change direction from the south to the ascent of Akrabbim and continue to Zin, and its termination shall be to the south of ^Kadeshbarnea; and it shall reach Hazaraddar and continue to Azmon. [5] Then the border shall change direction from Azmon to the brook

33:40 ^Num 21:1   33:43 ^Num 21:10, 11
33:47 ^Num 27:12   33:48 ^Num 22:1   33:49 ^Num 25:1
33:51 ^Josh 3:17   33:52 ^Deut 7:5; Ps 106:34-36
33:53 ^Deut 11:31; Josh 21:43   33:54 ^Num 26:53-56
33:55 ^Josh 23:13   34:2 ^Gen 17:8; Ps 78:54, 55
34:3 ^Josh 15:1-3   34:4 ^Num 32:8

of Egypt, and its termination shall be *at* ᴬthe sea.

⁶'As for the western border, you shall have the Great Sea, that is, *its* coastline; this shall be your western border.

⁷ᴬAnd this shall be your northern border: you shall draw your boundary from the Great Sea to Mount Hor. ⁸You shall draw a boundary from Mount Hor to ᴬthe Lebohamath, and the termination of the border shall be at Zedad; ⁹and the border shall proceed to Ziphron, and its termination shall be at Hazar-enan. This shall be your northern border.

¹⁰'For your eastern border you shall also draw a boundary from Hazar-enan to Shepham, ¹¹and the border shall go down from Shepham to ᴬRiblah on the east *side* of Ain; and the border shall go down and reach to the slope on the east side of the Sea of ᴮChinnereth. ¹²And the border shall go down to the Jordan, and its termination shall be at the Salt Sea. This shall be your land according to its borders on all sides.'"

¹³So Moses commanded the sons of Israel, saying, "ᴬThis is the land that you are to possess by lot, which the Lᴏʀᴅ has commanded to give to the nine and a half tribes. ¹⁴ᴬFor the tribe of the sons of Reuben have received *theirs* according to their fathers' households, and the tribe of the sons of Gad according to their fathers' households, and the half-tribe of Manasseh have received their possession. ¹⁵The two and a half tribes have received their possession across the Jordan *opposite* Jericho, eastward toward the sunrise."

¹⁶Then the Lᴏʀᴅ spoke to Moses, saying, ¹⁷ᴬThese are the names of the men who shall assign the land

to you as an inheritance: Eleazar the priest, and Joshua the son of Nun. ¹⁸And you shall take one leader of each tribe to assign the land as an inheritance. ¹⁹These are the names of the men: of the tribe of Judah, ᴬCaleb the son of Jephunneh. ²⁰Of the tribe of the sons of ᴬSimeon, Samuel the son of Ammihud. ²¹Of the tribe of ᴬBenjamin, Elidad the son of Chislon. ²²And of the tribe of the sons of Dan, a leader, Bukki the son of Jogli. ²³Of the sons of Joseph: of the tribe of the sons of Manasseh, a leader, Hanniel the son of Ephod. ²⁴Of the tribe of the sons of Ephraim, a leader, Kemuel the son of Shiphtan. ²⁵Of the tribe of the sons of Zebulun, a leader, Elizaphan the son of Parnach. ²⁶Of the tribe of the sons of Issachar, a leader, Paltiel the son of Azzan. ²⁷Of the tribe of the sons of Asher, a leader, Ahihud the son of Shelomi. ²⁸Of the tribe of the sons of Naphtali, a leader, Pedahel the son of Ammihud." ²⁹These are the ones whom the Lᴏʀᴅ commanded to apportion the inheritance to the sons of Israel in the land of Canaan.

CITIES FOR THE LEVITES

35 ᴬNow the Lᴏʀᴅ spoke to Moses in the plains of Moab, by the Jordan *opposite* Jericho, saying, ²"Command the sons of Israel that they give to the Levites from the inheritance of their possession cities to live in; and you shall give to the Levites pasture lands around the cities. ³The cities shall be theirs

34:5 ᴬJosh 15:4   34:7 ᴬEzek 47:15-17   34:8 ᴬJosh 13:5
34:11 ᴬ2 Kin 23:33   ᴮDeut 3:17   34:13 ᴬDeut 11:24;
Josh 14:1-5   34:14 ᴬNum 32:33   34:17 ᴬJosh 14:1, 2
34:19 ᴬNum 13:6, 30; Deut 1:36   34:20 ᴬGen 29:33;
Ezek 48:24   34:21 ᴬDeut 33:12; Ps 68:27
35:1 ᴬLev 25:32-34

to live in; and their pasture lands shall be for their cattle and for their equipment and for all their *other* animals.

⁴"The pasture lands of the cities which you are to give to the Levites *shall extend* from the wall of the city outward a thousand cubits around. ⁵You shall also measure outside the city on the east side two thousand cubits, on the south side two thousand cubits, on the west side two thousand cubits, and on the north side two thousand cubits, with the city in the center. This shall become theirs as pasture lands for the cities.

CITIES OF REFUGE

⁶The cities which you shall give to the Levites *shall be* the ᴬsix cities of refuge, which you shall provide for the one who commits manslaughter to flee to; and in addition to them you shall give forty-two cities. ⁷The total *number* of the cities which you are to give to the Levites *shall be*ᴬforty-eight cities, together with their pasture lands. ⁸ᴬAs for the cities which you shall give *them* from the possession of the sons of Israel, you shall take more from the larger, and you shall take fewer from the smaller; each shall give some of his cities to the Levites in proportion to his inheritance which he possesses."

⁹Then the LORD spoke to Moses, saying, ¹⁰"ᴬSpeak to the sons of Israel and say to them, 'When you cross the Jordan into the land of Canaan, ¹¹then you shall select for yourselves cities to be your ᴬcities of refuge, so that the one who commits manslaughter *by* killing a person unintentionally may flee there. ¹²ᴬThe cities shall serve you as a refuge from the avenger, so that the one who commits manslaughter does not die until he stands before the congregation for trial. ¹³So the cities which you are to provide shall be six cities of refuge for you. ¹⁴You ᴬshall provide three cities across the Jordan, and three cities in the land of Canaan; they are to be cities of refuge. ¹⁵These six cities shall be a refuge for the sons of Israel, for the stranger, and for the foreign resident among them; so that anyone who kills a person ᴬunintentionally may flee there.

¹⁶'ᴬBut if he struck him with an iron object, so that he died, he is a murderer; the murderer must be put to death. ¹⁷And if he struck him with a stone in the hand, by which he would die, and *as a result* he did die, he is a murderer; the murderer ᴬmust be put to death. ¹⁸Or *if* he struck him with a wooden object in the hand, by which he would die, and *as a result* he did die, he is a murderer; the murderer must be put to death. ¹⁹The blood avenger himself shall put the murderer to death; he himself shall put him to death when he meets him. ²⁰Now ᴬif he pushed him in hatred, or he threw *something* at him ᴮwith malicious intent, and *as a result* he died, ²¹or *if* he struck him with his hand with hostility, and *as a result* he died, the one who struck him must be put to death; he is a murderer. The blood avenger shall put the murderer to death when he meets him.

²²'ᴬBut if he pushed him suddenly, without hostility, or threw any

35:6ᴬJosh 20:7-9   35:7ᴬJosh 21:41   35:8ᴬLev 25:32-34; Josh 21:1-42   35:10ᴬJosh 20:1-9   35:11ᴬJosh 20:2f   35:12ᴬDeut 19:4-6; Josh 20:2, 3   35:14ᴬDeut 4:41   35:15ᴬNum 35:11   35:16ᴬEx 21:12, 14; Lev 24:17   35:17ᴬNum 35:31   35:20ᴬGen 4:8   ᴮEx 21:14   35:22ᴬNum 35:11

object at him without malicious intent, 23or had any deadly stone, and without looking he dropped *it* on him so that he died, while he was not his enemy nor was he seeking to harm him, 24then ^the congregation shall judge between the one who fatally struck *the victim* and the blood avenger in accordance with these ordinances. 25And the congregation shall save the one who committed manslaughter from the hand of the blood avenger, and the congregation shall return him to his city of refuge to which he fled; and he shall live in it until the death of the high priest who was anointed with the holy oil. 26But if at any time he goes beyond the border of his city of refuge to which he flees, 27and the blood avenger finds him outside the border of his city of refuge, and the blood avenger kills him, he will not be guilty of bloodshed, 28because he should have remained in his city of refuge until the death of the high priest. But after the death of the high priest the one who committed manslaughter may return to the land of his property.

29'These things shall be a ^statutory ordinance for you throughout your generations in all your dwelling places.

30'*If* anyone kills a person, the murderer shall be put to death on the testimony of witnesses, but no person shall be put to death on the testimony of *only* one witness. 31Moreover, you shall not accept a ransom for the life of a murderer who is condemned to death, but he must be put to death. 32And you shall not accept a ransom for one who has fled to his city of refuge, so that he may return to live in the land before the death of the priest. 33^So you shall not defile the land in which you *live;* for blood defiles the land, and no atonement can be made for the land for the blood that is shed on it, except ᴮby the blood of the one who shed it. 34So you shall not ^defile the land in which you live, in the midst of which ᴮI dwell; for I the Lᴏʀᴅ am dwelling in the midst of the sons of Israel.'"

INHERITANCE BY MARRIAGE

36 ^Now the heads of the fathers' *households* of the family of the sons of Gilead, the son of Machir, the son of Manasseh, of the families of the sons of Joseph, came forward and spoke before Moses and before the leaders, the heads of the fathers' *households* of the sons of Israel, 2and they said, "The Lᴏʀᴅ commanded my lord to give the land by lot to the sons of Israel as an inheritance, and my lord ^was commanded by the Lᴏʀᴅ to give the inheritance of our brother Zelophehad to his daughters. 3But *if* they marry one of the sons of the *other* tribes of the sons of Israel, their inheritance will be withdrawn from the inheritance of our fathers and will be added to the inheritance of the tribe to which they belong; so it will be withdrawn from our allotted inheritance. 4And when the ^jubilee of the sons of Israel takes place, then their inheritance will be added to the inheritance of the tribe to which they belong; so their inheritance will be withdrawn from the inheritance of the tribe of our fathers."

35:24^Josh 20:6   35:29^Num 27:11
35:30^Num 35:16   35:33^Ps 106:38   ᴮGen 9:6
35:34^Lev 18:24, 25   ᴮNum 5:3   36:1^Num 27:1
36:2^Num 27:5-7   36:4^Lev 25:10

⁵Then Moses commanded the sons of Israel in accordance with the word of the LORD, saying, "The tribe of the sons of Joseph is right in *its* statements. ⁶ᴬThis is what the LORD has commanded regarding the daughters of Zelophehad, saying, 'Let them marry whomever they wish; only they must marry within the family of the tribe of their father.' ⁷So ᴬno inheritance of the sons of Israel will be transferred from tribe to tribe, for the sons of Israel shall each retain possession of the inheritance of the tribe of his fathers. ⁸ᴬAnd every daughter who comes into possession of an inheritance of *any* tribe of the sons of Israel shall marry one of the family of the tribe of her father, so that the sons of Israel may each possess the inheritance of his fathers. ⁹So

no inheritance will be transferred from one tribe to another tribe, for the tribes of the sons of Israel shall each retain possession of its own inheritance."

¹⁰Just as the LORD had commanded Moses, so the daughters of Zelophehad did: ¹¹ᴬMahlah, Tirzah, Hoglah, Milcah, and Noah, the daughters of Zelophehad married their uncles' sons. ¹²They married *those* from the families of the sons of Manasseh the son of Joseph, and their inheritance remained with the tribe of the family of their father.

¹³ᴬThese are the commandments and the ordinances which the LORD commanded to the sons of Israel through Moses in the plains of Moab, by the Jordan *opposite* Jericho.

36:6ᴬNum 27:7   36:7ᴬ1 Kin 21:3   36:8ᴬ1 Chr 23:22
36:11ᴬNum 26:33   36:13ᴬLev 26:46; Num 22:1

DEUTERONOMY

1 These are the words that Moses spoke to all Israel ^across the Jordan in the wilderness, in the ^BArabah opposite Suph, between Paran and Tophel, Laban, Hazeroth, and Dizahab. ²It is eleven days' *journey* from ^Horeb by way of Mount Seir to Kadesh-barnea. ³In the fortieth year, on the first *day* of the eleventh month, Moses spoke to the sons of Israel, ^in accordance with everything that the Lord had commanded him *to declare* to them, ⁴after he had ^defeated Sihon the king of the Amorites, who lived in Heshbon, and ^BOg the king of Bashan, who lived in Ashtaroth and in Edrei. ⁵Across the Jordan in the land of Moab, Moses began to explain this Law, saying,

⁶"The Lord our God ^spoke to us at Horeb, saying, 'You have stayed long enough at this mountain. ⁷Turn and set out on your journey, and go to ^the hill country of the Amorites, and to all their neighbors in the Arabah, in the hill country, in the lowland, in the ¹Negev, by the seacoast, the land of the Canaanites, and Lebanon, as far as the great river, the river Euphrates. ⁸See, I have placed the land before you; go in and take possession of the land which the Lord ^swore to give to your fathers, to Abraham, to Isaac, and to Jacob, and their descendants after them.'

⁹"And I spoke to you at that time, saying, '^I am not able to endure you alone. ¹⁰The Lord your God has ^multiplied you, and behold, you are this day like the stars of heaven in number. ¹¹May the Lord, the God of your fathers increase you a thousand times more than you are, and bless you, ^just as He has promised you! ¹²How can I alone endure the burden and weight of you and your strife? ¹³^Obtain for yourselves men who are wise, discerning, and informed from your tribes, and I will appoint them as your heads.' ¹⁴And you answered me and said, 'The thing which you have said to do is good.' ¹⁵So I took the heads of your tribes, wise and informed men, and appointed them as heads over you, commanders of thousands, hundreds, fifties, and tens, and officers for your tribes.

¹⁶"Then I ordered your judges at that time, saying, 'Hear *the cases* between your fellow countrymen and ^judge righteously between a person and his fellow countryman, or the stranger who is with him. ¹⁷You are not to show partiality in judgment; you shall hear the small and the great alike. You are ^not to be afraid of any person, for the judgment is God's. ^BThe case that is too difficult for you, you shall bring to me, and I will hear it.' ¹⁸At that time ^I commanded you all the things that you were to do.

1:1 ^Deut 4:46   ^BDeut 2:8   1:2 ^Ex 3:1; 17:6
1:3 ^Deut 4:1, 2   1:4 ^Num 21:21-26   ^BNum 21:33-35
1:6 ^Num 10:11-13   1:7 ^Gen 15:18; Deut 11:24
1:8 ^Gen 12:7; 26:3   1:9 ^Ex 18:18, 24; Num 11:14
1:10 ^Gen 15:5; 22:17   1:11 ^Deut 1:8, 10
1:13 ^Ex 18:21   1:16 ^Deut 16:18; John 7:24
1:17 ^Prov 29:25   ^BEx 18:22, 26   1:18 ^Ex 18:20

1:7 ¹I.e., South country

¹⁹"Then we set out from ᴬHoreb, and went *through* all that great and terrible wilderness that you saw on the way to the hill country of the Amorites, just as the LORD our God had commanded us; and we came to ᴬKadesh-barnea. ²⁰And I said to you, 'You have come to the hill country of the Amorites, which the LORD our God is about to give us. ²¹See, the LORD your God has placed the land before you; go up, take possession, just as the LORD, the God of your fathers, has spoken to you. ᴬDo not fear or be dismayed.'

²²"ᴬThen all of you approached me and said, 'Let us send men ahead of us, so that they may spy out the land for us, and bring back to us word of the way by which we should go up, and the cities which we should enter.' ²³The plan pleased me, and I took twelve of your men, one man for each tribe. ²⁴Then ᴬthey turned and went up into the hill country, and came to the Valley of Eshcol, and spied it out. ²⁵And they took *some* of the fruit of the land in their hands and brought it down to us. They also brought us back a report and said, 'The land that the LORD our God is about to give us is good.'

²⁶"ᴬYet you were unwilling to go up; instead you rebelled against the command of the LORD your God; ²⁷and ᴬyou grumbled in your tents and said, 'Because the LORD hates us, He has brought us out of the land of Egypt, to hand us over to the Amorites to destroy us. ²⁸Where can we go up? Our brothers have made our hearts melt, *by* saying, "The people are bigger and taller than we; the cities are large and fortified *up* to heaven. And besides, we saw ᴬthe sons of the Anakim there."' ²⁹But I said to you, 'Do not be terrified, nor fear them. ³⁰The LORD your God, who goes before you, will ᴬHimself fight for you, just as He did for you in Egypt before your eyes, ³¹and in the wilderness where you saw how ᴬthe LORD your God carried you, just as a man carries his son, on all of the road which you have walked until you came to this place.' ³²Yet ᴬin spite of all this, you did not trust the LORD your God, ³³ᴬwho goes before you on *your* way, ᴮto seek out a place for you to make camp, in the fire by night to show you the way by which you should go, and in the cloud by day.

³⁴"Then the LORD heard the sound of your words, and He was angry and ᴬswore an oath, saying, ³⁵'ᴬNot one of these men, this evil generation, shall see the good land which I swore to give your fathers, ³⁶except Caleb the son of Jephunneh; he shall see it, and ᴬto him I will give the land on which he has set foot, and to his sons, because he has followed the LORD fully.' ³⁷The LORD was angry with me also on your account, saying, 'ᴬNot even you shall enter there. ³⁸Joshua the son of Nun, who stands before you, ᴬshall himself enter there; encourage him, for he will give it to Israel as an inheritance. ³⁹Moreover, ᴬyour little ones who, you said, would become plunder, and your sons, who this day have ᴮno knowledge of good and evil, shall enter

1:19ᴬDeut 1:2   1:21ᴬJosh 1:6, 9   1:22ᴬNum 13:1-3
1:24ᴬNum 13:21-25   1:26ᴬNum 14:1-4
1:27ᴬDeut 9:28; Ps 106:25   1:28ᴬNum 13:28, 33;
Deut 9:2   1:30ᴬEx 14:14; Deut 3:22   1:31ᴬDeut
32:10-12; Is 46:3, 4   1:32ᴬNum 14:11; Ps 106:24
1:33ᴬEx 13:21   ᴮNum 10:33   1:34ᴬNum 14:28-30;
Heb 3:18   1:35ᴬPs 95:11; 106:26   1:36ᴬNum 14:24;
Josh 14:9   1:37ᴬNum 27:13, 18   1:38ᴬNum 14:30
1:39ᴬNum 14:3, 31   ᴮIs 7:15, 16

there, and I will give it to them and they shall take possession of it. [40]But as for you, ^turn around and set out for the wilderness by the way of the Red Sea.'

[41]"^Then you replied to me, 'We have sinned against the LORD; we ourselves will go up and fight, just as the LORD our God commanded us.' And every man of you strapped on his weapons of war, and you viewed it as easy to go up into the hill country. [42]^But the LORD said to me, 'Say to them, "Do not go up nor fight, for I am not among you; otherwise you will be defeated by your enemies."' [43]So I spoke to you, but you would not listen. Instead, ^you rebelled against the command of the LORD, and acted presumptuously and went up into the hill country. [44]^And the Amorites who lived in that hill country came out against you and chased you as bees do, and they scattered you from Seir to Hormah. [45]Then you returned and wept before the LORD; but the ^LORD did not listen to your voice, nor pay attention to you. [46]So you remained at ^Kadesh for many days, the days that you spent *there*.

WANDERINGS IN THE WILDERNESS

2 "^Then we turned and set out for the wilderness by the way of the Red Sea, as the LORD spoke to me, and we circled Mount Seir for many days. [2]And the LORD spoke to me, saying, [3]'You have circled this mountain long enough. *Now* turn north, [4]and command the people, saying, "You are going to pass through the ^territory of your brothers the sons of Esau, who live in Seir; and ^they will be afraid of you. So be very careful; [5]do not provoke them, for I will not give you

any of their land, *not even* as much as a footprint, ^because I have given Mount Seir to Esau as a possession. [6]You are to buy food from them with money so that you may eat, and you shall also purchase water from them with money so that you may drink. [7]For the LORD your God has blessed you in all that you have done; He has known your wandering through this great wilderness. These ^forty years the LORD your God has been with you; you have not lacked anything."'

[8]"So we passed beyond our brothers the sons of Esau, who live in Seir, away from the Arabah road, away from Elath and ^Ezion-geber. And we turned and passed through by the way of the wilderness of Moab. [9]Then the LORD said to me, 'Do not attack Moab, nor provoke them to war, for I will not give you any of their land as a possession, because I have given Ar to ^the sons of Lot as a possession.' [10](The ^Emim lived there previously, a people as great, numerous, and tall as the Anakim. [11]Like the Anakim, they too are regarded as ^Rephaim, but the Moabites call them Emim. [12]^The Horites previously lived in Seir, but the sons of Esau dispossessed them and destroyed them from before 'them, and settled in their place; just as Israel did to the land of their possession which the LORD gave them.) [13]'Now arise and cross over the Wadi Zered

1:40 ^Num 14:25   1:41 ^Num 14:40
1:42 ^Num 14:41-43   1:43 ^Num 14:40
1:44 ^Num 14:45   1:45 ^Job 27:8, 9; Ps 66:18
1:46 ^Num 20:1, 22; Deut 2:7, 14   2:1 ^Num 21:4
2:4 ^Gen 36:8   ^Ex 15:15, 16   2:5 ^Gen 36:8; Josh 24:4
2:7 ^Num 14:33, 34; 32:13   2:8 ^Num 33:35; 1 Kin 9:26
2:9 ^Gen 19:36, 37   2:10 ^Gen 14:5   2:11 ^Gen 14:5;
Deut 2:20   2:12 ^Gen 36:20; Deut 2:22

2:12 ¹ I.e., the sons of Esau

yourselves.' So we crossed over the Wadi Zered. ¹⁴Now the time that it took for us to come from Kadesh-barnea until we crossed over the Wadi Zered was thirty-eight years, until ^all the generation of the men of war perished from within the camp, just as the Lᴏʀᴅ had sworn to them. ¹⁵^Indeed, the hand of the Lᴏʀᴅ was against them, to destroy them from within the camp until they all perished.

¹⁶"So it came about, when ^all the men of war had finally perished from among the people, ¹⁷that the Lᴏʀᴅ spoke to me, saying, ¹⁸'Today you shall cross over ^Ar, the border of Moab. ¹⁹When you come opposite the ^sons of Ammon, do not attack them nor provoke them, for I will not give you any of the land of the sons of Ammon as a possession, because I have given it to ᴮthe sons of Lot as a possession.' ²⁰(It is also regarded as the land of the ^Rephaim, *because the* Rephaim previously lived in it, but the Ammonites call them Zamzummin, ²¹a people as great, numerous, and tall as the Anakim; but the Lᴏʀᴅ destroyed them before ¹them. And they dispossessed them and settled in their place, ²²just as He did for the sons of Esau, who live in Seir, when He destroyed ^the Horites from before them; they dispossessed them and settled in their place, *where they remain* even to this day. ²³And *as for* the ^Avvim, who lived in villages as far as Gaza, the ¹Caphtorim, who came from ²Caphtor, destroyed them and lived in their place.) ²⁴'Arise, set out, and pass through the ^Valley of Arnon. Look! I have handed over to you Sihon the Amorite, king of Heshbon, and his land; start taking possession and

plunge into battle with him. ²⁵This day I will begin to put ^the dread and fear of you upon the faces of people everywhere, who, when they hear the news of you, will tremble and be in anguish because of you.'

²⁶"^So I sent messengers from the wilderness of Kedemoth to Sihon king of Heshbon with words of peace, saying, ²⁷'Let me pass through your land; I will travel only on the road. I will not turn aside to the right or to the left. ²⁸You will sell me food for money so that I may eat, and give me water for money so that I may drink, ^only let me pass through on foot, ²⁹just as the sons of Esau who live in Seir and the Moabites who live in ^Ar did for me, until I cross over the Jordan into the land that the Lᴏʀᴅ our God is giving us.' ³⁰But ^Sihon king of Heshbon was not willing for us to pass through his land; for the Lᴏʀᴅ your God hardened his spirit and made his heart obstinate, in order to hand him over to you, as *he is* today. ³¹And the Lᴏʀᴅ said to me, 'See, I have begun to turn Sihon and his land over to you. Begin taking possession, so that you may possess his land.'

³²"Then Sihon came out with all his people to meet us in battle at Jahaz. ³³And the Lᴏʀᴅ our God turned him over to us, and we ^defeated him with his sons and all his people. ³⁴So we captured all his cities at that time and ^utterly

2:14 ^Num 14:29-35; 26:64, 65   2:15 ^Jude 5
2:16 ^Deut 2:14   2:18 ^Deut 2:9   2:19 ^Gen 19:38
ᴮDeut 2:9   2:20 ^Deut 2:11   2:22 ^Deut 2:12
2:23 ^Josh 13:3   2:24 ^Num 21:13, 14; Judg 11:18
2:25 ^Ex 23:27; Deut 11:25   2:26 ^Num 21:21-32;
Deut 1:4   2:28 ^Num 20:19   2:29 ^Deut 2:9
2:30 ^Num 21:23   2:33 ^Deut 29:7   2:34 ^Deut 3:6; 7:2

2:21 ¹I.e., the Ammonites   2:23 ¹I.e., Philistines
²I.e., Crete

destroyed the men, women, and children of every city. We left no survivor. [35] We took ^only the animals as our plunder, and the spoils of the cities which we had captured. [36] From ^Aroer which is on the edge of the Valley of Arnon and *from* the city which is in the valley, even to Gilead, there was no city that was too high for us; the LORD our God turned it all over to us. [37] ^Only you did not go near the land of the sons of Ammon, all along the river Jabbok and the cities of the hill country, and wherever the LORD our God had commanded us *to avoid.*

CONQUESTS RECOUNTED

3 [1] "^Then we turned and went up the road to Bashan, and Og, king of Bashan, came out with all his people to meet us in battle at Edrei. [2] But the LORD said to me, 'Do not fear him, for I have handed him and all his people and his land over to you; and you shall do to him just as you did to Sihon king of the Amorites, who lived in Heshbon.' [3] So the LORD our God also handed over to us Og, king of Bashan, with all his people, and we struck them until no survivor was left. [4] We captured all his cities at that time; there was not a city which we did not take from them: sixty cities, all the region of ^Argob, the kingdom of Og in Bashan. [5] All these were cities fortified with high walls, gates, and bars, besides a great many unwalled towns. [6] We utterly destroyed them, as we did to ^Sihon king of Heshbon, [8] utterly destroying the men, women, and children of every city. [7] ^But all the animals and the spoils of the cities we took as our plunder.

[8] "^So at that time we took the land from the hand of the two kings of the Amorites who were beyond the Jordan, from the Valley of Arnon to Mount Hermon [9] (Sidonians call Hermon ^Sirion, and the Amorites call it [8] Senir): [10] all the cities of the plateau, all Gilead, and ^all Bashan, as far as Salecah and Edrei, cities of the kingdom of Og in Bashan. [11] (For only Og king of Bashan was left of the remnant of the ^Rephaim. Behold, his bed was a bed of iron; it is in Rabbah of the sons of Ammon. Its length was nine cubits, and its width four cubits by the usual cubit.)

[12] "So we took possession of this land at that time. From ^Aroer, which is by the Valley of Arnon, and half the hill country of [8] Gilead and its cities I gave to the Reubenites and to the Gadites. [13] The rest of Gilead and all Bashan, the kingdom of Og, I gave to the half-tribe of Manasseh, all the region of Argob. (As to all Bashan, it is called the land of Rephaim. [14] ^Jair the son of Manasseh took all the region of Argob as far as the border of the Geshurites and the Maacathites, *that is,* Bashan, and named it after his own name: Havvoth-jair, *as it is* to this day.) [15] ^To Machir I gave Gilead. [16] To the Reubenites and the Gadites I gave from Gilead even as far as the Valley of Arnon, the middle of the valley as a border, and as far as the river ^Jabbok, the border of the sons of Ammon; [17] the Arabah also, with the Jordan as a

2:35 ^Deut 3:7   2:36 ^Deut 3:12; 4:48   2:37 ^Deut 2:19
3:1 ^Num 21:33-35   3:4 ^Deut 3:13, 14; 1 Kin 4:13
3:6 ^Deut 1:4   [8] Deut 2:34   3:7 ^Deut 2:35
3:8 ^Num 32:33; Josh 12:1-7   3:9 ^Ps 29:6   [8] 1 Chr 5:23
3:10 ^Josh 13:11   3:11 ^Gen 14:5; Deut 2:11, 20
3:12 ^Deut 2:36   [8] Num 32:32-38   3:14 ^Num 32:41;
1 Chr 2:22   3:15 ^Num 32:39, 40
3:16 ^Num 21:24; Deut 2:37

border, from [1A]Chinnereth even as far as the sea of the Arabah, the Salt Sea, at the foot of the slopes of Pisgah on the east.

[18]"Then I commanded you at that time, saying, '[A]The LORD your God has given you this land to possess it; all you valiant men shall cross over armed ahead of your brothers, the sons of Israel. [19A]However, your wives, your little ones, and your livestock (I know that you have [B]much livestock) shall remain in your cities which I have given you, [20A]until the LORD gives rest to your fellow countrymen as to you, and they also take possession of the land which the LORD your God is giving them beyond the Jordan. Then you may return, each man to his possession which I have given you.' [21]And I commanded Joshua at that time, saying, 'Your eyes have seen everything that the LORD your God has done to these two kings; the LORD will do the same to all the kingdoms into which you are about to cross. [22]Do not fear them, for the LORD your God [A]is the One fighting for you.'

[23]"I also pleaded with the LORD at that time, saying, [24]'Lord GOD, You have begun to show Your servant [A]Your greatness and Your strong hand; for what god *is there* in heaven or on earth who can do such works and mighty acts as Yours? [25]Please let me cross over and see the [A]good land that is beyond the Jordan, that good hill country, and Lebanon.' [26]But [A]the LORD was angry with me on your account, and would not listen to me; instead, the LORD said to me, 'Enough! Do not speak to Me any more about this matter. [27]Go up to the top of [A]Pisgah and raise your eyes to the west, the north,

the south, and the east, and see *it* with your eyes; for you shall not cross over this Jordan. [28A]But commission Joshua and encourage him and strengthen him, for he shall go across leading this people, and he will give to them, as an inheritance, the land which you will see.' [29]So we remained in the valley opposite [A]Beth-peor.

ISRAEL URGED TO OBEY GOD'S LAW

4 "Now, Israel, listen to the statutes and the judgments which I am teaching you to perform, so that [A]you will live and go in and take possession of the land which the LORD, the God of your fathers, is giving you. [2A]You shall not add to the word which I am commanding you, nor take away from it, so that you may keep the commandments of the LORD your God which I am commanding you. [3A]Your eyes have seen what the LORD has done in the case of Baal-peor, for all the men who followed Baal-peor, the LORD your God has destroyed them from among you. [4]But you who clung to the LORD your God are alive today, every one of you.

[5]"See, I have taught you statutes and judgments [A]just as the LORD my God commanded me, that you are to do these things in the land where you are entering to take possession of it. [6]So keep and do *them*, [A]for that is your wisdom and your understanding in the sight of the peoples

3:17 [A]Num 34:11; Josh 13:27   3:18 [A]Josh 1:13
3:19 [A]Josh 1:14   [B]Num 32:1   3:20 [A]Josh 1:15
3:22 [A]Ex 14:14; Deut 1:30   3:24 [A]Deut 11:2
3:25 [A]Deut 4:22   3:26 [A]Deut 1:37   3:27 [A]Num 23:14;
27:12   3:28 [A]Num 27:18; Deut 31:3, 7, 8, 23
3:29 [A]Num 25:1–3; Deut 4:46   4:1 [A]Lev 18:5; Deut 5:33
4:2 [A]Deut 12:32; Prov 30:6   4:3 [A]Num 25:1–9
4:5 [A]Lev 26:46; 27:34   4:6 [A]Deut 30:19, 20; 32:46, 47

3:17 [1] I.e., the Sea of Galilee

who will hear all these statutes and say, 'Surely this great nation is a wise and understanding people.' [7]For what great nation *is there* that has a god ^so near to it as is the LORD our God whenever we call on Him? [8]Or what great nation *is there* that has ^statutes and judgments as righteous as this whole Law which I am setting before you today?

[9]"Only ^be careful for yourself and watch over your soul diligently, so that you do not forget the things which your eyes have seen and they do not depart from your heart all the days of your life; but [B]make them known to your sons and your grandsons. [10]*Remember* the day you stood before the LORD your God at Horeb, when the LORD said to me, 'Assemble the people to Me, that I may have them hear My words ^so that they may learn to fear Me all the days that they live on the earth, and that they may teach their children.' [11]You came forward and stood at the foot of the mountain, ^and the mountain was burning with fire to the heart of the heavens: darkness, cloud, and thick gloom. [12]Then the LORD spoke to you from the midst of the fire; you heard the sound of words, but you saw no form—*there was* only a voice. [13]So He declared to you His covenant which He commanded you to perform, *that is,* ^the Ten Commandments; and He wrote them on two tablets of stone. [14]The LORD commanded me at that time to teach you statutes and judgments, so that you would perform them in the land where you are going over to take possession of it.

[15]"So ^be very careful yourselves, since you did not see any form on the day the LORD spoke to you at Horeb from the midst of the fire, [16]so that you do not act corruptly and ^make a carved image for yourselves in the form of any figure, a representation of male or female, [17]a representation of any animal that is on the earth, a representation of ^any winged bird that flies in the sky, [18]a representation of anything that crawls on the ground, *or* a representation of any fish that is in the water below the earth. [19]And *be careful* not to raise your eyes to heaven and look at the sun, the moon, and the stars, all the heavenly lights, ^and *allow yourself* to be drawn away and worship them and serve them, *things* which the LORD your God has allotted to all the peoples under the whole heaven. [20]But the LORD has taken you and brought you out of ^the iron furnace, from Egypt, to be a people of His own possession, as today.

[21]"^Now the LORD was angry with me on your account, and He swore that I would not cross the Jordan, and that I would not enter the good land which the LORD your God is giving you as an inheritance. [22]For ^I am going to die in this land; I am not crossing the Jordan, but you are going to cross, and you will take possession of this [B]good land. [23]So be careful yourselves, ^that you do not forget the covenant of the LORD your God which He made with you, and make for yourselves a carved image in the form of anything *against* which the LORD your

4:7 ^Ps 34:17, 18; 145:18   4:8 ^Ps 89:14; 97:2
4:9 ^Deut 4:23   ᴮGen 18:19   4:10 ^Deut 14:23
4:11 ^Ex 19:18; Heb 12:18, 19   4:13 ^Ex 34:28;
Deut 10:4   4:15 ^Josh 23:11   4:16 ^Ex 20:4; Lev 26:1
4:17 ^Rom 1:23   4:19 ^Deut 13:5, 10; Job 31:26-28
4:20 ^1 Kin 8:51; Jer 11:4   4:21 ^Num 20:12; Deut 1:37
4:22 ^Num 27:13, 14   ᴮDeut 3:25   4:23 ^Deut 4:9

God has commanded you. ²⁴For the LORD your God is a ^consuming fire, a jealous God.

²⁵"When you father children and *have* grandchildren, and you grow old in the land, and you ^act corruptly, and ᴮmake an idol in the form of anything, and do what is evil in the sight of the LORD your God to provoke Him to anger, ²⁶I call heaven and earth as witnesses against you today, that you will ^certainly perish quickly from the land where you are going over the Jordan to take possession of it. You will not live long on it, but will be utterly destroyed. ²⁷The LORD will ^scatter you among the peoples, and you will be left few in number among the nations where the LORD drives you. ²⁸^There you will serve gods, the work of human hands, wood and stone, which neither see nor hear, nor eat nor smell *anything.* ²⁹But from there you will seek the LORD your God, and you will find *Him* if you search for Him ^with all your heart and all your soul. ³⁰When you are in distress and all these things happen to you, in the latter days ^you will return to the LORD your God and listen to His voice. ³¹For the LORD your God is a ^compassionate God; He will not abandon you nor destroy you, nor forget the covenant with your fathers which He swore to them.

³²"Indeed, ^ask now about the earlier days that were before your time, since the day that God created mankind on the earth, and *inquire* from one end of the heavens to the other. Has *anything* been done like this great thing, or has *anything* been heard like it? ³³^Has *any* people heard the voice of God speaking from the midst of the fire, as you have heard *it,* and survived? ³⁴Or has a god ventured to go to take for himself a nation from within *another* nation ^by trials, by signs and wonders, by war, ᴮby a mighty hand, by an outstretched arm, and by great terrors, just as the LORD your God did for you in Egypt before your eyes? ³⁵You were shown *these things* so that you might know that the LORD, He is God; ^there is no other besides Him. ³⁶Out of the heavens He let you hear His voice ^to discipline you; and on earth He let you see His great fire, and you heard His words from the midst of the fire. ³⁷Because He loved your fathers, He chose their descendants after them. And He ^personally brought you from Egypt by His great power, ³⁸driving out from before you nations greater and mightier than you, to bring you in *and* ^to give you their land as an inheritance, as *it is* today. ³⁹Therefore know today, and take it to your heart, that ^the LORD, He is God in heaven above and on the earth below; there is no other. ⁴⁰So you shall keep His statutes and His commandments which I am giving you today, so that ^it may go well for you and for your children after you, and that you may live long on the land which the LORD your God is giving you for all time."

⁴¹^Then Moses set apart three cities across the Jordan to the east, ⁴²for one to flee there who

4:24 ^Ex 24:17; Deut 9:3   4:25 ^Deut 4:16   ᴮDeut 4:23
4:26 ^Deut 7:4; 8:19, 20   4:27 ^Lev 26:33; Deut 28:64
4:28 ^Deut 28:36, 64; Jer 16:13   4:29 ^Deut 6:5; 10:12
4:30 ^Jer 4:1, 2   4:31 ^Ex 34:6; 2 Chr 30:9
4:32 ^Deut 32:7; Job 8:8   4:33 ^Ex 20:22; Deut 5:24, 26
4:34 ^Deut 7:19   ᴮDeut 5:15   4:35 ^Ex 8:10; 9:14
4:36 ^Deut 8:5   4:37 ^Ex 33:14; Is 63:9
4:38 ^Num 32:4; 34:14, 15   4:39 ^Deut 4:35; Josh 2:11
4:40 ^Deut 4:1; 5:16, 29, 33   4:41 ^Num 35:6;
Deut 19:2-13

unintentionally killed his neighbor, without having hatred for him in time past; and by fleeing to one of these cities he might live: [43]^A Bezer in the wilderness on the plateau for the Reubenites, Ramoth in Gilead for the Gadites, and Golan in Bashan for the Manassites.

[44] Now this is the Law which Moses set before the sons of Israel; [45] these are the testimonies and the statutes, and the ordinances which Moses spoke to the sons of Israel, when they came out of Egypt, [46] across the Jordan, in the valley ^A opposite Beth-peor, in the land of ^B Sihon king of the Amorites who lived in Heshbon, whom Moses and the sons of Israel defeated when they came out of Egypt. [47] And they took possession of his land and the land of ^A Og king of Bashan, the two kings of the Amorites, who *were* across the Jordan to the east, [48] from ^A Aroer, which is on the edge of the Valley of Arnon, even as far as ^B Mount Sion (that is, Hermon), [49] with all the Arabah across the Jordan to the east, even as far as the sea of the Arabah, at the foot of the slopes of Pisgah.

THE TEN COMMANDMENTS REPEATED

5 Now Moses summoned all Israel and said to them:

"Listen, Israel, to the statutes and ordinances which I am speaking today for you to hear, so that you may learn them and be careful to do them. [2] The LORD our God made ^A a covenant with us at Horeb. [3] ^A The LORD did not make this covenant with our fathers, but with us, all of us who are alive here today. [4] The LORD spoke with you face to face at the mountain ^A from the midst of the fire, [5] *while* ^A I was standing between the LORD and you at that time, to declare to you the word of the LORD; for you were afraid because of the fire, and you did not go up on the mountain. He said,

[6] '^A I am the LORD your God who brought you out of the land of Egypt, out of the house of slavery.

[7] '^A You shall have no other gods besides Me.

[8] '^A You shall not make for yourself a carved image, *or* any likeness *of* what is in heaven above or on the earth beneath or in the water under the earth. [9] You shall not worship them nor serve them; for I, the LORD your God, am a jealous God, ^A inflicting the [1] punishment of the fathers on the children, even on the third and fourth *generations* of those who hate Me, [10] but ^A showing favor to thousands, to those who love Me and keep My commandments.

[11] '^A You shall not take the name of the LORD your God in vain, for the LORD will not leave unpunished the one who takes His name in vain.

[12] '^A Keep the Sabbath day to treat it as holy, as the LORD your God commanded you. [13] For six days you shall labor and do all your work, [14] but ^A the seventh day is a Sabbath of the LORD your God; you shall not do any work *that day*, you or your son or your daughter, or your male slave or your female slave, or your ox, your donkey, or any of your cattle, or your resident who stays with you, so that your male slave and your female slave may rest as well

4:43 ^A Josh 20:8   4:46 ^A Deut 3:29   ^B Num 21:21-25
4:47 ^A Deut 1:4; 3:3, 4   4:48 ^A Deut 2:36   ^B Deut 3:9
5:2 ^A Ex 19:5; Mal 4:4   5:3 ^A Jer 31:32; Heb 8:9
5:4 ^A Deut 4:33   5:5 ^A Gal 3:19   5:6 ^A Ex 20:2-17;
Lev 26:1   5:7 ^A Ex 20:3   5:8 ^A Ex 20:4-6; Lev 26:1
5:9 ^A Ex 34:7; Num 14:18   5:10 ^A Num 14:18; Deut 7:9
5:11 ^A Ex 20:7; Lev 19:12   5:12 ^A Ex 16:23-30; 20:8-11
5:14 ^A Gen 2:2; Heb 4:4
5:9 [1] I.e., punishment for the wrongdoing

as you. ¹⁵ᴬAnd you shall remember that you were a slave in the land of Egypt, and the Lord your God brought you out of there by a mighty hand and an outstretched arm; therefore the Lord your God commanded you to celebrate the Sabbath day.

¹⁶ᴬHonor your father and your mother, just as the Lord your God has commanded you, ᴮso that your days may be prolonged and that it may go well for you on the land which the Lord your God is giving you.

¹⁷ᴬYou shall not murder.

¹⁸ᴬYou shall not commit adultery.

¹⁹ᴬYou shall not steal.

²⁰ᴬYou shall not give false testimony against your neighbor.

²¹ᴬYou shall not covet your neighbor's wife, nor desire your neighbor's house, his field, his male slave or his female slave, his ox, his donkey, or anything that belongs to your neighbor.'

MOSES INTERCEDED

²²"These words the Lord spoke to your whole assembly at the mountain from the midst of the fire, *from* the cloud, and *from* the thick darkness, with a great voice, and He added nothing more. ᴬHe wrote them on two tablets of stone and gave them to me. ²³And when you heard the voice from the midst of the darkness, while the mountain was burning with fire, you approached me, all the heads of your tribes and your elders. ²⁴You said, 'Behold, the Lord our God has shown us His glory and His greatness, and we have heard His voice from the midst of the fire; we have seen today that God speaks with mankind, yet he lives. ²⁵ᴬNow then,

why should we die? For this great fire will consume us; if we hear the voice of the Lord our God any longer, then we will die! ²⁶For ᴬwho *is there* of humanity who has heard the voice of the living God speaking from the midst of the fire, as we *have,* and lived? ²⁷Go near and listen to everything that the Lord our God says; then speak to us everything that the Lord our God speaks to you, and we will listen and do *it.*'

²⁸"Now the Lord heard the sound of your words when you spoke to me, ᴬand the Lord said to me, 'I have heard the sound of the words of this people which they have spoken to you. They have done well in all that they have spoken. ²⁹ᴬIf only they had such a heart in them, to fear Me and keep all My commandments always, so that it would go well with them and with their sons forever! ³⁰Go, say to them, "Return to your tents." ³¹ᴬBut as for you, stand here by Me, that I may speak to you all the commandments, the statutes, and the judgments which you shall teach them, so that they may follow *them* in the land which I am giving them to possess.' ³²So you shall be careful to do just as the Lord your God has commanded you; ᴬyou shall not turn aside to the right or to the left. ³³ᴬYou shall walk entirely in the way which the Lord your God has commanded you, so that you may live and that it may be well for you, and that you may prolong *your* days in the land which you will possess.

5:15ᴬEx 20:11   5:16ᴬEx 20:12   ᴮDeut 4:40
5:17ᴬGen 9:6; Ex 20:13   5:18ᴬEx 20:14; Lev 20:10
5:19ᴬEx 20:15; Lev 19:11   5:20ᴬEx 20:16; Matt 19:18
5:21ᴬEx 20:17; Rom 7:7   5:22ᴬEx 24:12; 31:18
5:25ᴬEx 20:18, 19; Deut 18:16   5:26ᴬDeut 4:33
5:28ᴬDeut 18:17   5:29ᴬPs 81:13; Is 48:18
5:31ᴬEx 24:12   5:32ᴬDeut 17:20; 28:14
5:33ᴬDeut 10:12; Jer 7:23

OBEY GOD AND PROSPER

6 "Now this is the commandment, the statutes, and the judgments which the LORD your God has commanded *me* to teach you, so that you may do *them* in the land where you are going over to take possession of it, ²so that you, your son, and your grandson will ^fear the LORD your God, to keep all His statutes and His commandments which I command you, ᴮall the days of your life, and that your days may be prolonged. ³Now Israel, you shall listen and be careful to do *them,* so that it may go well for you and that you may increase greatly, just as the LORD, the God of your fathers, has promised you, *in* ^a land flowing with milk and honey.

⁴"Hear, Israel! The LORD is our God, the ^LORD is one! ⁵And ^you shall love the LORD your God ᴮwith all your heart and with all your soul and with all your strength. ⁶^These words, which I am commanding you today, shall be on your heart. ⁷And ^you shall repeat them diligently to your sons and speak of them when you sit in your house, when you walk on the road, when you lie down, and when you get up. ⁸^You shall also tie them as a sign to your hand, and they shall be as frontlets on your forehead. ⁹^You shall also write them on the doorposts of your house and on your gates.

¹⁰"Then it shall come about when the LORD your God brings you into the land that He swore to your fathers, to Abraham, Isaac, and Jacob, to give you, ^great and splendid cities which you did not build, ¹¹and houses full of all good things which you did not fill, and carved cisterns which you did not carve out, vineyards and olive trees which you did not plant, and ^you eat and are satisfied, ¹²be careful that ^you do not forget the LORD who brought you out of the land of Egypt, out of the house of slavery. ¹³^You shall fear *only* the LORD your God; and you shall worship Him and swear by His name. ¹⁴^You shall not follow other gods, any of the gods of the peoples who surround you, ¹⁵for the LORD your God *who is* in the midst of you is a ^jealous God; *so follow Him,* or else the anger of the LORD your God will be kindled against you, and He will wipe you off the face of the earth.

¹⁶"^You shall not put the LORD your God to the test, ᴮas you tested *Him* at Massah. ¹⁷^You shall diligently keep the commandments of the LORD your God, and His provisions and His statutes which He has commanded you. ¹⁸You shall do what is right and good in the sight of the LORD, so that ^it may go well for you and that you may go in and take possession of the good land which the LORD swore to *give* your fathers, ¹⁹by driving out all your enemies from you, as the LORD has spoken.

²⁰"^When your son asks you in time to come, saying, 'What *do* the provisions and the statutes and the judgments *mean* which the LORD our God commanded you?' ²¹then you shall say to your son, 'We were slaves to Pharaoh in Egypt, and the LORD brought us out of Egypt with

6:2^Ex 20:20 ᴮDeut 4:9 **6:3**^Ex 3:8, 17
6:4^Deut 4:35, 39; John 10:30 **6:5**^Matt 22:37
ᴮDeut 4:29 **6:6**^Deut 11:18 **6:7**^Deut 4:9; 11:19
6:8^Ex 12:14; 13:9, 16 **6:9**^Deut 11:20 **6:10**^Deut 9:1;
Josh 24:13 **6:11**^Deut 8:10; 11:15 **6:12**^Deut 4:9
6:13^Deut 13:4; Matt 4:10 **6:14**^Jer 25:6
6:15^Deut 4:24; 5:9 **6:16**^Matt 4:7 ᴮEx 17:7
6:17^Deut 11:22; Ps 119:4 **6:18**^Deut 4:40
6:20^Ex 13:8, 14

a mighty hand. ²²Moreover, the Lord provided great and terrible signs and wonders before our eyes against Egypt, Pharaoh, and all his household; ²³He brought us out of there in order to bring us in, to give us the land which He had sworn to our fathers.' ²⁴So the Lord commanded us to follow all these statutes, ᴬto fear the Lord our God for our *own* good always and for our survival, as *it is* today. ²⁵And ᴬit will be righteousness for us if we are careful to follow all this commandment before the Lord our God, just as He commanded us.

WARNINGS

7 "ᴬWhen the Lord your God brings you into the land where you are entering to take possession of it, and He drives away many nations from before you, the Hittites, the Girgashites, the Amorites, the Canaanites, the Perizzites, the Hivites, and the Jebusites, seven nations greater and mightier than you, ²and when the Lord your God turns them over to you and you defeat them, ᴬyou shall utterly destroy them. You shall not make a covenant with them nor be gracious to them. ³Furthermore, ᴬyou shall not intermarry with them: you shall not give your daughters to their sons, nor shall you take their daughters for your sons. ⁴For they will turn your sons away from following Me, and they will serve other gods; then the anger of the Lord will be kindled against you and ᴬHe will quickly destroy you. ⁵But this is what you shall do to them: ᴬyou shall tear down their altars, smash their memorial stones, cut their ¹Asherim to pieces, and burn their carved images in the

fire. ⁶For you are ᴬa holy people to the Lord your God; the Lord your God has chosen you to be a people for His personal possession out of all the peoples who are on the face of the earth.

⁷"ᴬThe Lord did not make you His beloved nor choose you because you were greater in number than any of the peoples, since you were the fewest of all peoples, ⁸but because the Lord loved you and kept the ᴬoath which He swore to your forefathers, ᴮthe Lord brought you out by a mighty hand and redeemed you from the house of slavery, from the hand of Pharaoh king of Egypt. ⁹Know therefore that the Lord your God, He is God, ᴬthe faithful God, ᴮwho keeps His covenant and His faithfulness to a thousand generations for those who love Him and keep His commandments; ¹⁰but He ᴬrepays those who hate Him to their faces, to eliminate them; He will not hesitate toward him who hates Him, He will repay him to his face. ¹¹Therefore, you shall keep the commandment, the statutes, and the judgments which I am commanding you today, to do them.

PROMISES OF GOD

¹²"ᴬThen it shall come about, because you listen to these judgments and keep and do them, that the Lord your God will keep His covenant with you and His faithfulness which He swore to your forefathers. ¹³And He will ᴬlove you, bless you,

6:24ᴬDeut 10:12; Jer 32:39   6:25ᴬDeut 24:13; Rom 10:3
7:1ᴬDeut 20:16-18   7:2ᴬNum 31:17; Josh 11:11
7:3ᴬEx 34:15, 16; Josh 23:12   7:4ᴬDeut 4:26
7:5ᴬEx 23:24; 34:13   7:6ᴬEx 19:6; Deut 14:2, 21
7:7ᴬDeut 4:37   7:8ᴬEx 32:13   ᴮEx 13:3   7:9ᴬIs 49:7
ᴮEx 20:6   7:10ᴬIs 59:18; Nah 1:2   7:12ᴬLev 26:3-13;
Deut 28:1-14   7:13ᴬPs 146:8; Prov 15:9

7:5 ¹I.e., wooden symbols of a female deity (Asherah)

and make you numerous; He will also bless the fruit of your womb and the fruit of your ground, your grain, your new wine, and your oil, the newborn of your cattle and the offspring of your flock, in the land which He swore to your forefathers to give you. ¹⁴You shall be blessed above all peoples; there will be no sterile male or ᴬinfertile female among you or among your cattle. ¹⁵And ᴬthe Lᴏʀᴅ will remove from you all sickness; and He will not inflict upon you any of the harmful diseases of Egypt which you have known, but He will give them to all who hate you. ¹⁶You shall consume all the peoples whom the Lᴏʀᴅ your God will turn over to you; ᴬyour eye shall not pity them, nor shall you serve their gods, for that *would be* a snare to you.

¹⁷"If you say in your heart, 'These nations are greater than I; how can I ᴬdispossess them?' ¹⁸you are not to be afraid of them; you shall ᴬremember well what the Lᴏʀᴅ your God did to Pharaoh and to all Egypt: ¹⁹ᴬthe great trials which your eyes saw and the signs and the wonders, and the mighty hand and the outstretched arm by which the Lᴏʀᴅ your God brought you out. The Lᴏʀᴅ your God will do the same to all the peoples of whom you are afraid. ²⁰Indeed, the Lᴏʀᴅ your God will send ᴬthe hornet against them, until those who are left and hide themselves from you perish. ²¹You are not to be terrified of them, because ᴬthe Lᴏʀᴅ your God is in your midst, ᴮa great and awesome God. ²²ᴬAnd the Lᴏʀᴅ your God will drive away these nations from you little by little; you will not be able to put an end to them quickly, otherwise the wild animals

would become too numerous for you. ²³ᴬBut the Lᴏʀᴅ your God will turn them over to you, and will throw them into great confusion until they are destroyed. ²⁴ᴬAnd He will hand over their kings to you, so that you will eliminate their name from under heaven; no one will be able to stand against you until you have destroyed them. ²⁵The carved images of their gods you are to ᴬburn with fire; you shall not covet the silver or the gold that is on them, nor take it for yourselves, or you will be ᴮtrapped by it; for it is an abomination to the Lᴏʀᴅ your God. ²⁶And you shall not bring an abomination into your house and become ᴬdesignated for destruction, like it; you are to utterly detest it, and you are to utterly loathe it, for it is something designated for destruction.

GOD'S GRACIOUS DEALINGS

8 "All the commandments that I am commanding you today you shall be careful to do, so that you ᴬmay live and increase, and go in and take possession of the land which the Lᴏʀᴅ swore *to give* to your forefathers. ²ᴬAnd you shall remember all the way which the Lᴏʀᴅ your God has led you in the wilderness these forty years, in order to humble you, putting you to the test, to know what was in your heart, whether you would keep His commandments or not. ³And He humbled you and let you go hungry, and fed you with the manna which you did not know, nor did

7:14ᴬEx 23:26 7:15ᴬEx 15:26 7:16ᴬDeut 7:2
7:17ᴬNum 33:53 7:18ᴬPs 105:5 7:19ᴬDeut 4:34
7:20ᴬEx 23:28; Josh 24:12 7:21ᴬEx 29:45 ᴮDeut 10:17
7:22ᴬEx 23:29, 30 7:23ᴬEx 23:27; Josh 10:10
7:24ᴬJosh 6:2 7:25ᴬEx 32:20 ᴮDeut 7:16
7:26ᴬLev 27:28f 8:1ᴬDeut 4:1 8:2ᴬDeut 8:16

your fathers know, in order to make you understand that ^man shall not live on bread alone, but man shall live on everything that comes out of the mouth of the LORD. 4^Your clothing did not wear out on you, nor did your foot swell these forty years. 5^So you are to know in your heart that the LORD your God was disciplining you just as a man disciplines his son. 6Therefore, you shall keep the commandments of the LORD your God, to walk in His ways and to fear Him. 7For ^the LORD your God is bringing you into a good land, a land of streams of water, of fountains and springs, flowing out in valleys and hills; 8a land of wheat and barley, of vines, fig trees, and pomegranates, a land of olive oil and honey; 9a land where you will eat food without shortage, in which you will not lack anything; a land whose stones are iron, and out of whose hills you can dig copper. 10When ^you have eaten and are satisfied, you shall bless the LORD your God for the good land which He has given you.

11"Be careful that you do not ^forget the LORD your God by failing to keep His commandments, His ordinances, and His statutes which I am commanding you today; 12otherwise, ^when you eat and are satisfied, and you build good houses and live in them, 13and when your herds and your flocks increase, and your silver and gold increase, and everything that you have increases, 14then your heart will become proud and you will ^forget the LORD your God who brought you out of the land of Egypt, out of the house of slavery; 15He who led you through the great and terrible wilderness, with its ^fiery serpents and

scorpions, and its thirsty ground where there was no water; He who ^brought water for you out of the rock of flint. 16In the wilderness it was He who fed you manna which your fathers did not know, in order to humble you and in order to ^put you to the test, to do good for you in the end. 17Otherwise, ^you may say in your heart, 'My power and the strength of my hand made me this wealth.' 18But you are to remember the LORD your God, for ^it is He who is giving you power to make wealth, in order to confirm His covenant which He swore to your fathers, as it is this day. 19And it shall come about, if you ever forget the LORD your God and follow other gods and serve and worship them, ^I testify against you today that you will certainly perish. 20Like the nations that the LORD eliminates from you, so ^you shall perish, because you would not listen to the voice of the LORD your God.

ISRAEL PROVOKED GOD

9 "Hear, Israel! You are crossing the Jordan today, to go in to dispossess ^nations greater and mightier than you, cities that are great and fortified to heaven, 2a people who are great and tall, the sons of the Anakim, whom you know and of whom you have heard it said, '^Who can stand against the sons of Anak?' 3So be aware today that it is the LORD your God who is crossing over ahead of you as ^a consuming

8:3^Matt 4:4; Luke 4:4   8:4^Deut 29:5; Neh 9:21
8:5^Deut 4:36; 2 Sam 7:14   8:7^Deut 11:9–12; Jer 2:7
8:10^Deut 6:11   8:11^Deut 4:9   8:12^Prov 30:9;
Hos 13:6   8:14^Deut 8:11; Ps 106:21   8:15^Num 21:6
8Ex 17:6   8:16^Deut 8:2   8:17^Deut 9:4
8:18^Prov 10:22; Hos 2:8   8:19^Deut 4:26; 30:18
8:20^Ezek 5:5–17   9:1^Deut 4:38; 7:1
9:2^Num 13:22, 28, 33; Josh 11:21, 22
9:3^Deut 4:24; Heb 12:29

fire. He will destroy them and He will subdue them before you, so that you may drive them out and eliminate them quickly, just as the LORD has spoken to you.

4 "Do not say in your heart when the LORD your God has driven them away from you, 'Because of my righteousness the LORD has brought me in to take possession of this land.' Rather, *it is* ^because of the wickedness of these nations *that* the LORD is dispossessing them before you. 5 *It is* ^not because of your righteousness or the uprightness of your heart *that* you are going in to take possession of their land, but *it is* because of the wickedness of these nations *that* the LORD your God is driving them out from before you, and in order to confirm the oath which the LORD swore to your fathers, to Abraham, Isaac, and Jacob.

6 "Know, then, that *it is* not because of your righteousness *that* the LORD your God is giving you this good land to possess, for you are ^a stubborn people. 7 Remember, do not forget how you provoked the LORD your God to anger in the wilderness; ^from the day that you left the land of Egypt until you arrived at this place, you have been rebellious against the LORD. 8 Even ^at Horeb you provoked the LORD to anger, and the LORD was so angry with you that He would have destroyed you. 9 When I went up to the mountain to receive the tablets of stone, the tablets of the covenant which the LORD made with you, then I remained on the mountain for forty days and nights; ^I neither ate bread nor drank water. 10 The LORD gave me the two tablets of stone ^written by the finger of God; and on them *were* all the words which the LORD had spoken with you at the mountain from the midst of the fire on the day of the assembly. 11 It came about ^at the end of forty days and nights that the LORD gave me the two tablets of stone, the tablets of the covenant. 12 ^Then the LORD said to me, 'Arise, go down from here quickly, because your people, whom you brought out of Egypt, have behaved corruptly. They have quickly turned aside from the way that I commanded them; they have made a cast metal image for themselves.' 13 The LORD also said to me, 'I have seen this people, and indeed, it is a ^stubborn people. 14 Leave Me alone, that I may destroy them and ^wipe out their name from under heaven; and I will make of you a nation mightier and greater than they.'

15 "So I turned and came down from the mountain while the mountain was burning with fire, and the two tablets of the covenant were in my two hands. 16 And I saw that you had indeed sinned against the LORD your God. You had made for yourselves a cast metal image of a calf; you had quickly turned aside from the way that the LORD had commanded you. 17 So I took hold of the two tablets and threw them from my two hands, and smashed them to pieces before your eyes! 18 ^Then I fell down before the LORD like the first *time,* for forty days and nights; I neither ate bread nor drank water, ^because of all your sin which you had committed by doing what was evil in the sight of the LORD, to

9:4 ^Lev 18:3, 24–30; Deut 12:31 9:5 ^Titus 3:5
9:6 ^Deut 9:13; 10:16 9:7 ^Ex 14:10f; Num 14:22
9:8 ^Ex 32:7–10; Ps 106:19 9:9 ^Ex 24:18; 34:28
9:10 ^Deut 4:13 9:11 ^Deut 9:9 9:12 ^Ex 32:7, 8
9:13 ^Deut 10:16; 31:27 9:14 ^Ps 9:5; 109:13
9:15 ^Ex 32:15–19 9:18 ^Ex 34:28 B Ex 34:9

provoke Him to anger. ¹⁹For ᴬI was afraid of the anger and the rage with which the Lord was angry with you so as to destroy you; but the Lord listened to me that time as well. ²⁰The Lord was also angry enough with Aaron to destroy him; so I also prayed for Aaron at the same time. ²¹ᴬAnd I took your sinful *thing* which you had made, the calf, and burned it in the fire and crushed it, grinding it thoroughly until it was as fine as dust; and I threw its dust into the stream that came down from the mountain.

²²"Then at ᴬTaberah, at Massah, and at Kibroth-hattaavah you kept provoking the Lord to anger. ²³And when the Lord sent you from Kadesh-barnea, saying, 'Go up and take possession of the land which I have given you,' you rebelled against the command of the Lord your God; ᴬyou neither trusted Him nor listened to His voice. ²⁴ᴬYou have been rebellious toward the Lord since the day I knew you.

²⁵"ᴬSo I fell down before the Lord for the forty days and nights, which I did because the Lord said He would destroy you. ²⁶ᴬAnd I prayed to the Lord and said, 'Lord God, do not destroy Your people, Your inheritance, whom You have redeemed through Your greatness, whom You have brought out of Egypt with a mighty hand! ²⁷Remember Your servants, Abraham, Isaac, and Jacob; do not turn Your attention to the stubbornness of this people, or to their wickedness, or their sin. ²⁸Otherwise, the *people of the* land from which You brought us will say, "ᴬSince the Lord was not able to bring them into the land which He had promised them, and since He hated them, He has brought them out to kill them in the wilderness!" ²⁹Yet they are Your people, and ᴬYour inheritance, whom You brought out by Your great power and Your outstretched arm.'

THE TABLETS REWRITTEN

10 "At that time the Lord said to me, 'ᴬCut out for yourself two tablets of stone like the first *two*, and come up to Me on the mountain, and ᴮmake an ark of wood for yourself. ²Then ᴬI will write on the tablets the words that were on the first tablets which you smashed to pieces, and you shall put them in the ark.' ³So I made an ark of acacia wood and ᴬcut out two tablets of stone like the first *two*, and I went up on the mountain with the two tablets in my hand. ⁴Then He wrote on the tablets, like the first writing, ᴬthe Ten Commandments ᴮwhich the Lord had spoken to you on the mountain from the midst of the fire on the day of the assembly; and the Lord gave them to me. ⁵Then I turned and ᴬcame down from the mountain, and I ᴮput the tablets in the ark which I had made; and they are there, just as the Lord commanded me."

⁶(Now the sons of Israel set out from Beeroth Bene-jaakan to Moserah. ᴬThere Aaron died and there he was buried, and his son Eleazar served as priest in his place. ⁷ᴬFrom there they set out to Gudgodah, and from Gudgodah to Jotbathah, a land of streams of water. ⁸ᴬAt that

9:19 ᴬEx 32:10f; Heb 12:21   9:21 ᴬEx 32:20
9:22 ᴬNum 11:3   9:23 ᴬDeut 1:26; Ps 106:24
9:24 ᴬDeut 9:7; 31:27   9:25 ᴬDeut 9:18
9:26 ᴬEx 32:11-13; 1 Sam 7:9   9:28 ᴬEx 32:12;
Num 14:16   9:29 ᴬDeut 4:20   10:1 ᴬEx 34:1
ᴮEx 25:10   10:2 ᴬDeut 4:13   10:3 ᴬEx 34:4
10:4 ᴬEx 34:28   ᴮEx 20:1   10:5 ᴬEx 34:29   ᴮEx 40:20
10:6 ᴬNum 20:25-28; 33:38   10:7 ᴬNum 33:33, 34
10:8 ᴬNum 3:6

time the Lord singled out the tribe of Levi to carry the ark of the covenant of the Lord, to stand before the Lord ᴮto serve Him and to bless in His name, until this day. 9ᴬTherefore, Levi does not have a portion or inheritance with his brothers; the Lord is his inheritance, just as the Lord your God spoke to him.)

10 "ᴬI, moreover, stayed on the mountain for forty days and forty nights like the first time, and the Lord listened to me that time also; the Lord was not willing to destroy you. 11Then the Lord said to me, 'Arise, proceed on your journey ahead of the people, so that they may go in and take possession of the land which I swore to their fathers to give them.'

12 "ᴬAnd now, Israel, what does the Lord your God require of you, but to fear the Lord your God, to walk in all His ways and ᴮlove Him, and to serve the Lord your God with all your heart and with all your soul, 13 and to keep the Lord's commandments and His statutes which I am commanding you today for your good? 14Behold, ᴬto the Lord your God belong heaven and the highest heavens, ᴮthe earth and all that is in it. 15ᴬYet the Lord set His affection on your fathers, to love them, and He chose their descendants after them, you over all the other peoples, as it is this day. 16ᴬSo circumcise your heart, and do not ᴮstiffen your neck any longer. 17ᴬFor the Lord your God is the God of gods and the ᴮLord of lords, the great, the mighty, and the awesome God, who does not show partiality, nor take a bribe. 18He executes justice for ᴬthe orphan and the widow, and shows His love for the stranger by giving him food and clothing. 19ᴬSo show

your love for the stranger, for you were strangers in the land of Egypt. 20You shall fear the Lord your God; you shall serve Him, and ᴬcling to Him, and ᴮyou shall swear by His name. 21He is ᴬyour glory and He is your God, who has done these great and awesome things for you which your eyes have seen. 22ᴬYour fathers went down to Egypt seventy persons in all, and now the Lord your God has made you as numerous as the stars of heaven.

REWARDS OF OBEDIENCE

11 "You shall therefore ᴬlove the Lord your God, and always ᴮkeep His directive, His statutes, His ordinances, and His commandments. 2Know this day ᴬthat I am not speaking with your sons who have not known and who have not seen the discipline of the Lord your God—His greatness, His mighty hand, His outstretched arm, 3and ᴬHis signs and His works which He did in the midst of Egypt to Pharaoh the king of Egypt and to all his land; 4and what He did to Egypt's army, to its horses and its chariots, ᴬwhen He made the water of the Red Sea engulf them while they were pursuing you, and the Lord completely eliminated them; 5and what He did to you in the wilderness, until you came to this place; 6and ᴬwhat He did to Dathan and Abiram, the sons of Eliab, the son of Reuben, when the earth opened its mouth and swallowed them,

10:8 ᴮDeut 17:12 10:9ᴬNum 18:20, 24
10:10ᴬEx 34:28; Deut 9:18 10:12ᴬMic 6:8 ᴮDeut 6:5
10:14ᴬ1 Kin 8:27 ᴮPs 24:1 10:15ᴬDeut 4:37
10:16ᴬLev 26:41 ᴮDeut 9:6 10:17ᴬJosh 22:22
ᴮRev 17:14 10:18ᴬEx 22:22-24; Ps 68:5
10:19ᴬLev 19:34; Ezek 47:22, 23 10:20ᴬDeut 11:22
ᴮDeut 5:11 10:21ᴬPs 109:1; Jer 17:14 10:22ᴬGen 46:27
11:1ᴬDeut 6:5 ᴮLev 18:30 11:2ᴬDeut 4:34
11:3ᴬEx 7:8-21 11:4ᴬEx 14:28 11:6ᴬNum 16:1-35

their households, their tents, and [B]every living thing that followed them, among all Israel— [7]but your own eyes have seen all the great work of the LORD which He did.

[8]"You shall therefore keep every commandment which I am commanding you today, [A]so that you may be strong and go in and take possession of the land into which you are about to cross to possess it; [9]and [A]so that you may prolong *your* days on the land which the LORD swore to your fathers to give to them and to their descendants, [B]a land flowing with milk and honey. [10]For the land, into which you are entering to possess it, is not like the land of Egypt from which you came, where you used to sow your seed and water it [1]by your foot like a vegetable garden. [11]But [A]the land into which you are about to cross to possess it, a land of hills and valleys, drinks water from the rain of heaven, [12]a land for which the LORD your God cares; [A]the eyes of the LORD your God are continually on it, from the beginning even to the end of the year.

[13]"And it shall come about, [A]if you listen obediently to my commandments which I am commanding you today, to love the LORD your God and to serve Him with all your heart and all your soul, [14]that [A]He will provide rain for your land in its season, the [1]early and late rain, so that you may gather your grain, your new wine, and your oil. [15][A]He will also provide grass in your field for your cattle, and [B]you will eat and be satisfied. [16][A]Beware that your hearts are not easily deceived, and that you do not turn away and serve other gods, and worship them. [17]Otherwise, [A]the anger of the LORD will be kindled against you, and He

will [B]shut up the sky so that there will be no rain, and the ground will not yield its produce; then you will quickly perish from the good land which the LORD is giving you.

[18]"[A]You shall therefore take these words of mine to heart and to soul; and you shall tie them as a sign on your hand, and they shall be as frontlets on your forehead. [19][A]You shall also teach them to your sons, speaking of them when you sit in your house, when you walk along the road, when you lie down, and when you get up. [20][A]And you shall write them on the doorposts of your house and on your gates, [21]so that [A]your days and the days of your sons may be increased on the land which the LORD swore to your fathers to give them, as long as the heavens are above the earth. [22]For if you are careful to keep all of this commandment which I am commanding you to do, [A]to love the LORD your God, to walk in all His ways and [B]cling to Him, [23]then the LORD will [A]dispossess all these nations from you, and you will [B]dispossess nations greater and mightier than you. [24]Every place on which the sole of your foot steps shall be yours; [A]your border will be from the wilderness to Lebanon, *and* from the river, the river Euphrates, as far as [1]the western sea. [25][A]No one will *be able to* stand against you;

11:6 [B]Num 26:10, 11   11:8 [A]Deut 31:6, 7, 23; Josh 1:6, 7
11:9 [A]Deut 4:40   [B]Ex 3:8   11:11 [A]Deut 8:7
11:12 [A]1 Kin 9:3   11:13 [A]Lev 26:3; Deut 7:12
11:14 [A]Lev 26:4; Deut 28:12   11:15 [A]Ps 104:14
[B]Deut 6:11   11:16 [A]Job 31:27   11:17 [A]Deut 6:15
[B]1 Kin 8:35   11:18 [A]Ex 13:9, 16; Deut 6:8
11:19 [A]Deut 4:9, 10; 6:7   11:20 [A]Deut 6:9
11:21 [A]Prov 3:2; 4:10   11:22 [A]Deut 11:1   [B]Deut 10:20
11:23 [A]Deut 4:38   [B]Deut 9:1   11:24 [A]Gen 15:18;
Ex 23:31   11:25 [A]Ex 23:27; Deut 7:24

11:10 [1]I.e., use of foot to facilitate irrigation
11:14 [1]I.e., autumn   11:24 [1]I.e., the Mediterranean

the LORD your God will instill the dread of you and the fear of you in all the land on which you set foot, just as He has spoken to you.

26 "See, I am placing before you today a blessing and a curse: 27 the Ablessing, if you listen to the commandments of the LORD your God, which I am commanding you today; 28 and the Acurse, if you do not listen to the commandments of the LORD your God, but turn aside from the way which I am commanding you today, by following other gods which you have not known.

29 "And it shall come about, when the LORD your God brings you into the land where you are entering to possess it, Athat you shall place the blessing on Mount Gerizim and the curse on Mount Ebal. 30 Are they not across the Jordan, west of the road toward the sunset, in the land of the Canaanites who live in the Arabah, opposite AGilgal, beside Bthe oaks of Moreh? 31 For you are about to cross the Jordan to go in to take possession of the land which the LORD your God is giving you, and Ayou shall possess it and live in it, 32 and you shall be careful to do all the statutes and the judgments which I am placing before you today.

LAWS OF THE SANCTUARY

12 "These are the statutes and the judgments which you shall carefully follow in the land which the LORD, the God of your fathers, has given you to possess Aas long as you live on the earth. 2 You shall utterly destroy all the places where the nations whom you are going to dispossess serve their gods, on the Ahigh mountains, on the hills, and under every leafy

tree. 3 And Ayou shall tear down their altars and smash their memorial stones to pieces, and burn their IAsherim in the fire, and cut to pieces the carved images of their gods; and you shall Beliminate their name from that place. 4 You shall not act this way toward the LORD your God. 5 ABut you shall seek the LORD at the place which the LORD your God will choose from all your tribes, to establish His name there for His dwelling, and you shall come there. 6 You shall bring there your burnt offerings, your sacrifices, Ayour tithes, the contribution of your hand, your vowed offerings, your voluntary offerings, and the firstborn of your herd and of your flock. 7 There you and your households shall eat before the LORD your God, and Arejoice in all your undertakings in which the LORD your God has blessed you.

8 "You shall not do at all what we are doing here today, Aeveryone doing whatever is right in his own eyes; 9 for you have not as yet come to the resting place and the Ainheritance which the LORD your God is giving you. 10 When you cross the Jordan and live in the land which the LORD your God is giving you as an inheritance, and AHe gives you rest from all your enemies around you so that you live in security, 11 Athen it shall come about that the place in which the LORD your God will choose for His name to dwell,

11:26 ADeut 30:1, 19   11:27 ADeut 28:1-14
11:28 ADeut 28:15-68   11:29 ADeut 27:12; Josh 8:33
11:30 AJosh 4:19   BGen 12:6   11:31 ADeut 17:14;
Josh 21:43   12:1 ADeut 4:9, 10; 1 Kin 8:40
12:2 A2 Kin 16:4; 17:10, 11   12:3 ANum 33:52   BEx 23:13
12:5 AEx 20:24; Deut 12:11, 13   12:6 ADeut 14:22
12:7 ALev 23:40; Deut 12:12, 18   12:8 AJudg 17:6; 21:25
12:9 ADeut 4:21   12:10 AJosh 11:23
12:11 ADeut 12:5; 15:20

12:3 ¹I.e., wooden symbols of a female deity (Asherah)

there you shall bring everything that I command you: your burnt offerings and your sacrifices, your tithes and the contribution of your hand, and all your choice vowed offerings which you will vow to the LORD. ¹²And you shall rejoice before the LORD your God, you and your sons and daughters, your male and female slaves, and the ^Levite who is within your gates, since he has no portion or inheritance with you.

¹³ "^Be careful that you do not offer your burnt offerings in any *cultic* place that you see, ¹⁴but *only* in the place which the LORD chooses in one of your tribes: there you shall offer your burnt offerings, and there you shall do everything that I command you.

¹⁵ "^However, you may slaughter and eat meat within any of your gates, whatever you desire, according to the blessing of the LORD your God which He has given you; the unclean and the clean *alike* may eat it, as the gazelle and the deer. ¹⁶^Only you shall not eat the blood; ᴮyou are to pour it out on the ground like water. ¹⁷^You are not allowed to eat within your gates the tithe of your grain, new wine, or oil, or the firstborn of your herd or flock, or any of your vowed offerings which you vow, or your voluntary offerings, or the contribution of your hand. ¹⁸But you shall eat them before the LORD your God in the place which the LORD your God will choose, you and your son and daughter, and your male and female slaves, and the Levite who is within your gates; and you shall ^rejoice before the LORD your God in all your undertakings. ¹⁹^Be careful that you do not abandon the Levite as long as you live in your land.

²⁰ "When the LORD your God extends your border ^as He has promised you, and you say, 'I will eat meat,' because you desire to eat meat, *then* you may eat meat, whatever you desire. ²¹If the place where the LORD your God chooses to put His name is too far from you, then you may slaughter *animals* from your herd and flock which the LORD has given you, as I have commanded you; and you may eat within your gates whatever you desire. ²²Just as a gazelle or a deer is eaten, so you may eat it; the unclean and the clean alike may eat it. ²³Only be sure ^not to eat the blood, for the blood is the life, and you shall not eat the life with the flesh. ²⁴You shall not eat it; you shall pour it out on the ground like water. ²⁵You shall not eat it, so that it may go well for you and your sons after you, since ^you will be doing what is right in the sight of the LORD. ²⁶^Only your holy things which you may have and your vowed offerings, you shall take and go to the place which the LORD chooses. ²⁷And you shall offer your burnt offerings, the flesh and the blood, on the altar of the LORD your God; and the blood of your sacrifices shall be poured out on the altar of the LORD your God, and ^you shall eat the flesh.

²⁸ "Be careful and listen to all these words which I am commanding you, so that ^it may go well for you and your sons after you forever, for you will be doing what is

12:12^Deut 12:18, 19; 26:11-13   12:13^Deut 12:5, 11
12:15^Deut 12:20-23   12:16^Gen 9:4   ᴮDeut 15:23
12:17^Deut 12:26   12:18^Deut 12:7; Eccl 3:12f
12:19^Deut 14:27   12:20^Gen 15:18; Deut 11:24
12:23^Gen 9:4; Lev 17:10-14   12:25^Ex 15:26;
1 Kin 11:38   12:26^Num 5:9f; 18:19   12:27^Lev 3:1-17
12:28^Deut 4:40; Eccl 8:12

good and right in the sight of the LORD your God.

²⁹"When ᴬthe LORD your God cuts off from you the nations which you are going in to dispossess, and you dispossess them and live in their land, ³⁰be careful that you are not ensnared to follow them, after they are destroyed from your presence, and that you do not inquire about their gods, saying, 'How do these nations serve their gods, that I also may do likewise?' ³¹ᴬYou shall not behave this way toward the LORD your God, because every abominable act which the LORD hates, they have done for their gods; for ᴮthey even burn their sons and daughters in the fire for their gods.

³²"ᴬWhatever I command you, you shall be careful to do; ᴮyou shall not add to nor take *anything* away from it.

REJECT IDOLATRY

13 "ᴬIf a prophet or a dreamer of dreams arises among you and gives you a sign or a wonder, ²and the sign or the wonder comes *true,* of which he spoke to you, saying, 'ᴬLet's follow other gods (whom you have not known) and let's serve them,' ³you shall not listen to the words of that prophet or dreamer of dreams; for the LORD your God is ᴬtesting you to find out whether ᴮyou love the LORD your God with all your heart and with all your soul. ⁴You shall follow the LORD your God and fear Him; and you shall keep His commandments, listen to His voice, serve Him, and ᴬcling to Him. ⁵But that prophet or that dreamer of dreams shall be ᴬput to death, because he has spoken falsely against the LORD your God who brought you out of the land of Egypt and redeemed you from the house of slavery, to drive you from the way in which the LORD your God commanded you to walk. ᴮSo you shall eliminate the evil from among you.

⁶"ᴬIf your brother, your mother's son, or your son or daughter, or the wife you cherish, or your friend who is like your own soul, entices you secretly, saying, 'Let's go and serve other gods' (whom neither you nor your fathers have known, ⁷of the gods of the peoples who are around you, near you, or far from you, from one end of the earth to the other end), ⁸ᴬyou shall not consent to him or listen to him; and your eye shall not pity him, nor shall you spare or conceal him. ⁹Instead, you shall most certainly kill him; ᴬyour hand shall be first against him to put him to death, and afterward the hand of all the people. ¹⁰So you shall stone him to death, because he has attempted ᴬto drive you away from the LORD your God who brought you out of the land of Egypt, out of the house of slavery. ¹¹Then ᴬall Israel will hear *about it* and be afraid, and will not do such a wicked thing among you again.

¹²"If you hear in one of your cities, which the LORD your God is giving you to live in, *anyone* saying *that* ¹³some worthless men have gone out from among you and have seduced the inhabitants of their city, saying, 'ᴬLet's go and serve other gods' (whom you have not known),

12:29ᴬJosh 23:4   12:31ᴬDeut 9:5   ᴮLev 18:21
12:32ᴬDeut 4:2   ᴮProv 30:6   13:1ᴬMatt 24:24;
Mark 13:22   13:2ᴬDeut 13:6, 13   13:3ᴬEx 20:20
ᴮDeut 6:5   13:4ᴬDeut 10:20   13:5ᴬDeut 13:9, 15
ᴮ1 Cor 5:13   13:6ᴬDeut 17:2-7; 29:18   13:8ᴬProv 1:10
13:9ᴬLev 24:14; Deut 17:7   13:10ᴬDeut 13:5
13:11ᴬDeut 19:20   13:13ᴬDeut 13:2

¹⁴then you shall investigate, search out, and inquire thoroughly. And if it is true *and* the matter is certain that this abomination has been committed among you, ¹⁵ᴬyou shall most certainly strike the inhabitants of that city with the edge of the sword. Utterly destroy it and all who are in it and its cattle, with the edge of the sword. ¹⁶ᴬThen you shall gather all its plunder into the middle of its public square, and burn the city and all its plunder with fire as a whole burnt offering to the Lᴏʀᴅ your God; and it shall be a ruin forever. It shall never be rebuilt. ¹⁷Nothing at all from what is designated for destruction is to cling to your hand, in order that the Lᴏʀᴅ may turn from ᴬHis burning anger and ᴮshow mercy to you, and have compassion on you and make you increase, just as He has sworn to your fathers, ¹⁸if you will listen to the voice of the Lᴏʀᴅ your God, keeping all His commandments which I am commanding you today, and doing what is right in the sight of the Lᴏʀᴅ your God.

CLEAN AND UNCLEAN ANIMALS

14 "You are ᴬsons of the Lᴏʀᴅ your God; you shall not cut yourselves nor shave a bald spot above your forehead for the dead. ²For you are ᴬa holy people to the Lᴏʀᴅ your God, and the Lᴏʀᴅ has chosen you to be a people for His personal possession out of all the peoples who are on the face of the earth.

³"ᴬYou shall not eat any detestable thing. ⁴ᴬThese are the animals that you may eat: the ox, the sheep, the goat, ⁵the deer, the gazelle, the roebuck, the wild goat, the ibex, the antelope, and the mountain sheep. ⁶And any animal that has a divided hoof and has *its* hoofs split in two, *and* chews the cud, among the animals, that animal you may eat. ⁷However, you are not to eat these among the ones that chew the cud, or among those that have the hoof divided in two: the camel, the rabbit, and the rock hyrax, for though they chew the cud, they do not have a divided hoof; they are unclean to you. ⁸And the pig, because it has a divided hoof but *does* not *chew* the cud, it is unclean for you. You shall not eat any of their flesh, nor touch their carcasses.

⁹"These you may eat of everything that is in the water: anything that has fins and scales you may eat, ¹⁰but anything that does not have fins and scales, you shall not eat; it is unclean for you.

¹¹"You may eat any clean bird. ¹²But ᴬthese are the ones that you shall not eat: the eagle and the vulture and the buzzard, ¹³and the red kite, the falcon, and the kite in their kinds, ¹⁴and every raven in its kind, ¹⁵and the ostrich, the owl, the seagull, and the hawk in their kinds, ¹⁶the little owl, the great owl, the white owl, ¹⁷the pelican, the carrion vulture, the cormorant, ¹⁸the stork, and the heron in their kinds, and the hoopoe and the bat. ¹⁹And all the swarming insects with wings are unclean to you; they shall not be eaten. ²⁰You may eat any clean bird.

²¹"You shall not eat anything which dies *of itself*. You may give it to the stranger who is in your town, so that he may eat it, or you may sell it to a stranger; for you are ᴬa

13:15ᴬDeut 13:5　13:16ᴬDeut 7:25, 26
13:17ᴬEx 32:12　ᴮDeut 30:3　14:1ᴬRom 8:16; 9:8, 26
14:2ᴬLev 20:26; Deut 7:6　14:3ᴬEzek 4:14
14:4ᴬLev 11:2-45; Acts 10:14　14:12ᴬLev 11:13
14:21ᴬDeut 14:2

holy people to the Lord your God. [B]You shall not boil a young goat in its mother's milk.

[22]"You [A]shall certainly tithe all the produce from what you sow, which comes from the field every year. [23]You shall eat in the presence of the Lord your God, [A]at the place where He chooses to establish His name, the tithe of your grain, your new wine, your oil, and the firstborn of your herd and your flock, so that you may learn to fear the Lord your God always. [24]But if the distance is so great for you that you are not able to bring *the tithe*, since the place where the Lord your God chooses [A]to set His name is too far away from you when the Lord your God blesses you, [25]then you shall exchange *it* for money, and bind the money in your hand and go to the place which the Lord your God chooses. [26]And you may spend the money on whatever your heart desires: on oxen, sheep, wine, *other* strong drink, or whatever your heart desires; and [A]there you shall eat in the presence of the Lord your God and rejoice, you and your household. [27]Also you shall not neglect [A]the Levite who is in your town, for he has no portion or inheritance among you.

[28]"[A]At the end of every third year you shall bring out all the tithe of your produce in that year, and you shall deposit *it* in your town. [29]And the Levite, because he has no portion or inheritance among you, and [A]the stranger, the orphan, and the widow who are in your town, shall come and [B]eat and be satisfied, in order that the Lord your God may bless you in all the work of your hand which you do.

THE SABBATICAL YEAR

15 "[A]At the end of *every* seven years you shall grant a release of debts. [2]And this is the regulation for the release of debts: every creditor is to forgive what he has loaned to his neighbor; he shall not require it of his neighbor and his brother, because the Lord's release has been proclaimed. [3][A]From a foreigner you may require *it,* but your hand shall forgive whatever of yours is with your brother. [4]However, there will be no poor among you, since [A]the Lord will certainly bless you in the land which the Lord your God is giving you as an inheritance to possess, [5]if only you listen obediently to the voice of the Lord your God, to follow carefully all this commandment which I am commanding you today. [6][A]For the Lord your God will have blessed you just as He has promised you, and you will lend to many nations, but you will not borrow; and you will rule over many nations, but they will not rule over you.

[7]"If there is a poor person among you, one of your brothers, in any of your towns in your land which the Lord your God is giving you, [A]you shall not harden your heart, nor close your hand from your poor brother; [8]but [A]you shall fully open your hand to him, and generously lend him enough for his need *in* whatever he lacks. [9]Be careful that there is no mean-spirited thought in your heart, such as, 'The seventh year, the year of release of debts, is near,' and [A]your eye is malicious

14:21[B]Ex 23:19   14:22[A]Lev 27:30; Deut 12:6, 17
14:23[A]Deut 12:5   14:24[A]Deut 12:5, 21   14:26[A]Deut 12:7
14:27[A]Deut 12:12   14:28[A]Deut 26:12
14:29[A]Deut 16:11, 14   [B]Deut 6:11   15:1[A]Deut 31:10
15:3[A]Deut 23:20   15:4[A]Deut 28:8   15:6[A]Deut 28:12, 13
15:7[A]1 John 3:17   15:8[A]Matt 5:42; Luke 6:34
15:9[A]Matt 20:15

toward your poor brother, and you give him nothing; then he may cry out to the LORD against you, and it will be a sin in you. ¹⁰You shall generously give to him, and your heart shall not be grudging when you give to him, because ᴬfor this thing the LORD your God will bless you in all your work, and in all your undertakings. ¹¹ᴬFor the poor will not cease to exist in the land; therefore I am commanding you, saying, 'You shall fully open your hand to your brother, to your needy and poor in your land.'

¹²ᴬIf your fellow countryman, a Hebrew man or woman, is sold to you, then he shall serve you for six years, but in the seventh year you shall set him free. ¹³And when you set him free, you shall not send him away empty-handed. ¹⁴You shall give generously to him from your flock, your threshing floor, and from your wine vat; you shall give to him as the LORD your God has blessed you. ¹⁵And you are to remember that you were a slave in the land of Egypt, and the LORD your God redeemed you; therefore I am commanding this of you today. ¹⁶But it shall come about, ᴬif he says to you, 'I will not leave you,' because he loves you and your household, since he is doing well with you, ¹⁷then you shall take an ¹awl and pierce it through his ear into the door, and he shall be your servant permanently. You shall also do the same to your female slave.

¹⁸"It shall not seem difficult for you when you set him free, because he has given you six years *with* double the service of a hired worker; so the LORD your God will bless you in whatever you do.

¹⁹ᴬYou shall consecrate to the LORD your God all the firstborn males that are born in your herd and in your flock; you shall not work with the firstborn of your herd, nor shear the firstborn of your flock. ²⁰ᴬYou and your household shall eat it every year before the LORD your God in the place which the LORD chooses. ²¹ᴬBut if it has any impairment, *such as* a limp, or blindness, *or* any serious impairment, you shall not sacrifice it to the LORD your God. ²²You shall eat it within your gates; ᴬthe unclean and the clean alike *may eat it*, as ᴬa gazelle or a deer. ²³Only ᴬyou shall not eat its blood; you are to pour it out on the ground like water.

THE FEASTS OF PASSOVER, OF WEEKS, AND OF BOOTHS

16 "Observe the month of Abib and ᴬcelebrate the Passover to the LORD your God, for in the month of Abib the LORD your God brought you out of Egypt by night. ²You shall sacrifice the Passover to the LORD your God *from* the flock and the herd, in the place where the LORD chooses to establish His name. ³ᴬYou shall not eat leavened bread with it; for seven days you shall eat unleavened bread with it, the bread of affliction (for you came out of the land of Egypt in a hurry), so that you will remember the day when you came out of the land of Egypt ᴮall the days of your life. ⁴For seven days no leaven shall be seen with you in your entire territory, and ᴬnone of the meat which

15:10 ᴬDeut 14:29; Ps 41:1   15:11 ᴬMatt 26:11;
Mark 14:7   15:12 ᴬEx 21:2–6; Lev 25:39–43
15:16 ᴬEx 21:5, 6   15:19 ᴬEx 13:2, 12   15:20 ᴬLev
7:15–18; Deut 12:5   15:21 ᴬLev 22:19–25; Deut 17:1
15:22 ᴬDeut 12:15, 16, 22   15:23 ᴬGen 9:4; Lev 7:26
16:1 ᴬNum 28:16   16:3 ᴬEx 12:8, 15, 19, 39   ᴮDeut 4:9
16:4 ᴬEx 12:8, 10; 34:25

15:17 ¹I.e., a pointed tool

you sacrifice on the evening of the first day shall be left overnight until the morning. ⁵You are not allowed to sacrifice the Passover in any of your towns which the LORD your God is giving you; ⁶but *only* ᴬat the place where the LORD your God chooses to establish His name, you shall sacrifice the Passover in the evening at sunset, at the time that you came out of Egypt. ⁷You shall ᴬcook and eat *it* in the place which the LORD your God chooses. In the morning you are to return to your tents. ⁸For six days you shall eat unleavened bread, and ᴬon the seventh day there shall be a festive assembly to the LORD your God; you shall do no work *on it.*

⁹"ᴬYou shall count seven weeks for yourself; you shall begin to count seven weeks from *the time* you begin *to put* the sickle to the standing grain. ¹⁰Then you shall celebrate the Feast of Weeks to the LORD your God with a voluntary offering of your hand in a proportional amount, which you shall give just as the LORD your God blesses you; ¹¹and you shall ᴬrejoice before the LORD your God, you, your son and your daughter, and your male and female slaves, and the Levite who is in your town, and ᴮthe stranger, the orphan, and the widow who are in your midst, at the place where the LORD your God chooses to establish His name. ¹²ᴬYou shall also remember that you were a slave in Egypt, and you shall be careful and comply with these statutes.

¹³"ᴬYou shall celebrate the Feast of Booths for seven days when you have gathered in from your threshing floor and your wine vat; ¹⁴and you shall ᴬrejoice in your feast, you, your son and your daughter, and

your male and female slaves, and the Levite, the stranger, the orphan, and the widow who are in your towns. ¹⁵For seven days you shall celebrate a feast to the LORD your God in the place which the LORD chooses, because the LORD your God will bless you in all your produce and in all the work of your hands, so that you will be altogether joyful.

¹⁶"ᴬThree times a year all your males shall appear before the LORD your God at the place which He chooses: at the Feast of Unleavened Bread, at the Feast of Weeks, and at the Feast of Booths; and they are not to appear before the LORD empty-handed. ¹⁷Everyone shall give as he is able, in accordance with the blessing of the LORD your God which He has given you.

¹⁸"You shall appoint for yourself judges and officers in all your towns which the LORD your God is giving you, according to your tribes, and they shall judge the people with righteous judgment. ¹⁹ᴬYou shall not distort justice, you shall not show partiality; and you shall not accept a bribe, because a bribe blinds the eyes of the wise and distorts the words of the righteous. ²⁰Justice, *and only* justice, you shall pursue, so that ᴬyou may live and possess the land which the LORD your God is giving you.

²¹"ᴬYou shall not plant for yourself an Asherah of any kind of tree beside the altar of the LORD your God, which you shall make for yourself. ²²And ᴬyou shall not set

16:6 ᴬDeut 12:5   16:7 ᴬEx 12:8; 2 Chr 35:13
16:8 ᴬNum 28:25   16:9 ᴬEx 23:16; 34:22
16:11 ᴬDeut 12:7   ᴮDeut 14:29   16:12 ᴬDeut 15:15
16:13 ᴬLev 23:34-43   16:14 ᴬDeut 16:11
16:16 ᴬEx 23:14-17; 34:23, 24   16:19 ᴬEx 23:2; Lev 19:15
16:20 ᴬDeut 4:1   16:21 ᴬDeut 7:5; 2 Kin 17:16
16:22 ᴬLev 26:1

up for yourself a memorial stone, which the LORD your God hates.

ADMINISTRATION OF JUSTICE

17 "ᴬYou shall not sacrifice to the LORD your God an ox or a sheep which has a blemish *or* any defect, for that is a detestable thing to the LORD your God.

² "ᴬIf there is found in your midst, in any of your towns which the LORD your God is giving you, a man or a woman who does what is evil in the sight of the LORD your God, by violating His covenant, ³ and *that person* has gone and ᴬserved other gods and worshiped them, ᴮor the sun, the moon, or any of the heavenly lights, which I have commanded not to do, ⁴ and if it is reported to you and you have heard *about it,* then you shall investigate thoroughly. And if it is true and the report is trustworthy that this detestable thing has been done in Israel, ⁵ then you are to bring out to your gates that man or woman who has done this evil deed, *that is,* the man or the woman, and ᴬyou shall stone them to death. ⁶ᴬOn the testimony of two witnesses or three witnesses, the condemned shall be put to death; he shall not be put to death on the testimony of *only* one witness. ⁷ The hands of the witnesses shall be first against him to put him to death, and afterward the hands of all the people. ᴬSo you shall eliminate the evil from your midst.

⁸ "ᴬIf a case is too difficult for you to decide, between one kind of homicide or another, between one kind of lawsuit or another, and between one kind of assault or another, *that are* cases of dispute in your courts, then you shall arise and go up to the place which the LORD your God

chooses. ⁹ So you shall come to ᴬthe Levitical priests or the judge who is *in office* in those days, and you shall inquire *of them* and they will declare to you the verdict. ¹⁰ Then you shall act in accordance with the terms of the verdict which they declare to you from that place which the LORD chooses; and you shall be careful to act in accordance with everything that they instruct you *to do.* ¹¹ᴬIn accordance with the terms of the law about which they instruct you, and in accordance with the verdict which they tell you, you shall act; you shall not turn aside from the word which they declare to you, to the right or the left. ¹² But the person who acts ᴬinsolently by not listening to the priest who stands there to serve the LORD your God, nor to the judge, that person shall die; so you shall eliminate the evil from Israel. ¹³ Then all the people will hear and be afraid, and will not act ᴬinsolently again.

¹⁴ "When you enter the land which the LORD your God is giving you, and you take possession of it and live in it, and you say, 'I will appoint a king over me like all the nations who are around me,' ¹⁵ you shall in fact appoint a king over you whom the LORD your God chooses. *One* ᴬfrom among your countrymen you shall appoint as king over yourselves; you may not put a foreigner over yourselves, *anyone* who is not your countryman. ¹⁶ In any case, he is not to acquire many horses for himself, nor shall he ᴬmake the

17:1ᴬDeut 15:21   17:2ᴬDeut 13:6-11   17:3ᴬEx 22:20
ᴮJob 31:26-28   17:5ᴬLev 24:14; Josh 7:25
17:6ᴬNum 35:30; Deut 19:15   17:7ᴬ1 Cor 5:13
17:8ᴬ2 Chr 19:10; Hag 2:11   17:9ᴬDeut 19:17
17:11ᴬDeut 25:1   17:12ᴬNum 15:30; Deut 1:43
17:13ᴬDeut 17:12   17:14ᴬ1 Sam 8:5, 19, 20; 10:19
17:15ᴬJer 30:21   17:16ᴬIs 31:1; Ezek 17:15

people return to Egypt in order to acquire many horses, since the LORD has said to you, 'You shall never again return that way.' ¹⁷And ^he shall not acquire many wives for himself, so that his heart does not turn away; nor shall he greatly increase silver and gold for himself.

¹⁸"Now it shall come about, when he sits on the throne of his kingdom, that he shall write for himself a copy of this Law on a scroll ^in the presence of the Levitical priests. ¹⁹And it shall be with him, and he shall read it ^all the days of his life, so that he will learn to fear the LORD his God, by carefully following all the words of this Law and these statutes, ²⁰so that his heart will not be haughty toward his countrymen, ^and that he will not turn away from the commandment to the right or the left, so that he and his sons may live long in his kingdom in the midst of Israel.

PORTION FOR THE LEVITES

18 "^The Levitical priests, the whole tribe of Levi, shall not have a portion or inheritance with Israel; they shall eat the LORD's offerings by fire and His property. ²^They shall not have an inheritance among their countrymen; the LORD is their inheritance, as He promised them.

³"^Now this shall be the priests' portion from the people, from those who offer a sacrifice, either an ox or a sheep: they shall give the priest the shoulder, the two cheeks, and the stomach. ⁴You shall give him the ^first fruits of your grain, your new wine, and your oil, and the first fleece of your sheep. ⁵^For the LORD your God has chosen him and his sons from all your tribes,

to stand to serve in the name of the LORD always.

⁶"Now if a Levite comes from any of your towns throughout Israel where he ^resides, and he comes whenever he desires to the place which the LORD chooses, ⁷then he shall serve in the name of the LORD his God, like all his fellow Levites who stand there before the LORD. ⁸^They shall eat equal portions, except for *what they receive* from the sale of their fathers' *estates.*

SPIRITISM FORBIDDEN

⁹"When you enter the land which the LORD your God is giving you, you shall not learn to ^imitate the detestable things of those nations. ¹⁰There shall not be found among you *anyone* ^who makes his son or his daughter pass through the fire, one who uses divination, a soothsayer, one who interprets omens, or a sorcerer, ¹¹or one who casts a spell, ^or a medium, or a spiritist, or one who consults the dead. ¹²For whoever does these things is detestable to the LORD; and ^because of these detestable things the LORD your God is going to drive them out before you. ¹³^You are to be blameless before the LORD your God. ¹⁴For these nations, which you are going to dispossess, listen to ^soothsayers and diviners, but as for you, the LORD your God has not allowed you *to do* so.

¹⁵"^The LORD your God will raise up for you a prophet like me from

17:17 ^2 Sam 5:13; 12:11   17:18 ^Deut 31:24-26
17:19 ^Deut 4:9, 10; Josh 1:8   17:20 ^Deut 5:32;
1 Kin 15:5   18:1 ^Deut 10:9; 1 Cor 9:13
18:2 ^Num 18:20   18:3 ^Lev 7:32-34; Num 18:11, 12
18:4 ^Num 18:12   18:5 ^Ex 29:9   18:6 ^Num 35:2, 3
18:8 ^Lev 27:30-33; Num 18:21-24   18:9 ^Deut 9:5
18:10 ^Deut 12:31   18:11 ^Lev 19:31   18:12 ^Lev 18:24
18:13 ^Gen 6:9; 17:1   18:14 ^2 Kin 21:6
18:15 ^Matt 21:11; Luke 2:25-34

among you, from your countrymen; to him you shall listen. ¹⁶This is ᴬin accordance with everything that you asked of the LORD your God at Horeb on the day of the assembly, saying, 'Do not let me hear the voice of the LORD my God again, and do not let me see this great fire anymore, or I will die!' ¹⁷And ᴬthe LORD said to me, 'They have spoken well. ¹⁸I will raise up for them a prophet from among their countrymen like you, and ᴬI will put My words in his mouth, and he shall speak to them everything that I command him. ¹⁹ᴬAnd it shall come about that whoever does not listen to My words which he speaks in My name, I Myself will require it of him. ²⁰But the prophet who speaks a word presumptuously in My name, a word which I have not commanded him to speak, or ᴬwhich he speaks in the name of other gods, that prophet shall die.' ²¹And if you say in your heart, 'How will we recognize the word which the LORD has not spoken?' ²²ᴬWhen the prophet speaks in the name of the LORD, and the thing does not happen or come true, that is the thing which the LORD has not spoken. The prophet has spoken it presumptuously; you are not to be afraid of him.

CITIES OF REFUGE

19 ᴬ"When the LORD your God cuts off the nations whose land the LORD your God is giving you, and you dispossess them and settle in their cities and in their houses, ²ᴬyou shall set aside for yourself three cities in the midst of your land which the LORD your God is giving you to possess. ³You shall prepare the roads for yourself, and divide into three regions the territory of your land which the LORD your God will give you as an inheritance, so that anyone who commits manslaughter may flee there.

⁴"ᴬNow this is the case of the one who commits manslaughter, who may flee there and live: when he kills his friend unintentionally, not hating him previously— ⁵as when a person goes into the forest with his friend to cut wood, and his hand swings the axe to cut down the tree, and the iron head slips off the handle and strikes his friend so that he dies—he may flee to one of these cities and live. ⁶Otherwise, the avenger of blood might pursue him in the heat of his anger, and overtake him because the way is long, and take his life, though he was not sentenced to death since he had not hated him previously. ⁷Therefore I command you, saying, 'You shall set aside for yourself three cities.'

⁸"And if the LORD your God ᴬenlarges your territory, just as He has sworn to your fathers, and gives you all the land that He promised to give your fathers— ⁹if you carefully follow all of this commandment which I am commanding you today, ᴬto love the LORD your God, and to walk in His ways always— then you shall add three more cities for yourself, besides these three. ¹⁰So innocent blood will not be shed in the midst of your land which the LORD your God is giving you as an inheritance, and ᴬguilt for bloodshed will not be on you.

18:16 ᴬEx 20:18, 19; Deut 5:23-27   **18:17** ᴬDeut 5:28
18:18 ᴬIs 51:16; John 17:8   **18:19** ᴬActs 3:23; Heb 12:25
18:20 ᴬDeut 13:1, 2; Jer 14:14   **18:22** ᴬJer 28:9
19:1 ᴬDeut 6:10, 11   **19:2** ᴬDeut 4:41; Josh 20:2
19:4 ᴬNum 35:9-34   **19:8** ᴬGen 15:18   **19:9** ᴬDeut 6:5
19:10 ᴬNum 35:33; Deut 21:1-9

¹¹"But ^Aif there is a person who hates his neighbor, and waits in ambush for him and rises up against him and strikes him so that he dies, and he flees to one of these cities, ¹²then the elders of his city shall send *men* and take him from there, and hand him over to the avenger of blood, so that he may die. ^{13A}You shall not pity him, but ^Byou shall eliminate the guilt for the bloodshed of the innocent from Israel, so that it may go well for you.

LAWS OF LANDMARK AND TESTIMONY

¹⁴"^AYou shall not displace your neighbor's boundary marker, which the ancestors have set, in your inheritance which you will inherit in the land that the LORD your God is giving you to possess.

¹⁵"^AA single witness shall not rise up against a person regarding any wrongdoing or any sin that he commits; on the testimony of two or three witnesses a matter shall be confirmed. ^{16A}If a malicious witness rises up against a person to testify against him of wrongdoing, ¹⁷then both people who have the dispute shall stand ^Abefore the LORD, before the priests and the judges who will be *in office* in those days. ¹⁸And the judges ^Ashall investigate thoroughly, and if the witness is a false witness *and* he has testified against his brother falsely, ¹⁹then ^Ayou shall do to him just as he had planned to do to his brother. So you shall eliminate the evil from among you. ²⁰And ^Athe rest *of the people* will hear and be afraid, and will never again do such an evil thing among you. ²¹So you shall not show pity: ^Alife for life, ^Beye for eye, tooth for tooth, hand for hand, *and* foot for foot.

LAWS OF WARFARE

20 "When you go out to battle against your enemies and see horses, chariots, *and* people more numerous than you, ^Ado not be afraid of them; for the LORD your God, who brought you up from the land of Egypt, is with you. ²When you are approaching the battle, the priest shall come forward and speak to the people. ³He shall say to them, 'Hear, Israel, you are approaching the battle against your enemies today. Do not be fainthearted. ^ADo not be afraid, or panic, or be terrified by them, ⁴for the LORD your God ^Ais the One who is going with you, to fight for you against your enemies, to save you.' ⁵The officers also shall speak to the people, saying, 'Who is the man that has built a new house but has not ^Adedicated it? Let him go and return to his house, otherwise he might die in the battle and another man would dedicate it. ⁶And who is the man that has planted a vineyard but has not put it to use? Let him go and return to his house, otherwise he might die in the battle and another man would put it to use. ^{7A}And who is the man that is ¹betrothed to a woman and has not married her? Let him go and return to his house, otherwise he might die in the battle and another man would marry her.' ⁸Then the officers shall speak further to the people and say, '^AWho is the man that is

19:11 ^AEx 21:12; Num 35:16   19:13 ^ADeut 7:2   ^B1 Kin 2:31   19:14 ^ADeut 27:17; Job 24:2   19:15 ^ANum 35:30; Deut 17:6   19:16 ^AEx 23:1; Ps 27:12   19:17 ^ADeut 17:9   19:18 ^ADeut 25:1   19:19 ^AProv 19:5   19:20 ^ADeut 17:13; 21:21   19:21 ^AEx 21:23   ^BMatt 5:38   20:1 ^A2 Chr 32:7, 8; Ps 23:4   20:3 ^ADeut 20:1; Josh 23:10   20:4 ^ADeut 1:30; 3:22   20:5 ^ANeh 12:27   20:7 ^ADeut 24:5   20:8 ^AJudg 7:3

20:7 ¹A betrothed couple was considered legally married, but did not yet live together

afraid and fainthearted? Let him go and return to his house, so that he does not make his brothers' hearts melt like his heart!' 9 And when the officers have finished speaking to the people, they shall appoint commanders of armies at the head of the people.

10 "When you approach a city to fight against it, you shall offer it terms of peace. 11 And if it agrees to make peace with you and opens to you, then all the people who are found in it shall become your ᴬforced labor and serve you. 12 However, if it does not make peace with you, but makes war against you, then you shall besiege it. 13 When the LORD your God gives it into your hand, ᴬyou shall strike all the men in it with the edge of the sword. 14 However, the women, the children, ᴬthe animals, and everything that is in the city, all of its spoils, you shall take as plunder for yourself; and you shall use the spoils of your enemies which the LORD your God has given you. 15 This is what you shall do to all the cities that are very far from you, which are not of the cities of these nations nearby. 16ᴬOnly in the cities of these peoples that the LORD your God is giving you as an inheritance, you shall not leave anything that breathes alive. 17 Instead, you shall utterly destroy them, the Hittite and the Amorite, the Canaanite and the Perizzite, the Hivite and the Jebusite, just as the LORD your God has commanded you, 18 so that they will not teach you to do ᴬall the same detestable practices of theirs which they have done for their gods, by which you would sin against the LORD your God.

19 "When you besiege a city for a long time, to make war against it in order to capture it, you shall not destroy its trees by swinging an axe against them; for you may eat from them, so you shall not cut them down. For is the tree of the field a human, that it should be besieged by you? 20 Only the trees that you know are not fruit trees you shall destroy and cut down, so that you may construct siegeworks against the city that is making war against you until it falls.

EXPIATION OF A CRIME

21 "If a person who has been killed by someone is found lying in the open country in the land which the LORD your God is giving you to possess, and it is not known who struck him, 2 then your elders and your judges shall go out and measure the distance to the cities which are around the one who was killed. 3 And it shall be that the city which is nearest to the person killed, that is, that the elders of that city shall take a heifer of the herd that has not been worked and has not pulled in a yoke; 4 and the elders of that city shall bring the heifer down to a valley with running water, which has not been plowed or sown, and they shall break the heifer's neck there in the valley. 5 Then ᴬthe priests, the sons of Levi, shall come forward, because the LORD your God has chosen them to serve Him and to bless in the name of the LORD; and every dispute and violent crime shall be settled by them. 6 And all the elders of that city which is nearest to the person

20:11 ᴬ1 Kin 9:21   20:13 ᴬNum 31:7   20:14 ᴬJosh 8:2
20:16 ᴬEx 23:31-33; Num 21:2, 3   20:18 ᴬEx 34:12-16;
Deut 7:4   21:5 ᴬDeut 17:9-11; 19:17

killed shall ^wash their hands over the heifer whose neck was broken in the valley; ⁷and they shall respond and say, 'Our hands did not shed this blood, nor did our eyes see *who did.* ⁸Forgive Your people Israel whom You have redeemed, LORD, and do not place the guilt for ^innocent blood in the midst of Your people Israel.' And the guilt for bloodshed shall be forgiven them. ⁹^So you shall remove the guilt for innocent blood from your midst, when you do what is right in the eyes of the LORD.

DOMESTIC RELATIONS

¹⁰"When you go out to battle against your enemies, and ^the LORD your God hands them over to you and you take them away captive, ¹¹and you see among the captives a beautiful woman, and are strongly attracted to her and would take her as a wife for yourself, ¹²then you shall bring her into your home, and she shall ^shave her head and trim her nails. ¹³She shall also remove the clothes of her captivity and shall remain in your house, and ^weep for her father and mother a full month; and after that you may have relations with her and become her husband and she shall be your wife. ¹⁴But it shall be, if you are not pleased with her, then you shall let her go wherever she wishes; and you certainly shall not sell her for money, you shall not treat her as merchandise, since you have ¹,^humiliated her.

¹⁵"If a man has two wives, the one loved and ^the other unloved, and *both* the loved and the unloved have borne him sons, and the firstborn son belongs to the unloved, ¹⁶then it shall be on the day that he wills what he owns as an inheritance to his sons, he is not allowed to treat the son of the loved *wife* as the firstborn, at the expense of the son of the unloved, *who actually is* the firstborn *son.* ¹⁷On the contrary, he shall acknowledge the firstborn, the son of the unloved *wife,* by giving him a double portion of everything that he owns, for he *was* the beginning of his strength; ^to him belongs the right of the firstborn.

¹⁸"If any person has a stubborn and rebellious son who does ^not obey his father or his mother, and when they discipline him, he does not listen to them, ¹⁹then his father and mother shall seize him, and bring him out to the elders of his city at the gateway of his hometown. ²⁰And they shall say to the elders of his city, 'This son of ours is stubborn and rebellious; he does not obey us, he is thoughtless and given to drinking.' ²¹Then all the men of his city shall stone him to death; so ^you shall eliminate the evil from your midst, and ^all Israel will hear *about it* and fear.

²²"Now if a person has committed a sin *carrying* ^a sentence of death and he is put to death, and you hang him on ¹a tree, ²³^his body is not to be left overnight on the ¹tree, but you shall certainly bury him on the same day (for ^he who is hanged is cursed of God), so that you do not defile your land which the LORD your God is giving you as an inheritance.

21:6 ^Matt 27:24   21:8 ^Num 35:33, 34; Jon 1:14
21:9 ^Deut 19:13   21:10 ^Josh 21:44
21:12 ^Lev 14:8, 9; Num 6:9   21:13 ^Ps 45:10
21:14 ^Gen 34:2   21:15 ^Gen 29:33   21:17 ^Gen 25:31
21:18 ^Ex 20:12; Lev 19:3   21:21 ^Deut 19:19
^Deut 13:11   21:22 ^Deut 22:26; Matt 26:66
21:23 ^John 19:31   ^Gal 3:13

21:14 ¹I.e., by a forced marriage   21:22 ¹Lit *wood*
21:23 ¹Lit *wood*

VARIOUS LAWS

22 "^You shall not see your countryman's ox or his sheep straying away, and avoid them; you shall certainly bring them back to your countryman. ²And if your countryman is not near you, or if you do not know him, then you shall bring it to your house, and it shall remain with you until your countryman looks for it; then you shall restore it to him. ³You shall also do this with his donkey, and you shall do the same with his garment, and you shall do likewise with any lost property of your countryman, which has been lost by him and you have found. You are not allowed to avoid *them*. ⁴You shall not see your countryman's donkey or his ox fallen down on the road, and avoid them; you shall certainly help him raise *them* up.

⁵"A woman shall not wear a man's clothing, nor shall a man put on a woman's clothing; for whoever does these things is an abomination to the Lᴏʀᴅ your God.

⁶"If you happen to come upon a bird's nest along the way, in any tree or on the ground, with young ones or eggs *in it,* and the mother sitting on the young or on the eggs, ^you shall not take the mother with the young; ⁷you shall certainly let the mother go, but the young you may take for yourself, ^in order that it may go well for you and that you may prolong your days.

⁸"When you build a new house, you shall make a parapet for your roof, so that you will not bring guilt for bloodshed on your house if anyone falls from it.

⁹"^You shall not sow your vineyard with two kinds of seed, otherwise all the produce of the seed which you have sown and the yield of the vineyard will be forfeited to the sanctuary.

¹⁰"^You shall not plow with an ox and a donkey together.

¹¹"^You shall not wear a material of wool and linen combined together.

¹²"^You shall make yourself tassels on the four corners of your garment with which you cover yourself.

LAWS ON MORALITY

¹³"If any man takes a wife and goes in to her and *then* turns against her, ¹⁴and he charges her with shameful behavior and publicly defames her, and says, 'I took this woman, *but* when I came near her, I did not find her to have evidence of virginity,' ¹⁵then the girl's father and her mother shall take and bring out the evidence of the girl's virginity to the elders of the city at the gate. ¹⁶And the girl's father shall say to the elders, 'I gave my daughter to this man as a wife, but he turned against her; ¹⁷and behold, he has charged her with shameful behavior, saying, "I did not find your daughter to have evidence of virginity." But this is the evidence of my daughter's virginity.' And they shall spread out the garment before the elders of the city. ¹⁸Then ^the elders of that city shall take the man and rebuke him, ¹⁹and they shall fine him a hundred *shekels* of silver and give it to the girl's father, because he publicly defamed a virgin of Israel. And she shall remain his wife; he is not allowed to divorce her all his days.

22:1^Ex 23:4, 5; Prov 27:10   22:6^Lev 22:28
22:7^Deut 4:40   22:9^Lev 19:19   22:10^2 Cor
6:14-16   22:11^Lev 19:19   22:12^Num 15:37-41;
Matt 23:5   22:13^Gen 29:21; Deut 24:1
22:18^Ex 18:21; Deut 1:9-18

²⁰"But if this ^charge is true, *and* they did not find the girl to have evidence of virginity, ²¹then they shall bring the girl out to the doorway of her father's house, and the men of her city shall stone her to death, because she has ^committed a disgraceful sin in Israel by playing the prostitute in her father's house; so ᴮyou shall eliminate the evil from among you.

²²"^If a man is found sleeping with a married woman, then both of them shall die, the man who slept with the woman, and the woman; so you shall eliminate the evil from Israel.

²³"^If there is a girl who is a virgin ¹betrothed to a man, and *another* man finds her in the city and sleeps with her, ²⁴then you shall bring them both out to the gate of that city and you shall stone them to death: the girl, because she did not cry out for help *though she was* in the city, and the man, because he has violated his neighbor's wife. So you shall eliminate the evil from among you.

²⁵"But if the man finds the girl who is betrothed in the field, and the man seizes her and rapes her, then only the man who raped her shall die. ²⁶And you are not to do anything to the girl; there is no sin in the girl *worthy of* death, for just as a man rises against his neighbor and murders him, so is this case. ²⁷When he found her in the field, the betrothed girl cried out, but there was no one to save her.

²⁸"^If a man finds a girl who is a virgin, who is not betrothed, and he seizes her and has sexual relations with her, and they are discovered, ²⁹then the man who had sexual relations with her shall give the girl's father fifty *shekels* of silver, and she shall become his wife, because he has violated her; he is not allowed to divorce her all his days.

³⁰"^A man shall not take his father's wife *in marriage,* so that he does not ¹uncover his father's garment.

PERSONS EXCLUDED FROM THE ASSEMBLY

23 "^No one who is emasculated or has his male organ cut off may enter the assembly of the LORD. ²No one of illegitimate birth may enter the assembly of the LORD; none of his *descendants,* even to the tenth generation, may enter the assembly of the LORD. ³^No Ammonite or Moabite may enter the assembly of the LORD; none of their *descendants,* even to the tenth generation, may ever enter the assembly of the LORD, ⁴because they did not meet you with food and water on the way when you came out of Egypt, and because they hired against you ^Balaam the son of Beor from Pethor of Mesopotamia, to curse you. ⁵Nevertheless, the LORD your God was unwilling to listen to Balaam, but the LORD your God ^turned the curse into a blessing for you because the LORD your God loves you. ⁶^You shall never seek their peace or their prosperity all your days.

⁷"You shall not loathe an Edomite, for ^he is your brother; you shall not

22:20^Deut 17:4　**22:21**^Gen 34:7　ᴮDeut 13:5
22:22^Lev 20:10; Ezek 16:38　**22:23**^Lev 19:20–22;
Matt 1:18, 19　**22:28**^Ex 22:16　**22:30**^Lev 18:8; 20:11
23:1^Lev 21:20; 22:24　**23:3**^Neh 13:1, 2
23:4^Num 22:5; 23:7　**23:5**^Prov 26:2
23:6^Ezra 9:12　**23:7**^Gen 25:24–26; Obad 10, 12

22:23¹A betrothed couple was considered legally married, but did not yet live together　**22:30**¹Idiom for violating his father's marriage

loathe an Egyptian, because you were a stranger in his land. [8]The sons of the third generation who are born to them may enter the assembly of the LORD.

[9]"When you go out as an army against your enemies, you shall be on guard against every evil thing.

[10]"If there is among you any man who is unclean because of a nocturnal emission, then he must go outside the camp; he may not reenter the camp. [11]But when evening approaches, he shall bathe himself with water, and at sundown he may reenter the camp.

[12]"You shall also have a place *allocated* outside the camp, so that you may go out there *to relieve yourself,* [13]and you shall have a spade among your tools, and it shall be when you sit down outside, you shall dig with it and shall turn and cover up your excrement. [14]Since [A]the LORD your God walks in the midst of your camp to save you and to defeat your enemies before you, your camp must be [B]holy; so He must not see anything indecent among you or He will turn away from you.

[15]"You shall not hand over to his master a slave who has escaped from his master to you. [16]He shall live with you in your midst, in the place that he chooses in one of your towns where it pleases him; [A]you shall not mistreat him.

[17]"None of the daughters of Israel shall be a cult prostitute, [B]nor shall any of the sons of Israel be a cult prostitute. [18]You shall not bring the earnings of a prostitute or the money for a [1,A]dog into the house of the LORD your God *as payment* for any vowed offering, because both of these are an abomination to the LORD your God.

[19]"You are not to charge interest to your countrymen: interest on money, food, *or* anything that may be loaned on interest. [20]You may charge interest to a foreigner, but to your countrymen you shall not charge interest, so that [A]the LORD your God may bless you in all that you undertake in the land which you are about to enter to possess.

[21]"When you make a vow to the LORD your God, you shall not delay to pay it, for the LORD your God will certainly require it of you, and it will be a sin for you. [22]However, if you refrain from making vows, it will not be a sin for you. [23]You shall be careful and perform what goes out of your lips, since in fact you have vowed a voluntary offering to the LORD your God, whatever you have promised.

[24]"When you enter your neighbor's vineyard, you may eat grapes until you are satisfied; but you are not to put *any* in your basket.

[25]"When you enter your neighbor's standing grain, you may pluck the heads of grain with your hand, but you are not to use a sickle on your neighbor's standing grain.

LAW OF DIVORCE

24 "When a man takes a wife and marries her, and it happens, if she finds no favor in his eyes because he has found some indecency in her, that [A]he writes her a certificate of divorce, puts *it* in her hand, and sends her away from his house, [2]and she leaves

23:10 [A]Lev 15:16   23:14 [A]Lev 26:12   [B]Ex 3:5
23:15 [A]1 Sam 30:15   23:16 [A]Ex 22:21; Prov 22:22
23:17 [A]Lev 19:29   [B]2 Kin 23:7   23:18 [A]Lev 18:22; 20:13
23:19 [A]Ex 22:25; Lev 25:35–37   23:20 [A]Deut 15:10
23:21 [A]Num 30:1, 2; Job 22:27   23:25 [A]Matt 12:1;
Mark 2:23   24:1 [A]Matt 5:31; Mark 10:4, 5

23:18 [1] Prob. refers to a male prostitute

his house and goes and becomes another man's *wife,* ³and the latter husband turns against her, writes her a certificate of divorce and puts *it* in her hand, and sends her away from his house, or if the latter husband who took her to be his wife dies, ⁴*then* her ᴬformer husband who sent her away is not allowed to take her again to be his wife, after she has been defiled; for that is an abomination before the Lᴏʀᴅ, and you shall not bring sin on the land which the Lᴏʀᴅ your God is giving you as an inheritance.

⁵"When a man takes a new wife, he is not to go out with the army, nor be assigned any duty; he shall be free at home for one year and shall ᴬmake his wife whom he has taken happy.

VARIOUS LAWS

⁶"No one shall seize a handmill or an upper millstone as a pledge *for a loan,* since he would be seizing *the debtor's* means of life as a pledge.

⁷"ᴬIf someone is caught kidnapping any of his countrymen of the sons of Israel, and he treats him as merchandise and sells him, then that thief shall die; so you shall eliminate the evil from among you.

⁸"ᴬBe careful about an infestation of leprosy, that you are very attentive and act in accordance with everything that the Levitical priests teach you; just as I have commanded them, you shall be careful to act. ⁹Remember what the Lᴏʀᴅ your God did ᴬto Miriam on the way as you came out of Egypt.

¹⁰"ᴬWhen you make your neighbor a loan of any kind, you shall not enter his house to take his pledge. ¹¹You shall stand outside, and the person to whom you are making

the loan shall bring the pledge outside to you. ¹²And if he is a poor man, you shall not sleep with his pledge. ¹³ᴬWhen the sun goes down you shall certainly return the pledge to him, so that he may sleep in his cloak and bless you; and ᴮit will be righteousness for you before the Lᴏʀᴅ your God.

¹⁴"ᴬYou shall not exploit a hired worker *who is* poor and needy, whether *he is* one of your countrymen or one of your strangers who are in your land in your towns. ¹⁵ᴬYou shall give him his wages on his day before the sun sets—for he is poor and sets his heart on it—so that he does not cry out against you to the Lᴏʀᴅ, and it becomes a sin in you.

¹⁶"ᴬFathers shall not be put to death for *their* sons, nor shall sons be put to death for *their* fathers; everyone shall be put to death for his own sin *alone.*

¹⁷"ᴬYou shall not pervert the justice due a stranger *or* an orphan, nor seize a widow's garment as a pledge. ¹⁸But you are to remember that you were a slave in Egypt, and that the Lᴏʀᴅ your God redeemed you from there; therefore I am commanding you to do this thing.

¹⁹"When you reap your harvest in your field and forget a sheaf in the field, you are not to go back to get it; it shall belong ᴬto the stranger, the orphan, and to the widow, in order that the Lᴏʀᴅ your God ᴮmay bless you in all the work of your hands. ²⁰ᴬWhen you beat *the olives* off your olive tree, you are not to

24:4 ᴬJer 3:1   24:5 ᴬProv 5:18   24:7 ᴬEx 21:16
24:8 ᴬLev 13:1-14, 57   24:9 ᴬNum 12:10
24:10 ᴬEx 22:26, 27   24:13 ᴬEx 22:26   ᴮDeut 6:25
24:14 ᴬLev 25:35-43; Deut 15:7-18   24:15 ᴬLev 19:13;
Jer 22:13   24:16 ᴬ2 Kin 14:6; 2 Chr 25:4
24:17 ᴬEx 23:9; Lev 19:33   24:19 ᴬDeut 14:29
ᴮProv 19:17   24:20 ᴬLev 19:10

search through the branches again; *that* shall be *left* for the stranger, the orphan, and for the widow.

²¹"When you gather the grapes of your vineyard, you are not to go over it again; *that* shall be *left* for the stranger, the orphan, and the widow. ²²And you shall remember that you were a slave in the land of Egypt; therefore I am commanding you to do this thing.

VARIOUS LAWS

25 "If there is a dispute between people and they go to court, and the judges decide their case, ^and they declare the righteous innocent and pronounce the wicked guilty, ²then it shall be if the wicked person ^deserves to be beaten, the judge shall then make him lie down and have him beaten in his presence with the number *of lashes* according to his wrongful act. ³^He may have him beaten forty times, *but* not more, so that he does not have him beaten with many more lashes than these, and that your brother does not ᴮbecome contemptible in your eyes.

⁴"^You shall not muzzle the ox while it is threshing.

⁵"When brothers live together, and one of them dies and has no son, the wife of the deceased shall not be *married* outside *the family* to a strange man. ^Her husband's brother shall have relations with her and take her to himself as *his* wife, and perform the duty of a husband's brother to her. ⁶It shall then be that the firstborn to whom she gives birth shall assume the name of his *father's* deceased brother, so that ^his name will not be wiped out from Israel. ⁷^But if the man does not desire to take his

brother's widow, then his brother's widow shall go up to the gate to the elders, and say, 'My husband's brother refuses to establish a name for his brother in Israel; he is not willing to perform the duty of a husband's brother to me.' ⁸Then the elders of his city shall summon him and speak to him. And *if* he persists and says, 'I do not desire to take her,' ⁹^then his brother's widow shall come up to him in the sight of the elders, and pull his sandal off his foot and ᴮspit in his face; and she shall declare, 'This is what is done to the man who does not build up his brother's house!' ¹⁰And in Israel his family shall be called by the name, 'The house of him whose sandal was removed.'

¹¹"If *two* men, a man and his countryman, have a fight with each other, and the wife of one comes up to save her husband from the hand of the one who is hitting him, and she reaches out with her hand and grasps that man's genitals, ¹²then you shall cut off her hand; ^you shall not show pity.

¹³"^You shall not have in your bag differing weights, a large and a small. ¹⁴You shall not have in your house differing measures, a large and a small. ¹⁵You shall have a correct and honest weight; you shall have a correct and honest measure, ^so that your days may be prolonged in the land which the Lord your God is giving you. ¹⁶For ^everyone who does these things, everyone who acts unjustly is an abomination to the Lord your God.

25:1^Deut 1:16, 17 25:2^Prov 19:29; Luke 12:48
25:3^2 Cor 11:24 ᴮJob 18:3 25:4^Prov 12:10;
1 Cor 9:9 25:5^Matt 22:24; Mark 12:19
25:6^Ruth 4:5, 10 25:7^Ruth 4:5, 6 25:9^Ruth 4:7, 8
ᴮNum 12:14 25:12^Deut 7:2; 19:13 25:13^Lev
19:35-37; Prov 11:1 25:15^Ex 20:12 25:16^Prov 11:1

17 "^Remember what Amalek did to you on the way when you came out of Egypt, 18 how he confronted you on the way and attacked among you all the stragglers at your rear when you were tired and weary; and he ^did not fear God. 19 So it shall come about, when the LORD your God has given you ^rest from all your surrounding enemies in the land which the LORD your God is giving you as an inheritance to possess, that you shall wipe out the mention of *the name* Amalek from under heaven; you must not forget.

OFFERING FIRST FRUITS

26 "Then it shall be, when you enter the land which the LORD your God is giving you as an inheritance, and you take possession of it and live in it, 2 that you shall take some of ^the first of all the produce of the ground which you bring in from your land that the LORD your God gives you, and you shall put *it* in a basket and ^go to the place where the LORD your God chooses to establish His name. 3 And you shall go to the priest who is *in office* at that time and say to him, 'I declare today to the LORD my God that I have entered the land which the LORD swore to our fathers to give us.' 4 Then the priest shall take the basket from your hand and set it before the altar of the LORD your God. 5 And you shall respond and say before the LORD your God, '^My father was a wandering Aramean, and he went down to Egypt and resided there, few in number; but there he became a great, mighty, and populous nation. 6 And the ^Egyptians treated us badly and oppressed us, and imposed hard labor on us.

7 Then ^we cried out to the LORD, the God of our fathers, and the LORD heard our voice and saw our wretched condition, our trouble, and our oppression; 8 ^and the LORD brought us out of Egypt with a mighty hand, an outstretched arm, and with great terror, and with signs and wonders; 9 and He has brought us to this place, and has given us this land, ^a land flowing with milk and honey. 10 And now behold, I have brought the first of the produce of the ground ^which You, LORD have given me.' Then you shall set it before the LORD your God, and worship before the LORD your God; 11 and you, the Levite, and the stranger who is among you shall ^rejoice in all the good which the LORD your God has given you and your household.

12 "^When you have finished paying all the tithe of your produce in the third year, the year of the tithe, then you shall give it to the Levite, to the stranger, to the orphan, and to the widow, so that they may eat in your towns and be satisfied. 13 And you shall say before the LORD your God, 'I have removed the sacred *portion* from *my* house, and have also given it to the Levite, the stranger, the orphan, and the widow, in accordance with all Your commandments which You have commanded me; ^I have not violated or forgotten any of Your commandments. 14 I have not eaten of it while mourning, nor have I removed any of it while I was unclean, nor offered any of it to the

25:17 ^Ex 17:8-16   25:18 ^Ps 36:1; Rom 3:18
25:19 ^Deut 12:9   26:2 ^Ex 22:29   8 Deut 12:5
26:5 ^Gen 43:1-14   26:6 ^Ex 1:8-11   26:7 ^Ex 2:23-25;
3:9   26:8 ^Deut 4:34; 34:11, 12   26:9 ^Ex 3:8, 17
26:10 ^Deut 8:18; Prov 10:22   26:11 ^Deut 12:7; 16:11
26:12 ^Lev 27:30; Num 18:24   26:13 ^Ps 119:141, 153, 176

dead. I have listened to the voice of the LORD my God; I have acted in accordance with everything that You have commanded me. [15] ^Look down from Your holy dwelling place, from heaven, and bless Your people Israel, and the ground which You have given us, ^B a land flowing with milk and honey just as You swore to our fathers.'

[16] "This day the LORD your God commands you to perform these statutes and ordinances. Therefore you shall be careful to perform them ^with all your heart and with all your soul. [17] ^Today you have declared the LORD to be your God, and that you will walk in His ways and keep His statutes, His commandments, and His ordinances, and listen to His voice. [18] And the LORD has today declared you to be ^His people, *His* personal possession, just as He promised you, and that you are to keep all His commandments; [19] and that He will ^put you high above all the nations which He has made, for glory, fame, and honor; and that you shall be ^B a consecrated people to the LORD your God, just as He has spoken."

THE CURSES AT MOUNT EBAL

27 Then Moses and the elders of Israel commanded the people, saying, "Keep all the commandments which I am commanding you today. [2] ^So it shall be on the day when you cross the Jordan to the land which the LORD your God is giving you, that you shall set up for yourself large stones and coat them with lime [3] and write on them all the words of this Law, when you cross over, so that you may enter the land which the LORD your God is giving you, ^a land flowing with

milk and honey, just as the LORD, the God of your fathers, promised you. [4] So it shall be when you cross the Jordan, you shall set up these stones ^on Mount Ebal, as I am commanding you today, and you shall coat them with lime. [5] Moreover, you shall build there an altar to the LORD your God, an altar of stones; you ^shall not wield an iron *tool* on them. [6] You shall build the altar of the LORD your God of uncut stones, and you shall offer on it burnt offerings to the LORD your God; [7] and you shall sacrifice peace offerings and eat there, and ^rejoice before the LORD your God. [8] You shall write on the stones all the words of this Law very clearly."

[9] Then Moses and the Levitical priests spoke to all Israel, saying, "Be silent and listen, Israel! This day you have become a people for the LORD your God. [10] So you shall obey the LORD your God, and do His commandments and His statutes which I am commanding you today."

[11] Moses also commanded the people on that day, saying, [12] "When you cross the Jordan, these *tribes* shall stand on ^Mount Gerizim to bless the people: ^B Simeon, Levi, Judah, Issachar, Joseph, and Benjamin. [13] For the curse, these *tribes* shall stand on Mount Ebal: Reuben, Gad, Asher, Zebulun, Dan, and Naphtali. [14] The Levites shall then respond and say to all the people of Israel with a loud voice,

[15] 'Cursed is the person who makes ^a carved image or cast metal image, an abomination to the LORD, the

26:15 ^Ps 80:14   ^B Deut 26:9   26:16 ^Deut 4:29
26:17 ^Ps 48:14   26:18 ^Ex 6:7; 19:5   26:19 ^Deut 4:7, 8
^B Ex 19:6   27:2 ^Josh 8:30-32   27:3 ^Deut 26:9
27:4 ^Deut 11:29; Josh 8:30   27:5 ^Ex 20:25; Josh 8:31
27:7 ^Deut 26:11   27:12 ^Deut 11:29   ^B Josh 8:33-35
27:15 ^Ex 20:4, 23; 34:17

work of the hands of a craftsman, and sets *it* up in secret.' And all the people shall reply and say, 'Amen.'

¹⁶ 'ᴬCursed is one who treats his father or mother contemptuously.' And all the people shall say, 'Amen.'

¹⁷ 'ᴬCursed is one who displaces his neighbor's boundary marker.' And all the people shall say, 'Amen.'

¹⁸ 'ᴬCursed is one who misleads a person who is blind on the road.' And all the people shall say, 'Amen.'

¹⁹ 'ᴬCursed is one who distorts the justice *due* a stranger, an orphan, or a widow.' And all the people shall say, 'Amen.'

²⁰ 'ᴬCursed is he who sleeps with his father's wife, because he has ¹uncovered his father's garment.' And all the people shall say, 'Amen.'

²¹ 'ᴬCursed is one who has sexual intercourse with any animal.' And all the people shall say, 'Amen.'

²² 'ᴬCursed is he who sleeps with his sister, the daughter of his father or of his mother.' And all the people shall say, 'Amen.'

²³ 'ᴬCursed is he who sleeps with his mother-in-law.' And all the people shall say, 'Amen.'

²⁴ 'ᴬCursed is he who attacks his neighbor in secret.' And all the people shall say, 'Amen.'

²⁵ 'ᴬCursed is he who accepts a bribe to attack an innocent person.' And all the people shall say, 'Amen.'

²⁶ 'ᴬCursed is *anyone* who does not fulfill the words of this Law by doing them.' And all the people shall say, 'Amen.'

THE BLESSINGS AT MOUNT GERIZIM

28 "ᴬNow it shall be, if you diligently obey the Lᴏʀᴅ your God, being careful to do all His commandments which I am commanding you today, that the Lᴏʀᴅ your God will put you high above all the nations of the earth. ² And all these blessings will come to you and ᴬreach you if you obey the Lᴏʀᴅ your God:

³ "Blessed *will* you *be* in the city, and blessed *will* you *be* ᴬin the country.

⁴ "Blessed *will be* the children of your womb, the produce of your ground, and the offspring of your animals: the newborn of your herd and the young of your flock.

⁵ "Blessed *will be* your basket and your kneading bowl.

⁶ "Blessed *will* you *be* ᴬwhen you come in, and blessed *will* you *be* when you go out.

⁷ "The Lᴏʀᴅ will cause your enemies who rise up against you to be defeated by you; they will go out against you one way and will flee at your presence seven ways. ⁸ The Lᴏʀᴅ will command the blessing for you in your barns and in ᴬeverything that you put your hand to, and He will bless you in the land that the Lᴏʀᴅ your God is giving you. ⁹ ᴬThe Lᴏʀᴅ will establish you as a holy people to Himself, as He swore to you, if you keep the commandments of the Lᴏʀᴅ your God and walk in His ways. ¹⁰ So all the peoples of the earth will see that ᴬyou are called by the name of the Lᴏʀᴅ, and they will be afraid of you. ¹¹ ᴬAnd the Lᴏʀᴅ will give you more than enough prosperity, in the children of your womb, in the offspring of

27:16 ᴬEx 20:12; 21:17   27:17 ᴬDeut 19:14; Prov 22:28
27:18 ᴬLev 19:14   27:19 ᴬEx 22:21; 23:9
27:20 ᴬLev 18:8; 20:11   27:21 ᴬEx 22:19; Lev 18:23
27:22 ᴬLev 18:9; 20:17   27:23 ᴬLev 20:14
27:24 ᴬEx 21:12; Lev 24:17   27:25 ᴬEx 23:7; Deut 10:17
27:26 ᴬPs 119:21; Jer 11:3   28:1 ᴬEx 15:26; 23:22-27
28:2 ᴬZech 1:6   28:3 ᴬGen 39:5   28:6 ᴬPs 121:8
28:8 ᴬDeut 15:10   28:9 ᴬEx 19:5   28:10 ᴬ2 Chr 7:14
28:11 ᴬDeut 28:4; Prov 10:22

27:20 ¹Idiom for violated his father's marriage

your livestock, and in the produce of your ground, in the land which the LORD swore to your fathers to give you. ¹²The LORD will open for you His good storehouse, the heavens, to give rain to your land in its season and to bless every work of your hand; and ᴬyou will lend to many nations, but you will not borrow. ¹³ᴬAnd the LORD will make you the head and not the tail, and you will only be above, and not be underneath, if you listen to the commandments of the LORD your God which I am commanding you today, to follow *them* carefully, ¹⁴and ᴬdo not turn aside from any of the words which I am commanding you today, to the right or the left, to pursue other gods to serve them.

CONSEQUENCES OF DISOBEDIENCE

¹⁵ "ᴬBut it shall come about, if you do not obey the LORD your God, to be careful to follow all His commandments and His statutes which I am commanding you today, that all these curses will come upon you and overtake you:

¹⁶ "ᴬCursed *will* you *be* in the city, and cursed *will* you *be* in the country.

¹⁷ "ᴬCursed *will be* your basket and your kneading bowl.

¹⁸ "ᴬCursed *will be* the children of your womb, the produce of your ground, the newborn of your herd, and the offspring of your flock.

¹⁹ "ᴬCursed *will* you *be* when you come in, and cursed *will* you *be* when you go out.

²⁰ "ᴬThe LORD will send against you curses, panic, and rebuke, in everything you undertake to do, until you are destroyed and until you perish quickly, on account of the evil of your deeds, because you have abandoned Me. ²¹ᴬThe LORD

will make the plague cling to you until He has eliminated you from the land where you are entering to take possession of it. ²²ᴬThe LORD will strike you with consumption, inflammation, fever, feverish heat, and with ¹the sword, with blight, and with mildew, and they will pursue you until you perish. ²³The heaven which is over your head shall be bronze, and the earth which is under you, iron. ²⁴ᴬThe LORD will make the rain of your land powder and dust; from heaven it shall come down on you until you are destroyed.

²⁵ "ᴬThe LORD will cause you to be defeated by your enemies; you will go out one way against them, but you will flee seven ways from their presence, and you will be *an example of* terror to all the kingdoms of the earth. ²⁶ᴬYour dead bodies will serve as food for all birds of the sky and for the animals of the earth, and there will be no one to frighten *them away.*

²⁷ "ᴬThe LORD will strike you with the boils of Egypt and with ᴮtumors, the festering rash, and with scabies, from which you cannot be healed. ²⁸The LORD will strike you with insanity, blindness, and with confusion of mind; ²⁹and you will be ᴬgroping about at noon, just as a person who is blind gropes in the darkness, and you will not be successful in your ways; but you will only be oppressed and robbed all

28:12ᴬDeut 23:20   28:13ᴬDeut 28:1, 44
28:14ᴬDeut 5:32; Josh 1:7   28:15ᴬLev 26:14-43;
Josh 23:15   28:16ᴬDeut 28:3   28:17ᴬDeut 28:5
28:18ᴬDeut 28:4   28:19ᴬDeut 28:6
28:20ᴬDeut 28:8; Mal 2:2   28:21ᴬLev 26:25;
Num 14:12   28:22ᴬLev 26:16   28:24ᴬDeut 11:17; 28:12
28:25ᴬDeut 28:7; Is 30:17   28:26ᴬJer 7:33; 16:4
28:27ᴬEx 9:9   ᴮ1 Sam 5:6   28:29ᴬEx 10:21

28:22¹Another reading is *drought*

the time, with no one to save you. ³⁰ᴬYou will ¹betroth a woman, but another man will violate her; ᴮyou will build a house, but you will not live in it; you will plant a vineyard, but you will not make use of its fruit. ³¹Your ox *will be* slaughtered before your eyes, but you will not eat of it; your donkey *will be* snatched away from you, and will not be restored to you; your sheep *will be* given to your enemies, and you will have no one to save you. ³²ᴬYour sons and your daughters *will be* given to another people, while your eyes look on and long for them constantly; but there will be nothing you can do. ³³ᴬA people whom you do not know will eat the produce of your ground and every product of your labor, and you will never be anything but oppressed and mistreated continually. ³⁴You will also be driven insane by the sight of what you see. ³⁵ᴬThe LORD will strike you on the knees and thighs with severe boils from which you cannot be healed, *and strike you* from the sole of your foot to the top of your head. ³⁶ᴬThe LORD will bring you and your king, whom you appoint over you, to a nation that neither you nor your fathers have known, and there you shall serve other gods, *made of* wood and stone. ³⁷And ᴬyou will become an *object of* horror, a song of mockery, and an object of taunting among all the peoples where the LORD drives you.

³⁸"ᴬYou will bring out a great amount of seed to the field, but you will gather in little, because the locust will devour it. ³⁹ᴬYou will plant and cultivate vineyards, but you will neither drink of the wine nor bring in *the harvest,* because the worm will eat it. ⁴⁰ᴬYou will have olive trees throughout your territory

but you will not anoint yourself with the oil, because your olives will drop off *prematurely.* ⁴¹ᴬYou will father sons and daughters but they will not remain yours, because they will go into captivity. ⁴²ᴬThe cricket will take possession of all your trees and the produce of your ground. ⁴³ᴬThe stranger who is among you will rise above you higher and higher, and you will go down lower and lower. ⁴⁴ᴬHe will lend to you, but you will not lend to him; he will be the head, and you will be the tail.

⁴⁵"So all these curses shall come upon you and pursue you and overtake you ᴬuntil you are destroyed, because you would not obey the LORD your God by keeping His commandments and His statutes which He commanded you. ⁴⁶And they will become ᴬa sign and a wonder against you and your descendants forever.

⁴⁷"ᴬSince you did not serve the LORD your God with joy and a cheerful heart, *in gratitude* for the abundance of all *things,* ⁴⁸you will serve your enemies whom the LORD will send against you, ᴬin hunger, thirst, nakedness, and devoid of all *things;* and He ᴮwill put an iron yoke on your neck until He has destroyed you.

⁴⁹"ᴬThe LORD will bring a nation against you from far away, from

28:30 ᴬJob 31:10   ᴮAmos 5:11   28:32 ᴬDeut 28:41   28:33 ᴬJer 5:15, 17   28:35 ᴬDeut 28:27   28:36 ᴬ2 Kin 17:4, 6; 24:12, 14   28:37 ᴬ1 Kin 9:7, 8; Jer 19:8   28:38 ᴬIs 5:10; Mic 6:15   28:39 ᴬIs 5:10; 17:10, 11   28:40 ᴬJer 11:16; Mic 6:15   28:41 ᴬDeut 28:32   28:42 ᴬDeut 28:38   28:43 ᴬDeut 28:13   28:44 ᴬDeut 28:12   28:45 ᴬDeut 4:25, 26   28:46 ᴬNum 26:10; Is 8:18   28:47 ᴬDeut 12:7; Neh 9:35-37   28:48 ᴬLam 4:4-6   ᴮJer 28:13, 14   28:49 ᴬIs 5:26-30

28:30 ¹A betrothed couple was considered legally married, but did not yet live together

the end of the earth, ᴮas the eagle swoops down; a nation whose language you will not understand, ⁵⁰a nation with a defiant attitude, who will ᴬhave no respect for the old, nor show favor to the young. ⁵¹Furthermore, it will eat the offspring of your herd and the produce of your ground until you are destroyed; *a nation* that will leave you no grain, new wine, or oil, nor the newborn of your cattle or the young of your flock, until they have eliminated you. ⁵²ᴬAnd it will besiege you in all your towns until your high and fortified walls in which you trusted come down throughout your land, and it will besiege you in all your towns throughout your land which the LORD your God has given you. ⁵³ᴬThen you will eat the offspring of your own body, the flesh of your sons and of your daughters whom the LORD your God has given you, during the siege and the hardship by which your enemy will oppress you. ⁵⁴The man who is refined and very delicate among you will be hostile toward his brother, toward the wife he cherishes, and toward the rest of his children who are left, ⁵⁵so that he will not give *even* one of them any of the flesh of his children which he will eat, since he has nothing *else* left, during the siege and the hardship by which your enemy will oppress you in all your towns. ⁵⁶ᴬThe refined and delicate woman among you, who would not venture to set the sole of her foot on the ground because of her delicateness and tenderness, will be hostile toward the husband she cherishes and toward her son and daughter, ⁵⁷and toward her afterbirth that comes from between her legs, and toward her children to whom she

gives birth, because ᴬshe will eat them secretly for lack of anything *else,* during the siege and the hardship with which your enemy will oppress you in your towns.

⁵⁸"If you are not careful to follow all the words of this Law that are written in this book, to ᴬfear this honored and awesome name, the LORD your God, ⁵⁹then the LORD will bring extraordinary plagues on you and your descendants, severe and lasting plagues, and miserable and chronic sicknesses. ⁶⁰ᴬAnd He will bring back on you every disease of Egypt of which you were afraid, and they will cling to you. ⁶¹Also every sickness and every plague, which are not written in the book of this Law, the LORD will bring on you ᴬuntil you are destroyed. ⁶²Then you will be left few in number, ᴬwhereas you were as numerous as the stars of heaven, because you did not obey the LORD your God. ⁶³And it will come about that, just as the LORD ᴬrejoiced over you to be good to you, and make you numerous, so will the LORD ᴮrejoice over you to wipe you out and destroy you; and you will be torn away from the land which you are entering to possess. ⁶⁴Furthermore, the LORD will ᴬscatter you among all the peoples, from *one* end of the earth to the other; and there you will serve other gods, *made of* wood and stone, which you and your fathers have not known. ⁶⁵ᴬAmong those nations you will find no peace, and there will be no resting place for the sole of your

28:49 ᴮJer 48:40 28:50ᴬIs 47:6 28:52ᴬJer 10:17, 18; Zeph 1:15, 16 28:53ᴬLev 26:29; 2 Kin 6:28, 29 28:56ᴬLam 4:10 28:57ᴬ2 Kin 6:28, 29; Lam 4:10 28:58ᴬPs 99:3; Mal 1:14 28:60ᴬDeut 28:27 28:61ᴬDeut 4:25, 26 28:62ᴬDeut 1:10; Neh 9:23 28:63ᴬJer 32:41 ᴮProv 1:26 28:64ᴬLev 26:33; Deut 4:27 28:65ᴬLam 1:3 ᴮLev 26:36

foot; but there ᴮthe Lᴏʀᴅ will give you a trembling heart, failing of eyes, and despair of soul. ⁶⁶So your lives will be hanging in doubt before you; and you will be terrified night and day, and have no assurance of your life. ⁶⁷ᴬIn the morning you will say, 'If only it were evening!' And at evening you will say, 'If only it were morning!' because of the terror of your heart which you fear, and the sight of your eyes which you will see. ⁶⁸And the Lᴏʀᴅ will bring you back to Egypt in ships, by the way about which I said to you, 'You will never see it again!' And there you will offer yourselves for sale to your enemies as male and female slaves, but there will be no buyer."

THE COVENANT IN MOAB

29 ᴬThese are the words of the covenant which the Lᴏʀᴅ commanded Moses to make with the sons of Israel in the land of Moab, besides the covenant which He had made with them at Horeb.

² And Moses summoned all Israel and said to them, "You have seen all that the Lᴏʀᴅ did before your eyes in the land of Egypt to Pharaoh and all his servants, and to all his land; ³ᴬthe great trials which your eyes have seen, those great signs and wonders. ⁴Yet to this day ᴬthe Lᴏʀᴅ has not given you a heart to know, nor eyes to see, nor ears to hear. ⁵And I have led you in the wilderness for forty years; ᴬyour clothes have not worn out on you, and your sandal has not worn out on your foot. ⁶ᴬYou have not eaten bread, nor have you drunk wine or *other* strong drink, in order that you might know that I am the Lᴏʀᴅ your God. ⁷ᴬWhen you reached this place, Sihon the king of Heshbon

and Og the king of Bashan came out to meet us for battle, but we defeated them; ⁸and we took their land and ᴬgave it as an inheritance to the Reubenites, the Gadites, and the half-tribe of the Manassites. ⁹ᴬSo you will keep the words of this covenant and do them, in order that you may be successful in everything that you do.

¹⁰"You stand today, all of you, before the Lᴏʀᴅ your God: your heads, your tribes, your elders and your officers, *that is,* all the men of Israel, ¹¹your little ones, your wives, and the stranger who is within your camps, from ᴬthe one who gathers your firewood to the one who draws your water, ¹²so that you may enter into the covenant with the Lᴏʀᴅ your God, and into His oath which the Lᴏʀᴅ your God is making with you today, ¹³in order that He may establish you today as His people, and that ᴬHe may be your God, just as He spoke to you and as He swore to your fathers, to Abraham, Isaac, and Jacob.

¹⁴"Now *it is* not with you alone *that* I am ᴬmaking this covenant and this oath, ¹⁵ᴬbut *both* with those who stand here with us today in the presence of the Lᴏʀᴅ our God, and with those who are not with us here today ¹⁶(for you know how we lived in the land of Egypt, and how we passed through the midst of the nations through which you passed; ¹⁷moreover, you have seen their abominations and their idols *made of* ᴬwood and stone, silver and

28:67ᴬJob 7:4   29:1ᴬLev 26:46; 27:34
29:3ᴬDeut 4:34; 7:19   29:4ᴬIs 6:9, 10; Ezek 12:2
29:5ᴬDeut 8:4   29:6ᴬDeut 8:3   29:7ᴬNum
21:21-24, 33, 35; Deut 2:26-3:17   29:8ᴬNum 32:32, 33;
Deut 3:12, 13   29:9ᴬDeut 4:6; 1 Kin 2:3
29:11ᴬJosh 9:21, 23, 27   29:13ᴬGen 17:7; Ex 6:7
29:14ᴬJer 31:31; Heb 8:7, 8   29:15ᴬActs 2:39
29:17ᴬEx 20:23; Deut 4:28

gold, which *they had* with them); [18A]so that there will not be among you a man or woman, or family or tribe, whose heart turns away today from the LORD our God, to go to serve the gods of those nations; that there will not be among you a root bearing poisonous fruit and wormwood. [19]And it shall be when he hears the words of this curse, that he will consider himself fortunate in his heart, saying, 'I will do well though I walk in the stubbornness of my heart in order to destroy the watered *land* along with the dry.' [20]The LORD will not be willing to forgive him, but rather the anger of the LORD and His wrath will burn against that person, and every curse that is written in this book will lie upon him, and the LORD will [A]wipe out his name from under heaven. [21]Then the LORD will single him out for disaster from all the tribes of Israel, in accordance with all the curses of the covenant [A]which is written in this Book of the Law.

[22]"Now the future generation, your sons who rise up after you and [A]the foreigner who comes from a distant land, when they see the plagues of that land and the diseases with which the LORD has afflicted it, will say, [23]'All its land is [A]brimstone and salt, burned debris, unsown and unproductive, and no grass grows on it, like the overthrow of Sodom and Gomorrah, Admah and Zeboiim, which the LORD overthrew in His anger and in His wrath.' [24]All the nations will say, '[A]Why has the LORD done *all* this to this land? Why this great outburst of anger?' [25]Then *people* will say, '*It is* [A]because they abandoned the covenant of the LORD, the God of

their fathers, which He made with them when He brought them out of the land of Egypt. [26]And they went and served other gods and worshiped them, gods that they have not known and whom He had not assigned to them. [27]Therefore, the anger of the LORD burned against that land, [A]to bring upon it every curse which is written in this book; [28]and [A]the LORD uprooted them from their land in anger, fury, and in great wrath, and hurled them into another land, as *it is* this day.'

[29]"[A]The secret things belong to the LORD our God, but [B]the things revealed belong to us and to our sons forever, so that we may follow all the words of this Law.

RESTORATION PROMISED

30 "So it will be when all of these things have come upon you, [A]the blessing and the curse which I have placed before you, and you call *them* to mind [B]in all the nations where the LORD your God has scattered you, [2]and you [A]return to the LORD your God and obey Him with all your heart and soul in accordance with everything that I am commanding you today, you and your sons, [3]then the LORD your God will [A]restore you from captivity, and have compassion on you, and [B]will gather you again from all the peoples where the LORD your God has scattered you. [4]If any of your scattered *countrymen* are at the ends of the earth, [A]from there the LORD your God will

29:18 [A] Deut 13:6   29:20 [A] Ex 32:33; Deut 9:14
29:21 [A] Deut 30:10   29:22 [A] Jer 19:8; 49:17
29:23 [A] Gen 19:24; Is 34:9   29:24 [A] 1 Kin 9:8; Jer 22:8
29:25 [A] 2 Kin 17:9-23; 2 Chr 36:13-21   29:27 [A] Dan 9:11
29:28 [A] 2 Chr 7:20; Ps 52:5   29:29 [A] Acts 1:7
[B] John 5:39   30:1 [A] Deut 30:15, 19   [B] Lev 26:40-45
30:2 [A] Deut 4:29, 30; Neh 1:9   30:3 [A] Gen 28:15
[B] Ps 147:2   30:4 [A] Neh 1:9; Is 43:6

gather you, and from there He will bring you back. [5] The LORD your God will bring you into the land which your fathers possessed, and you shall possess it; and He will be good to you and [A]make you more numerous than your fathers.

[6] "Moreover, the LORD your God will circumcise your heart and the hearts of your descendants, [A]to love the LORD your God with all your heart and all your soul, so that you may live. [7][A]And the LORD your God will inflict all these curses on your enemies and on those who hate you, who persecuted you. [8] And you will again obey the LORD, and follow all His commandments which I am commanding you today. [9] Then the LORD your God will prosper you abundantly in every work of your hand, in the children of your womb, the offspring of your cattle, and in the produce of your ground, for [A]the LORD will again rejoice over you for good, just as He rejoiced over your fathers; [10] if you obey the LORD your God, to keep His commandments and His statutes which are written in this Book of the Law, if you turn to the LORD your God [A]with all your heart and soul.

[11] "For this commandment which I am commanding you today is not too difficult for you, nor is it far away. [12] It is not in heaven, that you could say, '[A]Who will go up to heaven for us and get it for us, and proclaim it to us, so that we may follow it?' [13] Nor is it beyond the sea, that you could say, 'Who will cross the sea for us and get it for us and proclaim it to us, so that we may follow it?' [14] On the contrary, the word is very near you, in your mouth and in your heart, that you may follow it.

CHOOSE LIFE

[15] "See, [A]I have placed before you today life and happiness, and death and adversity, [16] in that I am commanding you today [A]to love the LORD your God, to walk in His ways and to keep His commandments, His statutes, and His judgments, so that you may live and become numerous, and that the LORD your God may bless you in the land where you are entering to take possession of it. [17] But if your heart turns away and you will not obey, but allow yourself to be led astray and you worship other gods and serve them, [18] I declare to you today that [A]you will certainly perish. You will not prolong *your* days in the land where you are crossing the Jordan to enter and take possession of it. [19][A]I call heaven and earth to witness against you today, that I have placed before you life and death, [B]the blessing and the curse. So choose life in order that you may live, you and your descendants, [20][A]by loving the LORD your God, by obeying His voice, and [B]by holding close to Him; for this is your life and the length of your days, so that you may live in the land which the LORD swore to your fathers, to Abraham, Isaac, and Jacob, to give them."

MOSES' LAST COUNSEL

31 So Moses went and spoke these words to all Israel. [2] And he said to them, "I am 120 years old today; [A]I am no longer able to go out and come in, and the LORD has told me, 'You shall not cross this

30:5 [A]Deut 7:13; 13:17   30:6 [A]Deut 6:5   30:7 [A]Deut 7:15
30:9 [A]Jer 32:41   30:10 [A]Deut 4:29   30:12 [A]Rom 10:6-8
30:15 [A]Deut 11:26   30:16 [A]Deut 6:5   30:18 [A]Deut 4:26;
8:19   30:19 [A]Deut 4:26   [B]Deut 30:1   30:20 [A]Deut 6:5
[B]Deut 10:20   31:2 [A]Num 27:17; 1 Kin 3:7

Jordan.' ³It is the LORD your God who is going to cross ahead of you; He Himself will destroy these nations before you, and you shall dispossess them. ᴬJoshua is the one who is going to cross ahead of you, just as the LORD has spoken. ⁴And the LORD will do to them just as He did to Sihon and Og, the kings of the Amorites, and to their land, when He destroyed them. ⁵ᴬThe LORD will turn them over to you, and you will do to them in accordance with all the commandments which I have commanded you. ⁶Be strong and courageous, do not be afraid or in dread of them, for ᴬthe LORD your God is the One who is going with you. ᴮHe will not desert you or abandon you."

⁷Then Moses called to Joshua and said to him in the sight of all Israel, "ᴬBe strong and courageous, for you will go with this people into the land which the LORD has sworn to their fathers to give them, and you will give it to them as an inheritance. ⁸And ᴬthe LORD is the One who is going ahead of you; He will be with you. He will not desert you or abandon you. Do not fear and do not be dismayed."

⁹So Moses wrote this Law and gave it to the priests, the sons of Levi ᴬwho carried the ark of the covenant of the LORD, and to all the elders of Israel. ¹⁰Then Moses commanded them, saying, "At the end of *every* seven years, at the time of ᴬthe year of the release of debts, at the ᴮFeast of Booths, ¹¹when all Israel comes to appear before the LORD your God at the place which He will choose, ᴬyou shall read this Law before all Israel so that they hear *it*. ¹²Assemble the people, the men, the women, the children, and the stranger who

is in your town, so that they may hear and ᴬlearn and fear the LORD your God, and be careful to follow all the words of this Law. ¹³And their children, who have not known, will hear and learn to fear the LORD your God, as long as you live on the land which you are about to cross the Jordan to possess."

ISRAEL WILL FALL AWAY

¹⁴Then the LORD said to Moses, "Behold, ᴬthe time for you to die is near; call Joshua and present yourselves at the tent of meeting, and I will commission him." ᴮSo Moses and Joshua went and presented themselves at the tent of meeting. ¹⁵ᴬAnd the LORD appeared in the tent in a pillar of cloud, and the pillar of cloud stood at the entrance of the tent. ¹⁶The LORD said to Moses, "Behold, you are about to ¹lie down with your fathers; and ᴬthis people will arise and play the prostitute with the foreign gods of the land into the midst of which they are going, and ᴮthey will abandon Me and break My covenant which I have made with them. ¹⁷Then My anger will be kindled against them on that day, and I will abandon them and hide My face from them, and they will be consumed, and many evils and troubles will find them; so they will say on that day, 'ᴬIs it not because our God is not among us that these evils have found us?' ¹⁸But I will assuredly hide My face on that day because of

31:3 ᴬNum 27:18   31:5 ᴬDeut 7:2   31:6 ᴬDeut 20:4
ᴮJosh 1:5   31:7 ᴬDeut 1:38; 3:28   31:8 ᴬEx 13:21; 33:14
31:9 ᴬNum 4:5, 6, 15; Deut 10:8   31:10 ᴬDeut 15:1, 2
ᴮLev 23:34   31:11 ᴬJosh 8:34; 2 Kin 23:2
31:12 ᴬDeut 4:10   31:14 ᴬNum 27:12, 13   ᴮEx 33:9-11
31:15 ᴬEx 33:9   31:16 ᴬEx 34:15   ᴮJudg 10:6
31:17 ᴬNum 14:42

31:16 ¹I.e., die

all the evil that they will have done, for they will have turned away to other gods.

19 "Now then, ^write this song for yourselves, and teach it to the sons of Israel; put it on their lips, so that this song may be a witness for Me against the sons of Israel. 20 For when I bring them into the land flowing with milk and honey, which I swore to their fathers, and they eat and are satisfied and ^become prosperous, then they will turn to other gods and serve them, and spurn Me and break My covenant. 21 Then it will come about, when many evils and troubles find them, that this song will testify before them as a witness (for it shall not be forgotten from the mouth of their descendants); for ^I know their inclination which they are developing today, before I bring them into the land which I swore." 22 ^So Moses wrote down this song on the same day, and taught it to the sons of Israel.

JOSHUA IS COMMISSIONED

23 Then He commissioned Joshua the son of Nun, and said, "^Be strong and courageous, for you will bring the sons of Israel into the land which I swore to them, and ᴮI will be with you."

24 It came about, when Moses finished writing the words of this Law in a book until they were complete, 25 that Moses commanded the Levites ^who carried the ark of the covenant of the LORD, saying, 26 "Take this Book of the Law and place it beside the ark of the covenant of the LORD your God, so that it may remain there as a witness against you. 27 For I know ^your rebellion and your stubbornness;

behold, as long as I have been alive with you *until* today, you have been rebellious against the LORD; how much more, then, after my death? 28 Assemble to me all the elders of your tribes and your officers, that I may speak these words in their hearing and ^call the heavens and the earth as witnesses against them. 29 For I know that after my death you will ^behave very corruptly and turn from the way which I have commanded you; and evil will confront you in the latter days, because you will do that which is evil in the sight of the LORD, provoking Him to anger with the work of your hands."

30 Then Moses spoke in the hearing of all the assembly of Israel the words of this song, until they were complete:

THE SONG OF MOSES

32
"^Listen, you heavens, and I will speak;
And let the earth hear the words of my mouth!
2   "^May my teaching drip as the rain,
My speech trickle as the dew,
As droplets on the fresh grass,
And as the showers on the vegetation.
3   "For I proclaim the name of the LORD;
^Ascribe greatness to our God!
4   "The Rock! His work is perfect,
^For all His ways are just;
ᴮA God of faithfulness and without injustice,
Righteous and just is He.

31:19 ^Deut 31:22   31:20 ^Deut 32:15-17
31:21 ^1 Chr 28:9; John 2:24, 25   31:22 ^Deut 31:19
31:23 ^Josh 1:6   ᴮEx 3:12   31:25 ^Deut 31:9
31:27 ^Deut 9:7, 24   31:28 ^Deut 4:26; 30:19
31:29 ^Judg 2:19   32:1 ^Deut 4:26; Ps 50:4
32:2 ^Is 55:10, 11   32:3 ^Deut 3:24; 5:24
32:4 ^Gen 18:25   ᴮDeut 7:9

5 "They have acted corruptly
against Him,
They are not His children,
because of their defect;
^A*But are* a perverse and
crooked generation.
6 "*Is* this *what* you ^Ado to the LORD,
^BYou foolish and unwise people?
Is He not your Father *who has*
purchased you?
He has made you and
established you.
7 "Remember the days of old,
Consider the years of all
generations.
^AAsk your father and he will
inform you,
Your elders, and they will tell
you.
8 "^AWhen the Most High gave the
nations their inheritance,
When He separated the sons
of mankind,
He set the boundaries of the
peoples
According to the number of
the ¹sons of Israel.
9 "^AFor the LORD's portion is His
people;
Jacob is the allotment of His
inheritance.
10 "He found him in a desert land,
And in the howling wasteland
of a wilderness;
He encircled him, He cared for
him,
He guarded him as ^Athe apple
of His eye.
11 "As an eagle stirs up its nest,
And hovers over its young,
^AHe spread His wings, He
caught them,
He carried them on His
pinions.
12 "The LORD alone guided him,
^AAnd there was no foreign god
with him.

13 "^AHe had him ride on the high
places of the earth,
And he ate the produce of the
field;
And He had him suck honey
from the rock,
And oil from the flinty rock,
14 Curds of the herd, and milk of
the flock,
With fat of lambs
And rams, the breed of
Bashan, and *of* goats,
With the best of the wheat;
And you drank wine of the
^Ablood of grapes.

15 "But ¹Jeshurun became fat and
kicked—
You have become fat, thick,
and obstinate—
^AThen he abandoned God who
made him,
And rejected ^Bthe Rock of his
salvation.
16 "^AThey made Him jealous with
strange *gods;*
^BWith abominations they
provoked Him to anger.
17 "They sacrificed to demons,
who were not God,
^ATo gods *whom* they have not
known,
^BNew *gods* who came lately,
Whom your fathers did not
know.
18 "You forgot the Rock who
fathered you,
^AAnd forgot the God who gave
you birth.

32:5 ^AMatt 17:17   32:6 ^APs 116:12   ^BDeut 32:28
32:7 ^AEx 12:26; Ps 78:5-8   32:8 ^AActs 17:26
32:9 ^A1 Sam 10:1; 1 Kin 8:51, 53   32:10 ^APs 17:8; Prov 7:2
32:11 ^APs 18:10-18   32:12 ^ADeut 32:39; Is 43:12
32:13 ^AIs 58:14   32:14 ^AGen 49:11   32:15 ^AJudg 10:6
^BDeut 32:4   32:16 ^APs 78:58   ^BPs 106:29
32:17 ^ADeut 28:64   ^BJudg 5:8   32:18 ^APs 106:21

32:8 ¹As in MT; DSS *sons of God;* LXX *angels of God*
32:15 ¹I.e., Israel

19 "The Lord saw *this*, and
　　spurned *them*
　　ᴬBecause of the provocation *by*
　　His sons and daughters.
20 "Then He said, 'I will hide My
　　face from them,
　　I will see what their end *will be;*
　　For they are a perverse
　　generation,
　　ᴬSons in whom there is no
　　faithfulness.
21 'They have made Me jealous
　　with *what* is not God;
　　They have provoked Me to
　　anger with their idols.
　　ᴬSo I will make them jealous
　　with *those who are* not a
　　people;
　　I will provoke them to anger
　　with a foolish nation,
22 For a fire has flared in My anger,
　　And it burns to the lowest part
　　of ¹Sheol,
　　ᴬAnd devours the earth with
　　its yield,
　　And sets on fire the
　　foundations of the
　　mountains.
23 ᴬI will add misfortunes to
　　them;
　　ᴮI will use up My arrows on
　　them.
24 ᴬ*They will be* wasted by
　　famine, and emaciated by
　　plague
　　And a bitter epidemic;
　　And the teeth of beasts I will
　　send against them,
　　With the venom of crawling
　　things of the dust.
25 ᴬOutside the sword will make
　　them childless,
　　And inside, terror—
　　ᴮBoth young man and virgin,
　　The nursing child with the
　　man of gray hair.

26 'I would have said, "ᴬI will wipe
　　them out,
　　ᴮI will remove the mention of
　　their name from humanity,"
27 Had I not feared the
　　provocation by the enemy,
　　That their adversaries would
　　misjudge,
　　That they would say, "ᴬOur
　　hand is triumphant,
　　And the Lord has not
　　performed all this."'
28 "ᴬFor they are a nation destitute
　　of counsel,
　　And there is no understanding
　　in them.
29 "ᴬIf only they were wise *and*
　　they understood this;
　　ᴮ*If only* they would discern
　　their future!
30 "ᴬHow could one chase a
　　thousand,
　　And two put ten thousand to
　　flight,
　　Unless their Rock had sold
　　them,
　　And the Lord had given them
　　up?
31 "Indeed, their rock is not like
　　our Rock;
　　ᴬEven our enemies themselves
　　judge this.
32 "For their vine is from the vine
　　of Sodom,
　　And from the fields of
　　Gomorrah;
　　Their grapes are grapes of
　　ᴬpoison,
　　Their clusters, bitter.

32:19 ᴬJer 44:21-23　32:20 ᴬDeut 9:23
32:21 ᴬRom 10:19　32:22 ᴬLev 26:20
32:23 ᴬDeut 29:21　ᴮPs 18:14　32:24 ᴬDeut 28:22, 48
32:25 ᴬLam 1:20　ᴮ2 Chr 36:17　32:26 ᴬDeut 4:27
ᴮDeut 9:14　32:27 ᴬNum 15:30　32:28 ᴬDeut 32:6
32:29 ᴬDeut 5:29　ᴮDeut 31:29　32:30 ᴬLev 26:7, 8
32:31 ᴬEx 14:25　32:32 ᴬDeut 29:18

32:22 ¹I.e., the netherworld

33 "Their wine is the venom of
    serpents,
    And the deadly poison of
    vipers.

34 'AIs it not stored up with Me,
    Sealed up in My treasuries?
35 'AVengeance is Mine, and
    retribution;
    In *due* time their foot will slip.
    For the day of their disaster is
    near,
    And the impending things are
    hurrying to them.'
36 "AFor the LORD will vindicate
    His people,
    And will have compassion on
    His servants,
    When He sees that *their*
    strength is gone,
    And there is none *remaining*,
    bond or free.
37 "And He will say, 'AWhere are
    their gods,
    The rock in which they took
    refuge?
38 'AThose who ate the fat of their
    sacrifices,
    And drank the wine of their
    drink offering?
    BLet them rise up and help you,
    Let them be your protection!
39 'See now that I, I am He,
    AAnd there is no god besides Me;
    It is I *who* put to death and give
    life.
    I have wounded and *it is* I *who*
    heal,
    And there is no one who can
    save *anyone* from My hand.
40 'Indeed, AI raise My hand to
    heaven,
    And say, as I live forever,
41 AIf I have sharpened My
    flashing sword,
    And My hand has taken hold
    of justice,

BI will return vengeance on My
    adversaries,
    And I will repay those who
    hate Me.
42 'I will make My arrows drunk
    with blood,
    AAnd My sword will devour
    flesh,
    With the blood of the slain and
    the captives,
    From the long-haired leaders
    of the enemy.'
43 "Rejoice, you nations, *with* His
    people;
    AFor He will avenge the blood
    of His servants,
    And will return vengeance on
    His adversaries,
    And will atone for His land
    and His people."

44 Then Moses came and spoke all
the words of this song in the hearing of the people, he, with AJoshua
the son of Nun. 45 When Moses had
finished speaking all these words
to all Israel, 46 he said to them,
"ATake to your heart all the words
with which I am warning you
today, which you will command
Byour sons to follow carefully, all
the words of this Law. 47 For it is not
a trivial matter for you; indeed Ait
is your life. And by this word you
will prolong your days in the land,
which you are about to cross the
Jordan to possess."

48 Now Athe LORD spoke to Moses
that very same day, saying, 49 "AGo
up to this mountain of the Abarim,
Mount Nebo, which is in the land

32:34 AJob 14:17; Jer 44:21   32:35 APs 94:1; Rom 12:19
32:36 APs 135:14; Heb 10:30   32:37 AJudg 10:14;
Jer 2:28   32:38 ANum 25:1, 2   BJer 11:12
32:39 ADeut 32:12; Is 45:5   32:40 AEzek 20:5, 6;
21:4, 5   32:41 AIs 34:6-8   BJer 50:28-32
32:42 AJer 12:12; 46:10, 14   32:43 A2 Kin 9:7; Rev 6:10
32:44 ANum 13:8, 16   32:46 AEzek 40:4   BDeut 4:9
32:47 ADeut 8:3; 30:20   32:48 ANum 27:12
32:49 ANum 27:12-14; Deut 3:27

of Moab opposite Jericho, and look at the land of Canaan, which I am giving to the sons of Israel as a possession. ⁵⁰Then you are to die on the mountain where you ascend, and be ᴬgathered to your people, as Aaron your brother died on Mount Hor and was gathered to his people, ⁵¹ᴬbecause you broke faith with Me in the midst of the sons of Israel at the waters of Meribah-kadesh, in the wilderness of Zin, because you did not treat Me as holy in the midst of the sons of Israel. ⁵²ᴬFor you will see the land at a distance but you will not go there, into the land which I am giving the sons of Israel."

THE BLESSING BY MOSES

33 Now this is the blessing with which Moses ᴬthe man of God blessed the sons of Israel before his death. ²He said,
"ᴬThe Lᴏʀᴅ came from Sinai,
And dawned on them from Seir;
He shone from Mount Paran,
And He came from the midst of myriads of holy ones;
At His right hand there was flashing lightning for them.
³ "Indeed, He loves the people;
ᴬAll Your holy ones are in Your hand,
And they followed in Your steps;
Everyone takes of Your words.
⁴ "Moses issued to us *the* Law,
ᴬA possession for the assembly of Jacob.
⁵ "ᴬAnd He was king in Jeshurun,
When the heads of the people gathered,
The tribes of Israel together.

⁶ "ᴬMay Reuben live and not die,
Nor may his people be few."

⁷ᴬAnd this *was* regarding Judah; so he said:
"Hear, Lᴏʀᴅ, the voice of Judah,
And bring him to his people.
With his hands he contended for them,
And may You be a help against his adversaries."
⁸Of Levi he said,
"*Let* Your ᴬThummim and Your Urim *belong* to Your godly man,
Whom You tested at Massah,
With whom You contended at the waters of Meribah;
⁹ Who said of his father and his mother,
'I did not consider them';
And he did not acknowledge his brothers,
Nor did he regard his own sons,
For ᴬthey kept Your word,
And complied with Your covenant.
¹⁰ "ᴬThey will teach Your ordinances to Jacob,
And Your Law to Israel.
They shall put incense before You,
And whole burnt offerings on Your altar.
¹¹ "Lᴏʀᴅ, bless his strength,
And accept the work of his hands;
Smash the hips of those who rise up against him,
And those who hate him, so that they do not rise *again*."
¹²Of Benjamin he said,
"ᴬMay the beloved of the Lᴏʀᴅ live in security beside Him

32:50ᴬGen 25:8   32:51ᴬNum 20:12
32:52ᴬDeut 34:1-3   33:1ᴬJosh 14:6
33:2ᴬEx 19:18, 20; Ps 68:8, 17   33:3ᴬDeut 7:6; 14:2
33:4ᴬPs 119:111   33:5ᴬNum 23:21   33:6ᴬGen 49:3, 4
33:7ᴬGen 49:8-12   33:8ᴬEx 28:30; Lev 8:8
33:9ᴬMal 2:5   33:10ᴬLev 10:11; Deut 31:9-13
33:12ᴬDeut 4:37f; 12:10

Who shields him all the day
  long,
And he lives between His
  shoulders."

¹³ Of Joseph he said,
"^ABlessed of the LORD *be* his land,
With the choice things of
  heaven, with the dew,
And from the deep *waters*
  lying beneath,

¹⁴ And with the choice yield of
  the sun,
And the choice produce of the
  months;

¹⁵ And with the best things of
  ^Athe ancient mountains,
With the choice things of the
  everlasting hills,

¹⁶ And with the choice things of
  the earth and its fullness,
And the favor ^Aof Him who
  dwelt in the bush.
Let it come to the head of
  Joseph,
And to the top of the head
  of the *one who was* prince
  among his brothers.

¹⁷ "*As* the firstborn of his ox,
  majesty is his,
And his horns are the horns of
  ^Athe wild ox;
With them he will gore the
  peoples
All at once, *to* the ends of the
  earth.
And those are the ten
  thousands of Ephraim,
And those are the thousands
  of Manasseh."

¹⁸ ^AOf Zebulun he said,
"Rejoice, Zebulun, in your
  going out,
And, Issachar, in your tents.

¹⁹ "^AThey will call peoples *to* the
  mountain;
There they will offer righteous
  sacrifices;

For they will draw out ^Bthe
  abundance of the seas,
And the hidden treasures of
  the sand."

²⁰ Of Gad he said,
"Blessed is the one who
  enlarges Gad;
He lies down ^Aas a lion,
And tears the arm, also the
  crown of the head.

²¹ "Then he selected the choicest
  part for himself,
For there the ruler's portion
  was reserved;
And he came *with* the leaders
  of the people;
^AHe executed the justice of the
  LORD,
And His ordinances with
  Israel."

²² ^AOf Dan he said,
"Dan is ^Ba lion's cub;
He leaps out from Bashan."

²³ Of Naphtali he said,
"^ANaphtali, satisfied with
  favor,
And full of the blessing of the
  LORD,
Take possession of the sea
  and the south."

²⁴ ^AOf Asher he said,
"More blessed than sons is
  Asher;
May he be favored by his
  brothers,
And may he dip his foot in
  olive oil.

²⁵ "Your bars will be iron and
  bronze,
^AAnd as your days, *so will* your
  strength *be.*

33:13 ^AGen 27:27, 28; 49:22-26   33:15 ^AHab 3:6
33:16 ^AEx 2:2-6; 3:2, 4   33:17 ^ANum 23:22
33:18 ^AGen 49:13-15   33:19 ^AEx 15:17   ^BIs 60:5
33:20 ^AGen 49:9   33:21 ^AJosh 22:1-3
33:22 ^AGen 49:16   ^BEzek 19:2, 3   33:23 ^AGen 49:21
33:24 ^AGen 49:20   33:25 ^ADeut 4:40; 32:47

33:26 ¹I.e., Israel

26 "There is no one like the God
    of ¹Jeshurun,
  ᴬWho rides the heavens to
    your help,
  And the clouds in His majesty.
27 "ᴬThe eternal God is a hiding
    place,
  And underneath are the
    everlasting arms;
  And He drove out the enemy
    from you,
  And said, 'Destroy!'
28 "ᴬSo Israel lives in security,
  The fountain of Jacob
    secluded,
  ᴮIn a land of grain and new
    wine;
  His heavens also drip down
    dew.
29 "Blessed are you, Israel;
  ᴬWho is like you, a people
    saved by the Lᴏʀᴅ,
  The shield of your help,
  And He who is the sword of
    your majesty!
  So your enemies will cringe
    before you,
  And you will trample on their
    high places."

THE DEATH OF MOSES

34 ᴬNow Moses went up from
      the plains of Moab to Mount
Nebo, to the top of Pisgah, which
is opposite Jericho. And the Lᴏʀᴅ
ᴮshowed him all the land, Gilead as
far as Dan, ²and all Naphtali and
the land of Ephraim and Manasseh,
and all the land of Judah as far as
the ¹ᴬwestern sea, ³and the Negev
and the territory in the Valley of
Jericho, ᴬthe city of palm trees, as
far as Zoar. ⁴Then the Lᴏʀᴅ said

to him, "This is the land which
ᴬI swore to Abraham, Isaac, and
Jacob, saying, 'I will give it to your
descendants'; I have let you see *it*
with your eyes, but you will not
go over there." ⁵So Moses the servant of the Lᴏʀᴅ ᴬdied there in the
land of Moab, in accordance with
the word of the Lᴏʀᴅ. ⁶And He buried him in the valley in the land of
Moab, ᴬopposite Beth-peor; but
no one knows his burial place to
this day. ⁷Although Moses was 120
years old when he died, ᴬhis eyesight was not dim, nor *had* his vigor
left *him*. ⁸So the sons of Israel wept
for Moses in the plains of Moab for
thirty days; then the days of weeping *and* mourning for Moses came
to an end.

⁹Now Joshua the son of Nun was
ᴬfilled with the spirit of wisdom,
because Moses had laid his hands
on him; and the sons of Israel listened to him and did as the Lᴏʀᴅ
had commanded Moses. ¹⁰Since
that time ᴬno prophet has risen in
Israel like Moses, whom ᴮthe Lᴏʀᴅ
knew face to face, ¹¹for all the signs
and wonders which the Lᴏʀᴅ sent
him to perform in the land of Egypt
against Pharaoh, all his servants,
and all his land— ¹²and for all the
mighty power and all the great terror which Moses performed in the
sight of all Israel.

33:26ᴬDeut 10:14; Ps 68:33, 34   33:27ᴬPs 90:1, 2
33:28ᴬDeut 33:12   ᴮGen 27:28, 37   33:29ᴬDeut 4:32;
2 Sam 7:23   34:1ᴬDeut 32:49   ᴮDeut 32:52
34:2ᴬDeut 11:24   34:3ᴬJudg 1:16; 3:13   34:4ᴬGen 12:7;
26:3   34:5ᴬDeut 32:50   34:6ᴬDeut 3:29; 4:46
34:7ᴬGen 27:1; 48:10   34:9ᴬNum 27:18, 23; Is 11:2
34:10ᴬDeut 18:15, 18   ᴮEx 33:11

34:2¹I.e., Mediterranean Sea

JOSHUA

GOD'S ORDERS TO JOSHUA

1 Now it came about after the death of Moses the servant of the LORD, that the LORD spoke to Joshua the son of Nun, Moses' servant, saying, ²"Moses ᴬMy servant is dead; so now arise, cross this Jordan, you and all this people, to the land which I am giving to them, to the sons of Israel. ³ᴬEvery place on which the sole of your foot steps, I have given it to you, just as I spoke to Moses. ⁴ᴬFrom the wilderness and this Lebanon, even as far as the great river, the river Euphrates, all the land of the Hittites, and as far as the Great Sea toward the setting of the sun will be your territory. ⁵ᴬNo one will *be able to* oppose you all the days of your life. Just as I have been with Moses, I will be with you; I will not desert you nor abandon you. ⁶ᴬBe strong and courageous, for you shall give this people possession of the land which I swore to their fathers to give them. ⁷Only be strong and very courageous; ᴬbe careful to do according to all the Law which Moses My servant commanded you; do not turn from it to the right or to the left, so that you may achieve success wherever you go. ⁸ᴬThis Book of the Law shall not depart from your mouth, but you shall meditate on it day and night, so that you may be careful to do according to all that is written in it; for then you will make your way prosperous, and then you will achieve success. ⁹Have I not commanded you? Be strong and courageous! ᴬDo not be terrified nor dismayed, for the LORD your God is with you wherever you go."

JOSHUA ASSUMES COMMAND

¹⁰Then Joshua commanded the officers of the people, saying, ¹¹"Pass through the midst of the camp and command the people, saying, 'Prepare provisions for yourselves, for within ᴬthree days you are going to cross this Jordan, to go in to take possession of the land which the LORD your God is giving you, to possess it.'"

¹²But ᴬto the Reubenites, to the Gadites, and to the half-tribe of Manasseh, Joshua said, ¹³"Remember the word which Moses the servant of the LORD commanded you, saying, 'ᴬThe LORD your God is giving you rest, and will give you this land.' ¹⁴Your wives, your little ones, and your livestock shall remain in the land which Moses gave you beyond the Jordan, but you shall cross ahead of your brothers in battle formation, all your valiant warriors, and shall help them, ¹⁵until the LORD gives your brothers rest, as *He is giving* you, and they also possess the land which the LORD your God is giving them. ᴬThen you may return to your own land, and take possession of that which Moses the servant of the LORD gave you beyond the Jordan toward the sunrise."

1:2 ᴬNum 12:7; Deut 34:5   1:3 ᴬDeut 11:24
1:4 ᴬGen 15:18; Num 34:3   1:5 ᴬDeut 7:24
1:6 ᴬDeut 31:6, 7, 23   1:7 ᴬDeut 5:32   1:8 ᴬDeut 31:24;
Josh 8:34   1:9 ᴬDeut 31:8   1:11 ᴬJosh 3:2
1:12 ᴬNum 32:20-22   1:13 ᴬDeut 3:18-20   1:15 ᴬJosh 22:4

16They answered Joshua, saying, "All that you have commanded us we will do, and wherever you send us we will go. 17Just as we obeyed Moses in all things, so we will obey you; only ^may the LORD your God be with you as He was with Moses. 18Anyone who rebels against your command and does not obey your words in all that you command him, shall be put to death; only be strong and courageous."

RAHAB SHELTERS SPIES

2 Then Joshua the son of Nun sent two men as spies secretly from ^Shittim, saying, "Go, view the land, especially Jericho." So they went and entered the house of ^Ba prostitute whose name was Rahab, and rested there. 2But it was told to the king of Jericho, saying, "Behold, men from the sons of Israel have come here tonight to spy out the land." 3And the king of Jericho sent word to Rahab, saying, "Bring out the men who have come to you, who have entered your house, for they have come to spy out all the land." 4But the ^woman had taken the two men and hidden them, and she said, "Yes, the men came to me, but I did not know where they were from. 5It came about, when it was time to shut the gate at dark, that the men went out; I do not know where the men went. Pursue them quickly, for you will overtake them." 6But ^she had brought them up to the roof and hidden them in the stalks of flax which she had laid in order on the roof. 7So the men pursued them on the road to the Jordan, to the crossing places; and as soon as those who were pursuing them had gone out, they shut the gate.

8Now before the spies lay down, she came up to them on the roof, 9and said to the men, "^I know that the LORD has given you the land, and that the terror of you has fallen on us, and that all the inhabitants of the land have despaired because of you. 10^For we have heard how the LORD dried up the water of the Red Sea before you when you came out of Egypt, and what you did to the two kings of the Amorites who were beyond the Jordan, to Sihon and Og, whom you utterly destroyed. 11When we heard these reports, ^our hearts melted and no courage remained in anyone any longer because of you; for the ^BLORD your God, He is God in heaven above and on earth below. 12Now then, please swear to me by the LORD, since I have dealt kindly with you, that you also will deal kindly with my father's household, and give me a ^pledge of truth, 13and spare my father and my mother, and my brothers and my sisters, and all who belong to them, and save our lives from death." 14So the men said to her, "Our life for yours if you do not tell this business of ours; and it shall come about when the LORD gives us the land that we will ^deal kindly and faithfully with you."

THE PROMISE TO RAHAB

15Then she let them down by a rope through the window, for her house was on the city wall, so that she was living on the wall. 16And she said to them, "^Go to the hill

1:17^Josh 1:5, 9   2:1^Num 25:1   ^BHeb 11:31
2:4^2 Sam 17:19   2:6^James 2:25   2:9^Num 20:24;
Josh 9:24   2:10^Ex 14:21; Num 23:22   2:11^Josh 5:1
^BDeut 4:39   2:12^Josh 2:18, 19   2:14^Gen 24:49
2:16^James 2:25

country, so that the pursuers will not encounter you, and hide yourselves there for three days until the pursuers return. Then afterward you may go on your way." 17 And the men said to her, "^We *shall be* exempt from this oath to you which you have made us swear, 18 unless, when we come into the land, you tie this cord of scarlet thread in the window through which you let us down, and ^gather into your house your father, your mother, your brothers, and all your father's household. 19 And it shall come about that anyone who goes out of the doors of your house outside *will have* his blood on his own head, and we *will be* innocent; but anyone who is with you in the house, ^his blood *will be* on our head if a hand is *laid* on him. 20 But if you tell this business of ours, then we shall be exempt from the oath which you have made us swear." 21 She then said, "According to your words, so be it." So she sent them away, and they departed; and she tied the scarlet cord in the window.

22 So they departed and came to the hill country, and remained there for three days, until the pursuers returned. Now the pursuers had searched for *them* all along the road, but had not found *them*. 23 Then the two men returned and came down from the hill country, and they crossed over and came to Joshua the son of Nun. Then they reported to him all that had happened to them. 24 And they said to Joshua, "The Lord has indeed handed over to us all the land; furthermore, ^all the inhabitants of the land have despaired because of us."

ISRAEL CROSSES THE JORDAN

3 Then Joshua got up early in the morning; and he and all the sons of Israel set out from ^Shittim and came to the Jordan, and they spent the night there before they crossed. 2 Then ^at the end of three days the officers went through the midst of the camp; 3 and they commanded the people, saying, "When you see the ^ark of the covenant of the Lord your God with the Levitical priests carrying it, then you shall set out from your place and go after it. 4 However, there shall be a distance between you and it of about two thousand cubits by measurement. Do not come near it, so that you may know the way by which you shall go, for you have not passed this way before."

5 Then Joshua said to the people, "^Consecrate yourselves, for tomorrow the Lord will do miracles among you." 6 And Joshua spoke to the priests, saying, "Take up the ark of the covenant and cross over ahead of the people." So they took up the ark of the covenant and went ahead of the people.

7 Now the Lord said to Joshua, "This day I will begin to ^exalt you in the sight of all Israel, so that they will know that just as I have been with Moses, I will be with you. 8 So you shall command the priests who are carrying the ark of the covenant, saying, 'When you come to the edge of the waters of the Jordan, you shall stand *still* in the Jordan.'" 9 Then Joshua said to the sons of Israel, "Come here, and hear the words of the Lord your God."

2:17 ^Gen 24:8   2:18 ^Josh 2:12   2:19 ^Matt 27:25
2:24 ^Josh 2:9   3:1 ^Josh 2:1   3:2 ^Josh 1:11
3:3 ^Deut 31:9   3:5 ^Ex 19:10, 11; Josh 7:13
3:7 ^Josh 4:14

[10] And Joshua said, "By this you will know that the living God is among you, and that He will assuredly ^drive out from you the Canaanite, the Hittite, the Hivite, the Perizzite, the Girgashite, the Amorite, and the Jebusite. [11] Behold, the ark of the covenant of ^the Lord of all the earth is crossing over ahead of you into the Jordan. [12] Now then, ^take for yourselves twelve men from the tribes of Israel, one man for each tribe. [13] And it will come about when the soles of the feet of the priests who carry the ark of the LORD, the Lord of all the earth, rest in the waters of the Jordan, the waters of the Jordan will be cut off, *that is,* the waters which are flowing down from above; and they will ^stand in one heap."

[14] So when the people set out from their tents to cross the Jordan, with the priests carrying ^the ark of the covenant before the people, [15] and when those who were carrying the ark came up to the Jordan and the feet of the priests carrying the ark stepped down into the edge of the water (for the ^Jordan overflows all its banks all the days of harvest), [16] then the waters which were flowing down from above stood *and* rose up in ^one heap, a great distance away at Adam, the city that is beside Zarethan; and those which were flowing down toward the sea of the ^Arabah, the Salt Sea, were completely cut off. So the people crossed opposite Jericho. [17] And the priests who carried the ark of the covenant of the LORD stood firm ^on dry ground in the middle of the Jordan while all Israel crossed on dry ground, until all the nation had finished crossing the Jordan.

MEMORIAL STONES FROM THE JORDAN

4 Now when the entire nation had finished crossing the ^Jordan, the LORD spoke to Joshua, saying, [2] "^Take for yourselves twelve men from the people, one man from each tribe, [3] and command them, saying, 'Take up for yourselves twelve stones from here out of the middle of the Jordan, from the place where the priests' feet are standing firmly, and carry them over with you and lay them down in ^the encampment where you will spend the night.'"

[4] So Joshua called the twelve men whom he had appointed from the sons of Israel, one man from each tribe; [5] and Joshua said to them, "Cross again to the ark of the LORD your God into the middle of the Jordan, and each of you take up a stone on his shoulder, according to the number of the tribes of the sons of Israel. [6] This shall be a sign among you; ^when your children ask later, saying, 'What do these stones mean to you?' [7] then you shall say to them, 'That the ^waters of the Jordan were cut off before the ark of the covenant of the LORD; when it crossed the Jordan, the waters of the Jordan were cut off.' So these stones shall become a memorial to the sons of Israel forever."

[8] So the sons of Israel did exactly as Joshua commanded, and took up twelve stones from the middle of the Jordan, just as the LORD spoke to Joshua, according to the number of the tribes of the sons of Israel; and they carried them over with them to ^the encampment and put

3:10 ^Ex 33:2; Deut 7:1   3:11 ^Job 41:11; Ps 24:1   3:12 ^Josh 4:2   3:13 ^Ex 15:8   3:14 ^Ps 132:8; Acts 7:44f   3:15 ^1 Chr 12:15; Jer 12:5   3:16 ^Josh 3:13   ^B Deut 1:1   3:17 ^Ex 14:21, 22, 29   4:1 ^Deut 27:2; Josh 3:17   4:2 ^Josh 3:12   4:3 ^Josh 4:20   4:6 ^Ex 12:26; 13:14   4:7 ^Josh 3:13   4:8 ^Josh 4:20

them down there. [9]Then Joshua set up twelve ^stones in the middle of the Jordan at the place where the feet of the priests who carried the ark of the covenant were standing, and they are there to this day. [10]For the priests who carried the ark were standing in the middle of the Jordan until everything was completed that the Lord had commanded Joshua to speak to the people, according to all that Moses had commanded Joshua. And the people hurried and crossed; [11]and when all the people had finished crossing, then the ark of the Lord and the priests crossed in front of the people. [12]^The sons of Reuben, the sons of Gad, and the half-tribe of Manasseh crossed over in battle formation before the sons of Israel, just as Moses had spoken to them; [13]about forty thousand equipped for war, crossed for battle before the Lord to the desert plains of Jericho.

[14]^On that day the Lord exalted Joshua in the sight of all Israel, so that they revered him, just as they had revered Moses all the days of his life.

[15]Now the Lord said to Joshua, [16]"Command the priests who carry ^the ark of the testimony that they come up from the Jordan." [17]So Joshua commanded the priests, saying, "Come up from the Jordan." [18]It came about when the priests who carried the ark of the covenant of the Lord had come up from the middle of the Jordan, and the soles of the priests' feet were lifted up to the dry ground, that the waters of the Jordan returned to their place, and went over all its banks as before.

[19]Now the people came up from the Jordan on the ^tenth of the first month and camped at Gilgal, on the eastern edge of Jericho. [20]As for those twelve stones which they had taken from the Jordan, Joshua set *them* up ^at Gilgal. [21]And he said to the sons of Israel, "When your children ask their fathers in time to come, saying, 'What are these stones?' [22]then you shall inform your children, saying, 'Israel crossed this Jordan on ^dry ground.' [23]For the Lord your God dried up the waters of the Jordan before you until you had crossed, just as the Lord your God had done to the Red Sea, ^which He dried up before us until we had crossed; [24]so that ^all the peoples of the earth may know that the ^Bhand of the Lord is mighty, so that you may fear the Lord your God forever."

ISRAEL IS CIRCUMCISED

5 Now it came about when all the kings of the Amorites who *were* beyond the Jordan to the west, and all the kings of the ^Canaanites who *were* by the sea, heard how the Lord had dried up the waters of the Jordan before the sons of Israel until they had crossed, that their hearts melted, and there was no spirit in them any longer because of the sons of Israel.

[2]At that time the Lord said to Joshua, "Make for yourself ^flint knives and circumcise again the sons of Israel the second time." [3]So Joshua made himself flint knives and circumcised the sons of Israel at ¹Gibeath-haaraloth. [4]This is the

4:9 ^Gen 28:18; Josh 24:26f   4:12 ^Num 32:17
4:14 ^Josh 3:7   4:16 ^Ex 25:16   4:19 ^Deut 1:3
4:20 ^Josh 4:3, 8   4:22 ^Josh 3:17   4:23 ^Ex 14:21
4:24 ^1 Kin 8:42   ^BEx 15:16   5:1 ^Num 13:29
5:2 ^Ex 4:25

5:3 ¹I.e., the hill of the foreskins

reason why Joshua circumcised them: ^all the people who came out of Egypt who were males, all the men of war, died in the wilderness along the way after they came out of Egypt. ⁵For all the people who came out were circumcised, but all the people who were born in the wilderness along the way as they came out of Egypt had not been circumcised. ⁶For the sons of Israel walked ^forty years in the wilderness, until all the nation, *that is,* the men of war who came out of Egypt, perished because they did not listen to the voice of the Lord, to whom the Lord had sworn that He would not let them see the land which the Lord had sworn to their fathers to give us, a land flowing with milk and honey. ⁷So their children whom He raised up in their place, Joshua circumcised; for they were uncircumcised, because they had not circumcised them along the way.

⁸Now when they had finished circumcising all the nation, they remained in their places in the camp until they recovered. ⁹Then the Lord said to Joshua, "Today I have rolled away ^the shame of Egypt from you." So the name of that place is called ¹Gilgal to this day.

¹⁰While the sons of Israel camped at Gilgal ^they celebrated the Passover on the evening of the ᴮfourteenth day of the month on the desert plains of Jericho. ¹¹Then on the day after the Passover, on that very day, they ate some of the produce of the land, unleavened cakes and roasted *grain.* ¹²And ^the manna ceased on the day after they had eaten some of the produce of the land, so that the sons of Israel no longer had manna, but they ate some of the yield of the land of Canaan during that year.

¹³Now it came about when Joshua was by Jericho, he raised his eyes and looked, and behold, ^a man was standing opposite him with his sword drawn in his hand, and Joshua went to him and said to him, "Are you for us or for our enemies?" ¹⁴He said, "No; rather I have come now *as* captain of the army of the Lord." And Joshua ^fell on his face to the ground, and bowed down, and said to him, "What has my lord to say to his servant?" ¹⁵And the captain of the Lord's army said to Joshua, "^Remove your sandals from your feet, for the place where you are standing is holy." And Joshua did so.

THE CONQUEST OF JERICHO

6 Now Jericho was tightly shut because of the sons of Israel; no one went out and no one came in. ²But the Lord said to Joshua, "See, I have handed Jericho over to you, with ^its king *and* the valiant warriors. ³And you shall march around the city, all the men of war circling the city once. You shall do so for six days. ⁴Also seven priests shall carry seven ^trumpets of rams' horns in front of the ark; then on the seventh day you shall march around the city seven times, and the priests shall blow the trumpets. ⁵It shall be that when they make a long blast with the ram's horn, and when you hear the sound of the trumpet, all the people shall shout with a great

5:4 ^Deut 2:14   5:6 ^Deut 2:7, 14   5:9 ^Zeph 2:8
5:10 ^Ex 12:18   ᴮJosh 4:19   5:12 ^Ex 16:35
5:13 ^Gen 18:1, 2; 32:24, 30   5:14 ^Gen 17:3
5:15 ^Ex 3:5   6:2 ^Deut 7:24   6:4 ^Lev 25:9

5:9 ¹I.e., wheel, or stone circle

shout; and the wall of the city will fall down flat, and the people shall go up, everyone straight ahead."

⁶So Joshua the son of Nun called the priests and said to them, "Take up the ark of the covenant, and have seven priests carry seven trumpets of rams' horns in front of the ark of the Lᴏʀᴅ." ⁷Then he said to the people, "Go forward and march around the city, and the armed men shall go on ahead of the ark of the Lᴏʀᴅ." ⁸And it was *so,* that when Joshua had spoken to the people, the seven priests carrying the seven trumpets of rams' horns before the Lᴏʀᴅ went forward and blew the trumpets; and the ark of the covenant of the Lᴏʀᴅ followed them. ⁹And the armed men went ahead of the priests who blew the trumpets, and ᴬthe rear guard came after the ark, while they continued to blow the trumpets. ¹⁰But Joshua commanded the people, saying, "You shall not shout nor let your voice be heard, nor let a word proceed from your mouth, until the day I tell you, 'Shout!' Then you shall shout!" ¹¹So he had the ark of the Lᴏʀᴅ taken around the city, circling *it* once; then they came into the camp and spent the night in the camp.

¹²Now Joshua got up early in the morning, and the priests took up the ark of the Lᴏʀᴅ. ¹³Then ᴬthe seven priests carrying the seven trumpets of rams' horns in front of the ark of the Lᴏʀᴅ went on continually, and blew the trumpets; and the armed men went ahead of them, and ᴮthe rear guard came after the ark of the Lᴏʀᴅ, while they continued to blow the trumpets. ¹⁴So the second day they marched around the city once and returned to the camp; they did the same for six days.

¹⁵Then on the seventh day they got up early at the dawning of the day and marched around the city in the same way seven times; only on that day did they march around the city seven times. ¹⁶And at the seventh time, when the priests blew the trumpets, Joshua said to the people, "ᴬShout! For the Lᴏʀᴅ has given you the city. ¹⁷But the city shall be ᴬdesignated for ¹destruction, it and everything that is in it belongs to the Lᴏʀᴅ; only Rahab the prostitute and all who are with her in the house shall live, because she hid the messengers whom we sent. ¹⁸But as for you, only keep yourselves from the things designated for destruction, so that you do not covet *them* and ᴬtake some of the designated things, and turn the camp of Israel into something designated for destruction and bring disaster on it. ¹⁹ᴬBut all the silver and gold, and articles of bronze and iron are holy to the Lᴏʀᴅ; they shall go into the treasury of the Lᴏʀᴅ." ²⁰So the people shouted, and the priests blew the trumpets; and when the people heard the sound of the trumpet, the people shouted with a great shout, and the ᴬwall fell down flat, so that the people went up into the city, everyone straight ahead, and they took the city. ²¹ᴬThey utterly destroyed everything in the city, both man and woman, young and old, and ox, sheep, and donkey, with the edge of the sword.

6:9ᴬJosh 6:13; Is 52:12   6:13ᴬJosh 6:4   ⁸Josh 6:9
6:16ᴬ2 Chr 13:14f   6:17ᴬLev 27:28; Deut 20:17
6:18ᴬJosh 7:1   6:19ᴬNum 31:11, 12, 21-23
6:20ᴬHeb 11:30   6:21ᴬDeut 20:16

6:17¹I.e., as an offering to God

²² And Joshua said to the two men who had spied out the land, "ᴬGo into the prostitute's house and bring the woman and all she has out of there, just as you have sworn to her." ²³ So the young men who were spies went in and ᴬbrought out Rahab, her father, her mother, her brothers, and all she had; they also brought out all her relatives, and placed them outside the camp of Israel. ²⁴ Then ᴬthey burned the city with fire, and all that was in it. Only the silver and gold, and the articles of bronze and iron, they put into the treasury of the ¹house of the LORD. ²⁵ However, Rahab the prostitute and her father's household and all she had, Joshua spared; and she has lived in the midst of Israel to this day, because ᴬshe hid the messengers whom Joshua sent to spy out Jericho.

²⁶ Then Joshua made them take an oath at that time, saying, "ᴬCursed before the LORD is the man who rises up and builds this city Jericho; with *the loss of* his firstborn he will lay its foundation, and with *the loss of* his youngest son he will set up its gates." ²⁷ So the LORD was with Joshua, and his ᴬfame was in all the land.

ISRAEL IS DEFEATED AT AI

7 ᴬBut the sons of Israel acted unfaithfully regarding the things designated for destruction, for Achan, the son of Carmi, the son of Zabdi, the son of Zerah, from the tribe of Judah, took some of the designated things; therefore the anger of the LORD burned against the sons of Israel.

² Now Joshua sent men from Jericho to Ai, which is near ᴬBeth-aven, east of Bethel, and said to them,

"Go up and spy out the land." So the men went up and spied out Ai. ³ Then they returned to Joshua and said to him, "Do not have all the people go up; have *only* about two or three thousand men go up and attack Ai; do not trouble all the people there, for they are few." ⁴ So about three thousand men from the people went up there, but ᴬthey fled from the men of Ai. ⁵ And the men of Ai struck and killed about thirty-six of their men, and pursued them from the gate as far as Shebarim and struck them on the mountainside; and the ᴬhearts of the people melted and became like water.

⁶ Then Joshua ᴬtore his clothes and fell to the ground on his face before the ark of the LORD until the evening, *both* he and the elders of Israel; and they put dust on their heads. ⁷ And Joshua said, "Oh, Lord GOD! Why did You ever bring this people across the Jordan, *only* to hand us over to the Amorites, to eliminate us? If only we had been willing to live beyond the Jordan! ⁸ O Lord, what can I say since Israel has turned *their* back before their enemies? ⁹ ᴬFor the Canaanites and all the inhabitants of the land will hear about it, and they will surround us and eliminate our name from the earth. And what will You do for Your great name?"

¹⁰ So the LORD said to Joshua, "Stand up! Why is it that you have fallen on your face? ¹¹ Israel has sinned, and ᴬthey have also violated

---

6:22ᴬJosh 2:12-19   6:23ᴬHeb 11:31   6:24ᴬDeut 20:16-18   6:25ᴬJosh 2:6   6:26ᴬ1 Kin 16:34   6:27ᴬJosh 9:1, 3
7:1ᴬJosh 6:17-19   7:2ᴬJosh 18:12; 1 Sam 13:5
7:4ᴬLev 26:17; Deut 28:25   7:5ᴬLev 26:36; Josh 2:11
7:6ᴬJob 2:12   7:9ᴬEx 32:12; Deut 9:28
7:11ᴬJosh 6:18, 19

6:24 ¹I.e., tabernacle

My covenant which I commanded them. And they have even taken some of the things designated for destruction, and have both stolen and kept *it a* secret. Furthermore, they have also put *them* among their own things. ¹²Therefore the ^sons of Israel cannot stand against their enemies; they turn *their* backs before their enemies, because they have become designated for destruction. I will not be with you anymore unless you eliminate from your midst the things designated for destruction. ¹³Stand up! Consecrate the people and say, 'Consecrate yourselves for tomorrow, because the Lord, the God of Israel, has said this: "^There are things designated for destruction in your midst, Israel. You cannot stand against your enemies until you have removed the designated things from your midst." ¹⁴So in the morning you shall come forward by your tribes. And it shall be that the tribe which ^the Lord selects by lot shall come forward by families, and the family which the Lord selects shall come forward by households, and the household which the Lord selects shall come forward man by man. ¹⁵And ^it shall be that the one who is selected with the things designated for destruction shall be burned with fire, he and all that belongs to him, because he has violated the covenant of the Lord, and because he has committed a disgraceful thing in Israel.' "

THE SIN OF ACHAN

¹⁶So Joshua got up early in the morning and brought Israel forward by tribes, and the tribe of Judah was selected. ¹⁷So he brought the family of Judah forward, and he selected the family of the Zerahites; then he brought the family of the Zerahites forward man by man, and Zabdi was selected. ¹⁸And he brought his household forward man by man; and ^Achan, son of Carmi, son of Zabdi, son of Zerah, from the tribe of Judah, was selected. ¹⁹Then Joshua said to Achan, "My son, I implore you, ^give glory to the Lord, the God of Israel, and give praise to Him; and tell me now what you have done. Do not hide it from me." ²⁰So Achan answered Joshua and said, "Truly, I have sinned against the Lord, the God of Israel, and this is what I did: ²¹when I saw among the spoils a beautiful robe from Shinar, two hundred shekels of silver, and a bar of gold fifty shekels in weight, then I ^wanted them and took them; and behold, they are hidden in the ground inside my tent, with the silver underneath."

²²So Joshua sent messengers, and they ran to the tent; and behold, it was hidden in his tent with the silver underneath it. ²³So they took them from inside the tent and brought them to Joshua and to all the sons of Israel; and they laid them out before the Lord. ²⁴Then Joshua, and all Israel with him, took Achan the son of Zerah, the silver, the robe, the bar of gold, his sons, his daughters, his oxen, his donkeys, his sheep, his tent, and all that belonged to him; and they brought them up to ^the Valley of ¹Achor. ²⁵And Joshua said, "Why have you

7:12 ^Num 14:39, 45; Judg 2:14   7:13 ^Josh 6:18
7:14 ^Prov 16:33   7:15 ^1 Sam 14:38f
7:18 ^Num 32:23; Acts 5:1-10
7:19 ^1 Sam 6:5; 2 Chr 30:22   7:21 ^Eph 5:5;
1 Tim 6:10   7:24 ^Josh 15:7

7:24 ¹I.e., disaster

^Abrought disaster on us? The Lord will bring disaster on you this day." And all Israel stoned them with stones; and they burned them with fire after they had stoned them with stones. ²⁶Then they erected over him a large heap of stones *that stands* to this day, and the Lord turned from the fierceness of His anger. Therefore the name of that place has been called ^Athe Valley of ¹Achor to this day.

THE CONQUEST OF AI

8 Now the Lord said to Joshua, "Do not fear or be dismayed. Take all the people of war with you. Arise, go up to Ai; see, ^AI have handed over to you the king of Ai, his people, his city, and his land. ²You shall do to Ai and its king just as you did to Jericho and its king; you shall ^Atake only its spoils and its cattle as plunder for yourselves. Set an ambush for the city behind it."

³So Joshua rose up with all the people of war to go up to Ai; and Joshua chose thirty thousand men, valiant warriors, and sent them out at night. ⁴He commanded them, saying, "See, you are ^Agoing to ambush the city from behind it. Do not go very far from the city, but all of you be ready. ⁵Then I and all the people who are with me will approach the city. And when they come out to meet us as *they did* the first *time,* ^Awe will flee before them. ⁶They will come out after us until we have lured them away from the city, for they will say, '*They* are fleeing before us just as *they did* the first time.' So we will flee before them. ⁷Then you shall rise from *your* ambush and take possession of the city, for the Lord your God will hand it over to you. ⁸Then it

will be when you have seized the city, that you shall set the city on fire. You shall do *it* ^Ain accordance with the word of the Lord. See, I have commanded you." ⁹So Joshua sent them away, and they went to the *place of* ambush and remained between Bethel and Ai, on the west side of Ai; but Joshua spent that night among the people.

¹⁰Now Joshua ^Agot up early in the morning and mustered the people, and he went up with the elders of Israel before the people to Ai. ¹¹Then all the people of war who *were* with him went up and approached, and arrived in front of the city; and they camped on the north side of Ai. And *there was* a valley between him and Ai. ¹²Then he took about five thousand men and set them in ambush between ^ABethel and Ai, on the west side of the city. ¹³So they stationed the people, all the army that was on the north side of the city, and its rear guard on the west side of the city, and Joshua spent that night in the midst of the valley. ¹⁴And it came about, when the king of Ai saw *them,* that the men of the city hurried and got up early, and went out to meet Israel in battle, he and all his people at the appointed place before the desert plain. But he did not know that *there was* an ambush against him behind the city. ¹⁵Then Joshua and all Israel pretended to be defeated before them, and fled ^Aby the way of the wilderness. ¹⁶And all the people who were in

7:25 ^AJosh 6:18   7:26 ^AIs 65:10; Hos 2:15
8:1 ^AJosh 6:2   8:2 ^ADeut 20:14; Josh 8:27
8:4 ^AJudg 20:29   8:5 ^AJudg 20:32   8:8 ^ADeut
20:16-18; Josh 8:2   8:10 ^AGen 22:3   8:12 ^AGen 12:8;
Judg 1:22   8:15 ^AJosh 15:61; 16:1

7:26 ¹I.e., disaster

the city were called together to pursue them, and they pursued Joshua and ^were lured away from the city. ¹⁷So not a man was left in Ai or Bethel, but they had all gone out after Israel, and they left the city unguarded and pursued Israel.

¹⁸Then the LORD said to Joshua, "^Reach out with the sword that is in your hand toward Ai, for I will hand it over to you." So Joshua reached out with the sword that was in his hand toward the city. ¹⁹Then the *men in* ambush rose quickly from their place, and when he had reached out with his hand, they ran and entered the city and captured it, and they quickly set the city on fire. ²⁰When the men of Ai turned back and looked, behold, the smoke of the city ascended to the sky, and they had no place to flee this way or that, for the people who had been fleeing to the wilderness turned against the pursuers. ²¹When Joshua and all Israel saw that the *men in* ambush had captured the city and that the smoke of the city ascended, they turned back and killed the men of Ai. ²²The others came out from the city to confront them, so that they were *trapped* in the midst of Israel, some on this side and some on that side; and they killed them until there was not ^one left who escaped or survived. ²³But they captured the king of Ai alive and brought him to Joshua.

²⁴Now when Israel had finished killing all the inhabitants of Ai in the field in the wilderness where they pursued them, and all of them had fallen by the edge of the sword until they were destroyed, then all Israel returned to Ai and struck it with the edge of the sword. ²⁵So

^all who fell that day, both men and women, were twelve thousand—all the people of Ai. ²⁶For Joshua ^did not withdraw his hand with which he reached out with the sword until he had utterly destroyed all the inhabitants of Ai. ²⁷^Israel took only the cattle and the spoils of that city as plunder for themselves, in accordance with the word of the LORD which He had commanded Joshua. ²⁸So Joshua burned Ai and made it ^a refuse heap forever, a desolation until this day. ²⁹And ^he hanged the king of Ai on ¹a tree until evening; but at sunset Joshua gave the command and they took his body down from ¹the tree and threw it at the entrance of the city gate, and erected over it a large heap of stones *that stands* to this day.

³⁰Then Joshua built an altar to the LORD, the God of Israel, on ^Mount Ebal, ³¹just as Moses the servant of the LORD had commanded the sons of Israel, as it is written in the Book of the Law of Moses, ^an altar of uncut stones on which no one had wielded an iron *tool;* and they offered burnt offerings on it to the LORD, and sacrificed peace offerings. ³²And he ^wrote there on the stones a copy of the Law of Moses, which ¹he had written, in the presence of the sons of Israel. ³³And all Israel with their elders, officers, and their judges were standing on both sides of the ark before the Levitical priests who carried the ark of the covenant of the LORD, the stranger as well as

8:16 ^Judg 20:31   8:18 ^Ex 14:16; Josh 8:26
8:22 ^Josh 8:8   8:25 ^Deut 20:16-18
8:26 ^Ex 17:11, 12   8:27 ^Josh 8:2   8:28 ^Deut 13:16
8:29 ^Deut 21:22, 23   8:30 ^Deut 27:2-8
8:31 ^Ex 20:25   8:32 ^Deut 27:2, 3, 8

8:29 ¹Lit *the wood*   8:32 ¹I.e., Moses

the native. Half of them *stood* in front of ᴬMount Gerizim, and half of them in front of Mount Ebal, just as Moses the servant of the LORD had commanded at first to bless the people of Israel. ³⁴Then afterward he read all the words of the Law, the blessing and the curse, according to everything that is written in ᴬthe Book of the Law. ³⁵There was not a word of all that Moses had commanded which Joshua did not read before all the assembly of Israel ᴬwith the women, the little ones, and the strangers who were living among them.

DECEPTION BY THE GIBEONITES

9 Now it came about when ᴬall the kings who were beyond the Jordan, in the hill country, the lowland, and on all the coast of the Great Sea toward Lebanon, the Hittite and the Amorite, the Canaanite, the Perizzite, the Hivite, and the Jebusite, heard about it, ²that they met together with ᴬone purpose, to fight with Joshua and with Israel.

³The inhabitants of ᴬGibeon also heard what Joshua had done to Jericho and to Ai, ⁴but they on their part acted craftily and went and took provisions for a journey, and took worn-out sacks on their donkeys, and wineskins *that were* worn out, split open, and patched, ⁵and worn-out and patched sandals on their feet, and worn-out clothes on themselves; and all the bread of their provision was dry *and* had become crumbled. ⁶And they went to Joshua at the ᴬcamp at Gilgal and said to him and to the men of Israel, "We have come from a far country; now then, make a covenant with us." ⁷But the men of Israel said to

the ᴬHivites, "Perhaps you are living within our land; how then are we to make a covenant with you?" ⁸So they said to Joshua, "ᴬWe are your servants." Then Joshua said to them, "Who are you and where do you come from?" ⁹They said to him, "Your servants have come from ᴬa very distant country because of the fame of the LORD your God; for we have heard the report about Him and all that He did in Egypt, ¹⁰and all that He did to the two kings of the Amorites who were beyond the Jordan, to Sihon king of Heshbon and to Og king of Bashan who was in Ashtaroth. ¹¹So our elders and all the inhabitants of our country spoke to us, saying, 'Take provisions in your hand for the journey, and go to meet them, and say to them, "ᴬWe are your servants; now then, make a covenant with us."' ¹²This bread of ours *was* hot *when* we took it for our provisions from our houses on the day that we left to come to you; but now behold, it is dry and has become crumbled. ¹³And these wineskins which we filled were new, and behold, they are split open; and these clothes of ours and our sandals are worn out from the very long journey." ¹⁴So the men *of Israel* took some of their provisions, and ᴬdid not ask for the counsel of the LORD. ¹⁵And ᴬJoshua made peace with them and made a covenant with them, to let them live; and the leaders of the congregation swore *an oath* to them.

¹⁶However, it came about at the end of three days after they had made a covenant with them, that

8:33ᴬDeut 11:29 8:34ᴬJosh 1:8 8:35ᴬEx 12:38; Deut 31:12 9:1ᴬNum 13:29; Josh 3:10 9:2ᴬPs 83:3, 5 9:3ᴬJosh 9:17, 22; 10:2 9:6ᴬJosh 5:10 9:7ᴬJosh 9:1; 11:19 9:8ᴬDeut 20:11; 2 Kin 10:5 9:9ᴬJosh 9:16, 17 9:11ᴬJosh 9:8 9:14ᴬNum 27:21 9:15ᴬEx 23:32

they heard that they were neighbors and that they were living within their land. ¹⁷ Then the sons of Israel set out and came to their cities on the third day. Now their cities *were* ᴬGibeon, Chephirah, Beeroth, and Kiriath-jearim. ¹⁸ But the sons of Israel did not attack them because the leaders of the congregation had sworn to them by the LORD, the God of Israel. And the whole congregation grumbled against the leaders. ¹⁹ But all the leaders said to the whole congregation, "We have sworn to them by the LORD, the God of Israel, and now we cannot touch them. ²⁰ This we will do to them, even let them live, so that wrath will not be on us because of the oath which we swore to them." ²¹ So the leaders said to them, "Let them live." And they became ᴬgatherers of firewood and labor to draw water for the whole congregation, just as the leaders had spoken to them.

²² Then Joshua called for them and spoke to them, saying, "Why have you deceived us, saying, 'We are very far from you,' ᴬwhen you are living within our land? ²³ Now therefore, you are ᴬcursed, and you will never cease to be slaves, both gatherers of firewood and labor to draw water for the house of my God." ²⁴ So they answered Joshua and said, "ᴬSince your servants were fully informed that the LORD your God had commanded His servant Moses to give you all the land, and to destroy all the inhabitants of the land before you, we feared greatly for our lives because of you, and did this thing. ²⁵ And now behold, ᴬwe are in your hands; do to us as it seems good and right in your sight to do." ²⁶ This he did

to them, and saved them from the hands of the sons of Israel, and they did not kill them. ²⁷ But on that day Joshua made them gatherers of firewood and labor to draw water for the congregation and for the altar of the LORD, to this day, ᴬin the place which He would choose.

FIVE KINGS ATTACK GIBEON

10 Now it came about when Adoni-zedek king of Jerusalem heard that Joshua had captured Ai, and had utterly destroyed it (just ᴬas he had done to Jericho and its king, so he had done to Ai and its king), and that the inhabitants of Gibeon had ᴮmade peace with Israel and were within their land, ² that he ᴬfeared greatly because Gibeon *was* a great city, like one of the royal cities, and because it was greater than Ai, and all its men *were* mighty. ³ Therefore Adoni-zedek king of Jerusalem sent *word* ᴬto Hoham king of Hebron, to Piram king of Jarmuth, to Japhia king of Lachish, and to Debir king of Eglon, saying, ⁴ "Come up to me and help me, and let's attack Gibeon, for it has ᴬmade peace with Joshua and with the sons of Israel." ⁵ So the five kings of ᴬthe Amorites, the king of Jerusalem, the king of Hebron, the king of Jarmuth, the king of Lachish, *and* the king of Eglon, gathered together and went up, they with all their armies, and camped by Gibeon and fought against it.

⁶ Then the men of Gibeon sent *word* to Joshua at the camp at Gilgal, saying, "Do not abandon your servants; come up to us quickly and

9:17 ᴬJosh 18:25 9:21 ᴬDeut 29:11 9:22 ᴬJosh 9:16
9:23 ᴬGen 9:25 9:24 ᴬJosh 9:9 9:25 ᴬGen 16:6
9:27 ᴬDeut 12:5 10:1 ᴬJosh 8:21f ᴮJosh 9:15
10:2 ᴬEx 15:14-16 10:3 ᴬJosh 10:23 10:4 ᴬJosh 9:15
10:5 ᴬNum 13:29

save us and help us, for all the kings of the Amorites that live in the hill country have assembled against us." ⁷So Joshua went up from Gilgal, he and ᴬall the people of war with him, and all the valiant warriors. ⁸And the LORD said to Joshua, "ᴬDo not fear them, for I have handed them over to you; not one of them will stand against you." ⁹So Joshua came upon them suddenly by marching all night from Gilgal. ¹⁰ᴬAnd the LORD brought them into confusion before Israel, and He struck them down in a great defeat at Gibeon, and pursued them by the way of the ascent to Beth-horon and struck them as far as Azekah and Makkedah. ¹¹And as they fled from Israel, *while* they were at the descent of Beth-horon, ᴬthe LORD hurled large stones from heaven on them as far as Azekah, and they died; *there were* more who died from the hailstones than those whom the sons of Israel killed with the sword.

¹²Then Joshua spoke to the LORD on the day when the LORD turned the Amorites over to the sons of Israel, and he said in the sight of Israel,

"ᴬSun, stand still at Gibeon,
    And moon, at the Valley of
        Aijalon!"
¹³   So the sun stood still, and the
        moon stopped,
    Until the nation avenged
        themselves of their enemies.

Is it not written in ᴬthe Book of Jashar? And ᴮthe sun stopped in the middle of the sky and did not hurry to go *down* for about a whole day. ¹⁴There was no day like that before it or after it, when the LORD listened to the voice of a man; for ᴬthe LORD fought for Israel.

¹⁵Then Joshua and all Israel with him returned to the camp at Gilgal.

VICTORY AT MAKKEDAH

¹⁶Now these ᴬfive kings had fled and hidden themselves in the cave at Makkedah. ¹⁷And it was told to Joshua, saying, "The five kings have been found hidden in the cave at Makkedah." ¹⁸So Joshua said, "Roll large stones against the mouth of the cave, and post men by it to guard them, ¹⁹but do not stay *there* yourselves; pursue your enemies and attack them from behind. Do not allow them to enter their cities, for the LORD your God has handed them over to you." ²⁰It came about when Joshua and the sons of Israel had finished striking them down in a very great defeat, ᴬuntil they were destroyed, and the survivors of them *who* escaped had entered the fortified cities, ²¹that all the people returned to the camp, to Joshua at Makkedah in peace. No one uttered a word against any of the sons of Israel.

²²Then Joshua said, "Open the mouth of the cave and bring these five kings out to me from the cave." ²³They did so, and ᴬbrought these five kings out to him from the cave: the king of Jerusalem, the king of Hebron, the king of Jarmuth, the king of Lachish, *and* the king of Eglon. ²⁴When they brought these kings out to Joshua, Joshua called for all the men of Israel, and said to the leaders of the men of war who had gone with him, "Come forward, ᴬput your feet on the necks of these kings." So they came forward

10:7 ᴬJosh 8:1   10:8 ᴬJosh 1:5, 9   10:10 ᴬDeut 7:23
10:11 ᴬPs 18:12f; Is 28:2   10:12 ᴬHab 3:11
10:13 ᴬ2 Sam 1:18   ᴮIs 38:8   10:14 ᴬEx 14:14;
Deut 1:30   10:16 ᴬJosh 10:5   10:20 ᴬDeut 20:16
10:23 ᴬDeut 7:24   10:24 ᴬMal 4:3

and put their feet on their necks. ²⁵Joshua then said to them, "^Do not fear or be dismayed! Be strong and courageous, for the LORD will do this to all your enemies with whom you fight." ²⁶So afterward Joshua struck them and put them to death, and he ^hanged them on five 'trees; and they were hung on the 'trees until evening. ²⁷Then it came about at sunset that Joshua gave the command, and ^they took them down from the 'trees and threw them into the cave where they had hidden themselves, and put large stones over the mouth of the cave, to this very day.

²⁸Now Joshua captured Makkedah on that day, and struck it and its king with the edge of the sword; ^he utterly destroyed it and every 'person who was in it. He left no survivor. So he did to the king of Makkedah ^Bjust as he had done to the king of Jericho.

JOSHUA'S CONQUEST
OF SOUTHERN CANAAN

²⁹Then Joshua and all Israel with him passed on from Makkedah to ^Libnah, and fought against Libnah. ³⁰And the LORD also handed it over to Israel, with its king, and he struck it and every person who *was* in it with the edge of the sword. He left no survivor in it. So he did to its king just as he had done to the king of Jericho.

³¹And Joshua and all Israel with him passed on from Libnah to Lachish, and they camped by it and fought against it. ³²And the LORD handed Lachish over to Israel; and he captured it on the second day, and struck it and every person who *was* in it with the edge of the sword, according to all that he had done to Libnah.

³³Then Horam king of ^Gezer came up to help Lachish, and Joshua defeated him and his people until he had left him no survivor.

³⁴And Joshua and all Israel with him passed on from Lachish to Eglon, and they camped by it and fought against it. ³⁵They captured it on that day and struck it with the edge of the sword; and he utterly destroyed on that day every person who *was* in it, according to all that he had done to Lachish.

³⁶Then Joshua and all Israel with him went up from Eglon to ^Hebron, and they fought against it. ³⁷And they captured it and struck it and its king and all its cities and all the persons who *were* in it with the edge of the sword. He left no survivor, according to all that he had done to Eglon. And he utterly destroyed it and every person who *was* in it.

³⁸Then Joshua and all Israel with him returned to ^Debir, and they fought against it. ³⁹He captured it and its king and all its cities, and they struck them with the edge of the sword, and utterly destroyed every person *who was* in it. He left no survivor. Just as he had done to Hebron, so he did to Debir and its king, as he had also done to Libnah and its king.

⁴⁰So Joshua struck all the land, ^the hill country and the 'Negev and the lowland and the slopes, and ^Ball their kings. He left no survivor, but he utterly destroyed all

10:25 ^Josh 10:8   10:26 ^Josh 8:29
10:27 ^Deut 21:22, 23   10:28 ^Deut 20:16   ^BJosh 6:21
10:29 ^Josh 15:42; 21:13   10:33 ^Josh 16:3, 10; Judg 1:29
10:36 ^Num 13:22; Judg 1:10, 20   10:38 ^Josh 15:15; Judg 1:11   10:40 ^Deut 1:7   ^BDeut 7:24

10:26 'Or *wooden* posts   10:27 'Or *wooden* posts
10:28 'Lit *soul,* and so throughout the ch   10:40 'I.e., South country

who breathed, just as the LORD, the God of Israel, had commanded. ⁴¹Joshua struck them from Kadesh-barnea even as far as Gaza, and all the country of ᴬGoshen even as far as Gibeon. ⁴²Joshua captured all these kings and their lands at one time, because ᴬthe LORD, the God of Israel, fought for Israel. ⁴³So Joshua and all Israel with him returned to the camp at Gilgal.

NORTHERN CANAAN TAKEN

11 Then it came about, when Jabin king of ᴬHazor heard *about it,* that he sent *word* to Jobab king of Madon, to the king of Shimron, to the king of Achshaph, ²and to the kings who were of the north in the hill country, and in the ᴬArabah—south of ¹Chinneroth and in the lowland, and on the heights of Dor on the west— ³to the Canaanite on the east and on the west, and the Amorite, the Hittite, the Perizzite, and the Jebusite in the hill country, and the Hivite at the foot of ᴬHermon in the land of Mizpeh. ⁴Then they came out, they and all their armies with them, ᴬ*as* many people as the sand that is on the seashore, with very many horses and chariots. ⁵So all of these kings gathered together, and came and encamped together at the waters of Merom, to fight against Israel.

⁶Yet the LORD said to Joshua, "ᴬDo not be afraid because of them, for tomorrow at this time I am going to turn all of them over to Israel *as good as* dead; you shall ᴮhamstring their horses and burn their chariots with fire." ⁷So Joshua and all the people of war with him came upon them suddenly at the waters of Merom, and attacked them.

⁸And the LORD handed them over to Israel, so that they defeated them, and pursued them as far as Great Sidon, and ᴬMisrephoth-maim, and the Valley of Mizpeh to the east; and they struck them until no survivor was left to them. ⁹And Joshua did to them just as the LORD had told him; he ᴬhamstrung their horses and burned their chariots with fire.

¹⁰Then Joshua turned back at that time and captured ᴬHazor, and struck its king with the sword; for Hazor previously was the head of all these kingdoms. ¹¹ᴬThey struck every person who was in it with the edge of the sword, utterly destroying *them;* there was no one left who breathed. And he burned Hazor with fire. ¹²Joshua captured all the cities of these kings, and all their kings; and he struck them with the edge of the sword *and* utterly destroyed them, just ᴬas Moses the servant of the LORD had commanded. ¹³However, Israel did not burn any cities that stood on their mounds, except Hazor alone, *which* Joshua burned. ¹⁴And ᴬall the spoils of these cities and the cattle, the sons of Israel took as their plunder; but they struck every person with the edge of the sword, until they had destroyed them. They left no one breathing. ¹⁵Just as the LORD had commanded His servant Moses, so Moses commanded Joshua, and so Joshua did; he left nothing undone of all that the LORD had commanded Moses.

10:41ᴬJosh 11:16; 15:51   10:42ᴬJosh 10:14
11:1ᴬJosh 11:10   11:2ᴬJosh 12:3; 13:27
11:3ᴬJosh 11:17; 13:5, 11   11:4ᴬJudg 7:12
11:6ᴬJosh 10:8   ᴮ2 Sam 8:4   11:8ᴬJosh 13:6
11:9ᴬJosh 11:6   11:10ᴬJosh 11:1   11:11ᴬDeut 20:16
11:12ᴬNum 33:50–52; Deut 7:2   11:14ᴬNum 31:11, 12

11:2¹I.e., Sea of Galilee

¹⁶So Joshua took all that land: the hill country and all the Negev, all the land of Goshen, the lowland, ^the Arabah, the hill country of Israel and its lowland ¹⁷from Mount Halak, that rises toward Seir, even as far as Baal-gad in the Valley of Lebanon at the foot of Mount Hermon. And he captured ^all their kings, and struck them and put them to death. ¹⁸Joshua waged war a long time with all these kings. ¹⁹There was not a city which made peace with the sons of Israel except ^the Hivites living in Gibeon; they took them all in battle. ²⁰^For it was of the LORD to harden their hearts, to meet Israel in battle in order that he might utterly destroy them, that they might receive no mercy, but that he might destroy them, just as the LORD had commanded Moses.

²¹Then Joshua came at that time and eliminated ^the Anakim from the hill country, from Hebron, Debir, Anab, and from all the hill country of Judah and all the hill country of Israel. Joshua utterly destroyed them with their cities. ²²There were no Anakim left in the land of the sons of Israel; only in Gaza, ^Gath, and Ashdod *some* remained. ²³So Joshua took the whole land, in accordance with everything that the LORD had spoken to Moses; and ^Joshua gave it as an inheritance to Israel according to their divisions by their tribes. So the land was at rest from war.

KINGS DEFEATED BY ISRAEL

12 Now these are the ^kings of the land whom the sons of Israel defeated, and they took possession of their land beyond the Jordan toward the sunrise, from the Valley of the Arnon as far as Mount Hermon, and all the Arabah to the east: ²Sihon king of the Amorites, who lived in Heshbon *and* ruled ^from Aroer, which is on the edge of the Valley of the Arnon, both the middle of the valley and half of Gilead, even as far as the brook Jabbok, the border of the sons of Ammon; ³and the ^Arabah as far as the Sea of ¹Chinneroth toward the east, and as far as the Sea of the Arabah, *that is,* the Salt Sea, eastward toward ᴮBeth-jeshimoth, and on the south, at the foot of the slopes of Pisgah; ⁴and the territory of Og king of Bashan, one of ^the remnant of Rephaim, who lived at Ashtaroth and at Edrei, ⁵and ruled over Mount Hermon, Salecah, and all Bashan, as far as ^the border of the Geshurites and the Maacathites, and half of Gilead, *as far as* the border of Sihon king of Heshbon. ⁶Moses the servant of the LORD and the sons of Israel defeated them; and ^Moses the servant of the LORD gave it to the Reubenites, the Gadites, and the half-tribe of Manasseh as a possession.

⁷Now these are the kings of the land whom Joshua and the sons of Israel defeated beyond the Jordan toward the west, from Baal-gad in the Valley of Lebanon even as far as ^Mount Halak, which rises toward Seir; and Joshua gave it to the tribes of Israel as a possession according to their divisions, ⁸in ^the hill country, in the lowland, in the Arabah,

11:16 ^Josh 11:2   11:17 ^Deut 7:24   11:19 ^Josh 9:3, 7
11:20 ^Ex 14:17   11:21 ^Num 13:33; Deut 9:2
11:22 ^1 Sam 17:4; 1 Kin 2:39   11:23 ^Deut 1:38
12:1 ^Num 32:33; Deut 3:8-17   12:2 ^Deut 2:36
12:3 ^Josh 11:2   ᴮ Josh 13:20   12:4 ^Deut 3:11
12:5 ^Deut 3:14; 1 Sam 27:8   12:6 ^Num 32:33;
Deut 3:12   12:7 ^Josh 11:17   12:8 ^Josh 11:16

12:3 ¹ I.e., Galilee

on the slopes, in the wilderness, and in the Negev; the Hittite, the Amorite and the Canaanite, the Perizzite, the Hivite, and the Jebusite: ⁹the ᴬking of Jericho, one; the ᴮking of Ai, which is beside Bethel, one; ¹⁰the ᴬking of Jerusalem, one; the king of Hebron, one; ¹¹the king of Jarmuth, one; the king of Lachish, one; ¹²the king of Eglon, one; the king of Gezer, one; ¹³the king of Debir, one; the king of Geder, one; ¹⁴the king of Hormah, one; the king of ᴬArad, one; ¹⁵the king of Libnah, one; the king of Adullam, one; ¹⁶the king of Makkedah, one; the king of Bethel, one; ¹⁷the king of Tappuah, one; the ᴬking of Hepher, one; ¹⁸the king of ᴬAphek, one; the king of Lasharon, one; ¹⁹the king of Madon, one; the king of Hazor, one; ²⁰the king of Shimron-meron, one; the king of Achshaph, one; ²¹the king of Taanach, one; the king of Megiddo, one; ²²the king of ᴬKedesh, one; the king of Jokneam in Carmel, one; ²³the king of Dor in the heights of Dor, one; the king of ᴬGoiim in Gilgal, one; ²⁴the king of Tirzah, one: ᴬin all, thirty-one kings.

CANAAN DIVIDED AMONG THE TRIBES

13 Now ᴬJoshua was old *and* advanced in years when the LORD said to him, "You are old *and* advanced in years, and a very large *amount* of the land remains to be possessed. ²This is the land that remains: all the regions *of* the Philistines and all *those of* the ᴬGeshurites; ³from the Shihor which is east of Egypt, even as far as the border of Ekron to the north (it is counted as Canaanite); the ᴬfive governors of the Philistines: the Gazite, the Ashdodite, the Ashkelonite, the Gittite, the Ekronite;

and the Avvite ⁴to the south, all the land of the Canaanite, and Mearah that belongs to the Sidonians, as far as ᴬAphek, to the border of the Amorite; ⁵and the land of the ᴬGebalite, and all of Lebanon, toward the east, from Baal-gad below Mount Hermon as far as Lebo-hamath. ⁶All the inhabitants of the hill country from Lebanon as far as Misrephoth-maim, all the Sidonians, I will drive out from the sons of Israel; ᴬonly allot it to Israel as an inheritance as I have commanded you. ⁷Now therefore, apportion this land as an inheritance to the nine tribes and the half-tribe of Manasseh."

⁸With the other half-tribe, the Reubenites and the Gadites received their inheritance which Moses gave them ᴬbeyond the Jordan to the east, just as Moses the servant of the LORD gave to them; ⁹from Aroer, which is on the edge of the Valley of the Arnon, with the city which is in the middle of the valley, and all the plain of Medeba, as far as Dibon; ¹⁰and all the cities of Sihon king of the Amorites, who reigned in Heshbon, as far as the border of the sons of Ammon; ¹¹and ᴬGilead, and the territory of the Geshurites and Maacathites, and all Mount Hermon, and all Bashan as far as Salecah; ¹²all the kingdom of ᴬOg in Bashan, who reigned in Ashtaroth and in Edrei (he *alone* was left of the remnant of the Rephaim); for Moses ᴮstruck them and drove them out. ¹³But

12:9 ᴬJosh 6:2   ᴮJosh 8:29   12:10 ᴬJosh 10:23
12:14 ᴬNum 21:1   12:17 ᴬ1 Kin 4:10   12:18 ᴬJosh 13:4;
2 Kin 13:17   12:22 ᴬJosh 19:37; 20:7   12:23 ᴬGen 14:1
12:24 ᴬDeut 7:24   13:1 ᴬJosh 14:10   13:2 ᴬJosh 13:11;
1 Sam 27:8   13:3 ᴬ1 Sam 6:4, 16   13:4 ᴬJosh 12:18;
19:30   13:5 ᴬ1 Kin 5:18   13:6 ᴬNum 33:54
13:8 ᴬJosh 12:1-6   13:11 ᴬGen 37:25; Num 32:29
13:12 ᴬDeut 3:11   ᴮNum 21:24

the sons of Israel did not drive out the Geshurites or the Maacathites; instead, Geshur and Maacath live among Israel to this day. ¹⁴ᴬOnly to the tribe of Levi he did not give an inheritance; the offerings by fire to the Lᴏʀᴅ, the God of Israel, are their inheritance, as He spoke to him.

¹⁵So Moses gave *an inheritance* to the tribe of the sons of Reuben according to their families. ¹⁶Their territory was ᴬfrom Aroer, which is on the edge of the Valley of the Arnon, with the city which is in the middle of the valley and all the plain by Medeba; ¹⁷Heshbon and all its cities which are on the plain: Dibon, Bamoth-baal, Beth-baal-meon, ¹⁸ᴬJahaz, Kedemoth, Mephaath, ¹⁹ᴬKiriathaim, Sibmah, Zereth-shahar on the hill of the valley, ²⁰Beth-peor, the slopes of Pisgah, Beth-jeshimoth, ²¹even all the cities of the plain, and all the kingdom of Sihon king of the Amorites, who reigned in Heshbon, whom Moses struck with the leaders of Midian, ᴬEvi, Rekem, Zur, Hur, and Reba, the leaders of Sihon, who lived in the land. ²²The sons of Israel also killed ᴬBalaam the son of Beor, the diviner, with the sword among *the rest of* their dead. ²³The border of the sons of Reuben was the Jordan. This was the inheritance of the sons of Reuben according to their families, the cities and their villages.

²⁴Moses also gave *an inheritance* to the tribe of Gad, to the sons of Gad according to their families. ²⁵Their territory was ᴬJazer and all the cities of Gilead, and half the land of the sons of Ammon, as far as Aroer which is opposite Rabbah; ²⁶and from Heshbon as far as Ramath-mizpeh and Betonim,

and from Mahanaim as far as the border of Debir; ²⁷and in the valley, Beth-haram, Beth-nimrah, Succoth, and Zaphon, the rest of the kingdom of Sihon king of Heshbon, with the Jordan as a border, as far as the *lower* end of the Sea of ¹·ᴬChinnereth beyond the Jordan to the east. ²⁸This is the inheritance of the sons of Gad according to their families, the cities and their villages.

²⁹Moses also gave *an inheritance* to the half-tribe of Manasseh; and it was for the half-tribe of the sons of Manasseh according to their families. ³⁰Their territory was from Mahanaim, all Bashan, all the kingdom of Og king of Bashan, and all ᴬthe towns of Jair, which are in Bashan, sixty cities; ³¹also half of Gilead, with ᴬAshtaroth and Edrei, the cities of the kingdom of Og in Bashan, *were* for the sons of Machir the son of Manasseh, for half of the sons of Machir according to their families.

³²These are *the territories* which Moses apportioned as an inheritance in the plains of Moab, beyond the Jordan at Jericho to the east. ³³But ᴬto the tribe of Levi, Moses did not give an inheritance; the Lᴏʀᴅ, the God of Israel, is their inheritance, as He had promised to them.

CALEB'S REQUEST

14 Now these are *the territories* which the sons of Israel inherited in the land of Canaan, which ᴬEleazar the priest, Joshua the son of Nun, and the heads of

13:14ᴬDeut 18:1, 2   13:16ᴬJosh 13:9
13:18ᴬNum 21:23; Judg 11:20   13:19ᴬNum 32:37;
Jer 48:1, 23   13:21ᴬNum 31:8   13:22ᴬNum 31:8
13:25ᴬNum 21:32; Josh 21:39   13:27ᴬNum 34:11;
Deut 3:17   13:30ᴬNum 32:41
13:31ᴬJosh 9:10; Judg 10:6   13:33ᴬDeut 18:1f;
Josh 13:14   14:1ᴬNum 34:16-29

13:27¹I.e., Galilee

the fathers' *households* of the tribes of the sons of Israel apportioned to them as inheritances, ²by the ^lot of their inheritance, just as the LORD commanded through Moses, for the nine tribes and the half-tribe. ³For Moses had given the inheritance of the two tribes and the half-tribe beyond the Jordan; but ^he did not give an inheritance to the Levites among them. ⁴For the sons of Joseph were two tribes, ^Manasseh and Ephraim, and they did not give a portion to the Levites in the land, except cities to live in, with their pasture lands for their livestock and for their property. ⁵The sons of Israel did exactly ^as the LORD had commanded Moses, and they divided the land.

⁶Then the sons of Judah approached Joshua in Gilgal, and ^Caleb the son of Jephunneh the Kenizzite said to him, "You know the word which the LORD spoke to Moses the man of God on account of you and me in Kadesh-barnea. ⁷I was forty years old when ^Moses the servant of the LORD sent me from Kadesh-barnea to spy out the land, and I brought word back to him as *it was* in my heart. ⁸Nevertheless my brothers who went up with me made the heart of the people melt *with fear;* but ^I followed the LORD my God fully. ⁹So Moses swore on that day, saying, '^The land on which your foot has walked shall certainly be an inheritance to you and to your children forever, because you have followed the LORD my God fully.' ¹⁰And now behold, the LORD has let me live, just as He spoke, these forty-five years, from the time that the LORD spoke this word to Moses, when Israel walked in the wilderness; and now behold, I am

eighty-five years old today. ¹¹^I am still as strong today as I was on the day Moses sent me; as my strength was then, so my strength is now, for war and for ^going out and coming in. ¹²Now then, give me this hill country about which the LORD spoke on that day, for you heard on that day that ^Anakim *were* there, with great fortified cities; perhaps the LORD will be with me, and I will drive them out just as the LORD has spoken."

¹³So Joshua ^blessed him and ^gave Hebron to Caleb the son of Jephunneh as an inheritance. ¹⁴Therefore, Hebron became the inheritance of Caleb the son of Jephunneh the Kenizzite to this day, because he followed the LORD God of Israel fully. ¹⁵Now the name of Hebron was previously Kiriath-arba; *for Arba* was the greatest man among the Anakim. ^Then the land was at rest from war.

TERRITORY OF JUDAH

15 Now ^the lot for the tribe of the sons of Judah according to their families reached the border of Edom, southward to the wilderness of Zin at the extreme south. ²Their southern border was from the *lower* end of the Salt Sea, from the bay that turns to the south. ³Then it proceeded southward to the ascent of Akrabbim and continued to Zin, then went up by the south of Kadesh-barnea and continued to Hezron, and went up to Addar and turned to Karka.

14:2 ^Num 26:55; 33:54   14:3 ^Josh 13:14
14:4 ^Gen 41:51f; Num 26:28   14:5 ^Num 35:1f;
Josh 21:2   14:6 ^Num 13:6, 30; 14:6, 24, 30
14:7 ^Num 13:1-31   14:8 ^Num 14:24; Deut 1:36
14:9 ^Deut 1:36   14:11 ^Deut 34:7   ^Deut 31:2
14:12 ^Num 13:33   14:13 ^Josh 22:6   ^Judg 1:20
14:15 ^Josh 11:23   15:1 ^Num 34:3, 4

⁴It ^continued to Azmon and proceeded to the ^Bbrook of Egypt, and the border ended at the sea. This shall be your southern border. ⁵The ^eastern border *was* the Salt Sea, as far as the mouth of the Jordan. And the border of the north side was from the bay of the sea at the mouth of the Jordan. ⁶Then the border went up to Beth-hoglah, and continued on the north of Beth-arabah, and the border went up to the stone of Bohan the son of Reuben. ⁷And the border went up to Debir from ^the Valley of Achor, and turned northward toward Gilgal which is opposite the ascent of Adummim, which is on the south of the valley; and the border continued to the waters of En-shemesh and it ended at En-rogel. ⁸Then the border went up the Valley of Ben-hinnom to the slope of the ^Jebusite on the south (that is, Jerusalem); and the border went up to the top of the mountain which is opposite the Valley of Hinnom to the west, which is at the end of the Valley of Rephaim toward the north. ⁹And from the top of the mountain the border turned to the spring of the waters of Nephtoah and proceeded to the cities of Mount Ephron, then the border turned to ^Baalah (that is, ^BKiriath-jearim). ¹⁰The border turned from Baalah westward to Mount Seir, and continued to the slope of Mount Jearim on the north (that is, Chesalon), and went down to Beth-shemesh and continued through ^Timnah. ¹¹Then the border proceeded to the side of Ekron northward. And the border turned to Shikkeron and continued to Mount Baalah and proceeded to Jabneel, and the border ended at the sea. ¹²The western border *was*

^at the Great Sea, even *its* coastline. This is the border around the sons of Judah according to their families.

¹³Now ^he gave to Caleb the son of Jephunneh a portion among the sons of Judah, in accordance with the command of the LORD to Joshua, *namely,* Kiriath-arba, *Arba being* the father of Anak (that is, Hebron). ¹⁴And Caleb drove out from there the three ^sons of Anak: Sheshai, Ahiman, and Talmai, the children of Anak. ¹⁵Then ^he went up from there against the inhabitants of Debir; now the name of Debir previously was Kiriath-sepher. ¹⁶And Caleb said, "The one who attacks Kiriath-sepher and captures it, I will give him Achsah my daughter as a wife." ¹⁷^Othniel the son of Kenaz, the brother of Caleb, captured it; so he gave him Achsah his daughter as a wife. ¹⁸^And it happened that when she came *to him,* she incited him to ask her father for a field. So she dismounted from the donkey, and Caleb said to her, "What do you want?" ¹⁹Then she said, "Give me a blessing; since you have given me the land of the Negev, give me springs of water also." So he gave her the upper springs and the lower springs.

²⁰This is the inheritance of the tribe of the sons of Judah according to their families.

²¹Now the cities at the extremity of the tribe of the sons of Judah toward the border of Edom in the south were Kabzeel, ^Eder, and

15:4^Num 34:5   ^BGen 15:18   15:5^Num 34:3, 10-12
15:7^Josh 7:24   15:8^Josh 15:63   15:9^1 Chr 13:6
^BJudg 18:12   15:10^Gen 38:13; Judg 14:1
15:12^Num 34:6   15:13^Josh 14:13-15
15:14^Num 13:33; Deut 9:2   15:15^Josh 10:38
15:17^Judg 1:13; 3:9   15:18^Judg 1:14
15:21^Gen 35:21

Jagur, 22Kinah, Dimonah, and Ada-dah, 23Kedesh, Hazor, and Ith-nan, 24Ziph, Telem, and Bealoth, 25Hazor-hadattah, Kerioth-hezron (that is, Hazor), 26Amam, Shema, and Moladah, 27Hazar-gaddah, Heshmon, and Beth-pelet, 28Hazar-shual, ᴬBeersheba, and Biziothiah, 29Baalah, Iim, and Ezem, 30Elto-lad, Chesil, and Hormah, 31ᴬZiklag, Madmannah, and Sansannah, 32Lebaoth, Shilhim, Ain, and Rim-mon; in all, twenty-nine cities with their villages.

33In the lowland: ᴬEshtaol, Zorah, and Ashnah, 34Zanoah, En-gannim, Tappuah, and Enam, 35Jarmuth, ᴬAdullam, Socoh, and Azekah, 36Shaaraim, Adithaim, Gederah, and Gederothaim; four-teen cities with their villages.

37Zenan, Hadashah, and Migdal-gad, 38Dilean, Mizpeh, and Jok-theel, 39ᴬLachish, Bozkath, and Eglon, 40Cabbon, Lahmas, and Chitlish, 41Gederoth, Beth-dagon, Naamah, and Makkedah; sixteen cities with their villages.

42Libnah, Ether, and Ashan, 43Iphtah, Ashnah, and Nezib, 44Keilah, Achzib, and Mareshah; nine cities with their villages.

45Ekron, with its towns and its villages; 46from Ekron even to the sea, all that were by the side of Ash-dod, with their villages.

47Ashdod, its towns and its vil-lages; Gaza, its towns and its vil-lages, as far as ᴬthe brook of Egypt and the Great Sea, even its coast-line.

48In the hill country: Shamir, Jat-tir, and Socoh, 49Dannah, Kiriath-sannah (that is, Debir), 50Anab, Eshtemoh, Anim, 51Goshen, Holon, and Giloh; eleven cities with their villages.

52Arab, Dumah, and Eshan, 53Janum, Beth-tappuah, and Aphekah, 54Humtah, Kiriath-arba (that is, Hebron), and Zior; nine cit-ies with their villages.

55Maon, Carmel, Ziph, and Juttah, 56Jezreel, Jokdeam, and Zanoah, 57Kain, Gibeah, and Timnah; ten cities with their villages.

58Halhul, Beth-zur, and Gedor, 59Maarath, Beth-anoth, and Elte-kon; six cities with their villages.

60Kiriath-baal (that is, Kiriath-jearim), and Rabbah; two cities with their villages.

61In the wilderness: Beth-arabah, Middin, and Secacah, 62Nibshan, the City of Salt, and Engedi; six cit-ies with their villages.

63Now as for the ᴬJebusites, the inhabitants of Jerusalem, the sons of Judah could not drive them out; so the Jebusites live with the sons of Judah in Jerusalem to this day.

TERRITORY OF EPHRAIM

16 Then the lot for the sons of Joseph went from the Jordan at Jericho to the waters of Jericho on the east into ᴬthe wilderness, going up from Jericho through the hill country to Bethel. 2It went from Bethel to Luz, and ᴬcontin-ued to the border of the Archites at Ataroth. 3Then it went down west-ward to the territory of the Japhle-tites, as far as the territory of lower ᴬBeth-horon even to Gezer, and it ended at the sea.

4The ᴬsons of Joseph, Manasseh and Ephraim, received their inher-itance. 5Now this was the territory

15:28ᴬGen 21:31   15:31ᴬ1 Sam 27:6; 30:1
15:33ᴬJudg 13:25; 16:31   15:35ᴬ1 Sam 22:1
15:39ᴬJosh 10:3; 2 Kin 14:19   15:47ᴬJosh 15:4
15:63ᴬJudg 1:21; 2 Sam 5:6   16:1ᴬJosh 8:15; 18:12
16:2ᴬJosh 18:13   16:3ᴬJosh 18:13; 1 Kin 9:17
16:4ᴬJosh 17:14

of the sons of Ephraim according to their families: the border of their inheritance eastward was ^Ataroth-addar, as far as upper Beth-horon. ⁶Then the border went westward at ^Michmethath on the north, and the border turned eastward to Taanath-shiloh and continued *beyond* it to the east of Janoah. ⁷Then it went down from Janoah to Ataroth and to ^Naarah, then reached Jericho and came out at the Jordan. ⁸From ^Tappuah the border continued westward to the brook of Kanah, and it ended at the sea. This is the inheritance of the tribe of the sons of Ephraim according to their families, ⁹*together* with the cities which were set apart for the sons of Ephraim in the midst of the inheritance of the sons of Manasseh, all the cities with their villages. ¹⁰^But they did not drive out the Canaanites who lived in Gezer, so the Canaanites live in the midst of Ephraim to this day, and they became forced laborers.

TERRITORY OF MANASSEH

17 Now *this* was the lot for the tribe of ^Manasseh, for he was the firstborn of Joseph. To Machir the firstborn of Manasseh, the father of Gilead, were allotted Gilead and Bashan, because he was a man of war. ²So *the lot* was *made* for the rest of the sons of Manasseh according to their families: for the sons of Abiezer, the sons of Helek, the sons of Asriel, the sons of Shechem, the sons of Hepher, and the sons of Shemida; these *were* the male descendants of Manasseh the son of Joseph according to their families.

³However, ^Zelophehad, the son of Hepher, the son of Gilead, the son of Machir, the son of Manasseh, had no sons, only daughters; and these are the names of his daughters: Mahlah, Noah, Hoglah, Milcah, and Tirzah. ⁴They approached Eleazar the priest, Joshua the son of Nun, and the leaders, saying, "The LORD commanded Moses to give us an inheritance among our brothers." So ^in accordance with the command of the LORD he gave them an inheritance among their father's brothers. ⁵So ten portions fell to Manasseh, besides the land of Gilead and Bashan, which is beyond the Jordan, ⁶because the daughters of Manasseh received an inheritance among his sons. And the ^land of Gilead belonged to the rest of the sons of Manasseh.

⁷The border of Manasseh ran from Asher to Michmethath which was east of Shechem; then the border went southward to the inhabitants of En-tappuah. ⁸The land of Tappuah belonged to Manasseh, but ^Tappuah on the border of Manasseh *belonged* to the sons of Ephraim. ⁹And the ^border went down to the brook of Kanah, southward of the brook (these cities *belonged* to Ephraim among the cities of Manasseh), and the border of Manasseh *was* on the north side of the brook, and it ended at the sea. ¹⁰The south side *belonged* to Ephraim and the north side to Manasseh, and the sea was their border; and they reached to Asher on the north and to Issachar on the east. ¹¹In Issachar and in Asher, ^Manasseh had Beth-shean and its towns and Ibleam and its towns,

16:5 ^Josh 18:13   16:6 ^Josh 17:7   16:7 ^1 Chr 7:28
16:8 ^Josh 17:8   16:10 ^Judg 1:29; 1 Kin 9:16
17:1 ^Gen 41:51; 46:20   17:3 ^Num 26:33; 27:1-7
17:4 ^Num 27:5-7   17:6 ^Josh 13:30, 31
17:8 ^Josh 16:8   17:9 ^Josh 16:8f   17:11 ^1 Chr 7:29

and the inhabitants of Dor and its towns, and the inhabitants of Endor and its towns, and the inhabitants of Taanach and its towns, and the inhabitants of Megiddo and its towns; the third is Napheth. ¹²ᴬBut the sons of Manasseh could not take possession of these cities, because the Canaanites persisted in living in this land. ¹³And it came about when the sons of Israel became strong, ᴬthey put the Canaanites to forced labor, but they did not drive them out completely.

¹⁴Then the ᴬsons of Joseph spoke to Joshua, saying, "Why have you given me *only* one lot and one portion as an inheritance, though I am a numerous people whom the LORD has blessed up to this point?" ¹⁵And Joshua said to them, "If you are a numerous people, go up to the forest and clear *a place* for yourself there in the land of the Perizzites and of the Rephaim, since the hill country of Ephraim is too narrow for you." ¹⁶The sons of Joseph then said, "The hill country is not enough for us, but all the Canaanites who live in the valley land have ᴬiron chariots, both those who are in Beth-shean and its towns and those who are in the Valley of Jezreel." ¹⁷But Joshua spoke to the house of Joseph, to Ephraim and Manasseh, saying, "You are a numerous people and have great power; you shall not have one lot *only*, ¹⁸but the hill country shall be yours. For though it is a forest, you shall clear it, and to its farthest borders it shall be yours; for you shall drive out the Canaanites, even though they have ᴬiron chariots *and* though they are strong."

REST OF THE LAND DIVIDED

18 Then the whole congregation of the sons of Israel assembled at ᴬShiloh, and set up the tent of meeting there; and the land was subdued before them.

²But there remained among the sons of Israel seven tribes who had not divided their inheritance. ³So Joshua said to the sons of Israel, "ᴬHow long will you put off entering to take possession of the land which the LORD, the God of your fathers, has given you? ⁴Provide for yourselves three men from each tribe so that I may send them, and that they may arise and walk through the land and write *a description of* it according to their inheritance; then they shall return to me. ⁵And they shall divide it into seven portions; ᴬJudah shall stay in its territory on the south, and the house of Joseph shall stay in their territory on the north. ⁶And you shall write *a description of* the land in seven divisions, and bring *the description* here to me. ᴬThen I will cast lots for you here before the LORD our God. ⁷For ᴬthe Levites have no portion among you, because the priesthood of the LORD is their inheritance. Gad, Reuben, and the half-tribe of Manasseh also have received their inheritance eastward beyond the Jordan, which Moses the servant of the LORD gave them."

⁸Then the men arose and went, and Joshua commanded those who went to write *a description of* the land, saying, "Go and walk through the land and write *a description of* it, and return to me; then I will cast

17:12ᴬJudg 1:27   17:13ᴬJosh 16:10   17:14ᴬNum 13:7
17:16ᴬJosh 17:18; Judg 4:3, 13   17:18ᴬJosh 17:16
18:1ᴬJudg 21:19; Jer 7:12   18:3ᴬJudg 18:9
18:5ᴬJosh 15:1   18:6ᴬJosh 14:2   18:7ᴬNum 18:7, 20; Josh 13:33

lots for you here before the LORD in ^Shiloh." ⁹So the men went and passed through the land, and wrote *a description of* it by cities in seven divisions in a book; and they came to Joshua at the camp at Shiloh. ¹⁰^Joshua then cast lots for them in Shiloh before the LORD, and there Joshua divided the land for the sons of Israel according to their divisions.

THE TERRITORY OF BENJAMIN

¹¹Now the lot of the tribe of the sons of Benjamin came up according to their families, and the territory of their lot lay between the sons of Judah and the sons of Joseph. ¹²^Their border on the north side was from the Jordan, then the border went up to the side of Jericho on the north, and went up through the hill country westward, and it ended at the wilderness of Beth-aven. ¹³Then from there the border continued to ^Luz, to the side of Luz (that is, Bethel) southward; and the border went down to Ataroth-addar, near the hill which *lies* on the south of lower Beth-horon. ¹⁴And the border changed direction *from there* and turned around on the west side southward, from the hill which *lies* opposite Beth-horon southward; and it ended at Kiriath-baal (that is, Kiriath-jearim), a city of the sons of Judah. This *was* the west side. ¹⁵Then the ^south side *was* from the edge of Kiriath-jearim, and the border went westward and went to the fountain of the waters of Nephtoah. ¹⁶Then the border went down to the edge of the hill which is in the ^Valley of Ben-hinnom, which is in the Valley of Rephaim northward; and it went down to the Valley of Hinnom, to the slope of the Jebusite southward, and went down to En-rogel. ¹⁷Then it turned northward and went to En-shemesh, and went to Geli-loth, which is opposite the ascent of Adummim, and it went down to the ^stone of Bohan the son of Reuben. ¹⁸And it continued to the side in front of the Arabah north-ward, and went down to the Ara-bah. ¹⁹Then the border continued to the side of Beth-hoglah north-ward; and the border ended at the north bay of the Salt Sea, at the south end of the Jordan. This *was* the southern border. ²⁰Moreover, the Jordan was its border on the east side. This *was* the inheritance of the sons of Benjamin according to their families, *and* according to its borders all around.

²¹Now the cities of the tribe of the sons of Benjamin according to their families were Jericho, Beth-hoglah, and Emek-keziz, ²²Beth-arabah, Zemaraim, and Bethel, ²³Avvim, Parah, and Ophrah, ²⁴Chephar-ammoni, Ophni, and ^Geba; twelve cities with their villages. ²⁵Gibeon, Ramah, and Beeroth, ²⁶Mizpeh, Chephirah, and Mozah, ²⁷Rekem, Irpeel, and Taralah, ²⁸^Zelah, Haeleph, the Jebusite *city* (that is, Jerusalem), Gibeah, Kiriath; four-teen cities with their villages. This is the inheritance of the sons of Ben-jamin according to their families.

TERRITORY OF SIMEON

19 Then the second lot went to Simeon, to the tribe of the sons of Simeon according to their families; and their inheritance was

18:8 ^Josh 18:1   18:10 ^Num 34:16-29; Josh 19:51
18:12 ^Josh 16:1   18:13 ^Gen 28:19; Judg 1:23
18:15 ^Josh 15:5-9   18:16 ^2 Kin 23:10
18:17 ^Josh 15:6   18:24 ^Ezra 2:26; Is 10:29
18:28 ^2 Sam 21:14

in the midst of the inheritance of the sons of Judah. ²So they had in their inheritance Beersheba or Sheba and Moladah, ³Hazar-shual, Balah, and Ezem, ⁴Eltolad, Bethul, and Hormah, ⁵Ziklag, Beth-marcaboth, and Hazar-susah, ⁶Beth-lebaoth, and Sharuhen; thirteen cities with their villages; ⁷Ain, Rimmon, Ether, and Ashan; four cities with their villages; ⁸and all the villages which *were* around these cities as far as Baalath-beer, Ramah of the Negev. This *was* the inheritance of the tribe of the sons of Simeon according to their families. ⁹The inheritance of the sons of Simeon *was taken* from the portion of the sons of Judah, because the share of the sons of Judah was too large for them; so the sons of Simeon received an inheritance in the midst of Judah's inheritance.

TERRITORY OF ZEBULUN

¹⁰Now the third lot came up for the sons of Zebulun according to their families. And the territory of their inheritance was as far as Sarid. ¹¹Then their border went up to the west and to Maralah, and it reached Dabbesheth and reached to the brook that is opposite Jokneam. ¹²Then it turned from Sarid to the east toward the sunrise as far as the border of Chisloth-tabor, and it proceeded to Daberath and up to Japhia. ¹³From there it continued eastward toward the sunrise to Gath-hepher, to Eth-kazin, and it proceeded to Rimmon which stretches to Neah. ¹⁴Then the border circled around it on the north to Hannathon, and it ended at the Valley of Iphtahel. ¹⁵*Included* also *were* Kattah, Nahalal, Shimron, Idalah, and Bethlehem; twelve

cities with their villages. ¹⁶This *was* the inheritance of the sons of Zebulun according to their families, these cities with their villages.

TERRITORY OF ISSACHAR

¹⁷The fourth lot went to Issachar, to the sons of Issachar according to their families. ¹⁸Their territory was to Jezreel and *included* Chesulloth, ᴬShunem, ¹⁹Hapharaim, Shion, and Anaharath, ²⁰Rabbith, Kishion, and Ebez, ²¹Remeth, En-gannim, En-haddah, and Beth-pazzez. ²²The border reached to ᴬTabor, Shahazumah, and Beth-shemesh, and their border ended at the Jordan; sixteen cities with their villages. ²³This *was* the inheritance of the tribe of the sons of Issachar according to their families, the cities with their villages.

TERRITORY OF ASHER

²⁴Now the fifth lot went to the tribe of the sons of Asher according to their families. ²⁵Their territory was Helkath, Hali, Beten, and Achshaph, ²⁶Allammelech, Amad, and Mishal; and it reached to Carmel on the west and Shihor-libnath. ²⁷It turned toward the east to Beth-dagon and reached Zebulun, and to the Valley of Iphtahel northward to Beth-emek and Neiel; then it proceeded on north to ᴬCabul, ²⁸Ebron, Rehob, Hammon, and Kanah, as far as Great ᴬSidon. ²⁹The border turned to Ramah and to the fortified city of Tyre; then the border turned to Hosah, and it ended at the sea by the region of ᴬAchzib. ³⁰*Included* also *were* Ummah, Aphek, and Rehob; twenty-two

19:18 ᴬ1 Sam 28:4; 2 Kin 4:8   19:22 ᴬJudg 4:6; Ps 89:12
19:27 ᴬ1 Kin 9:13   19:28 ᴬGen 10:19; Judg 1:31
19:29 ᴬJudg 1:31

cities with their villages. ³¹ This *was* the inheritance of the tribe of the sons of Asher according to their families, these cities with their villages.

TERRITORY OF NAPHTALI

³² The sixth lot went to the sons of Naphtali; to the sons of Naphtali according to their families. ³³ Their border was from Heleph, from the oak in Zaanannim, and Adaminekeb and Jabneel, as far as Lakkum, and it ended at the Jordan. ³⁴ Then the border turned westward to Aznoth-tabor and proceeded from there to Hukkok; and it reached Zebulun on the south and reached Asher on the west, and Judah at the Jordan toward the east. ³⁵ The fortified cities *were* Ziddim, Zer, Hammath, Rakkath, and ^Chinnereth, ³⁶ Adamah, Ramah, and Hazor, ³⁷ Kedesh, Edrei, and En-hazor, ³⁸ Yiron, Migdal-el, Horem, Beth-anath, and Beth-shemesh; nineteen cities with their villages. ³⁹ This *was* the inheritance of the tribe of the sons of Naphtali according to their families, the cities with their villages.

TERRITORY OF DAN

⁴⁰ The seventh lot went to the tribe of the sons of Dan according to their families. ⁴¹ The territory of their inheritance was Zorah, Eshtaol, and Ir-shemesh, ⁴² Shaalabbin, Aijalon, and Ithlah, ⁴³ Elon, Timnah, and Ekron, ⁴⁴ Eltekeh, Gibbethon, and Baalath, ⁴⁵ Jehud, Bene-berak, and Gath-rimmon, ⁴⁶ Me-jarkon, and Rakkon, with the territory opposite Joppa. ⁴⁷ The territory of the ^sons of Dan proceeded beyond them; for the sons of Dan went up and fought with

Leshem and captured it. Then they struck it with the edge of the sword and took possession of it and settled in it; and they named Leshem Dan after the name of their father Dan. ⁴⁸ This *was* the inheritance of the tribe of the sons of Dan according to their families, these cities with their villages.

⁴⁹ When they finished apportioning the land for inheritance by its borders, the sons of Israel gave an inheritance among them to Joshua the son of Nun. ⁵⁰ In accordance with the command of the LORD, they gave him the city for which he asked, ^Timnath-serah in the hill country of Ephraim. So he built the city and settled in it.

⁵¹ ^These are the inheritances which Eleazar the priest, Joshua the son of Nun, and the heads of the fathers' *households* of the tribes of the sons of Israel apportioned by lot in Shiloh before the LORD at the doorway of the tent of meeting. So they finished dividing the land.

SIX CITIES OF REFUGE

20 Then the LORD spoke to Joshua, saying, ² "Speak to the sons of Israel, saying, 'Designate ^the cities of refuge, of which I spoke to you through Moses, ³ so that one who commits manslaughter *by* killing a person unintentionally, without premeditation, may flee there, and they shall become your refuge from the avenger of blood. ⁴ Then he shall flee to one of these cities, and shall stand at the entrance of the ^gate of the city, and state his case in the presence of the elders of that city; and they shall

19:35 ^Deut 3:17   **19:47** ^Judg 18:1   **19:50** ^Num 13:8; Josh 24:30   **19:51** ^Josh 18:10   **20:2** ^Num 35:6-34; Deut 4:41-43   **20:4** ^Ruth 4:1; Job 5:4

receive him into the city to them and give him a place, so that he may remain among them. 5Now ^if the avenger of blood pursues him, then they are not to hand the one who committed manslaughter over to him, since he struck his neighbor without premeditation and did not hate him previously. 6And he shall remain in that city ^until he stands before the congregation for judgment, until the death of the one who is high priest in those days. Then he shall return to his own city and to his own house, to the city from which he fled.'"

7So they set apart ^Kedesh in Galilee in the hill country of Naphtali, and Shechem in the hill country of Ephraim, and Kiriath-arba (that is, Hebron) in the hill country of Judah. 8And beyond the Jordan east of Jericho, they designated Bezer in the wilderness on the plain from the tribe of Reuben, and Ramoth in Gilead from the tribe of Gad, and Golan in Bashan from the tribe of Manasseh. 9^These were the designated cities for all the sons of Israel and for the stranger who resides among them, so that whoever kills a person unintentionally may flee there, and not die by the hand of the avenger of blood until he stands before the congregation.

FORTY-EIGHT CITIES OF THE LEVITES

21 Then the heads of fathers' *households* of ^the Levites approached Eleazar the priest, Joshua the son of Nun, and the heads of fathers' *households* of the tribes of the sons of Israel. 2And they spoke to them at Shiloh in the land of Canaan, saying, "^The LORD commanded through Moses to give us cities to live in, with their

pasture lands for our cattle." 3So the sons of Israel gave the Levites from their inheritance these cities with their pasture lands, in accordance with the command of the LORD. 4Then the lot came out for the families of the Kohathites. And to the sons of Aaron the priest, who were of the Levites, thirteen cities were *given* by lot from the tribe of Judah, from the tribe of the Simeonites, and from the tribe of Benjamin.

5And to the rest of the sons of Kohath ten cities *were given* by lot from the families of the tribe of Ephraim, from the tribe of Dan, and from the half-tribe of Manasseh.

6And to the sons of Gershon thirteen cities *were given* by lot from the families of the tribe of Issachar, from the tribe of Asher, from the tribe of Naphtali, and from the half-tribe of Manasseh in Bashan.

7To the sons of Merari according to their families twelve cities *were given* from the tribe of Reuben, from the tribe of Gad, and from the tribe of Zebulun.

8Now the ^sons of Israel gave by lot to the Levites these cities with their pasture lands, as the LORD had commanded through Moses.

9They gave these cities which are mentioned *here* by name from the tribe of the sons of Judah and from the tribe of the sons of Simeon; 10and they were for the sons of Aaron, one of the families of the Kohathites, of the sons of Levi, because the lot was theirs first. 11So ^they gave them Kiriath-arba (*Arba being* the father of Anak), that is, Hebron, in the hill country

20:5^Num 35:12   20:6^Num 35:12   20:7^Josh 21:32; 1 Chr 6:76   20:9^Num 35:13ff   21:1^Num 35:1-8 21:2^Num 35:2   21:8^Gen 49:5ff   21:11^1 Chr 6:55

of Judah, with its surrounding pasture lands. ¹²But the fields of the city and its villages they gave to Caleb the son of Jephunneh as his possession.

¹³So to the sons of Aaron the priest they gave ᴬHebron, the city of refuge for the one who commits manslaughter, with its pasture lands, ᴮLibnah with its pasture lands, ¹⁴ᴬJattir with its pasture lands, Eshtemoa with its pasture lands, ¹⁵Holon with its pasture lands, ᴬDebir with its pasture lands, ¹⁶Ain with its pasture lands, ᴬJuttah with its pasture lands, *and* ᴮBeth-shemesh with its pasture lands; nine cities from these two tribes. ¹⁷From the tribe of Benjamin, Gibeon with its pasture lands, ᴬGeba with its pasture lands, ¹⁸Anathoth with its pasture lands, and Almon with its pasture lands; four cities. ¹⁹All the cities of the sons of Aaron, the priests, were thirteen cities with their pasture lands.

²⁰Then the cities from the tribe of Ephraim were allotted to the ᴬfamilies of the sons of Kohath, the Levites, *that is, to* the rest of the sons of Kohath. ²¹They gave them ᴬShechem, the city of refuge for the one who commits manslaughter, with its pasture lands, in the hill country of Ephraim, and Gezer with its pasture lands, ²²and Kibzaim with its pasture lands, and Beth-horon with its pasture lands; four cities. ²³And from the tribe of Dan, Elteke with its pasture lands, Gibbethon with its pasture lands, ²⁴Aijalon with its pasture lands, Gath-rimmon with its pasture lands; four cities. ²⁵From the half-tribe of Manasseh, *they allotted* Taanach with its pasture lands and Gath-rimmon with

its pasture lands; two cities. ²⁶All the cities with their pasture lands for the families of the rest of the sons of Kohath were ten.

²⁷And ᴬto the sons of Gershon, one of the families of the Levites, from the half-tribe of Manasseh, *they gave* Golan in Bashan, the city of refuge for the one who commits manslaughter, with its pasture lands, and Be-eshterah with its pasture lands; two cities. ²⁸And from the tribe of Issachar *they gave* Kishion with its pasture lands, Daberath with its pasture lands, ²⁹Jarmuth with its pasture lands, *and* En-gannim with its pasture lands; four cities. ³⁰From the tribe of Asher, *they gave* Mishal with its pasture lands, Abdon with its pasture lands, ³¹Helkath with its pasture lands, and Rehob with its pasture lands; four cities. ³²And from the tribe of Naphtali, *they gave* ᴬKedesh in Galilee, the city of refuge for the one who commits manslaughter, with its pasture lands, Hammoth-dor with its pasture lands, and Kartan with its pasture lands; three cities. ³³All the cities of the Gershonites according to their families were thirteen cities with their pasture lands.

³⁴And to the families of ᴬthe sons of Merari, the rest of the Levites, *they gave* from the tribe of Zebulun, Jokneam with its pasture lands, Kartah with its pasture lands, ³⁵Dimnah with its pasture lands, *and* Nahalal with its pasture lands; four cities. ³⁶From the tribe of Reuben *they gave* ᴬBezer with its pasture lands, Jahaz with its pasture lands, ³⁷Kedemoth with its pasture

21:13ᴬJosh 15:54   ᴮJosh 15:42   21:14ᴬJosh 15:48
21:15ᴬJosh 15:49   21:16ᴬJosh 15:55   ᴮJosh 15:10
21:17ᴬJosh 18:24   21:20ᴬ1 Chr 6:66   21:21ᴬJosh 20:7
21:27ᴬ1 Chr 6:71   21:32ᴬJosh 20:7   21:34ᴬ1 Chr 6:77
21:36ᴬDeut 4:43; Josh 20:8

lands, and Mephaath with its pasture lands; four cities. ³⁸And from the tribe of Gad, *they gave* ^Ramoth in Gilead, the city of refuge for the one who commits manslaughter, with its pasture lands, ᴮMahanaim with its pasture lands, ³⁹Heshbon with its pasture lands, *and* Jazer with its pasture lands; four cities in all. ⁴⁰All *these were* the cities of the sons of Merari according to their families, the rest of the families of the Levites; and their lot was twelve cities.

⁴¹^All the cities of the Levites in the midst of the possession of the sons of Israel were forty-eight cities with their pasture lands. ⁴²These cities individually had their surrounding pasture lands; this is how *it was* with all these cities.

⁴³^So the LORD gave Israel all the land which He had sworn to give to their fathers, and they took possession of it and lived in it. ⁴⁴And the LORD gave them rest on every side, in accordance with everything that He had sworn to their fathers, and no one of all their enemies stood before them; ^the LORD handed all their enemies over to them. ⁴⁵^Not one of the good promises which the LORD had made to the house of Israel failed; everything came to pass.

TRIBES BEYOND JORDAN RETURN

22 ^Then Joshua summoned the Reubenites and the Gadites, and the half-tribe of Manasseh, ²and said to them, "You have kept all that Moses the servant of the LORD commanded you, ^and have listened to my voice in all that I commanded you. ³You have not abandoned your brothers these many days to this day, but have fulfilled the obligation of the commandment of the LORD your God. ⁴And now ^the LORD your God has given rest to your brothers, as He spoke to them; therefore turn now and go to your tents, to the land of your possession, which Moses the servant of the LORD gave you beyond the Jordan. ⁵Only be very careful to follow the commandment and the Law which Moses the servant of the LORD commanded you, to ^love the LORD your God and walk in all His ways, and keep His commandments and cling to Him, and serve Him ᴮwith all your heart and with all your soul." ⁶So Joshua ^blessed them and sent them away, and they went to their tents.

⁷Now ^to the one half-tribe of Manasseh Moses had given *a possession* in Bashan, but ᴮto the other half Joshua gave *a possession* among their brothers westward beyond the Jordan. So when Joshua sent them away to their tents, he also blessed them, ⁸and said to them, "Return to your tents with great riches and with very many livestock, with silver, gold, bronze, iron, and with very many clothes; ^divide the spoils of your enemies with your brothers." ⁹So the sons of Reuben, the sons of Gad, and the half-tribe of Manasseh returned *home,* leaving the sons of Israel at Shiloh, which is in the land of Canaan, to go to the ^land of Gilead, to the land of their possession in which they had settled, in accordance with the command of the LORD through Moses.

21:38 ^Deut 4:43   ᴮGen 32:2   21:41 ^Num 35:7
21:43 ^Deut 34:4   21:44 ^Ex 23:31   21:45 ^Josh 23:14;
1 Kin 8:56   22:1 ^Num 32:20-22   22:2 ^Josh 1:12-18
22:4 ^Num 32:18; Deut 3:20   22:5 ^Deut 5:10
ᴮDeut 4:29   22:6 ^Gen 47:7; Josh 14:13
22:7 ^Num 32:33   ᴮJosh 17:1-13   22:8 ^Num 31:27;
1 Sam 30:16   22:9 ^Num 32:1, 26, 29

THE OFFENSIVE ALTAR

¹⁰When they came to the region of the Jordan which is in the land of Canaan, the sons of Reuben, the sons of Gad, and the half-tribe of Manasseh built an altar there by the Jordan, a large altar in appearance. ¹¹But the sons of Israel heard a report: "Behold, the sons of Reuben, the sons of Gad, and the half-tribe of Manasseh have ^built an altar at the frontier of the land of Canaan, in the region of the Jordan, on the side *belonging to* the sons of Israel." ¹²And when the sons of Israel heard *about it,* the entire congregation of the sons of Israel assembled at ^Shiloh to go up against them in battle.

¹³Then the sons of Israel sent to the sons of Reuben, to the sons of Gad, and to the half-tribe of Manasseh, in the land of Gilead, ^Phinehas the son of Eleazar the priest, ¹⁴and with him ten leaders, one leader for each father's household from each of the tribes of Israel; and ^each one of them *was* the head of his father's household among the thousands of Israel. ¹⁵They came to the sons of Reuben, the sons of Gad, and to the half-tribe of Manasseh, in the land of Gilead, and they spoke with them, saying, ¹⁶"This is what the whole congregation of the LORD says: 'What is this unfaithful act which you have committed against the God of Israel, turning away from following the LORD this day, by ^building yourselves an altar, to rebel against the LORD this day? ¹⁷Is ^the wrongdoing of Peor not enough for us, from which we have not cleansed ourselves to this day, although a plague came on the congregation of the LORD, ¹⁸that

you must turn away this day from following the LORD? If you rebel against the LORD today, ^He will be angry with the entire congregation of Israel tomorrow. ¹⁹If, however, the land of your possession is unclean, then cross into the land of the possession of the LORD, where the LORD's tabernacle stands, and settle among us. Only do not rebel against the LORD, or rebel against us, by ^building an altar for yourselves besides the altar of the LORD our God. ²⁰Did ^Achan the son of Zerah not act unfaithfully in the things designated for destruction, and wrath fall on the entire congregation of Israel? So that man did not perish alone in his guilt.'"

²¹Then the sons of Reuben, the sons of Gad, and the half-tribe of Manasseh answered and spoke to the heads of the families of Israel. ²²"The Mighty One, God, the LORD, the Mighty One, God, the LORD! ^He knows, and may Israel itself know. If *it was* in rebellion, or if in an unfaithful act against the LORD, do not save us this day! ²³If we have built us an altar to turn away from following the LORD, or if to ^offer a burnt offering or grain offering on it, or if to offer sacrifices of peace offerings on it, may the LORD Himself demand it. ²⁴But truly we have done this out of concern, for a reason, saying, 'In time to come your sons may say to our sons, "What have you to do with the LORD, the God of Israel? ²⁵For the LORD has made the Jordan a border between us and you, *you* sons of Reuben and sons of Gad; you have no portion in

22:11 ^Deut 12:5; Josh 22:19   22:12 ^Josh 18:1
22:13 ^Num 25:7, 11; 31:6   22:14 ^Num 1:4
22:16 ^Josh 22:11   22:17 ^Num 25:1-9
22:18 ^Num 16:22   22:19 ^Josh 22:11   22:20 ^Josh 7:1-
26   22:22 ^1 Kin 8:39; Job 10:7   22:23 ^Deut 12:11

the LORD." So your sons may make our sons stop fearing the LORD.'

26 "Therefore we said, 'Let's build an altar, not for burnt offering or for sacrifice; 27 rather, it *shall be* ^a witness between us and you and between our generations after us, that we are to perform the service of the LORD before Him with our burnt offerings, our sacrifices, and with our peace offerings, so that your sons will not say to our sons in time to come, "You have no portion in the LORD."' 28 Therefore we said, 'It shall also come about if they say *this* to us or to our generations in time to come, then we shall say, "See the copy of the altar of the LORD which our fathers made, not for burnt offering or for sacrifice; rather, it is a witness between us and you."' 29 Far be it from us that we should rebel against the LORD and turn away from following the LORD this day, by ^building an altar for burnt offering, for grain offering, or for sacrifice, besides the altar of the LORD our God which is before His tabernacle."

30 So when Phinehas the priest and the leaders of the congregation, that is, the heads of the families of Israel who *were* with him, heard the words which the sons of Reuben, the sons of Gad, and the sons of Manasseh spoke, it pleased them. 31 And Phinehas the son of Eleazar the priest said to the sons of Reuben, the sons of Gad, and to the sons of Manasseh, "Today we know that the ^LORD is in our midst, because you have not committed this unfaithful act against the LORD; now you have saved the sons of Israel from the hand of the LORD."

32 Then Phinehas the son of Eleazar the priest and the leaders returned from the sons of Reuben and from the sons of Gad, from the land of Gilead to the land of Canaan, to the sons of Israel, and brought back word to them. 33 The word pleased the sons of Israel, and the sons of Israel ^blessed God; and they did not speak of going up against them in battle to destroy the land in which the sons of Reuben and the sons of Gad were living. 34 And the sons of Reuben and the sons of Gad ^called the altar *Witness;* "For," *they said,* "it is a witness between us that the LORD is God."

JOSHUA'S FAREWELL ADDRESS

23 Now it came about after many days, when the LORD had given ^rest to Israel from all their enemies on every side, and Joshua was old, advanced in years, 2 that ^Joshua called for all Israel, for their elders, their heads, their judges, and their officers, and said to them, "I am old, advanced in years. 3 And you have seen all that the LORD your God has done to all these nations because of you, for ^the LORD your God is He who has been fighting for you. 4 See, ^I have apportioned to you these nations which remain as an inheritance for your tribes, with all the nations which I have eliminated, from the Jordan even to the Great Sea toward the west. 5 And the LORD your God, He will thrust them away from you and ^drive them from you; and ^you will take possession of their land, just as the LORD your God promised you. 6 ^Be very determined, then, to keep and do everything that is

22:27 ^Gen 31:48; Josh 24:27 22:29 ^Deut 12:13f
22:31 ^Ex 25:8; Lev 26:11f 22:33 ^1 Chr 29:20;
Dan 2:19 22:34 ^Gen 31:47-49 23:1 ^Josh 21:44
23:2 ^Josh 24:1 23:3 ^Deut 1:30 23:4 ^Ex 23:30
23:5 ^Ex 23:20 ^Num 33:53 23:6 ^Deut 5:32; Josh 1:7

written in the Book of the Law of Moses, so that you will not turn aside from it to the right or to the left, ⁷so that you will not associate with these nations, these which remain with you, or mention the name of their gods, or ^make *anyone* swear *by them,* or ᴮserve them, or bow down to them. ⁸But you are to cling to the LORD your God, as you have done to this day. ⁹^For the LORD has driven out great and mighty nations from before you; and as for you, no one has stood against you to this day. ¹⁰One of your men puts to flight a thousand, for the LORD your God is ^He who fights for you, just as He promised you. ¹¹So take great care for yourselves that you love the LORD your God. ¹²For if you ever go back and ^cling to the rest of these nations, these which remain with you, and intermarry with them, so that you associate with them and they with you, ¹³know with certainty that the LORD your God will not continue to drive these nations out from before you; but they will be a ^snare and a trap to you, and a whip on your sides and thorns in your eyes, until you perish from this good land which the LORD your God has given you.

¹⁴"Now behold, today ^I am going the way of all the earth, and you know in all your hearts and in all your souls that ᴮnot one word of all the good words which the LORD your God spoke concerning you has failed; they all have been fulfilled for you, not one of them has failed. ¹⁵But it will come about that just as all the good words which the LORD your God spoke to you have come upon you, so ^the LORD will bring upon you all the warnings, until He

has eliminated you from this good land which the LORD your God has given you. ¹⁶^When you violate the covenant of the LORD your God, which He commanded you, and you go and serve other gods and bow down to them, then the anger of the LORD will burn against you, and you will perish quickly from the good land which He has given you."

JOSHUA REVIEWS ISRAEL'S HISTORY

24 Then ^Joshua gathered all the tribes of Israel at Shechem, and called for the elders of Israel, their heads, their judges, and their officers; and they presented themselves before God. ²Joshua said to all the people, "This is what the LORD, the God of Israel says: 'From ancient times your fathers lived beyond the *Euphrates* River, *namely,* ^Terah, the father of Abraham and the father of Nahor, and they served other gods. ³Then ^I took your father Abraham from beyond the *Euphrates* River and led him through all the land of Canaan, and multiplied his descendants and gave him Isaac. ⁴To Isaac I gave ^Jacob and Esau, and to Esau I gave Mount Seir, to possess it; but Jacob and his sons went down to Egypt. ⁵Then ^I sent Moses and Aaron, and I plagued Egypt by what I did in its midst; and afterward I brought you out. ⁶So I brought your fathers out of Egypt, and ^you came to the sea; and Egypt pursued your fathers with chariots and horsemen to the Red Sea. ⁷But when they cried

23:7^Deut 6:13   ᴮEx 20:5   23:9^Ex 23:23, 30
23:10^Deut 3:22; Josh 23:3   23:12^Ex 34:15, 16;
Ps 106:34, 35   23:13^Ex 23:33; 34:12   23:14^1 Kin 2:2
ᴮJosh 21:45   23:15^Lev 26:14-33; Deut 28:15
23:16^Deut 4:25, 26   24:1^Josh 23:2   24:2^Gen 11:27-
32   24:3^Gen 12:1; 24:7   24:4^Gen 25:25, 26
24:5^Ex 4:14-17   24:6^Ex 14:2-31

out to the Lord, He put darkness between you and the Egyptians, and brought the sea upon them and covered them; and your own eyes saw what I did in Egypt. And ^you lived in the wilderness for a long time. 8 Then ^I brought you into the land of the Amorites, who lived beyond the Jordan, and they fought with you; but I handed them over to you, and you took possession of their land when I eliminated them before you. 9 Then ^Balak the son of Zippor, king of Moab, rose up and fought against Israel, and he sent *messengers* and summoned Balaam the son of Beor to curse you. 10 But I ^was not willing to listen to Balaam. So he had to bless you, and I saved you from his hand. 11^You crossed the Jordan and came to Jericho; and the citizens of Jericho fought against you, *and* the Amorite, the Perizzite, the Canaanite, the Hittite, the Girgashite, the Hivite, and the Jebusite. Therefore ^BI handed them over to you. 12 Then I ^sent the hornet before you and it drove out the two kings of the Amorites from you—^Bnot by your sword nor your bow. 13 And ^I gave you a land on which you had not labored, and cities which you had not built, and you have lived in them; you are eating of vineyards and olive groves which you did not plant.'

"WE WILL SERVE THE LORD"

14 "Now, therefore, ^fear the Lord and serve Him in sincerity and truth; and do away with the gods which your fathers served beyond the *Euphrates* River and in Egypt, and serve the Lord. 15 But if it is disagreeable in your sight to serve the Lord, choose for yourselves today whom you will serve: whether the gods which your fathers served, which were beyond the *Euphrates* River, or ^the gods of the Amorites in whose land you are living; but as for me and my house, we will serve the Lord."

16 The people answered and said, "Far be it from us that we would abandon the Lord to serve other gods; 17 for the Lord our God is He who brought us and our fathers up out of the land of Egypt, from the house of slaves, and did these great signs in our sight and watched over us through all the way in which we went and among all the peoples through whose midst we passed. 18 The Lord drove out from before us all the peoples, even the Amorites who lived in the land. We also will serve the Lord, for He is our God."

19 Then Joshua said to the people, "You will not be able to serve the Lord, for He is a holy God. He is ^a jealous God; He will not forgive your wrongdoing or your sins. 20^If you abandon the Lord and serve foreign gods, then He will turn and do you harm and destroy you after He has done good to you." 21 And the people said to Joshua, "No, but we will serve the Lord." 22 So Joshua said to the people, "You are witnesses against yourselves that ^you have chosen for yourselves the Lord, to serve Him." And they said, "*We are* witnesses." 23 "Now then, do away with the foreign gods which are in your midst, and ^incline your hearts to the Lord, the God of Israel." 24 And ^the people

24:7 ^Deut 1:46; 2:14   24:8 ^Num 21:21-32
24:9 ^Num 22:2-6   24:10 ^Deut 23:5
24:11 ^Josh 3:14-17   ^BEx 23:31   24:12 ^Ex 23:28
^BPs 44:3   24:13 ^Deut 6:10, 11   24:14 ^Deut 10:12;
1 Sam 12:24   24:15 ^Judg 6:10   24:19 ^Ex 20:5; 34:14
24:20 ^Deut 4:25, 26   24:22 ^Ps 119:173
24:23 ^1 Kin 8:57, 58; Ps 119:36   24:24 ^Ex 19:8; 24:3, 7

said to Joshua, "We will serve the LORD our God and obey His voice." 25ᴬSo Joshua made a covenant with the people that day, and made for them a statute and an ordinance in Shechem. 26And Joshua ᴬwrote these words in the Book of the Law of God; and he took a large stone and set it up there under the oak that was by the sanctuary of the LORD. 27Then Joshua said to all the people, "Behold, ᴬthis stone shall be a witness against us, because it has heard all the words of the LORD which He spoke to us; so it shall be a witness against you, so that you do not deny your God." 28Then Joshua dismissed the people, each to his inheritance.

JOSHUA'S DEATH AND BURIAL

29Now it came about after these things that Joshua the son of Nun, the servant of the LORD, died, being 110 years old. 30And they buried him in the territory of his inheritance, in ᴬTimnath-serah, which is in the hill country of Ephraim, on the north of Mount Gaash.

31ᴬIsrael served the LORD all the days of Joshua and all the days of the elders who survived Joshua, and had known every deed of the LORD which He had done for Israel.

32Now ᴬthey buried the bones of Joseph, which the sons of Israel brought up from Egypt, at Shechem, in the plot of land which Jacob had bought from the sons of Hamor the father of Shechem for a hundred pieces of money; and they became the inheritance of Joseph's sons. 33And Eleazar the son of Aaron died; and they buried him at Gibeah, *the town* of his son ᴬPhinehas, which was given to him in the hill country of Ephraim.

24:25 ᴬEx 24:8   24:26 ᴬDeut 31:24
24:27 ᴬJosh 22:27, 34   24:30 ᴬJosh 19:50
24:31 ᴬJudg 2:6f   24:32 ᴬGen 50:24, 25; Ex 13:19
24:33 ᴬJosh 22:13

JUDGES

JERUSALEM IS CAPTURED

1 Now it came about after the death of Joshua that the sons of Israel inquired of the LORD, saying, "Who shall go up first for us ^against the Canaanites, to fight against them?" ²The LORD said, "^Judah shall go up; behold, I have handed the land over to him." ³Then Judah said to his brother Simeon, "Go up with me into the territory allotted me, and let's fight the Canaanites; and I in turn will go with you into the territory allotted you." So Simeon went with him. ⁴Judah went up, and ^the LORD handed over to them the Canaanites and the Perizzites, and they defeated ten thousand men at Bezek. ⁵They found Adoni-bezek in Bezek and fought against him, and they defeated the Canaanites and the Perizzites. ⁶But Adoni-bezek fled; and they pursued him and caught him, and cut off his thumbs and big toes. ⁷And Adoni-bezek said, "Seventy kings with their thumbs and their big toes cut off used to gather up *scraps* under my table; ^as I have done, so God has repaid me." So they brought him to Jerusalem, and he died there.

⁸Then the sons of Judah fought against ^Jerusalem and captured it, and struck it with the edge of the sword, and set the city on fire. ⁹Afterward, the sons of Judah went down to fight against the Canaanites living in the hill country, and in the ¹Negev, and in the lowland. ¹⁰^So Judah went against the Canaanites who lived in Hebron (the name of Hebron *was* previously Kirath-arba); and they struck Sheshai, Ahiman, and Talmai.

CAPTURE OF OTHER CITIES

¹¹Then ^from there he went against the inhabitants of Debir (the name of Debir *was* previously Kiriath-sepher). ¹²And Caleb said, "Whoever attacks Kiriath-sepher and captures it, I will give him my daughter Achsah as a wife." ¹³Now ^Othniel the son of Kenaz, Caleb's younger brother, captured it; so he gave him his daughter Achsah as a wife. ¹⁴Then ^it happened that when she came *to him,* she incited him to ask her father for a field. Then *later,* she dismounted from her donkey, and Caleb said to her, "What do you want?" ¹⁵She said to him, "Give me a blessing: since you have given me the land of the ¹Negev, give me springs of water also." So Caleb gave her the upper springs and the lower springs.

¹⁶Now the descendants of ^the Kenite, Moses' father-in-law, went up from the city of palms with the sons of Judah, to the wilderness of Judah which is in the south of Arad; and they went and lived with the people. ¹⁷Then Judah went with his brother Simeon, and they struck the Canaanites living in Zephath,

1:1 ^Judg 1:27; 2:21-23 1:2 ^Gen 49:8 1:4 ^Ps 44:2; 78:55 1:7 ^Lev 24:19 1:8 ^Josh 15:63; Judg 1:21 1:10 ^Josh 15:13-19 1:11 ^Josh 15:15 1:13 ^Judg 3:9 1:14 ^Josh 15:18 1:16 ^Num 10:29-32; Judg 4:11

1:9 ¹I.e., South country 1:15 ¹I.e., South country

and utterly destroyed it. So the name of the city was called ^Hormah. ¹⁸And Judah took ^Gaza with its territory, Ashkelon with its territory, and Ekron with its territory. ¹⁹Now the Lord was with Judah, and they took possession of the hill country; but *they could* not drive out the inhabitants of the valley, because they had ^iron chariots. ²⁰Then they gave Hebron to Caleb, ^as Moses had promised; and he drove out from there the three sons of Anak. ²¹But the sons of Benjamin did not drive out the ^Jebusites who lived in Jerusalem; so the Jebusites have lived with the sons of Benjamin in Jerusalem to this day.

²²Likewise the house of Joseph went up against Bethel, and the Lord was with them. ²³The house of Joseph had *men* spy out Bethel (^the name of the city previously was Luz). ²⁴And the spies saw a man coming out of the city, and they said to him, "Please show us the entrance to the city, and ^we will treat you kindly." ²⁵So he showed them the entrance to the city, and they struck the city with the edge of the sword, ^but they let the man and all his family go free. ²⁶Then the man went to the land of the Hittites and built a city, and named it Luz, which is its name to this day.

PLACES NOT CONQUERED

²⁷^But Manasseh did not take possession of Beth-shean and its villages, or Taanach and its villages, or the inhabitants of Dor and its villages, or the inhabitants of Ibleam and its villages, or the inhabitants of Megiddo and its villages; so ^Bthe Canaanites persisted in living in this land. ²⁸And it came about,

when Israel became strong, that they put the Canaanites to forced labor; but they did not drive them out completely.

²⁹And ^Ephraim did not drive out the Canaanites who were living in Gezer; so the Canaanites lived in Gezer among them.

³⁰Zebulun did not drive out the inhabitants of Kitron, or the inhabitants of ¹Nahalol; so the Canaanites lived among them and became subject to forced labor.

³¹Asher did not drive out the inhabitants of Acco, or the inhabitants of Sidon, or of Ahlab, or of Achzib, Helbah, Aphik, or of Rehob. ³²So the Asherites lived among the Canaanites, the inhabitants of the land; for they did not drive them out.

³³Naphtali did not drive out the inhabitants of Beth-shemesh, or the inhabitants of Beth-anath, but lived among the Canaanites, the inhabitants of the land; and the inhabitants of Beth-shemesh and Beth-anath became forced labor for them.

³⁴Then the Amorites forced the sons of Dan into the hill country, for they did not allow them to come down to the valley; ³⁵yet the Amorites persisted in living on Mount Heres, in Aijalon and Shaalbim; but when the power of the house of Joseph grew strong, they became forced labor. ³⁶The border of the Amorites *ran* from the ^ascent of Akrabbim, from Sela and upward.

1:17^Num 21:3   1:18^Josh 11:22   1:19^Josh 17:16; Judg 4:3, 13   1:20^Josh 14:9   1:21^1 Chr 11:4   1:23^Gen 28:19   1:24^Josh 2:12   1:25^Josh 6:25   1:27^Josh 17:12   ^BJudg 1:1   1:29^Josh 16:10   1:36^Josh 15:3

1:30¹Perhaps same as *Nahalal*

ISRAEL REBUKED

2 Now the angel of the LORD came up from Gilgal to Bochim. And he said, "ᴬI brought you up out of Egypt and led you into the land which I have sworn to your fathers; and I said, 'ᴮI will never break My covenant with you, ²and as for you, ᴬyou shall not make a covenant with the inhabitants of this land; you shall tear down their altars.' But you have not obeyed Me; what is this *thing that* you have done? ³Therefore I also said, 'I will not drive them out from you; but they will ¹become ᴬ*like thorns* in your sides, and their gods will be a snare to you.'" ⁴Now when the angel of the LORD spoke these words to all the sons of Israel, the people raised their voices and wept. ⁵So they named that place ¹Bochim; and there they sacrificed to the LORD.

JOSHUA DIES

⁶ᴬWhen Joshua had dismissed the people, the sons of Israel went, each one to his inheritance, to take possession of the land. ⁷The people served the LORD all the days of Joshua, and all the days of the elders who survived Joshua, who had seen all the great work of the LORD which He had done for Israel. ⁸Then Joshua the son of Nun, the servant of the LORD, died at the age of 110. ⁹And they buried him in the territory of ᴬhis inheritance in Timnath-heres, in the hill country of Ephraim, north of Mount Gaash. ¹⁰All that generation also were gathered to their fathers; and another generation rose up after them who ᴬdid not know the LORD, nor even the work which He had done for Israel.

ISRAEL SERVES THE BAALS

¹¹Then the sons of Israel did ᴬevil in the sight of the LORD and served the Baals, ¹²and ᴬthey abandoned the LORD, the God of their fathers, who had brought them out of the land of Egypt, and they followed other gods from the gods of the peoples who were around them, and bowed down to them; so they provoked the LORD to anger. ¹³They abandoned the LORD and ᴬserved Baal and the Ashtaroth. ¹⁴ᴬThen the anger of the LORD burned against Israel, and He handed them over to plunderers, and they plundered them; and He sold them into the hands of their enemies around *them*, so that they could no longer stand against their enemies. ¹⁵Wherever they went, the hand of the LORD was against them for evil, as the LORD had spoken and ᴬjust as the LORD had sworn to them, so that they were severely distressed.

¹⁶ᴬThen the LORD raised up judges who saved them from the hands of those who plundered them. ¹⁷Yet they did not listen to their judges, for they ¹committed infidelity with other gods and bowed down to them. They turned aside quickly from the way ᴬin which their fathers had walked in obeying the commandments of the LORD; they did not do the same *as their fathers*. ¹⁸And when the LORD raised up judges for them, ᴬthe LORD was with the judge and saved them from the hand of their enemies all the

2:1ᴬEx 20:2   ᴮGen 17:7, 8   2:2ᴬEx 23:32; Deut 7:2-5
2:3ᴬNum 33:55   2:6ᴬJosh 24:28-31   2:9ᴬJosh 19:49f
2:10ᴬEx 5:2; 1 Sam 2:12   2:11ᴬJudg 3:7, 12; 4:1
2:12ᴬDeut 31:16   2:13ᴬJudg 10:6   2:14ᴬDeut 31:17;
Ps 106:40-42   2:15ᴬLev 26:14-39; Deut 28:15-68
2:16ᴬPs 106:43-45   2:17ᴬJudg 2:7   2:18ᴬJosh 1:5

2:3¹Some ancient mss *become adversaries to you and*
2:5¹I.e., weepers   2:17¹I.e., against God

days of the judge; for the Lord was moved to pity by their groaning because of those who tormented and oppressed them. ¹⁹But it came about, when the judge died, that they would turn back and act more corruptly than their fathers, in following other gods to serve them and bow down to them; they did not abandon their practices or their obstinate ways. ²⁰ᴬSo the anger of the Lord burned against Israel, and He said, "Because this nation has violated My covenant which I commanded their fathers, and has not listened to My voice, ²¹ᴬI in turn will no longer drive out from them any of the nations which Joshua left when he died, ²²in order to ᴬtest Israel by them, whether they will keep the way of the Lord to walk in it as their fathers did, or not." ²³So the Lord allowed those nations to remain, not driving them out quickly; and He did not hand them over to Joshua.

IDOLATRY LEADS TO SERVITUDE

3 ᴬNow these are the nations that the Lord left, to test Israel by them (*that is,* all *the Israelites* who had not experienced any of the wars of Canaan; ²only in order that the generations of the sons of Israel might be taught war, those who had not experienced it previously). ³ *These nations are:* the five governors of the Philistines and all the Canaanites and the Sidonians, and ᴬthe Hivites who lived on Mount Lebanon, from Mount Baal-hermon as far as Lebo-hamath. ⁴They were *left* to ᴬtest Israel by them, to find out if they would obey the commandments of the Lord, which He had commanded their fathers through Moses. ⁵ᴬThe sons

of Israel lived among the Canaanites, the Hittites, the Amorites, the Perizzites, the Hivites, and the Jebusites; ⁶and ᴬthey took their daughters for themselves as wives, and gave their own daughters to their sons, and served their gods.

⁷So the sons of Israel did ᴬwhat was evil in the sight of the Lord, and they forgot the Lord their God and served the Baals and the ¹Asheroth. ⁸Then the anger of the Lord was kindled against Israel, so that He sold them into the hand of Cushan-rishathaim, king of Mesopotamia; and the sons of Israel served Cushan-rishathaim for eight years.

THE FIRST JUDGE FREES ISRAEL

⁹But the sons of Israel cried out to the Lord, and the Lord raised up a deliverer for the sons of Israel to set them free, ᴬOthniel the son of Kenaz, Caleb's younger brother. ¹⁰And ᴬthe Spirit of the Lord came upon him, and he judged Israel. When he went to war, the Lord handed over to him Cushan-rishathaim king of Mesopotamia, so that he prevailed over Cushan-rishathaim. ¹¹Then the land was at rest for forty years. And Othniel the son of Kenaz died.

¹²Now the sons of Israel again did evil in the sight of the Lord. So ᴬthe Lord strengthened Eglon the king of Moab against Israel, because they had done evil in the sight of the Lord. ¹³And he gathered to himself the sons of Ammon and Amalek; and he went and defeated

2:20ᴬJudg 2:14   2:21ᴬJosh 23:4, 5, 13   2:22ᴬDeut 8:2; 13:3   3:1ᴬJudg 1:1; 2:21, 22   3:3ᴬJosh 9:7; 11:19   3:4ᴬDeut 8:2   3:5ᴬPs 106:35   3:6ᴬEx 34:15, 16; Deut 7:3, 4   3:7ᴬJudg 2:11   3:9ᴬJudg 1:13   3:10ᴬNum 11:25-29; 24:2   3:12ᴬJudg 2:14

3:7¹I.e., wooden symbols of a female deity (Asherah)

Israel, and they took possession of ^the city of the palm trees. ¹⁴And the sons of Israel served Eglon the king of Moab for eighteen years.

EHUD KILLS EGLON

¹⁵But when the sons of Israel ^cried out to the LORD, the LORD raised up a deliverer for them, Ehud the son of Gera, the Benjaminite, a left-handed man. And the sons of Israel sent tribute by him to Eglon the king of Moab. ¹⁶Now Ehud made himself a sword which had two edges, a cubit in length, and he strapped it on his right thigh under his cloak. ¹⁷Then he presented the tribute to Eglon king of Moab. Now Eglon was a very fat man. ¹⁸And it came about, when he had finished presenting the tribute, that *Ehud* sent away the people who had carried the tribute. ¹⁹But he himself turned back from the idols which were at Gilgal, and said, "I have a secret message for you, O king." And *the king* said, "Silence!" And all who were attending him left him. ²⁰Then Ehud came to him while he was sitting in his cool roof chamber alone. And Ehud said, "I have a message from God for you." And he got up from his seat. ²¹Then Ehud reached out with his left hand and took the sword from his right thigh, and thrust it into his belly. ²²The hilt *of the sword* also went in after the blade, and the fat closed over the blade because he did not pull the sword out of his belly; and the refuse came out. ²³Then Ehud went out into the vestibule, and shut the doors of the roof chamber behind him, and locked *them.*

²⁴When he had left, the king's servants came and looked, and behold, the doors of the roof chamber were locked; and they said, "^Undoubtedly he is relieving himself in the cool room." ²⁵So they waited until it would have been shameful *to wait longer;* but behold, he did not open the doors of the roof chamber. So they took the key and opened *them,* and behold, their master had fallen to the floor dead.

²⁶Now Ehud escaped while they were hesitating, and he passed by the idols and escaped to Seirah. ²⁷And when he arrived, ^he blew the trumpet in the hill country of Ephraim; and the sons of Israel went down with him from the hill country, and he *was* leading them. ²⁸Then he said to them, "Pursue *them,* for the LORD has handed your enemies the Moabites over to you." So they went down after him and took control of ^the crossing places of the Jordan opposite Moab, and did not allow anyone to cross. ²⁹They struck and killed about ten thousand Moabites at that time, all robust and valiant men; and no one escaped. ³⁰So Moab was subdued that day under the hand of Israel. And the land was at rest for eighty years.

SHAMGAR SAVES ISRAEL

³¹Now after him came ^Shamgar the son of Anath, who struck and killed six hundred Philistines with an ¹oxgoad; and he also saved Israel.

DEBORAH AND BARAK

4 Then ^the sons of Israel again did evil in the sight of the LORD, after Ehud died. ²So the LORD sold them into the hand of

3:13^Deut 34:3; Judg 1:16   3:15^Ps 78:34
3:24^1 Sam 24:3   3:27^Judg 6:34; 1 Sam 13:3
3:28^Judg 7:24; 12:5   3:31^Judg 5:6   4:1^Judg 2:19

3:31 ¹I.e., a spiked stick for driving livestock

ᴬJabin king of Canaan, who reigned in Hazor; and the commander of his army was Sisera, who lived in Harosheth-hagoyim. ³The sons of Israel cried out to the Lᴏʀᴅ; for he had nine hundred ᴬiron chariots, and he oppressed the sons of Israel severely for twenty years.

⁴Now Deborah, a prophetess, the wife of Lappidoth, was judging Israel at that time. ⁵She used to sit under the ᴬpalm tree of Deborah between Ramah and Bethel in the hill country of Ephraim; and the sons of Israel went up to her for judgment. ⁶Now she sent *word* and summoned ᴬBarak the son of Abinoam from Kedesh-naphtali, and said to him, "The Lᴏʀᴅ, the God of Israel, has indeed commanded, 'Go and march to Mount Tabor, and take with you ten thousand men from the sons of Naphtali and from the sons of Zebulun. ⁷I will draw out to you Sisera, the commander of Jabin's army, with his chariots and his many *troops* to the river Kishon, and ᴬI will hand him over to you.'" ⁸Then Barak said to her, "If you will go with me, then I will go; but if you will not go with me, I will not go." ⁹She said, "I will certainly go with you; however, the fame shall not be yours on the journey that you are about to take, ᴬfor the Lᴏʀᴅ will sell Sisera into the hand of a woman." Then Deborah got up and went with Barak to Kedesh. ¹⁰Barak summoned Zebulun and Naphtali to Kedesh, and ten thousand men went up ᴬwith him; Deborah also went up with him.

¹¹Now Heber ᴬthe Kenite had separated himself from the Kenites, from the sons of Hobab the father-in-law of Moses, and had pitched his tent as far away as the oak in Zaanannim, which is near Kedesh.

¹²Then they told Sisera that Barak the son of Abinoam had gone up to Mount Tabor. ¹³Sisera summoned all his chariots, nine hundred iron chariots, and all the people who *were* with him, from ᴬHarosheth-hagoyim to the river Kishon. ¹⁴Then Deborah said to Barak, "Arise! For this is the day on which the Lᴏʀᴅ has handed Sisera over to you; behold, ᴬthe Lᴏʀᴅ has gone out before you." So Barak went down from Mount Tabor with ten thousand men following him. ¹⁵ᴬAnd the Lᴏʀᴅ routed Sisera and all *his* chariots and all *his* army with the edge of the sword before Barak; and Sisera got down from *his* chariot and fled on foot. ¹⁶But Barak pursued the chariots and the army as far as Harosheth-hagoyim, and all the army of Sisera fell by the edge of the sword; ᴬnot even one was left.

¹⁷Now Sisera fled on foot to the tent of Jael the wife of Heber the Kenite, because *there was* peace between Jabin the king of Hazor and the house of Heber the Kenite. ¹⁸And Jael went out to meet Sisera, and said to him, "Turn aside, my master, turn aside to me! Do not be afraid." So he turned aside to her into the tent, and she covered him with a rug. ¹⁹ᴬAnd he said to her, "Please give me a little water to drink, for I am thirsty." So she opened a leather bottle of milk and gave him a drink; then she covered him. ²⁰And he said to her, "Stand in the doorway of the tent,

4:2ᴬJosh 11:1, 10   4:3ᴬJudg 1:19   4:5ᴬGen 35:8
4:6ᴬHeb 11:32   4:7ᴬPs 83:9   4:9ᴬJudg 4:21
4:10ᴬJudg 4:14; 5:15   4:11ᴬJudg 1:16   4:13ᴬJudg 4:2
4:14ᴬDeut 9:3; 2 Sam 5:24   4:15ᴬDeut 7:23;
Josh 10:10   4:16ᴬEx 14:28; Ps 83:9   4:19ᴬJudg 5:24-27

and it shall be if anyone comes and inquires of you, and says, 'Is there anyone here?' that you shall say, 'No.'" ²¹But Jael, Heber's wife, ^took a tent peg and a hammer in her hand, and went secretly to him and drove the peg into his temple, and it went through into the ground; for he was sound asleep and exhausted. So he died. ²²And behold, while Barak was pursuing Sisera, Jael came out to meet him and said to him, "Come, and I will show you the man whom you are seeking." So he entered with her, and behold, Sisera was lying dead with the tent peg in his temple.

²³So ^God subdued Jabin the king of Canaan on that day before the sons of Israel. ²⁴And the hand of the sons of Israel pressed harder and harder upon Jabin the king of Canaan, until they had eliminated Jabin the king of Canaan.

THE SONG OF DEBORAH AND BARAK

5 ^Then Deborah and Barak the son of Abinoam sang on that day, saying,

² "^For the leaders leading in Israel,
For ^Bthe people volunteering,
Bless the Lord!
³ "Hear, you kings; listen, you dignitaries!
^I myself—to the Lord, I myself will sing,
I will sing praise to the Lord, the God of Israel!
⁴ "Lord, when You went out from Seir,
When You marched from the field of Edom,
^The earth quaked, the heavens also dripped,
The clouds also dripped water.

⁵ "^The mountains flowed *with water* at the presence of the Lord,
This Sinai, at the presence of the Lord, the God of Israel.

⁶ "In the days of ^Shamgar the son of Anath,
In the days of ^BJael, the roads were deserted,
And travelers went by roundabout ways.
⁷ "The peasantry came to an end, they came to an end in Israel,
Until I, Deborah, arose,
Until I arose, a mother in Israel.
⁸ "^New gods were chosen;
Then war *was in* the gates.
Not a shield or a spear was seen
Among forty thousand in Israel.
⁹ "My heart *goes out* to ^the commanders of Israel,
The volunteers among the people;
Bless the Lord!
¹⁰ "^You who ride on white donkeys,
You who sit on *rich* carpets,
And you who travel on the road—shout in praise!
¹¹ "At the sound of those who distribute *water* among ^the watering places,
There they will recount ^Bthe righteous deeds of the Lord,
The righteous deeds for His peasantry in Israel.
Then the people of the Lord went down to the gates.

4:21 ^Judg 5:26   4:23 ^Neh 9:24; Ps 18:47
5:1 ^Ex 15:1   5:2 ^Judg 5:9   ^BPs 110:3   5:3 ^Ps 27:6
5:4 ^Ps 68:8, 9   5:5 ^Ex 19:18   5:6 ^Judg 3:31
^BJudg 4:17   5:8 ^Deut 32:17   5:9 ^Judg 5:2
5:10 ^Judg 10:4; 12:14   5:11 ^Gen 24:11   ^B1 Sam 12:7

12 "^AAwake, awake, Deborah;
Awake, awake, sing a song!
Arise, Barak, and lead away
your captives, son of
Abinoam.

13 "Then survivors came down to
the nobles;
The people of the LORD came
down to me as warriors.

14 "From Ephraim those whose
root is ^Ain Amalek *came
down,*
Following you, Benjamin, with
your peoples;
From Machir commanders
came down,
And from Zebulun those who
wield the staff of office.

15 "And the princes of Issachar
were with Deborah;
As *was* Issachar, so *was* Barak;
Into the valley they rushed ^Aat
his heels;
Among the divisions of Reuben
There were great
determinations of heart.

16 "Why did you sit among ^Athe
¹sheepfolds,
To hear the piping for the
flocks?
Among the divisions of Reuben
There were great searchings of
heart.

17 "^AGilead remained across the
Jordan;
And why did Dan stay on
ships?
Asher sat at the seashore,
And remained by its landings.

18 "^AZebulun *was* a people who
risked their lives,
And Naphtali *too,* on the high
places of the field.

19 "The kings came *and* fought;
Then the kings of Canaan
fought

^AAt Taanach near the waters of
Megiddo;
^BThey took no plunder in
silver.

20 "^AThe stars fought from heaven,
From their paths they fought
against Sisera.

21 "The torrent of Kishon swept
them away,
The ancient torrent, the
torrent Kishon.
^AMy soul, march on with
strength!

22 "^AThen the horses' hoofs beat
From the galloping, the
galloping of his mighty
stallions.

23 'Curse Meroz,' said the angel of
the LORD,
'Utterly curse its inhabitants,
^ABecause they did not come to
the help of the LORD,
To the help of the LORD against
the warriors.'

24 "^AMost blessed of women is Jael,
The wife of Heber the Kenite;
Most blessed is she of women
in the tent.

25 "He asked for water, she gave
him milk;
In a magnificent bowl she
brought him curds.

26 "She reached out her hand for
the tent peg,
And her right hand for the
workmen's hammer.
Then she struck Sisera, she
smashed his head;
And she shattered and pierced
his temple.

5:12 ^APs 57:8   5:14 ^AJudg 12:15   5:15 ^AJudg 4:10
5:16 ^ANum 32:1, 2, 24, 36   5:17 ^AJosh 22:9
5:18 ^AJudg 4:6, 10   5:19 ^AJudg 1:27   ^BJudg 5:30
5:20 ^AJosh 10:12–14   5:21 ^AEx 15:2; Ps 44:5
5:22 ^AJob 39:19–25   5:23 ^AJudg 5:13
5:24 ^AJudg 4:19–21

5:16 ¹Or *saddlebags*

27 "Between her feet he bowed, he
  fell, he lay;
  Between her feet he bowed, he
  fell;
  Where he bowed, there he fell
  dead.

28 "Out of the window she looked
  and wailed,
  The mother of Sisera through
  the lattice,
  'Why does his chariot delay in
  coming?
  Why do the hoofbeats of his
  chariots delay?'
29 "Her wise princesses would
  answer her,
  Indeed she repeats her words
  to herself,
30 'Are they not finding, are they
  not dividing the spoils?
  A concubine, two concubines
  for every warrior;
  To Sisera a spoil of dyed cloth,
  A spoil of dyed cloth
  embroidered,
  Dyed cloth of double
  embroidery on the neck of
  the plunderer?'
31 "May all Your enemies perish
  in this way, LORD;
  But may those who love Him
  be like the rising of the sun
  in its might."

And the land was at rest for forty
years.

ISRAEL OPPRESSED BY MIDIAN

6 Then the sons of Israel ^did
what was evil in the sight of the
LORD; and the LORD handed them
over to Midian for seven years.
²The power of Midian prevailed
against Israel. Because of Midian
the sons of Israel made for themselves ^the dens which were in the
mountains and the caves and the

strongholds. ³For whenever Israel
had sown, the Midianites would
come up with the Amalekites and
the people of the east and march
against them. ⁴So they would camp
against them and ^destroy the produce of the earth as far as Gaza, and
ᴮleave no sustenance in Israel, nor
a sheep, ox, or donkey. ⁵For they
would come up with their livestock
and their tents, they would come
in ^like locusts in number, *and
both* they and their camels were
innumerable; and they came into
the land to ruin it. ⁶So Israel was
brought ^very low because of Midian, and the sons of Israel cried out
to the LORD.

⁷Now it came about, when the
sons of Israel cried out to the LORD
on account of Midian, ⁸that the
LORD sent a prophet to the sons of
Israel, and ^he said to them, "This
is what the LORD, the God of Israel
says: 'It was I who brought you up
from Egypt, and brought you out
of the house of slavery. ⁹And I rescued you from the hands of the
Egyptians, and from the hands of
all your oppressors, and I drove
them out from you and gave you
their land, ¹⁰and I said to you, "I
am the LORD your God; you ^shall
not fear the gods of the Amorites in
whose land you live." But you have
not obeyed Me.'"

GIDEON IS VISITED

¹¹Then ^the angel of the LORD came
and sat under the oak that was in
Ophrah, which belonged to Joash
the Abiezrite, as his son ᴮGideon
was beating out wheat in the wine

5:30 ^Ex 15:9   5:31 ^Ps 68:2; 92:9   6:1 ^Judg 2:11
6:2 ^1 Sam 13:6; Heb 11:38   6:4 ^Lev 26:16
ᴮDeut 28:31   6:5 ^Judg 7:12; 8:10   6:6 ^Deut 28:43
6:8 ^Judg 2:1, 2   6:10 ^2 Kin 17:35; Jer 10:2
6:11 ^Judg 2:1   ᴮHeb 11:32

press in order to save *it* from the Midianites. [12]And the angel of the LORD appeared to him and said to him, "The LORD is with you, valiant warrior." [13]Then Gideon said to him, "O my lord, if the LORD is with us, why then has all this happened to us? And where are all His miracles which our fathers told us about, saying, 'Did the LORD not bring us up from Egypt?' But ^now the LORD has abandoned us and handed us over to Midian." [14]And the LORD looked at him and said, "^Go in this strength of yours and save Israel from the hand of Midian. Have I not sent you?" [15]^But he said to Him, "O Lord, how am I to save Israel? Behold, my family is the least in ^BManasseh, and I am the youngest in my father's house." [16]^Yet the LORD said to him, "I will certainly be with you, and you will defeat Midian as one man." [17]So Gideon said to Him, "If now I have found favor in Your sight, then perform for me ^a sign that it is You speaking with me. [18]Please do not depart from here until I come *back* to You, and bring out my offering and lay it before You." And He said, "I will remain until you return."

[19]Then Gideon went in and ^prepared a young goat and unleavened bread *from* an 'ephah of flour; he put the meat in a basket and the broth in a pot, and brought *them* out to him under the oak and presented *them*. [20]And the angel of God said to him, "Take the meat and the unleavened bread and lay *them* on this rock, and pour out the broth." And he did so. [21]Then the angel of the LORD put out the end of the staff that was in his hand and touched the meat and the unleavened bread; and ^fire came up from

the rock and consumed the meat and the unleavened bread. Then the angel of the LORD vanished from his sight. [22]^When Gideon perceived that he was the angel of the LORD, he said, "Oh, Lord GOD! For I have seen the angel of the LORD face to face!" [23]But the LORD said to him, "Peace to you, do not be afraid; you shall not die." [24]Then Gideon built an altar there to the LORD and named it The LORD is Peace. To this day it is still ^in Ophrah of the Abiezrites.

[25]Now on the same night the LORD said to him, "Take your father's bull and a second bull seven years old, and tear down the altar of Baal which belongs to your father, and cut down the '^Asherah that is beside it; [26]and build an altar to the LORD your God on the top of this stronghold in an orderly way, and take a second bull and offer a burnt offering with the wood of the Asherah which you shall cut down." [27]Then Gideon took ten men from his servants and did as the LORD had spoken to him; and because he was too afraid of his father's household and the men of the city to do it by day, he did it by night.

THE ALTAR OF BAAL DESTROYED

[28]When the people of the city got up early in the morning, behold, the altar of Baal had been torn down, and the Asherah which had been beside it had been cut down, and the second bull had been

---

6:13^Judg 6:1; Ps 44:9   6:14^Heb 11:32-34
6:15^Ex 3:11   ^BJudg 6:11   6:16^Ex 3:12; Josh 1:5
6:17^Judg 6:37; Is 38:7, 8   6:19^Gen 18:6-8
6:21^Lev 9:24   6:22^Gen 32:30; Ex 33:20
6:24^Judg 8:32   6:25^Ex 34:13

6:19'About 1 cubic foot or 0.03 cubic meters
6:25'I.e., wooden symbol of a female deity; also vv 26, 28, 30

offered on the altar which had been built. ²⁹So they said to one another, "Who did this thing?" And when they searched and inquired, they said, "Gideon the son of Joash did this thing." ³⁰Then the men of the city said to Joash, "Bring out your son, that he may die, for he has torn down the altar of Baal, and indeed, he has cut down the Asherah which was beside it." ³¹But Joash said to all who stood against him, "Will you contend for Baal, or will you save him? Whoever will contend for him shall be put to death by morning. If he is a god, let him contend for himself, since *someone* has torn down his altar!" ³²Therefore on that day he named Gideon ^Jerubbaal, that is to say, "Let Baal contend against him," because he had torn down his altar.

³³Then all the Midianites, the Amalekites, and the people of the east assembled together; and they crossed over and camped in ^the Valley of Jezreel. ³⁴So ^the Spirit of the LORD covered Gideon like clothing; and he blew a trumpet, and the Abiezrites were called together to follow him. ³⁵And he sent messengers throughout Manasseh, and they also were called together to follow him; and he sent messengers to Asher, Zebulun, and Naphtali, and ^they came up to meet them.

SIGN OF THE FLEECE

³⁶Then Gideon said to God, "^If You are going to save Israel through me, as You have spoken, ³⁷behold, I am putting a fleece of wool on the threshing floor. If there is dew on the fleece only, and it is dry on all the ground, then I will know that You will save Israel through me, as You have spoken." ³⁸And it was so.

When he got up early the next morning and wrung out the fleece, he wrung the dew from the fleece, a bowl full of water. ³⁹Then Gideon said to God, "^Do not let Your anger burn against me, so that I may speak only one *more* time; please let me put *You* to the test only one *more* time with the fleece: let it now be dry only on the fleece, and let there be dew on all the ground." ⁴⁰And God did so that night; for it was dry only on the fleece, and dew was on all the ground.

GIDEON'S THREE HUNDRED CHOSEN MEN

7 Then ^Jerubbaal (that is, Gideon) and all the people who were with him got up early, and camped beside the spring of Harod; and the camp of Midian was on the north side of them by the hill of Moreh in the valley.

²And the LORD said to Gideon, "The people who are with you are too many for Me to hand Midian over to them, ^otherwise Israel would become boastful, saying, 'My own power has saved me.' ³Now therefore come, proclaim in the hearing of the people, saying, '^Whoever is afraid and worried, is to return and leave Mount Gilead.'" So twenty-two thousand from the people returned, but ten thousand remained.

⁴^Then the LORD said to Gideon, "The people are still too many; bring them down to the water and I will test them for you there. So it shall be that he of whom I say to you, 'This one shall go with you,'

6:32^Judg 7:1 6:33^Josh 17:16 6:34^Judg 3:10
6:35^Judg 7:3 6:36^Judg 6:14, 16, 17
6:39^Gen 18:32 7:1^Judg 6:32 7:2^Deut 8:17, 18
7:3^Deut 20:8 7:4^1 Sam 14:6

he shall go with you; but everyone of whom I say to you, 'This one shall not go with you,' he shall not go." ⁵So he brought the people down to the water. Then the LORD said to Gideon, "You shall put everyone who laps the water with his tongue as a dog laps in one group, and everyone who kneels down to drink *in another*." ⁶Now the number of those who lapped, putting their hand to their mouth, was three hundred men; but all the rest of the people kneeled down to drink water. ⁷And the LORD said to Gideon, "I will save you ^with the three hundred men who lapped, and will hand the Midianites over to you; so have all the *other* people go, each man to his home." ⁸So the three hundred men took the people's provisions and their trumpets in their hands. And Gideon dismissed all the *other* men of Israel, each to his tent, but retained the three hundred men; and the camp of Midian was below him in the valley.

⁹Now on the same night it came about that the LORD said to him, "Arise, go down against the camp, ^for I have handed it over to you. ¹⁰But if you are afraid to go down, go with Purah your servant down to the camp, ¹¹so that you will hear what they say; and ^afterward you will have the courage to go down against the camp." So he went down with Purah his servant to the outposts of the army that was in the camp. ¹²Now the Midianites, the Amalekites, and all the people of the east were lying in the valley ^as numerous as locusts; and their camels were without number, ᴮas numerous as the sand on the seashore. ¹³When Gideon

came, behold, a man was relating a dream to his friend. And he said, "Behold, I had a dream; a loaf of barley bread was tumbling into the camp of Midian, and it came to the tent and struck it so that it fell, and turned it upside down so that the tent collapsed." ¹⁴And his friend replied, "This is nothing other than the sword of Gideon the son of Joash, a man of Israel; God has ^handed over to him Midian and all the camp."

¹⁵When Gideon heard the account of the dream and its interpretation, he bowed in worship. Then he returned to the camp of Israel and said, "Arise, for the LORD has handed over to you the camp of Midian!" ¹⁶And he divided the three hundred men into three units, and he put trumpets and empty pitchers into the hands of all of them, with torches inside the pitchers. ¹⁷Then he said to them, "Look at me and do likewise. And behold, when I come to the outskirts of the camp, do as I do. ¹⁸When I and all who are with me blow the trumpet, then you also blow the trumpets around the entire camp and say, 'For the LORD and for Gideon!'"

CONFUSION OF THE ENEMY

¹⁹So Gideon and the hundred men who were with him came to the outskirts of the camp at the beginning of the middle night watch, when they had just posted the watch; and they blew the trumpets and smashed the pitchers that were in their hands. ²⁰When the three units blew the trumpets and broke the pitchers, they held the torches

7:7^1 Sam 14:6   7:9^Josh 2:24; 10:8   7:11^Judg 7:15; 1 Sam 14:9, 10   7:12^Judg 6:5   ᴮJosh 11:4   7:14^Josh 2:9

in their left hands and the trumpets in their right hands for blowing, and shouted, "A sword for the LORD and for Gideon!" 21 And each stood in his place around the camp; and ^all the army ran, crying out as they fled. 22 And when they blew the three hundred trumpets, the ^LORD set the sword of one against another even throughout the entire army; and the army fled as far as Beth-shittah toward Zererah, as far as the edge of Abel-meholah, by Tabbath. 23 And the men of Israel were summoned from ^Naphtali, Asher, and all Manasseh, and they pursued Midian.

24 Then Gideon sent messengers throughout the hill country of Ephraim, saying, "Come down against Midian and ^take control of the waters ahead of them, as far as Beth-barah and the Jordan." So all the men of Ephraim were summoned, and they took control of the waters as far as Beth-barah and the Jordan. 25 And they captured the two leaders of Midian, ^Oreb and Zeeb, and they killed Oreb at the rock of Oreb, and they killed Zeeb at the wine press of Zeeb, while they pursued Midian; and they brought the heads of Oreb and Zeeb to Gideon from across the Jordan.

ZEBAH AND ZALMUNNA ROUTED

8 Then the men of Ephraim said to Gideon, "^What is this thing *that* you have done to us, not calling upon us when you went to fight against Midian?" And they quarreled with him vehemently. 2 But he said to them, "What have I done now in comparison with you? Is the gleaning *of the grapes* of Ephraim not better than the vintage of Abiezer? 3 God has handed over

to you the leaders of Midian, Oreb and Zeeb; and what was I able to do in comparison with you?" Then their anger toward him subsided when he said that.

4 Then Gideon and the three hundred men who were with him came ^to the Jordan *and* crossed over, exhausted yet *still* pursuing. 5 And he said to the men of ^Succoth, "Please give loaves of bread to the people who are following me, for they are exhausted, and I am pursuing Zebah and Zalmunna, the kings of Midian." 6 But the leaders of Succoth said, "^Are the hands of Zebah and Zalmunna already in your hand, that we should give bread to your army?" 7 So Gideon said, "For this *answer,* ^when the LORD has handed over to me Zebah and Zalmunna, I will thrash your bodies with the thorns of the wilderness and with briers." 8 Then he went up from there to ^Penuel and spoke similarly to them; and the men of Penuel answered him just as the men of Succoth had answered. 9 So he said also to the men of Penuel, "When I return safely, ^I will tear down this tower."

10 Now Zebah and Zalmunna were in Karkor, and their armies with them, about fifteen thousand men, all who were left of the entire army of the people of the east; ^for the fallen were 120,000 swordsmen. 11 Gideon went up by the way of those who lived in tents to the east of Nobah and Jogbehah, and he attacked the camp when the camp was unsuspecting. 12 When Zebah and Zalmunna fled, he pursued

7:21 ^2 Kin 7:7   7:22 ^1 Sam 14:20   7:23 ^Judg 6:35
7:24 ^Judg 3:28   7:25 ^Ps 83:11; Is 10:26
8:1 ^Judg 12:1   8:4 ^Judg 7:25   8:5 ^Gen 33:17
8:6 ^Judg 8:15   8:7 ^Judg 7:15   8:8 ^Gen 32:31
8:9 ^Judg 8:17   8:10 ^Judg 6:5; 7:12

them and captured the two kings of Midian, Zebah and Zalmunna, and routed the entire army.

¹³Then Gideon the son of Joash returned from the battle by the ascent of Heres. ¹⁴And he captured a youth from Succoth and questioned him. Then *the youth* wrote down for him the leaders of Succoth and its elders, seventy-seven men. ¹⁵And he came to the men of Succoth and said, "Behold Zebah and Zalmunna, about whom you taunted me, saying, 'ᴬAre the hands of Zebah and Zalmunna already in your hand, that we should give bread to your men who are weary?'" ¹⁶Then he took the elders of the city, and thorns of the wilderness and briers, and he disciplined the men of Succoth with them. ¹⁷ᴬAnd he tore down the tower of Penuel and killed the men of the city.

¹⁸Then he said to Zebah and Zalmunna, "Where *were* the men whom you killed at Tabor?" But they said, "You and they were alike, each one resembling the son of a king." ¹⁹And he said, "They *were* my brothers, the sons of my mother. *As* the LORD lives, if only you had let them live, I would not kill you." ²⁰So he said to Jether his firstborn, "Rise, kill them." But the youth did not draw his sword, for he was afraid, because he was still a youth. ²¹Then Zebah and Zalmunna said, "Rise up yourself, and attack us; for as the man, so is his strength." ᴬSo Gideon arose and killed Zebah and Zalmunna, and took the crescent amulets which were on their camels' necks.

²²Then the men of Israel said to Gideon, "Rule over us, both you and your son, your son's son as well, for you have saved us from the hand of Midian!" ²³But Gideon said to them, "I will not rule over you, nor shall my son rule over you; ᴬthe LORD shall rule over you." ²⁴Yet Gideon said to them, "I would request of you, that each of you give me an earring from his plunder." (For they had gold earrings, because they were ᴬIshmaelites.) ²⁵And they said, "We will certainly give *them to you.*" So they spread out a garment, and every one of them tossed an earring there from his plunder. ²⁶The weight of the gold earrings that he requested was 1,700 *shekels* of gold, apart from the crescent amulets, the ear pendants, and the purple robes which *were* on the kings of Midian, and apart from the neck chains that *were* on their camels' necks. ²⁷Gideon made it into ᴬan ephod, and placed it in his city, Ophrah; but all Israel ¹committed infidelity with it there, and it became a snare to Gideon and his household.

FORTY YEARS OF PEACE

²⁸So Midian was subdued before the sons of Israel, and they did not lift up their heads anymore. And the land was undisturbed for forty years in the days of Gideon.

²⁹Then ᴬJerubbaal the son of Joash went and lived in his own house. ³⁰Now Gideon had ᴬseventy sons who were his direct descendants, for he had many wives. ³¹And his concubine who was in Shechem also bore him a son, and he named him Abimelech. ³²And

8:15 ᴬJudg 8:6   8:17 ᴬJudg 8:9   8:21 ᴬPs 83:11
8:23 ᴬ1 Sam 8:7; 10:19   8:24 ᴬGen 25:13-16
8:27 ᴬEx 28:6-35; Judg 17:5   8:29 ᴬJudg 7:1
8:30 ᴬJudg 9:2, 5
8:27 ¹I.e., against God

Gideon the son of Joash died at a good old age and was buried in the tomb of his father Joash, in Ophrah of the Abiezrites.

³³Then it came about, as soon as Gideon was dead, ᴬthat the sons of Israel again 'committed infidelity with the Baals, and made Baalberith their god. ³⁴So the sons of Israel ᴬdid not remember the LORD their God, who had saved them from the hands of all their enemies on every side; ³⁵ᴬnor did they show kindness to the household of Jerubbaal (*that is,* Gideon) in accordance with all the good that he had done for Israel.

ABIMELECH'S CONSPIRACY

9 Now ᴬAbimelech the son of Jerubbaal went to Shechem, to his mother's relatives, and spoke to them and to the entire family of the household of his mother's father, saying, ²"Speak, now, in the hearing of all the leaders of Shechem, 'Which is better for you: for seventy men, all the sons of Jerubbaal, to rule over you, or for one man to rule over you?' Also, remember that I am ᴬyour bone and your flesh." ³So his mother's relatives spoke all these words on his behalf in the hearing of all the leaders of Shechem; and they were inclined to follow Abimelech, for they said, "He is ᴬour relative." ⁴And they gave him seventy *pieces* of silver from the house of ᴬBaal-berith, with which Abimelech hired worthless and reckless men, and they followed him. ⁵Then he went to his father's house in Ophrah and ᴬkilled his brothers the sons of Jerubbaal, seventy men, on one stone. But Jotham the youngest son of Jerubbaal was left, because

he hid himself. ⁶All the leaders of Shechem and all Beth-millo assembled together, and they went and made Abimelech king, by the oak of the memorial stone which was in Shechem.

⁷Now when they told Jotham, he went and stood on the top of ᴬMount Gerizim, and raised his voice and called out. And he said to them, "Listen to me, you leaders of Shechem, that God may listen to you. ⁸Once the trees went to anoint a king over them, and they said to the olive tree, 'Reign over us!' ⁹But the olive tree said to them, 'Shall I give up my fatness with which God and mankind are honored, and go to wave over the trees?' ¹⁰Then the trees said to the fig tree, 'You, come, reign over us!' ¹¹But the fig tree said to them, 'Shall I give up my sweetness and my good fruit, and go to wave over the trees?' ¹²Then the trees said to the vine, 'You, come, reign over us!' ¹³But the vine said to them, 'Shall I give up my new wine, which cheers God and mankind, and go to wave over the trees?' ¹⁴Then all the trees said to the bramble, 'You, come, reign over us!' ¹⁵And the bramble said to the trees, 'If you really are anointing me as king over you, come and take refuge in my shade; but if not, may fire come out of the bramble and consume the cedars of Lebanon.'

¹⁶"Now then, if you have acted with honesty and integrity in making Abimelech king, and if you have dealt well with ᴬJerubbaal and his house, and have dealt with him

8:33 ᴬJudg 2:11, 12   8:34 ᴬDeut 4:9; Judg 3:7
8:35 ᴬJudg 9:16-18   9:1 ᴬJudg 8:31, 35   9:2 ᴬGen 29:14
9:3 ᴬGen 29:15   9:4 ᴬJudg 8:33   9:5 ᴬ2 Kin 11:1, 2
9:7 ᴬDeut 11:29, 30   9:16 ᴬJudg 8:35

8:33 ¹I.e., against God

as he deserved— ¹⁷for my father fought for you, and risked his life and saved you from the hand of Midian; ¹⁸but *in fact* you have risen against my father's house today and have killed ^his sons, seventy men, on one stone, and have made Abimelech, the son of his female slave, king over the leaders of Shechem, because he is your relative— ¹⁹so if you have acted with honesty and integrity toward Jerubbaal and his house this day, be joyful about Abimelech, and may he also be joyful about you. ²⁰But if not, may fire come out of Abimelech and consume the leaders of Shechem and Beth-millo; and may fire come out of the leaders of Shechem and from Beth-millo, and consume Abimelech." ²¹Then Jotham escaped and fled, and went to Beer; and he stayed there because of his brother Abimelech.

SHECHEM AND ABIMELECH FALL

²²Now Abimelech ruled over Israel for three years. ²³^Then God sent an evil spirit between Abimelech and the leaders of Shechem; and the leaders of Shechem ᴮdealt treacherously with Abimelech, ²⁴so that the violence done to the seventy sons of Jerubbaal would come, and *the responsibility for* ^their blood would be placed on their brother Abimelech, who killed them, and on the leaders of Shechem, who encouraged him to kill his brothers. ²⁵The leaders of Shechem set up men in ambush against him on the tops of the mountains, and they robbed everyone who would pass by them on the road; and it was reported to Abimelech. ²⁶Now Gaal the son of Ebed came with his relatives, and crossed over into Shechem; and the leaders of Shechem trusted him. ²⁷So they went out to the field and gathered the grapes of their vineyards and trampled *them*, and held a festival; and they went into the house of ^their god, and ate and drank and cursed Abimelech. ²⁸Then Gaal the son of Ebed said, "Who is Abimelech, and who is Shechem, that we should serve him? Is he not the son of Jerubbaal, and *is* Zebul *not* his governor? Serve the men of ^Hamor the father of Shechem; but why should we serve him? ²⁹^If only this people were under my authority! Then I would do away with Abimelech." And he said to Abimelech, "Enlarge your army and come out!"

³⁰When Zebul the leader of the city heard the words of Gaal the son of Ebed, his anger burned. ³¹So using deception, he *successfully* sent messengers to Abimelech, saying, "Behold, Gaal the son of Ebed and his relatives have come to Shechem; and behold, they are stirring up the city against you. ³²So now, arise by night, you and the people who are with you, and lie in wait in the field. ³³Then in the morning, as soon as the sun is up, you shall rise early and attack the city; and behold, when he and the people who are with him come out against you, you shall ^do to them whatever you can."

³⁴So Abimelech and all the people who *were* with him got up at night, and lay in wait against Shechem, in four units. ³⁵Now Gaal the son of Ebed went out and stood at the entrance of the city gate;

9:18^Judg 8:30; 9:2, 5   9:23^1 Sam 16:14   ᴮIs 33:1
9:24^Num 35:33   9:27^Judg 8:33; 9:46
9:28^Gen 34:2   9:29^2 Sam 15:4   9:33^1 Sam 10:7

and Abimelech and the people who *were* with him arose from the ambush. ³⁶When Gaal saw the people, he said to Zebul, "Look, people are coming down from the tops of the mountains." But Zebul said to him, "You are seeing the shadow of the mountains as *if they were* people." ³⁷And Gaal spoke yet again and said, "Look, people are coming down from ^the highest part of the land, and one unit is coming by way of the diviners' oak." ³⁸Then Zebul said to him, "Where then is your boasting with which you said, 'Who is Abimelech that we should serve him?' Is this not the people whom you rejected? Go out now and fight them!" ³⁹So Gaal went out in the sight of the leaders of Shechem and fought Abimelech. ⁴⁰But Abimelech chased him, and he fled from him; and many fell wounded up to the entrance of the gate. ⁴¹Then Abimelech stayed in Arumah, but Zebul drove out Gaal and his relatives so that they could not stay in Shechem.

⁴²Now it came about the next day, that the people went out to the field, and it was reported to Abimelech. ⁴³So he took his people and divided them into three units, and lay in wait in the field; when he looked and saw the people coming out from the city, he attacked them and killed them. ⁴⁴Then Abimelech and the company who was with him rushed forward and stood at the entrance of the city gate; the *other* two companies then attacked all who *were* in the field and killed them. ⁴⁵Abimelech fought against the city that whole day, and he captured the city and killed the people who *were* in it; then he ^tore down the city and sowed it with salt.

⁴⁶When all the leaders of the tower of Shechem heard *about it,* they entered the inner chamber of the temple of ^El-berith. ⁴⁷And it was reported to Abimelech that all the leaders of the tower of Shechem were gathered together. ⁴⁸So Abimelech went up to Mount ^Zalmon, he and all the people who *were* with him; and Abimelech took an axe in his hand and cut down a branch *from the* trees, and lifted it and put *it* on his shoulder. Then he said to the people who *were* with him, "What you saw me do, hurry *and* do likewise." ⁴⁹So all the people also cut down, each one, his branch and followed Abimelech, and put *them* on top of the inner chamber and set the inner chamber on fire over those *inside,* so that all the people of the tower of Shechem also died, about a thousand men and women.

⁵⁰Then Abimelech went to Thebez, and he camped against Thebez and captured it. ⁵¹But there was a strong tower in the center of the city, and all the men and women with all the leaders of the city fled there and shut themselves in; and they went up on the roof of the tower. ⁵²So Abimelech came to the tower and fought against it, and approached the entrance of the tower to burn it down with fire. ⁵³But ^a woman threw an upper millstone on Abimelech's head, crushing his skull. ⁵⁴Then ^he called quickly to the young man, his armor bearer, and said to him, "Draw your sword and kill me, so that it will not be said of me, 'A woman killed him.'" So the young man pierced him through,

9:37^Ezek 38:12   9:45^2 Kin 3:25   9:46^Judg 8:33
9:48^Ps 68:14   9:53^2 Sam 11:21   9:54^1 Sam 31:4

and he died. ⁵⁵Now when the men of Israel saw that Abimelech was dead, each left for his home. ⁵⁶So ^God repaid the wickedness of Abimelech, which he had done to his father in killing his seventy brothers. ⁵⁷God also returned all the wickedness of the men of Shechem on their heads, and the curse of Jotham the son of Jerubbaal came upon them.

OPPRESSION BY PHILISTINES AND AMMONITES

10 Now after Abimelech *died,* Tola the son of Puah, the son of Dodo, a man of Issachar, ^rose up to save Israel; and he lived in Shamir in the hill country of Ephraim. ²He judged Israel for twenty-three years. Then he died and was buried in Shamir.

³After him, Jair the Gileadite rose up and judged Israel for twenty-two years. ⁴And he had thirty sons who rode on thirty donkeys, and they had thirty cities in the land of Gilead ^that are called Havvoth-jair to this day. ⁵And Jair died and was buried in Kamon.

⁶Then the sons of Israel again did evil in the sight of the Lord, and ^they served the Baals and the Ashtaroth, the gods of Aram, the gods of Sidon, the gods of Moab, the gods of the sons of Ammon, and the gods of the Philistines; so ᴮthey abandoned the Lord and did not serve Him. ⁷And the anger of the Lord burned against Israel, and He ^sold them into the hands of the Philistines, and into the hands of the sons of Ammon. ⁸And they afflicted and oppressed the sons of Israel that year; for eighteen years they *oppressed* all the sons of Israel who were beyond the Jordan, in Gilead in the land of the Amorites. ⁹And the sons of Ammon crossed the Jordan to fight also against Judah, Benjamin, and the house of Ephraim, so that Israel was in great difficulty.

¹⁰Then the ^sons of Israel cried out to the Lord, saying, "We have sinned against You, for indeed, we have abandoned our God and served the Baals." ¹¹And the Lord said to the sons of Israel, "*Did I* not *save you* ^from the Egyptians, ᴮthe Amorites, the sons of Ammon, and the Philistines? ¹²And when the Sidonians, the Amalekites, and the Maonites ^oppressed you, you cried out to Me, and I saved you from their hands. ¹³Yet ^you abandoned Me and served other gods; therefore I will no longer save you. ¹⁴^Go and cry out to the gods which you have chosen; let them save you in the time of your distress." ¹⁵Then the sons of Israel said to the Lord, "We have sinned, ^do to us whatever seems good to You; only please save us this day." ¹⁶^So they removed the foreign gods from among them and served the Lord; and ᴮHe could no longer endure the misery of Israel.

¹⁷Then the sons of Ammon were summoned, and they camped in Gilead. And the sons of Israel gathered together and camped in ^Mizpah. ¹⁸And the people, the leaders of Gilead, said to one another, "Who is the man who will begin to fight against the sons of Ammon? He shall become head over all the inhabitants of Gilead."

9:56^Gen 9:5, 6; Ps 94:23   **10:1**^Judg 2:16
10:4^Num 32:41   **10:6**^Judg 2:13   ᴮDeut 31:16, 17
10:7^1 Sam 12:9   **10:10**^1 Sam 12:10
10:11^Judg 2:12   ᴮNum 21:21-25   **10:12**^Ps 106:42
10:13^Jer 2:13   **10:14**^Deut 32:37   **10:15**^1 Sam 3:18
10:16^Josh 24:23   ᴮDeut 32:36   **10:17**^Judg 11:29

JEPHTHAH, THE NINTH JUDGE

11 Now ^Jephthah the Gileadite was a valiant warrior, but he was the son of a prostitute. And Gilead had fathered Jephthah. ²Gilead's wife bore him sons; and when his wife's sons grew up, they drove Jephthah out and said to him, "You shall not have an inheritance in our father's house, for you are the son of another woman." ³So Jephthah fled from his brothers and lived in the land of ^Tob; and worthless men gathered around Jephthah, and they went wherever he did.

⁴Now it came about, after a while, that ^the sons of Ammon fought against Israel. ⁵When the sons of Ammon fought against Israel, the elders of Gilead went to get Jephthah from the land of Tob; ⁶and they said to Jephthah, "Come and be our leader, that we may fight against the sons of Ammon." ⁷But Jephthah said to the elders of Gilead, "^Did you not hate me and drive me from my father's house? So why have you come to me now when you are in trouble?" ⁸The elders of Gilead said to Jephthah, "For this reason we have now returned to you, that you may go with us and fight the sons of Ammon, and ^become our head over all the inhabitants of Gilead." ⁹So Jephthah said to the elders of Gilead, "If you bring me back to fight against the sons of Ammon and the Lord gives them up to me, will I become your head?" ¹⁰And the elders of Gilead said to Jephthah, "^The Lord is witness between us; be assured we will do as you have said." ¹¹Then Jephthah went with the elders of Gilead, and the people made him head and leader over them; and Jephthah spoke all his words before the Lord at ^Mizpah.

¹²So Jephthah sent messengers to the king of the sons of Ammon, saying, "What *conflict* do you and I have, that you have come to me to fight against my land?" ¹³And the king of the sons of Ammon said to the messengers of Jephthah, "*It is* because Israel ^took my land when they came up from Egypt, from the Arnon as far as the ^Jabbok and the Jordan; so return them peaceably now." ¹⁴But Jephthah sent messengers once again to the king of the sons of Ammon, ¹⁵and they said to him, "This is what Jephthah says: 'Israel did not take the land of Moab nor the land of the sons of Ammon. ¹⁶For when they came up from Egypt, and Israel went through the wilderness to the Red Sea, and ^came to Kadesh, ¹⁷then Israel ^sent messengers to the king of Edom, saying, "Please let us pass through your land"; but the king of Edom would not listen. ⁸And they also sent *messengers* to the king of Moab, but he would not consent. So Israel remained at Kadesh. ¹⁸Then they went through the wilderness and around the land of Edom and the land of Moab, and came to the east side of the land of Moab, and they camped beyond the Arnon; but they ^did not enter the territory of Moab, for the Arnon *was* the border of Moab. ¹⁹And Israel sent ^messengers to Sihon king of the Amorites, the king of Heshbon; and Israel said to him, "Please let us pass through your land to our place." ²⁰But Sihon did not trust Israel to pass through his territory;

11:1 ^Heb 11:32　11:3 ^2 Sam 10:6, 8　11:4 ^Judg 10:9, 17
11:7 ^Gen 26:27　11:8 ^Judg 10:18　11:10 ^Gen 31:50;
Jer 29:23　11:11 ^Judg 10:17; 11:29　11:13 ^Num 21:24
^Gen 32:22　11:16 ^Num 20:1, 4-21　11:17 ^Num
20:14-21　^Josh 24:9　11:18 ^Deut 2:9, 18, 19
11:19 ^Num 21:21-32; Deut 2:26-36

so Sihon gathered all his people and camped in Jahaz, and fought with Israel. ²¹And the LORD, the God of Israel, handed Sihon and all his people over to Israel, and they ^defeated them; so Israel took possession of all the land of the Amorites, the inhabitants of that country. ²²^So they possessed all the territory of the Amorites, from the Arnon as far as the Jabbok, and from the wilderness as far as the Jordan. ²³And now the LORD, the God of Israel, has driven out the Amorites from His people Israel; so should you possess it? ²⁴Do you not possess what ^Chemosh your god gives you to possess? So whatever the LORD our God has dispossessed before us, we will possess it. ²⁵Now then, are you any better than ^Balak the son of Zippor, king of Moab? Did he ever contend with Israel, or did he ever fight against them? ²⁶^While Israel was living in Heshbon and its villages, and in Aroer and its villages, and in all the cities that are on the banks of the Arnon, three hundred years, why did you not recover them within that time? ²⁷So I have not sinned against you, but you are doing me wrong by making war against me. ^May the LORD, the Judge, judge today between the sons of Israel and the sons of Ammon.'" ²⁸But the king of the sons of Ammon disregarded the message which Jephthah sent him.

JEPHTHAH'S TRAGIC VOW

²⁹Now ^the Spirit of the LORD came upon Jephthah, and he passed through Gilead and Manasseh; then he passed through Mizpah of Gilead, and from Mizpah of Gilead he went on to the sons of Ammon. ³⁰And Jephthah made a vow to the LORD and said, "If You will indeed hand over to me the sons of Ammon, ³¹then whatever comes out the doors of my house to meet me when I return safely from the sons of Ammon, it shall be the LORD's, and I will offer it up as a burnt offering." ³²So Jephthah crossed over to the sons of Ammon to fight against them; and the LORD handed them over to him. ³³He inflicted a very great defeat on them from Aroer to the entrance of ^Minnith, twenty cities, and as far as Abel-keramim. So the sons of Ammon were subdued before the sons of Israel.

³⁴But Jephthah came to his house at Mizpah, and behold, his daughter was coming out to meet him ^with tambourines and with dancing. And she was his one *and* only child; besides her he had no son or daughter. ³⁵So when he saw her, he tore his clothes and said, "Oh, my daughter! You have brought me disaster, and you are among those who trouble me; for I have given my word to the LORD, and ^I cannot take *it* back." ³⁶So she said to him, "My father, you have given your word to the LORD; ^do to me just as you have said, since the LORD has brought you vengeance on your enemies, the sons of Ammon." ³⁷And she said to her father, "Let this thing be done for me; allow me two months, so that I may go to the mountains and weep because of ^my virginity, I and my friends." ³⁸Then he said, "Go."

11:21^Num 21:24; Deut 2:32-34　11:22^Deut 2:36, 37
11:24^Num 21:29; 1 Kin 11:7　11:25^Num 22:2;
Josh 24:9　11:26^Num 21:25, 26; Deut 2:36
11:27^Gen 16:5; 1 Sam 24:12, 15　11:29^Judg 3:10
11:33^Ezek 27:17　11:34^Ex 15:20; 1 Sam 18:6
11:35^Num 30:2; Eccl 5:4, 5　11:36^Num 30:2
11:37^Gen 30:23; Luke 1:25

So he let her go for two months; and she left with her friends, and wept on the mountains because of her virginity. ³⁹And at the end of two months she returned to her father, who did to her what he had vowed; and she had no relations with a man. And it became a custom in Israel, ⁴⁰that the daughters of Israel went annually to commemorate the daughter of Jephthah the Gileadite for four days in the year.

JEPHTHAH AND HIS SUCCESSORS

12 Now the men of Ephraim were summoned, and they crossed to Zaphon; and ^they said to Jephthah, "Why did you cross over to fight against the sons of Ammon without calling us to go with you? We will burn your house down on you!" ²So Jephthah said to them, "I and my people were in a major dispute with the sons of Ammon; and I did call you, but you did not save me from their hand. ³When I saw that you were no deliverer, I ^took my life in my hands and crossed over against the sons of Ammon, and the LORD handed them over to me. Why then have you come up to me this day to fight against me?" ⁴Then Jephthah gathered all the men of Gilead and fought Ephraim; and the men of Gilead defeated Ephraim, because they said, "You are survivors of Ephraim, you Gileadites, in the midst of Ephraim *and* in the midst of Manasseh." ⁵And the Gileadites ^took control of the crossing places of the Jordan opposite Ephraim. And it happened whenever *any of* the survivors of Ephraim said, "Let me cross over," that the men of Gilead would say to him, "Are you an Ephraimite?" If he said, "No,"

⁶then they would say to him, "Just say, 'Shibboleth.'" But he said, "Sibboleth," for he was not prepared to pronounce it correctly. Then they seized him and slaughtered him at the crossing places of the Jordan. So at that time forty-two thousand from Ephraim fell.

⁷Jephthah judged Israel for six years. Then Jephthah the Gileadite died and was buried in *one of* the cities of Gilead.

⁸Now Ibzan of Bethlehem judged Israel after him. ⁹He had thirty sons, and thirty daughters *whom* he gave in marriage outside *the family,* and he brought in thirty daughters from outside for his sons. And he judged Israel for seven years. ¹⁰Then Ibzan died and was buried in Bethlehem.

¹¹Now Elon the Zebulunite judged Israel after him; he judged Israel for ten years. ¹²Then Elon the Zebulunite died and was buried at Aijalon in the land of Zebulun.

¹³Now Abdon the son of Hillel the Pirathonite judged Israel after him. ¹⁴He had forty sons and thirty grandsons who rode on seventy donkeys; and he judged Israel for eight years. ¹⁵Then Abdon the son of Hillel the Pirathonite died and was buried at Pirathon in the land of Ephraim, in the hill country of the Amalekites.

PHILISTINES OPPRESS AGAIN

13 Now the sons of Israel ^again did evil in the sight of the LORD, and the LORD handed them over to the Philistines for forty years.

²And there was a man of ^Zorah, of the family of the Danites, whose

12:1 ^Judg 8:1   12:3 ^1 Sam 19:5; Job 13:14
12:5 ^Judg 3:28   13:1 ^Judg 2:11   13:2 ^Josh 19:41

name was Manoah; and his wife was infertile and had not given birth *to any children.* [3]AThen the angel of the LORD appeared to the woman and said to her, "Behold now, you are infertile and have not given birth; but you will conceive and give birth to a son. [4]And now, be careful Anot to drink wine or strong drink, nor eat any unclean thing. [5]For behold, you will conceive and give birth to a son, and no razor shall come upon his head, for the boy shall be a ANazirite to God from the womb; and he will begin to save Israel from the hands of the Philistines." [6]Then the woman came and told her husband, saying, "AA man of God came to me, and his appearance was like the appearance of the angel of God, very awesome. So I did not ask him where he *came* from, nor did he tell me his name. [7]But he said to me, 'Behold, you shall conceive and give birth to a son, and now you shall not drink wine or strong drink, nor eat any unclean thing, for the boy shall be a Nazirite to God from the womb to the day of his death.'"

[8]Then Manoah pleaded with the LORD and said, "Lord, please let Athe man of God whom You have sent come to us again so that he may teach us what we are to do for the boy who is to be born." [9]And God listened to the voice of Manoah; and Athe angel of God came again to the woman as she was sitting in the field, but Manoah her husband was not with her. [10]So the woman hurried and ran, and told her husband, "Behold, Athe man who came the *other* day has appeared to me!" [11]So Manoah got up and followed his wife, and when he came to the man he said to him, "Are you Athe man

who spoke to the woman?" And he said, "I am." [12]Then Manoah said, "Now *when* your words are fulfilled, what shall be the boy's way of life and his vocation?" [13]And the angel of the LORD said to Manoah, "AThe woman shall pay attention to all that I said. [14]She shall not eat anything that comes from the Avine nor drink wine or strong drink, nor eat any unclean thing; she shall keep all that I commanded."

[15]Then Manoah said to Athe angel of the LORD, "Please let us detain you so that we may prepare a young goat for you." [16]But the angel of the LORD said to Manoah, "Though you detain me, AI will not eat your food, but if you prepare a burnt offering, offer it to the LORD." For Manoah did not know that he was the angel of the LORD. [17]And Manoah said to the angel of the LORD, "AWhat is your name, so that when your words are fulfilled, we may honor you?" [18]But the angel of the LORD said to him, "Why do you ask my name, for it is [1,A]wonderful?" [19]So AManoah took the young goat along with the grain offering and offered it on the rock to the LORD; and He performed wonders while Manoah and his wife looked on. [20]For it came about when the flame went up from the altar toward heaven, that the angel of the LORD ascended in the flame of the altar. When Manoah and his wife saw *this,* they Afell on their faces to the ground.

13:3 AJudg 6:11, 14; 13:6, 8, 10, 11   13:4 ANum 6:2, 3; Luke 1:15   13:5 ANum 6:2-5   13:6 AJudg 6:11; 13:8, 10, 11   13:8 AJudg 13:3, 7   13:9 AJudg 13:8   13:10 AJudg 13:9   13:11 AJudg 13:8   13:13 AJudg 13:4   13:14 ANum 6:4   13:15 AJudg 13:3   13:16 AJudg 6:20   13:17 AGen 32:29   13:18 AIs 9:6   13:19 AJudg 6:20, 21   13:20 ALev 9:24; 1 Chr 21:16

13:18 I.e., incomprehensible

²¹Now the angel of the Lord did not appear to Manoah or his wife again. ^Then Manoah knew that he was the angel of the Lord. ²²So Manoah said to his wife, "^We will certainly die, for we have seen God." ²³But his wife said to him, "If the Lord had desired to kill us, He would not have accepted a burnt offering and a grain offering from our hands, nor would He have ^shown us all these things, nor would He have let us hear *things* like this at this time."

²⁴So the woman gave birth to a son, and named him Samson; and the ^child grew up and the Lord blessed him. ²⁵And ^the Spirit of the Lord began to stir him *when he was* in 'Mahaneh-dan, between Zorah and Eshtaol.

SAMSON'S MARRIAGE

14 Then Samson went down to Timnah, and he saw a woman in Timnah, *one* of the daughters of the Philistines. ²So he came back and told his father and mother, "I saw a woman in Timnah, *one* of the daughters of the Philistines; so now, get her for me as a wife." ³But his father and his mother said to him, "Is there no woman among the daughters of your ^relatives, or among all our people, that you go to ^take a wife from the uncircumcised Philistines?" Yet Samson said to his father, "Get her for me, because she is right for me." ⁴However, his father and mother did not know that ^this was of the Lord, for He was seeking an occasion against the Philistines. And at that time the Philistines were ruling over Israel.

⁵Then Samson went down to Timnah with his father and mother, and came as far as the vineyards of Timnah; and behold, a young lion *came* roaring toward him. ⁶And ^the Spirit of the Lord rushed upon him, so that he tore it apart as one tears apart a young goat, though he had nothing in his hand; but he did not tell his father or mother what he had done. ⁷So he went down and talked to the woman; and she looked pleasing to Samson. ⁸When he returned later to take her, he turned aside to look at the carcass of the lion; and behold, a swarm of bees and honey were in the body of the lion. ⁹So he took out the honey on his hands and went on, eating as he went. When he came to his father and mother, he gave *some* to them and they ate *it;* but he did not tell them that he had taken the honey out of the body of the lion.

¹⁰Then his father went down to the woman; and Samson held a feast there, for the young men customarily did this. ¹¹When they saw him, they brought thirty companions to be with him.

SAMSON'S RIDDLE

¹²Then Samson said to them, "Let me now ^propose a riddle for you; if you actually tell me the answer within the seven days of the feast, and solve it, then I will give you thirty linen wraps and thirty outfits of clothes. ¹³But if you are unable to tell me, then you shall give me thirty linen wraps and thirty outfits of clothes." And they said to him, "Propose your riddle, so that we may hear it." ¹⁴So he said to them,

13:21 ^Judg 13:16   13:22 ^Gen 32:30; Deut 5:26
13:23 ^Ps 25:14   13:24 ^1 Sam 3:19; Luke 1:80
13:25 ^Judg 3:10   14:3 ^Gen 24:3, 4   ^Ex 34:16
14:4 ^Josh 11:20   14:6 ^Judg 3:10   14:12 ^Ezek 17:2

13:25 ¹I.e., the camp of Dan

"Out of the eater came
something to eat,
And out of the strong came
something sweet."
But they could not tell *the answer
to* the riddle in three days.

¹⁵Then it came about on the fourth day that they said to Samson's wife, "^Entice your husband, so that he will tell us the riddle, or we will burn you and your father's house with fire. Have you invited us to impoverish us? *Is this* not *so?*" ¹⁶So Samson's wife wept in front of him and said, "^You only hate me, and you do not love me; you have proposed a riddle to the sons of my people, and have not told *it* to me." And he said to her, "Behold, I have not told *it* to my father or mother; so should I tell you?" ¹⁷However she wept before him for seven days while their feast lasted. And on the seventh day he told her because she pressed him so hard. She then told the riddle to the sons of her people. ¹⁸So the men of the city said to him on the seventh day before the sun went down,

"What is sweeter than honey?
And what is stronger than a
lion?"
And he said to them,
"If you had not plowed with my
heifer,
You would not have found out
my riddle."

¹⁹Then ^the Spirit of the Lᴏʀᴅ rushed upon him, and he went down to Ashkelon and killed thirty men of them and took what they were wearing and gave the outfits of clothes to those who told the riddle. And his anger burned, and he went up to his father's house. ²⁰But Samson's wife was ^given to his companion who had been his friend.

SAMSON BURNS PHILISTINE CROPS

15 But after a while, in the time of wheat harvest, Samson visited his wife ^with a young goat, and said, "I will go in to my wife in *her* room." But her father did not let him enter. ²Her father said, "I really thought that you hated her intensely; so I ^gave her to your companion. Is her younger sister not more beautiful than she? Please let her be yours instead." ³Samson then said to them, "This time I will have been blameless regarding the Philistines when I do them harm." ⁴And Samson went and caught three hundred jackals, and took torches, and turned *the jackals* tail to tail and put one torch in the middle between two tails. ⁵When he had set fire to the torches, he released *the jackals* into the standing grain of the Philistines and set fire to both the bundled heaps and the standing grain, along with the vineyards *and* olive groves. ⁶Then the Philistines said, "Who did this?" And *some* said, "Samson, the son-in-law of the Timnite, because he took his wife and gave her to his companion." So the Philistines came up and ^burned her and her father *to death* with fire. ⁷Then Samson said to them, "If this is how you act, I will certainly take revenge on you, and *only* after *that* will I stop." ⁸So he struck them ruthlessly with a great slaughter; and *afterward* he went down and lived in the cleft of the rock of Etam.

⁹Then the Philistines went up and camped in Judah, and spread out in Lehi. ¹⁰So the men of Judah said,

14:15 ^Judg 16:5   14:16 ^Judg 16:15   14:19 ^Judg 3:10;
13:25   14:20 ^Judg 15:2   15:1 ^Gen 38:17
15:2 ^Judg 14:20   15:6 ^Judg 14:15

"Why have you come up against us?" And they said, "We have come up to bind Samson in order to do to him as he did to us." [11] Then three thousand men of Judah went down to the cleft of the rock of Etam and said to Samson, "Do you not know [A]that the Philistines are rulers over us? What then is this that you have done to us?" And he said to them, "Just as they did to me, so I have done to them." [12] Then they said to him, "We have come down to bind you so that we may hand you over to the Philistines." And Samson said to them, "Swear to me that you will not kill me." [13] So they said to him, "No, but we will bind you tightly and give you into their hands; but we certainly will not kill you." Then they bound him with two new ropes, and brought him up from the rock.

[14] When he came to Lehi, the Philistines shouted as they met him. And [A]the Spirit of the LORD rushed upon him so that the ropes that were on his arms were like flax that has burned with fire, and his restraints dropped from his hands. [15] Then he found a fresh jawbone of a donkey, so he reached out with his hand and took it, and killed [A]a thousand men with it. [16] And Samson said,

"With the jawbone of a donkey,
Heaps upon heaps,
With the jawbone of a donkey
I have killed a thousand men."

[17] When he had finished speaking, he threw the jawbone from his hand; and he named that place [1]Ramath-lehi. [18] Then he became very thirsty, and he [A]called to the LORD and said, "You have handed this great victory over to Your servant, and now am I to die of thirst

and fall into the hands of the uncircumcised?" [19] But God split the hollow place that is in Lehi so that water came out of it. When he drank, [A]his strength returned and he revived. Therefore he named it En-hakkore, which is in Lehi to this day. [20] So [A]he judged Israel for twenty years in the days of the Philistines.

SAMSON'S WEAKNESS

16 Now Samson went to [A]Gaza and saw a prostitute there, and had relations with her. [2] *When it was reported* to the Gazites, saying, "Samson has come here," they [A]surrounded *the place* and lay in wait for him all night at the gate of the city. And they kept silent all night, saying, "*Let's wait* until the morning light, then we will kill him." [3] Now Samson lay *asleep* until midnight, and at midnight he got up and took hold of the doors of the city gate and the two doorposts, and pulled them up along with the bars; then he put *them* on his shoulders, and carried them up to the top of the mountain which is opposite Hebron.

[4] After this it came about that he was in love with a woman in the Valley of Sorek, whose name was Delilah. [5] So the [A]governors of the Philistines came up to her and said to her, "Entice him, and see where his great strength *lies* and how we can overpower him so that we may bind him to humble him. Then we will each give you 1,100 *pieces* of

15:11[A]Lev 26:25; Deut 28:43f   15:14[A]Judg 14:19;
1 Sam 11:6   15:15[A]Lev 26:8; Josh 23:10
15:18[A]Judg 16:28   15:19[A]Is 40:29   15:20[A]Judg 16:31;
Heb 11:32   16:1[A]Josh 15:47   16:2[A]1 Sam 23:26;
Ps 118:10-12   16:5[A]Josh 13:3

15:17[1]I.e., the high place of the jawbone

silver." ⁶So Delilah said to Samson, "Please tell me where your great strength *lies,* and how you can be bound to humble you." ⁷And Samson said to her, "If they bind me with seven fresh ¹*animal* tendons that have not been dried, then I will become weak and be like any *other* man." ⁸Then the governors of the Philistines brought up to her seven fresh ¹*animal* tendons that had not been dried, and she bound him with them. ⁹Now she had *men* prepared for an ambush in an inner room. And she said to him, "The Philistines are upon you, Samson!" But he tore the tendons to pieces just like a thread of flax is torn apart when it comes too close to fire. So his strength was not discovered.

¹⁰Then Delilah said to Samson, "Behold, you have toyed with me and told me lies; now please tell me how you may be bound." ¹¹Then he said to her, "If they bind me tightly with new ropes which have not been used, then I will become weak and be like any *other* man." ¹²So Delilah took new ropes and bound him with them and said to him, "The Philistines are upon you, Samson!" For the *men* in the ambush *were* waiting in the inner room. But he tore the ropes from his arms like thread.

¹³Then Delilah said to Samson, "Up to now you have toyed with me and told me lies; tell me how you may be bound." And he said to her, "If you weave the seven locks of my hair with the ¹web ²[and fasten it with the pin, then I will be weak like any *other* man." ¹⁴So while he slept, Delilah wove the seven locks of his hair with the web]. And she fastened *it* with the pin and said

to him, "The Philistines are upon you, Samson!" But he awoke from his sleep and pulled out the pin of the loom and the web.

DELILAH EXTRACTS HIS SECRET

¹⁵Then she said to him, "^How can you say, 'I love you,' when your heart is not with me? You have toyed with me these three times and have not told me where your great strength is." ¹⁶And it came about, when she pressed him daily with her words and urged him, that his soul was annoyed to death. ¹⁷So he told her all *that was in* his heart and said to her, "A razor has never come on my head, for I have been a ^Nazirite to God from my mother's womb. If I am shaved, then my strength will leave me and I will become weak and be like any *other* man."

¹⁸When Delilah saw that he had told her all *that was in* his heart, she sent *word* and called the governors of the Philistines, saying, "Come up once more, for he has told me all *that is in* his heart." Then the governors of the Philistines came up to her and brought up the money in their hands. ¹⁹And she made him sleep on her knees, and called for a man and had him shave off the seven locks of his head. Then she began to humble him, and his strength left him. ²⁰She said, "The Philistines are upon you, Samson!" And he awoke from his sleep and said, "I will go out as at other times and shake myself free." But he did not know that ^the LORD

16:15^Judg 14:16   16:17^Num 6:2, 5; Judg 13:5
16:20^Num 14:42, 43; Josh 7:12

16:7¹I.e., of a butchered animal, that shrink and hold when drying   16:8¹See note v 7   16:13¹I.e., in weaving, the warp of a loom   ²The passage in brackets is found in LXX but not in any Heb mss

had departed from him. ²¹Then the Philistines seized him and gouged out his eyes; and they brought him down to Gaza and restrained him with bronze chains, and he became a grinder in the prison. ²²However, the hair of his head began to grow *again* after it was shaved off.

²³Now the governors of the Philistines assembled to offer a great sacrifice to ^ADagon their god, and to celebrate, for they said,

"Our god has handed Samson
    our enemy over to us."

²⁴When the people saw him, ^Athey praised their god, for they said,

"Our god has handed our
    enemy over to us,
Even the destroyer of our
    country,
Who has killed many of us."

²⁵It so happened when they were in high spirits, that they said, "Call for Samson, that he may amuse us." So they called for Samson from the prison, and he entertained them. And they made him stand between the pillars. ²⁶Then Samson said to the boy who was holding his hand, "Let me feel the pillars on which the house rests, so that I may lean against them." ²⁷Now the house was full of men and women, and all the governors of the Philistines were there. And about three thousand men and women were on the roof looking on while Samson was entertaining *them.*

SAMSON IS AVENGED

²⁸^AThen Samson called to the LORD and said, "Lord GOD, please remember me and please strengthen me just this time, O God, that I may at once ^Btake vengeance on the Philistines for my two eyes." ²⁹Then Samson grasped the two middle pillars on which the house rested, and braced himself against them, the one with his right hand and the other with his left. ³⁰And Samson said, "Let me die with the Philistines!" And he pushed outwards powerfully, so that the house fell on the governors and all the people who were in it. And the dead whom he killed at his death were more than those whom he killed during his lifetime. ³¹Then his brothers and all his father's household came down and took him, and brought him up and buried him between Zorah and Eshtaol in the tomb of his father Manoah. ^ASo he had judged Israel for twenty years.

MICAH'S IDOLATRY

17 Now there was a man of the hill country of Ephraim whose name was Micah. ²And he said to his mother, "The 1,100 *pieces* of silver that were taken from you, about which you uttered a curse and also spoke *it* in my hearing, behold, the silver is with me; I took it." And his mother said, "Blessed be my son by the LORD." ³He then returned the 1,100 *pieces* of silver to his mother, and his mother said, "I wholly consecrate the silver from my hand to the LORD for my son ^Ato make a carved image and a cast metal image; so now I will return them to you." ⁴So when he returned the silver to his mother, his mother took two hundred *pieces* of silver and gave them to the silversmith, who made them into a carved image and a cast metal image, and they were in the house of Micah. ⁵And

16:23^A1 Sam 5:2   16:24^A1 Sam 31:9; 1 Chr 10:9
16:28^AJudg 15:18   ^BJer 15:15   16:31^AJudg 15:20
17:3^AEx 20:4, 23; 34:17

the man Micah had a [1,A]shrine and he made an ephod and household idols, and consecrated one of his sons, [B]so that he might become his priest. 6 In those days [A]there was no king in Israel; [B]everyone did what was right in his own eyes.

7 Now there was a young man from [A]Bethlehem in Judah, of the family of Judah, who was a Levite; and he was staying there. 8 Then the man left the city, Bethlehem in Judah, to stay wherever he would find *a place;* and as he made his journey, he came to the [A]hill country of Ephraim, to the house of Micah. 9 Micah said to him, "Where do you come from?" And he said to him, "I am a Levite from Bethlehem in Judah, and I am going to stay wherever I may find *a place.*" 10 Micah then said to him, "Stay with me and be [A]a father and a priest to me, and I will give you ten *pieces* of silver a year, a supply of clothing, and your sustenance." So the Levite went *in.* 11 The Levite agreed to live with the man, and the young man became to him like one of his sons. 12 So Micah consecrated the Levite, and the young man [A]became his priest and lived in the house of Micah. 13 Then Micah said, "Now I know that the LORD will prosper me, because I have a Levite as a priest."

DANITES SEEK TERRITORY

18 In those days there was no king of Israel; and [A]in those days the tribe of the Danites was seeking an inheritance for themselves to live in, for until that day an inheritance had not been allotted to them as a possession among the tribes of Israel. 2 So the sons of Dan sent from their family five men out of their whole number, valiant men from [A]Zorah and Eshtaol, to spy out the land and to explore it; and they said to them, "Go, explore the land." And they came to [B]the hill country of Ephraim, to the house of Micah, and stayed overnight there. 3 When they were near the house of Micah, they recognized the voice of the young man, the Levite; and they turned aside there and said to him, "Who brought you here? And what are you doing in this *place?* And what do you have here?" 4 He said to them, "Micah has done this and that for me, and he has hired me and [A]I have become his priest." 5 Then they said to him, "Inquire of God, please, that we may know whether our way on which we are going will be successful." 6 And the priest said to them, "Go in peace; your way in which you are going has the LORD'S approval."

7 So the five men departed and came to [A]Laish, and saw the people who were in it living in security, in the way of the Sidonians, quiet and unsuspecting; for there was no oppressive ruler humiliating *them* for anything in the land, and they were far from the Sidonians and had no dealings with anyone. 8 When they came back to their brothers at Zorah and Eshtaol, their brothers said to them, "What *do* you *say?*" 9 And they said, "Arise, and let's go up against them; for we have seen the land, and behold, it is very good. And will you sit still? Do not hesitate to go, to enter, to take

---

17:5 [A]Judg 18:24   [B]Num 3:10   **17:6** [A]Judg 18:1
[B]Deut 12:8   **17:7** [A]Judg 19:1; Ruth 1:1, 2
17:8 [A]Josh 24:33   **17:10** [A]Judg 18:19
17:12 [A]Num 16:10; 18:1-7   **18:1** [A]Josh 19:40-48
18:2 [A]Judg 13:25   [B]Judg 17:1   **18:4** [A]Judg 17:12
18:7 [A]Josh 19:47; Judg 18:29

17:5 [1] Lit *house of gods*

possession of the land. ¹⁰When you enter, you will come to an unsuspecting people with a spacious land; for God has handed it over to you, ^a place where there is no lack of anything that is on the earth."

¹¹Then from the family of the Danites, from Zorah and from Eshtaol, six hundred men armed with weapons of war set out. ¹²They went up and camped at Kiriath-jearim in Judah. Therefore they called that place ¹·^Mahaneh-dan to this day; behold, it is west of Kiriath-jearim. ¹³And they passed from there to the hill country of Ephraim and came to the house of Micah.

DANITES TAKE MICAH'S IDOLS

¹⁴Then the five men who went to spy out the country of Laish said to their kinsmen, "Do you know that there are in these houses ^an ephod and ¹household idols, and a carved image and a cast metal image? Now then, consider what you should do." ¹⁵So they turned aside there and came to the house of the young man, the Levite, to the house of Micah, and asked him how he was doing. ¹⁶Meanwhile, the six hundred men armed with their weapons of war, who were of the sons of Dan, were positioned at the entrance of the gate. ¹⁷Now the five men who went to spy out the land went up *and* entered there; they took ^the carved image, the ephod, the household idols, and the cast metal image, while the priest was standing at the entrance of the gate with the six hundred men armed with weapons of war. ¹⁸When these *men* entered Micah's house and took the carved image, the ephod, household idols, and the cast metal image, the priest said to them, "What are you doing?" ¹⁹And they said to him, "Be silent, ^put your hand over your mouth, and go with us, and be to us ᴮa father and a priest. Is it better for you to be a priest to the house of one man, or to be priest to a tribe and a family in Israel?" ²⁰The priest's heart was glad, and he took the ephod, the household idols, and the carved image, and went among the people.

²¹Then they turned and left, and put the children, the livestock, and the valuables in front of them. ²²When they had distanced themselves from Micah's house, the men who *were* in the houses near Micah's house assembled by command and overtook the sons of Dan. ²³Then they called out to the sons of Dan, who turned around and said to Micah, "What is *the matter* with you, that you have assembled together?" ²⁴And he said, "You have taken my gods which I made, and the priest, and have gone away; what more do I have? So how can you say to me, 'What is *the matter* with you?'" ²⁵Then the sons of Dan said to him, "Do not let your voice be heard among us, or else fierce men will attack you, and you will lose your life and the lives of your household." ²⁶So the sons of Dan went on their way; and when Micah saw that they were too strong for him, he turned and went back to his house.

²⁷Then they took what Micah had made and the priest who had belonged to him, and came to ^Laish, to a people quiet and

18:10 ^Deut 8:9   18:12 ^Judg 13:25   18:14 ^Judg 17:5
18:17 ^Gen 31:19, 30; Is 41:29   18:19 ^Job 21:5
ᴮJudg 17:10   18:27 ^Josh 19:47; Judg 8:7
_____
18:12 ¹I.e., the camp of Dan   18:14 ¹Heb *teraphim*

unsuspecting, and struck them with the edge of the sword; and they burned the city with fire. ²⁸And there was no one to save *them,* because it was far from Sidon and they had no dealings with anyone, and it was in the valley which is near ᴬBeth-rehob. So they rebuilt the city and lived in it. ²⁹And ᴬthey named the city Dan, after the name of Dan their father who was born to Israel; however, the name of the city was previously Laish. ³⁰The sons of Dan set up for themselves ᴬthe carved image; and Jonathan, the son of Gershom, the son of ¹Manasseh, ᴬhe and his sons were priests to the tribe of the Danites until the day of the captivity of the land. ³¹So they set up for themselves Micah's carved image which he had made, all the time that the ᴬhouse of God was in Shiloh.

A LEVITE'S CONCUBINE
RAPED AND KILLED

19 Now it came about in those days, when ᴬthere was no king in Israel, that there was a certain Levite staying in the remote part of the hill country of Ephraim, who took a concubine for himself from Bethlehem in Judah. ²But his concubine ¹found him repugnant, and she left him *and went* to her father's house in Bethlehem in Judah, and remained there for a period of four months. ³Then her husband set out and went after her to ᴬspeak gently to her in order to bring her back, taking with him his servant and a pair of donkeys. And she brought him into her father's house, and when the girl's father saw him, he was glad to meet him. ⁴His father-in-law, the girl's father, prevailed upon him, and he

remained with him for three days. So they ate and drank and stayed there. ⁵Now on the fourth day they got up early in the morning, and he prepared to go; but the girl's father said to his son-in-law, "ᴬStrengthen yourself with a piece of bread, and afterward you may go." ⁶So both of them sat down and ate and drank together; and the girl's father said to the man, "Please be so kind as to spend the night, and ᴬlet your heart be cheerful." ⁷However, the man got up to go; but his father-in-law urged him, and he spent the night there again. ⁸Now on the fifth day he got up to go early in the morning, but the girl's father said, "Please strengthen yourself, and wait until late afternoon"; so both of them ate. ⁹When the man got up to go, along with his concubine and servant, his father-in-law, the girl's father, said to him, "Behold now, the day has drawn to a close; please spend the night. Behold, the day is coming to an end; spend the night here so that your heart may be cheerful. Then tomorrow you may arise early for your journey and go home."

¹⁰But the man was unwilling to spend the night, so he got up and left, and came to *a place* opposite ᴬJebus (that is, Jerusalem). And with him was a pair of saddled donkeys; his concubine also was with him. ¹¹When they *were* near Jebus, the day was almost gone; and ᴬthe servant said to his master, "Please

18:28ᴬ2 Sam 10:6   **18:29**ᴬJosh 19:47
18:30ᴬJudg 17:3, 5   **18:31**ᴬJosh 18:1   **19:1**ᴬJudg 18:1
19:3ᴬGen 34:3; 50:21   **19:5**ᴬGen 18:5; Judg 19:8
19:6ᴬJudg 16:25; 19:9, 22   **19:10**ᴬ1 Chr 11:4, 5
19:11ᴬJudg 19:19

18:30¹Some ancient versions *Moses*   **19:2**¹Or *was unfaithful to him* (a Hebrew homonym); LXX *became angry at him*

come, and let's turn aside into this city of the Jebusites and spend the night in it." [12]However, his master said to him, "We will not turn aside into a city of foreigners who are not of the sons of Israel; instead, we will go on as far as Gibeah." [13]And he said to his servant, "Come, and let's approach one of these places; and we will spend the night in Gibeah or Ramah." [14]So they passed along and went their way, and the sun set on them near Gibeah which belongs to Benjamin. [15]They turned aside there to enter *and* spend the night in Gibeah. When they entered, they sat down in the public square of the city, for no one took them into *his* house to spend the night.

[16]Then behold, an old man was coming out of the field from his work at evening. Now the man was from [A]the hill country of Ephraim, and he was staying in Gibeah, but the men of the place were Benjaminites. [17]And he raised his eyes and saw the traveler in the public square of the city; and the old man said, "Where are you going, and where do you come from?" [18]And he said to him, "We are passing from Bethlehem in Judah to the remote part of the hill country of Ephraim, *for* I am from there, and I went to Bethlehem in Judah. But I am *now* going to my house, and no one will take me into his house. [19]Yet there is both straw and feed for our donkeys, and also bread and wine for me, and your female slave, and [A]the young man who is with your servants; there is no lack of anything." [20]Then the old man said, "[A]Peace to you. Only let me *take care of* all your needs; however, do not spend the night in the public square." [21A]So he took him

into his house and fed the donkeys, and they washed their feet and ate and drank.

[22]While they were celebrating, behold, [A]the men of the city, certain worthless men, surrounded the house, pushing one another at the door; and they spoke to the owner of the house, the old man, saying, "Bring out the man who entered your house that we may have relations with him." [23]Then the man, the owner of the house, went out to them and said to them, "No, my brothers, please do not act *so* wickedly. Since this man has come into my house, [A]do not commit this vile sin. [24A]Here is my virgin daughter and the man's concubine. Please let me bring them out, then rape them and do to them whatever you wish. But do not commit this act of vile sin against this man." [25]But the men would not listen to him. So the man seized his concubine and brought *her* outside to them; and they raped her and abused her all night until morning, then let her go at the approach of dawn. [26]As the day began to dawn, the woman came and fell down at the doorway of the man's house where her master was, until *full* daylight.

[27]When her master got up in the morning and opened the doors of the house and went out to go on his way, then behold, his concubine was lying at the doorway of the house with her hands on the threshold. [28]And he said to her, "Get up and let's go," [A]but there was no answer. Then he put her on the donkey; and the man set out

and went to his home. ²⁹When he entered his house, he took a knife and seized his concubine, and ^cut her in twelve pieces, limb by limb. Then he sent her throughout the territory of Israel. ³⁰All who saw *it* said, "Nothing like this has *ever* happened or been seen from the day when the sons of Israel came up from the land of Egypt to this day. Consider it, ^make a plan, and speak up!"

RESOLVE TO PUNISH THE GUILTY

20 Then all the sons of Israel from Dan to Beersheba, including the land of Gilead, came out, and the congregation assembled as one person to the LORD at ^Mizpah. ²And the leaders of all the people, all the tribes of Israel, took their stand in the assembly of the people of God, four hundred thousand foot soldiers ^who drew the sword. ³(Now the sons of Benjamin heard that the sons of Israel had gone up to Mizpah.) And the sons of Israel said, "Tell *us,* how did this wickedness take place?" ⁴So the Levite, the husband of the woman who was murdered, answered and said, "I came with my concubine to spend the night at Gibeah which belongs to Benjamin. ⁵But the ^citizens of Gibeah rose up against me and surrounded the house at night, threatening me. They intended to kill me; instead, they raped my concubine so that she died. ⁶And I ^took hold of my concubine and cut her in pieces, and sent her throughout the land of Israel's inheritance; for ^Bthey have committed an outrageous sin and vile act in Israel. ⁷Behold, all you sons of Israel, ^give your response and advice here."

⁸Then all the people rose up as one person, saying, "Not one of us will go to his tent, nor will any of us go home. ⁹But now this is the thing which we will do to Gibeah; *we will go up* against it by lot. ¹⁰And we will take ten men out of a hundred throughout the tribes of Israel, and a hundred out of a thousand, and a thousand out of ten thousand to supply provisions for the people, so that when they come to Gibeah of Benjamin, they may punish *them* for all the vile sin that they have committed in Israel." ¹¹So all the men of Israel were gathered against the city, united as one man.

¹²Then the tribes of Israel sent men through the entire tribe of Benjamin, saying, "What is this wickedness that has taken place among you? ¹³Now then, turn over the men, the ^worthless men who are in Gibeah, so that we may put them to death and ^Bremove *this* wickedness from Israel." But the sons of Benjamin would not listen to the voice of their brothers, the sons of Israel. ¹⁴Instead, the sons of Benjamin gathered from the cities to Gibeah, to go out to battle against the sons of Israel. ¹⁵From the cities on that day the ^sons of Benjamin were counted, twenty-six thousand men who drew the sword, besides the inhabitants of Gibeah who were counted, seven hundred choice men. ¹⁶Out of all these people seven hundred ^choice men were left-handed; each one could sling a stone at a hair and not miss. ¹⁷Then the men of Israel besides Benjamin were counted, four

19:29^1 Sam 11:7   19:30^Judg 20:7; Prov 13:10
20:1^1 Sam 7:5   20:2^Judg 8:10   20:5^Judg 19:22
20:6^Judg 19:29   ᴮGen 34:7   20:7^Judg 19:30
20:13^2 Cor 6:15   ᴮDeut 13:5   20:15^Num 1:36, 37;
2:23   20:16^Judg 3:15; 1 Chr 12:2

hundred thousand men who drew the sword; all of these were men of war.

CIVIL WAR, BENJAMIN DEFEATED

[18] Now the sons of Israel set out, went up to Bethel, and ^inquired of God and said, "Who shall go up first for us to battle against the sons of Benjamin?" Then the LORD said, "Judah *shall go up* first."

[19] So the sons of Israel got up in the morning and camped against Gibeah. [20] The men of Israel went to battle against Benjamin, and the men of Israel lined up for battle against them at Gibeah. [21] Then the sons of Benjamin came out of Gibeah and ^struck to the ground on that day twenty-two thousand men of Israel. [22] But the people, the men of Israel, showed themselves courageous and lined up for battle again in the place where they had lined themselves up on the first day. [23] And ^the sons of Israel went up and wept before the LORD until evening, and ^Binquired of the LORD, saying, "Shall we again advance for battle against the sons of my brother Benjamin?" And the LORD said, "Go up against him."

[24] So the sons of Israel came against the sons of Benjamin on the second day. [25] And Benjamin went out against them from Gibeah the second day and struck to the ground again eighteen thousand men of the sons of Israel; all of these drew the sword. [26] Then ^all the sons of Israel and all the people went up and came to Bethel, and they wept and remained there before the LORD, and fasted that day until evening. And they offered burnt offerings and peace offerings before the LORD. [27] And the sons of Israel ^inquired of the LORD (for the ark of the covenant of God *was* there in those days, [28] and Phinehas the son of Eleazar, Aaron's son, stood before it *to minister* in those days), saying, "Shall I yet again go out to battle against the sons of my brother Benjamin, or shall I stop?" And the LORD said, "Go up, ^for tomorrow I will hand them over to you."

[29] ^So Israel set men in ambush around Gibeah. [30] And the sons of Israel went up against the sons of Benjamin on the third day and lined up against Gibeah as at other times. [31] ^When the sons of Benjamin went out against the people, they were lured away from the city, and they began to strike and kill some of the people as at other times, on the roads (one of which goes up to Bethel, and the other to Gibeah), *and* in the field, about thirty men of Israel. [32] And the sons of Benjamin said, "They are defeated before us, like the first time." But the sons of Israel said, "Let's flee, so that we may draw them away from the city to the roads." [33] Then all the men of Israel rose from their place and lined up at Baal-tamar; ^and the men of Israel in ambush charged from their place, from Maareh-geba. [34] When ten thousand choice men from all Israel came against Gibeah, the battle became fierce; ^but Benjamin did not know that disaster was close to them. [35] And the LORD struck Benjamin before Israel, so that the sons of Israel destroyed 25,100 men of Benjamin that day, all who drew the sword.

[36] So the sons of Benjamin saw that they were defeated. ^When

20:18 ^Num 27:21; Judg 20:23, 27   20:21 ^Judg 20:25
20:23 ^Josh 7:6, 7   ^BJudg 20:18   20:26 ^Judg 20:23;
21:2   20:27 ^Judg 20:18   20:28 ^Judg 7:9
20:29 ^Josh 8:4   20:31 ^Josh 8:16   20:33 ^Josh 8:19
20:34 ^Josh 8:14; Job 21:13   20:36 ^Josh 8:15

the men of Israel gave ground to Benjamin because they relied on the men in ambush whom they had set against Gibeah, ³⁷ᴬthe men in ambush hurried and rushed against Gibeah; the men in ambush also deployed and struck all the city with the edge of the sword. ³⁸ Now the agreed sign between the men of Israel and the men in ambush was ᴬthat they would make a great cloud of smoke rise from the city. ³⁹ Then the men of Israel turned in the battle, and Benjamin began to strike and kill about thirty men of Israel, ᴬfor they said, "Undoubtedly they are defeated before us, as in the first battle." ⁴⁰ But when the cloud began to rise from the city *in* a column of smoke, Benjamin looked ᴬbehind them; and behold, the entire city was going up *in smoke* to heaven. ⁴¹ Then the men of Israel turned, and the men of Benjamin were terrified; for they saw that ᴬdisaster was close to them. ⁴² Therefore, they turned their backs before the men of Israel *to flee* in the ᴬdirection of the wilderness, but the battle overtook them while those who *attacked* from the cities were annihilating them in the midst of them. ⁴³ᴬThey surrounded Benjamin, pursued them without rest, *and* trampled them down opposite Gibeah toward the east. ⁴⁴ So eighteen thousand men of Benjamin fell; all of these *were* valiant men. ⁴⁵ The rest turned and fled toward the wilderness to the rock of ᴬRimmon, but they caught five thousand of them on the roads and overtook them at Gidom, and killed two thousand of them. ⁴⁶ So all those of Benjamin who fell that day were twenty-five thousand men who drew the sword; all of these were valiant men. ⁴⁷ But six hundred men turned and fled toward the wilderness to the rock of Rimmon; and they remained at the rock of Rimmon for four months. ⁴⁸ The men of Israel then turned back against the sons of Benjamin and struck them with the edge of the sword, both the entire city with the cattle and all that they found; they also set on fire all the cities which they found.

MOURNING A LOST TRIBE

21 Now the men of Israel ᴬhad sworn in Mizpah, saying, "None of us shall give his daughter to Benjamin in marriage." ² ᴬSo the people came to Bethel and sat there before God until evening, and raised their voices and wept profusely. ³ And they said, "Why, Lᴏʀᴅ, God of Israel, has this happened in Israel, that one tribe is missing today from Israel?" ⁴ And it came about the next day that the people got up early and built ᴬan altar there, and offered burnt offerings and peace offerings.

⁵ Then the sons of Israel said, "Who is there among all the tribes of Israel who did not go up to the Lᴏʀᴅ in the assembly?" For they had taken a solemn oath concerning *anyone* ᴬwho did not go up to the Lᴏʀᴅ at Mizpah, saying, "He shall certainly be put to death." ⁶ And the sons of Israel were sorry for their brother Benjamin, and said, "Today one tribe is cut off from Israel! ⁷ What are we to do for wives for those who are left, since we have ᴬsworn by the Lᴏʀᴅ not to give them any of our daughters as wives?"

20:37 ᴬJosh 8:19   20:38 ᴬJosh 8:20   20:39 ᴬJudg 20:32   20:40 ᴬJosh 8:20   20:41 ᴬProv 5:22; 11:5, 6   20:42 ᴬJosh 8:15, 24   20:43 ᴬHos 9:9; 10:9   20:45 ᴬJudg 21:13   21:1 ᴬJudg 21:7, 18   21:2 ᴬJudg 20:26   21:4 ᴬDeut 12:5; 2 Sam 24:25   21:5 ᴬJudg 5:23   21:7 ᴬJudg 21:1

PROVISION FOR THEIR SURVIVAL

⁸And they said, "What one is there of the tribes of Israel that did not go up to the Lord at Mizpah?" And behold, no one had come to the camp from Jabesh-gilead to the assembly. ⁹For when the people were counted, behold, not one of the inhabitants of Jabesh-gilead was there. ¹⁰And the congregation sent twelve thousand of the valiant warriors there, and commanded them, saying, "Go and ^strike the inhabitants of Jabesh-gilead with the edge of the sword, along with the women and the children. ¹¹And this is the thing that you shall do: you ^shall utterly destroy every male, and every woman who has slept with a male." ¹²And they found among the inhabitants of Jabesh-gilead four hundred young virgins who had not known a man by sleeping with him; and they brought them to the camp at Shiloh, which is in the land of Canaan.

¹³Then the whole congregation sent *word* and spoke to the sons of Benjamin who were ^at the rock of Rimmon, and ᴮproclaimed peace to them. ¹⁴And *the tribe of* Benjamin returned at that time, and they gave them the women whom they had allowed to live from the women of Jabesh-gilead; but they were not enough for them. ¹⁵And the people were sorry for Benjamin, because the Lord had created a gap in the tribes of Israel.

¹⁶Then the elders of the congregation said, "What are we to do for wives for those who are left, since the women have been eliminated from Benjamin?" ¹⁷And they said, "*There must be* an inheritance for the survivors of Benjamin, so that a tribe will not be wiped out from

Israel. ¹⁸But we cannot give them wives from our daughters." For the sons of Israel ^had sworn, saying, "Cursed is he who gives a wife to Benjamin!"

¹⁹So they said, "Behold, there is a feast of the Lord from year to year in ^Shiloh, which is on the north side of Bethel, on the east side of the road that goes up from Bethel to Shechem, and on the south side of Lebonah." ²⁰And they commanded the sons of Benjamin, saying, "Go and lie in wait in the vineyards, ²¹and watch; and behold, if the daughters of Shiloh come out to ^take part in the dances, then you shall come out of the vineyards, and each of you shall seize his wife from the daughters of Shiloh, and go to the land of Benjamin. ²²And when their fathers or their brothers come to complain to us, we shall say to them, 'Give them to us voluntarily, because we did not take for each man *of Benjamin* a wife in battle, ^nor did you give *them* to them, otherwise you would now be guilty.'" ²³The sons of Benjamin did so, and took wives according to their number from those who danced, whom they seized. And they went and returned to their inheritance, and ^rebuilt the cities and lived in them. ²⁴And the sons of Israel departed from there at that time, every man to his tribe and family, and each one departed from there to his inheritance.

²⁵^In those days there was no king in Israel; everyone did what was right in his own eyes.

21:10 ^Num 31:17; Judg 5:23　21:11 ^Num 31:17
21:13 ^Judg 20:47　ᴮDeut 20:10　21:18 ^Judg 21:1
21:19 ^Josh 18:1; Judg 18:31　21:21 ^Ex 15:20;
Judg 11:34　21:22 ^Judg 21:1, 18　21:23 ^Judg 20:48
21:25 ^Judg 17:6; 18:1

RUTH

NAOMI WIDOWED

1 Now it came about in the days when the judges governed, that there was ^a famine in the land. And a man ^B of Bethlehem in Judah went to reside in the land of Moab with his wife and his two sons. ² The name of the man *was* Elimelech, and the name of his wife, Naomi; and the names of his two sons *were* Mahlon and Chilion, Ephrathites of Bethlehem in Judah. So they ^entered the land of Moab and remained there. ³ Then Elimelech, Naomi's husband, died; and she was left with her two sons. ⁴ And they took for themselves Moabite women *as* wives; the name of the one was Orpah, and the name of the other, Ruth. And they lived there about ten years. ⁵ Then both Mahlon and Chilion also died, and the woman was left without her two sons and her husband.

⁶ Then she arose with her daughters-in-law to return from the land of Moab, because she had heard in the land of Moab that the Lord had ^visited His people by giving them food. ⁷ So she departed from the place where she was, and her two daughters-in-law with her; and they went on the way to return to the land of Judah. ⁸ But Naomi said to her two daughters-in-law, "Go, return each of you to your mother's house. ^May the Lord deal kindly with you as you have dealt with the dead and with me. ⁹ May the Lord grant that you may find a place of rest, each one in the house of her husband." Then she kissed them, and they raised their voices and wept. ¹⁰ However, they said to her, "*No*, but we will return with you to your people." ¹¹ But Naomi said, "Return, my daughters. Why should you go with me? Do I still have sons in my womb, that ^they may be your husbands? ¹² Return, my daughters! Go, for I am too old to have a husband. If I said I have hope, if I were even to have a husband tonight and also give birth to sons, ¹³ would you therefore wait until they were grown? Would you therefore refrain from marrying? No, my daughters; for it is much more bitter for me than for you, because ^the hand of the Lord has come out against me."

RUTH'S LOYALTY

¹⁴ And they raised their voices and wept again; and Orpah kissed her mother-in-law, but Ruth clung to her.

¹⁵ Then she said, "Behold, your sister-in-law has gone back to her people and her ^gods; return after your sister-in-law." ¹⁶ But Ruth said, "Do not plead with me to leave you *or* to turn back from following you; for where you go, I will go, and where you sleep, I will sleep. Your people *shall be* my people, and your God, my God. ¹⁷ Where you die, I will die, and there I will be buried. May ^the Lord do so to me,

1:1 ^Gen 12:10   ^B Judg 17:8   1:2 ^Judg 3:30
1:6 ^Ex 4:31; Jer 29:10   1:8 ^2 Tim 1:16
1:11 ^Gen 38:11; Deut 25:5   1:13 ^Judg 2:15; Job 19:21
1:15 ^Josh 24:15; Judg 11:24   1:17 ^1 Sam 3:17; 2 Kin 6:31

and worse, if *anything but* death separates me from you." ¹⁸When ᴬshe saw that she was determined to go with her, she stopped speaking to her *about it.*

¹⁹So they both went on until they came to Bethlehem. And when they had come to Bethlehem, ᴬall the city was stirred because of them, and the women said, "Is this Naomi?" ²⁰But she said to them, "Do not call me ¹Naomi; call me ²Mara, for ᴬthe Almighty has dealt very bitterly with me. ²¹I went *away* full, but ᴬthe Lᴏʀᴅ has brought me back empty. Why do you call me Naomi, since the Lᴏʀᴅ has testified against me and the Almighty has afflicted me?"

²²So Naomi returned, and with her Ruth the Moabitess, her daughter-in-law, who returned from the land of Moab. And they came to Bethlehem at ᴬthe beginning of barley harvest.

RUTH GLEANS IN BOAZ'S FIELD

2 Now Naomi had a relative of her husband, a man of great wealth, of the family of ᴬElimelech, whose name was Boaz. ²And Ruth the Moabitess said to Naomi, "Please let me go to the field and ᴬglean among the ears of grain following one in whose eyes I may find favor." And she said to her, "Go, my daughter." ³So she left and went and gleaned in the field after the reapers; and she happened to come to the portion of the field belonging to Boaz, who was of the family of Elimelech. ⁴Now behold, Boaz came from Bethlehem and said to the reapers, "ᴬMay the Lᴏʀᴅ be with you." And they said to him, "May the Lᴏʀᴅ bless you." ⁵Then Boaz said to his servant who was in charge of the reapers, "Whose young woman is this?" ⁶And the servant in charge of the reapers replied, "She is the young Moabite woman who returned with Naomi from the land of Moab. ⁷And she said, 'Please let me glean and gather after the reapers among the sheaves.' So she came and has remained from the morning until now; she has been sitting in the house for a little while."

⁸Then Boaz said to Ruth, "Listen carefully, my daughter. Do not go to glean in another field; furthermore, do not go on from this one, but join my young women here. ⁹*Keep* your eyes on the field which they reap, and go after them. Indeed, I have ordered the servants not to touch you. When you are thirsty, go to the water jars and drink from what the servants draw." ¹⁰Then she ᴬfell on her face, bowing to the ground, and said to him, "Why have I found favor in your sight that you should take notice of me, since I am a foreigner?" ¹¹Boaz replied to her, "All that you have done for your mother-in-law after the death of your husband has been fully reported to me, and how you left your father and your mother and the land of your birth, and came to a people that you did not previously know. ¹²ᴬMay the Lᴏʀᴅ reward your work, and may your wages be full from the Lᴏʀᴅ, the God of Israel, under whose wings you have come to take refuge." ¹³Then she said, "I have found favor in your sight, my lord, for you have comforted me

---

1:18 ᴬActs 21:14   1:19 ᴬMatt 21:10   1:20 ᴬEx 6:3; Job 6:4   1:21 ᴬJob 1:21   1:22 ᴬEx 9:31; Lev 23:10, 11   2:1 ᴬRuth 1:2   2:2 ᴬLev 19:9, 10; 23:22   2:4 ᴬJudg 6:12; Ps 129:8   2:10 ¹1 Sam 25:23   2:12 ¹1 Sam 24:19

1:20 ¹I.e., pleasant   ²I.e., bitter

and indeed have spoken kindly to your servant, though I am not like one of your female servants."

¹⁴And at mealtime Boaz said to her, "Come here, that you may eat of the bread and dip your piece of bread in the vinegar." So she sat beside the reapers; and he served her roasted grain, and she ate and was satisfied ᴬand had some left. ¹⁵When she got up to glean, Boaz commanded his servants, saying, "Let her glean even among the sheaves, and do not insult her. ¹⁶Also you are to purposely slip out for her *some grain* from the bundles and leave *it* so that she may glean, and do not rebuke her."

¹⁷So she gleaned in the field until evening. Then she beat out what she had gleaned, and it was about an ¹ephah of barley. ¹⁸And she picked *it* up and went into the city, and her mother-in-law saw what she had gleaned. She also took *some* out and ᴬgave Naomi what she had left after she was satisfied. ¹⁹Her mother-in-law then said to her, "Where did you glean today and where did you work? May he who ᴬtook notice of you be blessed." So she told her mother-in-law with whom she had worked, and said, "The name of the man with whom I worked today is Boaz." ²⁰Naomi said to her daughter-in-law, "ᴬMay he be blessed of the LORD who has not withdrawn His kindness from the living and from the dead." Again Naomi said to her, "The man is our relative; he is one of our ᴮredeemers." ²¹Then Ruth the Moabitess said, "Furthermore, he said to me, 'You are to stay close to my servants until they have finished all my harvest.'" ²²And Naomi said to her daughter-in-law

Ruth, "It is good, my daughter, that you go out with his young women, so that *others* do not assault you in another field." ²³So she stayed close by the young women of Boaz in order to glean until ᴬthe end of the barley harvest and the wheat harvest. And she lived with her mother-in-law.

BOAZ WILL REDEEM RUTH

3 Then her mother-in-law Naomi said to her, "My daughter, shall I not seek security for you, that it may go well for you? ²Now then, is Boaz not ᴬour relative, with whose young women you were? Behold, he is winnowing barley at the threshing floor tonight. ³Wash yourself therefore, and anoint yourself, and put on your *best* clothes, and go down to the threshing floor; *but* do not reveal yourself to the man until he has finished eating and drinking. ⁴And it shall be when he lies down, that you shall take notice of the place where he lies, and you shall go and uncover his feet and lie down; then he will tell you what you should do." ⁵And she said to her, "ᴬAll that you say I will do."

⁶So she went down to the threshing floor and did according to all that her mother-in-law had commanded her. ⁷When Boaz had eaten and drunk and ᴬhis heart was cheerful, he went to lie down at the end of the heap of grain; and she came secretly, and uncovered his feet and lay down. ⁸And it happened in the middle of the night

2:14ᴬRuth 2:18   2:18ᴬRuth 2:14   2:19ᴬPs 41:1
2:20ᴬ2 Sam 2:5   ᴮLev 25:25; Deut 25:5-10
2:23ᴬDeut 16:9   3:2ᴬDeut 25:5-10   3:5ᴬEph 6:1;
Col 3:20   3:7ᴬJudg 19:6, 9; 2 Sam 13:28

2:17¹About 1 cubic foot or 0.03 cubic meters

that the man was startled and bent forward; and behold, a woman was lying at his feet. ⁹So he said, "Who are you?" And she answered, "I am Ruth your slave. Now spread your garment over your slave, for you are a redeemer." ¹⁰Then he said, "ᴬMay you be blessed of the LORD, my daughter. You have shown your last kindness to be better than the first, by not going after young men, whether poor or rich. ¹¹So now, my daughter, do not fear. I will do for you whatever you say, for all my people in the city know that you are ᴬa woman of excellence. ¹²But now, although it is true that I am a redeemer, yet there is also a redeemer more closely related than I. ¹³Remain this night, and when morning comes, ᴬif he will redeem you, good; let him redeem you. But if he does not wish to redeem you, then I will redeem you, as the LORD lives. Lie down until morning."

¹⁴So she lay at his feet until morning, and got up before one person could recognize another; and he said, "ᴬDo not let it be known that the woman came to the threshing floor." ¹⁵Again he said, "Give me the shawl that is on you and hold it." So she held it, and he measured six *measures* of barley and laid *it* on her. Then she went into the city. ¹⁶When she came to her mother-in-law, she said, "How did it go, my daughter?" And she told her all that the man had done for her. ¹⁷She also said, "These six *measures* of barley he gave to me, for he said, 'Do not go to your mother-in-law empty-handed.'" ¹⁸Then she said, "Wait, my daughter, until you know how the matter turns out; for the man will not rest until he has settled it today."

THE MARRIAGE OF RUTH

4 Now Boaz went up to the gate and sat down there, and behold, ᴬthe redeemer of whom Boaz spoke was passing by, so he said, "Come over here, friend, sit down here." And he came over and sat down. ²Then he took ten men of the ᴬelders of the city and said, "Sit down here." So they sat down. ³And he said to the redeemer, "Naomi, who has returned from the land of Moab, has to sell the plot of land ᴬwhich belonged to our brother Elimelech. ⁴So I thought that I would inform you, saying, 'Buy *it* before those who are sitting *here,* and before the elders of my people. If you will redeem *it,* redeem *it;* but if not, tell me so that I may know; for ᴬthere is no one except you to redeem *it,* and I am after you.'" And he said, "I will redeem *it.*" ⁵Then Boaz said, "On the day you buy the field from the hand of Naomi, you must also acquire Ruth the Moabitess, the widow of the deceased, in order ᴬto raise up the name of the deceased on his inheritance." ⁶Then ᴬthe redeemer said, "I cannot redeem *it* for myself, otherwise I would jeopardize my own inheritance. Redeem *it* for yourself; you *may have* my right of redemption, since I cannot redeem *it.*"

⁷Now this was ᴬ*the custom* in former times in Israel concerning the redemption and the exchange *of land* to confirm any matter: a man removed his sandal and gave *it* to another; and this was the *way of* confirmation in Israel. ⁸So the redeemer said to Boaz, "Buy *it* for

3:10ᴬRuth 2:20   3:11ᴬProv 12:4; 31:10   3:13ᴬDeut 25:5; Matt 22:24   3:14ᴬRom 14:16; 2 Cor 8:21   4:1ᴬRuth 3:12 4:2ᴬ1 Kin 21:8; Prov 31:23   4:3ᴬLev 25:25 4:4ᴬLev 25:25   4:5ᴬGen 38:8; Deut 25:5f 4:6ᴬLev 25:25   4:7ᴬDeut 25:8-10

yourself." And he removed his sandal. ⁹Then Boaz said to the elders and all the people, "You are witnesses today that I have bought from the hand of Naomi all that belonged to Elimelech and all that belonged to Chilion and Mahlon. ¹⁰Furthermore, I have acquired Ruth the Moabitess, the widow of Mahlon, to be my wife in order to raise up the name of the deceased on his inheritance, so ᴬthat the name of the deceased will not be eliminated from his brothers or from the court of his *birth* place; you are witnesses today." ¹¹And all the people who were in the court, and the elders, said, "*We are* witnesses. May the LORD make the woman who is coming into your home ᴬlike Rachel and Leah, both of whom built the house of Israel; and may you achieve wealth in Ephrathah and become famous in Bethlehem. ¹²Moreover, may your house be like the house of ᴬPerez whom Tamar bore to Judah, through the descendants whom the LORD will give you by this young woman."

¹³So Boaz took Ruth, and she became his wife, and he had relations with her. And ᴬthe LORD enabled her to conceive, and she gave birth to a son. ¹⁴Then the ᴬwomen said to Naomi, "Blessed is the LORD who has not left you without a redeemer today, and may his name become famous in Israel. ¹⁵May he also be to you one who restores life and sustains your old age; for your daughter-in-law, who loves you ᴬand is better to you than seven sons, has given birth to him."

THE LINE OF DAVID

¹⁶Then Naomi took the child and laid him in her lap, and became his nurse. ¹⁷And the neighbor women gave him a name, saying, "A son has been born to Naomi!" So they named him Obed. He is the father of Jesse, the father of David.

¹⁸Now these are the generations of Perez: ᴬPerez fathered Hezron, ¹⁹Hezron fathered Ram, and Ram fathered Amminadab, ²⁰and Amminadab fathered Nahshon, and Nahshon fathered Salmon, ²¹and Salmon fathered Boaz, and Boaz fathered Obed, ²²and Obed fathered Jesse, and Jesse fathered David.

4:10ᴬDeut 25:6 4:11ᴬGen 29:25-30
4:12ᴬGen 38:29; 46:12 4:13ᴬGen 29:31; 33:5
4:14ᴬLuke 1:58 4:15ᴬRuth 1:16, 17; 2:11, 12
4:18ᴬMatt 1:3-6

1 SAMUEL

ELKANAH AND HIS WIVES

1 Now there was a man from Ramathaim-zophim from the ᴬhill country of Ephraim, and his name was ᴮElkanah the son of Jeroham, the son of Elihu, the son of Tohu, the son of Zuph, an Ephraimite. ²And he had ᴬtwo wives: the name of one was ᴮHannah and the name of the other Peninnah; and Peninnah had children, but Hannah had no children.

³Now this man would go up from his city yearly ᴬto worship and to sacrifice to the LORD of armies in ᴮShiloh. And the two sons of Eli, Hophni and Phinehas, were priests to the LORD there. ⁴When the day came that Elkanah sacrificed, he ᴬwould give portions to his wife Peninnah and to all her sons and daughters; ⁵but to Hannah he would give a double portion, because he loved Hannah, ᴬbut the LORD had closed her womb. ⁶Her rival, moreover, ᴬwould provoke her bitterly to irritate her, because the LORD had closed her womb. ⁷And it happened year after year, as often as she went up to the house of the LORD, that she would provoke her; so she wept and would not eat. ⁸Then Elkanah her husband would say to her, "Hannah, why do you weep, and why do you not eat, and why is your heart sad? ᴬAm I not better to you than ten sons?"

⁹Then Hannah got up after eating and drinking in Shiloh. Now Eli the priest was sitting on the seat by the doorpost of ᴬthe temple of the LORD.

¹⁰She, greatly distressed, prayed to the LORD and wept bitterly. ¹¹And she ᴬmade a vow and said, "LORD of armies, if You will indeed look on the affliction of Your bond-servant and remember me, and not forget Your bond-servant, but will give Your bond-servant a son, then I will give him to the LORD all the days of his life, and ᴮa razor shall never come on his head."

¹²Now it came about, as she continued praying before the LORD, that Eli was watching her mouth. ¹³As for Hannah, ᴬshe was speaking in her heart, only her lips were quivering, but her voice was not heard. So Eli thought that she was drunk. ¹⁴Then Eli said to her, "ᴬHow long will you behave like a drunk? Get rid of your wine!" ¹⁵But Hannah answered and said, "No, my lord, I am a woman despairing in spirit; I have drunk neither wine nor strong drink, but I ᴬhave poured out my soul before the LORD. ¹⁶Do not consider your bond-servant a useless woman, for I have spoken until now out of my great concern and provocation." ¹⁷Then Eli answered and said, "Go in peace; and may the God of Israel ᴬgrant your request that you have asked of Him." ¹⁸She said, "ᴬLet your bond-servant find favor in your sight." So the woman

1:1 ᴬJosh 17:17, 18   ᴮ1 Chr 6:22-28, 33-38
1:2 ᴬDeut 21:15-17   ᴮLuke 2:36   1:3 ᴬEx 23:14
ᴮJosh 18:1   1:4 ᴬDeut 12:17, 18   1:5 ᴬGen 16:1; 30:1
1:6 ᴬJob 24:21   1:8 ᴬRuth 4:15   1:9 ᴬ1 Sam 3:3
1:11 ᴬNum 30:6-11   ᴮJudg 13:5   1:13 ᴬGen 24:42-45
1:14 ᴬActs 2:4, 13   1:15 ᴬPs 42:4; 62:8   1:17 ᴬPs 20:3-5
1:18 ᴬGen 33:15; Ruth 2:13

went on her way and ate, and her face was no longer *sad.*

SAMUEL IS BORN TO HANNAH

19 Then they got up early in the morning and worshiped before the LORD, and returned again to their house in ^Ramah. And Elkanah had relations with Hannah his wife, and the LORD remembered her. 20 It came about in due time, after Hannah had conceived, that she gave birth to a son; and she named him Samuel, *saying,* "^Because I have asked for him of the LORD."

21 Then the man Elkanah ^went up with all his household to offer to the LORD the yearly sacrifice and *to pay* his vow. 22 But Hannah did not go up, for she said to her husband, "*I will not go* until the child is weaned; then I will bring him, so that he may appear before the LORD and ^stay there for life." 23 ^Elkanah her husband said to her, "Do what seems best to you. Stay until you have weaned him; only may the LORD confirm His word." So the woman stayed and nursed her son until she weaned him. 24 Now when she had weaned him, ^she took him up with her, with a three-year-old bull, one ephah of flour, and a jug of wine, and brought him to the house of the LORD in Shiloh, although the child was young. 25 Then ^they slaughtered the bull, and ^brought the boy to Eli. 26 And she said, "Pardon me, my lord! ^As your soul lives, my lord, I am the woman who stood here beside you, praying to the LORD. 27 ^For this boy I prayed, and the LORD has granted me my request which I asked of Him. 28 ^So I have also dedicated him to the LORD; as long as he lives he is dedicated to the LORD." And ^he worshiped the LORD there.

HANNAH'S SONG OF THANKSGIVING

2 Then Hannah prayed and said,
"My heart rejoices in the LORD;
^My ¹horn is exalted in the LORD,
My mouth speaks boldly against my enemies,
Because I rejoice in Your salvation.
2 "^There is no one holy like the LORD,
Indeed, there is no one besides You,
Nor is there any rock like our God.
3 "Do not go on boasting so very proudly,
^Do not let arrogance come out of your mouth;
For the LORD is a God of knowledge,
And with Him actions are weighed.
4 "^The bows of the mighty are broken to pieces,
^But those who have stumbled strap on strength.
5 "Those who were full hire themselves out for bread,
But those who were hungry cease *to be hungry.*
Even the infertile woman gives birth to seven,
But ^she who has many children languishes.
6 "The LORD puts to death and makes alive;
^He brings down to ¹Sheol and brings up.

1:19 ^1 Sam 1:1; 2:11   1:20 ^Ex 2:10, 22; Matt 1:21
1:21 ^Deut 12:11; 1 Sam 1:3   1:22 ^1 Sam 1:11, 28
1:23 ^Num 30:7, 10, 11   1:24 ^Num 15:9, 10;
Deut 12:5, 6   1:25 ^Lev 1:5   ^Luke 2:22
1:26 ^2 Kin 2:2, 4, 6; 4:30   1:27 ^1 Sam 1:11-13; Ps 6:9
1:28 ^1 Sam 1:11, 22   ^Gen 24:26, 52   2:1 ^Deut 33:17;
Job 16:15   2:2 ^Ex 15:11; Lev 19:2   2:3 ^Prov 8:13
2:4 ^Ps 37:15   ^Heb 11:32-34   2:5 ^Jer 15:9
2:6 ^Is 26:19

2:1 ¹ I.e., strength   2:6 ¹ I.e., the netherworld

7 "ᴬThe Lᴏʀᴅ makes poor and rich;
   He humbles, He also exalts.
8 "ᴬHe raises the poor from the
      dust,
   He lifts the needy from the
      garbage heap
   To seat *them* with nobles,
   And He gives them a seat of
      honor as an inheritance;
   For the pillars of the earth are
      the Lᴏʀᴅ's,
   And He set the world on them.
9 "He watches over the feet of His
      godly ones,
   ᴬBut the wicked ones are
      silenced in darkness;
   ᴮFor not by might shall a
      person prevail.
10 "ᴬThose who contend with the
      Lᴏʀᴅ will be terrified;
   Against them He will thunder
      in the heavens,
   The Lᴏʀᴅ will judge the ends
      of the earth;
   And He will give strength to
      His king,
   ᴮAnd will exalt the ¹horn of His
      anointed."

11 Then Elkanah went to his home
at Ramah. ᴬBut the boy continued
to attend to the service of the Lᴏʀᴅ
before Eli the priest.

THE SIN OF ELI'S SONS

12 Now the sons of Eli were ᴬuseless
men; they did not know the Lᴏʀᴅ.
13 ᴬAnd *this was* the custom of the
priests with the people: *when* anyone was offering a sacrifice, the
priest's servant would come while
the meat was cooking, with a three-
pronged fork in his hand. 14 And he
would thrust it into the pan, or kettle, or caldron, or pot; everything
that the fork brought up, the priest
would take for himself. They did so
in Shiloh to all the Israelites who

came there. 15 Also, before ᴬthey
burned the fat, the priest's servant
would come and say to the man
who was sacrificing, "Give the priest
meat for roasting, as he will not take
cooked meat from you, only raw."
16 And *if* the man said to him, "They
must burn the fat first, then take
as much as you desire," then he
would say, "No, but you must give
it to me now; and if not, I am taking
it by force!" 17 And *so* the sin of the
young men was very great before
the Lᴏʀᴅ, for the men ᴬtreated the
offering of the Lᴏʀᴅ disrespectfully.

SAMUEL BEFORE THE LORD AS A BOY

18 Now Samuel was ministering
before the Lᴏʀᴅ, *as* a boy ᴬwearing
a linen ephod. 19 And his mother
would make for him a little ᴬrobe
and bring it up to him from year
to year when she would come up
with her husband to offer ᴮthe
yearly sacrifice. 20 Then Eli would
bless Elkanah and his wife, and say,
"May the Lᴏʀᴅ give you children
from this woman in place of the
one she ᴬrequested of the Lᴏʀᴅ."
And they went to their own home.
21 ᴬThe Lᴏʀᴅ indeed visited Hannah, and she conceived and gave
birth to three sons and two daughters. And the boy Samuel grew up
before the Lᴏʀᴅ.

ELI REBUKES HIS SONS

22 Now Eli was very old; and he
heard *about* ᴬeverything that his

2:7 ᴬDeut 8:17, 18   2:8 ᴬJob 42:10-12; Ps 75:7
2:9 ᴬMatt 8:12   ᴮPs 33:16, 17   2:10 ᴬEx 15:6
ᴮPs 89:24   2:11 ᴬ1 Sam 1:28; 3:1
2:12 ᴬJer 2:8; 2 Cor 6:15   2:13 ᴬLev 7:29-34
2:15 ᴬLev 3:3-5, 16   2:17 ᴬMal 2:7-9   2:18 ᴬ1 Sam 2:28;
1 Chr 15:27   2:19 ᴬEx 28:31   ᴮ1 Sam 1:3, 21
2:20 ᴬ1 Sam 1:11, 27, 28   2:21 ᴬGen 21:1
2:22 ᴬ1 Sam 2:13-17

2:10 ¹I.e., strength

sons were doing to all Israel, and that they slept with ᴮthe women who served at the doorway of the tent of meeting. ²³So he said to them, "Why are you doing such things as these, the evil things that I hear from all these people? ²⁴No, my sons; for the report is not good ᴬwhich I hear the Lᴏʀᴅ's people circulating. ²⁵If one person sins against another, ᴬGod will mediate for him; but if a person sins against the Lᴏʀᴅ, who can intercede for him?" But they would not listen to the voice of their father, for the ᴮLᴏʀᴅ desired to put them to death.

²⁶Now the boy ᴬSamuel was continuing to grow and to be in favor both with the Lᴏʀᴅ and with people.

²⁷Then ᴬa man of God came to Eli and said to him, "This is what the Lᴏʀᴅ says: 'Did I *not* indeed reveal Myself to the house of your father when they were in Egypt *in bondage* to Pharaoh's house? ²⁸Did I *not* choose them from all the tribes of Israel to be My priests, to go up to My altar, to burn incense, to carry an ephod before Me? And did I *not* ᴬgive to the house of your father all the fire *offerings* of the sons of Israel? ²⁹Why are you ᴬshowing contempt for My sacrifice and My offering which I have commanded *for My* dwelling, and *why* are you ᴮhonoring your sons above Me, by making yourselves fat with the choicest of every offering of My people Israel?' ³⁰Therefore the Lᴏʀᴅ God of Israel declares, 'I did indeed say that your house and the house of your father was to walk before Me forever'; but now the Lᴏʀᴅ declares, 'Far be it from Me—for ᴬthose who honor Me I will honor, and those ᴮwho despise Me will be insignificant. ³¹Behold,

ᴬthe days are coming when I will eliminate your strength and the strength of your father's house, so that there will not be an old man in your house. ³²And you will look at ᴬthe distress of *My* dwelling, in *spite of* all the good that I do for Israel; and there will never be an old man in your house. ³³Yet I will not cut off every man of yours from My altar, so that your eyes will fail *from weeping* and your soul grieve, and all the increase of your house will die in the prime of life. ³⁴And this will be the sign to you which will come in regard to your two sons, Hophni and Phinehas: ᴬon the same day both of them will die. ³⁵But ᴬI will raise up for Myself a faithful priest who will do according to what is in My heart and My soul; and I will build him an enduring house, and he will walk before My anointed always. ³⁶And everyone who is left in your house will come to bow down to him for a silver coin or a loaf of bread and say, "Please assign me to one of the priest's offices so that I may eat a piece of bread."'"

THE PROPHETIC CALL TO SAMUEL

3 Now ᴬthe boy Samuel was attending to the service of the Lᴏʀᴅ before Eli. And word from the Lᴏʀᴅ was rare in those days; visions were infrequent.

²But it happened at that time as Eli was lying down in his place (now ᴬhis eyesight had begun to be poor *and* he could not see *well*),

2:22 ᴮEx 38:8   2:24 ᴬ1 Kin 15:26   2:25 ᴬDeut 1:17
ᴮJosh 11:20   2:26 ᴬ1 Sam 2:21; Luke 2:52
2:27 ᴬDeut 33:1; Judg 13:6   2:28 ᴬLev 7:35, 36
2:29 ᴬ1 Sam 2:13-17   ᴮMatt 10:37   2:30 ᴬPs 50:23
ᴮMal 2:9   2:31 ᴬ1 Sam 4:11-18; 22:17-20
2:32 ᴬ1 Sam 2:26, 27   2:34 ᴬ1 Sam 4:11, 17
2:35 ᴬ1 Sam 3:1; 9:12, 13   3:1 ᴬ1 Sam 2:11, 18
3:2 ᴬGen 27:1; 1 Sam 4:15

³and ^the lamp of God had not yet gone out, and Samuel was lying down in the temple of the LORD where the ark of God *was,* ⁴that the LORD called Samuel; and he said, "^Here I am." ⁵Then he ran to Eli and said, "Here I am, for you called me." But he said, "I did not call, go back *and* lie down." So he went and lay down. ⁶And the LORD called yet again, "Samuel!" So Samuel got up and went to Eli and said, "Here I am, for you called me." But he said, "I did not call, my son, go back *and* lie down." ⁷^Now Samuel did not yet know the LORD, nor had the word of the LORD yet been revealed to him. ⁸So the LORD called Samuel again for the third time. And he got up and went to Eli and said, "Here I am, for you called me." Then Eli realized that the LORD was calling the boy. ⁹And Eli said to Samuel, "Go lie down, and it shall be if He calls you, that you shall say, 'Speak, LORD, for Your servant is listening.'" So Samuel went and lay down in his place.

¹⁰Then the LORD came and stood, and called as at *the* other times: "Samuel! Samuel!" And Samuel said, "Speak, for Your servant is listening." ¹¹Then the LORD said to Samuel, "Behold, ^I am going to do a thing in Israel, *and* both ears of everyone who hears *about* it will ring. ¹²On that day ^I will carry out against Eli everything that I have spoken in regard to his house, from beginning to end. ¹³For ^I have told him that I am going to judge his house forever for the wrongdoing that he knew, because his sons were bringing a curse on themselves and ^he did not rebuke them. ¹⁴Therefore I have sworn to the house of Eli that ^the wrongdoing of Eli's house shall never be atoned for by sacrifice or offering."

¹⁵So Samuel lay down until morning. Then he ^opened the doors of the house of the LORD. But Samuel was afraid to tell the vision to Eli. ¹⁶Then Eli called Samuel and said, "Samuel, my son." And he said, "Here I am." ¹⁷He said, "What is the word that He spoke to you? Please do not hide it from me. ^May God do the same to you, and more so, if you hide a *single* word from me of all the words that He spoke to you!" ¹⁸So Samuel told him everything and hid nothing from him. And he said, "^He is the LORD; let Him do what seems good to Him."

¹⁹Now ^Samuel grew, and ^the LORD was with him, and He let none of his words fail. ²⁰And all Israel ^from Dan even to Beersheba knew that Samuel was confirmed as a prophet of the LORD. ²¹And ^the LORD appeared again at Shiloh, ^because the LORD revealed Himself to Samuel at Shiloh by the word of the LORD.

PHILISTINES TAKE THE ARK IN VICTORY

4 So the word of Samuel came to all Israel. Now Israel went out to meet the Philistines in battle, and they camped beside ^Ebenezer, while the Philistines camped in Aphek. ²Then the Philistines drew up in battle formation to meet Israel. When the battle spread, Israel was defeated by the Philistines, who killed about four

3:3^Ex 25:31-37; Lev 24:2, 3   3:4^Is 6:8
3:7^Acts 19:2; 1 Cor 13:11   3:11^2 Kin 21:12; Jer 19:3
3:12^1 Sam 2:27-36   3:13^1 Sam 2:29-31   ^Deut 17:12
3:14^Lev 15:31; Is 22:14   3:15^1 Chr 15:23
3:17^2 Sam 3:35   3:18^Ex 34:5-7; Is 39:8
3:19^1 Sam 2:21   ^Gen 21:22   3:20^Judg 20:1
3:21^Gen 12:7   ^1 Sam 3:10   4:1^1 Sam 7:12

thousand men on the battlefield. [3]When the people came into the camp, the elders of Israel said, "^Why has the LORD defeated us today before the Philistines? Let's take the ark of the covenant of the LORD from Shiloh, so that He may come among us and save us from the power of our enemies." [4]So the people sent *men* to Shiloh, and from there they carried the ark of the covenant of the LORD of armies ^who is enthroned *above* the cherubim; and the two sons of Eli, Hophni and Phinehas, *were* there with the ark of the covenant of God.

[5]And as the ark of the covenant of the LORD was coming into the camp, ^all Israel shouted with a great shout, so that the earth resounded. [6]And when the Philistines heard the noise of the shout, they said, "What *does* the noise of this great shout in the camp of the Hebrews *mean?*" Then they understood that the ark of the LORD had come into the camp. [7]So the Philistines were afraid, for they said, "God has come into the camp!" And they said, "^Woe to us! For nothing like this has happened before. [8]Woe to us! Who will save us from the hand of these mighty gods? These are the gods who struck the Egyptians with all *kinds of* plagues in the wilderness. [9]^Take courage and be men, Philistines, or you will become slaves to the Hebrews, as they have been slaves to you; so be men and fight!"

[10]So the Philistines fought and ^Israel was defeated, and every man fled to his tent; and the defeat was very great, for thirty thousand foot soldiers of Israel fell. [11]Moreover, the ark of God was taken; and ^the

two sons of Eli, Hophni and Phinehas, died.

[12]Now a man of Benjamin ran from the battle line and came to Shiloh the same day with ^his clothes torn, and dust on his head. [13]When he came, behold, ^Eli was sitting on *his* seat by the road keeping watch, because his heart was anxious about the ark of God. And the man came to give a report in the city, and all the city cried out. [14]When Eli heard the noise of the outcry, he said, "What *does* the noise of this commotion *mean?*" Then the man came hurriedly and told Eli. [15]Now Eli was ninety-eight years old, and ^his eyes were fixed and he could not see. [16]The man said to Eli, "I am the one who came from the battle line. Indeed, I escaped from the battle line today." And he said, "^How are things, my son?" [17]Then the one who brought the news replied, "Israel has fled before the Philistines and there has also been a great defeat among the people, and your two sons, Hophni and Phinehas are also dead; and the ark of God has been taken." [18]When he mentioned the ark of God, ^Eli fell off the seat backward beside the gate, and his neck was broken and he died, for he was old and heavy. And *so* he judged Israel for forty years.

[19]Now his daughter-in-law, Phinehas' wife, was pregnant *and about* to give birth; and when she heard the news that the ark of God had been taken and that her father-in-law and her husband had died, she kneeled

4:3^Josh 7:7, 8   4:4^2 Sam 6:2; Ps 80:1
4:5^Josh 6:5, 20   4:7^Ex 15:14   4:9^1 Cor 16:13
4:10^Deut 28:15, 25; 1 Sam 4:2   4:11^1 Sam 2:34;
Ps 78:56-64   4:12^Josh 7:6; 2 Sam 1:2
4:13^1 Sam 1:9; 4:18   4:15^1 Sam 3:2; 1 Kin 14:4
4:16^2 Sam 1:4   4:18^1 Sam 4:13

down and gave birth, because her pains came upon her. ²⁰And about the time of her death the women who were standing by her said to her, "ᴬDo not be afraid, for you have given birth to a son." But she did not answer or pay attention. ²¹And she named the boy ¹Ichabod, saying, "The glory has departed from Israel," because ᴬthe ark of God had been taken and because of her father-in-law and her husband. ²²So she said, "The glory has departed from Israel, because the ark of God has been taken."

CAPTURE OF THE ARK PROVOKES GOD

5 Now the Philistines took the ark of God and brought it from Ebenezer to ᴬAshdod. ²Then the Philistines took the ark of God and brought it into ᴬthe house of Dagon, and placed it beside Dagon. ³When the Ashdodites got up early the next day, behold, ᴬDagon had fallen on his face to the ground before the ark of the Lord. So they took Dagon and set him back in his place. ⁴But when they got up early the next morning, behold, ᴬDagon had fallen on his face to the ground before the ark of the Lord. And the head of Dagon and both palms of his hands *were* cut off on the threshold; only the torso of Dagon was left. ⁵For that reason neither the priests of Dagon nor any who enter Dagon's house ᴬstep on the threshold of Dagon in Ashdod to this day.

⁶Now ᴬthe hand of the Lord was heavy on the Ashdodites, and He made them feel devastated and struck them with tumors, *both* Ashdod and its territories. ⁷When the men of Ashdod saw that it was so, they said, "The ark of the God

of Israel must not remain with us, because His hand is severe on us and on Dagon our god." ⁸So they sent *word* and ᴬgathered all the governors of the Philistines to them, and said, "What shall we do with the ark of the God of Israel?" And they said, "Have the ark of the God of Israel brought to Gath." So they took the ark of the God of Israel away. ⁹After they had taken it away, the hand of the Lord was against the city, *creating* a very great panic; and He struck the people of the city, from the young to the old, so that ᴬtumors broke out on them. ¹⁰So they sent the ark of God to Ekron. And as the ark of God came to Ekron, the Ekronites cried out, saying, "They have brought the ark of the God of Israel to us, to kill us and our people!" ¹¹Therefore they sent *word* and gathered all the governors of the Philistines, and said, "Send away the ark of the God of Israel and let it return to its own place, so that it will not kill us and our people!" For there was a deadly panic throughout the city; ᴬthe hand of God was very heavy there. ¹²And the people who did not die were struck with tumors, and ᴬthe outcry of the city went up to heaven.

THE ARK RETURNED TO ISRAEL

6 Now the ark of the Lord had been in the territory of the Philistines for seven months. ²And ᴬthe Philistines called for the priests and the diviners, saying, "What are we

4:20ᴬGen 35:16-19   4:21ᴬ1 Sam 4:11   5:1ᴬJosh 13:3   5:2ᴬJudg 16:23-30; 1 Chr 10:8-10   5:3ᴬIs 19:1; 46:1, 2   5:4ᴬEzek 6:4, 6; Mic 1:7   5:5ᴬZeph 1:9   5:6ᴬPs 145:20; Acts 13:11   5:8ᴬ1 Sam 5:11; 29:6-11   5:9ᴬ1 Sam 5:6   5:11ᴬ1 Sam 5:6, 9   5:12ᴬEx 12:30; Is 15:3   6:2ᴬEx 7:11; Is 2:6
4:21¹I.e., no glory, or where is the glory?

to do with the ark of the LORD? Tell us how we may send it to its place."

³ And they said, "If you are going to send the ark of the God of Israel away, ^do not send it empty; but you shall certainly ᴮreturn to Him a guilt offering. Then you will be healed, and it will be revealed to you why His hand does not leave you."

⁴ Then they said, "What is to be the guilt offering that we shall return to Him?" And they said, "Five gold tumors and five gold mice ^*corresponding to* the number of the governors of the Philistines, since one plague was on all of you and on your governors. ⁵ So you shall make likenesses of your tumors and likenesses of your mice that are ruining the land, and ^you shall give glory to the God of Israel; perhaps ᴮHe will lighten His hand from you, your gods, and your land. ⁶ Why then do you harden your hearts ^as the Egyptians and Pharaoh hardened their hearts? When He had severely dealt with them, ᴮdid they not let the people go, and they left? ⁷ Now then, take and prepare a new cart and two milk cows on which there ^has never been a yoke; and hitch the cows to the cart and take their calves back home, away from them. ⁸ Then take the ark of the LORD and place it on the cart; and put ^the articles of gold which you return to Him as a guilt offering in a saddlebag by its side. Then send it away that it may go. ⁹ But watch: if it goes up by the way of its own territory to ^Beth-shemesh, then He has done this great evil to us. But if not, then we will know that it was not His hand that struck us; it happened to us by chance."

¹⁰ Then the men did so: they took two milk cows and hitched them to

the cart, and shut in their calves at home. ¹¹ And they put the ark of the LORD on the cart, and the saddlebag with the gold mice and the likenesses of their tumors. ¹² Now the cows went straight in the direction of Beth-shemesh; they went on ^the same road, bellowing as they went, and did not turn off to the right or to the left. And the governors of the Philistines followed them to the border of Beth-shemesh.

¹³ Now *the people of* Beth-shemesh were gathering in their wheat harvest in the valley, and they raised their eyes and saw the ark, and rejoiced at seeing *it*. ¹⁴ And the cart came into the field of Joshua the Beth-shemite and stopped there where there *was* a large stone; and they split the wood of the cart and ^offered the cows as a burnt offering to the LORD. ¹⁵ And ^the Levites took down the ark of the LORD and the saddlebag that was with it, in which were the articles of gold, and put them on the large stone; and the men of Beth-shemesh offered burnt offerings and sacrificed sacrifices that day to the LORD. ¹⁶ When the ^five governors of the Philistines saw *it,* they returned to Ekron that day.

¹⁷ Now ^these are the gold tumors which the Philistines returned as a guilt offering to the LORD: one for Ashdod, one for Gaza, one for Ashkelon, one for Gath, *and* one for Ekron; ¹⁸ and the gold mice, *corresponding* to the number of all the cities of the Philistines belonging to the five governors, ^both of

6:3 ^Deut 16:16   ᴮLev 5:15, 16   6:4 ^Josh 13:3;
1 Sam 6:17, 18   6:5 ^Josh 7:19   ᴮ1 Sam 5:6, 11
6:6 ^Ex 7:13   ᴮEx 12:31   6:7 ^Num 19:2; Deut 21:3, 4
6:8 ^1 Sam 6:4, 5   6:9 ^Josh 15:10; 21:16
6:12 ^Num 20:19   6:14 ^2 Sam 24:22; 1 Kin 19:21
6:15 ^Josh 3:3   6:16 ^Josh 13:3; Judg 3:3
6:17 ^1 Sam 6:4   6:18 ^Deut 3:5

fortified cities and of country villages. ⁸The large stone on which they placed the ark of the LORD *is a witness* to this day in the field of Joshua the Beth-shemite.

¹⁹ᴬNow He fatally struck some of the men of Beth-shemesh because they had looked into the ark of the LORD. He struck 50,070 men among the people, and the people mourned because the LORD had struck the people with a great slaughter. ²⁰And the men of Beth-shemesh said, "ᴬWho is able to stand before the LORD, this holy God? And to whom will He go up from us?" ²¹So they sent messengers to the inhabitants of ᴬKiriath-jearim, saying, "The Philistines have brought back the ark of the LORD; come down and take it up to yourselves."

ISRAEL SAVED FROM THE PHILISTINES

7 And the men of Kiriath-jearim came and took the ark of the LORD and ᴬbrought it into the house of Abinadab on the hill, and they consecrated his son Eleazar to watch over the ark of the LORD. ²From the day that the ark remained at Kiriath-jearim, the time was long, for it was twenty years; and all the house of Israel mourned after the LORD.

³Then Samuel spoke to all the house of Israel, saying, "ᴬIf you are returning to the LORD with all your heart, then remove the foreign gods and the Ashtaroth from among you, and direct your hearts to the LORD and ᴮserve Him alone; and He will save you from the hand of the Philistines." ⁴So the sons of Israel removed the Baals and the Ashtaroth, and served the LORD alone.

⁵Then Samuel said, "Gather all Israel to ᴬMizpah and I will pray to the LORD for you." ⁶So they gathered to Mizpah, and drew water and poured it out before the LORD, and fasted on that day and said there, "ᴬWe have sinned against the LORD." And Samuel judged the sons of Israel at Mizpah.

⁷Now when the Philistines heard that the sons of Israel had gathered at Mizpah, the governors of the Philistines went up against Israel. And when the sons of Israel heard *about it,* ᴬthey were afraid of the Philistines. ⁸So the sons of Israel said to Samuel, "ᴬDo not stop crying out to the LORD our God for us, that He will save us from the hand of the Philistines!" ⁹Samuel took ᴬa nursing lamb and offered it as a whole burnt offering to the LORD; and Samuel cried out to the LORD for Israel, and the LORD answered him. ¹⁰Now Samuel was offering up the burnt offering, and the Philistines advanced to battle Israel. But ᴬthe LORD thundered with a great thunder on that day against the Philistines and confused them, so that they were struck down before Israel. ¹¹And the men of Israel came out of Mizpah and pursued the Philistines, and killed them as far as below Beth-car.

¹²Then Samuel ᴬtook a stone and placed it between Mizpah and Shen, and named it ¹Ebenezer, saying, "So far the LORD has helped us." ¹³So the Philistines were subdued,

6:18 ᴮ1 Sam 6:14, 15   6:19ᴬEx 19:21; Num 4:5, 15, 20
6:20ᴬMal 3:2; Rev 6:17   6:21ᴬJosh 15:9, 60;
1 Chr 13:5, 6   7:1ᴬ2 Sam 6:3, 4   7:3ᴬJoel 2:12-14
ᴮLuke 4:8   7:5ᴬJudg 10:17; 20:1   7:6ᴬJudg 10:10;
Ps 106:6   7:7ᴬ1 Sam 13:6; 17:11   7:8ᴬ1 Sam 12:19-24;
Is 37:4   7:9ᴬLev 22:27   7:10ᴬ2 Sam 22:14, 15;
Ps 29:3, 4   7:12ᴬGen 35:14; Josh 24:26

7:12¹I.e., the stone of help

and ^they did not come anymore within the border of Israel. And the hand of the LORD was against the Philistines all the days of Samuel. ¹⁴The cities which the Philistines had taken from Israel were restored to Israel, from Ekron even to Gath; and Israel recovered their territory from the hand of the Philistines. So there was peace between Israel and ^the Amorites.

SAMUEL'S MINISTRY

¹⁵Now Samuel ^judged Israel all the days of his life. ¹⁶And he used to go annually on a circuit to ^Bethel, Gilgal, and Mizpah, and he judged Israel in all these places. ¹⁷Then *he would make* his return to ^Ramah, because his house *was* there, and there he *also* judged Israel; and there he built an altar to the LORD.

ISRAEL DEMANDS A KING

8 Now it came about, when Samuel was old, that ^he appointed his sons as judges over Israel. ²The name of his firstborn was Joel, and the name of his second, Abijah; *they were* judging in ^Beersheba. ³His sons, however, did not walk in his ways but turned aside after dishonest gain, and they ^took bribes and perverted justice.

⁴Then all the elders of Israel gathered together and came to Samuel at ^Ramah; ⁵and they said to him, "Behold, you have grown old, and your sons do not walk in your ways. Now ^appoint us a king to judge us like all the nations." ⁶But the matter was ^displeasing in the sight of Samuel when they said, "Give us a king to judge us." And Samuel prayed to the LORD. ⁷And the LORD said to Samuel, "Listen to the voice of the people regarding all that they

say to you, because ^they have not rejected you, but they have rejected Me from being King over them. ⁸Like all the deeds which they have done since the day that I brought them up from Egypt even to this day—in that they have abandoned Me and served other gods—so they are doing to you as well. ⁹Now then, listen to their voice; however, you shall warn them strongly and tell them of ^the practice of the king who will reign over them."

WARNING CONCERNING A KING

¹⁰So Samuel spoke all the words of the LORD to ^the people who had asked him for a king. ¹¹And he said, "This will be the practice of the king who will reign over you: ^he will take your sons and put *them* in his chariots for himself and among his horsemen, and ^they will run before his chariots. ¹²^He will appoint for himself commanders of thousands and commanders of fifties, and *some* to do his plowing and to gather in his harvest, and to make his weapons of war and equipment for his chariots. ¹³He will also take your daughters *and use them* as perfumers, cooks, and bakers. ¹⁴^He will take the best of your fields, your vineyards, and your olive groves, and give *them* to his servants. ¹⁵And he will take a tenth of your seed and your vineyards and give *it* to his high officials and his servants. ¹⁶He will also take your male servants and your female servants, and your best young men, and your donkeys, and use *them* for

7:13^1 Sam 13:5   7:14^Num 13:29; Josh 10:5-10
7:15^1 Sam 7:6   7:16^Gen 28:19; 35:6
7:17^1 Sam 1:1, 19; 2:11   8:1^Deut 16:18, 19
8:2^1 Kin 19:3; Amos 5:5   8:3^Ex 23:6, 8; Deut 16:19
8:4^1 Sam 7:17   8:5^Deut 17:14, 15   8:6^1 Sam 12:17
8:7^Ex 16:8; 1 Sam 10:19   8:9^1 Sam 8:11-18; 10:25
8:10^1 Sam 8:4   8:11^1 Sam 14:52   ᴮ2 Sam 15:1
8:12^Num 31:14; 1 Sam 22:7   8:14^1 Kin 21:7; Ezek 46:18

his work. ¹⁷He will take a tenth of your flocks, and you yourselves will become his servants. ¹⁸Then ᴬyou will cry out on that day because of your king whom you have chosen for yourselves, but the LORD will not answer you on that day."

¹⁹Yet the people ᴬrefused to listen to the voice of Samuel, and they said, "No, but there shall be a king over us, ²⁰ᴬso that we also may be like all the nations, and our king may judge us and go out before us and fight our battles." ²¹Now after Samuel had heard all the words of the people, ᴬhe repeated them in the LORD's hearing. ²²And the LORD said to Samuel, "ᴬListen to their voice and appoint a king for them." So Samuel said to the men of Israel, "Go, every man to his city."

SAUL'S SEARCH

9 Now there was a man of Benjamin whose name was ᴬKish the son of Abiel, son of Zeror, son of Becorath, son of Aphiah, son of a Benjaminite, a ¹valiant mighty man. ²He had a son whose name was Saul, a young and handsome *man,* and there was not a more handsome man than he among the sons of Israel; ᴬfrom his shoulders and up he was taller than any of the people.

³Now the donkeys of Kish, Saul's father, had wandered off. So Kish said to his son Saul, "Now take with you one of the servants and arise, go search for the donkeys." ⁴So he passed through ᴬthe hill country of Ephraim and passed through the land of Shalishah, but they did not find *them.* Then they passed through the land of Shaalim, but they were not *there.* Then he passed through the land of the Benjaminites, but they did not find *them.*

⁵When they came to the land of ᴬZuph, Saul said to his servant who was with him, "Come, and let's return, or else my father will stop *being concerned* about the donkeys and will become anxious about us." ⁶But he said to him, "Behold now, *there is* ᴬa man of God in this city, and the man is held in honor; ᴮeverything that he says definitely comes *true.* Now let's go there, perhaps he can tell us about our journey on which we have set out." ⁷Then Saul said to his servant, "But look, if we go, what shall we bring the man? For the bread is gone from our sacks and there is ᴬno gift to bring to the man of God. What do we have?" ⁸The servant answered Saul again and said, "Look, I have in my hand a fourth of a shekel of silver; I will give *it* to the man of God and he will ᴬtell us our way." ⁹(Previously in Israel, when a man went to inquire of God, he used to say, "Come, and let's go to the seer"; for *he who is called* a prophet now was previously called ᴬa seer.) ¹⁰Then Saul said to his servant, "Good idea; come, let's go." So they went to the city where the man of God was.

¹¹As they went up the slope to the city, ᴬthey found young women going out to draw water, and they said to them, "Is the seer here?" ¹²They answered them and said, "He is; see, *he is* ahead of you. Hurry now, for he has come into the city today, because ᴬthe people have a sacrifice on the high place today.

8:18ᴬIs 8:21 8:19ᴬIs 66:4; Jer 44:16 8:20ᴬ1 Sam 8:5
8:21ᴬJudg 11:11 8:22ᴬ1 Sam 8:7 9:1ᴬ1 Sam 14:51;
1 Chr 9:36-39 9:2ᴬ1 Sam 10:23 9:4ᴬJosh 24:33
9:5ᴬ1 Sam 1:1 9:6ᴬDeut 33:1 ᴮ1 Sam 3:19
9:7ᴬ2 Kin 8:8, 9; Ezek 13:19 9:8ᴬ1 Sam 9:6
9:9ᴬIs 30:10; Amos 7:12 9:11ᴬGen 24:11, 15; Ex 2:16
9:12ᴬNum 28:11-15; 1 Kin 3:2

9:1¹Or *man of wealth and influence*

¹³As soon as you enter the city you will find him before he goes up to the high place to eat, for the people will not eat until he comes, because ᴬhe must bless the sacrifice; afterward those who are invited will eat. Now then, go up, for you will find him about this time." ¹⁴So they went up to the city. As they came into the city, behold, Samuel was coming out toward them to go up to the high place.

GOD'S CHOICE FOR KING

¹⁵Now a day before Saul's coming, ᴬthe LORD had revealed *this* to Samuel, saying, ¹⁶"About this time tomorrow I will send you a man from the land of Benjamin, and ᴬyou shall anoint him as ruler over My people Israel; and he will save My people from the hand of the Philistines. For ᴮI have considered My people, because their outcry has come to Me." ¹⁷When Samuel saw Saul, the LORD said to him, "ᴬBehold, the man of whom I spoke to you! This one shall rule over My people." ¹⁸Then Saul approached Samuel at the gateway and said, "Please tell me where the seer's house is." ¹⁹And Samuel answered Saul and said, "I am the seer. Go up ahead of me to the high place, for you shall eat with me today; and in the morning I will let you go, and will tell you everything that is on your mind. ²⁰And as for your donkeys that wandered off three days ago, do not be concerned about them, for they have been found. And ᴬfor whom is everything that is desirable in Israel? Is it not for you and for all your father's household?" ²¹Saul replied, "ᴬAm I not a Benjaminite, of the smallest of the tribes of Israel, and my family the

least of all the families of the tribe of Benjamin? Why then have you spoken to me in this way?"

²²Then Samuel took Saul and his servant and brought them into the hall, and gave them a place at the head of those who were invited, who were about thirty men. ²³And Samuel said to the cook, "Serve the portion that I gave you about which I said to you, 'Set it aside.'" ²⁴Then the cook ᴬtook up the leg with what was on it and placed *it* before Saul. And *Samuel* said, "Here is what has been reserved! Place *it* before you *and* eat, because it has been kept for you until the appointed time, since I said I have invited the people." So Saul ate with Samuel that day.

²⁵When they came down from the high place *into* the city, ¹*Samuel* spoke with Saul ᴬon the roof. ²⁶And they got up early; and at daybreak Samuel called to Saul on the roof, saying, "Get up, so that I may send you on your way." So Saul got up, and both he and Samuel went out into the street. ²⁷As they were going down to the edge of the city, Samuel said to Saul, "Speak to the servant and have him go on ahead of us and pass by; but you stand *here* now, so that I may proclaim the word of God to you."

SAUL AMONG THE PROPHETS

10 Then ᴬSamuel took the flask of oil, poured it on Saul's head, kissed him, and said, "Has ᴮthe LORD not anointed you as ruler over His inheritance? ²When you

9:13ᴬLuke 9:16; John 6:11   9:15ᴬ1 Sam 15:1; Acts 13:21
9:16ᴬ1 Sam 10:1   ᴮEx 3:7, 9   9:17ᴬ1 Sam 16:12
9:20ᴬ1 Sam 8:5; 12:13   9:21ᴬ1 Sam 15:17
9:24ᴬEx 29:22, 27; Lev 7:32, 33   9:25ᴬLuke 5:19;
Acts 10:9   10:1ᴬEx 30:23-33   ᴮ1 Sam 16:13

9:25¹LXX they spread a bed *for Saul on the roof*

leave me today, then you will find two men close to ᴬRachel's tomb in the territory of Benjamin at Zelzah; and they will say to you, 'The donkeys which you went to look for have been found. Now behold, your father has stopped talking about the donkeys and is anxious about you, saying, "What am I to do about my son?"' ³Then you will go on farther from there, and you will come as far as the oak of Tabor, and there three men going up ᴬto God at Bethel will meet you: one carrying three young goats, another carrying three loaves of bread, and another carrying a jug of wine. ⁴And they will greet you and give you two *loaves* of bread, *which* you will accept from their hand. ⁵Afterward you will come to ᴬthe hill of God where the Philistine garrison is; and it shall be as soon as you have come there to the city, that you will meet a group of prophets coming down from the high place with harp, tambourine, flute, and a lyre in front of them, and they will be prophesying. ⁶Then ᴬthe Spirit of the LORD will rush upon you, and you will prophesy with them and be changed into a different man. ⁷And it shall be when these signs come to you, ᴬdo for yourself what the occasion requires, because God is with you. ⁸And ᴬyou shall go down ahead of me to Gilgal; and behold, I will be coming down to you to offer burnt offerings and sacrifice peace offerings. You shall wait seven days until I come to you and inform you of what you should do."

⁹Then it happened, when he turned his back to leave Samuel, that God ᴬchanged his heart; and all those signs came about on that day. ¹⁰ᴬWhen they came there to the hill,

behold, a group of prophets met him; and the Spirit of God rushed upon him, so that he prophesied among them. ¹¹And it came about, when all who previously knew him saw that he was indeed prophesying with the prophets, that the people said to one another, "What is this that has happened to the son of Kish? ᴬIs Saul also among the prophets?" ¹²And a man from there responded and said, "And who is their father?" Therefore it became a saying: "ᴬIs Saul also among the prophets?" ¹³When he had finished prophesying, he came to the high place.

¹⁴Now Saul's uncle said to him and his servant, "Where did you go?" And he said, "ᴬTo look for the donkeys. When we saw that they were nowhere *to be found,* we went to Samuel." ¹⁵Saul's uncle said, "Please tell me what Samuel said to you." ¹⁶So Saul said to his uncle, "ᴬHe told us plainly that the donkeys had been found." But he did not tell him about the matter of the kingdom which Samuel had mentioned.

SAUL PUBLICLY CHOSEN KING

¹⁷Now Samuel called the ᴬpeople together to the LORD at Mizpah; ¹⁸and he said to the sons of Israel, "ᴬThis is what the LORD, the God of Israel says: 'I brought Israel up from Egypt, and I rescued you from the hand of the Egyptians and from the power of all the kingdoms that were oppressing you.' ¹⁹But today you ᴬhave rejected your God, who saves you from all your catastrophes and

10:2ᴬGen 35:16-20; 48:7   10:3ᴬGen 35:1, 3, 7
10:5ᴬ1 Sam 13:2, 3   10:6ᴬNum 11:25, 29; Judg 14:6
10:7ᴬEccl 9:10   10:8ᴬ1 Sam 11:14; 13:8
10:9ᴬ1 Sam 10:6   10:10ᴬ1 Sam 10:5, 6; 19:20
10:11ᴬAmos 7:14, 15; Matt 13:54-57
10:12ᴬ1 Sam 19:23, 24   10:14ᴬ1 Sam 9:3-6
10:16ᴬ1 Sam 9:20   10:17ᴬJudg 20:1; 1 Sam 7:5
10:18ᴬJudg 6:8, 9   10:19ᴬ1 Sam 8:6, 7

your distresses; yet you have said, 'No, but put a king over us!' Now then, ᴮpresent yourselves before the Lᴏʀᴅ by your tribes and by your groups of thousands."

²⁰ So Samuel brought all the tribes of Israel forward; and the tribe of Benjamin was selected by lot. ²¹ Then he brought the tribe of Benjamin forward by its families, and the Matrite family was selected by lot. And Saul the son of Kish was selected by lot; but when they looked for him, he could not be found. ²² Therefore ᴬthey inquired further of the Lᴏʀᴅ: "Has the man come here yet?" And the Lᴏʀᴅ said, "Behold, he is hiding himself among the baggage." ²³ So they ran and took him from there, and when he stood among the people, ᴬhe was taller than any of the people from his shoulders upward. ²⁴ Samuel said to all the people, "Do you see him ᴬwhom the Lᴏʀᴅ has chosen? Surely there is no one like him among all the people." So all the people shouted and said, "*Long* live the king!"

²⁵ Then Samuel told the people ᴬthe ordinances of the kingdom, and wrote *them* in the book, and placed *it* before the Lᴏʀᴅ. And Samuel sent all the people away, each one to his house. ²⁶ Saul also went ᴬto his house in Gibeah; and the valiant *men* whose hearts God had touched went with him. ²⁷ But certain ᴬuseless men said, "How can this one save us?" And they despised him and did not bring him a gift. But he kept silent *about it*.

SAUL DEFEATS THE AMMONITES

11 Now Nahash the Ammonite went up and besieged Jabesh-gilead; and all the men of Jabesh said to Nahash, "Make ᴬa covenant with us and we will serve you." ² But Nahash the Ammonite said to them, "I will make *it* with you on this condition, that I will gouge out the right eye of every one of you, and *thereby* I will inflict ᴬa disgrace on all Israel." ³ So ᴬthe elders of Jabesh said to him, "Allow us seven days to send messengers throughout the territory of Israel. Then, if there is no one to save us, we will come out to you." ⁴ Then the messengers came ᴬto Gibeah of Saul and spoke *these* words in the hearing of the people, and all the people raised their voices and wept.

⁵ Now behold, Saul was coming from the field ᴬbehind the oxen, and Saul said, "What is *the matter* with the people that they weep?" So they reported to him the words of the men of Jabesh. ⁶ Then ᴬthe Spirit of God rushed upon Saul when he heard these words, and he became very angry. ⁷ He then took a yoke of oxen and ᴬcut them in pieces, and sent *them* throughout the territory of Israel by the hand of messengers, saying, "Whoever does not come out after Saul and after Samuel, the same shall be done to his oxen." Then the dread of the Lᴏʀᴅ fell on the people, and they came out as one person. ⁸ He counted them in Bezek; and the ᴬsons of Israel were three hundred thousand, and the men of Judah, thirty thousand. ⁹ They said to the messengers who had come, "This is what you shall say to the men of Jabesh-gilead: 'Tomorrow,

10:19 ᴮJosh 7:14-18　**10:22**ᴬ1 Sam 23:2, 4
10:23ᴬ1 Sam 9:2　**10:24**ᴬDeut 17:15; 2 Sam 21:6
10:25ᴬDeut 17:14-20; 1 Sam 8:11-18　**10:26**ᴬ1 Sam 11:4;
15:34　**10:27**ᴬDeut 13:13; 1 Sam 25:17　**11:1**ᴬJob 41:4;
Ezek 17:13　**11:2**ᴬ1 Sam 17:26; Ps 44:13　**11:3**ᴬ1 Sam 8:4
11:4ᴬ1 Sam 10:26; 15:34　**11:5**ᴬ1 Kin 19:19
11:6ᴬJudg 3:10; 1 Sam 10:10　**11:7**ᴬJudg 19:29
11:8ᴬJudg 20:2

by the time the sun is hot, you will be saved.'" So the messengers went and told the men of Jabesh; and they rejoiced. ¹⁰Then the men of Jabesh said, "ᴬTomorrow we will come out to you, and you may do to us whatever seems good to you." ¹¹The next morning Saul put the people ᴬin three companies; and they came into the midst of the camp at the morning watch, and struck and killed the Ammonites until the heat of the day. And those who survived scattered, so that no two of them were left together.

¹²Then the people said to Samuel, "ᴬWho is he that said, 'Shall Saul reign over us?' ᴮBring the men, so that we may put them to death!" ¹³But Saul said, "Not a single person shall be put to death this day, for today ᴬthe Lᴏʀᴅ has brought about victory in Israel."

¹⁴Then Samuel said to the people, "Come, and let us go to Gilgal and ᴬrenew the kingdom there." ¹⁵So all the people went to Gilgal, and there they made Saul king ᴬbefore the Lᴏʀᴅ in Gilgal. There they also ᴮoffered sacrifices of peace offerings before the Lᴏʀᴅ; and there Saul and all the men of Israel rejoiced greatly.

SAMUEL ADDRESSES ISRAEL

12 Then Samuel said to all Israel, "Behold, ᴬI have listened to your voice for all that you said to me, and I ᴮhave appointed a king over you. ²Now, here is the king walking before you, but as for me, ᴬI am old and gray, and my sons are here with you. And ᴮI have walked before you since my youth to this day. ³Here I am; testify against me before the Lᴏʀᴅ and ᴬHis anointed. Whose ox have

I taken, or whose donkey have I taken, or whom have I exploited? Whom have I oppressed, or from whose hand have I taken a bribe to close my eyes with it? I will return *it* to you." ⁴And they said, "You have not exploited us or oppressed us, or taken anything from anyone's hand." ⁵So he said to them, "The Lᴏʀᴅ is witness against you, and His anointed is witness this day that you have found nothing ᴬin my hand." And they said, "*He is* witness."

⁶Then Samuel said to the people, "It is the Lᴏʀᴅ who ᴬappointed Moses and Aaron and who brought your fathers up from the land of Egypt. ⁷Now then, take your stand, ᴬso that I may enter into judgment with you before the Lᴏʀᴅ concerning all the righteous acts of the Lᴏʀᴅ that He did for you and your fathers. ⁸ᴬWhen Jacob went into Egypt and your fathers cried out to the Lᴏʀᴅ, then the Lᴏʀᴅ sent Moses and Aaron who brought your fathers out of Egypt and settled them in this place. ⁹But ᴬthey forgot the Lᴏʀᴅ their God, so He sold them into the hand of Sisera, commander of the army of Hazor, and into the hand of the Philistines, and into the hand of the king of Moab, and they fought against them. ¹⁰ᴬThey cried out to the Lᴏʀᴅ and said, 'We have sinned, because we have abandoned the Lᴏʀᴅ and have served the Baals and the Ashtaroth; but now save us from the hands of our enemies, and we will serve

11:10ᴬ1 Sam 11:3   11:11ᴬJudg 7:16, 20
11:12ᴬ1 Sam 10:27   ᴮLuke 19:27   11:13ᴬEx 14:13, 30;
1 Sam 19:5   11:14ᴬ1 Sam 10:25   11:15ᴬ1 Sam 10:17
ᴮ1 Sam 10:8   12:1ᴬ1 Sam 8:7, 9, 22   ᴮ1 Sam 11:14, 15
12:2ᴬ1 Sam 8:1, 5   ᴮ1 Sam 3:10, 19, 20   12:3ᴬ1 Sam 10:1;
2 Sam 1:14   12:5ᴬEx 22:4   12:6ᴬEx 6:26; Mic 6:4
12:7ᴬEzek 20:35; Mic 6:1-5   12:8ᴬGen 46:5, 6
12:9ᴬDeut 32:18; Judg 3:7   12:10ᴬJudg 10:10

You.' ¹¹Then the LORD sent ^Jerub-baal, ¹Bedan, ᴮJephthah, and Samuel, and saved you from the hands of your enemies all around, so that you lived in security.

THE KING CONFIRMED

¹²But when you saw that Nahash the king of the sons of Ammon was coming against you, you said to me, 'No, but a king shall reign over us!' ^Yet the LORD your God *was* your king. ¹³And now, ^behold, the king whom you have chosen, whom you have asked for, and behold, the LORD has put a king over you. ¹⁴^If you will fear the LORD and serve Him, and listen to His voice and not rebel against the command of the LORD, then both you and the king who reigns over you will follow the LORD your God. ¹⁵But if you do not listen to the voice of the LORD, but rebel against the command of the LORD, then ^the hand of the LORD will be against you, ᴮeven *as it was* against your fathers. ¹⁶Even now, ^take your stand and see this great thing which the LORD is going to do before your eyes. ¹⁷^Is it not the wheat harvest today? I will call to the LORD, that He will send thunder and rain. Then you will know and see that your wickedness is great which you have done in the sight of the LORD, by asking for yourselves a king." ¹⁸So Samuel called to the LORD, and the LORD sent thunder and rain that day; and ^all the people greatly feared the LORD and Samuel.

¹⁹Then all the people said to Samuel, "Pray to the LORD your God for your servants, so that we do not die; for we have added to all our sins ^*this* evil, by asking for ourselves a king." ²⁰Samuel said to the people, "Do not fear. You have committed all this evil, yet ^do not turn aside from following the LORD, but serve the LORD with all your heart. ²¹Indeed, you must not turn aside, for *then you would go* after ^useless things which cannot benefit or save, because they are useless. ²²For ^the LORD will not abandon His people on account of His great name, because the LORD has been pleased to make you a people for Himself. ²³Furthermore, as for me, far be it from me that I would sin against the LORD by ceasing to pray for you; but ^I will instruct you in the good and right way. ²⁴Only fear the LORD and serve Him in truth with all your heart; for consider ^what great things He has done for you. ²⁵^But if you still do evil, both you and your king ᴮwill be swept away."

WAR WITH THE PHILISTINES

13 Saul was ¹*thirty* years old when he began to reign, and he reigned for ²*forty*-two years over Israel.

²Now Saul chose for himself three thousand men of Israel, of whom two thousand were with Saul in ^Michmash and in the hill country of Bethel, while a thousand were with Jonathan at ᴮGibeah of Benjamin. But he sent the rest of the people away, each to his tent. ³And Jonathan attacked ^the garrison of the Philistines that was in Geba, and the Philistines heard

---

12:11 ¹Judg 6:31, 32 ᴮJudg 11:29 12:12 ^Judg 8:23; 1 Sam 8:7 12:13 ^1 Sam 10:24 12:14 ^Josh 24:14 12:15 ^1 Sam 5:9 ᴮ1 Sam 12:9 12:16 ^Ex 14:13, 31 12:17 ^Prov 26:1 12:18 ^Ex 14:31 12:19 ^1 Sam 12:17, 20 12:20 ^Deut 11:16 12:21 ^Is 41:29; Hab 2:18 12:22 ^Deut 31:6; 1 Kin 6:13 12:23 ^Ps 34:11; Prov 4:11 12:24 ^Deut 10:21; Is 5:12 12:25 ^Is 1:20 ᴮ1 Sam 31:1–5 13:2 ^1 Sam 13:5 ᴮ1 Sam 10:26 13:3 ^1 Sam 10:5

12:11 ¹LXX and Syriac *Barak* 13:1 ¹As in some LXX mss, but very uncertain; MT *one year old* ²See Acts 13:21; Heb *two years*

about it. Then Saul blew the trumpet throughout the land, saying, "Let the Hebrews hear!" 4And all Israel heard the news that Saul had attacked the garrison of the Philistines, and also that Israel ^had become repulsive to the Philistines. Then the people were summoned to Saul at Gilgal.

5Now the Philistines assembled to fight with Israel, thirty thousand chariots and six thousand horsemen, and ^people like the sand which is on the seashore in abundance; and they came up and camped in Michmash, east of Beth-aven. 6When the men of Israel saw that they were in trouble (for the people were hard-pressed), then ^the people kept themselves hidden in caves, in crevices, in cliffs, in crypts, and in pits. 7And *some of* the Hebrews crossed the Jordan *into* the land of ^Gad and Gilead. But as for Saul, he was still in Gilgal, and all the people followed him, trembling.

8Now ^he waited for seven days, until the appointed time that Samuel *had set,* but Samuel did not come to Gilgal; and the people were scattering from him. 9So Saul said, "Bring me the burnt offering and the peace offerings." And ^he offered the burnt offering. 10But as soon as he finished offering the burnt offering, behold, Samuel came; and ^Saul went out to meet him *and* to greet him. 11But Samuel said, "What have you done?" And Saul said, "Since I saw that the people were scattering from me, and that you did not come at the appointed time, and that ^the Philistines were assembling at Michmash, 12I thought, 'Now the Philistines will come down

against me at Gilgal, and I have not asked the favor of the LORD.' So I worked up the courage and offered the burnt offering." 13But Samuel said to Saul, "^You have acted foolishly! ^You have not kept the commandment of the LORD your God, which He commanded you, for the LORD would now have established your kingdom over Israel forever. 14But ^now your kingdom shall not endure. The LORD has sought for Himself a man after His own heart, and the LORD has appointed him ruler over His people, because you have not kept what the LORD commanded you."

15Then Samuel set out and went up from Gilgal to Gibeah of Benjamin. And Saul counted the people who were present with him, ^about six hundred men. 16Now Saul, his son Jonathan, and the people who were present with them were staying in ^Geba of Benjamin while the Philistines camped at Michmash. 17Then ^raiders came from the camp of the Philistines in three companies: one company turned toward ^Ophrah, to the land of Shual, 18and another company turned toward ^Beth-horon, and another company turned toward the border that overlooks the Valley of ^Zeboim toward the wilderness.

19Now ^no blacksmith could be found in all the land of Israel, because the Philistines said, "Otherwise the Hebrews will make swords or spears." 20So all Israel

13:4 ^Ex 5:21; 2 Sam 10:6   13:5 ^Josh 11:4
13:6 ^Judg 6:2   13:7 ^Num 32:33   13:8 ^1 Sam 10:8
13:9 ^Deut 12:5-14; 1 Kin 3:4   13:10 ^1 Sam 15:13
13:11 ^1 Sam 13:2, 5, 16, 23   13:13 ^2 Chr 16:9
^1 Sam 15:11, 22, 28   13:14 ^1 Sam 15:28
13:15 ^1 Sam 13:2, 6, 7; 14:2   13:16 ^1 Sam 13:2, 3
13:17 ^1 Sam 14:15   ^Josh 18:23   13:18 ^Josh 18:13, 14
^Neh 11:34   13:19 ^Judg 5:8; Jer 24:1

went down to the Philistines, each to sharpen his plowshare, his mattock, his axe; and his hoe. ²¹The charge was two-thirds of a shekel for the plowshares, the mattocks, the forks, and the axes, and to fix the ¹cattle goads. ²²So it came about on the day of battle that ᴬneither sword nor spear was found in the hands of any of the people who *were* with Saul and Jonathan, but they were found with Saul and his son Jonathan. ²³And ᴬthe garrison of the Philistines went out to the gorge of Michmash.

JONATHAN'S VICTORY

14 Now the day came that Jonathan, the son of Saul, said to the young man who was carrying his armor, "Come, and let's cross over to the Philistines' garrison that is on the other side." But he did not tell his father. ²Saul was staying on the outskirts of ᴬGibeah under the pomegranate tree that is in ᴮMigron. And the people who *were* with him *numbered* about six hundred men; ³and Ahijah, the son of Ahitub, ᴬIchabod's brother, the son of Phinehas, the son of Eli, the priest of the LORD at ᴮShiloh, was wearing an ephod. And the people did not know that Jonathan had gone. ⁴Now ᴬbetween the gorges by which Jonathan sought to cross over to the Philistines' garrison there was a rocky crag on the one side, and a rocky crag on the other side; and the name of the one was Bozez, and the name of the other, Seneh. ⁵The one crag *rose* on the north opposite Michmash, and the other on the south opposite Geba. ⁶Then Jonathan said to the young man who was carrying his armor, "Come, and let's cross over to the garrison of these uncircumcised *men;* perhaps the LORD will work for us, because ᴬthe LORD is not limited to saving by many or by few!" ⁷His armor bearer said to him, "Do everything that is in your heart; turn yourself *to it, and* here I am with you, as your heart *desires.*" ⁸Then Jonathan said, "ᴬBehold, we are going to cross over to the men and reveal ourselves to them. ⁹If they say to us, 'Wait until we come to you'; then we will stand in our place and not go up to them. ¹⁰But if they say, 'Come up to us,' then we will go up, for the LORD has handed them over to us; and ᴬthis *shall be* the sign to us." ¹¹When the two of them revealed themselves to the garrison of the Philistines, the Philistines said, "Behold, ᴬHebrews are coming out of the holes where they have kept themselves hidden." ¹²So the men of the garrison responded to Jonathan and his armor bearer and said, "Come up to us and we will inform you of something." And Jonathan said to his armor bearer, "Come up after me, for ᴬthe LORD has handed them over to Israel." ¹³Then Jonathan climbed up on his hands and feet, with his armor bearer behind him; and *the men* fell before Jonathan, and his armor bearer put some to death after him. ¹⁴Now that first slaughter which Jonathan and his armor bearer inflicted was about twenty men within about half a furrow in an acre of land. ¹⁵And there was a trembling in the camp, in the field,

13:22ᴬJudg 5:8　**13:23**ᴬ1 Sam 14:1; 2 Sam 23:14
14:2ᴬ1 Sam 13:15, 16　ᴮIs 10:28　**14:3**ᴬ1 Sam 4:21
ᴮ1 Sam 1:3　**14:4**ᴬ1 Sam 13:23　**14:6**ᴬZech 4:6;
Matt 19:26　**14:8**ᴬJudg 7:9-14　**14:10**ᴬGen 24:14;
Judg 6:36　**14:11**ᴬ1 Sam 13:6; 14:22　**14:12**ᴬ2 Sam 5:24

13:21¹I.e., spiked sticks for driving cattle

and among all the people. Even the garrison and ^the raiders trembled, and the earth quaked so that it became a great trembling.

¹⁶ Now Saul's watchmen in Gibeah of Benjamin looked, and behold, the multitude dissolved; they went here *and there.* ¹⁷ So Saul said to the people who *were* with him, "Look carefully now and see who has left us." And when they had looked, behold, Jonathan and his armor bearer were not *there.* ¹⁸ Then Saul said to Ahijah, "^Bring the ark of God here." For at that time the ark of God was with the sons of Israel. ¹⁹ ^While Saul talked to the priest, the commotion in the camp of the Philistines continued and increased; so Saul said to the priest, "Withdraw your hand." ²⁰ Then Saul and all the people who *were* with him rallied and came to the battle; and behold, ^every man's sword was against his fellow *Philistine, and there was* very great confusion. ²¹ Now the Hebrews *who* were with the Philistines previously, who went up with them all around in the camp, even ^they also *returned* to be with the Israelites who *were* with Saul and Jonathan. ²² When all the ^men of Israel who had kept themselves hidden in the hill country of Ephraim heard that the Philistines had fled, they also closely pursued them in the battle. ²³ So ^the Lᴏʀᴅ saved Israel that day, and the battle spread beyond Beth-aven.

SAUL'S FOOLISH ORDER

²⁴ Now the men of Israel were hardpressed on that day, for Saul had ^put the people under oath, saying, "Cursed be the man who eats food before evening, and *before* I

have avenged myself on my enemies." So none of the people tasted food. ²⁵ All *the people of* the land entered the forest, and there was honey on the ground. ²⁶ When the people entered the forest, behold, ^*there was* honey dripping; but no man put his hand to his mouth, because the people feared the oath. ²⁷ However, Jonathan had not heard *it* when his father put the people under oath; so he put out the end of the staff that *was* in his hand and dipped it in the honeycomb, and put his hand to his mouth, and ^his eyes brightened. ²⁸ Then one of the people responded and said, "Your father strictly put the people under oath, saying, 'Cursed be the man who eats food today.'" And the people were weary. ²⁹ Then Jonathan said, "^My father has troubled the land. See now that my eyes have brightened because I tasted a little of this honey. ³⁰ How much more, if only the people had freely eaten today of the spoils of their enemies which they found! For now the defeat among the Philistines has not been great."

³¹ They attacked the Philistines that day from Michmash to ^Aijalon. But the people were very tired. ³² So ^the people loudly rushed upon the spoils, and took sheep, oxen, and calves, and slaughtered *them* on the ground; and the people ate *them* ᴮwith the blood. ³³ Then *observers* informed Saul, saying, "Look, the people are ^sinning against the Lᴏʀᴅ by eating

14:15 ^1 Sam 13:17, 18   **14:18** ^1 Sam 23:9; 30:7
14:19 ^Num 27:21   **14:20** ^Judg 7:22; 2 Chr 20:23
14:21 ^1 Sam 29:4   **14:22** ^1 Sam 13:6
14:23 ^Ex 14:30; 1 Sam 10:19   **14:24** ^Josh 6:26
14:26 ^Matt 3:4   **14:27** ^1 Sam 30:12
14:29 ^Josh 7:25; 1 Kin 18:18   **14:31** ^Josh 10:12
14:32 ^1 Sam 15:19   ᴮLev 17:10-14
14:33 ^Lev 7:26, 27; Deut 12:16, 23-25

meat with the blood." And he said, "You have acted treacherously; roll a large rock to me today." ³⁴Then Saul said, "Disperse yourselves among the people and say to them, 'Each one of you bring me his ox or his sheep, and slaughter *it* here and eat; and do not sin against the LORD by eating *it* with the blood.'" So all the people brought *them* that night, each one his ox with him, and they slaughtered *them* there. ³⁵And ᴬSaul built an altar to the LORD; it was the first altar that he built to the LORD.

³⁶Then Saul said, "Let's go down after the Philistines by night and take plunder among them until the morning light, and let's not leave a man among them alive." And they said, "Do whatever seems good to you." So ᴬthe priest said, "Let's approach God here." ³⁷So Saul inquired of God: "Shall I go down after the Philistines? Will You hand them over to Israel?" But ᴬHe did not answer him on that day. ³⁸Then Saul said, "ᴬCome here, all you leaders of the people, and investigate and see how this sin has happened today. ³⁹For ᴬas the LORD lives, who saves Israel, even if it is in my son Jonathan, he shall assuredly die!" But not one of all the people answered him. ⁴⁰Then he said to all Israel, "You shall be on one side, and I and my son Jonathan will be on the other side." And the people said to Saul, "Do what seems good to you." ⁴¹Therefore, Saul said to the LORD, the God of Israel, "ᴬGive a perfect *lot*." And Jonathan and Saul were selected by lot, but the people were exonerated. ⁴²Then Saul said, "Cast *lots* between me and my son Jonathan." And Jonathan was selected by lot.

⁴³So Saul said to Jonathan, "ᴬTell me what you have done." And Jonathan told him, and said, "I did indeed taste a little honey with the end of the staff that was in my hand. Here I am, I must die!" ⁴⁴And Saul said, "May God do the same *to me* and more also, for ᴬyou shall certainly die, Jonathan!" ⁴⁵But the people said to Saul, "Must Jonathan die, he who has brought about this great victory in Israel? Far from it! As the LORD lives, ᴬnot *even* a hair of his head shall fall to the ground, because ᴮhe has worked with God this day." So the people rescued Jonathan and he did not die. ⁴⁶Then Saul went up from pursuing the Philistines, and the Philistines went to their own place.

CONSTANT WARFARE

⁴⁷Now when Saul had taken control of the kingdom over Israel, he fought against all his enemies on every side, against Moab, ᴬthe sons of Ammon, Edom, the kings of Zobah, and the Philistines; and wherever he turned, he inflicted punishment. ⁴⁸And he acted valiantly and ᴬdefeated the Amalekites, and saved Israel from the hands of those who plundered them.

⁴⁹Now ᴬthe sons of Saul were Jonathan, Ishvi, and Malchi-shua; and the names of his two daughters *were these:* the name of the firstborn *was* Merab, and the name of the younger, ᴮMichal. ⁵⁰And the name of Saul's wife was Ahinoam the daughter of Ahimaaz. And ᴬthe

14:35ᴬ1 Sam 7:12, 17; James 4:8
14:36ᴬ1 Sam 14:3, 18, 19   14:37ᴬ1 Sam 28:6
14:38ᴬJosh 7:11, 12; 1 Sam 10:19, 20
14:39ᴬ1 Sam 14:24, 44; 2 Sam 12:5   14:41ᴬActs 1:24
14:43ᴬJosh 7:19   14:44ᴬ1 Sam 14:39   14:45ᴬActs 27:34
ᴮ2 Cor 6:1   14:47ᴬ1 Sam 11:1-13   14:48ᴬ1 Sam 15:3, 7
14:49ᴬ1 Sam 31:2   ᴮ2 Sam 6:20-23   14:50ᴬ2 Sam 2:8

name of the commander of his army was Abner the son of Ner, Saul's uncle. ⁵¹ᴬKish *was* the father of Saul, and Ner the father of Abner *was* the son of Abiel.

⁵²Now the war against the Philistines was severe all the days of Saul; and when Saul saw any warrior or any valiant man, he ᴬattached him to his staff.

SAUL'S DISOBEDIENCE

15 Then Samuel said to Saul, "ᴬThe Lᴏʀᴅ sent me to anoint you as king over His people, over Israel; now therefore, listen to the words of the Lᴏʀᴅ. ²This is what the Lᴏʀᴅ of armies says: 'I will punish Amalek ᴬ*for* what he did to Israel, in that he obstructed him on the way while he was coming up from Egypt. ³Now go and strike Amalek and completely destroy everything that he has, and do not spare him; but ᴬput to death both man and woman, child and infant, ox and sheep, camel and donkey.'"

⁴Then Saul summoned the people and counted them in ᴬTelaim: two hundred thousand foot soldiers and ten thousand men of Judah. ⁵And Saul came to the city of Amalek and set an ambush in the ¹wadi. ⁶But Saul said to the Kenites, "Go, get away, go down from among the Amalekites, so that I do not destroy you along with them; for ᴬyou showed kindness to all the sons of Israel when they went up from Egypt." So the Kenites got away from among the Amalekites. ⁷Then Saul defeated the Amalekites, from ᴬHavilah going toward ᴮShur, which is east of Egypt. ⁸He captured ᴬAgag the king of the Amalekites alive, and completely destroyed all the people with the edge of the sword.

⁹But Saul and the people ᴬspared Agag and the best of the sheep, the oxen, the more valuable *animals,* the lambs, and everything that was good, and were unwilling to destroy them completely; but everything despicable and weak, that they completely destroyed.

SAMUEL REBUKES SAUL

¹⁰Then the word of the Lᴏʀᴅ came to Samuel, saying, ¹¹"ᴬI regret that I have made Saul king, because ᴮhe has turned back from following Me and has not carried out My commands." And Samuel was furious and cried out to the Lᴏʀᴅ all night. ¹²Samuel got up early in the morning to meet Saul; and it was reported to Samuel, saying, "Saul came to ᴬCarmel, and behold, he set up a monument for himself, then turned and proceeded on down to Gilgal." ¹³So Samuel came to Saul, and Saul said to him, "ᴬBlessed are you of the Lᴏʀᴅ! I have carried out the command of the Lᴏʀᴅ." ¹⁴But Samuel said, "ᴬWhat then is this bleating of the sheep in my ears, and the bellowing of the oxen which I hear?" ¹⁵Saul said, "They have brought them from the Amalekites, for ᴬthe people spared the best of the sheep and oxen to sacrifice to the Lᴏʀᴅ your God; but the rest we have completely destroyed." ¹⁶Then Samuel said to Saul, "Stop, and let me inform you of what the Lᴏʀᴅ said to me last night." And he said to him, "Speak!"

14:51ᴬ1 Sam 9:1, 21 **14:52**ᴬ1 Sam 8:11
15:1ᴬ1 Sam 9:16; 10:1 **15:2**ᴬEx 17:8-16; Deut 25:17-19
15:3ᴬ1 Sam 22:19 **15:4**ᴬJosh 15:24 **15:6**ᴬEx 18:9, 10; Num 10:29-32 **15:7**ᴬGen 25:18 ᴮEx 15:22
15:8ᴬ1 Sam 15:20; Esth 3:1 **15:9**ᴬ1 Sam 15:3, 15, 19
15:11ᴬEx 32:14 ᴮ1 Kin 9:6, 7 **15:12**ᴬJosh 15:55; 1 Sam 25:2 **15:13**ᴬRuth 3:10; 2 Sam 2:5
15:14ᴬEx 32:21-24 **15:15**ᴬEx 32:22, 23; 1 Sam 15:9, 21
15:5¹Or *valley*

¹⁷So Samuel said, "Is it not *true,* ᴬthough you were insignificant in your own eyes, *that* you *became* the head of the tribes of Israel? For the Lᴏʀᴅ anointed you as king over Israel. ¹⁸And the Lᴏʀᴅ sent you on a mission, and said, 'ᴬGo and completely destroy the sinners, the Amalekites, and fight against them until they are eliminated.' ¹⁹Why then did you not obey the voice of the Lᴏʀᴅ? ᴬInstead, you loudly rushed upon the spoils and did what was evil in the sight of the Lᴏʀᴅ!"

²⁰Then Saul said to Samuel, "ᴬI did obey the voice of the Lᴏʀᴅ, for I went on the mission on which the Lᴏʀᴅ sent me; and I have brought Agag the king of Amalek, and have completely destroyed the Amalekites. ²¹But ᴬthe people took *some* of the spoils, sheep and oxen, the choicest of the things designated for destruction, to sacrifice to the Lᴏʀᴅ your God at Gilgal." ²²Samuel said,

"ᴬDoes the Lᴏʀᴅ have as much
      delight in burnt offerings
      and sacrifices
As in obeying the voice of the
      Lᴏʀᴅ?
Behold, to obey is better than a
      sacrifice,
And to pay attention is *better*
      than the fat of rams.
²³ "For rebellion is *as*
      reprehensible *as* the sin of
      ᴬdivination,
And insubordination is
      as reprehensible as false
      religion and idolatry.
Since you have rejected the
      word of the Lᴏʀᴅ,
He has also rejected you from
      being king."

²⁴Then Saul said to Samuel, "I have sinned, for ᴬI have violated the command of the Lᴏʀᴅ and your words, because I feared the people and listened to their voice. ²⁵Now then, ᴬplease pardon my sin and return with me, so that I may worship the Lᴏʀᴅ." ²⁶But Samuel said to Saul, "I will not return with you; for ᴬyou have rejected the word of the Lᴏʀᴅ, and the Lᴏʀᴅ has rejected you from being king over Israel." ²⁷Then Samuel turned to go, but ᴬ*Saul* grasped the edge of his robe, and it tore off. ²⁸So Samuel said to him, "ᴬThe Lᴏʀᴅ has torn the kingdom of Israel from you today and has given it to your neighbor, who is better than you. ²⁹Also the Glory of Israel ᴬwill not lie nor change His mind; for He is not a man, that He would change His mind." ³⁰Then *Saul* said, "I have sinned; *but* please honor me now before the elders of my people and before *all* Israel, and go back with me, ᴬso that I may worship the Lᴏʀᴅ your God." ³¹So Samuel went back following Saul, and Saul worshiped the Lᴏʀᴅ.

³²Then Samuel said, "Bring me Agag, the king of the Amalekites." And Agag came to him cheerfully. And Agag said, "Surely the bitterness of death is gone!" ³³But Samuel said, "ᴬAs your sword has made women childless, so shall your mother be childless among women." And Samuel cut Agag to pieces before the Lᴏʀᴅ at Gilgal.

³⁴Then Samuel went to ᴬRamah, but Saul went up to his house at ᴮGibeah of Saul. ³⁵And ᴬSamuel did

15:17ᴬ1 Sam 9:21; 10:22   15:18ᴬ1 Sam 15:3
15:19ᴬ1 Sam 14:32   15:20ᴬ1 Sam 15:13
15:21ᴬEx 32:22, 23; 1 Sam 15:15   15:22ᴬIs 1:11-15;
Mic 6:6-8   15:23ᴬDeut 18:10   15:24ᴬProv 29:25;
Is 51:12, 13   15:25ᴬEx 10:17   15:26ᴬ1 Sam 13:14; 16:1
15:27ᴬ1 Kin 11:30, 31   15:28ᴬ1 Sam 28:17, 18;
1 Kin 11:31   15:29ᴬEzek 24:14; Titus 1:2
15:30ᴬIs 29:13   15:33ᴬJudg 1:7; Matt 7:2
15:34ᴬ1 Sam 7:17   ᴮ1 Sam 11:4   15:35ᴬ1 Sam 19:24

not see Saul again until the day of his death, though Samuel mourned for Saul. And the LORD regretted that He had made Saul king over Israel.

SAMUEL GOES TO BETHLEHEM

16 Now the LORD said to Samuel, "How long are you going to mourn for Saul, since I have rejected him from being king over Israel? Fill your horn with oil and go; I will send you to ^AJesse the Bethlehemite, because I have ^Bchosen a king for Myself among his sons." ²But Samuel said, "How can I go? When Saul hears *about it,* he will kill me." But the LORD said, "^ATake a heifer with you and say, 'I have come to sacrifice to the LORD.' ³And you shall invite Jesse to the sacrifice, and ^AI will let you know what you shall do; and ^Byou shall anoint for Me the one whom I designate to you." ⁴So Samuel did what the LORD told *him,* and he came to ^ABethlehem. Then the elders of the city came trembling to meet him and said, "Do you come in peace?" ⁵And he said, "In peace; I have come to sacrifice to the LORD. ^AConsecrate yourselves and come with me to the sacrifice." He also consecrated Jesse and his sons and invited them to the sacrifice.

⁶When they entered, he looked at ^AEliab and thought, "Surely the LORD's anointed is *standing* before Him." ⁷But the LORD said to Samuel, "Do not look at his appearance or at the height of his stature, because I have rejected him; for God does not *see* as man sees, since man looks at the outward appearance, ^Abut the LORD looks at the heart." ⁸Then Jesse called ^AAbinadab and had him pass before Samuel. But

he said, "The LORD has not chosen this one, either." ⁹Next Jesse had ^AShammah pass by. And he said, "The LORD has not chosen this one, either." ¹⁰So Jesse had seven of his sons pass before Samuel. But Samuel said to Jesse, "The LORD has not chosen these." ¹¹Then Samuel said to Jesse, "Are these all the boys?" And he said, "^AThe youngest is still left, but behold, he is tending the sheep." So Samuel said to Jesse, "Send *word* and bring him; for we will not take our places at the table until he comes here."

DAVID ANOINTED

¹²So he sent *word* and brought him in. Now he was reddish, with beautiful eyes and a handsome appearance. And the LORD said, "^AArise, anoint him; for this is he." ¹³So Samuel took the horn of oil and anointed him in the midst of his brothers; and ^Athe Spirit of the LORD rushed upon David from that day forward. And Samuel set out and went to Ramah.

¹⁴Now the Spirit of the LORD left Saul, and ^Aan evil spirit from the LORD terrified him. ¹⁵Saul's servants then said to him, "Behold now, an evil spirit from God is terrifying you. ¹⁶May our lord now command your servants who are before you. Have them search for a man who is a skillful musician on the harp; and it shall come about whenever the evil spirit from God is upon you, that ^Ahe shall play *the harp* with his hand, and you will

16:1 ^A Ruth 4:17-22   ^B Ps 78:70, 71   16:2 ^A 1 Sam 20:29
16:3 ^A Acts 9:6   ^B Deut 17:14, 15   16:4 ^A Gen 48:7;
Luke 2:4   16:5 ^A Gen 35:2; Ex 19:10   16:6 ^A 1 Sam 17:13
16:7 ^A 1 Sam 2:3; Luke 16:15   16:8 ^A 1 Sam 17:13
16:9 ^A 1 Sam 17:13   16:11 ^A 1 Sam 17:12; 2 Sam 13:3
16:12 ^A 1 Sam 9:17   16:13 ^A Num 27:18; 1 Sam 10:6, 9, 10
16:14 ^A 1 Sam 16:15, 16; 1 Kin 22:19-22
16:16 ^A 1 Sam 18:10; 2 Kin 3:15

become well." ¹⁷So Saul said to his servants, "Now select for me a man who can play well, and bring *him* to me." ¹⁸Then one of the young men responded and said, "Behold, I have seen a son of Jesse the Bethlehemite who is a skillful musician, ^a valiant mighty man, a warrior, skillful in speech, and a handsome man; and ^Bthe LORD is with him." ¹⁹So Saul sent messengers to Jesse to say, "Send me your son David, who is with the flock." ²⁰And Jesse ^took a donkey *loaded with* bread and a jug of wine, and *he took* a young goat, and sent *them* to Saul by his son David. ²¹Then David came to Saul and ^attended him; and *Saul* greatly loved him, and he became his armor bearer. ²²So Saul sent *word* to Jesse, saying, "Let David now be my attendant for he has found favor in my sight." ²³So it came about whenever ^the *evil* spirit from God came to Saul, David would take the harp and play *it* with his hand; and Saul would feel relieved and become well, and the evil spirit would leave him.

GOLIATH'S CHALLENGE

17 Now ^the Philistines gathered their armies for battle; and they were gathered at Socoh which belongs to Judah, and they camped between Socoh and Azekah, in Ephes-dammim. ²Saul and the men of Israel were assembled and camped in ^the Valley of Elah, and they drew up in battle formation to confront the Philistines. ³The Philistines were standing on the mountain on one side, while Israel was standing on the mountain on the other side, with the valley between them. ⁴Then a champion came forward from

the army encampment of the Philistines, named ^Goliath, from ^BGath. His height was ¹six cubits and a ²span. ⁵And *he had* a bronze helmet on his head, and he wore scale-armor which weighed five thousand shekels of bronze. ⁶*He* also *had* bronze ¹greaves on his legs and a ^bronze saber *slung* between his shoulders. ⁷The shaft of his spear was like a weaver's beam, and the head of his spear *weighed* six hundred shekels of iron; and ^his shield-carrier walked in front of him. ⁸He stood and shouted to the ranks of Israel and said to them, "Why do you come out to draw up in battle formation? Am I not the Philistine, and you the ^servants of Saul? Choose a man as your representative and have him come down to me. ⁹^If he is able to fight me and kill me, then we will become your servants; but if I prevail against him and kill him, then you shall become our servants and serve us." ¹⁰Then the Philistine said, "^I have defied the ranks of Israel this day! Give me a man, so that we may fight together." ¹¹When Saul and all Israel heard these words of the Philistine, they were dismayed and very fearful.

¹²Now David was ^the son of the Ephrathite of Bethlehem in Judah, *the man* whose name was Jesse, and he had eight sons. And Jesse was old in the days of Saul, advanced *in years* among men.

16:18^1 Sam 17:32-36   ^B1 Sam 3:19
16:20^1 Sam 10:4, 27; Prov 18:16   16:21^Gen 41:46;
Prov 22:29   16:23^1 Sam 16:14-16   17:1^1 Sam 13:5
17:2^1 Sam 21:9   17:4^2 Sam 21:19   ^BJosh 11:22
17:6^1 Sam 17:45   17:7^1 Sam 17:41   17:8^1 Sam 8:17
17:9^2 Sam 2:12-16   17:10^1 Sam 17:26, 36, 45;
2 Sam 21:21   17:12^Ruth 4:22; 1 Sam 16:18

17:4¹About 9 ft. or 2.7 m   ²About 9 in. or 23 cm
17:6¹I.e., shin guards

¹³The three older sons of Jesse had followed Saul to the battle. And ᴬthe names of his three sons who had gone into the battle were Eliab the firstborn, and second to him, Abinadab, and the third, Shammah. ¹⁴So ᴬDavid was the youngest. Now the three oldest followed Saul, ¹⁵ᴬbut David went back and forth from Saul to tend his father's flock at Bethlehem. ¹⁶And the Philistine came forward morning and evening, and took his stand for forty days.

¹⁷Then Jesse said to his son David, "ᴬTake now for your brothers an ephah of this roasted grain and these ten loaves, and run to the camp to your brothers. ¹⁸Bring also these ten slices of cheese to the commander of *their* thousand, ᴬand look into the well-being of your brothers and bring back confirmation from them. ¹⁹For Saul and they and all the men of Israel are in the Valley of Elah, fighting the Philistines."

DAVID ACCEPTS THE CHALLENGE

²⁰So David got up early in the morning and left the flock with a keeper, and took *the supplies* and went as Jesse had commanded him. And he came to the ᴬentrenchment encircling the camp while the army was going out in battle formation, shouting the war cry. ²¹Israel and the Philistines drew up in battle formation, army against army. ²²Then David left the ᴬbaggage in the care of the baggage keeper and ran to the battle line. And he entered and greeted his brothers. ²³As he was speaking with them, behold, the champion, the Philistine from Gath named Goliath, was coming up from the army of the Philistines,

and he spoke ᴬthese same words; and David heard *him*.

²⁴When all the men of Israel saw the man, they fled from him and were very fearful. ²⁵And the men of Israel said, "Have you seen this man who is coming up? Surely he is coming up to defy Israel. And it will be that the king will make the man who kills him wealthy with great riches, and ᴬwill give him his daughter and make his father's house ¹free in Israel."

²⁶Then David said to the men who were standing by him, "What will be done for the man who kills this Philistine and rids Israel of ᴬthe disgrace? For who is this uncircumcised Philistine, that he has *dared* to defy the armies of the living God?" ²⁷The people answered him in agreement with this statement, saying, "ᴬThis is what will be done for the man who kills him."

²⁸Now Eliab his oldest brother heard *him* when he spoke to the men; and ᴬEliab's anger burned against David and he said, "Why is it that you have come down? And with whom have you left those few sheep in the wilderness? I myself know your insolence and the wickedness of your heart; for you have come down in order to see the battle." ²⁹But David said, "What have I done now? Was it not *just* a question?" ³⁰Then he turned away from him to another and ᴬsaid the same thing; and the people replied with the same words as before.

17:13 ᴬ1 Sam 16:6, 8, 9   17:14 ᴬ1 Sam 16:11
17:15 ᴬ1 Sam 16:21-23   17:17 ᴬ1 Sam 25:18
17:18 ᴬGen 37:13, 14   17:20 ᴬ1 Sam 26:5, 7
17:22 ᴬJudg 18:21; Is 10:28   17:23 ᴬ1 Sam 17:8-10
17:25 ᴬJosh 15:16   17:26 ᴬ1 Sam 11:2   17:27 ᴬ1 Sam 17:25
17:28 ᴬProv 18:19; Matt 10:36   17:30 ᴬ1 Sam 17:26, 27

17:25 ¹I.e., exempt from taxes and public service

DAVID KILLS GOLIATH

³¹When the words that David spoke were heard, they informed Saul, and he sent for him. ³²And David said to Saul, "ᴬMay no one's heart fail on account of him; ᴮyour servant will go and fight this Philistine!" ³³But Saul said to David, "ᴬYou are not able to go against this Philistine to fight him; for you are *only* a youth, while he has been a warrior since his youth." ³⁴But David said to Saul, "Your servant was tending his father's sheep. When a lion or a bear came and took a sheep from the flock, ³⁵I went out after it and attacked it, and ᴬrescued *the sheep* from its mouth; and when it rose up against me, I grabbed *it* by its mane and struck it and killed it. ³⁶Your servant has killed both the lion and the bear; and this uncircumcised Philistine will be like one of them, since he has defied the armies of the living God." ³⁷And David said, "ᴬThe LORD who saved me from the paw of the lion and the paw of the bear, He will save me from the hand of this Philistine." So Saul said to David, "ᴮGo, and may the LORD be with you." ³⁸Then Saul clothed David with his military attire and put a bronze helmet on his head, and outfitted him with armor. ³⁹And David strapped on his sword over his military attire and struggled at walking, for he had not trained *with the armor*. So David said to Saul, "I cannot go with these, because I have not trained *with them*." And David took them off. ⁴⁰Then he took his staff in his hand and chose for himself five smooth stones from the brook, and put them in the shepherd's bag which he had, that is, in *his* shepherd's pouch, and ᴬhis sling was in his hand; and he approached the Philistine.

⁴¹Then the Philistine came and approached David, with the shield-bearer in front of him. ⁴²When the Philistine looked and saw David, ᴬhe was contemptuous of him; for he was *only* a youth, and reddish, with a handsome appearance. ⁴³So the Philistine said to David, "Am I a dog, that you come to me with sticks?" And ᴬthe Philistine cursed David by his gods. ⁴⁴The Philistine also said to David, "Come to me, and I will give your flesh ᴬto the birds of the sky and the wild animals." ⁴⁵But David said to the Philistine, "You come to me with a sword, a spear, and a saber, ᴬbut I come to you in the name of the LORD of armies, the God of the armies of Israel, whom you have defied. ⁴⁶This day the LORD will hand you over to me, and I will strike you and remove your head from you. Then I will give the ᴬdead bodies of the army of the Philistines this day to the birds of the sky and the wild animals of the earth, so that all the earth may know that there is a God in Israel, ⁴⁷and that this entire assembly may know that the LORD does not save by sword or by spear; ᴬfor the battle is the LORD's, and He will hand you over to us!"

⁴⁸Then it happened, when the Philistine came closer to meet David, that ᴬDavid ran quickly toward the battle line to meet the Philistine. ⁴⁹And David put his hand into his bag and took from it a stone and slung *it*, and struck the Philistine on his forehead. And the stone penetrated his forehead, and he fell on his face to the ground.

17:32 ᴬDeut 20:1-4   ᴮ1 Sam 16:18   17:33 ᴬNum 13:31
17:35 ᴬAmos 3:12   17:37 ᴬ2 Tim 4:17, 18
ᴮ1 Chr 22:11, 16   17:40 ᴬJudg 20:16   17:42 ᴬPs 123:4;
Prov 16:18   17:43 ᴬ1 Kin 20:10   17:44 ᴬ1 Sam 17:46
17:45 ᴬPs 124:8; Heb 11:32-34   17:46 ᴬDeut 28:26
17:47 ᴬ2 Chr 20:15   17:48 ᴬPs 27:3

⁵⁰So David prevailed over the Philistine with the sling and the stone: he struck the Philistine and killed him, and there was no sword in David's hand. ⁵¹Then David ran and stood over the Philistine, and took his sword and drew it out of its sheath and finished him, and cut off his head with it. ^When the Philistines saw that their champion was dead, they fled. ⁵²Then the men of Israel and Judah rose up and shouted, and they pursued the Philistines as far as the valley, and to the gates of ^Ekron. And the Philistine dead lay along the way to Shaaraim, even to Gath and Ekron. ⁵³Then the sons of Israel returned from their close pursuit of the Philistines, and plundered their camps. ⁵⁴And David took the Philistine's head and brought it to Jerusalem, but he put his weapons in his tent.

⁵⁵Now when Saul had seen David going out against the Philistine, he said to Abner the commander of the army, "Abner, whose son is ^this young man?" And Abner said, "By your life, O king, I do not know." ⁵⁶And the king said, "You then, ask whose son the youth is." ⁵⁷So when David returned from killing the Philistine, Abner took him and ^brought him before Saul with the Philistine's head in his hand. ⁵⁸Then Saul said to him, "Whose son are you, young man?" And David answered, "^I am the son of your servant Jesse the Bethlehemite."

JONATHAN AND DAVID

18 Now it came about, when he had finished speaking to Saul, that Jonathan committed himself to David, and ^Jonathan loved him as himself. ²And Saul took him that day and ^did not let

him return to his father's house. ³Then ^Jonathan made a covenant with David because he loved him as himself. ⁴^Jonathan stripped himself of the robe that was on him and gave it to David, with his military gear, including his sword, his bow, and his belt. ⁵And David went *into battle* wherever Saul sent him, *and always* achieved success; so Saul put him in charge of the men of war. And it was pleasing in the sight of all the people, and also in the sight of Saul's servants.

⁶Now it happened as they were coming, when David returned from killing the Philistine, that ^the women came out of all the cities of Israel, singing and dancing, to meet King Saul, with tambourines, with joy and with *other* ¹musical instruments. ⁷The women ^sang as they played, and said,

"Saul has slain his thousands,
   ^And David his ten thousands."
⁸Then Saul became very angry, for this lyric displeased him; and he said, "They have given David *credit for* ten thousands, but to me they have given *credit for only* thousands! Now *what* more can he have but the ^kingdom?" ⁹And Saul eyed David with suspicion from that day on.

SAUL TURNS AGAINST DAVID

¹⁰Now it came about on the next day that ^an evil spirit from God rushed upon Saul, and he raved in the midst of the house while

17:51 ^Heb 11:34   17:52 ^Josh 15:11
17:55 ^1 Sam 16:12, 21, 22   17:57 ^1 Sam 17:54
17:58 ^1 Sam 17:12   18:1 ^1 Sam 20:17; 2 Sam 1:26
18:2 ^1 Sam 17:15   18:3 ^1 Sam 20:8-17
18:4 ^1 Sam 17:38; Esth 6:8   18:6 ^Ps 68:25; 149:3
18:7 ^Ex 15:21   ²2 Sam 18:3   18:8 ^1 Sam 15:28
18:10 ^1 Sam 16:14

18:6 ¹Possibly three-stringed lutes

David was playing *the harp* with his hand, as usual; and a spear *was* in Saul's hand. [11]Then ^Saul hurled the spear, for he thought, "I will pin David to the wall." But David escaped from his presence, twice.

[12]Now Saul was afraid of David, because the LORD was with him but ^had left Saul. [13]So Saul removed him from his presence and appointed him as his commander of a thousand; and ^he went out and came in before the people. [14]David was successful in all his ways, for ^the LORD *was* with him. [15]When Saul saw that he was very successful, he was afraid of him. [16]But ^all Israel and Judah loved David, for he would go out *to battle* and return before them.

[17]Then Saul said to David, "^Here is my older daughter Merab; I will give her to you as a wife, only be a valiant man for me and fight the LORD's battles." For Saul thought, "My hand shall not be against him, but let the hand of the Philistines be against him." [18]But David said to Saul, "^Who am I, and who is my family, *or* my father's family in Israel, that I should be the king's son-in-law?" [19]So it came about at the time that Merab, Saul's daughter, was to be given to David, that she was given *instead* to ^Adriel the Meholathite as a wife.

DAVID MARRIES SAUL'S DAUGHTER

[20]Now ^Michal, Saul's daughter, loved David. When they informed Saul, the thing was pleasing to him. [21]For Saul thought, "I will give her to him so that she may become a trap for him, and that the hand of the Philistines may be against him." Therefore Saul said to David, "^For a second time you may become my son-in-law, today." [22]Then Saul commanded his servants, "Speak to David in secret, saying, 'Behold, the king delights in you, and all his servants love you; now then, become the king's son-in-law.'" [23]So Saul's servants spoke these words to David. But David said, "Is it trivial in your sight to become the king's son-in-law, ^since I am *only* a poor man and insignificant?" [24]Then Saul's servants reported to him, saying, "These are the words David spoke." [25]Saul then said, "This is what you shall say to David: 'The king does not desire any dowry except a hundred foreskins of the Philistines, ^to take vengeance on the king's enemies.'" But ^BSaul plotted to have David fall by the hand of the Philistines. [26]When his servants told David these words, it pleased David to become the king's son-in-law. So ^before the time had expired, [27]David set out and went, he and his men, and fatally struck two hundred men among the Philistines. Then ^David brought their foreskins, and they presented all *two hundred* of them to the king, so that he might become the king's son-in-law. And Saul gave him his daughter Michal as a wife. [28]When Saul saw and realized that the LORD was with David, and *that* Michal, Saul's daughter, loved him, [29]then Saul was even more afraid of David. So Saul was David's enemy continually.

[30]Then the commanders of the Philistines went *to battle,* and it happened as often as they went

18:11^1 Sam 19:10; 20:33   18:12^1 Sam 16:14; 28:15
18:13^1 Sam 18:16; 2 Sam 5:2   18:14^Gen 39:2, 3, 23;
1 Sam 16:18   18:16^1 Sam 18:5   18:17^1 Sam 17:25
18:18^1 Sam 9:21; 2 Sam 7:18   18:19^2 Sam 21:8
18:20^1 Sam 18:28   18:21^1 Sam 18:26
18:23^Gen 29:20; 34:12   18:25^1 Sam 14:24
^B1 Sam 18:17   18:26^1 Sam 18:21   18:27^2 Sam 3:14

out, that David ^was more successful than all the servants of Saul. So his name was held in high esteem.

DAVID PROTECTED FROM SAUL

19 Now Saul told his son Jonathan and all his servants to put David to death. But ^Jonathan, Saul's son, greatly delighted in David. ²So Jonathan informed David, saying, "My father Saul is seeking to put you to death. Now then, please be on your guard in the morning, and stay in a hiding place and conceal yourself. ³And as for me, I will go out and stand beside my father in the field where you are *hiding,* and I will speak with my father about you; and ^whatever I find out, I will tell you." ⁴Then Jonathan ^spoke well of David to his father Saul and said to him, "May the king not sin against his servant David, since he has not sinned against you, and since his deeds *have been* very beneficial to you. ⁵For he took his life in his hand and struck the Philistine, and ^the LORD brought about a great victory for all Israel; you saw *it* and rejoiced. Why then would you sin against innocent blood by putting David to death for no reason?" ⁶Saul listened to the voice of Jonathan, and Saul vowed, "As the LORD lives, *David* shall not be put to death." ⁷Then Jonathan called David, and Jonathan told him all these words. And Jonathan brought David to Saul, and he was in his presence as ^before.

⁸When there was war again, David went out and fought the Philistines and defeated them with great slaughter, so that they fled from him. ⁹Now there was ^an evil spirit from the LORD on Saul as he

was sitting in his house with his spear in his hand, and David was playing *the harp* with *his* hand. ¹⁰^And Saul tried to pin David to the wall with the spear, but he escaped from Saul's presence, so that he stuck the spear into the wall. And David fled and escaped that night.

¹¹Then ^Saul sent messengers to David's house to watch him, in order to put him to death in the morning. But Michal, David's wife, informed him, saying, "If you do not save your life tonight, tomorrow you will be put to death!" ¹²^So Michal let David down through a window, and he went and fled, and escaped. ¹³And Michal took ^the household idol and laid *it* on the bed, and put a quilt of goats' hair at its head, and covered *it* with clothing. ¹⁴When Saul sent messengers to take David, she said, "^He is sick." ¹⁵Then Saul sent messengers to see David, saying, "Bring him up to me on his bed, so that I may put him to death." ¹⁶When the messengers entered, behold, the household idol *was* on the bed with the quilt of goats' hair at its head. ¹⁷So Saul said to Michal, "Why have you betrayed me like this and let my enemy go, so that he has escaped?" And Michal said to Saul, "He said to me, 'Let me go! ^Why should I put you to death?'"

¹⁸So David fled and escaped, and came ^to Samuel at Ramah; and he informed him of everything that Saul had done to him. And he and Samuel went and stayed in Naioth. ¹⁹But it was reported to Saul,

18:30^1 Sam 18:5　19:1^1 Sam 18:1–3
19:3^1 Sam 20:9, 13　19:4^1 Sam 20:32; Prov 31:8, 9
19:5^1 Sam 11:13; 1 Chr 11:14　19:7^1 Sam 16:21;
18:2, 10, 13　19:9^1 Sam 16:14; 18:10, 11
19:10^1 Sam 18:11; Prov 1:16　19:11^Judg 16:2; Ps 59
19:12^Acts 9:25; 2 Cor 11:33　19:13^Gen 31:19;
Judg 18:14, 17　19:14^Josh 2:5　19:17^2 Sam 2:22
19:18^1 Sam 7:17

saying, "Behold, David is at Naioth in Ramah." ²⁰Then Saul sent messengers to take David, but when they saw the company of prophets prophesying, with Samuel standing *and* presiding over them, the Spirit of God came upon the messengers of Saul; and ^they also prophesied. ²¹When Saul was informed *of this,* he sent other messengers, but they also prophesied. So Saul sent messengers again the third time, yet they prophesied. ²²Then he went to Ramah himself and came as far as the large well that is in Secu; and he asked, "Where are Samuel and David?" And *someone* said, "Behold, they are at Naioth in Ramah." ²³So he proceeded there to Naioth in Ramah; but ^the Spirit of God came upon him also, so that he went along prophesying continually until he came to Naioth in Ramah. ²⁴He also stripped off his clothes, and he too prophesied before Samuel and lay down naked all that day and all night. Therefore they say, "^Is Saul also among the prophets?"

DAVID AND JONATHAN'S COVENANT

20 Then David fled from Naioth in Ramah, and he came and ^said to Jonathan, "What have I done? What is my guilt? And what is my sin before your father, that he is seeking my life?" ²He said to him, "Far from it, you shall not die! Behold, my father does nothing either great or small without informing me. So why would my father hide this thing from me? It is not so!" ³Yet David vowed again, saying, "Your father is well aware that I have found favor in your sight, and he has said, 'Jonathan is not to know this, otherwise he

will be worried.' But indeed ^as the LORD lives and as your soul lives, there is just a step between me and death." ⁴Then Jonathan said to David, "Whatever you say, I will do for you." ⁵So David said to Jonathan, "Behold, tomorrow is ^the new moon, and I am obligated to sit down to eat with the king. But let me go so that I may hide myself in the field until the third evening. ⁶If your father misses me at all, then say, 'David earnestly requested *leave* of me to run to ^Bethlehem, his city, because it is the yearly sacrifice there for the whole family.' ⁷If he says, '*That is* good,' your servant *will be* safe; but if he is very angry, ^be aware that he has decided on evil. ⁸So deal kindly with your servant, for ^you have brought your servant into a covenant of the LORD with you. But if I am guilty of wrongdoing, kill me yourself; for why then should you bring me to your father?" ⁹Jonathan said, "Far be it from you! For if I in fact learn that my father has decided to inflict harm on you, would I not inform you?" ¹⁰Then David said to Jonathan, "Who will inform me if your father answers you harshly?" ¹¹Jonathan said to David, "Come, and let's go out to the field." So both of them went out to the field.

¹²Then Jonathan said to David, "The LORD, the God of Israel, *is my witness!* When I have sounded out my father about this time tomorrow *or* the third day, behold, *if he has a* good *feeling* toward you, shall I not then send *word* to you and inform you? ¹³If it pleases my father *to do*

19:20^Num 11:25; Joel 2:28   19:23^1 Sam 10:10
19:24^1 Sam 10:10-12   20:1^1 Sam 24:9
20:3^1 Sam 25:26; 2 Kin 2:6   20:5^Num 28:11-15;
Amos 8:5   20:6^1 Sam 17:58   20:7^1 Sam 25:17
20:8^1 Sam 18:3; 23:18

you harm, may the LORD do so to me and more so, if I *fail to* inform you and send you away, so that you may go in safety. And ^may the LORD be with you as He has been with my father. ¹⁴And if I am still alive, will you not show me the faithfulness of the LORD, so that I do not die? ¹⁵And ^you shall never cut off your loyalty to my house, not even when the LORD cuts off every one of the enemies of David from the face of the earth." ¹⁶So Jonathan made a *covenant* with the house of David, *saying,* "^May the LORD demand *it* from the hands of David's enemies." ¹⁷And Jonathan made David vow again because of his love for him, because ^he loved him as he loved his own life.

¹⁸Then Jonathan said to him, "^Tomorrow is the new moon, and you will be missed since your seat will be empty. ¹⁹When you have stayed for three days, you shall go down quickly and come to the place where you hid yourself on that eventful day, and you shall remain beside the stone Ezel. ²⁰And I will shoot three arrows to the side, as though I shot at a target. ²¹Then behold, I will send the boy, *telling him,* 'Go, find the arrows.' If I specifically say to the boy, 'Behold, the arrows are on this side of you, get them,' then come, because it is safe for you and there is nothing *to harm you,* as the LORD lives. ²²But if I say to the youth, '^Behold, the arrows are beyond you,' go, because the LORD has sent you away. ²³As for the agreement of which you and I have spoken, behold, ^the LORD is between you and me forever."

²⁴So David hid himself in the field; and when the new moon came, the king sat down to eat food. ²⁵Now the king sat on his seat as usual, the seat by the wall; then Jonathan stood up and Abner sat down by Saul's side; but ^David's place was empty. ²⁶Nevertheless Saul did not say anything that day, because he thought, "It *must have been* an accident; ^he is not clean, undoubtedly *he is* not clean." ²⁷But it came about the next day, the second *day* of the new moon, that David's place was empty *again;* so Saul said to his son Jonathan, "Why has the son of Jesse not come to the meal, either yesterday or today?" ²⁸And Jonathan answered Saul, "^David earnestly requested leave of me *to go* to Bethlehem. ²⁹He said, 'Please let me go, because our family has a sacrifice in the city, and my brother has ordered me *to attend.* So now, if I have found favor in your sight, please let me slip away so that I may see my brothers.' For this reason he has not come to the king's table."

SAUL IS ANGRY WITH JONATHAN

³⁰Then Saul's anger burned against Jonathan, and he said to him, "You son of a perverse, rebellious woman! Do I not know that you are choosing the son of Jesse to your own shame, and to the shame of your mother's nakedness? ³¹For, as long as the son of Jesse lives on the earth, neither you nor your kingdom will be established. Now then, send *men* and bring him to me, for ^he is doomed to die!" ³²But Jonathan replied to his father Saul and said to him, "^Why must

20:13^Josh 1:5; 1 Chr 22:11, 16   20:15^2 Sam 9:1, 3
20:16^Deut 23:21; 1 Sam 25:22   20:17^1 Sam 18:1
20:18^1 Sam 20:5, 25   20:22^1 Sam 20:37
20:23^Gen 31:49, 53; 1 Sam 20:42
20:25^1 Sam 20:18   20:26^Lev 7:20, 21; 1 Sam 16:5
20:28^1 Sam 20:6   20:31^2 Sam 12:5
20:32^Prov 31:9; Matt 27:23

he be put to death? What has he done?" ³³Then ^ASaul hurled his spear at him to strike and kill him; so Jonathan knew that his father had decided to put David to death. ³⁴Then Jonathan got up from the table in the heat of anger, and did not eat food on the second day of the new moon, because he was worried about David since his father had insulted him.

³⁵Now it came about in the morning that Jonathan went out to the field at the time agreed upon with David, and a little boy *was* with him. ³⁶He said to his boy, "^ARun, find now the arrows which I am about to shoot." The boy ran, and he shot an arrow past him. ³⁷When the boy reached the location of the arrow which Jonathan had shot, Jonathan called after the boy and said, "^AIs the arrow not beyond you?" ³⁸Then Jonathan called after the boy, "Hurry, be quick, do not stay!" And Jonathan's boy picked up the arrow and came to his master. ³⁹But the boy was not aware of anything; only Jonathan and David knew about the matter. ⁴⁰Then Jonathan gave his weapons to his boy and said to him, "Go, bring *them* to the city." ⁴¹When the boy was gone, David got up from the south side, then he fell on his face to the ground and ^Abowed three times. And they kissed each other and wept together, until ^BDavid *wept* immeasurably. ⁴²Then Jonathan said to David, "Go in safety, since we have sworn to each other in the name of the LORD, saying, '^AThe LORD will be between me and you, and between my descendants and your descendants forever.'" So *David* set out and went *on his way*, while Jonathan went into the city.

DAVID TAKES CONSECRATED BREAD

21 Then David came to Nob, to Ahimelech the priest; and Ahimelech ^Acame trembling to meet David and said to him, "Why are you alone, and no one with you?" ²David said to Ahimelech the priest, "The king has commissioned me with a matter and has said to me, '^ANo one is to know anything about the matter on which I am sending you and with which I have commissioned you; and I have directed the young men to a certain place.' ³Now then, what do you have on hand? Give me five loaves of bread, or whatever can be found." ⁴The priest answered David and said, "There is no ordinary bread on hand, but there is consecrated bread, if only the young men have ^Akept themselves from women." ⁵David answered the priest and said to him, "Be assured, women have been denied to us as previously when I left and the ^Abodies of the young men were consecrated, though it was an ordinary journey; how much more then will their bodies be consecrated today?" ⁶So the priest gave him consecrated *bread;* for there was no bread there except the ^Abread of the Presence which was removed from *its place* before the LORD, in order to put hot bread *in its place* on the day it was taken away.

⁷Now one of the servants of Saul was there that day, detained before the LORD; and his name was ^ADoeg the Edomite, the ^Bchief of Saul's shepherds.

20:33 ^A1 Sam 18:11; 19:10   20:36 ^A1 Sam 20:20, 21
20:37 ^A1 Sam 20:22   20:41 ^AGen 42:6   ^B1 Sam 18:3
20:42 ^A1 Sam 20:15, 16, 23   21:1 ^A1 Sam 16:4
21:2 ^APs 141:3   21:4 ^AEx 19:15   21:5 ^A1 Thess 4:4
21:6 ^ALev 24:5-9   21:7 ^A1 Sam 14:47   ^B1 Chr 27:29, 31

⁸David said to Ahimelech, "Now is there no spear or sword on hand? For I brought neither my sword nor my weapons with me, because the king's matter was urgent." ⁹Then the priest said, "ᴬThe sword of Goliath the Philistine, whom you killed ᴮin the Valley of Elah, behold, it is wrapped in a cloth behind the ephod; if you would take it for yourself, take *it*. For there is no other except it here." And David said, "There is none like it; give it to me."

¹⁰Then David set out and fled that day from Saul, and went to ᴬAchish king of Gath. ¹¹But the servants of Achish said to him, "Is this not David, the king of the land? ᴬDid they not sing of this one as they danced, saying,

'Saul has slain his thousands,
    And David his ten
       thousands'?"

¹²David ᴬtook these words to heart and greatly feared Achish king of Gath. ¹³So he ᴬdisguised his sanity *while* in their sight and acted insanely in their custody, and he scribbled on the doors of the gate, and drooled on his beard. ¹⁴Then Achish said to his servants, "Look, you see the man is behaving like an insane person. Why do you bring him to me? ¹⁵Do I lack insane people, that you have brought this one to behave like an insane person in my presence? Shall this one come into my house?"

PRIESTS KILLED AT NOB

22 So David departed from there and escaped to ᴬthe cave of Adullam; and when his brothers and all his father's household heard *about it*, they went down there to him. ²Then everyone who was in distress, and everyone who was in debt, and everyone who was discontented gathered to him; and he became captain over them. Now there were ᴬabout four hundred men with him.

³And David went from there to Mizpah of Moab; and he said to the king of Moab, "Please let my father and my mother come *and stay* with you until I know what God will do for me." ⁴Then he left them with the king of Moab; and they stayed with him all the time that David was in the stronghold. ⁵But ᴬGad the prophet said to David, "Do not stay in the stronghold; leave, and go into the land of Judah." So David left and went into the forest of Hereth.

⁶Then Saul heard that David and the men who were with him had been discovered. Now ᴬSaul was in Gibeah, sitting under the tamarisk tree on the height with his spear in his hand, and all his servants were standing in front of him. ⁷Saul said to his servants who were standing in front of him, "Hear now, you Benjaminites! Will the son of Jesse really give all of you fields and vineyards? ᴬWill he make you all commanders of thousands and commanders of hundreds? ⁸For all of you have conspired against me so that there is no one who informs me ᴬwhen my son makes *a covenant* with the son of Jesse, and there is none of you who cares about me or informs me that my son has stirred up my servant against me to lie in ambush, as *it is* this day." ⁹Then Doeg the Edomite,

21:9ᴬ1 Sam 17:51, 54   ᴮ1 Sam 17:2   21:10ᴬPs 34
21:11ᴬ1 Sam 18:7; 29:5   21:12ᴬLuke 2:19   21:13ᴬPs 34
22:1ᴬJosh 12:15; 15:35   22:2ᴬ1 Sam 23:13; 25:13
22:5ᴬ2 Sam 24:11; 2 Chr 29:25   22:6ᴬJudg 4:5;
1 Sam 14:2   22:7ᴬ1 Sam 8:12; 1 Chr 12:16-18
22:8ᴬ1 Sam 18:3; 20:16

who was standing in front of the servants of Saul, responded and said, "⁹I saw the son of Jesse coming to Nob, to ᴮAhimelech the son of Ahitub. ¹⁰And he inquired of the LORD for him, ᴬgave him provisions, and ᴮgave him the sword of Goliath the Philistine."

¹¹Then the king sent *a messenger* to summon Ahimelech the priest, the son of Ahitub, and all his father's household, the priests who were in Nob; and all of them came to the king. ¹²Saul said, "Listen now, son of Ahitub." And he replied, "Here I am, my lord." ¹³Saul then said to him, "Why have you and the son of Jesse conspired against me, in that you have given him bread and a sword, and have inquired of God for him, so that he would rise up against me ᴬby lying in ambush as *it is* this day?"

¹⁴ᴬThen Ahimelech answered the king and said, "And who among all your servants is as faithful as David, the king's *own* son-in-law, who is commander over your bodyguard, and is honored in your house? ¹⁵Did I *just* begin ᴬto inquire of God for him today? Far be it from me! Do not let the king impute anything against his servant *or* against any of the household of my father, because your servant knows nothing at all of this whole affair." ¹⁶But the king said, "You shall certainly die, Ahimelech, you and all your father's household!" ¹⁷And the king said to the guards who were attending him, "Turn around and put the priests of the LORD to death, because their hand also is with David and because they knew that he was fleeing and did not inform me." But the ᴬservants of the king were unwilling to reach out with

their hands to attack the priests of the LORD. ¹⁸Then the king said to Doeg, "You, turn around and attack the priests!" And Doeg the Edomite turned around and attacked the priests, and ᴬhe killed on that day eighty-five men ᴮwho wore the linen ephod. ¹⁹ᴬHe also struck Nob the city of the priests with the edge of the sword, both men and women, children and infants; *he* also *struck* oxen, donkeys, and sheep with the edge of the sword.

²⁰But ᴬone son of Ahimelech the son of Ahitub, named Abiathar, escaped and fled to David. ²¹Abiathar informed David that Saul had killed the priests of the LORD. ²²Then David said to Abiathar, "I knew on that day, when ᴬDoeg the Edomite was there, that he would certainly tell Saul. I myself have turned against every person in your father's household. ²³Stay with me; do not be afraid, even though ᴬhe who is seeking my life is seeking your life. For you are safe with me."

DAVID SAVES KEILAH

23 Then they informed David, saying, "Behold, the Philistines are fighting against ᴬKeilah and are plundering the threshing floors." ²So David ᴬinquired of the LORD, saying, "Shall I go and attack these Philistines?" And the LORD said to David, "Go and attack the Philistines and save Keilah." ³But David's men said to him, "Behold, we are fearful here in Judah. How much more then if we go to Keilah

22:9 ᴬ1 Sam 21:1   ᴮ1 Sam 14:3   22:10 ᴬ1 Sam 21:6
ᴮ1 Sam 21:9   22:13 ᴬ1 Sam 22:8   22:14 ᴬ1 Sam 19:4, 5;
20:32   22:15 ᴬ2 Sam 5:19, 23   22:17 ᴬEx 1:17
22:18 ᴬ1 Sam 2:31   ᴮ1 Sam 2:18   22:19 ᴬ1 Sam 15:3
22:20 ᴬ1 Sam 23:6, 9; 1 Kin 2:26, 27   22:22 ᴬ1 Sam 21:7
22:23 ᴬ1 Kin 2:26   23:1 ᴬJosh 15:44; Neh 3:17, 18
23:2 ᴬ1 Sam 23:4, 6, 9–12; 2 Sam 5:19, 23

against the ranks of the Philistines?" ⁴So David inquired of the LORD once more. And the LORD answered him and said, "Arise, go down to Keilah, for ᴬI am going to hand the Philistines over to you." ⁵Then David and his men went to Keilah and fought the Philistines; and he drove away their livestock and struck them with a great slaughter. So David saved the inhabitants of Keilah.

⁶Now it came about, when Abiathar the son of Ahimelech ᴬfled to David at Keilah, *that* he came down *with* an ephod in his hand. ⁷When it was reported to Saul that David had come to Keilah, Saul said, "God has handed him over to me, for he shut himself in by entering a city with double gates and bars." ⁸So Saul summoned all the people for war, to go down to Keilah to besiege David and his men. ⁹But David knew that Saul was plotting evil against him; so he said to ᴬAbiathar the priest, "ᴮBring the ephod here." ¹⁰Then David said, "LORD God of Israel, Your servant has heard for certain that Saul is seeking to come to Keilah to destroy the city on my account. ¹¹Will the citizens of Keilah hand me over to him? Will Saul come down just as Your servant has heard? LORD God of Israel, please, tell Your servant." And the LORD said, "He will come down." ¹²Then David said, "Will the citizens of Keilah hand me and my men over to Saul?" And the LORD said, "ᴬThey will hand you over." ¹³Then David and his men, about six hundred, rose up and departed from Keilah, and they went ᴬwherever they could go. When it was reported to Saul that David had escaped from Keilah, he gave up the pursuit.

¹⁴David stayed in the wilderness in the strongholds, and remained in the hill country in the wilderness of Ziph. And Saul searched for him every day, but ᴬGod did not hand him over to him.

SAUL PURSUES DAVID

¹⁵Now David saw that Saul had come out to seek his life while David was in the wilderness of Ziph, at Horesh. ¹⁶And Jonathan, Saul's son, set out and went to David at Horesh, and ᴬencouraged him in God. ¹⁷He said to him, "Do not be afraid, because the hand of Saul my father will not find you, and you will be king over Israel, and I will be second in command to you; and ᴬSaul my father knows that as well." ¹⁸So ᴬthe two of them made a covenant before the LORD; and David stayed at Horesh, while Jonathan went to his house.

¹⁹Then ᴬZiphites came up to Saul at Gibeah, saying, "Is David not keeping himself hidden with us in the strongholds at Horesh, on the hill of Hachilah, which is south of Jeshimon? ²⁰Now then, O king, come down, since you fully desire to do so; and ᴬour part *shall be* to hand him over to the king." ²¹Saul said, "May you be blessed of the LORD, ᴬsince you have had compassion on me. ²²Go now, be more persistent, and investigate and see his place where he is hiding, *and* who has seen him there; for I am told that he is very cunning. ²³So look, and learn about all the hiding places where he keeps himself

23:4ᴬJosh 8:7; Judg 7:7   23:6ᴬ1 Sam 22:20
23:9ᴬ1 Sam 22:20   ᴮ1 Sam 23:6   23:12ᴬJudg 15:10-13;
1 Sam 23:20   23:13ᴬ2 Sam 15:20   23:14ᴬPs 32:7
23:16ᴬ1 Sam 30:6; Neh 2:18   23:17ᴬ1 Sam 20:31; 24:20
23:18ᴬ1 Sam 20:12-17, 42; 2 Sam 9:1   23:19ᴬ1 Sam 26:1
23:20ᴬ1 Sam 23:12   23:21ᴬ1 Sam 22:8

hidden, and return to me with certainty, and I will go with you; and if he is in the land, I will search him out among all the thousands of Judah."

24 So they set out and went to Ziph ahead of Saul. Now David and his men were in the wilderness of ^Maon, in the Arabah to the south of Jeshimon. 25 When Saul and his men went to seek *him,* they informed David, and he came down to the rock and stayed in the wilderness of Maon. And when Saul heard *about it,* he pursued David in the wilderness of Maon. 26 Saul went on one side of the mountain, and David and his men on the other side of the mountain; and David was hurrying to get away from Saul, while Saul and his men ^were surrounding David and his men to apprehend them. 27 But a messenger came to Saul, saying, "Hurry and come, for the Philistines have launched an attack against the land!" 28 So Saul returned from pursuing David and went to confront the Philistines; therefore they called that place the Rock of Division. 29 And David went up from there and stayed in the strongholds of ^Engedi.

DAVID SPARES SAUL'S LIFE

24 Now when Saul returned from pursuing the Philistines, ^it was reported to him, saying, "Behold, David is in the wilderness of Engedi." 2 Then ^Saul took three thousand chosen men from all Israel and went to search for David and his men in front of the Rocks of the Mountain Goats. 3 And he came to the sheepfolds on the way, where there *was* a cave; and Saul went in to relieve

himself. Now ^David and his men were sitting in the inner recesses of the cave. 4 Then David's men said to him, "Behold, *this is* the day of which the LORD said to you, 'Behold; ^I am about to hand your enemy over to you, and you shall do to him as it seems good to you.'" Then David got up and cut off the edge of Saul's robe secretly. 5 But it came about afterward that ^David's conscience bothered him because he had cut off the edge of Saul's *robe.* 6 So he said to his men, "^Far be it from me because of the LORD that I would do this thing to my lord, the LORD's anointed, to reach out with my hand against him, since he is the LORD's anointed." 7 And David rebuked his men with *these* words and did not allow them to rise up against Saul. And Saul got up, left the cave, and went on *his* way.

8 Afterward, however, David got up and went out of the cave, and called after Saul, saying, "My lord the king!" And when Saul looked behind him, ^David bowed with his face to the ground and prostrated himself. 9 And David said to Saul, "Why do you listen to the words of men who say, 'Behold, David is seeking to harm you'? 10 ^Behold, this day your eyes have seen that the LORD had handed you over to me today in the cave, and *someone* said to kill you, but I spared you; and I said, 'I will not reach out with my hand against my lord, because he is the LORD's anointed.' 11 So, ^my father, look! Indeed, look at the

23:24 ^Josh 15:55; 1 Sam 25:2　23:26 ^Ps 17:9
23:29 ^Josh 15:62; 2 Chr 20:2　24:1 ^1 Sam 23:19
24:2 ^1 Sam 26:2　24:3 ^Ps 57; 142
24:4 ^1 Sam 26:8, 11　24:5 ^2 Sam 24:10
24:6 ^1 Sam 26:11　24:8 ^1 Sam 25:23, 24; 1 Kin 1:31
24:10 ^Ps 7:3, 4　24:11 ^2 Kin 5:13

edge of your robe in my hand! For by *the fact* that I cut off the edge of your robe but did not kill you, know and understand that there is no evil or rebellion in my hands, and I have not sinned against you, though you are lying in wait for my life, to take it. [12]ᴬMay the Lᴏʀᴅ judge between you and me, and may the Lᴏʀᴅ take vengeance on you for me; but my hand shall not be against you. [13]As the proverb of the ancients says, 'ᴬOut of the wicked comes wickedness'; but my hand shall not be against you. [14]After whom has the king of Israel gone out? Whom are you pursuing? ᴬA dead dog, a single flea? [15]May ᴬthe Lᴏʀᴅ therefore be judge and decide between you and me; and may He see and plead my cause and save me from your hand."

[16]When David had finished speaking these words to Saul, Saul said, "ᴬIs this your voice, my son David?" Then Saul raised his voice and wept. [17]ᴬAnd he said to David, "You are more righteous than I; for you have dealt well with me, while I have dealt maliciously with you. [18]You have declared today that you have done good to me, that ᴬthe Lᴏʀᴅ handed me over to you and *yet* you did not kill me. [19]Though if a man ᴬfinds his enemy, will he let him go away unharmed? May the Lᴏʀᴅ therefore reward you with good in return for what you have done to me this day. [20]Now, behold, ᴬI know that you will certainly be king, and that ᴮthe kingdom of Israel will be established in your hand. [21]So now ᴬswear to me by the Lᴏʀᴅ that you will not cut off my descendants after me, and that you will not eliminate my name from my father's household."

[22]And David swore *an oath* to Saul. Then Saul went to his home, but David and his men went up to ᴬthe stronghold.

SAMUEL'S DEATH

25 ᴬThen Samuel died; and all Israel assembled and mourned for him, and they ᴮburied him at his house in Ramah. And David set out and went down to the wilderness of Paran.

NABAL AND ABIGAIL

[2]Now *there was* a man in Maon whose business was in ᴬCarmel; and the man was very rich, and he had three thousand sheep and a thousand goats. And it came about while he was shearing his sheep in Carmel [3](now the man's name was Nabal, and his ᴬwife's name was Abigail. And the woman was intelligent and beautiful in appearance, but the man was harsh and evil in *his* dealings, and he was a Calebite), [4]that David heard in the wilderness that Nabal was shearing his sheep. [5]So David sent ten young men; and David said to the young men, "Go up to Carmel and visit Nabal, and greet him in my name; [6]and this is what you shall say: 'Have a long life, ᴬpeace to you, and peace to your house, and peace to all that you have! [7]Now then, I have heard ᴬthat you have shearers. Now, your shepherds have been with us; we have not harmed them, nor has anything of theirs gone missing all

24:12ᴬGen 16:5; 31:53 24:13ᴬMatt 7:16–20
24:14ᴬ2 Sam 9:8 24:15ᴬ1 Sam 24:12
24:16ᴬ1 Sam 26:17 24:17ᴬ1 Sam 26:21
24:18ᴬ1 Sam 26:23 24:19ᴬ1 Sam 23:17
24:20ᴬ1 Sam 23:17 ᴮ1 Sam 13:14
24:21ᴬ1 Sam 20:14–17; 2 Sam 21:6–8
24:22ᴬ1 Sam 23:29 25:1ᴬ1 Sam 28:3 ᴮ2 Kin 21:18
25:2ᴬJosh 15:55 25:3ᴬProv 31:10 25:6ᴬPs 122:7;
Luke 10:5 25:7ᴬ2 Sam 13:23, 24

the days they were in Carmel. ⁸Ask your young men and they will tell you. Therefore let *my* young men find favor in your eyes, for we have come on ᴬa festive day. Please give whatever you find at hand to your servants and to your son David.'"

⁹When David's young men came, they spoke to Nabal in accordance with all these words in David's name; then they waited. ¹⁰But Nabal answered David's servants and said, "ᴬWho is David? And who is the son of Jesse? There are many servants today who are each breaking away from his master. ¹¹Shall I then ᴬtake my bread and my water and my meat that I have slaughtered for my shearers, and give it to men whose origin I do not know?" ¹²So David's young men made their way back and returned; and they came and informed him in accordance with all these words. ¹³Then David said to his men, "Each *of you* strap on his sword." So each man strapped on his sword. And David also strapped on his sword, and about ᴬfour hundred men went up behind David, while two hundred stayed with the baggage.

¹⁴Now one of the young men told Abigail, Nabal's wife, saying, "Behold, David sent messengers from the wilderness to ᴬgreet our master, and he spoke to them in anger. ¹⁵Yet the men were very good to us, and we were not ᴬharmed, nor did anything go missing as long as we went with them, while we were in the fields. ¹⁶ᴬThey were a wall to us both by night and by day, all the time we were with them tending the sheep. ¹⁷Now then, be aware and consider what you should do, because harm is plotted against our master and against all his household; and he is such a worthless man that no one can speak to him."

ABIGAIL INTERCEDES

¹⁸Then Abigail hurried and ᴬtook two hundred *loaves* of bread and two jugs of wine, and five sheep *already* prepared and five measures of roasted grain, and a hundred cakes of raisins and two hundred cakes of figs, and she loaded *them* on donkeys. ¹⁹Then she said to her young men, "ᴬGo on ahead of me; behold, I am coming after you." But she did not tell her husband Nabal. ²⁰And it happened as she was riding on her donkey and coming down by the hidden part of the mountain, that behold, David and his men were coming down toward her; so she met them. ²¹Now David had said, "It is certainly for nothing that I have guarded everything that this *man* has in the wilderness, so that nothing has gone missing of all that belonged to him! For he has ᴬreturned me evil for good. ²²ᴬMay God do so to the enemies of David, and more so, if by morning I leave alive *as much as* one male of any who belong to him."

²³When Abigail saw David, she hurried and dismounted from her donkey, and fell on her face in front of David ᴬand bowed herself to the ground. ²⁴She fell at his feet and said, "On me alone, my lord, be the blame. And please let your slave speak to you, and listen to the words of your slave. ²⁵Please

25:8ᴬNeh 8:10-12; Esth 9:19, 22   **25:10**ᴬJudg 9:28
25:11ᴬJudg 8:6, 15   **25:13**ᴬ1 Sam 23:13
25:14ᴬ1 Sam 13:10; 15:13   **25:15**ᴬ1 Sam 25:7, 21
25:16ᴬEx 14:22; Job 1:10   **25:18**ᴬ2 Sam 16:1;
1 Chr 12:40   **25:19**ᴬGen 32:16, 20   **25:21**ᴬPs 109:5;
Prov 17:13   **25:22**ᴬ1 Sam 3:17; 20:13
25:23ᴬ1 Sam 20:41

do not let my lord pay attention to this worthless man, Nabal, for as his name is, so is he. Nabal is his name, and stupidity is with him; but I your slave did not see the young men of my lord whom you sent.

26 "Now then, my lord, as the LORD lives, and as your soul lives, since the LORD has restrained you from shedding blood, and ᴬfrom avenging yourself by your own hand, now then, ᴮmay your enemies and those who seek evil against my lord, be like Nabal. 27 And now let ᴬthis gift which your servant has brought to my lord be given to the young men who accompany my lord. 28 Please forgive the offense of your slave; for the LORD will certainly make for my lord an enduring house, because my lord is ᴬfighting the battles of the LORD, and ᴮevil will not be found in you all your days. 29 Should anyone rise up to pursue you and to seek your life, then the life of my lord shall be bound in the bundle of the living with the LORD your God; but the lives of your enemies ᴬHe will sling out as from the hollow of a sling. 30 And when the LORD does for my lord in accordance with all the good that He has spoken concerning you, and ᴬappoints you ruler over Israel, 31 this will not become an obstacle to you, or a troubled heart to my lord, both by having shed blood without cause and by my lord's having avenged himself. ᴬWhen the LORD deals well with my lord, then remember your slave."

32 Then David said to Abigail, "ᴬBlessed be the LORD God of Israel, who sent you this day to meet me, 33 and blessed be your discernment, and blessed be you, ᴬwho have kept me this day from bloodshed and from avenging myself by my own hand. 34 Nevertheless, as the LORD God of Israel lives, ᴬwho has restrained me from harming you, if you had not come quickly to meet me, there certainly would not have been left to Nabal until the morning light as much as one male." 35 So David accepted from her hand what she had brought him, and said to her, "Go up to your house in peace. See, I have listened to you and ᴬgranted your request."

36 Then Abigail came to Nabal, and behold, he was having ᴬa feast in his house, like the feast of a king. And Nabal's heart was cheerful within him, for he was very drunk; so she did not tell him anything at all until the morning light. 37 But in the morning, when the wine had gone out of Nabal, his wife told him these things, and his heart died within him so that he became like a stone. 38 About ten days later, ᴬthe LORD struck Nabal and he died.

DAVID MARRIES ABIGAIL

39 When David heard that Nabal was dead, he said, "Blessed be the LORD, who has pleaded the cause of the shame inflicted on me by the hand of Nabal, and ᴬhas kept back His servant from evil. The LORD has also returned the evildoing of Nabal on his own head." Then David sent a proposal to Abigail, to take her as his wife. 40 When the servants of David came to Abigail at Carmel, they spoke to her, saying,

25:26 ᴬHeb 10:30   ᴮ2 Sam 18:32   25:27 ᴬGen 33:11; 1 Sam 30:26   25:28 ᴬ1 Sam 18:17   ᴮPs 7:3 25:29 ᴬJer 10:18   25:30 ᴬ1 Sam 13:14 25:31 ᴬGen 40:14; 1 Sam 25:30   25:32 ᴬPs 41:13; Luke 1:68   25:33 ᴬ1 Sam 25:26   25:34 ᴬ1 Sam 25:26 25:35 ᴬGen 19:21   25:36 ᴬ2 Sam 13:28 25:38 ᴬ1 Sam 26:10; Ps 104:29   25:39 ᴬ1 Sam 25:26, 34

"David has sent us to you to take you to him as *his* wife." [41]And she got up ^and bowed with her face to the ground, and said, "Behold, your slave is a servant [B]to wash the feet of my lord's servants." [42]Then ^Abigail got up quickly, and rode on a donkey, with her five female attendants who accompanied her; and she followed the messengers of David and became his wife.

[43]David had also taken Ahinoam of Jezreel, and ^they both became his wives.

[44]But Saul had given his daughter ^Michal, David's wife, to Palti the son of Laish, who was from Gallim.

DAVID AGAIN SPARES SAUL

26 Then the Ziphites came to Saul at Gibeah, saying, "^Is David not keeping himself hidden on the hill of Hachilah, *which is* opposite Jeshimon?" [2]So Saul set out and went down to the wilderness of Ziph, taking with him ^three thousand chosen men of Israel, to search for David in the wilderness of Ziph. [3]And Saul camped on the hill of Hachilah, which is opposite Jeshimon, beside the road, and David was staying in the wilderness. When ^he saw that Saul had come after him into the wilderness, [4]David sent out spies, and he learned that Saul was definitely coming. [5]David then set out and came to the place where Saul had camped. And David saw the place where Saul lay, and ^Abner the son of Ner, the commander of his army; and Saul was lying in the circle of the camp, and the people were camped around him.

[6]Then David said to Ahimelech the Hittite and to ^Abishai the son of Zeruiah, Joab's brother, saying,

"Who will go down with me to Saul in the camp?" And Abishai said, "I will go down with you." [7]So David and Abishai came to the people by night, and behold, Saul lay sleeping inside the circle of the camp with his spear stuck in the ground at his head; and Abner and the people were lying around him. [8]Then Abishai said to David, "Today God has handed your enemy over to you; now then, please let me pin him with the spear to the ground with one thrust, and I will not do it to him a second time." [9]But David said to Abishai, "Do not kill him, for ^who can reach out with his hand against the LORD's anointed and remain innocent?" [10]David also said, "As the LORD lives, the LORD certainly will strike him, or his day will come that he dies, or ^he will go down in battle and perish. [11]^The LORD forbid that I would reach out with my hand against the LORD's anointed! But now please take the spear that is at his head and the jug of water, and let's go." [12]So David took the spear and the jug of water *that were* at Saul's head, and they left; and no one saw or knew *about it,* nor did anyone awaken, for they were all asleep, because ^a deep sleep from the LORD had fallen on them.

[13]Then David crossed over to the other side and stood on top of the mountain at a distance *with* a large area between them. [14]And David called to the people and to Abner the son of Ner, saying, "Will you

25:41^1 Sam 25:23   [B]Mark 1:7   25:42^Gen 24:61-67
25:43^1 Sam 27:3; 30:5   25:44^1 Sam 18:27;
2 Sam 3:14   26:1^1 Sam 23:19   26:2^1 Sam 13:2; 24:2
26:3^1 Sam 23:15   26:5^1 Sam 14:50, 51; 17:55
26:6^1 Chr 2:16   26:9^1 Sam 24:6, 7; 2 Sam 1:14, 16
26:10^1 Sam 31:6   26:11^Rom 12:17, 19; 1 Pet 3:9
26:12^Gen 2:21; Is 29:10

not answer, Abner?" Then Abner replied, "Who are you who calls to the king?" ¹⁵ So David said to Abner, "Are you not a man? And who is like you in Israel? Why then have you not guarded your lord the king? For one of the people came to kill the king your lord! ¹⁶ This thing that you have done is not good. As the Lord lives, *all of* you undoubtedly ᴬmust die, because you did not guard your lord, the Lord's anointed. And now, see where the king's spear is and the jug of water that was at his head!"

¹⁷ Then Saul recognized David's voice and said, "ᴬIs this your voice, my son David?" And David said, "It is my voice, my lord the king." ¹⁸ He also said, "ᴬWhy then is my lord pursuing his servant? For what have I done? Or what evil is in my hand? ¹⁹ Now then, please let my lord the king listen to the words of his servant. If the Lord has incited you against me, may He accept an offering; but ᴬif it is people, cursed are they before the Lord, because ᴮthey have driven me out today so that I would have no share in the inheritance of the Lord, saying, 'Go, serve other gods.' ²⁰ Now then, do not let my blood fall to the ground far from the presence of the Lord; for the king of Israel has come out to search for ᴬa single flea, just as one hunts a partridge in the mountains."

²¹ Then Saul said, "ᴬI have sinned. Return, my son David, for I will not harm you again since my life was precious in your sight this day. Behold, I have played the fool and have made a very great mistake." ²² David replied, "Behold, the spear of the king! Now have one of the young men come over and take it.

²³ And ᴬthe Lord will repay each man *for* his righteousness and his faithfulness; for the Lord handed you over to me today, but I refused to reach out with my hand against the Lord's anointed. ²⁴ Therefore behold, just as your life was ᴬhighly valued in my sight this day, so may my life be highly valued in the sight of the Lord, and may He ᴮrescue me from all distress." ²⁵ Then Saul said to David, "ᴬBlessed are you, my son David; you will both accomplish much and assuredly prevail." So David went on his way, and Saul returned to his place.

DAVID FLEES TO THE PHILISTINES

27 Then David said to himself, "Now I will perish one day by the hand of Saul. ᴬThere is nothing better for me than to safely escape into the land of the Philistines. Then Saul will despair of searching for me anymore in all the territory of Israel, and I will escape from his hand." ² So David set out and went over, he and ᴬthe six hundred men who were with him, to Achish the son of Maoch, king of Gath. ³ And David lived with Achish in Gath, he and his men, ᴬeach with his *own* household—David with ᴮhis two wives, Ahinoam the Jezreelitess, and Abigail the Carmelitess, Nabal's widow. ⁴ Now it was reported to Saul that David had fled to Gath, so he no longer searched for him.

⁵ Then David said to Achish, "If now I have found favor in your sight, have them give me a place

26:16 ᴬ1 Sam 20:31 26:17 ᴬ1 Sam 24:16
26:18 ᴬ1 Sam 24:9, 11-14
26:19 ᴬ1 Sam 24:9 ᴮJosh 22:25-27
26:20 ᴬ1 Sam 24:14 26:21 ᴬEx 9:27; 1 Sam 15:24, 30
26:23 ᴬPs 7:8; 62:12 26:24 ᴬ1 Sam 18:30 ᴮPs 54:7
26:25 ᴬ1 Sam 24:19 27:1 ᴬ1 Sam 26:19
27:2 ᴬ1 Sam 25:13 27:3 ᴬ2 Sam 2:3 ᴮ1 Sam 25:42, 43

in one of the cities in the country, so that I may live there; for why should your servant live in the royal city with you?" ⁶So Achish gave him Ziklag that day; therefore ᴬZiklag has belonged to the kings of Judah to this day. ⁷The number of days that David lived in the country of the Philistines was ᴬa year and four months.

⁸Now David and his men went up and attacked the Geshurites, the Girzites, and the Amalekites; for they were the inhabitants of the land from ancient times, as you come to ᴬShur even as far as the land of Egypt. ⁹David attacked the land and did not leave a man or a woman alive, and he ᴬtook the sheep, the cattle, the donkeys, the camels, and the clothing. Then he returned and came to Achish. ¹⁰Now Achish said, "Where did you ᴬcarry out an attack today?" And David said, "Against the ᴵNegev of Judah, against the Negev of the Jerahmeelites, and against the Negev of the Kenites." ¹¹And David did not leave a man or a woman alive to bring to Gath, saying, "Otherwise they will tell about us, saying, 'This is what David has done, and this *has been* his practice all the time that he has lived in the country of the Philistines.'" ¹²So Achish believed David, saying, "He has undoubtedly made himself repulsive among his people Israel; therefore he will become my servant forever."

SAUL AND THE SPIRIT MEDIUM

28 Now it came about in those days that ᴬthe Philistines gathered their armed camps for war, to fight against Israel. And Achish said to David, "Know for certain that you will go out with me in the camp, you and your men." ²David said to Achish, "Very well, you will learn what your servant can do." So Achish said to David, "*Then* I will assuredly make you my bodyguard ᴬfor life!"

³Now ᴬSamuel was dead, and all Israel had mourned him and buried him in Ramah, his own city. And Saul had removed the mediums and spiritists from the land. ⁴So the Philistines assembled and came and camped in Shunem; and Saul gathered all Israel together, and they camped in ᴬGilboa. ⁵When Saul saw the camp of the Philistines, he was afraid and his heart trembled greatly. ⁶So Saul inquired of the LORD, but the LORD did not answer him, either in ᴬdreams, or by the ᴮUrim, or by the prophets. ⁷Then Saul said to his servants, "Find for me a woman who is a medium, so that I may go to her and inquire of her." And his servants said to him, "Behold, ᴬthere is a woman who is a medium at Endor."

⁸Then Saul disguised himself by putting on different clothes, and went, he and two men with him, and they came to the woman by night; and he said, "ᴬConsult the spirit for me, please, and ᴮbring up for me *the one* whom I shall name for you." ⁹But the woman said to him, "Behold, you know ᴬwhat Saul has done, that he has eliminated the mediums and spiritists

27:6 ᴬJosh 15:31; Neh 11:28   27:7 ᴬ1 Sam 29:3
27:8 ᴬEx 15:22   27:9 ᴬ1 Sam 15:3; Job 1:3
27:10 ᴬ1 Sam 23:27   28:1 ᴬ1 Sam 29:1
28:2 ᴬ1 Sam 1:22, 28   28:3 ᴬ1 Sam 25:1
28:4 ᴬ1 Sam 31:1   28:6 ᴬJoel 2:28   ᴮEx 28:30
28:7 ᴬActs 16:16   28:8 ᴬIs 8:19   ᴮDeut 18:10, 11
28:9 ᴬ1 Sam 28:3

27:10 ¹I.e., South country

from the land. Why are you then setting a trap for my life, to bring about my death?" [10] So Saul swore an oath to her by the LORD, saying, "As the LORD lives, no punishment shall come upon you for this thing." [11] Then the woman said, "Whom shall I bring up for you?" And he said, "Bring up Samuel for me." [12] When the woman saw Samuel, she cried out with a loud voice; and the woman spoke to Saul, saying, "Why have you deceived me? For you are Saul!" [13] But the king said to her, "Do not be afraid; but what do you see?" And the woman said to Saul, "I see a divine being coming up from the earth." [14] He said to her, "How does he appear?" And she said, "An old man is coming up, and [A]he is wrapped in a robe." Then Saul knew that it was Samuel, and [B]he bowed with his face to the ground and paid [1]homage.

[15] And Samuel said to Saul, "Why have you disturbed me by bringing me up?" Saul replied, "I am very distressed, for the Philistines are waging war against me, and [A]God has abandoned me and [B]no longer answers me, either through prophets or in dreams; therefore I have called you, so that you may let me know what I should do." [16] Samuel said, "But why ask me, since the LORD has abandoned you and has become your enemy? [17] And the LORD has done just [A]as He spoke through me; for the LORD has torn the kingdom from your hand and given it to your neighbor, to David. [18] Just as [A]you did not obey the LORD and did not execute His fierce wrath on Amalek, so the LORD has done this thing to you this day. [19] Furthermore, the LORD will also hand Israel along with you over to the Philistines; so tomorrow [A]you and your sons *will be* with me. Indeed, the LORD will hand the army of Israel over to the Philistines!"

[20] Then Saul immediately fell full length to the ground and was very afraid because of Samuel's words; there was no strength in him either, because he had eaten no food all day and all night. [21] The woman came to Saul and saw that he was utterly horrified, and she said to him, "Behold, your servant has obeyed you, and [A]I have taken my life in my hand and have listened to your words which you spoke to me. [22] So now you too, please listen to the voice of your servant, and let me serve you a piece of bread, and eat *it*, so that you will have strength when you go on *your* way." [23] But he refused and said, "[A]I will not eat." However, his servants together with the woman urged him, and he listened to them. So he got up from the ground and sat on the bed. [24] Now the woman had a [A]fattened calf in the house, and she quickly slaughtered it; then she took flour, kneaded it and baked unleavened bread *from it*. [25] She then served *it* to Saul and his servants, and they ate. Then they got up and left that night.

THE PHILISTINES MISTRUST DAVID

29 Now [A]the Philistines gathered together all their armies to Aphek, while the Israelites were camping by the spring which is in Jezreel. [2] And the governors of the Philistines were proceeding on,

28:14 [A]1 Sam 15:27   [B]1 Sam 24:8   28:15 [A]1 Sam 16:14
[B]1 Sam 28:6   28:17 [A]1 Sam 15:28
28:18 [A]1 Sam 15:20, 26; 1 Kin 20:42   28:19 [A]1 Sam 31:2;
Job 3:17-19   28:21 [A]Judg 12:3; Job 13:14   28:23 [A]1 Kin 21:4
28:24 [A]Gen 18:7; Luke 15:23, 27, 30   29:1 [A]1 Sam 28:1

28:14 [1]I.e., great respect and honor to a superior

leading hundreds and thousands, and ᴬDavid and his men were proceeding in the back with Achish. ³Then the commanders of the Philistines said, "What *are* these Hebrews *doing here?*" And Achish said to the commanders of the Philistines, "Is this not David, the servant of Saul the king of Israel, ᴬwho has been with me these days, or *rather* these years, and I have found nothing at all *suspicious* in him since the day he deserted *to me* to this day?" ⁴But the commanders of the Philistines were angry with him, and the commanders of the Philistines said to him, "Make the man go back, so that he will return ᴬto his place where you have assigned him, and do not let him go down to battle with us, ᴮor in the battle he may become an adversary to us. For how could this *man* find favor with his lord? *Would it* not *be* with the heads of these men? ⁵Is this not David, ᴬof whom they sing in the dances, saying,

'Saul has slain his thousands,
    And David his ten
        thousands'?"

⁶Then Achish called David and said to him, "*As* the Lᴏʀᴅ lives, you *have* indeed *been* honest, and your ¹going out and your coming in with me in the army are pleasing in my sight; ᴬfor I have not found evil in you since the day of your coming to me to this day. Nevertheless, you are not pleasing in the sight of the governors. ⁷Now then, return and go in peace, so that you will not do *anything* wrong in the sight of the governors of the Philistines." ⁸However, David said to Achish, "ᴬBut what have I done? And what have you found in your servant since the day that I came

before you, to this day, that I cannot go and fight against the enemies of my lord the king?" ⁹But Achish replied to David, "I know that you are pleasing in my sight, like an angel of God; nevertheless ᴬthe commanders of the Philistines have said, 'He must not go up with us into the battle.' ¹⁰Now then, rise early in the morning ᴬwith the servants of your lord who have come with you, and *as soon as* you have risen early in the morning and have light, leave." ¹¹So David got up early, he and his men, to leave in the morning to return to the land of the Philistines. And the Philistines went up to Jezreel.

DAVID'S VICTORY
OVER THE AMALEKITES

30 Then it happened, when David and his men came to Ziklag on the third day, that ᴬthe Amalekites had carried out an attack on the Negev and on ᴮZiklag, and had overthrown Ziklag and burned it with fire; ²and they took captive the women *and all* who were in it, from the small to the great, ᴬwithout killing anyone, and drove *them* off and went their way. ³When David and his men came to the city, behold, it was burned with fire, and their wives, their sons, and their daughters had been taken captive. ⁴Then David and the people who were with him ᴬraised their voices and wept until there was no strength in them to weep. ⁵Now ᴬDavid's two wives had been taken

29:2ᴬ1 Sam 28:1, 2   29:3ᴬ1 Sam 27:7
29:4ᴬ1 Sam 27:6   ᴮ1 Sam 14:21   29:5ᴬ1 Sam 18:7; 21:11
29:6ᴬ1 Sam 27:8-12; 29:3   29:8ᴬ1 Sam 27:10-12
29:9ᴬ1 Sam 29:4   29:10ᴬ1 Chr 12:19, 22
30:1ᴬ1 Sam 27:8-10   ᴮ1 Sam 27:6, 8   30:2ᴬ1 Sam 27:11
30:4ᴬNum 14:1   30:5ᴬ1 Sam 25:42, 43; 2 Sam 2:2

captive, Ahinoam the Jezreelitess and Abigail the widow of Nabal the Carmelite. ⁶Also, David was in great distress because ^the people spoke of stoning him, for all the people were embittered, each one because of his sons and his daughters. But ^David felt strengthened in the LORD his God.

⁷Then David said to ^Abiathar the priest, the son of Ahimelech, "Please bring me the ephod." So Abiathar brought the ephod to David. ⁸And ^David inquired of the LORD, saying, "Shall I pursue this band of raiders? Will I overtake them?" And He said to him, "Pursue, for you will certainly overtake them, and you will certainly rescue *everyone*." ⁹So David left, ^he and the six hundred men who were with him, and they came to the brook Besor, *where some* who were left behind stayed. ¹⁰But David pursued, he and four hundred men, for ^two hundred who were too exhausted to cross the brook Besor stayed *behind*.

¹¹Now they found an Egyptian in the field and brought him to David, and gave him bread and he ate, and they provided him water to drink. ¹²They also gave him a slice of fig cake and two cakes of raisins, and he ate; ^then his spirit revived. For he had not eaten bread or drunk water for three days and three nights. ¹³Then David said to him, "To whom do you belong? And where are you from?" And he said, "I am a young man of Egypt, a servant of an Amalekite; and my master abandoned me when I became sick three days ago. ¹⁴We carried out an attack on ^the Negev of the Cherethites, and on that which belongs to Judah, and on ^the Negev of Caleb, and we

burned Ziklag with fire." ¹⁵Then David said to him, "Will you bring me down to this band of raiders?" And he said, "Swear to me by God that you will not kill me or hand me over to my master, and I will bring you down to this band."

¹⁶Now when he had brought him down, behold, they were dispersed over all the land, eating and drinking and celebrating because of ^all the great plunder that they had taken from the land of the Philistines and from the land of Judah. ¹⁷And David slaughtered them ^from the twilight until the evening of the next day; and not a man of them escaped, except four hundred young men who rode on camels and fled. ¹⁸So David ^recovered all that the Amalekites had taken, and rescued his two wives. ¹⁹And nothing of theirs was missing, whether small or great, sons or daughters, plunder, or anything that they had taken for themselves; ^David brought *it* all back. ²⁰So David had captured all the sheep and the cattle *which the people* drove ahead of the *other* livestock, and they said, "^This is David's plunder."

THE PLUNDER IS DIVIDED

²¹When ^David came to the two hundred men who were too exhausted to follow David and had been left behind at the brook Besor, and they went out to meet David and to meet the people who were with him, then David approached the people and greeted them. ²²Then all the

30:6 ^John 8:59   ⁸1 Sam 23:16   30:7 ^1 Sam 22:20-23
30:8 ^1 Sam 23:2, 4; Ps 50:15   30:9 ^1 Sam 27:2
30:10 ^1 Sam 30:9, 21   30:12 ^Judg 15:19
30:14 ^Zeph 2:5   ⁸Josh 14:13   30:16 ^1 Sam 30:14
30:17 ^1 Sam 11:11   30:18 ^Gen 14:16
30:19 ^1 Sam 30:8   30:20 ^1 Sam 30:26-31
30:21 ^1 Sam 30:10

wicked and worthless men among those who went with David said, "Since they did not go with us, we will not give them any of the spoils that we have recovered, except to every man his wife and his children, so that they may lead *them* away and leave." 23 But David said, "You must not do so, my brothers, with what the LORD has given us, for He has protected us and handed over to us the band of raiders that came against us. 24 And who will listen to you in this matter? For ᴬas *is* the share of the one who goes down into the battle, so *shall be* the share of the one who stays by the baggage; they shall share alike." 25 So it has been from that day forward, that he made it a statute and an ordinance for Israel to this day.

26 Now when David came to Ziklag, he sent *some* of the spoils to the elders of Judah, to his friends, saying, "Behold, a gift for you from the spoils of ᴬthe enemies of the LORD: 27 to those who were in ᴬBethel, to those who were in Ramoth of the Negev, to those who were in Jattir, 28 to those who were in ᴬAroer, to those who were in Siphmoth, to those who were in Eshtemoa, 29 to those who were in Racal, to those who were in the cities of ᴬthe Jerahmeelites, to those who were in the cities of ᴮthe Kenites, 30 to those who were in ᴬHormah, to those who were in Bor-ashan, to those who were in Athach, 31 to those who were in ᴬHebron, and to all the places where David himself and his men ᴮwalked."

SAUL AND HIS SONS KILLED IN BATTLE

31 ᴬNow the Philistines were fighting against Israel, and the men of Israel fled from the Philistines but fell fatally wounded on Mount Gilboa. 2 And the Philistines also overtook Saul and his sons, and the Philistines killed ᴬJonathan, Abinadab, and Malchishua, the sons of Saul. 3 ᴬThe battle went heavily against Saul, and the archers found him; and he was gravely wounded by the archers. 4 Then Saul said to his armor bearer, "Draw your sword and pierce me through with it, otherwise these uncircumcised *Philistines* will come and pierce me through, and abuse me." But his armor bearer was unwilling, because he was very fearful. ᴬSo Saul took his sword and fell on it. 5 When his armor bearer saw that Saul was dead, he also fell on his sword and died with him. 6 So Saul died ᴬwith his three sons, his armor bearer, and all his men on that day together.

7 Now when the people of Israel who were on the other side of the valley, with those who were beyond the Jordan, saw that the men of Israel had fled and that Saul and his sons were dead, they abandoned the cities and fled; then the Philistines came and settled in them.

8 It came about on the next day, when the Philistines came to strip those killed, that they found Saul and his three sons fallen on Mount Gilboa. 9 They cut off his head and stripped off his weapons, and sent *them* throughout the land of the Philistines, to bring the good news ᴬto the house of their idols and to the people. 10 They put his weapons in the temple of ᴬAshtaroth,

30:24 ᴬNum 31:27; Josh 22:8 30:26 ᴬ1 Sam 18:17; 25:28 30:27 ᴬGen 12:8; Josh 7:2 30:28 ᴬJosh 13:16; 1 Chr 11:44 30:29 ᴬ1 Sam 27:10 ᴮJudg 1:16 30:30 ᴬNum 14:45; Josh 12:14 30:31 ᴬJosh 14:13-15 ᴮ1 Sam 23:22 31:1 ᴬ1 Chr 10:1-12 31:2 ᴬ1 Chr 8:33f 31:3 ᴬ2 Sam 1:6 31:4 ᴬ2 Sam 1:6, 10 31:9 ᴬJudg 16:23, 24 31:10 ᴬJudg 2:13; 1 Sam 7:3

and they nailed his body to the wall of Beth-shan. ¹¹Now when ^the inhabitants of Jabesh-gilead heard what the Philistines had done to Saul, ¹²^all the valiant men got up and walked all night, and they took the body of Saul and the bodies of his sons from the wall of Beth-shan, and they came to Jabesh and burned them there. ¹³And they took their bones and ^buried them under the tamarisk tree in Jabesh, and fasted for seven days.

31:11^1 Sam 11:1-13   **31:12**^2 Sam 2:4-7
31:13^2 Sam 21:12-14

2 SAMUEL

DAVID LEARNS OF SAUL'S DEATH

1 Now it came about after the death of Saul, when David had returned from ^the slaughter of the Amalekites, that David stayed two days in Ziklag. 2 And on the third day, behold, a man came from Saul's camp ^with his clothes torn and dust on his head. And it happened when he came to David, ^he fell to the ground and prostrated himself. 3 Then David said to him, "From where do you come?" And he said to him, "I have escaped from the camp of Israel." 4 David said to him, "^How did things go? Please tell me." And he said, "The people have fled from the battle, and many of the people also have fallen and are dead; and Saul and his son Jonathan are also dead." 5 Then David said to the young man who told him, "How do you know that Saul and his son Jonathan are dead?" 6 The young man who told him said, "By chance I happened to be on Mount Gilboa, and behold, ^Saul was leaning on his spear. And behold, the chariots and the horsemen had overtaken him. 7 When he looked behind himself, he saw me, and called to me. And I said, 'Here I am.' 8 Then he said to me, 'Who are you?' And I answered him, '^I am an Amalekite.' 9 And he said to me, 'Please stand next to me and finish me off, for agony has seized me because my life still lingers in me.' 10 So I stood next to him ^and finished him off, because I knew that he could not live after he had

fallen. And I took the crown which *was* on his head and the band which *was* on his arm, and I have brought them here to my lord."

11 Then ^David took hold of his clothes and tore them, and *so* also *did* all the men who *were* with him. 12 And they mourned and wept and ^fasted until evening for Saul and his son Jonathan, and for the people of the LORD and the house of Israel, because they had fallen by the sword. 13 Then David said to the young man who informed him, "Where are you from?" And he answered, "^I am the son of a stranger, an Amalekite." 14 And David said to him, "How is it you were not afraid ^to reach out with your hand to destroy the LORD's anointed?" 15 Then David called one of the young men and said, "Come forward, put him to death." ^So he struck him and he died. 16 And David said to him, "^Your blood is on your head, because ^your *own* mouth has testified against you, saying, 'I have finished off the LORD's anointed.'"

DAVID'S SONG OF MOURNING FOR SAUL AND JONATHAN

17 Then David ^sang this song of mourning over Saul and his son Jonathan, 18 and he told *them* to teach the sons of Judah *the*

1:1^1 Sam 30:1, 17, 26   1:2^1 Sam 4:12   ^B1 Sam 25:23
1:4^1 Sam 4:16   1:6^1 Sam 31:2-4   1:8^1 Sam 15:3;
30:1, 13, 17   1:10^Judg 9:54   1:11^2 Chr 34:27;
Ezra 9:3   1:12^2 Sam 3:35   1:13^2 Sam 1:8
1:14^1 Sam 24:6; 26:9, 11, 16   1:15^2 Sam 4:10, 12
1:16^2 Sam 1:10; Luke 19:22   1:17^2 Chr 35:25

1:16 ^I I.e., his death was his own responsibility

mourning song of the bow; behold, it is written in ^the Book of Jashar.

19 "Your beauty, Israel, is
    slaughtered on your high
    places!
    ^How the mighty have fallen!
20 "^Tell *it* not in Gath,
    Proclaim it not in the streets of
    Ashkelon,
    Or the daughters of the
    Philistines will rejoice,
    The daughters of the
    uncircumcised will
    celebrate.
21 "^Mountains of Gilboa,
    May there be no dew nor
    rain on you, or fields of
    offerings!
    For there the shield of the
    mighty was defiled,
    The shield of Saul, not
    anointed with oil.
22 "From the blood of those
    slaughtered, from the fat of
    the mighty,
    ^The bow of Jonathan did not
    turn back,
    And the sword of Saul did not
    return unstained.
23 "Saul and Jonathan, beloved
    and delightful in life,
    And in their deaths they were
    not separated;
    ^They were swifter than
    eagles,
    ^They were mightier than
    lions.
24 "Daughters of Israel, weep over
    Saul,
    Who clothed you in scarlet,
    with jewelry,
    Who put gold jewelry on your
    apparel.
25 "^How the mighty have fallen in
    the midst of the battle!
    Jonathan is slaughtered on
    your high places.

26 "I am distressed for you, my
    brother Jonathan;
    You have been a close friend
    to me.
    ^Your love for me was more
    wonderful
    Than the love of women.
27 "How the mighty have fallen,
    And ^the weapons of war have
    perished!"

DAVID MADE KING OVER JUDAH

2 Then it came about afterward that David inquired of the LORD, saying, "Shall I go up to one of the cities of Judah?" And the LORD said to him, "Go up." So David said, "Where shall I go up?" And He said, "^To Hebron." ²So David went up there, and ^his two wives also, Ahinoam the Jezreelitess and Abigail the widow of Nabal the Carmelite. ³And ^David brought up his men who *were* with him, each with his household; and they settled in the cities of Hebron. ⁴Then the men of Judah came, and there they ^anointed David king over the house of Judah.

And they told David, saying, "It was the men of Jabesh-gilead who buried Saul." ⁵So David sent messengers to the men of Jabesh-gilead, and said to them, "^May you be blessed of the LORD because you have shown this kindness to Saul your lord, and have buried him. ⁶And now ^may the LORD show kindness and truth to you; and I also will show this goodness to you, because you have done this

1:18^Josh 10:13   1:19^2 Sam 1:25, 27
1:20^1 Sam 31:8–13; Mic 1:10   1:21^1 Sam 31:1
1:22^1 Sam 18:4   1:23^Jer 4:13   ᴮJudg 14:18
1:25^2 Sam 1:19, 27   1:26^1 Sam 18:1–4   1:27^Is 13:5
2:1^Josh 14:13; 1 Sam 30:31   2:2^1 Sam 25:42, 43
2:3^1 Sam 30:9; 1 Chr 12:1   2:4^1 Sam 16:13;
2 Sam 5:3, 5   2:5^1 Sam 23:21; Ps 115:15
2:6^Ex 34:6; 2 Tim 1:16

thing. ⁷Now then, let your hands be strong and be valiant, since Saul your lord is dead, and also the house of Judah has anointed me king over them."

ISH-BOSHETH MADE
KING OVER ISRAEL

⁸But ^Abner the son of Ner, commander of Saul's army, had taken ¹Ish-bosheth the son of Saul and brought him over to Mahanaim. ⁹And he made him king over ^Gilead, over the Ashurites, over Jezreel, over Ephraim, and over Benjamin, even over all Israel. ¹⁰Ish-bosheth, Saul's son, was forty years old when he became king over Israel, and he was king for two years. The house of Judah, however, followed David. ¹¹And ^the time that David was king in Hebron over the house of Judah was seven years and six months.

CIVIL WAR

¹²Now Abner the son of Ner, went from Mahanaim to ^Gibeon with the servants of Ish-bosheth the son of Saul. ¹³And ^Joab the son of Zeruiah and the servants of David went out and met them by the pool of Gibeon; and they sat down, *Abner's men* on the one side of the pool and Joab's men on the other side of the pool. ¹⁴Then Abner said to Joab, "Now have the young men arise and ^hold a martial skills match in our presence." And Joab said, "Have them arise!" ¹⁵So they got up and went over by count, twelve for Benjamin and Ish-bosheth the son of Saul, and twelve from the servants of David. ¹⁶And each one of them seized his opponent by the head and *thrust* his sword in his opponent's side;

so they fell down together. Therefore that place was called ¹Helkath-hazzurim, which is in Gibeon. ¹⁷That day the battle was very severe, and ^Abner and the men of Israel were defeated by the servants of David.

¹⁸Now ^the three sons of Zeruiah were there, Joab, Abishai, and Asahel; and Asahel *was as* swift-footed as one of the gazelles that is in the field. ¹⁹Asahel pursued Abner and did not turn to the right or to the left from following Abner. ²⁰Then Abner looked behind himself and said, "Is that you, Asahel?" And he said, "It is I!" ²¹So Abner said to him, "Turn aside for your *own good* to your right or to your left, and take hold of one of the young men for yourself, and take for yourself his equipment." But Asahel was unwilling to turn aside from following him. ²²Then Abner repeated again to Asahel, "Turn aside for your *own good* from following me. Why should I strike you to the ground? ^How then could I show my face to your brother Joab?" ²³However, he refused to turn aside; so Abner struck him in the belly with the butt end of the spear, so that the spear came out at his back. And he fell there and died on the spot. And it happened that all who came *thereafter* to the place where ^Asahel had fallen and died, stood still.

²⁴But Joab and Abishai pursued Abner, and when the sun was going down, they came to the hill of Ammah, which is opposite Giah

2:8 ^1 Sam 14:50   2:9 ^Josh 22:9   2:11 ^2 Sam 5:5
2:12 ^Josh 10:12; 18:25   2:13 ^2 Sam 8:16; 1 Chr 2:16
2:14 ^2 Sam 2:16, 17   2:17 ^2 Sam 3:1   2:18 ^1 Chr 2:16
2:22 ^2 Sam 3:27   2:23 ^2 Sam 20:12

2:8 ¹I.e., man of shame; cf. 1 Chr 8:33, *Eshbaal*
2:16 ¹I.e., the field of sword-edges

by way of the wilderness of Gibeon. ²⁵And the sons of Benjamin gathered together behind Abner and became one troop, and they stood on the top of a hill. ²⁶Then Abner called to Joab and said, "Should the sword devour forever? Do you not realize that it will be bitter in the end? So how long will you refrain from telling the people to turn back from pursuing their kinsmen?" ²⁷Joab said, "As God lives, if you had not spoken, then the people *of Judah* certainly would have withdrawn in the morning, each from pursuing his brother." ²⁸So Joab blew the trumpet, and all the people halted and no longer pursued Israel, ᴬnor did they continue to fight anymore. ²⁹Abner and his men then went through the Arabah all that night; so they crossed the Jordan, walked all morning, and came to ᴬMahanaim.

³⁰Then Joab returned from pursuing Abner; but he gathered all the people together, and nineteen of David's servants were missing, besides Asahel. ³¹However, the servants of David had struck and killed *many* of Benjamin and Abner's men; 360 men were dead. ³²And they carried Asahel *away* and buried him ᴬin his father's tomb, which was in Bethlehem. Then Joab and his men traveled all night until *the day* dawned at Hebron.

THE HOUSE OF DAVID STRENGTHENED

3 Now ᴬthere was a long war between the house of Saul and the house of David; and David became steadily stronger, while the house of Saul became steadily weaker.

²ᴬSons were born to David in Hebron: his firstborn was Amnon, by Ahinoam the Jezreelitess; ³and his second, Chileab, by Abigail the widow of Nabal the Carmelite; and the third, Absalom the son of ᴬMaacah, the daughter of Talmai, king of Geshur; ⁴and the fourth, ᴬAdonijah the son of Haggith; and the fifth, Shephatiah the son of Abital; ⁵and the sixth, Ithream, by David's wife Eglah. These *sons* were born to David in Hebron.

ABNER JOINS DAVID

⁶Now it happened that while there was war between the house of Saul and the house of David, ᴬAbner was strengthening himself in the house of Saul. ⁷And Saul had a concubine whose name was ᴬRizpah, the daughter of Aiah; and Ishbosheth said to Abner, "Why have you gone in to my father's concubine?" ⁸Then Abner became very angry over Ish-bosheth's question and said, "ᴬAm I a dog's head that belongs to Judah? Today I show kindness to the house of Saul your father, to his brothers and to his friends, and have not let you fall into the hands of David; yet today you call me to account for wrongdoing with that woman? ⁹ᴬMay God do so to me, and more so, if as the LORD has sworn to David, I do not accomplish this for him: ¹⁰ᴬto transfer the kingdom from the house of Saul, and to establish the throne of David over Israel and over Judah, from Dan even to Beersheba!" ¹¹And *Ish-bosheth* could no longer say a word in response to Abner, because he was afraid of him.

2:28ᴬ2 Sam 3:1   2:29ᴬ2 Sam 2:8
2:32ᴬGen 47:29, 30; Judg 8:32   3:1ᴬ1 Kin 14:30;
Ps 46:9   3:2ᴬ1 Chr 3:1-3   3:3ᴬ1 Sam 27:8; 1 Chr 3:2
3:4ᴬ1 Kin 1:5   3:6ᴬ2 Sam 2:8, 9   3:7ᴬ2 Sam 21:8-11
3:8ᴬ1 Sam 24:14; 2 Sam 9:8   3:9ᴬ1 Kin 19:2
3:10ᴬ1 Sam 15:28

¹²Then Abner sent messengers to David at his place, saying, "Whose is the land? Make your covenant with me, and behold, my hand shall be with you to bring all Israel over to you." ¹³And he said, "Good! I will make a covenant with you, only I require one thing of you, namely, that you shall not see my face unless you ᴬfirst bring Michal, Saul's daughter, when you come to see me." ¹⁴So David sent messengers to Ish-bosheth, Saul's son, saying, "Give me my wife Michal, to whom I was betrothed ᴬfor a hundred foreskins of the Philistines." ¹⁵Ish-bosheth sent *men* and had her taken from *her* husband, from Paltiel the son of Laish. ¹⁶And her husband went with her, weeping as he went, following her as far as ᴬBahurim. Then Abner said to him, "Go, return." So he returned.

¹⁷Now Abner had a consultation with ᴬthe elders of Israel, saying, "In times past you were seeking for David to be king over you. ¹⁸Now then, do *it!* For the LORD has spoken regarding David, saying, 'ᴬBy the hand of My servant David I will save My people Israel from the hand of the Philistines, and from the hands of all their enemies.'" ¹⁹Abner also spoke to Benjamin; and in addition Abner went to speak to David in Hebron everything that seemed good to Israel and to ᴬthe entire house of Benjamin.

²⁰Then Abner and twenty men with him came to David at Hebron. And David held a feast for Abner and the men who were with him. ²¹Abner said to David, "Let me set out and go and ᴬgather all Israel to my lord the king, so that they may make a covenant with you, and that you may be king over all that your soul desires." So David let Abner go, and he went in peace.

²²And behold, ᴬthe servants of David and Joab came from a raid and brought a large amount of plunder with them; but Abner was not with David in Hebron, since he had let him go, and he had gone in peace. ²³When Joab and all the army that was with him arrived, they informed Joab, saying, "Abner the son of Ner came to the king, and he has let him go *on his way,* and he has gone in peace." ²⁴Then Joab came to the king and said, "What have you done? Behold, Abner came to you; why then have you let him go, so that he is already gone? ²⁵You know Abner the son of Ner, that he came to gain your confidence, and to learn of ᴬyour going out and coming in and to find out everything that you are doing."

JOAB MURDERS ABNER

²⁶When Joab left David's presence, he sent messengers after Abner, and they brought him back from the well of Sirah; but David did not know *about it.* ²⁷So when Abner returned to Hebron, Joab took him aside into the middle of the gate to speak with him privately, and there ᴬhe struck him in the belly, so that he died on account of the blood of his brother Asahel. ²⁸Afterward, when David heard *about* this, he said, "I and my kingdom are innocent before the LORD forever of the blood of Abner the son of Ner. ²⁹ᴬMay it turn upon the head of Joab and on all his father's house;

3:13 ᴬ1 Sam 18:20; 19:11   3:14 ᴬ1 Sam 18:25, 27
3:16 ᴬ2 Sam 16:5; 19:16   3:17 ᴬ1 Sam 8:4
3:18 ᴬ1 Sam 9:16; 15:28   3:19 ᴬ1 Sam 10:20, 21;
1 Chr 12:29   3:21 ᴬ2 Sam 3:10, 12   3:22 ᴬ1 Sam 27:8
3:25 ᴬDeut 28:6; Is 37:28   3:27 ᴬ2 Sam 2:23; 20:9, 10
3:29 ᴬDeut 21:6-9; 1 Kin 2:31-33

and may there not be eliminated from the house of Joab someone who suffers a discharge, or has leprosy, or holds the spindle, or falls by the sword, or lacks bread." ³⁰So Joab and his brother Abishai killed Abner ^because he had put their brother Asahel to death in the battle at Gibeon.

DAVID MOURNS ABNER

³¹Then David said to Joab and to all the people who were with him, "^Tear your clothes and put on sackcloth, and mourn before Abner." And King David walked behind the bier. ³²And they buried Abner in Hebron; and the king raised his voice and wept at ^the grave of Abner, and all the people wept. ³³And ^the king sang a song of mourning for Abner and said,

"Should Abner die as a fool
    dies?
³⁴ "Your hands were not bound,
      nor your feet put in bronze
      shackles;
   As one falls before the wicked,
      you have fallen."
And all the people wept over him again. ³⁵Then all the people came to provide food for David *in his distress* while it was still day; but David vowed, saying, "May God do so to me, and more so, if I taste bread or anything else ^before the sun goes down." ³⁶Now all the people took note *of David's vow,* and it pleased them, just as everything that the king did pleased all the people. ³⁷So all the people and all Israel understood on that day that it had not been *the desire* of the king to put Abner the son of Ner to death. ³⁸Then the king said to his servants, "Do you not know that a leader and a great man has fallen

in Israel this day? ³⁹And I am weak today, though anointed king; and these men, ^the sons of Zeruiah, are too difficult for me. ᴮMay the LORD repay the evildoer in proportion to his evil."

ISH-BOSHETH MURDERED

4 Now when Ish-bosheth, Saul's son, heard that ^Abner had died in Hebron, ᴮhis courage failed, and all Israel was horrified. ²And Saul's son had two men *who were* commanders of troops: the name of the one was Baanah, and the name of the other Rechab, sons of Rimmon the Beerothite, of the sons of Benjamin (for ^Beeroth is also considered ᴮ*part* of Benjamin, ³and the Beerothites fled to ^Gittaim and have lived there *as* strangers until this day).

⁴Now ^Jonathan, Saul's son, had a son who was disabled in both feet. He was five years old when the news of Saul and Jonathan came from Jezreel, and his nurse picked him up and fled. But it happened that in her hurry to flee, he fell and could no longer walk. And his name was Mephibosheth.

⁵So the sons of Rimmon the Beerothite, Rechab and Baanah, departed and came to the house of ^Ish-bosheth in the heat of the day, while he was taking his midday rest. ⁶And they came to the interior of the house *as if* to get wheat, and ^they struck him in the belly; and Rechab and his brother Baanah escaped. ⁷Now when they had come into the house, as he was

3:30^2 Sam 2:23   3:31^Gen 37:34; Judg 11:35
3:32^Job 31:28, 29; Prov 24:17   3:33^2 Sam 1:17;
2 Chr 35:25   3:35^2 Sam 1:12   3:39^2 Sam 19:5-7
ᴮ1 Kin 2:32-34   4:1^2 Sam 3:27   ᴮEzra 4:4
4:2^Josh 9:17   ᴮJosh 18:25   4:3^Neh 11:33
4:4^2 Sam 9:3, 6   4:5^2 Sam 2:8   4:6^2 Sam 2:23

lying on his bed in his bedroom, they struck him and killed him, and they beheaded him. And they took his head and ^traveled by way of the Arabah all night. [8] Then they brought the head of Ish-bosheth to David at Hebron, and said to the king, "Behold, the head of Ish-bosheth ^the son of Saul, your enemy, who sought your life; so the Lord has given my lord the king vengeance this day on Saul and his descendants."

[9] But David replied to Rechab and his brother Baanah, sons of Rimmon the Beerothite, and said to them, "As the Lord lives, ^who has redeemed my life from all distress, [10]^when the one who informed me, saying, 'Behold, Saul is dead,' also viewed himself as the bearer of good news, I seized him and killed him in Ziklag, which was the reward I gave him for *his* news. [11] How much more, when wicked men have killed a righteous man in his *own* house on his bed, shall I not now ^require his blood from your hands and eliminate you *both* from the earth?" [12] Then ^David commanded the young men, and they killed them and cut off their hands and feet, and hung them up beside the pool in Hebron. But they took the head of Ish-bosheth ^and buried it in the grave of Abner in Hebron.

DAVID KING OVER ALL ISRAEL

5 ^Then all the tribes of Israel came to David at Hebron and said, "Behold, we are ^your bone and your flesh. [2] Previously, when Saul was king over us, you were the one who led Israel out and in. And the Lord said to you, 'You will shepherd My people Israel, and you will be ^a leader over Israel.'"

[3] So all the elders of Israel came to the king at Hebron, and King David ^made a covenant with them before the Lord in Hebron; then ^they anointed David king over Israel. [4] David was ^thirty years old when he became king, *and* he reigned for forty years. [5] At Hebron ^he reigned over Judah for seven years and six months, and in Jerusalem he reigned for thirty-three years over all Israel and Judah.

[6]^Now the king and his men went to Jerusalem against the Jebusites, the inhabitants of the land; and they said to David, "You shall not come in here, but *even* those who are blind and those who limp will turn you away," thinking, "David cannot enter here." [7] Nevertheless, David captured the stronghold of Zion, that is, ^the city of David. [8] And David said on that day, "Whoever strikes the Jebusites is to reach those who limp and those who are blind, who are hated by David's soul, through the water tunnel." For that reason they say, "People who are blind and people who limp shall not come into the house." [9] So David lived in the stronghold, and called it ^the city of David. And David built all around from the ^Millo and inward. [10]^David became greater and greater, for the Lord God of armies was with him.

[11]^Then Hiram king of Tyre sent messengers to David with cedar trees, carpenters, and stonemasons;

4:7^2 Sam 2:29   4:8^1 Sam 24:4; 25:29
4:9^1 Kin 1:29; Ps 31:7   4:10^2 Sam 1:2, 4, 15
4:11^Gen 9:5; Ps 9:12   4:12^2 Sam 1:15   ^2 Sam 3:32
5:1^1 Chr 11:1-3   ^2 Sam 19:13   5:2^1 Sam 25:30
5:3^2 Sam 3:21   ^1 Sam 16:13   5:4^Num 4:3;
Luke 3:23   5:5^2 Sam 2:11; 1 Chr 3:4   5:6^1 Chr
11:4-9   5:7^2 Sam 6:12, 16; 1 Kin 2:10   5:9^2 Sam 5:7
5:10^2 Sam 3:1   5:11^1 Kin 5:1, 10, 18; 1 Chr 14:1

5:9 ^1 I.e., terraced structure

and they built a house for David. [12]And David realized that the LORD had appointed him as king over Israel, and that He had exalted his kingdom for the sake of His people Israel.

[13]Meanwhile ^David took more concubines and wives from Jerusalem, after he came from Hebron; and more sons and daughters were born to David. [14]Now ^these are the names of those who were born to him in Jerusalem: Shammua, Shobab, Nathan, Solomon, [15]Ibhar, Elishua, Nepheg, Japhia, [16]Elishama, Eliada, and Eliphelet.

WAR WITH THE PHILISTINES

[17]Now when the Philistines heard that they had anointed David king over Israel, ^all the Philistines went up to seek out David; and when David heard *about it,* he went down to the stronghold. [18]Now the Philistines came and overran ^the Valley of Rephaim. [19]So ^David inquired of the LORD, saying, "Shall I go up against the Philistines? Will You hand them over to me?" And ^Bthe LORD said to David, "Go up, for I will certainly hand the Philistines over to you." [20]Then David came to ^Baal-perazim and defeated them there; and he said, "The LORD has broken through my enemies before me like the breakthrough of waters." Therefore he named that place ^1Baal-perazim. [21]And *the Philistines* abandoned their idols there, so ^David and his men carried them away.

[22]Now ^the Philistines came up once again and overran the Valley of Rephaim. [23]So ^David inquired of the LORD, but He said, "You shall not go *directly* up; circle around behind them and come at them in front of the baka-shrubs. [24]And it shall be, when you hear the sound of marching in the tops of the baka-shrubs, then you shall act promptly, for then ^Athe LORD will have gone out before you to strike the army of the Philistines." [25]Then David did so, just as the LORD had commanded him; he struck and killed the Philistines from ^Geba as far as Gezer.

PERIL IN MOVING THE ARK

6 ^ANow David again gathered all the chosen men of Israel, thirty thousand. [2]And David departed from Baale-judah, with all the people who were with him, to bring up from there the ark of God which is called by the ^Name, the *very* name of the LORD of armies who is enthroned *above* the cherubim. [3]They had mounted the ark of God on ^Aa new cart and moved it from the house of Abinadab, which was on the hill; and Uzzah and Ahio, the sons of Abinadab, were leading the new cart. [4]So ^Athey brought it with the ark of God from the house of Abinadab, which was on the hill; and Ahio was walking ahead of the ark. [5]Meanwhile, David and all the house of Israel ^Awere celebrating before the LORD ^Bwith all kinds of *instruments made of* juniper wood, and with lyres, harps, tambourines, castanets, and cymbals.

[6]But when they came to the threshing floor of Nacon, Uzzah ^Areached out toward the ark of God

5:13^Deut 17:17; 1 Chr 3:9   5:14^1 Chr 3:5-8
5:17^1 Sam 29:1   5:18^Gen 14:5; Josh 15:8
5:19^1 Sam 23:2   ^B2 Sam 2:1   5:20^1 Chr 14:11;
Is 28:21   5:21^1 Chr 14:12   5:22^2 Sam 5:18
5:23^2 Sam 5:19   5:24^Judg 4:14   5:25^Is 28:21
6:1^1 Chr 13:5-14   6:2^Lev 24:16   ^A Num 7:4-9;
1 Sam 6:7   6:4^1 Sam 7:1; 1 Chr 13:7
6:5^1 Sam 18:6, 7   ^B1 Chr 13:8   6:6^Num 4:15, 19, 20

5:20 ^1 I.e., the master of breakthroughs

and took hold of it, because the oxen nearly overturned *it*. ⁷And the anger of the LORD burned against Uzzah, and ^God struck him down there for his irreverence; and he died there by the ark of God. ⁸Then David became angry because of the LORD's outburst against Uzzah; and that place has been called 'Perez-uzzah to this day. ⁹So ^David was afraid of the LORD that day; and he said, "How can the ark of the LORD come to me?" ¹⁰And David was unwilling to move the ark of the LORD into the city of David with him; but David took it aside to the house of ^Obed-edom, the Gittite. ¹¹The ark of the LORD remained in the house of Obed-edom the Gittite for three months, and the LORD ^blessed Obed-edom and all his household.

THE ARK IS BROUGHT TO JERUSALEM

¹²Now it was reported to King David, saying, "The LORD has blessed the house of Obed-edom and all that belongs to him, on account of the ark of God." ^So David went and brought the ark of God up from the house of Obed-edom to the city of David with joy. ¹³And *so* it was, that when ^those carrying the ark of the LORD marched six paces, he sacrificed an ox and a fattened steer. ¹⁴And David was dancing before the LORD with all *his* strength, and David was ^wearing a linen ephod. ¹⁵So David and all the house of Israel were bringing up the ark of the LORD with joyful shouting and the sound of the trumpet.

¹⁶Then it happened, *as* the ark of the LORD was coming into the city of David, that ^Michal the daughter of Saul looked down through the window and saw King David leaping and dancing before the LORD; and she was contemptuous of him in her heart.

¹⁷Now they brought in the ark of the LORD and set it ^in its place inside the tent which David had pitched for it; and David offered burnt offerings and peace offerings before the LORD. ¹⁸When David had finished offering the burnt offering and the peace offerings, ^he blessed the people in the name of the LORD of armies. ¹⁹Further, he distributed to all the people, to all the multitude of Israel, both to men and women, a cake of bread, one of dates, and one of raisins to each one. Then all the people left, each to his house.

²⁰But when David returned to bless his *own* household, Michal the daughter of Saul came out to meet David and said, "How the king of Israel dignified himself today! For ^he exposed himself today in the sight of his servants' female slaves, as one of the rabble shamelessly exposes himself!" ²¹But David said to Michal, "^*I was* before the LORD, who preferred me to your father and to all his house, to appoint me as ruler over the people of the LORD, over Israel. So I will celebrate before the LORD! ²²And I might demean myself *even* more than this and be lowly in my own sight, but with the female slaves of whom you have spoken, with them I am to be held in honor!" ²³And Michal the daughter of Saul had no child to the day of her death.

6:7^1 Sam 6:19   6:9^Ps 119:120; Luke 5:8
6:10^1 Chr 26:4-8   6:11^Gen 30:27; 39:5
6:12^1 Chr 15:25-16:3   6:13^Num 4:15; 1 Chr 15:2, 15
6:14^Ex 19:6; 1 Sam 2:18, 28   6:16^2 Sam 3:14
6:17^1 Chr 15:1; 2 Chr 1:4   6:18^1 Kin 8:14, 15
6:20^2 Sam 6:14, 16; Eccl 7:17   6:21^1 Sam 13:14; 15:28

6:8 'I.e., outburst *against* Uzzah

DAVID PLANS TO BUILD A TEMPLE

7 ᴬNow it came about, when the king lived in his house, and the Lᴏʀᴅ had given him rest on every side from all his enemies, ²that the king said to Nathan the prophet, "See now, I live in ᴬa house of cedar, but the ark of God ᴮremains within the tent." ³Nathan said to the king, "ᴬGo, do all that is in your mind, for the Lᴏʀᴅ is with you."

⁴But in the same night, the word of the Lᴏʀᴅ came to Nathan, saying, ⁵"Go and say to My servant David, 'This is what the Lᴏʀᴅ says: "ᴬShould you build Me a house for My dwelling? ⁶For I have not dwelt in a house since the day I brought up the sons of Israel from Egypt, even to this day; rather, I have been moving about ᴬin a tent, that is, in a dwelling place. ⁷ᴬWherever I have gone with all the sons of Israel, did I speak a word with one of the tribes of Israel, ᴮwhom I commanded to shepherd My people Israel, saying, 'Why have you not built Me a house of cedar?'"'

GOD'S COVENANT WITH DAVID

⁸Now then, this is what you shall say to My servant David: 'This is what the Lᴏʀᴅ of armies says: "ᴬI Myself took you from the pasture, from following the sheep, to be leader over My people Israel. ⁹And ᴬI have been with you wherever you have gone, and ᴮhave eliminated all your enemies from you; I will also make a great name for you, like the names of the great men who are on the earth. ¹⁰And I will establish a place for My people Israel, and ᴬwill plant them, so that they may live in their own place and not be disturbed again, nor will malicious people oppress them anymore as previously, ¹¹even from the day

that I appointed judges over My people Israel; and ᴬI will give you rest from all your enemies. The Lᴏʀᴅ also declares to you that the Lᴏʀᴅ will make a house for you. ¹²When your days are finished and you ¹lie down with your fathers, ᴬI will raise up your descendant after you, who will come from you, and I will establish his kingdom. ¹³ᴬHe shall build a house for My name, and ᴮI will establish the throne of his kingdom forever. ¹⁴ᴬI will be a father to him and he will be a son to Me; ᴮwhen he does wrong, I will discipline him with a rod of men and with strokes of sons of mankind, ¹⁵but My favor shall not depart from him, ᴬas I took *it* away from Saul, whom I removed from you. ¹⁶ᴬYour house and your kingdom shall endure before Me forever; your throne shall be established forever."'" ¹⁷In accordance with all these words and all of this vision, so Nathan spoke to David.

DAVID'S PRAYER

¹⁸Then David the king came in and sat before the Lᴏʀᴅ, and he said, "ᴬWho *am* I, Lord Gᴏᴅ, and who *are* the members of* my household, that You have brought me this far? ¹⁹And yet this was insignificant in Your eyes, Lord Gᴏᴅ, ᴬfor You have spoken also of the house of Your servant regarding the distant future. And ᴮthis is the custom of mankind, Lord Gᴏᴅ. ²⁰Again what more can

7:1 ᴬ1 Chr 17:1-27   7:2 ᴬ2 Sam 5:11   ᴮEx 26:1
7:3 ᴬ1 Kin 8:17, 18; 1 Chr 22:7   7:5 ᴬ1 Kin 5:3, 4; 8:19
7:6 ᴬEx 40:18, 34   7:7 ᴬLev 26:11, 12   ᴮ2 Sam 5:2
7:8 ᴬ1 Sam 16:11, 12; Ps 78:70, 71   7:9 ᴬ1 Sam 5:10
ᴮPs 18:37-42   7:10 ᴬEx 15:17; Is 5:2, 7   7:11 ᴬ2 Sam 7:1
7:12 ᴬ1 Kin 8:20; Ps 132:11   7:13 ᴬ1 Kin 6:12   ᴮIs 49:8
7:14 ᴬPs 89:26, 27   ᴮ1 Kin 11:34   7:15 ᴬ1 Sam 15:23;
16:14   7:16 ᴬ2 Sam 7:13; Ps 89:36, 37   7:18 ᴬEx 3:11;
1 Sam 18:18   7:19 ᴬ2 Sam 7:11-16   ᴮIs 55:8, 9
7:12 ¹I.e., die

David say to You? For ^You know Your servant, Lord GOD! ²¹^For the sake of Your word, and according to Your heart, You have done all this greatness, to let Your servant know. ²²For this reason You are great, Lord GOD; for ^there is no one like You, and there is no God except You, according to all that we have heard with our ears. ²³And ^what one nation on the earth is like Your people Israel, whom God went to redeem for Himself as a people, and to make a name for Himself, and to do a great thing for You and awesome things for Your land, because of Your people whom You have redeemed for Yourself from Egypt, *from other* nations and their gods? ²⁴For ^You have established for Yourself Your people Israel as Your *own* people forever, and You, LORD, have become their God. ²⁵Now then, LORD God, the word that You have spoken about Your servant and his house, confirm *it* forever, and do just as You have spoken, ²⁶^so that Your name may be great forever, by saying, 'The LORD of armies *is* God over Israel'; and may the house of Your servant David be established before You. ²⁷For You, LORD of armies, God of Israel, have given a revelation to Your servant, saying, '^I will build you a house'; therefore Your servant has found courage to pray this prayer to You. ²⁸Now then, Lord GOD, You are God, and ^Your words are truth; and You have promised this good thing to Your servant. ²⁹And now, may it please You to bless the house of Your servant, so that it may continue forever before You. For You, Lord GOD, have spoken; and ^with Your blessing may the house of Your servant be blessed forever."

DAVID'S TRIUMPHS

8 ^Now it happened afterward that David defeated the Philistines and subdued them; and David took control of the chief city from the hand of the Philistines.

²^And he defeated ^Moab, and measured them with the line, making them lie down on the ground; and he measured two lines to put to death, and a full line to keep alive. And the Moabites became servants to David, bringing tribute.

³Then David defeated Hadadezer, the son of Rehob king of Zobah, as ^he went to restore his power at the *Euphrates* River. ⁴And David captured from him 1,700 horsemen and twenty thousand foot soldiers; and David ^hamstrung *almost* all the chariot horses, but left *enough* of them *for* a hundred chariots. ⁵When ^the Arameans of Damascus came to help Hadadezer, king of Zobah, David killed twenty-two thousand men among the Arameans. ⁶Then David put garrisons among the Arameans of Damascus, and ^the Arameans became servants to David, bringing tribute. And the LORD helped David wherever he went. ⁷David took the shields of gold which were carried by the servants of Hadadezer, and brought them to Jerusalem. ⁸And from Betah and ^Berothai, cities of Hadadezer, King David took a very large amount of bronze.

⁹Now when Toi king of ^Hamath heard that David had defeated the whole army of Hadadezer, ¹⁰Toi

7:20^1 Sam 16:7; John 21:17   7:21^1 Chr 17:19; Eph 4:32   7:22^Ex 15:11; 1 Sam 2:2   7:23^Deut 4:32-38   7:24^Deut 32:6   7:26^Ps 72:18, 19; Matt 6:9   7:27^2 Sam 7:13   7:28^Ex 34:6; John 17:17 7:29^Num 6:24-26   8:1^1 Chr 18   8:2^Num 24:17 ^1 Sam 22:3, 4   8:3^2 Sam 10:15-19   8:4^Josh 11:6, 9 8:5^1 Kin 11:23-25   8:6^2 Sam 8:2   8:8^Ezek 47:16 8:9^1 Kin 8:65; 2 Chr 8:4

sent his son Joram to King David to greet him and bless him, because he had fought Hadadezer and defeated him; for Hadadezer had been at war with Toi. And *Joram* brought with him articles of silver, gold, and bronze. ¹¹King David also ^Aconsecrated these *gifts* to the LORD, with the silver and gold that he had consecrated from all the nations which he had subdued: ¹²from ¹Aram, ^AMoab, the sons of Ammon, the Philistines, Amalek, and from the spoils of Hadadezer, son of Rehob, king of Zobah.

¹³So ^ADavid made a name *for himself* when he returned from killing eighteen thousand ¹Arameans in ^Bthe Valley of Salt. ¹⁴He also put garrisons in Edom. In all Edom he put garrisons, and ^Aall the Edomites became servants to David. And the LORD helped David wherever he went.

¹⁵So David reigned over all Israel; and David administered justice and righteousness for all his people. ¹⁶^AJoab the son of Zeruiah *was commander* over the army, and Jehoshaphat the son of Ahilud *was* ^Bsecretary. ¹⁷^AZadok the son of Ahitub and Ahimelech the son of Abiathar *were* priests, and Seraiah *was* scribe. ¹⁸Benaiah the son of Jehoiada was over the ^ACherethites and the Pelethites; and David's sons were chief ministers.

DAVID'S KINDNESS TO MEPHIBOSHETH

9 Then David said, "Is there anyone still left of the house of Saul, ^Aso that I could show him kindness for Jonathan's sake?" ²Now *there was* a servant of the house of Saul whose name was Ziba, and they summoned him to David; and the king said to him, "Are you ^AZiba?"

And he said, "*I am* your servant." ³Then the king said, "Is there no one remaining of the house of Saul to whom I could show the kindness of God?" And Ziba said to the king, "^AThere is still a son of Jonathan, one who is disabled in both feet." ⁴So the king said to him, "Where is he?" And Ziba said to the king, "Behold, he is ^Ain the house of Machir the son of Ammiel, in Lo-debar." ⁵Then King David sent messengers who brought him from the house of Machir the son of Ammiel, from Lo-debar. ⁶^AMephibosheth, the son of Jonathan the son of Saul, came to David and fell on his face and prostrated himself. And David said, "Mephibosheth." And he said, "Here is your servant!" ⁷Then David said to him, "Do not be afraid, for I will assuredly show kindness to you for the sake of your father Jonathan, and I ^Awill restore to you all the land of your grandfather Saul; and you yourself shall eat at my table regularly." ⁸Again he prostrated himself, and said, "What is your servant, that you should be concerned about ^Aa dead dog like me?"

⁹Then the king summoned Saul's servant Ziba and said to him, "^AEverything that belonged to Saul and to all his house I have given to your master's grandson. ¹⁰You and your sons and your servants shall cultivate the land for him, and you shall bring in *the produce* so that

8:11^A1 Kin 7:51   **8:12**^A2 Sam 8:2   **8:13**^A2 Sam 7:9
^B2 Kin 14:7   **8:14**^AGen 27:37-40; Num 24:17, 18
8:16^A1 Chr 11:6   ^B2 Kin 18:18, 37   **8:17**^A1 Chr 6:4-8
8:18^A2 Sam 15:18; 1 Kin 1:38, 44   **9:1**^A1 Sam
20:14-17, 42   **9:2**^A2 Sam 16:1-4; 19:17, 29
9:3^A2 Sam 4:4   **9:4**^A2 Sam 17:27-29
9:6^A2 Sam 16:4; 19:24-30   **9:7**^A2 Sam 12:8
9:8^A2 Sam 16:9; 24:14   **9:9**^A2 Sam 16:4; 19:29

8:12¹Some mss *Edom*   **8:13**¹Some mss *Edom*

your master's grandson will have food to eat; nevertheless Mephibosheth, your master's grandson, ^shall eat at my table regularly." Now Ziba had fifteen sons and twenty servants. ¹¹Then Ziba said to the king, "In accordance ^with everything that my lord the king commands his servant, so your servant will do." So Mephibosheth ate at David's table as one of the king's sons. ¹²Mephibosheth had a young son whose name was Mica. And all who lived in the house of Ziba were servants to Mephibosheth. ¹³So Mephibosheth lived in Jerusalem, because ^he ate at the king's table regularly. And he was disabled in his two feet.

AMMON AND ARAM DEFEATED

10 ^Now it happened afterward that the king of the Ammonites died, and his son Hanun became king in his place. ²Then David said, "I will show kindness to Hanun the son of ^Nahash, just as his father showed kindness to me." So David sent some of his servants to console him about his father. But when David's servants came to the land of the Ammonites, ³the commanders of the Ammonites said to their lord Hanun, "Do you think that David is *simply* honoring your father since he has sent you *servants* to console you? ^Has David not sent his servants to you in order to explore the city, to spy it out and overthrow it?" ⁴So Hanun took David's servants and ^shaved off half of their beards, and ⁸cut off their robes in the middle as far as their buttocks, and sent them away. ⁵When *messengers* informed David, he sent *servants* to meet them, because the men

were extremely humiliated. And the king said, "Stay in Jericho until your beards grow *back,* and *then* you shall return."

⁶Now when the sons of Ammon saw that ^they had become repulsive to David, the sons of Ammon sent *messengers* and hired the Arameans of Beth-rehob and the Arameans of Zobah, twenty thousand foot soldiers, and the king of Maacah *with* a thousand men, and the men of Tob *with* twelve thousand men. ⁷When David heard *about this,* he sent Joab and all the army, the warriors. ⁸And the sons of Ammon came out and lined up for battle ^at the entrance of the city, while the Arameans of Zobah and of Rehob and the men of Tob and Maacah *were stationed* by themselves in the field.

⁹Now when Joab saw that the battle was set against him at the front and at the rear, he selected *warriors* from all the choice men in Israel, and lined *them* up against the Arameans. ¹⁰But the remainder of the people he placed under the command of his brother Abishai, and he lined *them* up against the sons of Ammon. ¹¹And he said, "If the Arameans are too strong for me, then you shall help me; but if the sons of Ammon are too strong for you, then I will come to help you. ¹²Be strong, and let's show ourselves courageous for the sake of our people and the cities of our God; and ^may the LORD do what is good in His sight." ¹³So Joab and the people who were with him advanced to the battle against the

9:10^2 Sam 19:28; 1 Kin 2:7   9:11^2 Sam 16:1-4; 19:24-30   9:13^2 Sam 9:7, 11   10:1^1 Chr 19:1-19   10:2^1 Sam 11:1   10:3^Gen 42:9, 16   10:4^Jer 41:5   ⁸Is 20:4   10:6^Gen 34:30; 1 Sam 27:12   10:8^1 Chr 19:9   10:12^1 Sam 3:18

Arameans, and ^they fled from him. ¹⁴When the sons of Ammon saw that the Arameans had fled, they *also* fled from Abishai and entered the city. ^Then Joab returned from *fighting* against the sons of Ammon and came to Jerusalem.

¹⁵When the Arameans saw that they had been defeated by Israel, they assembled together. ¹⁶^And Hadadezer sent *word* and brought out the Arameans who were beyond the *Euphrates* River, and they came to Helam; and Shobach the commander of the army of Hadadezer led them. ¹⁷Now when it was reported to David, he gathered all Israel together and crossed the Jordan, and came to Helam. And the Arameans lined up against David and fought him. ¹⁸But the Arameans fled from Israel, and David killed ^seven hundred charioteers of the Arameans and forty thousand horsemen, and struck Shobach the commander of their army, and he died there. ¹⁹When all the kings, servants of Hadadezer, saw that they had been defeated by Israel, ^they made peace with Israel and served them. So the Arameans were afraid to help the sons of Ammon anymore.

BATHSHEBA, DAVID'S GREAT SIN

11 ^Then it happened in the spring, at the time when kings go out *to battle,* that David sent Joab and his servants with him and all Israel, and they brought destruction on the sons of Ammon and besieged Rabbah. But David stayed in Jerusalem.

²Now at evening time David got up from his bed and walked around on ^the roof of the king's house, and from the roof he saw a woman bathing; and the woman was very beautiful in appearance. ³So David sent *servants* and inquired about the woman. And *someone* said, "Is this not ^Bathsheba, the daughter of Eliam, the wife of ^Uriah the Hittite?" ⁴Then David sent messengers and had her brought, and when she came to him, ^he slept with her; and when she had purified herself from her uncleanness, she returned to her house. ⁵But the woman conceived; so she sent *word* and informed David, and said, "^I am pregnant."

⁶Then David sent *word* to Joab: "Send me Uriah the Hittite." So Joab sent Uriah to David. ⁷When Uriah came to him, ^David asked about Joab's well-being and that of the people, and the condition of the war. ⁸Then David said to Uriah, "Go down to your house, and ^wash your feet." So Uriah left the king's house, and a gift from the king was sent after him. ⁹But Uriah slept ^at the door of the king's house with all the servants of his lord, and did not go down to his house. ¹⁰Now when they informed David, saying, "Uriah did not go down to his house," David said to Uriah, "Did you not come from a journey? Why did you not go down to your house?" ¹¹And Uriah said to David, "^The ark and Israel and Judah are staying in temporary shelters, and my lord Joab and ^the servants of my lord are camping in the open field. Should I then go to my house to eat and drink and to sleep with my wife? By your life

10:13^1 Kin 20:13-21   10:14^2 Sam 11:1
10:16^2 Sam 8:3-8   10:18^1 Chr 19:18
10:19^2 Sam 8:6   11:1^1 Chr 20:1   11:2^Matt 24:17;
Acts 10:9   11:3^1 Chr 3:5   ^2 Sam 23:39
11:4^James 1:14, 15   11:5^Lev 20:10; Deut 22:22
11:7^Gen 37:14; 1 Sam 17:22   11:8^Gen 43:24;
Luke 7:44   11:9^1 Kin 14:27, 28   11:11^2 Sam 7:2, 6
^2 Sam 20:6

and the life of your soul, I will not do this thing." ¹²Then David said to Uriah, "ᴬStay here today also, and tomorrow I will let you go *back*." So Uriah remained in Jerusalem that day and the day after. ¹³Now David summoned Uriah, and he ate and drank in his presence, and he ᴬmade Uriah drunk; and in the evening *Uriah* went out to lie on his bed with his lord's servants, and he *still* did not go down to his house.

¹⁴So in the morning David ᴬwrote a letter to Joab and sent *it* by the hand of Uriah. ¹⁵He had written in the letter the following: "Station Uriah on the front line of the fiercest battle and pull back from him, ᴬso that he may be struck and killed." ¹⁶So it was as Joab kept watch on the city, that he stationed Uriah at the place where he knew there *were* valiant men. ¹⁷And the men of the city went out and fought against Joab, and some of the people among David's servants fell; and ᴬUriah the Hittite also died. ¹⁸Then Joab sent *a messenger* and reported to David all the events of the war. ¹⁹He ordered the messenger, saying, "When you have finished telling all the events of the war to the king, ²⁰then it shall be that if the king's wrath rises and he says to you, 'Why did you move against the city to fight? Did you not know that they would shoot from the wall? ²¹Who ᴬstruck Abimelech the son of Jerubbesheth? Did a woman not throw an upper millstone on him from the wall so that he died at Thebez? Why did you move against the wall?'—then you shall say, 'Your servant Uriah the Hittite also died.'"

²²So the messenger departed and came and reported to David

everything that Joab had sent him *to tell*. ²³The messenger said to David, "The men prevailed against us and came out against us in the field, but we pressed them as far as the entrance of the gate. ²⁴Also, the archers shot at your servants from the wall; so some of the king's servants died, and your servant Uriah the Hittite also died." ²⁵Then David said to the messenger, "This is what you shall say to Joab: 'Do not let this thing displease you, for the sword devours one as well as another; fight with determination against the city and overthrow it'; and *thereby* encourage him."

²⁶Now when Uriah's wife heard that her husband Uriah was dead, ᴬshe mourned for her husband. ²⁷When the *time of* mourning was over, David sent *servants* and had her brought to his house and ᴬshe became his wife; then she bore him a son. But ᴮthe thing that David had done was evil in the sight of the Lᴏʀᴅ.

NATHAN REBUKES DAVID

12 Then the Lᴏʀᴅ sent ᴬNathan to David. And he came to him and said,

"There were two men in a city,
  the one wealthy and the
  other poor.
² "The wealthy man had a great
  many flocks and herds.
³ "But the poor man had nothing
  at all except ᴬone little ewe
  lamb
Which he bought and
  nurtured;
And it grew up together with
  him and his children.

11:12 ᴬJob 20:12-14   11:13 ᴬProv 20:1; 23:29-35
11:14 ᴬ1 Kin 21:8-10   11:15 ᴬ2 Sam 12:9
11:17 ᴬ2 Sam 11:21   11:21 ᴬJudg 9:50-54
11:26 ᴬDeut 34:8; 1 Sam 31:13   11:27 ᴬ2 Sam 12:9
ᴮPs 51:4, 5   12:1 ᴬ2 Sam 7:2, 4, 17   12:3 ᴬ2 Sam 11:3

It would eat scraps from him
and drink from his cup and
lie in his lap,
And was like a daughter to
him.
4 "Now a visitor came to the
wealthy man,
And he could not bring
himself to take *any animal*
from his own flock or his
own herd,
To prepare for the traveler who
had come to him;
So he took the poor man's ewe
lamb and prepared it for the
man who had come to him."
5 Then David's anger burned greatly
against the man, and he said to
Nathan, "As the Lord lives, the
man who has done this certainly
^Adeserves to die! 6 So he must make
restitution for the lamb ^Afour times
over, since he did this thing and
had no compassion."

7 Nathan then said to David, "^AYou
yourself are the man! This is what
the Lord, the God of Israel says: '^BIt
is I who anointed you as king over
Israel, and it is I who rescued you
from the hand of Saul. 8 I also gave
you ^Ayour master's house and *put*
your master's wives into your care,
and I gave you the house of Israel
and Judah; and if *that had been* too
little, I would have added to you
many more things like these! 9 Why
^Ahave you despised the word of the
Lord, by doing evil in His sight? You
have struck and killed Uriah the Hittite with the sword, you have taken
his wife as your wife, and you have
slaughtered him with the sword of
the sons of Ammon. 10 Now then,
^Athe sword shall never leave your
house, because you have despised
Me and have taken the wife of Uriah
the Hittite to be your wife.' 11 This is

what the Lord says: 'Behold, I am
going to raise up evil against you
from your own household; ^AI will
even take your wives before your
eyes and give *them* to your companion, and he will sleep with your
wives in broad daylight. 12 Indeed,
^Ayou did it secretly, but ^BI will do
this thing before all Israel, and in
open daylight.'" 13 Then David said
to Nathan, "^AI have sinned against
the Lord." And Nathan said to
David, "The Lord also has allowed
your sin to pass; you shall not die.
14 However, since by this deed you
have ^Ashown utter disrespect for the
Lord, the child himself who is born
to you shall certainly die." 15 Then
Nathan went to his house.

LOSS OF A CHILD

Later the Lord struck the child that
Uriah's widow bore to David, so that
he was *very* sick. 16 David therefore
pleaded with God for the child; and
David ^Afasted and went and ^Blay all
night on the ground. 17 ^AThe elders
of his household stood beside him
in order to help him up from the
ground, but he was unwilling and
would not eat food with them.
18 Then it happened on the seventh
day that the child died. And David's
servants were afraid to tell him that
the child was dead, for they said,
"Behold, while the child was *still*
alive, we spoke to him and he did
not listen to us. How then can we
tell him that the child is dead, since
he might do *himself* harm?" 19 But
when David saw that his servants

12:5 ^A1 Sam 26:16   12:6 ^AEx 22:1; Luke 19:8
12:7 ^A1 Kin 20:42   ^B1 Sam 16:13   12:8 ^A2 Sam 9:7
12:9 ^A1 Sam 15:23, 26   12:10 ^A2 Sam 13:28; 1 Kin 2:25
12:11 ^ADeut 28:30; 2 Sam 16:21, 22   12:12 ^A2 Sam
11:4-15   ^B2 Sam 16:22   12:13 ^A1 Sam 15:24, 30;
Luke 18:13   12:14 ^AIs 52:5; Rom 2:24   12:16 ^ANeh 1:4
^B2 Sam 13:31   12:17 ^AGen 24:2

were whispering together, David perceived that the child was dead; so David said to his servants, "Is the child dead?" And they said, "He is dead." ²⁰So David got up from the ground, ᴬwashed, anointed *himself,* and changed his clothes; and he went into the house of the LORD and worshiped. Then he went to his own house, and when he asked, they served him food, and he ate.

²¹Then his servants said to him, "What is this thing that you have done? You fasted and wept for the child *while he was* alive; but when the child died, you got up and ate food." ²²And he said, "While the child was still alive, I fasted and wept; for I said, 'ᴬWho knows, the LORD may be gracious to me, and the child may live.' ²³But now he has died; why should I fast? Can I bring him back again? I am going to him, but ᴬhe will not return to me."

SOLOMON BORN

²⁴Then David comforted his wife Bathsheba, and went in to her and slept with her; and she gave birth to a son, and ᴬhe named him Solomon. Now the LORD loved him, ²⁵and sent *word* through Nathan the prophet, and he named him ¹Jedidiah for the LORD's sake.

WAR AGAIN

²⁶ᴬNow Joab fought against Rabbah of the sons of Ammon, and captured the royal city. ²⁷Then Joab sent messengers to David and said, "I have fought against Rabbah, I have even captured the city of waters. ²⁸Now then, gather the rest of the people and camp opposite the city and capture it, or I will capture the city myself and it will be named after me." ²⁹So David

gathered all the people and went to Rabbah, and he fought against it and captured it. ³⁰Then ᴬhe took the crown of their king from his head; and its weight *was* a ¹talent of gold, and *it had* a precious stone; and it was *placed* on David's head. And he brought out the plunder of the city in great amounts. ³¹He also brought out the people who were in it, and ᴬput *some to work* at saws, iron picks, and iron axes, and made others serve at the brick works. And he did the same to all the cities of the sons of Ammon. Then David and all the people returned *to* Jerusalem.

AMNON AND TAMAR

13 Now it was after this that ᴬAbsalom the son of David had a beautiful sister whose name was Tamar, and Amnon the son of David was in love with her. ²But Amnon was so frustrated on account of his sister Tamar that he made himself ill, for she was a virgin, and it seemed too difficult to Amnon to do anything to her. ³But Amnon had a friend whose name was Jonadab, the son of ᴬShimeah, David's brother; and Jonadab was a very clever man. ⁴And he said to him, "Why are you, the king's son, so depressed morning after morning? Will you not tell me?" So Amnon said to him, "I am in love with Tamar, the sister of my brother Absalom." ⁵Jonadab then said to him, "Lie down on your bed and pretend to be ill; when your father comes to see you, say to him,

---

12:20 ᴬRuth 3:3; Matt 6:17   12:22 ᴬJon 3:9
12:23 ᴬJob 7:8-10   12:24 ᴬ1 Chr 22:9; Matt 1:6
12:26 ᴬ1 Chr 20:1-3   12:30 ᴬ1 Chr 20:2
12:31 ᴬ1 Chr 20:3; Heb 11:37   13:1 ᴬ2 Sam 3:2, 3;
1 Chr 3:2   13:3 ᴬ1 Sam 16:9

12:25 ¹I.e., beloved of the LORD   12:30 ¹About 75 lb. or 34 kg

'Please have my sister Tamar come and give me food to eat, and have her prepare the food in my sight, so that I may see *it* and eat from her hand.'" [6]So Amnon lay down and pretended to be ill; when the king came to see him, Amnon said to the king, "Please have my sister Tamar come and ^make me a couple of pastries in my sight, so that I may eat from her hand."

[7]Then David sent *a messenger* to the house for Tamar, saying, "Go now to your brother Amnon's house, and prepare food for him." [8]So Tamar went to her brother Amnon's house, and he was lying *in bed.* And she took dough, kneaded *it,* made pastries in his sight, and baked the pastries. [9]Then she took the tray and served *them* to him, but he refused to eat. And Amnon said, "^Have everyone leave me." So everyone left him. [10]Then Amnon said to Tamar, "Bring the food into the bedroom, so that I may eat from your hand." So Tamar took the pastries which she had made and brought them into the bedroom to her brother Amnon. [11]When she brought *them* to him to eat, he ^took hold of her and said to her, "Come, sleep with me, my sister." [12]But she said to him, "No, my brother, do not violate me, for ^such a thing is not done in Israel; do not do this disgraceful sin! [13]As for me, where could I get rid of my shame? And as for you, you will be like one of the fools in Israel. Now then, please speak to the king, for ^he will not withhold me from you." [14]However, he would not listen to her; since he was stronger than she, he ^violated her and slept with her.

[15]Then Amnon hated her with a very great hatred; indeed, the hatred with which he hated her was greater than the love with which he had loved her. And Amnon said to her, "Get up, go *away!*" [16]But she said to him, "No, because this wrong in sending me away is greater than the other that you have done to me!" Yet he would not listen to her. [17]Then he called his young man who attended him and said, "Now throw this woman out of my *presence,* and lock the door behind her!" [18]Now she had on ^a long-sleeved garment; for this is how the virgin daughters of the king dressed themselves in robes. Then his attendant took her out and locked the door behind her. [19]^Tamar took ashes *and put them* on her head, and ^Btore her long-sleeved garment which *was* on her; and she put her hand on her head and went *on her way,* crying out as she went.

[20]Then Absalom her brother said to her, "Has Amnon your brother been with you? But now keep silent, my sister, he is your brother; do not take this matter to heart." So Tamar remained and was isolated in her brother Absalom's house. [21]Now when King David heard about all these matters, he became very angry. [22]But Absalom did not speak with Amnon either good or bad; for ^Absalom hated Amnon because he had violated his sister Tamar.

[23]Now it came about after two full years that Absalom ^had sheepshearers in Baal-hazor, which is near Ephraim, and Absalom invited all the king's sons *to celebrate.*

13:6 ^Gen 18:6   13:9 ^Gen 45:1   13:11 ^Gen 39:12
13:12 ^Lev 20:17   13:13 ^Gen 20:12   13:14 ^Lev 18:9;
Deut 22:25   13:18 ^Gen 37:3, 23   13:19 ^Esth 4:1
^B 2 Sam 1:11   13:22 ^Lev 19:17; 1 John 3:10, 12, 15
13:23 ^1 Sam 25:7

ABSALOM AVENGES TAMAR

²⁴And Absalom came to the king and said, "Behold now, your servant has sheepshearers; may the king and his servants please go with your servant." ²⁵But the king said to Absalom, "No, my son, we should not all go, so that we will not be a burden to you." Though he urged him, he would not go; but he blessed him. ²⁶Then ᴬAbsalom said, "If not, please have my brother Amnon go with us." But the king said to him, "Why should he go with you?" ²⁷Nevertheless Absalom urged him, so he let Amnon and all the king's sons go with him.

²⁸Then Absalom commanded his servants, saying, "See now, ᴬwhen Amnon's heart is cheerful with wine, and I say to you, 'Strike Amnon,' then put him to death. Do not fear; have I not commanded you myself? Be courageous and be valiant." ²⁹And the servants of Absalom did to Amnon just as Absalom had commanded. Then all the king's sons got up and each mounted ᴬhis mule and fled.

³⁰Now it was while they were on the way that the report came to David, saying, "Absalom has struck and killed all the king's sons, and not one of them is left." ³¹Then the king stood up, ᴬtore his clothes, and lay on the ground; and all his servants were standing by with clothes torn. ³²And Jonadab, the son of Shimeah, David's brother, responded, "Let my lord not assume that they have put to death all the young men, the king's sons, for only Amnon is dead; because this has been set up by the intent of Absalom since the day that he violated his sister Tamar. ³³So now, may my lord the king not ᴬtake the report to heart, claiming, 'all the king's sons are dead'; but only Amnon is dead."

³⁴Now ᴬAbsalom had fled. And the young man who was the watchman raised his eyes and looked, and behold, many people were coming from the road behind him by the side of the mountain. ³⁵And Jonadab said to the king, "Behold, the king's sons have come; so it has happened according to your servant's word." ³⁶As soon as he had finished speaking, behold, the king's sons came and raised their voices and wept; and the king and all his servants also wept very profusely.

³⁷Now Absalom had fled and gone to ᴬTalmai the son of Ammihud, the king of ᴮGeshur. And *David* mourned for his son every day. ³⁸ᴬSo Absalom had fled and gone to Geshur, and was there for three years. ³⁹And *the heart of* King David longed to go out to Absalom; for ᴬhe was comforted regarding Amnon, since he was dead.

THE WOMAN OF TEKOA

14 Now Joab the son of Zeruiah perceived that ᴬthe king's heart *was drawn* toward Absalom. ²So Joab sent *a messenger* to ᴬTekoa and brought a wise woman from there, and said to her, "Please follow mourning rites, and put on mourning garments now, and do not anoint yourself with oil but be like a woman who has been mourning for the dead for many days.

13:26ᴬ2 Sam 3:27; 11:13-15   **13:28**ᴬJudg 19:6, 9, 22; 1 Sam 25:36-38   **13:29**ᴬ2 Sam 18:9; 1 Kin 1:33, 38
13:31ᴬ2 Sam 1:11   **13:32**ᴬ2 Sam 13:3-5
13:33ᴬ2 Sam 19:19   **13:34**ᴬ2 Sam 13:37, 38
13:37ᴬ2 Sam 3:3   ᴮ2 Sam 14:23, 32
13:38ᴬ2 Sam 13:34   **13:39**ᴬ2 Sam 12:19-23
14:1ᴬ2 Sam 13:39   **14:2**ᴬ2 Sam 23:26; Amos 1:1

³Then go to the king and speak to him in this way." So Joab put ᴬthe words in her mouth.

⁴Now when the woman of Tekoa ¹spoke to the king, she fell on her face to the ground and ᴬprostrated herself, and said, "Help, O king!" ⁵And the king said to her, "What is *troubling* you?" And she answered, "Truly I am a widow, for my husband is dead. ⁶And your servant had two sons, but the two of them fought in the field, and there was no one to save them from each other, so one struck the other and killed him. ⁷Now behold, the entire family has risen against your servant, and they have said, 'Hand over the one who struck his brother, so that we may put him to death for the life of his brother whom he killed, ᴬand eliminate the heir as well.' So they will extinguish my coal which is left, so as to leave my husband neither name nor remnant on the face of the earth."

⁸Then the king said to the woman, "Go to your home, and I will issue orders concerning you." ⁹The woman of Tekoa said to the king, "My lord, the king, the guilt is on me and my father's house, but ᴬthe king and his throne are guiltless." ¹⁰So the king said, "Whoever speaks to you, bring him to me, and he will not touch you anymore." ¹¹Then she said, "May the king please remember the Lᴏʀᴅ your God, ᴬso that the avenger of blood will not continue to destroy, otherwise they will destroy my son." And he said, "As the Lᴏʀᴅ lives, not one hair of your son shall fall to the ground."

¹²Then the woman said, "Please let your servant speak a word to my lord the king." And he said, "Speak." ¹³The woman said, "Why then have you planned such a thing against the people of God? For in speaking this word the king is like one who is guilty, *in that* the king does not bring back ᴬhis banished one. ¹⁴For we will surely die and are like water spilled on the ground, which cannot be gathered up. Yet God does not take away life, but makes plans so that ᴬthe banished one will not be cast out from Him. ¹⁵Now then, the reason I have come to speak this word to my lord the king is that the people have made me afraid; so your servant said, 'Let me now speak to the king, perhaps the king will perform the request of his slave. ¹⁶For the king will listen, to save his slave from the hand of the man who would eliminate both me and my son from ᴬthe inheritance of God.' ¹⁷Then your servant said, 'Please let the word of my lord the king be comforting, for as ᴬthe angel of God, so is my lord the king to discern good and evil. And may the Lᴏʀᴅ your God be with you.'"

¹⁸Then the king answered and said to the woman, "Please do not hide anything from me that I am about to ask you." And the woman said, "Let my lord the king please speak." ¹⁹So the king said, "Is the hand of Joab with you in all this?" And the woman replied, "As your soul lives, my lord the king, no one can turn to the right or to the left from anything that my lord the king has spoken. Indeed, it was ᴬyour servant Joab who commanded me, and it was he who put

14:3ᴬ2 Sam 14:19   14:4ᴬ1 Sam 25:23
14:7ᴬMatt 21:38   14:9ᴬ1 Kin 2:33
14:11ᴬNum 35:19, 21; Deut 19:4-10
14:13ᴬ2 Sam 13:37, 38   14:14ᴬNum 35:15, 25, 28
14:16ᴬDeut 32:9; 1 Sam 26:19   14:17ᴬ1 Sam 29:9;
2 Sam 14:20   14:19ᴬ2 Sam 14:3

14:4¹Many mss and ancient versions *came*

all these words in the mouth of your servant. 20 In order to change the appearance of things your servant Joab has done this thing. But my lord is wise, ^like the wisdom of the angel of God, to know all that is on the earth."

ABSALOM RETURNS

21 Then the king said to Joab, "Behold now, ^I will certainly do this thing; go then, bring back the young man Absalom." 22 And Joab fell on his face to the ground, prostrated himself, and blessed the king; then Joab said, "Today your servant knows that I have found favor in your sight, my lord the king, in that the king has performed the request of his servant." 23 So Joab arose and went to ^Geshur, and brought Absalom to Jerusalem. 24 However, the king said, "He shall return to ^his own house, but he shall not see my face." So Absalom returned to his own house and did not see the king's face.

25 Now in all Israel there was no one as handsome as Absalom, so highly praised; ^from the sole of his foot to the top of his head there was no impairment in him. 26 And when he ^cut the hair of his head (and it was at the end of every year that he cut *it*, because it was heavy on him, so he cut it), he weighed the hair of his head at ¹two hundred shekels by the king's weight. 27 And to Absalom there were born three sons, and one daughter whose name was ^Tamar; she was a woman of beautiful appearance.

28 Now Absalom lived two full years in Jerusalem, ^yet he did not see the king's face. 29 Then Absalom sent for Joab, to send him to the king, but he would not come to

him. So he sent *word* again a second time, but he would not come. 30 Therefore he said to his servants, "See, ^Joab's plot is next to mine, and he has barley there; go and set it on fire." So Absalom's servants set the plot on fire. 31 Then Joab got up, came to Absalom at his house, and said to him, "Why have your servants set my plot on fire?" 32 Absalom answered Joab, "Behold, I sent for you, saying, 'Come here, so that I may send you to the king, to say, "Why have I come from Geshur? It would be better for me still to be there."' Now then, let me see the king's face, ^and if there is guilt in me, he can have me executed." 33 So when Joab came to the king and told him, he summoned Absalom. Then *Absalom* came to the king and prostrated himself with his face to the ground before the king; and ^the king kissed Absalom.

ABSALOM'S CONSPIRACY

15 Now it came about after this that ^Absalom provided for himself a chariot and horses, and fifty men to run ahead of him. 2 And Absalom used to rise early and ^stand beside the road to the gate; and when any man who had a lawsuit was to come before the king for judgment, Absalom would call out to him and say, "From what city are you?" And he would say, "Your servant is from one of the tribes of Israel." 3 Then Absalom would say to him, "See, ^your

14:20 ^2 Sam 14:17; 19:27 14:21 ^2 Sam 14:11
14:23 ^Deut 3:14; 2 Sam 13:37, 38 14:24 ^2 Sam 13:20
14:25 ^Job 2:7; Is 1:6 14:26 ^Ezek 44:20
14:27 ^2 Sam 13:1 14:28 ^2 Sam 14:24
14:30 ^Judg 15:3–5 14:32 ^1 Sam 20:8; Prov 28:13
14:33 ^Gen 33:4; Luke 15:20 15:1 ^1 Kin 1:5
15:2 ^Ruth 4:1; 2 Sam 19:8 15:3 ^Prov 12:2

14:26 ¹About 4 lb. or 1.8 kg

claims are good and right, but you have no one to listen to you on the part of the king." [4]Moreover, Absalom would say, "^Oh that someone would appoint me judge in the land, then every man who has a lawsuit or claim could come to me, and I would give him justice!" [5]And whenever a man approached to prostrate himself before him, he would put out his hand and take hold of him and ^kiss him. [6]Absalom dealt this way with all Israel who came to the king for judgment; ^so Absalom stole the hearts of the people of Israel.

[7]Now it came about at the end of [1]four years that Absalom said to the king, "Please let me go and pay my vow which I have made to the LORD, in ^Hebron. [8]For your servant made a vow while I was living in Geshur in Aram, saying, '^If the LORD will indeed bring me back to Jerusalem, then I will serve the LORD.'" [9]The king said to him, "Go in peace." So he got up and went to Hebron. [10]But Absalom sent spies throughout the tribes of Israel, saying, "As soon as you hear the sound of the trumpet, then you shall say, '^Absalom is king in Hebron!'" [11]Then two hundred men went with Absalom from Jerusalem, ^who were invited and went innocently, for they did not know anything. [12]And Absalom sent for ^Ahithophel the Gilonite, David's counselor, from his city Giloh, while he was offering the sacrifices. And the conspiracy was strong, for [B]the people continually increased with Absalom.

DAVID FLEES JERUSALEM

[13]Then a messenger came to David, saying, "^The hearts of the people of Israel are with Absalom." [14]So David said to all his servants who were with him in Jerusalem, "^Arise and let's flee, for *otherwise* none of us will escape from Absalom. Go quickly, or he will hurry and overtake us, and bring disaster on us and strike the city with the edge of the sword." [15]Then the king's servants said to the king, "Behold, your servants *will do* whatever my lord the king chooses." [16]So the king left, and all his household with him; but ^the king left ten concubines behind to take care of the house. [17]The king left, and all the people with him, and they stopped at the last house. [18]Now all of his servants passed by beside him, and ^all the Cherethites, all the Pelethites, and all the Gittites, six hundred men who had come with him from Gath, passed by before the king.

[19]Then the king said to ^Ittai the Gittite, "Why should you go with us too? Return and stay with your king, since you are a foreigner and an exile as well; *return* to your own place. [20]You came *only* yesterday, so should I make you wander with us today, while ^I go wherever I go? Return and take your brothers back; [B]mercy and truth be with you." [21]But Ittai answered the king and said, "As the LORD lives, and as my lord the king lives, ^wherever my lord the king may be, whether for death or for life, there assuredly shall your servant be!"

15:4 ^Judg 9:29   15:5 ^2 Sam 14:33; 20:9
15:6 ^Rom 16:18   15:7 ^2 Sam 3:2, 3
15:8 ^Gen 28:20, 21   15:10 ^1 Kin 1:34; 2 Kin 9:13
15:11 ^1 Sam 9:13   15:12 ^2 Sam 15:31   [B]Ps 3:1
15:13 ^Judg 9:3; 2 Sam 15:6   15:14 ^2 Sam 12:11; Ps 3
15:16 ^2 Sam 16:21, 22   15:18 ^2 Sam 8:18
15:19 ^2 Sam 18:2   15:20 ^1 Sam 23:13   [B]2 Sam 2:6
15:21 ^Ruth 1:16, 17; Prov 17:17

15:7 [1]As in some ancient versions; MT *forty*

22Then David said to Ittai, "Go and cross over *the brook Kidron*." So Ittai the Gittite crossed over with all his men and all the ¹little ones who *were* with him. 23While all the country was weeping with a loud voice, all the people were crossing over. The king was also crossing over ᴬthe brook Kidron, and all the people were crossing over toward the way of the wilderness.

24Now behold, ᴬZadok also *came,* and all the Levites with him, carrying the ark of the covenant of God. And they set down the ark of God, and Abiathar came up until all the people had finished crossing over from the city. 25And the king said to Zadok, "Return the ark of God to the city. If I find favor in the sight of the LORD, then ᴬHe will bring me back and show me *both* it and ᴮHis habitation. 26But if He says this: 'ᴬI have no delight in you,' *then* here I am, ᴮlet Him do to me as seems good to Him." 27The king also said to Zadok the priest, "Are you *not* ᴬa seer? Return to the city in peace, and your two sons with you, your son Ahimaaz and Jonathan the son of Abiathar. 28See, I am going to wait ᴬat the river crossing places of the wilderness until word comes from you to inform me." 29So Zadok and Abiathar returned the ark of God to Jerusalem and remained there.

30And David was going up the ascent of the *Mount of* Olives, weeping as he went, and his head was covered, and he was walking ᴬbarefoot. Then all the people who were with him each covered his own head, and they were going up, weeping as they went. 31Now *someone* informed David, saying, "ᴬAhithophel is among the conspirators with Absalom." And David said, "LORD, please make the advice of Ahithophel foolish."

32It happened as David was coming to the summit, where God was worshiped, that behold, Hushai the ᴬArchite met him with his coat torn, and dust on his head. 33And David said to him, "If you go over with me, then you will become ᴬa burden to me. 34But if you return to the city and ᴬsay to Absalom, 'I will be your servant, O king; even *as* I was your father's servant in time past, so now I will also be your servant,' then you can foil the advice of Ahithophel for me. 35Are Zadok and Abiathar the priests not with you there? So it shall be that ᴬwhatever you hear from the king's house, you shall report to Zadok and Abiathar the priests. 36Behold their two sons are there with them, Ahimaaz, Zadok's *son* and Jonathan, Abiathar's *son;* and ᴬby them you shall send me everything that you hear." 37So Hushai, ᴬDavid's friend, came into the city, and Absalom came into Jerusalem.

ZIBA, A FALSE SERVANT

16 Now when David had gone on a little beyond the summit, behold, ᴬZiba the servant of Mephibosheth met him ᴮwith a team of saddled donkeys, and on them *were* two hundred loaves of bread, a hundred cakes of raisins, a hundred summer fruits, and a jug of wine.

15:23ᴬ1 Kin 15:13; 2 Chr 29:16   15:24ᴬ2 Sam 8:17; 20:25   15:25ᴬPs 43:3   ᴮEx 15:13   15:26ᴬ1 Chr 21:7   ᴮ1 Sam 3:18   15:27ᴬ1 Sam 9:6-9   15:28ᴬJosh 5:10; 2 Sam 17:16   15:30ᴬIs 20:2-4   15:31ᴬ2 Sam 15:12   15:32ᴬJosh 16:2   15:33ᴬ2 Sam 19:35   15:34ᴬ2 Sam 16:19   15:35ᴬ2 Sam 17:15, 16   15:36ᴬ2 Sam 17:17   15:37ᴬ2 Sam 16:16; 1 Chr 27:33   16:1ᴬ2 Sam 9:2-13   ᴮ1 Sam 25:18

15:22 ¹I.e., children; here, families of the men

²And the king said to Ziba, "Why do you have these?" And Ziba said, "ᴬThe donkeys are for the king's household to ride, the bread and summer fruit are for the young men to eat, and the wine, for whoever is weary in the wilderness to drink." ³Then the king said, "And where is ᴬyour master's son?" And Ziba said to the king, "Behold, he is staying in Jerusalem, for he said, 'Today the house of Israel will restore the kingdom of my father to me.'" ⁴So the king said to Ziba, "Behold, all that belongs to Mephibosheth is yours." And Ziba said, "I prostrate myself; may I find favor in your sight, my lord, the king!"

DAVID IS CURSED

⁵When King David came to Bahurim, behold, a man was coming out from there from the family of the house of Saul, and ᴬhis name was Shimei, the son of Gera; he was coming out, cursing as he came. ⁶He also threw stones at David and all the servants of King David; and all the people and all the warriors were on his right and on his left. ⁷This is what Shimei said when he cursed: "Go away, go away, ᴬyou man of bloodshed and worthless man! ⁸ᴬThe Lᴏʀᴅ has brought back upon you all the bloodshed of the house of Saul, in whose place you have become king; and the Lᴏʀᴅ has handed the kingdom over to your son Absalom. And behold, you are *caught* in your own evil, for you are a man of bloodshed!"

⁹Then Abishai the son of Zeruiah said to the king, "Why should ᴬthis dead dog ᴮcurse my lord the king? Now let me go over and cut off his head." ¹⁰But the king said, "What *business* of mine is yours, you sons of Zeruiah? ᴬIf he curses, and if the Lᴏʀᴅ has told him, 'Curse David,' ᴮthen who should say, 'Why have you done so?'" ¹¹Then David said to Abishai and to all his servants, "Behold, ᴬmy son who came out of my own body seeks my life; how much more now *this* Benjaminite? Leave him alone and let him curse, for the Lᴏʀᴅ has told him. ¹²Perhaps the Lᴏʀᴅ will look on my misery and ᴬreturn good to me instead of his cursing this day." ¹³So David and his men went on the road; and Shimei kept going on the hillside close beside him, and as he went he cursed and threw stones and dirt at him. ¹⁴And the king and all the people who were with him arrived exhausted, and he refreshed himself there.

ABSALOM ENTERS JERUSALEM

¹⁵ᴬThen Absalom and all the people, the men of Israel, entered Jerusalem, and Ahithophel with him. ¹⁶Now it came about, when ᴬHushai the Archite, David's friend, came to Absalom, that Hushai said to Absalom, "*Long* live the king! *Long* live the king!" ¹⁷But Absalom said to Hushai, "Is this your loyalty to your friend? ᴬWhy did you not go with your friend?" ¹⁸So Hushai said to Absalom, "No! For whomever the Lᴏʀᴅ, this people, and all the men of Israel have chosen, his I shall be, and with him I shall remain. ¹⁹Besides, ᴬwhom should I serve? *Should I* not *serve* in the presence of his son? Just as I have served in

16:2ᴬJudg 10:4   16:3ᴬ2 Sam 9:9, 10
16:5ᴬ2 Sam 19:16–23; 1 Kin 2:8, 9, 44
16:7ᴬ2 Sam 12:9   16:8ᴬ2 Sam 21:1–9
16:9ᴬ2 Sam 9:8   ᴮEx 22:28   16:10ᴬJohn 18:11
ᴮRom 9:20   16:11ᴬ2 Sam 12:11   16:12ᴬDeut 23:5;
Rom 8:28   16:15ᴬ2 Sam 15:12, 37   16:16ᴬ2 Sam 15:37
16:17ᴬ2 Sam 19:25   16:19ᴬ2 Sam 15:34

your father's presence, so I shall be in your presence."

²⁰Then Absalom said to Ahithophel, "Give your advice. What should we do?" ²¹Ahithophel said to Absalom, "ᴬHave relations with your father's concubines, whom he has left behind to take care of the house; then all Israel will hear that you have made yourself repulsive to your father. The hands of all who are with you will also be strengthened." ²²So they pitched a tent for Absalom on the roof, ᴬand Absalom had relations with his father's concubines ᴮin the sight of all Israel. ²³Now ᴬthe advice of Ahithophel, which he gave in those days, *was taken* as though one inquired of the word of God; ᴮso *was* all the advice of Ahithophel *regarded* by both David and Absalom.

HUSHAI'S COUNSEL

17 Furthermore, Ahithophel said to Absalom, "Please let me choose twelve thousand men and let me set out and pursue David tonight. ²ᴬAnd I will attack him while he is weary and exhausted and startle him, so that all the people who are with him will flee. Then ᴮI will strike and kill the king *when he is* alone, ³and I will bring all the people back to you. The return of everyone depends on the man whom you are seeking; *then* all the people will be at ᴬpeace." ⁴And the plan pleased Absalom and all the elders of Israel.

⁵Nevertheless, Absalom said, "Now call ᴬHushai the Archite also, and let's hear what he has to say." ⁶When Hushai had come to Absalom, Absalom said to him, "Ahithophel has proposed this plan. Should we carry out his plan? If not, say *so* yourself." ⁷So Hushai said to Absalom, "ᴬThis time the advice that Ahithophel has given is not good." ⁸Then Hushai said, "You yourself know your father and his men, that they are warriors and they are fierce, ᴬlike a bear deprived of her cubs in the field. And your father is an expert in warfare, and he will not spend the night with the people. ⁹Behold, he has now hidden himself in one of the ravines, or in another place; and it will be that when he falls on them at the first *attack,* whoever hears *it* will say, 'There has been a slaughter among the people who follow Absalom!' ¹⁰And even the one who is valiant, whose heart is like the heart of a lion, ᴬwill completely despair; for all Israel knows that your father is a mighty man, and those who are with him are valiant men. ¹¹But I advise that all Israel be fully gathered to you, ᴬfrom Dan even to Beersheba, like the sand that is by the sea in abundance; and that you personally go into battle. ¹²Then we will come to him in one of the places where he can be found, and we will fall on him ᴬjust as the dew falls on the ground; and of him and of all the men who are with him, not even one will be left. ¹³And if he withdraws into a city, then all Israel shall bring ropes to that city, and we will ᴬdrag it into the ¹valley until not even a pebble is found there." ¹⁴Then Absalom and all the men of Israel said, "The advice of Hushai the Archite is better than the advice of Ahithophel."

16:21ᴬ2 Sam 15:16; 20:3   16:22ᴬ2 Sam 15:16
ᴮ2 Sam 12:11, 12   16:23ᴬ2 Sam 17:14, 23   ᴮ2 Sam 15:12
17:2ᴬ2 Sam 16:14   ᴮ1 Kin 22:31   17:3ᴬJer 6:14
17:5ᴬ2 Sam 15:32–34   17:7ᴬ2 Sam 16:21
17:8ᴬHos 13:8   17:10ᴬJosh 2:9-11   17:11ᴬ1 Sam 3:20
17:12ᴬPs 110:3; Mic 5:7   17:13ᴬMic 1:6

17:13¹Or *wadi;* i.e., a dry stream bed

For ^the Lord had ordained to foil the good advice of Ahithophel, in order for the Lord to bring disaster on Absalom.

HUSHAI'S WARNING SAVES DAVID

¹⁵Then ^Hushai said to Zadok and to Abiathar the priests, "This is what Ahithophel advised Absalom and the elders of Israel *to do,* and this is what I have advised. ¹⁶Now then, send *a messenger* quickly and tell David, saying, '^Do not spend the night at the river crossing places of the wilderness, but by all means cross over, or else the king and all the people who are with him will be destroyed.'" ¹⁷Now Jonathan and Ahimaaz were staying at ^En-rogel, and a female servant would go and inform them, and they would go and inform King David, for they could not allow themselves to be seen entering the city. ¹⁸But a boy did see them, and he told Absalom; so the two of them left quickly and came to the house of a man ^in Bahurim, who had a well in his courtyard, and they went down into it. ¹⁹And ^the woman took a cover and spread it over the well's mouth and scattered barley meal on it, so that nothing was known. ²⁰Then Absalom's servants came to the woman at the house and said, "Where are Ahimaaz and Jonathan?" And ^the woman said to them, "They have crossed the brook of water." And when they searched and did not find *them,* they returned to Jerusalem.

²¹It came about after they had departed, that they came up out of the well and went and reported to King David; and they said to David, "^Set out and cross over the water quickly, because this is what Ahithophel has advised against you." ²²Then David and all the people who *were* with him set out and crossed the Jordan; by dawn not even one remained who had not crossed the Jordan.

²³Now when Ahithophel saw that his advice had not been followed, he saddled *his* donkey and set out and went to his home, to ^his city, and set his house in order, and ^hanged himself; so he died and was buried in his father's grave.

²⁴Then David came to ^Mahanaim. And Absalom crossed the Jordan, he and all the men of Israel with him. ²⁵Absalom put Amasa in command of the army in place of Joab. Now Amasa was the son of a man whose name was Ithra the Israelite, who had relations with Abigail the daughter of ^Nahash, sister of Zeruiah, Joab's mother. ²⁶And Israel and Absalom camped in the land of Gilead.

²⁷Now when David had come to Mahanaim, Shobi ^the son of Nahash from Rabbah of the sons of Ammon, Machir the son of Ammiel from Lo-debar, and Barzillai the Gileadite from Rogelim, ²⁸brought ^beds, basins, pottery, wheat, barley, flour, roasted *grain,* beans, lentils, roasted *seeds,* ²⁹honey, curds, sheep, and cheese of the herd, for David and the people who *were* with him, ^to eat. For they said, "The people are hungry and exhausted and thirsty in the wilderness."

17:14 ^2 Sam 15:31, 34; Ps 9:15, 16
17:15 ^2 Sam 15:35, 36   17:16 ^2 Sam 15:28
17:17 ^Josh 15:7; 18:16   17:18 ^2 Sam 3:16; 16:5
17:19 ^Josh 2:4-6   17:20 ^Josh 2:3-5; 1 Sam 19:12-17
17:21 ^2 Sam 17:15, 16   17:23 ^2 Sam 15:12   ^B Matt 27:5
17:24 ^Gen 32:2, 10; 2 Sam 2:8   17:25 ^1 Chr 2:16
17:27 ^1 Sam 11:1; 2 Sam 10:1, 2   17:28 ^Prov 11:25;
Matt 5:7   17:29 ^2 Sam 16:2, 14; Rom 12:13

ABSALOM KILLED

18 Then David took a count of the people who were with him and ^appointed over them commanders of thousands and commanders of hundreds. ²And David sent the people out, ^a third under the command of Joab, a third under the command of Abishai the son of Zeruiah, Joab's brother, and a third under the command of Ittai the Gittite. And the king said to the people, "I myself will certainly go out with you also." ³But the people said, "^You should not go out; for if in fact we flee, they will not care about us; and if half of us die, they will not care about us. But you are worth ten thousand of us; so now it is better that you will be *ready* to help us from the city." ⁴Then the king said to them, "Whatever seems best to you I will do." So ^the king stood beside the gate, and all the people went out by hundreds and thousands. ⁵But the king commanded Joab, Abishai, and Ittai, saying, "*Deal* gently with the young man Absalom for my sake." And ^all the people heard when the king commanded all the commanders regarding Absalom.

⁶Then the people went out to the field against Israel, and the battle took place in ^the forest of Ephraim. ⁷The people of Israel were defeated there by the servants of David, and the slaughter there that day was great, twenty thousand *men*. ⁸For the battle there was spread over the whole countryside, and the forest devoured more people that day than the sword devoured.

⁹Now Absalom encountered the servants of David. Absalom was riding on *his* mule, and the mule went under the branches of a massive oak. Then ^his head caught firmly in the oak, and he was left hanging between the sky and earth, while the mule that was under him kept going. ¹⁰When a certain man saw *him,* he informed Joab and said, "Behold, I saw Absalom hanging in an oak." ¹¹Then Joab said to the man who had informed him, "So behold, you saw *him!* Why then did you not strike him there to the ground? And *it would have been* my duty to give you ten *pieces* of silver and a belt." ¹²But the man said to Joab, "Even if I were to receive a thousand *pieces of* silver in my hand, I would not put out my hand against the king's son; for ^in our hearing the king commanded you, Abishai, and Ittai, saying, 'Protect the young man Absalom for me!' ¹³Otherwise, if I had dealt treacherously against his life (and ^there is nothing hidden from the king), then you yourself would have avoided *me.*" ¹⁴Then Joab said, "I will not waste time here with you." ^So he took three spears in his hand and thrust them through the heart of Absalom while he was still alive in the midst of the oak. ¹⁵And ten young men who carried Joab's armor gathered around and struck Absalom and killed him.

¹⁶Then ^Joab blew the trumpet, and the people returned from pursuing Israel, for Joab restrained the people. ¹⁷And they took Absalom and threw him into a deep pit in the forest, and ^erected over him a very large pile of stones. And all Israel fled, each to his *own* tent. ¹⁸Now

18:1^Ex 18:25; 1 Sam 22:7   18:2^Judg 7:16; 1 Sam 11:11
18:3^2 Sam 21:17   18:4^2 Sam 18:24   18:5^2 Sam 18:12
18:6^Josh 17:15, 18; 2 Sam 17:26   18:9^2 Sam 14:26
18:12^2 Sam 18:5   18:13^2 Sam 14:19, 20
18:14^2 Sam 14:30   18:16^2 Sam 2:28; 20:22
18:17^Deut 21:20, 21; Josh 7:26

Absalom in his lifetime had taken and ^set up for himself a memorial stone, which is in ᴮthe King's Valley, for he said, "I have no son to continue my name." So he named the memorial stone after his own name, and it is called Absalom's Monument to this day.

DAVID IS GRIEF-STRICKEN

¹⁹Then ^Ahimaaz the son of Zadok said, "Please let me run and bring the king news that the LORD has freed him from the hand of his enemies!" ²⁰But Joab said to him, "You are not the man *to bring* news this day, but you shall bring news another day; however, you shall bring no news this day, because the king's son is dead." ²¹Then Joab said to the Cushite, "Go, tell the king what you have seen." So the Cushite bowed to Joab and ran. ²²However, Ahimaaz the son of Zadok said once more to Joab, "But whatever happens, please let me also run after the Cushite." And Joab said, "Why would you run, my son, since ^you will have no messenger's reward for going?" ²³"But whatever happens," *he said,* "I will run." So he said to him, "Run." Then Ahimaaz ran by way of the plain and passed by the Cushite.

²⁴Now David was sitting between the two gates; and ^the watchman went to the roof of the gate by the wall, and raised his eyes and looked; and behold, a man was running by himself. ²⁵So the watchman called out and told the king. And the king said, "If he is by himself there is good news in his mouth." And he came nearer and nearer. ²⁶Then the watchman saw another man running; and the watchman called to the gatekeeper and said, "Behold, *another* man is running by himself." And the king said, "This one also is bringing good news." ²⁷The watchman said, "I think the running form of the first one is like the running form of Ahimaaz the son of Zadok." And the king said, "^This is a good man, and he is coming with good news."

²⁸Then Ahimaaz called out and said to the king, "All is well." And he prostrated himself before the king with his face to the ground. And he said, "^Blessed is the LORD your God, who has turned over the men who raised their hands against my lord the king." ²⁹But the king said, "^Is it well with the young man Absalom?" And Ahimaaz answered, "When Joab sent the king's servant, and your servant, I saw a great commotion, but I did not know what *it was.*" ³⁰Then the king said, "Turn aside and stand here." So he turned aside and stood still.

³¹Then behold, the Cushite arrived, and the Cushite said, "Let my lord the king receive good news, for ^the LORD has freed you this day from the hand of all those who rose up against you." ³²Then the king said to the Cushite, "Is it well with the young man Absalom?" And the Cushite answered, "^May the enemies of my lord the king, and all who rise up against you for evil, be like *that* young man!"

³³Then the king trembled and went up to the chamber over the gate and wept. And this is what he said as he walked: "My son Absalom, my son, my son Absalom! ^If only I had died instead of you, Absalom, my son, my son!"

18:18^1 Sam 15:12   ᴮGen 14:17   18:19^2 Sam 15:36
18:22^2 Sam 18:29   18:24^2 Sam 13:34; 2 Kin 9:17
18:27^1 Kin 1:42   18:28^1 Sam 17:46   18:29^2 Sam 20:9;
2 Kin 4:26   18:31^Judg 5:31; 2 Sam 18:19
18:32^1 Sam 25:26   18:33^Ex 32:32; Rom 9:3

JOAB DISAPPROVES OF DAVID'S MOURNING

19 Then it was reported to Joab, "Behold, ^the king is weeping and he mourns for Absalom." ²So the victory that day was turned into mourning for all the people, because the people heard *it* said that day, "The king is in mourning over his son." ³And the people entered the city surreptitiously that day, just as people who are humiliated surreptitiously flee in battle. ⁴And the king ^covered his face and cried out with a loud voice, "My son Absalom, Absalom, my son, my son!" ⁵Then Joab came into the house to the king and said, "Today you have shamed all your servants, who have saved your life today and the lives of your sons and daughters, the lives of your wives, and the lives of your concubines, ⁶by loving those who hate you, and by hating those who love you. For you have revealed today that commanders and servants are nothing to you; for I know today that if Absalom were alive and all of us were dead today, then it would be right as far as you are concerned. ⁷Now therefore arise, go out and speak kindly to your servants, for I swear by the Lord, if you do not go out, ^no man will stay the night with you, and this will be worse for you than all the misfortune that has happened to you from your youth until now!"

DAVID RESTORED AS KING

⁸So the king got up and sat at the gate. When they told all the people, saying, "Behold, the king is sitting at the gate," then all the people came before the king.

Now ^Israel had fled, each to his tent. ⁹And all the people were quarreling throughout the tribes of Israel, saying, "^The king rescued us from the hands of our enemies and saved us from the hands of the Philistines, but now ^he has fled out of the land from Absalom. ¹⁰However, Absalom, whom we anointed over us, has died in battle. Now then, why are you silent about bringing the king back?"

¹¹Then King David sent *word* to ^Zadok and Abiathar the priests, saying, "Speak to the elders of Judah, saying, 'Why are you the last to bring the king back to his house, since the word of all Israel has come to the king, *even* to his house? ¹²You are my brothers; ^you are my bone and my flesh. Why then should you be the last to bring back the king?' ¹³And say to Amasa, 'Are you not my bone and my flesh? May God do so to me, and more so, if you will not be ^commander of the army for me continually, ^in place of Joab.'" ¹⁴So he turned the hearts of all the men of Judah ^as one man, so that they sent *word* to the king, *saying,* "Return, you and all your servants." ¹⁵The king then returned and came as far as the Jordan. And *the men of* Judah came to ^Gilgal in order to go to meet the king, to escort the king across the Jordan.

¹⁶Then ^Shimei the son of Gera, the Benjaminite who was from Bahurim, hurried and came down with the men of Judah to meet King David. ¹⁷And there were a thousand men of Benjamin with him, and ^Ziba the servant of the house of Saul, and his fifteen sons and

19:1^2 Sam 18:5, 14   19:4^2 Sam 15:30
19:7^Prov 14:28   19:8^2 Sam 18:17   19:9^2 Sam 8:1-14
^2 Sam 15:14   19:11^2 Sam 15:29   19:12^2 Sam 5:1
19:13^2 Sam 8:16   ^2 Sam 3:27-39   19:14^Judg 20:1
19:15^Josh 5:9; 1 Sam 11:14, 15   19:16^2 Sam 16:5-13;
1 Kin 2:8   19:17^2 Sam 16:1-4; 19:26, 27

his twenty servants with him; and they rushed to the Jordan before the king. ¹⁸Then they crossed the shallow places *repeatedly* to bring over the king's household, and to do what was good in his sight. And Shimei the son of Gera fell down before the king as he was about to cross the Jordan. ¹⁹And he said to the king, "ᴬMay my lord not consider me guilty, nor call to mind what your servant did wrong on the day when my lord the king went out from Jerusalem, so that the king would take *it* to heart. ²⁰For your servant knows that I have sinned; so behold, I have come today, ᴬthe first of all the house of Joseph to go down to meet my lord the king." ²¹But Abishai the son of Zeruiah responded, "ᴬShould Shimei not be put to death for this, ᴮthe fact that he cursed the Lᴏʀᴅ's anointed?" ²²David then said, "What is there between you and me, you sons of Zeruiah, that you should be an adversary to me today? ᴬShould anyone be put to death in Israel today? For do I not know that I am king over Israel today?" ²³So the king said to Shimei, "ᴬYou shall not die." The king also swore to him.

²⁴Then ᴬMephibosheth the grandson of Saul came down to meet the king; but he had neither tended to his feet, nor trimmed his mustache, nor washed his clothes since the day the king departed until the day he came *home* in peace. ²⁵And it was when he came *from* Jerusalem to meet the king, that the king said to him, "ᴬWhy did you not go with me, Mephibosheth?" ²⁶So he said, "My lord the king, my servant betrayed me; for your servant said, 'I will saddle the donkey for myself so that I may ride on it and go with

the king,' ᴬsince your servant cannot walk. ²⁷Furthermore, ᴬhe has slandered your servant to my lord the king; but my lord the king is ᴮlike the angel of God, therefore do what is good in your sight. ²⁸For all my father's household was only people *worthy* of death to my lord the king; ᴬyet you placed your servant among those who ate at your own table. So what right do I still have, that I should complain anymore to the king?" ²⁹So the king said to him, "Why do you still speak of your affairs? I have decided, 'You and Ziba shall divide the land.'" ³⁰And Mephibosheth said to the king, "Let him even take it all, since my lord the king has come safely to his own house."

³¹Now ᴬBarzillai the Gileadite had come down from Rogelim; and he went on to the Jordan with the king to escort him over the Jordan. ³²Barzillai was very old: eighty years old; and he had ᴬprovided the king food while he stayed in Mahanaim, for he was a very great man. ³³So the king said to Barzillai, "You cross over with me, and I will provide you food in Jerusalem with me." ³⁴But Barzillai said to the king, "ᴬHow long do I still have to live, that I should go up with the king to Jerusalem? ³⁵I am now ᴬeighty years old. Can I distinguish between good and bad? Or can your servant taste what I eat or what I drink? Or can I still hear the voice of men and women singing? ᴮWhy then should your servant be an added burden

19:19 ᴬ1 Sam 22:15; 2 Sam 16:6-8   19:20 ᴬ2 Sam 16:5
19:21 ᴬ2 Sam 16:7, 8   ᴮEx 22:28   19:22 ᴬ1 Sam 11:13
19:23 ᴬ1 Kin 2:8   19:24 ᴬ2 Sam 9:6-10
19:25 ᴬ2 Sam 16:17   19:26 ᴬ2 Sam 9:3
19:27 ᴬ2 Sam 16:3, 4   ᴮ2 Sam 14:17, 20
19:28 ᴬ2 Sam 9:7, 10, 13   19:31 ᴬ2 Sam 17:27-29;
1 Kin 2:7   19:32 ᴬ2 Sam 17:27-29   19:34 ᴬGen 47:8
19:35 ᴬPs 90:10   ᴮ2 Sam 15:33

to my lord the king? ³⁶ Your servant would merely cross over the Jordan with the king. So why should the king compensate me *with* this reward? ³⁷ Please let your servant return, so that I may die in my *own* city near the grave of my father and my mother. However, here is your servant ᴬChimham; let him cross over with my lord the king, and do for him what is good in your sight." ³⁸ And the king answered, "Chimham shall cross over with me, and I will do for him what is good in your sight; and whatever you require of me, I will do for you." ³⁹ All the people crossed over the Jordan and the king crossed *too*. The king then ᴬkissed Barzillai and blessed him, and he returned to his place.

⁴⁰ Now the king went on to Gilgal, and Chimham went on with him; and all the people of Judah and also ᴬhalf the people of Israel accompanied the king. ⁴¹ And behold, all the men of Israel came to the king and said to the king, "Why have our brothers, ᴬthe men of Judah, abducted you and brought the king and his household and all David's men with him, over the Jordan?" ⁴² Then all the men of Judah answered the men of Israel, "Because ᴬthe king is a close relative to us. Why then are you angry about this matter? Have we eaten at all at the king's expense, or has anything been taken for us?" ⁴³ But the men of Israel answered the men of Judah and said, "ᴬWe have ten parts in the king, therefore we also *have* more *claim* on David than you. Why then did you treat us with contempt? Was it not our advice first to bring back our king?" Yet the words of the men of Judah were harsher than the words of the men of Israel.

SHEBA'S REVOLT

20 Now ᴬa worthless man happened to be there whose name was Sheba, the son of Bichri, a Benjaminite; and he blew the trumpet and said,

"ᴮWe have no share in David,
Nor do we have an inheritance
    in the son of Jesse;
Every man to his tents, Israel!"

² So all the men of Israel withdrew from following David *and* followed Sheba the son of Bichri; but the men of Judah remained loyal to their king, from the Jordan even to Jerusalem.

³ Then David came to his house in Jerusalem, and ᴬthe king took the ten women, the concubines whom he had left behind to take care of the house, and put them in custody and provided them with food, but did not have relations with them. So they were locked up until the day of their death, living as widows.

⁴ Now the king said to ᴬAmasa, "Summon the men of Judah for me *within* three days, and be present here yourself." ⁵ So Amasa went to summon *the men of* Judah, but he was ᴬdelayed longer than the set time which he had designated for him. ⁶ And David said to ᴬAbishai, "Now Sheba the son of Bichri will do us more harm than Absalom; take your lord's servants and pursue him, so that he does not find for himself fortified cities and escape from our sight." ⁷ So Joab's men went out after him, ᴬalong with the Cherethites, the Pelethites,

19:37 ᴬ1 Kin 2:7; Jer 41:17 19:39 ᴬRuth 1:14;
2 Sam 14:33   19:40 ᴬ2 Sam 19:9, 10
19:41 ᴬ2 Sam 19:11, 12   19:42 ᴬ2 Sam 19:12
19:43 ᴬ2 Sam 5:1; 1 Kin 11:30, 31   20:1 ᴬ2 Sam 16:7
ᴮ 1 Kin 12:16   20:3 ᴬ2 Sam 15:16; 16:21, 22
20:4 ᴬ2 Sam 17:25; 19:13   20:5 ᴬ1 Sam 13:8
20:6 ᴬ2 Sam 21:17   20:7 ᴬ2 Sam 8:18; 1 Kin 1:38

and all the warriors; and they left Jerusalem to pursue Sheba the son of Bichri. ⁸When they were at the large stone which is in ^Gibeon, Amasa came to meet them. Now Joab was dressed in his military attire, and over it *he had* a belt with a sword in its sheath strapped on at his waist; and as he went forward, it fell out. ⁹And Joab said to Amasa, "Is it going well for you, my brother?" And ^Joab took hold of Amasa by the beard with his right hand to kiss him.

AMASA MURDERED

¹⁰But Amasa was not on guard against the sword which was in Joab's hand, so ^he struck him in the belly with it and spilled out his intestines on the ground, and did not *strike* him again, and he died. Then Joab and his brother Abishai pursued Sheba the son of Bichri. ¹¹Now one of Joab's young men stood by him and said, "Whoever favors Joab and whoever is for David, ^follow Joab!" ¹²But Amasa was wallowing in *his own* blood in the middle of the road. And when the man saw that all the people stood still, he removed Amasa from the road to the field and threw a garment over him when he saw that everyone who came by him stood still.

REVOLT PUT DOWN

¹³As soon as he was removed from the road, all the men went on after Joab to pursue Sheba the son of Bichri. ¹⁴Now he went on through all the tribes of Israel to Abel, that is, Beth-maacah, and all the Berites; and they assembled and went after him as well. ¹⁵And they came and besieged him in Abel Beth-maacah, and ^they built up an assault ramp against the city, and it stood against the outer rampart; and all the people who were with Joab were wreaking destruction in order to topple the wall. ¹⁶Then ^a wise woman called out from the city, "Listen, listen! Please tell Joab, 'Come here that I may speak with you.'" ¹⁷So he approached her, and the woman said, "Are you Joab?" And he answered, "I am." Then she said to him, "Listen to the words of your slave." And he said, "I am listening." ¹⁸Then she spoke, saying, "In the past they used to say, 'They will undoubtedly ask *advice* at Abel,' and that is how they ended *a dispute.* ¹⁹I *am one* of those who are ready for peace *and* faithful in Israel. ^You are trying to destroy a city, even a mother in Israel. Why would you swallow up the inheritance of the LORD?" ²⁰Joab replied, "Far be it, far be it from me that I would consume or destroy! ²¹Such is not the case. But a man from the hill country of Ephraim, ^Sheba the son of Bichri by name, has raised his hand against King David. Only turn him over, and I will depart from the city." And the woman said to Joab, "Behold, his head will be thrown to you over the wall." ²²Then the woman wisely came to all the people. And they cut off the head of Sheba the son of Bichri and threw it to Joab. So ^he blew the trumpet, and they were dispersed from the city, each to his tent. Joab also returned to the king at Jerusalem.

20:8^2 Sam 2:13; 3:30   20:9^Matt 26:49
20:10^2 Sam 2:23; 1 Kin 2:5   20:11^2 Sam 20:13
20:15^2 Kin 19:32; Ezek 4:2   20:16^2 Sam 14:2
20:19^Deut 20:10   20:21^2 Sam 20:2
20:22^2 Sam 20:1

²³ᴬNow Joab was *in command* of the entire army of Israel, and Benaiah the son of Jehoiada was over the Cherethites and the Pelethites; ²⁴and Adoram was over the forced labor, and ᴬJehoshaphat the son of Ahilud was the secretary; ²⁵and Sheva was scribe, and Zadok and ᴬAbiathar were priests; ²⁶Ira the Jairite also was a priest to David.

GIBEONITE'S REVENGE

21 Now there was a famine in the days of David for three years, year after year; and ᴬDavid sought the presence of the LORD. And the LORD said, "*It is* because of Saul and his bloody house, because he put the Gibeonites to death." ²So the king called the Gibeonites and spoke to them (now the Gibeonites were not of the sons of Israel, but of the remnant of the Amorites, and ᴬthe sons of Israel had made a covenant with them, but Saul had sought to kill them in his zeal for the sons of Israel and Judah). ³David said to the Gibeonites, "What should I do for you? And how can I make amends, so that you will bless ᴬthe inheritance of the LORD?" ⁴Then the Gibeonites said to him, "ᴬFor us it is not *a matter* of silver or gold with Saul or his house, nor is it for us to put anyone to death in Israel." Nevertheless *David* said, "I will do for you whatever you say." ⁵So they said to the king, "ᴬThe man who destroyed us and who planned to eliminate us so that we would not exist within any border of Israel— ⁶let seven men from his sons be given to us, and we will hang them before the LORD in Gibeah of Saul, ᴬthe chosen of the LORD." And the king said, "I will give *them*."

⁷But the king spared Mephibosheth, the son of Jonathan, the son of Saul, ᴬbecause of the oath of the LORD which was between them, between David and Saul's son Jonathan. ⁸So the king took the two sons of ᴬRizpah the daughter of Aiah, Armoni and Mephibosheth whom she had borne to Saul, and the five sons of ᴮMerab the daughter of Saul, whom she had borne to Adriel the son of Barzillai the Meholathite. ⁹Then he handed them over to the Gibeonites, and they hanged them on the mountain before the LORD, so that the seven of them fell together; and they were put to death in the first days of harvest at ᴬthe beginning of barley harvest.

¹⁰ᴬAnd Rizpah the daughter of Aiah took sackcloth and spread it out for herself on the rock, from the beginning of harvest until it rained on them from the sky; and ᴮshe allowed neither the birds of the sky to rest on them by day nor the wild animals by night. ¹¹When it was reported to David what Rizpah the daughter of Aiah, the concubine of Saul, had done, ¹²then David went and took ᴬthe bones of Saul and the bones of his son Jonathan from the citizens of Jabesh-gilead, who had stolen them from the public square of Beth-shan, where the Philistines had hanged them on the day the Philistines struck and killed Saul in Gilboa. ¹³He brought up from there the bones of Saul and the bones of his son Jonathan, and they gathered the bones of those who had

20:23ᴬ2 Sam 8:16-18; 1 Kin 4:3-6 **20:24**ᴬ1 Kin 4:3 **20:25**ᴬ1 Kin 4:4 **21:1**ᴬNum 27:21 **21:2**ᴬJosh 9:3, 15-20 **21:3**ᴬ1 Sam 26:19; 2 Sam 20:19 **21:4**ᴬNum 35:31, 32 **21:5**ᴬ2 Sam 21:1 **21:6**ᴬ1 Sam 10:24 **21:7**ᴬ1 Sam 20:12-17; 2 Sam 9:1-7 **21:8**ᴬ2 Sam 3:7 ᴮ1 Sam 18:19 **21:9**ᴬEx 9:31, 32 **21:10**ᴬDeut 21:23 ᴮ1 Sam 17:44, 46 **21:12**ᴬ1 Sam 31:11-13

been hanged. ¹⁴Then they buried the bones of Saul and his son Jonathan in the country of Benjamin in ^Zela, in the grave of his father Kish; so they did everything that the king commanded, and after that ᴮGod responded to prayer for the land.

¹⁵Now when ^the Philistines were at war with Israel again, David went down, and his servants with him; and when they fought against the Philistines, David became weary. ¹⁶Then Ishbi-benob, who was ^among the descendants of the giant, the weight of whose spear was ¹three hundred *shekels* of bronze in weight, had strapped on a new *sword,* and he intended to kill David. ¹⁷But ^Abishai the son of Zeruiah helped him, and struck the Philistine and killed him. Then David's men swore to him, saying, "You shall not go out again with us to battle, so that you do not extinguish the lamp of Israel."

¹⁸^Now it came about after this that there was war again with the Philistines at Gob; then Sibbecai the Hushathite struck and killed Saph, who was among the descendants of the giant. ¹⁹And there was war with the Philistines again at Gob, and Elhanan the son of Jaareoregim the Bethlehemite killed ¹Goliath the Gittite, ^the shaft of whose spear was like a weaver's beam. ²⁰And there was war at Gath again, where there was a man of *great* stature who had six fingers on each hand and six toes on each foot, twenty-four in number; and he also had been born ^to the giant. ²¹When he defied Israel, Jonathan the son of Shimei, David's brother, struck and killed him. ²²^These four were born to the

giant at Gath, and they fell by the hand of David and by the hand of his servants.

DAVID'S PSALM OF DELIVERANCE

22 ^Now David spoke the words of this song to the Lᴏʀᴅ on the day that the Lᴏʀᴅ had saved him from the hand of all his enemies and from the hand of Saul. ²He said,

"^The Lᴏʀᴅ is my rock and my
   fortress and my deliverer;
3   ^My God, my rock, in whom I
   take refuge,
My shield and the horn of my
   salvation, my stronghold and
   my refuge;
My savior, You save me from
   violence.
4 "I call upon the Lᴏʀᴅ, ^who is
   worthy to be praised,
And I am saved from my
   enemies.
5 "For ^the waves of death
   encompassed me;
The floods of destruction
   terrified me;
6 ^The ropes of ¹Sheol
   surrounded me;
The snares of death
   confronted me.
7 "^In my distress I called upon
   the Lᴏʀᴅ,
Yes, I called out to my God;
And from His temple He heard
   my voice,
And my cry for help *came* into
   His ears.

21:14^Josh 18:28   ᴮ2 Sam 24:25   21:15^2 Sam
5:17-25   21:16^Num 13:22, 28; 2 Sam 21:18-22
21:17^2 Sam 20:6-10   21:18^1 Chr 20:4-8
21:19^1 Sam 17:7   21:20^2 Sam 21:16, 18
21:22^1 Chr 20:8   22:1^Ps 18:2-50   22:2^Ps 31:3;
71:3   22:3^Deut 32:4, 37; 1 Sam 2:2   22:4^Ps 48:1;
96:4   22:5^Ps 93:4; Jon 2:3   22:6^Ps 116:3
22:7^Ps 116:4; 120:1

21:16¹About 9 lb. or 4 kg   21:19¹In 1 Chr 20:5, *Lahmi,
the brother of Goliath*   22:6¹I.e., the netherworld

8 "Then the earth shook and
quaked,
^The foundations of heaven
were trembling
And were shaken, because He
was angry.
9 "Smoke went up out of His
nostrils,
^And fire from His mouth was
devouring;
Coals were kindled by it.
10 "He also bowed the heavens
down low, and came down
With ^thick darkness under
His feet.
11 "^He rode on a cherub and flew;
He appeared on ^Bthe wings of
the wind.
12 "^He made darkness canopies
around Him,
A mass of waters, thick clouds
of the sky.
13 "From the brightness before
Him
^Coals of fire were kindled.
14 "^The LORD thundered from
heaven,
And the Most High uttered His
voice.
15 "^And He shot arrows and
scattered them,
Lightning, and routed them.
16 "Then the channels of the sea
appeared,
The foundations of the world
were exposed
By the rebuke of the LORD,
^From the blast of the breath of
His nostrils.
17 "^He sent from on high, He took
me;
^BHe drew me out of many
waters.
18 "He rescued me from my strong
enemy,
From those who hated me, for
they were too strong for me.

19 "They confronted me on the
day of my disaster,
^But the LORD was my
support.
20 "He also brought me out into an
open place;
He rescued me, ^because He
delighted in me.
21 "^The LORD has treated me
in accordance with my
righteousness;
In accordance with the
cleanliness of my hands He
has repaid me.
22 "^For I have kept the ways of the
LORD,
And have not acted wickedly
against my God.
23 "^For all His ordinances *were*
before me,
And *as for* His statutes, I did
not deviate from them.
24 "^I was also blameless toward
Him,
And I have kept myself from
my wrongdoing.
25 "^So the LORD has repaid me
in accordance with my
righteousness,
In accordance with my
cleanliness before His eyes.
26 "^With *the one who is* faithful
You show Yourself faithful,
With the blameless one You
prove Yourself blameless;
27 ^With the *one who is* pure You
show Yourself pure,
But with the perverted You
show Yourself astute.

22:8 ^Job 26:11   22:9 ^Ps 97:3; Heb 12:29
22:10 ^Ps 97:2; Nah 1:3   22:11 ^2 Sam 6:2   ^B Ps 104:3
22:12 ^Job 36:29   22:13 ^2 Sam 22:9   22:14 ^Job
37:2-5; Ps 29:3   22:15 ^Deut 32:23; Josh 10:10
22:16 ^Ex 15:8; Nah 1:4   22:17 ^Ps 144:7   ^B Ex 2:10
22:19 ^Ps 23:4   22:20 ^2 Sam 15:26
22:21 ^1 Sam 26:23; 1 Kin 8:32   22:22 ^Ps 128:1;
Prov 8:32   22:23 ^Deut 6:6-9; Ps 119:30, 102
22:24 ^Eph 1:4; Col 1:21, 22   22:25 ^2 Sam 22:21
22:26 ^Matt 5:7   22:27 ^Matt 5:8; 1 John 3:3

28 "ᴬAnd You save an afflicted
  people;
  But Your eyes are on the
  haughty *whom* You
  humiliate.
29 "ᴬFor You are my lamp, Lᴏʀᴅ;
  And the Lᴏʀᴅ illuminates my
  darkness.
30 "ᴬFor by You I can run at a troop
  of warriors;
  By my God I can leap over a
  wall.
31 "ᴬAs for God, His way is
  blameless;
  The word of the Lᴏʀᴅ is
  refined;
  He is a shield to all who take
  refuge in Him.
32 "ᴬFor who is God, except the
  Lᴏʀᴅ?
  ᴮAnd who is a rock, except our
  God?
33 "ᴬGod is my strong fortress;
  And He sets the blameless on
  His way.
34 "ᴬHe makes my feet like deer's
  feet,
  And sets me on my high
  places.
35 "ᴬHe trains my hands for
  battle,
  So that my arms can bend a
  bow of bronze.
36 "You have also given me ᴬthe
  shield of Your salvation,
  And Your help makes me great.
37 "ᴬYou enlarge my steps under
  me,
  And my feet have not slipped.
38 "I pursued my enemies and
  ᴬeliminated them,
  And I did not turn back until
  they were finished off.
39 "And I have devoured them and
  smashed them, so that they
  would not rise;
  And ᴬthey fell under my feet.

40 "For You have encircled me
  with strength for battle;
  You have forced ᴬthose who
  rose up against me to bow
  down under me.
41 "You have also ᴬmade my enemies
  turn *their* backs to me,
  And I destroyed those who
  hated me.
42 "ᴬThey looked, but there was no
  one to save *them;*
  Even to the Lᴏʀᴅ, but He did
  not answer them.
43 "ᴬThen I pulverized them as the
  dust of the earth;
  ᴮI crushed *and* trampled them
  like the mud of the streets.
44 "ᴬYou have also saved me
  from the contentions of my
  people;
  ᴮYou have kept me as head of
  the nations;
  A people I have not known
  serve me.
45 "ᴬForeigners pretend to obey me;
  As soon as they hear, they
  obey me.
46 "Foreigners lose heart,
  ᴬAnd come trembling out of
  their fortresses.
47 "The Lᴏʀᴅ lives, and blessed be
  my Rock;
  And exalted be ᴬmy God, the
  rock of my salvation,
48 The God who executes
  vengeance for me,
  ᴬAnd brings down peoples
  under me,

22:28 ᴬEx 3:7, 8; Ps 72:12, 13 22:29 ᴬ1 Kin 11:36; Ps 27:1
22:30 ᴬ2 Sam 5:6-8 22:31 ᴬDeut 32:4; Matt 5:48
22:32 ᴬ1 Sam 2:2 ᴮ2 Sam 22:2 22:33 ᴬ2 Sam 22:2;
Ps 31:3, 4 22:34 ᴬ2 Sam 2:18; Hab 3:19
22:35 ᴬPs 144:1 22:36 ᴬEph 6:16, 17
22:37 ᴬ2 Sam 22:20; Prov 4:12 22:38 ᴬEx 15:9
22:39 ᴬMal 4:3 22:40 ᴬPs 44:5 22:41 ᴬEx 23:27;
Josh 10:24 22:42 ᴬIs 17:7, 8 22:43 ᴬ2 Kin 13:7
ᴮIs 10:6 22:44 ᴬ2 Sam 19:9, 14 ᴮ2 Sam 8:1-14
22:45 ᴬPs 66:3; 81:15 22:46 ᴬ1 Sam 14:11; Mic 7:17
22:47 ᴬ2 Sam 22:3; Ps 89:26 22:48 ᴬPs 144:2

⁴⁹ Who also brings me out from
　my enemies;
You also raise me above ^those
　who rise up against me;
You rescue me from the
　violent person.
⁵⁰ "^Therefore I will give thanks
　to You, Lᴏʀᴅ, among the
　nations,
And I will sing praises to Your
　name.
⁵¹ "^*He is* a tower of salvation *to*
　His king,
And ᴮshows favor to His
　anointed,
To David and his descendants
　forever."

DAVID'S LAST SONG

23 Now these are the last words
of David.
David the son of Jesse declares,
^The man who was raised on
　high,
ᴮThe anointed of the God of
　Jacob
And the sweet psalmist of
　Israel, declares,
² "^The Spirit of the Lᴏʀᴅ spoke
　through me,
And His word was on my
　tongue.
³ "The God of Israel said *it;*
^The Rock of Israel spoke to me:
'He who rules over mankind
　righteously,
Who rules *in* the fear of God,
⁴ ^Is like the light of the morning
　when the sun rises,
A morning without clouds,
When the fresh grass *springs*
　out of the earth
From sunshine after rain.'
⁵ "Is my house not indeed so with
　God?
For ^He has made an everlasting
　covenant with me,

Properly ordered in all things,
　and secured;
For will He not indeed make
All my salvation and all *my*
　delight grow?
⁶ "^But the worthless, every one
　of them, are like scattered
　thorns,
Because they cannot be taken
　in hand;
⁷ Instead, the man *who* touches
　them
Must be armed with iron and
　the shaft of a spear,
And ^they will be completely
　burned with fire in *their*
　place."

DAVID'S MIGHTY MEN

⁸^These are the names of the mighty men whom David had: Josheb-basshebeth, a Tahchemonite, chief of the captains; he was *called* Adino the Eznite because of eight hundred who were killed *by him* at one time. ⁹ And after him was Eleazar the son of ^Dodo the ᴮAhohite, one of the three mighty men with David when they defied the Philistines who were gathered there to battle and the men of Israel had withdrawn. ¹⁰^He rose up and struck the Philistines until his hand was weary and it clung to the sword, and the Lᴏʀᴅ brought about a great victory that day; and the people returned after him only to plunder *the dead.*
¹¹Now after him was Shammah the son of Agee, a ^Hararite. And the Philistines were gathered into

22:49^Ps 44:5　22:50^Rom 15:9　22:51^Ps 144:10
ᴮPs 89:24　23:1^2 Sam 7:8, 9　ᴮPs 89:20
23:2^Matt 22:43; 2 Pet 1:21　23:3^2 Sam 22:2, 3, 32
23:4^Judg 5:31; Ps 72:6　23:5^2 Sam 7:12-16; Is 55:3
23:6^Matt 13:41　23:7^Matt 3:10; Heb 6:8
23:8^1 Chr 11:11-47　23:9^1 Chr 27:4　ᴮ1 Chr 8:4
23:10^1 Chr 11:13　23:11^2 Sam 23:33

an army where there was a plot of land full of lentils, and the people fled from the Philistines. ¹²But he took his stand in the midst of the plot, defended it, and struck the Philistines; and ᴬthe Lᴏʀᴅ brought about a great victory.

¹³Then three of the thirty chief men went down and came to David at harvest time to the ᴬcave of Adullam, while the army of the Philistines was camping in ᴮthe Valley of Rephaim. ¹⁴David was then ᴬin the stronghold, while the garrison of the Philistines was then in Bethlehem. ¹⁵And ᴬDavid had a craving and said, "Oh that someone would give me water to drink from the well of Bethlehem which is by the gate!" ¹⁶ᴬSo the three mighty men forced their way into the camp of the Philistines, and drew water from the well of Bethlehem which was by the gate, and carried *it* and brought *it* to David. Yet he would not drink it, but poured it out as an offering to the Lᴏʀᴅ; ¹⁷and he said, "Far be it from me, Lᴏʀᴅ, that I would do this! ᴬ*Should I drink* the blood of the men who went at *the risk of* their lives?" So he would not drink it. These things the three mighty men did.

¹⁸Now ᴬAbishai, the brother of Joab, the son of Zeruiah, was ᴮchief of the thirty. And he swung his spear against three hundred and killed *them,* and had a name as well as the three. ¹⁹He was the most honored among the thirty, so he became their commander; however, he did not attain to *the reputation* of the three.

²⁰Then ᴬBenaiah the son of Jehoiada, the son of a valiant man of Kabzeel, who had done great deeds, killed the two *sons of* Ariel

of Moab. He also went down and killed a lion in the middle of a pit on a snowy day. ²¹And he killed an Egyptian, an impressive man. Now the Egyptian *had* a spear in his hand, but he went down to him with a club and snatched the spear from the Egyptian's hand, and killed him with his own spear. ²²These *things* ᴬBenaiah the son of Jehoiada did, and had a name as well as the three mighty men. ²³He was honored among the thirty, but he did not attain *the reputation* of the three. And David appointed him over his bodyguard.

²⁴ᴬAsahel the brother of Joab was among the thirty; *and there was* Elhanan the son of Dodo of Bethlehem, ²⁵ᴬShammah the Harodite, Elika the Harodite, ²⁶Helez the Paltite, Ira the son of Ikkesh the ᴬTekoite, ²⁷Abiezer the ᴬAnathothite, Mebunnai the Hushathite, ²⁸Zalmon the Ahohite, Maharai the ᴬNetophathite, ²⁹ᴬHeleb the son of Baanah the Netophathite, Ittai the son of Ribai of ᴮGibeah of the sons of Benjamin, ³⁰Benaiah a ᴬPirathonite, Hiddai of the brooks of Gaash, ³¹Abi-albon the Arbathite, Azmaveth the ᴬBarhumite, ³²Eliahba the ᴬShaalbonite, the sons of Jashen, Jonathan, ³³ᴬShammah the Hararite, Ahiam the son of Sharar the Ararite, ³⁴Eliphelet the son of Ahasbai, the son of the Maacathite, ᴬEliam the son of ᴮAhithophel the Gilonite, ³⁵ᴬHezro the Carmelite,

23:12ᴬ2 Sam 23:10   **23:13**ᴬ1 Sam 22:1   ᴮ2 Sam 5:18
23:14ᴬ1 Sam 22:4, 5   **23:15**ᴬ1 Chr 11:17
23:16ᴬ1 Chr 11:18   **23:17**ᴬLev 17:10
23:18ᴬ2 Sam 10:10, 14   ᴮ1 Chr 11:20, 21
23:20ᴬ2 Sam 8:18; 20:23   **23:22**ᴬ2 Sam 23:20
23:24ᴬ2 Sam 2:18; 1 Chr 27:7   **23:25**ᴬ1 Chr 11:27
23:26ᴬ2 Sam 14:2   **23:27**ᴬJosh 21:18
23:28ᴬ2 Kin 25:23   **23:29**ᴬ1 Chr 11:30   ᴮJosh 18:28
23:30ᴬJudg 12:13, 15   **23:31**ᴬ2 Sam 3:16
23:32ᴬJosh 19:42   **23:33**ᴬ2 Sam 23:11
23:34ᴬ2 Sam 11:3   ᴮ2 Sam 15:12   **23:35**ᴬ1 Chr 11:37

Paarai the Arbite, ³⁶Igal the son of Nathan of ^Zobah, Bani the Gadite, ³⁷Zelek the Ammonite, Naharai the ^Beerothite, armor bearers of Joab the son of Zeruiah, ³⁸Ira the ^Ithrite, Gareb the Ithrite, ³⁹ *and* ^Uriah the Hittite; thirty-seven in all.

THE CENSUS TAKEN

24 Now ^the anger of the LORD burned against Israel again, and He incited David against them to say, "^Go, count Israel and Judah." ²So the king said to Joab the commander of the army, who was with him, "Roam about now through all the tribes of Israel, ^from Dan to Beersheba, and conduct a census of the people, so that I may know the number of the people." ³But Joab said to the king, "^May the LORD your God add to the people a hundred times as many as they are, while the eyes of my lord the king *can still* see; but why does my lord the king delight in this thing?" ⁴Nevertheless, the king's order prevailed against Joab and against the commanders of the army. So Joab and the commanders of the army left the presence of the king to conduct a census of the people of Israel. ⁵They crossed the Jordan and camped in ^Aroer, on the right side of the city that is in the middle of the Valley of Gad and toward Jazer. ⁶Then they came to Gilead and to ¹the land of Tahtim-hodshi, and they came to Dan-jaan and around to ^Sidon, ⁷then they came to the ^fortress of Tyre and to all the cities of the Hivites and of the Canaanites, and they went out to the south of Judah, *to* Beersheba. ⁸So when they had roamed about through the whole land, they came to Jerusalem at the end of nine months and twenty days. ⁹And Joab gave the number of the census of the people to the king: in Israel there were ^eight hundred thousand valiant men who drew the sword, and the men of Judah were five hundred thousand men.

¹⁰Now ^David's heart troubled him after he had counted the people. So David said to the LORD, "I have sinned greatly in what I have done. But now, LORD, please overlook the guilt of Your servant, for I have acted very foolishly." ¹¹When David got up in the morning, the word of the LORD came to ^Gad the prophet, David's seer, saying, ¹²"Go and speak to David, 'This is what the LORD says: "I am imposing upon you three *choices;* choose for yourself one of them, and I will do *it* to you."'" ¹³So Gad came to David and told him, and said to him, "Shall ^seven years of famine come to you in your land? Or will you flee for three months before your enemies while they pursue you? Or shall there be three days of plague in your land? Now consider and see what answer I shall return to Him who sent me." ¹⁴Then David said to Gad, "I am in great distress. Let us now fall into the hand of the LORD, ^for His mercies are great; but do not let me fall into human hands."

PLAGUE SENT

¹⁵So ^the LORD sent a plague upon Israel from the morning until the

23:36 ^2 Sam 8:3   23:37 ^2 Sam 4:2   23:38 ^1 Chr 2:53
23:39 ^2 Sam 11:3, 6   24:1 ^2 Sam 21:1, 2
^B 1 Chr 27:23, 24   24:2 ^Judg 20:1; 2 Sam 3:10
24:3 ^Deut 1:11   24:5 ^Deut 2:36; Josh 13:9, 16
24:6 ^Josh 19:28; Judg 1:31   24:7 ^Josh 19:29
24:9 ^1 Chr 21:5   24:10 ^1 Sam 24:5   24:11 ^1 Sam 22:5;
1 Chr 29:29   24:13 ^1 Judg 21:12; Ezek 14:21
24:14 ^Ps 51:1; 130:4, 7   24:15 ^1 Chr 21:14; 27:24

24:6 ¹Another reading is *Kadesh in the land of the Hittite*

appointed time, and seventy thousand men of the people from Dan to Beersheba died. [16A]When the angel extended his hand *toward* Jerusalem to destroy it, [B]the LORD relented of the disaster and said to the angel who destroyed the people, "It is enough! Now drop your hand!" And the angel of the LORD was by the threshing floor of Araunah the Jebusite. [17]Then David spoke to the LORD when he saw the angel who was striking down the people, and said, "Behold, [A]it is I who have sinned, and it is I who have done wrong; but these sheep, what have they done? Please let Your hand be against me and against my father's house!"

DAVID BUILDS AN ALTAR

[18]So Gad came to David that day and said to him, "[A]Go up, erect an altar to the LORD on the threshing floor of Araunah the Jebusite." [19]Then David went up in accordance with the word of Gad, just as the LORD had commanded. [20]And Araunah looked down and saw the king and his servants crossing over toward him; so Araunah went out and bowed his face to the ground before the king. [21]Then Araunah said, "Why has my lord the king come to his servant?" And David said, "To buy the threshing floor from you, in order to build an altar to the LORD, [A]so that the plague may be withdrawn from the people." [22]Araunah then said to David, "Let my lord the king take and offer up what is good in his sight. Look, *here are* [A]the oxen for the burnt offering, the threshing sledges and the yokes of the oxen for the wood. [23]Everything, O king, Araunah gives to the king." And Araunah said to the king, "May the LORD your God be [A]favorable to you." [24]However, the king said to Araunah, "No, but I will certainly buy *it* from you for a price; for I will not offer burnt offerings to the LORD my God that cost me nothing." So [A]David bought the threshing floor and the oxen for fifty shekels of silver. [25]Then David built there an altar to the LORD, and he offered burnt offerings and peace offerings. And [A]the LORD responded to prayer for the land, and the plague was withdrawn from Israel.

24:16 [A]Acts 12:23   [B]Ex 32:14   24:17 [A]2 Sam 24:10
24:18 [A]1 Chr 21:18   24:21 [A]Num 16:44-50
24:22 [A]1 Sam 6:14; 1 Kin 19:21   24:23 [A]Ezek 20:40, 41
24:24 [A]1 Chr 21:24, 25   24:25 [A]2 Sam 21:14

1 KINGS

DAVID IN OLD AGE

1 Now King David was old, advanced in age; and they covered him with garments, but he could not keep warm. ²So his servants said to him, "Have them search for a young virgin for my lord the king, and have her attend the king and become his nurse; and have her lie on your chest, so that my lord the king may keep warm." ³So they searched for a beautiful girl throughout the territory of Israel, and found Abishag the ^Shunammite, and brought her to the king. ⁴The girl was very beautiful; and she became the king's nurse and served him, but the king did not become intimate with her.

⁵Now ^Adonijah the son of Haggith exalted himself, saying, "I will be king." So he prepared for himself chariots and horsemen, with fifty men to run before him. ⁶And his father had never rebuked him at any time by asking, "Why have you done so?" And he was also a very handsome man, and ^he was born after Absalom. ⁷Now he had conferred with ^Joab the son of Zeruiah and with ᴮAbiathar the priest; and they allied themselves with Adonijah. ⁸But ^Zadok the priest, Benaiah the son of Jehoiada, ᴮNathan the prophet, Shimei, Rei, and the mighty men who belonged to David, were not with Adonijah.

⁹Adonijah sacrificed sheep, oxen, and fattened steers by the stone of Zoheleth, which is beside ^En-rogel; and he invited all his brothers, the king's sons, and all the men of Judah, the king's servants. ¹⁰But he did not invite Nathan the prophet, Benaiah, the mighty men, or his brother ^Solomon.

NATHAN AND BATHSHEBA

¹¹Then Nathan spoke to ^Bathsheba the mother of Solomon, saying, "Have you not heard that Adonijah the son of Haggith has become king, and David our lord does not know *it?* ¹²So now come, please let me ^give you advice, and save your life and the life of your son Solomon. ¹³Go at once to King David and say to him, 'Have you not, my lord the king, sworn to your servant, saying, "^Solomon your son certainly shall be king after me, and he shall sit on my throne"? Why then has Adonijah become king?' ¹⁴Behold, while you are still there speaking with the king, I will come in after you and confirm your words."

¹⁵So Bathsheba entered to the king in the bedroom. Now ^the king was very old, and Abishag the Shunammite was serving the king. ¹⁶Then Bathsheba bowed and prostrated herself before the king. And the king said, "What is on your mind?" ¹⁷So she said to him, "My lord, you yourself swore to your servant by the LORD your God, *saying,* '^Your son Solomon

1:3^Josh 19:18; 1 Sam 28:4   1:5^2 Sam 3:4
1:6^2 Sam 3:3, 4   1:7^1 Chr 11:6   ᴮ1 Sam 22:20, 23
1:8^1 Chr 16:39   ᴮ2 Sam 12:1
1:9^Josh 15:7; 2 Sam 17:17   1:10^2 Sam 12:24
1:11^2 Sam 12:24   1:12^Prov 15:22   1:13^1 Kin 1:30;
1 Chr 22:9-13   1:15^1 Kin 1:1   1:17^1 Kin 1:13

certainly shall be king after me, and he shall sit on my throne.' ¹⁸But now, behold, Adonijah is king; and now, my lord the king, you do not know *it*. ¹⁹ᴬHe has sacrificed oxen and fattened steers and sheep in abundance, and has invited all the sons of the king, Abiathar the priest, and Joab the commander of the army, but he has not invited Solomon your servant. ²⁰And as for you, my lord the king, the eyes of all Israel are upon you, to announce to them who shall sit on the throne of my lord the king after him. ²¹Otherwise it will come about, ᴬas soon as my lord the king ¹lies down with his fathers, that I and my son Solomon will be *considered* offenders."

²²And behold, while she was still speaking with the king, Nathan the prophet came in. ²³They informed the king, saying, "Nathan the prophet is here." And when he came into the king's presence, he prostrated himself before the king with his face to the ground. ²⁴Then Nathan said, "My lord the king, have you yourself said, 'Adonijah shall be king after me, and he shall sit on my throne'? ²⁵ᴬFor he has gone down today and has sacrificed oxen and fattened steers and sheep in abundance, and has invited all the king's sons, the commanders of the army, and Abiathar the priest, and behold, they are eating and drinking in his presence; and they say, '*Long* live King Adonijah!' ²⁶ᴬBut me, *even* me your servant, Zadok the priest, Benaiah the son of Jehoiada, and your servant Solomon, he has not invited. ²⁷Has this thing been done by my lord the king, and you have not let your servants know who shall sit on the throne of my lord the king after him?"

²⁸Then King David responded and said, "Summon Bathsheba to me." And she came into the king's presence and stood before the king. ²⁹Then the king vowed and said, "ᴬAs the Lᴏʀᴅ lives, who has redeemed my life from all distress, ³⁰certainly as ᴬI vowed to you by the Lᴏʀᴅ, the God of Israel, saying, 'Your son Solomon certainly shall be king after me, and he shall sit on my throne in my place'; I will indeed do so this day." ³¹Then Bathsheba bowed with her face to the ground, and prostrated herself before the king and said, "ᴬMay my lord King David live forever."

³²Then King David said, "Summon to me ᴬZadok the priest, Nathan the prophet, and Benaiah the son of Jehoiada." And they came into the king's presence. ³³And the king said to them, "Take with you ᴬthe servants of your lord, and have my son Solomon ride on my own mule, and bring him down to Gihon. ³⁴And have Zadok the priest and Nathan the prophet anoint him there as king over Israel, and ᴬblow the trumpet and say, '*Long* live King Solomon!' ³⁵Then you shall come up after him, and he shall come and sit on my throne, and he shall be king in my place; for I have appointed him to be ruler over Israel and Judah." ³⁶Benaiah the son of Jehoiada answered the king and said, "Amen! May the Lᴏʀᴅ, the God of my lord the king, say the same. ³⁷ᴬJust as the Lᴏʀᴅ has been with my lord the king,

1:19ᴬ1 Kin 1:9   1:21ᴬDeut 31:16; 1 Kin 2:10
1:25ᴬ1 Kin 1:9   1:26ᴬ1 Kin 1:8, 10   1:29ᴬ2 Sam 4:9
1:30ᴬ1 Kin 1:13, 17   1:31ᴬDan 2:4; 3:9   1:32ᴬ1 Kin 1:8
1:33ᴬ2 Sam 20:6, 7   1:34ᴬ2 Sam 15:10
1:37ᴬJosh 1:5, 17; 1 Sam 20:13

1:21¹I.e., dies

so may He be with Solomon, and make his throne greater than the throne of my lord King David!"

SOLOMON ANOINTED KING

[38] So ^Zadok the priest, Nathan the prophet, Benaiah the son of Jehoiada, ^Bthe Cherethites, and the Pelethites went down and had Solomon ride on King David's mule, and brought him to Gihon. [39] And Zadok the priest then ^took the horn of oil from the tent and ^Banointed Solomon. Then they blew the trumpet, and all the people said, "*Long live King Solomon!*" [40] And all the people went up after him, and the people were playing on flutes and rejoicing with great joy, so that the earth shook at their noise.

[41] Now Adonijah and all the guests who *were* with him heard *this* as they finished eating. When Joab heard the sound of the trumpet, he said, "Why is the city making such an uproar?" [42] While he was still speaking, behold, ^Jonathan the son of Abiathar the priest came. Then Adonijah said, "Come in, for you are a valiant man and you bring good news." [43] But Jonathan replied to Adonijah, "On the contrary! Our lord King David has made Solomon king! [44] The king has also sent with him Zadok the priest, Nathan the prophet, Benaiah the son of Jehoiada, the Cherethites, and the Pelethites; and they have mounted him on the king's mule. [45] Furthermore, Zadok the priest and Nathan the prophet have anointed him king in Gihon, and they have come up from there rejoicing, ^so that the city is going wild. This is the noise which you have heard. [46] Besides, ^Solomon has even taken his seat on the

throne of the kingdom. [47] Moreover, the king's servants came to bless our lord King David, saying, 'May ^your God make the name of Solomon better than your name, and his throne greater than your throne!' And ^Bthe king bowed himself on the bed. [48] The king has also said this: 'Blessed be the LORD, God of Israel, who ^has granted one to sit on my throne today while my own eyes see *it.*'"

[49] Then all the guests of Adonijah trembled and got up, and each went on his way. [50] Adonijah also was afraid of Solomon, and he got up, and went, and ^took hold of the horns of the altar. [51] Now it was reported to Solomon, saying, "Behold, Adonijah is afraid of King Solomon, for behold, he has taken hold of the horns of the altar, saying, 'May King Solomon swear to me today that he will not put his servant to death with the sword.'" [52] And Solomon said, "If he is a worthy man, ^not one of his hairs will fall to the ground; but if wickedness is found in him, he will die." [53] So King Solomon sent *men,* and they brought him down from the altar. And he came and prostrated himself before King Solomon, and Solomon said to him, "Go to your house."

DAVID'S COMMAND TO SOLOMON

2 As David's ^time to die drew near, he commanded his son Solomon, saying, [2] "^I am going the way of all the earth. So be strong,

1:38 ^1 1 Kin 1:8   ^B 2 Sam 8:18   1:39 ^E Ex 30:23-32
^B 1 Chr 29:22   1:42 ^A 2 Sam 15:27, 36; 17:17
1:45 ^A 1 Kin 1:40   1:46 ^A 1 Chr 29:23   1:47 ^A 1 Kin 1:37
^B Gen 47:31   1:48 ^A 2 Sam 7:12; 1 Kin 3:6
1:50 ^A Ex 27:2; 1 Kin 2:28   1:52 ^A 1 Sam 14:45;
Acts 27:34   2:1 ^A Gen 47:29; Deut 31:14
2:2 ^A Josh 23:14

and prove yourself a man. ³Do your duty to the LORD your God, to walk in His ways, to keep His statutes, His commandments, His ordinances, and His testimonies, ^according to what is written in the Law of Moses, so that you may succeed in all that you do and wherever you turn, ⁴so that ^the LORD may fulfill His promise which He spoke regarding me, saying, 'If your sons are careful about their way, to walk before Me in truth with all their heart and all their soul, you shall not be deprived of a man to occupy the throne of Israel.'

⁵"Now you yourself also know what Joab the son of Zeruiah did to me, what he did to the two commanders of the armies of Israel, to ^Abner the son of Ner and to ^Amasa the son of Jether, whom he killed; he also shed the blood of war in peace. And he put the blood of war on his belt that was on his waist, and on his sandals that were on his feet. ⁶^So act as your wisdom dictates, and do not let his gray hair go down to ¹Sheol in peace. ⁷However, ^show kindness to the sons of Barzillai the Gileadite, and let them be among those who eat at your table; for they assisted me when I fled from Absalom your brother. ⁸And behold, you have with you ^Shimei the son of Gera the Benjaminite, of Bahurim; now it was he who cursed me with a painful curse on the day I went to Mahanaim. But when ^he came down to meet me at the Jordan, I swore to him by the LORD, saying, 'I will not put you to death with the sword.' ⁹But now do not leave him unpunished, ^for you are a wise man; and you will know what to do to him, and you will bring his gray hair down to Sheol with blood."

DEATH OF DAVID

¹⁰Then ^David ¹lay down with his fathers, and he was buried in ^the city of David. ¹¹Now ^the days that David reigned over Israel were forty years: in Hebron he reigned for seven years, and in Jerusalem he reigned for thirty-three years. ¹²Then ^Solomon sat on the throne of his father David, and his kingdom was firmly established.

¹³Now Adonijah the son of Haggith came to Bathsheba the mother of Solomon. So she said, "^Do you come peacefully?" And he said, "Peacefully." ¹⁴Then he said, "I have something to say to you." And she said, "Speak." ¹⁵So he said, "You yourself know that ^the kingdom was mine and that all Israel intended for me to be king; however, the kingdom has turned around and become my brother's, for it was his from the LORD. ¹⁶So now I am making one request of you; do not refuse me." And she said to him, "Speak." ¹⁷Then he said, "Please speak to Solomon the king—for he will not refuse you—that he may give me ^Abishag the Shunammite as a wife." ¹⁸And Bathsheba said, "Very well; I will speak to the king for you."

ADONIJAH EXECUTED

¹⁹So Bathsheba went to King Solomon, to speak to him for Adonijah. And the king stood to meet her, bowed to her, and sat on his throne; then he ^had a throne set up for the

2:3 ^Deut 17:18-20   2:4 ^2 Sam 7:25   2:5 ^1 Kin 2:32
^2 Sam 20:10   2:6 ^1 Kin 2:9   2:7 ^2 Sam 19:31-38
2:8 ^2 Sam 16:5-8   ^2 Sam 19:18-23   2:9 ^1 Kin 2:6
2:10 ^Acts 2:29   ^2 Sam 5:7   2:11 ^2 Sam 5:4, 5;
1 Chr 29:26, 27   2:12 ^1 Chr 29:23; 2 Chr 1:1
2:13 ^1 Sam 16:4   2:15 ^2 Sam 3:3, 4; 1 Kin 2:22
2:17 ^1 Kin 1:3, 4   2:19 ^1 Kin 15:13

2:6 ¹I.e., the netherworld   2:10 ¹I.e., died

king's mother, and [B]she sat on his right. [20] Then she said, "I am making one small request of you; [A]do not refuse me." And the king said to her, "Ask, my mother, for I will not refuse you." [21] So she said, "[A]Let Abishag the Shunammite be given to Adonijah your brother as a wife." [22] But King Solomon answered and said to his mother, "And why are you requesting Abishag the Shunammite for Adonijah? [A]Request for him the kingdom as well—since he is my older brother—for him, for [B]Abiathar the priest, and for Joab the son of Zeruiah!" [23] Then King Solomon swore by the LORD, saying, "May God do so to me and more so, if Adonijah has [A]not spoken this word against his own life! [24] Now then, as the LORD lives, who has established me and set me on the throne of David my father, and [A]has made me a house just as He promised, Adonijah certainly shall be put to death today!" [25] Then King Solomon [A]sent *the order* by Benaiah the son of Jehoiada; and he struck him so that he died.

[26] Then to Abiathar the priest the king said, "Go to Anathoth to your own field, for you deserve to die; but I will not put you to death at this time, because [A]you carried the ark of the Lord GOD before my father David, and because [B]you were afflicted in everything with which my father was afflicted." [27] So Solomon dismissed Abiathar from being priest to the LORD, to fulfill [A]the word of the LORD, which He had spoken regarding the house of Eli in Shiloh.

JOAB EXECUTED

[28] Now the news came to Joab [A]because Joab had followed Adonijah, though he had not followed Absalom. So Joab fled to the tent of the LORD and took hold of the horns of the altar. [29] And it was reported to King Solomon that Joab had fled to the tent of the LORD, and was beside the altar. Then Solomon sent Benaiah the son of Jehoiada, saying, "[A]Go, execute him." [30] So Benaiah came to the tent of the LORD and said to him, "This is what the king has said: 'Come out.'" But he said, "No, for I will die here." So Benaiah brought back word to the king, saying, "This is what Joab spoke, and so he answered me." [31] And the king said to him, "[A]Do just as he has spoken, and execute him and bury him, so that you may remove from me and from my father's house the blood which Joab shed without justification. [32] The LORD will return his blood on his own head, because he struck two men more righteous and better than he, and killed them with the sword, while my father David did not know *about it:* [A]Abner the son of Ner, commander of the army of Israel, and [B]Amasa the son of Jether, commander of the army of Judah. [33] [A]So their blood shall return on the head of Joab and on the head of his descendants forever; but for David and his descendants, and his house and his throne, may there be peace from the LORD forever." [34] Then [A]Benaiah the son of Jehoiada went up and struck him and put him to death, and he was buried at his own house in the wilderness. [35] And [A]the king appointed Benaiah the son of

2:19 [B]Ps 45:9   2:20 [A]1 Kin 2:16   2:21 [A]1 Kin 1:3, 4
2:22 [A]2 Sam 12:8   [B]1 Kin 1:7   2:23 [A]Ruth 1:17
2:24 [A]2 Sam 7:11, 13; 1 Chr 22:10   2:25 [A]2 Sam 8:18
2:26 [A]2 Sam 15:24-29   [B]1 Sam 22:20-23
2:27 [A]1 Sam 2:27-36   2:28 [A]1 Kin 1:7   2:29 [A]Ex 21:14
2:31 [A]Ex 21:14   2:32 [A]2 Sam 3:27   [B]2 Sam 20:9, 10
2:33 [A]2 Sam 3:29   2:34 [A]1 Kin 2:25   2:35 [A]1 Kin 4:4

Jehoiada over the army in his place, and the king appointed Zadok the priest in place of Abiathar.

SHIMEI EXECUTED

36 Now the king sent *men* and summoned ^Shimei, and said to him, "Build yourself a house in Jerusalem and live there, and do not leave there for any *other* place. 37 For on the day you leave and ^cross the brook Kidron, you will know for certain that you will assuredly die; your blood will be 'on your own head." 38 Shimei then said to the king, "The word is good. Just as my lord the king has spoken, so your servant shall do." So Shimei lived in Jerusalem for many days.

39 But it came about at the end of three years, that two of Shimei's servants ran away ^to Achish son of Maacah, king of Gath. And *others* told Shimei, saying, "Behold, your servants are in Gath." 40 Then Shimei got up and saddled his donkey, and went to Gath to Achish, to search for his servants. And Shimei went and brought his servants from Gath. 41 And it was reported to Solomon that Shimei had gone from Jerusalem to Gath, and had returned. 42 So the king sent *men* and summoned Shimei, and said to him, "Did I not make you swear by the LORD, and solemnly warn you, saying, 'Know for certain that on the day you depart and go anywhere, you shall assuredly die'? And you said to me, 'The word I have heard is good.' 43 Why then have you not kept the oath of the LORD, and the command which I imposed on you?" 44 The king also said to Shimei, "^You yourself know all the evil that you acknowledge in your heart, which you did to my father David;

therefore the LORD will return your evil on your own head. 45 But King Solomon will be blessed, and ^the throne of David will be established before the LORD forever." 46 ^So the king commanded Benaiah the son of Jehoiada, and he went out and struck him so that he died.

And the kingdom was established in the hands of Solomon.

SOLOMON'S RULE CONSOLIDATED

3 Now ^Solomon formed a marriage alliance with Pharaoh king of Egypt, and took Pharaoh's daughter and brought her to the city of David until he had finished building his own house and the house of the LORD, and the wall around Jerusalem. 2 ^The people were still sacrificing on the high places, because there was no house built for the name of the LORD until those days.

3 Now ^Solomon loved the LORD, ^walking in the statutes of his father David, except that he was sacrificing and burning incense on the high places. 4 And ^the king went to Gibeon to sacrifice there, because that was the great high place; Solomon offered a thousand burnt offerings on that altar. 5 In Gibeon the LORD appeared to Solomon ^in a dream at night; and God said, "^Ask what *you wish* Me to give you."

SOLOMON'S PRAYER

6 Then Solomon said, "^You have shown great faithfulness to Your servant David my father, ^according

2:36 ^2 Sam 16:5; 1 Kin 2:8　**2:37** ^2 Sam 15:23; John 18:1　**2:39** ^1 Sam 27:2　**2:44** ^2 Sam 16:5-13
2:45 ^2 Sam 7:13; Prov 25:5　**2:46** ^1 Kin 2:25, 34
3:1 ^1 Kin 9:16, 24; 2 Chr 8:11　**3:2** ^Lev 17:3-5;
Deut 12:2, 13, 14　**3:3** ^Deut 10:12, 13　^1 Kin 11:4, 6, 38
3:4 ^2 Chr 1:3　**3:5** ^Matt 1:20　^John 15:7
3:6 ^2 Sam 7:8-17　^1 Kin 9:4

2:37 ¹ I.e., your own responsibility

as he walked before You in truth, righteousness, and uprightness of heart toward You; and You have reserved for him this great faithfulness, that You have given him a son to sit on his throne, as *it is* this day. ⁷And now, Lᴏʀᴅ my God, ᴬYou have made Your servant king in place of my father David, yet I am *like* a little boy; I do not know how to ¹go out or come in. ⁸And ᴬYour servant is in the midst of Your people whom You have chosen, a great people who are too many to be numbered or counted. ⁹So ᴬgive Your servant an understanding heart to judge Your people, to discern between good and evil. For who is capable of judging this great people of Yours?"

GOD'S ANSWER

¹⁰Now it was pleasing in the sight of the Lord that Solomon had asked this thing. ¹¹And God said to him, "Because you have asked this thing, and have ᴬnot asked for yourself a long life, nor have asked riches for yourself, nor have you asked for the lives of your enemies, but have asked for yourself discernment to understand justice, ¹²behold, I have done according to your words. Behold, ᴬI have given you a wise and discerning heart, so that there has been no one like you before you, nor shall one like you arise after you. ¹³ᴬI have also given you what you have not asked, both riches and honor, so that there will not be any among the kings like you all your days. ¹⁴And ᴬif you walk in My ways, keeping My statutes and commandments, as your father David walked, then I will ᴮprolong your days."

¹⁵Then ᴬSolomon awoke, and behold, it was a dream. And he came to Jerusalem and stood before the ark of the covenant of the Lord, and offered burnt offerings and made peace offerings, and ᴮheld a feast for all his servants.

SOLOMON WISELY JUDGES

¹⁶Then two women who were prostitutes came to the king and stood before him. ¹⁷The one woman said, "Pardon me, my lord: this woman and I live in the same house; and I gave birth to a child while she was in the house. ¹⁸And it happened on the third day after I gave birth, that this woman also gave birth to a child, and we were together. There was no stranger with us in the house, only the two of us in the house. ¹⁹Then this woman's son died in the night, because she lay on him. ²⁰So she got up in the middle of the night and took my son from beside me while your servant was asleep, and she laid him at her breast, and laid her dead son at my breast. ²¹When I got up in the morning to nurse my son, behold, he was dead! But when I examined him closely in the morning, behold, he was not my son, whom I had borne!" ²²Then the other woman said, "No! For the living one is my son, and the dead one is your son." But the first woman said, "No! For the dead one is your son, and the living one is my son." So they spoke before the king.

²³Then the king said, "The one says, 'This is my son who is living, and your son is the dead one'; and the other says, 'No! For your

3:7 ¹1 Chr 22:9-13   3:8 ᴬEx 19:6; Deut 7:6
3:9 ²2 Chr 1:10; Ps 72:1, 2   3:11 ᴬJames 4:3
3:12 ᴬ1 Kin 4:29-31; Eccl 1:16   3:13 ᴬ1 Kin 4:21-24;
Matt 6:33   3:14 ᴬ1 Kin 3:6   ᴮPs 91:16   3:15 ᴬGen 41:7
ᴮ1 Kin 8:65

3:7 ¹I.e., conduct daily business

son is the dead one, and my son is the living one.'" [24]And the king said, "Get me a sword." So they brought a sword before the king. [25]And the king said, "Cut the living child in two, and give half to the one and half to the other." [26]But the woman whose child *was* the living one spoke to the king, for ^she was deeply stirred over her son, and she said, "Pardon me, my lord! Give her the living child, and by no means kill him!" But the other *woman* was saying, "He shall be neither mine nor yours; cut *him!*" [27]Then the king replied, "Give the first woman the living child, and by no means kill him. She is his mother." [28]When all Israel heard about the judgment which the king had handed down, they feared the king, because ^they saw that the wisdom of God was in him to administer justice.

SOLOMON'S OFFICIALS

4 Now King Solomon was king over all Israel. [2]These were his officials: Azariah the son of Zadok *was* ^the priest; [3]Elihoreph and Ahijah, the sons of Shisha *were* scribes; ^Jehoshaphat the son of Ahilud *was* the secretary; [4]and ^Benaiah the son of Jehoiada *was* over the army; and Zadok and Abiathar *were* priests; [5]and Azariah the son of Nathan *was* over ^the deputies; and Zabud the son of Nathan, a priest, *was* the king's confidant; [6]and Ahishar was over the household; and Adoniram the son of Abda *was* over the forced labor.

[7]Solomon had twelve deputies over all Israel, who provided food for the king and his household; each *deputy* had to provide food for a month in the year. [8]And these *were* their names: Ben-hur, in the ^hill

country of Ephraim; [9]Ben-deker in Makaz and ^Shaalbim, and [B]Bethshemesh, and Elonbeth-hanan; [10]Ben-hesed in Arubboth (^Socoh *was* his and all the land of [B]Hepher); [11]Ben-abinadab *in* all the ^hills of Dor (Taphath the daughter of Solomon was his wife); [12]Baana the son of Ahilud *in* ^Taanach and Megiddo, and all Beth-shean which is beside Zarethan below Jezreel, from Bethshean to Abel-meholah as far as the other side of Jokmeam; [13]Ben-geber in ^Ramoth-gilead (the villages of Jair, the son of Manasseh, which are in Gilead were his: the region of Argob, which is in Bashan, sixty great cities with walls and bronze bars *were* his); [14]Ahinadab the son of Iddo *in* ^Mahanaim; [15]^Ahimaaz in Naphtali (he also married Basemath the daughter of Solomon); [16]Baana the son of ^Hushai in Asher and Bealoth; [17]Jehoshaphat the son of Paruah in Issachar; [18]^Shimei the son of Ela in Benjamin; [19]Geber the son of Uri in the land of Gilead, ^the country of Sihon king of the Amorites and of Og king of Bashan; and *he was* the only deputy who *was* in the land.

SOLOMON'S POWER, WEALTH, AND WISDOM

[20]^Judah and Israel *were* as numerous as the sand that is on the seashore in abundance; *they* were eating, drinking, and rejoicing.

[21]Now Solomon was ruling over all the kingdoms from the *Euphrates* River *to* the land of the Philistines

3:26^Jer 31:20; Hos 11:8　**3:28**^Dan 1:17; Col 2:2, 3
4:2^1 Chr 6:10　**4:3**^2 Sam 8:16　**4:4**^1 Kin 2:35
4:5^1 Kin 4:7　**4:8**^Josh 24:33　**4:9**^Judg 1:35
[B]Josh 21:16　**4:10**^Josh 15:35　[B]Josh 12:17
4:11^Josh 11:1, 2　**4:12**^Judg 5:19　**4:13**^1 Kin 22:3-15
4:14^Josh 13:26　**4:15**^2 Sam 15:27
4:16^2 Sam 15:32　**4:18**^1 Kin 1:8　**4:19**^Deut 3:8-10
4:20^Gen 22:17; 1 Kin 3:8

and to the border of Egypt; ^they brought tribute and served Solomon all the days of his life.

²²Solomon's provision for one day was ¹thirty kors of fine flour and ²sixty kors of meal, ²³ten fat oxen, twenty pasture-fed oxen, and a hundred sheep, besides deer, gazelles, roebucks, and fattened geese. ²⁴For he was ruling over everything west of the *Euphrates* River, from Tiphsah even to Gaza, ^over all the kings west of the River; and ᴮhe had peace on all sides surrounding him. ²⁵^So Judah and Israel lived securely, everyone under his vine and his fig tree, ᴮfrom Dan even to Beersheba, all the days of Solomon. ²⁶^Solomon had forty thousand stalls of horses for his chariots, and twelve thousand horsemen. ²⁷And those deputies provided food for King Solomon and all who came to King Solomon's table, each in his month; they allowed nothing to be lacking. ²⁸They also brought barley and straw for the *war* horses and ^baggage horses to the place where it was *required,* each *deputy* according to his duty.

²⁹Now ^God gave Solomon wisdom and very great discernment and breadth of mind, like the sand that is on the seashore. ³⁰Solomon's wisdom surpassed the wisdom of all ^the people of the east and ᴮall the wisdom of Egypt. ³¹For ^he was wiser than all *other* people, *more* than Ethan the Ezrahite, Heman, Calcol, and Darda, the sons of Mahol; and his fame was *known* in all the surrounding nations. ³²^He also told three thousand proverbs, and his songs *numbered* 1,005. ³³He told of trees, from the cedar that is in Lebanon even to the hyssop that

grows on the wall; he told also of animals, birds, crawling things, and fish. ³⁴*People* ^came from all the nations to hear the wisdom of Solomon, from all the kings of the earth who had heard of his wisdom.

ALLIANCE WITH KING HIRAM

5 Now Hiram king of Tyre sent his servants to Solomon when he heard that they had anointed him king in place of his father, for ^Hiram had always been a friend of David. ²Then ^Solomon sent *word* to Hiram, saying, ³"You know that ^David my father was unable to build a house for the name of the Lᴏʀᴅ his God because of the wars which surrounded him, until the Lᴏʀᴅ put them under the soles of his feet. ⁴But now ^the Lᴏʀᴅ my God has secured me rest on every side; there is neither adversary nor misfortune. ⁵So behold, ^I intend to build a house for the name of the Lᴏʀᴅ my God, just as the Lᴏʀᴅ spoke to David my father, saying, 'Your son, whom I will put on your throne in your place, he will build the house for My name.' ⁶Now then, issue orders that they cut ^cedars from Lebanon for me, and my servants will be with your servants; and I will give you wages for your servants in accordance with all that you say, for you yourself know that there is no one among us who knows how to cut timber like the Sidonians."

4:21^2 Sam 8:2, 6   **4:24**^Ps 72:11   ᴮ1 Chr 22:9
4:25^Jer 23:6   ᴮ1 Sam 3:20   **4:26**^1 Kin 10:26;
2 Chr 1:14   **4:28**^Esth 8:10, 14; Mic 1:13
4:29^1 Kin 3:12   **4:30**^Gen 29:1   ᴮIs 19:11
4:31^1 Kin 3:12   **4:32**^Eccl 12:9; Song 1:1
4:34^1 Kin 10:1; 2 Chr 9:23   **5:1**^2 Sam 5:11; 1 Chr 14:1
5:2^2 Chr 2:3   **5:3**^2 Sam 7:5; 1 Chr 28:2, 3
5:4^1 Kin 4:24; 1 Chr 22:9
5:5^2 Sam 7:12, 13; 2 Chr 2:4   **5:6**^2 Chr 2:8

4:22¹About 231 cubic feet or 6.5 cubic meters
²About 462 cubic feet or 13 cubic meters

[7] When Hiram heard the words of Solomon, he greatly rejoiced; and he said, "Blessed be the LORD today, who has given to David a wise son over this great people." [8] So Hiram sent *word* to Solomon, saying, "I have heard *the message* which you sent me; I will do everything you wish concerning the cedar and juniper timber. [9] My servants will bring *the timbers* down from Lebanon to the sea; and I will have them made into rafts *to go* by sea ^to the place where you direct me, and I will have them broken up there, and you will carry *them* away. Then you shall do what I wish, by giving food to my household." [10] So Hiram gave Solomon all that he wished of the cedar and juniper timber. [11] ^Solomon then gave Hiram [1]twenty thousand kors of wheat as food for his household, and [2]twenty kors of pure oil; this is what Solomon would give Hiram year by year. [12] And ^the LORD gave wisdom to Solomon, just as He promised him; and there was peace between Hiram and Solomon, and the two of them made a covenant.

CONSCRIPTION OF LABORERS

[13] Now ^King Solomon conscripted forced laborers from all Israel; and the forced laborers *numbered* thirty thousand men. [14] Then he sent them to Lebanon, ten thousand a month in shifts; they were in Lebanon for a month, *and* two months at home. And ^Adoniram *was* in charge of the forced laborers. [15] Now ^Solomon had seventy thousand porters, and eighty thousand stonemasons in the mountains, [16] ^besides Solomon's 3,300 chief deputies who *were* in charge of the project *and* ruled over the

people who were doing the work. [17] Then ^the king issued orders, and they quarried large stones, valuable stones, to lay the foundation of the house with cut stones. [18] So Solomon's builders and Hiram's builders and ^the Gebalites cut *the stones,* and they prepared the timbers and the stones to build the house.

THE BUILDING OF THE TEMPLE

6 ^Now it came about in the four hundred and eightieth year after the sons of Israel came out of the land of Egypt, in the fourth year of Solomon's reign over Israel, in the month of Ziv, that is, the second month, that he began to build the house of the LORD. [2] And the house which King Solomon built for the LORD *was* [1]sixty cubits *in* its length, and twenty *cubits in* its width, and its height *was* thirty cubits. [3] The porch in front of the main room of the house *was* [1]twenty cubits in length, corresponding to the width of the house, *and* its width along the front of the house *was* ten cubits. [4] Also for the house ^he made windows with *artistic* frames. [5] ^Against the wall of the house he built stories encompassing the walls of the house around both the main room and the [B]inner sanctuary; so he made side chambers all around. [6] The lowest story *was* [1]five cubits wide, the middle

5:9 ^2 Chr 2:16   5:11 ^2 Chr 2:10   5:12 ^1 Kin 3:12
5:13 ^1 Kin 4:6; 9:15   5:14 ^1 Kin 4:6; 12:18
5:15 ^1 Kin 9:20-22; 2 Chr 2:17, 18   5:16 ^1 Kin 9:23
5:17 ^1 Kin 6:7; 1 Chr 22:2   5:18 ^Josh 13:5; Ezek 27:9
6:1 ^2 Chr 3:1, 2   6:4 ^Ezek 40:16; 41:16
6:5 ^Ezek 41:6   ^B 1 Kin 6:16, 19, 20

5:11 [1] About 154,000 cubic feet or 4,360 cubic
meters   [2] About 154 cubic feet or 4.4 cubic meters
6:2 [1] About 90 ft. long, 30 ft. wide, and 45 ft. high or
27 m, 9 m, and 14 m   6:3 [1] About 30 ft. long and 15 ft.
deep or 9 m and 4.6 m   6:6 [1] About 7.5 ft. wide, 9 ft.
wide, and 11 ft. wide or 2.3 m, 2.7 m, and 3.3 m

was six cubits wide, and the third *was* seven cubits wide; for on the outside he made offsets *in the wall* of the house all around so that *the beams* would not be inserted into the walls of the house.

7 ^The house, while it was being built, was built of stone finished at the quarry, and neither hammer, nor axe, nor any iron tool was heard in the house while it was being built.

8 The doorway for the 'lowest side chamber *was* on the right side of the house; and they would go up by a winding staircase to the middle *story,* and from the middle to the third. 9 So ^he built the house and finished it; and he covered the house with beams and planks of cedar. 10 He also built the stories against the whole house, *each* 'five cubits high; and they were attached to the house with timbers of cedar.

11 Now the word of the LORD came to Solomon, saying, 12 "*As for* this house which you are building, ^if you will walk in My statutes and execute My ordinances and keep all My commandments by walking in them, then I will fulfill My word with you which I spoke to David your father. 13 And ^I will dwell among the sons of Israel, and ^will not abandon My people Israel."

14 ^So Solomon built the house and finished it. 15 He ^built the walls of the house on the inside with boards of cedar; from the floor of the house to the ceiling he paneled *the walls* on the inside with wood, and he paneled the floor of the house with boards of juniper. 16 ^He also built 'twenty cubits on the rear part of the house with boards of cedar from the floor to the ceiling; he built *them* for it on the inside

as an inner sanctuary, as ^the Most Holy Place. 17 The house, that is, the main room in front of *the inner sanctuary,* was 'forty cubits *long.* 18 There was cedar inside the house, carved *in the shape* of ^gourds and open flowers; everything was cedar, there was no stone visible. 19 Then he prepared an inner sanctuary inside the house in order to place there the ark of the covenant of the LORD. 20 The inner sanctuary *was* twenty cubits in length, twenty cubits in width, and twenty cubits in height; and he overlaid it with pure gold. He also paneled the altar with cedar. 21 So Solomon overlaid the inside of the house with pure gold. And he extended chains of gold across the front of the inner sanctuary, and he overlaid it with gold. 22 He overlaid the entire house with gold, until all the house was finished. Also ^the entire altar which was by the inner sanctuary he overlaid with gold.

23 ^And in the inner sanctuary he made two 'cherubim of olive wood, each ten cubits high. 24 The one wing of the *first* cherub *was* five cubits, and the other wing of the *first* cherub *was* five cubits; from the end of one wing to the end of the other wing *were* ten cubits. 25 The second cherub *was* ten cubits; both of the cherubim were of the same measurement and the same form. 26 The height of the one cherub *was* ten cubits, and so *was that of* the other cherub. 27 He

6:7 ^Ex 20:25; Deut 27:5, 6   6:9 ^1 Kin 6:14, 38
6:12 ^2 Sam 7:5-16; 1 Kin 9:4   6:13 ^Ex 25:8
^Heb 13:5   6:14 ^1 Kin 6:9, 38   6:15 ^1 Kin 7:7
6:16 ^2 Chr 3:8   ^Heb 9:3   6:18 ^1 Kin 7:24
6:22 ^Ex 30:1, 3, 6   6:23 ^Ex 37:7-9; 2 Chr 3:10-12

6:8 'As in LXX and ancient versions; MT *middle*
6:10 'About 7.5 ft. or 2.3 m   6:16 'About 30 ft. or 9 m
6:17 'About 60 ft. or 18 m   6:23 'Heb plural of *cherub*

placed the cherubim in the midst of the inner house, and ^the wings of the cherubim spread out so that the wing of the one was touching the *one* wall, and the wing of the other cherub was touching the other wall. And their wings were touching end to end in the center of the house. ²⁸He also overlaid the cherubim with gold.

²⁹Then he carved all the surrounding walls of the house with engravings of cherubim, palm trees, and open flowers, for the inner and outer *sanctuaries.* ³⁰And he overlaid the floor of the house with gold, for the inner and outer *sanctuaries.*

³¹And for the entrance of the inner sanctuary he made doors of olive wood, the lintel, *and* five-sided doorposts. ³²So *he made* two doors of olive wood, and he carved on them carvings of cherubim, palm trees, and open flowers, and overlaid them with gold; and he overlaid the cherubim and the palm trees with gold.

³³So too he made for the entrance of the main room four-sided doorposts of olive wood, ³⁴and ^two doors of juniper wood; the two leaves of the one door turned on pivots, and the two leaves of the other door turned on pivots. ³⁵He carved *on it* cherubim, palm trees, and open flowers; and he overlaid *them* with gold plated on the carved work. ³⁶And ^he built the inner courtyard with three rows of cut stone and a row of cedar beams.

³⁷^In the fourth year the foundation of the house of the LORD was laid, in the month of Ziv. ³⁸And in the eleventh year, in the month of Bul, that is, the eighth month, the house was finished in all its parts

and in accordance with all its plans. So he was seven years in building it.

SOLOMON'S PALACE

7 Now ^Solomon built his own house *over the course of* thirteen years, and he finished all of his house. ²^He built the house of the timber from Lebanon; its length was ¹a hundred cubits, its width fifty cubits, and its height thirty cubits, on four rows of cedar pillars with cedar beams on the pillars. ³And it was paneled with cedar above the side chambers which were on the forty-five pillars, fifteen *in each* row. ⁴*There were artistic window* frames *in* three rows, and window was opposite window at three intervals. ⁵And all the doorways and doorposts *had* squared *artistic* frames, and window was opposite window at three intervals.

⁶Then he made ^the hall of pillars; its length was ¹fifty cubits and its width thirty cubits, and a porch *was* in front of them and pillars and a threshold in front of them.

⁷And he made the hall of the ^throne where he was to judge, the hall of judgment, and it was paneled with cedar from floor to floor.

⁸And his house where he was to live, the other courtyard inward from the hall, was of this *same* workmanship. He also made a house like this hall for Pharaoh's daughter, ^whom Solomon had married.

⁹All of these were *made* of valuable stones, of stone cut according

6:27 ^Ex 25:20; 1 Kin 8:7   6:34 ^Ezek 41:23-25
6:36 ^1 Kin 7:12; Jer 36:10   6:37 ^1 Kin 6:1
7:1 ^1 Kin 3:1; 2 Chr 8:1   7:2 ^1 Kin 10:17, 21; 2 Chr 9:16
7:6 ^1 Kin 7:12   7:7 ^Ps 122:5; Prov 20:8   7:8 ^1 Kin 3:1

7:2 ¹About 150 ft. long, 75 wide, and 45 high or 46 m long, 23 wide, and 14 high   7:6 ¹About 75 ft. long and 45 ft. wide or 23 m long and 7 m wide

to measure, sawed with saws, inside and outside; even from the foundation to the 'coping, and from the outside to the large courtyard.

[10] And the foundation was of valuable stones, large stones, stones of 'ten cubits and stones of eight cubits. [11] And above were valuable stones, cut according to measure, and cedar. [12] So ^the large courtyard all around *had* three rows of cut stone and a row of cedar beams as well as the inner courtyard of the house of the LORD, and ᴮthe porch of the house.

HIRAM'S WORK IN THE TEMPLE

[13] Now ^King Solomon sent *word* and had Hiram brought from Tyre. [14] ^He was a widow's son from the tribe of Naphtali, and his father was a man of Tyre, an artisan in bronze; and he was filled with wisdom, skill, and knowledge for doing any work in bronze. So he came to King Solomon and ᴮperformed all his work.

[15] He fashioned ^the two pillars of bronze; 'eighteen cubits was the height of each pillar, and a line of ²twelve cubits measured the circumference of both. [16] He also made two capitals of cast bronze to put on the tops of the pillars; the height of the one capital was 'five cubits and the height of the other capital was five cubits. [17] *There were* lattices of latticework and wreaths of chainwork for the capitals which were on the top of the pillars; seven for the one capital and seven for the other capital. [18] So he made the pillars, and two rows around on the one lattice to cover the capitals which were on the top of the pomegranates; and so he did for the other capital. [19] The capitals

which *were* on the tops of the pillars in the porch were of lily design, four cubits. [20] So *there were* capitals on the two pillars, also above *and* close to the rounded projection which was beside the lattice; and ^the pomegranates *totaled* two hundred in rows around both capitals. [21] ^And he set up the pillars at the porch of the main room: he set up the right pillar and named it 'Jachin, and he set up the left pillar and named it ²Boaz. [22] On the top of the pillars was *the* lily design. So the work of the pillars was finished.

[23] ^He also made the 'Sea of ᴮcast *metal* ²ten cubits from brim to brim, circular *in shape,* and its height was five cubits, and it was ³thirty cubits in circumference. [24] Under its brim ^gourds *went* around encircling it ten to a cubit, ᴮcompletely surrounding the Sea; the gourds were in two rows, cast with the rest. [25] ^It was standing on twelve oxen, three facing north, three facing west, three facing south, and three facing east; and the Sea *was set* on top of them, and all their rear parts *turned* inward. [26] And it was a 'hand width thick, and its brim was made like the brim of a cup, *like* a lily blossom; it could hold ²two thousand baths.

[27] Then ^he made the ten stands of bronze; the length of each stand was

7:12^1 Kin 6:36   ᴮ1 Kin 7:6   7:13^2 Chr 2:13, 14; 4:11
7:14^2 Chr 2:14   ᴮ2 Chr 4:11-16   7:15^2 Kin 25:17;
2 Chr 3:15   7:20^1 Kin 7:42; Jer 52:23   7:21^2 Chr 3:17
7:23^2 Chr 4:2   ᴮ2 Kin 16:17   7:24^1 Kin 6:18
ᴮ2 Chr 4:3   7:25^2 Chr 4:4, 5; Jer 52:20
7:27^1 Kin 7:38; 2 Chr 4:14

7:9 'I.e., top sloping course of stone   7:10 'About
15 and 12 ft. or 4.5 and 3.7 m   7:15 'About 27 ft. or 8
m   ²About 18 ft. or 5.5 m   7:16 'About 7.5 ft. or 2.3
m   7:21 'I.e., he shall establish   ²I.e., in it is strength
7:23 'I.e., large basin   ²About 15 ft. in diameter and
7.5 ft. high or 4.6 m and 2.3 m high   ³About 45 ft.
or 14 m   7:26 'About 3 in. or 7.6 cm   ²About 12,000
gallons or 45,424 liters

¹four cubits, its width four cubits, and its height was three cubits. ²⁸This was the design of the stands: they had borders, that is, borders between the crossbars, ²⁹and on the borders which were between the crossbars were lions, oxen, and cherubim; and on the crossbars there was a pedestal above, and beneath the lions and oxen were wreaths of hanging work. ³⁰Now each stand had four bronze wheels with bronze axles, and its four feet had supports; beneath the basin were cast supports with wreaths at each side. ³¹And its opening inside the crown at the top was a ¹cubit, and its opening was round like the design of a pedestal, a cubit and a half; and on its opening also there were engravings, and their borders were square, not round. ³²The four wheels were underneath the borders, and the axles of the wheels were on the stand. And the height of a wheel was a cubit and a half. ³³The workmanship of the wheels was like the workmanship of a chariot wheel. Their axles, their rims, their spokes, and their hubs were all cast. ³⁴Now there were four supports at the four corners of each stand; its supports were part of the stand itself. ³⁵And on the top of the stand there was a circular form half a cubit high, and on the top of the stand its stays and its borders were part of it. ³⁶And he engraved on the plates of its stays and on its borders cherubim, lions, and palm trees, as there was clear space on each, with wreaths all around. ³⁷ᴬHe made the ten stands like this: all of them had the same casting, same measure, and same form.

³⁸ᴬAnd he made ten basins of bronze, each holding ¹forty baths; each basin was ²four cubits, and on each of the ten stands was one basin. ³⁹Then he placed the stands, five on the right side of the house and five on the left side of the house; and he set the ¹Sea of cast metal on the right side of the house eastward toward the south.

⁴⁰Now Hiram made the basins and the shovels and the bowls. So Hiram finished doing all the work which he performed for King Solomon in the house of the LORD: ⁴¹the two pillars and the two bowls of the capitals which were on the top of the ᴬtwo pillars, and the two lattices to cover the two bowls of the capitals which were on the top of the pillars; ⁴²and the ᴬfour hundred pomegranates for the two lattices, two rows of pomegranates for each lattice to cover the two bowls of the capitals which were on the tops of the pillars; ⁴³and the ten stands with the ten basins on the stands; ⁴⁴and ᴬthe one ¹Sea and the twelve oxen under the Sea; ⁴⁵and ᴬthe buckets, the shovels, and the bowls; indeed, all these utensils which Hiram made for King Solomon in the house of the LORD were of polished bronze. ⁴⁶ᴬThe king had them cast in the plain of the Jordan, in the clay ground between Succoth and Zarethan. ⁴⁷However, Solomon left all the utensils unweighed, because they were too many; ᴬthe weight of the bronze could not be determined.

7:37 ¹2 Chr 4:14　7:38 ᴬEx 30:18; 2 Chr 4:6
7:41 ᴬ1 Kin 7:17, 18　7:42 ᴬ1 Kin 7:20
7:44 ᴬ1 Kin 7:23, 25　7:45 ᴬEx 27:3; 2 Chr 4:16
7:46 ᴬ2 Chr 4:17　7:47 ᴬ1 Chr 22:3, 14

7:27 ¹About 6 ft. long and wide and 4.5 ft. high
or 1.8 m and 1.4 m　7:31 ¹About 18 in. or 45 cm
7:38 ¹About 240 gallons or 908 liters　²About 6 ft. or
1.8 m　7:39 ¹I.e., large basin　7:44 ¹I.e., large basin

⁴⁸Solomon also made all the furniture that *was in* the house of the LORD: ᴬthe golden altar and the golden table on which *was set* the ᴮbread of the Presence; ⁴⁹and the lampstands of pure gold, five on the right side and five on the left, in front of the inner sanctuary; and ᴬthe flowers, the lamps, and the tongs, of gold; ⁵⁰also the cups, the shears, the bowls, the ladles, and the ᴬfirepans, of pure gold; and the hinges *both* for the doors of the inner house, the Most Holy Place, *and* for the doors of the house, *that is,* for the main room, of gold.

⁵¹So all the work that King Solomon performed *in* the house of the LORD was finished. And ᴬSolomon brought in the offerings vowed by his father David, the silver and the gold and the utensils, *and* he put them in the treasuries of the house of the LORD.

THE ARK BROUGHT INTO THE TEMPLE

8 ᴬThen Solomon assembled the elders of Israel and all the heads of the tribes, the leaders of the fathers' *households* of the sons of Israel, to King Solomon in Jerusalem, to bring up the ark of the covenant of the LORD from ᴮthe city of David, that is, Zion. ²So all the men of Israel assembled themselves before King Solomon at ᴬthe feast, in the month Ethanim, that is, the seventh month. ³Then all the elders of Israel came, and ᴬthe priests took up the ark. ⁴And they brought up the ark of the LORD, ᴬthe tent of meeting, and all the holy utensils which were in the tent; the priests and the Levites brought them up. ⁵And King Solomon and all the congregation of Israel, who were gathered together

to him, ᴬwere with him before the ark, sacrificing so many sheep and oxen that they could not be counted or numbered. ⁶Then the priests brought the ark of the covenant of the LORD ᴬto its place, into the inner sanctuary of the house, to the Most Holy Place, ᴮunder the wings of the cherubim. ⁷For the cherubim spread *their* wings over the place of the ark, and the cherubim made a covering over the ark and its carrying poles from above. ⁸But ᴬthe poles were so long that the ends of the poles could be seen from the holy place in front of the inner sanctuary, but they could not be seen outside; they are there to this day. ⁹ᴬThere was nothing in the ark except the two tablets of stone which Moses put there at Horeb, where the LORD made *a covenant* with the sons of Israel, when they came out of the land of Egypt. ¹⁰And it happened that when the priests came from the holy place, ᴬthe cloud filled the house of the LORD, ¹¹so that the priests could not stand to minister because of the cloud, for the glory of the LORD filled the house of the LORD.

SOLOMON ADDRESSES THE PEOPLE

¹²ᴬThen Solomon said,

"The LORD has said that He
     would dwell in the thick
     darkness.
¹³ "ᴬI have truly built You a lofty
     house,
   A place for Your dwelling
     forever."

7:48 ᴬEx 37:10-29   ᴮEx 25:30   7:49 ᴬEx 25:31-38
7:50 ᴬEx 27:3; 2 Kin 25:15   7:51 ᴬ2 Sam 8:11; 2 Chr 5:1
8:1 ᴬ2 Chr 5:2-10   ᴮ2 Sam 5:7   8:2 ᴬLev 23:34;
2 Chr 7:8-10   8:3 ᴬDeut 31:9; Josh 3:3, 6
8:4 ᴬ1 Kin 3:4; 2 Chr 1:3   8:5 ᴬ2 Sam 6:13; 2 Chr 1:6
8:6 ᴬ1 Kin 6:19   ᴮ1 Kin 6:27   8:8 ᴬEx 25:13-15; 37:4, 5
8:9 ᴬDeut 10:2-5; Heb 9:4   8:10 ᴬEx 40:34, 35;
2 Chr 7:1, 2   8:12 ᴬ2 Chr 6:1   8:13 ᴬ2 Sam 7:13

¹⁴Then the king turned around and ^blessed all the assembly of Israel, while all the assembly of Israel was standing. ¹⁵He said, "Blessed be the LORD, the God of Israel, ^who spoke with His mouth to my father David, and fulfilled *it* with His hands, saying, ¹⁶'^Since the day that I brought My people Israel from Egypt, I did not choose a city out of all the tribes of Israel *in which* to build a house so that My name would be there, but I chose David to be over My people Israel.' ¹⁷^Now it was in the heart of my father David to build a house for the name of the LORD, the God of Israel. ¹⁸But the LORD said to my father David, 'Because it was in your heart to build a house for My name, you did well that it was in your heart. ¹⁹^Nevertheless you shall not build the house, but your son who will be born to you, he will build the house for My name.' ²⁰Now the LORD has fulfilled His word which He spoke; for ^I have risen in place of my father David and I sit on the throne of Israel, just as the LORD promised, and I have built the house for the name of the LORD, the God of Israel. ²¹And there I have set a place for the ark, ^in which is the covenant of the LORD, which He made with our fathers when He brought them out of the land of Egypt."

THE PRAYER OF DEDICATION

²²Then ^Solomon stood before the altar of the LORD in the presence of all the assembly of Israel, and he spread out his hands toward heaven. ²³And he said, "LORD, God of Israel, ^there is no God like You in heaven above or on earth beneath, ^Bkeeping the covenant and *showing* faithfulness to Your servants who walk before You with all their heart, ²⁴You who have kept with Your servant, my father David, that which You promised him; You have spoken with Your mouth and have fulfilled it with Your hand, as *it is* this day. ²⁵Now then, LORD, God of Israel, keep with Your servant David my father that which You have promised him, saying, '^You shall not be deprived of a man to sit on the throne of Israel, if only your sons are careful about their way, to walk before Me as you have walked.' ²⁶Now then, God of Israel, let Your words, please, be confirmed, ^which You have spoken to Your servant, my father David.

²⁷"But will God indeed dwell on the earth? Behold, ^heaven and the highest heaven cannot contain You, how much less this house which I have built! ²⁸Nevertheless, turn Your attention to the ^prayer of Your servant and to his plea, LORD, my God, to listen to the cry and to the prayer which Your servant prays before You today, ²⁹^so that Your eyes may be open toward this house night and day, toward the place of which You have said, 'My name shall be there,' to listen to the prayer which Your servant will pray toward this place. ³⁰And ^listen to the plea of Your servant and of Your people Israel, ^Bwhen they pray toward this place; hear in heaven Your dwelling place; hear and forgive!

³¹"^If a person sins against his neighbor and is compelled to take

8:14^2 Sam 6:18; 1 Kin 8:55   8:15^2 Sam 7:12, 13; 1 Chr 22:10   8:16^2 Sam 7:4, 5; 1 Chr 17:3-10
8:17^2 Sam 7:2, 3; 1 Chr 17:1, 2
8:19^2 Sam 7:5, 12, 13; 1 Kin 5:3, 5   8:20^1 Chr 28:5, 6
8:21^Deut 31:26; 1 Kin 8:9   8:22^1 Kin 8:54;
2 Chr 6:12   8:23^1 Sam 2:2   ^BDeut 7:9
8:25^1 Kin 2:4   8:26^2 Sam 7:25   8:27^Ps 139:7-16;
Is 66:1   8:28^Phil 4:6   8:29^2 Chr 7:15; Neh 1:6
8:30^Neh 1:6   ^BDan 6:10   8:31^Ex 22:8-11

an oath *of innocence,* and he comes *and* takes an oath before Your altar in this house, ³²then hear in heaven and act and judge Your servants, ᴬcondemning the wicked by bringing his way on his own head, and acquitting the righteous by giving him according to his righteousness.

³³"When Your people Israel are defeated before an enemy because they have sinned against You, ᴬif they turn to You again and confess Your name and pray and implore Your favor in this house, ³⁴then hear in heaven, and forgive the sin of Your people Israel, and bring them back to the land which You gave their fathers.

³⁵"ᴬWhen the heavens are shut up and there is no rain because they have sinned against You, and they pray toward this place and praise Your name, and turn from their sin when You afflict them, ³⁶then hear in heaven and forgive the sin of Your servants and Your people Israel; ᴬindeed, teach them the good way in which they are to walk. And provide rain on Your land, which You have given to Your people as an inheritance.

³⁷"ᴬIf there is a famine in the land, if there is a plague, if there is blight *or* mildew, locust *or* grasshopper, if their enemy harasses them in the land of their cities, whatever plague, whatever sickness *there is,* ³⁸whatever prayer or plea is offered by any person *or* by all Your people Israel, each knowing the affliction of his own heart, and spreading his hands toward this house; ³⁹then hear in heaven, Your dwelling place, and forgive and act, and give to each in accordance with all his ways, ᴬwhose heart You know—for You alone know the hearts of all

mankind— ⁴⁰so that they will fear You all the days that they live on the land which You have given to our fathers.

⁴¹"Also regarding the foreigner who is not of Your people Israel, when he comes from a far country on account of Your name ⁴²(for they will hear of Your great name ᴬand Your mighty hand, and of Your outstretched arm); when he comes and prays toward this house, ⁴³hear in heaven Your dwelling place, and act in accordance with all for which the foreigner calls to You, in order ᴬthat all the peoples of the earth may know Your name, to fear You, as *do* Your people Israel, and that they may know that this house which I have built is called by Your name.

⁴⁴"When Your people go out to battle against their enemy, by whatever way You send them, and ᴬthey pray to the Lᴏʀᴅ toward the city which You have chosen and the house which I have built for Your name, ⁴⁵then hear in heaven their prayer and their pleading, and maintain their cause.

⁴⁶"When they sin against You (for ᴬthere is no person who does not sin) and You are angry with them and turn them over to an enemy, so that they take them away captive to the land of the enemy, distant or near; ⁴⁷if they take it to heart in the land where they have been taken captive, and repent and implore Your favor in the land of those who have taken them captive, saying, 'ᴬWe have sinned and done wrong,

---

8:32 ᴬDeut 25:1   8:33 ᴬLev 26:40–42
8:35 ᴬDeut 11:16, 17; 2 Sam 24:10-13   8:36 ᴬPs 5:8;
25:4, 5   8:37 ᴬLev 26:16, 25, 26; Deut 28:21-23, 38-42
8:39 ᴬ1 Sam 2:3; 16:7   8:42 ᴬEx 13:3; Deut 3:24
8:43 ᴬJosh 4:23, 24; Ps 67:2   8:44 ᴬ2 Chr 14:11
8:46 ᴬRom 3:23; 1 John 1:8-10   8:47 ᴬEzra 9:6, 7;
Neh 1:6

we have acted wickedly'; 48^if they return to You with all their heart and with all their soul in the land of their enemies who have taken them captive, and pray to You toward their land which You have given to their fathers, the city which You have chosen, and the house which I have built for Your name; 49then hear their prayer and their pleading in heaven, Your dwelling place, and maintain their cause, 50and forgive Your people who have sinned against You and all their wrongdoings which they have committed against You, and ^make them *objects of* compassion before those who have taken them captive, so that they will have compassion on them 51(for they are Your people and Your inheritance which You have brought out of Egypt, ^from the midst of the iron furnace), 52^so that Your eyes may be open to the pleading of Your servant and to the pleading of Your people Israel, to listen to them whenever they call to You. 53For You have singled them out from all the peoples of the earth as Your inheritance, ^just as You spoke through Moses Your servant, when You brought our fathers out of Egypt, Lord GOD."

SOLOMON'S BENEDICTION

54^When Solomon had finished praying this entire prayer and plea to the LORD, he stood up from the altar of the LORD, from kneeling on his knees with his hands spread toward heaven. 55And he stood and ^blessed all the assembly of Israel with a loud voice, saying:

56"Blessed be the LORD, who has given rest to His people Israel ^in accordance with everything that He promised; not one word

has failed of all His good promise, which He promised through Moses His servant. 57May the LORD our God be with us, as He was with our fathers; ^may He not leave us nor forsake us, 58so that ^He may guide our hearts toward Himself, to walk in all His ways and to keep His commandments, His statutes, and His ordinances, which He commanded our fathers. 59And may these words of mine, with which I have implored the favor of the LORD, be near to the LORD our God day and night, so that He will maintain the cause of His servant and the cause of His people Israel, as each day requires, 60so that all the peoples of the earth may know that ^the LORD is God; there is no one else. 61^Your hearts therefore shall be wholly devoted to the LORD our God, to walk in His statutes and to keep His commandments, as at this day."

DEDICATORY SACRIFICES

62^Then the king and all Israel with him offered sacrifice before the LORD. 63And Solomon offered for the sacrifice of peace offerings, which he offered to the LORD, twenty-two thousand oxen and 120,000 sheep. ^So the king and all the sons of Israel dedicated the house of the LORD. 64On the same day the king consecrated the middle of the courtyard that *was* in front of the house of the LORD, because there he offered the burnt offering, the grain offering, and

8:48^Deut 4:29; 1 Sam 7:3, 4 8:50^Ps 106:46; Acts 7:10 8:51^Deut 4:20; Jer 11:4 8:52^1 Kin 8:29 8:53^Ex 19:5, 6; Deut 9:26-29 8:54^2 Chr 7:1 8:55^Num 6:23-26; 1 Kin 8:14 8:56^Deut 12:10 8:57^Rom 8:31; Heb 13:5 8:58^Ps 119:36; Jer 31:33 8:60^Deut 4:35; Jer 10:10-12 8:61^Deut 18:13; 2 Kin 20:3 8:62^2 Chr 7:4-10 8:63^Ezra 6:15-18; Neh 12:27

the fat of the peace offerings; for ^the bronze altar that *was* before the LORD *was* too small to hold the burnt offering, the grain offering, and the fat of the peace offerings.

65 So Solomon held the 'feast at that time, and all Israel with him, a great assembly ^from the entrance of Hamath ᴮto the brook of Egypt, before the LORD our God, for seven days and seven *more* days, *that is,* fourteen days. 66 On the eighth day he dismissed the people, and they blessed the king. Then they went to their tents joyful and with happy hearts for all the goodness that the LORD had shown to David His servant, and to Israel His people.

GOD'S PROMISE AND WARNING

9 ^Now it came about when Solomon had finished building the house of the LORD and ᴮthe king's house, and all that Solomon desired to do, 2 that ^the LORD appeared to Solomon a second time, as He had appeared to him at Gibeon. 3 And the LORD said to him, "^I have heard your prayer and your plea which you have offered before Me; I have consecrated this house which you have built, by putting My name there forever, and My eyes and My heart will be there always. 4 As for you, ^if you walk before Me as your father David walked, in integrity of heart and honesty, acting in accordance with everything that I have commanded you, *and if* you keep My statutes and My ordinances, 5 then ^I will establish the throne of your kingdom over Israel forever, just as I promised to your father David, saying, 'You shall not be deprived of a man on the throne of Israel.'

6 "^But if you or your sons indeed turn away from following Me,

and do not keep My commandments and My statutes which I have placed before you, but you go and serve other gods and worship them, 7 ^then I will cut Israel off from the land which I have given them, and ᴮthe house which I have consecrated for My name, I will expel from My sight. So Israel will become a saying and an object of derision among all peoples. 8 And this house will become ^a heap of ruins; everyone who passes by it will be appalled and hiss and say, 'Why has the LORD done such a thing to this land and this house?' 9 And they will say, '^Because they abandoned the LORD their God, who brought their fathers out of the land of Egypt, and they adopted other gods and worshiped and served them, for that reason the LORD has brought all this adversity on them.'"

CITIES GIVEN TO HIRAM

10 ^Now it came about ᴮat the end of twenty years in which Solomon had built the two houses, the house of the LORD and the king's house 11 (Hiram king of Tyre had supplied Solomon with cedar and juniper timber and gold, satisfying all his desire), that King Solomon then gave Hiram twenty cities in the land of Galilee. 12 So Hiram left Tyre to see the cities which Solomon had given him, and they did not please him. 13 And he said, "What are these cities which you

8:64 ^2 Chr 4:1   8:65 ^Num 34:8   ᴮJosh 13:3
9:1 ^2 Chr 7:11   ᴮ1 Kin 7:1, 2   9:2 ^1 Kin 3:5; 2 Chr 1:7
9:3 ^Ps 10:17; 34:17   9:4 ^2 Kin 20:3; Ps 128:1
9:5 ^2 Sam 7:12, 16; 1 Chr 22:10   9:6 ^2 Sam 7:14-16;
Ps 89:30ff   9:7 ^Lev 18:24-29   ᴮJer 7:4-14
9:8 ^2 Kin 25:9; 2 Chr 36:19   9:9 ^Deut 29:25-28;
Jer 2:10-13   9:10 ^2 Chr 8:1   ᴮ1 Kin 6:37, 38

8:65 ¹I.e., of Booths

have given me, my brother?" So they have been called the land of [1,A]Cabul to this day. [14A]And Hiram sent to the king [1]120 talents of gold.

[15]Now this is the account of the forced labor which King Solomon [A]conscripted to build the house of the LORD, his own house, the [1]Millo, the wall of Jerusalem, Hazor, Megiddo, and Gezer. [16]For Pharaoh king of Egypt had gone up and overthrown Gezer and burned it with fire, and killed the [A]Canaanites who lived in the city; and he had given it *as* a dowry to his daughter, Solomon's wife. [17]So Solomon rebuilt Gezer and the lower [A]Beth-horon, [18]and [A]Baalath and Tamar in the wilderness, in the land *of Judah,* [19]and all the storage cities which Solomon had, that is, [A]the cities for his chariots and the cities for his horsemen, and everything that it pleased Solomon to build in Jerusalem, in Lebanon, and in all the land under his rule. [20]*As for* all the people who were left of the Amorites, the Hittites, the Perizzites, the Hivites, and the Jebusites, who were not of the sons of Israel, [21A]their descendants who were left after them in the land, whom the sons of Israel were unable to completely eliminate, from them Solomon conscripted forced laborers, *as they are* to this day. [22]But Solomon [A]did not make slaves of the sons of Israel; for they were men of war, his servants, his commanders, his charioteers, his chariot commanders, and his horsemen.

[23]These *were* the [A]chief officers who *were* in charge of Solomon's work, 550, who ruled over the people doing the work.

[24]As soon as [A]Pharaoh's daughter came up from the city of David to her house which *Solomon* had built for her, he then built the Millo.

[25]Now [A]three times a year Solomon offered burnt offerings and peace offerings on the altar which he had built for the LORD, burning incense with them *on the altar* which *was* before the LORD. So he finished the house.

[26]King Solomon also built a [A]fleet of ships in Ezion-geber, which is near Eloth on the shore of the Red Sea, in the land of Edom. [27A]And Hiram sent his servants with the fleet, sailors who knew the sea, along with the servants of Solomon. [28]And they went to [A]Ophir and received [1]420 talents of gold from there, and brought *it* to King Solomon.

THE QUEEN OF SHEBA

10 [A]Now when the queen of Sheba heard about the fame of Solomon *in relation* to the name of the LORD, she came to test him with riddles. [2]So she came to Jerusalem with a very large entourage, with camels [A]carrying balsam oil and a very large *quantity of* gold and precious stones. When she came to Solomon, she spoke to him about everything that was in her heart. [3]And Solomon answered all her questions; nothing was concealed from the king which he did not explain to her. [4]When the queen of Sheba saw all the wisdom

9:13[A]Josh 19:27   9:14[A]1 Kin 9:11   9:15[A]1 Kin 5:13
9:16[A]Josh 16:10   9:17[A]Josh 10:10; 2 Chr 8:5
9:18[A]Josh 19:44   9:19[A]1 Kin 10:26; 2 Chr 1:14
9:21[A]Judg 1:21-29; 3:1   9:22[A]Lev 25:39
9:23[A]2 Chr 8:10   9:24[A]1 Kin 3:1; 7:8   9:25[A]Ex
23:14-17; Deut 16:16   9:26[A]1 Kin 22:48
9:27[A]1 Kin 5:6, 9; 10:11   9:28[A]1 Chr 29:4; 2 Chr 8:18
10:1[A]Matt 12:42; Luke 11:31   10:2[A]1 Kin 10:10

9:13[1]I.e., like nothing   9:14[1]About 4.5 tons
or 4 metric tons   9:15[1]I.e., terraced structure
9:28[1]About 16 tons or 14 metric tons

of Solomon, and the house that he had built, ⁵and the food of his table, the seating of his servants, the service of his waiters and their attire, his cupbearers, and his burnt offerings which he offered at the house of the LORD, she was breathless. ⁶Then she said to the king, "It was a true story that I heard in my own land about your words and your wisdom. ⁷But I did not believe the stories until I came and my *own* eyes saw *it all.* And behold, the half *of it* was not reported to me. You have exceeded *in* wisdom and prosperity the report which I heard. ⁸ᴬBlessed are your men, *and* blessed are these servants of yours who stand before you continually *and* hear your wisdom! ⁹Blessed be the LORD your God who delighted in you to put you on the throne of Israel; ᴬbecause the LORD loves Israel forever, He made you king, ᴮto do justice and righteousness." ¹⁰Then ᴬshe gave the king ¹120 talents of gold, and a very large *amount* of balsam oil and precious stones. Never again did such a large quantity of balsam oil come in as that which the queen of Sheba gave King Solomon.

¹¹ᴬAnd the ships of Hiram as well, which brought gold from Ophir, brought in from Ophir a very great *number of* almug trees and precious stones. ¹²ᴬThe king made from the almug trees supports for the house of the LORD and for the king's house, and lyres and harps for the singers; such almug trees have not come in *again,* nor have they been seen to this day.

¹³And King Solomon granted the queen of Sheba everything she desired, whatever she requested, besides what he gave her in proportion to his royal bounty. Then she departed and went to her own land together with her servants.

WEALTH, SPLENDOR, AND WISDOM

¹⁴ᴬNow the weight of gold that came to Solomon in one year was ¹666 talents of gold, ¹⁵besides *that* from the traders, and the wares of the merchants and all the kings of the ᴬArabs and the governors of the country. ¹⁶ᴬKing Solomon made two hundred large shields of beaten gold, using six hundred *shekels of* gold on each large shield. ¹⁷And *he made* three hundred *small* shields of beaten gold, using ¹three minas of gold on each shield; and ᴬthe king put them in the house of the timber of Lebanon. ¹⁸Moreover, the king made a large throne of ᴬivory and overlaid it with fine gold. ¹⁹*There were* six steps to the throne and a round top to the throne at its back, and armrests on each side of the seat, and two lions standing beside the armrests. ²⁰Twelve lions were standing there on the six steps on the one side and on the other; nothing like *it* was made for any other kingdom. ²¹Now all King Solomon's drinking utensils *were* of gold, and all the utensils of the house of the timber of Lebanon *were* of pure gold. None was of silver; it was not considered *as amounting to* anything in the days of Solomon. ²²For ᴬthe

10:8 ᴬProv 8:34   10:9 ᴬ1 Chr 17:22   ᴮPs 72:2
10:10 ᴬ1 Kin 10:2   10:11 ᴬ1 Kin 9:27, 28; Job 22:24
10:12 ᴬ2 Chr 9:11   10:14 ᴬ2 Chr 9:13-28
10:15 ᴬ2 Chr 9:14   10:16 ᴬ1 Kin 14:26-28; 2 Chr 12:9, 10
10:17 ᴬ1 Kin 7:2   10:18 ᴬ2 Chr 9:17; Ps 45:8
10:22 ᴬ1 Kin 9:26-28; 2 Chr 20:36

10:10 ¹About 4.5 tons or 4 metric tons   10:14 ¹About 25 tons or 23 metric tons   10:17 ¹About 3.8 lb. or 1.7 kg

king had the ships of Tarshish at sea with Hiram's ships; once every three years the ships of Tarshish would come carrying gold and silver, ivory, monkeys, and peacocks. ²³ᴬSo King Solomon became greater than all the kings of the earth in wealth and wisdom. ²⁴And all the earth was seeking the attention of Solomon, ᴬto hear his wisdom, which God had put in his heart. ²⁵And ᴬthey were bringing, everyone, a gift: articles of silver and gold, garments, weapons, balsam oil, horses, and mules, so much year by year.

²⁶Now Solomon gathered chariots and horsemen; and he had 1,400 chariots and twelve thousand horsemen, and he stationed them in the ᴬchariot cities and with the king in Jerusalem. ²⁷ᴬAnd the king made silver *as common* as stones in Jerusalem, and he made cedars as plentiful as sycamore trees that are in the lowland. ²⁸ᴬAlso Solomon's import of horses was from Egypt and Kue, *and* the king's merchants acquired *them* from Kue for a price. ²⁹A chariot was imported from Egypt for six hundred *shekels* of silver, and a horse for 150; and by the same means they exported them ᴬto all the kings of the Hittites and to the kings of the Arameans.

SOLOMON TURNS FROM GOD

11 Now ᴬKing Solomon loved many foreign women along with the daughter of Pharaoh: Moabite, Ammonite, Edomite, Sidonian, *and* Hittite women, ²from the nations of which the Lᴏʀᴅ had said to the sons of Israel, "ᴬYou shall not associate with them, nor shall you associate with you; they will certainly turn your heart away to follow

their gods." Solomon clung to these in love. ³ᴬHe had seven hundred wives, *who were* princesses, and three hundred concubines; and his wives turned his heart away. ⁴For when Solomon was old, his wives turned his heart away to follow other gods; and ᴬhis heart was not wholly devoted to the Lᴏʀᴅ his God, as the heart of his father David *had been.* ⁵For Solomon became a follower of ᴬAshtoreth the goddess of the Sidonians, and of ᴮMilcom the abhorrent idol of the Ammonites. ⁶So Solomon did what was evil in the sight of the Lᴏʀᴅ, and did not follow the Lᴏʀᴅ fully, as his father David *had done.* ⁷Then Solomon built a high place for ᴬChemosh, the abhorrent idol of Moab, on the mountain that is east of Jerusalem, and for ᴮMolech, the abhorrent idol of the sons of Ammon. ⁸He also did the same for all his foreign wives, who burned incense and sacrificed to their gods.

⁹Now the Lᴏʀᴅ was angry with Solomon because his heart had turned away from the Lᴏʀᴅ, the God of Israel, ᴬwho had appeared to him twice, ¹⁰and ᴬhad commanded him regarding this thing, that he was not to follow other gods; but he did not comply with what the Lᴏʀᴅ had commanded. ¹¹So the Lᴏʀᴅ said to Solomon, "Since you have done this, and you have not kept My covenant and My statutes, which I have commanded you, ᴬI will certainly tear the kingdom away from you, and will give it to

10:23ᴬ1 Kin 3:12, 13; 4:30   10:24ᴬ1 Kin 3:9, 12, 28   10:25ᴬPs 68:29   10:26ᴬ1 Kin 9:19   10:27ᴬDeut 17:17; 2 Chr 1:15   10:28ᴬDeut 17:16; 2 Chr 1:16   10:29ᴬ2 Kin 7:6, 7   11:1ᴬDeut 17:17; Neh 13:23-27   11:2ᴬEx 23:31-33; 34:12-16   11:3ᴬ2 Sam 5:13-16   11:4ᴬ1 Kin 9:4   11:5ᴬ1 Sam 7:3, 4   ᴮ1 Kin 11:7   11:7ᴬNum 21:29   ᴮLev 20:2-5   11:9ᴬ1 Kin 3:5; 9:2   11:10ᴬ1 Kin 6:12; 9:6, 7   11:11ᴬ1 Sam 2:30; 1 Kin 11:29-31

your servant. ¹²However, I will not do it in your days, *only* for the sake of your father David; *but* I will tear it away from the hand of your son. ¹³Yet I will not tear away all the kingdom, *but* ᴬI will give one tribe to your son for the sake of My servant David, and for the sake of Jerusalem, which I have chosen."

GOD RAISES ADVERSARIES

¹⁴Then the LORD raised up an adversary against Solomon, Hadad the Edomite; he was of the royal line in Edom. ¹⁵For it came about, ᴬwhen David was in Edom and Joab the commander of the army had gone up to bury those killed *in battle*, and had struck and killed every male in Edom ¹⁶(for Joab and all Israel stayed there for six months, until he had eliminated every male in Edom), ¹⁷that Hadad fled to Egypt, he and certain Edomites of his father's servants with him, while Hadad *was* a young boy. ¹⁸They set out from Midian and came to ᴬParan; and they took men with them from Paran and came to Egypt, to Pharaoh king of Egypt, who gave him a house and assigned him food and gave him land. ¹⁹Now Hadad found great favor in the sight of Pharaoh, so that he gave him in marriage the sister of his own wife, the sister of Tahpenes the queen. ²⁰And the sister of Tahpenes gave birth to his son Genubath, whom Tahpenes weaned in Pharaoh's house; and Genubath was in Pharaoh's house among the sons of Pharaoh. ²¹But ᴬwhen Hadad heard in Egypt that David ¹lay down with his fathers and that Joab the commander of the army was dead, Hadad said to Pharaoh, "Let me go, so that I may go to my own country." ²²However,

Pharaoh said to him, "But what have you lacked with me that you are here, requesting to go to your own country?" And he answered, "Nothing; nevertheless you must let me go."

²³ᴬGod also raised up *another* adversary against him, Rezon the son of Eliada, who had fled from his master Hadadezer, king of Zobah. ²⁴And he gathered men to himself and became leader of a marauding band, ᴬafter David killed those *of Zobah;* and they went to Damascus and stayed there, and reigned in Damascus. ²⁵So he was an adversary to Israel all the days of Solomon, along with the harm that Hadad *inflicted;* and he felt disgust for Israel and reigned over Aram.

²⁶Then ᴬJeroboam the son of Nebat, an Ephraimite of Zeredah, Solomon's servant, whose mother's name was Zeruah, a widow, also rebelled against the king. ²⁷Now this was the reason why he rebelled against the king: ᴬSolomon built the ¹Millo, *and* closed up the breach of the city of his father David. ²⁸Now the man Jeroboam was a valiant warrior, and when ᴬSolomon saw that the young man was industrious, he appointed him over all the forced labor of the house of Joseph. ²⁹And it came about at that time, when Jeroboam went out of Jerusalem, that ᴬthe prophet Ahijah the Shilonite found him on the road. Now Ahijah had clothed himself with a new cloak; and both of them were alone in the field. ³⁰Then ᴬAhijah

11:13ᴬ1 Kin 11:32, 36; 12:20   11:15ᴬ2 Sam 8:14;
1 Chr 18:12, 13   11:18ᴬNum 10:12; Deut 1:1
11:21ᴬ1 Kin 2:10   11:23ᴬ1 Kin 11:14
11:24ᴬ2 Sam 10:8, 18   11:26ᴬ1 Kin 11:11, 28; 2 Chr 13:6
11:27ᴬ1 Kin 9:15, 24   11:28ᴬProv 22:29
11:29ᴬ1 Kin 12:15; 2 Chr 9:29   11:30ᴬ1 Sam 15:27, 28

11:21¹I.e., died   11:27¹I.e., terraced structure

took hold of the new cloak which was on him and tore it into twelve pieces. [31]And he said to Jeroboam, "Take for yourself ten pieces; for this is what the Lord, the God of Israel says: 'Behold, ^I am going to tear the kingdom away from the hand of Solomon and give you ten tribes [32](^but he shall have one tribe, for the sake of My servant David and for the sake of Jerusalem, ^Bthe city which I have chosen from all the tribes of Israel), [33]because they have abandoned Me, and ^have worshiped Ashtoreth the goddess of the Sidonians, ^BChemosh the god of Moab, and Milcom the god of the sons of Ammon; and they have not walked in My ways, doing what is right in My sight and *keeping* My statutes and My ordinances, as his father David *did*. [34]Nevertheless I will not take the whole kingdom out of his hand, but I will make him ruler all the days of his life, for the sake of My servant David whom I chose, who kept My commandments and My statutes; [35]but ^I will take the kingdom from his son's hand and give it to you; *that is*, ten tribes. [36]But to his son I will give one tribe, ^so that My servant David may always have a lamp before Me in Jerusalem, the city where I have chosen for Myself to put My name. [37]However I will take you, and you shall reign over all that you desire, and you shall be king over Israel. [38]Then it shall be, that if you listen to all that I command you and walk in My ways, and do what is right in My sight by keeping My statutes and My commandments, as My servant David did, then I will be with you and ^build you an enduring house as I built for David, and I will give Israel to you. [39]So I will oppress the descendants

of David for this, but not always.' " [40]Solomon sought therefore to put Jeroboam to death; but Jeroboam set out and fled to Egypt to ^Shishak king of Egypt, and he was in Egypt until the death of Solomon.

THE DEATH OF SOLOMON

[41]^ANow the rest of the acts of Solomon and whatever he did, and his wisdom, are they not written in the Book of the Acts of Solomon? [42]So ^the time that Solomon reigned in Jerusalem over all Israel was forty years. [43]Then Solomon [1]lay down with his fathers and was buried in the city of his father David, and his son ^Rehoboam reigned in his place.

KING REHOBOAM ACTS FOOLISHLY

12 ^AThen Rehoboam went to Shechem, because all Israel had come to ^BShechem to make him king. [2]Now ^when Jeroboam the son of Nebat heard *about this,* he was living in Egypt (for he was still in Egypt, where he had fled from the presence of King Solomon). [3]Then they sent *word* and summoned him, and Jeroboam and all the assembly of Israel came and spoke to Rehoboam, saying, [4]"^Your father made our yoke hard; but now, lighten the hard labor *imposed by* your father and his heavy yoke which he put on us, and we will serve you." [5]Then he said to them, "^Depart for three days, then return to me." So the people departed.

11:31^A1 Kin 11:11, 12　11:32^A1 Kin 12:21　^B1 Kin 14:21
11:33^A1 Kin 11:5–8　^BJer 48:7, 13　11:35^A1 Kin 11:12;
12:16, 17　11:36^A2 Kin 8:19; Ps 132:17
11:38^A2 Sam 7:11, 27　11:40^A1 Kin 14:25; 2 Chr 12:2–9
11:41^A2 Chr 9:29　11:42^A2 Chr 9:30
11:43^A1 Kin 14:21; Matt 1:7　12:1^A2 Chr 10:1
^BJudg 9:6　12:2^A1 Kin 11:26, 40　12:4^A1 Sam 8:11–18;
1 Kin 4:7, 21–25　12:5^A1 Kin 12:12

11:43[1]I.e., died

⁶And King Rehoboam ^consulted with the elders who had served his father Solomon while he was still alive, saying, "How do you advise *me* to answer this people?" ⁷Then they spoke to him, saying, "^If you will be a servant to this people today, and will serve them and grant them their request, and speak pleasant words to them, then they will be your servants always." ⁸But he ignored the advice of the elders which they had given him, and consulted with the young men who had grown up with him and served him. ⁹He said to them, "What advice do you give, so that we may answer this people who have spoken to me, saying, 'Lighten the yoke which your father put on us'?" ¹⁰And the young men who had grown up with him spoke to him, saying, "This is what you should say to this people who spoke to you, saying: 'Your father made our yoke heavy, now you make it lighter for us!' You should speak this way to them: 'My little finger is thicker than my father's waist! ¹¹Now then, my father loaded you with a heavy yoke; yet I will add to your yoke. My father disciplined you with whips, but I will discipline you with scorpions!'"

¹²Then Jeroboam and all the people came to Rehoboam on the third day, just as the king had directed, saying, "^Return to me on the third day." ¹³And the king answered the people harshly, for he ignored the advice of the elders which they had given him, ¹⁴and he spoke to them according to the advice of the young men, saying, "^My father made your yoke heavy, but I will add to your yoke; my father disciplined you with whips, but I will discipline you with scorpions!"

¹⁵So the king did not listen to the people; because it was a turn of events from the LORD, ^in order to establish His word which the LORD spoke through Ahijah the Shilonite to Jeroboam the son of Nebat.

THE KINGDOM DIVIDED; JEROBOAM RULES ISRAEL

¹⁶When all Israel saw that the king had not listened to them, the people replied to the king, saying,

"What share do we have in
   David?
We have no inheritance in the
   son of Jesse;
^To your tents, Israel!
Now look after your own
   house, David!"

So Israel went *away* to their tents. ¹⁷But ^as for the sons of Israel who lived in the cities of Judah, Rehoboam reigned over them. ¹⁸Then King Rehoboam sent ^Adoram, who was in charge of the forced labor, and all Israel stoned him to death. And King Rehoboam hurried to mount his chariot to flee to Jerusalem. ¹⁹^So Israel has broken with the house of David to this day.

²⁰And it came about, when all Israel heard that Jeroboam had returned, that they sent *word* and called him to the assembly, and made him king over all Israel. ^None except the tribe of Judah alone followed the house of David.

²¹^Now when Rehoboam had come to Jerusalem, he assembled all the house of Judah and the tribe of Benjamin, 180,000 chosen warriors, to fight against the house of Israel to

12:6^1 Kin 4:1-6; Job 12:12   12:7^2 Chr 10:7; Prov 15:1
12:12^1 Kin 12:5   12:14^Ex 1:13, 14; 5:5-9, 16-18
12:15^1 Kin 11:11, 31   12:16^2 Sam 20:1
12:17^1 Kin 11:13, 36   12:18^2 Sam 20:24; 1 Kin 4:6
12:19^2 Kin 17:21   12:20^1 Kin 11:13, 32, 36
12:21^2 Chr 11:1

restore the kingdom to Rehoboam the son of Solomon. ²²But the word of God came to ᴬShemaiah the man of God, saying, ²³"Tell Rehoboam the son of Solomon, king of Judah, and all the house of Judah and Benjamin, and the ᴬrest of the people, saying, ²⁴'This is what the LORD says: "You shall not go up nor fight against your relatives the sons of Israel; return, every man to his house, ᴬfor this thing has come from Me."'" So they listened to the word of the LORD, and returned to go *their way* in accordance with the word of the LORD.

JEROBOAM'S IDOLATRY

²⁵Then ᴬJeroboam built Shechem in the hill country of Ephraim, and lived there. And he went out from there and built ᴮPenuel. ²⁶And Jeroboam said in his heart, "Now the kingdom will return to the house of David. ²⁷ᴬIf this people go up to offer sacrifices in the house of the LORD in Jerusalem, then the heart of this people will return to their lord, to Rehoboam king of Judah; and they will kill me and return to Rehoboam king of Judah." ²⁸So the king consulted, and he ᴬmade two golden calves; and he said to the people, "It is too much for you to go up to Jerusalem; ᴮbehold your gods, Israel, that brought you up from the land of Egypt." ²⁹And he set up ᴬone in Bethel, and the other he put in Dan. ³⁰Now ᴬthis thing became a sin, for the people went *to worship* before the one as far as Dan. ³¹And he made houses on high places, and ᴬappointed priests from all the people who were not of the sons of Levi. ³²Jeroboam also instituted a feast in the eighth month on the fifteenth day of the month, ᴬlike the feast that is in Judah, and he went up to the altar. So he did in Bethel, sacrificing to the calves which he had made. And he stationed in Bethel the priests of the high places which he had made. ³³Then he went up to the altar which he had made in Bethel on the fifteenth day in the eighth month, the month that he had ᴬdevised in his own heart; and he instituted a feast for the sons of Israel and went up to the altar to burn incense.

JEROBOAM WARNED, STRICKEN

13 Now behold, ᴬa man of God came from Judah to Bethel by the word of the LORD, while Jeroboam was standing at the altar to burn incense. ²And he cried out against the altar by the word of the LORD and said, "Altar, altar, this is what the LORD says: 'Behold, a son shall be born to the house of David, ᴬJosiah by name; and on you he shall sacrifice the priests of the high places who burn incense on you, and human bones shall burn on you.'" ³Then he gave a sign on the same day, saying, "ᴬThis is the sign which the LORD has spoken: 'Behold, the altar shall be torn to pieces and the ashes which are on it shall be poured out.'" ⁴Now when the king heard the statement of the man of God which he cried out against the altar in Bethel, Jeroboam stretched out his hand from the altar, saying, "Seize him!" But his hand which he had

12:22 ᴬ2 Chr 11:2; 12:5-7   **12:23** ᴬ1 Kin 12:17
12:24 ᴬ1 Kin 12:15   **12:25** ᴬJudg 9:45-49
ᴮGen 32:30, 31   **12:27** ᴬDeut 12:5-7, 14
12:28 ᴬHos 8:4-7   ᴮEx 32:4, 8   **12:29** ᴬHos 10:5
12:30 ᴬ1 Kin 13:34; 2 Kin 17:21   **12:31** ᴬ1 Kin 13:33;
2 Kin 17:32   **12:32** ᴬLev 23:33, 34; 1 Kin 8:2, 5
12:33 ᴬNum 15:39   **13:1** ᴬ1 Kin 12:22; 2 Kin 23:17
13:2 ᴬ2 Kin 23:15, 16   **13:3** ᴬJohn 2:18; 1 Cor 1:22

stretched out toward him dried up, and he could not draw it back to himself. ⁵The altar also was torn to pieces and the ashes were poured out from the altar, in accordance with the sign which the man of God had given by the word of the LORD. ⁶And the king responded and said to the man of God, "Please appease the LORD your God and pray for me, so that my hand may be restored to me." So ^the man of God appeased the LORD, and the king's hand was restored to him, and it became as it was before. ⁷Then the king said to the man of God, "Come home with me and refresh yourself, and ^I will give you a gift." ⁸But the man of God said to the king, "^If you were to give me half your house, I would not go with you, nor would I eat bread or drink water in this place. ⁹For so it was commanded me by the word of the LORD, saying, 'You shall not eat bread nor drink water, nor return by the way that you came.'" ¹⁰So he went another way and did not return by the way that he had come to Bethel.

THE DISOBEDIENT PROPHET

¹¹Now ^an old prophet was living in Bethel; and his sons came and told him all the deeds which the man of God had done that day in Bethel; the words which he had spoken to the king, these also they reported to their father. ¹²And their father said to them, "Which way did he go?" Now his sons had seen the way that the man of God who came from Judah had gone. ¹³Then he said to his sons, "Saddle the donkey for me." So they saddled the donkey for him and he rode *away* on it. ¹⁴So he went after the man of God and found him sitting

under an oak; and he said to him, "Are you the man of God who came from Judah?" And he said, "I am." ¹⁵Then he said to him, "Come home with me and eat bread." ¹⁶But he said, "^I cannot return with you, nor come with you, nor will I eat bread or drink water with you in this place. ¹⁷For a command *came* to me ^by the word of the LORD: 'You shall not eat bread, nor drink water there; do not return by going the way that you came.'" ¹⁸Then he said to him, "I too am a prophet like you, and ^an angel spoke to me by the word of the LORD, saying, 'Bring him back with you to your house, so that he may eat bread and drink water.'" *But* he lied to him. ¹⁹So he went back with him, and ate bread in his house and drank water.

²⁰Now it came about, as they were sitting down at the table, that the word of the LORD came to the prophet who had brought him back; ²¹and he cried out to the man of God who came from Judah, saying, "This is what the LORD says: 'Because you have disobeyed the command of the LORD, and have not kept the commandment which the LORD your God commanded you, ²²but have returned and eaten bread and drunk water in the place of which He said to you, "You are not to eat bread nor drink water"; your dead body will not come to the grave of your fathers.'" ²³It came about after he had eaten bread and after he had drunk, that he saddled the donkey for him, for the prophet whom he had brought back. ²⁴Now when he had gone, ^a lion met him

13:6 ^Luke 6:27, 28   13:7 ^1 Sam 9:7, 8; 2 Kin 5:15
13:8 ^Num 22:18; 1 Kin 13:16, 17   13:11 ^1 Kin 13:25;
2 Kin 23:18   13:16 ^1 Kin 13:8, 9   13:17 ^1 Kin 20:35
13:18 ^Gal 1:8   13:24 ^1 Kin 20:36

on the way and killed him, and his body was thrown on the road, with the donkey standing beside it; the lion also was standing beside the body. ²⁵And behold, men passed by and saw the body thrown on the road, and the lion standing beside the body; so they came and told *about it* in the city where ᴬthe old prophet had lived.

²⁶Now when the prophet who had brought him back from the way heard *about it,* he said, "It is the man of God, who disobeyed the command of the Lᴏʀᴅ; therefore the Lᴏʀᴅ has given him to the lion, which has torn him and killed him, in accordance with the word of the Lᴏʀᴅ which He spoke to him." ²⁷Then he spoke to his sons, saying, "Saddle the donkey for me." And they saddled *it.* ²⁸Then he went and found his body thrown on the road, with the donkey and the lion standing beside the body; the lion had not eaten the body nor harmed the donkey. ²⁹So the prophet picked up the body of the man of God and laid it on the donkey and brought it back; and he came to the city of the old prophet to mourn and to bury him. ³⁰He laid his body in his own grave, and they mourned over him, *saying,* "ᴬOh, my brother!" ³¹And after he had buried him, he talked to his sons, saying, "When I die, bury me in the grave in which the man of God is buried; ᴬlay my bones beside his bones. ³²ᴬFor the thing will certainly come to pass which he cried out by the word of the Lᴏʀᴅ against the altar that is in Bethel, and against all the houses of the high places which are in the cities of Samaria."

³³After this event, Jeroboam did not abandon his evil way, but he ᴬagain appointed priests of the high places from all the people; ᴮanyone who wanted, he ordained, and he became *one of the* priests of the high places. ³⁴ᴬThis event also became a sin of the house of Jeroboam, even to wipe *it* out and eliminate *it* from the face of the earth.

AHIJAH PROPHESIES AGAINST THE KING

14 At that time Abijah the son of Jeroboam became sick. ²And Jeroboam said to his wife, "Now arise and disguise yourself so that they will not know that you are the wife of Jeroboam, and go to ᴬShiloh. Behold, Ahijah the prophet is there, who ᴮsaid regarding me *that I would be* king over this people. ³ᴬTake ten loaves with you, *some* pastries, and a jar of honey, and go to him. He will tell you what will happen to the boy."

⁴And Jeroboam's wife did so, and set out and went to Shiloh, and came to the house of ᴬAhijah. Now Ahijah could not see because his eyes were glossy from his old age. ⁵Now the Lᴏʀᴅ had said to Ahijah, "Behold, the wife of Jeroboam is coming to inquire of you about her son, because he is sick. You shall say such and such to her, for it will be when she arrives, that ᴬshe is going to make herself unrecognizable."

⁶So when Ahijah heard the sound of her feet coming in the doorway, he said, "Come in, wife of Jeroboam; why do you make yourself unrecognizable? Nevertheless, I am sent to you *with* a harsh *message.* ⁷Go, say

13:25ᴬ1 Kin 13:11   13:30ᴬJer 22:18   13:31ᴬRuth 1:17; 2 Kin 23:17, 18   13:32ᴬ1 Kin 13:2   13:33ᴬ1 Kin 12:31, 32   ᴮJudg 17:5   13:34ᴬ1 Kin 12:30; 2 Kin 17:21
14:2ᴬJosh 18:1   ᴮ1 Kin 11:29-31   14:3ᴬ1 Sam 9:7, 8; 1 Kin 13:7   14:4ᴬ1 Kin 11:29   14:5ᴬ2 Sam 14:2

to Jeroboam, 'This is what the Lord, the God of Israel says: "^Because I exalted you from among the people and made you leader over My people Israel, **8** and ^tore the kingdom away from the house of David and gave it to you—yet you have not been like My servant David, who kept My commandments and followed Me with all his heart, to do only that which was right in My sight; **9** you also have done more evil than all who were before you, and ^you have gone and made for yourself other gods and ^cast metal images to provoke Me to anger, and have thrown Me behind your back— **10** therefore behold, I am bringing disaster on the house of Jeroboam, and ^I will eliminate from Jeroboam every male person, both bond and free in Israel, and I will make a clean sweep of the house of Jeroboam, just as one sweeps away dung until it is all gone. **11** ^Anyone belonging to Jeroboam who dies in the city, the dogs will eat. And anyone who dies in the field, the birds of the sky will eat; for the Lord has spoken *it*."' **12** Now you, arise, go to your house. ^When your feet enter the city the child will die. **13** Then all Israel will mourn for him and bury him, for he alone of Jeroboam's *family* will come to the grave, because in him ^something good was found toward the Lord God of Israel in the house of Jeroboam. **14** Moreover, ^the Lord will raise up for Himself a king over Israel who will eliminate the house of Jeroboam this day and from now on.

15 "For the Lord will strike Israel, just as a reed sways in the water; and ^He will uproot Israel from this good land which He gave to their fathers, and ^will scatter them beyond the *Euphrates* River, because they have made their ^Asherim, provoking the Lord to anger. **16** He will give up Israel ^because of the sins of Jeroboam, which he committed and with which he misled Israel into sin."

17 Then Jeroboam's wife arose and departed, and came to Tirzah. ^As she was entering the threshold of the house, the child died. **18** ^Then all Israel buried him and mourned for him, in accordance with the word of the Lord which He had spoken through His servant Ahijah the prophet.

19 Now *as for* the rest of the acts of Jeroboam, ^how he made war and how he reigned, behold, they are written in the Book of the Chronicles of the Kings of Israel. **20** And the time that Jeroboam reigned *was* twenty-two years; and he ^lay down with his fathers, and his son Nadab reigned in his place.

REHOBOAM MISLEADS JUDAH

21 ^Now Rehoboam the son of Solomon reigned in Judah. Rehoboam was forty-one years old when he became king, and he reigned for seventeen years in Jerusalem, the city which the Lord had chosen from all the tribes of Israel to put His name there. And his mother's name was Naamah the Ammonitess. **22** And *the people of* ^Judah did evil in the sight of the Lord, and they ^provoked Him to jealousy with their sins which they committed, more

14:7 ^1 Kin 11:28-31; 16:2   **14:8** ^1 Kin 11:31
14:9 ^1 Kin 12:28   ^B Ex 34:17   **14:10** ^1 Kin 21:21;
2 Kin 9:8   **14:11** ^1 Kin 16:4; 21:24   **14:12** ^1 Kin 14:17
14:13 ^2 Chr 19:3   **14:14** ^1 Kin 15:27-29
14:15 ^Deut 29:28   ^B 2 Kin 15:29   **14:16** ^1 Kin 12:30;
15:30, 34   **14:17** ^1 Kin 14:12   **14:18** ^1 Kin 14:13
14:19 ^1 Kin 14:30; 2 Chr 13:2-20   **14:21** ^2 Chr 12:13
14:22 ^2 Chr 12:1, 14   ^B Deut 32:21

14:15 ^1 I.e., wooden symbols of a female deity (Asherah)   **14:20** ^1 I.e., died

than all that their fathers had done. [23] For they, too, built for themselves ^Ahigh places, ^Bmemorial stones, and [1]Asherim on every high hill and under every luxuriant tree. [24] There were also ^Amale cult prostitutes in the land. They committed all the same abominations of the nations which the LORD dispossessed before the sons of Israel.

[25] ^ANow it happened in the fifth year of King Rehoboam, that Shishak the king of Egypt marched against Jerusalem. [26] And he took away the treasures of the house of the LORD and the treasures of the king's house, and he took everything; ^Ahe even took all the shields of gold which Solomon had made. [27] So King Rehoboam made shields of bronze in their place, and ^Aentrusted them to the care of the commanders of the guard who guarded the doorway of the king's house. [28] And it happened as often as the king entered the house of the LORD, that the guards would carry them and would bring them back into the guards' room.

[29] ^ANow *as for* the rest of the acts of Rehoboam and all that he did, are they not written in the Book of the Chronicles of the Kings of Judah? [30] ^AAnd there was war between Rehoboam and Jeroboam continually. [31] And Rehoboam [1]lay down with his fathers and was buried with his fathers in the city of David; and ^Ahis mother's name was Naamah the Ammonitess. And his son Abijam became king in his place.

ABIJAM REIGNS OVER JUDAH

15 ^ANow in the eighteenth year of King Jeroboam, the son of Nebat, Abijam became king over Judah. [2] He reigned for three

years in Jerusalem; and his mother's name was ^AMaacah the daughter of ^BAbishalom. [3] He walked in all the sins of his father which he had committed before him; and ^Ahis heart was not wholly devoted to the LORD his God, like the heart of his father David. [4] But for David's sake the LORD his God gave him a ^Alamp in Jerusalem, to raise up his son after him and to establish Jerusalem, [5] ^Abecause David did what was right in the sight of the LORD, and did not deviate from anything that He commanded him all the days of his life, ^Bexcept in the case of Uriah the Hittite. [6] ^AAnd there was war between Rehoboam and Jeroboam all the days of his life.

[7] Now *as for* ^Athe rest of the acts of Abijam and all that he did, are they not written in the Book of the Chronicles of the Kings of Judah? ^BAnd there was war between Abijam and Jeroboam.

ASA SUCCEEDS ABIJAM

[8] ^AAnd Abijam [1]lay down with his fathers, and they buried him in the city of David; and his son Asa became king in his place.

[9] So in the twentieth year of Jeroboam the king of Israel, Asa began to reign as king of Judah. [10] He reigned for forty-one years in Jerusalem; and ^Ahis mother's name was Maacah the daughter of

14:23 ^AEzek 16:24　^BDeut 16:22　14:24 ^AGen 19:5;
Deut 23:17　14:25 ^A1 Kin 11:40; 2 Chr 12:2, 9
14:26 ^A1 Kin 10:17; 2 Chr 9:15, 16　14:27 ^A1 Sam 8:11;
22:17　14:29 ^A2 Chr 12:15, 16　14:30 ^A1 Kin 12:21; 15:6
14:31 ^A1 Kin 14:21　15:1 ^A2 Chr 13:1　15:2 ^A2 Chr 13:2
^B2 Chr 11:21　15:3 ^A1 Kin 11:4; Ps 119:80
15:4 ^A2 Sam 21:17; 1 Kin 11:36　15:5 ^ALuke 1:6
^B2 Sam 11:3f, 15–17　15:6 ^A1 Kin 14:30; 2 Chr
12:15–13:20　15:7 ^A2 Chr 13:2, 21, 22　^B2 Chr 13:3–20
15:8 ^A2 Chr 14:1　15:10 ^A1 Kin 15:2

14:23 [1]I.e., wooden symbols of a female deity
(Asherah)　14:31 [1]I.e., died　15:8 [1]I.e., died

Abishalom. [11]Now ^Asa did what was right in the sight of the LORD, like his father David. [12]^He also removed the male cult prostitutes from the land and ^removed all the idols which his fathers had made. [13]And even his mother Maacah, ^he also removed her from *the position of* queen mother, because she had made an abominable image [1]as an Asherah; and Asa cut down her abominable image and ^burned *it* at the brook Kidron. [14]But the high places were not eliminated; nevertheless ^Asa's heart was wholly devoted to the LORD all his days. [15]And ^he brought into the house of the LORD the holy gifts of his father and his own holy gifts: silver, gold, and *valuable* utensils.

[16]^Now there was war between Asa and Baasha king of Israel all their days. [17]^Baasha king of Israel marched against Judah and fortified Ramah in order to prevent *anyone* from going out or coming in to Asa king of Judah. [18]Then ^Asa took all the silver and the gold that was left in the treasuries of the house of the LORD and the treasuries of the king's house, and handed it over to his servants. And King Asa sent them to Ben-hadad the son of Tabrimmon, the son of Hezion, king of Aram, who lived in Damascus, saying, [19]"*Let's make* a ^treaty between you and me, *as there was* between my father and your father. Behold, I have sent you a gift of silver and gold; go, break your treaty with Baasha king of Israel so that he will withdraw from me." [20]So Ben-hadad listened to King Asa and sent the commanders of his armies against the cities of Israel, and conquered Ijon, ^Dan, Abel-beth-maacah, and all ^Chinneroth, besides all the

land of Naphtali. [21]When Baasha heard *about it,* he stopped fortifying Ramah and remained in ^Tirzah. [22]Then King Asa made a proclamation to all Judah—no one was exempt—and they carried away the stones of Ramah and its timber with which Baasha had built *fortifications.* And King Asa built with them ^Geba of Benjamin and Mizpah.

JEHOSHAPHAT SUCCEEDS ASA

[23]^Now *as for* the rest of all the acts of Asa and all his might, and all that he did and the cities which he built, are they not written in the Book of the Chronicles of the Kings of Judah? But in the time of his old age he was diseased in his feet. [24]And Asa [1]lay down with his fathers and was buried with his fathers in the city of his father David; and his son ^Jehoshaphat reigned in his place.

NADAB AND THEN BAASHA
RULE OVER ISRAEL

[25]Now ^Nadab the son of Jeroboam became king over Israel in the second year of Asa king of Judah, and he reigned over Israel for two years. [26]He did evil in the sight of the LORD, and ^walked in the way of his father and ^in his sin into which he misled Israel. [27]Then ^Baasha the son of Ahijah of the house of Issachar conspired against him, and Baasha struck and killed him at Gibbethon, which belonged to the Philistines,

---

15:11^2 Chr 14:2   15:12^Deut 23:17   ^2 Chr 14:2-5
15:13^2 Chr 15:16-18   ^Ex 32:20   15:14^1 Kin 8:61;
15:3   15:15^1 Kin 7:51   15:16^1 Kin 15:32
15:17^2 Chr 16:1-6   15:18^1 Kin 14:26; 15:15
15:19^2 Chr 16:7   15:20^Judg 18:29   ^Josh 11:2
15:21^1 Kin 14:17; 16:15-18   15:22^Josh 18:24; 21:17
15:23^2 Chr 16:11-14   15:24^1 Kin 22:41-44; Matt 1:8
15:25^1 Kin 14:20   15:26^1 Kin 12:28-33
^1 Kin 15:30, 34   15:27^1 Kin 14:14

15:13 [1]Or *for Asherah;* i.e., wooden symbol of a female deity   15:24 [1]I.e., died

while Nadab and all Israel were laying siege to Gibbethon.

²⁸So Baasha killed him in the third year of Asa king of Judah, and reigned in his place. ²⁹And as soon as he was king, he struck and killed all the household of Jeroboam. He did not leave Jeroboam any persons alive, *but kept killing* until he had eliminated them, ^in accordance with the word of the LORD which He spoke by His servant Ahijah the Shilonite, ³⁰*and* because of the sins of Jeroboam which he committed, and into ^which he misled Israel, because of his provocation with which he provoked the LORD God of Israel to anger.

³¹^Now *as for* the rest of the acts of Nadab and all that he did, are they not written in the Book of the Chronicles of the Kings of Israel?

WAR WITH JUDAH

³²^And there was war between Asa and Baasha king of Israel all their days.

³³In the third year of Asa king of Judah, Baasha the son of Ahijah became king over all Israel at Tirzah, *and he reigned* for twenty-four years. ³⁴And he did evil in the sight of the LORD, and ^walked in the way of Jeroboam and in his sin into which he misled Israel.

PROPHECY AGAINST BAASHA

16 Now the word of the LORD came to ^Jehu the son of Hanani against Baasha, saying, ²"Since I exalted you from the dust and made you leader over My people Israel, and ^you have walked in the way of Jeroboam and have misled My people Israel into sin, provoking Me to anger with their sins, ³behold, I am going to burn ^Baasha

and his house, and ⁸I will make your house like the house of Jeroboam the son of Nebat. ⁴^Anyone belonging to Baasha who dies in the city, the dogs will eat; and anyone belonging to him who dies in the field, the birds of the sky will eat."

⁵^Now *as for* the rest of the acts of Baasha and what he did and his might, are they not written in the Book of the Chronicles of the Kings of Israel?

THE ISRAELITE KINGS

⁶And Baasha ¹lay down with his fathers and was buried in ^Tirzah, and his son Elah became king in his place. ⁷Moreover, the word of the LORD through ^the prophet Jehu the son of Hanani came against Baasha and his household, both because of all the evil that he did in the sight of the LORD, provoking Him to anger with the work of his hands, by being like the house of Jeroboam, and because he struck it.

⁸In the twenty-sixth year of Asa king of Judah, Elah the son of Baasha became king over Israel at Tirzah, *and reigned* for two years. ⁹And his servant ^Zimri, commander of half his chariots, conspired against him. Now Elah *was* in Tirzah drinking himself drunk in the house of Arza, who *was* in charge of the household in Tirzah. ¹⁰Then Zimri came in and struck him and put him to death in the twenty-seventh year of Asa king of Judah, and he became king in his place. ¹¹And when he

15:29^1 Kin 14:9-16   15:30^1 Kin 15:26
15:31^1 Kin 14:19   15:32^1 Kin 15:16
15:34^1 Kin 15:26   16:1^1 Kin 16:7; 2 Chr 19:2
16:2^1 Kin 15:34   16:3^1 Kin 16:11   ⁸1 Kin 15:29
16:4^1 Kin 14:11; 21:24   16:5^1 Kin 14:19; 15:31
16:6^1 Kin 14:17; 15:21   16:7^1 Kin 16:1
16:9^2 Kin 9:30-33

16:6 ¹I.e., died

became king, as soon as he sat on his throne, ^he killed all the household of Baasha; he did not leave a single male alive, either of his relatives or of his friends.

¹²So Zimri eliminated all the household of Baasha, ^in accordance with the word of the LORD which He spoke against Baasha through ᴮJehu the prophet, ¹³for all the sins of Baasha and the sins of his son Elah, which they committed and into which they misled Israel, ^provoking the LORD God of Israel to anger with their idols. ¹⁴^Now *as for* the rest of the acts of Elah and all that he did, are they not written in the Book of the Chronicles of the Kings of Israel?

¹⁵In the twenty-seventh year of Asa king of Judah, Zimri reigned for seven days in Tirzah. Now the people were camped against ^Gibbethon, which belonged to the Philistines. ¹⁶And the people who were camped heard it being said, "Zimri has conspired and has also struck and killed the king!" Therefore all Israel made Omri, the commander of the army, king over Israel that day in the camp. ¹⁷Then Omri and all Israel with him went up from Gibbethon and besieged Tirzah. ¹⁸When Zimri saw that the city was taken, he went into the citadel of the king's house and burned the king's house over himself with fire, and ^died, ¹⁹because of his sins which he committed, doing evil in the sight of the LORD, ^walking in the way of Jeroboam, and in his sin which he committed, misleading Israel into sin. ²⁰^Now *as for* the rest of the acts of Zimri and his conspiracy which he carried out, are they not written in the Book of the Chronicles of the Kings of Israel?

²¹Then the people of Israel were divided into two parts: half of the people followed Tibni the son of Ginath, to make him king; the *other* half followed Omri. ²²But the people who followed Omri prevailed over the people who followed Tibni the son of Ginath. And Tibni died and Omri became king. ²³In the thirty-first year of Asa king of Judah, Omri became king over Israel *and reigned* for twelve years; he reigned for six years at ^Tirzah. ²⁴And he purchased the hill Samaria from Shemer for ¹two talents of silver; and he built on the hill, and named the city which he built ^Samaria, after the name of Shemer, the owner of the hill.

²⁵Now ^Omri did evil in the sight of the LORD, and acted more wickedly than all who *were* before him. ²⁶For he ^walked entirely in the way of Jeroboam the son of Nebat and in his sins into which he misled Israel, provoking the LORD God of Israel to anger with their idols. ²⁷Now *as for* the rest of the acts of Omri which he did and his might which he displayed, are they not written in the Book of the Chronicles of the Kings of Israel? ²⁸And Omri ¹lay down with his fathers and was buried in Samaria; and his son Ahab became king in his place.

²⁹Now Ahab the son of Omri became king over Israel in the thirty-eighth year of Asa king of Judah, and Ahab the son of Omri reigned over Israel in Samaria for twenty-two years. ³⁰Ahab the son

16:11^1 Kin 15:29; 16:3   16:12^1 Kin 16:3   ᴮ2 Chr 19:2
16:13^Deut 32:21; 1 Kin 15:30   16:14^1 Kin 16:5
16:15^1 Kin 15:27   16:18^1 Sam 31:4, 5; 2 Sam 17:23
16:19^1 Kin 12:28; 15:26   16:20^1 Kin 16:5, 14, 27
16:23^1 Kin 15:21   16:24^1 Kin 16:28, 29, 32
16:25^Mic 6:16   16:26^1 Kin 16:19

16:24¹About 150 lb. or 68 kg   16:28¹I.e., died

of Omri did evil in the sight of the LORD ^more than all who were before him.

31And as though it had been a trivial thing for him to walk in the sins of Jeroboam the son of Nebat, ^he married Jezebel the daughter of Ethbaal king of the Sidonians, and went and served Baal, and worshiped him. 32So he erected an altar for Baal at ^the house of Baal, which he built in Samaria. 33Ahab also made ^the 'Asherah. So Ahab did more to provoke the LORD God of Israel to anger than all the kings of Israel who were before him. 34^In his days Hiel the Bethelite rebuilt Jericho; he laid its foundations with *the loss of* Abiram his firstborn, and set up its gates with *the loss of* his youngest son Segub, in accordance with the word of the LORD, which He spoke by Joshua the son of Nun.

ELIJAH PREDICTS DROUGHT

17 Now Elijah the Tishbite, who was of ^the settlers of Gilead, said to Ahab, "As the LORD, the God of Israel lives, before whom I stand, ^there shall certainly be neither dew nor rain *during* these years, except by my word." 2Then the word of the LORD came to him, saying, 3"Go *away* from here and turn eastward, and hide yourself by the brook Cherith, which is east of the Jordan. 4And it shall be that you will drink from the brook, and ^I have commanded the ravens to provide food for you there." 5So he went and did *everything* according to the word of the LORD, for he went and lived by the brook Cherith, which is east of the Jordan. 6And the ravens brought him bread and meat in the morning and bread and meat in the evening, and he would

drink from the brook. 7But it happened after a while that the brook dried up, because there was no rain in the land.

8Then the word of the LORD came to him, saying, 9"Arise, go to ^Zarephath, which belongs to Sidon, and stay there; behold, I have commanded a widow there to provide food for you." 10So he arose and went to Zarephath, and when he came to the entrance of the city, behold, a widow was there gathering sticks; and ^he called to her and said, "Please get me a little water in a cup, so that I may drink." 11As she was going to get *it*, he called to her and said, "Please bring me a piece of bread in your hand." 12But she said, "As the LORD your God lives, ^I have no food, only a handful of flour in the bowl and a little oil in the jar; and behold, I am gathering a few sticks so that I may go in and prepare it for me and my son, so that we may eat it and ^die." 13However, Elijah said to her, "Do not fear; go, do as you have said. Just make me a little bread loaf from it first and bring *it* out to me, and afterward you may make *one* for yourself and for your son. 14For this is what the LORD, the God of Israel says: 'The bowl of flour shall not be used up, nor shall the jar of oil become empty, until the day that the LORD provides rain on the face of the earth.'" 15So she went and did *everything* in accordance with the word of Elijah, and she and he and her household ate for *many* days. 16The bowl of flour

16:30^1 Kin 14:9; 16:25   16:31^Deut 7:1-5
16:32^2 Kin 10:21, 26, 27   16:33^2 Kin 13:6
16:34^Josh 6:26   17:1^Judg 12:4   ^Luke 4:25
17:4^1 Kin 17:9   17:9^Obad 20; Luke 4:26
17:10^Gen 24:17; John 4:7
17:12^2 Kin 4:2-7   ^Gen 21:15, 16

16:33 ¹I.e., wooden symbol of a female deity

was not used up, nor did the jar of oil become empty, in accordance with the word of the LORD which He spoke through Elijah.

ELIJAH RAISES THE WIDOW'S SON

17 Now it happened after these things that the son of the woman, the mistress of the house, became sick; and his condition became very grave, until *at the end* he was no longer breathing. 18 So she said to Elijah, "Why is my *business any of* yours, you ᴬman of God? *Yet* you have come to me to bring my wrongdoing to remembrance, and to put my son to death!" 19 But he said to her, "Give me your son." Then he took him from her arms and carried him up to the upstairs room where he was living, and laid him on his own bed. 20 And he called to the LORD and said, "LORD, my God, have You also brought catastrophe upon the widow with whom I am staying, by causing her son to die?" 21ᴬThen he stretched himself out over the boy three times, and called to the LORD and said, "LORD, my God, please, let this boy's life return to him." 22 And the LORD listened to the voice of Elijah, ᴬand the life of the boy returned to him and he revived. 23 Elijah then took the boy and brought him down from the upstairs room into the house and gave him to his mother; and Elijah said, "See, your son is alive." 24 Then the woman said to Elijah, "ᴬNow I know that you are a man of God, and that the word of the LORD in your mouth is truth."

OBADIAH MEETS ELIJAH

18 Now it happened ᴬ*after* many days that the word of the LORD came to Elijah in the third year, saying, "Go, present yourself to Ahab, and I will provide rain on the face of the earth." 2 So Elijah went to present himself to Ahab. Now the famine *was* severe in Samaria. 3 Ahab summoned Obadiah, ᴬwho *was* in charge of the household. (Now Obadiah ᴮfeared the LORD greatly; 4 for ᴬwhen Jezebel killed the prophets of the LORD, Obadiah took a hundred prophets and hid them by fifties in a cave, and provided them with bread and water.) 5 Then Ahab said to Obadiah, "Go through the land to all the springs of water and to all the river valleys; perhaps we will find grass and keep the horses and mules alive, and not *have to* kill some of the cattle." 6 So they divided the land between them to survey it; Ahab went one way by himself, and Obadiah went another way by himself.

7 Now as Obadiah was on the way, behold, Elijah met him, ᴬand he recognized him and fell on his face and said, "Is it you, Elijah my master?" 8 And he said to him, "It is I. Go, say to your master, 'Behold, Elijah *is here.*'" 9 But he said, "What sin have I committed, that you are handing your servant over to Ahab, to put me to death? 10ᴬAs *surely as* the LORD your God lives, there is no nation or kingdom to which my master has not sent *word* to search for you; and whenever they say, 'He is not *here,*' he makes the kingdom or nation swear that they could not find you. 11 Yet now you are saying, 'Go, say to your master, "Behold, Elijah *is here!*"' 12 And it will come about when I leave you ᴬthat the Spirit of the LORD will carry you

17:18ᴬ1 Kin 12:22   17:21ᴬ2 Kin 4:34, 35; Acts 20:10
17:22ᴬLuke 7:14; Heb 11:35   17:24ᴬJohn 2:11; 3:2
18:1ᴬLuke 4:25; James 5:17   18:3ᴬ1 Kin 16:9
ᴮNeh 7:2   18:4ᴬ1 Kin 18:13   18:7ᴬ2 Kin 1:6-8
18:10ᴬ1 Kin 17:1   18:12ᴬEzek 3:12, 14; Acts 8:39

to where I do not know; so when I come and inform Ahab and he cannot find you, he will kill me, though *I*, your servant, have feared the LORD from my youth. [13]^AHas it not been reported to my master what I did when Jezebel killed the prophets of the LORD, that I hid a hundred prophets of the LORD by fifties in a cave, and provided them with bread and water? [14]Yet now you are saying, 'Go, say to your master, "Behold, Elijah *is here*"'; he will then kill me!" [15]Then Elijah said, "^AAs *surely as* the LORD of armies lives, before whom I stand, I will certainly present myself to him today." [16]So Obadiah went to meet Ahab and informed him; then Ahab went to meet Elijah.

[17]When Ahab saw Elijah, ^AAhab said to him, "Is this you, the cause of disaster to Israel?" [18]He said, "I have not brought disaster to Israel, but you and your father's house *have,* because ^Ayou have abandoned the commandments of the LORD and ^Byou have followed the Baals. [19]Now then, send *orders and* gather to me all Israel at ^AMount Carmel, *together* with 450 prophets of Baal and four hundred prophets of [1],Bthe Asherah, who eat at Jezebel's table."

GOD OR BAAL ON MOUNT CARMEL

[20]So Ahab sent *orders* among all the sons of Israel and brought the prophets together at Mount Carmel. [21]Then Elijah approached all the people and said, "^AHow long are you going to struggle with the two choices? ^BIf the LORD is God, follow Him; but if Baal, follow him." But the people did not answer him *so much as* a word. [22]Then Elijah said to the people, "I ^Aalone am left as a prophet of the LORD, while Baal's prophets are 450 men. [23]Now have them give us two oxen; and have them choose the one ox for themselves and cut it up, and place it on the wood, but put no fire *under it;* and I will prepare the other ox and lay it on the wood, and I will not put a fire *under it.* [24]Then you call on the name of your god, and I will call on the name of the LORD; and ^Athe God who answers by fire, He is God." And all the people replied, "That is a good idea."

[25]So Elijah said to the prophets of Baal, "Choose the one ox for yourselves and prepare it first, since *there are* many *of* you, and call on the name of your god, but put no fire *under the ox.*" [26]Then they took the ox which was given them and they prepared it, and they called on the name of Baal from morning until noon, saying, "O Baal, answer us!" But there was ^Ano voice and no one answered. And they ¹limped about the altar which they had made. [27]And at noon Elijah ridiculed them and said, "Call out with a loud voice, since he is a god; undoubtedly he is attending to business, or is on the way, or is on a journey. Perhaps he is asleep, and will awaken." [28]So they cried out with a loud voice, and ^Acut themselves according to their custom with swords and lances until blood gushed out on them. [29]When midday was past, they raved ^Auntil the time of the offering of the *evening* sacrifice; but there was no voice, no one answered, and no one paid attention.

18:13^A1 Kin 18:4　**18:15**^A1 Kin 17:1　**18:17**^AJosh 7:25; 1 Kin 21:20　**18:18**^A1 Kin 9:9　^B1 Kin 21:25, 26
18:19^AJosh 19:26　^B1 Kin 16:33　**18:21**^AMatt 6:24
^BJosh 24:15　**18:22**^A1 Kin 19:10, 14　**18:24**^A1 Kin 18:38
18:26^APs 115:4, 5; Jer 10:5　**18:28**^ALev 19:28; Deut 14:1
18:29^AEx 29:39, 41

18:19 ¹I.e., wooden symbol of a female deity
18:26 ¹I.e., in a type of ceremonial dance

³⁰Then Elijah said to all the people, "Come forward to me." So all the people came forward to him. And ^he repaired the altar of the LORD which had been torn down. ³¹Then Elijah took twelve stones, corresponding to the number of the tribes of the sons of Jacob, to whom the word of the LORD had come, saying, "^Israel shall be your name." ³²And with the stones he built an altar in ^the name of the LORD; and he made a trench around the altar, large enough to hold two measures of seed. ³³^Then he laid out the wood, and he cut the ox in pieces and placed *it* on the wood. ³⁴And he said, "Fill four large jars with water and pour *it* on the burnt offering and on the wood." And he said, "Do it a second time," so they did it a second time. Then he said, "Do it a third time," so they did it a third time. ³⁵The water flowed around the altar, and he also filled the trench with water.

ELIJAH'S PRAYER

³⁶Then at the time of the offering of the *evening* sacrifice, Elijah the prophet approached and said, "LORD, God of Abraham, Isaac, and Israel, today let it be known that ^You are God in Israel and that I am Your servant, and *that* ^B I have done all these things at Your word. ³⁷Answer me, LORD, answer me, so that this people may know that You, LORD, are God, and *that* You have turned their heart back." ³⁸Then the ^fire of the LORD fell and consumed the burnt offering and the wood, and the stones and the dust; and it licked up the water that was in the trench. ³⁹When all the people saw *this,* they fell on their faces; and they said, "^The LORD, He is God; the LORD, He is God!"

⁴⁰Then Elijah said to them, "Seize the prophets of Baal; do not let one of them escape." So they seized them; and Elijah brought them down to ^the brook Kishon, ᴮand slaughtered them there. ⁴¹Now Elijah said to Ahab, "Go up, eat and drink; for there is the sound of the roar of a *heavy* shower." ⁴²So Ahab went up to eat and drink. But Elijah went up to the top of ^Carmel; and he bent down to the earth and put his face between his knees. ⁴³And he said to his servant, "Go up now, look toward the sea." So he went up and looked, but he said, "There is nothing." Yet *Elijah* said, "Go back" seven times. ⁴⁴And *when he returned* the seventh *time,* he said, "Behold, ^a cloud as small as a person's hand is coming up from the sea." And *Elijah* said, "Go up, say to Ahab, 'Harness *your chariot horses* and go down, so that the *heavy* shower does not stop you.'" ⁴⁵Meanwhile the sky became dark with clouds and wind *came up,* and there was a heavy shower. And Ahab rode and went to ^Jezreel. ⁴⁶Then ^the hand of the LORD was on Elijah, and he belted *his cloak* around his waist and outran Ahab to Jezreel.

ELIJAH FLEES FROM JEZEBEL

19 Now Ahab told Jezebel everything that Elijah had done, and ^how he had killed all the prophets with the sword. ²Then Jezebel sent a messenger to Elijah, saying, "^So may the gods do to me and more so, if *by* about this time

18:30^1 Kin 19:10, 14; 2 Chr 33:16   18:31^Gen 32:28; 2 Kin 17:34   18:32^Col 3:17   18:33^Gen 22:9; Lev 1:7, 8   18:36^1 Kin 8:43   ᴮNum 16:28-32 18:38^Lev 10:1, 2; Job 1:16   18:39^1 Kin 18:21, 24 18:40^Judg 4:7   ᴮ2 Kin 10:24, 25 18:42^1 Kin 18:19, 20   18:44^Luke 12:54 18:45^Josh 17:16; Judg 6:33   18:46^Is 8:11; Ezek 3:14 19:1^1 Kin 18:40   19:2^Ruth 1:17; 2 Kin 6:31

tomorrow I do not make your life like the life of one of them." ³And he was afraid, and got up and ran for his life and came to ᴬBeersheba, which belongs to Judah; and he left his servant there. ⁴But he himself went a day's journey into the wilderness, and came and sat down under a broom tree; and ᴬhe asked for himself to die, and said, "Enough! Now, Lᴏʀᴅ, take my life, for I am no better than my fathers." ⁵Then he lay down and fell asleep under a broom tree; but behold, there was ᴬan angel touching him, and he said to him, "Arise, eat!" ⁶And he looked, and behold, there was at his head a round loaf of bread *baked on* hot coals, and a pitcher of water. So he ate and drank, and lay down again. ⁷But the angel of the Lᴏʀᴅ came back a second time and touched him, and said, "Arise, eat; because the journey is too long for you." ⁸So he arose and ate and drank, and he journeyed in the strength of that food for forty days and forty nights to ᴬHoreb, the mountain of God.

ELIJAH AT HOREB

⁹Then he came there to a cave and spent the night there; and behold, ᴬthe word of the Lᴏʀᴅ *came* to him, and He said to him, "What are you doing here, Elijah?" ¹⁰And he said, "ᴬI have been very zealous for the Lᴏʀᴅ, the God of armies; for the sons of Israel have abandoned Your covenant, ᴮtorn down Your altars, and killed Your prophets with the sword. And I alone am left; and they have sought to take my life."

¹¹So He said, "ᴬGo out and stand on the mountain before the Lᴏʀᴅ." And behold, the Lᴏʀᴅ was passing by! And a great and powerful wind was tearing out the mountains and breaking the rocks in pieces before the Lᴏʀᴅ; *but* the Lᴏʀᴅ *was* not in the wind. And after the wind *there was* an earthquake, *but* the Lᴏʀᴅ *was* not in the earthquake. ¹²And after the earthquake, a fire, *but* the Lᴏʀᴅ *was* not in the fire; and after the fire, ᴬa sound of a gentle blowing. ¹³When Elijah heard *it*, ᴬhe wrapped his face in his cloak and went out and stood in the entrance of the cave. And behold, a voice *came* to him and said, "What are you doing here, Elijah?" ¹⁴Then he said, "ᴬI have been very zealous for the Lᴏʀᴅ, the God of armies; for the sons of Israel have abandoned Your covenant, torn down Your altars, and killed Your prophets with the sword. And I alone am left; and they have sought to take my life."

¹⁵The Lᴏʀᴅ said to him, "Go, return on your way to the wilderness of Damascus; and when you have arrived, ᴬyou shall anoint Hazael king over Aram. ¹⁶You shall also anoint ᴬJehu the son of Nimshi king over Israel; and you shall anoint ᴮElisha the son of Shaphat of Abelmeholah as prophet in your place. ¹⁷And it shall come about that the ᴬone who escapes from the sword of Hazael, Jehu ᴮshall put to death, and the one who escapes from the sword of Jehu, Elisha shall put to death. ¹⁸ᴬYet I will leave seven thousand in Israel, all the knees that have not bowed to Baal and every mouth that has not kissed him."

¹⁹So he departed from there and found Elisha the son of Shaphat

19:3ᴬGen 21:31   **19:4**ᴬJer 20:14-18; Jon 4:3, 8
19:5ᴬGen 28:12   **19:8**ᴬEx 3:1; 4:27   **19:9**ᴬEx 33:21, 22
19:10ᴬEx 20:5   ᴮRom 11:3, 4
19:11ᴬEx 19:20; 24:12, 18   **19:12**ᴬJob 4:16; Zech 4:6
19:13ᴬEx 3:6   **19:14**ᴬ1 Kin 19:10   **19:15**ᴬ2 Kin 8:8-15
19:16ᴬ2 Kin 9:1-10   ᴮ1 Kin 19:19-21
19:17ᴬ2 Kin 13:3, 22   ᴮ2 Kin 9:14-10:25
19:18ᴬRom 11:4

while he was plowing, with twelve yoke *of oxen* in front of him, and he with the twelfth. And Elijah came over to him and threw ^his cloak on him. ²⁰Then he left the oxen behind and ran after Elijah, and said, "Please ^let me kiss my father and my mother, then I will follow you." And he said to him, "Go back, for ʲwhat have I done to you?" ²¹So he returned from following him, and took the pair of oxen and sacrificed them, and ^cooked their meat with the implements of the oxen, and gave *it* to the people and they ate. Then he got up and followed Elijah and served him.

WAR WITH ARAM

20 Now ^Ben-hadad, king of Aram, gathered all his army, ᴮand *there were* thirty-two kings with him, and horses and chariots. And he went up and besieged Samaria, and fought against it. ²Then he sent messengers to the city to Ahab, king of Israel, and said to him, "This is what Ben-hadad says: ³'Your silver and your gold are mine; your most beautiful wives and children are also mine.'" ⁴And the king of Israel replied, "As you say, my lord, O king; I am yours, as well as all that I have." ⁵Then the messengers returned and said, "Ben-hadad says this: 'I did indeed send *word* to you, saying, "You shall give me your silver, your gold, your wives, and your children"; ⁶but about this time tomorrow I will send my servants to you, and they will search your house and the houses of your servants; and they will take in their hands everything that is pleasing to your eyes, and take *it all* away.'"

⁷Then the king of Israel summoned all the elders of the land and said, "Please be aware and ^see that this man is looking for trouble; for he sent me *his demand* for my wives, my children, my silver, and my gold, and I did not refuse him." ⁸Then all the elders and all the people said to him, "Do not listen nor consent." ⁹So he said to the messengers of Ben-hadad, "Tell my lord the king, 'Everything that you sent *as a demand* to your servant at the first, I will do; but this thing I cannot do.'" Then the messengers departed, and brought him word again. ¹⁰Ben-hadad sent *word* to him and said, "May ^the gods do so to me and more so, ʲif the dust of Samaria will be enough for handfuls for all the people who follow me." ¹¹Then the king of Israel replied, "Tell *him,* ^He who straps on *his weapons* had better not boast like one who takes *them* off.'" ¹²And when *Ben-hadad* heard this message, while ^he was drinking with the kings in the temporary shelters, he said to his servants, "Take *your* positions." So they took *their* positions against the city.

AHAB VICTORIOUS

¹³Now behold, a prophet approached Ahab king of Israel, and said, "This is what the LORD says: 'Have you seen all this great multitude? Behold, I am going to hand them over to you today, and ^you shall know that I am the LORD.'" ¹⁴But Ahab said, "By whom?" So he

19:19 ^2 Kin 2:8, 13, 14   **19:20** ^Matt 8:21, 22; Luke 9:61, 62   **19:21** ^2 Sam 24:22
20:1 ^1 Kin 15:18, 20   ᴮ1 Kin 22:31   **20:7** ^2 Kin 5:7
20:10 ^1 Kin 19:2; 2 Kin 6:31   **20:11** ^Prov 27:1
20:12 ^1 Kin 16:9; Prov 31:4, 5   **20:13** ^1 Kin 18:36

19:20 ʲI.e., so as to influence Elisha's decision
20:10 ʲI.e., what is left of Samaria after it is destroyed

said, "The LORD says this: 'By the young men of the leaders of the provinces.'" Then he said, "Who will begin the battle?" And he said, "You *will.*" ¹⁵So he mustered the young men of the leaders of the provinces, and there were 232; and after them he mustered all the people, all the sons of Israel: seven thousand.

¹⁶They went out at noon, while ᴬBen-hadad was drinking himself drunk in the temporary shelters with the thirty-two kings who were helping him. ¹⁷The young men of the leaders of the provinces went out first; and Ben-hadad sent out *scouts,* and they reported to him, saying, "Men have come out from Samaria." ¹⁸ᴬThen he said, "If they have come out for peace, take them alive; or if they have come out for war, take them alive *as well.*"

¹⁹So these *men* went out from the city, the young men of the leaders of the provinces, and the army which followed them. ²⁰And they killed, each one, his man; and the Arameans fled and Israel pursued them, and Ben-hadad the king of Aram escaped on a horse with horsemen. ²¹The king of Israel also went out and struck the horses and chariots, and killed the Arameans in a great slaughter.

²²Then the prophet approached the king of Israel and said to him, "Go, show yourself courageous and be aware and see what you have to do; for ᴬat ¹the turn of the year the king of Aram will march against you."

²³Now the servants of the king of Aram said to him, "ᴬTheir gods are gods of the mountains; for that reason they were stronger than we. But let us fight them in the plain, *and* we will certainly be stronger than

they. ²⁴Carry out this plan: remove the kings, each from his place, and put governors in their place, ²⁵and muster an army like the army that you have lost, horse for horse and chariot for chariot. Then we will fight against them in the plain, *and* we will certainly be stronger than they." And he listened to their voice and did so.

ANOTHER ARAMEAN WAR

²⁶So at the turn of the year Ben-hadad mustered the Arameans and went up to ᴬAphek to fight against Israel. ²⁷And the sons of Israel were mustered and given provisions, and they went to meet them; and the sons of Israel camped opposite them like two little flocks of goats, ᴬwhile the Arameans filled the country. ²⁸Then ᴬa man of God approached and spoke to the king of Israel, and said, "This is what the LORD says: 'Since the Arameans have said, "The LORD is a god of mountains, but He is not a god of valleys," therefore I will hand over to you all this great multitude, and you shall know that I am the LORD.'" ²⁹So they camped, one opposite the other, for seven days. And on the seventh day the battle was joined, and the sons of Israel killed *of* the Arameans a hundred thousand foot soldiers in a single day. ³⁰But the rest fled to ᴬAphek into the city, and the wall fell on twenty-seven thousand men who were left. And Ben-hadad fled and came into the city, *going from one* ᴮinner room to another.

20:16 ᴬ1 Kin 16:9; Prov 20:1   20:18 ᴬ2 Kin 14:8-12   20:22 ᴬ2 Sam 11:1; 1 Kin 20:26   20:23 ᴬJer 16:19-21; Rom 1:21-23   20:26 ᴬ2 Kin 13:17   20:27 ᴬJudg 6:3-5; 1 Sam 13:5-8   20:28 ᴬ1 Kin 17:18   20:30 ᴬ1 Kin 20:26   ᴮ1 Kin 22:25

20:22 ¹I.e., spring

³¹But his servants said to him, "Behold now, we have heard that the kings of the house of Israel are merciful kings. Please let's ^put sackcloth around our waists and ropes on our heads, and go out to the king of Israel; perhaps he will let you live." ³²So they put sackcloth around their waists and ropes on their heads, and came to the king of Israel and said, "^Your servant Benhadad says, 'Please let me live.'" And *Ahab* said, "Is he still alive? He is my brother." ³³Now the men took this as a *good* omen, and quickly accepting it from him, they said, "Your brother Ben-hadad." Then he said, "Go, bring him." Then Benhadad came out to him, and he had him mount the chariot. ³⁴And *Ben-hadad* said to him, "^The cities which my father took from your father I will restore, and you can make streets for yourself in Damascus, as my father made in Samaria." *Ahab said,* "And I will let you go with this covenant." So he made a covenant with him and let him go.

³⁵Now a man from ^the sons of the prophets said to another by the word of the LORD, "Please strike me." But the man refused to strike him. ³⁶Then he said to him, "Because you have not listened to the voice of the LORD, behold, as soon as you leave me, ^a lion will kill you." And *as soon as* he left him a lion found him and killed him. ³⁷Then he found another man and said, "Please strike me." And the man struck him, injuring him. ³⁸So the prophet departed and waited for the king by the road, and ^disguised himself with a bandage over his eyes. ³⁹And as the king passed by, he cried out to the king and said, "Your servant went out into the midst of the battle; and behold, a man turned aside and brought a man to me and said, 'Guard this man; if for any reason he goes missing, ^then your life shall be *forfeited* in place of his life, or else you shall pay a 'talent of silver.' ⁴⁰Now while your servant was busy here and there, he disappeared." And the king of Israel said to him, "So shall your judgment be; you yourself determined *it.*" ⁴¹Then he quickly took the bandage away from his eyes, and the king of Israel recognized him, that he was *one* of the prophets. ⁴²And *the prophet* said to him, "This is what the LORD says: 'Since you have let go from *your* hand the man I had designated for destruction, ^your life shall be *forfeited* in place of his life, and your people in place of his people.'" ⁴³So ^the king of Israel went to his house sullen and furious, and came to Samaria.

AHAB COVETS NABOTH'S VINEYARD

21 Now it came about after these things that Naboth the Jezreelite had a vineyard which *was* in ^Jezreel beside the palace of Ahab, the king of Samaria. ²And Ahab spoke to Naboth, saying, "^Give me your vineyard so that I may have it for a vegetable garden, because it is close beside my house, and I will give you a better vineyard in place of it; if you prefer, I will give you what it is worth in money." ³But Naboth said to Ahab, "The LORD forbid me ^that I

20:31^Gen 37:34; 2 Sam 3:31   20:32^1 Kin 20:3-6
20:34^1 Kin 15:20   20:35^2 Kin 2:3-7
20:36^1 Kin 13:24   20:38^1 Kin 14:2
20:39^2 Kin 10:24   20:42^1 Kin 20:39
20:43^1 Kin 21:4   21:1^Judg 6:33; 1 Kin 18:45, 46
21:2^1 Sam 8:14   21:3^Lev 25:23; Ezek 46:18

20:39 'About 75 lb. or 34 kg

would give you the inheritance of my fathers!" ⁴ᴬSo Ahab entered his house sullen and furious because of the answer that Naboth the Jezreelite had given to him, since he said, "I will not give you the inheritance of my fathers." And he lay down on his bed and turned his face away, and ate no food.

⁵But Jezebel his wife came to him and said to him, "How is it that your spirit is so sullen that you are not eating food?" ⁶So he said to her, "*It is* because I was speaking to Naboth the Jezreelite and saying to him, 'Give me your vineyard for money; or else, if it pleases you, I will give you a vineyard in place of it.' But he said, 'I will not give you my vineyard.'" ⁷Jezebel his wife said to him, "ᴬDo you now reign over Israel? Arise, eat bread, and let your heart be joyful; I will give you the vineyard of Naboth the Jezreelite."

⁸ᴬSo she wrote letters in Ahab's name and sealed them with his seal, and sent the letters to the elders and to the nobles who were living with Naboth in his city. ⁹Now she had written in the letters, saying, "Proclaim a fast and seat Naboth at the head of the people; ¹⁰and seat two worthless men opposite him, and have them testify against him, saying, 'ᴬYou cursed God and the king.' Then take him out and ᴮstone him to death."

JEZEBEL'S PLOT

¹¹So the men of his city, the elders and the nobles who lived in his city, did just as Jezebel had sent *word* to them, just as it was written in the letters which she had sent them. ¹²They ᴬproclaimed a fast, and seated Naboth at the head of the people. ¹³Then the two worthless men came in and sat opposite him; and the worthless men testified against him, against Naboth, before the people, saying, "Naboth cursed God and the king." ᴬSo they took him outside the city and stoned him to death with stones. ¹⁴Then they sent *word* to Jezebel, saying, "Naboth has been stoned and is dead."

¹⁵And when Jezebel heard that Naboth had been stoned and was dead, Jezebel said to Ahab, "Arise, take possession of the vineyard of Naboth, the Jezreelite, which he refused to give you for money; for Naboth is not alive, but dead." ¹⁶When Ahab heard that Naboth was dead, Ahab got up to go down to the vineyard of Naboth the Jezreelite, to take possession of it.

¹⁷Then the word of the LORD came to Elijah the Tishbite, saying, ¹⁸"Arise, go down to meet Ahab king of Israel, ᴬwho is in Samaria; behold, he is in the vineyard of Naboth, where he has gone down to take possession of it. ¹⁹And you shall speak to him, saying, 'This is what the LORD says: "ᴬHave you murdered and also taken possession?"' And you shall speak to him, saying, 'The LORD says this: "In the place where the dogs licked up the blood of Naboth, the dogs will lick up your blood, yours as well."'"

²⁰Then Ahab said to Elijah, "ᴬHave you found me, enemy of mine?" And he answered, "I have found *you,* because you have given yourself over to do evil in the sight of the LORD. ²¹Behold, I am bringing

21:4ᴬ1 Kin 20:43   21:7ᴬ1 Sam 8:14   21:8ᴬEsth 3:12;
8:8, 10   21:10ᴬActs 6:11   ᴮLev 24:14   21:12ᴬIs 58:4
21:13ᴬActs 7:58, 59; Heb 11:37   21:18ᴬ1 Kin 16:29
21:19ᴬ2 Sam 12:9   21:20ᴬ1 Kin 18:17

disaster upon you, and I ^will utterly sweep you away, and will eliminate from Ahab every male, both bond and free in Israel; ²²and ^I will make your house ᴮlike the house of Jeroboam the son of Nebat, and like the house of Baasha the son of Ahijah, because of the provocation with which you have provoked *Me* to anger, and *because* you have misled Israel into sin. ²³The Lᴏʀᴅ has also spoken of Jezebel, saying, '^The dogs will eat Jezebel in the territory of Jezreel.' ²⁴^The one belonging to Ahab, who dies in the city, the dogs will eat; and the one who dies in the field, the birds of the sky will eat."

²⁵^There certainly was no one like Ahab who gave himself over to to do evil in the sight of the Lᴏʀᴅ, because Jezebel his wife incited him. ²⁶^He also acted very despicably in following idols, conforming to everything that the Amorites had done, whom the Lᴏʀᴅ drove out from the sons of Israel.

²⁷Yet it came about, when Ahab heard these words, that ^he tore his clothes and put on sackcloth and fasted, and he lay in sackcloth and went about despondently. ²⁸Then the word of the Lᴏʀᴅ came to Elijah the Tishbite, saying, ²⁹"Do you see how Ahab has humbled himself before Me? Because he has humbled himself before Me, I will not bring the disaster in his days; I will bring the disaster upon his house ^in his son's days."

AHAB'S THIRD CAMPAIGN
AGAINST ARAM

22 Now three years passed without war between Aram and Israel. ²In the third year, ^Jehoshaphat the king of Judah came down to the king of Israel. ³Now the king of Israel said to his servants, "Are you aware that ^Ramoth-gilead belongs to us, yet we are hesitant to take it out of the hand of the king of Aram?" ⁴So he said to Jehoshaphat, "Will you go to battle with me at Ramoth-gilead?" And Jehoshaphat said to the king of Israel, "^Consider me yours, my people yours, and my horses yours!"

⁵However, Jehoshaphat said to the king of Israel, "Please request the word of the Lᴏʀᴅ first." ⁶So ^the king of Israel assembled the ¹prophets, about four hundred men, and said to them, "Should I go to battle against Ramoth-gilead or should I refrain?" And they said, "Go up, for the Lord will hand *it* over to the king." ⁷But ^Jehoshaphat said, "Is there no longer a prophet of the Lᴏʀᴅ here, that we may inquire of him?" ⁸And the king of Israel said to Jehoshaphat, "There is still one man by whom we may inquire of the Lᴏʀᴅ, but I hate him, because he does not prophesy *anything* good regarding me, but *only* bad. *He is* Micaiah the son of Imlah." But Jehoshaphat said, "May the king not say so." ⁹Then the king of Israel summoned an officer and said, "Bring Micaiah son of Imlah quickly." ¹⁰Now the king of Israel and Jehoshaphat the king of Judah were sitting, each on his throne, dressed in *their* robes, at the threshing floor at the entrance of the gate of Samaria; and ^all the prophets were prophesying before

21:21^1 Kin 14:10; 2 Kin 9:8　21:22^1 Kin 15:29
ᴮ1 Kin 16:3, 11　21:23^2 Kin 9:10, 30-37
21:24^1 Kin 14:11; 16:4　21:25^1 Kin 16:30-33; 21:20
21:26^1 Kin 15:12; 2 Kin 17:12　21:27^Gen 37:34;
2 Kin 6:30　21:29^2 Kin 9:25-37　22:1^1 Kin 15:24
22:3^Deut 4:43; 1 Kin 4:13　22:4^2 Kin 3:7
22:6^1 Kin 18:19　22:7^2 Kin 3:1　22:10^1 Kin 22:6
22:6¹I.e., official prophets who at that time were false

them. [11]Then Zedekiah the son of Chenaanah made ^horns of iron for himself and said, "This is what the LORD says: 'With these you will gore the Arameans until they are destroyed!'" [12]All the prophets were prophesying this as well, saying, "Go up to Ramoth-gilead and succeed, for the LORD will hand *it* over to the king."

MICAIAH PREDICTS DEFEAT

[13]Then the messenger who went to summon Micaiah spoke to him saying, "Behold now, the words of the prophets are unanimously favorable to the king. Please let your word be like the word of one of them, and speak favorably." [14]But Micaiah said, "As the LORD lives, whatever ^the LORD says to me, I shall speak it."

[15]When he came to the king, the king said to him, "Micaiah, should we go to battle against Ramoth-gilead, or should we refrain?" And he said, "^Go up and succeed, for the LORD will hand *it* over to the king!" [16]Then the king said to him, "How many times must I make you swear that you will tell me nothing but the truth in the name of the LORD?" [17]So he said,

"I saw all Israel
Scattered on the mountains,
^Like sheep that have no shepherd.
And the LORD said,
'These *people* have no master.
Each of them is to return to his house in peace.'"

[18]Then the king of Israel said to Jehoshaphat, "^Did I not tell you that he would not prophesy *anything* good regarding me, but *only* bad?"

[19]And *Micaiah* said, "Therefore, hear the word of the LORD. ^I saw the LORD sitting on His throne, and all the angels of heaven standing by Him on His right and on His left. [20]And the LORD said, 'Who will entice Ahab to go up and fall at Ramoth-gilead?' And one *spirit* said this, while another said that. [21]Then a spirit came forward and stood before the LORD, and said, 'I will entice him.' [22]And the LORD said to him, 'How?' And he said, 'I will go out and ^be a deceiving spirit in the mouths of all his prophets.' Then He said, 'You shall entice *him*, and you will also prevail. Go and do so.' [23]Now then, behold, ^the LORD has put a deceiving spirit in the mouth of all these prophets of yours; and the LORD has declared disaster against you."

[24]Then Zedekiah the son of Chenaanah approached and struck Micaiah on the cheek; and he said, "^How did the Spirit of the LORD pass from me to speak to you?" [25]And Micaiah said, "Behold, you are going to see *how* on that day when you ^go *from one* inner room to another *trying* to hide yourself." [26]Then the king of Israel said, "Take Micaiah and return him to Amon the governor of the city, and to Joash the king's son; [27]and say, 'This is what the king says: "^Put this *man* in prison, and feed him enough bread and water to survive until I return safely."'" [28]But Micaiah said, "^If you actually return safely, the LORD has not spoken by me." And he said, "^Listen, all you people!"

22:11 ^Zech 1:18-21   22:14 ^Num 22:18; 24:13
22:15 ^1 Kin 22:12   22:17 ^Matt 9:36; Mark 6:34
22:18 ^1 Kin 22:8   22:19 ^Ezek 1:26-28; Dan 7:9, 10
22:22 ^Ezek 14:9; 2 Thess 2:11   22:23 ^Ezek 14:9
22:24 ^2 Chr 18:23   22:25 ^1 Kin 20:30
22:27 ^2 Chr 16:10; 18:25-27   22:28 ^Deut 18:22
^B Mic 1:2

DEFEAT AND DEATH OF AHAB

²⁹So ᴬthe king of Israel and Jehoshaphat king of Judah went up *against* Ramoth-gilead. ³⁰And the king of Israel said to Jehoshaphat, "ᴬI will disguise myself and go into the battle, but you put on your robes." So the king of Israel disguised himself and went into the battle. ³¹Now ᴬthe king of Aram had commanded the thirty-two commanders of his chariots, saying, "Do not fight with the small *or* great, but only with the king of Israel." ³²So when the commanders of the chariots saw Jehoshaphat, they said, "Surely he is the king of Israel!" And they turned aside to fight against him, and Jehoshaphat cried out. ³³Then, when the commanders of the chariots saw that it was not the king of Israel, they turned back from pursuing him.

³⁴Now one man drew his bow at random and struck the king of Israel in a joint of the armor. So he said to the driver of his chariot, "Turn around and take me out of the battle, ᴬfor I am severely wounded." ³⁵The battle raged on that day, and the king was propped up in his chariot in front of the Arameans, and he died at evening, and the blood from the wound ran into the bottom of the chariot. ³⁶ᴬThen the word passed throughout the army close to sunset, saying, "Every man to his city, and every man to his country!"

³⁷So the king died and was brought to Samaria, and they buried the king in Samaria. ³⁸They washed out the chariot by the pool of Samaria, and the dogs licked up his blood (*it was there that* the prostitutes bathed themselves) ᴬin accordance with the word of the Lᴏʀᴅ which He had spoken. ³⁹Now *as for* the rest of the acts of Ahab and everything that he did, and ᴬthe ivory house which he built and all the cities which he built, are they not written in the Book of the Chronicles of the Kings of Israel? ⁴⁰So Ahab ¹lay down with his fathers, and his son Ahaziah became king in his place.

THE NEW RULERS

⁴¹ᴬNow Jehoshaphat the son of Asa became king over Judah in the fourth year of Ahab king of Israel. ⁴²Jehoshaphat was thirty-five years old when he became king, and he reigned for twenty-five years in Jerusalem. And his mother's name was Azubah the daughter of Shilhi. ⁴³ᴬHe walked entirely in the way of his father Asa; he did not turn aside from it, doing what was right in the sight of the Lᴏʀᴅ. However, the high places were not taken away; the people still sacrificed and burned incense on the high places. ⁴⁴ᴬJehoshaphat also made peace with the king of Israel.

⁴⁵Now *as for* the rest of the acts of Jehoshaphat, and his might which he showed and how he made war, are they not written ᴬin the Book of the Chronicles of the Kings of Judah? ⁴⁶And the remnant of ᴬthe cult prostitutes who remained in the days of his father Asa, he eliminated from the land.

⁴⁷Now ᴬthere was no king in Edom; a governor *served as* king. ⁴⁸Jehoshaphat built ᴬships of Tarshish to go to ᴮOphir for gold,

22:29ᴬ1 Kin 22:3, 4   22:30ᴬ2 Chr 35:22
22:31ᴬ1 Kin 20:1, 16, 24; 2 Chr 18:30
22:34ᴬ2 Chr 35:23   22:36ᴬ2 Kin 14:12
22:38ᴬ1 Kin 21:19   22:39ᴬAmos 3:15
22:41ᴬ2 Chr 20:31   22:43ᴬ2 Chr 17:3
22:44ᴬ2 Kin 8:16, 18; 2 Chr 19:2   22:45ᴬ2 Chr 20:34
22:46ᴬDeut 23:17; Jude 7   22:47ᴬ2 Sam 8:14;
2 Kin 3:9   22:48ᴬ2 Chr 20:36   ᴮ1 Kin 9:28

22:40 ¹I.e., died

but they did not go, because the ships were destroyed at Ezion-geber. ⁴⁹Then Ahaziah the son of Ahab said to Jehoshaphat, "Let my servants go with your servants in the ships." But Jehoshaphat was not willing. ⁵⁰ᴬAnd Jehoshaphat ¹lay down with his fathers and was buried with his fathers in the city of his father David, and his son Jehoram became king in his place.

⁵¹Ahaziah the son of Ahab ᴬbe-came king over Israel in Samaria in the seventeenth year of Jeho-shaphat king of Judah, and he reigned over Israel for two years. ⁵²He did evil in the sight of the LORD and ᴬwalked in the way of his father and in the way of his mother, and in the way of Jeroboam the son of Nebat, who misled Israel into sin. ⁵³ᴬSo he served Baal and worshiped him, and provoked the LORD God of Israel to anger, according to all that his father had done.

22:50ᴬ2 Chr 21:1   22:51ᴬ1 Kin 22:40
22:52ᴬ1 Kin 15:26; 21:25   22:53ᴬJudg 2:11;
1 Kin 16:30-32

22:50 ¹I.e., died

2 KINGS

AHAZIAH'S MESSENGERS MEET ELIJAH

1 Now ^Moab broke with Israel after the death of Ahab. ²And Ahaziah fell through the *window* lattice in his upper chamber which *was* in Samaria, and became ill. So he sent messengers and said to them, "Go, ^inquire of Baal-zebub, the god of Ekron, ᴮwhether I will recover from this sickness." ³But the angel of the LORD said to ^Elijah the Tishbite, "Arise, go up to meet the messengers of the king of Samaria and say to them, 'Is it because there is no God in Israel *that* you are going to inquire of Baal-zebub, the god of Ekron?' ⁴Now therefore, this is what the LORD says: "^You will not get down from the bed upon which you have lain, but you shall certainly die.'" Then Elijah departed.

⁵When the messengers returned to Ahaziah, he said to them, "Why have you returned?" ⁶They said to him, "A man came up to meet us and said to us, 'Go, return to the king who sent you and say to him, "This is what the LORD says: 'Is it because there is no God in Israel *that* you are sending *messengers* ^to inquire of Baal-zebub, the god of Ekron? Therefore you will not get down from the bed upon which you have lain, but you shall certainly die.'"'" ⁷Then he said to them, "What did the man look like, who came up to meet you and spoke these words to you?" ⁸And they said to him, "^He *was* a hairy man with a leather belt worn around his waist." And he said, "It is Elijah the Tishbite."

⁹Then *the king* ^sent to him a captain of fifty with his fifty *men*. And he went up to him, and behold, he was sitting on the top of the hill. And he said to him, "You man of God, the king says, 'Come down.'" ¹⁰But Elijah replied to the captain of fifty, "If I am a man of God, ^may fire come down from heaven and consume you and your fifty." Then fire came down from heaven and consumed him and his fifty *men*.

¹¹So *the king* again sent to him another captain of fifty with his fifty *men*. And he said to him, "You man of God, this is what the king says: 'Come down quickly!'" ¹²But Elijah replied to them, "If I am a man of God, may fire come down from heaven and consume you and your fifty." Then the fire of God came down from heaven and consumed him and his fifty *men*.

¹³So *the king* ^again sent the captain of a third fifty with his fifty *men*. When the third captain of fifty went up, he came and bowed down on his knees before Elijah, and begged him and said to him, "You man of God, please let my life and the lives of these fifty servants of yours be precious in your sight. ¹⁴Behold, fire came down from heaven and consumed the first two captains of fifty with their fifties; but now let my life be precious in your sight." ¹⁵And the angel of

1:1^2 Sam 8:2; 2 Kin 3:5   1:2^2 Kin 1:3, 6, 16
ᴮ2 Kin 8:7-10   1:3^1 Kin 17:1; 21:17   1:4^2 Kin 1:6, 16
1:6^2 Kin 1:2   1:8^Zech 13:4; Matt 3:4
1:9^2 Kin 6:13, 14   1:10^1 Kin 18:36-38; Luke 9:54
1:13^Is 1:5; Jer 5:3

the LORD said to Elijah, "Go down with him; ^do not be afraid of him." So he got up and went down with him to the king. ¹⁶Then he said to him, "This is what the LORD says: 'Since you have sent messengers ^to inquire of Baal-zebub, the god of Ekron—is it because there is no God in Israel to inquire of His word? Therefore you will not get down from the bed upon which you have lain, but you shall certainly die.'"

JEHORAM REIGNS OVER ISRAEL

¹⁷So Ahaziah died in accordance with the word of the LORD which Elijah had spoken. And since he had no son, Jehoram became king in his place ^in the second year of Jehoram the son of Jehoshaphat, king of Judah. ¹⁸Now *as for* the rest of the acts of Ahaziah which he did, are they not written in the Book of the Chronicles of the Kings of Israel?

ELIJAH TAKEN TO HEAVEN

2 Now it came about, when the LORD was about to ^bring Elijah up by a whirlwind to heaven, that Elijah left Gilgal with ᴮElisha. ²And Elijah said to Elisha, "^Stay here please, for the LORD has sent me as far as Bethel." But Elisha said, "As *surely as* the LORD lives and as you yourself live, I will not leave you." So they went down to Bethel. ³Then ^the sons of the prophets who *were at* Bethel went out to Elisha and said to him, "Are you aware that the LORD will take away your master from over you today?" And he said, "Yes, I am aware; say nothing *about it.*"

⁴And Elijah said to him, "Elisha, please stay here, for the LORD has sent me to ^Jericho." But he said, "As *surely as* the LORD lives, and as you

yourself live, I will not leave you." So they came to Jericho. ⁵Then ^the sons of the prophets who *were* at Jericho approached Elisha and said to him, "Do you know that the LORD will take away your master from over you today?" And he answered, "Yes, I know; say nothing *about it.*" ⁶And Elijah said to him, "Please stay here, for the LORD has sent me to ^the Jordan." But he said, "As *surely as* the LORD lives, and as you yourself live, I will not leave you." So the two of them went on.

⁷Now ^fifty men of the sons of the prophets went and stood opposite *them* at a distance, while the two of them stood by the Jordan. ⁸And Elijah ^took his coat, folded it, and struck the waters, and they were divided here and there, so that the two of them crossed over on dry ground.

⁹When they had crossed over, Elijah said to Elisha, "Ask *me* what I should do for you before I am taken from you." And Elisha said, "Please let a ^double portion of your spirit be upon me." ¹⁰He said, "You have asked a hard thing. *Nevertheless,* if you ^see me when I am taken from you, it shall be so for you; but if not, it shall not be *so.*" ¹¹And as they were walking along and talking, behold, ^a chariot of fire *appeared* with horses of fire, and they separated the two of them. Then Elijah went up by a whirlwind to heaven. ¹²And Elisha was watching *it* and he was crying out, "^My father, my father, the chariot of Israel and its horsemen!" And he did not see Elijah

1:15 ^Is 51:12; Ezek 2:6   1:16 ^2 Kin 1:3   1:17 ^2 Kin 3:1; 8:16   2:1 ^Heb 11:5   ᴮJosh 4:19   2:2 ^Ruth 1:15 2:3 ^2 Kin 4:1, 38; 5:22   2:4 ^Josh 6:26   2:5 ^2 Kin 2:3 2:6 ^Josh 3:8, 15-17   2:7 ^2 Kin 2:15, 16 2:8 ^1 Kin 19:13, 19   2:9 ^Num 11:17-25; Deut 21:17 2:10 ^Acts 1:10   2:11 ^2 Kin 6:17   2:12 ^2 Kin 13:14

again. Then he took hold of his own clothes and tore them in two pieces. [13]He also took up the coat of Elijah that had fallen from him, and he went back and stood by the bank of the Jordan. [14]Then he took the coat of Elijah that had fallen from him and struck the waters, and said, "Where is the LORD, the God of Elijah?" And when he also had ^struck the waters, they were divided here and there; and Elisha crossed over.

ELISHA SUCCEEDS ELIJAH

[15]Now when ^the sons of the prophets who *were* at Jericho opposite *him* saw him, they said, "The spirit of Elijah has settled on Elisha." And they came to meet him and bowed down to the ground before him. [16]Then they said to him, "Behold now, there are with your servants fifty strong men; please let them go and search for your master, in case ^the Spirit of the LORD has taken him up and cast him on some mountain or into some valley." But he said, "You shall not send *anyone*." [17]Yet when ^they urged him until he was ashamed *to refuse,* he said, "Send *them*." So they sent fifty men; and they searched for three days, but did not find him. [18]They returned to him while he was staying in Jericho; and he said to them, "Did I not say to you, 'Do not go'?"

[19]Then the men of the city said to Elisha, "Behold now, the site of the city is pleasant, as my lord sees; but the water is bad and the land is unfruitful." [20]And he said, "Bring me a new jar, and put salt in it." So they brought *it* to him. [21]Then he went out to the spring of water and ^threw salt in it and said, "This is what the LORD says: 'I have purified these waters; there shall not come from there

death or unfruitfulness any longer.'" [22]So the waters have been purified to this day, in accordance with the word of Elisha which he spoke.

[23]Now he went up from there to Bethel; and as he was going up by the road, *some* young boys came out from the city and ^ridiculed him and said to him, "Go up, you baldhead; go up, you baldhead!" [24]When he looked behind him and saw them, he ^cursed them in the name of the LORD. Then two female bears came out of the woods and tore up forty-two of the boys. [25]He then went on from there to ^Mount Carmel, and from there he returned to Samaria.

JEHORAM MEETS MOABITE REBELLION

3 Now Jehoram the son of Ahab became king over Israel at Samaria ^in the eighteenth year of Jehoshaphat king of Judah, and he reigned for twelve years. [2]He did evil in the sight of the LORD, though not like his father and his mother; for ^he removed the memorial stone of Baal which his father had made. [3]Nevertheless, ^he clung to the sins of Jeroboam the son of Nebat, into which he misled Israel; he did not abandon them.

[4]Now Mesha the king of Moab was a sheep breeder, and he ^used to make *tribute* payments to the king of Israel of a hundred thousand lambs, and the wool of a hundred thousand rams. [5]However, ^when *King* Ahab died, the king of Moab broke with the [1]king of Israel.

2:14^2 Kin 2:8 2:15^2 Kin 2:7 2:16^1 Kin 18:12;
Acts 8:39 2:17^2 Kin 8:11 2:21^Ex 15:25, 26;
2 Kin 4:41 2:23^2 Chr 36:16; Ps 31:17, 18
2:24^Neh 13:25-27 2:25^1 Kin 18:19, 20; 2 Kin 4:25
3:1^2 Kin 1:17 3:2^Ex 23:24; 2 Kin 10:18, 26-28
3:3^1 Kin 12:28-32 3:4^2 Sam 8:2; Is 16:1, 2
3:5^2 Kin 1:1

3:5 [1]I.e., Jehoram, the new king

⁶So King Jehoram left Samaria *for battle* at that time and mustered all Israel. ⁷Then he went and sent *word* to Jehoshaphat the king of Judah, saying, "The king of Moab has broken away from me. Will you go with me to fight against Moab?" And he said, "I will go up. ^Consider me yours, my people as your people, my horses as your horses." ⁸Then he said, "Which way shall we go up?" And he answered, "The way of the wilderness of Edom."

⁹So the king of Israel went with the king of Judah and ^the king of Edom, and they made a circuit of seven days' journey. But there was no water for the army or for the cattle that followed them. ¹⁰Then the king of Israel said, "It is hopeless! For the LORD has called these three kings to hand them over to Moab!" ¹¹But Jehoshaphat said, "^Is there no prophet of the LORD here, that we may inquire of the LORD by him?" And one of the king of Israel's servants answered and said, "Elisha the son of Shaphat is here, who used to pour water on the hands of Elijah." ¹²And Jehoshaphat said, "The word of the LORD is with him." So the king of Israel and Jehoshaphat and the king of Edom went down to him.

¹³Now Elisha said to the king of Israel, "What business do you have with me? ^Go to your father's prophets and your mother's prophets." But the king of Israel said to him, "No, for the LORD has called these three kings *together* to hand them over to Moab." ¹⁴Elisha said, "^As *surely as* the LORD of armies lives, before whom I stand, if I did not respect Jehoshaphat the king of Judah, I would not look at you nor see you. ¹⁵But now bring me

a musician." And it came about, when the musician played, that ^the hand of the LORD came upon him. ¹⁶And he said, "This is what the LORD says: 'Make this valley full of trenches.' ¹⁷For the LORD says this: 'You will not see wind, nor will you see rain; yet that valley ^shall be filled with water, so that you will drink, you, your livestock, and your *other* animals. ¹⁸And this is an ^insignificant thing in the sight of the LORD; He will also give the Moabites into your hand. ¹⁹^Then you shall strike every fortified city and every choice city, and cut down every good tree and stop up all the springs of water, and spoil every good plot of land with stones.'" ²⁰And it happened in the morning ^about *the time of* offering the sacrifice, that behold, water came from the direction of Edom, and the country was filled with water.

²¹Now all the Moabites heard that the kings had come up to fight against them. And all who were able to put on armor and older were summoned and they took their positions on the border. ²²Then they got up early in the morning, and the sun shone on the water, and the Moabites saw the water opposite *them* as red as blood. ²³So they said, "This is blood; the kings must have fought each other, and they have killed one another. Now then, Moab, to the spoils!" ²⁴But when they came to the camp of Israel, the Israelites rose up and struck the Moabites, so that they fled from them; and *the Israelites* invaded the land, killing the

3:7^1 Kin 22:4   3:9^1 Kin 22:47   3:11^1 Kin 22:7
3:13^1 Kin 18:19; 22:6–11, 22–25   3:14^1 Kin 17:1;
2 Kin 5:16   3:15^1 Kin 18:46; Ezek 1:3   3:17^Ps 107:35
3:18^Jer 32:17, 27; Luke 1:37   3:19^2 Kin 3:25
3:20^Ex 29:39, 40

Moabites. ²⁵^So they destroyed the cities; and each one threw a stone on every plot of good land and filled it. So they stopped up every spring of water and cut down every good tree, until in Kir-hareseth *only* they left its stones; however, the rock slingers surrounded *it* and struck it. ²⁶When the king of Moab saw that the battle was too fierce for him, he took with him seven hundred men who drew swords, to break through to the king of Edom; but they could not. ²⁷Then *the king of Moab* took his oldest son who was to reign in his place, and ^offered him as a burnt offering on the wall. And great anger came upon Israel, and they departed from him and returned to their own land.

THE WIDOW'S OIL

4 Now a woman of the wives of ^the sons of the prophets cried out to Elisha, saying, "Your servant my husband is dead, and you know that your servant feared the Lord; and ^Bthe creditor has come to take my two children to be his slaves." ²So Elisha said to her, "What shall I do for you? Tell me, what do you have in the house?" And she said, "Your servant has nothing in the house except ^a jar of oil." ³Then he said, "Go, borrow containers elsewhere for yourself, empty containers from all your neighbors—do not get *too* few. ⁴Then you shall come in and shut the door behind you and your sons, and pour into all these containers; and you shall set aside what is full." ⁵So she left him and shut the door behind her and her sons; they *began* bringing *the containers* to her, and she poured *the oil.* ⁶When ^the containers were full, she said to her son,

"Bring me another container." But he said to her, "There are no more containers." Then the oil stopped. ⁷So she came and told ^the man of God. And he said, "Go, sell the oil and pay your debt, and you *and* your sons can live on the rest."

THE SHUNAMMITE WOMAN

⁸Now a day came when Elisha went over to ^Shunem, where there was a prominent woman, and she urged him to eat food. And so it was, as often as he passed by, *that* he turned in there to eat food. ⁹And she said to her husband, "Behold now, I am aware that this is a holy ^man of God passing by us repeatedly. ¹⁰Please, let's ^make a little walled upper room, and let's set up a bed for him there, and a table, a chair, and a lampstand; then it shall be, when he comes to us, *that* he can turn in there."

¹¹Now one day he came there, and turned in to the upper room and rested. ¹²Then he said to his servant ^Gehazi, "Call this Shunammite." And when he had called her, she stood before him. ¹³And he said to him, "Say now to her, 'Behold, you have taken trouble for us with all this care; what can I do for you? Would you like me to speak for you to the king or to the commander of the army?'" But she answered, "I live among my own people." ¹⁴So he said, "What then is to be done for her?" And Gehazi answered, "It is a fact that she has no son, and her husband is old." ¹⁵He then said, "Call her." When he had called her, she stood in the doorway. ¹⁶Then he said, "^At this season next year, you

3:25^2 Kin 3:19   3:27^Amos 2:1; Mic 6:7
4:1^2 Kin 2:3   ^BLev 25:39–41, 48   4:2^1 Kin 17:12
4:6^Matt 14:20   4:7^1 Kin 12:22   4:8^Josh 19:18
4:9^2 Kin 4:7   4:10^Matt 10:41, 42; Rom 12:13
4:12^2 Kin 4:29–31; 8:4, 5   4:16^Gen 18:14

are going to embrace a son." And she said, "No, my lord, you man of God, do not lie to your servant."

¹⁷Now the woman conceived and gave birth to a son at that season the next year, as Elisha had told her.

THE SHUNAMMITE'S SON

¹⁸When the child was grown, the day came that he went out to his father, to the reapers. ¹⁹And he said to his father, "My head, my head!" And *his father* said to his servant, "Carry him to his mother." ²⁰When he had carried him and brought him to his mother, he sat on her lap until noon, and *then* he died. ²¹And she went up and ᴬlaid him on the bed of ᴮthe man of God, and shut *the door* behind him and left. ²²Then she called to her husband and said, "Please send me one of the servants and one of the donkeys, so that I may run to the man of God and return." ²³But he said, "Why are you going to him today? It is neither ᴬnew moon nor Sabbath." So she *just* said, "*It will be* fine." ²⁴Then she saddled the donkey and said to her servant, "Drive *the donkey* and go on; do not slow down the pace for me unless I tell you." ²⁵So she went on and came to the man of God at ᴬMount Carmel.

When the man of God saw her at a distance, he said to Gehazi his servant, "Behold, that person there is the Shunammite. ²⁶Please run now to meet her and say to her, 'Is it *going* well for you? Is it *going* well for your husband? Is it *going* well for the child?'" Then she answered, "It is *going* well." ²⁷But she came to the man of God ᴬat the hill and took hold of his feet. And Gehazi came up to push her away, but the man of God said, "Leave her alone, for her

soul is troubled within her; and the LORD has concealed *it* from me and has not informed me." ²⁸Then she said, "Did I ask for a son from my lord? Did I not say, 'ᴬDo not give me false hope'?"

²⁹Then he said to Gehazi, "Get ready and ᴬtake my staff in your hand, and go; if you meet anyone, do not greet him, and if anyone greets you, do not reply to him. And ᴮlay my staff on the boy's face." ³⁰The mother of the boy said, "ᴬAs *surely as* the LORD lives and you yourself live, I will not leave you." So he got up and followed her. ³¹Then Gehazi went on ahead of them and laid the staff on the boy's face, but there was no sound or response. So he returned to meet him and informed him, saying, "The boy ᴬhas not awakened."

³²When Elisha entered the house, behold the boy was dead, laid on his bed. ³³So he entered and ᴬshut the door behind them both, and he prayed to the LORD. ³⁴Then ᴬhe got up *on the bed* and lay on the child, and put his mouth on his mouth, his eyes on his eyes, his hands on his hands, and he bent down on him; and the flesh of the child became warm. ³⁵Then he returned and walked in the house back and forth once, and went up and ᴬbent down on him; and the boy sneezed seven times, then the boy opened his eyes. ³⁶And he called Gehazi and said, "Call this Shunammite." So he called her. And when she came to him, he said, "Pick up your son." ³⁷Then she came in and fell at his feet and bowed down to the

4:21ᴬ2 Kin 4:32   ᴮ2 Kin 4:7   4:23ᴬNum 10:10; 1 Chr 23:31   4:25ᴬ2 Kin 2:25   4:27ᴬ2 Kin 4:25   4:28ᴬ2 Kin 4:16   4:29ᴬ2 Kin 2:14   ᴮEx 7:19, 20   4:30ᴬ2 Kin 2:2, 4   4:31ᴬJohn 11:11   4:33ᴬ2 Kin 4:4; Matt 6:6   4:34ᴬ1 Kin 17:21-23   4:35ᴬ1 Kin 17:21

ground, and ^she picked up her son and left.

THE POISONOUS STEW

38 When Elisha returned to Gilgal, *there was* ^a famine in the land. As the sons of the prophets were sitting in front of him, he said to his servant, "Put on the large pot and boil stew for the sons of the prophets." 39 Then one went out into the field to gather mallow, and found a wild vine and gathered from it his lap full of wild gourds; and he came and sliced them into the pot of stew, because they did not know *what they were.* 40 So they poured *it* out for the men to eat. But as they were eating the stew, they cried out and said, "You man of God, there is ^death in the pot!" And they were unable to eat. 41 Then he said, "Bring flour." ^And he threw it into the pot, and said, "Pour *it* out for the people that they may eat." Then there was nothing harmful in the pot.

42 Now a man came from Baal-shalishah, and brought the man of God bread of the first fruits, twenty loaves of barley and fresh grain in his sack. And *Elisha* said, "^Give *them* to the people that they may eat." 43 But his attendant said, "How ^am I to serve this to a hundred men?" Nevertheless he said, "Give *them* to the people that they may eat, for this is what the LORD says: 'They shall eat and have *some* left over.'" 44 So he served *it* to them, and they ate and ^had *some* left over, in accordance with the word of the LORD.

NAAMAN IS HEALED

5 Now ^Naaman, commander of the army of the king of Aram, was a great man in the view of his master, and eminent, because by

him the LORD had given victory to Aram. The man was also a valiant warrior, *but* afflicted with leprosy. 2 Now the Arameans had gone out ^in bands and had taken captive a little girl from the land of Israel; and she waited on Naaman's wife. 3 And she said to her mistress, "If only my master were with the prophet who is in Samaria! Then he would cure him of his leprosy." 4 And Naaman went in and told his master, saying, "The girl who is from the land of Israel spoke such and such." 5 Then the king of Aram said, "Go now, and I will send a letter to the king of Israel." So he departed and took with him ten ¹talents of silver, six thousand ²*shekels* of gold, and ten ^changes of clothes.

6 And he brought the letter to the king of Israel, which said, "And now as this letter comes to you, behold, I have sent Naaman my servant to you, so that you may cure him of his leprosy." 7 But when the king of Israel read the letter, he tore his clothes and said, "^Am I God, to kill and to keep alive, that this man is sending *word* to me to cure a man of his leprosy? But consider now, and see how he is seeking a quarrel against me."

8 Now it happened, when Elisha ^the man of God heard that the king of Israel had torn his clothes, that he sent *word* to the king, saying, "Why did you tear your clothes? Just have him come to me, and he shall learn that there is a prophet

4:37 ^Heb 11:35   4:38 ^2 Kin 8:1   4:40 ^Ex 10:17
4:41 ^Ex 15:25; 2 Kin 2:21   4:42 ^Matt 14:16–21;
15:32–38   4:43 ^Luke 9:13; John 6:9
4:44 ^Matt 14:20; John 6:13   5:1 ^Luke 4:27
5:2 ^2 Kin 6:23; 13:20   5:5 ^Judg 14:12; 2 Kin 5:22, 23
5:7 ^Gen 30:2; 1 Sam 2:6   5:8 ^1 Kin 12:22

5:5 ¹A talent was about 75 lb. or 34 kg   ²A shekel
was about 0.4 oz. or 11 gm

in Israel." ⁹So Naaman came with his horses and his chariots, and stood at the doorway of Elisha's house. ¹⁰And Elisha sent a messenger to him, saying, "ᴬGo and wash in the Jordan seven times, and your flesh will be restored to you and *you will* be clean." ¹¹But Naaman was furious and went away, and he said, "Behold, I thought, 'He will certainly come out to me, and stand and call on the name of the LORD his God, and wave his hand over the site and cure the leprosy.' ¹²Are Abanah and Pharpar, the rivers of Damascus, not better than all the waters of Israel? Could I not wash in them and be clean?" So he turned and ᴬwent away in a rage. ¹³Then his servants approached and spoke to him, saying, "ᴬMy father, had the prophet told you *to do some* great thing, would you not have done *it?* How much more *then,* when he says to you, 'Wash, and be clean'?" ¹⁴So he went down and dipped *himself* in the Jordan seven times, in accordance with the word of the man of God; and ᴬhis flesh was restored like the flesh of a little child, and he was clean.

GEHAZI'S GREED

¹⁵Then he returned to the man of God with all his company, and came and stood before him. And he said, "Behold now, ᴬI know that there is no God in all the earth, except in Israel; so please ᴮaccept a gift from your servant now." ¹⁶But he said, "As *surely as* the LORD lives, before whom I stand, ᴬI will accept nothing." And he urged him to accept *it,* but he refused. ¹⁷Then Naaman said, "If not, please let your servant be given two mules' load of ᴬearth; for your servant will no longer offer a burnt offering nor a sacrifice to other gods, but to the LORD. ¹⁸Regarding this matter may the LORD forgive your servant: when my master goes into the house of Rimmon to worship there, and ᴬhe leans on my hand and I bow down in the house of Rimmon, when I bow down in the house of Rimmon, may the LORD please forgive your servant in this matter." ¹⁹He said to him, "ᴬGo in peace." So he went some distance from him.

²⁰But ᴬGehazi, the servant of Elisha the man of God, thought, "Behold, my master has spared this Naaman the Aramean, by not accepting from his hand what he brought. As the LORD lives, I will run after him and take something from him." ²¹So Gehazi pursued Naaman. When Naaman saw *someone* running after him, he came down from the chariot to meet him and said, "*Is everything* well?" ²²And he said, "*Everything is* well. My master has sent me, saying, 'Behold, just now two young men of the sons of the prophets have come to me from ᴬthe hill country of Ephraim. Please give them a talent of silver and ᴮtwo changes of clothes.'" ²³Naaman said, "ᴬBe sure to take two talents." And he urged him, and tied up two talents of silver in two bags with two changes of clothes, and gave *them* to two of his servants; and they carried *them* before him. ²⁴When he came to the hill, he took them from their hand

5:10ᴬJohn 9:7 5:12ᴬProv 14:17; 19:11
5:13ᴬ2 Kin 2:12; 8:9 5:14ᴬ2 Kin 5:10; Job 33:25
5:15ᴬJosh 2:11 ᴮ1 Sam 25:27 5:16ᴬGen 14:22, 23;
2 Kin 5:20, 26 5:17ᴬEx 20:24 5:18ᴬ2 Kin 7:2, 17
5:19ᴬEx 4:18; Mark 5:34 5:20ᴬ2 Kin 4:12, 31, 36
5:22ᴬJosh 24:33 ᴮ2 Kin 5:5 5:23ᴬ2 Kin 6:3

and ^deposited them in the house, and he sent the men away, and they departed. 25 But he went in and stood before his master. And Elisha said to him, "Where have you been, Gehazi?" And he said, "^Your servant went nowhere."

26 Then he said to him, "Did my heart not go *with you,* when the man turned from his chariot to meet you? ^Is it a time to accept money and to accept clothes, olive groves, vineyards, sheep, oxen, and male and female slaves? 27 Therefore, the leprosy of Naaman shall cling to you and to your descendants forever." So he went out from his presence ^afflicted with leprosy, *as white* as snow.

THE AXE HEAD RECOVERED

6 Now ^the sons of the prophets said to Elisha, "Behold now, the place before you where we are living is too cramped for us. 2 Please let us go to the Jordan, and let us each take from there a beam, and let us construct a place there for ourselves, to live there." So he said, "Go." 3 Then one *of them* said, "Please agree and go with your servants." And he said, "I will go." 4 So he went with them; and when they came to the Jordan, they cut down trees. 5 But it happened that as one *of them* was cutting down a beam, the axe head fell into the water; and he cried out and said, "Oh, my master! It was borrowed!" 6 Then the man of God said, "Where did it fall?" And when he showed him the place, ^he cut off a stick and threw *it* in there, and made the iron float. 7 Then he said, "Pick it up for yourself." So he reached out his hand and took it.

THE ARAMEANS PLOT TO CAPTURE ELISHA

8 Now the king of Aram was making war against Israel; and he consulted with his servants, saying, "In such and such a place shall be my camp." 9 But ^the man of God sent *word* to the king of Israel, saying, "Be careful that you do not pass this place, because the Arameans are coming down there." 10 And the king of Israel sent *scouts* to the place about which the man of God had told him; so he warned him, so that he was on his guard there, more than once or twice.

11 Now the heart of the king of Aram was enraged over this matter; and he called his servants and said to them, "Will you not tell me which of us is for the king of Israel?" 12 One of his servants said, "No, my lord, the king; but Elisha, the prophet who is in Israel, tells the king of Israel the words that you speak in your bedroom." 13 So he said, "Go and see where he is, so that I may send *men* and take him." And it was told to him, saying, "Behold, *he is* in ^Dothan." 14 So he sent horses and chariots and a substantial army there, and they came by night and surrounded the city.

15 Now when the attendant of the man of God had risen early and gone out, behold, an army with horses and chariots was circling the city. And his servant said to him, "This is hopeless, my master! What are we to do?" 16 And he said, "^Do not be afraid, for ^those who are with us are greater than those who are with them." 17 Then Elisha

5:24 ^Josh 7:1, 11, 12, 21; 1 Kin 21:16   5:25 ^2 Kin 5:22
5:26 ^2 Kin 5:16   5:27 ^Ex 4:6; Num 12:10   6:1 ^2 Kin 2:3
6:6 ^Ex 15:25; 2 Kin 2:21   6:9 ^2 Kin 4:1, 7; 6:12
6:13 ^Gen 37:17   6:16 ^Ex 14:13   ^Rom 8:31

prayed and said, "Lord, please, open his eyes so that he may see." And the Lord opened the servant's eyes, and he saw; and behold, the mountain was full of ^horses and chariots of fire all around Elisha. ¹⁸And when they came down to him, Elisha prayed to the Lord and said, "Please strike this people with blindness." So He ^struck them with blindness in accordance with the word of Elisha. ¹⁹Then Elisha said to them, "This is not the way, nor is this the city; follow me and I will bring you to the man whom you seek." And he brought them to Samaria.

²⁰When they had come into Samaria, Elisha said, "^Lord, open the eyes of these *men*, so that they may see." So the Lord opened their eyes, and they saw; and behold, *they were* in the midst of Samaria. ²¹Then the king of Israel when he saw them, said to Elisha, "^My father, shall I kill them? Shall I kill them?" ²²But he answered, "You shall not kill *them*. Would you kill those whom you have taken captive with your sword and your bow? ^Set bread and water before them, so that they may eat and drink, and go to their master." ²³So he provided a large feast for them; and when they had eaten and drunk, he sent them away, and they went to their master. And ^the marauding bands of Arameans did not come again into the land of Israel.

THE SIEGE OF SAMARIA— CANNIBALISM

²⁴Now it came about after this, that ^Ben-hadad the king of Aram gathered all his army, and went up and besieged Samaria. ²⁵So there was a severe ^famine in Samaria; and

behold, they kept besieging it until a donkey's head was *sold* for eighty *shekels* of silver, and a fourth of a ¹kab of dove's dung for five *shekels* of silver. ²⁶And as the king of Israel was passing by on the wall, a woman cried out to him, saying, "Help, my lord the king!" ²⁷But he said, "If the Lord does not help you, from where am I to help you? From the threshing floor, or from the wine press?" ²⁸Then the king said to her, "^What is on your mind?" And she said, "This woman said to me, 'Give your son so that we may eat him today, and we will eat my son tomorrow.' ²⁹^So we cooked my son and ate him; and I said to her on the next day, 'Give your son, so that we may eat him'; but she has hidden her son." ³⁰When the king heard the woman's words, ^he tore his clothes—and he was passing by on the wall—and the people looked, and behold, *he had* sackcloth underneath on his body. ³¹Then he said, "May ^God do so to me and more so, if the head of Elisha the son of Shaphat remains on him today."

³²Now Elisha was sitting in his house, and ^the elders were sitting with him. And *the king* sent a man from his presence; but before the messenger came to him, he said to the elders, "Do you ^see how this son of a murderer has sent *a man* to cut off my head? Look, when the messenger comes, shut the door and hold the door shut against him. Is the sound of his master's

6:17^Ps 68:17; Zech 6:1-7   6:18^Gen 19:11
6:20^2 Kin 6:17   6:21^2 Kin 2:12; 8:9   6:22^Rom 12:20
6:23^2 Kin 5:2; 24:2   6:24^1 Kin 20:1   6:25^Lev 26:26
6:28^Judg 18:23   6:29^Lev 26:27-29; Lam 4:10
6:30^1 Kin 21:27   6:31^Ruth 1:17; 1 Kin 19:2
6:32^Ezek 8:1   ^B1 Kin 18:4, 13, 14

6:25¹One kab equals about 2 qt. or 1.9 liters

feet not behind him?" ³³While he was still talking with them, behold, the messenger came down to him and he said, "ᴬBehold, this evil is from the Lᴏʀᴅ; why should I wait for the Lᴏʀᴅ any longer?"

ELISHA PROMISES FOOD

7 Then Elisha said, "Listen to the word of the Lᴏʀᴅ; this is what the Lᴏʀᴅ says: 'ᴬAbout this time tomorrow a measure of fine flour *will be sold* for a shekel, and two measures of barley for a shekel, at the gate of Samaria.'" ²The royal officer on whose hand the king was leaning responded to the man of God and said, "ᴬEven if the Lᴏʀᴅ were to make windows in heaven, could this thing happen?" Then he said, "Behold, you are going to see it with your own eyes, but you will not eat any of it."

FOUR MEN WITH LEPROSY REPORT
ARAMEANS' FLIGHT

³Now there were four ᴬleprous men at the entrance of the gate; and they said to one another, "Why are we sitting here until we die? ⁴If we say, 'We will enter the city,' then the famine is in the city and we will die there; but if we sit here, we will also die. Now then come, and let's go over to ᴬthe camp of the Arameans. If they spare us, we will live; and if they kill us, then we will die." ⁵So they got up at twilight to go to the camp of the Arameans; when they came to the outskirts of the camp of the Arameans, behold, there was no one there. ⁶For the Lord had made the army of the Arameans hear a sound of chariots, a sound of horses, *that is,* the sound of a great army; and they said to one another, "Behold, the king of Israel has hired

ᴬthe kings of the Hittites and ᴮthe kings of the Egyptians against us, to attack us!" ⁷So they ᴬgot up and fled at twilight, and abandoned their tents, their horses, and their donkeys—*indeed* the camp *itself,* just as it was; and they fled for their lives. ⁸When these men with leprosy came to the outskirts of the camp, they entered one tent and ate and drank, and ᴬcarried from there silver, gold, and clothes, and they went and hid *them;* then they returned and entered another tent, and carried *valuables* from there *also,* and went and hid *them.*

⁹Then they said to one another, "We are not doing the right thing. This day is a day of good news, but we are keeping silent *about it;* if we wait until the morning light, punishment will overtake us. Now then come, let's go and inform the king's household." ¹⁰So they came and called to the gatekeepers of the city, and told them, saying, "We came to the camp of the Arameans, and behold, there was no one there, nor a human voice; only the horses tied and the donkeys tied, and the tents just as they were." ¹¹And the gatekeepers called and announced *it* inside the king's house. ¹²Then the king got up in the night and said to his servants, "I will now tell you what the Arameans have done to us. They know that we are hungry; so they have left the camp ᴬto hide themselves in the field, saying, 'When they come out of the city, we will capture them alive and get into the city.'" ¹³One of his servants responded and said, "Please, have

some *men* take five of the horses that remain, which are left in the city. Behold, they *will be in any case* like all the multitude of Israel who are left in it; behold, they *will be* like all the multitude of Israel who have *already* perished, so let us send *them* and see." [14] Therefore they took two chariots with horses, and the king sent *them* after the army of the Arameans, saying, "Go and see."

THE PROMISE FULFILLED

[15] They went after them to the Jordan, and behold, all the way was full of clothes and equipment which the Arameans had thrown away when they fled in a hurry. Then the messengers returned and informed the king.

[16] So the people went out and plundered the camp of the Arameans. Then a measure of fine flour *was sold* for a shekel, and two measures of barley for a shekel, [A]in accordance with the word of the LORD. [17] Now the king appointed the royal officer on whose hand he leaned to be in charge of the gate; but the people trampled on him at the gate, and he died, just as the man of God had said, [A]who spoke when the king came down to him. [18] So it happened just as the man of God had spoken to the king, saying, "[A]Two measures of barley for a shekel and a measure of fine flour for a shekel, will be *sold* about this time tomorrow at the gate of Samaria." [19] *At that time* the royal officer had responded to the man of God and said, "Now even if [A]the LORD were to make windows in heaven, could such a thing as this happen?" And he had said, "Behold, you are going to see it with your

own eyes, but you will not eat any of it." [20] And this is what happened to him, for the people trampled on him at the gate and he died.

JEHORAM RESTORES THE SHUNAMMITE'S LAND

8 Now Elisha spoke to the woman whose son he had restored to life, saying, "Arise and go with your household, and live wherever you can live; for the [A]LORD has called for a famine, and [B]it will indeed come on the land for seven years." [2] So the woman arose and acted in accordance with the word of the man of God: she went with her household and resided in the land of the Philistines for seven years. [3] Then at the end of seven years, the woman returned from the land of the Philistines; and she went to appeal to the king for her house and for her field. [4] Now the king was speaking with [A]Gehazi, the servant of the man of God, saying, "Please report to me all the great things that Elisha has done." [5] And as he was reporting to the king [A]how he had restored to life the one who was dead, behold, the woman whose son he had restored to life appealed to the king for her house and for her field. And Gehazi said, "My lord the king, this is the woman and this is her son, whom Elisha restored to life." [6] When the king asked the woman, she told *everything* to him. So the king appointed an officer for her, saying, "Restore all that was hers and all the produce of the field from the day that she left the land even until now."

7:16 [A]2 Kin 7:1   7:17 [A]2 Kin 6:32   7:18 [A]2 Kin 7:1
7:19 [A]2 Kin 7:2   8:1 [A]Ps 105:16   [B]Gen 41:27, 54
8:4 [A]2 Kin 4:12; 5:20-27   8:5 [A]2 Kin 4:35

ELISHA PREDICTS EVIL FROM HAZAEL

⁷Then Elisha came to Damascus. Now ᴬBen-hadad, the king of Aram, was sick, and it was told to him, saying, "ᴮThe man of God has come here." ⁸And the king said to Hazael, "ᴬTake a gift in your hand and go to meet the man of God, and ᴮinquire of the LORD by him, saying, 'Will I recover from this sickness?'" ⁹So Hazael went to meet him and took a gift in his hand, even every kind of good thing of Damascus, forty camels' loads; and he came and stood before him and said, "ᴬYour son Ben-hadad king of Aram has sent me to you, saying, 'Will I recover from this sickness?'" ¹⁰Then Elisha said to him, "ᴬGo, say to him, 'You will certainly recover'; but the LORD has shown me that he will certainly die." ¹¹And he stared steadily *at him* ᴬuntil *Hazael* was embarrassed, and *then* ᴮthe man of God wept. ¹²And Hazael said, "Why is my lord weeping?" And he answered, "Because I know the evil that you will do to the sons of Israel: you will set their fortified cities on fire, you will kill their young men with the sword, their little ones you ᴬwill smash to pieces, and you will rip up their pregnant women." ¹³Then Hazael said, "But what is your servant—a *lowly* dog—that he could do this great thing?" And Elisha answered, "ᴬThe LORD has shown me that you *will be* king over Aram." ¹⁴So he left Elisha and came to his master, who said to him, "What did Elisha say to you?" And he answered, "He told me that ᴬyou would certainly recover." ¹⁵But on the following day, he took the ¹cover and dipped it in water, and spread it over his face, ᴬso that he died. And Hazael became king in his place.

ANOTHER JEHORAM REIGNS IN JUDAH

¹⁶Now in the fifth year of ᴬJoram the son of Ahab king of Israel, when Jehoshaphat was the king of Judah, Jehoram the son of Jehoshaphat king of Judah became king. ¹⁷He was ᴬthirty-two years old when he became king, and he reigned for eight years in Jerusalem. ¹⁸He walked in the way of the kings of Israel, just as the house of Ahab had done, for ᴬAhab's daughter was his wife; and he did evil in the sight of the LORD. ¹⁹However, the LORD did not want to destroy Judah, for the sake of David His servant, ᴬsince He had promised him to give him a ¹lamp through his sons always.

²⁰In his days ᴬEdom broke away from the rule of Judah, and appointed a king over themselves. ²¹Then Joram crossed over to Zair, and all his chariots with him. And he got up at night and struck the Edomites who had surrounded him and the captains of the chariots; ᴬbut his army fled to their tents. ²²ᴬSo Edom has broken away from Judah to this day. Then Libnah broke away at the same time. ²³Now the rest of the acts of Joram and everything that he did, are they not written in the Book of the Chronicles of the Kings of Judah?

AHAZIAH SUCCEEDS JEHORAM IN JUDAH

²⁴So Joram ¹lay down with his fathers and ᴬwas buried with his fathers in

8:7 ᴬ2 Kin 6:24   ᴮ2 Kin 5:20
8:8 ᴬ1 Kin 14:3   ᴮ2 Kin 1:2   8:9 ᴬ2 Kin 5:13
8:10 ᴬ2 Kin 8:14   8:11 ᴬ2 Kin 2:17   ᴮLuke 19:41
8:12 ᴬ2 Kin 15:16; Nah 3:10   8:13 ᴬ1 Kin 19:15
8:14 ᴬ2 Kin 8:10   8:15 ᴬ2 Kin 8:10   8:16 ᴬ2 Kin 1:17; 3:1
8:17 ᴬ2 Chr 21:5-10   8:18 ᴬ2 Kin 8:27
8:19 ᴬ2 Sam 7:12-15; 1 Kin 11:36   8:20 ᴬ1 Kin 22:47;
2 Kin 3:9, 26, 27   8:21 ᴬ2 Sam 18:17; 19:8
8:22 ᴬGen 27:40   8:24 ᴬ2 Chr 21:20

8:15 ¹I.e., item of woven material   8:19 ¹I.e.,
descendant on the throne   8:24 ¹I.e., died

the city of David; and his ᴮAhaziah became king in his place.

²⁵ᴬIn the twelfth year of Joram the son of Ahab king of Israel, Ahaziah the son of Jehoram king of Judah began to reign. ²⁶ᴬAhaziah *was* twenty-two years old when he became king, and he reigned for one year in Jerusalem. And his mother's name *was* Athaliah the granddaughter of Omri king of Israel. ²⁷ᴬHe walked in the way of the house of Ahab and did evil in the sight of the Lᴏʀᴅ, like the house of Ahab, because he was a son-in-law of the house of Ahab.

²⁸Then he went with Joram the son of Ahab to war against ᴬHazael king of Aram at ᴮRamoth-gilead, and the Arameans wounded Joram. ²⁹So ᴬKing Joram returned to have himself healed in Jezreel of the wounds which the Arameans had inflicted on him at Ramah when he fought against Hazael king of Aram. Then Ahaziah the son of Jehoram king of Judah went down to see Joram the son of Ahab in Jezreel because he was sick.

JEHU REIGNS OVER ISRAEL

9 Now Elisha the prophet summoned one of ᴬthe sons of the prophets and said to him, "Get ready and ᴮtake this flask of oil in your hand, and go to Ramoth-gilead. ²When you arrive there, then look there for ᴬJehu the son of Jehoshaphat the son of Nimshi, and go in and have him get up from among his brothers, and bring him to an inner room. ³Then take the flask of oil and pour it on his head, and say, 'This is what the Lᴏʀᴅ says: "ᴬI have anointed you king over Israel."' Then open the door and flee, and do not wait."

⁴So ᴬthe young man, the servant of the prophet, went to Ramoth-gilead. ⁵When he arrived, behold, the commanders of the army were sitting, and he said, "I have a word for you, commander." And Jehu said, "For which *one* of us?" And he said, "For you, commander." ⁶He then got up and went into the house, and *the prophet's servant* poured the oil on his head and said to him, "This is what the Lᴏʀᴅ, the God of Israel says: 'ᴬI have anointed you king over the people of the Lᴏʀᴅ, over Israel. ⁷And you shall strike the house of Ahab your master, so that I may avenge ᴬthe blood of My servants the prophets, and the blood of all the servants of the Lᴏʀᴅ, at the hand of Jezebel. ⁸For the entire house of Ahab shall perish, and ᴬI will eliminate from Ahab every male person both slave and free in Israel. ⁹ᴬI will make the house of Ahab like the house of Jeroboam the son of Nebat, and ᴮlike the house of Baasha the son of Ahijah. ¹⁰ᴬThe dogs will eat Jezebel in the territory of Jezreel, and no one will bury *her*.'" Then he opened the door and fled.

¹¹Now Jehu went out to the servants of his master, and one said to him, "Is everything well? Why did this ᴬcrazy fellow come to you?" And he said to them, "You know *very well* the man and his talk." ¹²And they said, "It is a lie; tell us now." And he said, "Such and such he said to me, saying, 'This is what

8:24 ᴮ2 Chr 22:1   8:25 ᴬ2 Chr 22:1-6   8:26 ᴬ2 Chr 22:2
8:27 ᴬ2 Chr 22:3   8:28 ᴬ2 Kin 8:15   ᴮ1 Kin 22:3, 29
8:29 ᴬ2 Kin 9:15   9:1 ᴬ2 Kin 2:3   ᴮ1 Sam 10:1;
1 Kin 1:39   9:2 ᴬ1 Kin 19:16, 17; 2 Kin 9:14, 20
9:3 ᴬ2 Chr 22:7   9:4 ᴬ2 Kin 9:1   9:6 ᴬ1 Sam 2:7, 8;
2 Chr 22:7   9:7 ᴬ1 Kin 18:4; 21:15, 21, 25
9:8 ᴬ1 Kin 21:21; 2 Kin 10:17   9:9 ᴬ1 Kin 14:10, 11
ᴮ1 Kin 16:3-5, 11, 12   9:10 ᴬ1 Kin 21:23; 2 Kin 9:35, 36
9:11 ᴬJer 29:26; Hos 9:7

the LORD says: "I have anointed you king over Israel."'" [13]Then ^they hurried, and each man took his garment and put it under him on the bare steps, and ^Bblew the trumpet, saying, "Jehu is king!"

JEHU ASSASSINATES JEHORAM (JORAM)

[14]So Jehu the son of Jehoshaphat the son of Nimshi conspired against Joram. ^Now Joram with all Israel was defending Ramoth-gilead against Hazael king of Aram, [15]but ^King 'Joram had returned to Jezreel to have himself healed of the wounds which the Arameans had inflicted on him when he fought Hazael king of Aram. So Jehu said *to the other men,* "If *this* is your intent, *then* let no one escape from the city to go tell *about it* in Jezreel." [16]Then Jehu rode in a chariot and went to Jezreel, since Joram was lying there *recovering.* ^And Ahaziah the king of Judah had come down to see Joram.

[17]Now the watchman was standing on the tower in Jezreel and he saw the company of Jehu as he came, and he said, "I see a company." And 'Joram said, "Take a horseman and send him to meet them and have him ask, 'Is *your intention* peace?'" [18]So a horseman went to meet him and said, "This is what the king says: 'Is *your intention* peace?'" But Jehu said, "^How is peace any business of yours? Turn *and* follow me." And the watchman reported, "The messenger came to them, but he did not return." [19]Then he sent a second horseman, and he came to them and said, "This is what the king says: 'Is *your intention* peace?'" And Jehu answered, "How is peace

any business of yours? Turn *and* follow me." [20]And the watchman reported, "He came up to them, but he did not return; and ^the 'driving is like the driving of ^BJehu the son of Nimshi, for he drives furiously."

[21]Then Joram said, "Get ready." And they made his chariot ready. ^Then Joram king of Israel and Ahaziah king of Judah went out, each in his chariot, and they went out to meet Jehu and found him on the property of Naboth the Jezreelite. [22]When Joram saw Jehu, he said, "Is *your intention* peace, Jehu?" And he answered, "What 'peace,' ^so long as your mother Jezebel's acts of prostitution and witchcraft are so many?" [23]So Joram turned back and fled, and he said to Ahaziah, "^*There is* treachery, Ahaziah!" [24]Then ^Jehu drew his bow with his full strength and shot Joram between his arms; and the arrow went through his heart, and he sank in his chariot. [25]And *Jehu* said to Bidkar his officer, "Pick *him* up and ^throw him on the property of the field of Naboth the Jezreelite; for remember, *when* you and I were riding together after his father Ahab, that the LORD brought this pronouncement against him: [26]'^I have certainly seen yesterday the blood of Naboth and the blood of his sons,' declares the LORD, 'and I will repay you on this property,' declares the LORD. Now then, pick him up and throw him on the property, in accordance with the word of the LORD."

9:13^Matt 21:7, 8   ^B1 Kin 1:34, 39   9:14^1 Kin 22:3; 2 Kin 8:28   9:15^2 Kin 8:29   9:16^2 Kin 8:29 9:18^2 Kin 9:19, 22   9:20^2 Sam 18:27   ^B1 Kin 19:17 9:21^2 Chr 22:7   9:22^1 Kin 16:30-33; 2 Chr 21:13 9:23^2 Kin 11:14   9:24^1 Kin 22:34   9:25^1 Kin 21:1 9:26^1 Kin 21:13, 19

9:15'Heb *Jehoram*   9:17'Heb *Jehoram*   9:20'I.e., of the chariot

2 KINGS 9—10

JEHU ASSASSINATES AHAZIAH

27 ᴬWhen Ahaziah the king of Judah saw *this,* he fled by way of the garden house. But Jehu pursued him and said, "Shoot him too, in the chariot." *So they shot him* at the ascent of Gur, which is at ᴮIbleam. But he fled to Megiddo and died there. 28 ᴬThen his servants carried him in a chariot to Jerusalem, and buried him in his grave with his fathers in the city of David.

29 Now in ᴬthe eleventh year of Joram, the son of Ahab, Ahaziah became king over Judah.

30 When Jehu came to Jezreel, Jezebel heard *about it,* and ᴬshe put makeup on her eyes and adorned her head, and looked down through the window. 31 As Jehu entered the gate, she said, "ᴬIs *your intention* peace, Zimri, his master's murderer?" 32 Then he raised his face toward the window and said, "Who is with me, who?" And two *or* three officials looked down at him.

JEZEBEL IS KILLED

33 Then he said, "Throw her down." So they threw her down, and some of her blood spattered on the wall and on the horses, and he trampled her underfoot. 34 When he came in, he ate and drank; and he said, "See now to ᴬthis cursed woman and bury her, for ᴮshe is a king's daughter." 35 So they went to bury her, but they found nothing of her except the skull, the feet, and the palms of her hands. 36 Therefore they returned and informed him. And he said, "This is the word of the LORD, which He spoke by His servant Elijah the Tishbite, saying, 'ᴬOn the property of Jezreel the dogs shall eat the flesh of Jezebel; 37 and ᴬthe corpse of Jezebel will be like dung on the face of the field in the property of Jezreel, so they cannot say, "This is Jezebel."'"

JUDGMENT UPON AHAB'S HOUSE

10 Now Ahab had seventy sons in ᴬSamaria. And Jehu wrote letters and sent *them* to Samaria, to the officials of Jezreel, the elders, and to the guardians of *the children of* Ahab, saying, 2 "And now, ᴬwhen this letter comes to you, since your master's sons are with you, as well as the chariots and horses, and a fortified city and the weapons, 3 select the best and most capable of your master's sons and seat *him* on his father's throne, and fight for your master's house." 4 But they feared greatly and said, "Behold, ᴬthe two kings did not stand *firm* before him; how then can we stand?" 5 And the one who *was* in charge of the household, and the one who *was* in charge of the city, and the elders, and the guardians of *the children,* sent *word* to Jehu, saying, "ᴬWe are your servants, and everything that you tell us we will do. We will not appoint any man king; do what is good in your sight." 6 Then he wrote them a letter a second time, saying, "If you are on my side, and will listen to my voice, take the heads of the men, your master's sons, and come to me at Jezreel about this time tomorrow." Now the king's sons, seventy men, *were* with the great people of the city, *who* were raising them. 7 When the letter came to them, they took the king's sons and ᴬslaughtered

9:27ᴬ2 Chr 22:7, 9   ᴮJosh 17:11   9:28ᴬ2 Kin 23:30
9:29ᴬ2 Kin 8:25   9:30ᴬJer 4:30; Ezek 23:40
9:31ᴬ1 Kin 16:9–20; 2 Kin 9:18–22   9:34ᴬ1 Kin 21:25
ᴮ1 Kin 16:31   9:36ᴬ1 Kin 21:23   9:37ᴬJer 8:1–3
10:1ᴬ1 Kin 16:24–29   10:2ᴬ2 Kin 5:6
10:4ᴬ2 Kin 9:24, 27   10:5ᴬJosh 9:8, 11; 1 Kin 20:4, 32
10:7ᴬJudg 9:5; 2 Kin 11:1

them, seventy men, and put their heads in baskets, and sent them to him at Jezreel. ⁸When the messenger came and informed him, saying, "They have brought the heads of the king's sons," he said, "Put them in two heaps at the entrance of the gate until morning." ⁹Now in the morning he went out and stood and said to all the people, "You are innocent; behold, ᴬI conspired against my master and killed him, but who killed all these? ¹⁰Know then that ᴬnothing of the word of the LORD, which the LORD spoke concerning the house of Ahab, shall ¹fall to the earth, for the LORD has done ᴮwhat He spoke through His servant Elijah." ¹¹So Jehu killed all who remained of the house of Ahab in ᴬJezreel, and all his great men, his acquaintances, and his priests, until he left him without a survivor.

¹²Then he set out and went to Samaria. On the way while he was at ¹Beth-eked of the shepherds, ¹³ᴬJehu encountered the relatives of Ahaziah king of Judah, and he said, "Who are you?" And they answered, "We are the relatives of Ahaziah; and we have come down to greet the sons of the king and the sons of the queen mother." ¹⁴Then he said, "Take them alive." So they took them alive, and slaughtered them at the pit of Beth-eked, forty-two men; and he left none of them.

¹⁵Now when he had gone from there, he encountered ᴬJehonadab the son of ᴮRechab coming to meet him; and he greeted him and said to him, "Is your heart right, just as my heart is with your heart?" And Jehonadab answered, "It is." Jehu said, "If it is, give me your hand." And he gave him his hand, and he pulled him up to him into the chariot. ¹⁶Then he said, "Come with me and ᴬsee my zeal for the LORD." So he had him ride in his chariot. ¹⁷When he came to Samaria, ᴬhe killed all who remained to Ahab in Samaria, until he had eliminated them, ᴮin accordance with the word of the LORD which He spoke to Elijah.

JEHU DESTROYS BAAL WORSHIPERS

¹⁸Then Jehu gathered all the people and said to them, "ᴬAhab served Baal a little; Jehu will serve him much. ¹⁹Now, ᴬsummon to me all the prophets of Baal, all his worshipers and all his priests; let no one go missing, because I have a great sacrifice for Baal; whoever is missing shall not live." But Jehu did it in deception, in order to eliminate the worshipers of Baal. ²⁰And Jehu said, "ᴬProclaim a holy assembly for Baal." And ᴮthey proclaimed it. ²¹Then Jehu sent word throughout Israel, and all the worshipers of Baal came, so that there was not a person left who did not come. And when they entered ᴬthe house of Baal, the house of Baal was filled from one end to the other. ²²And he said to the one who was in charge of the wardrobe, "Bring out garments for all the worshipers of Baal." So he brought out the garments for them. ²³Then Jehu entered the house of Baal with Jehonadab the son of Rechab; and he said to the worshipers of Baal, "Search carefully and see to it that there is here with you

10:9ᴬ2 Kin 9:14-24   10:10ᴬ2 Kin 9:7-10   ᴮ1 Kin 21:19-29   10:11ᴬHos 1:4   10:13ᴬ2 Kin 8:24, 29; 2 Chr 21:17   10:15ᴬJer 35:6-19   ᴮ1 Chr 2:55   10:16ᴬ1 Kin 19:10   10:17ᴬ2 Kin 9:8   ᴮ2 Kin 10:10   10:18ᴬ1 Kin 16:31, 32   10:19ᴬ1 Kin 18:19; 22:6   10:20ᴬJoel 1:14   ᴮEx 32:4-6   10:21ᴬ1 Kin 16:32; 2 Kin 11:18

10:10¹I.e., fail to come true   10:12¹I.e., house of binding

none of the servants of the LORD, but only the worshipers of Baal." 24Then they entered to offer sacrifices and burnt offerings.

Now Jehu had stationed for himself eighty men outside, and he had said, "AThe one who allows any of the men whom I bring into your hands to escape shall give up his life in exchange."

25Then it came about, as soon as he had finished offering the burnt offering, that Jehu said to the guard and to the royal officers, "AGo in, kill them; let none come out." So they killed them with the edge of the sword; and the guard and the royal officers threw *them* out, and went to the sanctuary of the house of Baal. 26They brought out the Amemorial stones of the house of Baal and burned them. 27They also tore down the memorial stone of Baal and tore down the house of Baal, and Amade it a latrine *as it is* to this day.

28So Jehu eradicated Baal from Israel. 29However, A*as for* the sins of Jeroboam the son of Nebat, into which he misled Israel, from these Jehu did not desist, *including* the golden calves that *were* at Bethel and at Dan. 30Yet the LORD said to Jehu, "Because you have done well in performing what is right in My eyes, *and* have done to the house of Ahab in accordance with everything that *was* in My heart, Ayour sons to the fourth *generation* shall sit on the throne of Israel." 31But Jehu Awas not careful to walk in the Law of the LORD, the God of Israel, with all his heart; he did not desist from the sins of Jeroboam, into which he misled Israel.

32In those days the ALORD began to cut off *pieces* from Israel; and

Hazael defeated *them* throughout the territory of Israel: 33from the Jordan eastward, all the land of Gilead, the Gadites, the Reubenites, and the Manassites; from AAroer, which is by the Valley of the Arnon, that is, BGilead and Bashan.

JEHOAHAZ SUCCEEDS JEHU

34Now *as for* the rest of the acts of Jehu and everything that he did and all his might, are they not written in the Book of the Chronicles of the Kings of Israel? 35And Jehu 1lay down with his fathers, and they buried him in Samaria. And his son Jehoahaz became king in his place. 36So the time which Jehu reigned over Israel in Samaria *was* twenty-eight years.

ATHALIAH QUEEN OF JUDAH

11 AWhen Athaliah the mother of Ahaziah saw that her son was dead, she arose and eliminated all the royal children. 2But Jehosheba, the daughter of King Joram, sister of Ahaziah, Atook Joash the son of Ahaziah and abducted him from among the king's sons who were being put to death, *and put* him and his nurse in the bedroom. So they hid him from Athaliah, and he was not put to death. 3So he was kept hidden with her in the house of the LORD for six years, while Athaliah was reigning over the land.

4ANow in the seventh year Jehoiada sent *orders* and brought the captains of hundreds of Bthe Carites and of the guards, and

---

10:24A1 Kin 20:30-42   **10:25**A1 Kin 18:40
10:26A1 Kin 14:23; 2 Kin 3:2   **10:27**AEzra 6:11; Dan 2:5
10:29A1 Kin 12:28-30; 13:33, 34   **10:30**A2 Kin 15:12
10:31AProv 4:23   **10:32**A2 Kin 13:25; 14:25
10:33ADeut 2:36   BAmos 1:3-5   **11:1**A2 Chr 22:10-12
11:2A2 Kin 11:21; 12:1   **11:4**A2 Chr 23:1-21   B2 Sam 20:23

10:351 I.e., died

brought them to himself at the house of the LORD. Then he made a covenant with them and put them under oath at the house of the LORD, and showed them the king's son. ⁵And he commanded them, saying, "This is the thing that you shall do: ᴬa third of you, who come in on the Sabbath and keep watch over the king's house ⁶(a third also *shall be* at the gate Sur, and a third at the gate behind the guards), shall keep watch over the house for defense. ⁷And two parts of you, all who go out on the Sabbath, shall also keep watch over the house of the LORD for the king. ⁸Then you shall surround the king, each with his weapons in his hand; and whoever comes within the ranks shall be put to death. And ᴬyou are to be with the king when he goes out and when he comes in."

⁹So the captains of hundreds ᴬacted in accordance with everything that Jehoiada the priest commanded. And each one of them took his men who were to come in on the Sabbath, along with those who were to go out on the Sabbath, and they came to Jehoiada the priest. ¹⁰Then ᴬthe priest gave the captains of hundreds the spears and shields that *had been* King David's, which *were* in the house of the LORD. ¹¹The guards stood, each with his weapons in his hand, from the right side of the house to the left side of the house, by the altar and by the house, around the king. ¹²Then he brought the king's son out, and ᴬput the crown on him and *gave him* ᴮthe testimony; and they made him king and anointed him, and they clapped their hands and said, "*Long* live the king!"

¹³ᴬWhen Athaliah heard the noise of the guards *and of* the people, she came to the people at the house of the LORD. ¹⁴And she looked, and behold, the king was standing ᴬby the pillar according to the custom, with the captains and the trumpeters beside the king; and all the people of the land were joyful and were blowing trumpets. Then Athaliah ᴮtore her clothes and cried out, "Conspiracy! Conspiracy!" ¹⁵And Jehoiada the priest commanded the captains of hundreds who were appointed over the army and said to them, "Bring her out between the ranks, and whoever follows her, put to death with the sword!" For the priest said, "She is not to be put to death at the house of the LORD." ¹⁶So they seized her, and when they brought her to the horses' entrance of the king's house, she was ᴬput to death there.

¹⁷Then ᴬJehoiada made a covenant between the LORD, the king, and the people, that they would be the LORD's people, and between the king and the people. ¹⁸And all the people of the land came to ᴬthe house of Baal and tore it down; they thoroughly smashed his altars and his images in pieces, and they killed Mattan the priest of Baal before the altars. Then the priest appointed sentries over the house of the LORD. ¹⁹And he took the captains of hundreds and the ᴬCarites, and the guards and all the people of the land; and they brought the king down from the house of the LORD, and came by way of the gate of the

11:5ᴬ1 Chr 9:25   11:8ᴬNum 27:16, 17
11:9ᴬ2 Chr 23:8   11:10ᴬ2 Sam 8:7; 1 Chr 18:7
11:12ᴬ2 Sam 1:10   ᴮEx 25:16   11:13ᴬ2 Chr 23:12
11:14ᴬ2 Kin 23:3   ᴮGen 37:29   11:16ᴬGen 9:6;
Lev 24:17   11:17ᴬJosh 24:25; 2 Chr 15:12-14
11:18ᴬ2 Kin 10:26, 27   11:19ᴬ2 Kin 11:4

guards to the king's house. And he sat on the throne of the kings. [20]So ^all the people of the land rejoiced and the city was peaceful. For they had put Athaliah to death with the sword at the king's house.

[21,A]Jehoash was seven years old when he became king.

JEHOASH (JOASH) REIGNS OVER JUDAH

12 In the seventh year of Jehu, [1,A]Jehoash became king, and he reigned for forty years in Jerusalem; and his mother's name was Zibiah of Beersheba. [2]Jehoash did what was right in the sight of the LORD all his days that Jehoiada the priest instructed him. [3]Only ^the high places did not end; the people still sacrificed and burned incense on the high places.

THE TEMPLE TO BE REPAIRED

[4]Then Jehoash said to the priests, "All the money of the sacred offerings ^which is brought into the house of the LORD, in current money, *both* [B]the money of each man's assessment *and* all the money which anyone's heart prompts him to bring into the house of the LORD, [5]the priests are to take it for themselves, each from his acquaintance; and they shall repair damage to the house wherever any damage is found."

[6]But it came about that in the twenty-third year of King Jehoash, ^the priests had not repaired *any* damage to the house. [7]So King Jehoash summoned Jehoiada the priest, and the *other* priests, and said to them, "Why do you not repair damage to the house? Now then, you are not to take *any more* money from your acquaintances, but give it up for the damage to the

house." [8]The priests then agreed that they would not take *any more* money from the people, nor would they repair damage to the house.

[9]Instead, ^Jehoiada the priest took a chest and drilled a hole in its lid and put it beside the altar, on the right side as one comes into the house of the LORD; and the priests who guarded the threshold put in it all the money that was brought into the house of the LORD. [10]When they saw that there was a great *amount of* money in the chest, ^the king's scribe and the high priest went up and tied *it* up in bags, and counted the money that was found in the house of the LORD. [11]And they handed the money which was assessed over to those who did the work, who had the oversight of the house of the LORD; and they paid it out to the carpenters and the builders who worked on the house of the LORD; [12]and ^to the masons and the stonecutters, and for buying timber and cut stone to repair the damage to the house of the LORD, and for everything that was laid out for the house to repair it. [13]However ^there were not made for the house of the LORD silver cups, shears, bowls, trumpets, any receptacles of gold, or receptacles of silver from the money which was brought into the house of the LORD; [14]for they gave that to those who did the work, and with it they repaired the house of the LORD. [15]Moreover, ^they did not require

11:20 ^Prov 11:10   11:21 ^2 Chr 24:1-14
12:1 ^2 Chr 24:1   12:3 ^2 Kin 14:4; 15:35
12:4 ^2 Kin 22:4   [B]Ex 30:13-16   12:6 ^2 Chr 24:5
12:9 ^Mark 12:41; Luke 21:1   12:10 ^2 Sam 8:17;
2 Kin 22:3, 4, 12   12:12 ^2 Kin 22:5, 6
12:13 ^2 Chr 24:14   12:15 ^2 Kin 22:7; 2 Cor 8:20

11:21 [1]Ch 12:1 in Heb; Jehoash is another spelling of
Joash in Heb   12:1 [1]Jehoash is another spelling of
Joash in Heb

an accounting from the men into whose hands they gave the money to pay to those who did the work, because they acted faithfully. ¹⁶The money from the guilt offerings and the money from the sin offerings was not brought into the house of the LORD; ᴬit belonged to the priests.

¹⁷Then Hazael the king of Aram went up and fought against Gath and captured it, and ᴬHazael was intent on going up against Jerusalem. ¹⁸So ᴬJehoash king of Judah took all the sacred offerings that Jehoshaphat, Jehoram, and Ahaziah, his fathers, kings of Judah, had consecrated, and his own sacred offerings, and all the gold that was found among the treasuries of the house of the LORD and of the king's house, and sent *them* to Hazael king of Aram. Then he withdrew from Jerusalem.

JOASH (JEHOASH) SUCCEEDED BY AMAZIAH IN JUDAH

¹⁹Now *as for* the rest of the acts of Joash and everything that he did, are they not written in the Book of the Chronicles of the Kings of Judah? ²⁰And ᴬhis servants rose up and formed a conspiracy; and they struck and killed Joash at the house of Millo *as he was* going down to Silla. ²¹For Jozacar the son of Shimeath and Jehozabad the son of ᴬShomer, his servants, struck *him* and he died; and they buried him with his fathers in the city of David, and his son ᴮAmaziah became king in his place.

KINGS OF ISRAEL: JEHOAHAZ AND JEHOASH

13 In the twenty-third year of Joash the son of Ahaziah, king of Judah, Jehoahaz the son of Jehu became king over Israel at Samaria,

and he reigned for seventeen years. ²He did evil in the sight of the LORD, and followed the sins of Jeroboam the son of Nebat, ᴬinto which he misled Israel; he did not turn from them. ³ᴬSo the anger of the LORD was kindled against Israel, and He continually handed them over to Hazael king of Aram, and to Ben-hadad, the son of Hazael. ⁴Then ᴬJehoahaz appeased the LORD, and the LORD listened to him; for ᴮHe saw the oppression of Israel, how the king of Aram oppressed them. ⁵And the LORD gave Israel a ᴬsavior, so that they escaped from under the hand of the Arameans; and the sons of Israel lived in their tents as previously. ⁶Nevertheless they did not abandon the sins of the house of Jeroboam, into which he misled Israel; *rather,* they walked in them; and ᴬthe ¹Asherah also remained standing in Samaria. ⁷For he left to Jehoahaz no more of the army than fifty horsemen, ten chariots, and ten thousand infantry, because the king of Aram had eliminated them and ᴬmade them like the dust at threshing. ⁸Now *as for* the rest of the acts of Jehoahaz, and all that he did and his might, are they not written in the Book of the Chronicles of the Kings of Israel? ⁹And Jehoahaz ¹lay down with his fathers, and they buried him in Samaria; and his son Joash became king in his place.

¹⁰In the thirty-seventh year of Joash king of Judah, ¹Jehoash the

12:16 ᴬLev 7:7; Num 18:19   12:17 ᴬ2 Chr 24:23, 24   12:18 ᴬ1 Kin 14:26; 2 Kin 18:15, 16   12:20 ᴬ2 Chr 24:25-27   12:21 ᴬ2 Chr 24:26   ᴮ2 Kin 14:1   13:2 ᴬ1 Kin 12:26-33   13:3 ᴬJudg 2:14   13:4 ᴬNum 21:7-9   ᴮEx 3:7, 9   13:5 ᴬ2 Kin 13:25; 14:25, 27   13:6 ᴬ1 Kin 16:33   13:7 ᴬAmos 1:3

13:6 ¹I.e., wooden symbol of a female deity   13:9 ¹I.e., died   13:10 ¹In Heb Jehoash is another spelling of Joash

son of Jehoahaz became king over Israel in Samaria, *and he reigned* for sixteen years. ¹¹He did evil in the sight of the LORD; he did not turn away from all the sins of Jeroboam the son of Nebat, into which he misled Israel; *rather,* he walked in them. ¹²ᴬNow *as for* the rest of the acts of Joash and all that he did, and his might with which he fought against Amaziah king of Judah, are they not written in the Book of the Chronicles of the Kings of Israel? ¹³So Joash ¹lay down with his fathers, and Jeroboam sat on his throne; and Joash was buried in Samaria with the kings of Israel.

DEATH OF ELISHA

¹⁴When Elisha became sick with the illness of which he was to die, Joash the king of Israel came down to him, and wept over him and said, "ᴬMy father, my father, the chariots of Israel and its horsemen!" ¹⁵And Elisha said to him, "Take a bow and arrows." So he took a bow and arrows. ¹⁶Then *Elisha* said to the king of Israel, "Lay your hand on the bow." And he laid his hand *on it,* then Elisha put his hands on the king's hands. ¹⁷And he said, "Open the window toward the east," and he opened *it.* Then Elisha said, "Shoot!" So he shot. And he said, "The LORD's arrow of victory, and the arrow of victory over Aram; for you will defeat the Arameans at ᴬAphek until you have put an end *to them.*" ¹⁸Then he said, "Take the arrows," and he took *them.* And he said to the king of Israel, "Strike the ground," and he struck *it* three times and stopped. ¹⁹Then ᴬthe man of God became angry at him and said, "You should have struck five or six times, then you would

have struck Aram until you put an end *to it.* But now you shall strike Aram *only* three times."

²⁰And Elisha died, and they buried him. Now ᴬthe marauding bands of the Moabites would invade the land in the spring of the year. ²¹And as they were burying a man, behold, they saw a marauding band; and they threw the man into the grave of Elisha. And when the man touched the bones of Elisha he ᴬrevived and stood up on his feet.

²²Now ᴬHazael king of Aram had oppressed Israel all the days of Jehoahaz. ²³But the ᴬLORD was gracious to them and ᴮhad compassion on them and turned to them because of His covenant with Abraham, Isaac, and Jacob; and He was unwilling to eliminate them or cast them away from His presence until now.

²⁴When Hazael king of Aram died, his son Ben-hadad became king in his place. ²⁵Then Jehoash the son of Jehoahaz again took from the hand of Ben-hadad the son of Hazael the cities which he had taken in war from the hand of his father Jehoahaz. ᴬThree times Joash defeated him and recovered the cities of Israel.

AMAZIAH REIGNS OVER JUDAH

14 ᴬIn the second year of Joash son of Joahaz king of Israel, ᴮAmaziah the son of Joash king of Judah became king. ²He was twenty-five years old when he became king, and he reigned for twenty-nine years in Jerusalem. And his mother's name was

---

13:12 ᴬ2 Kin 13:14-19; 14:8-15　13:14 ᴬ2 Kin 2:12
13:17 ᴬ1 Kin 20:26　13:19 ᴬ2 Kin 5:20　13:20 ᴬ2 Kin 3:7;
24:2　13:21 ᴬMatt 27:52　13:22 ᴬ2 Kin 8:12, 13
13:23 ᴬ2 Kin 14:27　ᴮ1 Kin 8:22　13:25 ᴬ2 Kin 13:18, 19
14:1 ᴬ2 Chr 25:1　ᴮ2 Kin 13:10

13:13 ¹I.e., died

Jehoaddin of Jerusalem. ³He did what was right in the sight of the LORD, yet not like his father David; he acted in accordance with everything that his father Joash had done. ⁴Only ^the high places were not eliminated; the people still sacrificed and burned incense on the high places. ⁵Now it came about, as soon as the kingdom was firmly in his hand, that he ^killed his servants who had killed the king, his father. ⁶But he did not put the sons of the murderers to death, in obedience to what is written in the Book of the Law of Moses, as the LORD commanded, saying, "^The fathers shall not be put to death for the sons, nor the sons be put to death for the fathers; but each shall be put to death for his own sin."

⁷He killed ten thousand *of* the Edomites in the Valley of Salt, and took ^Sela by war, and named it ᴮJoktheel, *as it is* to this day.

⁸^Then Amaziah sent messengers to ʲJehoash, the son of Jehoahaz son of Jehu, king of Israel, saying, "Come, let's face each other *in combat.*" ⁹But Jehoash king of Israel sent *messengers* to Amaziah king of Judah, saying, "^The thorn bush that was in Lebanon sent *word* to the cedar that was in Lebanon, saying, 'Give your daughter to my son in marriage.' But a wild animal that was in Lebanon passed by and trampled the thorn bush. ¹⁰^You have indeed defeated Edom, and your heart is elated. Enjoy the glory and stay home; for why should you get involved in trouble so that you would fall, you and Judah with you?"

¹¹But Amaziah would not listen. So Jehoash king of Israel went up; and they faced each other, he and Amaziah king of Judah, at

^Beth-shemesh, which belongs to Judah. ¹²And Judah was defeated by Israel, and ^they fled, every man to his tent. ¹³Then Jehoash king of Israel captured Amaziah king of Judah, the son of Jehoash the son of Ahaziah, at Beth-shemesh, and came to Jerusalem and tore down the wall of Jerusalem from ^the Gate of Ephraim to ᴮthe Corner Gate, ˡfour hundred cubits. ¹⁴And ^he took all the gold and silver and all the utensils which were found in the house of the LORD, and in the treasuries of the king's house, the hostages as well, and returned to Samaria.

JEROBOAM II SUCCEEDS JEHOASH (JOASH) IN ISRAEL

¹⁵^Now *as for* the rest of the acts of Jehoash that he did, and his might and how he fought with Amaziah king of Judah, are they not written in the Book of the Chronicles of the Kings of Israel? ¹⁶So Jehoash ˡlay down with his fathers and was buried in Samaria with the kings of Israel; and his son Jeroboam became king in his place.

AZARIAH (UZZIAH) SUCCEEDS AMAZIAH IN JUDAH

¹⁷^Amaziah the son of Joash king of Judah lived for fifteen years after the death of Jehoash son of Jehoahaz king of Israel. ¹⁸Now *as for* the rest of the acts of Amaziah, are they not written in the Book of the Chronicles of the Kings of Judah? ¹⁹They formed a conspiracy against

14:4 ^2 Kin 12:3   14:5 ^2 Kin 12:20   14:6 ^Deut 24:16
14:7 ^Is 16:1   ᴮJosh 15:38   14:8 ^2 Chr 25:17-24
14:9 ^Judg 9:8-15   14:10 ^2 Kin 14:7   14:11 ^Josh 19:38
14:12 ^2 Sam 18:17   14:13 ^Neh 8:16   ᴮ2 Chr 25:23
14:14 ^1 Kin 14:26; 2 Kin 12:18   14:15 ^2 Kin 13:12, 13
14:17 ^2 Chr 25:25-28

14:8 ˡIn Heb Jehoash is another spelling of Joash   14:13 ˡAbout 600 ft. or 183 m   14:16 ˡI.e., died

him in Jerusalem, and he fled to ^La-chish; but they sent *men* to Lachish after him and they killed him there. ²⁰Then they carried him on horses, and he was buried in Jerusalem with his fathers in the city of David. ²¹And all the people of Judah took Azariah, who *was* sixteen years old, and made him king in place of his father Amaziah. ²²^He built Elath and restored it to Judah after the king ¹lay down with his fathers.

²³In the fifteenth year of Ama-ziah the son of Joash king of Judah, Jeroboam the son of Joash king of Israel became king in Samaria, *and reigned* for forty-one years. ²⁴He did evil in the sight of the Lord; he did not abandon all the sins of Jeroboam the son of Nebat, into which he misled Israel. ²⁵He restored the border of Israel from the entrance of Hamath as far as the Sea of the Arabah, in accor-dance with the word of the Lord, the God of Israel, which He spoke through His servant ^Jonah the son of Amittai, the prophet, who was from ᴮGath-hepher. ²⁶For the ^Lord saw the misery of Israel, *which was* very bitter; for there was neither bond nor free *spared,* nor was there any helper for Israel. ²⁷Yet the ^Lord did not say that He would wipe out the name of Israel from under heaven, but He saved them by the hand of Jeroboam the son of Joash.

ZECHARIAH REIGNS OVER ISRAEL

²⁸Now *as for* the rest of the acts of Jeroboam and all that he did and his might, how he fought and how he recovered for Israel ^Damascus and ᴮHamath, *which had belonged* to Judah, are they not written in the Book of the Chronicles of the Kings of Israel? ²⁹And Jeroboam

¹lay down with his fathers, with the kings of Israel, and his son Zecha-riah became king in his place.

SERIES OF KINGS: AZARIAH (UZZIAH) OVER JUDAH

15 ^In the twenty-seventh year of Jeroboam king of Israel, Azariah son of Amaziah king of Judah became king. ²He was ^six-teen years old when he became king, and he reigned for fifty-two years in Jerusalem; and his moth-er's name was Jecoliah of Jerusalem. ³He did what was right in the sight of the Lord, in accordance with everything that his father Amaziah had done. ⁴Only ^the high places were not eliminated; the people still sacrificed and burned incense on the high places. ⁵^And the Lord afflicted the king, so that he had leprosy to the day of his death. And he lived in a separate house, while Jotham the king's son was in charge of the household, judging the peo-ple of the land. ⁶Now *as for* the rest of the acts of Azariah and all that he did, are they not written in the Book of the Chronicles of the Kings of Judah? ⁷And Azariah ¹lay down with his fathers, and they buried him with his fathers in the city of David, and his son Jotham became king in his place.

ZECHARIAH OVER ISRAEL

⁸^In the thirty-eighth year of Aza-riah king of Judah, Zechariah the son of Jeroboam became king over Israel in Samaria for six months.

14:19^Josh 10:31; 2 Kin 18:14, 17 14:22^1 Kin 9:26; 2 Chr 8:17 14:25^Matt 12:39, 40 ᴮJosh 19:13
14:26^2 Kin 13:4 14:27^2 Kin 13:23
14:28^1 Kin 11:24 ᴮ2 Chr 8:3 15:1^2 Kin 14:17
15:2^2 Chr 26:3, 4 15:4^2 Kin 12:3
15:5^2 Chr 26:21-23 15:8^2 Kin 15:1

14:22 ¹I.e., died 14:29 ¹I.e., died 15:7 ¹I.e., died

⁹He did evil in the sight of the LORD, just as his fathers had done; he did not desist from the sins of Jeroboam the son of Nebat, into which he misled Israel. ¹⁰Then Shallum the son of Jabesh conspired against him, and ^struck him in the presence of the people and killed him, and reigned in his place. ¹¹Now *as for* the rest of the acts of Zechariah, behold they are written in the Book of the Chronicles of the Kings of Israel. ¹²This is ^the word of the LORD which He spoke to Jehu, saying, "Your sons *to* the fourth *generation* shall sit on the throne of Israel." And so it was.

¹³Shallum the son of Jabesh became king in the thirty-ninth year of Uzziah king of Judah, and he reigned for one month in ^Samaria. ¹⁴Then Menahem the son of Gadi went up from ^Tirzah and came to Samaria, and struck Shallum son of Jabesh in Samaria, and killed him and became king in his place. ¹⁵Now *as for* the rest of the acts of Shallum and his conspiracy which he formed, behold, they are written in the Book of the Chronicles of the Kings of Israel. ¹⁶Then Menahem attacked Tiphsah and all who were in it and its borders from Tirzah, because they did not open up *to him;* so he attacked *it* and ripped up ^all its women who were pregnant.

MENAHEM OVER ISRAEL

¹⁷In the ^thirty-ninth year of Azariah king of Judah, Menahem the son of Gadi became king over Israel *and reigned* for ten years in Samaria. ¹⁸He did evil in the sight of the LORD; for all his days he did not desist from the sins of Jeroboam the son of Nebat, into which he misled Israel.

¹⁹^Pul, the king of Assyria, came against the land, and Menahem gave Pul a ¹thousand talents of silver so that his hand might be with him to strengthen the kingdom under his rule. ²⁰Then Menahem collected the money from Israel, from all the ¹mighty men of wealth, from each man fifty shekels of silver to pay the king of Assyria. So the king of Assyria returned and did not stay there in the land. ²¹Now *as for* the rest of the acts of Menahem and all that he did, are they not written in the Book of the Chronicles of the Kings of Israel? ²²And Menahem ¹lay down with his fathers, and his son Pekahiah became king in his place.

PEKAHIAH OVER ISRAEL

²³In ^the fiftieth year of Azariah king of Judah, Pekahiah the son of Menahem became king over Israel in Samaria, *and reigned* for two years. ²⁴He did evil in the sight of the LORD; he did not desist from the sins of Jeroboam son of Nebat, into which he misled Israel. ²⁵Then Pekah the son of Remaliah, his officer, conspired against him and struck him in Samaria, in ^the castle of the king's house with Argob and Arieh; and with him were fifty men of the Gileadites, and he killed him and became king in his place. ²⁶Now *as for* the rest of the acts of Pekahiah and everything that he did, behold, they are written in the Book of the Chronicles of the Kings of Israel.

15:10^Amos 7:9   15:12^2 Kin 10:30
15:13^1 Kin 16:24   15:14^1 Kin 14:17
15:16^2 Kin 8:12; Hos 13:16   15:17^2 Kin 15:1, 8, 13
15:19^1 Chr 5:25, 26   15:23^2 Kin 15:1, 8, 13, 17
15:25^1 Kin 16:18

15:19¹About 38 tons or 34 metric tons   15:20¹I.e.,
landowners   15:22¹I.e., died

PEKAH OVER ISRAEL

²⁷In the fifty-second year of Azariah king of Judah, ^Pekah the son of Remaliah became king over Israel in Samaria, *and he reigned* for twenty years. ²⁸He did evil in the sight of the Lord; he did not desist from the sins of Jeroboam son of Nebat, into which he misled Israel.

²⁹In the days of Pekah king of Israel, Tiglath-pileser the king of Assyria came and took Ijon, Abelbeth-maacah, Janoah, Kedesh, Hazor, Gilead, and Galilee, all the land of Naphtali; and ^he led their populations into exile to Assyria. ³⁰And Hoshea the son of Elah formed a conspiracy against Pekah the son of Remaliah, and struck him and put him to death, and he became king in his place, in the twentieth year of Jotham the son of Uzziah. ³¹Now *as for* the rest of the acts of Pekah and all that he did, behold, they are written in the Book of the Chronicles of the Kings of Israel.

JOTHAM OVER JUDAH

³²In the second year of Pekah the son of Remaliah king of Israel, Jotham the son of Uzziah king of Judah became king. ³³^He was twenty-five years old when he became king, and he reigned for sixteen years in Jerusalem; and his mother's name *was* Jerusha the daughter of Zadok. ³⁴^He did what was right in the sight of the Lord; he acted in accordance with everything that his father Uzziah had done. ³⁵Only ^the high places were not eliminated; the people still sacrificed and burned incense on the high places. ᴮHe built the upper gate of the house of the Lord. ³⁶Now *as for* the rest of the acts of Jotham which he did, are they not written in the Book of the Chronicles of the Kings of Judah? ³⁷In those days ^the Lord began to send Rezin the king of Aram and Pekah the son of Remaliah against Judah. ³⁸And Jotham ¹lay down with his fathers, and he was buried with his fathers in the city of his father David; and his son Ahaz became king in his place.

AHAZ REIGNS OVER JUDAH

16 In the seventeenth year of Pekah the son of Remaliah, ^Ahaz the son of Jotham, king of Judah, became king. ²^Ahaz *was* twenty years old when he became king, and he reigned for sixteen years in Jerusalem; and he did not do what was right in the sight of the Lord his God, as his father David *had done.* ³But he walked in the way of the kings of Israel, ^and he even made his son pass through the fire, in accordance with the abominations of the nations whom the Lord had driven out before the sons of Israel. ⁴And he ^sacrificed and burned incense on the high places, on the hills, and under every green tree.

⁵Then ^Rezin the king of Aram and Pekah the son of Remaliah, king of Israel, went up to Jerusalem for war; and they besieged Ahaz, ᴮbut were not capable of fighting him. ⁶At that time Rezin king of Aram restored ^Elath to Aram, and drove the Judeans away from Elath; and the Arameans came to Elath and have lived there to this day.

15:27^2 Chr 28:6; Is 7:1   15:29^2 Kin 17:6
15:33^2 Chr 27:1   15:34^2 Kin 15:3, 4; 2 Chr 26:4, 5
15:35^2 Kin 12:3   ᴮ2 Chr 23:20   15:37^2 Kin 16:5; Is 7:1
16:1^2 Chr 28:1   16:2^2 Chr 28:1-4   16:3^Lev 18:21;
2 Kin 17:17   16:4^Deut 12:2; 2 Kin 14:4   16:5^Is 7:1
ᴮ2 Chr 28:5, 6   16:6^2 Kin 14:22; 2 Chr 26:2

15:38 ¹I.e., died

AHAZ SEEKS HELP OF ASSYRIA

7 ^A So Ahaz sent messengers to Tiglath-pileser king of Assyria, saying, "I am your servant and your son; come up and save me from the hand of the king of Aram, and from the hand of the king of Israel, who are rising up against me." **8** And ^A Ahaz took the silver and gold that was found in the house of the LORD and in the treasuries of the king's house, and sent a gift to the king of Assyria. **9** So the king of Assyria listened to him; and the king of Assyria went up against Damascus and captured it, and led *the people of* it into exile to ^A Kir, and put Rezin to death.

DAMASCUS FALLS

10 Now King Ahaz went to Damascus to meet Tiglath-pileser king of Assyria, and he saw the altar which *was* at Damascus; and King Ahaz sent to ^A Urijah the priest the pattern of the altar and its model, according to all its workmanship. **11** So Urijah the priest built an altar; according to everything that King Ahaz had sent from Damascus, in that way Urijah the priest made *it,* before the coming of King Ahaz from Damascus. **12** And when the king came from Damascus, the king saw the altar; then ^A the king approached the altar and went up to it, **13** and burned his burnt offering and his meal offering, and poured out his drink offering and sprinkled the blood of his peace offerings on the altar. **14** And ^A the bronze altar, which *was* before the LORD, he brought from the front of the house, from between ^B *his* altar and the house of the LORD, and he put it on the north side of *his* altar. **15** Then King Ahaz commanded Urijah the priest, saying, "Upon the great altar burn ^A the

morning burnt offering, the evening meal offering, the king's burnt offering and his meal offering, with the burnt offering of all the people of the land, their meal offering, and their drink offerings; and sprinkle on it all the blood of the burnt offering and all the blood of the sacrifice. But ^B the bronze altar shall be for me, for making inquiries." **16** So Urijah the priest acted in accordance with everything that King Ahaz commanded.

17 Then King Ahaz cut off the borders of the stands, and removed the wash basin from them; he also ^A took down the ^1 Sea from the bronze oxen which were under it and put it on a pavement of stone. **18** And the covered way for the Sabbath which they had built in the house, and the outer entry of the king, he removed *from* the house of the LORD because of the king of Assyria.

HEZEKIAH REIGNS OVER JUDAH

19 Now *as for* the rest of the acts of Ahaz which he did, are they not written ^A in the Book of the Chronicles of the Kings of Judah? **20** So ^A Ahaz ^1 lay down with his fathers, and ^B was buried with his fathers in the city of David; and his son Hezekiah reigned in his place.

HOSHEA REIGNS OVER ISRAEL

17 In the twelfth year of Ahaz king of Judah, ^A Hoshea the son of Elah became king over Israel in Samaria, *and reigned* for nine years. **2** He did evil in the sight of the

16:7 ^A 2 Chr 28:16   16:8 ^A 2 Kin 12:17, 18; 18:15
16:9 ^A Is 22:6; Amos 9:7   16:10 ^A Is 8:2
16:12 ^A 2 Chr 26:16, 19   16:14 ^A Ex 27:1, 2   ^B 2 Kin 16:11
16:15 ^A Ex 29:39-41   ^B 2 Kin 16:14   16:17 ^A 1 Kin 7:23, 25
16:19 ^A 2 Chr 28:26   16:20 ^A Is 14:28   ^B 2 Chr 28:27
17:1 ^A 2 Kin 15:30

16:17 ^1 I.e., a very large basin   16:20 ^1 I.e., died

Lord, only not as the kings of Israel who preceded him. ³ᴬShalmaneser the king of Assyria marched against him, and Hoshea became his servant and paid him tribute. ⁴But the king of Assyria uncovered a conspiracy by Hoshea, who had sent messengers to So, king of Egypt, and had *then* brought no tribute to the king of Assyria, as *he had done* year by year; so the king of Assyria arrested him and confined him in prison.

⁵Then the king of Assyria invaded the entire land, and went up to ᴬSamaria and besieged it for three years.

ISRAEL CAPTIVE

⁶In the ninth year of Hoshea, the king of Assyria captured Samaria and led *the people of* Israel into exile to Assyria, and ᴬsettled them in Halah and Habor, *on* the river of ᴮGozan, and in the cities of the Medes.

WHY ISRAEL FELL

⁷Now ᴬ*this* came about because the sons of Israel had sinned against the Lord their God, who had brought them up from the land of Egypt, from under the hand of Pharaoh, king of Egypt; ⁸and they had feared other gods. ⁸They also ᴬfollowed the customs of the nations whom the Lord had driven out from the sons of Israel, and *in the customs* of the kings of Israel which they had introduced. ⁹And the sons of Israel did things secretly against the Lord their God which were not right. Moreover, they built for themselves high places in all their towns, from ᴬwatchtower to fortified city. ¹⁰And ᴬthey set up for themselves memorial stones and ᴵAsherim on every high hill and

under every green tree, ¹¹and there they burned incense on all the high places as the nations *did* that the Lord had taken into exile before them; and they did evil things, provoking the Lord. ¹²They served idols, ᴬconcerning which the Lord had said to them, "You shall not do this thing." ¹³Yet the ᴬLord warned Israel and Judah ᴮthrough all His prophets *and* every seer, saying, "Turn back from your evil ways and keep My commandments *and* My statutes in accordance with all the Law which I commanded your fathers, and which I sent to you through My servants the prophets." ¹⁴However, they did not listen, but ᴬstiffened their neck like their fathers, who did not believe in the Lord their God. ¹⁵They rejected His statutes and ᴬHis covenant which He made with their fathers, and His warnings which He gave them. And ᴮthey followed idols and became empty, and followed the nations that surrounded them, *about* which the Lord had commanded them not to do as they *did*. ¹⁶And they abandoned all the commandments of the Lord their God and made for themselves cast metal images: two calves. And they made an ᴵAsherah, and ᴬworshiped all the heavenly lights, and ᴮserved Baal. ¹⁷Then they made their sons and their daughters pass through the fire, and they ᴬpracticed divination and interpreting omens, and gave

17:3 ᴬHos 10:14   17:5 ᴬHos 13:16   17:6 ᴬ2 Kin 18:11
ᴮIs 37:12   17:7 ᴬJosh 23:16   ᴮJudg 6:10   17:8 ᴬLev 18:3;
Deut 18:9   17:9 ᴬ2 Kin 18:8   17:10 ᴬEx 34:12-14
17:12 ᴬEx 20:4   17:13 ᴬNeh 9:29, 30   ᴮ2 Kin 17:23
17:14 ᴬEx 32:9; Acts 7:51   17:15 ᴬEx 24:6-8
ᴮDeut 32:21   17:16 ᴬDeut 4:19   ᴮ1 Kin 16:31
17:17 ᴬLev 19:26; Deut 18:10-12

17:10 ᴵI.e., wooden symbols of a female deity (Asherah)
17:16 ᴵI.e., a wooden symbol of a female deity

themselves over to do evil in the sight of the Lord, provoking Him. ¹⁸So the Lord was very angry with Israel, and He ^removed them from His sight; no one was left except the tribe of Judah.

¹⁹^Judah did not keep the commandments of the Lord their God either, but they followed the customs which Israel had introduced. ²⁰So the Lord rejected all the descendants of Israel and afflicted them and ^handed them over to plunderers, until He had cast them out of His sight.

²¹When ^He had torn Israel from the house of David, they made Jeroboam the son of Nebat king. Then ^BJeroboam drove Israel away from following the Lord and misled them into a great sin. ²²And the sons of Israel walked in all the sins of Jeroboam which he committed; they did not desist from them ²³^until the Lord removed Israel from His sight, just as He had spoken through all His servants the prophets. ^So Israel went into exile from their own land to Assyria until this day.

CITIES OF ISRAEL FILLED WITH STRANGERS

²⁴^Then the king of Assyria brought *people* from Babylon, Cuthah, Avva, Hamath, and Sepharvaim, and settled *them* in the cities of Samaria in place of the sons of Israel. So they took possession of Samaria and lived in its cities. ²⁵And at the beginning of their living there, they ^did not fear the Lord; therefore the Lord sent lions among them that were killing some of them. ²⁶So they spoke to the king of Assyria, saying, "The nations whom you have taken into exile and settled in the cities of Samaria do not know the custom of the God of the land; so He has sent lions among them, and behold, they are killing them because they do not know the custom of the God of the land."

²⁷Then the king of Assyria issued commands, saying, "Take one of the priests there whom you led into exile, and have him go and live there; and have him teach them the custom of the God of the land." ²⁸So one of the priests whom they had led into exile from Samaria came and lived in Bethel, and taught them how they were to fear the Lord.

²⁹But every nation was *still* making gods of its own, and they put them ^in the houses of the high places which the people of Samaria had made, every nation in their cities in which they lived. ³⁰^The men of Babylon made Succoth-benoth, the men of Cuth made Nergal, the men of Hamath made Ashima, ³¹and the Avvites made Nibhaz and Tartak; and ^the Sepharvites were burning their children in the fire to ^BAdrammelech and Anammelech, the gods of Sepharvaim. ³²They also feared the Lord and ^appointed from their entire population priests of the high places, who acted for them in the houses of the high places. ³³They feared the Lord, yet they were serving their own gods in accordance with the custom of the nations from among whom they had been taken into exile.

³⁴To this day they act in accordance with the earlier customs:

17:18^2 Kin 17:6   17:19^1 Kin 14:22, 23
17:20^2 Kin 15:29   17:21^1 Kin 11:11, 31   ^B1 Kin 12:28-33   17:23^2 Kin 17:6   17:24^Ezra 4:2, 10
17:25^2 Kin 17:32-41   17:29^1 Kin 12:31; 13:32
17:30^2 Kin 17:24   17:31^2 Kin 17:17   ^B2 Kin 19:37
17:32^1 Kin 12:31

they do not fear the Lord, nor do they follow their statutes, their ordinances, the Law, or the commandments which the Lord commanded the sons of Jacob, ^whom He named Israel. ³⁵The Lord made a covenant with them and commanded them, saying, "^You shall not fear other gods, nor bow down to them, nor serve them, nor sacrifice to them. ³⁶But the Lord, ^who brought you up from the land of Egypt with great power and with an outstretched arm, ^Him you shall fear, and to Him you shall bow down, and to Him you shall sacrifice. ³⁷And the statutes, the ordinances, the Law, and the commandment which He wrote for you, ^you shall take care to do always; and you shall not fear other gods. ³⁸The covenant that I have made with you, ^you shall not forget, nor shall you fear other gods. ³⁹But you shall fear the Lord your God; and He will save you from the hand of all your enemies." ⁴⁰However, they did not listen, but they kept acting in accordance with their earlier custom. ⁴¹^So while these nations feared the Lord, they also served their idols; their children likewise and their grandchildren, just as their fathers did, they do to this day.

HEZEKIAH REIGNS OVER JUDAH

18 Now it came about in the third year of Hoshea, the son of Elah king of Israel, that ^Hezekiah the son of Ahaz king of Judah became king. ²He was ^twenty-five years old when he became king, and he reigned for twenty-nine years in Jerusalem; and his mother's name was Abi the daughter of Zechariah. ³^He did what was right in the sight of the Lord, in accordance with everything that his father David

had done. ⁴^He removed the high places and smashed the memorial stones to pieces, and cut down the ¹Asherah. He also crushed to pieces ^Bthe bronze serpent that Moses had made, for until those days the sons of Israel had been burning incense to it; and it was called ²Nehushtan. ⁵^He trusted in the Lord, the God of Israel; and ^Bafter him there was no one like him among all the kings of Judah, nor *among those* who came before him. ⁶For he ^clung to the Lord; he did not desist from following Him, but kept His commandments, which the Lord had commanded Moses.

HEZEKIAH VICTORIOUS

⁷And the Lord was with him; wherever he went he was successful. And ^he revolted against the king of Assyria and did not serve him. ⁸^He defeated the Philistines as far as Gaza and its territory, from watchtower to fortified city.

⁹Now in the fourth year of King Hezekiah, which was the seventh year of Hoshea son of Elah king of Israel, ^Shalmaneser king of Assyria marched against Samaria and besieged it. ¹⁰And at the end of three years they captured it; in the sixth year of Hezekiah, which was ^the ninth year of Hoshea king of Israel, Samaria was captured. ¹¹Then the king of Assyria led Israel into exile to Assyria, and put them in ^Halah and on the

17:34 ^Gen 32:28; 35:10   17:35 ^Judg 6:10
17:36 ^Ex 14:15-30   ^BLev 19:32   17:37 ^Deut 5:32
17:38 ^Deut 4:23; 6:12   17:41 ^Zeph 1:5; Matt 6:24
18:1 ^2 Chr 28:27   18:2 ^2 Chr 29:1, 2
18:3 ^2 Kin 20:3; 2 Chr 31:20   18:4 ^2 Kin 18:22
^BNum 21:8, 9   18:5 ^2 Kin 19:10   ^B2 Kin 23:25
18:6 ^Deut 10:20; Josh 23:8   18:7 ^2 Kin 16:7
18:8 ^2 Chr 28:18; Is 14:29   18:9 ^2 Kin 17:3-7
18:10 ^2 Kin 17:6   18:11 ^1 Chr 5:26

18:4 ¹I.e., a wooden symbol of a female deity   ²I.e., a bronze sculpture

Habor, the river of Gozan, and in the cities of the Medes. ¹²*This happened* because they ᴬdid not obey the voice of the LORD their God, but violated His covenant, all that Moses the servant of the LORD had commanded; they would neither listen nor do *it.*

INVASION OF JUDAH

¹³ᴬNow in the fourteenth year of King Hezekiah, Sennacherib king of Assyria marched against all the fortified cities of Judah and seized them. ¹⁴Then Hezekiah king of Judah sent *messengers* to the king of Assyria at Lachish, saying, "ᴬI have done wrong. Withdraw from me; whatever you impose on me I will endure." So the king of Assyria imposed on Hezekiah king of Judah *the payment of* three hundred ¹talents of silver and thirty talents of gold. ¹⁵ᴬHezekiah then gave *him* all the silver that was found in the house of the LORD, and in the treasuries of the king's house. ¹⁶At that time Hezekiah cut off *the gold from* the doors of the temple of the LORD, and *from* the doorposts, which Hezekiah king of Judah had overlaid, and he gave it to the king of Assyria.

¹⁷Then the king of Assyria sent ᴬTartan, Rab-saris, and Rabshakeh from Lachish to King Hezekiah with a large army to Jerusalem. So they went up and came to Jerusalem. And when they went up, they came and stood by the conduit of the upper pool, which is on the road of the ¹fuller's field. ¹⁸Then they called to the king, and ᴬEliakim the son of Hilkiah, who was in charge of the household, Shebnah the scribe, and Joah the son of Asaph the secretary, went out to them.

¹⁹And Rabshakeh said to them, "Say now to Hezekiah, 'This is what the great king, the king of Assyria says: "ᴬWhat is this confidence that you have? ²⁰You say—*but they are* only empty words—'*I have* a plan and strength for the war.' Now on whom have you relied, ᴬthat you have revolted against me? ²¹Now behold, you have ᴬrelied on the support of this broken reed, on Egypt; on which if a man leans, it will go into his hand and pierce it. That is how Pharaoh king of Egypt is to all who rely on him. ²²However, if you say to me, 'We have trusted in the LORD our God,' is it not He whose high places and ᴬwhose altars Hezekiah has removed, and has said to Judah and to Jerusalem, 'You shall worship before this altar in Jerusalem'? ²³Now then, come make a wager with my master the king of Assyria: I will give you two thousand horses, if you are able on your part to put riders on them! ²⁴How then can you drive back *even* one official of the least of my master's servants, and rely on Egypt for chariots and horsemen? ²⁵Have I now come up without the LORD's approval against this place to destroy it? The LORD said to me, 'Go up against this land and destroy it.'"'"

²⁶Then Eliakim the son of Hilkiah, Shebnah, and Joah, said to Rabshakeh, "Speak now to your servants in Aramaic, because we understand *it;* and do not speak with us in ¹·ᴬJudean so that the people who are on

18:12^1 Kin 9:6; Dan 9:6, 10   18:13^2 Chr 32:1;
Is 36:1-39:8   18:14^2 Kin 18:7   18:15^1 Kin 15:18, 19;
2 Kin 12:18   18:17^Is 20:1   18:18^2 Kin 19:2; Is 22:20
18:19^2 Chr 32:10   18:20^2 Kin 18:7
18:21^Is 30:2, 3, 7; Ezek 29:6, 7   18:22^2 Kin 18:4;
2 Chr 31:1   18:26^Ezra 4:7; Dan 2:4

18:14¹A talent was about 75 lb. or 34 kg   18:17¹I.e.,
launderer's   18:26¹I.e., Hebrew

the wall hear *you*." ²⁷But Rabshakeh said to them, "Has my master sent me *only* to your master and to you to speak these words? *Has he* not *also sent me* to the men who sit on the wall, *doomed* to eat their own dung and drink their own urine with you?"

²⁸Then Rabshakeh stood up and shouted with a loud voice in Judean, saying, "Hear the word of the great king, the king of Assyria! ²⁹This is what the king says: 'ᴬDo not let Hezekiah deceive you, for he will not be able to save you from my hand. ³⁰And do not let Hezekiah lead you to trust in the LORD by saying, "The LORD will certainly save us, and this city will not be handed over to the king of Assyria." ³¹Do not listen to Hezekiah, for this is what the king of Assyria says: "Make your peace with me and come out to me, and eat, ᴬeach one, *from* his vine and each *from* his fig tree, and drink, each one, the waters of his own cistern, ³²until I come and take you ᴬto a land like your own land, a land of grain and new wine, a land of bread and vineyards, a land of olive trees *producing* oil, and of honey, so that you will live and not die." But do not listen to Hezekiah, because he misleads you by saying, "The LORD will save us." ³³ᴬHas any of the gods of the nations actually saved his land from the hand of the king of Assyria? ³⁴ᴬWhere are the gods of Hamath and Arpad? Where are the gods of Sepharvaim, Hena, and Ivvah? Have they saved Samaria from my hand? ³⁵Who among all the gods of the lands *are there* who have saved their land from my hand, ᴬthat the LORD would save Jerusalem from my hand?'"

³⁶But the people were silent and did not answer him *with even* a word, because it was the king's command: "Do not answer him." ³⁷Then Eliakim the son of Hilkiah, who was in charge of the household, and Shebna the scribe and Joah the son of Asaph, the secretary, came to Hezekiah ᴬwith their clothes torn, and they reported to him the words of Rabshakeh.

ISAIAH ENCOURAGES HEZEKIAH

19 ᴬNow when King Hezekiah heard *the report*, he tore his clothes, ᴮcovered himself with sackcloth, and entered the house of the LORD. ²Then he sent Eliakim, who was in charge of the household, with Shebna the scribe and the elders of the priests, covered with sackcloth, to ᴬIsaiah the prophet, the son of Amoz. ³And they said to him, "This is what Hezekiah says: 'This day is a day of distress, rebuke, and humiliation; for children have come to the point of birth, and there is no strength to deliver *them*. ⁴Perhaps the LORD your God will hear all the words of Rabshakeh, whom his master the king of Assyria has sent ᴬto taunt the living God, and will avenge the words which the LORD your God has heard. Therefore, offer a prayer for ᴮthe remnant that is left.'" ⁵So the servants of King Hezekiah came to Isaiah. ⁶And Isaiah said to them, "This is what you shall say to your master: 'The LORD says this: "Do not be fearful because of the words that you have heard, with which the ᴬservants of the king

18:29ᴬ2 Chr 32:15   18:31ᴬ1 Kin 4:20, 25
18:32ᴬDeut 8:7-9; 11:12   18:33ᴬ2 Kin 19:12; Is 10:10, 11
18:34ᴬ2 Kin 19:13   18:35ᴬPs 2:1-3; 59:7
18:37ᴬ2 Kin 6:30   19:1ᴬIs 37:1   ᴮ1 Kin 21:27
19:2ᴬIs 1:1; 2:1   19:4ᴬ2 Kin 18:35   ᴮIs 1:9
19:6ᴬ2 Kin 18:17

of Assyria ᴮhave blasphemed Me. ⁷Behold, I am going to put a spirit in him so that he will hear news and return to his own land. And ᴬI will make him fall by the sword in his own land."'"

SENNACHERIB DEFIES GOD

⁸Then Rabshakeh returned and found the king of Assyria fighting against Libnah, for he had heard that *the king* had left ᴬLachish. ⁹When he heard *them* say about Tirhakah king of Cush, "Behold, he has come out to fight you," he sent messengers again to Hezekiah, saying, ¹⁰"This is what you shall say to Hezekiah king of Judah: 'Do not let your God in whom you trust deceive you by saying, "ᴬJerusalem will not be handed over to the king of Assyria." ¹¹Behold, you yourself have heard what the kings of Assyria have done to all the lands, destroying them completely. So will you be saved? ¹²Did the gods of the nations which my fathers destroyed save them: Gozan, ᴬHaran, Rezeph, and ᴮthe sons of Eden who *were* in Telassar? ¹³ᴬWhere is the king of Hamath, the king of Arpad, the king of the city of Sepharvaim, and *of* Hena and Ivvah?'"

HEZEKIAH'S PRAYER

¹⁴Then ᴬHezekiah took the letter from the hand of the messengers and read it, and he went up to the house of the Lᴏʀᴅ and spread it out before the Lᴏʀᴅ. ¹⁵Hezekiah prayed before the Lᴏʀᴅ and said, "Lᴏʀᴅ, God of Israel, enthroned *above* the cherubim, ᴬYou are the God, You alone, of all the kingdoms of the earth. You have made heaven and earth. ¹⁶Incline Your ear, Lᴏʀᴅ, and hear; ᴬopen Your eyes, Lᴏʀᴅ, and see; and

listen to the words of Sennacherib, which he has sent ᴮto taunt the living God. ¹⁷It is true, Lᴏʀᴅ; the kings of Assyria have laid waste the nations and their lands, ¹⁸and have hurled their gods into the fire; ᴬfor they were not gods, but *only* the work of human hands, wood and stone. So they have destroyed them. ¹⁹But now, Lᴏʀᴅ our God, please, save us from his hand, ᴬso that all the kingdoms of the earth may know that You alone, Lᴏʀᴅ, are God."

GOD'S ANSWER THROUGH ISAIAH

²⁰Then Isaiah the son of Amoz sent *word* to Hezekiah, saying, "This is what the Lᴏʀᴅ, the God of Israel says: 'Because you have prayed to Me about Sennacherib king of Assyria, ᴬI have heard *you*.' ²¹This is the word that the Lᴏʀᴅ has spoken against him:

'She, ᴬthe virgin daughter of
    Zion, has shown contempt
    for you *and* mocked you;
 She, the daughter of
    Jerusalem, ᴮhas shaken *her*
    head behind you!
²² 'Whom have you taunted and
    blasphemed?
 And against whom have you
    raised *your* voice,
 And haughtily raised your
    eyes?
 Against the ᴬHoly One of
    Israel!
²³ 'ᴬThrough your messengers
    you have taunted the Lord,
 And you have said, "With my
    many chariots

19:6 ᴮ2 Kin 18:22-25, 30, 35   19:7 ᴬ2 Kin 19:37
19:8 ᴬ2 Kin 18:14   19:10 ᴬ2 Kin 18:30   19:12 ᴬGen 11:31
ᴮIs 37:12   19:13 ᴬ2 Kin 18:34   19:14 ᴬIs 37:14
19:15 ᴬ2 Kin 5:15   19:16 ᴬ2 Chr 6:40   ᴮ2 Kin 19:4
19:18 ᴬIs 44:9-20; Acts 17:29   19:19 ᴬ1 Kin 8:42, 43
19:20 ᴬ2 Kin 20:5   19:21 ᴬJer 14:17   ᴮPs 109:25
19:22 ᴬIs 5:24; 30:11-15   19:23 ᴬ2 Kin 18:17

I went up to the heights of the
mountains,
To the remotest parts of
Lebanon;
And I cut down its tall cedars
and its choicest junipers.
And I entered its farthest
resting place, its thickest
forest.
24 "I dug *wells* and drank foreign
waters,
And with the soles of my feet I
^dried up
All the streams of Egypt."

25 "^Have you not heard?
Long ago I did it;
From ancient times I
planned it.
^BNow I have brought it about,
That you would turn fortified
cities into ruined heaps.
26 'Therefore their inhabitants
were powerless,
They were shattered and put
to shame.
They were ^*like* the vegetation
of the field and the green
grass,
Like grass on the housetops
that is scorched before it has
grown.
27 'But ^I know your sitting down,
Your going out, your coming in,
And your raging against Me.
28 'Because of your raging
against Me,
And because your
complacency has come up to
My ears,
I ^will put My hook in your
nose,
And My bridle in your lips,
And I will turn you back by the
way by which you came.
29 'Then this shall be ^the sign
for you: you will eat this year what

grows of itself, in the second year
what grows by itself, and in the
third year sow, harvest, plant
vineyards, and eat their fruit.
30^AThe survivors that are left of
the house of Judah will again *take*
root downward and bear fruit
upward. 31For out of Jerusalem will
go a remnant, and survivors ^out
of Mount Zion. ^BThe zeal of 'the
LORD will perform this.

32 'Therefore this is what the LORD
says about the king of Assyria: "^He
will not come to this city nor shoot
an arrow there; and he will not
come before it with a shield nor
heap up an assault ramp against it.
33^ABy the way that he came, by the
same he will return, and he shall
not come to this city," ' declares the
LORD. 34 '^For I will protect this city
to save it for My own sake, and for
My servant David's sake.' "

35^AThen it happened that night
that the angel of the LORD went
out and struck 185,000 in the
camp of the Assyrians; and when
the rest got up early in the morning, behold, all of the 185,000 were
dead. 36So ^ASennacherib the king
of Assyria departed and returned
home, and lived at ^BNineveh.
37Then it came about, as he was
worshiping in the house of Nisroch his god, that ^Adrammelech
and Sharezer killed him with the
sword; and they escaped to the
land of Ararat. And his son Esar-
haddon became king in his place.

19:24^AIs 19:6   19:25^AIs 45:7   ^BIs 10:5
19:26^APs 129:6   19:27^APs 139:1   19:28^AEzek 19:9;
29:4   19:29^AEx 3:12; 2 Kin 20:8, 9   19:30^A2 Kin 19:4;
2 Chr 32:22, 23   19:31^AIs 10:20   ^BIs 9:7
19:32^AIs 8:7-10   19:33^A2 Kin 19:28
19:34^A2 Kin 20:6; Is 31:5   19:35^A2 Sam 24:16;
2 Chr 32:21   19:36^A2 Kin 19:7, 28, 33   ^BJon 1:2
19:37^A2 Kin 17:31
19:31 ¹Some ancient mss *the* LORD *of armies*

HEZEKIAH'S ILLNESS AND RECOVERY

20 ^AIn those days Hezekiah became mortally ill. And Isaiah the prophet, the son of Amoz, came to him and said to him, "This is what the LORD says: 'Set your house in order, for you are going to die and not live.'" ²Then he turned his face to the wall and prayed to the LORD, saying, ³"Please, LORD, just remember ^Ahow I have walked before You wholeheartedly and in truth, and have done what is good in Your sight!" And ᴮHezekiah wept profusely. ⁴And even before Isaiah had left the middle courtyard, the word of the LORD came to him, saying, ⁵"Return and say to Hezekiah the leader of My people, 'This is what the LORD, the God of your father David says: "^AI have heard your prayer, ᴮI have seen your tears; behold, I am going to heal you. On the third day you shall go up to the house of the LORD. ⁶And I will add fifteen years to your life, and I will save you and this city from the hand of the king of Assyria; and ^AI will protect this city for My own sake and for My servant David's sake."'" ⁷Then Isaiah said, "Take a cake of figs." And they took *it* and placed *it* on the inflamed spot, and he recovered.

⁸Now Hezekiah said to Isaiah, "What *will be* the sign that the LORD will heal me, and that I will go up to the house of the LORD on the third day?" ⁹Isaiah said, "^AThis shall be the sign to you from the LORD, that the LORD will perform the word that He has spoken: shall the shadow go forward ten steps or go back ten steps?" ¹⁰So Hezekiah said, "It is easy for the shadow to decline ten steps; no, but have the shadow turn backward ten steps."

¹¹Then Isaiah the prophet called out to the LORD, and ^AHe brought the shadow on the stairway back ten steps by which it had gone down on the stairway of Ahaz.

HEZEKIAH SHOWS BABYLON HIS TREASURES

¹²^AAt that time Berodach-baladan, a son of Baladan, king of Babylon, sent letters and a gift to Hezekiah, because he heard that Hezekiah had been sick. ¹³And Hezekiah listened to ¹them, and showed them ^Aall his treasure house, the silver, the gold, the balsam oil, the scented oil, the house of his armor, and everything that was found in his treasuries. There was nothing in his house nor in all his realm that Hezekiah did not show them. ¹⁴Then Isaiah the prophet came to King Hezekiah and said to him, "What did these men say, and from where have they come to you?" And Hezekiah said, "They have come from a far country, from Babylon." ¹⁵*Isaiah* said, "What have they seen in your house?" So Hezekiah answered, "They have seen everything that is in my house; there is nothing among my treasuries that I have not shown them."

¹⁶Then Isaiah said to Hezekiah, "Hear the word of the LORD: ¹⁷'Behold, the days are coming when ^Aeverything that is in your house, and what your fathers have stored up to this day, will be carried to Babylon; nothing will be left,' says the LORD. ¹⁸'And some of your sons who will come from you, whom you will

20:1^2 Chr 32:24; Is 38:1-22   **20:3**^2 Kin 18:3-6
ᴮ2 Sam 12:21, 22   **20:5**^2 Kin 19:20   ᴮPs 39:12
20:6^2 Kin 19:34   **20:9**^Is 38:7   **20:11**^Josh 10:12-14;
Is 38:8   **20:12**^2 Chr 32:31; Is 39:1-8
20:13^2 Chr 32:27   **20:17**^2 Chr 36:10; Jer 52:17-19

20:13 ¹I.e., messengers

father, will be taken away; and they will become ^officials in the palace of the king of Babylon.'" ¹⁹Then Hezekiah said to Isaiah, "The word of the LORD which you have spoken is ^good." For he thought, "Is it not *good,* if there will be peace and security in my days?"

²⁰^Now the rest of the acts of Hezekiah and all his might, and how he ᴮconstructed the pool and the conduit and brought water into the city, are they not written in the Book of the Chronicles of the Kings of Judah? ²¹^So Hezekiah ¹lay down with his fathers, and his son Manasseh became king in his place.

MANASSEH SUCCEEDS HEZEKIAH

21 ^Manasseh was twelve years old when he became king, and he reigned for fifty-five years in Jerusalem; and his mother's name was Hephzibah. ²He did evil in the sight of the LORD, ^in accordance with the abominations of the nations whom the LORD dispossessed before the sons of Israel. ³For ^he rebuilt the high places which his father Hezekiah had destroyed; and ᴮhe erected altars for Baal and made an ¹Asherah, just as Ahab king of Israel had done, and he worshiped all the heavenly lights and served them. ⁴And ^he built altars in the house of the LORD, of which the LORD had said, "In Jerusalem I will put My name." ⁵He built altars for all the heavenly lights in ^the two courtyards of the house of the LORD. ⁶And ^he made his son pass through the fire, ᴮinterpreted signs, practiced divination, and used mediums and spiritists. He did great evil in the sight of the LORD, provoking *Him* to anger. ⁷Then ^he put the carved image of Asherah that

he had made in the house of which the LORD had said to David and to his son Solomon, "In this house and in Jerusalem, which I have chosen from all the tribes of Israel, I will put My name forever. ⁸And I ^will not make the feet of Israel wander anymore from the land which I gave their fathers, if only they will take care to act in accordance with everything that I have commanded them, and with all the Law that My servant Moses commanded them." ⁹But they did not listen, and Manasseh ^encouraged them to do evil, more than the nations whom the LORD eliminated from the presence of the sons of Israel.

THE KING'S IDOLATRIES REBUKED

¹⁰Now the LORD spoke through His servants the prophets, saying, ¹¹"Since Manasseh king of Judah has committed these abominations, ^having done more evil than all that the Amorites did who *were* before him, and ᴮhas also misled Judah into sin with his idols, ¹²therefore this is what the LORD, the God of Israel says: 'Behold, I am bringing *such a* disaster on Jerusalem and Judah that whoever hears about it, ^both of his ears will ring. ¹³^I will stretch over Jerusalem the line of Samaria and the plummet of the house of Ahab, and I will wipe Jerusalem clean just as one wipes a bowl, wiping it and turning it upside down. ¹⁴And I will

20:18^Dan 1:3-7   20:19^1 Sam 3:18   20:20^2 Chr 32:32
ᴮNeh 3:16   20:21^2 Chr 32:33   21:1^2 Chr 33:1-9
21:2^2 Kin 16:3   21:3^2 Kin 18:4   ᴮ1 Kin 16:31-33
21:4^2 Kin 16:10-16   21:5^1 Kin 7:12; 2 Kin 23:12
21:6^2 Kin 16:3   ᴮLev 19:26, 31   21:7^Deut 16:21;
2 Kin 23:6   21:8^2 Sam 7:10; 2 Kin 18:11, 12
21:9^Prov 29:12   21:11^Gen 15:16   ᴮ2 Kin 21:16
21:12^1 Sam 3:11; Jer 19:3   21:13^Is 34:11; Amos 7:7, 8

20:21 ¹I.e., died   21:3 ¹I.e., a wooden symbol of a
female deity

abandon the remnant of My inheritance and hand them over to their enemies, and they will become as plunder and spoils to all their enemies, [15]because they have done evil in My sight, and have been provoking Me to anger since the day their fathers came from Egypt, even to this day.'"

[16^A]Furthermore, Manasseh shed very much innocent blood until he had filled Jerusalem from one end to another, besides his sin into which he misled Judah, in doing evil in the sight of the LORD. [17^A]Now the rest of the acts of Manasseh and all that he did, and his sin which he committed, are they not written in the Book of the Chronicles of the Kings of Judah? [18^A]And Manasseh [1]lay down with his fathers and was buried in the garden of his own house, in the garden of Uzza, and his son Amon became king in his place.

AMON SUCCEEDS MANASSEH

[19^A]Amon was twenty-two years old when he became king, and he reigned for two years in Jerusalem; and his mother's name *was* Meshullemeth the daughter of Haruz of Jotbah. [20]He did evil in the sight of the LORD, ^just as his father Manasseh had done. [21]For he walked entirely in the way that his father had walked, and served the idols that his father had served, and worshiped them. [22]So ^he abandoned the LORD, the God of his fathers, and did not walk in the way of the LORD. [23]And ^the servants of Amon conspired against him and killed the king in his own house. [24]Then ^the people of the land killed all those who had conspired against King Amon, and the people of the land made his son Josiah

king in his place. [25]Now the rest of the acts of Amon which he did, are they not written in the Book of the Chronicles of the Kings of Judah? [26]He was buried in his grave ^in the garden of Uzza, and his son Josiah became king in his place.

JOSIAH SUCCEEDS AMON

22 ^Josiah was eight years old when he became king, and he reigned for thirty-one years in Jerusalem; and his mother's name *was* Jedidah the daughter of Adaiah of Bozkath. [2]He did what was right in the sight of the LORD and walked entirely in the way of his father David, and did not ^turn aside to the right or to the left.

[3]Now ^in the eighteenth year of King Josiah, the king sent Shaphan, the son of Azaliah the son of Meshullam the scribe, to the house of the LORD, saying, [4]"^Go up to Hilkiah the high priest, and have him count all the money brought into the house of the LORD, which the doorkeepers have collected from the people. [5]^And have them hand it over to the workmen who have the oversight of the house of the LORD, and have them give it to the workmen who are in the house of the LORD to repair the damage to the house: [6]to the carpenters, the builders, the masons, and for buying timber and cut stone to repair the house. [7]However, ^no accounting shall be made with them for

21:16^2 Kin 24:4   21:17^2 Chr 33:11–19
21:18^2 Chr 33:20   21:19^2 Chr 33:21–23
21:20^2 Kin 21:2–6, 11, 16   21:22^2 Kin 22:17;
1 Chr 28:9   21:23^2 Kin 12:20; 14:19
21:24^2 Kin 14:5   21:26^2 Kin 21:18   22:1^2 Chr 34:1
22:2^Deut 5:32; Josh 1:7   22:3^2 Kin 34:8
22:4^2 Kin 12:4, 9, 10   22:5^2 Kin 12:11–14
22:7^2 Kin 12:15; 1 Cor 4:2

21:18 [1]I.e., died

the money handed over to them, because they deal honestly."

THE LOST BOOK

⁸Then Hilkiah the high priest said to Shaphan the scribe, "ᴬI have found the Book of the Law in the house of the LORD." And Hilkiah gave the book to Shaphan, who read it. ⁹Then Shaphan the scribe came to the king and brought back word to the king and said, "Your servants have emptied out the money that was found in the house, and have handed it over to the workmen who have the oversight of the house of the LORD." ¹⁰Moreover, Shaphan the scribe informed the king, saying, "Hilkiah the priest has given me a book." And Shaphan read it in the presence of the king.

¹¹When the king heard the words of the Book of the Law, ᴬhe tore his clothes. ¹²Then the king commanded Hilkiah the priest, ᴬAhikam the son of Shaphan, ᴮAchbor the son of Micaiah, Shaphan the scribe, and Asaiah the king's servant, saying, ¹³"Go, inquire of the LORD for me and for the people and all Judah concerning the words of this book that has been found, for ᴬthe wrath of the LORD that burns against us is great, because our fathers did not listen to the words of this book, to act in accordance with everything that is written regarding us."

HULDAH PREDICTS

¹⁴So Hilkiah the priest, Ahikam, Achbor, Shaphan, and Asaiah went to Huldah the prophetess, the wife of Shallum the son of Tikvah, the son of Harhas, keeper of the wardrobe (and she lived in Jerusalem in the ᴬSecond Quarter); and they spoke to her. ¹⁵Then she said to

them, "This is what the LORD, the God of Israel says: 'Tell the man who sent you to Me, ¹⁶"This is what the LORD says: 'Behold, I am going to ᴬbring disaster on this place and on its inhabitants, all the words of the book which the king of Judah has read. ¹⁷ᴬSince they have abandoned Me and have burned incense to other gods so that they may provoke Me to anger with all the work of their hands, My wrath burns against this place, and it shall not be quenched.'" ¹⁸But to ᴬthe king of Judah who sent you to inquire of the LORD, this is what you shall say to him: "This is what the LORD, the God of Israel says: '*Regarding* the words which you have heard, ¹⁹ᴬsince your heart was tender and ᴮyou humbled yourself before the LORD when you heard what I spoke against this place and against its inhabitants, that they would become an object of horror and a curse, and you have torn your clothes and wept before Me, I have indeed heard you,' declares the LORD." ²⁰Therefore, behold, I am going to gather you to your fathers, and ᴬyou will be gathered to your grave in peace, and your eyes will not look at all the devastation that I am going to bring on this place.'" So they brought back word to the king.

JOSIAH'S COVENANT

23 ᴬThen the king sent *messengers*, and they gathered to him all the elders of Judah and Jerusalem. ²And the king went up

22:8ᴬDeut 31:24-26; 2 Chr 34:14, 15
22:11ᴬGen 37:34; Josh 7:6   22:12ᴬ2 Kin 25:22
ᴮ2 Chr 34:20   22:13ᴬDeut 29:23-28; 31:17, 18
22:14ᴬZeph 1:10   22:16ᴬDeut 29:27; Dan 9:11-14
22:17ᴬDeut 29:25, 26; 2 Kin 21:22   22:18ᴬ2 Chr 34:26
22:19ᴬPs 51:17   ᴮEx 10:3   22:20ᴬ2 Kin 23:30
23:1ᴬ2 Chr 34:29-32

to the house of the LORD and every man of Judah and all the inhabitants of Jerusalem with him, and the priests, the prophets, and all the people, from the small to the great; and ^he read in their presence all the words of the Book of the Covenant ^Bwhich was found in the house of the LORD. ³And ^the king stood by the pillar and made a covenant before the LORD, ^Bto walk after the LORD, and to keep His commandments, His provisions, and His statutes with all *his* heart and all *his* soul, to carry out the words of this covenant that were written in this book. And all the people entered into the covenant.

REFORMS UNDER JOSIAH

⁴Then the king commanded Hilkiah the high priest, the priests of the second order, and the doorkeepers ^to bring out of the temple of the LORD all the utensils that had been made for Baal, for ¹Asherah, and for all the heavenly lights; and he burned them outside Jerusalem in the fields of the Kidron *Valley,* and carried their ashes to Bethel. ⁵Then he did away with the idolatrous priests whom the kings of Judah had appointed to burn incense on the high places in the cities of Judah and in the surrounding area of Jerusalem, as well as those who burned incense to Baal, to the sun, to the moon, to the constellations, and to all the *remaining* ^heavenly lights. ⁶He also brought out the Asherah from the house of the LORD outside Jerusalem to the brook Kidron, and burned it at the brook Kidron, and ground *it* to dust, and ^threw its dust on the graves of the common people. ⁷And he tore down the cubicles of the ^*male* cult prostitutes which

were in the house of the LORD, where the women were weaving hangings for the Asherah. ⁸Then he brought all the priests from the cities of Judah, and defiled the high places where the priests had burned incense, from ^Geba to Beersheba; and he tore down the high places of the gates that *were* at the entrance of the gate of Joshua the governor of the city, which *were* on one's left at the city gate. ⁹Nevertheless ^the priests of the high places did not go up to the altar of the LORD in Jerusalem, but they ate unleavened bread among their brothers. ¹⁰He also defiled ¹Topheth, which is in the Valley of the Son of Hinnom, ^so that no one would make his son or his daughter pass through the fire for ^BMolech. ¹¹And he did away with the horses that the kings of Judah had given to the ^sun, at the entrance of the house of the LORD, by the chamber of Nathan-melech the official, which *was* at the covered courtyard; and he burned the chariots of the sun with fire. ¹²The king also tore down ^the altars that *were* on the roof, the upper chamber of Ahaz, which the kings of Judah had made, and ^Bthe altars which Manasseh had made in the two courtyards of the house of the LORD; and he smashed them there and threw their dust into the brook Kidron. ¹³And the king defiled the high places that *were* opposite Jerusalem, which *were* on the right of ^the mount of destruction which

23:2^Deut 31:10-13   ^B2 Kin 22:8   23:3^2 Kin 11:14, 17
^BDeut 13:4   23:4^2 Kin 21:3, 7; 2 Chr 33:3
23:5^2 Kin 21:3   23:6^2 Chr 34:4   23:7^1 Kin 14:24;
15:12   23:8^Josh 21:17; 1 Kin 15:22   23:9^Ezek 44:10-14
23:10^Lev 18:21   ^B1 Kin 11:7   23:11^Job 31:26; Ezek 8:16
23:12^Zeph 1:5   ^B2 Chr 33:5   23:13^1 Kin 11:7

23:4 ¹I.e., a wooden symbol of a female deity, and so throughout the ch   23:10 ¹I.e., place of burning

Solomon the king of Israel had built for Ashtoreth the abomination of the Sidonians, for Chemosh the abomination of Moab, and for Milcom the abomination of the sons of Ammon. [14]ᴬHe also smashed to pieces the memorial stones and cut down the ¹Asherim, and filled their places with human bones.

[15]Furthermore, ᴬthe altar that *was* at Bethel *and* the ᴮhigh place which Jeroboam the son of Nebat, who misled Israel into sin, had made, even that altar and the high place he tore down. Then he burned the high place, ground *the remains* to dust, and burned the Asherah. [16]Now when Josiah turned, he saw the graves that *were* there on the mountain, and he sent *men* and took the bones from the graves, and burned *them* on the altar and defiled it ᴬin accordance with the word of the Lᴏʀᴅ which the man of God proclaimed, *the one* who proclaimed these things. [17]Then he said, "What is this gravestone there that I see?" And the men of the city told him, "ᴬ*It is* the grave of the man of God who came from Judah and proclaimed these things which you have done against the altar of Bethel." [18]And he said, "Leave him alone; no one is to disturb his bones." So they left his bones undisturbed ᴬwith the bones of the prophet who came from Samaria. [19]Then Josiah also removed all the houses of the high places which *were* ᴬin the cities of Samaria, which the kings of Israel had constructed, provoking the Lᴏʀᴅ to anger; and he did to them just as he had done in Bethel. [20]And ᴬhe slaughtered all the priests of the high places who *were* there on the altars, and burned human bones

on them; then he returned to Jerusalem.

PASSOVER REINSTITUTED

[21]Then the king commanded all the people, saying, "ᴬCelebrate the Passover to the Lᴏʀᴅ your God ᴮas it is written in this Book of the Covenant." [22]ᴬTruly such a Passover had not been celebrated since the days of the judges who judged Israel, nor in all the days of the kings of Israel and the kings of Judah. [23]But in the eighteenth year of King Josiah, this Passover was celebrated to the Lᴏʀᴅ in Jerusalem.

[24]Moreover, Josiah removed ᴬthe mediums, the spiritists, the ¹·ᴮhousehold idols, the idols, and all the abominations that were seen in the land of Judah and in Jerusalem, so that he might fulfill the words of the Law which were written in the book that Hilkiah the priest found in the house of the Lᴏʀᴅ. [25]Before him there was no king ᴬlike him who turned to the Lᴏʀᴅ with all his heart, all his soul, and all his might, in conformity to all the Law of Moses; nor did any like him arise after him.

[26]Nevertheless, the Lᴏʀᴅ did not turn from the fierceness of His great wrath with which His anger burned against Judah, ᴬbecause of all the provocations with which Manasseh had provoked Him. [27]And the Lᴏʀᴅ said, "I will also remove Judah from My sight, ᴬjust as I have removed Israel. And I will

23:14ᴬDeut 7:5, 25   23:15ᴬ1 Kin 13:1   ᴮ1 Kin 12:28-33
23:16ᴬ1 Kin 13:2   23:17ᴬ1 Kin 13:1, 30, 31
23:18ᴬ1 Kin 13:11, 31   23:19ᴬ2 Chr 34:6, 7
23:20ᴬ2 Kin 10:25; 11:18   23:21ᴬ2 Chr 35:1-17
ᴮDeut 16:2-8   23:22ᴬ2 Chr 35:18, 19
23:24ᴬLev 19:31   ᴮGen 31:19   23:25ᴬ2 Kin 18:5
23:26ᴬ2 Kin 21:11-13; Jer 15:4   23:27ᴬ2 Kin 18:11

23:14 ¹I.e., wooden symbols of a female deity (Asherah)   23:24 ¹Heb *teraphim*

reject this city which I have chosen, Jerusalem, and the temple of which I said, 'My name shall be there!'"

JEHOAHAZ SUCCEEDS JOSIAH

28 Now the rest of the acts of Josiah and all that he did, are they not written in the Book of the Chronicles of the Kings of Judah? 29 AIn his days BPharaoh Neco king of Egypt went up to the king of Assyria at the river Euphrates. And King Josiah went to meet him, and when *Pharaoh Neco* saw him he killed him at Megiddo. 30 AHis servants carried his body in a chariot from Megiddo, and brought him to Jerusalem and buried him in his own tomb. BThen the people of the land took Jehoahaz the son of Josiah and anointed him and made him king in place of his father.

31 AJehoahaz was twenty-three years old when he became king, and he reigned for three months in Jerusalem; and his mother's name was Hamutal the daughter of Jeremiah of Libnah. 32 He did evil in the sight of the LORD, Ain accordance with all that his forefathers had done. 33 And Pharaoh Neco imprisoned him at ARiblah in the land of BHamath, so that he would not reign in Jerusalem; and he imposed on the land a fine of ¹a hundred talents of silver and ²a talent of gold.

JEHOIAKIM MADE KING BY PHARAOH

34 Then Pharaoh Neco made AEliakim the son of Josiah king in the place of his father Josiah, and he Bchanged his name to Jehoiakim. But he took Jehoahaz and brought *him* to Egypt, and he died there. 35 So Jehoiakim Agave the silver and gold to Pharaoh, but he assessed the land in order to give the money at the command of Pharaoh. He

collected the silver and gold from the people of the land, each according to his assessment, to give to Pharaoh Neco.

36 AJehoiakim was twenty-five years old when he became king, and he reigned for eleven years in Jerusalem; and his mother's name *was* Zebidah the daughter of Pedaiah of Rumah. 37 He did evil in the sight of the LORD, Ain accordance with all that his forefathers had done.

BABYLON CONTROLS JEHOIAKIM

24 AIn his days Nebuchadnezzar king of Babylon came up, and Jehoiakim became his servant for three years; then he turned and revolted against him. 2 And the LORD sent against him bands of Chaldeans, bands of Arameans, bands of Moabites, and bands of Ammonites. He sent them against Judah to destroy it, Ain accordance with the word of the LORD which He had spoken through His servants the prophets. 3 It indeed came upon Judah at the command of the LORD, to remove *them* from His sight Adue to the sins of Manasseh, in accordance with everything that he had done, 4 and Aalso for the innocent blood which he shed, for he filled Jerusalem with innocent blood; and the LORD was unwilling to forgive. 5 Now the rest of the acts of Jehoiakim and all that he did, are they not written in the Book of the Chronicles of the Kings of Judah?

23:29 A2 Chr 35:20-24   BJer 46:2   23:30 A2 Kin 9:28   B2 Chr 36:1-4   23:31 A1 Chr 3:15; Jer 22:11   23:32 A2 Kin 21:2-7   23:33 A2 Kin 25:6   B1 Kin 8:65   23:34 A1 Chr 3:15   B2 Kin 24:17   23:35 A2 Kin 23:33   23:36 AJer 22:18, 19; 26:1   23:37 A2 Kin 23:32   24:1 AJer 25:1; Dan 1:1, 2   24:2 A2 Kin 23:27   24:3 A2 Kin 23:26   24:4 A2 Kin 21:16
23:33 ¹About 3.75 tons or 3.4 metric tons   ²About 75 lb. or 34 kg

JEHOIACHIN REIGNS

⁶So ᴬJehoiakim ¹lay down with his fathers, and his son Jehoiachin became king in his place. ⁷Now the king of Egypt did not come out of his land again, ᴬbecause the king of Babylon had taken everything that belonged to the king of Egypt from ᴮthe brook of Egypt to the river Euphrates.

⁸ᴬJehoiachin was ᴮeighteen years old when he became king, and he reigned for three months in Jerusalem; and his mother's name *was* Nehushta the daughter of Elnathan of Jerusalem. ⁹He did evil in the sight of the Lᴏʀᴅ, ᴬin accordance with all that his father had done.

DEPORTATION TO BABYLON

¹⁰At that time the servants of Nebuchadnezzar the king of Babylon went up to Jerusalem, and the city came under siege. ¹¹And Nebuchadnezzar the king of Babylon came to the city, while his servants were besieging it. ¹²Then Jehoiachin the king of Judah went out to the king of Babylon, he, his mother, his servants, his commanders, and his officials. And ᴬthe king of Babylon took him *prisoner* in the eighth year of his reign. ¹³ᴬHe also brought out from there all the treasures of the house of the Lᴏʀᴅ, and the treasures of the king's house, and he smashed all the articles of gold that Solomon king of Israel had made in the temple of the Lᴏʀᴅ, just as the Lᴏʀᴅ had said. ¹⁴Then he led into exile all *the people of* Jerusalem and all the commanders and all the valiant warriors, ᴬten thousand exiles, and ᴮall the craftsmen and the smiths. None were left except the poorest people of the land.

¹⁵So ᴬhe led Jehoiachin into exile to Babylon; also the king's mother, the king's wives, and his officials and the leading men of the land, he led into exile from Jerusalem to Babylon. ¹⁶And all the valiant men, ᴬseven thousand, and the craftsmen and the smiths, a thousand, all strong *and* fit for war, these too the king of Babylon brought into exile to Babylon.

ZEDEKIAH MADE KING

¹⁷ᴬThen the king of Babylon made his uncle Mattaniah king in his place, and changed his name to Zedekiah.

¹⁸ᴬZedekiah was twenty-one years old when he became king, and he reigned for eleven years in Jerusalem; and his mother's name was Hamutal the daughter of Jeremiah of Libnah. ¹⁹He did evil in the sight of the Lᴏʀᴅ, ᴬin accordance with everything that Jehoiakim had done. ²⁰For *it was* ᴬdue to the anger of the Lᴏʀᴅ *that this* happened in Jerusalem and Judah, until He cast them out of His presence. And Zedekiah revolted against the king of Babylon.

NEBUCHADNEZZAR BESIEGES JERUSALEM

25 ᴬNow in the ninth year of his reign, on the tenth day of the tenth month, Nebuchadnezzar the king of Babylon came, he and all his army, against Jerusalem,

24:6 ᴬJer 22:18, 19   24:7 ᴬJer 46:2   ᴮGen 15:18
24:8 ᴬ1 Chr 3:16   ᴮ2 Chr 36:9   24:9 ᴬ2 Kin 21:2-7
24:12 ᴬ2 Chr 36:10   24:13 ᴬ2 Kin 20:17; Is 39:6
24:14 ᴬ2 Kin 24:16   ᴮJer 24:1   24:15 ᴬJer 22:24-28;
Ezek 17:12   24:16 ᴬ2 Kin 24:14   24:17 ᴬ2 Chr 36:10-13;
Jer 37:1   24:18 ᴬJer 27:1; 52:1   24:19 ᴬ2 Kin 23:37
24:20 ᴬDeut 4:24; 2 Kin 23:26   25:1 ᴬ2 Chr 36:17-20;
Jer 39:1-7
24:6 ¹I.e., died

camped against it, and built a siege wall all around it. ²So the city was under siege until the eleventh year of King Zedekiah. ³On the ninth day of the *fourth* month ᴬthe famine was so severe in the city that there was no food for the people of the land. ⁴ᴬThen the city was broken into, and all the men of war *fled* by night by way of the gate between the two walls that were beside ᴮthe king's garden, though the Chaldeans were all around the city. And they went by way of the Arabah. ⁵But the army of the Chaldeans pursued the king and overtook him in the plains of Jericho, and all his army was scattered from him. ⁶Then ᴬthey captured the king and ᴮbrought him up to the king of Babylon at Riblah, and he passed sentence on him. ⁷And ᴬthey slaughtered the sons of Zedekiah before his eyes, then ᴮput out Zedekiah's eyes and bound him with bronze shackles, and brought him to Babylon.

JERUSALEM BURNED AND PLUNDERED

⁸ᴬNow on the seventh *day* of the fifth month, which was the nineteenth year of King Nebuchadnezzar, king of Babylon, Nebuzaradan the captain of the bodyguards, a servant of the king of Babylon, came to Jerusalem. ⁹And ᴬhe burned the house of the LORD, the king's house, and all the houses of Jerusalem; even every great house he burned with fire. ¹⁰So all the army of the Chaldeans who *were with* the captain of the bodyguards ᴬtore down the walls around Jerusalem. ¹¹Then Nebuzaradan, the captain of the bodyguards, led into exile ᴬthe rest of the people who were left in the city and the deserters who had deserted to the king of Babylon, and the rest of the people.

¹²But the captain of the bodyguards left some of ᴬthe poorest of the land to be vinedressers and farmers.

¹³ᴬNow the Chaldeans smashed to pieces the bronze pillars which were in the house of the LORD, and the stands and the bronze ¹Sea which were in the house of LORD, and carried the bronze to Babylon. ¹⁴ᴬAnd they took away the pots, the shovels, the shears, the spoons, and all the bronze utensils which were used in temple service. ¹⁵The captain of the bodyguards also took away the firepans and the basins, what was fine gold and what was fine silver. ¹⁶The two pillars, the one Sea, and the stands which Solomon had made for the house of the LORD—ᴬthe bronze of all these articles was too heavy to weigh. ¹⁷ᴬThe height of the one pillar was ¹eighteen cubits, and a bronze capital was on it; the height of the capital was ²three cubits, with latticework and pomegranates on the capital all around, all of bronze. And the second pillar was like these, same *features* with latticework.

¹⁸Then the captain of the bodyguards took ᴬSeraiah the chief priest and ᴮZephaniah the second priest, with the three doorkeepers. ¹⁹And from the city he took one official who was overseer of the men of war, and ᴬfive of the king's advisers who were found in the city; and the scribe of the captain of the army who mustered the

---

25:3ᴬ2 Kin 6:24, 25; Lam 4:9, 10   25:4ᴬEzek 33:21
ᴮNeh 3:15   25:6ᴬJer 34:21, 22   ᴮJer 32:4
25:7ᴬJer 39:6, 7   ᴮEzek 12:13   25:8ᴬJer 52:12
25:9ᴬ1 Kin 9:8; Ps 74:3-7   25:10ᴬ2 Kin 14:13; Neh 1:3
25:11ᴬ2 Chr 36:20   25:12ᴬ2 Kin 24:14; Jer 40:7
25:13ᴬ1 Kin 7:15-22; 2 Chr 3:15-17   25:14ᴬ1 Kin 7:47-50;
2 Chr 4:16   25:16ᴬ1 Kin 7:47   25:17ᴬ1 Kin 7:15-22
25:18ᴬEzra 7:1   ᴮJer 29:25, 29   25:19ᴬEsth 1:14

25:13¹I.e., a very large basin   25:17¹About 27 ft. or 8 m
²About 4.5 ft. or 1.3 m

people of the land; and sixty men of the people of the land who were found in the city. ²⁰Nebuzaradan the captain of the bodyguards took them and brought them to the king of Babylon at ^Riblah. ²¹Then the king of Babylon struck them down and put them to death at Riblah in the land of Hamath. ^So Judah went into exile from its land.

GEDALIAH MADE GOVERNOR

²²Now *as for* the people who were left in the land of Judah, whom Nebuchadnezzar king of Babylon had left, he appointed ^Gedaliah the son of Ahikam, the son of Shaphan over them. ²³^When all the captains of the forces, they and *their* men, heard that the king of Babylon had appointed Gedaliah *governor,* they came to Gedaliah at Mizpah, namely, Ishmael the son of Nethaniah, Johanan the son of Kareah, Seraiah the son of Tanhumeth the Netophathite, and Jaazaniah the son of the Maacathite, they and their men. ²⁴And Gedaliah swore to them and their men and said to them, "Do not be afraid of the servants of the Chaldeans; live in the land and serve the king of Babylon, and it will go well for you."

²⁵^But it happened in the seventh month, that Ishmael the son of Nethaniah, the son of Elishama, of the royal family, came with ten men and struck Gedaliah down so that he died along with the Jews and the Chaldeans who were with him at Mizpah. ²⁶^Then all the people, from the small to the great, and the captains of the forces set out and came to Egypt; for they were afraid of the Chaldeans.

²⁷^Now it came about in the thirty-seventh year of ᴮthe exile of Jehoiachin king of Judah, in the twelfth month, on the twenty-seventh *day* of the month, that Evil-merodach king of Babylon, in the year that he became king, released Jehoiachin king of Judah from prison; ²⁸and he ^spoke kindly to him and set his throne above the throne of the kings who *were* with him in Babylon. ²⁹So Jehoiachin changed his prison clothes, and ^had his meals in the king's presence regularly all the days of his life; ³⁰and as his ^allowance, a regular allowance was given to him by the king, a portion for each day, all the days of his life.

25:20^2 Kin 23:33   25:21^Deut 28:64; 2 Kin 23:27
25:22^Jer 39:14; 40:7-9   25:23^Jer 40:7-9
25:25^Jer 41:1, 2   25:26^Jer 43:4-7   25:27^Jer
52:31-34   ᴮ2 Kin 24:12, 15   25:28^Dan 2:37; 5:18, 19
25:29^2 Sam 9:7   25:30^Neh 11:23; 12:47

1 CHRONICLES

GENEALOGY FROM ADAM

1 ^AAdam, Seth, Enosh, ²Kenan, Mahalalel, Jared, ³Enoch, Methuselah, Lamech, ⁴Noah, Shem, Ham, and Japheth.

⁵^AThe sons of Japheth were Gomer, Magog, Madai, Javan, Tubal, Meshech, and Tiras. ⁶The sons of Gomer were Ashkenaz, Diphath, and Togarmah. ⁷The sons of Javan were Elishah, Tarshish, Kittim, and Rodanim.

⁸The sons of Ham were Cush, Mizraim, Put, and Canaan. ⁹The sons of Cush were Seba, Havilah, Sabta, Raama, and Sabteca; and the sons of Raama were Sheba and Dedan. ¹⁰Cush fathered Nimrod; he began to be a mighty one on the earth.

¹¹^AMizraim fathered the people of Lud, Anam, Lehab, Naphtuh, ¹²Pathrus, and Casluh, from whom the Philistines came, and the Caphtorim.

¹³Canaan fathered Sidon his firstborn, and Heth, ¹⁴and the Jebusites, the Amorites, the Girgashites, ¹⁵the Hivites, the Arkites, the Sinites, ¹⁶the Arvadites, the Zemarites, and the Hamathites.

¹⁷^AThe sons of Shem were Elam, Asshur, Arpachshad, Lud, Aram, Uz, Hul, Gether, and Meshech. ¹⁸Arpachshad fathered Shelah, and Shelah fathered Eber. ¹⁹Two sons were born to Eber: the name of the one was Peleg, for in his days the earth was divided; and his brother's name was Joktan. ²⁰Joktan fathered Almodad, Sheleph, Hazarmaveth, Jerah, ²¹Hadoram, Uzal, Diklah,

²²Ebal, Abimael, Sheba, ²³Ophir, Havilah, and Jobab; all these were the sons of Joktan.

²⁴^AShem, Arpachshad, Shelah, ²⁵Eber, Peleg, Reu, ²⁶Serug, Nahor, Terah, ²⁷and Abram, that is Abraham.

DESCENDANTS OF ABRAHAM

²⁸The sons of Abraham were Isaac and Ishmael. ²⁹^AThese are their genealogies: the firstborn of Ishmael was Nebaioth, then Kedar, Adbeel, Mibsam, ³⁰Mishma, Dumah, Massa, Hadad, Tema, ³¹Jetur, Naphish, and Kedemah; these were the sons of Ishmael. ³²^AThe sons of Keturah, Abraham's concubine, to whom she gave birth, were Zimran, Jokshan, Medan, Midian, Ishbak, and Shuah. And the sons of Jokshan were Sheba and Dedan. ³³The sons of Midian were Ephah, Epher, Hanoch, Abida, and Eldaah. All these were the sons of Keturah.

³⁴Abraham fathered Isaac. The sons of Isaac were ^AEsau and ¹Israel. ³⁵^AThe sons of Esau were Eliphaz, Reuel, Jeush, Jalam, and Korah. ³⁶The sons of Eliphaz were Teman, Omar, Zephi, Gatam, Kenaz, Timna, and Amalek. ³⁷The sons of Reuel were Nahath, Zerah, Shammah, and Mizzah. ³⁸^AThe sons of Seir were Lotan, Shobal, Zibeon,

---

1:1 ^AGen 4:25–5:32   1:5 ^AGen 10:2–4   1:11 ^AGen 10:13–18   1:17 ^AGen 10:22–29   1:24 ^AGen 11:10–26; Luke 3:34–36   1:29 ^AGen 25:13–16   1:32 ^AGen 25:1–4   1:34 ^AGen 25:25, 26; 32:28   1:35 ^AGen 36:4–10   1:38 ^AGen 36:20–28

1:34 ¹I.e., Jacob

Anah, Dishon, Ezer, and Dishan. ³⁹The sons of Lotan *were* Hori and Homam; and Lotan's sister *was* Timna. ⁴⁰The sons of Shobal *were* Alian, Manahath, Ebal, Shephi, and Onam. And the sons of Zibeon *were* Aiah and Anah. ⁴¹The son of Anah *was* Dishon. And the sons of Dishon *were* Hamran, Eshban, Ithran, and Cheran. ⁴²The sons of Ezer *were* Bilhan, Zaavan, and Jaakan. The sons of Dishan *were* Uz and Aran.

⁴³ᴬNow these are the kings who reigned in the land of Edom before *any* king from the sons of Israel reigned. Bela was the son of Beor, and the name of his city was Din-habah. ⁴⁴When Bela died, Jobab the son of Zerah of ᴬBozrah became king in his place. ⁴⁵When Jobab died, Husham of the land of ᴬthe Temanites became king in his place. ⁴⁶When Husham died, Hadad the son of Bedad, who defeated Midian in the field of Moab, became king in his place; and the name of his city *was* Avith. ⁴⁷When Hadad died, Samlah of Masrekah became king in his place. ⁴⁸When Samlah died, Shaul of Rehoboth by the *Euphrates* River became king in his place. ⁴⁹When Shaul died, Baal-hanan the son of Achbor became king in his place. ⁵⁰When Baal-hanan died, Hadad became king in his place; and the name of his city was Pai, and his wife's name was Mehetabel, the daughter of Matred, the daughter of Mezahab. ⁵¹Then Hadad died.

Now the tribal chiefs of Edom were chief Timna, chief Aliah, chief Jetheth, ⁵²chief Oholibamah, chief Elah, chief Pinon, ⁵³chief Kenaz, chief Teman, chief Mibzar, ⁵⁴chief Magdiel, *and* chief Iram. These *were* the chiefs of Edom.

GENEALOGY: TWELVE SONS OF ISRAEL (JACOB)

2 ᴬThese *were* the sons of Israel: Reuben, Simeon, Levi, Judah, Issachar, Zebulun, ²Dan, Joseph, Benjamin, Naphtali, Gad, and Asher.

³ᴬThe sons of Judah *were* Er, Onan, and Shelah; *these* three were born to him by Bath-shua the Canaanitess. But Er, Judah's firstborn, was evil in the sight of the Lᴏʀᴅ, so He put him to death. ⁴ᴬHis daughter-in-law Tamar bore him Perez and Zerah. Judah had five sons in all.

⁵The sons of Perez *were* Hezron and Hamul. ⁶The sons of Zerah *were* Zimri, Ethan, Heman, Calcol, and Dara; five of them in all. ⁷The son of Carmi *was* ᴬAchar, the one who brought disaster on Israel by violating the ¹ban. ⁸The son of Ethan *was* Azariah.

GENEALOGY OF DAVID

⁹Now the sons of Hezron who were born to him *were* Jerahmeel, Ram, and Chelubai. ¹⁰Ram fathered Amminadab, and Amminadab fathered Nahshon, leader of the sons of Judah; ¹¹Nahshon fathered Salma, Salma fathered Boaz, ¹²Boaz fathered Obed, and Obed fathered Jesse; ¹³and Jesse fathered Eliab his firstborn, then Abinadab, the second, Shimea, the third, ¹⁴Nethanel, the fourth, Raddai, the fifth, ¹⁵Ozem, the sixth, *and* David, the seventh. ¹⁶Their sisters *were* Zeruiah and Abigail. And the three sons of Zeruiah *were* Abshai, Joab, and Asahel. ¹⁷Abigail gave birth to Amasa, and the father of Amasa was Jether the Ishmaelite.

1:43ᴬGen 36:31-43   **1:44**ᴬIs 34:6   **1:45**ᴬJob 2:11
2:1ᴬGen 35:22-26; 46:8-25   **2:3**ᴬGen 38:2-10
2:4ᴬGen 38:13-30   **2:7**ᴬJosh 7:1

2:7¹I.e., the ban against forbidden spoils

18 Now Caleb the son of Hezron had sons by Azubah *his* wife, and by Jerioth; and these were her sons: Jesher, Shobab, and Ardon. 19 When Azubah died, Caleb married Ephrath, who bore to him Hur. 20 Hur fathered Uri, and Uri fathered Bezalel.

21 Later, Hezron had relations with the daughter of Machir the father of Gilead, whom he married when he was sixty years old; and she bore to him Segub. 22 Segub fathered Jair, who had twenty-three cities in the land of Gilead. 23 But Geshur and Aram took the villages of Jair from them, with Kenath and its villages, sixty settlements. All of these were the sons of Machir, the father of Gilead. 24 After the death of Hezron in Caleb-ephrathah, Abijah, Hezron's wife, bore to him Ashhur the father of Tekoa.

25 Now the sons of Jerahmeel, the firstborn of Hezron, were Ram the firstborn, then Bunah, Oren, Ozem, *and* Ahijah. 26 Jerahmeel had another wife, whose name was Atarah; she was the mother of Onam. 27 The sons of Ram, the firstborn of Jerahmeel, were Maaz, Jamin, and Eker. 28 The sons of Onam were Shammai and Jada. And the sons of Shammai *were* Nadab and Abishur. 29 The name of Abishur's wife *was* Abihail, and she bore to him Ahban and Molid. 30 The sons of Nadab *were* Seled and Appaim, and Seled died without sons. 31 The son of Appaim *was* Ishi. And the son of Ishi *was* Sheshan, and the son of Sheshan, Ahlai. 32 The sons of Jada the brother of Shammai *were* Jether and Jonathan, and Jether died without sons. 33 The sons of Jonathan *were* Peleth and Zaza. These were the descendants of Jerahmeel. 34 Now Sheshan had no sons, only daughters. Sheshan also had an Egyptian servant, whose name was Jarha. 35 Sheshan gave his daughter to his servant Jarha in marriage, and she bore to him Attai. 36 Attai fathered Nathan, Nathan fathered Zabad, 37 Zabad fathered Ephlal, Ephlal fathered Obed, 38 Obed fathered Jehu, Jehu fathered Azariah, 39 Azariah fathered Helez, Helez fathered Eleasah, 40 Eleasah fathered Sismai, Sismai fathered Shallum, 41 Shallum fathered Jekamiah, and Jekamiah fathered Elishama.

42 Now the sons of Caleb, the brother of Jerahmeel, *were* Mesha his firstborn, who was the father of Ziph; and his son was Mareshah, the father of Hebron. 43 The sons of Hebron *were* Korah, Tappuah, Rekem, and Shema. 44 Shema fathered Raham, the father of Jorkeam; and Rekem fathered Shammai. 45 The son of Shammai was Maon, and Maon *was* the father of Bethzur. 46 Ephah, Caleb's concubine, gave birth to Haran, Moza, and Gazez; and Haran fathered Gazez. 47 The sons of Jahdai *were* Regem, Jotham, Geshan, Pelet, Ephah, and Shaaph. 48 Maacah, Caleb's concubine, gave birth to Sheber and Tirhanah. 49 She also gave birth to Shaaph the father of Madmannah, Sheva the father of Machbena and the father of Gibea; and the daughter of Caleb *was* Achsah. 50 These were the sons of Caleb.

The sons of Hur, the firstborn of Ephrathah, *were* Shobal the father of Kiriath-jearim, 51 Salma the father of Bethlehem, *and* Hareph the father of Beth-gader. 52 Shobal the father of Kiriath-jearim had sons: Haroeh, half of the Manahathites, 53 and the families of Kiriath-jearim:

the Ithrites, the Puthites, the Shu-mathites, and the Mishraites; from these came the Zorathites and the Eshtaolites. ⁵⁴The sons of Salma *were* Bethlehem and the Netopha-thites, Atroth-beth-joab, and half of the Manahathites, the Zorites. ⁵⁵The families of scribes who lived at Jabez *were* the Tirathites, the Shimeathites, *and* the Sucathites. Those are the Kenites who came from Hammath, the father of the house of Rechab.

FAMILY OF DAVID

3 ^Now these were the sons of David who were born to him in Hebron: the firstborn *was* Amnon, by Ahinoam the Jezreelitess; the second *was* Daniel, by Abigail the Carmelitess; ²the third *was* Absa-lom the son of Maacah, the daugh-ter of Talmai king of Geshur; the fourth *was* Adonijah the son of Hag-gith; ³the fifth *was* Shephatiah, by Abital; the sixth *was* Ithream, by his wife Eglah. ⁴Six were born to him in Hebron, and ^he reigned there for seven years and six months. And in Jerusalem he reigned for thirty-three years. ⁵These were *the children* born to him in Jeru-salem: Shimea, Shobab, Nathan, and ^Solomon, four by ᴮBath-shua the daughter of Ammiel; ⁶and Ibhar, Elishama, Eliphelet, ⁷Nogah, Nepheg, Japhia, ⁸Elishama, Eliada, and Eliphelet, nine. ⁹All *of these were* the sons of David, besides the sons of the concubines; and ^Tamar *was* their sister.

¹⁰Now Solomon's son *was* Rehoboam, *then* Abijah *was* his son, Asa, his son, Jehoshaphat, his son, ¹¹Joram, his son, Ahaziah, his son, Joash, his son, ¹²Ama-ziah, his son, Azariah, his son,

Jotham, his son, ¹³Ahaz, his son, Hezekiah, his son, Manasseh, his son, ¹⁴Amon, his son, *and* Josiah, his son. ¹⁵The sons of Josiah *were* Johanan, the firstborn, the second *was* Jehoiakim, the third, Zedekiah, *and* the fourth, Shallum. ¹⁶The sons of Jehoiakim *were* his son Jeconiah *and* his son Zedekiah. ¹⁷The sons of Jeconiah, the prisoner, *were* his son Shealtiel ¹⁸and Mal-chiram, Pedaiah, Shenazzar, Jeka-miah, Hoshama, and Nedabiah. ¹⁹The sons of Pedaiah *were* Zerub-babel and Shimei. And the sons of Zerubbabel *were* Meshullam and Hananiah, and Shelomith *was* their sister; ²⁰and Hashubah, Ohel, Bere-chiah, Hasadiah, and Jushab-hesed, five. ²¹The sons of Hananiah *were* Pelatiah and Jeshaiah, the sons of Rephaiah, the sons of Arnan, the sons of Obadiah, the sons of Sheca-niah. ²²The descendants of Sheca-niah *were* Shemaiah, and the sons of Shemaiah: Hattush, Igal, Bariah, Neariah, and Shaphat, six. ²³The sons of Neariah *were* Elioenai, Hiz-kiah, and Azrikam, three. ²⁴The sons of Elioenai *were* Hodaviah, Eliashib, Pelaiah, Akkub, Johanan, Delaiah, and Anani, seven.

DESCENDANTS OF JUDAH

4 ^The sons of Judah *were* Perez, Hezron, Carmi, Hur, and Shobal. ²Reaiah the son of Sho-bal fathered Jahath, and Jahath fathered Ahumai and Lahad. These *were* the families of the Zorathites. ³These *were* the sons of Etam: Jezreel, Ishma, and Idbash; and the name of their sister *was* Haz-zelelponi. ⁴Penuel *was* the father

3:1^2 Sam 3:2-5   3:4^2 Sam 5:4, 5; 1 Kin 2:11
3:5^2 Sam 12:24, 25   ᴮ2 Sam 11:3   3:9^2 Sam 13:1
4:1^1 Chr 2:3

of Gedor, and Ezer the father of Hushah. These *were* the sons of Hur, the firstborn of Ephrathah, the father of Bethlehem. [5]Ashhur, the father of Tekoa, had two wives, Helah and Naarah. [6]Naarah bore to him Ahuzzam, Hepher, Temeni, and Haahashtari. These were the sons of Naarah. [7]The sons of Helah *were* Zereth, Izhar, and Ethnan. [8]Koz fathered Anub and Zobebah, and the families of Aharhel, the son of Harum. [9]Jabez was more honorable than his brothers, and his mother named him Jabez, saying, "Because I gave birth *to him* in pain." [10]Now Jabez called on the God of Israel, saying, "Oh that You would greatly bless me and extend my border, and that Your hand might be with me, and that You would keep *me* from harm so that *it* would not hurt me!" And God brought about what he requested.

[11]Chelub the brother of Shuhah fathered Mehir, who was the father of Eshton. [12]Eshton fathered Bethrapha and Paseah, and Tehinnah the father of Ir-nahash. These are the men of Recah.

[13]Now the sons of Kenaz *were* Othniel and Seraiah. And the sons of Othniel *were* Hathath and Meonothai. [14]Meonothai fathered Ophrah, and Seraiah fathered Joab the father of Ge-harashim, for they were craftsmen. [15]The sons of Caleb the son of Jephunneh *were* Iru, Elah, and Naam; and the son of Elah *was* Kenaz. [16]The sons of Jehallelel *were* Ziph and Ziphah, Tiria and Asarel. [17]The sons of Ezrah *were* Jether, Mered, Epher, and Jalon. And *Mered's wife* conceived *and gave birth to* Miriam, Shammai, and Ishbah the father of Eshtemoa. [18](His Jewish wife gave birth to Jered, the father of Gedor, Heber the father of Soco, and Jekuthiel the father of Zanoah.) These were the sons of Bithia the daughter of Pharaoh, whom Mered married. [19]The sons of the wife of Hodiah, the sister of Naham, *were* the fathers of Keilah the Garmite and Eshtemoa the Maacathite. [20]The sons of Shimon *were* Amnon and Rinnah, *and* Benhanan and Tilon. And the sons of Ishi *were* Zoheth and Ben-zoheth. [21]The sons of Shelah the son of Judah *were* Er the father of Lecah and Laadah the father of Mareshah, and the families of the house of the linen workers at Bethashbea; [22]and Jokim, the men of Cozeba, Joash, Saraph, who ruled in Moab, and Jashubi-lehem. And the records are ancient. [23]These were the potters and the inhabitants of Netaim and Gederah; they lived there with the king for his work.

DESCENDANTS OF SIMEON

[24]The sons of Simeon *were* Nemuel and Jamin, Jarib, Zerah, *and* Shaul; [25]Shallum *was* his son, Mibsam his son, *and* Mishma his son. [26]The sons of Mishma *were* Hammuel his son, Zaccur his son, *and* Shimei his son. [27]Now Shimei had sixteen sons and six daughters; but his brothers did not have many sons, nor did all their family increase like the sons of Judah. [28]They lived in Beersheba, Moladah, and Hazarshual, [29]in Bilhah, Ezem, Tolad, [30]Bethuel, Hormah, Ziklag, [31]Bethmarcaboth, Hazar-susim, Bethbiri, and Shaaraim. These *were* their cities until the reign of David. [32]Their villages *were* Etam, Ain, Rimmon, Tochen, and Ashan, five cities, [33]and all their settlements that *were* around the same cities as

far as Baal. These *were* their dwellings, and they have their genealogy. ³⁴Meshobab, Jamlech, Joshah the son of Amaziah, ³⁵Joel, Jehu the son of Joshibiah, the son of Seraiah, the son of Asiel, ³⁶and Elioenai, Jaakobah, Jeshohaiah, Asaiah, Adiel, Jesimiel, Benaiah, ³⁷and Ziza the son of Shiphi, the son of Allon, the son of Jedaiah, the son of Shimri, the son of Shemaiah— ³⁸these mentioned by name *were* leaders in their families; and their fathers' houses spread out greatly. ³⁹They went to the entrance of Gedor, as far as the east side of the valley, to seek pasture for their flocks. ⁴⁰They found pasture that was rich and good, and ^the land was spread out on both sides, and peaceful and undisturbed; for those who lived there previously *were* Hamites. ⁴¹^These *people,* recorded by name, came in the days of Hezekiah king of Judah, and they attacked their tents and the Meunites who were found there, and utterly destroyed them to this day; and they lived in their place, because there was pasture there for their flocks. ⁴²From them, from the sons of Simeon, five hundred men went to ^Mount Seir, with Pelatiah, Neariah, Rephaiah, and Uzziel, the sons of Ishi, as their leaders. ⁴³^They destroyed the remnant of the Amalekites who escaped, and they have lived there to this day.

GENEALOGY FROM REUBEN

5 Now the sons of Reuben, the firstborn of Israel (for he was the firstborn, but because ^he defiled his father's bed, his birthright was given to the sons of Joseph, the son of Israel; so he is not enrolled in the genealogy according to the birthright. ²Though Judah prevailed over his brothers, and ^from him *came* the leader, yet the birthright belonged to Joseph), ³^the sons of Reuben the firstborn of Israel *were* Hanoch and Pallu, *and* Hezron and Carmi. ⁴The sons of Joel *were* Shemaiah his son, Gog his son, ^Shimei his son, ⁵Micah his son, Reaiah his son, Baal his son, ⁶*and* Beerah his son, whom Tilgath-pilneser king of Assyria took into exile; he was leader of the Reubenites. ⁷His relatives by their families, ^in the genealogy of their generations, *were* Jeiel the chief, then Zechariah ⁸and Bela, the son of Azaz, the son of Shema, the son of Joel, who lived in ^Aroer, as far as Nebo and Baal-meon. ⁹Toward the east he settled as far as the entrance of the wilderness from the river Euphrates, ^because their livestock had increased in the land of Gilead. ¹⁰In the days of Saul ^they made war with the Hagrites, who fell by their hand, so that they occupied their tents throughout the land east of Gilead.

¹¹Now the sons of Gad lived opposite them in the land of ^Bashan, as far as Salecah. ¹²Joel *was* the head and Shapham the second, then Janai and Shaphat in Bashan. ¹³Their relatives of their fathers' households *were* Michael, Meshullam, Sheba, Jorai, Jacan, Zia, and Eber, seven. ¹⁴These *were* the sons of Abihail, the son of Huri, the son of Jaroah, the son of Gilead, the son of Michael, the son of Jeshishai, the son of Jahdo, the son of Buz; ¹⁵Ahi the son of Abdiel, the son of Guni, *was* head of their fathers' households. ¹⁶They

4:40 ^Judg 18:7-10   4:41 ^1 Chr 4:33-38
4:42 ^Gen 36:8, 9   4:43 ^1 Sam 15:7, 8; 30:17
5:1 ^Gen 35:22; 49:4   5:2 ^Mic 5:2; Matt 2:6
5:3 ^Ex 6:14; Num 26:5-9   5:4 ^1 Chr 5:8
5:7 ^1 Chr 5:17   5:8 ^Num 32:34; Josh 12:2
5:9 ^Josh 22:8, 9   5:10 ^1 Chr 5:18-21   5:11 ^Josh 13:11

lived in Gilead, in Bashan and in its towns, and in all the pasture lands of ^Sharon, as far as their borders. [17]All of these were enrolled in the genealogies in the days of ^Jotham king of Judah, and in the days of [B]Jeroboam king of Israel.

[18]The sons of Reuben, the Gadites, and the half-tribe of Manasseh, *consisting* of valiant men, men who carried shield and sword and shot with a bow and *were* skillful in battle, *totaled* 44,760 who ^went to war. [19]They made war against the Hagrites, ^Jetur, Naphish, and Nodab. [20]They were helped against them, and the Hagrites and all who *were* with them were handed over to them; for ^they cried out to God in the battle, and He answered their prayers because they trusted in Him. [21]They took away their livestock: their fifty thousand camels, 250,000 sheep, *and* two thousand donkeys; and a hundred thousand people. [22]For many fell mortally wounded, because ^the war *was* of God. And they settled in their place until the exile.

[23]Now the sons of the half-tribe of Manasseh lived in the land; from Bashan to Baal-hermon, ^Senir, and Mount Hermon they were numerous. [24]These were the heads of their fathers' households: Epher, Ishi, Eliel, Azriel, Jeremiah, Hodaviah, and Jahdiel, valiant mighty men, famous men, heads of their fathers' households.

[25]But they were ^untrue to the God of their fathers and prostituted themselves with the gods of the peoples of the land, whom God had destroyed before them. [26]So the God of Israel stirred up the spirit of ^Pul, king of Assyria, that is, the spirit of Tilgath-pilneser

king of Assyria, and he took them into exile, namely the Reubenites, the Gadites, and the half-tribe of Manasseh, and brought them to Halah, Habor, Hara, and to the river of Gozan, *where they are* to this day.

GENEALOGY: THE PRIESTLY LINE

6 ^The sons of Levi *were* Gershon, Kohath, and Merari. [2]The sons of Kohath *were* Amram, Izhar, Hebron, and Uzziel. [3]The children of Amram *were* Aaron, Moses, and Miriam. And the sons of Aaron *were* Nadab, Abihu, Eleazar, and Ithamar. [4]Eleazar fathered Phinehas, Phinehas fathered Abishua, [5]Abishua fathered Bukki, Bukki fathered Uzzi, [6]Uzzi fathered Zerahiah, Zerahiah fathered Meraioth, [7]Meraioth fathered Amariah, Amariah fathered Ahitub, [8]^Ahitub fathered Zadok, Zadok [B]fathered Ahimaaz, [9]Ahimaaz fathered Azariah, Azariah fathered Johanan, [10]Johanan fathered Azariah (^it was he who served as the priest in the house which Solomon built in Jerusalem), [11]^Azariah fathered Amariah, Amariah fathered Ahitub, [12]Ahitub fathered Zadok, Zadok fathered Shallum, [13]Shallum fathered Hilkiah, Hilkiah fathered Azariah, [14]Azariah fathered ^Seraiah, and Seraiah fathered Jehozadak; [15]Jehozadak went *along* when the Lord led Judah and Jerusalem into exile by Nebuchadnezzar.

[16]^The sons of Levi *were* Gershom, Kohath, and Merari. [17]These are the names of the sons of Gershom: Libni

5:16 ^Is 35:2; 65:10   5:17 ^2 Kin 15:5, 32
[B]2 Kin 14:16, 28   5:18 ^Num 1:3   5:19 ^Gen 25:15;
1 Chr 1:31   5:20 ^2 Chr 14:11-13   5:22 ^Josh 23:10;
Rom 8:31   5:23 ^Deut 3:9   5:25 ^Deut 32:15-18
5:26 ^2 Kin 15:19, 29; 2 Chr 28:20
6:1 ^Gen 46:11; Ex 6:16-25   6:8 ^2 Sam 8:17
[B]2 Sam 15:27   6:10 ^2 Chr 26:17   6:11 ^Ezra 7:3
6:14 ^Neh 11:11   6:16 ^Gen 46:11; Ex 6:16

and Shimei. [18]The sons of Kohath *were* Amram, Izhar, Hebron, and Uzziel. [19]The sons of ^Merari *were* Mahli and Mushi. And these are the families of the Levites according to their fathers' *households.* [20]Of Gershom: Libni his son, Jahath his son, Zimmah his son, [21]Joah his son, Iddo his son, Zerah his son, *and* Jeatherai his son. [22]The sons of Kohath *were* Amminadab his son, Korah his son, Assir his son, [23]Elkanah his son, Ebiasaph his son, Assir his son, [24]Tahath his son, Uriel his son, Uzziah his son, and Shaul his son. [25]The sons of Elkanah *were* Amasai and Ahimoth. [26]*As for* Elkanah, the sons of Elkanah *were* Zophai his son, Nahath his son, [27]Eliab his son, Jeroham his son, *and* Elkanah his son. [28]The sons of Samuel *were* ^Joel, the firstborn, and Abijah, the second. [29]The sons of Merari *were* Mahli, Libni his son, Shimei his son, Uzzah his son, [30]Shimea his son, Haggiah his son, *and* Asaiah his son.

[31]^Now these are the ones whom David appointed over the service of song in the house of the Lord, after the ark rested *there.* [32]They were ministering in song in front of the tabernacle of the tent of meeting until Solomon's building of the house of the Lord in Jerusalem; and they served in their office according to their order. [33]These are the ones who served with their sons: From the sons of the Kohathites *were* Heman the singer, the son of Joel, the son of Samuel, [34]the son of Elkanah, the son of Jeroham, the son of Eliel, the son of Toah, [35]the son of Zuph, the son of Elkanah, the son of Mahath, the son of Amasai, [36]the son of Elkanah, the son of Joel, the son of Azariah,

the son of Zephaniah, [37]the son of Tahath, the son of Assir, the son of Ebiasaph, the son of Korah, [38]the son of Izhar, the son of Kohath, the son of Levi, the son of Israel. [39]*Heman's* brother Asaph stood at his right hand, Asaph the son of Berechiah, the son of Shimea, [40]the son of Michael, the son of Baaseiah, the son of Malchijah, [41]the son of Ethni, the son of Zerah, the son of Adaiah, [42]the son of Ethan, the son of Zimmah, the son of Shimei, [43]the son of Jahath, the son of Gershom, the son of Levi. [44]On the left hand *were* their kinsmen the sons of Merari: Ethan the son of Kishi, the son of Abdi, the son of Malluch, [45]the son of Hashabiah, the son of Amaziah, the son of Hilkiah, [46]the son of Amzi, the son of Bani, the son of Shemer, [47]the son of Mahli, the son of Mushi, the son of Merari, the son of Levi. [48]Their kinsmen the Levites were appointed for all the service of the tabernacle of the house of God.

[49]But Aaron and his sons ^offered on the altar of burnt offering and on the altar of incense, for all the work of the Most Holy Place, and to make atonement for Israel, in accordance with everything that Moses the servant of God had commanded. [50]^These are the sons of Aaron: Eleazar his son, Phinehas his son, Abishua his son, [51]Bukki his son, Uzzi his son, Zerahiah his son, [52]Meraioth his son, Amariah his son, Ahitub his son, [53]Zadok his son, *and* Ahimaaz his son.

[54]Now these are their settlements according to their camps within their borders. To the sons of Aaron

6:19 ^Num 3:33; 1 Chr 23:21
6:28 ^1 Sam 8:2; 1 Chr 6:33   6:31 ^1 Chr 15:16-22, 27;
16:4-6   6:49 ^Ex 27:1-8   6:50 ^1 Chr 6:4-8; Ezra 7:5

of the families of the Kohathites (for theirs was the ^first lot), ⁵⁵to them they gave ^Hebron in the land of Judah and its pasture lands around it; ⁵⁶^but they gave the fields of the city and its settlements to Caleb the son of Jephunneh. ⁵⁷^To the sons of Aaron they gave the *following* cities of refuge: Hebron, Libnah *together* with its pasture lands, Jattir, Eshtemoa with its pasture lands, ⁵⁸Hilen with its pasture lands, Debir with its pasture lands, ⁵⁹Ashan with its pasture lands, and Beth-shemesh with its pasture lands; ⁶⁰and from the tribe of Benjamin: Geba with its pasture lands, Allemeth with its pasture lands, and Anathoth with its pasture lands. Their cities throughout their families were thirteen cities in all.

⁶¹^Then to the rest of the sons of Kohath *were given* by lot, from the family of the tribe, from the half-tribe, the half of Manasseh, ten cities. ⁶²To the sons of Gershom, according to their families, *were given* from the tribe of Issachar, the tribe of Asher, the tribe of Naphtali, and the tribe of Manasseh, thirteen cities in Bashan. ⁶³^To the sons of Merari *were given* by lot, according to their families, from the tribe of Reuben, the tribe of Gad, and the tribe of Zebulun, twelve cities. ⁶⁴^So the sons of Israel gave the Levites the cities with their pasture lands. ⁶⁵They gave by lot from the tribe of the sons of Judah, the tribe of the sons of Simeon, and the tribe of the sons of Benjamin, ^these cities which are mentioned by name.

⁶⁶^Now some of the families of the sons of Kohath had cities of their territory from the tribe of Ephraim. ⁶⁷They gave to them the *following*

cities of refuge: Shechem in the hill country of Ephraim with its pasture lands, Gezer with its pasture lands, ⁶⁸Jokmeam with its pasture lands, Beth-horon with its pasture lands, ⁶⁹Aijalon with its pasture lands, and Gath-rimmon with its pasture lands; ⁷⁰and from the half-tribe of Manasseh: Aner with its pasture lands and Bileam with its pasture lands, for the rest of the family of the sons of Kohath.

⁷¹To the sons of Gershom *were given,* from the family of the half-tribe of Manasseh: Golan in Bashan with its pasture lands and Ashtaroth with its pasture lands; ⁷²and from the tribe of Issachar: Kedesh with its pasture lands, Daberath with its pasture lands, ⁷³Ramoth with its pasture lands, and Anem with its pasture lands; ⁷⁴and from the tribe of Asher: Mashal with its pasture lands, Abdon with its pasture lands, ⁷⁵Hukok with its pasture lands, and Rehob with its pasture lands; ⁷⁶and from the tribe of Naphtali: Kedesh in Galilee with its pasture lands, Hammon with its pasture lands, and Kiriathaim with its pasture lands.

⁷⁷To the rest of *the Levites,* the sons of Merari, *were given,* from the tribe of Zebulun: Rimmono with its pasture lands, Tabor with its pasture lands, ⁷⁸and beyond the Jordan at Jericho, on the east side of the Jordan, *were given them,* from the tribe of Reuben: Bezer in the wilderness with its pasture lands, Jahzah with its pasture lands, ⁷⁹Kedemoth with its pasture lands, and Mephaath with its pasture lands; ⁸⁰and from the tribe of Gad: Ramoth in

6:54^Josh 21:4, 10   6:55^Josh 14:13; 21:11f
6:56^Josh 15:13   6:57^Josh 21:13, 19   6:61^Josh 21:5;
1 Chr 6:66-70   6:63^Josh 21:7, 34-40
6:64^Num 35:1-8; Josh 21:3, 41, 42   6:65^1 Chr
6:57-60   6:66^Josh 21:20-26

Gilead with its pasture lands, Mahanaim with its pasture lands, [81]Heshbon with its pasture lands, and Jazer with its pasture lands.

GENEALOGY FROM ISSACHAR

7 Now the sons of Issachar *were* four: Tola, Puah, Jashub, and Shimron. [2]The sons of Tola *were* Uzzi, Rephaiah, Jeriel, Jahmai, Ibsam, and Samuel, heads of their fathers' households. *The sons* of Tola *were* valiant warriors in their generations. ^Their number in the days of David was 22,600. [3]The son of Uzzi *was* Izrahiah. And the sons of Izrahiah *were* Michael, Obadiah, Joel, *and* Isshiah; all five of them *were* ^chief men. [4]And with them by their generations according to their fathers' households were thirty-six thousand troops of the army for war; for they had many wives and sons. [5]Their relatives among all the families of Issachar *were* valiant warriors, registered by genealogy, eighty-seven thousand in all.

DESCENDANTS OF BENJAMIN

[6]^Benjamin *had* three *sons:* Bela, Becher, and Jediael. [7]The sons of Bela were five: Ezbon, Uzzi, Uzziel, Jerimoth, and Iri. They *were* heads of fathers' households, valiant warriors, 22,034 registered by genealogy. [8]The sons of Becher *were* Zemirah, Joash, Eliezer, Elioenai, Omri, Jeremoth, Abijah, Anathoth, and Alemeth. All these *were* the sons of Becher. [9]They were registered by genealogy according to their generations, heads of their fathers' households, 20,200 valiant warriors. [10]The son of Jediael *was* Bilhan. And the sons of Bilhan *were* Jeush, Benjamin, Ehud, Chenaanah, Zethan, Tarshish, and Ahishahar. [11]All these *were* sons of Jediael, according to the heads of their fathers' households, 17,200 valiant warriors who were ready to go out with the army to war. [12]Shuppim and Huppim *were* the sons of Ir; Hushim *was* the son of Aher.

SONS OF NAPHTALI

[13]The sons of Naphtali *were* Jahziel, Guni, Jezer, and Shallum, the sons of Bilhah.

DESCENDANTS OF MANASSEH

[14]The sons of Manasseh *were* Asriel, to whom his Aramean concubine gave birth; she *also* gave birth to Machir, the father of Gilead. [15]Machir took a wife from Huppim and Shuppim, whose name was Maacah. And the name of the second was Zelophehad, and Zelophehad had daughters. [16]Maacah the wife of Machir gave birth to a son, and she named him Peresh; the name of his brother *was* Sheresh, and his sons *were* Ulam and Rakem. [17]The son of Ulam *was* Bedan. These *were* the sons of Gilead the son of Machir, the son of Manasseh. [18]His sister Hammolecheth gave birth to Ishhod, Abiezer, and Mahlah. [19]The sons of Shemida were Ahian, Shechem, Likhi, and Aniam.

DESCENDANTS OF EPHRAIM

[20]^The sons of Ephraim *were* Shuthelah and Bered his son, Tahath his son, Eleadah his son, Tahath his son, [21]Zabad his son, Shuthelah his son, and Ezer and Elead, whom the men of Gath who were born in the land killed, because they came down to take their livestock. [22]Their

father Ephraim ^mourned for many days, and his relatives came to comfort him. ²³Then he went in to his wife, and she conceived and gave birth to a son, and he named him Beriah, because misfortune had come upon his house. ²⁴His daughter was Sheerah, ^who built lower and upper Beth-horon, as well as Uzzen-sheerah. ²⁵Rephah was his son *along* with Resheph, Telah his son, Tahan his son, ²⁶Ladan his son, Ammihud his son, Elishama his son, ²⁷Non his son, and ^Joshua his son.

²⁸^Their possessions and dwelling places *were* Bethel with its towns, and to the east, Naaran, and to the west, Gezer with its towns, and Shechem with its towns, as far as Ayyah with its towns, ²⁹and along the borders of the sons of Manasseh, Beth-shean with its towns, Taanach with its towns, Megiddo with its towns, *and* Dor with its towns. In these *regions* lived the ^sons of Joseph the son of Israel.

DESCENDANTS OF ASHER

³⁰^The sons of Asher *were* Imnah, Ishvah, Ishvi, and Beriah, and Serah *was* their sister. ³¹The sons of Beriah *were* Heber and Malchiel, who was the father of Birzaith. ³²Heber fathered Japhlet, Shomer, and Hotham, and their sister Shua. ³³The sons of Japhlet *were* Pasach, Bimhal, and Ashvath. These were the sons of Japhlet. ³⁴The sons of Shemer *were* Ahi and Rohgah, *and* Jehubbah and Aram. ³⁵The sons of his brother Helem *were* Zophah, Imna, Shelesh, and Amal. ³⁶The sons of Zophah *were* Suah, Harnepher, Shual, Beri, Imrah, ³⁷Bezer, Hod, Shamma, Shilshah, Ithran, and Beera. ³⁸The sons of Jether

were Jephunneh, Pispa, and Ara. ³⁹The sons of Ulla *were* Arah, Hanniel, and Rizia. ⁴⁰All these *were* the sons of Asher, heads of the fathers' houses, choice, valiant mighty men, *and* heads of the leaders. And the number of them registered by genealogy for service in war was twenty-six thousand men.

GENEALOGY FROM BENJAMIN

8 And ^Benjamin fathered Bela his firstborn, Ashbel the second, Aharah the third, ²Nohah the fourth, and Rapha the fifth. ³Bela had sons: Addar, Gera, Abihud, ⁴Abishua, Naaman, Ahoah, ⁵Gera, Shephuphan, and Huram. ⁶These are the sons of Ehud: these are the heads of fathers' *households* of the inhabitants of Geba, and they took them into exile to Manahath, ⁷namely, Naaman, Ahijah, and Gera—he exiled them; and he fathered Uzza and Ahihud. ⁸Shaharaim fathered children in the country of Moab after he had sent his wives Hushim and Baara away. ⁹By Hodesh his wife he fathered Jobab, Zibia, Mesha, Malcam, ¹⁰Jeuz, Sachia, and Mirmah. These were his sons, heads of fathers' *households*. ¹¹By Hushim he fathered Abitub and Elpaal. ¹²The sons of Elpaal *were* Eber, Misham, and Shemed, who built Ono and Lod, with its towns; ¹³and Beriah and Shema, who were heads of fathers' *households* of the inhabitants of Aijalon, who put the inhabitants of Gath to flight; ¹⁴and Ahio, Shashak, and Jeremoth. ¹⁵Zebadiah, Arad, Eder, ¹⁶Michael, Ishpah, and

7:22^Gen 37:34   7:24^Josh 16:3, 5; 2 Chr 8:5
7:27^Ex 17:9–14; 24:13   7:28^Josh 16:2
7:29^Judg 1:22–29   7:30^Gen 46:17; Num 26:44–46
8:1^Gen 46:21; 1 Chr 7:6–12

Joha *were* the sons of Beriah. ¹⁷Zebadiah, Meshullam, Hizki, Heber, ¹⁸Ishmerai, Izliah, and Jobab *were* the sons of Elpaal. ¹⁹Jakim, Zichri, Zabdi, ²⁰Elienai, Zillethai, Eliel, ²¹Adaiah, Beraiah, and Shimrath *were* the sons of Shimei. ²²Ishpan, Eber, Eliel, ²³Abdon, Zichri, Hanan, ²⁴Hananiah, Elam, Anthothijah, ²⁵Iphdeiah, and Penuel *were* the sons of Shashak. ²⁶Shamsherai, Shehariah, Athaliah, ²⁷Jaareshiah, Elijah, and Zichri *were* the sons of Jeroham. ²⁸These were heads of the fathers' *households* according to their generations, chief men who lived in Jerusalem.

²⁹ᴬNow, *Jeiel,* the father of Gibeon lived in Gibeon, and his wife's name was Maacah; ³⁰and his firstborn son *was* Abdon, then Zur, Kish, Baal, Nadab, ³¹Gedor, Ahio, and Zecher. ³²Mikloth fathered Shimeah. They also lived with their relatives in Jerusalem opposite their *other* relatives.

GENEALOGY FROM KING SAUL

³³ᴬNer fathered Kish, Kish fathered Saul, and Saul fathered Jonathan, Malchi-shua, Abinadab, and Eshbaal. ³⁴The son of Jonathan *was* Merib-baal, and Merib-baal fathered Micah. ³⁵The sons of Micah *were* Pithon, Melech, Tarea, and Ahaz. ³⁶Ahaz fathered Jehoaddah, Jehoaddah fathered Alemeth, Azmaveth, and Zimri; and Zimri fathered Moza. ³⁷Moza fathered Binea; Raphah *was* his son, Eleasah, his son, *and* Azel, his son. ³⁸Azel had six sons, and these *were* their names: Azrikam, Bocheru, Ishmael, Sheariah, Obadiah, and Hanan. All these *were* the sons of Azel. ³⁹The sons of his brother Eshek *were* Ulam his firstborn,

Jeush the second, and Eliphelet the third. ⁴⁰The sons of Ulam were valiant mighty men, archers, and they had many sons and grandsons, 150 *of them.* All these *were* among the sons of Benjamin.

PEOPLE OF JERUSALEM

9 So all Israel was enrolled in genealogies; and behold, they are written in the Book of the Kings of Israel. And ᴬJudah was taken into exile to Babylon for their infidelity.

²ᴬNow the first inhabitants who *lived* on their own property in their cities *were people of* Israel, *including* the priests, the Levites, and the temple servants. ³Some of the sons of Judah, some of the sons of Benjamin, and some of the sons of Ephraim and Manasseh lived in ᴬJerusalem: ⁴Uthai the son of Ammihud, the son of Omri, the son of Imri, the son of Bani, from the sons of Perez the ᴬson of Judah. ⁵From the Shilonites *were* Asaiah the firstborn and his sons. ⁶From the sons of Zerah *were* Jeuel and their relatives, 690 *of them.* ⁷From the sons of Benjamin *were* Sallu the son of Meshullam, the son of Hodaviah, the son of Hassenuah, ⁸and Ibneiah the son of Jeroham, and Elah the son of Uzzi, the son of Michri, and Meshullam the son of Shephatiah, the son of Reuel, the son of Ibnijah; ⁹and their relatives according to their generations, ᴬ956. All these men *were* heads of fathers' *households* according to their fathers' houses.

¹⁰ᴬFrom the priests *were* Jedaiah, Jehoiarib, Jachin, ¹¹and Azariah the

son of Hilkiah, the son of Meshullam, the son of Zadok, the son of Meraioth, the son of Ahitub, ^the chief officer of the house of God; ¹²and Adaiah the son of Jeroham, the son of Pashhur, the son of Malchijah, and Maasai the son of Adiel, the son of Jahzerah, the son of Meshullam, the son of Meshillemith, the son of Immer; ¹³and their relatives, heads of their fathers' households, 1,760 competent men for the work of the service of the house of God.

¹⁴^Of the Levites, *there were* Shemaiah the son of Hasshub, the son of Azrikam, the son of Hashabiah, of the sons of Merari; ¹⁵and Bakbakkar, Heresh, and Galal; and Mattaniah the son of Mica, the son of Zichri, the son of Asaph, ¹⁶and Obadiah the son of Shemaiah, the son of Galal, the son of Jeduthun; and Berechiah the son of Asa, the son of Elkanah, who lived in the settlements of the Netophathites.

¹⁷Now the gatekeepers *were* Shallum, Akkub, Talmon, Ahiman, and their relatives (Shallum the chief ¹⁸*being stationed* until now at ^the king's gate to the east). These *were* the gatekeepers for the camp of the sons of Levi. ¹⁹Shallum the son of Kore, the son of Ebiasaph, the son of Korah, and his relatives of his father's house, the Korahites, *were* in charge of the work of the service, doorkeepers of the tent; and their fathers had been in charge of the camp of the LORD, keepers of the entrance. ²⁰^Phinehas the son of Eleazar was supervisor over them previously, *and* the LORD was with him. ²¹^Zechariah the son of Meshelemiah was gatekeeper of the entrance of the tent of meeting. ²²Those who were chosen to be gatekeepers at the thresholds were

212 in all. They were registered by genealogy in their settlements, ^those whom David and Samuel the seer appointed ᴮin their official capacity. ²³So they and their sons were in charge of the gates of the house of the LORD, the house of the tent, in their divisions of service. ²⁴The gatekeepers were on the four sides, to the east, west, north, and south. ²⁵Their relatives in their settlements ^*were* to come in every seven days from time to time *to be* with them; ²⁶for the four chief gatekeepers, who *were* Levites, *served* in an official capacity, and were in charge of the chambers and in charge of the treasuries in the house of God. ²⁷They spent the night around the house of God, ^because the watch was committed to them; and they were in charge of opening *it* morning by morning.

²⁸Now some of them were in charge of the utensils of the service, for they counted them when they brought them in and when they took them out. ²⁹Some of them also were appointed over the furniture and over all the utensils of the sanctuary, and ^over the finely milled flour, the wine, the olive oil, the frankincense, and the balsam oil. ³⁰Some of ^the sons of the priests prepared the mixing of the balsam oil. ³¹Mattithiah, one of the Levites, who was the firstborn of Shallum the Korahite, had ^the responsibility for the baking of cakes in pans. ³²Some of their relatives of the sons of the Kohathites ^were in charge of the showbread to prepare it every Sabbath.

9:11^Jer 20:1   9:14^Neh 11:15-19   9:18^Ezek 44:1; 46:1, 2   9:20^Num 25:7-13   9:21^1 Chr 26:2, 14   9:22^1 Chr 26:1   ᴮ2 Chr 31:15, 18   9:25^2 Kin 11:5, 7; 2 Chr 23:8   9:27^1 Chr 23:30-32   9:29^1 Chr 23:29   9:30^Ex 30:23-25   9:31^1 Chr 9:22   9:32^Lev 24:5-8

33 Now these are ^the singers, heads of fathers' *households* of the Levites, *who lived* in the chambers *of the temple* free *of other duties;* for they were engaged in their work day and night. 34 These were heads of fathers' *households* of the Levites according to their generations, chief men who lived in Jerusalem.

ANCESTRY AND DESCENDANTS OF SAUL

35 ^Jeiel the father of Gibeon lived in Gibeon, and his wife's name was Maacah, 36 and his firstborn son *was* Abdon, then Zur, Kish, Baal, Ner, Nadab, 37 Gedor, Ahio, Zechariah, and Mikloth. 38 Mikloth fathered Shimeam. And they also lived with their relatives in Jerusalem opposite their *other* relatives. 39 ^Ner fathered Kish, Kish fathered Saul, and Saul fathered Jonathan, Malchi-shua, Abinadab, and Eshbaal. 40 The son of Jonathan *was* Merib-baal; and Merib-baal fathered Micah. 41 The sons of Micah *were* Pithon, Melech, Tahrea, ^*and Ahaz.* 42 Ahaz fathered Jarah, Jarah fathered Alemeth, Azmaveth, and Zimri; and Zimri fathered Moza. 43 Moza fathered Binea, and Rephaiah *was* his son, Eleasah his son, Azel his son. 44 Azel had six sons whose names were these: Azrikam, Bocheru, Ishmael, Sheariah, Obadiah, and Hanan. These were the sons of Azel.

DEFEAT AND DEATH OF SAUL AND HIS SONS

10 ^Now the Philistines fought against Israel, and the men of Israel fled from the Philistines but fell fatally wounded on Mount Gilboa. 2 And the Philistines also overtook Saul and his sons, and

the Philistines killed Jonathan, ^Abinadab, and Malchi-shua, the sons of Saul. 3 The battle became severe against Saul, and the archers found him; and he was wounded by the archers. 4 Then Saul said to his armor bearer, "Draw your sword and thrust me through with it, otherwise these uncircumcised *Philistines* will come and abuse me." But his armor bearer would not, for he was very afraid. ^So Saul took his *own* sword and fell on it. 5 When his armor bearer saw that Saul was dead, he likewise fell on his sword and died. 6 ^So Saul died with his three sons, and all *those* of his house died together.

7 When all the people of Israel who were in the valley saw that they had fled, and that Saul and his sons were dead, they abandoned their cities and fled; and the Philistines came and lived in them.

8 It came about the next day, when the Philistines came to strip those killed, that they found Saul and his sons fallen on Mount Gilboa. 9 ^So they stripped him and took his head and his armor and sent *messengers* around the land of the Philistines to carry the good news to their idols and to the people. 10 They put his armor in the house of their gods and impaled his head in the house of Dagon.

JABESH-GILEAD'S TRIBUTE TO SAUL

11 When all Jabesh-gilead heard everything that the Philistines had done to Saul, 12 ^all the valiant men got up and took away the body of Saul and the bodies of his sons, and

9:33^1 Chr 6:31-47; 25:1   9:35^1 Chr 8:29-32
9:39^1 Chr 8:33-38   9:41^1 Chr 8:35-37
10:1^1 Sam 31:1-13   10:2^1 Sam 31:2   10:4^1 Sam 31:4
10:6^1 Sam 31:6   10:9^1 Sam 31:9   10:12^1 Sam 31:12f

brought them to Jabesh; and they buried their bones under the oak in Jabesh, and fasted for seven days.

13ᴬSo Saul died for his unfaithfulness which he committed against the LORD, because of the word of the LORD which he did not keep; and also ᴮbecause he asked *counsel* of a medium, making inquiry *of her,* 14and did not inquire of the LORD. Therefore He killed him and ᴬturned the kingdom over to David, the son of Jesse.

DAVID MADE KING OVER ALL ISRAEL

11 ᴬThen all Israel gathered to David at Hebron and said, "Behold, we are your bone and your flesh. 2In times past, even when Saul was king, you *were* the one who led out and brought in Israel; and the LORD your God said to you, 'ᴬYou shall shepherd My people Israel, and you shall be leader over My people Israel.'" 3So all the elders of Israel came to the king at Hebron, and David made a covenant with them in Hebron before the LORD; and ᴬthey anointed David king over Israel, ᴮin accordance with the word of the LORD through Samuel.

JERUSALEM IS THE CAPITAL CITY

4Then David and all Israel went to Jerusalem (ᴬthat is, Jebus); and the Jebusites, the inhabitants of the land, *were* there. 5The inhabitants of Jebus said to David, "You shall not enter here." Nevertheless David took the mountain stronghold of Zion (that is, the city of David). 6Now David had said, "Whoever is first to kill a Jebusite shall be chief and commander." ᴬJoab the son of Zeruiah went up first, so he became chief. 7Then David lived in the stronghold; therefore it was called

the city of David. 8He built the city all around, from the ¹Millo to the surrounding area; and Joab repaired the rest of the city. 9ᴬAnd David became greater and greater, for the LORD of armies *was* with him.

DAVID'S MIGHTY MEN

10ᴬNow these are the heads of the mighty men whom David had, who remained faithful to him in his kingdom, together with all Israel, to make him king, in accordance with the word of the LORD concerning Israel. 11These *constitute* the list of David's mighty men: ᴬJashobeam, the son of a Hachmonite, the chief of the thirty; he wielded his spear against three hundred whom he killed at one time.

12After him was Eleazar the son of ᴬDodo, the Ahohite, who *was* one of the three mighty men. 13He was with David at Pas-dammim ᴬwhen the Philistines were gathered together there to battle, and there was a plot of land full of barley; and the people fled from the Philistines. 14But they took their stand in the midst of the plot and defended it, and defeated the Philistines; and the LORD saved them with a great victory.

15Now three of the thirty chief men went down to the rock to David, into the cave of Adullam, while ᴬthe army of the Philistines was camping in the Valley of Rephaim. 16David was then in the stronghold, while ᴬthe garrison of

10:13ᴬ1 Sam 13:13, 14   ᴮLev 19:31   10:14ᴬ1 Sam 15:28;
1 Chr 12:23   11:1ᴬ2 Sam 5:1, 3, 6-10   11:2ᴬ2 Sam 5:2; 7:7
11:3ᴬ2 Sam 5:3, 5   ᴮ1 Sam 16:1, 3, 12, 13
11:4ᴬJosh 15:8, 63; Judg 1:21   11:6ᴬ2 Sam 8:16
11:9ᴬ2 Sam 3:1   11:10ᴬ2 Sam 23:8-39   11:11ᴬ2 Sam 23:8
11:12ᴬ1 Chr 27:4   11:13ᴬ2 Sam 23:11, 12
11:15ᴬ1 Chr 14:9   11:16ᴬ1 Sam 10:5

11:8 ¹I.e., terraced structure

the Philistines *was* then in Bethlehem. ¹⁷And David had a craving and said, "Oh that someone would give me water to drink from the well of Bethlehem, which is by the gate!" ¹⁸So the three broke through the camp of the Philistines and drew water from the well of Bethlehem which *was* by the gate, and took *it* and brought *it* to David; however, David would not drink it, but poured it out to the LORD; ¹⁹and he said, "Far be it from me before my God that I would do this. Shall I drink the blood of these men *who went* at the risk of their lives? For they brought it at the risk of their lives." Therefore he would not drink it. The three mighty men did these things.

²⁰As for Abshai the brother of Joab, he was chief of the thirty, and he wielded his spear against three hundred and killed them; and he had a name as well as the thirty. ²¹Of the three in the second *rank* he was the most honored, and he became their commander; however, he did not attain *the reputation* of the *first* three.

²²ᴬBenaiah the son of Jehoiada, the son of a warrior of Kabzeel, mighty in deeds, struck and killed the two *sons of* Ariel of Moab. He also went down and struck and killed a lion inside a pit on a snowy day. ²³And he killed an Egyptian, a man of *great* stature ¹five cubits tall. Now in the Egyptian's hand *was* ᴬa spear like a weaver's beam, but he went down to him with a club and snatched the spear from the Egyptian's hand and killed him with his own spear. ²⁴Benaiah the son of Jehoiada did these things, and had a name as well as the three mighty men. ²⁵Behold, he

was honored among the thirty, but he did not attain *the reputation* of the *first* three; and David appointed him over his bodyguard.

²⁶Now the mighty men of the armies *were* Asahel the brother of Joab, Elhanan the son of Dodo of Bethlehem, ²⁷Shammoth the Harorite, Helez the Pelonite, ²⁸Ira the son of Ikkesh the Tekoite, Abiezer the Anathothite, ²⁹Sibbecai the Hushathite, Ilai the Ahohite, ³⁰Maharai the Netophathite, Heled the son of Baanah the Netophathite, ³¹Ithai the son of Ribai of Gibeah of the sons of Benjamin, Benaiah the Pirathonite, ³²Hurai of the brooks of Gaash, Abiel the Arbathite, ³³Azmaveth the Baharumite, Eliahba the Shaalbonite, ³⁴the sons of Hashem the Gizonite, Jonathan the son of Shagee the Hararite, ³⁵Ahiam the son of Sacar the Hararite, Eliphal the son of Ur, ³⁶Hepher the Mecherathite, Ahijah the Pelonite, ³⁷Hezro the Carmelite, Naarai the son of Ezbai, ³⁸Joel the brother of Nathan, Mibhar the son of Hagri, ³⁹Zelek the Ammonite, Naharai the Berothite, the armor bearer of Joab the son of Zeruiah, ⁴⁰Ira the Ithrite, Gareb the Ithrite, ⁴¹Uriah the Hittite, Zabad the son of Ahlai, ⁴²Adina the son of Shiza the Reubenite, a chief of the Reubenites, and thirty with him, ⁴³Hanan the son of Maacah and Joshaphat the Mithnite, ⁴⁴Uzzia the Ashterathite, Shama and Jeiel the sons of Hotham the Aroerite, ⁴⁵Jediael the son of Shimri and his brother Joha the Tizite, ⁴⁶Eliel the Mahavite, and Jeribai and Joshaviah, the sons of Elnaam,

---

11:22ᴬ2 Sam 8:18   11:23ᴬ1 Sam 17:7

11:23¹About 7.5 ft. or 2.3 m

Ithmah the Moabite, ⁴⁷Eliel, Obed, and Jaasiel the Mezobaite.

DAVID'S SUPPORTERS IN ZIKLAG

12 ᴬNow these are the *men* who came to David at Ziklag, while he was still restricted because of Saul the son of Kish; and they were among the mighty men who helped *him* in war. ²They were equipped with bows, using both the right hand and the left *to sling* stones and *shoot* arrows with the bow; ᴬ*they were* Saul's kinsmen from Benjamin. ³The chief was Ahiezer, then Joash, the sons of Shemaah the Gibeathite; and Jeziel and Pelet, the sons of Azmaveth, and Beracah, and Jehu the Anathothite, ⁴and Ishmaiah the Gibeonite, a mighty man among the thirty, and in charge of the thirty. Then Jeremiah, Jahaziel, Johanan, Jozabad the Gederathite, ⁵Eluzai, Jerimoth, Bealiah, Shemariah, Shephatiah the Haruphite, ⁶Elkanah, Isshiah, Azarel, Joezer, Jashobeam, the Korahites, ⁷and Joelah and Zebadiah, the sons of Jeroham of Gedor.

⁸From the Gadites valiant mighty men went over to David at the stronghold in the wilderness, men trained for war who could handle a large shield and spear, whose faces were *like* the faces of lions, and ᴬ*they were* as swift as the gazelles on the mountains. ⁹Ezer *was* the first, Obadiah the second, Eliab the third, ¹⁰Mishmannah the fourth, Jeremiah the fifth, ¹¹Attai the sixth, Eliel the seventh, ¹²Johanan the eighth, Elzabad the ninth, ¹³Jeremiah the tenth, *and* Machbannai, the eleventh. ¹⁴These men from the sons of Gad were captains of the army; ᴬthe one who was least was *equal* to a hundred, and the greatest, to a thousand. ¹⁵ᴬThese are the ones who crossed the Jordan in the first month, when it was overflowing all its banks, and they put to flight all those in the valleys, to the east and to the west.

¹⁶Then some of the sons of Benjamin and Judah came to the stronghold to David. ¹⁷David went out to meet them, and said to them, "If you come peacefully to help me, my heart shall be united with you; but if to betray me to my enemies, since there is no wrong in my hands, may the God of our fathers look on *it* and decide." ¹⁸Then ᴬthe Spirit covered ᴮAmasai like clothing, the chief of the thirty; *and he said,*

"*We are* yours, David,
   And *are* with you, son of Jesse!
   Peace, peace to you,
   And peace to him who helps you;
   Indeed, your God helps you!"
Then David received them and made them captains of the troops.

¹⁹ᴬFrom Manasseh some also defected to David when he was about to go to battle with the Philistines against Saul. But they did not help them, because the governors of the Philistines sent him away after consultation, saying, "At *the cost of* our heads he might defect to his master Saul." ²⁰As he was going to Ziklag, *men* from Manasseh defected to him: Adnah, Jozabad, Jediael, Michael, Jozabad, Elihu, and Zillethai, captains of thousands who belonged to Manasseh. ²¹They helped David against ᴬthe band of raiders, for they were all valiant mighty men, and were captains in the army. ²²For day by day

12:1ᴬ1 Sam 27:2-6   12:2ᴬ1 Chr 12:29   12:8ᴬ2 Sam 2:18   12:14ᴬDeut 32:30   12:15ᴬJosh 3:15; 4:18   12:18ᴬJudg 3:10   ᴮ1 Chr 2:17   12:19ᴬ1 Sam 29:2-9   12:21ᴬ1 Sam 30:1

men came to David to help him, until there was a great army ^like the army of God.

SUPPORTERS GATHERED AT HEBRON

²³Now these are the numbers of the divisions equipped for war, ^who came to David at Hebron, to turn the kingdom of Saul to him, according to the word of the LORD. ²⁴The sons of Judah who carried shield and spear *numbered* 6,800, equipped for war. ²⁵From the sons of Simeon, valiant mighty men of war, 7,100. ²⁶From the sons of Levi, 4,600. ²⁷Now Jehoiada was the leader of *the house of* Aaron, and with him were 3,700, ²⁸also ^Zadok, a young valiant mighty man, and *from* his father's house, twenty-two captains. ²⁹From the sons of Benjamin, ^Saul's kinsmen, three thousand; for until now ᴮthe majority of them had kept their allegiance to the house of Saul. ³⁰From the sons of Ephraim 20,800, valiant mighty men, famous men in their fathers' households. ³¹From the half-tribe of Manasseh eighteen thousand, who were designated by name to come and make David king. ³²From the sons of Issachar, ^men who understood the times, with knowledge of what Israel should do, their chiefs *were* two hundred; and all their kinsmen *were* at their command. ³³From Zebulun, there were fifty thousand who went out in the army, who could draw up in battle formation with all kinds of weapons of war and helped *David* with ^an undivided heart. ³⁴From Naphtali *there were* a thousand captains, and with them thirty-seven thousand with shield and spear. ³⁵From the Danites who could draw up in battle formation, *there were* 28,600.

³⁶From Asher *there were* forty thousand who went out in the army to draw up in battle formation. ³⁷From the other side of the Jordan, from the Reubenites, the Gadites, and the half-tribe of Manasseh, *there were* 120,000 with all *kinds* of weapons of war for the battle.

³⁸All of these, being men of war who helped in battle formation, came to Hebron with ^a perfect heart to make David king over all Israel; and all the rest of Israel also were of one mind to make David king. ³⁹They were there with David for three days, eating and drinking, for their kinsmen had prepared for them. ⁴⁰Moreover, those who were near to them, as far as Issachar, Zebulun, and Naphtali, ^brought food on donkeys, camels, mules, and on oxen, great quantities of flour cakes, fig cakes and bunches of raisins, wine, oil, oxen, and sheep. There was joy indeed in Israel.

PERIL IN TRANSPORTING THE ARK

13 Then David consulted with the captains of the thousands and the hundreds, with every leader. ²David said to all the assembly of Israel, "If it *seems* good to you, and if it is from the LORD our God, ¹let us send *word* everywhere to our kinsmen who remain in all the land of Israel, and to the priests and Levites who are with them in their cities with pasture lands, that they meet with us; ³and ¹let us bring back the ark of our God to us, ^since we did not seek it in the

---

12:22^Gen 32:2; Josh 5:13-15　12:23^2 Sam 2:3, 4
12:28^2 Sam 8:17; 1 Chr 6:8, 53　12:29^1 Chr 12:2
ᴮ2 Sam 2:8, 9　12:32^Esth 1:13　12:33^Ps 12:2
12:38^2 Sam 5:1-3; 1 Chr 12:33　12:40^1 Sam 25:18
13:3^1 Sam 7:1, 2

13:2 ¹Indicating a proposal, not a request　13:3 ¹See note v 2

days of Saul." ⁴Then all the assembly said that they would do so, for this was right in the eyes of all the people.

⁵So David assembled all Israel together, from the Shihor of Egypt to the entrance of Hamath, ᴬto bring the ark of God from Kiriath-jearim. ⁶ᴬDavid and all Israel went up to Baalah, *that is,* to Kiriath-jearim, which belongs to Judah, to bring up from there the ark of God, the LORD who is enthroned *above* the cherubim, where His name is called. ⁷And they carried the ark of God on a new cart from ᴬthe house of Abinadab, and Uzza and Ahio drove the cart. ⁸David and all Israel were celebrating before God with all *their* might, ᴬwith songs and with lyres, harps, tambourines, cymbals, and trumpets.

⁹When they came to ᴬthe threshing floor of Chidon, Uzza put out his hand to hold the ark, because the oxen nearly overturned *it.* ¹⁰But the anger of the LORD burned against Uzza, so He struck him ᴬbecause he had put out his hand toward the ark; and he died there before God. ¹¹Then David became angry because of the LORD's outburst against Uzza; and he called that place ¹Perez-uzza *as it is* to this day. ¹²David was afraid of God that day, saying, "How can I bring the ark of God *home* to me?" ¹³So David did not take the ark with him to the city of David, but took it aside ᴬto the house of Obed-edom the Gittite. ¹⁴And the ark of God remained with the family of Obed-edom in his house for three months; and ᴬthe LORD blessed the family of Obed-edom and all that he had.

DAVID'S FAMILY ENLARGED

14 ᴬNow Hiram king of Tyre sent messengers to David with cedar trees, masons, and carpenters, to build a house for him. ²And David realized that the LORD had established him as king over Israel, *and* that his kingdom was highly exalted, for the sake of His people Israel.

³Then David took more wives in Jerusalem, and David fathered more sons and daughters. ⁴ᴬThese are the names of the children born to him in Jerusalem: Shammua, Shobab, Nathan, Solomon, ⁵Ibhar, Elishua, Elpelet, ⁶Nogah, Nepheg, Japhia, ⁷Elishama, Beeliada, and Eliphelet.

PHILISTINES DEFEATED

⁸When the Philistines heard that David had been anointed king over all Israel, all the Philistines went up in search of David; and David heard about it and went out against them. ⁹Now the Philistines had come and ᴬcarried out a raid in the Valley of Rephaim. ¹⁰David inquired of God, saying, "Shall I go up against the Philistines? And will You hand them over to me?" Then the LORD said to him, "Go up, for I will hand them over to you." ¹¹So they came up to Baal-perazim, and David defeated them there; and David said, "God has broken through my enemies by my hand, like the breakthrough of waters." Therefore they named that place ¹Baal-perazim. ¹²They abandoned their gods there; so David gave the order and they were burned with fire.

13:5ᴬ1 Sam 6:21; 7:1   13:6ᴬ2 Sam 6:2-11
13:7ᴬ1 Sam 7:1   13:8ᴬ1 Chr 15:16   13:9ᴬ2 Sam 6:6
13:10ᴬ1 Chr 15:13, 15   13:13ᴬ1 Chr 15:25
13:14ᴬ1 Chr 26:4, 5   14:1ᴬ2 Sam 5:11
14:4ᴬ1 Chr 3:5-8   14:9ᴬ1 Chr 11:15; 14:13

13:11¹l.e., the outburst *against* Uzza   14:11¹l.e., the master of breakthroughs

¹³The Philistines carried out ^yet another raid in the valley. ¹⁴David inquired again of God, and God said to him, "You shall not go up after them; circle around behind them and come at them in front of the baka-shrubs. ¹⁵When you hear the sound of marching in the tops of the baka-shrubs, then you shall go out to battle, for God will have gone out before you to strike the army of the Philistines." ¹⁶David did just as God had commanded him, and they defeated the army of the Philistines from Gibeon even as far as Gezer. ¹⁷Then the fame of David spread in all the lands; and ^the Lord brought the fear of him on all the nations.

PLANS TO MOVE THE ARK TO JERUSALEM

15 Now *David* built houses for himself in the city of David; and he prepared a place for the ark of God and ^pitched a tent for it. ²Then David said, "^No one is to carry the ark of God except the Levites; for the Lord chose them to carry the ark of the Lord and to serve Him forever." ³And ^David assembled all Israel at Jerusalem to bring up the ark of the Lord to its place which he had prepared for it. ⁴David gathered together the sons of Aaron and ^the Levites: ⁵of the sons of Kohath, Uriel the chief, and 120 of his relatives; ⁶of the sons of Merari, Asaiah the chief, and 220 of his relatives; ⁷of the sons of Gershom, Joel the chief, and 130 of his relatives; ⁸of the sons of Elizaphan, Shemaiah the chief, and two hundred of his relatives; ⁹of the sons of Hebron, Eliel the chief, and eighty of his relatives; ¹⁰of the sons of Uzziel, Amminadab the chief, and 112 of his relatives.

¹¹Then David called for the priests ^Zadok and ^Abiathar, and for the Levites, for Uriel, Asaiah, Joel, Shemaiah, Eliel, and Amminadab; ¹²and he said to them, "You are the heads of the fathers' *households* of the Levites; ^consecrate yourselves, you and your relatives, so that you may bring up the ark of the Lord God of Israel to *the place* that I have prepared for it. ¹³^Because you did not *carry it* at the first, the Lord our God made an outburst against us, since we did not seek Him according to the ordinance." ¹⁴^So the priests and the Levites consecrated themselves to bring up the ark of the Lord God of Israel. ¹⁵The sons of ^the Levites carried the ark of God on their shoulders with the poles on them, just as Moses had commanded in accordance with the word of the Lord.

¹⁶Then David spoke to the chiefs of the Levites ^to appoint their relatives *as* the singers, with musical instruments, harps, lyres, and cymbals, playing to raise sounds of joy. ¹⁷So ^the Levites appointed Heman the son of Joel, and from his relatives, Asaph the son of Berechiah; and from the sons of Merari their relatives, Ethan the son of Kushaiah, ¹⁸and with them their relatives of the second rank, Zechariah, Ben, Jaaziel, Shemiramoth, Jehiel, Unni, Eliab, Benaiah, Maaseiah, Mattithiah, Eliphelehu, Mikneiah, Obed-edom, and Jeiel, the gatekeepers. ¹⁹So the singers, Heman, Asaph, and Ethan, *were*

14:13^1 Chr 14:9   14:17^Ex 15:14-16; Deut 2:25
15:1^1 Chr 15:3; 17:1-5   15:2^Num 4:15; Deut 10:8
15:3^1 Kin 8:1; 1 Chr 13:5   15:4^1 Chr 6:16-30; 12:26
15:11^1 Chr 12:28   ^1 Sam 22:20-23   15:12^Ex 19:14, 15;
2 Chr 35:6   15:13^2 Sam 6:3; 1 Chr 13:7
15:14^1 Chr 15:12   15:15^Ex 25:14; Num 4:5f
15:16^1 Chr 13:8; 25:1   15:17^1 Chr 25:1

appointed to sound aloud cymbals of bronze; [20] and Zechariah, Aziel, Shemiramoth, Jehiel, Unni, Eliab, Maaseiah, and Benaiah, with harps *tuned* to ^alamoth; [21] and Mattithiah, Eliphelehu, Mikneiah, Obed-edom, Jeiel, and Azaziah, to lead with lyres *tuned* to ^the sheminith. [22] Chenaniah, chief of the Levites, was *in charge of* the singing; he gave instruction in singing because he was skillful. [23] Berechiah and Elkanah were gatekeepers for the ark. [24] Shebaniah, Joshaphat, Nethanel, Amasai, Zechariah, Benaiah, and Eliezer, the priests, ^blew the trumpets before the ark of God. Obed-edom and Jehiah also *were* gatekeepers for the ark.

[25] ^So *it was* David, with the elders of Israel and the captains of thousands, who went to bring up the ark of the covenant of the LORD from the house of Obed-edom with joy. [26] Because God was helping the Levites who were carrying the ark of the covenant of the LORD, they sacrificed ^seven bulls and seven rams. [27] Now David was clothed with a robe of fine linen with all the Levites who were carrying the ark, and the singers, and Chenaniah the leader of the singing *with* the singers. ^David also wore an ephod of linen. [28] So all Israel brought up the ark of the covenant of the LORD with shouting, and with *the* sound of the horn, with trumpets, with loud-sounding cymbals, with harps, and lyres.

[29] When the ark of the covenant of the LORD came to the city of David, ^Michal the daughter of Saul looked out of the window and saw King David dancing and celebrating; and she despised him in her heart.

A TENT FOR THE ARK

16 And they brought in the ark of God and ^placed it inside the tent which David had pitched for it, and they offered burnt offerings and peace offerings before God. [2] When David had finished offering the burnt offering and the peace offerings, he blessed the people in the name of the LORD. [3] Then he distributed to everyone of Israel, both men and women, to everyone a loaf of bread, a portion *of meat,* and a raisin cake.

[4] He appointed some of the Levites *as* ministers before the ark of the LORD, to celebrate and to thank and praise the LORD God of Israel: [5] Asaph the chief, and second to him Zechariah, *then* Jeiel, Shemiramoth, Jehiel, Mattithiah, Eliab, Benaiah, Obed-edom, and Jeiel, with *musical* instruments, harps, *and* lyres; also Asaph *played* loud-sounding cymbals, [6] and the priests Benaiah and Jahaziel *blew* trumpets continually before the ark of the covenant of God.

[7] Then on that day David ^first assigned Asaph and his relatives to give thanks to the LORD.

PSALM OF THANKSGIVING

8   ^Give thanks to the LORD, call
    upon His name;
    Make His deeds known among
    the peoples.
9   Sing to Him, sing praises to
    Him;
    Speak of all His wonders.
10 Boast in His holy name;
    Let the heart of those who
    seek the LORD be joyful.

15:20 ^Ps 46: title   **15:21** ^Ps 6: title
15:24 ^1 Chr 15:28; 16:6   **15:25** ^2 Sam 6:12, 15
15:26 ^Num 23:1–4, 29   **15:27** ^2 Sam 6:14
15:29 ^2 Sam 3:13f; 6:16   **16:1** ^1 Chr 15:1
16:7 ^2 Sam 22:1; 23:1   **16:8** ^1 Chr 16:8–36; Ps 105:1–15

11 ^ASeek the Lord and His
      strength;
   Seek His face continually.
12 ^ARemember His wonderful
      deeds which He has done,
   ^BHis marvels and the
      judgments from His mouth,
13 *You* descendants of Israel His
      servant,
   Sons of Jacob, His chosen ones!
14 He is the Lord our God;
   ^AHis judgments are in all the
      earth.
15 Remember His covenant
      forever,
   The word which He
      commanded to a thousand
      generations,
16 ^A*The covenant* which He made
      with Abraham,
   And His oath to Isaac.
17 ^AHe also confirmed it to Jacob
      as a statute,
   To Israel as an everlasting
      covenant,
18 Saying, "^ATo you I will give the
      land of Canaan,
   As the portion of your
      inheritance."
19 ^AWhen they were only a few in
      number,
   Very few, and strangers in it,
20 And they wandered from
      nation to nation,
   And from *one* kingdom to
      another people,
21 He allowed no one to oppress
      them,
   And ^AHe rebuked kings for
      their sakes, *saying,*
22 "Do not touch My anointed
      ones,
   And ^Ado not harm My
      prophets."
23 ^ASing to the Lord, all the earth;
   Proclaim good news of His
      salvation from day to day.

24 Tell of His glory among the
      nations,
   His wonderful deeds among
      all the peoples.
25 For ^Agreat is the Lord, and
      greatly to be praised;
   He also is ^Bto be feared above
      all gods.
26 For all the gods of the peoples
      are ^Aidols,
   ^BBut the Lord made the
      heavens.
27 Splendor and majesty are
      before Him,
   Strength and joy are in His
      place.
28 Ascribe to the Lord, you
      families of the peoples,
   Ascribe to the Lord glory and
      strength.
29 Ascribe to the Lord the glory
      due His name;
   Bring an offering, and come
      before Him;
   ^AWorship the Lord in holy
      attire.
30 Tremble before Him, all the
      earth;
   Indeed, the world is firmly
      established, it will not be
      moved.
31 ^1,^ALet the heavens be joyful,
      and the earth rejoice;
   And let them say among the
      nations, "^BThe Lord reigns."
32 ^ALet the sea roar, and
      everything it contains;
   Let the field rejoice, and
      everything that is in it.

16:11 ^APs 24:6   16:12 ^APs 103:2   ^BPs 78:43-68
16:14 ^APs 48:10   16:16 ^AGen 12:7; 22:16-18
16:17 ^AGen 35:11, 12   16:18 ^AGen 13:15
16:19 ^AGen 34:30; Deut 7:7   16:21 ^AGen 12:17; Ex 7:15-18
16:22 ^AGen 20:7   16:23 ^APs 96:1-13   16:25 ^APs 144:3-6
^BPs 89:7   16:26 ^ALev 19:4   ^BPs 102:25   16:29 ^APs 29:2
16:31 ^AIs 44:23   ^BPs 93:1   16:32 ^APs 98:7

16:31 ^1 Hopeful command or wish, not a request; and
so through v 32

33 Then the trees of the forest
    will sing for joy in the
    presence of the LORD;
  For He is coming to judge the
    earth.
34 ^Give thanks to the LORD, for
    He is good;
  For His faithfulness is
    everlasting.
35 ^Then say, "Save us, God of our
    salvation,
  And gather us and save us
    from the nations,
  To give thanks to Your holy
    name,
  And glory in Your praise."
36 ^Blessed be the LORD, the God
    of Israel,
  From everlasting to
    everlasting!
Then all the people said, "Amen,"
and praised the LORD.

WORSHIP BEFORE THE ARK

37 So he left Asaph and his relatives there before the ark of the
covenant of the LORD, to minister
before the ark continually, ^as every
day's work required, 38 and ^Obed-
edom with his sixty-eight relatives;
Obed-edom, the son of Jeduthun,
and Hosah as gatekeepers. 39 *He left*
^Zadok the priest and his relatives
the priests ^Bbefore the tabernacle
of the LORD in the high place which
was at Gibeon, 40 to offer burnt
offerings to the LORD on the altar
of burnt offering continually morning and evening, ^even according
to everything that is written in the
Law of the LORD, which He commanded Israel. 41 With them *were*
^Heman and Jeduthun, and ^Bthe rest
who were chosen, who were designated by name, to give thanks to
the LORD, because His kindness is
everlasting. 42 And with them *were*

Heman and Jeduthun *with* trumpets and cymbals for those who
were to play *them,* and *with* instruments *for* ^the songs of God, and
the sons of Jeduthun for the gate.

43 ^AThen all the people departed,
each to his house; and David
returned to bless his household.

GOD'S COVENANT WITH DAVID

17 ^AAnd it came about, when
    David lived in his house, that
David said to Nathan the prophet,
"Look, I am living in a house of
cedar, but the ark of the covenant
of the LORD is under tent curtains."
2 Then Nathan said to David, "Do
whatever is in your heart, for God
is with you."

3 But it happened that same night,
that the word of God came to
Nathan, saying, 4 "Go and tell David
My servant, 'This is what the LORD
says: "^AYou shall not build a house
for Me to dwell in; 5 for I have not
dwelt in a house since the day that
I brought up Israel to this day, ^but
I have gone from tent to tent and
from *one* dwelling place *to another.*
6 In all places where I have walked
with all Israel, have I spoken a word
^with any of the judges of Israel,
whom I commanded to shepherd
My people, saying, 'Why have you
not built Me a house of cedar?'"'
7 Now, therefore, this is what you
shall say to My servant David: 'This
is what the LORD of armies says: "I
took you from the pasture, from
following the sheep, to be leader
over My people Israel. 8 I have been

16:34 ^APs 106:1; Jer 33:11   16:35 ^APs 106:47, 48
16:36 ^A1 Kin 8:15; Ps 72:18   16:37 ^A2 Chr 8:14;
Ezra 3:4   16:38 ^A1 Chr 13:14   16:39 ^A1 Chr 15:11
^B1 Kin 3:4   16:40 ^AEx 29:38-42; Num 28:3, 4
16:41 ^A1 Chr 6:33   ^B1 Chr 25:1-6   16:42 ^A1 Chr 25:7;
2 Chr 7:6   16:43 ^A2 Sam 6:19   17:1 ^A2 Sam 7:1-29
17:4 ^A1 Chr 28:2, 3   17:5 ^AEx 40:2, 3; 2 Sam 7:6
17:6 ^A2 Sam 7:7

with you wherever you have gone, and have eliminated all your enemies from you; and I will make for you a name like the name of the great ones who are on the earth. ⁹And I will appoint a place for My people Israel, and will plant them *there,* so that they may live in their own place and not tremble *with anxiety* again; and the wicked will not make them waste away anymore as *they did* previously, ¹⁰even from the day that I commanded judges *to be* over My people Israel. And I will subdue all your enemies.

Moreover, I tell you that the LORD will build a house for you. ¹¹When your days are fulfilled that you must ¹go *to be* with your fathers, then I will set up *one of* your descendants after you, who will be from your sons; and I will establish his kingdom. ¹²He shall build for Me a house, and I will establish his throne forever. ¹³ᴬI will be his father and he shall be My son; and I will not take My favor away from him, ᴮas I took it from him who was before you. ¹⁴But I will settle him in My house and in My kingdom forever, and his throne will be established forever.'"' ¹⁵According to all these words and according to all of this vision, so Nathan spoke to David.

DAVID'S PRAYER IN RESPONSE

¹⁶Then King David came in and sat before the LORD, and said, "ᴬWho am I, LORD God, and what is my house that You have brought me this far? ¹⁷This was a small thing in Your eyes, God; but You have spoken of Your servant's house for a great while to come, and have viewed me according to the standard of a person of high degree,

LORD God. ¹⁸What more can David still *say* to You concerning the honor *bestowed* on Your servant? For You know Your servant. ¹⁹LORD, ᴬfor Your servant's sake, and according to Your own heart, You have accomplished all this greatness, to make known all these great things. ²⁰LORD, there is none like You, nor is there any God besides You, according to everything that we have heard with our ears. ²¹And what one nation on the earth is like Your people Israel, whom God went to redeem for Himself *as* a people, to make for You a name by great and awesome things, by driving out nations from before Your people, whom You redeemed from Egypt? ²²ᴬFor You have made Your people Israel Your own people forever, and You, LORD, became their God.

²³"Now, LORD, let the word that You have spoken concerning Your servant and concerning his house be established forever, and do just as You have spoken. ²⁴Let Your name be established and be great forever, saying, 'The LORD of armies is the God of Israel, a God to Israel; and the house of Your servant David is established before You.' ²⁵For You, my God, have revealed to Your servant that You will build him a house; therefore Your servant has found *courage* to pray before You. ²⁶Now, LORD, You are God, and have promised this good thing to Your servant. ²⁷And now You have decided to bless the house of Your servant, that it may continue forever before You; for You, LORD, have blessed, and it is blessed forever."

17:13 ᴬHeb 1:5   ᴮ1 Chr 10:14   17:16 ᴬ2 Sam 7:18
17:19 ᴬ2 Sam 7:21; Is 37:35   17:22 ᴬEx 19:5, 6

17:11 ¹I.e., die

DAVID'S KINGDOM STRENGTHENED

18 Now after this ^it came about that David defeated the Philistines and subdued them and took Gath and its towns from the hand of the Philistines. ²And he defeated Moab, and the Moabites became servants to David, bringing tribute.

³David also defeated Hadadezer king of Zobah *as far as* Hamath, as he went to establish his rule to the river Euphrates. ⁴David took from him a thousand chariots and seven thousand horsemen and twenty thousand foot soldiers, and David hamstrung *almost* all the chariot horses, but left *enough* of them for a hundred chariots.

⁵When the Arameans of Damascus came to help Hadadezer king ^of Zobah, David killed twenty-two thousand men of the Arameans. ⁶Then David put *garrisons* among the Arameans of Damascus; and the Arameans became servants to David, bringing tribute. And the LORD helped David wherever he went. ⁷And David took the shields of gold which were carried by the servants of Hadadezer, and brought them to Jerusalem. ⁸Also from Tibhath and Cun, cities of Hadadezer, David took a very large amount of bronze, with which ^Solomon made the bronze ¹Sea and the pillars and the bronze utensils.

⁹Now when Tou king of Hamath heard that David had defeated all the army of Hadadezer king of Zobah, ¹⁰he sent Hadoram his son to King David to greet him and to bless him, because he had fought against Hadadezer and had defeated him; for Hadadezer had been at war with Tou. And *Hadoram brought* all kinds

of articles of gold and silver and bronze. ¹¹King David also dedicated these to the LORD, with the silver and the gold which he had carried away from all the nations: from Edom, Moab, the sons of Ammon, the Philistines, and from Amalek.

¹²Moreover, Abishai the son of Zeruiah defeated eighteen thousand Edomites in the Valley of Salt. ¹³Then he put garrisons in Edom, and all the Edomites became servants to David. And the LORD helped David wherever he went.

¹⁴So David reigned over all Israel; and he administered justice and righteousness for all his people. ¹⁵^Joab the son of Zeruiah *was* over the army, and Jehoshaphat the son of Ahilud *was* secretary; ¹⁶and Zadok the son of Ahitub and Abimelech the son of Abiathar *were* priests, and Shavsha *was* secretary; ¹⁷and Benaiah the son of Jehoiada *was* over the Cherethites and the Pelethites, and the sons of David *were* chiefs at the king's side.

DAVID'S MESSENGERS ABUSED

19 ^Now it came about after this, that Nahash the king of the sons of Ammon died, and his son became king in his place. ²Then David said, "I will show kindness to Hanun the son of Nahash, because his father showed kindness to me." So David sent messengers to console him concerning his father. And David's servants came into the land of the sons of Ammon to Hanun to console him. ³But the commanders among the sons of Ammon said to Hanun, "Do you think that David

18:1^2 Sam 8:1-18   18:5^1 Chr 19:6   18:8^1 Kin 7:40-47; 2 Chr 4:11-18   18:15^1 Chr 11:6   19:1^2 Sam 10:1-19

18:8 ¹I.e., large basin

is honoring your father, in that he has sent comforters to you? Have his servants not come to you to search, to demolish, and to spy out the land?" ⁴So Hanun took David's servants and shaved them, and cut off their robes in the middle as far as their buttocks, and sent them away. ⁵Then *certain people* went and told David about the men. And he sent *messengers* to meet them, because the men were very humiliated. And the king said, "Stay at Jericho until your beards grow *back,* then return."

⁶When the sons of Ammon saw that they had made themselves repulsive to David, Hanun and the sons of Ammon sent ¹a thousand talents of silver to hire for themselves chariots and horsemen from Mesopotamia, Aram-maacah, and ᴬZobah. ⁷So they hired for themselves thirty-two thousand chariots, and the king of Maacah and his people, who came and camped opposite ᴬMedeba. And the sons of Ammon gathered together from their cities and came to the battle. ⁸When David heard *about it,* he sent Joab and all the army, the mighty men. ⁹The sons of Ammon came out and drew up in battle formation at the entrance of the city; and the kings who had come were by themselves in the field.

AMMON AND ARAM DEFEATED

¹⁰Now when Joab saw that the battle was set against him at the front and at the rear, he selected *warriors* from all the choice men in Israel and lined *them* up against the Arameans. ¹¹But the remainder of the people he placed under the command of Abshai his brother; and they lined up against the sons of Ammon. ¹²He said, "If the Arameans are too strong for me, then you shall help me; but if the sons of Ammon are too strong for you, then I will help you. ¹³Be strong, and let's show ourselves courageous for the benefit of our people and the cities of our God; and may the LORD do what is good in His sight." ¹⁴So Joab and the people who were with him advanced to battle against the Arameans, and they fled from him. ¹⁵When the sons of Ammon saw that the Arameans had fled, they also fled from his brother Abshai and entered the city. Then Joab came to Jerusalem.

¹⁶When the Arameans saw that they had been defeated by Israel, they sent messengers and brought out the Arameans who were beyond the *Euphrates* River, with Shophach the commander of the army of Hadadezer leading them. ¹⁷When it was reported to David, he gathered all Israel together and crossed the Jordan, and came upon them and drew up in formation against them. And when David drew up in battle formation against the Arameans, they fought against him. ¹⁸And the Arameans fled from Israel, and David killed of the Arameans seven thousand charioteers and forty thousand foot soldiers; and he put Shophach the commander of the army to death. ¹⁹So when the servants of Hadadezer saw that they had been defeated by Israel, they made peace with David and served him. So the Arameans were not willing to help the sons of Ammon anymore.

19:6 ᴬ1 Chr 18:5, 9   **19:7** ᴬNum 21:30; Josh 13:9, 16

19:6 ¹About 38 tons or 34 metric tons

WAR WITH PHILISTINE GIANTS

20 Then it happened in the spring, at the time when kings go out *to battle*, that Joab led out the army and ravaged the land of the sons of Ammon, and came and besieged Rabbah. But David stayed in Jerusalem. And ^Joab struck Rabbah and overthrew it. ^2^David took the crown of their king from his head, and he found it to weigh a ^1^talent of gold, and there was a precious stone in it; and it was placed on David's head. And he brought out the spoils of the city, a very great amount. ^3^He brought out the people who *were* in it, ^and ^1^put *them to work* at saws, iron picks, and axes. And David did the same to all the cities of the sons of Ammon. Then David and all the people returned *to* Jerusalem.

^4^Now it came about after this, that war broke out at Gezer with the Philistines; then Sibbecai the Hushathite killed Sippai, one of the descendants of the giants, and they were subdued. ^5^And there was war with the Philistines again, and Elhanan the son of ^Jair killed Lahmi the brother of Goliath the Gittite, the shaft of whose spear *was* like a weaver's beam. ^6^Again there was war at Gath, where there was a man of *great* stature who had twenty-four fingers and toes, six *fingers on each hand* and six *toes on each foot;* and he also was descended from the giants. ^7^When he taunted Israel, Jonathan the son of Shimea, David's brother, killed him. ^8^These were descended from the giants in Gath, and they fell by the hand of David and by the hand of his servants.

CENSUS BRINGS PLAGUE

21 ^Then Satan stood up against Israel and incited David to count Israel. ^2^So David said to Joab and to the leaders of the people, "^Go, count Israel from Beersheba to Dan, and bring me *word* so that I may know their number." ^3^But Joab said, "^May the LORD add to His people a hundred times as many as they are! My lord the king, are they not all my lord's servants? Why does my lord seek this thing? Why should he be a cause of guilt to Israel?" ^4^Nevertheless, the king's word prevailed against Joab. Therefore, Joab departed and went throughout Israel, and came to Jerusalem. ^5^Then Joab gave the number of the census of the people to David. ^Israel was 1,100,000 men in all who drew the sword; and Judah *was* 470,000 men who drew the sword. ^6^But he did not count Levi and Benjamin among them, because the king's command was abhorrent to Joab.

^7^Now God was displeased with this thing, so He struck Israel. ^8^David said to God, "I have sinned greatly, by doing this thing. ^But now, please overlook Your servant's guilt, for I have behaved very foolishly."

^9^The LORD spoke to ^Gad, David's seer, saying, ^10^"Go and speak to David, saying, 'This is what the LORD says: "I extend to you three *choices;* choose for yourself one of them, which I will do to you."'" ^11^So Gad came to David and said to him, "This is what the LORD says: 'Take

20:1^2 Sam 12:26   20:2^2 Sam 12:30, 31
20:3^2 Sam 12:31   20:4^2 Sam 21:18-22
20:5^2 Sam 21:19   21:1^2 Sam 24:1-25
21:2^1 Chr 27:23, 24   21:3^Deut 1:11
21:5^2 Sam 24:9   21:6^1 Chr 27:24
21:8^2 Sam 12:13   21:9^2 Sam 24:11; 1 Chr 29:29

20:2 ^1 About 75 lb. or 34 kg   20:3 ^1 So 2 Sam 12:31; MT *sawed* them *apart with*

for yourself ¹²ᴬthree years of famine, or three months to be swept away before your foes while the sword of your enemies overtakes *you*, or else three days of the sword of the Lᴏʀᴅ: a plague in the land, and the angel of the Lᴏʀᴅ destroying throughout the territory of Israel.' Now, therefore, consider what answer I shall bring back to Him who sent me."
¹³David said to Gad, "I am in great distress; please let me fall into the hand of the Lᴏʀᴅ, ᴬfor His mercies are very great. But do not let me fall into human hands."

¹⁴ᴬSo the Lᴏʀᴅ sent a plague on Israel; seventy thousand men of Israel fell. ¹⁵And God sent an angel to Jerusalem to destroy it; but as he was about to destroy *it*, the Lᴏʀᴅ saw and ᴬwas sorry about the catastrophe, and said to the destroying angel, "It is enough; now relax your hand." And the angel of the Lᴏʀᴅ was standing by the threshing floor of Ornan the Jebusite. ¹⁶Then David raised his eyes and saw the angel of the Lᴏʀᴅ standing between earth and heaven, with his drawn sword in his hand stretched out over Jerusalem. Then David and the elders, ᴬcovered with sackcloth, fell on their faces. ¹⁷And David said to God, "Is it not I who commanded to count the people? Indeed, I am the one who has sinned and acted very wickedly, ᴬbut these sheep, what have they done? Lᴏʀᴅ, my God, just let Your hand be against me and my father's household, and not against Your people as a plague."

DAVID'S ALTAR

¹⁸ᴬThen the angel of the Lᴏʀᴅ commanded Gad to say to David, that David was to go up and build an altar to the Lᴏʀᴅ on the threshing floor of Ornan the Jebusite. ¹⁹So David went up at the word of Gad, which he spoke in the name of the Lᴏʀᴅ. ²⁰Now Ornan turned back and saw the angel, and his four sons *who were* with him hid themselves. And Ornan was threshing wheat. ²¹As David came to Ornan, Ornan looked and saw David, and went out from the threshing floor and prostrated himself to David with his face to the ground. ²²Then David said to Ornan, "Give me the site of *this* threshing floor, so that I may build on it an altar to the Lᴏʀᴅ; you shall give it to me for the full price, so that the plague may be brought to a halt from the people." ²³But Ornan said to David, "Take *it* for yourself, and may my lord the king do what is good in his sight. See, I am giving the oxen for burnt offerings, and the threshing sledges for wood and the wheat for the grain offering; I am giving *it* all." ²⁴Nevertheless, King David said to Ornan, "No, but I will certainly buy *it* for the full price; for I will not take what is yours for the Lᴏʀᴅ, nor offer a burnt offering which costs me nothing." ²⁵So ᴬDavid gave Ornan six hundred shekels of gold by weight for the site. ²⁶Then David built an altar there to the Lᴏʀᴅ, and offered burnt offerings and peace offerings. And he called to the Lᴏʀᴅ, and ᴬHe answered him with fire from heaven on the altar of burnt offering. ²⁷The Lᴏʀᴅ commanded the angel, and he returned his sword to its sheath.

21:12ᴬ2 Sam 24:13   21:13ᴬPs 51:1; 130:4, 7
21:14ᴬ1 Chr 27:24   21:15ᴬEx 32:14; 1 Sam 15:11
21:16ᴬ1 Kin 21:27   21:17ᴬ2 Sam 7:8; Ps 74:1
21:18ᴬ2 Chr 3:1   21:25ᴬ2 Sam 24:24   21:26ᴬLev 9:24; Judg 6:21

²⁸At that time, when David saw that the LORD had answered him on the threshing floor of Ornan the Jebusite, he offered sacrifice there. ²⁹ᴬFor the tabernacle of the LORD, which Moses had made in the wilderness, and the altar of burnt offering *were* on the high place at Gibeon at that time. ³⁰But David could not go before it to inquire of God, for he was terrified by the sword of the angel of the LORD.

DAVID PREPARES FOR TEMPLE BUILDING

22 Then David said, "ᴬThis is the house of the LORD God, and this is the altar of burnt offering for Israel."

²So David gave orders to gather the strangers who were in the land of Israel, and ᴬhe set stonecutters to cut out stones to build the house of God. ³And David ᴬprepared large quantities of iron to make the nails for the doors of the gates and for the clamps, and more bronze than could be weighed; ⁴and timbers of cedar beyond number, for ᴬthe Sidonians and Tyrians brought large quantities of cedar timber to David. ⁵David said, "My son ᴬSolomon is young and inexperienced, and the house that is to be built for the LORD shall be exceedingly magnificent, famous, and glorious throughout the lands. *Therefore* I now will make preparations for it." So David made ample preparations before his death.

SOLOMON COMMANDED TO BUILD THE TEMPLE

⁶Then ᴬhe called for his son Solomon, and commanded him to build a house for the LORD God of Israel. ⁷David said to Solomon, "ᴬMy son,

I had intended to build a house for the name of the LORD my God. ⁸But the word of the LORD came to me, saying, 'ᴬYou have shed much blood and have waged great wars; you shall not build a house to My name, because you have shed *so* much blood on the earth before Me. ⁹Behold, a son will be born to you, who shall be a man of rest, and ᴬI will give him rest from all his enemies on every side; for his name will be ¹Solomon, and I will give peace and quiet to Israel in his days. ¹⁰ᴬHe shall build a house for My name, and he shall be My son and I will be his Father; and I will establish the throne of his kingdom over Israel forever.' ¹¹Now, my son, ᴬthe LORD be with you that you may be successful, and build the house of the LORD your God just as He has spoken concerning you. ¹²ᴬOnly the LORD give you discretion and understanding, and put you in charge of Israel, so that you may keep the Law of the LORD your God. ¹³ᴬThen you will prosper, if you are careful to follow the statutes and the ordinances which the LORD commanded Moses concerning Israel. ᴮBe strong and courageous, do not fear nor be dismayed. ¹⁴Now behold, with great pains I have prepared for the house of the LORD ᴬa hundred thousand ¹talents of gold and a million talents of silver, and bronze and iron beyond measure, for they are in great quantity; I have

21:29ᴬ1 Kin 3:4; 1 Chr 16:39 22:1ᴬ1 Chr 21:18-28; 2 Chr 3:1 22:2ᴬ1 Kin 5:17, 18 22:3ᴬ1 Chr 29:2, 7 22:4ᴬ1 Kin 5:6-10 22:5ᴬ1 Kin 3:7; 1 Chr 29:1 22:6ᴬ1 Kin 2:1 22:7ᴬ2 Sam 7:2, 3; 1 Chr 17:1 22:8ᴬ1 Chr 28:3 22:9ᴬ1 Kin 4:20, 25 22:10ᴬ2 Sam 7:13, 14; 1 Chr 17:12 22:11ᴬ1 Chr 22:16 22:12ᴬ1 Kin 3:9-12; 2 Chr 1:10 22:13ᴬ1 Chr 28:7 ᴮJosh 1:6-9 22:14ᴬ1 Chr 29:4

22:9 ¹I.e., peaceful 22:14 ¹A talent was about 75 lb. or 34 kg

also prepared timber and stone, and you may add to that. ¹⁵Moreover there are many workmen with you, stonecutters, masons of stone, and carpenters; and all *of them* are skillful in every kind of work. ¹⁶Of the gold, silver, bronze, and iron there is no limit. Arise and work, and may ^the LORD be with you."

¹⁷^David also commanded all the leaders of Israel to help his son Solomon, *saying,* ¹⁸"Is the LORD your God not with you? And ^has He not given you rest on every side? For He has handed over to me the inhabitants of the land, and the land is subdued before the LORD and before His people. ¹⁹Now ^set your heart and your soul to seek the LORD your God; then arise, and build the sanctuary of the LORD God, so that you may bring the ark of the covenant of the LORD and the holy vessels of God into the house that is to be built for the name of the LORD."

SOLOMON REIGNS

23 ^Now when David reached old age, he made his son Solomon king over Israel. ²And he gathered together all the leaders of Israel with the priests and the Levites.

OFFICES OF THE LEVITES

³Now the Levites were counted from thirty years old and upward, and ^their number by head count of men was thirty-eight thousand. ⁴Of these, twenty-four thousand were ^to oversee the work of the house of the LORD; and six thousand *were* ᴮofficers and judges, ⁵and four thousand *were* gatekeepers, and ^four thousand *were* praising the LORD with the instruments which David made for giving praise.

⁶David divided them into divisions ^according to the sons of Levi: Gershon, Kohath, and Merari.

GERSHONITES

⁷Of the Gershonites *there were* Ladan and Shimei. ⁸The sons of Ladan *were* Jehiel the first, and Zetham and Joel, three. ⁹The sons of Shimei *were* Shelomoth, Haziel, and Haran, three. These were the heads of the fathers' *households* of Ladan. ¹⁰The sons of Shimei *were* Jahath, Zina, Jeush, and Beriah. These four *were* the sons of Shimei. ¹¹Jahath was the first and Zizah the second; but Jeush and Beriah did not have many sons, so they became a father's household, one group for duty.

KOHATHITES

¹²The sons of Kohath were four *in number:* Amram, Izhar, Hebron, and Uzziel. ¹³^The sons of Amram were Aaron and Moses. And Aaron was set apart to sanctify him as most holy, he and his sons forever, to burn incense before the LORD, to serve Him and bless in His name forever. ¹⁴But *as for* ^Moses, the man of God, his sons were named among the tribe of Levi. ¹⁵The sons of Moses *were* Gershom and Eliezer. ¹⁶The son of Gershom *was* Shebuel the chief. ¹⁷The son of Eliezer was Rehabiah the chief; and Eliezer had no other sons, but the sons of Rehabiah were very many. ¹⁸The son of Izhar was Shelomith the chief. ¹⁹The sons of Hebron *were* Jeriah the first, Amariah the

22:16 ^1 Chr 22:11   **22:17** ^1 Chr 28:1-6
22:18 ^1 Chr 22:9; 23:25   **22:19** ^1 Chr 28:9
23:1 ^1 Chr 29:28   **23:3** ^Num 4:48; 1 Chr 23:24
23:4 ^Ezra 3:8, 9   ᴮ1 Chr 26:29   **23:5** ^1 Chr 15:16
23:6 ^1 Chr 6:1   **23:13** ^Ex 6:20   **23:14** ^Deut 33:1;
Ps 90: title

second, Jahaziel the third, and Jekameam the fourth. ²⁰The sons of Uzziel *were* Micah the first and Isshiah the second.

MERARITES

²¹The sons of Merari were Mahli and Mushi. The sons of Mahli *were* Eleazar and Kish. ²²Eleazar died and had no sons, but only daughters; so their relatives, the sons of Kish, took them *as wives.* ²³The sons of Mushi *were* three: Mahli, Eder, and Jeremoth.

DUTIES REVISED

²⁴ᴬThese were the sons of Levi according to their fathers' households, the heads of the fathers' *households* of those among them who were counted, in the number of names by their head count, doing the work for the service of the house of the LORD, from twenty years old and upward. ²⁵For David said, "The LORD God of Israel ᴬhas given rest to His people, and He dwells in Jerusalem forever. ²⁶Also, ᴬthe Levites will no longer need to carry the tabernacle and all its utensils for its service." ²⁷For by the last words of David, the sons of Levi *were* counted from twenty years old and upward. ²⁸For their office is to assist the sons of Aaron with the service of the house of the LORD, in the courtyards and in the chambers, and in the purification of all holy things, and the work of the service of the house of God, ²⁹ᴬand with the showbread, and the fine flour for a grain offering, and unleavened wafers, or *what is baked in* the pan or what is well-mixed, and ᴮall measures of volume and size. ³⁰They are to stand every morning to thank and to praise

the LORD, and likewise at evening, ³¹and to offer all burnt offerings to the LORD, ᴬon the Sabbaths, the new moons and ᴮthe appointed festivals, in the number *determined* by the ordinance concerning them, continually before the LORD. ³²So ᴬthey are to perform the duties of the tent of meeting, the holy place, and *of assisting* the sons of Aaron their relatives, for the service of the house of the LORD.

DIVISIONS OF THE LEVITES

24 Now the divisions of the descendants of Aaron *were these:* ᴬthe sons of Aaron *were* Nadab, Abihu, Eleazar, and Ithamar. ²ᴬBut Nadab and Abihu died before their father and had no sons. So Eleazar and Ithamar served as priests. ³David, with ᴬZadok of the sons of Eleazar and Ahimelech of the sons of Ithamar, divided them according to their offices for their ministry. ⁴Since more chief men were found from the descendants of Eleazar than the descendants of Ithamar, they divided them this way: *there were* sixteen heads of fathers' households of the descendants of Eleazar, and eight of the descendants of Ithamar according to their fathers' households. ⁵ᴬSo they were divided by lot, the one as the other; for they were officers of the sanctuary and officers of God, both from the descendants of Eleazar and the descendants of Ithamar. ⁶Shemaiah, the son of Nethanel the scribe, from the Levites, recorded them in the presence of the king,

23:24 ᴬNum 10:17, 21   23:25 ᴬ1 Chr 22:18
23:26 ᴬNum 4:5, 15; Deut 10:8   23:29 ᴬLev 24:5-9
ᴮLev 19:35, 36   23:31 ᴬIs 1:13, 14   ᴮLev 23:2-4
23:32 ᴬNum 1:53; 1 Chr 9:27   24:1 ᴬEx 6:23
24:2 ᴬLev 10:2   24:3 ᴬ1 Chr 6:8   24:5 ᴬ1 Chr 24:31

the leaders, Zadok the priest, ^Ahimelech the son of Abiathar, and the heads of the fathers' *households* of the priests and the Levites; one father's household taken for Eleazar and one taken for Ithamar.

7 Now the first lot came out for Jehoiarib, the second for Jedaiah, 8 the third for Harim, the fourth for Seorim, 9 the fifth for Malchijah, the sixth for Mijamin, 10 the seventh for Hakkoz, the eighth for ^Abijah, 11 the ninth for Jeshua, the tenth for Shecaniah, 12 the eleventh for Eliashib, the twelfth for Jakim, 13 the thirteenth for Huppah, the fourteenth for Jeshebeab, 14 the fifteenth for Bilgah, the sixteenth for Immer, 15 the seventeenth for Hezir, the eighteenth for Happizzez, 16 the nineteenth for Pethahiah, the twentieth for Jehezkel, 17 the twenty-first for Jachin, the twenty-second for Gamul, 18 the twenty-third for Delaiah, *and* the twenty-fourth for Maaziah. 19 ^These were their offices for their ministry when *they* entered the house of the LORD according to the ordinance *given* to them through their father Aaron, just as the LORD God of Israel had commanded him.

20 Now for the rest of the sons of Levi: of the sons of Amram, Shubael; of the sons of Shubael, Jehdeiah. 21 Of Rehabiah: of the sons of Rehabiah, Isshiah, the first. 22 Of the Izharites, Shelomoth; of the sons of Shelomoth, Jahath. 23 The sons ^of Hebron: Jeriah *the first,* Amariah the second, Jahaziel the third, Jekameam the fourth. 24 Of the sons of Uzziel, Micah; of the sons of Micah, Shamir. 25 The brother of Micah, Isshiah; of the sons of Isshiah, Zechariah. 26 The sons of Merari, Mahli and Mushi; the sons of Jaaziah, Beno. 27 The sons of Merari: by Jaaziah *were* Beno, Shoham, Zaccur, and Ibri. 28 By Mahli: Eleazar, who had no sons. 29 By Kish: the sons of Kish, Jerahmeel. 30 The sons of Mushi: Mahli, Eder, and Jerimoth. These *were* the sons of the Levites according to their fathers' households. 31 ^These also cast lots just as their relatives, the sons of Aaron *did* in the presence of David the king, Zadok, Ahimelech, and the heads of the fathers' *households* of the priests and of the Levites—the head of fathers' *households* as well as those of his younger brother.

NUMBER AND SERVICES OF MUSICIANS

25 Moreover, David and the commanders of the army set apart for the service *some* of the sons of ^Asaph, Heman, and Jeduthun, who *were* to ^Bprophesy with lyres, harps, and cymbals; and the number of those who performed this service was: 2 Of the sons of Asaph: Zaccur, Joseph, Nethaniah, and Asharelah; the sons of Asaph *were* under the direction of Asaph, who prophesied under the direction of the king. 3 ^Of Jeduthun, the sons of Jeduthun: Gedaliah, Zeri, Jeshaiah, Shimei, Hashabiah, and Mattithiah, six *in all,* under the direction of their father Jeduthun with the harp, who prophesied in giving thanks and praising the LORD. 4 Of Heman, the sons of Heman: Bukkiah, Mattaniah, Uzziel, Shebuel and Jerimoth, Hananiah, Hanani, Eliathah, Giddalti and

24:6 ^1 Chr 18:16   24:10 ^Neh 12:4; Luke 1:5
24:19 ^1 Chr 9:25   24:23 ^1 Chr 23:19
24:31 ^1 Chr 24:5, 6   25:1 ^1 Chr 6:33, 39   ^B 2 Kin 3:15
25:3 ^1 Chr 16:41, 42

Romamti-ezer, Joshbekashah, Mallothi, Hothir, *and* Mahazioth. ⁵All these *were* the sons of Heman ^the king's seer to exalt him according to the words of God, for God gave fourteen sons and three daughters to Heman. ⁶All of these were under the direction of their father to sing in the house of the LORD, ^with cymbals, harps, and lyres, for the service of the house of God. ᴮAsaph, Jeduthun, and Heman *were* under the direction of the king. ⁷Their number who were trained in singing to the LORD, with their relatives, all who were skillful, *was* ^288.

DIVISIONS OF THE MUSICIANS

⁸^They cast lots for their duties, all alike, the small as well as the great, the teacher *as well* as the pupil.

⁹Now the first lot came out for Asaph to Joseph, the second for Gedaliah, he with his relatives and sons *were* twelve; ¹⁰the third to Zaccur, his sons and his relatives, twelve; ¹¹the fourth to Izri, his sons and his relatives, twelve; ¹²the fifth to Nethaniah, his sons and his relatives, twelve; ¹³the sixth to Bukkiah, his sons and his relatives, twelve; ¹⁴the seventh to Jesharelah, his sons and his relatives, twelve; ¹⁵the eighth to Jeshaiah, his sons and his relatives, twelve; ¹⁶the ninth to Mattaniah, his sons and his relatives, twelve; ¹⁷the tenth to Shimei, his sons and his relatives, twelve; ¹⁸the eleventh to Azarel, his sons and his relatives, twelve; ¹⁹the twelfth to Hashabiah, his sons and his relatives, twelve; ²⁰for the thirteenth, Shubael, his sons and his relatives, twelve; ²¹for the fourteenth, Mattithiah, his sons and his relatives, twelve; ²²for the fifteenth to Jeremoth, his sons and his relatives, twelve; ²³for the sixteenth to Hananiah, his sons and his relatives, twelve; ²⁴for the seventeenth to Joshbekashah, his sons and his relatives, twelve; ²⁵for the eighteenth to Hanani, his sons and his relatives, twelve; ²⁶for the nineteenth to Mallothi, his sons and his relatives, twelve; ²⁷for the twentieth to Eliathah, his sons and his relatives, twelve; ²⁸for the twenty-first to Hothir, his sons and his relatives, twelve; ²⁹for the twenty-second to Giddalti, his sons and his relatives, twelve; ³⁰for the twenty-third to Mahazioth, his sons and his relatives, twelve; ³¹for the twenty-fourth to Romamti-ezer, his sons and his relatives, twelve.

DIVISIONS OF THE GATEKEEPERS

26 For the divisions of the gatekeepers *there were* of the Korahites, Meshelemiah the son of Kore, of the sons of Asaph. ²Meshelemiah had sons: Zechariah the firstborn, Jediael the second, Zebadiah the third, Jathniel the fourth, ³Elam the fifth, Johanan the sixth, *and* Eliehoenai the seventh. ⁴^Obed-edom had sons: Shemaiah the firstborn, Jehozabad the second, Joah the third, Sacar the fourth, Nethanel the fifth, ⁵Ammiel the sixth, Issachar the seventh, *and* Peullethai the eighth; God had indeed blessed him. ⁶Also to his son Shemaiah sons were born who ruled over the house of their father, for they were valiant mighty men. ⁷The sons of Shemaiah *were* Othni, Rephael, Obed, and Elzabad, whose brothers, Elihu and Semachiah, were valiant men. ⁸All

25:5 ^2 Sam 24:11; 1 Chr 21:9   25:6 ^1 Chr 15:16   ᴮ1 Chr 15:19   25:7 ^1 Chr 23:5   25:8 ^1 Chr 26:13   26:4 ^2 Sam 6:11; 1 Chr 13:14

these *were* of the sons of Obed-edom; they and their sons and relatives *were* able men with strength for the service, sixty-two from Obed-edom. ⁹Meshelemiah had sons and relatives, eighteen valiant men. ¹⁰Also ᴬHosah, *one* of the sons of Merari had sons: Shimri the first (although he was not the firstborn, his father made him first), ¹¹Hilkiah the second, Tebaliah the third, *and* Zechariah the fourth; the sons and relatives of Hosah *were* thirteen in all.

¹²To these divisions of the gatekeepers, to the chief men, *were given* duties like their relatives, to serve in the house of the LORD. ¹³ᴬThey cast lots, the small and the great alike, according to their fathers' households, for every gate. ¹⁴The lot to the east fell to Shelemiah. Then they cast lots *for* his son Zechariah, a counselor with insight, and his lot came out to the north. ¹⁵For Obed-edom *it fell* to the south, and to his sons went the storehouse. ¹⁶For Shuppim and Hosah *it was* to the west, by the gate of Shallecheth, on the ascending highway. Guard corresponded to guard. ¹⁷On the east there were six Levites, on the north four daily, on the south four daily, and at the storehouse two by two. ¹⁸At the ¹,ᴬannex on the west *there were* four at the highway and two at the annex. ¹⁹These were the divisions of the gatekeepers of the sons of Korah and of the sons of Merari.

KEEPERS OF THE TREASURE

²⁰¹The Levites, their relatives, were in ᴬcharge of the treasures of the house of God and of the treasures of the dedicated gifts. ²¹The sons of Ladan, the sons of the Gershonites belonging to Ladan, *namely,* the Jehielites, *were* the heads of the fathers' *households,* belonging to Ladan the Gershonite.

²²The sons of Jehieli, Zetham, and his brother Joel, were in charge of the treasures of the house of the LORD. ²³As for the Amramites, the Izharites, the Hebronites, and the Uzzielites, ²⁴Shebuel the son of Gershom, the son of Moses, was officer over the treasures. ²⁵His relatives by Eliezer *were* Rehabiah his son, Jeshaiah his son, Joram his son, Zichri his son, and Shelomoth his son. ²⁶This Shelomoth and his relatives were in charge of all the treasures of the dedicated gifts ᴬwhich King David and the heads of the fathers' *households,* the commanders of thousands and hundreds, and the commanders of the army, had dedicated. ²⁷They dedicated part of the spoils won in battles to repair the house of the LORD. ²⁸And all that Samuel the seer had dedicated, and Saul the son of Kish, Abner the son of Ner, and Joab the son of Zeruiah, everyone who had dedicated *anything, all of this* was under the care of Shelomoth and his relatives.

OUTSIDE DUTIES

²⁹As for the Izharites, Chenaniah and his sons ᴬwere *assigned* to outside duties for Israel, as ᴮofficers and judges. ³⁰As for the Hebronites, ᴬHashabiah and his relatives, 1,700 capable men, were responsible for the affairs of Israel west of the

26:10 ᴬ1 Chr 16:38   26:13 ᴬ1 Chr 24:5, 31; 25:8
26:18 ᴬ2 Kin 23:11   26:20 ᴬ1 Chr 26:22, 24, 26;
Ezra 2:69   26:26 ᴬ2 Sam 8:11   26:29 ᴬNeh 11:16
ᴮ1 Chr 23:4   26:30 ᴬ1 Chr 27:17

26:18 ¹Possibly *court* or *colonnade*   26:20 ¹As in LXX;
MT *As for the Levites, Ahijah had*

Jordan, for all the work of the LORD and the service of the king. ³¹As for the Hebronites, ^Jerijah the chief (these Hebronites were sought out according to their genealogies and fathers' *households,* in the fortieth year of David's reign, and men of outstanding capability were found among them at ⁸Jazer of Gilead) ³²and his relatives, capable men, *numbered* 2,700, heads of fathers' *households.* And King David appointed them as overseers of the Reubenites, the Gadites, and the half-tribe of the Manassites ^concerning all the affairs of God and of the king.

COMMANDERS OF THE ARMY

27 Now *this is* the number of the sons of Israel, the heads of fathers' *households,* the commanders of thousands and of hundreds, and their officers who served the king in all the affairs of the divisions which came in and went out month by month throughout the months of the year, each division *numbering* twenty-four thousand: ²Jashobeam the son of Zabdiel ^was in charge of the first division for the first month; and in his division *were* twenty-four thousand. ³*He was* from the sons of Perez, *and was* chief of all the commanders of the army for the first month. ⁴Dodai the Ahohite and his division was in charge of the division for the second month, Mikloth *being* the chief officer; and in his division *were* twenty-four thousand. ⁵The third commander of the army for the third month *was* Benaiah, the son of Jehoiada the priest, *as* chief; and in his division *were* twenty-four thousand. ⁶This Benaiah *was* the mighty man of the thirty, and was in charge of thirty; and over his

division was his son Ammizabad. ⁷The fourth, for the fourth month *was* Asahel the brother of Joab, and Zebadiah his son after him; and in his division *were* twenty-four thousand. ⁸The fifth, for the fifth month *was* the commander Shamhuth the Izrahite; and in his division *were* twenty-four thousand. ⁹The sixth, for the sixth month *was* Ira the son of Ikkesh the Tekoite; and in his division *were* twenty-four thousand. ¹⁰The seventh, for the seventh month *was* Helez the Pelonite of the sons of Ephraim; and in his division *were* twenty-four thousand. ¹¹The eighth, for the eighth month *was* Sibbecai the Hushathite of the Zerahites; and in his division *were* twenty-four thousand. ¹²The ninth, for the ninth month *was* Abiezer the Anathothite of the Benjaminites; and in his division *were* twenty-four thousand. ¹³The tenth, for the tenth month *was* Maharai the Netophathite of the Zerahites; and in his division *were* twenty-four thousand. ¹⁴The eleventh, for the eleventh month *was* Benaiah the Pirathonite of the sons of Ephraim; and in his division *were* twenty-four thousand. ¹⁵The twelfth, for the twelfth month *was* Heldai the Netophathite of Othniel; and in his division *were* twenty-four thousand.

CHIEF OFFICERS OF THE TRIBES

¹⁶Now in charge of the tribes of Israel: chief officer for the Reubenites was Eliezer the son of Zichri; for the Simeonites, Shephatiah the son of Maacah; ¹⁷for Levi, Hashabiah the son of Kemuel; for Aaron, Zadok; ¹⁸for Judah, Elihu,

26:31 ^1 Chr 23:19   ⁸1 Chr 6:81   26:32 ^2 Chr 19:11
27:2 ^2 Sam 23:8-30; 1 Chr 11:11-31

one of David's brothers; for Issachar, Omri the son of Michael; [19]for Zebulun, Ishmaiah the son of Obadiah; for Naphtali, Jeremoth the son of Azriel; [20]for the sons of Ephraim, Hoshea the son of Azaziah; for the half-tribe of Manasseh, Joel the son of Pedaiah; [21]for the half-tribe of Manasseh in Gilead, Iddo the son of Zechariah; for Benjamin, Jaasiel the son of Abner; [22]for Dan, Azarel the son of Jeroham. ^These *were* the leaders of the tribes of Israel. [23]But David did not count those twenty years of age and under, ^because the LORD had said He would multiply Israel as the stars of heaven. [24]Joab the son of Zeruiah had begun to count *them,* but did not finish; and because of ^this, wrath came upon Israel, and the number was not included in the account of the chronicles of King David.

VARIOUS OVERSEERS

[25]Now Azmaveth the son of Adiel was responsible for the king's storehouses. And Jonathan the son of Uzziah was responsible for the storehouses in the country, the cities, the villages, and the towers. [26]Ezri the son of Chelub was responsible for the agricultural workers who tilled the soil. [27]Shimei the Ramathite was responsible for the vineyards; and Zabdi the Shiphmite was responsible for the produce of the vineyards *stored* in the wine cellars. [28]Baalhanan the Gederite was responsible for the olive and ^sycamore trees in the ¹Shephelah; and Joash was responsible for the stores of oil. [29]Shitrai the Sharonite was responsible for the cattle which were grazing in ^Sharon; and Shaphat the son of Adlai was responsible for the cattle in the valleys. [30]Obil the Ishmaelite

was responsible for the camels; and Jehdeiah the Meronothite was responsible for the donkeys. [31]Jaziz the ^Hagrite was responsible for the flocks. All these were overseers of the property which belonged to King David.

COUNSELORS

[32]Also Jonathan, David's uncle, *was* a counselor, a man of understanding, and a scribe; and Jehiel the son of Hachmoni tutored the king's sons. [33]^Ahithophel *was* counselor to the king; and Hushai the Archite *was* the king's friend. [34]Jehoiada the son of Benaiah, and ^Abiathar succeeded Ahithophel; and Joab was the ᴮcommander of the king's army.

DAVID'S ADDRESS ABOUT THE TEMPLE

28 Now David assembled at Jerusalem all the officials of Israel, the leaders of the tribes, and the commanders of the divisions that served the king, the commanders of thousands, and the commanders of hundreds, and the overseers of all the property and livestock belonging to the king and his sons, with the officials and ^the mighty men, all the valiant warriors. [2]Then King David rose to his feet and said, "Listen to me, my brothers and my people; I ^*had* intended to build a permanent home for the ark of the covenant of the LORD and for the footstool of our God. So I had made preparations to build *it.* [3]But God said to me, '^You shall not build a house for

27:22^1 Chr 28:1   27:23^1 Chr 21:2-5
27:24^2 Sam 24:12-15; 1 Chr 21:1-7   27:28^1 Kin 10:27;
2 Chr 1:15   27:29^1 Chr 5:16   27:31^1 Chr 5:10
27:33^2 Sam 15:12   27:34^1 Kin 1:7   ᴮ1 Chr 11:6
28:1^1 Chr 11:10-47   28:2^1 Chr 17:1, 2
28:3^1 Chr 22:8

27:28 ¹Or *lowlands*

My name, because you are a man of war and have shed blood.' [4]Yet, the LORD, the God of Israel, ^chose me from all the household of my father to be king over Israel [B]forever. For He has chosen Judah to be a leader; and in the house of Judah, my father's house, and among the sons of my father He took pleasure in me to make *me* king over all Israel. [5]Of all my sons (for the LORD has given me many sons), ^He has chosen my son Solomon to sit on the throne of the kingdom of the LORD over Israel. [6]He said to me, 'Your son ^Solomon is the one who shall build My house and My courtyards; for I have chosen him to be a son to Me, and I will be a Father to him. [7]I will establish his kingdom forever ^if he resolutely performs My commandments and My ordinances, as is done now.' [8]So now, in the sight of all Israel, the assembly of the LORD, and in the presence of our God, keep and seek after all the commandments of the LORD your God so that you may possess the good land and leave it as an inheritance to your sons after you forever.

[9]"As for you, my son Solomon, know the God of your father, and ^serve Him wholeheartedly and with a willing mind; for the LORD searches all hearts, and understands every intent of the thoughts. If you seek Him, He will let you find Him; but if you forsake Him, He will reject you forever. [10]Consider now, for the LORD has chosen you to build a house for the sanctuary; ^be courageous and act."

[11]Then David gave to his son Solomon ^the plan of the porch *of the temple,* its buildings, its storehouses, its upper rooms, its inner rooms, and the room for the [1]atoning cover;

[12]and the plan of all that he had in mind, for the courtyards of the house of the LORD, and for all the surrounding rooms, for ^the storehouses of the house of God and for the storehouses of the dedicated things; [13]also for ^the divisions of the priests and the Levites and for all the work of the service of the house of the LORD and for all the utensils of service in the house of the LORD; [14]for the golden *utensils,* by weight of gold for all utensils for every service; for all the silver utensils, by weight *of silver* for all utensils for every service; [15]and the weight *of gold* for the ^golden lampstands and their golden lamps, with the weight of each lampstand and its lamps; and *the weight of silver* for the silver lampstands, with the weight of each lampstand and its lamps according to the use of each lampstand; [16]and the gold by weight for the tables of the showbread, for each table; and silver for the silver tables; [17]and the forks, the basins, and the pitchers of pure gold; and for the golden bowls with the weight for each bowl; and for the silver bowls with the weight for each bowl; [18]and for ^the altar of incense, refined gold by weight; and gold for the model of the chariot, and [B]the cherubim that spread out *their wings* and covered the ark of the covenant of the LORD.

[19]"All *this,*" said David, "the LORD made me understand in writing by *His* hand upon me, ^all the details of this pattern."

28:4^1 Sam 16:6-13   [B]1 Chr 17:23, 27
28:5^1 Chr 22:9, 10   **28:6**^2 Sam 7:13, 14
28:7^1 Chr 22:13   **28:9**^1 Kin 8:61; 1 Chr 29:17-19
28:10^1 Chr 22:13   **28:11**^Ex 25:40; 1 Chr 28:12, 19
28:12^1 Chr 26:20, 28   **28:13**^1 Chr 24:1
28:15^Ex 25:31-39   **28:18**^Ex 30:1-10   [B]Ex 25:18-22
28:19^1 Chr 28:11, 12

28:11[1]Also called *mercy seat;* i.e., where blood was sprinkled on the Day of Atonement

²⁰ Then David said to his son Solomon, "ᴬBe strong and courageous, and act; do not fear nor be dismayed, for the LORD God, my God, is with you. He will not fail you nor forsake you until all the work for the service of the house of the LORD is finished. ²¹ Now behold, *there are* the divisions of the priests and the Levites for all the service of the house of God, and ᴬevery willing man of any skill will be with you in all the work for all kinds of service. The officials also and all the people will be entirely at your command."

OFFERINGS FOR THE TEMPLE

29 Then King David said to the entire assembly, "My son Solomon, whom alone God has chosen, ᴬis still young and inexperienced, and the work is great; for the temple is not for mankind, but for the LORD God. ² Now ᴬwith all my ability I have provided for the house of my God the gold for the *things of* gold, the silver for the *things of* silver, the bronze for the *things of* bronze, the iron for the *things of* iron, wood for the *things of* wood, onyx stones and inlaid *stones,* stones of antimony and stones of various colors, and all kinds of precious stones and alabaster in abundance. ³ In addition, in my delight in the house of my God, the treasure I have of gold and silver, I give to the house of my God, over and above all that I have *already* provided for the holy temple, ⁴ *namely,* ᴬthree thousand ¹talents of gold, from ᴮthe gold of Ophir, and seven thousand talents of refined silver, to overlay the walls of the buildings; ⁵ gold for the *things of* gold and silver for the *things of* silver, that is, for all the work done by the craftsmen. Who

then is willing to consecrate himself this day to the LORD?"

⁶ Then ᴬthe rulers of the fathers' *households,* the leaders of the tribes of Israel, and the commanders of thousands and hundreds, with ᴮthe supervisors of the king's work, offered willingly; ⁷ and for the service of the house of God they gave five thousand talents and ten thousand ¹'ᴬdarics of gold, ten thousand talents of silver, eighteen thousand talents of brass, and a hundred thousand talents of iron. ⁸ Whoever possessed *precious* stones gave *them* to the treasury of the house of the LORD, in care of ᴬJehiel the Gershonite. ⁹ Then the people rejoiced because they had offered so willingly, for they made their offering to the LORD ᴬwholeheartedly, and King David also rejoiced greatly.

DAVID'S PRAYER

¹⁰ So David blessed the LORD in the sight of all the assembly; and David said, "Blessed are You, LORD God of Israel our father, forever and ever. ¹¹ ᴬYours, LORD, is the greatness, the power, the glory, the victory, and the majesty, indeed everything that is in the heavens and on the earth; Yours is the dominion, LORD, and You exalt Yourself as head over all. ¹² ᴬBoth riches and honor *come* from You, and You rule over all, and ᴮin Your hand is power and might; and it lies in Your hand to make great and to strengthen everyone. ¹³ Now

---

28:20ᴬ1 Chr 22:13   28:21ᴬEx 35:25-35; 36:1, 2
29:1ᴬ1 Chr 22:5   29:2ᴬ1 Chr 22:3-5   29:4ᴬ1 Chr 22:14
ᴮ1 Kin 9:28   29:6ᴬ1 Chr 27:1   ᴮ1 Chr 27:25-31
29:7ᴬEzra 2:69; Neh 7:70   29:8ᴬ1 Chr 23:8
29:9ᴬ1 Kin 8:61; 2 Cor 9:7   29:11ᴬMatt 6:13; Rev 5:13
29:12ᴬ2 Chr 1:12   ᴮ2 Chr 20:6

29:4¹A talent was about 75 lb. or 34 kg   29:7¹A coin weighing about 0.25 oz. or 7 gm

therefore, our God, we thank You, and praise Your glorious name.

14"But who am I and who are my people that we should be able to offer as generously as this? For all things come from You, and from Your hand we have given to You. 15For ^we are strangers before You, and temporary residents, as all our fathers were; our days on the earth are like a shadow, and there is no hope. 16LORD our God, all this abundance that we have provided to build You a house for Your holy name, it is from Your hand, and everything is Yours. 17Since I know, my God, that ^You put the heart to the test and ^Bdelight in uprightness, I, in the integrity of my heart, have willingly offered all these *things;* so now with joy I have seen Your people, who are present here, make *their* offerings willingly to You. 18LORD, God of Abraham, Isaac, and Israel, our fathers, keep this forever in the intentions of the hearts of Your people, and direct their hearts to You; 19and ^give my son Solomon a perfect heart to keep Your commandments, Your testimonies, and Your statutes, and to do *them* all, and to build the temple for which I have made provision."

20Then David said to all the assembly, "Now bless the LORD your God." And ^all the assembly blessed the LORD, the God of their fathers, and ^Bbowed down and paid ¹homage to the LORD and the king.

SACRIFICES

21On the next day ^they made sacrifices to the LORD and offered burnt offerings to the LORD, a thousand bulls, a thousand rams, *and* a thousand lambs, with their drink offerings and sacrifices in abundance for all Israel. 22So they ate and drank that day before the LORD with great gladness.

SOLOMON AGAIN MADE KING

And they made Solomon the son of David king ^a second time, and they ^Banointed *him* as ruler for the LORD and Zadok as priest. 23Then ^Solomon sat on the throne of the LORD as king instead of his father David; and he prospered, and all Israel obeyed him. 24And all the officials, the mighty men, and also all the sons of King David pledged allegiance to King Solomon. 25The LORD highly honored Solomon in the sight of all Israel, and ^bestowed on him royal majesty which had not been *bestowed* on any king before him in Israel.

26Now ^David the son of Jesse reigned over all Israel. 27^The period which he reigned over Israel *was* forty years; he reigned in Hebron seven years and in Jerusalem thirty-three *years.*

DEATH OF DAVID

28Then he died at ^a good old age, full of days, riches, and honor; and his son Solomon reigned in his place. 29Now the acts of King David, from the first to the last, are written in the chronicles of Samuel the seer, in the chronicles of ^Nathan the prophet, and in the chronicles of ^BGad the seer, 30with all of his reign, his power, and the circumstances which came upon him, Israel, and all the kingdoms of the lands.

29:15^Lev 25:23   29:17^1 Chr 28:9   ᴮPs 15:2
29:19^1 Chr 28:9; Ps 72:1   29:20^Josh 22:33
ᴮEx 4:31   29:21^1 Kin 8:62, 63   29:22^1 Chr 23:1
ᴮ1 Kin 1:33-39   29:23^1 Kin 2:12   29:25^1 Kin 3:13;
2 Chr 1:12   29:26^1 Chr 18:14   29:27^2 Sam 5:4, 5;
1 Chr 3:4   29:28^Gen 15:15; Acts 13:36
29:29^2 Sam 7:2-4   ᴮ1 Sam 22:5
29:20¹I.e., great respect and honor to a superior

2 CHRONICLES

SOLOMON WORSHIPS AT GIBEON

1 Now ^Solomon the son of David established himself securely over his kingdom, and the LORD his God *was* with him and exalted him greatly.

² And Solomon spoke to all Israel, ^to the commanders of thousands, of hundreds, and to the judges and to every leader in all Israel, the heads of the fathers' *households*. ³ Then Solomon and all the assembly with him went to ^the high place which was at Gibeon, ^because God's tent of meeting was there which Moses, the servant of the LORD had made in the wilderness. ⁴ However, David had brought up ^the ark of God from Kiriath-jearim to the place he had prepared for it, for he had pitched a tent for it in Jerusalem. ⁵ Now ^the bronze altar which Bezalel, the son of Uri, the son of Hur, had made was there before the tabernacle of the LORD, and Solomon and the assembly sought it *out*. ⁶ And Solomon went up there before the LORD to the bronze altar which *was* at the tent of meeting, and ^offered a thousand burnt offerings on it.

⁷ ^In that night God appeared to Solomon and said to him, "Ask what I shall give you."

SOLOMON'S PRAYER FOR WISDOM

⁸ And Solomon said to God, "You have dealt with my father David with great faithfulness, and ^have made me king in his place. ⁹ Now, LORD God, ^Your promise to my father David is fulfilled, for You

have made me king over a people as numerous as the dust of the earth. ¹⁰ ^Now give me wisdom and knowledge, so that I may go out and come in before this people, for who can rule this great people of Yours?" ¹¹ ^Then God said to Solomon, "Because this was in your heart, and you did not ask for riches, wealth, or honor, or the life of those who hate you, nor did you even ask for long life, but you asked for yourself wisdom and knowledge so that you may rule My people over whom I have made you king, ¹² wisdom and knowledge have been granted to you. ^I will also give you riches, wealth, and honor, such as none of the kings who were before you has possessed, nor *will* those who will come after you." ¹³ ^So Solomon went from the high place which was at Gibeon, from the tent of meeting, to Jerusalem, and he reigned over Israel.

SOLOMON'S WEALTH

¹⁴ ^Solomon amassed chariots and horsemen. He had 1,400 chariots and twelve thousand horsemen, and he stationed them in the chariot cities and with the king in Jerusalem. ¹⁵ ^The king made ^silver and gold as plentiful in Jerusalem as stones, and he made cedars as plentiful as sycamores in the

1:1 ^1 Kin 2:12, 46   1:2 ^1 Chr 28:1   1:3 ^1 Kin 3:4
^B Ex 36:8   1:4 ^1 Chr 15:25-28   1:5 ^A Ex 31:9; 38:1-7
1:6 ^1 Kin 3:4   1:7 ^1 Kin 3:5-14   1:8 ^1 Chr 28:5
1:9 ^2 Sam 7:12-16   1:10 ^1 Kin 3:9   1:11 ^1 Kin 3:11
1:12 ^1 Chr 29:25; 2 Chr 9:22   1:13 ^2 Chr 1:3
1:14 ^1 Kin 10:26-29   1:15 ^1 Kin 10:27   ^B Deut 17:17

lowland. ¹⁶Solomon's ^horses were imported from Egypt and from Kue; the king's traders acquired them from Kue for a price. ¹⁷They imported chariots from Egypt for six hundred *shekels* of silver apiece, horses for 150 apiece, and by the same means they exported them to all the kings of the Hittites and the kings of Aram.

SOLOMON WILL BUILD A TEMPLE AND A PALACE

2 ^Now Solomon decided to build a house for the name of the LORD, and a royal palace for himself. ²So ^Solomon assigned seventy thousand men to carry loads, eighty thousand men to quarry *stone* in the mountains, and 3,600 to supervise them.

³^Then Solomon sent *word* to Huram the king of Tyre, saying, "ᴮAs you dealt with my father David and sent him cedars to build him a house to live in, *do it for me*. ⁴Behold, I am about to build a house for the name of the LORD my God, dedicating it to Him, to burn fragrant incense before Him and *to set out* the showbread continually, and to offer ^burnt offerings morning and evening, ᴮon Sabbaths, on new moons, and on the appointed feasts of the LORD our God. This *is to be done* in Israel forever. ⁵The house which I am about to build *will be* great, for our God is ^greater than all the gods. ⁶But ^who is able to build a house for Him, since the heavens and the highest heavens cannot contain Him? And who am I, that I should build a house for Him, except to burn *incense* before Him? ⁷Now send me a skilled man to work in gold, silver, brass, iron, and in purple, crimson, and violet *fabrics*, one who knows

how to make engravings, to *work* with the skilled workers ^whom I have in Judah and Jerusalem, whom my father David provided. ⁸^Send me also cedar, juniper, and algum timber from Lebanon, for I know that your servants know how to cut timber of Lebanon; and indeed ᴮmy servants *will work* with your servants, ⁹to prepare timber in abundance for me, for the house which I am about to build *will be* great and wonderful. ¹⁰Now behold, ^I will give your servants, the woodsmen who cut the timber, ¹twenty thousand kors of crushed wheat, twenty thousand kors of barley, ²twenty thousand baths of wine, and twenty thousand baths of oil."

HURAM TO ASSIST

¹¹Then Huram, king of Tyre, answered in a letter sent to Solomon: "^Because the LORD loves His people, He has made you king over them." ¹²Then Huram continued, "Blessed be ^the LORD, the God of Israel, who made heaven and earth, who has given King David a wise son, endowed with discretion and understanding, who will build a house for the LORD and a royal palace for himself.

¹³"Now then, I am sending Huram-abi, a skilled man, endowed with understanding, ¹⁴^the son of a Danite woman and a Tyrian father, who knows how to work in gold, silver, bronze, iron, stone, and wood, *and*

1:16^Deut 17:16   2:1^1 Kin 5:5   2:2^1 Kin 5:15, 16; 2 Chr 2:18   2:3^1 Kin 5:2-11   ᴮ1 Chr 14:1 2:4^Ex 29:38-42   ᴮNum 28:9, 10   2:5^Ex 15:11; 1 Chr 16:25   2:6^1 Kin 8:27; 2 Chr 6:18 2:7^1 Chr 22:15   2:8^1 Kin 5:6   ᴮ2 Chr 9:10, 11 2:10^1 Kin 5:11   2:11^1 Kin 10:9; 2 Chr 9:8 2:12^Ps 33:6; 102:25   2:14^1 Kin 7:14

2:10 ¹About 154,000 cubic feet or 4,360 cubic meters ²About 120,000 gallons or 454,249 liters

in purple, violet, linen, and crimson fabrics, and *who knows how* to make all kinds of engravings and to execute any design which is assigned to him, *to work* with your skilled workers and with those of my lord, your father David. ¹⁵Now then, let my lord send his servants wheat and barley, oil and wine, of ^which he has spoken. ¹⁶^We will cut whatever timber you need from Lebanon and bring it to you as rafts by sea to Joppa, so that you may carry it up to Jerusalem."

¹⁷Solomon counted all the foreigners who *were* in the land of Israel, ^following the census which his father David had taken; and 153,600 were found. ¹⁸^He appointed seventy thousand of them to carry loads and eighty thousand to quarry *stones* in the mountains, and 3,600 supervisors to make the people work.

THE TEMPLE CONSTRUCTION IN JERUSALEM

3 ^Then Solomon began to build the house of the Lᴏʀᴅ in Jerusalem on Mount Moriah, where *the* Lᴏʀᴅ had appeared to his father David, at the place that David had prepared ᴮon the threshing floor of Ornan the Jebusite. ²He began to build on the second *day* in the second month of the fourth year of his reign.

DIMENSIONS AND MATERIALS OF THE TEMPLE

³Now these are the foundations which ^Solomon laid for building the house of God. The length in cubits, according to the old standard, *was* ¹sixty cubits, and the width, twenty cubits. ⁴The porch which was in front *of the house* ^was as long as the width of the house, ¹twenty cubits, and the

height ²twenty; and inside he overlaid it with pure gold. ⁵He overlaid ^the main room with juniper wood and overlaid it with fine gold; and he ornamented it with palm trees and chains. ⁶Further, he overlaid the house with precious stones; and the gold was gold from Parvaim. ⁷^He also overlaid the house with gold—the beams, the thresholds, and its walls and doors; and he ᴮcarved cherubim on the walls.

⁸Then he made ^the room of the Most Holy Place: its length across the width of the house *was* ¹twenty cubits, and its width *was* twenty cubits; and he overlaid it with fine gold, *amounting* to ²six hundred talents. ⁹The weight of the nails was fifty shekels of gold. He also overlaid ^the upper rooms with gold.

¹⁰^Then he made two sculptured cherubim in the room of the Most Holy Place and overlaid them with gold. ¹¹The wingspan of the ¹cherubim *was* twenty ²cubits; the wing of one, of five cubits, touched the wall of the house, and *its* other wing, of five cubits, touched the wing of the other cherub. ¹²The wing of the other cherub, of five cubits, touched the wall of the house; and *its* other wing, of five cubits, was attached to the wing of the first cherub. ¹³The wings of these cherubim extended twenty cubits, and they stood on their feet facing the *main* room. ¹⁴^He made

2:15^2 Chr 2:10   2:16^1 Kin 5:8, 9   2:17^1 Chr 22:2
2:18^2 Chr 2:2   3:1^1 Kin 6:1   ᴮ1 Chr 21:18
3:3^1 Kin 6:2   3:4^1 Kin 6:3   3:5^1 Kin 6:17
3:7^1 Kin 6:20-22   ᴮ1 Kin 6:29-35   3:8^Ex 26:33;
1 Kin 6:16   3:9^1 Chr 28:11   3:10^Ex 25:18-20;
1 Kin 6:23-28   3:14^Ex 26:31

3:3¹About 90 ft. long and 30 ft. wide or 27 m long and 9 m wide   3:4¹About 30 ft. or 9 m   ²As in ancient versions; MT *120 cubits* or about 180 ft. or 55 m
3:8¹About 30 ft. or 9 m   ²About 23 tons or 21 metric tons   3:11¹Heb plural of *cherub*   ²About 18 in. or 45 cm

the veil of violet, purple, crimson, and fine linen, and he worked cherubim into it.

15ᴬHe also made two pillars for the front of the house, thirty-five cubits high, and the capital on the top of each *was* five cubits. 16He made chains in the inner sanctuary and placed *them* on the tops of the pillars; and he made a hundred pomegranates and placed *them* on the chains. 17ᴬHe erected the pillars in front of the temple, one on the right and the other on the left, and named the one on the right Jachin and the one on the left Boaz.

FURNISHINGS OF THE TEMPLE

4 Then ᴬhe made a bronze altar, 1twenty cubits in length, twenty cubits in width, and 2ten cubits in height. 2ᴬHe also made the 1Sea of cast *metal,* 2ten cubits from brim to brim, circular in form, and its height *was* 3five cubits and its circumference 4thirty cubits. 3Now figures like oxen *were* under it *and* all around it, 1ten cubits, entirely encircling the Sea. The oxen *were* in two rows, cast in one piece. 4It was standing on twelve oxen, three facing north, three facing west, three facing south, and three facing east; and the Sea *was set* on top of them and all their hindquarters turned inward. 5It was a 1hand width thick, and its brim was made like the brim of a cup, *like* a lily blossom; it ᴬcould hold three thousand 2baths. 6ᴬHe also made ten basins in which to wash, and he set five on the right side and five on the left to rinse things for the burnt offering; but the Sea *was* for the priests to wash in.

7Then ᴬhe made the ten golden lampstands in the way prescribed for them, and he set them in the temple, five on the right side and five on the left. 8He also made ᴬten tables and placed them in the temple, five on the right side and five on the left. And he made a hundred golden bowls. 9Then he made ᴬthe courtyard of the priests and ᴮthe great courtyard, and doors for the courtyard, and overlaid their doors with bronze. 10ᴬHe put the Sea on the right side *of the house* toward the southeast.

11ᴬHuram also made the pails, the shovels, and the bowls. So Huram finished the work that he did for King Solomon in the house of God: 12the two pillars, the bowls and the two capitals on top of the pillars, and the two latticeworks to cover the two bowls of the capitals which were on top of the pillars, 13and ᴬthe four hundred pomegranates for the two latticeworks, two rows of pomegranates for each latticework to cover the two bowls of the capitals which were on the pillars. 14ᴬHe also made the stands and he made the basins on the stands, 15*and* the one Sea with the twelve oxen under it. 16The pails, the shovels, the forks, and all its utensils, ᴬHuram-abi made of polished bronze for King Solomon, for the house of the Lord. 17On the plain of the Jordan the king cast them in the clay ground between Succoth and

---

3:15ᴬ1 Kin 7:15-20   3:17ᴬ1 Kin 7:21   4:1ᴬEx 27:1, 2; 2 Kin 16:14   4:2ᴬ1 Kin 7:23-26   4:5ᴬ1 Kin 7:26 4:6ᴬEx 30:17-21; 1 Kin 7:38, 40   4:7ᴬEx 25:31-40; 1 Kin 7:49   4:8ᴬ1 Kin 7:48   4:9ᴬ1 Kin 6:36 ᴮ2 Kin 21:5   4:10ᴬ1 Kin 7:39   4:11ᴬ1 Kin 7:40-51 4:13ᴬ1 Kin 7:20   4:14ᴬ1 Kin 7:27-43 4:16ᴬ1 Kin 7:14; 2 Chr 2:13

4:1¹About 30 ft. or 9 m   ²About 15 ft. or 4.6 m 4:2¹I.e., large basin   ²About 15 ft. or 4.6 m   ³About 7.5 ft. or 2.3 m   ⁴About 45 ft. or 14 m   4:3¹About 15 ft. or 4.6 m   4:5¹About 3 in. or 7.6 cm   ²About 18,000 gallons or 68,137 liters

Zeredah. ¹⁸ᴬSo Solomon made all these utensils in great quantities, for the weight of the bronze could not be determined.

¹⁹Solomon also made all the things that *were* in the house of God: the golden altar, ᴬthe tables with the bread of the Presence on them, ²⁰the lampstands with their lamps of pure gold, ᴬto burn in front of the inner sanctuary in the way prescribed; ²¹the flowers, the lamps, and the tongs of gold, that is, of purest gold; ²²and the snuffers, the bowls, the spoons, and the firepans of pure gold; and the entrance of the house, its inner doors for the Most Holy Place and the doors of the house, *that is,* of the main room, of gold.

THE ARK IS BROUGHT
INTO THE TEMPLE

5 ᴬSo all the work that Solomon performed for the house of the LORD was finished. And Solomon brought in the things that his father David had dedicated, the silver, the gold, and all the utensils, *and he* put *them* in the treasuries of the house of God.

²ᴬThen Solomon assembled at Jerusalem the elders of Israel, all the heads of the tribes, *and the* leaders of the fathers' *households* of the sons of Israel, to bring the ark of the covenant of the LORD up from the city of David, which is Zion. ³ᴬAll the men of Israel assembled themselves before the king at ᴮthe feast, that is *in* the seventh month. ⁴Then all the elders of Israel came, and ᴬthe Levites picked up the ark. ⁵They brought up the ark, the tent of meeting, and all the holy utensils that *were* in the tent. The Levitical priests brought them up. ⁶And King

Solomon and all the congregation of Israel who had assembled with him before the ark were sacrificing so many sheep and oxen that they could not be counted or numbered. ⁷Then the priests brought the ark of the covenant of the LORD to its place, into the inner sanctuary of the house, to the Most Holy Place, under the wings of the cherubim. ⁸For the cherubim spread their wings over the place of the ark, so that the cherubim made a covering over the ark and its poles. ⁹The poles were so long that ᴬthe ends of the poles of the ark could be seen in front of the inner sanctuary, but they could not be seen outside; and they are there to this day. ¹⁰ᴬThere was nothing in the ark except the two tablets which Moses put *there* at Horeb, where the LORD made *a covenant* with the sons of Israel, when they came out of Egypt.

THE GLORY OF GOD FILLS THE TEMPLE

¹¹When the priests came out from the holy place (for all the priests who were present had sanctified themselves, without regard ᴬto divisions), ¹²and all the Levitical singers, ᴬAsaph, Heman, Jeduthun, and their sons and kinsmen, clothed in fine linen, with cymbals, harps, and lyres, standing east of the altar, and with them 120 priests ᴮblowing trumpets ¹³in unison when the trumpeters and the singers were to make themselves heard with one voice to praise and to glorify the LORD, and when they raised their voices ᴬaccompanied by trumpets,

4:18ᴬ1 Kin 7:47   4:19ᴬ2 Chr 4:8   4:20ᴬEx 25:31-37;
2 Chr 5:7   5:1ᴬ1 Kin 7:51   5:2ᴬ1 Kin 8:1-9
5:3ᴬ1 Kin 8:2   ᴮ2 Chr 7:8-10   5:4ᴬJosh 3:6; 2 Chr 5:7
5:9ᴬ1 Kin 8:8, 9   5:10ᴬDeut 10:2-5; Heb 9:4
5:11ᴬ1 Chr 24:1-5   5:12ᴬ1 Chr 25:1-4   ᴮ2 Chr 7:6
5:13ᴬ1 Chr 16:42

cymbals, and *other* musical instruments, and when they praised the LORD *saying*, "He indeed is good for His kindness is everlasting," then the house, the house of the LORD, was filled with a cloud, ¹⁴so that the priests could not rise to minister because of the cloud, for ᴬthe glory of the LORD filled the house of God.

SOLOMON'S DEDICATION OF THE TEMPLE

6 ᴬThen Solomon said, "The LORD has said that He would dwell in the thick darkness.

² "I have built You a lofty house, And a place for Your dwelling forever."

³Then the king turned around and blessed all the assembly of Israel, while all the assembly of Israel was standing. ⁴He said, "Blessed be the LORD, the God of Israel, who spoke with His mouth to my father David, and fulfilled *it* with His hands, saying, ⁵'Since the day that I brought My people from the land of Egypt, I did not choose a city out of all the tribes of Israel *in which* to build a house, so that My name might be there, nor did I choose a man to be *the* leader over My people Israel; ⁶but ᴬI have chosen Jerusalem so that My name might be there, and I ᴮhave chosen David to be over My people Israel.' ⁷ᴬNow it was in the heart of my father David to build a house for the name of the LORD, the God of Israel. ⁸But the LORD said to my father David, 'Because it was in your heart to build a house for My name, you did well that it was in your heart. ⁹Nevertheless you shall not build the house, but your son who will be born to you, he shall build the house for My name.'

¹⁰Now the LORD has fulfilled His word which He spoke; for I have risen in place of my father David and sit on the throne of Israel, as the LORD promised, and have built the house for the name of the LORD, the God of Israel. ¹¹There I have placed the ark ᴬin which is the covenant of the LORD, which He made with the sons of Israel."

SOLOMON'S PRAYER OF DEDICATION

¹²Then he stood before the altar of the LORD in the presence of all the assembly of Israel and spread out his hands. ¹³For Solomon had made a bronze platform, ¹five cubits long, five cubits wide, and three cubits high, and had set it in the midst of the courtyard; and he stood on it, ᴬknelt on his knees in the presence of all the assembly of Israel and spread out his hands toward heaven. ¹⁴He said, "LORD, God of Israel, ᴬthere is no god like You in heaven or on earth, ᴮkeeping Your covenant and Your faithfulness to Your servants who walk before You with all their heart; ¹⁵ᴬYou who have kept with Your servant, my father David, that which You promised him; You have spoken with Your mouth and have fulfilled it with Your hand, as *it is* this day. ¹⁶Now then, LORD, God of Israel, keep to Your servant David, my father, that which You promised him, saying, 'ᴬYou shall not lack a man to sit on the throne of Israel, if only your sons pay attention to their way, to walk in My Law

5:14 ᴬEx 40:35; 1 Kin 8:11   6:1 ᴬ1 Kin 8:12-50
6:6 ᴬ2 Chr 12:13   ᴮ1 Chr 28:4   6:7 ᴬ1 Kin 5:3;
1 Chr 28:2   6:11 ᴬ2 Chr 5:7, 10   6:13 ᴬ1 Kin 8:54
6:14 ᴬEx 15:11   ᴮDeut 7:9   6:15 ᴬ1 Chr 22:9, 10
6:16 ᴬ1 Kin 2:4; 2 Chr 7:18

6:13 ¹About 7.5 ft. long and wide and 4.5 ft. high or
2.3 m and 1.4 m

as you have walked before Me.' [17]Now then, LORD, God of Israel, let Your word be confirmed which You have spoken to Your servant David.

[18]"But ^will God really dwell with mankind on the earth? Behold, heaven and the highest heaven cannot contain You; how much less this house which I have built! [19]Nevertheless, turn Your attention to the prayer of Your servant and to his plea, LORD, my God, to listen to the cry and to the prayer which Your servant prays before You; [20]that Your eye will be open toward this house day and night, toward ^the place of which You have said that *You would* put Your name there, to listen to the prayer which Your servant shall pray toward this place. [21]Listen to the pleadings of Your servant and of Your people Israel when they pray toward this place; hear from Your dwelling place, from heaven; ^hear and forgive.

[22]"If someone sins against his neighbor and is made to take an oath, and he comes *and* takes an oath before Your altar in this house, [23]then hear from heaven and take action and judge Your servants, ^punishing the wicked by bringing his way on his own head, and justifying the righteous by repaying him according to his righteousness.

[24]"If Your people Israel are defeated before an enemy because ^they have sinned against You, and they return *to You* and praise Your name, and pray and plead before You in this house, [25]then hear from heaven and forgive the sin of Your people Israel, and bring them back to the land which You have given to them and to their fathers.

[26]"When the ^heavens are shut up and there is no rain because they have sinned against You, and they pray toward this place and praise Your name, and turn from their sin when You afflict them, [27]then hear in heaven and forgive the sin of Your servants and Your people Israel; indeed, ^teach them the good way in which they are to walk. And provide rain on Your land, which You have given to Your people as an inheritance.

[28]"If there is a ^famine in the land, if there is a plague, if there is blight or mildew, if there is locust or grasshopper, if their enemies besiege them in the land of their cities, whatever plague or whatever sickness *there is,* [29]whatever prayer or plea is made by anyone or by all Your people Israel, each knowing his own affliction and his own pain, and spreading his hands toward this house, [30]then hear from heaven, Your dwelling place, and forgive, and render to each according to all his ways, whose heart You know—^for You alone know the hearts of the sons of mankind— [31]so that they may fear You, to walk in Your ways as long as they live in the land which You have given to our fathers.

[32]"Also concerning ^the foreigner who is not from Your people Israel, when he comes from a far country on account of Your great name and Your mighty hand and Your outstretched arm, when they come and pray toward this house, [33]then hear from heaven, from Your dwelling place, and do according to all

6:18 ^Ps 113:5, 6   6:20 ^Deut 12:11   6:21 ^Is 43:25; Mic 7:18   6:23 ^Is 3:11; Rom 2:8, 9   6:24 ^Ps 51:4   6:26 ^1 Kin 17:1   6:27 ^Ps 94:12   6:28 ^2 Chr 20:9   6:30 ^1 Sam 16:7; 1 Chr 28:9   6:32 ^Is 56:3-8

for which the foreigner calls to You, so that all the peoples of the earth may know Your name, and fear You as *do* Your people Israel, and that they may know that this house which I have built is ^called by Your name.

³⁴"When Your people go out to battle against their enemies, by whatever way You send them, and they pray to You toward this city which You have chosen and the house which I have built for Your name, ³⁵then hear from heaven their prayer and their pleading, and maintain their cause.

³⁶"When they sin against You (^for there is no one who does not sin), and You are angry with them and turn them over to an enemy, so that they take them away captive to a land far off or near, ³⁷if they take it to heart in the land where they are taken captive, and repent and plead to You in the land of their captivity, saying, 'We have sinned, we have done wrong and have acted wickedly'; ³⁸^*if* they return to You with all their heart and with all their soul in the land of their captivity, where they have been taken captive, and pray toward their land which You have given to their fathers and the city which You have chosen, and toward the house which I have built for Your name, ³⁹then hear from heaven, from Your dwelling place, their prayer and pleadings, and maintain their cause, and forgive Your people who have sinned against You.

⁴⁰"Now, my God, please, ^let Your eyes be open and ^ᴮYour ears attentive to the prayer *offered* in this place.

⁴¹"^Now then arise, Lᴏʀᴅ God, to Your resting place, You and the ark of Your might; let Your priests, Lᴏʀᴅ God, be clothed with salvation, and let Your godly ones rejoice in what is good.

⁴²"Lᴏʀᴅ God, do not turn away the face of Your anointed; ^remember *Your* faithfulness to Your servant David."

THE SHEKINAH GLORY

7 ^Now when Solomon had finished praying, ᴮfire came down from heaven and consumed the burnt offering and the sacrifices, and the glory of the Lᴏʀᴅ filled the house. ²^And the priests could not enter the house of the Lᴏʀᴅ because the glory of the Lᴏʀᴅ filled the Lᴏʀᴅ's house. ³All the sons of Israel, seeing the fire come down and the glory of the Lᴏʀᴅ upon the house, bowed down on the pavement with their faces to the ground, and they worshiped and gave praise to the Lᴏʀᴅ, *saying,* "^Certainly He is good, certainly His faithfulness is everlasting."

SACRIFICES OFFERED

⁴^Then the king and all the people offered sacrifice before the Lᴏʀᴅ. ⁵King Solomon offered a sacrifice of twenty-two thousand oxen and 120,000 sheep. So the king and all the people dedicated the house of God. ⁶The priests stood at their posts, and ^the Levites also, with the musical instruments for the Lᴏʀᴅ, which King David had made for giving praise to the Lᴏʀᴅ—"for His faithfulness is everlasting"— whenever David gave praise through their ministry; ᴮthe priests

6:33^2 Chr 7:14   6:36^Job 15:14-16; 1 John 1:8-10
6:38^Jer 29:12, 13   6:40^Neh 1:6, 11   ᴮPs 17:1
6:41^Ps 132:8, 9   6:42^Ps 132:10-12; Is 55:3
7:1^1 Kin 8:54   ᴮLev 9:23f   7:2^2 Chr 5:14
7:3^2 Chr 5:13; 20:21   7:4^1 Kin 8:62, 63
7:6^1 Chr 15:16-21   ᴮ2 Chr 5:12

on the other side blew trumpets and all Israel was standing.

7 ᴬThen Solomon consecrated the middle of the courtyard that *was* before the house of the Lord, for he offered the burnt offerings and the fat of the peace offerings there, because the bronze altar which Solomon had made was not able to contain the burnt offering, the grain offering, and the fat.

THE FEAST OF DEDICATION

8 So ᴬSolomon held the feast at that time for seven days, and all Israel with him, a very great assembly *that came* from the entrance of Hamath to the ᴮbrook of Egypt. 9 And on the eighth day they held ᴬa solemn assembly, because they held the dedication of the altar for seven days, and the feast for seven days. 10 Then on the twenty-third day of the seventh month he sent the people to their tents, rejoicing and happy in heart because of the goodness that the Lord had shown to David, to Solomon, and to His people Israel.

GOD'S PROMISE AND WARNING

11 ᴬSo Solomon finished the house of the Lord and the king's palace, and successfully completed everything that he had planned on doing in the house of the Lord and in his palace.

12 Then the Lord appeared to Solomon at night and said to him, "I have heard your prayer and ᴬhave chosen this place for Myself as a house of sacrifice. 13 ᴬIf I shut up the heavens so that there is no rain, or if I command the locust to devour the land, or if I send a plague among My people, 14 ᴬand My people who are called by My name

humble themselves, and pray and seek My face, and turn from their wicked ways, then I will hear from heaven, and I will forgive their sin and will heal their land. 15 ᴬNow My eyes will be open and My ears attentive to the prayer *offered in* this place. 16 For ᴬnow I have chosen and consecrated this house so that My name may be there forever, and My eyes and My heart will be there always. 17 As for you, if you walk before Me as your father David walked, to do according to everything that I have commanded you, and keep My statutes and My ordinances, 18 then I will establish your royal throne as I covenanted with your father David, saying, 'ᴬYou shall not lack a man *to be* ruler in Israel.'

19 "ᴬBut if you turn away and abandon My statutes and My commandments which I have set before you, and go and serve other gods and worship them, 20 ᴬthen I will uproot you from My land which I have given you, and this house which I have consecrated for My name I will cast out of My sight; and I will make it ᴮa proverb and an object of scorn among all peoples. 21 As for this house, which was exalted, everyone who passes by it will be astonished and say, 'ᴬWhy has the Lord done these things to this land and to this house?' 22 And they will say, 'Because ᴬthey abandoned the Lord, the God of their fathers, who brought them from the land of Egypt, and they adopted other

7:7 ᴬ1 Kin 8:64-66   7:8 ᴬ1 Kin 8:65   ᴮGen 15:18
7:9 ᴬLev 23:36   7:11 ᴬ1 Kin 9:1-9   7:12 ᴬDeut 12:5, 11
7:13 ᴬ2 Chr 6:26-28   7:14 ᴬ2 Chr 6:37-39; James 4:10
7:15 ᴬ2 Chr 6:20, 40   7:16 ᴬ2 Chr 7:12   7:18 ᴬ1 Kin 2:4;
2 Chr 6:16   7:19 ᴬLev 26:14, 33; Deut 28:15
7:20 ᴬ1 Kin 14:15   ᴮDeut 28:37   7:21 ᴬDeut 29:24-27
7:22 ᴬJudg 2:13

gods, and worshiped and served them; therefore He has brought all this adversity on them.'"

SOLOMON'S ACTIVITIES
AND ACCOMPLISHMENTS

8 ^ANow it came about at the end of the twenty years in which Solomon had built the house of the LORD and his own house, ²that he built the cities which Huram had given him, and settled the sons of Israel there.

³Then Solomon went to Hamath-zobah and captured it. ⁴He built Tadmor in the wilderness and all the storage cities which he had built in Hamath. ⁵He also built upper ^ABeth-horon and lower Beth-horon, *which were* fortified cities *with* walls, gates, and bars; ⁶and Baalath and all the storage cities that Solomon had, and all the cities for his chariots and cities for his horsemen, and everything that it pleased Solomon to build in Jerusalem, Lebanon, and all the land under his rule.

⁷^AAll of the people who were left of the Hittites, the Amorites, the Perizzites, the Hivites, and the Jebusites, who were not of Israel, ⁸*that is,* from their descendants who were left after them in the land, whom the sons of Israel had not destroyed, ^ASolomon raised them as forced laborers to this day. ⁹But Solomon did not make slaves from the sons of Israel for his work; for they were men of war, his chief captains and commanders of his chariots and his horsemen. ¹⁰These were the chief officers of King Solomon, 250 who ruled over the people.

¹¹^AThen Solomon brought Pharaoh's daughter up from the city of David to the house which he had built for her, for he said, "My wife shall not live in the house of David king of Israel, because the places where the ark of the LORD has entered are holy."

¹²Then Solomon offered burnt offerings to the LORD on ^Athe altar of the LORD which he had built in front of the porch; ¹³and *he did so* according to the daily rule, offering *them* up according to the commandment of Moses, for ^Athe Sabbaths, the new moons, and the ^Bthree annual feasts—the Feast of Unleavened Bread, the Feast of Weeks, and the Feast of Booths.

¹⁴Now according to the ordinance of his father David, he appointed the divisions of the priests for their service, and the Levites for their duties of praise and ministering before the priests according to the daily rule, and the gatekeepers by their divisions at every gate; for this is what ^ADavid, the man of God, had commanded. ¹⁵And they did not deviate from the commandment of the king to the priests and Levites in any matter or regarding the storehouses.

¹⁶So all the work of Solomon was carried out from the day of the foundation of the house of the LORD, until it was finished. *So* the house of the LORD was completed.

¹⁷Then Solomon went to ^AEzion-geber and to ^BEloth on the seashore in the land of Edom. ¹⁸And by his servants Huram sent him ships and servants who knew the sea; and they went with Solomon's servants to Ophir and ^Atook from there ¹450

8:1^A1 Kin 9:10-28   8:5^A1 Chr 7:24   8:7^AGen 15:18-21;
1 Kin 9:20   8:8^A1 Kin 4:6; 9:21   8:11^A1 Kin 3:1; 7:8
8:12^A2 Chr 4:1   8:13^ANum 28:9, 10   ^BEx 23:14-17
8:14^ANeh 12:24, 36   8:17^A1 Kin 9:26   ^B2 Kin 14:22
8:18^A2 Chr 9:10, 13

8:18 ¹About 17 tons or 15 metric tons

talents of gold, and brought it to King Solomon.

VISIT OF THE QUEEN OF SHEBA

9 ^Now when the queen of Sheba heard about the fame of Solomon, she came to Jerusalem to test Solomon with riddles. She had a very large entourage, with camels carrying balsam oil and a large amount of gold and precious stones; and when she came to Solomon, she spoke with him about everything that was on her heart. ²Solomon answered all her questions; nothing was hidden from Solomon which he did not explain to her. ³When the queen of Sheba had seen the wisdom of Solomon, the house which he had built, ⁴the food at his table, the seating of his servants, the attendance of his ministers and their attire, his cupbearers and their attire, and his stairway by which he went up to the house of the LORD, she was breathless. ⁵Then she said to the king, "It was a true story that I heard in my own land about your words and your wisdom. ⁶But I did not believe their stories until I came and my *own* eyes saw *it all.* And behold, not *even* half of the greatness of your wisdom was reported to me. You have surpassed the report that I heard. ⁷How blessed are your men, how blessed are these servants of yours, who stand before you continually and hear your wisdom! ⁸Blessed be the LORD your God who delighted in you, setting you on His throne as king for the LORD your God; ^because your God loved Israel, establishing them forever, He made you king over them, to carry out justice and righteousness." ⁹Then she gave the king ¹120

talents of gold and a very great *amount of* balsam oil and precious stones; there had never been balsam oil like that which the queen of Sheba gave King Solomon.

¹⁰The servants of Huram and the servants of Solomon ^who brought gold from Ophir, also brought algum trees and precious stones. ¹¹From the algum trees the king made steps to the house of the LORD and for the king's palace, and lyres and harps for the singers; and nothing like them was seen before in the land of Judah.

¹²King Solomon gave the queen of Sheba her every desire, whatever she requested, besides *gifts equal to* what she had brought to the king. Then she turned and went to her own land with her servants.

SOLOMON'S WEALTH AND POWER

¹³^Now the weight of gold that came to Solomon in one year was ¹666 talents of gold, ¹⁴besides *what* the traders and merchants brought; and all ^the kings of Arabia and the governors of the country brought gold and silver to Solomon. ¹⁵King Solomon made two hundred large shields of beaten gold, using six hundred *shekels of* beaten gold on each large shield. ¹⁶*He made* three hundred shields of beaten gold, using three hundred *shekels of* gold on each shield; and the king put them in the house of the forest of Lebanon.

¹⁷Moreover, the king made a great throne of ivory, and overlaid it with pure gold. ¹⁸*There were* six steps to the throne and a footstool in gold

9:1^1 Kin 10:1-13; Luke 11:31   9:8^Deut 7:8; 2 Chr 2:11
9:10^1 Kin 10:11; 2 Chr 8:18   9:13^1 Kin 10:14-28
9:14^Ps 68:29; 72:10

9:9¹About 4.5 tons or 4 metric tons   9:13¹About 25 tons or 23 metric tons

attached to the throne, and arms on each side of the seat, and two lions standing beside the arms. ¹⁹Twelve lions were standing there on the six steps on the one side and on the other; nothing like *it* was made for any *other* kingdom. ²⁰All King Solomon's drinking vessels *were* of gold, and all the vessels of the house of the forest of Lebanon *were* of pure gold; silver was not considered valuable in the days of Solomon. ²¹ᴬFor the king had ships which went to Tarshish with the servants of Huram; once *every* three years the ships of Tarshish came bringing gold and silver, ivory, apes, and peacocks.

²²ᴬSo King Solomon became greater than all the kings of the earth in wealth and wisdom. ²³And all the kings of the earth were seeking the presence of Solomon, to hear his wisdom which God had put in his heart. ²⁴ᴬThey were bringing, each *of them* his gift: articles of silver and gold, garments, weapons, balsam oil, horses, and mules, so much year by year.

²⁵Now Solomon had ᴬfour thousand stalls for horses and chariots and twelve thousand horsemen, and he stationed them in the chariot cities and with the king in Jerusalem. ²⁶ᴬHe was ruler over all the kings from the *Euphrates* River to the land of the Philistines, and as far as the border of Egypt. ²⁷ᴬAnd the king made silver *as common* as stones in Jerusalem, and he made cedars as plentiful as sycamore trees that are in the lowland. ²⁸ᴬAnd they were bringing horses for Solomon from Egypt and from all countries.

²⁹ᴬNow the rest of the acts of Solomon, *from* the first to the last, ᴮare they not written in the records of Nathan the prophet, in the prophecy of Ahijah the Shilonite, and in the visions of Iddo the seer concerning Jeroboam the son of Nebat? ³⁰ᴬSolomon reigned in Jerusalem over all Israel for forty years.

DEATH OF SOLOMON

³¹And Solomon ¹lay down with his fathers and was buried in ᴬthe city of his father David; and his son Rehoboam reigned in his place.

REHOBOAM'S REIGN OF FOOLISHNESS

10 ᴬThen Rehoboam went to Shechem, because all Israel had come to Shechem to make him king. ²When Jeroboam the son of Nebat heard *about it* (ᴬhe was in Egypt where he had fled from the presence of King Solomon), Jeroboam returned from Egypt. ³So they sent *word* and summoned him. When Jeroboam and all Israel came, they spoke to Rehoboam, saying, ⁴"Your father made our ᴬyoke hard; but now, lighten the hard labor *imposed by* your father and his heavy yoke which he put on us, and we will serve you." ⁵He said to them, "Return to me again in three days." So the people departed.

⁶And then King Rehoboam ᴬconsulted with the elders who had served his father Solomon while he was still alive, saying, "How do you advise *me* to answer this people?" ⁷They spoke to him, saying, "If you are kind to this people and please them and ᴬspeak pleasant words to

9:21ᴬ2 Chr 20:36, 37   9:22ᴬ1 Kin 3:13; 2 Chr 1:12   9:24ᴬPs 72:10   9:25ᴬDeut 17:16; 2 Chr 1:14   9:26ᴬGen 15:18; 1 Kin 4:21, 24   9:27ᴬ2 Chr 1:15-17   9:28ᴬ2 Chr 1:16   9:29ᴬ1 Kin 11:41-43   ᴮ1 Chr 29:29   9:30ᴬ1 Kin 11:42, 43   9:31ᴬ1 Kin 2:10   10:1ᴬ1 Kin 12:1-20   10:2ᴬ1 Kin 11:40   10:4ᴬ1 Kin 5:13-16   10:6ᴬJob 8:8, 9; 32:7   10:7ᴬProv 15:1

9:31¹I.e., died

them, then they will be your servants always." 8 But he ^ignored the advice of the elders which they had given him, and consulted with the young men who had grown up with him and served him. 9 He said to them, "What advice do you give, so that we may answer this people, who have spoken to me, saying, 'Lighten the yoke which your father put on us'?" 10 The young men who had grown up with him spoke to him, saying, "This is what you should say to the people who spoke to you, saying: 'Your father made our yoke heavy, but you make it lighter for us!' You should speak this way to them: 'My little finger is thicker than my father's waist! 11 Now then, my father loaded you with a heavy yoke; yet I will add to your yoke. My father disciplined you with whips, but I *will discipline you* with 'scorpions!'"

12 So Jeroboam and all the people came to Rehoboam on the third day, just as the king had directed, saying, "Return to me on the third day." 13 The king answered them harshly, and King Rehoboam ignored the advice of the elders. 14 He spoke to them according to the advice of the young men, saying, "My father made your yoke heavy, but I will add to it; my father disciplined you with whips, but I *will discipline you* with 'scorpions." 15 So the king did not listen to the people, because it was a turn of events from God ^so that the LORD might establish His word, which He spoke through Ahijah the Shilonite to Jeroboam the son of Nebat.

16 When all Israel *saw* that the king had not listened to them, the people replied to the king, saying,

"^What share do we have in
   David?
We have no inheritance in the
   son of Jesse.
Everyone to your tents, Israel!
Now look after your own
   house, David!"

So all Israel went *away* to their tents. 17 But as for the sons of Israel who lived in the cities of Judah, Rehoboam reigned over them. 18 Then King Rehoboam sent Hadoram, who was in ^charge of the forced labor, and the sons of Israel stoned him to death. And King Rehoboam hurried to mount his chariot to flee to Jerusalem. 19 So ^Israel has been in rebellion against the house of David to this day.

REHOBOAM REIGNS OVER JUDAH AND BUILDS CITIES

11 ^Now when Rehoboam had come to Jerusalem, he assembled the house of Judah and Benjamin, 180,000 chosen warriors, to fight against Israel to restore the kingdom to Rehoboam. 2 But the word of the LORD came to ^Shemaiah the man of God, saying, 3 "Tell Rehoboam the son of Solomon, king of Judah, and all Israel in Judah and Benjamin, saying, 4 'This is what the LORD says: "You shall not go up nor fight against ^your relatives; return, every man, to his house, for this event is from Me."'" So they listened to the words of the LORD and returned from going against Jeroboam.

10:8 ^2 Sam 17:14; Prov 13:20   10:15 ^1 Kin 11:29-39
10:16 ^2 Sam 20:1   10:18 ^1 Kin 4:6; 5:14
10:19 ^1 Kin 12:19   11:1 ^1 Kin 12:21-24
11:2 ^2 Chr 12:5-7, 15   11:4 ^2 Chr 28:8-11

10:11 ¹ Prob. a brutal type of whip   10:14 ¹ Prob. a brutal type of whip

⁵Rehoboam lived in Jerusalem and ^built cities for defense in Judah. ⁶He built Bethlehem, Etam, Tekoa, ⁷Beth-zur, Soco, Adullam, ⁸Gath, Mareshah, Ziph, ⁹Adoraim, Lachish, Azekah, ¹⁰Zorah, Aijalon, and Hebron, which are fortified cities in Judah and Benjamin. ¹¹He also strengthened the fortresses and put officers in them and supplies of food, oil, and wine. ¹²*He put* shields and spears in every city and strengthened them greatly. So he held Judah and Benjamin.

¹³Moreover, the priests and the Levites who were in all Israel also stood with him from all their districts.

JEROBOAM APPOINTS FALSE PRIESTS

¹⁴For ^the Levites left their pasture lands and their property and went to Judah and Jerusalem, because Jeroboam and his sons had excluded them from serving as priests to the LORD. ¹⁵^He set up priests of his own for the high places, for the satyrs and the calves which he had made. ¹⁶^Those from all the tribes of Israel who set their hearts on seeking the LORD God of Israel followed them to Jerusalem, to sacrifice to the LORD God of their fathers. ¹⁷^They strengthened the kingdom of Judah and supported Rehoboam the son of Solomon for three years, for they walked in the way of David and Solomon for three years.

REHOBOAM'S FAMILY

¹⁸Then Rehoboam married Mahalath the daughter of Jerimoth the son of David *and of* Abihail the daughter of ^Eliab the son of Jesse, ¹⁹and she bore to him sons: Jeush, Shemariah, and Zaham. ²⁰After her he married ^Maacah the daughter

of Absalom, and she bore to him Abijah, Attai, Ziza, and Shelomith. ²¹Rehoboam loved Maacah the daughter of Absalom more than all his *other* wives and concubines. For ^he had taken eighteen wives and sixty concubines, and fathered twenty-eight sons and sixty daughters. ²²^Rehoboam appointed Abijah the son of Maacah as head and leader among his brothers, for he *intended* to make him king. ²³He acted wisely and distributed some of his sons through all the territories of Judah and Benjamin to all the fortified cities, and he gave them plenty of provisions. And he sought many wives *for them.*

SHISHAK OF EGYPT INVADES JUDAH

12 When the kingdom of Rehoboam was established and strong, ^he and all Israel with him abandoned the Law of the LORD. ²^And it came about in King Rehoboam's fifth year, because they had been unfaithful to the LORD, that Shishak king of Egypt came up against Jerusalem ³with 1,200 chariots and sixty thousand horsemen. And the people who came with him from Egypt were innumerable: ^the Lubim, the Sukkiim, and the Ethiopians. ⁴And he captured ^the fortified cities of Judah and came as far as Jerusalem. ⁵Then ^Shemaiah the prophet came to Rehoboam and the princes of Judah who had gathered at Jerusalem because of Shishak, and he said to them, "This is what the LORD

11:5^2 Chr 8:2-6; 11:23   11:14^Num 35:2-5
11:15^1 Kin 12:31; 13:33   11:16^2 Chr 15:9
11:17^2 Chr 12:1   11:18^1 Sam 16:6   11:20^1 Kin 15:2;
2 Chr 13:2   11:21^Deut 17:17   11:22^Deut 21:15-17
12:1^2 Chr 26:13-16   12:2^1 Kin 14:25
12:3^2 Chr 16:8; Nah 3:9   12:4^2 Chr 11:5-12
12:5^2 Chr 11:2

says: 'You have abandoned Me, so I also have abandoned you to Shishak.'" [6]So the princes of Israel and the king humbled themselves and said, "The ᴬLORD is righteous."

[7]When the LORD saw that they had humbled themselves, the word of the LORD came to Shemaiah, saying, "ᴬThey have humbled themselves, *so* I will not destroy them; and I will grant them a little deliverance, and My wrath will not be poured out on Jerusalem by means of Shishak. [8]But they will become his slaves, so ᴬthat they may learn *the difference between* My service and the service of the kingdoms of the countries."

PLUNDER IMPOVERISHES JUDAH

[9]ᴬSo Shishak king of Egypt went up against Jerusalem, and he took the treasures of the house of the LORD and the treasures of the king's palace. He took everything; he even took the gold shields which Solomon had made. [10]Then King Rehoboam made shields of bronze in their place and committed them to the care of the commanders of the guards who guarded the entrance of the king's house. [11]As often as the king entered the house of the LORD, the guards came and carried them and *then* brought them back into the guards' room. [12]And when he humbled himself, the anger of the LORD turned away from him, so as not to destroy *him* completely; and conditions ᴬwere also good in Judah.

[13]ᴬSo King Rehoboam became powerful in Jerusalem and reigned *there.* For Rehoboam was forty-one years old when he began to reign, and he reigned for seventeen years in Jerusalem, the city which

the LORD had chosen from all the tribes of Israel, to put His name there. And his mother's name was Naamah the Ammonitess. [14]But he did evil ᴬbecause he did not set his heart to seek the LORD.

[15]ᴬNow the acts of Rehoboam, from the first to the last, are they not written in the records of Shemaiah the prophet and of ᴮIddo the seer, according to genealogical enrollment? And *there were* wars between Rehoboam and Jeroboam continually. [16]And Rehoboam ¹lay down with his fathers and was buried in the city of David; and his son ᴬAbijah became king in his place.

ABIJAH SUCCEEDS REHOBOAM

13 ᴬIn the eighteenth year of King Jeroboam, Abijah became king over Judah. [2]He reigned in Jerusalem for three years; and his mother's name was Micaiah the daughter of Uriel of Gibeah.

ᴬNow there was war between Abijah and Jeroboam. [3]Abijah began the battle with an army of warriors, four hundred thousand chosen men, while Jeroboam drew up in battle formation against him with eight hundred thousand chosen men *who were* valiant warriors.

CIVIL WAR

[4]Then Abijah stood on Mount ᴬZemaraim, which is in the hill country of Ephraim, and said, "Listen to me, Jeroboam and all Israel: [5]Do you not know that ᴬthe LORD God of Israel gave the rule over Israel forever to

---

12:6 ᴬEx 9:27; Dan 9:14   12:7 ᴬ1 Kin 21:29
12:8 ᴬDeut 28:47, 48   12:9 ᴬ1 Kin 14:26-28
12:12 ᴬ2 Chr 19:3   12:13 ᴬ1 Kin 14:21   12:14 ᴬ2 Chr 19:3
12:15 ᴬ1 Kin 14:29   ᴮ2 Chr 9:29   12:16 ᴬ2 Chr 11:20
13:1 ᴬ1 Kin 15:1, 2   13:2 ᴬ1 Kin 15:7   13:4 ᴬJosh 18:22
13:5 ᴬ2 Sam 7:12-16

12:16 ¹I.e., died

David and his sons by ᴮa covenant of salt? ⁶Yet ᴬJeroboam the son of Nebat, the servant of Solomon the son of David, rose up and rebelled against his master, ⁷and worthless men gathered to him, wicked men, who proved too strong for Rehoboam, the son of Solomon, when ᴬhe was young and timid and could not hold his own against them.

⁸"So now you intend to assert yourselves against the kingdom of the Lᴏʀᴅ through the sons of David, being a great multitude and *having* with you ᴬthe golden calves which Jeroboam made for you as gods. ⁹ᴬHave you not driven out the priests of the Lᴏʀᴅ, the sons of Aaron and the Levites, and made for yourselves priests like the peoples of *other* lands? Whoever comes to consecrate himself with a bull and seven rams, even he may become a priest of *things that are* not gods. ¹⁰But as for us, the Lᴏʀᴅ is our God, and we have not abandoned Him; and the sons of Aaron are ministering to the Lᴏʀᴅ as priests, and the Levites attend to their work. ¹¹Every morning and evening ᴬthey burn to the Lᴏʀᴅ burnt offerings and fragrant incense, and the showbread is *set* on the clean table, and the golden lampstand with its lamps is *ready* to light every evening; for we perform *our* duty to the Lᴏʀᴅ our God, but you have abandoned Him. ¹²Now behold, God is with us at *our* head, and ᴬHis priests with the signal trumpets to sound the war cry against you. Sons of Israel, do not fight against the Lᴏʀᴅ God of your fathers, for you will not succeed."

¹³But Jeroboam ᴬhad set an ambush to come from behind, so that *Israel* was in front of Judah and the ambush was behind them.

¹⁴When Judah turned around, behold, they were attacked both from front and rear; so ᴬthey cried out to the Lᴏʀᴅ, and the priests blew the trumpets. ¹⁵Then the men of Judah raised a war cry, and when the men of Judah raised the war cry, God ᴬdefeated Jeroboam and all Israel before Abijah and Judah. ¹⁶When the sons of Israel fled from Judah, ᴬGod handed them over to them. ¹⁷Abijah and his people defeated them with a great slaughter, so that five hundred thousand chosen men of Israel fell slain. ¹⁸The sons of Israel were subdued at that time, and the sons of Judah conquered ᴬbecause they trusted in the Lᴏʀᴅ, the God of their fathers. ¹⁹Abijah pursued Jeroboam and captured from him *several* cities, Bethel with its villages, Jeshanah with its villages, and Ephron with its villages.

DEATH OF JEROBOAM

²⁰Jeroboam did not again recover strength in the days of Abijah; and the Lᴏʀᴅ struck him and ᴬhe died.

²¹But Abijah became powerful, and he took fourteen wives for himself, and fathered twenty-two sons and sixteen daughters. ²²Now the rest of the acts of Abijah, and his ways and his words are written in the treatise of ᴬIddo the prophet.

ASA SUCCEEDS ABIJAH IN JUDAH

14 ᴬSo Abijah ¹lay down with his fathers, and they buried him in the city of David, and his son Asa became king in his place. The

13:5 ᴮLev 2:13   13:6 ᴬ1 Kin 11:26   13:7 ᴬ2 Chr 12:13
13:8 ᴬ1 Kin 12:28; 2 Chr 11:15   13:9 ᴬ2 Chr 11:14, 15
13:11 ᴬEx 29:38; 2 Chr 2:4   13:12 ᴬNum 10:8, 9
13:13 ᴬJosh 8:4–9   13:14 ᴬ2 Chr 14:11   13:15 ᴬ2 Chr 14:12
13:16 ᴬ2 Chr 16:8   13:18 ᴬ2 Chr 14:11
13:20 ᴬ1 Kin 14:20   13:22 ᴬ2 Chr 9:29   14:1 ᴬ1 Kin 15:8

14:1 ¹I.e., died

land was undisturbed for ten years during his days.

2 And Asa did *what was* good and right in the sight of the LORD his God, 3 for he removed the foreign altars and ^high places, tore down the memorial stones, cut down the 1,B Asherim, 4 and commanded Judah to seek the LORD God of their fathers and to comply with the Law and the commandment. 5 He also removed the high places and the ^incense altars from all the cities of Judah. And the kingdom was undisturbed under him. 6 He built fortified cities in Judah, since the land was undisturbed, and there was no one at war with him during those years, ^because the LORD had given him rest. 7 For he said to Judah, "^Let's build these cities and surround *them* with walls and towers, gates and bars. The land is still ours because we have sought the LORD our God; we have sought Him, and He has given us rest on every side." So they built and prospered. 8 Now Asa had an army of ^three hundred thousand from Judah, carrying large shields and spears, and 280,000 from Benjamin, carrying shields and wielding bows; all of them were valiant warriors.

9 Now Zerah the Ethiopian went out against them with an army of a million men and three hundred chariots, and he came to ^Mareshah. 10 So Asa went out to meet him, and they drew up in battle formation in the Valley of Zephathah at Mareshah. 11 Then Asa called to the LORD his God and said, "LORD, there is no one besides You to help *in the battle* between the powerful and those who have no strength; help us, LORD our God, ^for we trust in You, and in Your name have

come against this multitude. LORD, You are our God; do not let man prevail against You." 12 So ^the LORD routed the Ethiopians before Asa and before Judah, and the Ethiopians fled. 13 Asa and the people who *were* with him pursued them as far as ^Gerar; and so many Ethiopians fell that they could not recover, for they were shattered before the LORD and before His army. And they carried away a very large *amount of* plunder. 14 They destroyed all the cities around Gerar, ^for the dread of the LORD had fallen on them; and they pillaged all the cities, for there was much plunder in them. 15 They also fatally struck those who owned livestock, and they led away large numbers of sheep and camels. Then they returned to Jerusalem.

AZARIAH THE PROPHET WARNS ASA

15 Now ^the Spirit of God came on Azariah the son of Oded, 2 and he went out to meet Asa and said to him, "Listen to me, Asa, and all Judah and Benjamin: ^the LORD is with you when you are with Him. And if you seek Him, He will let you find Him; but if you abandon Him, He will abandon you. 3 ^For many days Israel was without the true God and without a teaching priest and without *the* Law. 4 But ^in their distress they turned to the LORD God of Israel, and they sought Him, and He let them find Him. 5 ^In those times there was no peace for him who went out or him who came in, because

14:3 ^1 Kin 15:12-14   B Ex 34:13   14:5 ^2 Chr 34:4, 7
14:6 ^2 Chr 15:15   14:7 ^2 Chr 8:5   14:8 ^2 Chr 13:3
14:9 ^2 Chr 11:8   14:11 ^2 Chr 13:18   14:12 ^2 Chr 13:15
14:13 ^Gen 10:19   14:14 ^2 Chr 17:10
15:1 ^2 Chr 20:14; 24:20   15:2 ^2 Chr 20:17
15:3 ^1 Kin 12:28-33   15:4 ^Deut 4:29   15:5 ^Judg 5:6

14:3 1 I.e., wooden symbols of a female deity (Asherah)

many disturbances afflicted all the inhabitants of the lands. [6]^A Nation was crushed by nation, and city by city, for God troubled them with every kind of distress. [7]But you, ^A be strong and do not lose courage, for there is a ^B reward for your work."

ASA'S REFORMS

[8]Now when Asa heard these words and the prophecy which Azariah the son of Oded the prophet spoke, he took courage and removed the abominable idols from all the land of Judah and Benjamin, and from ^A the cities which he had captured in the hill country of Ephraim. [B]He then restored the altar of the LORD which was in front of the porch of the LORD. [9]And he gathered all Judah and Benjamin, and those from Ephraim, Manasseh, and Simeon ^A who resided with them, for many defected to him from Israel when they saw that the LORD his God was with him. [10]So they assembled at Jerusalem in the third month of the fifteenth year of Asa's reign. [11]^A They sacrificed to the LORD on that day seven hundred oxen and seven thousand sheep from the spoils they had brought. [12]^A They entered into the covenant to seek the LORD God of their fathers with all their heart and soul; [13]and whoever would not seek the LORD God of Israel ^A was to be put to death, whether small or great, man or woman. [14]Moreover, they made an oath to the LORD with a loud voice, with shouting, trumpets, and with horns. [15]All Judah rejoiced concerning the oath, for they had sworn with all their heart and had sought Him earnestly, and He let them find Him. So ^A the LORD gave them rest on every side.

[16]^A He also removed Maacah, the mother of King Asa, from the *position of* queen mother, because she had made an abominable image [1]as an Asherah, and Asa cut down her abominable image, crushed *it,* and burned *it* at the brook Kidron. [17]But the high places were not removed from Israel; nevertheless Asa's heart was blameless all his days. [18]He brought into the house of God the dedicated things of his father and his own dedicated things: silver, gold, and utensils. [19]And there was no *more* war until the thirty-fifth year of Asa's reign.

ASA WARS AGAINST BAASHA

16 In the thirty-sixth year of Asa's reign, ^A Baasha king of Israel came up against Judah and fortified Ramah in order to prevent *anyone* from going out or coming in to Asa king of Judah. [2]Then Asa brought out silver and gold from the treasuries of the house of the LORD and the king's house, and sent it to Ben-hadad king of Aram, who lived in Damascus, saying, [3]"A treaty *must be made* between you and me, *as there was* between my father and your father. Behold, I have sent you silver and gold; go, break your treaty with Baasha king of Israel so that he will withdraw from me." [4]And Ben-hadad listened to King Asa, and he sent the commanders of his armies against the cities of Israel, and they conquered Ijon, Dan, Abel-maim, and all ^A the storage cities of Naphtali.

15:6 ^A Matt 24:7   15:7 ^A Josh 1:7, 9   ^B Ps 58:11
15:8 ^A 2 Chr 13:19   ^B 2 Chr 4:1   15:9 ^A 2 Chr 11:16
15:11 ^A 2 Chr 14:13-15   15:12 ^A 2 Chr 23:16
15:13 ^A Ex 22:20; Deut 13:6-9   15:15 ^A 2 Chr 14:7
15:16 ^A 1 Kin 15:13-15   16:1 ^A 1 Kin 15:17-22   16:4 ^A Ex 1:11

15:16 [1]Or for *Asherah;* i.e., a wooden symbol of a female deity

⁵When Baasha heard *about it,* he stopped fortifying Ramah and put an end to his work. ⁶Then King Asa brought all Judah, and they carried away the stones of Ramah and its timber with which Baasha had been building, and with it he fortified Geba and Mizpah.

ASA IMPRISONS THE PROPHET

⁷At that time ^Hanani the seer came to Asa king of Judah and said to him, "Because you have relied on the king of Aram and have not relied on the LORD your God, for that reason the army of the king of Aram has escaped from your hand. ⁸Were not the Ethiopians and the Lubim an immense army with very many chariots and horsemen? Yet ^because you relied on the LORD, He handed them over to you. ⁹For the eyes of the LORD roam throughout the earth, so that He may strongly support those ^whose heart is completely His. You have acted foolishly in this. Indeed, from now on you will have wars." ¹⁰Then Asa was angry with the seer and put him in prison, for he was enraged at him for this. And Asa mistreated some of the people at the same time.

¹¹^Now, the acts of Asa *from* the first to the last, behold, they are written in the Book of the Kings of Judah and Israel. ¹²In the thirty-ninth year of his reign Asa became diseased in his feet. His disease was severe, yet even in his disease he ^did not seek the LORD, but the physicians. ¹³So Asa ¹lay down with his fathers, and died in the forty-first year of his reign. ¹⁴They buried him in his own tomb which he had cut out for himself in the city of David, and they laid him in the resting place which he had filled ^with spices of various kinds blended by the perfumers' art; and they made a very great fire for him.

JEHOSHAPHAT SUCCEEDS ASA

17 His son ^Jehoshaphat then became king in his place, and he proved himself strong over Israel. ²He placed troops in all ^the fortified cities of Judah, and placed garrisons in the land of Judah and in the cities of Ephraim ᴮwhich his father Asa had captured.

HIS GOOD REIGN

³And the LORD was with Jehoshaphat because he followed the example of his father David's earlier days and did not seek the Baals, ⁴but sought the God of his father, followed His commandments, ^and did not *act* as Israel did. ⁵So the LORD established the kingdom in his control, and all Judah gave tribute to Jehoshaphat, and ^he had great riches and honor. ⁶He took great pride in the ways of the LORD, and again ^removed the high places and the ¹Asherim from Judah.

⁷Then in the third year of his reign he sent his officials, Ben-hail, Obadiah, Zechariah, Nethanel, and Micaiah, ^to teach in the cities of Judah; ⁸and with them ^the Levites, Shemaiah, Nethaniah, Zebadiah, Asahel, Shemiramoth, Jehonathan, Adonijah, Tobijah, and Tobadonijah, the Levites; and with them the priests Elishama and Jehoram. ⁹They taught in Judah, *having* ^the

16:7^1 Kin 16:1; 2 Chr 19:2   16:8^2 Chr 13:16, 18
16:9^2 Chr 15:17   16:11^1 Kin 15:23, 24   16:12^Jer 17:5
16:14^Gen 50:2; John 19:39, 40   17:1^1 Kin 15:24
17:2^2 Chr 11:5   ᴮ2 Chr 15:8   17:4^1 Kin 12:28
17:5^2 Chr 18:1   17:6^2 Chr 15:17   17:7^2 Chr 15:3;
35:3   17:8^2 Chr 19:8   17:9^Deut 6:4-9

16:13 ¹I.e., died   17:6 ¹I.e., wooden symbols of a female deity (Asherah)

Book of the Law of the LORD with them; and they went throughout the cities of Judah and taught among the people.

¹⁰Now ᴬthe dread of the LORD was on all the kingdoms of the lands which *were* around Judah, so that they did not make war against Jehoshaphat. ¹¹Some of the Philistines ᴬbrought gifts and silver as tribute to Jehoshaphat; the Arabians also brought him flocks, 7,700 rams and 7,700 male goats. ¹²So Jehoshaphat grew greater and greater, and he built fortresses and storage cities in Judah. ¹³He had large supplies in the cities of Judah, and warriors, valiant mighty men, in Jerusalem. ¹⁴This was their muster according to their fathers' households: of Judah, commanders of thousands, Adnah *was* the commander, and with him three hundred thousand valiant warriors; ¹⁵and next to him *was* Johanan the commander, and with him 280,000; ¹⁶and next to him Amasiah the son of Zichri, ᴬwho volunteered for the LORD, and with him two hundred thousand valiant warriors; ¹⁷and of Benjamin, Eliada, a valiant warrior, and with him two hundred thousand armed with bow and shield; ¹⁸and next to him Jehozabad, and with him 180,000 equipped for war. ¹⁹These are the ones who served the king, apart from ᴬthose whom the king put in the fortified cities throughout Judah.

JEHOSHAPHAT ALLIES WITH AHAB

18 Now ᴬJehoshaphat had great riches and honor; and he allied himself by marriage to Ahab. ²ᴬSome years later he went down to *visit* Ahab at Samaria, and Ahab slaughtered many sheep and oxen for him and the people who were with him. And he incited him to go up against Ramoth-gilead. ³Ahab king of Israel said to Jehoshaphat king of Judah, "Will you go with me *against* Ramoth-gilead?" And he said to him, "I am as you are, and my people as your people, and *we will be* with you in the battle."

⁴However, Jehoshaphat said to the king of Israel, "Please request the word of the LORD first." ⁵So the king of Israel assembled the ¹prophets, four hundred men, and said to them, "Should we go to battle against Ramoth-gilead, or should I refrain?" And they said, "Go up, for God will hand *it* over to the king." ⁶But Jehoshaphat said, "Is there no longer a prophet of the LORD here, that we may inquire of him?" ⁷And the king of Israel said to Jehoshaphat, "There is still one man by whom we may inquire of the LORD, but I hate him, for he never prophesies *anything* good regarding me, but always bad. He is Micaiah the son of Imlah." But Jehoshaphat said, "May the king not say so."

AHAB'S FALSE PROPHETS ASSURE VICTORY

⁸Then the king of Israel summoned an officer and said, "Bring Micaiah son of Imlah quickly." ⁹Now the king of Israel and Jehoshaphat the king of Judah were sitting, each on his throne, dressed in *their* robes, and *they* were sitting ᴬat the threshing floor at the entrance of the gate of Samaria; and all the prophets were prophesying before them. ¹⁰Then Zedekiah the son of

17:10ᴬ2 Chr 14:14   17:11ᴬ2 Chr 9:14; 26:8
17:16ᴬJudg 5:2, 9; 1 Chr 29:9   17:19ᴬ2 Chr 17:2
18:1ᴬ2 Chr 17:5   18:2ᴬ1 Kin 22:2-35   18:9ᴬRuth 4:1

18:5 ¹I.e., official prophets who at that time were false

Chenaanah made horns of iron for himself and said, "This is what the LORD says: 'With these you will gore the Arameans until they are destroyed!'" ¹¹All the prophets were prophesying this as well, saying, "Go up to Ramoth-gilead and be successful, for the LORD will hand *it* over to the king."

MICAIAH BRINGS WORD FROM GOD

¹²Then the messenger who went to summon Micaiah spoke to him saying, "Behold, the words of the prophets are unanimously favorable to the king. So please let your word be like one of them, and speak favorably." ¹³But Micaiah said, "As the LORD lives, ^whatever my God says, I will speak it."

¹⁴When he came to the king, the king said to him, "Micaiah, should we go to battle against Ramoth-gilead, or should I refrain?" He said, "Go up and succeed, for they will be handed over to you!" ¹⁵Then the king said to him, "How many times must I make you swear that you will tell me nothing but the truth in the name of the LORD?" ¹⁶So he said,

"I saw all Israel
    Scattered on the mountains,
    ^Like sheep that have no
        shepherd.
And the LORD said,
    'These *people* have no master.
    Each of them is to return to his
        house in peace.'"

¹⁷Then the king of Israel said to Jehoshaphat, "Did I not tell you that he would not prophesy *anything* good regarding me, but *only* bad?"

¹⁸And *Micaiah* said, "Therefore, hear the word of the LORD. ^I saw the LORD sitting on His throne, and all the angels of heaven standing on His right and on His left. ¹⁹And

the LORD said, 'Who will entice Ahab king of Israel to go up and fall at Ramoth-gilead?' And one *spirit* said this, while another said that. ²⁰Then a ^spirit came forward and stood before the LORD and said, 'I will entice him.' And the LORD said to him, 'How?' ²¹He said, 'I will go out and be ^a deceiving spirit in the mouths of all his prophets.' Then He said, 'You shall entice *him,* and you will also prevail. Go out and do so.' ²²Now therefore, behold, ^the LORD has put a deceiving spirit in the mouths of these prophets of yours, for the LORD has declared disaster against you."

²³Then Zedekiah the son of Chenaanah approached and ^struck Micaiah on the cheek; and he said, "How did the Spirit of the LORD pass from me to speak to you?" ²⁴And Micaiah said, "Behold, you are going to see *how* on that day when you go *from one* inner room to another *trying* to hide yourself." ²⁵Then the king of Israel said, "^Take Micaiah and return him to Amon the governor of the city, and to Joash the king's son; ²⁶and say, 'This is what the king says: "^Put this *man* in prison, and feed him enough bread and water to survive until I return safely."'" ²⁷But Micaiah said, "If you actually return safely, the LORD has not spoken by me." And he said, "^Listen, all you people!"

AHAB'S DEFEAT AND DEATH

²⁸So the king of Israel and Jehoshaphat king of Judah went up against Ramoth-gilead. ²⁹And the king of Israel said to Jehoshaphat,

18:13^Num 22:18-20, 35   18:16^Ezek 35:4-8;
Matt 9:36   18:18^Is 6:1-5; Dan 7:9, 10
18:20^Job 1:6; 2 Thess 2:9   18:21^John 8:44
18:22^Is 19:14; Ezek 14:9   18:23^Jer 20:2; Acts 23:2
18:25^2 Chr 18:8   18:26^2 Chr 16:10   18:27^Mic 1:2

"I will disguise myself and go into battle, but you put on your robes." So the king of Israel disguised himself, and they went into battle. 30 Now the king of Aram had commanded the commanders of his chariots, saying, "Do not fight with the small *or* great, but only with the king of Israel." 31 So when the commanders of the chariots saw Jehoshaphat, they said, "He is the king of Israel!" And they turned aside to fight against him. But Jehoshaphat ^cried out, and the LORD helped him, and God diverted them from him. 32 When the commanders of the chariots saw that it was not the king of Israel, they turned back from pursuing him. 33 Now one man drew his bow at random and struck the king of Israel in a joint of the armor. So he said to the driver of his chariot, "Turn around and take me out of the battle, for I am severely wounded." 34 The battle raged on that day, and the king of Israel propped himself up in his chariot in front of the Arameans until the evening; and at sunset he died.

JEHU REBUKES JEHOSHAPHAT

19 Then Jehoshaphat the king of Judah returned in safety to his house in Jerusalem. 2 And Jehu the son of Hanani the seer went out to meet him and said to King Jehoshaphat, "^Should you help the wicked and love those who hate the LORD, and ^Bby doing so *bring* wrath on yourself from the LORD? 3 But ^there is *some* good in you, for ^Byou have removed the ¹Asheroth from the land and you have set your heart to seek God."

4 So Jehoshaphat lived in Jerusalem and went out again among the people from Beersheba to the hill country of Ephraim, and ^brought them back to the LORD, the God of their fathers.

REFORMS INSTITUTED

5 He appointed ^judges in the land in all the fortified cities of Judah, city by city. 6 He said to the judges, "Consider what you are doing, for ^you do not judge for mankind but for the LORD who is with you when you render judgment. 7 Now then, let the fear of the LORD be upon you; be careful about what you do, for the LORD our God will have no part in injustice ^or partiality, or in the taking of a bribe."

8 In Jerusalem Jehoshaphat also appointed some ^of the Levites and priests, and some of the heads of the fathers' *households* of Israel, for the judgment of the LORD, and to judge disputes among the inhabitants of Jerusalem. 9 Then he commanded them, saying, "This is what you shall do in the fear of the LORD, faithfully and wholeheartedly. 10 ^Whenever any dispute comes to you from your countrymen who live in their cities, between blood and blood, between law and commandment, statutes and ordinances, you shall warn them so that they will not be guilty before the LORD, and wrath will *not* come on you and your countrymen. This you shall do and you will not be guilty. 11 Behold, Amariah the chief priest will be over you in every matter that pertains to the LORD, and

18:31^2 Chr 13:14, 15   19:2^2 Chr 18:1, 3
^B2 Chr 24:18   19:3^2 Chr 12:12   ^B2 Chr 17:6
19:4^2 Chr 15:8–13   19:5^Deut 16:18–20
19:6^Lev 19:15; Deut 1:17   19:7^Deut 10:17, 18
19:8^2 Chr 17:8, 9   19:10^Deut 17:8

19:3 ¹I.e., wooden symbols of a female deity

Zebadiah the son of Ishmael, the ruler of the house of Judah, in all that pertains to the king. Also the Levites shall be officers before you. ^Act resolutely, and may the LORD be with the upright."

JUDAH INVADED

20 Now it came about after this, that the sons of Moab and the sons of Ammon, together with some of the ^Meunites, came to make war against Jehoshaphat. ²Then some came and reported to Jehoshaphat, saying, "A great multitude is coming against you from beyond the sea, from Aram; and behold, they are in ^Hazazon-tamar (that is Engedi)." ³Jehoshaphat was afraid and ^turned his attention to seek the LORD; and he proclaimed a period of fasting throughout Judah. ⁴So Judah gathered together to ^seek help from the LORD; they even came from all the cities of Judah to seek the LORD.

JEHOSHAPHAT'S PRAYER

⁵Then Jehoshaphat stood in the assembly of Judah and Jerusalem, in the house of the LORD in front of the new courtyard; ⁶and he said, "LORD, God of our fathers, are You not God in the heavens? And ^are You not ruler over all the kingdoms of the nations? Power and might are in Your hand so that no one can stand against You. ⁷Did You not, our God, drive out the inhabitants of this land from Your people Israel, and ^give it to the descendants of Your friend Abraham forever? ⁸They have lived in it, and have built You a sanctuary in it for Your name, saying, ⁹'^If disaster comes upon us, the sword, *or* judgment, or plague, or famine, we will stand before

this house and before You (for Your name is in this house), and cry out to You in our distress, and You will hear and save *us*.' ¹⁰Now behold, the sons of Ammon, Moab, and Mount Seir, ^whom You did not allow Israel to invade when they came out of the land of Egypt (for they turned aside from them and did not destroy them), ¹¹see *how* they are rewarding us by ^coming to drive us out from Your possession which You have given us as an inheritance. ¹²Our God, ^will You not judge them? For we are powerless before this great multitude that is coming against us; nor do we know what to do, but our eyes are on You."

¹³All Judah was standing before the LORD, with their infants, their wives, and their children.

JAHAZIEL ANSWERS THE PRAYER

¹⁴Then in the midst of the assembly ^the Spirit of the LORD came upon Jahaziel the son of Zechariah, the son of Benaiah, the son of Jeiel, the son of Mattaniah, the Levite of the sons of Asaph; ¹⁵and he said, "Listen, all *you of* Judah and the inhabitants of Jerusalem, and King Jehoshaphat: This is what the LORD says to you: 'Do not fear or be dismayed because of this great multitude, for ^the battle is not yours but God's. ¹⁶Tomorrow, go down against them. Behold, they will come up by the ascent of Ziz, and you will find them at the end of the valley in front of the wilderness of Jeruel. ¹⁷You *need* not fight in this *battle;* take your position, ^stand

19:11^1 Chr 28:20   20:1^1 Chr 4:41; 2 Chr 26:7
20:2^Gen 14:7   20:3^2 Chr 19:3   20:4^Joel 1:14
20:6^1 Chr 29:11   20:7^Is 41:8   20:9^2 Chr 6:28-30
20:10^Num 20:17-21   20:11^Ps 83:12
20:12^Judg 11:27   20:14^2 Chr 15:1; 24:20
20:15^1 Sam 17:47   20:17^Ex 14:13

and watch the salvation of the LORD in your behalf, Judah and Jerusalem.' Do not fear or be dismayed; tomorrow, go out to face them, for the LORD is with you."

¹⁸Jehoshaphat ^bowed his head with *his* face to the ground, and all Judah and the inhabitants of Jerusalem fell down before the LORD, worshiping the LORD. ¹⁹The Levites, from the sons of the Kohathites and from the sons of the Korahites, stood up to praise the LORD God of Israel, with a very loud voice.

ENEMIES DESTROY THEMSELVES

²⁰They rose early in the morning and went out to the wilderness of Tekoa; and when they went out, Jehoshaphat stood and said, "Listen to me, Judah and inhabitants of Jerusalem: ^Put your trust in the LORD your God and you will endure. Put your trust in His prophets, and succeed." ²¹When he had consulted with the people, he appointed those who sang to the LORD and those who ^praised *Him* in holy attire, as they went out before the army and said, "Give thanks to the LORD, for His faithfulness is everlasting." ²²When they began singing and praising, the LORD ^set ambushes against the sons of Ammon, Moab, and Mount Seir, who had come against Judah; so they were struck down. ²³For the sons of Ammon and Moab rose up against the inhabitants of Mount Seir, completely destroying *them;* and when they had finished with the inhabitants of Seir, ^they helped to destroy one another.

²⁴When Judah came to the watchtower of the wilderness, they turned toward the multitude, and behold, they *were* corpses lying on the ground, and there was no survivor. ²⁵When Jehoshaphat and his people came to take their spoils, they found much among them, *including* goods, garments, and valuable things which they took for themselves, more than they could carry. And they were taking the spoils for three days because there was *so* much.

TRIUMPHANT RETURN TO JERUSALEM

²⁶Then on the fourth day they assembled in the Valley of Beracah, for they blessed the LORD there. Therefore they have named that place "The Valley of 'Beracah" until today. ²⁷Every man of Judah and Jerusalem returned, with Jehoshaphat at their head, returning to Jerusalem with joy, ^for the LORD had helped them to rejoice over their enemies. ²⁸They came to Jerusalem with harps, lyres, and trumpets, to the house of the LORD. ²⁹And ^the dread of God was on all the kingdoms of the lands when they heard that the LORD had fought against the enemies of Israel. ³⁰So the kingdom of Jehoshaphat was at peace, ^for his God gave him rest on all sides.

³¹^Now Jehoshaphat reigned over Judah. He *was* thirty-five years old when he became king, and he reigned in Jerusalem for twenty-five years. And his mother's name *was* Azubah the daughter of Shilhi. ³²He walked in the way of his father Asa and did not deviate from it, doing right in the sight of the LORD. ³³^The high places, however, were not removed; the people had not

20:18 ^Ex 4:31   20:20 ^Is 7:9
20:21 ^1 Chr 16:29; Ps 29:2   20:22 ^2 Chr 13:13
20:23 ^Judg 7:22; 1 Sam 14:20   20:27 ^Neh 12:43
20:29 ^2 Chr 14:14; 17:10   20:30 ^2 Chr 14:6, 7; 15:15
20:31 ^1 Kin 22:41-43   20:33 ^2 Chr 17:6

20:26 ¹I.e., blessing

yet directed their hearts to the God of their fathers.

34 Now the rest of the acts of Jehoshaphat, first to last, behold, they are written in the annals of ^Jehu the son of Hanani, which is recorded in the Book of the Kings of Israel.

ALLIANCE DISPLEASES GOD

35 ^After this Jehoshaphat king of Judah allied himself with Ahaziah king of Israel. He acted wickedly in so doing. 36 So he allied himself with him to make ships to go ^to Tarshish, and they made the ships in Ezion-geber. 37 Then Eliezer the son of Dodavahu of Mareshah prophesied against Jehoshaphat, saying, "Because you have allied yourself with Ahaziah, the LORD has destroyed your works." So the ships were wrecked and could not go to Tarshish.

JEHORAM SUCCEEDS JEHOSHAPHAT IN JUDAH

21 ^Then Jehoshaphat 'lay down with his fathers and was buried with his fathers in the city of David, and his son Jehoram became king in his place. 2 He had brothers, the sons of Jehoshaphat: Azariah, Jehiel, Zechariah, Azaryahu, Michael, and Shephatiah. All these *were* the sons of Jehoshaphat king ^of Israel. 3 Their father gave them many gifts of silver, gold, and precious things, ^with fortified cities in Judah; but he gave the kingdom to Jehoram because he was the firstborn.

4 Now when Jehoram had taken over the kingdom of his father and gathered courage, he ^killed all his brothers with the sword, and some of the leaders of Israel as well.

5 ^Jehoram *was* thirty-two years old when he became king, and he reigned for eight years in Jerusalem. 6 ^He walked in the way of the kings of Israel, just as the house of Ahab had done, ^for Ahab's daughter was his wife; and he did evil in the sight of the LORD. 7 Yet the LORD was not willing to destroy the house of David because of the covenant which He had made with David, ^and because He had promised to give a lamp to him and his sons forever.

REVOLT AGAINST JUDAH

8 In his days ^Edom broke away from the rule of Judah, and appointed a king over themselves. 9 Then Jehoram crossed over with his commanders and all his chariots with him. And he got up at night and struck and killed the Edomites who were surrounding him, and the commanders of the chariots. 10 So Edom revolted against Judah to this day. Then Libnah revolted at the same time against his rule because he had abandoned the LORD God of his fathers. 11 Furthermore, ^he made high places in the mountains of Judah, and caused the inhabitants of Jerusalem ^to be unfaithful, and led Judah astray.

12 Then a letter came to him from Elijah the prophet, saying, "This is what the LORD, the God of your father David says: 'Because ^you have not walked in the ways of your father Jehoshaphat and the ways of Asa king of Judah, 13 but have walked

20:34^2 Chr 19:2   20:35^1 Kin 22:48, 49
20:36^2 Chr 9:21   21:1^1 Kin 22:50   21:2^2 Chr 12:6;
23:2   21:3^2 Chr 11:5   21:4^Gen 4:8; Judg 9:5
21:5^2 Kin 8:17-22   21:6^1 Kin 12:28-30   ^B 2 Chr 18:1
21:7^2 Sam 7:12-17; 1 Kin 11:13, 36   21:8^2 Chr 20:22, 23;
21:10   21:11^1 Kin 11:7   ^B Lev 20:5   21:12^2 Chr 17:3, 4
21:1 'I.e., died

in the way of the kings of Israel, and have caused Judah and the inhabitants of Jerusalem to be unfaithful ^as the house of Ahab was unfaithful, and you have also killed your brothers, your own family, who were better than you, ¹⁴behold, the LORD is going to strike your people, your sons, your wives, and all your possessions with a great plague; ¹⁵and ^you will suffer severe sickness, a disease of your bowels, until your bowels come out because of the sickness, day by day.'"

¹⁶Then the LORD stirred up against Jehoram the spirit of the Philistines and ^the Arabs who bordered the Ethiopians; ¹⁷and they came against Judah and invaded it, and carried away all the possessions found in the king's house together with his sons and his wives, so that no son was left to him except ^Jehoahaz, the youngest of his sons.

¹⁸So after all this the LORD struck him ^in his intestines with an incurable sickness. ¹⁹Now it came about in the course of time, at the end of two years, that his bowels came out because of his sickness, and he died in great pain. And his people did not make a *funeral* fire for him like ^the fire for his fathers. ²⁰He was thirty-two years old when he became king, and he reigned in Jerusalem for eight years; and he departed ^with no one's regret, and they buried him in the city of David, ᴮbut not in the tombs of the kings.

AHAZIAH SUCCEEDS JEHORAM IN JUDAH

22 ^Then the inhabitants of Jerusalem made Ahaziah, his youngest son, king in his place, for the band of men who came with the Arabs to the camp had killed all the older *sons*. So Ahaziah the son of Jehoram king of Judah began to reign. ²Ahaziah *was* twenty-two years old when he became king, and he reigned for one year in Jerusalem. And his mother's name was Athaliah, the granddaughter of Omri. ³He also walked in the ways of the house of Ahab, for his mother was his counselor to act wickedly. ⁴So he did evil in the sight of the LORD like the house of Ahab, for they were his counselors after the death of his father, to ^his own destruction.

AHAZIAH ALLIES WITH JEHORAM OF ISRAEL

⁵He also walked by their counsel, and went with Jehoram the son of Ahab king of Israel to wage war against Hazael king of Aram at Ramoth-gilead. But the ^Arameans wounded Joram. ⁶So he returned to be healed in Jezreel of the wounds which they had inflicted on him at Ramah, when he fought against Hazael king of Aram. And Ahaziah, the son of Jehoram king of Judah, went down to see Jehoram the son of Ahab in Jezreel, because he was sick.

⁷Now the destruction of Ahaziah was from God, in that he went to Joram. For when he arrived, ^he went out with Jehoram against Jehu the son of Nimshi, ᴮwhom the LORD had anointed to eliminate the house of Ahab.

JEHU MURDERS PRINCES OF JUDAH

⁸^And it came about, when Jehu was executing judgment on the

21:13^1 Kin 16:31-33   21:15^2 Chr 21:18, 19
21:16^2 Chr 17:11; 22:1   21:17^2 Chr 25:23
21:18^2 Chr 21:15   21:19^2 Chr 16:14
21:20^Jer 22:18, 28   ᴮ2 Chr 24:25   22:1^2 Kin
8:24-29   22:4^Prov 13:20   22:5^2 Kin 8:28
22:7^2 Kin 9:21   ᴮ2 Kin 9:6, 7   22:8^2 Kin 10:11-14

house of Ahab, that he found the princes of Judah and the sons of Ahaziah's brothers attending to Ahaziah, and killed them. 9^He also searched for Ahaziah, and they caught him while he was hiding in Samaria; they brought him to Jehu, put him to death, and buried him. For they said, "He is the son of Jehoshaphat, who sought the LORD with all his heart." So there was no one of the house of Ahaziah to retain the power of the kingdom. 10^Now when Athaliah the mother of Ahaziah saw that her son was dead, she rose and eliminated all the royal children of the house of Judah. 11But Jehoshabeath the king's daughter took Joash the son of Ahaziah, and stole him from among the king's sons who were being put to death, and placed him and his nurse in the bedroom. So Jehoshabeath, the daughter of King Jehoram, the wife of Jehoiada the priest (for she was the sister of Ahaziah), hid him from Athaliah so that she would not put him to death. 12He kept himself hidden with them in the house of God for six years while Athaliah reigned over the land.

JEHOIADA SETS JOASH ON THE THRONE OF JUDAH

23 ^Now in the seventh year, Jehoiada gathered his courage, and took captains of hundreds: Azariah the son of Jeroham, Ishmael the son of Johanan, Azariah the son of Obed, Maaseiah the son of Adaiah, and Elishaphat the son of Zichri, *and they entered* into a covenant with him. 2And they went throughout Judah and gathered the Levites from all the cities of Judah, and the heads of the

fathers' *households* of ^Israel, and they came to Jerusalem. 3Then all the assembly made a covenant with the king in the house of God. And Jehoiada said to them, "Behold, the king's son shall reign, ^as the LORD has spoken concerning the sons of David. 4This is the thing which you shall do: a third of you, of the priests and Levites ^who come in on the Sabbath, *shall be* gatekeepers, 5and a third *shall be* at the king's house, and a third at the Gate of the Foundation; and all the people *shall be* in the courtyards of the house of the LORD. 6But no one is to enter the house of the LORD except the priests and ^the ministering Levites; they may enter, for they are holy. And all the people are to keep the command of the LORD. 7The Levites will surround the king, each man with his weapons in his hand; and whoever enters the house is to be put to death. Therefore be with the king when he comes in and when he goes out."

8The Levites and all Judah did according to all that Jehoiada the priest commanded. And each one of them took his men who were to come in on the Sabbath, with those who were to go out on the Sabbath, for Jehoiada the priest did not dismiss *any of* ^the divisions. 9Then Jehoiada the priest gave the captains of hundreds the spears and the shields and quivers which had been King David's, which were in the house of God. 10He stationed all the people, each man with his weapon in his hand, from the right side of the house to the left side of

22:9^2 Kin 9:27   22:10^2 Kin 11:1-3   23:1^2 Kin 11:4-20   23:2^2 Chr 11:13-17; 21:2   23:3^2 Sam 7:12; 2 Chr 21:7   23:4^1 Chr 9:25   23:6^1 Chr 23:28-32   23:8^1 Chr 24:1

the house, by the altar and by the house, around the king. ¹¹Then they brought out the king's son and put the crown on him, and *gave him* ᴬthe testimony and made him king. And Jehoiada and his sons anointed him and said, "*Long* live the king!"

ATHALIAH MURDERED

¹²When Athaliah heard the noise of the people running and praising the king, she went into the house of the Lord to the people. ¹³She looked, and behold, the king was standing by his pillar at the entrance, and the captains and the trumpeters *were* beside the king. And all the people of the land rejoiced and blew trumpets, the singers with *their* musical instruments leading the praise. Then Athaliah tore her clothes and said, "Conspiracy! Conspiracy!" ¹⁴And Jehoiada the priest brought out the captains of hundreds who were appointed over the army, and said to them, "Bring her out between the ranks, and whoever follows her is to be put to death with the sword." For the priest said, "You shall not put her to death in the house of the Lord." ¹⁵So they seized her, and when she arrived at the entrance of ᴬthe Horse Gate of the king's house, they put her to death there.

REFORMS CARRIED OUT

¹⁶Then ᴬJehoiada made a covenant between himself and all the people and the king, that they would be the Lord's people. ¹⁷And all the people went to the house of Baal and tore it down, and they broke in pieces his altars and his images, and ᴬkilled Mattan the priest of Baal before the altars. ¹⁸Moreover, Jehoiada placed the offices of the house of the Lord under the authority of ᴬthe Levitical priests, ᴮwhom David had assigned over the house of the Lord, to offer the burnt offerings of the Lord, as it is written in the Law of Moses— with rejoicing and singing according to the order of David. ¹⁹He stationed ᴬthe gatekeepers of the house of the Lord, so that no one would enter *who was* in any way unclean. ²⁰ᴬHe took the captains of hundreds, the nobles, the rulers of the people, and all the people of the land, and brought the king down from the house of the Lord, and went through the upper gate to the king's house. And they seated the king upon the royal throne. ²¹So ᴬall of the people of the land rejoiced and the city was at rest. For they had put Athaliah to death with the sword.

YOUNG JOASH INFLUENCED BY JEHOIADA

24 ᴬJoash *was* seven years old when he became king, and he reigned for forty years in Jerusalem; and his mother's name *was* Zibiah from Beersheba. ²ᴬJoash did what was right in the sight of the Lord all the days of Jehoiada the priest. ³Jehoiada took two wives for him, and he fathered sons and daughters.

FAITHLESS PRIESTS

⁴Now it came about after this that Joash decided ᴬto restore the house of the Lord. ⁵He gathered the priests and Levites and said to them, "Go out to the cities of

23:11ᴬEx 25:16, 21   23:15ᴬNeh 3:28; Jer 31:40
23:16ᴬ2 Kin 11:17   23:17ᴬDeut 13:6–9; 1 Kin 18:40
23:18ᴬ2 Chr 5:5   ᴮ1 Chr 23:6, 25–31
23:19ᴬ1 Chr 9:22   23:20ᴬ2 Kin 11:19
23:21ᴬ2 Kin 11:20   24:1ᴬ2 Kin 11:21; 12:1–15
24:2ᴬ2 Chr 26:4, 5   24:4ᴬ2 Chr 24:7

Judah and collect money from all ^Israel to repair the house of your God annually, and you shall do the work quickly." But the Levites did not act quickly. [6]So the king summoned Jehoiada, the chief *priest,* and said to him, "Why have you not required the Levites to bring in from Judah and from Jerusalem ^the contribution of Moses, the servant of the LORD, and the congregation of Israel, [B]for the tent of the testimony?" [7]For ^the sons of the wicked Athaliah had broken into the house of God, and even used the holy things of the house of the LORD for the Baals.

TEMPLE REPAIRED

[8]So the king commanded, and ^they made a chest and set it outside by the gate of the house of the LORD. [9]^And they made a proclamation in Judah and Jerusalem to bring to the LORD the contribution *commanded by* Moses the servant of God on Israel in the wilderness. [10]All the officers and all the people rejoiced, and they brought in *their contribution* and dropped *it* into the chest until they had finished. [11]It happened that whenever the chest was brought to the king's officer by the Levites, and ^they saw that the money was substantial, the king's scribe and the chief priest's officer would come and empty the chest, and pick it up and return it to its place. They did this daily and collected a large amount of money. [12]The king and Jehoiada gave it to those who did the work of the service of the house of the LORD; and they hired masons and carpenters to restore the house of the LORD, and also workers in iron and bronze to repair the house of the

LORD. [13]So the workmen labored, and the repair work progressed in their hands, and they restored the house of God according to its specifications and strengthened it. [14]When they had finished, they brought the rest of the money before the king and Jehoiada; and it was made into utensils for the house of the LORD, utensils for the service and the burnt offerings, and pans and utensils of gold and silver. And they offered burnt offerings in the house of the LORD continually, all the days of Jehoiada.

[15]Now Jehoiada reached a good old age and he died; he was 130 years old at his death. [16]And they buried him ^in the city of David with the kings, because he had done well in Israel and for God and His house.

[17]But after the death of Jehoiada the officials of Judah came and bowed down to the king, and the king listened to them. [18]And they abandoned the house of the LORD, the God of their fathers, and ^served the [1]Asherim and the idols; so [B]wrath came upon Judah and Jerusalem for this guilt of theirs. [19]Yet ^He sent prophets to them to bring them back to the LORD; and they testified against them, but they would not listen.

JOASH MURDERS SON OF JEHOIADA

[20]^Then the Spirit of God covered Zechariah, the son of Jehoiada the priest like clothing; and he stood above the people and said to them, "This is what God has said, 'Why do you break the commandments

24:5 ^2 Chr 21:2   24:6 ^Ex 30:12-16   [B]Num 1:50
24:7 ^2 Chr 21:17   24:8 ^2 Kin 12:9   24:9 ^2 Chr 36:22
24:11 ^2 Kin 12:10   24:16 ^2 Chr 21:20
24:18 ^Ex 34:12-14   [B]Josh 22:20   24:19 ^Jer 7:25
24:20 ^2 Chr 20:14

24:18 [1]I.e., wooden symbols of a female deity (Asherah)

of the LORD and do not prosper? [B]Because you have abandoned the LORD, He has also abandoned you.'" [21]So [A]they conspired against him, and at the command of the king they stoned him to death in the courtyard of the house of the LORD. [22]So Joash the king did not remember the kindness which *Zechariah's* father Jehoiada had shown him, but he murdered his son. And as *Zechariah* died he said, "May [A]the LORD see and avenge!"

ARAM INVADES AND DEFEATS JUDAH

[23]Now it happened at the turn of the year that [A]the army of the Arameans came up against *Joash;* and they came to Judah and Jerusalem, destroyed all the officials of the people from among the people, and sent all their spoils to the king of Damascus. [24]Indeed, the army of the Arameans came with a small number of men; yet [A]the LORD handed a very great army over to them, because Judah and Joash had abandoned the LORD, the God of their fathers. So they executed judgment on Joash.

[25][A]When they left him (for they left him very sick), his own servants conspired against him because of the blood of the son of Jehoiada the priest, and they murdered him on his bed. So he died, and they buried him in the city of David, but they did not bury him in the tombs of the kings. [26]Now these are the men who conspired against him: Zabad the son of Shimeath the Ammonitess, and Jehozabad the son of Shimrith the Moabitess. [27]As to his sons and the many pronouncements against him and the rebuilding of the house of God, behold, they are written in the [A]treatise of

the Book of the Kings. Then his son Amaziah became king in his place.

AMAZIAH SUCCEEDS JOASH IN JUDAH

25 [A]Amaziah was twenty-five years old when he became king, and he reigned for twenty-nine years in Jerusalem. And his mother's name was Jehoaddan of Jerusalem. [2]He did what was right in the sight of the LORD, [A]only not wholeheartedly. [3]Now [A]it came about, as soon as the kingdom was firmly in his grasp, that he killed his servants who had killed his father the king. [4]However, he did not put their children to death, but *did* as it is written in the Law in the Book of Moses, which the LORD commanded, saying, "[A]Fathers shall not be put to death for sons, nor sons be put to death for fathers; but each shall be put to death for his own sin."

AMAZIAH DEFEATS EDOMITES

[5]Moreover, Amaziah assembled Judah and appointed them according to *their* fathers' households under commanders of thousands and commanders of hundreds throughout Judah and Benjamin; and he took a census of those [A]from twenty years old and upward and found them to be three hundred thousand choice men, *able* to go to war *and* handle spear and shield. [6]He also hired a hundred thousand valiant warriors from Israel for [1]a hundred talents of silver. [7]But [A]a man of God came to him saying,

24:20 [B]2 Chr 15:2   24:21[A]Neh 9:26; Matt 23:34, 35
24:22[A]Gen 9:5   24:23[A]2 Kin 12:17
24:24[A]2 Chr 16:7, 8   24:25[A]2 Kin 12:20, 21
24:27[A]2 Chr 13:22   25:1[A]2 Kin 14:1–6
25:2[A]2 Chr 25:14   25:3[A]2 Kin 14:5   25:4[A]Deut 24:16
25:5[A]Num 1:3   25:7[A]2 Kin 4:9

25:6[1]About 3.75 tons or 3.4 metric tons

"O king, do not let the army of Israel come with you, for the LORD is not with Israel *nor with* any of the sons of Ephraim. [8]But if you do go, do *it*, be strong for the battle; *yet* God will bring you down before the enemy, ^for God has the power to help and to bring down." [9]Amaziah said to the man of God, "But what *are we* to do about the ⁱhundred talents which I have given to the troops of Israel?" And the man of God answered, "^The LORD has much more to give you than this." [10]Then Amaziah dismissed the troops which came to him from Ephraim, to go home; so their anger burned against Judah, and they returned home in fierce anger.

[11]Now Amaziah gathered his courage and led his people out, and went to ^the Valley of Salt, and struck and killed ten thousand of the sons of Seir. [12]The sons of Judah also captured ten thousand alive and brought them to the top of the cliff, and threw them down from the top of the cliff so that they were all dashed to pieces. [13]But the troops whom Amaziah sent back, *those* not going with him to battle, raided the cities of Judah from Samaria to Beth-horon, and struck and killed three thousand of them, and plundered a large amount of spoils.

AMAZIAH REBUKED FOR IDOLATRY

[14]Now after Amaziah came from slaughtering the Edomites, ^he brought the gods of the sons of Seir and set them up as his gods. Then he bowed down before them and burned incense to them. [15]So the anger of the LORD burned against Amaziah, and He sent him a prophet who said to him, "Why have you sought the gods of the people ^who have not saved their own people from your hand?" [16]As he was talking with him, the king said to him, "Have we appointed you to be a royal counselor? Stop! Why should you be put to death?" Then the prophet stopped and said, "I know that God has planned to destroy you, because you have done this and have not listened to my counsel."

AMAZIAH DEFEATED BY JOASH OF ISRAEL

[17]^Then Amaziah king of Judah took counsel and sent *word* to Joash the son of Jehoahaz the son of Jehu, the king of Israel, saying, "Come, let's face each other." [18]But Joash the king of Israel sent *a reply* to Amaziah king of Judah, saying, "^The thorn bush that was in Lebanon sent *word* to the cedar that was in Lebanon, saying, 'Give your daughter to my son in marriage.' But a wild beast that was in Lebanon passed by and trampled the thorn bush. [19]You said, 'Behold, you have defeated Edom.' And ^your heart has lifted you up in boasting. Now stay home; why should you provoke trouble so that you, would fall, you and Judah with you?"

[20]But Amaziah would not listen, for it was from God, so that He might hand them over *to Joash*, because they had sought the gods of Edom. [21]So Joash king of Israel went up, and he and Amaziah king of Judah faced each other at Beth-shemesh, which belonged to Judah. [22]And Judah was defeated by

25:8 ^2 Chr 14:11; 20:6   25:9 ^Deut 8:18; Prov 10:22
25:11 ^2 Kin 14:7   25:14 ^2 Chr 28:23
25:15 ^2 Chr 25:11, 12   25:17 ^2 Kin 14:8-14
25:18 ^Judg 9:8-15   25:19 ^2 Chr 26:16; 32:25
25:9 ¹About 3.75 tons or 3.4 metric tons

Israel, and they fled, every man to his tent. 23 Then Joash king of Israel captured Amaziah king of Judah, the son of Joash the son of ^Jehoahaz, at Beth-shemesh, and brought him to Jerusalem and tore down the wall of Jerusalem from the Gate of Ephraim to the Corner Gate, 1four hundred cubits. 24 *He took* all the gold and silver and all the utensils which were found in the house of God with ^Obed-edom, and the treasures of the king's house, the hostages too, and returned to Samaria.

25 ^And Amaziah, the son of Joash king of Judah, lived fifteen years after the death of Joash, son of Jehoahaz, king of Israel. 26 Now the rest of the acts of Amaziah, from the first to the last, behold, are they not written in the Book of the Kings of Judah and Israel? 27 From the time that Amaziah turned away from following the LORD they conspired against him in Jerusalem, and he fled to Lachish; but they sent *men* after him to Lachish, and they killed him there. 28 Then they brought him on horses and buried him with his fathers in the city of Judah.

UZZIAH SUCCEEDS AMAZIAH IN JUDAH

26 Now all the people of Judah took Uzziah, who *was* sixteen years old, and made him king in place of his father Amaziah. 2 He built Eloth and restored it to Judah after the king 1lay down with his fathers. 3 Uzziah was ^sixteen years old when he became king, and he reigned for fifty-two years in Jerusalem; and his mother's name was Jechiliah of Jerusalem. 4 He did what was right in the sight of the LORD, in accordance with

everything that his father Amaziah had done. 5 ^He continued to seek God in the days of Zechariah, bwho had understanding through the vision of God; and as long as he sought the LORD, God made him successful.

UZZIAH SUCCEEDS IN WAR

6 Now he went out and ^fought against the Philistines, and broke down the wall of Gath, the wall of Jabneh, and the wall of Ashdod; and he built cities in *the area of* Ashdod and among the Philistines. 7 ^God helped him against the Philistines, and against the Arabians who lived in Gur-baal, and the Meunites. 8 The Ammonites gave ^tribute to Uzziah, and his fame extended to the border of Egypt, for he became very strong. 9 Moreover, Uzziah built towers in Jerusalem at ^the Corner Gate, the Valley Gate, and at the corner buttress, and he fortified them. 10 He also built towers in the wilderness and ^carved out many cisterns, for he had much livestock, both in the lowland and in the plain. *He also had* plowmen and vinedressers in the hill country and the fertile fields, for he loved the soil. 11 Moreover, Uzziah had an army ready for battle, which entered combat by divisions according to the number of their muster, recorded by Jeiel the scribe and Maaseiah the official, under the direction of Hananiah, one of the king's officers. 12 The total number of the heads of the

25:23 ^2 Chr 21:17; 22:1   25:24 ^1 Chr 26:15
25:25 ^2 Kin 14:17-22   26:3 ^2 Kin 15:2, 3
26:5 ^2 Chr 24:2   b Dan 1:17   26:6 ^Is 14:29
26:7 ^2 Chr 21:16   26:8 ^2 Chr 17:11
26:9 ^2 Chr 25:23   26:10 ^Gen 26:18-21

25:23 1About 600 ft. or 183 m   26:2 1I.e., died

households, of valiant warriors, was 2,600. ¹³Under their direction was an army of ^307,500, who could wage war with great power, to help the king against the enemy. ¹⁴Moreover, Uzziah prepared for all the army shields, spears, helmets, body armor, bows, and slingstones. ¹⁵In Jerusalem he made machines *of war* invented by skillful workmen to be on the towers and the corners, for the purpose of shooting arrows and great stones. So his fame spread far, for he was marvelously helped until he *was* strong.

PRIDE IS UZZIAH'S UNDOING

¹⁶But when he became strong, his heart was so proud that he acted corruptly, and he was untrue to the LORD his God, for ^he entered the temple of the LORD to burn incense on the altar of incense. ¹⁷Then ^Azariah the priest entered after him, and with him eighty priests of the LORD, valiant men. ¹⁸^They opposed Uzziah the king and said to him, "It is not for you, Uzziah, to burn incense to the LORD, ^Bbut for the priests, the sons of Aaron who have been consecrated to burn incense. Leave the sanctuary, for you have been untrue and will have no honor from the LORD God." ¹⁹But Uzziah, with a censer in his hand for burning incense, was enraged; and while he was enraged with the priests, ^leprosy broke out on his forehead in the presence of the priests in the house of the LORD, beside the altar of incense. ²⁰Azariah the chief priest and all the priests looked at him, and behold, he *was* leprous on his forehead; and they quickly removed him from there, and he himself also hurried to get out because the LORD

had stricken him. ²¹^King Uzziah had leprosy to the day of his death; and he lived in a separate house, afflicted *as he was* with leprosy, for he was cut off from the house of the LORD. And his son Jotham *was* over the king's house, judging the people of the land.

²²Now the rest of the acts of Uzziah, the first to the last, the prophet ^Isaiah, the son of Amoz, has written. ²³So Uzziah ¹lay down with his fathers, and they buried him with his fathers ^in the field of the grave which belonged to the kings, for they said, "He had leprosy." And his son Jotham became king in his place.

JOTHAM SUCCEEDS UZZIAH IN JUDAH

27 ^Jotham was twenty-five years old when he became king, and he reigned for sixteen years in Jerusalem. And his mother's name was Jerushah the daughter of Zadok. ²He did what was right in the sight of the LORD, according to all that his father Uzziah had done; ^however he did not enter the temple of the LORD. But the people continued acting corruptly. ³He built the upper gate of the house of the LORD, and he built the wall of ^Ophel extensively. ⁴Moreover, he built ^cities in the hill country of Judah, and he built fortresses and towers on the wooded *hills*. ⁵He fought with the king of the Ammonites and prevailed over them so that during that year the Ammonites gave him ¹a hundred

26:13^2 Chr 25:5 26:16^1 Kin 13:1–4
26:17^1 Chr 6:10 26:18^2 Chr 19:2 ᴮEx 30:7, 8
26:19^2 Kin 5:25–27 26:21^2 Kin 15:5–7
26:22^Is 1:1 26:23^2 Chr 21:20; Is 6:1
27:1^2 Chr 15:33–35 27:2^2 Chr 26:16
27:3^2 Chr 33:14; Neh 3:26 27:4^2 Chr 11:5

26:23¹I.e., died 27:5¹About 3.75 tons or 3.4 metric tons

talents of silver, ²ten thousand kors of wheat, and ten thousand of barley. The Ammonites also paid him this *amount* in the second year and in the third. ⁶ᴬSo Jotham became powerful because he directed his ways before the LORD his God. ⁷ᴬNow the rest of the acts of Jotham, all his wars and his ways, behold, they are written in the Book of the Kings of Israel and Judah. ⁸He was ᴬtwenty-five years old when he became king, and he reigned in Jerusalem for sixteen years. ⁹And Jotham ¹lay down with his fathers, and they buried him in the city of David; and his son Ahaz became king in his place.

AHAZ SUCCEEDS JOTHAM IN JUDAH

28 ᴬAhaz *was* twenty years old when he became king, and he reigned in Jerusalem for sixteen years. He did not do what was right in the sight of the LORD as his father David *had done.* ²But he walked in the ways of the kings of Israel; he also ᴬmade cast metal images for the Baals. ³Furthermore, ᴬhe burned incense in the Valley of Ben-hinnom, and ᴮburned his sons in fire, according to the abominations of the nations whom the LORD had driven out from the sons of Israel. ⁴He sacrificed and ᴬburned incense on the high places, on the hills, and under every green tree.

JUDAH IS INVADED

⁵Therefore ᴬthe LORD his God handed him over to the king of Aram; and they defeated him and carried from him a great number of captives, and brought *them* to Damascus. And he was also handed over to the king of Israel, who struck him with heavy casualties.

⁶For ᴬPekah the son of Remaliah killed 120,000 in Judah in one day, all valiant men, because they had abandoned the LORD God of their fathers. ⁷And Zichri, a mighty man of Ephraim, killed Maaseiah the king's son, Azrikam the ruler of the house, and Elkanah the second to the king.

⁸ᴬThe sons of Israel led away captive two hundred thousand of their relatives, women, sons, and daughters; and they also took a great deal of spoils from them, and brought the spoils to Samaria. ⁹But a prophet of the LORD was there, whose name *was* Oded; and ᴬhe went out to meet the army which came to Samaria and said to them, "Behold, because the LORD, the God of your fathers, ᴮwas angry with Judah, He has handed them over to you, and you have killed them in a rage *which* has even reached heaven. ¹⁰Now you are proposing to ᴬsubjugate the people of Judah and Jerusalem as male and female slaves for yourselves. *Are* you not, however guilty yourselves of offenses against the LORD your God? ¹¹Now then, listen to me and return the captives whom you captured from your brothers, ᴬfor the burning anger of the LORD is against you." ¹²Then some of the leading men of the sons of Ephraim—Azariah the son of Johanan, Berechiah the son of Meshillemoth, Jehizkiah the son of Shallum, and Amasa the son of Hadlai—rose up against those who

27:6 ᴬ2 Chr 26:5   27:7 ᴬ2 Kin 15:36   27:8 ᴬ2 Chr 27:1
28:1 ᴬ2 Kin 16:2-4   28:2 ᴬEx 34:17   28:3 ᴬJosh 15:8
ᴮLev 18:21   28:4 ᴬ2 Chr 28:25
28:5 ᴬ2 Chr 24:24; Is 7:1   28:6 ᴬ2 Kin 16:5
28:8 ᴬDeut 28:25, 41   28:9 ᴬ2 Chr 25:15   ᴮIs 47:6
28:10 ᴬLev 25:39   28:11 ᴬJames 2:13

27:5 ²About 77,000 cubic feet or 2,180 cubic meters
27:9 ¹I.e., died

were coming from the battle, [13]and said to them, "You must not bring the captives in here, for you are proposing *to bring* guilt upon us before the Lord, adding to our sins and our guilt; for our guilt is great, and *His* burning anger is against Israel." [14]So the armed men left the captives and the spoils before the officers and all the assembly. [15]Then the men who were designated by name got up, took the captives, and they clothed all their naked people from the spoils; they gave them clothes and sandals, fed them and ^gave them drink, anointed them *with oil,* led all their feeble ones on donkeys, and brought them to Jericho, ᴮthe city of palm trees, to their brothers; then they returned to Samaria.

COMPROMISE WITH ASSYRIA

[16]^At that time King Ahaz sent *word* to the ¹kings of Assyria for help. [17]^For the Edomites had come again and attacked Judah, and led away captives. [18]^The Philistines had also invaded the cities of the lowland and of the Negev of Judah, and had taken Bethshemesh, Aijalon, Gederoth, and Soco with its villages, Timnah with its villages, and Gimzo with its villages; and they had settled there. [19]For the Lord had humbled Judah because of Ahaz king of ^Israel, for he had brought about a lack of restraint in Judah and was very unfaithful to the Lord. [20]So ^Tilgath-pilneser king of Assyria came against him and afflicted him instead of strengthening him. [21]^Although Ahaz took a portion out of the house of the Lord and out of the palace of the king and of the princes, and gave *it* to the king of Assyria, it did not help him.

[22]Now during the time of his distress, this same King Ahaz ^became even more unfaithful to the Lord. [23]^For he sacrificed to the gods of Damascus who had defeated him, and said, "ᴮBecause the gods of the kings of Aram helped them, I will sacrifice to them so that they may help me." But they became the downfall of him and all Israel. [24]Moreover, when Ahaz gathered together the utensils of the house of God, he ^cut the utensils of the house of God in pieces; and he closed the doors of the house of the Lord, and made altars for himself in every corner of Jerusalem. [25]In every city of Judah he made high places to burn incense to other gods, and provoked the Lord, the God of his fathers, to anger. [26]^Now the rest of his acts and all his ways, from the first to the last, behold, they are written in the Book of the Kings of Judah and Israel. [27]^So Ahaz ¹lay down with his fathers, and they buried him in the city, in Jerusalem, for they did not bring him to the tombs of the kings of ᴮIsrael; and his son Hezekiah reigned in his place.

HEZEKIAH SUCCEEDS AHAZ IN JUDAH

29 ^Hezekiah became king *when he was* twenty-five years old; and he reigned for twenty-nine years in Jerusalem. And his mother's name *was* Abijah, the daughter of Zechariah. [2]^He did what was right in the sight of the Lord,

28:15 ^Prov 25:21, 22   ᴮDeut 34:3   **28:16** ^2 Kin 16:7
28:17 ^Obad 10, 14   **28:18** ^Ezek 16:57
28:19 ^2 Chr 21:2   **28:20** ¹1 Chr 5:26
28:21 ^2 Kin 16:8, 9   **28:22** ^Jer 5:3; Rev 16:11
28:23 ^2 Chr 25:14   ᴮJer 44:17, 18   **28:24** ^2 Kin 16:17
28:26 ^2 Kin 16:19, 20   **28:27** ^Is 14:28   ᴮ2 Chr 21:2
29:1 ^2 Kin 18:1-3   **29:2** ^2 Chr 28:1; 34:2

28:16 ¹Ancient versions *king*   **28:27** ¹I.e., died

in accordance with everything that his father David had done.

³In the first year of his reign, in the first month, he ^opened the doors of the house of the LORD and repaired them. ⁴He brought in the priests and the Levites and gathered them into the public square on the east.

REFORMS BEGUN

⁵Then he said to them, "Listen to me, you Levites. ^Consecrate yourselves now, and consecrate the house of the LORD, the God of your fathers, and carry the uncleanness out of the holy place. ⁶For our fathers have been unfaithful and have done evil in the sight of the LORD our God, and they have abandoned Him and ^turned their faces away from the dwelling place of the LORD, and have turned *their* backs. ⁷They have also ^shut the doors of the porch and extinguished the lamps, and have not burned incense nor offered burnt offerings in the holy place to the God of Israel. ⁸Therefore ^the wrath of the LORD was against Judah and Jerusalem, and He has made them an object of terror, of horror, and of hissing, as you see with your own eyes. ⁹For behold, ^our fathers have fallen by the sword, and our sons, our daughters, and our wives are in captivity because of this. ¹⁰Now it is in my heart ^to make a covenant with the LORD God of Israel, so that His burning anger may turn away from us. ¹¹My sons, do not be negligent now, for ^the LORD has chosen you to stand before Him, to serve Him, and to be His ministers and burn incense."

¹²Then the Levites arose: ^Mahath the son of Amasai and Joel the son of Azariah, from the sons

of the Kohathites; and from the sons of Merari, Kish the son of Abdi and Azariah the son of Jehallelel; and from the Gershonites, Joah the son of Zimmah and Eden the son of Joah; ¹³and from the sons of Elizaphan, Shimri and Jeiel; and from the sons of Asaph, Zechariah and Mattaniah; ¹⁴and from the sons of Heman, Jehiel and Shimei; and from the sons of Jeduthun, Shemaiah and Uzziel. ¹⁵They assembled their brothers, ^consecrated themselves, and went in ᴮto cleanse the house of the LORD, according to the commandment of the king by the words of the LORD. ¹⁶So the priests went into the inner part of the house of the LORD to cleanse *it,* and they brought every unclean thing which they found in the temple of the LORD out to the courtyard of the house of the LORD. Then the Levites received *it* to carry out to ^the Kidron Valley. ¹⁷Now they began the consecration ^on the first *day* of the first month, and on the eighth day of the month they entered the porch of the LORD. Then they consecrated the house of the LORD in eight days, and finished on the sixteenth day of the first month. ¹⁸Then they went in to King Hezekiah and said, "We have cleansed the whole house of the LORD, the altar of burnt offering with all its utensils, and the table of the showbread with all of its utensils. ¹⁹Moreover, ^all the utensils which King Ahaz had discarded during his reign in his unfaithfulness, we have prepared

29:3^2 Chr 28:24; 29:7   29:5^2 Chr 29:15, 34; 35:6
29:6^Ezek 8:16   29:7^2 Chr 28:24   29:8^2 Chr 24:20
29:9^2 Chr 28:5-8, 17   29:10^2 Chr 23:16
29:11^Num 3:6; 8:6   29:12^2 Chr 31:13
29:15^2 Chr 29:5   ᴮ1 Chr 23:28   29:16^2 Chr 15:16
29:17^2 Chr 29:3   29:19^2 Chr 28:24

and consecrated; and behold, they are before the altar of the LORD."

HEZEKIAH RESTORES
TEMPLE WORSHIP

²⁰Then King Hezekiah got up early and assembled the princes of the city, and went up to the house of the LORD. ²¹They brought seven bulls, seven rams, seven lambs, and seven male goats ᴬas a sin offering for the kingdom, the sanctuary, and Judah. And he ordered the priests, the sons of Aaron, to offer *them* on the altar of the LORD. ²²So they slaughtered the bulls, and the priests took the blood and sprinkled it on the altar. They also slaughtered the rams and sprinkled the blood on the altar; they slaughtered the lambs as well, and ᴬsprinkled the blood on the altar. ²³Then they brought the male goats of the sin offering before the king and the assembly, and ᴬthey laid their hands on them. ²⁴The priests slaughtered them and purified the altar with their blood ᴬto atone for all Israel, because the king ordered the burnt offering and the sin offering for all Israel.

²⁵He then stationed the Levites in the house of the LORD with cymbals, harps, and lyres, ᴬaccording to the command of David and of ᴮGad, the king's seer, and of Nathan the prophet; for the command was from the LORD through His prophets. ²⁶The Levites stood with ᴬthe *musical* instruments of David, and ᴮthe priests with the trumpets. ²⁷Then Hezekiah gave the order to offer the burnt offering on the altar. When the burnt offering began, ᴬthe song to the LORD *also* began with the trumpets, *accompanied* by the instruments of David, king of Israel. ²⁸While the whole assembly worshiped, the singers also sang and the trumpets sounded; all this *continued* until the burnt offering was finished.

²⁹Now at the completion of the burnt offerings, ᴬthe king and all who were present with him bowed down and worshiped. ³⁰Moreover, King Hezekiah and the officials ordered the Levites to sing praises to the LORD with the words of David and Asaph the seer. ᴬSo they sang praises with joy, and bowed down and worshiped.

³¹Then Hezekiah said, "Now *that* you have consecrated yourselves to the LORD, come forward and bring sacrifices and thanksgiving offerings to the house of the LORD." So the assembly brought sacrifices and thanksgiving offerings, and ᴬeveryone who was willing *brought* burnt offerings. ³²The number of the burnt offerings which the assembly brought was seventy bulls, a hundred rams, and two hundred lambs; all of these were for a burnt offering to the LORD. ³³The consecrated *offerings* were six hundred bulls and three thousand sheep. ³⁴But the priests were too few, so that they were unable to skin all the burnt offerings; ᴬtherefore their brothers the Levites helped them until the work was finished and the *other* priests had consecrated themselves. For ᴮthe Levites were more conscientious to consecrate themselves than the priests. ³⁵There *were* also

29:21ᴬLev 4:3–14   29:22ᴬLev 4:18   29:23ᴬLev 4:15
29:24ᴬLev 4:26   29:25ᴬ2 Chr 8:14   ᴮ2 Sam 24:11
29:26ᴬ1 Chr 23:5   ᴮ2 Chr 5:12   29:27ᴬ2 Chr 23:18
29:29ᴬ2 Chr 20:18   29:30ᴬPs 100:1; 106:12
29:31ᴬEx 35:5, 22   29:34ᴬ2 Chr 35:11   ᴮ2 Chr 30:3

many burnt offerings with ^the fat of the peace offerings and ^Bthe drink offerings for the burnt offerings. So the service of the house of the LORD was established *again*. ^36 Then Hezekiah and all the people rejoiced over what God had prepared for the people, because the thing came about suddenly.

ALL ISRAEL INVITED
TO THE PASSOVER

30 Now Hezekiah sent *word* to all Israel and Judah and also wrote letters to Ephraim and Manasseh, that they should come to the house of the LORD in Jerusalem to celebrate the Passover to the LORD God of Israel. ^2 For the king and his princes and all the assembly in Jerusalem had decided ^to celebrate the Passover in the second month, ^3 since they could not celebrate it ^at that time, because the priests had not consecrated themselves in sufficient numbers, nor had the people been gathered to Jerusalem. ^4 So the decision was right in the sight of the king and all the assembly. ^5 So they established a decree to circulate a proclamation throughout Israel ^from Beersheba to Dan, that they are to come to celebrate the Passover to the LORD God of Israel in Jerusalem. For they had not celebrated *it* in great numbers as was written. ^6 ^The couriers went throughout Israel and Judah with the letters from the hand of the king and his princes, even according to the command of the king, saying, "Sons of Israel, return to the LORD God of Abraham, Isaac, and Israel, that He may return to those of you who escaped *and* are left from the hand of the kings of Assyria. ^7 ^Do not be like your fathers and your

brothers, who were untrue to the LORD God of their fathers, so that He made them an object of horror, just as you see. ^8 Now do not ^stiffen your neck like your fathers, *but* yield to the LORD and enter His sanctuary which He has consecrated forever, and serve the LORD your God, that His burning anger may turn away from you. ^9 For ^if you return to the LORD, your brothers and your sons *will find* compassion in the presence of those who led them captive, and will return to this land. ^BFor the LORD your God is gracious and compassionate, and will not turn *His* face away from you if you return to Him."

^10 So the couriers passed from city to city through the country of Ephraim and Manasseh, and as far as Zebulun, but ^they laughed at them with scorn and mocked them. ^11 Nevertheless, ^some men of Asher, Manasseh, and Zebulun humbled themselves and came to Jerusalem. ^12 The ^hand of God was also on Judah to give them one heart to do what the king and the princes commanded by the word of the LORD.

PASSOVER REINSTITUTED

^13 Now many people were gathered at Jerusalem to celebrate the Feast of Unleavened Bread ^in the second month, a very large assembly. ^14 They got up and removed the altars which *were* in Jerusalem; they also ^removed all the incense altars and threw *them* into the brook Kidron. ^15 Then ^they

29:35 ^A Lev 3:16   ^B Num 15:5-10   30:2 ^A Num 9:10, 11; 2 Chr 30:13, 15   30:3 ^2 Chr 29:17, 34   30:5 ^Judg 20:1 30:6 ^Job 9:25; Jer 51:31   30:7 ^Ezek 20:13 30:8 ^Ex 32:9   30:9 ^Deut 30:2   ^B Ex 34:6, 7 30:10 ^2 Chr 36:16   30:11 ^2 Chr 30:18, 21, 25 30:12 ^Phil 2:13; Heb 13:20, 21   30:13 ^2 Chr 30:2 30:14 ^2 Chr 28:24   30:15 ^2 Chr 30:2, 3

slaughtered the Passover *lambs* on the fourteenth of the second month. And the priests and Levites were ashamed of themselves, and consecrated themselves and brought burnt offerings to the house of the LORD. [16]^They stood at their stations following their custom, according to the Law of Moses the man of God; the priests sprinkled the blood *which they received* from the hand of the Levites. [17]For *there were* many in the assembly who had not consecrated themselves; therefore, ^the Levites *were* in charge of the slaughter of the Passover *lambs* for everyone who *was* unclean, in order to consecrate *them* to the LORD. [18]For a multitude of the people, many from Ephraim and Manasseh, *and* Issachar and Zebulun, had not purified themselves, ^yet they ate the Passover ^Bcontrary to *what was* written. For Hezekiah prayed for them, saying, "May the good LORD pardon [19]^everyone who prepares his heart to seek God, the LORD God of his fathers, though not according to the purification *rules* of the sanctuary." [20]So the LORD heard Hezekiah and ^healed the people. [21]The sons of Israel present in Jerusalem ^celebrated the Feast of Unleavened Bread for seven days with great joy, and the Levites and the priests were praising the LORD day after day with loud instruments to the LORD. [22]Then Hezekiah ^spoke encouragingly to all the Levites who showed good insight *in the things* of the LORD. So they ate for the appointed seven days, sacrificing peace offerings and giving thanks to the LORD God of their fathers.

[23]Then the whole assembly ^decided to celebrate *the feast* another seven days, so they celebrated the seven days with joy. [24]For ^Hezekiah king of Judah had contributed to the assembly a thousand bulls and seven thousand sheep, and the princes had contributed to the assembly a thousand bulls and ten thousand sheep; and a large number of priests consecrated themselves. [25]All the assembly of Judah rejoiced, with the priests and the Levites and ^all the assembly that came from Israel, both the strangers who came from the land of Israel and those living in Judah. [26]So there was great joy in Jerusalem, because there was nothing like this in Jerusalem ^since the days of Solomon the son of David, king of Israel. [27]Then the Levitical priests stood and blessed the people; and their voice was heard and their prayer came to ^His holy dwelling place, to heaven.

IDOLS ARE DESTROYED

31 Now when all this was finished, all Israel who were present went out to the cities of Judah, ^broke the memorial stones in pieces, cut down the [1]Asherim and pulled down the high places and the altars throughout Judah and Benjamin, as well as in Ephraim and Manasseh, until they had destroyed them all. Then all the sons of Israel returned to their cities, each to his possession.

30:16^2 Chr 35:10, 15   30:17^2 Chr 29:34
30:18^Num 9:10   ^BEx 12:43-49   30:19^2 Chr 19:3
30:20^James 5:16   30:21^Ex 12:15; 13:6
30:22^2 Chr 32:6   30:23^1 Kin 8:65
30:24^2 Chr 35:7, 8   30:25^2 Chr 30:11, 18
30:26^2 Chr 7:8-10   30:27^Deut 26:15; Ps 68:5
31:1^2 Kin 18:4

31:1[1]I.e., wooden symbols of a female deity (Asherah)

² And Hezekiah appointed ^the divisions of the priests and the Levites by their divisions, each according to his service, *both* the priests and the Levites, for burnt offerings and for peace offerings, to serve and to give thanks and to praise in the gates of the camp of the LORD.

REFORMS CONTINUED

³ *He* also *appointed* ^the king's portion of his property for the burnt offerings, *namely,* for the morning and evening burnt offerings, and the burnt offerings for the Sabbaths and for the new moons and for the appointed festivals, ᴮas it is written in the Law of the LORD. ⁴ Also he told the people who lived in Jerusalem to give ^the portion due to the priests and the Levites, so that they might devote themselves to ᴮthe Law of the LORD. ⁵ As soon as the order spread, the sons of Israel abundantly provided the first fruits of grain, new wine, oil, honey, and of all the produce of the field; and they brought in abundantly ^the tithe of everything. ⁶ The sons of Israel and Judah who lived in the cities of Judah also brought in the tithe of oxen and sheep, and ^the tithe of sacred gifts which were consecrated to the LORD their God, and placed *them* in heaps. ⁷ In the third month they began to make the heaps, and they finished *them* by the seventh month. ⁸ When Hezekiah and the rulers came and saw the heaps, they blessed the LORD and ^His people Israel. ⁹ Then Hezekiah questioned the priests and the Levites concerning the heaps. ¹⁰ Azariah, the chief priest of the house of Zadok, said to him, "^Since the contributions started coming into the house of the LORD, we have had enough to eat with plenty left over, for the LORD has blessed His people, and this great quantity is left over."

¹¹ Then Hezekiah commanded *them* to prepare ^rooms in the house of the LORD, and they prepared *them.* ¹² They faithfully brought in the contributions, the tithes, and the consecrated things; and Conaniah the Levite *was* the officer in charge ^of them, and his brother Shimei *was* second. ¹³ Jehiel, Azaziah, Nahath, Asahel, Jerimoth, Jozabad, Eliel, Ismachiah, Mahath, and Benaiah *were* overseers under the authority of Conaniah and his brother Shimei by the appointment of King Hezekiah, and ^Azariah *was* the *chief* officer of the house of God. ¹⁴ Kore the son of Imnah the Levite, the keeper of the eastern *gate, was* in charge of the voluntary offerings for God, to distribute the contributions for the LORD and the most holy things. ¹⁵ Under his authority *were* Eden, Miniamin, Jeshua, Shemaiah, Amariah, and Shecaniah, in ^the cities of the priests, to distribute *their portions* faithfully to their brothers by divisions, whether great or small, ¹⁶ without regard to their genealogical enrollment, to the males from ^thirty years old and upward—everyone who entered the house of the LORD for his daily obligations—for their work in their duties according to their divisions; ¹⁷ as well as the priests who were enrolled genealogically according to their fathers' households, and the Levites ^from twenty years old

31:2 ^1 Chr 24:1   31:3 ^2 Chr 35:7   ᴮNum 28:1-29:40
31:4 ^Num 18:8   ᴮMal 2:7   31:5 ^Neh 13:12
31:6 ^Lev 27:30; Deut 14:28   31:8 ^Deut 33:29;
Ps 144:15   31:10 ^Mal 3:10   31:11 ^1 Kin 6:5, 8
31:12 ^2 Chr 35:9   31:13 ^2 Chr 31:10   31:15 ^Josh
21:9-19   31:16 ^1 Chr 23:3   31:17 ^1 Chr 23:24

and upward, by their duties *and* their divisions. ¹⁸The genealogical enrollment *included* all their little children, their wives, their sons, and their daughters, for the whole assembly, for they consecrated themselves faithfully in holiness. ¹⁹Also for the sons of Aaron, the priests, *who were* in ᴬthe pasture lands of their cities, *or* in each and every city, *there were* men who were designated by name to distribute portions to every male among the priests and to everyone genealogically enrolled among the Levites.

²⁰Hezekiah did this throughout Judah; and ᴬhe did what *was* good, right, and true before the LORD his God. ²¹Every work which he began in the service of the house of God in the Law and in the commandment, seeking his God, he did with all his heart and ᴬprospered.

SENNACHERIB INVADES JUDAH

32 After these acts of faithfulness ᴬSennacherib king of Assyria came and invaded Judah and besieged the fortified cities, and intended to break into them for himself. ²Now when Hezekiah saw that Sennacherib had come and that he intended to *wage* war against Jerusalem, ³he decided with his officers and his warriors to cut off the *supply of* water from the springs which *were* outside the city, and they helped him. ⁴So many people assembled ᴬand stopped up all the springs and the stream which flowed through the region, saying, "Why should the kings of Assyria come and find abundant water?" ⁵And he resolutely set to work and rebuilt all of the wall that had been broken down and erected towers on it, and *built* ᴬanother

outside wall and strengthened the ¹ˑᴮMillo *in* the city of David, and made weapons and shields in great numbers. ⁶He appointed military officers over the people and gathered them to him in the public square at the city gate, and ᴬspoke encouragingly to them, saying, ⁷"Be strong and courageous, do not fear or be dismayed because of the king of Assyria nor because of all the horde that is with him; ᴬfor *the One* with us is greater than *the one* with him. ⁸With him is *only* an arm of flesh, but ᴬwith us is the LORD our God to help us and to fight our battles." And the people relied on the words of Hezekiah king of Judah.

SENNACHERIB UNDERMINES HEZEKIAH

⁹After this ᴬSennacherib king of Assyria sent his servants to Jerusalem while he *was* besieging Lachish with all his forces with him, against Hezekiah king of Judah and against all of Judah who *were* in Jerusalem, saying, ¹⁰"This is what Sennacherib king of Assyria says: 'On what are you trusting that you are staying in Jerusalem under siege? ¹¹Is Hezekiah not misleading you to give yourselves over to die by hunger and by thirst, saying, "The LORD our God will save us from the hand of the king of Assyria"? ¹²ᴬIs it not the same Hezekiah who removed His high places and His altars, and said to Judah and Jerusalem, "You shall worship before one altar, and on it you shall burn

---

31:19ᴬLev 25:34; Num 35:2-5   31:20ᴬ2 Kin 20:3; 22:2
31:21ᴬDeut 29:9; Prov 3:9, 10   32:1ᴬ2 Kin
18:13-19, 37; Is 36:1-37:38   32:4ᴬ2 Kin 20:20
32:5ᴬ2 Kin 25:4   ᴮ1 Kin 9:24   32:6ᴬ2 Chr 30:22
32:7ᴬ2 Kin 6:16   32:8ᴬ2 Chr 20:17   32:9ᴬ2 Kin 18:17
32:12ᴬ2 Chr 31:1

32:5 ¹ I.e., terraced structure

incense"? [13] Do you not know what I and my fathers have done to all the peoples of the lands? ^Were the gods of the nations of those lands at all able to save their land from my hand? [14] ^Who *was there* among all the gods of those nations which my fathers utterly destroyed who could save his people from my hand, that your God would be able to save you from my hand? [15] Now then, do not let Hezekiah deceive you or mislead you like this, and do not believe him, for ^no god of any nation or kingdom was able to save his people from my hand or from the hand of my fathers. How much less will your God save you from my hand?'"

[16] His servants spoke further against the LORD God and against His servant Hezekiah. [17] He also wrote letters to insult the LORD God of Israel, and to speak against Him, saying, "^As the gods of the nations of the lands have not saved their people from my hand, so the God of Hezekiah will not save His people from my hand." [18] ^They called *this* out with a loud voice in the language of Judah to the people of Jerusalem who were on the wall, to frighten and terrify them, so that they might take the city. [19] They spoke of the God of Jerusalem as *they did* against ^the gods of the peoples of the earth, the work of human hands.

HEZEKIAH'S PRAYER IS ANSWERED

[20] But King Hezekiah and Isaiah the prophet, the son of Amoz, prayed about this and called out to heaven for help. [21] And the LORD sent an angel who destroyed every warrior, commander, and officer in the camp of the king of Assyria. So he returned in shame to his own land. And when he had entered the temple of his god, some of his own sons killed him there with the sword. [22] So the LORD ^saved Hezekiah and the inhabitants of Jerusalem from the hand of Sennacherib the king of Assyria and from the hand of all *others,* and guided them on every side. [23] And ^many were bringing gifts to the LORD at Jerusalem and valuable presents to Hezekiah king of Judah; so thereafter he rose in the sight of all nations.

[24] ^In those days Hezekiah became mortally ill; and he prayed to the LORD, and the LORD spoke to him and gave him a sign. [25] But Hezekiah did nothing in return for the benefit he received, ^because his heart was proud; ^B therefore wrath came upon him and upon Judah and Jerusalem. [26] However, ^Hezekiah humbled the pride of his heart, both he and the inhabitants of Jerusalem, so that the wrath of the LORD did not come on them in the days of Hezekiah.

[27] Now Hezekiah had immense riches and honor; and he made for himself treasuries for silver, gold, precious stones, spices, shields, and all kinds of valuable articles, [28] also storehouses for the produce of grain, wine, and oil; stalls for all kinds of cattle, and sheepfolds for the flocks. [29] He made cities for himself and acquired flocks and herds in abundance, because ^God had given him very great wealth. [30] It was Hezekiah who ^stopped the upper outlet of the waters of Gihon and directed them to the west side of

32:13^2 Kin 18:33-35   32:14^Is 10:9-11
32:15^Is 36:18-20; Dan 3:15   32:17^2 Chr 32:14
32:18^2 Kin 18:28   32:19^Ps 115:4-8   32:22^Is 31:5
32:23^2 Sam 8:10   32:24^2 Kin 20:1-11; Is 38:1-8
32:25^2 Chr 26:16   ^B 2 Chr 24:18   32:26^Jer 26:18, 19
32:29^1 Chr 29:12   32:30^2 Kin 20:20

the city of David. And Hezekiah was successful in everything that he did. [31]Even *in the matter of* ^Athe messengers of the rulers of Babylon, who were sent to him to inquire about the wonder that had happened in the land; God left him alone *only* ^Bto test him, so that He might know everything that was in his heart.

[32]Now the rest of the acts of Hezekiah and his deeds of devotion, behold, they are written in the vision of Isaiah the prophet, the son of Amoz, in the Book of the Kings of Judah and Israel. [33]So Hezekiah ¹lay down with his fathers, and they buried him in the upper section of the tombs of the sons of David; and all Judah and the inhabitants of Jerusalem ^Ahonored him at his death. And his son Manasseh became king in his place.

MANASSEH SUCCEEDS HEZEKIAH IN JUDAH

33 ^AManasseh was twelve years old when he became king, and he reigned for fifty-five years in Jerusalem. [2]^AHe did evil in the sight of the LORD according to the abominations of the nations whom the LORD dispossessed before the sons of Israel. [3]For ^Ahe rebuilt the high places which his father Hezekiah had torn down; he also set up altars for the Baals and made ¹Asherim, and he worshiped all the heavenly lights and served them. [4]^AHe built altars in the house of the LORD of which the LORD had said, "My name shall be in Jerusalem forever." [5]He built altars for all the heavenly lights in ^Athe two courtyards of the house of the LORD. [6]^AHe also made his sons pass through the fire in the Valley of Ben-hinnom; and he practiced witchcraft, used divination,

practiced sorcery, and dealt with mediums and spiritists. He did much evil in the sight of the LORD, provoking Him to anger. [7]Then he put ^Athe carved image of the idol which he had made in the house of God, of which God had said to David and his son Solomon, "In this house and in Jerusalem, which I have chosen from all the tribes of Israel, I will put My name forever; [8]and I will not remove the foot of Israel again from the land ^Awhich I have appointed for your fathers, if only they will take care to do everything that I have commanded them according to all the Law, the statutes, and the ordinances *given* through Moses." [9]So Manasseh encouraged Judah and the inhabitants of Jerusalem to do more evil than the nations whom the LORD destroyed before the sons of Israel.

MANASSEH'S IDOLATRY REBUKED

[10]So the LORD spoke to Manasseh and his people, but ^Athey paid no attention. [11]Therefore the LORD brought the commanders of the army of the king of Assyria against them, and they captured Manasseh with hooks, ^Abound him with bronze *chains,* and led him to Babylon. [12]When ^Ahe was in distress, he appeased the LORD his God and ^Bhumbled himself greatly before the God of his fathers. [13]When he prayed to Him, ^AHe was moved by him and heard his pleading, and

32:31 ^AIs 39:1   ^BDeut 8:16   32:33 ^APs 112:6; Prov 10:7
33:1 ^A2 Kin 21:1–9   33:2 ^A2 Chr 28:3; Jer 15:4
33:3 ^A2 Chr 31:1   33:4 ^A2 Chr 28:24   33:5 ^A2 Chr 4:9
33:6 ^A2 Chr 28:3   33:7 ^A2 Chr 33:15   33:8 ^A2 Sam 7:10
33:10 ^ANeh 9:29; Jer 25:4   33:11 ^A2 Chr 36:6
33:12 ^APs 130:1, 2   ^B2 Chr 32:26   33:13 ^A1 Chr 5:20; Ezra 8:23

32:33 ¹I.e., died   33:3 ¹I.e., wooden symbols of a female deity (Asherah)

brought him back to Jerusalem to his kingdom. Then Manasseh knew that the LORD *alone is* God.

[14] Now after this he built the outer wall of the city of David on the west side of ^Gihon, in the valley, up to the entrance of the Fish Gate; and he encircled the Ophel *with it* and made it very high. Then he put army commanders in all the fortified cities in Judah. [15] He also ^removed the foreign gods and the idol from the house of the LORD, as well as all the altars which he had built on the mountain of the house of the LORD and in Jerusalem, and he threw *them* outside the city. [16] He set up the altar of the LORD and sacrificed ^peace offerings and thanksgiving offerings on it; and he ordered Judah to serve the LORD God of Israel. [17] However, ^the people still sacrificed on the high places, *although* only to the LORD their God.

[18] Now the rest of the acts of Manasseh and ^his prayer to his God, and the words of the seers who spoke to him in the name of the LORD God of Israel, behold, they are among the records of the kings of Israel. [19] His prayer also and ^*how God* was moved by him, and all his sin, his unfaithfulness, and ^B^the sites on which he built high places and erected the ^1^Asherim and the carved images, before he humbled himself, behold, they are written in the records of ^2^Hozai. [20] So Manasseh ^1^lay down with his fathers, and they buried him in his own house. And his son Amon became king in his place.

AMON BECOMES KING IN JUDAH

[21] ^Amon *was* twenty-two years old when he became king, and he reigned for two years in Jerusalem.

[22] He did evil in the sight of the LORD, just as his father Manasseh had done, and Amon sacrificed to all ^the carved images which his father Manasseh had made, and he served them. [23] Furthermore, he did not humble himself before the LORD ^as his father Manasseh had done, but Amon multiplied *his* guilt. [24] Finally, ^his servants conspired against him and put him to death in his own house. [25] But the people of the land killed all the conspirators against King Amon, and the people of the land made his son Josiah king in his place.

JOSIAH SUCCEEDS AMON IN JUDAH

34 ^Josiah *was* eight years old when he became king, and he reigned for thirty-one years in Jerusalem. [2] ^He did what was right in the sight of the LORD, and walked in the ways of his father David and did not turn aside to the right or the left. [3] For in the eighth year of his reign while he was still a youth, he began to seek the God of his father David; and in the twelfth year he began ^to purge Judah and Jerusalem of the high places, the ^1^Asherim, the carved images, and the cast metal images. [4] They tore down the altars of the Baals in his presence, and he chopped down ^the incense altars that were high above them; also he broke in pieces the Asherim, the carved images, and the cast metal images, and ground

33:14^1 Kin 1:33　33:15^2 Chr 33:3-7　33:16^Lev 7:11-18　33:17^2 Chr 32:12　33:18^2 Chr 33:12, 13　33:19^2 Chr 33:13　^B 2 Chr 33:3　33:21^2 Kin 21:19-24　33:22^2 Chr 34:3, 4　33:23^2 Chr 33:12, 19　33:24^2 Chr 25:27　34:1^2 Kin 22:1, 2; Jer 1:2　34:2^2 Chr 29:2　34:3^1 Kin 13:2; 2 Chr 33:22　34:4^2 Kin 23:4, 5, 11

33:19 ^1 I.e., wooden symbols of a female deity (Asherah)　^2 LXX *seers*　33:20 ^1 I.e., died　34:3 ^1 I.e., wooden symbols of a female deity (Asherah)

them to powder, and scattered *it* on the graves of those who had sacrificed to them. ⁵Then ᴬhe burned the bones of the priests on their altars and purged Judah and Jerusalem. ⁶ᴬIn the cities of Manasseh, Ephraim, Simeon, and as far as Naphtali, in their surrounding spaces, ⁷he also tore down the altars and ᴬcrushed the Asherim and the carved images into powder, and chopped down all the incense altars throughout the land of Israel. Then he returned to Jerusalem.

JOSIAH REPAIRS THE TEMPLE

⁸ᴬNow in the eighteenth year of his reign, when he had purged the land and the house, he sent Shaphan the son of Azaliah, Maaseiah an official of the city, and Joah the son of Joahaz the secretary, to repair the house of the Lᴏʀᴅ his God. ⁹They came to Hilkiah the high priest and gave him the money that was brought into the house of God, which the Levites, the doorkeepers, had collected from ᴬManasseh and Ephraim, and from all the remnant of Israel, from all Judah and Benjamin and the inhabitants of Jerusalem. ¹⁰Then they handed it over to the workmen who had the oversight of the house of the Lᴏʀᴅ, and the workmen who were working in the house of the Lᴏʀᴅ used it to restore and repair the house. ¹¹They in turn gave *it* to the carpenters and the builders to buy quarried stone and timber for couplings, and to make beams for the houses ᴬwhich the kings of Judah had let go to ruin. ¹²ᴬThe men did the work faithfully with foremen over them to supervise: Jahath and Obadiah, the Levites of the sons of Merari, Zechariah and Meshullam

of the sons of the Kohathites, and the Levites, all who were skillful with musical instruments. ¹³*They were* also in charge of ᴬthe burden bearers, and supervised all the workmen from job to job; and some of the Levites *were* scribes, and officials, and gatekeepers.

HILKIAH DISCOVERS THE LOST BOOK OF THE LAW

¹⁴When they were bringing out the money which had been brought into the house of the Lᴏʀᴅ, ᴬHilkiah the priest found the Book of the Law of the Lᴏʀᴅ *given* by Moses. ¹⁵Hilkiah responded and said to Shaphan the scribe, "I have found the Book of the Law in the house of the Lᴏʀᴅ." And Hilkiah gave the book to Shaphan. ¹⁶Then Shaphan brought the book to the king and reported further word to the king, saying, "Everything that was entrusted to your servants, they are doing. ¹⁷They have also emptied out the money which was found in the house of the Lᴏʀᴅ, and have handed it over to the supervisors and the workmen." ¹⁸Moreover, Shaphan the scribe informed the king, saying, "Hilkiah the priest gave me a book." And Shaphan read from it in the presence of the king.

¹⁹When the king heard ᴬthe words of the Law, ᴮhe tore his clothes. ²⁰Then the king commanded Hilkiah, Ahikam the son of Shaphan, Abdon the son of Micah, Shaphan the scribe, and Asaiah the king's servant, saying, ²¹"Go, inquire of the Lᴏʀᴅ for me

34:5 ᴬ1 Kin 13:2; 2 Kin 23:20   34:6 ᴬ2 Kin 23:15, 19
34:7 ᴬ2 Chr 31:1   34:8 ᴬ2 Kin 22:3-20
34:9 ᴬ2 Chr 30:10, 18   34:11 ᴬ2 Chr 33:4-7
34:12 ᴬ2 Kin 12:15   34:13 ᴬNeh 4:10
34:14 ᴬ2 Chr 34:9   34:19 ᴬDeut 28:3-68   ᴮJosh 7:6

and for those who are left in Israel and Judah, concerning the words of the book which has been found; for ^the wrath of the LORD which has poured out on us is great, because our fathers have not kept the word of the LORD, to act in accordance with everything that is written in this book."

HULDAH, THE PROPHETESS, SPEAKS

22 So Hilkiah and *those* whom the king had told went to Huldah the prophetess, the wife of Shallum the son of Tokhath, the son of Hasrah, the keeper of the wardrobe (she lived in Jerusalem in the Second Quarter); and they spoke to her regarding this. 23 Then she said to them, "This is what the LORD, the God of Israel says: 'Tell the man who sent you to Me, 24 this is what the LORD says: "Behold, ^I am bringing evil on this place and on its inhabitants, all ^B the curses written in the book which they have read in the presence of the king of Judah. 25 ^Since they have abandoned Me and have burned incense to other gods, so that they may provoke Me to anger with all the works of their hands, My wrath will be poured out on this place and it will not be quenched."' 26 But to the king of Judah who sent you to inquire of the LORD, this is what you shall say to him: 'This is what the LORD, the God of Israel says: *In regard to* the words which you have heard, 27 "^Because your heart was tender and you humbled yourself before God when you heard His words against this place and its inhabitants, and *because* you humbled yourself before Me, tore your clothes, and wept before Me,

I have indeed heard you," declares the LORD. 28 "Behold, I will gather you to your fathers, and you will be gathered to your grave in peace, so your eyes will not see all the evil which I am bringing on this place and its inhabitants."'" And they brought back word to the king.

29 ^Then the king sent *word* and gathered all the elders of Judah and Jerusalem. 30 The king went up to the house of the LORD with ^all the men of Judah, the inhabitants of Jerusalem, the priests, the Levites, and all the people, from the greatest to the least; and he read in their presence all the words of the Book of the Covenant which was found in the house of the LORD.

JOSIAH'S GOOD REIGN

31 Then the king stood in his place and ^made a covenant before the LORD to walk after the LORD, and to keep His commandments, His testimonies, and His statutes with all his heart and with all his soul, to perform the words of the covenant that are written in this book. 32 Furthermore, he made all who were present in Jerusalem and Benjamin stand *with him*. So the inhabitants of Jerusalem acted in accordance with the covenant of God, the God of their fathers. 33 Josiah ^removed all the abominations from all the lands belonging to the sons of Israel, and made all who were present in Israel serve the LORD their God. Throughout his lifetime they did not turn from following the LORD God of their fathers.

34:21 ^2 Chr 29:8   34:24 ^2 Chr 36:14-20
^B Deut 28:15-68   34:25 ^2 Chr 33:3
34:27 ^2 Kin 22:19; 2 Chr 12:7   34:29 ^2 Kin 23:1-3
34:30 ^Neh 8:1-3   34:31 ^2 Chr 23:16; 29:10
34:33 ^2 Chr 34:3-7

THE PASSOVER HELD AGAIN

35 Then Josiah ^celebrated the Passover to the LORD in Jerusalem, and they slaughtered the Passover *animals* on the fourteenth *day* of the first month. ²He appointed the priests to their offices and ^encouraged them in the service of the house of the LORD. ³He also said to the Levites who taught all Israel *and* who were holy to the LORD, "Put the holy ark in the house which Solomon the son of David king of Israel built; ^it will not be a burden on *your* shoulders. Now serve the LORD your God and His people Israel. ⁴^Prepare *yourselves* by your fathers' households in your divisions, according to the writing of David king of Israel and according to the writing of his son Solomon. ⁵Furthermore, ^stand in the holy place according to the sections of the fathers' households of your countrymen, the lay people, and according to the Levites, by division of a father's household. ⁶Now slaughter the Passover *animals,* ^keep one another consecrated, and prepare for your countrymen to act in accordance with the word of the LORD by Moses."

⁷Josiah contributed to the lay people, to all who were present, flocks of lambs and young goats, all for the Passover offerings, numbering thirty thousand, plus three thousand bulls; these were from the king's property. ⁸His officers also contributed a voluntary offering to the people, the priests, and the Levites. Hilkiah, Zechariah, and Jehiel, ^the officials of the house of God, gave the priests 2,600 *from the flocks* and three hundred bulls, for the Passover offerings. ⁹^Conaniah also, and his brothers Shemaiah and Nethanel, and Hashabiah and Jeiel and Jozabad, the officers of the Levites, contributed five thousand *from the flocks* and five hundred bulls to the Levites for the Passover offerings.

¹⁰So the service was prepared, and ^the priests stood at their positions and the Levites by their divisions according to the king's command. ¹¹They slaughtered the Passover *animals,* and while ^the priests sprinkled the blood *received* from their hand, ᴮthe Levites skinned *the animals.* ¹²Then they removed the burnt offerings so that *they* might give them to the sections of the fathers' households of the lay people to present to the LORD, as it is written in the Book of Moses. *They did* this with the bulls as well. ¹³So ^they roasted the Passover *animals* on the fire according to the ordinance, and they boiled ᴮthe holy things in pots, in kettles, and in pans and carried *them* quickly to all the lay people. ¹⁴Afterward they prepared for themselves and for the priests, because the priests, the sons of Aaron, *were* offering the burnt offerings and the fat until night; so the Levites prepared for themselves and for the priests, the sons of Aaron. ¹⁵The singers, the sons of Asaph, *were* also at their positions according to the command of David, Asaph, Heman, and Jeduthun the king's seer; and ^the gatekeepers at each gate did not have to leave their service, because their kinsmen the Levites prepared for them.

35:1^2 Kin 23:21   35:2^2 Chr 29:11   35:3^1 Chr 23:26
35:4^1 Chr 9:10-13   35:5^Ezra 6:18   35:6^2 Chr 29:5
35:8^2 Chr 31:13   35:9^2 Chr 31:12
35:10^2 Chr 35:5   35:11^2 Chr 29:22   ᴮ2 Chr 29:34
35:13^Ex 12:8, 9   ᴮLev 6:28   35:15^1 Chr 26:12-19

16 So all the service of the LORD was prepared on that day to celebrate the Passover, and to offer burnt offerings on the altar of the LORD according to the command of King Josiah. 17 And ᴬthe sons of Israel who were present celebrated the Passover at that time, and the Feast of Unleavened Bread for seven days. 18ᴬThere had not been a Passover celebrated like it in Israel since the days of Samuel the prophet; nor had any of the kings of Israel celebrated such a Passover as Josiah did with the priests, the Levites, all Judah and Israel who were present, and the inhabitants of Jerusalem. 19 In the eighteenth year of Josiah's reign this Passover was celebrated.

JOSIAH DIES IN BATTLE

20ᴬAfter all this, when Josiah had set the temple in order, Neco king of Egypt came up to wage war at Carchemish on the Euphrates, and Josiah went out to engage him. 21 But Neco sent messengers to him, saying, "ᴬWhat business do you have with me, King of Judah? *I am* not *coming* against you today, but against the house with which I am at war, and God has told me to hurry. For your own sake, stop *interfering with* God who is with me, so that He does not destroy you." 22 However, Josiah would not turn away from him, but ᴬdisguised himself in order to fight against him; nor did he listen to the words of Neco from the mouth of God, but he came to wage war on the plain of Megiddo. 23 The archers shot King Josiah, and the king said to his servants, "Take me away, for I am badly wounded." 24 So his servants took him out of the chariot and carried him on the second chariot which he had, and brought him to Jerusalem where he died and was buried in the tombs of his fathers. ᴬAll Judah and Jerusalem mourned for Josiah. 25 Then ᴬJeremiah chanted a song of mourning for Josiah. And all the male and female singers speak about Josiah in their songs of mourning to this day. And they made them an ordinance in Israel; behold, they are also written in the Lamentations. 26 Now the rest of the acts of Josiah and his deeds of devotion as written in the Law of the LORD, 27 and his acts, the first to the last, behold, they are written in the Book of the Kings of Israel and Judah.

JOAHAZ, JEHOIAKIM, THEN JEHOIACHIN RULE

36 ᴬThen the people of the land took ¹Joahaz the son of Josiah and made him king in place of his father in Jerusalem. 2 Joahaz was twenty-three years old when he became king, and he reigned for three months in Jerusalem. 3 Then the king of Egypt deposed him in Jerusalem, and imposed a fine on the land of ¹a hundred talents of silver and ²one talent of gold. 4 The king of Egypt made Joahaz's brother Eliakim king over Judah and Jerusalem, and changed his name to Jehoiakim. But ᴬNeco took his brother Joahaz and brought him to Egypt.

5ᴬJehoiakim was twenty-five years old when he became king, and he reigned for eleven years in

---

35:17 ᴬEx 12:1-20; 2 Chr 30:21   35:18 ᴬ2 Kin 23:21; 2 Chr 30:5   35:20 ᴬ2 Kin 23:29, 30
35:21 ᴬ2 Chr 25:19   35:22 ᴬ2 Chr 18:29
35:24 ᴬZech 12:11   35:25 ᴬJer 22:10; Lam 4:20
36:1 ᴬ2 Kin 23:30-34   36:4 ᴬJer 22:10-12
36:5 ᴬ2 Kin 23:36, 37; Jer 22:13-19

36:1 ¹I.e., short form of Jehoahaz   36:3 ¹About 3.75 tons or 3.4 metric tons   ²About 75 lb. or 34 kg

Jerusalem; and he did evil in the sight of the LORD his God. ⁶Nebuchadnezzar king of Babylon came up against him and ᴬbound him with bronze *chains* to take him to Babylon. ⁷ᴬNebuchadnezzar also brought *some* of the articles of the house of the LORD to Babylon, and he put them in his temple in Babylon. ⁸ᴬNow the rest of the acts of Jehoiakim and the abominations which he committed, and what was found against him, behold, they are written in the Book of the Kings of Israel and Judah. And his son Jehoiachin became king in his place.

⁹ᴬJehoiachin was ¹eighteen years old when he became king, and he reigned for three months and ten days in Jerusalem. He did evil in the sight of the LORD.

CAPTIVITY IN BABYLON BEGUN

¹⁰At the turn of the year King Nebuchadnezzar sent *men* and had him brought to Babylon with the valuable articles of the house of the LORD; and he made his relative ᴬZedekiah king over Judah and Jerusalem.

ZEDEKIAH RULES IN JUDAH

¹¹ᴬZedekiah was twenty-one years old when he became king, and he reigned for eleven years in Jerusalem. ¹²He did evil in the sight of the LORD his God; he did not humble himself ᴬbefore Jeremiah the prophet who spoke for the LORD. ¹³ᴬHe also rebelled against King Nebuchadnezzar, who had made him swear *allegiance* by God. But ᴮhe stiffened his neck and hardened his heart against turning to the LORD God of Israel. ¹⁴Furthermore, all the officials of the priests and the people were very unfaithful, *following* all the abominations

of the nations; and they defiled the house of the LORD which He had sanctified in Jerusalem.

¹⁵Yet the LORD, the God of their fathers, ᴬsent *word* to them again and again by His messengers, because He had compassion on His people and on His dwelling place; ¹⁶but they *continually* ᴬmocked the messengers of God, despised His words, and scoffed at His prophets, until the wrath of the LORD rose against His people, until there was no remedy. ¹⁷ᴬSo He brought up against them the king of the Chaldeans, who killed their young men with the sword in the house of their sanctuary, and had no compassion on young man or virgin, old man or frail; He handed *them* all over to him. ¹⁸ᴬHe brought all the articles of the house of God, great and small, and the treasures of the house of the LORD, and the treasures of the king and his officers, to Babylon. ¹⁹Then ᴬthey burned the house of God and broke down the wall of Jerusalem, and burned all its fortified buildings with fire and destroyed all its valuable articles. ²⁰He ᴬtook into exile those who had escaped from the sword to Babylon; and ᴮthey were servants to him and to his sons until the rule of the kingdom of Persia, ²¹ᴬto fulfill the word of the LORD by the mouth of Jeremiah, until the land had enjoyed its Sabbaths. All the days of its desolation it kept the Sabbath ᴮuntil seventy years were complete.

36:6 ᴬ2 Chr 33:11   36:7 ᴬ2 Kin 24:13   36:8 ᴬ2 Kin 24:5
36:9 ᴬ2 Kin 24:8-17   36:10 ᴬJer 37:1   36:11 ᴬ2 Kin
24:18-20; Jer 27:1   36:12 ᴬJer 21:3-7   36:13 ᴬJer 52:3
ᴮ2 Chr 30:8   36:15 ᴬJer 7:13; 25:3   36:16 ᴬ2 Chr 30:10;
Jer 5:12, 13   36:17 ᴬ2 Kin 25:1-7; Jer 21:1-10
36:18 ᴬ2 Chr 36:7, 10   36:19 ᴬ1 Kin 9:8; Jer 52:13
36:20 ᴬ2 Kin 25:11   ᴮJer 27:7   36:21 ᴬJer 29:10   ᴮJer 25:11
36:9 ¹As in LXX and some Heb mss; MT *eight years*

CYRUS PERMITS RETURN

22 Now in the first year of Cyrus king of Persia—in order to fulfill the word of the LORD ^by the mouth of Jeremiah—the LORD stirred up the spirit of Cyrus king of Persia so that he sent a proclamation throughout his kingdom, and also *put it* in writing, saying, 23 "This is what Cyrus king of Persia says: 'The LORD, the God of heaven, has given me all the kingdoms of the earth, and He has appointed me to build Him a house in Jerusalem, which is in Judah. Whoever there is among you of all His people, may the LORD his God be with him; 'go up then!'"

36:22 ^Jer 25:12; 29:10

36:23 ¹ Lit *and he is to go up*; i.e., go to Jerusalem

EZRA

CYRUS' PROCLAMATION

1 Now in the first year of Cyrus king of Persia, in order to fulfill the word of the LORD by the mouth of Jeremiah, the LORD stirred up the spirit of Cyrus king of Persia, so that he ^sent a proclamation throughout his kingdom, and also *put it* in writing, saying:

2 "This is what Cyrus king of Persia says: 'The LORD, the God of heaven, has given me all the kingdoms of the earth, and ^He has appointed me to rebuild for Him a house in Jerusalem, which is in Judah. 3 Whoever there is among you of all His people, may his God be with him! Go up to Jerusalem which is in Judah and rebuild the house of the LORD, the God of Israel; ^He is the God who is in Jerusalem. 4 And every survivor, at whatever place he may live, the people of that place are to support him with silver and gold, with equipment and cattle, together with a voluntary offering for the house of God which is in Jerusalem.'"

HOLY VESSELS RESTORED

5 Then the heads of fathers' *households* of Judah and Benjamin and the priests and the Levites rose up, ^everyone whose spirit God had stirred to go up to rebuild the house of the LORD which is in Jerusalem. 6 And all of those around them ^encouraged them with articles of silver, with gold, with equipment, cattle, and with valuables, aside from everything that was given as a voluntary offering. 7 Also

King Cyrus brought out the articles of the house of the LORD, ^which Nebuchadnezzar had carried away from Jerusalem and put in the house of his gods; 8 and Cyrus, king of Persia, had them brought out by the hand of Mithredath the treasurer, and he counted them out to ^Sheshbazzar, the leader of Judah. 9 Now this *was* their number: thirty ^gold dishes, a thousand silver dishes, twenty nine duplicates; 10 thirty gold bowls, 410 silver bowls of a second *kind, and* a thousand other articles. 11 All the articles of gold and silver *totaled* 5,400. Sheshbazzar brought them all up with the exiles who went up from Babylon to Jerusalem.

NUMBER OF THOSE RETURNING

2 ^Now these are the people of the province who came up out of the captivity of the exiles whom Nebuchadnezzar the king of Babylon had taken into exile to Babylon, and they returned to Jerusalem and Judah, each to his city. 2 These came with Zerubbabel, Jeshua, Nehemiah, Seraiah, Reelaiah, Mordecai, Bilshan, Mispar, Bigvai, Rehum, *and* Baanah.

This is the number of the men of the people of Israel: 3 the sons of Parosh, 2,172; 4 the sons of Shephatiah, 372; 5 the sons of ^Arah, 775; 6 the sons of ^Pahath-moab of the

1:1 ^Ezra 5:13   1:2 ^Is 44:28; 45:1, 12, 13   1:3 ^Is 37:16;
Dan 6:26   1:5 ^Ezra 1:1, 2   1:6 ^Neh 6:9; Is 35:3
1:7 ^2 Kin 24:13; 2 Chr 36:7   1:8 ^Ezra 5:14
1:9 ^Ezra 8:27   2:1 ^2 Kin 24:14-16; Neh 7:6-73
2:5 ^Neh 7:10   2:6 ^Neh 7:11

sons of Jeshua *and* Joab, 2,812; [7]the sons of Elam, 1,254; [8]the sons of Zattu, 945; [9]the sons of Zaccai, 760; [10]the sons of Bani, 642; [11]the sons of Bebai, 623; [12]the sons of Azgad, 1,222; [13]the sons of ^Adonikam, 666; [14]the sons of Bigvai, 2,056; [15]the sons of Adin, 454; [16]the sons of Ater, of Hezekiah, 98; [17]the sons of Bezai, 323; [18]the sons of Jorah, 112; [19]the sons of Hashum, 223; [20]the sons of Gibbar, 95; [21]the men of ^Bethlehem, 123; [22]the men of Netophah, 56; [23]the men of Anathoth, 128; [24]the sons of Azmaveth, 42; [25]the sons of Kiriath-arim, Chephirah, and Beeroth, 743; [26]the sons of ^Ramah and Geba, 621; [27]the men of Michmas, 122; [28]the men of Bethel and Ai, 223; [29]the sons of Nebo, 52; [30]the sons of Magbish, 156; [31]the sons of the other Elam, 1,254; [32]the sons of Harim, 320; [33]the sons of Lod, Hadid, and Ono, 725; [34]the men of ^Jericho, 345; [35]the sons of Senaah, 3,630.

PRIESTS RETURNING

[36]^The priests: the sons of Jedaiah of the house of Jeshua, 973; [37]the sons of ^Immer, 1,052; [38]^the sons of Pashhur, 1,247; [39]the sons of ^Harim, 1,017.

LEVITES RETURNING

[40]The Levites: the sons of Jeshua and Kadmiel, of the sons of Hodaviah, 74. [41]The singers: the sons of Asaph, 128. [42]The sons of the gatekeepers: the sons of Shallum, the sons of Ater, the sons of Talmon, the sons of Akkub, the sons of Hatita, *and* the sons of Shobai, 139 in all.

[43]The ^temple servants: the sons of Ziha, the sons of Hasupha, the sons of Tabbaoth, [44]the sons of Keros, the sons of Siaha, the sons

of Padon, [45]the sons of Lebanah, the sons of Hagabah, the sons of Akkub, [46]the sons of Hagab, the sons of Shalmai, the sons of Hanan, [47]the sons of Giddel, the sons of Gahar, the sons of Reaiah, [48]the sons of Rezin, the sons of Nekoda, the sons of Gazzam, [49]the sons of Uzza, the sons of Paseah, the sons of Besai, [50]the sons of Asnah, the sons of Meunim, the sons of Nephisim, [51]the sons of Bakbuk, the sons of Hakupha, the sons of Harhur, [52]the sons of Bazluth, the sons of Mehida, the sons of Harsha, [53]the sons of Barkos, the sons of Sisera, the sons of Temah, [54]the sons of Neziah, *and* the sons of Hatipha.

[55]The sons of ^Solomon's servants: the sons of Sotai, the sons of Hassophereth, the sons of Peruda, [56]the sons of Jaalah, the sons of Darkon, the sons of Giddel, [57]the sons of Shephatiah, the sons of Hattil, the sons of Pochereth-hazzebaim, *and* the sons of Ami.

[58]All the ^temple servants and the sons of ^BSolomon's servants *totaled* 392.

[59]Now these *were* the ones who came up from Tel-melah, Tel-harsha, Cherub, Addan, *and* Immer, but they were not able to provide evidence of their fathers' households and their descendants, whether they *were* of Israel: [60]the sons of Delaiah, the sons of Tobiah, *and* the sons of Nekoda, 652.

PRIESTS REMOVED

[61]Of the sons of the priests: the sons of Hobaiah, the sons of Hakkoz, the sons of ^Barzillai, who took

2:13 ^Ezra 8:13   2:21 ^Gen 35:19; Matt 2:6
2:26 ^Josh 18:25   2:34 ^1 Kin 16:34; 2 Chr 28:15
2:36 ^1 Chr 24:7-18   2:37 ^1 Chr 24:14   2:38 ^1 Chr 9:12
2:39 ^1 Chr 24:8   2:43 ^1 Chr 9:2   2:55 ^1 Kin 9:21
2:58 ^1 Chr 9:2   ^B1 Kin 9:21   2:61 ^2 Sam 17:27; 1 Kin 2:7

a wife from the daughters of Barzillai the Gileadite, and he was called by their name. 62 These searched *among* their genealogical registration but they could not be located; ^so they were considered defiled *and excluded* from the priesthood. 63 The governor said to them that they were not to eat from the most holy things until a priest stood up with ^Urim and Thummim.

64 The whole assembly together *totaled* 42,360, 65 besides their male and female slaves who *totaled* 7,337; and they had two hundred ^singing men and women. 66 Their horses *numbered* 736; their mules, 245; 67 their camels, 435; *their* donkeys, 6,720.

68 Some of the heads of fathers' *households,* when they arrived at the house of the LORD which is in Jerusalem, offered willingly for the house of God to erect it on its site. 69 According to their ability they gave ^to the treasury *for* the work sixty-one thousand gold drachmas, five thousand silver minas, and a hundred priestly garments.

70 ^Now the priests and the Levites, some of the people, the singers, the gatekeepers, and the temple servants lived in their cities, and all Israel in their cities.

ALTAR AND SACRIFICES RESTORED

3 Now when the seventh month came, and ^the sons of Israel *were* in the cities, the people gathered together as one person to Jerusalem. 2 Then ^Jeshua the son of Jozadak and his brothers the priests, and Zerubbabel the son of Shealtiel and his brothers, rose up and built the altar of the God of Israel to offer burnt offerings on it, as it is written in the Law of Moses, the man of God. 3 So they set up the altar on its foundation, because ^they were terrified of the peoples of the lands; and they offered burnt offerings on it to the LORD, burnt offerings morning and evening. 4 They also celebrated the ^Feast of Booths, as it is written, and *offered* the prescribed number of burnt offerings daily, according to the ordinance, as each day required; 5 and afterward *there was* a ^continual burnt offering, also for the new moons and for all the appointed festivals of the LORD that were consecrated, and from everyone who offered a voluntary offering to the LORD. 6 From the first day of the seventh month they began to offer burnt offerings to the LORD, but the foundation of the temple of the LORD had not been laid. 7 Then they gave money to the masons and carpenters, and food, drink, and oil to the Sidonians and the Tyrians ^to bring cedar wood from Lebanon to the sea at ᴮJoppa, according to the permission they had from Cyrus king of Persia.

TEMPLE RESTORATION BEGUN

8 Now in the second year of their coming to the house of God at Jerusalem, in the second month, Zerubbabel the son of Shealtiel, Jeshua the son of Jozadak, and the rest of their brothers the priests and the Levites, and all who came from the captivity to Jerusalem, began *the work* and ^appointed the Levites who were twenty years old and upward to oversee the work

2:62 ^Num 16:39, 40   2:63 ^Ex 28:30; Num 27:21
2:65 ^2 Chr 35:25   2:69 ^Ezra 8:25-34
2:70 ^1 Chr 9:2; Neh 11:3   3:1 ^Neh 7:73; 8:1
3:2 ^Neh 12:1, 8   3:3 ^Ezra 4:4
3:4 ^Neh 8:14; Zech 14:16   3:5 ^Ex 29:38; Num 28:3
3:7 ^2 Chr 2:16   ᴮActs 9:36   3:8 ^1 Chr 23:4, 24

of the house of the LORD. ⁹Then ^Jeshua *with* his sons and brothers stood united *with* Kadmiel and his sons, the sons of Judah *and* the sons of Henadad *with* their sons and brothers the Levites, to oversee the workmen in the temple of God.

¹⁰Now when the builders had ^laid the foundation of the temple of the LORD, the priests stood in their apparel with trumpets, and the Levites, the sons of Asaph, with cymbals, to praise the LORD according to the directions of King David of Israel. ¹¹And they sang, praising and giving thanks to the LORD, *saying,* "^For *He is* good, for His favor *is* upon Israel forever." And all the people shouted with a great shout of joy when they praised the LORD, because the foundation of the house of the LORD was laid. ¹²Yet many of the priests and Levites and heads of fathers' *households,* ^the old men who had seen the first temple, wept with a loud voice when the foundation of this house was laid before their eyes, while many shouted aloud for joy, ¹³so that the people could not distinguish the sound of the shout of joy from the sound of the weeping of the people, because the people were shouting with a loud shout, and the sound was heard far away.

ENEMIES HINDER THE WORK

4 Now when the enemies of Judah and Benjamin heard that ^the people of the exile were building a temple to the LORD God of Israel, ²they approached Zerubbabel and the heads of fathers' *households,* and said to them, "Let us build with you, for like you, we seek your God; and we have been sacrificing to Him since the days of ^Esarhaddon king of Assyria, who brought us up here." ³But Zerubbabel and Jeshua and the rest of the heads of fathers' *households* of Israel said to them, "^You have nothing *in common* with us in building a house to our God; but we ourselves will together build for the LORD God of Israel, ^just as King Cyrus, the king of Persia, has commanded us."

⁴Then ^the people of the land discouraged the people of Judah, and frightened them from building, ⁵and bribed advisers against them to frustrate their advice all the days of Cyrus king of Persia, even until the reign of Darius king of Persia.

⁶Now in the reign of ¹·^Ahasuerus, in the beginning of his reign, they wrote an accusation against the inhabitants of Judah and Jerusalem.

⁷And in the days of Artaxerxes, Bishlam, Mithredath, Tabeel, and the rest of his colleagues wrote to Artaxerxes king of Persia; and the text of the letter was written in Aramaic and translated ^*from* Aramaic.

THE LETTER TO KING ARTAXERXES

⁸Rehum the commander and Shimshai the scribe wrote a letter against Jerusalem to King Artaxerxes, as follows— ⁹Rehum the commander, Shimshai the scribe, and the rest of their colleagues, the judges and ^the lesser governors, the officials, the secretaries, the men of Erech, the Babylonians, the men of Susa, that is, the Elamites, ¹⁰and the rest of the nations which the great and honorable Osnappar deported and

3:9^Ezra 2:40   3:10^Zech 4:6-10   3:11^Ps 100:5; Jer 33:11   3:12^Hag 2:3   4:1^Ezra 1:11 4:2^2 Kin 19:37   4:3^Neh 2:20   ^Ezra 1:1, 2 4:4^Ezra 3:3   4:6^Esth 1:1; Dan 9:1   4:7^2 Kin 18:26; Dan 2:4   4:9^Ezra 5:6; 6:6

4:6 ¹Or *Xerxes*; Heb *Ahash-verosh*

settled in the city of Samaria, and in the rest of the region beyond the *Euphrates* River. ^And now ¹¹this is a copy of the letter which they sent to him:

"To King Artaxerxes: Your servants, the men of the region beyond the *Euphrates* River; and now ¹²let it be known to the king that the Jews who came up from you have come to us at Jerusalem; they are rebuilding the rebellious and evil city and ^are finishing the walls and repairing the foundations. ¹³Now let it be known to the king, that if that city is rebuilt and the walls are finished, ^they will not pay tribute, custom tax, or toll, and it will be detrimental to the revenue of the kings. ¹⁴Now because we are in the service of the palace, and it is not fitting for us to see the king's shame, for this reason we have sent *word* and informed the king, ¹⁵so that a search may be conducted in the record books of your fathers. And you will discover in the record books and learn that that city is a rebellious city and detrimental to kings and provinces, and that they have revolted within it in past days; for this reason that city was laid waste. ¹⁶We are informing the king that if that city is rebuilt and the walls finished, then as a result of this you will have no possession in *the province* beyond the *Euphrates* River."

THE KING REPLIES AND WORK STOPS

¹⁷*Then* the king sent a response to Rehum the commander, Shimshai the scribe, and to the rest of their colleagues who live in Samaria and in the rest of *the provinces* beyond the *Euphrates* River: "Peace. And now, ¹⁸the document which you sent to us has been ^translated *and*

read before me. ¹⁹And a decree has been issued by me, and a search has been conducted and it has been discovered that that city has risen up against the kings in past days, and that rebellion and revolt have been perpetrated in it, ²⁰^that mighty kings have ruled over Jerusalem, governing all *the provinces* beyond the *Euphrates* River, and that tribute, custom tax, and toll were paid to them. ²¹Now issue a decree to make those men stop *work,* so that this city will not be rebuilt until a decree is issued by me. ²²And beware of being negligent in carrying out this *matter;* why should there be great damage, to the detriment of the kings?"

²³Then as soon as the copy of King Artaxerxes' decree was read before Rehum and Shimshai the scribe and their colleagues, they went in a hurry to Jerusalem to the Jews and stopped them by military force.

²⁴Then work on the house of God in Jerusalem was discontinued, and it was stopped until the second year of the reign of Darius king of Persia.

TEMPLE WORK RESUMED

5 When the prophets, ^Haggai the prophet and ᴮZechariah the son of Iddo, prophesied to the Jews who were in Judah and Jerusalem in the name of the God of Israel, who was over them, ²then Zerubbabel the son of Shealtiel and Jeshua the son of Jozadak rose up and began to rebuild the house of God which is in Jerusalem; and ^the prophets of God were with them, supporting them.

4:10^Ezra 4:11, 17; 7:12   **4:12**^Ezra 5:3, 9
4:13^Ezra 4:20; 7:24   **4:18**^Neh 8:8   **4:20**^1 Kin 4:21;
1 Chr 18:3   **5:1**^Hag 1:1   ᴮZech 1:1   **5:2**^Ezra 6:14;
Zech 3:1

³At that time ^Tattenai, the governor of *the province* beyond the *Euphrates* River, and Shethar-bozenai and their colleagues came to them and spoke to them as follows: "⁸Who issued you a decree to rebuild this temple and to finish this structure?" ⁴^Then we told them accordingly what the names of the men were who were reconstructing this building. ⁵But ^the eye of their God was on the elders of the Jews, and they did not stop them until the report could reach Darius, and then the decree concerning it could be sent back.

ENEMIES WRITE TO DARIUS

⁶ *This is* the copy of the letter that Tattenai, the governor of *the province* beyond the *Euphrates* River, and Shethar-bozenai and his colleagues ^the officials, who were beyond the River, sent to Darius the king. ⁷They sent the report to him in which it was written as follows: "To Darius the king, all peace. ⁸May it be known to the king that we have gone to the province of Judah, to the house of the great God which is being built with large stones, and beams are being laid in the walls; and this work is being performed with great care and is succeeding in their hands. ⁹Then we asked those elders and said to them as follows: 'Who issued you a decree to rebuild this temple and to finish this structure?' ¹⁰We also asked them their names so as to inform you, in order that we might write down the names of the men who were in charge. ¹¹So they answered us as follows, saying, 'We are the servants of the God of heaven and earth, and are rebuilding the temple that was built many years ago,

^which a great king of Israel built and finished. ¹²But because our fathers provoked the God of heaven to wrath, ^He handed them over to Nebuchadnezzar king of Babylon, the Chaldean, *who* destroyed this temple and deported the people to Babylon. ¹³However, in the first year of Cyrus king of Babylon, King Cyrus ^issued a decree to rebuild this house of God. ¹⁴Also ^the gold and silver utensils of the house of God which Nebuchadnezzar had taken from the temple in Jerusalem and brought them to the temple of Babylon, King Cyrus took them from the temple of Babylon and they were given to one whose name was Sheshbazzar, whom he had appointed governor. ¹⁵And he said to him, "Take these utensils, go *and* deposit them in the temple in Jerusalem, and have the house of God rebuilt in its place." ¹⁶Then that Sheshbazzar came *and* ^laid the foundations of the house of God in Jerusalem; and from then until now it has been under construction and it is not *yet* completed.' ¹⁷And now, if it pleases the king, ^let a search be conducted in the king's treasure house, which is there in Babylon, as to whether a decree was issued by King Cyrus to rebuild this house of God in Jerusalem; and let the king send to us his decision concerning this *matter.*"

DARIUS FINDS CYRUS' DECREE

6 Then King Darius issued a decree, and a ^search was conducted in the archives, where the treasures were stored in Babylon.

5:3^Ezra 6:6, 13 ⁸Ezra 1:3 5:4^Ezra 5:10
5:5^Ezra 7:6, 28 5:6^Ezra 4:9 5:11^1 Kin 6:1, 38
5:12^2 Kin 25:8-11; Jer 52:12-15 5:13^Ezra 1:1-4
5:14^Ezra 1:7; 6:5 5:16^Ezra 3:8, 10 5:17^Ezra 6:1, 2
6:1^Ezra 5:17

² And in ¹Ecbatana, in the fortress which is ^in the province of Media, a scroll was found; and the following was written in it: "Memorandum— ³^In the first year of King Cyrus, Cyrus the king issued a decree: 'Concerning the house of God in Jerusalem, let the temple, the place where sacrifices are offered, be rebuilt, and let its foundations be repaired, its height being ¹sixty cubits and its width sixty cubits, ⁴^with three layers of large stones and one layer of timber. And the cost is to be paid from the royal treasury. ⁵ Also ^the gold and silver utensils of the house of God, which Nebuchadnezzar took from the temple in Jerusalem and brought to Babylon, are to be returned and brought to their places in the temple in Jerusalem; and you shall put them in the house of God.'

⁶ "Now as for you, ^Tattenai, governor of the province beyond the Euphrates River, Shethar-bozenai, and your colleagues, the officials of the provinces beyond the River, stay away from there. ⁷ Leave that work on the house of God alone; let the governor of the Jews and the elders of the Jews rebuild that house of God on its site. ⁸ Furthermore, ^I issue a decree concerning what you are to do for these elders of Judah in the rebuilding of that house of God: the full cost is to be paid to those people from the royal treasury out of the taxes of the provinces beyond the Euphrates River, and that without interruption. ⁹ And whatever is needed, bulls, rams, and lambs for burnt offerings to the God of heaven, and wheat, salt, wine, and anointing oil, as the priests in Jerusalem order, it is to be given to them daily without fail, ¹⁰ so that they

may offer acceptable sacrifices to the God of heaven and ^pray for the lives of the king and his sons. ¹¹ And I issued a decree that ^any person who violates this decree, a timber shall be pulled out of his house and he shall be impaled on it; and his house shall be turned into a refuse heap on account of this. ¹² May the God who ^has caused His name to dwell there overthrow any king or people who attempts to change it, so as to destroy that house of God in Jerusalem. I, Darius, have issued this decree; it is to be carried out with all diligence!"

THE TEMPLE COMPLETED AND DEDICATED

¹³ Then ^Tattenai, the governor of the province beyond the Euphrates River, Shethar-bozenai, and their colleagues carried out the decree with all diligence, just as King Darius had ordered. ¹⁴ And ^the elders of the Jews were successful in building through the prophecy of Haggai the prophet and Zechariah the son of Iddo. And they finished building following the command of the God of Israel and the decree of Cyrus, Darius, and Artaxerxes king of Persia. ¹⁵ Now this temple was completed on the third day of the ^month Adar; it was the sixth year of the reign of King Darius.

¹⁶ And the sons of Israel, the priests, the Levites, and the rest of the exiles, ^celebrated the dedication of this house of God with joy. ¹⁷ They offered for the dedication of

6:2 ^2 Kin 17:6   6:3 ^Ezra 1:1; 5:13   6:4 ^1 Kin 6:36
6:5 ^Ezra 1:7; 5:14   6:6 ^Ezra 5:3; 6:13   6:8 ^Ezra 6:4;
7:14-22   6:10 ^Ezra 7:23; 1 Tim 2:1, 2   6:11 ^Ezra 7:26
6:12 ^Deut 12:5, 11; 1 Kin 9:3   6:13 ^Ezra 6:6
6:14 ^Ezra 5:1, 2   6:15 ^Esth 3:7   6:16 ^1 Kin 8:63;
2 Chr 7:5

6:2 ¹Aram Achmetha   6:3 ¹About 90 ft. or 27 m

this temple of God a hundred bulls, two hundred rams, four hundred lambs, and as a sin offering for all Israel ^twelve male goats, corresponding to the number of the tribes of Israel. ¹⁸ Then they appointed the priests to their divisions and the Levites in their sections for the service of God in Jerusalem, ^as it is written in the Book of Moses.

THE PASSOVER HELD

¹⁹ The exiles held the Passover on ^the fourteenth of the first month. ²⁰ For the priests and the Levites had purified themselves together; all of them were pure. Then ^they slaughtered the Passover *lambs* for all the exiles, both for their brothers the priests and for themselves. ²¹ And the sons of Israel who returned from exile and ^all those who had separated themselves from the impurity of the nations of the land to *join* them, to seek the LORD God of Israel, ate *the Passover.* ²² And ^they held the Feast of Unleavened Bread for seven days with joy, because the LORD had made them happy, and ᴮhad turned the heart of the king of Assyria toward them to encourage them in the work of the house of God, the God of Israel.

EZRA JOURNEYS FROM BABYLON TO JERUSALEM

7 Now after these things, in the reign of ^Artaxerxes king of Persia, Ezra *went up to Jerusalem; Ezra was* the son of Seraiah, son of Azariah, son of Hilkiah, ²son of Shallum, son of Zadok, son of Ahitub, ³son of Amariah, son of Azariah, son of Meraioth, ⁴son of Zerahiah, son of Uzzi, son of Bukki, ⁵son of Abishua, son of Phinehas, son of Eleazar, son of Aaron the chief

priest. ⁶ *So* this Ezra went up from Babylon, and he was a ^scribe skilled in the Law of Moses, which the LORD God of Israel had given; and the king granted him all he requested because the hand of the LORD his God *was* upon him. ⁷^Some of the sons of Israel and some of the priests, the Levites, the singers, the gatekeepers, and the temple servants went up to Jerusalem in the seventh year of King Artaxerxes.

⁸ And he came to Jerusalem in the fifth month, which was in the seventh year of the king. ⁹ For on the first *day* of the first month he began to go up from Babylon; and on the first of the fifth month he came to Jerusalem, ^because the good hand of his God *was* upon him. ¹⁰ For Ezra had firmly resolved to study the Law of the LORD and to practice *it,* and ^to teach *His* statutes and ordinances in Israel.

KING'S DECREE ON BEHALF OF EZRA

¹¹ Now this is the copy of the letter which King Artaxerxes gave to Ezra the priest, the scribe, learned in the words of the commandments of the LORD and His statutes to Israel: ¹² "Artaxerxes, ^king of kings, to Ezra the priest, the scribe of the Law of the God of heaven, perfect *peace.* And now ¹³^I have issued a decree that any of the people of Israel and their priests and the Levites in my kingdom who are willing to go to Jerusalem, may go with you. ¹⁴ Since you are sent on the part of the king and his ^seven advisers to inquire about Judah and Jerusalem

6:17^Ezra 8:35   6:18^Num 3:6; 8:9   6:19^Ex 12:6
6:20^2 Chr 35:11   6:21^Neh 9:2; 10:28
6:22^Ex 12:15   ᴮEzra 7:27   7:1^Ezra 7:12, 21; Neh 2:1
7:6^Ezra 7:11, 12, 21   7:7^Ezra 8:1-20   7:9^Ezra 7:6;
Neh 2:8   7:10^Ezra 7:25; Neh 8:1   7:12^Ezek 26:7;
Dan 2:37   7:13^Ezra 6:1   7:14^Ezra 7:15, 28; 8:25

according to the Law of your God which is in your hand, [15]and to bring the silver and gold, which the king and his advisers have voluntarily given to the God of Israel, ^whose dwelling is in Jerusalem, [16]with all the silver and gold which you find in the entire province of Babylon, along ^with the voluntary offering of the people and of the priests, who ᴮoffered willingly for the house of their God which is in Jerusalem; [17]with this money, therefore, you shall diligently buy bulls, rams, *and* lambs, with their grain offerings and their drink offerings, and ^offer them on the altar of the house of your God which is in Jerusalem. [18]And whatever seems good to you and your brothers to do with the rest of the silver and gold, you may do according to the will of your God. [19]Also the utensils which are given to you for the service of the house of your God, deliver in full before the God of Jerusalem. [20]And the rest of the needs of the house of your God, for which it may be incumbent upon you to provide, ^provide *for them* from the royal treasury.

[21]"I myself, King Artaxerxes, issue a decree to all the treasurers who are *in the provinces* beyond the *Euphrates* River, that whatever Ezra the priest, ^the scribe of the Law of the God of heaven, may require of you, it shall be done diligently, [22]up to [1]a hundred talents of silver, [2]a hundred kors of wheat, [3]a hundred baths of wine, a hundred baths of anointing oil, and salt as needed. [23]Whatever is commanded by the God of heaven, it shall be done with zeal for the house of the God of heaven, ^so that there will not be wrath against the kingdom of the king and his sons. [24]We also inform you that ^it is not allowed

to impose tax, tribute, or toll *on* any of the priests, Levites, singers, doorkeepers, temple servants, or *other* servants of this house of God.

[25]"And you, Ezra, according to the wisdom of your God which is in your hand, ^appoint magistrates and judges so that they may judge all the people who are in *the province* beyond the *Euphrates* River, that is, all those who know the laws of your God; and you may ᴮteach anyone who is ignorant *of them*. [26]And ^whoever does not comply with the Law of your God and the law of the king, judgment is to be executed upon him strictly, whether for death or for banishment, or for confiscation of property or for imprisonment."

THE KING'S KINDNESS

[27]Blessed be the Lᴏʀᴅ, the God of our fathers, ^who has put *such a thing* as this in the king's heart, to glorify the house of the Lᴏʀᴅ which is in Jerusalem, [28]and ^has extended favor to me before the king and his counselors and before all the king's mighty officials. So I was strengthened according to ᴮthe hand of the Lᴏʀᴅ my God *that was* upon me, and I gathered leading men from Israel to go up with me.

PEOPLE WHO WENT WITH EZRA

8 Now these are the heads of their fathers' *households* and the genealogical enrollment of those who went up with me from

7:15 ^Ezra 6:12; Ps 135:21　7:16 ^Ezra 1:4, 6　ᴮ1 Chr 29:6　7:17 ^Deut 12:5-11　7:20 ^Ezra 6:4　7:21 ^Ezra 7:6　7:23 ^Ezra 6:10　7:24 ^Ezra 4:13, 20　7:25 ^Ex 18:21　ᴮMal 2:7　7:26 ^Ezra 6:11, 12　7:27 ^Ezra 6:22　7:28 ^Ezra 9:9　ᴮEzra 5:5

7:22 [1]About 3.75 tons or 3.4 metric tons　[2]About 770 cubic feet or 22 cubic meters　[3]About 600 gallons or 2,271 liters

Babylon in the reign of King Arta-xerxes: [2]of the sons of Phinehas, Gershom; of the sons of Ithamar, Daniel; of the sons of David, ^Hattush; [3]of the sons of Shecaniah *who was* of the sons of ^Parosh, Zechariah, and with him 150 males *who were in* the genealogical list; [4]of the sons of Pahath-moab, Eliehoenai the son of Zerahiah and two hundred males with him; [5]of the sons of Zattu, Shecaniah, the son of Jahaziel and three hundred males with him; [6]and of the sons of ^Adin, Ebed the son of Jonathan and fifty males with him; [7]and of the sons of Elam, Jeshaiah the son of Athaliah and seventy males with him; [8]and of the sons of Shephatiah, Zebadiah the son of Michael and eighty males with him; [9]of the sons of Joab, Obadiah the son of Jehiel and 218 males with him; [10]and of the sons of Bani, Shelomith, the son of Josiphiah and 160 males with him; [11]and of the sons of Bebai, Zechariah the son of Bebai and twenty-eight males with him; [12]and of the sons of Azgad, Johanan the son of Hakkatan and 110 males with him; [13]and of the sons of Adonikam, the last ones, these being their names: Eliphelet, Jeiel, and Shemaiah, and sixty males with them; [14]and of the sons of Bigvai, Uthai and Zabbud, and seventy males with them.

EZRA SENDS FOR LEVITES

[15]Now I assembled them at ^the river that runs to Ahava, where we camped for three days; and when I paid close attention to the people and the priests, I did not find any Levites there. [16]So I sent for Eliezer, Ariel, Shemaiah, Elnathan, Jarib, Elnathan, Nathan, Zechariah, and Meshullam, leading men, and

for Joiarib and Elnathan, teachers. [17]And I sent them to Iddo the leading man at the place *called* Casiphia; and I told them what to say to Iddo and his brothers, ^the temple servants at the place Casiphia, *that is,* to bring ministers to us for the house of our God. [18]And as the good hand of our God *was* upon us, they brought us a ^man of insight from the sons of Mahli, the son of Levi, the son of Israel, namely Sherebiah, and his sons and brothers, eighteen men; [19]and Hashabiah and Jeshaiah of the sons of Merari, *with* his brothers and their sons, twenty men; [20]and 220 of ^the temple servants, whom David and the officials had provided for the service of the Levites, all of them designated by name.

PROTECTION OF GOD INVOKED

[21]Then I proclaimed a fast there at the river of Ahava, to ^humble ourselves before our God, to seek from Him a safe journey for us, our little ones, and all our possessions. [22]For I was ashamed to request from the king troops and horsemen to protect us from the enemy on the way, because we had said to the king, "The hand of our God is favorably disposed to all who seek Him, but ^His power and His anger are against all those who [B]abandon Him." [23]So we fasted and sought our God concerning this *matter,* and He ^listened to our pleading.

[24]Then I selected twelve of the leading priests: ^Sherebiah, Hashabiah, and with them ten of their

8:2 ^1 Chr 3:22   8:3 ^Ezra 2:3   8:6 ^Ezra 2:15;
Neh 7:20   8:15 ^Ezra 8:21, 31   8:17 ^Ezra 2:43
8:18 ^2 Chr 30:22   8:20 ^Ezra 2:43; 7:7
8:21 ^Lev 16:29; Is 58:3, 5   8:22 ^Josh 22:16
[B]2 Chr 15:2   8:23 ^1 Chr 5:20; 2 Chr 33:13
8:24 ^Ezra 8:18, 19

brothers; 25and I weighed out to them ^the silver, the gold, and the utensils, the offering for the house of our God which the king, his counselors, his officials, and all Israel who were present *there* had contributed. 26^So I weighed into their hands '650 talents of silver, and silver utensils *worth* ²a hundred talents, *and* a hundred gold talents, 27and twenty gold bowls *worth* a thousand 'darics, and two utensils of fine shiny bronze, precious as gold. 28Then I said to them, "^You are holy to the LORD, and the utensils are holy; and the silver and the gold are a voluntary offering to the LORD God of your fathers. 29Watch and keep *them* ^until you weigh *them* before the leading priests, the Levites, and the leaders of the fathers' *households* of Israel in Jerusalem, *in* the chambers of the house of the LORD." 30So the priests and the Levites ^accepted the weight of silver and gold and the utensils, to bring *them* to Jerusalem to the house of our God.

31Then we journeyed from ^the river Ahava on the twelfth of the first month to go to Jerusalem; and the hand of our God was upon us, and He rescued us from the hand of the enemy and the ambushes by the road. 32^So we came to Jerusalem and remained there for three days.

TREASURE PLACED IN THE TEMPLE

33And on the fourth day the silver, the gold, and the utensils ^were weighed out in the house of our God into the hand of Meremoth the son of Uriah the priest, and with him *was* Eleazar the son of Phinehas; and with them *were* the Levites, Jozabad the son of Jeshua and Noadiah the son of Binnui. 34*A notation was made* for everything

by number and weight, and all the weight was recorded at that time.

35^The exiles who had come from the captivity offered burnt offerings to the God of Israel: twelve bulls for all Israel, ninety-six rams, seventy-seven lambs, twelve male goats for a sin offering, all as a burnt offering to the LORD. 36Then ^they delivered the king's edicts to ᴮthe king's satraps and the governors *in the provinces* beyond the *Euphrates* River, and they supported the people and the house of God.

MIXED MARRIAGES

9 Now when these things had been completed, the officials approached me, saying, "The people of Israel and the priests and the Levites have not separated themselves from the peoples of the lands, ^as to their abominations, *those* of the Canaanites, the Hittites, the Perizzites, the Jebusites, the Ammonites, the Moabites, the Egyptians, and the Amorites. 2For ^they have taken some of their daughters *as wives* for themselves and for their sons, so that the holy line has intermingled with the peoples of the lands; indeed, the hands of the officials and the leaders have taken the lead in this unfaithfulness." 3When I heard about this matter, I ^tore my garment and my robe, and pulled out some of the hair from my head and my beard, and ᴮsat down appalled. 4Then

8:25^Ezra 7:15, 16   8:26^Ezra 1:9-11   8:28^Lev 21:6-8   8:29^Ezra 8:33, 34   8:30^Ezra 1:9 8:31^Ezra 8:15, 21   8:32^Neh 2:11   8:33^Ezra 8:30 8:35^Ezra 2:1   8:36^Ezra 7:21-24   ᴮEzra 4:7 9:1^Lev 18:24-30   9:2^Deut 7:3; Ezra 10:2, 18 9:3^2 Kin 18:37   ᴮNeh 1:4

8:26 ¹About 24 tons or 22 metric tons   ²About 3.75 tons or 3.4 metric tons   8:27 ¹A coin weighing about 0.25 oz. or 7 gm

everyone who was frightened by the words of the God of Israel on account of the unfaithfulness of the exiles gathered to me, and I sat appalled until ^the evening offering.

PRAYER OF CONFESSION

5 But at the evening offering I stood up from my humiliation, even with my garment and my robe torn, and I bowed down on my knees and ^spread out my hands to the LORD my God; 6 and I said, "My God, I am ashamed and humiliated to lift up my face to You, my God, for our wrongful deeds have risen above our heads, and our ^guilt has grown even to the heavens. 7 ^Since the days of our fathers to this day we *have been* in great guilt, and because of our wrongful deeds we, our kings, *and* our priests have been handed over to the kings of the lands, to the sword, to captivity, to plunder, and to open shame, as *it is* this day. 8 But now for a brief moment grace has been *shown* from the LORD our God, to leave us an escaped remnant and to give us a 1,^peg in His holy place, so that our God may ^Benlighten our eyes and grant us a little reviving in our bondage. 9 ^For we are slaves; yet in our bondage our God has not abandoned us, but has extended favor to us in the sight of the kings of Persia, to give us reviving to erect the house of our God, to restore its ruins, and to give us a wall in Judah and Jerusalem.

10 "And now, our God, what shall we say after this? For we have abandoned Your commandments, 11 which You have commanded by Your servants the prophets, saying, 'The land which you are entering to possess is an unclean land with the uncleanness of the peoples of the lands, with their abominations which have filled it from end to end, *and* ^with their impurity. 12 So now do not ^give your daughters to their sons nor take their daughters for your sons, and ^Bnever seek their peace or their prosperity, so that you may be strong and may eat the good *things* of the land, and leave *it* as an inheritance to your sons forever.' 13 And after everything that has come upon us for our evil deeds and ^our great guilt, since You our God have spared *us by inflicting* less than our wrongdoing *deserves,* and have given us *such* an escaped remnant as this, 14 shall we again break Your commandments and intermarry with the peoples who commit these abominations? ^Would You not be angry with us to the point of destruction, until there would be no remnant nor any who would escape? 15 LORD God of Israel, ^You are righteous, for we have been left an escaped remnant, as *it is* this day; behold, we are before You in our guilt, for ^Bno one can stand before You because of this."

RECONCILIATION WITH GOD

10 Now ^while Ezra was praying and making confession, weeping and prostrating himself before the house of God, a very large assembly, men, women, and children, gathered to him from Israel; for the people wept greatly. 2 Shecaniah the son of Jehiel, one of the sons of Elam, said to Ezra, "^We have been unfaithful to our God

9:4^Ex 29:39   9:5^Ex 9:29   9:6^Ezra 9:13, 15; Rev 18:5   9:7^2 Chr 29:6; Ps 106:6   9:8^Is 22:23   ^BPs 13:3   9:9^Neh 9:36   9:11^Ezra 6:21   9:12^Ex 34:15, 16   ^BDeut 23:6   9:13^Ezra 9:6, 7   9:14^Deut 9:8, 14   9:15^Neh 9:33   ^BPs 130:3   10:1^Dan 9:4, 20   10:2^Ezra 9:2; Neh 13:27

9:8 1 I.e., a foothold

and have married foreign women from the peoples of the land; yet now there is hope for Israel in spite of this. ³So now ᴬlet's make a covenant with our God to send away all the wives and their children, following the counsel of ¹my lord and of those who fear the commandment of our God; and let it be done ᴮaccording to the Law. ⁴Arise! For *this* matter is your responsibility, but we will be with you; ᴬbe courageous and act."

⁵Then Ezra stood and ᴬmade the leading priests, the Levites, and all Israel take an oath that they would do according to this proposal; so they took the oath. ⁶Then Ezra rose from before the house of God and went into the chamber of Jehohanan the son of Eliashib. Although he went there, ᴬhe did not eat bread nor drink water, because he was mourning over the unfaithfulness of the exiles. ⁷So they made a proclamation throughout Judah and Jerusalem to all the exiles, that they were to assemble at Jerusalem, ⁸and that whoever did not come within three days, in accordance with the counsel of the leaders and the elders, all his property would be forfeited, and he himself would be excluded from the assembly of the exiles.

⁹So all the men of Judah and Benjamin assembled at Jerusalem within the three days. It was the ninth month on the twentieth of the month, and all the people sat in the public square *before* the house of God, ᴬtrembling because of this matter and the *heavy* rain. ¹⁰Then Ezra the priest stood up and said to them, "You have been unfaithful and have married foreign wives, adding to the guilt of Israel. ¹¹Now therefore, ᴬmake confession to the LORD God of your fathers and do His will; and separate yourselves from the peoples of the land and from the foreign wives." ¹²Then all the assembly replied with a loud voice, "It is our duty to do exactly as you have said! ¹³However, there are many people, it is the rainy season, and we are not able to stand in the open. Nor *can* the task *be done* in one or two days, because we have done a great wrong in this matter. ¹⁴Please let our leaders represent all the assembly and have all those in our cities who have married foreign wives come at appointed times, together with the elders and judges of each city, until the ᴬfierce anger of our God on account of this matter is turned away from us." ¹⁵Only Jonathan the son of Asahel and Jahzeiah the son of Tikvah opposed this, with Meshullam and Shabbethai the Levite supporting them.

¹⁶But the exiles did so. And Ezra the priest selected men *who were* the heads of fathers' *households* for *each of* their father's households, all of them by name. So they convened on the first day of the tenth month to investigate the matter. ¹⁷And they finished *investigating* all the men who had married foreign wives by the first day of the first month.

LIST OF OFFENDERS

¹⁸Now among the sons of the priests who had married foreign wives were found of the sons of ᴬJeshua the son of Jozadak, and his

10:3ᴬ2 Chr 34:31   ᴮDeut 7:2, 3   10:4ᴬ1 Chr 28:10
10:5ᴬNeh 5:12; 13:25   10:6ᴬDeut 9:18
10:9ᴬ1 Sam 12:18; Ezra 9:4
10:11ᴬLev 26:40; Prov 28:13   10:14ᴬ2 Kin 23:26;
2 Chr 28:11-13   10:18ᴬHag 1:1, 12; Zech 3:1

10:3¹Or *the Lord*

brothers: Maaseiah, Eliezer, Jarib, and Gedaliah. [19] They pledged to send away their wives, and being guilty, ^*they offered* a ram of the flock for their guilt. [20] Of the sons of Immer, *there were* Hanani and Zebadiah; [21] and of the sons of Harim: Maaseiah, Elijah, Shemaiah, Jehiel, and Uzziah; [22] and of the sons of Pashhur: Elioenai, Maaseiah, Ishmael, Nethanel, Jozabad, and Elasah.

[23] Of the Levites *there were* Jozabad, Shimei, Kelaiah (that is, Kelita), Pethahiah, Judah, and Eliezer.

[24] Of the singers *there was* Eliashib; and of the gatekeepers: Shallum, Telem, and Uri.

[25] Of Israel, of the sons of ^Parosh *there were* Ramiah, Izziah, Malchijah, Mijamin, Eleazar, Malchijah, and Benaiah; [26] and of the sons of Elam: Mattaniah, Zechariah, Jehiel, Abdi, Jeremoth, and Elijah; [27] and of the sons of ^Zattu: Elioenai, Eliashib, Mattaniah, Jeremoth, Zabad, and Aziza; [28] and of the sons of Bebai: Jehohanan, Hananiah, Zabbai, *and* Athlai; [29] and of the sons of Bani: Meshullam, Malluch

and Adaiah, Jashub, Sheal, *and* Jeremoth; [30] and of the sons of Pahathmoab: Adna and Chelal, Benaiah, Maaseiah, Mattaniah, Bezalel, Binnui, and Manasseh; [31] and *of* the sons of Harim: Eliezer, Isshijah, ^Malchijah, Shemaiah, Shimeon, [32] Benjamin, Malluch, *and* Shemariah; [33] of the sons of Hashum: Mattenai, Mattattah, Zabad, Eliphelet, Jeremai, Manasseh, *and* Shimei; [34] of the sons of Bani: Maadai, Amram, Uel, [35] Benaiah, Bedeiah, Cheluhi, [36] Vaniah, Meremoth, Eliashib, [37] Mattaniah, Mattenai, Jaasu, [38] Bani, Binnui, Shimei, [39] Shelemiah, Nathan, Adaiah, [40] Machnadebai, Shashai, Sharai, [41] Azarel, Shelemiah, Shemariah, [42] Shallum, Amariah, *and* Joseph. [43] Of the sons of ^Nebo *there were* Jeiel, Mattithiah, Zabad, Zebina, Jaddai, Joel, *and* Benaiah. [44] All of these men had married ^foreign wives, and some of them had wives *by whom* they had children.

10:19 ^Lev 5:15; 6:6   10:25 ^Ezra 2:3; Neh 7:8
10:27 ^Ezra 2:8; Neh 7:13   10:31 ^Neh 3:11
10:43 ^Num 32:38; Ezra 2:29   10:44 ^1 Kin 11:1-3; Ezra 10:3

NEHEMIAH

NEHEMIAH'S GRIEF FOR THE EXILES

1 The words of ^Nehemiah the son of Hacaliah.

Now it happened in the month Chislev, *in* the twentieth year, while I was in ^Susa the capitol, ²that ^Hanani, one of my brothers, and some men from Judah came; and I asked them about the Jews who had escaped and had survived the captivity, and about Jerusalem. ³And they said to me, "The remnant there in the province who survived the captivity are in great distress and ^disgrace, and ^the wall of Jerusalem is broken down and ^its gates have been burned with fire."

⁴Now when I heard these words, ^I sat down and wept and mourned for days; and I was fasting and praying before the God of heaven. ⁵I said, "Please, LORD God of heaven, ^the great and awesome God, who keeps the covenant and faithfulness for those who love Him and keep His commandments: ⁶let Your ear now be attentive and Your eyes open, to hear the prayer of Your servant which I am praying before You now, day and night, on behalf of the sons of Israel Your servants, ^confessing the sins of the sons of Israel which we have committed against You; I and my father's house have sinned. ⁷^We have acted very corruptly against You and have not kept the commandments, nor the statutes, nor the ordinances which You commanded Your servant Moses. ⁸Remember, please, the word which You commanded Your servant

Moses, saying, '^If you are unfaithful, I will scatter you among the peoples; ⁹^but *if* you return to Me and keep My commandments and do them, though those of you who have been scattered were in the most remote part of the heavens, I will gather them from there and bring them ^to the place where I have chosen to have My name dwell.' ¹⁰^They are Your servants and Your people whom You redeemed by Your great power and by Your strong hand. ¹¹Please, Lord, may Your ear be attentive to the prayer of Your servant and the prayer of Your servants who delight to revere Your name, and please make Your servant successful today and grant him mercy before this man."

Now I was the ^cupbearer to the king.

NEHEMIAH'S PRAYER ANSWERED

2 And it came about in the month Nisan, in the twentieth year of King ^Artaxerxes, that wine *was* before him, and I picked up the wine and gave it to the king. Now I had not been sad in his presence. ²So the king said to me, "Why is your face sad, though you are not ill? ^This is nothing but sadness of heart." Then I was very much afraid. ³And I said to the king, "May the king live forever. Why should

---

1:1 ^Neh 10:1   ᴮEsth 1:2   1:2 ^Neh 7:2   1:3 ^Neh 2:17
ᴮNeh 2:3   1:4 ^Ezra 9:3; 10:1   1:5 ^Neh 4:14; Dan 9:4
1:6 ^Ezra 10:1; Dan 9:20   1:7 ^Dan 9:5   1:8 ^Lev 26:33
1:9 ^Deut 30:2, 3   ᴮDeut 12:5   1:10 ^Ex 32:11;
Deut 9:29   1:11 ^Gen 40:21; Neh 2:1   2:1 ^Ezra 7:1
2:2 ^Prov 15:13

my face not be sad ^when the city, the site of my fathers' tombs, is desolate and its gates have been consumed by fire?" ⁴Then the king said to me, "What would you request?" ^So I prayed to the God of heaven. ⁵Then I said to the king, "If it pleases the king, and if your servant has found favor before you, *I request* that you send me to Judah, to the city of my fathers' tombs, that I may rebuild it." ⁶Then the king said to me, with the queen sitting beside him, "How long will your journey be, and when will you return?" So it pleased the king to send me, and ^I gave him a definite time. ⁷And I said to the king, "If it pleases the king, let letters be given me ^for the governors *of the provinces* beyond the River, so that they will allow me to pass through until I come to Judah, ⁸and a letter to Asaph the keeper of the king's forest, so that he will give me timber to make beams for the gates of ^the citadel which is by the temple, for the wall of the city, and for the house to which I will go." And the king granted *them* to me because ᴮthe good hand of my God *was* on me.

⁹Then I came to the governors *of the provinces* beyond the *Euphrates* River and gave them the king's letters. Now ^the king had sent with me officers of the army and horsemen. ¹⁰And when ^Sanballat the Horonite and Tobiah the Ammonite official heard *about it,* it was very displeasing to them that someone had come to seek the welfare of the sons of Israel.

NEHEMIAH INSPECTS JERUSALEM'S WALLS

¹¹So I ^came to Jerusalem and was there for three days. ¹²And I got up in the night, I and a few men with me. I did not tell anyone what my God was putting into my mind to do for Jerusalem, and there was no animal with me except the animal on which I was riding. ¹³So I went out at night by ^the Valley Gate in the direction of the Dragon's Spring and *on* to the Dung Gate, and I was inspecting the walls of Jerusalem which were broken down and its gates which had been consumed by fire. ¹⁴Then I passed on to the Fountain Gate and ^the King's Pool, but there was no place for my mount to pass. ¹⁵So I was going up at night by the ^ravine and inspecting the wall. Then I entered the Valley Gate again and returned. ¹⁶However, the officials did not know where I had gone or what I was doing; nor had I as yet told the Jews, the priests, the nobles, the officials, or the rest who were doing the work.

¹⁷Then I said to them, "You see the bad situation we are in, that ^Jerusalem is desolate and its gates have been burned by fire. Come, let's rebuild the wall of Jerusalem so that we will no longer be a disgrace." ¹⁸And I told them how the hand of my God had been favorable to me and also about the king's words which he had spoken to me. Then they said, "Let's arise and build." ^So they put their hands to the good *work.* ¹⁹But when Sanballat the Horonite and Tobiah the Ammonite official, and ^Geshem the Arab heard *about it,* they mocked us and despised us, and said, "What is this thing that

2:3 ^Neh 1:3; Jer 52:12-14   2:4 ^Neh 1:4
2:6 ^Neh 13:6   2:7 ^Ezra 7:21; 8:36   2:8 ^Neh 7:2
ᴮEzra 7:6   2:9 ^Ezra 8:22   2:10 ^Neh 2:19; 4:1
2:11 ^Ezra 8:32   2:13 ^Neh 3:13   2:14 ^2 Kin 20:20
2:15 ^John 18:1   2:17 ^Neh 1:3   2:18 ^2 Sam 2:7
2:19 ^Neh 6:6

you are doing? ^Are you rebelling against the king?" ²⁰So I answered them and said to them, "^The God of heaven will make us successful; therefore we His servants will arise and build, but you have no part, right, or memorial in Jerusalem."

BUILDERS OF THE WALLS

3 Then Eliashib the high priest arose with his brothers the priests and built the Sheep Gate; they consecrated it and installed its doors. They consecrated the wall to ^the Tower of the Hundred *and* ᴮthe Tower of Hananel. ²And next to him ^the men of Jericho built, and next to them Zaccur the son of Imri built.

³Now the sons of Hassenaah built ^the Fish Gate; they laid its beams and installed its doors with its bolts and bars. ⁴Next to them Meremoth the son of Uriah the son of Hakkoz made repairs. And next to him Meshullam the son of Berechiah the son of Meshezabel made repairs. And next to him Zadok the son of Baana *also* made repairs. ⁵Moreover, next to him the Tekoites made repairs, but their nobles did not support the work of their masters.

⁶Now Joiada the son of Paseah and Meshullam the son of Besodeiah repaired ^the Ancient Gate; they laid its beams and installed its doors with its bolts and its bars. ⁷Next to them Melatiah the Gibeonite and Jadon the Meronothite, the men of Gibeon and of Mizpah, also made repairs for the official seat of the ^governor *of the province* beyond the *Euphrates* River. ⁸Next to him Uzziel the son of Harhaiah of the goldsmiths made repairs. And next to him Hananiah, one of the perfumers, made repairs,

and they restored Jerusalem as far as ^the Broad Wall. ⁹And next to them Rephaiah the son of Hur, ^the official of half the district of Jerusalem, made repairs. ¹⁰Next to them Jedaiah the son of Harumaph made repairs opposite his house. And next to him Hattush the son of Hashabneiah made repairs. ¹¹Malchijah the son of Harim and Hasshub the son of Pahath-moab repaired another section and ^the Tower of Furnaces. ¹²Next to him Shallum the son of Hallohesh, ^the official of half the district of Jerusalem, made repairs, he and his daughters.

¹³Hanun and the inhabitants of Zanoah repaired ^the Valley Gate. They built it and installed its doors with its bolts and its bars, and a ¹thousand cubits of the wall to the Dung Gate.

¹⁴And Malchijah the son of Rechab, the official of the district of ^Beth-haccherem repaired the Dung Gate. He built it and installed its doors with its bolts and its bars.

¹⁵Shallum the son of Col-hozeh, the official of the district of Mizpah, repaired the Fountain Gate. He built it, made a roof for it, and installed its doors with its bolts and its bars, and the wall of the Pool of Shelah at ^the king's garden as far as ᴮthe steps that descend from the city of David. ¹⁶After him Nehemiah the son of Azbuk, official of half the district of Beth-zur, made repairs as far as *a point* opposite the tombs of David, and as far as

2:20 ^Ezra 4:3   3:1 ^Neh 12:39   ᴮJer 31:38
3:2 ^Neh 7:36   3:3 ^Neh 12:39   3:6 ^Neh 12:39
3:7 ^Neh 2:7   3:8 ^Neh 12:38   3:9 ^Neh 3:12, 17
3:11 ^Neh 12:38   3:12 ^Neh 3:9   3:13 ^Neh 2:13
3:14 ^Jer 6:1   3:15 ^2 Kin 25:4   ᴮNeh 12:37

3:13 ¹About 1,500 ft. or 457 m

^the artificial pool and the house of the mighty men. 17 After him the Levites carried out repairs *under* Rehum the son of Bani. Next to him Hashabiah, the official of half the district of Keilah, carried out repairs for his district. 18 After him their brothers carried out repairs *under* Bavvai the son of Henadad, official of *the other* half of the district of Keilah. 19 And next to him Ezer the son of Jeshua, the official of Mizpah, repaired another section in front of the ascent of the armory ^at the Angle. 20 After him Baruch the son of Zabbai zealously repaired another section, from the Angle to the doorway of the house of ^Eliashib the high priest. 21 After him Meremoth the son of Uriah the son of Hakkoz repaired another section, from the doorway of Eliashib's house even as far as the end of his house. 22 And after him the priests, ^the men of the 'vicinity, carried out repairs. 23 After them Benjamin and Hasshub carried out repairs in front of their house. After them Azariah the son of Maaseiah, son of Ananiah, carried out repairs beside his house. 24 After him Binnui the son of Henadad repaired another section, from the house of Azariah as far as ^the Angle and as far as the corner. 25 Palal the son of Uzai *made repairs* in front of the Angle and the tower projecting from the upper house of the king, which is by ^the courtyard of the guard. After him Pedaiah the son of Parosh *made repairs*. 26 Now the temple servants living in ^Ophel *made repairs* as far as the front of the Water Gate toward the east and the projecting tower. 27 After them ^the Tekoites repaired another section in front of the great projecting tower and as far as the wall of Ophel.

28 Above ^the Horse Gate the priests carried out repairs, each in front of his house. 29 After them Zadok the son of Immer carried out repairs in front of his house. And after him Shemaiah the son of Shecaniah, the keeper of the East Gate, carried out repairs. 30 After him Hananiah the son of Shelemiah, and Hanun the sixth son of Zalaph, repaired another section. After him Meshullam the son of Berechiah carried out repairs in front of his own quarters. 31 After him Malchijah, one of ^the goldsmiths, carried out repairs as far as the house of the temple servants and of the merchants, in front of the Inspection Gate and as far as the upper room of the corner. 32 And between the upper room of the corner and ^the Sheep Gate the goldsmiths and the merchants carried out repairs.

WORK IS RIDICULED

4 Now it came about that when ^Sanballat heard that we were rebuilding the wall, he became furious and very angry, and he mocked the Jews. 2 And he spoke in the presence of his brothers and ^the wealthy people of Samaria and said, "What are these feeble Jews doing? Are they going to restore *the temple* for themselves? Can they offer sacrifices? Can they finish *it* in a day? Can they revive the stones from the heaps of rubble, even the burned ones?" 3 Now Tobiah

3:16 ^2 Kin 20:20; Is 7:3   3:19 ^2 Chr 26:9
3:20 ^Neh 3:1   3:22 ^Neh 12:28   3:24 ^Neh 3:19
3:25 ^Jer 32:2   3:26 ^Neh 11:21   3:27 ^Neh 3:5
3:28 ^2 Chr 23:15; Jer 31:40   3:31 ^Neh 3:8, 32
3:32 ^Neh 3:1; 12:39   4:1 ^Neh 2:10   4:2 ^Ezra 4:9, 10

3:22 'I.e., the lower Jordan Valley

the Ammonite *was* near him, and he said, "Even what they are building—^if a fox were to jump *on it,* it would break their stone wall down!"

⁴Hear, O our God, how we are *an object of* contempt! ^Return their taunting on their own heads, and turn them into plunder in a land of captivity. ⁵Do not ^forgive their guilt and do not let their sin be wiped out before You, for they have demoralized the builders.

⁶So we built the wall, and the entire wall was joined together to half its *height,* for the people had a mind to work.

⁷Now when Sanballat, Tobiah, the Arabs, the Ammonites, and the Ashdodites heard that the repair of the walls of Jerusalem went on, *and* that the breaches began to be closed, they were very angry. ⁸So all of them ^conspired together to come to fight against Jerusalem and to cause confusion in it.

DISCOURAGEMENT OVERCOME

⁹But we prayed to our God, and because of them we ^set up a guard against them day and night.

¹⁰And so in Judah it was said:
"The strength of the burden
    bearers is failing,
Yet there is much rubble;
And we ourselves are unable
To rebuild the wall."

¹¹And our enemies said, "They will not know or see until we come among them, kill them, and put a stop to the work." ¹²When the Jews who lived near them came and told us ten times, "They will come up against us from every place where you may turn," ¹³then I stationed *men* in the lowest parts of the space behind the wall, the exposed places, and I ^stationed the people in families with their swords, spears, and bows. ¹⁴When I saw *their fear,* I stood and said to the nobles, the officials, and the rest of the people: "Do not be afraid of them; remember the Lord who is great and awesome, and ^fight for your brothers, your sons, your daughters, your wives, and your houses."

¹⁵Now when our enemies heard that it was known to us, and that ^God had frustrated their plan, then all of us returned to the wall, each one to his work. ¹⁶And from that day *on,* half of my servants carried on the work while half of them kept hold of the spears, the shields, the bows, and the coats of mail; and the captains *were* behind all the house of Judah. ¹⁷Those who were rebuilding the wall and those who carried burdens carried with one hand doing the work, and the other keeping hold of a weapon. ¹⁸As for the builders, each *wore* his sword strapped to his waist as he built, while the trumpeter *stood* near me. ¹⁹And I said to the nobles, the officials, and the rest of the people, "The work is great and extensive, and we are separated on the wall far from one another. ²⁰At whatever place you hear the sound of the trumpet, assemble to us there. ^Our God will fight for us."

²¹So we carried on the work with half of them holding spears from dawn until the stars appeared. ²²At that time I also said to the people, "Each man with his servant shall spend the night within Jerusalem,

4:3 ^Lam 5:18   4:4 ^Ps 79:12   4:5 ^Ps 69:27, 28; Jer 18:23   4:8 ^Ps 83:3   4:9 ^Neh 4:11   4:13 ^Neh 4:17, 18   4:14 ^2 Sam 10:12   4:15 ^2 Sam 17:14   4:20 ^Ex 14:14; Deut 1:30

so that they may be a guard for us by night and a laborer by day." [23]So neither I, my brothers, my servants, nor the men of the guard who followed me—none of us removed our clothes; each *took* his weapon *even to* the water.

CHARGING INTEREST ABOLISHED

5 Now ^there was a great outcry of the people and of their wives against their Jewish brothers. [2]For there were those who said, "We, our sons, and our daughters are many; therefore let's ^get grain so that we may eat and live." [3]And there were *others* who said, "We are mortgaging our fields, our vineyards, and our houses so that we might get grain because of the famine." [4]There also were those who said, "We have borrowed money ^for the king's tax *on* our fields and our vineyards. [5]And now our flesh is like the flesh of our brothers, our children like their children. Yet behold, ^we are forcing our sons and our daughters to be slaves, and some of our daughters are forced into bondage *already,* and we are helpless because our fields and vineyards belong to others."

[6]Then I was very ^angry when I heard their outcry and these words. [7]So I thought it over and contended with the nobles and the leading people, and said to them, "^You are lending at interest, each to his brother!" Therefore, I held a great assembly against them. [8]And I said to them, "We, according to our ability, ^have redeemed our Jewish brothers who were sold to the nations; now would you even sell your brothers that they may be sold to us?" Then they were silent and could not find a word *to say.*

[9]So I said, "The thing which you are doing is not good; should you not walk in the fear of our God because of ^the taunting of the nations, our enemies? [10]And likewise I, my brothers, and my servants are lending them money and grain. Please, let's do without this interest. [11]Please, give back to them this very day their fields, their vineyards, their olive groves, and their houses, as well as the hundredth *part* of the money and of the grain, the new wine, and the oil that you are charging as interest from them." [12]Then they said, "We will give *it* back and will require nothing from them; we will do exactly as you say." So I called the priests and made them ^take an oath to act in accordance with this promise. [13]I ^also shook out the front of my garment and said, "So may God shake out every person from his house and from his possessions who does not keep this promise; just so may he be shaken out and emptied." And all the assembly said, "Amen!" And they praised the LORD. Then the people acted in accordance with this promise.

NEHEMIAH'S EXAMPLE

[14]Furthermore, since the day that I was appointed to be their governor in the land of Judah, from the twentieth year to the ^thirty-second year of King Artaxerxes, for twelve years, neither I nor my kinsmen have eaten the governor's food *allowance.* [15]But the previous governors who were before me laid burdens on the people and took

5:1 ^Lev 25:35   5:2 ^Hag 1:6   5:4 ^Ezra 4:13; 7:24
5:5 ^Lev 25:39   5:6 ^Ex 11:8   5:7 ^Lev 25:36;
Deut 23:19, 20   5:8 ^Lev 25:48   5:9 ^Neh 4:4
5:12 ^Ezra 10:5   5:13 ^Acts 18:6   5:14 ^Neh 13:6

from them bread and wine besides forty shekels of silver; even their servants domineered the people. But I did not do so ^because of *my* fear of God. [16] I also applied myself to the work on this wall; we did not buy any land, and all my servants were gathered there for the work. [17] Moreover, ^*there were* at my table 150 Jews and officials, besides those who came to us from the nations that were around us. [18] Now ^that which was prepared for each day was one ox *and* six choice sheep; also birds were prepared for me, and every ten days all *sorts of* wine *were provided* in abundance. Yet for *all* this I did not request the governor's food *allowance,* because the forced labor was heavy on this people. [19] ^Remember me, my God, for good, *in return for* all that I have done for this people.

THE ENEMY'S PLOT

6 Now when it was reported to Sanballat, Tobiah, Geshem the Arab, and to the rest of our enemies that I had rebuilt the wall, and *that* no breach was left in it, ^although at that time I had not installed the doors in the gates, [2] Sanballat and Geshem sent *a message* to me, saying, "Come, let's meet together [1]at Chephirim in the plain of ^Ono." But they were plotting to harm me. [3] So I sent messengers to them, saying, "I am doing a great work and am unable to come down. Why should the work stop while I leave it and come down to you?" [4] Then they sent *messages* to me four times worded in this way, and I answered them with the same wording. [5] Then Sanballat sent his servant to me in the same way a fifth time with an open letter in his hand. [6] In

it was written: "It is reported among the nations, and Gashmu says, that ^you and the Jews intend to rebel; for that reason you are rebuilding the wall. And you are to be their king, according to these reports. [7] You have also appointed prophets to proclaim in Jerusalem concerning you, 'A king is in Judah!' And now it will be reported to the king according to these reports. So come now, let's consult together." [8] Then I sent *a message* to him saying, "*Nothing* like these things that you are saying has been done, but you are ^inventing them in your own mind." [9] For all of them were *trying* to frighten us, thinking, "They will become discouraged with the work and it will not be done." But now, ^*God,* strengthen my hands.

[10] When I entered the house of Shemaiah the son of Delaiah, son of Mehetabel, ^who was confined *at home,* he said, "Let's meet together in the house of God, within the temple, and let's close the doors of the temple, for they are coming to kill you, and they are coming to kill you at night." [11] But I said, "^Should a man like me flee? And who is there like me who would go into the temple to save his own life? I will not go in." [12] Then I realized that God certainly had not sent him, but he uttered *his* prophecy against me because Tobiah and Sanballat had hired him. [13] He was hired for this reason, ^that I would become frightened and act accordingly and sin, so that they might

---

5:15 ^Neh 5:9; Job 31:23   5:17 ^1 Kin 18:19
5:18 ^1 Kin 4:22, 23   5:19 ^Neh 13:14, 22, 31
6:1 ^Neh 3:1, 3   6:2 ^1 Chr 8:12   6:6 ^Neh 2:19
6:8 ^Job 13:4; Ps 52:2   6:9 ^Ps 138:3   6:10 ^Jer 36:5
6:11 ^Prov 28:1   6:13 ^Neh 6:6

6:2 [1] LXX *in the villages in*

have an evil report in order that they could taunt me. [14]Remember, my God, Tobiah and Sanballat in accordance with these works of theirs, and also Noadiah the prophetess and the rest of the prophets, who were *trying* to frighten me.

THE WALL IS FINISHED

[15]So [A]the wall was completed on the twenty-fifth of *the month* Elul, in fifty-two days. [16]When all our enemies heard *about it,* and all the nations surrounding us saw *it,* they lost their confidence; for [A]they realized that this work had been accomplished with the help of our God. [17]Also in those days many letters went from the nobles of Judah to Tobiah, and Tobiah's letters came to them. [18]For many in Judah were bound by oath to him because he was the son-in-law of Shecaniah the son of Arah, and his son Jehohanan had married the daughter of Meshullam the son of Berechiah. [19]Moreover, they were speaking about his good deeds in my presence, and were reporting my words to him. Then Tobiah sent letters to frighten me.

CENSUS OF FIRST RETURNED EXILES

7 Now when [A]the wall was rebuilt and I had installed the doors, and the gatekeepers, the singers, and the Levites were appointed, [2]then I put [A]Hanani my brother, and Hananiah the commander of the citadel, in charge of Jerusalem, for he was a faithful man and feared God more than many. [3]Then I said to them, "The gates of Jerusalem are not to be opened until the sun is hot, and while they are standing *guard, the gatekeepers* are to keep the doors shut and bolted. Also appoint guards from the inhabitants of Jerusalem, each at his post, and each in front of his own house." [4]Now the city was large and spacious, but the people in it were few and the houses were not built.

[5A]Then my God put it into my heart to assemble the nobles, the officials, and the *other* people to be enrolled by genealogies. Then I found the book of the genealogy of those who came up first, in which I found the following record:

[6A]These are the people of the province who came up from the captivity of the exiles whom Nebuchadnezzar the king of Babylon had taken into exile, and who returned to Jerusalem and Judah, each to his city, [7]who came with Zerubbabel, Jeshua, Nehemiah, Azariah, Raamiah, Nahamani, Mordecai, Bilshan, Mispereth, Bigvai, Nehum, *and* Baanah.

The number of men of the people of Israel: [8]the sons of Parosh, 2,172; [9]the sons of Shephatiah, 372; [10]the sons of Arah, 652; [11]the sons of Pahath-moab of the sons of Jeshua and Joab, 2,818; [12]the sons of Elam, 1,254; [13]the sons of Zattu, 845; [14]the sons of Zaccai, 760; [15]the sons of Binnui, 648; [16]the sons of Bebai, 628; [17]the sons of Azgad, 2,322; [18]the sons of Adonikam, 667; [19]the sons of Bigvai, 2,067; [20]the sons of Adin, 655; [21]the sons of Ater, of Hezekiah, 98; [22]the sons of Hashum, 328; [23]the sons of Bezai, 324; [24]the sons of Hariph, 112; [25]the sons of Gibeon, 95; [26]the men of Bethlehem and Netophah, 188; [27]the men of Anathoth, 128; [28]the

men of Beth-azmaveth, 42; [29]the men of Kiriath-jearim, Chephirah, and Beeroth, 743; [30]the men of Ramah and Geba, 621; [31]the men of Michmas, 122; [32]the men of Bethel and Ai, 123; [33]the men of the other Nebo, 52; [34]the sons of the other Elam, 1,254; [35]the sons of Harim, 320; [36]the men of Jericho, 345; [37]the sons of Lod, Hadid, and Ono, 721; [38]the sons of Senaah, 3,930.

[39]The priests: the sons of Jedaiah of the house of Jeshua, 973; [40]the sons of Immer, 1,052; [41]the sons of Pashhur, 1,247; [42]the sons of Harim, 1,017.

[43]The Levites: the sons of Jeshua, of Kadmiel, of the sons of Hodevah, 74. [44]The singers: the sons of Asaph, 148. [45]The gatekeepers: the sons of Shallum, the sons of Ater, the sons of Talmon, the sons of Akkub, the sons of Hatita, the sons of Shobai, 138.

[46]The temple servants: the sons of Ziha, the sons of Hasupha, the sons of Tabbaoth, [47]the sons of Keros, the sons of Sia, the sons of Padon, [48]the sons of Lebana, the sons of Hagaba, the sons of Shalmai, [49]the sons of Hanan, the sons of Giddel, the sons of Gahar, [50]the sons of Reaiah, the sons of Rezin, the sons of Nekoda, [51]the sons of Gazzam, the sons of Uzza, the sons of Paseah, [52]the sons of Besai, the sons of Meunim, the sons of Nephushesim, [53]the sons of Bakbuk, the sons of Hakupha, the sons of Harhur, [54]the sons of Bazlith, the sons of Mehida, the sons of Harsha, [55]the sons of Barkos, the sons of Sisera, the sons of Temah, [56]the sons of Neziah, the sons of Hatipha.

[57]The sons of Solomon's servants: the sons of Sotai, the sons of Sophereth, the sons of Perida, [58]the sons of Jaala, the sons of Darkon, the sons of Giddel, [59]the sons of Shephatiah, the sons of Hattil, the sons of Pochereth-hazzebaim, *and* the sons of Amon.

[60]All the temple servants and the sons of Solomon's servants *totaled* 392.

[61]These *were* the ones who came up from Tel-melah, Tel-harsha, Cherub, Addon, and Immer; but they could not provide evidence for their fathers' households or their descendants, whether they *were* of Israel: [62]the sons of Delaiah, the sons of Tobiah, the sons of Nekoda, 642. [63]And of the priests: the sons of Hobaiah, the sons of Hakkoz, the sons of Barzillai, who took a wife of the daughters of Barzillai, the Gileadite, and was named after them. [64]These searched *among* their ancestral registration, but it could not be located; therefore they were considered unclean *and disqualified* from the priesthood. [65]And the governor said to them that they were not to eat from the most holy things until a priest arose with ^Urim and Thummim.

TOTAL OF PEOPLE AND GIFTS

[66]The whole assembly together *totaled* 42,360, [67]besides their male slaves and their female slaves, of whom *there were* 7,337; and they had 245 male and female singers. [68]^*Their* horses were 736; *their* mules, 245; [69]*their* camels, 435; *their* donkeys, 6,720.

[70]Some of the heads of fathers' *households* gave to the work. The ^governor gave to the treasury a thousand gold drachmas, fifty basins, *and* 530 priests'

7:65 ^Ex 28:30; Deut 33:8   7:68 ^Ezra 2:66
7:70 ^Neh 7:65; 8:9

garments. [71]And some of the heads of fathers' *households* gave to the treasury *for* the work twenty thousand gold drachmas and 2,200 silver minas. [72]What the rest of the people gave was twenty thousand gold drachmas, two thousand silver minas, and sixty-seven priests' garments.

[73]Now [A]the priests, the Levites, the gatekeepers, the singers, some of the people, the temple servants, and all Israel lived in their cities.

And when the seventh month came, the sons of Israel *were* in their cities.

EZRA READS THE LAW

8 And all the people gathered as one person at the public square which was in front of the Water Gate, and they asked Ezra the scribe to bring [A]the Book of the Law of Moses which the LORD had given to Israel. [2]Then Ezra the priest brought the Law before the assembly of men, women, and all who *could* listen with understanding, on [A]the first day of the seventh month. [3]And he read from it before the public square which was in front of [A]the Water Gate, from early morning until midday, in the presence of men and women, those who could understand; and all the people were attentive to the Book of the Law. [4]Ezra the scribe stood at a wooden podium which they had made for the purpose. And beside him stood Mattithiah, Shema, Anaiah, Uriah, Hilkiah, and Maaseiah on his right; and Pedaiah, Mishael, Malchijah, Hashum, Hashbaddanah, Zechariah, *and* Meshullam on his left. [5]Then Ezra opened the book in the sight of all the people, for he was *standing*

above all the people; and when he opened it, all the people [A]stood up. [6]Then Ezra blessed the LORD, the great God. And all the people answered, "Amen, Amen!" with the raising of their hands; then [A]they kneeled down and worshiped the LORD with *their* faces to the ground. [7]Also Jeshua, Bani, Sherebiah, Jamin, Akkub, Shabbethai, Hodiah, Maaseiah, Kelita, Azariah, Jozabad, Hanan, Pelaiah, and the Levites explained the Law to the people while the people *remained* in their place. [8]They read from the book, from the Law of God, translating to give the sense so that they understood the reading.

THIS DAY IS HOLY

[9]Then Nehemiah, who was the governor, and Ezra the priest *and* scribe, and the Levites who taught the people said to all the people, "[A]This day is holy to the LORD your God; [B]do not mourn or weep." For all the people were weeping when they heard the words of the Law. [10]Then he said to them, "Go, eat the festival foods, drink the sweet drinks, and [A]send portions to him who has nothing prepared; for this day is holy to our Lord. Do not be grieved, for the joy of the LORD is your refuge." [11]So the Levites silenced all the people, saying, "Be still, for the day is holy; do not be grieved." [12]Then all the people went away to eat, drink, to send portions, and to celebrate a great feast, [A]because they understood the words which had been made known to them.

7:73[A]1 Chr 9:2   8:1[A]2 Chr 34:15   8:2[A]Lev 23:24
8:3[A]Neh 8:1   8:5[A]Judg 3:20; 1 Kin 8:12-14
8:6[A]Ex 4:31   8:9[A]Neh 8:2   [B]Deut 12:7, 12
8:10[A]Deut 26:11-13   8:12[A]Neh 8:7, 8

FEAST OF BOOTHS RESTORED

¹³ Then on the second day the heads of fathers' *households* of all the people, the priests, and the Levites were gathered to Ezra the scribe so that they might gain insight into the words of the Law. ¹⁴ And they found written in the Law how the Lord had commanded through Moses that the sons of Israel ^were to live in booths during the feast of the seventh month. ¹⁵ And that they were to proclaim and circulate a proclamation in all their cities and in Jerusalem, saying, "^Go out to the hills, and bring olive branches and wild olive branches, myrtle branches, palm branches, and branches of *other* trees with thick branches, to make booths, as it is written." ¹⁶ So the people went out and brought *them* and made booths for themselves, each ^on his roof, and in their courtyards and in the courtyards of the house of God, and in the public square at the Water Gate, and in the square at the Gate of Ephraim. ¹⁷ The entire assembly of those who had returned from the captivity made booths and lived in the booths. Indeed, the sons of Israel ^had not done so since the days of Joshua the son of Nun to that day. And there was very great rejoicing. ¹⁸^He read from the Book of the Law of God daily, from the first day to the last day. And they celebrated the feast seven days, and on the eighth day *there was* a festive assembly in accordance with the ordinance.

THE PEOPLE CONFESS THEIR SIN

9 Now on the twenty-fourth day of this month the sons of Israel assembled ^with fasting, in sackcloth and with ^dirt upon them.

² The ^descendants of Israel separated themselves from all foreigners, and they stood and confessed their sins and the wrongdoings of their fathers. ³ While ^they stood in their place, they read from the Book of the Law of the Lord their God for a fourth of the day; and for *another* fourth they confessed and worshiped the Lord their God. ⁴^Now on the Levites' platform stood Jeshua, Bani, Kadmiel, Shebaniah, Bunni, Sherebiah, Bani, *and* Chenani, and they cried out with a loud voice to the Lord their God.

⁵ Then the Levites, Jeshua, Kadmiel, Bani, Hashabneiah, Sherebiah, Hodiah, Shebaniah, *and* Pethahiah said, "Arise, bless the Lord your God forever and ever!

May Your glorious name be blessed
And exalted above all blessing and praise!
⁶   "You alone are the Lord.
You have made the heavens,
The heaven of heavens with all their ¹lights,
The earth and everything that is on it,
The seas and everything that is in them.
^You give life to all of them,
And the heavenly lights bow down before You.
⁷   "You are the Lord God,
Who chose Abram
And brought him out from ^Ur of the Chaldees,
And ^gave him the name Abraham.

8:14 ^Lev 23:34, 40, 42   8:15 ^Lev 23:40
8:16 ^Jer 32:29   8:17 ^2 Chr 7:8; 8:13   8:18 ^Deut 31:11
9:1 ^Ezra 8:23   ^1 Sam 4:12   9:2 ^Ezra 10:11; Neh 13:3
9:3 ^Neh 8:4   9:4 ^Neh 8:7   9:6 ^Col 1:16f
9:7 ^Gen 11:31   ^Gen 17:5

9:6 ¹ Lit *host;* i.e., sun, stars, etc.

8 "You found his heart faithful
   before You,
And made a covenant with
   him
To give *him* the land of the
   Canaanite,
Of the Hittite and the Amorite,
Of the Perizzite, the Jebusite,
   and the Girgashite—
To give *it* to his descendants.
And You ᴬhave fulfilled Your
   promise,
Because You are righteous.

9 "ᴬYou saw the affliction of our
   fathers in Egypt,
And heard their cry by the Red
   Sea.

10 "Then You performed ᴬsigns
   and wonders against
   Pharaoh,
Against all his servants and all
   the people of his land;
For You knew that they acted
   arrogantly toward them,
And You made a name for
   Yourself as *it is* this day.

11 "ᴬYou divided the sea before
   them,
So they passed through the
   midst of the sea on dry
   ground;
And You hurled ᴮtheir pursuers
   into the depths,
Like a stone into raging waters.

12 "And with a pillar of cloud ᴬYou
   led them by day,
And with a pillar of fire by
   night
To light for them the way
In which they were to go.

13 "Then ᴬYou came down on
   Mount Sinai,
And spoke with them from
   heaven;
You gave them ᴮjust ordinances
   and true laws,

Good statutes and
   commandments.

14 "So You made known to them
   ᴬYour holy Sabbath,
And gave them
   commandments, statutes,
   and law,
Through Your servant Moses.

15 "You ᴬprovided bread from
   heaven for them for their
   hunger,
You brought out water from a
   rock for them for their thirst,
And You told them to enter in
   order to take possession of
The land which You swore to
   give them.

16 "But they, our fathers, acted
   arrogantly;
They ᴬbecame stubborn and
   would not listen to Your
   commandments.

17 "They refused to listen,
And did not remember Your
   wondrous deeds which You
   performed among them;
So they became stubborn and
   ᴬappointed a leader to return
   to their slavery in Egypt.
But You are a God of
   forgiveness,
Gracious and compassionate,
Slow to anger and abounding
   in mercy;
And You did not abandon them.

18 "Even when they ᴬmade for
   themselves
A calf of cast metal
And said, 'This is your ¹god
Who brought you up from
   Egypt,'

9:8 ᴬJosh 21:43-45   9:9 ᴬEx 3:7   9:10 ᴬEx 7:8-12:32
9:11 ᴬEx 14:21   ᴮEx 15:1, 5, 10   9:12 ᴬEx 13:21, 22
9:13 ᴬEx 19:11, 18-20   ᴮPs 19:7-9   9:14 ᴬEx 16:23; 20:8
9:15 ᴬEx 16:4, 14, 15   9:16 ᴬDeut 1:26-33; Neh 9:29
9:17 ᴬNum 14:4   9:18 ᴬEx 32:4-8, 31

9:18 ¹Or *God;* i.e., an idol intended to represent God

And committed great
blasphemies,
19 ᴬYou, in Your great
compassion,
Did not abandon them in the
wilderness;
The pillar of cloud did not
leave them by day,
To guide them on their way,
Nor the pillar of fire by night,
to light for them the way in
which they were to go.
20 "Instead, ᴬYou gave Your good
Spirit to instruct them,
You did not withhold Your
manna from their mouth,
And You gave them water for
their thirst.
21 "Indeed, for ᴬforty years You
provided for them in the
wilderness *and* they were
not lacking;
Their clothes did not wear
out, nor did their feet swell
up.
22 "You also gave them kingdoms
and peoples,
And allotted *them* to them as a
boundary.
ᴬThey took possession of the
land of Sihon the king of
Heshbon
And the land of Og the king of
Bashan.
23 "You made their sons *as*
numerous as ᴬthe stars of
heaven,
And You brought them into
the land
Which You had told their
fathers to enter and
possess.
24 "ᴬSo their sons entered and
took possession of the land.
And ᴮYou subdued before them
the inhabitants of the land,
the Canaanites,

And You handed them over to
them, with their kings and
the peoples of the land,
To do with them as they
desired.
25 "They captured fortified cities
and a fertile land.
They took possession of
ᴬhouses full of every good
thing,
Carved out cisterns, vineyards,
olive groves,
Fruit trees in abundance.
So they ate, were filled and
ᴮput on fat,
And lived luxuriously in Your
great goodness.

26 "ᴬBut they became rebellious
and revolted against You,
And ᴮthrew Your Law behind
their backs
And killed Your prophets who
had admonished them
In order to bring them back to
You,
And they committed great
blasphemies.
27 "Therefore You ᴬhanded them
over to their enemies who
oppressed them,
But when they cried out to
You in the time of their
distress,
You heard from heaven, and
according to Your great
compassion
You gave them people who
saved them from the hand of
their enemies.
28 "But ᴬas soon as they had rest,
they did evil again before
You;

9:19 ᴬDeut 8:2-4; Neh 9:27, 31   9:20 ᴬNum 11:17;
Is 63:11-14   9:21 ᴬDeut 2:7   9:22 ᴬNum 21:21-35
9:23 ᴬGen 15:5; 22:17   9:24 ᴬJosh 11:23   ᴮJosh 18:1
9:25 ᴬDeut 6:11   ᴮDeut 32:15   9:26 ᴬJudg 2:11
ᴮ1 Kin 14:9   9:27 ᴬJudg 2:14   9:28 ᴬJudg 3:11

Therefore You abandoned them to the hand of their enemies, so that they ruled over them.

When they cried out again to You, You heard from heaven,

And [B]many times You rescued them according to Your compassion,

29 And admonished them in order to turn them back to Your Law.

Yet they acted arrogantly and did not listen to Your commandments but sinned against Your ordinances,

[A]Which, *if* a person follows them, then he will live by them.

And they [B]turned a stubborn shoulder and stiffened their neck, and would not listen.

30 "However, You remained patient with them for many years,

And [A]admonished them by Your Spirit through Your prophets,

Yet they would not listen.

Therefore You handed them over to the peoples of the lands.

31 "Nevertheless, in Your great compassion You [A]did not make an end of them or abandon them,

For You are a gracious and compassionate God.

32 "Now then, our God, [A]the great, the mighty, and the awesome God, who keeps *His* covenant and faithfulness,

Do not let all the hardship seem insignificant before You,

Which has happened to us, our kings, our leaders, our priests, our prophets, our fathers, and to all Your people,

From the days of the kings of Assyria to this day.

33 "However, [A]You are righteous in everything that has happened to us;

For You have dealt faithfully, but we have acted wickedly.

34 "For our kings, our leaders, our priests, and our fathers have not kept Your Law

Or paid attention to Your commandments and Your admonitions with which You have admonished them.

35 "But [A]they, in their own kingdom,

With Your great goodness which You gave them,

With the broad and rich land which You placed before them,

Did not serve You or turn from their evil deeds.

36 "Behold, [A]we are slaves today,

And as for the land which You gave to our fathers to eat its fruit and its bounty,

Behold, we are slaves on it.

37 "And [A]its abundant produce is for the kings

Whom You have set over us because of our sins;

They also rule over our bodies

And over our cattle as they please,

So we are in great distress.

9:28 [B]Ps 106:43   9:29 [A]Lev 18:5   [B]Zech 7:11
9:30 [A]2 Chr 36:15, 16; Neh 9:26, 29   9:31 [A]Jer 4:27
9:32 [A]Neh 1:5   9:33 [A]Gen 18:25; Jer 12:1
9:35 [A]Deut 28:47   9:36 [A]Deut 28:48
9:37 [A]Deut 28:33

A COVENANT RESULTS

38 "Now because of all this
ᴬWe are making an agreement
in writing;
And on the ᴮsealed *document
are the names of* our leaders,
our Levites, *and* our priests."

SIGNERS OF THE DOCUMENT

10 Now on the ᴬsealed *document
were the names of:*
Nehemiah the governor, the son of
Hacaliah, and Zedekiah, ²Seraiah,
Azariah, Jeremiah, ³Pashhur, Amariah, Malchijah, ⁴Hattush, Sheba-
niah, Malluch, ⁵Harim, Meremoth,
Obadiah, ⁶Daniel, Ginnethon,
Baruch, ⁷Meshullam, Abijah, Mijamin, ⁸Maaziah, Bilgai, *and* She-
maiah. These *were* the priests.
⁹And the Levites: Jeshua the son
of Azaniah, Binnui of the sons of
Henadad, *and* Kadmiel; ¹⁰also
their brothers Shebaniah, Hodiah,
Kelita, Pelaiah, Hanan, ¹¹Mica,
Rehob, Hashabiah, ¹²Zaccur,
Sherebiah, Shebaniah, ¹³Hodiah,
Bani, *and* Beninu. ¹⁴The leaders
of the people: Parosh, Pahath-
moab, Elam, Zattu, Bani, ¹⁵Bunni,
Azgad, Bebai, ¹⁶Adonijah, Bigvai,
Adin, ¹⁷Ater, Hezekiah, Azzur,
¹⁸Hodiah, Hashum, Bezai, ¹⁹Har-
iph, Anathoth, Nebai, ²⁰Magpiash,
Meshullam, Hezir, ²¹Meshezabel,
Zadok, Jaddua, ²²Pelatiah, Hanan,
Anaiah, ²³Hoshea, Hananiah, Has-
shub, ²⁴Hallohesh, Pilha, Shobek,
²⁵Rehum, Hashabnah, Maaseiah,
²⁶Ahiah, Hanan, Anan, ²⁷Malluch,
Harim, *and* Baanah.

OBLIGATIONS OF THE DOCUMENT

²⁸Now the rest of the people, the
priests, the Levites, the gatekeepers, the singers, the temple servants, and ᴬall those who had
separated themselves from the
peoples of the lands to the Law of
God, their wives, their sons, and
their daughters, all those who had
knowledge and understanding,
²⁹are joining with their kinsmen,
their nobles, and are ᴬtaking on
themselves a curse and an oath to
walk in God's Law, which was given
through Moses, God's servant, and
to keep and to comply with all the
commandments of Gᴏᴅ our Lord,
and His ordinances and statutes;
³⁰and ᴬthat we will not give our
daughters to the peoples of the
land or take their daughters for
our sons. ³¹As for the peoples of
the land who bring wares or any
grain on the Sabbath day to sell, we
will not buy from them on the Sabbath or on *any* holy day; and we will
forgo *the crops of* the seventh year
and ᴬevery debt.

³²We also imposed on ourselves
the obligation to contribute yearly
ᴬa third of a shekel for the service
of the house of our God: ³³for the
ᴬshowbread, for the continual grain
offering, for the continual burnt
offering, the Sabbaths, the new
moons, for the appointed times,
for the holy things, and for the sin
offerings to make atonement for
Israel, and all the work of the house
of our God.

³⁴Likewise we cast lots ᴬfor the
supply of wood *among* the priests,
the Levites, and the people so that
they could bring it to the house of
our God, according to our fathers'
households, at set times annually,
to burn on the altar of the Lᴏʀᴅ
our God, as it is written in the Law;

9:38ᴬNeh 10:29 ᴮNeh 10:1 10:1ᴬNeh 9:38
10:28ᴬNeh 9:2 10:29ᴬNeh 5:12 10:30ᴬEx 34:16;
Deut 7:3 10:31ᴬDeut 15:1, 2 10:32ᴬEx 30:11-16;
Matt 17:24 10:33ᴬLev 24:5, 6; 2 Chr 2:4
10:34ᴬNeh 13:31

³⁵and so that they could bring the first fruits of our ground and ^the first fruits of all the fruit of every tree to the house of the LORD annually, ³⁶and ^bring to the house of our God the firstborn of our sons and of our cattle, and the firstborn of our herds and our flocks as it is written in the Law, for the priests who are ministering in the house of our God. ³⁷^We will also bring the first of our dough, our contributions, the fruit of every tree, the new wine, and the oil to the priests at the chambers of the house of our God, and the ᴮtithe of our ground to the Levites, for the Levites are they who receive the tithes in all the rural towns. ³⁸And ^the priest, the son of Aaron, shall be with the Levites when the Levites receive tithes, and the Levites shall bring up the tenth of the tithes to the house of our God, to the chambers of the storehouse. ³⁹For the sons of Israel and the sons of Levi shall bring the contribution of the grain, the new wine, and the oil to the chambers; the utensils of the sanctuary, the priests who are ministering, the gatekeepers, and the singers are there. So ^we will not neglect the house of our God.

TIME PASSES; HEADS OF PROVINCES

11 Now ^the leaders of the people lived in Jerusalem, but the rest of the people cast lots to bring one out of ten to live in Jerusalem, the holy city, while nine-tenths *remained* in the *other* cities. ²And the people blessed all the men who ^volunteered to live in Jerusalem.

³^Now these are the heads of the provinces who lived in Jerusalem, but in the cities of Judah each lived on his own property in their cities—the Israelites, the priests, the Levites, the temple servants, and the descendants of Solomon's servants. ⁴Some of the sons of Judah and some of the sons of Benjamin lived in Jerusalem. From the sons of Judah: Athaiah the son of Uzziah, the son of Zechariah, the son of Amariah, the son of Shephatiah, the son of Mahalalel, of the sons of Perez; ⁵and Maaseiah the son of Baruch, the son of Colhozeh, the son of Hazaiah, the son of Adaiah, the son of Joiarib, the son of Zechariah, the son of the Shilonite. ⁶All the sons of Perez who lived in Jerusalem were 468 able men.

⁷Now these are the sons of Benjamin: Sallu the son of Meshullam, the son of Joed, the son of Pedaiah, the son of Kolaiah, the son of Maaseiah, the son of Ithiel, the son of Jeshaiah; ⁸and after him Gabbai *and* Sallai, 928. ⁹Joel the son of Zichri was their overseer, and Judah the son of Hassenuah was second in command of the city.

¹⁰From the priests: Jedaiah the son of Joiarib, Jachin, ¹¹Seraiah the son of Hilkiah, the son of Meshullam, the son of Zadok, the son of Meraioth, the son of Ahitub, the overseer of the house of God, ¹²and their kinsmen who did the work of the temple, 822; and Adaiah the son of Jeroham, the son of Pelaliah, the son of Amzi, the son of Zechariah, the son of Pashhur, the son of Malchijah, ¹³and his kinsmen, heads of fathers' *households*, 242; and Amashsai the son of Azarel, the son of Ahzai, the son of

10:35^Ex 23:19; Deut 26:2   **10:36**^Ex 13:2
10:37^Lev 23:17   ᴮNum 18:21   **10:38**^Num 18:26
10:39^Neh 13:10, 11   **11:1**^Neh 7:4   **11:2**^Judg 5:9
11:3^1 Chr 9:2-34

Meshillemoth, the son of Immer, [14]and their brothers, valiant warriors, 128. And their overseer was Zabdiel, the son of Haggedolim.

[15]Now from the Levites: Shemaiah the son of Hasshub, the son of Azrikam, the son of Hashabiah, the son of Bunni; [16]and Shabbethai and Jozabad, from the leaders of the Levites, who were in charge of ^the outside work of the house of God; [17]and Mattaniah the son of Mica, the son of Zabdi, the son of Asaph, who was the leader in beginning the thanksgiving at prayer, and Bakbukiah, the second among his kinsmen; and Abda the son of Shammua, the son of Galal, the son of Jeduthun. [18]All the Levites in ^the holy city were 284.

[19]Also the gatekeepers: Akkub, Talmon, and their kinsmen who kept watch at the gates, were 172.

OUTSIDE JERUSALEM

[20]The rest of Israel, of the priests and of the Levites, were in all the cities of Judah, each ^on his own inheritance. [21]But ^the temple servants were living in Ophel, and Ziha and Gishpa were in charge of the temple servants.

[22]Now ^the overseer of the Levites in Jerusalem was Uzzi the son of Bani, the son of Hashabiah, the son of Mattaniah, the son of Mica, from the sons of Asaph, who were the singers for the service of the house of God. [23]^For there was a commandment from the king concerning them and a royal command for the singers day by day. [24]And Pethahiah the son of Meshezabel, of the sons ^of Zerah the son of Judah, was the [B]king's representative for every matter concerning the people.

[25]Now as for the villages with their fields, some of the sons of Judah lived in ^Kiriath-arba and its towns, in Dibon and its towns, and in Jekabzeel and its villages, [26]and in Jeshua, in Moladah, and Beth-pelet, [27]and in Hazar-shual, in Beersheba and its towns, [28]and in Ziklag, in Meconah and in its towns, [29]and in En-rimmon, in Zorah, and in Jarmuth, [30]Zanoah, Adullam, and their villages, Lachish and its fields, Azekah and its towns. So they camped from Beersheba as far as the Valley of Hinnom. [31]The sons of Benjamin also lived from Geba onward, at Michmash and Aija, at Bethel and its towns, [32]at Anathoth, Nob, Ananiah, [33]Hazor, Ramah, Gittaim, [34]Hadid, Zeboim, Neballat, [35]Lod, and Ono, the Valley of Craftsmen. [36]And from the Levites, some divisions in Judah belonged to Benjamin.

PRIESTS AND LEVITES WHO RETURNED TO JERUSALEM WITH ZERUBBABEL

12 Now these are ^the priests and the Levites who came up with Zerubbabel the son of Shealtiel, and Jeshua: Seraiah, Jeremiah, Ezra, [2]Amariah, Malluch, Hattush, [3]Shecaniah, Rehum, Meremoth, [4]Iddo, Ginnethoi, Abijah, [5]Mijamin, Maadiah, Bilgah, [6]Shemaiah and Joiarib, Jedaiah, [7]Sallu, Amok, Hilkiah, and Jedaiah. These were the heads of the priests and their kinsmen in the days of Jeshua.

[8]And the Levites were Jeshua, Binnui, Kadmiel, Sherebiah, Judah, and Mattaniah who was in charge of the songs of thanksgiving,

11:16 ^1 Chr 26:29   11:18 ^Neh 11:1   11:20 ^Neh 11:3
11:21 ^Neh 3:26   11:22 ^Neh 11:9, 14   11:23 ^Ezra 6:8;
7:20   11:24 ^Gen 38:30   [B]1 Chr 18:17
11:25 ^Josh 14:15   12:1 ^Ezra 2:1; 7:7

he and his brothers. ⁹Also Bakbukiah and Unni, their brothers, *stood* opposite them ᴬin *their* service divisions. ¹⁰Jeshua fathered Joiakim, Joiakim fathered Eliashib, Eliashib *fathered* Joiada, ¹¹Joiada fathered Jonathan, and Jonathan fathered Jaddua.

¹²Now in the days of Joiakim, the priests, the heads of fathers' *households* were: of Seraiah, Meraiah; of Jeremiah, Hananiah; ¹³of Ezra, Meshullam; of Amariah, Jehohanan; ¹⁴of Malluchi, Jonathan; of Shebaniah, Joseph; ¹⁵of Harim, Adna; of Meraioth, Helkai; ¹⁶of Iddo, Zechariah; of Ginnethon, Meshullam; ¹⁷of Abijah, Zichri; of Miniamin, of Moadiah, Piltai; ¹⁸of Bilgah, Shammua; of Shemaiah, Jehonathan; ¹⁹of Joiarib, Mattenai; of Jedaiah, Uzzi; ²⁰of Sallai, Kallai; of Amok, Eber; ²¹of Hilkiah, Hashabiah; *and* of Jedaiah, Nethanel.

THE CHIEF LEVITES

²²As for the Levites, the heads of fathers' *households* were registered in the days of Eliashib, Joiada, and Johanan, and Jaddua; so *were* the priests in the reign of Darius the Persian. ²³The sons of Levi, the heads of fathers' *households,* were registered in the Book of the Chronicles up to the days of Johanan the son of Eliashib. ²⁴And the heads of the Levites *were* Hashabiah, Sherebiah, and Jeshua the son of Kadmiel, with their brothers opposite them, ᴬto praise *and* give thanks, as prescribed by David the man of God, division corresponding to division. ²⁵Mattaniah, Bakbukiah, Obadiah, Meshullam, Talmon, *and* Akkub *were* gatekeepers keeping watch at ᴬthe storerooms of the gates. ²⁶These men *served* in the days of Joiakim the son of Jeshua, the son of Jozadak, and in the days of ᴬNehemiah the governor and Ezra the priest *and* scribe.

DEDICATION OF THE WALL

²⁷Now at the dedication of the wall of Jerusalem they sought out the Levites from all their places, to bring them to Jerusalem so that they could celebrate the dedication with joy, with songs of thanksgiving and with songs ᴬto the accompaniment of cymbals, harps, and lyres. ²⁸So the sons of the singers were assembled from the territory around Jerusalem, and from ᴬthe villages of the Netophathites, ²⁹from Beth-gilgal and from *their* fields in Geba and Azmaveth, because the singers had built themselves villages around Jerusalem. ³⁰The priests and the Levites ᴬpurified themselves; they also purified the people, the gates, and the wall.

PROCEDURES FOR THE TEMPLE

³¹Then I had the leaders of Judah come up on top of the wall, and I appointed two large choirs, the first proceeding to the right on top of the wall toward ᴬthe Dung Gate. ³²Hoshaiah and half of the leaders of Judah followed them, ³³with Azariah, Ezra, Meshullam, ³⁴Judah, Benjamin, Shemaiah, Jeremiah, ³⁵and some of the sons of the priests with trumpets; *and* Zechariah the son of Jonathan, the son of Shemaiah, the son of Mattaniah, the son of Micaiah, the son of Zaccur, the son of Asaph, ³⁶and his kinsmen, Shemaiah, Azarel,

12:9 ᴬNeh 12:24   12:24 ᴬNeh 11:17   12:25 ᴬ1 Chr 26:15
12:26 ᴬNeh 8:9   12:27 ᴬ1 Chr 15:16, 28
12:28 ᴬ1 Chr 9:16   12:30 ᴬNeh 13:22, 30
12:31 ᴬNeh 2:13

Milalai, Gilalai, Maai, Nethanel, Judah, *and* Hanani, ^with the musical instruments of David the man of God. And Ezra the scribe *went* before them. ³⁷At the Fountain Gate they went directly up ^the steps of the city of David by the stairway of the wall, above the house of David to the Water Gate on the east.

³⁸The second choir proceeded to the left, while I followed them with half of the people on the wall, ^above the Tower of Furnaces, to ᴮthe Broad Wall, ³⁹and above ^the Gate of Ephraim, by the Ancient Gate, by the Fish Gate, ᴮthe Tower of Hananel, and the Tower of the Hundred, as far as the Sheep Gate; and they stopped at the Gate of the Guard. ⁴⁰Then the two choirs took their positions in the house of God. So did I and half of the officials with me; ⁴¹and the priests, Eliakim, Maaseiah, Miniamin, Micaiah, Elioenai, Zechariah, and Hananiah, with the trumpets; ⁴²and Maaseiah, Shemaiah, Eleazar, Uzzi, Jehohanan, Malchijah, Elam, and Ezer. And the singers sang, with Jezrahiah *their* leader, ⁴³and on that day they offered great sacrifices and rejoiced because ^God had given them great joy, and the women and children rejoiced as well, so that the joy of Jerusalem was heard from far away.

⁴⁴On that day ^men were also appointed over the chambers for the supplies, the contributions, the first fruits, and the tithes, to gather into them from the fields of the cities the portions *required by* the Law for the priests and Levites; for Judah rejoiced over the priests and the Levites who served. ⁴⁵For they performed the worship of their God and the service of purification, together with the singers

and the gatekeepers ^in accordance with the command of David *and* of his son Solomon. ⁴⁶For in the days of David and ^Asaph, in ancient times, *there were* ᴮleaders of the singers, songs of praise and songs of thanksgiving to God. ⁴⁷So all Israel in the days of Zerubbabel and Nehemiah gave the portions *due* the singers and the gatekeepers as each day required, and they ^set apart the consecrated *portion* for the Levites, and the Levites set apart the consecrated *portion* for the sons of Aaron.

FOREIGNERS EXCLUDED

13 On that day the Book of Moses was ^read aloud as the people listened; and there was found written in it that no Ammonite or Moabite was ever to enter the assembly of God, ²because they did not meet the sons of Israel with bread and water, but ^hired Balaam against them to curse them. However, ᴮour God turned the curse into a blessing. ³So when they heard the Law, they excluded ^all foreigners from Israel.

TOBIAH EXPELLED AND THE TEMPLE CLEANSED

⁴Now prior to this, Eliashib the priest, ^who was appointed over the chambers of the house of our God, being related to Tobiah, ⁵had prepared a large room for him, where previously they used to put the grain offerings, the frankincense, the utensils and the tithes of grain, wine, and oil ^prescribed

12:36 ^Neh 12:24　12:37 ^Neh 3:15　12:38 ^Neh 3:11　ᴮNeh 3:8　12:39 ^Neh 8:16　ᴮNeh 3:1　12:43 ^Ps 9:2; 92:4　12:44 ^Neh 13:4, 5, 12, 13　12:45 ^1 Chr 25:1　12:46 ^2 Chr 29:30　ᴮ1 Chr 9:33　12:47 ^Num 18:21　13:1 ^Neh 9:3　13:2 ^Num 22:3-11　ᴮDeut 23:5　13:3 ^Ex 12:38　13:4 ^Neh 12:44　13:5 ^Num 18:21

for the Levites, the singers, and the gatekeepers, and the contributions for the priests. ⁶But during all this *time* I was not in Jerusalem, for in the thirty-second year of ^Artaxerxes king of Babylon I had come to the king. After some time, however, I requested a leave of absence from the king, ⁷and I came to Jerusalem and learned about the evil that Eliashib had committed for Tobiah, ^by preparing a room for him in the courtyards of the house of God. ⁸It was very displeasing to me, so I ^threw all of Tobiah's household articles out of the room. ⁹Then I gave an order, and ^they cleansed the rooms; and I returned the utensils of the house of God there with the grain offering and the frankincense.

TITHES RESTORED

¹⁰I also discovered that ^the portions of the Levites had not been given *to them,* so the Levites and the singers who performed the service had gone away, each to his own field. ¹¹So I reprimanded the officials and said, "^Why has the house of God been neglected?" Then I gathered them together and stationed them at their posts. ¹²All Judah then brought ^the tithe of the grain, wine, and oil into the storehouses. ¹³ *To be* in charge of the storehouses, I appointed Shelemiah the priest, Zadok the scribe, and Pedaiah from the Levites, and in addition to them was Hanan the son of Zaccur, the son of Mattaniah; for ^they were considered reliable, and it was their task to distribute to their kinsmen. ¹⁴^Remember me for this, my God, and do not wipe out my loyal deeds which I have performed for the house of my God and its services.

SABBATH RESTORED

¹⁵In those days I saw in Judah *people* who were treading wine presses ^on the Sabbath, and bringing in sacks of grain and loading *them* on donkeys, as well as wine, grapes, figs, and every *kind of* load, and they were bringing *them* into Jerusalem on the Sabbath day. So I admonished *them* on the day they sold food. ¹⁶Also people of Tyre were living there *who* imported fish and all *kinds of* merchandise, and sold *them* to the sons of Judah on the Sabbath, even in Jerusalem. ¹⁷Then ^I reprimanded the nobles of Judah and said to them, "What is this evil thing that you are doing, by profaning the Sabbath day? ¹⁸^Did your fathers not do the same, so that our God brought on us and on this city all this trouble? Yet you are adding to the wrath against Israel by profaning the Sabbath."

¹⁹And ^it came about that just as it became dark at the gates of Jerusalem before the Sabbath, I ordered that the doors be shut, and that they were not to open them until after the Sabbath. Then I stationed some of my servants at the gates *so that* no load would enter on the Sabbath day. ²⁰Once or twice the traders and merchants of every *kind of* merchandise spent the night outside Jerusalem. ²¹Then ^I warned them and said to them, "Why do you spend the night in front of the wall? If you do so again, I will use force against you." From that time *on* they did not come on the Sabbath. ²²And I ordered the Levites that ^they were

13:6 ^Ezra 6:22   13:7 ^Neh 13:5   13:8 ^John 2:13-16
13:9 ^2 Chr 29:5, 15, 16   13:10 ^Deut 12:19; Neh 10:37
13:11 ^Neh 10:39   13:12 ^Neh 10:37; Mal 3:10
13:13 ^Neh 7:2   13:14 ^Neh 5:19; 13:22, 31
13:15 ^Deut 5:12-14; Jer 17:22   13:17 ^Neh 13:11, 25
13:18 ^Ezra 9:13; Jer 17:21   13:19 ^Lev 23:32
13:21 ^Neh 13:15   13:22 ^1 Chr 15:12; Neh 12:30

to purify themselves and come as gatekeepers to sanctify the Sabbath day. *For* this also remember me, my God, and have compassion on me according to the greatness of Your mercy.

MIXED MARRIAGES FORBIDDEN

23 In those days I also saw that the Jews had ^married women from Ashdod, Ammon, *and* Moab. 24 As for their children, half spoke in the language of Ashdod, and none of them knew how to speak the language of Judah, but only the language of his own people. 25 So I quarreled with them and cursed them, and struck some of them and pulled out their hair, and ^made them swear by God, "You shall not give your daughters to their sons, nor take *any* of their daughters for your sons or for yourselves. 26 ^Did Solomon the king of Israel not sin regarding these things? ᴮYet among the many nations there was no king like him, and he was loved by his God, and God made him king over all Israel; *yet* the foreign women caused even him to sin. 27 Has it not then been reported about you that you have committed all this great evil ^by acting unfaithfully against our God, by marrying foreign women?" 28 Even one of the sons of Joiada, the son of Eliashib the high priest, *became* a son-in-law of ^Sanballat the Horonite, so I chased him away from me. 29 Remember them, my God, because they have defiled the priesthood and the ^covenant of the priesthood and the Levites.

30 ^So I purified them from everything foreign, and assigned duties to the priests and the Levites, each in his work, 31 and *I arranged* ^for the delivery of wood at appointed times and for the first fruits. Remember me, my God, for good.

13:23 ^Ezra 9:2; Neh 10:30 **13:25** ^Neh 10:29, 30
13:26 ^1 Kin 11:1 ᴮ1 Kin 3:13 **13:27** ^Ezra 10:2;
Neh 13:23 **13:28** ^Neh 2:10, 19; 4:1
13:29 ^Num 25:13 **13:30** ^Neh 10:30
13:31 ^Neh 10:34

ESTHER

THE BANQUETS OF THE KING

1 Now it happened in the days of ^Ahasuerus, the Ahasuerus who reigned from India to Cush over 127 provinces, ²in those days as King Ahasuerus sat on his royal throne which *was* at the citadel in ^Susa, ³in the third year of his reign ^he held a banquet for all his officials and attendants, the army *officers* of Persia and Media, the nobles and the officials of his provinces, in his presence. ⁴At that time he displayed the riches of his royal glory and the splendor of his great majesty for many days, 180 days.

⁵When these days were finished, the king held a banquet lasting seven days for all the people who were present at the citadel in Susa, from the greatest to the least, in the courtyard of ^the garden of the king's palace. ⁶*There were curtains of* fine white and violet linen held by cords of fine purple linen on silver rings and marble columns, *and* ^couches of gold and silver on a mosaic floor of porphyry, marble, mother-of-pearl, and mineral stones. ⁷Drinks were served in golden vessels of various kinds, and the royal wine was plentiful ^in proportion to the king's bounty. ⁸But the drinking was *done* according to the *royal* law; there was no compulsion, for so the king had given orders to each official of his household, that he was to do as each person pleased. ⁹Queen Vashti also held a banquet for the women in the palace which belonged to King Ahasuerus.

QUEEN VASHTI'S REFUSAL

¹⁰On the seventh day, when the heart of the king was ^cheerful with wine, he ordered Mehuman, Biztha, Harbona, Bigtha, Abagtha, Zethar, and Carkas, the seven eunuchs who served in the presence of King Ahasuerus, ¹¹to bring Queen Vashti before the king with *her* royal ^turban in order to display her beauty to the people and the officials, for she was beautiful. ¹²But Queen Vashti refused to come at the king's order delivered by the eunuchs. So the king became very angry, and his wrath burned within him.

¹³Then the king said to ^the wise men who understood the times— for it was the custom of the king *to speak* this way before all who knew *Persian* law and justice ¹⁴and were close to him, *namely,* Carshena, Shethar, Admatha, Tarshish, Meres, Marsena, and Memucan, the seven officials of Persia and Media ^who had access to the king's presence and sat in the first place in the kingdom— ¹⁵"According to law, what is to be done with Queen Vashti, since she did not obey the command of King Ahasuerus delivered by the eunuchs?" ¹⁶And in the presence of the king and the *other* officials, Memucan said, "Queen Vashti has wronged not only the king but *also* all the officials and all the peoples who are in all the

1:1^Ezra 4:6; Dan 9:1 1:2^Neh 1:1; Dan 8:2
1:3^Esth 2:18 1:5^Esth 7:7, 8 1:6^Ezek 23:41;
Amos 6:4 1:7^Esth 2:18 1:10^Judg 16:25
1:11^Esth 2:17; 6:8 1:13^Jer 10:7; Dan 2:2
1:14^2 Kin 25:19; Matt 18:10

provinces of King Ahasuerus. [17]For the queen's conduct will become known to all the women so as to make their own husbands despicable in their sight, when they say, 'King Ahasuerus commanded that Queen Vashti be brought in to his presence, but she did not come.' [18]And this day the wives of the officials of Persia and Media who have heard about the queen's conduct will talk *about it* to all the king's officials, and there will be plenty of contempt and anger. [19]If it pleases the king, let a royal edict be issued by him and let it be written in the laws of Persia and Media so ^that it cannot be repealed, that Vashti may not come into the presence of King Ahasuerus, and let the king give her royal position to another who is more worthy than she. [20]When the king's edict which he will make is heard throughout his kingdom, great as it is, then ^all women will give honor to their husbands, great and small."

[21]Now *this* word pleased the king and the officials, and the king did as Memucan proposed. [22]So he sent letters to all the king's provinces, to each province according to its script and to every people according to their language, that every man was to ^be the ruler in his own house and the one who speaks in the language of his own people.

VASHTI'S SUCCESSOR SOUGHT

2 After these things, when the anger of King Ahasuerus had subsided, he remembered Vashti and what she had done, and ^what had been decided regarding her. [2]Then the king's attendants, who served him, said, "^Let beautiful young virgins be sought for the king. [3]And may the king appoint overseers in ^all the provinces of his kingdom, and have them bring every beautiful young virgin to the citadel of Susa, to the harem, into the custody of Hegai, the king's eunuch, who is in charge of the women; and let their cosmetics be given *to them*. [4]Then let the young woman who pleases the king be queen in place of Vashti." And the suggestion pleased the king, and he did accordingly.

[5]There was a Jew at the citadel in Susa whose name was ^Mordecai, the son of Jair, the son of Shimei, the son of Kish, a Benjaminite, [6]^who had been taken from Jerusalem with the exiles who had been deported with Jeconiah king of Judah, whom Nebuchadnezzar the king of Babylon had deported. [7]He was the guardian to Hadassah, that is ^Esther, his uncle's daughter, for she had no father or mother. Now the young woman was beautiful of form and face, and when her father and her mother died, Mordecai took her as his own daughter.

ESTHER FINDS FAVOR

[8]So it came about, when the command and decree of the king were heard and many young ladies were gathered to the citadel of Susa into the custody of ^Hegai, that Esther was taken to the king's palace into the custody of Hegai, who was in charge of the women. [9]Now the young lady pleased him and found favor with him. So he quickly provided her with her ^cosmetics and food, gave her seven choice female

1:19^Esth 8:8; Dan 6:8 **1:20**^Eph 5:22;
Col 3:18 **1:22**^Eph 5:22-24 **2:1**^Esth 1:19, 20
2:2^1 Kin 1:2 **2:3**^Esth 1:1, 2 **2:5**^Esth 3:2
2:6^2 Kin 24:14, 15; 2 Chr 36:10 **2:7**^Esth 2:15
2:8^Esth 2:3, 15 **2:9**^Esth 2:3, 12

attendants from the king's palace, and transferred her and her attendants to the best place in the harem. ¹⁰ᴬEsther did not reveal her people or her kindred, because Mordecai had instructed her that she was not to reveal *them*. ¹¹And every day Mordecai walked back and forth in front of the courtyard of the harem to learn how Esther was and what was happening to her.

¹²Now when the turn came for each young woman to go in to King Ahasuerus, after the end of her twelve months under the regulations for the women—for the days of their beauty treatment were completed as follows: six months with oil of myrrh and six months with balsam oil and the cosmetics for women— ¹³the young woman would go in to the king in this way: anything that she desired was given her to take with her from the harem to the king's palace. ¹⁴In the evening she would enter and in the morning she would return to the second harem, to the custody of Shaashgaz, the king's eunuch who was in charge of the concubines. She would not go in to the king again, unless the king delighted in her and she was summoned by name.

¹⁵Now when the turn of Esther, ᴬthe daughter of Abihail the uncle of Mordecai who had taken her as his daughter, came to go in to the king, she did not request anything except what Hegai, the king's eunuch who was in charge of the women, advised. And Esther was finding favor in the eyes of all who saw her. ¹⁶So Esther was taken to King Ahasuerus in his royal palace in the tenth month, which is the month Tebeth, in the seventh year of his reign.

ESTHER BECOMES QUEEN

¹⁷The king loved Esther more than all the women, and she found favor and kindness with him more than all the virgins, so that ᴬhe set the royal turban on her head and made her queen in place of Vashti. ¹⁸Then the king held a great banquet, Esther's banquet, for all his officials and his servants; he also made a holiday for the provinces and gave gifts ᴬin proportion to the king's bounty.

¹⁹Now when the virgins were gathered together for the second time, then Mordecai ᴬwas sitting at the king's gate. ²⁰Esther *still* had not revealed her relatives or her people, just as Mordecai had instructed her; for Esther did what Mordecai told her just as she had ᴬwhen under his care.

MORDECAI SAVES THE KING

²¹In those days, while Mordecai was sitting at the king's gate, ᴬBigthan and Teresh, two of the king's officials from those who guarded the door, became angry and sought to attack King Ahasuerus. ²²But the plot became known to Mordecai and ᴬhe informed Queen Esther, and Esther told the king in Mordecai's name. ²³Then when the plot was investigated and found *to be so,* they were both hanged on a wooden *gallows;* and it was written in ᴬthe Book of the Chronicles in the king's presence.

HAMAN'S PLOT AGAINST THE JEWS

3 After these events King Ahasuerus ᴬhonored Haman, the son of Hammedatha the Agagite, and ᴬpromoted him and established his

2:10ᴬEsth 2:20   2:15ᴬEsth 2:7; 9:29   2:17ᴬEsth 1:11
2:18ᴬEsth 1:7   2:19ᴬEsth 2:21; 3:2   2:20ᴬEsth 2:7
2:21ᴬEsth 6:2   2:22ᴬEsth 6:1, 2   2:23ᴬEsth 10:2
3:1ᴬEsth 5:11

authority over all the officials who *were* with him. [2] All the king's servants who were at the king's gate bowed down and paid ¹homage to Haman; for so the king had commanded regarding him. But ᴬMordecai neither bowed down nor paid ¹homage. [3] Then the king's servants who were at ᴬthe king's gate said to Mordecai, "Why are you violating the king's command?" [4] Now it was when they had spoken daily to him and he would not listen to them, that they told Haman to see whether Mordecai's reason would stand; for he had told them that he was a Jew. [5] When Haman saw that ᴬMordecai neither bowed down nor paid ¹homage to him, Haman was filled with rage. [6] But he considered it beneath his dignity to kill Mordecai alone, for they had told him *who* the people of Mordecai *were;* so Haman ᴬsought to annihilate all the Jews, the people of Mordecai, who *were found* throughout the kingdom of Ahasuerus.

[7] In the first month, which is the month Nisan, in the twelfth year of King Ahasuerus, Pur, that is the lot, was cast before Haman from day to day and from month *to month,* until the twelfth month, that is ᴬthe month Adar. [8] Then Haman said to King Ahasuerus, "There is a certain people scattered and dispersed among the peoples in all the provinces of your kingdom; ᴬtheir laws are different from *those* of all *other* people and they do not comply with the king's laws, so it is not in the king's interest to let them remain. [9] If it is pleasing to the king, let it be decreed that they be eliminated, and I will pay ¹ten thousand talents of silver into the hands of those who carry out the *king's* business, to put into the king's treasuries." [10] Then ᴬthe king took his signet ring from his hand and gave it to Haman, the son of Hammedatha the Agagite, the enemy of the Jews. [11] And the king said to Haman, "The silver is yours, and the people *also,* to do with them as you please."

[12] Then the king's scribes were summoned on the thirteenth day of the first month, and it was written just as Haman commanded to ᴬthe king's satraps, to the governors who were over each province and to the officials of each people, each province according to its script, each people according to its language, being written in the name of King Ahasuerus and sealed with the king's signet ring. [13] Letters were sent by couriers to all the king's provinces ᴬto annihilate, kill, and destroy all the Jews, both young and old, women and children, in one day, the thirteenth *day* of the twelfth month, which is the month Adar, and to ᴮseize their possessions as plunder. [14] ᴬA copy of the edict to be issued as law in every province was published to all the peoples so that they would be ready for this day. [15] The couriers went out, speeded by the king's order while the decree was issued at the citadel in Susa; and while the king and Haman sat down to drink, ᴬthe city of Susa was agitated.

3:2 ᴬEsth 2:19; 5:9   3:3 ᴬEsth 2:19   3:5 ᴬEsth 5:9
3:6 ᴬPs 83:4   3:7 ᴬEzra 6:15   3:8 ᴬEzra 4:12-15;
Acts 16:20, 21   3:10 ᴬGen 41:42; Esth 8:2
3:12 ᴬEzra 8:36   3:13 ᴬEsth 7:4   ᴮEsth 8:11
3:14 ᴬEsth 8:13, 14   3:15 ᴬEsth 8:15

3:2 ¹I.e., great respect and honor to a superior
3:5 ¹I.e., great respect and honor to a superior
3:9 ¹About 375 tons or 340 metric tons

ESTHER LEARNS OF HAMAN'S PLOT

4 When Mordecai learned of ^everything that had been done, he tore his clothes, put on sackcloth and ashes, and went out into the midst of the city and wailed loudly and bitterly. ²And he came as far as the king's gate, for no one was to enter the king's gate clothed in sackcloth. ³In each and every province where the command and decree of the king came, there was great mourning among the Jews, with ^fasting, weeping, and mourning rites; and many had sackcloth and ashes spread out as a bed.

⁴Then Esther's attendants and her eunuchs came and informed her, and the queen was seized by great fear. And she sent garments to clothe Mordecai so that he would remove his sackcloth from him, but he did not accept *them*. ⁵Then Esther summoned Hathach from the king's eunuchs, whom the king had appointed to attend her, and ordered him *to go* to Mordecai to learn what this *mourning was* and why it *was happening*. ⁶So Hathach went out to Mordecai in the city square, in front of the king's gate. ⁷Mordecai told him everything that had happened to him, and ^the exact amount of money that Haman had promised to pay to the king's treasuries for the elimination of the Jews. ⁸He also gave him ^a copy of the text of the edict which had been issued in Susa for their annihilation, so that he might show Esther and inform her, and to order her to go in to the king to implore his favor and plead with him for her people.

⁹So Hathach came back and reported Mordecai's words to Esther. ¹⁰Then Esther spoke to Hathach and ordered him *to reply* to Mordecai: ¹¹"All the king's servants and the people of the king's provinces know that for any man or woman who ^comes to the king in the inner courtyard, who is not summoned, he has *only* one law, that he be put to death, unless the king holds out to him the golden scepter so that he may live. And I have not been summoned to come to the king for these thirty days." ¹²And they reported Esther's words to Mordecai.

¹³Then Mordecai told *them* to reply to Esther, "Do not imagine that you in the king's palace can escape any more than all the *other* Jews. ¹⁴For if you keep silent at this time, liberation and ^rescue will arise for the Jews from another place, and you and your father's house will perish. And who knows whether you have not attained royalty for such a time as this?"

ESTHER PLANS TO INTERCEDE

¹⁵Then Esther told *them* to reply to Mordecai, ¹⁶"Go, gather all the Jews who are found in Susa, and fast for me; ^do not eat or drink for three days, night or day. I and my attendants also will fast in the same way. And then I will go in to the king, which is not in accordance with the law; and if I perish, I perish." ¹⁷So Mordecai went away and did just as Esther had commanded him.

ESTHER PLANS A BANQUET

5 Now it came about on the third day that Esther put on her royal robes and stood ^in the inner courtyard of the king's palace in front of

4:1^Esth 3:8-10; Jon 3:5, 6   4:3^Esth 4:16
4:7^Esth 3:9   4:8^Esth 3:14   4:11^Esth 5:1; 6:4
4:14^Lev 26:42; 2 Kin 13:5   4:16^Joel 1:14; 2:12
5:1^Esth 4:11; 6:4

the king's rooms, and the king was sitting on his royal throne in the throne room, opposite the entrance to the palace. [2] When the king saw Esther the queen standing in the courtyard, [A] she obtained favor in his sight; and [B] the king extended to Esther the golden scepter which *was* in his hand. So Esther approached and touched the top of the scepter. [3] Then the king said to her, "What is *troubling* you, Queen Esther? And what is your request? [A] Up to half of the kingdom it shall be given to you." [4] Esther said, "If it pleases the king, may the king and Haman come this day to the banquet that I have prepared for him."

[5] Then the king said, "[A] Bring Haman quickly so that we may do as Esther desires." So the king and Haman came to the banquet which Esther had prepared. [6] As they drank their wine at the banquet, [A] the king said to Esther, "What is your request, for it shall be granted to you. And what is your wish? Up to half of the kingdom it shall be done." [7] So Esther replied, "My request and my wish is: [8][A] if I have found favor in the sight of the king, and if it pleases the king to grant my request and do what I wish, may the king and Haman come to the banquet which I will prepare for them, and tomorrow I will do as the king says."

HAMAN'S PRIDE

[9] Then Haman went out that day joyful and pleased of heart; but when Haman saw Mordecai [A] at the king's gate and [B] that he did not stand up or tremble before him, Haman was filled with anger against Mordecai. [10] Haman controlled himself, however, and went to his house. But he sent for his friends and his wife [A] Zeresh. [11] Then Haman told them of the glory of his riches, and his many sons, and every *occasion on* which the king had honored him and how he had [A] promoted him above the officials and servants of the king. [12] Haman also said, "Even Esther the queen let no one except me come with the king to the banquet which she had prepared; and [A] tomorrow also I am invited by her with the king. [13] Yet all of this does not satisfy me every time I see Mordecai the Jew sitting at [A] the king's gate." [14] Then Zeresh his wife and all his friends said to him, "[A] Have a wooden *gallows* [1] fifty cubits high made, and in the morning ask the king to have Mordecai hanged on it; then go joyfully with the king to the banquet." And the advice pleased Haman, so he had the wooden *gallows* made.

THE KING PLANS TO HONOR MORDECAI

6 During that night the king [A] could not sleep, so he gave an order to bring the book of records, the chronicles, and they were read before the king. [2] And it was found written what [A] Mordecai had reported about Bigthana and Teresh, two of the king's eunuchs who were doorkeepers, that they had sought to attack King Ahasuerus. [3] Then the king said, "What honor or dignity has been bestowed on Mordecai for this?" And the king's servants who

5:2 [A] Esth 2:9   [B] Esth 4:11   5:3 [A] Esth 7:2; Mark 6:23
5:5 [A] Esth 6:14   5:6 [A] Esth 7:2   5:8 [A] Esth 7:3;
8:5   5:9 [A] Esth 2:19   [B] Esth 3:5   5:10 [A] Esth 6:13
5:11 [A] Esth 3:1   5:12 [A] Esth 5:8   5:13 [A] Esth 5:9
5:14 [A] Esth 6:4; 7:9, 10   6:1 [A] Dan 6:18   6:2 [A] Esth 2:21, 22

5:14 [1] About 75 ft. or 23 m

attended him said, "Nothing has been done for him." [4]So the king said, "Who is in the courtyard?" Now Haman had *just* entered the outer courtyard of the king's palace in order to speak to the king about [A]hanging Mordecai on the wooden *gallows* which he had prepared for him. [5]So the king's servants said to him, "Behold, Haman is standing in the courtyard." And the king said, "Have him come in." [6]Haman then came in and the king said to him, "What is to be done for the man [A]whom the king desires to honor?" And Haman said to himself, "Whom would the king desire to honor more than me?" [7]Therefore Haman said to the king, "For the man whom the king desires to honor, [8]have them bring a royal robe which the king has worn, and [A]the horse on which the king has ridden, and on whose head a royal turban has been placed; [9]then *order them* to hand the robe and the horse over to one of the king's noble officials, and have them dress the man whom the king desires to honor, and lead him on horseback through the city square, [A]and proclaim before him, 'So it shall be done for the man whom the king desires to honor.'"

HAMAN MUST HONOR MORDECAI

[10]Then the king said to Haman, "Quickly, take the robe and the horse just as you have said, and do so for Mordecai the Jew, who is sitting at the king's gate; do not fail to do anything of all that you have said." [11]So Haman took the robe and the horse, and dressed Mordecai, and led him *on horseback* through the city square, and proclaimed before him, "So it shall be

done for the man whom the king desires to honor."

[12]Then Mordecai returned to the king's gate, while Haman hurried home, mourning, [A]with *his* head covered. [13]And Haman informed [A]Zeresh his wife and all his friends of everything that had happened to him. Then his wise men and Zeresh his wife said to him, "If Mordecai, before whom you have begun to fall, is of Jewish origin, you will not prevail over him, but will certainly fall before him."

[14]While they were still talking with him, the king's eunuchs arrived and quickly [A]brought Haman to the banquet which Esther had prepared.

ESTHER'S PLEA

7 Now the king and Haman came to drink *wine* with Esther the queen. [2]And the king said to Esther on the second day also as they drank their wine at the banquet, "[A]What is your request, Queen Esther? It shall be granted you. And what is your wish? Up to half of the kingdom it shall be done." [3]Then Queen Esther replied, "[A]If I have found favor in your sight, O king, and if it pleases the king, let my life be given me as my request, and my people as my wish; [4]for [A]we have been sold, I and my people, to be destroyed, [B]killed, and eliminated. Now if we had only been sold as slaves, men and women, I would have kept silent, because the distress would not be sufficient *reason* to burden the king." [5]Then King Ahasuerus asked Queen

6:4 [A]Esth 5:14   6:6 [A]Esth 6:7, 9, 11   6:8 [A]1 Kin 1:33
6:9 [A]Gen 41:43   6:12 [A]2 Sam 15:30   6:13 [A]Esth 5:10
6:14 [A]Esth 5:8   7:2 [A]Esth 5:6; 9:12   7:3 [A]Esth 5:8; 8:5
7:4 [A]Esth 3:9   [B]Esth 3:13

Esther, "Who is he, and where is he, who would presume to do such *a thing?*" 6 And Esther said, "'A foe and an enemy is this wicked Haman!" Then Haman became terrified before the king and queen.

HAMAN IS HANGED

7 The king then got up ^in his anger from drinking wine *and went* into the palace garden; but Haman stayed to beg for his life from Queen Esther, for he saw that harm had been determined against him by the king. 8 Now when the king returned from the palace garden into the place where they had been drinking wine, Haman was falling on ^the couch where Esther was. Then the king said, "Will he even assault the queen with me in the house?" As the word went out of the king's mouth, they covered Haman's face. 9 Then Harbonah, one of the eunuchs who *stood* before the king, said, "Indeed, behold, ^the wooden *gallows* standing at Haman's house 'fifty cubits high, which Haman made for Mordecai who spoke good in behalf of the king!" And the king said, "Hang him on it." 10 ^So they hanged Haman on the wooden *gallows* which he had prepared for Mordecai, and the king's anger subsided.

MORDECAI PROMOTED

8 On that day King Ahasuerus gave the house of Haman, the enemy of the Jews, to Queen Esther; and Mordecai came before the king, because Esther had disclosed ^what he was to her. 2 Then ^the king took off his signet ring, which he had taken away from Haman, and gave it to Mordecai. And Esther set Mordecai over the house of Haman.

3 Then Esther spoke again to the king, fell at his feet, wept, and pleaded for his compassion to avert the evil *scheme* of Haman the Agagite and his plot which he had devised against the Jews. 4 And ^the king extended the golden scepter to Esther. So Esther got up and stood before the king. 5 Then she said, "If it pleases the king and if I have found favor before him, and the matter *seems* proper to the king and I am pleasing in his sight, let it be written to revoke the ^letters devised by Haman, the son of Hammedatha the Agagite, which he wrote to eliminate the Jews who are in all the king's provinces. 6 For ^how can I endure to see the disaster which will happen to my people, and how can I endure to see the destruction of my kindred?" 7 So King Ahasuerus said to Queen Esther and to Mordecai the Jew, "Behold, ^I have given the house of Haman to Esther, and they have hanged him on the wooden *gallows* because he had reached out with his hand against the Jews.

THE KING'S DECREE
AVENGES THE JEWS

8 Now you write to the Jews as you see fit, in the king's name, and seal *it* with the king's signet ring; for a decree which is written in the name of the king and sealed with the king's signet ring ^may not be revoked."

9 So the king's scribes were summoned at that time in the third month (that is, the month Sivan),

---

7:6 ^Esth 3:10   7:7 ^Esth 1:12   7:8 ^Esth 1:6
7:9 ^Esth 5:14   7:10 ^Ps 7:16; 94:23   8:1 ^Esth 2:7, 15
8:2 ^Esth 3:10   8:4 ^Esth 4:11; 5:2   8:5 ^Esth 3:13
8:6 ^Esth 7:4; 9:1   8:7 ^Esth 8:1   8:8 ^Esth 1:19

7:9 'About 75 ft. or 23 m

on the twenty-third day; and it was written in accordance with everything that Mordecai commanded the Jews, the satraps, the governors, and the officials of the provinces which *extended* from India to Cush, 127 provinces, to ^every province according to its script, and to every people according to their language, as well as to the Jews according to their script and their language. ¹⁰He wrote in the name of King Ahasuerus, and sealed it with the king's signet ring, and sent letters by couriers on ^horses, riding on royal relay horses, offspring of racing mares. ¹¹In the letters the king granted the Jews who were in each and every city *the right* ^to assemble and to defend their lives, ᴮto destroy, kill, and eliminate the entire army of *any* people or province which was going to attack them, *including* children and women, and to plunder their spoils, ¹²on ^one day in all the provinces of King Ahasuerus, on the thirteenth *day* of the twelfth month (that is, the month Adar). ¹³^A copy of the edict to be issued as law in each and every province was published to all the peoples, so that the Jews would be ready for this day to avenge themselves on their enemies. ¹⁴The couriers, hurrying and speeded by the king's command, left, riding on the royal relay horses; and the decree was issued at the citadel in Susa.

¹⁵Then Mordecai went out from the presence of the king in a royal robe of violet and white, with a large crown of gold and a garment of fine linen and purple; and ^the city of Susa shouted and rejoiced. ¹⁶For the Jews there was ^light, joy, jubilation, and honor. ¹⁷In each

and every province and in each and every city, wherever the king's commandment and his decree arrived, there was joy and jubilation for the Jews, a feast and a ^holiday. And ᴮmany among the peoples of the land became Jews, because the dread of the Jews had fallen on them.

THE JEWS DESTROY THEIR ENEMIES

9 Now in the twelfth month (that is, the month Adar), on the thirteenth day, ^when the king's command and edict were to be put into effect, on the day when the enemies of the Jews hoped to gain the mastery over them, it turned out to the contrary so that the Jews themselves gained mastery over those who hated them. ²The Jews assembled in their cities throughout the provinces of King Ahasuerus to attack those who sought to harm them; and no one could stand against them, ^because the dread of them had fallen on all the peoples. ³Even all the officials of the provinces, ^the satraps, the governors, and those who were doing the king's business were supporting the Jews, because the dread of Mordecai had fallen on them. ⁴For Mordecai was great in the king's house, and the news about him spread throughout the provinces; for the man Mordecai ^became greater and greater. ⁵So ^the Jews struck all their enemies with the sword, killing and destroying; and they did as they pleased to those who hated them. ⁶At the citadel in

8:9 ^Esth 1:22; 3:12   8:10 ^1 Kin 4:28
8:11 ^Esth 9:2   ᴮEsth 3:13   8:12 ^Esth 3:13; 9:1
8:13 ^Esth 3:14   8:15 ^Esth 3:15   8:16 ^Ps 97:11;
112:4   8:17 ^Esth 9:19   ᴮEsth 9:27   9:1 ^Esth 3:13
9:2 ^Esth 8:17   9:3 ^Ezra 8:36   9:4 ^2 Sam 3:1;
1 Chr 11:9   9:5 ^Esth 3:13

Susa the Jews killed and eliminated five hundred men, [7] and they killed Parshandatha, Dalphon, Aspatha, [8] Poratha, Adalia, Aridatha, [9] Parmashta, Arisai, Aridai, and Vaizatha, [10] ^the ten sons of Haman the son of Hammedatha, the Jews' enemy; but they did not lay their hands on the plunder.

[11] On that day the number of those who were killed at the citadel in Susa was reported to the king. [12] And the king said to Queen Esther, "The Jews have killed and eliminated five hundred men and the ten sons of Haman at the citadel in Susa. What have they done in the rest of the king's provinces! ^Now what is your request? It shall also be granted you. And what is your further wish? It shall also be done."

[13] Then Esther said, "If it pleases the king, ^let tomorrow also be granted to the Jews who are in Susa to do according to the edict of today; and let Haman's ten sons be hanged on the wooden *gallows*." [14] So the king commanded that it was to be done so; and an edict was issued in Susa, and Haman's ten sons were hanged. [15] The Jews who were in Susa assembled also on the fourteenth day of the month Adar and killed three hundred men in Susa, but ^they did not lay their hands on the plunder.

[16] Now the rest of the Jews who *were* in the king's provinces ^assembled, to defend their lives and rid themselves of their enemies, and to kill seventy-five thousand of those who hated them; but they did not lay their hands on the plunder. [17] *This was done* on ^the thirteenth day of the month Adar, and on the fourteenth day they rested and made it a day of feasting and rejoicing.

[18] But the Jews who were in Susa ^assembled on the thirteenth and the fourteenth of the same month, and they rested on the fifteenth day and made it a day of feasting and rejoicing. [19] Therefore the Jews of the rural areas, who live in ^the rural towns, make the fourteenth day of the month Adar *a* holiday for rejoicing and feasting and sending portions *of food* to one another.

THE FEAST OF PURIM INSTITUTED

[20] Then Mordecai recorded these events, and he sent letters to all the Jews who were in all the provinces of King Ahasuerus, *both* near and far, [21] obliging them to celebrate the fourteenth day of the month Adar, and the fifteenth day of the same month, annually, [22] because on those days the Jews rid themselves of their enemies, and *it was a* month which was ^turned for them from grief into joy, and from mourning into a holiday; that they were to make them days of feasting and rejoicing, and ^Bsending portions *of food* to one another, and gifts to the poor.

[23] So the Jews undertook what they had started to do, and what Mordecai had written to them. [24] For Haman the son of Hammedatha, the Agagite, the adversary of all the Jews, had schemed against the Jews to eliminate them, and ^had cast Pur, that is the lot, to disturb them and eliminate them. [25] But when it came to the king's attention, he commanded by letter ^that his wicked scheme which he had devised against the Jews was

9:10 ^Esth 5:11   **9:12** ^Esth 5:6; 7:2   **9:13** ^Esth 8:11; 9:15   **9:15** ^Esth 9:10   **9:16** ^Lev 26:7, 8; Esth 8:11   **9:17** ^Esth 9:1   **9:18** ^Esth 8:11; 9:2   **9:19** ^Deut 3:5; Zech 2:4   **9:22** ^Ps 30:11   ^BNeh 8:12   **9:24** ^Esth 3:7   **9:25** ^Esth 3:6-15

to return on his own head, and that he and his sons were to be hanged on the wooden *gallows*. [26] Therefore they called these days Purim after the name of Pur. And ^because of the instructions in this letter, both what they had seen in this regard and what had happened to them, [27] the Jews established and made a custom for themselves, their descendants, and for all those who allied themselves with them, so that they would not fail ^to celebrate these two days according to their regulation and according to their appointed time annually. [28] So these days were to be remembered and celebrated throughout every generation, every family, every province, and every city; and these days of Purim were not to be neglected by the Jews, or their memory fade from their descendants.

[29] Then Queen Esther, ^daughter of Abihail, with Mordecai the Jew, wrote with full authority to confirm this second letter about Purim. [30] He sent letters to all the Jews, ^to the 127 provinces of the kingdom of Ahasuerus, *namely,* words of peace and truth, [31] to establish these days of Purim at their appointed times, just as Mordecai the Jew and Queen Esther had established for them, and just as they had established for themselves and for their descendants, *with* instructions ^for their times of fasting and their mourning. [32] The command of Esther established these customs for ^Purim, and it was written in the book.

MORDECAI'S GREATNESS

10 Now King Ahasuerus imposed a tax on the land and the ^coastlands of the sea. [2] And every accomplishment of his authority and power, and the full account of the greatness of Mordecai ^with which the king honored him, are they not written in the Book of the Chronicles of the Kings of Media and Persia? [3] For Mordecai the Jew was ^second *only* to King Ahasuerus, and great among the Jews and in favor with his many kinsmen, ^Bone who sought the good of his people and one who spoke for the welfare of his entire nation.

9:26 ^Esth 9:20   9:27 ^Esth 9:20, 21
9:29 ^Esth 2:15   9:30 ^Esth 1:1   9:31 ^Esth 4:3
9:32 ^Esth 9:26   10:1 ^Is 11:11; 24:15   10:2 ^Esth 8:15; 9:4
10:3 ^Gen 41:43, 44   ^BNeh 2:10

JOB

JOB'S CHARACTER AND WEALTH

1 There was a man in the ^land of Uz whose name was Job; and that man was blameless, upright, fearing God and turning away from evil. ² ^Seven sons and three daughters were born to him. ³ His possessions were seven thousand sheep, three thousand camels, five hundred yoke of oxen, five hundred female donkeys, and very many servants; and that man was ^the greatest of all the men of the east. ⁴ His sons used to go and hold a feast in the house of each one on his day, and they would send *word* and invite their three sisters to eat and drink with them. ⁵ When the days of feasting had completed their cycle, Job would send *word to them* and consecrate them, getting up early in the morning and offering ^burnt offerings *according to* the number of them all; for Job said, "Perhaps my sons have sinned and cursed God in their hearts." Job did so continually.

⁶ Now there was a day when the [1,A]sons of God came to present themselves before the LORD, and ²Satan also came among them. ⁷ The LORD said to Satan, "From where do you come?" Satan answered the LORD and said, "^From roaming about on the earth and walking around on it." ⁸ The LORD said to Satan, "Have you considered ^My servant Job? For there is no one like him on the earth, a blameless and upright man, fearing God and turning away from evil." ⁹ Then ^Satan answered the LORD, "Does Job fear God for nothing? ¹⁰ Have You not made a fence around him and his house and all that he has, on every side? You have blessed the work of his hands, and his ^possessions have increased in the land. ¹¹ ^But reach out with Your hand now and touch all that he has; he will certainly curse You to Your face." ¹² Then the LORD said to Satan, "Behold, all that he has is in your power; only do not reach out *and put* your hand on him." So Satan departed from the presence of the LORD.

SATAN ALLOWED TO TEST JOB

¹³ Now on the day when his sons and his daughters were eating and drinking wine in their oldest brother's house, ¹⁴ a messenger came to Job and said, "The oxen were plowing and the female donkeys feeding beside them, ¹⁵ and the ^Sabeans attacked and took them. They also killed the servants with the edge of the sword, and I alone have escaped to tell you." ¹⁶ While he was still speaking, another came and said, "^The fire of God fell from heaven and burned up the sheep and the servants and consumed them, and I alone have escaped to tell you." ¹⁷ While he was still speaking, another came and said, "The

---

1:1 ^Jer 25:20; Lam 4:21   1:2 ^Job 42:13
1:3 ^Job 29:25   1:5 ^Gen 8:20; Job 42:8   1:6 ^Job 38:7
1:7 ^1 Pet 5:8   1:8 ^Josh 1:2, 7; Job 42:7, 8
1:9 ^Rev 12:9f   1:10 ^Job 1:3; 31:25   1:11 ^Job 2:5
1:15 ^Gen 10:7; Job 6:19   1:16 ^Lev 10:2; Num 11:1-3

1:6 ¹ I.e., prob. angels   ² Heb *ha-satan;* i.e., the adversary, and so throughout the ch

^Chaldeans formed three units and made a raid on the camels and took them, and killed the servants with the edge of the sword, and I alone have escaped to tell you." [18]While he was still speaking, another also came and said, "Your sons and your daughters were eating and drinking wine in their oldest brother's house, [19]and behold, a great wind came from across the wilderness and struck the four corners of the house, and it fell on the young people and they died, and I alone have escaped to tell you."

[20]Then Job got up, ^tore his robe, and shaved his head; then he fell to the ground and worshiped. [21]He said,

"^Naked I came from my
　　mother's womb,
And naked I shall return there.
The Lord gave and the Lord
　　has taken away.
Blessed be the name of the
　　Lord."

[22]^Despite all this, Job did not sin, nor did he blame God.

JOB LOSES HIS HEALTH

2 ^Again, there was a day when the sons of God came to present themselves before the Lord, and 'Satan also came among them to present himself before the Lord. [2]The Lord said to Satan, "Where have you come from?" Then Satan answered the Lord and said, "From roaming about on the earth and walking around on it." [3]The Lord said to Satan, "Have you considered My servant Job? For there is no one like him on the earth, a blameless and upright man fearing God and turning away from evil. And he still ^holds firm to his integrity, although you incited Me

against him to ruin him without cause." [4]Satan answered the Lord and said, "Skin for skin! Yes, all that a man has, he will give for his life. [5]However, reach out with Your hand now, and ^touch his bone and his flesh; he will curse You to Your face!" [6]So the Lord said to Satan, "Behold, he is in your power, only spare his life."

[7]Then Satan went out from the presence of the Lord and struck Job with ^severe boils from the sole of his foot to the top of his head. [8]And *Job* took a piece of pottery to scrape himself while ^he was sitting in the ashes.

[9]Then his wife said to him, "Do you still hold firm your integrity? Curse God and die!" [10]But he said to her, "You are speaking as one of the foolish women speaks. ^Shall we actually accept good from God but not accept adversity?" Despite all this, Job did not sin with his lips.

[11]Now when Job's three friends heard about all this adversity that had come upon him, they came, each one from his own place—Eliphaz the ^Temanite, Bildad the Shuhite, and Zophar the Naamathite; and they made an appointment together to come to sympathize with him and comfort him. [12]When they looked from a distance and did not recognize him, they raised their voices and wept. And each of them tore his robe, and they ^threw dust over their heads toward the sky. [13]^Then they sat down on the ground with him for

1:17^Gen 11:28, 31　1:20^Gen 37:29, 34; Josh 7:6
1:21^Eccl 5:15　1:22^Job 2:10　2:1^Job 1:6-8
2:3^Job 27:5, 6　2:5^Job 19:20　2:7^Deut 28:35;
Job 7:5　2:8^Ezek 27:30; Jon 3:6　2:10^Job 1:21
2:11^Job 6:19; Jer 49:7　2:12^Lam 2:10; Ezek 27:30
2:13^Gen 50:10; Ezek 3:15

2:1 [1] Heb *ha-satan;* i.e., the adversary, and so throughout the ch

seven days and seven nights, with no one speaking a word to him, for they saw that *his* pain was very great.

JOB'S LAMENT

3 Afterward Job opened his mouth and cursed the day of his *birth.* ² And Job said,

³ "ᴬMay the day on which I was to be born perish,
As well as the night *which* said,
'A boy is conceived.'

⁴ "May that day be darkness;
May God above not care for it,
Nor light shine on it.

⁵ "May ᴬdarkness and black gloom claim it;
May a cloud settle on it;
May the blackness of the day terrify it.

⁶ "*As for* that night, may darkness seize it;
May it not rejoice among the days of the year;
May it not come into the number of the months.

⁷ "Behold, may that night be barren;
May no joyful shout enter it.

⁸ "May those curse it who curse the day,
Who are prepared to ᴬdisturb Leviathan.

⁹ "May the stars of its twilight be darkened;
May it wait for light but have none,
And may it not see the breaking dawn;

¹⁰ Because it did not shut the opening of my *mother's* womb,
Or hide trouble from my eyes.

¹¹ "ᴬWhy did I not die at birth,
Come out of the womb and pass away?

¹² "Why were the knees *there* in front of me,
And why the breasts, that I would nurse?

¹³ "For now I ᴬwould have lain down and been quiet;
I would have slept then, I would have been at rest,

¹⁴ With ᴬkings and counselors of the earth,
Who rebuilt ruins for themselves;

¹⁵ Or with rulers ᴬwho had gold,
Who were filling their houses *with* silver.

¹⁶ "Or like a miscarriage which is hidden, I would not exist,
As infants that never saw light.

¹⁷ "There the wicked cease from raging,
And there the weary are at ᴬrest.

¹⁸ "The prisoners are at ease together;
They do not hear the voice of the taskmaster.

¹⁹ "The small and the great are there,
And the slave is free from his master.

²⁰ "Why is ᴬlight given to one burdened with grief,
And life to the bitter of soul,

²¹ Who ᴬlong for death, but there is none,
And dig for it more than for hidden treasures;

²² Who are filled with jubilation,
And rejoice when they find the grave?

²³ "*Why is light given* to a man ᴬwhose way is hidden,
And whom God has shut off?

3:3 ᴬJer 20:14-18   3:5 ᴬJer 13:16   3:8 ᴬJob 41:1, 25
3:11 ᴬJob 10:18, 19   3:13 ᴬJob 3:13-19; 7:8-10, 21
3:14 ᴬJob 12:18   3:15 ᴬJob 27:16, 17   3:17 ᴬJob 17:16
3:20 ᴬJer 20:18   3:21 ᴬRev 9:6   3:23 ᴬJob 19:6, 8, 12

24 "For ^my groaning comes at the sight of my food,
   And my cries pour out like water.
25 "For ^what I fear comes upon me,
   And what I dread encounters me.
26 "I ^am not at ease, nor am I quiet,
   And I am not at rest, but turmoil comes."

ELIPHAZ SAYS THE INNOCENT DO NOT SUFFER

4 Then Eliphaz the Temanite responded,
2 "If one ventures a word with you, will you become impatient?
   But ^who can refrain from speaking?
3 "Behold, ^you have taught many,
   And you have strengthened weak hands.
4 "Your words have helped the stumbling to stand,
   And you have strengthened feeble knees.
5 "But now it comes to you, and you ^are impatient;
   It touches you, and you are horrified.
6 "Is your ^fear of God not ᴮyour confidence,
   And the integrity of your ways your hope?
7 "Remember now, ^who ever perished being innocent?
   Or where were the upright destroyed?
8 "According to what I have seen, ^those who ¹plow wrongdoing
   And those who sow trouble harvest it.

9 "By ^the breath of God they perish,
   And by the blast of His anger they come to an end.
10 "The ^roaring of the lion and the voice of the fierce lion,
   And the teeth of the young lions are broken out.
11 "The ^lion perishes for lack of prey,
   And the cubs of the lioness are scattered.
12 "Now a word was brought to me secretly,
   And my ear received a ^whisper of it.
13 "Amid disquieting ^thoughts from visions of the night,
   When deep sleep falls on people,
14 Dread came upon me, and trembling,
   And made all my bones shake.
15 "Then a spirit passed by my face;
   The hair of my flesh stood up.
16 "Something was standing still, but I could not recognize its appearance;
   A form was before my eyes;
   There was silence, then I heard a voice:
17 'Can ^mankind be righteous before God?
   Can a man be pure before his Maker?
18 '^He puts no trust even in His servants;
   And He accuses His angels of error.

3:24 ^Job 6:7; 33:20   3:25 ^Job 9:28; 30:15
3:26 ^Job 7:13, 14   4:2 ^Job 32:18-20   4:3 ^Job 4:3, 4;
29:15, 16, 21, 25   4:5 ^Job 6:14   4:6 ^Job 1:1
ᴮProv 3:26   4:7 ^Job 36:6, 7; Ps 37:25   4:8 ^Hos 10:13;
Gal 6:7   4:9 ^Is 11:4; 2 Thess 2:8   4:10 ^Job 5:15;
Ps 58:6   4:11 ^Job 29:17; Ps 34:10   4:12 ^Job 26:14
4:13 ^Job 33:15   4:17 ^Job 9:2; 25:4   4:18 ^Job 15:15

4:8 ¹I.e., devise

19 'How much more those who
      live in houses of clay,
   Whose ^foundation is in the
      dust,
   Who are crushed before the
      moth!
20 '^Between morning and
      evening they are broken in
      pieces;
   Unregarded, they perish
      forever.
21 'Is their ^tent-cord not pulled
      out within them?
   They die, yet without wisdom.'

GOD IS JUST

5 "Call now, is there anyone who
      will answer you?
   And to which of the ^holy ones
      will you turn?
2 "For ^irritation kills the fool,
   And jealousy brings death to
      the simple.
3 "I have seen the ^fool taking
      root,
   And I cursed his home
      immediately.
4 "His ^sons are far from safety,
   They are also oppressed at the
      gate,
   And there is no one to save
      them.
5 "The hungry devour his harvest
   And take it to a *place of* thorns,
   And the ^schemer is eager for
      their wealth.
6 "For ^disaster does not come
      from the dust,
   Nor does trouble sprout from
      the ground,
7 For ^man is born for trouble,
   As sparks fly upward.
8 "But as for me, I would ^seek
      God,
   And I would make my plea
      before God,

9 Who ^does great and
      unsearchable things,
   Wonders without number.
10 "He ^gives rain on the earth,
   And sends water on the fields,
11 So that ^He sets on high those
      who are lowly,
   And those who mourn are
      lifted to safety.
12 "He ^frustrates the schemes of
      the shrewd,
   So that their hands cannot
      attain success.
13 "He ^captures the wise by their
      own cleverness,
   And the advice of the cunning
      is quickly thwarted.
14 "By day they ^meet with
      darkness,
   And grope at noon as in the
      night.
15 "But He saves from ^the sword
      of their mouth,
   And the poor from the hand of
      the strong.
16 "So the helpless has hope,
   And ^injustice has shut its
      mouth.
17 "Behold, ^happy is the person
      whom God disciplines,
   So do not reject the ^Bdiscipline
      of the Almighty.
18 "For ^He inflicts pain, and gives
      relief;
   He wounds, but His hands *also*
      heal.
19 "In six troubles ^He will save you;
   Even in seven, evil will not
      touch you.

4:19 ^Gen 2:7; Job 22:16   4:20 ^Job 14:2
4:21 ^Job 8:22   5:1 ^Job 15:15   5:2 ^Prov 12:16; 27:3
5:3 ^Jer 12:2   5:4 ^Job 4:11   5:5 ^Job 18:8-10; 22:10
5:6 ^Job 15:35   5:7 ^Job 14:1   5:8 ^Job 13:2, 3; Ps 50:15
5:9 ^Job 37:14, 16; 42:3   5:10 ^Job 36:27-29; 38:26
5:11 ^Job 22:29; 36:7   5:12 ^Ps 33:10   5:13 ^Job 37:24;
1 Cor 3:19   5:14 ^Job 12:25; 15:30   5:15 ^Job 4:10, 11;
Ps 35:10   5:16 ^Ps 107:42   5:17 ^Ps 94:12   ^BHeb
12:5-11   5:18 ^Is 30:26; Hos 6:1   5:19 ^Ps 34:19

20 "In famine He will redeem you
    from death,
    And ^in war, from the power of
    the sword.
21 "You will be hidden from the
    scourge of the tongue,
    ^And you will not be afraid of
    violence when it comes.
22 "You will ^laugh at violence and
    hunger,
    And you will not be afraid of
    wild animals.
23 "For you will be in league with
    the stones of the field,
    And ^the animals of the field
    will be at peace with you.
24 "You will know that your ^tent
    is secure,
    For you will visit your home
    and have nothing missing.
25 "You will also know that your
    ^descendants will be many,
    And ^Byour offspring as the
    grass of the earth.
26 "You will ^come to the grave at a
    ripe age,
    Like the stacking of grain in its
    season.
27 "Behold this; we have
    investigated it, *and* so it is.
    Hear it, and know for yourself."

JOB'S FRIENDS ARE NO HELP

6 Then Job responded,
2 "^Oh if only my grief were
    actually weighed
    And laid in the balances
    together with my disaster!
3 "For then it would be ^heavier
    than the sand of the seas;
    For that reason my words have
    been rash.
4 "For the ^arrows of the
    Almighty are within me,
    My spirit drinks their poison;
    The terrors of God line up
    against me.

5 "Does the ^wild donkey bray
    over *his* grass,
    Or does the ox low over his
    feed?
6 "Can something tasteless be
    eaten without salt,
    Or is there any taste in the
    juice of an alkanet *plant?*
7 "My soul ^refuses to touch *them;*
    They are like loathsome food
    to me.
8 "Oh, that my request might
    come to pass,
    And that God would grant my
    hope!
9 "*Oh,* that God would ^decide to
    crush me,
    That He would let loose His
    hand and cut me off!
10 "But it is still my comfort,
    And I rejoice in unsparing pain,
    That I ^have not denied the
    words of the Holy One.
11 "What is my strength, that I
    should wait?
    And what is my end, that I
    should ^endure?
12 "Is my strength the strength of
    stones,
    Or is my flesh bronze?
13 "Is it that my ^help is not within
    me,
    And that a good outcome is
    driven away from me?

14 "For the ^despairing man *there
    should be* kindness from his
    friend;
    So that he does not ^Babandon
    the fear of the Almighty.

5:20 ^Ps 144:10   5:21 ^Ps 91:5, 6   5:22 ^Job 8:21
5:23 ^Is 11:6-9; 65:25   5:24 ^Job 8:6   5:25 ^Ps 112:2
^BIs 44:3, 4   5:26 ^Job 42:17   6:2 ^Job 31:6
6:3 ^Job 23:2   6:4 ^Job 16:13; Ps 38:2   6:5 ^Job 39:5-8
6:7 ^Job 3:24; 33:20   6:9 ^Num 11:15; 1 Kin 19:4
6:10 ^Job 22:22; 23:11, 12   6:11 ^Job 21:4
6:13 ^Job 26:2   6:14 ^Job 4:5   ^BJob 1:5

¹⁵ "My brothers have acted
^deceitfully like a ¹wadi,
Like the torrents of wadis
which drain away,

¹⁶ Which are darkened because
of ice,
And into which the snow melts.

¹⁷ "When ^they dry up, they
vanish;
When it is hot, they disappear
from their place.

¹⁸ "The paths of their course wind
along,
They go up into wasteland and
perish.

¹⁹ "The caravans of ^Tema looked,
The travelers of Sheba hoped
for them.

²⁰ "They ^were put to shame, for
they had trusted,
They came there and were
humiliated.

²¹ "Indeed, you have now become
such,
^You see terrors and are afraid.

²² "Have I said, 'Give me
something,'
Or, 'Offer a bribe for me from
your wealth,'

²³ Or, 'Save me from the hand of
the enemy,'
Or, 'Redeem me from the hand
of the tyrants'?

²⁴ "Teach me, and ^I will be silent;
And show me how I have done
wrong.

²⁵ "How painful are honest words!
But what does your argument
prove?

²⁶ "Do you intend to rebuke *my*
words,
When the ^words of one in
despair belong to the wind?

²⁷ "You would even ^cast *lots* for
the orphans,
And barter over your friend.

²⁸ "Now please look at me,
And *see* if I am ^lying to your
face.

²⁹ "Please turn away, let there be
no injustice;
Turn away, ^my righteousness
is still in it.

³⁰ "Is there injustice on my tongue?
Does ^my palate not discern
disasters?

JOB'S LIFE SEEMS FUTILE

7 "Is a person not ^forced to
labor on earth,
And *are* his days not like the
days of ᴮa hired worker?

² "As a slave pants for the shade,
And as a hired worker who
eagerly waits for his wages,

³ So I am allotted worthless
months,
And ^nights of trouble are
apportioned to me.

⁴ "When I ^lie down, I say,
'When shall I arise?'
But the night continues,
And I am continually tossing
until dawn.

⁵ "My ^flesh is clothed with
maggots and a crust of dirt,
My skin hardens and oozes.

⁶ "My days are ^swifter than a
weaver's shuttle,
And they come to an end
ᴮwithout hope.

⁷ "Remember that my life ^is a
mere breath;
My eye will ᴮnot see goodness
again.

6:15 ^Jer 15:18   **6:17** ^Job 24:19   **6:19** ^Is 21:14;
Jer 25:23   **6:20** ^Jer 14:3   **6:21** ^Ps 38:11
6:24 ^Ps 39:1   **6:26** ^Job 8:2; 16:3   **6:27** ^Joel 3:3;
Nah 3:10   **6:28** ^Job 27:4; 36:4   **6:29** ^Job 13:18; 19:6
6:30 ^Job 12:11   **7:1** ^Job 5:7   ᴮJob 14:6   **7:3** ^Job 16:7
7:4 ^Deut 28:67; Job 7:13, 14   **7:5** ^Job 2:7; 17:14
7:6 ^Job 9:25   ᴮJob 13:15   **7:7** ^Ps 78:39   ᴮJob 9:25

6:15 ¹I.e., dry stream bed(s), except in the rainy season

8 "The ^eye of him who sees me
    will no *longer* look at me;
    Your eyes *will be* on me, but ^I
    will not exist.
9 "When a cloud vanishes, it is
    gone;
    In the same way ^one who goes
    down to [1,]^Sheol does not
    come up.
10 "He will not return to his house
    again,
    Nor will ^his place know about
    him anymore.

11 "Therefore ^I will not restrain
    my mouth;
    I will speak in the anguish of
    my spirit,
    I will complain in the
    bitterness of my soul.
12 "Am I the sea, or ^the sea
    monster,
    That You set a guard over me?
13 "If I say, '^My couch will comfort
    me,
    My bed will ease my complaint,'
14 Then You frighten me with
    dreams,
    And terrify me by visions,
15 So that my soul would choose
    suffocation,
    Death rather than my pains.
16 "I ^waste away; I will not live
    forever.
    Leave me alone, for my days
    are *only* a breath.
17 "^What is man that You exalt him,
    And that You are concerned
    about him,
18 That ^You examine him every
    morning
    And put him to the test every
    moment?
19 "^Will You never turn Your gaze
    away from me,
    Nor leave me alone until I
    swallow my spittle?

20 "^Have I sinned? What have I
    done to You,
    ^Watcher of mankind?
    Why have You made me Your
    target,
    So that I am a burden to
    myself?
21 "Why then ^do You not forgive
    my wrongdoing
    And take away my guilt?
    For now I will lie down in the
    dust;
    And You will search for
    me, but I will no *longer*
    exist."

BILDAD SAYS GOD REWARDS THE GOOD

8 Then Bildad the Shuhite re-
    sponded,
2 "How long will you say these
    things,
    And the ^words of your mouth
    be a mighty wind?
3 "Does ^God pervert justice?
    Or does the Almighty pervert
    what is right?
4 "^If your sons sinned against
    Him,
    Then He turned them over
    to the power of their
    wrongdoing.
5 "If you will ^search for God
    And implore the compassion
    of the Almighty,
6 If you are pure and upright,
    Surely now ^He will stir
    Himself for you
    And restore your righteous
    estate.

7:8 ^Job 8:18   ^Job 7:21   7:9 ^Job 3:13-19
^2 Sam 12:23   7:10 ^Job 8:18; 27:21, 23   7:11 ^Job 10:1;
Ps 40:9   7:12 ^Ezek 32:2, 3   7:13 ^Job 7:4; Ps 6:6
7:16 ^Job 6:9; 10:1   7:17 ^Ps 8:4; Heb 2:6
7:18 ^Job 14:3   7:19 ^Job 9:18; 14:6   7:20 ^Job 35:3, 6
^Ps 36:6   7:21 ^Job 9:28; 10:14   8:2 ^Job 6:26
8:3 ^Gen 18:25; Deut 32:4   8:4 ^Job 1:5, 18, 19
8:5 ^Job 5:17-27   8:6 ^Job 22:27; Ps 7:6

7:9 [1] I.e., the netherworld

7 "Though your beginning was
    insignificant,
  Yet your ^end will increase
    greatly.

8 "Please ^inquire of past
    generations,
  And consider the things
    searched out by their fathers.

9 "For we are *only* of yesterday
    and know nothing,
  Because ^our days on earth are
    as a shadow.

10 "Will they not teach you *and*
    tell you,
  And bring forth words from
    their minds?

11 "Can papyrus grow tall without
    a marsh?
  Can the rushes grow without
    water?

12 "While it is still green *and* not
    cut down,
  Yet it withers before any *other*
    plant.

13 "So are the paths of ^all who
    forget God;
  And the hope of the godless
    will perish,

14 His confidence is fragile,
  And his trust is a ^spider's
    web.

15 "He depends on his ^house, but
    it does not stand;
  He holds on to it, but it does
    not endure.

16 "He ^flourishes before the sun,
  And his shoots spread out over
    his garden.

17 "His roots wrap around a rock
    pile,
  He grasps a house of stones.

18 "If he is removed from ^his
    place,
  Then it will deny him, *saying*,
    'I never saw you.'

19 "Behold, ^this is the joy of His
    way;
  And out of the dust others will
    spring.

20 "Behold, ^God will not reject *a
    person of* integrity,
  Nor will He help evildoers.

21 "He will yet fill ^your mouth
    with laughter,
  And your lips with joyful
    shouting.

22 "Those who hate you will be
    ^clothed with shame,
  And the tent of the wicked will
    no *longer* exist."

JOB SAYS THERE IS NO ARBITRATOR BETWEEN GOD AND MANKIND

9 Then Job responded,
2 "In truth I know that this is so;
  But how can a ^person be in
    the right with God?

3 "If one wished to ^dispute with
    Him,
  He could not answer Him once
    in a thousand *times.*

4 "Wise in heart and mighty in
    strength,
  Who has ^defied Him without
    harm?

5 "^*It is God* who removes the
    mountains, and they do not
    know *how*,
  When He overturns them in
    His anger.

6 "*It is He* who ^shakes the earth
    from its place,
  And its ^B pillars tremble;

7 Who commands the ^sun not
    to shine,
  And puts a seal on the stars;

8:7 ^A Job 42:12   8:8 ^A Deut 4:32; Job 15:18
8:9 ^A Job 14:2   8:13 ^A Ps 9:17   8:14 ^A Is 59:5, 6
8:15 ^A Job 8:22; Ps 49:11   8:16 ^A Ps 37:35; Jer 11:16
8:18 ^A Job 7:10   8:19 ^A Job 20:5   8:20 ^A Job 4:7
8:21 ^A Job 5:22; Ps 126:1, 2   8:22 ^A Ps 132:18
9:2 ^A Job 4:17; 25:4   9:3 ^A Job 10:2; 13:19
9:4 ^A 2 Chr 13:12; Prov 29:1   9:5 ^A Job 9:5-10; 26:6-14
9:6 ^A Is 2:19, 21   ^B Ps 75:3   9:7 ^A Is 13:10; Ezek 32:7, 8

8   Who alone ^stretches out the
    heavens,
    And tramples down the waves
    of the sea;
9   Who makes the ^Bear, Orion,
    and the Pleiades,
    And the constellations of the
    south.
10 "*It is He* who ^does great things,
    the unfathomable,
    And wondrous works without
    number.
11 "If He were to pass by me, ^I
    would not see *Him;*
    Were He to move past *me,* I
    would not perceive Him.
12 "If He were to snatch away, who
    could ^restrain Him?
    Who could say to Him, '^What
    are You doing?'
13 "God will not turn back His
    anger;
    Beneath Him the helpers of
    ^1,^Rahab cower.
14 "How then can ^I answer Him,
    And choose my words before
    Him?
15 "For though I were right, I could
    not answer;
    I would have to ^implore the
    mercy of my Judge.
16 "If I called and He answered me,
    I could not believe that He was
    listening to my voice.
17 "For He ^bruises me with a
    storm
    And multiplies my wounds
    without cause.
18 "He will ^not allow me to get my
    breath,
    But He saturates me with
    ^bitterness.
19 "If *it is a matter* of power,
    ^behold, *He is* the strong one!
    And if *it is a matter* of justice,
    who can summon Him?

20 "^Though I am righteous, my
    mouth will ^condemn me;
    Though I am guiltless, He will
    declare me guilty.
21 "I am ^guiltless;
    I do not take notice of myself;
    I ^reject my life.
22 "It is *all* one; therefore I say,
    'He ^destroys the guiltless and
    the wicked.'
23 "If the whip kills suddenly,
    He ^mocks the despair of the
    innocent.
24 "The earth ^is handed over to
    the wicked;
    He ^covers the faces of its judges.
    If *it is* not *He,* then who is it?

25 "Now ^my days are swifter than
    a runner;
    They flee away, they see no
    good.
26 "They slip by like ^reed boats,
    Like an ^eagle that swoops on
    its prey.
27 "Though I say, 'I will forget ^my
    complaint,
    I will put my face in order and
    be cheerful,'
28 I am afraid of all my pains,
    I know that ^You will not
    acquit me.
29 "I am ^guilty,
    Why then should I struggle in
    vain?
30 "If I ^washed myself with snow,
    And cleansed my hands
    with lye,

9:8^APs 104:2; Is 40:22   **9:9**^AJob 38:31, 32; Amos 5:8
9:10^AJob 5:9   **9:11**^AJob 23:8, 9; 35:14   **9:12**^AJob 10:7
^BIs 45:9   **9:13**^AIs 30:7; 51:9   **9:14**^AJob 9:3, 32
9:15^AJob 8:5   **9:17**^AJob 16:12, 14; 30:22   **9:18**^AJob 7:19
^BJob 13:26   **9:19**^AJob 9:4   **9:20**^AJob 9:15   ^BJob 9:29
9:21^AJob 1:1   ^BJob 7:16   **9:22**^AJob 10:7, 8
9:23^AJob 24:12   **9:24**^AJob 10:3   ^BJob 12:17   **9:25**^AJob 7:6
9:26^AIs 18:2   ^BHab 1:8   **9:27**^AJob 7:11   **9:28**^AJob 7:21;
10:14   **9:29**^AJob 10:2; Ps 37:33   **9:30**^AJer 2:22

9:13^1 I.e., a sea monster, not to be confused with
Rahab in Joshua 2

31 Then You would plunge me
　　into the pit,
　And my own clothes would
　　loathe me.
32 "For ^He is not a man, as I am,
　　that ᴮI may answer Him—
　That we may go to court
　　together!
33 "There is no ^arbitrator
　　between us,
　Who can place his hand upon
　　us both.
34 "Let Him ^remove His rod from
　　me,
　And let not the dread of Him
　　terrify me.
35 "Then I ^would speak and not
　　fear Him;
　But I am not like that in myself.

JOB DESPAIRS OF GOD'S DEALINGS

10 "^I am disgusted with my
　　own life;
　I will express ᴮmy complaint
　　freely;
　I will speak in the bitterness of
　　my soul.
2 "I will say to God, '^Do not
　　condemn me;
　Let me know why You contend
　　with me.
3 'Is it right for You indeed to
　　^oppress,
　To reject the work of Your
　　hands,
　And to look favorably on the
　　plan of the wicked?
4 'Do You have eyes of flesh?
　Or do You ^see as mankind
　　sees?
5 'Are Your days like the days of a
　　mortal,
　Or ^Your years like a man's
　　year,
6 That ^You should search for
　　my guilt
　And carefully seek my sin?

7 'According to Your knowledge I
　　am indeed not guilty,
　Yet there is ^no one to save me
　　from Your hand.
8 '^Your hands fashioned and
　　made me altogether,
　ᴮYet would You destroy me?
9 'Remember that You have made
　　me as ^clay;
　Yet would You turn me into
　　dust again?
10 'Did You not pour me out like
　　milk,
　And curdle me like cheese,
11 Clothe me with skin and
　　flesh,
　And intertwine me with bones
　　and tendons?
12 'You have ^granted me life and
　　goodness;
　And Your care has guarded my
　　spirit.
13 'Yet You have concealed ^these
　　things in Your heart;
　I know that this is within
　　You:
14 If I have sinned, You will take
　　note of me,
　And ^will not acquit me of my
　　guilt.
15 'If I am wicked, woe to me!
　But if ^I am righteous, I dare
　　not lift up my head.
　I am full of shame, and
　　conscious of my misery.
16 'And should my head be high,
　　^You would hunt me like a
　　lion;
　And You would show Your
　　ᴮpower against me again.

9:32 ^Eccl 6:10   ᴮRom 9:20   9:33 ^Job 9:19; Is 1:18
9:34 ^Job 13:21   9:35 ^Job 13:22   10:1 ^Job 7:16
ᴮJob 7:11   10:2 ^Job 9:29   10:3 ^Job 9:22–24; 16:11
10:4 ^1 Sam 16:7; Job 28:24   10:5 ^Job 36:26
10:6 ^Job 14:16   10:7 ^Job 9:12; 27:22   10:8 ^Ps 119:73
ᴮJob 9:22   10:9 ^Job 4:19; 33:6   10:12 ^Job 33:4
10:13 ^Job 23:13   10:14 ^Job 7:21; 9:28   10:15 ^Job 6:29
10:16 ^Is 38:13   ᴮJob 5:9

17 'You renew ^Your witnesses
     against me
   And increase Your anger
     toward me;
   Hardship after hardship is
     with me.

18 '^Why then did You bring me
     out of the womb?
   If only I had died and no eye
     had seen me!

19 'I should have been as though I
     had not been,
   Brought from womb to tomb.'

20 "Would He not leave ^my few
     days alone?
   Withdraw from me so
     that I may have a little
     cheerfulness

21 Before I go—^and I shall not
     return—
   ^BTo the land of darkness and
     deep shadow,

22 The land of utter gloom like
     darkness *itself*,
   Of deep shadow without
     order,
   And it shines like darkness."

ZOPHAR REBUKES JOB

11 Then Zophar the Naamathite
       responded,

2 "Shall a multitude of words go
     unanswered,
   And a ^talkative man be
     acquitted?

3 "Shall your boasts silence
     people?
   And will you ^scoff, and no one
     rebuke?

4 "For you have said, 'My
     teaching is pure,
   And ^I am innocent in your
     eyes.'

5 "But if only God would speak,
   And open His lips against
     you,

6 And show you the secrets of
     wisdom!
   For sound wisdom ^has two
     sides.
   Know then that God forgets
     part of your guilt.

7 "^Can you discover the depths
     of God?
   Can you discover the limits of
     the Almighty?

8 "*They are as* ^high *as* the
     heavens; what can
     you do?
   Deeper than ^1,BSheol; what
     can you know?

9 "Its measurement is longer
     than the earth
   And broader than the sea.

10 "If He passes by or apprehends
     people,
   Or calls an assembly, ^who
     can restrain Him?

11 "For ^He knows false people,
   And He sees injustice without
     investigating.

12 "^An idiot will become
     intelligent
   When a ^Bwild donkey is born
     a human.

13 "If you would ^direct your
     heart *rightly*
   And ^Bspread out your hands
     to Him,

14 If wrongdoing is in your
     hand, ^put it far away,
   And do not let malice dwell
     in your tents;

10:17 ^Ruth 1:21; Job 16:8   10:18 ^Job 3:11-13
10:20 ^Job 14:1   10:21 ^Job 3:13-19   ^B Ps 88:12
11:2 ^Job 8:2; 18:2   11:3 ^Job 17:2; 21:3
11:4 ^Job 10:7   11:6 ^Job 9:4   11:7 ^Job 33:12, 13;
Rom 11:33   11:8 ^Job 22:12   ^B Job 26:6
11:10 ^Job 9:12   11:11 ^Job 34:21-23
11:12 ^Ps 39:5, 11   ^B Job 39:5   11:13 ^1 Sam 7:3
^B Ps 88:9   11:14 ^Job 22:23

11:8 ^1 I.e., the netherworld

15 Then, indeed, you could ^lift
up your face without *moral*
blemish,
And you would be firmly
established and ^not fear.

16 "For you would ^forget *your*
trouble;
Like waters that have passed
by, you would remember *it*.

17 "Your life would be ^brighter
than noonday;
Darkness would be like the
morning.

18 "Then you would trust, because
there is hope;
And you would look around
and rest securely.

19 "You would ^lie down and none
would disturb *you*,
And many would ^flatter you.

20 "But the ^eyes of the wicked
will fail,
And there will ^be no escape
for them;
And their hope is to breathe
their last."

JOB CHIDES HIS ACCUSERS

12 Then Job responded,
2 "Truly then ^you are the
people,
And with you wisdom will
die!

3 "But ^I have intelligence as well
as you;
I am not inferior to you.
And who does not know such
things as these?

4 "I am a joke to my friends,
The one who called on God
and He answered him;
The just *and* ^blameless *man*
is a joke.

5 "He who is at ease holds
disaster in contempt,
As prepared for those whose
feet slip.

6 "The ^tents of the destroyers
prosper,
And those who provoke God
are secure,
Whom God brings into their
power.

7 "But just ask the animals, and
have them teach you;
And the birds of the sky, and
have them tell you.

8 "Or speak to the earth, and have
it teach you;
And have the fish of the sea
tell you.

9 "Who among all these does not
know
That ^the hand of the LORD has
done this,

10 ^In whose hand is the life of
every living thing,
And ^the breath of all
mankind?

11 "Does ^the ear not put words to
the test,
As the palate tastes its food?

12 "Wisdom is with the ^aged,
And with long life *comes*
understanding.

JOB SPEAKS OF THE POWER OF GOD

13 "^Wisdom and might are with
Him;
Advice and ^understanding
belong to Him.

14 "Behold, He ^tears down, and it
cannot be rebuilt;
He imprisons a person, and
there is no release.

15 "Behold, He restrains the
waters, and they dry up;

11:15 ^Job 22:26   ^Ps 27:3   11:16 ^Is 65:16
11:17 ^Job 22:26   11:19 ^Zeph 3:13   ^Is 45:14
11:20 ^Deut 28:65   ^Job 27:22   12:2 ^Job 17:10
12:3 ^Job 13:2   12:4 ^Job 6:29   12:6 ^Job 9:24; 21:7-9
12:9 ^Is 41:20   12:10 ^Acts 17:28   ^Job 27:3
12:11 ^Job 34:3   12:12 ^Job 15:10; 32:7   12:13 ^Job 9:4
^Job 11:6   12:14 ^Job 19:10; Is 25:2

And He ^sends them out, and
they inundate the earth.

16 "Strength and sound wisdom
are with Him.
One who ^goes astray and one
who leads astray belong to
Him.

17 "He makes ^advisers walk
barefoot
And makes fools of ^Bjudges.

18 "He ^undoes the binding of
kings,
And ties a loincloth around
their waist.

19 "He makes priests walk barefoot,
And overthrows ^the secure
ones.

20 "He deprives the trusted ones
of speech,
And ^takes away the
discernment of the elders.

21 "He ^pours contempt on nobles,
And loosens the belt of the
strong.

22 "He ^reveals mysteries from the
darkness,
And brings the deep darkness
into light.

23 "He ^makes the nations great,
then destroys them;
He enlarges the nations, then
leads them away.

24 "He ^deprives the leaders of the
earth's people of intelligence
And makes them wander in a
pathless wasteland.

25 "They ^grope in darkness with
no light,
And He makes them ^Bstagger
like a drunken person.

JOB SAYS HIS FRIENDS' PROVERBS ARE ASHES

13 "^Behold, my eye has seen
all *this,*
My ear has heard and
understood it.

2 "^What you know I also know;
I am not inferior to you.

3 "But ^I would speak to the
Almighty,
And I desire to argue with
God.

4 "But you ^smear *me* with lies;
You are all ^Bworthless
physicians.

5 "Oh that you would ^be
completely silent,
And that it would become
your wisdom!

6 "Please hear my argument,
And give your attention to the
contentions of my lips.

7 "Will you ^speak what is unjust
for God,
And speak what is deceitful for
Him?

8 "Will you ^show partiality for
Him?
Will you contend for God?

9 "*Will it go* well when He
examines you?
Or ^will you deceive Him as
one deceives a man?

10 "He will certainly punish you
If you secretly ^show
partiality.

11 "Will ^His majesty not terrify
you,
And the dread of Him fall
upon you?

12 "Your memorable sayings are
proverbs of ashes,
Your defenses are defenses
of clay.

12:15 ^Gen 7:11-24   12:16 ^Job 13:7, 9   12:17 ^Job 3:14
^B Job 9:24   12:18 ^Ps 116:16   12:19 ^Job 34:24-28; 35:9
12:20 ^Job 17:4; 32:9   12:21 ^Job 34:19; Ps 107:40
12:22 ^Dan 2:22; 1 Cor 4:5   12:23 ^Is 9:3; 26:15
12:24 ^Job 12:20   12:25 ^Job 5:14   ^B Is 24:20
13:1 ^Job 12:9   13:2 ^Job 12:3   13:3 ^Job 13:22; 23:4
13:4 ^Ps 119:69   ^B Jer 23:32   13:5 ^Job 13:13; Prov 17:28
13:7 ^Job 27:4   13:8 ^Lev 19:15; Prov 24:23
13:9 ^Job 12:16   13:10 ^Job 13:8; 34:19
13:11 ^Job 31:23

JOB IS SURE HE WILL BE VINDICATED

13 "^ABe silent before me so that I
     may speak;
     Then let come upon me what
     may.

14 "Why should I take my flesh in
     my teeth,
     And ^Aput my life in my hands?

15 "^AThough He slay me,
     I will hope in Him.
     Nevertheless I ^Bwill argue my
     ways before Him.

16 "This also *will be* my ^Asalvation,
     For a godless person cannot
     come before His presence.

17 "Listen carefully to my speech,
     And let my declaration *fill*
     your ears.

18 "Behold now, I have prepared
     my case;
     I know that ^AI will be
     vindicated.

19 "^AWho could contend with me?
     For then I would be silent and
     die.

20 "Only two things *I ask that You*
     do not do to me,
     Then I will not hide from Your
     face:

21 ^ARemove Your hand from me,
     And may the dread of You not
     terrify me.

22 "Then call and ^AI will answer;
     Or let me speak, then reply to
     me.

23 "^AHow many are my guilty
     deeds and sins?
     Make known to me my
     wrongdoing and my sin.

24 "Why do You ^Ahide Your face
     And consider me ^BYour
     enemy?

25 "Will You scare away a
     ^Ascattered leaf?
     Or will You pursue the dry
     chaff?

26 "For You write ^Abitter things
     against me
     And ^Bmake me inherit the
     guilty deeds of my youth.

27 "You ^Aput my feet in the stocks
     And watch all my paths;
     You set a limit for the soles of
     my feet,

28 While I am decaying like a
     ^Arotten thing,
     Like a garment that is moth-
     eaten.

JOB SPEAKS OF THE FINALITY OF DEATH

14 "Man, who is born of
     woman,
     Is short-lived and ^Afull of
     turmoil.

2 "Like a flower he comes out and
     withers.
     He also flees like ^Aa shadow
     and does not remain.

3 "You also open Your eyes on
     him
     And ^Abring him into judgment
     with Yourself.

4 "^AWho can make the clean out
     of the unclean?
     No one!

5 "Since his days are
     determined,
     The ^Anumber of his months is
     with You;
     And You have set his limits so
     that he cannot pass.

6 "^ALook away from him so that
     he may rest,
     Until he fulfills his day like a
     hired worker.

13:13 ^AJob 13:5   13:14 ^APs 119:109   13:15 ^AJob 7:6
^BJob 27:5   13:16 ^AJob 23:7; Is 12:1, 2   13:18 ^AJob 9:21;
12:4   13:19 ^AIs 50:8   13:21 ^AJob 9:34; Ps 39:10
13:22 ^AJob 9:16; 14:15   13:23 ^AJob 7:21   13:24 ^APs 13:1
^BLam 2:5   13:25 ^ALev 26:36   13:26 ^AJob 9:18
^BPs 25:7   13:27 ^AJob 33:11   13:28 ^AJob 2:7
14:1 ^AEccl 2:23   14:2 ^AJob 8:9   14:3 ^APs 143:2
14:4 ^AJob 15:14; Ps 51:5   14:5 ^AJob 21:21
14:6 ^AJob 7:19; Ps 39:13

7 "For there is hope for a tree,
      When it is cut down, that it
         will sprout again,
      And its shoots will not fail.

8 "Though its roots grow old in
         the ground,
      And its stump dies in the dry
         soil,

9 At the scent of water it will
         flourish
      And produce sprigs like a plant.

10 "But ^a man dies and lies
         prostrate.
      A person passes away, and
         where is he?

11 "*As* ^water evaporates from the
         sea,
      And a river becomes parched
         and dried up,

12 So ^a man lies down and does
         not rise.
      Until the heavens no longer
         exist,
      He will not awake nor be
         woken from his sleep.

13 "Oh that You would hide me in
      ¹Sheol,
      That You would conceal me
         ^until Your wrath returns *to
         You,*
      That You would set a limit for
         me and remember me!

14 "If a man dies, will he live
      again?
      All the days of my struggle I
         will wait
      Until my relief comes.

15 "You will call, and I will answer
         You;
      You will long for ^the work of
         Your hands.

16 "For now You number my steps,
      You do not ^observe my sin.

17 "My wrongdoing is ^sealed up in
         a bag,
      And You cover over my guilt.

18 "But the falling mountain
         crumbles away,
      And the rock moves from its
         place;

19 Water wears away stones,
      Its torrents wash away the
         dust of the earth;
      So You ^destroy a man's
         hope.

20 "You forever overpower him
         and he ^departs;
      You change his appearance
         and send him away.

21 "His sons achieve honor, but
         ^he does not know *it;*
      Or they become
         insignificant, and he does
         not perceive it.

22 "However, his body pains him,
      And his soul mourns for
         himself."

ELIPHAZ SAYS JOB PRESUMES MUCH

15 Then Eliphaz the Temanite
         responded,

2 "Should a wise man answer
         with windy knowledge,
      ^And fill himself with the east
         wind?

3 "Should he argue with useless
         talk,
      Or with words which do not
         benefit?

4 "Indeed, you do away with
         reverence,
      And hinder meditation before
         God.

5 "For ^your wrongdoing teaches
         your mouth,
      And you choose the language
         of the cunning.

14:10 ^Job 3:13; 14:10-15   14:11 ^Is 19:5
14:12 ^Job 3:13   14:13 ^Is 26:20   14:15 ^Job 10:3
14:16 ^Job 10:6   14:17 ^Deut 32:32-34   14:19 ^Job 7:6
14:20 ^Job 4:20; 20:7   14:21 ^Eccl 9:5   15:2 ^Job 6:26
15:5 ^Job 22:5

14:13 ¹I.e., the netherworld

6 "Your ^own mouth condemns
   you, and not I;
   And your own lips testify
   against you.

7 "Were you the first person to be
   born,
   Or ^were you brought forth
   before the hills?

8 "Do you hear the ^secret
   discussion of God,
   And limit wisdom to yourself?

9 "^What do you know that we do
   not know?
   What do you understand that
   we do not?

10 "Both the ^gray-haired and the
    aged are among us,
    Older than your father.

11 "Are the consolations of God
    too little for you,
    Or the ^word *spoken* gently to
    you?

12 "Why does your ^heart take you
    away?
    And why do your eyes wink,

13 That you can turn your spirit
    against God
    And produce *such* words from
    your mouth?

14 "What is man, that ^he would
    be pure,
    Or ^he who is born of a woman,
    that he would be righteous?

15 "Behold, He has no trust in His
    ^holy ones,
    And the heavens are not pure
    in His sight;

16 How much less one who is
    detestable and corrupt:
    A person who ^drinks malice
    like water!

WHAT ELIPHAZ HAS SEEN OF LIFE

17 "I will tell you, listen to me;
    And what I have seen I will
    also declare;

18 What wise people have told,
    And have not concealed from
    ^their fathers,

19 To whom alone the land was
    given,
    And no stranger passed among
    them.

20 "The wicked person writhes ^in
    pain all *his* days,
    And the years reserved for the
    ruthless are numbered.

21 "Sounds of terror are in his
    ears;
    ^*While he is* at peace the
    destroyer comes upon him.

22 "He does not believe that he
    will ^return from darkness,
    And he is destined for ^Bthe
    sword.

23 "He wanders about for food,
    saying, 'Where *is it?*'
    He knows that a day of
    ^darkness is at hand.

24 "Distress and anguish terrify
    him,
    They overpower him like a
    king ready for the attack,

25 Because he has reached out
    with his hand against God,
    And is ^arrogant toward the
    Almighty.

26 "He rushes headlong at Him
    With his massive shield.

27 "For he has ^covered his face
    with his fat,
    And put fat on his waist.

28 "He has ^lived in desolate cities,
    In houses no one would inhabit,
    Which are destined to become
    ruins.

15:6 ^Job 18:7   15:7 ^Job 38:4, 21; Prov 8:25
15:8 ^Rom 11:34; 1 Cor 2:11   15:9 ^Job 12:3; 13:2
15:10 ^Job 12:12; 32:6, 7   15:11 ^Job 6:10; 23:12
15:12 ^Job 11:13; 36:13   15:14 ^Eccl 7:20   ^BJob 25:4
15:15 ^Job 5:1   15:16 ^Job 34:7; Prov 19:28
15:18 ^Job 8:8; 20:4   15:20 ^Job 15:24
15:21 ^Job 20:21; 1 Thess 5:3   15:22 ^Job 15:30
^BJob 19:29   15:23 ^Job 15:22, 30   15:25 ^Job 36:9
15:27 ^Ps 73:7; 119:70   15:28 ^Job 3:14; Is 5:8, 9

29 "He ^will not become rich, nor
will his wealth endure;
And his property will not
stretch out on the earth.
30 "He will ^not escape from
darkness;
The flame will dry up his
shoot,
And he will go away by ^Bthe
breath of His mouth.
31 "Let him not ^trust in
emptiness, deceiving
himself;
For his reward will be
emptiness.
32 "It will be accomplished ^before
his time,
And his palm branch will not
be green.
33 "He will drop off his unripe
grape like the vine,
And will ^cast off his flower
like the olive tree.
34 "For the company of ^the
godless is barren,
And fire consumes ^Bthe tents
of the corrupt.
35 "They ^conceive harm and give
birth to wrongdoing,
And their mind prepares
deception."

JOB SAYS FRIENDS ARE MISERABLE COMFORTERS

16 Then Job responded,
2 "I have heard many things
like these;
^Miserable comforters are you
all!
3 "Is there *no* end to ^windy
words?
Or what provokes you that you
answer?
4 "I too could speak like you,
If only I were in your place.
I could compose words against
you

And ^shake my head at you.
5 "*Or* I could strengthen you with
my mouth,
And the condolence of my lips
could lessen *your pain*.

JOB SAYS GOD SHATTERED HIM

6 "If I speak, ^my pain is not
lessened,
And if I refrain, what *pain*
leaves me?
7 "But now He has ^exhausted me;
You have laid ^Bwaste all my
group *of loved ones*.
8 "And You have shriveled me up,
It has become a witness;
And my ^infirmity rises up
against me,
It testifies to my face.
9 "His anger has ^torn me and
hunted me down,
He has gnashed at me with His
teeth;
My ^Benemy glares at me.
10 "They have ^gaped at me with
their mouths,
They have slapped me on the
cheek with contempt;
They have massed themselves
against me.
11 "God hands me over to
criminals,
And tosses me into the hands
of the wicked.
12 "I was at ease, but ^He shattered
me,
And He has grasped me by
my neck and shaken me to
pieces;
He has also set me up as His
target.

15:29 ^Job 27:16, 17   15:30 ^Job 5:14   ^BJob 4:9
15:31 ^Job 35:13; Is 59:4   15:32 ^Job 22:16; Eccl 7:17
15:33 ^Job 14:2   15:34 ^Job 8:13   ^BJob 8:22
15:35 ^Ps 7:14; Is 59:4   16:2 ^Job 13:4; 21:34
16:3 ^Job 6:26   16:4 ^Zeph 2:15; Matt 27:39
16:6 ^Job 9:27, 28   16:7 ^Job 7:3   ^BJob 19:13-15
16:8 ^Job 19:20; Ps 109:24   16:9 ^Hos 6:1   ^BJob 13:24
16:10 ^Ps 22:13   16:12 ^Job 9:17

¹³ "His ^arrows surround me.
　He splits my kidneys open
　　without mercy;
　He pours out ^Bmy bile on the
　　ground.
¹⁴ "He ^breaks through me with
　　breach after breach;
　He ^Bruns at me like a warrior.
¹⁵ "I have sewed ^sackcloth over
　　my skin,
　And thrust my horn in the
　　dust.
¹⁶ "My face is flushed from
　　^weeping,
　And deep darkness is on my
　　eyelids,
¹⁷ Although there is no ^violence
　　in my hands,
　And my prayer is pure.

¹⁸ "Earth, do not cover my blood,
　And may there be no *resting*
　　place for my cry.
¹⁹ "Even now, behold, ^my witness
　　is in heaven,
　And my advocate is on high.
²⁰ "My friends are my scoffers;
　^My eye weeps to God,
²¹ That one might plead for a
　　man with God
　As a son of man with his
　　neighbor!
²² "For when a few years are past,
　I shall go the way ^of no return.

JOB SAYS HE HAS BECOME A PROVERB

17 "My spirit is broken, my days
　　are extinguished,
　The ^grave is *ready* for me.
² "^Mockers are certainly with me,
　And my eye gazes on their
　　provocation.

³ "Make a pledge ^for me with
　　Yourself;
　Who is there that will be my
　　guarantor?

⁴ "For You have ^kept their
　　hearts away from
　　understanding;
　Therefore You will not exalt
　　them.
⁵ "He who ^informs against
　　friends for a share *of the*
　　spoils,
　The eyes of his children also
　　will perish.

⁶ "But He has made me a ^proverb
　　among the people,
　And I am one at whom people
　　^Bspit.
⁷ "My eye has also become
　　^inexpressive because of
　　grief,
　And all my body parts are like
　　a shadow.
⁸ "The upright will be appalled at
　　this,
　And the ^innocent will stir
　　himself up against the
　　godless.
⁹ "Nevertheless ^the righteous
　　will hold to his way,
　And ^Bthe one who has clean
　　hands will grow stronger and
　　stronger.
¹⁰ "But come again all of you now,
　For I ^do not find a wise man
　　among you.
¹¹ "My ^days are past, my plans are
　　torn apart,
　The wishes of my heart.
¹² "They make night into day,
　　saying,
　'The light is near,' in the
　　presence of darkness.

16:13 ^Job 6:4   ^B Job 20:25   16:14 ^Job 9:17   ^B Joel 2:7
16:15 ^Gen 37:34; Ps 69:11   16:16 ^Job 16:20
16:17 ^Is 59:6; Jon 3:8   16:19 ^Rom 1:9; Phil 1:8
16:20 ^Job 17:7   16:22 ^Job 3:13   17:1 ^Ps 88:3, 4
17:2 ^Job 12:4; 17:6   17:3 ^Ps 119:122; Is 38:14
17:4 ^Job 12:20   17:5 ^Lev 19:13, 16   17:6 ^Job 17:2
^B Job 30:10   17:7 ^Job 16:16   17:8 ^Job 22:19
17:9 ^Prov 4:18   ^B Job 22:30   17:10 ^Job 12:2
17:11 ^Job 7:6

13 "If I hope for [1,A]Sheol as my
　　home,
　　I make my bed in the darkness;
14 *If* I call to the ^grave, 'You are
　　my father';
　　To the ^B^maggot, 'my mother
　　and my sister';
15 Where then is ^my hope?
　　And who looks at my hope?
16 "Will it go down with me to
　　Sheol?
　　Shall we together ^go down
　　into the dust?"

BILDAD SPEAKS OF THE WICKED

18 Then Bildad the Shuhite
responded,
2 "How long will you hunt for
　　words?
　　Show understanding, and
　　then we can talk.
3 "Why are we ^regarded as
　　animals,
　　As stupid in your eyes?
4 "You who tear yourself in your
　　anger—
　　Should the earth be
　　abandoned for your sake,
　　Or the rock moved from its
　　place?
5 "Indeed, the ^light of the
　　wicked goes out,
　　And the spark from his fire
　　does not shine.
6 "The light in his tent is
　　^darkened,
　　And his lamp goes out above
　　him.
7 "His vigorous stride is shortened,
　　And his ^own plan brings him
　　down.
8 "For he is ^thrown into the net
　　by his own feet,
　　And he steps on the webbing.
9 "A snare seizes *him* by the heel,
　　And a trap snaps shut on him.

10 "A noose for him is hidden in
　　the ground,
　　And a trap for him on the
　　pathway.
11 "All around ^sudden terrors
　　frighten him,
　　And harass him at every step.
12 "His strength is ^famished,
　　And disaster is ready at his side.
13 "It devours parts of his skin,
　　The firstborn of death
　　^devours his limbs.
14 "He is ^torn from the security of
　　his tent,
　　And they march him before
　　the king of terrors.
15 "Nothing of his dwells in his tent;
　　^Brimstone is scattered on his
　　home.
16 "His ^roots are dried below,
　　And his ^B^branch withers above.
17 "^A^The memory of him perishes
　　from the earth,
　　And he has no name abroad.
18 "He is driven from light ^into
　　darkness,
　　And chased from the
　　inhabited world.
19 "He has no ^offspring or
　　descendants among his
　　people,
　　Nor any survivor where he
　　resided.
20 "Those in the west are appalled
　　at ^his fate,
　　And those in the east are
　　seized with horror.
21 "Certainly these are the
　　^dwellings of the wicked,

17:13 ^Job 3:13　17:14 ^Job 7:5　^B^ Job 21:26
17:15 ^Job 7:6　17:16 ^Job 3:17; 21:33　18:3 ^Ps 73:22
18:5 ^Job 21:17; Prov 13:9　18:6 ^Job 12:25
18:7 ^Job 15:6　18:8 ^Is 24:17, 18　18:11 ^Job 15:21
18:12 ^Is 8:21　18:13 ^Zech 14:12　18:14 ^Job 8:22; 18:6
18:15 ^Ps 11:6　18:16 ^Mal 4:1　^B^ Job 15:30, 32
18:17 ^Ps 34:16; Prov 10:7　18:18 ^Job 5:14; Is 8:22
18:19 ^Job 27:14, 15; Is 14:22
18:20 ^Jer 50:27; Obad 12　18:21 ^Job 21:28

17:13 [1] I.e., the netherworld

And this is the place of him
who does not know God."

JOB FEELS INSULTED

19 Then Job responded,
² "How long will you
torment me
And crush me with words?
³ "These ten times you have
insulted me;
You are not ashamed to wrong
me.
⁴ "Even *if* I have truly done wrong,
My error stays with me.
⁵ "If indeed you ^exalt yourselves
against me
And prove my disgrace to me,
⁶ Know then that ^God has
wronged me
And has surrounded me with
ᴮHis net.

EVERYTHING IS AGAINST HIM

⁷ "Behold, ^I cry, 'Violence!' but I
get no answer;
I shout for help, but there is no
justice.
⁸ "He has ^blocked my way so
that I cannot pass,
And He has put darkness on
my paths.
⁹ "He has ^stripped my honor
from me
And removed the crown from
my head.
¹⁰ "He ^breaks me down on every
side, and I am gone;
And He has uprooted my hope
like a tree.
¹¹ "He has also ^kindled His anger
against me
And ᴮconsidered me as His
enemy.
¹² "His troops come together
And ^build up their way
against me
And camp around my tent.

¹³ "He has ^removed my brothers
far from me,
And my ᴮacquaintances have
completely turned away
from me.
¹⁴ "My relatives have failed,
And my ^close friends have
forgotten me.
¹⁵ "Those who live in my house
and my servant women
consider me a stranger.
I am a foreigner in their
sight.
¹⁶ "I call to my servant, but he
does not answer;
I have to implore his favor with
my mouth.
¹⁷ "My breath is offensive to my
wife,
And I am loathsome to my
own brothers.
¹⁸ "Even young children despise
me;
I stand up and they speak
against me.
¹⁹ "All my ^associates loathe
me,
And those I love have turned
against me.
²⁰ "My ^bone clings to my skin and
my flesh,
And I have escaped *only* by the
skin of my teeth.
²¹ "Pity me, pity me, you friends
of mine,
For the ^hand of God has
struck me.
²² "Why do you ^persecute me as
God *does,*
And are not satisfied with my
flesh?

19:5 ^Ps 35:26; 55:12, 13   19:6 ^Job 16:11   ᴮLam 1:13
19:7 ^Job 30:20, 24; Hab 1:2   19:8 ^Job 3:23; Lam 3:7, 9
19:9 ^Job 12:17, 19; Ps 89:44   19:10 ^Job 12:14
19:11 ^Job 16:9   ᴮJob 13:24   19:12 ^Job 30:12
19:13 ^Job 16:7   ᴮPs 88:8, 18   19:14 ^Job 19:19
19:19 ^Ps 38:11; 55:12, 13   19:20 ^Ps 102:5; Lam 4:8
19:21 ^Job 1:11; Ps 38:2   19:22 ^Job 13:24, 25; Ps 69:26

JOB SAYS MY REDEEMER LIVES

23 "Oh that my words were
    written!
    Oh that they were ^recorded in
    a book!
24 "That with an iron stylus and
    lead
    They were engraved in the
    rock forever!
25 "Yet as for me, I know that ^my
    Redeemer lives,
    And at the last, He will take
    His stand on the earth.
26 "Even after my skin is
    destroyed,
    Yet from my flesh I will ^see God,
27 Whom I, on my part, shall
    behold for myself,
    And *whom* my eyes will see,
    and not another.
    My heart ^faints within me!
28 "If you say, 'How shall we
    ^persecute him?'
    And 'What pretext for a case
    against him can we find?'
29 "*Then* be afraid of ^the sword
    for yourselves,
    For wrath *brings* the
    punishment of the sword,
    So that you may know ^there is
    judgment."

ZOPHAR SAYS THE REJOICING
OF THE WICKED IS SHORT

20 Then Zophar the Naama-
    thite responded,
2 "Therefore my disquieting
    thoughts make me respond,
    Even because of my inward
    agitation.
3 "I listened to ^the reprimand
    which insults me,
    And the spirit of my
    understanding makes me
    answer.
4 "Do you know this from
    ^ancient times,

From the establishment of
    mankind on earth,
5 That the ^rejoicing of the
    wicked is short,
    And ^the joy of the godless
    momentary?
6 "Though his arrogance ^reaches
    the heavens,
    And his head touches the
    clouds,
7 He ^perishes forever like his
    refuse;
    Those who have seen him will
    say, 'Where is he?'
8 "He flies away like a ^dream,
    and they cannot find him;
    Like a vision of the night he is
    ^chased away.
9 "The ^eye which saw him sees
    him no longer,
    And his place no longer
    beholds him.
10 "His ^sons favor the poor,
    And his hands ^give back his
    wealth.
11 "His ^bones are full of his
    youthful strength,
    But it lies down with him in
    the dust.
12 "Though ^evil tastes sweet in
    his mouth
    And he hides it under his tongue,
13 *Though* he desires it and will
    not let it go,
    But holds it ^in his mouth,
14 *Yet* his food in his stomach is
    changed
    To the venom of cobras
    within him.

19:23 ^Is 30:8; Jer 36:2 19:25 ^Is 43:14; Jer 50:34
19:26 ^1 Cor 13:12; 1 John 3:2 19:27 ^Ps 73:26
19:28 ^Job 19:22 19:29 ^Job 15:22 ^Eccl 12:14
20:3 ^Job 19:3 20:4 ^Job 8:8 20:5 ^Ps 37:35, 36
^Job 8:13 20:6 ^Is 14:13, 14; Obad 3, 4
20:7 ^Job 4:20; 14:20 20:8 ^Ps 73:20 ^Job 27:21-23
20:9 ^Job 7:8; 8:18 20:10 ^Job 5:4 ^Job 27:16, 17
20:11 ^Job 21:23, 24 20:12 ^Job 15:16
20:13 ^Num 11:18-20, 33; Job 20:23

¹⁵ "He swallows riches,
  But will ᴬvomit them up;
  God will expel them from his
    belly.
¹⁶ "He sucks ᴬthe poison of cobras;
  The viper's tongue kills him.
¹⁷ "He does not look at ᴬthe
    streams,
  The rivers flowing with honey
    and curds.
¹⁸ "He ᴬreturns the product of his
    labor
  And cannot swallow *it;*
  As to the riches of his trading,
  He cannot even enjoy *them.*
¹⁹ "For he has ᴬoppressed *and*
    neglected the poor;
  He has seized a house which
    he has not built.

²⁰ "Because he knew no quiet
    within him,
  He does ᴬnot retain anything
    he desires.
²¹ "Nothing remains for him to
    devour,
  Therefore ᴬhis prosperity does
    not endure.
²² "In the fullness of his excess he
    will be cramped;
  The ᴬhand of everyone who
    suffers will come *against*
    him.
²³ "When he ᴬfills his belly,
  God will send His fierce anger
    on him
  And rain *it* on him while he is
    eating.
²⁴ "He may ᴬflee from the iron
    weapon,
  But the bronze bow will pierce
    him.
²⁵ "It is drawn and comes out of
    his back,
  Even the flashing *point* from
    his gallbladder;
  ᴬTerrors come upon him,

²⁶ Complete darkness is held in
    reserve for his treasures,
  And unfanned ᴬfire will
    devour him;
  It will consume the survivor in
    his tent.
²⁷ "The ᴬheavens will reveal his
    guilt,
  And the earth will rise up
    against him.
²⁸ "The ᴬincrease of his house will
    disappear;
  His possessions will flow away
    ᴮon the day of His anger.
²⁹ "This is a wicked person's
    ᴬportion from God,
  The inheritance decreed to
    him by God."

JOB SAYS GOD WILL DEAL WITH THE WICKED

21 Then Job responded,
  ² "Listen carefully to my
    speech,
  And let this be your *way of*
    consolation.
³ "Bear with me that I may speak;
  Then after I have spoken, you
    may ᴬmock *me.*
⁴ "As for me, is ᴬmy complaint to a
    mortal?
  Or ᴮwhy should I not be
    impatient?
⁵ "Look at me, and be astonished,
  And ᴬput *your* hand over *your*
    mouth.
⁶ "Even when I remember, I am
    disturbed,
  And ᴬhorror takes hold of my
    flesh.

20:15 ᴬJob 20:10, 20, 21   20:16 ᴬDeut 32:24, 33
20:17 ᴬDeut 32:13, 14; Job 29:6   20:18 ᴬJob 20:10, 15
20:19 ᴬJob 24:2-4; 35:9   20:20 ᴬEccl 5:13-15
20:21 ᴬJob 15:29   20:22 ᴬJob 5:5   20:23 ᴬJob 20:13, 14
20:24 ᴬIs 24:18; Amos 5:19   20:25 ᴬJob 18:11, 14
20:26 ᴬJob 15:30; Ps 21:9   20:27 ᴬDeut 31:28; Is 26:21
20:28 ᴬDeut 28:31   ᴮJob 20:15   20:29 ᴬJob 27:13;
31:2, 3   21:3 ᴬJob 11:3; 17:2   21:4 ᴬJob 7:11   ᴮJob 6:11
21:5 ᴬJudg 18:19; Job 13:5   21:6 ᴬPs 55:5

7 "Why ^do the wicked *still* live,
Grow old, *and* also become
very powerful?

8 "Their ^descendants endure
with them in their sight,
And their offspring before
their eyes,

9 Their houses ^are safe from fear,
And the rod of God is not on
them.

10 "His ox mates without fail;
His cow calves and does not
miscarry.

11 "They send out their boys like
the flock,
And their children dance.

12 "They sing with the tambourine
and harp,
And rejoice at the sound of the
flute.

13 "They ^spend their days in
prosperity,
And suddenly they go down to
¹Sheol.

14 "Yet they say to God, '^Go away
from us!
We do not even desire the
knowledge of Your ways.

15 'Who is the Almighty, that we
should serve Him,
And ^what would we gain if we
plead with Him?'

16 "Behold, their prosperity is not
in their hand;
The ^advice of the wicked is far
from me.

17 "How often is ^the lamp of the
wicked put out,
Or does their ^Bdisaster fall on
them?
Does God apportion
destruction in His anger?

18 "Are they as ^straw before the
wind,
And like chaff which the storm
carries away?

19 "*You say,* '^God saves up a
person's wrongdoing for his
sons.'
Let God repay him so that he
may know *it.*

20 "Let his ^own eyes see his
destruction,
And let him drink of the wrath
of the Almighty.

21 "For what does he care about
his household after him,
When the number of his
months is at an end?

22 "Can anyone ^teach God
knowledge,
In that He ^Bjudges those on
high?

23 "One ^dies in his full strength,
Being wholly undisturbed and
at ease;

24 His sides are filled with fat,
And the ^marrow of his bones
is wet,

25 While another dies with a
bitter soul,
Never even tasting *anything*
good.

26 "Together they ^lie down in the
dust,
And maggots cover them.

27 "Behold, I know your thoughts,
And the plots you devise
against me.

28 "For you say, 'Where is the
house of ^the nobleman,
And where is the tent, the
dwelling places of the
wicked?'

21:7 ^Jer 12:1; Hab 1:13   21:8 ^Ps 17:14   21:9 ^Job 12:6
21:13 ^Job 21:23; 36:11   21:14 ^Job 22:17
21:15 ^Job 22:17; 34:9   21:16 ^Job 22:18
21:17 ^Job 18:5, 6   ᴮJob 31:2, 3   21:18 ^Job 13:25;
Ps 83:13   21:19 ^Jer 31:29; Ezek 18:2   21:20 ^Jer 31:30;
Ezek 18:4   21:22 ^Rom 11:34   ᴮPs 82:1
21:23 ^Job 20:11; 21:13   21:24 ^Prov 3:8
21:26 ^Job 3:13; Eccl 9:2   21:28 ^Job 1:3; 31:37

21:13 ¹I.e., the netherworld

²⁹ "Have you not asked travelers,
　　And do you not examine their
　　　evidence?
³⁰ "For the ^wicked person is
　　spared a day of disaster;
　　They are led *away* from ᴮa day
　　　of fury.
³¹ "Who confronts him with his
　　actions,
　　And who repays him for what
　　　he has done?
³² "When he is carried to the grave,
　　People will keep watch over *his*
　　　tomb.
³³ "The clods of the valley will
　　gently cover him;
　　Moreover, ^all mankind will
　　　follow after him,
　　While countless *others go*
　　　before him.
³⁴ "So how dare you give me
　　empty ^comfort?
　　For your answers remain
　　　nothing but falsehood!"

ELIPHAZ ACCUSES AND EXHORTS JOB

22 Then Eliphaz the Temanite
　　responded,
² "Can a strong ^man be of use to
　　God,
　　Or a wise one be useful to
　　　himself?
³ "Is *it any* pleasure to the
　　Almighty if you are righteous,
　　Or gain if you make your ways
　　　blameless?
⁴ "Is it because of your reverence
　　that He punishes you,
　　That He ^enters into judgment
　　　against you?
⁵ "Is ^your wickedness not
　　abundant,
　　And is there no end to your
　　　guilty deeds?
⁶ "For you have ^seized pledges
　　from your brothers without
　　cause,

And stripped people naked.
⁷ "You have ^given the weary no
　　water to drink,
　　And you have ᴮwithheld bread
　　　from the hungry.
⁸ "But the earth belongs to the
　　powerful man,
　　And ^the one who is honorable
　　　dwells on it.
⁹ "You have sent ^widows away
　　empty,
　　And the strength of ᴮorphans
　　　has been crushed.
¹⁰ "Therefore ^traps surround you,
　　And sudden ᴮdread terrifies
　　　you,
¹¹ Or ^darkness, *so that* you
　　cannot see,
　　And a flood of water covers you.
¹² "Is God not ^*in* the height of
　　heaven?
　　Look also at the highest stars,
　　how high they are!
¹³ "But you say, '^What does God
　　know?
　　Can He judge through the
　　thick darkness?
¹⁴ '^Clouds are a hiding place for
　　Him, so that He cannot see;
　　And He walks on the vault of
　　heaven.'
¹⁵ "Will you keep to the ancient
　　path
　　Which ^wicked people have
　　walked,
¹⁶ Who were snatched away
　　before their time,
　　Whose ^foundations were
　　washed away *by* a river?

21:30 ^2 Pet 2:9   ᴮJob 40:11   21:33 ^Job 3:19; 24:24
21:34 ^Job 16:2   22:2 ^Job 35:7; Luke 17:10
22:4 ^Job 14:3; 19:29   22:5 ^Job 11:6; 15:5
22:6 ^Job 24:3, 9; Ezek 18:16   22:7 ^Job 31:16, 17
ᴮJob 31:31   22:8 ^Is 3:3; 9:15   22:9 ^Job 24:3, 21
ᴮJob 6:27   22:10 ^Job 18:8   ᴮJob 15:21
22:11 ^Job 5:14   22:12 ^Job 11:7-9   22:13 ^Is 29:15;
Ezek 8:12   22:14 ^Job 26:9   22:15 ^Job 34:36
22:16 ^Is 28:2; Matt 7:26, 27

17 "They ^said to God, 'Go away
     from us!'
   And 'What can the Almighty
     do to them?'
18 "Yet He ^filled their houses with
     good *things*;
   But ^Bthe advice of the wicked is
     far from me.
19 "The ^righteous see and are
     glad,
   And the innocent mock them,
     saying,
20 'Truly our enemies are
     eliminated,
   And ^fire has consumed their
     abundance.'

21 "^Be reconciled with Him, and
     be at peace;
   Thereby good will come to
     you.
22 "Please receive ^instruction
     from His mouth,
   And put His words in your
     heart.
23 "If you ^return to the Almighty,
     you will be restored;
   If you ^Bremove injustice far
     from your tent,
24 And ^put *your* gold in the
     dust,
   And *the gold of* Ophir among
     the stones of the brooks,
25 Then the Almighty will be
     your gold
   And abundant silver to you.
26 "For then you will ^take
     pleasure in the Almighty
   And lift up your face to God.
27 "You will pray to Him, and ^He
     will hear you;
   And you will pay your vows.
28 "You will also decide
     something, and it will be
     established for you;
   And ^light will shine on your
     ways.

29 "When they have brought *you*
     low, you will speak with
     confidence,
   And He will save the ^humble
     person.
30 "He will rescue one who is not
     innocent,
   And he will be ^rescued due
     to the cleanness of your
     hands."

JOB SAYS HE LONGS FOR GOD

23 Then Job responded,
   2 "Even today my ^complaint
     is rebellion;
   His hand is heavy despite my
     groaning.
3 "Oh that I knew how to find Him,
   That I might come to His home!
4 "I would ^present *my* case
     before Him
   And fill my mouth with
     arguments.
5 "I would learn the words *which*
     He would answer,
   And perceive what He would
     tell me.
6 "Would He contend with me by
     ^the greatness of *His* power?
   No, surely He would pay
     attention to me.
7 "There the upright would
     ^argue with Him;
   And I would be ^Bfree of my
     Judge forever.

8 "Behold, I go forward but He is
     not *there,*
   And backward, but I ^cannot
     perceive Him;

22:17 ^Job 21:14, 15   22:18 ^Job 12:6   ^B Job 21:16
22:19 ^Ps 52:6; 107:42   22:20 ^Job 15:30
22:21 ^Ps 34:10   22:22 ^Job 6:10; Prov 2:6
22:23 ^Is 19:22   ^B Job 11:14   22:24 ^Job 31:24, 25
22:26 ^Ps 37:4; Is 58:14   22:27 ^Job 34:28
22:28 ^Job 11:17; Ps 112:4   22:29 ^James 4:6; 1 Pet 5:5
22:30 ^Job 42:7, 8; Ps 24:3, 4   23:2 ^Job 7:11
23:4 ^Job 13:18   23:6 ^Job 9:4   23:7 ^Job 13:3
^B Job 23:10   23:8 ^Job 9:11; 35:14

9 When He acts on the left, I
   cannot see *Him;*
   He turns to the right, but I
   cannot see Him.
10 "But He knows the way I take;
   When He has ^put me to the
   test, I will come out as gold.
11 "My foot has ^held on to His
   path;
   I have kept His way and not
   turned aside.
12 "I have not failed the command
   of His lips;
   I have treasured the ^words
   of His mouth more than my
   necessary food.
13 "But He is unique, and who can
   make Him turn?
   Whatever His soul desires, He
   does *it.*
14 "For He carries out what is
   destined for me,
   And many such *destinies* are
   with Him.
15 "Therefore, I would be terrified
   at His presence;
   When I consider *this,* I am
   frightened of Him.
16 "*It is* God *who* has made my
   ^heart faint,
   And the Almighty *who* has
   terrified me,
17 But I ^am not destroyed by
   darkness,
   Nor by ^deep gloom *which*
   covers me.

JOB SAYS GOD SEEMS TO IGNORE WRONGS

24 "^Why are ¹times not stored
   up by the Almighty,
   And *why* do those who know
   Him not see ^His ¹days?
2 "*People* ^remove landmarks;
   They seize and devour flocks.
3 "They drive away the donkeys
   of ^orphans;

They seize the widow's ox as
   a pledge.
4 "They push ^the needy aside
   from the road;
   The poor of the land have
   to hide themselves
   together.
5 "Behold, *like* ^wild donkeys in
   the wilderness
   They ^go out scavenging for
   food in their activity,
   As bread for *their* children in
   the desert.
6 "They harvest their feed in the
   field
   And glean the vineyard of the
   wicked.
7 "^They spend the night naked,
   without clothing,
   And have no covering against
   the cold.
8 "They are wet from the
   mountain rains,
   And they hug the rock for lack
   of a shelter.
9 "*Others* snatch an ^orphan from
   the breast,
   And they seize *it* as a pledge
   against the poor.
10 "*The poor* move about naked
   without clothing,
   And they carry sheaves, *while*
   going hungry.
11 "Within the walls they
   produce oil;
   They tread wine presses but go
   thirsty.
12 "From the city people groan,
   And the souls of the wounded
   cry for help;

23:10 ^Zech 13:9; 1 Pet 1:7   23:11 ^Job 31:7; Ps 17:5
23:12 ^Job 6:10; 22:22   23:16 ^Deut 20:3; Jer 51:46
23:17 ^Job 10:18, 19   ^Job 19:8   24:1 ^Acts 1:7
^Is 2:12   24:2 ^Deut 19:14; Prov 23:10
24:3 ^Job 6:27   24:4 ^Job 24:14; 29:16
24:5 ^Job 39:5-8   ^Ps 104:23
24:7 ^Ex 22:26; Job 22:6   24:9 ^Job 6:27

24:1 ¹I.e., of judgment for the wicked

Yet God ^does not
  pay attention to the
  offensiveness.

13 "Others have been with those
  who rebel against the light;
  They do not want to know its
    ways
  Nor stay in its paths.

14 "The murderer ^arises at dawn;
  He ^Bkills the poor and the needy,
  And at night he is like a thief.

15 "The eye of the ^adulterer
    watches for twilight,
  Saying, 'No eye will see me.'
  And he disguises his face.

16 "In the darkness they ^dig into
    houses,
  They ^Bshut themselves up by
    day;
  They do not know the light.

17 "For the morning is the same to
    him as thick darkness,
  For he is familiar with the
    ^terrors of thick darkness.

18 "They are insignificant on the
    surface of the water;
  Their plot of land on the earth
    is ^cursed.
  They do not turn toward the
    vineyards.

19 "Dryness and heat ^snatch away
    the snow waters,
  As [1,B]Sheol snatches those who
    have sinned.

20 "A ^mother will forget him;
  The maggot feeds sweetly
    until he is no longer
    remembered.
  And injustice will be broken
    like a tree.

21 "He wrongs the infertile woman,
  And does no good for ^the
    widow.

22 "But He drags off the mighty by
    His power;

He rises, but ^no one has
    assurance of life.

23 "He provides them with
    security, and they are
    supported;
  And His ^eyes are on their ways.

24 "They are exalted a ^little while,
    then they are gone;
  Moreover, they are ^Bbrought
    low, and like everything they
    are gathered up;
  Like the heads of grain they
    wither.

25 "Now if it is not so, ^who can
    prove me a liar,
  And make my speech
    worthless?"

BILDAD SAYS MANKIND IS INFERIOR

25 Then Bildad the Shuhite
   responded,

2 "^Dominion and awe belong to
    Him
  Who makes peace in His heights.

3 "Is there any number to ^His
    troops?
  And upon whom does His light
    not rise?

4 "How then can mankind be
    ^righteous with God?
  Or how can anyone who is
    born of woman be ^Bpure?

5 "If even ^the moon has no
    brightness
  And the ^Bstars are not pure in
    His sight,

6 How much less ^man, that
    maggot,
  And a son of man, that worm!"

24:12 ^Job 9:23, 24   24:14 ^Mic 2:1   ^B Ps 10:8
24:15 ^Prov 7:9   24:16 ^Ex 22:2   ^B John 3:20
24:17 ^Job 15:21   24:18 ^Job 5:3   24:19 ^Job 6:16, 17
^B Job 21:13   24:20 ^Is 49:15   24:21 ^Job 22:9
24:22 ^Job 18:20   24:23 ^Job 10:4; 11:11
24:24 ^Ps 37:10   ^B Job 14:21   24:25 ^Job 6:28; 27:4
25:2 ^Job 9:4; 36:5, 22   25:3 ^Job 16:13   25:4 ^Job 4:17
^B Job 14:4   25:5 ^Job 31:26   ^B Job 15:15   25:6 ^Job 7:17

24:19 [1] I.e., the netherworld

JOB REBUKES BILDAD

26 Then Job responded,
² "What a help you are to
ᴬthe weak!
You have saved the arm
ᴮwithout strength!

³ "What advice you have given to
one without wisdom!
What helpful insight you have
abundantly provided!

⁴ "To whom have you uttered
words?
And whose spirit was
expressed through you?

THE GREATNESS OF GOD

⁵ "The ᴬdeparted spirits are made
to tremble
Under the waters and their
inhabitants.

⁶ "¹·ᴬSheol is naked before Him,
And ²·ᴮAbaddon has no
covering.

⁷ "He ᴬstretches out the north
over empty space
And hangs the earth on nothing.

⁸ "He ᴬwraps up the waters in His
clouds,
And the cloud does not burst
under them.

⁹ "He ᴬobscures the face of the
full moon
And spreads His cloud over it.

¹⁰ "He has inscribed a ᴬcircle on
the surface of the waters
At the ᴮboundary of light and
darkness.

¹¹ "The pillars of heaven tremble
And are amazed at His rebuke.

¹² "With His power He ᴬquieted
the sea,
And by His understanding He
shattered ¹·ᴮRahab.

¹³ "By His breath the ᴬheavens are
cleared;
His hand has pierced the
fleeing serpent.

¹⁴ "Behold, these are the fringes of
His ways;
And how faint ᴬa word we hear
of Him!
But His mighty thunder, who
can understand?"

JOB AFFIRMS HIS RIGHTEOUSNESS

27 Job again took up his ᴬdis-
course and said,
² "As God lives, ᴬwho has taken
away my right,
And the Almighty, ᴮwho has
embittered my soul,

³ For as long as life is in me,
And the ᴬbreath of God is in
my nostrils,

⁴ My lips certainly will not speak
unjustly,
Nor will ᴬmy tongue mutter
deceit.

⁵ "Far be it from me that I should
declare you right;
Until I die, ᴬI will not give up
my integrity.

⁶ "I have ᴬkept hold of my
righteousness and will not
let it go.
My heart does not rebuke any
of my days.

THE STATE OF THE GODLESS

⁷ "May my enemy be as the wicked,
And my opponent as the
criminal.

⁸ "For what is ᴬthe hope of the
godless when he makes an
end *of life,*

26:2 ᴬJob 6:11, 12   ᴮPs 71:9   26:5 ᴬJob 3:13; Ps 88:10
26:6 ᴬJob 26:6-14   ᴮJob 28:22   26:7 ᴬJob 9:8
26:8 ᴬJob 37:11; Prov 30:4   26:9 ᴬJob 22:14; Ps 97:2
26:10 ᴬJob 38:1-11   ᴮJob 38:19, 20, 24   26:12 ᴬIs 51:15
ᴮJob 9:13   26:13 ᴬJob 9:8   ᴬJob 4:12
27:1 ᴬJob 13:12; 29:1   27:2 ᴬJob 34:5   ᴮJob 9:18
27:3 ᴬJob 32:8; 33:4   27:4 ᴬJob 6:28; 33:3   27:5 ᴬJob 6:29
27:6 ᴬJob 2:3; 13:18   27:8 ᴬJob 8:13; 11:20

26:6 ¹I.e., the netherworld   ²I.e., the place of
destruction   26:12 ¹I.e., a sea monster, not to be
confused with Rahab in Joshua 2

When God requires his life?

9 "Will God hear his cry
   When ^distress comes upon
      him?
10 "Or will he take ^pleasure in the
      Almighty?
   Will he call on God at all
      times?
11 "I will instruct you in the power
      of God;
   What is with the Almighty I
      will not conceal.
12 "Behold, all of you have
      seen *it;*
   Why then do you talk of
      nothing?

13 "This is ^the portion of a wicked
      person from God,
   And the inheritance *which*
      ^Btyrants receive from the
      Almighty:
14 Though his sons are many,
      they are destined for the
      sword;
   And his ^descendants will not
      be satisfied with bread.
15 "His survivors will be buried
      because of the plague,
   And their ^widows will not *be
      able to* weep.
16 "Though he piles up silver like
      dust,
   And prepares garments as
      plentiful as the clay,
17 He may prepare *it,* ^but the
      righteous will wear *it*
   And the innocent will divide
      the silver.
18 "He has built his ^house like the
      spider's web,
   Or a hut *which* the watchman
      has made.
19 "He lies down rich, but never
      again;
   He opens his eyes, and ^it no
      longer exists.

20 "^ATerrors overtake him like a
      flood;
   A storm steals him away in the
      night.
21 "The east ^wind carries him
      away, and he is gone;
   For it sweeps him ^Baway from
      his place.
22 "For it will hurl at him without
      mercy;
   He will certainly try to ^flee
      from its power.
23 "*People* will ¹clap their hands at
      him,
   And will ^whistle at him from
      their places.

JOB TELLS OF EARTH'S TREASURES

28 "Certainly there is a mine
      for silver
   And a place for refining gold.
2 "Iron is taken from the dust,
   And copper is smelted from
      rock.
3 "*Man* puts an end to
      darkness,
   And ^to the farthest limit he
      searches out
   The rock in gloom and deep
      shadow.
4 "He sinks a shaft away from
      inhabited areas,
   Forgotten by the foot;
   They hang *and* swing, away
      from people.
5 "From the earth comes food,
   And underneath, it is turned
      over like fire.
6 "Its rocks are the source of
      sapphires,
   And its dust *contains* gold.

27:9 ^Prov 1:27   27:10 ^Ps 37:4; Is 58:14
27:13 ^Job 20:29   ᴮJob 15:20   27:14 ^Job 20:10
27:15 ^Ps 78:64   27:17 ^Job 20:18-21   27:18 ^Job 8:15;
18:14   27:19 ^Job 7:8, 21; 20:7   27:20 ^Job 15:21
27:21 ^Job 21:18   ᴮJob 7:10   27:22 ^Job 11:20
27:23 ^Job 18:18; 20:8   28:3 ^Eccl 1:13

27:23 ¹I.e., mock and ridicule him

7 "No bird of prey knows the path,
Nor has the falcon's eye caught sight of it.
8 "The proud animals have not trodden it,
Nor has the lion passed over it.
9 "He puts his hand on the flint;
He overturns the mountains at the base.
10 "He carves out channels through the rocks,
And his eye sees anything precious.
11 "He dams up the streams from flowing,
And brings to light what is hidden.

THE SEARCH FOR WISDOM IS HARDER

12 "But ^Awhere can wisdom be found?
And where is the place of understanding?
13 "^AMankind does not know its value,
Nor is it found in the land of the living.
14 "The ocean depth says, 'It is not in me';
And the sea says, 'It is not with me.'
15 "^APure gold cannot be given in exchange for it,
Nor can silver be weighed as its price.
16 "It cannot be valued in the gold of Ophir,
In precious onyx, or sapphire.
17 "^AGold or glass cannot equal it,
Nor can it be exchanged for articles of pure gold.
18 "Coral and crystal are not to be mentioned;
And the acquisition of ^Awisdom is more *valuable* than pearls.

19 "The topaz of Cush cannot equal it,
Nor can it be valued in ^Apure gold.
20 "^AWhere then does wisdom come from?
And where is this place of understanding?
21 "It is hidden from the eyes of every living *creature,*
And concealed from the birds of the sky.
22 "^1,^AAbaddon and Death say,
'With our ears we have heard a report of it.'

23 "^AGod understands its way,
And He knows its place.
24 "For He ^Alooks to the ends of the earth;
He sees everything under the heavens.
25 "When He imparted ^Aweight to the wind,
And ^Bassessed the waters by measure,
26 When He made a ^Alimit for the rain,
And a course for the thunderbolt,
27 Then He saw it and declared it;
He established it and also searched it out.
28 "And to mankind He said,
'Behold, the ^Afear of the Lord, that is wisdom;
And to turn away from evil is understanding.'"

28:12 ^AJob 28:23, 28; Eccl 7:24　28:13 ^AMatt 13:44-46
28:15 ^AProv 3:13, 14; 8:10, 11　28:17 ^AProv 8:10; 16:16
28:18 ^AProv 8:11　28:19 ^AProv 8:19
28:20 ^AJob 28:23, 28　28:22 ^AJob 26:6; Prov 8:32-36
28:23 ^AJob 9:4; Prov 8:22-36　28:24 ^APs 11:4; 33:13, 14
28:25 ^APs 135:7　^BJob 38:8-11　28:26 ^AJob 37:6, 11, 12; 38:26-28　28:28 ^AProv 9:10; Eccl 12:13

28:22 ^1 I.e., Destruction

JOB'S PAST WAS GLORIOUS

29 Job again took up his ^dis-course and said,

2 "Oh that I were as in months gone by,
As in the days when God ^watched over me;

3 When ^His lamp shone over my head,
And ^by His light I walked *through* darkness;

4 Just as I was in the days of my youth,
When the ^protection of God *was* over my tent;

5 When the Almighty was still with me,
And my children were around me;

6 When my steps were bathed in cream,
And the ^rock poured out streams of oil for me!

7 "When I went out to ^the gate of the city,
When I took my seat in the public square,

8 The young men saw me and hid themselves,
And the old men arose *and* stood.

9 "The leaders stopped talking
And ^put *their* hands on their mouths;

10 The voices of the prominent people were hushed,
And their ^tongues stuck to their palates.

11 "For *when* ^an ear heard, it called me blessed,
And when an eye saw, it testified in support of me,

12 Because I saved the poor who cried for help,
And the ^orphan who had no helper.

13 "The blessing of the one who was about to perish came upon me,
And I made the ^widow's heart sing for joy.

14 "I ^put on righteousness, and it clothed me;
My justice was like a robe and a headband.

15 "I was ^eyes to those who were blind,
And feet to those who could not walk.

16 "I was a father to ^the poor,
And I investigated the case which I did not know.

17 "I ^broke the jaws of the wicked
And rescued the prey from his teeth.

18 "Then I thought, 'I will die with my family,
And I will multiply *my* days as the sand.

19 'My ^root is spread out to the waters,
And ^dew lies on my branch all night.

20 'My glory is *ever* new with me,
And my ^bow is renewed in my hand.'

21 "To me ^they listened and waited,
And they kept silent for my advice.

22 "After my words they did not *speak* again,
And ^my speech dropped on them.

29:1 ^Num 23:7; Job 13:12   29:2 ^Jer 31:28
29:3 ^Job 18:6   ^Job 11:17   29:4 ^Ps 25:14; Prov 3:32
29:6 ^Deut 32:13; Ps 81:16   29:7 ^Job 31:21
29:9 ^Job 21:5   29:10 ^Ps 137:6   29:11 ^Job 4:3, 4
29:12 ^Job 31:17, 21   29:13 ^Job 22:9   29:14 ^Is 61:10;
Eph 6:14   29:15 ^Num 10:31
29:16 ^Job 24:4; Prov 29:7   29:17 ^Ps 3:7
29:19 ^Jer 17:8   ^Hos 14:5   29:20 ^Gen 49:24;
Ps 18:34   29:21 ^Job 4:3; 29:9   29:22 ^Deut 32:2

23 "They waited for me as for the
   rain,
   And opened their mouths as
   for the late rain.
24 "I smiled at them *when* they did
   not believe,
   And they did not look at my
   kindness ungraciously.
25 "I chose a way for them and sat
   as ^chief,
   And lived as a king among the
   troops,
   As one who comforted the
   mourners.

JOB'S PRESENT STATE IS HUMILIATING

30 "But now those who are
       younger than I ^mock me,
   Whose fathers I refused to put
   with the dogs of my flock.
2 "Indeed, what *good was* the
   strength of their hands to
   me?
   Vigor had perished from
   them.
3 "From poverty and famine they
   are gaunt,
   They who gnaw at the dry
   ground by night in waste and
   desolation,
4   Who pluck saltweed by the
    bushes,
    And whose food is the root of
    the broom shrub.
5 "They are driven from the
   community;
   They shout against them as
   against a thief,
6   So that they live on the slopes
    of ravines,
    In holes *in* the ground and
    among the rocks.
7 "Among the bushes they cry
   out;
   Under the weeds they are
   gathered together.

8 "Worthless fellows, even those
   without a name,
   They were cast out from the
   land.
9 "And now I have become their
   ^taunt,
   And I have become a ¹byword
   to them.
10 "They loathe me *and* stand
   aloof from me,
   And they do not refrain from
   ^spitting in my face.
11 "Because He has undone my
   bowstring and afflicted me,
   They have cast off ^the bridle
   before me.
12 "On the right hand their mob
   arises;
   They ^push aside my feet
   and pile up their ways of
   destruction against me.
13 "They ^break up my path,
   They promote my destruction;
   No one restrains them.
14 "As *through* a wide gap they
   come,
   Amid the storm they roll on.
15 "^Sudden terrors are turned
   upon me;
   They chase *away* my dignity
   like the wind,
   And my prosperity has passed
   away like a cloud.

16 "And now ^my soul is poured
   out within me;
   Days of misery have seized me.
17 "At night it pierces ^my bones
   within me,
   And my gnawing *pains* do not
   rest.

29:25 ^Job 1:3; 31:37   30:1 ^Job 12:4   30:9 ^Job 12:4
30:10 ^Is 50:6; Matt 26:67   30:11 ^Ps 32:9
30:12 ^Ps 140:4, 5   30:13 ^Is 3:12   30:15 ^Job 3:25;
Ps 55:3-5   30:16 ^Ps 42:4; Is 53:12   30:17 ^Job 30:30

30:9 ¹I.e., prob. a word of insult

18 "By a great force my garment is
     ^distorted;
     It ties me up like the collar of
        my coat.
19 "He has thrown me into the
     ^mire,
     And I have become like dust
        and ashes.
20 "I ^cry out to You for help, but
        You do not answer me;
     I stand up, and You turn Your
        attention against me.
21 "You have become cruel to me;
     With the strength of Your
        hand You ^persecute me.
22 "You ^lift me up to the wind *and*
        make me ride *it;*
     And You dissolve me in a storm.
23 "For I know that You ^will bring
        me to death,
     And to the ^Bhouse of meeting
        for all living.

24 "Yet does one in a heap of ruins
        not reach out *with his* hand,
     Or in his disaster does he not
        ^cry out for help?
25 "Have I not ^wept for the one
        whose life is hard?
     Was my soul not grieved for
        ^Bthe needy?
26 "When I ^expected good, evil
        came;
     When I waited for light,
        darkness came.
27 "I am seething ^within and
        cannot rest;
     Days of misery confront me.
28 "I go about mourning without
        comfort;
     I stand up in the assembly *and*
        ^cry out for help.
29 "I have become a brother to
     ^jackals,
     And a companion of ostriches.
30 "My ^skin turns black on me,
     And my ^Bbones burn with fever.

31 "Therefore my ^harp is turned
        to mourning,
     And my flute to the sound of
        those who weep.

JOB ASSERTS HIS INTEGRITY

31 "I have made a covenant
        with my ^eyes;
     How then could I look at a
        virgin?
2 "And what is ^the portion of
        God from above,
     Or the inheritance of the
        Almighty from on high?
3 "Is it not ^disaster to the criminal,
     And misfortune to ^Bthose who
        practice injustice?
4 "Does He not ^see my ways,
     And count all my steps?

5 "If I have ^walked with
        deception,
     And my foot has hurried after
        deceit,
6   Let Him ^weigh me with
        accurate scales,
     And let God know my integrity.
7 "If my step has ^turned from the
        way,
     Or my heart followed my eyes,
     Or *if any* spot has stuck to my
        hands,
8   Let me ^sow and another eat,
     And let my crops be uprooted.

9 "If my heart has been ^enticed
        by a woman,
     Or I have lurked at my
        neighbor's doorway,

30:18^AJob 2:7   30:19^APs 69:2, 14   30:20^AJob 19:7
30:21^AJob 16:9, 14; 19:6, 22   30:22^AJob 9:17; 27:21
30:23^AJob 9:22   ^BEccl 12:5   30:24^AJob 19:7
30:25^ARom 12:15   ^BJob 24:4   30:26^AJob 3:25, 26;
Jer 8:15   30:27^ALam 2:11   30:28^AJob 19:7
30:29^APs 44:19; Mic 1:8   30:30^AJob 2:7   ^BPs 102:3
30:31^AIs 24:8   31:1^AMatt 5:28   31:2^AJob 20:29
31:3^AJob 21:30   ^BJob 34:22   31:4^A2 Chr 16:9; Job 24:23
31:5^AJob 15:31; Mic 2:11   31:6^AJob 6:2, 3   31:7^AJob 23:11
31:8^ALev 26:16; Mic 6:15   31:9^AJob 24:15; 31:1

¹⁰ May my wife ^grind *grain* for
another,
And let ^Bothers ¹kneel down
over her.

¹¹ "For that would be a ^lustful
crime;
Moreover, it would be
^Bwrongdoing *punishable by*
judges.

¹² "For it would be ^fire that
consumes to ¹,^BAbaddon,
And would uproot all my
increase.

¹³ "If I have ^rejected the claim of
my male or female slaves
When they filed a complaint
against me,

¹⁴ What then could I do when
God arises?
And when He calls me to
account, how am I to answer
Him?

¹⁵ "Did ^He who made me in the
womb not make him,
And the same One create us in
the womb?

¹⁶ "If I have kept ^the poor from
their desire,
Or have caused the eyes of the
widow to fail,

¹⁷ Or have ^eaten my morsel alone,
And ^Bthe orphan has not
shared it

¹⁸ (But from my youth he grew up
with me as with a father,
And from my infancy I guided
her),

¹⁹ If I have seen anyone perish
for lack of clothing,
Or that ^the needy had no
covering,

²⁰ If his waist has not ¹thanked me,
And if he has not been
warmed with the fleece of
my sheep,

²¹ If I have lifted up my hand
against ^the orphan,
Because I saw I had support in
the gate,

²² May my shoulder fall from *its*
socket,
And my ^arm be broken off at
the elbow.

²³ "For ^disaster from God is a
terror to me,
And because of ^BHis majesty I
can do nothing.

²⁴ "If I have put my confidence *in*
^gold,
And called fine gold my trust,

²⁵ If I have ^gloated because my
wealth was great,
And because my hand had
obtained *so* much;

²⁶ If I have ^looked at the sun
when it shone,
Or the moon going in splendor,

²⁷ And my heart was secretly
enticed,
And my hand threw a kiss
from my mouth,

²⁸ That too would have been
a guilty deed *calling for*
judgment,
For I would have ^denied God
above.

²⁹ "Have I ^rejoiced at the
misfortune of my enemy,
Or become excited when evil
found him?

31:10 ^Is 47:2 ^BDeut 28:30 31:11 ^Lev 20:10
^BJob 31:28 31:12 ^Job 15:30 ^BJob 26:6
31:13 ^Deut 24:14, 15 31:15 ^Job 10:3 31:16 ^Job 5:16;
20:19 31:17 ^Job 22:7 ^BJob 29:12 31:19 ^Job 24:4
31:21 ^Job 29:12; 31:17 31:22 ^Job 38:15
31:23 ^Job 31:3 ^BJob 13:11 31:24 ^Job 22:24;
Mark 10:23-25 31:25 ^Job 1:3, 10; Ps 62:10
31:26 ^Deut 4:19; Ezek 8:16 31:28 ^Josh 24:27;
Is 59:13 31:29 ^Prov 17:5; Obad 12

31:10 ¹I.e., have sexual relations with her 31:12 ¹I.e.,
the place of destruction 31:20 ¹Lit *blessed*; i.e., for
clothing

30 "No, ^I have not allowed my
　　mouth to sin
　　By asking for his life in ^Ba curse.
31 "Have the people of my tent not
　　said,
　　'Who can find one who has
　　　not been ^satisfied with his
　　　meat'?
32 "The stranger has not spent the
　　night outside,
　　For I have opened my doors to
　　　the traveler.
33 "Have I ^covered my
　　wrongdoings like a man,
　　By hiding my guilt in my shirt
　　　pocket,
34 Because I ^feared the great
　　multitude
　　And the contempt of families
　　　terrified me,
　　And I kept silent and did not
　　　go out of doors?
35 "Oh that I had one to hear me!
　　Here is my signature;
　　Let the Almighty answer me!
　　And the indictment which my
　　　^adversary has written,
36 I would certainly carry it on
　　my shoulder,
　　I would tie it to myself *like* a
　　　garland.
37 "I would declare to Him ^the
　　number of my steps;
　　Like ^Ba prince, I would
　　　approach Him.

38 "If my ^land cries out against me,
　　And its furrows weep together;
39 If I have eaten its fruit without
　　money,
　　Or have ^caused its owners to
　　　lose their lives,
40 May the ^thorn-bush grow
　　instead of wheat,
　　And stinkweed instead of
　　　barley."
The words of Job are ended.

ELIHU REBUKES JOB IN ANGER

32 Then these three men
stopped answering Job,
because he was ^righteous in his
own eyes. 2 But the anger of Elihu
the son of Barachel the ^Buzite, of
the family of Ram, burned against
Job; his anger burned because he
justified himself before God. 3 And
his anger burned against his three
friends because they had found no
answer, yet they had condemned
Job. 4 Now Elihu had waited to speak
to Job because they were years older
than he. 5 But when Elihu saw that
there was no answer in the mouth
of the three men, his anger burned.
6 So Elihu the son of Barachel the
Buzite spoke out and said,
　　"I am young in years and you
　　　are ^old;
　　Therefore I was shy and afraid
　　　to tell you what I think.
7 "I thought ^age should speak,
　　And increased years should
　　　teach wisdom.
8 "But it is a spirit *that is* in
　　mankind,
　　And the ^breath of the
　　　Almighty gives them
　　　^Bunderstanding.
9 "The abundant *in years* may
　　not be wise,
　　Nor may ^elders understand
　　　justice.
10 "So I say, 'Listen to me,
　　I too will tell what I think.'

11 "Behold, I waited for your words,
　　I listened to your skillful speech,
　　While you pondered what to say.

31:30 ^Ps 7:4　^BJob 5:3　31:31 ^Job 22:7
31:33 ^Gen 3:10; Prov 28:13　31:34 ^Ex 23:2
31:35 ^Job 27:7　31:37 ^Job 31:4　^BJob 1:3
31:38 ^Job 24:2　31:39 ^1 Kin 21:19　31:40 ^Job 32:13;
Is 5:6　32:1 ^Job 10:7; 27:5, 6　32:2 ^Gen 22:21
32:6 ^Job 15:10　32:7 ^Job 8:8, 9　32:8 ^Job 33:4
^BJob 38:36　32:9 ^Job 32:7

¹² "I also paid close attention to
        you;
    But indeed, there was no one
        who refuted Job,
    Not one of you who answered
        his words.
¹³ "So do not say,
    'ᴬWe have found wisdom:
    God will defeat him, not man.'
¹⁴ "But he has not presented *his*
        words against me,
    Nor will I reply to him with
        your arguments.

¹⁵ "They are dismayed, they no
        longer answer;
    Words have failed them.
¹⁶ "Should I wait, because they are
        not speaking,
    Because they have stopped
        and no longer answer?
¹⁷ "I too will give my share of
        answers;
    I also will tell my opinion.
¹⁸ "For I am full of words;
    The spirit within me compels
        me.
¹⁹ "Behold, my belly is like
        unvented wine;
    Like new wineskins, it is about
        to burst.
²⁰ "Let me speak so that I may get
        relief;
    Let me open my lips and
        answer.
²¹ "Let me ᴬbe partial to no one,
    Nor flatter *any* man.
²² "For I do not know how to
        flatter,
    Otherwise my Maker would
        quickly take me away.

ELIHU CLAIMS TO SPEAK FOR GOD

33

"However, please ᴬhear my
        speech, Job,
    And listen to all my words.
² "Behold now, I open my mouth,

My tongue in my mouth
        speaks.
³ "My words are *from* the
        integrity of my heart,
    And my lips speak ᴬknowledge
        sincerely.
⁴ "The ᴬSpirit of God has made
        me,
    And the ᴮbreath of the
        Almighty gives me life.
⁵ "ᴬRefute me if you can;
    Line up against me, take your
        stand.
⁶ "Behold, I belong to God, like
        you;
    I too have been formed out of
        the ᴬclay.
⁷ "Behold, ᴬno fear of me should
        terrify you,
    Nor should my pressure weigh
        heavily on you.

⁸ "You have in fact spoken while I
        listened,
    And I heard the sound of *your*
        words:
⁹ 'I am pure, without
        wrongdoing;
    I am innocent and there ᴬis no
        guilt in me.
¹⁰ 'Behold, He invents criticisms
        against me;
    He ᴬcounts me as His enemy.
¹¹ 'He ᴬputs my feet in the stocks;
    He watches all my paths.'
¹² "Behold, let me respond to you,
    ᴬyou are not right in this,
    For God is greater than
        mankind.

¹³ "Why do you ᴬcomplain to Him
    That He does not give an
        account of all His doings?

32:13 ᴬJer 9:23   **32:21** ᴬLev 19:15; Job 13:8, 10
33:1 ᴬJob 13:6   **33:3** ᴬJob 6:28; 36:4   **33:4** ᴬGen 2:7
ᴮJob 27:3   **33:5** ᴬJob 33:32   **33:6** ᴬJob 4:19
33:7 ᴬJob 13:21   **33:9** ᴬJob 10:14   **33:10** ᴬJob 13:24
33:11 ᴬJob 13:27   **33:12** ᴬEccl 7:20   **33:13** ᴬJob 40:2; Is 45:9

14 "Indeed ^God speaks once,
   Or twice, *yet* no one notices it.
15 "In a ^dream, a vision of the night,
   When deep sleep falls on
     people,
   While they slumber in their
     beds,
16 Then ^He opens the ears of
     people,
   And horrifies them with
     warnings,
17 So that He may turn a person
     away *from bad* conduct,
   And keep a man from pride;
18 He ^keeps his soul back from
     the pit,
   And his life from perishing by
     the ^Bspear.

19 "*A person* is also rebuked by
     ^pain in his bed,
   And with constant complaint
     in his bones,
20 So that his life ^loathes bread,
   And his soul, food that he
     should crave.
21 "His ^flesh wastes away from
     sight,
   And his bones, *which* were not
     seen, stick out.
22 "Then ^his soul comes near to
     the pit,
   And his life to those who bring
     death.

23 "If there is an ^interceding angel
     for him,
   One out of a thousand,
   To remind a person of what is
     right for him,
24 And he is gracious to him, and
     says,
   'Free him from going down to
     the pit,
   I have found a ^ransom';
25 Let his flesh become fresher
     than in youth,

Let him return to the days of
     his youthful vigor;
26 *Then* he will ^pray to God, and
     He will accept him,
   So that he may see His face
     with joy,
   And He will restore His
     righteousness to *that*
     person.
27 "He will sing to people and say,
   'I have sinned and perverted
     what is right,
   And it is not ^proper for me.
28 'He has redeemed my soul from
     going to the pit,
   And my life will ^see the light.'

29 "Behold, God does ^all these
     things for a man two or three
     times,
30 To ^bring back his soul from
     the pit,
   So that he may be enlightened
     with the light of life.
31 "Pay attention, Job, listen to me;
   Keep silent, and let me speak.
32 "*Then* if you have anything to
     say, answer me;
   Speak, for I would take
     pleasure in justifying you.
33 "If not, ^listen to me;
   Keep silent, and I will teach
     you wisdom."

ELIHU VINDICATES GOD'S JUSTICE

34 Then Elihu continued and
   said,
2 "Hear my words, you wise men,
   And listen to me, you who
     understand.
3 "For ^the ear tests words

33:14 ^Job 33:29; Ps 62:11   33:15 ^Job 4:12-17; 33:15-18
33:16 ^Job 36:10, 15   33:18 ^Job 33:22, 24, 28, 30
^B Job 15:22   33:19 ^Job 30:17   33:20 ^Job 3:24; Ps 107:18
33:21 ^Job 16:8   33:22 ^Job 33:18, 28   33:23 ^Gen 40:8
33:24 ^Job 36:18; Ps 49:7   33:26 ^Job 22:27; Ps 50:14, 15
33:27 ^Rom 6:21   33:28 ^Job 22:28   33:29 ^Eph 1:11;
Phil 2:13   33:30 ^Job 33:18; Zech 9:11   33:33 ^Ps 34:11
34:3 ^Job 12:11

As the palate tastes food.

4 "Let us choose for ourselves
    what is right;
  Let us understand among
    ourselves what is good.

5 "For Job has said, 'I am
    righteous,
  But ᴬGod has taken away my
    right;

6 Should I lie about my right?
  My ᴬwound is incurable,
    though I am without
    wrongdoing.'

7 "What man is like Job,
  Who ᴬdrinks up derision like
    water,

8 Who goes ᴬin company with
    the workers of injustice,
  And walks with wicked
    people?

9 "For he has said, 'ᴬIt is of no use
    to a man
  When he becomes friends
    with God.'

10 "Therefore, listen to me, you
    men of understanding.
  Far be it from God to ᴬdo evil,
  And from the Almighty to do
    wrong.

11 "For He repays a person for ᴬhis
    work,
  And lets *things* happen in
    correspondence to a man's
    behavior.

12 "ᴬGod certainly will not act
    wickedly,
  And the Almighty will not
    pervert justice.

13 "Who ᴬgave Him authority over
    the earth?
  And who has placed the whole
    world *on Him*?

14 "If He were to determine to
    do so,
  If He were to ᴬgather His spirit
    and His breath to Himself,

15 ᴬHumanity would perish
    together,
  And mankind would ᴮreturn
    to dust.

16 "But if *you have* understanding,
    hear this;
  Listen to the sound of my
    words.

17 "Shall ᴬone who hates justice
    rule?
  And ᴮwill you condemn the
    righteous mighty One,

18 Who says to a king, 'You
    worthless one,'
  To nobles, 'You wicked one';

19 Who shows no ᴬpartiality to
    the prominent,
  Nor regards the rich as above
    the poor,
  Since they are all the ᴮwork of
    His hands?

20 "In a moment they die, and ᴬat
    midnight
  People are shaken and pass
    away,
  And ᴮthe powerful are taken
    away without a hand.

21 "For ᴬHis eyes are upon the
    ways of a person,
  And He sees all his steps.

22 "There is ᴬno darkness or deep
    shadow
  Where the workers of injustice
    can hide themselves.

23 "For He does not ᴬ*need to*
    consider a person further,
  That he should go before God
    in judgment.

34:5 ᴬJob 27:2   34:6 ᴬJob 6:4   34:7 ᴬJob 15:16
34:8 ᴬJob 22:15   34:9 ᴬJob 21:15; Ps 50:18
34:10 ᴬJob 8:3; Rom 9:14   34:11 ᴬ2 Cor 5:10; Rev 22:12
34:12 ᴬJob 34:10   34:13 ᴬJob 38:4   34:14 ᴬPs 104:29;
Eccl 12:7   34:15 ᴬGen 7:21   ᴮJob 10:9
34:17 ᴬ2 Sam 23:3   ᴮJob 40:8   34:19 ᴬ1 Pet 1:17
ᴮJob 10:3   34:20 ᴬEx 12:29   ᴮJob 12:19
34:21 ᴬProv 15:3; Jer 16:17   34:22 ᴬPs 139:11, 12;
Amos 9:2, 3   34:23 ᴬJob 11:11

24 "He breaks in pieces
      the ^mighty without
      investigation,
   And sets others in their place.
25 "Therefore He ^knows their
      deeds,
   And He overthrows *them* in
      the night,
   And they are crushed.
26 "He ^strikes them like the
      wicked
   In a public place,
27 Because they ^turned aside
      from following Him,
   And had no regard for any of
      His ways,
28 So that they caused ^the cry of
      the poor to come to Him,
   And that He would hear the
      cry of the afflicted—
29 When He keeps quiet, who can
      condemn?
   And when He hides His face,
      who then can look at Him,
   That is, regarding both nation
      and a person?—
30 "So that ^godless people would
      not rule,
   Nor be snares for the people.

31 "For has anyone said to God,
   'I have endured *punishment;*
   I will not offend *anymore;*
32 Teach me what I do not see;
   If I have ^done wrong,
   I will not do it again'?
33 "Shall *God* ^repay on your
      terms, because you have
      rejected *His?*
   For you must choose,
      and not I;
   Therefore declare what you
      know.
34 "Men of understanding will say
      to me,
   And a wise man who hears
      me,

35 'Job ^speaks without
      knowledge,
   And his words are without
      wisdom.
36 'Oh that Job were tested to the
      limit,
   Because he answers ^like
      sinners.
37 'For he adds ^rebellion to his
      sin;
   He claps his hands among us,
   And multiplies his words
      against God.'"

ELIHU SHARPLY REBUKES JOB

35 Then Elihu continued and
      said,
2 "Do you think this is in
      accordance with ^justice?
   Do you say, 'My righteousness
      is more than God's'?
3 "For you say, '^What advantage
      will it be to You?
   ^What benefit will I have, more
      than *if* I had sinned?'
4 "I will answer you,
   And your friends with you.
5 "^Look at the heavens and
      see;
   And look at the clouds—they
      are higher than you.
6 "If you have sinned, ^what do
      you accomplish against
      Him?
   And if your wrongdoings are
      many, what do you do to
      Him?
7 "If you are righteous, ^what do
      you give to Him,
   Or what does He receive from
      your hand?

34:24 ^Job 12:19   34:25 ^Job 34:11   34:26 ^Ps 9:5; 11:5
34:27 ^1 Sam 15:11   34:28 ^Job 35:9; James 5:4
34:30 ^Job 5:15; Prov 29:2-12   34:32 ^Job 33:27
34:33 ^Job 41:11   34:35 ^Job 35:16; 38:2
34:36 ^Job 22:15   34:37 ^Job 23:2   35:2 ^Job 27:2
35:3 ^Job 34:9   ᴮJob 9:30, 31   35:5 ^Gen 15:5; Ps 8:3
35:6 ^Prov 8:36; Jer 7:19   35:7 ^Luke 17:10; Rom 11:35

8 "Your wickedness is for a man
    like yourself,
  And your righteousness is for
    a son of man.

9 "Because of the ^multitude of
    oppressions they cry out;
  They cry for help because of
    the arm of the mighty.

10 "But ^no one says, 'Where is
    God my Maker,
  Who gives songs in the night,

11 Who ^teaches us more than
    the animals of the earth
  And makes us wiser than the
    birds of the sky?'

12 "There ^they cry out, but He
    does not answer
  Because of the pride of evil
    people.

13 "^God certainly will not listen to
    an empty *cry,*
  Nor will the Almighty
    regard it.

14 "How much less when you say
    you do not look at Him,
  The ^case is before Him, and
    you must wait for Him!

15 "And now, because He has not
    avenged His anger,
  Nor has He acknowledged
    wrongdoing well,

16 So Job opens his mouth *with*
    empty *words;*
  He multiplies words ^without
    knowledge."

ELIHU SPEAKS OF GOD'S DEALINGS
WITH MANKIND

36
Then Elihu continued and
said,

2 "Wait for me a little, and I will
    show you
  That there is still more to be
    said on God's behalf.

3 "I will bring my knowledge
    from afar,

And ascribe ^righteousness to
    my Maker.

4 "For truly ^my words are not
    false;
  One who is ^perfect in
    knowledge is with you.

5 "Behold, God is mighty but does
    not ^reject *anyone;*
  He is ^mighty in strength of
    understanding.

6 "He does not keep the wicked
    alive,
  But gives justice to ^the afflicted.

7 "He does not ^withdraw His
    eyes from the righteous,
  But with kings on the throne
  He has seated them forever,
    and they are exalted.

8 "And if they are bound in
    shackles,
  And are caught in the snares of
    ^misery,

9 Then He declares to them
    their work
  And their wrongdoings, that
    they have ^been arrogant.

10 "^He opens their ears to
    instruction,
  And commands that they
    return from injustice.

11 "If they listen and serve *Him,*
  They will ^end their days in
    prosperity,
  And their years in ^happiness.

12 "But if they do not listen, they
    will perish ^by the sword,
  And ^die without knowledge.

13 "But the godless in heart
    nurture anger;
  They do not call for help when
    He binds them.

35:9 ^Ex 2:23   35:10 ^Job 21:14; Is 51:13
35:11 ^Ps 94:12; Jer 32:33   35:12 ^Prov 1:28
35:13 ^Jer 11:11; Mic 3:4   35:14 ^Job 31:35
35:16 ^Job 34:35; 38:2   36:3 ^Job 8:3; 37:23
36:4 ^Job 33:3   ^Job 37:16   36:5 ^Ps 22:24   ^Job 12:13
36:6 ^Job 5:15   36:7 ^Ps 33:18; 34:15   36:8 ^Job 36:15, 21
36:9 ^Job 15:25   36:10 ^Job 33:16; 36:15
36:11 ^1 Tim 4:8   ^Ps 16:11   36:12 ^Job 15:22   ^Job 4:21

14 "They die in youth,
　　And their life *perishes* among
　　the ^cult prostitutes.
15 "He rescues the afflicted in
　　their ^misery,
　　And opens their ears in *time of*
　　oppression.
16 "Then indeed, He induced you
　　away from the mouth of
　　distress,
　　And instead of it, a broad place
　　with no constraint;
　　And your table was full of rich
　　food.
17 "But you were full of ^judgment
　　on the wicked;
　　Judgment and justice take hold
　　of you.
18 "*Beware* that ^wrath does not
　　entice you to mockery;
　　And do not let the greatness of
　　the ^Bransom turn you aside.
19 "Will your cry for help keep you
　　from distress,
　　Or all the exertions of *your*
　　strength?
20 "Do not long for ^the night,
　　When people vanish in their
　　places.
21 "Be careful, do ^not turn to
　　evil,
　　For you preferred this to
　　misery.
22 "Behold, God is exalted in His
　　power;
　　Who is a ^teacher like Him?
23 "Who has appointed Him His
　　way,
　　And who has said, '^You have
　　done wrong'?
24 "Remember that you are to
　　^exalt His work,
　　Of which people have sung.
25 "All people have seen it;
　　Mankind looks at it from afar.

26 "Behold, God is exalted, and
　　^we do not know *Him;*
　　The ^Bnumber of His years is
　　unsearchable.
27 "For ^He draws up the drops of
　　water;
　　They distill rain from its
　　celestial stream,
28 Which clouds pour down;
　　They drip upon mankind
　　abundantly.
29 "Can anyone understand the
　　^spreading of the clouds,
　　The thundering of His
　　pavilion?
30 "Behold, He spreads His
　　lightning about Him,
　　And He covers the depths of
　　the sea.
31 "For by them He ^judges
　　peoples;
　　He ^Bgives food in abundance.
32 "He covers *His* hands with the
　　lightning,
　　And ^commands it to strike the
　　target.
33 "Its ^thundering voice declares
　　His presence;
　　The livestock also, concerning
　　what is coming up.

ELIHU SAYS GOD HAS AUTHORITY OVER THE STORM

37 "At this also my heart
　　　trembles,
　　And leaps from its place.
2 "Listen closely to the ^thunder
　　of His voice,
　　And the rumbling that goes
　　out from His mouth.

36:14 ^Deut 23:17　36:15 ^Job 36:8, 21
36:17 ^Job 22:5, 10, 11　36:18 ^Jon 4:4, 9　^B Job 33:24
36:20 ^Job 34:20, 25　36:21 ^Job 36:10; Ps 31:6
36:22 ^Job 35:11　36:23 ^Deut 32:4; Job 8:3
36:24 ^Ps 92:5; Rev 15:3　36:26 ^1 Cor 13:12
^B Heb 1:12　36:27 ^Ps 147:8　36:29 ^Job 37:11, 16
36:31 ^Job 37:13　^B Acts 14:17　36:32 ^Job 37:11, 12, 15
36:33 ^Job 37:2　37:2 ^Job 37:4, 5; Ps 29:3-9

3 "Under the whole heaven He
    lets it loose,
    And His lightning *travels* to
    the ^ends of the earth.
4 "After it, a voice roars;
    He thunders with His majestic
    voice,
    And He does not restrain the
    lightning when His voice is
    heard.
5 "God thunders wondrously
    with His voice,
    Doing ^great things which we
    do not comprehend.
6 "For to ^the snow He says, 'Fall
    on the earth,'
    And to the ^downpour and the
    rain, 'Be strong.'
7 "He seals the hand of every
    person,
    So that ^all people may know
    His work.
8 "Then the animal goes into its
    ^lair
    And remains in its den.
9 "From the ^south comes the
    storm,
    And from the north wind the
    cold.
10 "From the breath of God ^ice is
    made,
    And the expanse of the waters
    is frozen.
11 "He also ^loads the clouds with
    moisture;
    He disperses ^the cloud of His
    lightning.
12 "It changes direction, turning
    around by His guidance,
    That it may do whatever He
    commands it
    On the ^face of the inhabited
    earth.
13 "Whether for ^correction, or for
    His earth,
    Or for ^goodness, He causes it
    to happen.

14 "Listen to this, Job;
    Stand and consider the
    wonders of God.
15 "Do you know how God
    establishes them,
    And makes the lightning of His
    clouds to shine?
16 "Do you know about the
    hovering of the clouds,
    The wonders of One who is
    ^perfect in knowledge,
17   You whose garments are hot
    When the land is still because
    of the south wind?
18 "Can you, with Him, ^spread out
    the skies,
    Strong as a cast metal mirror?
19 "Teach us what we are to say to
    Him;
    We ^cannot present *our case*
    because of darkness.
20 "Shall it be told Him that I
    would speak?
    Or should a man say that he
    would be swallowed up?

21 "Now *people* do not see the
    light which is bright in the
    skies;
    But the wind has passed and
    cleared them.
22 "From the north comes golden
    splendor;
    Around God is awesome
    majesty.
23 "The Almighty—we cannot
    find Him;
    He is exalted in power
    And ^He will not violate
    ^justice and abundant
    righteousness.

37:3^Job 28:24; 37:11, 12   37:5^Job 5:9; 37:14, 16, 23
37:6^Job 38:22   ^Job 36:27   37:7^Ps 111:2
37:8^Job 38:40; Ps 104:21, 22   37:9^Job 9:9
37:10^Job 38:29; Ps 147:17   37:11^Job 36:27
^Job 37:15   37:12^Is 14:21; 27:6   37:13^Ex 9:18, 23
^1 Kin 18:41–46   37:16^Job 36:4   37:18^Jer 10:12;
Zech 12:1   37:19^Job 9:14; Rom 8:26
37:23^Ezek 18:23, 32   ^Job 8:3

24 "Therefore people fear Him;
He does not ^regard any who
are wise of heart.'"

GOD SPEAKS NOW TO JOB

38 Then the LORD ^answered
Job from the whirlwind and
said,
2 "Who is this who ^darkens *the
divine* plan
By words without
knowledge?
3 "Now ^tighten the belt on your
waist like a man,
And ^BI shall ask you, and you
inform Me!
4 "Where were you ^when I
laid the foundation of the
earth?
Tell *Me*, if you have
understanding,
5 Who set its ^measurements?
Since you know.
Or who stretched the
measuring line over it?
6 "On what ^were its bases sunk?
Or who laid its cornerstone,
7 When the morning stars sang
together
And all the ^sons of God
shouted for joy?

8 "Or *who* ^enclosed the sea with
doors
When it went out from the
womb, bursting forth;
9 When I made a cloud its
garment,
And thick darkness its
swaddling bands,
10 And I ^placed boundaries on it
And set a bolt and doors,
11 And I said, 'As far as this point
you shall come, but no
farther;
And here your proud waves
shall stop'?

GOD'S MIGHTY POWER

12 "Have you ever in your life
commanded the morning,
And made the dawn know its
place,
13 So that it would take hold of
^the ends of the earth,
And ^Bthe wicked would be
shaken off from it?
14 "It is changed like clay *under*
the seal;
And they stand out like a
garment.
15 "^Their light is withheld from
the wicked,
And the uplifted arm is broken.

16 "Have you entered ^the springs
of the sea,
And walked in the depth of the
ocean?
17 "Have the gates of death been
revealed to you,
And have you seen the gates of
^deep darkness?
18 "Have you understood the
expanse of ^the earth?
Tell *Me*, if you know all this.

19 "Where is the way to the
dwelling of light?
And darkness, where is its
place,
20 That you would take it to ^its
territory,
And discern the paths to its
home?
21 "You know, for ^you were born
then,
And the number of your days
is great!

37:24 ^Matt 11:25; 1 Cor 1:26 38:1 ^Job 40:6
38:2 ^Job 35:16; 42:3 38:3 ^Job 40:7 ^BJob 42:4
38:4 ^Ps 104:5; Prov 30:4 38:5 ^Prov 8:29; Is 40:12
38:6 ^Job 26:7 38:7 ^Job 1:6 38:8 ^Ps 104:6-9;
Jer 5:22 38:10 ^Prov 8:29; Jer 5:22 38:13 ^Job 28:24
^BJob 34:25, 26 38:15 ^Job 5:14 38:16 ^Gen 7:11;
Prov 8:24, 28 38:17 ^Job 10:21; 34:22
38:18 ^Job 28:24 38:20 ^Job 26:10 38:21 ^Job 15:7

²² "Have you entered the
 storehouses ^Aof the snow,
 And have you seen the
 storehouses of the hail,
²³ Which I have reserved for a
 time of distress,
 For a day of war and battle?
²⁴ "Where is the way that ^Athe
 light is divided,
 And the east wind scattered on
 the earth?

²⁵ "Who has split *open* a channel
 for the flood,
 And a way for the
 thunderbolt,
²⁶ To bring ^Arain on a land
 without people,
 On a desert without a person
 in it,
²⁷ To ^Asatisfy the waste and
 desolate land,
 And to make the seeds of grass
 to sprout?
²⁸ "Does ^Athe rain have a father?
 Or who has fathered the drops
 of dew?
²⁹ "From whose womb has come
 the ^Aice?
 And the frost of heaven, who
 has given it birth?
³⁰ "Water becomes hard like
 stone,
 And the surface of the deep is
 imprisoned.

³¹ "Can you tie up the chains of
 the ^APleiades,
 Or untie the cords of Orion?
³² "Can you bring out a
 constellation in its season,
 And guide the Bear with her
 satellites?
³³ "Do you know the ^Aordinances
 of the heavens,
 Or do you establish their rule
 over the earth?

³⁴ "Can you raise your voice to
 the clouds,
 So that an ^Aabundance of
 water will cover you?
³⁵ "Can you ^Asend flashes of
 lightning, so that they
 may go
 And say to you, 'Here we are'?
³⁶ "Who has ^Aput wisdom in the
 innermost being,
 Or given ^Bunderstanding to
 the mind?
³⁷ "Who can count the clouds by
 wisdom,
 And ^Apour out the water jars
 of the heavens,
³⁸ When the dust hardens into a
 mass
 And the clods stick together?

³⁹ "Can you hunt the ^Aprey for the
 lioness,
 Or satisfy the appetite of
 young lions,
⁴⁰ When they ^Acrouch in *their*
 hiding places,
 And lie in wait in *their* lair?
⁴¹ "Who prepares feed for ^Athe
 raven
 When its young cry to God,
 And wander about without
 food?

**GOD SPEAKS OF NATURE
AND ITS BEINGS**

39 "Do you know the time the
 ^Amountain goats give birth?
 Do you observe the calving of
 the ^Bdeer?
² "Can you count the months
 they fulfill,

38:22 ^AJob 37:6   38:24 ^AJob 26:10   38:26 ^AJob 36:27
38:27 ^APs 104:13, 14; 107:35   38:28 ^APs 147:8; Jer 14:22
38:29 ^AJob 37:10; Ps 147:17   38:31 ^AJob 9:9; Amos 5:8
38:33 ^APs 148:6; Jer 31:35, 36
38:34 ^AJob 22:11; 36:27, 28   38:35 ^AJob 36:32; 37:3
38:36 ^APs 51:6   ^BJob 32:8   38:37 ^AJob 38:34
38:39 ^APs 104:21   38:40 ^AJob 37:8   38:41 ^APs 147:9;
Luke 12:24   39:1 ^APs 104:18   ^BPs 29:9

Or do you know the time they
give birth?
3 "They kneel down, they deliver
their young,
They get rid of their labor pains.
4 "Their offspring become strong,
they grow up in the open
field;
They leave and do not return
to them.

5 "Who sent the ᴬwild donkey out
free?
And who opened the bonds of
the swift donkey,
6 To whom I gave ᴬthe
wilderness as his home,
And the salt land as his
dwelling place?
7 "He laughs at the turmoil of the
city,
He does not hear the shouting
of the taskmaster.
8 "He explores the mountains of
his pasture,
And searches after every green
thing.
9 "Will the ᴬwild bull be willing to
serve you,
Or will he spend the night at
your feeding trough?
10 "Can you tie down the wild bull
in a furrow with ropes,
Or will he plow the valleys
after you?
11 "Will you trust him because his
strength is great,
And leave your labor to him?
12 "Will you have faith in him that
he will return your grain
And gather *it from* your
threshing floor?

13 "The wings of the ostrich flap
joyously,
With the pinion and feathers
of love,

14 For she abandons her eggs to
the earth
And warms them in the dust,
15 And she forgets that a foot
may crush them,
Or that a wild animal may
trample them.
16 "She treats her young ᴬcruelly,
as if *they* were not hers;
Though her labor is for
nothing, *she* is unconcerned,
17 Because God has made her
forget wisdom,
And has not given her a share
of understanding.
18 "When she rushes away on
high,
She laughs at the horse and his
rider.

19 "Do you give the horse *his*
might?
Do you clothe his neck with a
mane?
20 "Do you make him ᴬleap like
locusts?
His majestic ᴮsnorting is
frightening.
21 "He paws in the valley, and
rejoices in *his* strength;
He ᴬgoes out to meet the battle.
22 "He laughs at fear and is not
dismayed;
And he does not turn back
from the sword.
23 "The quiver rattles against him,
The flashing spear and javelin.
24 "He races over the ground with
a roar and fury,
And he does not stand still
when *he hears* the sound of
the trumpet.
25 "As often as the trumpet *sounds*
he says, 'Aha!'

39:5 ᴬJob 6:5; Ps 104:11   39:6 ᴬJer 2:24; Hos 8:9
39:9 ᴬPs 22:21; Is 34:7   39:16 ᴬLam 4:3
39:20 ᴬJoel 2:5   ᴮJer 8:16   39:21 ᴬJer 8:6

And he senses the battle from
    afar,
And the thunder of the
    captains and the war cry.

26 "Is it by your understanding
    that the hawk soars,
Stretching his wings toward
    the south?
27 "Is it at your command that the
    eagle flies high,
And makes ^his nest on high?
28 "He dwells and spends his
    nights on the cliff,
On the rocky cliff, an
    inaccessible place.
29 "From there he ^tracks food;
His eyes look at *it* from afar.
30 "His young ones also lick up
    blood greedily;
And ^where the slain are, there
    he is."

JOB SAYS WHAT CAN I SAY?

40 Then the Lord said to Job,
2 "Will the faultfinder
^contend with the Almighty?
Let him who ^Brebukes God give
an answer."

3 Then Job answered the Lord and
said,
4 "Behold, I am insignificant;
    what can I say in response to
    You?
I ^put my hand on my mouth.
5 "I have spoken once, and ^I will
    not reply;
Or twice, and I will add
    nothing *more*."

GOD QUESTIONS JOB

6 Then the ^Lord answered Job
from the whirlwind and said,
7 "Now tighten the belt on your
    waist like a man;
I will ^ask you, and you
    instruct Me.

8 "Will you really ^nullify My
    judgment?
Will you condemn Me so that
    you may be justified?
9 "Or do you have an arm like
    God,
And can you ^thunder with a
    voice like His?
10 "^Adorn yourself with pride and
    dignity,
And clothe yourself with
    honor and majesty.
11 "Let out your ^outbursts of
    anger,
And look at everyone who is
    arrogant, and humble him.
12 "Look at everyone who is
    arrogant, *and* ^humble him,
And trample down the wicked
    where they stand.
13 "^Hide them together in the
    dust;
Imprison them in the hidden
    place.
14 "Then I will also confess to you,
That your own right hand can
    save you.

GOD'S POWER SHOWN IN CREATURES

15 "Behold, ¹Behemoth, which ^I
    made as well as you;
He eats grass like an ox.
16 "Behold, his strength in his
    waist,
And his power in the muscles
    of his belly.
17 "He hangs his tail like a cedar;
The tendons of his thighs are
    knit together.

39:27 ^Jer 49:16; Obad 4   39:29 ^Job 9:26
39:30 ^Matt 24:28; Luke 17:37   40:2 ^Is 45:9
^BJob 13:3   40:4 ^Job 21:5; 29:9   40:5 ^Job 9:3, 15
40:6 ^Job 38:1   40:7 ^Job 38:3; 42:4   40:8 ^Rom 3:4
40:9 ^Job 37:5; Ps 29:3   40:10 ^Ps 93:1; 104:1
40:11 ^Is 42:25; Nah 1:6, 8   40:12 ^1 Sam 2:7; Is 2:12
40:13 ^Is 2:10-12   40:15 ^Job 40:19

40:15 ¹I.e., a powerful animal, possibly a hippopotamus

¹⁸ "His bones are tubes of
bronze;
His limbs are like bars of iron.

¹⁹ "He is the ^first of the ways of
God;
Let his Maker bring His sword
near.

²⁰ "Indeed the ¹mountains ^bring
him food,
And all the animals of the field
play there.

²¹ "He lies down under the lotus
plants,
In the hiding place of the reeds
and the marsh.

²² "The lotus plants cover him
with shade;
The willows of the brook
surround him.

²³ "If a river rages, he is not
alarmed;
He is confident, though
the ^Jordan rushes to his
mouth.

²⁴ "Can anyone capture him when
he is on watch,
Can anyone pierce *his* nose
with barbs?

GOD'S POWER SHOWN IN CREATURES

41 "Can you drag out
¹,^Leviathan with a fishhook,
And press down his tongue
with a rope?

² "Can you ^put a rope in his
nose,
And pierce his jaw with a
hook?

³ "Will he make many pleas to
you,
Or will he speak to you gentle
words?

⁴ "Will he make a covenant with
you?
Will you take him as a servant
forever?

⁵ "Will you play with him as with
a bird,
And tie him down for your
young girls?

⁶ "Will the traders bargain for
him?
Will they divide him among
the merchants?

⁷ "Can you fill his skin with
harpoons,
Or his head with fishing
spears?

⁸ "Lay your hand on him.
Remember the battle; you will
not do it again!

⁹ "Behold, your expectation is
false;
Will you be hurled down even
at the sight of him?

¹⁰ "No one is so reckless that he
dares to ^stir him;
Who then is he who opposes
Me?

¹¹ "Who has ^been first *to give* to
Me, that I should repay *him?*
Whatever is under the entire
heaven is Mine.

¹² "I will not be silent about his
limbs,
Or his mighty strength, or his
graceful frame.

¹³ "Who can strip off his outer
covering?
Who can pierce his double
armor?

¹⁴ "Who can open the doors of his
face?
Around his teeth there is
terror.

¹⁵ "*His* strong scales are *his* pride,
Locked *as with* a tight seal.

40:19 ^Job 41:33   40:20 ^Ps 104:14   40:23 ^Gen 13:10
41:1 ^Ps 74:14; Is 27:1   41:2 ^2 Kin 19:28; Is 37:29
41:10 ^Job 3:8   41:11 ^Rom 11:35

40:20 ¹I.e., the mountain streams   41:1 ¹I.e., a sea
monster or crocodile

16 "One is so close to another
   That no air can come between
   them.

17 "They are joined one to another;
   They clasp each other and
   cannot be separated.

18 "His sneezes flash forth light,
   And his eyes are like the ^eye
   of dawn.

19 "From his mouth go burning
   torches;
   Sparks of fire leap forth.

20 "From his nostrils smoke goes
   out
   As *from* a boiling pot and
   burning reeds.

21 "His breath sets coals aglow,
   And a flame goes forth from
   his mouth.

22 "In his neck dwells strength,
   And dismay leaps before him.

23 "The folds of his flesh are
   joined together,
   Firm and immovable on him.

24 "His heart is as firm as a stone,
   And as firm as a lower millstone.

25 "When he rises up, the mighty
   are afraid;
   Because of the crashing they
   are bewildered.

26 "The sword that reaches him
   cannot prevail,
   Nor the spear, the dart, or the
   javelin.

27 "He regards iron as straw,
   Bronze as rotten wood.

28 "The arrow cannot make him
   flee;
   Slingstones are turned into
   stubble for him.

29 "Clubs are regarded as stubble;
   He laughs at the rattling of the
   javelin.

30 "His underparts are *like* sharp
   pieces of pottery;
   He spreads out *like* a threshing
   sledge on the mud.

31 "He makes the depths boil like
   a pot;
   He makes the sea like a jar of
   ointment.

32 "Behind him he illuminates a
   pathway;
   One would think the deep to
   be gray-haired.

33 "^Nothing on earth is like him,
   One made without fear.

34 "He looks on everything that is
   high;
   He is king over all the ^sons of
   pride."

JOB'S CONFESSION

42 Then Job answered the Lord
   and said,

2 "I know that ^You can *do* all
   things,
   And that no plan is impossible
   for You.

3 'Who is this who ^conceals
   advice without knowledge?'
   Therefore I have declared that
   which I did not understand,
   Things too wonderful for me,
   which I do not know.

4 'Please listen, and I will speak;
   I will ^ask You, and You
   instruct me.'

5 "I have ^heard of You by the
   hearing of the ear;
   But now my ^Beye sees You;

6 Therefore I retract,
   And I repent, *sitting* on dust
   and ashes."

GOD IS DISPLEASED WITH JOB'S FRIENDS

7 It came about after the Lord had
spoken these words to Job, that the
Lord said to Eliphaz the Temanite,
"My wrath is kindled against you

41:18 ^Job 3:9   41:33 ^Job 40:19   41:34 ^Job 28:8
42:2 ^Gen 18:14; Matt 19:26   42:3 ^Job 38:2
42:4 ^Job 38:3; 40:7   42:5 ^Rom 10:17   ^BEph 1:17, 18

and against your two friends, because you have not spoken of Me what is trustworthy, ^as My servant Job *has*. ⁸Now therefore, take for yourselves seven bulls and seven rams, and go to My servant Job, and offer up a ^burnt offering for yourselves, and My servant Job will pray for you. ⁸For I will accept him so as not to do with you *as your* foolishness *deserves*, because you have not spoken of Me what is trustworthy, as My servant Job *has*." ⁹So Eliphaz the Temanite, Bildad the Shuhite, *and* Zophar the Naamathite went and did as the Lord told them; and the Lord accepted Job.

GOD RESTORES JOB'S FORTUNES

¹⁰The Lord also ^restored the fortunes of Job when he prayed for his friends, and the Lord increased double all that Job had. ¹¹Then all his ^brothers, all his sisters, and all who had known him before came to him, and they ate bread with him in his house; and they sympathized with him and comforted him for all the adversities that the Lord had brought on him. And each one gave him a piece of money, and each a ring of gold. ¹²^The Lord blessed the latter *days* of Job more than his beginning; and he had fourteen thousand sheep, six thousand camels, a thousand yoke of oxen, and a thousand female donkeys. ¹³^He also had seven sons and three daughters. ¹⁴He named the first Jemimah, the second Keziah, and the third Keren-happuch. ¹⁵In all the land no women were found as beautiful as Job's daughters; and their father gave them inheritances among their brothers. ¹⁶After this, Job lived 140 years, and saw his sons and his grandsons, four generations. ¹⁷^And Job died, an old man and full of days.

42:7^Job 40:3-5; 42:1-6   **42:8**^Job 1:5   ⁸Job 22:30
42:10^Ps 85:1-3; 126:1-6   **42:11**^Job 19:13
42:12^Job 1:10; James 5:11   **42:13**^Job 1:2
42:17^Gen 15:15; Job 5:26

THE PSALMS

The following expressions occur often in the Psalms:
Selah Might mean *Higher pitch, Pause, Always,* or *From the beginning*
Maskil Possibly *Contemplative,* or *Didactic,* or *Skillful Psalm*
Mikhtam Possibly *Epigrammatic Poem,* or *Atonement Psalm*
Sheol The netherworld

BOOK 1

THE RIGHTEOUS AND THE WICKED CONTRASTED.

1 Blessed is the person who ^does not walk in the counsel of the wicked,
Nor stand in the path of sinners,
Nor sit in the seat of scoffers!

2 But his ^delight is ^Bin the Law of the LORD,
And on His Law he meditates day and night.

3 He will be like ^a tree planted by streams of water,
Which yields its fruit in its season,
And its leaf does not wither;
And in whatever he does, he prospers.

4 The wicked are not so,
But they are like ^chaff which the wind blows away.

5 Therefore ^the wicked will not stand in the ^Bjudgment,
Nor sinners in the assembly of the righteous.

6 For the LORD ^knows the way of the righteous,
But the way of the wicked will perish.

THE REIGN OF THE LORD'S ANOINTED.

2 Why are the nations restless
And the peoples ^plotting in vain?

2 The kings of the earth take their stand
And the rulers conspire together
^Against the LORD and against His ^1,BAnointed, *saying,*

3 "Let's ^tear their shackles apart
And throw their ropes away from us!"

4 He who sits in the heavens ^laughs,
The Lord scoffs at them.

5 Then He will speak to them in His ^anger
And terrify them in His fury, *saying,*

6 "But as for Me, I have installed ^My King
Upon Zion, ^BMy holy mountain."

7 "I will announce the decree of the LORD:
He said to Me, 'You are ^My Son,
Today I have fathered You.

1:1^Prov 4:14   1:2^Ps 119:14, 16, 35   ^BJosh 1:8
1:3^Ps 92:12-14; Jer 17:8   1:4^Ps 35:5; Is 17:13
1:5^Ps 5:5   ^BPs 9:7, 8, 16   1:6^Nah 1:7; 2 Tim 2:19
2:1^Ps 21:11   2:2^Ps 74:18, 23   ^BJohn 1:41
2:3^Jer 5:5   2:4^Ps 37:13   2:5^Ps 21:8, 9; 76:7
2:6^Ps 45:6   ^BPs 48:1, 2   2:7^Acts 13:33; Heb 1:5
───────────────────────────────
2:2 ^1Or *Messiah*

8   'Ask *it* of Me, and I will
     certainly give ^the nations as
     Your inheritance,
     And the ^Bends of the earth as
     Your possession.
9   'You shall ^1,^Abreak them with a
     rod of iron,
     You shall ^Bshatter them like
     earthenware.'"

10   Now then, you kings, ^use
     insight;
     Let yourselves be instructed,
     you judges of the earth.
11   Serve the Lord with
     ^reverence
     And rejoice with ^Btrembling.
12   ^1Kiss the Son, that He not be
     angry and you perish *on* the
     way,
     For His wrath may be kindled
     quickly.
     How blessed are all who ^take
     refuge in Him!

MORNING PRAYER OF TRUST IN GOD.
A Psalm of David, when he fled
from his son Absalom.

3   Lord, how ^my enemies have
     increased!
     Many are rising up against
     me.
2   Many are saying of my soul,
     "There is no ^salvation for him
     in God."   *Selah*

3   But You, Lord, are ^a shield
     around me,
     My glory, and the One who
     ^Blifts my head.
4   I was crying out to the Lord
     with my voice,
     And He ^answered me from
     His holy mountain.   *Selah*
5   I ^lay down and slept;
     I awoke, for the Lord sustains
     me.

6   I will not be afraid of ten
     thousands of people
     Who have ^set themselves
     against me all around.
7   Arise, Lord; save me, my God!
     For You have ^struck all my
     enemies on the cheek;
     You have ^Bshattered the teeth
     of the wicked.
8   ^Salvation belongs to the Lord;
     May Your blessing *be* upon
     Your people!   *Selah*

EVENING PRAYER OF TRUST IN GOD.
For the music director; on stringed
instruments. A Psalm of David.

4   Answer me when I call, God of
     my righteousness!
     You have ^relieved me in my
     distress;
     Be ^Bgracious to me and hear
     my prayer.

2   You sons of man, how long will
     my honor be *treated as* an
     insult?
     How long will you love ^what
     is worthless and strive for a
     ^Blie?   *Selah*
3   But know that the Lord has set
     apart the godly person for
     Himself;
     The Lord ^hears when I call to
     Him.

4   Tremble, ^and do not sin;
     ^BMeditate in your heart upon
     your bed, and be still. *Selah*

2:8^Ps 22:27 ^BPs 67:7 2:9^Rev 2:26, 27 ^BPs 28:5
2:10^Prov 8:15; 27:11 2:11^Ps 5:7 ^BPs 119:119, 120
2:12^Ps 5:11; 34:22 3:1^2 Sam 15:12; Ps 69:4
3:2^Ps 22:7, 8; 71:11 3:3^Ps 28:7 ^BPs 27:6 3:4^Ps 4:3;
34:4 3:5^Lev 26:6; Prov 3:24 3:6^Ps 118:10-13
3:7^Job 16:10 ^BPs 57:4 3:8^Ps 28:8; Is 43:11
4:1^Ps 18:18, 19 ^BPs 25:16 4:2^Ps 12:2 ^BPs 31:18
4:3^Ps 6:8, 9; 17:6 4:4^Eph 4:26 ^BPs 77:6

2:9^1 Another reading is *rule* 2:12^1 I.e., probably kiss
the feet of the Son

5 Offer the sacrifices of
   righteousness,
   And ^trust in the Lord.

6 Many are saying, "^Who will
   show us *anything* good?"
   Lift up the light of Your face
   upon us, Lord!
7 You have put ^joy in my heart,
   More than when their grain
   and new wine are abundant.
8 In peace I will both ^lie down
   and sleep,
   For You alone, Lord, have me
   ^dwell in safety.

**PRAYER FOR PROTECTION
FROM THE WICKED.**
For the music director; for flute
accompaniment. A Psalm of David.

5 ^Listen to my words, Lord,
   Consider my sighing.
2 Listen to the sound of my cry for
   help, ^my King and my God,
   For to You I pray.
3 In the morning, Lord, You will
   hear my voice;
   In the ^morning I will present
   my prayer to You and be on
   the ^watch.

4 For You are not a God
   ^who takes pleasure in
   wickedness;
   ^No evil can dwell with You.
5 The boastful will not stand
   before Your eyes;
   You ^hate all who do injustice.
6 You ^destroy those who speak
   lies;
   The Lord loathes the person
   of bloodshed and deceit.
7 But as for me, ^by Your
   abundant graciousness I will
   enter Your house,
   At Your holy temple I will bow
   in reverence for You.

8 Lord, ^lead me ^in Your
   righteousness because of my
   enemies;
   Make Your way straight
   before me.
9 For there is nothing
   trustworthy in their mouth;
   Their ^inward part is
   destruction *itself.*
   Their ^throat is an open
   grave;
   They flatter with their
   tongue.
10 Make them pay, God;
   ^Have them fall by their own
   schemes!
   Scatter them in the multitude
   of their wrongdoings,
   For they are ^rebellious against
   You.

11 But ^rejoice, all who ^take
   refuge in You,
   Sing for joy forever!
   And may You shelter them,
   That those who love Your
   name may rejoice in You.
12 For You ^bless the righteous
   person, Lord,
   You ^surround him with favor
   as with a shield.

**PRAYER FOR MERCY IN TIME
OF TROUBLE.**
For the music director; with stringed
instruments, upon an eight-string lyre.
A Psalm of David.

6 Lord, ^do not rebuke me in
   Your anger,
   Nor discipline me in Your
   wrath.

4:5 ^Ps 37:3, 5; 62:8   4:6 ^Job 7:7; 9:25   4:7 ^Is 9:3;
Acts 14:17   4:8 ^Ps 3:5   ^Lev 25:18   5:1 ^Ps 54:2
5:2 ^Ps 84:3   5:3 ^Ps 88:13   ^Ps 130:5   5:4 ^Ps 34:16
^Ps 92:15   5:5 ^Ps 11:5; 45:7   5:6 ^Ps 52:4, 5
5:7 ^Ps 69:13   5:8 ^Ps 31:3   ^Ps 31:1   5:9 ^Ps 7:14
^Rom 3:13   5:10 ^Ps 9:16   ^Ps 107:10, 11   5:11 ^Ps 64:10
^Ps 2:12   5:12 ^Ps 29:11   ^Ps 32:7, 10   6:1 ^Ps 38:1; 118:18

2 Be gracious to me, LORD, for I
   am frail;
   ^Heal me, LORD, for ^B^my bones
   are horrified.
3 And my ^soul is greatly horrified;
   But You, LORD—how long?
4 Return, LORD, ^rescue my soul;
   Save me because of Your mercy.
5 For ^there is no mention of You
   in death;
   In ^1^Sheol, who will praise You?

6 I am weary with my sighing;
   Every night I make my bed
   swim,
   I flood my couch with ^my tears.
7 My ^eye has wasted away with
   grief;
   It has grown old because of all
   my enemies.

8 ^Leave me, all you who
   practice injustice,
   For the LORD has heard the
   sound of my weeping.
9 The LORD ^has heard my
   pleading,
   The LORD ^B^receives my prayer.
10 All my enemies will be put to
   shame and greatly horrified;
   They shall turn back, they will
   ^suddenly be put to shame.

**THE LORD IMPLORED TO DEFEND THE
PSALMIST AGAINST THE WICKED.**

A †Shiggaion of David, which
he sang to the LORD concerning
Cush, a Benjaminite.

7 O LORD my God, ^in You I have
   taken refuge;
   Save me from all those who
   pursue me, and rescue me,
2 Or he will tear my soul ^like a
   lion,
   Dragging me away, while there
   is no one to rescue *me.*

3 O LORD my God, if I have done
   this,
   If there is ^injustice in my
   hands,
4 If I have ^done evil to my
   friend,
   Or have ^B^plundered my enemy
   for no reason,
5 Let the enemy pursue my soul
   and overtake *it;*
   And let him trample my life to
   the ground
   And lay my glory in the
   dust.   *Selah*

6 Arise, LORD, in Your anger;
   ^Raise Yourself against ^B^the
   rage of my enemies,
   And stir Yourself for me; You
   have ordered judgment.
7 Let the assembly of the
   ^peoples encompass You,
   And return on high over it.
8 The LORD judges the peoples;
   ^Vindicate me, LORD, according
   to my righteousness and my
   integrity that is in me.
9 Please let the evil of the
   wicked come to an end, but
   establish the righteous;
   For the righteous God ^puts
   hearts and minds to the test.
10 My shield is with God,
   Who ^saves the upright in
   heart.
11 God is a ^righteous judge,
   And a God who ^B^shows
   indignation every day.

6:2 ^A^Hos 6:1   ^B^Ps 22:14   6:3 ^A^Ps 88:3; John 12:27
6:4 ^A^Ps 17:13   6:5 ^A^Eccl 9:10; Is 38:18   6:6 ^A^Ps 42:3
6:7 ^A^Job 17:7; Ps 38:10   6:8 ^A^Matt 7:23; Luke 13:27
6:9 ^A^Ps 116:1   ^B^Ps 66:19, 20   6:10 ^A^Ps 73:19
7:1 ^A^Ps 31:1; 71:1   7:2 ^A^Ps 57:4; Is 38:13
7:3 ^A^1 Sam 24:11   7:4 ^A^Ps 109:4, 5   ^B^1 Sam 24:7
7:6 ^A^Ps 94:2   ^B^Ps 138:7   7:7 ^A^Ps 22:27   7:8 ^A^Ps 18:20;
43:1   7:9 ^A^Jer 11:20; Rev 2:23   7:10 ^A^Ps 97:10, 11; 125:4
7:11 ^A^Ps 50:6   ^B^Ps 90:9

6:5 ^1^I.e., the netherworld   7:1 †I.e., Dithyrambic
rhythm; or wild, passionate song

¹² If one does not repent, He will
   ^sharpen His sword;
   He has ^Bbent His bow and
   taken aim.
¹³ He has also prepared deadly
   weapons for Himself;
   He makes His ^arrows fiery
   shafts.
¹⁴ Behold, *an evil person* is
   pregnant with injustice,
   And he ^conceives harm and
   gives birth to lies.
¹⁵ He has dug a pit and hollowed
   it out,
   And has ^fallen into the hole
   which he made.
¹⁶ His ^harm will return on his
   own head,
   And his violence will descend
   on the top of his own head.

¹⁷ I will give thanks to the
   LORD ^according to His
   righteousness
   And will sing praise to the
   name of the LORD Most High.

THE LORD'S GLORY AND MANKIND'S DIGNITY.
For the music director; on the
Gittith. A Psalm of David.

8 LORD, our Lord,
   How majestic is Your name in
   all the earth,
   You who have ^displayed Your
   splendor above the heavens!
² ^From the mouths of infants
   and nursing babies You have
   established strength
   Because of Your enemies,
   To do away with the enemy
   and the revengeful.

³ When I consider ^Your heavens,
   the work of Your fingers,
   The ^Bmoon and the stars,
   which You have set in place;

⁴ ^What is man that You think
   of him,
   And a son of man that You are
   concerned about him?
⁵ Yet You have made him a ^little
   lower than ¹God,
   And You crown him with glory
   and majesty!
⁶ You have him rule over the
   works of Your hands;
   You have ^put everything
   under his feet,
⁷ All sheep and oxen,
   And also the animals of the
   field,
⁸ The birds of the sky, and the
   fish of the sea,
   Whatever passes through the
   paths of the seas.

⁹ ^LORD, our Lord,
   How majestic is Your name in
   all the earth!

THANKSGIVING FOR GOD'S JUSTICE.
For the music director; on †Muth-
labben. A Psalm of David.

9 I will give thanks to the LORD
   with all ^my heart;
   I will tell of all Your wonders.
² I will rejoice and be jubilant in
   You;
   I will ^sing praise to Your
   name, O ^BMost High.

³ When my enemies turn
   back,
   They stumble and ^perish
   before You.

7:12 ^Deut 32:41   ^BPs 64:7   7:13 ^Ps 18:14; 45:5
7:14 ^Is 59:4; James 1:15   7:15 ^Job 4:8; Ps 57:6
7:16 ^Esth 9:25; Ps 140:9   7:17 ^Ps 71:15, 16
8:1 ^Ps 57:5, 11; 148:13   8:2 ^Matt 21:16; 1 Cor 1:27
8:3 ^Ps 89:11   ^BPs 136:9   8:4 ^Ps 144:3; Heb 2:6-8
8:5 ^Gen 1:26; Ps 82:6   8:6 ^Eph 1:22; Heb 2:8
8:9 ^Ps 8:1   9:1 ^Ps 86:12   9:2 ^Ps 66:2, 4   ^BPs 83:18
9:3 ^Ps 27:2

8:5 ¹LXX *angels*   9:1 †Meaning of the Heb uncertain

4 For You have ^maintained my
just cause;
You have sat on the throne
^Bjudging righteously.
5 You have rebuked the nations,
You have eliminated the
wicked;
You have ^wiped out their
name forever and ever.
6 The enemy has come to an end
in everlasting ruins,
And You have uprooted the
cities;
The very ^memory of them has
perished.

7 But the LORD sits *as King*
forever;
He has established His ^throne
for judgment,
8 And He will ^judge the world
in righteousness;
He will execute judgment for
the peoples fairly.
9 The LORD will also be
a ^stronghold for the
oppressed,
A stronghold in times of
trouble;
10 And those who ^know Your
name will put their trust in
You,
For You, LORD, have not
^Babandoned those who seek
You.

11 Sing praises to the LORD, who
^dwells in Zion;
Declare His deeds among the
peoples.
12 For ^He who ¹requires blood
remembers them;
He does not forget the cry of
the needy.
13 Be gracious to me, LORD;
See my oppression from those
who hate me,

You who ^lift me up from the
gates of death,
14 So that I may tell of all Your
praises,
That in the gates of the
daughter of Zion
I may ^rejoice in Your salvation.
15 The nations have sunk down
^into the pit *which* they have
made;
In the ^Bnet which they hid, their
own foot has been caught.
16 The LORD has ^made Himself
known;
He has ^Bexecuted judgment.
A wicked one is ensnared in
the work of his own
hands.   *Higgaion Selah*

17 The wicked will ^return to
¹Sheol,
All the nations who forget God.
18 For the ^needy will not always
be forgotten,
Nor the hope of the afflicted
perish forever.
19 ^Arise, LORD, do not let
mankind prevail;
Let the nations be judged
before You.
20 Put them ^in fear, LORD;
Let the nations know that they
are ^Bmerely human.   *Selah*

A PRAYER FOR THE OVERTHROW
OF THE WICKED.

10
Why ^do You stand far away,
LORD?
Why do You hide *Yourself* in
times of trouble?

9:4 ^Ps 140:12   ^BPs 50:6   9:5 ^Ps 69:28; Prov 10:7
9:6 ^Ps 34:16   9:7 ^Ps 89:14   9:8 ^Ps 96:13; 98:9
9:9 ^Ps 32:7; 59:9, 16, 17   9:10 ^Ps 91:14   ^BPs 37:28
9:11 ^Ps 76:2   9:12 ^Gen 9:5; Ps 72:14   9:13 ^Ps 30:3;
86:13   9:14 ^Ps 13:5; 20:5   9:15 ^Ps 7:15, 16   ^BPs 57:6
9:16 ^Ex 7:5   ^BPs 9:4   9:17 ^Ps 49:14   9:18 ^Ps 9:12; 12:5
9:19 ^Num 10:35   9:20 ^Ps 14:5   ^BPs 62:9   10:1 ^Ps 22:1

9:12 ¹I.e., avenges bloodshed   9:17 ¹I.e., the netherworld

2 In arrogance the wicked hotly
pursue the needy;
Let them be ^caught in the plots
which they have devised.

3 For the wicked ^boasts of his
^Bsoul's desire,
And the greedy person curses
and shows disrespect to the
Lord.

4 The wicked, in his haughtiness,
does not seek *Him.*
^There is no God *in* all his
schemes.

5 His ways ^succeed at all times;
Yet Your judgments are on
high, out of his sight;
As for all his enemies, he
snorts at them.

6 He says to himself, "^I will not
be moved;
Throughout the generations ^BI
will not be in adversity."

7 His ^mouth is full of cursing,
deceit, and ^Boppression;
Under his tongue is harm and
injustice.

8 He sits in the lurking places of
the villages;
He ^kills the innocent in the
secret places;
His eyes surreptitiously watch
for the ^Bunfortunate.

9 He lurks in secret like ^a lion in
his lair;
He lurks to catch the needy;
He catches the needy when he
pulls him into his ^Bnet.

10 Then he crushes *the needy
one, who* cowers;
And unfortunate people fall by
his mighty *power.*

11 He ^says to himself, "God has
forgotten;
He has hidden His face; He will
never see it."

12 Arise, Lord; God, ^lift up Your
hand.
Do not forget the humble.

13 Why has the wicked ^treated
God disrespectfully?
He has said to himself, "You
will not require *an account.*"

14 You have seen *it,* for You
have looked at harm and
provocation to take it into
Your hand.
The ^unfortunate commits
himself to You;
You have been the ^Bhelper of
the orphan.

15 ^Break the arm of the wicked
and the evildoer,
Seek out his wickedness until
You find none.

16 The Lord is ^King forever and
ever;
^BNations have perished from
His land.

17 Lord, You have heard the
^desire of the humble;
You will strengthen their
heart, You will make Your ear
attentive

18 To vindicate the ^orphan and
the ^Boppressed,
So that mankind, which is
of the earth, will no longer
cause terror.

THE LORD, A REFUGE AND DEFENSE.
For the music director. *A Psalm* of David.

11 In the Lord I ^take refuge;
How can you say to my
soul, "Flee *as* a bird to your
mountain?

10:2^A Ps 7:16; 9:16   10:3^A Ps 94:3, 4   ^B Ps 112:10
10:4^A Ps 14:1; 36:1   10:5^A Ps 52:7   10:6^A Eccl 8:11
^B Rev 18:7   10:7^A Rom 3:14   ^B Ps 73:8   10:8^A Ps 94:6
^B Ps 72:12   10:9^A Ps 17:12   ^B Ps 140:5   10:11^A Ps 10:4
10:12^A Ps 7:7; Mic 5:9   10:13^A Ps 10:3
10:14^A Ps 22:11   ^B Ps 68:5   10:15^A Ps 37:17
10:16^A Ps 29:10   ^B Deut 8:20   10:17^A Ps 9:18
10:18^A Ps 146:9   ^B Ps 9:9   11:1^A Ps 2:12

2 "For, behold, the wicked ^bend
the bow,
They have ^Bset their arrow on
the string
To shoot in darkness at the
upright in heart.

3 "If the ^foundations are
destroyed,
What can the righteous do?"

4 The LORD is in His ^holy
temple; the LORD's ^Bthrone is
in heaven;
His eyes see, His eyelids test
the sons of mankind.

5 The LORD ^tests the righteous
and the wicked,
And His soul hates one who
loves violence.

6 He will ^rain ^1coals of fire upon
the wicked,
And brimstone and burning
wind will be the portion of
their cup.

7 For the LORD is righteous, He
loves righteousness;
The upright will ^see His face.

GOD, A HELPER AGAINST
THE TREACHEROUS.

For the music director; upon an eight-
stringed lyre. A Psalm of David.

12 Help, LORD, for ^the godly
person has come to an end,
For the faithful have
disappeared from the sons of
mankind.

2 They ^speak lies to one
another;
They speak with ^Bflattering lips
and a double heart.

3 May the LORD cut off all
flattering lips,
The tongue that ^speaks great
things;

4 Who ^have said, "With our
tongue we will prevail;

Our lips are our own; who is
lord over us?"

5 "Because of the devastation
of the poor, because of the
groaning of the needy,
Now ^I will arise," says the
LORD; "I will ^Bput him in the
safety for which he longs."

6 The words of the LORD are
pure words;
Like silver ^refined in a furnace
on the ground, filtered seven
times.

7 You, LORD, will keep them;
You will ^protect him from this
generation forever.

8 The ^wicked strut about on
every side
When ^Bvileness is exalted
among the sons of mankind.

PRAYER FOR HELP IN TROUBLE.

For the music director. A Psalm of David.

13 How long, LORD? Will You
^forget me forever?
How long ^Bwill You hide Your
face from me?

2 How long am I to ^feel anxious
in my soul,
With grief in my heart all the
day?
How long will my enemy be
exalted over me?

3 Consider *and* answer me,
O LORD my God;
^Enlighten my eyes, or I will
sleep the *sleep of* death,

11:2 ^Ps 37:14   ^BPs 64:3   11:3 ^Ps 82:5; 119:152
11:4 ^Hab 2:20   ^BRev 4:2   11:5 ^Gen 22:1; James 1:12
11:6 ^Ps 18:13, 14   11:7 ^Ps 16:11; 17:15   12:1 ^Is 57:1;
Mic 7:2   12:2 ^Ps 41:6   ^BRom 16:18   12:3 ^Dan 7:8;
Rev 13:5   12:4 ^Ps 73:8, 9   12:5 ^Is 33:10   ^BPs 34:6
12:6 ^Prov 30:5   12:7 ^Ps 37:28; 97:10
12:8 ^Ps 55:10, 11   ^BIs 32:5   13:1 ^Ps 44:24
^BJob 13:24   13:2 ^Ps 42:4   13:3 ^Ezra 9:8; Job 33:30

11:6 ^1As in a Gr version; MT *snares; Fire and*

4 And my enemy will say, "I have
    overcome him,"
  And ^my adversaries will
    rejoice when I am shaken.

5 But I have ^trusted in Your
    faithfulness;
  My heart shall rejoice in Your
    salvation.
6 I will ^sing to the LORD,
  Because He has ᴮlooked after
    me.

**FOOLISHNESS AND WICKEDNESS
OF PEOPLE.**
For the music director. *A Psalm* of David.

14 The fool has ^said in his
      heart, "There is no God."
  They are corrupt, they have
    committed detestable acts;
  There is ᴮno one who does
    good.
2 The LORD has looked down
    from heaven upon the sons
    of mankind
  To see if there are any who
    ^understand,
  Who ᴮseek God.
3 They have all turned aside,
    together they are corrupt;
  There is ^no one who does
    good, not even one.

4 Do all the workers of injustice
    not know,
  Who ^devour my people *as*
    they eat bread,
  And do not call upon the LORD?
5 There they are in great dread,
  For God is with a ^righteous
    generation.
6 You would put to shame the
    plan of the poor,
  But the LORD is his ^refuge.

7 Oh, that the salvation of Israel
  would come out of Zion!

When the LORD ^restores the
    fortunes of His people,
  Jacob will rejoice, Israel will be
    glad.

DESCRIPTION OF A CITIZEN OF ZION.
A Psalm of David.

15 LORD, who may reside ^in
      Your tent?
  Who may settle on Your ᴮholy
    hill?
2 One who walks with integrity,
    practices righteousness,
  And ^speaks truth in his heart.
3 He ^does not slander with his
    tongue,
  Nor do evil to his neighbor,
  Nor bring shame on his friend;
4 A despicable person is
    despised in his eyes,
  But he ^honors those who fear
    the LORD;
  He takes an oath to his own
    detriment, and does not
    change;
5 He does not lend his money ¹at
    interest,
  Nor ^does he take a bribe
    against the innocent.
  One who does these things
    will never be shaken.

**THE LORD, THE PSALMIST'S PORTION
IN LIFE AND SALVATION IN DEATH.**
A †Mikhtam of David.

16 Protect me, God, for ^I take
      refuge in You.
2 I said to the LORD, "You are my
    Lord;

13:4 ^Ps 25:2; 38:16   13:5 ^Ps 52:8   13:6 ^Ps 96:1, 2
ᴮPs 116:7 14:1 ^Ps 10:4   ᴮRom 3:10-12 14:2 ^Ps 92:6
ᴮ1 Chr 22:19   14:3 ^Ps 143:2   14:4 ^Jer 10:25; Mic 3:3
14:5 ^Ps 73:15; 112:2 14:6 ^Ps 46:1; 142:5
14:7 ^Ps 85:1, 2 15:1 ^Ps 27:5, 6   ᴮPs 24:3
15:2 ^Zech 8:16; Eph 4:25 15:3 ^Ps 50:20
15:4 ^Acts 28:10 15:5 ^Ex 23:8; Deut 16:19 16:1 ^Ps 7:1

15:5 ¹I.e., to a fellow Israelite 16:1 †Possibly
Epigrammatic Poem or *Atonement Psalm*

I ^have nothing good besides
You."

3 As for the 'saints who are on
the earth,
They are the majestic ones;
^all my delight is in them.

4 The ^pains of those who have
acquired another *god* will be
multiplied;
I will not pour out their drink
offerings of blood,
Nor will I ^take their names
upon my lips.

5 The LORD is the ^portion of
my inheritance and my
cup;
You support my lot.

6 The measuring ^lines have
fallen for me in pleasant
places;
Indeed, my inheritance is
^beautiful to me.

7 I will bless the LORD who has
^advised me;
Indeed, my ^mind instructs
me in the night.

8 ^I have set the LORD
continually before me;
Because He is at my right
hand, I will not be shaken.

9 Therefore ^my heart is glad
and my glory rejoices;
My flesh also will dwell
securely.

10 For You will not abandon my
soul to 'Sheol;
You will not ^allow Your
Holy One to undergo
decay.

11 You will make known to me
^the way of life;
In Your presence is fullness
of joy;
In Your right hand there are
pleasures forever.

PRAYER FOR PROTECTION
AGAINST OPPRESSORS.
A Prayer of David.

17 Hear a ^just cause, LORD, give
Your attention to my cry;
Listen to my prayer, which is
not from ^deceitful lips.

2 Let ^my judgment come forth
from Your presence;
Let Your eyes look with integrity.

3 You have ^put my heart to the
test;
You have visited *me* by night;
You have ^sifted me and You
find nothing;
My intent is that my mouth
will not offend.

4 As for the works of mankind,
^by the word of Your lips
I have kept from the ways of
the violent.

5 My ^steps have held to Your
paths.
My feet have not slipped.

6 I have ^called upon You, for
You will answer me, God;
Incline Your ear to me, hear
my speech.

7 ^Show Your wonderful
faithfulness,
^Savior of those who take
refuge at Your right hand
From those who rise up
against them.

8 Keep me as the ^apple of the eye;
Hide me in the shadow of Your
wings

16:2 ^Ps 73:25   16:3 ^Ps 119:63   16:4 ^Ps 32:10
^Ex 23:13   16:5 ^Ps 73:26; Lam 3:24   16:6 ^Ps 78:55
^Jer 3:19   16:7 ^Ps 73:24   ^Ps 77:6   16:8 ^Ps 16:8-11;
Acts 2:25-28   16:9 ^Ps 4:7; 13:5   16:10 ^Acts 13:35
16:11 ^Ps 139:24; Matt 7:14   17:1 ^Ps 9:4   ^Is 29:13
17:2 ^Ps 103:6   17:3 ^Ps 26:1, 2   ^1 Pet 1:7
17:4 ^Ps 119:9, 101   17:5 ^Job 23:11; Ps 119:133
17:6 ^Ps 86:7; 116:2   17:7 ^Ps 31:21   ^Ps 20:6
17:8 ^Deut 32:10; Zech 2:8

16:3 ^1 Lit *holy ones*; i.e., God's people   16:10 ^1 I.e., the
netherworld

739 PSALMS 17—18

9 From the ᴬwicked who deal
   violently with me,
   My ᴮdeadly enemies who
   surround me.
10 They have ᴬclosed their
   unfeeling *hearts,*
   With their mouths they speak
   proudly.
11 They have now ᴬsurrounded
   us in our steps;
   They set their eyes ᴮto cast *us*
   down to the ground.
12 He is ᴬlike a lion that is eager to
   tear,
   And as a young lion ᴮlurking in
   secret places.

13 Arise, Lᴏʀᴅ, confront him,
   make him bow down;
   ᴬSave my soul from the wicked
   with ᴮYour sword,
14 From people by Your hand,
   Lᴏʀᴅ,
   From people of the world,
   ᴬwhose portion is in *this* life,
   And whose belly You fill with
   Your treasure;
   They are satisfied with children,
   And leave their abundance to
   their babies.
15 As for me, I shall ᴬbehold Your
   face in righteousness;
   I shall be satisfied with Your
   likeness when I awake.

THE Lᴏʀᴅ PRAISED FOR RESCUING DAVID.

For the music director. A *Psalm* of David, the servant of the Lᴏʀᴅ, who spoke to the Lᴏʀᴅ the words of this song on the day that the Lᴏʀᴅ rescued him from the hand of all his enemies and from the hand of Saul. And he said,

18 "I love You, Lᴏʀᴅ, ᴬmy
      strength."
2 The Lᴏʀᴅ is ᴬmy rock and ᴮmy
   fortress and my savior,

My God, my rock, in whom I
take refuge;
My shield and the horn of my
salvation, my stronghold.
3 I call upon the Lᴏʀᴅ, who is
worthy to be praised,
And I am ᴬsaved from my
enemies.

4 The ᴬropes of death
encompassed me,
And the torrents of
destruction terrified me.
5 The ᴬropes of ¹Sheol
surrounded me;
The snares of death
confronted me.
6 In my distress I called upon
the Lᴏʀᴅ,
And cried to my God for help;
He heard my voice from His
temple,
And my ᴬcry for help before
Him came into His ears.

7 Then the ᴬearth shook and
quaked;
And the ᴮfoundations of the
mountains were trembling
And were shaken, because He
was angry.
8 Smoke went up out of His
nostrils,
And ᴬfire from His mouth was
devouring;
Coals burned from it.
9 He also ᴬbowed the heavens
down low, and came down
With thick ᴮdarkness under
His feet.

17:9 ᴬPs 31:20 ᴮPs 27:12 17:10 ᴬJob 15:27; Ps 73:7
17:11 ᴬPs 88:17 ᴮPs 37:14 17:12 ᴬPs 7:2 ᴮPs 10:9
17:13 ᴬPs 22:20 ᴮPs 7:12 17:14 ᴬPs 73:3-7; Luke 16:25
17:15 ᴬPs 11:7; 1 John 3:2 18:1 ᴬPs 59:17 18:2 ᴬDeut 32:18
ᴮPs 144:2 18:3 ᴬPs 34:6 18:4 ᴬPs 116:3 18:5 ᴬPs 116:3
18:6 ᴬPs 34:15 18:7 ᴬHag 2:6 ᴮPs 114:4, 6
18:8 ᴬPs 50:3 18:9 ᴬPs 144:5 ᴮPs 97:2

18:5 ¹I.e., the netherworld

¹⁰ He rode on a cherub and flew;
And He sped on the ^wings of
the wind.

¹¹ He made ^darkness His hiding
place, ^His canopy around
Him,
Darkness of waters, thick
clouds.

¹² From the ^brightness before
Him passed His thick clouds,
Hailstones and coals of fire.

¹³ The LORD also ^thundered in
the heavens,
And the Most High uttered His
voice,
Hailstones and coals of fire.

¹⁴ He ^sent out His arrows, and
scattered them,
And lightning flashes in
abundance, and routed them.

¹⁵ Then the ^channels of water
appeared,
And the foundations of the
world were exposed
By Your rebuke, LORD,
At the blast of the breath of
Your nostrils.

¹⁶ He ^sent from on high, He took
me;
He drew me out of many waters.

¹⁷ He ^saved me from my strong
enemy,
And from those who hated me,
for they were too mighty for
me.

¹⁸ They confronted me in ^the
day of my disaster,
But ^the LORD was my support.

¹⁹ He also brought me out into an
open place;
He rescued me, because ^He
delighted in me.

²⁰ The LORD has ^rewarded
me according to my
righteousness;

According to the cleanness of
my hands He has repaid me.

²¹ For I have kept the ways of the
LORD,
And have ^not acted wickedly
against my God.

²² For all ^His judgments were
before me,
And I did not put away His
statutes from me.

²³ I was also ^blameless with
Him,
And I ^kept myself from my
wrongdoing.

²⁴ Therefore the LORD has
^repaid me according to my
righteousness,
According to the cleanness of
my hands in His eyes.

²⁵ With ^the faithful You show
Yourself faithful;
With the blameless You prove
Yourself blameless;

²⁶ With the pure You show
Yourself ^pure,
And with the crooked You
show Yourself astute.

²⁷ For You ^save an afflicted
people,
But You humiliate ^haughty
eyes.

²⁸ For You light my lamp;
The LORD my God ^illumines
my darkness.

²⁹ For by You I can run at a troop
of warriors;
And by my God I can ^leap over
a wall.

18:10 ^Ps 104:3   18:11 ^Deut 4:11   ^Ps 97:2
18:12 ^Ps 104:2   18:13 ^Ps 29:3; 104:7
18:14 ^Ps 144:6; Hab 3:11   18:15 ^Ps 106:9
18:16 ^Ps 144:7   18:17 ^Ps 59:1   18:18 ^Ps 59:16
^Ps 16:8   18:19 ^Ps 37:23; 41:11   18:20 ^1 Sam 24:19;
Ps 7:8   18:21 ^2 Chr 34:33; Ps 119:102
18:22 ^Ps 119:30   18:23 ^Ps 18:32   ^Ps 19:12, 13
18:24 ^1 Sam 26:23; Ps 18:20   18:25 ^1 Kin 8:32;
Matt 5:7   18:26 ^Job 25:5; Hab 1:13   18:27 ^Ps 72:12
^Prov 6:17   18:28 ^Ps 27:1   18:29 ^Ps 18:33; 40:2

30 As for God, His way is
   ᴬblameless;
   The ᴮword of the Lᴏʀᴅ is
   refined;
   He is a shield to all who take
   refuge in Him.
31 For ᴬwho is God, but the Lᴏʀᴅ?
   And who is a rock, except our
   God,
32 The God who ᴬencircles me
   with strength,
   And makes my way
   ᴮblameless?
33 He ᴬmakes my feet like deer's
   feet,
   And ᴮsets me up on my high
   places.
34 He ᴬtrains my hands for battle,
   So that my arms can ᴮbend a
   bow of bronze.
35 You have also given me ᴬthe
   shield of Your salvation,
   And Your right hand upholds
   me;
   And Your gentleness makes
   me great.
36 You ᴬenlarge my steps under
   me,
   And my feet have not slipped.
37 I ᴬpursued my enemies and
   overtook them,
   And I did not turn back until
   they were consumed.
38 I shattered them, so that they
   were ᴬnot able to rise;
   They fell ᴮunder my feet.
39 For You have encircled me
   with strength for battle;
   You have forced those who
   rose up against me ᴬto bow
   down under me.
40 You have also made my
   enemies ᴬturn their backs to
   me,
   And I ᴮdestroyed those who
   hated me.

41 They cried for help, but there
   was ᴬno one to save,
   They cried to the Lᴏʀᴅ, but He
   did not answer them.
42 Then I beat them fine like the
   ᴬdust before the wind;
   I emptied them out like the
   mud of the streets.
43 You have rescued me from the
   contentions of the people;
   You have placed me as ᴬhead of
   the nations;
   A ᴮpeople whom I have not
   known serve me.
44 As soon as they hear, they
   obey me;
   Foreigners ᴬpretend to obey me.
45 Foreigners lose heart,
   And ᴬcome trembling out of
   their fortresses.

46 The Lᴏʀᴅ ᴬlives, and blessed
   be my rock;
   And exalted be the God of my
   salvation,
47 The God who ᴬexecutes
   vengeance for me,
   And subdues peoples under me.
48 He rescues me from my
   enemies;
   You indeed ᴬlift me above those
   who rise up against me;
   You rescue me from a ᴮviolent
   man.
49 Therefore I will ᴬgive thanks
   to You among the nations,
   Lᴏʀᴅ,
   And I will sing praises to Your
   name.

18:30 ᴬRev 15:3   ᴮPs 12:6   18:31 ᴬPs 86:8-10; Is 45:5
18:32 ᴬIs 45:5   ᴮPs 18:23   18:33 ᴬHab 3:19   ᴮDeut 32:13
18:34 ᴬPs 144:1   ᴮJob 29:20   18:35 ᴬPs 33:20
18:36 ᴬPs 18:33   18:37 ᴬPs 44:5   18:38 ᴬPs 36:12
ᴮPs 47:3   18:39 ᴬPs 18:47   18:40 ᴬPs 21:12   ᴮPs 94:23
18:41 ᴬPs 50:22   18:42 ᴬPs 83:13   18:43 ᴬ2 Sam 8:1-18
Is 55:5   ᴮPs 66:3   18:44 ᴬPs 66:3   18:45 ᴬMic 7:17
18:46 ᴬJob 19:25   18:47 ᴬPs 94:1   18:48 ᴬPs 27:6
ᴮPs 11:5   18:49 ᴬRom 15:9

50 He gives great ¹salvation to His
   king,
   And shows faithfulness to ᴬHis
   anointed,
   To David and ᴮhis descendants
   forever.

THE WORKS AND THE WORD OF GOD.
For the music director. A Psalm of David.

19 The ᴬheavens tell of the
   glory of God;
   And their expanse declares the
   work of His hands.

2 Day to ᴬday pours forth
   speech,
   And ᴮnight to night reveals
   knowledge.

3 There is no speech, nor are
   there words;
   Their voice is not heard.

4 Their ¹,ᴬline has gone out into
   all the earth,
   And their words to the end of
   the world.
   In them He has placed a tent
   for the sun,

5 Which is like a groom coming
   out of his chamber;
   It rejoices like a strong person
   to run his course.

6 Its ᴬrising is from one end of
   the heavens,
   And its circuit to the other end
   of them;
   And there is nothing hidden
   from its heat.

7 ᴬThe Law of the Lᴏʀᴅ is
   ¹,ᴮperfect, restoring the soul;
   The testimony of the Lᴏʀᴅ
   is sure, making wise the
   simple.

8 The precepts of the Lᴏʀᴅ are
   right, ᴬrejoicing the heart;
   The commandment of the
   Lᴏʀᴅ is pure, ᴮenlightening
   the eyes.

9 The fear of the Lᴏʀᴅ is clean,
   enduring forever;
   The judgments of the Lᴏʀᴅ
   are ᴬtrue; they are ᴮrighteous
   altogether.

10 They are more desirable than
   ᴬgold, yes, than much pure
   gold;
   ᴮSweeter also than honey and
   drippings of the honeycomb.

11 Moreover, Your servant is
   warned by them;
   In keeping them there is great
   ᴬreward.

12 Who can discern *his* errors?
   ᴬAcquit me of ᴮhidden *faults*.

13 Also keep Your servant back
   from presumptuous *sins;*
   Let them not ᴬrule over me;
   Then I will be innocent,
   And I will be blameless of
   ᴮgreat wrongdoing.

14 May the words of my mouth
   and ᴬthe meditation of my
   heart
   Be acceptable in Your sight,
   Lᴏʀᴅ, my rock and my
   Redeemer.

PRAYER FOR VICTORY OVER ENEMIES.
For the music director. A Psalm of David.

20 May the Lᴏʀᴅ answer you
   ᴬon a day of trouble!
   May the name of the God of
   Jacob protect you!

2 May He send you help ᴬfrom
   the sanctuary,
   And ᴮsupport you from Zion!

18:50 ᴬPs 28:8 ᴮPs 89:4 19:1 ᴬPs 8:1; Rom 1:19, 20
19:2 ᴬPs 74:16 ᴮPs 139:12 19:4 ᴬRom 10:18
19:6 ᴬPs 113:3; Eccl 1:5 19:7 ᴬPs 111:7 ᴮPs 119:160
19:8 ᴬPs 119:14 ᴮPs 36:9 19:9 ᴬPs 119:142
ᴮPs 119:138 19:10 ᴬPs 119:72, 127 ᴮPs 119:103
19:11 ᴬPs 24:5, 6; Prov 29:18 19:12 ᴬPs 51:1, 2
ᴮPs 139:23, 24 19:13 ᴬPs 119:133 ᴮPs 25:11
19:14 ᴬPs 104:34 20:1 ᴬPs 50:15
20:2 ᴬPs 3:4 ᴮPs 110:2

18:50 ¹I.e., victories; lit *salvations* 19:4 ¹Another
reading is *sound* 19:7 ¹I.e., blameless

3 May He ^remember all your
meal offerings
And ^Baccept your burnt
offering!   *Selah*

4 May He grant you your ^heart's
desire
And ^Bfulfill your whole plan!

5 We will sing for joy over your
victory,
And in the name of our God
we will ^set up our banners.
May the LORD ^Bfulfill all your
desires.

6 Now ^I know that the LORD
saves His anointed;
He will ^Banswer him from His
holy heaven
With the saving strength of
His right hand.

7 Some *praise their* chariots and
some *their* horses,
But ^we will praise the name of
the LORD, our God.

8 They have bowed down and
fallen,
But we have ^risen and stood
upright.

9 ^Save, LORD;
May the ^BKing answer us on
the day we call.

PRAISE FOR SALVATION.
For the music director. A Psalm of David.

21 LORD, in Your strength the
king will ^be glad,
And in Your salvation how
greatly he will rejoice!

2 You have ^given him his heart's
desire,
And You have not withheld the
request of his lips.   *Selah*

3 For You ^meet him with the
blessings of good things;
You set a ^Bcrown of pure gold
on his head.

4 He asked for life from You,
You gave it to him,
^Length of days forever and
ever.

5 His ^glory is great through
Your salvation,
^BSplendor and majesty You
place upon him.

6 For You make him most
blessed forever;
You make him joyful ^with the
joy of Your presence.

7 For the king ^trusts in the
LORD,
And through the faithfulness
of the Most High ^Bhe will not
be shaken.

8 Your hand will ^find all your
enemies;
Your right hand will find those
who hate you.

9 You will make them ^as a fiery
oven in the time of your
anger;
The LORD will ^Bswallow them
up in His wrath,
And fire will devour them.

10 You will eliminate their
descendants from the earth,
And their ^children from
among the sons of mankind.

11 Though they ^intended evil
against You
And ^Bdevised a plot,
They will not succeed.

12 For You will make them turn
their back;
You will take aim at their faces
^with Your bowstrings.

20:3 ^Acts 10:4 ^BPs 51:19   20:4 ^Ps 21:2   ^BPs 145:19
20:5 ^Ps 60:4   ^B1 Sam 1:17   20:6 ^Ps 41:11   ^BIs 58:9
20:7 ^2 Chr 32:8   20:8 ^Ps 37:24; Mic 7:8   20:9 ^Ps 3:7
^BPs 17:6   21:1 ^Ps 59:16, 17   21:2 ^Ps 20:4; 37:4
21:3 ^Ps 59:10   ^B2 Sam 12:30   21:4 ^Ps 91:16
21:5 ^Ps 20:5   ^BPs 96:6   21:6 ^Ps 43:4   21:7 ^Ps 125:1
^BPs 112:6   21:8 ^Is 10:10   21:9 ^Mal 4:1   ^BLam 2:2
21:10 ^Ps 37:28   21:11 ^Ps 2:1-3   ^BPs 10:2
21:12 ^Ps 7:12, 13

13 Be exalted, LORD, in Your
       strength;
   We will ^sing and praise Your
       power.

**A CRY OF ANGUISH AND A SONG
OF PRAISE.**
For the music director; upon Aijeleth
Hashshahar. A Psalm of David.

22 ^My God, my God, why have
       You forsaken me?
   Far from my help are the
       words of my groaning.
2 My God, I ^cry out by day, but
       You do not answer;
   And by night, but I have no rest.
3 Yet ^You are holy,
   You who are enthroned upon
       ^the praises of Israel.
4 In You our fathers ^trusted;
   They trusted and You ^rescued
       them.
5 To You they cried out and they
       fled to safety;
   ^In You they trusted and were
       not disappointed.

6 But I am a ^worm and not a
       person,
   A disgrace of mankind and
       despised by the people.
7 All who see me deride me;
   They sneer, they ^shake their
       heads, *saying,*
8 "Turn *him* over to the LORD; ^let
       Him save him;
   Let Him rescue him, because
       He delights in him."

9 Yet You are He who ^brought
       me forth from the womb;
   You made me trust *when* upon
       my mother's breasts.
10 I was cast upon You ^from
       birth;
   You have been my God from
       my mother's womb.

11 ^Do not be far from me, for
       trouble is near;
   For there is no one to help.
12 Many bulls have surrounded
       me;
   Strong *bulls* of ^Bashan have
       encircled me.
13 They ^open their mouths wide
       at me,
   As a ravening and roaring
       ^lion.
14 I am ^poured out like water,
   And all my bones are out of
       joint;
   My ^heart is like wax;
   It is melted within me.
15 My strength is dried up like a
       piece of pottery,
   And ^my tongue clings to my
       jaws;
   And You ^lay me in the dust of
       death.
16 For dogs have surrounded me;
   A band of evildoers has
       encompassed me;
   They ^pierced my hands and
       my feet.
17 I can count all my bones.
   ^They look, they stare at me;
18 They ^divide my garments
       among them,
   And they cast lots for my
       clothing.

19 But You, LORD, do not be far
       away;
   You who are my help, ^hurry to
       my assistance.

21:13 ^Ps 59:16; 81:1   22:1 ^Matt 27:46; Mark 15:34
22:2 ^Ps 42:3; 88:1   22:3 ^Ps 99:9   ^Deut 10:21
22:4 ^Ps 78:53   ^Ps 107:6   22:5 ^Is 49:23
22:6 ^Job 25:6; Is 41:14   22:7 ^Matt 27:39; Mark 15:29
22:8 ^Ps 91:14; Matt 27:43   22:9 ^Ps 71:5, 6
22:10 ^Is 46:3; 49:1   22:11 ^Ps 71:12
22:12 ^Deut 32:14; Amos 4:1   22:13 ^Lam 2:16
^Ps 10:9   22:14 ^Job 30:16   ^Nah 2:10
22:15 ^John 19:28   ^Ps 104:29   22:16 ^Matt 27:35;
John 20:25   22:17 ^Luke 23:27, 35   22:18 ^Matt 27:35;
Luke 23:34   22:19 ^Ps 70:5

20 Save my soul from ^the sword,
My ^Bonly *life* from the power of
the dog.
21 Save me from the ^lion's
mouth;
From the horns of the wild
oxen You answer me.

22 I will ^proclaim Your name to
my brothers;
In the midst of the assembly I
will praise You.
23 ^You who fear the Lord, praise
Him;
All you descendants of Jacob,
glorify Him,
And stand in awe of Him, all
you descendants of Israel.
24 For He has not despised nor
scorned the suffering of the
afflicted;
Nor has He hidden His face
from him;
But ^when he cried to Him for
help, He heard.

25 From You *comes* my praise in
the great assembly;
I shall ^pay my vows before
those who fear Him.
26 The afflicted will eat and ^be
satisfied;
Those who seek Him will
praise the Lord.
May your heart live forever!
27 All the ^ends of the earth will
remember and turn to the
Lord,
And all the families of the
nations will worship before
You.
28 For the ^kingdom is the Lord's
And He rules over the nations.
29 All the ^prosperous of the
earth will eat and worship,
All those who go down to the
dust will kneel before Him,

Even he who ^Bcannot keep his
soul alive.
30 A posterity will serve Him;
It will be told of the Lord to
^the *coming* generation.
31 They will come and will
declare His righteousness
To a people ^who will be born,
that He has performed *it.*

THE LORD, THE PSALMIST'S
SHEPHERD.
A Psalm of David.

23 The Lord is my ^shepherd,
I will ^Bnot be in need.
2 He lets me lie down in green
pastures;
He ^leads me beside quiet
waters.
3 He restores my soul;
He ^guides me in the ^Bpaths of
righteousness
For the sake of His name.

4 Even though I walk through
the valley of the shadow of
death,
I fear no evil, for ^You are with
me;
Your ^Brod and Your staff, they
comfort me.
5 You prepare a table before
me in the presence of my
enemies;
You have ^anointed my head
with oil;
My ^Bcup overflows.
6 Certainly goodness and
faithfulness will follow me
all the days of my life,

22:20 ^Ps 37:14 ^B Ps 35:17 22:21 ^Ps 22:13
22:22 ^Ps 40:10; Heb 2:12 22:23 ^Ps 135:19, 20
22:24 ^Ps 31:22; Heb 5:7 22:25 ^Ps 61:8; Eccl 5:4
22:26 ^Ps 107:9 22:27 ^Ps 2:8; 82:8
22:28 ^Zech 14:9; Matt 6:13
22:29 ^Hab 1:16 ^B Ps 89:48 22:30 ^Ps 102:18
22:31 ^Ps 78:6 23:1 ^Ezek 34:11-13 ^B Phil 4:19
23:2 ^Rev 7:17 23:3 ^Ps 5:8 ^B Prov 4:11 23:4 ^Is 43:2
^B Mic 7:14 23:5 ^Luke 7:46 ^B Ps 16:5

And my ^dwelling *will be* in the house of the LORD forever.

THE KING OF GLORY ENTERING ZION.
A Psalm of David.

24 The ^earth is the LORD's,
and all it contains,
The world, and those who live in it.
2 For He has ^founded it upon the seas
And established it upon the rivers.
3 Who may ascend onto the ^hill of the LORD?
And who may stand in His holy ^Bplace?
4 One who has clean hands and a pure heart,
Who has not ^lifted up his soul to deceit
And has not ^Bsworn deceitfully.
5 He will receive a ^blessing from the LORD
And ^Brighteousness from the God of his salvation.
6 This is the generation of those who ^seek Him,
Who seek Your face—*even* Jacob. *Selah*

7 Lift up your heads, you gates,
And be lifted up, you ancient doors,
That the King of ^glory may come in!
8 Who is the King of glory?
The LORD ^strong and mighty,
The LORD ^Bmighty in battle.
9 Lift up your heads, you gates,
And lift *them* up, you ancient doors,
That the King of ^glory may come in!
10 Who is this King of glory?
The LORD of ^armies,
He is the King of glory. *Selah*

PRAYER FOR PROTECTION, GUIDANCE, AND PARDON.
A Psalm of David.

25 To You, LORD, I ^lift up my soul.
2 My God, in You ^I trust,
Do not let me be ashamed;
Do not let my ^Benemies rejoice over me.
3 Indeed, ^none of those who wait for You will be ashamed;
Those who ^Bdeal treacherously without cause will be ashamed.

4 ^Make me know Your ways, LORD;
Teach me Your paths.
5 Lead me in ^Your truth and teach me,
For You are the ^BGod of my salvation;
For You I wait all the day.
6 Remember, LORD, Your compassion and Your faithfulness,
For they have been ^from of old.
7 Do not remember the ^sins of my youth or my wrongdoings;
Remember me according to Your faithfulness,
For Your goodness' sake, LORD.

8 The LORD is good and upright;
Therefore He ^instructs sinners in the way.
9 He ^leads the humble in justice,
And He teaches the humble His way.

23:6 ^A Ps 27:4-6   24:1 ^A 1 Cor 10:26   24:2 ^A Ps 104:3, 5;
136:6   24:3 ^A Ps 2:6   ^B Ps 65:4   24:4 ^A Ezek 18:15
^B Ps 15:4   24:5 ^A Ps 115:13   ^B Ps 36:10   24:6 ^A Ps 27:4, 8
24:7 ^A Acts 7:2; 1 Cor 2:8   24:8 ^A Deut 4:34   ^B Ps 76:3-6
24:9 ^A Ps 26:8; 57:11   24:10 ^A 2 Sam 5:10; Neh 9:6
25:1 ^A Ps 86:4; 143:8   25:2 ^A Ps 31:1   ^B Ps 13:4
25:3 ^A Is 49:23   ^B Hab 1:13   25:4 ^A Ex 33:13; Ps 27:11
25:5 ^A Ps 43:3   ^B Ps 79:9   25:6 ^A Ps 103:17
25:7 ^A Job 13:26; 20:11   25:8 ^A Ps 32:8   25:9 ^A Ps 23:3

10 All the paths of the LORD are
   ^faithfulness and truth
   To ^Bthose who comply with
      His covenant and His
      testimonies.
11 For the sake of Your name, LORD,
   ^Forgive my wrongdoing, for it
      is great.

12 Who is the person who ^fears
      the LORD?
   He will ^Binstruct him in the
      way he should choose.
13 His soul will ^dwell in
      prosperity,
   And his descendants will
      inherit the land.
14 The ^secret of the LORD is for
      those who fear Him,
   And He will make them know
      His covenant.
15 My ^eyes are continually
      toward the LORD,
   For He will ^Brescue my feet
      from the net.

16 ^Turn to me and be gracious to
      me,
   For I am lonely and afflicted.
17 The ^troubles of my heart are
      enlarged;
   Bring me ^Bout of my distresses.
18 Look at my misery and my
      trouble,
   And ^forgive all my sins.
19 Look at my enemies, for they
   ^are many,
   And they ^Bhate me with violent
      hatred.
20 Guard my soul and save me;
   Do not let me ^be ashamed, for
      I take refuge in You.
21 Let ^integrity and uprightness
      protect me,
   For I wait for You.
22 ^Redeem Israel, God,
   From all his distress.

PROTESTATION OF INTEGRITY AND PRAYER FOR PROTECTION.

A Psalm of David.

26
^Vindicate me, LORD, for
   I have ^Bwalked in my
   integrity,
And I have trusted in the LORD
   without wavering.
2 Examine me, LORD, and put me
   to the test;
   ^Refine my mind and my
      heart.
3 For Your goodness is before my
      eyes,
   And I have ^walked in Your
      truth.
4 I do not ^sit with deceitful
      people,
   Nor will I go with pretenders.
5 I ^hate the assembly of
      evildoers,
   And I will not sit with the
      wicked.
6 I will ^wash my hands in
      innocence,
   And I will go around Your
      altar, LORD,
7 That I may proclaim with the
      voice of ^thanksgiving
   And declare all Your wonders.
8 LORD, I ^love the dwelling of
      Your house,
   And the place where Your
      ^Bglory remains.
9 ^Do not take my soul away
   along with sinners,
   Nor my life with ^Bmen of
      bloodshed,

25:10 ^Ps 40:11   ^BPs 103:18   25:11 ^Ex 34:9
25:12 ^Ps 31:19   ^BPs 25:8   25:13 ^Prov 1:33; Jer 23:6
25:14 ^Prov 3:32; John 7:17   25:15 ^Ps 141:8   ^BPs 124:7
25:16 ^Ps 69:16   25:17 ^Ps 40:12   ^BPs 107:6
25:18 ^Ps 103:3   25:19 ^Ps 3:1   ^BPs 9:13
25:20 ^Ps 25:2   25:21 ^Ps 41:12   25:22 ^Ps 130:8
26:1 ^Ps 7:8   ^B2 Kin 20:3   26:2 ^Ps 7:9
26:3 ^2 Kin 20:3; Ps 86:11   26:4 ^Ps 5:5 ^APs 31:6;
139:21   26:6 ^Ps 73:13   26:7 ^Ps 9:1   26:8 ^Ps 27:4
^BPs 24:7   26:9 ^Ps 28:3   ^BPs 139:19

10 In whose hands is a ^wicked
    scheme,
    And whose right hand is full of
    ^Bbribes.
11 But as for me, I will walk in my
    integrity;
    ^Redeem me, and be gracious
    to me.
12 My foot stands on level ground;
    In the ^congregations I will
    bless the LORD.

A PSALM OF FEARLESS TRUST IN GOD.
A Psalm of David.

27 The LORD is my ^light and
    my ^Bsalvation;
    Whom should I fear?
    The LORD is the defense of my
    life;
    Whom should I dread?
2 When evildoers came upon
    me to devour my flesh,
    My adversaries and my enemies,
    they ^stumbled and fell.
3 If an ^army encamps against
    me,
    My heart will not fear;
    If war arises against me,
    In *spite of* this I am ^Bconfident.

4 One thing I have asked from
    the LORD, that I shall seek:
    That I may ^dwell in the house
    of the LORD all the days of
    my life,
    To behold ^Bthe beauty of the
    LORD
    And to meditate in His temple.
5 For on the ^day of trouble
    He will ^Bconceal me in His
    tabernacle;
    He will hide me in the secret
    place of His tent;
    He will lift me up on a rock.
6 And now ^my head will be
    lifted up above my enemies
    around me,

And I will offer sacrifices in
    His tent with shouts of joy;
    I will sing, yes, I will sing
    praises to the LORD.

7 ^Hear, LORD, when I cry with
    my voice,
    And be gracious to me and
    answer me.
8 *When You said,* "^Seek My
    face," my heart said to You,
    "I shall seek Your face, LORD."
9 Do not hide Your face from
    me,
    Do not turn Your servant away
    in anger;
    You have been my help;
    ^Do not abandon me nor
    ^Bforsake me,
    God of my salvation!
10 For my father and ^my mother
    have forsaken me,
    But ^Bthe LORD will take me
    up.

11 ^Teach me Your way, LORD,
    And lead me on a level path
    Because of my enemies.
12 Do not turn me over to the
    ^desire of my enemies,
    For ^Bfalse witnesses have risen
    against me,
    And *the* violent witness.
13 I certainly believed that I
    would see the ^goodness of
    the LORD
    In the land of the living.
14 ^Wait for the LORD;
    Be ^Bstrong and let your heart
    take courage;
    Yes, wait for the LORD.

26:10 ^Ps 37:7 ^BPs 15:5 26:11 ^Ps 44:26; 69:18
26:12 ^Ps 22:22 27:1 ^Mic 7:8 ^BIs 33:2 27:2 ^Ps 9:3
27:3 ^Ps 3:6 ^BJob 4:6 27:4 ^Ps 23:6 ^BPs 90:17
27:5 ^Ps 50:15 ^BPs 31:20 27:6 ^Ps 3:3 27:7 ^Ps 4:3;
61:1 27:8 ^Ps 105:4; Amos 5:6 27:9 ^Ps 94:14
^BPs 37:28 27:10 ^Is 49:15 ^BIs 40:11 27:11 ^Ps 25:4;
86:11 27:12 ^Ps 41:2 ^BMatt 26:60 27:13 ^Ps 31:19
27:14 ^Is 25:9 ^BPs 31:24

A PRAYER FOR HELP, AND PRAISE FOR ITS ANSWER.
A Psalm of David.

28

To You, Lord, I call;
My ^rock, do not be deaf to me,
For if You ^Bare silent to me,
I will become like those who go down to the pit.

2 Hear the ^sound of my pleadings when I cry to You for help,
When I raise my hands toward Your holy sanctuary.

3 ^Do not drag me away with the wicked
And with those who practice injustice,
Who speak peace with their neighbors,
While evil is in their hearts.

4 Give *back* to them ^according to their work and according to the evil of their practices;
Give *back* to them according to the work of their hands;
Repay them what is due them.

5 Because they ^do not regard the works of the Lord
Nor the deeds of His hands,
He will tear them down and not build them up.

6 Blessed be the Lord,
Because He ^has heard the sound of my pleading.

7 The Lord is my strength and my shield;
My heart ^trusts in Him, and I am helped;
Therefore my heart triumphs,
And with my song I shall thank Him.

8 The Lord is their ^strength,
And He is a refuge of salvation to His anointed.

9 ^Save Your people and bless Your inheritance;
Be their ^Bshepherd also, and carry them forever.

THE VOICE OF THE LORD IN THE STORM.
A Psalm of David.

29

^Ascribe to the Lord, sons of the mighty,
Ascribe to the Lord glory and strength.

2 Ascribe to the Lord the glory due His name;
Worship the Lord ^in holy attire.

3 The ^voice of the Lord is on the waters;
The God of glory ^Bthunders,
The Lord is over many waters.

4 The voice of the Lord is ^powerful,
The voice of the Lord is majestic.

5 The voice of the Lord breaks the cedars;
Yes, the Lord breaks ^the cedars of Lebanon in pieces.

6 He makes Lebanon skip like a calf,
And ^Sirion like a young wild ox.

7 The voice of the Lord divides ^1flames of fire.

8 The voice of the Lord shakes the wilderness;
The Lord shakes the wilderness of ^Kadesh.

28:1^Ps 18:2 ᴮPs 83:1 **28:2**^Ps 140:6 **28:3**^Ps 26:9 **28:4**^Rev 18:6; 22:12 **28:5**^Is 5:12 **28:6**^Ps 28:2 **28:7**^Ps 13:5; 112:7 **28:8**^Ps 20:6; 89:17 **28:9**^Ps 106:40 ᴮPs 80:1 **29:1**^1 Chr 16:28, 29; Ps 96:7-9 **29:2**^2 Chr 20:21; Ps 110:3 **29:3**^Ps 104:7 ᴮJob 37:4, 5 **29:4**^Ps 68:33 **29:5**^Ps 104:16; Is 2:13 **29:6**^Deut 3:9 **29:8**^Num 13:26

29:7 ¹I.e., lightning

9   The voice of the LORD makes
    ^the deer give birth
    And strips the forests bare;
    And ^Bin His temple everything
    says, "Glory!"

10 The LORD sat *as King* at the
    ^flood;
    Yes, the LORD sits as ^BKing
    forever.

11 The LORD will give ^strength to
    His people;
    The LORD will bless His people
    with ^Bpeace.

**THANKSGIVING FOR RESCUE
FROM DEATH.**
A Psalm; a Song at the Dedication
of the House. *A Psalm* of David.

30 I will exalt You, LORD, for
    You have ^lifted me up,
    And have not let my enemies
    rejoice over me.

2   LORD my God,
    I ^cried to You for help, and
    You ^Bhealed me.

3   LORD, You have ^brought up my
    soul from ^1Sheol;
    You have kept me alive, that I
    would not ^Bgo down to the pit.

4   Sing praise to the LORD, you
    ^His godly ones,
    And praise the mention of His
    holiness.

5   For His anger is but for a
    moment,
    His ^favor is for a lifetime;
    Weeping may ^Blast for the night,
    But a shout of joy *comes* in the
    morning.

6   Now as for me, I said in my
    prosperity,
    "I will ^never be moved."

7   LORD, by Your favor You have
    made my mountain to stand
    strong;

You ^hid Your face, I was
    dismayed.

8   To You, LORD, I called,
    And to the Lord I pleaded for
    compassion:

9   "What gain is there in my
    blood, if I ^go down to the
    pit?
    Will the dust praise You? Will
    it declare Your faithfulness?

10 "Hear, LORD, and be gracious to
    me;
    LORD, be my ^helper."

11 You have turned my mourning
    into dancing for me;
    You have ^untied my sackcloth
    and encircled me with ^Bjoy,

12 That *my* soul may sing praise
    to You and not be silent.
    LORD my God, I will ^give
    thanks to You forever.

**A PSALM OF COMPLAINT
AND OF PRAISE.**
For the music director. A Psalm of David.

31 In You, LORD, I have taken
    refuge;
    Let me never ^be put to shame;
    ^BIn Your righteousness rescue
    me.

2   Incline Your ear to me, rescue
    me quickly;
    Be a ^rock of strength for me,
    A stronghold to save me.

3   For You are my rock and ^my
    fortress;
    For the sake of Your name You
    will lead me and guide me.

29:9 ^Job 39:1   ^BPs 26:8   29:10^Gen 6:17   ^BPs 10:16
29:11^Is 40:29   ^BPs 72:3   30:1^Ps 3:3
30:2^Ps 88:13   ^BIs 53:5   30:3^Ps 86:13   ^BPs 28:1
30:4^Ps 50:5   30:5^Ps 118:1   ^B2 Cor 4:17
30:6^Ps 10:6; 62:2, 6   30:7^Deut 31:17; Ps 104:29
30:9^Ps 28:1   30:10^Ps 27:9; 54:4   30:11^Is 20:2
^BPs 4:7   30:12^Ps 44:8   31:1^Ps 25:2   ^BPs 143:1
31:2^Ps 18:2; 71:3   31:3^Ps 18:2

30:3 ^1I.e., the netherworld

4 You will ^pull me out of the net
   which they have secretly laid
   for me,
   For You are my strength.
5 ^Into Your hand I entrust my
   spirit;
   You have redeemed me, Lord,
   God of truth.

6 I hate those who devote
   themselves to worthless idols,
   But I ^trust in the Lord.
7 I will rejoice and be glad in
   Your faithfulness,
   Because You have ^seen my
   misery;
   You have known the troubles
   of my soul,
8 And You have not ^handed me
   over to the enemy;
   You have set my feet in a large
   place.

9 Be gracious to me, Lord, for I
   am in distress;
   My ^eye is wasted away from
   grief, ^my soul and my body
   too.
10 For my life is spent with
   sorrow
   And my years with sighing;
   My ^strength has failed
   because of my guilt,
   And my body has wasted away.
11 Because of all my adversaries, I
   have become a ^disgrace,
   Especially to my neighbors,
   And an object of dread to my
   acquaintances;
   Those who see me in the street
   flee from me.
12 I am ^forgotten like a dead
   person, out of mind;
   I am like a broken vessel.
13 For I have heard the ^slander
   of many,
   Terror is on every side;

While they ^took counsel
   together against me,
   They schemed to take away
   my life.

14 But as for me, I trust in You,
   Lord,
   I say, "^You are my God."
15 My ^times are in Your hand;
   ^Rescue me from the hand of
   my enemies and from those
   who persecute me.
16 Make Your face shine upon
   Your servant;
   ^Save me in Your faithfulness.
17 Let me not be put to shame,
   Lord, for I call upon You;
   Let the ^wicked be put to
   shame, let them ^be silent in
   ^Sheol.
18 Let the ^lying lips be speechless,
   Which ^speak arrogantly
   against the righteous
   With pride and contempt.

19 How great is Your ^goodness,
   Which You have stored up for
   those who fear You,
   Which You have performed
   for those who take refuge in
   You,
   Before the sons of mankind!
20 You hide them in the ^secret
   place of Your presence
   from the ^conspiracies of
   mankind;
   You keep them secretly in a
   shelter from the strife of
   tongues.

31:4 ^Ps 25:15   31:5 ^Luke 23:46; Acts 7:59
31:6 ^Ps 52:8   31:7 ^Ps 10:14   31:8 ^Deut 32:30;
Ps 37:33   31:9 ^Ps 6:7   ^Ps 63:1   31:10 ^Ps 39:11
31:11 ^Ps 69:19   31:12 ^Ps 88:5   31:13 ^Jer 20:10
^Matt 27:1   31:14 ^Ps 140:6
31:15 ^Job 14:5   ^Ps 143:9   31:16 ^Ps 6:4
31:17 ^Ps 25:3   ^1 Sam 2:9   31:18 ^Ps 120:2   ^Jude 15
31:19 ^Is 64:4; Rom 11:22   31:20 ^Ps 27:5   ^Ps 37:12

31:17 ^1 I.e., the netherworld

21 Blessed be the LORD,
For He has shown His
^marvelous faithfulness to
me in a besieged ᴮcity.
22 As for me, ^I said in my alarm,
"I am ᴮcut off from Your eyes";
Nevertheless You heard the
sound of my pleadings
When I called to You for help.

23 Love the LORD, all His godly
ones!
The LORD ^watches over the
faithful
But fully repays the one who
acts arrogantly.
24 ^Be strong and let your heart
take courage,
All you who wait for the
LORD.

**BLESSEDNESS OF FORGIVENESS
AND OF TRUST IN GOD.**
A Psalm of David. A †Maskil.

32 ^How blessed is he whose
wrongdoing is forgiven,
Whose sin is covered!
2 How blessed is a person whose
guilt the LORD ^does not take
into account,
And in whose spirit there is
ᴮno deceit!

3 When ^I kept silent *about my
sin,* my body wasted away
Through my groaning all day
long.
4 For day and night ^Your hand
was heavy upon me;
My vitality failed *as* with the
dry heat of summer.   *Selah*
5 I acknowledged my sin to You,
And I did not hide my guilt;
I said, "^I will confess my
wrongdoings to the LORD";
And You ᴮforgave the guilt of
my sin.   *Selah*

6 Therefore, let everyone who is
godly pray to You ^in a time
when You may be found;
Certainly in a flood of great
waters, they will not reach him.
7 You are ^my hiding place; You
ᴮkeep me from trouble;
You surround me with songs of
deliverance.   *Selah*

8 I will ^instruct you and teach
you in the way which you
should go;
I will advise you with My eye
upon you.
9 Do not be ^like the horse or
like the mule, which have no
understanding,
Whose trappings include bit
and bridle to hold them in
check,
Otherwise they will not come
near to you.
10 The ^sorrows of the wicked are
many,
But ᴮthe one who trusts in
the LORD, goodness will
surround him.
11 Be glad in the LORD and
rejoice, you righteous ones;
And shout for joy, all you who
are ^upright in heart.

**PRAISE TO THE CREATOR
AND PROTECTOR.**

33 Sing for joy in the LORD, you
righteous ones;
Praise is ^becoming to the
upright.

31:21^Ps 17:7 ᴮ1 Sam 23:7 31:22^Ps 116:11
ᴮIs 38:11, 12 31:23^Ps 145:20; Rev 2:10
31:24^Ps 27:14 32:1^Ps 85:2; Rom 4:7, 8
32:2^2 Cor 5:19 ᴮJohn 1:47 32:3^Ps 39:2, 3
32:4^1 Sam 5:6; Job 23:2 32:5^1 John 1:9 ᴮPs 103:12
32:6^Ps 69:13; Is 55:6 32:7^Ps 119:114 ᴮPs 121:7
32:8^Ps 25:8 32:9^Prov 26:3 32:10^Rom 2:9
ᴮProv 16:20 32:11^Ps 7:10; 64:10 33:1^Ps 92:1; 147:1

32:1†Possibly *Contemplative;* or *Didactic;* or *Skillful Psalm*

2 Give thanks to the Lord with
     the ^lyre;
   Sing praises to Him with a
     ^Bharp of ten strings.
3 Sing to Him a new song;
   Play skillfully with ^a shout of
     joy.
4 For the word of the Lord ^is
     right,
   And all His work is *done* ^Bin
     faithfulness.
5 He ^loves righteousness and
     justice;
   The earth is full of the
     goodness of the Lord.

6 By the word of the Lord the
     heavens were made,
   And ^by the breath of His
     mouth ^Ball their ¹lights.
7 He gathers the ^waters of the
     sea together as a heap;
   He puts the depths in
     storehouses.
8 Let ^all the earth fear the Lord;
   Let all the inhabitants of the
     world ^Bstand in awe of Him.
9 For ^He spoke, and it was
     done;
   He commanded, and it stood
     firm.
10 The Lord ^nullifies the plan of
     nations;
   He frustrates the plans of
     peoples.
11 The ^plan of the Lord stands
     forever,
   The plans of His heart from
     generation to generation.
12 Blessed is the ^nation whose
     God is the Lord,
   The people He has ^Bchosen for
     His own inheritance.

13 The Lord ^looks from heaven;
   He ^Bsees all the sons of
     mankind;

14 From ^His dwelling place He
     looks out
   On all the inhabitants of the
     earth,
15 He who ^fashions the hearts of
     them all,
   He who understands all their
     works.
16 ^The king is not saved by a
     mighty army;
   A warrior is not rescued by
     great strength.
17 A ^horse is a false hope for
     victory;
   Nor does it rescue anyone by
     its great strength.

18 Behold, the eye of the Lord is
     on those who fear Him,
   On those who ^wait for His
     faithfulness,
19 To ^rescue their soul from
     death
   And to keep them alive in
     famine.
20 Our soul ^waits for the
     Lord;
   He is our ^Bhelp and our
     shield.
21 For our ^heart rejoices in
     Him,
   Because we trust in His holy
     name.
22 Let Your favor, Lord, be upon
     us,
   Just as we have waited for
     You.

33:2 ^Ps 71:22   ^BPs 144:9   33:3 ^Ps 98:4
33:4 ^Ps 19:8   ^BPs 119:90   33:5 ^Ps 11:7; 37:28
33:6 ^Ps 104:30   ^BGen 2:1   33:7 ^Ex 15:8; Ps 78:13
33:8 ^Ps 67:7   ^BPs 96:9   33:9 ^Gen 1:3; Ps 148:5
33:10 ^Ps 2:1-3; Is 8:10   33:11 ^Job 23:12; Prov 19:21
33:12 ^Ps 144:15   ^BEx 19:5   33:13 ^Job 28:24   ^BPs 11:4
33:14 ^1 Kin 8:39, 43; Ps 102:19   33:15 ^Job 10:8;
Ps 119:73   33:16 ^Ps 44:6; 60:11   33:17 ^Ps 20:7;
Prov 21:31   33:18 ^Ps 32:10; 147:11   33:19 ^Ps 56:13;
Acts 12:11   33:20 ^Is 8:17   ^BPs 115:9
33:21 ^Zech 10:7; John 16:22

33:6 ¹Lit *host*; i.e., sun, stars, etc.

THE LORD, A PROVIDER AND
THE ONE WHO RESCUES ME.

A Psalm of David, when he pretended
to be insane before Abimelech, who
drove him away, and he departed.

34 I will ᴬbless the LORD at all
times;
His ᴮpraise shall continually be
in my mouth.
2 My soul will ᴬmake its boast in
the LORD;
The humble will hear it and
rejoice.
3 Exalt the LORD with me,
And let's ᴬexalt His name
together.

4 I ᴬsought the LORD and He
answered me,
And ᴮrescued me from all my
fears.
5 They looked to Him and were
radiant,
And their faces will ᴬnever be
ashamed.
6 This wretched man cried out,
and ᴬthe LORD heard *him,*
And saved him out of all his
troubles.
7 The ᴬangel of the LORD
encamps around those who
fear Him,
And rescues them.

8 Taste and see that the LORD is
good;
How ᴬblessed is the man who
takes refuge in Him!
9 Fear the LORD, you ᴬHis saints;
For to those who fear
Him there is ᴮno lack *of
anything.*
10 The young lions do without
and suffer hunger;
But they who seek the LORD
will ᴬnot lack any good
thing.

11 Come, you children, listen to
me;
ᴬI will teach you ᴮthe fear of the
LORD.
12 Who is the person who desires
life
And loves *length of* days, that
he may ᴬsee good?
13 Keep ᴬyour tongue from evil
And your lips from speaking
deceit.
14 ᴬTurn from evil and do good;
Seek peace and ᴮpursue it.

15 The ᴬeyes of the LORD are
toward the righteous,
And His ears are toward their
cry for help.
16 The ᴬface of the LORD is against
evildoers,
To ᴮeliminate the memory of
them from the earth.
17 *The righteous* ᴬcry out, and the
LORD hears
And rescues them from all
their troubles.
18 The LORD is near to the
ᴬbrokenhearted
And saves those who are
ᴮcrushed in spirit.

19 The ᴬafflictions of the
righteous are many,
But the LORD ᴮrescues him
from them all.
20 He protects all his bones,
ᴬNot one of them is broken.
21 ᴬEvil will bring death to the
wicked,

34:1 ᴬEph 5:20   ᴮPs 71:6   34:2 ᴬJer 9:24; 1 Cor 1:31
34:3 ᴬPs 18:46   34:4 ᴬMatt 7:7   ᴮPs 34:6, 17, 19
34:5 ᴬPs 25:3   34:6 ᴬPs 34:4   34:7 ᴬPs 91:11; Dan 6:22
34:8 ᴬPs 2:12   34:9 ᴬPs 31:23   ᴮPs 23:1   34:10 ᴬPs 84:11
34:11 ᴬPs 32:8   ᴮPs 111:10   34:12 ᴬEccl 3:13
34:13 ᴬProv 13:3; James 1:26   34:14 ᴬIs 1:16, 17
ᴮHeb 12:14   34:15 ᴬJob 36:7; Ps 33:18   34:16 ᴬAmos 9:4
ᴮJob 18:17   34:17 ᴬPs 34:6; 145:19   34:18 ᴬPs 147:3
ᴮIs 57:15   34:19 ᴬ2 Tim 3:11f   ᴮPs 34:4, 6, 17
34:20 ᴬJohn 19:33, 36   34:21 ᴬPs 94:23; Prov 24:16

And those who hate the
righteous will suffer for their
guilt.
22 The LORD ^redeems the souls
of His servants,
And none of those who ^Btake
refuge in Him will suffer for
their guilt.

PRAYER FOR RESCUE FROM ENEMIES.
A Psalm of David.

35 Contend, LORD, with those
who contend with me;
Fight against those who ^fight
against me.
2 Take hold of ^1,^buckler and
shield
And rise up as ^Bmy help.
3 Draw also the spear and the
battle-axe to meet those who
pursue me;
Say to my soul, "I am ^your
salvation."
4 Let those be ^ashamed and
dishonored who seek my
life;
Let those be ^Bturned back and
humiliated who devise evil
against me.
5 Let them be ^like chaff before
the wind,
With the angel of the LORD
driving *them* on.
6 Let their way be dark and
^slippery,
With the angel of the LORD
pursuing them.
7 For they ^hid their net for me
without cause;
Without cause they dug a pit
for my soul.
8 Let ^destruction come upon
him when he is unaware,
And let the net which he hid
catch him;
Let him fall into that very
^Bdestruction.

9 So my soul shall rejoice in the
LORD;
It shall ^rejoice in His
salvation.
10 All my bones will say, "LORD,
^who is like You,
Who rescues the afflicted from
one who is too strong for him,
And the afflicted and the poor
from one who robs him?"
11 ^Malicious witnesses rise up;
They ask me things that I do
not know.
12 They ^repay me evil for good,
To the bereavement of my
soul.
13 But as for me, ^when they
were sick, my ^Bclothing was
sackcloth;
I humbled my soul with
fasting,
But my prayer kept returning
to me.
14 I went about as though it were
my friend or brother;
I ^bowed down in mourning,
like one who mourns for a
mother.
15 But ^at my stumbling they
rejoiced and gathered
themselves together;
The afflicted people whom
I did not know gathered
together against me,
They ^Bslandered me without
ceasing.
16 Like godless jesters at a feast,
They ^gnashed at me with
their teeth.

34:22 ^1 Kin 1:29 ^B Ps 37:40 35:1 ^Ps 56:2
35:2 ^Ps 91:4 ^B Ps 44:26 35:3 ^Ps 62:2 35:4 ^Ps 70:2
^B Ps 40:14 35:5 ^Ps 83:13; Is 29:5
35:6 ^Ps 73:18; Jer 23:12 35:7 ^Ps 9:15
35:8 ^1 Thess 5:3 ^B Ps 73:18 35:9 ^Ps 9:14; Luke 1:47
35:10 ^Ex 15:11; Mic 7:18 35:11 ^Ps 27:12
35:12 ^Jer 18:20; John 10:32 35:13 ^Job 30:25
^B Ps 69:11 35:14 ^Ps 38:6 35:15 ^Obad 12 ^B Ps 7:2
35:16 ^Ps 37:12; Lam 2:16

35:2 ^1 I.e., small shield

17 Lord, ^how long will You look
    on?
  Rescue my soul ᴮfrom their
    ravages,
  My only *life* from the lions.
18 I will ^give You thanks in the
    great congregation;
  I will praise You among a
    mighty people.
19 Do not let those who are
    wrongfully my enemies
    rejoice over me;
  Nor let those ^who hate
    me for no reason ᴮwink
    maliciously.
20 For they do not speak peace,
  But they devise ^deceitful
    words against those who are
    quiet in the land.
21 They ^opened their mouth
    wide against me;
  They said, "ᴮAha, aha! Our
    eyes have seen it!"

22 You have seen it, Lᴏʀᴅ, ^do not
    keep silent;
  Lord, ᴮdo not be far from me.
23 ^Stir Yourself, and awake to my
    right
  And to my cause, my God and
    my Lord.
24 ^Judge me, Lᴏʀᴅ my
    God, according to Your
    righteousness,
  And do not let them rejoice
    over me.
25 Do not let them say in their
    heart, "Aha, our desire!"
  Do not let them say, "We have
    ^swallowed him up!"
26 May those be ashamed and
    altogether humiliated who
    rejoice at my distress;
  May those who exalt
    themselves over me be
    ^clothed with shame and
    dishonor.

27 May those shout for joy and
    rejoice, who take delight in
    ^my vindication;
  And may they say continually,
    "The Lᴏʀᴅ be exalted,
  Who ᴮdelights in the
    prosperity of His servant."
28 And ^my tongue
    shall proclaim Your
    righteousness
  And Your praise all day long.

WICKEDNESS OF HUMANITY
AND GOODNESS OF GOD.

For the music director. *A Psalm* of
David the servant of the Lᴏʀᴅ.

36
Wrongdoing speaks to the
    ungodly within his heart;
  There is ^no fear of God before
    his eyes.
2 For it ^flatters him in his *own*
    eyes
  Concerning the discovery of
    his wrongful deed *and* the
    hatred *of it.*
3 The ^words of his mouth are
    wickedness and deceit;
  He has ceased to be wise *and*
    to do good.
4 He ^plans wickedness on his
    bed;
  He sets himself on a path that
    is not good;
  He ᴮdoes not reject evil.

5 Your ^mercy, Lᴏʀᴅ, extends to
    the heavens,
  Your faithfulness *reaches* to
    the skies.

35:17^Hab 1:13   ᴮPs 35:7   35:18^Ps 22:22
35:19^John 15:25   ᴮProv 6:13   35:20^Jer 9:8;
Mic 6:12   35:21^Job 16:10   ᴮPs 40:15   35:22^Ps 28:1
ᴮPs 10:1   35:23^Ps 7:6; 44:23   35:24^Ps 9:4; 43:1
35:25^Prov 1:12; Lam 2:16   35:26^Ps 109:29
35:27^Ps 9:4   ᴮPs 147:11   35:28^Ps 51:14; 71:15, 24
36:1^Hab 3:18   36:2^Deut 29:19; Ps 10:11
36:3^Ps 10:7; 12:2   36:4^Mic 2:1   ᴮRom 12:9
36:5^Ps 57:10; 108:4

6 Your ^righteousness is like the
  mountains of God;
  Your ^judgments are *like* the
  great deep.
  LORD, You protect mankind
  and animals.
7 How precious is Your mercy,
  God!
  And the sons of mankind ^take
  refuge in the shadow of Your
  wings.
8 They ^drink their fill of the
  abundance of Your house;
  And You allow them to drink
  from the river of Your
  delights.
9 For the ^fountain of life is with
  You;
  In Your light we see light.

10 Prolong Your mercy to ^those
   who know You,
   And Your ^righteousness to the
   upright of heart.
11 May the foot of pride not come
   upon me,
   And may the hand of the
   wicked not drive me away.
12 Those who do injustice have
   fallen there;
   They have been thrust down
   and ^cannot rise.

SECURITY OF THOSE WHO TRUST IN THE LORD, AND INSECURITY OF THE WICKED.

A Psalm of David.

37 Do not get upset because of
   evildoers,
   Do not be ^envious of
   wrongdoers.
2 For they will ^wither quickly
  like the grass,
  And decay like the green plants.
3 ^Trust in the LORD and do good;
  Live in the land and ^cultivate
  faithfulness.

4 Delight yourself in the LORD;
  And He will ^give you the
  desires of your heart.
5 ^Commit your way to the LORD,
  Trust also in Him, and He will
  do it.
6 He will bring out ^your
  righteousness as the light,
  And your judgment ^as the
  noonday.

7 Rest in the LORD and ^wait
  patiently for Him;
  Do not get upset because of one
  who is successful in his way,
  Because of the person who
  carries out wicked schemes.
8 Cease from anger and
  ^abandon wrath;
  Do not get upset; *it leads* only
  to evildoing.
9 For ^evildoers will be
  eliminated,
  But those who wait for the LORD,
  they will inherit the land.
10 Yet ^a little while and the wicked
   person will be no more;
   And you will look carefully for
   his place and he will not be
   there.
11 But ^the humble will inherit
   the land
   And will delight themselves in
   ^abundant prosperity.

12 The wicked ^plots against the
   righteous,
   And gnashes at him with his
   teeth.

36:6 ^Ps 71:19   ^Rom 11:33   36:7 ^Ruth 2:12; Ps 17:8
36:8 ^Is 25:6; Jer 31:12-14   36:9 ^Jer 2:13
36:10 ^Jer 22:16   ^Ps 24:5   36:12 ^Ps 140:10; Is 26:14
37:1 ^Ps 73:3; Prov 3:31   37:2 ^Job 14:2; James 1:11
37:3 ^Ps 62:8   ^Ezek 34:13, 14   37:4 ^Ps 145:19;
Matt 7:7, 8   37:5 ^Prov 16:3; 1 Pet 5:7   37:6 ^Mic 7:9
^Job 11:17   37:7 ^Ps 40:1; Lam 3:26
37:8 ^Eph 4:31; Col 3:8   37:9 ^Ps 37:2, 22
37:10 ^Job 24:24   37:11 ^Matt 5:5   ^Ps 72:7
37:12 ^Ps 31:13, 20

13 The Lord ^Alaughs at him,
   For He sees that ^Bhis day is
      coming.
14 The wicked have drawn the
      sword and ^Abent their bow
   To take down the afflicted and
      the needy,
   To ^Bkill off those who are
      upright in conduct.
15 Their sword will enter their
      own heart,
   And their ^Abows will be broken.

16 ^ABetter is the little of the
      righteous
   Than the abundance of many
      wicked.
17 For the arms of the wicked will
      be broken,
   But the Lord ^Asustains the
      righteous.
18 The Lord ^Aknows the days of
      the blameless,
   And their inheritance will be
      forever.
19 They will not be ashamed in
      the time of evil,
   And ^Ain the days of famine
      they will have plenty.
20 But the ^Awicked will perish;
   And the enemies of the Lord
      will be like the ¹glory of the
      pastures,
   They vanish—^Blike smoke
      they vanish away.
21 The wicked borrows and does
      not pay back,
   But the righteous ^Ais gracious
      and gives.
22 For ^Athose blessed by Him will
      inherit the land,
   But those ^Bcursed by Him will
      be eliminated.

23 ^AThe steps of a man are
      established by the Lord,
   And He delights in his way.

24 When ^Ahe falls, he will not be
      hurled down,
   Because the Lord is the One
      who holds his hand.
25 I have been young and now I
      am old,
   Yet ^AI have not seen the
      righteous forsaken
   Or ^Bhis descendants begging
      for bread.
26 All day long ^Ahe is gracious and
      lends,
   And his descendants are a
      blessing.

27 ^ATurn from evil and do good,
   So that you will dwell
      ^Bforever.
28 For the Lord loves justice
   And does not abandon His
      godly ones;
   They are ^Aprotected forever,
   But the ^Bdescendants of the
      wicked will be eliminated.
29 The righteous will ^Ainherit the
      land
   And dwell in it forever.
30 The mouth of the righteous
      ^Autters wisdom,
   And his tongue ^Bspeaks
      justice.
31 The ^ALaw of his God is in his
      heart;
   His ^Bsteps do not slip.
32 The wicked spies upon the
      righteous
   And ^Aseeks to kill him.

37:13 ^APs 2:4   ^B1 Sam 26:10   37:14 ^ALam 2:4   ^BPs 11:2
37:15 ^A1 Sam 2:4; Ps 46:9   37:16 ^AProv 15:16; 16:8
37:17 ^APs 71:6; 145:14   37:18 ^APs 1:6; 31:7
37:19 ^AJob 5:20; Ps 33:19   37:20 ^APs 73:27   ^BPs 68:2
37:21 ^APs 112:5, 9   37:22 ^AProv 3:33   ^BJob 5:3
37:23 ^A1 Sam 2:9; Ps 119:5   37:24 ^AProv 24:16; Mic 7:8
37:25 ^AHeb 13:5   ^BPs 109:10   37:26 ^ADeut 15:8;
Ps 37:21   37:27 ^APs 34:14   ^BPs 102:28
37:28 ^APs 31:23   ^BIs 14:20   37:29 ^APs 37:9; Prov 2:21
37:30 ^AProv 10:13   ^BPs 119:13
37:31 ^ADeut 6:6   ^BPs 26:1   37:32 ^APs 37:14

37:20 ¹I.e., flowers

33 The LORD will ^not leave him in
his hand
Or ^Blet him be condemned
when he is judged.
34 ^Wait for the LORD and keep
His way,
And He will exalt you to
inherit the land;
When the ^Bwicked are
eliminated, you will see it.

35 I have ^seen a wicked, violent
person
Spreading himself like a
luxuriant tree in its native
soil.
36 Then he passed away, and
behold, he ^was no more;
I searched for him, but he
could not be found.
37 Observe the blameless
person, and look at the
^upright;
For the person of peace will
have ^Ba future.
38 But wrongdoers will altogether
be ^destroyed;
The future of the wicked will
be ^Beliminated.
39 But the ^salvation of the
righteous is from the
LORD;
He is their strength in time of
trouble.
40 ^The LORD helps them and
rescues them;
He rescues them from the
wicked and saves them,
Because they ^Btake refuge in
Him.

PRAYER OF A SUFFERING PENITENT.
A Psalm of David, for a memorial.

38
LORD, ^do not rebuke me in
Your wrath,
And do not punish me in Your
burning anger.

2 For Your ^arrows have sunk
deep into me,
And ^BYour hand has pressed
down on me.
3 There is ^no healthy part in
my flesh ^Bbecause of Your
indignation;
There is no health in my bones
because of my sin.
4 For my ^guilty deeds have gone
over my head;
Like a heavy burden they
weigh too much for me.
5 My wounds grow foul *and*
fester
Because of ^my foolishness.
6 I am bent over and ^greatly
bowed down;
I go in mourning all day
long.
7 For my sides are filled with
^burning,
And there is no healthy part in
my flesh.
8 I feel ^faint and badly
crushed;
I groan because of the
agitation of my heart.
9 Lord, all ^my desire is before
You;
And my ^Bsighing is not hidden
from You.
10 My heart throbs, ^my strength
fails me;
And the light of my eyes, even
that has gone from me.
11 My ^loved ones and my
friends stand aloof from my
plague;

37:33 ^Ps 31:8   ^BPs 34:22   37:34 ^Ps 27:14
^BPs 52:5, 6   37:35 ^Job 5:3; Jer 12:2   37:36 ^Job 20:5;
Ps 37:10   37:37 ^Ps 7:10   ^BIs 57:1, 2   37:38 ^Ps 1:4-6
^BPs 37:9   37:39 ^Ps 3:8; 62:1   37:40 ^Ps 54:4
^B1 Chr 5:20   38:1 ^Ps 6:1   38:2 ^Job 6:4   ^BPs 32:4
38:3 ^Is 1:6   ^BPs 102:10   38:4 ^Ezra 9:6; Ps 40:12
38:5 ^Ps 69:5   38:6 ^Ps 35:14   38:7 ^Ps 102:3
38:8 ^Lam 1:13, 20f; 2:11   38:9 ^Ps 10:17   ^BPs 6:6
38:10 ^Ps 31:10   38:11 ^Ps 31:11

And my kinsmen ^Bstand far away.

12 Those who ^Aseek my life ^Blay snares *for me;*
And those who seek to injure me have threatened destruction,
And they plot deception all day long.

13 But I, like a person who is deaf, do not hear;
And *I am* like a ^Aperson who cannot speak, *who* does not open his mouth.

14 Yes, I am like a person who does not hear,
And in whose mouth are no arguments.

15 For I wait for You, LORD;
You ^Awill answer, Lord my God.

16 For I said, "May they not rejoice over me,
Who, when my foot slips,
^Awould exalt themselves over me."

17 For I am ready to fall,
And ^Amy sorrow is continually before me.

18 For I ^Aadmit my guilt;
I am full of ^Banxiety because of my sin.

19 But my enemies are vigorous *and* strong,
And those who wrongfully ^Ahate me are many.

20 And those who repay evil for good,
They ^Abecome my enemies, because I follow what is good.

21 Do not abandon me, LORD;
My God, ^Ado not be far from me!

22 ^AHurry to help me,
Lord, my salvation!

THE FUTILITY OF LIFE.

For the music director, for Jeduthun. A Psalm of David.

39

I said, "I will keep watch over my ways
So that I ^Ado not sin with my tongue;
I will keep watch over ^Bmy mouth as with a muzzle
While the wicked are in my presence."

2 I was ^Amute and silent,
I refused to say *even something* good,
And my pain was stirred up.

3 My ^Aheart was hot within me,
While I was musing the fire burned;
Then I spoke with my tongue:

4 "LORD, let me know ^Amy end,
And what is the extent of my days;
Let me know how transient I am.

5 "Behold, You have made ^Amy days *like* ¹hand widths,
And my lifetime as nothing in Your sight;
Certainly all mankind standing is a mere breath.   *Selah*

6 "Certainly every person ^Awalks around as a fleeting shadow;
They certainly make an ^Buproar for nothing;
He amasses *riches* and does not know who will gather them.

38:11 ^BLuke 23:49   **38:12** ^APs 54:3   ^BPs 140:5
38:13 ^APs 39:2, 9   **38:15** ^APs 17:6   **38:16** ^APs 35:26
38:17 ^APs 13:2   **38:18** ^APs 32:5   ^B2 Cor 7:9, 10
38:19 ^APs 35:19   **38:20** ^APs 109:5; 1 John 3:12
38:21 ^APs 22:19; 35:22   **38:22** ^APs 40:13, 17
39:1 ^AJob 2:10   ^BPs 141:3   **39:2** ^APs 38:13
39:3 ^APs 32:4; Jer 20:9   **39:4** ^AJob 6:11; Ps 90:12
39:5 ^APs 89:47   **39:6** ^A1 Cor 7:31   ^BPs 127:2

39:5 ¹I.e., short

7 "And now, Lord, for what do I
    wait?
    My ^hope is in You.
8 "^Save me from all my
    wrongdoings;
    Do not make me an *object of*
    reproach for the foolish.
9 "I have become mute, I do not
    open my mouth,
    Because it is ^You who have
    done *it.*
10 "^Remove Your plague from me;
    Because of ^Bthe opposition of
    Your hand I am perishing.
11 "With ^rebukes You punish a
    person for wrongdoing;
    You ^Bconsume like a moth
    what is precious to him;
    Certainly all mankind is mere
    breath!   *Selah*

12 "Hear my prayer, Lord, and
    listen to my cry for help;
    Do not be silent ^to my tears;
    For I am ^Ba stranger with You,
    One who lives abroad, like all
    my fathers.
13 "^Turn Your eyes away from me,
    that I may become cheerful
    again
    Before I depart and am no
    more."

GOD SUSTAINS HIS SERVANT.
For the music director. A Psalm of David.

40 I ^waited patiently for the
         Lord;
    And He reached down to me
    and heard my cry.
2 He brought me up out of the
    pit of destruction, out of the
    mud;
    And ^He set my feet on a rock,
    ^Bmaking my footsteps firm.
3 He put a ^new song in my
    mouth, a song of praise to
    our God;

Many will see and fear
And will trust in the Lord.

4 How ^blessed is the man
    who has made the Lord
    his trust,
    And has not turned to
    the proud, nor to those
    who become involved in
    falsehood.
5 Many, Lord my God, are ^the
    wonders which You have
    done,
    And Your ^Bthoughts toward us;
    There is no one to compare
    with You.
    If I would declare and speak of
    them,
    They would be too numerous
    to count.

6 ^You have not desired sacrifice
    and meal offering;
    You have opened my ears;
    You have not required burnt
    offering and sin offering.
7 Then I said, "Behold, I have
    come;
    It is written of me in the scroll
    of the book.
8 "^I delight to do Your will, my
    God;
    Your Law is within my heart."

9 I have ^proclaimed good news
    of righteousness in the great
    congregation;
    Behold, I will not restrain my
    lips,
    Lord, You know.

39:7 ^Ps 38:15   39:8 ^Ps 51:9, 14; 79:9
39:9 ^2 Sam 16:10; Job 2:10   39:10 ^Job 9:34
^B Ps 32:4   39:11 ^Ezek 5:15   ^B Job 13:28
39:12 ^2 Kin 20:5   ^B Lev 25:23   39:13 ^Job 7:19;
10:20, 21   40:1 ^Ps 25:5; 27:14
40:2 ^Ps 27:5   ^B Ps 37:23   40:3 ^Ps 32:7; 33:3
40:4 ^Ps 34:8; 84:12   40:5 ^Ps 6:9   ^B Ps 139:17
40:6 ^1 Sam 15:22; Ps 51:16   40:8 ^John 4:34
40:9 ^Ps 22:22, 25

10   I have ^not hidden Your
righteousness within my
heart;
I have ᴮspoken of Your
faithfulness and Your
salvation;
I have not concealed Your
mercy and Your truth from
the great congregation.

11   You, Lᴏʀᴅ, will not withhold
Your compassion from me;
Your ^mercy and Your truth
will continually watch over
me.

12   For evils beyond number have
surrounded me;
My ^guilty deeds have
overtaken me, so that I am
not able to see;
They are ᴮmore numerous
than the hairs of my head,
And my heart has failed me.

13   Be pleased, Lᴏʀᴅ, to rescue
me;
^Hurry, Lᴏʀᴅ, to help me.

14   May those be ashamed and
humiliated together
Who ^seek my life to destroy it;
May those be turned back and
dishonored
Who delight in my hurt.

15   May those be appalled because
of their shame
Who ^say to me, "Aha, aha!"

16   May all who seek You rejoice
and be glad in You;
May those who love Your
salvation continually ^say,
"The Lᴏʀᴅ be exalted!"

17   But I am afflicted and needy;
^May the Lord be mindful of
me.
You are my help and my
savior;
Do not delay, my God.

THE PSALMIST IN SICKNESS COMPLAINS OF ENEMIES AND FALSE FRIENDS.

For the music director. A Psalm of David.

41 Blessed is one who
considers the helpless;
The Lᴏʀᴅ will save him ^on a
day of trouble.

2   The Lᴏʀᴅ will ^protect him and
keep him alive,
And he will be called blessed
upon the earth;
And ᴮdo not turn him over to
the desire of his enemies.

3   The Lᴏʀᴅ will sustain him
upon his sickbed;
In his illness, You restore him
to health.

4   As for me, I said, "Lᴏʀᴅ, be
gracious to me;
^Heal my soul, for ᴮI have
sinned against You."

5   My enemies ^speak evil against
me,
"When will he die, and his
name perish?"

6   And when he comes to see *me*,
he ^speaks empty words;
His heart gathers wickedness
to itself;
When he goes outside, he tells
it.

7   All who hate me whisper
together against me;
They ^plot my harm against
me, *saying*,

8   "A wicked thing is poured out
upon him,
So that when he lies down, he
will ^not get up again."

40:10 ^Acts 20:20, 27   ᴮPs 89:1   **40:11** ^Ps 43:3; 57:3
40:12 ^Ps 38:4   ᴮPs 69:4   **40:13** ^Ps 22:19; 71:12
40:14 ^Ps 63:9   **40:15** ^Ps 35:21; 70:3   **40:16** ^Ps 35:27
40:17 ^Ps 40:5; 1 Pet 5:7   **41:1** ^Ps 27:5; 37:19
41:2 ^Ps 37:28   ᴮPs 27:12   **41:4** ^Ps 6:2   ᴮPs 51:4
41:5 ^Ps 38:12   **41:6** ^Ps 12:2; 62:4   **41:7** ^Ps 56:5
41:8 ^Ps 71:10, 11

⁹ Even my ^close friend in whom
    I trusted,
  Who ate my bread,
  Has lifted up his heel against
    me.

¹⁰ But You, Lᴏʀᴅ, be gracious to
    me and ^raise me up,
  That I may repay them.
¹¹ By this I know that ^You are
    pleased with me,
  Because ᴮmy enemy does not
    shout in triumph over me.
¹² As for me, ^You uphold me in
    my integrity,
  And You place me ᴮin Your
    presence forever.

¹³ ^Blessed be the Lᴏʀᴅ, the God
    of Israel,
  From everlasting to
    everlasting.
  Amen and Amen.

BOOK 2

THIRSTING FOR GOD IN TROUBLE AND EXILE.

For the music director. A Maskil
of the sons of Korah.

42
As the deer pants for the
water brooks,
  So my soul ^pants for You, God.
² My soul ^thirsts for God, for
    the living God;
  When shall I come and ᴮappear
    before God?
³ My tears have been my food
    day and night,
  While *they* ^say to me all day
    long, "Where is your God?"
⁴ I remember these things and
    ^pour out my soul within me.
  For I used to go over with the
    multitude *and* walk them to
    the house of God,

With a voice of joy and
    thanksgiving, a multitude
    celebrating a festival.

⁵ Why are you in despair, my
    soul?
  And *why* are you restless
    within me?
  ^Wait for God, for I will again
    praise Him
  For the ᴮhelp of His presence,
    my God.
⁶ My soul is in despair within me;
  Therefore I ^remember You
    from the land of the Jordan
  And the peaks of Hermon,
    from Mount Mizar.
⁷ Deep calls to deep at the sound
    of Your waterfalls;
  All Your ^breakers and Your
    waves have passed over me.
⁸ The Lᴏʀᴅ will ^send His
    goodness in the daytime;
  And His song will be with me
    ᴮin the night,
  A prayer to the God of my life.

⁹ I will say to God my rock,
    "Why have You forgotten
    me?
  Why do I go about ^mourning
    because of the ᴮoppression
    of the enemy?"
¹⁰ As a shattering of my bones,
    my adversaries taunt me,
  While they ^say to me all day
    long, "Where is your God?"
¹¹ ^Why are you in despair, my
    soul?
  And why are you restless
    within me?

41:9 ^2 Sam 15:12; Job 19:13, 19   41:10 ^Ps 3:3
41:11 ^Ps 37:23   ᴮPs 25:2   41:12 ^Ps 18:32   ᴮJob 36:7
41:13 ^Ps 72:18, 19; 89:52   42:1 ^Ps 119:131
42:2 ^Ps 63:1   ᴮEx 23:17   42:3 ^Ps 79:10; 115:2
42:4 ^1 Sam 1:15; Job 30:16   42:5 ^Ps 71:14   ᴮPs 44:3
42:6 ^Ps 61:2   42:7 ^Ps 69:1, 2; 88:7   42:8 ^Ps 57:3
ᴮJob 35:10   42:9 ^Ps 38:6   ᴮPs 17:9   42:10 ^Ps 42:3;
Joel 2:17   42:11 ^Ps 42:5; 43:5

Wait for God, for I will again
    praise ¹Him
For the ²help of His presence,
    my God.

PRAYER FOR HELP.

43 ^Vindicate me, God, and
    plead my case against an
    ungodly nation;
Save me from the deceitful
    and unjust person!
2 For You are the God of my
    strength; why have You
    rejected me?
   Why do I go about ^mourning
    because of the oppression of
    the enemy?

3 Send out Your ^light and Your
    truth, they shall lead me;
   They shall bring me to Your
    holy hill
   And to Your dwelling places.
4 Then I will go to ^the altar of God,
   To God my exceeding ᴮjoy;
   And I will praise You on the
    lyre, God, my God.

5 ^Why are you in despair, my
    soul?
   And why are you restless
    within me?
   Wait for God, for I will again
    praise ¹Him
   For the ²help of His presence,
    my God.

**FORMER TIMES OF HELP AND
PRESENT TROUBLES.**

For the music director. A Maskil
of the sons of Korah.

44 God, we have heard with
    our ears,
   Our fathers have told us
   The ^work that You did in their
    days,
   In the ᴮdays of old.

2 You with Your own hand
    ^drove out the nations;
   Then You planted them;
   You afflicted the peoples,
   Then You let them go free.
3 For by their own sword they
    ^did not possess the land,
   And their own arm did not
    save them,
   But Your right hand and Your
    ᴮarm and the light of Your
    presence,
   For You favored them.

4 You are ^my King, God;
   Command victories for Jacob.
5 Through You we will push
    back our adversaries;
   Through Your name we will
    ^trample down those who
    rise up against us.
6 For I will ^not trust in my bow,
   Nor will my sword save me.
7 But You ^have saved us from
    our adversaries,
   And You have put to shame
    those who hate us.
8 In God we have ^boasted all
    day long,
   And we will give thanks to
    Your name forever.   *Selah*

9 Yet You have rejected *us* and
    brought us to dishonor,
   And ^do not go out with our
    armies.
10 You cause us to ^turn back
    from the enemy;

43:1 ^Ps 26:1; 35:24   43:2 ^Ps 42:9   43:3 ^Ps 36:9
43:4 ^Ps 26:6   ᴮPs 21:6   43:5 ^Ps 42:5, 11
44:1 ^Ps 78:12   ᴮDeut 32:7   44:2 ^Josh 3:10; Neh 9:24
44:3 ^Deut 8:17, 18   ᴮPs 77:15   44:4 ^Ps 74:12
44:5 ^Ps 108:13; Zech 10:5   44:6 ^1 Sam 17:47;
Ps 33:16   44:7 ^Ps 136:24   44:8 ^Ps 34:2
44:9 ^Ps 60:10; 108:11   44:10 ^Lev 26:17

42:11 ¹As in some ancient mss, cf. v 5; MT *Him, the
help of my face and my God*   ²Or *saving acts of*
43:5 ¹As in some ancient mss; MT *Him, the help of my
face and my God*   ²Or *saving acts of*

And those who hate us ᴮhave taken spoils for themselves.
11 You turn us over to be eaten like ᴬsheep,
And have ᴮscattered us among the nations.
12 You ᴬsell Your people cheaply,
And have not profited by their sale.
13 You make us an *object of* reproach to our neighbors,
Of scoffing and ᴬridicule to those around us.
14 You make us a proverb among the nations,
A ᴬlaughingstock among the peoples.
15 All day long my dishonor is before me
And I am covered with my ᴬhumiliation,
16 Because of the voice of one who ᴬtaunts and reviles,
Because of the presence of the enemy and the avenger.

17 All this has come upon us, but we have ᴬnot forgotten You,
And we have not ᴮdealt falsely with Your covenant.
18 Our heart has not ᴬturned back,
And our steps ᴮhave not deviated from Your way,
19 Yet You have crushed us in a place of jackals
And covered us with ᴬdeep darkness.

20 If we had ᴬforgotten the name of our God
Or extended our hands to ᴮa strange god,
21 Would God not ᴬfind this out?
For He knows the secrets of the heart.

22 But ᴬfor Your sake we are killed all day long;
We are regarded as ᴮsheep to be slaughtered.
23 Wake Yourself up, why do You sleep, Lord?
Awake, ᴬdo not reject us forever.
24 Why do You ᴬhide Your face
And forget our affliction and oppression?
25 For our ᴬsouls have sunk down into the dust;
Our bodies cling to the earth.
26 ᴬRise up, be our help,
And redeem us because of Your mercy.

A SONG CELEBRATING THE KING'S MARRIAGE.

For the music director; according to the Shoshannim. A Maskil of the sons of Korah. A Song of Love.

45 My heart is moved with a good theme;
I address my verses to the King;
My tongue is the pen of ᴬa ready writer.
2 You are the most handsome of the sons of mankind;
ᴬGrace is poured upon Your lips;
Therefore God has blessed You forever.

3 Strap ᴬYour sword on *Your* thigh, Mighty One,
In Your splendor and majesty!

44:10 ᴮPs 89:41   44:11 ᴬPs 44:22   ᴮLev 26:33
44:12 ᴬDeut 32:30; Judg 2:14
44:13 ᴬPs 80:6; Ezek 23:32   44:14 ᴬ2 Kin 19:21;
Ps 109:25   44:15 ᴬ2 Chr 32:21; Ps 69:7
44:16 ᴬPs 74:10   44:17 ᴬPs 78:7   ᴮPs 78:57
44:18 ᴬPs 78:57   ᴮJob 23:11   44:19 ᴬJob 3:5; Ps 23:4
44:20 ᴬPs 78:11   ᴮDeut 6:14   44:21 ᴬPs 139:1, 2;
Jer 17:10   44:22 ᴬRom 8:36   ᴮIs 53:7   44:23 ᴬPs 77:7
44:24 ᴬJob 13:24; Ps 88:14   44:25 ᴬPs 119:25
44:26 ᴬPs 35:2   45:1 ᴬEzra 7:6   45:2 ᴬLuke 4:22
45:3 ᴬHeb 4:12; Rev 1:16

4 And in Your majesty ride on
victoriously,
For the cause of truth,
   ᴬhumility, *and* righteousness;
Let Your right hand teach You
awesome things.

5 Your ᴬarrows are sharp;
The peoples fall under You;
Your arrows are ᴮin the heart
of the King's enemies.

6 ᴬYour throne, God, is forever
and ever;
  ᴮThe scepter of Your kingdom
is a scepter of justice.

7 You have ᴬloved righteousness
and hated wickedness;
Therefore God, Your God, has
  ᴮanointed You
With the oil of joy above Your
companions.

8 All Your garments are *fragrant
with* ᴬmyrrh, aloes, *and*
cassia;
From ivory palaces stringed
instruments have made You
joyful.

9 Kings' daughters are among
  ᴬYour noble women;
At Your ᴮright hand stands the
queen in gold from Ophir.

10 Listen, daughter, look and
incline your ear:
  ᴬForget your people and your
father's house;

11 Then the King will crave your
beauty.
Because He is your Lord, ᴬbow
down to Him.

12 The daughter of ᴬTyre *will
come* with a gift;
The wealthy among the people
will seek your favor.

13 The King's daughter is all
glorious within;

Her clothing is ᴬinterwoven
with gold.

14 She will be ᴬbrought to the
King in colorful garments;
The ᴮvirgins, her companions
who follow her,
Will be brought to You.

15 They will be brought with joy
and rejoicing;
They will enter into the King's
palace.

16 In place of your fathers will be
your sons;
You shall make them princes
in all the earth.

17 I will make ᴬYour name known
among all generations;
Therefore the peoples ᴮwill
praise You forever and ever.

GOD, THE REFUGE OF HIS PEOPLE.
For the music director. *A Psalm* of the
sons of Korah, †set to Alamoth. A Song.

46

God is our ᴬrefuge and
strength,
A very ready help in trouble.

2 Therefore we will ᴬnot fear,
though the earth shakes
And the mountains slip into
the heart of the sea;

3 Though its ᴬwaters roar *and*
foam,
Though the mountains quake
at its swelling pride.   *Selah*

4 There is a river whose
streams make the ᴬcity of
God happy,

45:4ᴬ Zeph 2:3   45:5ᴬ Ps 18:14 ᴮ 2 Sam 18:14
45:6ᴬ Ps 93:2   ᴮ Ps 98:9   45:7ᴬ Ps 11:7 ᴮ Ps 2:2
45:8ᴬ Song 4:14; John 19:39   45:9ᴬ Song 6:8
ᴮ 1 Kin 2:19   45:10ᴬ Deut 21:13; Ruth 1:16, 17
45:11ᴬ Eph 5:33   45:12ᴬ Ps 87:4   45:13ᴬ Ex 39:2, 3
45:14ᴬ Song 1:4 ᴮ Ps 45:9   45:17ᴬ Mal 1:11
ᴮ Ps 138:4   46:1ᴬ Ps 14:6; 62:7, 8   46:2ᴬ Ps 23:4; 27:1
46:3ᴬ Ps 93:3, 4; Jer 5:22   46:4ᴬ Ps 48:1

46:1† Possibly *for soprano voices*

The holy [B]dwelling places of
the Most High.
5 God is [A]in the midst of her, she
will not be moved;
God will help her when
morning dawns.
6 The nations made an uproar,
the kingdoms tottered;
He [A]raised His voice, the earth
[B]quaked.
7 The LORD of armies [A]is with us;
The God of Jacob is [B]our
stronghold.   *Selah*
8 Come, [A]behold the works of
the LORD,
Who has inflicted [B]horrific
events on the earth.
9 He [A]makes wars to cease to the
end of the earth;
He [B]breaks the bow and cuts
the spear in two;
He burns the chariots with fire.
10 "Stop *striving* and [A]know that I
am God;
I will be exalted among the
nations, I will be exalted on
the earth."
11 The LORD of armies is with us;
The God of Jacob is our
stronghold.   *Selah*

GOD, THE KING OF THE EARTH.
For the music director. A Psalm
of the sons of Korah.

47 Clap your hands, all you
peoples;
[A]Shout to God with a voice of joy.
2 For the LORD Most High is to
be feared,
A [A]great King over all the earth.
3 He [A]subdues peoples under us
And nations under our feet.
4 He chooses our [A]inheritance
for us,
The [B]pride of Jacob whom He
loves.   *Selah*

5 God has ascended with a shout,
The LORD, with the [A]sound of a
trumpet.
6 Sing praises to God, sing
praises;
Sing praises to [A]our King, sing
praises.
7 For God is the [A]King of all the
earth;
Sing praises [B]with a psalm of
wisdom.
8 God [A]reigns over the nations,
God sits on [B]His holy throne.
9 The [A]princes of the people
have assembled *as* the
[B]people of the God of
Abraham,
For the shields of the earth
belong to God;
He is highly exalted.

THE BEAUTY AND GLORY OF ZION.
A Song; a Psalm of the sons of Korah.

48 [A]Great is the LORD, and
greatly to be praised
In the city of our God, His
[B]holy mountain.
2 Beautiful in elevation, [A]the joy
of the whole earth,
Is Mount Zion *in* the far north,
The [B]city of the great King.
3 In its palaces,
God has made Himself known
as a [A]stronghold.

4 For, behold, the [A]kings arrived,
They passed by together.
5 They saw *it*, then they were
amazed;

46:4 [B]Ps 43:3   46:5 [A]Deut 23:14; Is 12:6   46:6 [A]Ps 18:13
[B]Amos 9:5   46:7 [A]Num 14:9   [B]Ps 9:9   46:8 [A]Ps 66:5
[B]Is 61:4   46:9 [A]Is 2:4; Mic 4:3   [B]1 Sam 2:4; Ps 76:3
46:10 [A]Ps 100:3   47:1 [A]Ps 106:47   47:2 [A]Mal 1:14
47:3 [A]Ps 18:47   47:4 [A]1 Pet 1:4   [B]Amos 6:8
47:5 [A]Ps 98:6   47:6 [A]Ps 89:18   47:7 [A]Zech 14:9
[B]1 Cor 14:15   47:8 [A]1 Chr 16:31   [B]Ps 97:2
47:9 [A]Ps 72:11   [B]Rom 4:11, 12   48:1 [A]1 Chr 16:25
[B]Ps 2:6   48:2 [A]Lam 2:15   [B]Matt 5:35   48:3 [A]Ps 46:7
48:4 [A]2 Sam 10:6-19

They were ^terrified, they fled
in a hurry.

6 Panic seized them there,
Anguish, as *that* of ^a woman
in childbirth.

7 With the ^east wind
You smash the ships of
Tarshish.

8 Just as we have heard, so have
we seen
In the city of the Lᴏʀᴅ of
armies, in the city of our God;
God will ^establish her
forever.   *Selah*

9 We have thought over ^Your
goodness, God,
In the midst of Your temple.

10 As is Your ^name, God,
So is Your praise to the ends of
the earth;
Your right hand is full of
righteousness.

11 Mount ^Zion shall be glad,
The ^daughters of Judah shall
rejoice
Because of Your judgments.

12 Walk around Zion and encircle
her;
Count her ^towers;

13 Consider her ^ramparts;
Go through her palaces,
So that you may ^tell *of her* to
the next generation.

14 For such is God,
Our God forever and ever;
He will ^lead us until death.

**THE FOOLISHNESS OF TRUSTING
IN RICHES.**

For the music director. A Psalm
of the sons of Korah.

49
Hear this, all peoples;
Listen, all ^inhabitants of
the world,

2 Both ^low and high,
Rich and poor together.

3 My mouth will ^speak
wisdom,
And the meditation
of my heart *will be*
understanding.

4 I will incline my ear to ^a
proverb;
I will express my ^riddle on the
harp.

5 Why should I ^fear in days of
adversity,
When the injustice of those
who betray me surrounds
me,

6 Those who ^trust in their
wealth
And boast in the abundance of
their riches?

7 No one can by any means
^redeem another
Or give God a ransom for
him—

8 For ^the redemption of his soul
is priceless,
And he should cease
imagining forever—

9 That he might ^live on
eternally,
That he might not ^undergo
decay.

10 For he sees *that even* wise
people die;
The ^foolish and the stupid
alike perish
And ^leave their wealth to
others.

11 Their inner thought is *that*
their houses are forever

48:5 ^Ex 15:15   48:6 ^Is 13:8   48:7 ^Jer 18:17
48:8 ^Ps 87:5   48:9 ^Ps 26:3; 40:10
48:10 ^Deut 28:58; Josh 7:9   48:11 ^Ps 97:8
48:12 ^Neh 3:1, 11, 25–27   48:13 ^Ps 122:7   ^Ps 78:5–7
48:14 ^Ps 23:4; Is 58:11   49:1 ^Ps 33:8   49:2 ^Ps 62:9
49:3 ^Ps 37:30   49:4 ^Ps 78:2   ^Num 12:8
49:5 ^Ps 23:4; 27:1   49:6 ^Job 31:24; Ps 52:7
49:7 ^Matt 25:8, 9   49:8 ^Matt 16:26   49:9 ^Ps 22:29
^Ps 16:10   49:10 ^Ps 92:6   ^Ps 39:6

And their dwelling places to all generations;
They have ^named their lands after their own names.

12 But ^man in *his* splendor will not endure;
He is like the animals that perish.

13 This is the ^way of those who are foolish,
And of those after them who approve their words.   *Selah*

14 Like sheep they sink down to ¹Sheol;
Death will be their shepherd;
And the ^upright will rule over them in the morning,
And their form shall be for Sheol ᴮto consume
So that they have no lofty home.

15 But God will ^redeem my soul from the power of Sheol,
For ᴮHe will receive me.   *Selah*

16 Do not be afraid ^when a person becomes rich,
When the splendor of his house is increased;

17 For when he dies, he will ^take nothing *with him;*
His wealth will not descend after him.

18 Though while he lives he ^congratulates himself—
And though *people* praise you when you do well for yourself—

19 He will go to the generation of his fathers;
They will never see ^the light.

20 ^Mankind in *its* splendor, yet without understanding,
Is ᴮlike the animals *that* perish.

GOD, THE JUDGE OF THE RIGHTEOUS AND THE WICKED.

A Psalm of Asaph.

50 ^The Mighty One, God, the LORD, has spoken
And summoned the earth,
  ᴮfrom the rising of the sun to its setting.

2 Out of Zion, ^the perfection of beauty,
God has shone.

3 May our God ^come and not keep silent;
Fire devours before Him,
And a storm is violently raging around Him.

4 He ^summons the heavens above,
And the earth, to judge His people:

5 "Gather My godly ones to Me,
Those who have made a ^covenant with Me by ᴮsacrifice."

6 And the ^heavens declare His righteousness,
For ᴮGod Himself is judge.   *Selah*

7 "Hear, My people, and I will speak;
Israel, I will testify against you;
I am God, ^your God.

8 "I do ^not rebuke you for your sacrifices,
And your burnt offerings are continually before Me.

49:11 ^Gen 4:17; Deut 3:14   49:12 ^Ps 49:20
49:13 ^Jer 17:11   49:14 ^Dan 7:18   ᴮJob 24:19
49:15 ^Ps 16:10   ᴮGen 5:24   49:16 ^Ps 37:7
49:17 ^Ps 17:14; 1 Tim 6:7   49:18 ^Deut 29:19;
Ps 10:3, 6   49:19 ^Job 33:30; Ps 56:13
49:20 ^Ps 49:12   ᴮEccl 3:19   50:1 ^Josh 22:22
ᴮPs 113:3   50:2 ^Ps 48:2; Lam 2:15   50:3 ^Ps 96:13
50:4 ^Deut 4:26; 31:28   50:5 ^Ex 24:7   ᴮPs 50:8
50:6 ^Ps 89:5   ᴮPs 75:7   50:7 ^Ex 20:2; Ps 48:14
50:8 ^Ps 40:6; 51:16

49:14 ¹I.e., the netherworld

9 "I will not take a ^bull from your
    house,
   Nor male goats from your folds.
10 "For ^every animal of the forest
    is Mine,
   The cattle on a thousand hills.
11 "I know every ^bird of the
    mountains,
   And everything that moves in
    the field is Mine.
12 "If I were hungry I would not
    tell you,
   For the ^world is Mine, and
    everything it contains.
13 "Shall I eat the flesh of ^bulls
   Or drink the blood of male
    goats?
14 "Offer God ^a sacrifice of
    thanksgiving
   And pay your vows to the Most
    High;
15 Call upon Me on the day of
    trouble;
   I will ^rescue you, and you will
    ^honor Me."

16 But to the wicked God says,
   "What *right* do you have to tell
    of My statutes
   And to take ^My covenant in
    your mouth?
17 "For you yourself ^hate
    discipline,
   And you throw My words
    behind you.
18 "When you see a thief, you
    become friends with him,
   And you ^associate with
    adulterers.
19 "You ^let your mouth loose in
    evil,
   And your ^tongue harnesses
    deceit.
20 "You sit and ^speak against your
    brother;
   You slander your own
    mother's son.

21 "These things you have done
    and I kept silent;
   You thought that I was *just* like
    you;
   I will ^rebuke you and present
    the case before your eyes.

22 "Now consider this, you who
    ^forget God,
   Or I will tear *you* in pieces, and
    there will be no one to save
    you.
23 "He who offers a sacrifice of
    thanksgiving honors Me;
   And to him who ^sets *his* way
    properly
   I will ^show the salvation of
    God."

A CONTRITE SINNER'S PRAYER FOR PARDON.

For the music director. A Psalm of David,
when Nathan the prophet came to him,
after he had gone in to Bathsheba.

51 Be gracious to me, God,
    according to Your
    faithfulness;
   According to the greatness of
    Your compassion, ^wipe out
    my wrongdoings.
2 ^Wash me thoroughly from my
   guilt
   And ^cleanse me from my sin.
3 For I ^know my wrongdoings,
   And my sin is constantly
    before me.
4 ^Against You, You only, I have
   sinned
   And done what is evil in Your
    sight,

50:9 ^Ps 69:31   50:10 ^Ps 104:24   50:11 ^Matt 6:26
50:12 ^Ex 19:5; Deut 10:14   50:13 ^Ps 50:9
50:14 ^Ps 27:6; 69:30   50:15 ^Ps 81:7   ^Ps 22:23
50:16 ^Is 29:13   50:17 ^Prov 5:12; 12:1
50:18 ^1 Tim 5:22   50:19 ^Ps 10:7   ^Ps 36:3
50:20 ^Job 19:18; Matt 10:21   50:21 ^Ps 90:8
50:22 ^Job 8:13; Ps 9:17   50:23 ^Ps 85:13   ^Ps 91:16
51:1 ^Ps 51:9; Is 43:25   51:2 ^Ps 51:7   ^Jer 33:8
51:3 ^Is 59:12   51:4 ^Gen 20:6

So that ^BYou are justified when
You speak
And blameless when You judge.

5 Behold, I was ^brought forth in
guilt,
And in sin my mother
conceived me.
6 Behold, You desire ^truth in
the innermost being,
And in secret You will ^Bmake
wisdom known to me.
7 Purify me with hyssop, and I
will be clean;
Cleanse me, and I will be
^whiter than snow.
8 Let me hear joy and gladness,
Let the ^bones You have
broken rejoice.
9 ^Hide Your face from my sins
And wipe out all my guilty
deeds.

10 Create in me a ^clean heart, God,
And renew a ^Bsteadfast spirit
within me.
11 Do not cast me away from Your
presence,
And do not take Your ^Holy
Spirit from me.
12 Restore to me the ^joy of Your
salvation,
And sustain me with a ^Bwilling
spirit.
13 *Then* I will ^teach wrongdoers
Your ways,
And sinners will be ^Bconverted
to You.
14 Save me from ^the guilt of
bloodshed, God, the God of
my salvation;
Then my tongue will joyfully
sing of Your righteousness.
15 Lord, ^open my lips,
So that my mouth may declare
Your praise.

16 For You ^do not delight in
sacrifice, otherwise I would
give it;
You do not take pleasure in
burnt offering.
17 The sacrifices of God are a
^broken spirit;
A broken and a contrite heart,
God, You will not despise.

18 ^By Your favor do good to
Zion;
Build the walls of Jerusalem.
19 Then You will delight in
^righteous sacrifices,
In burnt offering and whole
burnt offering;
Then bulls will be offered on
Your altar.

FUTILITY OF BOASTFUL WICKEDNESS.
For the music director. A Maskil of
David, when Doeg the Edomite came
and told Saul and said to him, "David
has come to the house of Ahimelech."

52 Why do you boast in evil,
you mighty man?
The faithfulness of God
endures all day long.
2 Your tongue devises
^destruction,
Like a ^Bsharp razor, you worker
of deceit.
3 You ^love evil more than
good,
Lies more than speaking what
is right.   *Selah*
4 You love all words that
devour,
You ^deceitful tongue.

51:4 ^BRom 3:4 51:5 ^Job 14:4; 15:14 51:6 ^Job 38:36
^BProv 2:6 51:7 ^Is 1:18 51:8 ^Ps 35:10 51:9 ^Jer 16:17
51:10 ^Ps 24:4 ^BPs 78:37 51:11 ^Is 63:10, 11
51:12 ^Ps 13:5 ^BPs 110:3 51:13 ^Acts 9:21, 22
^BPs 22:27 51:14 ^2 Sam 12:9; Ps 26:9 51:15 ^Ex 4:15
51:16 ^1 Sam 15:22; Ps 40:6 51:17 ^Ps 34:18
51:18 ^Ps 69:35; Is 51:3 51:19 ^Ps 4:5 52:2 ^Ps 5:9
^BPs 57:4 52:3 ^Ps 36:4 52:4 ^Ps 120:3

5 But God will break you down
   forever;
   He will snatch you up and ^tear
   you away from *your* tent,
   And ^Buproot you from the land
   of the living.   *Selah*
6 The righteous will ^see and fear,
   And they will laugh at him,
   saying,
7 "Behold, the man who would
   not make God his refuge,
   But ^trusted in the abundance
   of his riches
   And was strong in his *evil*
   desire."

8 But as for me, I am like a ^green
   olive tree in the house of God;
   I ^Btrust in the faithfulness of
   God forever and ever.
9 I will ^praise You forever,
   because You have done *it,*
   And I will wait on Your name,
   for *it is* good, in the presence
   of Your godly ones.

FOOLISHNESS AND WICKEDNESS
OF PEOPLE.

For the music director; according
to †Mahalath. A Maskil of David.

53
^The fool has said in his
heart, "There is no God."
They are corrupt, and have
   committed abominable
   injustice;
^BThere is no one who does good.
2 God has looked down from
   heaven upon the sons of
   mankind
   To see if there is ^anyone who
   understands,
   Who ^Bseeks after God.
3 ^Every one of them has turned
   aside; together they have
   become corrupt;
   There is no one who does
   good, not even one.

4 Have the workers of injustice
   ^no knowledge,
   Who eat up My people *like*
   they ate bread,
   And have not called upon
   God?
5 They were in great fear there,
   where no fear had been;
   For God ^scattered the bones
   of him who encamped
   against you;
   You put *them* to shame,
   because ^BGod had rejected
   them.
6 Oh, that ^the salvation of Israel
   would come from Zion!
   When God restores the
   fortunes of His people,
   Jacob shall rejoice, Israel shall
   be glad.

PRAYER FOR DEFENSE
AGAINST ENEMIES.

For the music director; on stringed
instruments. A Maskil of David, when the
Ziphites came and said to Saul, "Is David
not keeping himself hidden among us?"

54
Save me, God, by ^Your
name,
And vindicate me by ^BYour
   power.
2 Hear my prayer, God;
   ^Listen to the words of my
   mouth.
3 For strangers have ^risen
   against me
   And violent men have sought
   my life;
   They have ^Bnot set God before
   them.   *Selah*

52:5 ^Is 22:18, 19   ^B Prov 2:22   52:6 ^Ps 37:34; 40:3
52:7 ^Ps 49:6   52:8 ^Ps 92:12   ^B Ps 13:5
52:9 ^Ps 30:12   53:1 ^Ps 10:4   ^B Rom 3:10
53:2 ^Rom 3:11   ^B 2 Chr 15:2   53:3 ^Rom 3:12
53:4 ^Jer 4:22   53:5 ^Ps 141:7   ^B 2 Kin 17:20
53:6 ^Ps 14:7   54:1 ^Ps 20:1   ^B 2 Chr 20:6
54:2 ^Ps 5:1   54:3 ^Ps 86:14   ^B Ps 36:1

53:1 †I.e., sickness, a sad tone

4 Behold, ^God is my helper;
  The Lord is the ^Bsustainer of
  my soul.
5 He will pay back the evil to my
  enemies;
  ^ADestroy them ^Bin Your
  faithfulness.

6 ^AWillingly I will sacrifice to
  You;
  I will praise Your name, Lord,
  for it is good.
7 For He has ^saved me from all
  trouble,
  And my eye has looked
  with satisfaction upon my
  enemies.

**PRAYER FOR THE DESTRUCTION
OF THE TREACHEROUS.**
For the music director; on stringed
instruments. A Maskil of David.

55 Listen to my prayer, God;
     And ^do not hide Yourself
     from my pleading.
2 Give *Your* attention to me and
  answer me;
  I am restless in my
  ^Acomplaint and ^Bseverely
  distracted,
3 Because of the voice of the
  enemy,
  Because of the pressure of the
  wicked;
  For they ^bring down trouble
  upon me
  And in anger they hold a
  grudge against me.

4 My ^heart is in anguish within
  me,
  And the terrors of death have
  fallen upon me.
5 Fear and ^trembling come
  upon me,
  And ^Bhorror has
  overwhelmed me.

6 I said, "Oh, that I had wings
  like a dove!
  I would fly away and ^be at
  rest.
7 "Behold, I would flee far
  away,
  I would ^spend my nights in
  the wilderness.   *Selah*
8 "I would hurry to my place of
  refuge
  From the ^stormy wind *and*
  heavy gale."

9 Confuse them, Lord, ^divide
  their tongues,
  For I have seen ^Bviolence and
  strife in the city.
10 Day and night they go around
   her upon her walls,
   And evil and harm are in her
   midst.
11 Destruction is in her midst;
   ^Oppression and deceit do not
   depart from her streets.

12 For it is ^not an enemy who
   taunts me,
   Then I could endure *it;*
   Nor is it one who hates me
   who has exalted himself
   against me,
   Then I could hide myself from
   him.
13 But it is you, a man my equal,
   My ^companion and my
   ^Bconfidant;
14 We who had sweet fellowship
   together,
   ^Walked in the house of God
   among the commotion.

54:4 ^A Ps 30:10   ^B Ps 37:17, 24   54:5 ^A Ps 143:12
^B Ps 89:49   54:6 ^A Num 15:3; Ps 116:17   54:7 ^A Ps 34:6
55:1 ^A Ps 27:9   55:2 ^A 1 Sam 1:16   ^B Is 38:14
55:3 ^A 2 Sam 16:7, 8   55:4 ^A Ps 38:8   55:5 ^A Ps 119:120
^B Job 21:6   55:6 ^A Job 3:13   55:7 ^A 1 Sam 23:14
55:8 ^A Is 4:6; 25:4   55:9 ^A Gen 11:9   ^B Ps 11:5
55:11 ^A Ps 10:7; 17:9   55:12 ^A Ps 41:9
55:13 ^A 2 Sam 15:12   ^B Job 19:14   55:14 ^A Ps 42:4

15 *May* death *come* ^deceitfully
upon them;
May they ^B^go down alive to
¹Sheol,
For evil is in their dwelling, in
their midst.

16 As for me, I shall ^call upon God,
And the Lord will save me.

17 ^Evening and morning and at
noon, I will complain and
moan,
And He will hear my voice.

18 He will ^redeem my soul in
peace from the battle *which
is* against me,
For they are ^B^many *who are
aggressive* toward me.

19 God will ^hear and humiliate
them—
Even the one ^B^who sits
enthroned from ancient
times—   *Selah*
With whom there is no
change,
And who do not fear God.

20 He has put forth his hands
against ^those who were at
peace with him;
He has ^B^violated his covenant.

21 His speech was ^smoother
than butter,
But his heart was war;
His words were ^softer than oil,
Yet they were drawn swords.

22 ^Cast your burden upon the
Lord and He will sustain you;
He will never allow the
righteous to be shaken.

23 But You, God, will bring
them down to the ^pit of
destruction;
^B^Men of bloodshed and deceit
will not live out half their
days.
But I will trust in You.

PLEADING FOR HELP AND GRATEFUL TRUST IN GOD.

For the music director; according to
Jonath elem rehokim. A Mikhtam of David,
when the Philistines seized him in Gath.

56 Be gracious to me, God, for
a man has trampled upon
me;
Fighting all day long he
^oppresses me.

2 My enemies have ^trampled
upon me all day long,
For they are many who fight
proudly against me.

3 When I am afraid,
I will ^put my trust in You.

4 In God, whose word I praise,
In God I have put my trust;
I shall not be afraid.
^What can *mere* mortals do to
me?

5 All day long they ^distort my
words;
All their ^B^thoughts are against
me for evil.

6 They ^attack, they lurk,
They watch my steps,
As they have ^B^waited *to take*
my life.

7 Because of *their* wickedness,
will there be an ^escape for
them?
In anger make the peoples fall
down, God!

8 You ^have taken account of my
miseries;
Put my tears in Your bottle.
Are they not in ^B^Your book?

55:15 ^Ps 64:7   ^B^Num 16:30, 33   55:16 ^Ps 57:2, 3
55:17 ^Ps 141:2; Dan 6:10   55:18 ^Ps 103:4   ^B^Ps 56:2
55:19 ^Ps 78:59   ^B^Ps 36:1   55:20 ^Ps 7:4   ^B^Num 30:2
55:21 ^Ps 12:2; 28:3   55:22 ^Ps 37:5; 1 Pet 5:7
55:23 ^Ps 73:18   ^B^Ps 5:6   56:1 ^Ps 17:9   56:2 ^Ps 35:25;
57:3   56:3 ^Ps 11:1   56:4 ^Ps 118:6; Heb 13:6
56:5 ^2 Pet 3:16   ^B^Ps 41:7   56:6 ^Ps 59:3   ^B^Ps 71:10
56:7 ^Ps 36:12   56:8 ^Ps 139:3   ^B^Mal 3:16

55:15 ¹I.e., the netherworld

9 Then my enemies will turn
   back on the day when I call;
   This I know, that ^God is for
   me.
10 In God, *whose* word I praise,
   In the LORD, *whose* word I
   praise,
11 In God I have put my trust, I
   shall not be afraid.
   What can mankind do to me?
12 Your ^vows are *binding* upon
   me, God;
   I will render thanksgiving
   offerings to You.
13 For You have ^saved my soul
   from death,
   Indeed ᴮmy feet from
   stumbling,
   So that I may walk before
   God
   In the light of the living.

**PRAYER FOR RESCUE
FROM PERSECUTORS.**

For the music director; *set to* Al-
tashheth. A Mikhtam of David, when
he fled from Saul in the cave.

57 Be gracious to me, God, be
     gracious to me,
   For my soul takes refuge in
   You;
   And in the ^shadow of Your
   wings I will take refuge
   Until destruction passes by.
2 I will cry to God Most High,
   To God who ^accomplishes *all
   things* for me.
3 He will ^send from heaven and
   save me;
   He rebukes the one who
   tramples upon me.   *Selah*
   God will send His favor and
   His truth.

4 My soul is among ^lions;
   I must lie *among* those who
   devour,

Among sons of mankind whose
   teeth are spears and arrows,
   And their tongue is a sharp
   sword.
5 ^Be exalted above the heavens,
   God;
   May Your glory *be* above all
   the earth.
6 They have prepared a net for
   my steps;
   My soul is bowed down;
   They ^dug a pit before me;
   They *themselves* have ᴮfallen
   into the midst of it.   *Selah*

7 My ^heart is steadfast, God, my
   heart is steadfast;
   I will sing, yes, I will sing
   praises!
8 Awake, ^my glory!
   Awake, harp and lyre!
   I will awaken the dawn.
9 ^I will praise You, Lord, among
   the peoples;
   I will sing praises to You
   among the nations.
10 For Your ^goodness is great to
   the heavens
   And Your truth to the clouds.
11 ^Be exalted above the heavens,
   God;
   May Your glory *be* above all
   the earth.

**PRAYER FOR THE PUNISHMENT
OF THE WICKED.**

For the music director; *set to* Al-
tashheth. A Mikhtam of David.

58 Do you indeed speak
     righteousness, you gods?
   Do you ^judge fairly, you sons
   of mankind?

56:9 ^Ps 41:11; 118:6   56:12 ^Ps 50:14   56:13 ^Ps 33:19
ᴮPs 116:8   57:1 ^Ruth 2:12; Ps 17:8   57:2 ^Ps 138:8
57:3 ^Ps 18:16   57:4 ^Ps 35:17; 58:6   57:5 ^Ps 57:11;
108:5   57:6 ^Ps 7:15   ᴮProv 26:27   57:7 ^Ps 112:7
57:8 ^Ps 16:9; 30:12   57:9 ^Ps 108:3   57:10 ^Ps 36:5;
103:11   57:11 ^Ps 57:5; 108:5   58:1 ^Ps 82:2

² No, in heart you ^practice
injustice;
On earth you clear a way for
the violence of your
hands.
³ The wicked have turned away
from the womb;
These who speak lies ^go
astray from birth.
⁴ They have venom like the
^venom of a serpent;
Like a deaf cobra that stops
up its ear,
⁵ So that it ^does not hear the
voice of ᴮcharmers,
Or a skillful caster of spells.
⁶ God, ^shatter their teeth in
their mouth;
Break out the fangs of the
young lions, Lᴏʀᴅ.
⁷ May they ^flow away like
water that runs off;
When he ᴮaims his arrows,
may they be as headless
shafts.
⁸ *May they be* like a snail which
goes along in slime,
Like the ^miscarriage of a
woman that never sees the
sun.
⁹ Before your pots can feel *the*
fire of thorns
He will ^sweep them away
with a whirlwind, the
green and the burning
alike.
¹⁰ The ^righteous will rejoice
when he ᴮsees vengeance;
He will wash his feet in the
blood of the wicked.
¹¹ And people will say, "There
certainly is ^a reward for the
righteous;
There certainly is a God who
ᴮjudges on the earth!"

PRAYER FOR RESCUE FROM ENEMIES.
For the music director; *set to* Al-
tashheth. A Mikhtam of David, when
Saul sent *men* and they watched
the house in order to kill him.

59 ^Rescue me from my
enemies, my God;
Set me *securely* on high away
from those who rise up
against me.
² Rescue me from ^those who
practice injustice,
And save me from ᴮmen of
bloodshed.
³ For behold, they ^have set an
ambush for my life;
Fierce men ^attack me,
Not for my wrongdoing nor for
my sin, Lᴏʀᴅ,
⁴ For no guilt *of mine,* they run
and take their stand against
me.
^Stir Yourself to help me, and
see!
⁵ You, Lᴏʀᴅ God of armies, the
God of Israel,
Awake to ^punish all the
nations;
ᴮDo not be gracious to any
who deal treacherously in
wrongdoing.   *Selah*
⁶ They ^return at evening, they
howl like a ᴮdog,
And prowl around the city.
⁷ Behold, they gush forth with
their mouths;
^Swords are in their lips,
For, *they say,* "Who hears?"
⁸ But You, Lᴏʀᴅ, ^laugh at them;
You scoff at all the nations.

58:2 ^Mal 3:15   58:3 ^Ps 53:3   58:4 ^Deut 32:33;
Ps 140:3   58:5 ^Jer 8:17   ᴮEccl 10:11   58:6 ^Job 4:10;
Ps 3:7   58:7 ^Josh 2:11   ᴮPs 64:3   58:8 ^Job 3:16;
Eccl 6:3   58:9 ^Job 27:21; Ps 83:15   58:10 ^Job 22:19
ᴮDeut 32:43   58:11 ^Ps 18:20   ᴮPs 9:8   59:1 ^Ps 143:9
59:2 ^Ps 28:3   ᴮPs 26:9   59:3 ^Ps 56:6   59:4 ^Ps 7:6;
35:23   59:5 ^Ps 9:5   ᴮIs 2:9   59:6 ^Ps 59:14   ᴮPs 22:16
59:7 ^Ps 57:4; Prov 12:18   59:8 ^Ps 37:13; Prov 1:26

9 *Because of* ¹his strength I will
   watch for You,
   For God is my ^refuge.
10 My God ^in His faithfulness
   will meet me;
   God will let me ᴮlook
   triumphantly upon my
   enemies.
11 Do not kill them, ^or my
   people will forget;
   Scatter them by Your power
   and bring them down,
   Lord, our shield.
12 *On account of* the ^sin of their
   mouths *and* the words of
   their lips,
   May they even be ᴮcaught in
   their pride,
   And on account of curses and
   lies which they tell.
13 ^Destroy *them* in wrath,
   destroy *them* so that they
   will no longer exist;
   So that *people* may ᴮknow that
   God rules in Jacob,
   To the ends of the earth. *Selah*
14 They ^return at evening, they
   howl like a dog,
   And prowl around the city.
15 They ^wander about for
   food
   And murmur if they are not
   satisfied.

16 But as for me, I will sing of
   Your strength;
   Yes, I will joyfully sing of
   Your faithfulness in the
   morning,
   For You have been my
   ^refuge
   And a ᴮplace of refuge on the
   day of my distress.
17 ^My strength, I will sing
   praises to You;
   For God is my refuge, the God
   who shows me favor.

GRIEVING OVER DEFEAT IN BATTLE, AND PRAYER FOR HELP.

For the music director; according to
Shushan Eduth. A Mikhtam of David,
to teach; when he fought with Aram-
naharaim and Aram-zobah, and Joab
returned, and killed twelve thousand
of Edom in the Valley of Salt.

60 God, ^You have rejected us.
   You have broken us;
   You have been angry; restore
   us!
2 You have made the ^land
   quake, You have split it
   open;
   Heal its cracks, for it sways.
3 You have ^made Your people
   experience hardship;
   You have given us wine to
   drink that makes us stagger.
4 You have given a ^banner to
   those who fear You,
   That it may be displayed
   because of the truth.   *Selah*
5 That Your ^beloved may be
   rescued,
   Save *us* with Your right hand,
   and answer us!

6 God has spoken in His
   holiness:
   "I will triumph, I will divide up
   ^Shechem, and measure out
   the Valley of ᴮSuccoth.
7 "Gilead is Mine, and Manasseh
   is Mine;
   ^Ephraim also is the helmet of
   My head;
   Judah is My ᴮscepter.

59:9 ^Ps 9:9; 62:2 **59:10** ^Ps 21:3   ᴮPs 54:7
59:11 ^Deut 4:9; 6:12   **59:12** ^Prov 12:13   ᴮZeph 3:11
59:13 ^Ps 104:35   ᴮPs 83:18   **59:14** ^Ps 59:6
59:15 ^Job 15:23   **59:16** ^Ps 59:9   ᴮ2 Sam 22:3
59:17 ^Ps 59:9   **60:1** ^Ps 44:9   **60:2** ^Ps 18:7
60:3 ^Ps 66:12; 71:20   **60:4** ^Ps 20:5; Is 5:26
60:5 ^Deut 33:12; Ps 127:2   **60:6** ^Gen 12:6
ᴮGen 33:17   **60:7** ^Deut 33:17   ᴮGen 49:10

59:9 ¹LXX, some mss and some ancient versions *my strength* (cf. v 17)

8 "ᴬMoab is My washbowl;
  I will throw My sandal over
    ᴮEdom;
  Shout loud, Philistia, because
    of Me!"

9 Who will bring me into the
    besieged city?
  Who will lead me to Edom?
10 Have You Yourself not
    ᴬrejected us, God?
  And will You not go out with
    our armies, God?
11 Oh give us help against the
    enemy,
  For ᴬrescue by man is
    worthless.
12 Through God we will ᴬdo
    valiantly,
  And it is He who will ᴮtrample
    down our enemies.

CONFIDENCE IN GOD'S PROTECTION.
For the music director; on a stringed
instrument. *A Psalm* of David.

61 ᴬHear my cry, God;
      ᴮGive *Your* attention to my
      prayer.
2 From the ᴬend of the earth I
    call to You when my heart is
    ᴮfaint;
  Lead me to the rock that is
    higher than I.
3 For You have been a ᴬrefuge for
    me,
  A ᴮtower of strength against
    the enemy.
4 Let me ᴬdwell in Your tent
    forever;
  Let me take refuge in the
    shelter of Your wings.   *Selah*

5 For You have heard my ᴬvows,
    God;
  You have given *me* the
    inheritance of those who
    ᴮfear Your name.

6 You will ᴬprolong the king's life;
  His years will be like
    generations.
7 He will sit *enthroned* ᴬbefore
    God forever;
  Appoint ᴮfaithfulness and
    truth that they may watch
    over him.
8 So I will sing praise to Your
    name forever,
  That I may ᴬpay my vows day
    by day.

**GOD ALONE A REFUGE FROM
TREACHERY AND OPPRESSION.**
For the music director; according
to Jeduthun. A Psalm of David.

62 ᴬMy soul *waits in* silence for
      God alone;
    From Him ᴮ*comes* my
      salvation.
2 He alone is my ᴬrock and my
    salvation,
  My ᴮstronghold; I will not be
    greatly shaken.

3 How long will you attack a man,
  That you may murder *him*, all
    of you,
  Like a ᴬleaning wall, like a
    tottering fence?
4 They have planned only to
    thrust him down from his
    high position;
  They ᴬdelight in falsehood;
  They bless with their mouth,
  But inwardly they curse.   *Selah*

5 My soul, ᴬwait in silence for
    God alone,
  For my hope is from Him.

60:8 ᴬ2 Sam 8:2   ᴮ2 Sam 8:14   60:10 ᴬPs 60:1;
108:11   60:11 ᴬPs 146:3   60:12 ᴬNum 24:18
ᴬPs 44:5   61:1 ᴬPs 64:1   ᴮPs 86:6   61:2 ᴬPs 42:6
ᴮPs 77:3   61:3 ᴬPs 62:7   ᴮPs 59:9   61:4 ᴬPs 23:6;
27:4   61:5 ᴬJob 22:27   ᴮDeut 28:58   61:6 ᴬPs 21:4
61:7 ᴬPs 41:12   ᴮPs 40:11   61:8 ᴬPs 65:1; Is 19:21
62:1 ᴬPs 33:20   ᴮPs 37:39   62:2 ᴬPs 89:26   ᴮPs 59:17
62:3 ᴬIs 30:13   62:4 ᴬPs 4:2   62:5 ᴬPs 62:1

6 He alone is ^my rock and my
    salvation,
    My refuge; I will not be
    shaken.
7 My ^salvation and my glory
    rest on God;
    The rock of my strength, my
    ^refuge is in God.
8 ^Trust in Him at all times, you
    people;
    ^Pour out your hearts before
    Him;
    God is a refuge for us.   *Selah*

9 People of ^low standing are
    only ^breath, and people of
    rank are a lie;
    In the balances they go up.
    Together they are *lighter* than
    breath.
10 ^Do not trust in oppression,
    And do not vainly rely on
    ^robbery;
    If wealth increases, do not set
    your heart *on it.*

11 God has spoken ¹once;
    ²Twice I have heard this:
    That ^power belongs to God;
12 And faithfulness is Yours,
    Lord,
    For You ^reward a person
    according to his work.

THE THIRSTING SOUL SATISFIED IN GOD.

A Psalm of David, when he was
in the wilderness of Judah.

63 God, You are my God; I shall
    be watching for You;
    My soul ^thirsts for You, my
    flesh yearns for You,
    In a ^dry and exhausted land
    where there is no water.
2 So have I ^seen You in the
    sanctuary,
    To see Your power and glory.

3 Because Your ^favor is better
    than life,
    My lips will praise You.
4 So I will bless You ^as long as I
    live;
    I will lift up my hands in Your
    name.
5 My soul is ^satisfied as with fat
    and fatness,
    And my mouth offers praises
    with joyful lips.

6 When I remember You ^on my
    bed,
    I meditate on You in the ^night
    watches,
7 For You have been my help,
    And in the ^shadow of Your
    wings I sing for joy.
8 My soul ^clings to You;
    Your ^right hand takes hold
    of me.

9 But those who ^seek my life to
    destroy it,
    Will go into the ^depths of the
    earth.
10 They will be ^turned over to
    the power of the sword;
    They will be a prey for
    foxes.
11 But the ^king will rejoice in
    God;
    Everyone who swears by Him
    will boast,
    For the mouths of those
    who speak lies will be
    stopped.

62:6 ^Ps 62:2   62:7 ^Ps 85:9   ^Ps 46:1
62:8 ^Ps 37:3, 5   ^1 Sam 1:15   62:9 ^Ps 49:2
^Job 7:16   62:10 ^Is 30:12   ^Is 61:8
62:11 ^Ps 59:17; Rev 19:1   62:12 ^Job 34:11; Ps 28:4
63:1 ^Ps 42:2   ^Ps 143:6   63:2 ^Ps 27:4
63:3 ^Ps 69:16   63:4 ^Ps 104:33; 146:2
63:5 ^Ps 36:8   63:6 ^Ps 4:4   ^Ps 16:7
63:7 ^Ps 17:8   63:8 ^Num 32:12   ^Ps 18:35
63:9 ^Ps 40:14   ^Ps 55:15   63:10 ^Jer 18:21
63:11 ^Ps 21:1

62:11 ¹Or *one thing*   ²Or *These two things I have heard*

PRAYER FOR RESCUE FROM SECRET
ENEMIES.
For the music director. A Psalm of David.

64

Hear my voice, God, in ^my
¹complaint;
ᴮProtect my life from dread of
the enemy.

2 Hide me from the ^secret
discussion of evildoers,
From the restlessness of ᴮthe
workers of injustice,

3 Who ^have sharpened their
tongues like a sword.
They ᴮaimed bitter speech *as*
their arrows,

4 To ^shoot from concealment at
the innocent;
Suddenly they shoot at him,
and do not fear.

5 They make firm for
themselves an evil purpose;
They talk of ^setting snares
secretly;
They say, "Who can see them?"

6 They devise injustices, *saying,*
"We are ready *with* a
well-conceived plot";
For the ^inward thought and the
heart of a person are deep.

7 But ^God will shoot an arrow at
them;
Suddenly they will be
wounded.

8 So they will ^make him stumble;
Their own tongue is against
them;
All who see *them* will shake
their heads.

9 Then all people will fear,
And they will ^declare the
work of God,
And will consider what He has
done.

10 The righteous person will be
^glad in the Lᴏʀᴅ and take
refuge in Him;

And all the upright in heart
will boast.

GOD'S ABUNDANT FAVOR TO EARTH
AND MANKIND.
For the music director. A Psalm
of David. A Song.

65

There will be silence before
You, *and* praise in Zion,
God,
And the ^vow will be fulfilled
for You.

2 You who hear prayer,
To You ^all mankind comes.

3 ^Wrongdoings prevail against
me;
As for our offenses, You
ᴮforgive them.

4 ^Blessed *is the one* You ᴮchoose
and allow to approach *You;*
He will dwell in Your courtyards.
We will be satisfied with the
goodness of Your house,
Your holy temple.

5 By ^awesome *deeds* You answer
us in righteousness, God of
our salvation,
You who are the trust of all the
ends of the earth and the
farthest sea;

6 Who ^establishes the
mountains by His strength,
Who is ᴮencircled with might;

7 Who ^stills the roaring of the
seas,
The roaring of their waves,
And the turmoil of the
nations.

64:1 ^Ps 55:2   ᴮPs 140:1   64:2 ^Ps 56:6   ᴮPs 59:2
64:3 ^Ps 140:3   ᴮPs 58:7   64:4 ^Ps 10:8; 11:2
64:5 ^Ps 140:5   64:6 ^Ps 49:11   64:7 ^Ps 7:12, 13
64:8 ^Ps 9:3   64:9 ^Jer 51:10   64:10 ^Job 22:19;
Ps 32:11   65:1 ^Ps 116:18   65:2 ^Ps 86:9; 145:21
65:3 ^Ps 38:4   ᴮPs 79:9   65:4 ^Ps 33:12   ᴮPs 4:3
65:5 ^Ps 45:4; 66:3   65:6 ^Ps 95:4   ᴮPs 93:1
65:7 ^Ps 89:9; 93:3, 4

64:1 ¹Or *concern*

8 They who dwell at the ^ends
   of the earth stand in awe of
   Your signs;
   You make the sunrise and the
   sunset shout for joy.

9 You visit the earth and ^cause
   it to overflow;
   You greatly ^Benrich it;
   The stream of God is full of
   water;
   You prepare their grain, for so
   You prepare the earth.

10 You water its furrows
   abundantly,
   You settle its ridges,
   You soften it ^with showers,
   You bless its growth.

11 You have crowned the year
   with Your ^goodness,
   And Your paths drip *with*
   fatness.

12 ^The pastures of the
   wilderness drip,
   And the hills encircle
   themselves with rejoicing.

13 The meadows are ^clothed
   with flocks
   And the valleys are ^Bcovered
   with grain;
   They shout for joy, yes, they
   sing.

PRAISE FOR GOD'S MIGHTY DEEDS
AND FOR HIS ANSWER TO PRAYER.
For the music director. A Song. A Psalm.

66
^Shout joyfully to God, all
the earth;

2 Sing the ^glory of His name;
   Make His praise glorious.

3 Say to God, "How ^awesome
   are Your works!
   Because of the greatness of
   Your power Your enemies
   will pretend to obey You.

4 "^All the earth will worship You,
   And will sing praises to You;

They will sing praises to
Your name."   *Selah*

5 ^Come and see the works of
   God,
   Who is ^Bawesome in *His* deeds
   toward the sons of mankind.

6 He ^turned the sea into dry
   land;
   They passed through ^Bthe river
   on foot;
   Let's rejoice there, in Him!

7 He ^rules by His might forever;
   His ^Beyes keep watch on the
   nations;
   The rebellious shall not exalt
   themselves!   *Selah*

8 Bless our God, you peoples,
   And ^sound His praise abroad,

9 Who ^keeps us in life,
   And ^Bdoes not allow our feet
   to slip.

10 For You have ^put us to the
   test, God;
   You have ^Brefined us as silver is
   refined.

11 You ^brought us into the net;
   You laid an oppressive burden
   upon us.

12 You made men ^ride over our
   heads;
   We went through ^Bfire and
   through water.
   Yet You brought us out into *a*
   place of abundance.

13 I shall ^come into Your house
   with burnt offerings;
   I shall ^Bpay You my vows,

65:8 ^Ps 2:8; 139:9   65:9 ^Lev 26:4   ^Ps 104:24
65:10 ^Deut 32:2; Ps 72:6   65:11 ^Ps 104:28
65:12 ^Job 38:26, 27; Joel 2:22   65:13 ^Ps 144:13
^Ps 72:16   66:1 ^Ps 81:1; 95:1   66:2 ^Ps 79:9; Is 42:8
66:3 ^Ps 47:2; 65:5   66:4 ^Ps 22:27; 67:7
66:5 ^Ps 46:8   ^Ps 106:22   66:6 ^Ex 14:21
^Josh 3:16   66:7 ^Ps 145:13   ^Ps 11:4   66:8 ^Ps 98:4
66:9 ^Ps 30:3   ^Ps 121:3   66:10 ^Job 23:10   ^Is 48:10
66:11 ^Lam 1:13; Ezek 12:13   66:12 ^Is 51:23   ^Ps 78:21
66:13 ^Ps 96:8   ^Ps 22:25

14 Which my lips uttered
    And my mouth spoke when I
        was ^in distress.
15 I shall ^offer to You burnt
        offerings of fat animals,
    With the smoke of ᴮrams;
    I shall make *an offering of*
        bulls with male goats.   *Selah*

16 Come *and* hear, all who fear
        God,
    And I will ^tell of what He has
        done for my soul.
17 I cried to Him with my mouth,
    And He was ^exalted with my
        tongue.
18 If I ^regard wickedness in my
        heart,
    The ᴮLord will not hear;
19 But ^God has heard;
    He has given attention to the
        sound of my prayer.
20 Blessed be God,
    Who ^has not turned away my
        prayer
    Nor His favor from me.

THE NATIONS EXHORTED
TO PRAISE GOD.
For the music director; with stringed
instruments. A Psalm. A Song.

67 God be gracious to us and
        ^bless us,
    And cause His face to shine
        upon us—   *Selah*
2 That ^Your way may be known
        on the earth,
    ᴮYour salvation among all
        nations.
3 May the ^peoples praise You,
        God;
    May all the peoples praise
        You.
4 May the nations be glad and
        sing for joy;
    For You will ^judge the peoples
        with fairness

And ᴮguide the nations on the
        earth.   *Selah*
5 May the ^peoples praise You,
        God;
    May all the peoples praise You.
6 The ^earth has yielded its
        produce;
    God, our God, blesses us.
7 God blesses us,
    So that ^all the ends of the
        earth may fear Him.

THE GOD OF SINAI AND
OF THE SANCTUARY.
For the music director.
A Psalm of David. A Song.

68 May ^God arise, may His
        enemies be scattered,
    And may those who hate Him
        flee from His presence.
2 As smoke is driven away, *so*
        drive *them* away;
    As ^wax melts before a fire,
    So the ᴮwicked will perish
        before God.
3 But the ^righteous will be
        joyful; they will rejoice
        before God;
    Yes, they will rejoice with
        gladness.
4 Sing to God, sing praises to His
        name;
    Exalt Him who ^rides through
        the deserts,
    Whose ᴮname is the Lᴏʀᴅ, and
        be jubilant before Him.

5 A ^father of the fatherless and
        a judge for the widows,
    Is God in His holy dwelling.

66:14^Ps 18:6   66:15^Ps 51:19   ᴮNum 6:14
66:16^Ps 71:15, 24   66:17^Ps 30:1   66:18^Job 36:21
ᴮJob 27:9   66:19^Ps 18:6; 116:1, 2   ᴮ66:20^Ps 22:24
67:1^Num 6:25   67:2^Ps 98:2   ᴮIs 52:10
67:3^Ps 66:4   67:4^Ps 9:8   ᴮPs 47:8   67:5^Ps 67:3
67:6^Lev 26:4; Ps 85:12   67:7^Ps 22:27; 33:8
68:1^Num 10:35; Ps 12:5   68:2^Ps 22:14   ᴮPs 9:3
68:3^Ps 32:11; 64:10   68:4^Deut 33:26   ᴮEx 6:3
68:5^Ps 10:14; 146:9

6 God ^makes a home for the
      lonely;
   He ^Bleads out the prisoners
      into prosperity,
   Only the rebellious live in
      parched lands.

7 God, when You ^went forth
      before Your people,
   When You marched through
      the desert,   *Selah*
8 The ^earth quaked;
   The ^Bheavens also dropped
      rain at the presence of God;
   Sinai itself *quaked* at the
      presence of God, the God of
      Israel.
9 You ^made plentiful rain fall,
      God;
   You confirmed Your
      inheritance when it was
      parched.
10 Your creatures settled in it;
   In Your kindness You
      ^provided for the poor, God.

11 The Lord gives the command;
   The ^women who proclaim
      good news are a great army:
12 "^Kings of armies flee, they
      flee,
   And she who remains at home
      will ^Bdivide the spoils!"
13 When you lie down ^among
      the sheepfolds,
   You are like the wings of a dove
      covered with silver,
   And its pinions with glistening
      gold.
14 When the Almighty ^scattered
      the kings there,
   It was snowing in ^BZalmon.

15 ^The mountain of Bashan is a
      mountain of God;
   The mountain of Bashan is a
      mountain of many peaks.

16 Why do you look with envy,
      you mountains of many
      peaks,
   At the mountain God has
      ^desired as His dwelling?
   Indeed, the Lord will dwell
      there forever.
17 The ^chariots of God are
      myriads, thousands upon
      thousands;
   The Lord is among them *as at*
      Sinai, in holiness.
18 You have ^ascended on high,
   You have ^Bled captive *Your*
      captives;
   You have received gifts among
      people,
   Even *among* the rebellious as
      well, that the Lord God may
      dwell *there*.

19 Blessed be the Lord, who daily
      ^bears our burden,
   The God *who* is our
      salvation.   *Selah*
20 God is to us a ^God of
      salvation;
   And to God the Lord belong
      ways of escape from death.
21 God certainly will ^shatter the
      heads of His enemies,
   The hairy head of one who
      goes about in his guilt.
22 The Lord said, "^I will bring
      them back from Bashan.
   I will bring *them* back from the
      depths of the sea,
23 So that your foot may shatter
      them in blood,

68:6 ^Ps 107:4-7   ^B Ps 69:33   68:7 ^Ex 13:21; Ps 78:14
68:8 ^Ex 19:18   ^B Judg 5:4   68:9 ^Lev 26:4; Deut 11:11
68:10 ^Ps 65:9; 74:19   68:11 ^Ex 15:20; 1 Sam 18:6
68:12 ^Josh 10:16   ^B Judg 5:30   68:13 ^Gen 49:14;
Judg 5:16   68:14 ^Josh 10:10   ^B Judg 9:48
68:15 ^Ps 36:6   68:16 ^Deut 12:5; Ps 87:1, 2
68:17 ^2 Kin 6:17; Hab 3:8   68:18 ^Ps 7:7   ^B Judg 5:12
68:19 ^Ps 55:22; Is 46:4   68:20 ^Ps 106:43
68:21 ^Ps 110:6; Hab 3:13   68:22 ^Num 21:33;
Amos 9:1-3

And the tongue of your ^dogs
may have its portion from
your enemies."

24 They have seen ^Your
procession, God,
The procession of my God, my
King, into the sanctuary.

25 The singers went on, the
musicians after *them,*
In the midst of the
^young women beating
tambourines.

26 Bless God in the congregations,
Even the Lord, *you who are* of
the ^fountain of Israel.

27 ^Benjamin, the youngest, is
there, ruling them,
The leaders of Judah *in* their
company,
The leaders of Zebulun, the
leaders of Naphtali.

28 Your God has ^commanded
your strength;
Show Yourself strong, God,
You ^Bwho acted in our behalf.

29 Because of Your temple at
Jerusalem
^Kings will bring gifts to You.

30 Rebuke the animals in the reeds,
The herd of ^bulls with the
calves of the peoples,
Trampling the pieces of silver;
He has ^Bscattered the peoples
who delight in war.

31 ¹Messengers will come from
^Egypt;
^BCush will quickly stretch out
her hands to God.

32 Sing to God, you ^kingdoms of
the earth,
Sing praises to the Lord,   *Selah*

33 To Him who ^rides upon the
^Bhighest heavens, which are
from ancient times;

Behold, He speaks with His
voice, a mighty voice.

34 ^Ascribe strength to God;
His majesty is over Israel,
And ^BHis strength is in the
skies.

35 God, *You are* ^awesome from
Your sanctuary.
The God of Israel Himself
^Bgives strength and power to
the people.
Blessed be God!

A CRY OF DISTRESS AND A CURSE ON ADVERSARIES.

For the music director; according to
†Shoshannim. *A Psalm* of David.

69 Save me, God,
For the ^waters have
threatened my life.

2 I have sunk in deep mud, and
there is no foothold;
I have come into deep
waters, and a ^flood
overflows me.

3 I am ^weary with my crying;
my throat is parched;
My eyes fail while I wait for my
God.

4 Those ^who hate me without
a cause are more than the
hairs of my head;
Those who would destroy me
^Bare powerful, those who
oppose me with lies;
What I did not steal, I then
have to restore.

68:23 ^A 1 Kin 21:19; Jer 15:3   68:24 ^A Ps 77:13
68:25 ^A Ex 15:20; Judg 11:34   68:26 ^A Deut 33:28; Is 48:1
68:27 ^A Judg 5:14; 1 Sam 9:21   68:28 ^A Ps 29:11
^B Is 26:12   68:29 ^A 1 Kin 10:10, 25; 2 Chr 32:23
68:30 ^A Ps 22:12   ^B Ps 18:14   68:31 ^A Is 19:19, 21
^B Is 45:14   68:32 ^A Ps 102:22   68:33 ^A Deut 33:26
^B Deut 10:14   68:34 ^A Ps 29:1   ^B Ps 150:1
68:35 ^A Deut 7:21   ^B Ps 29:11   69:1 ^A Job 22:11; Ps 32:6
69:2 ^A Jon 2:3   69:3 ^A Ps 6:6   69:4 ^A Ps 35:19   ^B Ps 38:19

68:31 ¹ As in LXX; MT uncertain, possibly, Articles
of *bronze;* or Articles of *red cloth*   69:1 † Or possibly
Lilies

5   God, You know ^my
    foolishness,
    And ^B^my guilt is not hidden
    from You.
6   May those who wait for You
    not ^be ashamed because of
    me, Lord GOD of armies;
    May those who seek You not
    be dishonored because of
    me, God of Israel,
7   Because ^for Your sake I have
    endured disgrace;
    Dishonor has covered my
    face.
8   I have become ^estranged from
    my brothers,
    And a stranger to my mother's
    sons.
9   For ^zeal for Your house has
    consumed me,
    And ^B^the taunts of those who
    taunt You have fallen on
    me.
10 When I wept ^in my soul with
    fasting,
    It became my disgrace.
11 When I made ^sackcloth my
    clothing,
    I became a proverb to them.
12 Those who ^sit in the gate talk
    about me,
    And songs of mockery by
    those habitually drunk *are
    about me.*
13 But as for me, my prayer is to
    You, LORD, ^at an acceptable
    time;
    God, in the greatness of Your
    mercy,
    Answer me with Your saving
    truth.
14 Rescue me from the ^mud and
    do not let me sink;
    May I be ^B^rescued from those
    who hate me, and from the
    ^depths of water.

15 May the ^flood of water not
    overflow me
    Nor the deep swallow me up,
    Nor the pit close its mouth on
    me.
16 Answer me, LORD, for Your
    mercy is good;
    According to the greatness of
    Your compassion, ^turn to me,
17 And ^do not hide Your face
    from Your servant,
    For I am ^B^in distress; answer
    me quickly.
18 Come near to my soul *and*
    redeem it;
    ^Ransom me because of my
    enemies!
19 You know my ^disgrace, my
    shame, and my dishonor;
    All my enemies are ^1^known to
    You.
20 Disgrace has ^broken my heart,
    and I am so sick.
    And I waited for sympathy, but
    there was none;
    And for ^B^comforters, but I
    found none.
21 They also gave me ^1,^A^a bitter
    herb in my food,
    And for my thirst they ^B^gave
    me vinegar to drink.
22 May ^their table before them
    become a snare;
    And when they are at peace,
    may it become a trap.

69:5 ^Ps 38:5   ^B^Ps 44:21   69:6 ^2 Sam 12:14
69:7 ^Jer 15:15   69:8 ^Job 19:13-15   69:9 ^Ps 119:139
^B^Ps 89:41, 50   69:10 ^Ps 35:13; Heb 12:2
69:11 ^1 Kin 20:31; Ps 35:13   69:12 ^Gen 19:1; Ruth 4:1
69:13 ^Ps 32:6; Is 49:8   69:14 ^Ps 69:2   ^B^Ps 144:7
69:15 ^Ps 124:4, 5   69:16 ^Ps 25:16; 86:16
69:17 ^Ps 27:9   ^B^Ps 31:9   69:18 ^Ps 119:134
69:19 ^Ps 22:6; 31:11   69:20 ^Jer 23:9   ^B^Job 16:2
69:21 ^Deut 29:18   ^B^Matt 27:34, 48
69:22 ^Rom 11:9, 10

69:19 ^1 Lit *before You*   69:21 ^1 Or *poison*

23 May their ^eyes grow dim so
that they cannot see,
And make their ^Bhips shake
continually.
24 ^Pour out Your indignation on
them,
And may Your burning anger
overtake them.
25 May their ^camp be desolated;
May there be none living in
their tents.
26 For they have ^persecuted him
whom ^BYou Yourself struck,
And they tell of the pain
of those whom You have
wounded.
27 Add guilt to their guilt,
And ^may they not come into
^BYour righteousness.
28 May they be ^wiped out of the
^Bbook of life,
And may they not be recorded
with the righteous.

29 But I am ^afflicted and in
pain;
May Your salvation, God, set
me *safely* on high.
30 I will ^praise the name of God
with song,
And ^Bexalt Him with
thanksgiving.
31 And it will ^please the Lord
better than an ox
Or bull with horns and hoofs.
32 The ^humble have seen *it and*
are glad;
You who seek God, ^Blet your
heart revive.
33 For ^the Lord hears the needy,
And ^Bdoes not despise *those of*
His *who are* prisoners.

34 Heaven and earth shall praise
Him,
The seas and ^everything that
moves in them.

35 For God will ^save Zion and
^Bbuild the cities of Judah,
So that they may live there and
possess it.
36 The descendants of His
servants will inherit it,
And those who love His name
^will live in it.

PRAYER FOR HELP AGAINST PERSECUTORS.

For the music director. *A Psalm*
of David; for a memorial.

70 ^God, *hurry* to save me;
Lord, hurry to help me!
2 ^May those who seek my life
Be put to shame and humiliated;
May those who delight in my
harm
Be turned back and dishonored.
3 ^May those who say, "Aha,
aha!" be turned back
Because of their shame.

4 May all who seek You rejoice
and be glad in You;
And may those who love Your
salvation say continually,
"May God be exalted!"
5 But ^I am afflicted and needy;
^BHurry to me, God!
You are my help and my savior;
Lord, do not delay.

PRAYER OF AN OLD MAN FOR RESCUE.

71 ^In You, Lord, I have taken
refuge;
Let me never be put to
shame.

69:23^Is 6:10   ^BDan 5:6   **69:24**^Ps 79:6; Jer 10:25
69:25^Matt 23:38; Luke 13:35   **69:26**^2 Chr 28:9
^BIs 53:4   **69:27**^Is 26:10   ^BPs 103:17
69:28^Ex 32:32, 33   ^BPhil 4:3   **69:29**^Ps 70:5
69:30^Ps 28:7   ^BPs 34:3   **69:31**^Ps 50:13, 14; 51:16
69:32^Ps 34:2   ^BPs 22:26   **69:33**^Ps 12:5   ^BPs 68:6
69:34^Is 55:12   **69:35**^Ps 46:5   ^BPs 147:2
69:36^Ps 37:29   **70:1**^Ps 40:13-17; 70:1-5
70:2^Ps 35:4, 26   **70:3**^Ps 40:15   **70:5**^Ps 40:17
^BPs 141:1   **71:1**^Ps 25:2, 3; 31:1-3

2 ^In Your righteousness rescue
     me and save me;
   Extend Your ear to me and
     help me.
3 ^Be to me a rock of dwelling
     to which I may continually
     come;
   You have given the
     commandment to save me,
   For You are ^Bmy rock and my
     fortress.
4 ^Save me, my God, from the
     hand of the wicked,
   From the grasp of the
     wrongdoer and the ruthless,
5 For You are my hope;
   Lord GOD, *You are* my
     ^confidence from my youth.
6 I have ^leaned on You since *my*
     birth;
   You are He who took me from
     my mother's womb;
   My praise is continually of
     You.

7 I have become a ^marvel to
     many,
   For You are ^Bmy strong refuge.
8 My mouth is filled with Your
     praise
   And with ^Your glory all day
     long.
9 Do not cast me away at the
     ^time of *my* old age;
   Do not abandon me when my
     strength fails.
10 For my enemies have spoken
     against me;
   And those who watch for my
     life ^have consulted together,
11 Saying, "^God has abandoned
     him;
   Pursue and seize him, for there
     is ^Bno one to save *him*."

12 God, ^do not be far from me;
   My God, ^Bhurry to my aid!

13 May those who are enemies
     of my soul be ^put to shame
     and consumed;
   May they be covered with
     disgrace and dishonor, who
     ^Bseek to injure me.
14 But as for me, I will ^wait
     continually,
   And will ^Bpraise You yet more
     and more.
15 My mouth shall tell of Your
     righteousness
   And of ^Your salvation all day
     long;
   For I ^Bdo not know the art of
     writing.
16 I will come ^with the mighty
     deeds of the Lord GOD;
   I will ^Bmake mention of Your
     righteousness, Yours alone.

17 God, You ^have taught me from
     my youth,
   And I still declare Your
     wondrous deeds.
18 And even when *I am* ^old and
     gray, God, do not abandon me,
   Until I ^Bdeclare Your strength
     to *this* generation,
   Your power to all who are to
     come.
19 For Your ^righteousness, God,
     reaches to the heavens,
   You who have done great things;
   God, ^Bwho is like You?
20 You who have shown me many
     troubles and distresses
   Will ^revive me again,
   And will bring me up again
     ^Bfrom the depths of the earth.

71:2 ^Ps 31:1   71:3 ^Ps 31:2, 3   ^B Ps 18:2
71:4 ^Ps 140:1, 4   71:5 ^Ps 22:9   71:6 ^Ps 22:10; Is 46:3
71:7 ^Is 8:18   ^B Ps 61:3   71:8 ^Ps 96:6; 104:1
71:9 ^Ps 71:18; 92:14   71:10 ^Ps 31:13; 83:3   71:11 ^Ps 3:2
^B Ps 7:2   71:12 ^Ps 10:1   ^B Ps 38:22   71:13 ^Ps 35:4, 26
^B Esth 9:2   71:14 ^Ps 130:7   ^B Ps 71:8   71:15 ^Ps 96:2
^B Ps 40:5   71:16 ^Ps 106:2   ^B Ps 51:14   71:17 ^Deut 4:5;
6:7   71:18 ^Ps 71:9   ^B Ps 22:31   71:19 ^Ps 36:6
^B Deut 3:24   71:20 ^Ps 80:18   ^B Ps 86:13

²¹ May You increase my
     greatness
And turn *to* ᴬcomfort me.

²² I will also praise You with ᴬa
     harp,
And Your truth, my God;
I will sing praises to You with
     the lyre,
ᴮHoly One of Israel.

²³ My lips will shout for joy when
     I sing praises to You;
And my ᴬsoul, which You have
     redeemed.

²⁴ My tongue also will tell of Your
     righteousness all day long;
For they are ᴬput to shame,
     for they are humiliated who
     seek my harm.

THE REIGN OF THE RIGHTEOUS KING.

A Psalm of Solomon.

72 Give the king ᴬYour
          judgments, God,
And ᴮYour righteousness to the
     king's son.

² May he ᴬjudge Your people
     with righteousness
And ᴮYour afflicted with
     justice.

³ May the mountains bring
     ᴬpeace to the people,
And the hills, in righteousness.

⁴ May he ᴬvindicate the afflicted
     of the people,
Save the children of the needy,
And crush the oppressor.

⁵ May they fear You ᴬwhile the
     sun *shines*,
And as long as the moon
     shines, throughout all
     generations.

⁶ May he come down ᴬlike rain
     upon the mown grass,
Like showers that water the
     earth.

⁷ May the ᴬrighteous flourish in
     his days,
As well as an ᴮabundance of
     peace, until the moon is no
     more.

⁸ May he also rule ᴬfrom sea to
     sea,
And from the *Euphrates* River
     to the ends of the earth.

⁹ May the nomads of the desert
     bow before him,
And his enemies ᴬlick the dust.

¹⁰ May the kings of Tarshish and
     of the ᴬislands bring gifts;
May the kings of Sheba and
     ᴮSeba offer tributes.

¹¹ And may all ᴬkings bow down
     before him,
All ᴮnations serve him.

¹² For he will ᴬsave the needy
     when he cries for help,
The afflicted also, and him
     who has no helper.

¹³ He will have ᴬcompassion on
     the poor and needy,
And he will save the lives of
     the needy.

¹⁴ He will ᴬrescue their life from
     oppression and violence,
And their blood will be
     ᴮprecious in his sight;

¹⁵ So may he live, and may the
     ᴬgold of Sheba be given to
     him;
And they are to pray for him
     continually;
They are to bless him all day
     long.

71:21 ᴬPs 23:4; 86:17 **71:22** ᴬPs 33:2 ᴮ2 Kin 19:22
71:23 ᴬPs 34:22; 55:18 **71:24** ᴬPs 71:13 **72:1** ᴬ1 Kin 3:9
ᴮPs 24:5 **72:2** ᴬIs 9:7 **72:3** ᴬIs 2:4; 9:5, 6
72:4 ᴬIs 11:4 **72:5** ᴬPs 72:17; 89:36, 37
72:6 ᴬDeut 32:2; 2 Sam 23:4 **72:7** ᴬPs 92:12 ᴮIs 2:4
72:8 ᴬEx 23:31; Zech 9:10 **72:9** ᴬIs 49:23; Mic 7:17
72:10 ᴬPs 97:1 ᴮGen 10:7 **72:11** ᴬPs 138:4 ᴮPs 86:9
72:12 ᴬJob 29:12; Ps 72:4 **72:13** ᴬProv 19:17; 28:8
72:14 ᴬPs 69:18 ᴮ1 Sam 26:21 **72:15** ᴬIs 60:6

16 May there be abundance of
grain on the earth on top of
the mountains;
Its fruit will wave like *the
cedars of* Lebanon;
And may those from the city
flourish like the ᴬvegetation
of the earth.

17 May his ᴬname endure forever;
May his name produce
descendants ᴮas long as the
sun *shines;*
And may *people* wish blessings
on themselves by him;
May all nations call him
blessed.

18 Blessed be the Lᴏʀᴅ God, the
God of Israel,
Who alone ᴬworks wonders.

19 And blessed be His ᴬglorious
name forever;
And may the whole ᴮearth be
filled with His glory.
Amen and Amen.

20 The prayers of David the son of
Jesse are ended.

BOOK 3

**THE END OF THE WICKED
CONTRASTED WITH THAT
OF THE RIGHTEOUS.**
A Psalm of Asaph.

73 God certainly is good to
Israel,
To those who are ᴬpure in
heart!

2 But as for me, ᴬmy feet came
close to stumbling,
My steps had almost slipped.

3 For I was ᴬenvious of the
arrogant
As I saw the ᴮprosperity of the
wicked.

4 For there are no pains in their
death,
And their belly is fat.

5 They are ᴬnot in trouble like
other people,
Nor are they ᴮtormented
together with *the rest of*
mankind.

6 Therefore arrogance is ᴬtheir
necklace;
The garment of violence
covers them.

7 Their eye bulges from ᴬfatness;
The imaginations of *their*
heart overflow.

8 They ᴬmock and wickedly
speak of oppression;
They ᴮspeak from on high.

9 They have ᴬset their mouth
against the heavens,
And their tongue parades
through the earth.

10 Therefore his people return
here,
And ᴬabundant waters are
drunk by them.

11 They say, "ᴬHow does God
know?
And is there knowledge with
the Most High?"

12 Behold, these are the wicked;
And always ᴬat ease, they have
increased *in* wealth.

13 Surely ᴬin vain I have kept my
heart pure
And ᴮwashed my hands in
innocence;

14 For I have been stricken ᴬall
day long,
And ᴮpunished every morning.

72:16 ᴬJob 5:25   **72:17** ᴬEx 3:15   ᴮPs 89:36
72:18 ᴬEx 15:11; Job 5:9   **72:19** ᴬNeh 9:5   ᴮNum 14:21
73:1 ᴬPs 24:4; 51:10   **73:2** ᴬPs 94:18   **73:3** ᴬPs 37:1
ᴮJob 21:7   **73:5** ᴬJob 21:9   ᴮPs 73:14   **73:6** ᴬGen 41:42;
Prov 1:9   **73:7** ᴬJob 15:27; Ps 17:10
73:8 ᴬPs 1:1   ᴮPs 17:10   **73:9** ᴬRev 13:6   **73:10** ᴬPs 23:5
73:11 ᴬJob 22:13   **73:12** ᴬJer 49:31; Ezek 23:42
73:13 ᴬJob 21:15   ᴮPs 26:6   **73:14** ᴬPs 38:6   ᴮJob 33:19

15 If I had said, "I will speak this
      way,"
    Behold, I would have betrayed
      the ^generation of Your
      children.
16 When I ^thought of
      understanding this,
    It was troublesome in my sight
17 Until I entered the sanctuary
      of God;
    Then I perceived their ^end.
18 You indeed put them on
      ^slippery ground;
    You dropped them into ᴮruin.
19 How they are ^destroyed in a
      moment!
    They are utterly swept away by
      ᴮsudden terrors!
20 Like a dream when one awakes,
    Lord, when stirred, You will
      ^despise their image.

21 When my ^heart was
      embittered
    And I was ᴮpierced within,
22 Then I was ^stupid and
      ignorant;
    I was *like* an ᴮanimal before
      You.
23 Nevertheless ^I am continually
      with You;
    You have taken hold of my
      right hand.
24 You will ^guide me with Your
      plan,
    And afterward ᴮreceive me to
      glory.

25 ^Whom do I have in heaven
      but You?
    And with You, I desire nothing
      on earth.
26 My ^flesh and my heart *may*
      fail,
    But God is the strength of
      my heart and my portion
      forever.

27 For, behold, those who are far
      from You will ^perish;
    You have destroyed all those
      who are unfaithful to You.
28 But as for me, ^the nearness of
      God is good for me;
    I have made the Lord GOD my
      ᴮrefuge,
    So that I may tell of all Your
      works.

AN APPEAL AGAINST THE
DEVASTATION OF THE LAND
BY THE ENEMY.

A Maskil of Asaph.

74 God, why have You rejected
    us forever?
    Why does Your anger ^smoke
      against the ᴮsheep of Your
      pasture?
2   Remember Your
      congregation, *which* You
      ^purchased of old,
    Which You have ᴮredeemed
      to be the tribe of Your
      inheritance;
    And this Mount Zion, where
      You have dwelt.
3   Step toward the irreparable
      ruins;
    The enemy ^has damaged
      everything in the sanctuary.
4   Your adversaries have roared
      in the midst of Your meeting
      place;
    They have set up their ^own
      signs as ᴮsigns.
5   It seems like one bringing up
      His ^axe into a forest of trees.

73:15 ^Ps 14:5   73:16 ^Eccl 8:17   73:17 ^Ps 37:38
73:18 ^Ps 35:6   ᴮPs 35:8   73:19 ^Num 16:21
ᴮJob 18:11   73:20 ^1 Sam 2:30   73:21 ^Judg 10:16
ᴮActs 2:37   73:22 ^Ps 49:10   ᴮJob 18:3
73:23 ^Ps 16:8   73:24 ^Ps 32:8   ᴮGen 5:24
73:25 ^Ps 16:2; Phil 3:8   73:26 ^Ps 38:10; 40:12
73:27 ^Ps 37:20   73:28 ^Ps 65:4   ᴮPs 14:6
74:1 ^Deut 29:20   ᴮPs 79:13   74:2 ^Ex 15:16
ᴮEx 15:13   74:3 ^Ps 79:1   74:4 ^Num 2:2   ᴮPs 74:9
74:5 ^Jer 46:22

6 And now they break down all
    its ^carved work
   With axe and hammers.
7 They have ^burned Your
    sanctuary to the ground;
   They have ^defiled the
    dwelling place of Your name.
8 They ^said in their heart, "Let's
    completely subdue them."
   They have burned all the
    meeting places of God in the
    land.
9 We do not see our ^signs;
   There is ^no longer any prophet,
   Nor is there *anyone* among us
    who knows how long.
10 How long, God, will the enemy
    ^taunt *You?*
   Shall the enemy ^treat Your
    name disrespectfully forever?
11 Why ^do You withdraw Your
    hand, even Your right hand?
   Extend it from Your chest *and*
    ^destroy *them!*
12 Yet God is ^my King from long
    ago,
   Who performs acts of salvation
    in the midst of the earth.
13 You divided the sea by Your
    strength;
   You ^broke the heads of the
    ^sea monsters in the waters.
14 You crushed the heads of
    ^Leviathan;
   You gave him as food for the
    creatures of the wilderness.
15 You ^broke open springs and
    torrents;
   You ^dried up ever-flowing
    streams.
16 Yours is the day, Yours also is
    the night;
   You have ^prepared the light
    and the sun.
17 You have ^established all the
    boundaries of the earth;

You have created ^summer and
    winter.
18 Remember this, LORD, that the
    enemy has taunted *You,*
   And a ^foolish people
    has treated Your name
    disrespectfully.
19 Do not give the soul of Your
    ^turtledove to the wild animal;
   Do not forget the life of Your
    afflicted forever.
20 Consider the covenant;
   For the ^dark places of the
    land are full of the places of
    violence.
21 May the ^oppressed person not
    return dishonored;
   May the afflicted and the
    needy praise Your name.
22 Arise, God, *and* plead Your
    own cause;
   Remember how the ^foolish
    person taunts You all day long.
23 Do not forget the voice of Your
    adversaries,
   The ^uproar of those who rise
    against You, which ascends
    continually.

**GOD HUMBLES THE PROUD, BUT
EXALTS THE RIGHTEOUS.**
For the music director; *set to* Al-
tashheth. A Psalm of Asaph, a Song.

75

We give thanks to You, God,
    we give thanks,
For Your name is ^near;
People declare ^Your wondrous
    works.

74:6 ^1 Kin 6:18, 29, 32, 35   **74:7** ^2 Kin 25:9   ^Ps 89:39
74:8 ^Ps 83:4   **74:9** ^Ps 78:43   ^1 Sam 3:1
74:10 ^Ps 44:16   ^Lev 24:16   **74:11** ^Lam 2:3   ^Ps 59:13
74:12 ^Ps 44:4   **74:13** ^Is 51:9   ^Ps 148:7   **74:14** ^Job 41:1;
Ps 104:26   **74:15** ^Ex 17:5, 6   ^Ex 14:21, 22
74:16 ^Gen 1:14-18; Ps 104:19   **74:17** ^Deut 32:8
^Gen 8:22   **74:18** ^Deut 32:6; Ps 14:1   **74:19** ^Song 2:14
74:20 ^Ps 88:6; 143:3   **74:21** ^Ps 103:6   **74:22** ^Ps 14:1;
53:1   **74:23** ^Ps 65:7   **75:1** ^Ps 145:18   ^Ps 26:7

2   "When I select an ^appointed
        time,
     It is I who ^Bjudge fairly.
3   "The ^earth and all who inhabit
        it are unsteady;
     It is I who have firmly set its
        ^Bpillars.   *Selah*
4   "I said to the boastful, 'Do not
        boast,'
     And to the wicked, '^Do not lift
        up the horn;
5   Do not lift up your horn on
        high,
     ^Do not speak with insolent
        pride.'"

6   For not from the east, nor from
        the west,
     Nor from the ^desert *comes*
        exaltation;
7   But ^God is the Judge;
     He ^Bputs down one and exalts
        another.
8   For a cup is in the hand of the
        Lord, and the wine foams;
     It is ^well mixed, and He pours
        out of this;
     Certainly all the wicked of the
        earth must drain *and* ^Bdrink
        its dregs.

9   But as for me, I will ^declare *it*
        forever;
     I will sing praises to the God of
        Jacob.
10   And He will cut off all the
        horns of the wicked,
     But ^the horns of the righteous
        will be lifted up.

THE VICTORIOUS POWER
OF THE GOD OF JACOB.

For the music director; on stringed
instruments. A Psalm of Asaph, a Song.

76 God is ^known in Judah;
        His name is ^Bgreat in Israel.
2   His ^tabernacle is in Salem;

His ^Bdwelling place also is in
        Zion.
3   There He ^broke the flaming
        arrows,
     The shield, the sword, and the
        weapons of war.   *Selah*
4   You are resplendent,
     More majestic than the
        mountains of prey.
5   The ^stouthearted were
        plundered,
     They sank into sleep;
     And none of the warriors
        could use his hands.
6   At Your rebuke, God of Jacob,
     Both ^rider and horse were
        cast into a dead sleep.
7   You, You *indeed* are to be feared,
     And ^who may stand in Your
        presence, once You are
        angry?
8   You caused judgment to be
        heard from heaven;
     The earth ^feared and was still
9   When God ^arose to judgment,
     To save all the humble of the
        earth.   *Selah*
10   For the ^wrath of mankind
        shall praise You;
     You will encircle Yourself with
        a remnant of wrath.

11   ^Make vows to the Lord your
        God and ^Bfulfill *them;*
     All who are around Him are to
        bring gifts to Him who is to
        be feared.

75:2 ^Ps 102:13   ^BPs 9:8   75:3 ^Ps 46:6   ^B1 Sam 2:8
75:4 ^Zech 1:21   75:5 ^1 Sam 2:3; Ps 94:4
75:6 ^Ps 3:3   75:7 ^Ps 50:6   ^B1 Sam 2:7
75:8 ^Prov 23:30   ^BObad 16   75:9 ^Ps 22:22; 40:10
75:10 ^1 Sam 2:1; Ps 89:17   76:1 ^Ps 48:3   ^BPs 99:3
76:2 ^Ps 27:5   ^BPs 9:11   76:3 ^Ps 46:9   76:5 ^Is 10:12;
46:12   76:6 ^Ex 15:1; 21; Ps 78:53   76:7 ^Ezra 9:15;
Ps 130:3   76:8 ^1 Chr 16:30; 2 Chr 20:29, 30
76:9 ^Ps 9:7, 8; 74:22   76:10 ^Ex 9:16; Rom 9:17
76:11 ^Eccl 5:4-6   ^BPs 50:14

12 He will cut off the spirit of
      princes;
   He is ^feared by the kings of
      the earth.

**COMFORT IN TROUBLE FROM
RECALLING GOD'S MIGHTY DEEDS.**
For the music director; according
to Jeduthun. A Psalm of Asaph.

77 My voice *rises* to God, and I
      will ^cry aloud;
   My voice *rises* to God, and He
      will listen to me.
2 In the ^day of my trouble I
      sought the Lord;
   In the night my hand was
      stretched out and did not
      grow weary;
   My soul ^Brefused to be
      comforted.
3 *When* I remember God, then I
      am ^restless;
   When I sigh, then ^Bmy spirit
      feels weak.   *Selah*
4 You have held my eyelids
      open;
   I am so troubled that I ^cannot
      speak.
5 I have considered the ^days of
      old,
   The years of long ago.
6 I will remember my song in the
      night;
   I ^will meditate with my
      heart,
   And my spirit ponders:
7 Will the Lord ^reject forever?
   And will He ^Bnever be
      favorable again?
8 Has His ^favor ceased forever?
   Has *His* ^Bpromise come to an
      end forever?
9 Has God forgotten to be
      gracious,
   Or has He in anger withdrawn
      His ^compassion?   *Selah*

10 Then I said, "It is my grief,
   That the ^right hand of the
      Most High has changed."
11 I shall remember the ^deeds of
      the LORD;
   I will certainly ^remember
      Your wonders of old.
12 I will ^meditate on all Your
      work,
   And on Your deeds with
      thanksgiving.
13 Your way, God, is holy;
   ^What god is great like our
      God?
14 You are the ^God who works
      wonders;
   You have made known
      Your strength among the
      peoples.
15 By Your power You have
      ^redeemed Your people,
   The sons of Jacob and
      ^BJoseph.   *Selah*
16 The ^waters saw You, God;
   The waters saw You, they were
      in anguish;
   The ocean depths also
      trembled.
17 The ^clouds poured out water;
   The skies sounded out;
   Your arrows flashed here and
      there.
18 The ^sound of Your thunder
      was in the whirlwind;
   The lightning lit up the
      world;
   The earth trembled and
      shook.

76:12 ^A Ps 47:2   77:1 ^A Ps 3:4; 142:1   77:2 ^A Ps 50:15
^B Gen 37:35   77:3 ^A Ps 42:5, 11   ^B Ps 61:2
77:4 ^A Ps 39:9   77:5 ^A Deut 32:7; Ps 44:1   77:6 ^A Ps 4:4
77:7 ^A Ps 44:9   ^B Ps 85:1, 5   77:8 ^A Ps 89:49   ^B 2 Pet 3:9
77:9 ^A Ps 25:6; 40:11   77:10 ^A Ps 44:2, 3
77:11 ^A Ps 105:5; 143:5   77:12 ^A Ps 145:5
77:13 ^A Ex 15:11; Ps 71:19   77:14 ^A Ps 72:18
77:15 ^A Ex 6:6   ^B Ps 80:1   77:16 ^A Ex 14:21; Ps 114:3
77:17 ^A Judg 5:4   77:18 ^A Ps 18:13; 104:7

¹⁹ Your ^Away was in the sea
And Your paths in the mighty
   waters,
And Your footprints were not
   known.
²⁰ You ^Aled Your people like a flock
By the hand of ^BMoses and
   Aaron.

**GOD'S GUIDANCE OF HIS PEOPLE IN
SPITE OF THEIR UNFAITHFULNESS.**
A Maskil of Asaph.

78 ^AListen, my people, to my
   instruction;
Incline your ears to the words
   of my mouth.
² I will ^Aopen my mouth in a
   parable;
I will tell riddles of old,
³ Which we have heard and
   known,
And ^Aour fathers have told us.
⁴ We will ^Anot conceal them
   from their children,
But we will ^Btell the generation
   to come the praises of the
   Lord,
And His power and His
   wondrous works that He has
   done.

⁵ For He established a
   ^Atestimony in Jacob,
And appointed a law in Israel,
Which He commanded our
   fathers
That they were to ^Bteach them
   to their children,
⁶ So that the generation to come
   would know, the children *yet*
   to be born,
That they would arise and ^Atell
   them to their children,
⁷ So that they would put their
   confidence in God
And ^Anot forget the works of
   God,

But ^Bcomply with His
   commandments,
⁸ And ^Anot be like their fathers,
A stubborn and rebellious
   generation,
A generation that did not
   prepare its heart
And whose spirit was not
   faithful to God.

⁹ The sons of Ephraim were
   archers equipped with bows,
Yet ^Athey turned back on the
   day of battle.
¹⁰ They ^Adid not keep the
   covenant of God
And refused to ^Bwalk in His Law;
¹¹ They ^Aforgot His deeds
And His miracles that He had
   shown them.
¹² ^AHe performed wonders before
   their fathers
In the land of Egypt, *in* the
   ^Bfield of Zoan.
¹³ He ^Adivided the sea and caused
   them to pass through,
And He made the waters stand
   ^Bup like a heap.
¹⁴ Then He led them with the
   cloud by day
And all the night with a ^Alight
   of fire.
¹⁵ He ^Asplit the rocks in the
   wilderness
And gave *them* plenty to drink
   like the ocean depths.
¹⁶ He ^Abrought forth streams
   from the rock
And made waters run down
   like rivers.

77:19 ^AIs 51:10; Hab 3:15   77:20 ^AEx 13:21   ^BEx 6:26
78:1 ^AIs 51:4   78:2 ^APs 49:4; Matt 13:35   78:3 ^APs 44:1
78:4 ^AEx 12:26   ^BEx 13:8, 14   78:5 ^APs 19:7   ^BDeut 4:9
78:6 ^ADeut 11:19   78:7 ^ADeut 4:9   ^BDeut 4:2
78:8 ^A2 Kin 17:14; 2 Chr 30:7   78:9 ^AJudg 20:39;
Ps 78:57   78:10 ^AJudg 2:20   ^BPs 119:1
78:11 ^APs 106:13   78:12 ^AEx chs 7-12   ^BNum 13:22
78:13 ^AEx 14:21   ^BEx 15:8   78:14 ^AEx 14:24
78:15 ^AEx 17:6; Num 20:11   78:16 ^ANum 20:8, 10, 11

17 Yet they still continued to sin
   against Him,
   To ^rebel against the Most
   High in the desert.
18 And in their heart they ^put
   God to the test
   By asking for ^Bfood that suited
   their taste.
19 Then they spoke against God;
   They said, "^ACan God prepare a
   table in the wilderness?
20 "Behold, He ^struck the rock so
   that waters gushed out,
   And streams were overflowing;
   Can He also provide bread?
   Will He prepare ^Bmeat for His
   people?"

21 Therefore the LORD heard and
   was ^full of wrath;
   And a fire was kindled against
   Jacob,
   And anger also mounted
   against Israel,
22 Because they ^did not believe
   in God
   And did not trust in His
   salvation.
23 Yet He commanded the clouds
   above
   And ^opened the doors of
   heaven;
24 He ^rained down manna upon
   them to eat,
   And gave them food from
   heaven.
25 Man ate the bread of angels;
   He sent them food ^in
   abundance.
26 He ^made the east wind blow
   in the sky
   And by His power He directed
   the south wind.
27 When He rained meat upon
   them like the dust,
   Even ^winged fowl like the
   sand of the seas,

28 He let *them* fall in the midst of
   their camp,
   All around their dwellings.
29 So they ^ate and were well
   filled,
   And He satisfied their
   longing.
30 Yet before they had
   abandoned their longing,
   ^While their food was in their
   mouths,
31 The ^anger of God rose against
   them
   And killed some of their
   ^Bstrongest ones,
   And subdued the choice men
   of Israel.
32 In spite of all this they ^still
   sinned
   And ^Bdid not believe in His
   wonderful works.
33 So He brought ^their days to an
   end in futility,
   And their years *to an end* in
   sudden terror.

34 When He killed them, then
   they ^sought Him,
   And they returned and
   searched ^Bdiligently for God;
35 And they remembered that
   God was their ^rock,
   And the Most High God their
   ^BRedeemer.
36 But they ^flattered Him with
   their mouth
   And lied to Him with their
   tongue.

78:17 ^Deut 9:22; Is 63:10   78:18 ^Ex 17:6   ^B Num 11:4
78:19 ^Ex 16:3; Num 11:4   78:20 ^Num 20:11
^B Num 11:18   78:21 ^Num 11:1   78:22 ^Deut 1:32; 9:23
78:23 ^Gen 7:11; Mal 3:10   78:24 ^Ex 16:4
78:25 ^Ex 16:3   78:26 ^Num 11:31   78:27 ^Ex 16:13;
Ps 105:40   78:29 ^Num 11:19, 20   78:30 ^Num 11:33
78:31 ^Num 11:33, 34   ^B Is 10:16
78:32 ^Num chs 14, 16, 17   ^B Num 14:11
78:33 ^Num 14:29, 35   78:34 ^Num 21:7   ^B Ps 63:1
78:35 ^Deut 32:4   ^B Ex 15:13
78:36 ^Ex 24:7, 8; Ezek 33:31

37 For their heart was not
^steadfast toward Him,
Nor were they faithful with
His covenant.
38 But He, being ^compassionate,
^forgave *their* wrongdoing
and did not destroy *them;*
And often He restrained His
anger
And did not stir up all His wrath.
39 So He remembered that they
were *only* ^flesh,
A ^wind that passes and does
not return.

40 How often they ^rebelled
against Him in the
wilderness
And ^grieved Him in the
desert!
41 Again and again they ^tempted
God,
And pained the Holy One of
Israel.
42 They ^did not remember ^His
power,
The day when He redeemed
them from the enemy,
43 When He performed His ^signs
in Egypt
And His ^marvels in the field
of Zoan,
44 And ^turned their rivers to
blood,
And their streams, *so that* they
could not drink.
45 He sent swarms of ^flies
among them that devoured
them,
And ^frogs that destroyed
them.
46 He also gave their crops to the
grasshopper
And the product of their labor
to the ^locust.
47 He destroyed their vines with
^hailstones

And their sycamore trees with
frost.
48 He also turned their ^cattle
over to the hailstones,
And their herds to bolts of
lightning.
49 He ^sent His burning anger
upon them,
Fury and indignation and
trouble,
A band of destroying angels.
50 He leveled a path for His
anger;
He did not spare their souls
from death,
But ^turned their lives over to
the plague,
51 And ^struck all the firstborn in
Egypt,
The ^first and best of their
vigor in the tents of Ham.
52 But He ^led His own people out
like sheep,
And guided them in the
wilderness ^like a flock;
53 He led them ^safely, so that
they did not fear;
But ^the sea engulfed their
enemies.

54 So ^He brought them to His
holy land,
To this hill country which His
right hand had gained.
55 He also ^drove out the nations
from them
And ^apportioned them
as an inheritance by
measurement,

78:37 ^Ps 51:10; 78:8   78:38 ^Ex 34:6   ^Num 14:18-20
78:39 ^Gen 6:3   ^Job 7:7, 16   78:40 ^Ps 95:8, 9
^Ps 95:10   78:41 ^Num 14:22   78:42 ^Judg 8:34
^Ps 44:3   78:43 ^Ps 105:27   ^Ex 4:21   78:44 ^Ex 7:20;
Ps 105:29   78:45 ^Ex 8:24   ^Ex 8:6   78:46 ^Ex 10:14
78:47 ^Ex 9:23-25; Ps 105:32   78:48 ^Ex 9:19
78:49 ^Ex 15:7   78:50 ^Ex 12:29, 30   78:51 ^Ex 12:29
^Gen 49:3   78:52 ^Ex 15:22   ^Ps 77:20
78:53 ^Ex 14:19, 20   ^Ex 14:27, 28   78:54 ^Ex 15:17
78:55 ^Josh 11:16-23   ^Josh 13:7

And had the tribes of Israel
dwell in their tents.
56 Yet they tempted and ^rebelled
against the Most High God
And did not keep His
testimonies,
57 But turned back and ^acted
treacherously like their
fathers;
They turned aside like a
treacherous bow.
58 For they provoked Him with
their ^high places
And moved Him to jealousy
with their ^Bcarved images.
59 When God heard *them,* He was
filled with ^wrath
And He utterly ^Brejected Israel;
60 So that He ^abandoned the
dwelling place at Shiloh,
The tent which He had pitched
among people,
61 And He gave up His strength to
captivity
And His glory ^into the hand
of the enemy.
62 He also ^turned His people
over to the sword,
And was filled with wrath at
His inheritance.
63 ^Fire devoured His young men,
And His ^Bvirgins had no
wedding songs.
64 His ^priests fell by the sword,
And His widows could not
weep.

65 Then the Lord awoke as *if
from* sleep,
Like a ^warrior overcome by
wine.
66 He ^drove His adversaries
backward;
He put on them an everlasting
disgrace.
67 He also ^rejected the tent of
Joseph,

And did not choose the tribe
of Ephraim,
68 But chose the tribe of Judah,
Mount ^Zion, which He loved.
69 And He ^built His sanctuary
like the heights,
Like the earth which He has
established forever.
70 He also ^chose His servant
David
And took him from the
sheepfolds;
71 From the care of the ewes with
nursing lambs He brought
him
To ^shepherd Jacob His
people,
And Israel ^BHis inheritance.
72 So he shepherded them
according to the ^integrity of
his heart,
And guided them with his
skillful hands.

**GRIEVING OVER THE DESTRUCTION OF
JERUSALEM, AND PRAYER FOR HELP.**
A Psalm of Asaph.

79

God, the ^nations have
invaded Your inheritance;
They have defiled Your holy
temple;
They have ^Blaid Jerusalem in
ruins.
2 They have given the ^dead
bodies of Your servants to
the birds of the sky as food,
The flesh of Your godly ones to
the animals of the earth.

78:56 ^Judg 2:11-13; Ps 78:40   78:57 ^Ezek 20:27, 28
78:58 ^Lev 26:30   ^BEx 20:4   78:59 ^Deut 1:34
^BLev 26:30   78:60 ^1 Sam 4:11; Ps 78:67
78:61 ^1 Sam 4:17   78:62 ^Judg 20:21; 1 Sam 4:10
78:63 ^Num 11:1   ^BJer 7:34   78:64 ^1 Sam 4:17; 22:18
78:65 ^Is 42:13   78:66 ^1 Sam 5:6   78:67 ^Ps 78:60
78:68 ^Ps 87:2; 132:13   78:69 ^1 Kin 6:1-38
78:70 ^1 Sam 16:11, 12   78:71 ^2 Sam 5:2   ^B1 Sam 10:1
78:72 ^1 Kin 9:4   79:1 ^Lam 1:10   ^B2 Kin 25:9, 10
79:2 ^Deut 28:26; Jer 7:33

3 They have poured out their
   blood like water all around
   Jerusalem;
   And there was ^no one to bury
   them.
4 We have become a ^disgrace
   before our neighbors,
   An *object of* derision and
   ridicule to those around us.
5 How long, LORD? Will You be
   angry forever?
   Will Your ^jealousy ᴮburn like
   fire?
6 ^Pour out Your wrath upon the
   nations which do not know
   You,
   And upon the kingdoms which
   do not call upon Your name.
7 For they have ^devoured Jacob
   And laid waste his settlement.

8 ^Do not hold us responsible
   for the guilty deeds of *our*
   forefathers;
   Let Your compassion come
   quickly to meet us,
   For we have become very low.
9 ^Help us, God of our salvation,
   for the glory of Your name;
   And save us and forgive our
   sins for the sake of Your
   name.
10 ^Why should the nations say,
   "Where is their God?"
   Let vengeance for the blood
   of Your servants which has
   been shed
   Be known among the nations
   in our sight.
11 Let ^the groaning of the
   prisoner come before You;
   According to the greatness of
   Your power, let those who
   are ^doomed to die remain.
12 And return to our neighbors
   ^seven times *as much* ᴮinto
   their lap

Their taunts with which they
   have taunted You, Lord.
13 So we Your people and the
   ^sheep of Your pasture
   Will give thanks to You
   forever;
   To all generations we will tell
   of Your praise.

**GOD IMPLORED TO RESCUE HIS
PEOPLE FROM THEIR CALAMITIES.**

For the music director; *set to* El
Shoshannim; Eduth. A Psalm of Asaph.

80 Listen, Shepherd of Israel,
   Who leads Joseph like a
   flock;
   You who ^are enthroned *above*
   the cherubim, shine forth!
2 Before Ephraim, Benjamin,
   and Manasseh, ^awaken Your
   power,
   And come to save us!
3 God, ^restore us
   And ᴮmake Your face shine
   upon us, and we will be
   saved.

4 LORD God of armies,
   ^How long will You be angry
   with the prayer of Your
   people?
5 You have fed them with the
   ^bread of tears,
   And You have made them
   drink tears in large measure.
6 You make us an object
   of contention ^to our
   neighbors,
   And our enemies laugh among
   themselves.

79:3 ^Jer 14:16; 16:4   79:4 ^Ps 44:13; 80:6
79:5 ^Deut 29:20   ᴮPs 89:46   79:6 ^Ps 69:24;
Jer 10:25   79:7 ^Ps 53:4   79:8 ^Ps 106:6; Is 64:9
79:9 ^2 Chr 14:11   79:10 ^Ps 42:10; 115:2
79:11 ^Ps 102:20   79:12 ^Gen 4:15   ᴮPs 35:13
79:13 ^Ps 74:1; 95:7   80:1 ^Ex 25:22; 1 Sam 4:4
80:2 ^Ps 35:23   80:3 ^Ps 60:1   ᴮNum 6:25
80:4 ^Ps 79:5; 85:5   80:5 ^Ps 42:3; 102:9
80:6 ^Ps 44:13; 79:4

7 God of armies, restore us
   And make Your face shine
   upon us, and we will be
   saved.

8 You removed a vine from
   Egypt;
   You ^drove out the nations and
   ^planted it.
9 You ^cleared *the ground* before
   it,
   And it ^took deep root and
   filled the land.
10 The mountains were covered
   with its shadow,
   And the cedars of God with its
   ^branches.
11 It was sending out its branches
   ^to the sea
   And its shoots to the
   Euphrates River.
12 Why have You ^broken down
   its hedges,
   So that all who pass *that* way
   pick its *fruit?*
13 A boar from the forest ^eats it
   away,
   And whatever moves in the
   field feeds on it.

14 God of armies, do ^turn back;
   ^Look down from heaven and
   see, and take care of this
   vine,
15 The ^shoot which Your right
   hand has planted,
   And of the son whom You have
   strengthened for Yourself.
16 It is ^burned with fire, it is cut
   down;
   They perish from the rebuke
   of Your face.
17 Let ^Your hand be upon the
   man of Your right hand,
   Upon the son of man whom
   You made strong for
   Yourself.

18 Then we will not ^turn back
   from You;
   ^Revive us, and we will call
   upon Your name.
19 Lord God of armies, ^restore us;
   Make Your face shine *upon us,*
   and we will be saved.

GOD'S GOODNESS AND ISRAEL'S WAYWARDNESS.

For the music director; on the
Gittith. *A Psalm* of Asaph.

81

Sing for joy to God our
   ^strength;
   Shout joyfully to the ^God of
   Jacob.
2 Raise a song, strike ^the
   tambourine,
   The sweet sounding lyre with
   the harp.
3 Blow the trumpet at the ^new
   moon,
   At the full moon, on our ^feast
   day.
4 For it is a statute for Israel,
   An ordinance of the God of
   Jacob.
5 He established it as a
   testimony in Joseph
   When he ^went throughout
   the land of Egypt.
   I heard a language I did not
   know:

6 "I ^relieved his shoulder of the
   burden,
   His hands were freed from the
   basket.
7 "You ^called in trouble and I
   rescued you;

80:8 ^Josh 13:6   ^Jer 11:17   80:9 ^Ex 23:28
^Hos 14:5   80:10 ^Gen 49:22   80:11 ^Ps 72:8
80:12 ^Ps 89:40; Is 5:5   80:13 ^Jer 5:6
80:14 ^Ps 90:13   ^Ps 102:19   80:15 ^Ps 80:8
80:16 ^2 Chr 36:19; Ps 74:8   80:17 ^Ps 89:21
80:18 ^Is 50:5   ^Ps 71:20   80:19 ^Ps 80:3
81:1 ^Ps 46:1   ^Ps 84:8   81:2 ^Ex 15:20; Ps 149:3
81:3 ^Num 10:10   ^Lev 23:24   81:5 ^Ex 11:4
81:6 ^Is 9:4; 10:27   81:7 ^Ex 2:23; 14:10

I answered you in the hiding
    place of thunder;
I put you to the test at the
    waters of Meribah.   *Selah*

8 "Hear, My people, and I will
    admonish you;
    Israel, if you ^would listen to
    Me!

9 "There shall be no ^strange god
    among you;
    Nor shall you worship a
    foreign god.

10 "^I, the LORD, am your God,
    Who brought you up from the
    land of Egypt;
    Open your mouth wide and I
    will fill it.

11 "But My people ^did not listen
    to My voice,
    And Israel did not obey Me.

12 "So I ^gave them over to the
    stubbornness of their heart,
    To walk by their own plans.

13 "Oh that My people would
    listen to Me,
    That Israel would ^walk in My
    ways!

14 "I would quickly ^subdue their
    enemies
    And ^Bturn My hand against
    their adversaries.

15 "^AThose who hate the LORD
    would ^Bpretend to obey Him,
    And their time *of punishment*
    would be forever.

16 "But I would feed you with the
    ^finest of the wheat,
    And with honey from the rock
    I would satisfy you."

UNJUST JUDGMENTS REBUKED.
A Psalm of Asaph.

82 God takes His position in
    His assembly;
He ^judges in the midst of the
    ^Bgods.

2 How long will you ^judge
    unjustly
    And ^Bshow partiality to the
    wicked?   *Selah*

3 ^AVindicate the weak and
    fatherless;
    Do justice to the afflicted and
    destitute.

4 ^ARescue the weak and needy;
    Save *them* from the hand of
    the wicked.

5 They ^do not know nor do they
    understand;
    They ^Bwalk around in
    darkness;
    All the foundations of the
    earth are shaken.

6 I ^said, "You are gods,
    And all of you are sons of the
    Most High.

7 "Nevertheless ^you will die like
    men,
    And fall like one of the
    princes."

8 Arise, God, ^judge the earth!
    For You ^Bpossess all the
    nations.

**GOD IMPLORED TO CONFOUND
HIS ENEMIES.**
A Song, a Psalm of Asaph.

83 God, ^do not remain quiet;
    Do not be silent and, God,
    do not be still.

2 For behold, Your enemies
    ^make an uproar,
    And those who hate You have
    ^Bexalted themselves.

81:8 ^Ps 95:7   81:9 ^Ex 20:3; Deut 5:7   81:10 ^Ex 20:2;
Deut 5:6   81:11 ^Deut 32:15; Ps 106:25   81:12 ^Job 8:4;
Acts 7:42   81:13 ^Ps 128:1; Is 42:24   81:14 ^Ps 18:47
^BAmos 1:8   81:15 ^Rom 1:30   ^BPs 18:44
81:16 ^Deut 32:14; Ps 147:14   82:1 ^2 Chr 19:6
^BEx 21:6   82:2 ^Ps 58:1   ^BDeut 1:17   82:3 ^Deut 24:17;
Ps 10:18   82:4 ^Job 29:12   82:5 ^Ps 14:4   ^BProv 2:13
82:6 ^Ps 82:1; John 10:34   82:7 ^Job 21:32; Ps 49:12
82:8 ^Ps 58:1   ^BPs 2:8   83:1 ^Ps 28:1; 35:22
83:2 ^Ps 2:1   ^BJudg 8:28

3   They ^make shrewd plans
    against Your people,
    And conspire together against
    ^BYour treasured ones.
4   They have said, "Come, and
    ^let's wipe them out as a
    nation,
    So that the ^Bname of Israel will
    no longer be remembered."
5   For they have ^conspired
    together with one mind;
    They make a covenant against
    You:
6   The tents of ^Edom and the
    Ishmaelites,
    Moab and the ^BHagrites;
7   ^Gebal, Ammon, and Amalek,
    Philistia with the inhabitants
    of Tyre;
8   Assyria also has joined them;
    They have become a help to
    the ^children of Lot.   *Selah*
9   Deal with them ^as with Midian,
    As with Sisera *and* Jabin at the
    river of Kishon,
10 Who were destroyed at En-dor,
    Who ^became *like* dung for the
    ground.
11 Make their nobles like ^Oreb
    and Zeeb,
    And all their leaders like
    ^BZebah and Zalmunna,
12 Who said, "^Let's possess for
    ourselves
    The ^Bpastures of God."
13 My God, make them like the
    ^whirling dust,
    Like chaff before the wind.
14 Like ^fire that burns the forest,
    And like a flame that sets the
    mountains on fire,
15 So pursue them ^with Your
    heavy gale,
    And terrify them with Your
    storm.

16 ^Fill their faces with dishonor,
    So that they will seek Your
    name, LORD.
17 May they be ^ashamed and
    dismayed forever,
    And may they be humiliated
    and perish,
18 So that they will know that
    ^You alone, whose name is
    the LORD,
    Are the ^BMost High over all the
    earth.

LONGING FOR THE TEMPLE WORSHIP.
For the music director; on the Gittith.
A Psalm of the sons of Korah.

84 How lovely are Your
    ^dwelling places,
    LORD of armies!
2   My ^soul longed and even
    yearned for the courtyards of
    the LORD;
    My heart and my flesh sing for
    joy to the living God.
3   The bird also has found a house,
    And the swallow a nest for
    herself, where she may put
    her young:
    Your altars, LORD of armies,
    ^My King and my God.
4   ^Blessed are those who dwell
    in Your house!
    They are ever praising
    You.   *Selah*

5   Blessed is the person whose
    ^strength is in You,
    In whose heart are the roads
    to Zion!

83:3 ^Ps 64:2   ^BPs 27:5   83:4 ^Esth 3:6   ^BPs 41:5
83:5 ^Ps 2:2; Dan 6:7   83:6 ^2 Chr 20:10
^B1 Chr 5:10   83:7 ^Josh 13:5; Ezek 27:9
83:8 ^Deut 2:9   83:9 ^Judg 7:1-24   83:10 ^Zeph 1:17
83:11 ^Judg 7:25   ^BJudg 8:12, 21   83:12 ^2 Chr 20:11
^BPs 132:13   83:13 ^Is 17:13   83:14 ^Is 9:18
83:15 ^Job 9:17; Ps 58:9   83:16 ^Job 10:15; Ps 109:29
83:17 ^Ps 35:4; 70:2   83:18 ^Ps 86:10   ^BPs 9:2
84:1 ^Ps 43:3; 132:5   84:2 ^Ps 42:1, 2; 63:1
84:3 ^Ps 5:2   84:4 ^Ps 65:4   84:5 ^Ps 81:1

6 Passing through the Valley of
    [1]Baca they make it a spring;
  The ^early rain also covers it
    with blessings.
7 They ^go from strength to
    strength,
  Every one of them ^Bappears
    before God in Zion.

8 LORD God of armies, hear my
    prayer;
  Listen, ^God of Jacob!   *Selah*
9 See our shield, God,
  And look at the face of ^Your
    anointed.
10 For ^a day in Your courtyards
    is better than a thousand
    elsewhere.
  I would rather stand at the
    threshold of the house of my
    God
  Than live in the tents of
    wickedness.
11 For the LORD God is ^a sun and
    shield;
  The LORD gives grace and glory;
  ^BHe withholds no good thing
    from those who walk with
    integrity.
12 LORD of armies,
  ^Blessed is the person who
    trusts in You!

**PRAYER FOR GOD'S MERCY
UPON THE NATION.**
For the music director. A Psalm
of the sons of Korah.

85 LORD, You showed favor to
    Your land;
  You ^restored the fortunes of
    Jacob.
2 You ^forgave the guilt of Your
    people;
  You ^Bcovered all their sin. *Selah*
3 You withdrew all Your fury;
  You ^turned away from Your
    burning anger.

4 ^Restore us, God of our
    salvation,
  And ^Bcause Your indignation
    toward us to cease.
5 Will ^You be angry with us
    forever?
  Will You prolong Your anger
    to all generations?
6 Will You not ^revive us again,
  So that Your people may
    rejoice in You?
7 Show us Your mercy, LORD,
  And ^grant us Your
    salvation.

8 I will hear what God the LORD
    will say;
  For He will ^speak peace to
    His people, to His godly
    ones;
  And may they not turn back to
    foolishness.
9 Certainly His salvation is
    near to those who fear
    Him,
  That ^glory may dwell in our
    land.
10 ^Graciousness and truth have
    met together;
  ^BRighteousness and peace
    have kissed each other.
11 Truth ^sprouts from the
    earth,
  And righteousness looks
    down from heaven.
12 Indeed, the LORD will give
    what is good,
  And our ^land will yield its
    produce.

84:6 ^Ps 107:35; Joel 2:23 84:7 ^Prov 4:18 ^BEx 34:23
84:8 ^Ps 81:1 84:9 ^1 Sam 16:6; 2 Sam 19:21
84:10 ^Ps 27:4 84:11 ^Is 60:19, 20 ^BPs 34:9, 10
84:12 ^Ps 2:12; 40:4 85:1 ^Ezra 1:11; Ps 14:7
85:2 ^Num 14:19 ^BPs 32:1 85:3 ^Ex 32:12; Deut 13:17
85:4 ^Ps 80:3, 7 ^BDan 9:16 85:5 ^Ps 74:1; 79:5
85:6 ^Ps 71:20; 80:18 85:7 ^Ps 106:4 85:8 ^Ps 29:11;
Hag 2:9 85:9 ^Ps 84:11; Hag 2:7 85:10 ^Ps 25:10
^BPs 72:3 85:11 ^Is 45:8 85:12 ^Lev 26:4; Ps 67:6

84:6 [1]Prob. *Weeping;* or *Balsam-shrubs*

13 ^Righteousness will go before
 Him
 And will make His footsteps
 into a way.

PLEADING AND TRUST.
A Prayer of David.

86

Incline Your ear, Lord, *and*
 answer me;
 For I am ^afflicted and needy.

2 ^Protect my soul, for I am godly;
 You my God, save Your servant
 who trusts in You.

3 Be gracious to me, Lord,
 For ^I call upon You all day long.

4 Make the soul of Your servant
 joyful,
 For to You, Lord, ^I lift up my
 soul.

5 For You, Lord, are ^good, and
 ^Bready to forgive,
 And abundant in mercy to all
 who call upon You.

6 ^Listen, Lord, to my prayer;
 And give *Your* attention to the
 sound of my pleading!

7 On the day of my trouble I will
 call upon You,
 For ^You will answer me.

8 There is no one like You
 among the gods, Lord,
 Nor are there any works ^like
 Yours.

9 ^All nations whom You have
 made will come and worship
 before You, Lord,
 And they will glorify Your name.

10 For You are ^great, and You ^Bdo
 wondrous deeds;
 You alone are God.

11 ^Teach me Your way, Lord;
 I will walk in Your truth;
 ^BUnite my heart to fear Your
 name.

12 I will ^give thanks to You, Lord
 my God, with all my heart,

And I will glorify Your name
 forever.

13 For Your graciousness toward
 me is great,
 And You have ^saved my soul
 from the depths of ¹Sheol.

14 God, arrogant men have ^risen
 up against me,
 And a gang of violent men
 have sought my life,
 And they have not set You
 before them.

15 But You, Lord, are a
 ^compassionate and gracious
 God,
 Slow to anger and abundant in
 mercy and truth.

16 Turn to me, and be gracious
 to me;
 ^Grant Your strength to Your
 servant,
 And save the son of Your
 maidservant.

17 Show me a sign of good,
 That those who hate me may
 see *it* and be ashamed,
 Because You, Lord, ^have
 helped me and comforted me.

THE PRIVILEGES OF CITIZENSHIP
IN ZION.
A Psalm of the sons of Korah. A Song.

87

His ^foundation is in the
 holy mountains.

2 The Lord ^loves the gates of
 Zion
 More than all the *other*
 dwelling places of Jacob.

85:13 ^Ps 89:14   86:1 ^Ps 40:17; 70:5   86:2 ^Ps 25:20
86:3 ^Ps 25:5; 88:9   86:4 ^Ps 25:1; 143:8
86:5 ^Ps 25:8   ^BPs 130:4   86:6 ^Ps 55:1
86:7 ^Ps 17:6   86:8 ^Deut 3:24   86:9 ^Ps 22:27; 66:4
86:10 ^Ps 77:13   ^BEx 15:11   86:11 ^Ps 25:5   ^BJer 32:39
86:12 ^Ps 111:1   86:13 ^Ps 30:3   86:14 ^Ps 54:3
86:15 ^Ps 86:5   86:16 ^Ps 68:35   86:17 ^Ps 118:13
87:1 ^Ps 78:69; Is 28:16   87:2 ^Ps 78:67, 68

86:13 ¹I.e., the netherworld

3   Glorious things are spoken of
       you,
      ^City of God.   *Selah*
4   "I shall mention ¹·^Rahab and
       Babylon among those who
       know Me;
    Behold, Philistia and Tyre with
       Cush:
    'This one was born there.'"
5   But of Zion it will be said,
       "This one and that one were
       born in her";
    And the Most High Himself
       will ^establish her.
6   The LORD will count when He
       ^registers the peoples,
    "This one was born
       there."   *Selah*
7   Then those who sing as *well*
       as those who play the flutes
       will say,
    "All my ^springs *of joy* are in
       you."

A PETITION TO BE SAVED FROM DEATH.
A Song. A Psalm of the sons of
Korah. For the music director;
according to Mahalath Leannoth.
A Maskil of Heman the Ezrahite.

88 LORD, the God of my
       salvation,
    I have cried out by day and in
       the night before You.
2   Let my prayer ^come before
       You;
    Incline Your ear to my cry!
3   For my ^soul has had enough
       troubles,
    And ^my life has approached
       ¹Sheol.
4   I am counted among those
       who ^go down to the pit;
    I have become like a man
       without strength,
5   Abandoned among the dead,
    Like the slain who lie in the
       grave,

Whom You no longer
       remember,
    And they are ^cut off from
       Your hand.
6   You have put me in ^the lowest
       pit,
    In dark places, in the depths.
7   Your wrath ^has rested upon
       me,
    And You have afflicted me
       with all Your waves.   *Selah*
8   You have removed my
       acquaintances far from me;
    You have made me an ^object
       of loathing to them;
    I am ^shut up and cannot go out.
9   My ^eye grows dim from misery;
    I have called upon You every
       day, LORD;
    I have spread out my hands to
       You.
10 Will You perform wonders for
       the dead?
    Or will ^the departed spirits
       rise *and* praise You?   *Selah*
11 Will Your graciousness be
       declared in the grave,
    Your faithfulness in ¹Abaddon?
12 Will Your wonders be made
       known in the ^darkness?
    And Your righteousness in the
       land of forgetfulness?
13 But I, LORD, have cried out ^to
       You for help,
    And ^in the morning my prayer
       comes before You.

87:3 ^Ps 46:4; 48:8   87:4 ^Job 9:13; Ps 89:10
87:5 ^Ps 48:8   87:6 ^Ps 69:28; Is 4:3   87:7 ^Ps 36:9
88:2 ^Ps 18:6   88:3 ^Ps 107:26   ^Ps 107:18
88:4 ^Ps 28:1; 143:7   88:5 ^Ps 31:22; Is 53:8
88:6 ^Ps 86:13; Lam 3:55   88:7 ^Ps 32:4; 39:10
88:8 ^Job 30:10   ^Ps 142:7   88:9 ^Ps 6:7; 31:9
88:10 ^Ps 6:5; 30:9   88:12 ^Job 10:21; Ps 88:6
88:13 ^Ps 30:2   ^Ps 5:3

87:4 ¹I.e., Egypt, as a sea monster; not to be confused
with Rahab in Joshua 2   88:3 ¹I.e., the netherworld
88:11 ¹I.e., place of destruction

14 LORD, why ^do You reject my
    soul?
    Why do You ^Bhide Your face
    from me?
15 I was miserable and ^about to
    die from my youth on;
    I suffer Your terrors; I grow
    weary.
16 Your ^burning anger has
    passed over me;
    Your terrors have ^Bdestroyed
    me.
17 They have ^surrounded me
    like water all day long;
    They have ^Bencircled me
    altogether.
18 You have removed ^lover and
    friend far from me;
    My acquaintances are *in* a
    hiding place.

THE LORD'S COVENANT WITH DAVID AND ISRAEL'S AFFLICTIONS.

A Maskil of Ethan the Ezrahite.

89 I will sing of the
    graciousness of the LORD
    forever;
    To all generations I will make
    Your faithfulness known
    with my mouth.
2 For I have said, "Graciousness
    will be built up forever;
    In the heavens You will
    establish Your ^faithfulness."
3 "I have made a covenant with
    ^My chosen;
    I have ^Bsworn to My servant
    David,
4 I will establish your
    ^descendants forever
    And build up your throne to all
    generations."   *Selah*
5 The heavens will praise Your
    wonders, LORD;
    Your faithfulness also ^in the
    assembly of the ^Bholy ones.

6 For who in the skies is
    comparable to the LORD?
    Who among the ^sons of the
    mighty is like the LORD,
7 A God ^greatly feared in the
    council of the holy ones,
    And ^Bawesome above all those
    who are around Him?
8 LORD God of armies, ^who is
    like You, mighty LORD?
    Your faithfulness also
    surrounds You.
9 You rule the surging of the
    sea;
    When its waves rise, You ^calm
    them.
10 You Yourself crushed ^1,^ARahab
    like one who is slain;
    You scattered Your enemies
    with Your mighty arm.
11 The ^heavens are Yours, the
    earth also is Yours;
    The world and all it contains,
    You have established them.
12 The ^north and the south, You
    have created them;
    ^BTabor and Hermon shout for
    joy at Your name.
13 You have a strong arm;
    Your hand is mighty, Your
    ^right hand is exalted.
14 ^Righteousness and justice
    are the foundation of Your
    throne;
    ^BMercy and truth go before
    You.

88:14 ^Ps 43:2   ^BJob 13:24   88:15 ^Prov 24:11
88:16 ^2 Chr 28:11   ^BLam 3:54   88:17 ^Ps 118:10-12
^BPs 17:11   88:18 ^Job 19:13; Ps 88:8   89:2 ^Ps 36:5;
119:90   89:3 ^1 Kin 8:16   ^BPs 132:11
89:4 ^2 Sam 7:16   89:5 ^Ps 149:1   ^BJob 5:1
89:6 ^Ps 29:1; 82:1   89:7 ^Ps 47:2   ^BPs 96:4
89:8 ^Ps 35:10; 71:19   89:9 ^Ps 65:7; 107:29
89:10 ^Ps 87:4; Is 30:7   89:11 ^Gen 1:1; 1 Chr 29:11
89:12 ^Job 26:7   ^BJosh 19:22   89:13 ^Ps 98:1; 118:16
89:14 ^Ps 97:2   ^BPs 85:13

89:10 ^1 I.e., Egypt, as a sea monster; not to be
confused with Rahab in Joshua 2

15 Blessed are the people who
     know the joyful sound!
   LORD, they walk in the ^light of
     Your face.
16 In ^Your name they rejoice all
     the day,
   And by Your righteousness
     they are exalted.
17 For You are the glory of ^their
     strength,
   And by Your favor our horn is
     exalted.
18 For our ^shield belongs to the
     LORD,
   And our king to the ^Holy One
     of Israel.

19 Once You spoke in vision to
     Your godly ones,
   And said, "I have given help to
     one who is ^mighty;
   I have exalted one ^chosen
     from the people.
20 "I have ^found My servant
     David;
   With My holy oil I have
     anointed him,
21 With whom ^My hand will be
     established;
   My arm also will strengthen
     him.
22 "The enemy will not deceive
     him,
   Nor will the ^son of
     wickedness afflict him.
23 "But I will ^crush his adversaries
     before him,
   And strike those who hate
     him.
24 "My ^faithfulness and My favor
     will be with him,
   And in My name his ^horn will
     be exalted.
25 "I will also place his hand ^on
     the sea,
   And his right hand on the
     rivers.

26 "He will call to Me, 'You are ^my
     Father,
   My God, and the ^rock of my
     salvation.'
27 "I will also make him *My*
     ^firstborn,
   The ^highest of the kings of
     the earth.
28 "I will maintain My favor for
     him forever,
   And My ^covenant shall be
     confirmed to him.
29 "So I will establish his
     ^descendants forever,
   And his throne ^as the days of
     heaven.

30 "If his sons ^abandon My Law
   And do not walk in My
     judgments,
31 If they violate My statutes
   And do not keep My
     commandments,
32 Then I will punish their
     wrongdoing with the ^rod,
   And their guilt with
     afflictions.
33 "But I will not withhold ^My
     favor from him,
   Nor deal falsely in My
     faithfulness.
34 "I will not violate My ^covenant,
   Nor will I ^alter the utterance
     of My lips.
35 "¹Once I have ^sworn by My
     holiness;
   I will not lie to David.

89:15 ^Ps 4:6; 44:3   89:16 ^Ps 105:3   89:17 ^Ps 28:8
89:18 ^Ps 47:9   ^Ps 71:22   89:19 ^2 Sam 17:10
^1 Kin 11:34   89:20 ^1 Sam 13:14; 16:1-12
89:21 ^Ps 18:35; 80:17   89:22 ^2 Sam 7:10; Ps 125:3
89:23 ^2 Sam 7:9; Ps 18:40   89:24 ^Ps 89:1
^Ps 132:17   89:25 ^Ps 72:8   89:26 ^2 Sam 7:14
^2 Sam 22:47   89:27 ^Ex 4:22   ^Num 24:7
89:28 ^Ps 89:3, 34   89:29 ^Ps 18:50   ^Deut 11:21
89:30 ^2 Sam 7:14; Ps 119:53   89:32 ^Job 9:34; 21:9
89:33 ^2 Sam 7:15   89:34 ^Deut 7:9   ^Num 23:19
89:35 ^Ps 60:6; Amos 4:2

89:35 ¹Or *One thing*

36 "His descendants shall endure
    forever,
    And his ᴬthrone ᴮas the sun
    before Me.
37 "It shall be established forever
    ᴬlike the moon,
    And a ᴮwitness in the sky is
    faithful."   *Selah*

38 But You have ᴬrejected and
    ᴮrefused,
    You have been full of wrath
    against Your anointed.
39 You have ¹,ᴬrepudiated the
    covenant of Your servant;
    You have profaned his crown
    in the dust.
40 You have ᴬbroken down all his
    walls;
    You have ᴮbrought his
    strongholds to ruin.
41 ᴬAll who pass along the way
    plunder him;
    He has become a disgrace to
    his neighbors.
42 You have ᴬexalted the right
    hand of his adversaries;
    You have ᴮmade all his enemies
    rejoice.
43 You also turn back the edge of
    his sword,
    And have ᴬnot made him stand
    in battle.
44 You have put an end to his
    ᴬsplendor
    And cast his throne to the
    ground.
45 You have ᴬshortened the days
    of his youth;
    You have covered him with
    shame.   *Selah*

46 ᴬHow long, Lᴏʀᴅ?
    Will You hide Yourself
    forever?
    Will Your ᴮwrath burn like
    fire?

47 ᴬRemember what my lifespan is;
    For what ᴮfutility You have
    created all the sons of
    mankind!
48 What man can live and not
    ᴬsee death?
    Can he save his soul from the
    power of ¹Sheol?   *Selah*

49 Where are Your former acts of
    favor, Lord,
    Which You ᴬswore to David in
    Your faithfulness?
50 Remember, Lord, the ᴬtaunt
    against Your servants;
    How I carry in my heart *the
    taunts of* all the many peoples,
51 With which ᴬYour enemies
    have taunted, Lᴏʀᴅ,
    With which they have taunted
    the footsteps of Your anointed.

52 ᴬBlessed be the Lᴏʀᴅ forever!
    Amen and Amen.

BOOK 4

GOD'S ETERNITY AND THE BREVITY OF HUMAN LIFE.
A Prayer of Moses, the man of God.

90 Lord, You have been our
    ᴬdwelling place in all
    generations.
2   Before ᴬthe mountains were
    born
    Or You gave birth to the earth
    and the world,

89:36 ᴬPs 72:5   ᴮPs 72:17   89:37 ᴬPs 72:5   ᴮJob 16:19
89:38 ᴬPs 44:9   ᴮDeut 32:19   89:39 ᴬPs 78:59; Lam 2:7
89:40 ᴬPs 80:12   ᴮLam 2:2, 5   89:41 ᴬPs 80:12
89:42 ᴬPs 13:2   ᴮPs 80:6   89:43 ᴬPs 44:10
89:44 ᴬEzek 28:7   89:45 ᴬPs 102:23   89:46 ᴬPs 13:1
ᴮPs 79:5   89:47 ᴬJob 7:7   ᴮPs 39:5   89:48 ᴬPs 22:29;
49:9   89:49 ᴬ2 Sam 7:15; Jer 30:9   89:50 ᴬPs 69:9;
74:18, 22   89:51 ᴬPs 74:10, 18, 22   89:52 ᴬPs 41:13; 72:19
90:1 ᴬDeut 33:27; Ps 71:3   90:2 ᴬJob 15:7

89:39 ¹I.e., scornfully rejected   89:48 ¹I.e., the
netherworld

Even ᴮfrom everlasting to
everlasting, You are God.

3 You ᴬturn mortals back into dust
And say, "Return, you sons of
mankind."

4 For ᴬa thousand years in Your
sight
Are like ᴮyesterday when it
passes by,
Or *like* a watch in the night.

5 You ᴬhave swept them away
like a flood, they fall asleep;
In the morning they are like
grass that sprouts anew.

6 In the morning it ᴬflourishes
and sprouts anew;
Toward evening it wilts and
ᴮwithers away.

7 For we have been ᴬconsumed
by Your anger,
And we have been terrified by
Your wrath.

8 You have ᴬplaced our guilty
deeds before You,
Our ᴮhidden *sins* in the light of
Your presence.

9 For ᴬall our days have
dwindled away in Your fury;
We have finished our years like
a sigh.

10 As for the days of our life, they
contain seventy years,
Or if due to strength, eighty
years,
Yet their pride is *only* ᴬtrouble
and tragedy;
For it quickly passes, and we
ᴮdisappear.

11 Who understands the ᴬpower
of Your anger
And Your fury, according to
the fear that is due You?

12 So ᴬteach *us* to number our days,
That we may ᴮpresent *to You* a
heart of wisdom.

13 Do ᴬreturn, Lᴏʀᴅ; how long
will it be?
And be sorry for Your servants.

14 ᴬSatisfy us in the morning with
Your graciousness,
That we may sing for joy and
rejoice all our days.

15 ᴬMake us glad according to the
days You have afflicted us,
And the ᴮyears we have seen evil.

16 Let Your ᴬwork appear to Your
servants
And Your ᴮmajesty to their
children.

17 May the ᴬkindness of the Lord
our God be upon us;
And ᴮconfirm for us the work
of our hands;
Yes, confirm the work of our
hands.

SECURITY OF ONE WHO TRUSTS IN THE LORD.

91 One who dwells in the
ᴬshelter of the Most High
Will lodge in the ᴮshadow of
the Almighty.

2 I will say to the Lᴏʀᴅ, "My
ᴬrefuge and my fortress,
My God, in whom I ᴮtrust!"

3 For it is He who rescues you
from the ᴬnet of the trapper
And from the deadly ᴮplague.

4 He will ᴬcover you with His
pinions,
And under His wings you may
take refuge;
His ᴮfaithfulness is a shield
and wall.

90:2 ᴮPs 93:2 90:3ᴬGen 3:19; Job 34:14, 15
90:4ᴬ2 Pet 3:8 ᴮPs 39:5 90:5ᴬJob 22:16; 27:20
90:6ᴬJob 14:2 ᴮJames 1:11 90:7ᴬPs 39:11
90:8ᴬPs 50:21 ᴮPs 19:12 90:9ᴬPs 78:33
90:10ᴬEccl 12:2-7 ᴮJob 20:8 90:11ᴬPs 76:7
90:12ᴬDeut 32:29 ᴮProv 2:1-6 90:13ᴬPs 6:4; 80:14
90:14ᴬPs 36:8; 65:4 90:15ᴬPs 86:4 ᴮDeut 2:14-16
90:16ᴬDeut 32:4 ᴮ1 Kin 8:11 90:17ᴬPs 27:4 ᴮPs 37:23
91:1ᴬPs 27:5 ᴮPs 17:8 91:2ᴬPs 14:6 ᴮPs 25:2
91:3ᴬPs 124:7 ᴮ1 Kin 8:37 91:4ᴬIs 51:16 ᴮPs 40:11

5   You ^will not be afraid of the
    terror by night,
    Or of the ^Barrow that flies by
    day;
6   Of the ^plague that stalks in
    darkness,
    Or of the destruction that
    devastates at noon.
7   A thousand may fall at your
    side
    And ten thousand at your
    right hand,
    But ^it shall not approach you.
8   You will only look on with
    your eyes
    And ^see the retaliation
    against the wicked.
9   For you have made the LORD,
    ^my refuge,
    The Most High, ^Byour dwelling
    place.
10 ^No evil will happen to you,
    Nor will any plague come near
    your tent.

11 For He will give ^His angels
    orders concerning you,
    To protect you in all your ways.
12 On their hands they will ^lift
    you up,
    So that you do not strike your
    foot against a stone.
13 You will ^walk upon the lion
    and cobra,
    You will trample the young
    lion and the serpent.

14 "^Because he has loved Me, I
    will save him;
    I will ^Bset him *securely* on high,
    because he has known My
    name.
15 "He will ^call upon Me, and I
    will answer him;
    I will be with him in trouble;
    I will rescue him and honor
    him.

16 "I will satisfy him with a ^long
    life,
    And ^Bshow him My salvation."

PRAISE FOR THE LORD'S GOODNESS.
A Psalm, a Song for the Sabbath day.

92 It is ^good to give thanks to
        the LORD
    And to sing praises to Your
    name, Most High;
2   To ^declare Your goodness in
    the morning
    And Your ^Bfaithfulness by
    night,
3   With the ^ten-stringed lute
    and with the harp,
    With resounding music on the
    ^lyre.
4   For You, LORD, have made me
    joyful by what You ^have
    done,
    I will sing for joy over the
    ^Bworks of Your hands.

5   How ^great are Your works,
    LORD!
    Your thoughts are very deep.
6   A ^stupid person has no
    knowledge,
    Nor does a ^foolish person
    understand this:
7   When the wicked ^sprouted up
    like grass
    And all who did injustice
    flourished,
    It *was only* that they might be
    ^Bdestroyed forevermore.
8   But You, LORD, are ^on high
    forever.

91:5 ^Job 5:19-23   ^B Ps 64:4   91:6 ^2 Kin 19:35;
Ps 91:10   91:7 ^Gen 7:23; Josh 14:10   91:8 ^Ps 37:34;
58:10   91:9 ^Ps 91:2   ^B Ps 90:1   91:10 ^Prov 12:21
91:11 ^Ps 34:7; Matt 4:6   91:12 ^Matt 4:6; Luke 4:11
91:13 ^Judg 14:6; Dan 6:22   91:14 ^Ps 145:20
^B Ps 59:1   91:15 ^Job 12:4; Ps 50:15   91:16 ^Deut 6:2
^B Ps 50:23   92:1 ^Ps 147:1   92:2 ^Ps 59:16   ^B Ps 89:1
92:3 ^1 Sam 10:5; 1 Chr 13:8   92:4 ^Ps 40:5   ^B Ps 8:6
92:5 ^Ps 40:5; 111:2   92:6 ^Ps 49:10; 73:22
92:7 ^Job 12:6   ^B Ps 37:38   92:8 ^Ps 83:18; 93:4

9 For, behold, Your enemies,
  Lord,
  For, behold, ^Your enemies will
    perish;
  All who do injustice will be
    ^Bscattered.

10 But You have exalted my horn
   like *that of* the wild ox;
   I have been ^anointed with
     fresh oil.

11 And my eye has ^looked at my
   enemies,
   My ears hear of the evildoers
     who rise up against me.

12 The ^righteous person will
   flourish like the palm tree,
   He will grow like a cedar in
     Lebanon.

13 ^Planted in the house of the
   Lord,
   They will flourish in the
     courtyards of our God.

14 They will still ^yield fruit in
   advanced age;
   They will be full of sap and
     very green,

15 To declare that the Lord is just;
   He is my rock, and there is ^no
     malice in Him.

THE MAJESTY OF THE LORD.

93 ^The Lord reigns, He is
   clothed with majesty;
   The Lord has ^Bclothed and
     encircled Himself with
     strength.
   Indeed, the world is *firmly*
     established; it will not be
     moved.

2 Your ^throne is established
  from of old;
  You ^Bare from eternity.

3 The ^floods have lifted up, Lord,
  The floods have lifted up their
    voice,

The floods lift up their
  pounding waves.

4 More than the sounds of
  many waters,
  Than the mighty breakers of
    the sea,
  The Lord ^on high is mighty.

5 Your ^testimonies are fully
  confirmed;
  Holiness is pleasing to Your
    house,
  Lord, forevermore.

THE LORD IMPLORED TO AVENGE HIS PEOPLE.

94 Lord, God of ^vengeance,
   God of vengeance, shine
   forth!

2 Rise up, ^Judge of the earth,
  Pay back retribution to the
    proud.

3 How long, Lord, shall the
  wicked—
  How long shall the ^wicked
    triumph?

4 They pour out *words,* they
  speak arrogantly;
  All who do injustice ^boast.

5 They ^crush Your people, Lord,
  And ^Bafflict Your inheritance.

6 They ^kill the widow and the
  stranger
  And murder the orphans.

7 ^They have said, "The Lord
  does not see,
  Nor does the God of Jacob
    perceive."

8 Pay attention, you ^stupid ones
  among the people;

92:9 ^Ps 37:20 ^B Ps 68:1 92:10 ^Ps 23:5; 45:7
92:11 ^Ps 54:7; 91:8 92:12 ^Num 24:6; Ps 1:3
92:13 ^Ps 80:15; Is 60:21 92:14 ^Prov 11:30; Is 37:31
92:15 ^Rom 9:14 93:1 ^Ps 96:10 ^B Ps 65:6
93:2 ^Ps 45:6 ^B Ps 90:2 93:3 ^Ps 96:11; 98:7, 8
93:4 ^Ps 65:7; 89:6, 9 93:5 ^Ps 19:7 94:1 ^Deut 32:35;
Is 35:4 94:2 ^Gen 18:25 94:3 ^Job 20:5
94:4 ^Ps 10:3; 52:1 94:5 ^Is 3:15 ^B Ps 79:1
94:6 ^Is 10:2 94:7 ^Job 22:13; Ps 10:11 94:8 ^Ps 92:6

And when will you understand, ^foolish ones?

9 He who ^planted the ear, does He not hear?
Or He who formed the eye, does He not see?

10 He who ^disciplines the nations, will He not rebuke,
He who ^Bteaches mankind knowledge?

11 The Lord ^knows human thoughts,
That they are *mere* breath.

12 Blessed is the man whom You discipline, Lord,
And ^whom You teach from Your Law,

13 So that You may grant him ^relief from the ^Bdays of adversity,
Until a pit is dug for the wicked.

14 For the Lord will not abandon His people,
Nor will He ^abandon His inheritance.

15 For ^judgment will again be righteous,
And all the upright in heart will follow it.

16 Who will ^stand up for me against evildoers?
Who will take his stand for me ^Bagainst those who do injustice?

17 If ^the Lord had not been my help,
My soul would soon have dwelt *in the land of* silence.

18 If I should say, "^My foot has slipped,"
Your faithfulness, Lord, will support me.

19 When my anxious thoughts multiply within me,
Your ^comfort delights my soul.

20 Can a ^throne of destruction be allied with You,
One ^Bwhich devises mischief by decree?

21 They band themselves together against the life of the righteous
And ^condemn the innocent to death.

22 But the Lord has been my ^refuge,
And my God the ^Brock of my refuge.

23 He has ^brought back their injustice upon them,
And He will ^Bdestroy them in their evil;
The Lord our God will destroy them.

PRAISE TO THE LORD AND WARNING AGAINST UNBELIEF.

95

Come, let's sing for joy to the Lord,
Let's shout joyfully to ^the rock of our salvation.

2 Let's ^come before His presence ^Bwith a song of thanksgiving,
Let's shout joyfully to Him in songs *with instruments*.

3 For the Lord is a ^great God
And a great King ^Babove all gods,

4 In whose hand are the ^depths of the earth,
The peaks of the mountains are also His.

94:9 ^Ex 4:11; Prov 20:12   94:10 ^Ps 44:2   ^BJob 35:11
94:11 ^Job 11:11; 1 Cor 3:20   94:12 ^Ps 119:171
94:13 ^Job 34:29   ^BPs 49:5   94:14 ^Ps 37:28
94:15 ^Ps 97:2; Is 42:3   94:16 ^Num 10:35   ^BPs 17:13
94:17 ^Ps 124:1, 2   94:18 ^Ps 38:16; 73:2
94:19 ^Is 57:18; 66:13   94:20 ^Amos 6:3   ^BPs 50:16
94:21 ^Ex 23:7; Ps 106:38   94:22 ^Ps 9:9   ^BPs 18:2
94:23 ^Ps 7:16   ^BGen 19:15   95:1 ^Ps 89:26
95:2 ^Mic 6:6   ^BPs 100:4   95:3 ^Ps 48:1   ^BPs 96:4
95:4 ^Ps 135:6

⁵ The sea is His, for it was He
  ᴬwho made it,
  And His hands formed the
  dry land.

⁶ Come, let's worship and bow
  down,
  Let's kneel before the Lᴏʀᴅ our
  ᴬMaker.

⁷ For He is our God,
  And we are the people of His
  pasture and the sheep of His
  hand.
  ᴬToday, if you will hear His
  voice,

⁸ Do not harden your hearts as
  at ᴬMeribah,
  As on the day of Massah in the
  wilderness,

⁹ "When your fathers ᴬput Me to
  the test,
  They tested Me, though they
  had seen My work.

¹⁰ "For ᴬforty years I was disgusted
  with *that* generation,
  And said they are a people
  who err in their heart,
  And they do not know My
  ways.

¹¹ "Therefore I ᴬswore in My
  anger,
  They certainly shall not enter
  My ᴮrest."

A CALL TO WORSHIP THE LORD
THE RIGHTEOUS JUDGE.

96 Sing to the Lᴏʀᴅ a ᴬnew
  song;
  Sing to the Lᴏʀᴅ, all the earth.

² Sing to the Lᴏʀᴅ, bless His
  name;
  ᴬProclaim the good news of His
  salvation from day to day.

³ Tell of ᴬHis glory among the
  nations,
  His wonderful deeds among
  all the peoples.

⁴ For great is the Lᴏʀᴅ, and
  greatly to be praised;
  He is to be ᴬfeared ᴮabove all
  gods.

⁵ For ᴬall the gods of the peoples
  are idols,
  But ᴮthe Lᴏʀᴅ made the
  heavens.

⁶ ᴬSplendor and majesty are
  before Him,
  Strength and beauty are in His
  sanctuary.

⁷ Ascribe to the Lᴏʀᴅ, you
  families of the peoples,
  ᴬAscribe to the Lᴏʀᴅ glory and
  strength.

⁸ Ascribe to the Lᴏʀᴅ the ᴬglory
  of His name;
  Bring an offering and come
  into His courtyards.

⁹ Worship the Lᴏʀᴅ in holy attire;
  ᴬTremble before Him, all the
  earth.

¹⁰ Say among the nations, "ᴬThe
  Lᴏʀᴅ reigns;
  Indeed, the ᴬworld is *firmly*
  established, it will not be
  moved;
  He will judge the peoples fairly."

¹¹ May the ᴬheavens be joyful,
  and may the earth rejoice;
  May the sea roar, and all it
  contains;

¹² May the ᴬfield be jubilant, and
  all that is in it.
  Then all the ᴮtrees of the forest
  will sing for joy

95:5 ᴬGen 1:9, 10; Ps 146:6   95:6 ᴬPs 100:3; 149:2
95:7 ᴬHeb 3:7-11, 15; 4:7   95:8 ᴬEx 17:2-7; Num 20:13
95:9 ᴬNum 14:22; Ps 78:18   95:10 ᴬActs 7:36; 13:18
95:11 ᴬNum 14:23, 28-30   ᴮDeut 12:9   96:1 ᴬPs 40:3
96:2 ᴬPs 71:15   96:3 ᴬPs 145:12   96:4 ᴬPs 89:7
ᴮPs 95:3   96:5 ᴬ1 Chr 16:26   ᴮPs 115:15
96:6 ᴬPs 104:1   96:7 ᴬ1 Chr 16:28, 29; Ps 29:1, 2
96:8 ᴬPs 79:9; 115:1   96:9 ᴬPs 33:8; 114:7
96:10 ᴬPs 93:1; 97:1   96:11 ᴬPs 69:34; Is 49:13
96:12 ᴬPs 65:13   ᴮIs 44:23

13 Before the LORD, ^for He is
   coming,
   For He is coming to judge the
   earth.
   ^BHe will judge the world in
   righteousness,
   And the peoples in His
   faithfulness.

THE LORD'S POWER AND DOMINION.

97 ^AThe LORD reigns, may the
         earth rejoice;
   May the many ^Bislands be
   joyful.
2 Clouds and thick darkness
   surround Him;
   ^ARighteousness and justice
   are the foundation of His
   throne.
3 ^AFire goes before Him
   And ^Bburns up His enemies all
   around.
4 His ^Alightning lit up the world;
   The earth saw *it* and trembled.
5 The mountains ^Amelted like wax
   at the presence of the LORD,
   At the presence of the ^BLord of
   the whole earth.
6 The ^Aheavens declare His
   righteousness,
   And all the peoples have seen
   His glory.

7 May all those be ashamed who
   serve ^Acarved images,
   Who boast in ^Bidols;
   Worship Him, all you gods.
8 Zion heard *this* and ^Awas
   joyful,
   And the daughters of Judah
   have rejoiced
   Because of Your judgments,
   LORD.
9 For You are the LORD ^AMost
   High over all the earth;
   You are exalted far ^Babove all
   gods.

10 ^AHate evil, you who love the
   LORD,
   Who watches over the souls of
   His godly ones;
   He saves them from the hand
   of the wicked.
11 ^ALight is sown *like seed* for the
   righteous,
   And ^Bgladness for the upright
   in heart.
12 Be joyful in the LORD, you
   righteous ones,
   And ^Apraise the mention of His
   holy name.

A CALL TO PRAISE THE LORD
FOR HIS RIGHTEOUSNESS.

A Psalm.

98 Sing a new song to the LORD,
         For He has done wonderful
   things,
   His ^Aright hand and His ^Bholy
   arm have gained the victory
   for Him.
2 ^AThe LORD has made His
   salvation known;
   He has ^Brevealed His
   righteousness in the sight of
   the nations.
3 He has ^Aremembered His
   graciousness and His
   faithfulness to the house of
   Israel;
   ^BAll the ends of the earth have
   seen the salvation of our God.

4 ^AShout joyfully to the LORD, all
   the earth;
   Be cheerful and sing for joy
   and sing praises.

96:13 ^APs 98:9   ^BRev 19:11   97:1 ^APs 96:10
^BIs 42:10, 12   97:2 ^APs 89:14   97:3 ^APs 18:8   ^BMal 4:1
97:4 ^AEx 19:16; Ps 77:18   97:5 ^APs 46:6   ^BJosh 3:11
97:6 ^APs 19:1; 50:6   97:7 ^APs 78:58   ^BPs 106:36
97:8 ^APs 48:11; Zeph 3:14   97:9 ^APs 83:18   ^BEx 18:11
97:10 ^APs 34:14; Prov 8:13   97:11 ^AJob 22:28
^BPs 64:10   97:12 ^APs 30:4   98:1 ^AEx 15:6   ^BIs 52:10
98:2 ^AIs 52:10   ^BIs 62:2   98:3 ^ALuke 1:54, 72
^BPs 22:27   98:4 ^APs 100:1

5 Sing praises to the Lord with
   the lyre,
   With the lyre and the ^sound
   of melody.
6 With ^trumpets and the sound
   of the horn
   Shout joyfully before the King,
   the Lord.

7 May the ^sea roar and all it
   contains,
   The world and those who
   dwell in it.
8 May the ^rivers clap their hands,
   May the mountains sing
   together for joy
9 Before the Lord, for He is
   coming to ^judge the earth;
   He will judge the world with
   righteousness
   And ^Bthe peoples with fairness.

PRAISE TO THE LORD FOR HIS
FAITHFULNESS TO ISRAEL.

99 ^The Lord reigns, the
   peoples tremble!
   He ^Bsits *enthroned above* the
   cherubim, the earth quakes!
2 The Lord is great in Zion,
   And He is ^exalted above all
   the peoples.
3 May they praise Your ^great
   and awesome name;
   ^BHoly is He.
4 The strength of the King ^loves
   justice;
   You have established order;
   You have ^Bexecuted justice and
   righteousness in Jacob.
5 ^Exalt the Lord our God
   And ^Bworship at His footstool;
   Holy is He.

6 ^Moses and Aaron were among
   His priests,
   And ^Samuel was among those
   who called on His name;

They ^Bcalled upon the Lord
   and He answered them.
7 He ^spoke to them in the pillar
   of cloud;
   They kept His testimonies
   And the statute that He gave
   them.
8 Lord our God, You answered
   them;
   You were a ^forgiving God to
   them,
   And *yet* an ^Bavenger of their
   evil deeds.
9 Exalt the Lord our God
   And worship at His holy hill,
   For the Lord our God is holy.

ALL PEOPLE EXHORTED
TO PRAISE GOD.
A Psalm for Thanksgiving.

100 ^Shout joyfully to the
   Lord, all the earth.
2 ^Serve the Lord with
   jubilation;
   Come before Him with
   rejoicing.
3 Know that the Lord Himself is
   God;
   It is He who has ^made us, and
   ^1not we ourselves;
   We are His people and the
   sheep of His pasture.

4 Enter His gates ^with
   thanksgiving,
   And His courtyards with
   praise.
   Give thanks to Him, bless His
   name.

98:5 ^Is 51:3   98:6 ^Num 10:10; 2 Chr 15:14
98:7 ^Ps 96:11   98:8 ^Ps 93:3; Is 55:12   98:9 ^Ps 96:13
^BPs 96:10   99:1 ^Ps 97:1   ^BEx 25:22   99:2 ^Ps 97:9;
113:4   99:3 ^Deut 28:58   ^BLev 19:2   99:4 ^Ps 11:7
^BPs 103:6   99:5 ^Ps 34:3   ^BPs 132:7   99:6 ^Jer 15:1
^BEx 15:25   99:7 ^Ex 33:9; Num 12:5
99:8 ^Num 14:20   ^BEx 32:28   100:1 ^Ps 95:1; 98:4, 6
100:2 ^Deut 12:11, 12; 28:47   100:3 ^Job 10:3, 8;
Ps 95:6   100:4 ^Ps 95:2; 116:17

100:3 ^1Some mss *His we are*

5 For the LORD is good;
His mercy is everlasting
And His ^faithfulness is to all
generations.

**THE PSALMIST'S PROFESSION
OF UPRIGHTNESS.**
A Psalm of David.

101
I will ^sing of mercy and
justice;
To You, LORD, I will sing
praises.

2 I will ^carefully attend to the
blameless way.
When will You come to me?
I will walk within my house in
the ^Bintegrity of my heart.

3 I will set no ^worthless thing
before my eyes;
I hate the work of those who
^Bfall away;
It shall not cling to me.

4 A ^perverse heart shall leave
me;
I will know no evil.

5 Whoever secretly ^slanders his
neighbor, him I will destroy;
I will not endure one who
has a ^Bhaughty look and an
arrogant heart.

6 My eyes shall be upon the
faithful of the land, that they
may dwell with me;
One who walks in a ^blameless
way is one who will serve me.

7 One who ^practices deceit
shall not dwell within my
house;
One who speaks lies shall not
maintain his position before
me.

8 Every morning I will destroy
all the wicked of the land,
So as to ^eliminate from the
^Bcity of the LORD all those
who do injustice.

**PRAYER OF AN AFFLICTED MAN FOR
MERCY ON HIMSELF AND ON ZION.**
A Prayer of the afflicted when
he is weak and pours out his
complaint before the LORD.

102
Hear my prayer, LORD!
And let my cry for help
^come to You.

2 ^Do not hide Your face from
me on the day of my
distress;
Incline Your ear to me;
On the day when I call ^answer
me quickly.

3 For my days ^have ended in
smoke,
And my bones have been
scorched like a hearth.

4 My heart ^has been struck like
grass and has withered,
Indeed, I forget to eat my bread.

5 Because of the loudness of my
groaning
My ^bones cling to my flesh.

6 I resemble a ^pelican of the
wilderness;
I have become like an owl of
the ruins.

7 I ^lie awake,
I have become like a solitary
bird on a housetop.

8 My enemies have taunted me
all day long;
Those who ^deride me have
used my *name* as a ^Bcurse.

9 For I have eaten ashes like
bread,
And ^mixed my drink with
weeping

100:5 ^Ps 119:90   101:1 ^Ps 51:14; 89:1
101:2 ^1 Sam 18:5, 14   ^B1 Kin 9:4   101:3 ^Deut 15:9
^BJosh 23:6   101:4 ^Prov 11:20   101:5 ^Ps 50:20
^BPs 10:4   101:6 ^Ps 119:1   101:7 ^Ps 43:1; 52:2
101:8 ^Ps 118:10-12   ^BPs 46:4   102:1 ^Ex 2:23;
1 Sam 9:16   102:2 ^Ps 69:17   102:3 ^Ps 37:20;
James 4:14   102:4 ^Ps 90:5, 6   102:5 ^Job 19:20;
Lam 4:8   102:6 ^Is 34:11; Zeph 2:14   102:7 ^Ps 77:4
102:8 ^Acts 26:11   ^B2 Sam 16:5   102:9 ^Ps 42:3; 80:5

¹⁰ Because of Your indignation
and Your wrath;
For You have ^lifted me up and
thrown me away.
¹¹ My days are like a ^lengthened
shadow,
And I wither away like grass.

¹² But You, LORD, ^remain forever,
And Your ᴮname *remains* to all
generations.
¹³ You will arise *and* have
^compassion on Zion;
For it is time to be gracious to
her,
For the appointed time has
come.
¹⁴ Surely Your servants take
pleasure in her stones,
And feel pity for her dust.
¹⁵ So the ^nations will fear the
name of the LORD,
And all the kings of the earth,
Your glory.
¹⁶ For the LORD has ^built up
Zion;
He has appeared in His glory.
¹⁷ He has ^turned His attention
to the prayer of the destitute
And has not despised their
prayer.

¹⁸ This will be written for the
^generation to come,
That ᴮa people yet to be
created may praise the LORD:
¹⁹ For He looked down from His
holy height;
^From heaven the LORD looked
upon the earth,
²⁰ To hear the groaning of the
prisoner,
To ^set free those who were
doomed to death,
²¹ So that *people* may ^tell of the
name of the LORD in Zion,
And His praise in Jerusalem,

²² When ^the peoples are
gathered together,
And the kingdoms, to serve
the LORD.

²³ He has broken my strength in
the way;
He has ^shortened my days.
²⁴ I say, "My God, ^do not take
me away in the middle of
my days,
Your years are throughout all
generations.
²⁵ "In time of old You ^founded
the earth,
And the heavens are the work
of Your hands.
²⁶ "Even they will ^perish, but You
endure;
All of them will wear out like a
garment;
Like clothing You will change
them and they will pass away.
²⁷ "But You are ^the same,
And Your years will not come
to an end.
²⁸ "The ^children of Your servants
will continue,
And their descendants will be
established before You."

PRAISE FOR THE LORD'S MERCIES.
A Psalm of David.

103 ^Bless the LORD, my soul,
And all that is within me,
bless His holy name.
² Bless the LORD, my soul,
And ^do not forget any of His
benefits;

102:10 ^Job 27:21; 30:22 102:11 ^Job 14:2; Ps 109:23
102:12 ^Ps 9:7 ᴮEx 3:15 102:13 ^Is 60:10; Zech 1:12
102:15 ^1 Kin 8:43; Ps 67:7 102:16 ^Ps 147:2
102:17 ^Neh 1:6; Ps 22:24 102:18 ^Ps 22:30
ᴮPs 22:31 102:19 ^Ps 33:13 102:20 ^Ps 146:7
102:21 ^Ps 22:22 102:22 ^Ps 22:27; 86:9
102:23 ^Ps 39:5 102:24 ^Ps 39:13; Is 38:10
102:25 ^Gen 1:1; Neh 9:6 102:26 ^Is 34:4; 51:6
102:27 ^Is 41:4; 43:10 102:28 ^Ps 69:36
103:1 ^Ps 104:1, 35 103:2 ^Deut 6:12; 8:11

3 Who ^pardons all your guilt,
  Who heals all your diseases;
4 Who ^redeems your life from
    the pit,
  Who ^Bcrowns you with favor
    and compassion;
5 Who ^satisfies your years with
    good things,
  So that your youth is ^Brenewed
    like the eagle.

6 The LORD ^performs righteous
    deeds
  And judgments for all who are
    oppressed.
7 He ^made known His ways to
    Moses,
  His ^Bdeeds to the sons of
    Israel.
8 The LORD is ^compassionate
    and gracious,
  Slow to anger and abounding
    in mercy.
9 He will not always contend
    with us,
  Nor will He ^keep *His anger*
    forever.
10 He has ^not dealt with us
    according to our sins,
   Nor rewarded us according to
    our guilty deeds.
11 For as high ^as the heavens are
    above the earth,
   So great is His mercy toward
    those who fear Him.
12 As far as the east is from the
    west,
   So far has He ^removed our
    wrongdoings from us.
13 Just ^as a father has
    compassion on *his* children,
   So the LORD has compassion
    on those who fear Him.
14 For He Himself knows ¹our
    form;
   He ^is mindful that we are
    nothing but ^Bdust.

15 As for man, his days are ^like
    grass;
   Like a flower of the field, so he
    flourishes.
16 When the ^wind has passed
    over it, it is no more,
   And its place no longer knows
    about it.
17 But the ^mercy of the LORD
    is from everlasting to
    everlasting for those who
    fear Him,
   And His justice to the
    children's children,
18 To ^those who keep His
    covenant
   And remember His precepts,
    so as to do them.

19 The LORD has established His
    ^throne in the heavens,
   And His ^Bsovereignty rules
    over all.
20 Bless the LORD, you ^His
    angels,
   Mighty in strength, who
    perform His word,
   ^BObeying the voice of His
    word!
21 Bless the LORD, all you His
    angels,
   You ^who serve Him, doing His
    will.
22 Bless the LORD, ^all you works
    of His,
   In all places of His dominion;
   Bless the LORD, my soul!

103:3 ^Ex 34:7; Ps 86:5   103:4 ^Ps 49:15   ^BPs 5:12
103:5 ^Ps 107:9   ^BIs 40:31   103:6 ^Ps 99:4; 146:7
103:7 ^Ex 33:13   ^BPs 78:11   103:8 ^Ex 34:6; Num 14:18
103:9 ^Jer 3:5, 12; Mic 7:18   103:10 ^Ezra 9:13;
Lam 3:22   103:11 ^Ps 36:5; 57:10
103:12 ^2 Sam 12:13; Is 38:17   103:13 ^Mal 3:17
103:14 ^Ps 78:39   ^BGen 3:19   103:15 ^Ps 90:5; Is 40:6
103:16 ^Is 40:7   103:17 ^Ps 25:6   103:18 ^Deut 7:9;
Ps 25:10   103:19 ^Ps 11:4   ^BPs 47:2, 8
103:20 ^Ps 148:2   ^BHeb 1:14   103:21 ^Ps 104:4
103:22 ^Ps 145:10

103:14 ¹ I.e., what we are made of

THE LORD'S CARE OVER ALL HIS WORKS.

104 Bless the LORD, my soul!
LORD my God, You are
very great;
You are ^clothed with splendor
and majesty,

2 Covering Yourself with ^light
as with a cloak,
^Stretching out heaven like a
tent curtain.

3 He lays the beams of His upper
chambers in the waters;
He makes the ^clouds His
chariot;
He walks on the ^wings of the
wind;

4 He makes ^the winds His
messengers,
Flaming ^fire His ministers.

5 He ^established the earth upon
its foundations,
So that it will not totter forever
and ever.

6 You ^covered it with the deep
sea as with a garment;
The waters were standing
above the mountains.

7 They fled from Your rebuke,
At the ^sound of Your thunder
they hurried away.

8 The mountains rose; the
valleys sank down
To the ^place which You
established for them.

9 You set a ^boundary *so that*
they will not pass over,
So that they will not return to
cover the earth.

10 He sends forth ^springs in the
valleys;
They flow between the
mountains;

11 They give drink to every
animal of the field;
The ^wild donkeys quench
their thirst.

12 The birds of the sky ^dwell
beside them;
They lift up *their* voices from
among the branches.

13 He waters the mountains from
His upper chambers;
^The earth is satisfied with the
fruit of His works.

14 He causes the ^grass to grow
for the cattle,
And vegetation for the labor of
mankind,
So that they may produce food
from the earth,

15 And wine, which makes a
human heart cheerful,
So that he makes *his* face
gleam with oil,
And food, which ^sustains a
human heart.

16 The trees of the LORD drink
their fill,
The cedars of Lebanon which
He planted,

17 Where the ^birds build their
nests,
And the ^stork, whose home is
the juniper trees.

18 The high mountains are for
the ^wild goats;
The cliffs are a refuge for the
^rock hyrax.

19 He made the moon ^for the
seasons;
The sun knows the place of its
setting.

104:1 ^Ps 93:1   104:2 ^Dan 7:9   ^Is 40:22
104:3 ^Is 19:1   ^Ps 18:10   104:4 ^Ps 148:8   ^2 Kin 2:11
104:5 ^Job 38:4; Ps 24:2   104:6 ^Gen 1:2
104:7 ^Ps 29:3; 77:18   104:8 ^Ps 33:7
104:9 ^Job 38:10, 11; Jer 5:22   104:10 ^Ps 107:35; Is 41:18
104:11 ^Job 39:5   104:12 ^Matt 8:20   104:13 ^Jer 10:13
104:14 ^Job 38:27; Ps 147:8   104:15 ^Gen 18:5;
Judg 19:5, 8   104:17 ^Ps 104:12   ^Lev 11:19
104:18 ^Job 39:1   ^Lev 11:5   104:19 ^Gen 1:14

20 You appoint darkness and it
  becomes night,
  In which all the ^animals of the
  forest prowl about.
21 The young lions roar for their
  prey
  And ^seek their food from God.
22 *When* the sun rises they
  withdraw,
  And they lie down in their
  ^dens.
23 A person goes out to ^his work
  And to his labor until
  evening.

24 Lord, how ^many are Your
  works!
  In wisdom You have made
  them all;
  The ^Bearth is full of Your
  possessions.
25 There is the ^sea, great and
  broad,
  In which are swarms without
  number,
  Animals both small and
  great.
26 The ships move along there,
  And ^Leviathan, which You
  have formed to have fun in it.

27 They all ^wait for You
  To ^Bgive them their food in due
  season.
28 You give to them, they gather
  it up;
  You ^open Your hand, they are
  satisfied with good.
29 You hide Your face, they are
  terrified;
  You ^take away their breath,
  they perish
  And ^Breturn to their dust.
30 You send forth Your ^Spirit,
  they are created;
  And You renew the face of the
  ground.

31 May the ^glory of the Lord
  endure forever;
  May the Lord rejoice in His
  works;
32 He looks at the earth, and it
  ^trembles;
  He ^Btouches the mountains,
  and they smoke.
33 I will sing to the Lord ^as long
  as I live;
  I will sing praise to my God
  while I have my being.
34 May my ^praise be pleasing to
  Him;
  As for me, I shall rejoice in the
  Lord.
35 May sinners be ^removed
  from the earth
  And *may* the ^Bwicked be no
  more.
  Bless the Lord, my soul.
  Praise the Lord!

THE LORD'S WONDERFUL WORKS IN BEHALF OF ISRAEL.

105 Give thanks to the
  Lord, call upon His
  name;
  ^Make His deeds known
  among the peoples.
2 Sing to Him, sing praises to
  Him;
  ^Tell of all His wonders.
3 Boast in His holy name;
  May the ^heart of those who
  seek the Lord be joyful.
4 Seek the Lord and ^His
  strength;
  ^BSeek His face continually.

104:20 ^Ps 50:10; Is 56:9   104:21 ^Ps 145:15; Joel 1:20
104:22 ^Job 37:8   104:23 ^Gen 3:19   104:24 ^Ps 40:5
^BPs 65:9   104:25 ^Ps 8:8; 69:34   104:26 ^Job 41:1;
Ps 74:14   104:27 ^Ps 145:15   ^BJob 36:31
104:28 ^Ps 145:16   104:29 ^Job 34:14, 15   ^BGen 3:19
104:30 ^Job 33:4; Ezek 37:9   104:31 ^Ps 86:12; 111:10
104:32 ^Hab 3:10   ^BEx 19:18   104:33 ^Ps 63:4
104:34 ^Ps 19:14   104:35 ^Ps 59:13   ^BPs 37:10
105:1 ^Ps 145:12   105:2 ^Ps 77:12; 119:27
105:3 ^Ps 33:21   105:4 ^Ps 63:2   ^BPs 27:8

5 Remember His wonders which
  He has done,
  His marvels and the ^judgments
  spoken by His mouth,
6 You descendants of Abraham,
  His servant,
  You sons of ^Jacob, His ^chosen
  ones!
7 He is the LORD our God;
  His ^judgments are in all the
  earth.

8 He has ^remembered His
  covenant forever,
  The word which He
  commanded to a ^thousand
  generations,
9 *The covenant* which He made
  with Abraham,
  And His ^oath to Isaac.
10 Then He ^confirmed it to Jacob
   as a statute,
   To Israel as an everlasting
   covenant,
11 Saying, "^To you I will give the
   land of Canaan
   As the ^portion of your
   inheritance,"
12 When they were *only* a ^few
   people in number,
   Very few, and ^strangers in it.
13 And they wandered from
   nation to nation,
   From *one* kingdom to another
   people,
14 He ^allowed no one to oppress
   them,
   And He ^rebuked kings for
   their sakes, *saying,*
15 "^Do not touch My anointed
   ones,
   And do not harm My prophets."

16 And He ^called for a famine
   upon the land;
   He broke the whole staff of
   bread.

17 He ^sent a man before them,
   Joseph, *who* was ^sold as a slave.
18 They forced his ^feet into
   shackles,
   He was put in irons;
19 Until the time that his ^word
   came to pass,
   The word of the LORD ^refined
   him.
20 The ^king sent and released him,
   The ruler of peoples, and set
   him free.
21 He ^made him lord of his house,
   And ruler over all his
   possessions,
22 To imprison his high officials
   ^at will,
   That he might teach his elders
   wisdom.
23 ^Israel also came into Egypt;
   So Jacob ^lived in the land of
   Ham.
24 And He ^made His people very
   fruitful,
   And made them stronger than
   their enemies.

25 He ^turned their heart to hate
   His people,
   To deal cunningly with His
   servants.
26 He ^sent His servant Moses,
   And ^Aaron, whom He had
   chosen.
27 They ^performed His
   wondrous acts among them,
   And miracles in the land of
   Ham.

105:5 ^Ps 119:13   105:6 ^Ps 135:4   ^1 Chr 16:13
105:7 ^Is 26:9   105:8 ^Ps 105:42   ^Deut 7:9
105:9 ^Gen 26:3   105:10 ^Gen 28:13-15
105:11 ^Gen 13:15   ^Josh 23:4   105:12 ^Gen 34:30
^Gen 23:4   105:14 ^Gen 20:7   ^Gen 12:17
105:15 ^Gen 26:11   105:16 ^Gen 41:54
105:17 ^Gen 45:5   ^Gen 37:28, 36   105:18 ^Gen 39:20;
40:15   105:19 ^Gen 40:20, 21   ^Ps 66:10
105:20 ^Gen 41:14   105:21 ^Gen 41:40-44
105:22 ^Gen 41:44   105:23 ^Gen 46:6   ^Acts 13:17
105:24 ^Ex 1:7, 9   105:25 ^Ex 1:8; 4:21   105:26 ^Ex 3:10
^Ex 4:14   105:27 ^Ps 78:43-51; 105:27-36

28 He ^sent darkness and made *it*
  dark;
  And they did not rebel against
  His words.
29 He ^turned their waters into
  blood,
  And caused their fish to die.
30 Their land swarmed with
  ^frogs
  Even in the ᴮchambers of their
  kings.
31 He spoke, and a ^swarm of
  flies
  And ᴮgnats invaded all their
  territory.
32 He gave them ^hail for rain,
  And flaming fire in their land.
33 He also ^struck their vines and
  their fig trees,
  And smashed the trees of their
  territory.
34 He spoke, and ^locusts came,
  And creeping locusts, beyond
  number,
35 And they ate all the vegetation
  in their land,
  And ate the fruit of their
  ground.
36 He also ^fatally struck all the
  firstborn in their land,
  The ᴮfirst fruits of all their
  vigor.
37 Then He brought ¹the
  Israelites out with ^silver
  and gold,
  And among His tribes there
  was not one who stumbled.
38 Egypt was ^glad when they
  departed,
  For the dread of them had
  fallen upon ¹the Egyptians.
39 He spread out a ^cloud as a
  covering,
  And ᴮfire to illumine by night.
40 They asked, and He brought
  ^quail,

And satisfied them with the
  ᴮbread of heaven.
41 He opened the rock and
  ^water flowed out;
  It ran in the dry places *like* a
  river.
42 For He ^remembered His holy
  word
  With His servant Abraham;
43 And He led out His people
  with joy,
  His chosen ones with a joyful
  ^shout.
44 He also ^gave them the lands
  of the nations,
  So that they might take
  possession of *the fruit of*
  the peoples' labor,
45 *And* that they might ^keep His
  statutes
  And comply with His laws;
  Praise the Lᴏʀᴅ!

ISRAEL'S REBELLIOUSNESS AND THE LORD'S HELP.

106 Praise the Lᴏʀᴅ!
  Oh give thanks to the
  Lᴏʀᴅ, for He ^is good;
  For ᴮHis mercy is everlasting.
2 Who can speak of the ^mighty
  deeds of the Lᴏʀᴅ,
  Or can proclaim all His
  praise?
3 How blessed are those who
  maintain justice,
  Who ^practice righteousness
  at all times!

105:28 ^Ex 10:21, 22   105:29 ^Ex 7:20, 21
105:30 ^Ex 8:6   ᴮEx 8:3   105:31 ^Ex 8:21   ᴮEx 8:16, 17
105:32 ^Ex 9:23-25   105:33 ^Ps 78:47
105:34 ^Ex 10:12-15   105:36 ^Ex 12:29   ᴮGen 49:3
105:37 ^Ex 12:35, 36   105:38 ^Ex 12:33   105:39 ^Ex 13:21
ᴮEx 40:38   105:40 ^Ex 16:13   ᴮEx 16:15
105:41 ^Ex 17:6; Num 20:11   105:42 ^Gen 15:13, 14;
Ps 105:8   105:43 ^Ex 15:1; Ps 106:12
105:44 ^Josh 11:16-23; 13:7   105:45 ^Deut 4:1, 40
106:1 ^2 Chr 5:13; 7:3   ᴮ1 Chr 16:34, 41
106:2 ^Ps 145:4, 12; 150:2   106:3 ^Ps 15:2

105:37 ¹Lit *them*   105:38 ¹Lit *them*

4 Remember me, LORD, in *Your*
   ^favor toward Your people.
   Visit me with Your salvation,
5 So that I may see the ^prosperity
   of Your chosen ones,
   That I may rejoice in the joy of
   Your nation,
   That I may ^boast with Your
   ¹inheritance.

6 ^We have sinned ^like our
   fathers,
   We have gone astray, we have
   behaved wickedly.
7 Our fathers in Egypt did not
   understand Your wonders;
   They did not remember Your
   abundant kindnesses,
   But ^rebelled by the sea, at the
   Red Sea.
8 Nevertheless He saved them
   ^for the sake of His name,
   So that He might ^make His
   power known.
9 So He rebuked the Red Sea and
   it dried up,
   And He ^led them through the
   mighty waters, as *through*
   the wilderness.
10 So He ^saved them from the
   hand of one who hated *them,*
   And ^redeemed them from the
   hand of the enemy.
11 ^The waters covered their
   adversaries;
   Not one of them was left.
12 Then they ^believed His
   words;
   They sang His praise.

13 They quickly ^forgot His
   works;
   They ^did not wait for His plan,
14 But ^became lustfully greedy
   in the wilderness,
   And put God to the test in the
   desert.

15 So He ^gave them their
   request,
   But ^sent a wasting disease
   among them.

16 When they became ^envious
   of Moses in the camp,
   And of Aaron, the holy one of
   the LORD,
17 The ^earth opened and
   swallowed up Dathan,
   And engulfed the company of
   Abiram.
18 And a ^fire blazed up in their
   company;
   The flame consumed the
   wicked.

19 They ^made a calf in Horeb,
   And worshiped a cast metal
   image.
20 So they ^exchanged their glory
   For the image of an ox that
   eats grass.
21 They ^forgot God their Savior,
   Who had done great things in
   Egypt,
22 ^Wonders in the land of Ham,
   And awesome things by the
   Red Sea.
23 Therefore He said that He
   would destroy them,
   If ^Moses, His chosen one, had
   not stood in the gap before
   Him,
   To turn away His wrath from
   destroying *them.*

106:4 ^Ps 44:3; 119:132   106:5 ^Ps 1:3   ^Ps 105:3
106:6 ^1 Kin 8:47   ^2 Chr 30:7   106:7 ^Ex 14:11, 12;
Ps 78:17   106:8 ^Ezek 20:9   ^Ex 9:16
106:9 ^Is 63:11-13   106:10 ^Ex 14:30   ^Ps 78:42
106:11 ^Ex 14:27, 28; 15:5   106:12 ^Ex 14:31
106:13 ^Ex 15:24   ^Ps 107:11   106:14 ^Num 11:4;
Ps 78:18   106:15 ^Num 11:31   ^Is 10:16
106:16 ^Num 16:1-3   106:17 ^Num 16:32; Deut 11:6
106:18 ^Num 16:35   106:19 ^Ex 32:4; Deut 9:8
106:20 ^Jer 2:11; Rom 1:23   106:21 ^Ps 78:11; 106:7, 13
106:22 ^Ps 105:27   106:23 ^Ex 32:11-14; Deut 9:25-29

106:5 ¹I.e., people

24 Then they rejected the
    pleasant land;
    They ^did not believe His
    word,
25 But ^grumbled in their tents;
    They did not listen to the voice
    of the Lord.
26 Therefore He ^swore to them
    That He would have them fall
    in the wilderness,
27 And that He would ^bring
    down their descendants
    among the nations,
    And ^Bscatter them in the
    lands.

28 They also ^followed Baal-peor,
    And ate sacrifices *offered to*
    the dead.
29 So they ^provoked *Him* to
    anger with their deeds,
    And a plague broke out among
    them.
30 Then Phinehas ^stood up and
    intervened,
    And so the plague was brought
    to a halt.
31 And it was ^credited to him as
    righteousness,
    To all generations forever.

32 They also ^provoked *Him*
    to wrath at the waters of
    Meribah,
    So that it went badly for Moses
    on their account.
33 Because they ^were rebellious
    against His Spirit,
    He spoke rashly with his lips.

34 They ^did not destroy the
    peoples,
    As ^Bthe Lord had commanded
    them,
35 But ^they got involved with the
    nations
    And learned their practices,

36 And ^served their idols,
    ^BWhich became a snare to
    them.
37 They even ^sacrificed their
    sons and their daughters to
    the demons,
38 And shed ^innocent blood,
    The blood of their ^Bsons and
    their daughters
    Whom they sacrificed to the
    idols of Canaan;
    And the land was defiled with
    the blood.
39 So they became ^unclean in
    their practices,
    And were unfaithful in their
    deeds.

40 Therefore the anger of the
    Lord was kindled against His
    people,
    And He ^loathed His
    ^Binheritance.
41 So ^He handed them over to
    the nations,
    And those who hated them
    ruled over them.
42 Their enemies also ^oppressed
    them,
    And they were subdued under
    their power.
43 Many times He would ^rescue
    them;
    They, however, were rebellious
    in their plan,
    And they ^Bsank down into
    their guilt.

106:24 ^Deut 1:32; 9:23   106:25 ^Num 14:2; Deut 1:27
106:26 ^Num 14:28–35; Ps 95:11   106:27 ^Deut 4:27
^BLev 26:33   106:28 ^Num 25:3; Deut 4:3
106:29 ^Num 25:4   106:30 ^Num 25:7
106:31 ^Gen 15:6; Num 25:11-13   106:32 ^Num
20:2-13; Ps 81:7   106:33 ^Num 20:3, 10; Ps 78:40
106:34 ^Judg 1:21, 27-36   ^BDeut 7:2, 16
106:35 ^Judg 3:5, 6   106:36 ^Judg 2:12   ^BDeut 7:16
106:37 ^Deut 12:31; 32:17   106:38 ^Ps 94:21
^BDeut 18:10   106:39 ^Lev 18:24; Ezek 20:18
106:40 ^Lev 26:30   ^BDeut 9:29   106:41 ^Judg 2:14;
Neh 9:27   106:42 ^Judg 4:3; 10:12
106:43 ^Judg 2:16-18   ^BJudg 6:6

44 Nevertheless He looked at
their distress
When He ^heard their cry;
45 And He ^remembered His
covenant for their sake,
And relented according to the
greatness of His mercy.
46 He also made them ^*objects* of
compassion
In the presence of all their
captors.

47 ^Save us, Lord our God,
And ^gather us from the nations,
To give thanks to Your holy
name
And glory in Your praise.
48 ^Blessed be the Lord, the God
of Israel,
From everlasting to everlasting.
And all the people shall say,
"Amen."
Praise the Lord!

BOOK 5

THE LORD RESCUES PEOPLE
FROM MANY TROUBLES.

107 Give thanks to the Lord,
for ^He is good,
For His mercy is everlasting.
2 ^The redeemed of the Lord
shall say *so,*
Those whom He has redeemed
from the hand of the enemy
3 And ^gathered from the lands,
From the east and from the
west,
From the north and from the
south.

4 They ^wandered in the
wilderness in a desert
region;
They did not find a way to an
inhabited city.

5 *They were* hungry and thirsty;
Their ^souls felt weak within
them.
6 Then they ^cried out to the
Lord in their trouble;
He saved them from their
distresses.
7 He also had them walk on a
^straight way,
To go to ^an inhabited city.
8 ^They shall give thanks to the
Lord for His mercy,
And for His wonders to the
sons of mankind!
9 For He has ^satisfied the
thirsty soul,
And He has filled the ^hungry
soul with what is good.

10 There were those who ^lived in
darkness and in the shadow
of death,
^Prisoners in misery and chains,
11 Because they had rebelled
against the words of God
And ^rejected the ^plan of the
Most High.
12 Therefore He humbled their
heart with labor;
They stumbled and there was
^no one to help.
13 Then they ^cried out to the
Lord in their trouble;
He saved them from their
distresses.
14 He ^brought them out of
darkness and the shadow of
death
And ^broke their bands apart.

106:44 ^Judg 3:9; 6:7   106:45 ^Lev 26:42; Ps 105:8
106:46 ^1 Kin 8:50; 2 Chr 30:9   106:47 ^1 Chr 16:35, 36
^Ps 147:2   106:48 ^Ps 41:13; 72:18   107:1 ^2 Chr 5:13;
7:3   107:2 ^Is 35:9, 10; 62:12   107:3 ^Deut 30:3;
Neh 1:9   107:4 ^Num 14:33; 32:13   107:5 ^Ps 77:3
107:6 ^Ps 50:15; 107:13, 19, 28   107:7 ^Ezra 8:21
^Ps 107:4, 36   107:8 ^Ps 107:15, 21, 31   107:9 ^Ps 22:26
^Ps 146:7   107:10 ^Ps 143:3   ^Job 36:8
107:11 ^Num 15:31   ^Ps 73:24   107:12 ^Ps 22:11; 72:12
107:13 ^Ps 107:6   107:14 ^Ps 86:13   ^Ps 116:16

¹⁵ ᴬThey shall give thanks to the
LORD for His mercy,
And for His wonders to the
sons of mankind!
¹⁶ For He has ᴬshattered gates of
bronze
And cut off bars of iron.

¹⁷ Fools, because of their
rebellious way,
And ᴬbecause of their guilty
deeds, were afflicted.
¹⁸ Their souls loathed all kinds
of food,
And they ᴬcame close to the
ᴮgates of death.
¹⁹ Then they cried out to the
LORD in their trouble;
He saved them from their
distresses.
²⁰ He sent His word and ᴬhealed
them,
And ᴮsaved *them* from their
destruction.
²¹ ᴬThey shall give thanks to the
LORD for His mercy,
And for His wonders to the
sons of mankind!
²² They shall also offer ᴬsacrifices
of thanksgiving,
And tell of His works with
joyful singing.

²³ Those who ᴬgo down to the sea
in ships,
Who do business on great
waters;
²⁴ They have seen the works of
the LORD,
And His wonders in the deep.
²⁵ For He spoke and raised a
ᴬstormy wind,
Which ᴮlifted the waves of
the sea.
²⁶ They rose up to the heavens,
they went down to the
depths;

Their soul ᴬmelted away in
their misery.
²⁷ They reeled and ᴬstaggered
like a drunken person,
And were at their wits' end.
²⁸ Then they cried out to the
LORD in their trouble,
And He brought them out of
their distresses.
²⁹ He ᴬcaused the storm to be
still,
So that the waves of the sea
were hushed.
³⁰ Then they were glad because
they were quiet,
So He guided them to their
desired harbor.
³¹ They shall give thanks to the
LORD for His mercy,
And for His ᴬwonders to the
sons of mankind!
³² They shall also ᴬexalt Him
ᴮin the congregation of the
people,
And praise Him at the seat of
the elders.

³³ He ᴬturns rivers into a
wilderness,
And springs of water into a
thirsty ground;
³⁴ *And* a ᴬfruitful land into a ᴮsalt
waste,
Because of the wickedness of
those who dwell in it.
³⁵ He ᴬturns a wilderness into a
pool of water,
And a dry land into springs of
water;

107:15 ᴬPs 107:8, 21, 31 107:16 ᴬIs 45:1, 2
107:17 ᴬIs 65:6, 7; Jer 30:14, 15 107:18 ᴬJob 33:22
ᴮJob 38:17 107:20 ᴬ2 Kin 20:5 ᴮJob 33:28, 30
107:21 ᴬPs 107:8, 15, 31 107:22 ᴬLev 7:12; Ps 50:14
107:23 ᴬIs 42:10; Jon 1:3 107:25 ᴬPs 148:8
ᴮPs 93:3, 4 107:26 ᴬPs 22:14; 119:28
107:27 ᴬJob 12:25; Is 24:20 107:29 ᴬPs 65:7; 89:9
107:31 ᴬPs 78:4; 111:4 107:32 ᴬPs 34:3 ᴮPs 22:22, 25
107:33 ᴬ1 Kin 17:1, 7; Ps 74:15 107:34 ᴬGen 13:10
ᴮJob 39:6 107:35 ᴬPs 105:41; 114:8

36 And He has the hungry live
there,
So that they may establish ^an
inhabited city,
37 And sow fields and ^plant
vineyards,
And gather a fruitful harvest.
38 He also blesses them and they
^multiply greatly,
And He does not let their
cattle decrease.

39 When they ^become few and
lowly
Because of oppression, misery,
and sorrow,
40 He ^pours contempt upon
noblemen
And makes them wander ^Bin a
pathless wasteland.
41 But He ^sets the needy
securely on high, away from
affliction,
And makes *his* families like a
flock.
42 The ^upright see it and are
glad;
But all injustice shuts its
mouth.
43 Who is ^wise? He is to pay
attention to these things,
And consider the mercy of the
Lord.

**GOD PRAISED AND PLEAS
TO GIVE VICTORY.**
A Song, a Psalm of David.

108 ^My heart is steadfast,
God;
I will sing, I will sing praises
also with my soul.
2 Awake, harp and lyre;
I will awaken the dawn!
3 I will give thanks to You, Lord,
among the peoples,
And I will sing praises to You
among the nations.

4 For Your ^mercy is great ^Babove
the heavens,
And Your truth *reaches* to the
skies.
5 ^Be exalted above the heavens,
God,
And *may* Your glory *be* above
all the earth.
6 ^So that Your beloved may be
rescued,
Save with Your right hand, and
answer me!

7 God has spoken in His
holiness:
"I will triumph, I will divide up
Shechem,
And measure out the Valley of
Succoth.
8 "Gilead is Mine, Manasseh is
Mine;
Ephraim also is the helmet of
My head;
^Judah is My scepter.
9 "Moab is My washbowl;
I will throw My sandal over
Edom;
I will shout aloud over
Philistia."

10 ^Who will bring me into the
fortified city?
Who will lead me to Edom?
11 God, have You Yourself not
^rejected us?
And will You not go forth with
our armies, God?
12 Give us help against the
enemy,
For ^deliverance by man is
worthless.

107:36 ^A Ps 107:4, 7   107:37 ^A 2 Kin 19:29; Is 65:21
107:38 ^A Gen 12:2; 17:20   107:39 ^A 2 Kin 10:32; Ezek 5:11
107:40 ^A Job 12:21   ^B Deut 32:10   107:41 ^A 1 Sam 2:8;
Ps 59:1   107:42 ^A Job 22:19; Ps 52:6   107:43 ^A Ps 64:9;
Jer 9:12   108:1 ^A Ps 57:7-11; 108:1-5   108:4 ^A Num 14:18
^B Ps 113:4   108:5 ^A Ps 57:5   108:6 ^A Ps 60:5-12;
108:6-13   108:8 ^A Gen 49:10   108:10 ^A Ps 60:9
108:11 ^A Ps 44:9   108:12 ^A Is 30:3

13 Through God we will do
   valiantly,
   And ^it is He who will trample
   down our enemies.

**VENGEANCE INVOKED
UPON ADVERSARIES.**
For the music director. A Psalm of David.

109 God of my praise,
   ^Do not be silent!
2 For they have opened a wicked
   and ^deceitful mouth against
   me;
   They have spoken against me
   with a ^Blying tongue.
3 They have also surrounded me
   with words of hatred,
   And have fought against me
   ^without cause.
4 In return ^for my love they act
   as my accusers;
   But I am *in* prayer.
5 So they have ^repaid me evil
   for good,
   And ^Bhatred for my love.

6 Appoint a wicked person over
   him,
   And may an ^accuser stand at
   his right hand.
7 When he is judged, may he
   ^come out guilty,
   And may his ^Bprayer become
   sin.
8 May ^his days be few;
   May ^Banother take his office.
9 May his ^children be
   fatherless,
   And his ^Bwife a widow.
10 May his ^children wander
   about and beg;
   And may they seek *sustenance*
   far from their ruined homes.
11 May ^the creditor seize
   everything that he has,
   And may ^Bstrangers plunder
   the product of his labor.

12 May there be none to ^extend
   kindness to him,
   Nor any to be gracious to his
   fatherless children.
13 May his descendants be
   eliminated;
   May their ^name be wiped out
   in a following generation.
14 May ^the guilt of his fathers be
   remembered before the LORD,
   And do not let the sin of his
   mother be wiped out.
15 May they be before the LORD
   continually,
   So that He may ^eliminate their
   memory from the earth;
16 Because he did not remember
   to show mercy,
   But persecuted the afflicted
   and needy person,
   And the ^despondent in heart,
   to ^Bput *them* to death.
17 He also loved cursing, so ^it
   came to him;
   And he did not delight in
   blessing, so it was far from
   him.
18 But he clothed himself with
   cursing as with his garment,
   And it ^entered his body like
   water,
   And like oil into his bones.
19 May it be to him as ^a garment
   with which he covers himself,
   And as a belt which he
   constantly wears around
   himself.

108:13 ^Is 60:12; 63:1-4 109:1 ^Ps 28:1; 83:1
109:2 ^Ps 10:7 ^BPs 120:2 109:3 ^Ps 35:7; 69:4
109:4 ^Ps 38:20 109:5 ^Ps 35:12 ^BJohn 7:7
109:6 ^Zech 3:1 109:7 ^Ps 1:5 ^BProv 28:9
109:8 ^Ps 55:23 ^BActs 1:20 109:9 ^Ex 22:24
^BJer 18:21 109:10 ^Gen 4:12; Job 30:5-8
109:11 ^Neh 5:7 ^BIs 1:7 109:12 ^Ezra 7:28; 9:9
109:13 ^Ps 9:5; Prov 10:7 109:14 ^Ex 20:5; Num 14:18
109:15 ^Job 18:17; Ps 34:16 109:16 ^Ps 34:18
^BPs 37:32; 94:6 109:17 ^Prov 14:14; Ezek 35:9
109:18 ^Num 5:22 109:19 ^Ps 73:6; 109:29

20 *May* this *be* the ^reward of my
     accusers from the Lᴏʀᴅ,
   And of those who ᴮspeak evil
     against my soul.

21 But You, Gᴏᴅ, the Lord, deal
     kindly with me ^for the sake
     of Your name;
   Because Your mercy is good,
     rescue me;
22 For ^I am afflicted and needy,
   And my heart is ᴮwounded
     within me.
23 I am passing like a shadow
     when it lengthens;
   I am shaken off ^like the
     locust.
24 My ^knees are weak from
     ᴮfasting,
   And my flesh has grown lean,
     without fatness.
25 I also have become a disgrace
     to them;
   When they see me, they
     ^shake their head.

26 ^Help me, Lᴏʀᴅ my God;
   Save me according to Your
     mercy.
27 And may they ^know that this
     is Your hand;
   You, Lᴏʀᴅ, have done it.
28 ^They will curse, but You bless;
   When they arise, they will be
     ashamed,
   But Your ᴮservant will be glad.
29 May ^my accusers be clothed
     with dishonor,
   And may they ᴮcover
     themselves with their own
     shame as with a robe.

30 With my mouth I will give
     thanks abundantly to the
     Lᴏʀᴅ;
   And ^I will praise Him in the
     midst of many.

31 For He stands ^at the right
     hand of the needy,
   To save him from those who
     ᴮjudge his soul.

**THE LORD GIVES DOMINION
TO THE KING.**
A Psalm of David.

110
^The Lᴏʀᴅ says to my
     Lord:
   "Sit at My right hand
   Until I make Your enemies a
     footstool for Your feet."
2 The Lᴏʀᴅ will stretch out Your
     strong ^scepter from Zion,
     saying,
   "Rule in the midst of Your
     enemies."
3 Your ^people will volunteer
     freely on the day of Your
     power;
   In holy splendor, from the
     womb of the dawn,
   Your youth are to You *as* the
     ᴮdew.

4 The Lᴏʀᴅ has sworn and will
     ^not change His mind,
   "You are a ᴮpriest forever
   According to the order of
     Melchizedek."
5 The Lord is at Your right hand;
   He will ^shatter kings in the
     ᴮday of His wrath.
6 He will ^judge among the
     nations,
   He will fill *them* with corpses,
   He will ᴮshatter the chief men
     over a broad country.

109:20 ^Ps 54:5   ᴮPs 41:5   109:21 ^Ps 23:3; 25:11
109:22 ^Ps 40:17   ᴮJob 24:12   109:23 ^Ex 10:19;
Job 39:20   109:24 ^Heb 12:12   ᴮPs 35:13
109:25 ^Ps 22:7; Jer 18:16   109:26 ^Ps 119:86
109:27 ^Job 37:7   109:28 ^2 Sam 16:11, 12   ᴮIs 65:14
109:29 ^Job 8:22   ᴮPs 35:26   109:30 ^Ps 22:22; 35:18
109:31 ^Ps 16:8   ᴮPs 37:33   110:1 ^Matt 22:44;
Mark 12:36   110:2 ^Ps 45:6; Jer 48:17   110:3 ^Judg 5:2
ᴮ2 Sam 17:12   110:4 ^Num 23:19   ᴮZech 6:13
110:5 ^Ps 68:14   ᴮPs 2:5, 12   110:6 ^Is 2:4   ᴮPs 68:21

7 He will ᴬdrink from the brook
  by the wayside;
  Therefore He will lift up *His*
  head.

**THE LORD PRAISED FOR HIS
GOODNESS.**

111 Praise the LORD!
  I will give thanks to the
  LORD with all *my* heart,
  In the ᴬcompany of the upright
  and in the assembly.
2 ᴬGreat are the works of the
  LORD;
  They are ᴮstudied by all who
  delight in them.
3 ᴬSplendid and majestic is His
  work,
  And His righteousness
  endures forever.
4 He has caused His wonders to
  be remembered;
  The LORD is ᴬgracious and
  compassionate.
5 He has ᴬgiven food to those
  who fear Him;
  He will ᴮremember His
  covenant forever.
6 He has made known to His
  people the power of His
  works,
  In giving them the inheritance
  of the nations.
7 The works of His hands are
  ᴬtruth and justice;
  All His precepts are trustworthy.
8 They are ᴬupheld forever and
  ever;
  They are performed in ᴮtruth
  and uprightness.
9 He has sent ᴬredemption to
  His people;
  He has ordained His covenant
  forever;
  Holy and awesome is His
  name.

10 The ᴬfear of the LORD is the
  beginning of wisdom;
  All those who follow His
  commandments have a good
  understanding;
  His praise endures forever.

**PROSPERITY OF ONE WHO
FEARS THE LORD.**

112 Praise the LORD!
  ᴬBlessed is a person who
  fears the LORD,
  Who greatly delights in His
  commandments.
2 His ᴬdescendants will be
  mighty on the earth;
  The generation of the ᴮupright
  will be blessed.
3 ᴬWealth and riches are in his
  house,
  And his righteousness endures
  forever.
4 Light shines in the darkness
  ᴬfor the upright;
  He is gracious,
  compassionate, and
  righteous.
5 It *goes* well for a person who
  ᴬis gracious and lends;
  He will maintain his cause in
  judgment.
6 For he will ᴬnever be shaken;
  The ᴮrighteous will be
  remembered forever.
7 He will not fear bad news;
  His ᴬheart is steadfast,
  ᴮtrusting in the LORD.
8 His ᴬheart is firm, he ᴮwill not
  fear,

110:7 ᴬJudg 7:5, 6   111:1 ᴬPs 89:7; 149:1
111:2 ᴬPs 92:5   ᴮPs 143:5   111:3 ᴬPs 96:6; 145:5
111:4 ᴬPs 86:5, 15; 103:8   111:5 ᴬMatt 6:31-33
ᴮPs 105:8   111:7 ᴬRev 15:3   111:8 ᴬPs 119:160
ᴮPs 19:9   111:9 ᴬLuke 1:68   111:10 ᴬJob 28:28; Prov 1:7
112:1 ᴬPs 128:1   112:2 ᴬPs 102:28   ᴮPs 128:4
112:3 ᴬProv 3:16; 8:18   112:4 ᴬJob 11:17; Ps 97:11
112:5 ᴬPs 37:21   112:6 ᴬPs 15:5   ᴮProv 10:7
112:7 ᴬPs 57:7   ᴮPs 56:4   112:8 ᴬHeb 13:9   ᴮPs 27:1

But will look *with satisfaction*
on his enemies.

9 He ^has given freely to the poor,
His righteousness endures
forever;
His horn will be exalted in
honor.

10 The ^wicked will see it and be
vexed,
He will ^gnash his teeth and
melt away;
The desire of the wicked will
perish.

THE LORD EXALTS THE HUMBLE.

113 Praise the LORD!
Praise *Him,* you ^servants
of the LORD,
Praise the name of the LORD.

2 ^Blessed be the name of the
LORD
From this time *on* and forever.

3 ^From the rising of the sun to
its setting,
The name of the LORD is to be
praised.

4 The LORD is ^high above all
nations;
His ^glory is above the
heavens.

5 ^Who is like the LORD our God,
Who is enthroned on high,

6 Who ^looks far down to
The heavens and the earth?

7 He ^raises the poor from the
dust,
He lifts the needy from the
garbage heap,

8 To ^seat *them* with noblemen,
With the noblemen of His
people.

9 He ^has the infertile woman
live in the house
As a joyful mother of children.
Praise the LORD!

GOD'S RESCUE OF ISRAEL FROM EGYPT.

114 When Israel went forth
^from Egypt,
The house of Jacob from a
people of a foreign language,

2 Judah became ^His sanctuary;
Israel, ^His dominion.

3 The ^sea looked and fled;
The ^Jordan turned back.

4 The mountains ^skipped like
rams,
The hills, like lambs.

5 What ^ails you, sea, that you
flee?
Jordan, that you turn back?

6 Mountains, that you skip like
rams?
Hills, like lambs?

7 ^Tremble, earth, before the Lord,
Before the God of Jacob,

8 Who turned the rock into a
^pool of water,
The ^flint into a fountain of
water.

HEATHEN IDOLS CONTRASTED
WITH THE LORD.

115 Not to us, LORD, not to us,
But ^to Your name give
glory,
Because of Your mercy,
because of Your truth.

2 Why should the nations say,
"^Where, then, is their God?"

3 But our ^God is in the heavens;
He ^does whatever He pleases.

112:9^2 Cor 9:9   112:10^Ps 86:17   ^Ps 35:16
113:1^Ps 34:22; 69:36; 145:21; Dan 2:20
113:2^Ps 145:21   113:3^Ps 50:1; Is 59:19   113:4^Ps 97:9   ^Ps 8:1
113:5^Ex 15:11; Ps 35:10   113:6^Ps 11:4; 138:6
113:7^1 Sam 2:8; Ps 107:41   113:8^Job 36:7
113:9^1 Sam 2:5; Ps 68:6   114:1^Ex 12:51; 13:3
114:2^Ex 15:17   ^Ex 19:6   114:3^Ex 14:21
^Josh 3:13, 16   114:4^Ex 19:18; Judg 5:5
114:5^Hab 3:8   114:7^Ps 96:9   114:8^Ps 107:35
^Deut 8:15   115:1^Ps 29:2; 96:8   115:2^Ps 42:3, 10
115:3^Ps 103:19   ^Ps 135:6

4 Their ^idols are silver and
gold,
The ^Bwork of human hands.
5 They have mouths, but they
^cannot speak;
They have eyes, but they
cannot see;
6 They have ears, but they
cannot hear;
They have noses, but they
cannot smell;
7 They have hands, but they
cannot feel;
They have feet, but they
cannot walk;
They cannot make a sound
with their throat.
8 ^Those who make them will
become like them,
Everyone who trusts in them.

9 Israel, ^trust in the Lord;
He is their ^Bhelp and their
shield.
10 House of ^Aaron, trust in the
Lord;
He is their help and their
shield.
11 You who ^fear the Lord, trust
in the Lord;
He is their help and their
shield.
12 The Lord ^has been mindful of
us; He will bless us.
He will bless the house of
Israel;
He will bless the house of
Aaron.
13 He will bless those who fear
the Lord,
^The small together with the
great.
14 May the Lord ^increase you,
You and your children.
15 May you be blessed of the
Lord,
^Maker of heaven and earth.

16 The heavens are ^the heavens
of the Lord,
But ^Bthe earth He has given to
the sons of mankind.
17 The ^dead do not praise the
Lord,
Nor do any who go down into
silence;
18 But as for us, we will ^bless the
Lord
From this time and forever.
Praise the Lord!

**THANKSGIVING FOR RESCUE
FROM DEATH.**

116

I love the Lord, because
He ^hears
My voice and my pleas.
2 Because He has ^inclined His
ear to me,
Therefore I will call upon Him
as long as I live.
3 The ^snares of death
encompassed me
And the terrors of ^1Sheol came
upon me;
I found distress and sorrow.
4 Then ^I called upon the name
of the Lord:
"Please, Lord, ^Bsave my life!"

5 ^Gracious is the Lord, and
righteous;
Yes, our God is ^Bcompassionate.
6 The Lord watches over ^the
simple;
I was brought low, and He
saved me.

115:4 ^Ps 115:4-8   ^B Deut 4:28   115:5 ^Jer 10:5
115:8 ^Ps 135:18; Is 44:9-11   115:9 ^Ps 37:3   ^B Ps 33:20
115:10 ^Ps 118:3; 135:19   115:11 ^Ps 22:23; 103:11
115:12 ^Ps 98:3   115:13 ^Rev 11:18; 19:5
115:14 ^Deut 1:11   115:15 ^Gen 1:1; Neh 9:6
115:16 ^Ps 89:11   ^B Ps 8:6   115:17 ^Ps 6:5; 88:10-12
115:18 ^Ps 113:2; Dan 2:20   116:1 ^Ps 6:8; 66:19
116:2 ^Ps 17:6; 31:2   116:3 ^Ps 18:4, 5   116:4 ^Is 18:6
^B Ps 17:13   116:5 ^Ps 86:15   ^B Ex 34:6   116:6 ^Ps 19:7;
Prov 1:4

116:3 ^1 I.e., the netherworld

7 Return to your ^rest, my soul,
 For the Lord has dealt
  generously with you.
8 For You have ^rescued my soul
  from death,
 My eyes from tears,
 And my feet from stumbling.
9 I shall walk before the Lord
 In the ^land of the living.
10 I ^believed when I said,
 "I am greatly afflicted."
11 I said in my alarm,
 "^All people are liars."

12 What shall I ^repay to the
  Lord
 For all His ^Bbenefits to me?
13 I will lift up the ^cup of
  salvation,
 And call upon the name of the
  Lord.
14 I will ^pay my vows to the
  Lord;
 May it be in the presence of all
  His people!
15 ^Precious in the sight of the
  Lord
 Is the death of His godly ones.
16 O Lord, I surely am Your
  slave,
 I am Your slave, the ^son of
  Your female slave,
 You have ^Bunfastened my
  restraints.
17 I will offer You ^a sacrifice of
  thanksgiving,
 And call upon the name of
  the Lord.
18 I will ^pay my vows to the
  Lord,
 May it be in the presence of all
  His people,
19 In the ^courtyards of the
  Lord's house,
 In the midst of you,
  Jerusalem!
 Praise the Lord!

A PSALM OF PRAISE.

117
^Praise the Lord, all
  nations;
 Sing His praises, all peoples!
2 For His mercy toward us is
  great,
 And the ^truth of the Lord is
  everlasting.
 Praise the Lord!

THANKSGIVING FOR THE LORD'S
SAVING GOODNESS.

118
^Give thanks to the Lord,
  for ^BHe is good;
 For His mercy is everlasting.
2 Let ^Israel say,
 "His mercy is everlasting."
3 Oh let the ^house of Aaron say,
 "His mercy is everlasting."
4 Let those ^who fear the Lord
  say,
 "His mercy is everlasting."

5 From *my* ^distress I called
  upon the Lord;
 The Lord answered me *and
  put me* in an open space.
6 The Lord is for me; I will not
  fear;
 ^What can man do to me?
7 The Lord is for me ^among
  those who help me;
 Therefore I will look *with
  satisfaction* on those who
  hate me.
8 It is ^better to take refuge in
  the Lord
 Than to trust in people.

116:7 ^Jer 6:16; Matt 11:29   116:8 ^Ps 49:15; 56:13
116:9 ^Ps 27:13   116:10 ^2 Cor 4:13   116:11 ^Ps 62:9;
Rom 3:4   116:12 ^2 Chr 32:25   ^BPs 103:2
116:13 ^Ps 16:5   116:14 ^Ps 50:14; 116:18
116:15 ^Ps 72:14   116:16 ^Ps 86:16   ^BPs 107:14
116:17 ^Lev 7:12; Ps 50:14   116:18 ^Ps 116:14
116:19 ^Ps 92:13; 96:8   117:1 ^Rom 15:11
117:2 ^Ps 100:5; 146:6   118:1 ^1 Chr 16:8, 34
^B2 Chr 5:13   118:2 ^Ps 115:9   118:3 ^Ps 115:10
118:4 ^Ps 115:11   118:5 ^Ps 18:6; 86:7   118:6 ^Ps 56:4, 11
118:7 ^Ps 54:4   118:8 ^2 Chr 32:7, 8; Ps 40:4

9 It is ^better to take refuge in
   the LORD
   Than to trust in noblemen.

10 All nations ^surrounded me;
   In the name of the LORD I will
   certainly fend them off.

11 They ^surrounded me, yes,
   they surrounded me;
   In the name of the LORD I will
   certainly fend them off.

12 They surrounded me ^like
   bees;
   They were extinguished like a
   ^Bfire of thorn bushes;
   In the name of the LORD I will
   certainly fend them off.

13 You ^pushed me violently so
   that I was falling,
   But the LORD ^Bhelped me.

14 ^The LORD is my strength and
   song,
   And He has become ^Bmy
   salvation.

15 The sound of joyful shouting
   and salvation is in the tents
   of the righteous;
   The ^right hand of the LORD
   performs valiantly.

16 The ^right hand of the LORD is
   exalted;
   The right hand of the LORD
   performs valiantly.

17 I will not die, but live,
   And ^tell of the works of the
   LORD.

18 The LORD has ^disciplined me
   severely,
   But He has ^Bnot turned me
   over to death.

19 ^Open the gates of
   righteousness to me;
   I will enter through them,
   I will give thanks to the
   LORD.

20 This is the gate of the
   LORD;
   The ^righteous will enter
   through it.

21 I will give thanks to You, for
   You have ^answered me,
   And You have become my
   salvation.

22 A ^stone which the builders
   rejected
   Has become the chief
   cornerstone.

23 This came about from the
   LORD;
   It is marvelous in our eyes.

24 This is the day which the
   LORD has made;
   Let's ^rejoice and be glad in it.

25 Please, O LORD, do save *us*;
   Please, O LORD, do send
   ^prosperity!

26 ^Blessed is the one who
   comes in the name of the
   LORD;
   We have blessed you from
   the house of the LORD.

27 The LORD is God, and He has
   given us ^light;
   Bind the festival sacrifice to
   the horns of the altar with
   cords.

28 You are my God, and I give
   thanks to You;
   You are my God, ^I exalt You.

29 ^Give thanks to the LORD,
   for He is good;
   For His mercy is
   everlasting.

118:9 ^Ps 146:3   118:10 ^Ps 3:6; 88:17   118:11 ^Ps 88:17
118:12 ^Deut 1:44   ^BPs 58:9   118:13 ^Ps 140:4
^BPs 86:17   118:14 ^Ex 15:2   ^BPs 27:1   118:15 ^Ex 15:6;
Ps 89:13   118:16 ^Ex 15:6; Ps 89:13   118:17 ^Ps 73:28;
107:22   118:18 ^Ps 73:14   ^BPs 86:13   118:19 ^Is 26:2
118:20 ^Ps 15:1, 2; 24:3–6   118:21 ^Ps 116:1; 118:5
118:22 ^Matt 21:42; Mark 12:10, 11   118:24 ^Ps 31:7
118:25 ^Ps 122:6, 7   118:26 ^Matt 21:9; 23:39
118:27 ^Esth 8:16; Ps 18:28   118:28 ^Ex 15:2; Is 25:1
118:29 ^Ps 118:1

MEDITATIONS AND PRAYERS
RELATING TO THE LAW OF GOD.

ALEPH א

119
Blessed are those whose
way is blameless,
Who ^walk in the Law of the
LORD.

2 Blessed are those who
comply with His
testimonies,
And ^seek Him ^B^with all *their*
heart.

3 They also ^do no injustice;
They walk in His ways.

4 You have ^ordained Your
precepts,
That we are to keep *them*
diligently.

5 Oh that my ^ways may be
established
To keep Your statutes!

6 Then I ^will not be ashamed
When I look at all Your
commandments.

7 I will ^give thanks to You with
uprightness of heart,
When I learn Your righteous
judgments.

8 I will keep Your statutes;
Do not utterly ^abandon me!

BETH ב

9 How can a young man keep
his way pure?
By ^keeping *it* according to
Your word.

10 With ^all my heart I have
sought You;
Do not let me wander from
Your commandments.

11 I have ^treasured Your word in
my heart,
So that I may not sin against
You.

12 Blessed are You, LORD;
^Teach me Your statutes.

13 With my lips I have ^told of
All the ordinances of Your
mouth.

14 I have ^rejoiced in the way of
Your testimonies,
As much as in all riches.

15 I will ^meditate on Your
precepts
And regard Your ways.

16 I shall ^delight in Your
statutes;
I will not forget Your word.

GIMEL ג

17 ^Deal *generously* with Your
servant,
That I may live and keep Your
word.

18 Open my eyes, that I may
behold
Wonderful things from Your
Law.

19 I am a ^stranger on the
earth;
Do not hide Your
commandments from me.

20 My soul is crushed ^with
longing
For Your ordinances at all
times.

21 You ^rebuke the arrogant, the
^B^cursed,
Who wander from Your
commandments.

22 ^Take disgrace and contempt
away from me,
For I comply with Your
testimonies.

119:1 ^Ps 128:1; Ezek 11:20   119:2 ^Deut 4:29
^B^Deut 6:5   119:3 ^1 John 3:9; 5:18   119:4 ^Deut 4:13;
Neh 9:13   119:5 ^Ps 40:2; Prov 4:26
119:6 ^Job 22:26; Ps 119:80   119:7 ^Ps 119:62
119:8 ^Ps 38:21; 71:9, 18   119:9 ^1 Kin 2:4; 8:25
119:10 ^2 Chr 15:15; Ps 119:2, 145   119:11 ^Ps 37:31;
40:8   119:12 ^Ps 119:26, 64, 108, 124, 135, 171
119:13 ^Ps 40:9   119:14 ^Ps 119:111, 162
119:15 ^Ps 1:2; 119:23, 48, 78, 97, 148   119:16 ^Ps 1:2;
119:24   119:17 ^Ps 13:6; 116:7   119:19 ^Gen 47:9;
Lev 25:23   119:20 ^Ps 42:1, 2; 63:1   119:21 ^Ps 68:30
^B^Deut 27:26   119:22 ^Ps 39:8; 119:39

23 Even though ^rulers sit *and*
   speak against me,
   Your servant meditates on
   Your statutes.
24 Your testimonies also are my
   ^delight;
   They are my advisers.

DALETH ד

25 My ^soul clings to the dust;
   ^BRevive me according to Your
   word.
26 I have told of my ways, and
   You have answered me;
   ^Teach me Your statutes.
27 Make me understand the way
   of Your precepts,
   And I will ^meditate on Your
   wonders.
28 My ^soul weeps because of
   grief;
   ^BStrengthen me according to
   Your word.
29 Remove the false way from me,
   And graciously grant me Your
   Law.
30 I have chosen the faithful way;
   I have placed Your judgments
   before me.
31 I ^cling to Your testimonies;
   LORD, do not put me to shame!
32 I shall run the way of Your
   commandments,
   For You will ^enlarge my heart.

HE ה

33 ^Teach me the way of Your
   statutes, LORD,
   And I shall comply with it to
   the end.
34 ^Give me understanding, so
   that I may comply with Your
   Law
   And keep it with all *my* heart.
35 Make me walk in the ^path of
   Your commandments,
   For I delight in it.

36 Incline my heart to Your
   testimonies,
   And not to ^*dishonest* gain.
37 Turn my ^eyes away from
   looking at what is worthless,
   And ^Brevive me in Your ways.
38 ^Establish Your word to Your
   servant
   As that which produces
   reverence for You.
39 ^Take away my disgrace which
   I dread,
   For Your judgments are good.
40 Behold, I ^long for Your
   precepts;
   Revive me through Your
   righteousness.

VAV ו

41 May Your ^favor also come to
   me, LORD,
   Your salvation according to
   Your word;
42 So that I will have an ^answer
   for one who ^Btaunts me,
   For I trust in Your word.
43 And do not take the word
   of truth utterly out of my
   mouth,
   For I ^wait for Your judgments.
44 So I will ^keep Your Law
   continually,
   Forever and ever.
45 And I will ^walk at liberty,
   For I seek Your precepts.
46 I will also speak of Your
   testimonies ^before kings
   And shall not be ashamed.

119:23 ^Ps 119:161   119:24 ^Ps 119:16   119:25 ^Ps 44:25
^BPs 119:37   119:26 ^Ps 25:4; 27:11   119:27 ^Ps 105:2;
145:5   119:28 ^Ps 22:14   ^BPs 20:2   119:31 ^Deut 11:22
119:32 ^1 Kin 4:29; Is 60:5   119:33 ^Ps 119:5, 12
119:34 ^Ps 119:27, 73, 125, 144, 169   119:35 ^Ps 25:4;
Is 40:14   119:36 ^Ezek 33:31; Mark 7:21, 22
119:37 ^Is 33:15   ^BPs 71:20   119:38 ^2 Sam 7:25
119:39 ^Ps 119:22   119:40 ^Ps 119:20   119:41 ^Ps 119:77
119:42 ^Prov 27:11   ^BPs 102:8
119:43 ^Ps 119:49, 74, 81, 114, 147   119:44 ^Ps 119:33
119:45 ^Prov 4:12   119:46 ^Matt 10:18; Acts 26:1, 2

47 I will ^delight in Your
   commandments,
   Which I love.
48 And I shall lift up my hands to
   Your commandments,
   Which I ^love;
   And I will meditate on Your
   statutes.

ZAYIN ז

49 Remember the word to Your
   servant,
   In which You have made me
   hope.
50 This is my ^comfort in my
   misery,
   That Your word has revived
   me.
51 The arrogant ^utterly deride
   me,
   Yet I do not ^Bturn aside from
   Your Law.
52 I have ^remembered Your
   judgments from of old,
   LORD,
   And comfort myself.
53 Burning ^indignation has
   seized me because of the
   wicked,
   Who ^Babandon Your Law.
54 Your statutes are my songs
   In the house of my ^pilgrimage.
55 LORD, I ^remember Your name
   in the night,
   And keep Your Law.
56 This has become mine,
   That I ^comply with Your
   precepts.

HETH ח

57 The LORD is my ^portion;
   I have promised to ^Bkeep Your
   words.
58 I ^sought Your favor ^Bwith all
   my heart;
   Be gracious to me according to
   Your word.

59 I ^considered my ways
   And turned my feet to Your
   testimonies.
60 I hurried and did not delay
   To keep Your
   commandments.
61 The ^snares of the wicked have
   surrounded me,
   But I have not forgotten Your
   Law.
62 At midnight I will rise to give
   thanks to You
   Because of Your ^righteous
   judgments.
63 I am a ^companion to all those
   who fear You,
   And to those who keep Your
   precepts.
64 ^The earth is full of Your
   goodness, LORD;
   ^BTeach me Your statutes.

TETH ט

65 You have treated Your servant
   well,
   LORD, according to Your word.
66 Teach me good ^discernment
   and knowledge,
   For I believe in Your
   commandments.
67 ^Before I was afflicted I went
   astray,
   But now I keep Your word.
68 You are ^good and You ^Bdo
   good;
   Teach me Your statutes.
69 The arrogant have ^forged a lie
   against me;

119:47 ^Ps 119:16   119:48 ^Ps 119:97, 127, 159
119:50 ^Job 6:10; Rom 15:4   119:51 ^Job 30:1
^BJob 23:11   119:52 ^Ps 103:18   119:53 ^Ex 32:19
^BPs 89:30   119:54 ^Gen 47:9; Ps 119:19
119:55 ^Ps 63:6   119:56 ^Ps 119:22, 69, 100
119:57 ^Ps 16:5   ^BDeut 33:9
119:58 ^1 Kin 13:6   ^BPs 119:2   119:59 ^Mark 14:72;
Luke 15:17   119:61 ^Job 36:8; Ps 140:5   119:62 ^Ps 119:7
119:63 ^Ps 101:6   119:64 ^Ps 33:5   ^BPs 119:12
119:66 ^Phil 1:9   119:67 ^Ps 119:71, 75; Jer 31:18, 19
119:68 ^Ps 86:5   ^BDeut 8:16   119:69 ^Job 13:4; Ps 109:2

With all *my* heart I will comply with Your precepts.
70 Their heart is ^insensitive, like fat,
But I delight in Your Law.
71 It is ^good for me that I was afflicted,
So that I may learn Your statutes.
72 The ^Law of Your mouth is better to me
Than thousands of gold and silver *pieces*.

YODH ＇

73 ^Your hands made me and fashioned me;
^Give me understanding, so that I may learn Your commandments.
74 May those who fear You ^see me and be glad,
Because I wait for Your word.
75 I know, Lord, that Your judgments are righteous,
And that You have afflicted me ^in faithfulness.
76 May Your favor comfort me, According to Your word to Your servant.
77 May ^Your compassion come to me so that I may live,
For Your Law is my delight.
78 May ^the arrogant be put to shame, because they lead me astray with a lie;
But I shall meditate on Your precepts.
79 May those who fear You turn to me,
And those who know Your testimonies.
80 May my heart be ^blameless in Your statutes,
So that I will not be ashamed.

KAPH כ

81 My ^soul languishes for Your salvation;
I wait for Your word.
82 My ^eyes fail *with longing* for Your word,
While I say, "When will You comfort me?"
83 Though I have ^become like a wineskin in the smoke,
I do not forget Your statutes.
84 How many are the ^days of Your servant?
When will You ^execute judgment on those who persecute me?
85 The arrogant have ^dug pits for me,
People who are not in accord with Your Law.
86 All Your commandments are faithful;
They have ^persecuted me with a lie; help me!
87 They almost destroyed me on earth,
But as for me, I ^did not abandon Your precepts.
88 Revive me according to Your faithfulness,
So that I may keep the testimony of Your mouth.

LAMEDH ל

89 ^Forever, Lord,
Your word stands in heaven.
90 Your ^faithfulness *continues* throughout generations;
You established the earth, and it stands.

119:70 ^Deut 32:15; Job 15:27　119:71 ^Ps 119:67, 75
119:72 ^Ps 19:10; 119:127　119:73 ^Job 10:8　^Ps 119:34
119:74 ^Ps 34:2; 35:27　119:75 ^Heb 12:10
119:77 ^Ps 119:41　119:78 ^Jer 50:32　119:80 ^Ps 119:1
119:81 ^Ps 84:2　119:82 ^Ps 69:3; 119:123
119:83 ^Job 30:30　119:84 ^Ps 39:4　^Rev 6:10
119:85 ^Ps 7:15; 35:7　119:86 ^Ps 35:19; 119:78, 161
119:87 ^Is 58:2　119:89 ^Ps 89:2; 119:160
119:90 ^Ps 36:5; 89:1, 2

91 They stand this day by Your
ᴬordinances,
For all things are Your
servants.

92 If Your Law had not been my
delight,
Then I would have perished
ᴬin my misery.

93 I will never forget Your
precepts,
For by them You have
ᴬrevived me.

94 I am Yours, ᴬsave me;
For I have ᴮsought Your
precepts.

95 The wicked ᴬwait for me to
destroy me;
I will diligently consider Your
testimonies.

96 I have seen a limit to all
perfection;
Your commandment is
exceedingly broad.

MEM מ

97 How I ᴬlove Your Law!
It is my ᴮmeditation all the
day.

98 Your ᴬcommandments make
me wiser than my
enemies,
For they are ever mine.

99 I have more insight than all
my teachers,
For Your testimonies are my
ᴬmeditation.

100 I understand ᴬmore than
those who are old,
Because I have complied with
Your precepts.

101 I have ᴬrestrained my feet
from every evil way,
So that I may keep Your word.

102 I have not ᴬturned aside from
Your judgments,
For You Yourself have taught
me.

103 How ᴬsweet are Your words to
my taste!
Yes, sweeter than honey to my
mouth!

104 From Your precepts I ᴬget
understanding;
Therefore I ᴮhate every false
way.

NUN נ

105 Your word is a ᴬlamp to my feet
And a light to my path.

106 I have ᴬsworn and I will
confirm it,
That I will keep Your righteous
judgments.

107 I am exceedingly ᴬafflicted;
ᴮRevive me, Lᴏʀᴅ, according to
Your word.

108 Be pleased to accept the
ᴬvoluntary offerings of my
mouth, Lᴏʀᴅ,
And teach me Your judgments.

109 My ᴬlife is continually ¹in my
hand,
Yet I do not forget Your Law.

110 The wicked have ᴬset a trap
for me,
Yet I have not wandered from
Your precepts.

111 I have ᴬinherited Your
testimonies forever,
For they are the joy of my
heart.

112 I have ᴬinclined my heart to
perform Your statutes
Forever, *even* to the end.

119:91 ᴬJer 31:35; 33:25 **119:92** ᴬPs 119:50
119:93 ᴬPs 119:25 **119:94** ᴬPs 119:146 ᴮPs 119:45
119:95 ᴬPs 40:14; Is 32:7 **119:97** ᴬPs 119:47 ᴮPs 1:2
119:98 ᴬDeut 4:6; Ps 119:130 **119:99** ᴬPs 119:15
119:100 ᴬJob 32:7–9 **119:101** ᴬProv 1:15
119:102 ᴬDeut 17:20; Josh 23:6 **119:103** ᴬPs 19:10;
Prov 8:11 **119:104** ᴬPs 119:130 ᴮPs 119:128
119:105 ᴬProv 6:23 **119:106** ᴬNeh 10:29
119:107 ᴬPs 119:25, 50 ᴮPs 119:25 **119:108** ᴬHos 14:2;
Heb 13:15 **119:109** ᴬJudg 12:3; Job 13:14
119:110 ᴬPs 91:3; 140:5 **119:111** ᴬDeut 33:4
119:112 ᴬPs 119:36

119:109 ¹I.e., in danger

SAMEKH ס

113 I hate those who are
^double-minded,
But I love Your Law.

114 You are my ^hiding place and
my ᴮshield;
I wait for Your word.

115 ^Leave me, you evildoers,
So that I may comply with the
commandments of my God.

116 Sustain me according to Your
word, that I may live;
And ^do not let me be
ashamed of my hope.

117 Sustain me so that I may be
^safe,
That I may have regard for
Your statutes continually.

118 You have rejected all those
^who stray from Your statutes,
For their deceitfulness is
useless.

119 You have removed all the wicked
of the earth *like* ^impurities;
Therefore I love Your
testimonies.

120 My flesh ^trembles from the
fear of You,
And I am afraid of Your
judgments.

AYIN ע

121 I have ^done justice and
righteousness;
Do not leave me to my
oppressors.

122 Be ^a guarantor for Your
servant for good;
Do not let the arrogant
oppress me.

123 My ^eyes fail *with longing* for
Your salvation,
And for Your righteous word.

124 Deal with Your servant
^according to Your
graciousness,
And ᴮteach me Your statutes.

125 ^I am Your servant; ᴮgive me
understanding,
So that I may know Your
testimonies.

126 It is time for the Lᴏʀᴅ to ^act,
For they have broken Your
Law.

127 Therefore I ^love Your
commandments
Above gold, yes, above pure
gold.

128 Therefore I carefully follow all
Your ^precepts concerning
everything,
I ᴮhate every false way.

PE פ

129 Your testimonies are
^wonderful;
Therefore my soul ᴮcomplies
with them.

130 The ^unfolding of Your words
gives light;
It gives ᴮunderstanding to the
simple.

131 I ^opened my mouth wide and
panted,
For I longed for Your
commandments.

132 ^Turn to me and be gracious
to me,
As is right for those who love
Your name.

133 Establish my ^footsteps in Your
word,
And do not let any wrongdoing
ᴮhave power over me.

119:113 ^1 Kin 18:21; James 1:8   119:114 ^Ps 31:20
ᴮPs 84:9   119:115 ^Ps 6:8; 139:19   119:116 ^Ps 25:2, 20;
31:1, 17   119:117 ^Ps 12:5; Prov 29:25
119:118 ^Ps 119:10, 21   119:119 ^Is 1:22, 25; Ezek 22:18, 19
119:120 ^Job 4:14; Hab 3:16   119:121 ^2 Sam 8:15;
Job 29:14   119:122 ^Job 17:3; Heb 7:22
119:123 ^Ps 119:82   119:124 ^Ps 51:1   ᴮPs 119:12
119:125 ^Ps 116:16   ᴮPs 119:27   119:126 ^Jer 18:23;
Ezek 31:11   119:127 ^Ps 19:10; 119:47   119:128 ^Ps 19:8
ᴮPs 119:104   119:129 ^Ps 119:18   ᴮPs 119:22
119:130 ^Prov 6:23   ᴮPs 19:7   119:131 ^Job 29:23;
Ps 81:10   119:132 ^Ps 25:16; 106:4   119:133 ^Ps 17:5
ᴮPs 19:13

134 ᴬRedeem me from oppression
by man,
So that I may keep Your
precepts.
135 ᴬMake Your face shine upon
Your servant,
And teach me Your statutes.
136 My eyes shed ᴬstreams of
water,
Because they ᴮdo not keep
Your Law.

TSADHE צ

137 ᴬYou are righteous, Lᴏʀᴅ,
And Your judgments are right.
138 You have commanded
Your testimonies in
ᴬrighteousness
And great ᴮfaithfulness.
139 My ᴬzeal has consumed me,
Because my enemies have
forgotten Your words.
140 Your ᴬword is very pure,
Therefore Your servant loves it.
141 I am small and ᴬdespised,
Yet I do not forget Your
precepts.
142 Your righteousness is an
everlasting righteousness,
And ᴬYour Law is truth.
143 Trouble and anguish have
come upon me,
Yet Your commandments are
my ᴬdelight.
144 Your ᴬtestimonies are
righteous forever;
ᴮGive me understanding that I
may live.

QOPH ק

145 I cried out ᴬwith all my heart;
answer me, Lᴏʀᴅ!
I will ᴮcomply with Your
statutes.
146 I cried to You; ᴬsave me
And I shall keep Your
testimonies.

147 I ᴬrise before dawn and cry for
help;
I wait for Your words.
148 My eyes anticipate the ᴬnight
watches,
So that I may meditate on
Your word.
149 Hear my voice ᴬaccording to
Your faithfulness;
Revive me, Lᴏʀᴅ, according to
Your judgments.
150 Those who follow after
wickedness approach;
They are far from Your Law.
151 You are ᴬnear, Lᴏʀᴅ,
And all Your commandments
are truth.
152 From long ago I have ᴬknown
from Your testimonies
That You have founded them
forever.

RESH ר

153 ᴬLook at my ᴮaffliction and
rescue me,
For I have not forgotten Your
Law.
154 ᴬPlead my cause and redeem
me;
Revive me according to Your
word.
155 Salvation is ᴬfar from the
wicked,
For they do not seek Your
statutes.
156 ᴬGreat are Your mercies, Lᴏʀᴅ;
Revive me according to Your
judgments.

119:134 ᴬPs 119:84; 142:6   119:135 ᴬNum 6:25; Ps 4:6
119:136 ᴬJer 9:1, 18; 14:17   ᴮPs 119:158
119:137 ᴬEzra 9:15; Neh 9:33   119:138 ᴬPs 19:7-9
ᴮPs 119:86, 90   119:139 ᴬPs 69:9; John 2:17
119:140 ᴬPs 12:6; 19:8   119:141 ᴬPs 22:6
119:142 ᴬPs 19:9; 119:151, 160   119:143 ᴬPs 119:24
119:144 ᴬPs 19:9   ᴮPs 119:27   119:145 ᴬPs 119:10
ᴮPs 119:22, 55   119:146 ᴬPs 3:7   119:147 ᴬPs 5:3; 57:8
119:148 ᴬPs 63:6   119:149 ᴬPs 119:124
119:151 ᴬPs 34:18; 145:18   119:152 ᴬPs 119:125
119:153 ᴬLam 5:1   ᴮPs 119:50   119:154 ᴬ1 Sam 24:15;
Ps 35:1   119:155 ᴬJob 5:4   119:156 ᴬ2 Sam 24:14

157 Many are my ^persecutors and
my enemies,
Yet I do not turn aside from
Your testimonies.
158 I see the ^treacherous and
^loathe *them,*
Because they do not keep Your
word.
159 Consider how I ^love Your
precepts;
Revive me, Lord, according to
Your faithfulness.
160 The ^sum of Your word is ^truth,
And every one of Your
righteous judgments is
everlasting.

SHIN ש

161 ^Rulers persecute me without
cause,
But my heart stands in awe of
Your words.
162 I rejoice at Your word,
Like one who ^finds great
plunder.
163 I ^hate and loathe falsehood,
But I love Your Law.
164 Seven times a day I praise You
Because of Your ^righteous
judgments.
165 Those who love Your Law have
^great peace,
And ^nothing causes them to
stumble.
166 I ^hope for Your salvation, Lord,
And do Your commandments.
167 My ^soul keeps Your
testimonies,
And I love them exceedingly.
168 I keep Your precepts and Your
testimonies,
For all my ^ways are before
You.

TAV ת

169 Let my ^cry come before You,
Lord;

Give me understanding
according to Your word.
170 Let my pleading come before
You;
^Save me according to Your
word.
171 Let my lips pour out praise,
For You ^teach me Your
statutes.
172 Let my tongue sing about Your
word,
For all Your ^commandments
are righteousness.
173 Let Your hand be ready to help
me,
For I have ^chosen Your
precepts.
174 I ^long for Your salvation, Lord,
And Your Law is my ^delight.
175 Let my ^soul live that it may
praise You,
And let Your ordinances help
me.
176 I have ^wandered about like a
lost sheep; search for Your
servant,
For I do not forget Your
commandments.

**PRAYER FOR RESCUE FROM
THE TREACHEROUS.**
A Song of Ascents.

120 ^I cried to the Lord in my
trouble,
And He answered me.
2 Rescue my soul, Lord, from
^lying lips,
From a deceitful tongue.

119:157 ^Ps 7:1; 119:86, 161   119:158 ^Is 21:2   ^Ps 139:21
119:159 ^Ps 119:47   119:160 ^Ps 139:17   ^Ps 119:142
119:161 ^1 Sam 24:11; 26:18   119:162 ^1 Sam 30:16; Is 9:3
119:163 ^Ps 31:6; 119:104, 128   119:164 ^Ps 119:7, 160
119:165 ^Ps 37:11   ^Prov 3:23   119:166 ^Gen 49:18;
Ps 119:81, 174   119:167 ^Ps 119:129   119:168 ^Job 24:23;
Ps 139:3   119:169 ^Job 16:18; Ps 18:6
119:170 ^Ps 22:20; 31:2   119:171 ^Ps 94:12; 119:12
119:172 ^Ps 119:138   119:173 ^Josh 24:22; Luke 10:42
119:174 ^Ps 119:166   ^Ps 119:16, 24   119:175 ^Is 55:3
119:176 ^Is 53:6; Jer 50:6   120:1 ^Ps 18:6; 66:14
120:2 ^Ps 109:2; Prov 12:22

³ What will *He* give to you, and
what more will *He* do to you,
You ^deceitful tongue?

⁴ ^Sharp arrows of the warrior,
With the *burning* ^Bcoals of the
broom tree!

⁵ Woe to me, for I reside in
^Meshech,
For I have settled among the
^Btents of Kedar!

⁶ Too long has my soul had its
dwelling
With those who ^hate peace.

⁷ I ^am *for* peace, but when I
speak,
They are for war.

THE LORD, THE KEEPER OF ISRAEL.

A Song of Ascents.

121
I will ^raise my eyes to ^Bthe
mountains;
From where will my help
come?

² My ^help *comes* from the LORD,
Who ^Bmade heaven and earth.

³ He will not ^allow your foot to
slip;
He who ^Bwatches over you will
not slumber.

⁴ Behold, He who watches over
Israel
Will neither slumber nor
sleep.

⁵ The LORD is your ^protector;
The LORD is your shade on
your right hand.

⁶ The ^sun will not beat down on
you by day,
Nor the moon by night.

⁷ The LORD will ^protect you
from all evil;
He will keep your soul.

⁸ The LORD will ^guard your
going out and your coming in
From this time and forever.

PRAYER FOR THE PEACE OF JERUSALEM.

A Song of Ascents, of David.

122
I was glad when they said
to me,
"Let's ^go to the house of the
LORD."

² Our feet are standing
Within your ^gates,
Jerusalem,

³ Jerusalem, that has been built
As a city that is ^firmly joined
together;

⁴ To which the tribes ^go up, the
tribes of the LORD—
An ordinance for Israel—
To give thanks to the name of
the LORD.

⁵ For ^thrones were set there for
judgment,
The thrones of the house of
David.

⁶ Pray for the ^peace of
Jerusalem:
"May they prosper who ^Blove
you.

⁷ "May peace be within your
^walls,
And prosperity within your
^Bpalaces."

⁸ For the sake of my brothers
and my friends,
I will now say, "^May peace be
within you."

⁹ For the sake of the house of
the LORD our God,
I will ^seek your good.

120:3 ^Ps 52:4; Zeph 3:13   120:4 ^Ps 45:5   ^BPs 140:10
120:5 ^Gen 10:2   ^BSong 1:5   120:6 ^Ps 35:20
120:7 ^Ps 109:4   121:1 ^Ps 123:1   ^BPs 87:1
121:2 ^Ps 124:8   ^BPs 115:15   121:3 ^1 Sam 2:9   ^BPs 41:2
121:5 ^Ps 91:4   121:6 ^Ps 91:5; Is 49:10   121:7 ^Ps 41:2;
91:10–12   121:8 ^Deut 28:6   122:1 ^Ps 42:4; Is 2:3
122:2 ^Ps 9:14; 87:2   122:3 ^2 Sam 5:9; Neh 4:6
122:4 ^Ex 23:17; Deut 16:16   122:5 ^Deut 17:8;
2 Chr 19:8   122:6 ^Ps 29:11   ^BPs 102:14   122:7 ^Ps 51:18
^BPs 48:3, 13   122:8 ^1 Sam 25:6; John 20:19
122:9 ^Neh 2:10; Esth 10:3

PRAYER FOR THE LORD'S HELP.
A Song of Ascents.

123 To You I have ^raised my eyes,
You who ^Bare enthroned in the heavens!

2 Behold, as the eyes of
^servants *look* to the hand of their master,
As the eyes of a female servant to the hand of her mistress,
So our eyes *look* to the LORD our God,
Until He is gracious to us.

3 ^Be gracious to us, LORD, be gracious to us,
For we have had much more than enough of ^Bcontempt.

4 Our soul has had much more than enough
Of the ^scoffing of ^Bthose who are at ease,
And of the contempt of the proud.

PRAISE FOR RESCUE FROM ENEMIES.
A Song of Ascents, of David.

124 "^Had it not been the LORD who was on our side,"
Let Israel say,

2 "Had it not been the LORD who was on our side
When people rose up against us,

3 Then they would have ^swallowed us alive,
When their anger was kindled against us;

4 Then the ^waters would have flooded over us,
The stream would have swept over our souls;

5 Then the ^raging waters would have swept over our souls."

6 Blessed be the LORD,
Who has not given us to be ^torn by their teeth.

7 Our souls have escaped ^like a bird from the trapper's ^Bsnare;
The snare is broken and we have escaped.

8 Our help is in the name of the LORD,
Who ^made heaven and earth.

THE LORD SURROUNDS HIS PEOPLE.
A Song of Ascents.

125 Those who trust in the LORD
Are like Mount Zion, *which* ^cannot be moved *but* remains forever.

2 *As* the mountains surround Jerusalem,
So ^the LORD surrounds His people
From this time and forever.

3 For the ^scepter of wickedness will not rest upon the land of the righteous,
So that the righteous will not extend their hands to do wrong.

4 ^Do good, LORD, to those who are good
And to those who are ^Bupright in their hearts.

5 But as for those who ^turn aside to their ^Bcrooked ways,
The LORD will lead them away with those who practice injustice.
Peace be upon Israel.

123:1 ^Ps 121:1 ^BPs 2:4   123:2 ^Prov 27:18; Mal 1:6
123:3 ^Ps 4:1 ^BNeh 4:4   123:4 ^Neh 2:19 ^BJob 12:5
124:1 ^Ps 94:17   124:3 ^Num 16:30; Ps 35:25
124:4 ^Job 22:11; Ps 18:16   125:1 ^Job 38:11
124:6 ^Ps 27:2; Prov 30:14   124:7 ^Prov 6:5 ^BPs 91:3
124:8 ^Gen 1:1; Ps 134:3   125:1 ^Ps 46:5
125:2 ^Zech 2:5   125:3 ^Ps 89:22; Prov 22:8
125:4 ^Ps 119:68 ^BPs 7:10   125:5 ^Job 23:11 ^BProv 2:15

THANKSGIVING FOR RETURN FROM CAPTIVITY.

A Song of Ascents.

126 When the Lord ᴬbrought back the captives of Zion,
We were ᴮlike those who dream.

2 Then our ᴬmouth was filled with laughter
And our tongue with joyful shouting;
Then they said among the nations,
"The Lord has ᴮdone great things for them."

3 The Lord has done great things for us;
We are ᴬjoyful.

4 Restore our fortunes, Lord,
As the ᴬstreams in the South.

5 Those who sow in ᴬtears
shall harvest with ᴮjoyful shouting.

6 One who goes here and there weeping, carrying *his* bag of seed,
Shall indeed come again with a shout of joy, bringing his sheaves *with him*.

PROSPERITY COMES FROM THE LORD.

A Song of Ascents, of Solomon.

127 Unless the Lord ᴬbuilds a house,
They who build it labor in vain;
Unless the Lord ᴮguards a city,
The watchman stays awake in vain.

2 It is futile for you to rise up early,
To stay up late,
To ᴬeat the bread of painful labor;
This is how He gives to His beloved ᴮsleep.

3 Behold, children are a gift of the Lord,
The ᴬfruit of the womb is a reward.

4 Like arrows in the hand of a ᴬwarrior,
So are the children of one's youth.

5 ᴬBlessed is the man whose quiver is full of them;
They will not be ashamed
When they speak with their enemies in the gate.

BLESSEDNESS OF THE FEAR OF THE LORD.

A Song of Ascents.

128 ᴬBlessed is everyone who fears the Lord,
Who walks in His ways.

2 When you eat the ᴬfruit of the labor of your hands,
You will be happy and ᴮit will go well for you.

3 Your wife will be like a ᴬfruitful vine
Within your house,
Your children like olive plants
Around your table.

4 Behold, for so shall a man
Who fears the Lord be blessed.

5 ᴬThe Lord bless you from Zion,
And may you see the prosperity of Jerusalem all the days of your life.

6 Indeed, may you see your ᴬchildren's children.
Peace be upon Israel!

126:1 ᴬPs 85:1   ᴮActs 12:9   126:2 ᴬJob 8:21
ᴮ1 Sam 12:24   126:3 ᴬIs 25:9; Zeph 3:14   126:4 ᴬIs 35:6;
43:19   126:5 ᴬPs 80:5   ᴮIs 35:10   127:1 ᴬPs 78:69
ᴮPs 121:4   127:2 ᴬGen 3:17, 19   ᴮJob 11:18, 19
127:3 ᴬDeut 7:13; 28:4   127:4 ᴬPs 112:2; 120:4
127:5 ᴬPs 128:2, 3   128:1 ᴬPs 112:1; 119:1
128:2 ᴬPs 109:11   ᴮEccl 8:12   128:3 ᴬEzek 19:10
128:5 ᴬPs 134:3   128:6 ᴬGen 48:11; 50:23

PRAYER FOR THE OVERTHROW OF ZION'S ENEMIES.

A Song of Ascents.

129 "Many times they have ^attacked me from my ^Byouth up,"
Let Israel say,

2 "Many times they have attacked me from my youth up;
Yet they have ^not prevailed against me.

3 "The plowers plowed upon my back;
They lengthened their furrows."

4 The Lord ^is righteous;
He has cut up the ^Bropes of the wicked.

5 May all who ^hate Zion
Be put to shame and turned backward;

6 May they be like ^grass upon the housetops,
Which withers before it grows up;

7 With which the harvester does not fill his hand,
Or the binder of sheaves his ^arms;

8 Nor do those who pass by say,
"The ^blessing of the Lord be upon you;
We bless you in the name of the Lord."

HOPE IN THE LORD'S FORGIVING LOVE.

A Song of Ascents.

130 Out of the ^depths I have cried to You, Lord.

2 Lord, hear my voice!
Let Your ears be attentive
To the ^sound of my pleadings.

3 If You, Lord, were to keep *account of* guilty deeds,
Lord, who could ^stand?

4 But there is ^forgiveness with You,
So that You may be ^Brevered.

5 I wait for the Lord, my soul waits,
And I wait ^for His word.

6 My soul *waits in hope* for the Lord
More than the watchmen ^for the morning;
Yes, more than the watchmen for the morning.

7 Israel, wait for the Lord;
For with the Lord there is mercy,
And with Him is ^abundant redemption.

8 And He will ^redeem Israel
From all his guilty deeds.

CHILDLIKE TRUST IN THE LORD.

A Song of Ascents, of David.

131 Lord, my heart is not ^proud, nor my eyes ^Barrogant;
Nor do I involve myself in great matters,
Or in things too difficult for me.

2 I have certainly soothed and quieted my soul;
Like a weaned ^child *resting* against his mother,
My soul within me is like a weaned child.

3 Israel, ^wait for the Lord
From this time *on* and forever.

129:1^Ex 1:11 ^BIs 47:12 129:2^Jer 1:19; 15:20
129:4^Ps 119:137 ^BPs 140:5 129:5^Mic 4:11
129:6^2 Kin 19:26; Ps 37:2 129:7^Ps 79:12
129:8^Ruth 2:4; Ps 118:26 130:1^Ps 42:7; 69:2
130:2^Ps 28:2; 140:6 130:3^Ps 76:7; 143:2
130:4^Ex 34:7 ^B1 Kin 8:39, 40 130:5^Ps 119:74, 81
130:6^Ps 63:6; 119:147 130:7^Ps 111:9; Rom 3:24
130:8^Ps 103:3, 4; Luke 1:68 131:1^2 Sam 22:28
^BProv 30:13 131:2^Matt 18:3; 1 Cor 14:20
131:3^Ps 130:7

**PRAYER FOR THE LORD'S BLESSING
UPON THE SANCTUARY.**
A Song of Ascents.

132

Remember, LORD, in
David's behalf,
All ^his affliction;

2 How he swore to the LORD
And vowed to ^the Mighty One
of Jacob,

3 "I certainly will not enter ^my
house,
Nor lie on my bed;

4 I will not ^give sleep to my eyes
Or slumber to my eyelids,

5 Until I find a ^place for the LORD,
A dwelling place for the
Mighty One of Jacob."

6 Behold, we heard *about* it in
^Ephrathah,
We found it in the field of Jaar.

7 Let's go into His ^dwelling place;
Let's ^Bworship at His footstool.

8 Arise, LORD, to Your ^resting
place,
You and the ark of Your
^Bstrength.

9 May Your priests be ^clothed
with righteousness,
And may Your godly ones sing
for joy.

10 For the sake of Your servant
David,
Do not turn away the face of
Your ^anointed.

11 The LORD has sworn to David
A truth from which He will not
turn back:
"I will set upon your throne *one*
^from the fruit of your body.

12 "If your sons will keep My
covenant
And My testimony which I will
teach them,
Their sons also will ^sit upon
your throne forever."

13 For the LORD has ^chosen Zion;
He has desired it as His
dwelling place.

14 "This is My ^resting place
forever;
Here I will ^Bdwell, for I have
desired it.

15 "I will abundantly ^bless her
food;
I will ^Bsatisfy her needy with
bread.

16 "I will also clothe her ^priests
with salvation,
And her ^godly ones will sing
aloud for joy.

17 "I will make the horn of David
spring forth there;
I have prepared a ^lamp for My
anointed.

18 "I will clothe his enemies with
shame,
But upon himself his ^crown
will gleam."

**THE EXCELLENCY OF BROTHERLY
UNITY.**
A Song of Ascents, of David.

133

Behold, how good and
how pleasant it is
For ^brothers to live together
in unity!

2 It is like the precious ^oil on
the head,
Running down upon the
beard,
As on Aaron's beard,
The oil which ran down upon
the edge of his robes.

132:1 ^Gen 49:24; 2 Sam 16:12 132:2 ^Gen 49:24;
Is 49:26 132:3 ^Job 21:28 132:4 ^Prov 6:4
132:5 ^1 Kin 8:17; 1 Chr 22:7 132:6 ^Gen 35:19;
1 Sam 17:12 132:7 ^Ps 43:3 ^B Ps 5:7 132:8 ^Ps 132:14
^B Ps 78:61 132:9 ^Job 29:14 132:10 ^Ps 2:2; 132:17
132:11 ^2 Sam 7:12-16; 1 Chr 17:11-14
132:12 ^Luke 1:32; Acts 2:30 132:13 ^Ps 48:1, 2; 78:68
132:14 ^Ps 132:8 ^B Ps 68:16 132:15 ^Ps 147:14
^B Ps 107:9 132:16 ^2 Chr 6:41; Ps 132:9
132:17 ^1 Kin 11:36; 15:4 132:18 ^Ps 21:3
133:1 ^Gen 13:8; Heb 13:1 133:2 ^Ex 29:7; 30:25, 30

3 It is like the ^dew of Hermon
Coming down upon the
mountains of Zion;
For the LORD commanded
the blessing there—^Blife
forever.

GREETINGS OF NIGHT WATCHERS.
A Song of Ascents.

134 Behold, ^bless the LORD,
all you ^Bservants of the
LORD,
Who serve by night in the
house of the LORD!
2 ^Lift up your hands to the
sanctuary
And bless the LORD.
3 May the LORD ^bless you from
Zion,
He who ^Bmade heaven and
earth.

**PRAISE THE LORD'S WONDERFUL
WORKS. FUTILITY OF IDOLS.**

135 ^Praise the LORD!
Praise the name of the
LORD;
Praise *Him,* you servants of
the LORD,
2 You who stand in the house of
the LORD,
In the ^courtyards of the house
of our God!
3 Praise the LORD, for ^the LORD
is good;
Sing praises to His name, for it
is lovely.
4 For the LORD has ^chosen Jacob
for Himself,
Israel as His ^Bown possession.

5 For I know that ^the LORD is
great
And that our Lord is ^Babove all
gods.
6 ^Whatever the LORD pleases,
He does,

In heaven and on earth, in
the seas and in all the ocean
depths.
7 He ^causes the mist to ascend
from the ends of the earth,
He makes lightning for the rain;
He ^brings forth the wind from
His treasuries.
8 He ^struck the firstborn of
Egypt,
Both human *firstborn* and
animal.
9 He sent ^signs and wonders
into your midst, Egypt,
Upon Pharaoh and all his
servants.
10 ^He ^Bstruck many nations
And brought death to mighty
kings,
11 ^Sihon, king of the Amorites,
^BOg, king of Bashan,
And all the kingdoms of
Canaan;
12 And He ^gave their land as an
inheritance,
An inheritance to His people
Israel.
13 Your ^name, LORD, is
everlasting,
The mention of You, LORD, is
throughout all generations.
14 For the LORD will ^judge His
people
And ^Bwill have compassion on
His servants.
15 The ^idols of the nations are
nothing but silver and gold,
The work of human hands.

133:3^AProv 19:12   ^BPs 21:4   134:1^APs 103:21   ^BPs 135:1, 2
134:2^APs 28:2; 1 Tim 2:8   134:3^APs 128:5   ^BPs 124:8
135:1^APs 113:1   135:2^APs 92:13; 116:19   135:3^APs 100:5;
119:68   135:4^ADeut 7:6   ^BEx 19:5   135:5^APs 48:1
^BPs 97:9   135:6^APs 115:3   135:7^AJer 10:13; 51:16
135:8^AEx 12:12; Ps 78:51   135:9^AEx 7:10; Deut 6:22
135:10^ANum 21:24   ^BPs 44:2   135:11^ANum 21:21-26
^BNum 21:33-35   135:12^ADeut 29:8; Ps 78:55
135:13^AEx 3:15; Ps 102:12   135:14^ADeut 32:36   ^BPs 90:13
135:15^APs 115:4-8; 135:15-18

16 They have mouths, but they
 do not speak;
 They have eyes, but they do
 not see;
17 They have ears, but they do
 not hear,
 Nor is there any breath at all in
 their mouths.
18 Those who make them will
 become like them,
 Yes, everyone who trusts in
 them.

19 House of ᴬIsrael, bless the Lᴏʀᴅ;
 House of Aaron, bless the
 Lᴏʀᴅ;
20 House of Levi, bless the Lᴏʀᴅ;
 You ᴬwho revere the Lᴏʀᴅ,
 bless the Lᴏʀᴅ.
21 Blessed be the Lᴏʀᴅ ᴬfrom Zion,
 Who dwells in Jerusalem.
 Praise the Lᴏʀᴅ!

**THANKS FOR THE LORD'S
GOODNESS TO ISRAEL.**

136

ᴬGive thanks to the Lᴏʀᴅ,
for ᴮHe is good,
 For His ¹faithfulness is
 everlasting.
2 Give thanks to the ᴬGod of
 gods,
 For His faithfulness is
 everlasting.
3 Give thanks to the ᴬLord of
 lords,
 For His faithfulness is
 everlasting.
4 To Him who ᴬalone does great
 wonders,
 For His faithfulness is
 everlasting;
5 To Him who made the heavens
 ᴬwith skill,
 For His faithfulness is
 everlasting;
6 To Him who ᴬspread out the
 earth above the waters,

 For His faithfulness is
 everlasting;
7 To Him who ᴬmade *the* great
 lights,
 For His faithfulness is
 everlasting:
8 The ᴬsun to rule by day,
 For His faithfulness is
 everlasting,
9 The ᴬmoon and stars to rule by
 night,
 For His faithfulness is
 everlasting.

10 To Him who ᴬstruck the
 Egyptians, that is, their
 firstborn,
 For His faithfulness is
 everlasting,
11 And ᴬbrought Israel out from
 their midst,
 For His faithfulness is
 everlasting,
12 With a ᴬstrong hand and an
 ᴮoutstretched arm,
 For His faithfulness is
 everlasting.
13 To Him who ᴬdivided the Red
 Sea in parts,
 For His faithfulness is
 everlasting,
14 And ᴬallowed Israel to pass
 through the midst of it,
 For His faithfulness is
 everlasting;
15 But ᴬHe overthrew Pharaoh
 and his army in the Red Sea,
 For His faithfulness is
 everlasting.

135:19 ᴬPs 115:9 135:20 ᴬPs 118:4 135:21 ᴬPs 128:5;
134:3 ¹1 Chr 16:34 ᴮ2 Chr 5:13
136:2 ᴬDeut 10:17 136:3 ᴬDeut 10:17
136:4 ᴬDeut 6:22; Job 9:10 136:5 ᴬPs 104:24; Prov 3:19
136:6 ᴬGen 1:2, 6, 9; Ps 24:2 136:7 ᴬGen 1:14–18;
Ps 74:16 136:8 ᴬGen 1:16 136:9 ᴬGen 1:16
136:10 ᴬEx 12:29; Ps 78:51 136:11 ᴬEx 12:51; 13:3
136:12 ᴬEx 6:1 ᴮEx 6:6 136:13 ᴬEx 14:21; Ps 66:6
136:14 ᴬEx 14:22; Ps 106:9 136:15 ᴬEx 14:27; Ps 78:53

136:1 ¹Or *mercy,* and so throughout the Psalm

16 To Him who ᴬled His people
   through the wilderness,
   For His faithfulness is
   everlasting;

17 To Him who ᴬstruck great kings,
   For His faithfulness is
   everlasting,

18 And ᴬbrought death to mighty
   kings,
   For His faithfulness is
   everlasting:

19 ᴬSihon, king of the Amorites,
   For His faithfulness is
   everlasting,

20 And ᴬOg, king of Bashan,
   For His faithfulness is
   everlasting,

21 And ᴬgave their land as an
   inheritance,
   For His faithfulness is
   everlasting,

22 An inheritance to His ᴬservant
   Israel,
   For His faithfulness is
   everlasting.

23 Who ᴬremembered us in our
   lowliness,
   For His faithfulness is
   everlasting,

24 And has ᴬrescued us from our
   enemies,
   For His faithfulness is
   everlasting;

25 Who ᴬgives food to all flesh,
   For His faithfulness is
   everlasting.

26 Give thanks to the ᴬGod of
   heaven,
   For His faithfulness is
   everlasting.

AN EXPERIENCE OF THE CAPTIVITY.

137 By the ᴬrivers of Babylon,
There we sat down and
ᴮwept,
When we remembered Zion.

2 Upon the ᴬwillows in the
   midst of it
   We hung our harps.

3 For there our captors
   ᴬdemanded of us songs,
   And ᴮour tormentors,
   jubilation, *saying,*
   "Sing for us one of the songs of
   Zion!"

4 How can we sing ᴬthe Lᴏʀᴅ's
   song
   In a foreign land?

5 If I ᴬforget you, Jerusalem,
   May my right hand forget *its
   skill.*

6 May my ᴬtongue cling to the
   roof of my mouth
   If I do not remember you,
   If I do not ᴮexalt Jerusalem
   Above my chief joy.

7 Remember, Lᴏʀᴅ, against the
   sons of ᴬEdom
   The day of Jerusalem,
   Those who said, "Lay it bare,
   lay it bare
   ᴮTo its foundation!"

8 Daughter of Babylon, you
   ᴬdevastated one,
   Blessed will be one who
   repays you
   With the retribution with
   which you have repaid us.

9 Blessed will be one who
   seizes and ᴬdashes your
   children
   Against the rock.

136:16 ᴬEx 13:18; 15:22   136:17 ᴬPs 135:10-12; 136:17-22
136:18 ᴬDeut 29:7   136:19 ᴬNum 21:21-24
136:20 ᴬNum 21:33-35   136:21 ᴬJosh 12:1
136:22 ᴬPs 105:6; Is 41:8   136:23 ᴬPs 9:12; 103:14
136:24 ᴬJudg 6:9; Neh 9:28   136:25 ᴬPs 104:27; 145:15
136:26 ᴬGen 24:3, 7; 2 Chr 36:23   137:1 ᴬEzek 1:1, 3
ᴮNeh 1:4   137:2 ᴬLev 23:40; Is 44:4   137:3 ᴬPs 80:6
ᴮIs 49:17   137:4 ᴬ2 Chr 29:27; Neh 12:46
137:5 ᴬIs 65:11   137:6 ᴬJob 29:10   ᴮNeh 2:3
137:7 ᴬPs 83:4-8   ᴮPs 74:7   137:8 ᴬIs 13:1-22; 47:1-15
137:9 ᴬ2 Kin 8:12; Is 13:16

THANKSGIVING FOR THE LORD'S FAVOR.

A Psalm of David.

138 ^A^I will give You thanks with all my heart;
I will sing Your praises before the gods.

2 I will bow down ^A^toward Your holy temple
And give thanks to Your name for Your mercy and Your truth;
For You have made Your word great according to all Your name.

3 On the day I called, You answered me;
You made me bold *with* ^A^strength in my soul.

4 ^A^All the kings of the earth will give thanks to You, LORD,
When they have heard the words of Your mouth.

5 And they will sing of the ways of the LORD,
For ^A^great is the glory of the LORD.

6 For the LORD is exalted,
Yet He ^A^looks after the lowly,
But He knows the ^B^haughty from afar.

7 Though I ^A^walk in the midst of trouble, You will ^B^revive me;
You will reach out with Your hand against the wrath of my enemies,
And Your right hand will save me.

8 The LORD will ^A^accomplish what concerns me;
Your faithfulness, LORD, is everlasting;
Do not abandon the works of Your hands.

GOD'S OMNIPRESENCE AND OMNISCIENCE.

For the music director. A Psalm of David.

139 LORD, You have ^A^searched me and known *me*.

2 You ^A^know when I sit down and when I get up;
You ^B^understand my thought from far away.

3 You ^A^scrutinize my path and my lying down,
And are acquainted with all my ways.

4 Even before there is a word on my tongue,
Behold, LORD, You ^A^know it all.

5 You have encircled me behind and in front,
And ^A^placed Your hand upon me.

6 *Such* ^A^knowledge is too wonderful for me;
It is *too* high, I cannot comprehend it.

7 ^A^Where can I go from Your Spirit?
Or where can I flee from Your presence?

8 ^A^If I ascend to heaven, You are there;
If I make my bed in ¹Sheol, behold, You are there.

9 *If* I take up the wings of the dawn,
If I dwell in the remotest part of the sea,

10 Even there Your hand will ^A^lead me,
And Your right hand will take hold of me.

138:1 ^A^Ps 111:1   **138:2** ^A^1 Kin 8:29; Ps 5:7   **138:3** ^A^Ps 28:7;
46:1   **138:4** ^A^Ps 72:11; 102:15   **138:5** ^A^Ps 21:5
138:6 ^A^Prov 3:34   ^B^Ps 40:4   **138:7** ^A^Ps 23:4   ^B^Ezra 9:8, 9
138:8 ^A^Ps 57:2; Phil 1:6   **139:1** ^A^Ps 17:3; 44:21
139:2 ^A^2 Kin 19:27   ^B^Matt 9:4   **139:3** ^A^Job 14:16; 31:4
139:4 ^A^Heb 4:13   **139:5** ^A^Job 9:33   **139:6** ^A^Rom 11:33
139:7 ^A^Jer 23:24   **139:8** ^A^Amos 9:2-4   **139:10** ^A^Ps 23:2, 3

139:8 ¹I.e., the netherworld

11 *If* I say, "Surely the ᴬdarkness
will overwhelm me,
And the light around me will
be night,"
12 Even ᴬdarkness is not dark to
You,
And the night is as bright as
the day.
ᴮDarkness and light are alike
to You.

13 For You ᴬcreated my innermost
parts;
You ᴮwove me in my mother's
womb.
14 I will give thanks to You,
because ¹I am awesomely
and wonderfully *made;*
ᴬWonderful are Your works,
And my soul knows it very
well.
15 My ᴬframe was not hidden
from You
When I was made in secret,
And skillfully formed in the
depths of the earth;
16 Your ᴬeyes have seen my
formless substance;
And in ᴮYour book were
written
All the days that were ordained
for me,
When as yet there was not one
of them.

17 How precious also are Your
ᴬthoughts for me, God!
How vast is the sum of them!
18 Were I to count them, they
would ᴬoutnumber the sand.
When ᴮI awake, I am still with
You.

19 If only You would ᴬput the
wicked to death, God;
Leave me, you men of
bloodshed.

20 For they ᴬspeak against You
wickedly,
And Your enemies take *Your
name* in vain.
21 Do I not ᴬhate those who hate
You, Lᴏʀᴅ?
And do I not loathe those who
rise up against You?
22 I hate them with the utmost
hatred;
They have become my
enemies.

23 ᴬSearch me, God, and know my
heart;
Put me to the test and know
my anxious thoughts;
24 And see if there is *any* hurtful
way in me,
And ᴬlead me in the
ᴮeverlasting way.

**PRAYER FOR PROTECTION
AGAINST THE WICKED.**
For the music director. A Psalm of David.

140
ᴬRescue me, Lᴏʀᴅ, from
evil people;
Protect me from violent men
2 Who ᴬdevise evil things in
their hearts;
They ᴮcontinually stir up
wars.
3 They sharpen their tongues
like a snake;
ᴬThe venom of a viper is under
their lips.   *Selah*

4 ᴬKeep me, Lᴏʀᴅ, from the
hands of the wicked;

139:11 ᴬJob 22:13   139:12 ᴬJob 34:22   ᴮ1 John 1:5
139:13 ᴬPs 119:73   ᴮJob 10:11   139:14 ᴬPs 40:5
139:15 ᴬJob 10:8-10; Eccl 11:5   139:16 ᴬJob 10:8-10
ᴮPs 56:8   139:17 ᴬPs 40:5; 92:5   139:18 ᴬPs 40:5
ᴮPs 3:5   139:19 ᴬIs 11:4   139:20 ᴬJude 15
139:21 ᴬ2 Chr 19:2; Ps 26:5   139:23 ᴬJob 31:6; Ps 26:2
139:24 ᴬPs 5:8   ᴮPs 16:11   140:1 ᴬPs 17:13; 59:2
140:2 ᴬPs 7:14   ᴮPs 56:6   140:3 ᴬPs 58:4; Rom 3:13
140:4 ᴬPs 71:4

139:14 ¹Some ancient versions *You are fearfully wonderful*

Protect me from violent men
Who intend to ᴮtrip up my
feet.

5 The proud have hidden a trap
for me, and snares;
They have spread a net at the
wayside;
They have set ᴬsnares for
me.   *Selah*

6 I said to the Lᴏʀᴅ, "You are my
God;
ᴬListen, Lᴏʀᴅ, to the ᴮsound of
my pleadings.

7 "Gᴏᴅ the Lord, ᴬthe strength of
my salvation,
You have ᴮcovered my head on
the day of battle.

8 "Do not grant, Lᴏʀᴅ, the
ᴬdesires of the wicked;
Do not bring about ᴮhis evil
planning, *so that* they *are*
not exalted.   *Selah*

9 "As for the head of those who
surround me,
May the ᴬharm of their lips
cover them.

10 "May ᴬburning coals fall upon
them;
May they be ᴮcast into the
fire,
Into bottomless pits from
which they cannot rise.

11 "May a slanderer not endure
on the earth;
ᴬMay evil hunt a violent
person violently."

12 I know that the Lᴏʀᴅ will
maintain the cause of the
afflicted,
And ᴬjustice for the poor.

13 Certainly the ᴬrighteous will
give thanks to Your name;
The ᴮupright will dwell in Your
presence.

AN EVENING PRAYER FOR
SANCTIFICATION AND PROTECTION.
A Psalm of David.

141
Lᴏʀᴅ, I call upon You;
ᴬhurry to me!
Listen to my voice when I call
to You!

2 May my prayer be counted as
ᴬincense before You;
The ᴮraising of my hands as
the evening offering.

3 Set a ᴬguard, Lᴏʀᴅ, over my
mouth;
Keep watch over the ᴮdoor of
my lips.

4 ᴬDo not incline my heart to *any*
evil thing,
To practice deeds of
wickedness
With people who ᴮdo wrong;
And may I not taste their
delicacies.

5 May the ᴬrighteous strike me
with mercy and discipline
me;
It is oil for the head;
My head shall not refuse it,
For my prayer is still against
their evil deeds.

6 Their judges are ᴬthrown down
by the sides of the rock,
And they hear my words, for
they are pleasant.

7 As when one plows and breaks
open the earth,
Our ᴬbones have been
scattered at the ᴮmouth of
¹Sheol.

140:4 ᴮPs 36:11   140:5 ᴬPs 141:9; Is 8:14
140:6 ᴬPs 143:1   ᴮPs 116:1   140:7 ᴬPs 28:8   ᴮPs 144:10
140:8 ᴬPs 112:10   ᴮEsth 9:25   140:9 ᴬPs 7:16;
Prov 18:7   140:10 ᴬPs 11:6   ᴮPs 21:9   140:11 ᴬPs 34:21
140:12 ᴬPs 12:5; 35:10   140:13 ᴬPs 97:12   ᴮPs 11:7
141:1 ᴬPs 22:19; 38:22   141:2 ᴬEx 30:8   ᴮ1 Tim 2:8
141:3 ᴬPs 34:13   ᴮMic 7:5   141:4 ᴬPs 119:36   ᴮIs 32:6
141:5 ᴬProv 9:8; 19:25   141:6 ᴬ2 Chr 25:12
141:7 ᴬPs 53:5   ᴮNum 16:32, 33

141:7 ¹I.e., the netherworld

8 For my ^eyes are toward You,
   God, the Lord;
   In You I ^Btake refuge; do not
   leave me defenseless.
9 Keep me from the ^jaws of the
   trap which they have set for
   me,
   And from the ^Bsnares of those
   who do wrong.
10 May the wicked ^fall into their
   own nets,
   While I pass by safely.

PRAYER FOR HELP IN TROUBLE.

Maskil of David, when he was
in the cave. A Prayer.

142 I cry out with my voice to
the Lord;
   With my voice I ^implore the
   Lord for compassion.
2 I pour out my complaint
   before Him;
   I declare my ^trouble before
   Him.
3 When ^my spirit felt weak
   within me,
   You knew my path.
   In the way where I walk
   They have hidden a trap for me.
4 Look to the right and see;
   For there is ^no one who
   regards me *favorably*;
   There is no escape for me;
   ^BNo one cares for my soul.
5 I cried out to You, Lord;
   I said, "You are ^my refuge,
   My portion in the land of the
   living.
6 "Give *Your* attention to my cry,
   For I have been ^brought very
   low;
   Rescue me from my persecutors,
   For they are too ^Bstrong for me.
7 "^Bring my soul out of prison,
   So that I may give thanks to
   Your name;

The righteous will surround me,
For You will ^Blook after me."

PRAYER FOR HELP AND GUIDANCE.

A Psalm of David.

143 Hear my prayer, Lord,
Listen to my pleadings!
   Answer me in Your
   ^faithfulness, in Your
   ^Brighteousness!
2 And ^do not enter into
   judgment with Your servant,
   For ^Bno person living is
   righteous in Your sight.
3 For the enemy has persecuted
   my soul;
   He has crushed my life to the
   ground;
   He ^has made me dwell in dark
   places, like those who have
   long been dead.
4 Therefore my spirit feels weak
   within me;
   My heart is ^appalled within
   me.
5 I ^remember the days of old;
   I meditate on all Your
   accomplishments;
   I ^Breflect on the work of Your
   hands.
6 I ^spread out my hands to You;
   My ^Bsoul *longs* for You, like a
   weary land.   *Selah*
7 Answer me quickly, Lord, my
   spirit fails;
   ^Do not hide Your face from me,
   Or I will be the same as ^Bthose
   who go down to the pit.

141:8 ^A Ps 25:15   ^B Ps 2:12   141:9 ^A Ps 38:12   ^B Ps 140:5
141:10 ^A Ps 7:15; 35:8   142:1 ^A Ps 30:8   142:2 ^A Ps 77:2
142:3 ^A Ps 77:3; 143:4   142:4 ^A Ps 31:11   ^B Jer 30:17
142:5 ^A Ps 91:2, 9   142:6 ^A Ps 79:8   ^B Ps 18:17
142:7 ^A Ps 143:11   ^B Ps 13:6   143:1 ^A Ps 89:1, 2   ^B Ps 71:2
143:2 ^A Job 14:3   ^B 1 Kin 8:46   143:3 ^A Ps 88:6; Lam 3:6
143:4 ^A Lam 3:11   143:5 ^A Ps 77:5, 10, 11   ^B Ps 105:2
143:6 ^A Job 11:13   ^B Ps 42:2   143:7 ^A Ps 27:9   ^B Ps 28:1

8 Let me hear Your faithfulness
     in the morning,
   For I trust in You;
   Teach me the ^way in which I
     should walk;
   For to You I ^Blift up my soul.
9 ^Save me, Lord, from my
     enemies;
   I take refuge in You.

10 ^Teach me to do Your will,
    For You are my God;
    Let ^BYour good Spirit lead me
      on level ground.
11 ^For the sake of Your name,
    Lord, revive me.
    In Your righteousness bring
      my soul out of trouble.
12 And in Your faithfulness,
    ^destroy my enemies,
    And ^Beliminate all those who
      attack my soul,
    For I am Your servant.

PRAYER FOR RESCUE AND PROSPERITY.
A Psalm of David.

144 Blessed be the Lord, my
      rock,
    Who ^trains my hands for war,
    And my fingers for battle;
2 My faithfulness and ^my
     fortress,
   My ^Bstronghold and my savior,
   My shield and He in whom I
     take refuge,
   Who subdues my people
     under me.
3 Lord, ^what is man, that You
     look after him?
   Or a son of man, that You
     think of him?
4 ^Man is like the breath;
   His ^Bdays are like a passing
     shadow.

5 ^Bend down Your heavens,
   Lord, and come down;

^BTouch the mountains, that
   they may smoke.
6 Flash forth ^lightning and
     scatter them;
   Send out Your ^Barrows and
     confuse them.
7 Reach out with Your hand
     from on high;
   Rescue me and ^save me from
     great waters,
   From the hand of ^Bforeigners
8 Whose mouth ^speaks deceit,
   And whose ^Bright hand is a
     right hand of falsehood.

9 God, I will sing a ^new song to
     You;
   On a ^Bharp of ten strings I will
     sing praises to You,
10 Who ^gives salvation to kings,
    Who ^Brescues His servant
      David from the evil sword.
11 Rescue me and save me from
      the hand of ^foreigners,
    Whose mouth ^Bspeaks deceit
    And whose right hand is a
      right hand of falsehood.

12 When our sons in their youth
      are like growing plants,
    And our daughters like ^corner
      pillars fashioned for a
      palace,
13 Our ^granaries *are* full,
      providing every kind *of
      produce,*
    And our flocks deliver
      thousands and ten
      thousands in our fields;

143:8 ^Ps 27:11   ^B Ps 86:4   143:9 ^Ps 31:15; 59:1
143:10 ^Ps 25:4, 5   ^B Neh 9:20   143:11 ^Ps 25:11
143:12 ^Ps 54:5   ^B Ps 52:5   144:1 ^2 Sam 22:35;
Ps 18:34   144:2 ^Ps 18:2   ^B Ps 59:9   144:3 ^Job 7:17;
Ps 8:4   144:4 ^Ps 39:11   ^B Job 8:9   144:5 ^Ps 18:9
^B Ps 104:32   144:6 ^Ps 18:14   ^B Ps 7:13
144:7 ^Ps 69:1, 14   ^B Ps 18:44   144:8 ^Ps 12:2
^B Gen 14:22   144:9 ^Ps 33:3   ^B Ps 33:2
144:10 ^Ps 18:50   ^B 2 Sam 18:7   144:11 ^Ps 18:44
^B Ps 41:6   144:12 ^Song 4:4; 7:4   144:13 ^Prov 3:9, 10

14 *May* our ^cattle be bred
Without mishap and without
    ¹loss,
May there be no ᴮoutcry in our
    streets!
15 Blessed are the people who are
    so situated;
^Blessed are the people whose
    God is the LORD!

**THE LORD EXALTED FOR HIS
GOODNESS.**
A Psalm of Praise, of David.

145 I will ^exalt You, my God,
    the King,
And I will ᴮbless Your name
    forever and ever.
2 Every day I will bless You,
And I will ^praise Your name
    forever and ever.
3 Great is the LORD, and highly
    to be praised;
And His ^greatness is
    unsearchable.
4 One ^generation will praise
    Your works to another,
And will declare Your mighty
    acts.
5 On the ^glorious splendor of
    Your majesty
And ᴮon Your wonderful
    works, I will meditate.
6 People will speak of the
    power of Your ^awesome
    acts,
And I will tell of Your
    greatness.
7 They will burst forth in
    speaking of Your ^abundant
    goodness,
And will shout joyfully of Your
    righteousness.
8 The LORD is ^gracious and
    compassionate;
Slow to anger and great in
    mercy.

9 The LORD is ^good to all,
And His ᴮmercies are over all
    His works.
10 ^All Your works will give
    thanks to You, LORD,
And Your godly ones will bless
    You.
11 They will speak of the ^glory of
    Your kingdom,
And talk of Your might,
12 To ^make known to the sons
    of mankind Your mighty
    acts,
And the glory of the majesty of
    Your kingdom.
13 Your kingdom is an
    ^everlasting kingdom,
And Your dominion *endures*
    throughout all generations.
ⁱThe LORD is faithful in His
    words,
And holy in all His works.

14 The LORD ^supports all who
    fall,
And ᴮraises up all who are
    bowed down.
15 The eyes of all look to You,
And You ^give them their food
    in due time.
16 You ^open Your hand
And satisfy the desire of every
    living thing.

17 The LORD is ^righteous in all
    His ways,
And kind in all His works.

144:14^Prov 14:4   ᴮIs 24:11   144:15^Ps 33:12
145:1^Ps 30:1   ᴮPs 34:1   145:2^Ps 71:6
145:3^Job 5:9; Rom 11:33   145:4^Ps 22:30, 31; Is 38:19
145:5^Ps 145:12   ᴮPs 119:27
145:6^Deut 10:21; Ps 66:3   145:7^Ps 31:19; Is 63:7
145:8^Ex 34:6; Num 14:18   145:9^Ps 100:5
ᴮPs 145:15   145:10^Ps 19:1; 103:22   145:11^Jer 14:21
145:12^Ps 105:1   145:13^Ps 10:16; 29:10
145:14^Ps 37:24   ᴮPs 146:8   145:15^Ps 104:27;
136:25   145:16^Ps 104:28   145:17^Ps 116:5

144:14¹Lit *going out;* i.e., miscarriage   145:13¹*The
LORD...His works* in LXX (cf. DSS); not found in MT

18 The LORD is ^near to all who
call on Him,
To all who call on Him ^Bin
truth.

19 He will ^fulfill the desire of
those who fear Him;
He will also hear their cry for
help and save them.

20 The LORD ^watches over all
who love Him,
But He will destroy all the
^Bwicked.

21 My mouth will speak the
praise of the LORD,
And ^all flesh will bless His
holy name forever and ever.

THE LORD, AN ABUNDANT HELPER.

146

Praise the LORD!
^Praise the LORD, my
soul!

2 I will praise the LORD ^while I
live;
I will sing praises to my God
while I have my being.

3 ^Do not trust in noblemen,
In mortal man, in whom there
is ^Bno salvation.

4 His ^spirit departs, he ^Breturns
to the earth;
On that *very* day his plans
perish.

5 ^Blessed is he whose help is
the God of Jacob,
Whose ^Bhope is in the LORD his
God,

6 Who ^made heaven and earth,
The ^Bsea and everything that is
in them;
Who keeps faith forever;

7 Who ^executes justice for the
oppressed;
Who gives food to the hungry.
The LORD ^Bfrees the prisoners.

8 The LORD ^opens *the eyes of*
those who are blind;

The LORD raises up those who
are bowed down;
The LORD ^Bloves the
righteous.

9 The LORD ^watches over
strangers;
He ^Bsupports the fatherless
and the widow,
But He thwarts the way of the
wicked.

10 The LORD will ^reign forever,
Your God, Zion, to all
generations.
Praise the LORD!

PRAISE FOR JERUSALEM'S RESTORATION AND PROSPERITY.

147

Praise the LORD!
For it is good to sing
praises to our God;
For it is pleasant *and* praise is
^beautiful.

2 The LORD builds up
Jerusalem;
He ^gathers the outcasts of
Israel.

3 He heals the ^brokenhearted
And binds up their wounds.

4 He ^counts the number of the
stars;
He ^Bgives names to all of them.

5 Great is our Lord and
abundant in strength;
His ^understanding is infinite.

6 The LORD ^supports the
afflicted;
He brings the wicked down to
the ground.

145:18 ^Deut 4:7   ^B John 4:7   145:19 ^Ps 21:2; 37:4
145:20 ^Ps 31:23   ^B Ps 9:5   145:21 ^Ps 65:2; 150:6
146:1 ^Ps 103:1   146:2 ^Ps 63:4   146:3 ^Ps 118:9
^B Ps 60:11   146:4 ^Ps 104:29   ^B Eccl 12:7
146:5 ^Ps 144:15   ^B Ps 71:5   146:6 ^Ps 115:15
^B Acts 14:15   146:7 ^Ps 103:6   ^B Ps 68:6
146:8 ^Matt 9:30   ^B Ps 11:7   146:9 ^Ex 22:21
^B Deut 10:18   146:10 ^Ex 15:18; Ps 10:16
147:1 ^Ps 33:1   147:2 ^Deut 30:3; Ps 106:47
147:3 ^Ps 34:18; 51:17   147:4 ^Gen 15:5   ^B Is 40:26
147:5 ^Is 40:28   147:6 ^Ps 37:24; 146:8, 9

[7] ᴬSing to the Lᴏʀᴅ with
     thanksgiving;
   Sing praises to our God on the
     lyre;

[8] *It is* He who ᴬcovers the
     heavens with clouds,
   Who ᴮprovides rain for the earth,
   Who makes grass sprout on the
     mountains.

[9] *It is* He who gives an animal its
     food,
   And feeds ᴬyoung ravens that
     cry.

[10] He does not delight in ¹the
     strength of the ᴬhorse;
   He ᴮdoes not take pleasure in
     the ¹legs of a man.

[11] The Lᴏʀᴅ ᴬfavors those who
     fear Him,
   ᴮThose who wait for His
     faithfulness.

[12] Praise the Lᴏʀᴅ, Jerusalem!
   Praise your God, Zion!

[13] For He has strengthened the
     bars of your gates;
   He has ᴬblessed your sons
     among you.

[14] He ᴬmakes peace in your
     borders;
   He satisfies you with the finest
     of the wheat.

[15] He sends His ᴬcommand to the
     earth;
   His ᴮword runs very swiftly.

[16] He showers snow like wool;
   He scatters the ᴬfrost like ashes.

[17] He hurls His ice as fragments;
   Who can stand before His ᴬcold?

[18] He ᴬsends His word and makes
     them melt;
   He ᴮmakes His wind blow, and
     the waters flow.

[19] He ᴬdeclares His words to
     Jacob,
   His statutes and His
     judgments to Israel.

[20] He ᴬhas not dealt this way with
     any *other* nation;
   And as for His judgments, they
     have not known them.
   Praise the Lᴏʀᴅ!

**THE WHOLE CREATION INVOKED
TO PRAISE THE LORD.**

148

Praise the Lᴏʀᴅ!
Praise the Lᴏʀᴅ ᴬfrom the
   heavens;
Praise Him in the heights!

[2] Praise Him, ᴬall His angels;
   Praise Him, ᴮall His *heavenly*
     armies!

[3] Praise Him, sun and moon;
   Praise Him, all stars of light!

[4] Praise Him, highest heavens,
   And the ᴬwaters that are above
     the heavens!

[5] They are to praise the name of
     the Lᴏʀᴅ,
   For ᴬHe commanded and they
     were created.

[6] He has also established them
     forever and ever;
   He has made a ᴬdecree, and it
     will not pass away.

[7] Praise the Lᴏʀᴅ from the earth,
   ᴬSea monsters, and all the
     ocean depths;

[8] Fire and hail, snow and clouds;
   Stormy wind, ᴬfulfilling His
     word;

[9] ᴬMountains and all hills;
   Fruit ᴮtrees and all cedars;

147:7ᴬPs 33:2; 95:1, 2   147:8ᴬJob 26:8   ᴮJob 5:10
147:9ᴬJob 38:41; Matt 6:26   147:10ᴬPs 33:17
ᴮ1 Sam 16:7   147:11ᴬPs 149:4   ᴮPs 33:18
147:13ᴬPs 37:26   147:14ᴬPs 29:11; Is 54:13
147:15ᴬJob 37:12   ᴮPs 104:4   147:16ᴬJob 38:29
147:17ᴬJob 37:9   147:18ᴬPs 33:9   ᴮPs 107:25
147:19ᴬDeut 33:3, 4   147:20ᴬDeut 4:7, 8, 32–34;
Rom 3:1, 2   148:1ᴬPs 69:34   148:2ᴬPs 103:20
ᴮPs 103:21   148:4ᴬGen 1:7   148:5ᴬGen 1:1; Ps 33:6, 9
148:6ᴬJob 38:33   148:7ᴬGen 1:21; Ps 74:13
148:8ᴬJob 37:12; Ps 103:20   148:9ᴬIs 44:23   ᴮIs 55:12

147:10 ¹I.e., as a military asset

10 ^Animals and all cattle;
   ^BCrawling things and winged
   fowl;
11 ^Kings of the earth and all
   peoples;
   Rulers and all judges of the
   earth;
12 Both young men and virgins;
   Old men and children.

13 They are to praise the name of
   the LORD,
   For His ^name alone is exalted;
   His ^Bmajesty is above earth
   and heaven.
14 And He has ^lifted up a horn
   for His people,
   Praise for all His godly ones,
   For the sons of Israel, a people
   near to Him.
   Praise the LORD!

ISRAEL INVOKED TO PRAISE THE LORD.

149 Praise the LORD!
Sing a new song to the
LORD,
And His praise ^in the
congregation of the godly
ones.
2 Israel shall be joyful in ^his
Maker;
The sons of Zion shall rejoice
in their ^BKing.
3 They shall praise His name
with ^dancing;
They shall sing praises to Him
with ^Btambourine and lyre.
4 For the LORD takes pleasure in
His people;
He will ^glorify the lowly with
salvation.

5 The ^godly ones shall be
jubilant in glory;
They shall sing for joy on their
beds.

6 The ^high praises of God *shall
be* in their mouths,
And a two-edged sword in
their hands,
7 To ^execute vengeance on the
nations,
And punishment on the
peoples,
8 To bind their kings ^with chains,
And their ^Bdignitaries with
shackles of iron,
9 To ^execute against them the
judgment written.
This is an honor for all His
godly ones.
Praise the LORD!

A PSALM OF PRAISE.

150 Praise the LORD!
Praise God in His
^sanctuary;
Praise Him in His mighty
^Bexpanse.
2 Praise Him for His ^mighty
deeds;
Praise Him according to His
excellent greatness.

3 Praise Him with ^trumpet sound;
Praise Him with harp and lyre.
4 Praise Him with ^tambourine
and dancing;
Praise Him with stringed
instruments and flute.
5 Praise Him with loud ^cymbals;
Praise Him with resounding
cymbals.
6 ^Everything that has breath
shall praise the LORD.
Praise the LORD!

148:10 ^Is 43:20 ^BHos 2:18 148:11 ^Ps 102:15
148:13 ^Is 12:4 ^BPs 8:1 148:14 ^1 Sam 2:1; Ps 75:10
149:1 ^Ps 35:18; 89:5 149:2 ^Ps 95:6 ^BJudg 8:23
149:3 ^2 Sam 6:14 ^BEx 15:20 149:4 ^Ps 132:16; Is 61:3
149:5 ^Ps 132:16 149:6 ^Ps 66:17 149:7 ^Ezek 25:17;
Mic 5:15 149:8 ^Job 36:8 ^BNah 3:10
149:9 ^Deut 7:12; Ezek 28:26 150:1 ^Ps 73:17 ^BPs 19:1
150:2 ^Ps 145:12 150:3 ^Ps 98:6 150:4 ^Ps 149:3
150:5 ^2 Sam 6:5; 1 Chr 13:8 150:6 ^Ps 103:22; 145:21

THE PROVERBS

THE USEFULNESS OF PROVERBS

1 The ᴬproverbs of Solomon the son of David, king of Israel:

2 To know ᴬwisdom and instruction,
To discern the sayings of ᴮunderstanding,

3 To ᴬreceive instruction in wise behavior,
Righteousness, justice, and integrity;

4 To give ᴬprudence to the naive,
To the youth knowledge and discretion,

5 A wise person will hear and ᴬincrease in learning,
And a ᴮperson of understanding will acquire wise counsel,

6 To understand a proverb and a saying,
The words of the wise and their ᴬriddles.

7 ᴬThe fear of the Lᴏʀᴅ is the beginning of knowledge;
Fools despise wisdom and instruction.

THE ENTICEMENT OF SINNERS

8 ᴬListen, my son, to your father's instruction,
And ᴮdo not ignore your mother's teaching;

9 For they are a ᴬgraceful wreath for your head
And ᴮnecklaces for your neck.

10 My son, if sinners entice you,
ᴬDo not consent.

11 If they say, "Come with us,
Let's ᴬlie in wait for blood,
Let's ambush the innocent without cause;

12 Let's ᴬswallow them alive like Sheol,
Even whole, like those who go down to the pit;

13 We will find all *kinds* of precious wealth,
We will fill our houses with plunder;

14 Throw in your lot with us;
We will all have one money bag,"

15 My son, ᴬdo not walk on the way with them.
Keep your feet from their path,

16 For ᴬtheir feet run to evil,
And they are quick to shed blood.

17 Indeed, it is useless to spread the *baited* net
In the sight of any bird;

18 But they ᴬlie in wait for their own blood;
They ambush their own lives.

19 Such are the ways of everyone who ᴬmakes unjust gain;
It takes away the life of its possessors.

WISDOM WARNS

20 ᴬWisdom shouts in the street,
She raises her voice in the public square;

1:1 ᴬ1 Kin 4:32; Prov 10:1   1:2 ᴬProv 15:33   ᴮProv 4:1
1:3 ᴬProv 2:1; 19:20   1:4 ᴬProv 8:5, 12   1:5 ᴬProv 9:9
ᴮProv 14:6   1:6 ᴬNum 12:8; Ps 49:4   1:7 ᴬJob 28:28;
Ps 111:10   1:8 ᴬProv 4:1   ᴮProv 6:20   1:9 ᴬProv 4:9
ᴮGen 41:42   1:10 ᴬGen 39:7-10; Deut 13:8
1:11 ᴬProv 12:6; Jer 5:26   1:12 ᴬPs 124:3   1:15 ᴬPs 1:1;
Prov 4:14   1:16 ᴬProv 6:17, 18; Is 59:7   1:18 ᴬProv 11:19
1:19 ᴬProv 15:27   1:20 ᴬProv 8:1-3; 9:3

21 At the head of the noisy *streets*
   she cries out;
   At the entrance of the gates
   in the city she declares her
   sayings:
22 "How long, you naive ones, will
   you love simplistic thinking?
   And *how long will* ᴬscoffers
   delight themselves in
   scoffing
   And fools ᴮhate knowledge?
23 "Turn to my rebuke,
   Behold, I will ᴬpour out my
   spirit on you;
   I will make my words known
   to you.
24 "Because I called and you
   ᴬrefused,
   I ᴮstretched out my hand and
   no one paid attention;
25 And you ᴬneglected all my
   advice
   And did not ᴮwant my rebuke;
26 I will also laugh at your ᴬdisaster;
   I will mock when your ᴮdread
   comes,
27 When your dread comes like a
   storm
   And your disaster comes like a
   ᴬwhirlwind,
   When distress and anguish
   come upon you.
28 "Then they will call on me, but I
   will not answer;
   They will ᴬseek me diligently
   but will not find me,
29 Because they ᴬhated
   knowledge
   And did not choose the fear of
   the LORD.
30 "They ᴬdid not accept my advice,
   They disdainfully rejected
   every rebuke from me.
31 "So they shall ᴬeat of the fruit of
   their own way,
   And be ᴮfilled with their own
   schemes.

32 "For the ᴬfaithlessness of the
   naive will kill them,
   And the complacency of fools
   will destroy them.
33 "But ᴬwhoever listens to me will
   live securely
   And will be at ease from the
   dread of evil."

THE PURSUIT OF WISDOM
BRINGS SECURITY

2 My son, if you will receive my
  words
  And ᴬtreasure my
  commandments within you,
2 ᴬMake your ear attentive to
  wisdom;
  Incline your heart to
  understanding.
3 For if you cry out for insight,
  And raise your voice for
  understanding;
4 If you seek her as silver
  And search for her as for
  ᴬhidden treasures;
5 Then you will understand the
  ᴬfear of the LORD,
  And discover the knowledge
  of God.
6 For ᴬthe LORD gives wisdom;
  From His mouth *come*
  knowledge and
  understanding.
7 He stores up sound wisdom
  for the upright;
  He is a ᴬshield to those who
  walk in integrity,
8 Guarding the paths of justice,
  And He ᴬwatches over the way
  of His godly ones.

1:22 ᴬPs 1:1   ᴮProv 1:29   1:23 ᴬIs 32:15; Joel 2:28
1:24 ᴬZech 7:11   ᴮIs 65:2   1:25 ᴬPs 107:11   ᴮProv 15:10
1:26 ᴬProv 6:15   ᴮProv 10:24   1:27 ᴬProv 10:25
1:28 ᴬProv 8:17   1:29 ᴬJob 21:14; Prov 1:22
1:30 ᴬPs 81:11; Prov 1:25   1:31 ᴬJob 4:8   ᴮProv 14:14
1:32 ᴬJer 2:19   1:33 ᴬPs 25:12, 13; Prov 3:24-26
2:1 ᴬProv 3:1   2:2 ᴬProv 22:17   2:4 ᴬJob 3:21;
Matt 13:44   2:5 ᴬProv 1:7   2:6 ᴬ1 Kin 3:12; Job 32:8
2:7 ᴬPs 84:11; Prov 30:5   2:8 ᴬ1 Sam 2:9; Ps 66:9

9 Then you will discern
    ^righteousness, justice,
  And integrity, *and* every good
    path.
10 For ^wisdom will enter your
    heart,
  And ^Bknowledge will be
    delightful to your soul;
11 Discretion will ^watch over you,
  Understanding will guard you,
12 To ^rescue you from the way of
    evil,
  From a person who speaks
    perverse things;
13 *From* those who ^leave the
    paths of uprightness
  To walk in the ways of
    darkness;
14 Who ^delight in doing evil
  And rejoice in the perversity
    of evil;
15 Whose paths are ^crooked,
  And who are devious in their
    ways;
16 To rescue you from the
    strange woman,
  From the ^foreign woman who
    flatters with her words,
17 Who leaves the ^companion of
    her youth
  And forgets the covenant of
    her God;
18 For ^her house sinks down to
    death,
  And her tracks *lead* to the
    dead;
19 None ^who go to her return,
  Nor do they reach the ^Bpaths
    of life.
20 So you will ^walk in the way of
    good people
  And keep to the paths of the
    righteous.
21 For ^the upright will live in the
    land,
  And ^Bthe blameless will
    remain in it;

22 But the wicked will be
    eliminated from the land,
  And ^the treacherous will be
    ^Btorn away from it.

THE REWARDS OF WISDOM

3 My son, ^do not forget my
    teaching,
  But have your heart ^Bcomply
    with my commandments;
2 For ^length of days and years
    of life
  And peace they will add to
    you.
3 Do not let ^kindness and truth
    leave you;
  Bind them around your neck,
  ^BWrite them on the tablet of
    your heart.
4 So you will find favor and a
    ^good reputation
  In the sight of God and man.
5 ^Trust in the LORD with all
    your heart
  And ^Bdo not lean on your own
    understanding.
6 In all your ways acknowledge
    Him,
  And He will ^make your paths
    straight.
7 ^Do not be wise in your own
    eyes;
  Fear the LORD and turn away
    from evil.
8 It will be ^healing to your
    body
  And refreshment to your
    bones.

2:9 ^Prov 8:20   2:10 ^Prov 14:33   ^BProv 22:18
2:11 ^Prov 4:6; 6:22   2:12 ^Prov 28:26
2:13 ^Prov 21:16   2:14 ^Prov 10:23; Jer 11:15
2:15 ^Ps 125:5; Prov 21:8   2:16 ^Prov 23:27
2:17 ^Mal 2:14, 15   2:18 ^Prov 7:27   2:19 ^Eccl 7:26
^BPs 16:11   2:20 ^Heb 6:12   2:21 ^Ps 37:9, 29
^BProv 28:10   2:22 ^Prov 11:3   ^BDeut 28:63
3:1 ^Ps 119:61   ^BEx 20:6   3:2 ^Ps 91:16; Prov 3:16
3:3 ^2 Sam 15:20   ^BProv 7:3   3:4 ^Ps 111:10
3:5 ^Ps 37:3, 5   ^BProv 23:4   3:6 ^Is 45:13; Jer 10:23
3:7 ^Rom 12:16   3:8 ^Prov 4:22

9 ^Honor the LORD from your
      wealth,
    And from the ^Bfirst of all your
      produce;
10 Then your ^barns will be filled
      with plenty,
    And your ^Bvats will overflow
      with new wine.
11 ^My son, do not reject the
      discipline of the LORD
    Or loathe His rebuke,
12 For ^whom the LORD loves He
      disciplines,
    Just ^Bas a father *disciplines* the
      son in whom he delights.

13 ^Blessed is a person who finds
      wisdom,
    And one who obtains
      understanding.
14 For ^1her ^profit is better than
      the profit of silver,
    And her produce better than
      gold.
15 She is ^more precious than
      jewels,
    And nothing you desire
      compares with her.
16 ^Long life is in her right hand;
    In her left hand are ^Briches
      and honor.
17 Her ^ways are pleasant ways,
    And all her paths are peace.
18 She is a ^tree of life to those
      who take hold of her,
    And happy are those who hold
      on to her.
19 The LORD founded the earth
      ^by wisdom,
    He established the heavens by
      understanding.
20 By His knowledge the ^ocean
      depths were burst open,
    And the clouds drip with
      dew.
21 My son, *see that* ^they do not
      escape from your sight;

Comply with sound wisdom
      and discretion,
22 And they will be ^life to your
      soul
    And adornment to your neck.
23 Then you will ^walk in your
      way securely,
    And your foot will not ^Bstumble.
24 When you ^lie down, you will
      not be afraid;
    When you lie down, your sleep
      will be sweet.
25 Do not be afraid of sudden
      danger,
    Nor of ^trouble from the
      wicked when it comes;
26 For the LORD will be your
      confidence,
    And will ^keep your foot from
      being caught.

27 ^Do not withhold good from
      those to whom it is due,
    When it is in your power to
      do *it*.
28 ^Do not say to your neighbor,
    "Go, and come back,
    And tomorrow I will give *it to
      you*,"
    When you have it with you.
29 ^Do not devise harm against
      your neighbor,
    While he lives securely beside
      you.
30 ^Do not contend with a person
      for no reason,
    If he has done you no harm.

3:9 ^Is 43:23   ^BEx 23:19   3:10^Deut 28:8   ^BJoel 2:24
3:11^Job 5:17; Heb 12:5, 6   3:12^Rev 3:19   ^BDeut 8:5
3:13^Prov 8:32, 34   3:14^Job 28:15-19; Prov 8:10, 19
3:15^Job 28:18; Prov 8:11   3:16^Prov 3:2   ^BProv 8:18
3:17^Matt 11:29   3:18^Gen 2:9; Prov 11:30
3:19^Ps 104:24; Prov 8:27   3:20^Gen 7:11
3:21^Prov 4:21   3:22^Deut 32:47; Prov 4:22
3:23^Prov 4:12   ^BPs 91:12   3:24^Job 11:19; Ps 3:5
3:25^Job 5:21   3:26^1 Sam 2:9   3:27^Rom 13:7;
Gal 6:10   3:28^Lev 19:13; Deut 24:15   3:29^Prov 6:14;
14:22   3:30^Prov 26:17; Rom 12:18

3:14 ^1 I.e., the profit from Wisdom (personified)

31 ^Do not envy a violent person,
And do not choose any of his
ways.
32 For the ^devious are an
abomination to the Lord;
But He is ^Bintimate with the
upright.
33 The ^curse of the Lord is on
the house of the wicked,
But He ^Bblesses the home of
the righteous.
34 Though ^He scoffs at the
scoffers,
Yet ^BHe gives grace to the
needy.
35 ^The wise will inherit honor,
But fools increase dishonor.

A FATHER'S INSTRUCTION

4 Listen, *my* sons, to the
^instruction of a father,
And pay attention so that you
may gain understanding,
2 For I give you good ^teaching;
^BDo not abandon my
instruction.
3 When I was a son to my father,
Tender and ^the only son in
the sight of my mother,
4 He ^taught me and said to me,
"Let your heart take hold of my
words;
Keep my commandments and
live;
5 ^Acquire wisdom! ^BAcquire
understanding!
Do not forget nor turn away
from the words of my
mouth.
6 "Do not abandon her, and she
will guard you;
^Love her, and she will watch
over you.
7 "The beginning of wisdom *is*:
^Acquire wisdom;
And with all your possessions,
acquire understanding.

8 "^Prize her, and she will exalt
you;
She will honor you if you
embrace her.
9 "She will place ^on your head a
garland of grace;
She will present you with a
crown of beauty."

10 Listen, my son, and ^accept my
sayings,
And the years of your life will
be many.
11 I have ^instructed you in the
way of wisdom;
I have led you in upright
paths.
12 When you walk, your ^steps
will not be hampered;
And if you run, you ^Bwill not
stumble.
13 ^Take hold of instruction; do
not let go.
Guard her, for she is your life.
14 ^Do not enter the path of the
wicked
And do not proceed in the way
of evil people.
15 Avoid it, do not pass by it;
Turn away from it and pass on.
16 For they ^cannot sleep unless
they do evil;
And they are robbed of sleep
unless they make *someone*
stumble.
17 For they ^eat the bread of
wickedness,
And drink the wine of
violence.

3:31 ^Ps 37:1; Prov 24:1 3:32 ^Prov 11:20 ^BJob 29:4
3:33 ^Lev 26:14, 16 ^BJob 8:6 3:34 ^James 4:6
^B1 Pet 5:5 3:35 ^Dan 12:3 4:1 ^Ps 34:11; Prov 1:8
4:2 ^Deut 32:2 ^BPs 89:30 4:3 ^Zech 12:10
4:4 ^Eph 6:4 4:5 ^Prov 4:7 ^BProv 16:16
4:6 ^2 Thess 2:10 4:7 ^Prov 23:23 4:8 ^1 Sam 2:30
4:9 ^Prov 1:9 4:10 ^Prov 2:1 4:11 ^1 Sam 12:23
4:12 ^Job 18:7 ^BPs 91:11 4:13 ^Prov 3:18
4:14 ^Ps 1:1; Prov 1:15 4:16 ^Ps 36:4; Mic 2:1
4:17 ^Prov 13:2

18 But the ᴬpath of the righteous
   is like the light of dawn
   That ᴮshines brighter and
   brighter until the full day.
19 The ᴬway of the wicked is like
   darkness;
   They do not know over what
   they stumble.

20 My son, ᴬpay attention to my
   words;
   Incline your ear to my sayings.
21 They are not to escape from
   your sight;
   ᴬKeep them in the midst of
   your heart.
22 For they are ᴬlife to those who
   find them,
   And ᴮhealing to all their body.
23 Watch over your heart with all
   diligence,
   For ᴬfrom it *flow* the springs
   of life.
24 Rid yourself of a ᴬdeceitful
   mouth
   And ᴮkeep devious speech far
   from you.
25 Let your eyes look directly
   ahead
   And let your gaze be fixed
   straight in front of you.
26 ᴬWatch the path of your feet,
   And all your ways will be
   established.
27 ᴬDo not turn to the right or to
   the left;
   ᴮTurn your foot from evil.

PITFALLS OF IMMORALITY

5 My son, pay attention to my
   wisdom,
   ᴬIncline your ear to my
   understanding,
2 So that you may ᴬmaintain
   discretion
   And your ᴮlips may comply
   with knowledge.

3 For the lips of an adulteress
   ᴬdrip honey,
   And her speech is ᴮsmoother
   than oil;
4 But in the end she is ᴬbitter as
   wormwood,
   ᴮSharp as a two-edged sword.
5 Her feet ᴬgo down to death,
   Her steps take hold of Sheol.
6 She does not ponder the path
   of life;
   Her ways are ᴬunstable, she
   ᴮdoes not know *it*.

7 Now then, *my* sons, listen to me
   And ᴬdo not turn away from
   the words of my mouth.
8 ᴬKeep your way far from her,
   And do not go near the ᴮdoor
   of her house,
9 Otherwise you will give your
   vigor to others,
   And your years to the cruel one;
10 And strangers will be filled
   with your strength,
   And your hard-earned
   possessions *will go* to the
   house of a foreigner;
11 And you will groan in the end,
   When your flesh and your
   body are consumed;
12 And you say, "How I ᴬhated
   instruction!
   And my heart disdainfully
   rejected rebuke!
13 "I did not listen to the voice of
   my ᴬteachers,
   Nor incline my ear to my
   instructors!

4:18 ᴬIs 26:7   ᴮDan 12:3   4:19 ᴬJob 18:5, 6; Prov 2:13
4:20 ᴬProv 5:1   4:21 ᴬProv 7:1, 2   4:22 ᴬProv 3:22
ᴮProv 3:8   4:23 ᴬMatt 12:34; 15:18, 19
4:24 ᴬProv 6:12   ᴮProv 19:1   4:26 ᴬProv 5:21;
Heb 12:13   4:27 ᴬDeut 5:32   ᴮProv 1:15
5:1 ᴬProv 22:17   5:2 ᴬProv 3:21   ᴮMal 2:7
5:3 ᴬSong 4:11   ᴮPs 55:21   5:4 ᴬEccl 7:26   ᴮPs 57:4
5:5 ᴬProv 7:27   5:6 ᴬ2 Pet 2:14   ᴮProv 30:20
5:7 ᴬPs 119:102   5:8 ᴬProv 7:25   ᴮProv 9:14
5:12 ᴬProv 1:7, 22, 29   5:13 ᴬProv 1:8

14 "I was almost in total ruin
In the midst of the assembly
and congregation."

15 Drink water from your own
cistern,
And fresh water from your
own well.
16 Should your ^springs overflow
into the street,
Streams of water in the public
squares?
17 Let them be yours alone,
And not for strangers with
you.
18 Let your ^fountain be blessed,
And rejoice in the ^Bwife of your
youth.
19 *Like* a loving ^doe and a
graceful mountain goat,
Let her breasts satisfy you at
all times;
Be exhilarated always with her
love.
20 For why should you, my son,
be exhilarated with an
adulteress,
And embrace the breasts of a
^foreigner?
21 For the ways of everyone are
before the eyes of the LORD,
And He ^observes all his paths.
22 His ^own wrongdoings will
trap the wicked,
And he will be held by the
ropes of his sin.
23 He will ^die for lack of
instruction,
And in the greatness of his
foolishness he will go astray.

PARENTAL COUNSEL

6 My son, if you have become
a ^guarantor for your
neighbor,
Or have given a handshake for
a stranger,

2 *If* you have been ensnared by
the words of your mouth,
Or caught by the words of your
mouth,
3 Then do this, my son, and save
yourself:
Since you have come into the
hand of your neighbor,
Go, humble yourself, and be
urgent with your neighbor *to
free yourself.*
4 Give no ^sleep to your eyes,
Nor slumber to your eyelids;
5 Save yourself like a gazelle
from *the hunter's* hand,
And like a ^bird from the hand
of the fowler.

6 Go to the ^ant, you lazy one,
Observe its ways and be wise,
7 Which, having ^no chief,
Officer, or ruler,
8 Prepares its food ^in the summer
And gathers its provision in
the harvest.
9 How long will you lie down,
you lazy one?
When will you arise from your
sleep?
10 "^A little sleep, a little slumber,
A little folding of the hands to
rest,"
11 ^Then your poverty will come
in like a drifter,
And your need like an armed
man.

12 A ^worthless person, a wicked
man,
Is one who walks with a
^Bperverse mouth,

5:16 ^Prov 5:18; 9:17　5:18 ^Prov 9:17　^BMal 2:14
5:19 ^Song 2:9, 17; 4:5　5:20 ^Prov 2:16; 6:24
5:21 ^Prov 4:26　5:22 ^Num 32:23; Ps 7:15
5:23 ^Job 4:21; 36:12　6:1 ^Prov 11:15; 17:18
6:4 ^Ps 132:4　6:5 ^Ps 91:3; 124:7　6:6 ^Prov 30:24, 25
6:7 ^Prov 30:27　6:8 ^Prov 10:5　6:10 ^Prov 24:33
6:11 ^Prov 24:34　6:12 ^Prov 16:27　^BProv 4:24

13 Who ^winks with his eyes, who
      signals with his feet,
   Who points with his fingers;
14 Who, *with* perversion in his
      heart, continually ^devises
      evil,
   Who ^Bspreads strife.
15 Therefore ^his disaster will
      come suddenly;
   Instantly he will be broken and
      there will be no healing.

16 There are six things that the
      LORD hates,
   Seven that are an abomination
      to Him:
17 Haughty eyes, a ^lying
      tongue,
   And hands that shed innocent
      blood,
18 A heart that devises ^wicked
      plans,
   ^BFeet that run rapidly to evil,
19 A ^false witness *who* declares
      lies,
   And one who spreads strife
      among brothers.

20 ^My son, comply with the
      commandment of your
      father,
   And do not ignore the
      teaching of your mother;
21 ^Bind them continually on
      your heart;
   Tie them around your neck.
22 When you ^walk, they will
      guide you;
   When you sleep, they will
      watch over you;
   And when you awake, they
      will talk to you.
23 For ^the commandment is a
      lamp and the teaching is
      light;
   And rebukes for discipline are
      the way of life

24 To ^keep you from the evil
      woman,
   From the smooth tongue of
      the foreign woman.
25 ^Do not desire her beauty in
      your heart,
   Nor let her capture you with
      her eyelids.
26 For ^the price of a prostitute
      reduces one to a loaf of
      bread,
   And an adulteress ^Bhunts for a
      precious life.
27 Can anyone take fire in his lap
   And his clothes not be
      burned?
28 Or can a person walk on hot
      coals
   And his feet not be scorched?
29 So is the one who ^goes in to
      his neighbor's wife;
   Whoever touches her will not
      go unpunished.
30 *People* do not despise a thief if
      he steals
   To ^satisfy himself when he is
      hungry;
31 But when he is found, he
      must ^repay seven times *as*
      much;
   He must give up all the
      property of his house.
32 One who commits adultery
      with a woman is lacking
      sense;
   He who would ^destroy
      himself commits it.
33 He will find wounds and
      disgrace,
   And his shame will not be
      removed.

6:13 ^Job 15:12; Ps 35:19   6:14 ^Prov 3:29   ^B Prov 6:19
6:15 ^Prov 24:22   6:17 ^Ps 31:18; 120:2   6:18 ^Gen 6:5
^B Prov 1:16   6:19 ^Ps 27:12; Prov 12:17   6:20 ^Eph 6:1
6:21 ^Prov 3:3   6:22 ^Prov 3:23   6:23 ^Ps 19:8;
119:105   6:24 ^Prov 5:3; 7:5, 21   6:25 ^Matt 5:28
6:26 ^Prov 5:9, 10   ^B Prov 7:23   6:29 ^Ezek 18:6; 33:26
6:30 ^Job 38:39   6:31 ^Ex 22:1-4   6:32 ^Prov 7:22, 23

34 For ^jealousy enrages a man,
   And he will not have
      compassion on the ^Bday of
      vengeance.
35 He will not accept any
      settlement,
   Nor will he be satisfied though
      you make *it* a large gift.

THE LURES OF THE PROSTITUTE

7 My son, ^keep my words
   And treasure my
      commandments within you.
2 Keep my commandments and
      live,
   And my teaching ^as the ¹apple
      of your eye.
3 Bind them on your fingers;
   ^Write them on the tablet of
      your heart.
4 Say to wisdom, "You are my
      sister,"
   And call understanding *your*
      intimate friend,
5 So that they may keep you
      from an adulteress,
   From the foreigner who
      flatters with her words.

6 For ^at the window of my house
   I looked out ^Bthrough my
      lattice,
7 And I saw among the ^naive,
   And discerned among the
      youths
   A young man ^Blacking sense,
8 Passing through the street
      near her corner;
   And he walks along the way to
      ^her house,
9 In the ^twilight, in the evening,
   In the middle of the night and
      the darkness.
10 And behold, a woman *comes*
      to meet him,
   ^Dressed as a prostitute and
      cunning of heart.

11 She is boisterous and
      rebellious,
   Her ^feet do not remain at
      home;
12 *She is* now in the streets, now
      in the public squares,
   And ^lurks by every corner.
13 So she seizes him and kisses
      him,
   And with a ^brazen face she
      says to him:
14 "I was due to offer ^peace
      offerings;
   Today I have ^Bpaid my vows.
15 "Therefore I have come out to
      meet you,
   To seek your presence
      diligently, and I have found
      you.
16 "I have spread my couch with
      coverings,
   With colored ^linens of Egypt.
17 "I have sprinkled my bed
   With ^myrrh, aloes, and
      ^Bcinnamon.
18 "Come, let's drink our fill of
      love until morning;
   Let's delight ourselves with
      caresses.
19 "For my husband is not at home;
   He has gone on a long journey;
20 "He has taken a ^bag of money
      with him.
   At the full moon he will come
      home."
21 With her many persuasions
      she entices him;
   With her ^flattering lips she
      seduces him.

6:34 ^Prov 27:4   ᴮProv 11:4   7:1 ^Prov 2:1; 6:20
7:2 ^Deut 32:10; Ps 17:8   7:3 ^Prov 3:3   7:6 ^Judg 5:28
ᴮSong 2:9   7:7 ^Prov 1:22   ᴮProv 6:32   7:8 ^Prov 7:27
7:9 ^Job 24:15   7:10 ^Gen 38:14, 15; 1 Tim 2:9
7:11 ^1 Tim 5:13; Titus 2:5   7:12 ^Prov 23:28
7:13 ^Prov 21:29   7:14 ^Lev 7:11   ᴮLev 7:16
7:16 ^Is 19:9; Ezek 27:7   7:17 ^Ps 45:8   ᴮEx 30:23
7:20 ^Gen 42:35   7:21 ^Prov 5:3; 6:24

7:2 ¹Lit *pupil*

22 Suddenly he follows her
   As an ox goes to the slaughter,
   Or as *one* walks in ankle
      bracelets to the discipline of
      a fool,
23 Until an arrow pierces through
      his liver;
   As a ^bird hurries to the snare,
   So he does not know that it
      will cost him his life.

24 Now therefore, *my* sons,
      ^listen to me,
   And pay attention to the words
      of my mouth.
25 Do not let your heart ^turn
      aside to her ways,
   Do not stray into her paths.
26 For many are the victims she
      has brought to ruin,
   And ^numerous are all those
      slaughtered by her.
27 Her ^house is the way to
      Sheol,
   Descending to the chambers
      of death.

THE COMMENDATION OF WISDOM

8 Does not ^wisdom call,
   And understanding raise her
      voice?
2 On top of ^the heights beside
      the way,
   Where the paths meet, she
      takes her stand;
3 Beside the ^gates, at the
      opening to the city,
   At the entrance of the doors,
      she cries out:
4 "To you, people, I call,
   And my voice is to mankind.
5 "You ^naive ones, understand
      prudence;
   And, you ^Bfools, understand
      wisdom!
6 "Listen, for I will speak ^noble
      things;

And the opening of my lips
   will reveal ^Bright things.
7 "For my ^mouth will proclaim
      truth;
   And wickedness is an
      abomination to my lips.
8 "All the words of my mouth are
      in righteousness;
   There is nothing ^crooked or
      perverted in them.
9 "They are all ^straightforward
      to him who understands,
   And right to those who ^Bfind
      knowledge.
10 "Accept my ^instruction and not
      silver,
   And knowledge rather than
      choice gold.
11 "For wisdom is ^better than
      jewels;
   And all desirable things
      cannot compare with her.
12 "I, wisdom, dwell with prudence,
   And I find ^knowledge *and*
      discretion.
13 "The ^fear of the LORD is to hate
      evil;
   Pride, arrogance, the evil way,
   And the perverted mouth, I
      hate.
14 "^Advice is mine and ^Bsound
      wisdom;
   I am understanding, power is
      mine.
15 "By me ^kings reign,
   And rulers decree justice.
16 "By me princes rule, and nobles,
   All who judge rightly.

7:23 ^Eccl 9:12 7:24 ^Prov 5:7 7:25 ^Prov 5:8
7:26 ^Prov 9:18 7:27 ^Prov 2:18; 5:5
8:1 ^Prov 1:20, 21; 8:1-3 8:2 ^Prov 9:3, 14
8:3 ^Job 29:7 8:5 ^Prov 1:4 ^BProv 1:22, 32
8:6 ^Prov 22:20 ^BProv 23:16 8:7 ^Ps 37:30;
John 8:14 8:8 ^Deut 32:5; Prov 2:15 8:9 ^Prov 14:6
^BProv 3:13 8:10 ^Prov 3:14, 15; 8:19
8:11 ^Job 28:15, 18; Ps 19:10 8:12 ^Prov 1:4
8:13 ^Prov 3:7; 16:6 8:14 ^Prov 1:25 ^BProv 2:7
8:15 ^2 Chr 1:10; Prov 29:4

¹⁷ "I ^Alove those who love me;
   And ^Bthose who diligently seek
      me will find me.
¹⁸ "^ARiches and honor are with me,
   Enduring wealth and
      righteousness.
¹⁹ "My fruit is ^Abetter than gold,
      even pure gold;
   And my yield *better* than
      choice silver.
²⁰ "I walk in the way of
      righteousness,
   In the midst of the paths of
      justice,
²¹ To endow those who love me
      with wealth,
   That I may ^Afill their treasuries.

²² "The LORD created me ^Aat the
      beginning of His way,
   Before His works of old.
²³ "From eternity I was
      ^Aestablished,
   From the beginning, ^Bfrom the
      earliest times of the earth.
²⁴ "When there were no ^Aocean
      depths, I was born,
   When there were no springs
      abounding with water.
²⁵ "^ABefore the mountains were
      settled,
   Before the hills, I was born;
²⁶ While He had not yet made the
      earth and the fields,
   Nor the first dust of the world.
²⁷ "When He ^Aestablished the
      heavens, I was there;
   When ^BHe inscribed a circle on
      the face of the deep,
²⁸ When He made firm the skies
      above,
   When the springs of the deep
      became fixed,
²⁹ When He set a boundary for
      the sea
   So that the water would not
      violate His command,

When He marked out ^Athe
      foundations of the earth;
³⁰ Then ^AI was beside Him, *as* a
      master workman;
   And I was *His* delight daily,
   Rejoicing always before Him,
³¹ Rejoicing in the world, His earth,
   And *having* ^Amy delight in the
      sons of mankind.

³² "Now then, sons, ^Alisten to me,
   For blessed are those who
      keep my ways.
³³ "^AListen to instruction and be
      wise,
   And do not neglect *it*.
³⁴ "^ABlessed is the person who
      listens to me,
   Watching daily at my gates,
   Waiting at my doorposts.
³⁵ "For ^Aone who finds me finds life,
   And obtains favor from the
      LORD.
³⁶ "But one who sins against me
      ^Ainjures himself;
   All those who hate me ^Blove
      death."

WISDOM'S INVITATION

9 Wisdom has ^Abuilt her house,
   She has carved out her seven
      pillars;
² She has ^Aprepared her food,
      she has mixed her wine;
   She has also set her table;
³ She has ^Asent out her
      attendants, she calls out
   From the ^Btops of the heights
      of the city:

8:17^A1 Sam 2:30   ^BProv 2:4, 5   8:18^AProv 3:16
8:19^AJob 28:15; Prov 3:14   8:21^AProv 24:4
8:22^AJob 28:26-28; Ps 104:24   8:23^AJohn 1:1-3
^BJohn 17:5   8:24^AGen 1:2; Ex 15:5   8:25^AJob 15:7;
Ps 90:2   8:27^AProv 3:19   ^BJob 26:10   ^AJob 38:6;
Ps 104:5   8:30^AJohn 1:2, 3   8:31^APs 16:3; John 13:1
8:32^AProv 5:7; 7:24   8:33^AProv 4:1   8:34^AProv 3:13, 18
8:35^AProv 4:22; John 17:3   8:36^AProv 1:31, 32
^BProv 21:6   9:1^A1 Cor 3:9, 10; Eph 2:20-22
9:2^AMatt 22:4   9:3^APs 68:11   ^BProv 9:14

4 "ᴬWhoever is naive, let him turn in here!"
To him who ᴮlacks understanding she says,

5 "Come, ᴬeat of my food And drink of the wine I have mixed.

6 "Abandon *your* foolishness and live,
And ᴬproceed in the way of understanding."

7 One who ᴬcorrects a scoffer gets dishonor for himself,
And one who rebukes a wicked person *gets* insults for himself.

8 Do not rebuke a scoffer, or he will hate you;
ᴬRebuke a wise person and he will love you.

9 Give *instruction* to a wise person and he will become still wiser;
Teach a righteous person and he will ᴬincrease *his* insight.

10 The ᴬfear of the Lᴏʀᴅ is the beginning of wisdom,
And the knowledge of the Holy One is understanding.

11 For ᴬby me your days will be multiplied,
And years of life will be added to you.

12 If you are wise, you are wise ᴬfor yourself,
And if you scoff, you alone will suffer *from it*.

13 A woman of foolishness is ᴬboisterous,
She has a lack of understanding and ᴮknows nothing.

14 She sits at the doorway of her house,
On a seat by ᴬthe high places of the city,

15 Calling to those who pass by, Who are going straight on their paths:

16 "ᴬWhoever is naive, let him turn in here,"
And to him who lacks understanding she says,

17 "Stolen water is sweet; And ᴬbread *eaten* in secret is pleasant."

18 But he does not know that the dead are there,
That her guests are in the ᴬdepths of Sheol.

CONTRAST OF THE RIGHTEOUS AND THE WICKED

10 The proverbs of Solomon.
ᴬA wise son makes a father glad,
But ᴮa foolish son is a grief to his mother.

2 ᴬIll-gotten gains do not benefit,
But righteousness rescues from death.

3 The Lᴏʀᴅ ᴬwill not allow the righteous to hunger,
But He ᴮwill reject the craving of the wicked.

4 Poor is one who works with a lazy hand,
But the ᴬhand of the diligent makes rich.

5 He who gathers in summer is a son who acts wisely,
But he who sleeps in harvest is a son who acts shamefully.

9:4 ᴬProv 8:5   ᴮProv 6:32   9:5 ᴬSong 5:1; Is 55:1
9:6 ᴬEzek 11:20; 37:24   9:7 ᴬProv 23:9   9:8 ᴬPs 141:5;
Prov 10:8   9:9 ᴬProv 1:5   9:10 ᴬJob 28:28; Ps 111:10
9:11 ᴬProv 3:16; 10:27   9:12 ᴬJob 22:2; Prov 14:14
9:13 ᴬProv 7:11   ᴮProv 5:6   9:14 ᴬProv 9:3
9:16 ᴬProv 9:4   9:17 ᴬProv 20:17   9:18 ᴬProv 7:27
10:1 ᴬProv 15:20   ᴮProv 17:25   10:2 ᴬPs 49:7;
Prov 11:4   10:3 ᴬPs 34:9, 10   ᴮPs 112:10
10:4 ᴬProv 13:4; 21:5

6   Blessings are on the head of
    the righteous,
    But ^the mouth of the wicked
    conceals violence.
7   The ^mentioning of the
    righteous is a blessing,
    But ^Bthe name of the wicked
    will rot.
8   The ^wise of heart will receive
    commands,
    But a babbling fool will come
    to ruin.
9   One ^who walks in integrity
    walks securely,
    But ^Bone who perverts his ways
    will be found out.
10 He ^who winks the eye causes
    trouble,
    And a babbling fool will come
    to ruin.
11 The ^mouth of the righteous is
    a fountain of life,
    But the mouth of the wicked
    conceals violence.
12 Hatred stirs up strife,
    But ^love covers all offenses.
13 On ^the lips of the
    discerning, wisdom is
    found,
    But ^Ba rod is for the back of
    him who has no sense.
14 Wise people ^store up
    knowledge,
    But with ^Bthe mouth of the
    foolish, ruin is at hand.
15 The rich person's wealth is his
    fortress,
    The ^ruin of the poor is their
    poverty.
16 The ^wages of the righteous is
    life,
    The income of the wicked,
    punishment.
17 One who ^is *on* the path of life
    follows instruction,
    But one who ignores a rebuke
    goes astray.

18 One ^who conceals hatred *has*
    lying lips,
    And one who spreads slander
    is a fool.
19 When there are many
    words, wrongdoing is
    unavoidable,
    But ^one who restrains his lips
    is wise.
20 The tongue of the righteous is
    like ^choice silver,
    The heart of the wicked is
    worth little.
21 The ^lips of the righteous feed
    many,
    But fools ^Bdie for lack of
    understanding.
22 It is the ^blessing of the Lord
    that makes rich,
    And He adds no sorrow to it.
23 Doing wickedness is like
    ^sport to a fool,
    And *so is* wisdom to a person
    of understanding.
24 What the wicked fears will
    come upon him,
    But the ^desire of the
    righteous will be granted.
25 When the whirlwind passes,
    the wicked is no more,
    But the ^righteous *has* an
    everlasting foundation.
26 Like vinegar to the teeth and
    smoke to the eyes,
    So is the ^lazy one to those
    who send him.
27 The ^fear of the Lord
    prolongs life,

10:6 ^Prov 10:11; Obad 10   10:7 ^Ps 112:6   ^BPs 9:5, 6
10:8 ^Prov 9:8; Matt 7:24   10:9 ^Ps 23:4   ^BProv 26:26
10:10 ^Ps 35:19; Prov 6:13   10:11 ^Ps 37:30; Prov 13:14
10:12 ^Prov 17:9; 1 Cor 13:4-7   10:13 ^Prov 10:31
^BProv 19:29   10:14 ^Prov 9:9   ^BProv 10:8, 10
10:15 ^Prov 19:7   10:16 ^Prov 11:18, 19
10:17 ^Prov 6:23   10:18 ^Prov 26:24   10:19 ^Prov 17:27;
James 1:19   10:20 ^Prov 8:19   10:21 ^Prov 10:11
^BProv 5:23   10:22 ^Gen 24:35; 26:12   10:23 ^Prov 2:14;
15:21   10:24 ^Ps 145:19; Prov 15:8   10:25 ^Ps 15:5;
Prov 12:3   10:26 ^Prov 26:6   10:27 ^Prov 3:2; 9:11

But the years of the wicked
will be shortened.

28 The ᴬhope of the righteous is
gladness,
But the ᴮexpectation of the
wicked perishes.

29 The ᴬway of the Lᴏʀᴅ is a
stronghold for the upright,
But ᴮruin to the workers of
injustice.

30 The righteous will never be
shaken,
But ᴬthe wicked will not live in
the land.

31 The ᴬmouth of the righteous
flows with wisdom,
But the perverted tongue will
be cut out.

32 The lips of the righteous know
ᴬwhat is acceptable,
But the mouth of the wicked,
what is perverted.

CONTRAST OF THE UPRIGHT
AND THE WICKED

11 A ᴬfalse balance is an
abomination to the Lᴏʀᴅ,
But a just weight is His
delight.

2 When ᴬpride comes, then
comes dishonor;
But with the humble there is
wisdom.

3 The ᴬintegrity of the upright
will guide them,
But the ᴮperversity of the
treacherous will destroy
them.

4 ᴬRiches do not benefit on the
day of wrath,
But ᴮrighteousness rescues
from death.

5 The righteousness of the
blameless will smooth his
way,
But ᴬthe wicked will fall by his
own wickedness.

6 The righteousness of the
upright will rescue them,
But the treacherous will ᴬbe
caught by *their own* greed.

7 When a wicked person dies,
his ᴬexpectation will perish,
And the hope of strong people
perishes.

8 The righteous is rescued from
trouble,
But the wicked takes his place.

9 With *his* mouth the godless
person destroys his
neighbor,
But through knowledge the
ᴬrighteous will be rescued.

10 When things ᴬgo well for the
righteous, the city rejoices,
And when the wicked perish,
there is joyful shouting.

11 By the blessing of the upright a
city is exalted,
But by the mouth of the
wicked, it is torn down.

12 One who despises his
neighbor lacks sense,
But a person of understanding
keeps silent.

13 One who goes about as a
slanderer reveals secrets,
But one who is trustworthy
ᴬconceals a matter.

14 Where there is no ᴬguidance
the people fall,
But in an abundance of
counselors there is victory.

15 One who is a ᴬguarantor for a
stranger will certainly suffer
for it,
But one who hates being a
guarantor is secure.

10:28 ᴬProv 11:23 ᴮJob 8:13 10:29 ᴬProv 13:6
ᴮProv 21:15 10:30 ᴬProv 2:22
10:31 ᴬPs 37:30; Prov 10:13 10:32 ᴬEccl 12:10
11:1 ᴬLev 19:35, 36; Deut 25:13-16 11:2 ᴬProv 16:18; 18:12
11:3 ᴬProv 13:6 ᴮProv 19:3 11:4 ᴬProv 10:2 ᴮGen 7:1
11:5 ᴬProv 5:22 11:6 ᴬPs 7:15, 16; 9:15 11:7 ᴬProv 10:28
11:9 ᴬProv 11:6 11:10 ᴬProv 28:12 11:13 ᴬProv 19:11
11:14 ᴬProv 15:22; 20:18 11:15 ᴬProv 6:1; 27:13

16 A ^gracious woman attains
  honor,
  And ruthless men attain riches.
17 A ^merciful person does
  himself *good,*
  But the cruel person does
  himself harm.
18 A wicked person earns
  deceptive wages,
  But one who ^sows
  righteousness *gets* a true
  reward.
19 One who is steadfast in
  ^righteousness *attains* life,
  But one who pursues evil
  attains his own death.
20 The perverse in heart are an
  abomination to the LORD,
  But the blameless in *their* walk
  are His ^delight.
21 Be assured, the evil person will
  not go unpunished,
  But the descendants of the
  righteous will be rescued.
22 *As* a ^ring of gold in a pig's
  snout
  So is a beautiful woman who
  lacks discretion.
23 The desire of the righteous is
  only good,
  But the ^expectation of the
  wicked is wrath.
24 There is one who scatters, and
  yet increases all the more,
  And there is one who
  withholds what is justly
  due, *and yet it results* only in
  poverty.
25 A ^generous person will be
  prosperous,
  And one who gives *others*
  plenty of water will himself
  be given plenty.
26 One who withholds grain, the
  ^people will curse him,
  But blessing will be on the
  head of him who sells *it.*

27 One who diligently seeks good
  seeks favor,
  But ^one who seeks evil, evil
  will come to him.
28 One who ^trusts in his riches
  will fall,
  But the righteous will flourish
  like the *green* leaf.
29 One who ^troubles his own
  house will ^inherit wind,
  And the foolish will be servant
  to the wise-hearted.
30 The fruit of the righteous is ^a
  tree of life,
  And ^one who is wise gains
  souls.
31 If ^the righteous will be repaid
  on the earth,
  How much more the wicked
  and the sinner!

CONTRAST OF THE UPRIGHT AND THE WICKED

12 One who loves discipline
  loves knowledge,
  But one who hates rebuke is
  stupid.
2 A ^good person will obtain
  favor from the LORD,
  But He will condemn a person
  who devises evil.
3 A person will not be
  established by wickedness,
  But the root of the ^righteous
  will not be moved.
4 An ^excellent wife is the crown
  of her husband,
  But she who shames *him* is like
  ^rottenness in his bones.

11:16 ^Prov 31:28, 30   11:17 ^Matt 5:7; 25:34-36
11:18 ^Hos 10:12; Gal 6:8, 9   11:19 ^Prov 10:16; 12:28
11:20 ^1 Chr 29:17   11:22 ^Gen 24:47
11:23 ^Prov 10:28; Rom 2:8, 9   11:25 ^Prov 3:9, 10;
2 Cor 9:6, 7   11:26 ^Prov 24:24   11:27 ^Esth 7:10;
Ps 7:15, 16   11:28 ^Ps 49:6; Mark 10:25
11:29 ^Prov 15:27   ^Eccl 5:16   11:30 ^Prov 3:18
^Prov 14:25   11:31 ^2 Sam 22:21; Prov 13:21
12:2 ^Prov 3:4; 8:35   12:3 ^Prov 10:25
12:4 ^Prov 31:11   ^Prov 14:30

5 The thoughts of the righteous
   are just,
   But the counsels of the wicked
   are deceitful.
6 The words of the wicked wait
   in ambush for blood,
   But the ^mouth of the upright
   will rescue them.
7 The ^wicked are overthrown
   and are no more,
   But the ^Bhouse of the righteous
   will stand.
8 A person will be praised
   according to his insight,
   But one of perverse mind will
   be despised.
9 Better is one who is lightly
   esteemed and has a servant,
   Than one who honors himself
   and lacks bread.
10 A ^righteous person has regard
   for the life of his animal,
   But *even* the compassion of
   the wicked is cruel.
11 One ^who works his land will
   have plenty of bread,
   But one who pursues
   worthless *things* lacks sense.
12 The ^wicked person desires the
   plunder of evil people,
   But the root of the righteous
   ^Byields *fruit.*
13 An evil person is ensnared by
   the offense of his lips,
   But the ^righteous will escape
   from trouble.
14 A person will be satisfied with
   good by the fruit of his words,
   And the ^deeds of a person's
   hands will return to him.
15 The ^way of a fool is right in his
   own eyes,
   But a person who listens to
   advice is wise.
16 A ^fool's anger is known at once,
   But a prudent person conceals
   dishonor.

17 One *who* declares truth tells
   what is right,
   But a false witness, deceit.
18 There is one who ^speaks
   rashly like the thrusts of a
   sword,
   But the ^Btongue of the wise
   brings healing.
19 Truthful lips will endure
   forever,
   But a ^lying tongue is only for a
   moment.
20 Deceit is in the heart of those
   who devise evil,
   But counselors of peace *have*
   joy.
21 ^No harm happens to the
   righteous,
   But the wicked are filled with
   trouble.
22 ^Lying lips are an abomination
   to the Lord,
   But those who deal faithfully
   are His delight.
23 A ^prudent person conceals
   knowledge,
   But the heart of fools
   proclaims foolishness.
24 The hand of the diligent will
   rule,
   But the lazy *hand* will be ^put
   to forced labor.
25 ^Anxiety in a person's heart
   weighs it down,
   But a ^Bgood word makes it
   glad.
26 The righteous person is a
   guide to his neighbor,
   But the way of the wicked
   leads them astray.

12:6 ^Prov 14:3   12:7 ^Job 34:25   ^B Matt 7:24-27
12:10 ^Deut 25:4   12:11 ^Prov 28:19   12:12 ^Prov 21:10
^B Prov 11:30   12:13 ^Prov 11:8; 21:23   12:14 ^Job 34:11;
Prov 1:31   12:15 ^Prov 14:12; 16:2   12:16 ^Prov 14:33;
27:3   12:18 ^Ps 57:4   ^B Prov 4:22   12:19 ^Ps 52:4, 5;
Prov 19:9   12:21 ^Ps 91:10; 121:7   12:22 ^Rev 22:15
12:23 ^Prov 10:14; 11:13   12:24 ^Gen 49:15; Judg 1:28
12:25 ^Prov 15:13   ^B Is 50:4

27 A lazy person does not roast
his prey,
But the ^precious possession
of a person *is* diligence.
28 ^In the way of righteousness
there is life,
And in *its* pathway there is no
death.

CONTRAST OF THE UPRIGHT AND THE WICKED

13 A ^wise son *accepts his*
father's discipline,
But a scoffer does not listen to
rebuke.
2 From the fruit of a person's
mouth he ^enjoys good,
But the desire of the
treacherous is violence.
3 One who ^guards his mouth
protects his life;
One who opens wide his lips
comes to ruin.
4 The soul of the lazy one craves
and *gets* nothing,
But the soul of the diligent is
made prosperous.
5 A righteous person ^hates a
false statement,
But a wicked person
acts disgustingly and
shamefully.
6 Righteousness ^guards the one
whose way is blameless,
But wickedness brings the
sinner to ruin.
7 There is one who pretends to
be rich but has nothing;
Another pretends to be ^poor,
but has great wealth.
8 The ransom of a person's life is
his wealth,
But the poor hears no rebuke.
9 The light of the righteous
¹rejoices,
But the ^lamp of the wicked
goes out.

10 Through overconfidence
comes nothing but strife,
But wisdom is with those who
receive counsel.
11 Wealth *obtained* from
¹nothing dwindles,
But one who gathers by labor
increases *it*.
12 Hope deferred makes the
heart sick,
But desire fulfilled is a tree of
life.
13 One who ^despises the word
will do badly,
But one who fears the
commandment will be
rewarded.
14 The teaching of the wise is a
^fountain of life,
To turn aside from the snares
of death.
15 ^Good understanding
produces favor,
But the way of the treacherous
is their own disaster.
16 Every ^prudent person acts
with knowledge,
But a fool displays foolishness.
17 A wicked messenger falls into
adversity,
But ^a faithful messenger
brings healing.
18 Poverty and shame *will come* to
one who ^neglects discipline,
But one who complies with
rebuke will be honored.
19 Desire realized is sweet to the
soul,
But it is an abomination to
fools to turn away from evil.

12:27 ^Prov 10:4; 13:4   12:28 ^Deut 30:15f; 32:46f
13:1 ^Prov 10:1; 15:20   13:2 ^Prov 12:14
13:3 ^Prov 18:21; 21:23   13:5 ^Col 3:9   13:6 ^Prov 11:3
13:7 ^Luke 12:33; 2 Cor 6:10   13:9 ^Job 18:5; Prov 24:20
13:13 ^Num 15:31; 2 Chr 36:16   13:14 ^Prov 10:11; 14:27
13:15 ^Ps 111:10; Prov 3:4   13:16 ^Prov 12:23
13:17 ^Prov 25:13   13:18 ^Prov 15:5, 32

13:9 ¹I.e., shines brightly   13:11 ¹Prob. referring to fraud

20 ᴬOne who walks with wise
    people will be wise,
    But a companion of fools will
    suffer harm.
21 ᴬAdversity pursues sinners,
    But the ᴮrighteous will be
    rewarded with prosperity.
22 A good person ᴬleaves
    an inheritance to his
    grandchildren,
    And the wealth of a sinner is
    stored up for the righteous.
23 ᴬAbundant food *is in* the
    uncultivated ground of the
    poor,
    But it is swept away by injustice.
24 He who ᴬwithholds his rod
    hates his son,
    But he who loves him
    ᴮdisciplines him diligently.
25 The ᴬrighteous has enough to
    satisfy his appetite,
    But the stomach of the ᴮwicked
    is in need.

CONTRAST OF THE UPRIGHT
AND THE WICKED

14 The ᴬwise woman builds her
    house,
    But the foolish tears it down
    with her own hands.
2 One who ᴬwalks in his
    uprightness fears the LORD,
    But one who is ᴮdevious in his
    ways despises Him.
3 In the mouth of the foolish is a
    rod for *his* back,
    But ᴬthe lips of the wise will
    protect them.
4 Where there are no oxen, the
    manger is clean;
    But much revenue *comes* by
    the strength of the ox.
5 A ᴬtrustworthy witness will
    not lie,
    But a ᴮfalse witness declares
    lies.

6 A scoffer seeks wisdom and
    finds none,
    But knowledge is easy for one
    who has understanding.
7 Leave the ᴬpresence of a fool,
    Or you will not discern words
    of knowledge.
8 The wisdom of the sensible is
    to understand his way,
    But ᴬthe foolishness of fools is
    deceit.
9 Fools mock at sin,
    But ᴬamong the upright there
    is goodwill.
10 The heart knows its own
    ᴬbitterness,
    And a stranger does not share
    its joy.
11 The ᴬhouse of the wicked will
    be destroyed,
    But the tent of the upright will
    flourish.
12 There is a way *which seems*
    right to a person,
    But its ᴬend is the way of death.
13 Even in laughter the heart may
    be in pain,
    And the ᴬend of joy may be
    grief.
14 One with a wayward heart will
    have his ᴬfill of his own ways,
    But a good person will *be
    satisfied* with his.
15 The naive believes everything,
    But the sensible person
    considers his steps.
16 A wise person is cautious and
    ᴬturns away from evil,
    But a fool is arrogant and
    careless.

13:20 ᴬProv 2:20; 15:31   **13:21** ᴬPs 32:10   ᴮProv 11:31
13:22 ᴬEzra 9:12; Ps 37:25   **13:23** ᴬProv 12:11
13:24 ᴬProv 19:18   ᴮDeut 8:5   **13:25** ᴬPs 34:10
ᴮProv 13:18   **14:1** ᴬRuth 31:10–27
14:2 ᴬProv 19:1   ᴮProv 2:15   **14:3** ᴬProv 12:6
14:5 ᴬRev 1:5   ᴮEx 23:1   **14:7** ᴬProv 23:9   **14:8** ᴬ1 Cor 3:19
14:9 ᴬProv 3:34; 11:20   **14:10** ᴬ1 Sam 1:10; Job 21:25
14:11 ᴬJob 8:15   **14:12** ᴬRom 6:21   **14:13** ᴬEccl 2:1, 2
14:14 ᴬProv 1:31; 12:21   **14:16** ᴬJob 28:28; Ps 34:14

17 A quick-tempered person acts
   foolishly,
   And a person of evil devices is
   hated.
18 The naive inherit foolishness,
   But the sensible are crowned
   with knowledge.
19 The ^evil will bow down before
   the good,
   And the wicked at the gates of
   the righteous.
20 The ^poor is hated even by his
   neighbor,
   But those who love the rich are
   many.
21 One who ^despises his
   neighbor sins,
   But ^one who is gracious to the
   poor is blessed.
22 Will they who ^devise evil not
   go astray?
   But kindness and truth *will be
   to* those who devise good.
23 In all labor there is profit,
   But mere talk *leads* only to
   poverty.
24 The ^crown of the wise is their
   riches,
   But the foolishness of fools is
   simply foolishness.
25 A truthful witness saves lives,
   But one *who* ^declares lies *is*
   deceitful.
26 In ^the fear of the LORD there is
   strong confidence,
   And his children will have
   refuge.
27 The fear of the LORD is a
   fountain of life,
   By which one may avoid the
   snares of death.
28 In a multitude of people is a
   king's glory,
   But in the scarcity of people is
   a prince's ruin.
29 One who is ^slow to anger has
   great understanding;

But one who is quick-tempered
exalts foolishness.
30 A ^tranquil heart is life to the
   body,
   But jealousy is ^rottenness to
   the bones.
31 One ^who oppresses the poor
   taunts ^his Maker,
   But one who is gracious to the
   needy honors Him.
32 The wicked is ^thrust down by
   his own wrongdoing,
   But the ^righteous has a refuge
   when he dies.
33 Wisdom rests in the heart of
   one who has understanding,
   But among fools it is made
   known.
34 Righteousness exalts a nation,
   But sin is a disgrace to *any*
   people.
35 The king's favor is toward a
   ^servant who acts wisely,
   But his anger is toward him
   who acts shamefully.

CONTRAST OF THE UPRIGHT
AND THE WICKED

15 A ^gentle answer turns away
   wrath,
   But a ^harsh word stirs up
   anger.
2 The ^tongue of the wise makes
   knowledge pleasant,
   But the mouth of fools spouts
   foolishness.
3 The ^eyes of the LORD are in
   every place,
   Watching the evil and the
   good.

14:19 ^1 Sam 2:36; Prov 11:29   **14:20** ^Prov 19:7
14:21 ^Prov 11:12   ^Ps 41:1   **14:22** ^Ps 36:4; Prov 3:29
14:24 ^Prov 10:22; 13:8   **14:25** ^Prov 14:5
14:26 ^Prov 18:10; 19:23   **14:29** ^Prov 16:32; 19:11
14:30 ^Prov 15:13   ^Prov 12:4   **14:31** ^Prov 17:5
^Job 31:15   **14:32** ^Prov 6:15   ^Gen 49:18
14:35 ^Matt 24:45, 47; 25:21, 23   **15:1** ^Judg 8:1-3
^1 Sam 25:10-13   **15:2** ^Prov 15:7   **15:3** ^2 Chr 16:9;
Job 31:4

4   A soothing tongue is a tree of
    life,
    But perversion in it crushes
    the spirit.
5   A fool rejects his father's
    discipline,
    But he who complies with
    rebuke is sensible.
6   Great wealth is *in* the house of
    the ^righteous,
    But trouble is in the income of
    the wicked.
7   The lips of the wise spread
    knowledge,
    But the hearts of fools are not
    so.
8   The sacrifice of the wicked
    is an abomination to the
    LORD,
    But ^the prayer of the upright
    is His delight.
9   The way of the wicked is an
    abomination to the LORD,
    But He loves the one who
    ^pursues righteousness.
10 There is severe punishment
    for one who abandons the
    way;
    One who hates a rebuke will
    die.
11 ^1,^Sheol and ^2Abaddon *lie open*
    before the LORD,
    How much more the ^Bhearts of
    mankind!
12 A ^scoffer does not love one
    who rebukes him;
    He will not go to the wise.
13 A joyful heart makes a
    cheerful face,
    But when the heart is ^sad, the
    ^Bspirit is broken.
14 The ^mind of the intelligent
    seeks knowledge,
    But the mouth of fools feeds
    on foolishness.
15 All the days of the needy are
    bad,

But a cheerful heart *has* a
    continual feast.
16 ^Better is a little with the fear
    of the LORD
    Than great treasure, and
    turmoil with the treasure.
17 ^Better is a portion of
    vegetables where there is
    love,
    Than a ^Bfattened ox *served*
    with hatred.
18 A hot-tempered person stirs
    up strife,
    But the ^slow to anger ^Bcalms a
    dispute.
19 The way of the lazy one is like
    a hedge of thorns,
    But the path of the upright is a
    highway.
20 A ^wise son makes a father
    glad,
    But a foolish man despises his
    mother.
21 Foolishness is joy to one who
    lacks sense,
    But a person of understanding
    ^walks straight.
22 Without consultation, plans
    are frustrated,
    But with many counselors
    they succeed.
23 A ^person has joy in an apt
    answer,
    And how delightful is a timely
    word!
24 The ^path of life *leads* upward
    for the wise,
    So that he may keep away from
    ^1Sheol below.

15:6 ^Prov 8:21   15:8 ^Prov 15:29   15:9 ^1 Tim 6:11
15:11 ^Job 26:6   ^B1 Sam 16:7
15:12 ^Prov 13:1; Amos 5:10   15:13 ^Prov 12:25
^BProv 17:22   15:14 ^Prov 18:15   15:16 ^Ps 37:16;
Prov 16:8   15:17 ^Prov 17:1   ^BMatt 22:4
15:18 ^Prov 14:29   ^BGen 13:8   15:20 ^Prov 10:1; 29:3
15:21 ^Prov 14:8; Eph 5:15   15:23 ^Prov 12:14
15:24 ^Prov 4:18

15:11 ^1 I.e., The netherworld   ^2 I.e., place of
destruction   15:24 ^1 I.e., the netherworld

25 The Lord will ᴬtear down the
   house of the proud,
   But He will ᴮset the boundary
   of the widow.

26 Evil plans are an abomination
   to the Lord,
   But pleasant words are pure.

27 He who ᴬprofits illicitly
   troubles his own house,
   But he who ᴮhates bribes will
   live.

28 The heart of the righteous
   ᴬponders how to answer,
   But the mouth of the wicked
   pours out evil things.

29 The Lord is far from the
   wicked,
   But He ᴬhears the prayer of the
   righteous.

30 Bright eyes gladden the heart;
   Good news refreshes the bones.

31 *One whose* ear listens to a
   life-giving rebuke
   Will stay among the wise.

32 One who ᴬneglects discipline
   rejects himself,
   But one who ᴮlistens to a rebuke
   acquires understanding.

33 The fear of the Lord is the
   instruction for wisdom,
   And before honor *comes*
   humility.

CONTRAST OF THE UPRIGHT
AND THE WICKED

16 The ᴬplans of the heart
   belong to a person,
   But the answer of the tongue is
   from the Lord.

2 All the ways of a person are
   clean in his own sight,
   But the ᴬLord examines the
   motives.

3 ᴬCommit your works to the
   Lord,
   And your plans will be
   established.

4 The Lord ᴬhas made
   everything for its own
   purpose,
   Even the ᴮwicked for the day
   of evil.

5 Everyone who is proud in
   heart is an abomination to
   the Lord;
   Be assured, he will not go
   unpunished.

6 By ᴬmercy and truth
   atonement is made for
   wrongdoing,
   And by the ᴮfear of the Lord
   one keeps away from evil.

7 When a person's ways are
   pleasing to the Lord,
   He ᴬcauses even his enemies to
   make peace with him.

8 Better is a little with
   righteousness
   Than great income with
   injustice.

9 The mind of a ᴬperson plans
   his way,
   But ᴮthe Lord directs his
   steps.

10 A divine ᴬverdict is on the lips
   of the king;
   His mouth should not err in
   judgment.

11 A ᴬjust balance and scales
   belong to the Lord;
   All the weights of the bag are
   His concern.

12 It is an abomination for kings
   to commit wicked acts,
   Because a ᴬthrone
   is established on
   righteousness.

15:25 ᴬProv 12:7   ᴮDeut 19:14   15:27 ᴬProv 1:19
ᴮEx 23:8   15:28 ᴬ1 Pet 3:15   15:29 ᴬPs 145:18, 19
15:32 ᴬProv 1:7   ᴮProv 15:5   16:1 ᴬProv 16:9
16:2 ᴬ1 Sam 16:7   16:3 ᴬPs 37:5; 55:22   16:4 ᴬGen 1:31
ᴮRom 9:22   16:6 ᴬDan 4:27   ᴮProv 8:13
16:7 ᴬGen 33:4; 2 Chr 17:10   16:9 ᴬProv 16:1
ᴮPs 37:23   16:10 ᴬ1 Kin 3:28   16:11 ᴬProv 11:1
16:12 ᴬProv 25:5

13 Righteous lips are the delight of kings,
And one who speaks right is loved.
14 The fury of a king is *like* messengers of death;
But a wise person will appease it.
15 In the light of a king's face is life,
And his favor is like a cloud *with* the ^spring rain.
16 How much ^better it is to get wisdom than gold!
And to get understanding is to be chosen above silver.
17 The ^highway of the upright is to turn away from evil;
One who watches his way protects his life.
18 ^Pride *goes* before destruction,
And a haughty spirit before stumbling.
19 It is better to be ^humble in spirit with the needy
Than to divide the spoils with the proud.
20 One who pays attention to the word will ^find good,
And blessed is one who trusts in the LORD.
21 The ^wise in heart will be called understanding,
And sweetness of speech increases persuasiveness.
22 Understanding is a fountain of life to those who have it,
But the discipline of fools is foolishness.
23 The ^heart of the wise instructs his mouth
And adds persuasiveness to his lips.
24 ^Pleasant words are a honeycomb,
Sweet to the soul and healing to the bones.
25 ^There is a way *which seems* right to a person,
But its end is the way of death.
26 A worker's appetite works for him,
For his hunger urges him *on*.
27 A ^worthless person digs up evil,
While his words are like scorching fire.
28 A perverse person spreads strife,
And a slanderer separates close friends.
29 A person of violence ^entices his neighbor
And leads him in a way that is not good.
30 He who winks his eyes *does so* to devise perverse things;
He who compresses his lips brings evil to pass.
31 A ^gray head is a crown of glory;
It is found in the way of righteousness.
32 One who is slow to anger is better than the mighty,
And one who rules his spirit, than one who captures a city.
33 The lot is cast into the lap,
But its every ^decision is from the LORD.

CONTRAST OF THE UPRIGHT AND THE WICKED

17 ^Better is a dry morsel and quietness with it
Than a house full of feasting with strife.

16:15 ^Job 29:23   16:16 ^Prov 8:10, 19   16:17 ^Is 35:8
16:18 ^Prov 11:2; 18:12   16:19 ^Prov 3:34; 29:23
16:20 ^Prov 19:8   16:21 ^Hos 14:9   16:23 ^Ps 37:30;
Prov 15:28   16:24 ^Ps 19:10; Prov 15:26
16:25 ^Prov 12:15; 14:12   16:27 ^Prov 6:12, 14, 18
16:29 ^Prov 1:10; 12:26   16:31 ^Prov 20:29
16:33 ^Prov 29:26   17:1 ^Prov 15:17

2   A servant who acts wisely
    will rule over a son who acts
    shamefully,
    And will share in the
    inheritance among brothers.
3   The refining pot is for silver
    and the furnace for gold,
    But ^the LORD tests hearts.
4   An ^evildoer listens to wicked
    lips;
    A liar pays attention to a
    destructive tongue.
5   One who mocks the ^poor
    taunts his Maker;
    One who rejoices at disaster
    will not go unpunished.
6   ^Grandchildren are the crown
    of the old,
    And the ^Bglory of sons is their
    fathers.
7   ^Excellent speech is not fitting
    for a fool,
    Much less are ^Blying lips to a
    prince.
8   A ^bribe is a charm in the sight
    of its owner;
    Wherever he turns, he
    prospers.
9   One who ^conceals an offense
    seeks love,
    But one who repeats a matter
    separates close friends.
10 A rebuke goes deeper into one
    who has understanding
    Than a hundred blows into a
    fool.
11 A rebellious person seeks only
    evil,
    So a cruel messenger will be
    sent against him.
12 Let a person meet a ^bear
    robbed of her cubs,
    Rather than a fool in his
    foolishness.
13 One who ^returns evil for good,
    Evil will not depart from his
    house.

14 The beginning of strife is *like*
    letting out water,
    So ^abandon the quarrel
    before it breaks out.
15 One who ^justifies the wicked
    and one who condemns the
    righteous,
    Both of them alike are an
    abomination to the LORD.
16 Why is there money in the hand
    of a fool to ^buy wisdom,
    When he has no sense?
17 A ^friend loves at all times,
    And a brother is born for
    adversity.
18 A person lacking in sense
    ^shakes hands
    And becomes guarantor in the
    presence of his neighbor.
19 One who loves wrongdoing
    loves strife;
    One who ^makes his doorway
    high seeks destruction.
20 One who has a crooked mind
    ^finds nothing good,
    And one who is corrupted in
    his language falls into evil.
21 He who ^fathers a fool *does so*
    to his sorrow,
    And the father of a fool has no
    joy.
22 A ^joyful heart is good
    medicine,
    But a broken spirit ^Bdries up
    the bones.
23 A wicked person accepts a
    bribe ^1from an inside pocket
    To ^pervert the ways of justice.

17:3 ^1 Chr 29:17; Ps 26:2   17:4 ^Prov 14:15
17:5 ^Prov 14:31   17:6 ^Gen 48:11   ^BEx 20:12
17:7 ^Prov 24:7   ^BPs 31:18   17:8 ^Prov 21:14; Is 1:23
17:9 ^Prov 10:12; James 5:20   17:12 ^2 Sam 17:8;
Hos 13:8   17:13 ^Ps 35:12; 109:5   17:14 ^Prov 20:3; 25:8
17:15 ^Ex 23:7; Prov 18:5   17:16 ^Prov 23:23
17:17 ^Ruth 1:16; Prov 18:24   17:18 ^Prov 6:1; 11:15
17:19 ^Prov 16:18; 29:23   17:20 ^Prov 24:20
17:21 ^Prov 10:1; 17:25   17:22 ^Prov 15:13   ^BPs 22:15
17:23 ^Ex 23:8; Mic 3:11

17:23 ^1 Lit *a fold in a robe*; i.e., secretly

24 Wisdom is in the presence of
   one who has understanding,
   But the ^eyes of a fool are on
   the ends of the earth.
25 A ^foolish son is a grief to his
   father,
   And ^bitterness to her who
   gave birth to him.
26 It is also not good to ^fine the
   righteous,
   Nor to strike the noble for
   their uprightness.
27 One who ^withholds his words
   has knowledge,
   And one who has a ^cool spirit
   is a person of understanding.
28 Even a fool, when he ^keeps
   silent, is considered wise;
   When he closes his lips, he is
   considered prudent.

CONTRAST OF THE UPRIGHT AND THE WICKED

18 One who separates himself
   seeks *his own* desire;
   He ^quarrels against all sound
   wisdom.
2 A fool does not delight in
   understanding,
   But ^in revealing his own mind.
3 When a wicked person comes,
   contempt also comes,
   And with dishonor *comes*
   taunting.
4 The words of a person's mouth
   are ^deep waters;
   The fountain of wisdom is a
   bubbling brook.
5 To ^show partiality to the
   wicked is not good,
   Nor to ^suppress the righteous
   in judgment.
6 A fool's lips bring strife,
   And his mouth invites ^beatings.
7 A ^fool's mouth is his ruin,
   And his lips are the snare of
   his soul.

8 The words of a gossiper are
   like dainty morsels,
   And they go down into the
   innermost parts of the body.
9 He also who is ^lax in his work
   ^Is a brother to him who
   destroys.
10 The ^name of the LORD is a
   strong tower;
   The righteous runs into it and
   is safe.
11 A ^rich person's wealth is his
   strong city,
   And like a high wall in his own
   imagination.
12 ^Before destruction the heart
   of a person is haughty,
   But ^humility *goes* before
   honor.
13 One who ^gives an answer
   before he hears,
   It is foolishness and shame to
   him.
14 The ^spirit of a person can
   endure his sickness,
   But *as for* a ^broken spirit, who
   can endure it?
15 The ^mind of the discerning
   acquires knowledge,
   And the ear of the wise seeks
   knowledge.
16 A person's ^gift makes room
   for him
   And brings him before great
   people.
17 The first to plead his case
   seems right,
   Until another comes and
   examines him.

17:24 ^Eccl 2:14   17:25 ^Prov 19:13   ^Prov 10:1
17:26 ^Prov 17:15; 18:5   17:27 ^Prov 10:19
^Prov 14:29   17:28 ^Job 13:5   18:1 ^Prov 3:21; 8:14
18:2 ^Prov 12:23; 13:16   18:4 ^Prov 20:5
18:5 ^Lev 19:15   ^Ex 23:2, 6   18:6 ^Prov 19:29
18:7 ^Ps 64:8; 140:9   18:9 ^Prov 10:4   ^Prov 28:24
18:10 ^Ex 3:15   18:11 ^Prov 10:15   18:12 ^Prov 11:2
^Prov 15:33   18:13 ^Prov 20:25; John 7:51
18:14 ^Prov 17:22   ^Prov 15:13   18:15 ^Prov 15:14;
Eph 1:17   18:16 ^Gen 32:20; 1 Sam 25:27

18 The *cast* ^lot puts an end to quarrels,
And decides between the mighty ones.

19 A brother who is offended *is harder to be won* than a strong city,
And quarrels are like the bars of a citadel.

20 With the fruit of a person's mouth his stomach will be satisfied;
^He will be satisfied *with* the product of his lips.

21 ^Death and life are in the power of the tongue,
And those who love it will eat its fruit.

22 He who finds a ^wife finds a good thing
And ^obtains favor from the Lord.

23 A ^poor person utters pleadings,
But a rich person answers defiantly.

24 A person of *too many* friends *comes* to ruin,
But there is ^a friend who sticks *closer* than a brother.

ON LIFE AND CONDUCT

19 ^Better is a poor person who walks in his integrity
Than a person who is perverse in speech and is a fool.

2 Also it is not good for a person to be without knowledge,
And one who hurries ^his footsteps errs.

3 The ^foolishness of a person ruins his way,
And his heart rages against the Lord.

4 ^Wealth adds many friends,
But a poor person is separated from his friend.

5 A ^false witness will not go unpunished,
And one *who* ^declares lies will not escape.

6 ^Many will seek the favor of a generous person,
And every person is a friend to him who *gives* gifts.

7 All the brothers of a poor person hate him;
How much more do his ^friends abandon him!
He ^pursues *them with* words, *but* they are gone.

8 One who gets wisdom loves his own soul;
One who keeps understanding will ^find good.

9 A ^false witness will not go unpunished,
And one *who* declares lies will perish.

10 Luxury is not fitting for a fool;
Much less for a ^slave to rule over princes.

11 A person's ^discretion makes him slow to anger,
And it is his glory ^to overlook an offense.

12 A ^king's wrath is like the roaring of a lion,
But his favor is like dew on the grass.

13 A ^foolish son is destruction to his father,
And the ^quarrels of a wife are a constant dripping.

14 House and wealth are an ^inheritance from fathers,

18:18 ^Prov 16:33   18:20 ^Prov 14:14
18:21 ^Prov 12:13; 13:3   18:22 ^Gen 2:18   ^Prov 8:35
18:23 ^Prov 19:7   18:24 ^Prov 17:17; John 15:14, 15
19:1 ^Prov 28:6   19:2 ^Prov 21:5; 28:20
19:3 ^Prov 11:3   19:4 ^Prov 14:20   19:5 ^Ex 23:1
^Prov 6:19   19:6 ^Prov 29:26   19:7 ^Ps 38:11
^Prov 18:23   19:8 ^Prov 16:20
19:9 ^Prov 19:5; Dan 6:24   19:10 ^Prov 30:22
19:11 ^Prov 14:29   ^Matt 5:44   19:12 ^Prov 16:14
19:13 ^Prov 17:25   ^Prov 21:9, 19   19:14 ^2 Cor 12:14

But a prudent wife is from the LORD.

15 ^Laziness casts *one* into a deep sleep,
And a lazy person will suffer hunger.

16 One who ^keeps the commandment keeps his soul,
But one who is careless of conduct will die.

17 One who ^is gracious to a poor person lends to the LORD,
And He will repay him for his ^good deed.

18 ^Discipline your son while there is hope,
And do not desire his death.

19 *A person of* great anger will suffer the penalty,
For if you rescue *him,* you will only have to do it again.

20 ^Listen to advice and accept discipline,
So that you may be wise the rest of your days.

21 Many ^plans are in a person's heart,
But the ^advice of the LORD will stand.

22 What is desirable in a person is his kindness,
And *it is* better to be a poor person than a liar.

23 The ^fear of the LORD *leads* to life,
So that one may sleep satisfied, untouched by evil.

24 The lazy one buries his hand ^in the dish,
But will not even bring it back to his mouth.

25 Strike a scoffer and the naive may become clever,
But ^rebuke one who has understanding, *and* he will gain knowledge.

26 He ^who assaults *his* father *and* drives *his* mother away
Is a shameful and disgraceful son.

27 Stop listening, my son, to discipline,
And you will stray from the words of knowledge.

28 A worthless witness makes a mockery of justice,
And the mouth of the wicked ^swallows wrongdoing.

29 Judgments are prepared for ^scoffers,
And ^beatings for the backs of fools.

ON LIFE AND CONDUCT

20 Wine is a mocker,
^intoxicating drink a brawler,
And whoever is intoxicated by it is not wise.

2 The terror of a king is like the roaring of a lion;
One who provokes him to anger ^forfeits his own life.

3 ^Avoiding strife is an honor for a person,
But any fool will quarrel.

4 The ^lazy one does not plow after the autumn,
So he begs during the harvest and has nothing.

5 A plan in the heart of a person is *like* deep water,
But a person of understanding draws it out.

6 Many a person proclaims his own loyalty,

19:15 ^Prov 6:9, 10; 24:33   19:16 ^Prov 13:13; 16:17
19:17 ^Deut 15:7, 8   ^B Prov 12:14   19:18 ^Prov 13:24;
23:13   19:20 ^Prov 4:1; 8:33   19:21 ^Prov 16:1, 9
^B Ps 33:10, 11   19:23 ^Prov 14:27; 1 Tim 4:8
19:24 ^Matt 26:23; Mark 14:20   19:25 ^Prov 9:8
19:26 ^Prov 28:24   19:28 ^Job 15:16; 20:12, 13
19:29 ^Ps 1:1   ^B Prov 10:13   20:1 ^Prov 31:4; Is 5:22
20:2 ^Num 16:38; 1 Kin 2:23   20:3 ^Gen 13:7f;
Prov 17:14   20:4 ^Prov 13:4; 21:25

But who can find a
^trustworthy person?

7 A righteous person who walks
in his integrity—
^How blessed are his sons after
him.

8 ^A king who sits on the throne
of justice
Disperses all evil with his eyes.

9 ^Who can say, "I have cleansed
my heart,
I am pure from my sin"?

10 ^Differing weights and
differing measures,
Both of them are abominable
to the Lord.

11 It is by his deeds that a boy
^distinguishes himself,
If his conduct is pure and
right.

12 The hearing ^ear and the
seeing eye,
The Lord has made both of
them.

13 ^Do not love sleep, or you will
become poor;
Open your eyes, *and you will*
be satisfied with food.

14 "Bad, bad," says the buyer,
But when he goes his way, then
he boasts.

15 There is gold, and an
abundance of jewels;
But lips of knowledge are a
more precious thing.

16 Take his garment when he
becomes guarantor for a
stranger;
And for foreigners, seize a
pledge from him.

17 ^Bread *obtained by* a lie is
sweet to a person,
But afterward his mouth will
be filled with gravel.

18 Prepare ^plans by consultation,
And ^make war by wise
guidance.

19 One who goes about as a
slanderer reveals secrets;
Therefore do not associate
with ^a gossip.

20 He who ^curses his father or
his mother,
His lamp will go out in time of
darkness.

21 An inheritance gained in a
hurry at the beginning
Will not be blessed in the
end.

22 ^Do not say, "I will repay evil";
^Wait for the Lord, and He will
save you.

23 Differing weights are an
abomination to the Lord,
And a ^false scale is not
good.

24 ^A man's steps are *ordained* by
the Lord;
How then can a person
understand his way?

25 It is a trap for a person to say
carelessly, "It is holy!"
And ^after the vows to make
inquiry.

26 A ^wise king scatters the
wicked,
And drives a ^*threshing* wheel
over them.

27 The ^spirit of a person is the
lamp of the Lord,
Searching all the innermost
parts of his being.

28 Loyalty and ^truth watch over
the king,
And he upholds his throne by
loyalty.

20:6 ^Ps 12:1; Luke 18:8   20:7 ^Ps 37:26; 112:2
20:8 ^Prov 20:26; 25:5   20:9 ^1 Kin 8:46; 2 Chr 6:36
20:10 ^Prov 11:1; 20:23   20:11 ^Matt 7:16
20:12 ^Ex 4:11; Ps 94:9   20:13 ^Prov 6:9, 10; 19:15
20:17 ^Prov 9:17   20:18 ^Prov 11:14   ^Prov 24:6
20:19 ^Prov 13:3   20:20 ^Ex 21:17; Lev 20:9
20:22 ^Prov 24:29   ^Ps 27:14   20:23 ^Prov 11:1
20:24 ^Prov 16:9   20:25 ^Eccl 5:4, 5
20:26 ^Prov 20:8   ^Is 28:27   20:27 ^1 Cor 2:11
20:28 ^Prov 29:14

29 The glory of young men is
 their strength,
 And the ^honor of old men is
 their gray hair.
30 ^Bruising wounds clean away
 evil,
 And blows *cleanse* the
 innermost parts.

ON LIFE AND CONDUCT

21 The king's heart is *like*
 channels of water in the
 hand of the LORD;
 He ^turns it wherever He
 pleases.
2 Every person's way is right in
 his own eyes,
 But the LORD ^examines the
 hearts.
3 To do ^righteousness and
 justice
 Is preferred by the LORD more
 than sacrifice.
4 Haughty eyes and a proud
 heart,
 The ^lamp of the wicked, is sin.
5 The plans of the ^diligent
 certainly *lead* to advantage,
 But everyone who is in a
 hurry certainly *comes* to
 poverty.
6 The ^acquisition of treasures
 by a lying tongue
 Is a fleeting vapor, the pursuit
 of death.
7 The violence of the wicked
 will sweep them away,
 Because they ^refuse to act
 with justice.
8 The way of a guilty person is
 ^crooked,
 But as for the pure, his
 conduct is upright.
9 It is better to live on a corner
 of a roof
 Than in a house shared with a
 contentious woman.

10 The soul of the wicked desires
 evil;
 His ^neighbor is shown no
 compassion in his eyes.
11 When the ^scoffer is punished,
 the naive becomes wise;
 But when the wise is
 instructed, he receives
 knowledge.
12 The righteous one considers
 the house of the wicked,
 Bringing the ^wicked to ruin.
13 One who ^shuts his ear to the
 outcry of the poor
 Will also call out himself, and
 not be ^Banswered.
14 A ^gift in secret subdues anger,
 And a bribe ¹in an inside
 pocket, strong wrath.
15 The exercise of justice is joy
 for the righteous,
 But ^terror to those who
 practice injustice.
16 A person who wanders from
 the way of understanding
 Will ^rest in the assembly of
 the dead.
17 One who ^loves pleasure *will
 become* a poor person;
 One who loves wine and oil
 will not become rich.
18 The wicked is a ^ransom for
 the righteous,
 And the treacherous is in the
 place of the upright.
19 ^It is better to live in a desert
 land
 Than with a contentious and
 irritating woman.

20:29 ^Prov 16:31   20:30 ^Ps 89:32; Prov 22:15
21:1 ^Ezra 6:22   21:2 ^Prov 16:2; 24:12   21:3 ^1 Sam 15:22;
Prov 15:8   21:4 ^Prov 24:20; Luke 11:34   21:5 ^Prov 10:4;
13:4   21:6 ^Prov 13:11; 20:21   21:7 ^Amos 5:7; Mic 3:9
21:8 ^Prov 2:15   21:10 ^Ps 52:3; Prov 2:14
21:11 ^Prov 19:25   21:12 ^Prov 14:11   21:13 ^Matt
18:30-34   ^BJames 2:13   21:14 ^Prov 18:16; 19:6
21:15 ^Prov 10:29   21:16 ^Ps 49:14   21:17 ^Prov 23:21
21:18 ^Is 43:3   21:19 ^Prov 21:9

21:14 ¹Lit *a fold in a robe*; i.e., secretly

20 There is precious ^treasure
   and oil in the home of the
   wise,
   But a foolish person ^Bswallows
   it up.
21 One who ^pursues
   righteousness and loyalty
   Finds life, righteousness, and
   honor.
22 A ^wise person scales the city
   of the mighty
   And brings down the
   stronghold in which they
   trust.
23 One who ^guards his mouth
   and his tongue,
   Guards his soul from
   troubles.
24 "Proud," "Arrogant," "Scoffer,"
   are his names,
   One who acts with ^insolent
   pride.
25 The ^desire of the lazy one
   puts him to death,
   For his hands refuse to work;
26 All day long he is craving,
   While the righteous ^gives and
   does not hold back.
27 The ^sacrifice of the wicked is
   an abomination,
   How much more when he
   brings it with evil intent!
28 A ^false witness will perish,
   But a person who listens will
   speak forever.
29 A wicked person displays a
   bold face,
   But as for the ^upright, he
   makes his way sure.
30 There is ^no wisdom, no
   understanding,
   And no plan against the
   LORD.
31 The horse is prepared for the
   day of battle,
   But the ^victory belongs to the
   LORD.

ON LIFE AND CONDUCT

22 A ^*good* name is to be more
   desired than great wealth;
   Favor is better than silver and
   gold.
2 The rich and the poor have a
   common bond,
   The LORD is the ^Maker of
   them all.
3 A ^prudent person sees evil
   and hides himself,
   But the naive proceed, and pay
   the penalty.
4 The reward of humility *and*
   the fear of the LORD
   Are riches, honor, and life.
5 ^Thorns *and* snares are in the
   way of the perverse;
   One who guards himself will
   be far from them.
6 ^Train up a child in the way he
   should go,
   Even when he grows older he
   will not abandon it.
7 The ^rich rules over the poor,
   And the borrower *becomes* the
   lender's slave.
8 One who ^sows injustice will
   reap disaster,
   And the rod of his fury will
   perish.
9 One who is ^generous will be
   blessed,
   Because he gives some of his
   food to the poor.
10 ^Drive out the scoffer, and
   strife will leave,
   Even quarreling and dishonor
   will cease.

21:20 ^A Ps 112:3   ^B Job 20:15, 18   21:21 ^A Prov 15:9; Matt 5:6
21:22 ^A 2 Sam 5:6-9; Prov 24:5   21:23 ^A Prov 12:13; 13:3
21:24 ^A Is 16:6; Jer 48:29   21:25 ^A Prov 13:4
21:26 ^A Ps 37:26; 112:5, 9   21:27 ^A Prov 15:8; Is 66:3
21:28 ^A Prov 19:5, 9   21:29 ^A Ps 119:5; Prov 11:5
21:30 ^A Jer 9:23; Acts 5:38, 39   21:31 ^A Ps 3:8; Jer 3:23
22:1 ^A Prov 10:7; Eccl 7:1   22:2 ^A Job 31:15; Prov 14:31
22:3 ^A Prov 14:16; 27:12   22:5 ^A Prov 15:19   22:6 ^A Eph 6:4
22:7 ^A Prov 18:23; James 2:6   22:8 ^A Job 4:8
22:9 ^A Prov 19:17; 2 Cor 9:6   22:10 ^A Gen 21:9, 10; Prov 18:6

11 One who loves ^purity of heart
   And whose speech is gracious,
   the king is his friend.
12 The eyes of the LORD protect
   knowledge,
   But He overthrows the words
   of the treacherous person.
13 The ^lazy one says, "There is a
   lion outside;
   I will be killed in the streets!"
14 The mouth of ^an adulteress is
   a deep pit;
   He who is cursed of the LORD
   will fall into it.
15 Foolishness is bound up in the
   heart of a child;
   The ^rod of discipline will
   remove it far from him.
16 One ^who oppresses the poor
   to make more for himself,
   Or gives to the rich, ^B^*will* only
   come to poverty.

17 ^Extend your ear and hear the
   words of the wise,
   And apply your mind to my
   knowledge;
18 For it will be ^pleasant if you
   keep them within you,
   So that they may be ready on
   your lips.
19 So that your ^trust may be in
   the LORD,
   I have taught you today, you
   indeed.
20 Have I not written to you
   ^excellent things
   Of counsels and knowledge,
21 To make you ^know the
   certainty of the words of truth,
   So that you may ^B^correctly
   answer him who sent you?

22 ^Do not rob the poor because
   he is poor,
   Nor ^B^crush the needy at the
   gate;

23 For the LORD will ^plead their
   case
   And take the life of those who
   rob them.

24 Do not make friends with a
   person *given* to anger,
   Or go with a ^hot-tempered
   person,
25 Or you will ^learn his ways
   And find a snare for yourself.

26 Do not be among those who
   ^shake hands,
   Among those who become
   guarantors for debts.
27 If you have nothing with
   which to repay,
   Why should he ^take your bed
   from under you?

28 ^Do not move the ancient
   boundary
   Which your fathers have set.

29 Do you see a person skilled in
   his work?
   He will ^stand before kings;
   He will not stand before
   obscure people.

ON LIFE AND CONDUCT

23 When you sit down to dine
   with a ruler,
   Consider carefully what is
   before you,
2 And put a knife to your throat
   If you are a ^person of *great*
   appetite.

22:11 ^A Ps 24:4; Matt 5:8   22:13 ^A Prov 26:13
22:14 ^A Prov 2:16; 5:3   22:15 ^A Prov 13:24; 23:14
22:16 ^A Eccl 5:8   ^B Prov 28:22   22:17 ^A Prov 5:1
22:18 ^A Prov 2:10   22:19 ^A Prov 3:5   22:20 ^A Prov 8:6
22:21 ^A Luke 1:3, 4   ^B Prov 25:13   22:22 ^A Ex 23:6
^B Zech 7:10   22:23 ^A 1 Sam 25:39; Ps 12:5
22:24 ^A Prov 29:22   22:25 ^A 1 Cor 15:33
22:26 ^A Prov 17:18   22:27 ^A Ex 22:26; Prov 20:16
22:28 ^A Deut 19:14; 27:17   22:29 ^A Gen 41:46; 1 Kin 10:8
23:2 ^A Prov 23:20

3 Do not ^desire his delicacies,
   For it is deceptive food.

4 ^Do not weary yourself to gain
   wealth;
   ^BStop dwelling *on it.*
5 When you set your eyes on it,
   it is gone.
   For ^*wealth* certainly makes
   itself wings
   Like an eagle that flies *toward*
   the heavens.

6 Do not eat the bread of a
   ^selfish person;
   Or desire his delicacies;
7 For as he thinks within
   himself, so he is.
   He says to you, "Eat and drink!"
   But ^his heart is not with you.
8 You will ^vomit up the morsel
   you have eaten
   And waste your compliments.

9 ^Do not speak to be heard by a
   fool,
   For he will despise the wisdom
   of your words.

10 Do not move the ancient
   boundary
   Or ^go into the fields of the
   fatherless,
11 For their ^Redeemer is strong;
   ^BHe will plead their case
   against you.
12 Apply your heart to discipline,
   And your ears to words of
   knowledge.

13 ^Do not withhold discipline
   from a child;
   Though you strike him with
   the rod, he will not die.
14 You shall strike him with the rod
   And ^rescue his soul from
   Sheol.

15 My son, if your heart is ^wise,
   My own heart also will be glad,
16 And my innermost being will
   rejoice
   When your lips speak ^what is
   right.

17 ^Do not let your heart envy
   sinners,
   But *live* in the fear of the LORD
   always.
18 Certainly there is a future,
   And your ^hope will not be cut
   off.
19 Listen, my son, and ^be wise,
   And ^Bdirect your heart in the
   way.
20 Do not be with ^heavy drinkers
   of wine,
   Or with ^Bgluttonous eaters of
   meat;
21 For the ^heavy drinker and the
   glutton will come to poverty,
   And ^Bdrowsiness will clothe
   one with rags.

22 ^Listen to your father, who
   fathered you,
   And do not despise your
   mother when she is old.
23 ^Buy truth, and do not sell *it,*
   Get wisdom, instruction, and
   understanding.

24 The father of the righteous
   will greatly rejoice,
   And ^he who fathers a wise
   son will be glad in him.

23:3 ^Ps 141:4; Prov 23:6
23:4 ^Prov 15:27   ^BProv 3:5, 7   23:5 ^Prov 27:24;
1 Tim 6:17   23:6 ^Deut 15:9; Prov 28:22
23:7 ^Prov 26:24, 25   23:8 ^Prov 25:16
23:9 ^Matt 7:6   23:10 ^Jer 22:3; Zech 7:10
23:11 ^Job 19:25   ^BProv 22:23   23:13 ^Prov 13:24;
19:18   23:14 ^1 Cor 5:5   23:15 ^Prov 23:24f; 27:11
23:16 ^Prov 8:6   23:17 ^Ps 37:1; Prov 24:1, 19
23:18 ^Ps 9:18   23:19 ^Prov 6:6   ^BProv 4:23
23:20 ^Prov 20:1   ^BDeut 21:20   23:21 ^Prov 21:17
^BProv 6:10, 11   23:22 ^Prov 1:8; Eph 6:1
23:23 ^Prov 4:7; 18:15   23:24 ^Prov 10:1; 15:20

²⁵ Let your ^father and your
     mother be glad,
     And let her rejoice who gave
        birth to you.

²⁶ ^Give me your heart, my son,
     And let your eyes ^Bdelight in
        my ways.

²⁷ For a prostitute is a ^deep pit,
     And a ^Bstrange woman is a
        narrow well.

²⁸ Certainly she ^lurks as a
        robber,
     And increases the treacherous
        among mankind.

²⁹ Who has ^woe? Who has
        sorrow?
     Who has contentions? Who
        has complaining?
     Who has wounds without
        cause?
     Who has red eyes?

³⁰ Those who ^linger long over
        wine,
     Those who go to taste mixed
        wine.

³¹ Do not look at wine when it is
        red,
     When it sparkles in the cup,
     When it ^goes down smoothly;

³² In the end it ^bites like a snake
     And stings like a viper.

³³ Your eyes will see strange things
     And your mind will ^say
        perverse things.

³⁴ And you will be like one who
        lies down in the middle of
        the sea,
     Or like one who lies down on
        the top of a ¹mast.

³⁵ "They struck me, *but* I did not
        become ill;
     They beat me, *but* I did not
        know *it*.
     When will I awake?
     I will ^seek another drink."

PRECEPTS AND WARNINGS

24 Do not be ^envious of evil
        people,
     Nor desire to ^Bbe with them;

² For their minds plot ^violence,
     And their lips ^Btalk of trouble.

³ ^By wisdom a house is built,
     And by understanding it is
        established;

⁴ And by knowledge the rooms
        are ^filled
     With all precious and pleasant
        riches.

⁵ A ^wise man is strong,
     And a person of knowledge
        increases power.

⁶ For by wise guidance you will
        wage war,
     And ^in an abundance of
        counselors there is victory.

⁷ Wisdom is ^*too* exalted for a
        fool,
     He does not open his mouth at
        the gate.

⁸ One who ^plans to do evil,
     People will call a schemer.

⁹ The ^devising of foolishness is
        sin,
     And the scoffer is an
        abomination to humanity.

¹⁰ *If* you ^show yourself lacking
        courage on the day of distress,
     Your strength is meager.

23:25 ^Prov 27:11   23:26 ^Prov 3:1   ^BPs 1:2
23:27 ^Prov 22:14   ^BProv 5:20   23:28 ^Prov 6:26; 7:12
23:29 ^Is 5:11, 22   23:30 ^1 Sam 25:36; Prov 20:1
23:31 ^Song 7:9   23:32 ^Job 20:16; Prov 20:1
23:33 ^Prov 2:12   23:35 ^Prov 26:11; Is 56:12
24:1 ^Ps 37:1   ^BPs 1:1   24:2 ^Is 30:12   ^BJob 15:35
24:3 ^Prov 9:1; 14:1   24:4 ^Prov 8:21   24:5 ^Prov 21:22
24:6 ^Prov 11:14   24:7 ^Ps 10:5; Prov 14:6
24:8 ^Prov 6:14; 14:22   24:9 ^Matt 15:19; Acts 8:22
24:10 ^Deut 20:8; Job 4:5

23:34 ¹Or *lookout*

11 ^Rescue those who are being
taken away to death,
And those who are staggering
to the slaughter, Oh hold
them back!

12 If you say, "See, we did not
know this,"
Does He ^who weighs the
hearts not ^consider *it?*
And does He who watches
over your soul not know *it?*
And will He not repay a person
according to his work?

13 My son, eat ^honey, for it is
good;
Yes, the honey from the comb
is sweet to your taste;

14 Know *that* ^wisdom is the
same for your soul;
If you find *it,* then there will be
a ^future,
And your hope will not be cut
off.

15 ^Do not lie in ambush, you
wicked person, against the
home of the righteous;
Do not destroy his resting
place;

16 For a ^righteous person falls
seven times and rises again,
But the wicked stumble in *time
of* disaster.

17 ^Do not rejoice when your
enemy falls,
And do not let your heart
rejoice when he stumbles,

18 Otherwise, the Lord will see
and be displeased,
And turn His anger away from
him.

19 ^Do not get upset because of
evildoers
Or be ^envious of the wicked;

20 For ^there will be no ^future for
the evil person;
The lamp of the wicked will be
put out.

21 My son, ^fear the Lord and the
king;
Do not get involved with those
of high rank,

22 For their ^disaster will rise
suddenly,
And who knows the ruin
that can come from both of
them?

23 These also are *sayings* of the
wise:
To ^show partiality in
judgment is not good.

24 One ^who says to the wicked,
"You are righteous,"
^Peoples will curse him,
nations will scold him;

25 But ^for those who rebuke the
wicked there will be delight,
And a good blessing will come
upon them.

26 One who gives a right answer
Kisses the lips.

27 Prepare your work outside,
And ^make it ready for yourself
in the field;
Afterward, then, build your
house.

28 Do not be a witness against
your neighbor for no reason,
And ^do not deceive with your
lips.

24:11 ^Ps 82:4; Is 58:6, 7   24:12 ^1 Sam 16:7   ^Eccl 5:8
24:13 ^Ps 19:10; 119:103   24:14 ^Prov 2:10
^Prov 23:18   24:15 ^Ps 10:9, 10   24:16 ^Job 5:19;
Ps 37:24   24:17 ^Job 31:29; Ps 35:15, 19   24:19 ^Ps 37:1
^Prov 23:17   24:20 ^Job 15:31   ^Prov 23:18
24:21 ^Rom 13:1-7; 1 Pet 2:17   24:22 ^Prov 24:16
24:23 ^Prov 18:5; 28:21   24:24 ^Prov 17:15
^Prov 11:26   24:25 ^Prov 28:23   24:27 ^Prov 27:23-27
24:28 ^Lev 6:2, 3; 19:11

29 ^Do not say, "I shall do the same to him as he has done to me;
I will repay the person according to his work."

30 I passed by the field of a lazy one,
And by the vineyard of a person ^lacking sense,

31 And behold, it was completely overgrown with weeds;
Its surface was covered with ^weeds,
And its stone ^Bwall was broken down.

32 When I saw, I reflected upon it;
I looked, *and* received instruction.

33 "^A little sleep, a little slumber,
A little folding of the hands to rest,"

34 Then your poverty will come like a drifter,
And your need like an armed man.

SIMILITUDES AND INSTRUCTIONS

25 These also are ^proverbs of Solomon which the men of Hezekiah, king of Judah, transcribed.

2 It is the glory of God to ^conceal a matter,
But the glory of ^Bkings is to search out a matter.

3 *As* the heavens for height and the earth for depth,
So the heart of kings is unsearchable.

4 Take away the ^impurities from the silver,
And there comes out a vessel for the smith;

5 Take away the ^wicked before the king,
And his throne will be established in righteousness.

6 Do not boast in the presence of the king,
And do not stand in the *same* place as great people;

7 For ^it is better that it be said to you, "Come up here,"
Than for you to be placed lower in the presence of the prince,
Whom your eyes have seen.

8 Do not go out ^hastily to argue *your case;*
Otherwise, what will you do in the end,
When your neighbor humiliates you?

9 ^Argue your case with your neighbor,
And do not reveal the secret of another,

10 Or one who hears *it* will put you to shame,
And the evil report about you will not pass away.

11 *Like* apples of gold in settings of silver,
Is a ^word spoken at the proper time.

12 *Like* an ^earring of gold and a jewelry piece of fine gold,
Is a wise person who offers rebukes to a ^Blistening ear.

13 Like the cold of snow in the time of harvest
Is a ^faithful messenger to those who send him,
For he refreshes the soul of his masters.

14 *Like* ^clouds and ^Bwind without rain

24:29 ^Prov 20:22; Matt 5:39   24:30 ^Prov 6:32
24:31 ^Job 30:7   ^BIs 5:5   24:33 ^Prov 6:10
25:1 ^Prov 1:1   25:2 ^Deut 29:29   ^BEzra 6:1
25:4 ^Prov 26:23; Ezek 22:18   25:5 ^Prov 20:8
25:7 ^Luke 14:7-11   25:8 ^Prov 17:14; Matt 5:25
25:9 ^Matt 18:15   25:11 ^Prov 15:23   25:12 ^Ex 32:2
^BProv 15:31   25:13 ^Prov 13:17   25:14 ^Jude 12   ^BJer 5:13

Is a person who boasts of his gifts falsely.

15 Through ^patience a ruler may be persuaded,
And a gentle tongue breaks bone.

16 Have you ^found honey? Eat *only* what you need,
So that you do not have it in excess and vomit it.

17 Let your foot rarely be in your neighbor's house,
Or he will become weary of you and hate you.

18 *Like* a club, a sword, and a sharp arrow
Is a person who gives ^false testimony against his neighbor.

19 *Like* a bad tooth and an unsteady foot
Is confidence in a ^treacherous person in time of trouble.

20 *Like* one who takes off a garment on a cold day, *or like* vinegar on soda,
Is one who sings songs to a troubled heart.

21 ^If your enemy is hungry, give him food to eat;
And if he is thirsty, give him water to drink;

22 For you will heap burning coals on his head,
And ^the LORD will reward you.

23 The north wind brings rain,
And a ^gossiping tongue *brings* an angry face.

24 It is ^better to live on a corner of the roof,
Than in a house shared with a contentious woman.

25 *Like* cold water to a weary soul,
So is ^good news from a distant land.

26 *Like* a ^trampled spring and a polluted well,
So is a righteous person who gives way before the wicked.

27 It is not good to eat much honey,
Nor is it glory to ^search out one's own glory.

28 *Like* a ^city that is broken into *and* without walls
So is a person ^B who has no self-control over his spirit.

SIMILITUDES AND INSTRUCTIONS

26 Like snow in summer and like ^rain in harvest,
So honor is not ^B fitting for a fool.

2 Like a sparrow in *its* flitting, like a swallow in *its* flying,
So a ^curse without cause does not come *to rest*.

3 A whip is for the horse, a bridle for the donkey,
And a ^rod for the back of fools.

4 ^Do not answer a fool according to his foolishness,
Or you will also be like him.

5 ^Answer a fool as his foolishness *deserves*,
So that he will not be ^B wise in his own eyes.

6 One who sends a message by the hand of a fool
Chops off *his own* feet *and* drinks violence.

7 *Like* useless legs to one who cannot walk,
So is a proverb in the mouths of fools.

25:15 ^Gen 32:4; 1 Sam 25:24
25:16 ^Judg 14:8; 1 Sam 14:25
25:18 ^Ex 20:16; Prov 24:28   25:19 ^Job 6:15; Is 36:6
25:21 ^Ex 23:4, 5; 2 Kin 6:22   25:22 ^2 Sam 16:12;
Matt 6:4, 6   25:23 ^Ps 101:5   25:24 ^Prov 21:9
25:25 ^Prov 15:30   25:26 ^Ezek 32:2; 34:18, 19
25:27 ^Prov 27:2; Luke 14:11   25:28 ^Prov 16:32
^B 2 Chr 32:5   26:1 ^1 Sam 12:17   ^B Prov 17:7
26:2 ^Num 23:8; Deut 23:5   26:3 ^Prov 10:13; 19:29
26:4 ^Prov 23:9; 29:9   26:5 ^Matt 16:1-4   ^B Prov 3:7

8 Like one who binds a stone in
a sling,
So is one who gives honor to
a fool.

9 *Like* a thorn *that* sticks in the
hand of a heavy drinker,
So is a proverb in the mouths
of fools.

10 *Like* an archer who wounds
everyone,
So is one who hires a fool or
hires those who pass by.

11 Like ^a dog that returns to its
vomit,
So is a fool who ^Brepeats his
foolishness.

12 Do you see a person ^wise in
his own eyes?
^BThere is more hope for a fool
than for him.

13 A ^lazy one says, "There is a
lion on the road!
A lion is in the public
square!"

14 *As* the door turns on its
hinges,
So *does* a ^lazy one on his
bed.

15 A ^lazy one buries his hand in
the dish;
He is weary of bringing it to
his mouth again.

16 A lazy one is ^wiser in his own
eyes
Than seven *people* who can
give a discreet answer.

17 *Like* one who takes a dog by
the ears,
So is one who passes by *and*
meddles with ^strife not
belonging to him.

18 Like a maniac who shoots
^Flaming arrows, arrows, and
death,

19 So is a person who ^deceives
his neighbor,
And says, "^BWas I not joking?"

20 For lack of wood the fire goes
out,
And where there is no
^gossiper, ^Bquarreling quiets
down.

21 *Like* charcoal to hot embers
and wood to fire,
So is a ^contentious person to
kindle strife.

22 The ^words of a gossiper are
like dainty morsels,
And they go down into the
innermost parts of the
body.

23 *Like* an earthenware ^vessel
overlaid with silver
impurities
Are burning lips and a wicked
heart.

24 One who ^hates disguises *it*
with his lips,
But he harbors ^Bdeceit in his
heart.

25 When he ^speaks graciously,
do not believe him,
Because there are seven
abominations in his heart.

26 *Though his* hatred ^covers
itself with deception,
His wickedness will be
^Brevealed in the assembly.

27 One who ^digs a pit will fall
into it,
And one who rolls a stone, it
will come back on him.

28 A lying tongue hates those it
crushes,
And a ^flattering mouth works
ruin.

26:11 ^2 Pet 2:22   ^B Ex 8:15   26:12 ^Prov 3:7
^B Prov 29:20   26:13 ^Prov 22:13   26:14 ^Prov 6:9
26:15 ^Prov 19:24   26:16 ^Prov 27:11
26:17 ^Prov 3:30   26:18 ^Is 50:11   26:19 ^Prov 24:28
^B Eph 5:4   26:20 ^Prov 16:28   ^B Prov 22:10
26:21 ^Prov 15:18; 29:22   26:22 ^Prov 18:8
26:23 ^Matt 23:27; Luke 11:39   26:24 ^Ps 41:6
^B Prov 12:20   26:25 ^Ps 28:3; Prov 26:23
26:26 ^Matt 23:28   ^B Luke 8:17   26:27 ^Esth 7:10;
Prov 28:10   26:28 ^Prov 29:5

WARNINGS AND INSTRUCTIONS

27 ^ADo not boast about tomorrow,
For you ^Bdo not know what a day may bring.

2 Let ^Aanother praise you, and not your own mouth;
A stranger, and not your own lips.

3 A stone is heavy and the sand weighty,
But the provocation of a fool is heavier than both of them.

4 Wrath is fierce and anger is a flood,
But ^Awho can stand before jealousy?

5 Better is ^Aopen rebuke
Than love that is concealed.

6 Faithful are the wounds of a friend,
But deceitful are the ^Akisses of an enemy.

7 A satisfied person despises honey,
But to a hungry person any bitter thing is sweet.

8 Like a ^Abird that wanders from its nest,
So is a person who wanders from his home.

9 ^AOil and perfume make the heart glad,
And a person's advice is sweet to his friend.

10 Do not abandon your ^Afriend or ^Byour father's friend,
And do not go to your brother's house on the day of your disaster;
Better is a neighbor who is near than a brother far away.

11 ^ABe wise, my son, and make my heart glad,
So that I may reply to one who taunts me.

12 A prudent person sees evil *and* hides himself;
But the naive proceed, *and* pay the penalty.

13 ^ATake his garment when he becomes a guarantor for a stranger;
And for a foreign woman seize a pledge from him.

14 ^AOne who blesses his friend with a loud voice early in the morning,
It will be considered a curse to him.

15 A ^Aconstant dripping on a day of steady rain
And a contentious woman are alike;

16 He who would restrain her restrains the wind,
And grasps oil with his right hand.

17 *As* iron sharpens iron,
So one person sharpens another.

18 One who tends the fig tree will eat its fruit,
And one who ^Acares for his master will be honored.

19 As in water a face *reflects* the face,
So the heart of a person *reflects the* person.

20 ^{1,A}Sheol and ²Abaddon are ^Bnever satisfied,
Nor are the eyes of a person ever satisfied.

21 The ^Acrucible is for silver and the furnace for gold,

27:1 ^AJames 4:13-16   ^BLuke 12:19, 20   27:2 ^AProv 25:27;
2 Cor 10:12, 18   27:4 ^AProv 6:34; 1 John 3:12
27:5 ^AProv 28:23; Gal 2:14   27:6 ^AMatt 26:49
27:8 ^AProv 26:2; Is 16:2   27:9 ^APs 23:5; 141:5
27:10 ^AProv 18:24   ^B1 Kin 12:6-8   27:11 ^AProv 10:1;
23:15   27:13 ^AProv 20:16   27:14 ^APs 12:2
27:15 ^AProv 19:13   27:18 ^ALuke 12:42-44; 19:17
27:20 ^AJob 26:6   ^BProv 30:15, 16   27:21 ^AProv 17:3

27:20 ¹I.e., The netherworld   ²I.e., the place of destruction

And each *is tested* by the
praise accorded him.

22 Though you ^pound the fool in
a mortar with a pestle along
with crushed grain,
His foolishness *still* will not
leave him.

23 ^Know well the condition of
your flocks,
And pay attention to your herds;

24 For riches are not forever,
Nor does a ^crown *endure* to
all generations.

25 *When* the grass disappears, the
new growth is seen,
And the herbs of the
mountains are ^gathered in,

26 The lambs *will be* for your
clothing,
And the goats *will bring* the
price of a field,

27 And *there will be* enough
goats' milk for your food,
For the food of your
household,
And sustenance for your
attendants.

WARNINGS AND INSTRUCTIONS

28 The wicked ^flee when no
one is pursuing,
But the righteous are bold as
a lion.

2 Due to a wrongdoing of a land
its leaders are ^many,
But ^by a person of
understanding *and*
knowledge, so it endures.

3 A ^poor man who oppresses
the helpless
Is *like* a driving rain which
leaves no food.

4 Those who abandon the Law
^praise the wicked,
But those who keep the Law
strive against them.

5 Evil people ^do not understand
justice,
But those who seek the Lord
understand everything.

6 ^Better is a poor person who
walks in his integrity,
Than a person who is crooked,
though he is rich.

7 He who keeps the Law is a
discerning son,
But he who is a companion
of ^gluttons humiliates his
father.

8 One who increases his wealth
by [1],^interest *of any kind,*
Collects it for one who is
gracious to the poor.

9 One who turns his ear away
from listening to the Law,
Even his ^prayer is an
abomination.

10 One who leads the upright
astray in an evil way
Will ^himself fall into his own
pit,
But the ^Bblameless will inherit
good.

11 The rich person is ^wise in his
own eyes,
But the poor who has
understanding sees through
him.

12 When the righteous triumph,
there is great glory,
But ^when the wicked rise,
people hide themselves.

13 One who ^conceals his
wrongdoings will not
prosper,

27:22 ^Prov 23:35; 26:11   27:23 ^Jer 31:10; Ezek 34:12
27:24 ^Job 19:9; Ps 89:39   27:25 ^Is 17:5; Jer 40:10, 12
28:1 ^Lev 26:17, 36; Ps 53:5   28:2 ^1 Kin 16:8-28
^B Prov 11:11   28:3 ^Matt 18:28   28:4 ^Ps 49:18;
Rom 1:32   28:5 ^Ps 92:6; Is 6:9   28:6 ^Prov 19:1
28:7 ^Prov 23:20   28:8 ^Ex 22:25; Lev 25:36
28:9 ^Ps 66:18; 109:7   28:10 ^Ps 7:15   ^B Matt 6:33
28:11 ^Prov 3:7; 26:5, 12   28:12 ^Prov 28:28;
Eccl 10:5, 6   28:13 ^Job 31:33

28:8 [1] Possibly interest on money and food loans

But one who ᴮconfesses and abandons *them* will find compassion.

14 How blessed is the person who ᴬfears always,
But one who hardens his heart will fall into disaster.

15 *Like* a ᴬroaring lion and a rushing bear
Is a ᴮwicked ruler over a poor people.

16 A ᴬleader who is a great oppressor lacks understanding,
But a person who hates unjust gain will prolong *his* days.

17 A person who is ᴬburdened with the guilt of human blood
Will be a fugitive until death; no one is to support him!

18 One who walks blamelessly will receive help,
But one who is ᴬcrooked will fall all at once.

19 ᴬOne who works his land will ᴮhave plenty of food,
But one who follows empty *pursuits* will have plenty of poverty.

20 A ᴬfaithful person will abound with blessings,
But one who hurries to be rich will not go unpunished.

21 To ᴬshow partiality is not good,
Because for a piece of bread a man will do wrong.

22 A person with an ᴬevil eye hurries after wealth
And does not know that poverty will come upon him.

23 One who ᴬrebukes a person will afterward find *more* favor
Than one who ᴮflatters with the tongue.

24 He who ᴬrobs his father or his mother
And says, "There is no wrong done,"
Is the ᴮcompanion of a person who destroys.

25 An arrogant person ᴬstirs up strife,
But one who trusts in the Lᴏʀᴅ will prosper.

26 One who ᴬtrusts in his own heart is a fool,
But one who walks wisely will flee to safety.

27 One who ᴬgives to the poor will never lack *anything*,
But one who shuts his eyes will have many curses.

28 When the wicked rise, people hide themselves;
But when they perish, the righteous increase.

WARNINGS AND INSTRUCTIONS

29 A person often rebuked who becomes obstinate
Will ᴬsuddenly be broken beyond remedy.

2 When the ᴬrighteous increase, the people rejoice,
But when a wicked person rules, people groan.

3 A man who ᴬloves wisdom makes his father glad,
But he who involves himself with prostitutes wastes *his* wealth.

4 The ᴬking gives stability to the land by justice,
But a person who takes bribes ruins it.

28:13 ᴮ Ps 32:5 28:14 ᴬ Prov 23:17 28:15 ᴬ Prov 19:12
ᴮ Ex 1:14 28:16 ᴬ Eccl 10:16; Is 3:12 28:17 ᴬ Gen 9:6;
Ex 21:14 28:18 ᴬ Prov 10:27 28:19 ᴬ Prov 12:11
ᴮ Prov 20:13 28:20 ᴬ Prov 10:6; Matt 24:45
28:21 ᴬ Prov 24:23 28:22 ᴬ Prov 23:6
28:23 ᴬ Prov 27:5, 6 ᴮ Prov 29:5 28:24 ᴬ Prov 19:26
ᴮ Prov 18:9 28:25 ᴬ Prov 15:18 28:26 ᴬ Prov 3:5
28:27 ᴬ Prov 11:24; 19:17 29:1 ᴬ Prov 6:15
29:2 ᴬ Esth 8:15; Prov 11:10 29:3 ᴬ Prov 10:1; 15:20
29:4 ᴬ 2 Chr 9:8; Prov 8:15

5 A man who ^flatters his
   neighbor
   Is spreading a net for his steps.
6 By wrongdoing an evil person
   is ^ensnared,
   But the righteous sings and
   rejoices.
7 The ^righteous is concerned
   for the rights of the poor;
   The wicked does not
   understand *such* concern.
8 Arrogant people ^inflame a city,
   But ^wise people turn away
   anger.
9 When a wise person has a
   controversy with a foolish
   person,
   The foolish person either rages
   or laughs, and there is no rest.
10 People of ^bloodshed hate the
   blameless person,
   But the upright are concerned
   for his life.
11 A fool always loses his temper,
   But a ^wise person holds it back.
12 If a ^ruler pays attention to
   falsehood,
   All his ministers *become*
   wicked.
13 The poor person and the
   oppressor have this in
   common:
   The LORD gives ^light to the
   eyes of both.
14 If a ^king judges the poor with
   truth,
   His throne will be established
   forever.
15 The ^rod and a rebuke give
   wisdom,
   But a child who gets his own
   way brings shame to his
   mother.
16 When the wicked increase,
   wrongdoing increases;
   But the ^righteous will see
   their downfall.

17 ^Correct your son, and he will
   give you comfort;
   He will also ^delight your
   soul.
18 Where there is ^no vision, the
   people ^are unrestrained,
   But happy is one who keeps
   the Law.
19 A slave will not be instructed
   by words *alone;*
   For *though* he understands,
   there will be no response.
20 Do you see a person who is
   ^hasty with his words?
   There is more hope for a fool
   than for him.
21 One who pampers his slave
   from childhood
   Will in the end *find* him to be
   rebellious.
22 An ^angry person stirs up
   strife,
   And a hot-tempered person
   abounds in wrongdoing.
23 A person's ^pride will bring
   him low,
   But a ^humble spirit will obtain
   honor.
24 One who is a partner with a
   thief hates his own life;
   He ^hears the oath but tells
   nothing.
25 The fear of man brings a
   snare,
   But one who ^trusts in the
   LORD will be protected.
26 Many seek the ruler's favor,
   But ^justice for mankind *comes*
   from the LORD.

29:5 ^Ps 5:9   29:6 ^Prov 22:5; Eccl 9:12
29:7 ^Job 29:16; Ps 41:1   29:8 ^Prov 11:11   ^Prov 16:14
29:10 ^Gen 4:5-8; 1 John 3:12   29:11 ^Prov 19:11
29:12 ^1 Kin 12:14   29:13 ^Ezra 9:8; Ps 13:3
29:14 ^Ps 72:4; Is 11:4   29:15 ^Prov 13:24; 22:15
29:16 ^Ps 37:34, 36; 58:10   29:17 ^Prov 13:24
^Prov 10:1   29:18 ^1 Sam 3:1   ^Ex 32:25
29:20 ^James 1:19   29:22 ^Prov 15:18; 26:21
29:23 ^Prov 11:2   ^Prov 15:33   29:24 ^Lev 5:1
29:25 ^Ps 91:1-16; Prov 18:10   29:26 ^Is 49:4; 1 Cor 4:4

27 An ᴬunjust person is an
abomination to the
righteous,
And one who is upright in the
way is an abomination to the
wicked.

THE WORDS OF AGUR

30 The words of Agur the son of
Jakeh, the pronouncement.
The man declares to Ithiel, to Ith-
iel and Ucal:

2 I am certainly more ᴬstupid
than any man,
And I do not have the
understanding of a man;

3 Nor have I learned wisdom,
Nor do I have the ᴬknowledge
of the Holy One.

4 Who has ᴬascended into
heaven and descended?
Who has gathered the wind in
His fists?
Who has wrapped the waters
in His garment?
Who has established all the
ends of the earth?
What is His ᴮname or His Son's
name?
Surely you know!

5 Every ᴬword of God is pure;
He is a shield to those who
take refuge in Him.

6 ᴬDo not add to His words
Or He will rebuke you, and you
will be proved a liar.

7 Two things I have asked of
You;
Do not refuse me before I die:

8 Keep deception and lies far
from me,
Give me neither poverty nor
riches;
Feed me with the ᴬfood that is
my portion,

9 So that I will not be ᴬfull and
deny *You* and say, "Who is
the LORD?"
And that I will not become
ᴮimpoverished and steal,
And profane the name of my
God.

10 Do not slander a slave to his
master,
Or he will ᴬcurse you and you
will be found guilty.

11 There is a kind *of person* who
ᴬcurses his father
And does not bless his mother.

12 There is a kind who is ᴬpure in
his own eyes,
Yet is not washed from his
filthiness.

13 There is a kind—oh how ᴬlofty
are his eyes!
And his eyelids are raised *in
arrogance.*

14 There is a kind *of person*
whose teeth are *like* swords
And his jaw teeth *like* knives,
To ᴬdevour the poor from the
earth
And the needy from among
mankind.

15 The leech has two daughters:
"Give" *and* "Give."
There are three things that will
not be satisfied,
Four that will not say,
"Enough":

16 ᴬSheol, the ᴮinfertile womb,
Earth that is never satisfied
with water,

29:27ᴬPs 6:8; 139:21, 22 **30:2**ᴬPs 49:10; 73:22
30:3ᴬProv 9:10 **30:4**ᴬPs 68:18 ᴮRev 19:12
30:5ᴬPs 12:6; 18:30 **30:6**ᴬDeut 4:2; 12:32
30:8ᴬJob 23:12; Matt 6:11 **30:9**ᴬDeut 8:12 ᴮProv 6:30
30:10ᴬEccl 7:21 **30:11**ᴬEx 21:17; Prov 20:20
30:12ᴬProv 16:2; Is 65:5 **30:13**ᴬProv 6:17; Is 2:11
30:14ᴬPs 14:4; Amos 8:4 **30:16**ᴬProv 27:20 ᴮGen 30:1

And fire that never says,
"Enough."

17 The eye that mocks a father
And scorns a mother,
The ^ravens of the valley will
pick it out,
And the young ^eagles will eat it.

18 There are three things which
are too wonderful for me,
Four which I do not understand:
19 The way of the ^eagle in the sky,
The way of a snake on a rock,
The way of a ship in the
middle of the sea,
And the way of a man with a
virgin.
20 This is the way of an
^adulterous woman:
She eats and wipes her mouth,
And says, "I have done no
wrong."

21 Under three things the earth
quakes,
And under four, it cannot
endure:
22 Under a ^slave when he
becomes king,
And a fool when he is satisfied
with food,
23 Under an unloved woman
when she gets a husband,
And a female servant when she
dispossesses her mistress.

24 Four things are small on the
earth,
But they are exceedingly wise:
25 The ^ants are not a strong
people,
But they prepare their food in
the summer;
26 The ^rock hyraxes are not a
mighty people,
Yet they make their houses in
the rocks;

27 The locusts have no king,
Yet all of them go out in ^ranks;
28 The lizard you may grasp with
the hands,
Yet it is in kings' palaces.

29 There are three things which
are stately in *their* march,
Even four which are stately
when they walk:
30 The lion, *which* is ^mighty
among animals
And does not retreat from
anything,
31 The strutting rooster or the
male goat,
And a king *when his* army is
with him.

32 If you have been foolish in
exalting yourself,
Or if you have plotted *evil*,
^*put your* hand on your
mouth.
33 For the churning of milk
produces butter,
And pressing the nose
produces blood;
So the churning of ^anger
produces strife.

THE WORDS OF LEMUEL

31 The words of King Lemuel,
the pronouncement which
his mother taught him:
2 What, my son?
And what, son of my womb?
And what, son of my ^vows?
3 ^Do not give your strength to
women,
Or your ways to that which
destroys kings.

30:17 ^Deut 28:26 30:19 ^Deut 28:49; Jer 48:40
30:20 ^Prov 5:6 30:22 ^Prov 19:10; Eccl 10:7
30:25 ^Prov 6:6 30:26 ^Lev 11:5; Ps 104:18
30:27 ^Joel 2:7 30:30 ^Judg 14:18; 2 Sam 1:23
30:32 ^Job 21:5; 40:4 30:33 ^Prov 10:12; 29:22
31:2 ^1 Sam 1:11 31:3 ^Prov 5:9

4   It is not for ^kings, Lemuel,
    It is not for kings to drink wine,
    Or for rulers to desire
        intoxicating drink,
5   Otherwise they will drink and
        forget what is decreed,
    And ^pervert the rights of all
        the needy.
6   Give intoxicating drink to one
        who is ^perishing,
    And wine to one whose life is
        bitter.
7   Let him drink and forget his
        poverty,
    And remember his trouble no
        more.
8   ^Open your mouth for the
        people who cannot speak,
    For the rights of all the
        unfortunate.
9   Open your mouth, ^judge
        righteously,
    And defend the ᴮrights of the
        poor and needy.

DESCRIPTION OF A WORTHY WOMAN

10 An ^excellent wife, who can
        find *her*?
    For her worth is far above
        jewels.
11 The heart of her husband
        trusts in her,
    And he will have no lack of
        gain.
12 She does him good and not evil
    All the days of her life.
13 She looks for wool and linen,
    And works with her hands in
        delight.
14 She is like ^merchant ships;
    She brings her food from afar.
15 And she rises while it is still
        night
    And ^gives food to her
        household,
    And portions to her
        attendants.

16 She considers a field and buys it;
    From her earnings she plants a
        vineyard.
17 She ^surrounds her waist with
        strength
    And makes her arms strong.
18 She senses that her profit is
        good;
    Her lamp does not go out at
        night.
19 She stretches out her hands to
        the distaff,
    And her hands grasp the
        spindle.
20 She ^extends her hand to the
        poor,
    And she stretches out her
        hands to the needy.
21 She is not afraid of the snow
        for her household,
    For all her household are
        ^clothed with scarlet.
22 She makes ^coverings for
        herself;
    Her clothing is fine linen and
        purple.
23 Her husband is known ^in the
        gates,
    When he sits among the elders
        of the land.
24 She makes ^linen garments
        and sells *them,*
    And supplies belts to the
        tradesmen.
25 Strength and ^dignity are her
        clothing,
    And she smiles at the future.
26 She ^opens her mouth in
        wisdom,
    And the teaching of kindness
        is on her tongue.

31:4 ^Eccl 10:17   31:5 ^Ex 23:6; Deut 16:19
31:6 ^Job 29:13   31:8 ^Job 29:12-17; Ps 82   31:9 ^Lev 19:15
ᴮIs 1:17   31:10 ^Ruth 3:11; Prov 12:4   31:14 ^Ezek 27:25
31:15 ^Luke 12:42   31:17 ^1 Kin 18:46; 2 Kin 4:29
31:20 ^Deut 15:11; Job 31:16-20   31:21 ^2 Sam 1:24
31:22 ^Prov 7:16   31:23 ^Deut 16:18; Ruth 4:1, 11
31:24 ^Judg 14:12   31:25 ^1 Tim 2:9, 10   31:26 ^Prov 10:31

27 She watches over the activities
    of her household,
    And does not eat the ^bread of
    idleness.
28 Her children rise up and bless
    her;
    Her husband *also,* and he
    praises her, *saying:*
29 "Many daughters have done
    nobly,
    But you excel them all."

30 Charm is deceitful and beauty
    is vain,
    But a woman who ^fears
    the Lord, she shall be
    praised.
31 Give her the product of her
    hands,
    And let her works praise her in
    the gates.

31:27 ^Prov 19:15   31:30 ^Ps 112:1; Prov 22:4

ECCLESIASTES

THE FUTILITY OF ALL ENDEAVORS

1 The words of the ^Preacher, the son of David, king in Jerusalem.
² "^Futility of futilities," says the Preacher,
"Futility of futilities! All is futility."

³ ^What advantage does a person have in all his work
Which he does under the sun?
⁴ A generation goes and a generation comes,
But the ^earth remains forever.
⁵ Also, ^the sun rises and the sun sets;
And hurrying to its place it rises there *again*.
⁶ ^Blowing toward the south,
Then turning toward the north,
The wind continues swirling along;
And on its circular courses the wind returns.
⁷ All the rivers flow into the sea,
Yet the sea is not full.
To the place where the rivers flow,
There they flow again.
⁸ All things are wearisome;
No one can tell *it*.
^The eye is not satisfied with seeing,
Nor is the ear filled with hearing.
⁹ ^What has been, it is what will be,
And what has been done, it is what will be done.
So there is nothing new under the sun.

¹⁰ Is there anything of which one might say,
"See this, it is new"?
It has already existed for ages
Which were before us.
¹¹ There is ^no remembrance of the earlier things,
And of the later things as well, which will occur,
There will be no remembrance of them
Among those who will come later *still*.

THE FUTILITY OF WISDOM

¹² I, the ^Preacher, have been king over Israel in Jerusalem. ¹³ And I set my mind to seek and ^explore by wisdom about everything that has been done under heaven. *It* is a ^B^sorry task with which God has given the sons of mankind to be troubled. ¹⁴ I have seen all the works which have been done under the sun, and behold, all is ^futility and striving after wind. ¹⁵ What is ^crooked cannot be straightened, and what is lacking cannot be counted.

¹⁶ I said to myself, "Behold, I have magnified and increased ^wisdom more than all who were over Jerusalem before me; and my mind has observed a wealth of wisdom and knowledge." ¹⁷ And I applied my mind to know wisdom and to

1:1 ^Eccl 1:12; 7:27   1:2 ^Ps 39:5, 6; 62:9   1:3 ^Eccl 2:11;
3:9   1:4 ^Ps 104:5; 119:90   1:5 ^Ps 19:6   1:6 ^Eccl 11:5;
John 3:8   1:8 ^Prov 27:20; Eccl 4:8   1:9 ^Eccl 1:10; 2:12
1:11 ^Eccl 2:16; 9:5   1:12 ^Eccl 1:1; 7:27
1:13 ^Eccl 3:10, 11   ^B Eccl 2:23, 26   1:14 ^Eccl 2:11, 17;
4:4   1:15 ^Eccl 7:13   1:16 ^1 Kin 3:12; 4:30

^Aknow insanity and foolishness; I realized that this also is ^Bstriving after wind. [18] Because ^Ain much wisdom there is much grief; and increasing knowledge *results in* increasing pain.

THE FUTILITY OF PLEASURE
AND POSSESSIONS

2 I said to myself, "Come now, I will test you with ^Apleasure. So enjoy yourself." And behold, it too was futility. [2]^AI said of laughter, "*It is* senseless," and of pleasure, "What does this accomplish?" [3]I explored with my mind *how* to refresh my body with wine while my mind was guiding *me* wisely; and how to seize ^Afoolishness, until I could see ^Bwhat good there is for the sons of mankind to do under heaven for the few years of their lives. [4]I enlarged my works: I ^Abuilt houses for myself, I planted vineyards for myself; [5]I made ^Agardens and ^Bparks for myself, and I planted in them all kinds of fruit trees; [6]I made ^Aponds of water for myself from which to irrigate a forest of growing trees. [7]I bought male and female slaves, and I had ^Aslaves *born* at home. I also possessed flocks and herds larger than all who preceded me in Jerusalem. [8]I also amassed for myself silver and ^Agold, and the treasure of kings and provinces. I provided for myself male and female singers, and the pleasures of the sons of mankind: many concubines.

[9]Then I became ^Agreat and increased more than all who preceded me in Jerusalem. My wisdom also stood by me. [10]^AAll that my eyes desired, I did not refuse them. I did not restrain my heart from any pleasure, for my heart was pleased because of all my labor; and this was my ^Breward for all my labor. [11]So I considered all my activities which my hands had done and the labor which I had exerted, and behold, all was ^Afutility and striving after wind, and there was no benefit under the sun.

WISDOM SURPASSES FOOLISHNESS

[12]So I turned to ^Aconsider wisdom, insanity, and foolishness; for what *will* the man *do* who will come after the king, *except* what has already been done? [13]Then I saw that ^Awisdom surpasses foolishness as light surpasses darkness. [14]The wise person's eyes are in his head, but the ^Afool walks in darkness. And yet I know that ^Bone *and the same* fate happens to both of them. [15]Then I said to myself, "As is the fate of the fool, it will also happen to me. ^AWhy then have I been extremely wise?" So I said to myself, "This too is futility." [16]For there is ^Ano lasting remembrance of the wise, along with the fool, since *in* the coming days everything will soon be forgotten. And how the wise and the fool alike die! [17]So I ^Ahated life, for the work which had been done under the sun was unhappy to me; because everything is futility and striving after wind.

THE FUTILITY OF LABOR

[18]So I hated ^Aall the fruit of my labor for which I had labored under the sun, because I must ^Bleave it to the man who will come after me.

1:17^AEccl 2:12　^BEccl 1:14　1:18^AEccl 2:23; 12:12
2:1^AEccl 7:4; 8:15　2:2^AProv 14:13; Eccl 7:3, 6
2:3^AEccl 7:25　^BEccl 2:24　2:4^A1 Kin 7:1-12
2:5^ASong 4:16　^BNeh 2:8　2:6^ANeh 2:14; 3:15, 16
2:7^AGen 14:14; 15:3　2:8^A1 Kin 9:28; 10:10, 14, 21
2:9^A1 Chr 29:25; Eccl 1:16　2:10^AEccl 6:2　^BEccl 3:22
2:11^AEccl 1:14; 2:22, 23　2:12^AEccl 1:17
2:13^AEccl 7:11, 12, 19; 9:18　2:14^A1 John 2:11
^BPs 49:10　2:15^AEccl 6:8, 11　2:16^AEccl 1:11; 9:5
2:17^AEccl 4:2, 3　2:18^AEccl 1:3　^BPs 39:6

[19] And who knows whether he will be wise or ^a fool? Yet he will have control over all the fruit of my labor for which I have labored by acting wisely under the sun. This too is futility. [20] Therefore I completely despaired over all the fruit of my labor for which I had labored under the sun. [21] When there is a person who has labored with wisdom, knowledge, and ^skill, and then gives his legacy to one who has not labored for it; this too is futility and a great evil. [22] For what does a person get in ^all his labor and in his striving with which he labors under the sun? [23] Because all his days his activity is painful and irritating; even at night his mind ^does not rest. This too is futility.

[24] There is nothing better for a person *than* to eat and drink, and show himself *some* good in his trouble. This too I have seen, that it is ^from the hand of God. [25] For who can eat and who can have enjoyment without Him? [26] For to a person who is good in His sight, ^He has given wisdom and knowledge and joy, while to the sinner He has given the task of gathering and collecting so that he may give to one who is good in God's sight. This too is futility and striving after wind.

A TIME FOR EVERYTHING

3 There is an appointed time for everything. And there is a ^time for every matter under heaven—

[2]   A time to give birth and a
      ^time to die;
      A time to plant and a time to
      uproot what is planted.
[3]   A ^time to kill and a time to
      heal;
      A time to tear down and a
      time to build up.

[4]   A time to ^weep and a time to
      ^laugh;
      A time to mourn and a time to
      dance.
[5]   A time to throw stones and a
      time to gather stones;
      A time to embrace and a time
      to shun embracing.
[6]   A time to search and a time to
      give up as lost;
      A time to keep and a time to
      throw away.
[7]   A time to tear apart and a time
      to sew together;
      A time to ^be silent and a time
      to speak.
[8]   A time to love and a time to
      ^hate;
      A time for war and a time for
      peace.

[9] ^What benefit *is there for* the worker *from that* in which he labors? [10] I have seen the ^task which God has given the sons of mankind with which to occupy themselves.

GOD SET ETERNITY IN THE HEART OF MANKIND

[11] He has ^made everything appropriate in its time. He has also set eternity in their heart, without *the possibility that* mankind will find out the work which God has done from the beginning even to the end.

[12] I know that there is ^nothing better for them than to rejoice and to do good in one's lifetime; [13] moreover, that every person who eats and drinks sees good in all his labor—this is the ^gift of God.

2:19 ^1 Kin 12:13   2:21 ^Eccl 4:4   2:22 ^Eccl 1:3; 2:11
2:23 ^Ps 127:2   2:24 ^Eccl 3:13   2:26 ^Job 32:8;
Prov 2:6   3:1 ^Eccl 3:17; 8:6   3:2 ^Job 14:5; Heb 9:27
3:3 ^Gen 9:6; 1 Sam 2:6   3:4 ^Rom 12:15   ^Ps 126:2
3:7 ^Amos 5:13   3:8 ^Ps 101:3   3:9 ^Eccl 1:3; 2:11
3:10 ^Eccl 1:13; 2:26   3:11 ^Gen 1:31   3:12 ^Eccl 2:24
3:13 ^Eccl 2:24; 5:19

¹⁴I know that everything God does will remain forever; there is nothing to add to it and there is nothing to take from it. And God has *so* worked, that *people* will ᴬfear Him. ¹⁵ᴬThat *which is,* is what has already been, and that which will be has already been; and God seeks what has passed by.

¹⁶Furthermore, I have seen under the sun *that* in the place of justice there is ᴬwickedness and in the place of righteousness there is wickedness. ¹⁷I said to myself, "ᴬGod will judge the righteous and the wicked," for a time for every matter and for every deed ¹is there. ¹⁸I said to myself regarding the sons of mankind, "God is testing them in order for them to see that they are *as* ᴬanimals, they to themselves." ¹⁹ᴬFor the fate of the sons of mankind and the fate of animals is the same. As one dies, so dies the other; indeed, they all have the same breath, and there is no advantage for mankind over animals, for all is futility. ²⁰All go to the same place. All came from the ᴬdust and all return to the dust. ²¹Who knows that the ᴬspirit of the sons of mankind ascends upward and the spirit of the animal descends downward to the earth? ²²I have seen that ᴬnothing is better than when a person is happy in his activities, for that is his lot. For who will bring him to see ᴮwhat will occur after him?

THE EVILS OF OPPRESSION

4 Then I looked again at all the acts of oppression which were being done under the sun. And behold, *I saw* the tears of the oppressed and *that* they had ᴬno one to comfort *them;* and power was on the side of their oppressors,

but they had no one to comfort *them.* ²So ᴬI congratulated the dead who are already dead, more than the living who are still living. ³But ᴬbetter *off* than both of them is the one who has never existed, who has never seen the evil activity that is done under the sun.

⁴I have seen that every labor and every ᴬskill which is done is *the result of* rivalry between a person and his neighbor. This too is ᴮfutility and striving after wind. ⁵The fool ᴬfolds his hands and consumes his own flesh. ⁶One hand full of rest is ᴬbetter than two fists full of labor and striving after wind.

⁷Then I looked again at futility under the sun. ⁸There was a man without a dependent, having neither a son nor a brother, yet there was no end to all his labor. Indeed, ᴬhis eyes were not satisfied with riches, *and he never asked,* "And ᴮfor whom do I labor and deprive myself of pleasure?" This too is futility, and it is an unhappy task.

⁹Two are better than one because they have a good return for their labor; ¹⁰for if either of them falls, the one will lift up his companion. But woe to the one who falls when there is not another to lift him up! ¹¹Furthermore, if two lie down together they keep warm, but ᴬhow can one be warm *alone?* ¹²And if one can overpower him who is alone, two can resist him. A cord of three *strands* is not quickly torn apart.

3:14ᴬEccl 5:7; 7:18   3:15ᴬEccl 1:9; 6:10
3:16ᴬEccl 4:1; 5:8   3:17ᴬGen 18:25; Ps 96:13
3:18ᴬPs 49:12, 20; 73:22   3:19ᴬPs 49:12; Eccl 9:12
3:20ᴬGen 3:19; Ps 103:14   3:21ᴬEccl 12:7
3:22ᴬEccl 2:24   ᴮEccl 2:18   4:1ᴬJer 16:7; Lam 1:9
4:2ᴬJob 3:11-26; Eccl 2:17   4:3ᴬJob 3:11-22; Eccl 6:3
4:4ᴬEccl 2:21   ᴮEccl 1:14   4:5ᴬProv 6:10; 24:33
4:6ᴬProv 15:16, 17; 16:8   4:8ᴬProv 27:20   ᴮEccl 2:21
4:11ᴬ1 Kin 1:1-4

3:17 ¹I.e., exists with God

[13] A ^poor yet wise youth is better than an old and foolish king who no longer knows *how* to receive instruction— [14] for he has come ^out of prison to become king, even though he was born poor in his kingdom. [15] I have seen all those living under the sun move to the side of the second youth who replaces him. [16] There is no end to all the people, to all who were before them. Even the ones who will come later will not be happy with him; for this too is ^futility and striving after wind.

YOUR ATTITUDE TOWARD GOD

5 Guard your steps as you go to the house of God, and approach to listen rather than to offer the ^sacrifice of fools; for they do not know that they are doing evil. [2] Do not be ^quick with your mouth or impulsive in thought to bring up a matter in the presence of God. For God is in heaven and you are on the earth; therefore let your ^Bwords be few. [3] For the dream comes through much effort, and the voice of a ^fool through many words.

[4] When you ^make a vow to God, do not be late in paying it; for *He takes* no delight in fools. Pay what you vow! [5] It is ^better that you not vow, than vow and not pay. [6] Do not let your speech cause you to sin, and do not say in the presence of the messenger *of God* that it was a ^mistake. Why should God be angry on account of your voice, and destroy the work of your hands? [7] For in many dreams and in many words there is futility. Rather, ^fear God.

[8] If you see ^oppression of the poor and ^Bdenial of justice and righteousness in the province, do not be shocked at the sight; for one official watches over another official, and there are higher officials over them. [9] After all, a king who cultivates the field is beneficial to the land.

THE FOOLISHNESS OF RICHES

[10] ^One who loves money will not be satisfied with money, nor one who loves abundance *with its* income. This too is futility. [11] ^When good things increase, those who consume them increase. So what is the advantage to their owners except to look *at them?* [12] The sleep of the laborer is ^sweet, whether he eats little or much; but the full stomach of the rich person does not allow him to sleep.

[13] There is a sickening evil *which* I have seen under the sun: ^wealth being hoarded by its owner to his detriment. [14] When that wealth was lost through bad business and he had fathered a son, then there was nothing to support him. [15] As he came naked from his mother's womb, so he will return as he came. He will ^take nothing from the fruit of his labor that he can carry in his hand. [16] This also is a sickening evil: exactly as a person is born, so will he die. ^What then is the advantage for him who labors for the wind? [17] All his life ^*he* also eats in darkness with ^Bgreat irritation, sickness, and anger.

[18] Here is what I have seen to be good and fitting: to eat, to drink, and enjoy oneself in all one's labor in which he labors under the sun

4:13 ^Eccl 7:19; 9:15 4:14 ^Gen 41:14, 41-43
4:16 ^Eccl 1:14 5:1 ^1 Sam 15:22; Prov 15:8
5:2 ^Prov 20:25 ^B Prov 10:19 5:3 ^Job 11:2; Prov 15:2
5:4 ^Num 30:2; Ps 50:14 5:5 ^Prov 20:25; Acts 5:4
5:6 ^Lev 4:2, 22; Num 15:25 5:7 ^Eccl 3:14; 7:18
5:8 ^Eccl 4:1 ^B Ezek 18:18 5:10 ^Eccl 1:8; 2:10, 11
5:11 ^Eccl 2:9 5:12 ^Prov 3:24 5:13 ^Eccl 6:2
5:15 ^Ps 49:17; 1 Tim 6:7 5:16 ^Eccl 1:3; 2:11
5:17 ^Ps 127:2 ^B Eccl 2:23

during the few years of his life which God has given him; for this is his ^reward. ¹⁹Furthermore, as for every person to whom ^God has given riches and wealth, He has also given him the opportunity to enjoy them and to receive his reward and rejoice in his labor; this is the ᴮgift of God. ²⁰For he will not often call to mind the years of his life, because ^God keeps him busy with the joy of his heart.

THE FUTILITY OF LIFE

6 There is an ^evil which I have seen under the sun, and it is widespread among mankind: ²a person to whom God has ^given riches, wealth, and honor, so that his soul lacks nothing of all that he desires, yet God has not given him the opportunity to enjoy these things, but a foreigner enjoys them. This is futility and a severe affliction. ³If a man fathers a hundred *children* and lives many years, however many they may be, but his soul is not satisfied with good things and he does not even have a *proper* burial, *then* I say, "Better ^the miscarriage than he, ⁴for *a miscarriage* comes in futility and goes into darkness; and its name is covered in darkness. ⁵It has not even seen the sun nor does it know *it; yet* it is better off than that *man.* ⁶Even if *the man* lives a thousand years twice, but does not see good things—^do not all go to one *and the same* place?"

⁷^All a person's labor is for his mouth, and yet his appetite is not satisfied. ⁸For ^what advantage does the wise person have over the fool? What does the poor person have, knowing *how* to walk before the living? ⁹What the eyes ^see is better than what the soul desires. This too is futility and striving after wind.

¹⁰Whatever exists has already been named, and it is known what man is; for he ^cannot dispute with the one who is mightier than he is. ¹¹For there are many words which increase futility. What *then* is the advantage to a person? ¹²For who knows what is good for a person during *his* lifetime, *during* the few years of his futile life? He will spend them like a shadow. For who can tell a person ^what will happen after him under the sun?

WISDOM AND FOOLISHNESS CONTRASTED

7 A ^good name is better than good ¹oil,
　And the ᴮday of *one's* death *is
　　better* than the day of one's
　　birth.
²　It is better to go to a house of
　　mourning
　Than to go to a house of
　　feasting,
　Because ¹that is the ^end of
　　every person,
　And the living ᴮtakes *it* to heart.
³　Sorrow is better than laughter,
　For ^when a face is sad a heart
　　may be happy.
⁴　The mind of the wise is in the
　　house of mourning,
　While the mind of fools is in
　　the house of pleasure.
⁵　It is better to ^listen to the
　　rebuke of a wise person
　Than for one to listen to the
　　song of fools.

5:18 ^Eccl 2:10　5:19 ^2 Chr 1:12　ᴮEccl 3:13
5:20 ^Ex 3:25　6:1 ^Eccl 5:13　6:2 ^1 Kin 3:13
6:3 ^Job 3:16; Eccl 4:3　6:6 ^Eccl 2:14　6:7 ^Prov 16:26
6:8 ^Eccl 2:15　6:9 ^Eccl 11:9　6:10 ^Job 9:32; 40:2
6:12 ^Eccl 3:22　7:1 ^Prov 22:1　ᴮEccl 4:2
7:2 ^Eccl 2:14, 16　ᴮPs 90:12　7:3 ^2 Cor 7:10
7:5 ^Ps 141:5; Prov 6:23
7:1 ¹I.e., olive oil　7:2 ¹I.e., death

6   For as the crackling of thorn
     bushes under a pot,
   So is the ^laughter of the fool;
   And this too is futility.
7   For ^oppression makes a wise
     person look foolish,
   And a ^Bbribe corrupts the
     heart.
8   The ^end of a matter is better
     than its beginning;
   Patience of spirit is better than
     arrogance of spirit.
9   Do not be ^eager in your spirit
     to be angry,
   For anger resides in the heart
     of fools.
10   Do not say, "Why is it that the
     former days were better than
     these?"
   For it is not from wisdom that
     you ask about this.
11   Wisdom along with an
     inheritance is good,
   And an ^advantage to those
     who see the sun.
12   For ^wisdom is protection *just
     as* money is protection,
   But the advantage of
     knowledge is that ^Bwisdom
     keeps its possessors alive.
13   Consider the work of God,
   For who is ^able to straighten
     what He has bent?
14   On the day of prosperity be
     happy,
   But ^on the day of adversity
     consider:
   God has made the one as well
     as the other
   So that a person will ^Bnot
     discover anything *that will
     come* after him.

15 I have seen everything during
my ^lifetime of futility; there is a
righteous person who perishes in
his righteousness, and there is a
wicked person who prolongs *his*
life in his wickedness. 16 Do not be
excessively righteous, and do not
^be overly wise. Why should you
ruin yourself? 17 Do not be excessively wicked, and do not be foolish. Why should you ^die before
your time? 18 It is good that you
grasp one thing while not letting
go of the other; for one who ^fears
God comes out with both of them.
19 ^Wisdom strengthens a wise
person more than ten rulers who
are in a city. 20 Indeed, ^there is not
a righteous person on earth who
always does good and does not *ever*
sin. 21 Also, do not take seriously all
the words which are spoken, so
that you do not hear your servant
^cursing you, 22 for you know that
even you have cursed others many
times as well.

23 I tested all this with wisdom,
and I said, "I will be wise," ^but *wisdom* was far from me. 24 What has
been is remote and ^very mysterious. Who can discover it? 25 I ^di-
rected my mind to know and to
investigate, and to seek wisdom
and an explanation, and to know
the evil of foolishness and the foolishness of insanity. 26 And I discovered as more bitter than death the
woman whose heart is snares and
nets, whose hands are chains. ^One
who is pleasing to God will escape
from her, but ^Bthe sinner will be
captured by her.
27 "Behold, I have discovered
this," says the Preacher, "*by adding* one thing to another to find

7:6 ^Eccl 2:2   7:7 ^Eccl 4:1   ^BEx 23:8   7:8 ^Eccl 7:1
7:9 ^Prov 14:17; James 1:19   7:11 ^Prov 8:10, 11; Eccl 2:13
7:12 ^Eccl 7:19   ^BProv 3:18   7:13 ^Eccl 1:15
7:14 ^Deut 8:5   ^BEccl 3:22   7:15 ^Eccl 6:12; 9:9
7:16 ^Rom 12:3   7:17 ^Job 22:16; Ps 55:23
7:18 ^Eccl 3:14; 5:7   7:19 ^Eccl 7:12; 9:13–18
7:20 ^1 Kin 8:46; 2 Chr 6:36   7:21 ^Prov 30:10
7:23 ^Eccl 3:11; 8:17   7:24 ^Rom 11:33   7:25 ^Eccl 1:15, 17;
10:13   7:26 ^Prov 6:23, 24   ^BProv 22:14

an explanation, 28which I am still seeking but have not found. I have found one man among a thousand, but I have not found a ^woman among all these. 29Behold, I have found only this, that ^God made people upright, but they have sought out many schemes."

OBEY RULERS

8 Who is like the wise person and who knows the meaning of a matter? A person's wisdom ^illuminates his face and makes his stern face brighten up.

2I say, "Keep the command of the king because of the ^oath before God. 3Do not be in a hurry ^to leave him. Do not join in an evil matter, for he will do whatever he pleases." 4Since the word of the king is authoritative, ^who will say to him, "What are you doing?"

5One who keeps a *royal* command ^experiences no trouble, for a wise heart knows the proper time and procedure. 6For ^there is a proper time and procedure for every delight, though a person's trouble is heavy upon him. 7If no one ^knows what will happen, who can tell him when it will happen? 8No one has authority over the wind to restrain the wind, nor authority over the day of death; and there is no *military* discharge in the time of war, and ^evil will not save those who practice it. 9All this I have seen, and have applied my mind to every deed that has been done under the sun at a time when one person has exercised ^authority over *another* person to his detriment.

10So then, I have seen the wicked buried, those who used to go in and out of the holy place, and they are ^*soon* forgotten in the city where

they did such things. This too is futility. 11Because the sentence against an evil deed is not executed quickly, therefore ^the hearts of the sons of mankind among them are fully given to do evil. 12Although a sinner does evil a hundred *times* and may lengthen his *life,* still I know that it will go ^well for those who fear God, who fear Him openly. 13But it will ^not go well for the evil person and he will not lengthen his days like a shadow, because he does not fear God.

14There is futility which is done on the earth, that is, there are ^righteous people to whom it happens according to the deeds of the wicked. On the other hand, there are evil people to whom it happens according to the deeds of the righteous. I say that this too is futility. 15So I commended pleasure, for there is nothing good for ^a person under the sun except to eat, drink, and be joyful, and this will stand by him in his labor *throughout* the days of his life which God has given him under the sun.

16When I ^devoted my mind to know wisdom and to see the business which has been done on the earth (even though one should never sleep day or night), 17and I saw every work of God, *I concluded* that ^one cannot discover the work which has been done under the sun. Even though a person laboriously seeks, he will not discover; and even if the wise person claims to know, he cannot discover.

7:28^1 Kin 11:3   7:29^Gen 1:27   8:1^Ex 34:29, 30
8:2^Ex 22:11; 2 Sam 21:7   8:3^Eccl 10:4
8:4^Job 9:12; Dan 4:35   8:5^Prov 12:21
8:6^Eccl 3:1, 17   8:7^Eccl 3:22; 6:12   8:8^Eccl 8:13
8:9^Eccl 4:1; 5:8   8:10^Eccl 1:11; 2:16   8:11^Eccl 9:3
8:12^Deut 4:40; 12:25   8:13^Eccl 8:8; Is 3:11
8:14^Ps 73:14; Eccl 7:15   8:15^Eccl 2:24; 3:12, 13
8:16^Eccl 1:13, 14   8:17^Eccl 3:11

PEOPLE ARE IN THE HAND OF GOD

9 For I have taken all this to my heart, even to examine it all, that righteous people, wise people, and their deeds are ^in the hand of God. ^BPeople do not know whether *it will be* love or hatred; anything awaits them.

²^It is the same for all. There is one fate for the righteous and for the wicked; for the good, for the clean and the unclean; for the person who offers a sacrifice and for the one who does not sacrifice. As the good person is, so is the sinner; the one who swears *an oath* is just as the one who is afraid to swear an oath. ³This is an evil in everything that is done under the sun, that there is one fate for everyone. Furthermore, ^the hearts of the sons of mankind are full of evil, and ^Binsanity is in their hearts throughout their lives. Afterward *they go* to the dead. ⁴For whoever is joined to all the living, there is hope; for better a live dog, than a dead lion. ⁵For the living know that they will die; but the dead ^do not know anything, nor do they have a reward any longer, for their memory is forgotten. ⁶Indeed their love, their hate, and their zeal have already perished, and they will no longer have a ^share in all that is done under the sun.

⁷Go *then*, ^eat your bread in happiness, and drink your wine with a cheerful heart; for God has already approved your works. ⁸See that your ^clothes are white all the time, and that there is no lack of oil on your head. ⁹Enjoy life with the wife whom you love all the days of your futile life which He has given you under the sun, all the days of your futility; for this is your ^reward in life and in your work which you have labored under the sun.

WHATEVER YOUR HAND FINDS TO DO

¹⁰Whatever your hand finds to do, ^do *it* with *all* your might; for there is no activity, planning, knowledge, or wisdom in Sheol where you are going.

¹¹I again saw under the sun that the ^race is not to the swift and the battle is not to the warriors, and neither is bread to the wise nor wealth to the discerning, nor favor to the skillful; for time and ^Bchance overtake them all. ¹²For indeed, a person does not ^know his time: like fish that are caught in a treacherous net and birds caught in a snare, so the sons of mankind are ensnared at an evil time when it ^Bsuddenly falls on them.

¹³This too I saw as wisdom under the sun, and it impressed me: ¹⁴there ^was a small city with few men in it, and a great king came to it, surrounded it, and constructed large siegeworks against it. ¹⁵But there was found in it a ^poor wise man, and he saved the city ^Bby his wisdom. Yet no one remembered that poor man. ¹⁶So I said, "^Wisdom is better than strength." But the wisdom of the poor man is despised, and his words are ignored. ¹⁷The ^words of the wise heard in calm are *better* than the shouting of a ruler among fools. ¹⁸^Wisdom is better than weapons of war, but ^Bone sinner destroys much good.

9:1^Deut 33:3   ^BEccl 10:14   9:2^Job 9:22; Eccl 9:11
9:3^Eccl 8:11   ^BEccl 1:17   9:5^Job 14:21
9:6^Eccl 2:10; 3:22   9:7^Eccl 2:24; 8:15   9:8^Rev 3:4
9:9^Eccl 2:10   9:10^Eccl 11:6; Rom 12:11
9:11^Amos 2:14, 15   ^B1 Sam 6:9   9:12^Eccl 8:7
^BLuke 21:34, 35   9:14^2 Sam 20:16-22   9:15^Eccl 4:13
^B2 Sam 20:22   9:16^Prov 21:22; Eccl 7:12, 19
9:17^Eccl 7:5; 10:12   9:18^Eccl 9:16   ^BJosh 7:1-26

A LITTLE FOOLISHNESS

10 Dead flies turn a ^perfumer's oil rancid, *so* a little foolishness is more potent than wisdom *and* honor. ²A wise person's heart *directs him* toward the right, but the foolish ^person's heart *directs him* toward the left. ³Even when the fool walks along the road, his sense is lacking, and he ^demonstrates to everyone *that* he is a fool. ⁴If the ruler's temper rises against you, ^do not abandon your place, because ᴮcomposure puts great offenses to rest.

⁵There is an evil I have seen under the sun, like a mistake that proceeds from the ruler: ⁶^foolishness is set in many exalted places while the rich sit in humble places. ⁷I have seen slaves *riding* ^on horses and princes walking like slaves on the land.

⁸^One who digs a pit may fall into it, and a serpent may bite one who breaks through a wall. ⁹One who quarries stones may be hurt by them, and one who splits logs may be endangered by them. ¹⁰If the axe is dull and he does not sharpen *its* edge, then he must exert *more* strength. Wisdom *has* the advantage of bringing success. ¹¹If the serpent bites ^before being charmed, there is no benefit for the charmer. ¹²^Words from the mouth of a wise person are gracious, while the lips of a fool consume him; ¹³the beginning of his talking is foolishness, and the end of it is evil ^insanity. ¹⁴Yet the fool multiplies words. No person knows what will happen, and who can tell him ^what will come after him? ¹⁵The labor of a fool makes him *so* weary that he does not *even* know how to go to a city. ¹⁶Woe to you, land whose ^king is a boy, and whose princes feast in the morning. ¹⁷Blessed are you, land whose king is of nobility, and whose princes eat at the appropriate time—for strength and not for ^drunkenness. ¹⁸Through ^extreme laziness the rafters sag, and through idleness the house leaks. ¹⁹*People* prepare a meal for enjoyment, ^wine makes life joyful, and ᴮmoney is the answer to everything. ²⁰Furthermore, in your bedroom do not ^curse a king, and in your sleeping rooms do not curse a rich person; for a bird of the sky will bring the sound, and the winged one will make *your* word known.

CAST YOUR BREAD ON THE WATERS

11 ^Cast your bread on the surface of the waters, for you ^will find it after many days. ²Divide your portion to seven, or even to eight, for you do not know what ^misfortune may occur on the earth. ³If the clouds are full, they pour out rain on the earth; and whether a tree falls toward the south or toward the north, wherever the tree falls, there it lies. ⁴One who watches the wind will not sow and one who looks at the clouds will not harvest. ⁵Just as you do not know the path of the wind, and ^how bones *are formed* in the womb of the pregnant woman, so you do not ᴮknow the activity of God who makes everything.

⁶Sow your seed ^in the morning and do not be idle in the evening,

10:1 ^Ex 30:25   10:2 ^Matt 6:33; Col 3:1   10:3 ^Prov 13:16; 18:2   10:4 ^Eccl 8:3   ᴮ1 Sam 25:24-33   10:6 ^Esth 3:1, 5f; Prov 28:12   10:7 ^Esth 6:8-10   10:8 ^Ps 7:15; Prov 26:27   10:11 ^Ps 58:4, 5; Jer 8:17   10:12 ^Prov 10:32; 22:11   10:13 ^Eccl 7:25   10:14 ^Eccl 3:22; 6:12   10:16 ^Is 3:4, 12   10:17 ^Prov 31:4; Is 5:11   10:18 ^Prov 24:30-34   10:19 ^Judg 9:13   ᴮEccl 7:12   10:20 ^Ex 22:28; Acts 23:5   11:1 ^Deut 15:10; Prov 19:17   11:2 ^Eccl 11:8; 12:1   11:5 ^Ps 139:13-16   ᴮEccl 1:13   11:6 ^Eccl 9:10

for you do not know whether one or the other will succeed, or whether both of them alike will be good.

7The light is pleasant, and *it is* good for the eyes to ^see the sun. 8Indeed, if a person lives many years, let him ^rejoice in them all; but let him remember the ᴮdays of darkness, for they will be many. Everything that is to come *will be* futility.

9Rejoice, young man, during your childhood, and let your heart be pleasant during the days of young manhood. And follow the impulses of your heart and the desires of your eyes. Yet know that ^God will bring you to judgment for all these things. 10So remove sorrow from your heart and keep ^pain away from your body, because childhood and the prime of life are fleeting.

REMEMBER GOD IN YOUR YOUTH

12 ^Remember also your Creator in the days of your youth, before the ᴮevil days come and the years approach when you will say, "I have no pleasure in them"; 2before the ^sun and the light, the moon and the stars are darkened, and clouds return after the rain; 3on the day that the watchmen of the house tremble, and strong men are ^bent over, the grinders stop working because they are few, and those who look through windows grow ¹dim; 4and the doors on the street are shut as the ^sound of the grinding mill is low, and one will arise at the sound of the bird, and all the daughters of song will sing softly. 5Furthermore, *people* are afraid of a high place and of terrors on the road; the almond tree blossoms,

the grasshopper drags itself along, and the caper berry is ineffective. For man goes to his eternal ^home while the mourners move around in the street. 6*Remember your Creator* before the silver cord is broken and the ^golden bowl is crushed, the pitcher by the spring is shattered and the wheel at the cistern is crushed; 7then the ^dust will return to the earth as it was, and the spirit will return to ᴮGod who gave it. 8"^Futility of futilities," says the Preacher, "all is futility!"

PURPOSE OF THE PREACHER

9In addition to being wise, the Preacher also taught the people knowledge; and he pondered, searched out, and arranged ^many proverbs. 10The Preacher sought to find delightful words and to write ^words of truth correctly.

11The ^words of the wise are like ¹,ᴮgoads, and masters of *these* collections are like driven nails; they are given by one Shepherd. 12But beyond this, my son, be warned: the writing of ^many books is endless, and excessive ᴮstudy is wearying to the body.

13The conclusion, when everything has been heard, *is:* ^fear God and keep His commandments, because this *applies to* every person. 14For ^God will bring every act to judgment, everything which is hidden, whether it is good or evil.

11:7 ^Eccl 6:5; 7:11   11:8 ^Eccl 9:7   ᴮEccl 12:1
11:9 ^Eccl 3:17; 12:14   11:10 ^2 Cor 7:1; 2 Tim 2:22
12:1 ^Deut 8:18   ᴮEccl 11:8   12:2 ^Is 5:30; 13:10
12:3 ^Ps 35:14; 38:6   12:4 ^Jer 25:10; Rev 18:22
12:5 ^Job 17:13; 30:23   12:6 ^Zech 4:2, 3
12:7 ^Gen 3:19   ᴮNum 16:22   12:8 ^Eccl 1:2
12:9 ^1 Kin 4:32   12:10 ^Prov 22:20, 21   12:11 ^Prov 1:6
ᴮActs 2:37   12:12 ^1 Kin 4:32   ᴮEccl 1:18
12:13 ^Eccl 3:14; 5:7   12:14 ^Eccl 3:17; 11:9

12:3 ¹I.e., in their eyesight   12:11 ¹I.e., spiked sticks for driving cattle

THE SONG OF SOLOMON

1 The ¹Song of ᴬSongs, which is Solomon's.

†The Bride

2 "May he kiss me with the kisses of his mouth!
For your ᴬlove is sweeter than wine.
3 "Your oils have a pleasing fragrance,
Your ᴬname is *like* purified oil;
Therefore the young women love you.
4 "Draw me after you *and* let's run *together!*
The ᴬking has brought me into his chambers."

The Chorus

"We will rejoice in you and be joyful;
We will praise your love more than wine.
Rightly do they love you."

The Bride

5 "I am black and beautiful,
You daughters of Jerusalem,
Like the ᴬtents of ᴮKedar,
Like the curtains of Solomon.
6 "Do not stare at me because I am dark,
For the sun has tanned me.
My ᴬmother's sons were angry with me;
They made me ᴮcaretaker of the vineyards,
But I have not taken care of my own vineyard.

7 "Tell me, you ᴬwhom my soul loves,
Where do you pasture *your flock,*
Where do you have *it* lie down at noon?
For why should I be like one who veils herself
Beside the flocks of your ᴮcompanions?"

SOLOMON, THE LOVER, SPEAKS

8 "If you yourself do not know,
ᴬMost beautiful among women,
Go out on the trail of the flock,
And pasture your young goats
By the tents of the shepherds.

9 "To me, my darling, you are like
My ᴬmare among the chariots of Pharaoh.
10 "Your ᴬcheeks are delightful with jewelry,
Your neck with strings of ᴮbeads."

The Chorus

11 "We will make for you jewelry of gold
With beads of silver."

1:1ᴬ1 Kin 4:32   1:2ᴬSong 1:4; 4:10   1:3ᴬEccl 7:1
1:4ᴬSong 1:4; 4:10   1:5ᴬPs 120:5   ᴮIs 60:7
1:6ᴬPs 69:8   ᴮSong 8:11   1:7ᴬSong 3:1-4
ᴮSong 8:13   1:8ᴬSong 5:9; 6:1   1:9ᴬ2 Chr 1:16, 17
1:10ᴬSong 5:13   ᴮGen 24:53

1:1¹Or *Best of the Songs*   1:2†The speaker identifications are not from the Hebrew text nor the Septuagint, but reflect an ancient tradition which appears in some manuscripts.

The Bride

12 "While the king was at his
    table,
  My ^perfume gave forth its
    fragrance.
13 "My beloved is to me a pouch
    of ^myrrh
  Which lies all night between
    my breasts.
14 "My beloved is to me a cluster
    of ^henna blossoms
  In the vineyards of ^Engedi."

The Groom

15 "How beautiful you are, my
    darling,
  How beautiful you are!
  Your ^eyes are *like* doves."

The Bride

16 "How handsome you are,
    ^my beloved,
  And so delightful!
  Indeed, our bed is
    luxuriant!
17 "The beams of our house are
    ^cedars,
  Our rafters, junipers.

THE BRIDE'S ADMIRATION

2 "I am the rose of ^Sharon,
  The lily of the valleys."

The Groom

2 "Like a lily among the thorns,
  So is ^my darling among the
    young women."

The Bride

3 "Like an ^apple tree among the
    trees of the forest,
  So is my beloved among the
    young men.
  In his shade I took great
    delight and sat down,
  And his fruit was sweet to
    my taste.

4 "He has ^brought me to *his*
    banquet hall,
  And his ^banner over me is
    love.
5 "Refresh me with ^raisin cakes,
  Sustain me with apples,
  Because I am lovesick.
6 "^His left hand is under my
    head,
  And ^his right hand
    ^embraces me."

The Groom

7 "^Swear to me, you daughters
    of Jerusalem,
  By the gazelles or by the does
    of the field,
  ^That you will not disturb or
    awaken *my* love
  Until she pleases."

The Bride

8 "Listen! My beloved!
  Behold, he is coming,
  Leaping ^on the mountains,
  Jumping on the hills!
9 "My beloved is like a ^gazelle or
    a young stag.
  Behold, he is standing behind
    our wall,
  He is looking through the
    windows,
  He is peering through the
    lattice.

10 "My beloved responded and
    said to me,
  '^Arise, my darling, my
    beautiful one,
  And come along.

1:12 ^Song 4:14; Mark 14:3   1:13 ^Ps 45:8; John 19:39
1:14 ^Song 4:13   ^1 Sam 23:29   1:15 ^Song 4:1; 5:12
1:16 ^Song 2:3, 9, 17; 5:2, 5, 6, 8   1:17 ^1 Kin 6:9, 10;
Jer 22:14   2:1 ^Is 33:9; 35:2   2:2 ^Song 1:9
2:3 ^Song 8:5   2:4 ^Song 1:4   ^Ps 20:5
2:5 ^2 Sam 6:19; 1 Chr 16:3   2:6 ^Song 8:3   ^Prov 4:8
2:7 ^Song 3:5; 5:8, 9   2:8 ^Song 2:17; Is 52:7
2:9 ^Prov 6:5; Song 2:17   2:10 ^Song 2:13

¹¹ 'For behold, the winter is
     past,
     The rain is over *and* gone.
¹² 'The blossoms have *already*
     appeared in the land;
     The time has arrived for
     pruning *the vines,*
     And the voice of the
     ^Aturtledove has been heard
     in our land.
¹³ 'The ^Afig tree has ripened its
     fruit,
     And the vines in blossom
     have given forth *their*
     fragrance.
     Arise, my darling, my
     beautiful one,
     And come along!'"

The Groom

¹⁴ "^AMy dove, ^Bin the clefts of the
     rock,
     In the hiding place of the
     mountain pathway,
     Let me see how you look,
     Let me hear your voice;
     For your voice is pleasant,
     And you look delightful."

The Chorus

¹⁵ "^ACatch the foxes for us,
     The little foxes that are
     ruining the vineyards,
     While our vineyards are in
     blossom."

The Bride

¹⁶ "^AMy beloved is mine, and I am
     his;
     He pastures *his flock* among
     the lilies.
¹⁷ "^AUntil the cool of the day,
     when the shadows flee,
     Turn, my beloved, and be like
     a ^Bgazelle
     Or a young stag on the
     mountains of Bether."

THE BRIDE'S TROUBLED DREAM

3 "On my bed night after night I
     sought him
     ^AWhom my soul loves;
     I sought him but did not find
     him.
² 'I must arise now and go
     around in the city;
     In the ^Astreets and in the
     public squares
     I must seek him whom my soul
     loves.'
     I sought him but did not find
     him.
³ "^AThe watchmen who make the
     rounds in the city found me,
     And I said, 'Have you seen him
     whom my soul loves?'
⁴ "^AHardly had I left them
     When I found him whom my
     soul loves;
     I ^Bheld on to him and would
     not let him go
     Until I had brought him to my
     mother's house,
     And into the room of her who
     conceived me."

The Groom

⁵ "^ASwear to me, you daughters of
     Jerusalem,
     By the gazelles or by the does
     of the field,
     That you will not disturb or
     awaken *my* love
     Until she pleases."

SOLOMON'S WEDDING DAY

The Bride

⁶ "What is this coming up from
     the wilderness
     Like ^Acolumns of smoke,

2:12 ^AGen 15:9; Ps 74:19   2:13 ^AMatt 24:32
2:14 ^ASong 5:2   ^BJer 48:28   2:15 ^AEzek 13:4;
Luke 13:32   2:16 ^ASong 6:3; 7:10   2:17 ^ASong 4:6
^BSong 2:9   3:1 ^ASong 1:7   3:2 ^AJer 5:1   3:3 ^ASong 5:7;
Is 21:6-8, 11, 12   3:4 ^AProv 8:17   ^BProv 4:13
3:5 ^ASong 2:7; 5:8   3:6 ^AEx 13:21

Perfumed with myrrh and
  [B]frankincense,
With all the scented powders
  of the merchant?

The Chorus

7 "Behold, it is the *traveling*
  couch of Solomon;
Sixty warriors around it,
Of the warriors of Israel.
8 "All of them are wielders of the
  sword,
  [A]Expert in war;
Each man has his sword at his
  side,
Guarding against the terrors of
  the night.
9 "King Solomon has made for
  himself a sedan chair
From the timber of Lebanon.
10 "He made its posts of silver,
Its back of gold
And its seat of purple fabric,
With its interior lovingly inlaid
By the [A]daughters of Jerusalem.
11 "Go out, you [A]daughters of Zion,
And look at King Solomon
  with the crown
With which his mother has
  crowned him
On the [B]day of his wedding,
And on the day of the joy of
  his heart."

SOLOMON'S LOVE EXPRESSED

4 "How beautiful you are, my
  darling,
How beautiful you are!
Your [A]eyes are *like* doves
  behind your veil;
Your [B]hair is like a flock of goats
That have descended from
  Mount Gilead.
2 "Your [A]teeth are like a flock of
  newly shorn *sheep*
Which have come up from
  their watering place,

All of which bear twins,
And not one among them has
  lost her young.
3 "Your lips are like a [A]scarlet
  thread,
And your mouth is beautiful.
Your temples are like a slice of
  a pomegranate
Behind your veil.
4 "Your [A]neck is like the tower of
  David,
Built with layers of stones
On which are hung a
  thousand shields,
All the round shields of the
  warriors.
5 "Your [A]two breasts are like two
  fawns,
Twins of a gazelle
That graze among the lilies.
6 "[A]Until the cool of the day
When the shadows flee,
I will go my way to the
  mountain of [B]myrrh
And to the hill of
  [B]frankincense.

7 "[A]You are altogether beautiful,
  my darling,
And there is no blemish on
  you.
8 "*Come* with me from [A]Lebanon,
  my bride,
You shall come with me from
  Lebanon.
You shall come down from the
  summit of Amana,
From the summit of Senir and
  Hermon,
From the dens of lions,
From the mountains of
  leopards.

3:6 [B]Ex 30:34   3:8 [A]Jer 50:9   3:10 [A]Song 1:5
3:11 [A]Is 3:16, 17   [B]Is 62:5   4:1 [A]Song 1:15
[B]Song 6:5   4:2 [A]Song 6:6   4:3 [A]Josh 2:18
4:4 [A]Song 7:4   4:5 [A]Song 7:3   4:6 [A]Song 2:17
[B]Song 4:14   4:7 [A]Song 1:15; Eph 5:27
4:8 [A]1 Kin 4:33; Ps 72:16

9 "You have enchanted my heart,
   my sister, *my* bride;
   You have enchanted my heart
   with a single *glance* of your
   eyes,
   With a single strand of your
   ^necklace.

10 "^How beautiful is your love,
   my sister, *my* bride!
   How much sweeter is your
   love than wine,
   And the fragrance of your
   oils
   Than *that of* all *kinds of*
   balsam oils!

11 "Your lips drip honey, *my*
   bride;
   Honey and milk are under
   your tongue,
   And the fragrance of your
   garments is like the
   ^fragrance of Lebanon.

12 "A locked garden is my sister,
   my bride,
   A locked spring, a sealed
   ^fountain.

13 "Your branches are an ^orchard
   of ^Bpomegranates
   With delicious fruits, henna
   with nard plants,

14 Nard and saffron, spice reed
   and cinnamon,
   With all the trees of
   ^frankincense,
   ^BMyrrh, and aloes, along with
   all the finest balsam oils.

15 "*You are* a garden spring,
   A well of ^fresh water,
   And flowing *streams* from
   Lebanon."

The Bride

16 "Awake, north *wind*,
   And come, *wind of* the south;
   Make my garden breathe out
   fragrance,
   May its balsam oils flow.

May ^my beloved come into
his garden
And eat its ^Bdelicious fruits!"

THE TORMENT OF SEPARATION

The Groom

5 "I have come into my garden,
   my sister, *my* bride;
   I have gathered my ^myrrh
   along with my balsam.
   I have eaten my honeycomb
   with my honey;
   I have drunk my wine with my
   milk.
   Eat, ^Bfriends;
   Drink and drink deeply,
   lovers."

The Bride

2 "I was asleep but my heart was
   awake.
   A voice! My beloved was
   knocking:
   'Open to me, my sister, my
   darling,
   ^My dove, my perfect one!
   For my head is drenched with
   dew,
   My ^Blocks with the dew drops
   of the night.'

3 "I have ^taken off my dress,
   How can I put it on *again*?
   I have ^Bwashed my feet,
   How can I dirty them *again*?

4 "My beloved extended his hand
   through the opening,
   And my ^feelings were stirred
   for him.

5 "I arose to open to my beloved;
   And my hands ^dripped with
   myrrh,

4:9 ^Gen 41:42; Prov 1:9   **4:10** ^Song 7:6
4:11 ^Gen 27:27; Hos 14:6   **4:12** ^Gen 29:3
4:13 ^Eccl 2:5   ^BSong 6:11   **4:14** ^Song 4:6   ^BPs 45:8
4:15 ^Zech 14:8; John 4:10   **4:16** ^Song 1:13
^BSong 4:13   **5:1** ^Song 1:13   ^BJudg 14:11, 20
5:2 ^Song 2:14   ^BSong 5:11   **5:3** ^Luke 11:7
^BGen 19:2   **5:4** ^Jer 31:20   **5:5** ^Song 5:13

And my fingers with drops of
  myrrh,
On the handles of the bolt.
6 "I opened to my beloved,
But my beloved had ^turned
  away *and* had gone!
My heart went out *to him* as he
  spoke.
I searched for him but I did not
  find him;
I called him but he did not
  answer me.
7 "The ^watchmen who make
  the rounds in the city
  found me,
They struck me *and* wounded
  me;
The guards of the walls took
  my shawl away from me.
8 "Swear to me, you daughters of
  Jerusalem,
If you find my beloved,
As to what you will tell him:
For ^I am lovesick."

The Chorus

9 "What kind of beloved is your
  beloved,
O ^most beautiful among
  women?
What kind of beloved is your
  beloved,
That you make us swear in this
  way?"

ADMIRATION BY THE BRIDE
The Bride

10 "My beloved is dazzling and
  ^reddish,
^Outstanding among ten
  thousand.
11 "His head is *like* gold, pure gold;
His ^locks are *like* clusters of
  dates
And black as a raven.
12 "His ^eyes are like doves
Beside streams of water,

Bathed in milk,
And perched in *their* ^setting.
13 "His cheeks are like a ^bed of
  balsam,
Banks of herbal spices;
His lips are ^lilies
Dripping with drops of myrrh.
14 "His hands are rods of gold
Set with ^topaz;
His abdomen is panels of ivory
Covered with ^sapphires.
15 "His thighs are pillars of
  alabaster
Set on pedestals of pure gold;
His appearance is like
  ^Lebanon,
Choice as the cedars.
16 "His ^mouth is *full of*
  sweetness.
And he is wholly ^desirable.
This is my beloved and this is
  my friend,
You daughters of Jerusalem."

MUTUAL DELIGHT IN EACH OTHER
The Chorus

6 "^Where has your beloved
  gone,
O most beautiful among
  women?
Where has your beloved
  turned,
That we may seek him with
  you?"

The Bride

2 "My beloved has gone down to
  his garden,
To the beds of balsam,
To pasture *his flock* in the
  gardens
And gather ^lilies.

5:6 ^Song 6:1   5:7 ^Song 3:3   5:8 ^Song 2:5
5:9 ^Song 1:8; 6:1   5:10 ^1 Sam 16:12   ^Ps 45:2
5:11 ^Song 5:2   5:12 ^Song 1:15   ^Ex 25:7
5:13 ^Song 6:2   ^Song 2:1   5:14 ^Ex 28:20
^Ex 24:10   5:15 ^Song 7:4   5:16 ^Song 7:9
^2 Sam 1:23   6:1 ^Song 5:6   6:2 ^Song 2:1; 5:13

3 "^AI am my beloved's and my
   beloved is mine,
   He who pastures *his flock*
   among the lilies."

The Groom

4 "^AYou are as beautiful as
   ^BTirzah, my darling,
   As lovely as Jerusalem,
   As awesome as an army with
   banners.

5 "Turn your eyes away from me,
   For they have confused me;
   ^AYour hair is like a flock of
   goats
   That have descended from
   Gilead.

6 "^AYour teeth are like a flock of
   ewes
   That have come up from *their*
   watering place,
   All of which bear twins,
   And not one among them has
   lost her young.

7 "^AYour temples are like a slice
   of a pomegranate
   Behind your veil.

8 "There are sixty queens and
   eighty concubines,
   And ^Ayoung women without
   number;

9 *But* ^Amy dove, my perfect one,
   is unique:
   She is her mother's only
   daughter;
   She is the pure *child* of the
   one who gave birth to her.
   The ^Byoung women saw her
   and called her blessed,
   The queens and the
   concubines *also,* and they
   praised her, *saying,*

10 'Who is this who looks down
   like the dawn,
   As beautiful as the full
   ^Amoon,

As pure ^Bas the sun,
   As awesome as an army with
   banners?'

11 "I went down to the orchard of
   nut trees
   To see the plants of the valley,
   To see whether the vine had
   grown
   Or the ^Apomegranates had
   bloomed.

12 "Before I was aware, my soul
   set me
   Over the chariots of my noble
   people."

The Chorus

13 "Come back, come back,
   O Shulammite;
   Come back, come back, so
   that we may look at you!"

The Groom

"Why should you look at the
   Shulammite,
   As at the ^Adance of the two
   armies?

ADMIRATION BY THE GROOM

7 "How beautiful are your feet
   in sandals,
   ^APrince's daughter!
   The curves of your hips are
   like jewels,
   The work of the hands of an
   artist.

2 "Your navel is *like* a round goblet
   That never lacks mixed wine;
   Your belly is *like* a heap of
   wheat,
   Surrounded with lilies.

3 "Your ^Atwo breasts are like two
   fawns,
   Twins of a gazelle.

6:3 ^ASong 2:16; 7:10   6:4 ^ASong 1:15   ^B1 Kin 14:17
6:5 ^ASong 4:1   6:6 ^ASong 4:2   6:7 ^ASong 4:3
6:8 ^ASong 1:3   6:9 ^ASong 2:14   ^BGen 30:13
6:10 ^AJob 31:26   ^BMatt 17:2   6:11 ^ASong 4:13
6:13 ^AJudg 21:21   7:1 ^APs 45:13   7:3 ^ASong 4:5

4 "Your ^neck is like a tower of
      ivory,
   Your eyes *like the* pools in
      ᴮHeshbon
   By the gate of Bath-rabbim;
   Your nose is like the tower of
      Lebanon,
   Which looks toward Damascus.
5 "Your head crowns you like
      ^Carmel,
   And the flowing hair of your
      head is like purple threads;
   The king is captivated by *your*
      tresses.
6 "How ^beautiful and how
      delightful you are,
   My love, with *all* your delights!
7 "Your stature is like a palm tree,
   And your breasts are *like its*
      clusters.
8 "I said, 'I will climb the palm tree,
   I will grasp its fruit stalks.'
   Oh, may your breasts be like
      clusters of the vine,
   And the fragrance of your
      breath like ^apples,
9   And your ^mouth like the best
      wine!"

The Bride

   "It ᴮgoes *down* smoothly for my
      beloved,
   Flowing gently *through* the
      lips of those who are asleep.

THE UNION OF LOVE

10 "^I am my beloved's,
   And his ᴮdesire is for me.
11 "Come, my beloved, let's go out
      to the country,
   Let's spend the night in the
      villages.
12 "Let's rise early *and go* to the
      vineyards;
   Let's ^see whether the vine has
      grown
   And its buds have opened,

And whether the
      pomegranates have bloomed.
   There I will give you my love.
13 "The ^mandrakes have given
      forth fragrance;
   And over our doors are all
      delicious *fruits,*
   New as well as old,
   Which I have saved for you, my
      beloved.

THE LOVERS SPEAK

8 "Oh that you were like a
      brother to me
   Who nursed at my mother's
      breasts.
   If I found you outdoors, I
      would kiss you;
   No one would despise me,
      either.
2 "I would lead you *and* ^bring you
   Into the house of my mother,
      who used to instruct me;
   I would give you spiced wine
      to drink from the juice of my
      pomegranates.
3 "*Let* ^his left hand *be* under my
      head,
   And his right hand embrace
      me."

The Groom

4 "^Swear to me, you daughters of
      Jerusalem:
   Do not disturb or awaken *my*
      love
   Until she pleases."

The Chorus

5 "^Who is this coming up from
      the wilderness,
   Leaning on her beloved?"

7:4 ^Song 4:4   ᴮNum 21:26   7:5 ^Is 35:2
7:6 ^Song 1:15, 16; 4:10   7:8 ^Song 2:5
7:9 ^Song 5:16   ᴮProv 23:31
7:10 ^Song 2:16   ᴮPs 45:11   7:12 ^Song 6:11
7:13 ^Gen 30:14   8:2 ^Song 3:4   8:3 ^Song 2:6
8:4 ^Song 2:7; 3:5   8:5 ^Song 3:6

The Bride

"Beneath the ᴮapple tree I
   awakened you;
There your mother went into
   labor with you,
There she was in labor *and*
   gave birth to you.
6 "Put me like a seal over your
      heart,
Like a ᴬseal on your arm.
For love is as strong as death,
ᴮJealousy is as severe as
   Sheol;
Its flames are flames of fire,
The flame of the Lᴏʀᴅ.
7 "Many waters cannot quench
      love,
Nor will rivers flood over it;
ᴬIf a man were to give all the
   riches of his house for love,
It would be utterly despised."

The Chorus

8 "We have a little sister,
And she ᴬhas no breasts;
What shall we do for our
   sister
On the day when she is
   spoken for?
9 "If she is a wall,
We will build on her a
   battlement of silver;
But if she is a door,
We will barricade her with
   ᴬplanks of cedar."

The Bride

10 "I was a wall, and ᴬmy breasts
      were like towers;
Then I became in his eyes as
   one who finds peace.
11 "Solomon had a ᴬvineyard at
      Baal-hamon;
He ᴮentrusted the vineyard to
   caretakers.
Each one was to bring a
   thousand *shekels* of silver for
   its fruit.
12 "My very own vineyard is at my
      disposal;
The thousand *shekels* are for
   you, Solomon,
And two hundred are for those
   who take care of its fruit."

The Groom

13 "You who sit in the gardens:
My ᴬcompanions are listening
   for your voice—
ᴮLet me hear it!"

The Bride

14 "Hurry, my beloved,
And be ᴬlike a gazelle or a
   young stag
On the ᴮmountains of balsam
   trees!"

8:5 ᴮSong 2:3   8:6 ᴬIs 49:16   ᴮProv 6:34
8:7 ᴬProv 6:35   8:8 ᴬEzek 16:7   8:9 ᴬ1 Kin 6:15
8:10 ᴬEzek 16:7   8:11 ᴬEccl 2:4   ᴮMatt 21:33
8:13 ᴬSong 1:7   ᴮSong 2:14   8:14 ᴬSong 2:7, 9, 17
ᴮSong 4:6

ISAIAH

REBELLION OF GOD'S PEOPLE

1 The vision of Isaiah the son of Amoz concerning Judah and Jerusalem, which he saw during the reigns of Uzziah, Jotham, ^Ahaz, *and* ^BHezekiah, kings of Judah.

2 Listen, heavens, and hear, earth;
    For the LORD has spoken:
    "^ASons I have raised and
        brought up,
    But they have ^Brevolted against
        Me.

3 "An ox knows its owner,
    And a donkey its master's
        manger,
    But Israel ^Adoes not know,
    My people ^Bdo not understand."

4 Oh, sinful nation,
    People weighed down with
        guilt,
    ^AOffspring of evildoers,
    Sons who act corruptly!
    They have abandoned the
        LORD,
    They have despised the Holy
        One of Israel,
    They have turned away from
        Him.

5 Where will you be stricken
        again,
    As you ^Acontinue in *your*
        rebellion?
    The entire head is sick
    And the entire heart is faint.

6 ^AFrom the sole of the foot even
        to the head
    There is nothing healthy in it,
    Only bruises, slashes, and raw
        wounds;
    Not pressed out nor bandaged,
    Nor softened with oil.

7 Your ^Aland is desolate,
    Your cities are burned with
        fire;
    As for your fields, strangers
        are devouring them in front
        of you;
    It is desolation, as overthrown
        by strangers.

8 The daughter of Zion is left
        like a shelter in a vineyard,
    Like a watchman's hut in a
        cucumber field, like a city
        under watch.

9 ^AIf the LORD of armies
    Had not left us a few
        ^Bsurvivors,
    We would be like Sodom,
    We would be like Gomorrah.

GOD HAS HAD ENOUGH

10 Hear ^Athe word of the LORD,
    You rulers of ^BSodom;
    Listen to the instruction of our
        God,
    You people of Gomorrah!

11 "^AWhat are your many sacrifices
        to Me?"
    Says the LORD.
    "I have had enough of burnt
        offerings of rams
    And the fat of fattened cattle;
    And I take no pleasure in the
        blood of bulls, lambs, or
        goats.

1:1 ^A 2 Kin 16:1-20   ^B 2 Kin 18:1-20:21   1:2 ^A Jer 3:22
^B Is 30:1, 9   1:3 ^A Jer 9:3, 6   ^B Is 44:18   1:4 ^A Is 14:20
1:5 ^A Is 31:6   1:6 ^A Job 2:7   1:7 ^A Lev 26:33; Jer 44:6
1:9 ^A Rom 9:29   ^B Is 10:20-22   1:10 ^A Is 8:20   ^B Is 3:9
1:11 ^A Ps 50:8; Jer 6:20

12 "When you come ^to appear
before Me,
Who requires of you
this trampling of My
courtyards?
13 "Do not go on bringing your
worthless offerings,
Incense is an abomination to
Me.
New moon and Sabbath,
the proclamation of an
assembly—
I cannot ^endure wrongdoing
and the festive assembly.
14 "I hate your new moon
festivals and your
^appointed feasts,
They have become a burden
to Me;
I am ^Btired of bearing *them.*
15 "So when you spread out your
hands *in prayer,*
^I will hide My eyes from you;
Yes, even though you offer
many prayers,
I will not be listening.
^BYour hands are covered with
blood.

16 "Wash yourselves, make
yourselves clean;
^Remove the evil of your
deeds from My sight.
^BStop doing evil,
17 Learn to do good;
^Seek justice,
Rebuke the oppressor,
^BObtain justice for the
orphan,
Plead for the widow's case.

INVITATION TO DEBATE

18 "Come now, and ^let us debate
your case,"
Says the LORD,
"Though your sins are as
scarlet,

They shall become as white as
snow;
Though they are red like
crimson,
They shall be like wool.
19 "^If you are willing and
obedient,
You will ^Beat the best of the
land;
20 But if you refuse and rebel,
You will be ^devoured by the
sword."
For ^Bthe mouth of the LORD
has spoken.

ZION CORRUPTED; WILL BE REDEEMED

21 How the faithful city has
become a ^prostitute,
She *who* was full of justice!
Righteousness *once* dwelt in
her,
But now murderers.
22 Your silver has become waste
matter,
Your drink diluted with water.
23 Your ^rulers are rebels
And companions of thieves;
Everyone loves a bribe
And chases after gifts.
They do not obtain justice for
the orphan,
Nor does the widow's case
come before them.

24 Therefore the Lord GOD of
armies,
The Mighty One of Israel,
declares,
"Ah, I will have satisfaction
against My adversaries,
And ^avenge Myself on My
enemies.

1:12 ^Ex 23:17   1:13 ^Jer 7:9, 10   1:14 ^Is 29:1, 2
^BIs 7:13   1:15 ^Is 8:17   ^BIs 59:3   1:16 ^Is 55:7
^BJer 25:5   1:17 ^Jer 22:3   ^BPs 82:3   1:18 ^Is 41:1, 21;
43:26   1:19 ^Deut 28:1   ^BIs 55:2   1:20 ^Is 3:25
^BIs 40:5   1:21 ^Is 57:3-9; Jer 2:20   1:23 ^Hos 5:10;
Mic 7:3   1:24 ^Deut 28:63; Is 35:4

25 "I will also turn My hand
        against you,
    And ^smelt away your
        impurities as with lye;
    And I will remove all your slag.
26 "Then I will restore your ^judges
        as at first,
    And your counselors as at the
        beginning;
    After that you will be called
        the city of righteousness,
    A faithful city."

27 Zion will be ^redeemed with
        justice
    And her repentant ones with
        righteousness.
28 But wrongdoers and sinners
        together will be ^broken,
    And those who abandon the
        LORD will come to an end.
29 You certainly will be ashamed
        of the ^oaks which you have
        desired,
    And you will be embarrassed
        by the ^gardens which you
        have chosen.
30 For you will be like an oak
        whose ^leaf withers away,
    Or like a garden that has no
        water.
31 The strong man will become
        like flax fiber,
    And his work a spark.
    So they shall both burn
        together
    And there will be ^no one to
        extinguish *them.*

GOD'S UNIVERSAL REIGN

2   The word which ^Isaiah the son
    of Amoz saw concerning Judah
and Jerusalem.
2   Now it will come about that
        ^In the last days
    The mountain of the house of
        the LORD

    Will be established as the
        chief of the mountains,
    And will be raised above the
        hills;
    And all the nations will
        stream to it.
3   And many peoples will come
        and say,
    "Come, let's go up to the
        mountain of the LORD,
    To the house of the God of
        Jacob;
    So that He may teach us about
        His ways,
    And that we may walk in His
        paths."
    For the law will go out ^from
        Zion
    And the word of the LORD
        from Jerusalem.
4   And He will judge between
        the nations,
    And will mediate for many
        peoples;
    And ^they will beat their swords
        into plowshares, and their
        spears into pruning knives.
    Nation will not lift up a sword
        against nation,
    And never again will they
        learn war.

5   Come, house of Jacob, and let's
        walk in the ^light of the LORD.
6   For You have ^abandoned Your
        people, the house of Jacob,
    Because they are filled *with
        influences* from the east,
    And *they are* soothsayers like
        the Philistines.
    They also strike *bargains* with
        the children of foreigners.

1:25 ^Ezek 22:19–22; Mal 3:3   1:26 ^Is 60:17
1:27 ^Is 35:9f; 62:12   1:28 ^Ps 9:5; Is 66:24
1:29 ^Is 57:5   ^BIs 65:3   1:30 ^Is 64:6   1:31 ^Is 66:24;
Matt 3:12   2:1 ^Is 1:1   2:2 ^Mic 4:1–3   2:3 ^Is 51:4, 5;
Luke 24:47   2:4 ^Is 32:17, 18; Joel 3:10
2:5 ^Is 60:1, 2, 19, 20; 1 John 1:5   2:6 ^Deut 31:17

7 Their land has also been filled
with silver and gold
And there is no end to their
treasures;
Their land has also been filled
with ^horses,
And there is no end to their
chariots.
8 Their land has also been ^filled
with idols;
They worship the work of
their hands,
That which their fingers have
made.
9 So *the common* person has
been humbled
And *the* person *of importance*
has been brought low,
But ^do not forgive them.
10 ^Enter the rocky *place* and
hide in the dust
^BFrom the terror of the LORD
and from the splendor of His
majesty.
11 The ^proud look of humanity
will be brought low,
And the arrogance of people
will be humbled;
And the LORD alone will be
exalted on that day.

A DAY OF RECKONING COMING

12 For the LORD of armies will
have a day *of reckoning*
Against ^everyone who is
arrogant and haughty,
And against everyone who is
lifted up,
That he may be brought low.
13 And *it will be* against all the
cedars of Lebanon that are
lofty and lifted up,
Against all the ^oaks of Bashan,
14 Against all the ^lofty
mountains,
And against all the hills that are
lifted up,

15 Against every ^high tower,
Against every fortified wall,
16 Against all the ^ships of Tarshish
And against all the delightful
ships.
17 And the pride of humanity will
be humbled
And the arrogance of people
will be brought low;
And the LORD alone will be
exalted on that day,
18 And the ^idols will completely
vanish.
19 *People* will ^go into caves of the
rocks
And into holes in the ground
Away from the terror of the
LORD
And the splendor of His
majesty,
When He arises to terrify the
earth.
20 On that day people will ^throw
away to the moles and the
^Bbats
Their idols of silver and their
idols of gold,
Which they made for
themselves to worship,
21 In order to ^go into the clefts of
the rocks and the crannies of
the cliffs
Before the terror of the LORD
and the splendor of His
majesty,
When He arises to terrify the
earth.
22 ^Take no account of man, whose
breath *of life* is in his nostrils;
For ^Bwhy should he be
esteemed?

2:7 ^Deut 17:16; Is 30:16   **2:8** ^Is 10:11   **2:9** ^Neh 4:5
2:10 ^Is 2:19, 21   ^B2 Thess 1:9   **2:11** ^Is 5:15; 37:23
2:12 ^Job 40:11, 12; Is 24:4, 21   **2:13** ^Zech 11:2
2:14 ^Is 40:4   **2:15** ^Is 25:12   **2:16** ^1 Kin 10:22;
Is 23:1, 14   **2:18** ^Is 21:9; Mic 1:7   **2:19** ^Is 2:10
2:20 ^Is 30:22   ^BLev 11:19   **2:21** ^Is 2:19
2:22 ^Ps 146:3   ^BIs 40:15, 17

GOD WILL REMOVE THE LEADERS

3 For behold, the Lord GOD of armies ^is going to remove from Jerusalem and Judah
Both supply and support, the entire supply of bread
And the entire supply of water;

2 ^The mighty man and the warrior,
The judge and the prophet,
The diviner and the elder,

3 The captain of fifty and the esteemed *person,*
The counselor and the expert artisan,
And the skillful enchanter.

4 And I will make *mere* ^boys their leaders,
And mischievous *children* will rule over them,

5 And the people will be ^oppressed,
Each one by another, and each one by his neighbor;
The youth will assault the elder,
And the contemptible *person will assault* the one honored.

6 When a man ^lays hold of his brother in his father's house, *saying,*
"You have a cloak, you shall be our ruler!
And these ruins will be under your authority,"

7 He will protest on that day, saying,
"I will not be *your* ^healer,
For in my house there is neither bread nor cloak;
You should not appoint me ruler of the people."

8 For Jerusalem has stumbled and Judah has fallen,
Because their ^speech and their actions are against the LORD,
To ^Brebel against His glorious presence.

9 The expression of their faces testifies against them,
And they display their sin like Sodom;
They do not *even* conceal *it.*
Woe to them!
For they have ^done evil to themselves.

10 Say to the ^righteous that *it will go* well *for them,*
For they will eat the fruit of their actions.

11 Woe to the wicked! *It will go* badly *for him,*
For ^what he deserves will be done to him.

12 My people! Their oppressors ^treat them violently,
And women rule over them.
My people! ^BThose who guide you lead *you* astray
And confuse the direction of your paths.

GOD WILL JUDGE

13 ^The LORD arises to contend,
And stands to judge the people.

14 The LORD ^enters into judgment with the elders and leaders of His people,
"It is you who have devoured the vineyard;
The goods stolen from the poor are in your houses.

15 "What do you mean by ^crushing My people
And oppressing the face of the poor?"
Declares the Lord GOD of armies.

3:1 ^Lev 26:26; Is 5:13   3:2 ^2 Kin 24:14; Is 9:14, 15
3:4 ^Eccl 10:16   3:5 ^Mic 7:3–6   3:6 ^Is 4:1
3:7 ^Ezek 34:4; Hos 5:13   3:8 ^Ps 73:9–11   ^BIs 65:3
3:9 ^Prov 8:36; 15:32   3:10 ^Deut 28:1–14; Eccl 8:12
3:11 ^Deut 28:15–68; Is 65:6, 7   3:12 ^Is 3:4   ^BIs 9:16
3:13 ^Is 66:16; Hos 4:1   3:14 ^Job 22:4; Ps 143:2
3:15 ^Ps 94:5

JUDAH'S WOMEN DENOUNCED

16 Moreover, the LORD said,
   "Because the ^daughters of
       Zion are haughty
   And walk with heads held
       high and seductive eyes,
   And go along with mincing
       steps
   And jingle the anklets on
       their feet,
17 The Lord will afflict the scalp
       of the daughters of Zion
       with scabs,
   And the LORD will make their
       foreheads bare."

18 On that day the Lord will take
away the beauty of *their* anklets,
headbands, ^crescent ornaments,
19 dangling earrings, bracelets,
veils, 20^headdresses, ankle chains,
sashes, perfume boxes, amulets,
21 finger rings, ^nose rings, 22 festive robes, outer garments, shawls,
purses, 23 papyrus garments, undergarments, headbands, and veils.

24 Now it will come about that
       instead of balsam oil there
       will be a stench;
   Instead of a belt, a rope;
   Instead of ^well-set hair, a
       ^plucked-out scalp;
   Instead of fine clothes, a robe
       of sackcloth;
   And branding instead of
       beauty.
25 Your men will ^fall by the sword
   And your mighty ones in battle.
26 And her gates will lament and
       mourn,
   And she will ^sit deserted on
       the ground.

A REMNANT PREPARED

4 For seven women will take hold
of ^one man on that day, saying, "We will eat our own bread and
wear our own clothes, only let us
be called by your name; ^take away
our disgrace!"

2 On that day the ^Branch of the
LORD will be beautiful and glorious,
and the ^fruit of the earth *will be*
the pride and the beauty of the survivors of Israel. 3 And it will come
about that the one who is left in
Zion and remains behind in Jerusalem will be called ^holy—everyone
who is ^recorded for life in Jerusalem. 4 When the Lord has washed
away the filth of the daughters of
Zion and purged the bloodshed of
Jerusalem from her midst, by the
^spirit of judgment and the ^spirit of
burning, 5 then the LORD will create
over the entire area of Mount Zion
and over her assemblies ^a cloud
by day, and smoke, and the brightness of a flaming fire by night; for
over all the glory will be a canopy.
6 And there will be a ^shelter to *give*
shade from the heat by day, and refuge and protection from the storm
and the rain.

PARABLE OF THE VINEYARD

5 Let me sing now for my beloved
   A song of my beloved about
       His vineyard.
   My beloved had a ^vineyard on
       a fertile hill.
2   He dug it all around, cleared it
       of stones,
   And planted it with the
       ^choicest vine.
   And He built a tower in the
       middle of it,
   And also carved out a wine vat
       in it;

3:16 ^Song 3:11; Is 3:16-4:1, 4   3:18 ^Judg 8:21, 26
3:20 ^Ex 39:28   3:21 ^Gen 24:47; Ezek 16:12
3:24 ^1 Pet 3:3   ^Is 22:12   3:25 ^Is 1:20; 65:12
3:26 ^Lam 2:10   4:1 ^Is 13:12   ^Gen 30:23   4:2 ^Is 11:1
^Ps 72:16   4:3 ^Is 52:1   ^Ex 32:32   4:4 ^Is 28:6
^Is 1:31   4:5 ^Ex 13:21, 22; 24:16   4:6 ^Ps 27:5; Is 25:4
5:1 ^Ps 80:8; Jer 12:10   5:2 ^Jer 2:21

Then He expected *it* to
produce *good* grapes,
But it produced *only* worthless
ones.

3 "And now, you inhabitants of
Jerusalem and people of
Judah,
^Judge between Me and My
vineyard.

4 "^What more was there to do for
My vineyard that I have not
done in it?
Why, *when* I expected *it* to
produce *good* grapes did it
produce worthless ones?

5 "So now let Me tell you what
I am going to do to My
vineyard:
I will ^remove its hedge and it
will be consumed;
I will break down its wall and
it will become trampled
ground.

6 "I will ^lay it waste;
It will not be pruned nor hoed,
But briars and thorns will
come up.
I will also command the
clouds not to ^rain on it."

7 For the ^vineyard of the Lord of
armies is the house of Israel,
And the people of Judah are
His delightful plant.
So He waited for justice,
but behold, *there was*
bloodshed;
For righteousness, but behold,
a cry for help.

WOES FOR THE WICKED

8 Woe to those who ^attach house
to house *and* join field to field,
Until there is no more room,
And you alone are a landowner
in the midst of the land!

9 In my ears the Lord of armies
has sworn, "^Many houses
shall certainly become
^desolate,
Even great and fine ones,
without occupants.

10 "For ten acres of vineyard will
yield *only* one ^1bath *of wine,*
And a ^2,^homer of seed will
yield *only* an ^3ephah of grain."

11 Woe to those who rise early
in the morning so that they
may pursue ^intoxicating
drink,
Who stay up late in the
evening so that wine may
inflame them!

12 Their banquets are
accompanied by lyre and
harp, *by* tambourine and
flute, and *by* wine;
But they ^do not pay attention
to the deeds of the Lord,
Nor do they consider the work
of His hands.

13 Therefore My people go
into exile for their ^lack of
knowledge;
And their nobles are famished,
And their multitude is parched
with thirst.

14 Therefore ^Sheol has enlarged
its throat and opened its
mouth beyond measure;
And Jerusalem's splendor,
her multitude, her noise
of revelry, and the jubilant
within her, descend *into it.*

5:3 ^Matt 21:40   **5:4** ^2 Chr 36:16; Jer 2:5
5:5 ^Ps 89:40   **5:6** ^2 Chr 36:19-21   ^B1 Kin 8:35
5:7 ^Ps 80:8-11   **5:8** ^Jer 22:13-17; Mic 2:2
5:9 ^Is 6:11, 12   ^B Matt 23:38   **5:10** ^Ezek 45:11
5:11 ^Prov 23:29, 30; Eccl 10:16, 17   **5:12** ^Job 34:27;
Ps 28:5   **5:13** ^Is 1:3; 27:11   **5:14** ^Prov 30:16; Hab 2:5

5:10 ^1About 6 gallons or 23 liters   ^2About 7.7 cubic
feet or 0.22 cubit meters or more   ^3About 1 cubic
foot or 0.03 cubic meters

15 So *the common* people will be humbled and *the* person *of importance* brought low,
^The eyes of the haughty also will be brought low.

16 But the Lord of armies will be ^exalted in judgment,
And the holy God will show Himself ᴮholy in righteousness.

17 ^Then the lambs will graze as in their pasture,
And strangers will eat in the ruins of the wealthy.

18 Woe to those who drag ^wrongdoing with the cords of deceit,
And sin as if with cart ropes;

19 ^Who say, "Let Him hurry, let Him do His work quickly, so that we may see *it;*
And let the plan of the Holy One of Israel approach
And come to pass, so that we may know *it!*"

20 Woe to those who ^call evil good, and good evil;
Who ᴮsubstitute darkness for light and light for darkness;
Who substitute bitter for sweet and sweet for bitter!

21 Woe to those who are ^wise in their own eyes
And clever in their own sight!

22 ^Woe to those who are heroes in drinking wine,
And valiant men in mixing intoxicating drink,

23 ^Who declare the wicked innocent for a bribe,
And ᴮtake away the rights of the ones who are in the right!

24 Therefore, as a tongue of fire consumes stubble,
And dry grass collapses in the flame,
So their root will become like rot, and their blossom blow away like dust;
For they have ^rejected the Law of the Lord of armies,
And discarded the word of the Holy One of Israel.

25 For this reason the ^anger of the Lord has burned against His people,
And He has stretched out His hand against them and struck them.
And the mountains quaked, and their corpses lay like refuse in the middle of the streets.
ᴮDespite all this, His anger is not spent,
But His hand is still stretched out.

26 He will also lift up a ^flag to the distant nation,
And whistle for it from the ends of the earth;
And behold, it will come with speed swiftly.

27 ^No one in it is tired or stumbles,
No one slumbers or sleeps;
Nor is the ᴮundergarment at his waist loosened,
Nor his sandal strap broken.

28 ^Its arrows are sharp and all its bows are bent;

5:15^Is 2:11; 10:33   **5:16**^Is 2:11, 17   ᴮIs 8:13
5:17^Is 7:25; Mic 2:12   **5:18**^Is 59:4-8; Jer 23:10-14
5:19^Ezek 12:22; 2 Pet 3:4   **5:20**^Prov 17:15
ᴮJob 17:12   **5:21**^Prov 3:7; Rom 12:16
5:22^Prov 23:20; Is 5:11   **5:23**^Ex 23:8   ᴮPs 94:21
5:24^Is 8:6; 30:9, 12   **5:25**^2 Kin 22:13, 17
ᴮIs 9:12, 17, 19, 21   **5:26**^Is 13:2, 3   **5:27**^Joel 2:7, 8
ᴮJob 12:18   **5:28**^Ps 7:12, 13

The hoofs of its horses seem
like flint, and its *chariot*
wheels like a storm wind.
29 Its ^roaring is like a lioness,
and it roars like young lions;
It growls as it ^Bseizes the prey
And carries *it* off with no one
to save *it*.
30 And it will roar against it on that
day like the roaring of the sea.
If one ^looks across to the land,
behold, there is darkness
and distress;
Even the light is darkened by
its clouds.

ISAIAH'S VISION

6 In the year of King Uzziah's
death ^I saw the Lord sitting on
a throne, lofty and exalted, with
the train of His robe filling the
temple. 2 Seraphim were standing
above Him, ^each having six wings:
with two *each* covered his face,
and with two *each* covered his feet,
and with two *each* flew. 3 And one
called out to another and said,
"Holy, Holy, Holy, is the LORD of
armies.
The ^whole earth is full of His
glory."
4 And the foundations of the thresholds trembled at the voice of him
who called out, while the ^temple
was filling with smoke. 5 Then I said,
"^AWoe to me, for I am ruined!
Because I am a man of
^Bunclean lips,
And I live among a people of
unclean lips;
For my eyes have seen the
King, the LORD of armies."
6 Then one of the seraphim flew to
me with a burning coal in his hand,
which he had taken from the ^altar
with tongs. 7 He touched my mouth
with it and said, "Behold, this has

touched your lips; and ^your guilt is
taken away and atonement is made
for your sin."

ISAIAH'S COMMISSION

8 Then I heard the voice of the Lord,
saying, "Whom shall I send, and who
will go for Us?" Then ^I said, "Here
am I. Send me!" 9 And He said, "Go,
and tell this people:
'Keep on ^listening, but do not
understand;
And keep on looking, but do
not gain knowledge.'
10 "^AMake the hearts of this people
^Binsensitive,
Their ears dull,
And their eyes blind,
So that they will not see with
their eyes,
Hear with their ears,
Understand with their hearts,
And return and be healed."
11 Then I said, "Lord, ^how long?"
And He answered,
"Until cities are devastated *and*
without inhabitant,
Houses are without people
And the land is utterly desolate,
12 The LORD has ^completely
removed people,
And there are many ^Bforsaken
places in the midst of the land.
13 "Yet there will still be a tenth
portion in it,
And it will again be *subject* to
burning,
Like a terebinth or an ^oak
Whose stump remains when it
is cut down.
The ^Bholy seed is its stump."

5:29 ^Jer 51:38 ^BIs 10:6   5:30 ^Is 8:22; Jer 4:23-28
6:1 ^John 12:41; Rev 4:2, 3   6:2 ^Rev 4:8
6:3 ^Num 14:21; Ps 72:19   6:4 ^Rev 15:8
6:5 ^Ex 33:20   ^BEx 6:12, 30   6:6 ^Rev 8:3
6:7 ^Is 40:2; 53:5, 6, 11   6:8 ^Acts 26:19   6:9 ^Is 43:8;
Matt 13:14   6:10 ^Matt 13:15   ^BDeut 31:20
6:11 ^Ps 79:5   6:12 ^Deut 28:64   ^BJer 4:29
6:13 ^Job 14:7   ^BDeut 7:6

WAR AGAINST JERUSALEM

7 Now it came about in the days of Ahaz, the son of Jotham, the son of Uzziah, king of Judah, that Rezin the king of Aram and Pekah the son of Remaliah, king of Israel, went up to Jerusalem to *wage* war against it, but ^could not conquer it. 2When it was reported to the ^house of David, saying, "The Arameans have taken a stand by Ephraim," his heart and the hearts of his people shook as the trees of the forest shake from the wind.

3Then the LORD said to Isaiah, "Go out now to meet Ahaz, you and your son Shear-jashub, at the end of the ^conduit of the upper pool, on the road to the 1fuller's field, 4and say to him, 'Take care and be calm, have no fear and do not be fainthearted because of these two stumps of smoldering ^logs, on account of the fierce anger of Rezin and Aram and the son of Remaliah. 5Because ^Aram, *with* Ephraim and the son of Remaliah, has planned evil against you, saying, 6"Let's go up against Judah and terrorize it, and take it for ourselves by assault and set up the son of Tabeel as king in the midst of it," 7this is what the Lord GOD says: "^It shall not stand nor shall it come to pass. 8For the head of Aram is ^Damascus, and the head of Damascus is Rezin (now within another sixty-five years Ephraim will be broken to pieces, *so that it is* no longer a people), 9and the head of Ephraim is Samaria, and the head of Samaria is the son of Remaliah. ^If you will not believe, you certainly shall not last."'"

THE CHILD IMMANUEL

10Then the LORD spoke again to Ahaz, saying, 11"Ask for a ^sign for yourself from the LORD your God; make *it* deep as Sheol or high as heaven." 12But Ahaz said, "I will not ask, nor will I put the LORD to the test!" 13Then he said, "Listen now, house of David! Is it too trivial a thing for you to try the patience of men, that you will ^try the patience of Bmy God as well? 14Therefore the Lord Himself will give you a sign: Behold, ^the 1virgin will conceive and give birth to a son, and she will name Him 2,BImmanuel. 15He will eat ^curds and honey at the time He knows *enough* to refuse evil and choose good. 16^For before the boy knows *enough* to refuse evil and choose good, Bthe land whose two kings you dread will be abandoned.

TRIALS TO COME FOR JUDAH

17The LORD will bring on you, on your people, and on your father's house such days as have not come since the day that ^Ephraim separated from Judah—*the days of* the king of Assyria."

18On that day the LORD will ^whistle for the fly that is in the Bremotest part of the canals of Egypt and for the bee that is in the land of Assyria. 19They will all come and settle on the steep ravines, on the ^ledges of the cliffs, on all the thorn bushes, and on all the watering places.

20On that day the Lord will ^shave with a razor, hired from regions

7:1^Is 7:6, 7   7:2^Is 7:13; 22:22   7:3^2 Kin 18:17; Is 36:2   7:4^Amos 4:11; Zech 3:2   7:5^Is 7:2
7:7^Is 8:10; 28:18   7:8^Gen 14:15; Is 17:1-3
7:9^2 Chr 20:20; Is 5:24   7:11^2 Kin 19:29; Is 37:30
7:13^Is 1:14   BIs 25:1   7:14^Matt 1:23   BIs 8:8, 10
7:15^Is 7:22   7:16^Is 8:4   BIs 8:14   7:17^1 Kin 12:16
7:18^Is 5:26   BIs 13:5   7:19^Is 2:19; Jer 16:16
7:20^2 Kin 18:13-16; Is 24:1

7:3 1I.e., launderer's   7:14 1As in LXX; MT *young unmarried woman*   2I.e., God is with us

beyond the *Euphrates* River (*that is,* with the king of Assyria), the head and the hair of the legs; and it will also remove the beard.

²¹Now on that day a person may keep alive *only* a ^heifer and a pair of sheep; ²²and because of the abundance of the milk produced he will eat curds, for everyone who is left within the land will eat ^curds and honey.

²³And it will come about on that day, ^that every place where there used to be a thousand vines, *valued* at a thousand *shekels* of silver, will become ᴮbriars and thorns. ²⁴*People* will come there with bows and arrows, because all the land will be briars and thorns. ²⁵As for all the hills which used to be cultivated with the plow, you will not go there for fear of briars and thorns; but they will become a place for ^pasturing oxen and for sheep to trample.

DAMASCUS AND SAMARIA FALL

8 Then the LORD said to me, "Take for yourself a large tablet and ^write on it in ordinary letters: ¹'ᴮMaher-shalal-hash-baz. ²And I will take to Myself faithful witnesses for testimony, ^Uriah the priest and Zechariah the son of Jeberechiah." ³So I approached the prophetess, and she conceived and gave birth to a son. Then the LORD said to me, "Name him ¹'^Maher-shalal-hash-baz; ⁴for ^before the boy knows how to cry out 'My father' or 'My mother,' the wealth of Damascus and the spoils of Samaria will be carried away before the king of Assyria."

⁵Again the LORD spoke to me further, saying,

⁶ "Inasmuch as these people have ^rejected the gently flowing waters of Shiloah
And rejoice in Rezin and the son of Remaliah;
⁷ Now therefore, behold, the Lord is about to bring on them the strong and abundant waters of the *Euphrates* River,
That is, the ^king of Assyria and all his glory;
And it will ᴮrise over all its channels and go over all its banks.
⁸ "Then ^it will sweep on into Judah, it will overflow and pass through,
It will ᴮreach as far as the neck;
And the spread of its wings will fill the expanse of your land, Immanuel.

A BELIEVING REMNANT

⁹ "^Be broken, you peoples, and be ᴮshattered;
And listen, all remote places of the earth.
Get ready, yet be shattered;
Get ready, yet be shattered.
¹⁰ "^Devise a plan, but it will fail;
State a proposal, but it will not stand,
For God is with us."

¹¹For so the LORD spoke to me with mighty power and instructed me ^not to walk in the way of this people, saying,

7:21 ^Is 14:30; 27:10   7:22 ^Is 8:15   7:23 ^Is 5:10
ᴮIs 5:6   7:25 ^Is 5:17   8:1 ^Is 30:8   ᴮIs 8:3
8:2 ^2 Kin 16:10, 11, 15, 16   8:3 ^Is 8:1   8:4 ^Is 7:16
8:6 ^Is 1:20; 5:24   8:7 ^Is 7:17   ᴮAmos 8:8
8:8 ^Is 10:6   ᴮIs 30:28   8:9 ^Is 17:12-14
ᴮDan 2:34, 35   8:10 ^Job 5:12; Is 28:18
8:11 ^Ezek 2:8

8:1 ¹I.e., swift is the plunder, speedy is the prey
8:3 ¹I.e., swift is the plunder, speedy is the prey

12 "You are not to say, '*It is* a
　　conspiracy!'
　　Regarding everything that this
　　　people call a conspiracy,
　　And ^you are not to fear what
　　　they fear or be in dread of *it*.
13 "It is the Lord of armies ^whom
　　you are to regard as holy.
　　And He shall be your fear,
　　And He shall be your dread.
14 "Then He will become a
　　^sanctuary;
　　But to both houses of Israel, *He
　　will be* a ^B^stone of stumbling
　　and a rock ¹of offense,
　　And a snare and a trap for the
　　　inhabitants of Jerusalem.
15 "Many ^will stumble over them,
　　Then they will fall and be
　　broken;
　　They will be snared and
　　caught."

16 Bind up the testimony, ^seal the
Law among ^B^my disciples. 17 And I
will ^wait for the Lord who is hiding
His face from the house of Jacob; I
will wait eagerly for Him. 18 Behold,
I and the children whom the Lord
has given me are for ^signs and
wonders in Israel from the Lord of
armies, who ^B^dwells on Mount Zion.
19 When they say to you, "Consult
the mediums and the spiritists who
whisper and mutter," should a people not ^consult their God? *Should
they consult* the dead in behalf of the
living? 20 To the Law and to the testimony! If they do not speak in accordance with this word, it is because
^they have no dawn. 21 They will pass
through the land ^dejected and hungry, and it will turn out that when
they are hungry, they will become
enraged and curse their king and
their God as they face upward.
22 Then they will look to the earth,
and behold, distress and darkness,

the gloom of anguish; and *they will
be* ^driven away into darkness.

BIRTH AND REIGN OF THE PRINCE
OF PEACE

9 But there will be no *more* gloom
　for her who was in anguish. In
earlier times He ^treated the ^B^land
of Zebulun and the land of Naphtali with contempt, but later on He
will make *it* glorious, by the way of
the sea, on the other side of the Jordan, Galilee of the Gentiles.
2　^The people who walk in
　　darkness
　　Will see a great light;
　　Those who live in a dark land,
　　The light will shine on them.
3　^You will multiply the nation,
　　You ^B^will increase their joy;
　　They will rejoice in Your
　　presence
　　As with the joy of harvest,
　　As *people* rejoice when they
　　divide the spoils.
4　For ^You will break the yoke of
　　their burden and the staff on
　　their shoulders,
　　The rod of their ^B^oppressor, as
　　at the battle of Midian.
5　For every boot of the marching
　　warrior in the roar *of battle,*
　　And cloak rolled in blood, will
　　be for burning, fuel for the
　　fire.
6　For a Child will be born to us,
　　a ^Son will be given to us;
　　And the ^B^government will rest
　　on His shoulders;

8:12 ^A 1 Pet 3:14, 15　8:13 ^A Num 20:12　8:14 ^A Is 4:6
^B Luke 2:34　8:15 ^A Is 28:13; 59:10　8:16 ^A Dan 12:4
^B Is 50:4　8:17 ^A Is 25:9; 30:18　8:18 ^A Luke 2:34
^B Ps 9:11　8:19 ^A Is 30:2; 45:11　8:20 ^A Is 8:22; Mic 3:6
8:21 ^A Is 9:20, 21　8:22 ^A Is 8:20　9:1 ^A 2 Kin 15:29
^B Matt 4:15, 16　9:2 ^A Matt 4:16; Luke 1:79
9:3 ^A Is 26:15　^B Is 35:10　9:4 ^A Is 10:27　^B Is 14:4
9:6 ^A John 3:16　^B Matt 28:18

8:14 ¹Or *to trip on*

And His name will be called
Wonderful Counselor,
Mighty God,
Eternal Father, Prince of Peace.
7 There will be ^no end to the
increase of *His* government
or of peace
On the ^Bthrone of David and
over 'his kingdom,
To establish it and to
uphold it with justice and
righteousness
From then on and
forevermore.
The zeal of the LORD of armies
will accomplish this.

GOD'S ANGER WITH ISRAEL'S ARROGANCE

8 The Lord sends a message
against Jacob,
And it falls on Israel.
9 And all the people know *it*,
That is, ^Ephraim and the
inhabitants of Samaria,
Asserting in pride and in
^Barrogance of heart:
10 "The bricks have fallen down,
But we will ^rebuild with
smooth stones;
The sycamores have been cut
down,
But we will replace *them* with
cedars."
11 Therefore the LORD raises
superior adversaries against
them from ^Rezin
And provokes their enemies,
12 The Arameans from the east
and the ^Philistines from the
west;
And they ^Bdevour Israel with
gaping jaws.
In *spite of* all this, His anger
does not turn away,
And His hand is still
stretched out.

13 Yet the people ^do not turn
back to Him who struck
them,
Nor do they ^Bseek the LORD of
armies.
14 So the LORD cuts off ^head and
tail from Israel,
Both palm branch and bulrush
in a single day.
15 The head is ^the elder and
esteemed man,
And the prophet who teaches
falsehood is the tail.
16 ^For those who guide this
people are leading *them*
astray;
And those who are guided by
them are confused.
17 Therefore the Lord does not
rejoice over their young
men,
^Nor does He have compassion
on their orphans or their
widows;
For every one of them is
godless and an evildoer,
And every ^Bmouth is speaking
foolishness.
In *spite of* all this, His anger
does not turn away,
And His hand is still
stretched out.

18 ^For wickedness burns like a
fire;
It consumes briars and
thorns;
It also sets the thickets of the
forest aflame
And they roll upward in a
column of smoke.

9:7 ^Dan 2:44 ^BIs 16:5 9:9 ^Is 7:8, 9 ^BIs 46:12
9:10 ^Mal 1:4 9:11 ^Is 7:1, 8 9:12 ^2 Chr 28:18
^BPs 79:7 9:13 ^Jer 5:3 ^BIs 31:1 9:14 ^Is 19:15
9:15 ^Is 3:2, 3 9:16 ^Is 3:12; Matt 15:14 9:17 ^Is 27:11
^BMatt 12:34 9:18 ^Ps 83:14; Is 1:7
9:7 'I.e., David's

19 By the wrath of the LORD of
armies the ^land is burned,
And the people are like fuel
for the fire;
No ^Bone spares his brother.

20 They devour *what is* on the
right hand but are *still*
hungry,
And they eat *what is* on the
left hand, but they are not
satisfied;
Each of them eats the ^flesh of
his own arm.

21 Manasseh *devours* Ephraim,
and Ephraim Manasseh,
And together they are against
Judah.
^In *spite of* all this, His anger
does not turn away
And His hand is still
stretched out.

ASSYRIA IS GOD'S INSTRUMENT

10 Woe to those who ^enact
unjust statutes
And to those who constantly
record harmful decisions,

2 So as ^to deprive the needy of
justice
And rob the poor among My
people of *their* rights,
So ^Bthat widows may be their
spoil
And that they may plunder
the orphans.

3 Now ^what will you do in the
^Bday of punishment,
And in the devastation which
will come from afar?
To whom will you flee for
help?
And where will you leave your
wealth?

4 Nothing *remains* but to
crouch among the
^captives
Or fall among those killed.

^BIn *spite of* all this, His anger
does not turn away
And His hand is still stretched
out.

5 Woe to Assyria, the ^rod of My
anger
And the staff in whose hands
is ^BMy indignation,

6 I send it against a ^godless
nation
And commission it against the
people of My fury
To capture spoils and to seize
plunder,
And to trample them down
like ^Bmud in the streets.

7 Yet it ^does not so intend,
Nor does it plan so in its heart,
But rather it is its purpose to
destroy
And to eliminate many nations.

8 For it says, "Are not my officers
all kings?

9 "Is not ^Calno like ^BCarchemish,
Or Hamath like Arpad,
Or Samaria like Damascus?

10 "As my hand has reached to the
^kingdoms of the idols,
Whose carved images *were*
greater than those of
Jerusalem and Samaria,

11 Shall I not do the same to
Jerusalem and her images
Just as I have done to Samaria
and ^her idols?"

12 So it will be that when the Lord
has completed all His ^work on
Mount Zion and on Jerusalem, *He*
will say, "I will punish the fruit of
the arrogant heart of the king of

9:19 ^Joel 2:3   ^B Mic 7:2, 6   **9:20** ^Is 49:26
9:21 ^Is 5:25   **10:1** ^Ps 94:20; Is 29:21   **10:2** ^Is 5:23
^B Is 1:23   **10:3** ^Job 31:14   ^B Is 13:6   **10:4** ^Is 24:22
^B Is 5:25   **10:5** ^Jer 51:20   ^B Is 13:5   **10:6** ^Is 9:17
^B Is 5:25   **10:7** ^Gen 50:20; Mic 4:11, 12
10:9 ^Gen 10:10   ^B 2 Chr 35:20   **10:10** ^2 Kin 19:17, 18
10:11 ^Is 2:8   **10:12** ^2 Kin 19:31; Is 28:21, 22

Assyria and the arrogant pride of his eyes." ¹³For he has said,

"By the power of my hand and
by my wisdom I did *this*,
Because I have understanding;
And I ^removed the
boundaries of the peoples
And plundered their treasures,
And like a powerful man
I brought down *their*
inhabitants,
¹⁴ And my hand reached to the
riches of the peoples like a
^nest,
And as one gathers abandoned
eggs, I gathered all the earth;
And there was not one that
flapped its wing, opened *its*
beak, or chirped."

¹⁵ Is the ^axe to ᴮboast itself over
the one who chops with it?
Is the saw to exalt itself over
the one who wields it?
That would be like a club
wielding those who lift it,
Or like a rod lifting *the one
who* is not wood.
¹⁶ Therefore the Lord, the Gᴏᴅ of
armies, will send a ^wasting
disease among his stout
warriors;
And under his glory a fire will
be kindled like a burning
flame.
¹⁷ And the ^Light of Israel will
become a fire and Israel's
ᴮHoly One a flame,
And it will burn and devour
his thorns and his briars in a
single day.
¹⁸ And He will ^destroy the
glory of his forest and of his
fruitful garden, both soul
and body,
And it will be as when a sick
person wastes away.

¹⁹ And the ^rest of the trees of
his forest will be so small in
number
That a child could write them
down.

A REMNANT WILL RETURN

²⁰ Now on that day the remnant of
Israel, and those of the house of
Jacob who have escaped, will no
longer rely on the one who struck
them, but will truly ^rely on the
Lᴏʀᴅ, the Holy One of Israel.
²¹ A ^remnant will return, the
remnant of Jacob, to the
ᴮmighty God.
²² For though your people,
Israel, may be like the sand
of the sea,
Only a remnant within them
will return;
A ^destruction is determined,
overflowing with
righteousness.
²³For a complete destruction, one
that is determined, ^the Lord Gᴏᴅ
of armies will execute in the midst
of the whole land.

²⁴Therefore this is what the Lord
Gᴏᴅ of armies says: "My people,
you who dwell in Zion, ^do not fear
the Assyrian who ᴮstrikes you with
the rod, and lifts up his staff against
you the way Egypt *did*. ²⁵For in a
very ^little while My indignation
against you will be ended and My
anger *will be directed* toward their
destruction." ²⁶The Lᴏʀᴅ of armies
will wield a whip against him like
the defeat of ^Midian at the rock
of Oreb; and His staff will be over

10:13^Hab 2:6-11   10:14^Jer 49:16; Obad 4
10:15^Jer 51:20   ᴮIs 29:16   10:16^Ps 106:15
10:17^Is 30:33   ᴮIs 37:23   10:18^Is 10:33, 34
10:19^Is 21:17   10:20^2 Chr 14:11; Is 17:7, 8
10:21^Is 7:3   ᴮIs 9:6   10:22^Is 28:22; Dan 9:27
10:23^Is 28:22; Dan 9:27   10:24^Is 7:4   ᴮEx 5:14-16
10:25^Is 17:14; Hag 2:6   10:26^Judg 7:25

the sea, and He will lift it up ᴮthe way *He did in* Egypt. ²⁷ So it will be on that day, that his ᴬburden will be removed from your shoulders, and his yoke from your neck; and the yoke will be broken because of fatness.

28 He has come against Aiath,
He has passed through Migron;
At ᴬMichmash he deposited
his ᴮbaggage.

29 They have gone through ᴬthe
pass, *saying,*
"ᴮGeba will be our encampment
for the night."
Ramah is terrified, and Gibeah
of Saul has fled.

30 Cry aloud with your voice,
daughter of ᴬGallim!
Pay attention, Laishah *and*
wretched Anathoth!

31 Madmenah has fled.
The inhabitants of Gebim have
sought refuge.

32 Yet today he will halt at Nob;
He ᴬshakes his fist at the
mountain of the daughter of
Zion, the hill of Jerusalem.

33 Behold, the Lord, the Goᴅ
of armies, will lop off the
branches with terrifying
power;
Those also who are ᴬtall in
stature will be cut down,
And those who are lofty will
be brought low.

34 He will cut down the thickets
of the forest with an iron *axe,*
And ᴬLebanon will fall by the
Mighty One.

RIGHTEOUS REIGN OF THE BRANCH

11 Then a shoot will spring
from the stem of Jesse,
And a ᴬBranch from ᴮhis roots
will bear fruit.

2 The ᴬSpirit of the Loʀᴅ will
rest on Him,
The spirit of ᴮwisdom and
understanding,
The spirit of counsel and
strength,
The spirit of knowledge and
the fear of the Loʀᴅ.

3 And He will delight in the fear
of the Loʀᴅ,
And He will not judge by what
His eyes ᴬsee,
Nor make decisions by what
His ears hear;

4 But with ᴬrighteousness He
will judge the poor,
And decide with fairness for
the humble of the earth;
And He will strike the earth
with the rod of His mouth,
And with the ᴮbreath of His
lips He will slay the wicked.

5 Also ᴬrighteousness will be
the belt *around* His hips,
And ᴮfaithfulness the belt
around His waist.

6 And the ᴬwolf will dwell with
the lamb,
And the leopard will lie down
with the young goat,
And the calf and the young
lion ¹and the fattened steer
will be together;
And a little boy will lead them.

7 Also the cow and the bear will
graze,
Their young will lie down
together,

10:26 ᴮEx 14:27   10:27 ᴬIs 9:4; 14:25
10:28 ᴬ1 Sam 13:2, 5   ᴮJudg 18:21   10:29 ᴬ1 Sam 13:23
ᴮJosh 21:17   10:30 ᴬ1 Sam 25:44   10:32 ᴬIs 19:16;
Zech 2:9   10:33 ᴬIs 37:24, 36–38; Ezek 31:3
10:34 ᴬIs 2:13; 33:9   11:1 ᴬIs 6:13   ᴮRev 5:5
11:2 ᴬIs 42:1   ᴮJohn 16:13   11:3 ᴬJohn 2:25; 7:24
11:4 ᴬIs 9:7   ᴮJob 4:9   11:5 ᴬEph 6:14   ᴮIs 25:1
11:6 ᴬIs 65:25

11:6 ¹Some ancient versions *will feed together*

And the ^lion will eat straw
    like the ox.
8   The nursing child will play by
    the hole of the cobra,
    And the weaned child will put
    his hand on the viper's den.
9   They will not hurt or destroy
    in all My holy mountain,
    For the ^earth will be full of the
    knowledge of the Lord
    As the waters cover the sea.

10 Then on that day
    The ^nations will resort to the
    root of Jesse,
    Who will stand as a ^signal flag
    for the peoples;
    And His resting place will be
    glorious.

THE RESTORED REMNANT

11 Then it will happen on that
    day that the Lord
    Will again recover with His
    hand the second time
    The remnant of His people
    who will remain,
    From ^Assyria, ^Egypt, Pathros,
    Cush, Elam, Shinar, Hamath,
    And from the islands of the
    sea.
12 And He will lift up a flag for
    the nations
    And ^assemble the banished
    ones of Israel,
    And will gather the dispersed
    of Judah
    From the four corners of the
    earth.
13 Then the ^jealousy of Ephraim
    will depart,
    And those who harass Judah
    will be eliminated;
    Ephraim will not be jealous of
    Judah,
    And Judah will not harass
    Ephraim.

14 They will ^swoop down on the
    slopes of the Philistines on
    the west;
    Together they will plunder the
    people of the east;
    They will possess Edom and
    Moab,
    And the sons of Ammon will
    be subject to them.
15 And the Lord will utterly
    destroy
    The tongue of the Sea of
    Egypt;
    And He will wave His hand
    over the ^*Euphrates* River
    With His scorching wind;
    And He will strike it into seven
    streams
    And make *people* walk over in
    dry sandals.
16 And there will be a ^highway
    from Assyria
    For the remnant of His people
    who will be left,
    Just as there was for Israel
    On ^the day that they came up
    out of the land of Egypt.

THANKSGIVING EXPRESSED

12 Then you will say on that day,
    "I will give thanks to You,
    Lord;
    For *although* ^You were angry
    with me,
    Your anger is turned away,
    And You comfort me.
2   "Behold, ^God is my salvation,
    I will ^trust and not be afraid;
    For the Lord God is my
    strength and song,
    And He has become my
    salvation."

11:7^Is 65:25   11:9^Ps 98:2, 3; Is 45:6
11:10^Luke 2:32   ^Is 11:12   11:11^Is 19:23-25
^Is 19:21, 22   11:12^Is 56:8; Zeph 3:10   11:13^Is 9:21;
Jer 3:18   11:14^Jer 48:40; 49:22   11:15^Is 7:20; 8:7
11:16^Is 19:23   ^Ex 14:26-29   12:1^Ps 30:5; Is 40:1, 2
12:2^Is 32:2   ^Is 26:3

3 Therefore you will joyously
  ^draw water
  From the ^Bsprings of salvation.
4 And on that day you will say,
  "^AGive thanks to the LORD, call
  on His name.
  ^BMake known His deeds
  among the peoples;
  Make *them* remember that His
  name is exalted."
5 ^APraise the LORD in song, for
  He has done glorious things;
  Let this be known throughout
  the earth.
6 Rejoice and shout for joy, you
  inhabitant of Zion,
  For ^Agreat in your midst is the
  Holy One of Israel.

PROPHECIES ABOUT BABYLON

13 The ^Apronouncement concerning ^BBabylon which Isaiah the son of Amoz saw:
2 ^ALift up a flag on the ^Bbare hill,
  Raise your voice to them,
  Wave the hand that they may
  enter the doors of the nobles.
3 I have commanded My
  consecrated ones,
  I have also called for My
  ^Awarriors
  Who boast in My eminence,
  To *execute* My anger.
4 A ^Asound of a roar on the
  mountains,
  Like that of many people!
  A sound of an uproar of
  kingdoms,
  Of nations gathered together!
  The LORD of armies is
  mustering the army for battle.
5 They are coming from a
  distant country,
  From the farthest horizons,
  The LORD and the weapons of
  His ^Aindignation,
  To ^Bdestroy the whole land.

JUDGMENT ON THE DAY OF THE LORD

6 Wail, for the ^Aday of the LORD
  is near!
  It will come as destruction
  from the Almighty.
7 Therefore all hands will fall
  limp,
  And every human ^Aheart will
  melt.
8 They will be ^Aterrified,
  Pains and anguish will take
  hold of *them;*
  They will ^Bwrithe like a woman
  in labor,
  They will look at one another
  in astonishment,
  Their faces aflame.
9 Behold, ^Athe day of the LORD is
  coming,
  Cruel, with fury and burning
  anger,
  To make the land a
  desolation;
  And He will exterminate its
  sinners from it.
10 For the ^Astars of heaven and
  their constellations
  Will not flash their light;
  The ^Bsun will be dark when it
  rises
  And the moon will not shed
  its light.
11 So I will ^Apunish the world for
  its evil
  And the ^Bwicked for their
  wrongdoing;
  I will also put an end to the
  audacity of the proud
  And humiliate the arrogance
  of the tyrants.

12:3 ^A John 4:10 ^B Is 41:18 **12:4** ^A Ps 105:1
^B Ps 145:4 **12:5** ^A Ex 15:1; Ps 98:1 **12:6** ^A Is 1:24;
49:26 **13:1** ^A Is 14:28 ^B Is 47:1-15 **13:2** ^A Is 5:26
^B Jer 51:25 **13:3** ^A Joel 3:11 **13:4** ^A Is 5:30; 17:12
13:5 ^A Is 10:5 ^B Is 24:1 **13:6** ^A Is 2:12; 10:3
13:7 ^A Is 19:1; Ezek 21:7 **13:8** ^A 2 Kin 19:26 ^B Is 26:17
13:9 ^A Is 13:6 **13:10** ^A Is 5:30 ^B Is 24:23
13:11 ^A Is 26:21 ^B Is 3:11

12   I will make mortal man
        ^scarcer than pure gold
      And mankind than the gold of
        Ophir.
13   Therefore I will make the
        heavens tremble,
      And ^the earth will be shaken
        from its place
      At the fury of the Lord of
        armies
      In ^Bthe day of His burning
        anger.
14   And it will be that, like a
        hunted gazelle,
      Or like ^sheep with no one to
        gather *them,*
      Each of them will turn to his
        own people,
      And each of them will flee to
        his own land.
15   Anyone who is found will be
        ^thrust through,
      And anyone who is captured
        will fall by the sword.
16   Their ^little ones also will be
        dashed to pieces
      Before their eyes;
      Their houses will be plundered
      And their wives raped.

BABYLON WILL FALL TO THE MEDES

17   Behold, I am going to ^stir up
        the Medes against them,
      Who will not value silver or
        take pleasure in gold.
18   And *their* bows will mow
        down the young men,
      They will not even have
        compassion on the fruit of
        the womb,
      Nor will their ^eye pity
        children.
19   And ^Babylon, the ^Bbeauty of
        kingdoms, the glory of the
        Chaldeans' pride,
      Will be as when God overthrew
        Sodom and Gomorrah.

20   It will ^never be inhabited or
        lived in from generation to
        generation;
      Nor will the Arab pitch *his*
        tent there,
      Nor will shepherds allow *their
        flocks* to lie down there.
21   But ^desert creatures will lie
        down there,
      And their houses will be full
        of owls;
      Ostriches also will live there,
        and shaggy goats will frolic
        there.
22   Hyenas will howl in their
        fortified towers
      And jackals in their luxurious
        ^palaces.
      Her *fateful* time also will soon
        come,
      And her days will not be
        prolonged.

ISRAEL'S TAUNT AGAINST BABYLON

14 When the Lord ^has com-
      passion on Jacob and again
^Bchooses Israel, and settles them on
their own land, then strangers will
join them and attach themselves
to the house of Jacob. ²The peoples will take them along and bring
them to their place, and the house
of Israel will make them their own
possession in the land of the Lord
^as male and female servants; and
they will take their captors captive
and will rule over their oppressors.

³And it will be on the day when
the Lord gives you ^rest from your
hardship, your turmoil, and from
the harsh service in which you

13:12 ^Is 4:1; 6:11, 12   13:13 ^Ps 18:7   ^BLam 1:12
13:14 ^1 Kin 22:17; Matt 9:36   13:15 ^Is 14:19; Jer 50:25
13:16 ^Ps 137:8, 9; Is 13:18   13:17 ^Jer 51:11; Dan 5:28
13:18 ^Ezek 9:5, 10   13:19 ^Is 21:9   ^BDan 4:30
13:20 ^Is 14:23; 34:10-15   13:21 ^Is 34:11-15; Zeph 2:14
13:22 ^Is 25:2; 32:14   14:1 ^Ps 102:13   ^BIs 41:8, 9
14:2 ^Is 60:10; 61:5   14:3 ^Ezra 9:8, 9; Is 11:10

have been enslaved, [4]that you will
[A]take up this taunt against the king
of Babylon, and say,

"How the oppressor has
    ceased,
And how the onslaught has
    ceased!

5 "The LORD has broken the staff
    of the wicked,
The scepter of rulers,

6 [A]Which used to strike the
    peoples in fury with
    unceasing strokes,
Which subdued the nations
    in anger with unrestrained
    persecution.

7 "The whole earth is at rest *and*
    is quiet;
They [A]break forth into shouts
    of joy.

8 "Even the [A]juniper trees rejoice
    over you, *and* the cedars of
    Lebanon, *saying,*
'Since you have been laid low,
    no *tree* cutter comes up
    against us.'

9 "[A]Sheol below is excited about
    you, to meet you when you
    come;
It stirs the spirits of the dead
    for you, all the leaders of the
    earth;
It raises all the kings of the
    nations from their thrones.

10 "[A]They will all respond and say
    to you,
'Even you have become weak
    as we,
You have become like us.

11 'Your [A]pride *and* the music of
    your harps
Have been brought down to
    Sheol;
Maggots are spread out *as your
    bed* beneath you
And worms are your
    covering.'

12 "How you have fallen from
    heaven,
You [A]star of the morning, son
    of the dawn!
You have been cut down to the
    earth,
You who defeated the nations!

13 "But you said in your heart,
'I will [A]ascend to heaven;
I will [B]raise my throne above
    the stars of God,
And I will sit on the mount of
    assembly
In the recesses of the north.

14 'I will ascend above the heights
    of the clouds;
[A]I will make myself like the
    Most High.'

15 "Nevertheless you [A]will be
    brought down to Sheol,
To the recesses of the pit.

16 "Those who see you will stare
    at you,
They will closely examine
    you, *saying,*
'Is this the man who made the
    earth tremble,
Who shook kingdoms,

17 Who made the world like a
    [A]wilderness
And overthrew its cities,
Who [B]did not allow his
    prisoners to *go* home?'

18 "All the kings of the nations lie
    in glory,
Each in his own tomb.

19 "But you have been hurled out
    of your tomb
Like a rejected branch,
Clothed with those killed who
    have been pierced with a
    sword,

14:4 [A]Hab 2:6   14:6 [A]Is 10:14; 47:6   14:7 [A]Ps 47:1-3;
98:1-9   14:8 [A]Is 55:12; Ezek 31:16   14:9 [A]Is 5:14
14:10 [A]Ezek 32:21   14:11 [A]Is 5:14   14:12 [A]2 Pet 1:19;
Rev 2:28   14:13 [A]Ezek 28:2   [B]Dan 5:22, 23
14:14 [A]Is 47:8; 2 Thess 2:4   14:15 [A]Ezek 28:8;
Matt 11:23   14:17 [A]Joel 2:3   [B]Is 45:13

Who go down to the stones of
the ^pit
Like a ^Btrampled corpse.
20 "You will not be united with
them in burial,
Because you have ruined your
country,
You have killed your people.
May the ^descendants
of evildoers never be
mentioned.
21 "Prepare a place of slaughter
for his sons
Because of the ^wrongdoing
of their fathers.
They must not arise and take
possession of the earth,
And fill the surface of the
world with cities."
22"I will rise up against them,"
declares the Lord of armies, "and
eliminate from Babylon ^name and
survivors, ^Boffspring and descendants," declares the Lord. 23"I will
also make it the property of the
^hedgehog and swamps of water,
and I will sweep it away with the
broom of destruction," declares the
Lord of armies.

JUDGMENT ON ASSYRIA

24The Lord of armies has sworn,
saying, "Certainly, ^just as I have
intended, so it has happened, and
just as I have planned, so it will
stand, 25to ^break Assyria in My
land, and I will trample him on My
mountains. Then his ^Byoke will be
removed from them, and his burden removed from their shoulders.
26This is the ^plan devised against
the entire earth; and this is the hand
that is stretched out against all the
nations. 27For ^the Lord of armies
has planned, and who can frustrate it? And as for His stretched-
out hand, who can turn it back?"

JUDGMENT ON PHILISTIA

28In the ^year that King Ahaz died,
this pronouncement came:
29 "Do not rejoice, Philistia, all of
you,
Because the rod that struck
you is broken;
For from the serpent's root a
^viper will come out,
And its fruit will be a ^Bwinged
serpent.
30 "Those who are most helpless
will eat,
And the poor will lie down in
security;
I will kill your root with
^famine,
And it will kill your survivors.
31 "Wail, you gate; cry, you city;
Melt away, Philistia, all of you!
For smoke comes from the
^north,
And ^Bthere is no straggler in
his ranks.
32 "What answer will one give the
^messengers of the nation?
That the Lord has founded
Zion,
And ^Bthe poor of His people
will take refuge in it."

JUDGMENT ON MOAB

15 The pronouncement con-
cerning Moab:
Certainly in a night ^Ar of
Moab is devastated and
ruined;
Certainly in a night Kir of
Moab is devastated and
ruined.

14:19^Jer 41:7, 9   ^BIs 5:25   14:20^Job 18:16, 19;
Ps 21:10   14:21^Ex 20:5; Lev 26:39   14:22^Prov 10:7
^BIs 18:19   14:23^Is 34:11; Zeph 2:14
14:24^Job 23:13; Is 46:11   14:25^Is 10:12   ^BIs 9:4
14:26^Is 23:9; Zeph 3:6, 8   14:27^2 Chr 20:6; Is 43:13
14:28^2 Kin 16:20; 2 Chr 28:27   14:29^Is 11:8
^BIs 30:6   14:30^Is 8:21; 9:20   14:31^Jer 1:14
^BIs 34:16   14:32^Is 37:9   ^BIs 4:6   15:1^Num 21:28

2　The people have gone up to
　　the temple and *to* ^Dibon, to
　　the high places to weep.
　Moab wails over Nebo and
　　Medeba;
　Everyone's head is bald *and*
　　every beard is cut off.

3　In their streets they have put
　　on ^sackcloth;
　On their housetops and in
　　their public squares
　Everyone is wailing, overcome
　　with weeping.

4　^Heshbon and Elealeh also cry
　　out,
　Their voice is heard all the way
　　to Jahaz;
　Therefore the armed men of
　　Moab cry aloud;
　His soul trembles within him.

5　My heart cries out for Moab;
　His fugitives are as far as ^Zoar
　　and Eglath-shelishiyah,
　For they go up the ascent of
　　Luhith weeping;
　Indeed, on the road to
　　Horonaim they raise a
　　cry of distress ^B^over *their*
　　collapse.

6　For the waters of Nimrim are
　　desolate.
　Indeed, the grass is withered,
　　the new growth has died,
　There is ^no greenery.

7　Therefore the ^abundance
　　which they have acquired
　　and stored up,
　They carry *it* off over the
　　brook of Arabim.

8　For the cry of distress has
　　gone around the territory of
　　Moab,
　Its wailing *goes* as far as
　　Eglaim and its howling to
　　Beer-elim.

9　For the waters of Dimon are
　　full of blood;

I will certainly bring added
　　woes upon Dimon,
A ^lion upon the fugitives of
　　Moab and the remnant of
　　the land.

PROPHECY OF MOAB'S DEVASTATION

16　^Send the *tribute* lamb to
　　the ruler of the land,
　From Sela by way of the
　　wilderness to the mountain
　　of the daughter of Zion.

2　Then, like ^fluttering birds *or*
　　scattered nestlings,
　The daughters of Moab will be
　　at the crossing places of the
　　Arnon.

3　"Give *us* advice, make a decision;
　Cast your shadow like night at
　　high noon;
　^Hide the outcasts, do not
　　betray the fugitive.

4　"Let the outcasts of Moab stay
　　with you;
　Be a hiding place to them from
　　the destroyer."
　For the oppressor has come
　　to an end, destruction has
　　ceased,
　^Oppressors have been
　　removed from the land.

5　A ^throne will be established
　　in faithfulness,
　And a judge will sit on it in
　　trustworthiness in the tent
　　of ^B^David;
　Moreover, he will seek justice,
　And be prompt in
　　righteousness.

6　^We have heard of the pride of
　　Moab, an excessive pride;

15:2 ^Jer 48:18, 22　15:3 ^Jon 3:6-8　15:4 ^Num 21:28;
32:3　15:5 ^Jer 48:34　^B^Is 59:7　15:6 ^Joel 1:10-12; 2:3
15:7 ^Is 30:6; Jer 48:36　15:9 ^2 Kin 17:25; Jer 50:17
16:1 ^2 Kin 3:4; Ezra 7:17　16:2 ^Prov 27:8
16:3 ^1 Kin 18:4　16:4 ^Is 9:4; 14:4　16:5 ^Is 9:6, 7
^B^Is 9:7　16:6 ^Jer 48:29; Amos 2:1

Even of his arrogance, pride,
    and fury;
His idle boasts are false.

7 Therefore Moab will wail;
    everyone of Moab will wail.
You will moan for the ^raisin
    cakes of Kir-hareseth
As those who are utterly
    stricken.
8 For the fields of ^Heshbon
    have withered, the vines of
    ^Sibmah *as well;*
The lords of the nations have
    trampled down its choice
    clusters
Which reached as far as Jazer
    and wandered to the deserts;
Its ¹tendrils spread
    themselves out *and* passed
    over the sea.
9 Therefore I will ^weep bitterly
    for Jazer, for the vine of
    Sibmah;
I will drench you with my
    tears, Heshbon and Elealeh;
For the shouting over your
    summer fruits and your
    harvest has fallen away.
10 ^Gladness and joy are taken
    away from the fruitful field;
In the vineyards also there will
    be no cries of joy or jubilant
    shouting,
No treader treads out wine in
    the presses,
For I have made the shouting
    to cease.
11 Therefore my ^inner being
    sounds like a harp for Moab.
And my heart for Kir-hareseth.
12 So it will come about when
    Moab presents himself,
When he ^tires himself upon
    his ^high place
And comes to his sanctuary to
    pray,
That he will not prevail.

13 This is the word which the LORD
spoke earlier concerning Moab.
14 But now the LORD has spoken,
saying, "Within three years, as ^a
hired worker would count them,
the glory of ^Moab will become
contemptible along with all *his*
great population, and *his* remnant
will be very small *and* impotent."

PROPHECY ABOUT DAMASCUS

17 The pronouncement concern-
    ing Damascus:
"Behold, Damascus is about to
    be ^removed from being a
    city
And will become a ^fallen
    ruin.
2 "The cities of ^Aroer are
    abandoned;
They will be for herds to lie
    down in,
And there will be no one to
    frighten *them.*
3 "The ^fortified city will
    disappear from Ephraim,
And sovereignty from
    Damascus
And the remnant of Aram;
They will be like the glory of
    the sons of Israel,"
Declares the LORD of armies.

4 Now on that day the ^glory of
    Jacob will fade,
And ^the fatness of his flesh
    will become lean.
5 It will be like the reaper
    gathering the standing grain,
As his arm harvests the ears,

16:7 ^1 Chr 16:3   16:8 ^Is 15:4   ^Num 32:38
16:9 ^Jer 48:32   16:10 ^Is 24:8; Jer 48:33
16:11 ^Is 15:5; 63:15   16:12 ^1 Kin 18:29   ^Is 15:2
16:14 ^Job 7:1; 14:6   ^Is 25:10   17:1 ^Is 7:16
^Is 25:2   17:2 ^Num 32:34   17:3 ^Is 7:8, 16; 8:4
17:4 ^Is 10:3   ^Is 10:16

16:8 ¹ I.e., parts of a climbing plant that attach to its
support

Or it will be like one gleaning
ears of grain
In the ^Valley of Rephaim.
6 Yet ^gleanings will be left in it
like the shaking of an olive
tree,
Two *or* three olives on the
topmost branch,
Four *or* five on the branches of
a fruitful tree,
Declares the LORD, the God of
Israel.
7 On that day man will ^look to
his Maker
And his eyes will look to the
Holy One of Israel.
8 And he will not look to the
^altars, the work of his
hands,
Nor will he look to that which
his fingers have made,
Even the [1,B]Asherim and
incense altars.
9 On that day their strong cities
will be like abandoned
places in the forest,
Or like branches which they
abandoned before the sons
of Israel;
And the land will be a
desolation.
10 For ^you have forgotten the
[B]God of your salvation
And have not remembered the
rock of your refuge.
Therefore you plant delightful
plants
And set them with vine shoots
of a strange *god*.
11 On the day that you plant *it*
you carefully fence *it* in,
And in the ^morning you
bring your seed to
blossom;
But the harvest will flee
On a day of illness and
incurable pain.

12 Oh, the uproar of many
peoples
^Who roar like the roaring of
the seas,
And the rumbling of nations
Who rush on like the rumbling
of mighty waters!
13 The ^nations rumble on
like the rumbling of many
waters,
But He will rebuke them, and
they will flee far away,
And be chased like chaff on
the mountains before the
wind,
Or like whirling dust before a
gale.
14 At evening time, behold, *there
is* terror!
Before morning ^they are gone.
This *will be* the fate of those
who plunder us
And the lot of those who
pillage us.

MESSAGE TO ETHIOPIA

18 Woe, land of whirring wings
Which lies beyond the
rivers of [1,A]Cush,
2 Which sends messengers by
the sea,
Even in ^papyrus vessels on
the surface of the waters.
Go, swift messengers, to a
nation [B]tall and smooth,
To a people feared far and
wide,
A powerful and oppressive
nation
Whose land the rivers divide.

17:5 ^2 Sam 5:18, 22   17:6 ^Deut 4:27; Is 24:13
17:7 ^Is 10:20; Hos 3:5   17:8 ^2 Chr 34:7   ^B Ex 34:13
17:10 ^Is 51:13   ^B Ps 68:19   17:11 ^Ps 90:6
17:12 ^Is 5:30; Jer 6:23   17:13 ^Is 33:3
17:14 ^2 Kin 19:35; Is 41:12   18:1 ^2 Kin 19:9; Is 20:3–5
18:2 ^Ex 2:3   ^B Is 18:7

17:8 [1]I.e., wooden symbols of a female deity
(Asherah)   18:1 [1]Or *Ethiopia*

³ All you who inhabit the world,
 and live on earth,
As soon as a flag is raised on
 the mountains, ^you will
 see *it,*
And as soon as the trumpet is
 blown, you will hear *it.*
⁴For this is what the Lord has told
me:
"I will quietly look from My
 ^dwelling place
Like dazzling heat in the
 sunshine,
Like a cloud of dew in the
 heat of harvest."
⁵ For ^before the harvest, as
 soon as the bud blossoms
And the flower becomes a
 ripening grape,
He will cut off the shoots with
 pruning knives,
And remove *and* tear away
 the spreading branches.
⁶ They will be left together for
 mountain birds ^of prey,
And for the animals of the
 earth;
And the birds of prey will
 spend the summer *feeding*
 on them,
And all the animals of the
 earth will spend harvest
 time on them.
⁷ At that time a gift of tribute
 will be brought to the Lord
 of armies
From a ^people tall and
 smooth,
From a people feared far and
 wide,
A powerful and oppressive
 nation,
Whose land the rivers
 divide—
To the place of the name
 of the Lord of armies, *to*
 Mount Zion.

MESSAGE TO EGYPT

19 The pronouncement concerning Egypt:
Behold, the Lord is ^riding on
 a swift cloud and is about to
 come to Egypt;
The idols of Egypt will tremble
 at His presence,
And the ᴮheart of the
 Egyptians will melt within
 them.
² "So I will incite Egyptians
 against Egyptians;
And they will fight, ^each
 against his brother and each
 against his neighbor,
City against city *and* kingdom
 against kingdom.
³ "Then the spirit of the
 Egyptians will be
 demoralized within them;
And I will confuse their
 strategy,
So that ^they will resort to
 idols and ghosts of the dead,
And to mediums and spiritists.
⁴ "Furthermore, I will hand the
 Egyptians over to a ^cruel
 master,
And a mighty king will rule
 over them," declares the
 Lord God of armies.
⁵ ^The waters from the sea will
 dry up,
And the river will be parched
 and dry.
⁶ The ^canals will emit a stench,
The streams of Egypt will thin
 out and dry up;
ᴮThe reeds and rushes will rot
 away.

18:3 ^Is 26:11   18:4 ^Is 26:21; Hos 5:15
18:5 ^Is 17:10, 11; Ezek 17:6-10   18:6 ^Is 46:11; 56:9
18:7 ^Ps 68:31; Is 45:14   19:1 ^Ps 18:9, 10   ᴮJosh 2:11
19:2 ^Judg 7:22; 1 Sam 14:20   19:3 ^1 Chr 10:13; Is 8:19
19:4 ^Is 20:4; Jer 46:26   19:5 ^Is 50:2; Jer 51:36
19:6 ^Ex 7:18   ᴮJob 8:11

7 The bulrushes by the ^Nile, by
the edge of the Nile
And all the sown fields by the
Nile
Will become dry, be driven
away, and be no more.

8 And the ^fishermen will grieve,
And all those who cast a line
into the Nile will mourn,
And those who spread nets on
the waters will dwindle away.

9 Moreover, the manufacturers
of linen made from combed
flax
And the weavers of white
^cloth will be utterly dejected.

10 And the ^pillars *of Egypt* will
be crushed;
All the hired laborers will be
grieved in soul.

11 The officials of ^Zoan are mere
fools;
The advice of Pharaoh's wisest
advisers has become stupid.
How can you say to Pharaoh,
"I am a son of the wise, a son of
ancient kings"?

12 Well then, where are your wise
men?
Please let them tell you,
And let them understand what
the LORD of armies
Has ^planned against Egypt.

13 The officials of Zoan have
turned out to be fools,
The officials of ^Memphis are
deluded;
Those who are the
^cornerstone of her tribes
Have led Egypt astray.

14 The LORD has mixed within
her a spirit of ^distortion;
^They have led Egypt astray in
all that it does,
As a drunken person staggers
in his vomit.

15 There will be no work for Egypt
^Which *its* head or tail, *its* palm
branch or bulrush, may do.

16 On that day the Egyptians will
become like women, and they
will tremble and be in great fear
because of the ^waving of the hand
of the LORD of armies, which He
is going to wave over them. 17 The
land of Judah will become a cause
of shame to Egypt; everyone to
whom it is mentioned will be in
great fear because of the ^plan of
the LORD of armies which He is
making against them.

18 On that day five cities in the
land of Egypt will be speaking the
language of Canaan and ^swearing
allegiance to the LORD of armies;
one will be called the City of
¹Destruction.

19 On that day there will be an
^altar to the LORD in the midst of
the land of Egypt, and a memorial
stone to the LORD beside its border. 20 And it will become a sign and
a witness to the LORD of armies in
the land of Egypt; for they will cry
out to the LORD because of oppressors, and He will send them a ^Sav-
ior and a ^Champion, and He will
save them. 21 So the LORD will make
Himself known to Egypt, and the
Egyptians will know the LORD on
that day. They will even worship
with ^sacrifice and offering, and
will make a vow to the LORD and
perform it. 22 And the LORD will
strike Egypt, striking but ^healing;

19:7 ^Is 23:3, 10   19:8 ^Ezek 47:10; Hab 1:15
19:9 ^Prov 7:16; Ezek 27:7   19:10 ^Ps 11:3
19:11 ^Num 13:22; Ps 78:12, 43   19:12 ^Is 14:24;
Rom 9:17   19:13 ^Jer 2:16   ^B Zech 10:4
19:14 ^Prov 12:8   ^B Is 3:12   19:15 ^Is 9:14, 15
19:16 ^Is 11:15   19:17 ^Is 14:24; Dan 4:35
19:18 ^Is 45:23; 65:16   19:19 ^Is 56:7; 60:7
19:20 ^Is 43:3, 11   ^B Is 49:25   19:21 ^Is 56:7; 60:7
19:22 ^Deut 32:39; Is 30:26

19:18 ¹ Some mss and ancient versions *the Sun*

so they will return to the LORD, and He will respond to their pleas and heal them.

²³On that day there will be a ^road from Egypt to Assyria, and the Assyrians will come into Egypt and the Egyptians into Assyria; and the Egyptians will ᴮworship with the Assyrians.

²⁴On that day Israel will be the third *party* to Egypt and Assyria, a blessing in the midst of the earth, ²⁵whom the LORD of armies has blessed, saying, "Blessed is ^Egypt My people, and Assyria the work of My hands, and Israel My inheritance."

PROPHECY ABOUT EGYPT AND ETHIOPIA

20 In the year that the commander came to ^Ashdod, when Sargon the king of Assyria sent him and he fought against Ashdod and captured it, ²at that time the LORD spoke through Isaiah the son of Amoz, saying, "Go and loosen the ^sackcloth from your hips and take your ᴮsandals off your feet." And he did so, going naked and barefoot. ³Then the LORD said, "Even as My servant Isaiah has gone naked and barefoot for three years as a ^sign and symbol against Egypt and Cush, ⁴so the ^king of Assyria will lead away the captives of Egypt and the exiles of Cush, ᴮyoung and old, naked and barefoot with buttocks uncovered, to the shame of Egypt. ⁵Then they will be ^terrified and ashamed because of Cush their hope and Egypt their pride. ⁶So the inhabitants of this coastland will say on that day, 'Behold, such is our hope, where we fled for help to be saved from the king of Assyria; and ^how are we ourselves to escape?'"

GOD COMMANDS THAT BABYLON BE TAKEN

21 The pronouncement concerning the ^wilderness of the sea:

As ᴮwindstorms in the Negev come in turns,
It comes from the wilderness, from a terrifying land.
2 A ^harsh vision has been shown to me;
The ᴮtreacherous one *still* deals treacherously, and the destroyer *still* destroys.
Go up, Elam, lay siege, Media;
I have put an end to all the groaning she has caused.
3 For this reason my ^loins are full of anguish;
Pains have seized me like the pains of a woman in labor.
I am so bewildered I cannot hear, so terrified I cannot see.
4 My mind reels, horror overwhelms me;
The twilight I longed for has been ^turned into trembling for me.
5 They ^set the table, they spread out the cloth, they eat, they drink;
"Rise up, captains, oil the shields!"
⁶For this is what the Lord says to me:
"Go, station the lookout, have him ^report what he sees.
7 "When he sees a ^column of chariots, horsemen in pairs,

19:23 ^Is 11:16   ᴮIs 27:13   19:25 ^Is 45:14
20:1 ^1 Sam 5:1   20:2 ^Zech 13:4   ᴮEzek 24:17, 23
20:3 ^Is 8:18   20:4 ^Is 19:4   ᴮIs 47:2, 3
20:5 ^2 Kin 18:21; Is 30:3-5   20:6 ^Matt 23:33;
1 Thess 5:3   21:1 ^Is 13:20-22   ᴮZech 9:14
21:2 ^Ps 60:3   ᴮIs 24:16   21:3 ^Is 13:8; 16:11
21:4 ^Deut 28:67   21:5 ^Jer 51:39, 57; Dan 5:1-4
21:6 ^2 Kin 9:17-20   21:7 ^Is 21:9

A train of donkeys, a train of
    camels,
He is to pay close attention,
    very close attention."

⁸Then the lookout called,
  "^Lord, I stand continually by
    day on the watchtower,
  And I am stationed every night
    at my guard post.
⁹   "Now behold, here comes a
    troop of riders, horsemen in
    pairs."
  And one said, "^Fallen, fallen is
    Babylon;
  And all the ᴮimages of her gods
    are shattered on the ground."
¹⁰ My ^downtrodden *people,* and
    my afflicted of the threshing
    floor!
  What I have heard from the
    Lᴏʀᴅ of armies,
  The God of Israel, I make
    known to you.

PRONOUNCEMENTS ABOUT
EDOM AND ARABIA

¹¹The pronouncement concerning
Edom:
  One keeps calling to me from
    ^Seir,
  "Watchman, how far gone is the
    night?
  Watchman, how far gone is
    the night?"
¹²   The watchman says,
  "Morning comes but also night.
  If you would inquire, inquire;
  Come back again."
¹³The pronouncement about
^Arabia:
  In the thickets of Arabia you
    must spend the night,
  You caravans of ᴮDedanites.
¹⁴   Bring water for the thirsty,
  You inhabitants of the land of
    ^Tema;
  Meet the fugitive with bread.

¹⁵ For they have ^fled from the
    swords,
  From the drawn sword, and
    from the bent bow,
  And from the press of battle.
¹⁶For this is what the Lord said to
me: "In a ^year, as a hired worker
would count it, all the splendor of
ᴮKedar will come to an end; ¹⁷and
the ^remainder of the number of
bowmen, the warriors of the sons
of Kedar, will be few; for the Lᴏʀᴅ
God of Israel has spoken."

THE VALLEY OF VISION

22 The pronouncement con-
cerning the ^valley of vision:
  What is the matter with you
    now, that you have all gone
    up to the ᴮhousetops?
²   You who were full of noise,
  You tumultuous town, you
    jubilant city;
  Your dead were ^not killed
    with the sword,
  Nor did they die in battle.
³   ^All your rulers have fled
    together,
  And have been captured
    without the bow;
  All of you who were found
    were taken captive
    together,
  Though they had fled far
    away.
⁴   Therefore I say, "Look away
    from me,
  Let me ^weep bitterly,
  Do not try to comfort me
    concerning the destruction
    of the daughter of my
    people."

21:8^Hab 2:1   21:9^Is 13:19   ᴮIs 46:1   21:10^Jer 51:33;
Mic 4:13   21:11^Gen 32:3   21:13^Jer 25:23, 24
ᴮGen 10:7   21:14^Gen 25:15; Job 6:19
21:15^Is 13:14, 15; 17:13   21:16^Is 16:14   ᴮPs 120:5
21:17^Is 10:19   22:1^Ps 125:2   ᴮIs 15:3   22:2^Jer 14:18;
Lam 2:20   22:3^Is 21:15   22:4^Is 15:3; Jer 9:1

5 For the Lord God of armies has
   a ^day of panic, ^Bsubjugation,
   and confusion
   In the valley of vision,
   A breaking down of walls
   And a crying to the mountain.
6 ^Elam picked up the quiver,
   With the chariots, infantry,
   and horsemen;
   And ^BKir uncovered the shield.
7 Then your choicest valleys
   were full of chariots,
   And the horsemen took
   positions at the gate.
8 And He removed the defense
   of Judah.
   On that day you depended on
   the weapons of the ^house of
   the forest,
9 And you saw that the
   breaches
   In the *wall* of the city of David
   were many;
   And you ^collected the waters
   of the lower pool.
10 Then you counted the houses
   of Jerusalem
   And tore down houses to
   fortify the wall.
11 And you made a reservoir
   ^between the two walls
   For the waters of the ^Bold pool.
   But you did not depend on
   Him who made it,
   Nor did you take into
   consideration Him who
   planned it long ago.

12 Therefore on that day the Lord
   God of armies called *you* to
   weeping, to wailing,
   To ^shaving the head, and to
   wearing sackcloth.
13 Instead, there is joy and
   jubilation,
   Killing of cattle and
   slaughtering of sheep,

Eating of meat and drinking of
   wine:
   "^Let's eat and drink, for
   tomorrow we may die."
14 But the Lord of armies
   revealed Himself to me:
   "Certainly this wrongdoing ^will
   not be forgiven you
   ^BUntil you die," says the Lord
   God of armies.

15 This is what the Lord God of
armies says:
   "Come, go to this steward,
   To ^Shebna who is in charge of
   the *royal* household,
16 'What right do you have here,
   And whom do you have here,
   That you have ^cut out a tomb
   for yourself here,
   You who cut out a tomb on the
   height,
   You who carve a resting place
   for yourself in the rock?
17 'Behold, the Lord is about
   to hurl you violently, you
   strong man.
   And He is about to grasp you
   firmly
18 *And* wrap you up tightly like a
   ball,
   To be ^driven into a vast
   country;
   There you will die,
   And there your splendid
   chariots will be,
   You shame of your master's
   house!'
19 "I will ^depose you from your
   office,
   And I will pull you down from
   your position.

22:5 ^Is 37:3   ^B Is 10:6   22:6 ^Is 21:2   ^B 2 Kin 16:9
22:8 ^1 Kin 7:2; 10:17   22:9 ^2 Kin 20:20; Neh 3:16
22:11 ^2 Kin 25:4   ^B 2 Kin 20:20   22:12 ^Mic 1:16
22:13 ^Is 56:12; 1 Cor 15:32   22:14 ^1 Sam 3:14
^B Is 65:20   22:15 ^2 Kin 18:18, 26, 37; Is 36:3, 11, 22
22:16 ^2 Sam 18:18; 2 Chr 16:14   22:18 ^Job 18:18;
Is 17:13   22:19 ^Job 40:11, 12; Ezek 17:24

²⁰ "Then it will come about on
    that day,
    That I will summon My
    servant ^AEliakim the son of
    Hilkiah,
²¹ And I will clothe him with
    your tunic
    And tie your sash securely
    around him.
    I will hand your authority over
    to him,
    And he will become a ^Afather
    to the inhabitants of
    Jerusalem and to the house
    of Judah.
²² "Then I will put ^Athe key of
    the ^Bhouse of David on his
    shoulder;
    When he opens, no one will
    shut,
    When he shuts, no one will
    open.
²³ "I will drive him *like* a ^Apeg in a
    firm place,
    And he will become a ^Bthrone
    of glory to his father's house.
²⁴So they will hang on him all the
glory of his father's house, the offspring and the descendants, all the
least of vessels, from bowls to all
the jars. ²⁵On that day," declares the
LORD of armies, "the ^Apeg driven
into a firm place will give way; it
will even ^Bbreak off and fall, and the
load that is *hanging* on it will be cut
off, for the LORD has spoken."

THE FALL OF TYRE

23
The pronouncement con-
cerning ^ATyre:
    Wail, you ships of ^BTarshish,
    For *Tyre* is destroyed, without
    house *or* harbor;
    It is reported to them from the
    land of Cyprus.
² ^ABe silent, you inhabitants of
    the coastland,

    You merchants of Sidon;
    Your messengers crossed the
    sea
³ And *were* on many waters.
    The grain of the ^ANile, the
    harvest of the River was her
    revenue;
    And she was the ^Bmarket of
    nations.
⁴ Be ashamed, ^ASidon,
    For the sea speaks, the
    stronghold of the sea, saying,
    "I have neither been in labor
    nor given birth,
    I have neither brought up
    young men *nor* raised
    virgins."
⁵ When the report *reaches*
    Egypt,
    They will be in ^Aanguish over
    the report of Tyre.
⁶ Pass over to ^ATarshish;
    Wail, you inhabitants of the
    coastland.
⁷ Is this your ^Ajubilant *city*,
    Whose origin is from
    antiquity,
    Whose feet used to bring her
    to colonize distant places?
⁸ Who has planned this against
    Tyre, ^Athe bestower of
    crowns,
    Whose merchants were
    princes, whose traders were
    the honored of the earth?
⁹ The LORD of armies has
    planned it, to ^Adefile the
    pride of all beauty,
    To despise all the ^Bhonored of
    the earth.

22:20 ^A2 Kin 18:18; Is 36:3, 22   22:21 ^AGen 45:8;
Job 29:16   22:22 ^ARev 3:7   ^BIs 7:2, 13
22:23 ^AEzra 9:8   ^B1 Sam 2:8   22:25 ^AIs 22:23
^BEsth 9:24, 25   23:1 ^AJosh 19:29   ^BGen 10:4
23:2 ^AIs 47:5   23:3 ^AJosh 13:3   ^BEzek 27:3-23
23:4 ^AGen 10:15, 19; Josh 11:8   23:5 ^AEx 15:14-16;
Josh 2:9-11   23:6 ^AIs 23:1   23:7 ^AIs 22:2; 32:13
23:8 ^AEzek 28:2   23:9 ^AJob 40:11, 12   ^BIs 5:13

¹⁰ Overflow your land like
　　the Nile, you daughter of
　　Tarshish,
　　There is no more restraint.
¹¹ He has stretched His hand out
　　over the sea,
　　He has ᴬmade the kingdoms
　　tremble;
　　The LORD has given a command
　　concerning Canaan to
　　ᴮdemolish its strongholds.

¹² He has said, "You shall not
　　be jubilant anymore, you
　　crushed virgin daughter of
　　Sidon.
　　Arise, pass over to ᴬCyprus; even
　　there you will find no rest."

¹³ Behold, the land of the
Chaldeans—this is the people *that*
did not exist; Assyria allocated it
for ᴬdesert creatures—they erected
their siege towers, they stripped its
palaces, ᴮthey made it a ruin.
¹⁴ Wail, you ᴬships of Tarshish,
　　For your stronghold is
　　destroyed.
¹⁵ Now on that day Tyre will be forgotten for ᴬseventy years like the
days of one king. At the end of seventy years it will happen to Tyre as
in the song of the prostitute:
¹⁶ Take *your* harp, wander
　　around the city,
　　You forgotten prostitute;
　　Pluck the strings skillfully,
　　sing many songs,
　　That you may be remembered.
¹⁷ It will come about at ᴬthe end of
seventy years that the LORD will
visit Tyre. Then she will go back to
her prostitute's wages and commit
prostitution with all the kingdoms
on the face of the earth. ¹⁸ Her profit
and her prostitute's wages will be
ᴬsacred to the LORD; it will not be
stored up or hoarded, but her profit

will become sufficient food and
magnificent attire for those who
dwell in the presence of the LORD.

JUDGMENT ON THE EARTH

24 Behold, the LORD ᴬlays the
earth waste, devastates it,
twists its surface, and scatters its
inhabitants. ² And the people will
be like the priest, the servant like
his master, the female servant
like her mistress, the buyer like
the seller, the lender like the borrower, the ᴬcreditor like the debtor.
³ The earth will be completely laid
waste and completely plundered,
for the LORD has spoken this word.
⁴ The ᴬearth dries up *and* crumbles away, the mainland dries out
and crumbles away, the exalted
of the people of the earth dwindle. ⁵ The earth is also defiled by
its inhabitants, for they violated
laws, altered statutes, *and* ᴬbroke
the everlasting covenant. ⁶ Therefore, a ᴬcurse devours the earth,
and those who live on it suffer for
their guilt. Therefore, the inhabitants of the earth decrease in number, and few people are left.
⁷ The ᴬnew wine mourns,
　　The vine decays,
　　All the joyful-hearted sigh.
⁸ The ᴬjoy of tambourines
　　ceases,
　　The noise of revelers stops,
　　The joy of the harp ceases.
⁹ They do not drink wine with
　　song;
　　ᴬIntoxicating drink is ᴮbitter to
　　those who drink it.

23:11 ᴬIs 13:13   ᴮIs 25:2   23:12 ᴬIs 23:1   23:13 ᴬIs 13:21
ᴮIs 10:7   23:14 ᴬIs 2:16; Ezek 27:25, 26
23:15 ᴬJer 25:11, 22   23:17 ᴬIs 23:15   23:18 ᴬEx 28:36;
Zech 14:20   24:1 ᴬIs 2:19; 13:13   24:2 ᴬLev 25:36, 37;
Deut 23:19, 20   24:4 ᴬIs 33:9   24:5 ᴬIs 33:8
24:6 ᴬJosh 23:15; Is 34:5   24:7 ᴬIs 16:10; Joel 1:10, 12
24:8 ᴬIs 5:12, 14; Ezek 26:13   24:9 ᴬIs 5:11, 22   ᴮIs 5:20

¹⁰ The ^Acity of chaos is broken
down;
^BEvery house is shut up so that
no one may enter.

¹¹ There is an outcry in the
streets concerning the wine;
^AAll joy turns to gloom.
The joy of the earth is banished.

¹² Desolation is left in the city
And the ^Agate is battered to
ruins.

¹³ For ^Aso it will be in the midst of
the earth among the peoples,
As the shaking of an olive tree,
As the gleanings when the
grape harvest is over.

¹⁴ ^AThey raise their voices, they
shout for joy;
They cry out from the west
concerning the majesty of
the Lord.

¹⁵ Therefore glorify the Lord in
the east,
The ^Aname of the Lord, the
God of Israel,
In the ^Bcoastlands of the sea.

¹⁶ From the ^Aends of the earth we
hear songs: "^BGlory to the
Righteous One,"
But I say, "I am finished! I am
finished! Woe to me!
The treacherous deal
treacherously,
And the treacherous deal very
treacherously."

¹⁷ ^ATerror and pit and snare
Confront you, you inhabitant
of the earth.

¹⁸ Then it will be that the one
who flees the sound of terror
will fall into the pit,
And the one who climbs out of
the pit will be caught in the
snare;
For the ^Awindows above are
opened, and the foundations
of the earth shake.

¹⁹ ^AThe earth is broken apart,
The earth is ^Bsplit through,
The earth is shaken violently.

²⁰ The earth trembles like a
heavy drinker
And sways like a hut,
For its wrongdoing is heavy
upon it,
And it will fall, ^Anever to rise
again.

²¹ So it will happen on that day,
That the Lord will ^Apunish the
rebellious angels of heaven
on high,
And the ^Bkings of the earth on
earth.

²² They will be gathered
together
Like ^Aprisoners in the
dungeon,
And will be confined in
prison;
And after many days they *will*
^B*be* punished.

²³ Then the ^Amoon will be
ashamed and the sun be put
to shame,
For the Lord of armies will
reign on ^BMount Zion and in
Jerusalem,
And *His* glory will be before
His elders.

SONG OF PRAISE FOR GOD'S FAVOR

25 Lord, You are my God;
I will exalt You, I will give
thanks to Your name;
For You have ^Aworked
wonders,
^BPlans *formed* long ago, with
perfect faithfulness.

24:10 ^AIs 34:11   ^BIs 23:1   24:11 ^AIs 16:10; 32:13
24:12 ^AIs 14:31; 45:2   24:13 ^AIs 17:6; 27:12
24:14 ^AIs 12:6; 48:20   24:15 ^AMal 1:11   ^BIs 11:11
24:16 ^AIs 11:12   ^BIs 28:5   24:17 ^AJer 48:43; Amos 5:19
24:18 ^AGen 7:11   24:19 ^AIs 24:1   ^BNum 16:31, 32
24:20 ^ADan 11:19; Amos 8:14   24:21 ^AIs 10:12
^BPs 76:12   24:22 ^AIs 10:4   ^BEzek 38:8   24:23 ^AIs 13:10
^BMic 4:7   25:1 ^APs 40:5   ^BEph 1:11

2 For You have turned a city
   into a heap,
  A fortified city into a ruin;
  A ^palace of strangers is no
   longer a city,
  It will never be rebuilt.
3 Therefore a strong people will
   glorify You;
  ^Cities of ruthless nations will
   revere You.
4 For You have been a
   stronghold for the helpless,
  A stronghold for the poor in
   his distress,
  A refuge from the storm, a
   shade from the heat;
  For the breath of the
   ^ruthless
  Is like a *rain* storm *against* a
   wall.
5 Like heat in a dry land, You
   subdue the ^uproar of
   foreigners;
  Like heat by the shadow of
   a cloud, the song of the
   ruthless is silenced.

6 Now the LORD of armies will
   prepare a lavish banquet
   for ^all peoples on this
   mountain;
  A banquet of aged wine,
   choice pieces with marrow,
  And refined, aged wine.
7 And on this mountain He will
   destroy the ^covering which
   is over all peoples,
  The veil which is stretched
   over all nations.
8 He will [1,]^swallow up death
   for all time,
  And the Lord GOD will ^Bwipe
   tears away from all faces,
  And He will remove the
   disgrace of His people from
   all the earth;
  For the LORD has spoken.

9 And it will be said on that day,
  "Behold, ^this is our God for
   whom we have waited that
   He might save us.
  This is the LORD for whom we
   have waited;
  Let's rejoice and be glad in His
   salvation."
10 For the hand of the LORD will
   rest on this mountain,
  And ^Moab will be trampled
   down in his place
  As straw is trampled down in
   the water of a manure pile.
11 And he will spread out his
   hands in the middle of it
  As a swimmer spreads out *his*
   hands to swim,
  But *the Lord* will ^lay low his
   pride together with the
   trickery of his hands.
12 The ^unassailable
   fortifications of your walls
   He will bring down,
  Lay low, *and* throw to the
   ground, to the dust.

SONG OF TRUST IN GOD'S PROTECTION

26 ^On that day this song will
be sung in the land of Judah:
  "We have a strong city;
  He sets up walls and ramparts
   for ^B security.
2 "Open the ^gates, that the
   righteous nation may enter,
  The one that remains
   faithful.
3 "The steadfast of mind You will
   keep in perfect ^peace,
  Because he trusts in You.

25:2 ^Is 13:22; 32:14 25:3 ^Is 13:11 25:4 ^Is 29:5, 20;
49:25 25:5 ^Jer 51:54-56 25:6 ^Is 2:2-4; 56:7
25:7 ^2 Cor 3:15, 16; Eph 4:18 25:8 ^Hos 13:14
^B Is 30:19 25:9 ^Is 35:2; 40:9 25:10 ^Is 16:14;
Jer 48:1-47 25:11 ^Job 40:11; Is 2:10-12, 15-17
25:12 ^Is 15:1; 25:2 26:1 ^Is 4:2 ^B Is 60:18
26:2 ^Is 60:11, 18; 62:10 26:3 ^Is 26:12; 27:5

25:8 [1] I.e., destroy

4 "ATrust in the LORD forever,
    For in GOD the LORD, *we have*
    an everlasting BRock.
5 "For He has brought low those
    who dwell on high, the
    unassailable city;
    AHe lays it low, He lays it low
    to the ground, He casts it to
    the dust.
6 "AThe foot will trample it,
    The feet of the poor, the steps
    of the helpless."

7 The Away of the righteous is
    smooth;
    O Upright One, make the path
    of the righteous level.
8 Indeed, *while following* the
    way of Your judgments,
    LORD,
    We have waited for You
    eagerly;
    Your name, and Aremembering
    You, is the desire of *our*
    souls.
9 AAt night my soul longs for You,
    Indeed, my spirit within me
    seeks You diligently;
    For when the earth
    experiences Your judgments,
    The inhabitants of the world
    learn righteousness.
10 *Though* the wicked person is
    shown compassion,
    He does not learn
    righteousness;
    He Adeals unjustly in the land
    of uprightness,
    And does not perceive the
    majesty of the LORD.

11 LORD, Your hand is lifted up,
    yet they Ado not see it.
    They see *Your* zeal for the
    people and are put to shame;
    Indeed, fire will devour Your
    enemies.

12 LORD, You will establish Apeace
    for us,
    Since You have also performed
    for us all our works.
13 LORD, our God, Aother masters
    besides You have ruled us;
    But through You alone we
    Bconfess Your name.
14 AThe dead will not live, the
    departed spirits will not rise;
    Therefore You have punished
    and destroyed them,
    And You have eliminated all
    remembrance of them.
15 AYou have increased the
    nation, LORD,
    You have increased the nation,
    You are glorified;
    You have Bextended all the
    borders of the land.
16 LORD, they sought You Ain
    distress;
    They could only whisper a
    prayer,
    Your discipline was upon
    them.
17 AAs the pregnant woman
    approaches *the time* to give
    birth,
    She writhes *and* cries out in
    her labor pains;
    This is how we were before
    You, LORD.
18 We were pregnant, we writhed
    in labor,
    We gave birth, as it seems, *only*
    to wind.
    We could not accomplish
    deliverance for the earth,
    Nor were Ainhabitants of the
    world born.

26:4 AIs 12:2   BIs 17:10   **26:5** AJob 40:11-13
26:6 AIs 28:3   **26:7** AIs 57:2   **26:8** AEx 3:15
26:9 APs 63:5, 6; 77:2   **26:10** AHos 11:7; John 5:37, 38
26:11 AIs 44:9, 18   **26:12** AIs 26:3
26:13 AIs 2:8   BIs 63:7   **26:14** ADeut 4:28; Ps 135:17
26:15 AIs 9:3   BIs 33:17   **26:16** AIs 37:3; Hos 5:15
26:17 AIs 13:8; 21:3   **26:18** APs 17:14

19 Your ᴬdead will live;
   Their corpses will rise.
   You who lie in the dust, ᴮawake
      and shout for joy,
   For your dew *is as* the dew of
      the dawn,
   And the earth will give birth to
      the departed spirits.

20 Come, my people, enter your
      rooms
   And close your doors behind
      you;
   Hide for a little while
   Until ᴬindignation runs *its*
      course.

21 For behold, the Lᴏʀᴅ is about
      to ᴬcome out from His place
   To punish the inhabitants of the
      earth for their wrongdoing;
   And the earth will reveal her
      bloodshed
   And will no longer cover her
      slain.

GOD'S BLESSINGS FOR ISRAEL

27 On that day the Lᴏʀᴅ will
   punish ᴬLeviathan the
   fleeing serpent,
   With His fierce and great and
      mighty sword,
   Even Leviathan the twisted
      serpent;
   And ᴮHe will kill the dragon
      who *lives* in the sea.

2 On that day,
   "A ᴬvineyard of beauty, sing of it!

3 "I, the Lᴏʀᴅ, am its keeper;
   ᴬI water it every moment.
   So that no one will damage it,
   I ᴮguard it night and day.

4 "I have no wrath.
   Should someone give Me
      briars *and* thorns in battle,
   Then I would step on them, ᴬI
      would burn them completely.

5 "Or let him ᴬrely on My
      protection,
   Let him make peace with Me,
   Let him make peace with Me."

6 In the days to come Jacob
   ᴬwill take root,
   Israel will blossom and
      sprout,
   And they will fill the whole
      world with ᴮfruit.

7 Like the striking of Him who
      has struck them, has ᴬHe
      struck them?
   Or like the slaughter of His
      slain, have they been
      slain?

8 You contended with them by
      banishing them, by ᴬdriving
      them away.
   With His fierce wind He has
      expelled *them* on the day of
      the ᴮeast wind.

9 Therefore through this
      Jacob's wrongdoing will be
      ᴬforgiven;
   And this will be the full price
      of the ᴮpardoning of his sin:
   When he makes all the altar
      stones like pulverized chalk
      stones;
   When ¹Asherim and incense
      altars will not stand.

10 For the fortified city is
      ᴬisolated,
   A homestead deserted and
      abandoned like the desert;
   ᴮThere the calf will graze,
   And there it will lie down and
      feed on its branches.

26:19 ᴬIs 25:8   ᴮEph 5:14   26:20 ᴬIs 10:5, 25; 13:5
26:21 ᴬMic 1:3; Jude 14   27:1 ᴬJob 3:8   ᴮIs 51:9
27:2 ᴬPs 80:8; Is 5:7   27:3 ᴬIs 58:11   ¹1 Sam 2:9
27:4 ᴬIs 33:12; Matt 3:12   27:5 ᴬIs 12:2; 25:4
27:6 ᴬIs 37:31   ᴮIs 4:2   27:7 ᴬIs 10:12, 17; 30:31-33
27:8 ᴬIs 50:1   ᴮJer 4:11   27:9 ᴬIs 1:25   ᴮRom 11:27
27:10 ᴬIs 32:13, 14   ᴮIs 17:2

27:9 ¹I.e., wooden symbols of a female deity (Asherah)

11 When its limbs are dry, they
   are broken off;
   Women come *and* make a fire
   with them,
   For they are not a people of
   discernment,
   Therefore ^their Maker ^Bwill
   not have compassion on
   them.
   And their Creator will not be
   gracious to them.
12 On that day the LORD will thresh
from the flowing stream of the
Euphrates River to the brook of
Egypt, and you will be ^gathered up
one by one, you sons of Israel. 13 It
will come about also on that day
that a great ^trumpet will be blown,
and those who were perishing in
the land of Assyria and who were
scattered in the land of Egypt will
come and ^Bworship the LORD on the
holy mountain in Jerusalem.

EPHRAIM'S CAPTIVITY PREDICTED

28 Woe to the proud crown of
   the ^habitually drunk of
   ^BEphraim,
   And to the fading flower of its
   glorious beauty,
   Which is at the head of the
   fertile valley
   Of those who are overcome
   with wine!
2 Behold, the Lord has a strong
   and ^mighty *agent;*
   As a storm of hail, a tempest of
   destruction,
   Like a storm of mighty
   overflowing waters,
   He has thrown *it* down to the
   earth with *His* hand.
3 The splendid crown of the
   habitually drunk of Ephraim
   is ^trampled underfoot.
4 And the fading flower of its
   glorious beauty,

Which is at the head of the
   fertile valley,
   Will be like the ^first-ripe fig
   prior to the summer,
   Which one sees,
   And as soon as it is in his hand,
   He swallows it.
5 On that day the LORD of armies
   will become a beautiful
   ^crown
   And a glorious wreath to the
   remnant of His people;
6 A ^spirit of justice for him who
   sits in judgment,
   A strength to those who repel
   the onslaught at the gate.
7 And these also ^reel with
   wine and stagger from
   intoxicating drink:
   The priest and the prophet reel
   with intoxicating drink,
   They are confused by
   wine, they stagger from
   intoxicating drink;
   They reel while having
   ^Bvisions,
   They stagger *when rendering* a
   verdict.
8 For all the tables are full of
   filthy ^vomit, without a
   single clean place.
9 "To whom would He teach
   knowledge,
   And to whom would He
   interpret the message?
   Those *just* ^weaned from milk?
   Those *just* taken from the
   breast?
10 "For *He says,*
   '^Order on order, order on order,

27:11 ^Deut 32:18   ^BIs 9:17   27:12 ^Deut 30:3, 4;
Neh 1:9   27:13 ^Lev 25:9   ^BIs 19:21, 23   28:1 ^Is 28:7
^BIs 9:9   28:2 ^Is 8:7; 40:10   28:3 ^Is 26:6; 28:18
28:4 ^Hos 9:10; Mic 7:1   28:5 ^Is 62:3
28:6 ^1 Kin 3:28; Is 11:2   28:7 ^Is 5:11, 22   ^BIs 29:11
28:8 ^Jer 48:26   28:9 ^Ps 131:2   28:10 ^2 Chr 36:15;
Neh 9:30

Line on line, line on line,
A little here, a little there.'"
11 Indeed, He will speak to this
people
Through ^stammering lips and
a foreign tongue,
12 He who said to them, "This is
the ^place of quiet, give rest
to the weary,"
And, "This is the resting place,"
but they would not listen.
13 So the word of the LORD to
them will be,
"Order on order, order on order,
Line on line, line on line,
A little here, a little there,"
That they may go and ^stumble
backward, be broken,
snared, and taken captive.

JUDAH IS WARNED

14 Therefore, hear the word of
the LORD, you ^scoffers,
Who rule this people who are
in Jerusalem,
15 Because you have said, "We
have made a ^covenant with
death,
And with Sheol we have made
a pact.
The gushing flood will not
reach us when it passes by,
Because we have made
falsehood our refuge and we
have ^concealed ourselves
with deception."
16 Therefore this is what the Lord
GOD says:
"^Behold, I am laying a stone in
Zion, a tested stone,
A precious cornerstone *for* the
foundation, firmly placed.
The one who believes *in it* will
not be disturbed.
17 "I will make ^justice the
measuring line
And righteousness the level;

Then ^hail will sweep away the
refuge of lies,
And the waters will overflow
the secret place.
18 "Your ^covenant with death will
be canceled,
And your pact with Sheol will
not stand;
When the ^gushing flood
passes through,
Then you will become its
^trampling *ground*.
19 "As ^often as it passes through,
it will seize you;
For ^morning after morning
it will pass through,
anytime during the day
or night,
And it will be sheer terror
to understand what it
means."
20 The bed is too short on which
to stretch out,
And the ^blanket is too small
to wrap oneself in.
21 For the LORD will rise up as *at*
Mount ^Perazim,
He will be stirred up as in the
Valley of ^Gibeon,
To do His task, His unusual
task,
And to work His work, His
extraordinary work.
22 And now do not carry on as
^scoffers,
Or your shackles will be made
stronger;
For I have heard from the
Lord GOD of armies
Of decisive ^destruction on
all the earth.

28:11 ^Is 33:19; 1 Cor 14:21   **28:12** ^Is 11:10; 30:15
28:13 ^Is 8:15; Matt 21:44   **28:14** ^Is 29:20
28:15 ^Is 28:18   ^Is 29:15   **28:16** ^Rom 9:33; 10:11
28:17 ^2 Kin 21:13   ^Is 28:2   **28:18** ^Is 28:15   ^Is 28:3
28:19 ^2 Kin 24:2   ^Is 50:4   **28:20** ^Is 59:6
28:21 ^2 Sam 5:20   ^Josh 10:10, 12   **28:22** ^Is 28:14
^Is 10:22, 23

23 Listen and hear my voice,
  Pay attention and hear my
    words.
24 Does the farmer plow
    continually to plant seed?
  Does he *continually* turn and
    break up his ground?
25 Does he not level its surface
  And sow dill and scatter ^Acumin
  And plant ^Bwheat in rows,
  Barley in its place and rye
    within its area?
26 For his God instructs and
    teaches him properly.
27 For dill is not threshed with a
    ^Athreshing sledge,
  Nor is the cartwheel driven
    over cumin;
  But dill is beaten out with a
    rod, and cumin with a club.
28 *Grain for* bread is crushed,
  Indeed, he does not continue
    to thresh it forever.
  Because the wheel of *his* cart
    and his horses *eventually*
    damage *it,*
  He does not thresh it *longer.*
29 This also comes from the LORD
    of armies,
  Who has made *His* counsel
    ^Awonderful and *His* wisdom
    ^Bgreat.

JERUSALEM IS WARNED

29 Woe, ¹Ariel, Ariel the city
    where David *once* ^Acamped!
  Add year to year, keep *your*
    feasts on schedule.
2 I will bring distress to Ariel,
  And she will be *a city of*
    grieving and ^Amourning;
  And she will be like an ¹Ariel
    to me.
3 I will ^Acamp against you
    encircling *you,*
  And I will set up siegeworks
    against you,

And I will raise up battle
  towers against you.
4 Then you will ^Abe brought low;
  From the earth you will speak,
  And from the dust *where* you
    are prostrate
  Your words *will come.*
  Your voice will also be like that
    of a spirit from the ground,
  And your speech will whisper
    from the dust.
5 But the multitude of your
    enemies will become like
    fine ^Adust,
  And the multitude of the
    ruthless ones like the chaff
    which blows away;
  And it will happen instantly,
    suddenly.
6 From the LORD of armies
    you will be ^Apunished with
    ^Bthunder and earthquake
    and loud noise,
  With whirlwind and
    tempest and the flame of a
    consuming fire.
7 And the ^Amultitude of all
    the nations who wage war
    against Ariel,
  Even all who wage war against
    her and her stronghold, and
    who distress her,
  Will be like a dream, a vision
    of the night.
8 It will be as when a hungry
    person dreams—
  And behold, he is eating;
  But when he awakens, his
    hunger is not satisfied,

28:25 ^AMatt 23:23   ^BEx 9:32   28:27 ^AAmos 1:3
28:29 ^AIs 9:6   ^BIs 31:2   29:1 ^A2 Sam 5:9   29:2 ^AIs 3:26;
Lam 2:5   29:3 ^ALuke 19:43, 44   29:4 ^AIs 8:19
29:5 ^AIs 17:13; 41:15, 16   29:6 ^AIs 10:3   ^B1 Sam 2:10
29:7 ^AMic 4:11, 12; Zech 12:9

29:1 ¹ I.e., Lion of God, or Jerusalem   29:2 ¹Ariel (i.e.,
Jerusalem) is a Heb word for "altar hearth" where
offerings were burned

Or as when a thirsty person
dreams—
And behold, he is drinking,
But when he awakens, behold,
he is faint
And his thirst is not quenched.
^So will the multitude of all the
nations be
Who wage war against Mount
Zion.

9 ^Be delayed and horrified,
Blind yourselves and be blind;
They become drunk, but not
with wine,
They stagger, but not with
intoxicating drink.
10 For the Lord has poured over
you a spirit of deep ^sleep,
He has shut your eyes—the
prophets;
And He has covered your
heads—the seers.
11 The entire vision will be to you
like the words of a sealed ^book,
which, when they give it to the one
who is literate, saying, "Please read
this," he will say, "I cannot, because
it is sealed." 12 Then the book will be
given to the one who is illiterate,
saying, "Please read this." And he
will say, "I cannot read."
13 Then the Lord said,
"Because ^this people
approaches Me with their
words
And honors Me with their lips,
But their heart is far away
from Me,
And their reverence
for Me consists of the
commandment of men that
is taught;
14 Therefore behold, I will once
again deal marvelously with
this people, wondrously
marvelous;

And ^the wisdom of their wise
men will perish,
And the understanding
of their men who have
understanding will be
concealed."

15 Woe to those who deeply
^hide their plans from the
Lord,
And whose ^deeds are done in
a dark place,
And they say, "Who sees us?"
or "Who knows us?"
16 You turn things around!
Shall the potter be considered
as equal with the clay,
That ^what is made would say
to its maker, "He did not
make me";
Or what is formed say to him
who formed it, "He has no
understanding"?

BLESSING AFTER DISCIPLINE

17 Is it not yet just a little while
Before Lebanon will be
turned into a ^fertile field,
And the fertile field will be
considered as a forest?
18 On that day those who are
^deaf will hear ^words of a
book,
And out of their gloom and
darkness the eyes of those
who are blind will see.
19 The ^afflicted also will
increase their joy in the
Lord,
And the ^needy of mankind
will rejoice in the Holy One
of Israel.

29:8 ^Is 54:17   29:9 ^Is 29:1   29:10 ^Ps 69:23;
Is 6:9, 10   29:11 ^Is 8:16; Dan 12:4, 9
29:13 ^Ezek 33:31; Matt 15:8, 9   29:14 ^Is 44:25; Jer 8:9
29:15 ^Ps 10:11, 13   ^Job 22:13   29:16 ^Is 45:9; 64:8
29:17 ^Ps 84:6; 107:33, 35   29:18 ^Is 35:5   ^Is 29:11
29:19 ^Ps 25:9   ^Is 3:14, 15

20 For the ruthless will come to
   an end and the scorner will
   be finished,
   Indeed ^all who are intent on
   doing evil will be eliminated,
21 Who cause a person to be
   indicted by a word,
   And set a trap for the
   arbitrator at the gate,
   And ^defraud the one in the
   right with meaningless
   arguments.
22 Therefore this is what the LORD,
who redeemed Abraham, says concerning the house of Jacob:
   "Jacob ^will not be ashamed
   now, nor will his face turn
   pale now;
23 But when he sees his ^children,
   the work of My hands, in his
   midst,
   They will sanctify My name;
   Indeed, they will ^Bsanctify the
   Holy One of Jacob,
   And will stand in awe of the
   God of Israel.
24 "Those who err in mind will
   ^know the truth,
   And those who criticize will
   ^Baccept instruction.

JUDAH WARNED AGAINST
EGYPTIAN ALLIANCE

30 "Woe to the rebellious
   children," declares the
   LORD,
   "Who ^execute a plan, but not
   Mine,
   And ^Bmake an alliance, but not
   of My Spirit,
   In order to add sin to sin;
2 Who proceed down to Egypt
   Without ^consulting Me,
   ^BTo take refuge in the safety of
   Pharaoh,
   And to seek shelter in the
   shadow of Egypt!

3 "Therefore the safety of
   Pharaoh will be ^your shame,
   And the shelter in the shadow
   of Egypt, your humiliation.
4 "For ^their officials are at Zoan
   And their ambassadors arrive
   at Hanes.
5 "Everyone will be ^ashamed
   because of a people who do
   not benefit them,
   Who are not a help or benefit,
   but a source of shame and
   also disgrace."

6 The pronouncement concerning the animals of the ^Negev:
   Through a land of distress and
   anguish,
   From where come lioness
   and lion, viper and ^Bflying
   serpent,
   They carry their riches on the
   backs of young donkeys,
   And their treasures on camels'
   humps,
   To a people who will not
   benefit them;
7 Even Egypt, whose ^help is
   vain and empty.
   Therefore, I have called her
   "^1,BRahab who has been
   exterminated."

8 Now go, ^write it on a tablet in
   their presence
   And inscribe it on a scroll,
   That it may serve in the time
   to come
   As a witness forever.
9 For this is a ^rebellious people,
   false sons,

29:20 ^Is 59:4; Mic 2:1   29:21 ^Is 32:7; Amos 5:12
29:22 ^Is 45:17; 49:23   29:23 ^Is 49:20-26   ^BIs 5:16
29:24 ^Is 41:20   ^BIs 54:13   30:1 ^Is 29:15   ^BIs 8:11, 12
30:2 ^Is 8:19   ^BIs 36:9   30:3 ^Is 20:5, 6; 36:6
30:4 ^Is 19:11   30:5 ^Jer 2:36   30:6 ^Gen 12:9
^BDeut 8:15   30:7 ^Is 30:5   ^BJob 9:13   30:8 ^Is 8:1
30:9 ^Is 30:1

30:7 ¹MT They are Rahab or arrogance, to remain; i.e.,
Egypt, as a sea monster; see note Job 26:12

Sons who refuse to ^Blisten
To the instruction of the LORD;

10 Who say to the seers, "You
must not see *visions*";
And to the prophets, "You must
not prophesy the truth to us.
^ASpeak to us pleasant words,
Prophesy illusions.

11 "Get out of the way, ^Aturn aside
from the path,
^BStop *speaking* before us *about*
the Holy One of Israel!"

12 Therefore this is what the Holy
One of Israel says:
"^ASince you have rejected this
word
And have put your trust in
oppression and crookedness,
and have relied on them,

13 Therefore this ^Awrongdoing
will be to you
Like a breach about to fall,
A bulge in a high wall,
Whose collapse comes
^Bsuddenly in an instant,

14 Whose collapse is like the
smashing of a ^Apotter's jar,
So ruthlessly shattered
That a shard will not be found
among its pieces
To take fire from a hearth
Or to scoop water from a
cistern."

15 For this is what the Lord GOD, the
Holy One of Israel, has said:
"In repentance and ^Arest you
will be saved,
In quietness and trust is your
strength."
But you were not willing,

16 And you said, "No, for we will
flee on ^Ahorses!"
Therefore you shall flee!
"And we will ride on swift
horses!"
Therefore those who pursue
you shall be swift.

17 ^AOne thousand *will flee* at the
threat of one *man;*
You will flee at the threat of
five,
Until you are left like a signal
post on a mountain top,
And like a flag on a hill.

GOD IS GRACIOUS AND JUST

18 Therefore the LORD ^Alongs to
be gracious to you,
And therefore He waits on
high to have compassion on
you.
For the LORD is a God of
justice;
How blessed are all those who
^Blong for Him.

19 For, you people in Zion, inhabitant in Jerusalem, you will ^Aweep no longer. He will certainly be gracious to you at the sound of your cry; when He hears it, He will answer you. 20 Although the Lord has given you bread of deprivation and water of oppression, *He,* your Teacher, will no longer ^Ahide Himself, but your eyes will see your Teacher. 21 Your ears will hear a word behind you, saying, "This is the ^Away, walk in it," whenever you turn to the right or to the left. 22 And you will desecrate your carved ^Aimages plated with silver, and your cast metal ^Aimages plated with gold. You will scatter them as a filthy thing, *and* say to them, "^BBe gone!"

23 Then He will ^Agive *you* rain for your seed which you will sow in the ground, and bread *from* the yield of the ground, and it will be rich

30:9 ^B Is 1:10 30:10 ^A 1 Kin 22:8, 13; Jer 6:14
30:11 ^A Acts 13:8 ^B Job 21:14 30:12 ^A Is 5:24; 7:9
30:13 ^A Is 26:21 ^B Is 29:5 30:14 ^A Ps 2:9; Jer 19:10, 11
30:15 ^A Ps 116:7; Is 28:12 30:16 ^A Is 2:7; 31:1, 3
30:17 ^A Lev 26:36; Deut 28:25 30:18 ^A Is 42:14, 16
^B Is 8:17 30:19 ^A Is 25:8; 60:20 30:20 ^A Ps 74:9;
Amos 8:11 30:21 ^A Ps 25:8, 9; Prov 3:6 30:22 ^A Ex 32:2, 4
^B Matt 4:10 30:23 ^A Ps 65:9-13; 104:13, 14

and plentiful; on that day your livestock will graze in a wide pasture.
24 Also the oxen and the donkeys that work the ground will eat seasoned feed, which has been ^winnowed with shovel and pitchfork.
25 And on every lofty mountain and ^every high hill there will be streams running with water on the day of the great ᴮslaughter, when the towers fall. 26 ^And the light of the full moon will be like the light of the sun, and the light of the sun will be seven times *brighter,* like the light of seven days, on the day the LORD binds up the fracture of His people and heals the wound He has inflicted.
27 Behold, ^the name of the LORD comes from a remote place;
ᴮHis anger is burning and dense with smoke;
His lips are filled with indignation,
And His tongue is like a consuming fire;
28 His breath is like an overflowing river,
Which reaches to the neck,
To ^shake the nations back and forth in a sieve,
And to *put* in the jaws of the peoples ᴮthe bridle which leads astray.
29 You will have songs as in the night when you keep the festival,
And gladness of heart as when one marches to *the sound of* the flute,
To go to the mountain of the LORD, to the Rock of Israel.
30 And the LORD will cause His voice of authority to be heard,
And the descending of His arm to be seen in fierce anger,

And *in* the flame of a consuming fire
In cloudburst, downpour, and hailstones.
31 For at the voice of the LORD Assyria will be terrified,
When He strikes with the ^rod.
32 And every blow of the ^rod of punishment,
Which the LORD will lay on him,
Will be with *the music of* tambourines and lyres;
And in battles, ᴮbrandishing weapons, He will fight them.
33 For ¹,^Topheth has long been ready,
Indeed, it has been prepared for the king.
He has made it deep and large,
A pyre of fire with plenty of wood;
The breath of the LORD, like a torrent of brimstone, sets it afire.

HELP NOT IN EGYPT BUT IN GOD

31 Woe to those who go down to Egypt for help
And rely on horses,
And trust in chariots because they are many
And in horsemen because they are very strong,
But they do not ^look to the ᴮHoly One of Israel, nor seek the LORD!
2 Yet He also is ^wise and will bring disaster,
And does ᴮnot retract His words,

30:24 ^Matt 3:12; Luke 3:17   30:25 ^Is 35:6, 7
ᴮIs 34:2   30:26 ^Is 24:23; 60:19, 20   30:27 ^Is 59:19
ᴮIs 10:17   30:28 ^Amos 9:9   ᴮ2 Kin 19:28
30:31 ^Is 10:26; 11:4   30:32 ^Is 10:24   ᴮEzek 32:10
30:33 ^2 Kin 23:10; Jer 7:31   31:1 ^Is 9:13   ᴮIs 10:17
31:2 ^Is 28:29   ᴮNum 23:19

30:33 ¹I.e., the place of human sacrifice to Molech

But will arise against the house
   of evildoers,
And against the help of the
   workers of injustice.
3 Now the Egyptians are ᴬhuman
   and not God,
And their ᴮhorses are flesh and
   not spirit;
So the LORD will stretch out
   His hand,
And *any* helper will stumble,
And one who is helped will fall.
And all of them will come to
   an end together.

4 For this is what the LORD says
   to me:
"As the lion or the young lion
   growls over his prey,
Against which a band of
   shepherds is called out,
And he will not be terrified at
   their voice nor disturbed at
   their noise,
So will the LORD of armies
   come down to wage ᴬwar on
   Mount Zion and on its hill."
5 Like flying birds so the LORD
   of armies will protect
   Jerusalem.
He will ᴬprotect and save *it;*
He will pass over and rescue *it.*
6 ᴬReturn to Him against whom
you have been ᴮprofoundly obstinate, you sons of Israel. 7 For on that
day every person will ᴬreject his silver idols and his gold idols, which
your hands have made for you as
ᴮa sin.
8 And the Assyrian will fall by a
   sword not *wielded by* a man,
And a ᴬsword not of man will
   devour him.
So he will ᴮnot escape the
   sword,
And his young men will
   become forced laborers.

9 "His rock will pass away
   because of panic,
And his officers will be
   terrified by the flag,"
Declares the LORD, whose ᴬfire
   is in Zion and whose furnace
   is in Jerusalem.

THE GLORIOUS FUTURE

32 Behold, a ᴬking will reign
   righteously,
And officials will rule justly.
2 Each will be like a ᴬrefuge from
   the wind
And a shelter from the storm,
Like streams of water in a dry
   country,
Like the ᴬshade of a huge rock
   in an exhausted land.
3 Then ᴬthe eyes of those who
   see will not be blinded,
And the ears of those who
   hear will listen.
4 The mind of the ᴬrash will
   discern the truth,
And the tongue of the
   stammerers will hurry to
   speak clearly.
5 No longer will the ᴬfool be
   called noble,
Or the rogue be spoken of *as*
   generous.
6 For a fool speaks nonsense,
And his heart inclines toward
   wickedness:
To practice ᴬungodliness and
   to speak error against the
   LORD,
To ᴮkeep the hungry person
   unsatisfied
And to withhold drink from
   the thirsty.

31:3 ᴬEzek 28:9   ᴮIs 36:9   31:4 ᴬIs 42:13; Zech 12:8
31:5 ᴬIs 37:35; 38:6   31:6 ᴬIs 44:22   ᴮIs 1:2, 5
31:7 ᴬIs 2:20   ᴮ1 Kin 12:30   31:8 ᴬIs 66:16   ᴮIs 21:15
31:9 ᴬIs 10:16, 17; 30:33   32:1 ᴬPs 72:1–4; Is 9:6, 7
32:2 ᴬIs 4:6; 25:4   32:3 ᴬIs 29:18   32:4 ᴬIs 29:24
32:5 ᴬ1 Sam 25:25   32:6 ᴬIs 9:17   ᴮIs 3:15

7 As for a rogue, his weapons
  are evil;
He ^devises wicked schemes
To destroy *the* poor with
  slander,
Even though *the* needy one
  speaks what is right.
8 But ^the noble person devises
  noble plans;
And by noble plans he stands.

9 Rise up, you ^women who are
  at ease,
And hear my voice;
Listen to my word,
You complacent daughters.
10 Within a year and *a few* days
  You will be troubled, you
    complacent *daughters;*
  ^For the vintage is ended,
  And the *fruit* gathering will
    not come.
11 Tremble, you *women* who are
  at ease;
^Be troubled, you complacent
  daughters;
^Strip, undress, and put
  sackcloth on *your* waist,
12 ^Beat your breasts for the
  pleasant fields, for the
  fruitful vine,
13 ^For the land of my people *in
  which* thorns *and* briars will
  come up;
Indeed, for all the joyful houses
  and for the ^jubilant city.
14 For ^the palace has been
  neglected, the populated
  ^city abandoned.
Hill and watch-tower have
  become caves forever,
A delight for wild donkeys, a
  pasture for flocks,
15 Until the ^Spirit is poured out
  upon us from on high,
And the wilderness becomes a
  fertile field,

And the fertile field is
  considered as a forest.
16 Then ^justice will dwell in the
  wilderness,
And righteousness will remain
  in the fertile field.
17 And the ^work of
  righteousness will be peace,
And the service of
  righteousness, quietness and
  confidence forever.
18 Then my people will live in a
  ^peaceful settlement,
In secure dwellings, and in
  undisturbed ^resting places;
19 And it will hail when the forest
  comes down,
And ^the city will be utterly
  laid low.
20 How ^blessed will you be, you
  who sow beside all waters,
Who let the ox and the donkey
  out freely.

THE JUDGMENT OF GOD

33 Woe to you, destroyer,
While you were not
  destroyed;
And he who is treacherous,
  while *others* did not deal
  treacherously with him.
As soon as you finish
  destroying, ^you will be
  destroyed;
As soon as you cease to deal
  treacherously, *others* will
  ^deal treacherously with you.
2 Lord, ^be gracious to us; we
  have ^waited for You.
Be their strength every
  morning,

32:7 ^Jer 5:26-28; Mic 7:3   32:8 ^Prov 11:25
32:9 ^Is 47:8; Amos 6:1   32:10 ^Is 5:5, 6; 7:23
32:11 ^Is 22:12   ^Is 47:2   32:12 ^Nah 2:7
32:13 ^Is 5:6, 10, 17   ^Is 22:2   32:14 ^Is 13:22   ^Is 6:11
32:15 ^Is 11:2; 44:3   32:16 ^Is 33:5; Zech 8:3
32:17 ^Ps 72:2, 3; 85:8   32:18 ^Is 26:3, 12   ^Is 11:10
32:19 ^Is 24:10, 12; 26:5   32:20 ^Eccl 11:1; Is 30:23, 24
33:1 ^Is 10:12   ^Jer 25:12-14   33:2 ^Is 30:18, 19   ^Is 25:9

Our salvation also in the time
of distress.

3 At the sound of a roar,
^peoples flee;
At the lifting up of Yourself,
nations disperse.

4 Your plunder is gathered *as*
the caterpillar gathers;
Like an infestation of locusts,
people storm it.

5 The LORD is exalted, for He
dwells on high;
He has ^filled Zion with justice
and righteousness.

6 And He will be the stability of
your times,
A ^wealth of salvation,
wisdom, and ^Bknowledge;
The fear of the LORD is his
treasure.

7 Behold, their brave men cry
out in the streets,
The ^ambassadors of peace
weep bitterly.

8 The highways are desolate, the
^traveler has ceased,
He has ^Bbroken the covenant,
he has despised the cities,
He has no regard for mankind.

9 ^The land mourns *and* wastes
away,
Lebanon is shamed *and*
withers;
Sharon is like a desert plain,
And Bashan and Carmel lose
their foliage.

10 "Now ^I will arise," says the LORD,
"Now I will be exalted, now I
will be lifted up.

11 "You have conceived chaff, you
will give birth to stubble;
My ^breath will consume you
like a fire.

12 "The peoples will be burned to
lime,
^Like cut thorns which are
burned in the fire.

13 "You who are far away, ^hear
what I have done;
And you who are near,
acknowledge My might."

14 ^Sinners in Zion are terrified;
^BTrembling has seized the
godless.
"Who among us can live with
the consuming fire?
Who among us can live with
everlasting burning?"

15 One who ^walks righteously
and speaks with integrity,
One who rejects unjust gain
And shakes his hands so that
they hold no bribe;
One who stops his ears from
hearing about bloodshed
And ^Bshuts his eyes from
looking at evil;

16 He will dwell on the heights,
^His refuge will be the
impregnable rock;
His bread will be given *him,*
His water will be sure.

17 Your eyes will see ^the King in
His beauty;
They will see ^Ba distant land.

18 Your heart will meditate on
^terror:
"Where is one who counts?
Where is one who weighs?
Where is one who counts the
towers?"

19 You will no longer see a fierce
people,
A people of ^unintelligible
speech which no one
comprehends,

33:3 ^Is 17:13; 21:15   33:5 ^Is 1:26; 28:6   33:6 ^Is 45:17
^B Is 11:9   33:7 ^2 Kin 18:18, 37   33:8 ^Is 35:8   ^B Is 24:5
33:9 ^Is 3:26; 24:4   33:10 ^Ps 12:5; Is 2:19, 21
33:11 ^Is 1:31   33:12 ^2 Sam 23:6, 7; Is 10:17
33:13 ^Ps 48:10; Is 49:1   33:14 ^Is 1:28   ^B Is 32:11
33:15 ^Ps 15:2   ^B Ps 119:37   33:16 ^Is 25:4
33:17 ^Is 6:5   ^B Is 26:15   33:18 ^Is 17:14
33:19 ^Deut 28:49, 50; Is 28:11

Of a stammering tongue
which no one understands.
20 ᴬLook at Zion, the city of our
appointed feasts;
Your eyes will see Jerusalem,
an undisturbed settlement,
ᴮA tent which will not be folded;
Its stakes will never be pulled
up,
Nor any of its ropes be torn
apart.
21 But there the majestic *One*,
the Lᴏʀᴅ, will be for us
A place of ᴬrivers *and* wide
canals
On which no boat with oars
will go,
And on which no mighty ship
will pass—
22 For the Lᴏʀᴅ is our ᴬjudge,
The Lᴏʀᴅ is ᴮour lawgiver,
The Lᴏʀᴅ is our king;
He will save us—
23 Your *ship's* tackle hangs slack;
It cannot hold the base of its
mast firmly,
Nor spread out the sail.
Then the prey of an abundant
spoil will be divided;
ᴬThose who limp will take the
plunder.
24 And no resident will say, "I am
ᴬsick";
The people who live there will
be ᴮforgiven *their* wrongdoing.

GOD'S WRATH AGAINST NATIONS

34 Come near, you nations,
to hear; and listen, you
peoples!
ᴬLet the earth and all it
contains hear, and the world
and all that springs from it.
2 For the Lᴏʀᴅ's ᴬanger is against
all the nations,
And *His* wrath against all their
armies.

He has utterly destroyed
them,
He has turned them over to
slaughter.
3 So their slain will be ᴬthrown
out,
And their corpses will give off
their stench,
And the mountains will be
drenched with their blood.
4 And ᴬall the heavenly ¹lights
will wear away,
And the ᴮsky will be rolled up
like a scroll;
All its lights will also wither
away
As a leaf withers from the
vine,
Or as *one* withers from the fig
tree.
5 For ᴬMy sword has drunk its
fill in heaven;
Behold it shall descend for
judgment upon Edom,
And upon the people whom
I have designated for
destruction.
6 The sword of the Lᴏʀᴅ is filled
with blood,
It drips with fat, with the
blood of lambs and goats,
With the fat of the kidneys of
rams.
For the Lᴏʀᴅ has a sacrifice in
ᴬBozrah,
And a great slaughter in the
land of Edom.
7 Wild oxen will also fall with
them
And young bulls with strong
ones;

33:20 ᴬPs 48:12   ᴮIs 54:2   33:21 ᴬIs 41:18; 43:19, 20
33:22 ᴬIs 2:4   ᴮIs 1:10   33:23 ᴬ2 Kin 7:8; Is 35:6
33:24 ᴬIs 30:26   ᴮIs 40:2   34:1 ᴬDeut 32:1; Is 1:2
34:2 ᴬIs 26:20   34:3 ᴬIs 14:19   34:4 ᴬIs 13:13
ᴮRev 6:12-14   34:5 ᴬDeut 32:41, 42; Jer 46:10
34:6 ᴬIs 63:1; Jer 49:13

34:4 ¹ Lit *host*; i.e., sun, stars, etc.

So their land will be ^soaked
   with blood,
And their dust become greasy
   with fat.
8 For the LORD has a day of
   ^vengeance,
A year of retribution for the
   cause of Zion.
9 Its streams will be turned into
   pitch,
And its loose earth into
   ^brimstone,
And its land will become
   burning pitch.
10 It will ^not be extinguished
   night or day;
Its ^Bsmoke will go up forever.
From generation to
   generation it will be
   desolate;
None will pass through it
   forever and ever.
11 But ^pelican and hedgehog will
   possess it,
And owl and raven will dwell
   in it;
And He will stretch over it the
   line of desolation
And the plumb line of
   emptiness.
12 Its nobles—there is ^no one
   there
Whom they may proclaim
   king—
And all its officials will be
   nothing.
13 Thorns will come up in its
   ^fortified towers,
Weeds and thistles in its
   fortified cities;
It will also be a haunt of
   jackals
And a habitat of ostriches.
14 The desert ^creatures will meet
   with the wolves,
The ^goat also will cry to its
   kind.

Yes, the night-bird will settle
   there
And will find herself a resting
   place.
15 The tree snake will make its
   nest and lay *eggs* there,
And it will hatch and gather
   them under its protection.
Yes, ^the hawks will be
   gathered there,
Every one with its kind.
16 Seek from the ^book of the LORD,
and read:
Not one of these will be missing;
None will lack its mate.
For ^BHis mouth has
   commanded,
And His Spirit has gathered
   them.
17 He has cast the ^lot for them,
And His hand has divided it to
   them by the ^Bmeasuring line.
They shall possess it forever;
From generation to generation
   they will dwell in it.

ZION'S HAPPY FUTURE

35 The wilderness and the
   desert will rejoice,
And the ^desert will shout for
   joy and blossom;
Like the crocus
2 It will blossom profusely
And rejoice with joy and
   jubilation.
The ^glory of Lebanon will be
   given to it,
The majesty of Carmel and
   Sharon.
They will see the ^Bglory of the
   LORD,
The majesty of our God.

34:7 ^Is 63:6   34:8 ^Is 13:6; 35:4   34:9 ^Deut 29:23;
Ps 11:6   34:10 ^Is 1:31   ^BRev 14:11   34:11 ^Zeph 2:14
34:12 ^Jer 27:20; 39:6   34:13 ^Is 13:22; 25:2
34:14 ^Is 13:21   34:15 ^Deut 14:13   34:16 ^Is 30:8
^BIs 1:20   34:17 ^Is 17:13, 14   ^BIs 34:11   35:1 ^Is 41:19;
51:3   35:2 ^Is 60:13   ^BIs 25:9

3 ᴬStrengthen the exhausted,
   and make the feeble
   strong.
4 Say to those with ᴬanxious
   heart,
   "Take courage, fear not.
   Behold, your God will come
   with ᴮvengeance;
   The retribution of God will
   come,
   But He will save you."
5 Then the ᴬeyes of those who
   are blind will be opened,
   And the ears of those who are
   deaf will be unstopped.
6 Then those who ᴬlimp will
   leap like a deer,
   And the ᴮtongue of those who
   cannot speak will shout for
   joy.
   For waters will burst forth in
   the wilderness,
   And streams in the desert.
7 The scorched land will
   become a pool
   And the thirsty ground
   ᴬsprings of water;
   In the haunt of jackals, its
   resting place,
   Grass *becomes* reeds and
   rushes.
8 A highway will be there, ᴬa
   roadway,
   And it will be called the
   Highway of Holiness.
   The unclean will not travel
   on it,
   But it *will* be for the one who
   walks *that* way,
   And ᴮfools will not wander *on
   it.*
9 No ᴬlion will be there,
   Nor will any vicious animal go
   up on it;
   They will not be found there.
   But ᴮthe redeemed will walk
   there,

10 And ᴬthe redeemed of the
   LORD will return
   And come to Zion with joyful
   shouting,
   And everlasting joy will be on
   their heads.
   They will obtain gladness and
   joy,
   And sorrow and sighing will
   flee away.

SENNACHERIB INVADES JUDAH

36 ᴬNow in the fourteenth year
of King Hezekiah, ᴮSennacherib king of Assyria marched
against all the fortified cities of
Judah and seized them. ²And the
ᴬking of Assyria sent Rabshakeh
from Lachish to Jerusalem to King
Hezekiah with a large army. And
he stood by the ᴮconduit of the
upper pool on the road to the ¹fuller's field. ³Then ᴬEliakim the son of
Hilkiah, who was over the household, and Shebna the scribe, and
Joah the son of Asaph, the secretary, went out to him.

⁴And ᴬRabshakeh said to them,
"Say now to Hezekiah, 'This is what
the great king, the king of Assyria
says: "What is this confidence
that you have? ⁵I say, 'Your plan
and strength for the war are only
empty words.' Now on whom have
you relied, that ᴬyou have revolted
against me? ⁶Behold, you have relied
on the staff of this broken reed, on
Egypt, on which if a man leans, it
will go into his hand and pierce it.
ᴬSo is Pharaoh king of Egypt to all

35:3 ᴬJob 4:3, 4; Heb 12:12 35:4 ᴬIs 32:4 ᴮIs 1:24
35:5 ᴬIs 29:18; 32:3, 4 35:6 ᴬMatt 15:30 ᴮMatt 9:32
35:7 ᴬIs 41:10 35:8 ᴬIs 30:21 ᴮIs 33:8 35:9 ᴬIs 5:29
ᴮIs 51:10 35:10 ᴬIs 1:27; 51:11 36:1 ᴬ2 Kin 18:13
ᴮ2 Chr 32:1 36:2 ᴬ2 Kin 18:17-20:11 ᴮIs 7:3
36:3 ᴬIs 22:20 36:4 ᴬ2 Kin 18:19 36:5 ᴬ2 Kin 18:7
36:6 ᴬPs 146:3; Is 30:3, 5, 7

36:2 ¹I.e., launderer's

who rely on him. **7**But if you say to me, 'We trust in the LORD our God,' is it not He ^whose high places and whose altars Hezekiah has taken away and has said to Judah and to Jerusalem, 'You shall worship before this altar'? **8**Now then, come make a wager with my master the king of Assyria: I will give you two thousand horses, if you are able on your part to put riders on them! **9**How then can you drive back *even* one official of the least of my master's servants and ^rely on Egypt for chariots and horsemen? **10**And have I now come up without the LORD's approval against this land to destroy it? ^The LORD said to me, 'Go up against this land and destroy it.'"'"

11Then Eliakim, Shebna, and Joah said to Rabshakeh, "Please speak to your servants in ^Aramaic, for we understand *it;* and do not speak to us in ¹,ᴮJudean so that the people who are on the wall hear *you*." **12**But Rabshakeh said, "Has my master sent me *only* to your master and to you to speak these words, *and* not to the men who sit on the wall, *doomed* to eat their own dung and drink their own urine with you?"

13Then Rabshakeh stood and ^called out with a loud voice in Judean and said, "Hear the words of the great king, the king of Assyria! **14**This is what the king says: 'Do not let Hezekiah ^deceive you, for he will not be able to save you; **15**and do not let Hezekiah lead you to ^rely on the LORD, saying, "The LORD will certainly save us. This city will not be handed over to the king of Assyria!" **16**Do not listen to Hezekiah,' for this is what the king of Assyria says: 'Surrender to me and come out to me, and eat, each one, of his ^vine and each of

his fig tree, and each drink of the ᴮwaters of his own cistern, **17**until I come and take you away to a land like your own land, a land of grain and new wine, a land of bread and vineyards. **18***Beware* that Hezekiah does not mislead you, saying, "^The LORD will save us." Has any one of the gods of the nations saved his land from the hand of the king of Assyria? **19**Where are the gods of Hamath and Arpad? Where are the gods of Sepharvaim? And when have they ^saved Samaria from my hand? **20**Who among all the ^gods of these lands have saved their land from my hand, that the ᴮLORD would save Jerusalem from my hand?'"

21But they were silent and did not ^answer him *so much as* a word; for the king's command was, "Do not answer him." **22**Then ^Eliakim the son of Hilkiah, who was over the household, and Shebna the scribe, and Joah the son of Asaph, the secretary, came to Hezekiah with their clothes torn, and reported to him the words of Rabshakeh.

HEZEKIAH SEEKS ISAIAH'S HELP

37 Now ^when King Hezekiah heard *the report,* he tore his clothes, covered himself with sackcloth, and entered the house of the LORD. **2**Then he sent ^Eliakim, who was in charge of the household, with Shebna the scribe and the elders of the priests, covered with sackcloth, to ᴮIsaiah the prophet,

36:7^Deut 12:2–5; 2 Kin 18:4, 5 **36:9**^Is 20:5; 30:2–5, 7 **36:10**^1 Kin 13:18; 22:6, 12 **36:11**^Ezra 4:7 ᴮIs 36:13 **36:13**^2 Chr 32:18 **36:14**^Is 37:10 **36:15**^Is 36:18, 20; 37:10, 11 **36:16**^1 Kin 4:25 ᴮProv 5:15 **36:18**^Is 36:15 **36:19**^2 Kin 17:6 **36:20**^1 Kin 20:23, 28 ᴮIs 36:15 **36:21**^Prov 9:7, 8; 26:4 **36:22**^Is 22:20; 36:3 **37:1**^2 Kin 19:1–37; Is 37:1–38 **37:2**^Is 22:20 ᴮIs 1:1

36:11¹I.e., Hebrew

the son of Amoz. ³And they said to him, "This is what Hezekiah says: 'This day is a ^day of distress, rebuke, and humiliation; for children have come to the point of birth, and there is no strength to deliver *them*. ⁴Perhaps the LORD your God will hear the words of Rabshakeh, whom his master the king of Assyria has sent to ^taunt the living God, and will avenge the words which the LORD your God has heard. Therefore, offer a prayer for the remnant that is left.'"

⁵So the servants of King Hezekiah came to Isaiah. ⁶And Isaiah said to them, "This is what you shall say to your master: 'This is what the LORD says: "^Do not be afraid because of the words that you have heard, with which the servants of the king of Assyria have blasphemed Me. ⁷Behold, I am going to put a spirit in him so that he will hear news and ^return to his own land. And I will make him fall by the sword in his own land."'"

⁸Then Rabshakeh returned and found the king of Assyria fighting against ^Libnah, for he had heard that the king had left ^Lachish. ⁹Now he heard *them* say regarding Tirhakah king of ^Cush, "He has come out to fight against you," and when he heard *it* he sent messengers to Hezekiah, saying, ¹⁰"This is what you shall say to Hezekiah king of Judah: '^Do not let your God in whom you trust deceive you by saying, "Jerusalem will not be handed over to the king of Assyria." ¹¹^Behold, you yourself have heard what the kings of Assyria have done to all the lands, destroying them completely. So will you be saved? ¹²Did the gods of the nations which my fathers destroyed save them: ^Gozan, ^Haran, Rezeph,

and the sons of Eden who *were* in Telassar? ¹³Where is the king of Hamath, the king of Arpad, the king of the city of Sepharvaim, *and of* Hena and Ivvah?'"

HEZEKIAH'S PRAYER IN THE TEMPLE

¹⁴Then Hezekiah took the letter from the hand of the messengers and read it, and he went up to the house of the LORD and spread it out before the LORD. ¹⁵Hezekiah prayed to the LORD, saying, ¹⁶"LORD of armies, God of Israel, who is enthroned *above* the cherubim, You are the ^God, You alone, of all the kingdoms of the earth. ^You made heaven and earth. ¹⁷Incline Your ear, LORD, and hear; open Your eyes, LORD, and see; and ^listen to all the words of Sennacherib, who sent *them* to ^taunt the living God. ¹⁸Truly, LORD, the ^kings of Assyria have laid waste all the countries and their lands, ¹⁹and have thrown their gods into the fire, for they were not gods but *only* the ^work of human hands, wood and stone. So they have destroyed them. ²⁰But now LORD, our God, ^save us from his hand, so that all the kingdoms of the earth may know that You alone, LORD, are God."

GOD ANSWERS THROUGH ISAIAH

²¹Then ^Isaiah the son of Amoz sent *word* to Hezekiah, saying, "This is what the LORD, the God of Israel says: 'Because you have prayed to Me about Sennacherib king of Assyria, ²²this is the word that the LORD has spoken against him:

37:3 ^Is 22:5; 26:16　37:4 ^Is 36:13-15, 18, 20
37:6 ^Is 7:4; 35:4　37:7 ^Is 37:37, 38　37:8 ^Num 33:20
^Josh 10:31, 32　37:9 ^Is 18:1; 20:5　37:10 ^Is 36:15
37:11 ^Is 10:9-11; 36:18-20　37:12 ^2 Kin 17:6
^Gen 11:31　37:16 ^Deut 10:17　^Is 42:5
37:17 ^Ps 74:22　^Is 37:4　37:18 ^2 Kin 15:29; 16:9
37:19 ^Is 2:8; 17:8　37:20 ^Is 25:9; 33:22　37:21 ^Is 37:2

"She has shown contempt for
you *and* derided you,
The ^virgin ^Bdaughter of Zion;
The daughter of Jerusalem
has shaken *her* head behind
you!
23 "Whom have you ^taunted and
blasphemed?
And against whom have you
raised *your* voice
And haughtily raised your
eyes?
Against the ^BHoly One of
Israel!
24 "Through your servants you
have taunted the Lord,
And you have said, 'With
my many chariots I came
up to the heights of the
mountains,
To the remotest parts of
Lebanon;
And I cut down its tall ^cedars
and its choice junipers.
And I will come to its highest
peak, its thickest forest.
25 'I dug *wells* and drank waters,
And ^with the sole of my feet I
dried up
All the canals of Egypt.'
26 "Have you not heard?
Long ago I did it,
From ancient times I
^planned it.
Now ^BI have brought it about
That you would turn fortified
cities into ruined heaps.
27 "Therefore their inhabitants
were powerless,
They were shattered and put
to shame;
They were *like* the ^vegetation
of the field and the green
grass,
Like ^Bgrass on the housetops
that is scorched before it
has grown.

28 "But I ^know your sitting down,
Your going out, your coming in,
And your raging against Me.
29 "Because of your raging
against Me
And because your ^complacency
has come up to My ears,
I will put My ^Bhook in your nose
And My bridle in your lips,
And I will turn you back by the
way that you came.
30 "Then this shall be the sign
for you: you will eat this year what
^grows of itself, in the second year
what grows from the same, and in
the third year sow, harvest, plant
vineyards, and eat their fruit. 31 The
survivors that are left of the house
of Judah will again ^*take* root downward and bear fruit upward. 32 For
out of Jerusalem a ^remnant will go,
and out of Mount Zion survivors.
The ^Bzeal of the Lord of armies will
perform this.'"

33 "Therefore, this is what the
Lord says about the king of Assyria:
'He will not come to this city nor
shoot an arrow there; and he will
not come before it with a shield, nor
heap up an ^assault ramp against
it. 34 ^By the way that he came, by
the same he will return, and he will
not come to this city,' declares the
Lord. 35 'For I will ^protect this city
to save it ^Bfor My own sake, and for
My servant David's sake.'"

ASSYRIANS DESTROYED

36 Then the ^angel of the Lord went
out and struck 185,000 in the camp
of the Assyrians; and when *the rest*

37:22 ^Jer 14:17   ^BPs 9:14   37:23 ^Is 37:4   ^BEzek 39:7
37:24 ^Is 14:8   37:25 ^Deut 11:10; 1 Kin 20:10
37:26 ^Acts 2:23   ^BIs 46:11   37:27 ^Is 40:7   ^BPs 129:6
37:28 ^Ps 139:1   37:29 ^Is 10:12   ^BEzek 29:4
37:30 ^Lev 25:5, 11   37:31 ^Is 27:6   37:32 ^Is 37:4
^B2 Kin 19:31   37:33 ^Jer 6:6; 32:24   37:34 ^Is 37:29
37:35 ^2 Kin 20:6   ^BIs 43:25   37:36 ^2 Kin 19:35;
Is 10:12, 33, 34

got up early in the morning, behold, all of the 185,000 were dead. ³⁷So Sennacherib the king of Assyria departed and returned *home* and lived in ^Nineveh. ³⁸Then it came about, as he was worshiping in the house of Nisroch his god, that his sons Adrammelech and Sharezer killed him with the sword; and they escaped to the land of Ararat. And his son ^Esarhaddon became king in his place.

HEZEKIAH HEALED

38 ^In those days Hezekiah became mortally ill. And Isaiah the prophet, the son of Amoz, came to him and said to him, "This is what the LORD says: '^BSet your house in order, for you are going to die and not live.'" ²Then Hezekiah turned his face to the wall and prayed to the LORD, ³and said, "Please, LORD, just remember how I have ^walked before You wholeheartedly and in truth, and ^Bhave done what is good in Your sight." And Hezekiah wept profusely.

⁴Then the word of the LORD came to Isaiah, saying, ⁵"Go and say to Hezekiah, 'This is what the LORD, the God of your father David says: "I have heard your prayer, I have seen your tears; behold, I will add ^fifteen years to your life. ⁶And I will ^save you and this city from the hand of the king of Assyria; and I will protect this city."'

⁷"And this shall be the ^sign to you from the LORD, that the LORD will perform this word that He has spoken: ⁸Behold, I will ^make the shadow on the stairway, which has gone down with the sun on the stairway of Ahaz, go back ten steps." So the ^Bsun's *shadow* went back ten steps on the stairway on which it had gone down.

⁹*This is* a writing of Hezekiah king of Judah after his illness and recovery:
¹⁰   I said, "^AIn the middle of my life
        I am to enter the ^Bgates of Sheol;
        I have been deprived of the
            rest of my years."
¹¹   I said, "I will not see the LORD,
        The LORD ^Ain the land of the
            living;
        I will no longer look on
            mankind among the
            inhabitants of the world.
¹²   "Like a shepherd's ^tent my
            dwelling is pulled up and
            removed from me;
        As a weaver I rolled up my life.
        He cuts me off from the loom;
        From day until night You make
            an end of me.
¹³   "I composed *my soul* until
            morning.
        ^Like a lion—so He ^Bbreaks all
            my bones,
        From day until night You make
            an end of me.
¹⁴   "Like a swallow, *like* a crane, so
            I twitter;
        I moan like a dove;
        My ^eyes look wistfully to the
            heights;
        Lord, I am oppressed, be my
            ^Bsecurity.

¹⁵   "What shall I say?
        For He has spoken to me, and
            He Himself has done it;
        I will ^walk quietly all my years
            because of the ^Bbitterness of
            my soul.

37:37^Gen 10:11; Jon 1:2   **37:38**^Ezra 4:2
38:1^2 Kin 20:1-6, 9-11   ^B2 Sam 17:23
38:3^2 Kin 18:5, 6   ^BDeut 6:18   **38:5**^2 Kin 18:2, 13
38:6^Is 31:5; 37:35   **38:7**^Judg 6:17, 21, 36-40;
Is 7:11, 14   **38:8**^2 Kin 20:9-11   ^BJosh 10:12-14
38:10^Ps 102:24   ^BPs 107:18   **38:11**^Ps 27:13; 116:9
38:12^2 Cor 5:1, 4; 2 Pet 1:13, 14   **38:13**^Job 10:16
^BPs 51:8   **38:14**^Ps 119:123   ^BJob 17:3
38:15^1 Kin 21:27   ^BJob 7:11

16 "Lord, by *these* things *people* live,
  And in all these is the life of
    my spirit;
  ^ARestore me to health and ^Blet
    me live!
17 "Behold, for *my own* welfare I
    had great bitterness;
  But You have ^Akept my soul
    from the pit of nothingness,
  For You have ^Bhurled all my
    sins behind Your back.
18 "For Sheol cannot thank You,
  Death cannot praise You;
  Those who go down ^Ato the
    pit cannot hope for Your
    faithfulness.
19 "It is the ^Aliving who give
    thanks to You, as I do today;
  A father tells his sons about
    Your faithfulness.
20 "The LORD is *certain* to save me;
  So we will play my songs on
    stringed instruments
  ^AAll *the* days of our life at the
    house of the LORD."

21 Now ^AIsaiah had said, "Have
them take a cake of figs and apply it
to the boil, so that he may recover."
22 Then Hezekiah had said, "What
is the ^Asign that I will go up to the
house of the LORD?"

HEZEKIAH SHOWS HIS TREASURES

39 ^AAt that time Merodach-
baladan son of Baladan,
king of Babylon, sent letters and a
gift to Hezekiah, for he heard that
he had been sick and had recovered. 2 Hezekiah was ^Apleased, and
let them see *all* his treasure house,
the silver, the gold, the balsam oil,
the excellent olive oil, his entire
armory, and everything that was
found in his treasuries. There was
nothing in his house nor in all his
realm that Hezekiah did not let
them see. 3 Then Isaiah the prophet

came to King Hezekiah and said to
him, "What did these men say, and
from where did they come to you?"
And Hezekiah said, "They came to
me from a far ^Acountry, from Babylon." 4 Then he said, "What have
they seen in your house?" So Hezekiah answered, "They have seen
everything that is in my house;
there is nothing among my treasuries that I have not let them see."

5 Isaiah then said to Hezekiah,
"Hear the ^Aword of the LORD of
armies, 6 'Behold, the days are
coming when ^Aeverything that is in
your house, and what your fathers
have stored up to this day, will be
carried to Babylon; nothing will
be left,' says the LORD. 7 'And some
of your sons who will come from
you, whom you will father, ^Awill be
taken away, and ^Bthey will become
eunuchs in the palace of the king
of Babylon.'" 8 Then Hezekiah said
to Isaiah, "The word of the LORD
which you have spoken is good."
For he thought, "For there will be
peace and truth ^Ain my days."

THE GREATNESS OF GOD

40 "^AComfort, comfort My
     people," says your God.
2 "Speak kindly to Jerusalem;
   And call out to her, that her
     ^Awarfare has ended,
   That her ^Bguilt has been
     removed,
   That she has received of the
     LORD's hand
   Double for all her sins."

38:16 ^APs 39:13   ^BPs 119:25   38:17 ^APs 30:3   ^BIs 43:25
38:18 ^ANum 16:33; Ps 28:1   38:19 ^APs 118:17; 119:175
38:20 ^APs 104:33; 116:2   38:21 ^A2 Kin 20:7, 8
38:22 ^AIs 38:7   39:1 ^A2 Kin 20:12–19; 2 Chr 32:31
39:2 ^A2 Chr 32:25, 31; Job 31:25   39:3 ^ADeut 28:49;
Jer 5:15   39:5 ^A1 Sam 13:13, 14; 15:16
39:6 ^A2 Kin 24:13; 25:13–15   39:7 ^A2 Kin 24:10–16
^BDan 1:1–7   39:8 ^A2 Chr 34:28   40:1 ^AIs 12:1; 49:13
40:2 ^AIs 41:11–13   ^BIs 33:24

³ ᴬThe voice of one calling out,
"Clear the way for the LORD in
the wilderness;
Make straight in the desert a
highway for our God.

⁴ "Let every valley be lifted up,
And every mountain and hill
be made low;
And let the uneven ground
become a plain,
And the rugged terrain a broad
valley;

⁵ Then the ᴬglory of the LORD
will be revealed,
And ᴮall flesh will see *it* together;
For the mouth of the LORD has
spoken."

⁶ A voice says, "Call out."
Then he answered, "What
shall I call out?"
ᴬAll flesh is grass, and all its
loveliness is like the flower
of the field.

⁷ The ᴬgrass withers, the flower
fades,
When the breath of the LORD
blows upon it;
The people are indeed grass!

⁸ The grass withers, the flower
fades,
But ᴬthe word of our God
stands forever.

⁹ Go up on a high mountain,
Zion, messenger of good news,
Raise your voice forcefully,
Jerusalem, messenger of good
news;
Raise *it* up, do not fear.
Say to the ᴬcities of Judah,
"ᴮHere is your God!"

¹⁰ Behold, the Lord GOD will
come ᴬwith might,
With His arm ruling for Him.
Behold, His ᴮcompensation is
with Him,
And His reward before Him.

¹¹ Like a shepherd He will ᴬtend
His flock,
In His arm He will gather the
lambs
And carry *them* in the fold of
His robe;
He will gently lead the
nursing *ewes*.

¹² Who has ᴬmeasured the waters
in the hollow of His hand,
And measured the heavens
with a span,
And calculated the dust of the
earth with a measure,
And weighed the mountains
in a balance
And the hills in a pair of
scales?

¹³ ᴬWho has directed the Spirit
of the LORD,
Or as His ᴮcounselor has
informed Him?

¹⁴ With whom did He consult
and *who* ᴬgave Him
understanding?
And *who* taught Him in the
path of justice and taught
Him knowledge,
And informed Him of the way
of understanding?

¹⁵ Behold, the ᴬnations are like a
drop from a bucket,
And are regarded as a speck of
ᴮdust on the scales;
Behold, He lifts up the islands
like fine dust.

¹⁶ Even Lebanon is not enough
to burn,
Nor its ᴬanimals enough for a
burnt offering.

40:3 ᴬMatt 3:3; Mark 1:3   **40:5** ᴬIs 6:3   ᴮIs 52:10
40:6 ᴬJob 14:2; Ps 102:11   **40:7** ᴬPs 90:5, 6;
James 1:10, 11   **40:8** ᴬIs 55:11; 59:21   **40:9** ᴬIs 44:26
ᴮIs 25:9   **40:10** ᴬIs 9:6, 7   ᴮIs 62:11   **40:11** ᴬJer 31:10;
Ezek 34:12-14, 23, 31   **40:12** ᴬJob 38:8-11;
Ps 102:25, 26   **40:13** ᴬRom 11:34   ᴮIs 41:28
40:14 ᴬJob 21:22; Col 2:3   **40:15** ᴬJer 10:10   ᴮIs 17:13
40:16 ᴬPs 50:9-11; Mic 6:6, 7

17 ᴬAll the nations are as nothing
   before Him,
   They are regarded by Him
   as less than nothing and
   meaningless.
18 ᴬTo whom then will you liken
   God?
   Or what likeness will you
   compare with Him?
19 *As for* the idol, a craftsman
   casts it,
   A goldsmith ᴬplates it with
   gold,
   And a silversmith *fashions*
   chains of silver.
20 He who is too impoverished
   for *such* an offering
   Selects a ᴬtree that does not rot;
   He seeks out for himself a
   skillful craftsman
   To prepare an idol that ᴮwill
   not totter.
21 ᴬDo you not know? Have you
   not heard?
   Has it not been declared to you
   from the beginning?
   Have you not understood from
   the foundations of the earth?
22 It is He who sits above the
   ᴬcircle of the earth,
   And its inhabitants are like
   ᴮgrasshoppers,
   Who stretches out the heavens
   like a curtain
   And spreads them out like a
   tent to live in.
23 *It is* He who reduces rulers to
   nothing,
   Who ᴬmakes the judges of the
   earth meaningless.
24 Scarcely have they been
   planted,
   Scarcely have they been sown,
   Scarcely has their stock taken
   root in the earth,

But He merely blows on them,
and they wither,
And the ᴬstorm carries them
away like stubble.
25 "ᴬTo whom then will you
   compare Me
   That I would be *his* equal?"
   says the Holy One.
26 ᴬRaise your eyes on high
   And see ᴮwho has created
   these *stars,*
   The One who brings out their
   multitude by number,
   He calls them all by name;
   Because of the greatness of His
   might and the strength of
   His power,
   Not one *of them* is missing.

27 Why do you say, Jacob, and you
   assert, Israel,
   "My way is ᴬhidden from the
   LORD,
   And the ᴮjustice due me escapes
   the notice of my God"?
28 Do you not know? Have you
   not heard?
   The ᴬEverlasting God, the
   LORD, the Creator of the ends
   of the earth
   Does not become weary or tired.
   His understanding is
   ᴮunsearchable.
29 He gives strength to the
   ᴬweary,
   And to *the one who* lacks
   might He ᴮincreases power.
30 Though ᴬyouths grow weary
   and tired,
   And vigorous ᴮyoung men
   stumble badly,

40:17ᴬIs 29:7   **40:18**ᴬEx 8:10; 15:11   **40:19**ᴬIs 2:20;
30:22   **40:20**ᴬIs 44:14   ᴮ1 Sam 5:3, 4   **40:21**ᴬPs 19:1;
50:6   **40:22**ᴬJob 22:14   ᴮNum 13:33   **40:23**ᴬIs 5:21;
Jer 25:18-27   **40:24**ᴬIs 17:13; 41:16   **40:25**ᴬIs 40:18
40:26ᴬIs 51:6   ᴮIs 42:5   **40:27**ᴬIs 54:8   ᴮJob 27:2
40:28ᴬGen 21:33   ᴮPs 147:5   **40:29**ᴬIs 50:4
ᴮIs 41:10   **40:30**ᴬJer 6:11   ᴮIs 9:17

³¹ Yet those who wait for the
    LORD
Will ^Again new strength;
They will ^Bmount up *with*
    wings like eagles,
They will run and not get tired,
They will walk and not
    become weary.

ISRAEL ENCOURAGED

41 "^AListen to Me ^Bin silence,
    you coastlands,
And let the peoples gain new
    strength;
Let them come forward, then
    let them speak;
Let's come together for
    judgment.

² "Who has stirred one from the
    east
Whom He calls in
    righteousness to His feet?
He ^Aturns nations over to him
And subdues kings.
He makes them like ^Bdust with
    his sword,
Like the wind-driven chaff
    with his bow.

³ "He pursues them, passing on
    in safety,
By a way he had not been
    traversing with his feet.

⁴ "Who has performed and
    accomplished *it,*
Summoning the generations
    from the beginning?
'^AI, the LORD, am the first, and
    with the last. I am He.'"

⁵ The coastlands have seen and
    are afraid;
The ^Aends of the earth tremble;
They have approached and
    have come.

⁶ Each one helps his neighbor
And says to his brother, "Be
    strong!"

⁷ So the ^Acraftsman encourages
    the smelter,
And he who smooths
    metal with the hammer
    encourages him who beats
    the anvil,
Saying of the soldering, "It is
    good";
And he fastens it with nails,
^B*So that* it will not totter.

⁸ "But you, Israel, ^AMy servant,
Jacob whom I have chosen,
Descendant of Abraham My
    friend,

⁹ You whom I have ^Ataken from
    the ends of the earth
And called from its ^Bremotest
    parts,
And said to you, 'You are My
    servant,
I have chosen you and have
    not rejected you.

¹⁰ 'Do not ^Afear, for I am with
    you;
Do not be afraid, for I am your
    God.
I will strengthen you, I will
    also help you,
I will also uphold you with My
    righteous right hand.'

¹¹ "Behold, ^Aall those who are
    angered at you will be
    shamed and dishonored;
^BThose who contend with you
    will be as nothing and will
    perish.

¹² "^AYou will seek those who
    quarrel with you, but will
    not find them,
Those who war with you will
    be as nothing and non-
    existent.

40:31 ^A Job 17:9   ^B Ex 19:4   41:1 ^A Is 11:11   ^B Hab 2:20
41:2 ^A 2 Chr 36:23   ^B 2 Sam 22:43   41:4 ^A Is 43:10; 44:6
41:5 ^A Josh 5:1; Ps 67:7   41:7 ^A Is 44:12, 13   ^B Is 40:20
41:8 ^A Is 42:19; 43:10   41:9 ^A Is 11:11   ^B Is 43:5-7
41:10 ^A Deut 20:1; 31:6   41:11 ^A Is 45:24   ^B Is 17:13
41:12 ^A Job 20:7-9; Ps 37:35, 36

13 "For I am the LORD your God
   ^who takes hold of your right
   hand,
   Who says to you, 'Do not fear, I
   will help you.'
14 "Do not fear, you ^worm Jacob,
   you people of Israel;
   I will help you," declares the
   LORD, "and your Redeemer is
   the Holy One of Israel.
15 "Behold, I turned you into a
   new, sharp threshing sledge
   with double edges;
   ^You will thresh the mountains
   and pulverize *them,*
   And make the hills like chaff.
16 "You will ^winnow them, and the
   wind will carry them away,
   And the storm will scatter them;
   But you will rejoice in the LORD,
   You will boast in the Holy One
   of Israel.

17 "The poor and needy are seeking
   water, but there is none,
   And their tongues are parched
   with thirst.
   I, the LORD, ^will answer them
   Myself;
   As the God of Israel I ^will not
   abandon them.
18 "I will open ^rivers on the bare
   heights,
   And springs in the midst of the
   valleys;
   I will make ^the wilderness a
   pool of water,
   And the dry land fountains of
   water.
19 "I will put the cedar in the
   wilderness,
   The acacia, the ^myrtle, and
   the olive tree;
   I will place the ^juniper in the
   desert,
   Together with the elm tree and
   the cypress,

20 So that they may see and
   recognize,
   And consider and gain insight
   as well,
   That the ^hand of the LORD has
   done this,
   And the Holy One of Israel has
   created it.

21 "Present your case," the LORD
   says.
   "Bring forward your evidence,"
   The ^King of Jacob says.
22 Let them bring *them* forward
   and declare to us what is
   going to take place;
   As for the ^former *events,*
   declare what they *were,*
   So that we may consider them
   and know their outcome.
   Or announce to us what is
   coming;
23 ^Declare the things that are
   going to come afterward,
   So that we may know that you
   are gods;
   Indeed, ^do good or evil, that
   we may be afraid and fear
   together.
24 Behold, you are less than
   nothing,
   And your work is less than
   nothing!
   He who chooses you is an
   ^abomination.

25 "I have put ^one from the north
   into motion, and he has
   come;
   From the rising of the sun he
   will call on My name;

41:13 ^Is 42:6; 45:1   41:14 ^Job 25:6; Ps 22:6
41:15 ^Mic 4:13; Hab 3:12   41:16 ^Jer 51:2
41:17 ^Is 30:19   ^Is 42:16   41:18 ^Is 30:25
^Ps 107:35   41:19 ^Is 35:1; 55:13   41:20 ^Job 12:9;
Is 66:14   41:21 ^Is 44:6   41:22 ^Is 43:9
41:23 ^Is 42:9   ^Jer 10:5   41:24 ^Prov 3:32; 28:9
41:25 ^Is 41:2; Jer 50:3

And he will come upon rulers
as *upon* mortar,
As the potter treads on clay."
²⁶ Who has ^declared *this* from
the beginning, that we might
know?
Or from former times, that we
may say, "*He is* right!"?
There was no one at all who
declared,
There was no one at all who
proclaimed,
There was no one at all who
heard your words.
²⁷ "Previously *I said* to Zion,
'Behold, here they are.'
And to Jerusalem, 'I will give a
^messenger of good news.'
²⁸ "But ^when I look, there is no
one,
And there is no ᴮcounselor
among them
Who, if I ask, can give an
answer.
²⁹ "Behold, all of them are ¹false;
Their works are nothing,
Their cast metal images are
^wind and emptiness.

GOD'S PROMISE CONCERNING
HIS SERVANT

42 "Behold, My Servant,
whom I uphold;
My ^chosen one *in whom* My
ᴮsoul delights.
I have put My Spirit upon Him;
He will bring forth justice to
the nations.
² "He will not cry out nor raise
His voice,
Nor make His voice heard in
the street.
³ "A bent reed He will not break *off*
And a dimly burning wick He
will not extinguish;
He will faithfully bring forth
^justice.

⁴ "He will not be ^disheartened or
crushed
Until He has established
justice on the earth;
And the coastlands will wait
expectantly for His law."
⁵ This is what God the Lᴏʀᴅ says,
Who ^created the heavens and
stretched them out,
Who spread out the earth and
its offspring,
Who gives breath to the people
on it
And spirit to those who walk
in it:
⁶ "I am the Lᴏʀᴅ, I have ^called
You in righteousness,
I will also hold You by the
hand and watch over You,
And I will appoint You as a
covenant to the people,
As a ᴮlight to the nations,
⁷ To ^open blind eyes,
To bring out prisoners from
the dungeon
And those who dwell in
darkness from the prison.
⁸ "I am the Lᴏʀᴅ, that is My name;
I will not give My ^glory to
another,
Nor My praise to idols.
⁹ "Behold, the ^former things
have come to pass,
Now I declare ᴮnew things;
Before they sprout I proclaim
them to you."

¹⁰ Sing to the Lᴏʀᴅ a new song,
Sing His praise from the ^end
of the earth!

41:26 ^Is 41:22; 44:7   41:27 ^Is 40:9; 44:28
41:28 ^Is 50:2   ᴮIs 40:13, 14   41:29 ^Jer 5:13
42:1 ^Luke 9:35   ᴮMatt 3:17   42:3 ^Ps 72:2, 4; 96:13
42:4 ^Is 40:28   42:5 ^Ps 102:25, 26; Is 45:18
42:6 ^Is 41:2   ᴮIs 49:6   42:7 ^Is 29:18; 35:5
42:8 ^Ex 20:3–5; Is 48:11   42:9 ^Is 48:3   ᴮIs 48:6
42:10 ^Is 49:6

41:29 ¹ Another reading is *nothing*

You who go down to the sea,
and all that is in it;
You ᴮislands, and those who
live on them.

11 Let the ᴬwilderness and its
cities raise *their voices,*
The settlements which Kedar
inhabits.
Let the inhabitants of Sela
sing aloud,
Let them shout for joy from
the tops of the ᴮmountains.

12 Let them ᴬgive glory to the
Lᴏʀᴅ
And declare His praise in the
coastlands.

13 ᴬThe Lᴏʀᴅ will go out like a
warrior,
He will stir *His* ᴮzeal like a
man of war.
He will shout, indeed, He will
raise a war cry.
He will prevail against His
enemies.

THE BLINDNESS OF THE PEOPLE

14 "ᴬI have kept silent for a long
time,
I have kept still and restrained
Myself.
Now like a woman in labor I
will groan,
I will both gasp and pant.

15 "I will ᴬlay waste the
mountains and hills
And wither all their
vegetation;
I will turn the rivers into
coastlands
And dry up the ponds.

16 "I will ᴬlead those who are
blind by a way they have not
known,
In paths they have not known I
will guide them.
I will turn darkness into light
before them

And uneven land into plains.
These are the things I will do,
And I will not leave them
undone."

17 They will be turned back *and*
be ᴬutterly put to shame,
Who trust in idols,
Who say to cast metal images,
"You are our gods."

18 ᴬHear, you who are deaf!
And look, you who are blind,
so that you may see.

19 Who is blind but My ᴬservant,
Or so deaf as My ᴮmessenger
whom I send?
Who is so blind as one who is
at peace *with Me,*
Or so blind as the servant of
the Lᴏʀᴅ?

20 ᴬYou have seen many things,
but you do not retain *them;*
Your ears are open, but no one
hears.

21 The Lᴏʀᴅ was pleased for His
righteousness' sake
To make the Law ᴬgreat and
glorious.

22 But this is a people plundered
and pillaged;
All of them are ᴬtrapped in
caves,
Or are ᴮhidden away in prisons;
They have become plunder,
with no one to save *them,*
And spoils with no one to say,
"Give *them* back!"

23 Who among you will listen to
this?
Who will pay attention and
listen in the time to come?

42:10 ᴮIs 42:4   42:11ᴬIs 32:16   ᴮIs 52:7   42:12ᴬIs 24:15
42:13ᴬEx 15:3   ᴮIs 9:7   42:14ᴬPs 50:21; Is 57:11
42:15ᴬIs 2:12-16; Ezek 38:19, 20   42:16ᴬIs 29:18; 30:21
42:17ᴬPs 97:7; Is 1:29   42:18ᴬIs 29:18; 35:5
42:19ᴬIs 41:8   ᴮIs 44:26   42:20ᴬRom 2:21
42:21ᴬIs 42:4; 51:4   42:22ᴬIs 24:18   ᴮIs 24:22

²⁴ Who gave Jacob up for spoils,
and Israel to plunderers?
Was it not the LORD, against
whom we have sinned,
And in whose ways they ^were
not willing to walk,
And whose Law did not
obey?
²⁵ So He poured out on him the
heat of His anger
And the ^fierceness of battle;
And it set him aflame all
around,
Yet he did not recognize *it*;
And it burned him, but he paid
no attention.

ISRAEL REDEEMED

43 But now, this is what the
LORD says, *He who is* your
^Creator, Jacob,
And He who formed you, Israel:
"Do not fear, for I have
^redeemed you;
I have called you by name; you
are Mine!
² "When you ^pass through the
waters, I will be with you;
And through the rivers, they
will not overflow you.
When you ^walk through the
fire, you will not be scorched,
Nor will the flame burn you.
³ "For I am the LORD your God,
The Holy One of Israel, your
^Savior;
I have given Egypt as your
ransom,
^Cush and Seba in exchange
for you.
⁴ "Since you are ^precious in My
sight,
Since you are honored and I
love you,
I will give *other* people in your
place and *other* nations in
exchange for your life.

⁵ "Do not fear, for ^I am with you;
I will bring ^your offspring
from the east,
And gather you from the west.
⁶ "I will say to the ^north, 'Give
them up!'
And to the south, 'Do not hold
them back.'
Bring My sons from afar
And My daughters from the
ends of the earth,
⁷ Everyone who is called by My
name,
And whom I have ^created for
My ^glory,
Whom I have formed, even
whom I have made."

ISRAEL IS GOD'S WITNESS

⁸ Bring out the people who are
^blind, even though they
have eyes,
And those who are deaf, even
though they have ears.
⁹ All the nations have ^gathered
together
So that the peoples may be
assembled.
Who among them can declare
this
And proclaim to us the former
things?
Let them present their
witnesses so that they may
be justified,
Or let them hear and say, "It is
true."
¹⁰ "You are My witnesses,"
declares the LORD,
"And My servant whom I have
chosen,
So that you may know and
believe Me

42:24 ^Is 30:15   42:25 ^Is 5:25; 9:19   43:1 ^Is 43:15
^Is 44:22, 23   43:2 ^Ps 66:12   ^Is 29:6   43:3 ^Is 19:20
^Is 20:3-5   43:4 ^Ex 19:5, 6   43:5 ^Is 8:10   ^Is 41:8
43:6 ^Ps 107:3   43:7 ^Ps 100:3   ^Is 44:23
43:8 ^Is 6:9; Ezek 12:2   43:9 ^Is 34:1; 41:1

And understand that ^AI am He.
^BBefore Me there was no God formed,
And there will be none after Me.
11 "I, *only* I, am the LORD,
And there is no ^Asavior besides Me.
12 "It is I who have declared and saved and proclaimed,
And there was no ^Astrange *god* among you;
So you are My witnesses," declares the LORD,
"And I am God.
13 "Even from eternity I am He,
And there is ^Ano one who can rescue from My hand;
^BI act, and who can reverse it?"

BABYLON TO BE DESTROYED

14This is what the LORD your ^ARedeemer, the Holy One of Israel says:
"For your sake I have sent to Babylon,
And will bring them all down as fugitives,
Even the Chaldeans, into the ships over which they rejoice.
15 "I am the LORD, your Holy One,
^AThe Creator of Israel, your King."
16This is what the LORD says,
He who ^Amakes a way through the sea
And a path through the mighty waters,
17 Who brings out the ^Achariot and the horse,
The army and the mighty man
(They will lie down together *and* not rise again;
They have been extinguished, *and* have gone out like a wick):
18 "^ADo not call to mind the former things,
Or consider things of the past.

19 "Behold, I am going to do something ^Anew,
Now it will spring up;
Will you not be aware of it?
I will even make a roadway in the wilderness,
Rivers in the desert.
20 "The animals of the field will glorify Me,
The jackals and the ostriches,
Because I have ^Agiven waters in the wilderness
And rivers in the desert,
To give drink to My chosen people.
21 "The people whom ^AI formed for Myself
Will declare My praise.

THE SHORTCOMINGS OF ISRAEL

22 "Yet you have not called on Me, Jacob;
But you have become ^Aweary of Me, Israel.
23 "You have ^Anot brought to Me the sheep of your burnt offerings,
Nor have you ^Bhonored Me with your sacrifices.
I have not burdened you with offerings,
Nor wearied you with incense.
24 "You have not bought Me sweet cane with money,
Nor have you satisfied Me with the fat of your sacrifices;
Rather, you have burdened Me with your sins,
You have ^Awearied Me with your wrongdoings.

43:10^A Is 41:4   ^B Is 45:5, 6   **43:11**^A Is 43:3; 45:21
43:12^A Deut 32:16; Ps 81:9   **43:13**^A Ps 50:22   ^B Job 9:12
43:14^A Is 41:14   **43:15**^A Is 43:1   **43:16**^A Ex 14:21, 22;
Ps 77:19   **43:17**^A Ex 15:19   **43:18**^A Is 65:17; Jer 23:7
43:19^A Is 42:9; 48:6   **43:20**^A Is 41:17, 18; 48:21
43:21^A Is 43:1   **43:22**^A Mic 6:3; Mal 1:13
43:23^A Amos 5:25   ^B Zech 7:5, 6
43:24^A Ps 95:10; Is 1:14

25 "I, I *alone,* am the one who
    ^wipes out your wrongdoings
    for My own sake,
    And I will not remember your
    sins.
26 "Meet Me in court, ^let's argue
    our case together;
    State your *cause,* so that you
    may be proved right.
27 "Your ^first forefather sinned,
    And your spokesmen have
    rebelled against Me.
28 "So I will profane the officials of
    the sanctuary,
    And I will turn Jacob over to
    destruction and Israel to
    ^abuse.

THE BLESSINGS OF ISRAEL

44 "But now listen, Jacob, My
    ^servant,
    And Israel, whom I have
    chosen:
2 This is what the Lord says, *He*
    who made you
    And formed you from the
    womb, who ^will help you:
    'Do not fear, Jacob My servant,
    And ¹,ᴮJeshurun, whom I have
    chosen.
3 'For I will pour water on the
    thirsty *land*
    And streams on the dry ground;
    I will ^pour out My Spirit on
    your ᴮoffspring,
    And My blessing on your
    descendants;
4 And they will spring up among
    the grass
    Like ^poplars by streams of
    water.'
5 "This one will say, 'I am the
    Lord's';
    And that one will call on the
    name of Jacob;
    And another will ^write *on* his
    hand, 'Belonging to the Lord,'

And will give himself Israel's
    name with honor.
6 "This is what the Lord says, *He
who is* the King of Israel and his
^Redeemer, the Lord of armies:
    'I am the ᴮfirst and I am the last,
    And there is no God besides
    Me.
7 'Who is like Me? ^Let him
    proclaim and declare it;
    And, let him confront Me
    Beginning with My
    establishing of the ancient
    nation.
    Then let them declare to them
    the things that are coming
    And *the events* that are going
    to take place.
8 'Do not tremble and do not be
    afraid;
    Have I not long since
    announced *it* to you and
    declared *it?*
    And you are My witnesses.
    Is there any God ^besides Me,
    Or is there any *other* ᴮRock?
    I know of none.'"

THE FOOLISHNESS OF IDOLATRY

9 Those who fashion an idol are all
futile, and their treasured things
are of no benefit; even their own
witnesses fail to see or know, so
that they will be ^put to shame.
10 Who has fashioned a god or cast
an idol to ^no benefit? 11 Behold,
all his companions will be ^put to
shame, for the craftsmen themselves are mere men. Let them all

43:25 ^Is 44:22; 55:7   43:26 ^Is 1:18; 41:1
43:27 ^Is 51:2; Ezek 16:3   43:28 ^Ps 79:4; Ezek 5:15
44:1 ^Is 41:8; Jer 30:10   44:2 ^Is 41:10   ᴮDeut 32:15
44:3 ^Is 32:15   ᴮIs 61:9   44:4 ^Lev 23:40; Job 40:22
44:5 ^Ex 13:9; Neh 9:38   44:6 ^Is 41:14   ᴮIs 43:10
44:7 ^Is 41:22, 26   44:8 ^Deut 4:35, 39   ᴮIs 17:10
44:9 ^Ps 97:7; Is 42:17   44:10 ^Is 41:29; Jer 10:5
44:11 ^Ps 97:7; Is 42:17

44:2 ¹I.e., Israel

assemble themselves, let them stand up, let them tremble, let them be put to shame together.

¹²The ᴬcraftsman of iron *shapes* a cutting tool and does his work over the coals, fashioning it with hammers and working it with his strong arm. He also gets hungry and his strength fails; he drinks no water and becomes weary. ¹³ᴬThe craftsman of wood extends a measuring line; he outlines it with a marker. He works it with carving knives and outlines it with a compass, and makes it like the form of a man, like the beauty of mankind, so that it may sit in a house. ¹⁴He will cut cedars for himself, and he takes a holm-oak or *another* oak and lets *it* grow strong for himself among the trees of the forest. He plants a laurel tree, and the rain makes it grow. ¹⁵Then it becomes *something* for a person to burn, so he takes one of them and gets warm; he also makes a fire and bakes bread. He also ᴬmakes a god and worships it; he makes it a carved image and ᴮbows down before it. ¹⁶Half of it he burns in the fire; over *this* half he eats meat, he roasts a roast, and is satisfied. He also warms himself and says, "Aha! I am warm, I have seen the fire." ¹⁷Yet the rest of it he makes into a god, his carved image. He bows down before it and worships; he also ᴬprays to it and says, "Save me, for you are my god."

¹⁸They do not know, nor do they understand, for He has ᴬsmeared over their eyes so that they cannot see, and their hearts so that they cannot comprehend. ¹⁹No one remembers, nor is there knowledge or understanding to say, "I have burned half of it in the fire and also have baked bread over its coals. I

roast meat and eat *it*. Then I make the rest of it into an ᴬabomination, I bow down before a block of wood!" ²⁰He feeds on ashes; a ᴬdeceived heart has misled him. And he cannot save himself, nor say, "ᴮIs there not a lie in my right hand?"

GOD FORGIVES AND REDEEMS

21 "ᴬRemember these things, Jacob,
    And Israel, for you are My
        servant;
    I have formed you, you are My
        servant,
    Israel, you will ᴮnot be
        forgotten by Me.
22 "I have ᴬwiped out your
        wrongdoings like a thick
        cloud
    And your sins like a heavy mist.
    Return to Me, for I have
        redeemed you."
23 Shout for joy, you heavens, for
        the Lᴏʀᴅ has done *it!*
    Shout joyfully, you lower parts
        of the earth;
    Break into a shout of
        jubilation, you mountains,
    Forest, and every tree in it;
    For ᴬthe Lᴏʀᴅ has redeemed
        Jacob,
    And in Israel He ᴮshows His
        glory.

²⁴This is what the Lᴏʀᴅ says, *He who is* your Redeemer, and the One who formed you from the womb:
    "I, the Lᴏʀᴅ, am the Maker of all
        things,
    ᴬStretching out the heavens by
        Myself
    And spreading out the earth
        alone,

44:12ᴬIs 40:19, 20; 41:6, 7   44:13ᴬIs 41:7
44:15ᴬIs 44:17   ᴮ2 Chr 25:14   44:17ᴬ1 Kin 18:26, 28;
Is 45:20   44:18ᴬPs 81:12; Is 6:9, 10   44:19ᴬDeut 27:15;
1 Kin 11:5, 7   44:20ᴬJob 15:31   ᴮIs 57:11
44:21ᴬIs 46:8   ᴮIs 49:15   44:22ᴬPs 51:1, 9; Is 43:25
44:23ᴬIs 43:1   ᴮIs 49:3   44:24ᴬIs 40:22; 42:5

25 ᴬCausing the omens of
   diviners to fail,
   Making fools of fortune-tellers;
   Causing wise men to turn back
   And making their knowledge
   ridiculous,
26 ᴬConfirming the word of His
   servant
   And carrying out the purpose
   of His messengers.
   It is I who says of Jerusalem,
   'She shall be inhabited!'
   And of the cities of Judah,
   'They shall be built.'
   And I will raise her ruins *again.*
27 "*I am* the One who says to the
   depth of the sea, 'Dry up!'
   And I will make your rivers
   ᴬdry up.
28 "*It is I* who says of Cyrus, '*He is*
   My shepherd,
   And he will carry out all My
   desire.'
   And he says of Jerusalem, 'ᴬShe
   will be built,'
   And of the temple, 'Your
   foundation will be laid.'"

GOD USES CYRUS

45 This is what the Lord says
to Cyrus His anointed,
Whom I have taken by the
   right ᴬhand,
To ᴮsubdue nations before him
And to undo *the weapons belt
   on* the waist of kings;
To open doors before him so
   that gates will not be shut:
2 "I will go before you and ᴬmake
   the rough places smooth;
   I will ᴮshatter the doors of
   bronze and cut through their
   iron bars.
3 "I will give you the ᴬtreasures of
   darkness
   And hidden wealth of secret
   places,

So that you may know that it is I,
The Lord, the God of Israel,
   who calls you by your name.
4 "For the sake of Jacob My
   servant,
   And Israel My chosen *one,*
   I have also ᴬcalled you by your
   name;
   I have given you a title of
   honor
   Though you have ᴮnot known
   Me.
5 "I am the Lord, and there is no
   one else;
   ᴬThere is no God except Me.
   I will ¹,ᴮarm you, though you
   have not known Me,
6 So that ᴬ*people* may know from
   the rising to the setting of
   the sun
   That there is no one besides
   Me.
   I am the Lord, and there is no
   one else,
7 The One forming light and
   creating darkness,
   Causing well-being and
   ᴬcreating disaster;
   I am the Lord who does all
   these things.

GOD'S SUPREME POWER

8 "Drip down, heavens, from
   above,
   And let the clouds pour down
   righteousness;
   Let the ᴬearth open up and
   salvation bear fruit,
   ᴮAnd righteousness sprout
   with it.
   I, the Lord, have created it.

44:25 ᴬIs 47:13   44:26 ᴬZech 1:6; Matt 5:18
44:27 ᴬIs 42:15; 50:2   44:28 ᴬ2 Chr 36:22, 23; Ezra 1:1
45:1 ᴬPs 73:23   ᴮIs 41:2, 25   45:2 ᴬIs 40:4   ᴮPs 107:16
45:3 ᴬJer 41:8; 50:37   45:4 ᴬIs 43:1   ᴮActs 17:23
45:5 ᴬIs 44:6, 8   ᴮPs 18:39   45:6 ᴬPs 102:15; Mal 1:11
45:7 ᴬIs 31:2; 47:11   45:8 ᴬPs 85:11   ᴮIs 60:21

45:5 ¹Or *embrace*

9 "Woe to *the one* who quarrels
   with his Maker—
   A piece of pottery among the
   other earthenware pottery
   pieces!
   Will the ^clay say to the potter,
   'What are you doing?'
   Or the thing you are making
   say, 'He has no hands'?

10 "Woe to him who says to a father,
   'What are you fathering?'
   Or to a woman, 'To what are
   you giving birth?'"

11 This is what the LORD says, the
Holy One of Israel and his Maker:
   "^Ask Me about the things to
   come concerning My ^Bsons,
   And you shall commit to Me
   the work of My hands.

12 "It is I who made the earth, and
   created mankind upon it.
   I stretched out the heavens
   with My hands,
   And I ordained ^all their ¹lights.

13 "I have stirred him in
   ^righteousness,
   And I will ^Bmake all his ways
   smooth.
   He will build My city and let
   My exiles go free,
   Without any payment or
   reward," says the LORD of
   armies.

14 This is what the LORD says:
   "The products of Egypt and the
   merchandise of Cush
   And the Sabeans, men of
   stature,
   Will ^come over to you and will
   be yours;
   They will walk behind you,
   they will come over in chains
   And will bow down to you;
   They will plead with you:
   '^BGod certainly is with you, and
   there is no one else,
   No other God.'"

15 Truly, You are a God who
   ^hides Himself,
   God of Israel, ^BSavior!

16 They will be ^put to shame
   and even humiliated, all of
   them;
   The manufacturers of idols
   will go away together in
   humiliation.

17 Israel has been saved by the
   LORD
   With an everlasting salvation;
   You ^will not be put to shame
   or humiliated
   To all eternity.

18 For this is what the LORD says,
He who created the heavens (He is
the God who ^formed the earth and
made it, He established it *and* did
not create it as a ^Bwaste place, *but*
formed it to be inhabited):
   "I am the LORD, and there is no
   one else.

19 "I have not spoken in secret,
   In some dark land;
   I did not say to the offspring of
   Jacob,
   'Seek Me in a wasteland';
   I, the LORD, ^speak
   righteousness,
   ^BDeclaring things that are
   right.

20 "^Gather yourselves and come;
   Come together, you survivors
   of the nations!
   They have no knowledge,
   Who carry around their
   wooden idol
   And ^Bpray to a god who cannot
   save.

45:9 ^A Is 29:16; 64:8   45:11 ^A Is 8:19   ^B Jer 31:9
45:12 ^A Gen 2:1; Neh 9:6   45:13 ^A Is 41:2   ^B Is 45:2
45:14 ^A Is 14:1, 2   ^B Jer 16:19   45:15 ^A Ps 44:24   ^B Is 43:3
45:16 ^A Is 42:17; 44:9   45:17 ^A Is 49:23; 50:7
45:18 ^A Is 45:12   ^B Gen 1:2   45:19 ^A Ps 19:8   ^B Is 43:12
45:20 ^A Is 43:9   ^B Is 44:17

45:12 ¹ Lit *host;* i.e., sun, stars, etc.

21 "Declare and present *your case;*
　　Indeed, let them consult
　　　together.
　　Who has announced this long
　　　ago?
　　Who has long since declared it?
　　Is it not I, the LORD?
　　And there is ^no other God
　　　besides Me,
　　A righteous God and a ^B^Savior;
　　There is none except Me.
22 "^A^Turn to Me and be saved, all
　　　the ends of the earth;
　　For I am God, and there is no
　　　other.
23 "I have sworn by Myself;
　　The word has gone out from
　　　My mouth in righteousness
　　And will not turn back,
　　That to Me ^A^every knee will
　　　bow, every tongue will
　　　^B^swear *allegiance.*
24 "They will say of Me, 'Only ^A^in
　　　the LORD are righteousness
　　　and strength.'
　　People will come to Him,
　　And ^B^all who were angry at
　　　Him will be put to shame.
25 "In the LORD all the offspring of
　　　Israel
　　Will be ^A^justified and will boast."

BABYLON'S IDOLS AND THE TRUE GOD

46 ^A^Bel has bowed down,
　　　Nebo stoops over;
　　Their idols have become *loads*
　　　for the animals and the
　　　cattle.
　　The things that you carry are
　　　burdensome,
　　A load for the weary *animal.*
2 　　They stooped over, they have
　　　bowed down together;
　　They could not rescue the
　　　burden,
　　But have themselves ^A^gone
　　　into captivity.

3 "Listen to Me, house of Jacob,
　　And all ^A^the remnant of the
　　　house of Israel,
　　You who have been ^B^carried *by*
　　　Me from birth
　　And have been carried from
　　　the womb;
4 Even to *your* old age ^A^I will be
　　　the same,
　　And even to *your* ^B^graying
　　　years I will carry *you!*
　　I have done *it,* and I will bear
　　　you;
　　And I will carry *you* and I will
　　　save *you.*

5 "^A^To whom would you liken Me
　　And make Me equal, and
　　　compare Me,
　　That we would be alike?
6 "Those who ^A^lavish gold from
　　　the bag
　　And weigh silver on the scale,
　　Hire a goldsmith, and he
　　　makes it *into* a god;
　　They bow down, indeed they
　　　worship it.
7 "They lift it on the shoulder,
　　　carry it,
　　And set it in its place, and it
　　　stands *there.*
　　It does not move from its place.
　　Though one may shout to it, it
　　　^A^cannot answer;
　　It ^B^cannot save him from his
　　　distress.

8 "Remember this, and be
　　　assured;
　　^A^Recall it to mind, you
　　　^B^wrongdoers.

45:21 ^A^Is 45:5　^B^Is 43:3, 11　45:22 ^A^Num 21:8, 9;
2 Chr 20:12　45:23 ^A^Rom 14:11　^B^Deut 6:13
45:24 ^A^Jer 33:16　^B^Is 41:11　45:25 ^A^1 Kin 8:32; Is 53:11
46:1 ^A^Is 2:18; 21:9　46:2 ^A^Judg 18:17, 18, 24; 2 Sam 5:21
46:3 ^A^Is 10:21, 22　^B^Ps 71:6　46:4 ^A^Is 41:4　^B^Ps 71:18
46:5 ^A^Is 40:18, 25　46:6 ^A^Is 40:19; 41:7　46:7 ^A^Is 41:28
^B^Is 45:20　46:8 ^A^Is 44:19　^B^Is 50:1

9 "Remember the ^former things
  long past,
  For I am God, and there is no
  other;
  I am God, and there is no one
  like Me,
10 Declaring the end from the
   beginning,
   And from ancient times things
   which have not been done,
   Saying, '^My plan will be
   established,
   And I will accomplish all My
   good pleasure';
11 Calling a bird of prey from the
   east,
   The man of My purpose from a
   distant country.
   Truly I have ^spoken; truly I
   will bring it to pass.
   I have planned *it*, I will
   certainly do it.

12 "Listen to Me, you ^stubborn-
   minded,
   Who are ^far from
   righteousness.
13 "I bring near My righteousness,
   it is not far off;
   And My salvation will not delay.
   And I will grant ^salvation in
   Zion,
   And My glory for Israel.

MOURNING FOR BABYLON

47 "Come down and sit in the
   dust,
   ^Virgin ^daughter of Babylon;
   Sit on the ground without a
   throne,
   Daughter of the Chaldeans!
   For you will no longer be
   called tender and delicate.
2 "Take the millstones and grind
  flour.
  Remove your ^veil, ^strip off
  the skirt,

Uncover the leg, cross the rivers.
3 "Your ^nakedness will be
  uncovered,
  Your shame will also be
  exposed;
  I will ^take vengeance and will
  not spare anyone."
4 Our ^Redeemer, the Lord of
  armies is His name,
  The Holy One of Israel.

5 "^Sit silently, and go into
  ^darkness,
  Daughter of the Chaldeans;
  For you will no longer be called
  The queen of kingdoms.
6 "I was angry with My people,
  I profaned My heritage
  And handed them over to you.
  You did not show mercy to
  them,
  On the ^aged you made your
  yoke very heavy.
7 "Yet you said, 'I will be a ^queen
  forever.'
  These things you did not
  consider
  Nor remember the outcome of
  them.

8 "Now, then, hear this, you
  luxuriant one,
  Who lives securely,
  Who says in her heart,
  '^I am, and there is no one
  besides me.
  I will ^not sit as a widow,
  Nor know the loss of children.'
9 "But these two things will come
  on you ^suddenly in one day:
  Loss of children and
  widowhood.

46:9 ^Deut 32:7; Is 42:9   **46:10** ^Ps 33:11; Prov 19:21
46:11 ^Num 23:19; Is 14:24   **46:12** ^Ps 76:5   ^Ps 119:150
46:13 ^Is 61:3; 62:11   **47:1** ^Is 23:12   ^Ps 137:8
47:2 ^Gen 24:65   ^Is 32:11   **47:3** ^Ezek 16:37   ^Is 34:8
47:4 ^Is 41:14   **47:5** ^Is 23:2   ^Is 13:10
47:6 ^Deut 28:50   **47:7** ^Is 47:5   **47:8** ^Is 45:5, 6, 18
^Rev 18:7   **47:9** ^Ps 73:19

They will come on you in full
measure
In spite of your many
[B]sorceries,
In spite of the great power of
your spells.

10 "You felt [A]secure in your
wickedness and said,
'No one sees me,'
Your wisdom and your
knowledge, they have led
you astray;
For you have said in your
heart,
'I am, and there is no one
besides me.'

11 "But [A]evil will come on you
Which you will not know how
to charm away;
And disaster will fall on you
For which you cannot atone;
And [B]destruction about which
you do not know
Will come on you suddenly.

12 "Persist now in your [A]spells
And in your many sorceries
With which you have labored
from your youth;
Perhaps you will be able to
benefit,
Perhaps you may cause
trembling.

13 "You are [A]wearied with your
many counsels;
Let now the astrologers,
Those who prophesy by the
stars,
Those who predict by the new
moons,
Stand up and save you from
what will come upon you.

14 "Behold, they have become [A]like
stubble,
Fire burns them;
They cannot save themselves
from the power of the flame;

There will be no coal to warm by
Nor a fire to sit before!

15 "So have those become to
you with whom you have
labored,
Those who have [A]done
business with you from your
youth;
Each has wandered in his own
way;
There is [B]no one to save you.

ISRAEL'S OBSTINACY

48 "Hear this, house of Jacob,
who are named Israel
And who came from the
waters of Judah,
Who [A]swear by the name of
the LORD
And invoke the God of Israel,
But not in truth nor in
[B]righteousness.

2 "For they name themselves
after the holy city,
And [A]lean on the God of Israel;
The LORD of armies is His
name.

3 "I [A]declared the former things
long ago,
And they went out of My
mouth, and I proclaimed
them.
Suddenly I acted, and they
came to pass.

4 "Because I know that you are
[A]obstinate,
And your [B]neck is an iron
tendon
And your forehead bronze,

5 Therefore I declared *them* to
you long ago,
Before they took place I
proclaimed *them* to you,

47:9 [B] Is 47:13   47:10 [A] Ps 52:7; 62:10   47:11 [A] Is 57:1
[B] Is 13:6   47:12 [A] Is 47:9   47:13 [A] Jer 51:58, 64
47:14 [A] Is 5:24; Nah 1:10   47:15 [A] Rev 18:11   [B] Is 5:29
48:1 [A] Deut 6:13   [B] Is 58:2   48:2 [A] Is 10:20; Jer 7:4
48:3 [A] Is 41:22; 42:9   48:4 [A] Ex 32:9   [B] 2 Chr 36:13

So that you would not say, 'My
   ^Aidol has done them,
And my carved image and
   my cast metal image have
   commanded them.'
6 "You have heard; look at all this.
   And you, will you not declare it?
   I proclaim to you ^Anew things
   from this time,
   Hidden things which you have
   not known.
7 "They are created now and not
   long ago;
   And before today you have not
   heard them,
   So that you will not say,
   'Behold, I knew them.'
8 "You have not heard, you have
   not known.
   Even from long ago your ear
   has not been open,
   Because I knew that
   you would deal very
   treacherously;
   And you have been called a
   ^Arebel from birth.
9 "^AFor the sake of My name I
   ^Bdelay My wrath,
   And for My praise I restrain it
   for you,
   In order not to cut you off.
10 "Behold, I have refined you, but
   not as silver;
   I have tested you in the
   ^Afurnace of affliction.
11 "For My own sake, for My own
   sake, I will act;
   For how can My name be
   profaned?
   And I will not give My ^Aglory
   to another.

RESCUE PROMISED

12 "Listen to Me, Jacob, Israel
   whom I called;
   I am He, ^AI am the first, I am
   also the last.

13 "Assuredly My hand ^Afounded
   the earth,
   And My right hand spread out
   the heavens;
   When I ^Bcall to them, they
   stand together.
14 "Assemble, all of you, and
   listen!
   Who among them has
   declared these things?
   The LORD loves him; he will
   ^Acarry out His good pleasure
   against ^BBabylon,
   And His arm will be against
   the Chaldeans.
15 "I, yes I, have spoken; indeed I
   have ^Acalled him,
   I have brought him, and
   He will make his ways
   successful.
16 "Come near to Me, listen to this:
   From the beginning I have ^Anot
   spoken in secret,
   From the time it took place, I
   was there.
   And now ^Bthe Lord GOD has
   sent Me, and His Spirit."

17 This is what the LORD says, He
who is your Redeemer, the Holy
One of Israel:
   "I am the LORD your God, who
   teaches you to benefit,
   Who ^Aleads you in the way you
   should go.
18 "If only you had ^Apaid attention
   to My commandments!
   Then your well-being would
   have been like a river,
   And your righteousness like
   the waves of the sea.

48:5 ^A Jer 44:15-18   48:6 ^A Is 42:9; 43:19
48:8 ^A Deut 9:7, 24; Ps 58:3   48:9 ^A Is 48:11
^B Neh 9:30, 31   48:10 ^A Deut 4:20; 1 Kin 8:51
48:11 ^A Deut 32:26, 27; Is 42:8   48:12 ^A Is 44:6; Rev 1:17
48:13 ^A Ex 20:11   ^B Is 40:26   48:14 ^A Is 46:10, 11
^B Is 13:4, 5, 17-19   48:15 ^A Is 41:2; 45:1, 2
48:16 ^A Is 45:19   ^B Zech 2:9, 11   48:17 ^A Ps 32:8;
Is 30:21   48:18 ^A Deut 5:29; 32:29

19 "Your descendants would have
     been like the sand,
   And your offspring like its
     grains;
   ᴬTheir name would never be
     eliminated or destroyed
     from My presence."

20 ᴬGo out from Babylon! Flee
     from the Chaldeans!
   Declare with the sound of joyful
     shouting, proclaim this,
   Send it out to the end of the
     earth;
   Say, "The Lᴏʀᴅ has redeemed
     His servant Jacob."
21 They did not thirst when
     He led them through the
     deserts.
   He ᴬmade the water flow out of
     the rock for them;
   He split the rock and ᴮthe
     water gushed out.
22 "ᴬThere is no peace for the
     wicked," says the Lᴏʀᴅ.

SALVATION REACHES TO THE ENDS OF THE EARTH

49 Listen to Me, you ᴬislands,
     And pay attention, you
   peoples from afar.
   The Lᴏʀᴅ called Me from the
     womb;
   From the body of My mother
     He named Me.
2 He has made My mouth like a
     sharp sword,
   In the ᴬshadow of His hand He
     has concealed Me;
   And He has also made Me a
     sharpened ᴮarrow,
   He has hidden Me in His
     quiver.
3 He said to Me, "ᴬYou are My
     Servant, Israel,
   ᴮIn whom I will show My
     glory."

4 But I said, "I have ᴬlabored in
     vain,
   I have spent My strength for
     nothing and futility;
   Nevertheless, the justice *due*
     to Me is with the Lᴏʀᴅ,
   And My ᴮreward is with My
     God."

5 And now says the Lᴏʀᴅ, who
     formed Me from the womb
     to be His Servant,
   To bring Jacob back to Him,
     so that Israel might be
     gathered to Him
   (For I am ᴬhonored in the
     sight of the Lᴏʀᴅ,
   And My God is My
     ᴮstrength),
6 He says, "It is too small a
     thing that You should be My
     Servant
   To raise up the tribes of Jacob
     and to restore the protected
     ones of Israel;
   I will also make You a ᴬlight of
     the nations
   So that My salvation may
     reach to the end of the
     earth."
7 This is what the Lᴏʀᴅ, the
     ᴬRedeemer of Israel *and* its
     Holy One,
   Says to the ᴮdespised One,
   To the One abhorred by the
     nation,
   To the Servant of rulers:
   "Kings will see and arise,
     Princes will also bow down,
   Because of the Lᴏʀᴅ who is
     faithful, the Holy One of
     Israel who has chosen You."

48:19 ᴬIs 56:5; 66:22   48:20 ᴬJer 50:8; 51:6, 45
48:21 ᴬEx 17:6   ᴮPs 78:20   48:22 ᴬIs 57:21
49:1 ᴬIs 42:4   49:2 ᴬIs 51:16   ᴮHab 3:11
49:3 ᴬZech 3:8   ᴮIs 44:23   49:4 ᴬIs 65:23   ᴮIs 35:4
49:5 ᴬIs 43:4   ᴮIs 12:2   49:6 ᴬIs 42:6; 51:4
49:7 ᴬIs 48:17   ᴮPs 22:6-8

8   This is what the LORD says:
    "At a favorable time I
        answered You,
    And on a day of salvation I
        helped You;
    And I will watch over You and
        ^make You a covenant of the
        people,
    To ^Brestore the land, to give as
        inheritances the deserted
        hereditary lands;
9   Saying to those who are
        ^bound, 'Go free,'
    To those who are in darkness,
        'Show yourselves.'
    They will feed along the
        roads,
    And their pasture *will be* on
        all bare heights.
10 "They will not hunger or
        thirst,
    Nor will the scorching heat or
        sun strike them down;
    For ^He who has
        compassion on them will
        ^Blead them,
    And He will guide them to
        springs of water.
11 "I will make all ^My mountains
        a road,
    And My highways will be
        raised up.
12 "Behold, these will come from
        afar;
    And behold, these *will come*
        from the ^north and from
        the west,
    And these from the land of
        Aswan."
13 Shout for joy, you heavens!
        And rejoice, you earth!
    Break forth into joyful
        shouting, mountains!
    For the ^LORD has comforted
        His people
    And will ^Bhave compassion
        on His afflicted.

PROMISE TO ZION

14 But Zion said, "The LORD has
        abandoned me,
    And the Lord has forgotten me."
15 "Can a woman forget her
        nursing child
    And have no compassion on
        the son of her womb?
    Even these may forget, but ^I
        will not forget you.
16 "Behold, I have ^inscribed you
        on the palms *of My hands;*
    Your walls are continually
        before Me.
17 "Your builders hurry;
    Your ^destroyers and
        devastators
    Will leave you.
18 "Raise your eyes and look
        around;
    All of them gather together,
        they come to you.
    ^As I live," declares the LORD,
    "You will certainly ^Bput them all
        on as jewelry and bind them
        on as a bride.
19 "For your ruins and deserted
        places and your destroyed
        land—
    Now you will certainly
        be ^too cramped for the
        inhabitants,
    And those who ^Bswallowed
        you will be far away.
20 "The ^children you lost will yet
        say in your ears,
    'The place is too cramped for me;
    Make room for me that I may
        live *here.*'
21 "Then you will say in your
        heart,
    'Who has fathered these for me,

49:8 ^Is 42:6   ^BIs 44:26   49:9 ^Is 42:7; 61:1
49:10 ^Is 14:1   ^BPs 23:2   49:11 ^Is 40:4
49:12 ^Is 43:5, 6   49:13 ^Is 40:1   ^BIs 54:7, 8, 10
49:15 ^Is 44:21   49:16 ^Song 8:6; Hag 2:23
49:17 ^Is 10:6; 37:18   49:18 ^Is 45:23   ^BIs 52:1
49:19 ^Is 54:1, 2   ^BPs 56:1, 2   49:20 ^Is 54:1–3

Since I have been bereaved of
my children
And cannot conceive, *and I am*
an ^exile, and a wanderer?
And who has raised these?
Behold, I was left alone;
^BWhere are these from?'"

22 This is what the Lord GOD says:
"Behold, I will lift up My hand
to the nations
And set up My flag to the
peoples;
And they will ^bring your sons
in their arms,
And your daughters will be
carried on *their* shoulders.

23 "Kings will be your guardians,
And their princesses your
nurses.
They will bow down to you
with their faces to the ground
And lick the dust from your
feet;
And you will know that I am
the LORD;
Those who hopefully ^wait for
Me will ^Bnot be put to shame.

24 "^ACan the prey be taken from a
mighty man,
Or the captives of a tyrant be
rescued?"

25 Indeed, this is what the LORD
says:
"Even the ^captives of the
mighty man will be taken
away,
And the prey of a tyrant will be
rescued;
For I will contend with the one
who contends with you,
And I will ^Bsave your sons.

26 "I will feed your oppressors
with their own flesh,
And they will become drunk
with their own blood as with
sweet wine;

And ^humanity will know
that I, the LORD, am your
Savior
And your ^BRedeemer, the
Mighty One of Jacob."

GOD HELPS HIS SERVANT

50 This is what the LORD says:
"Where is the certificate of
divorce
By which I have sent your
mother away?
Or to whom of My creditors
did I ^sell you?
Behold, you were sold for your
^Bwrongdoings,
And for your wrongful acts
your mother was sent away.

2 "Why was there no one when I
came?
When I called, *why* was there
no one to answer?
Is My hand so short that it
cannot redeem?
Or do I have no power to
rescue?
Behold, I ^dry up the sea with
My rebuke,
I ^Bturn rivers into a
wilderness;
Their fish stink for lack of
water,
And die of thirst.

3 "I ^clothe the heavens with
blackness,
And make sackcloth their
covering."

4 The Lord GOD has given Me
the tongue of ^disciples,
So that I may know how to
sustain the weary one with
a word.

49:21 ^AIs 5:13 ^BIs 60:8 49:22 ^AIs 14:2; 43:6
49:23 ^APs 37:9 ^BPs 25:3 49:24 ^AMatt 12:29; Luke 11:21
49:25 ^AIs 10:6 ^BIs 25:9 49:26 ^AIs 45:6 ^BIs 49:7
50:1 ^ADeut 32:30 ^BIs 52:3 50:2 ^AEx 14:21 ^BJosh 3:16
50:3 ^AIs 13:10; Rev 6:12 50:4 ^AIs 8:16; 54:13

He awakens *Me* morning by
  morning,
He awakens My ear to listen as
  a disciple.
5 The Lord GOD has ^opened
  My ear,
And I was ᴮnot disobedient,
Nor did I turn back.
6 I ^gave My back to those who
  strike *Me,*
And My cheeks to those who
  pull out My beard;
I did not hide My face from
  insults and spitting.
7 For the Lord GOD ^helps Me,
Therefore, I am ᴮnot disgraced;
Therefore, I have made My
  face like flint,
And I know that I will not be
  ashamed.
8 He who ^vindicates Me is near;
Who will contend with Me?
Let us stand up to each other.
Who has a case against Me?
Let him approach Me.
9 Behold, ^the Lord GOD helps
  Me;
ᴮWho is he who condemns
  Me?
Behold, they will all wear out
  like a garment;
A moth will eat them.
10 Who is among you who fears
  the LORD,
Who obeys the voice of His
  ^servant,
Who walks in darkness and
  has no light?
Let him trust in the name of
  the LORD and rely on his God.
11 Behold, all you who ^kindle a
  fire,
Who encircle yourselves with
  flaming arrows,
Walk in the light of your fire
And among the flaming
  arrows you have set ablaze.

This you will have from My
  hand:
You will ᴮlie down in torment.

ISRAEL EXHORTED

51 "^Listen to Me, you who
    ᴮpursue righteousness,
Who seek the LORD:
Look to the rock from which
  you were cut,
And to the quarry from which
  you were dug.
2 "Look to ^Abraham your
  father
And to Sarah who gave birth
  to you in pain;
When *he was only* one I called
  him,
Then I blessed him and
  multiplied him."
3 Indeed, the LORD will comfort
  Zion;
He will comfort all her ruins.
And He will make her
  wilderness like ^Eden,
And her desert like the ᴮgarden
  of the LORD.
Joy and gladness will be found
  in her,
Thanksgiving and the sound
  of a melody.
4 "Pay attention to Me, My
  people,
And listen to Me, My nation;
For a law will go out from Me,
And I will bring My ^justice as
  a ᴮlight of the peoples.
5 "My ^righteousness is near, My
  salvation has gone forth,
And My arms will judge the
  peoples;

50:5 ^Ps 40:6   ᴮMatt 26:39   50:6 ^Matt 26:67; 27:30
50:7 ^Is 42:1   ᴮIs 45:17   50:8 ^Is 45:25; Rom 8:33, 34
50:9 ^Is 41:10   ᴮIs 54:17   50:10 ^Is 49:2, 3; 50:4
50:11 ^Prov 26:18   ᴮIs 8:22   51:1 ^Is 46:3   ᴮPs 94:15
51:2 ^Is 29:22; 41:8   51:3 ^Gen 2:8   ᴮGen 13:10
51:4 ^Is 1:27   ᴮIs 42:6   51:5 ^Is 46:13

The ᴮcoastlands will wait for Me,
And they will wait expectantly
for My arm.

6 "Raise your eyes to the sky,
Then look to the earth
beneath;
For the ᴬsky will vanish like
smoke,
And the ᴬearth will wear out
like a garment
And its inhabitants will die in
the same way.
But My ᴮsalvation will be
forever,
And My righteousness will
not fail.

7 "Listen to Me, you who know
righteousness,
A people in whose ᴬheart is
My Law;
Do not fear the ᴮtaunting of
people,
Nor be terrified of their
abuses.

8 "For the moth will eat them like
a garment;
Yes, the ᴬmoth will eat them
like wool.
But My ᴮrighteousness will be
forever,
And My salvation to all
generations."

9 Awake, awake, put on
strength, O arm of the Lᴏʀᴅ;
Awake as in the days of old,
the generations of long ago.
ᴬWas it not You who cut ¹Rahab
in pieces,
Who pierced the ᴮdragon?

10 Was it not You who dried up
the sea,
The waters of the great deep;
Who made the depths of the
sea a pathway
For the ᴬredeemed to cross
over?

11 And the redeemed of the Lᴏʀᴅ
will return
And come to Zion with joyful
shouting,
And ᴬeverlasting joy *will be* on
their heads.
They will obtain gladness and
joy,
And ᴮsorrow and sighing will
flee away.

12 "I, I Myself, am He who
ᴬcomforts you.
Who are you that you are
afraid of mortal man,
And of a son of man *who* is
made *like* grass,

13 That you have ᴬforgotten the
Lᴏʀᴅ your Maker,
Who stretched out the heavens
And laid the foundations of
the earth,
That you fear continually all
day long because of the fury
of the oppressor,
As he makes ready to destroy?
And where is the rage of the
oppressor?

14 The ᴬexile will soon be set free,
and will not die in the dungeon,
nor will his bread be lacking. 15 For
I am the Lᴏʀᴅ your God, who ᴬstirs
up the sea so that its waves roar
(the Lᴏʀᴅ of armies is His name).
16 And I have ᴬput My words in your
mouth and have covered you with
the shadow of My hand, to ᴮestab-
lish the heavens, to found the
earth, and to say to Zion, 'You are
My people.'"

51:5 ᴬIs 42:4   51:6 ᴬPs 102:25, 26   ᴮIs 45:17
51:7 ᴬPs 37:31   ᴮIs 25:8   51:8 ᴬIs 14:11   ᴮIs 51:6
51:9 ᴬJob 26:12   ᴮPs 74:13   51:10 ᴬEx 15:13; Ps 106:10
51:11 ᴬIs 60:19   ᴮIs 25:8   51:12 ᴬIs 51:3
51:13 ᴬDeut 6:12; 8:11   51:14 ᴬIs 48:20; 52:2
51:15 ᴬPs 107:25; Jer 31:35   51:16 ᴬDeut 18:18   ᴮIs 66:22

51:9 ¹ I.e., a sea monster, not to be confused with
Rahab in Joshua 2

17 ᴬPull yourself up! Pull
    yourself up! Arise,
    Jerusalem!
    You who have drunk from the
    Lᴏʀᴅ's hand the cup of His
    anger;
    The chalice of staggering you
    have drunk to the dregs.

18 There is ᴬno one to guide her
    among all the sons *to whom*
    she has given birth,
    Nor is there anyone to take her
    by the hand among all the
    sons she has raised.

19 These two things have
    happened to you;
    Who will mourn for you?
    The ᴬdevastation and
    destruction, famine and
    sword;
    How shall I comfort you?

20 Your sons have fainted,
    They lie *helpless* at the head
    of every street,
    Like an antelope in a net,
    Full of the wrath of the
    Lᴏʀᴅ,
    The ᴬrebuke of your God.

21 Therefore, listen to this, you
    ᴬafflicted,
    Who are drunk, but not with
    wine:

22 This is what your Lord, the
    Lᴏʀᴅ, your God
    Who contends for His people
    says:
    "Behold, I have taken from
    your hand the ᴬcup of
    staggering,
    The chalice of My anger;
    You will never drink it again.

23 "I will put it into the hand of
    your tormentors,
    Who have said to you, 'ᴬLie
    down so that we may walk
    over *you*.'

You have also made your back
    like the ground,
And like the street for those
    who walk over *it*."

CHEER FOR PROSTRATE ZION

52 ᴬAwake, awake,
    Clothe yourself in your
    strength, Zion;
    Clothe yourself with your
    ᴮbeautiful garments,
    Jerusalem, the holy city;
    For the uncircumcised and the
    unclean
    Will no longer come into you.

2 Shake yourself ᴬfrom the dust,
    rise up,
    Captive Jerusalem;
    ᴮRelease yourself from the
    chains around your neck,
    Captive daughter of Zion.

3 For this is what the Lᴏʀᴅ says:
"You were sold for nothing, and you
will be ᴬredeemed ᴮwithout money."
4 For this is what the Lord Gᴏᴅ says:
"My people ᴬwent down to Egypt
first to reside there; then the Assyrian oppressed them without reason.
5 And now, what do I have here,"
declares the Lᴏʀᴅ, "seeing that
My people have been taken away
without reason?" *Again* the Lᴏʀᴅ
declares, "Those who rule over them
howl, and My ᴬname is continually
reviled all day long. 6 Therefore, My
people shall ᴬknow My name; therefore on that day I am the one who is
speaking, 'Here I am.'"

7 How delightful on the
    mountains
    Are the feet of one who brings
    ᴬgood news,

51:17 ᴬIs 51:9; 52:1   51:18 ᴬPs 88:18; 142:4
51:19 ᴬIs 8:21; 9:20   51:20 ᴬIs 66:15   51:21 ᴬIs 54:11
51:22 ᴬIs 51:17   51:23 ᴬJosh 10:24   52:1 ᴬIs 51:9, 17
ᴮEx 28:2, 40   52:2 ᴬIs 29:4   ᴮIs 9:4   52:3 ᴬIs 1:27
ᴮIs 45:13   52:4 ᴬGen 46:6   52:5 ᴬEzek 36:20, 23;
Rom 2:24   52:6 ᴬIs 49:23   52:7 ᴬIs 40:9; 61:1

Who announces peace
And brings good news of
    happiness,
Who announces salvation,
And says to Zion, "Your God
    reigns!"
8 Listen! Your watchmen raise
    their ^voices,
They shout joyfully together;
For they will see with their
    own eyes
When the Lord restores
    Zion.
9 Be cheerful, shout joyfully
    together,
You ruins of Jerusalem;
For the Lord has comforted
    His people,
He has ^redeemed Jerusalem.
10 The Lord has bared His holy
    arm
In the sight of all the nations,
So that ^all the ends of the
    earth may see
The salvation of our God.

11 ^Depart, depart, go out from
    there,
Do not touch what is
    unclean;
Go out of the midst of her,
    purify yourselves,
You who carry the vessels of
    the Lord.
12 But you will not go out in a
    hurry,
Nor will you go as fugitives;
For the ^Lord will go before
    you,
And ^Bthe God of Israel *will be*
    your rear guard.

THE EXALTED SERVANT

13 Behold, My ^Servant will
    prosper,
He will be high and lifted up
    and greatly exalted.

14 Just as many were appalled at
    you, *My people,*
So His ^appearance was marred
    beyond *that of a* man,
And His form beyond the sons
    of mankind.
15 So He will sprinkle many
    nations,
Kings will shut their mouths
    on account of Him;
For ^what they had not been
    told, they will see,
And what they had not heard,
    they will understand.

THE SUFFERING SERVANT

53 ^Who has believed our
    report?
And to whom has the arm of
    the Lord been revealed?
2 For He grew up before Him
    like a ^tender shoot,
And like a root out of dry
    ground;
He has ^Bno *stately* form or
    majesty
That we would look at Him,
Nor an appearance that we
    would take pleasure in Him.
3 He was ^despised and
    abandoned by men,
A man of great pain and
    familiar with sickness;
And like one from whom
    people hide their faces,
He was ^Bdespised, and we had
    no regard for Him.

4 However, *it was* our sicknesses
    that He Himself ^bore,
And our pains *that* He
    carried;

52:8 ^Is 62:6   52:9 ^Is 43:1; 48:20   52:10 ^Is 45:22;
48:20   52:11 ^Is 48:20; Jer 50:8
52:12 ^Is 26:7   ^BEx 14:19, 20   52:13 ^Is 42:1; 49:1-7
52:14 ^Is 53:2, 3   52:15 ^Rom 15:21; Eph 3:5
53:1 ^John 12:38; Rom 10:16   53:2 ^Is 11:1   ^BIs 52:14
53:3 ^Ps 22:6   ^BMark 10:33, 34   53:4 ^Matt 8:17

Yet we ourselves assumed that
  He had been afflicted,
Struck down by ᴮGod, and
  humiliated.
⁵ But He was pierced for our
  offenses,
He was crushed for ᴬour
  wrongdoings;
The punishment for our
  well-being *was laid* upon
  Him,
And by ᴮHis wounds we are
  healed.
⁶ All of us, like sheep, have gone
  astray,
Each of us has turned to his
  own way;
But the Lᴏʀᴅ has caused the
  wrongdoing of us all
To fall on Him.

⁷ He was oppressed and
  afflicted,
Yet He did not open His
  mouth;
ᴬLike a lamb that is led to
  slaughter,
And like a sheep that is silent
  before its shearers,
So He did not open His mouth.
⁸ By oppression and judgment
  He was taken away;
And as for His generation, who
  considered
That He was cut off from the
  land of the living
ᴬFor the wrongdoing of my
  people, to whom the blow
  was due?
⁹ And His grave was assigned
  with wicked men,
Yet He was with a ᴬrich man in
  His death,
Because He had ᴮdone no
  violence,
Nor was there any deceit in
  His mouth.

¹⁰ But the Lᴏʀᴅ desired
To ᴬcrush Him, ᴮcausing *Him*
  grief;
If He renders Himself *as* a guilt
  offering,
He will see *His* offspring,
He will prolong *His* days,
And the good pleasure of the
  Lᴏʀᴅ will prosper in His hand.
¹¹ As a result of the anguish of
  His soul,
He will ᴬsee *it and* be satisfied;
By His ᴮknowledge the
  Righteous One,
My Servant, will justify the
  many,
For He will bear their
  wrongdoings.
¹² Therefore, I will allot Him a
  portion with the great,
And He will divide the plunder
  with the strong,
Because He poured out His
  ᴬlife unto death,
And was ᴮcounted with
  wrongdoers;
Yet He Himself bore the sin of
  many,
And interceded for the
  wrongdoers.

THE FERTILITY OF ZION

54

"Shout for joy, infertile one,
  you who have not given
  birth *to any child;*
Break forth into joyful
  shouting and cry aloud, you
  who have not been in labor;
For the sons of the ᴬdesolate
  one *will be* ᴮmore numerous
Than the sons of the married
  woman," says the Lᴏʀᴅ.

53:4 ᴮJohn 19:7   **53:5** ᴬIs 53:10   ᴮ1 Pet 2:24, 25
53:7 ᴬActs 8:32, 33; Rev 5:6   **53:8** ᴬIs 53:5, 12
53:9 ᴬMatt 27:57-60   ᴮ1 Pet 2:22   **53:10** ᴬIs 53:5
ᴮIs 53:3, 4   **53:11** ᴬJohn 10:14-18   ᴮIs 45:25
53:12 ᴬMatt 26:38, 39, 42   ᴮLuke 22:37   **54:1** ᴬIs 62:4
ᴮ1 Sam 2:5

2 "Enlarge the place of your tent;
  Stretch out the curtains of
    your dwellings, do not
    spare *them;*
  Lengthen your ^ropes
  And strengthen your ^pegs.
3 "For you will ^spread out to the
    right and to the left.
  And your descendants will
    possess nations
  And will resettle the desolate
    cities.

4 "Fear not, for you will ^not be
    put to shame;
  And do not feel humiliated, for
    you will not be disgraced;
  But you will forget the shame
    of your youth,
  And no longer remember
    the disgrace of your
    widowhood.
5 "For your ^husband is your
    Maker,
  Whose name is the LORD of
    armies;
  And your Redeemer is the
    Holy One of Israel,
  Who is called the ^BGod of all
    the earth.
6 "For the LORD has called you,
  Like a wife ^forsaken and
    grieved in spirit,
  Even like a wife of *one's* youth
    when she is rejected,"
  Says your God.
7 "For a ^brief moment I
    abandoned you,
  But with great compassion I
    will ^Bgather you.
8 "In an ^outburst of anger
  I hid My face from you for a
    moment,
  But with everlasting favor I
    will ^Bhave compassion on
    you,"
  Says the LORD your Redeemer.

9 "For this is like the days of
    Noah to Me,
  When I swore that the waters
    of Noah
  Would ^not flood the earth
    again;
  So I have sworn that I will not
    be angry with you
  Nor rebuke you.
10 "For the mountains may be
    removed and the hills may
    shake,
  But My favor will not be
    removed from you,
  Nor will My ^covenant of
    peace be shaken,"
  Says the LORD who has
    compassion on you.

11 "Afflicted one, storm-tossed,
    and ^not comforted,
  Behold, I will set your stones
    in antimony,
  And I will lay your
    foundations with
    sapphires.
12 "Moreover, I will make your
    battlements of rubies,
  And your gates of crystal,
  And your entire wall of
    precious stones.
13 "^All your sons will be taught
    by the LORD;
  And the well-being of your
    sons will be great.
14 "In ^righteousness you will be
    established;
  You will be far from
    oppression, for you will not
    fear;
  And from terror, for it will not
    come near you.

54:2 ^Ex 35:18; 39:40   54:3 ^Gen 28:14; Is 43:5, 6
54:4 ^Is 45:17   54:5 ^Jer 3:14   ^BIs 6:3   54:6 ^Is
49:14-21; 50:1, 2   54:7 ^Is 26:20   ^BIs 11:12
54:8 ^Is 60:10   ^BIs 49:10, 13   54:9 ^Gen 9:11
54:10 ^2 Sam 23:5; Ps 89:34   54:11 ^Is 51:18, 19
54:13 ^John 6:45   54:14 ^Is 1:26, 27; 9:7

15 "If anyone fiercely attacks *you*,
    it will not be from Me.
    ᴬWhoever attacks you will fall
    because of you.
16 "Behold, I Myself have created
    the smith who blows on the
    fire of coals
    And produces a weapon for its
    work;
    And I have created the
    destroyer to inflict ruin.
17 "No weapon that is formed
    against you will succeed;
    And you will condemn every
    tongue that accuses you in
    judgment.
    This is the heritage of the
    servants of the Lᴏʀᴅ,
    And their ᴬvindication is from
    Me," declares the Lᴏʀᴅ.

THE FREE OFFER OF MERCY

55
"You there! Everyone who
    ᴬthirsts, come to the
    waters;
    And you who have no money
    come, buy and eat.
    Come, buy wine and milk
    ᴮWithout money and without
    cost.
2 "Why do you spend money for
    what is not bread,
    And your wages for what does
    not satisfy?
    Listen carefully to Me, and
    ᴬeat what is good,
    And ᴮdelight yourself in
    abundance.
3 "Incline your ear and come to
    Me.
    Listen, that you may ᴬlive;
    And I will make an everlasting
    covenant with you,
    According to the ᴮfaithful
    mercies shown to David.
4 "Behold, I have made ᴬhim a
    witness to the peoples,

A leader and commander for
    the peoples.
5 "Behold, you will call a ᴬnation
    you do not know,
    And a nation which does not
    know you will ᴮrun to you,
    Because of the Lᴏʀᴅ your God,
    the Holy One of Israel;
    For He has glorified you."

6   ᴬSeek the Lᴏʀᴅ while He may
    be found;
    Call upon Him while He is near.
7   ᴬLet the wicked abandon his
    way,
    And the unrighteous person
    his ᴮthoughts;
    And let him return to the Lᴏʀᴅ,
    And He will have compassion
    on him,
    And to our God,
    For He will abundantly
    pardon.
8 "For My thoughts are not ᴬyour
    thoughts,
    Nor are ᴮyour ways My ways,"
    declares the Lᴏʀᴅ.
9 "For ᴬ*as* the heavens are higher
    than the earth,
    So are My ways higher than
    your ways
    And My thoughts than your
    thoughts.
10 "For as the ᴬrain and the snow
    come down from heaven,
    And do not return there
    without watering the earth
    And making it produce and
    sprout,
    And providing ᴮseed to the
    sower and bread to the
    eater;

54:15 ᴬIs 41:11–16   54:17 ᴬIs 45:24; 46:13
55:1 ᴬPs 42:1, 2   ᴮHos 14:4   55:2 ᴬPs 22:26   ᴮIs 25:6
55:3 ᴬLev 18:5   ᴮActs 13:34   55:4 ᴬPs 18:43; Jer 30:9
55:5 ᴬIs 45:14, 22–24   ᴮZech 8:22   55:6 ᴬPs 32:6;
Is 45:19, 22   55:7 ᴬIs 1:16, 19   ᴮIs 32:7   55:8 ᴬIs 65:2
ᴮIs 53:6   55:9 ᴬPs 103:11   55:10 ᴬIs 30:23   ᴮ2 Cor 9:10

11 So will My word be which goes
    out of My mouth;
    It will ^not return to Me empty,
    Without ^Baccomplishing what
        I desire,
    And without succeeding *in the
        purpose* for which I sent it.
12 "For you will go out with ^joy
    And be led in ^Bpeace;
    The mountains and the hills
        will break into shouts of joy
        before you,
    And all the trees of the field
        will clap *their* hands.
13 "Instead of the thorn bush, the
        juniper will come up,
    And instead of the ^stinging
        nettle, the myrtle will come
        up;
    And it will be a ^Bmemorial to
        the LORD,
    An everlasting sign which will
        not be eliminated."

REWARDS FOR OBEDIENCE TO GOD

56 This is what the LORD says:
    "^AGuard justice and do
        righteousness,
    For My ^Bsalvation is about to
        come
    And My righteousness to be
        revealed.
2 "^ABlessed is a man who does
        this,
    And a son of man who takes
        hold of it;
    Who ^Bkeeps from profaning
        the Sabbath,
    And keeps his hand from
        doing any evil."
3 Let not the ^Aforeigner who has
        joined himself to the LORD say,
    "The LORD will certainly
        separate me from His
        people."
    Nor let the ^Beunuch say,
        "Behold, I am a dry tree."

4 For this is what the LORD says:
    "To the eunuchs who ^Akeep My
        Sabbaths,
    And choose what pleases Me,
    And hold firmly to My covenant,
5 To them I will give in My
        house and within My walls a
        memorial,
    And a name better than that of
        sons and daughters;
    I will give them an everlasting
        ^Aname which ^Bwill not be
        eliminated.
6 "Also the ^Aforeigners who join
        themselves to the LORD,
    To attend to His service and to
        love the name of the LORD,
    To be His servants, every one
        who keeps the Sabbath so as
        not to profane it,
    And holds firmly to My
        covenant;
7 Even those I will bring to My
        holy mountain,
    And make them joyful in My
        house of prayer.
    Their burnt offerings and their
        sacrifices will be acceptable
        on My altar;
    For ^AMy house will be called
        a house of prayer for all the
        peoples."
8 The Lord GOD, who ^Agathers
        the dispersed of Israel,
        declares,
    "I will yet gather *others* to them,
        to those *already* gathered."

9   All you ^Awild animals,
    All you animals in the forest,
    Come to eat.

55:11 ^Is 44:26   ^BIs 46:10   55:12 ^APs 105:43
^BIs 54:10, 13   55:13 ^AIs 5:6   ^BIs 63:12, 14   56:1 ^AIs 1:17
^BPs 85:9   56:2 ^APs 112:1   ^BEx 20:8-11   56:3 ^AIs 14:1
^BDeut 23:1   56:4 ^AIs 56:2, 6   56:5 ^AIs 62:2   ^BIs 48:19
56:6 ^AIs 56:3; 60:10   56:7 ^AMatt 21:13; Mark 11:17
56:8 ^AIs 11:12   56:9 ^AIs 18:6; 46:11

10 His ᴬwatchmen are ᴮblind,
All of them know nothing.
All of them are mute dogs
    unable to bark,
Dreamers lying down, who
    love to slumber;

11 And the dogs are greedy, they
    are never satisfied.
And they are shepherds who
    have no understanding;
They have all ᴬturned to their
    own way,
Each one to his unjust gain,
    without exception.

12 "Come," *they say,* "let's get
    wine, and let's drink heavily
    of intoxicating drink;
And ᴬtomorrow will be like
    today, only more so."

EVIL LEADERS REBUKED

57 The righteous person
perishes, and no one takes
    it to heart;
And devout people are
    taken away, while no one
    understands.
For the righteous person is
    taken away from ᴬevil,

2   He enters into peace;
They rest in their ¹beds,
Each one who ᴬwalked in his
    upright way.

3   "But come here, you sons of a
    sorceress,
ᴬOffspring of an adulterer and
    a ᴮprostitute!

4   "Of whom do you make fun?
Against whom do you open
    wide your mouth
And stick out your tongue?
Are you not children of
    ᴬrebellion,
Offspring of deceit,

5   Who inflame yourselves
    among the oaks,
Under every luxuriant tree,

Who ᴬslaughter the children in
    the ravines,
Under the clefts of the rocks?

6   "Among the ¹·ᴬsmooth *stones* of
    the ravine
Is your portion, they are your
    lot;
Even to them you have poured
    out a drink offering,
You have made a grain
    offering.
Should I relent of these
    things?

7   "On a high and lofty mountain
You have ᴬmade your bed.
You also went up there to offer
    sacrifice.

8   "Behind the door and the
    doorpost
You have set up your sign;
Indeed, far removed from
    Me, you have ᴬuncovered
    yourself,
And have gone up and made
    your bed wide.
And you have made an
    agreement for yourself with
    them,
You have loved their bed,
You have looked at *their*
    manhood.

9   "You have journeyed to the
    king with oil
And increased your
    perfumes;
You have ᴬsent your
    messengers a great
    distance
And made *them* go down to
    ¹Sheol.

56:10ᴬEzek 3:17   ᴮIs 29:9-14   **56:11**ᴬIs 57:17;
Jer 22:17   **56:12**ᴬPs 10:6; Luke 12:19, 20
57:1²2 Kin 22:20; Is 47:11   **57:2**ᴬIs 26:7   **57:3**ᴬIs 1:4
ᴮIs 1:21   **57:4**ᴬIs 48:8   **57:5**ᴬ2 Kin 23:10; Ps 106:37, 38
57:6ᴬJer 3:9; Hab 2:19   **57:7**ᴬEzek 23:41
57:8ᴬEzek 23:18   **57:9**ᴬEzek 23:16, 40

57:2¹I.e., graves   **57:6**¹I.e., symbols of fertility gods
57:9¹I.e., the netherworld

10 "You were tired out by the
    length of your road,
    Yet you did not say, '^It is
    hopeless!'
    You found renewed strength,
    Therefore you did not faint.

11 "Of ^whom were you worried
    and fearful
    When you lied, and did not
    remember Me
    Nor give *Me* a thought?
    Was I not silent, even for a
    long time,
    So you do not fear Me?

12 "I will ^declare your
    righteousness and your
    ^Bdeeds,
    And they will not benefit you.

13 "When you cry out, ^let your
    collection *of idols* save you.
    But the wind will carry them
    all up,
    And a breath will take *them*
    away.
    But the one who takes refuge
    in Me will inherit the land
    And possess My holy
    mountain."

14 And it will be said,
    "^Build up, build up, prepare the
    way,
    Remove *every* obstacle from
    the way of My people."

15 For this is what the high and
    exalted One
    Who lives forever, whose
    name is Holy, says:
    "I dwell *in* a high and holy
    place,
    And *also* with the ^contrite
    and lowly of spirit
    In order to ^Brevive the spirit of
    the lowly
    And to revive the heart of the
    contrite.

16 "For I will not contend forever,
    ^Nor will I always be angry;
    For the spirit would grow
    faint before Me,
    And the breath *of those whom*
    I have made.

17 "Because of the wrongful act of
    his ^unjust gain I was angry
    and struck him;
    I hid *My face* and was angry,
    And he went on turning away,
    in the way of his heart.

18 "I have seen his ways, but I will
    ^heal him;
    I will ^Blead him and restore
    comfort to him and to his
    mourners,

19 Creating the praise of the
    lips.
    Peace, peace to him who is
    ^far away and to him who is
    near,"
    Says the LORD, "and I will heal
    him."

20 But the ^wicked are like the
    tossing sea,
    For it cannot be quiet,
    And its waters toss up refuse
    and mud.

21 "^There is no peace," says my
    God, "for the wicked."

OBSERVANCES OF FASTS

58 "^Cry loudly, do not hold
    back;
    Raise your voice like a
    trumpet,
    And declare to My people
    their wrongdoing,
    And to the house of Jacob
    their sins.

57:10 ^Jer 2:25; 18:12 **57:11** ^Prov 29:25; Is 51:12, 13
57:12 ^Is 58:1, 2 ^BIs 29:15 **57:13** ^Jer 22:20; 30:14
57:14 ^Is 62:10; Jer 18:15 **57:15** ^Ps 34:18 ^BPs 147:3
57:16 ^Ps 85:5; 103:9 **57:17** ^Is 2:7; 56:11
57:18 ^Is 19:22 ^BIs 52:12 **57:19** ^Acts 2:39; Eph 2:17
57:20 ^Job 18:5-14; Is 3:9, 11 **57:21** ^Is 48:22; 59:8
58:1 ^Is 40:6

2 "Yet they ^seek Me day by day
  and delight to know My
  ways,
  As a nation that has done
  righteousness
  And has not forsaken the
  ordinance of their God.
  They ask Me *for* just decisions,
  They delight ^Bin the nearness
  of God.
3 'Why have we ^fasted and You
  do not see?
  Why have we humbled
  ourselves and You do not
  notice?'
  Behold, on the day of your fast
  you find *your* desire,
  And oppress all your workers.
4 "Behold, you fast for contention
  and ^strife, and to strike with
  a wicked fist.
  You do not fast like *you have
  done* today to ^Bmake your
  voice heard on high!
5 "Is it a fast like this that I
  choose, a day for a person to
  humble himself?
  Is it for bowing one's head like
  a reed
  And for spreading out
  ^sackcloth and ashes as a
  bed?
  Will you call this a fast, even
  an ^Bacceptable day to the
  LORD?
6 "Is this not the fast that I
  choose:
  To ^release the bonds of
  wickedness,
  To undo the ropes of the yoke,
  And to let the oppressed go
  free,
  And break every yoke?
7 "Is it not to break your bread
  with the hungry
  And bring the homeless poor
  into the house;

When you see the ^naked, to
  cover him;
  And not to ^Bhide yourself from
  your own flesh?
8 "Then your light will break out
  like the dawn,
  And your ^recovery will spring
  up quickly;
  And your righteousness will
  go before you;
  The glory of the ^BLORD will be
  your rear guard.
9 "Then you will call, and the
  LORD will answer;
  You will cry for help, and He
  will say, 'Here I am.'
  If you remove the yoke from
  your midst,
  The ^pointing of the finger and
  ^Bspeaking wickedness,
10 And *if* you offer yourself to the
  hungry
  And satisfy the need of the
  afflicted,
  Then your ^light will rise in
  darkness,
  And your gloom *will become*
  like midday.
11 "And the LORD will continually
  guide you,
  And satisfy your desire in
  scorched places,
  And give strength to your
  bones;
  And you will be like a ^watered
  garden,
  And like a ^Bspring of water
  whose waters do not fail.
12 "Those from among you will
  ^rebuild the ancient ruins;
  You will raise up the age-old
  foundations;

58:2^Is 1:11   ^BPs 119:151   **58:3**^Mal 3:14; Luke 18:12
58:4^Is 3:14, 15   ^BIs 59:2   **58:5**^1 Kin 21:27   ^BIs 49:8
58:6^Neh 5:10-12; Jer 34:8   **58:7**^Matt 25:35, 36
^BDeut 22:1-4   **58:8**^Is 30:26   ^BEx 14:19
58:9^Prov 6:13   ^BPs 12:2   **58:10**^Job 11:17; Ps 37:6
58:11^Song 4:15   ^BJohn 4:14   **58:12**^Is 49:8

And you will be called the
　　repairer of the ᴮbreach,
The restorer of the streets in
　　which to dwell.

KEEPING THE SABBATH

13 "If, because of the Sabbath, you
　　restrain your foot
　　From doing as you wish on My
　　holy day,
　　And call the Sabbath a
　　pleasure, *and* the holy *day* of
　　the Lᴏʀᴅ honorable,
　　And honor it, desisting from
　　your ^own ways,
　　From seeking your *own*
　　pleasure
　　And ᴮspeaking *your own* word,
14 Then you will take delight in
　　the Lᴏʀᴅ,
　　And I will make you ride ^on
　　the heights of the earth;
　　And I will feed you *with*
　　the heritage of Jacob your
　　father,
　　For the mouth of the Lᴏʀᴅ has
　　spoken."

SEPARATION FROM GOD

59 Behold, ^the Lᴏʀᴅ's hand is
　　not so short
　　That it cannot save;
　　Nor is His ear so dull
　　That it cannot hear.
2 But your ^wrongdoings have
　　caused a separation between
　　you and your God,
　　And your sins have hidden
　　His face from you so that He
　　does not hear.
3 For your ^hands are defiled
　　with blood,
　　And your fingers with
　　wrongdoing;
　　Your lips have spoken ᴮdeceit,
　　Your tongue mutters
　　wickedness.

4 ^No one sues righteously and
　　no one pleads honestly.
　　They trust in confusion and
　　speak lies;
　　They ᴮconceive trouble and
　　give birth to disaster.
5 They hatch vipers' eggs and
　　^weave the spider's web;
　　The one who eats of their eggs
　　dies,
　　And *from* what is crushed, a
　　snake breaks out.
6 Their webs will not become
　　clothing,
　　Nor will they ^cover themselves
　　with their works;
　　Their ᴮworks are works of
　　wrongdoing,
　　And an act of violence is in
　　their hands.
7 ^Their feet run to evil,
　　And they hurry to shed
　　innocent blood;
　　Their thoughts are thoughts of
　　wrongdoing,
　　Devastation and destruction
　　are in their paths.
8 They do not know the ^way of
　　peace,
　　And there is no justice in their
　　tracks;
　　They have made their paths
　　crooked,
　　Whoever walks on them does
　　not know peace.

A CONFESSION OF WICKEDNESS

9 Therefore justice is far from us,
　　And righteousness does not
　　reach us;
　　We ^hope for light, but there is
　　darkness,

58:12 ᴮ Is 30:13   58:13 ^ Is 55:8   ᴮ Is 59:13
58:14 ^Deut 32:13; 33:29   59:1 ^Num 11:23; Is 50:2
59:2 ^Is 1:15; 50:1   59:3 ^Is 1:15, 21   ᴮ Is 28:15
59:4 ^Is 5:7   ᴮ Job 15:35   59:5 ^Job 8:14
59:6 ^Is 28:20   ᴮ Is 57:12   59:7 ^Prov 1:16; 6:17
59:8 ^Luke 1:79   59:9 ^Is 5:30; 8:21, 22

For brightness, but we walk
in gloom.
10 We ^grope for the wall like
people who are blind,
We grope like those who have
no eyes.
We ^Bstumble at midday as in
the twilight;
Among those who are healthy
we are like the dead.
11 All of us growl like bears,
And ^moan sadly like doves;
We hope for ^Bjustice, but there
is none;
For salvation, *but* it is far from
us.
12 For our wrongful acts have
multiplied before You,
And our ^sins have testified
against us;
For our wrongful acts are with
us,
And we know our
wrongdoings:
13 Offending and ^denying the
Lord,
And turning away from our God,
Speaking oppression and revolt,
Conceiving and uttering lying
words from the heart.
14 ^Justice is turned back,
And ^Brighteousness stands far
away;
For truth has stumbled in the
street,
And uprightness cannot enter.
15 Truth is lacking,
And one who turns aside from
evil ^makes himself a prey.

Now the Lord saw,
And it was displeasing in His
sight that there was no justice.
16 And He saw that there was no
one,
And was amazed that there
was not one to intercede;

Then His ^own arm brought
salvation to Him,
And His righteousness
upheld Him.
17 He put on righteousness like a
breastplate,
And a ^helmet of salvation on
His head;
And He put on ^Bgarments of
vengeance for clothing
And wrapped Himself with
zeal as a cloak.
18 ^According to *their* deeds, so
will He repay:
Wrath to His adversaries,
retribution to His
enemies;
To the coastlands He will deal
retribution.
19 So they will fear the name of
the Lord from the west
And His glory from the rising
of the sun,
For He will ^come like a
rushing stream
Which the wind of the Lord
drives.
20 "A ^Redeemer will come to
Zion,
And to those in Jacob who turn
from wrongdoing," declares
the Lord.

21 "As for Me, this is My ^covenant
with them," says the Lord: "My Spirit
who is upon you, and My words
which I have put in your mouth
shall not depart from your mouth,
nor from the mouth of your offspring, nor from the mouth of your
offspring's offspring," says the Lord,
"from now and forever."

59:10 ^Deut 28:29 ^BIs 8:14, 15
59:11 ^Is 38:14 ^BIs 59:9, 14 59:12 ^Is 3:9; Jer 14:7
59:13 ^Josh 24:27; Prov 30:9 59:14 ^Is 1:21 ^BIs 46:12
59:15 ^Is 5:23 59:16 ^Ps 98:1; Is 52:10
59:17 ^Eph 6:17 ^BIs 63:2, 3 59:18 ^Job 34:11;
Is 65:6, 7 59:19 ^Is 30:28; 66:12 59:20 ^Rom 11:26
59:21 ^Jer 31:31-34; Rom 11:27

A GLORIFIED ZION

60
"Arise, shine; for your light
has come,
And the ᴬglory of the LORD has
risen upon you.

2 "For behold, ᴬdarkness will
cover the earth
And deep darkness the
peoples;
But the LORD will rise upon
you
And His glory will appear
upon you.

3 "ᴬNations will come to your
light,
And kings to the brightness of
your rising.

4 "ᴬRaise your eyes all around
and see;
They all gather together, they
come to you.
Your sons will come from afar,
And your ᴮdaughters will be
carried on the hip.

5 "Then you will see and be
ᴬradiant,
And your heart will thrill and
rejoice;
Because the abundance of the
sea will be turned to you,
The ᴮwealth of the nations will
come to you.

6 "A multitude of camels will
cover you,
The young camels of Midian
and Ephah;
All those from ᴬSheba will
come;
They will bring ᴮgold and
frankincense,
And proclaim good news of
the praises of the LORD.

7 "All the flocks of Kedar will be
gathered to you,
The rams of Nebaioth will
serve you;

They will go up on My altar
with acceptance,
And I will ᴬglorify My glorious
house.

8 "ᴬWho are these who fly like a
cloud
And like the doves to their
windows?

9 "Certainly the coastlands will
wait for Me;
And the ᴬships of Tarshish
will come first,
To ᴮbring your sons from afar,
Their silver and their gold
with them,
For the name of the LORD
your God,
And for the Holy One of Israel
because He has glorified
you.

10 "ᴬForeigners will build up your
walls,
And their kings will serve
you;
For in My wrath I struck you,
And in My favor I have had
compassion on you.

11 "Your ᴬgates will be open
continually;
They will not be closed day or
night,
So that *people* may bring
you the wealth of the
nations,
With their kings led in
procession.

12 "For the ᴬnation and the
kingdom which will not
serve you will perish,
And the nations will be
utterly ruined.

60:1 ᴬIs 24:23; 35:2   60:2 ᴬIs 58:10; Jer 13:16
60:3 ᴬIs 2:3; 45:14, 22-25   60:4 ᴬIs 11:12   ᴮIs 43:6
60:5 ᴬPs 34:5   ᴮIs 61:6   60:6 ᴬGen 25:3   ᴮIs 60:9
60:7 ᴬIs 60:13; Hag 2:7, 9   60:8 ᴬIs 49:21
60:9 ᴬPs 48:7   ᴮIs 14:2   60:10 ᴬIs 14:1, 2; 61:5
60:11 ᴬIs 26:2; 60:18   60:12 ᴬIs 14:2; Zech 14:17

13 "The ^glory of Lebanon will
    come to you,
   The juniper, the elm tree and
    the cedar together,
   To beautify the place of My
    sanctuary;
   And I will make the ^Bplace of
    My feet glorious.
14 "The ^sons of those who
    afflicted you will come
    bowing to you,
   And all those who despised
    you will bow down at the
    soles of your feet;
   And they will call you the city
    of the LORD,
   The Zion of the Holy One of
    Israel.
15 "Whereas you have been
    forsaken and hated
   With no one passing through,
   I will make you an ^object of
    pride forever,
   A joy from generation to
    generation.
16 "You will also suck the milk of
    nations,
   And suck the breast of kings;
   Then you will know that I, the
    LORD, am your ^Savior
   And your ^BRedeemer, the
    Mighty One of Jacob.
17 "Instead of bronze I will bring
    gold,
   And instead of iron I will bring
    silver,
   And instead of wood, bronze,
   And instead of stones, iron.
   And I will make peace your
    administrators,
   And righteousness your
    overseers.
18 "^AViolence will not be heard
    again in your land,
   Nor ^Bdevastation or destruction
    within your borders;

   But you will call your walls
    salvation, and your gates
    praise.
19 "No longer will you have the
    ^Asun for light by day,
   Nor will the moon give you
    light for brightness;
   But you will have the LORD as
    an everlasting light,
   And your ^BGod as your
    glory.
20 "Your ^Asun will no longer set,
   Nor will your moon wane;
   For you will have the LORD as
    an everlasting light,
   And the days of your
    mourning will be over.
21 "Then all your people *will be*
    righteous;
   They will ^Apossess the land
    forever,
   The branch of My planting,
   The ^Bwork of My hands,
   That I may be glorified.
22 "The ^Asmallest one will
    become a thousand,
   And the least one a mighty
    nation.
   I, the LORD, will bring it about
    quickly in its time."

EXALTATION OF THE AFFLICTED

61 The ^ASpirit of the Lord GOD
   is upon me,
   Because the LORD anointed me
   To ^Bbring good news to the
    humble;
   He has sent me to bind up the
    brokenhearted,
   To proclaim release to
    captives
   And freedom to prisoners;

60:13 ^AIs 35:2   ^B1 Chr 28:2   60:14 ^AIs 14:1, 2; 45:14, 23
60:15 ^AIs 4:2; 65:18   60:16 ^AIs 19:20   ^BIs 59:20
60:18 ^AIs 54:14   ^BIs 51:19   60:19 ^ARev 21:23
^BIs 41:16   60:20 ^AIs 30:26   60:21 ^APs 37:11, 22
^BIs 19:25   60:22 ^AIs 10:22; 51:2   61:1 ^AIs 11:2
^BMatt 11:5

2 To ^proclaim the favorable
      year of the LORD
   And the day of vengeance of
      our God;
   To ^Bcomfort all who mourn,
3 To grant those who mourn *in*
      Zion,
   Giving them a garland instead
      of ashes,
   The ^oil of gladness instead of
      mourning,
   The cloak of praise instead of a
      disheartened spirit.
   So they will be called ^Boaks of
      righteousness,
   The planting of the LORD, that
      He may be glorified.

4 Then they will ^rebuild the
      ancient ruins,
   They will raise up the former
      devastations;
   And they will repair the ruined
      cities,
   The desolations of many
      generations.
5 ^Strangers will stand and
      pasture your flocks,
   And foreigners will be
      your farmers and your
      vinedressers.
6 But you will be called the
      ^priests of the LORD;
   You will be spoken of *as*
      ^Bministers of our God.
   You will eat the wealth of
      nations,
   And you will boast in their
      riches.
7 Instead of your shame *you will
      have a* ^double *portion,*
   And *instead of* humiliation
      they will shout for joy over
      their portion.
   Therefore they will possess a
      double *portion* in their land,
   Everlasting joy will be theirs.

8 For I, the LORD, ^love justice,
   I hate robbery in the burnt
      offering;
   And I will faithfully give them
      their reward,
   And make an everlasting
      covenant with them.
9 Then their offspring will be
      known among the nations,
   And their descendants in the
      midst of the peoples.
   All who see them will
      recognize them
   Because they are the ^offspring
      whom the LORD has blessed.

10 I will rejoice greatly in the LORD,
   My soul will be joyful in my God;
   For He has ^clothed me with
      garments of salvation,
   He has wrapped me with a
      robe of righteousness,
   As a groom puts on a turban,
   And ^Bas a bride adorns herself
      with her jewels.
11 For as the earth produces its
      sprouts,
   And as a garden causes the
      things sown in it to spring up,
   So the Lord GOD will ^cause
      ^Brighteousness and praise
   To spring up before all the
      nations.

ZION'S GLORY AND NEW NAME

62 For Zion's sake I will not
      keep silent,
   And for Jerusalem's sake I will
      not keep quiet,
   Until her ^righteousness goes
      forth like brightness,
   And her salvation like a torch
      that is burning.

61:2 ^A Is 49:8   ^B Is 57:18   61:3 ^A Ps 23:5   ^B Is 60:21
61:4 ^A Is 49:8; 58:12   61:5 ^A Is 14:2; 60:10   61:6 ^A Is 66:21
^B Is 56:6   61:7 ^A Is 40:2; Zech 9:12   61:8 ^A Is 5:16; 28:17
61:9 ^A Is 44:3   61:10 ^A Is 49:18   ^B Rev 21:2
61:11 ^A Is 45:23, 24   ^B Ps 72:3   62:1 ^A Is 1:26; 58:8

2 The ^nations will see your
    righteousness,
  And all kings your glory;
  And you will be called by a
    new ^Bname
  Which the mouth of the LORD
    will designate.
3 You will also be a ^crown of
    beauty in the hand of the
    LORD,
  And a royal headband in the
    hand of your God.
4 It will no longer be said to you,
    "^Forsaken,"
  Nor to your land will it any
    longer be said, "Desolate";
  But you will be called, "My
    delight is in her,"
  And your land, "^BMarried";
  For the LORD delights in you,
  And *to Him* your land will be
    married.
5 For *as* a young man marries a
    virgin,
  So your sons will marry you;
  And *as* the groom rejoices over
    the bride,
  So your ^God will rejoice over
    you.

6 On your walls, Jerusalem, I
    have appointed ^watchmen;
  All day and all night they will
    never keep silent.
  You who profess the LORD, take
    no rest for yourselves;
7 And give Him no rest until He
    establishes
  And makes ^Jerusalem an
    object of praise on the
    earth.
8 ^The LORD has sworn by His
    right hand and by His mighty
    arm:
  "I will never again give your
    grain *as* food for your
    enemies,

  Nor will foreigners drink your
    new wine for which you have
    labored."
9 But those who ^harvest it will
    eat it and praise the LORD;
  And those who gather it will
    drink it in the courtyards of
    My sanctuary.

10 Go through, go through the
    gates,
  Clear a way for the people!
  ^Build up, build up the ^Bhighway,
  Remove the stones, lift up a
    flag over the peoples.
11 Behold, the LORD has
    proclaimed to the end of the
    earth:
  Say to the daughter of Zion,
    "Behold, your ^salvation is
    coming;
  ^BBehold His reward is with
    Him, and His compensation
    before Him."
12 And they will call them, "^The
    holy people,
  The redeemed of the LORD";
  And you will be called, "Sought
    Out, A City Not Abandoned."

GOD'S VENGEANCE ON THE NATIONS

63 Who is this who comes
    from Edom,
  With garments of glowing
    colors from Bozrah,
  This One who is majestic in
    His apparel,
  Marching in the greatness of
    His strength?
  "It is I, the One who speaks in
    righteousness, ^mighty to
    save."

62:2 ^Is 60:3   ^BIs 56:5   62:3 ^Is 28:5; Zech 9:16
62:4 ^Is 54:6, 7   ^BHos 2:19, 20   62:5 ^Is 65:19
62:6 ^Is 52:8; Jer 6:17   62:7 ^Is 60:18; Jer 33:9
62:8 ^Is 45:23; 54:9   62:9 ^Is 65:13, 21-23
62:10 ^Is 57:14   ^BIs 11:16   62:11 ^Is 51:5   ^BIs 40:10
62:12 ^Deut 7:6; Is 4:3   63:1 ^Zeph 3:17

2 Why is Your apparel red,
And Your garments like one
who ^treads in the wine press?
3 "I have trodden the wine trough
alone,
And from the peoples there
was no one with Me.
I also ^trod them in My anger
And ^Btrampled them in My
wrath;
And their lifeblood is
sprinkled on My garments,
And I stained all My clothes.
4 "For the ^day of vengeance was
in My heart,
And My year of redemption
has come.
5 "I looked, but there was ^no one
to help,
And I was astonished and
there was no one to uphold;
So My ^Bown arm brought
salvation to Me,
And My wrath upheld Me.
6 "I ^trampled down the peoples
in My anger
And made them drunk with
My wrath,
And I poured out their
lifeblood on the earth."

GOD'S ANCIENT MERCIES RECALLED

7 I will make mention of the
^mercies of the Lord, *and* the
praises of the Lord,
According to all that the Lord
has granted us,
And the great goodness toward
the house of Israel,
Which He has granted them
according to His compassion
And according to the
abundance of His mercies.
8 For He said, "Certainly they
are My people,
Sons who will not deal falsely."
So He became their ^Savior.

9 In all their distress ^He was
distressed,
And the ^Bangel of His
presence saved them;
In His love and in His mercy
He redeemed them,
And He lifted them and
carried them all the days of
old.
10 But they rebelled
And grieved His ^Holy Spirit;
Therefore He turned Himself
to become their enemy,
He fought against them.
11 Then His people remembered
the days of old, of Moses.
Where is He who brought
them up out of the sea with
the shepherds of His flock?
Where is He who ^put His
Holy Spirit in the midst of
them,
12 Who caused His glorious arm
to go at the right hand of
Moses,
Who ^divided the waters
before them to make for
Himself an everlasting
name,
13 Who led them through the
depths?
Like the horse in the
wilderness, they did not
^stumble;
14 Like the cattle which go down
into the valley,
The Spirit of the Lord gave
them rest.
So You ^led Your people,
To make for Yourself a
glorious name.

63:2 ^Rev 19:13, 15   63:3 ^Is 22:5   ^BMic 7:10
63:4 ^Is 34:8; 35:4   63:5 ^Is 59:16   ^BPs 44:3
63:6 ^Is 22:5; 34:2   63:7 ^Ps 25:6; 92:2   63:8 ^Is 60:16
63:9 ^Judg 10:16   ^BEx 23:20-23   63:10 ^Ps 51:11;
Is 63:11   63:11 ^Num 11:17, 25, 29; Hag 2:5
63:12 ^Ex 14:21, 22; Is 11:15   63:13 ^Jer 31:9
63:14 ^Deut 32:12

YOU ARE OUR FATHER

15 Look down from heaven and
   see from Your holy and
   glorious lofty habitation;
   Where are Your zeal and Your
   mighty deeds?
   The ^stirrings of Your heart
   and Your compassion are
   restrained toward me.

16 For You are our ^Father,
   though Abraham does not
   know us
   And Israel does not recognize
   us.
   You, LORD, are our Father,
   Our ^BRedeemer from ancient
   times is Your name.

17 Why, LORD, do You ^cause us to
   stray from Your ways
   And ^Bharden our heart from
   fearing You?
   Return for the sake of Your
   servants, the tribes of Your
   heritage.

18 Your holy people possessed
   Your sanctuary for a little
   while,
   Our adversaries have
   ^trampled it down.

19 We have become like those
   over whom You have never
   ruled,
   Like those who were not called
   by Your name.

PRAYER FOR MERCY AND HELP

64 Oh, that You would tear
   open the heavens and
   come down,
   That the mountains would
   ^quake at Your presence—

2 As fire kindles brushwood, as
   fire causes water to boil—
   To make Your name known to
   Your adversaries,
   That the ^nations may tremble
   at Your presence!

3 When You did ^awesome things
   which we did not expect,
   You came down, the mountains
   quaked at Your presence.

4 For from days of old ^they have
   not heard or perceived by ear,
   Nor has the eye seen a God
   besides You,
   Who acts in behalf of one who
   waits for Him.

5 You meet him who rejoices in
   doing righteousness,
   Who remembers You in Your
   ways.
   Behold, ^You were angry, for
   we sinned,
   We continued in our sins for a
   long time;
   Yet shall we be saved?

6 For all of us have become like
   one who is unclean,
   And all our ^righteous deeds
   are like a filthy garment;
   And all of us wither like a leaf,
   And our ^Bwrongdoings, like
   the wind, take us away.

7 There is ^no one who calls on
   Your name,
   Who stirs himself to take hold
   of You;
   For You have ^Bhidden Your face
   from us
   And have surrendered
   us to the power of our
   wrongdoings.

8 But now, LORD, You are our
   Father;
   We are the ^clay, and You our
   potter,
   And all of us are the ^Bwork of
   Your hand.

63:15 ^Jer 31:20; Hos 11:8   63:16 ^Is 1:2   ^BIs 41:14
63:17 ^Is 30:28   ^BIs 29:13, 14   63:18 ^Ps 74:3-7;
Is 64:11   64:1 ^Judg 5:5; Ps 68:8   64:2 ^Ps 99:1;
Jer 5:22   64:3 ^Ps 65:5; 66:3, 5   64:4 ^1 Cor 2:9
64:5 ^Is 12:1   64:6 ^Is 46:12   ^BIs 50:1   64:7 ^Is 59:4
^BDeut 31:18   64:8 ^Is 29:16   ^BPs 100:3

9 Do not be angry beyond
measure, Lord,
^ANor remember wrongdoing
forever.
Behold, please look, all of us
are Your people.

10 Your ^Aholy cities have become
a ^Bwilderness,
Zion has become a wilderness,
Jerusalem a desolation.

11 Our holy and beautiful ^Ahouse,
Where our fathers praised You,
Has been burned *by* fire;
And all our precious things
have become a ruin.

12 Will You ^Arestrain Yourself at
these things, Lord?
Will You keep silent and afflict
us beyond measure?

A REBELLIOUS PEOPLE

65 "I permitted Myself to be
sought by ^Athose who did
not ask *for Me;*
I permitted Myself to be found
by those who did not seek
Me.
I said, 'Here am I, here am I,'
To a nation which ^Bdid not call
on My name.

2 "^AI have spread out My hands
all day long to a ^Brebellious
people,
Who walk *in* the way which
is not good, following their
own thoughts,

3 A people who continually
^Aprovoke Me to My face,
Offering sacrifices in gardens
and burning incense on
bricks;

4 Who sit among graves and
spend the night in secret
places;
Who ^Aeat pig's flesh,
And the broth of unclean meat
is *in* their pots.

5 "Who say, '^AKeep to yourself, do
not come near me,
For I am holier than you!'
These are smoke in My nostrils,
A fire that burns all the day.

6 "Behold, it is written before Me:
I will not keep silent, but ^AI will
repay;
I will even repay ¹into their laps,

7 Both your own ^Awrongdoings
and the wrongdoings of your
fathers together," says the
Lord.
"Because they have burned
incense on the mountains
And scorned Me on the hills,
Therefore I will ^Bmeasure their
former work ¹into their laps."

8 This is what the Lord says:
"Just as the new wine is found
in the cluster,
And one says, 'Do not destroy
it, for there is benefit in it,'
So I will act in behalf of My
servants
In order ^Anot to destroy all of
them.

9 "I will bring forth offspring
from Jacob,
And an heir of My mountains
from Judah;
^AMy chosen ones shall inherit it,
And ^BMy servants will live
there.

10 "Sharon will be a pasture land
for flocks,
And the Valley of Achor a
resting place for herds,
For My people who ^Aseek Me.

64:9 ^AIs 43:25; Mic 7:18   64:10 ^AIs 48:2   ^BIs 1:7
64:11 ^A2 Kin 25:9; Ps 74:5-7   64:12 ^APs 74:10; Is 42:14
65:1 ^ARom 9:24-26   ^BIs 63:19   65:2 ^ARom 10:21
^BIs 1:2, 23   65:3 ^AJob 1:11; 2:5   65:4 ^ALev 11:7;
Is 66:3, 17   65:5 ^AMatt 9:11; Luke 7:39   65:6 ^AJer 16:18
65:7 ^AIs 13:11   ^BJer 5:29   65:8 ^AIs 1:9; 10:21, 22
65:9 ^AIs 57:13   ^BIs 32:18   65:10 ^AIs 51:1; 55:6

65:6 ¹I.e., individually and fully   65:7 ¹I.e., individually
and fully

11 "But as for you who ^abandon
    the LORD,
  Who forget My holy mountain,
  Who set a table for Fortune,
  And fill a jug of mixed wine for
    Destiny,
12 I will destine you for the sword,
  And all of you will bow down
    to the slaughter.
  Because I called, but you ^did
    not answer;
  I spoke, but you did not listen.
  Instead, you did evil in My sight
  And chose that in which I did
    not delight."

13 Therefore, this is what the
    Lord GOD says:
  "Behold, My servants will ^eat,
    but you will be ᴮhungry.
  Behold, My servants will
    drink, but you will be thirsty.
  Behold, My servants will rejoice,
    but you will be put to shame.
14 "Behold, My servants will shout
    joyfully with a glad heart,
  But you will ^cry out from a
    painful heart,
  And you will wail from a
    broken spirit.
15 "You will leave your name as a
    curse to My chosen ones,
  And the Lord GOD will put you
    to death.
  But My servants will be called
    by ^another name.
16 "Because the one who is
    blessed on the earth
  Will be blessed by the ^God of
    truth;
  And the one who swears *an
    oath* on the earth
  Will swear by the God of truth;
  Because the former troubles
    are forgotten,
  And because they are hidden
    from My sight!

NEW HEAVENS AND A NEW EARTH

17 "For behold, I create ^new
    heavens and a new earth;
  And the former things will not
    be remembered or come to
    mind.
18 "But be ^glad and rejoice forever
    in what I create;
  For behold, I create Jerusalem
    for rejoicing
  And her people *for* gladness.
19 "I will also ^rejoice in Jerusalem
    and be glad in My people;
  And there will no longer be
    heard in her
  The voice of weeping and the
    sound of crying.
20 "No longer will there be in it an
    infant *who lives only a few*
    days,
  Or an old person who does
    ^not live out his days;
  For the youth will die at the
    age of a hundred,
  And the ᴮone who does not
    reach the age of a hundred
  Will be *thought* accursed.
21 "They will ^build houses and
    inhabit *them;*
  They will also ᴮplant vineyards
    and eat their fruit.
22 "They will not build and
    another inhabit,
  They will not plant and
    another eat;
  For ^as the lifetime of a tree,
    so will be the days of My
    people,
  And My chosen ones will
    ᴮfully enjoy the work of their
    hands.

65:11 ^Deut 29:24, 25; Is 1:4, 28
65:12 ^2 Chr 36:15, 16; Prov 1:24   65:13 ^Is 1:19
ᴮIs 8:21   65:14 ^Is 13:6; Matt 8:12   65:15 ^Is 62:2
65:16 ^Ex 34:6; Ps 31:5   65:17 ^Is 66:22; 2 Pet 3:13
65:18 ^Ps 98; Is 12:1, 2   65:19 ^Is 62:4, 5; Jer 32:41
65:20 ^Deut 4:40   ᴮEccl 8:12, 13   65:21 ^Is 32:18
ᴮIs 30:23   65:22 ^Ps 92:12-14   ᴮPs 21:4

23 "They will ^not labor in vain,
  Or give birth *to children* for
    disaster;
  For they are the ^Bdescendants
    of those blessed by the Lord,
  And their descendants with
    them.
24It will also come to pass that
before they call, I will ^answer; while
they are still speaking, I will listen.
25The ^wolf and the lamb will graze
together, and the lion will eat straw
like the ox; and dust will be the serpent's food. They will ^Bdo no evil or
harm on all My holy mountain," says
the Lord.

HEAVEN IS GOD'S THRONE

66 This is what the Lord says:
  "^Heaven is My throne and
  the earth is the footstool for
  My feet.
  Where then is a house you
    could build for Me?
  And where is a place that I
    may rest?
2 "For ^My hand made all these
    things,
  So all these things came into
    being," declares the Lord.
  "But I will look to this one,
  At one who is humble and
    contrite in spirit, and who
    trembles at My word.

HYPOCRISY REBUKED

3 "*But* the one who slaughters
    an ox is *like* one who kills a
    person;
  The one who sacrifices a lamb
    is *like* one who breaks a
    dog's neck;
  One who offers a grain offering
    is like one who offers pig's
    blood;
  One who burns incense is *like*
    one who blesses an idol.

As they have chosen their
    ^own ways,
  And their souls delight in their
    ^Babominations,
4 So I will ^choose their
    punishments
  And bring on them what they
    dread.
  Because I called, but no one
    answered;
  I spoke, but they did not
    listen.
  Instead, they did ^Bevil in My
    sight
  And chose that in which I did
    not delight."
5 Hear the word of the Lord, you
    who tremble at His word:
  "Your brothers who ^hate you,
    who ^Bexclude you on account
    of My name,
  Have said, 'Let the Lord be
    glorified, so that we may see
    your joy.'
  But they will be put to shame.
6 "A sound of uproar from the
    city, a voice from the temple,
  The voice of the Lord who is
    ^dealing retribution to His
    enemies.

7 "Before she was in labor, she
    delivered;
  Before her pain came, ^she
    gave birth to a boy.
8 "^Who has heard such a thing?
  Who has seen such things?
  Can a land be born in one day?
  Can a nation be given birth all
    at once?
  As soon as Zion was in labor,
    she also delivered her sons.

65:23 ^Deut 28:3-12   ^BIs 61:9   65:24 ^Ps 91:15;
Is 55:6   65:25 ^Is 11:6   ^BIs 11:9   66:1 ^1 Kin 8:27;
Ps 11:4   66:2 ^Is 40:26   66:3 ^Is 57:17   ^BIs 44:19
66:4 ^Prov 1:31, 32   ^B2 Kin 21:2, 6   66:5 ^Ps 38:20
^BMatt 5:10-12   66:6 ^Is 59:18; 65:6   66:7 ^Rev 12:5
66:8 ^Is 64:4

9 "Shall I bring to the point of
     birth but ᴬnot give delivery?"
     says the Lᴏʀᴅ.
  "Or shall I who gives delivery
     shut *the womb?*" says your
     God.

JOY IN JERUSALEM'S FUTURE

10 "Be ᴬjoyful with Jerusalem and
     rejoice for her, all you who
     love her;
  Be exceedingly glad with
     her, all you who mourn
     over her,
11 So that you may nurse and ᴬbe
     satisfied with her comforting
     breasts,
  So that you may drink fully
     and be delighted with her
     bountiful breasts."
12 For this is what the Lᴏʀᴅ says:
  "Behold, I extend ᴬpeace to
     her like a river,
  And the ᴮglory of the nations
     like an overflowing stream;
  And you will be nursed, you
     will be carried on the hip
     and rocked back and forth
     on the knees.
13 "As one whom his mother
     comforts, so I will ᴬcomfort
     you;
  And you will be comforted in
     Jerusalem."
14 Then you will see *this,* and
     your ᴬheart will be glad,
  And your bones will flourish
     like the new grass;
  And the hand of the Lᴏʀᴅ
     will be made known to His
     servants,
  But He will be ᴮindignant
     toward His enemies.
15 For behold, the Lᴏʀᴅ will
     come in fire,
  And His ᴬchariots like the
     whirlwind,

To render His anger with fury,
  And His rebuke with flames of
     fire.
16 For the Lᴏʀᴅ will execute
     judgment by ᴬfire
  And by His sword on
     humanity,
  And those put to death by the
     Lᴏʀᴅ will be many.
17 "Those who sanctify and purify
     themselves *to go* to the
     gardens,
  Following one in the center,
  Who eat pig's flesh, detestable
     things, and mice,
  Will ᴬcome to an end
     altogether," declares the
     Lᴏʀᴅ.

18 "For I know their works and
their ᴬthoughts; the time is coming to gather all the nations and
tongues. And they shall come and
see My glory. 19 And I will put a sign
among them and send survivors
from them to the nations: Tarshish, Put, Lud, Meshech, Tubal,
and Javan, to the distant ᴬcoast-
lands that have neither heard of My
fame nor seen My glory. And they
will ᴮdeclare My glory among the
nations. 20 Then they shall ᴬbring
all your countrymen from all the
nations as a grain offering to the
Lᴏʀᴅ, on horses, in chariots, in lit-
ters, on mules, and on camels, to
My holy mountain Jerusalem," says
the Lᴏʀᴅ, "just as the sons of Israel
bring their grain offering in a clean
vessel to the house of the Lᴏʀᴅ.
21 I will also take some of them as
ᴬpriests *and* Levites," says the Lᴏʀᴅ.

66:9 ᴬ Is 37:3   66:10 ᴬ Deut 32:43; Is 65:18
66:11 ᴬ Is 49:23; 60:16   66:12 ᴬ Ps 72:3, 7   ᴮ Is 60:5
66:13 ᴬ Is 12:1; 40:1, 2   66:14 ᴬ Zech 10:7   ᴮ Is 10:5
66:15 ᴬ Ps 68:17; Is 5:28   66:16 ᴬ Is 30:30; Ezek 38:22
66:17 ᴬ Is 1:28, 31   66:18 ᴬ Is 59:7; 65:2
66:19 ᴬ Is 11:11   ᴮ 1 Chr 16:24   66:20 ᴬ Is 43:6; 49:22
66:21 ᴬ Ex 19:6; Is 61:6

22 "For just as the ᴬnew heavens
   and the new earth,
      Which I make, will endure
      before Me," declares the
      Lord,
   "So will your descendants and
      your name endure.
23 "And it shall be from new moon
      to new moon
      And from Sabbath to Sabbath,
      All mankind will come to ᴬbow
      down before Me," says the
      Lord.

24 "Then they will go out and
      look
      At the corpses of the people
      Who have rebelled against
      Me.
      For their ᴬworm will not die
      ᴮAnd their fire will not be
      extinguished;
      And they will be an
      abhorrence to all
      mankind."

66:22 ᴬIs 65:17; Heb 12:26, 27   **66:23** ᴬIs 19:21, 23;
27:13   **66:24** ᴬIs 14:11   ᴮIs 1:31

JEREMIAH

JEREMIAH'S CALL AND COMMISSION

1 The words of ᴬJeremiah the son of Hilkiah, of the priests who were in ᴮAnathoth in the land of Benjamin, ²to whom the word of the LORD came in the days of ᴬJosiah the son of Amon, king of Judah, in the thirteenth year of his reign. ³It came also in the days of ᴬJehoiakim the son of Josiah, king of Judah, until the end of the eleventh year of ᴮZedekiah the son of Josiah, king of Judah, until the exile of Jerusalem in the fifth month.

⁴Now the word of the LORD came to me, saying,

5 "Before I formed you in the
    womb I knew you,
   And before you were born I
    consecrated you;
   I have ᴬappointed you as a
    prophet to the nations."
6 Then I said, "Oh, Lord GOD!
    Behold, I do not know how
    to speak,
   Because ᴬI am a youth."
7 But the LORD said to me,
   "Do not say, 'I am a youth,'
   ᴬBecause everywhere I send
    you, you shall go,
   And ᴮall that I command you,
    you shall speak.
8 "ᴬDo not be afraid of them,
   For ᴮI am with you to save
    you," declares the LORD.

⁹Then the LORD stretched out His hand and ᴬtouched my mouth, and the LORD said to me,

   "Behold, I have ᴮput My words
    in your mouth.

10 "See, ᴬI have appointed you this
     day over the nations and
     over the kingdoms,
    To root out and to tear down,
    To destroy and to overthrow,
    To build and to plant."

THE ALMOND BRANCH
AND BOILING POT

¹¹And the word of the LORD came to me, saying, "What do you see, ᴬJeremiah?" And I said, "I see a branch of an almond tree." ¹²Then the LORD said to me, "You have seen well, for ᴬI am watching over My word to perform it."

¹³And the word of the LORD came to me a second time, saying, "ᴬWhat do you see?" And I said, "I see a boiling pot, facing away from the north." ¹⁴Then the LORD said to me, "ᴬOut of the north the evil will be unleashed on all the inhabitants of the land. ¹⁵For, behold, I am calling all the families of the kingdoms of the north," declares the LORD; "and they will come and ᴬplace, each one *of them,* his throne at the entrance of the gates of Jerusalem, and against all its walls around, and against all the cities of Judah. ¹⁶And I will pronounce My judgments against them concerning all their wickedness, since they have abandoned Me and have ᴬoffered sacrifices to other

1:1 ᴬ2 Chr 35:25   ᴮJosh 21:18   1:2 ᴬ1 Kin 13:2;
2 Kin 21:24   1:3 ᴬ2 Kin 23:34   ᴮ2 Kin 24:17
1:5 ᴬJer 1:10; 25:15-26   1:6 ᴬ1 Kin 3:7   1:7 ᴬEzek 2:3, 4
ᴮNum 22:20   1:8 ᴬEx 3:12   ᴮEzek 2:6   1:9 ᴬIs 6:7
ᴮEx 4:11-16   1:10 ᴬRev 11:3-6   1:11 ᴬJer 24:3; Amos 7:8
1:12 ᴬJer 31:28   1:13 ᴬZech 4:2   1:14 ᴬIs 41:25; Jer 4:6
1:15 ᴬIs 22:7; Jer 39:3   1:16 ᴬJer 7:9

gods, and worshiped the ᴮworks of their own hands. ¹⁷Now, ᴬbelt *your garment* around your waist and arise, and speak to them all that I command you. ᴮDo not be dismayed before them, or I will make you dismayed before them. ¹⁸Now behold, I have made you today like a fortified city and like a pillar of iron and walls of bronze against the whole land, to the kings of Judah, to its leaders, to its priests, and to the people of the land. ¹⁹And they will fight against you but they will not overcome you, for ᴬI am with you to save you," declares the Lᴏʀᴅ.

JUDAH'S APOSTASY

2 Now the word of the Lᴏʀᴅ came to me, saying, ²"Go and proclaim in the ears of Jerusalem, saying, 'This is what the Lᴏʀᴅ says:
"I remember regarding you the
   ᴬdevotion of your youth,
Your love when you were a
   bride,
ᴮYour following after Me in the
   wilderness,
Through a land not sown.
³ "Israel was holy to the Lᴏʀᴅ,
The ᴬfirst of His harvest.
All who ate of it became guilty;
Evil came upon them,"
   declares the Lᴏʀᴅ.'"

⁴Hear the word of the Lᴏʀᴅ, house of Jacob, and all the families of the house of Israel. ⁵This is what the Lᴏʀᴅ says:
"ᴬWhat injustice did your
   fathers find in Me,
That they went far from Me,
And walked after emptiness
   and became empty?
⁶ "They did not say, 'Where is the
   Lᴏʀᴅ
Who ᴬbrought us up out of the
   land of Egypt,

Who ᴮled us through the
   wilderness,
Through a land of deserts and
   of pits,
Through a land of drought
   and of deep darkness,
Through a land that no one
   crossed
And where no person lived?'
⁷ "I brought you into the fruitful
   land
To eat its fruit and its good
   things.
But you came and ᴬdefiled My
   land,
And you made My
   inheritance an
   abomination.
⁸ "The priests did not say,
   'Where is the Lᴏʀᴅ?'
And those who handle the
   Law ᴬdid not know Me;
The rulers also revolted
   against Me,
And the prophets prophesied
   by Baal
And walked after ᴮthings that
   were of no benefit.
⁹ "Therefore I will still ᴬcontend
   with you," declares the
   Lᴏʀᴅ,
"And I will contend with your
   sons' sons.
¹⁰ "For ᴬcross to the coastlands of
   Kittim and see,
And send to Kedar and
   observe closely,
And see if there has been
   anything like this!
¹¹ "Has a nation changed gods,
   When they were not gods?

1:16 ᴮIs 2:8   1:17ᴬ1 Kin 18:46   ᴮEzek 2:6
1:19ᴬNum 14:9; Jer 1:8   2:2ᴬEzek 16:8   ᴮDeut 2:7
2:3ᴬJames 1:18; Rev 14:4   2:5ᴬIs 5:4; Mic 6:3
2:6ᴬEx 20:2   ᴮDeut 8:15   2:7ᴬPs 106:38; Jer 3:2
2:8ᴬJer 4:22   ᴮJer 16:19   2:9ᴬJer 2:35; Ezek 20:35, 36
2:10ᴬIs 23:12

But My people have
^exchanged their glory
For that which is of no benefit.
12 "Be appalled at this, ^you
heavens,
And shudder, be very
desolate," declares the LORD.
13 "For My people have committed
two evils:
They have abandoned Me,
The ^fountain of living
waters,
To carve out for themselves
cisterns,
Broken cisterns
That do not hold water.
14 "Is Israel ^a slave? Or is he a
servant born in the home?
Why has he become plunder?
15 "The young ^lions have roared
at him,
They have roared loudly.
And they have made his land
a waste;
His cities have been destroyed,
without inhabitant.
16 "Also the men of Memphis and
Tahpanhes
Have shaved ^your head.
17 "Have you not ^done this to
yourself
By your abandoning the LORD
your God
When He ^led you in the way?
18 "But now what are you doing
^on the road to Egypt,
Except to drink the waters of
the Nile?
Or what are you doing on the
road to Assyria,
Except to drink the waters of
the Euphrates River?
19 "^Your own wickedness will
correct you,
And your ^apostasies will
punish you;

Know therefore and see that it
is evil and bitter
For you to abandon the LORD
your God,
And the fear of Me is not in
you," declares the Lord GOD
of armies.

20 "For long ago ^I broke your yoke
And tore off your restraints;
But you said, 'I will not serve!'
For on every high hill
And under every leafy tree
You have lain down as a
prostitute.
21 "Yet I planted you as a choice
vine,
A completely faithful seed.
How then have you turned
yourself before Me
Into the ^degenerate shoots of
a foreign vine?
22 "Although you wash yourself
with lye
And use much soap,
The ^stain of your guilt is
before Me," declares the
Lord GOD.
23 "^How can you say, 'I am not
defiled,
I have not gone after the
^Baals'?
Look at your way in the valley!
Know what you have done!
You are a swift young camel
running about senselessly
on her ways,
24 A ^wild donkey accustomed to
the wilderness,
That sniffs the wind in her
passion.

2:11 ^Ps 106:20; Rom 1:23   2:12 ^Is 1:2; Jer 4:23
2:13 ^Ps 36:9; Jer 17:13   2:14 ^Jer 5:19; 17:4
2:15 ^Jer 50:17   2:16 ^Deut 33:20; Jer 48:45
2:17 ^Deut 32:10; Jer 4:18   2:18 ^Is 30:2   2:19 ^Is 3:9
^Jer 3:6, 8, 11, 14   2:20 ^Lev 26:13   2:21 ^Is 5:4
2:22 ^Job 14:17; Hos 13:12   2:23 ^Prov 30:12   ^Jer 9:14
2:24 ^Jer 14:6

Who can turn her away *in* her
mating season?
None who seek her will grow
weary;
In her month they will find her.
25 "Keep your feet from being bare,
And your throat from thirst;
But you said, 'It is hopeless!
No! For I have loved strangers,
And I will walk after them.'

26 "Like the shame of a ^thief
when he is discovered,
So the house of Israel is
shamed;
They, their kings, their leaders,
Their priests, and their
prophets,
27 Who say to a tree, 'You are my
father,'
And to a stone, 'You gave me
birth.'
For they have turned *their*
^backs to Me,
And not *their* faces;
But in the time of their trouble
they will say,
'Arise and save us!'
28 "But where are your ^gods
Which you made for
yourself?
Let them arise, if they can save
you
In the time of your trouble!
For *as many as* the number of
your cities
Are your gods, Judah.

29 "Why do you contend with Me?
You have ^all revolted against
Me," declares the LORD.
30 "^In vain I have struck your
sons;
They did not accept discipline.
Your ^Bsword has devoured
your prophets
Like a destroying lion.

31 "You generation, look to the
word of the LORD.
Have I been a wilderness to
Israel,
Or a land of thick darkness?
Why do My people say, '^We
are free to roam;
We will no longer come to
You'?
32 "Can a virgin forget her jewelry,
Or a bride her attire?
Yet My people have ^forgotten
Me
For days without number.
33 "How well you prepare your way
To seek love!
Therefore even to the wicked
women
You have taught your ways.
34 "Also on your skirts is found
The ^lifeblood of the innocent
poor;
You did not find them
^Bbreaking in.
But in spite of all these
things,
35 You said, 'I am innocent;
Surely His anger is turned
away from me.'
Behold, I will ^enter into
judgment with you
Because you ^Bsay, 'I have not
sinned.'
36 "Why do you go around so
much
Changing your way?
Also, ^you will be put to shame
by Egypt,
Just as you were put to shame
by ^BAssyria.
37 "From this *place* as well you will
go out

2:25 ^Jer 18:12   2:26 ^Jer 48:27   2:27 ^Jer 18:17; 32:33
2:28 ^Deut 32:37; Judg 10:14   2:29 ^Jer 5:1; 6:13
2:30 ^Is 1:5   ^BNeh 9:26   2:31 ^Deut 32:15; Jer 2:20, 25
2:32 ^Ps 106:21; Is 17:10   2:34 ^2 Kin 21:16   ^BEx 22:2
2:35 ^Jer 25:31   ^BProv 28:13   2:36 ^Is 30:3
^B2 Chr 28:16, 20, 21

With your hands on your
    head;
For the LORD has rejected
    ^those in whom you trust,
And you will not prosper with
    them."

THE DEFILED LAND

3 *God* says, "^If a husband
    divorces his wife
And she leaves him
And becomes another man's
    wife,
Will he return to her again?
Would that land not be
    completely defiled?
But you are a prostitute *with*
    many lovers;
Yet you turn to Me," declares
    the LORD.

2 "Raise your eyes to the bare
    heights and see;
Where have you not been
    violated?
You have sat for them by the
    roads
Like an Arab in the desert,
And you have ^defiled a land
With your prostitution and
    your wickedness.

3 "Therefore the ^showers have
    been withheld,
And there has been no spring
    rain.
Yet you had a ᴮprostitute's
    forehead;
You refused to be ashamed.

4 "Have you not just now called
    to Me,
'My Father, You are the ^friend
    of my ᴮyouth?

5 '^Will He be angry forever,
    Or keep *His anger* to the end?'
Behold, you have spoken
And have done evil things,
And you have had your own
    way."

FAITHLESS ISRAEL

6 Then the LORD said to me in the days of King Josiah, "Have you seen what faithless Israel did? She ^went up on every high hill and under every leafy tree, and she prostituted herself there. 7 Yet ^I thought, 'After she has done all these things she will return to Me'; but she did not return, and her treacherous sister Judah saw it. 8 And I saw that for all the adulteries of faithless Israel, I had sent her away and given her a certificate of divorce, yet her ^treacherous sister Judah did not fear; but she went and prostituted herself also. 9 And because of the thoughtlessness of her prostitution, she defiled the land and committed adultery with ^stones and trees. 10 Yet in spite of all this her treacherous sister Judah did not return to Me with all her heart, but rather in ^deception," declares the LORD.

GOD INVITES REPENTANCE

11 And the LORD said to me, "^Faithless Israel has proved herself to be more righteous than treacherous Judah. 12 Go and proclaim these words toward the north and say,
    '^Return, faithless Israel,'
      declares the LORD;
    'I will not look at you in anger.
     For I am gracious,' declares the
      LORD;
    'I will not be angry forever.
13 'Only ^acknowledge your
    wrongdoing,
    That you have revolted against
    the LORD your God,

2:37 ^Jer 37:7-10   3:1 ^Deut 24:1-4   3:2 ^Jer 2:7
3:3 ^Lev 26:19   ᴮJer 6:15   3:4 ^Ps 71:17   ᴮJer 2:2
3:5 ^Ps 103:9; Is 57:16   3:6 ^Jer 17:2; Ezek 23:4-10
3:7 ^2 Kin 17:13   3:8 ^Ezek 16:46, 47; 23:11
3:9 ^Is 57:6; Jer 2:27   3:10 ^Jer 12:2; Hos 7:14
3:11 ^Ezek 16:51, 52; 23:11   3:12 ^Jer 3:14, 22;
Ezek 33:11   3:13 ^Deut 30:1-3; Jer 3:25

And have scattered your favors
  to the strangers under every
  leafy tree,
And you have not obeyed My
  voice,' declares the LORD.
14 'Return, you faithless sons,'
  declares the LORD;
'For I am a ^master to you,
  And I will take you, one from a
  city and two from a family,
  And bring you to Zion.'
15 "Then I will give you shepherds
after My own heart, who will ^feed
you knowledge and understanding.
16 And it shall be in those days when
you become numerous and are
fruitful in the land," declares the
LORD, "they will ^no longer say, 'The
ark of the covenant of the LORD.'
And it will not come to mind, nor
will they remember it, nor miss *it,*
nor will it be made again. 17 At that
time they will call Jerusalem 'The
^Throne of the LORD,' and ^Ball the
nations will assemble at it, at Jerusalem, for the name of the LORD;
and they will no longer follow the
stubbornness of their evil heart.
18 In those days the house of Judah
will walk with the house of Israel,
and they will come together ^from
the land of the north to the ^Bland
that I gave your fathers as an inheritance.
19 "Then I said,

'How I would set you among
  My sons
And give you a pleasant land,
The most ^beautiful
  inheritance of the nations!'
And I said, 'You shall call Me,
  My Father,
And not turn away from
  following Me.'
20 "However, *as* a woman
  treacherously leaves her
  lover,

So you have ^dealt
  treacherously with Me,
House of Israel," declares the
  LORD.
21 A voice is heard on the bare
  heights,
The weeping, the pleading of
  the sons of Israel.
Because they have perverted
  their way,
They have ^forgotten the LORD
  their God.
22 "Return, you faithless sons,
  ^I will heal your
  faithlessness."

"Behold, we come to You;
  For You are the LORD our
  God.
23 "Certainly ^the hills are a
  deception,
  ¹Commotion *on* the
  mountains.
Certainly in the LORD our God
Is the salvation of Israel.
24 "But ^the shame has consumed
the product of our fathers' labor
since our youth—their flocks and
their herds, their sons and their
daughters. 25 Let us lie down in
our shame, and let our humiliation cover us; for we have sinned
against the LORD our God, we and
our fathers, ^from our youth even
to this day. And we have not obeyed
the voice of the LORD our God."

JUDAH THREATENED WITH INVASION

4 "If you will ^return, Israel,"
  declares the LORD,
  "*Then* you should return to Me.

3:14 ^Jer 31:32; Hos 2:19   3:15 ^Acts 20:28
3:16 ^Is 65:17   3:17 ^Jer 17:12   ^Jer 16:19
3:18 ^Jer 16:15   ^Amos 9:15   3:19 ^Ps 106:6
3:20 ^Is 48:8   3:21 ^Is 17:10; Jer 2:32   3:22 ^Jer 30:17;
33:6   3:23 ^Jer 17:2   3:24 ^Hos 9:10   3:25 ^Jer 22:21
4:1 ^Jer 3:22; 15:19

3:23 ¹I.e., from idolatrous rituals

And if you will put away your detestable things from My presence,
And will not waver,

2 And *if* you will swear, 'As the LORD lives,'
^In truth, in justice, and in righteousness;
Then the nations will bless themselves in Him,
And in Him they will boast."

3 For this is what the LORD says to the men of Judah and to Jerusalem:

"^Break up your uncultivated ground,
And ^Bdo not sow among thorns.

4 "Circumcise yourselves to the LORD
And remove the foreskins of your hearts,
Men of Judah and inhabitants of Jerusalem,
Or else My wrath will spread like fire
And burn with ^no one to quench it,
Because of the evil of your deeds."

5 Declare in Judah and proclaim in Jerusalem, and say,
"Blow the trumpet in the land;
Cry aloud and say,
'^Assemble, and let's go
Into the fortified cities.'

6 "Raise a flag toward Zion!
Take refuge, do not stand *still,*
For I am bringing ^evil from the north,
And great destruction.

7 "A ^lion has gone up from his thicket,
And a destroyer of nations has set out;
He has gone out from his place
To make your land a waste.

Your cities will be ruins,
Without an inhabitant.

8 "For this, ^put on sackcloth,
Mourn and wail;
For the fierce anger of the LORD
Has not turned away from us."

9 "And it shall come about on that day," declares the LORD, "that the heart of the king and the hearts of the leaders will fail; and the priests will tremble, and the ^prophets will be astonished."

10 Then I said, "Oh, Lord GOD! Surely You have utterly ^deceived this people and Jerusalem, saying, 'You will have peace'; yet a sword touches the throat."

11 At that time it will be said to this people and to Jerusalem, "A ^scorching wind from the bare heights in the wilderness, in the direction of the daughter of My people—not to winnow and not to cleanse, 12 a wind too strong for this—will come at My command; now I will also pronounce judgments against them."

13 "Behold, he goes up like clouds,
And his chariots like the whirlwind;
His horses are ^swifter than eagles.
Woe to us, for we are ruined!"

14 Wash your heart from evil, Jerusalem,
So that you may be saved.
How long will your ^wicked thoughts
Lodge within you?

4:2 ^Is 48:1   4:3 ^Hos 10:12   ^BMatt 13:7
4:4 ^Amos 5:6; Mark 9:43, 48   4:5 ^Josh 10:20;
Jer 8:14   4:6 ^Jer 1:14, 15; 6:1, 22   4:7 ^Jer 5:6; 25:38
4:8 ^Is 22:12; Jer 6:26   4:9 ^Is 29:9, 10; Ezek 13:9-16
4:10 ^Ezek 14:9; 2 Thess 2:11   4:11 ^Jer 13:24; 51:1
4:13 ^Lam 4:19; Hab 1:8   4:14 ^Prov 1:22; Jer 6:19

15 For a voice declares from ^Dan,
   And proclaims wickedness
      from Mount Ephraim.
16 "Report *it* to the nations, now!
   Proclaim to Jerusalem,
   'Enemies are coming from a
      ^remote country,
   And they raise their voices
      against the cities of Judah.
17 'Like watchmen of a field they
      are against her all around,
   Because she has ^rebelled
      against Me,' declares the
      LORD.
18 "Your ^ways and your deeds
   Have brought these things
      upon you.
   This is your evil. How bitter!
   How it has touched your
      heart!"

GRIEF OVER JUDAH'S DEVASTATION

19 ^My soul, my soul! I am in
      anguish! Oh, my heart!
   My ^Bheart is pounding in me;
   I cannot keep silent,
   Because, 'my soul, you have
      heard
   The sound of the trumpet,
   The alarm of war.
20 ^Disaster upon disaster is
      proclaimed,
   For the whole land is
      devastated;
   Suddenly my tents are
      devastated,
   And my curtains in an instant.
21 How long must I see the flag
   And hear the sound of the
      trumpet?
22 "For My people are foolish,
   They do not know Me;
   They are foolish children
   And have no understanding.
   They are skillful at ^doing evil,
   But they do not know how to
      do good."

23 I looked at the earth, and
   behold, *it was* a ¹·^formless
      and desolate emptiness;
   And to the heavens, and they
      had no light.
24 I looked on the mountains, and
   behold, they were ^quaking,
   And all the hills jolted back
      and forth.
25 I looked, and behold, there
      was no human,
   And all the ^birds of the sky
      had fled.
26 I looked, and behold,
      the ^fruitful land was a
      wilderness,
   And all its cities were pulled
      down
   Before the LORD, before His
      fierce anger.

27 For this is what the LORD says:
   "The ^whole land shall be a
      desolation,
   Yet I will ^Bnot execute a
      complete destruction.
28 "For this the ^earth will mourn,
   And the ^Bheavens above will
      become dark,
   Because I have spoken, I have
      purposed,
   And I have not changed My
      mind, nor will I turn from it."
29 At the sound of the horseman
      and archer ^every city flees;
   They ^Bgo into the thickets and
      climb among the rocks;
   Every city is abandoned,
   And no one lives in them.

4:15 ^Jer 8:16   4:16 ^Is 39:3; Jer 5:15   4:17 ^Is 1:20, 23;
Jer 5:23   4:18 ^Ps 107:17; Is 50:1   4:19 ^Is 15:5
^BHab 3:16   4:20 ^Ps 42:7; Ezek 7:26   4:22 ^Jer 9:3,
13:23   4:23 ^Gen 1:2; Is 24:19   4:24 ^Is 5:25; Jer 10:10
4:25 ^Jer 9:10; Zeph 1:3   4:26 ^Jer 9:10
4:27 ^Jer 12:11, 12   ^BJer 5:10, 18   4:28 ^Jer 12:4, 11
^BIs 5:30   4:29 ^2 Kin 25:4   ^BIs 2:19-21

4:16 ¹As indicated in LXX; MT *watchmen*
4:19 ¹Another reading is *I have heard*   4:23 ¹Or *waste*

30 And you, desolate one, ^what
will you do?
Although you dress in
scarlet,
Although you adorn
yourself with jewelry of
gold,
Although you enlarge your
eyes with makeup,
In vain you make yourself
beautiful.
Your lovers despise you;
They seek your life.

31 For I heard a voice *cry* as of a
woman in labor,
The anguish as of one giving
birth to her first child.
The voice of the daughter of
Zion ^gasping for breath,
^Stretching out her hands,
saying,
"Ah, woe to me, for I faint
before murderers."

JERUSALEM'S GODLESSNESS

5 "Roam about through the
streets of Jerusalem,
And look and take notice.
And seek in her public
squares,
If you can ^find a person,
^If there is one who does
justice, who seeks honesty,
Then I will forgive ¹her.

2 "And ^although they say, 'As
the LORD lives,'
Certainly they swear falsely."

3 LORD, do ^Your eyes not *look*
for honesty?
You have struck them,
But they did not weaken;
You have consumed them,
But they ^refused to accept
discipline.
They have made their faces
harder than rock;
They have refused to repent.

4 Then I said, "They are only
the poor,
They are foolish;
For they ^do not know the way
of the LORD
Or the judgment of their God.

5 "I will go to the great
And speak to them,
For ^they know the way of the
LORD
And the judgment of their
God."
But together they *too* have
broken the yoke
And burst the restraints.

6 Therefore a lion from the
forest will kill them,
A wolf of the deserts will
destroy them,
A ^leopard is watching their
cities.
Everyone who goes out of
them will be torn in pieces,
Because their ^wrongdoings
are many,
Their apostasies are
numerous.

7 "Why should I forgive you?
Your sons have forsaken Me
And ^sworn by those who are
^not gods.
When I had fed them to the
full,
They committed adultery
And stayed at the prostitute's
house.

8 "They were well-fed lusty
horses,
Each one neighing at his
^neighbor's wife.

4:30 ^Is 10:3; 20:6   4:31 ^Is 42:14   ^Is 1:15
5:1 ^Ezek 22:30   ^Gen 18:26, 32   5:2 ^Is 48:1;
Titus 1:16   5:3 ^2 Chr 16:9   ^Jer 7:28   5:4 ^Is 27:11;
Jer 8:7   5:5 ^Mic 3:1   5:6 ^Hos 13:7   ^Jer 30:14, 15
5:7 ^Josh 23:7   ^Deut 32:21   5:8 ^Jer 13:27; 29:23

5:1 ¹I.e., Jerusalem

9 "Shall I not punish *them* for these
   things?" declares the LORD,
   "And ^shall I not avenge Myself
   On a nation such as this?

10 "Go up through her vine rows
   and destroy,
   But do not execute a complete
   destruction;
   Strip away her branches,
   For they are not the LORD's.

11 "For the ^house of Israel and the
   house of Judah
   Have dealt very treacherously
   with Me," declares the LORD.

12 They have lied about the LORD
   And said, "Not He;
   Misfortune will ^not come
   upon us,
   ^BNor will we see sword or
   famine.

13 "The ^prophets are *as* wind,
   And the word is not in them.
   So it will be done to them!"

JUDGMENT PROCLAIMED

14 Therefore, this is what the
   LORD, the God of armies says:
   "Because you have spoken this
   word,
   Behold, I am ^making My
   words fire in your mouth,
   And this people wood, and it
   will consume them.

15 "Behold, I am ^bringing a nation
   against you from far away,
   you house of Israel," declares
   the LORD.
   "It is an enduring nation,
   It is an ancient nation,
   A nation whose ^Blanguage you
   do not know,
   Nor can you understand what
   they say.

16 "Their quiver is like an ^open
   grave,
   All of them are warriors.

17 "They will devour your harvest
   and your food;
   They will devour your sons
   and your daughters;
   They will devour your flocks
   and your herds;
   They will devour your ^vines
   and your fig trees;
   They will demolish your
   ^Bfortified cities, in which you
   trust, with the sword.

18 "Yet even in those days," declares
the LORD, "I will not make a complete destruction of you. 19 And it
shall come about when they say,
'Why has the LORD our God done
all these things to us?' then you
shall say to them, 'Just as you have
abandoned Me and served foreign gods in your land, so you will
^serve strangers in a land that is not
yours.'

20 "Declare this in the house of
   Jacob
   And proclaim it in Judah,
   saying,

21 'Now hear this, you foolish and
   senseless people,
   Who have ^eyes but do not see,
   Who have ears but do not
   hear.

22 'Do you not ^fear Me?' declares
   the LORD.
   'Do you not tremble in My
   presence?
   For I have placed the sand as a
   boundary for the sea,
   An eternal limit, and it will not
   cross over it.
   Though the waves toss, they
   cannot prevail;
   Though they roar, they will
   not cross over it.

5:9 ^Jer 9:9   **5:11** ^Jer 3:6, 7, 20   **5:12** ^Jer 23:17
^BJer 14:13   **5:13** ^Job 8:2; Jer 14:13, 15   **5:14** ^Is 24:6;
Jer 1:9   **5:15** ^Deut 28:49   ^BIs 28:11   **5:16** ^Ps 5:9
5:17 ^Jer 8:13   ^BHos 8:14   **5:19** ^Deut 28:48; Jer 16:13
5:21 ^Is 6:9; 43:8   **5:22** ^Deut 28:58; Ps 119:120

23 'But this people has a ^stubborn
    and rebellious heart;
    They have turned aside and
    departed.
24 'They do not say in their heart,
    "Let us now fear the Lord our
    God,
    Who ^gives rain in its season,
    Both ^Bthe autumn rain and the
    spring rain,
    Who keeps for us
    The appointed weeks of the
    harvest."
25 'Your ^wrongdoings have
    turned these away,
    And your sins have kept good
    away from you.
26 'For wicked people are found
    among My people,
    They ^watch like fowlers lying
    in wait;
    They set a trap,
    They catch people.
27 'Like a cage full of birds,
    So their houses are full of
    ^deceit;
    Therefore they have become
    great and rich.
28 'They are ^fat, they are sleek,
    They also excel in deeds of
    wickedness;
    They do not plead the cause,
    The cause of the ^Borphan, so
    that they may be successful;
    And they do not defend the
    rights of the poor.
29 '^Shall I not punish *them* for
    these *things?*' declares the
    Lord,
    'Or shall I not avenge Myself
    On a nation such as this?'

30 "An appalling and ^horrible thing
    Has happened in the land:
31 The ^prophets prophesy falsely,
    And the priests rule on their
    own authority;

And My people love it this way!
    But what will you do when the
    end comes?

THE COMING DESTRUCTION
OF JERUSALEM

6 "Flee to safety, you sons of
    ^Benjamin,
    From the midst of Jerusalem!
    Blow a trumpet in Tekoa
    And raise a *warning* signal
    over [1,B]Beth-haccerem;
    For evil looks down from the
    north,
    Along with a great destruction.
2 "The beautiful and delicate
    one, ^the daughter of Zion, I
    will destroy.
3 "'^Shepherds and their flocks
    will come to her,
    They will ^Bpitch *their* tents
    around her,
    They will pasture, each in his
    place.
4 '^Prepare for war against her;
    Arise, and let's attack at noon.
    Woe to us, for the day declines,
    For the shadows of the
    evening lengthen!
5 'Arise, and let's attack by night
    And ^destroy her palaces!'"
6 For this is what the Lord of
    armies says:
    "Cut down her trees
    And pile up an ^assault ramp
    against Jerusalem.
    This is the city to be punished,
    In whose midst there is only
    ^Boppression.

5:23 ^Deut 21:18; Ps 78:8   5:24 ^Ps 147:8   ^BJoel 2:23
5:25 ^Jer 2:17; 4:18   5:26 ^Ps 10:9; Prov 1:11
5:27 ^Jer 9:6   5:28 ^Deut 32:15   ^BIs 1:23
5:29 ^Jer 5:9; Mal 3:5   5:30 ^Jer 23:14; Hos 6:10
5:31 ^Ezek 13:6   6:1 ^Josh 18:28   ^BNeh 3:14
6:2 ^Is 1:8; Jer 4:31   6:3 ^Jer 12:10   ^B2 Kin 25:1
6:4 ^Jer 6:23; Joel 3:9   6:5 ^Is 32:14; Jer 52:13
6:6 ^Jer 32:24   ^BJer 22:17

6:1 [1] I.e., house of the vineyard

7 "As a well keeps its waters fresh,
  So she keeps fresh her
    wickedness.
  ^AViolence and destruction are
    heard in her;
  ^BSickness and wounds are
    constantly before Me.

8 "Be warned, Jerusalem,
  Or ^AI shall be alienated from
    you,
  And make you a desolation,
  An uninhabited land."

9 This is what the LORD of
    armies says:
  "They will ^Athoroughly glean
    the ^Bremnant of Israel like
    the vine;
  Pass your hand over the
    branches again
  Like a grape gatherer."

10 To whom shall I speak and
    give warning,
  That they may hear?
  Behold, their ears are closed
  And they cannot listen.
  Behold, ^Athe word of the LORD
    has become for them a
    rebuke;
  They take no delight in it.

11 But I am ^Afull of the wrath of
    the LORD;
  I am weary of holding it in.
  "Pour it out on the children in
    the street
  And on the gathering of young
    men together;
  For both husband and wife
    shall be taken,
  The old and the very old.

12 "Their ^Ahouses shall be turned
    over to others,
  Their fields and their wives
    together;
  For I will stretch out My hand
  Against the inhabitants of the
    land," declares the LORD.

13 "For ^Afrom the least of them to
    the greatest of them,
  Everyone is ^Bgreedy for gain,
  And from the prophet to the
    priest
  Everyone deals falsely.

14 "They have ^Ahealed the
    brokenness of My people
    superficially,
  Saying, 'Peace, peace,'
  But there is no peace.

15 "Were they ^Aashamed because
    of the abomination they had
    done?
  They were not ashamed at all,
  Nor did they know even how
    to be ashamed.
  Therefore they will fall among
    those who fall;
  At the time that I punish
    them,
  They will collapse," says the
    LORD.

16 This is what the LORD says:
  "Stand by the ways and see and
    ask for the ^Aancient paths,
  Where the good way is, and
    walk in it;
  Then ^Byou will find a resting
    place for your souls.
  But they said, 'We will not
    walk in it.'

17 "And I set ^Awatchmen over you,
    saying,
  'Listen to the sound of the
    trumpet!'
  But they said, 'We will not
    listen.'

18 "Therefore hear, you nations,
  And know, you congregation,
    what is among them.

6:7 ^AJer 20:8   ^BJer 30:12, 13   6:8 ^AEzek 23:18;
Hos 9:12   6:9 ^AJer 16:16   ^BJer 8:3   6:10 ^AJer 20:8
6:11 ^AJob 32:18, 19; Mic 3:8   6:12 ^ADeut 28:30; Jer 8:10
6:13 ^AJer 8:10   ^BIs 56:11   6:14 ^AJer 8:11; Ezek 13:10
6:15 ^AJer 3:3; 8:12   6:16 ^AIs 8:20   ^BMatt 11:29
6:17 ^AIs 21:11; 58:1

¹⁹ "Hear, earth: behold, I am
    bringing disaster on this
    people,
  The ^fruit of their plans,
  Because they have not listened
    to My words,
  And as for My Law, they have
    ^Brejected it also.
²⁰ "For what purpose does
    ^frankincense come to Me
    from Sheba,
  And the ^Bsweet cane from a
    distant land?
  Your burnt offerings are not
    acceptable
  And your sacrifices are not
    pleasing to Me."
²¹ Therefore, this is what the
    LORD says:
  "Behold, ^I am placing stumbling
    blocks before this people.
  And they will stumble against
    them,
  Fathers and sons together;
  Neighbor and friend will
    perish."

THE ENEMY FROM THE NORTH

²² This is what the LORD says:
  "Behold, *there is* ^a people
    coming from the north land,
  And a great nation will be
    stirred up from the ^Bremote
    parts of the earth.
²³ "They seize ^bow and spear;
  They are ^Bcruel and have no
    mercy;
  Their voice roars like the sea,
  And they ride on horses,
  Lined up as a man for the
    battle
  Against you, daughter of Zion!"
²⁴ We have heard the report of it;
  Our hands are limp.
  ^Anguish has seized us,
  Pain like *that of* a woman in
    childbirth.

²⁵ Do not go out into the field,
  And do not walk on the road;
  For the enemy has a sword,
  ^Terror is on every side.
²⁶ Daughter of my people, put
    on sackcloth
  And ^roll in ashes;
  ^BMourn as for an only son,
  A most bitter mourning.
  For suddenly the destroyer
  Will come against us.
²⁷ "I have ^made you an assayer
    and an examiner among My
    people,
  So that you may know and put
    their way to the test."
²⁸ All of them are stubbornly
    rebellious,
  ^Going about as a slanderer;
  They are ^Bbronze and iron.
  They are, all of them, corrupt.
²⁹ The bellows blow fiercely,
  The lead is consumed by the
    fire;
  In vain the refining goes on,
  But the ^wicked are not
    separated.
³⁰ They call them rejected silver,
  Because the ^LORD has rejected
    them.

MESSAGE AT THE TEMPLE GATE

7 The word that came to Jeremiah
  from the LORD, saying, ²"^Stand
at the gate of the LORD's house and
proclaim there this word, and say,
'Hear the word of the LORD, all you
of Judah, who enter by these gates
to worship the LORD!'" ³This is what
the LORD of armies, the God of Israel

6:19 ^Prov 1:31   ^BJer 8:9   **6:20** ^Is 60:6   ^BEx 30:23
6:21 ^Is 8:14; Jer 13:16   **6:22** ^Jer 1:15   ^BNeh 1:9
6:23 ^Is 13:18   ^BJer 50:42   **6:24** ^Is 21:3; Jer 4:31
6:25 ^Jer 20:10; 46:5   **6:26** ^Jer 25:34   ^BAmos 8:10
6:27 ^Jer 1:18; 15:20   **6:28** ^Jer 9:4   ^BEzek 22:18
6:29 ^Jer 15:19   **6:30** ^Jer 7:29; Hos 9:17
7:2 ^Jer 17:19; 26:2

says: "^Amend your ways and your deeds, and I will let you live in this place. 4^Do not trust in deceptive words, saying, 'This is the temple of the LORD, the temple of the LORD, the temple of the LORD.' 5For if you truly amend your ways and your deeds, if you truly ^practice justice between a person and his neighbor, 6*if* you do not oppress the stranger, the orphan, or the widow, and do not shed ^innocent blood in this place, nor ^Bfollow other gods to your own ruin, 7then I will let you live in this place, in the ^land that I gave to your fathers forever and ever.

8"Behold, you are trusting in ^deceptive words to no avail. 9Will you steal, murder, commit adultery, swear falsely, offer sacrifices to Baal, and follow ^other gods that you have not known, 10then ^come and stand before Me in ^Bthis house which is called by My name, and say, 'We are saved!'—so that you may do all these abominations? 11Has this house, which is called by My name, become a ^den of robbers in your sight? Behold, I Myself have seen *it*," declares the LORD.

12"But go now to My place which was in ^Shiloh, where I made My name dwell at the beginning, and ^Bsee what I did to it because of the wickedness of My people Israel. 13And now, because you have done all these things," declares the LORD, "and I spoke to you, ^speaking again and again, but you did not listen, and I called you but you did not answer, 14therefore I will do to the ^house which is called by My name, in which you trust, and to the place which I gave to you and your fathers, just as I did to Shiloh. 15I will ^hurl you out of My sight, just

as I have hurled out all your brothers, all the descendants of Ephraim.

16"As for you, ^do not pray for this people, and do not lift up a cry or prayer for them, and do not plead with Me; for I am not listening to you. 17Do you not see what they are doing in the cities of Judah and in the streets of Jerusalem? 18The children gather wood, the fathers kindle the fire, and the women knead dough to make sacrificial cakes for the queen of heaven; and *they* pour out drink offerings to other gods in order to ^provoke Me to anger. 19^Are they provoking Me?" declares the LORD. "Is it not themselves *instead,* to their own shame?" 20Therefore this is what the Lord GOD says: "Behold, My ^anger and My wrath will be poured out on this place, on human and animal *life,* and on the trees of the field and the fruit of the ground; and it will burn and not be quenched."

21This is what the LORD of armies, the God of Israel says: "Add your burnt offerings to your sacrifices and ^eat flesh. 22For I did not ^speak to your fathers, or command them on the day that I brought them out of the land of Egypt, concerning burnt offerings and sacrifices. 23But this is what I commanded them, saying, '^Obey My voice, and ^BI will be your God, and you will be My people; and you shall walk entirely in the way which I command you,

7:3^Jer 4:1; 7:5   7:4^Jer 7:8; Mic 3:11   7:5^1 Kin 6:12; Jer 21:12   7:6^Jer 2:34   BDeut 6:14, 15   7:7^Jer 3:18
7:8^Jer 7:4; 28:15   7:9^Ex 20:3; Jer 7:6
7:10^Ezek 23:39   BJer 7:11, 14, 30   7:11^Matt 21:13; Mark 11:17   7:12^Judg 18:31   B1 Sam 4:10, 11, 22
7:13^Jer 35:17   7:14^Deut 12:5; 1 Kin 9:7   7:15^Jer 15:1; 52:3   7:16^Ex 32:10; Deut 9:14   7:18^Deut 32:16, 21; 1 Kin 14:9   7:19^Job 35:6; 1 Cor 10:22   7:20^Is 42:25; Jer 6:11, 12   7:21^Ezek 33:25; Hos 8:13
7:22^1 Sam 15:22; Ps 51:16   7:23^Ex 15:26   BEx 19:5, 6

so that it may go well for you.' ²⁴Yet they did not obey or incline their ear, but walked by *their own* advice *and* in the stubbornness of their evil hearts, and they ^went backward and not forward. ²⁵Since the day that your fathers came out of the land of Egypt until this day, I have ^sent you all My servants the prophets, sending *them* daily, again and again. ²⁶Yet they did not listen to Me or incline their ear, but stiffened their neck; they ^did more evil than their fathers.

²⁷"So you shall ^speak all these words to them, but they will not listen to you; and you shall call to them, but they will ᴮnot answer you. ²⁸And you shall say to them, 'This is the nation that ^did not obey the voice of the LORD their God or accept discipline; trustworthiness has perished and has been eliminated from their mouth.
²⁹ 'Cut off your hair and throw *it*
       away,
     And take up a song of
       mourning on the bare
       heights;
     For the LORD has ^rejected and
       forsaken
     The generation of His wrath.'
³⁰For the sons of Judah have done that which is evil in My sight," declares the LORD. "They have ^put their detestable things in the house which is called by My name, to defile it. ³¹They have built the high places of Topheth, which is in the Valley of Ben-hinnom, to ^burn their sons and their daughters in the fire, which I did not command, and it did not come into My mind. ³²"^Therefore, behold, days are coming," declares the LORD, "when it will no longer be called Topheth, or the Valley of Ben-hinnom, but

the Valley of the Slaughter; for they will bury in Topheth because there is no *other* place. ³³The ^dead bodies of this people will be food for the birds of the sky and for the animals of the earth; and no one will frighten *them away*. ³⁴Then I will eliminate from the cities of Judah and from the streets of Jerusalem the voice of joy and the voice of gladness, the voice of the groom and the voice of the bride; for the ^land will become a site of ruins.

THE SIN AND TREACHERY OF JUDAH

8 "At that time," declares the LORD, "they will ^bring out the bones of the kings of Judah, the bones of its leaders, the bones of the priests, the bones of the prophets, and the bones of the inhabitants of Jerusalem from their graves. ²They will spread them out to the sun, the moon, and to all the ^heavenly lights, which they have loved, which they have served, which they have followed, which they have sought, and which they have worshiped. They will not be gathered nor buried; they will be like dung on the face of the ground. ³And ^death will be chosen rather than life by all the remnant that remains of this evil family, that remains in all the places to which I have driven them," declares the LORD of armies. ⁴"You shall say to them, 'This is what the LORD says:
   "Do *people* ^fall and not get up?
    Does one turn away and not
      repent?

7:24 ^Jer 15:6   7:25 ^2 Chr 36:15; Jer 25:4
7:26 ^Jer 16:12; Matt 23:32   7:27 ^Jer 1:7   ᴮIs 50:2
7:28 ^Jer 6:17; 11:10   7:29 ^Jer 6:30; 14:19
7:30 ^2 Kin 21:3f; 2 Chr 33:3-5, 7   7:31 ^Lev 18:21;
2 Kin 17:17   7:32 ^Jer 19:6, 11   7:33 ^Deut 28:26;
Ps 79:2   7:34 ^Lev 26:33; Is 1:7   8:1 ^Ezek 6:5
8:2 ^2 Kin 23:5; Jer 19:13   8:3 ^Job 3:21, 22; 7:15, 16
8:4 ^Prov 24:16; Amos 5:2

5 "Why has this people,
    Jerusalem,
  ᴬTurned away in continual
    apostasy?
  They ᴮhold on to deceit,
  They refuse to return.
6 "I have listened and heard,
  They have spoken what is not
    right;
  ᴬNo one repented of his
    wickedness,
  Saying, 'What have I done?'
  Everyone turned to his own
    course,
  Like a ᴮhorse charging into the
    battle.
7 "Even the stork in the sky
  ᴬKnows her seasons;
  And the turtledove, the
    swallow, and the crane
  Keep to the time of their
    migration;
  But ᴮMy people do not know
  The judgment of the LORD.

8 "ᴬHow can you say, 'We are wise,
  And the Law of the LORD is
    with us'?
  But behold, the lying pen of
    the scribes
  Has made it into a lie.
9 "The wise men are ᴬput to
    shame,
  They are dismayed and caught;
  Behold, they have rejected the
    word of the LORD,
  So what kind of wisdom do
    they have?
10 "Therefore I will give their
    wives to others,
  Their fields to new owners;
  Because from the least even to
    the greatest
  Everyone is ᴬgreedy for gain;
  From the prophet even to the
    priest,
  Everyone practices deceit.

11 "They have ᴬhealed the
    brokenness of the daughter
    of My people superficially,
  Saying, 'Peace, peace,'
  But there is no peace.
12 "Were they ashamed because
    of the abomination they
    had done?
  They were not ashamed at
    all,
  And they did not know how to
    be ashamed;
  Therefore they will ᴬfall
    among those who fall;
  At the time of their
    punishment they will
    collapse,"
  Says the LORD.

13 "I will ᴬcertainly snatch them
    away," declares the LORD.
  "There will be no grapes on the
    vine
  And no figs on the fig tree,
  And the leaf will wither;
  And what I have given them
    will pass away."'"
14 Why are we sitting still?
  Assemble yourselves, and
    let's go into the fortified
    cities
  And perish there,
  For the LORD our God has
    doomed us
  And given us ᴬpoisoned water
    to drink,
  Because ᴮwe have sinned
    against the LORD.
15 We ᴬwaited for peace, but no
    good came;
  For a time of healing, but
    behold, terror!

8:5ᴬJer 5:6   ᴮJer 5:27   8:6ᴬEzek 22:30   ᴮJob
39:21-25   8:7ᴬProv 6:6-8   ᴮJer 5:4   8:8ᴬJob 5:12, 13;
Jer 4:22   8:9ᴬIs 19:11; Jer 6:15   8:10ᴬIs 56:11; 57:17
8:11ᴬJer 6:14; 14:13, 14   8:12ᴬIs 9:14; Jer 6:21
8:13ᴬJer 14:12; Ezek 22:20, 21   8:14ᴬDeut 29:18
ᴮJer 3:25   8:15ᴬJer 8:11; 14:19

16 From Dan there is heard the
    snorting of his horses;
  At the sound of the neighing
    of his stallions
  The whole land quakes;
  For they come and ^devour the
    land and its fullness,
  The city and its inhabitants.
17 "For behold, I am ^sending
    serpents among you,
  Vipers for which there is no
    charm;
  And they will bite you,"
    declares the LORD.

18 My ^sorrow is beyond healing,
  My ^heart is faint within me!
19 Behold, listen! The cry of the
    daughter of my people from
    a distant land:
  "Is the LORD not in Zion? Is her
    King not within her?"
  "Why have they ^provoked Me
    with their carved images,
    with foreign ^idols?"
20 "Harvest is past, summer is
    over,
  And we are not saved."
21 I am broken over the
    brokenness of the daughter
    of my people.
  I ^mourn, dismay has taken
    hold of me.
22 Is there no balm in Gilead?
  Is there no physician there?
  ^Why then has not the health
    of the daughter of my people
    been restored?

GRIEF OVER ZION

9 Oh, that my head were waters
  And my eyes a fountain of
    tears,
  That I might weep day and
    night
  For those slain of the
    ^daughter of my people!

2 Oh that I had in the desert
  A travelers' lodging place;
  So that I might leave my
    people
  And go away from them!
  For all of them are ^adulterers,
  An assembly of ^treacherous
    people.
3 "They ^bend their tongues *like*
    their bows;
  Lies and not truth prevail in
    the land;
  For they ^proceed from evil to
    evil,
  And they do not know Me,"
    declares the LORD.
4 "Let everyone ^be on guard
    against his neighbor,
  And do not trust any brother;
  Because every brother utterly
    betrays,
  And every neighbor goes
    about as a slanderer.
5 "Everyone ^deceives his
    neighbor
  And does not speak the truth.
  They have taught their tongue
    to speak lies;
  They weary themselves
    committing wrongdoing.
6 "Your dwelling is in the midst
    of deceit;
  Through deceit they ^refuse to
    know Me," declares the LORD.
7 Therefore this is what the LORD
  of armies says:
  "Behold, I will refine them and
    ^put them to the test;
  For ^what *else* can I do,
    because of the daughter of
    My people?

8:16 ^Jer 3:24; 10:25   8:17 ^Num 21:6; Deut 32:24
8:18 ^Is 22:4   ^Jer 23:9   8:19 ^Deut 32:21   ^Ps 31:6
8:21 ^Jer 14:2; Joel 2:6   8:22 ^Jer 14:19; 30:13
9:1 ^Jer 6:26; 8:21, 22   9:2 ^Jer 5:7, 8   ^Jer 5:11
9:3 ^Ps 64:3   ^Jer 4:22   9:4 ^Ps 12:2; Prov 26:24, 25
9:5 ^Mic 6:12   9:6 ^Job 21:14, 15; Prov 1:24
9:7 ^Is 1:25   ^Hos 11:8

8 "Their tongue is a deadly arrow;
   It speaks deceit;
   With his mouth one ^speaks
      peace to his neighbor,
   But inwardly he ^Bsets an
      ambush for him.
9 "^AShall I not punish them for
      these things?" declares the
      LORD.
   "Shall I not avenge Myself
   On a nation such as this?

10 "I will take up a weeping and
      wailing for the mountains,
   And for the pastures of
      the wilderness a song of
      mourning,
   Because they are ^laid waste so
      that no one passes through,
   And the sound of the livestock
      is not heard;
   Both the ^Bbirds of the sky and
      the animals have fled; they
      are gone.
11 "I will make Jerusalem a ^heap
      of ruins,
   A haunt of jackals;
   And I will make the cities of
      Judah a ^Bdesolation without
      inhabitant."

12 Who is the wise person who
may understand this? And *who is*
he to whom the mouth of the LORD
has spoken, that he may declare
it? ^AWhy is the land destroyed, laid
waste like the desert, so that no one
passes through? 13 The LORD said,
"Because they have ^Aabandoned
My Law which I put before them,
and have not obeyed My voice nor
walked according to it, 14 but have
^Afollowed the stubbornness of their
heart and the Baals, as their ^Bfa-
thers taught them," 15 therefore this
is what the LORD of armies, the God
of Israel says: "Behold, ^AI will feed
this people wormwood; and I will

give them poisoned water to drink.
16 I will also ^Ascatter them among
the nations, whom neither they
nor their fathers have known; and I
will send the sword after them until
I have put an end to them."

17 This is what the LORD of armies
says:
   "Consider and call for the
      ^Amourning women, that they
      may come;
   And send for the ^1,Bskillful
      women, that they may come!
18 "Have them hurry and take up a
      wailing for us,
   So that our ^Aeyes may shed tears,
   And our eyelids flow with water.
19 "For a voice of wailing is heard
      from Zion:
   '^AHow devastated we are!
   We are put to great shame,
   For we have ^Babandoned the
      land
   Because they have torn down
      our homes.'"
20 Now hear the word of the
      LORD, you ^Awomen,
   And let your ears receive the
      word of His mouth;
   Teach your daughters wailing,
   And *have every* woman *teach*
      her neighbor a song of
      mourning.
21 For ^Adeath has come up
      through our windows;
   It has entered our palaces
   To eliminate the ^Bchildren
      from the streets,
   The young men from the
      public squares.

9:8 ^APs 28:3   ^BJer 5:26   9:9 ^AIs 1:24; Jer 5:9, 29
9:10 ^AJer 12:4, 10   ^BJer 4:25   9:11 ^AIs 25:2   ^BJer 4:27
9:12 ^APs 107:34; Jer 23:10   9:13 ^A2 Chr 7:19; Ps 89:30
9:14 ^AJer 7:24   ^BGal 1:14   9:15 ^APs 80:5
9:16 ^ALev 26:33; Deut 28:64   9:17 ^A2 Chr 35:25
^BAmos 5:16   9:18 ^AIs 22:4; Jer 9:1   9:19 ^ADeut 28:29
^BJer 7:15   9:20 ^AIs 32:9   9:21 ^A2 Chr 36:17   ^BJer 6:11
9:17 ^1 I.e., professional mourners

22 Speak, "This is what the Lord says:
'The corpses of people will fall ^like dung on the open field,
And like the sheaf after the reaper,
But no one will gather *them*.'"

23 This is what the Lord says: "^Let no wise man boast of his wisdom, nor let the mighty man boast of his might, nor a rich man boast of his riches; 24 but let the one who boasts ^boast of this, that he understands and knows Me, that I am the Lord who exercises mercy, justice, and righteousness on the earth; for I delight in these things," declares the Lord.

25 "Behold, the days are coming," declares the Lord, "that I will punish all who are circumcised and yet ^uncircumcised— 26 Egypt, Judah, Edom, the sons of Ammon, Moab, and ^all those inhabiting the desert who trim the hair on their temples; for all the nations are uncircumcised, and all the house of Israel are ^uncircumcised of heart."

A SATIRE ON IDOLATRY

10 Hear the word which the Lord speaks to you, house of Israel. 2 This is what the Lord says:
"^Do not learn the way of the nations,
And do not be terrified by the signs of the heavens,
Although the nations are terrified by them;
3 For the customs of the peoples are ^futile;
For ^it is wood cut from the forest,
The work of the hands of a craftsman with a cutting tool.

4 "They decorate *the idol* with silver and gold;
They ^fasten it with nails and hammers
So that it will not totter.
5 "They are like a scarecrow in a cucumber field,
And they ^cannot speak;
They must be ^carried,
Because they cannot walk!
Do not fear them,
For they can do no harm,
Nor can they do any good."

6 ^There is none like You, Lord;
You are great, and Your name is great in might.
7 ^Who would not fear You,
O ^King of the nations?
For it is Your due!
For among all the wise men of the nations
And in all their kingdoms,
There is none like You.
8 But they are altogether ^stupid and foolish;
The instruction *from* idols is *nothing but* wood!
9 Beaten silver is brought from Tarshish,
And gold from Uphaz,
The work of a craftsman and of the hands of a goldsmith;
Their clothing is of violet and purple;
They are all the ^work of skilled people.
10 But the Lord is the ^true God;
He is the ^living God and the everlasting King.

9:22 ^Ps 83:10; Is 5:25   9:23 ^Eccl 9:11; Is 47:10
9:24 ^Ps 20:7; 44:8   9:25 ^Jer 4:4; Rom 2:28, 29
9:26 ^Jer 25:23   ^Lev 26:41   10:2 ^Lev 18:3; 20:23
10:3 ^Jer 14:22   ^Is 44:9-20   10:4 ^Is 40:20; 41:7
10:5 ^Ps 115:5   ^Ps 115:7   10:6 ^Ex 15:11; Deut 33:26
10:7 ^Rev 15:4   ^Ps 22:28   10:8 ^Jer 4:22; 5:4
10:9 ^Ps 115:4   10:10 ^Is 65:16   ^Jer 4:2

The earth quakes at His wrath,
And the nations cannot
    endure His indignation.

¹¹This is what you shall say to
them: "The ᴬgods that did not make
the heavens and the earth will ᴮper-
ish from the earth and from under
these heavens."

¹² *It is* He who made the earth by
    His power,
Who ᴬestablished the world by
    His wisdom;
And by His understanding
    He has ᴮstretched out the
    heavens.

¹³ When He utters His voice,
    there is a roar of waters in
    the heavens,
And He makes the ᴬclouds
    ascend from the end of the
    earth;
He makes lightning for the rain,
And brings out the ᴮwind from
    His storehouses.

¹⁴ Every person is ᴬstupid, devoid
    of knowledge;
Every goldsmith is put to
    shame by his idols,
For his cast metal images are
    deceitful,
And there is no breath in them.

¹⁵ They are ᴬworthless, a work of
    mockery;
At the time of their
    punishment they will perish.

¹⁶ The Portion of Jacob is not like
    these;
For He is the ᴬMaker of
    everything,
And ᴮIsrael is the tribe of His
    inheritance;
The Lᴏʀᴅ of armies is His
    name.

¹⁷ ᴬPick up your bundle from the
    ground,
You who live under siege!

¹⁸ For this is what the Lᴏʀᴅ says:
"Behold, I am ᴬslinging out the
    inhabitants of the land
At this time,
And I will cause them distress,
So that they may be found."

¹⁹ Woe to me, because of my
    injury!
My ᴬwound is incurable.
But I said, "This certainly is a
    sickness,
And I ᴮmust endure it."

²⁰ My ᴬtent is destroyed,
And all my ropes are broken.
My ᴮsons have gone from me
    and are no more.
There is no one to stretch out
    my tent again
Or to set up my curtains.

²¹ For the shepherds have
    become stupid
And ᴬhave not sought the Lᴏʀᴅ.
Therefore they have not
    prospered,
And ᴮall their flock is scattered.

²² The sound of a report! Behold,
    it is coming—
A great roar ᴬfrom the land of
    the north—
To ᴮmake the cities of Judah
A desolation, a haunt of jackals.

²³ I know, Lᴏʀᴅ, that ᴬa person's
    way is not in himself,
ᴮNor is it in a person who
    walks to direct his steps.

²⁴ ᴬCorrect me, Lᴏʀᴅ, but with
    justice;
Not with Your anger, or You
    will bring me to nothing.

10:11 ᴬPs 96:5   ᴮIs 2:18   10:12 ᴬPs 78:69   ᴮJob 9:8
10:13 ᴬJob 36:27-29   ᴮPs 135:7   10:14 ᴬJer 10:8;
51:17, 18   10:15 ᴬIs 41:24; Jer 8:19   10:16 ᴬIs 45:7
ᴮDeut 32:9   10:17 ᴬEzek 12:3-12   10:18 ᴬ1 Sam 25:29
10:19 ᴬJer 14:17   ᴮMic 7:9   10:20 ᴬJer 4:20   ᴮJer 31:15
10:21 ᴬJer 2:8   ᴮJer 23:2   10:22 ᴬJer 1:14   ᴮJer 9:11
10:23 ᴬProv 16:1   ᴮIs 26:7   10:24 ᴬPs 6:1; 38:1

25 ᴬPour out Your wrath on the
nations that ᴮdo not know
You,
And on the families who do
not call upon Your name;
For they have devoured Jacob;
They have devoured him and
consumed him,
And have laid waste his
settlement.

THE BROKEN COVENANT

11 The word that came to Jeremiah from the Lᴏʀᴅ, saying, ²"Hear the words of this ᴬcovenant, and speak to the men of Judah and to the inhabitants of Jerusalem; ³and say to them, 'This is what the Lᴏʀᴅ, the God of Israel says: "ᴬCursed is the one who does not obey the words of this covenant ⁴which I commanded your forefathers on the day that I brought them out of the land of Egypt, from the ᴬiron furnace, saying, 'Listen to My voice, and do according to all that I command you; so you shall be ᴮMy people, and I will be your God,' ⁵in order to confirm the ᴬoath which I swore to your forefathers, to give them a land flowing with milk and honey, as *it is* this day." ' " Then I replied, "Amen, Lᴏʀᴅ."

⁶And the Lᴏʀᴅ said to me, "Proclaim all these words in the cities of Judah and in the streets of Jerusalem, saying, 'Hear the words of this covenant and ᴬdo them. ⁷For I solemnly ᴬwarned your fathers on the day I brought them up from the land of Egypt, even to this day, ᴮwarning *them* persistently, saying, "Listen to My voice." ⁸Yet they did not obey or incline their ear, but walked in the stubbornness of their evil heart, each one *of them;* therefore I brought on them all the ᴬwords of

this covenant which I commanded *them* to do, but they did not.' "

⁹Then the Lᴏʀᴅ said to me, "A ᴬconspiracy has been found among the men of Judah and among the inhabitants of Jerusalem. ¹⁰They have turned back to the wrongdoings of their ancestors who refused to hear My words, and they ᴬhave followed other gods to serve them. The house of Israel and the house of Judah have ᴮbroken My covenant which I made with their fathers." ¹¹Therefore this is what the Lᴏʀᴅ says: "Behold, I am ᴬbringing disaster on them which they will ᴮnot be able to escape; though they will cry out to Me, I will not listen to them. ¹²Then the cities of Judah and the inhabitants of Jerusalem will ᴬgo and cry out to the gods to whom they burn incense, but they certainly will not save them in the time of their disaster. ¹³For your gods are as many as your cities, Judah; and as many as the streets of Jerusalem are the altars you have set up to the ᴬshameful thing, altars for ᴮburning incense to Baal.

¹⁴"So *as for* you, do not pray for this people, nor lift up a cry or prayer for them; for I will ᴬnot listen when they call to Me because of their disaster.

15 "What right has My ᴬbeloved in
My house
When ᴮshe has carried out
many evil schemes?
Can the sacrificial flesh take
away from you your disaster,
So *that* you can rejoice?"

10:25 ᴬPs 79:6, 7   ᴮJob 18:21   11:2 ᴬEx 19:5
11:3 ᴬDeut 27:26; Jer 17:5   11:4 ᴬDeut 4:20   ᴮJer 24:7
11:5 ᴬEx 13:5; Deut 7:12   11:6 ᴬJohn 13:17; Rom 2:13
11:7 ᴬ1 Sam 8:9   ᴮEx 15:26   11:8 ᴬLev 26:14-43
11:9 ᴬEzek 22:25; Hos 6:9   11:10 ᴬJudg 2:11-13
ᴮJer 3:6-11   11:11 ᴬ2 Kin 22:16   ᴮIs 24:17
11:12 ᴬDeut 32:37; Jer 44:17   11:13 ᴬJer 3:24   ᴮJer 7:9
11:14 ᴬPs 66:18; Jer 11:11   11:15 ᴬJer 13:27   ᴮEzek 16:25

16 The Lord named you
"A green olive tree, beautiful in
    fruit and form";
With the ^noise of a great
    ¹tumult
He has ^Bset fire to it,
And its branches are worthless.
17 The Lord of armies, who planted
you, has pronounced evil against
you because of the evil of the house
of Israel and the house of Judah,
which they have done to provoke
Me by ^offering sacrifices to Baal.

PLOTS AGAINST JEREMIAH

18 Moreover, the Lord ^made it
    known to me and I knew it;
Then You showed me their
    deeds.
19 But I was like a gentle ^lamb
    led to the slaughter;
And I did not know that they
    had devised plots against
    me, *saying,*
"Let's destroy the tree with its
    fruit,
And ^Blet's cut him off from the
    land of the living,
So that his name will no longer
    be remembered."
20 But, Lord of armies, who
    ^judges righteously,
Who ^Bputs the feelings and the
    heart to the test,
Let me see Your vengeance on
    them,
For to You I have committed
    my cause.
21 Therefore this is what the Lord
says concerning the people of
^Anathoth, who are seeking your
life, saying: "Do not prophesy in
the name of the Lord, so that you
do not die by our hand"; 22 therefore, this is what the Lord of armies
says: "Behold, I am going to ^punish
them! The ^Byoung men will die by

the sword, their sons and daughters will die by famine; 23 and a
remnant ^will not be *left* to them,
because I will ^Bbring disaster on the
people of Anathoth—the year of
their punishment."

JEREMIAH'S PRAYER

12 Righteous are You, Lord,
    when I plead *my* case with
    You;
Nevertheless I would discuss
    matters of justice with You:
Why has the ^way of the
    wicked prospered?
Why are all those who ^Bdeal in
    treachery at ease?
2 You have planted them, they
    have also taken root;
They grow, they have also
    produced fruit.
You are ^near to their lips
But far from their mind.
3 But You know me, Lord;
You see me
And examine my heart's
    attitude toward You.
Drag them off like sheep for
    the slaughter,
And set them apart for a ^day
    of slaughter!
4 How long is the land to mourn,
And the ^vegetation of the
    countryside to dry up?
Due to the wickedness of
    those who live in it,
^BAnimals and birds have been
    snatched away,
Because *people* have said, "He
    will not see our final end."

11:16 ^Ps 83:2   ^BPs 80:16   11:17 ^Jer 7:9; 11:13
11:18 ^1 Sam 23:11, 12; 2 Kin 6:9, 10   11:19 ^Is 53:7
^BPs 83:4   11:20 ^Gen 18:25   ^B1 Sam 16:7
11:21 ^Jer 1:1   11:22 ^Jer 21:14   ^B2 Chr 36:17
11:23 ^Jer 6:9   ^BJer 23:12   12:1 ^Job 12:6   ^BJer 3:7, 20
12:2 ^Is 29:13; Jer 3:10   12:3 ^Jer 17:18; 50:27
12:4 ^Joel 1:10-17   ^BJer 4:25

11:16 ¹I.e., confused noise

5 "If you have run with
     infantrymen and they have
     tired you out,
  How can you compete with
     horses?
  If you fall down in a land of
     peace,
  How will you do in the ^thicket
     by the Jordan?
6 "For even your ^brothers and
     the household of your father,
  Even they have dealt
     treacherously with you,
  Even they have called aloud
     after you.
  Do not believe them, though
     they say nice things to you."

GOD'S ANSWER

7 "I have forsaken My house,
  I have abandoned My
     inheritance;
  I have handed the ^beloved of
     My soul
  Over to her enemies.
8 "My inheritance has become to
     Me
  Like a lion in the forest;
  She has roared against Me;
  Therefore I have come to ^hate
     her.
9 "Is My inheritance *like* a
     speckled bird of prey to Me?
  Are the ^birds of prey against
     her on every side?
  Go, gather all the animals of
     the field,
  Bring them to devour!
10 "Many ^shepherds have ruined
     My ^vineyard,
   They have trampled down My
     field;
   They have made My pleasant
     field
   A desolate wilderness.
11 "It has been made a desolation;
   Desolate, it mourns before Me;

  The whole land has been made
     desolate,
  Because no one ^takes it to
     heart.
12 "On all the ^bare heights in the
     wilderness
   Destroyers have come,
   For the sword of the LORD is
     devouring
   From one end of the land even
     to the other;
   There is no peace for anyone.
13 "They have ^sown wheat but
     have harvested thorns,
   They have strained themselves
     to no profit.
   So be ashamed of your produce
   Because of the fierce anger of
     the LORD."

14 This is what the LORD says concerning all My ^wicked neighbors
who ^do harm to the inheritance
with which I have endowed My
people Israel: "Behold, I am going
to drive them out of their land,
and I will drive the house of Judah
out from among them. 15 And it
will come about that after I have
driven them out, I will again have
compassion on them; and I will
^bring them back, each one to his
inheritance and each one to his
land. 16 Then, if they will really
^learn the ways of My people, to
swear by My name, 'As the LORD
lives,' just as they taught My people to swear by Baal, they will be
^built up in the midst of My people.
17 But if they do not listen, then I will
^drive out that nation, drive *it* out
and destroy *it*," declares the LORD.

12:5 ^Jer 49:19; 50:44   12:6 ^Gen 37:4-11; Job 6:15
12:7 ^Jer 11:15; Hos 11:1-8   12:8 ^Hos 9:15; Amos 6:8
12:9 ^2 Kin 24:2; Ezek 23:22-25   12:10 ^Jer 6:3
^Ps 80:8-16   12:11 ^Is 42:25   12:12 ^Jer 3:2, 21
12:13 ^Lev 26:16; Deut 28:38   12:14 ^Jer 49:1, 7
^Jer 2:3   12:15 ^Amos 9:14   12:16 ^Is 42:6   ^Jer 3:17
12:17 ^Ps 2:8-12; Is 60:12

THE RUINED UNDERGARMENT

13 This is what the LORD said to me: "Go and ^buy yourself a linen undergarment and put it around your waist, but do not put it in water." ²So I bought the undergarment in accordance with the ^word of the LORD, and put it around my waist. ³Then the word of the LORD came to me a second time, saying, ⁴"Take the undergarment that you bought, which is around your waist, and arise, go to the ^Euphrates and hide it there in a crevice of the rock." ⁵So I went and hid it by the Euphrates, ^as the LORD had commanded me. ⁶After many days the LORD said to me, "Arise, go to the Euphrates and take from there the undergarment which I commanded you to hide there." ⁷Then I went to the Euphrates and dug, and I took the undergarment from the place where I had hidden it; and behold, the undergarment was ruined, it was completely useless.

⁸Then the word of the LORD came to me, saying, ⁹"This is what the LORD says: 'To the same extent I will destroy the ^pride of Judah and the great pride of Jerusalem. ¹⁰This wicked people, who refuse to listen to My words, who ^walk in the stubbornness of their hearts and have followed other gods to serve them and to bow down to them, let them be just like this undergarment which is completely useless. ¹¹For as the undergarment clings to the waist of a man, so I made the entire household of Israel and the entire household of Judah ^cling to Me,' declares the LORD, 'so that they might be My people, for renown, for praise, and for glory; but they ᴮdid not listen.'

CAPTIVITY THREATENED

¹²"Therefore you are to speak this word to them. 'This is what the LORD, the God of Israel says: "Every jug is to be filled with wine."' And *when* they say to you, 'Do we not very well know that every jug is to be filled with wine?' ¹³then say to them, 'This is what the LORD says: "Behold, I am going to fill all the inhabitants of this land—the kings who sit for David on his throne, the priests, the prophets, and all the inhabitants of Jerusalem—with ^drunkenness! ¹⁴Then I will smash them against each other, both the fathers and the sons together," declares the LORD. "I will ^not have compassion nor be troubled nor take pity so as to keep from destroying them."'"

15   Listen and pay attention, do
      not be ^haughty;
     For the LORD has spoken.
16   Give glory to the LORD your
      God
     Before He brings ^darkness
     And before your feet stumble
     On the mountains in the
      dark,
     And while you are hoping for
      light
     He makes it into ᴮgloom,
     And turns *it* into thick
      darkness.
17   But ^if you do not listen to it,
     My soul will weep in secret for
      such pride;
     And my eyes will shed
     And stream down tears,
     Because the ᴮflock of the LORD
      has been taken captive.

13:1^Jer 13:11   **13:2**^Is 20:2; Ezek 2:8   **13:4**^Jer 51:63
13:5^Ex 39:42, 43; 40:16   **13:9**^Lev 26:19; Is 2:10–17
13:10^Jer 9:14; 11:8   **13:11**^Ex 19:5, 6 ᴮPs 81:11
13:13^Ps 60:3; 75:8   **13:14**^Deut 29:20; Is 27:11
13:15^Prov 16:5; Is 28:14–22   **13:16**^Is 5:30
ᴮPs 44:19   **13:17**^Mal 2:2 ᴮPs 80:1

18 Say to the ^king and the queen
    mother,
  "^BTake a lowly seat,
  For your beautiful crown
  Has come down from your
    head."
19 The ^cities of the Negev have
    been locked up,
  And there is no one to open
    them;
  All ^BJudah has been taken into
    exile,
  Wholly taken into exile.
20 "Raise your eyes and see
  Those coming ^from the
    north.
  Where is the flock that was
    given you,
  Your beautiful sheep?
21 "What will you say when He
    appoints over you—
  And you yourself had taught
    them—
  Former ^companions to be
    head over you?
  Will sharp pains not take hold
    of you
  Like a woman in childbirth?
22 "If you say in your heart,
  '^Why have these things
    happened to me?'
  Because of the ^Bmagnitude of
    your wrongdoing
  Your skirts have been
    removed
  And your ¹heels have suffered
    violence.
23 "^Can the Ethiopian change his
    skin,
  Or the leopard his spots?
  Then you as well can ^Bdo good
  Who are accustomed to doing
    evil.
24 "Therefore I will ^scatter them
    like drifting straw
  To the desert wind.

25 "This is your ^lot, the portion
    measured to you
  From Me," declares the LORD,
  "Because you have ^Bforgotten Me
  And trusted in falsehood.
26 "So I Myself have ^stripped your
    skirts off over your face,
  So that your shame will be
    seen.
27 "As for your ^adulteries and
    your lustful neighings,
  The ^Boutrageous sin of your
    prostitution
  On the hills in the field,
  I have seen your
    abominations.
  Woe to you, Jerusalem!
  How long will you remain
    unclean?"

DROUGHT AND A PRAYER FOR MERCY

14 That which came as the word
    of the LORD to Jeremiah regard-
ing the ^drought:
2 "Judah mourns
  And her gates languish;
  Her people sit on the ground in
    mourning garments,
  And the ^cry of Jerusalem has
    ascended.
3 "Their nobles have ^sent their
    servants for water;
  They have come to the cisterns
    and found no water.
  They have returned with their
    containers empty;
  They have been put to shame
    and humiliated,
  And they ^Bcover their heads,

13:18^2 Kin 24:12, 15   ^B2 Chr 33:12, 19
13:19^Jer 32:44   ^BJer 20:4   13:20^Jer 1:15; 6:22
13:21^Jer 2:25; 38:22   13:22^Jer 5:19   ^BJer 2:17-19
13:23^Prov 27:22   ^BJer 4:22; 9:5   13:24^Lev 26:33;
Jer 9:16   13:25^Job 20:29   ^BPs 9:17   13:26^Lam 1:8;
Ezek 23:29   13:27^Jer 5:7, 8   ^BJer 11:15   14:1^Jer 17:8
14:2^1 Sam 5:12; Jer 11:11   14:3^1 Kin 18:5
^B2 Sam 15:30

13:22 ¹I.e., a euphemism for private parts

4 Because the ^ground is
    cracked,
For there has been ^Bno rain on
    the land.
The farmers have been put to
    shame,
They have covered their heads.
5 "For even the doe in the field
    has given birth only to
    abandon *her young,*
Because there is ^no grass.
6 "The ^wild donkeys stand on
    the bare heights;
They pant for air like jackals,
Their eyes fail
Because there is ^Bno
    vegetation.
7 "Though our ^wrongdoings
    testify against us,
Lord, act for the sake of Your
    name!
Our ^Bapostasies have indeed
    been many,
We have sinned against You.
8 "Hope of Israel,
Its ^Savior in ^Btime of distress,
Why are You like a stranger in
    the land,
Or like a traveler who has
    pitched *his tent* for the
    night?
9 "Why are You like a confused
    person,
Like a warrior who cannot
    save?
Yet ^You are in our midst,
Lord,
And we are ^Bcalled by Your
    name;
Do not leave us!"

10 This is what the Lord says to
this people: "So much they have
loved to wander; they have not
restrained their feet. Therefore the
Lord does ^not accept them; now
He will ^Bremember their wrongdoing and call their sins to account."

11 So the Lord said to me, "^Do not
pray for a good outcome on behalf
of this people. 12 When they fast, I
am ^not going to listen to their cry;
and when they offer burnt offering and grain offering, I am not
going to accept them. Rather, I am
going to ^Bput an end to them by the
sword, famine, and plague."

FALSE PROPHETS

13 But I said, "Oh, Lord God! Behold,
the prophets are telling them, 'You
^will not see a sword, nor will you
have famine; on the contrary, I
will give you lasting ^Bpeace in this
place.'" 14 Then the Lord said to
me, "The ^prophets are prophesying falsehood in My name. ^BI have
neither sent them nor commanded
them, nor spoken to them; they are
prophesying to you a false vision,
divination, futility, and the deception of their own minds. 15 Therefore this is what the Lord says
concerning the prophets who are
prophesying in My name, although
it was not I who sent them—yet
they keep saying: 'There will be no
sword or famine in this land'—^Aby
sword and famine those prophets shall meet their end! 16 And the
people to whom they are prophesying will be thrown out into the
streets of Jerusalem because of the
famine and the sword; and there
will be no one to bury them—
neither them, *nor* their wives, nor
their sons, nor their daughters. For
I will ^pour out their *own* wickedness upon them.

14:4 ^Joel 1:19, 20   ^BJer 3:3   14:5 ^Is 15:6
14:6 ^Job 39:5, 6   ^BJoel 1:18   14:7 ^Is 59:12   ^BJer 5:6
14:8 ^Is 43:3   ^BPs 9:9   14:9 ^Ex 29:45   ^BIs 63:19
14:10 ^Jer 6:20   ^BJer 44:21-23   14:11 ^Ex 32:10;
Jer 7:16   14:12 ^Prov 1:28   ^BJer 8:13   14:13 ^Jer 5:12
^BJer 6:14   14:14 ^Jer 5:31   ^BJer 23:21   14:15 ^Jer 23:15;
Ezek 14:10   14:16 ^Prov 1:31; Jer 13:22-25

17 "You will say this word to them,
    'Let my eyes stream down tears
        night and day,
    And let them not cease;
    For the virgin ^daughter of my
        people has been crushed
        with a mighty blow,
    With a sorely ^Binfected wound.
18 'If I go out to the country,
    There are those killed by the
        sword!
    Or if I enter the city,
    There are diseases from
        famine!
    For ^both prophet and priest
    Have wandered around in the
        land that they do not know.'"

19 Have You completely rejected
        Judah?
    Or have You loathed Zion?
    Why have You stricken us
        so that we ^are beyond
        healing?
    We waited for peace, but
        nothing good *came;*
    And for a time of healing, but
        behold, terror!
20 We know our wickedness,
        LORD,
    The wrongdoing of our
        fathers, for ^we have sinned
        against You.
21 Do not despise *us,* ^for the sake
        of Your own name;
    Do not disgrace the ^Bthrone of
        Your glory.
    Remember *and* do not annul
        Your covenant with us.
22 Are there any among the idols
        of the nations who give rain?
    Or can the heavens grant
        showers?
    Is it not You, LORD our God?
    Therefore we ^wait for You,
    For You are the one who has
        done all these things.

JUDGMENT MUST COME

15 Then the LORD said to me,
"*Even* if ^Moses and ^BSam-
uel were to stand before Me, My
heart would not be with this people. Send them away from My
presence and have them go! 2 And
it shall be that when they say to
you, 'Where should we go?' then
you are to tell them, 'This is what
the LORD says:

    "Those *destined* ^for death, to
        death;
    And those *destined* for the
        sword, to the sword;
    And those *destined* for
        famine, to famine;
    And those *destined* for
        captivity, to captivity."'

3 And I will ^appoint over them four
kinds *of doom,*" declares the LORD:
"the sword to kill, the dogs to drag
away, and the birds of the sky and
the animals of the earth to devour
and destroy. 4 I will ^make them
an object of terror among all the
kingdoms of the earth because of
^BManasseh, the son of Hezekiah,
the king of Judah, for what he did
in Jerusalem.

5   "Indeed, who will have pity on
        you, Jerusalem,
    Or who will ^mourn for you,
    Or who will turn aside to ask
        about your welfare?
6   "You who have forsaken Me,"
        declares the LORD,
    "You keep ^going backward.
    So I will ^Bstretch out My hand
        against you and destroy
        you;
    I am tired of relenting!

14:17 ^Is 37:22   ^B Jer 10:19   14:18 ^Jer 6:13; 8:10
14:19 ^Jer 30:13   14:20 ^Jer 8:14; 14:7   14:21 ^Ps 25:11
^B Jer 3:17   14:22 ^Lam 3:26   15:1 ^Ex 32:11-14
^B 1 Sam 7:9   15:2 ^Jer 14:12; 24:10
15:3 ^Lev 26:16, 22, 25; Ezek 14:21   15:4 ^Lev 26:33
^B 2 Kin 21:1-18   15:5 ^Nah 3:7   15:6 ^Is 1:4   ^B Jer 6:12

7 "I will winnow them with a
        winnowing fork
    At the gates of the land;
    I will ᴬbereave *them* of children,
        I will destroy My people;
    ᴮThey did not repent of their
        ways.

8 "Their ᴬwidows will be more
        numerous before Me
    Than the sand of the seas;
    I will bring against them,
        against the mother of a
        young man,
    A ᴮdestroyer at noon;
    I will suddenly bring down on
        her
    Shock and horror.

9 "She who ᴬgave birth to seven
        sons withers away;
    Her breathing is labored.
    Her ᴮsun has set while it was
        still day;
    She has been shamed and
        humiliated.
    So I will turn over their
        survivors to the sword
    Before their enemies,"
        declares the LORD.

10 Woe to me, my mother, that
        you have given birth to me
    As a ᴬman of strife and a man
        of contention to all the land!
    I have not lent, nor have
        people lent money to me,
    Yet everyone curses me.

11 The LORD said, "I will certainly
        ᴬset you free for *purposes of*
        good;
    I will certainly make the
        enemy plead with you
    In a time of disaster and a time
        of distress.

12 "Can *anyone* smash iron,
    ᴬIron from the north, or
        bronze?

13 "I will give your ᴬwealth and
        your treasures
    As plunder ᴮwithout cost,
    For all your sins
    And within all your borders.

14 "Then I will make your enemies
        bring *your possessions*
    Into a ᴬland *that* you do not
        know;
    For a ᴮfire has been kindled in
        My anger,
    And it will burn upon you."

JEREMIAH'S PRAYER
AND GOD'S ANSWER

15 ᴬYou know, LORD;
    Remember me, take notice of
        me,
    And ᴮtake vengeance for me on
        my persecutors.
    Do not, in view of Your
        patience, take me away;
    Know that for Your sake I
        endure reproach.

16 Your words were found and I
        ᴬate them,
    And Your words became a joy
        to me and the delight of my
        heart;
    For I have been ᴮcalled by Your
        name,
    LORD God of armies.

17 I ᴬdid not sit in a circle of
        revelers and celebrate.
    Because of Your hand *upon me*
        I sat alone,
    For You filled me with
        indignation.

18 Why has my pain been endless
    And my ᴬwound incurable,
        refusing to be healed?

15:7 ᴬJer 18:21   ᴮIs 9:13   15:8 ᴬIs 3:25, 26   ᴮJer 22:7
15:9 ᴬ1 Sam 2:5   ᴮJer 6:4   15:10 ᴬJer 1:18, 19; 15:20
15:11 ᴬPs 138:3; Is 41:10   15:12 ᴬJer 28:14
15:13 ᴬJer 17:3   ᴮPs 44:12   15:14 ᴬDeut 28:36, 64
ᴮDeut 32:22   15:15 ᴬJer 12:3   ᴮJer 11:20
15:16 ᴬEzek 3:3   ᴮJer 14:9   15:17 ᴬPs 1:1; Jer 16:8
15:18 ᴬJob 34:6; Jer 30:12, 15

Will You indeed be to me like a
  deceptive *stream*
With water that is unreliable?

19 Therefore, this is what the
      LORD says:
    "ᴬIf you return, then I will
      restore you—
    You will stand before Me;
    And if you extract the precious
      from the worthless,
    You will become My
      spokesman.
    They, for their part, may turn
      to you,
    But as for you, you are not to
      turn to them.
20 "Then I will make you to this
      people
    A fortified wall of bronze;
    And though they fight against
      you,
    They will not prevail over you;
    For ᴬI am with you to save you
    And rescue you," declares the
      LORD.
21 "So I will ᴬrescue you from the
      hand of the wicked,
    And I will ᴮredeem you from
      the grasp of the violent."

DISTRESSES FORETOLD

16 The word of the LORD also
came to me, saying, 2"You
shall not take a wife for yourself
nor have sons or daughters in this
place." 3For this is what the LORD
says concerning the sons and
daughters born in this place, and
concerning their ᴬmothers who
give birth to them, and their ᴮfa-
thers who father them in this land:
4"They will ᴬdie of deadly diseases,
they ᴮwill not be mourned or buried; they will be like dung on the
surface of the ground. And they
will perish by sword and famine,

and their dead bodies will become
food for the birds of the sky and for
the animals of the earth."

5For this is what the LORD says:
"Do not enter a house of ᴬmourning, or go to mourn or to console
them; for I have withdrawn My
peace from this people," declares
the LORD, "*and My* favor and compassion. 6Both great people and
small will die in this land; they
will not be buried, *people* will not
mourn for them, nor will anyone
ᴬmake cuts on himself or have his
head ᴮshaved for them. 7*People* will
not ᴬbreak *bread* in mourning for
them, to comfort anyone for the
dead, nor give them a cup of consolation to drink for anyone's father
or mother. 8Moreover, you shall
ᴬnot go into a house of feasting to
sit with them to eat and drink." 9For
this is what the LORD of armies, the
God of Israel says: "Behold, I am
going to ᴬeliminate from this place,
before your eyes and in your time,
the voice of rejoicing and the voice
of joy, the voice of the groom and
the voice of the bride.

10"Now it will happen that, when
you tell this people all these words,
they will say to you, 'ᴬFor what reason has the LORD declared all this
great disaster against us? And what
is our wrongdoing, or what is our
sin that we have committed against
the LORD our God?' 11Then you are
to say to them, '*It is* ᴬbecause your
forefathers have abandoned Me,'
declares the LORD, 'and have followed other gods, and served and

15:19ᴬJer 4:1; Zech 3:7   15:20ᴬPs 46:7; Is 41:10
15:21ᴬPs 37:40   ᴮGen 48:16   16:3ᴬJer 15:8   ᴮJer 6:21
16:4ᴬJer 15:2   ᴮJer 25:33   16:5ᴬEzek 24:16-23
16:6ᴬDeut 14:1   ᴮIs 22:12   16:7ᴬDeut 26:14;
Ezek 24:17   16:8ᴬEccl 7:2-4; Is 22:12-14
16:9ᴬJer 7:34; 25:10   16:10ᴬDeut 29:24; 1 Kin 9:8
16:11ᴬDeut 29:25; 1 Kin 9:9

worshiped them; but they have abandoned Me and have not kept My Law. [12] You too have done evil, *even* ^more than your forefathers; for behold, each one of you is following the stubbornness of his own evil heart, without listening to Me. [13] So I will ^hurl you off this land to the ^Bland which you have not known, *neither* you nor your fathers; and there you will serve other gods day and night, because I will show you no compassion.'

GOD WILL RESTORE THEM

[14] "Therefore behold, days are coming," declares the LORD, "when it will no longer be said, 'As the LORD lives, who ^brought up the sons of Israel out of the land of Egypt,' [15] but, 'As the LORD lives, who brought up the sons of Israel from the ^land of the north and from all the lands where He had banished them.' For I will restore them to their own land which I gave to their fathers.

[16] "Behold, I am going to send for many ^fishermen," declares the LORD, "and they will fish for them; and afterward I will send for many hunters, and they will hunt them from every mountain and every hill and from the clefts of the rocks. [17] For My eyes are on all their ways; they are not hidden from My face, ^nor is their wrongdoing concealed from My eyes. [18] I will first repay them double for their wrongdoing and their sin, because they have ^defiled My land; they have filled My inheritance with the carcasses of their ^Bdetestable idols and their abominations."

[19] LORD, my ^strength and my
      stronghold,
    And my ^Brefuge in the day of
      distress,

To You the nations will come
From the ends of the earth
  and say,
"Our fathers have inherited
  nothing but falsehood,
Futility, and things of no
  benefit."
[20] Can a person make gods for
      himself?
    But they are ^not gods!

[21] "Therefore behold, I am going
      to make them know—
    This time I will ^make them
      know
    My power and My might;
    And they will know that My
      name is the LORD."

THE DECEITFUL HEART

17

The sin of Judah is written
  with an iron stylus;
With a diamond point it is
  ^engraved on the tablet of
  their hearts
And on the horns of their
  altars,
[2] As they remember their
     ^children,
   So they *remember* their altars
     and their [1,B]Asherim
   By green trees on the high
     hills.
[3] ^Mountain of Mine in the
     countryside,
   I will turn over your wealth
     and all your treasures as
     plunder,
   Your high places for sin
     throughout your borders.

16:12 ^Jer 7:26   **16:13** ^Deut 4:26, 27   ^B Jer 15:14
16:14 ^Ex 20:2; Deut 15:15   **16:15** ^Ps 106:47; Is
11:11-16   **16:16** ^Amos 4:2; Hab 1:14, 15
16:17 ^Jer 2:22   **16:18** ^Num 35:33, 34   ^B Jer 7:30
16:19 ^Ps 18:1, 2   ^B Nah 1:7   **16:20** ^Ps 115:4-8; Is 37:19
16:21 ^Ps 9:16   **17:1** ^Prov 3:3; 7:3   **17:2** ^Jer 7:18
^B Ex 34:13   **17:3** ^Jer 26:18; Mic 3:12

17:2 [1] I.e., wooden symbols of a female deity (Asherah)

4 And you will, even of
   yourself, ^let go of your
   inheritance
   That I gave you;
   And I will make you serve
   your enemies
   In the ^Bland which you do not
   know;
   For you have kindled a fire in
   My anger
   Which will burn forever.

5 This is what the LORD says:
   "^Cursed is the man who trusts
   in mankind
   And makes flesh his
   strength,
   And whose heart turns away
   from the LORD.

6 "For he will be like a ^bush in
   the desert,
   And will not see when
   prosperity comes,
   But will live in stony wastes in
   the wilderness,
   A ^Bland of salt that is not
   inhabited.

7 "Blessed is the man who trusts
   in the LORD,
   And whose ^trust is the LORD.

8 "For he will be like a tree
   planted by the water
   That extends its roots by a
   stream,
   And does not fear when the
   heat comes;
   But its leaves will be green,
   And it will not be anxious in a
   year of ^drought,
   Nor cease to yield fruit.

9 "The ^heart is more ^Bdeceitful
   than all else
   And is desperately sick;
   Who can understand it?

10 "I, the LORD, search the heart,
   I test the mind,

^To give to each person
   according to his ways,
   According to the results of his
   deeds.

11 "As a partridge that hatches
   eggs which it has not laid,
   So is a person who ^makes a
   fortune, but unjustly;
   In the middle of his days it will
   abandon him,
   And in the end he will be a
   ^Bfool."

12 ^A glorious throne on high
   from the beginning
   Is the place of our sanctuary.

13 LORD, the hope of Israel,
   All who ^abandon You will be
   put to shame.
   Those who turn away on earth
   will be ^Bwritten down,
   Because they have forsaken
   the fountain of living water,
   that is the LORD.

14 ^Heal me, LORD, and I will be
   healed;
   ^BSave me and I will be saved,
   For You are my praise.

15 Look, they keep ^saying to me,
   "Where is the word of the
   LORD?
   Let it come now!"

16 But as for me, I have not
   hurried away from being a
   shepherd following after
   You,
   Nor have I longed for the
   disastrous day;
   ^You Yourself know that the
   utterance of my lips
   Was in Your presence.

17:4 ^Jer 12:7   ^BJer 16:13   17:5 ^Ps 146:3; Is 2:22
17:6 ^Jer 48:6   ^BDeut 29:23   17:7 ^Ps 40:4
17:8 ^Jer 14:1-6   17:9 ^Eccl 9:3   ^BRom 7:11
17:10 ^Ps 62:12; Jer 32:19   17:11 ^Jer 6:13   ^BLuke 12:20
17:12 ^Jer 3:17; 14:21   17:13 ^Is 1:28   ^BLuke 10:20
17:14 ^Jer 30:17   ^BPs 54:1   17:15 ^Is 5:19; 2 Pet 3:4
17:16 ^Jer 12:3

17 Do not be a ^terror to me;
   You are my ^Brefuge in a day of
   disaster.
18 Let those who persecute me be
   put to shame, but as for me,
   ^let me not be put to shame;
   Let them be dismayed, but let
   me not be dismayed.
   ^BBring on them a day of
   disaster,
   And crush them with double
   destruction!

THE SABBATH MUST BE KEPT

19 This is what the LORD said to me:
"Go and stand at the public gate,
through which the kings of Judah
come in and go out, as well as at all
the gates of Jerusalem; 20 and say
to them, '^Listen to the word of the
LORD, you kings of Judah, and all
Judah, and all inhabitants of Jerusalem who come in through these
gates. 21 This is what the LORD says:
"Take care for yourselves, and ^do
not carry *any* load on the Sabbath
day or bring *anything* in through
the gates of Jerusalem. 22 You shall
not bring a load out of your houses
on the Sabbath day ^nor do any
work, but keep the Sabbath day
holy, just as I commanded your
forefathers. 23 Yet they did not listen or incline their ears, but ^stiff-
ened their necks so as not to listen
or accept discipline.

24 "But it will come about, if
you ^give your attention to Me,"
declares the LORD, "to bring no load
in through the gates of this city on
the Sabbath day, but to keep the
Sabbath day holy by doing no work
on it, 25 ^then there will come in
through the gates of this city kings
and officials ^Bsitting on the throne
of David, riding in chariots and on
horses, they and their officials, the

men of Judah and the inhabitants
of Jerusalem, and this city will be
inhabited forever. 26 They will come
in from the ^cities of Judah and
from the areas surrounding Jerusalem, from the land of Benjamin,
from the ^Blowland, from the hill
country, and from the Negev, bringing burnt offerings, sacrifices, grain
offerings, and frankincense, and
bringing sacrifices of thanksgiving
to the house of the LORD. 27 But ^if
you do not listen to Me, to keep the
Sabbath day holy by not carrying
a load and coming in through the
gates of Jerusalem on the Sabbath
day, then I will set fire to its gates,
and it will devour the palaces of
Jerusalem and not go out."'"

THE POTTER AND THE CLAY

18 The word that came to Jeremiah from the LORD, saying,
2 "Arise and ^go down to the potter's
house, and there I will announce
My words to you." 3 So I went down
to the potter's house, and there
he was, making something on the
wheel. 4 But the vessel that he was
making of clay was spoiled in the
hand of the potter; so he remade
it into another vessel, as it pleased
the potter to make.

5 Then the word of the LORD
came to me, saying, 6 "Am I not
able, house of Israel, to deal with
you as this potter *does*?" declares
the LORD. "Behold, like the ^clay
in the potter's hand, so are you in
My hand, house of Israel. 7 At one
moment I might speak concerning
a nation or concerning a kingdom

17:17 ^Ps 88:15   ^BJer 16:19   17:18 ^Jer 1:17   ^BPs 35:8
17:20 ^Ezek 2:7   17:21 ^Num 15:32-36; Neh 13:15-21
17:22 ^Ex 16:23-29; 20:8-10   17:23 ^Prov 29:1; Jer 7:26
17:24 ^Ex 15:26; Deut 11:13   17:25 ^Jer 22:4   ^B2 Sam 7:16
17:26 ^Jer 32:44   ^BZech 7:7   17:27 ^Is 1:20; Jer 22:5
18:2 ^Jer 19:1, 2   18:6 ^Is 45:9; 64:8

to ^uproot *it*, to tear *it* down, or to destroy *it*; ⁸^if that nation against which I have spoken turns from its evil, I will ᴮrelent of the disaster that I planned to bring on it. ⁹Or at *another* moment I might speak concerning a nation or concerning a kingdom to ^build up or to plant *it*; ¹⁰if it does ^evil in My sight by not obeying My voice, then I will ᴮrelent of the good with which I said that I would bless it. ¹¹So now, speak to the men of Judah and against the inhabitants of Jerusalem, saying, 'This is what the Lᴏʀᴅ says: "Behold, I am forming a disaster against you and devising a plan against you. Now ^turn back, each of you from his evil way, and correct your ways and your deeds!"' ¹²But they will say, 'It's hopeless! For we are going to follow our own plans, and each of us will persist in the ^stubbornness of his evil heart.'

¹³ "Therefore this is what the
        Lᴏʀᴅ says:
    'Just ask among the nations,
    Who *ever* heard *anything* like
        this?
    The ^virgin of Israel
    Has done a most ᴮappalling
        thing.
¹⁴ 'Does the snow of Lebanon
        leave the rock of the open
        country alone?
    Or is the cold flowing water
        from a foreign *land* ever
        dried up?
¹⁵ 'For ^My people have forgotten
        Me,
    ᴮThey burn incense to
        worthless *gods*.
    And they have stumbled in
        their ways,
    In the ancient roads,
    To walk on paths,
    Not on a highway,

¹⁶ To make their land a
        ^desolation,
    An object of perpetual hissing;
    Everyone who passes by it will
        be astonished
    And shake his head.
¹⁷ 'Like an east wind I will ^scatter
        them
    Before the enemy;
    I will show them ᴮMy back and
        not *My* face
    In the day of their disaster.'"

¹⁸Then they said, "Come and let's ^devise plans against Jeremiah. Certainly the Law is not going to be lost by the priest, nor advice by the wise, nor *the divine* word by the prophet! Come, and let's ᴮstrike at him with *our* tongue, and let's pay no attention to any of his words."

¹⁹ Give *Your* attention to me, Lᴏʀᴅ,
    And listen to what my
        opponents are saying!
²⁰ ^Should good be repaid with
        evil?
    For they have dug a pit for me.
    Remember how I ᴮstood
        before You
    To speak good in their behalf,
    So as to turn Your wrath away
        from them.
²¹ Therefore, ^give their children
        over to famine
    And turn them over to the
        power of the sword;
    And let their wives become
        childless and widowed.
    Let their men also be
        slaughtered to death,
    Their ᴮyoung men struck and
        killed by the sword in battle.

18:7^Jer 1:10   18:8^Jer 7:3-7   ᴮPs 106:45
18:9^Jer 1:10; 31:28   18:10^Ps 125:5   ᴮ1 Sam 2:30
18:11^2 Kin 17:13; Is 1:16-19   18:12^Deut 29:19;
Jer 7:24   18:13^Jer 14:17   ᴮJer 5:30   18:15^Jer 2:32
ᴮIs 65:7   18:16^Jer 25:9; 49:13   18:17^Job 27:21
ᴮJer 2:27   18:18^Jer 11:19   ᴮPs 52:2   18:20^Ps 109:4
ᴮPs 106:23   18:21^Ps 109:9-20   ᴮJer 9:21

22 May a cry be heard from their
     houses
   When You suddenly bring
     raiders upon them;
   ^For they have dug a pit to
     capture me
   And ^Bhidden snares for my feet.
23 But You, LORD, know
   All their deadly schemes
     against me;
   ^Do not forgive their
     wrongdoing
   Or wipe out their sin from
     Your sight.
   But may they be overthrown
     before You;
   Deal with them in the time of
     Your anger!

THE BROKEN JAR

19 This is what the LORD says:
   "Go and buy a potter's earthenware jar, and *take* some of the
^elders of the people and some of
the ^Bsenior priests. ² Then go out to
the ^Valley of Ben-hinnom, which
is by the entrance of the ¹Pot-
sherd Gate, and proclaim there
the words that I tell you, ³ and say,
'Hear the word of the LORD, you
kings of Judah and inhabitants of
Jerusalem. This is what the LORD
of armies, the God of Israel says:
"Behold I am going to bring a ^di-
saster upon this place, at which
the ^Bears of everyone that hears
of it will tingle. ⁴ Since they have
abandoned Me and have ^made
this place foreign, and have burned
sacrifices in it to other gods that
neither they nor their forefathers
nor the kings of Judah had *ever*
known, and *since* they have filled
this place with the ^Bblood of the
innocent ⁵ and have built the ^high
places of Baal to burn their ^Bsons in
the fire as burnt offerings to Baal,

a thing which I did not command
nor speak of, nor did it *ever* enter
My mind; ⁶ therefore, behold, days
are coming," declares the LORD,
"when this place will no longer be
called ^Topheth or ^Bthe Valley of
Ben-hinnom, but rather the Valley
of Slaughter. ⁷ And I will ^frustrate
the planning of Judah and Jerusalem in this place, and ^BI will make
them fall by the sword before their
enemies and by the hand of those
who seek their life; and I will make
their carcasses food for the birds
of the sky and the animals of the
earth. ⁸ I will also turn this city into
an object of ^horror and hissing;
^Beveryone who passes by it will be
appalled and hiss because of all its
disasters. ⁹ And I will make them
^eat the flesh of their sons and the
flesh of their daughters, and they
will eat one another's flesh during
the siege and in the hardship with
which their enemies and those who
seek their life will torment them.'

¹⁰ "Then you are to break the ^jar
in the sight of the men who accompany you, ¹¹ and say to them, 'This
is what the LORD of armies says:
"To the same extent I will ^break
this people and this city, just as
one breaks a potter's vessel, which
cannot again be repaired; and they
will ^Bbury *their dead* in Topheth,
because there is no *other* place for
burial. ¹² This is how I will treat this
place and its inhabitants," declares
the LORD, "so as to make this city

18:22 ^Jer 18:20   ^BPs 140:5   18:23 ^Neh 4:5; Ps 109:14
19:1 ^Num 11:16   ^B2 Kin 9:2   19:2 ^Josh 15:8;
2 Kin 23:10   19:3 ^Jer 6:19   ^B1 Sam 3:11
19:4 ^Ezek 7:22   ^B2 Kin 21:6, 16   19:5 ^Num 22:41
^BLev 18:21   19:6 ^Is 30:33   ^BJosh 15:8
19:7 ^Ps 33:10, 11   ^BLev 26:17   19:8 ^Jer 18:16
^B1 Kin 9:8   19:9 ^Lev 26:29; Deut 28:53, 55
19:10 ^Jer 19:1   19:11 ^Ps 2:9   ^BJer 7:32

19:2 ¹ I.e., pottery fragment

like Topheth. ¹³The houses of Jerusalem and the houses of the kings of Judah will be ^defiled like the place Topheth, because of all the houses on whose rooftops they burned sacrifices to ᴮall the heavenly ¹lights and poured out drink offerings to other gods.""

¹⁴Then Jeremiah came from Topheth, where the Lᴏʀᴅ had sent him to prophesy; and he stood in the ^courtyard of the Lᴏʀᴅ's house and said to all the people, ¹⁵"This is what the Lᴏʀᴅ of armies, the God of Israel says: 'Behold, I am going to bring on this city and all its towns the entire disaster that I have declared against it, because they have stiffened their necks so ^as not to listen to My words.'"

PASHHUR PERSECUTES JEREMIAH

20 When Pashhur the priest, the son of Immer, who was ^chief overseer in the house of the Lᴏʀᴅ, heard Jeremiah prophesying these things, ²Pashhur had Jeremiah the prophet ^beaten and put him in the ᴮstocks that were at the upper Benjamin Gate, which was by the house of the Lᴏʀᴅ. ³Then on the next day, when Pashhur released Jeremiah from the stocks, Jeremiah said to him, "Pashhur is not the name the Lᴏʀᴅ has ^called you, but rather ¹,ᴮMagor-missabib. ⁴For this is what the Lᴏʀᴅ says: 'Behold, I am going to make you a horror to yourself and to all your friends; and while your eyes look on, they will fall by the sword of their enemies. So I will ^hand all Judah over to the king of Babylon, and he will take them away as ᴮexiles to Babylon and will kill them with the sword. ⁵I will also give all the ^wealth of this city, all

its produce and all its valuable things—even all the treasures of the kings of Judah I will ᴮhand over to their enemies, and they will plunder them, take them away, and bring them to Babylon. ⁶And you, Pashhur, and all who live in your house will go into captivity; and you will enter Babylon, and there you will die and there you will be buried, you and all your ^friends to whom you have ᴮfalsely prophesied.'"

JEREMIAH'S COMPLAINT

7   Lᴏʀᴅ, You persuaded me and I
        let myself be persuaded;
    You have overcome me and
        prevailed.
    I have become a
        ^laughingstock all day long;
    Everyone ᴮmocks me.
8   For each time I speak, I cry
        aloud;
    I proclaim violence and
        destruction,
    Because for me the ^word of
        the Lᴏʀᴅ has resulted
    In taunting and derision all
        day long.
9   But *if* I say, "I will not
        remember Him
    Nor speak anymore in His
        name,"
    Then in ^my heart it becomes
        like a burning fire
    Shut up in my bones;
    And I am tired of holding *it* in,
    And ᴮI cannot endure *it*.

19:13^2 Kin 23:10   ᴮDeut 4:19   **19:14**^2 Chr 20:5; Jer 26:2   **19:15**^Ps 58:4   **20:1**^2 Kin 25:18   **20:2**^1 Kin 22:27   ᴮJob 13:27   **20:3**^Is 8:3   ᴮJer 6:25   **20:4**^Jer 21:4-10   ᴮJer 13:10   **20:5**^Jer 15:13   ᴮ2 Kin 20:17, 18   **20:6**^Jer 20:4   ᴮJer 14:14, 15   **20:7**^Job 12:4   ᴮPs 22:7   **20:8**^2 Chr 36:16; Jer 6:10   **20:9**^Ezek 3:14   ᴮJob 32:18-20

19:13¹Lit *host*; i.e., sun, stars, etc.   **20:3**¹I.e., horror on every side

10 For I have heard the
    whispering of many,
    "^ATerror on every side!
    ^BDenounce *him;* let's
    denounce him!"
   All my trusted friends,
   Watching for my fall, say:
   "Perhaps he will be persuaded,
    so that we may prevail
    against him
   And take our revenge on him."
11 But the ^ALᴏʀᴅ is with me like a
    powerful champion;
   Therefore my persecutors will
    stumble and not prevail.
   They will be put to great shame
    because they have failed,
   An ^Beverlasting disgrace that
    will not be forgotten.
12 Yet, Lᴏʀᴅ of armies, who ^Atests
    the righteous,
   Who sees the mind and the
    heart;
   Let me see Your vengeance on
    them,
   For ^Bto You I have disclosed my
    cause.
13 Sing to the Lᴏʀᴅ, praise the
    Lᴏʀᴅ!
   For He has ^Asaved the soul of
    the needy one
   From the hand of evildoers.

14 Cursed be the ^Aday when I was
    born;
   May the day when my mother
    gave birth to me not be
    blessed!
15 Cursed be the man who
    brought the news
   To my father, saying,
   "A ^Aboy has been born to you!"
   And made him very happy.
16 But may that man be like the
    cities
   Which the Lᴏʀᴅ ^Aoverthrew
    without relenting,

   And may he hear an outcry in
    the morning
   And an alarm for war at noon;
17 Because he did not ^Akill me
    before birth,
   So that my mother would have
    been my grave,
   And her womb forever
    pregnant.
18 Why did I ever come out of the
    womb
   To ^Alook at trouble and sorrow,
   So that my days have been
    spent in shame?

JEREMIAH'S MESSAGE FOR ZEDEKIAH

21 The word that came to Jeremiah from the Lᴏʀᴅ when ^AKing Zedekiah sent to him Pashhur the son of Malchijah and Zephaniah the priest, the son of Maaseiah, saying, 2 "Please inquire of the Lᴏʀᴅ in our behalf, because ^ANebuchadnezzar king of ^BBabylon is making war against us; perhaps the Lᴏʀᴅ will deal with us in accordance with all His wonderful acts, so that *the enemy* will withdraw from us."

3 But Jeremiah said to them, "You shall say to Zedekiah as follows: 4 'This is what the Lᴏʀᴅ, the God of Israel says: "Behold, I am going to ^Aturn back the weapons of war that are in your hands, with which you are making war against the king of Babylon and the Chaldeans who are besieging you outside the wall; and I will gather them into the middle of this city. 5 And I ^AMyself will make war against you with an ^Boutstretched hand and a mighty

20:10 ^AJer 6:25   ^BNeh 6:6-13   20:11 ^AJer 1:8
^BJer 23:40   20:12 ^APs 7:9   ^BPs 62:8   20:13 ^APs 34:6;
69:33   20:14 ^AJob 3:3-6; Jer 15:10   20:15 ^AGen 21:6, 7
20:16 ^AGen 19:25   20:17 ^AJob 3:10, 11, 16; 10:18, 19
20:18 ^AJob 3:20; 5:7   21:1 ^A2 Kin 24:17, 18; Jer 32:1-3
21:2 ^A2 Kin 25:1   ^BGen 10:10   21:4 ^AJer 32:5; 33:5
21:5 ^AIs 63:10   ^BEx 6:6

arm, and in anger, wrath, and great indignation. ⁶I will also strike the inhabitants of this city, both the people and the animals; they will die of a great ^plague. ⁷Then afterward," declares the LORD, "^I will hand Zedekiah king of Judah, his servants, and the people, that is, those who survive in this city from the plague, the sword, and the famine, over to Nebuchadnezzar king of Babylon, to their enemies, and to those who seek their lives; and he will strike and kill them with the edge of the sword. He will not spare them nor have pity nor compassion."'

⁸"You shall also say to this people, 'This is what the LORD says: "Behold, I am ^setting before you the way of life and the way of death. ⁹*Anyone* who ^stays in this city will die by the ᴮsword, by famine, or by plague; but *anyone* who leaves and goes over to the Chaldeans who are besieging you will live, and he will have his own life as plunder. ¹⁰For I have ^set My face against this city for harm and not for good," declares the LORD. "It will be handed over to the king of Babylon and he will burn it with fire."'

¹¹"Then *say* to the household of the ^king of Judah, 'Hear the word of the LORD, ¹²house of David, this is what the LORD says:

"^Administer justice every
　　morning;
And save the *person* who has
　　been robbed from the power
　　of *his* oppressor,
ᴮSo that My wrath will not
　　spread like fire
And burn, with no one to
　　extinguish *it*,
Because of the evil of their
　　deeds.

¹³ "Behold, ^I am against you, you
　　inhabitant of the ᴮvalley,
　　You rocky plain," declares the
　　LORD,
"You who say, 'Who will come
　　down against us?
Or who will enter our
　　dwellings?'

¹⁴ "But I will punish you ^according
　　to the results of your deeds,"
　　declares the LORD,
"And I will kindle a fire in its
　　forest
So that it may devour all its
　　surroundings."'"

WARNING OF JERUSALEM'S FALL

22 This is what the LORD says: "Go down to the house of the king of Judah and there speak this word, ²and say, 'Hear the word of the LORD, O king of Judah, who ^sits on David's throne, you and your servants and your people who enter these gates. ³This is what the LORD says: "^Do justice and righteousness, and save one who has been robbed from the power of *his* oppressor. And ᴮdo not mistreat *or* do violence to the stranger, the orphan, or the widow; and do not shed innocent blood in this place. ⁴For if you will indeed perform this instruction, then ^kings will enter the gates of this house, sitting in David's place on his throne, riding in chariots and on horses, *the king* himself, his servants, and his people. ⁵^But if you will not obey these words, I ᴮswear by Myself," declares the LORD, "that this house

21:6 ^Jer 14:12; 32:24　21:7 ^2 Kin 25:5-7, 18-21;
Jer 37:17　21:8 ^Deut 30:15, 19; Is 1:19, 20
21:9 ^Jer 38:2, 17-23　ᴮJer 14:12
21:10 ^Lev 17:10; Jer 44:11, 27　21:11 ^Jer 17:20
21:12 ^Ps 72:1　ᴮJer 4:4　21:13 ^Jer 23:30-32
ᴮPs 125:2　21:14 ^Is 3:10, 11　22:2 ^Is 9:7; Jer 17:25
22:3 ^Is 58:6, 7　ᴮEx 22:21-24　22:4 ^Jer 17:25
22:5 ^Jer 17:27　ᴮGen 22:16

will become a place of ruins.”’” ⁶For this is what the LORD says concerning the house of the king of Judah:

"You are *like* Gilead to Me,
Like the summit of Lebanon;
Yet most assuredly I will make
    you a ᴬwilderness,
Cities that are not inhabited.
7 "For I will set apart ᴬdestroyers
    against you,
Each with his weapons;
And they will cut down your
    choicest cedars
And throw *them* on the fire.

⁸"Many nations will pass by this city; and they will ᴬsay to one another, ‘Why has the LORD done this to this great city?’ ⁹Then they will answer, ‘Because they ᴬabandoned the covenant of the LORD their God and bowed down to other gods and served them.’"

10 ᴬDo not weep for the dead or
    mourn for him,
But weep deeply for the one
    who goes away;
For ᴮhe will never return
Or see his native land.

¹¹For this is what the LORD says regarding ᴬShallum the son of Josiah, king of Judah, who became king in the place of his father Josiah, who went out from this place: "He will never return there; ¹²but in the place where they took him into exile, there he will ᴬdie and he will not see this land again.

MESSAGES ABOUT THE KINGS

13 "Woe to him who builds his
    house ᴬwithout righteousness,
And his upstairs rooms
    without justice,
Who uses his neighbor's
    services without pay
And does not give him his
    wages,

14 Who says, ‘I will ᴬbuild myself
    a large house
With spacious upstairs rooms,
And cut out its windows,
Paneling *it* with ᴮcedar and
    painting *it* bright red.’
15 "Do you become a king
    because you are competing
    in cedar?
Did your father not eat and
    drink
And ᴬdo justice and
    righteousness?
Then it was ᴮwell for him.
16 "He pled the cause of the
    afflicted and the poor,
Then it was well.
ᴬIs that not *what it means* to
    know Me?"
Declares the LORD.
17 "But your eyes and your heart
Are *intent* only upon your
    own ᴬdishonest gain,
And on ᴮshedding innocent
    blood,
And on practicing oppression
    and extortion."

¹⁸Therefore this is what the LORD says regarding ᴬJehoiakim the son of Josiah, king of Judah:

"They will not mourn for him:
‘Oh, my brother!’ or, ‘Oh, sister!’
They will not mourn for him:
‘Oh, for the master!’ or, ‘Oh, for
    his splendor!’
19 "He will be ᴬburied with a
    donkey's burial,
Dragged off and thrown
    out beyond the gates of
    Jerusalem.

22:6 ᴬPs 107:34; Is 6:11   22:7 ᴬIs 10:3-6; Jer 4:6, 7
22:8 ᴬDeut 29:24-26; 1 Kin 9:8, 9   22:9 ᴬ2 Kin 22:17;
2 Chr 34:25   22:10 ᴬEccl 4:2   ᴮJer 25:27
22:11 ᴬ2 Kin 23:30-34; 1 Chr 3:15   22:12 ᴬ2 Kin 23:34;
Jer 22:18   22:13 ᴬJer 17:11; Mic 3:10   22:14 ᴬIs 5:8
ᴮ2 Sam 7:2   22:15 ᴬ2 Kin 23:25   ᴮPs 128:2
22:16 ᴬ1 Chr 28:9; Jer 9:24   22:17 ᴬJer 6:13
ᴮ2 Kin 24:4   22:18 ᴬ2 Kin 23:36-24:6; 2 Chr 36:5
22:19 ᴬ1 Kin 21:23, 24; Jer 36:30

20 "Go up to Lebanon and cry out,
   And raise your voice in Bashan;
   Cry out also from ^Abarim,
   For all your lovers have been
      crushed.
21 "I spoke to you in your
      prosperity;
   But ^you said, 'I will not listen!'
   This has been your way ^Bfrom
      your youth,
   That you have not obeyed My
      voice.
22 "The wind will sweep away all
      your shepherds,
   And your ^lovers will go into
      captivity;
   Then you will certainly be
      ^Bashamed and humiliated
   Because of all your wickedness.
23 "You who live in Lebanon,
   Nested in the cedars,
   How you will groan when
      sharp pains come on you,
   ^Pain like a woman in
      childbirth!
24 "As I live," declares the LORD,
"even if ^1,^AConiah the son of
Jehoiakim king of Judah were a
signet *ring* on My right hand, yet I
would pull you off; 25 and I will ^hand
you over to those who are seeking
your life, yes, to those of whom you
are frightened, that is, to Nebuchadnezzar king of Babylon and the Chaldeans. 26 I will ^hurl you and your
^Bmother who gave birth to you into
another country where you were not
born, and there you will die. 27 But as
for the land to which they long to
return, they will not return to it.
28 "Is this man Coniah a despised,
      shattered jar?
   Or is he an undesirable vessel?
   Why have he and his
      descendants been ^hurled out
   And cast into a ^Bland that they
      had not known?

29 "^AO land, land, land,
   Hear the word of the LORD!
30 This is what the LORD says:
   'Write this man down *as*
      ^Achildless,
   A man who will not prosper
      in his days;
   For no man among his
      descendants will prosper
   Sitting on the throne of
      David
   Or ruling again in Judah.'"

THE COMING MESSIAH:
THE RIGHTEOUS BRANCH

23 "Woe to the shepherds who
are causing the ^sheep of
My pasture to ^Bperish and are scattering *them!*" declares the LORD.
2 Therefore this is what the LORD,
the God of Israel says concerning
the shepherds who are tending
My people: "You have scattered My
flock and driven them away, and
have not been concerned about
them; behold, I am going to ^call
you to account for the ^Bevil of your
deeds," declares the LORD. 3 "Then
I Myself will ^gather the remnant
of My flock out of all the countries where I have driven them,
and bring them back to their pasture, and they will be fruitful and
multiply. 4 I will also raise up shepherds over them and they will tend
them; and they will ^not be afraid
any longer, nor be terrified, ^Bnor
will any be missing," declares the
LORD.

22:20 ^Num 27:12; Deut 32:49   22:21 ^Jer 13:10
^B Jer 3:24   22:22 ^Jer 30:14   ^B Is 65:13   22:23 ^Jer 4:31;
6:24   22:24 ^2 Kin 24:6; 1 Chr 3:16
22:25 ^2 Kin 24:15, 16; Jer 21:7   22:26 ^2 Kin 24:15
^B 2 Kin 24:8   22:28 ^Jer 15:1   ^B Jer 17:4
22:29 ^Deut 4:26; Jer 6:19   22:30 ^1 Chr 3:17;
Matt 1:12   23:1 ^Ezek 34:31   ^B Is 56:9-12
23:2 ^Ex 32:34   ^B Jer 21:12   23:3 ^Is 11:11, 12, 16;
Jer 31:7, 8   23:4 ^Jer 30:10   ^B John 6:39

22:24 ¹ I.e., Jehoiachin

5 "Behold, *the* days are coming,"
    declares the LORD,
  "When I will raise up for David
    a righteous ᴬBranch;
  And He will ᴮreign as king and
    act wisely
  And do justice and
    righteousness in the land.
6 "In His days Judah will be saved,
    And Israel will live securely;
  And this is His ᴬname by which
    He will be called,
  'The ᴮLORD Our Righteousness.'
7 "ᴬTherefore behold, *the* days are
coming," declares the LORD, "when
they will no longer say, 'As the LORD
lives, who brought the sons of Israel
up from the land of Egypt,' 8but, 'As
the LORD lives, who ᴬbrought up and
led the descendants of the household of Israel *back* from *the* north
land and from all the countries
where I had driven them.' Then
they will live on their own soil."

FALSE PROPHETS DENOUNCED

9 As for the prophets:
  My ᴬheart is broken within me,
    All my bones tremble;
  I have become like a drunken
    man,
  And like a man overcome by
    wine,
  Because of the LORD
  And because of His holy words.
10 For the land is full of ᴬadulterers;
  For the land mourns because
    of the curse.
    The ᴮpastures of the
      wilderness have dried up.
  Their course is evil
  And their might is not right.
11 "For ᴬboth prophet and priest
    are defiled;
  Even in My house I have found
    their wickedness," declares
    the LORD.

12 "Therefore their way will be
    like slippery paths to
    them,
  They will be driven away into
    the gloom and fall down in
    it;
  For I will bring ᴬdisaster upon
    them,
  The year of their
    punishment," declares the
    LORD.

13 "Moreover, among the prophets
    of Samaria I saw an offensive
    thing:
  They ᴬprophesied by Baal and
    ᴮled My people Israel astray.
14 "Also among the prophets of
    Jerusalem I have seen a
    horrible thing:
  The committing of ᴬadultery
    and walking in deceit;
  And they strengthen the
    hands of ᴮevildoers,
  So that no one has turned
    back from his wickedness.
  All of them have become to
    Me like Sodom,
  And her inhabitants like
    Gomorrah.
15Therefore this is what the LORD
of armies says concerning the
prophets:
  'Behold, I am going to ᴬfeed
    them wormwood
  And make them drink
    poisonous water,
  For from the prophets of
    Jerusalem
  Ungodliness has spread into
    all the land.'"

23:5 ᴬIs 4:2 ᴮIs 9:7 23:6 ᴬIs 7:14 ᴮIs 45:24
23:7 ᴬIs 43:18, 19; Jer 16:14, 15 23:8 ᴬIs 43:5, 6;
Ezek 34:13 23:9 ᴬJer 8:18; Hab 3:16 23:10 ᴬJer 9:2
ᴮPs 107:34 23:11 ᴬJer 6:13; Zeph 3:4
23:12 ᴬJer 11:23 23:13 ᴬ1 Kin 18:18-21 ᴮIs 9:16
23:14 ᴬJer 29:23 ᴮJer 23:22
23:15 ᴬDeut 29:18; Jer 8:14

16 This is what the LORD of
   armies says:
"ᴬDo not listen to the words
   of the prophets who are
   prophesying to you.
They are ᴮleading you into
   futility;
They tell a vision of their own
   imagination,
Not from the mouth of the
   LORD.
17 "They keep saying to those who
   despise Me,
   'The LORD has said, "ᴬYou will
      have peace"';
   And as for everyone who
      walks in the stubbornness of
      his own heart,
   They say, 'ᴮDisaster will not
      come on you.'
18 "But who has stood in the
   council of the LORD,
   That he should see and hear
      His word?
   Who has paid ᴬattention to His
      word and listened?
19 "Behold, the ᴬstorm of the LORD
   has gone forth in wrath,
   Even a whirling tempest;
   It will swirl down on the head
      of the wicked.
20 "The ᴬanger of the LORD will not
   turn back
   Until He has ᴮperformed and
      carried out the purposes of
      His heart;
   In the last days you will clearly
      understand it.
21 "ᴬI did not send these prophets,
   But they ran.
   I did not speak to them,
   But they prophesied.
22 "But if they had ᴬstood in My
   council,
   Then they would have
      ᴮannounced My words to My
      people,

And would have turned them
   back from their evil way
And from the evil of their deeds.

23 "Am I a God who is ᴬnear,"
   declares the LORD,
   "And not a God far off?
24 "Can a person hide himself in
   hiding places
   So that I do not see him?"
      declares the LORD.
"ᴬDo I not fill the heavens and
   the earth?" declares the LORD.
25 "I have heard what the prophets
have said who ᴬprophesy falsely in
My name, saying, 'I had a dream,
I had a dream!' 26 How long? Is
there *anything* in the hearts of the
prophets who prophesy falsehood,
these prophets of the ᴬdeceitfulness
of their own heart, 27 who intend to
ᴬmake My people forget My name
by their dreams which they report
to one another, just as their fathers
forgot My name because of Baal?
28 The prophet who has a dream
may report *his* dream, but let him
who has ᴬMy word speak My word
truthfully. ᴮWhat does straw have
in common with grain?" declares
the LORD. 29 "Is My word not like
ᴬfire?" declares the LORD, "and like
a ᴮhammer *which* shatters a rock?
30 Therefore behold, ᴬI am against
the prophets," declares the LORD,
"who steal My words from each
other. 31 Behold, I am against the
prophets," declares the LORD, "who
use their tongues and declare,
'*The Lord* declares!' 32 Behold, I am
against those who have prophesied

23:16 ᴬJer 27:9, 10, 14-17 ᴮMatt 7:15 23:17 ᴬJer 8:11
ᴮJer 5:12 23:18 ᴬJob 33:31 23:19 ᴬJer 25:32; 30:23
23:20 ᴬ2 Kin 23:26, 27 ᴮIs 55:11 23:21 ᴬJer 14:14;
23:32 23:22 ᴬJer 9:12 ᴮJer 35:15 23:23 ᴬPs 139:1-10
23:24 ᴬ1 Kin 8:27; 2 Chr 2:6 23:25 ᴬJer 14:14
23:26 ᴬ1 Tim 4:1, 2 23:27 ᴬDeut 13:1-3; Jer 29:8
23:28 ᴬJer 9:12, 20 ᴮ1 Cor 3:12, 13 23:29 ᴬJer 5:14
ᴮ2 Cor 10:4, 5 23:30 ᴬDeut 18:20; Ps 34:16

^false dreams," declares the LORD, "and reported them and led My people astray by their lies and reckless boasting; yet ^BI did not send them nor command them, nor do they provide this people the slightest benefit," declares the LORD.

33 "Now when this people or the prophet or a priest asks you, saying, 'What is the ¹,^pronouncement of the LORD?' then you shall say to them, 'What pronouncement?' The LORD declares, 'I will abandon you.' 34 Then as for the prophet or the priest or the people who say, 'The ^pronouncement of the LORD,' I will bring punishment upon that person and his household. 35 This is what each one of you will say to his neighbor and to his brother: '^What has the LORD answered?' or, 'What has the LORD spoken?' 36 For you will no longer remember the pronouncement of the LORD, because every person's own word will become the pronouncement, and you have ^perverted the words of the living God, the LORD of armies, our God. 37 This is what you will say to that prophet: 'What has the LORD answered you?' and, 'What has the LORD spoken?' 38 And if you say, 'The pronouncement of the LORD!' for that reason the LORD says this: 'Because you said this word, "The pronouncement of the LORD!" I have also sent word to you, saying, "You shall not say, 'The pronouncement of the LORD!'"' 39 Therefore behold, ^I will certainly forget you and thrust you away from My presence, along with the city which I gave you and your fathers. 40 I will put an everlasting ^disgrace on you and an everlasting humiliation which will not be forgotten."

BASKETS OF FIGS AND THE RETURNEES

24 After ^Nebuchadnezzar king of Babylon had taken into exile Jeconiah the son of Jehoiakim, king of Judah, and the officials of Judah with the craftsmen and metalworkers from Jerusalem and had brought them to Babylon, the LORD showed me: behold, two baskets of figs placed before the temple of the LORD. 2 One basket had very good figs, like ^first-ripe figs, and the other basket had ^Bvery bad figs which could not be eaten due to rottenness. 3 Then the LORD said to me, "^What do you see, Jeremiah?" And I said, "Figs: the good figs *are* very good, and the bad *ones,* very bad, which cannot be eaten due to rottenness."

4 Then the word of the LORD came to me, saying, 5 "This is what the LORD, the God of Israel says: 'Like these good figs, so I will regard ^as good the captives of Judah, whom I have sent out of this place *into* the land of the Chaldeans. 6 For I will set My eyes on them for good, and I will ^bring them back to this land; and I will build them up and not overthrow them, and I will ^Bplant them and not uproot them. 7 I will also give them a ^heart to know Me, for I am the LORD; and they will be My people, and I will be their God, for they will return to Me wholeheartedly.

8 'But like the bad figs which cannot be eaten due to rottenness,' indeed, this is what the LORD says, 'so will I give up Zedekiah king of

23:32 ^Deut 13:1, 2   ^BJer 23:21   23:33 ^Is 13:1; Nah 1:1
23:34 ^Lam 2:14; Zech 13:3   23:35 ^Jer 33:3; 42:4
23:36 ^Gal 1:7, 8; 2 Pet 3:16   23:39 ^Jer 7:14, 15; 23:33
23:40 ^Jer 20:11; 42:18   24:1 ^2 Kin 24:10–16;
2 Chr 36:10   24:2 ^Mic 7:1   ^BIs 5:4, 7
24:3 ^Jer 1:11, 13; Amos 8:2   24:5 ^Nah 1:7; Zech 13:9
24:6 ^Jer 12:15   ^BJer 32:41   24:7 ^Deut 30:6; Jer 31:33

23:33 ¹Or *burden,* and so throughout the ch

Judah and his officials, and the ᴬremnant of Jerusalem who remain in this land, and the ones who live in the land of ᴮEgypt. ⁹I will ᴬmake them an object of terror *and an* evil for all the kingdoms of the earth, as a disgrace and a proverb, a taunt and a ᴮcurse in all the places where I will scatter them. ¹⁰And I will send the ᴬsword, the famine, and the plague upon them until they are eliminated from the land which I gave to them and their forefathers.'"

PROPHECY OF THE CAPTIVITY

25 The word that came to Jeremiah concerning all the people of Judah, in the fourth year of ᴬJehoiakim the son of Josiah, king of Judah (that was the ᴮfirst year of Nebuchadnezzar king of Babylon), ²*the word* which Jeremiah the prophet spoke to all the ᴬpeople of Judah and to all the inhabitants of Jerusalem, saying, ³"From the thirteenth year of ᴬJosiah the son of Amon, king of Judah, even to this day, these ᴮtwenty-three years the word of the Lᴏʀᴅ has come to me, and I have spoken to you again and again, but you have not listened. ⁴And the Lᴏʀᴅ has sent to you all His ᴬservants the prophets again and again, but you have not listened nor inclined your ear to hear, ⁵saying, 'ᴬTurn now, everyone from his evil way and from the evil of your deeds, and live on the land which the Lᴏʀᴅ has given to you and your forefathers forever and ever; ⁶and ᴬdo not follow other gods to serve them and to worship them, and do not provoke Me to anger with the work of your hands, then I will do you no harm.' ⁷Yet you have not listened to Me,"

declares the Lᴏʀᴅ, "in order to ᴬprovoke Me to anger with the work of your hands to your own harm.

⁸"Therefore this is what the Lᴏʀᴅ of armies says: 'Because you have not obeyed My words, ⁹behold, I will send and take all the families of the north,' declares the Lᴏʀᴅ, 'and *I will send* to Nebuchadnezzar king of Babylon, ᴬMy servant, and will bring them against this land and against its inhabitants and against all these surrounding nations; and I will completely destroy them and ᴮmake them an object of horror and hissing, and an everlasting place of ruins. ¹⁰Moreover, I will ᴬeliminate from them the voice of jubilation and the voice of joy, the voice of the groom and the voice of the bride, the sound of the millstones and the light of the lamp. ¹¹This entire land will be a place of ruins and an object of horror, and these nations will serve the king of Babylon for ᴬseventy years.

BABYLON WILL BE JUDGED

¹²'Then it will be ᴬwhen seventy years are completed I will ᴮpunish the king of Babylon and that nation,' declares the Lᴏʀᴅ, 'for their wrongdoing, and the land of the Chaldeans; and I will make it an everlasting desolation. ¹³I will bring upon that land all My words which I have pronounced against it, all that is written in ᴬthis book which Jeremiah has prophesied against all the nations. ¹⁴(For ᴬmany nations and great kings will make

24:8 ᴬJer 39:9   ᴮJer 44:1, 26–30   24:9 ᴬJer 15:4
ᴮIs 65:15   24:10 ᴬIs 51:19; Jer 21:9   25:1 ᴬ2 Kin 24:1, 2
ᴮJer 32:1   25:2 ᴬJer 18:11   25:3 ᴬ2 Chr 34:1–3, 8
ᴮJer 36:2   25:4 ᴬ2 Chr 36:15; Jer 26:5   25:5 ᴬ2 Kin 17:13;
Is 55:6, 7   25:6 ᴬDeut 6:14; 8:19   25:7 ᴬ2 Kin 17:17; 21:15
25:9 ᴬIs 13:3   ᴮ1 Kin 9:7, 8   25:10 ᴬIs 24:8–11; Jer 7:34
25:11 ᴬ2 Chr 36:21; Jer 29:10   25:12 ᴬEzra 1:1   ᴮIs 13:14
25:13 ᴬJer 36:4, 29, 32   25:14 ᴬJer 27:7

slaves of them, even them; and I will ᴮrepay them according to their deeds and according to the work of their hands.)'"

15 For this is what the LORD, the God of Israel, says to me: "Take this ᴬcup of the wine of wrath from My hand and give it to all the nations to whom I send you, to drink *from it.* 16 Then they will ᴬdrink and loudly vomit and act insanely because of the sword that I am going to send among them."

17 So I took the cup from the LORD's hand and ᴬgave it to all the nations to whom the LORD sent me, to drink *from it:* 18 To ᴬJerusalem and the cities of Judah, and its kings *and* its officials, to make them places of ruins, objects of horror, hissing, and a curse, as it is this day; 19 To ᴬPharaoh king of Egypt, his servants, his officials, and all his people; 20 and *to* all the ᴬforeign people, all the kings of the ᴮland of Uz, all the kings of the land of the Philistines (that is, Ashkelon, Gaza, Ekron, and the remnant of Ashdod); 21 *To* Edom, ᴬMoab, and the sons of ᴮAmmon; 22 and *to* all the kings of Tyre, all the kings of Sidon, and the kings of ᴬthe coastlands which are beyond the sea; 23 and *to* Dedan, Tema, ᴬBuz, and all who ᴮtrim the corners *of their hair;* 24 and *to* all the kings of ᴬArabia and all the kings of the ᴮforeign people who live in the desert; 25 and *to* all the kings of Zimri, all the kings of ᴬElam, and all the kings of Media; 26 and *to* all the kings of the north, near and far, one with another; and ᴬall the kingdoms of the earth which are on the face of the ground; and the king of Sheshach shall drink *it* after them.

27 "And you shall say to them, 'This is what the LORD of armies, the God of Israel says: "Drink, be drunk, vomit, fall down, and do not get up, because of the ᴬsword which I am sending among you."' 28 And if they ᴬrefuse to take the cup from your hand to drink, then you shall say to them, 'This is what the LORD of armies says: "You shall certainly drink! 29 For behold, I am beginning to inflict disaster on *this* city which is ᴬcalled by My name, so should you be completely free from punishment? You will not be free from punishment, for ᴮI am summoning a sword against all the inhabitants of the earth," declares the LORD of armies.'

30 "Therefore you shall prophesy against them all these words, and you shall say to them,

'The LORD will ᴬroar from on
    high
And raise His voice from His
    holy dwelling;
He will roar forcefully against
    His fold.
He will shout like those who
    tread *the grapes,*
Against all the inhabitants of
    the earth.
31 'A clamor has come to the end
    of the earth,
Because the LORD has ᴬa
    controversy with the
    nations.

25:14 ᴮJer 51:6, 24, 56   25:15 ᴬJob 21:20; Ps 75:8
25:16 ᴬNah 3:11   25:17 ᴬJer 1:10; 25:28
25:18 ᴬPs 60:3; Is 51:17   25:19 ᴬJer 46:2-28; Nah
3:8-10   25:20 ᴬJer 25:24   25:21 ᴬJob 1:1   25:21 ᴬJer
48:1-47   ᴮJer 49:1-6   25:22 ᴬJer 31:10
25:23 ᴬGen 22:21   ᴮJer 9:26   25:24 ᴬ2 Chr 9:14
ᴮJer 25:20   25:25 ᴬGen 10:22; Is 11:11
25:26 ᴬJer 25:9; 50:9   25:27 ᴬEzek 21:4, 5
25:28 ᴬJob 34:33   25:29 ᴬ1 Kin 8:43
ᴮEzek 38:21   25:30 ᴬJoel 2:11; 3:16
25:31 ᴬHos 4:1; Mic 6:2

He is entering into judgment
　with humanity;
As for the wicked, He has
　turned them over to the
　sword,' declares the LORD."

³² This is what the LORD of
　armies says:
"Behold, evil is going out
　From nation to nation,
And a great ^storm is being
　stirred up
From the remotest parts of the
　earth.
³³ "Those ^put to death by the
LORD on that day will be from one
end of the earth to the other. They
will not be mourned, gathered, or
buried; they will be like dung on
the face of the ground.
³⁴ "Wail, you shepherds, and cry
　out;
^Wallow *in the dust,* you
　masters of the flock;
For the days of your
　ᴮslaughter and your
　dispersions have come,
And you will fall like a
　precious vessel.
³⁵ "There will be ^no sanctuary
　for the shepherds,
Nor escape for the masters of
　the flock.
³⁶ "*Hear* the sound of the cry of
　the shepherds,
And the wailing of the
　masters of the flock!
For the LORD is destroying
　their pasture,
³⁷ And the peaceful ^grazing
　places are devastated
Because of the ᴮfierce anger
　of the LORD.
³⁸ "He has left His hiding place
^like the lion;
For their land has become a
　horror

Because of the fierceness of
　the oppressing *sword*
And because of His fierce
　anger."

CITIES OF JUDAH WARNED

26 In the beginning of the
reign of ^Jehoiakim the son
of Josiah, king of Judah, this word
came from the LORD, saying, ²"This
is what the LORD says: 'Stand in the
courtyard of the LORD's house, and
speak to all the cities of Judah who
have come to worship *in* the LORD's
house ^all the words that I have
commanded you to speak to them.
ᴮDo not omit a word! ³Perhaps they
will listen and everyone will turn
from his evil way, and ^I will relent
of the disaster which I am planning
to inflict on them because of the
evil of their deeds.' ⁴And you shall
say to them, 'This is what the LORD
says: "^If you do not listen to Me,
to ᴮwalk in My Law which I have
set before you, ⁵to listen to the
words of ^My servants the prophets, whom I have been sending to
you again and again, but you have
not listened; ⁶then I will make this
house like Shiloh, and I will make
this city a ^curse to all the nations
of the earth."'"

A PLOT TO MURDER JEREMIAH

⁷The ^priests and the prophets
and all the people heard Jeremiah
speaking these words in the house
of the LORD. ⁸Yet when Jeremiah
finished speaking everything that
the LORD had commanded *him* to

25:32 ^Is 30:30; Jer 23:19　25:33 ^Is 34:2, 3; 66:16
25:34 ^Jer 6:26　ᴮIs 34:6, 7　25:35 ^Job 11:20; Jer 11:11
25:37 ^Is 27:10, 11　ᴮPs 97:1-3　25:38 ^Jer 4:7; 5:6
26:1 ^2 Kin 23:36; 2 Chr 36:4, 5　26:2 ^Jer 1:17
ᴮDeut 4:2　26:3 ^Jer 18:8; Jon 3:8　26:4 ^Lev 26:14
ᴮJer 32:23　26:5 ^2 Kin 9:7; Ezra 9:11
26:6 ^2 Kin 22:19; Is 65:15　26:7 ^Jer 5:31; Mic 3:11

speak to all the people, *then* the priests and the prophets and all the people seized him, saying, "^You must die! ⁹Why have you prophesied in the name of the Lord, saying, 'This house will be like Shiloh and this city will be in ruins, without inhabitant'?" And ^all the people gathered to Jeremiah at the house of the Lord.

¹⁰When the ^officials of Judah heard these things, they came up from the king's house to the house of the Lord and sat at the ᴮentrance of the New Gate of the Lord's *house.* ¹¹Then the priests and the prophets spoke to the officials and to all the people, saying, "A ^death sentence for this man! For he has prophesied ᴮagainst this city, just as you have heard with your own ears!"

¹²Then Jeremiah spoke to all the officials and to all the people, saying, "^The Lord sent me to prophesy against this house and against this city all the words that you have heard. ¹³Now then, ^reform your ways and your deeds and obey the voice of the Lord your God; and the Lord will relent of the disaster which He has pronounced against you. ¹⁴But as for me, behold, ^I am in your hands; do with me as is good and right in your sight. ¹⁵Only know for certain that if you put me to death, you will bring ^innocent blood on yourselves, and on this city and its inhabitants; for truly the Lord has sent me to you to speak all these words so that you hear them."

JEREMIAH IS SPARED

¹⁶Then the officials and all the people said to the priests and the prophets, "No ^death sentence for this man! For he has spoken to us

in the name of the Lord our God." ¹⁷Then ^some of the elders of the land rose up and spoke to all the assembly of the people, saying, ¹⁸ "^Micah of Moresheth used to prophesy in the days of Hezekiah king of Judah; and he spoke to all the people of Judah, saying, 'This is what the Lord of armies has said:

"ᴮZion will be plowed *like* a field,
And Jerusalem will become
    heaps of ruins,
And the mountain of the
    house like the high places of
    a forest."'

¹⁹Did Hezekiah king of Judah and all Judah actually put him to death? Did he not ^fear the Lord and plead for the favor of the Lord, and the Lord relented of the disaster which He had pronounced against them? But we are ᴮcommitting a great evil against our own lives!"

²⁰Indeed, *there was* also a man *who* used to prophesy in the name of the Lord, Uriah the son of Shemaiah from ^Kiriath-jearim; and he prophesied against this city and against this land words similar to all those of Jeremiah. ²¹When King Jehoiakim and all his warriors and all the officials heard his words, then the king sought to put him to death; but Uriah heard *about it,* and he was afraid, so he ^fled and went to Egypt. ²²Then King Jehoiakim sent men to Egypt: ^Elnathan the son of Achbor and *certain* men with him, to Egypt. ²³And they brought Uriah from Egypt and

26:8^Jer 11:19; 18:23 **26:9**^Acts 3:11; 5:12
26:10^Jer 26:21 ᴮJer 36:10 **26:11**^Deut 18:20
ᴮJer 38:4 **26:12**^Jer 1:17, 18; 26:15 **26:13**^Jer 7:3, 5;
18:8, 11 **26:14**^Jer 38:5 **26:15**^Num 35:33;
Prov 6:16, 17 **26:16**^Acts 5:34-39; 23:9, 29
26:17^Acts 5:34 **26:18**^Mic 1:1 ᴮNeh 4:2
26:19^2 Chr 29:6-11 ᴮJer 44:7 **26:20**^Josh 9:17;
1 Sam 6:21 **26:21**^1 Kin 19:2-4; Matt 10:23
26:22^Jer 36:12

led him to King Jehoiakim, who ^killed him with a sword and threw his dead body into the burial place of the common people.

²⁴But the hand of Ahikam the son of Shaphan was with Jeremiah, so that he was ^not handed over to the people to put him to death.

THE NATIONS TO SUBMIT TO NEBUCHADNEZZAR

27 In the beginning of the reign of ^Zedekiah the son of Josiah, king of Judah, this word came to Jeremiah from the LORD, saying— ²this is what the LORD has said to me: "Make for yourself ^restraints and ᴮyokes and put them on your neck, ³and send word to the king of ^Edom, the king of ^Moab, the king of the sons of Ammon, the king of ^Tyre, and to the king of Sidon by the messengers who come to Jerusalem to Zedekiah king of Judah. ⁴Order them *to go* to their masters, saying, 'This is what the LORD of armies, the God of Israel says: "This is what you shall say to your masters: ⁵'I have made the earth, mankind, and the animals which are on the face of the earth ^by My great power and by My outstretched arm, and I will ᴮgive it to the one who is pleasing in My sight. ⁶And now I ^have handed all these lands over to Nebuchadnezzar king of Babylon, My servant, and I have also given him the ᴮanimals of the field to serve him. ⁷^All the nations shall serve him and his son and his grandson until the time of his own land comes; then many nations and great kings will make him their servant.

⁸'And it will be *that* the nation or the kingdom which will not serve him, Nebuchadnezzar king of Babylon, and will not put its neck under the yoke of the king of Babylon, I will punish that nation with the ^sword, with famine, and with plague,' declares the LORD, 'until I have eliminated it by his hand. ⁹And as for you, ^do not listen to your prophets, your diviners, your dreamers, your soothsayers, or your sorcerers who talk to you, saying, "You will not serve the king of Babylon." ¹⁰For they are prophesying a ^lie to you in order to remove you far from your land; and I will drive you away and you will perish. ¹¹But the nation that will ^bring its neck under the yoke of the king of Babylon and serve him, I will ᴮlet remain on its land,' declares the LORD, 'and they will cultivate it and live in it.'"'"

¹²I spoke words like all these to ^Zedekiah king of Judah, saying, "Bring your necks under the yoke of the king of Babylon and serve him and his people, and live! ¹³Why should you ^die, you and your people, by the sword, famine, and plague, as the LORD has spoken to the nation that will not serve the king of Babylon? ¹⁴So ^do not listen to the words of the prophets who talk to you, saying, 'You will not serve the king of Babylon,' for they are prophesying a lie to you; ¹⁵for ^I have not sent them," declares the LORD, "but they are ᴮprophesying falsely in My name, so that I will drive you away and that you will perish, you and the prophets who prophesy to you."

26:23 ^Jer 2:30   26:24 ^1 Kin 18:4; Jer 1:18, 19
27:1 ^2 Kin 24:18-20; 2 Chr 36:11-13   27:2 ^Jer 30:8
ᴮJer 28:10, 13   27:3 ^Jer 25:21, 22   27:5 ^Deut 9:29
ᴮPs 115:15, 16   27:6 ^Jer 21:7   ᴮJer 28:14
27:7 ^2 Chr 36:20; Jer 44:30   27:8 ^Jer 24:10; 27:13
27:9 ^Ex 22:18; Deut 18:10   27:10 ^Jer 23:25
27:11 ^Jer 27:2, 8, 12   ᴮJer 21:9   27:12 ^Jer 27:3; 28:1
27:13 ^Prov 8:36; Jer 27:8   27:14 ^Jer 27:9; 2 Cor
11:13-15   27:15 ^Jer 23:21   ᴮJer 23:25

16 *Then* I spoke to the priests and to all this people, saying: "This is what the Lord says: 'Do not listen to the words of your prophets who prophesy to you, saying, "Behold, the ^Avessels of the Lord's house will now shortly be brought back from Babylon"; for they are prophesying a lie to you. 17 Do not listen to them; serve the king of Babylon, and live! Why should this city ^Abecome a place of ruins? 18 But ^Aif they are prophets, and if the word of the Lord is with them, have them now ^Bplead with the Lord of armies that the vessels which are left in the house of the Lord and the house of the king of Judah and in Jerusalem do not go to Babylon. 19 For this is what the Lord of armies says concerning the ^Apillars, concerning the sea, concerning the kettle stands, and concerning the rest of the vessels that are left in this city, 20 which Nebuchadnezzar king of Babylon did not take when he ^Aled into exile Jeconiah the son of Jehoiakim, king of Judah, from Jerusalem to Babylon, and all the nobles of Judah and Jerusalem— 21 Yes, this is what the Lord of armies, the God of Israel, says concerning the vessels that are left in the house of the Lord and in the house of the king of Judah and in Jerusalem: 22 "They will be ^Abrought to Babylon and will be there until the day I visit them," declares the Lord. "Then I will ^Bbring them back and restore them to this place."'"

HANANIAH'S FALSE PROPHECY

28 Now in the same year, in the beginning of the reign of ^AZedekiah king of Judah, in the fourth year, in the fifth month, ^BHananiah the prophet the son of Azzur, who was from Gibeon, spoke to me at the house of the Lord in the sight of the priests and all the people, saying, 2 "^AThis is what the Lord of armies, the God of Israel says: 'I have broken the yoke of the king of Babylon. 3 Within two years I am going to bring back to this place ^Aall the vessels of the Lord's house, which Nebuchadnezzar king of Babylon took from this place and brought to Babylon. 4 I am also going to bring back to this place ^AJeconiah the son of Jehoiakim, king of Judah, and all the ^Bexiles of Judah who went to Babylon,' declares the Lord, 'for I will break the yoke of the king of Babylon.'"

5 Then Jeremiah the prophet spoke to the prophet Hananiah in the sight of the priests and in the sight of all the people who were standing at the ^Ahouse of the Lord, 6 and Jeremiah the prophet said, "^AAmen! May the Lord do so; may the Lord fulfill your words which you have prophesied, to bring back the vessels of the Lord's house and all the exiles, from Babylon to this place. 7 Yet ^Ahear now this word which I am going to speak so that you and all the people can hear it! 8 The prophets who were before me and before you from ancient times also ^Aprophesied against many lands and against great kingdoms regarding war, disaster, and plague. 9 *As for* the prophet who prophesies of peace, ^Awhen the word of the prophet comes to pass, then

27:16 ^A 2 Kin 24:13; 2 Chr 36:7, 10　27:17 ^A Jer 7:34
27:18 ^A 1 Kin 18:24　^B 1 Sam 7:8　27:19 ^A 1 Kin 7:15;
2 Kin 25:13, 17　27:20 ^A 2 Kin 24:12, 14–16;
2 Chr 36:10, 18　27:22 ^A Jer 34:2, 3　^B Ezra 1:7–11
28:1 ^A 2 Kin 24:18–20　^B Jer 28:17　28:2 ^A Jer 27:12; 28:11
28:3 ^A 2 Kin 24:13; 2 Chr 36:10　28:4 ^A 2 Kin 25:27
^B Jer 22:10　28:5 ^A Jer 28:1　28:6 ^A 1 Kin 1:36; Ps 41:13
28:7 ^A 1 Kin 22:28　28:8 ^A Lev 26:14–39; 1 Kin 14:15
28:9 ^A Deut 18:22

that prophet will be known *as* one whom the LORD has truly sent."

¹⁰Then Hananiah the prophet took the ^yoke from the neck of Jeremiah the prophet and broke it. ¹¹Hananiah spoke in the sight of all the people, saying, "^This is what the LORD says: 'Even so within two full years I will break the yoke of Nebuchadnezzar king of Babylon from the neck of all the nations.'" Then Jeremiah the prophet went his way.

¹²Then the ^word of the LORD came to Jeremiah after Hananiah the prophet had broken the yoke from the neck of Jeremiah the prophet, saying, ¹³"Go and speak to Hananiah, saying, 'This is what the LORD says: "You have broken the yokes of wood, but in their place you have made ^yokes of iron." ¹⁴For this is what the LORD of armies, the God of Israel says: "I have put a ^yoke of iron on the neck of all these nations, to serve Nebuchadnezzar king of Babylon; and they shall ^Bserve him. And I have also given him the animals of the field."'" ¹⁵Then Jeremiah the prophet said to Hananiah the prophet, "Listen now, Hananiah: the LORD has not sent you, and ^you have made this people trust in a lie. ¹⁶Therefore, this is what the LORD says: 'Behold, I am going to remove you from the face of the earth. This year you are going to ^die, because you ^Bspoke falsely against the LORD.'"

¹⁷So Hananiah the prophet died in the same year, in the seventh month.

MESSAGE TO THE EXILES

29 Now these are the words of the ^letter which Jeremiah the prophet sent from Jerusalem to the rest of the elders of the exile,

the priests, the prophets, and all the people whom Nebuchadnezzar had taken into exile from Jerusalem to Babylon. ²(*This was* after King ^Jeconiah and the queen mother, the high officials, the leaders of Judah and Jerusalem, the craftsmen, and the metalworkers had departed from Jerusalem.) ³ *The letter was sent* by the hand of Elasah the son of Shaphan and Gemariah the son of ^Hilkiah, whom Zedekiah king of Judah sent to Babylon to Nebuchadnezzar king of Babylon, saying, ⁴"This is what the LORD of armies, the God of Israel, says to all the exiles whom I have ^sent into exile from Jerusalem to Babylon: ⁵^Build houses and live *in them;* and plant gardens and eat their produce. ⁶Take ^wives and father sons and daughters, and take wives for your sons and give your daughters to husbands, so that they may give birth to sons and daughters; and grow in numbers there and do not decrease. ⁷^Seek the prosperity of the city where I have sent you into exile, and pray to the LORD in its behalf; for in its prosperity will be your prosperity.' ⁸For this is what the LORD of armies, the God of Israel says: 'Do not let your ^prophets who are in your midst or your diviners ^Bdeceive you, and do not listen to *their interpretations of* your dreams which you dream. ⁹For they ^prophesy falsely to you in My name; ^BI have not sent them,' declares the LORD.

28:10^Jer 27:2　**28:11**^Jer 14:14; 27:10　**28:12**^Jer 1:2
28:13^Ps 107:16; Is 45:2　**28:14**^Deut 28:48
^BJer 25:11　**28:15**^Jer 20:6; 29:31　**28:16**^Jer 20:6
^BDeut 13:5　**29:1**^2 Chr 30:1, 6; Esth 9:20
29:2^2 Kin 24:12-16; 2 Chr 36:9, 10　**29:3**^1 Chr 6:13
29:4^Jer 24:5　**29:5**^Jer 29:28　**29:6**^Jer 16:2-4
29:7^Dan 4:27; 6:4, 5　**29:8**^Jer 27:9　^BJer 14:14
29:9^Jer 27:15　^BJer 29:31

¹⁰"For this is what the LORD says: 'When ^seventy years have been completed for Babylon, I will visit you and fulfill My ᴮgood word to you, to bring you back to this place. ¹¹For I know the ^plans that I have for you,' declares the LORD, 'plans for prosperity and not for disaster, to give you a future and a hope. ¹²Then you will ^call upon Me and come and pray to Me, and I will ᴮlisten to you. ¹³And you will ^seek Me and find *Me* when you search for Me with all your heart. ¹⁴I will let Myself be ^found by you,' declares the LORD, 'and I will restore your fortunes and gather you from all the nations and all the places where I have driven you,' declares the LORD, 'and I will bring you back to the place from where I sent you into exile.'

¹⁵"Because you have said, 'The LORD has raised up ^prophets for us in Babylon'— ¹⁶for this is what the LORD says concerning the king who sits on the throne of David, and concerning all the people who live in this city, your brothers who did ^not go with you into exile— ¹⁷this is what the LORD of armies says: 'Behold, I am sending upon them the ^sword, famine, and plague; and I will make them like rotten figs that cannot be eaten due to rottenness. ¹⁸I will pursue them with the sword, with famine, and with plague; and I will make them an object of terror to all the kingdoms of the earth, to be a ^curse and an object of horror and hissing, and a disgrace among all the nations where I have driven them, ¹⁹because they have ^not listened to My words,' declares the LORD, 'which I sent to them again and again by My servants the prophets; but you did not listen,' declares the LORD. ²⁰'You, therefore, hear the word of the LORD, all you exiles, whom I have ^sent away from Jerusalem to Babylon.

²¹'This is what the LORD of armies, the God of Israel says concerning Ahab the son of Kolaiah and concerning Zedekiah the son of Maaseiah, who are ^prophesying to you falsely in My name: "Behold, I am going to hand them over to Nebuchadnezzar king of Babylon, and he will kill them before your eyes. ²²Because of them a ^curse will be used by all the exiles from Judah who are in Babylon, saying, 'May the LORD make you like Zedekiah and Ahab, whom the king of Babylon roasted in the fire,' ²³because they acted foolishly in Israel, and ^committed adultery with their neighbors' wives, and falsely ᴮspoke words in My name which I did not command them. I am He who knows, and a witness," declares the LORD.'"

²⁴Now you shall speak to ^Shemaiah the Nehelamite, saying, ²⁵"This is what the LORD of armies, the God of Israel says: 'Because you have sent ^letters in your own name to all the people who are in Jerusalem, and to the priest Zephaniah the son of Maaseiah, and to all the priests, saying, ²⁶"The LORD has made you priest instead of Jehoiada the priest, to be the ^overseer of the house of the LORD for every insane person who prophesies, to ᴮput him in the stocks and in the iron

29:10^2 Chr 36:21-23   ᴮJer 24:6, 7   **29:11**^Ps 40:5; Jer 23:5, 6   **29:12**^Ps 50:15   ᴮPs 145:19
29:13^Deut 4:29; Ps 32:6   **29:14**^Deut 30:1-10; Ps 32:6   **29:15**^Jer 29:21, 24   **29:16**^Jer 38:2, 3, 17-23
29:17^Jer 27:8; 29:18   **29:18**^Is 65:15; Jer 42:18
29:19^Jer 6:19   **29:20**^Jer 24:5; Ezek 11:9
29:21^Deut 14:14, 15; 29:8, 9   **29:22**^Is 65:15
29:23^Jer 5:8   ᴮJer 29:8, 9, 21   **29:24**^Jer 29:31, 32
29:25^Jer 29:1   **29:26**^Jer 20:1   ᴮActs 16:24

collar. ²⁷So now, why have you not rebuked Jeremiah of ᴬAnathoth who prophesies to you, ²⁸seeing that he has ᴬsent *word* to us in Babylon, saying, 'The exile will be ᴮlong; build houses and live *in them*, and plant gardens and eat their produce'?"'"

²⁹Now ᴬZephaniah the priest read this letter to Jeremiah the prophet. ³⁰Then the word of the Lᴏʀᴅ came to Jeremiah, saying, ³¹"Send *word* to all the exiles, saying, 'This is what the Lᴏʀᴅ says concerning Shemaiah the Nehelamite: "Because Shemaiah has ᴬprophesied to you, although I did not send him, and he has ᴮmade you trust in a lie," ³²therefore this is what the Lᴏʀᴅ says: "Behold, I am going to ᴬpunish Shemaiah the Nehelamite and his descendants; he will ᴮnot have anyone living among this people, and he will not see the good that I am going to do for My people," declares the Lᴏʀᴅ, "because he has spoken falsely against the Lᴏʀᴅ."'"

LIBERATION FROM CAPTIVITY PROMISED

30 The word that came to Jeremiah from the Lᴏʀᴅ, saying, ²"This is what the Lᴏʀᴅ, the God of Israel says: 'ᴬWrite all the words which I have spoken to you in a book. ³For behold, days are coming,' declares the Lᴏʀᴅ, 'when I will restore the fortunes of My people ᴬIsrael and Judah.' The Lᴏʀᴅ says, 'I will also ᴮbring them back to the land that I gave to their forefathers, and they shall take possession of it.'"

⁴Now these are the words which the Lᴏʀᴅ spoke concerning Israel and Judah:

⁵"For this is what the Lᴏʀᴅ says:
'I have heard a sound of ᴬterror,
Of fear, and there is no peace.

⁶ 'Ask now, and see
If a male can give birth.
Why do I see every man
With his hands on his waist,
ᴬas a woman in childbirth?
And *why* have all faces
turned pale?

⁷ 'Woe, for that day is great,
There is none like it;
And it is the time of Jacob's
ᴬdistress,
Yet he will be ᴮsaved from it.

⁸'It shall come about on that day,' declares the Lᴏʀᴅ of armies, 'that I will ᴬbreak his yoke from their necks and will tear to pieces their ᴮrestraints; and strangers will no longer make them their slaves. ⁹But they shall serve the Lᴏʀᴅ their God and ᴬDavid their king, whom I will raise up for them.

¹⁰ 'And do not fear, Jacob My
servant,' declares the Lᴏʀᴅ,
'And do not be dismayed,
Israel;
For behold, I am going to save
you from far away,
And your descendants
from the land of their
captivity.
And Jacob will return and be
ᴬat peace, without anxiety,
And ᴮno one will make him
afraid.

¹¹ 'For ᴬI am with you,' declares
the Lᴏʀᴅ, 'to save you;
For I will completely ᴮdestroy
all the nations where I have
scattered you,
Only I will not destroy you
completely.

29:27ᴬJer 1:1　29:28ᴬJer 29:1　ᴮJer 29:10
29:29ᴬJer 29:25　29:31ᴬJer 14:14, 15　ᴮJer 28:15
29:32ᴬJer 36:31　ᴮ1 Sam 2:30-34　30:2ᴬIs 30:8;
Jer 25:13　30:3ᴬJer 3:18　ᴮJer 16:15　30:5ᴬIs 5:30;
Jer 6:25　30:6ᴬJer 4:31; 6:24　30:7ᴬJer 2:27, 28
ᴮJer 30:10　30:8ᴬIs 9:4　ᴮJer 27:2　30:9ᴬIs 55:3-5;
Ezek 34:23, 24　30:10ᴬIs 35:9　ᴮMic 4:4
30:11ᴬJer 1:8, 19　ᴮJer 46:28

But I will discipline you fairly
And will by no means leave
    you unpunished.'

12 "For this is what the LORD says:
'Your broken *limb* is
    irreparable,
And your ^wound is incurable.
13 'There is no one to plead your
    cause;
No healing for *your* sore,
^No recovery for you.
14 'All your lovers have forgotten
    you,
They do not seek you;
For I have ^wounded you with
    the wound of an enemy,
With the ^Bpunishment of a
    cruel one,
Because your wrongdoing is
    great,
And your sins are numerous.
15 'Why do you cry out over your
    injury?
Your pain is incurable.
Because your wrongdoing is
    great
And your sins are numerous,
I have done these things to
    you.
16 'Therefore all who ^devour you
    will be devoured;
And all your adversaries,
    every one of them, will go
    into captivity;
And those who plunder you
    will become plunder,
And all who plunder you I will
    turn into plunder.
17 'For I will restore you to
    ^health
And I will heal you of your
    wounds,' declares the LORD,
'Because they have called you
    an outcast, saying:
"It is Zion; no one cares for
    her."'

RESTORATION OF JACOB

18 "This is what the LORD says:
'Behold, I will restore the
    fortunes of the tents of Jacob
And have compassion on his
    dwellings;
And the ^city will be rebuilt on
    its ruins,
And the ^Bpalace will stand on
    its rightful place.
19 'From them will come a song of
    thanksgiving
And the voices of those who
    celebrate;
And I will ^multiply them and
    they will not decrease;
I will ^Bhonor them and they
    will not be insignificant.
20 'Their children also will be as
    before,
And their congregation will be
    ^established before Me;
And I will punish all their
    oppressors.
21 'Their ^leader shall be one of
    them,
And their ruler will come out
    from their midst;
And I will ^Bbring him near and
    he shall approach Me;
For who would dare to risk
    his life to approach Me?'
    declares the LORD.
22 'You shall be ^My people,
And I will be your God.'"

23 Behold, the ^tempest of the
    LORD!
Wrath has gone forth,
A sweeping tempest;
It will whirl upon the head of
    the wicked.

30:12 ^2 Chr 36:16; Jer 15:18   30:13 ^Jer 14:19; 46:11
30:14 ^Lam 2:4, 5   ^BJob 30:21   30:16 ^Jer 2:3; 8:16
30:17 ^Ex 15:26; Ps 107:20   30:18 ^Jer 31:4, 38-40
^B1 Chr 29:1, 19   30:19 ^Jer 33:22   ^BIs 55:5
30:20 ^Is 54:14   30:21 ^Jer 30:9   ^BNum 16:5
30:22 ^Ex 6:7; Jer 32:38   30:23 ^Jer 23:19

24 The ^fierce anger of the LORD
    will not turn back
Until He has performed and
    accomplished
The intent of His heart.
In the ^Blatter days you will
    understand this.

ISRAEL'S MOURNING TURNED TO JOY

31 "At that time," declares the
LORD, "I will be the ^God of all
the families of Israel, and they shall
be My people."

2 This is what the LORD says:
"The people who survived the
    sword
    ^Found grace in the
    wilderness—
Israel, when it went to find its
    rest."

3 The LORD appeared to him
    long ago, *saying,*
"I have loved you with an
    everlasting love;
Therefore I have drawn you
    out with ^kindness.

4 "^I will build you again and you
    will be rebuilt,
Virgin of Israel!
You will take up your
    tambourines again,
And go out to the dances of
    the ^Brevelers.

5 "Again you will ^plant vineyards
On the hills of Samaria;
The planters will plant
And will enjoy *the fruit.*

6 "For there will be a day when
    watchmen
On the hills of Ephraim call out,
'Arise, and ^let's go up *to* Zion,
To the LORD our God.'"

7 For this is what the LORD says:
"Sing aloud with joy for Jacob,
And be joyful with the ^chief
    of the nations;

Proclaim, give praise, and say,
'LORD, ^Bsave Your people,
The remnant of Israel!'

8 "Behold, I am bringing them
    from the north country,
And I will gather them from
    the remote parts of the earth,
Among them those who are
    ^blind and those who ^Blimp,
The pregnant woman and she
    who is in labor, together;
They will return here as a great
    assembly.

9 "They will come with weeping,
And by pleading I will bring
    them;
I will lead them by streams of
    waters,
On a straight path on which
    they will ^not stumble;
For I am a ^Bfather to Israel,
And Ephraim is My firstborn."

10 Hear the word of the LORD, you
    nations,
And declare *it* in the
    coastlands far away,
And say, "He who scattered
    Israel will ^gather him,
And He will keep him as a
    ^Bshepherd *keeps* his flock."

11 For the LORD has ^ransomed
    Jacob
And redeemed him from
    the hand of him who was
    stronger than he.

12 "They will ^come and shout for
    joy on the ^Bheight of Zion,
And they will be radiant over
    the bounty of the LORD—
Over the grain, the new wine,
    the oil,

30:24 ^Jer 4:8   ^BJer 23:20   **31:1** ^Jer 30:22
31:2 ^Num 14:20   **31:3** ^Ps 25:6   **31:4** ^Jer 24:6
^BJer 30:19   **31:5** ^Ps 107:37; Is 65:21   **31:6** ^Is 2:3; Jer 31:12
31:7 ^Deut 28:13   ^BPs 28:9   **31:8** ^Is 42:16   ^BEzek 34:16
31:9 ^Is 63:13   ^BJer 3:4, 19   **31:10** ^Jer 50:19   ^BIs 40:11
31:11 ^Is 44:23; 48:20   **31:12** ^Jer 31:6, 7   ^BEzek 17:23

And over the young of the
flock and the herd.
And their life will be like a
watered garden,
And they will never languish
again.
13 "Then the virgin will rejoice in
the dance,
And the young men and the
old together;
For I will ᴬturn their mourning
into joy
And comfort them, and give
them ᴮjoy for their sorrow.
14 "I will refresh the soul of the
priests with abundance,
And My people will be
ᴬsatisfied with My
goodness," declares the
LORD.

15   This is what the LORD says:
"ᴬA voice is heard in ᴮRamah,
Lamenting *and* bitter weeping.
Rachel is weeping for her
children;
She refuses to be comforted
for her children,
Because they are no more."
16 This is what the LORD says:
"Restrain your voice from
weeping
And your eyes from tears;
For your ᴬwork will be
rewarded," declares the
LORD,
"And they will ᴮreturn from the
land of the enemy.
17 "There is ᴬhope for your
future," declares the LORD,
"And *your* children will return
to their own territory.
18 "I have certainly heard Ephraim
ᴬgrieving,
'You have ᴮdisciplined me, and I
was corrected,
Like an untrained calf;

Bring me back that I may be
restored,
For You are the LORD my God.
19   'For after I turned back, I
ᴬrepented;
And after I was instructed, I
¹slapped *my* thigh;
I was ᴮashamed and also
humiliated
Because I bore the shame of
my youth.'
20 "Is ᴬEphraim My dear son?
Is he a delightful child?
Indeed, as often as I have
spoken against him,
I certainly *still* remember him;
Therefore My ᴮheart yearns
for him;
I will certainly have mercy on
him," declares the LORD.

21 "Set up roadmarks for yourself,
Place guideposts for yourself;
ᴬDirect your mind to the
highway,
The way by which you went.
ᴮReturn, O virgin of Israel,
Return to these your cities.
22 "How long will you waver,
You ᴬrebellious daughter?
For the LORD has created a new
thing on the earth:
A woman will shelter a man."
23 This is what the LORD of armies,
the God of Israel says: "Once again
they will speak this word in the
land of Judah and in its cities when
I restore their fortunes,
'The LORD bless you, O ᴬplace of
righteousness,
O ᴮholy hill!'

31:13 ᴬIs 61:3   ᴮIs 51:11   31:14 ᴬJer 50:19
31:15 ᴬMatt 2:18   ᴮJosh 18:25   31:16 ᴬRuth 2:12
ᴮJer 30:3   31:17 ᴬJer 29:11   31:18 ᴬJer 3:21   ᴮJob 5:17
31:19 ᴬEzek 36:31   ᴮJer 3:25   31:20 ᴬHos 11:8
ᴮGen 43:30   31:21 ᴬJer 50:5   ᴮIs 48:20
31:22 ᴬJer 3:6; 49:4   31:23 ᴬIs 1:26   ᴮPs 48:1

31:19 ¹I.e., in regret

²⁴Judah and all its cities will ^live together in it, the farmers and those who travel with flocks. ²⁵^For I give plenty of water to the weary ones, and refresh everyone who languishes." ²⁶At this I ^awoke and looked, and my sleep had been pleasant to me.

A NEW COVENANT

²⁷"Behold, days are coming," declares the LORD, "when I will ^sow the house of Israel and the house of Judah with the seed of mankind and the seed of animals. ²⁸And just as I have watched over them to uproot *them,* tear *them* down, ruin, destroy, and bring disaster *on them,* so I will watch over them to ^build and to plant *them,*" declares the LORD.

²⁹ "In those days they will no
　　longer say,
'^The fathers have eaten sour
　　grapes,
¹But *it is* the children's teeth
　　that have become blunt.'

³⁰But ^everyone will die for his own wrongdoing; each person who eats the sour grapes, his *own* teeth will become blunt.

³¹"Behold, days are coming," declares the LORD, "when I will make a ^new covenant with the house of Israel and the house of Judah, ³²not like the ^covenant which I made with their fathers on the day I took them by the hand to bring them out of the land of Egypt, My covenant which they broke, although I was a husband to them," declares the LORD. ³³"For this is the covenant which I will make with the house of Israel after those days," declares the LORD: "^I will put My law within them and write it on their heart; and I will be their God,

and they shall be My people. ³⁴They will not teach again, each one his neighbor and each one his brother, saying, 'Know the LORD,' for they will all know Me, from the least of them to the greatest of them," declares the LORD, "for I will ^forgive their wrongdoing, and their ᴮsin I will no longer remember."

³⁵ This is what the LORD says,
　　He who ^gives the sun for light
　　　　by day
　　And the fixed order of the
　　　　moon and the stars for light
　　　　by night,
　　Who ᴮstirs up the sea so that
　　　　its waves roar—
　　The LORD of armies is His name:
³⁶ "^If this fixed order departs
　　From Me," declares the LORD,
　　"Then the descendants of Israel
　　　　also will ᴮcease
　　To be a nation before Me
　　　　forever."
³⁷ This is what the LORD says:
　　"^If the heavens above can be
　　　　measured
　　And the foundations of the
　　　　earth searched out below,
　　Then I will also reject all the
　　　　descendants of Israel
　　For everything that they have
　　　　done," declares the LORD.

³⁸"Behold, days are coming," declares the LORD, "when the ^city will be rebuilt for the LORD from the Tower of Hananel to the Corner Gate. ³⁹The ^measuring line will go out farther straight ahead,

31:24 ^Jer 31:12; Ezek 36:10　31:25 ^Ps 107:9;
Jer 31:12, 14　31:26 ^Zech 4:1　31:27 ^Ezek 36:9, 11;
Hos 2:23　31:28 ^Jer 24:6　31:29 ^Lam 5:7; Ezek 18:2
31:30 ^Deut 24:16; Is 3:11　31:31 ^Jer 32:40; 33:14
31:32 ^Ex 19:5; 24:6-8　31:33 ^Ps 40:8; 2 Cor 3:3
31:34 ^Jer 33:8　ᴮIs 43:25　31:35 ^Gen 1:14-18
ᴮIs 51:15　31:36 ^Ps 89:36, 37　ᴮAmos 9:8, 9
31:37 ^Is 40:12; Jer 33:22　31:38 ^Jer 30:18; 31:4
31:39 ^Zech 2:1

31:29 ¹I.e., the children suffer for the fathers' sins

to the hill Gareb; then it will turn to Goah. ⁴⁰And ^the entire valley of the dead bodies and of the ashes, and all the fields as far as the brook ᴮKidron to the corner of the Horse Gate toward the east, shall be holy to the Lᴏʀᴅ; it will not be uprooted or overthrown ever again."

JEREMIAH IMPRISONED

32 The word that came to Jeremiah from the Lᴏʀᴅ in the ^tenth year of Zedekiah king of Judah, which was the eighteenth year of Nebuchadnezzar. ²Now at that time the army of the king of Babylon was besieging Jerusalem, and Jeremiah the prophet was imprisoned in the ^courtyard of the guard, which *was at* the house of the king of Judah, ³because Zedekiah king of Judah had ^imprisoned him, saying, "Why do you prophesy, saying, 'This is what the Lᴏʀᴅ says: "Behold, I am going to ᴮhand this city over to the king of Babylon, and he will take it; ⁴and Zedekiah king of Judah will not escape from the hand of the Chaldeans, but he will certainly be handed over to the king of Babylon, and he will ^speak with him face to face and see him eye to eye. ⁵Then he will take Zedekiah to Babylon, and he will be there until I visit him," declares the Lᴏʀᴅ. "If you fight against the Chaldeans, you will ^not succeed"'?"

⁶And Jeremiah said, "The word of the Lᴏʀᴅ came to me, saying, ⁷'Behold, Hanamel the son of Shallum your uncle is coming to you, saying, "Buy for yourself my field which is at Anathoth, for you have the ^right of redemption to buy *it*."' ⁸Then my uncle's son Hanamel came to me in the ^courtyard of the guard in accordance with the word

of the Lᴏʀᴅ and said to me, 'Buy my field, please, that is at Anathoth, which is in the land of Benjamin; for you have the right of possession and the redemption is yours; buy *it* for yourself.' Then I knew that this was the word of the Lᴏʀᴅ.

⁹"So I bought the field which was in Anathoth from Hanamel my uncle's son, and I ^weighed out the silver for him, seventeen shekels of silver. ¹⁰And I ^signed and ᴮsealed the deed, and called in witnesses, and weighed out the silver on the scales. ¹¹Then I took the deeds of purchase, both the sealed *copy containing* the ^terms and conditions and the open *copy;* ¹²and I gave the deed of purchase to ^Baruch the son of ᴮNeriah, the son of Mahseiah, in the sight of Hanamel my uncle's *son* and in the sight of the witnesses who signed the deed of purchase, in the sight of all the Jews who were sitting in the courtyard of the guard. ¹³And I commanded Baruch in their sight, saying, ¹⁴'This is what the Lᴏʀᴅ of armies, the God of Israel says: "Take these deeds, this sealed deed of purchase and this open deed, and put them in an earthenware jar, so that they may last a long time." ¹⁵For this is what the Lᴏʀᴅ of armies, the God of Israel says: "^Houses and fields and vineyards will again be purchased in this land."'

JEREMIAH PRAYS AND GOD EXPLAINS

¹⁶"After giving the deed of purchase to Baruch the son of Neriah, I ^prayed to the Lᴏʀᴅ, saying, ¹⁷'Oh,

31:40^Jer 7:32; 8:2   ᴮ2 Sam 15:23   **32:1**^2 Kin 25:1, 2; Jer 39:1, 2   **32:2**^Neh 3:25; Jer 33:1   **32:3**^2 Kin 6:32   ᴮJer 21:4-7   **32:4**^Jer 39:5   **32:5**^Ezek 17:9, 10, 15   **32:7**^Lev 25:25; Ruth 4:3, 4   **32:8**^Jer 32:2; 33:1   **32:9**^Gen 23:16; Zech 11:12   **32:10**^Is 44:5   ᴮDeut 32:34   **32:11**^Luke 2:27   **32:12**^Jer 32:16   ᴮJer 51:59   **32:15**^Jer 30:18; 31:5, 12, 24   **32:16**^Gen 32:9-12; Jer 12:1

Lord GOD! Behold, You Yourself have ^made the heavens and the earth by Your great power and by Your outstretched arm! ^BNothing is too difficult for You, ^18who ^shows mercy to thousands, but ^Brepays the wrongdoing of fathers into the laps of their children after them, great and mighty God. The LORD of armies is His name; ^19^Agreat in counsel and mighty in deed, whose ^Beyes are open to all the ways of the sons of mankind, giving to everyone according to his ways and according to the fruit of his deeds; ^20who has ^accomplished signs and wonders in the land of Egypt, *and* even to this day both in Israel and among mankind; and You have made a name for Yourself, as at this day. ^21You ^brought Your people Israel out of the land of Egypt with signs and with wonders, and with a strong hand and an outstretched arm, and with great terror; ^22and You gave them this land, which You ^swore to their forefathers to give them, a land flowing with milk and honey. ^23They came in and took possession of it, but they ^did not obey Your voice or ^Bwalk in Your Law; they did not do anything that You commanded them to do; therefore You have made all this disaster happen to them. ^24Behold, the ^assault ramps have reached the city to take it; and the city has been ^Bhanded over to the Chaldeans who fight against it, because of the sword, the famine, and the plague; and what You have spoken has come to pass; and behold, You see *it*. ^25Yet You have said to me, Lord GOD, "Buy for yourself the field with money and call in witnesses"— although the city has been handed over to the Chaldeans.'"

^26Then the word of the LORD came to Jeremiah, saying, ^27"Behold, I am the LORD, the ^God of all flesh; is anything ^Btoo difficult for Me?" ^28Therefore this is what the LORD says: "Behold, I am going to ^hand this city over to the Chaldeans and to Nebuchadnezzar king of Babylon, and he will take it. ^29And the Chaldeans who are fighting against this city will enter and ^set this city on fire and burn it, with the ^Bhouses where *people* have offered incense to Baal on their roofs and poured out drink offerings to other gods, to provoke Me to anger. ^30For the sons of Israel and the sons of Judah have been doing only ^evil in My sight since their youth; for the sons of Israel have been only ^Bprovoking Me to anger by the work of their hands," declares the LORD. ^31"Indeed this city has been to Me a provocation of My anger and My wrath since the day that they built it, even to this day, so that it should be ^removed from My sight, ^32because of all the evil of the sons of Israel and the sons of Judah which they have done to provoke Me to anger— they, their ^kings, their leaders, their priests, their prophets, the men of Judah, and the inhabitants of Jerusalem. ^33They have turned *their* back to Me and not *their* face; though *I* taught them, ^teaching again and again, they would not listen to accept discipline. ^34But they ^put their detestable things in the

32:17^A2 Kin 19:15   ^BGen 18:14   32:18^AEx 20:6
^B1 Kin 14:9, 10   32:19^AIs 9:6   ^BJob 34:21
32:20^APs 78:43; 105:27   32:21^AEx 6:6; Deut 4:34
32:22^AEx 3:8, 17; 13:5   32:23^ANeh 9:26   ^BEzra 9:7
32:24^AJer 33:4   ^BJer 20:5   32:27^ANum 16:22
^BJer 32:17   32:28^A2 Kin 25:11; 2 Chr 36:17-21
32:29^A2 Chr 36:19   ^BJer 19:13   32:30^ADeut 9:7-12
^BJer 8:19   32:31^A2 Kin 23:27; 24:3, 4   32:32^AEzra 9:7;
Is 1:4-6, 23   32:33^A2 Chr 36:15, 16; Jer 7:13
32:34^A2 Kin 21:1-7; Jer 7:30

house which is called by My name, to defile it. ³⁵They built the ^high places of Baal that are in the Valley of Ben-hinnom to make their sons and their daughters pass through *the fire* to ^BMolech, which I had not commanded them, nor had it entered My mind that they should do this abomination, to mislead Judah to sin.

³⁶"Now therefore the LORD God of Israel says the following concerning this city of which you say, 'It has been ^handed over to the king of Babylon by sword, by famine, and by plague': ³⁷Behold, I am going to gather them out of all the lands to which I have driven them in My anger, in My wrath, and in great indignation; and I will bring them back to this place and ^have them live in safety. ³⁸They shall be ^My people, and I will be their God; ³⁹and I will ^give them one heart and one way, so that they will fear Me always, for their own ^Bgood and for *the good of* their children after them. ⁴⁰I will make an everlasting covenant with them that I will ^not turn away from them, to do them good; and I will ^Bput the fear of Me in their hearts, so that they will not turn away from Me. ⁴¹I will rejoice over them to do them good and will faithfully ^plant them in this land with ^Ball My heart and all My soul. ⁴²For this is what the LORD says: '^Just as I brought all this great disaster on this people, so I am going to ^Bbring on them all the good that I am promising them. ⁴³And ^fields will be purchased in this land of which you say, "It is a desolation, without man or animal; it has been handed over to the Chaldeans." ⁴⁴*People* will buy fields for money, ^sign and seal deeds,

and call in witnesses in the ^Bland of Benjamin, in the areas surrounding Jerusalem, in the cities of Judah, in the cities of the hill country, in the cities of the lowland, and in the cities of the ¹Negev; for I will restore their fortunes,' declares the LORD."

RESTORATION PROMISED

33 Then the word of the LORD came to Jeremiah the second time, while he was still ^confined in the courtyard of the guard, saying, ²"This is what ^the LORD says, *He* who made the earth, the LORD who formed it to create it, *He* whose name is the LORD: ³'^Call to Me and I will answer you, and I will tell you great and mighty things, which you do not know.' ⁴For this is what the LORD, the God of Israel says concerning the houses of this city, and concerning the houses of the kings of Judah which have been torn down *to make a defense* against the ^assault ramps and the sword: ⁵'While *they* are coming to fight the Chaldeans and to fill their houses with the bodies of people whom I have struck down in My anger and My wrath, and I have ^hidden My face from this city because of all their wickedness: ⁶Behold, I am going to bring to it ^healing and a remedy, and I will heal them; and I will reveal to them an ^Babundance of peace and truth. ⁷And I will restore the fortunes of Judah and the fortunes of Israel,

32:35^2 Chr 28:2   ^BLev 18:21   **32:36**^Jer 32:24
32:37^Jer 23:6; Ezek 34:25, 28   **32:38**^Jer 24:7
32:39^2 Chr 30:12   ^BDeut 11:18-21
32:40^Deut 31:6, 8   ^BJer 24:7   **32:41**^Jer 24:6
^BHos 2:19, 20   **32:42**^Jer 31:28   ^BJer 33:14
32:43^Jer 32:15, 25; Ezek 37:11-14   **32:44**^Jer 32:10
^BJer 17:26   **33:1**^Jer 32:2, 8; 37:21   **33:2**^Jer 51:19
33:3^Ps 50:15; 91:15   **33:4**^Jer 32:24; Ezek 4:2
33:5^Is 8:17; Jer 21:10   **33:6**^Jer 17:14   ^BIs 66:12

32:44¹I.e., South country

and will ^rebuild them as *they were* at first. ⁸And I will ^cleanse them from all their wrongdoing by which they have sinned against Me, and I will forgive all their wrongdoings by which they have sinned against Me and revolted against Me. ⁹'It will be to Me a name of joy, praise, and glory before ^all the nations of the earth, which will hear of all the ᴮgood that I do for them, and they will be frightened and tremble because of all the good and all the peace that I make for it.'

¹⁰"This is what the Lᴏʀᴅ says: '*Yet* again there will be heard in this place, of which you say, "It is a ^waste, without man and without animal," *that is,* in the cities of Judah and in the streets of Jerusalem that are ᴮdeserted, without man and without inhabitant and without animal, ¹¹the voice of joy and the voice of gladness, the voice of the groom and the voice of the bride, the voice of those who say,

"Give thanks to the Lᴏʀᴅ of armies,

For the Lᴏʀᴅ is good,

For His mercy is everlasting,"

as they bring a ^thanksgiving offering into the house of the Lᴏʀᴅ. For I will restore the fortunes of the land as *they were* at first,' says the Lᴏʀᴅ.

¹²"This is what the Lᴏʀᴅ of armies says: 'There will again be in this place which is waste, ^without man or animal, and in all its cities, a pasture for shepherds who rest their flocks. ¹³In the cities of the hill country, in the cities of the lowland, in the cities of the Negev, in the land of Benjamin, in the areas surrounding Jerusalem, and in the cities of Judah, the flocks will again ^pass under the hands of the one who counts them,' says the Lᴏʀᴅ.

THE DAVIDIC KINGDOM

¹⁴'Behold, ^days are coming,' declares the Lᴏʀᴅ, 'when I will ᴮfulfill the good word which I have spoken concerning the house of Israel and the house of Judah. ¹⁵In those days and at that time I will make a ^righteous Branch of David sprout; and He shall execute ᴮjustice and righteousness on the earth. ¹⁶In those days Judah will be saved and Jerusalem will live in safety; and this is *the name* by which it will be called: the ^Lᴏʀᴅ is our righteousness.' ¹⁷For this is what the Lᴏʀᴅ says: 'David shall ^not lack a man to sit on the throne of the house of Israel; ¹⁸and the ^Levitical priests shall not lack a man before Me to offer burnt offerings, to burn grain offerings, and to prepare sacrifices continually.'"

¹⁹And the word of the Lᴏʀᴅ came to Jeremiah, saying, ²⁰"This is what the Lᴏʀᴅ says: 'If you can ^break My covenant for the day and My covenant for the night, so that day and night do not occur at their proper time, ²¹then ^My covenant with David My servant may also be broken, so that he will not have a son to reign on his throne, and with the Levitical priests, My ministers. ²²As the heavenly ¹lights cannot be counted, and the sand of the sea cannot be measured, so I will ^multiply the descendants of My servant David and the ᴮLevites who serve Me.'"

33:7 ^Is 1:26; Jer 30:18   **33:8** ^Ps 51:2; Is 44:22
33:9 ^Jer 3:17, 19   ᴮJer 24:6   **33:10** ^Jer 32:43
ᴮJer 26:9   **33:11** ^Lev 7:12, 13; Ps 107:22
33:12 ^Jer 32:43; 36:29   **33:13** ^Lev 27:32; Luke 15:4
33:14 ^Jer 23:5   ᴮIs 32:1, 2   **33:15** ^Is 4:2   ᴮPs 72:1-5
33:16 ^Is 45:24, 25; Jer 23:6   **33:17** ^2 Sam 7:16;
1 Kin 2:4   **33:18** ^Num 3:5-10; Deut 18:1
33:20 ^Ps 89:37; 104:19-23   **33:21** ^2 Sam 23:5;
2 Chr 7:18   **33:22** ^Ezek 37:24-27   ᴮIs 66:21

33:9 ¹I.e., This city   **33:22** ¹Lit *host*; i.e., sun, stars, etc.

²³And the word of the LORD came to Jeremiah, saying, ²⁴"Have you not observed what these people have asserted, saying, 'The ᴬtwo families which the LORD chose, He has ᴮrejected them'? So they despise My people as no longer being a nation in their sight. ²⁵This is what the LORD says: 'If My ᴬcovenant *for* day and night *does* not *continue, and* I have ᴮnot established the fixed patterns of heaven and earth, ²⁶then I would ᴬreject the descendants of Jacob and David My servant, so as not to take from his descendants ᴮrulers over the descendants of Abraham, Isaac, and Jacob. But I will restore their fortunes and have mercy on them.'"

A PROPHECY AGAINST ZEDEKIAH

34 The word that came to Jeremiah from the LORD, when Nebuchadnezzar king of Babylon and all his army, with ᴬall the kingdoms of the earth that were *under* his control and all the peoples, were fighting against Jerusalem and all its cities, saying, ²"This is what the LORD, the God of Israel says: 'Go and speak to Zedekiah king of Judah and say to him, "This is what the LORD says: 'Behold, ᴬI am handing this city over to the king of Babylon, and ᴮhe will burn it with fire. ³And as for you, ᴬyou will not escape from his hand, for you will assuredly be caught and handed over to him; and you will see the king of Babylon eye to eye, and he will speak with you face to face, and you will go to Babylon.'"' ⁴Yet hear the word of the LORD, Zedekiah king of Judah! This is what the LORD says concerning you: 'You will not die by the sword. ⁵You will die in peace; and as *spices*

were burned for your fathers, the former kings who were before you, so they will burn *spices* for you; and ᴬthey will mourn for you, *crying,* "Oh, *my* lord!"' For I have spoken the word," declares the LORD.

⁶Then Jeremiah the prophet spoke ᴬall these words to Zedekiah king of Judah in Jerusalem ⁷when the army of the king of Babylon was fighting against Jerusalem and all the remaining cities of Judah, *that is,* Lachish and Azekah, for they *alone* remained as ᴬfortified cities among the cities of Judah.

⁸The word that came to Jeremiah from the LORD after King Zedekiah had ᴬmade a covenant with all the people who were in Jerusalem, to proclaim release to them: ⁹that each person was to set his male servant free and each his female servant, a Hebrew man or a Hebrew woman, so that ᴬno one would keep them, his Jewish brother *or sister,* in bondage. ¹⁰And all the ᴬofficials and all the people obeyed who had entered into the covenant that each person was to set his male servant free and each his female servant, so that no one would keep them in bondage any longer; they obeyed, and set *them free.* ¹¹But afterward they turned around and took back the male servants and the female servants whom they had set free, and brought them into subjection as male servants and as female servants.

¹²Then the word of the LORD came to Jeremiah from the LORD, saying, ¹³"This is what the LORD, the God

33:24 ᴬIs 7:17   ᴮJer 30:17   33:25 ᴬGen 8:22
ᴮPs 74:16, 17   33:26 ᴬJer 31:37   ᴮGen 49:10
34:1 ᴬJer 1:15; 27:7   34:2 ᴬJer 21:10   ᴮJer 32:29
34:3 ᴬ2 Kin 25:4, 5; Jer 21:7   34:5 ᴬJer 22:18
34:6 ᴬ1 Sam 3:18; 15:16-24   34:7 ᴬ2 Chr 11:5-10
34:8 ᴬ2 Kin 11:17; 23:2, 3   34:9 ᴬLev 25:39
34:10 ᴬJer 26:10, 16

of Israel says: 'I ^made a covenant with your forefathers on the day that I ^Bbrought them out of the land of Egypt, from the house of bondage, saying, ¹⁴"^At the end of seven years each of you shall set free his Hebrew brother who has been sold to you and has served you for six years, and you shall send him out free from you." But your forefathers did not obey Me nor incline their ear to Me. ¹⁵Although recently you *had* turned and ^done what is right in My sight, each one proclaiming release to his neighbor, and you had made a covenant before Me in the house which is called by My name. ¹⁶Yet you turned and ^profaned My name, and each person took back his male servant and each his female servant whom you had set free according to their desire, and you brought them into subjection to be your male and female servants.'

¹⁷"Therefore this is what the LORD says: 'You have not obeyed Me in proclaiming release, each one to his brother and each to his neighbor. Behold, I am proclaiming a release to you,' declares the LORD, 'to the ^sword, to the plague, and to the famine; and I will make you a ^Bterror to all the kingdoms of the earth. ¹⁸I will give the people who have violated My covenant, who have not fulfilled the words of the covenant which they made before Me, *when* they ^cut the calf in two and passed between its parts— ¹⁹the ^officials of Judah and the officials of Jerusalem, the high officials and the priests, and all the people of the land who passed between the parts of the calf— ²⁰I will hand them over to their enemies and to those who ^seek their lives. And their dead bodies will be food for

the birds of the sky and the animals of the earth. ²¹Zedekiah king of Judah and his officials I will also hand over to their enemies and to those who seek their lives, and to the army of the king of Babylon which has ^withdrawn from you. ²²Behold, I am going to give a command,' declares the LORD, 'and I will bring them back to this city, and they will fight against it and take it and burn it with fire; and I will make the cities of Judah a ^desolation ^Bwithout inhabitant.'"

THE RECHABITES' OBEDIENCE

35 The word that came to Jeremiah from the LORD in the days of ^Jehoiakim the son of Josiah, king of Judah, saying, ²"Go to the house of the ^Rechabites and speak to them, and bring them into the house of the LORD, into one of the chambers, and give them wine to drink." ³So I took Jaazaniah the son of Jeremiah, son of Habazziniah, and his brothers and all his sons, and all the household of the Rechabites, ⁴and I brought them into the house of the LORD, into the chamber of the sons of Hanan the son of Igdaliah, the man of God, which was next to the chamber of the officials, which was above the chamber of Maaseiah the son of Shallum, ^the doorkeeper. ⁵Then I set before the men of the house of the Rechabites pitchers full of wine, and cups; and I said to them, "^Drink wine!" ⁶But they said, "We will not drink wine, for Jonadab the son of

34:13^Ex 24:3, 7, 8   ᴮEx 20:2   34:14^Ex 21:2;
Deut 15:12   34:15^Jer 34:8   34:16^Ex 20:7; Lev 19:12
34:17^Jer 32:24   ᴮDeut 28:25   34:18^Gen 15:10
34:19^Jer 34:10; Ezek 22:27   34:20^Jer 11:21; 21:7
34:21^Jer 37:5-11   34:22^Jer 4:7   ᴮJer 33:10
35:1^2 Kin 23:34-36; 24:1   35:2^2 Kin 10:15; 1 Chr 2:55
35:4^1 Chr 9:18f   35:5^Amos 2:12

Rechab, our father, commanded us, saying, 'You shall ^not drink wine, you or your sons, forever. ⁷You shall not build a house, and you shall not sow seed nor plant a vineyard, nor own one; but you shall live in tents all your days, so that you may live ^many days in the land where you ᴮlive as strangers.' ⁸And we have ^obeyed the voice of Jonadab the son of Rechab, our father, in all that he commanded us, not to drink wine all our days, we, our wives, our sons, or our daughters, ⁹nor to build ourselves houses to live in; and we ^do not have a vineyard, a field, or seed. ¹⁰But we have ^lived *only* in tents, and have obeyed and have done according to all that our father Jonadab commanded us. ¹¹However, when Nebuchadnezzar king of Babylon came up against the land, we said, 'Come, and let's ^go to Jerusalem away from the army of the Chaldeans and the army of the Arameans.' So we have lived in Jerusalem."

JUDAH REBUKED

¹²Then the word of the Lᴏʀᴅ came to Jeremiah, saying, ¹³"This is what the Lᴏʀᴅ of armies, the God of Israel says: 'Go and say to the people of Judah and the inhabitants of Jerusalem, "^Will you not accept instruction by listening to My words?" declares the Lᴏʀᴅ. ¹⁴"The ^words of Jonadab the son of Rechab have been followed, which he commanded his sons: not to drink wine. And they do not drink *wine* to this day, for they have obeyed their father's command. But I have spoken to you again and again, yet you have ᴮnot listened to Me. ¹⁵Also I have sent to you all My servants the prophets, sending

them again and again, saying: "^Turn now every person from his evil way and amend your deeds, and ᴮdo not follow other gods to worship them. Then you will live in the land which I have given to you and to your forefathers; but you have not inclined your ear or listened to Me. ¹⁶Indeed, the sons of Jonadab the son of Rechab have ^followed the command of their father which he commanded them, but this people has not listened to Me."'" ¹⁷Therefore this is what the Lᴏʀᴅ says, the God of armies, the God of Israel: 'Behold, ^I am bringing on Judah and on all the inhabitants of Jerusalem all the disaster that I have pronounced against them; because I spoke to them but they did not listen, and I have called them but they did not answer.'"

¹⁸Then Jeremiah said to the house of the Rechabites, "This is what the Lᴏʀᴅ of armies, the God of Israel says: 'Because you have ^obeyed the command of Jonadab your father, kept all his commands, and done according to all that he commanded you, ¹⁹therefore this is what the Lᴏʀᴅ of armies, the God of Israel says: "Jonadab the son of Rechab ^will not lack a man to ᴮstand before Me always."'"

JEREMIAH'S SCROLL READ IN THE TEMPLE

36 In the ^fourth year of Jehoiakim the son of Josiah, king of Judah, this word came to Jeremiah from the Lᴏʀᴅ, saying, ²"Take

35:6 ^Lev 10:9; Num 6:2-4　35:7 ^Ex 20:12　ᴮGen 36:7　35:8 ^Prov 1:8, 9; 4:1, 2, 10　35:9 ^Ps 37:16; Jer 35:7　35:10 ^Jer 35:7　35:11 ^Jer 4:5-7; 8:14　35:13 ^Is 28:9-12; Jer 5:3　35:14 ^Jer 35:6-10　ᴮIs 30:9　35:15 ^Is 1:16, 17　ᴮDeut 6:14　35:16 ^Jer 35:14; Mal 1:6　35:17 ^Josh 23:15; Jer 19:3, 15　35:18 ^Ex 20:12; Eph 6:1-3　35:19 ^1 Chr 2:55　ᴮJer 15:19　36:1 ^2 Kin 24:1; 2 Chr 36:5-7

a scroll and write on it all the words which I have spoken to you concerning ^Israel, Judah, and all the ^Bnations, from the day I *first* spoke to you, from the days of Josiah, even to this day. ³Perhaps the house of Judah will listen to all the disaster which I plan to carry out against them, so that every person will ^turn from his evil way; then I will ^Bforgive their wrongdoing and their sin."

⁴Then Jeremiah called Baruch the son of Neriah, and Baruch wrote on a ^scroll at the dictation of Jeremiah all the words of the LORD which He had spoken to him. ⁵Jeremiah then commanded Baruch, saying, "I am ^restricted; I cannot go into the house of the LORD. ⁶So you go and read from the scroll, which you have written at my dictation, the words of the LORD to the people at the LORD's house on a day of ^fasting. And you shall also read them to all *the people of* Judah who come from their cities. ⁷^Perhaps their pleading will come before the LORD, and everyone will turn from his evil way; for great is the anger and the wrath that the LORD has pronounced against this people." ⁸So Baruch the son of Neriah acted in accordance with all that Jeremiah the prophet commanded him, ^reading from the book the words of the LORD in the LORD's house.

⁹Now in the fifth year of Jehoiakim the son of Josiah, king of Judah, in the ninth month, all the people in Jerusalem and all the people who ^came from the cities of Judah to Jerusalem proclaimed a ^Bfast before the LORD. ¹⁰Then Baruch read to all the people from the book the words of Jeremiah in the house of the LORD in the ^chamber of ^BGemariah the son of Shaphan the scribe, in the upper courtyard, at the entry of the New Gate of the LORD's house.

¹¹Now when ^Micaiah the son of Gemariah, the son of Shaphan, had heard all the words of the LORD from the book, ¹²he went down to the king's house, into the scribe's chamber. And behold, all the officials were sitting there—^Elishama the scribe, Delaiah the son of Shemaiah, Elnathan the son of Achbor, Gemariah the son of Shaphan, Zedekiah the son of Hananiah, and all the *other* officials. ¹³And Micaiah ^declared to them all the words that he had heard when Baruch read from the book to the people. ¹⁴Then all the officials sent Jehudi the son of Nethaniah, *who was* the son of Shelemiah, the son of Cushi, to Baruch, saying, "Take in your hand the scroll from which you have read to the people and come." So Baruch the son of Neriah ^took the scroll in his hand and came to them. ¹⁵And they said to him, "Sit down, please, and read it to us." So Baruch ^read it to them. ¹⁶When they had heard all the words, they turned in ^fear one to another. And they said to Baruch, "We will certainly ^Breport all these words to the king." ¹⁷Then they asked Baruch, saying, "Tell us, please, ^how did you write all these words? *Was it* at Jeremiah's dictation?" ¹⁸And Baruch said to them, "He ^dictated all these words to me, and I wrote them with ink on the

36:2^Jer 3:3-10   ^BJer 1:5, 10   36:3^Deut 30:2, 8
^BJon 3:10   36:4^Jer 36:14; Ezek 2:9   36:5^Jer 32:2; 33:1
36:6^Jer 36:9; Zech 8:19   36:7^1 Kin 8:33; 2 Chr 33:12, 13
36:8^Jer 1:17; 36:6   36:9^Jer 36:6   ^BJudg 20:26
36:10^Jer 35:4   ^BJer 36:11, 25   36:11^Jer 36:13
36:12^Jer 36:20   36:13^2 Kin 22:10   36:14^Jer 36:2;
Ezek 2:7-10   36:15^Jer 36:21   36:16^Jer 36:24
^BJer 13:18   36:17^John 9:10, 15, 26   36:18^Jer 36:4

book." ¹⁹Then the officials said to Baruch, "Go, ^hide yourself, you and Jeremiah, and do not let anyone know where you are."

THE SCROLL IS BURNED

²⁰So they came to the ^king in the courtyard, but they had deposited the scroll in the chamber of ^Elishama the scribe; and they reported all the words to the king. ²¹Then the king sent Jehudi to get the scroll, and he took it out of the chamber of Elishama the scribe. And Jehudi ^read it to the king as well as to all the officials who were standing beside the king. ²²Now the king was sitting in the ^winter house in the ninth month, with *a fire* burning in the brazier before him. ²³And when Jehudi had read three or four columns, *the king* cut it with a scribe's knife and ^threw *it* into the fire that was in the brazier, until all of the scroll was consumed in the fire that was in the brazier. ²⁴Yet the king and all his servants who heard all these words did ^not tremble in fear, nor did they tear their garments. ²⁵Even though Elnathan, Delaiah, and Gemariah ^urged the king not to burn the scroll, he would not listen to them. ²⁶And the king commanded Jerahmeel the king's son, Seraiah the son of Azriel, and Shelemiah the son of Abdeel to ^seize Baruch the scribe and Jeremiah the prophet, but the ^LORD hid them.

THE SCROLL IS REPLACED

²⁷Then the word of the LORD came to Jeremiah after the king had ^burned the scroll and the words which Baruch had written at the dictation of Jeremiah, saying, ²⁸"^Take again another scroll and write on it all the previous words that were ^on the first scroll, which Jehoiakim the king of Judah burned. ²⁹And concerning Jehoiakim king of Judah you shall say, 'This is what the LORD says: "You have burned this scroll, saying, '^Why have you written on it that the ^king of Babylon will certainly come and destroy this land, and will make mankind and animals disappear from it?'" ³⁰Therefore this is what the LORD says concerning Jehoiakim king of Judah: "He shall have ^no one to sit on the throne of David, and his ^dead body shall be thrown out to the heat of the day and the frost of the night. ³¹I will also ^punish him, his descendants, and his servants for their wrongdoing, and I will bring on them and the inhabitants of Jerusalem and the people of Judah all the disaster that I have declared to them—but they did not listen."'"

³²Then Jeremiah took another scroll and gave it to the scribe Baruch the son of Neriah, and he ^wrote on it at the dictation of Jeremiah all the words of the book which Jehoiakim king of Judah had burned in the fire; and many similar words were added to them.

JEREMIAH WARNS AGAINST TRUST IN PHARAOH

37 Now ^Zedekiah the son of Josiah whom Nebuchadnezzar king of Babylon had ^made king in the land of Judah, reigned as king in place of Coniah the son of

36:19^1 Kin 17:3; 18:4, 10   **36:20**^Jer 36:12
36:21^2 Kin 22:10; 2 Chr 34:18   **36:22**^Judg 3:20;
Amos 3:15   **36:23**^1 Kin 22:8, 27; Prov 1:30
36:24^Ps 36:1; 64:5   **36:25**^Gen 37:22, 26, 27;
Acts 5:34-39   **36:26**^1 Kin 19:1-3, 10, 14   ^Ps 91:1
36:27^Jer 36:23   **36:28**^Zech 1:5, 6   ^Jer 36:4, 23
36:29^Is 29:21   ^Jer 25:9-11   **36:30**^2 Kin 24:12-15
^Jer 22:19   **36:31**^Jer 23:34   **36:32**^Ex 4:15, 16; 34:1
37:1^2 Kin 24:17   ^Ezek 17:12-21

Jehoiakim. ²But ^neither he nor his servants nor the people of the land listened to the words of the LORD which He spoke through Jeremiah the prophet.

³Yet King Zedekiah sent Jehucal the son of Shelemiah, and the priest Zephaniah the son of Maaseiah, to Jeremiah the prophet, saying, "^Please pray to the LORD our God in our behalf." ⁴Now Jeremiah was *still* coming and going among the people, for they had not *yet* ^put him in prison. ⁵Meanwhile, ^Pharaoh's army had set out from Egypt; and when the Chaldeans who had been besieging Jerusalem heard the report about them, they ᴮwithdrew from Jerusalem.

⁶Then the word of the LORD came to Jeremiah the prophet, saying, ⁷"This is what the LORD, the God of Israel says: 'This is what you are to say to the king of Judah, who sent you to Me to inquire of Me: "Behold, ^Pharaoh's army, which has come out to help you, is going to return to its own land of Egypt. ⁸Then the Chaldeans will ^return and fight against this city, and they will capture it and burn it with fire."' ⁹This is what the LORD says: 'Do not ^deceive yourselves, saying, "The Chaldeans will certainly go *away* from us," for they will not go. ¹⁰For ^even if you had defeated the entire army of Chaldeans who were fighting against you, and there were *only* wounded men left among them, each man in his tent, they would rise up and ᴮburn this city with fire.'"

JEREMIAH IMPRISONED

¹¹Now it happened when the army of the Chaldeans had withdrawn from Jerusalem because of Pharaoh's army, ¹²that Jeremiah left Jerusalem to go to the land of Benjamin in order to ^take possession of *some* property there among the people. ¹³While he was at the Gate of Benjamin, a captain of the guard whose name was Irijah, the son of Shelemiah the son of Hananiah was there; and he ^arrested Jeremiah the prophet, saying, "You are deserting to the Chaldeans!" ¹⁴But Jeremiah said, "^A lie! I am not deserting to the Chaldeans"; yet he would not listen to him. So Irijah arrested Jeremiah and brought him to the officials. ¹⁵Then the officials were ^angry at Jeremiah and they beat him, and ᴮput him in prison in the house of Jonathan the scribe, for they had made it into the prison. ¹⁶For Jeremiah had come into the ^dungeon, that is, the vaulted cell; and Jeremiah stayed there many days.

¹⁷Now King Zedekiah sent *men* and took him *out;* and in his palace the king ^secretly asked him and said, "Is there a word from the LORD?" And Jeremiah said, "There is!" Then he said, "You will be ᴮhanded over to the king of Babylon!" ¹⁸Moreover, Jeremiah said to King Zedekiah, "^*In* what *way* have I sinned against you, or your servants, or this people, that you have put me in prison? ¹⁹And where are your prophets who prophesied to you, saying, 'The ^king of Babylon will not come against you or against this land'? ²⁰But now, please listen, my lord the king; please let my ^plea

37:2 ^2 Kin 24:19, 20; 2 Chr 36:12-16   37:3 ^1 Kin 13:6; Jer 2:27   37:4 ^Jer 32:2, 3; 37:15   37:5 ^2 Kin 24:7
ᴮ Jer 37:11   37:7 ^Is 30:1-3; 31:1-3   37:8 ^Jer 34:22; 38:23   37:9 ^Jer 29:8; Obad 3   37:10 ^Lev 26:36-38
ᴮ Jer 37:8   37:12 ^Jer 32:8   37:13 ^Jer 18:18; 20:10
37:14 ^Ps 27:12; 52:1, 2   37:15 ^Jer 18:23   ᴮ Gen 39:20
37:16 ^Jer 38:6   37:17 ^1 Kin 14:1-4   ᴮ Jer 21:7
37:18 ^1 Sam 24:9; 26:18   37:19 ^Jer 27:14; 28:1-4, 10-17
37:20 ^Jer 36:7; 38:26

come before you and do not make me return to the house of Jonathan the scribe, so that I will not die there." 21 Then King Zedekiah gave a command, and they placed Jeremiah in custody in the ^courtyard of the guardhouse, and gave him a loaf of bread daily from the bakers' street, until all the bread in the city was gone. So Jeremiah remained in the courtyard of the guardhouse.

JEREMIAH THROWN INTO THE CISTERN

38 Now Shephatiah the son of Mattan, Gedaliah the son of Pashhur, Jucal the son of Shelemiah, and ^Pashhur the son of Malchijah heard the words that Jeremiah was speaking to all the people, saying, 2 "This is what the LORD says: 'Anyone who ^stays in this city will die by the ^sword, by famine, or by plague; but anyone who surrenders to the Chaldeans will live and have his own life as plunder, and stay alive.' 3 This is what the LORD says: 'This city will certainly be ^handed over to the army of the king of Babylon and he will capture it.'" 4 Then the officials said to the king, "Please have this man put to death, since he is ^discouraging the men of war who are left in this city and all the people, by speaking words like these to them; for this man ^is not seeking the well-being of this people, but rather their harm." 5 And King Zedekiah said, "Behold, he is in your hands; for the king ^can do nothing against you." 6 So they took Jeremiah and threw him into the ^cistern of Malchijah the king's son, which was in the courtyard of the guardhouse; and they let Jeremiah down with ropes. Now

in the cistern there was no water but only mud, and Jeremiah sank into the mud. 7 But ^Ebed-melech the Ethiopian, a ^eunuch, while he was in the king's palace, heard that they had put Jeremiah in the cistern. Now the king was sitting at the Gate of Benjamin; 8 and Ebed-melech went out from the king's palace and spoke to the king, saying, 9 "My lord the king, these men have acted wickedly in all that they have done to Jeremiah the prophet whom they have thrown into the cistern; and he will die right where he is because of the famine, for there is ^no more bread in the city." 10 Then the king commanded Ebed-melech the Ethiopian, saying, "Take thirty men from here under your authority and bring Jeremiah the prophet up from the cistern before he dies." 11 So Ebed-melech took the men under his authority and went into the king's palace to a place beneath the storeroom, and took from there worn-out clothes and worn-out rags, and let them down by ropes into the cistern to Jeremiah. 12 Then Ebed-melech the Ethiopian said to Jeremiah, "Now put these worn-out clothes and rags under your armpits under the ropes"; and Jeremiah did so. 13 So they pulled Jeremiah out with the ropes and lifted him out of the cistern, and Jeremiah stayed in the ^courtyard of the guardhouse.

ZEDEKIAH SEEKS AN ANSWER FROM GOD

14 Then King Zedekiah sent word and had Jeremiah the prophet

37:21 ^Jer 32:2; 38:13, 28   38:1 ^Jer 21:1   38:2 ^Jer 21:9
^Jer 34:17   38:3 ^Jer 21:10; 32:3-5   38:4 ^Ex 5:4
^Jer 29:7   38:5 ^2 Sam 3:39   38:6 ^Jer 37:16, 21;
Acts 16:24   38:7 ^Jer 39:16   ^Jer 29:2
38:9 ^Jer 37:21; 52:6   38:13 ^Neh 3:25; Jer 32:2

brought to him at the third entrance that is in the house of the LORD; and the king said to Jeremiah, "I am going to ^ask you something; do not hide anything from me." ¹⁵And Jeremiah said to Zedekiah, "^If I tell you, will you not certainly put me to death? Besides, if I give you advice, you will not listen to me." ¹⁶But King Zedekiah swore to Jeremiah in ^secret, saying, "As the LORD lives, who made this ᴮlife for us, I certainly will not put you to death, nor will I hand you over to these men who are seeking your life."

¹⁷So Jeremiah said to Zedekiah, "This is what the LORD God of armies, the God of Israel says: 'If you will indeed ^surrender to the officers of the king of Babylon, then you will live, this city will not be burned with fire, and you and your household will survive. ¹⁸But if you do ^not surrender to the officers of the king of Babylon, then this city will be handed over to the Chaldeans; and they will burn it with fire, and ᴮyou yourself will not escape from their hands.'" ¹⁹Then King Zedekiah said to Jeremiah, "I am ^in fear of the Jews who have ᴮdeserted to the Chaldeans, for they may hand me over to them, and they will abuse me." ²⁰But Jeremiah said, "They will not turn you over. Please ^obey the LORD in what I am saying to you, so that it may go well for you and you may live. ²¹But if you keep refusing to surrender, this is the word which the LORD has shown me: ²²'Behold, all of the ^women who have been left in the palace of the king of Judah are going to be brought out to the officers of the king of Babylon; and those women will say,

"Your close friends
    Have misled and overpowered
       you;
While your feet were sunk in
       the mire,
    They turned back."

²³They are also going to bring out all your wives and your sons to the Chaldeans, and ^you yourself will not escape from their hand, but will be seized by the hand of the king of Babylon, and ^this city will be burned with fire.'"

²⁴Then Zedekiah said to Jeremiah, "Let no one know about these words, and you will not die. ²⁵But if the ^officials hear that I have talked with you and come to you and say to you, 'Tell us now what you said to the king and what the king said to you; do not hide *it* from us and we will not put you to death,' ²⁶then you are to say to them, 'I was ^presenting my plea before the king, not to make me return to the house of Jonathan to die there.'" ²⁷Then all the officials came to Jeremiah and questioned him. So he reported to them in accordance with all these words which the king had commanded; and they stopped speaking with him, since the conversation had not been overheard. ²⁸So Jeremiah ^stayed in the courtyard of the guard until the day that Jerusalem was captured.

JERUSALEM CAPTURED

39 Now when Jerusalem was captured ^in the ninth year of Zedekiah king of Judah, in the tenth month, Nebuchadnezzar king of

38:14 ^1 Sam 3:17, 18; 1 Chr 22:16   38:15 ^Luke 22:67, 68
38:16 ^Jer 37:17   ᴮNum 16:22   38:17 ^2 Kin 24:12;
25:27-30   38:18 ^Jer 27:8   ᴮJer 32:4   38:19 ^Is 51:12, 13
ᴮJer 39:9   38:20 ^2 Chr 20:20; Jer 11:4, 8
38:22 ^Jer 6:12; 8:10   38:23 ^Jer 38:18   38:25 ^Jer
38:4-6, 27   38:26 ^Jer 37:20   38:28 ^Ps 23:4;
Jer 15:20, 21   39:1 ^2 Kin 25:1-12; Jer 52:4

Babylon and all his army came to Jerusalem and laid siege to it; ²in the eleventh year of Zedekiah, in the fourth month, in the ninth *day* of the month, the city *wall* was ^breached. ³Then all the ^officials of the king of Babylon came in and sat down at the ^BMiddle Gate: Nergal-sar-ezer, Samgar-nebu, Sar-sekim the Rab-saris, Nergal-sar-ezer *the* Rab-mag, and all the rest of the officials of the king of Babylon. ⁴And when Zedekiah the king of Judah and all the men of war saw them, they fled and left the city at night by way of the king's garden through the gate ^between the two walls; and he went out toward the ¹Arabah. ⁵But the army of the Chaldeans pursued them and overtook Zedekiah in the plains of Jericho; and they took him and brought him up to Nebuchadnezzar king of Babylon at ^Riblah in the land of Hamath, and he passed sentence on him. ⁶Then the king of Babylon slaughtered the sons of Zedekiah ^before his eyes at Riblah; the king of Babylon also slaughtered all the ^Bnobles of Judah. ⁷He then ^blinded Zedekiah's eyes and bound him in shackles of bronze to bring him to Babylon. ⁸The Chaldeans also ^burned the king's palace and the houses of the people with fire, and they ^Btore down the walls of Jerusalem. ⁹And as for the rest of the people who were left in the city, the ^deserters who had deserted to him and ^Bthe rest of the people who remained, Nebuzaradan the captain of the bodyguard took *them* into exile in Babylon. ¹⁰But some of the ^poorest people, who had nothing, ^Nebuzaradan the captain of the bodyguard left behind in the land of Judah, and gave them vineyards and fields at that time.

JEREMIAH SPARED

¹¹Now Nebuchadnezzar king of Babylon gave orders regarding ^Jeremiah through Nebuzaradan the captain of the bodyguard, saying, ¹²"Take him and look after him, and ^do not do anything harmful to him, but rather deal with him just as he tells you." ¹³So Nebuzaradan the captain of the bodyguard sent *word*, along with Nebushazban the Rab-saris, Nergal-sar-ezer the Rab-mag, and all the leading officers of the king of Babylon; ¹⁴they even sent *word* and ^took Jeremiah out of the courtyard of the guardhouse and entrusted him to Gedaliah, the son of Ahikam, the son of Shaphan, to take him home. So he stayed among the people.

¹⁵Now the word of the LORD had come to Jeremiah while he was ^confined in the courtyard of the guardhouse, saying, ¹⁶"Go and speak to Ebed-melech the Ethiopian, saying, 'This is what the LORD of armies, the God of Israel says: "Behold, I am going to bring My words on this city ^for disaster and not for prosperity; and they will ^Btake place before you on that day. ¹⁷But I will ^save you on that day," declares the LORD, "and you will not be handed over to the men of whom you are afraid. ¹⁸For I will assuredly rescue you, and you will not fall by the sword; but you will have your *own* life as plunder, because you have ^trusted in Me," declares the LORD.'"

39:2^2 Kin 25:4; Jer 52:7   **39:3**^Jer 38:17   ᴮJer 21:4
39:4^2 Chr 32:5   **39:5**^2 Kin 23:33; Jer 52:9, 26, 27
39:6^Deut 28:34   ᴮJer 21:7   **39:7**^2 Kin 25:7; Jer 52:11
39:8^2 Kin 25:9   ᴮ2 Kin 25:10   **39:9**^Jer 38:19
ᴮJer 24:8   **39:10**^2 Kin 25:12; Jer 52:16
39:11^Job 5:15, 16; Jer 1:8   **39:12**^Ps 105:14, 15;
Prov 16:7   **39:14**^Jer 38:28; 40:1-6   **39:15**^Jer 38:28
39:16^Jer 21:10   ᴮPs 91:8   **39:17**^Ps 41:1, 2; 50:15
39:18^Ps 34:22; Jer 17:7, 8

39:4 ¹I.e., Jordan valley

JEREMIAH REMAINS IN JUDAH

40 The word that came to Jeremiah from the LORD after Nebuzaradan captain of the bodyguard had released him from ^Ramah, when he had taken him bound in ^Bchains among all the exiles of Jerusalem and Judah who were being exiled to Babylon. ²Now the captain of the bodyguard had taken Jeremiah and said to him, "The ^LORD your God promised this disaster against this place; ³and the LORD has brought *it* and done just as He promised. Because you *people* ^sinned against the LORD and did not listen to His voice, this thing has happened to you. ⁴But now, behold, I am ^setting you free today from the chains that are on your hands. If you would prefer to come with me to Babylon, come *along,* and I will look after you; but if you would prefer not to come with me to Babylon, do not *come.* Look, the whole land is before you; go wherever it seems good and right for you to go." ⁵As Jeremiah was still not going back, ¹*he said,* "Go on back then to ^Gedaliah the son of Ahikam, the son of Shaphan, whom the king of Babylon has ^Bappointed over the cities of Judah, and stay with him among the people; or else go anywhere it seems right for you to go." So the captain of the bodyguard gave him a ration and a gift, and let him go. ⁶Then Jeremiah went to ^Mizpah to Gedaliah the son of Ahikam and stayed with him among the people who were left in the land.

⁷Now all the commanders of the forces that were in the field, they and their men, heard that the king of Babylon had appointed Gedaliah the son of Ahikam over the land, and that he had put him in charge of the men, women, and children, those of the ^poorest of the land who had not been exiled to Babylon. ⁸So they came to Gedaliah at Mizpah, along with Ishmael the son of Nethaniah, Johanan and Jonathan the sons of Kareah, Seraiah the son of Tanhumeth, the sons of Ephai the ^Netophathite, and ^BJezaniah the son of the Maacathite, *both* they and their men. ⁹Then Gedaliah the son of Ahikam, the son of Shaphan, ^swore to them and to their men, saying, "^BDo not be afraid of serving the Chaldeans; stay in the land and serve the king of Babylon, so that it may go well for you. ¹⁰Now as for me, behold, I am going to stay in Mizpah to ^stand *for you* before the Chaldeans who come to us; but as for you, gather wine, summer fruit, and oil, and put *them* in your *storage* vessels, and live in your cities that you have taken over." ¹¹Likewise, also all the Jews who were in ^Moab and among the sons of Ammon and in Edom, and who were in all the *other* countries, heard that the king of Babylon had left a remnant for Judah, and that he had appointed over them Gedaliah the son of Ahikam, the son of Shaphan. ¹²Then all the Jews ^returned from all the places to which they had been scattered and came to the land of Judah, to Gedaliah at Mizpah, and gathered wine and summer fruit in great abundance.

40:1^Jer 31:15   ^BActs 12:6, 7   40:2^Lev 26:14-38; Deut 28:15-68   40:3^Jer 50:7; Dan 9:11
40:4^Jer 39:11, 12   40:5^Jer 39:14   ^B2 Kin 25:23
40:6^Judg 20:1; 21:1   40:7^Jer 39:10; 52:16
40:8^2 Sam 23:28, 29   ^BJer 42:1   40:9^1 Sam 20:16, 17
^BJer 27:11   40:10^Deut 1:38; 1 Kin 10:8
40:11^Num 22:1; 25:1, 2   40:12^Jer 43:5
40:5 ¹I.e., Nebuzaradan

[13] Now Johanan the son of Kareah and all the commanders of the forces that were in the field came to Gedaliah at Mizpah, [14] and said to him, "Are you well aware that Baalis the king of the sons of ^Ammon has sent Ishmael the son of Nethaniah to take your life?" But Gedaliah the son of Ahikam did not believe them. [15] Then Johanan the son of Kareah spoke secretly to Gedaliah in Mizpah, saying, "^Let me go and kill Ishmael the son of Nethaniah, and no one will know! Why should he take your life, so that all the Jews who are gathered to you would be scattered and the remnant of Judah would perish?" [16] But Gedaliah the son of Ahikam said to Johanan the son of Kareah, "^Do not do this thing, for you are telling a lie about Ishmael."

GEDALIAH IS MURDERED

41 Now in the seventh month Ishmael the son of Nethaniah, the son of Elishama, of the royal family and *one* of the chief officers of the king, along with ten men, came to Mizpah to Gedaliah the son of Ahikam. While they ^were eating bread together there in Mizpah, [2] Ishmael the son of Nethaniah and the ten men who were with him rose up, and ^struck and killed Gedaliah the son of Ahikam, the son of Shaphan, with the sword and put to death the one ^whom the king of Babylon had appointed over the land. [3] Ishmael also struck and killed all the Jews who were with him, *that is* with Gedaliah in Mizpah, and the Chaldeans who were found there, the men of war.

[4] Now it happened on the next day after the killing of Gedaliah, when no one knew *about it*, [5] that eighty men came from Shechem, from Shiloh, and from Samaria with ^their beards shaved off, their clothes torn, and their bodies ^gashed, having grain offerings and incense in their hands to bring to the house of the LORD. [6] Then Ishmael the son of Nethaniah left Mizpah to meet them, ^weeping as he went; and as he met them, he said to them, "Come to Gedaliah the son of Ahikam!" [7] Yet it turned out that as soon as they came inside the city, Ishmael the son of Nethaniah and the men who were with him ^slaughtered them *and threw them* into the cistern. [8] But ten men who were found among them said to Ishmael, "Do not put us to death, for we have ^supplies of wheat, barley, oil, and honey hidden in the field." So he refrained and did not put them to death along with their companions.

[9] Now as for the cistern where Ishmael had thrown all the bodies of the men whom he had struck and killed because of Gedaliah, it was the ^one that King Asa had constructed on account of Baasha, king of Israel; Ishmael the son of Nethaniah filled it with the dead. [10] Then Ishmael took captive all the ^remnant of the people who were in Mizpah, the ^king's daughters and all the people who were left in Mizpah, whom Nebuzaradan the captain of the bodyguard had put in the custody of Gedaliah the son of Ahikam. Ishmael the son of Nethaniah took them captive and proceeded to cross over to the sons of Ammon.

40:14 ^1 Sam 11:1-3; 2 Sam 10:1-6   40:15 ^1 Sam 26:8
40:16 ^Matt 10:16; 1 Cor 13:5   41:1 ^Ps 41:9; Jer 40:13, 14
41:2 ^2 Sam 3:27   ^Jer 40:5   41:5 ^Lev 19:27
^Deut 14:1   41:6 ^2 Sam 3:16; Jer 50:4   41:7 ^Ps 55:23;
Is 59:7   41:8 ^Is 45:3   41:9 ^1 Kin 15:17-22; 2 Chr 16:1-6
41:10 ^Jer 40:11, 12   ^Jer 43:6

JOHANAN RESCUES THE PEOPLE

¹¹But Johanan the son of Kareah and all the ^commanders of the forces that were with him heard about all the evil that Ishmael the son of Nethaniah had done. ¹²So they took all the men and went to fight with Ishmael the son of Nethaniah and they found him by the ^large pool that is in Gibeon. ¹³Now as soon as all the people who were with Ishmael saw Johanan the son of Kareah and all the commanders of the forces that were with him, they were joyful. ¹⁴So all the people whom Ishmael had taken captive from Mizpah turned around and came back, and went to Johanan the son of Kareah. ¹⁵But Ishmael the son of Nethaniah ^escaped from Johanan with eight men, and went to the sons of Ammon. ¹⁶Then Johanan the son of Kareah and all the commanders of the forces that were with him took from Mizpah ^all the remnant of the people whom he had recovered from Ishmael the son of Nethaniah, after he had struck and killed Gedaliah the son of Ahikam, *that is,* the men who were soldiers, *the* women, *the* children, and *the* high officials, whom he had brought back from Gibeon. ¹⁷And they went and stayed in ^Geruth Chimham, which is beside Bethlehem, in order to ^proceed into Egypt ¹⁸because of the Chaldeans; for they were afraid of them, since Ishmael the son of Nethaniah had struck and killed Gedaliah the son of Ahikam, whom ^the king of Babylon had appointed over the land.

WARNING AGAINST GOING TO EGYPT

42 Then all the commanders of the forces, ^Johanan the son of Kareah, Jezaniah the son of Hoshaiah, and all the people from the small to the great approached ²and said to Jeremiah the prophet, "Please let our ^pleading come before you, and pray for us to the Lord your God for all this remnant— since we have been left *only* a ^few out of many, just as your own eyes *now* see us— ³that the Lord your God will tell us the ^way in which we should walk, and the thing that we should do." ⁴Then Jeremiah the prophet said to them, "I have heard *you.* Behold, I am going to pray to the Lord your God in accordance with your words; and I will tell you the whole message which the ^Lord gives you as an answer. I will ^not withhold a word from you." ⁵Then they said to Jeremiah, "May the ^Lord be a true and faithful witness against us if we do not act in accordance with the whole message with which the Lord your God will send you to us. ⁶Whether *it is* pleasant or unpleasant, we will ^listen to the voice of the Lord our God to whom we are sending you, so that it may go well for us when we listen to the voice of the Lord our God."

⁷Now at the ^end of ten days the word of the Lord came to Jeremiah. ⁸Then he called for Johanan the son of Kareah and all the commanders of the forces that were with him, and for all the people from the small to the great, ⁹and said to them, "This is what the Lord ^says, the God of Israel, to whom you sent me to present your plea before Him: ¹⁰'If you will indeed stay in this land, then I will ^build

41:11^Jer 40:7, 8, 13–16   41:12^2 Sam 2:13
41:15^1 Sam 30:17; 1 Kin 20:20   41:16^Jer 42:8; 43:4-7
41:17^2 Sam 19:37, 38, 40   ^Jer 42:14   41:18^Jer 40:5
42:1^Jer 40:8, 13; 41:11, 18   42:2^Jer 36:7   ^Lev 26:22
42:3^Ps 86:11; Prov 3:6   42:4^1 Kin 22:14
^1 Sam 3:17, 18   42:5^Gen 31:50; Judg 11:10
42:6^Ex 24:7; Deut 5:27   42:7^Ps 27:14; Is 30:18
42:9^2 Kin 19:4, 6, 20; 22:15   42:10^Jer 24:6; 31:28

you up and not tear you down, and I will plant you and not uproot you; for I will relent of the disaster that I have inflicted on you. [11]ᴬDo not be afraid of the king of Babylon, whom you are *now* fearing; do not be afraid of him,' declares the Lᴏʀᴅ, 'for ᴮI am with you to save you and rescue you from his hand. [12]I will also show you compassion, so that ᴬhe will have compassion on you and restore you to your own soil. [13]But if you are going to say, "We will ᴬnot stay in this land," so as not to listen to the voice of the Lᴏʀᴅ your God, [14]saying, "No, but we will ᴬgo to the land of Egypt, where we will not see war, or hear the sound of a trumpet, or hunger for bread, and we will stay there"; [15]then in that case listen to the word of the Lᴏʀᴅ, you remnant of Judah. This is what the Lᴏʀᴅ of armies, the God of Israel says: "If you really set your minds to enter ᴬEgypt and go in to reside there, [16]then the ᴬsword, of which you are afraid, will overtake you there in the land of Egypt; and the famine, about which you are anxious, will follow closely after you there *in* Egypt, and you will die there. [17]So all the people who set their minds to go to Egypt to reside there will die by the sword, by famine, or by plague; and they will ᴬhave no refugees or survivors from the disaster that I am going to bring on them."'"

[18]For this is what the Lᴏʀᴅ of armies, the God of Israel says: "As My anger and wrath have gushed out on the inhabitants of Jerusalem, so My wrath will gush out on you when you enter Egypt. And you will become a ᴬcurse, an object of horror, ¹an imprecation, and a disgrace; and ᴮyou will not see this place

again." [19]The Lᴏʀᴅ has spoken to you, you remnant of Judah, "Do not ᴬgo to Egypt!" You know for certain that I have admonished you today. [20]For you have *only* ᴬdeceived yourselves; for it is you who sent me to the Lᴏʀᴅ your God, saying, "Pray for us to the Lᴏʀᴅ our God; and whatever the Lᴏʀᴅ our God says, tell us so, and we will do it." [21]So I have told you today, but you have ᴬnot obeyed the Lᴏʀᴅ your God in whatever He has sent me to *tell* you. [22]And now you shall know for certain that you will ᴬdie by the sword, by famine, or by plague in the ᴮplace where you desire to go to reside.

IN EGYPT JEREMIAH WARNS OF JUDGMENT

43 But as soon as Jeremiah, whom the Lᴏʀᴅ their God had sent to them, had ᴬfinished telling all the people all the words of the Lᴏʀᴅ their God—that is, all these words— [2]Azariah the ᴬson of Hoshaiah, Johanan the son of Kareah, and all the arrogant men said to Jeremiah, "You are telling a lie! The Lᴏʀᴅ our God has not sent you to say, 'You are not to enter Egypt to reside there'; [3]but ᴬBaruch the son of Neriah is inciting you against us in order to hand us over to the Chaldeans, so they will put us to death or exile us to Babylon!" [4]So Johanan the son of Kareah and all the commanders of the forces, and all the people, ᴬdid

42:11ᴬJer 1:8   ᴮNum 14:9   42:12ᴬNeh 1:11; Ps 106:46
42:13ᴬEx 5:2; Jer 44:16   42:14ᴬIs 31:1; Jer 41:17
42:15ᴬDeut 17:16; Jer 42:17   42:16ᴬJer 44:13, 27;
Ezek 11:8   42:17ᴬJer 44:14, 28   42:18ᴬDeut 29:21
ᴮJer 22:10, 27   42:19ᴬDeut 17:16; Is 30:1-7
42:20ᴬJer 43:2; Ezek 14:3   42:21ᴬJer 43:4
42:22ᴬJer 43:11   ᴮHos 9:6   43:1ᴬJer 26:8; 51:63
43:2ᴬJer 42:1   43:3ᴬJer 36:4, 10, 26, 32; 43:6
43:4ᴬ2 Chr 25:16

42:18 ¹Lit *a curse-formula*

not obey the voice of the Lord to ᴮstay in the land of Judah. ⁵Instead, Johanan the son of Kareah and all the commanders of the forces took the ᴬentire remnant of Judah who had returned from all the nations to which they had been scattered, in order to reside in the land of Judah— ⁶the men, the women, the children, the ᴬking's daughters, and ᴮevery person whom Nebuzaradan the captain of the bodyguard had left with Gedaliah the son of Ahikam and grandson of Shaphan, together with Jeremiah the prophet and Baruch the son of Neriah— ⁷and they entered the land of Egypt (for they did not obey the voice of the Lord) and went in as far as ᴬTahpanhes.

⁸Then the word of the Lord came to Jeremiah in ᴬTahpanhes, saying, ⁹"Take *some* large stones in your hands and hide them in the mortar in the brick *terrace* which is at the entrance of Pharaoh's palace in Tahpanhes, in the sight of some *of the* Jews; ¹⁰and say to them, 'This is what the Lord of armies, the God of Israel says: "Behold, I am going to send *men* and get ᴬMy servant ᴮNebuchadnezzar the king of Babylon, and I am going to set his throne over these stones that I have hidden; and he will spread his canopy over them. ¹¹He will also come and strike the land of Egypt; those who are *meant* for death *will be given over* to death, and those for captivity to captivity, and ᴬthose for the sword to the sword. ¹²And I shall set fire to the temples of the ᴬgods of Egypt, and he will burn them and take them captive. So he will wrap himself with the land of Egypt as a shepherd wraps himself with his garment, and he will depart from

there safely. ¹³He will also smash to pieces the obelisks of Heliopolis, which is in the land of Egypt; and the temples of the gods of Egypt he will burn with fire."'"

CONQUEST OF EGYPT PREDICTED

44 The word that came to Jeremiah for all the Jews living in the land of Egypt, those who were living in ᴬMigdol, Tahpanhes, ᴮMemphis, and the land of Pathros, saying, ²"This is what the Lord of armies, the God of Israel says: 'You yourselves have seen all the disaster that I have brought on Jerusalem and all the cities of Judah; and behold, this day they are in ᴬruins and no one lives in them, ³because of their wickedness which they committed to ᴬprovoke Me to anger by continuing to ᴮburn sacrifices *and* to serve other gods whom they had not known, *neither* they, you, nor your fathers. ⁴Yet I ᴬsent you all My servants the prophets again and again, saying, "Oh, do not do this ᴮabominable thing which I hate." ⁵But ᴬthey did not listen or incline their ears to turn from their wickedness, so as not to burn sacrifices to other gods. ⁶Therefore My wrath and My anger gushed out and burned in the ᴬcities of Judah and in the streets of Jerusalem, so they have become ruins and a ᴮdesolation as *it is* this day. ⁷Now then, this is what the Lord God of armies, the God of Israel says: "Why are you doing great harm to yourselves, to

43:4 ᴮPs 37:3   43:5 ᴬJer 40:11   43:6 ᴬJer 41:10
ᴮJer 39:10   43:7 ᴬJer 2:16; 44:1
43:8 ᴬJer 46:14; Ezek 30:18   43:10 ᴬIs 44:28
ᴮJer 25:9, 11   43:11 ᴬJer 15:2   43:12 ᴬEx 12:12; Is 19:1
44:1 ᴬEx 14:2   ᴮIs 19:13   44:2 ᴬIs 6:11; Jer 4:7
44:3 ᴬIs 3:8   ᴮJer 19:4   44:4 ᴬJer 7:13, 25   ᴮJer 16:18
44:5 ᴬJer 11:8, 10; 13:10   44:6 ᴬJer 7:17, 34   ᴮJer 4:27

^eliminate from yourselves man and woman, child and infant from among Judah, leaving yourselves without a remnant, ⁸provoking Me to anger with the works of your hands, ^burning sacrifices to other gods in the land of Egypt where you are entering to reside, so that you may be eliminated and become a curse and a disgrace among all the nations of the earth? ⁹Have you forgotten the ^wickedness of your fathers, the wickedness of the kings of Judah and the wickedness of their wives, your own wickedness and the wickedness of your wives, which they committed in the land of Judah and in the streets of Jerusalem? ¹⁰*Yet* they have not become contrite *even* to this day, nor have they feared, nor ^walked in My Law or My statutes, which I placed before you and before your fathers."'

¹¹"Therefore this is what the LORD of armies, the God of Israel says: 'Behold, I am going to ^set My face against you for a disaster, even to eliminate all Judah. ¹²And I will ^take away the remnant of Judah who have set their minds on entering the land of Egypt to reside there, and they will all meet their end in the land of Egypt; they will fall by the sword *or* meet their end by famine. From the small to the great, they will die by the sword and famine; and they will become a curse, an object of horror, ¹an imprecation, and a disgrace. ¹³And I will ^punish those who live in the land of Egypt, just as I have punished Jerusalem, with the sword, with famine, and with plague. ¹⁴So there will be ^no survivor or refugee for the remnant of Judah who have entered the land of Egypt to

reside there and *then* to return to the land of Judah, to which they are longing to return to live; for none will return except *a few* refugees.'"

¹⁵Then ^all the men who were aware that their wives were burning sacrifices to other gods, along with all the women who were standing by, *as* a large assembly, including all the people who were living in Pathros in the land of Egypt, responded to Jeremiah, saying, ¹⁶"As for the ^message that you have spoken to us in the name of the LORD, ᴮwe are not going to listen to you! ¹⁷But we will certainly carry out every word that has proceeded from our mouths, by burning sacrifices to the ^queen of heaven and pouring out drink offerings to her, just as we ourselves, our forefathers, our kings, and our leaders did in the cities of Judah and in the streets of Jerusalem; for *then* we had ᴮplenty of food and were well off and saw no misfortune. ¹⁸But since we stopped burning sacrifices to the queen of heaven and pouring out drink offerings to her, we have ^lacked everything, and have met our end by the sword and by famine." ¹⁹"And," *said the women*, "when we were ^burning sacrifices to the queen of heaven and pouring out drink offerings to her, was it ᴮwithout our husbands that we made for her sacrificial cakes in her image, and poured out drink offerings to her?"

44:7^Jer 3:24; 9:21   **44:8**^Jer 7:9; 11:12, 17
44:9^Jer 7:9, 10, 17, 18; 44:17, 21   **44:10**^Jer 26:4;
32:23   **44:11**^Lev 17:10; 20:5, 6   **44:12**^Jer
42:15-18, 22   **44:13**^Jer 11:22; 44:27, 28
44:14^Jer 22:10; 44:27   **44:15**^Prov 11:21; Is 1:5
44:16^Jer 43:2   ᴮProv 1:24-27   **44:17**^2 Kin 17:16
ᴮEx 16:3   **44:18**^Num 11:5, 6; Jer 40:12
44:19^Jer 7:18   ᴮNum 30:6, 7

44:12¹Lit *a curse-formula*

DISASTER FOR THE JEWS

²⁰Then Jeremiah said to all the people, to the men and women—even to all the people who were giving him *such* an answer—saying, ²¹"As for the ^smoking sacrifices that you burned in the cities of Judah and in the streets of Jerusalem, you and your forefathers, your kings and your leaders, and the people of the land, did the Lord not remember them, and did *all of this* not come into His mind? ²²So the Lord was ^no longer able to endure *it*, ᴮbecause of the evil of your deeds, because of the abominations which you have committed; so your land has become a place of ruins, an object of horror, and a curse, without an inhabitant, as *it is* this day. ²³Since you have burned sacrifices and have sinned against the Lord and not obeyed the voice of the Lord nor walked in His Law, His statutes, or His testimonies, therefore this ^disaster has happened to you, as *it has* this day."

²⁴Then Jeremiah said to all the people, including all the women, "Hear the word of the Lord, all Judah who are ^in the land of Egypt! ²⁵This is what the Lord of armies, the God of Israel says: 'As for you and your wives, you have spoken with your mouths and fulfilled *it* with your hands, saying, "We will certainly perform our vows that we have vowed, to burn sacrifices to the queen of heaven and pour out drink offerings to her." ^By all means fulfill your vows, and be sure to perform your vows!' ²⁶In return, hear the word of the Lord, all Judah who are living in the land of Egypt: 'Behold, I have sworn by My great name,' says the Lord, 'that My name shall ^never

be invoked again by the mouth of anyone of Judah in all the land of Egypt, saying, "As the Lord God lives." ²⁷Behold, I am watching over them for harm and not for good, and ^all the people of Judah who are in the land of Egypt will meet their end by the sword or by famine until they are completely gone. ²⁸^Those who escape the sword will return from the land of Egypt to the land of Judah ᴮfew in number. Then all the remnant of Judah who have gone to the land of Egypt to reside there will know whose word will stand, Mine or theirs. ²⁹And this will be the sign to you,' declares the Lord, 'that I am going to punish you in this place, so that you may know that ^My words will assuredly stand against you for harm.' ³⁰This is what the Lord says: 'Behold, I am going to hand ^Pharaoh Hophra king of Egypt over to his enemies, to those who seek his life, just as I handed ᴮZedekiah king of Judah over to Nebuchadnezzar king of Babylon, *who was* his enemy and was seeking his life.'"

MESSAGE TO BARUCH

45 *This is* the message which Jeremiah the prophet spoke to Baruch the son of Neriah, when he had ^written these words in a book at Jeremiah's dictation, in the ᴮfourth year of Jehoiakim the son of Josiah, king of Judah, saying: ²"This is what the Lord, the God of Israel says to you, Baruch: ³'You said, "Oh, woe to me! For the

44:21^Ezek 8:10, 11 44:22^Is 7:13 ᴮJer 4:4
44:23^1 Kin 9:9; Neh 13:18 44:24^Jer 43:7; 44:15, 26
44:25^Ezek 20:39 44:26^Ps 50:16; Ezek 20:39
44:27^2 Kin 21:14; Jer 44:14 44:28^Jer 44:14
ᴮIs 10:19 44:29^Prov 19:21; Is 40:8 44:30^Jer
43:9-13 ᴮ2 Kin 25:4-7 45:1^Jer 36:4, 18, 32
ᴮ2 Kin 24:1

LORD has added grief to my pain; I am ^weary with my groaning and have found no rest."' ⁴This is what you are to say to him: 'This is what the LORD says: "Behold, ^what I have built I am going to tear down, and what I have planted I am going to uproot, that is, all *the people of* the land." ⁵But as for you, are you seeking great things for yourself? Do not seek *them;* for behold, I am going to ^bring disaster on all flesh,' declares the LORD, 'but I will ^Bgive your life to you as plunder in all the places where you may go.'"

DEFEAT OF PHARAOH FORETOLD

46 That which came as the word of the LORD to Jeremiah the prophet ^concerning the nations.

²To Egypt, concerning the army of ^Pharaoh Neco king of Egypt, which was by the river Euphrates at Carchemish, which Nebuchadnezzar king of Babylon defeated in the fourth year of Jehoiakim the son of Josiah, king of Judah:

3 "^Set up the ¹buckler and shield,
    And advance to the battle!

4 "Harness the horses,
    And mount the steeds,
    Take your stand with helmets *on!*
    ^Polish the spears,
    Put on the coats of armor!

5 "Why have I seen *it?*
    They are terrified,
    They are ^retreating,
    And their warriors are defeated
    And have taken refuge in flight,
    Without facing back.
    ^BTerror is on every side!"
    Declares the LORD.

6 Let not the ^swift man flee,
    Nor the warrior escape.

In the north beside the river Euphrates
    They have stumbled and fallen.

7 Who is this that ^rises like the Nile,
    Like the rivers whose waters surge?

8 Egypt rises like the Nile,
    And like the rivers whose waters surge;
    And He has said, "I will ^rise and cover *that* land;
    I will ^Bdestroy the city and its inhabitants."

9 Go up, you horses, and ^drive wildly, you chariots,
    So that the warriors may march forward:
    Cush and Put, who handle the shield,
    And the ^BLydians, who handle *and* bend the bow.

10 For ^that day belongs to the Lord GOD of armies,
    A day of vengeance, so as to avenge Himself on His foes;
    And the sword will devour and be satisfied,
    And drink its fill of their blood;
    For there will be a ^Bslaughter for the Lord GOD of armies,
    In the land of the north at the river Euphrates.

11 Go ^up to Gilead and obtain balm,
    Virgin daughter of Egypt!
    You have used many remedies in vain;
    There is ^Bno healing for you.

45:3 ^Ps 6:6; 69:3   45:4 ^Is 5:5; Jer 1:10
45:5 ^Is 66:16   ^BJer 21:9   46:1 ^Jer 1:10; 25:15-38
46:2 ^2 Kin 18:21; 23:29, 33–35   46:3 ^Is 21:5; Jer 51:11
46:4 ^Ezek 21:9-11   46:5 ^Is 42:17   ^BJer 6:25
46:6 ^Is 30:16   46:7 ^Jer 47:2   46:8 ^Is 37:24
^BIs 10:13   46:9 ^Jer 47:3   ^BIs 66:19   46:10 ^Joel 1:15
^BIs 34:6   46:11 ^Jer 8:22   ^BJer 30:13

46:3 ¹I.e., small shield

12 The nations have heard of
      your ^shame,
    And the earth is full of your
      ᴮcry *of distress;*
    For one warrior has stumbled
      over another,
    And both of them have fallen
      down together.

13 *This is* the message which the
LORD spoke to Jeremiah the prophet
about the ^coming of Nebuchadnezzar king of Babylon to ᴮstrike
the land of Egypt:

14 "Declare in Egypt and proclaim
      in Migdol,
    Proclaim also in Memphis and
      ^Tahpanhes;
    Say, 'Take your stand and get
      yourself ready,
    For the sword has devoured
      those around you.'

15 "Why have your powerful ones
      been cut down?
    They do not stand because the
      LORD has ^thrust them away.

16 "They have repeatedly
      ^stumbled;
    Indeed, they have fallen, one
      against another.
    Then they said, 'Get up, and
      ᴮlet's go back
    To our own people and our
      native land,
    Away from the sword of the
      oppressor!'

17 "They shouted there, 'Pharaoh
      king of Egypt *is nothing but*
      ^a big noise;
    He has let the appointed time
      pass by!'

18 "As I live," declares the ^King,
    Whose name is the LORD of
      armies,
    "One certainly shall come *who
      is* like Tabor among the
      mountains,
    Or like Carmel by the sea.

19 "Make your baggage *ready for*
      ^exile,
    ᴮDaughter living in Egypt,
    For Memphis will become a
      desolation;
    It will be destroyed *and*
      deprived of inhabitants.

20 "Egypt is a pretty heifer,
    But a horsefly is coming ^from
      the north—it is coming!

21 "Also her mercenaries in her
      midst
    Are like fattened calves,
    For they too have turned away
      and have fled together;
    They did not stand *their
      ground.*
    For the day of their disaster
      has come upon them,
    The time of their ^punishment.

22 "Its sound moves along like a
      serpent;
    For they move on like an army
    And come to her as
      woodcutters with axes.

23 "They have cut down her
      forest," declares the LORD;
    "Certainly it will no *longer* be
      found,
    Even though they are more
      numerous than ^locusts
    And are without number.

24 "The daughter of Egypt has
      been put to shame,
    Turned over to the power of
      the ^people of the north."

25 The LORD of armies, the God of
Israel says: "Behold, I am going to
punish Amon of ^Thebes, and Pharaoh, and Egypt along with her gods
and her kings, indeed, Pharaoh and

46:12 ^Jer 2:36   ᴮJer 14:2   46:13 ^Jer 43:10-13
ᴮIs 19:1   46:14 ^Jer 43:8   46:15 ^Ps 18:14, 39; 68:1, 2
46:16 ^Lev 26:36, 37   ᴮJer 51:9   46:17 ^Ex 15:9, 10;
1 Kin 20:10, 11   46:18 ^Jer 48:15; Mal 1:14
46:19 ^Is 20:4   ᴮJer 48:18   46:20 ^Jer 1:14; 47:2
46:21 ^Jer 48:44; Hos 9:7   46:23 ^Judg 6:5; 7:12
46:24 ^Jer 1:15   46:25 ^Ezek 30:14-16; Nah 3:8

those who trust in him. ²⁶I shall hand them over to those who are ^seeking their lives, that is, to Nebuchadnezzar king of Babylon and to his officers. Afterward, however, it will be inhabited as in the days of old," declares the LORD.

²⁷ "But as for you, Jacob My
    servant, do not fear,
Nor be dismayed, Israel!
For, see, I am going to ^save
    you from far away,
And your descendants from
    the land of their captivity;
And Jacob will return and be
    undisturbed
And secure, with no one
    making *him* afraid.

²⁸ "Jacob My servant, do not fear,"
    declares the LORD,
"For I am with you.
For I will make a complete
    destruction of all the nations
Where I have driven you,
Yet I will ^not make a complete
    destruction of you;
But I will ᴮcorrect you properly
And by no means leave you
    unpunished."

PROPHECY AGAINST PHILISTIA

47 The word of the LORD that came to Jeremiah the prophet concerning the ^Philistines, before Pharaoh conquered Gaza. ²This is what the LORD says:

"Behold, waters are going to rise
    from ^the north
And become an overflowing
    torrent,
And ᴮoverflow the land and
    everything that is in it,
The city and those who live
    in it;
And the people will cry out,
And every inhabitant of the
    land will wail.

³ "Because of the noise of the
    ^galloping hoofs of his
    stallions,
The roar of his chariots, *and*
    the rumbling of his wheels,
The fathers have not turned
    back for *their* children,
Because of the debility of *their*
    hands,

⁴ Because of the day that is
    coming
To ^destroy all the Philistines,
To eliminate from Tyre and
    Sidon
Every surviving ally;
For the LORD is going to
    destroy the Philistines,
The remnant of the coastland
    of Caphtor.

⁵ "^Baldness has come upon Gaza;
ᴮAshkelon has been destroyed.
Remnant of their valley,
How long will you gash
    yourself?

⁶ "Ah, ^sword of the LORD,
How long will you not be
    quiet?
Withdraw into your sheath;
Rest and stay still.

⁷ "How can it be quiet,
When the LORD has given it an
    order?
Against Ashkelon and against
    the sea shore—
There He has ^summoned it."

PROPHECY AGAINST MOAB

48 Concerning ^Moab. This is what the LORD of armies, the God of Israel says:

"Woe to ᴮNebo, for it has been
    destroyed;

46:26 ^Jer 44:30; Ezek 32:11 **46:27** ^Is 11:11;
Jer 23:3, 4 **46:28** ^Jer 4:27 ᴮJer 10:24
47:1 ^Jer 25:20; Zech 9:6 **47:2** ^Is 14:31 ᴮIs 8:7, 8
47:3 ^Judg 5:22; Jer 8:16 **47:4** ^Is 14:31
47:5 ^Jer 48:37 ᴮJudg 1:18 **47:6** ^Judg 7:20; Jer 12:12
47:7 ^Mic 6:9 **48:1** ^Is 15:1 ᴮNum 32:3, 38

Kiriathaim has been put to
   shame, it has been captured;
   The high stronghold has been
   put to shame and shattered.
2 "There is no longer praise for
   Moab;
   In ^Heshbon they have devised
   disaster against her:
   'Come and let's cut her off from
   being a nation!'
   You too, ¹Madmen, will be
   silenced;
   The sword will follow you.
3 "The sound of an outcry from
   ^Horonaim,
   'Devastation and great
   destruction!'
4 "Moab is broken,
   Her little ones have sounded
   out a cry *of distress.*
5 "For they will go up by the
   ascent of ^Luhith
   With continual weeping;
   For at the descent of
   Horonaim
   They have heard the
   anguished cry of
   destruction.
6 "^Flee, save yourselves,
   So that you may be like a
   juniper in the wilderness.
7 "For because of your ^trust in
   your own achievements and
   treasures,
   You yourself will also be
   captured;
   And ᴮChemosh will go off into
   exile
   Together with his priests and
   his leaders.
8 "A destroyer will come to every
   city,
   So that no city will escape;
   The valley also will be ruined
   And the ^plateau will be
   destroyed,
   As the LORD has said.

9 "Give wings to Moab,
   For she will flee away;
   And her cities will become a
   ^desolation,
   Without inhabitants in them.
10 "^Cursed is the one who does
   the LORD's work ᴮnegligently,
   And cursed is the one who
   restrains his sword from
   blood.

11 "Moab has been ^at ease since
   his youth;
   He has also been peaceful, *like
   wine* on its dregs,
   And he has not been poured
   from vessel to vessel,
   Nor has he gone into exile.
   Therefore he retains his flavor,
   And his aroma has not changed.
12 Therefore behold, the days are
   coming," declares the LORD, "when
   I will send to him those who tip *vessels,* and they will tip him over, and
   they will pour out his vessels and
   smash his jars. 13 And Moab will be
   ashamed of ^Chemosh, just as the
   house of Israel was ashamed of
   ᴮBethel, their confidence.
14 "How can you say, 'We are
   ^warriors,
   And men competent for battle'?
15 "Moab has been destroyed and
   men have gone up to his
   cities;
   His choicest ^young men
   have also gone down to the
   slaughter,"
   Declares the King, whose
   name is the LORD of armies.

48:2 ^Num 21:25; Jer 48:34, 45   48:3 ^Is 15:5;
Jer 48:5, 34   48:5 ^Is 15:5   48:6 ^Jer 51:6
48:7 ^Ps 52:7   ᴮNum 21:29   48:8 ^Josh 13:9, 17, 21
48:9 ^Jer 44:22   48:10 ^Jer 11:3   ᴮ1 Kin 20:39, 40, 42
48:11 ^Jer 22:21; Ezek 16:49   48:13 ^Judg 11:24
ᴮ1 Kin 12:29   48:14 ^Ps 33:16; Is 10:13-16
48:15 ^Is 40:30, 31; Jer 50:27

48:2 ¹Heb *Madmen*; i.e., a city of Moab

16 "The disaster of Moab will
      ^soon come,
   And his catastrophe has
      hurried quickly.
17 "Mourn for him, all you who
      live around him,
   And all of you who know his
      name;
   Say, 'How the mighty ^scepter
      has been broken,
   A staff of splendor!'
18 "^Come down from your glory
   And sit on the parched ground,
   O daughter living in Dibon,
   For the destroyer of Moab has
      come up against you,
   He has ruined your strongholds.
19 "Stand by the road and keep
      watch,
   You inhabitant of ^Aroer;
   Ask him who flees and her
      who escapes
   And say, 'What has happened?'
20 "Moab has been put to shame,
      for it has been shattered.
   Wail and cry out;
   Declare by the ^Arnon
   That Moab has been
      destroyed.
21 "Judgment has also come upon
the plain, upon Holon, ^Jahzah,
and against ^BMephaath, 22 against
Dibon, Nebo, and Beth-diblathaim,
23 against Kiriathaim, Beth-gamul,
and ^Beth-meon, 24 against ^Keri-
oth, Bozrah, and all the cities of the
land of Moab, far and near. 25 The
^horn of Moab has been cut off, and
his arm broken," declares the LORD.
26 "^Make him drunk, for he has
become arrogant toward the LORD;
so Moab will vomit, and he also will
become a laughingstock. 27 Now was
Israel not a ^laughingstock to you?
Or was he ^Bcaught among thieves?
For whenever you speak about him
you shake *your head in scorn.*

28 "Leave the cities and live
      among the ^rocky cliffs,
   You inhabitants of Moab,
   And be like a dove that nests
   Beyond the mouth of the
      chasm.
29 "^We have heard of the pride of
      Moab—he *is* very proud—
   Of his haughtiness, his pride,
      his arrogance, and his self-
      exaltation.
30 "I know his ^fury," declares the
      LORD,
   "But it is futile;
   His idle boasts have
      accomplished nothing.
31 "Therefore I will ^wail for Moab,
   For all of Moab I will cry out;
   I will moan for the men of Kir-
      heres.
32 "More than the ^weeping for
      ^BJazer
   I will weep for you, O vine of
      Sibmah!
   Your tendrils stretched across
      the sea,
   They reached to the sea of Jazer;
   Upon your summer fruits and
      your grape harvest
   The destroyer has fallen.
33 "So ^joy and rejoicing are
      removed
   From the fruitful field, and
      from the land of Moab.
   And I have eliminated the
      wine from the wine presses;
   No one will tread *them* with
      shouting,
   The shouting will not be
      shouts *of joy.*

48:16 ^Is 13:22   48:17 ^Is 9:4; 14:5   48:18 ^Is 47:1
48:19 ^Deut 2:36; Josh 12:2   48:20 ^Num 21:13
48:21 ^Num 21:23   ^BJosh 13:18   48:23 ^Josh 13:17
48:24 ^Jer 48:41; Amos 2:2   48:25 ^Ps 75:10; Zech
1:19-21   48:26 ^Jer 25:15   48:27 ^Lam 2:15-17
^BJer 2:26   48:28 ^Judg 6:2; Is 2:19   48:29 ^Is 16:6;
Zeph 2:8   48:30 ^Is 37:28   48:31 ^Is 15:5; 16:7, 11
48:32 ^Is 16:8, 9   ^BNum 21:32   48:33 ^Is 16:10; Jer 25:10

³⁴ᴬFrom the outcry at Heshbon to ᴮElealeh, to Jahaz they have raised their voice, from Zoar to Horonaim, *and to* Eglath-shelishiyah; for even the waters of Nimrim will become desolate. ³⁵And I will put an end to Moab," declares the Lᴏʀᴅ, "the one who offers *sacrifice* on the high place and the one who ᴬburns incense to his gods.

³⁶"Therefore My ᴬheart makes a sound like flutes for Moab; My heart also makes a sound like flutes for the men of Kir-heres. Therefore they have lost the abundance it produced. ³⁷For ᴬevery head is *shaved* bald, and every beard cut short; there are gashes on all the hands, and sackcloth around the waists. ³⁸On all the ᴬhousetops of Moab and in its public squares there is mourning everywhere; for I have broken Moab like an undesirable vessel," declares the Lᴏʀᴅ. ³⁹"How shattered it is! *How* they have wailed! How Moab has turned his back—he is ashamed! So Moab will become a laughingstock and an ᴬobject of terror to all around him."

⁴⁰ For this is what the Lᴏʀᴅ says:
"Behold, one will fly swiftly like an eagle
And ᴬspread out his wings against Moab.

⁴¹ "Kerioth has been captured
And the strongholds have been seized,
So the ᴬhearts of the warriors of Moab on that day
Will be like the heart of a woman in labor.

⁴² "Moab will be ᴬdestroyed from *being* a people
Because he has become ᴮarrogant toward the Lᴏʀᴅ.

⁴³ "ᴬTerror, pit, and snare are *coming* upon you,
Inhabitant of Moab," declares the Lᴏʀᴅ.

⁴⁴ "The one who flees from the terror
Will fall into the pit,
And the one who climbs up out of the pit
Will be caught in the snare;
For I will bring upon her, upon Moab,
The year of their ᴬpunishment," declares the Lᴏʀᴅ.

⁴⁵ "In the shadow of Heshbon
The fugitives stand without strength;
For a fire has spread out from Heshbon
And a ᴬflame from the midst of Sihon,
And it has devoured the ᴮforehead of Moab
And the scalps of the loud revelers.

⁴⁶ "Woe to you, Moab!
The people of ᴬChemosh have perished;
For your sons have been taken away captive,
And your daughters into captivity.

⁴⁷ "Yet I will ᴬrestore the fortunes of Moab
In the latter days," declares the Lᴏʀᴅ.
This is the extent of the judgment on Moab.

48:34 ᴬIs 15:4-6   ᴮNum 32:3, 37   48:35 ᴬJer 7:9; 11:13
48:36 ᴬIs 15:5; 16:11   48:37 ᴬIs 15:2; Jer 16:6
48:38 ᴬIs 22:1   48:39 ᴬEzek 26:16   48:40 ᴬIs 8:8
48:41 ᴬJer 49:22   48:42 ᴬPs 83:4   ᴮIs 37:23
48:43 ᴬIs 24:17, 18; Lam 3:47   48:44 ᴬJer 46:21
48:45 ᴬNum 21:28, 29   ᴮNum 24:17
48:46 ᴬJudg 11:24; 1 Kin 11:7   48:47 ᴬJer 12:14-17; 49:6, 39

PROPHECY AGAINST AMMON

49
Concerning the sons of ^Ammon. This is what the LORD says:

"Does Israel have no sons?
Or has he no heirs?
Why *then* has Malcam taken
possession of Gad,
And his people settled in its
cities?

2 "Therefore behold, the days are
coming," declares the LORD,
"When I will cause an alarm of
^war to be heard
Against Rabbah of the sons of
Ammon;
And it will become a desolate
heap,
And her ^Btowns will be set on
fire.
Then Israel will take possession
of his possessors,"
Says the LORD.

3 "Wail, Heshbon, for Ai has been
destroyed!
Cry out, daughters of Rabbah,
^Put on sackcloth and mourn,
And move about inside the
walls;
For Malcam will ^Bgo into exile
Together with his priests and
his leaders.

4 "How you boast about the
valleys!
Your valley is flowing *away,*
You backsliding daughter
Who trusts in her ^treasures,
saying,
'^BWho can come against me?'

5 "Behold, I am going to bring
terror upon you,"
Declares the Lord GOD of armies,
"From all *directions* around you;
And you will be ^driven away
one after another,
With no one to gather the
^Bfugitives together.

6 "But afterward I will ^restore
The fortunes of the sons of
Ammon,"
Declares the LORD.

PROPHECY AGAINST EDOM

7 Concerning Edom.
This is what the LORD of
armies says:
"Is there no longer *any* ^wisdom
in ^BTeman?
Has *good* advice been lost by
the prudent?
Has their wisdom decayed?

8 "Flee away, turn back, dwell in
the depths,
You inhabitants of Dedan,
For I will bring the ^disaster of
Esau upon him
At the time I punish him.

9 "^AIf grape pickers came to you,
Would they not leave
gleanings?
If thieves *came* by night,
They would destroy *only* what
was sufficient for them.

10 "But I have ^stripped Esau bare,
I have uncovered his hiding
places
So that he will not be able to
conceal himself;
His offspring have been
destroyed along with his
¹brothers
And his neighbors, and ^Bhe no
longer exists.

11 "Leave your ^orphans behind, I
will keep *them* alive;
And let your ^Bwidows trust in
Me."

49:1 ^Deut 23:3, 4; 2 Chr 20:1　**49:2** ^Num 10:9
^BJosh 17:11, 16　**49:3** ^Is 32:11　^BJer 46:25
49:4 ^Ps 62:10　^BJer 21:13　**49:5** ^Jer 16:16
^BLam 4:15　**49:6** ^Jer 48:47; 49:39　**49:7** ^Job 2:11
^BGen 36:11, 15, 34　**49:8** ^Jer 46:21; Mal 1:3, 4
49:9 ^Obad 5　**49:10** ^Jer 13:26　^BIs 17:14
49:11 ^Ps 68:5　^BZech 7:10

49:10 ¹Or *relatives*

¹²For this is what the LORD says: "Behold, those who were not sentenced to drink the ^cup will certainly drink *it,* so are you the one who will be held completely blameless? You will not be held blameless, but you will certainly drink *it.* ¹³For I have ^sworn by Myself," declares the LORD, "that Bozrah will become an object of horror, a disgrace, a wasteland, and a curse; and all its cities will become permanent ruins."

¹⁴ I have heard a message from
the LORD,
And a ^messenger is being sent
among the nations, *saying,*
"ᴮGather yourselves together
and come against her,
And rise up for battle!"
¹⁵ "For behold, I have made you
small among the nations,
Despised among people.
¹⁶ "As for the terror you cause,
The arrogance of your heart
has deceived you,
You who live in the clefts of
the rock,
Who occupy the height of the
hill.
Though you make your nest as
^high as an eagle's,
I will ᴮbring you down from
there," declares the LORD.

¹⁷"Edom will become an ^object of horror; everyone who passes by it will be appalled and will hiss at all its wounds. ¹⁸Like the ^overthrow of Sodom and Gomorrah with its neighbors," says the LORD, "ᴮno one will live there, nor will anyone of mankind reside in it. ¹⁹Behold, one will come up like a lion from the thicket of the Jordan to a perennially watered pasture; for in an instant I will chase him away from it, and I will appoint over it whoever is ^chosen. For who is ᴮlike

Me, and who will summon Me *into court?* And who then is the shepherd who can stand against Me?"

²⁰Therefore hear the ^plan of the LORD which He has planned against Edom, and His purposes which He has in mind against the inhabitants of Teman: they will certainly drag them off, *even* the little ones of the flock; He will certainly make their pasture desolate because of them. ²¹The ^earth has quaked at the noise of their downfall. There is an outcry! The noise of it has been heard at the Red Sea. ²²Behold, He will mount up and swoop like an eagle, and spread out His wings against Bozrah; and the ^hearts of the warriors of Edom on that day will be like the heart of a woman in labor.

PROPHECY AGAINST DAMASCUS

²³ Concerning ^Damascus:
"ᴮHamath and Arpad are put to
shame,
For they have heard bad
news;
They despair.
There is anxiety at the sea,
It cannot be calmed.
²⁴ "Damascus has become
helpless;
She has turned away to flee,
And panic has gripped her;
^Distress and labor pains have
seized her
Like a woman in childbirth.
²⁵ "How the ^city of praise has not
been deserted,
The town of My joy!

49:12^Jer 25:15   49:13^Gen 22:16; Is 45:23
49:14^Is 18:2   ᴮJer 50:14   49:16^Job 39:27   ᴮAmos 9:2
49:17^Jer 18:16; 49:13   49:18^Gen 19:24, 25
ᴮJob 18:15-18   49:19^Num 16:5   ᴮEx 15:11
49:20^Is 14:24, 27; Jer 50:45   49:21^Jer 50:46;
Ezek 26:15, 18   49:22^Is 13:8   49:23^Gen 14:15
ᴮNum 13:21   49:24^Is 13:8   49:25^Jer 33:9; 51:41

26 "Therefore, her ^young men
will fall in her streets,
And all the men of war will
perish on that day," declares
the Lord of armies.

27 "I will ^set fire to the wall of
Damascus,
And it will devour the fortified
palace of Ben-hadad."

PROPHECY AGAINST
KEDAR AND HAZOR

28 Concerning Kedar and the kingdoms of Hazor, which Nebuchadnezzar king of Babylon defeated.
This is what the Lord says:

"Arise, go up to Kedar
And devastate the ^people of
the east.

29 "They will take away their tents
and their flocks;
They will carry off for
themselves
Their tent ^curtains, all their
goods and their ^camels,
And they will call out to one
another, 'Horror on every
side!'

30 "Run away, flee! Dwell in the
depths,
You inhabitants of Hazor,"
declares the Lord;
"For ^Nebuchadnezzar king of
Babylon has formed a plan
against you
And devised a scheme against
you.

31 "Arise, go up against a nation
which is ^at ease,
Which lives securely," declares
the Lord.
"It has ^no gates or bars;
They dwell alone.

32 "Their camels will become
plunder,
And their many livestock for
spoils,

And I will ^scatter to all the
winds those who ^cut the
corners *of their hair*;
And I will bring their disaster
from every side," declares
the Lord.

33 "Hazor will become a ^haunt of
jackals,
A desolation forever;
No one will live there,
Nor will anyone of mankind
reside in it."

PROPHECY AGAINST ELAM

34 The word of the Lord that came
to Jeremiah the prophet concerning ^Elam, ^at the beginning of the
reign of Zedekiah king of Judah,
saying:

35 "This is what the Lord of
armies says:
'Behold, I am going to ^break
the bow of Elam,
The finest of their might.

36 'I will bring upon Elam the four
winds
From the four ends of
heaven,
And will ^scatter them to all
these winds;
And there will be no nation
To which the outcasts of Elam
will not go.

37 'So I will shatter Elam before
their enemies
And before those who seek
their lives;
And I will ^bring disaster
upon them,
Even My fierce anger,'
declares the Lord,

49:26 ^Jer 11:22; 50:30   49:27 ^Jer 43:12; Amos 1:3-5
49:28 ^Job 1:3; Is 11:14   49:29 ^Hab 3:7   ^1 Chr 5:21
49:30 ^Jer 25:9; 27:6   49:31 ^Judg 18:7   ^Is 42:11
49:32 ^Ezek 5:10   ^Jer 9:26   49:33 ^Is 13:20-22;
Jer 9:11   49:34 ^Gen 14:17, 18   ^2 Kin 24:17, 18
49:35 ^Ps 46:9; Is 22:6   49:36 ^Jer 49:32; Ezek 5:10
49:37 ^Jer 6:19

'And I will ᴮsend the sword
  after them
Until I have consumed them.
38 'Then I will set My throne in
  Elam,
  And eliminate from there *the*
  king and officials,'
  Declares the Lᴏʀᴅ.
39 'But it will come about in the
  last days
  That I will ᴬrestore the
  fortunes of Elam,'"
  Declares the Lᴏʀᴅ.

PROPHECY AGAINST BABYLON

50 The word which the Lᴏʀᴅ spoke concerning ᴬBabylon, the land of the Chaldeans, through Jeremiah the prophet:
2 "Declare and proclaim among
  the nations.
  Proclaim it and lift up a flag,
  Do not conceal *it*. Say,
  'ᴬBabylon has been captured,
  ᴮBel has been put to shame,
  Marduk has been shattered;
  Her idols have been put to
  shame, her images have
  been shattered.'

3 For a nation has come up against her from the ᴬnorth; it will make her land an object of horror, and there will be no inhabitant in it. Whether people or animals, they have wandered off, they have gone!

4 "In those days and at that time," declares the Lᴏʀᴅ, "the sons of Israel will come, they and the sons of Judah as well; they will go along ᴬweeping as they go, and *it will be* ᴮthe Lᴏʀᴅ their God *whom* they will seek. 5 They will ᴬask for the way to Zion, *turning* their faces in its direction; they will come so that they may join themselves to the Lᴏʀᴅ *in* an everlasting covenant *that* will not be forgotten.

6 "My people have become ᴬlost
  sheep;
  ᴮTheir shepherds have led
  them astray.
  They have made them turn
  aside *on* the mountains.
  They have gone from
  mountain to hill,
  They have forgotten their
  resting place.
7 "All who found them have
  devoured them;
  And their adversaries have
  said, 'ᴬWe are not guilty,
  Since they have sinned
  against the Lᴏʀᴅ *who is* the
  habitation of righteousness,
  The Lᴏʀᴅ, the hope of their
  fathers.'
8 "Wander away from the ᴬmidst
  of Babylon
  And go out from the land of
  the Chaldeans;
  Be like male goats at the head
  of the flock.
9 "For behold, I am going to
  ᴬrouse and bring up against
  Babylon
  A contingent of great nations
  from the land of the north,
  And they will draw up *their*
  battle lines against her;
  From there she will be taken
  captive.
  Their arrows will be like an
  expert warrior
  Who does not return empty-
  handed.
10 "ᴬChaldea will become plunder;
  All who plunder her will have
  enough," declares the Lᴏʀᴅ.

49:37 ᴮ Jer 9:16   49:39 ᴬ Jer 48:47   50:1 ᴬ Gen 10:10;
11:9   50:2 ᴬ Jer 51:31   ᴮ Is 46:1   50:3 ᴬ Is 13:17; Jer 50:9
50:4 ᴬ Ezra 3:12, 13   ᴮ Hos 3:5   50:5 ᴬ Is 35:8; Jer 6:16
50:6 ᴬ Is 53:6   ᴮ Jer 23:11-14   50:7 ᴬ Jer 2:3; Zech 11:5
50:8 ᴬ Is 48:20; Jer 51:6   50:9 ᴬ Jer 51:1
50:10 ᴬ Jer 51:24, 35; Ezek 11:24

11 "Because you are glad, because
     you are jubilant,
   You who ^pillage My heritage,
   Because you skip about like a
     threshing heifer
   And neigh like stallions,
12 Your ^mother will be greatly
     ashamed,
   She who gave you birth will be
     humiliated.
   Behold, *she will be* the least of
     the nations,
   A ^Bwilderness, a dry land and
     a desert.
13 "Because of the wrath of
     the LORD she will not be
     inhabited,
   But she will be completely
     desolate;
   Everyone who passes by
     Babylon ^will be horrified
   And will hiss because of all her
     wounds.
14 "Draw up your battle lines
     against Babylon on every side,
   All of you who bend the bow;
   Shoot at her, do not spare *your*
     arrows,
   For she has ^sinned against the
     LORD.
15 "Raise your battle cry against
     her on every side!
   She has given herself up, her
     towers have fallen,
   Her walls have been torn
     down.
   For this is the ^vengeance of
     the LORD:
   Take vengeance on her;
   ^BAs she has done *to others, so*
     do to her.
16 "Eliminate the ^sower from
     Babylon
   And the one who wields the
     sickle at the time of harvest;
   From the sword of the
     oppressor

^BEach of them will turn back to
   his own people
And each of them will flee to
   his own land.

17 "Israel is a ^scattered flock,
the ^Blions have driven *them* away.
The first one *who* devoured him
was the king of Assyria, and this
last one *who* has gnawed his
bones is Nebuchadnezzar king of
Babylon. 18 Therefore this is what
the LORD of armies, the God of
Israel says: 'Behold, I am going to
punish the king of Babylon and
his land, just as I ^punished the
king of Assyria. 19 And I will ^bring
Israel back to his pasture and he
will graze on Carmel and Bashan,
and his desire will be satisfied in
the ^Bhill country of Ephraim and
Gilead. 20 In those days and at that
time,' declares the LORD, 'search
will be made for the wrongdoing
of Israel, but ^there will be none;
and for the sins of Judah, but they
will not be found; for I will forgive those ^Bwhom I leave as a remnant.'
21 "Against the land of
   ^1Merathaim, go up against it,
   And against the inhabitants
     of ^2,^APekod.
   Kill and completely destroy
     them," declares the LORD,
   "And do according to
     everything that I have
     commanded you.
22 "The ^noise of battle is in the
     land,
   And great destruction.

50:11^A Jer 12:14   50:12^A Jer 15:9   ^B Jer 22:6
50:13^A Jer 18:16; 49:17   50:14^A Hab 2:8, 17
50:15^A Jer 46:10   ^B Ps 137:8   50:16^A Joel 1:11
^B Is 13:14   50:17^A Joel 3:2   ^B Jer 2:15   50:18^A Is 10:12;
Ezek 31:3, 11, 12   50:19^A Is 65:10   ^B Jer 31:6
50:20^A Is 43:25   ^B Is 1:9   50:21^A Ezek 23:23
50:22^A Jer 4:19-21; 51:54-56

50:21 ^1 Or *double rebellion*   ^2 I.e., punishment (uncertain)

23 "How the ^hammer of the
    whole earth
  Has been cut off and broken!
  How Babylon has become
  An object of horror among the
    nations!
24 "I ^set a trap for you and you
    were also ᴮcaught, Babylon,
  While you yourself were not
    aware;
  You have been found and also
    seized
  Because you have engaged in
    conflict with the Lᴏʀᴅ."
25 The Lᴏʀᴅ has opened His
    armory
  And has brought out the
    ^weapons of His indignation,
  For it is a work of the Lord Gᴏᴅ
    of armies
  In the land of the Chaldeans.
26 Come to her from the farthest
    border;
  Open up her barns,
  Pile her up like heaps of grain
  And ^completely destroy her,
  Let nothing be left to her.
27 ^Put all her bulls to the sword;
  Let them ᴮgo down to the
    slaughter!
  Woe be upon them, for their
    day has come,
  The time of their punishment.

28 There is a ^sound of fugitives
    and refugees from the land
    of Babylon,
  To declare in Zion the
    vengeance of the Lᴏʀᴅ our
    God,
  Vengeance for His temple.

29 "Summon ¹many against
    Babylon,
  All those who bend the bow:
  Encamp against her on every
    side,

  Let there be no escape.
  Repay her according to her
    work;
  According to all that she has
    done, *so* do to her;
  For she has become ^arrogant
    against the Lᴏʀᴅ,
  Against the Holy One of Israel.
30 "Therefore her ^young men will
    fall in her streets,
  And all her men of war will
    ᴮperish on that day," declares
    the Lᴏʀᴅ.
31 "Behold, ^I am against you,
    arrogant one,"
  Declares the Lord Gᴏᴅ of
    armies,
  "For your day has come,
  The time when I will punish
    you.
32 "The ^arrogant one will stumble
    and fall
  With no one to raise him up;
  And I will ᴮset fire to his cities,
  And it will devour all his
    surroundings."

33 This is what the Lᴏʀᴅ of
    armies says:
  "The sons of Israel are
    oppressed,
  And the sons of Judah as well;
  And ^all who took them
    captive have held them
    firmly,
  They have refused to let
    them go.
34 "Their ^Redeemer is strong, the
    Lᴏʀᴅ of armies is His name;
  He will vigorously plead their
    case

50:23 ^Jer 51:20-24   50:24 ^Jer 48:43, 44   ᴮJer 51:31
50:25 ^Is 13:5   50:26 ^Is 14:23   50:27 ^Is 34:7
ᴮJer 48:10   50:28 ^Is 48:20   50:29 ^Ex 10:3; Jer 49:16
50:30 ^Is 13:17, 18   ᴮJer 51:57   50:31 ^Jer 21:13;
Nah 2:13   50:32 ^Is 10:12-15   ᴮJer 21:14
50:33 ^Is 14:17; 58:6   50:34 ^Prov 23:11; Is 43:14

50:29 ¹Another reading is *archers*

So that He may bring rest to
their land,
But turmoil to the inhabitants
of Babylon.
35 "A sword against the Chaldeans,"
declares the LORD,
"And against the inhabitants of
Babylon
And against her ᴬleaders and
her ᴮwise men!
36 "A sword against the ᴬoracle
priests, and they will become
fools!
A sword against her ᴮwarriors,
and they will be shattered!
37 "A sword against their ᴬhorses,
against their chariots,
And against all the ᴮforeigners
who are in the midst of her,
And they will become women!
A sword against her treasures,
and they will be plundered!
38 "A drought on her waters, and
they will be dried up!
For it is a land of ᴬidols,
And they go insane at frightful
images.

39 "Therefore the ᴬdesert creatures
will live there with the
jackals;
The ostriches also will live in it.
It will ᴮnever again be
inhabited
Nor lived in from generation
to generation.
40 "As when God overthrew ᴬSodom
And Gomorrah with its
neighbors," declares the LORD,
"No one will live there,
Nor will anyone of mankind
reside in it.

41 "Behold, a people is coming
ᴬfrom the north,
And a great nation and many
kings

Will be roused from the
remote parts of the earth.
42 "They seize their bow and
javelin;
They are cruel and have no
mercy.
Their ᴬvoice roars like the sea;
And they ride on ᴮhorses,
Drawn up like a man for the
battle
Against you, daughter of
Babylon.
43 "The king of Babylon has
heard the report about
them,
And his hands hang limp;
ᴬDistress has gripped him,
Agony like a woman in
childbirth.

44 "Behold, one will come up like
a lion from the thicket of the Jordan to a perennially watered pasture; for in an instant I will chase
them away from it, and I will
appoint over it whoever is ᴬcho-
sen. For who is ᴮlike Me, and who
will summon Me into court? And
who then is the shepherd who can
stand against Me?" 45 Therefore
hear the ᴬplan of the LORD which
He has planned against Babylon,
and His purposes which He has in
mind against the land of the Chaldeans: ᴮthey will certainly drag
them off, even the little ones of the
flock; He will certainly make their
pasture desolate because of them.
46 At the shout, "Babylon has been
conquered!" the earth quakes,
and an ᴬoutcry is heard among the
nations.

50:35 ᴬDan 5:1, 2   ᴮDan 5:7, 8   50:36 ᴬIs 44:25
ᴮJer 49:22   50:37 ᴬPs 20:7, 8   ᴮJer 25:20
50:38 ᴬIs 46:1, 6, 7   50:39 ᴬIs 13:21   ᴮIs 13:20
50:40 ᴬGen 19:24, 25; Is 13:19   50:41 ᴬIs 13:2-5;
Jer 6:22   50:42 ᴬIs 5:30   ᴮJer 8:16   50:43 ᴬJer 30:6;
49:24   50:44 ᴬNum 16:5   ᴮIs 46:9   50:45 ᴬPs 33:11
ᴮJer 49:20   50:46 ᴬIs 5:7; 15:5

BABYLON JUDGED FOR SINS
AGAINST ISRAEL

51 This is what the LORD says:
    "Behold, I am going to stir up
    The ^spirit of a destroyer
        against Babylon
    And against the inhabitants of
        [1]Leb-kamai.
2   "I will send foreigners to Babylon
        so that they may ^winnow her
    And devastate her land;
    For they will be opposed to her
        on every side
    On the day of *her* disaster.
3   "Let not him who ^bends his
        bow bend *it,*
    Nor let him rise up in his coat
        of armor.
    Do not spare her young men;
    Devote all her army to
        destruction.
4   "They will fall down dead in the
        land of the Chaldeans,
    And ^pierced through in their
        streets."

5   For neither Israel nor Judah
        has been forsaken
    By his God, the LORD of armies,
    Although their land is ^full of
        guilt
    Before the Holy One of Israel.
6   ^Flee from the midst of Babylon,
    And each of you save his life!
    Do not perish in her
        punishment,
    For this is the LORD's time of
        vengeance;
    He is going to repay to her
        what she deserves.
7   Babylon has been a golden
        ^cup in the hand of the LORD,
    Intoxicating all the earth.
    The nations have drunk of her
        wine;
    Therefore the nations are
        ^going insane.

8   Suddenly ^Babylon has fallen
        and been broken;
    ^Wail over her!
    Bring balm for her pain;
    Perhaps she may be healed.
9   We applied healing to
        Babylon, but she was not
        healed;
    Abandon her and let's each go
        to his own country,
    For her judgment has ^reached
        to heaven
    And it rises to the clouds.
10 The LORD has ^brought about
        our vindication;
    Come and let's recount in Zion
    The work of the LORD our God!

11 ^Sharpen the arrows, fill the
        quivers!
    The LORD has stirred up the
        spirit of the kings of the
        Medes,
    Because His plan is against
        Babylon to destroy it;
    For it is the vengeance of the
        LORD, vengeance for His
        temple.
12 Lift up a signal flag against
        the walls of Babylon;
    Post a strong guard,
    Station sentries,
    Set up an ambush!
    For the LORD has both
        ^planned and performed
    What He spoke concerning the
        inhabitants of Babylon.
13 You who live by many
        waters,
    Abundant in treasures,

51:1 ^Jer 4:11, 12; 23:19   51:2 ^Is 41:16; Jer 15:7
51:3 ^Jer 50:14, 29   51:4 ^Is 13:15; 14:19
51:5 ^Hos 4:1, 2   51:6 ^Jer 50:8, 28; Rev 18:4
51:7 ^Jer 25:15   ^B Jer 25:16   51:8 ^Is 21:9   ^B Is 13:6
51:9 ^Ezra 9:6; Rev 18:5   51:10 ^Ps 37:6; Mic 7:9
51:11 ^Jer 46:4, 9; Joel 3:9, 10   51:12 ^Jer 4:28; 23:20

51:1 [1]Cryptic name for Chaldea; or *the heart of those
who rise up against Me*

Your end has come,
The measure of your ^end.
14 The ^LORD of armies has sworn
by Himself:
"I will certainly fill you with a
population like locusts,
And they will cry out with
shouts of victory over you."

15 *It is* He who made the earth by
His power,
Who established the world by
His wisdom,
And by His understanding He
^stretched out the heavens.
16 When He utters His ^voice,
there is a roar of waters in
the heavens,
And He makes the clouds
ascend from the end of the
earth.
He makes lightning for the rain
And brings out wind from His
storehouses.
17 ^Every person is stupid, devoid
of knowledge;
Every goldsmith is put to
shame by his idols,
For his cast metal images are
^deceitful,
And there is no breath in them.
18 They are ^worthless, a work of
mockery;
At the time of their
punishment they will perish.
19 The ^portion of Jacob is not
like these;
For He is the Maker of
everything,
And of the tribe of His
inheritance;
The LORD of armies is His name.
20 *He says,* "You are My war-club,
My weapon of war;
And with you I ^shatter nations,
And with you I destroy
kingdoms.

21 "With you I ^shatter the horse
and his rider,
And with you I shatter the
chariot and its rider,
22 And with you I shatter ^man
and woman,
And with you I shatter the old
man and youth,
And with you I shatter the
young man and virgin,
23 And with you I shatter the
shepherd and his flock,
And with you I shatter the
farmer and his team,
And with you I shatter
governors and officials.
24 "But I will repay Babylon and all
the inhabitants of Chaldea for ^all
their evil that they have done in Zion
before your eyes," declares the LORD.
25 "Behold, ^I am against you,
mountain of ^destruction
That destroys the whole
earth," declares the LORD,
"And I will stretch out My hand
against you,
And roll you down from the
rocky cliffs,
And I will make you a burnt
out mountain.
26 "They will not take from you
even a stone for a corner
Nor a stone for foundations,
But you will be ^desolate
forever," declares the LORD.

27 Lift up a signal flag in the land,
Blow a trumpet among the
nations!
Consecrate the nations
against her,

51:13 ^Is 57:17; Hab 2:9-11   51:14 ^Jer 49:13
51:15 ^Job 9:8; Ps 146:5, 6   51:16 ^Job 37:2-6; Ps 18:13
51:17 ^Is 44:18-20 ^B Hab 2:18, 19   51:18 ^Jer 18:15
51:19 ^Ps 73:26; Jer 10:16   51:20 ^Is 8:9; 41:15, 16
51:21 ^Ex 15:1   51:22 ^2 Chr 36:17; Is 13:15, 16
51:24 ^Jer 50:15, 29   51:25 ^Jer 50:31 ^B Is 13:2
51:26 ^Is 13:19-22; Jer 50:13

Summon against her the
kingdoms of ᴬArarat, Minni,
and ᴮAshkenaz;
Appoint an officer against her,
Bring up the horses like bristly
locusts.
28 Consecrate the nations against
her,
The kings of the Medes,
Their governors and all their
officials,
And every land under their
control.
29 So the ᴬland quakes and
writhes,
For the plans of the Lᴏʀᴅ
against Babylon stand,
To make the land of Babylon
A desolation without
inhabitants.
30 The warriors of Babylon have
ceased fighting,
They stay in the strongholds;
ᴬTheir strength is exhausted,
They are becoming ᴬ*like*
women;
Their homes are set on fire,
The ᴮbars of her *gates* are
broken.
31 One ᴬcourier runs to meet
another,
And one ᴮmessenger to meet
another,
To tell the king of Babylon
That his city has been
captured from end *to end;*
32 The river crossing places have
been seized,
And they have burned the
marshes with fire,
And the men of war are
terrified.

33 For this is what the Lᴏʀᴅ of
armies, the God of Israel says:
"The daughter of Babylon is like
a ᴬthreshing floor

At the time that it is tread down;
In just a little while the time of
harvest will come for her."

34 "Nebuchadnezzar the king of
Babylon has ᴬdevoured me,
he has crushed me,
He has set me down *like* an
empty vessel;
He has ᴮswallowed me like a
monster,
He has filled his stomach with
my delicacies;
He has washed me away.
35 "May the ᴬviolence *done* to me
and to my flesh be upon
Babylon,"
The inhabitant of Zion will say;
And, "May my blood be upon
the inhabitants of Chaldea,"
Jerusalem will say.
36 Therefore this is what the Lᴏʀᴅ
says:
"Behold, I am going to ᴬplead
your case
And ᴮtake vengeance for you;
And I will dry up her sea
And make her fountain dry.
37 "ᴬBabylon will become a heap *of
ruins,* a haunt of jackals,
An ᴮobject of horror
and hissing, without
inhabitants.
38 "They will roar together like
ᴬyoung lions,
They will growl like lions' cubs.
39 "When they become heated
up, I will serve *them* their
banquet
And make them drunk, so
that they may rejoice in
triumph,

51:27 ᴬGen 8:4   ᴮGen 10:3   51:29 ᴬJer 8:16; 10:10
51:30 ᴬIs 13:7, 8   ᴮIs 45:1, 2   51:31 ᴬ2 Chr 30:6
ᴮ2 Sam 18:19-31   51:33 ᴬIs 21:10; 41:15, 16
51:34 ᴬJer 50:17   ᴮJob 20:15   51:35 ᴬPs 137:8
51:36 ᴬPs 140:12   ᴮJer 51:6, 11   51:37 ᴬRev 18:2
ᴮJer 25:9   51:38 ᴬJer 2:15

And may ^sleep a perpetual
sleep
And not wake up," declares the
Lord.

40 "I will bring them down like
lambs ^to the slaughter,
Like rams together with male
goats.

41 "How ¹^Sheshak has been
captured,
And the praise of the whole
earth has been seized!
How Babylon has become an
object of horror among the
nations!

42 "The ^sea has come up over
Babylon;
She has been engulfed by its
roaring waves.

43 "Her cities have become an
^object of horror,
A dry land and a desert,
A land in which ᴮno one lives
And through which no one of
mankind passes.

44 "^I will punish Bel in Babylon,
And I will make what he has
swallowed ᴮcome out of his
mouth;
And the nations will no longer
stream toward him.
Even the wall of Babylon has
fallen down!

45 "^Come out from her midst, My
people,
And each of you save yourselves
From the fierce anger of the
Lord.

46 "Now, so that your heart does
not grow faint,
And you are not afraid at the
^report that *will be* heard in
the land—
For the report will come in one
year,

And after that another report
in another year,
And violence *will be* in the land
With ᴮruler against ruler—

47 Therefore behold, days are
coming
When I will punish the ^idols
of Babylon;
And her whole land will be
ᴮput to shame.
And all her slain will fall in her
midst.

48 "Then heaven and earth and
everything that is in them
Will shout for joy over Babylon,
Because ^the destroyers will
come to her from the north,"
Declares the Lord.

49 Indeed, Babylon is to fall *for*
the slain of Israel,
As ^the slain of all the earth
have also fallen for Babylon.

50 You ^who have escaped the
sword,
Go! Do not stay!
ᴮRemember the Lord from far
away,
And let Jerusalem come to
your mind.

51 ^We are ashamed because we
have heard rebuke;
Disgrace has covered our faces,
Because strangers have entered
The holy places of the Lord's
house.

52 "Therefore behold, the days are
coming," declares the Lord,
"When I will punish her ^idols,

51:39 ^Ps 76:5   51:40 ^Jer 48:15; 50:27
51:41 ^Jer 25:26   51:42 ^Is 8:7, 8; Jer 51:55
51:43 ^Jer 50:12   ᴮIs 13:20   51:44 ^Is 46:1   ᴮEzra 1:7, 8
51:45 ^Is 48:20; Jer 50:8, 28   51:46 ^2 Kin 19:7
ᴮIs 19:2   51:47 ^Is 21:9   ᴮJer 50:12, 35–37
51:48 ^Jer 50:3   51:49 ^Rev 18:24   51:50 ^Jer 44:28
ᴮDeut 4:29–31   51:51 ^Ps 44:15   51:52 ^Jer 50:38

51:41 ¹Cryptic name for Babylon

And the mortally wounded
will groan throughout her
land.
⁵³ "Though Babylon ascends to
the heavens,
And though she fortifies her
lofty stronghold,
Destroyers will come from
ᴬMe to her," declares the
Lᴏʀᴅ.

⁵⁴ The ᴬsound of an outcry from
Babylon,
And of great destruction from
the land of the Chaldeans!
⁵⁵ For the Lᴏʀᴅ is going to
destroy Babylon,
And He will make *her* loud
noise vanish from her.
And their ᴬwaves will roar like
many waters;
The clamor of their voices
sounds forth.
⁵⁶ For the ᴬdestroyer is coming
against her, against Babylon,
And her warriors will be
captured,
Their ᴮbows shattered;
For the Lᴏʀᴅ is a God of
retribution,
He will fully repay.
⁵⁷ "I will ᴬmake her leaders and
her wise men drunk,
Her governors, her officials,
and her warriors,
So that they will sleep a
ᴮperpetual sleep and not
wake up,"
Declares the King, whose
name is the Lᴏʀᴅ of armies.
⁵⁸This is what the Lᴏʀᴅ of armies
says:

"The broad wall of Babylon
will be completely
demolished,
And her high ᴬgates will be set
on fire;

So the peoples will ᴮlabor for
nothing,
And the nations become
exhausted *only* for fire."

⁵⁹The command that Jeremiah the prophet gave Seraiah the son of Neriah, the grandson of Mahseiah, when he went with ᴬZedekiah the king of Judah to Babylon in the fourth year of his reign. (And Seraiah was quartermaster.) ⁶⁰Jeremiah ᴬwrote on a single scroll all the disaster which would come against Babylon, *that is,* all these words which have been written concerning Babylon. ⁶¹Then Jeremiah said to Seraiah, "As soon as you come to Babylon, see that you read all these words aloud, ⁶²and say, 'You, Lᴏʀᴅ, have promised concerning this place to cut it off, so that there will be ᴬnothing living in it, whether man or animal; but it will be a permanent desolation.' ⁶³And as soon as you finish reading this scroll, you shall tie a stone to it and ᴬthrow it into the middle of the Euphrates, ⁶⁴and say, 'Just so shall Babylon sink down and ᴬnot rise *again,* because of the disaster that I am going to bring upon her; and they will become ᴮexhausted.'" To this point are the words of Jeremiah.

THE FALL OF JERUSALEM

52 ᴬZedekiah was twenty-one years old when he became king, and he reigned for eleven years in Jerusalem; and his mother's name was ᴮHamutal the daughter of Jeremiah of Libnah. ²He did

51:53ᴬIs 13:3 51:54ᴬJer 48:3-5; 50:22, 46
51:55ᴬPs 18:4; 69:2 51:56ᴬJer 51:48 ᴮPs 46:9
51:57ᴬJer 25:27 ᴮPs 76:5, 6 51:58ᴬIs 45:1, 2
ᴮHab 2:13 51:59ᴬJer 28:1; 52:1 51:60ᴬIs 30:8;
Jer 30:2, 3 51:62ᴬJer 51:43; Ezek 35:9
51:63ᴬJer 19:10, 11; Rev 18:21 51:64ᴬNah 1:8, 9
ᴮJer 51:58 52:1ᴬ2 Kin 24:18 ᴮ2 Kin 23:31

evil in the sight of the Lord, in accordance with everything that ^Jehoiakim had done. ³For because of the anger of the Lord *this* came about in Jerusalem and Judah, until He drove them out from His presence. And Zedekiah ^revolted against the king of Babylon. ⁴Now it came about in the ninth year of his reign, on the tenth *day* of the tenth month, that Nebuchadnezzar king of Babylon came, he and all his army, against Jerusalem, camped against it, and built a ¹,^bulwark all around it. ⁵^So the city was under siege until the eleventh year of King Zedekiah. ⁶On the ninth *day* of the fourth month the ^famine was so severe in the city that there was no food for the people of the land. ⁷Then the city was ^breached, and all the ᴮwarriors fled and left the city at night by way of the gate between the two walls which *was* by the king's garden, though the Chaldeans were all around the city. And they went by way of the Arabah. ⁸But the army of the Chaldeans pursued the king and ^overtook Zedekiah in the desert plains of Jericho, and all his army was scattered from him. ⁹Then they captured the king and brought him up to the king of Babylon at ^Riblah in the land of ᴮHamath, and he passed sentence on him. ¹⁰And the king of Babylon ^slaughtered the sons of Zedekiah before his eyes, and he also slaughtered all the commanders of Judah in Riblah. ¹¹Then he ^blinded the eyes of Zedekiah; and the king of Babylon bound him with bronze shackles and brought him to Babylon and put him in prison until the day of his death.

¹²Now on the tenth *day* of the fifth month, which was the nineteenth year of King Nebuchadnezzar, king of Babylon, ^Nebuzaradan the captain of the bodyguard, who was in the service of the king of Babylon, came to Jerusalem. ¹³And he ^burned the house of the Lord, the ᴮking's house, and all the houses of Jerusalem; even every large house he burned with fire. ¹⁴So the entire army of the Chaldeans who *were* with the captain of the guard ^tore down all the walls around Jerusalem. ¹⁵Then Nebuzaradan the captain of the guard ^took into exile some of the poorest of the people, the rest of the people who were left in the city, the ᴮdeserters who had deserted to the king of Babylon, and the rest of the craftsmen. ¹⁶But ^Nebuzaradan the captain of the guard left some of the poorest of the land to be vinedressers and farmers.

¹⁷Now the bronze pillars which belonged to the house of the Lord and the ^stands and the bronze ᴮsea, which were in the house of the Lord, the Chaldeans smashed to pieces and carried all their bronze to Babylon. ¹⁸They also took the ^pots, the shovels, the snuffers, the basins, the pans, and all the bronze vessels which were used in temple service. ¹⁹The captain of the guard also took the ^bowls, the firepans, the basins, the pots,

52:2 ^Jer 36:30, 31   52:3 ^2 Chr 36:13; Ezek 17:12-16
52:4 ^Jer 32:24   52:5 ^2 Kin 25:2   52:6 ^2 Kin 25:3;
Is 3:1   52:7 ^2 Kin 25:4   ᴮJer 39:4-7   52:8 ^Jer 21:7;
32:4   52:9 ^Num 34:11   ᴮJosh 13:5
52:10 ^2 Kin 25:7; Jer 22:30   52:11 ^Jer 39:7; Ezek 12:13
52:12 ^Jer 39:9   52:13 ^1 Kin 9:8   ᴮJer 39:8
52:14 ^2 Kin 25:10; Neh 1:3   52:15 ^2 Kin 25:11
ᴮJer 39:9   52:16 ^2 Kin 25:12; Jer 39:10
52:17 ^1 Kin 7:27-37   ᴮ1 Kin 7:23-26   52:18 ^Ex 27:3;
1 Kin 7:40, 45   52:19 ^1 Kin 7:49, 50; 2 Kin 25:15

52:4 ¹I.e., a defensive wall

the lampstands, the pans, and the drink offering bowls, whatever was fine gold, and whatever was fine silver. ²⁰The two pillars, the one sea, and the twelve bronze bulls that were under the sea, *and* the stands, which King Solomon had made for the house of the LORD— the bronze of all these vessels was ^beyond weight. ²¹As for the pillars, the ^height of each pillar *was* ¹eighteen cubits, and it *was* twelve cubits in ^circumference and four fingers in thickness, *and* hollow. ²²Also, a ^capital of bronze was on top of it; and the height of each capital was ¹five cubits, with latticework and pomegranates on the capital all around, all of bronze. And the second pillar was like these, including pomegranates. ²³There were ninety-six exposed pomegranates; all ^the pomegranates *numbered* a hundred on the latticework all around.

²⁴Then the captain of the guard took Seraiah the chief priest and Zephaniah the second priest, with the three ^officers of the temple. ²⁵He also took from the city one official who was overseer of the warriors, seven of the ^king's advisers who were found in the city, the scribe of the commander of the army who mustered the people of the land, and sixty men from the people of the land who were found inside the city. ²⁶Nebuzaradan the captain of the bodyguards took them and ^brought them to the king of Babylon at Riblah. ²⁷Then the king of Babylon ^struck them

and put them to death in Riblah in the land of Hamath. So Judah was led into exile from its land.

²⁸These are the people whom ^Nebuchadnezzar took into exile: in the seventh year 3,023 Jews; ²⁹in the eighteenth year of Nebuchadnezzar 832 persons from Jerusalem; ³⁰in the twenty-third year of Nebuchadnezzar, ^Nebuzaradan the captain of the guard took into exile 745 Jewish people; *there were* 4,600 people in all.

³¹Now it came about in the thirty-seventh year of the exile of Jehoiachin king of Judah, in the twelfth month, on the twenty-fifth of the month, that Evil-merodach king of Babylon, in the *first* year of his reign, ^showed favor to Jehoiachin king of Judah and brought him out of prison. ³²^Then he spoke kindly to him and set his throne above the thrones of the kings who *were* with him in Babylon. ³³So Jehoiachin changed his prison clothes, and ^had his meals in the king's presence regularly all the days of his life. ³⁴And as his allowance, a ^regular allowance was given to him by the king of Babylon, a portion for each day, all the days of his life until the day of his death.

52:20 ^1 Kin 7:47; 2 Kin 25:16   52:21 ^1 Kin 7:15; 2 Kin 25:17   52:22 ^1 Kin 7:16; 2 Kin 25:17
52:23 ^1 Kin 7:20   52:24 ^1 Chr 9:19; Jer 35:4
52:25 ^2 Kin 25:19; Esth 1:14   52:26 ^2 Kin 25:20
52:27 ^2 Kin 25:21; Ezek 8:11-18
52:28 ^2 Kin 24:2, 3, 12-16; 2 Chr 36:20
52:30 ^2 Kin 25:11; Jer 39:9   52:31 ^Gen 40:13, 20; Ps 3:3   52:32 ^2 Kin 25:28   52:33 ^2 Sam 9:7, 13; 1 Kin 2:7   52:34 ^2 Sam 9:10; 2 Kin 25:30

52:21 ¹About 27 ft. high and 18 ft. in circumference or 8 m and 5.4 m   52:22 ¹About 7.5 ft. or 2.3 m

THE LAMENTATIONS

THE SORROWS OF ZION

1 How ᴬlonely sits the city
That *once* had ᴮmany people!
She has become like a widow
Who was once great among the
nations!
She who was a princess among
the provinces
Has become a forced laborer!

2 She weeps bitterly in the night,
And her tears are on her cheeks;
She has no one to comfort her
Among all her ᴬlovers.
All her friends have ᴮdealt
treacherously with her;
They have become her enemies.

3 ᴬJudah has gone into exile out
of affliction
And harsh servitude;
She lives among the nations,
But she has not found a resting
place;
All those who pursued her
have overtaken her
In the midst of distress.

4 The roads of Zion are in
mourning
Because no one comes to an
appointed feast.
All her gates are deserted;
Her priests groan,
Her ᴬvirgins are worried,
And as for *Zion* herself, it is
ᴮbitter for her.

5 Her adversaries have become
her masters,
Her enemies are secure;
For the Lord has ᴬcaused her
grief
Because of the multitude of
her wrongdoings;

Her little ones have gone away
As captives led by the enemy.

6 All of her ᴬsplendor
Is gone from the daughter of
Zion;
Her leaders have become like
deer
That have found no pasture,
And they have fled without
strength
From the pursuer.

7 *In* the days of her affliction
and homelessness
Jerusalem remembers all her
treasures
That were *hers* since the days
of old,
When her people fell into the
hand of the adversary
And ᴬno one helped her.
The adversaries saw her,
They ᴮlaughed at her ruin.

8 Jerusalem sinned ᴬgreatly,
Therefore she has become an
object of ridicule.
All who honored her despise
her
Because they have seen her
nakedness;
Even she herself groans and
turns away.

9 Her uncleanness was in her
garment's seams;
She did not think of her future.
So she has ᴬfallen in an
astonishing way;
ᴮShe has no comforter.

1:1 ᴬIs 3:26   ᴮIs 22:2   1:2 ᴬJer 2:25   ᴮJob 19:13, 14
1:3 ᴬJer 13:19   1:4 ᴬLam 2:10, 21   ᴮJoel 1:8-13
1:5 ᴬPs 90:7, 8; Ezek 8:17, 18   1:6 ᴬJer 13:18
1:7 ᴬJer 37:7   ᴮPs 79:4   1:8 ᴬIs 59:2-13; Lam 1:5, 20
1:9 ᴬIs 3:8   ᴮEccl 4:1

"See, Lord, my affliction,
For the enemy has honored
    himself!"

10 The adversary has stretched
    out his hand
Over all her precious things,
For she has seen the nations
    enter her sanctuary,
The ones whom You
    commanded
That they were ᴬnot to enter
Your congregation.

11 All her people groan, ᴬseeking
    bread;
They have given their
    treasures for food
To ᴮrestore their lives.
"See, Lord, and look,
For I am despised."

12 "*Is it* nothing to all you who
    pass *this* way?
Look and see if there is *any*
    pain like my pain
Which was inflicted on me,
With which the ᴬLord
    tormented *me* on the day of
    His ᴮfierce anger.

13 "From ¹the height He sent fire
    into my ᴬbones,
And it dominated *them*.
He has spread a ᴮnet for my feet;
He has turned me back;
He has made me desolate,
Faint all day long.

14 "The yoke of my wrongdoings is
    bound;
By His hand they are woven
    together.
They have come upon my
    neck;
He has made my strength fail.
The Lord ᴬhas handed me over
To *those against whom* I am
    not able to stand.

15 "The Lord has thrown away all
    my strong men
In my midst;

He has called an appointed
    time against me
To crush my ᴬyoung men;
The Lord has ᴮtrodden *as in* a
    wine press
The virgin daughter of Judah.

16 "For these things I weep;
My eyes run down with water;
Because far from me is a
    ᴬcomforter,
One to restore my soul.
My children are desolate
Because the enemy has
    prevailed."

17 Zion stretches out with her
    hands;
There is no one to comfort her;
The Lord has commanded
    regarding Jacob
That those around him
    become his adversaries;
ᴬJerusalem has become a filthy
    thing among them.

18 "The Lord is ᴬrighteous,
For I have ᴮrebelled against His
    command;
Hear now, all peoples,
And see my pain;
My virgins and my young men
Have gone into captivity.

19 "I called to my lovers, *but* they
    deserted me;
My ᴬpriests and my elders
    perished in the city
While they sought food
    to restore their strength
    themselves.

20 "See, Lord, for I am in distress;
My ᴬspirit is greatly troubled;
My heart is overturned within
    me,

1:10 ᴬDeut 23:3   1:11 ᴬJer 38:9   ᴮ1 Sam 30:12
1:12 ᴬJer 30:23, 24   ᴮIs 13:13   1:13 ᴬJob 30:30
ᴮJob 19:6   1:14 ᴬJer 32:3, 5; Ezek 25:4, 7   1:15 ᴬJer 6:11
ᴮMal 4:3   1:16 ᴬPs 69:20; Eccl 4:1   1:17 ᴬLam 1:8
1:18 ᴬPs 119:75   ᴮ1 Sam 12:14, 15   1:19 ᴬJer 14:15;
Lam 2:20   1:20 ᴬIs 16:11

1:13 ¹I.e., heaven

For I have been very
  ᴮrebellious.
In the street the sword has
  made *women* childless;
In the house it is like death.

21 "They have heard that I groan;
  There is no one to comfort me,
  All my enemies have heard of
    my disaster;
  They are ᴬjoyful that You have
    done *it*.
  Oh, that You would bring
    the day which You have
    proclaimed,
  So that they will become like
    me.

22 "May all their wickedness come
    before You;
  And ᴬdeal with them just as
    You have dealt with me
  For all my wrongdoings.
  For my groans are many and
    my heart is faint."

GOD'S ANGER OVER ISRAEL

2 How the Lord has covered the
    daughter of Zion
  With a cloud in His anger!
  He has ᴬhurled
  The ᴮglory of Israel from
    heaven to earth,
  And has not remembered His
    footstool
  In the day of His anger.

2 The Lord has destroyed; He
    has not spared
  All the settlements of Jacob.
  In His wrath He has
    ᴬoverthrown
  The strongholds of the
    daughter of Judah,
  He has ᴮhurled *them* down to
    the ground;
  He has profaned the kingdom
    and its leaders.

3 In fierce anger He has cut off
  All the strength of Israel;

He has pulled back His right
  hand
From the enemy.
And He has ᴬburned in Jacob
  like a flaming fire
Consuming on all sides.

4 He has bent His ᴬbow like an
    enemy;
  His right hand is positioned
    like an adversary,
  And He has killed everything
    that was pleasant to the eye.
  In the tent of the daughter of
    Zion
  He has ᴮpoured out His wrath
    like fire.

5 The Lord has become like an
    ᴬenemy.
  He has engulfed Israel;
  He has engulfed all its palaces,
  He has destroyed its
    strongholds
  And caused great mourning
    and grieving in the daughter
    of Judah.

6 And He has treated His
    tabernacle violently, like a
    despised garden;
  He has ᴬdestroyed His
    appointed meeting place.
  The LORD has caused
  The appointed feast and
    Sabbath in Zion to be
    forgotten,
  And He has ᴮdespised king and
    priest
  In the indignation of His anger.

7 The Lord has ᴬrejected His altar,
  He has ¹repudiated His
    sanctuary;
  He ᴮhas handed over

1:20 ᴮJer 14:20 1:21ᴬPs 35:15; Jer 50:11
1:22ᴬNeh 4:4; Ps 137:7 2:1ᴬIs 14:12–15 ᴮIs 64:11
2:2ᴬLam 2:5 ᴮIs 25:12 2:3ᴬIs 42:25; Jer 21:14
2:4ᴬJob 6:4 ᴮIs 42:25 2:5ᴬJer 30:14 2:6ᴬJer 52:13
ᴮLam 4:16 2:7ᴬPs 78:59–61 ᴮJer 33:4, 5

2:7 ¹I.e., scornfully rejected

The walls of her palaces to the
  enemy.
They have made a noise in the
  house of the Lord
As on the day of an appointed
  feast.

8 The Lord determined to
  destroy
The wall of the daughter of
  Zion.
He has ^stretched out a line,
He has not restrained His
  hand from destroying,
And He has caused rampart
  and wall to mourn;
They have languished
  together.

9 Her ^gates have sunk into the
  ground,
He has destroyed and broken
  her bars.
Her king and her leaders are
  among the nations;
The Law is gone.
Her prophets, too, find
^No vision from the Lord.

10 The elders of the daughter of
  Zion
Sit on the ground *and* ¹are
  silent.
They have thrown ^dust on
  their heads;
They have put on ^sackcloth.
The virgins of Jerusalem
Have bowed their heads to the
  ground.

11 My eyes fail because of tears,
My ^spirit is greatly troubled;
My ^heart is poured out on the
  earth
Because of the destruction of
  the daughter of my people,
When little ones and infants
  languish
In the streets of the city.

12 They say to their mothers,
"^Where is grain and wine?"

As they faint like a wounded
  person
In the streets of the city,
As their ^lives are poured out
In their mothers' arms.

13 How shall I admonish you?
What ^shall I compare to you,
Daughter of Jerusalem?
What shall I liken to you as I
  comfort you,
Virgin daughter of Zion?
For your collapse is as vast as
  the sea;
Who can ^heal you?

14 Your prophets have seen for
  you
Worthless and deceptive
  visions;
And they have not ^exposed
  your wrongdoing
So as to restore you from
  captivity,
But they have ^seen for you
  worthless and misleading
  pronouncements.

15 All who pass along the way
^Clap their hands *in ridicule*
  at you;
They ^hiss and shake their
  heads
At the daughter of Jerusalem:
"Is this the city of which they
  said,
'Perfect in beauty,
A joy to all the earth'?"

16 All your enemies
Have opened their mouths
  wide against you;
They hiss and gnash *their*
  teeth.
They say, "We have ^engulfed
  her!

2:8 ^2 Kin 21:13; Is 34:11   2:9 ^Neh 1:3   ^Jer 14:14
2:10 ^Job 2:12   ^Is 15:3   2:11 ^Jer 4:19   ^Job 16:13
2:12 ^Jer 5:17   ^Job 30:16   2:13 ^Lam 1:12   ^Jer 8:22
2:14 ^Is 58:1   ^Jer 23:36   2:15 ^Job 27:23   ^Ps 22:7
2:16 ^Ps 56:2

2:10 ¹Another reading is *wail*

This certainly is the ^Bday
which we awaited;
We have reached *it*, we have
seen *it!*"

17 The LORD has ^done what He
determined;
He has accomplished His word
Which He commanded from
days of old.
He has torn down without
sparing,
And He has helped the enemy
to rejoice over you;
He has exalted the might of
your adversaries.

18 Their ^heart cried out to the
Lord:
"You ^Bwall of the daughter of
Zion,
Let *your* tears stream down
like a river day and night;
Give yourself no relief,
Let your eyes have no rest.

19 "Arise, whimper in the night
At the beginning of the night
watches;
^Pour out your heart like water
Before the presence of the Lord;
Raise your hands to Him
For the ^Blife of your little ones
Who languish because of
hunger
At the head of every street.

20 "See, LORD, and look!
With whom have You dealt
this way?
Should women really ^eat their
children,
The little ones who were born
healthy?
Should ^Bpriest and prophet
really be killed
In the sanctuary of the Lord?

21 "On the ground in the streets
Lie ^young and old;
My ^Bvirgins and my young men
Have fallen by the sword.

You have put *them* to death on
the day of Your anger,
You have slaughtered,
without sparing.

22 "You called as on the day of an
appointed feast
My terrors on every side;
And there was ^no one who
survived or escaped
On the day of the LORD's anger.
As for those ^Bwhom I brought
forth healthy and whom I
raised,
My enemy annihilated them."

JEREMIAH SHARES ISRAEL'S MISERY

3 I am the man who has ^seen
misery
Because of the rod of His wrath.

2 He has driven me and made
me walk
In ^darkness and not in light.

3 Indeed, He has ^turned His
hand against me
Repeatedly all the day.

4 He has consumed my flesh
and my skin,
He has ^broken my bones.

5 He has ^besieged and
surrounded me with
bitterness and hardship.

6 He has made me live in ^dark
places,
Like those who have long been
dead.

7 He has ^walled me in so that I
cannot go out;
He has made my chain heavy.

8 Even when I cry out and call
for help,
He ^shuts out my prayer.

2:16 ^BObad 12-15 2:17^Jer 4:28 2:18^Ps 119:145
^BLam 2:8 2:19^1 Sam 1:15 ^BLam 2:11 2:20^Jer 19:9
^BPs 78:64 2:21^2 Chr 36:17 ^BPs 78:62, 63
2:22^Jer 11:11 ^BJer 16:2-4 3:1^Ps 88:7, 15, 16
3:2^Job 30:26; Is 59:9 3:3^Ps 38:2; Is 5:25
3:4^Ps 51:8; Is 38:13 3:5^Job 19:8 3:6^Ps 88:5, 6;
143:3 3:7^Job 3:23; 19:8 3:8^Job 30:20; Ps 22:2

9 He has ^blocked my ways with
   cut stone;
   He has twisted my paths.
10 He is to me *like* a bear lying in
   wait,
   Like a lion in secret places.
11 He has made my ways deviate,
   and ^torn me to pieces;
   He has made me desolate.
12 He bent His bow
   And ^took aim at me as a target
   for the arrow.
13 He made the arrows of His
   ^quiver
   Enter my inward parts.
14 I have become a ^laughingstock
   to all my people,
   Their song of ridicule all the
   day.
15 He has ^filled me with
   bitterness,
   He has made me drink plenty
   of wormwood.
16 He has also ^made my teeth
   grind with ^Bgravel;
   He has made me cower in the
   dust.
17 My soul has been excluded
   ^from peace;
   I have forgotten happiness.
18 So I say, "My strength has
   failed,
   And *so has* my ^hope from the
   LORD."

HOPE OF RELIEF IN GOD'S MERCY

19 Remember my misery and
   my homelessness, the
   ^wormwood and bitterness.
20 ^My soul certainly remembers,
   And is ^Bbent over within me.
21 I recall this to my mind,
   Therefore I ^wait.
22 The LORD's acts of mercy
   indeed do not end,
   ^For His compassions do not
   fail.

23 *They* are new every morning;
   Great is ^Your faithfulness.
24 "The LORD is my ^portion," says
   my soul,
   "Therefore I ^Bwait for Him."
25 The LORD is good to those who
   ^await Him,
   To the person *who* ^Bseeks Him.
26 *It is* good that he ^waits
   silently
   For the salvation of the LORD.
27 *It is* good for a man to bear
   The yoke in his youth.
28 Let him ^sit alone and keep
   quiet,
   Since He has laid *it* on him.
29 Let him put his mouth in the
   ^dust;
   Perhaps there is ^Bhope.
30 Let him give *his* ^cheek to the
   one who is going to strike
   him;
   Let him be filled with shame.
31 For the Lord will ^not reject
   forever,
32 For if He causes grief,
   Then He will have
   ^compassion
   In proportion to His abundant
   mercy.
33 For He ^does not afflict
   willingly
   Or grieve the sons of mankind.
34 To crush under one's feet
   All the prisoners of the land,
35 To deprive a man of ^justice
   In the presence of the Most
   High,

3:9 ^Is 63:17; Hos 2:6   3:11 ^Job 16:12, 13; Jer 15:3
3:12 ^Job 6:4; 7:20   3:13 ^Jer 5:16   3:14 ^Ps 22:6, 7;
123:4   3:15 ^Jer 9:15   3:16 ^Ps 3:7   ^BProv 20:17
3:17 ^Is 59:11; Jer 12:12   3:18 ^Job 17:15; Ezek 37:11
3:19 ^Jer 9:15; Lam 3:5, 15   3:20 ^Job 21:6
^BPs 42:5, 6, 11   3:21 ^Ps 130:7   3:22 ^Mal 3:6
3:23 ^Heb 10:23   3:24 ^Ps 16:5   ^BPs 33:18
3:25 ^Ps 27:14   ^BIs 26:9   3:26 ^Ps 37:7   3:28 ^Jer 15:17
3:29 ^Job 16:15   ^BJer 31:17   3:30 ^Job 16:10; Is 50:6
3:31 ^Ps 77:7; 94:14   3:32 ^Ps 78:38; 106:43-45
3:33 ^Ps 119:67, 71, 75; Ezek 33:11
3:35 ^Ps 140:12; Prov 17:15

36 To ^defraud someone in his
   lawsuit—
   Of these things the Lord does
   not approve.
37 Who is there who speaks and
   it ^comes to pass,
   Unless the Lord has
   commanded *it?*
38 *Is it* not from the mouth of the
   Most High
   That ^both adversity and good
   proceed?
39 Of what can *any* living mortal,
   or any man,
   ^Complain in view of his sins?
40 Let's ^examine and search out
   our ways,
   And let's return to the Lord.
41 We ^raise our heart and hands
   Toward God in heaven;
42 We have ^done wrong and
   rebelled;
   You have ^not pardoned.
43 You have covered *Yourself* with
   ^anger
   And pursued us;
   You have slain *and* ^have not
   spared.
44 You have ^veiled Yourself with
   a cloud
   So that ^no prayer can pass
   through.
45 You have made us *mere* ^refuse
   and rubbish
   In the midst of the peoples.
46 All our enemies have ^opened
   their mouths against us.
47 ^Panic and pitfall have come
   upon us,
   Devastation and destruction;
48 My ^eyes run down *with*
   streams of water
   Because of the destruction of
   the daughter of my people.
49 My eyes flow ^unceasingly,
   Without stopping,

50 Until the Lord ^looks down
   And sees from heaven.
51 My eyes bring pain to my soul
   Because of all the daughters of
   my city.
52 My enemies ^without reason
   Hunted me down ^like a bird;
53 They have silenced me ^in the
   pit
   And have ^thrown stones on me.
54 Waters flowed ^over my head;
   I said, "I am cut off!"
55 I ^called on Your name, Lord,
   Out of the lowest pit.
56 You have ^heard my voice,
   "^Do not cover Your ear from
   my *plea for* relief,
   From my cry for help."
57 You ^came near on the day I
   called to You;
   You said, "^Do not fear!"
58 Lord, You ^have pleaded my
   soul's cause;
   You have ^redeemed my life.
59 Lord, You have ^seen my
   oppression;
   ^Judge my case.
60 You have seen all their
   vengeance,
   All their ^schemes against me.
61 You have heard their
   ^reproach, Lord,
   All their schemes against me.
62 The ^lips of my assailants and
   their talk
   Are against me all day long.

3:36 ^A Jer 22:3; Hab 1:13   3:37 ^A Ps 33:9-11
3:38 ^A Job 2:10; Is 45:7   3:39 ^A Jer 30:15; Mic 7:9
3:40 ^A Ps 119:59; 139:23, 24   3:41 ^A Ps 25:1; 28:2
3:42 ^A Neh 9:26   ^B 2 Kin 24:4   3:43 ^A Lam 2:21
^B Lam 2:2, 17, 21   3:44 ^A Ps 97:2   ^B Lam 3:8
3:45 ^A 1 Cor 4:13   3:46 ^A Job 30:9, 10; Ps 22:6-8
3:47 ^A Is 24:17, 18; Jer 48:43, 44   3:48 ^A Ps 119:136;
Jer 9:1, 18   3:49 ^A Ps 77:2; Jer 14:17   3:50 ^A Ps 80:14;
Is 63:15   3:52 ^A Ps 35:7, 19   ^B 1 Sam 26:20
3:53 ^A Jer 37:16   ^B Dan 6:17   3:54 ^A Ps 69:2; Jon 2:3-5
3:55 ^A Ps 130:1; Jon 2:2   3:56 ^A Job 34:28   ^B Ps 55:1
3:57 ^A Ps 145:18   ^B Is 41:10, 14   3:58 ^A Jer 50:34
^B Ps 34:22   3:59 ^A Jer 18:19, 20   ^B Ps 26:1   3:60 ^A Jer 11:19
3:61 ^A Ps 74:18; 89:50   3:62 ^A Ps 59:7, 12; 140:3

⁶³ Look at their ᴬsitting and their
      rising;
      ᴮI am their mocking song.
⁶⁴ You will ᴬrepay them, Lᴏʀᴅ,
      In accordance with the work
         of their hands.
⁶⁵ You will give them
      ᴬshamelessness of heart,
      Your curse will be on them.
⁶⁶ You will ᴬpursue them in
      anger and eliminate them
      From under the ᴮheavens of
         the Lᴏʀᴅ!

DISTRESS OF THE SIEGE DESCRIBED

4 How ᴬdark the gold has
      become,
      How the pure gold has
         changed!
      The sacred stones are spilled
         out
      At the corner of every street.
² The precious sons of Zion,
      Weighed against pure gold,
      How they are regarded as
         ᴬearthenware jars,
      The work of a potter's hands!
³ Even jackals offer the breast,
      They nurse their young;
      But the daughter of my
         people has proved herself
         ᴬcruel,
      Like ᴮostriches in the
         wilderness.
⁴ The ᴬtongue of the infant
      clings
      To the roof of its mouth
         because of ᴮthirst;
      The children ask for bread,
      But no one breaks *it* for them.
⁵ Those who used to eat
      ᴬdelicacies
      Are made to tremble in the
         streets;
      Those who were raised in
         crimson *clothing*
      Embrace garbage heaps.

⁶ For the wrongdoing of the
      daughter of my people
      Is greater than the sin of Sodom,
      Which was ᴬoverthrown as in a
         moment,
      And no hands were turned
         toward her.
⁷ Her consecrated ones were
      ᴬpurer than snow,
      They shined more than milk;
      They were more ruddy *in* body
         than pearls of coral,
      Their form *was like* lapis lazuli.
⁸ Their appearance is ᴬdarker
      than soot,
      They are not recognized in
         the streets;
      Their skin is shriveled on
         their bones,
      It is dry, it has become like
         wood.
⁹ Better *off* are those ᴬkilled by
      the sword
      Than those killed by hunger;
      For they waste away, stricken
      By the lack of the produce of
         the field.
¹⁰ The hands of compassionate
      women
      Boiled their own children;
      They became ᴬfood for them
      Due to the destruction of the
         daughter of my people.
¹¹ The Lᴏʀᴅ has ᴬexpended His
      wrath,
      He has poured out His fierce
         anger;
      And He has kindled a fire in
         Zion,
      And it has consumed its
         foundations.

3:63 ᴬPs 139:2 ᴮJob 30:9 3:64 ᴬPs 28:4; Jer 51:6, 24, 56
3:65 ᴬEx 14:8; Deut 2:30 3:66 ᴬLam 3:43 ᴮPs 8:3
4:1 ᴬEzek 7:19-22 4:2 ᴬIs 30:14; Jer 19:1, 11
4:3 ᴬIs 49:15 ᴮJob 39:14-17 4:4 ᴬPs 22:15 ᴮJer 14:3
4:5 ᴬJer 6:2; Amos 6:3-7 4:6 ᴬGen 19:25; Jer 20:16
4:7 ᴬPs 51:7 4:8 ᴬJob 30:30; Lam 5:10 4:9 ᴬJer 16:4
4:10 ᴬDeut 28:53-55 4:11 ᴬJer 7:20; Lam 2:17

12 The kings of the earth did not
believe,
Nor *did* any of the inhabitants
of the world,
That the adversary and the
enemy
Would ^enter the gates of
Jerusalem.

13 Because of the sins of her
prophets
And the wrongdoings of her
priests,
Who have shed in her midst
The ^blood of the righteous,

14 They wandered, blind, in the
streets;
They were defiled with ^blood,
Such that no one could touch
their ^Bgarments.

15 "Keep away! ^Unclean!" they
cried out of themselves.
"Keep away, keep away, do not
touch!"
For they ^Bdistanced themselves
as well as wandered;
People among the nations said,
"They shall not continue to
reside *with us.*"

16 The presence of the LORD has
scattered them,
He will not continue to look at
them;
They did not ^honor the
priests,
They did not favor the elders.

17 Yet our eyes failed,
Looking for help was ^useless;
At our observation point we
have watched
For a ^Bnation that could not
save.

18 They ^hunted our steps
So that we could not walk in
our streets;
Our end drew near,
Our days were finished
For our end had come.

19 Our pursuers were ^swifter
Than the eagles of the sky;
They chased us on the
mountains,
They waited in ambush for us
in the wilderness.

20 The breath of our nostrils, the
^LORD's anointed,
Was ^Bcaptured in their pits,
Of whom we had said, "In his
shadow
We shall live among the
nations."

21 Rejoice and be joyful,
daughter of ^Edom,
Who lives in the land of Uz;
But the ^Bcup will pass to you
as well,
You will become drunk and
expose yourself.

22 *The punishment* of your
wrongdoing has been
^completed, daughter of
Zion;
He will no longer exile you.
But He ^Bwill punish your
wrongdoing, daughter of
Edom;
He will expose your sins!

A PRAYER FOR MERCY

5 Remember, LORD, what has
come upon us;
Look, and see our ^disgrace!

2 Our inheritance has been
turned over to ^strangers,
Our ^Bhouses to foreigners.

3 We have become orphans,
^without a father;
Our mothers are like
widows.

4:12 ^Jer 21:13   4:13 ^Jer 2:30; 26:8, 9   4:14 ^Is 1:15
^B Jer 2:34   4:15 ^Lev 13:45, 46   ^B Jer 49:5
4:16 ^Is 9:14-16; Jer 52:24-27   4:17 ^Jer 37:7
^B Ezek 29:6, 7, 16   4:18 ^Jer 16:16   4:19 ^Is 5:26-28;
30:16, 17   4:20 ^2 Sam 1:14   ^B Jer 39:5   4:21 ^Ps 137:7
^B Obad 16   4:22 ^Is 40:2   ^B Jer 49:10   5:1 ^Ps 44:13-16
5:2 ^Is 1:7   ^B Zeph 1:13   5:3 ^Ex 22:24; Jer 15:8

4 We have to pay for our
   drinking ^water,
  Our wood comes *to us* at a
   price.
5 Our pursuers are at our necks;
  We are worn out, we are given
   ^no rest.
6 We have submitted to ^Egypt
   and Assyria to get enough
   bread.
7 Our ^fathers sinned, *and* are
   gone;
  It is we *who* have been
   burdened with the
   punishment for their
   wrongdoings.
8 ^Slaves rule over us;
  There is ^Bno one to rescue us
   from their hand.
9 We get our bread at the ^risk
   of our lives
  Because of the sword in the
   wilderness.
10 Our skin has become as ^hot
   as an oven,
  Because of the ravages of
   hunger.
11 They violated the ^women in
   Zion,
  The virgins in the cities of
   Judah.
12 Leaders were hung by their
   hands;
  ^Elders were not respected.
13 Young men ^worked at the
   grinding mill,
  And youths ^Bstaggered under
   loads of wood.

14 Elders are absent from the gate,
  Young men from their ^music.
15 The joy of our hearts has
   ^ended;
  Our dancing has been turned
   into mourning.
16 The crown has fallen from our
   head;
  ^Woe to us, for we have sinned!
17 Because of this our ^heart is
   faint,
  Because of these things our
   eyes are dim;
18 Because of ^Mount Zion which
   lies desolate,
  ^BJackals prowl in it.
19 You, LORD, rule forever;
  Your ^throne is from
   generation to generation.
20 Why will You ^forget us
   forever?
  Why do You abandon us for so
   long?
21 ^Restore us to You, LORD, so
   that we may be restored;
  Renew our days as of old,
22 Unless ^You have utterly
   rejected us
  And are exceedingly angry
   with us.

5:4 ^A Is 3:1   5:5 ^A Neh 9:36, 37   5:6 ^A Hos 9:3; 12:1
5:7 ^A Jer 14:20; 16:12   5:8 ^A Neh 5:15   ^B Ps 7:2
5:9 ^A Jer 40:9-12   5:10 ^A Job 30:30; Lam 4:8
5:11 ^A Is 13:16; Zech 14:2   5:12 ^A Is 47:6; Lam 4:16
5:13 ^A Judg 16:21   ^B Jer 7:18   5:14 ^A Is 24:8; Jer 7:34
5:15 ^A Jer 25:10; Amos 8:10   5:16 ^A Is 3:9-11
5:17 ^A Is 1:5   5:18 ^A Mic 3:12   ^B Neh 4:3   5:19 ^A Ps 45:6
5:20 ^A Ps 13:1; 44:24   5:21 ^A Ps 80:3; Jer 31:18
5:22 ^A Ps 60:1, 2; Jer 7:29

EZEKIEL

THE VISION OF FOUR FIGURES

1 Now it came about in the thirtieth year, on the fifth *day* of the fourth month, while I was by the ^river Chebar among the exiles, the ^heavens were opened and I saw visions of God. ²(On the fifth of the month in the ^fifth year of King Jehoiachin's exile, ³the ^word of the Lord came expressly to Ezekiel the priest, son of Buzi, in the ^land of the Chaldeans by the river Chebar; and there the hand of the Lord came upon him.)

⁴As I looked, behold, a ^high wind was coming from the north, a great cloud with fire flashing intermittently and a bright light around it, and in its midst *something* like ^gleaming metal in the midst of the fire. ⁵And within it there were figures resembling ^four living beings. And this was their appearance: they had human form. ⁶Each of them had ^four faces and four wings. ⁷Their legs were straight and their feet were like a calf's hoof, and they sparkled like ^polished bronze. ⁸Under their wings on their four sides *were* human ^hands. As for the faces and wings of the four of them, ⁹their wings touched one another; *their faces* did not turn when they moved, each ^went straight forward. ¹⁰As for the ^form of their faces, *each had* a human ^face; all four had the face of a lion on the right and the face of a bull on the left, and all four had the face of an eagle. ¹¹Such were their faces. Their wings were spread out above;

each had two touching another *being,* and ^two covering their bodies. ¹²And each went straight forward; ^wherever the spirit was about to go, they would go, without turning as they went. ¹³In the midst of the living beings there was something that looked like burning coals of ^fire, like torches moving among the living beings. The fire was bright, and lightning was flashing from the fire. ¹⁴And the living beings ^ran back and forth like bolts of lightning.

¹⁵Now as I looked at the living beings, behold, there was one ^wheel on the ground beside the living beings, for each of the four of them. ¹⁶The appearance of the wheels and their workmanship *was* like sparkling ^topaz, and all four of them had the same form, their appearance and workmanship *being* as if one wheel were within another. ¹⁷Whenever they moved, they moved in *any* of their four directions without ^turning as they moved. ¹⁸As for their rims, they were high and awesome, and the rims of all four of them were ^covered with eyes all around. ¹⁹Whenever the living beings moved, the wheels moved

1:1 ^Ezek 3:23   ^B Matt 3:16
1:2 ^2 Kin 24:12–15; Ezek 8:1   1:3 ^2 Pet 1:21
^B Ezek 12:13   1:4 ^Is 21:1   ^B Ezek 1:27
1:5 ^Ezek 10:15, 17, 20; Rev 4:6–8   1:6 ^Ezek 1:10;
10:14, 21   1:7 ^Dan 10:6; Rev 1:15   1:8 ^Ezek 10:8, 21
1:9 ^Ezek 1:12; 10:22   1:10 ^Rev 4:7   ^B Ezek 10:14
1:11 ^Is 6:2; Ezek 1:23   1:12 ^Ezek 1:20   1:13 ^Ps 104:4;
Rev 4:5   1:14 ^Zech 4:10   1:15 ^Ezek 1:19–21; 10:9
1:16 ^Ezek 10:9; Dan 10:6   1:17 ^Ezek 1:9, 12; 10:11
1:18 ^Ezek 10:12; Rev 4:6, 8

with them. And whenever the living beings ^rose from the earth, the wheels rose *also*. ²⁰^Wherever the spirit was about to go, they would go in that direction. And the wheels rose just as they *did;* for the spirit of the living beings *was* in the wheels. ²¹^Whenever those went, they went; and whenever those stopped, they stopped. And whenever those rose from the earth, the wheels rose just as they *did;* for the spirit of the living beings *was* in the wheels.

VISION OF DIVINE GLORY

²²Now ^over the heads of the living beings *there was* something like an expanse, like the awesome gleam of crystal, spread out over their heads. ²³Under the expanse their wings *were stretched out* straight, one toward the other; each one also had ^two *wings* covering its body on the one side and on the other. ²⁴And I also heard the sound of their wings, like the ^sound of abundant waters as they went, like the ᴮvoice of the Almighty, a sound of a crowd like the sound of an army camp; whenever they stopped, they let down their wings. ²⁵And a voice came from above the ^expanse that was over their heads; whenever they stood still, they let down their wings.

²⁶Now above the expanse that was over their heads there was something ^resembling a throne, like lapis lazuli in appearance; and on that which resembled a throne, high up, *was* a figure with the appearance of a ᴮman. ²⁷Then I noticed from the appearance of His waist and upward *something* ^like gleaming metal that looked like fire all around within it, and

from the appearance of His waist and downward I saw something like fire; and *there was* a radiance around Him. ²⁸Like the appearance of the ^rainbow in the clouds on a rainy day, so *was* the appearance of the surrounding radiance. Such *was* the appearance of the likeness of the ᴮglory of the Lᴏʀᴅ. And when I saw *it,* I fell on my face and heard a voice speaking.

THE PROPHET'S CALL

2 Then He said to me, "Son of man, ^stand on your feet, and I will speak with you." ²And as He spoke to me the ^Spirit entered me and set me on my feet; and I heard *Him* speaking to me. ³Then He said to me, "Son of man, I am sending you to the sons of Israel, to a rebellious people who have rebelled against Me; ^they and their fathers have revolted against Me to this very day. ⁴So I am sending you to those who are ^impudent and obstinate children, and you shall say to them, 'This is what the Lord Gᴏᴅ says:' ⁵As for them, whether they listen or not—for they are a rebellious house—they will ^know that a prophet has been among them. ⁶And as for you, son of man, you are ^not to fear them nor fear their words, though thistles and thorns are with you and you sit on scorpions; you are not to fear their words nor be dismayed at their presence, since they are a rebellious house. ⁷But you shall ^speak My words to

1:19^Ezek 10:19   1:20^Ezek 1:12   1:21^Ezek 10:17
1:22^Ezek 10:1   1:23^Ezek 1:6, 11   1:24^Ezek 43:2
ᴮEzek 10:5   1:25^Ezek 1:22; 10:1   1:26^Is 6:1
ᴮEzek 43:6, 7   1:27^Ezek 1:4; 8:2   1:28^Gen 9:13
ᴮEx 24:16   2:1^Dan 10:11; Acts 9:6   2:2^Ezek 3:24;
Dan 8:18   2:3^Ezek 20:18, 30   2:4^Ps 95:8; Is 48:4
2:5^Ezek 33:33; Luke 10:10, 11   2:6^Is 51:12; Jer 1:8, 17
2:7^Jer 1:7, 17; Ezek 3:10, 17

them whether they listen or not, for they are rebellious.

⁸"Now you, son of man, listen to what I am speaking to you; do not be rebellious like that rebellious house. Open your mouth wide and ᴬeat what I am giving you." ⁹Then I looked, and behold, a ᴬhand was extended to me; and behold, a ᴮscroll *was* in it. ¹⁰When He spread it out before me, it was written on the front and back, and written on it were songs of mourning, sighing, and ᴬwoe.

EZEKIEL'S COMMISSION

3 Then He said to me, "Son of man, eat what you find; ᴬeat this scroll, and go, speak to the house of Israel." ²So I ᴬopened my mouth, and He fed me this scroll. ³And He said to me, "Son of man, feed your stomach and ᴬfill your body with this scroll which I am giving you." Then I ate it, and it was as sweet as honey in my mouth.

⁴Then He said to me, "Son of man, go to the house of Israel and speak with My words to them. ⁵For ᴬyou are not being sent to a people of unintelligible speech or difficult language, *but* to the house of Israel, ⁶nor to many peoples of unintelligible speech or difficult language, whose words you cannot understand. But I have sent you to the people who understand you; ⁷yet the house of Israel will not be willing to listen to you, since they are ᴬnot willing to listen to Me. The entire house of Israel certainly is stubborn and obstinate. ⁸Behold, I have made your face just as hard as their faces, and your forehead just as hard as their foreheads. ⁹Like emery harder than flint I have made your forehead. Do not

be afraid of them or be dismayed before them, since they are a rebellious house." ¹⁰Moreover, He said to me, "Son of man, take into your heart all My ᴬwords which I will speak to you and listen closely. ¹¹Go to the exiles, to the sons of your people, and speak to them and tell them, whether they listen or not, 'This is what the Lord GOD says.'"

¹²Then the ᴬSpirit lifted me up, and I heard a great rumbling sound behind me: "Blessed be the glory of the LORD from His place!" ¹³And *I heard* the sound of the wings of the living beings touching one another and the sound of the ᴬwheels beside them, even a great rumbling sound. ¹⁴So the Spirit lifted me up and took me away; and I went embittered in the rage of my spirit, and ᴬthe hand of the LORD was strong on me. ¹⁵Then I came to the exiles who lived beside the river Chebar *at* Tel-abib, and I sat there for ᴬseven days where they were living, causing consternation among them.

¹⁶Now ᴬat the end of seven days the word of the LORD came to me, saying, ¹⁷"Son of man, I have appointed you as a ᴬwatchman for the house of Israel; whenever you hear a word from My mouth, ᴮwarn them from Me. ¹⁸When I say to the wicked, 'You will certainly die,' and you do not warn him or speak out to warn the wicked from his wicked way so that he may live, that wicked person shall die for wrongdoing, but his ᴬblood I will require from

2:8ᴬJer 15:16; Ezek 3:3 2:9ᴬEzek 8:3 ᴮJer 36:2
2:10ᴬIs 3:11; Rev 8:13 3:1ᴬEzek 2:9 3:2ᴬJer 25:17
3:3ᴬJer 6:11; 20:9 3:5ᴬJon 1:2; Acts 14:11
3:7ᴬ1 Sam 8:7 3:10ᴬJob 22:22; Ezek 2:8
3:12ᴬEzek 3:14; 8:3 3:13ᴬEzek 1:15; 10:16, 17
3:14ᴬ2 Kin 3:15 3:15ᴬJob 2:13 3:16ᴬJer 42:7
3:17ᴬIs 52:8 ᴮ2 Chr 19:10 3:18ᴬEzek 3:20; 33:6, 8

your hand. ¹⁹However if you have warned the wicked and he does not turn from his wickedness or from his wicked way, he shall die for wrongdoing, but you have ^saved yourself. ²⁰Again, ^when a righteous person turns away from his righteousness and commits sin, and I place an obstacle before him, he will die; since you have not warned him, he shall die in his sin, and his righteous deeds which he has done shall not be remembered; but his blood I will require from your hand. ²¹However, if you have ^warned the righteous person that the righteous is not to sin, and he does not sin, he shall certainly live because he took warning; and you have saved yourself."

²²Now the hand of the Lord was on me there, and He said to me, "Get up, go out to the plain, and there I will ^speak to you." ²³So I got up and went out to the plain; and behold, the ^glory of the Lord was standing there, like the glory that I saw by the river Chebar, and I fell on my face. ²⁴But the ^Spirit entered me and set me up on my feet; and He spoke with me and said to me, "Go, shut yourself inside your house. ²⁵And as for you, son of man, they will ^put ropes around you and bind you with them so that you do not go out among them. ²⁶Moreover, ^I will make your tongue stick to the roof of your mouth so that you will be unable to speak and will not be a man who reprimands them, since they are a rebellious house. ²⁷But ^when I speak to you, I will open your mouth and you will say to them, 'This is what the Lord God says:' The one who hears, let him hear; and the one who refuses, let him refuse; for they are a rebellious house.

SIEGE OF JERUSALEM PREDICTED

4 "Now you, son of man, ^get yourself a brick, place it before you, and inscribe a city on it—Jerusalem. ²Then ^lay siege against it, build a siege wall, pile up an assault ramp, set up camps, and place battering rams against it all around. ³Then get yourself an iron plate and set it up as an iron wall between yourself and the city, and direct your face toward it so that it is under siege, and besiege it. This *will be* a ^sign to the house of Israel.

⁴"Then you are to lie down on your left side and put the wrongdoing of the house of Israel on it; you shall ^bear their wrongdoing for the number of days that you lie on it. ⁵For I have assigned you a number of days corresponding to the years of their wrongdoing, 390 days; so ^you shall bear the wrongdoing of the house of Israel. ⁶When you have completed these *days,* you shall lie down a second time, *but* on your right side, and bear the wrongdoing of the house of Judah; I have assigned it to you for forty days, a day for ^each year. ⁷Then you shall direct your face toward the siege of Jerusalem with your arm bared, and ^prophesy against it. ⁸Now behold, I will ^put ropes around you so that you cannot turn from your one side to your other until you have completed the days of your siege.

3:19 ^Ezek 14:14, 20; Acts 18:6
3:20 ^Ps 125:5; Ezek 18:24   3:21 ^Acts 20:31
3:22 ^Acts 9:6   3:23 ^Ezek 1:28; Acts 7:55
3:24 ^Ezek 2:2   3:25 ^Ezek 4:8   3:26 ^Luke 1:20, 22
3:27 ^Ezek 24:27; 33:22   4:1 ^Is 20:2; Jer 13:1
4:2 ^Jer 6:6; Ezek 21:22   4:3 ^Is 8:18; 20:3
4:4 ^Lev 10:17; 16:22   4:5 ^Num 14:34
4:6 ^Num 14:34; Dan 9:24-26   4:7 ^Ezek 21:2
4:8 ^Ezek 3:25

DEFILED BREAD

9 "But as for you, take wheat, barley, beans, lentils, millet, and ᴬspelt, and put them in one vessel and make them into bread for yourself; you shall eat it according to the number of the days that you lie on your side, 390 days. 10 Your food which you eat *shall be* ᴬtwenty shekels a day by weight; you shall eat it from time to time. 11 The water you drink shall be a ¹sixth of a hin by measure; you shall drink it from time to time. 12 You shall eat it as a barley cake, having baked *it* in their sight over human ᴬdung." 13 Then the LORD said, "In this way the sons of Israel will eat their bread ᴬunclean among the nations where I will scatter them." 14 But I said, "Oh, Lord GOD! Behold, I have ᴬnever been defiled; for from my youth until now I have never eaten what died of itself or was torn by animals, nor has any ᴮunclean meat ever entered my mouth!" 15 Then He said to me, "See, I will give you cow's dung in place of human dung, so that you may prepare your bread over it." 16 Moreover, He said to me, "Son of man, behold, I am going to ᴬbreak the staff of bread in Jerusalem, and they will eat bread by weight and with anxiety, and drink water by measure and in horror, 17 because bread and water will be scarce; and they will tremble with one another and ᴬwaste away in their guilt.

JERUSALEM'S DESOLATION FORETOLD

5 "As for you, son of man, take a ᴬsharp sword; take and use it *as* a barber's razor on your head and beard. Then take ᴮscales for weighing and divide the hair. 2 A third you shall burn in the fire at the center of the city, when the ᴬdays of the siege

are completed. Then you shall take a third and strike *it* with the sword all around the city, and a third you shall scatter to the wind; for I will unsheathe a sword behind them. 3 Take also a few *hairs* in number from them and bind them in the hems of your *robes.* 4 Take again some of them and throw them into the fire and burn them in the fire; from it a fire will spread to all the house of Israel.

5 "This is what the Lord GOD says: 'This is Jerusalem; I have placed her at the ᴬcenter of the nations, with lands around her. 6 But she has rebelled against My ordinances more wickedly than the nations, and against My statutes ᴬmore than the lands which surround her; for they have rejected My ordinances and have not walked in My statutes.' 7 Therefore, this is what the Lord GOD says: 'Because you have ᴬmore turmoil than the nations that surround you *and* have not walked in My statutes, nor executed My ordinances, nor acted in accordance with the ordinances of the nations around you,' 8 therefore, this is what the Lord GOD says: 'Behold, I, even I, am against you, and I will ᴬexecute judgments among you in the sight of the nations. 9 And because of all your abominations I will do among you what I have ᴬnot done, and the like of which I will never do again. 10 Therefore, ᴬfathers will

4:9ᴬEx 9:32; Is 28:25   4:10ᴬEzek 45:12
4:12ᴬIs 36:12   4:13¹Dan 1:8; Hos 9:3
4:14ᴬActs 10:14   ᴮDeut 14:3   4:16ᴬLev 26:26; Is 3:1
4:17ᴬLev 26:39; Ezek 24:23   5:1ᴬLev 21:5   ᴮDan 5:27
5:2ᴬJer 39:1, 2; Ezek 4:2-8   5:5ᴬDeut 4:6; Lam 1:1
5:6ᴬ2 Kin 17:8-20; Ezek 16:47, 48, 51   5:7ᴬ2 Kin
21:9-11; 2 Chr 33:9   5:8ᴬJer 24:9; Ezek 5:15
5:9ᴬDan 9:12; Amos 3:2   5:10ᴬLev 26:29
4:11¹About 0.6 qt. or 0.6 liter

eat *their* sons among you, and sons will eat their fathers; for I will execute judgments on you and ^Bscatter all your remnant to every wind. ¹¹Therefore as I live,' declares the Lord God, 'Because you have ^Adefiled My sanctuary with all your ^Bdetestable idols and with all your abominations, I definitely will also withdraw and My eye will have no pity, and I also will not spare. ¹²A third of you will die by plague or perish by famine among you, a third will fall by the sword around you, and a third I will ^Ascatter to every wind, and I will ^Bunsheathe a sword behind them.

¹³'Then My anger will be spent and I will satisfy My wrath on them, and I will be ^Aappeased; then they will know that I, the Lord, have spoken in My zeal, when I have spent My wrath upon them. ¹⁴Moreover, I will make you a site of ruins and a ^Adisgrace among the nations that surround you, in the sight of everyone who passes by. ¹⁵So it will be a disgrace, an *object of* abuse, a warning, and an object of horror to the nations that surround you when I ^Aexecute judgments against you in anger, wrath, and raging reprimands. I, the Lord, have spoken. ¹⁶When I send against them the deadly arrows of famine which were for the destruction of those whom I will send to destroy you, then I will also intensify the famine upon you and break off your provision of bread. ¹⁷^AI will send on you famine and vicious animals, and they will bereave you of children; ^Bplague and bloodshed also will pass through you, and I will bring the sword on you. I, the Lord, have spoken.'"

IDOLATROUS WORSHIP DENOUNCED

6 Now the word of the Lord came to me, saying, ²"Son of man, set your face toward the ^Amountains of Israel, and prophesy against them ³and say, 'Mountains of Israel, listen to the word of the Lord God! This is what the Lord God says to the mountains, the hills, the ravines, and the valleys: "Behold, I Myself am going to bring a sword against you, and ^AI will destroy your high places. ⁴So your ^Aaltars will become deserted and your incense altars will be smashed; and I will make your slain fall in front of your idols. ⁵I will also lay the dead bodies of the sons of Israel in front of their idols; and I will scatter your ^Abones around your altars. ⁶Everywhere you live, ^Acities will be in ruins and the high places will be deserted, so that your altars will be in ruins and deserted, your ^Bidols will be broken and brought to an end, your incense altars will be cut down, and your works wiped out. ⁷The slain will fall among you, and you will know that I am the Lord.

⁸"However, I will leave a ^Aremnant, in that you will have those who escaped the sword among the nations when you are scattered among the countries. ⁹Then those of you who escape will remember Me among the nations to which they will be taken captive, how I have ^Abeen hurt by their adulterous hearts which turned away from Me, and by their eyes which committed infidelity with their idols; and they

5:10 ^BPs 44:11   5:11 ^AJer 7:9-11   ^BJer 16:18
5:12 ^AEzek 5:2, 10   ^BJer 43:10, 11   5:13 ^AIs 1:24
5:14 ^APs 74:3-10; 79:1-4   5:15 ^AIs 66:15, 16; Ezek 5:8
5:17 ^ALev 26:22   ^BEzek 38:22   6:2 ^AEzek 36:1
6:3 ^ALev 26:30   6:4 ^ALev 26:30; 2 Chr 14:5
6:5 ^A2 Kin 23:14, 16, 20; Jer 8:1, 2   6:6 ^ALev 26:31
^BEzek 6:4   6:8 ^AIs 6:13; Jer 30:11   6:9 ^APs 78:40; Is 7:13

will loathe themselves in their own sight for the evils which they have committed, for all their abominations. ¹⁰Then they will know that I am the Lord; I have not said in vain that I would inflict this disaster on them."'

¹¹"This is what the Lord God says: 'Clap your hands, stamp your foot and say, "Woe, because of all the evil abominations of the house of Israel, which will fall by the ᴬsword, famine, and plague! ¹²*Anyone* who is far away will die by the plague, *anyone* who is near will fall by the sword, and *anyone* who remains and is spared *from these* will die by the famine. So I will ᴬexpend My wrath on them. ¹³Then you will know that I am the Lord, when their ᴬdead are among their idols around their altars, on every high hill, on all the tops of the mountains, under every leafy tree and under every massive oak with thick branches—the places where they offered a soothing aroma to all their idols. ¹⁴So through all their dwelling places I will ᴬstretch out My hand against them and make the land more desolate and waste than the wilderness toward Diblah; so they will know that I am the Lord."'"

PUNISHMENT FOR WICKEDNESS FORETOLD

7 Moreover, the word of the Lord came to me, saying, ²"And you, son of man, this is what the Lord God says to the land of Israel: 'An ᴬend! The end is coming on the four corners of the land. ³Now the end is upon you, for I will send My anger against you; I will judge you according to your ways and bring all your abominations upon you. ⁴And My eye will have no pity on

you, nor will I spare *you*, but I will ᴬbring your ways upon you, and your abominations will be among you; then you will know that I am the Lord!'

⁵"This is what the Lord God says: 'A ᴬdisaster, a unique disaster, behold, it is coming! ⁶An end is coming; the end has come! It has ᴬawakened against you; behold, it has come! ⁷Your doom has come to you, you inhabitant of the land. The time has come, the ᴬday is near—panic rather than joyful shouting *on the* mountains. ⁸Now I will shortly pour out My wrath on you and expend My anger against you; I will ᴬjudge you according to your ways and bring on you all your abominations. ⁹My eye will have no pity nor will I spare *you*. I will repay you according to your ways, while your abominations are in your midst; then you will know that I, the Lord, am striking.

¹⁰'Behold, the day! Behold, it is coming! *Your* doom has gone forth; the ᴬrod has budded, arrogance has blossomed. ¹¹Violence has grown into a rod of ᴬwickedness. None of them *shall remain*, none of their people, none of their ᴮwealth, nor *anything* eminent among them. ¹²The time has come, the day has arrived. Let neither the ᴬbuyer rejoice nor the seller mourn; for ᴮwrath is against all their multitude. ¹³Indeed, the seller will not ᴬregain what he sold as long as they *both* live; for the vision regarding all their multitude will not be

6:11ᴬEzek 5:12; 7:15   6:12ᴬLam 4:11, 22; Ezek 5:13
6:13ᴬEzek 6:4-7   6:14ᴬIs 5:25; 9:12
7:2ᴬEzek 7:3, 5, 6; 11:13   7:4ᴬEzek 11:21; 22:31
7:5ᴬ2 Kin 21:12, 13; Nah 1:9   7:6ᴬZech 13:7
7:7ᴬIs 22:5   7:8ᴬEzek 7:3; 33:20
7:10ᴬPs 89:32; Is 10:5   7:11ᴬPs 73:8   ᴮZeph 1:18
7:12ᴬProv 20:14   ᴮIs 5:13, 14   7:13ᴬLev 25:24-28, 31

averted, nor will any of them maintain his life by his wrongdoing.

¹⁴"They have ^blown the trumpet and made everything ready, but no one is going to the battle, for My wrath is against all their multitude. ¹⁵The ^sword is outside *the city* and the plague and the famine are within. *Anyone* who is in the field will die by the sword, while famine and the plague will consume those in the city. ¹⁶Even when their survivors escape, they will be on the mountains like ^doves of the valleys, all of them ^moaning, each over his own wrongdoing. ¹⁷All ^hands will hang limp, and all knees will drip with water. ¹⁸They will ^put on sackcloth and shuddering will overwhelm them; and shame *will be* on all faces, and a ^bald patch on all their heads. ¹⁹They will fling their silver into the streets, and their gold will become an abhorrent thing; their ^silver and their gold will not be able to save them on the day of the wrath of the Lord. They cannot satisfy their appetite, nor can they fill their stomachs, because their wrongdoing has become a cause of stumbling.

THE TEMPLE PROFANED

²⁰Moreover, they transformed the splendor of His jewels into pride, and ^they made the images of their abominations *and* their detestable things with it; therefore I will make it an abhorrent thing to them. ²¹And I will hand it over to the ^foreigners as plunder, and to the wicked of the earth as spoils; and they will profane it. ²²I will also turn My ^face away from them, and they will profane My treasure; then robbers will enter and profane it.

²³'Make the ¹chain, for the land is full of ^bloody crimes, and the city is ^full of violence. ²⁴Therefore, I will bring the worst of the ^nations, and they will take possession of their houses. I will also put an end to the pride of the strong ones, and their ^holy places will be profaned. ²⁵When anguish comes, they will seek ^peace, but there will be none. ²⁶^Disaster will come upon disaster and rumor will be *added* to rumor; then they will seek a vision from a prophet, but the ^Law will be lost from the priest, and counsel from the elders. ²⁷The king will mourn, the prince will be ^clothed in horror, and the hands of the people of the land will tremble. I will deal with them because of their conduct, and by their judgments I will judge them. And they will know that I am the Lord.'"

VISION OF ABOMINATIONS IN JERUSALEM

8 Now it came about in the sixth year, on the fifth *day* of the sixth month, as I was sitting in my house with the elders of Judah sitting before me, that the hand of the Lord God fell upon me there. ²Then I looked, and behold, something like the appearance of a man; from His waist and downward *there was* the appearance of fire, and from His waist and upward like the appearance of a glow, like ^gleaming metal. ³And He extended the form

7:14 ^Num 10:9; Jer 4:5   7:15 ^Jer 14:18; Ezek 5:12
7:16 ^Is 38:14   ^Is 59:11   7:17 ^Is 13:7; Ezek 21:7
7:18 ^Is 15:3   ^Ezek 27:31   7:19 ^Prov 11:4; Zeph 1:18
7:20 ^Jer 7:30   7:21 ^2 Kin 24:13; Ps 74:2-8
7:22 ^Jer 18:17; Ezek 39:23, 24   7:23 ^Ezek 9:9
^Ezek 8:17   7:24 ^Ezek 21:31   ^2 Chr 7:20
7:25 ^Ezek 13:10, 16   7:26 ^Is 47:11   ^Ps 74:9
7:27 ^Job 8:22; Ps 35:26   8:2 ^Ezek 1:4, 27

7:23 ¹I.e., used for imprisonment

of a hand and took me by the hair of my head; and the ^Spirit lifted me up between earth and heaven and brought me in the visions of God to Jerusalem, to the entrance of the north gate of the inner *courtyard,* where the seat of the idol of jealousy, which ^provokes to jealousy, *was located.* ⁴And behold, the ^glory of the God of Israel *was* there, like the appearance which I saw in the plain.

⁵Then He said to me, "Son of man, raise your eyes now toward the north." So I raised my eyes toward the north, and behold, to the north of the altar gate *was* this ^idol of jealousy at the entrance. ⁶And He said to me, "Son of man, do you see what they are doing, the great ^abominations which the house of Israel are committing here, so that I would be far from My sanctuary? But yet you will see still greater abominations!"

⁷Then He brought me to the entrance of the courtyard, and when I looked, behold, a hole in the wall. ⁸And He said to me, "Son of man, now ^dig through the wall." So I dug through the wall, and behold, an entrance. ⁹Then He said to me, "Go in and see the wicked abominations that they are committing here." ¹⁰So I entered and looked, and behold, every form of crawling things and animals *and* detestable things, with all the idols of the house of Israel, were carved on the wall all around. ¹¹And standing in front of them were ^seventy ᴮelders of the house of Israel, with Jaazaniah the son of Shaphan standing among them, each man *with* his censer in his hand; and the fragrance of the cloud of incense was rising. ¹²Then He said to me, "Do you see,

son of man, what the elders of the house of Israel are doing in the dark, each man in the rooms of his carved images? For they say, '^The LORD does not see us; the LORD has ᴮabandoned the land.'" ¹³And He said to me, "Yet you will see still greater abominations which they are committing!"

¹⁴Then He brought me to the entrance of the ^gate of the LORD's house which *was* toward the north; and behold, women were sitting there weeping for Tammuz. ¹⁵And He said to me, "Do you see *this,* son of man? Yet you will see still greater abominations than these!"

¹⁶Then He brought me into the inner courtyard of the LORD's house. And behold, at the entrance to the temple of the LORD, between the porch and the altar, *were* about twenty-five men *with* their backs to the temple of the LORD while their faces were toward the east; and ^they were ¹prostrating themselves eastward toward the sun. ¹⁷And He said to me, "Do you see *this,* son of man? Is it a trivial thing for the house of Judah to commit the abominations which they have committed here, that they have ^filled the land with violence and provoked Me to anger repeatedly? Yet behold, they are putting the twig to their nose! ¹⁸Therefore, I indeed will deal in wrath. My eye will have no pity nor will I spare; and ^though they cry out in My ears with a loud voice, yet I will not listen to them."

8:3 ^Ezek 3:12   ᴮEx 20:4   8:4 ^Ezek 1:28; 3:22, 23
8:5 ^Ps 78:58; Jer 7:30   8:6 ^2 Kin 23:4, 5; Ezek 5:11
8:8 ^Is 29:15   8:11 ^Num 11:16, 25   ᴮJer 19:1
8:12 ^Ps 14:1   ᴮPs 10:11   8:14 ^Ezek 44:4; 46:9
8:16 ^Deut 4:19; 17:3   8:17 ^Ezek 7:11, 23; 9:9
8:18 ^Is 1:15; Jer 11:11

8:16 ¹I.e., worshiping

THE VISION OF SLAUGHTER

9 Then He cried out in my presence with a loud ^voice, saying, "Come forward, you executioners of the city, each *with* his weapon of destruction in his hand." ²And behold, six men came from the direction of the upper gate which faces north, each *with* his smashing weapon in his hand; and among them was ^one man clothed in linen with a scribe's kit at his waist. And they came in and stood beside the bronze altar.

³Then the ^glory of the God of Israel ascended from the cherub on which it had been, to the threshold of the temple. And He called to the man clothed in linen at whose waist was the scribe's kit. ⁴And the LORD said to him, "Go through the midst of the city, through the midst of Jerusalem, and make a mark on the foreheads of the people who ^groan and sigh over all the abominations which are being committed in its midst." ⁵But to the others He said in my presence, "Go through the city after him and strike; do not let your eye have pity and do not spare. ⁶Utterly ^kill old men, young men, *female* virgins, little children, and women, but do not ᴮtouch any person on whom is the mark; and you shall start from My sanctuary." So they started with the elders who *were* before the temple. ⁷He also said to them, "^Defile the temple and fill the courtyards with the dead. Go out!" So they went out and struck and killed *the people* in the city. ⁸And as they were striking *the people* and I *alone* was left, I ^fell on my face and cried out, saying, "Oh, Lord GOD! Are You going to destroy the entire remnant of Israel by pouring out Your wrath on Jerusalem?"

⁹Then He said to me, "The guilt of the house of Israel and Judah is very, very great, and the land is ^filled with blood, and the city is ᴮfull of perversion; for they say, 'The LORD has abandoned the land, and the LORD does not see!' ¹⁰But as for Me, ^My eye will have no pity nor will I spare, but ᴮI will bring their conduct upon their heads."

¹¹Then behold, the man clothed in linen, at whose waist was the *scribe's* kit, reported, saying, "I have done just as You have commanded me."

VISION OF GOD'S GLORY DEPARTING FROM THE TEMPLE

10 Then I looked, and behold, in the ¹,^expanse that was over the heads of the cherubim *something* like a ᴮsapphire stone, in appearance resembling a throne, appeared above them. ²And He spoke to the man clothed in linen and said, "Enter between the ^whirling wheels under the cherubim and fill your hands with coals of fire from between the cherubim, and scatter *them* over the city." And he entered in my sight.

³Now the cherubim were standing on the right side of the temple when the man entered, and the cloud filled the ^inner courtyard. ⁴Then the ^glory of the LORD went up from the cherub to the threshold of the temple, and the temple was filled with the cloud, and the courtyard was filled with the

9:1^Is 6:8   9:2^Lev 16:4   9:3^Ezek 10:4; 11:22, 23
9:4^Ps 119:53, 136; Jer 13:17   9:6^2 Chr 36:17
ᴮEx 12:23   9:7^2 Chr 36:17; Ezek 7:20–22
9:8^1 Chr 21:16   9:9^2 Kin 21:16   ᴮEzek 22:29
9:10^Is 65:6   ᴮEzek 7:4   10:1^Ezek 1:22, 26
ᴮEx 24:10   10:2^Ezek 1:15–21; 10:13
10:3^Ezek 8:3, 16   10:4^Ezek 9:3

10:1 ¹Or *firmament;* i.e., atmosphere and space

8brightness of the glory of the Lord. 5Moreover, the sound of the wings of the cherubim was heard as far as the outer courtyard, like the ^voice of God Almighty when He speaks.

6And it came about when He commanded the man clothed in linen, saying, "Take fire from between the whirling wheels, from between the cherubim," he entered and stood beside a wheel. 7Then the cherub reached out with his hand from between the cherubim to the fire which was between the cherubim, took *some coals* and put *them* into the hands of the one clothed in linen; and he took *them* and went out. 8The cherubim appeared to have something like a human hand under their wings.

9Then I looked, and behold, ^four wheels beside the cherubim, one wheel beside each cherub; and the appearance of the wheels *was* like the gleam of a Tarshish stone. 10And as for their appearance, *all* four of them had the same likeness, as if one wheel were within another wheel. 11When they moved, they went ^in *any of* their four directions without turning as they went; but they followed in the direction which they faced, without turning as they went. 12And their ^whole body, their backs, their hands, their wings and the wheels were covered with eyes all around, the wheels belonging to *all* four of them. 13The wheels were called, as I heard, the whirling wheels. 14And ^each one had four faces. The first face *was* the face of a cherub, the second face *was* the face of a human, the third, the face of a lion, and the fourth, the face of an eagle.

15Then the cherubim rose up. They are the ^living beings that I saw by the river Chebar. 16Now when the cherubim moved, the wheels would move beside them; also when the cherubim lifted up their wings to rise from the ground, the wheels themselves would not turn away from beside them. 17When the cherubim ^stood still, the wheels would stand still; and when they rose up, the wheels would rise with them, because the spirit of the living beings *was* in them.

18Then the glory of the Lord departed from the threshold of the temple and stood ^over the cherubim. 19When ^the cherubim departed, they lifted their wings and rose up from the ground in my sight with the wheels beside them; and they stood still at the entrance of the east gate of the Lord's house, and the glory of the God of Israel hovered over them.

20These are the ^living beings that I saw beneath the God of Israel by the river Chebar; so I knew that they *were* cherubim. 21^Each one had four faces and each one four wings, and beneath their wings *was* the form of human hands. 22As for the likeness of their faces, they were the same faces whose appearance I had seen by the river Chebar. Each one went straight ahead.

EVIL RULERS TO BE JUDGED

11 Now the ^Spirit lifted me up and brought me to the east gate of the Lord's house which faced eastward. And behold, *there were* twenty-five men at the entrance of the gate, and among them I saw

10:4 8Ezek 1:28   10:5^Job 40:9; Ezek 1:24
10:9^Ezek 1:15-17   10:11^Ezek 1:17   10:12^Rev 4:6, 8
10:14^1 Kin 7:29, 36; Ezek 1:6, 10   10:15^Ezek 1:3, 5
10:17^Ezek 1:21   10:18^Ps 18:10   10:19^Ezek 11:22
10:20^Ezek 1:5, 22, 26; 10:15   10:21^Ezek 1:6, 8;
10:14   11:1^Ezek 3:12, 14; 8:3

Jaazaniah son of Azzur and Pelatiah son of Benaiah, leaders of the people. ²Then He said to me, "Son of man, these are the men who devise wrongdoing and ^give evil advice in this city, ³who say, '*The time* is not near to build houses. This ^*city* is the pot and we are the meat.' ⁴Therefore, ^prophesy against them, prophesy, son of man!"

⁵Then the Spirit of the LORD fell upon me, and He said to me, "Say, 'This is what the LORD says: "This is how you think, house of Israel, for ^I know your thoughts. ⁶You have ^multiplied your slain in this city, and filled its streets with them." ⁷Therefore, this is what the Lord GOD says: "Your ^slain whom you have laid in the midst of the city are the meat and this *city* is the pot; but I will bring you out of it. ⁸You have ^feared a sword; so I will ^Bbring a sword upon you," the Lord GOD declares. ⁹"And I will bring you out of the midst of the city, and hand you over to strangers, and ^execute judgments against you. ¹⁰You will ^fall by the sword. I will judge you to the border of Israel; so you shall know that I am the LORD. ¹¹This *city* will ^not be a pot for you, nor will you be meat in the midst of it; I will judge you to the border of Israel. ¹²So you will know that I am the LORD; for you have not walked in My statutes, nor have you ^executed My ordinances, but you have acted in accordance with the ordinances of the nations around you."'"

¹³Now it came about, as I prophesied, that ^Pelatiah son of Benaiah died. Then I fell on my face and cried out with a loud voice, and said, "Oh, Lord GOD! Will You bring the remnant of Israel to a complete destruction?"

PROMISE OF RESTORATION

¹⁴Then the word of the LORD came to me, saying, ¹⁵"Son of man, your brothers, your relatives, your fellow exiles, and the entire house of Israel, all of them, *are those* to whom the inhabitants of Jerusalem have said, 'Keep far from the LORD; this land has been given ^to us as a possession.' ¹⁶Therefore say, 'This is what the Lord GOD says: "Though I had removed them far away among the nations, and though I had scattered them among the countries, yet I was a ^sanctuary for them for a little while in the countries where they had gone."' ¹⁷Therefore say, 'This is what the Lord GOD says: "I will ^gather you from the peoples and assemble you from the countries among which you have been scattered, and I will give you the land of Israel."' ¹⁸When they come there, they will ^remove all its ^Bdetestable things and all its abominations from it. ¹⁹And I will give them one heart, and put a new spirit within them. And I will remove the ^heart of stone from their flesh and give them a ^Bheart of flesh, ²⁰so that they may ^walk in My statutes, and keep My ordinances and do them. Then they will be My people, and I shall be their God. ²¹But as for those whose hearts go after their detestable things and abominations, I will ^bring their conduct down on their heads," declares the Lord GOD.

11:2 ^Ps 2:1; Is 30:1   11:3 ^Jer 1:13; Ezek 11:7, 11
11:4 ^Ezek 3:4, 17   11:5 ^Jer 11:20; 17:10   11:6 ^Is 1:15;
Ezek 7:23   11:7 ^Ezek 24:3-13; Mic 3:2, 3
11:8 ^Prov 10:24   ^BJob 3:25   11:9 ^Ezek 5:8; 16:41
11:10 ^Jer 52:9, 10   11:11 ^Ezek 11:3, 7; 24:3, 6
11:12 ^Ezek 18:8, 9   11:13 ^Ezek 11:1   11:15 ^Ezek 33:24
11:16 ^Ps 31:20; 90:1   11:17 ^Is 11:11-16; Jer 3:12, 18
11:18 ^Ezek 37:23   ^BEzek 5:11   11:19 ^Zech 7:12
^B2 Cor 3:3   11:20 ^Ps 105:45; Ezek 36:27
11:21 ^Ezek 9:10; 16:43

22 Then the cherubim ^lifted up their wings with the wheels beside them, and ^Bthe glory of the God of Israel hovered over them. 23 The ^glory of the LORD went up from the midst of the city and ^Bstood over the mountain which is east of the city. 24 And the ^Spirit lifted me up and brought me in a vision by the Spirit of God to Chaldea, to the exiles. Then the vision that I had seen ^Bleft me. 25 And I ^told the exiles all the things that the LORD had shown me.

EZEKIEL PREPARES FOR EXILE

12 Then the word of the LORD came to me, saying, 2 "Son of man, you live in the ^midst of the ^Brebellious house, who have eyes to see but do not see, ears to hear but do not hear; for they are a rebellious house. 3 So as for you, son of man, prepare for yourself baggage for exile and go into exile by day in their sight; that is, go into exile from your place to another place in their sight. ^Perhaps they will understand, though they are a rebellious house. 4 Bring your baggage out by day in their sight, as baggage for exile. Then you shall go out ^at evening in their sight, as those who are going into exile. 5 Dig a hole through the wall in their sight and go out through it. 6 Load the baggage on your shoulder in their sight and carry it out in the dark. You shall cover your face so that you cannot see the land, for I have set you as a ^sign to the house of Israel."

7 Then I ^did so, just as I had been commanded. By day I brought out my baggage like the baggage of an exile. Then in the evening I dug through the wall with my hands; I went out in the dark and carried the baggage on my shoulder in their sight.

8 And in the morning the word of the LORD came to me, saying, 9 "Son of man, has the house of Israel, the rebellious house, not said to you, '^What are you doing?' 10 Say to them, 'This is what the Lord GOD says: "This ^pronouncement concerns the prince in Jerusalem as well as all the house of Israel who are in it."' 11 Say, 'I am a sign to you. Just as I have done, so it will be done to them; they will ^go into exile, into captivity.' 12 The ^prince who is among them will load his baggage on his shoulder in the dark and go out. They will dig a hole through the wall to bring it out through it. He will cover his face so that he cannot see the land with his eyes. 13 I will also spread My net over him, and he will be caught in My net. And I will bring him to Babylon in the land of the Chaldeans; yet he will ^not see it, though he will die there. 14 And I will ^scatter to every wind all who are around him, his helpers and all his troops; and I will draw out a sword after them. 15 So they will ^know that I am the LORD, when I disperse them among the nations and scatter them among the countries. 16 But I will spare a few of them from the sword, the famine, and plague so that they may tell of all their abominations among the nations where they go, and may ^know that I am the LORD."

11:22 ^Ezek 10:19   ^BEzek 43:2   11:23 ^Ezek 8:4
^BZech 14:4   11:24 ^Ezek 8:3   ^BActs 10:16
11:25 ^Ezek 2:7; 3:4, 17, 27   12:2 ^Is 6:5   ^BPs 78:40
12:3 ^Jer 26:3; 36:3, 7   12:4 ^2 Kin 25:4; Jer 39:4
12:6 ^Is 8:18; 20:3   12:7 ^Ezek 24:18; 37:7, 10
12:9 ^Ezek 17:12; 20:49   12:10 ^2 Kin 9:25; Is 13:1
12:11 ^Jer 15:2; 52:15, 28–30   12:12 ^2 Kin 25:4; Jer 39:4
12:13 ^Jer 39:7; 52:11   12:14 ^2 Kin 25:4, 5; Ezek 5:2
12:15 ^Ezek 6:7, 14; 12:16, 20   12:16 ^Jer 22:8, 9

¹⁷Moreover, the word of the LORD came to me, saying, ¹⁸"Son of man, ^eat your bread with trembling, and drink your water with quivering and anxiety. ¹⁹Then say to the people of the land, 'This is what the Lord GOD says concerning the inhabitants of Jerusalem in the land of Israel: "They will eat their bread with anxiety and drink their water with horror, because their land will be ^stripped of its fullness on account of the violence of all who live in it. ²⁰The inhabited ^cities will be in ruins, and the land will be a desolation. So you will know that I am the LORD."'"

²¹Then the word of the LORD came to me, saying, ²²"Son of man, what is this proverb you *people* have about the land of Israel, saying, 'The ^days are long, and every ^vision fails'? ²³Therefore say to them, 'This is what the Lord GOD says: "I will put an end to this proverb so that they will no longer use it as a proverb in Israel." But tell them, "^The days are approaching as well as the fulfillment of every vision. ²⁴For there will no longer be any ^false vision or deceptive divination within the house of Israel. ²⁵For I the LORD will speak whatever ^word I speak, and it will be performed. It will no longer be delayed, for in your days, you rebellious house, I will speak the word and perform it," declares the Lord GOD.'"

²⁶Furthermore, the word of the LORD came to me, saying, ²⁷"Son of man, behold, the house of Israel is saying, 'The vision that he sees is for ^many years *from now,* and he prophesies of times far off.' ²⁸Therefore say to them, 'This is what the Lord GOD says: "None of My words will be delayed any longer.

Whatever word I speak will be performed,"'" declares the Lord GOD.

FALSE PROPHETS CONDEMNED

13 Then the word of the LORD came to me, saying, ²"Son of man, prophesy against the ^prophets of Israel who prophesy, and say to those who prophesy from their own inspiration, 'Listen to the word of the LORD! ³This is what the Lord GOD says: "Woe to the ^foolish prophets who are following their own spirit and have ^seen nothing! ⁴Israel, your prophets have been like jackals among ruins. ⁵You have not gone up into the breaches, nor did you build up a stone wall around the house of Israel to stand in the battle on the ^day of the LORD. ⁶They see ^deceit and lying divination, those who are saying, 'The LORD declares,' when the LORD has not sent them; yet they wait for the fulfillment of *their* word! ⁷^Did you not see a false vision and tell a lying divination when you said, 'The LORD declares,' but it is not I who have spoken?"'"

⁸Therefore, this is what the Lord GOD says: "Because you have spoken deceit and have seen a lie, therefore behold, ^I am against you," declares the Lord GOD. ⁹"So My hand will be against the ^prophets who see false visions and utter lying divinations. They will have no place in the council of My people, ^nor will they be written down in the register of the house of Israel,

12:18^Lam 5:9; Ezek 4:16　12:19^Jer 10:22; Ezek 6:6, 7, 14　12:20^Is 3:26; Jer 4:7　12:22^Jer 5:12　^Ezek 7:26　12:23^Ps 37:13; Joel 2:1　12:24^Jer 14:13-16; Ezek 13:6, 23　12:25^Num 14:28-34; Is 14:24　12:27^Ezek 12:22; Dan 10:14　13:2^Is 9:15; Jer 37:19　13:3^Lam 2:14　^Jer 23:28-32　13:5^Is 13:6, 9; Ezek 7:19　13:6^Jer 29:8; Ezek 22:28　13:7^Ezek 22:28　13:8^Ezek 5:8; 21:3　13:9^Jer 20:3-6　^Ps 69:28

nor will they enter the land of Israel, so that you may know that I am the Lord GOD. [10]It is definitely because they have ^misled My people by saying, 'Peace!' when there is no peace. And when anyone builds a wall, behold, they plaster it over with whitewash; [11]*so* tell those who plaster *it* over with whitewash, that it will fall. A ^flooding rain will come, and you, hailstones, will fall, and a violent wind will break out. [12]Behold, *when* the wall has fallen, will you not be asked, 'Where is the plaster with which you plastered *it?*'" [13]Therefore, this is what the Lord GOD says: "I will make a violent wind break out in My wrath. There will also be in My anger a flooding rain and ^hailstones to consume *it* in wrath. [14]So I will tear down the wall which you plastered over with whitewash and hurl it down to the ground, so that its ^foundation is exposed; and when it falls, you will perish in its midst. And you will know that I am the LORD. [15]So I will expend My wrath on the wall and on those who have plastered it over with whitewash; and I will say to you, 'The wall is gone and those who plastered it are gone, [16]*along with* the prophets of Israel who prophesy to Jerusalem, and who ^see a vision of peace for her when there is [B]no peace,' declares the Lord GOD.

[17]"Now you, son of man, set your face against the daughters of your people who are talking like prophets ^from their own imagination. Prophesy against them [18]and say, 'This is what the Lord GOD says: "Woe to the women who sew *magic* bands on all wrists and make veils for the heads *of persons* of every stature to ^capture souls! Will you

capture the souls of My people, but keep the souls *of others* alive for yourselves? [19]^For handfuls of barley and pieces of bread, you have profaned Me to My people, to put to death some who should not die, and to [B]keep others alive who should not live, by your lying to My people who listen to lies."'"

[20]Therefore, this is what the Lord GOD says: "Behold, I am against your *magic* bands by which you capture souls there as birds, and I will tear them from your arms; and I will let them go, those souls whom you capture as birds. [21]I will also tear off your veils and ^save My people from your hands, and they will no longer be in your hands as prey; and you will know that I am the LORD. [22]Because you ^disheartened the righteous with falsehood when I did not cause him pain, but *you* have [B]encouraged the wicked not to turn from his wicked way to keep him alive, [23]therefore you women will no longer see deceitful visions or practice divination, and I will ^save My people from your hands. So you will [B]know that I am the LORD."

IDOLATROUS ELDERS CONDEMNED

14 Then some ^elders of Israel came to me and sat down before me. [2]And the word of the LORD came to me, saying, [3]"Son of man, these men have ^set up their idols in their hearts and have [B]put in front of their faces the stumbling block of their wrongdoing. Should I

13:10^Jer 23:32; 50:6   13:11^Ezek 38:22
13:13^Ex 9:24, 25; Ps 18:12, 13   13:14^Mic 1:6; Hab 3:13
13:16^Jer 6:14   [B]Is 57:21   13:17^Ezek 13:2; Rev 2:20
13:18^2 Pet 2:14   13:19^Prov 28:21   [B]Jer 23:14, 17
13:21^Ps 91:3; 124:7   13:22^Amos 5:12   [B]Jer 23:14
13:23^Ezek 13:21   [B]Ezek 13:9, 21   14:1^2 Kin 6:32;
Ezek 8:1   14:3^Ezek 20:16   [B]Ezek 7:19

let Myself be consulted by them at all? ⁴Therefore speak to them and tell them, 'This is what the Lord God says: "Anyone of the house of Israel who sets up his idols in his heart, puts in front of his face the stumbling block of his wrongdoing, and *then* comes to the prophet, I the Lord will let Myself answer him in the matter in view of the ᴬmultitude of his idols, ⁵in order to take hold of ᴬthe hearts of the house of Israel who have ᴮturned away from Me due to all their idols."'

⁶"Therefore say to the house of Israel, 'This is what the Lord God says: "ᴬRepent and turn away from your idols, and turn your faces away from all your abominations. ⁷For anyone of the house of Israel, or of the ᴬstrangers who reside in Israel, who deserts Me, sets up his idols in his heart, puts in front of his face the stumbling block of his wrongdoing, and *then* comes to the prophet to request something of Me for himself, I the Lord will let Myself answer him Myself. ⁸I will ᴬset My face against that person and make him a sign and a proverb, and I will eliminate him from among My people. So you will know that I am the Lord.

⁹"But if the prophet is persuaded so that he speaks a word, it is I, the Lord, who have persuaded that prophet; and I will stretch out My hand against him and ᴬeliminate him from among My people Israel. ¹⁰And they will bear *the punishment for* their wrongdoing; as the wrongdoing of the inquirer is, so the wrongdoing of the prophet will be, ¹¹in order that the house of Israel may no longer ᴬstray from Me and no longer ᴮdefile themselves with all their offenses. So they will

be My people, and I shall be their God,"' declares the Lord God."

THE CITY WILL NOT BE SPARED

¹²Then the word of the Lord came to me, saying, ¹³"Son of man, if a country sins against Me by ᴬbeing unfaithful, and I stretch out My hand against it, destroy its supply of bread, send famine against it, and eliminate from it *both* human and animal *life,* ¹⁴even ᴬ*though* these three men, Noah, Daniel, and Job, were in its midst, by their *own* righteousness they could *only* save ᴮthemselves," declares the Lord God. ¹⁵"If I were to cause ᴬvicious animals to pass through the land and they depopulated it, and it became desolate so that no one would pass through it because of the animals, ¹⁶*though* these three men were in its midst, as I live," declares the Lord God, "they could not save either *their* sons or *their* daughters. ᴬThey alone would be saved, but the country would be desolate. ¹⁷Or *if* I were to ᴬbring a sword on that country and say, 'A sword is to pass through the country,' and I eliminated human and animal *life* from it, ¹⁸even *though* these three men were in its midst, as I live," declares the Lord God, "they could not save either *their* sons or *their* daughters, but they alone would be saved. ¹⁹Or *if* I were to send a ᴬplague against that country and pour out My wrath on it in blood to eliminate man and animal from it, ²⁰even *though* Noah,

14:4 ᴬ1 Kin 21:20-24; 2 Kin 1:16   14:5 ᴬJer 17:10   ᴮIs 1:4
14:6 ᴬ1 Sam 7:3; Neh 1:9   14:7 ᴬEx 12:48   14:8 ᴬJer 44:11;
Ezek 15:7   14:9 ᴬJer 6:14, 15; 14:15   14:11 ᴬEzek 44:10, 15
ᴮEzek 11:18   14:13 ᴬEzek 15:8; 20:27   14:14 ᴬJer 15:1
ᴮEzek 16:18, 20   14:15 ᴬLev 26:22; Num 21:6
14:16 ᴬGen 19:29; Ezek 18:20   14:17 ᴬLev 26:25;
Ezek 5:12   14:19 ᴬJer 14:12; Ezek 5:12

Daniel, and Job were in its midst, as I live," declares the Lord GOD, "they could not save either *their* son or *their* daughter. They would save only themselves by their righteousness."

²¹For this is what the Lord GOD says: "How much more when ^I send My four severe judgments against Jerusalem: sword, famine, vicious animals, and plague to eliminate human and animal *life* from it! ²²Yet, behold, survivors will be left in it who will be brought out, *both* sons and daughters. Behold, they are going to come out to you, and you will ^see their conduct and actions; then you will be comforted for the disaster which I have brought against Jerusalem for everything which I have brought upon it. ²³Then they will comfort you when you see their conduct and actions, for you will know that I have not done ^without reason whatever I did to it," declares the Lord GOD.

JERUSALEM LIKE A USELESS VINE

15 Then the word of the LORD came to me, saying, ²"Son of man, how is the wood of the ^vine *better* than any wood of a branch which is among the trees of the forest? ³Can wood be taken from it to make anything, or can *even* a peg be taken from it on which to hang any utensil? ⁴If it has been put into the ^fire for fuel, *and* the fire has consumed both of its ends and its middle part has been charred, is it *then* good for anything? ⁵Behold, while it is intact, it is not made into anything. How much less, when the fire has consumed it and it is charred, can it still be made into anything! ⁶Therefore, this is what the Lord GOD says: 'As the

wood of the vine among the trees of the forest, which I have given to the fire for fuel, so have I given up the inhabitants of Jerusalem; ⁷and I set My face against them. *Though* they have ^come out of the fire, yet the fire will consume them. Then you will know that I am the LORD, when I set My face against them. ⁸So I will make the land desolate, because they have ^acted unfaithfully,'" declares the Lord GOD.

GOD'S GRACE TO UNFAITHFUL JERUSALEM

16 Then the word of the LORD came to me, saying, ²"Son of man, ^make known to Jerusalem her abominations, ³and say, 'This is what the Lord GOD says to Jerusalem: "Your origin and your birth are from the land of the Canaanite; your father was an Amorite and your mother a Hittite. ⁴As for your birth, ^on the day you were born your navel cord was not cut, nor were you washed with water for cleansing; you were not rubbed with salt or even wrapped in cloths. ⁵No eye looked with pity on you to do any of these things for you, to have compassion on you. Rather you were thrown out into the ^open field, for you were abhorred on the day you were born.

⁶"When I passed by you and saw you squirming in your blood, I said to you *while you were* in your blood, 'Live!' Yes, I said to you *while you were* in your blood, 'Live!' ⁷^made you very numerous, like plants of the field. Then you grew up, became tall and reached *the age*

14:21^Ezek 5:17; 33:27   14:22^Ezek 12:16; 36:20
14:23^Jer 22:8, 9   15:2^Ps 80:8-16; Is 5:1-7
15:4^Is 27:11; Ezek 15:6   15:7^1 Kin 19:17; Is 24:18
15:8^Ezek 14:13; 17:20   16:2^Is 58:1; Ezek 20:4
16:4^Hos 2:3   16:5^Deut 32:10   16:7^Ex 1:7; Deut 1:10

for fine jewelry; *your* breasts were formed and your hair had grown. Yet you were naked and bare.

8 "Then I passed by you and saw you, and behold, you were at the time for love; so I spread My garment over you and covered your nakedness. I also ^swore an oath to you and ^Bentered into a covenant with you so that you became Mine," declares the Lord God. 9 "Then I bathed you with water, washed off your blood from you, and ^anointed you with oil. 10 I also clothed you with ^colorfully woven cloth and put sandals of ¹fine leather on your feet; and I wrapped you with fine linen and covered you with silk. 11 I adorned you with jewelry, put bracelets on your wrists, and a ^necklace around your neck. 12 I also put a ring in your nose, earrings in your ears, and a ^beautiful crown on your head. 13 So you were adorned with gold and silver, and your dress was of fine linen, silk, and colorfully woven cloth. You ate fine flour, honey, and oil; so you were exceedingly beautiful and advanced to ^royalty. 14 Then your fame spread among the nations on account of your beauty, for it was ^perfect because of My splendor which I bestowed on you," declares the Lord God.

15 "But you ^trusted in your beauty and ^Bbecame unfaithful because of your fame, and you poured out your obscene practices on every passerby to whom it might be *tempting*. 16 You took some of your clothes, made for yourself high places of various colors, and committed prostitution on them, *which* should not come about nor happen. 17 You also took your beautiful ^jewels *made* of My gold and of My silver, which I

had given you, and made for yourself male images so that you might commit prostitution with them. 18 Then you took your colorfully woven cloth and covered them, and offered My oil and My incense before them. 19 Also ^My bread which I gave you, fine flour, oil, and honey with which I fed you, you would offer before them for a soothing aroma; so it happened," declares the Lord God. 20 "Furthermore, you took your sons and daughters whom you had borne to Me and ^sacrificed them to idols to be devoured. Were your obscene practices a trivial matter? 21 You slaughtered ^My children and offered them to idols by ^Bmaking them pass through *the fire*. 22 And besides all your abominations and obscene practices, you did not remember the days of ^your youth, when you were naked and bare and squirming in your blood.

23 "Then it came about after all your wickedness ('Woe, woe to you!' declares the Lord God), 24 that you built yourself a shrine and made yourself a ^high place in every public square. 25 You built yourself a high place at the beginning of ^every street and made your beauty abominable, and you spread your legs to every passer-by and multiplied your obscene practice. 26 You also committed prostitution with the Egyptians, your lustful neighbors, and multiplied your obscene practice to ^provoke Me to anger.

16:8 ^Gen 22:16-18　ᴮEx 24:7, 8　16:9 ^Ruth 3:3
16:10 ^Ex 26:36; Ezek 16:13, 18　16:11 ^Gen 41:42
16:12 ^Is 28:5; Jer 13:18　16:13 ^1 Sam 10:1; 1 Kin 4:21
16:14 ^Ps 50:2; Lam 2:15　16:15 ^Ezek 16:25　ᴮIs 57:8
16:17 ^Ezek 16:11, 12　16:19 ^Hos 2:8
16:20 ^Ps 106:37, 38; Jer 7:31　16:21 ^Ex 13:2
ᴮ2 Kin 17:17　16:22 ^Jer 2:2　16:24 ^Ps 78:58; Is 57:7
16:25 ^Prov 9:14　16:26 ^Jer 7:18, 19; Ezek 8:17

16:10 ¹Meaning of the Heb uncertain

²⁷So behold, I have stretched out My hand against you and cut back your rations. And I turned you over to the desire of those who hate you, the ^daughters of the Philistines, who are ashamed of your outrageous conduct. ²⁸Moreover, you committed prostitution with the ^Assyrians because you were not satisfied; you committed prostitution with them and still were not satisfied. ²⁹You also multiplied your obscene practice with the land of merchants, Chaldea; yet even with this you were not satisfied."'"

³⁰"How feverish is your heart," declares the Lord God, "while you do all these things, the action of a ^bold prostitute! ³¹When you built your shrine at the beginning of every street and made your high place in every public square, in ^spurning a prostitute's fee, you were not like a prostitute. ³²You adulteress wife, who takes strangers instead of her husband! ³³*Men* give gifts to all prostitutes, but you ^give your gifts to all your lovers and lavish favors on them so that they will come to you from every direction for your obscene practices. ³⁴So it is the opposite for you from those women in your obscene practices, in that you are not approached for prostitution, and in *the fact* that you pay a prostitute's fee, and no fee is paid to you; so you are the opposite."

³⁵Therefore, you prostitute, hear the word of the Lord. ³⁶This is what the Lord God says: "Because your lewdness was poured out and your nakedness uncovered through your obscene practices with your lovers and with all your detestable ^idols, and because of the blood of your sons that you gave to idols,

³⁷therefore, behold, I am going to ^gather all your lovers whom you pleased, all those whom you loved as well as all those whom you hated. So I will gather them against you from every direction and ^expose your nakedness to them so that they may see all your nakedness. ³⁸So I will ^judge you as women who commit adultery or shed blood are judged; and I will bring on you the blood of wrath and jealousy. ³⁹I will also hand you over to your lovers, and they will tear down your shrines, demolish your high places, ^strip you of your clothing, take away your jewels, and will leave you naked and bare. ⁴⁰They will incite a ^crowd against you, and they will stone you and cut you to pieces with their swords. ⁴¹And they will ^burn your houses with fire and execute judgments against you in the sight of many women. Then I will put an end to your prostitution, and you will also no longer pay your lovers. ⁴²So I ^will satisfy My fury against you and My jealousy will leave you, and I will be pacified and no longer be angry. ⁴³Since you have not remembered the days of your youth but have ^caused Me unrest by all these things, behold, I in turn will ^bring your conduct *down* on your own head," declares the Lord God, "so that you will not commit this outrageous sin in addition to all your *other* abominations.

⁴⁴"Behold, everyone who quotes ^proverbs will quote *this* proverb

16:27^Is 9:12; Ezek 16:57   16:28^2 Kin 16:7, 10-18; 2 Chr 28:16, 20-23   16:30^Is 3:9; Jer 3:3   16:31^Is 52:3 16:33^Is 57:9; Ezek 16:41   16:36^Jer 19:5; Ezek 20:31 16:37^Jer 13:22, 26   ᴮIs 47:3   16:38^Ezek 23:45 16:39^Ezek 23:26; Hos 2:3   16:40^Ezek 23:47; Hab 1:6-10   16:41^2 Kin 25:9; Jer 39:8 16:42^2 Sam 24:25; Ezek 5:13   16:43^Is 63:10 ᴮEzek 11:21   16:44^1 Sam 24:13; Ezek 12:22, 23

about you, saying, 'Like mother, like daughter.' ⁴⁵You are the daughter of your mother, who loathed her husband and children. You are also the sister of your sisters, who ᴬloathed their husbands and children. Your mother was a Hittite and your father an Amorite. ⁴⁶Now your ᴬolder sister is Samaria, who lives north of you with her daughters; and your younger sister, who lives south of you, is Sodom with her daughters. ⁴⁷Yet you have not *merely* walked in their ways and committed their abominations; *but,* as *if that were* too little, you also acted ᴬmore corruptly in all your conduct than they. ⁴⁸As I live," declares the Lord Gᴏᴅ, "Sodom, your sister and her daughters have ᴬnot done as you and your daughters have done! ⁴⁹Behold, this was the guilt of your sister Sodom: she and her daughters had ᴬarrogance, plenty of food, and ᴮcarefree ease, but she did not help the poor and needy. ⁵⁰So they were haughty and committed ᴬabominations before Me. Therefore I ᴮremoved them when I saw *it.* ⁵¹Furthermore, Samaria did not commit half of your sins, for you have multiplied your abominations more than they. So you have made your sisters appear ᴬinnocent by all your abominations which you have committed. ⁵²Also, bear your disgrace in that you have made judgment favorable for your sisters. Because of your sins in which you acted ᴬmore abominably than they, they are more in the right than you. Yes, be also ashamed and bear your disgrace, in that you made your sisters appear innocent.

⁵³"Nevertheless, I will restore their fortunes, the fortunes of Sodom and her daughters, the fortunes of Samaria and her daughters, and along with them your own fortunes, ⁵⁴so that you will bear your disgrace and feel ᴬashamed for all that you have done when you become ᴮa consolation to them. ⁵⁵Your sisters, Sodom with her daughters and Samaria with her daughters, will return to their former state, and you with your daughters will *also* return to your former state. ⁵⁶As *the name of* your sister Sodom was not heard from your lips in your day of pride, ⁵⁷before your ᴬwickedness was uncovered, so now *you have become* the disgrace of the daughters of Edom and of all who are around her, of the daughters of the Philistines—those surrounding *you* who despise you. ⁵⁸You have ᴬsuffered *the penalty of* your outrageous sin and abominations," the Lᴏʀᴅ declares. ⁵⁹For this is what the Lord Gᴏᴅ says: "I will also do with you as you have done, you who have ᴬdespised the oath by breaking the covenant.

THE COVENANT REMEMBERED

⁶⁰"Nevertheless, I will remember My covenant with you in the days of your youth, and I will establish an ᴬeverlasting covenant with you. ⁶¹Then you will ᴬremember your ways and be ashamed when you receive your sisters, *both* your older and your younger; and I will give them to you as daughters, but not because of your covenant. ⁶²So I will ᴬestablish My covenant with

16:45 ᴬIs 1:4; Ezek 23:37-39   **16:46** ᴬJer 3:8-11;
Ezek 23:4   **16:47** ᴬ2 Kin 21:9; Ezek 5:6
16:48 ᴬMatt 10:15; 11:23, 24   **16:49** ᴬGen 19:9
ᴮLuke 12:16-20   **16:50** ᴬGen 13:13   ᴮGen 19:24, 25
16:51 ᴬJer 3:8-11   **16:52** ᴬEzek 16:47, 48, 51
16:54 ᴬJer 2:26   ᴮEzek 14:22, 23   **16:57** ᴬEzek 16:36, 37
16:58 ᴬEzek 23:49   **16:59** ᴬIs 24:5; Ezek 17:19
16:60 ᴬIs 55:3; Jer 32:38-41   **16:61** ᴬJer 50:4, 5;
Ezek 6:9   **16:62** ᴬEzek 20:37; 34:25

you, and you shall know that I am the Lord, [63] so that you may ^remember and be ashamed, and not open your mouth again because of your disgrace, when I have forgiven you for all that you have done," the Lord God declares.

PARABLE OF TWO EAGLES AND A VINE

17 Now the word of the Lord came to me, saying, [2] "Son of man, ask a riddle and present a ^parable to the house of Israel, [3] saying, 'This is what the Lord God says: "A great eagle with ^great wings, long pinions, and a full plumage of many colors came to ^BLebanon and took away the top of the cedar. [4] He broke off the topmost of its young twigs and brought it to a land of merchants; he set it in a city of traders. [5] He also took from the seed of the land and planted it in ^fertile soil, a meadow beside abundant waters; he set it *like* a willow. [6] Then it sprouted and became a low, spreading vine with its branches turned toward him, but its roots remained under it. So it became a vine and produced shoots and sent out branches.

[7] "But there was another great eagle with great wings and much plumage; and behold, this vine turned its roots toward him and sent out its branches toward him from the beds where it was ^planted, so that he might water it. [8] It was planted in good soil beside abundant waters, so that it would produce branches and bear fruit, *and* become a splendid vine."' [9] Say, 'This is what the Lord God says: "Will it thrive? Will he not pull up its roots and cut off its fruit, so that it withers—so that all its sprouting shoots wither? And neither by great strength nor by many people can it be raised from

its roots *again.* [10] Behold, though it is planted, will it thrive? Will it not ^completely wither as soon as the east wind strikes it—wither on the beds where it grew?"'"

ZEDEKIAH'S REBELLION

[11] Moreover, the word of the Lord came to me, saying, [12] "Say now to the rebellious house, 'Do you not know what these things *mean?*' Say, 'Behold, the ^king of Babylon came to Jerusalem, took its king and leaders, and brought them to him in Babylon. [13] Then he took one of the royal ^family and made a covenant with him, putting him under oath. He also took away the mighty of the land, [14] so that the kingdom would ^be humbled, not exalting itself, *but* keeping his covenant so that it might continue. [15] But he ^revolted against him by sending his messengers to Egypt so that they might give him horses and many troops. Will he succeed? Will he who does these things escape? Can he indeed break the covenant and escape? [16] As I live,' declares the Lord God, 'In the country of the king who put him on the throne, whose oath he despised and whose covenant he broke, ^in Babylon he shall certainly die. [17] ^Pharaoh with *his* mighty army and great contingent will not help him in the war, when they pile up assault ramps and build siege walls to eliminate many lives. [18] Now he despised the oath by breaking the covenant, and behold, he ^pledged his allegiance,

16:63 ^Ezek 36:31, 32; Dan 9:7, 8   17:2 ^Ezek 20:49;
24:3   17:3 ^Dan 4:22   ^BJer 22:23   17:5 ^Deut 8:7-9
17:7 ^Ezek 31:4   17:10 ^Ezek 19:14; Hos 13:15
17:12 ^2 Kin 24:11, 12, 15; Ezek 1:2   17:13 ^2 Kin 24:17;
Ezek 17:5   17:14 ^Ezek 29:14   17:15 ^2 Kin 24:20;
2 Chr 36:13   17:16 ^Jer 52:11; Ezek 12:13
17:17 ^Is 36:6; Jer 37:5, 7   17:18 ^1 Chr 29:24

yet did all these things; he shall not escape.'" [19]Therefore, this is what the Lord God says: "As I live, My oath which he despised and My covenant which he broke, I will certainly inflict on his head. [20]And I will spread My net over him, and he will be caught in My net. Then I will bring him to Babylon and [A]enter into judgment with him there *regarding* the unfaithful act which he has committed against Me. [21]All the [A]choice men in all his troops will fall by the sword, and the survivors will be scattered to every wind; and you will know that I, the Lord, have spoken."

[22]This is what the Lord God says: "I will also take *a sprig* from the lofty top of the cedar and set *it* out; I will break off from the topmost of its young twigs a tender one, and I will plant *it* on a [A]high and lofty mountain. [23]On the high mountain of Israel I will plant it, so that it may bring forth branches and bear fruit, and become a stately [A]cedar. And birds of every kind will nest under it; they will nest in the shade of its branches. [24]All the trees of the field will know that I am the Lord; I bring down the high tree, exalt the low tree, dry up the green tree, and make the dry tree [A]flourish. I am the Lord; I have spoken, and I will perform *it*."

GOD DEALS JUSTLY WITH INDIVIDUALS

18 Then the word of the Lord came to me, saying, [2]"[A]What do you *people* mean by using this proverb about the land of Israel, saying,

> [B]The fathers eat sour grapes,
> [1]But *it is* the children's teeth
>   *that* have become blunt'?

[3]As I live," declares the Lord God, "you certainly are not going to use this proverb in Israel anymore. [4]Behold, all souls are Mine; the soul of the father as well as the soul of the son is Mine. The soul who [A]sins will die.

[5]"But if a man is righteous and practices justice and righteousness, [6]*if* he does not eat at the mountain *shrines* or [A]raise his eyes to the idols of the house of Israel, or [B]defile his neighbor's wife or approach a woman during her menstrual period— [7]and *if* a man does not oppress *anyone, but* restores to the debtor his pledge, [A]does not commit robbery, *but* [B]gives his bread to the hungry and covers the naked with clothing, [8]*and if* he does not lend *money* at [A]interest or take [1]interest, *if* he keeps his hand from injustice *and* executes true justice between one person and another, [9]*if* he walks in [A]My statutes and keeps My ordinances so as to deal faithfully—he is righteous *and* will certainly live," declares the Lord God.

[10]"However, he may father a violent son who sheds blood, and does any one of these things to a brother [11](though he himself did not do any of these things), that is, he even eats at the mountain *shrines,* and [A]defiles his neighbor's wife, [12]oppresses the poor and needy, [A]commits robbery, does not restore a pledge, but raises his eyes to the idols *and* [B]commits abomination,

17:20 [A]Jer 2:35; Ezek 20:35, 36   17:21 [A]2 Kin 25:5, 11; Ezek 5:2, 10, 12-14   17:22 [A]Ps 72:16; Ezek 20:40   17:23 [A]Ps 92:12   17:24 [A]Amos 9:11   18:2 [A]Is 3:15   [B]Jer 31:29   18:4 [A]Ezek 18:20; Rom 6:23   18:6 [A]Deut 4:19   [B]Ezek 18:15   18:7 [A]Lev 19:13   [B]Deut 15:11   18:8 [A]Ex 22:25; Deut 23:19, 20   18:9 [A]Lev 18:5   18:11 [A]1 Cor 6:9   18:12 [A]Is 59:6, 7   [B]2 Kin 21:11

18:2 [1]Lit *I.e., the children suffer for the fathers' sins*
18:8 [1]Or *usury,* and so throughout the ch; i.e., on other kinds of loans

¹³ᴬlends *money* at interest and takes ¹interest; will he live? He will not live! He has committed all these abominations, he shall certainly be put to death; his ᴮblood will be on himself.

¹⁴"Now behold, he has fathered a son who saw all his father's sins which he committed, but he has ᴬseen *them* and does not do likewise. ¹⁵He does not eat at the mountain *shrines* or raise his eyes to the idols of the house of Israel; he has not defiled his neighbor's wife, ¹⁶nor oppressed anyone, nor retained a pledge, nor committed robbery; *instead,* he ᴬgives his bread to the hungry and covers the naked with clothing, ¹⁷he keeps his hand from the poor, does not take *any kind of* interest *on loans, but* executes My ordinances, *and* walks in My statutes; ᴬhe will not die for his father's guilt, he will certainly live. ¹⁸As for his father, because he practiced extortion, robbed *his* brother, and did what was not good among his people, behold, he will die for his guilt.

¹⁹"Yet you say, 'Why should the son not suffer *the punishment* for the father's guilt?' When the son has practiced ᴬjustice and righteousness *and* has kept all My statutes and done them, he shall certainly live. ²⁰The person who sins will die. A son will not suffer *the punishment* for the father's guilt, nor will a father suffer *the punishment* for the son's guilt; the ᴬrighteousness of the righteous will be upon himself, and the wickedness of the wicked will be upon himself.

²¹"But if the ᴬwicked person turns from all his sins which he has committed and keeps all My statutes and practices justice and righteousness,

he shall certainly live; he shall not die. ²²All his offenses which he has committed will not be remembered against him; because of his ᴬrighteousness which he has practiced, he will live. ²³Do I take any pleasure in the death of the wicked," declares the Lord Goᴅ, "rather than that he would ᴬturn from his ways and live?

²⁴"But when a righteous person turns away from his righteousness, commits injustice *and* does according to all the abominations that the wicked person does, will he live? ᴬAll his righteous deeds which he has done will not be remembered for his treachery which he has committed and his sin which he has committed; for them he will die. ²⁵Yet you say, 'The way of the Lord is not right.' Hear now, house of Israel! Is ᴬMy way not right? Is it not your ways that are not right? ²⁶When a righteous person turns away from his righteousness, commits injustice and dies because of it, for his injustice which he has committed he dies. ²⁷But when a wicked person turns away ᴬfrom his wickedness which he has committed and practices justice and righteousness, he will save his life. ²⁸Since he understood and turned away from all his offenses which he had committed, he shall certainly live; he shall not die. ²⁹But the house of Israel says, 'The way of the Lord is not right.' Are My ways not right, house of Israel? Is it not your ways that are not right?

18:13 ᴬ Ex 22:25   ᴮ Ezek 33:4, 5   18:14 ᴬ 2 Chr 29:6-10; 34:21   18:16 ᴬ Job 31:16, 20; Ps 41:1   18:17 ᴬ Rom 2:7
18:19 ᴬ Ezek 18:9; 20:18-20
18:20 ᴬ 1 Kin 8:32; Is 3:10, 11   18:21 ᴬ Ezek 18:27, 28; 33:12, 19   18:22 ᴬ Ps 18:20-24   18:23 ᴬ Ps 147:11; Mic 7:18   18:24 ᴬ Ezek 18:22; Gal 3:3, 4
18:25 ᴬ Gen 18:25; Jer 12:1   18:27 ᴬ Is 1:18; 55:7

18:13 ¹ I.e., on other kinds of loans

³⁰"Therefore I will judge you, house of Israel, each according to his conduct," declares the Lord GOD. "ᴬRepent and turn away from all your offenses, so that wrongdoing does not become a stumbling block to you. ³¹ᴬHurl away from you all your offenses which you have committed and make yourselves a ᴮnew heart and a new spirit! For why should you die, house of Israel? ³²For I take ᴬno pleasure in the death of anyone who dies," declares the Lord GOD. "Therefore, repent and live!"

SONG OF MOURNING
FOR THE LEADERS OF ISRAEL

19 "As for you, take up a song of mourning for the ᴬleaders of Israel ²and say,

'What was your mother?
  A lioness among lions!
  She lay down among young
    lions,
  She raised her cubs.
³ 'When she brought up one of
    her cubs,
  He became a young lion,
  And he learned to tear *his* prey;
  He devoured people.
⁴ 'Then nations heard about him;
  He was caught in their trap,
  And they ᴬbrought him with
    hooks
  To the land of Egypt.
⁵ 'When she saw, as she waited,
  That her hope was lost,
  She took another of her cubs
  And made him a young lion.
⁶ 'And he ᴬwalked about among
    the lions,
  He became a young lion;
  He learned to tear *his* prey;
  He devoured people.
⁷ 'He destroyed their palaces
  And laid waste their cities;

And the land and its fullness
    were appalled
  Because of the sound of his
    roaring.
⁸ 'Then ᴬnations set against
    him
  On every side from *their*
    provinces,
  And they spread their net
    over him;
  He was caught in their trap.
⁹ 'They put him in a wooden
    collar with hooks
  And ᴬbrought him to the king
    of Babylon;
  They brought him in hunting
    nets
  So that his voice would no
    longer be heard
  On the mountains of Israel.
¹⁰ 'Your mother was ᴬlike a vine
    in your vineyard,
  Planted by the waters;
  It was fruitful and thick with
    branches
  Because of abundant waters.
¹¹ 'And it had ᴬstrong stems *fit*
    for scepters of rulers,
  And its ᴮheight was raised
    above the clouds
  So that it was seen in its
    height with the mass of its
    branches.
¹² 'But it was ᴬuprooted in fury;
  It was ᴮthrown down to the
    ground;
  And the east wind dried up its
    fruit.
  Its strong stem was torn out
  So that it withered;
  The fire consumed it.

18:30 ᴬEzek 14:6; 33:11   18:31 ᴬIs 1:16, 17   ᴮPs 51:10
18:32 ᴬEzek 18:23; 33:11   19:1 ᴬ2 Kin 23:29, 30, 34;
24:6, 12   19:4 ᴬ2 Kin 23:34; 2 Chr 36:4, 6
19:6 ᴬ2 Kin 24:9; 2 Chr 36:9   19:8 ᴬ2 Kin 24:8-15
19:9 ᴬ2 Kin 24:15   19:10 ᴬPs 80:8-11
19:11 ᴬPs 80:15   ᴮEzek 31:3   19:12 ᴬJer 31:28
ᴮLam 2:1

¹³ 'And now it is planted in the
    ^Awilderness,
    In a dry and thirsty land.
¹⁴ 'And ^Afire has gone out from *its*
    stem;
    It has consumed its shoots
    and fruit,
    So that there is no strong
    stem in it,
    A scepter to rule.'"

This is a song of mourning, and has become a song of mourning.

GOD'S DEALINGS WITH ISRAEL REHEARSED

20 Now in the seventh year, in the fifth *month,* on the tenth of the month, men from the ^Aelders of Israel came to inquire of the LORD, and they sat before me. ²Then the word of the LORD came to me, saying, ³"Son of man, speak to the elders of Israel and say to them, 'This is what the Lord GOD says: "Do you yourselves come to inquire of Me? As I live," declares the Lord GOD, "^AI certainly will not be inquired of by you."' ⁴Will you judge them, will you judge *them,* son of man? ^AMake known to them the abominations of their fathers; ⁵and say to them, 'This is what the Lord GOD says: "On the day when I ^Achose Israel and swore to the descendants of the house of Jacob and made Myself known to them in the land of Egypt, when I swore to them, saying, I am the LORD your God, ⁶on that day I swore to them, ^Ato bring them out from the land of Egypt into a land that I had selected for them, flowing with milk and honey, which is ^Bthe glory of all the lands. ⁷And I said to them, '^AThrow away, each of you, the detestable things of his eyes, and ^Bdo not defile yourselves with the idols of Egypt;

I am the LORD your God.' ⁸But they rebelled against Me and were not willing to listen to Me; they did not throw away, each of them, the detestable things of their eyes, nor did they abandon the ^Aidols of Egypt.

"Then I resolved to ^Bpour out My wrath on them, to use up My anger against them in the midst of the land of Egypt. ⁹But I acted ^Afor the sake of My name, that it would ^Bnot be defiled in the sight of the nations among whom they *lived,* in whose sight I made Myself known to them by bringing them out of the land of Egypt. ¹⁰So I took them out of the land of Egypt and brought them into the ^Awilderness. ¹¹I gave them My ^Astatutes and informed them of My ordinances, which, *if* a person follows them, then he will live by them. ¹²Also I gave them My Sabbaths to be a ^Asign between Me and them, so that they might know that I am the LORD who sanctifies them. ¹³But the house of Israel rebelled against Me in the wilderness. They did not walk in My statutes and they rejected My ordinances, ^Awhich, *if* a person follows them, then he will live by them; and they greatly profaned My ^BSabbaths. Then I resolved to pour out My wrath on them in the wilderness, to annihilate them. ¹⁴But I acted for the sake of My name, so that it would not be defiled before the eyes of the nations, before whose eyes I had brought them out. ¹⁵Also ^AI swore to them in the wilderness that I would

19:13^A2 Kin 24:12-16; Ezek 19:10   **19:14**^AEzek 15:4; 20:47, 48   **20:1**^AEzek 8:1, 11, 12   **20:3**^AEzek 14:3   **20:4**^AEzek 16:2; 22:2   **20:5**^AEx 6:6-8   **20:6**^AJer 32:22   ^BPs 48:2   **20:7**^AEx 20:4, 5   ^BLev 18:3   **20:8**^AEx 32:1-9   ^BEzek 5:13   **20:9**^AEx 32:11-14   ^BEzek 39:7   **20:10**^AEzek 19:1   **20:11**^AEx 20:1-23:33   **20:12**^AEx 31:13, 17; Ezek 20:20   **20:13**^ALev 18:5   ^BIs 56:6   **20:15**^ANum 14:30; Ps 95:11

not bring them into the land which I had given *them,* flowing with milk and honey, which is the glory of all the lands, ¹⁶because they rejected My ordinances, and as for My statutes, they did not walk in them; they also profaned My Sabbaths, because their ^heart continually followed their idols. ¹⁷Yet My eye spared them rather than destroying them, and I did not bring about their ^annihilation in the wilderness.

¹⁸"Instead, I said to their ^children in the wilderness, '^BDo not walk in the statutes of your fathers or keep their ordinances or defile yourselves with their idols. ¹⁹I am the Lord your God; ^walk in My statutes and keep My ordinances and follow them. ²⁰^Sanctify My Sabbaths; and they shall be a sign between Me and you, so that you may know that I am the Lord your God.' ²¹But the ^children rebelled against Me; they did not walk in My statutes, nor were they careful to follow My ordinances which, *if* a person follows them, then he will live by them; they profaned My Sabbaths. So I resolved to pour out My wrath on them, to use up My anger against them in the wilderness. ²²But I withdrew My hand and acted ^for the sake of My name, so that it would not be defiled in the sight of the nations in whose sight I had brought them out. ²³Also I swore to them in the wilderness that I would ^scatter them among the nations and disperse them among the lands, ²⁴because they had not complied with My ordinances, but had rejected My statutes and had profaned My Sabbaths, and ^their eyes were on the idols of their fathers. ²⁵I also gave them statutes that were ^not good,

and ordinances by which they could not live; ²⁶and I pronounced them ^unclean because of their gifts, in that they ^Bmade all their firstborn pass through *the fire* so that I might make them desolate, in order that they might know that I am the Lord."'

²⁷"Therefore speak to the house of Israel, son of man, and say to them, 'This is what the Lord God says: "Again, in this your fathers have ^blasphemed Me by ^Bbeing disloyal to Me. ²⁸When I had brought them into the land which I swore to give to them, then they saw every ^high hill and every tree thick with branches, and there they offered their sacrifices and there they presented the provocation of their offering. There also they made their soothing aroma and there they poured out their drink offerings. ²⁹Then I said to them, 'What is the high place to which you go?' So its name is called ¹Bamah to this day."' ³⁰Therefore, say to the house of Israel, 'This is what the Lord God says: "Will you defile yourselves in the way of your ^fathers and adulterously pursue their detestable things? ³¹And when you offer your gifts, when you ^make your sons pass through the fire, you are defiling yourselves with all your idols to this day. So shall I be inquired of by you, house of Israel? As I live," declares the Lord God, "I certainly will not be

20:16 ^Ezek 11:21; 14:3-7   20:17 ^Jer 4:27; 5:18
20:18 ^Num 14:31   ᴮZech 1:4   20:19 ^Deut 5:32, 33;
6:1, 2   20:20 ^Jer 17:22   20:21 ^Num 21:5; 25:1-3
20:22 ^Is 48:9-11; Jer 14:7, 21   20:23 ^Lev 26:33;
Deut 4:27   20:24 ^Ezek 6:9   20:25 ^Ps 81:12; Is 66:4
20:26 ^Lev 18:21   ᴮJer 7:31   20:27 ^Num 15:30
ᴮEzek 18:24   20:28 ^1 Kin 14:23; Ps 78:58
20:30 ^Judg 2:19; Jer 7:26   20:31 ^Ps 106:37-39; Jer 7:31

20:29 ¹Or *High Place*

inquired of by you. ³²And whatever ^comes into your mind certainly will not come about, when you say: 'We will be like the nations, like the families of the lands, ᴮserving wood and stone.'

GOD WILL RESTORE ISRAEL
TO HER LAND

³³"As I live," declares the Lord Goᴅ, "with a mighty hand and with an ^outstretched arm and with wrath poured out, I assuredly shall be ᴮking over you. ³⁴I will bring you out from the peoples and gather you from the lands where you are scattered, with a mighty hand and with an outstretched arm and with ^wrath poured out; ³⁵and I will bring you into the ^wilderness of the peoples, and there I will enter into judgment with you face to face. ³⁶Just as I ^entered into judgment with your fathers in the ᴮwilderness of the land of Egypt, so I will enter into judgment with you," declares the Lord Goᴅ. ³⁷"I will make you ^pass under the rod, and I will bring you into the bond of the covenant; ³⁸and I will purge from you the rebels and those who revolt against Me; I will bring them out of the land where they reside, but they will ^not enter the land of Israel. So you will know that I am the Loʀᴅ.

³⁹"As for you, house of Israel," this is what the Lord Goᴅ says: "Go, serve, everyone *of you* his idols; but later you will certainly listen to Me, and My holy name you will no longer ^defile with your gifts and your idols. ⁴⁰For on My holy mountain, on the high mountain of Israel," declares the Lord Goᴅ, "there the entire house of Israel, ^all of them, will serve Me in the land; there I will ᴮaccept them and there I will

demand your contributions and the choicest of your gifts, with all your holy things. ⁴¹As a soothing aroma I will accept you when I ^bring you out from the peoples and gather you from the lands where you are scattered; and I will show Myself to be holy among you in the sight of the nations. ⁴²And you will know that I am the Loʀᴅ, ^when I bring you into the land of Israel, into the land which I swore to give to your forefathers. ⁴³And there you will remember your ways and all your deeds by which you have defiled yourselves; and you will ^loathe yourselves in your own sight for all the evil things that you have done. ⁴⁴Then you will know that I am the Loʀᴅ, when I have dealt with you ^in behalf of My name, not according to your evil ways or according to your corrupt deeds, house of Israel," declares the Lord Goᴅ.'"

⁴⁵Now the word of the Loʀᴅ came to me, saying, ⁴⁶"Son of man, set your face toward the south, and speak prophetically against the south and ^prophesy against the ᴮforest land of the Negev, ⁴⁷and say to the forest of the Negev, 'Hear the word of the Loʀᴅ: this is what the Lord Goᴅ says: "Behold, I am going to ^kindle a fire in you, and it will consume every green tree in you, as well as every dry tree; the blazing flame will not go out and the entire surface from south to north will be scorched by it. ⁴⁸And all mankind will see that I, the Loʀᴅ, have

20:32 ^Ezek 11:5   ᴮJer 2:25   20:33 ^Jer 21:5
ᴮJer 51:57   20:34 ^Jer 42:18; 44:6   20:35 ^Ezek 19:13;
20:36   20:36 ^Num 11:1-35   ᴮDeut 32:10
20:37 ^Lev 27:32; Jer 33:13   20:38 ^Num 14:29, 30;
Ps 95:11   20:39 ^Is 1:13-15; Ezek 23:38, 39
20:40 ^Is 66:23   ᴮIs 56:7   20:41 ^Is 27:12, 13;
Ezek 11:17   20:42 ^Ezek 11:17; 34:13   20:43 ^Jer 31:18;
Ezek 36:31   20:44 ^Ezek 36:22   20:46 ^Ezek 21:2
ᴮIs 30:6-11   20:47 ^Is 9:18, 19; Jer 21:14

kindled it; it will ^not go out."'"
⁴⁹Then I said, "Oh, Lord God! They are saying of me, 'Is he not *just* speaking in ^riddles?'"

PARABLE OF THE SWORD OF THE LORD

21 And the word of the Lord came to me, saying, ²"Son of man, ^set your face against Jerusalem, and ᴮspeak prophetically against the sanctuaries and prophesy against the land of Israel; ³and say to the land of Israel, 'This is what the Lord says: "Behold, ^I am against you; and I will draw My sword from its sheath and cut off from you the ᴮrighteous and the wicked. ⁴Because I will cut off from you the righteous and the wicked, therefore My sword will go out from its sheath against ^humanity from south *to* north. ⁵So humanity will know that I, the Lord, have drawn My sword from its sheath. It will ^not return *to its sheath* again."' ⁶As for you, son of man, groan with a breaking heart and bitter grief; you shall groan in their sight. ⁷And when they say to you, 'Why are you groaning?' you shall say, 'Because of the ^news, for it is coming; and ᴮevery heart will melt, all hands will go limp, every spirit will be disheartened, and all knees will drip with water. Behold, it is coming and it will happen,' declares the Lord God."

⁸And the word of the Lord came to me, saying, ⁹"Son of man, prophesy and say, 'This is what the Lord says:' Say,

^"A sword, a sword sharpened
And also polished!
¹⁰ 'Sharpened to make a
^slaughter,
Polished to flash like
lightning!'

Or shall we rejoice, the rod of My son despising every tree? ¹¹And it is given to be polished, so that it may be handled; the sword is sharpened and polished, to hand it over to the slaughterer. ¹²Cry out and wail, son of man; for it is against My people, it is against all the ^officials of Israel. They are turned over to the sword with My people, therefore slap *your* thigh. ¹³For *there is* a testing; and what if even the rod which despises will cease to be?" declares the Lord God.

¹⁴"You therefore, son of man, prophesy and clap *your* hands; and let the sword be ^doubled the third time, the sword for the slain. It is the sword for the great one slain, which surrounds them, ¹⁵so that *their* hearts will waver, and many ^fall at all their ᴮgates. I have granted the slaughter of the sword. Oh! It is made for *striking like* lightning, it is sharpened *in readiness* for slaughter. ¹⁶Prove yourself sharp, go to the right; set yourself; go to the left, wherever your edge is ordered. ¹⁷I will also clap My hands, and I will ^satisfy My wrath; I, the Lord, have spoken."

THE INSTRUMENT OF GOD'S JUDGMENT

¹⁸And the word of the Lord came to me, saying, ¹⁹"Now as for you, son of man, ^make two ways for the sword of the king of Babylon to come; both of them will go out of one land. And make a signpost; make it at the head of the way to

20:48 ^Jer 7:20; 17:27   20:49 ^Ezek 17:2; Matt 13:13
21:2 ^Ezek 20:46   ᴮJob 29:22   21:3 ^Jer 21:13   ᴮIs 57:1
21:4 ^Jer 12:12; Ezek 7:2   21:5 ^1 Sam 3:12; Jer 23:20
21:7 ^Ezek 7:26   ᴮIs 13:7   21:9 ^Deut 32:41
21:10 ^Is 34:5, 6   21:12 ^Ezek 21:25; 22:6
21:14 ^Lev 26:21, 24; 2 Kin 24:1, 10-16   21:15 ^Is 59:10
ᴮJer 17:27   21:17 ^Ezek 5:13   21:19 ^Jer 1:10; Ezek 4:1-3

the city. ²⁰You shall mark a way for the sword to come to Rabbah of the sons of Ammon, and to Judah into ^fortified Jerusalem. ²¹For the king of Babylon stands at the parting of the way, at the head of the two ways, to use divination; he shakes the arrows, he consults the ^household idols, he looks at the liver. ²²Into his right hand came the divination, 'Jerusalem,' to ^set up battering rams, to open the mouth for slaughter, to raise the voice with a battle cry, to set up battering rams against the gates, to pile up assault ramps, to build a siege wall. ²³And it will be to them like a false divination in their eyes; they have *sworn* solemn oaths. But he ^makes guilt known, so that they may be seized.

²⁴"Therefore, this is what the Lord God says: 'Because you have made your guilt known, in that your offenses are uncovered, so that in all your deeds your sins are seen—because you have come to mind, you will be seized by the hand. ²⁵And you, slain, wicked one, the prince of Israel, whose ^day has come, in the time of the punishment of the end,' ²⁶this is what the Lord God says: 'Remove the turban and take off the crown; this *will* no *longer be* the same. ^Exalt that which is low, and humble that which is high. ²⁷^Ruins, ruins, ruins, I will make it! This also will be no *longer* until ^He comes whose right it is, and I will give it *to Him*.'

²⁸"And you, son of man, prophesy and say, 'This is what the Lord God says concerning the sons of Ammon and their ^taunting,' and say: 'A sword, a sword is drawn, sharpened for the slaughter, to make it consume, so that *it may be like* lightning— ²⁹while they see ^false

visions for you, while they divine lies for you—to place you on the necks of the wicked who are killed, whose day has come, in the ^Btime of the punishment of the end. ³⁰Return *it* to its sheath. In the ^place where you were created, in the land of your origin, I will judge you. ³¹I will ^pour out My indignation on you; I will ^Bblow on you with the fire of My wrath, and I will hand you over to brutal men, craftsmen of destruction. ³²You will be ^fuel for the fire; your blood will be in the midst of the land. You will not be remembered, for I, the Lord, have spoken.'"

THE SINS OF ISRAEL

22 Then the word of the Lord came to me, saying, ²"And you, son of man, will you judge, will you judge the bloody city? Then inform her of all her abominations. ³And you shall say, 'This is what the Lord God says: "A city ^shedding blood in her midst, so that her time is coming; and *a city* that makes idols, contrary to her *own good*, for defilement! ⁴You have become ^guilty by the blood which you have shed, and you have become defiled by your idols which you have made. So you have brought your days closer and have come to your years; therefore I have made you a disgrace to the nations, and an object of mocking to all the lands. ⁵Those who are near and those who are far from you will make fun of you, you of ill repute, full of ^turmoil.

21:20 ^Ps 48:12, 13; 125:1, 2   21:21 ^Gen 31:19, 30; Judg 17:5   21:22 ^Ezek 4:2; 26:9   21:23 ^Num 5:15; Ezek 21:24   21:25 ^Ps 37:13; Ezek 7:2, 3, 7   21:26 ^Ps 75:7; Ezek 17:24   21:27 ^Hag 2:21, 22   ^BPs 2:6   21:28 ^Ezek 36:15; Zeph 2:8-10   21:29 ^Jer 27:9   ^BEzek 21:25   21:30 ^Ezek 25:5   21:31 ^Ezek 14:19   ^BPs 18:15   21:32 ^Ezek 20:47, 48; Mal 4:1   22:3 ^Ezek 22:6, 27; 23:37, 45   22:4 ^2 Kin 21:16; Ezek 24:7, 8   22:5 ^Is 22:2

⁶"Behold, the ᴬrulers of Israel, each according to his power, have been among you for the purpose of shedding blood. ⁷They have ᴬtreated father and mother with contempt among you. They have oppressed the ᴮstranger in your midst; they have oppressed the orphan and the widow among you. ⁸You have despised My holy things and ᴬprofaned My Sabbaths. ⁹Slanderous men have been among you for the purpose of shedding blood, and among you they have eaten at the mountain *shrines*. In your midst they have ᴬcommitted outrageous sin. ¹⁰Among you they have ᴬuncovered *their* fathers' nakedness; among you they have abused her who was unclean in her menstruation. ¹¹And one has committed abomination with his ᴬneighbor's wife, another has outrageously defiled his ᴮdaughter-in-law, and another among you has *sexually* abused his sister, his father's daughter. ¹²Among you they have ᴬtaken bribes to shed blood; you have taken interest, you have injured your neighbors by ᴮoppression, and you have forgotten Me," declares the Lord Goᴅ.

¹³"Behold, then, I strike with My hand your ᴬprofit which you have made and the bloodshed which is among you. ¹⁴Can ᴬyour heart endure, or can your hands be strong for the days that I will deal with you? ᴮI, the Lᴏʀᴅ, have spoken and will act. ¹⁵And I will scatter you among the nations and disperse you among the lands, and I will ᴬeliminate your uncleanness from you. ¹⁶Then you will defile yourself in the sight of the nations, and you will ᴬknow that I am the Lᴏʀᴅ."'"

¹⁷And the word of the Lᴏʀᴅ came to me, saying, ¹⁸"Son of man, the house of Israel has become waste metal to Me; all of them are ᴬbronze, tin, iron, and lead in the ᴮsmelting furnace; they are the waste metal of silver. ¹⁹Therefore, this is what the Lord Goᴅ says: 'Because all of you have become waste metal, therefore, behold, I am going to gather you into the midst of Jerusalem. ²⁰As they gather silver, bronze, iron, lead, and tin into the ᴬsmelting furnace to blow fire on it in order to melt *it*, so I will gather *you* in My anger and in My wrath, and I will place you *there* and melt you. ²¹And I will gather you and blow on you with the fire of My wrath, and you will be melted in the midst of it. ²²As silver is melted in the furnace, so you will be melted in the midst of it; and you will know that I, the Lᴏʀᴅ, have ᴬpoured out My wrath on you.'"

²³And the word of the Lᴏʀᴅ came to me, saying, ²⁴"Son of man, say to her, 'You are a land that is ᴬnot clean or rained on in the day of indignation.' ²⁵There is a conspiracy of her prophets in her midst like a roaring lion tearing the prey. They have ᴬdevoured lives; they have taken treasure and precious things; they have made many widows in the midst of her. ²⁶Her priests have done violence to My Law and have profaned My holy things; they have made no ᴬdistinction between the holy and

22:6 ᴬIs 1:23; Ezek 22:27 22:7 ᴬEx 20:12 ᴮEx 22:21f
22:8 ᴬEzek 20:13, 21, 24; 23:38, 39 22:9 ᴬEzek 23:29;
Hos 4:2, 10, 14 22:10 ᴬLev 18:8 22:11 ᴬEzek 18:11
ᴮLev 18:15 22:12 ᴬEx 23:8 ᴮLev 19:13
22:13 ᴬIs 33:15; Amos 2:6–8 22:14 ᴬEzek 21:7
ᴮEzek 17:24 22:15 ᴬEzek 23:27, 48 22:16 ᴬPs 83:18;
Ezek 6:7 22:18 ᴬJer 6:28–30 ᴮProv 17:3
22:20 ᴬIs 1:25 22:22 ᴬEzek 20:8, 33; Hos 5:10
22:24 ᴬIs 9:13; Jer 2:30 22:25 ᴬJer 2:34; Ezek 13:19
22:26 ᴬLev 10:10

the common, and they have not taught the difference between the ᴮunclean and the clean; and they have closed their eyes from My Sabbaths, and I am defiled among them. ²⁷Her leaders within her are like wolves tearing the prey, by shedding blood *and* ᴬdestroying lives in order to make ᴮdishonest profit. ²⁸And her prophets have coated with whitewash for them, seeing ᴬfalse visions and divining lies for them, saying, 'This is what the Lord Gᴏᴅ says,' when the Lᴏʀᴅ has not spoken. ²⁹The people of the land have practiced ᴬextortion and committed robbery, and they have oppressed the poor and needy, and have ᴮoppressed the stranger without justice. ³⁰I ᴬsearched for a man among them who would build up a wall and stand in the gap before Me for the land, so that I would not destroy it; but I found no one. ³¹So I have poured out My indignation on them; I have consumed them with the fire of My wrath; I have brought ᴬtheir way upon their heads," declares the Lord Gᴏᴅ.

OHOLAH AND OHOLIBAH'S SIN AND ITS CONSEQUENCES

23 The word of the Lᴏʀᴅ came to me again, saying, ²"Son of man, there were ᴬtwo women, the daughters of one mother; ³and they prostituted themselves in Egypt. They ᴬprostituted themselves in their youth; there their breasts were squeezed and there their virgin breasts were handled. ⁴Their names were Oholah the elder and Oholibah her sister. And they became Mine, and they gave birth to sons and daughters. And *as for* their names, Samaria is Oholah and Jerusalem is Oholibah.

⁵"Oholah prostituted herself while she was Mine; and she lusted after her lovers, after the ᴬAssyrians, *her* neighbors, ⁶who were clothed in purple, ᴬgovernors and officials, all of them handsome young men, horsemen riding on horses. ⁷She bestowed her obscene practices on them, all of whom *were* the choicest men of Assyria; and with all whom she lusted after, with all their idols she ᴬdefiled herself. ⁸She did not abandon her obscene practices ᴬfrom *the time in* Egypt; for in her youth men had slept with her, and they handled her virgin breasts and poured out their obscene practice on her. ⁹Therefore, I handed her over to her ᴬlovers, to the Assyrians, after whom she lusted. ¹⁰They ᴬuncovered her nakedness; they took her sons and her daughters, but they killed her with the sword. So she became a subject of gossip among women, and they executed judgments on her.

¹¹"Now her sister Oholibah saw *this,* yet she was ᴬmore corrupt in her lust than she, and her obscene practices were more than the prostitution of her sister. ¹²She lusted after the ᴬAssyrians, governors and officials, the ones near, opulently dressed, horsemen riding on horses, all of them handsome young men. ¹³And I saw that she had defiled herself; they both took the same way. ¹⁴So she increased her obscene practices. And she saw

22:26 ᴮ Hag 2:11-14   **22:27** ᴬ Ezek 22:25
ᴮ Ezek 22:13   **22:28** ᴬ Jer 23:25-32; Ezek 13:6
22:29 ᴬ Is 5:7   ᴮ Ezek 23:9   **22:30** ᴬ Is 59:16; 63:5
22:31 ᴬ Ezek 7:3, 8, 9; 9:10   **23:2** ᴬ Ezek 16:46
23:3 ᴬ Lev 17:7; Jer 3:9   **23:5** ᴬ 2 Kin 15:19; 16:7
23:6 ᴬ Ezek 23:12, 13   **23:7** ᴬ Ezek 20:7; 22:3, 4
23:8 ᴬ Ex 32:4; 1 Kin 12:28   **23:9** ᴬ Ezek 16:37; 23:22
23:10 ᴬ Ezek 16:37, 41   **23:11** ᴬ Jer 3:8-11; Ezek 16:51
23:12 ᴬ 2 Kin 16:7

men ^carved on the wall, images of the ^BChaldeans drawn in bright red, ^15wearing belts around their waists, with flowing turbans on their heads, all of them looking like officers, like the Babylonians *in* Chaldea, the land of their birth. ^16And when she saw them she ^lusted after them and sent messengers to them in Chaldea. ^17And the ^Babylonians came to her to the bed of love and defiled her with their obscene practice. And when she had been defiled by them, she turned away from them in disgust. ^18She exposed her obscene practices and exposed her nakedness; then I turned away from her in ^disgust, just as I had turned away from her ^Bsister in disgust. ^19Yet she multiplied her obscene practices, remembering the days of her youth, when she prostituted herself in the land of Egypt. ^20She ^lusted after their lovers, whose flesh is *like* the flesh of donkeys and whose discharge is *like* the discharge of horses. ^21So you longed for the ^outrageous sin of your youth, when the Egyptians handled your breasts because of the breasts of your youth.

^22"Therefore, Oholibah, this is what the Lord God says: 'Behold I am going to incite your lovers against you, from whom you turned away in disgust, and I will bring them against you from every side: ^23the ^Babylonians and all the ^BChaldeans, Pekod and Shoa and Koa, *and* all the Assyrians with them; handsome young men, governors and officials all of them, officers and men of renown, all of them riding on horses. ^24And they will come against you with weapons, chariots, and wagons, and

with a contingent of peoples. They will attack you on every side with shield, ^1buckler, and helmet; and I will commit the ^judgment to them, and they will judge you according to their customs. ^25I will set My ^jealousy against you, so that they may deal with you in wrath. They will remove your nose and your ears; and your survivors will fall by the sword. They will take your sons and your daughters; and your survivors will be consumed by the fire. ^26They will also ^strip you of your clothes and take away your ^Bbeautiful jewelry. ^27So ^I will remove from you your outrageous sin and your prostitution *that you brought* from the land of Egypt, so that you will not raise your eyes to them or remember Egypt anymore.' ^28For this is what the Lord God says: 'Behold, I am going to hand you over to those whom you ^hate, to those from whom you turned away in disgust. ^29They will ^deal with you in hatred, take all your property, and leave you naked and bare. And the nakedness of your prostitution will be exposed, both your outrageous sin and your obscene practices. ^30These things will be done to you because you have ^adulterously pursued the nations, because you have defiled yourself with their idols. ^31You have walked in the way of your sister; therefore I will put ^her cup in your hand.' ^32This is what the Lord God says:

23:14 ^Ezek 8:10   ^BEzek 16:29   23:16 ^Ezek 23:20;
Matt 5:28   23:17 ^2 Kin 24:17   23:18 ^Ps 78:59
^BEzek 23:9   23:20 ^Ezek 16:26; 17:15   23:21 ^Jer 3:9;
Ezek 23:3   23:23 ^2 Kin 20:14-17   ^B2 Kin 24:2
23:24 ^Jer 39:5, 6; Ezek 16:38   23:25 ^Ex 34:14;
Ezek 5:13   23:26 ^Jer 13:22   ^BIs 3:18-23
23:27 ^Ezek 16:41   23:28 ^Jer 21:7-10; 34:20
23:29 ^Deut 28:48; Ezek 23:25, 26, 45-47
23:30 ^Ezek 6:9   23:31 ^2 Kin 21:13; Jer 7:14, 15

23:24 ^1I.e., small shield

'You will ^drink your sister's cup,
Which is deep and wide.
You will be laughed at and held
in derision;
Because it contains much.

33 'You will be filled with
^drunkenness and grief,
A cup of horror and
desolation,
The cup of your sister Samaria.

34 'And you will ^drink it and
drain it.
Then you will gnaw on its
fragments
And tear your breasts;
for I have spoken,' declares the Lord
God. 35 Therefore, this is what the
Lord God says: 'Because you have
forgotten Me and ^discarded Me
behind your back, suffer on your
own part *the punishment for* your
outrageous sin and your obscene
practices.'"

36 Moreover, the Lord said to me,
"Son of man, will you judge Oholah
and Oholibah? Then ^declare to
them their abominations. 37 For they
have committed adultery, and blood
is on their hands. So they have committed adultery with their idols, and
even made their sons, ^whom they
bore to Me, pass through *the fire* to
them as food. 38 Again, they have
done this to Me: they have ^defiled
My sanctuary on the same day, and
have ^Bprofaned My Sabbaths. 39 For
when they slaughtered their children for their idols, they entered My
^sanctuary on the same day to profane it; and behold, this is what they
did within My house.

40 "Furthermore, they have even
sent for men who come from a
great distance, to whom a messenger was sent; and behold, they
came—for whom you bathed, ^put
makeup on your eyes, and adorned

yourselves with jewelry; 41 and you
sat on a splendid ^couch with a table
arranged in front of it on which
you had set My ^Bincense and My
oil. 42 And the sound of a ^carefree
multitude was with her; and ^Bheavy
drinkers were brought from the wilderness with people from the multitude of humanity. And they put
bracelets on the wrists of the women
and beautiful crowns on their heads.

43 "Then I said concerning her
who was ^worn out by adulteries, 'Will they now commit adultery with her when she is *like this?'*
44 But they went in to her as they
would go in to a prostitute. This is
how they went in to Oholah and to
Oholibah, the lewd women. 45 But
they, righteous people, will ^judge
them with the judgment of adulteresses and with the judgment of
women who shed blood, because
they are adulteresses and blood is
on their hands.

46 "For this is what the Lord God
says: 'Bring up a contingent against
them and turn them over to ^terror
and plunder. 47 The contingent will
^stone them with stones and cut
them down with their swords; they
will kill their sons and their daughters and ^Bburn their houses with
fire. 48 So I will eliminate outrageous
conduct from the land, so that all
women will take warning and not
commit outrageous sin as you have
done. 49 Your outrageous conduct
will be ^repaid to you, and you will
bear the guilt for your idols; so you
will know that I am the Lord God.'"

23:32 ^Ps 60:3; Is 51:17　23:33 ^Jer 25:15, 16, 27; Hab 2:16
23:34 ^Ps 75:8; Is 51:17　23:35 ^1 Kin 14:9; Jer 2:27
23:36 ^Is 58:1; Ezek 16:2　23:37 ^Ezek 16:20; 20:26
23:38 ^2 Kin 21:4, 7　^BJer 17:27　23:39 ^Jer 7:9-11
23:40 ^2 Kin 9:30; Jer 4:30　23:41 ^Esth 1:6　^BJer 44:17
23:42 ^Ezek 16:49　^BJer 51:7　23:43 ^Ezek 23:3
23:45 ^Ezek 16:38　23:46 ^Jer 15:4; 24:9
23:47 ^Lev 20:10　^BJer 39:8　23:49 ^Is 59:18; Ezek 7:4, 9

PARABLE OF THE BOILING POT

24 Now the word of the Lord came to me in the ninth year, in the tenth month, on the tenth of the month, saying, ²"Son of man, write the name of the day, this very day. The king of Babylon has ^laid siege to Jerusalem this very day. ³Present a ^parable to the rebellious house and say to them, 'This is what the Lord God says:

"Put on the pot, put *it* on and
    also pour water into it;
⁴   ^Put in it the pieces of meat,
    Every good piece, the thigh
        and the shoulder;
    Fill *it* with choice bones.
⁵ "Take the ^choicest of the flock,
    And also stack wood under
        the pot.
    Make it boil vigorously.
    Also boil its bones in it."

⁶'Therefore, this is what the Lord God says:

"Woe to the ^bloody city,
    To the pot in which there is
        rust
    And whose rust has not gone
        out of it!
    Take out of it piece after piece,
    Without making a choice.
⁷ "For her blood is in her midst;
    She placed it on the bare
        rock;
    She did not ^pour it on the
        ground
    To cover it with dust.
⁸ "So that it may ^cause wrath to
        come up to take vengeance,
    I have put her blood on the
        bare rock,
    So that it will not be covered."

⁹Therefore, this is what the Lord God says:

"^Woe to the bloody city!
    I also will make the wood pile
        great.

¹⁰ "Heap on the wood, kindle the
        fire,
    Cook the meat thoroughly
    And mix in the spices,
    And let the bones be burned up.
¹¹ "Then set it empty on its
        burning coals
    So that it may be hot
    And its bronze may glow,
    And its ^filthiness may be
        melted in it,
    Its rust eliminated.
¹² "She has ^wearied *Me* with
        work,
    Yet her great rust has not gone
        from her;
    Let her rust *be* in the fire!
¹³ "In your filthiness is
        outrageous sin.
    Because I *would* have cleansed
        you,
    Yet you are not clean,
    You will not be cleansed from
        your filthiness again
    Until I have ^expended My
        wrath on you.

¹⁴I, the Lord, have spoken; it is coming and I will act. I will not overlook, I will not ^pity, and I will not be sorry; ᴮaccording to your ways and according to your deeds I will judge you," declares the Lord God.'"

DEATH OF EZEKIEL'S WIFE IS A SIGN

¹⁵And the word of the Lord came to me, saying, ¹⁶"Son of man, behold, I am about to take from you ^what is precious to your eyes with a ᴮfatal blow; but you shall not mourn and you shall not weep, and your tears

24:2 ^2 Kin 25:1; Jer 39:1   24:3 ^Ps 78:2; Ezek 17:2
24:4 ^Mic 3:2, 3   24:5 ^Jer 39:6; 52:10, 24-27
24:6 ^2 Kin 24:3, 4; Ezek 22:2, 3, 27   24:7 ^Lev 17:13;
Deut 12:16   24:8 ^Is 26:21   24:9 ^Ezek 24:6; Hab 2:12
24:11 ^Ezek 22:15; 23:27   24:12 ^Jer 9:5
24:13 ^Ezek 5:13; 8:18   24:14 ^Jer 13:14   ᴮIs 3:11
24:16 ^Song 7:10   ᴮJob 23:2

shall not come. [17]Groan silently; do no mourning for the dead. Bind on your turban and put your sandals on your feet, and do not cover *your* mustache, and ^do not eat the bread of *other* people." [18]So I spoke to the people in the morning, and in the evening my wife died. And in the morning I did as I was commanded. [19]And the people said to me, "Will you not tell us what these things *mean* for us, that you are doing?" [20]Then I said to them, "The word of the LORD came to me, saying, [21]'Speak to the house of Israel, "This is what the Lord GOD says: 'Behold, I am about to profane My sanctuary, the pride of your power, that which is precious in your eyes and the longing of your soul; and your ^sons and your daughters whom you have left behind will fall by the sword. [22]And you will do just as I have done; you will not cover *your* mustache, and you will not eat the bread of *other* people. [23]Your turbans will be on your heads, and your sandals on your feet. You will not mourn and you will not weep; but ^you will rot away in your guilty deeds, and you will groan to one another. [24]So Ezekiel will be a ^sign to you; according to all that he has done, you will do. When it comes, then you will know that I am the Lord GOD.'"

[25]'As for you, son of man, will *it* not be on the day when I take from them their ^stronghold, the joy of their splendor, that which is precious in their eyes and their heart's longing, their sons and their daughters, [26]that on that day the one who ^escapes will come to you with information for *your* ears? [27]On that day your ^mouth will be opened to him who escaped, and

you will speak and no longer be silenced. So you will be a sign to them, and they will know that I am the LORD.'"

JUDGMENT ON GENTILE NATIONS—AMMON

25 And the word of the LORD came to me, saying, [2]"Son of man, set your face against the ^sons of Ammon and prophesy against them, [3]and say to the sons of Ammon, 'Hear the word of the Lord GOD! This is what the Lord GOD says: "Because you said, '^Aha!' against My sanctuary when it was profaned, and against the land of Israel when it was made desolate, and against the house of Judah when they went into exile, [4]therefore, behold, I am going to give you to the ^people of the east as a possession, and they will set up their encampments among you and make their dwellings among you; they will eat your fruit and drink your milk. [5]I will make ^Rabbah a pasture for camels, and the sons of Ammon a resting place for flocks. Then you will know that I am the LORD." [6]For this is what the Lord GOD says: "Because you have ^clapped your hands and stamped your feet, and have ^Brejoiced with all the malice in your soul against the land of Israel, [7]therefore, behold, I have reached out with My hand against you and I will give you as ^plunder to the nations. And I will cut you off from the peoples and ^Beliminate you from the lands.

24:17^Jer 16:7; Hos 9:4   24:21^Jer 6:11; 16:3, 4
24:23^Lev 26:39; Ezek 33:10   24:24^Ezek 4:3;
Luke 11:29, 30   24:25^Ps 48:2; 50:2
24:26^1 Sam 4:12; Job 1:15-19   24:27^Ezek 3:26; 33:22
25:2^Jer 49:1-6; Amos 1:13-15   25:3^Ps 70:2, 3;
Ezek 21:28   25:4^Judg 6:3, 33; 1 Kin 4:30
25:5^Deut 3:11; 2 Sam 12:26   25:6^Job 27:23
^BObad 12   25:7^Is 33:4   ^BAmos 1:14, 15

I will exterminate you. So you will know that I am the LORD."

MOAB

8'The Lord GOD says this: "Because ^Moab and Seir say, 'Behold, the house of Judah is like all the nations,' 9therefore, behold, I am going to deprive the flank of Moab of *its* cities, of its cities which are on its frontiers, the glory of the land, ^Beth-jeshimoth, ^Baal-meon, and Kiriathaim; 10and I will give it as a possession along with the sons of Ammon to the ^people of the east, so that the sons of Ammon will not be remembered among the nations. 11So I will execute judgments on Moab, and they will know that I am the LORD."

EDOM

12'The Lord GOD says this: "Because ^Edom has acted against the house of Judah by taking vengeance, and has incurred great guilt, and avenged themselves upon them," 13therefore this is what the Lord GOD says: "I will also ^reach out with My hand against Edom and ^eliminate human and animal *life* from it. And I will turn it into ruins; from Teman even to Dedan they will fall by the sword. 14And ^I will inflict My vengeance on Edom by the hand of My people Israel. Therefore, they will act in Edom in accordance with My anger and My wrath; so they will know My vengeance," declares the Lord GOD.

PHILISTIA

15'This is what the Lord GOD says: "Because the Philistines have acted in ^revenge, and have taken vengeance with malice in *their* souls to destroy with everlasting hostility,"

16therefore this is what the Lord GOD says: "Behold, I am going to reach out with My hand against the Philistines and eliminate the ^Cherethites; and I will destroy the remnant of the seacoast. 17I will execute great vengeance on them with wrathful rebukes; and they will ^know that I am the LORD, when I inflict My vengeance on them."'"

JUDGMENT ON TYRE

26 Now in the eleventh year, on the first of the month, the word of the LORD came to me, saying, 2"Son of man, because Tyre has said in regard to Jerusalem, 'Aha! The ^gateway of the peoples is broken; it has ^opened to me. I shall be filled, *now that* she is laid waste,' 3therefore this is what the Lord GOD says: 'Behold, I am against you, Tyre, and I will bring up ^many nations against you, as the sea brings up its waves. 4They will ^destroy the walls of Tyre and tear down her towers; and I will sweep her debris away from her and make her a bare rock. 5She will become a dry place for *the spreading of* nets in the midst of the sea, for I have spoken,' declares the Lord GOD; 'and she will become ^plunder for the nations. 6Also her ^daughters who are on the mainland will be killed by the sword, and they will know that I am the LORD.'"

7For the Lord GOD says this: "Behold, I am going to bring upon Tyre from the north Nebuchadnezzar king of Babylon, ^king of

25:8^Is 15:1; Jer 48:1   25:9^Num 33:49   ^Num 32:3, 38
25:10^Ezek 25:4   25:12^2 Chr 28:17; Ps 137:7
25:13^Jer 49:8, 13   ^Ezek 29:8   25:14^Is 11:14
25:15^Is 14:29-31; Ezek 25:6, 12   25:16^1 Sam 30:14;
Zeph 2:5   25:17^Ps 9:16   26:2^Is 62:10   ^Ezek 25:8
26:3^Mic 4:11   26:4^Is 23:11; Ezek 26:9
26:5^Ezek 25:7; 29:19   26:6^Ezek 16:46, 53; 26:8
26:7^Ezra 7:12; Is 10:8

kings, with horses, chariots, cavalry, and a great army. [8]He will kill your daughters on the mainland with the sword; and he will make siege walls against you, pile up an ^assault ramp against you, and raise up a large shield against you. [9]And he will direct the blow of his battering rams against your walls, and he will tear down your towers with his axes. [10]Because of the multitude of his horses, the dust *raised by* them will cover you; your walls will ^shake from the noise of cavalry, wagons, and chariots when he ^Benters your gates as *warriors* enter a city that is breached. [11]With the hoofs of his ^horses he will trample all your streets. He will kill your people with the sword, and your strong pillars will go down to the ground. [12]Also they will take your riches as spoils and plunder your merchandise, ^tear down your walls and destroy your ^Bdelightful houses, and throw your stones, your timbers, and your debris into the water. [13]So I will put an end to the sound of your songs, and the sound of your ^harps will no longer be heard. [14]I will turn you into a bare rock; you will become a dry place for *the spreading of* nets. You will not be ^rebuilt, for I the Lord have spoken," declares the Lord God.

[15]The Lord God says this to Tyre: "Will the ^coastlands not ^Bshake from the sound of your downfall when the wounded groan, when the slaughter takes place in your midst? [16]Then all the princes of the sea will ^descend from their thrones, remove their robes, and strip off their colorfully woven garments. They will ^Bclothe themselves with trembling; they will sit on the ground, tremble again and

again, and be appalled at you. [17]And they will take up a ^song of mourning over you and say to you,

'How you have perished, you inhabited one,
From the seas, you famous city,
Which was mighty on the sea,
She and her inhabitants,
Who imposed her terror
On all her inhabitants!
[18] 'Now the ^coastlands will tremble
On the day of your downfall;
Yes, the coastlands which are by the sea
Will be horrified at your passing.'"

[19]For this is what the Lord God says: "When I make you a desolate city, like the cities which are not inhabited, when I ^bring up the deep over you and the great waters cover you, [20]then I will bring you down with those who ^go down to the pit, to the people of old, and I will make you remain in the lower parts of the earth, like the ancient ruins, with those who go down to the pit, so that you will not be inhabited; but I will put ^Bglory in the land of the living. [21]I will cause you ^sudden terrors and you will no longer exist; though you will be sought, you will never be found again," declares the Lord God.

GRIEF OVER TYRE

27 Moreover, the word of the Lord came to me, saying, [2]"And you, son of man, ^take up a song of mourning over Tyre;

26:8 ^Jer 32:24   26:10 ^Ezek 26:15   ^BJer 39:3
26:11 ^Is 5:28; Hab 1:8   26:12 ^Jer 52:14   ^B2 Chr 32:27
26:13 ^Is 5:12; Rev 18:22   26:14 ^Deut 13:16; Job 12:14
26:15 ^Ezek 26:18   ^BJer 49:21   26:16 ^Jon 3:6
^BJob 8:22   26:17 ^Ezek 19:1, 14; 27:2, 32
26:18 ^Is 41:5; Ezek 26:15   26:19 ^Is 8:7, 8; Ezek 26:3
26:20 ^Is 14:9, 10   ^BJer 33:9   26:21 ^Ezek 26:15, 16;
27:36   27:2 ^Jer 9:10, 17-20; Ezek 28:12

³and say to Tyre, ^who sits at the entrance to the sea, merchant of the peoples to many coastlands, 'This is what the Lord God says:

> "Tyre, you have said, 'I am perfect in beauty.'

⁴ "Your borders are in the heart of the seas;
> Your builders have perfected your beauty.

⁵ "They have made all *your* planks of juniper trees from ^Senir;
> They have taken a cedar from Lebanon to make a mast for you.

⁶ "Of ^oaks from ᴮBashan they have made your rudders;
> With ivory they have inlaid your deck of boxwood from the coastlands of Cyprus.

⁷ "Your sail was of colorfully embroidered linen from Egypt
> So that it became your flag;
> Your awning was ^violet and purple from the coastlands of ᴮElishah.

⁸ "The inhabitants of Sidon and Arvad were your rowers;
> Your ^wise men, Tyre, were aboard; they were your sailors.

⁹ "The elders of ^Gebal and her wise men were with you repairing your leaks;
> All the ships of the sea and their sailors were with you in order to deal in your merchandise.

¹⁰ "^Persia, Lud, and Put were in your army, your men of war. They hung up shield and helmet on you; they presented your splendor. ¹¹The sons of Arvad and your army were on your walls, *all* around, and the Gammadim were in your towers. They hung their shields on your walls *all* around; they perfected your beauty.

¹² "Tarshish was your customer because of the abundance of all *kinds of* wealth; with silver, iron, tin, and lead they paid for your merchandise. ¹³Javan, Tubal, and Meshech, they were your traders; with human ^lives and vessels of bronze they paid for your merchandise. ¹⁴Those from ^Beth-togarmah gave horses, war horses, and mules for your merchandise. ¹⁵The sons of ^Dedan were your traders. Many coastlands were your market; they brought ᴮivory tusks and ebony as your payment. ¹⁶^Aram was your customer because of the abundance of your goods; they paid for your merchandise with emeralds, purple, colorfully woven cloth, fine linen, coral, and rubies. ¹⁷Judah and the land of Israel, they were your traders; with the wheat of ^Minnith, cakes, honey, oil, and balsam they paid for your merchandise. ¹⁸^Damascus was your customer because of the abundance of your goods, because of the abundance of all *kinds of* wealth, because of the wine of Helbon and white wool. ¹⁹Vedan and Javan paid for your merchandise from Uzal; wrought iron, cassia, and spice reed were among your merchandise. ²⁰^Dedan traded with you in saddlecloths for riding. ²¹^Arabia and all the princes of Kedar, they were your customers for lambs, rams, and goats; for these they were your

27:3^Ezek 28:2   27:5^Deut 3:9; 1 Chr 5:23
27:6^Is 2:13   ᴮNum 21:33   27:7^Ex 25:4   ᴮGen 10:4
27:8^1 Kin 9:27   27:9^Josh 13:5; 1 Kin 5:18
27:10^Ezek 30:5; 38:5   27:13^Joel 3:3; Rev 18:13
27:14^Gen 10:3; Ezek 38:6   27:15^Jer 25:23
ᴮ1 Kin 10:22   27:16^Judg 10:6; Is 7:1-8
27:17^Judg 11:33   27:18^Gen 14:15; Is 7:8
27:20^Gen 25:3   27:21^Is 21:13

customers. ²²The traders of ^Sheba and Raamah, they traded with you; they paid for your merchandise with the best of all balsam oil, and with all *kinds of* precious stones, and gold. ²³Haran, Canneh, ^Eden, the traders of Sheba, Asshur, *and* Chilmad traded with you. ²⁴They traded with you in choice garments, in clothes of violet and colorfully woven cloth, and in blankets of two colors, *and* tightly wound cords, *which were* among your merchandise. ²⁵The ^ships of Tarshish were the carriers for your merchandise.

> And you were filled and were
>   very glorious
> In the heart of the seas.

²⁶ "Your rowers have brought you
   Into ^great waters;
   The ^Beast wind has broken you
   In the heart of the seas.
²⁷ "Your wealth, your wares, your
   merchandise,
   Your seamen and your sailors,
   Your repairers of leaks, your
   dealers in merchandise,
   And all your men of war who
   are in you,
   With all your contingent that
   is in your midst,
   Will fall into the heart of the
   seas
   On the day of your overthrow.
²⁸ "At the sound of the cry of your
   sailors,
   The pasture lands will ^shake.
²⁹ "All who handle the oar,
   The ^seamen *and* all the sailors
   of the sea
   Will come down from their
   ships;
   They will stand on the land,
³⁰ And they will make their voice
   heard over you
   And cry out bitterly.

> They will ^throw dust on their
>   heads,
> They will ^Bwallow in ashes.

³¹ "Also they will shave
   themselves ^bald for you
   And ^Bput on sackcloth;
   And they will weep for you in
   bitterness of soul
   With bitter mourning.
³² "Moreover, in their wailing
   they will take up a ^song of
   mourning for you
   And sing a song of mourning
   over you:
'Who is like Tyre,
   Like her who is silent in the
   midst of the sea?
³³ 'When your merchandise went
   out from the seas,
   You satisfied many peoples;
   With the ^abundance of your
   wealth and your merchandise
   You enriched the kings of the
   earth.
³⁴ 'Now that you are broken by
   the seas
   In the depths of the waters,
   Your ^merchandise and all
   your company
   Have fallen in the midst of you.
³⁵ 'All the ^inhabitants of the
   coastlands
   Are appalled at you,
   And their kings are horribly
   afraid;
   They have a troubled look.
³⁶ 'The merchants among the
   peoples hiss at you;
   You have become terrified
   And you ^will cease to be
   forever.'"'"

27:22 ^Gen 10:7; Is 60:6   27:23 ^2 Kin 19:12; Is 37:12
27:25 ^Is 2:16   27:26 ^Ezek 26:19   ^BPs 48:7
27:28 ^Ezek 26:10, 15, 18   27:29 ^Rev 18:17-19
27:30 ^1 Sam 4:12   ^BJer 6:26   27:31 ^Is 15:2   ^BIs 22:12
27:32 ^Ezek 26:17; 27:2   27:33 ^Ezek 27:12, 18; 28:4, 5
27:34 ^Zech 9:3, 4   27:35 ^Is 23:6; Ezek 26:16
27:36 ^Ps 37:10, 36

TYRE'S KING OVERTHROWN

28 The word of the LORD came again to me, saying, [2] "Son of man, say to the leader of Tyre, 'The Lord GOD says this:

"Because your heart is haughty
  And you have said, 'I am a god,
  I sit in the seat of gods
  In the heart of the seas';
  Yet you are a ^mortal and not
    God,
  Although you make your heart
    like the heart of God—
[3] Behold, you are wiser than
    ^Daniel;
  There is no secret that is a
    match for you!
[4] "By your wisdom and
    understanding
  You have acquired ^riches for
    yourself
  And have acquired gold and
    silver for your treasuries.
[5] "By your great wisdom, by your
    trade
  You have increased your riches,
  And your ^heart is haughty
    because of your riches—
[6] Therefore this is what the Lord
  GOD says:
  'Because you have ^made your
    heart
  Like the heart of God,
[7] Therefore, behold, I am going
    to bring ^strangers against
    you,
  The most ruthless of the
    nations.
  And they will draw their swords
  Against the beauty of your
    wisdom
  And profane your splendor.
[8] 'They will bring you down to
    the pit,
  And you will die the ^death of
    those who are killed
  In the heart of the seas.

[9] 'Will you still say, "I am a god,"
  In the presence of one who
    kills you,
  Though you are a mortal and
    not God,
  In the hands of those who
    wound you?
[10] 'You will die the death of the
    ^uncircumcised
  By the hand of strangers,
  For I have spoken!' declares
    the Lord GOD!"'"

[11] Again the word of the LORD came to me, saying, [12] "Son of man, ^take up a song of mourning over the king of Tyre and say to him, 'This is what the Lord GOD says:

"You had the seal of
    perfection,
  Full of wisdom and perfect in
    beauty.
[13] "You were in ^Eden, the garden
    of God;
  Every precious stone was your
    covering:
  The ruby, the topaz and the
    diamond;
  The beryl, the onyx and the
    jasper;
  The lapis lazuli, the
    turquoise and the
    emerald;
  And the gold, the
    workmanship of your
    settings and sockets,
  Was in you.
  On the day that you were
    created
  They were prepared.
[14] "You were the ^anointed
    cherub who covers,
  And I placed you *there*.

28:2 ^Ps 9:20; 82:6, 7   28:3 ^Dan 1:20; 2:20-23, 28
28:4 ^Ezek 27:33; Zech 9:2, 3   28:5 ^Job 31:24, 25;
Ps 52:7   28:6 ^Ex 9:17; Ezek 28:2   28:7 ^Ezek 26:7
28:8 ^Ezek 27:26, 27, 34   28:10 ^1 Sam 17:26, 36;
Ezek 31:18   28:12 ^Ezek 19:1; 26:17   28:13 ^Gen 2:8;
Is 51:3   28:14 ^Ex 25:17-20; 30:26

You were on the holy
mountain of God;
You walked in the midst of the
stones of fire.
15 "You were ^blameless in your
ways
From the day you were
created
Until unrighteousness was
found in you.
16 "By the ^abundance of your
trade
You were internally ^Bfilled with
violence,
And you sinned;
Therefore I have cast you as
profane
From the mountain of God.
And I have destroyed you, you
covering cherub,
From the midst of the stones
of fire.
17 "Your heart was haughty
because of your ^beauty;
You ^Bcorrupted your wisdom
by reason of your splendor.
I threw you to the ground;
I put you before kings,
That they may see you.
18 "By the multitude of your
wrongdoings,
In the unrighteousness of
your trade
You profaned your
sanctuaries.
Therefore I have brought ^fire
from the midst of you;
It has consumed you,
And I have turned you to
^Bashes on the earth
In the eyes of all who see you.
19 "All who know you among the
peoples
Are appalled at you;
You have become ^terrified
And you will cease to be
^Bforever."'"

JUDGMENT OF SIDON

20 And the word of the LORD came
to me, saying, 21"Son of man, set
your face toward ^Sidon, prophesy
against her 22 and say, 'This is what
the Lord GOD says:
"Behold, I am against you, Sidon,
And I will appear in My glory
in your midst.
Then they will know that I am
the LORD, when I ^execute
judgments against her,
And I will reveal Myself as holy
in her.
23 "For ^I will send a plague to her
And blood to her streets,
And the ^Bwounded will fall in
her midst
By the sword upon her on
every side;
Then they will know that I am
the LORD.
24 And there will no longer be for
the house of Israel a ^painful thorn
or a hurtful thorn bush from any
surrounding them who despised
them; then they will know that I
am the Lord GOD."

ISRAEL REGATHERED

25 'This is what the Lord GOD says:
"When I ^gather the house of Israel
from the peoples among whom
they are scattered, and show
Myself holy among them in the
sight of the nations, then they will
^Blive on their land which I gave to
My servant Jacob. 26 They will live
on it securely; and they will ^build
houses, plant vineyards, and live
securely when I ^Bexecute judgments

28:15 ^Ezek 27:3, 4; 28:3-6, 12   28:16 ^Ezek 27:12
^BEzek 8:17   28:17 ^Ezek 27:3, 4   ^BIs 19:11
28:18 ^Amos 1:9, 10   ^BMal 4:3   28:19 ^Ezek 26:21
^BJer 51:64   28:21 ^Gen 10:15, 19; Is 23:2, 4
28:22 ^Ezek 28:26; 30:19   28:23 ^Ezek 38:22   ^BJer 51:52
28:24 ^Num 33:55; Josh 23:13   28:25 ^Ps 106:47
^BJer 23:8   28:26 ^Jer 32:15, 43, 44   ^BEzek 25:11

upon all around them who despise them. Then they will know that I am the LORD their God.""'"

JUDGMENT OF EGYPT

29 In the ^tenth year, in the tenth *month,* on the twelfth of the month, the word of the LORD came to me, saying, ²"Son of man, set your face against ^Pharaoh king of Egypt, and prophesy against him and against all Egypt. ³Speak and say, 'This is what the Lord GOD says:

"Behold, I am against you,
     Pharaoh king of Egypt,
The great ^monster that lies in
     the midst of his canals,
That has said, 'My Nile is
     mine, and I myself have
     made *it.'*
⁴ "I will put ^hooks in your jaws
And make the fish of your
     canals cling to your scales.
And I will bring you up out of
     the midst of your canals,
And all the fish of your canals
     will cling to your scales.
⁵ "I will ^abandon you to the
     wilderness, you and all the
     fish of your canals;
You will fall on the open field;
     you will not be brought
     together or ^gathered.
I have given you for food to the
     animals of the earth and to
     the birds of the sky.
⁶ "Then all the inhabitants of
     Egypt will know that I am
     the LORD,
Because they have been *only*
     a ^staff *made* of reed to the
     house of Israel.
⁷ "When they took hold of you
     with the hand,
You ^broke and tore all their
     hands;

And when they leaned on you,
     You broke and made all their
     hips shake."

⁸'Therefore the Lord GOD says this: "Behold, I am going to ^bring upon you a sword, and I will cut off from you human and animal *life.* ⁹The land of Egypt will become a desolation and place of ruins. Then they will know that I am the LORD.

"Because you ^said, 'The Nile is mine, and I have made *it,*' ¹⁰therefore, behold, I am ^against you and against your canals, and I will make the land of Egypt an utter waste *and* desolation, from Migdol *to* Syene and as far as the border of Cush. ¹¹A human foot will ^not pass through it, nor will the foot of an animal pass through it, and it will not be inhabited for forty years. ¹²So I will make the land of Egypt a desolation in the midst of deserted lands. And her cities, in the midst of cities that are laid waste, will be desolate for forty years; and I will ^scatter the Egyptians among the nations and disperse them among the lands."

¹³'For this is what the Lord GOD says: "At the end of forty years I will ^gather the Egyptians from the peoples among whom they were scattered. ¹⁴And I will restore the fortunes of Egypt and bring them back to the land of ^Pathros, to the land of their origin, and there they will be a lowly kingdom. ¹⁵It will be the lowest of the kingdoms, and it will not raise itself above the nations again. And I will make them small so that they will not ^rule over

29:1^Ezek 26:1; 29:17   29:2^Jer 44:30   29:3^Is 27:1; Ezek 32:2   29:4^2 Kin 19:28; Ezek 38:4
29:5^Ezek 32:4-6   ᴮJer 8:2   29:6^2 Kin 18:21; Is 36:6
29:7^2 Kin 18:21; Is 36:6   29:8^Jer 46:13; Ezek 14:17
29:9^Prov 16:18; 18:12   29:10^Ezek 13:8; 21:3
29:11^Jer 43:11, 12; 46:19   29:12^Jer 46:19;
Ezek 30:23, 26   29:13^Is 19:22; Jer 46:26
29:14^Is 11:11; Jer 44:1, 15   29:15^Ezek 31:2; 32:2

the nations. ¹⁶And it will no longer be *a kingdom* on which the house of Israel relies, ^bringing to mind the guilt of their having turned to Egypt. Then they will know that I am the Lord GOD.”’”

¹⁷Now in the ^twenty-seventh year, in the first *month,* on the first of the month, the word of the LORD came to me, saying, ¹⁸“Son of man, ^Nebuchadnezzar king of Babylon made his army labor hard against Tyre; every head had a bald spot and every shoulder was rubbed raw. But he and his army acquired no wages from Tyre for the labor that he had performed against it.” ¹⁹Therefore this is what the Lord GOD says: “Behold, I am going to ^give the land of Egypt to Nebuchadnezzar king of Babylon. And he will carry off her ᴮwealth and capture her spoils and seize her plunder; and it will be wages for his army. ²⁰I have given him the land of Egypt *for* his labor which he ^performed, because they acted for Me,” declares the Lord GOD.

²¹“On that day I will make a ^horn sprout for the house of Israel, and I will open your mouth among them. Then they will know that I am the LORD.”

GRIEF OVER EGYPT

30 The word of the LORD came again to me, saying, ²“Son of man, prophesy and say, ‘This is what the Lord GOD says:

“^Wail, ‘Woe for the day!’

³ “For the day is near,
    Indeed, ^the day of the LORD is
        near;
    It will be a day of clouds,
    A time *of doom* for the nations.
⁴ “A sword will come upon Egypt,
    And there will be trembling in
        Cush;

When the slain fall in Egypt,
    They will ^take away her wealth,
    And her foundations will be
        torn down.
⁵Cush, Put, Lud, all ^Arabia, Libya and the people of the land that is in league will fall with them by the sword.”

⁶ ‘This is what the LORD says:
    “Indeed, those who support
        ^Egypt will fall
    And the pride of her power
        will come down;
    From Migdol *to* Syene
    They will fall within her by
        the sword,”
    Declares the Lord GOD.
⁷ “They will be desolate
    In the ^midst of the desolated
        lands;
    And her cities will be
    In the midst of the devastated
        cities.
⁸ “And they will know that I am
        the LORD,
    When I set a ^fire in Egypt
    And all her helpers are broken.
⁹On that day ^messengers will go out from Me in ships to frighten ᴮcarefree Cush; and trembling will come on them *as* on the day of Egypt; for behold, it is coming!”

¹⁰‘This is what the Lord GOD says:
    “^I will also make the hordes of
        Egypt cease
    By the hand of
        Nebuchadnezzar king of
        Babylon.
¹¹ “He and his people with him,
    ^The most ruthless of the
        nations,

29:16^Is 64:9; Jer 14:10 **29:17**^Ezek 24:1; 26:1
29:18^Jer 25:9; 27:6 **29:19**^Ezek 30:10, 24, 25
ᴮJer 43:10–13 **29:20**^Is 10:6, 7; 45:1–3
29:21^1 Sam 2:10; Ps 92:10 **30:2**^Is 13:6; 15:2
30:3^Ezek 7:19; 13:5 **30:4**^Ezek 29:19
30:5^Jer 25:20, 24 **30:6**^Is 20:3–6 **30:7**^Jer 25:18–26;
Ezek 29:12 **30:8**^Ezek 22:31; 30:14, 16 **30:9**^Is 18:1, 2
ᴮIs 47:8 **30:10**^Ezek 29:19 **30:11**^Ezek 28:7

Will be brought in to destroy
the land;
And they will draw their
swords against Egypt
And fill the land with the slain.

12 "Moreover, I will make the Nile
canals dry
And ^sell the land into the
hands of evil men.
And I will make the land
desolate
And all that is in it,
By the hand of strangers; I the
LORD have spoken."

13 'This is what the Lord GOD says:
"I will also ^destroy the idols
And make the images cease
from Memphis.
And there will no longer be a
prince in the land of Egypt;
And I will put fear in the land
of Egypt.

14 "I will make Pathros desolate,
Set a fire in ^Zoan
And execute judgments on
1,BThebes.

15 "I will pour out My wrath on
1Sin,
The stronghold of Egypt;
I will also eliminate the hordes
of Thebes.

16 "I will set a fire in Egypt;
Sin will writhe in anguish,
Thebes will be breached
And 1Memphis *will have*
distresses daily.

17 "The young men of 1,AOn and of
Pi-beseth
Will fall by the sword,
And the women will go into
captivity.

18 "In ^Tehaphnehes the day will
be Bdark
When I break there the yoke
bars of Egypt.
Then the pride of her power
will cease in her;

A cloud will cover her,
And her daughters will go into
captivity.

19 "So I will ^execute judgments
on Egypt,
And they will know that I am
the LORD."'"

VICTORY FOR BABYLON

20 In the ^eleventh year, in the
first *month,* on the seventh of the
month, the word of the LORD came
to me, saying, 21 "Son of man, I have
^broken the arm of Pharaoh king of
Egypt; and, behold, it has not been
bound up for healing or wrapped
with a bandage, so that it may be
strong to wield the sword. 22 Therefore this is what the Lord GOD says:
'Behold, I am against Pharaoh king
of Egypt, and I will break his arms,
both the strong and the ^broken;
and I will make the sword Bfall from
his hand. 23 And I will ^scatter the
Egyptians among the nations and
disperse them among the lands.
24 For I will strengthen the arms
of the king of Babylon and put
^My sword in his hand; and I will
break the arms of Pharaoh, so that
he will groan before him with the
groans of a wounded man. 25 So I
will strengthen the arms of the king
of Babylon, but the arms of Pharaoh will fail. Then they will know
that I am the LORD, when I put My
sword into the hand of the king of
Babylon and he ^reaches out with it
against the land of Egypt. 26 When

30:12 1Is 19:4   **30:13** AIs 2:18   **30:14** APs 78:12, 43
BJer 46:25   **30:17** AGen 41:45; 46:20   **30:18** AJer
43:8-13   BEzek 30:3   **30:19** APs 9:16; Ezek 5:8, 15
30:20 AEzek 26:1; 29:1, 17   **30:21** APs 10:15; 37:17
30:22 A2 Kin 24:7   BJer 46:21   **30:23** AEzek 29:12;
30:17, 18, 26   **30:24** AEzek 30:11, 25; Zeph 2:12
30:25 1Josh 8:18; 1 Chr 21:16

30:14 1Or No   **30:15** 1Or *Pelusium*   **30:16** 1Or *Noph*
30:17 1Or *Aven*

I scatter the Egyptians among the nations and disperse them among the lands, then they will know that I am the LORD.'"

PHARAOH WARNED OF ASSYRIA'S FATE

31 In the ^eleventh year, in the third *month,* on the first of the month, the word of the LORD came to me, saying, 2 "Son of man, say to Pharaoh king of Egypt and to his ^hordes,

'Whom are you like in your greatness?
3   'Behold, Assyria *was* a ^cedar in Lebanon
With beautiful branches and forest shade,
And very high,
And its top was among the clouds.
4   'The ^waters made it grow, the deep made it high.
With its rivers it continually extended all around its planting place,
And sent out its channels to all the trees of the field.
5   'Therefore ^its height was loftier than all the trees of the field
And its boughs became many and its branches long
Because of ^Bmany waters as it spread them out.
6   'All the ^birds of the sky nested in its twigs,
And under its branches all the animals of the field gave birth,
And all great nations lived under its shade.
7   'So it was beautiful in its greatness, in the length of its branches;
For its roots extended to many waters.

8   'The cedars in ^God's garden could not match it;
The junipers could not compare with its branches,
And the plane trees could not match its branches.
No tree in ^God's garden could compare with it in its beauty.
9   'I made it beautiful with the multitude of its branches,
And all the trees of ^Eden, which were in the garden of God, were jealous of it.

10 "Therefore this is what the Lord GOD says: "Because it is tall in stature and has put its top among the clouds, and its ^heart is haughty in its loftiness, 11 I will hand it over to a ^ruler of the nations; he will thoroughly deal with it. In accordance with its wickedness I have driven it out. 12 ^Foreign tyrants of the nations have cut it down and left it; on the mountains and in all the valleys its branches have fallen, and its branches have been broken in all the ravines of the land. And all the peoples of the earth have gone down from its shade and left it. 13 All the ^birds of the sky will nest on its fallen trunk, and all the animals of the field will rest on its *fallen* branches, 14 so that all the trees *by* the waters will not be exalted in their stature, nor put their tops among the clouds, nor will any of their well-watered mighty ones stand *straight* in their height. For they have all been turned over to death, to the ^earth beneath, among mankind, with those who go down to the pit."

31:1 ^Jer 52:5, 6; Ezek 30:20   31:2 ^Ezek 29:19; 30:10
31:3 ^Is 10:33, 34; Ezek 17:3, 4, 22   31:4 ^Ezek 17:5, 8;
Rev 17:1, 15   31:5 ^Dan 4:11   ^BPs 1:3   31:6 ^Ezek 17:23;
31:13   31:8 ^Gen 2:8, 9; 13:10   31:9 ^Gen 2:8, 9; 13:10
31:10 ^2 Chr 32:25; Is 10:12   31:11 ^Ezek 30:10, 11;
32:11, 12   31:12 ^Ezek 7:21; 28:7   31:13 ^Is 18:6;
Ezek 29:5   31:14 ^Num 16:30, 33; Ps 63:9

¹⁵'This is what the Lord God says: "On the day when it went down to Sheol I ^caused mourning; I closed the deep over it and held back its rivers. And *its* many waters were stopped up, and I made Lebanon mourn for it, and all the trees of the field wilted away on account of it. ¹⁶I made the nations ^quake from the sound of its fall when I made it ᴮgo down to Sheol with those who go down to the pit; and all the well-watered trees of Eden, the choicest and best of Lebanon, were comforted in the earth beneath. ¹⁷They also ^went down with it to Sheol to those who were slain by the sword; and *those who were* its strength lived ᴮin its shade among the nations.

¹⁸"To which among the trees of Eden are you so alike in glory and greatness? Yet you will be brought down with the trees of Eden to the earth beneath; you will lie in the midst of the uncircumcised with those who were killed by the sword. ^This is Pharaoh and all his hordes!"' declares the Lord God."

GRIEF OVER PHARAOH AND EGYPT

32 In the ^twelfth year, in the twelfth month, on the first of the month, the word of the Lord came to me, saying, ²"Son of man, take up a song of mourning over Pharaoh king of Egypt, and say to him,

'You compared yourself to a
    young ^lion of the nations,
Yet you are like the ᴮmonster in
    the seas;
And you burst forth in your
    rivers
And muddied the waters with
    your feet
And fouled their rivers.'"

³This is what the Lord God says:
"Now I will ^spread My net over
    you
With a contingent of many
    peoples,
And they will lift you up in My
    net.
⁴ "I will leave you on the land;
    I will hurl you on the open field.
    And I will cause all the ^birds
        of the sky to nest on you,
    And I will satisfy the animals
        of the whole earth with you.
⁵ "I will lay your flesh ^on the
        mountains
    And fill the valleys with your
        refuse.
⁶ "I will also make the land drink
        the discharge of your ^blood
    As far as the mountains,
    And the ravines will be full of
        you.
⁷ "And when I ^extinguish you,
    I will cover the heavens and
        darken their stars;
    I will cover the sun with a cloud
    And the moon will not give its
        light.
⁸ "All the shining ^lights in the
        heavens
    I will darken over you
    And will set darkness on your
        land,"
    Declares the Lord God.
⁹"I will also trouble the hearts of many peoples when I ^bring your destruction among the nations, into lands which you have not known. ¹⁰And I will make many peoples ^appalled at you, and their kings will be horribly afraid

31:15^Ezek 32:7; Nah 2:10   31:16^Ezek 26:15
ᴮIs 14:15   31:17^Ps 9:17   ᴮEzek 31:3, 6
31:18^Ps 52:7; Matt 13:19   32:1^Ezek 30:20; 31:1
32:2^Jer 4:7   ᴮIs 27:1   32:3^Ezek 12:13   32:4^Is 18:6
32:5^Ezek 31:12   32:6^Ex 7:17; Is 34:3, 7
32:7^Job 18:5, 6; Prov 13:9   32:8^Gen 1:14
32:9^Ex 15:14-16   32:10^Ezek 27:35

of you when I brandish My sword before them; and ᴮthey will tremble again and again, every person for his own life, on the day of your fall."

¹¹For ᴬthe Lord Gᴏᴅ says ᴬthis: "The sword of the king of Babylon will attack you. ¹²By the swords of the warriors I will make your multitude fall; all of them are ᴬtyrants of the nations,

And they will ᴮdevastate the
    pride of Egypt,
And all its multitude will be
    destroyed.
¹³ "I will also eliminate all its
    cattle from beside many
    waters;
And ᴬa human foot will not
    muddy them anymore,
And the hoofs of animals will
    not muddy them.
¹⁴ "Then I will make their waters
    settle,
And make their rivers run
    like oil,"
Declares the Lord Gᴏᴅ.
¹⁵ "When I make the land of
    Egypt a ᴬdesolation,
And the land is destitute of
    that which filled it,
When I strike all those who
    live in it,
Then they shall know that I
    am the Lᴏʀᴅ.

¹⁶This is a ᴬsong of mourning, and they shall sing it. The daughters of the nations shall sing it. Over Egypt and over all her hordes they shall sing it," declares the Lord Gᴏᴅ.

¹⁷In the ᴬtwelfth year, on the fifteenth of the month, the word of the Lᴏʀᴅ came to me, saying, ¹⁸"Son of man, lament for the hordes of Egypt and ᴬbring it down, her and the daughters of the mighty

nations, to the ᴮnetherworld, with those who go down to the pit;
¹⁹ 'Whom do you surpass in
        beauty?
    Go down and make your bed
        with the ᴬuncircumcised.'
²⁰They shall fall in the midst of those who are killed by the sword. She is turned over to the sword; they have ᴬdragged her and all her hordes away. ²¹The ᴬstrong among the mighty ones shall speak of him *and* his helpers from the midst of Sheol: 'They have gone down, they lie still, the uncircumcised, killed by the sword.'

²²"ᴬAssyria is there and all her company; her graves are all around her. All of them killed, fallen by the sword, ²³whose ᴬgraves are set in the remotest parts of the pit, and her company is all around her grave. All of them killed, fallen by the sword, who spread terror in the land of the living.

²⁴"ᴬElam is there and all her hordes around her grave; all of them killed, fallen by the sword, who went down uncircumcised to the lower parts of the earth, who inflicted their terror on the land of the living, and bore their disgrace with those who go down to the pit. ²⁵They have made a ᴬbed for her among the slain with all her hordes. Her graves are around it, they are all uncircumcised, killed by the sword (although their terror was inflicted on the land of the living), and they bore their disgrace with those who go down to

32:10 ᴮEzek 26:16   32:11 ᴬJer 46:26   32:12 ᴬEzek 28:7
ᴮEzek 28:19   32:13 ᴬEzek 29:11   32:15 ᴬPs 107:33, 34;
Ezek 29:12, 19, 20   32:16 ᴬ2 Sam 1:17; 3:33, 34
32:17 ᴬEzek 31:1; 32:1   32:18 ᴬJer 1:10
ᴮEzek 31:14, 16, 18   32:19 ᴬJer 9:25, 26; Ezek 31:18
32:20 ᴬPs 28:3   32:21 ᴬIs 14:9–12; Ezek 32:27
32:22 ᴬEzek 27:23; 31:3, 16   32:23 ᴬIs 14:15
32:24 ᴬGen 10:22; 14:1   32:25 ᴬPs 139:8

the pit; they were put in the midst of the slain.

26 "ᴬMeshech, ᴮTubal, and all their hordes are there; their graves surround them. All of them were killed by the sword uncircumcised, though they inflicted their terror on the land of the living. 27ᴬNor do they lie beside the fallen heroes of the uncircumcised, who went down to Sheol with their weapons of war and whose swords were placed under their heads; but the punishment for their ᴮwrongdoing rested on their bones, though the terror of *these* heroes *was once* in the land of the living. 28But in the midst of the uncircumcised you will be broken and lie with those killed by the sword.

29"There *also is* ᴬEdom, its kings and all its princes, who despite *all* their might are laid with those killed by the sword; they will lie with the uncircumcised and with those who go down to the pit.

30"There *also are* the chiefs of the ᴬnorth, all of them, and all the ᴮSidonians, who in *spite of* the terror *resulting* from their might, in shame went down with the slain. So they lay down uncircumcised with those killed by the sword and bore their disgrace with those who go down to the pit.

31"These Pharaoh will see, and he will ᴬfind consolation regarding all his hordes killed by the sword, Pharaoh and all his army," declares the Lord Goᴅ. 32"Though I inflicted the terror of him on the land of the living, yet he will be laid to rest among *the* uncircumcised *along* with those killed by the sword, Pharaoh and all his hordes," declares the Lord Goᴅ.

THE WATCHMAN'S DUTY

33 Now the word of the Lᴏʀᴅ came to me, saying, 2"Son of man, speak to the ᴬsons of your people and say to them, 'If I bring a sword upon a land, and the people of the land take one man from among them and make him their watchman, 3and he sees the sword coming upon the land and ᴬblows the horn and warns the people, 4then someone who hears the sound of the horn but ᴬdoes not take warning, and a sword comes and takes him away, his blood will be on his *own* head. 5He heard the sound of the horn but did not take warning; his blood will be on himself. But had he taken warning, he would have ᴬsaved his life. 6But if the watchman sees the sword coming and does not blow the horn and the people are not warned, and a sword comes and takes a person from them, he is ᴬtaken away for his wrongdoing; but I will require his ᴮblood from the watchman's hand.'

7"Now as for you, son of man, I have appointed you as a watchman for the house of Israel; so you will hear a message from My mouth and give them a ᴬwarning from Me. 8When I say to the wicked, 'You wicked person, you will ᴬcertainly die,' and you do not speak to warn the wicked about his way, that wicked person shall die for his wrongdoing, but I will require his blood from your hand. 9But if you on your part warn a wicked person to turn from his way and he ᴬdoes

32:26ᴬGen 10:2   ᴮIs 66:19   32:27ᴬIs 14:18, 19
ᴮJob 20:11   32:29ᴬIs 34:5-15; Jer 49:7-22
32:30ᴬJer 1:15   ᴮJer 25:22   32:31ᴬEzek 14:22; 31:16
33:2ᴬEzek 3:11; 33:12, 17, 30   33:3ᴬNeh 4:18-20;
Is 58:1   33:4ᴬ2 Chr 25:16; Jer 6:17   33:5ᴬEx 9:19-21;
Heb 11:7   33:6ᴬEzek 18:20, 24   ᴮEzek 3:18, 20
33:7ᴬJer 1:17; 26:2   33:8ᴬIs 3:11; Ezek 18:4, 13, 18, 20
33:9ᴬActs 13:40, 41, 46

not turn from his way, he will die for his wrongdoing, but you have ᴮsaved your life.

10 "Now as for you, son of man, say to the house of Israel, 'This is what you have said: "Surely our offenses and our sins are upon us, and we are ᴬrotting away in them; ᴮhow then can we survive?"' 11 Say to them, 'As I live!' declares the Lord GOD, 'I take ᴬno pleasure at all in the death of the wicked, but rather that the wicked ᴮturn from his way and live. Turn back, turn back from your evil ways! Why then should you die, house of Israel?' 12 And you, son of man, say to your fellow citizens, 'The righteousness of a righteous one will not save him on the day of his offense, and as for the wickedness of a wicked one, he will ᴬnot stumble because of it on the day when he turns from his wickedness; whereas a righteous one will not be able to live by his righteousness on the day when he commits sin.' 13 When I say to the righteous *that* he will certainly live, and he *so* trusts in his righteousness that he ᴬcommits injustice, none of his righteous deeds will be remembered; but for that same injustice of his which he has committed he will die. 14 But when I say to the wicked, 'You will certainly die,' and he ᴬturns from his sin and practices ᴮjustice and righteousness, 15 *if a* wicked person returns a pledge, ᴬpays back what he has taken by robbery, walks by the statutes which ensure life without committing injustice, he shall certainly live; he shall not die. 16 ᴬNone of his sins that he has committed will be remembered against him. He has practiced

justice and righteousness; he shall certainly live.

17 "Yet your fellow citizens say, 'The way of the Lord is not right,' when it is their own way that is not right. 18 When the righteous turns from his righteousness and ᴬcommits injustice, then he shall die in it. 19 But when the wicked turns from his wickedness and practices justice and righteousness, he will live by them. 20 Yet you say, 'ᴬThe way of the Lord is not right.' I will judge each of you according to his ways, house of Israel."

WORD OF JERUSALEM'S CAPTURE

21 Now in the twelfth year of our exile, on the fifth of the tenth month, the survivor from Jerusalem came to me, saying, "ᴬThe city has been taken." 22 Now the ᴬhand of the LORD had been upon me in the evening, before the survivors came. And He ᴮopened my mouth at the time *they* came to me in the morning; so my mouth was opened and I was no longer speechless.

23 Then the word of the LORD came to me, saying, 24 "Son of man, they who ᴬlive in these ruins in the land of Israel are saying, 'Abraham was *only* one, yet he possessed the land; so to ᴮus who are many the land has been given as a possession.' 25 Therefore say to them, 'This is what the Lord GOD says: "You eat *meat* with the ᴬblood *in it,* raise your eyes to your idols as you shed blood. Should you then

33:9 ᴮEzek 3:19, 21   33:10 ᴬLev 26:39   ᴮIs 49:14
33:11 ᴬEzek 18:23, 32   ᴮJer 31:20   33:12 ᴬ2 Chr 7:14;
Ezek 18:21   33:13 ᴬEzek 18:26; Heb 10:38
33:14 ᴬIs 55:7   ᴮMic 6:8   33:15 ᴬEx 22:1-4; Lev 6:4, 5
33:16 ᴬIs 1:18; 43:25   33:18 ᴬEzek 3:20; 18:24
33:20 ᴬEzek 18:25   33:21 ᴬ2 Kin 25:10; Jer 39:8
33:22 ᴬEzek 1:3   ᴮEzek 3:26, 27   33:24 ᴬJer 39:10
ᴮEzek 11:15   33:25 ᴬLev 17:10, 12, 14; Deut 12:16, 23

possess the land? ²⁶You ^rely on your sword, you commit abominations, and each of you defiles his neighbor's wife. Should you then possess the land?"' ²⁷You shall say this to them: 'This is what the Lord GOD says: "As I live, those who are in the places of ruins certainly will ^fall by the sword, and whoever is in the open field I will give to the animals to be devoured, and those who are in the strongholds and in the ^Bcaves will die of plague. ²⁸And I will ^make the land a desolation and a waste, and the pride of her power will be brought to an end; and the mountains of Israel will be deserted so that no one will pass through. ²⁹Then they will know that I am the LORD, when I make the land a desolation and a waste because of all their abominations which they have committed."'

³⁰"But as for you, son of man, your fellow citizens who talk with one another about you by the walls and in the doorways of the houses, speak one with another, each with his brother, saying, '^Come now and hear what the message is that comes from the LORD.' ³¹And they come to you as people come, and sit before you *as* My people and hear your words, but they do not do them; for they do the lustful desires *expressed* by their ^mouth, *and* their heart follows their unlawful gain. ³²And behold, you are to them like a love song *by one who has* a ^beautiful voice and plays well on an instrument; for they hear your words but they do not practice them. ³³So when it ^comes—as it certainly will—then they will know that a prophet has been among them."

PROPHECY AGAINST THE SHEPHERDS OF ISRAEL

34 Then the word of the LORD came to me, saying, ²"Son of man, prophesy against the ^shepherds of Israel. Prophesy and say to those shepherds, 'This is what the Lord GOD says: "Woe, shepherds of Israel who have been ^Bfeeding themselves! Should the shepherds not feed the flock? ³You ^eat the fat and clothe yourselves with the wool, you ^Bslaughter the fat *sheep* without feeding the flock. ⁴Those who are sickly you have not strengthened, the diseased you have not healed, ^the broken you have not bound up, the scattered you have not brought back, nor have you searched for the lost; but with force and with violence you have dominated them. ⁵They scattered for lack of a shepherd, and they became ^food for every animal of the field and scattered. ⁶My flock ^strayed through all the mountains and on every high hill; My flock was scattered over all the surface of the earth, and there was ^Bno one to search or seek *for them*."'"

⁷Therefore, you shepherds, hear the word of the LORD: ⁸"As I live," declares the Lord GOD, "certainly, because My flock has become ^plunder, and My flock has become food for all the animals of the field for lack of a shepherd, and My shepherds did not search for My flock, but *rather* the shepherds fed themselves and did not feed My flock, ⁹therefore, you shepherds,

33:26^Mic 2:1, 2; Zeph 3:3 **33:27**^Jer 15:2, 3 ^B1 Sam 13:6 **33:28**^Ezek 5:14; 6:14 **33:30**^Is 29:13; 58:2 **33:31**^Ps 78:36, 37; Is 29:13 **33:32**^Mark 6:20 **33:33**^Jer 28:9; Ezek 33:29 **34:2**^Jer 2:8 ^BEzek 22:25 **34:3**^Zech 11:16 ^BEzek 22:25, 27 **34:4**^Zech 11:16 **34:5**^Ezek 34:8, 28 **34:6**^Jer 40:11, 12 ^BPs 142:4 **34:8**^Acts 20:29

hear the word of the LORD: [10] 'This is what the Lord GOD says: "Behold, I am against the shepherds, and I will demand My sheep from them and make them ^stop tending sheep. So the shepherds will not feed themselves anymore, but I will ^Bsave My sheep from their mouth, so that they will not be food for them."'"

THE RESTORATION OF ISRAEL

[11] For the Lord GOD says this: "Behold, I Myself will ^search for My sheep and look after them. [12] As a shepherd cares for his flock on a day when he is among his scattered sheep, so I will ^care for My sheep and will rescue them from all the places where they were scattered on a ^Bcloudy and gloomy day. [13] I will bring them out from the peoples and gather them from the countries and bring them to their own land; and I will ^feed them on the mountains of Israel, by the ^Bstreams, and in all the inhabited places of the land. [14] I will feed them in a ^good pasture, and their grazing place will be on the mountain heights of Israel. There they will lie down in a good grazing place and feed in rich pasture on the mountains of Israel. [15] I Myself will ^feed My flock and I Myself will lead them to rest," declares the Lord GOD. [16] "I will seek the lost, bring back the scattered, bind up the broken, and strengthen the sick; but the ^fat and the strong I will eliminate. I will ^Bfeed them with judgment.

[17] "As for you, My flock, this is what the Lord GOD says: 'Behold, I am going to ^judge between one sheep and another, between the rams and the male goats. [18] Is it too ^little a thing for you to feed in the good pasture, that you must

trample with your feet the rest of your pastures? Or *too little for you* to drink the clear waters, that you must muddy the rest with your feet? [19] But as for My flock, they must eat what you trample with your feet, and drink what you muddy with your feet!'"

[20] Therefore, this is what the Lord GOD says to them: "Behold, I, I Myself will also judge between the fat sheep and the lean sheep. [21] Since you push away with *your* side and shoulder, and ^gore all the weak with your horns until you have scattered them abroad, [22] therefore, I will ^save My flock, and they will no longer be plunder; and I will judge between one sheep and another.

[23] "Then I will ^appoint over them one ^Bshepherd, My servant David, and he will feed them; he will feed them himself and be their shepherd. [24] And I, the LORD, will be their God, and My servant ^David will be prince among them; I the LORD have spoken.

[25] "And I will make a covenant of peace with them and ^eliminate harmful animals from the land, so that they may ^Blive securely in the wilderness and sleep in the woods. [26] I will make them and the places around My hill a ^blessing. And I will make ^Bshowers fall in their season; they will be showers of blessing. [27] Also the tree of the field will yield its fruit and the earth will yield its produce, and they will be ^secure on their land. Then they will know

34:10 ^1 Sam 2:29, 30　^BPs 72:12-14　34:11 ^Ezek 11:17; 20:41　34:12 ^Is 40:11　^BJer 13:16　34:13 ^Ezek 34:23　^BIs 30:25　34:14 ^Ps 23:2; Jer 31:12-14, 25 34:15 ^Ps 23:1, 2; Ezek 34:23　34:16 ^Is 10:16　^BIs 49:26 34:17 ^Ezek 20:38; 34:20-22　34:18 ^Num 16:9, 13; 2 Sam 7:19　34:21 ^Deut 33:17; Dan 8:4 34:22 ^Ps 72:12-14; Jer 23:3　34:23 ^Rev 7:17　^BIs 40:11 34:24 ^Is 55:3; Jer 30:9　34:25 ^Job 5:22, 23　^BJer 33:16 34:26 ^Gen 12:2　^BDeut 11:13-15　34:27 ^Ezek 38:8, 11

that I am the LORD, when I have broken the bars of their yoke and have saved them from the hand of those who enslaved them. 28 They will no longer be plunder to the nations, and the animals of the earth will not devour them; but they will ᴬlive securely, and no one will make *them* afraid. 29 I will establish for them a ᴬrenowned planting place, and they will not again be victims of famine in the land, and they will not ᴮendure the insults of the nations anymore. 30 Then they will know that ᴬI, the LORD their God, am with them, and that they, the house of Israel, are My people," declares the Lord GOD. 31 "As for you, My ᴬsheep, the sheep of My pasture, you are mankind, *and* I am your God," declares the Lord GOD.

PROPHECY AGAINST MOUNT SEIR

35 Now the word of the LORD came to me, saying, 2 "Son of man, set your face against ᴬMount Seir, and prophesy against it 3 and say to it, 'This is what the Lord GOD says:

"Behold, I am against you,
    Mount Seir,
And I will reach out with My
    hand against you
And make you a ᴬdesolation
    and a waste.
4 "I will ᴬturn your cities to ruins,
    And you will become a
    desolation.
Then you will know that I am
    the LORD.

5 Since you have had everlasting ᴬhostility and have turned over the sons of Israel to the power of the sword at the time of their disaster, at the time of the ᴮpunishment of the end, 6 therefore as I live," declares the Lord GOD, "I will certainly doom you to ᴬbloodshed, and bloodshed

will pursue you; since you have not hated bloodshed, therefore bloodshed will pursue you. 7 I will make Mount Seir a waste and a desolation and I will eliminate from it one who passes through and returns. 8 I will ᴬfill its mountains with its slain; those killed by the sword will fall on your hills, in your valleys, and in all your ravines. 9 I will make you a permanent ᴬdesolation, and your cities will not be inhabited. Then you will know that I am the LORD.

10 "Since you have ᴬsaid, 'These two nations and these two lands will be mine, and we will possess them,' although the LORD was there, 11 therefore as I live," declares the Lord GOD, "I will deal *with you* ᴬaccording to your anger and according to your envy which you displayed because of your hatred for them; so I will make Myself known among them when I judge you. 12 Then you will know that I, the LORD, have heard all your insults which you have spoken against the mountains of Israel saying, 'They are desolate; they have been ᴬgiven to us as food.' 13 And you have ᴬspoken arrogantly against Me and have multiplied your words against Me; I Myself have heard *it*." 14 This is what the Lord GOD says: "As all the ᴬearth rejoices, I will make you a desolation. 15 As you rejoiced over the inheritance of the house of Israel because it was desolate, ᴬso I will do to you. You will be a ᴮdesolation,

34:28 ᴬJer 30:10; Ezek 39:26   34:29 ᴬIs 4:2
ᴮEzek 36:6, 15   34:30 ᴬPs 46:7, 11; Ezek 14:11
34:31 ᴬPs 78:52; 80:1   35:2 ᴬGen 36:8; Ezek 25:12
35:3 ᴬJer 49:13, 17, 18; Ezek 35:7   35:4 ᴬEzek 6:6; 35:9
35:5 ᴬPs 137:7   ᴮEzek 7:2   35:6 ᴬIs 63:2-6; Ezek 16:38
35:8 ᴬIs 34:5, 6; Ezek 31:12   35:9 ᴬJer 49:13; Ezek 25:13
35:10 ᴬPs 83:4-12; Ezek 36:2, 5   35:11 ᴬPs 137:7;
Ezek 25:14   35:12 ᴬJer 50:7; Ezek 36:2
35:13 ᴬIs 10:13, 14; 36:20   35:14 ᴬIs 44:23; 49:13
35:15 ᴬObad 15   ᴮIs 34:5, 6

Mount Seir, and all Edom, all of it. Then they will know that I am the LORD."'

THE MOUNTAINS OF ISRAEL
TO BE BLESSED

36 "Now you, son of man, prophesy to the mountains of Israel and say, 'You mountains of Israel, hear the word of the LORD. ²This is what the Lord GOD says: "Since the enemy has spoken against you, 'Aha!' and, 'The everlasting ^heights have become our possession,' ³therefore prophesy and say, 'This is what the Lord GOD says: "For good reason they have made you ^desolate and harassed you from every side, so that you would become a possession of the rest of the nations; and you have been taken up in the talk and the rumor of the people."'" ⁴Therefore, you mountains of Israel, hear the word of the Lord GOD. This is what the Lord GOD says to the mountains and to the hills, to the ravines and to the valleys, to the desolate ruins and to the abandoned cities which have become ^plunder and an object of ridicule to the rest of the nations which are all around— ⁵therefore the Lord GOD says this: "Certainly in the fire of My ^jealousy I have spoken against the ^Brest of the nations, and against all Edom, who appropriated My land for themselves as a possession with wholehearted joy *and* with contempt of soul, in order to *make* its pastureland plunder." ⁶Therefore prophesy in regard to the land of Israel and say to the mountains and to the hills, to the ravines and to the valleys, "This is what the Lord GOD says: 'Behold, I have spoken in My jealousy and in My wrath because

you have ^endured the insults of the nations.' ⁷Therefore the Lord GOD says this: 'I have sworn that the nations that are around you will certainly endure their insults themselves. ⁸But as for you, mountains of Israel, you will ^grow your branches and bear fruit for My people Israel; for they are about to come. ⁹For, behold, I am for you, and I will ^turn to you, and you will be ^Bcultivated and sown. ¹⁰And I will multiply people on you, ^all the house of Israel, all of it; and the cities will be inhabited and the ruins will be rebuilt. ¹¹I will multiply on you people and animals, and they will increase and be fruitful; and I will populate you as you were previously, and treat you ^better than at the beginning. Then you will know that I am the LORD. ¹²Yes, I will have ^people—My people Israel—walk on you and possess you, so that you will become their ^Binheritance and never again bereave them of children.'

¹³"The Lord GOD says this: 'Since they say to you, "You are a ^devourer of people and have bereaved your nation of children," ¹⁴for that reason you will no longer devour people and no longer bereave your nation of children,' declares the Lord GOD. ¹⁵I will not let you hear insults from the nations anymore, nor will you suffer disgrace from the peoples any longer, nor will you make your nation ^stumble any longer," declares the Lord GOD.'"

¹⁶Then the word of the LORD came to me, saying, ¹⁷"Son of man, when the house of Israel was living

36:2^Deut 32:13; Ps 78:69   **36:3**^Jer 2:15
36:4^Ezek 34:8, 28   **36:5**^Ezek 5:13   ^BJer 25:9, 15-29
36:6^Ps 74:10; 123:3, 4   **36:8**^Is 4:2; Ezek 17:23
36:9^Lev 26:9   ^BEzek 28:26   **36:10**^Is 27:6; 49:17-23
36:11^Job 42:12; Is 51:3   **36:12**^Ezek 34:13, 14
^BEzek 47:14   **36:13**^Num 13:32   **36:15**^Is 63:13; Jer 13:16

on their own land, they ^defiled it by their ways and their deeds; their way before Me was like the uncleanness of a woman in her impurity. ¹⁸Therefore I ^poured out My wrath on them for the blood which they had shed on the land, because they had defiled it with their idols. ¹⁹I also ^scattered them among the nations, and they were dispersed throughout the lands. According to their ways and their deeds I judged them. ²⁰When they came to the nations where they went, they ^profaned My holy name, because it was said of them, 'These are the ^Bpeople of the Lord, yet they have left His land.' ²¹But I had concern for My ^holy name, which the house of Israel had profaned among the nations where they went.

ISRAEL TO BE RENEWED
FOR HIS NAME'S SAKE

²²"Therefore say to the house of Israel, 'This is what the Lord God says: "It is ^not for your sake, house of Israel, that I am about to act, but for My holy name, which you have profaned among the nations where you went. ²³And I will ^vindicate the holiness of My great name which has been profaned among the nations, which you have profaned among them. Then the ^Bnations will know that I am the Lord," declares the Lord God, "when I show Myself holy among you in their sight. ²⁴For I will ^take you from the nations, and gather you from all the lands; and I will bring you into your own land. ²⁵Then I will sprinkle clean water on you, and you will be clean; I will cleanse you from all your ^filthiness and from all your ^Bidols. ²⁶Moreover, I will give you a new

heart and put a new spirit within you; and I will remove the ^heart of stone from your flesh and give you a heart of flesh. ²⁷And I will ^put My Spirit within you and bring it about that you walk in My statutes, and are careful and follow My ordinances. ²⁸And you will live in the land that I gave to your forefathers; so you will be ^My people, and I will be your God. ²⁹Moreover, I will save you from all your uncleanness; and I will call for the grain and multiply it, and I ^will not bring a famine on you. ³⁰Instead, I will ^multiply the fruit of the tree and the produce of the field, so that you will not receive again the disgrace of famine among the nations. ³¹Then you will ^remember your evil ways and your deeds that were not good, and you will loathe yourselves in your own sight for your wrongdoings and your abominations. ³²I am not doing *this* ^for your sake," declares the Lord God; "let *that* be known to you. Be ashamed and humiliated for your ways, house of Israel!"

³³'This is what the Lord God says: "On the day that I cleanse you from all your wrongdoings, I will populate the ^cities, and the ^Bplaces of ruins will be rebuilt. ³⁴The desolated land will be cultivated instead of being a desolation in the sight of everyone who passes by. ³⁵And they will say, 'This desolated land has become like the ^Garden of Eden; and the waste, desolated

36:17^Jer 2:7   36:18^2 Chr 34:21, 25; Lam 2:4
36:19^Deut 28:64; Ezek 5:12   36:20^Is 52:5
^BJer 33:24   36:21^Ps 74:18; Is 48:9   36:22^Deut 7:7, 8;
9:5, 6   36:23^Is 5:16   ^BPs 102:15   36:24^Is 43:5, 6;
Ezek 34:13   36:25^Is 4:4   ^BIs 2:18, 20
36:26^Ezek 11:19; Zech 7:12   36:27^Is 44:3; 59:21
36:28^Ezek 14:11; 37:23, 27   36:29^Ezek 34:27, 29;
Hos 2:21-23   36:30^Lev 26:4; Ezek 34:27
36:31^Ezek 16:61-63; 20:43   36:32^Deut 9:5
36:33^Ezek 36:10   ^BIs 58:12   36:35^Is 51:3; Ezek 31:9

and ruined cities are fortified *and* inhabited.' [36]Then the nations around you that are left will know that I, the LORD, have rebuilt the ruined places *and* planted that which was desolated; I, the LORD, have spoken, and I ^will do it."

[37]'This is what the Lord GOD says: "This too I will let the house of Israel ask Me to do for them: I will increase their people like a flock. [38]Like the flock for sacrifices, like the flock at Jerusalem during her appointed feasts, so will the waste cities be filled with ^flocks of people. Then they will know that I am the LORD."'

VISION OF THE VALLEY OF DRY BONES

37 The hand of the LORD was upon me, and He ^brought me out by the Spirit of the LORD and set me down in the middle of the valley; and it was full of bones. [2]He had me pass among them all around, and behold, *there were* very many on the surface of the valley; and behold, *they were* very dry. [3]Then He said to me, "Son of man, ^can these bones live?" And I answered, "Lord GOD, ^BYou Yourself know." [4]Again He said to me, "^Prophesy over these bones and say to them, 'You dry bones, hear the word of the LORD.' [5]This is what the Lord GOD says to these bones: 'Behold, I am going to make [1],^breath enter you so that you may come to life. [6]And I will attach tendons to you, make flesh grow back on you, cover you with skin, and put breath in you so that you may come to life; and you will ^know that I am the LORD.'"

[7]So I prophesied ^as I was commanded; and as I prophesied, there was a *loud* noise, and behold, a rattling; and the bones came together, bone to its bone. [8]And I looked, and behold, tendons were on them, and flesh grew and skin covered them; but there was no breath in them. [9]Then He said to me, "Prophesy to the breath, prophesy, son of man, and say to the breath, 'The Lord GOD says this: "Come from the four winds, breath, and ^breathe on these slain, so that they come to life."'" [10]So I prophesied as He commanded me, and the ^breath entered them, and they came to life and stood on their feet, an ^Bexceedingly great army.

THE VISION EXPLAINED

[11]Then He said to me, "Son of man, these bones are the ^entire house of Israel; behold, they say, 'Our bones are dried up and our hope has perished. We are completely cut off.' [12]Therefore prophesy and say to them, 'This is what the Lord GOD says: "Behold, I am going to open your graves and ^cause you to come up out of your graves, My people; and I will bring you into the land of Israel. [13]Then you will know that I am the LORD, when I have opened your graves and caused you to come up out of your graves, My people. [14]And I will ^put My ¹Spirit within you and you will come to life, and I will place you on your own land. Then you will know that I, the LORD, have spoken and done it," declares the LORD.'"

36:36^Ezek 17:24; 22:14   **36:38**^Ps 74:1; 100:3
37:1^Ezek 8:3; 11:24   **37:3**^Ezek 26:19   ^BDeut 32:39
37:4^Ezek 37:9, 12   **37:5**^Gen 2:7; Ps 104:29, 30
37:6^Is 49:23; Ezek 35:9   **37:7**^Jer 13:5-7
37:9^Ps 104:30   **37:10**^Rev 11:11   ^BJer 30:19
37:11^Jer 33:24; Ezek 36:10   **37:12**^Deut 32:39;
1 Sam 2:6   **37:14**^Is 32:15; Ezek 11:19

37:5¹Or *spirit,* and so throughout the ch   **37:14**¹Or *breath*

REUNION OF JUDAH AND ISRAEL

¹⁵The word of the LORD came again to me, saying, ¹⁶"Now you, son of man, take for yourself one stick and write on it, 'For ᴬJudah and for the sons of Israel, his companions'; then take another stick and write on it, 'For ᴮJoseph, the stick of Ephraim and all the house of Israel, his companions.' ¹⁷Then ᴬput them together for yourself one to another into one stick, so that they may become one in your hand. ¹⁸And when the sons of your people speak to you, saying, 'Will you not declare to us ᴬwhat you mean by these?' ¹⁹say to them, 'This is what the Lord GOD says: "Behold, I am going to take the stick of Joseph, which is in the hand of Ephraim, and the tribes of Israel, his companions; and I will put them with it, with the stick of Judah, and make them one stick, and they will be one in My hand."' ²⁰The sticks on which you write will be in your hand before their eyes. ²¹And say to them, 'This is what the Lord GOD says: "Behold, I am going to ᴬtake the sons of Israel from among the nations where they have gone, and I will gather them from every side and bring them into their own land; ²²and I will make them ᴬone nation in the land, on the mountains of Israel; and ᴮone king will be king for all of them; and they will no longer be two nations, and no longer be divided into two kingdoms. ²³They will no longer defile themselves with their idols, or with their detestable things, or with any of their offenses; but ᴬI will rescue them from all their ¹dwelling places in which they have sinned, and will cleanse them. And they will be My people, and I will be their God.

THE DAVIDIC KINGDOM

²⁴"And My servant ᴬDavid will be king over them, and they will all have one shepherd; and they will walk in My ordinances, and keep My statutes and follow them. ²⁵And they will live on the land that I gave to My servant Jacob, in which your fathers lived; and they will live on it, they, and their sons and their sons' sons, forever; and My servant ᴬDavid will be their leader forever. ²⁶And I will make a covenant of peace with them; it will be an ᴬeverlasting covenant with them. And I will place them and multiply them, and set My ᴮsanctuary in their midst forever. ²⁷My ᴬdwelling place also will be among them; and I will be their God, and they will be My people. ²⁸And the nations will know that I am the LORD ᴬwho sanctifies Israel, when My sanctuary is in their midst forever."'"

PROPHECY ABOUT GOG AND FUTURE INVASION OF ISRAEL

38 Now the word of the LORD came to me, saying, ²"Son of man, set your face toward ᴬGog of the land of ᴮMagog, the chief prince of Meshech and Tubal, and prophesy against him, ³and say, 'This is what the Lord GOD says: "Behold, I am against you, Gog, chief prince of Meshech and Tubal. ⁴So I will turn you around and put hooks into your jaws, and I will ᴬbring you out, and all your army, horses

---

37:16 ᴬ2 Chr 10:17   ᴮ1 Kin 12:16-20   37:17 ᴬIs 11:13; Jer 50:4   37:18 ᴬEzek 12:9; 17:12   37:21 ᴬIs 43:5, 6; Jer 29:14   37:22 ᴬJer 3:18   ᴮEzek 34:23, 24
37:23 ᴬEzek 36:28, 29   37:24 ᴬJer 30:9; Ezek 34:24
37:25 ᴬIs 11:1; Ezek 37:24   37:26 ᴬPs 89:3, 4
ᴮEzek 20:40   37:27 ᴬJohn 1:14; Rev 21:3
37:28 ᴬEx 31:13; Ezek 20:12   38:2 ᴬEzek 38:3, 14, 16, 18
ᴮGen 10:2   38:4 ᴬIs 43:17

37:23 ¹Another reading is offenses

and horsemen, all of them magnificently dressed, a great contingent *with* shield and ¹buckler, all of them wielding swords; ⁵ᴬPersia, ᴮCush, and Put with them, all of them *with* buckler and helmet; ⁶Gomer with all its troops; ᴬBethtogarmah *from* the remote parts of the north with all its troops—many peoples with you.

⁷"ᴬBe ready, and be prepared, you and all your contingents that are assembled around you, and be a guard for them. ⁸After many days you will be summoned; in the latter years you will come into the land that is restored from the sword, *whose inhabitants* have been ᴬgathered from many nations to the mountains of Israel which had been a continual place of ruins; but its people were brought out from the nations, and they are living securely, all of them. ⁹And you will go up, you will come ᴬlike a storm; you will be like a ᴮcloud covering the land, you and all your troops, and many peoples with you."

¹⁰'This is what the Lord GOD says: "It will come about on that day, that thoughts will come into your mind and you will ᴬdevise an evil plan, ¹¹and you will say, 'I will go up against the land of ᴬunwalled villages. I will go against those who are ᴮat rest, who live securely, all of them living without walls and having no bars or gates, ¹²to ᴬcapture spoils and to seize plunder, to turn your hand against the ruins that are *now* inhabited, and against the people who are gathered from the nations, who have acquired livestock and goods, who live at the center of the world.' ¹³Sheba and Dedan and the merchants of ᴬTarshish with all its villages will say to you, 'Have you come to capture spoils? Have you assembled your contingent to seize plunder, to carry away silver and gold, to take away livestock and goods, to capture great ᴮspoils?'"'

¹⁴"Therefore prophesy, son of man, and say to Gog, 'This is what the Lord GOD says: "On that day when My people Israel are ᴬliving securely, will you not know *it*? ¹⁵ᴬYou will come from your place out of the remote parts of the north, you and many peoples with you, all of them riding horses, a large assembly and a mighty army; ¹⁶and you will come up against My people Israel like a cloud to cover the land. It shall come about in the last days that I will bring you against My land, so that the nations may know Me when I ᴬshow Myself holy through you before their eyes, Gog."

¹⁷'This is what the Lord GOD says: "Are you the one of whom I spoke in former days through My servants the prophets of Israel, who ᴬprophesied in those days for *many* years that I would bring you against them? ¹⁸It will come about on that day, when Gog comes against the land of Israel," declares the Lord GOD, "that My fury will mount up in My ᴬanger. ¹⁹In My zeal and in My blazing wrath I declare *that* on that day there will certainly be a great ᴬearthquake in the land of Israel. ²⁰ᴬThe fish of the sea, the birds of the sky, the animals of the field, all

---

38:5ᴬ2 Chr 36:20   ᴮGen 10:6-8   38:6ᴬGen 10:3;
Ezek 27:14   38:7ᴬIs 8:9   38:8ᴬIs 11:11; Ezek 36:24
38:9ᴬIs 5:28   ᴮEzek 30:18   38:10ᴬPs 36:4; Mic 2:1
38:11ᴬZech 2:4   ᴮJer 49:31   38:12ᴬIs 10:6; Ezek 29:19
38:13ᴬEzek 27:12   ᴮIs 10:6   38:14ᴬJer 23:6;
Ezek 38:8, 11   38:15ᴬEzek 39:2   38:16ᴬIs 5:16; 8:13
38:17ᴬIs 5:26-29; 34:1-6   38:18ᴬPs 18:8, 15
38:19ᴬJoel 3:16; Hag 2:6, 7, 21   38:20ᴬJer 4:24, 25

38:4 ¹ I.e., small shield

the crawling things that crawl on the earth, and all mankind who are on the face of the earth will shake at My presence; and the ᴮmountains will be thrown down, the steep pathways will collapse, and every wall will fall to the ground. ²¹And I will call for a ᴬsword against ¹him on all My mountains," declares the Lord Gᴏᴅ. "ᴮEvery man's sword will be against his brother. ²²With plague and with blood I will enter into ᴬjudgment with him; and I will rain on him and on his troops, and on the many peoples who are with him, a torrential rain, hailstones, fire, and brimstone. ²³So I will prove Myself great, show Myself holy, and ᴬmake Myself known in the sight of many nations; and they will know that I am the Lᴏʀᴅ."'

PROPHECY AGAINST GOG— INVADERS DESTROYED

39 "And ᴬyou, son of man, prophesy against Gog and say, 'This is what the Lord Gᴏᴅ says: "Behold, I am against you, Gog, chief prince of Meshech and Tubal; ²and I will turn you around, lead you on a rope, take you up from the remotest parts of the north, and bring you against the mountains of Israel. ³Then I will ᴬstrike your bow from your left hand and make your arrows fall from your right hand. ⁴You will ᴬfall on the mountains of Israel, you and all your troops, and the peoples who are with you; I will give you as food to every kind of predatory bird and animal of the field. ⁵You will fall on the open field; for it is I who have spoken," declares the Lord Gᴏᴅ. ⁶"And I will send ᴬfire upon Magog and those who inhabit the ᴮcoastlands in safety; and they will know that I am the Lᴏʀᴅ.

⁷"And I will make My holy name known in the midst of My people Israel; and I will not allow My holy name to be ᴬprofaned anymore. But the nations will know that I am the Lᴏʀᴅ, the Holy One in Israel. ⁸Behold, it is coming and it shall be done," declares the Lord Gᴏᴅ. "That is the day of which I have spoken.

⁹"Then those who inhabit the cities of Israel will ᴬgo out and make ᴮfires with the weapons and burn *them,* both ¹bucklers and shields, bows and arrows, war clubs and spears, and for seven years they will make fires of them. ¹⁰They will not take wood from the field or gather firewood from the forests, because they will make fires with the weapons; and they will take the spoils of those who plundered them and seize the ᴬplunder of those who plundered them," declares the Lord Gᴏᴅ.

¹¹"On that day I will give Gog a burial place there in Israel, the valley of those who pass by east of the sea, and it will block the way of those who would pass by. So they will bury Gog there with all his horde, and they will call *it* the Valley of Hamongog. ¹²For seven months the house of Israel will be burying them in order to ᴬcleanse the land. ¹³And all the people of the land will bury *them;* and it will be to their ᴬrenown *on* the day that I ᴮappear in My glory," declares the Lord Gᴏᴅ. ¹⁴"They will

38:20 ᴮZech 14:4   **38:21** ᴬEzek 14:17   ¹Judg 7:22
38:22 ᴬIs 66:16; Jer 25:31   **38:23** ᴬPs 9:16; Ezek 37:28
39:1 ᴬEzek 38:2   **39:3** ᴬPs 76:3; Jer 21:4, 5
39:4 ᴬIs 14:24, 25; Ezek 39:17-20   **39:6** ᴬEzek 30:8, 16
ᴮPs 72:10   **39:7** ᴬEx 20:7; Ezek 20:9, 14, 39
39:9 ᴬIs 66:24   ᴮJosh 11:6   **39:10** ᴬIs 14:2; 33:1
39:12 ᴬDeut 21:23; Ezek 39:14, 16   **39:13** ᴬJer 33:9
ᴮEzek 28:22

38:21 ¹I.e., Gog   **39:9** ¹I.e., small shields

also select men who will constantly pass through the land, ^burying those who were passing through, those left on the surface of the ground, in order to cleanse it. At the end of seven months they will conduct a search. ¹⁵As those who pass through the land pass through and anyone sees a human bone, then he will set up a marker by it until the burial detail has buried it in the Valley of Hamon-gog. ¹⁶And even *the* name of *the* city will be Hamonah. So they will cleanse the land."'

¹⁷"Now as for you, son of man, this is what the Lord God says: 'Say to every kind of ^bird and to every animal of the field: "Assemble and come, gather from every direction to My sacrifice, which I am going to sacrifice for you as a great sacrifice on the mountains of Israel; and you will eat flesh and drink blood. ¹⁸You will eat the flesh of warriors and drink the blood of the leaders of the earth, *as though they were* ^rams, lambs, goats, *and* ^bulls, all of them fattened livestock of Bashan. ¹⁹So you will eat fat until you are full, and drink blood until you are drunk, from My sacrifice which I have sacrificed for you. ²⁰You will eat your fill at My table *with* ^horses and charioteers, *with* warriors and all the men of war," declares the Lord God.

²¹"And I will place My ^glory among the nations; and all the nations will see My judgment which I have executed, and My hand which I have laid on them. ²²And the house of Israel will ^know that I am the Lord their God, from that day onward. ²³The nations will know that the house of Israel went into exile for their ^wrongdoing, because they were disloyal to Me, and I hid My face from them; so I handed them over to their adversaries, and all of them fell by the sword. ²⁴^In accordance with their uncleanness and their offenses I dealt with them, and I hid My face from them."''

ISRAEL RESTORED

²⁵Therefore this is what the Lord God says: "Now I will ^restore the fortunes of Jacob and have mercy on all the house of Israel; and I will be jealous for My holy name. ²⁶They will ¹forget their disgrace and all their treachery which they perpetrated against Me, when they ^live securely on their *own* land with ^no one to make *them* afraid. ²⁷When I ^bring them back from the peoples and gather them from the lands of their enemies, then I shall show Myself holy through them in the sight of the many nations. ²⁸Then they will know that I am the Lord their God because I made them go into exile among the nations, and *then* I gathered them *again* to their own land; and I will leave none of them there any longer. ²⁹I will not hide My face from them any longer, for I will have ^poured out My Spirit on the house of Israel," declares the Lord God.

VISION OF THE MAN WITH A MEASURING ROD

40 In the twenty-fifth year of our exile, at the beginning of the year, on the tenth of the month, in the fourteenth year after the ^city was taken, on this

39:14 ^Jer 14:16   39:17 ^Is 56:9; Jer 12:9   39:18 ^Jer 51:40
^Jer 50:27   39:20 ^Ps 76:5, 6; Ezek 38:4   39:21 ^Ex 9:16;
Is 37:20   39:22 ^Jer 24:7   39:23 ^Jer 22:8, 9; 44:22
39:24 ^2 Kin 17:7; Jer 2:17, 19   39:25 ^Is 27:12, 13; Jer 33:7
39:26 ^1 Kin 4:25   ^Is 17:2   39:27 ^Ezek 36:24; 37:21
39:29 ^Is 32:15; Ezek 36:27   40:1 ^2 Kin 25:1-7

39:26 ¹Another reading is *bear*

very day the [B]hand of the LORD was upon me and He brought me there. [2]In the visions of God He brought me into the land of Israel and set me on a very [A]high mountain, and on it to the south *there was something* like a [B]structure of a city. [3]So He brought me there; and behold, there was a man whose appearance was like the appearance of [A]bronze, with a thread of flax and a [B]measuring rod in his hand; and he was standing in the gateway. [4]And the man said to me, "Son of man, [A]see with your eyes, hear with your ears, and pay attention to all that I am going to show you; for you have been brought here in order to show *it* to you. [B]Declare to the house of Israel all that you see."

MEASUREMENTS RELATING TO THE TEMPLE

[5]And behold, there was a [A]wall on the outside of the temple all around, and in the man's hand was a measuring rod of six [1]cubits, each of which was a [2]cubit and a hand width. So he measured the thickness of the wall, one rod; and the height, one rod. [6]Then he went to the gate which faced [A]east, went up its steps, and measured the threshold of the gate, one rod in width; and the other threshold *was* one rod in width. [7]The [A]guardroom *was* one rod long and one rod wide; and *there were* five cubits between the guardrooms. And the threshold of the gate by the porch of the gate facing inward *was* one rod. [8]Then he measured the porch of the gate facing inward, one rod. [9]And he measured the porch of the gate, eight cubits; and its side pillars, two cubits. And the porch of the gate was faced inward. [10]The

guardrooms of the gate toward the east *numbered* three on each side; the three of them had the same measurement. The side pillars also had the same measurement on each side. [11]And he measured the width of the gateway, ten cubits, *and* the length of the gate, thirteen cubits. [12]*There was* a barrier *wall* one cubit *wide* in front of the guardrooms on each side; and the guardrooms *were* six cubits *square* on each side. [13]And he measured the gate from the roof of the one guardroom to the roof of the other, a width of twenty-five cubits, from *one* door to *the* door opposite. [14]He made the side pillars sixty cubits *high;* the gate *extended* all around to the side pillar of the [A]courtyard. [15]And *from* the front of the entrance gate to the front of the inner porch of the gate *was* fifty cubits. [16]And *there were* [A]shuttered windows *looking* toward the guardrooms, and toward their side pillars within the gate all around, and likewise for the porches. And *there were* windows all around inside; and on *each* side pillar *were* palm tree decorations.

[17]Then he brought me into the outer courtyard, and behold, *there were* [A]chambers and a stone pavement made for the courtyard all around; thirty chambers faced the pavement. [18]And the pavement (*that is,* the lower pavement) *was* by the side of the gates, corresponding to the length of the gates. [19]Then he

40:1 [B]Ezek 1:3   40:2 [A]Is 2:2, 3   [B]1 Chr 28:12, 19
40:3 [A]Ezek 1:7   [B]Rev 11:1   40:4 [A]Ezek 2:7, 8   [B]Is 21:10
40:5 [A]Is 26:1; Ezek 42:20   40:6 [A]Ezek 8:16; 11:1
40:7 [A]Ezek 40:10-16, 21   40:14 [A]Ex 27:9; 1 Chr 28:6
40:16 [A]1 Kin 6:4; Ezek 41:16, 26   40:17 [A]2 Kin 23:11;
1 Chr 9:26

40:5 [1]I.e., "long" cubits, see note 2   [2]A cubit and
hand width equals about 21 in. or 53 cm

measured the width from the front of the ᴬlower gate to the front of the exterior of the inner courtyard, a hundred cubits on the east and on the north.

²⁰ And *as for* the ᴬgate of the outer courtyard which faced north, he measured its length and its width. ²¹ It had three ᴬguardrooms on each side; and its ᴮside pillars and its porches had the same measurement as the first gate. Its length *was* fifty cubits, and the width twenty-five cubits. ²² Its ᴬwindows, its porches, and its palm tree decorations *had* the same measurements as the ᴮgate which faced east; and it was reached by seven steps, and its porch *was* in front of them. ²³ The inner courtyard had a gate opposite the gate on the north as well as *the gate* on the east; and he measured a ᴬhundred cubits from gate to gate.

²⁴ Then he led me toward the south, and behold, there was a ᴬgate toward the south; and he measured its side pillars and its porches according to those same measurements. ²⁵ The gate and its porches had ᴬwindows all around like those other windows; the length *was* fifty cubits and the width, twenty-five cubits. ²⁶ *There were* seven ᴬsteps going up to it, and its porches *were* in front of them; and it had palm tree decorations on its side pillars, one on each side. ²⁷ The inner courtyard had a gate toward the ᴬsouth; and he measured from gate to gate toward the south, a hundred cubits.

²⁸ Then he brought me to the inner courtyard by the south gate; and he measured the south gate ᴬaccording to those same measurements. ²⁹ Its ᴬguardrooms also, its side pillars, and its ᴮporches *were* according to those same measurements. And

the gate and its porches had ᴮwindows all around; it *was* fifty cubits long and twenty-five cubits wide. ³⁰ *There were* ᴬporches all around, twenty-five cubits long and five cubits wide. ³¹ And its porches *were* toward the outer courtyard; and palm tree decorations *were* on its side pillars, and its stairway *had* eight ᴬsteps.

³² Then he brought me into the ᴬinner courtyard toward the east. And he measured the gate according to those same measurements. ³³ Its ᴬguardrooms also, its side pillars, and its porches *were* according to those same measurements. And the gate and its porches had ᴮwindows all around; it *was* fifty cubits long and twenty-five cubits wide. ³⁴ Its ᴬporches *were* toward the outer courtyard; and ᴬpalm tree decorations *were* on its side pillars, on each side, and its stairway *had* eight steps.

³⁵ Then he brought me to the ᴬnorth gate; and he measured *it* according to those same measurements, ³⁶ *with* its ᴬguardrooms, its side pillars, and its ᴮporches. And the gate had windows all around; the length *was* fifty cubits and the width twenty-five cubits. ³⁷ And its side pillars *were* toward the outer courtyard; and palm tree decorations *were* on its side pillars, on each side, and its stairway had eight ᴬsteps.

40:19 ᴬEzek 40:23, 27; 46:1, 2   **40:20** ᴬEzek 40:6
40:21 ᴬEzek 40:7   ᴮEzek 40:16, 30   **40:22** ᴬEzek 40:16
ᴮEzek 40:6   **40:23** ᴬEzek 40:19, 27
40:24 ᴬEzek 40:6, 20, 35; 46:9   **40:25** ᴬEzek 40:16, 22, 29
40:26 ᴬEzek 40:6, 22   **40:27** ᴬEzek 40:23, 32
40:28 ᴬEzek 40:32, 35   **40:29** ᴬEzek 40:7, 10, 21
ᴮEzek 40:16, 22, 25   **40:30** ᴬEzek 40:16, 21
40:31 ᴬEzek 40:22, 26, 34, 37   **40:32** ᴬEzek 40:28-31, 35
40:33 ᴬEzek 40:29   ᴮEzek 40:16   **40:34** ᴬEzek 40:16
40:35 ᴬEzek 40:27, 32; 44:4   **40:36** ᴬEzek 40:7, 29
ᴮEzek 40:16   **40:37** ᴬEzek 40:34

³⁸ A ^chamber with its doorway was by the side pillars at the gates; there they ^Brinse the burnt offering. ³⁹ And in the porch of the gate *were* two ^tables on each side, on which to slaughter the ^Bburnt offering, the sin offering, and the guilt offering. ⁴⁰ On the outer side, as one went up to the gateway toward the north, *were* two tables; and on the other side of the porch of the gate *were* two tables. ⁴¹ Four ^tables *were* on each side next to the gate; eight tables on which they slaughter *sacrifices.* ⁴² For the burnt offering *there were* four tables of ^cut stone, a cubit and a half long, a cubit and a half wide, and one cubit high, on which they set the utensils with which they slaughter the burnt offering and the sacrifice. ⁴³ And the double hooks, ^1one hand width *in length,* were installed in the house all around; and on the tables *was* the flesh of the offering.

⁴⁴ From the outside to the inner gate were chambers for the ^singers in the inner courtyard, *one of* which was at the side of the north gate, with its front toward the south, *and* one at the side of the south gate facing north. ⁴⁵ Then he said to me, "This is the chamber which faces south, *intended* for the priests who are ^responsible for the temple; ⁴⁶ but the chamber which faces north is for the priests who are responsible for the altar. They are the ^sons of Zadok, who from the sons of Levi ^Bcome near to the LORD to serve Him." ⁴⁷ He measured the courtyard, a *perfect* square, a ^hundred cubits long and a hundred cubits wide; and the altar was in front of the temple.

⁴⁸ Then he brought me to the ^porch of the temple and measured *each* side pillar of the porch, five cubits on each side; and the width of the gate was three cubits on each side. ⁴⁹ The length of the porch *was* twenty cubits, and the width eleven cubits; and at the ^stairway by which it was ascended *were* ^Bcolumns *belonging* to the side pillars, one on each side.

THE INNER TEMPLE

41 Then he brought me to the ^sanctuary, and he measured the ^Bside pillars: six ^1cubits wide on each side *was* the width of the side pillar. ² The width of the entrance *was* ten cubits and the sides of the entrance *were* five cubits on each side. He also measured the length of the sanctuary, ^forty cubits, and the width, ^twenty cubits. ³ Then he went ^inside and measured *each* side pillar of the doorway, two cubits, and the doorway, six cubits *high;* and the width of the doorway, seven cubits. ⁴ And he measured its length, twenty cubits, and the width, twenty cubits, before the ^sanctuary; and he said to me, "This is the ^BMost Holy Place."

⁵ Then he measured the wall of the temple, six cubits; and the width of the ^side chambers, four cubits, all around the house on every side. ⁶ ^The side chambers were in three *stories,* one above another, and thirty in each story;

40:38 ^1 Chr 28:12   ^B 2 Chr 4:6   **40:39** ^Ezek 40:42
^B Lev 1:3–17   **40:41** ^Ezek 40:39, 40   **40:42** ^Ex 20:25
40:44 ^1 Chr 6:31, 32; 16:41–43   **40:45** ^1 Chr 9:23;
Ps 134:1   **40:46** ^1 Kin 2:35   ^B Lev 10:3
40:47 ^Ezek 40:19, 23, 27   **40:48** ^1 Kin 6:3; 2 Chr 3:4
40:49 ^Ezek 40:31, 34, 37   ^B 1 Kin 7:15–22
41:1 ^Ezek 41:21, 23   ^B Ezek 40:9   **41:2** ^1 Kin 6:2, 17;
2 Chr 3:3   **41:3** ^Ezek 40:16   **41:4** ^1 Kin 6:5
^B Ex 26:33, 34   **41:5** ^1 Kin 6:5; Ezek 41:6–11
41:6 ^1 Kin 6:5–10

40:43 ^1 About 3 in. or 7.5 cm   **41:1** ^1 Each of these
cubits equals about 21 in. or 53 cm

and the side chambers extended to the wall which *stood* on their inward side all around, so that they could be attached, but not be attached to the wall of the temple *itself*. 7 And the side chambers surrounding *the temple* were wider at each successive story. Because the ^structure surrounding the temple *went* upward by stages on all sides of the temple, for that reason the width of the temple *increased* as it went higher; and so one went up from the lowest *story* to the highest by way of the second *story*. 8 I saw also that the house had a raised platform all around; the foundations of the side chambers were a full rod of ^six long cubits *in height*. 9 The thickness of the outer wall of the side chambers *was* five cubits. But the ^free space between the side chambers belonging to the temple 10 and the *outer* ^chambers *was* twenty cubits in width around the temple on every side. 11 The doorways of the side chambers toward the ^free space *consisted of* one doorway toward the north, and another doorway toward the south; and the width of the ^free space *was* five cubits all around.

12 The ^building that *was* in front of the separate area at the side toward the west *was* seventy cubits wide; and the wall of the building *was* five cubits thick all around, and its length *was* ninety cubits. 13 Then he measured the temple, a hundred cubits long; the ^separate area with the ^building and its walls *were* also a hundred cubits long. 14 Also the width of the front of the temple and *that of* the separate areas along the east *side totaled* a hundred cubits.

15 And he measured the length of the ^building along the front of the separate area behind it, with a ^gallery on each side, a hundred cubits; *he* also *measured* the inner sanctuary and the porches of the courtyard. 16 The ^thresholds, the latticed windows, and the galleries all around their three *stories,* opposite the threshold, were ^paneled with wood all around, and *from* the ground to the windows (but the windows were covered), 17 over the entrance, and to the inner house, and on the outside, and on all the wall all around inside and outside, *by* measurement. 18 It was carved with ^cherubim and palm trees; and a palm tree was between cherub and cherub, and *every* cherub had two faces: 19 a ^human face toward the palm tree on one side and a young ^lion's face toward the palm tree on the other side; they were carved on all the house all around. 20 From the ground to above the entrance ^cherubim and ^palm trees were carved, as well as *on* the wall of the sanctuary.

21 The ^doorposts of the sanctuary were square; as for the front of the *inner* sanctuary, the appearance *of one doorpost was* like that *of the other.* 22 The ^altar *was* of wood, three cubits high, and its length two cubits; its corners, its base, and its sides *were* of wood. And he said to me, "This is the table that is before the LORD." 23 The sanctuary and the *inner* sanctuary *each* had a double ^door. 24 *Each of* the

41:7 ^1 Kin 6:8   41:8 ^Ezek 40:5   41:9 ^Ezek 41:11
41:10 ^Ezek 40:17   41:11 ^Ezek 41:9
41:12 ^Ezek 41:13, 15; 42:1   41:13 ^Ezek 41:13-15
^Ezek 41:12   41:15 ^Ezek 41:12, 13   ^Ezek 41:16
41:16 ^Is 6:4   ^1 Kin 6:15   41:18 ^1 Kin 6:29, 32, 35;
7:36   41:19 ^Ezek 1:10; 10:14   41:20 ^Ezek 41:18
41:21 ^1 Kin 6:33; Ezek 40:9, 14, 16   41:22 ^Ex 30:1-3;
1 Kin 6:20   41:23 ^1 Kin 6:31-35

doors had two leaves, two ^swinging leaves; two *leaves* for one door and two leaves for the other. ²⁵ Also there were carved on them, on the doors of the main room, ^cherubim and palm trees like those carved on the walls; and *there was* a ᴮthreshold of wood on the front of the porch outside. ²⁶ *And there were* ^latticed windows and palm trees on one side and on the other, on the sides of the ᴮporch; *the same were on* the side chambers of the house and the thresholds.

CHAMBERS OF THE TEMPLE

42 Then he brought me out into the outer courtyard, the way toward the north; and he brought me to the ^chamber which *was* opposite the ᴮseparate area and opposite the building toward the north. ² Along the length, *which was* a ^hundred ¹cubits, *was* the north door; the width *was* fifty cubits. ³ Opposite the twenty *cubits* which *belonged* to the inner courtyard, and opposite the ^stone pavement which *belonged* to the outer courtyard, *was* ᴮgallery corresponding to gallery in three *stories.* ⁴ In front of the ^chambers *was* an inner passage ten cubits wide, a way of one *hundred* cubits; and their openings *were* on the north. ⁵ Now the upper chambers *were* smaller because the ^galleries took more *space* away from them than from the lower and middle ones in the building. ⁶ For they *were* in ^three *stories* and had no pillars like the pillars of the courtyards; for that reason *the upper chambers* were set back from the ground *upward,* more than the lower and middle ones. ⁷ As for the ^outer wall by the side of the chambers, toward the

outer courtyard facing the chambers, its length *was* fifty cubits. ⁸ For the length of the chambers which *were* in the outer courtyard *was* fifty cubits; and behold, *the length of those* facing the main room *was* a ^hundred cubits. ⁹ And below these chambers *was* the ^entrance on the east side, as one enters them from the outer courtyard.

¹⁰ In the thickness of the wall of the courtyard toward the east, facing the separate area and facing the building, *there were* ^chambers. ¹¹ And the ^way in front of them *was* like the appearance of the chambers which *were* on the north; according to their length, so was their width, and all their exits *were* according to their building plans and openings. ¹² Corresponding to the openings of the chambers which were toward the south was an opening at the head of the way, the way in front of the ^wall toward the east, as one enters them.

¹³ Then he said to me, "The north chambers *and* the south chambers, which are opposite the separate area, they are the ^holy chambers where the priests who are ᴮnear to the Lᴏʀᴅ shall eat the most holy things. There they shall set the most holy things, the grain offering, the sin offering, and the guilt offering; for the place is holy. ¹⁴ When the priests enter, they shall not go out into the outer courtyard from the sanctuary without ^laying

41:24 ^1 Kin 6:34   41:25 ^Ezek 41:18   ᴮEzek 41:16
41:26 ^Ezek 41:16   ᴮEzek 40:9, 48   42:1 ^Ezek 40:17
ᴮEzek 41:12   42:2 ^Ezek 41:13   42:3 ^Ezek 40:17
ᴮEzek 41:15, 16   42:4 ^Ezek 46:19   42:5 ^Ezek 42:3
42:6 ^Ezek 41:6   42:7 ^Ezek 42:10, 12
42:8 ^Ezek 41:13, 14   42:9 ^Ezek 44:5; 46:19
42:10 ^Ezek 40:17   42:11 ^Ezek 42:4
42:12 ^Ezek 42:7   42:13 ^Ex 29:31   ᴮLev 10:3
42:14 ^Ezek 44:19

42:2 ¹ Each of these cubits equals about 21 in. or 53 cm

their ᴮgarments there in which they minister, for they are holy. They shall put on other garments; then they shall approach that which is for the people."

¹⁵ Now when he had finished measuring the inner house, he brought me out by way of the ᴬgate which faced east, and measured it all around. ¹⁶ He measured on the east side with the measuring rod: five hundred rods by the ᴬmeasuring rod. ¹⁷ He measured on the north side: five hundred rods by the measuring rod. ¹⁸ On the south side he measured five hundred rods with the measuring rod. ¹⁹ He turned to the west side *and* measured five hundred rods with the measuring rod. ²⁰ He measured it on the four sides; it had a ᴬwall all around, the length five hundred *rods* and the width five hundred, to ᴮdivide between the holy and the common.

VISION OF THE GLORY OF GOD FILLING THE TEMPLE

43 Then he led me to the ᴬgate, the gate facing east; ² and behold, the ᴬglory of the God of Israel was coming from the way of the east. And His ᴮvoice was like the sound of many waters; and the earth shone from His glory. ³ And *it was* like the appearance of the vision which I saw, like the ᴬvision which I saw when He came to ᴮdestroy the city. And the visions *were* like the vision which I saw by the river Chebar; and I fell on my face. ⁴ And the glory of the Lᴏʀᴅ entered the house by way of the gate facing ᴬeast. ⁵ And the ᴬSpirit lifted me up and brought me into the inner courtyard; and behold, the glory of the Lᴏʀᴅ filled the house.

⁶ Then I heard *Him* speaking to me from the house, while a ᴬman was standing beside me. ⁷ And He said to me, "Son of man, *this is* the place of My ᴬthrone and the place of the soles of My feet, where I will ᴮdwell among the sons of Israel forever. And the house of Israel will not again defile My holy name, neither they nor their kings, by their prostitution and by the corpses of their kings when they die, ⁸ by putting their threshold by My threshold, and their door post beside My door post, with *only* the wall between Me and them. And they have ᴬdefiled My holy name by their abominations which they have committed. So I have consumed them in My anger. ⁹ Now let them ᴬremove their prostitution and the corpses of their kings far from Me, and I will dwell among them forever.

¹⁰ "As for you, son of man, ᴬinform the house of Israel of the temple, so that they will be ashamed of their wrongdoings; and have them measure the ᴮplan. ¹¹ And if they are ashamed of everything that they have done, make known to them the plan of the house, its layout, its exits, its entrances, all its plans, all its statutes, and all its laws. And write *it* ᴬin their sight, so that they may observe its entire plan and all its statutes and ᴮexecute them. ¹² This is the law of the house: its entire area on the top of the ᴬmountain all around *shall be* most holy. Behold, this is the law of the house.

42:14 ᴮEx 29:4-9   42:15 ᴬEzek 40:6; 43:1
42:16 ᴬEzek 40:3   42:20 ᴬIs 60:18   ᴮEzek 22:26
43:1 ᴬEzek 10:19; 40:6   43:2 ᴬIs 6:3   ᴮEzek 1:24
43:3 ᴬEzek 1:4-28   ᴮJer 1:10   43:4 ᴬEzek 10:19; 11:23
43:5 ᴬEzek 3:14; 8:3   43:6 ᴬEzek 1:26; 40:3
43:7 ᴬPs 47:8   ᴮEzek 37:26, 28   43:8 ᴬEzek 8:3, 16
43:9 ᴬEzek 18:30, 31   43:10 ᴬEzek 40:4   ᴮEzek 28:12
43:11 ᴬEzek 12:3   ᴮEzek 11:20   43:12 ᴬEzek 40:2

THE ALTAR OF SACRIFICE

¹³"And these are the measurements of the ᴬaltar by cubits (the ᴮcubit *being* a ¹cubit and a hand width): the base *shall be* a cubit and the width a cubit, and its border on its edge all around one span; and this *shall be the height of* the base of the altar. ¹⁴And from the base on the ground to the lower ᴬledge *shall be* two cubits, and the width one cubit; and from the smaller ledge to the larger ledge *shall be* four cubits, and the width one cubit. ¹⁵The altar hearth *shall be* four cubits; and from the altar hearth *shall extend* upward four ᴬhorns. ¹⁶Now the altar hearth *shall be* twelve *cubits* long by twelve wide, ᴬsquare in its four sides. ¹⁷And the ledge *shall be* fourteen *cubits* long by fourteen wide in its four sides, the border around it *shall be* half a cubit, and its base *shall be* a cubit all around; and its ᴬsteps shall ᴮface east."

THE OFFERINGS

¹⁸And He said to me, "Son of man, this is what the Lord Gᴏᴅ says: 'These are the statutes for the altar on the day it is built, to offer ᴬburnt offerings on it and to ᴮsprinkle blood on it. ¹⁹You shall give to the Levitical priests who are from the descendants of ᴬZadok, who come ᴮnear to Me to serve Me,' declares the Lord Gᴏᴅ, 'a bull as a sin offering. ²⁰And you shall take some of its blood and put it on its four ᴬhorns and on the four corners of the ledge, and on the border all around; so you shall ᴮcleanse it and make atonement for it. ²¹You shall also take the bull as the sin offering, and it shall be ᴬburned in the appointed place of the house, outside the sanctuary.

²²'And on the second day you shall offer a male goat without blemish as a sin offering, and they shall ᴬcleanse the altar from sin as they cleansed *it* with the bull. ²³When you have finished cleansing *it,* you shall offer a ᴬbull without blemish and a ram without blemish from the flock. ²⁴You shall offer them before the Lᴏʀᴅ, and the priests shall throw ᴬsalt on them, and they shall offer them up as a burnt offering to the Lᴏʀᴅ. ²⁵ᴬFor seven days you shall prepare a goat as a sin offering daily; also a bull and a ram from the flock, *both* without blemish, shall be prepared. ²⁶For seven days they shall make atonement for the altar and purify it; so shall they consecrate it. ²⁷When they have completed the days, it shall be that on the ᴬeighth day and onward, the priests shall offer your burnt offerings on the altar, and your peace offerings; and I will ᴮaccept you,' declares the Lord Gᴏᴅ."

GATE FOR THE PRINCE

44 Then He brought me back by way of the ᴬouter gate of the sanctuary, which faces east; and it was shut. ²And the Lᴏʀᴅ said to me, "This gate shall be shut; it shall not be opened, and no one shall enter by it, for the ᴬLᴏʀᴅ God of Israel has entered by it; therefore it shall be shut. ³As for the ᴬprince, he shall

43:13ᴬEx 27:1-8   ᴮEzek 40:5   **43:14**ᴬEzek 43:17, 20; 45:19   **43:15**ᴬEx 27:2; Lev 9:9   **43:16**ᴬEx 27:1
43:17ᴬEx 20:26   ᴮEzek 40:6   **43:18**ᴬEx 40:29
ᴮLev 1:5, 11   **43:19**ᴬ1 Kin 2:35   ᴮNum 16:5, 40
43:20ᴬLev 8:15   ᴮLev 16:19   **43:21**ᴬEx 29:14; Lev 4:12
43:22ᴬEzek 43:20, 26   **43:23**ᴬEx 29:1, 10; Ezek 45:18
43:24ᴬLev 2:13; Num 18:19   **43:25**ᴬEx 29:35–37;
Lev 8:33, 35   **43:27**ᴬLev 9:1   ᴮEzek 20:40
44:1ᴬEzek 40:6, 17; 42:14   **44:2**ᴬEzek 43:2-4
44:3ᴬEzek 34:24

43:13 ¹A cubit and hand width equals about 21 in. or 53 cm

sit in it as prince to eat bread before the LORD; he shall ᴮenter by way of the porch of the gate and shall go out by the same way."

⁴Then He brought me by way of the ᴬnorth gate to the front of the house; and I looked, and behold, the ᴮglory of the LORD filled the house of the LORD, and I fell on my face. ⁵And the LORD said to me, "Son of man, pay attention, see with your eyes and hear with your ears everything that I say to you concerning all the ᴬstatutes of the house of the LORD and all its laws; and pay attention to the entrance of the house, with all the exits of the sanctuary. ⁶You shall say to the ᴬrebellious ones, to the house of Israel, 'This is what the Lord GOD says: "ᴮEnough of all your abominations, house of Israel, ⁷when you brought in foreigners, ᴬuncircumcised in heart and uncircumcised in flesh, to be in My sanctuary to profane it, My house, when you offered My food, the fat, and the blood and they ᴮbroke My covenant—*this* in addition to all your abominations. ⁸And you have not ᴬtaken responsibility for My holy things yourselves, but you have appointed *foreigners* to take responsibility for My sanctuary."

⁹'This is what the Lord GOD says: "ᴬNo foreigner uncircumcised in heart and uncircumcised in flesh, of all the foreigners who are among the sons of Israel, shall enter My sanctuary. ¹⁰But the Levites who went far from Me when Israel went astray, who ᴬwent astray from Me following their idols, shall ᴮsuffer the punishment for their wrongdoing. ¹¹Yet they shall be ᴬministers in My sanctuary, having ᴮoversight at the gates of the house and ministering *in* the house; they shall

slaughter the burnt offering and the sacrifice for the people, and they shall stand before them to minister to them. ¹²Since they ministered to them ᴬbefore their idols and became a ᴮstumbling block of wrongdoing to the house of Israel, for that reason I have sworn against them," declares the Lord GOD, "that they shall suffer the punishment for their wrongdoing. ¹³And they shall ᴬnot approach Me to serve as priests for Me, nor approach any of My holy things, to the things that are most holy; but they will bear their shame and their abominations which they have committed. ¹⁴Nevertheless I will appoint them to ᴬtake responsibility for the house, of all its service and of everything that shall be done in it.

ORDINANCES FOR THE LEVITES

¹⁵"But the ᴬLevitical priests, the sons of Zadok, who ᴮtook responsibility for My sanctuary when the sons of Israel went astray from Me, shall come near to Me to serve Me; and they shall stand before Me to offer Me the fat and the blood," declares the Lord GOD. ¹⁶"They shall ᴬenter My sanctuary; they shall come near to My ᴮtable to serve Me and assume the responsibility I give them. ¹⁷And it shall be that when they enter at the gates of the inner courtyard, they shall be clothed with ᴬlinen garments; and wool shall not be worn by them

44:3 ᴮEzek 46:2, 8-10　**44:4**ᴬEzek 40:20, 40
ᴮIs 6:3, 4　**44:5**ᴬDeut 12:32; Ezek 43:10, 11
44:6ᴬEzek 2:5-7　ᴮEzek 45:9　**44:7**ᴬLev 26:41
ᴮGen 17:14　**44:8**ᴬLev 22:2; Num 18:7
44:9ᴬEzek 44:7; Joel 3:17　**44:10**ᴬ2 Kin 23:8, 9
ᴮNum 18:23　**44:11**ᴬNum 3:5-37　ᴮ1 Chr 26:1-19
44:12ᴬ2 Kin 16:10-16　ᴮEzek 14:3, 4　**44:13**ᴬNum 18:3
44:14ᴬNum 18:4; 1 Chr 23:28-32　**44:15**ᴬJer 33:18-22
ᴮNum 18:7　**44:16**ᴬNum 18:5, 7, 8　ᴮEzek 41:22
44:17ᴬEx 28:42, 43; 39:27-29

while they are ministering in the gates of the inner courtyard or in the house. [18]Linen ^turbans shall be on their heads and linen undergarments shall be around their waists; they shall not put on *anything that makes them* sweat. [19]And when they go out into the outer courtyard, into the outer courtyard to the people, they shall ^take off their garments in which they have been ministering and lay them in the holy chambers; then they shall put on other garments, so that they will ^Bnot transfer holiness to the people with their garments. [20]Also they shall ^not shave their heads, yet they shall not ^Blet their locks grow long; they shall only trim *the hair of* their heads. [21]^ANor shall any of the priests drink wine when they enter the inner courtyard. [22]And they shall not marry a widow or a ^divorced woman, but shall take virgins from the descendants of the house of Israel, or a widow who is the widow of a priest. [23]Moreover, they shall teach My people *the ^difference* between the holy and the common, and teach them to distinguish between the unclean and the clean. [24]In a dispute they shall take their stand to judge; they shall judge it according to My ordinances. They shall also keep My laws and My statutes in all My ^Aappointed feasts, and ^Bsanctify My Sabbaths. [25]^AThey shall not go to a dead person to defile *themselves;* however, for father, for mother, for son, for daughter, for brother, or for a sister who has not had a husband, they may defile themselves. [26]And after he is ^cleansed, seven days [1]shall elapse for him. [27]On the day that he goes into the sanctuary, to the ^inner courtyard to minister in

the sanctuary, he shall offer his ^Bsin offering," declares the Lord God.

[28]"And it shall be regarding an inheritance for them, *that* ^AI am their inheritance; and you shall give them no property in Israel—I am their property. [29]They shall ^eat the grain offering, the sin offering, and the guilt offering; and everything ^Bbanned from secular use in Israel shall be theirs. [30]And the first of all the ^Afirst fruits of every kind and every contribution of every kind, from all your contributions, shall be for the priests; you shall also give to the priest the first of your dough, to make a ^Bblessing rest on your house. [31]The priests shall not eat any bird or animal that has ^died a natural death or has been torn to pieces by animals.

THE LORD'S PORTION OF THE LAND

45 "Now when you ^Adivide the land by lot for inheritance, you shall offer an ^Ballotment to the Lord, a holy portion of the land; the length shall be a length of twenty-five thousand [1]*cubits,* and the width shall be twenty thousand. It shall be holy within its entire surrounding boundary. [2]Out of this there shall be for the sanctuary a square encompassing ^Afive hundred by five hundred *cubits,* and fifty cubits for its ^Bopen space round about. [3]From this area you shall measure a length

---

44:18 ^A Ex 28:40; Is 3:20   44:19 ^A Lev 6:10   ^B Lev 6:27
44:20 ^A Lev 21:5   ^B Num 6:5   44:21 ^A Lev 10:9
44:22 ^A Lev 21:7, 14   44:23 ^A Lev 10:10; Ezek 22:26
44:24 ^A Lev 23:2, 4, 44   ^B Ezek 20:12, 20
44:25 ^A Lev 21:1-4   44:26 ^A Num 19:13-19
44:27 ^A Ezek 44:17   ^B Lev 5:3, 6   44:28 ^A Num 18:20;
Deut 10:9   44:29 ^A Num 18:9, 14   ^B Lev 27:21, 28
44:30 ^A Num 18:12, 13   ^B Mal 3:10   44:31 ^A Lev 22:8;
Deut 14:21   45:1 ^A Num 34:13   ^B Ezek 48:8, 9
45:2 ^A Ezek 42:20   ^B Ezek 27:28

44:26 [1]Lit *they shall count*   45:1 [1]Each of these cubits equals about 21 in. or 53 cm

of twenty-five thousand *cubits* and a width of ten thousand *cubits;* and in it shall be the sanctuary, the Most Holy Place. ⁴It shall be the holy portion of the land; it shall be for the ^priests, the ministers of the sanctuary, who come near to serve the Lᴏʀᴅ, and it shall be a place for their houses and a holy place for the sanctuary. ⁵*An area*^twenty-five thousand *cubits* in length and ten thousand in width shall be for the Levites, the ministers of the house, *and* for their possession cities in which to live.

⁶"And you shall give the ^city possession of *an area* five thousand *cubits* wide and twenty-five thousand *cubits* long, alongside the allotment of the holy portion; it shall be for the entire house of Israel.

PORTION FOR THE PRINCE

⁷"And the ^prince shall have *land* on either side of the holy allotment and the property of the city, adjacent to the holy allotment and the property of the city, on the west side toward the west and on the east side toward the east, and in length comparable to one of the portions, from the west border to the east border. ⁸*This* shall be his land as a possession in Israel; so My princes shall no longer ^oppress My people, but they shall give *the rest of* the land to the house of Israel according to their tribes."

⁹'This is what the Lord Gᴏᴅ says: "Enough, you princes of Israel; get rid of violence and destruction, and ^practice justice and righteousness. Revoke your ᴮevictions of My people," declares the Lord Gᴏᴅ.

¹⁰"You shall have ^accurate balances, an accurate ¹·ᴮephah, and an accurate ²·ᴮbath. ¹¹The ephah and

the bath shall be the same quantity, so that the bath will contain a tenth of a ^homer, and the ephah a tenth of a ¹homer; their standard shall be according to the homer. ¹²And the ^shekel shall be twenty gerahs; twenty shekels, twenty-five shekels, *and* fifteen shekels shall be your mina.

¹³"This is the offering that you shall offer: a sixth of an ephah from *each* homer of wheat; a sixth of an ephah from *each* homer of barley; ¹⁴and the prescribed portion of oil (*namely,* the bath of oil), a tenth of a bath from *each* kor (*which is* ten baths *or* a homer, for ten baths are a homer); ¹⁵and one sheep from *each* flock of two hundred from the watering places of Israel—for a ^grain offering, for a burnt offering, and for peace offerings, to ᴮmake atonement for them," declares the Lord Gᴏᴅ. ¹⁶"^All the people of the land shall give to this offering for the ᴮprince in Israel. ¹⁷And it shall be the ^prince's part *to provide* the burnt offerings, the grain offerings, and the drink offerings, at the feasts, on the new moons, and on the Sabbaths, at all the appointed feasts of the house of Israel; he shall provide the sin offering, the grain offering, the burnt offering, and the peace offerings, to make atonement for the house of Israel."

¹⁸'This is what the Lord Gᴏᴅ says: "In the first *month,* on the first of

45:4^Ezek 48:10, 11   45:5^Ezek 48:13
45:6^Ezek 48:15-18, 30-35   45:7^Ezek 34:24; 37:24
45:8^Is 11:3-5; Jer 23:5   45:9^Jer 22:3   ᴮNeh 5:1-5
45:10^Lev 19:36   ᴮIs 5:10   45:11^Is 5:10
45:12^Ex 30:13; Lev 27:25   45:15^Ezek 45:17
ᴮLev 1:4; 6:30   45:16^Ex 30:14, 15   ᴮIs 16:1
45:17^Ezek 46:4-12

45:10 ¹I.e., a dry measure, about 1 cubic foot or 0.03 cubic meters   ²I.e., a liquid measure, about 6 gallons or 23 liters   45:11 ¹About 7.7 cubic feet or 0.22 cubic meters

the month, you shall take a bull ^without blemish and ^Bcleanse the sanctuary from sin. ¹⁹And the priest shall take some of the blood from the sin offering and put *it* on the door posts of the house, on the ^four corners of the ledge of the altar, and on the posts of the gate of the inner courtyard. ²⁰And you shall do this on the seventh *day* of the month for everyone who does ^wrong inadvertently or is naive; so you shall make ^Batonement for the house.

²¹"In the first *month,* on the fourteenth day of the month, you shall have the ^Passover, a feast of seven days; unleavened bread shall be eaten. ²²On that day the prince shall provide for himself and all the people of the land a ^bull as a sin offering. ²³And *during* the ^seven days of the feast he shall provide as a burnt offering to the LORD ^Bseven bulls and seven rams without blemish on every day of the seven days, and a male goat daily as a sin offering. ²⁴And he shall provide as a ^grain offering an ¹ephah with a bull, an ephah with a ram, and a ²hin of oil with an ephah. ²⁵In the ^seventh *month,* on the fifteenth day of the month, at the feast, he shall provide like these, seven days for the sin offering, the burnt offering, the grain offering, and the oil."

THE PRINCE'S OFFERINGS

46 ¹This is what the Lord GOD says: "The gate of the inner courtyard facing east shall be shut for the six ^working days; but it shall be opened on the ^BSabbath day and opened on the day of the new moon. ²The ^prince shall enter by way of the porch of the gate from outside and stand by the post of the

gate. Then the priests shall provide his burnt offering and his peace offerings, and he shall worship at the threshold of the gate and *then* go out; but the gate shall not be shut until the evening. ³The ^people of the land shall also worship at the doorway of that gate before the LORD on the Sabbaths and on the new moons. ⁴The burnt offering which the prince shall offer to the LORD on the Sabbath day shall be ^six lambs without blemish and a ram without blemish; ⁵and the ^grain offering shall be an ¹ephah with the ram, and the grain offering with the lambs as much as he is able to give, and a ²hin of oil with an ephah. ⁶On the day of the ^new moon *he shall offer* a bull without blemish, and six lambs and a ram, *which* shall be without blemish. ⁷And he shall provide a grain offering, an ephah with the bull and an ephah with the ram, and with the lambs as much as he is ^able, and a hin of oil with an ephah. ⁸When the ^prince enters, he shall go in by way of the porch of the gate, and go out by the same way. ⁹But when the people of the land come ^before the LORD at the appointed feasts, one who enters by way of the north gate to worship shall go out by way of the south gate. And one who enters by way of the south gate shall go out by

45:18 ^A Lev 22:20   ^B Lev 16:16, 33   **45:19** ^A Lev 16:18-20; Ezek 43:20   **45:20** ^A Lev 4:27   ^B Lev 16:20
45:21 ^A Ex 12:1-24; Lev 23:5-8   **45:22** ^A Lev 4:14
45:23 ^A Lev 23:8   ^B Num 23:1, 2   **45:24** ^A Num 28:12-15; Ezek 46:5-7   **45:25** ^A Lev 23:33-43; Num 29:12-38
46:1 ^A Ex 20:9   ^B Is 66:23   **46:2** ^A Ezek 44:3; 46:8
46:3 ^A Luke 1:10   **46:4** ^A Num 28:9   **46:5** ^A Num 28:12; Ezek 45:24   **46:6** ^A Ezek 46:1   **46:7** ^A Lev 14:21; Deut 16:17   **46:8** ^A Ezek 44:3; 46:2
46:9 ^A Ex 34:23; Ps 84:7

45:24 ¹About 1 cubic foot or 0.03 cubic meters
²About 1 gallon or 3.8 liters   **46:5** ¹About 1 cubic foot or 0.03 cubic meters, and so throughout the ch
²About 1 gallon or 3.8 liters, and so throughout the ch

way of the north gate. No one shall return by way of the gate by which he entered, but shall go straight out. ¹⁰And when they go in, the prince shall go in ^among them; and when they go out, he shall go out.

¹¹"At the ^festivals and the appointed feasts, the grain offering shall be an ephah with a bull and an ephah with a ram, and with the lambs as much as one is able to give, and a hin of oil with an ephah. ¹²And when the prince provides a ^voluntary offering, a burnt offering, or peace offerings *as* a voluntary offering to the LORD, the gate facing east shall be opened for him. And he shall provide his burnt offering and his peace offerings as he does on the Sabbath day. Then he shall go out, and the gate shall be shut after he goes out.

¹³"And you shall provide a ^lamb a year old without blemish as a burnt offering to the LORD daily; ᴮmorning by morning you shall provide it. ¹⁴You shall also provide a grain offering with it morning by morning, a ^sixth of an ephah and a third of a hin of oil to moisten the fine flour, a grain offering to the LORD continually by a permanent ordinance. ¹⁵So they shall provide the lamb, the grain offering, and the oil, morning by morning, as a ^continual burnt offering."

¹⁶"This is what the Lord GOD says: "If the prince gives a ^gift *from* his inheritance to any of his sons, it shall belong to his sons; it is their possession by inheritance. ¹⁷But if he gives a gift from his inheritance to one of his servants, it shall be his until the ^year of release; then it shall return to the prince. His inheritance *shall be* only his sons'; it shall belong to them. ¹⁸And the

prince shall ^not take from the people's inheritance, depriving them of their property; he shall give his sons inheritance from his own property, so that My people will not be scattered, anyone from his property.""

THE BOILING PLACES

¹⁹Then he brought me through the ^entrance, which *was* at the side of the gate, into the holy chambers for the priests, which faced north; and behold, a place was there at the extreme rear toward the west. ²⁰And he said to me, "This is the place where the priests shall boil the ^guilt offering and the sin offering, *and* where they shall ᴮbake the grain offering, so that they do not bring *them* out into the outer courtyard and transfer holiness to the people."

²¹Then he brought me out into the outer courtyard and led me across to the four corners of the courtyard; and behold, in every corner of the courtyard *there was* a *small* courtyard. ²²In the four corners of the courtyard *there were* enclosed courtyards, forty ¹*cubits* long and thirty wide; these four in the corners *were* the same size. ²³And *there was* a row *of masonry* all around in them, around the four of them, and cooking hearths were made under the rows all around. ²⁴Then he said to me, "These are the cooking places where the ministers of the house shall cook the sacrifices of the people."

46:10 ^2 Sam 6:14, 15; 1 Chr 29:20, 22
46:11 ^Ezek 45:17   46:12 ^Lev 23:38; 2 Chr 29:31
46:13 ^Num 28:3-5   ᴮIs 50:4   46:14 ^Num 28:5
46:15 ^Ex 29:42; Num 28:6   46:16 ^2 Chr 21:3
46:17 ^Lev 25:10   46:18 ^Ezek 45:8   46:19 ^Ezek 42:9;
44:5   46:20 ^2 Chr 35:13   ᴮLev 2:4-7
46:22 ¹Each of these cubits equals about 21 in. or 53 cm

WATER FROM THE TEMPLE

47 Then he brought me back to the ^door of the house; and behold, ^water was flowing from under the threshold of the house toward the east, for the house faced east. And the water was flowing down from under, from the right side of the house, from south of the altar. ²And he brought me out by way of the north gate and led me around on the outside to the outer gate, by the way facing east. And behold, water was spurting out from the south side.

³When the man went out toward the east with a line in his hand, he measured a thousand ¹cubits, and he led me through the water, water *reaching* the ankles. ⁴Again he measured a thousand and led me through the water, water *reaching* the knees. Again he measured a thousand and led me through *the water,* water *reaching* the hips. ⁵Again he measured a thousand; *and it was* a river that I could not wade across, because the water had risen, *enough* water to swim in, a ^river that could not be crossed *by wading.* ⁶And he said to me, "Son of man, have you ^seen *this?*" Then he brought me back to the bank of the river. ⁷Now when I had returned, behold, on the bank of the river *there were* very many ^trees on the one side and on the other. ⁸Then he said to me, "These waters go out toward the eastern region and go down into the ^Arabah; then they go toward the sea, being made to flow into the ^sea, and the waters *of the sea* become fresh. ⁹And it will come about that every living creature which swarms in every place where the river goes, will live. And there will be very many fish, for

these waters go there and *the others* become fresh; so ^everything will live where the river goes. ¹⁰And it will come about that ^fishermen will stand beside it; from ^Engedi to Eneglaim there will be a place for the spreading of nets. Their fish will be according to their kinds, like the fish of the Great Sea, very many. ¹¹But its swamps and marshes will not become fresh; they will be left for ^salt. ¹²And by the river on its bank, on one side and on the other, will grow all *kinds of* ^trees for food. Their leaves will not wither and their fruit will not fail. They will bear fruit every month because their water flows from the sanctuary, and their fruit will be for food and their ^leaves for healing."

BOUNDARIES AND DIVISION OF THE LAND

¹³This is what the Lord GOD says: "This *shall be* the ^boundary by which you shall divide the land for an inheritance among the twelve tribes of Israel; Joseph *shall have* two portions. ¹⁴And you shall divide it for an inheritance, each one equally with the other; for I ^swore to give it to your forefathers, and this land shall fall to you as an inheritance.

¹⁵"And this *shall be* the boundary of the land: on the ^north side, from the Great Sea *by* the way of Hethlon, to the entrance of Zedad; ¹⁶^Hamath, Berothah, Sibraim, which is between the border of Damascus and the border of Hamath;

47:1 ^Ezek 41:2, 23-25   ᴮPs 46:4
47:5 ^Is 11:9; Hab 2:14   47:6 ^Ezek 8:6; 40:4
47:7 ^Is 60:13, 21; 61:3   47:8 ^Deut 3:17   ᴮJosh 3:16
47:9 ^Is 12:3; 55:1   47:10 ^Matt 4:19   ᴮGen 14:7
47:11 ^Deut 29:23   47:12 ^Gen 2:9   ᴮRev 22:2
47:13 ^Num 34:2-12   47:14 ^Deut 1:8; Ezek 20:6
47:15 ^Num 34:7-9   47:16 ^Num 13:21; Is 10:9

47:3 ¹Each of these cubits equals about 21 in. or 53 cm

Hazer-hatticon, which is by the border of Hauran. ¹⁷The boundary shall extend from the sea *to* ᴬHazar-enan *at* the border of Damascus, and on the north toward the north is the border of Hamath. This is the north side.

¹⁸"The ᴬeast side, from between Hauran, Damascus, ᴮGilead, and the land of Israel, *shall be* the Jordan; from the *north* border to the eastern sea you shall measure. This is the east side.

¹⁹"The south side toward the south *shall extend* from Tamar as far as the waters of ᴬMeribath-kadesh, to the ᴮbrook *of Egypt and* to the Great Sea. This is the south side toward the south.

²⁰"And the ᴬwest side *shall be* the Great Sea, from the *south* border to a point opposite ᴮLebo-hamath. This is the west side.

²¹"So you shall divide this land among yourselves according to the tribes of Israel. ²²You shall divide it by lot for an inheritance among yourselves and among the ᴬstrangers who stay in your midst, who bring forth sons in your midst. And they shall be to you as the native-born among the sons of Israel; they shall be allotted an ᴮinheritance with you among the tribes of Israel. ²³And in the tribe with which the stranger resides, there you shall give *him* his inheritance," declares the Lord Gᴏᴅ.

DIVISION OF THE LAND

48 "Now ᴬthese are the names of the tribes: from the northern extremity, beside the way of Hethlon to Lebo-hamath, *as far as* Hazar-enan *at* the border of Damascus, toward the north beside Hamath, running from east to west,

ᴮDan, one *portion*. ²Beside the border of Dan, from the east side to the west side, ᴬAsher, one *portion*. ³Beside the border of Asher, from the east side to the west side, ᴬNaphtali, one *portion*. ⁴Beside the border of Naphtali, from the east side to the west side, ᴬManasseh, one *portion*. ⁵Beside the border of Manasseh, from the east side to the west side, ᴬEphraim, one *portion*. ⁶Beside the border of Ephraim, from the east side to the west side, ᴬReuben, one *portion*. ⁷Beside the border of Reuben, from the east side to the west side, ᴬJudah, one *portion*.

⁸"And beside the border of Judah, from the east side to the west side, shall be the allotment which you shall set apart, twenty-five thousand ¹cubits in width, and in length like one of the portions, from the east side to the west side; and the ᴬsanctuary shall be in the middle of it. ⁹The allotment that you shall set apart to the Lᴏʀᴅ *shall be* twenty-five thousand *cubits* in length and ten thousand in width.

PORTION FOR THE PRIESTS

¹⁰The holy allotment shall be for these, *namely* for the ᴬpriests, toward the north twenty-five thousand *cubits in length,* toward the west ten thousand in width, toward the east ten thousand in width, and toward the south twenty-five thousand in length; and the sanctuary of the Lᴏʀᴅ shall be in its midst. ¹¹*It shall*

47:17ᴬNum 34:9   47:18ᴬNum 34:10-12   ᴮGen 37:25
47:19ᴬDeut 32:51   ᴮNum 34:5   47:20ᴬNum 34:6
ᴮJudg 3:3   47:22ᴬIs 14:1   ᴮActs 11:18   48:1ᴬEx 1:1
ᴮJosh 19:40-48   48:2ᴬJosh 19:24-31
48:3ᴬJosh 19:32-39   48:4ᴬJosh 13:29-31; 17:1-11
48:5ᴬJosh 16:5-9; 17:8-10, 14-18   48:6ᴬJosh 13:15-21
48:7ᴬJosh 15:1-63; 19:9   48:8ᴬIs 12:6; 33:20-22
48:10ᴬEzek 44:28; 45:4
48:8 ¹Each of these cubits equals about 21 in. or 53 cm

be for the priests who are sanctified of the ^sons of Zadok, who have taken the responsibility I gave them, who did not go astray when the sons of Israel went astray as the Levites went astray. 12 It shall be an allotment to them from the allotment of the land, a most holy reserve, by the border of the Levites. 13 And alongside the border of the priests, the Levites *shall have* twenty-five thousand *cubits* in length and ten thousand in width. The entire length *shall be* twenty-five thousand *cubits* and the width ten thousand. 14 Moreover, they ^shall not sell or exchange any of it, or allow this choice *portion* of land to pass *to others;* for it is holy to the Lord.

15 "The remainder, five thousand *cubits* in width *and* twenty-five thousand in length, shall be for ^common use for the city, for homes and for open spaces; and the city shall be in its midst. 16 And these *shall be* its measurements: the north side, 4,500 *cubits,* the south side ^4,500 *cubits,* the east side 4,500 *cubits,* and the west side, 4,500 *cubits.* 17 The city shall have open spaces: on the north 250 *cubits,* on the south 250 *cubits,* on the east 250 *cubits,* and on the west 250 *cubits.* 18 The remainder of the length alongside the holy allotment shall be ten thousand *cubits* toward the east and ten thousand toward the west; and it shall be alongside the holy allotment. And its produce shall be food for the workers of the city. 19 And the workers of the city, out of all the tribes of Israel, shall cultivate it. 20 The whole allotment *shall be* twenty-five thousand by twenty-five thousand *cubits;* you shall set apart the holy allotment, a square, with the property of the city.

PORTION FOR THE PRINCE

21 "The ^remainder *shall be* for the prince, on the one side and on the other of the holy allotment and of the property of the city; in front of the twenty-five thousand *cubits* of the allotment toward the east border and westward in front of the twenty-five thousand toward the west border, alongside the portions, *it shall be* for the prince. And the holy allotment and the sanctuary of the house shall be in the middle of it. 22 And exclusive of the property of the Levites and the property of the city, *which are* in the middle of that which belongs to the prince, *everything* between the border of Judah and the border of Benjamin shall belong to the prince.

PORTION FOR OTHER TRIBES

23 "As for the rest of the tribes: from the east side to the west side, ^Benjamin, one *portion.* 24 Beside the border of Benjamin, from the east side to the west side, ^Simeon, one *portion.* 25 Beside the border of Simeon, from the east side to the west side, ^Issachar, one *portion.* 26 Beside the border of Issachar, from the east side to the west side, ^Zebulun, one *portion.* 27 Beside the border of Zebulun, from the east side to the west side, ^Gad, one *portion.* 28 And beside the border of Gad, at the south side toward the south, the border shall be from ^Tamar to the waters of Meribath-kadesh, to the brook *of Egypt,* to the Great Sea. 29 This is the ^land

48:11 ^Ezek 40:46; 44:15   48:14 ^Lev 25:32-34; 27:10, 28, 33   48:15 ^Ezek 42:20; 45:6
48:16 ^Rev 21:16   48:21 ^Ezek 34:24; 45:7
48:23 ^Josh 18:21-28   48:24 ^Josh 19:1-9
48:25 ^Josh 19:17-23   48:26 ^Josh 19:10-16
48:27 ^Josh 13:24-28   48:28 ^Gen 14:7; 2 Chr 20:2
48:29 ^Ezek 47:13-20

which you shall divide by lot to the tribes of Israel for an inheritance, and these are their *several* portions," declares the Lord GOD.

THE CITY GATES

30 "Now these are the exits of the city: on the ^north side, 4,500 *cubits* by measurement, 31shall be the gates of the city, ^named for the tribes of Israel, three gates toward the north: the gate of Reuben, one; the gate of Judah, one; *and* the gate of Levi, one. 32On the east side, 4,500 *cubits,* shall be three gates: the gate of Joseph, one; the gate

of Benjamin, one; *and* the gate of Dan, one. 33On the south side, 4,500 *cubits* by measurement, shall be three gates: the gate of Simeon, one; the gate of Issachar, one; *and* the gate of Zebulun, one. 34On the west side, 4,500 *cubits, shall be* three gates: the gate of Gad, one; the gate of Asher, one; *and* the gate of Naphtali, one. 35 *The city shall be* eighteen thousand *cubits* all around; and the ^name of the city from *that* day *shall be,* 'The LORD is there.'"

48:30 ^Ezek 48:32-34   48:31 ^Rev 21:12, 13
48:35 ^Jer 23:6; 33:16

DANIEL

THE CHOICE YOUNG MEN

1 In the third year of the reign of ^Jehoiakim king of Judah, Nebuchadnezzar king of Babylon came to Jerusalem and besieged it. ²And the Lord handed Jehoiakim king of Judah over to him, along with some of the ^vessels of the house of God; and he brought them to the land of ^Shinar, to the house of his god, and he brought the vessels into the treasury of his god.

³Then the king told Ashpenaz, the chief of his officials, to bring in some of the sons of Israel, including some of the royal ^family and of the nobles, ⁴youths in whom there was ^no impairment, who were good-looking, suitable for instruction in every *kind of* expertise, endowed with understanding and discerning knowledge, and who had ability to serve in the king's court; and *he ordered Ashpenaz* to teach them the literature and ^language of the Chaldeans. ⁵The king also allotted for them a daily ration from the ^king's choice food and from the wine which he drank, and *ordered* that they be educated for three years, at the end of which they were to ^enter the king's personal service. ⁶Now among them from the sons of Judah were ^Daniel, Hananiah, Mishael, and Azariah. ⁷Then the commander of the officials assigned *new* names to them; and to Daniel he assigned *the name* ^Belteshazzar, to Hananiah ^Shadrach, to Mishael Meshach, and to Azariah ^Abed-nego.

DANIEL'S RESOLVE

⁸But Daniel made up his mind that he would not ^defile himself with the king's choice food or with the wine which he drank; so he sought *permission* from the commander of the officials that he might not defile himself. ⁹Now God granted Daniel ^favor and compassion in the sight of the commander of the officials. ¹⁰The commander of the officials said to Daniel, "I am afraid of my lord the king, who has allotted your food and your drink; for why should he see your faces looking gaunt in comparison to the youths who are your own age? Then you would make me forfeit my head to the king." ¹¹But Daniel said to the overseer whom the commander of the officials had appointed over Daniel, Hananiah, Mishael, and Azariah, ¹²"Please put your servants to the test for ten days, and let us be ^given some vegetables to eat and water to drink. ¹³Then let our appearance be examined in your presence and the appearance of the youths who are eating the king's choice food; and deal with your servants according to what you see."

¹⁴So he listened to them in this matter, and put them to the test for ten days. ¹⁵And at the end of ten days their appearance seemed ^better, and they were fatter than all

1:1 ^2 Kin 24:1; 2 Chr 36:5, 6   1:2 ^2 Chr 36:7
^Gen 10:10   1:3 ^2 Kin 24:15; Is 39:7   1:4 ^2 Sam 14:25
^Is 36:11   1:5 ^Dan 1:8   ^1 Sam 16:22
1:6 ^Ezek 14:14, 20; 28:3   1:7 ^Dan 2:26   ^Dan 2:49
1:8 ^Lev 11:47; Ezek 4:13, 14   1:9 ^Gen 39:21;
1 Kin 8:50   1:12 ^Dan 1:16   1:15 ^Ex 23:25; Prov 10:22

the youths who had been eating the king's choice food. ¹⁶So the overseer continued to withhold their choice food and the wine they were to drink, and kept ᴬgiving them vegetables.

¹⁷And as for these four youths, ᴬGod gave them knowledge and intelligence in every *kind of* literature and expertise; Daniel even understood all *kinds of* ᴮvisions and dreams.

¹⁸Then at the end of the days which the king had specified for presenting them, the commander of the officials presented them before Nebuchadnezzar. ¹⁹And the king talked with them, and out of them all not one was found like Daniel, Hananiah, Mishael, and Azariah; so they ᴬentered the king's personal service. ²⁰As for every matter of ᴬexpertise and understanding about which the king consulted them, he found them ᴮten times better than all the soothsayer priests *and* conjurers who *were* in all his realm. ²¹And Daniel continued until the ᴬfirst year of Cyrus the king.

THE KING'S DREAM

2 Now in the second year of the reign of Nebuchadnezzar, Nebuchadnezzar ᴬhad dreams; and his spirit was troubled and his sleep left him. ²Then the king gave orders to call in the ᴬsoothsayer priests, the conjurers, the sorcerers, and the ¹Chaldeans, to tell the king his dreams. So they came in and stood before the king. ³The king said to them, "I ᴬhad a dream, and my spirit is anxious to understand the dream."

⁴Then the Chaldeans spoke to the king in ᴬAramaic: "O king, live forever! Tell the dream to your servants, and we will declare the interpretation." ⁵The king replied to the Chaldeans, "The command from me is firm: if you do not make known to me the dream and its interpretation, you will be ᴬtorn limb from limb and your houses will be turned into a rubbish heap. ⁶But if you declare the dream and its interpretation, you will receive from me ᴬgifts and a reward and great honor; therefore declare to me the dream and its interpretation." ⁷They answered a second time and said, "Let the king ᴬtell the dream to his servants, and we will declare the interpretation." ⁸The king replied, "I know for certain that you are trying to buy time, because you have perceived that the command from me is firm, ⁹that if you do not make the dream known to me, there is only ᴬone decree for you. For you have agreed together to speak lying and corrupt words before me until the situation is changed; therefore tell me the dream, so that I may ᴮknow that you can declare to me its interpretation." ¹⁰The Chaldeans answered the king and said, "There is no person on earth who could declare the matter to the king, because no great king or ruler has *ever* asked anything like this of any ᴬsoothsayer priest, sorcerer, or Chaldean. ¹¹Moreover, the thing which the king demands is difficult, and there is no one else who could declare it to the king except ᴬgods, whose ᴮdwelling place is not with *mortal* flesh."

1:16ᴬDan 1:12   1:17ᴬ1 Kin 3:12, 28   ᴮDan 2:19
1:19ᴬGen 41:46; Dan 1:5   1:20ᴬ1 Kin 4:30, 31   ᴮGen 31:7
1:21ᴬDan 6:28; 10:1   2:1ᴬGen 40:5-8; 41:1, 8
2:2ᴬGen 41:8; Ex 7:11   2:3ᴬGen 40:8; 41:15
2:4ᴬEzra 4:7; Is 36:11   2:5ᴬEzra 6:11; Dan 2:12
2:6ᴬDan 2:48; 5:7, 16, 29   2:7ᴬDan 2:4   2:9ᴬEsth 4:11
ᴮIs 41:23   2:10ᴬDan 2:2, 27   2:11ᴬGen 41:39   ᴮEx 29:45

¹²Because of this, the king became ᴬangry and extremely furious, and he gave orders to kill all the wise men of Babylon. ¹³So the decree was issued that the wise men be killed; and they looked for ᴬDaniel and his friends, to kill *them*.

¹⁴Then Daniel replied with discretion and discernment to ᴬArioch, the captain of the king's bodyguard, who had gone out to kill the wise men of Babylon; ¹⁵he said to Arioch, the king's officer, "For what reason is the decree from the king *so* harsh?" Then Arioch informed Daniel of the matter. ¹⁶So Daniel went in and requested of the king that he would give him a grace period, so that he might declare the interpretation to the king.

¹⁷Then Daniel went to his house and informed his friends, ᴬHananiah, Mishael and Azariah, about the matter, ¹⁸so that they might ᴬrequest compassion from the God of heaven concerning this secret, so that Daniel and his friends would not be ᴮkilled with the rest of the wise men of Babylon.

THE SECRET IS REVEALED TO DANIEL

¹⁹Then the secret was revealed to Daniel in a night ᴬvision. Then Daniel blessed the God of heaven; ²⁰Daniel said,

"May the name of God be blessed forever and ever,
For ᴬwisdom and power belong to Him.
²¹"It is He who ᴬchanges the times and the periods;
He removes kings and appoints kings;
He gives ᴮwisdom to wise men,
And knowledge to people of understanding.

²²"It is He who ᴬreveals the profound and hidden things;
He knows what is in the darkness,
And the ᴮlight dwells with Him.
²³"To You, ᴬGod of my fathers, I give thanks and praise,
For You have given me ᴮwisdom and power;
Even now You have made known to me what we requested of You,
For You have made known to us the king's matter."

²⁴Thereupon, Daniel went to Arioch, whom the king had appointed to kill the wise men of Babylon; he went and said this to him: "ᴬDo not kill the wise men of Babylon! Take me into the king's presence, and I will declare the interpretation to the king."

²⁵Then Arioch hurriedly ᴬbrought Daniel into the king's presence and spoke to him as follows: "I have found a man among the exiles from Judah who can make the interpretation known to the king!" ²⁶The king said to Daniel, whose name was ᴬBelteshazzar, "Are you able to make known to me the dream which I have seen and its interpretation?" ²⁷Daniel answered before the king and said, "As for the secret about which the king has inquired, neither ᴬwise men, sorcerers, soothsayer priests, *nor* diviners are able to declare *it* to the king. ²⁸However, there is a God in

2:12ᴬPs 76:10; Dan 2:5   **2:13**ᴬDan 1:19, 20
2:14ᴬDan 2:24   **2:17**ᴬDan 1:6   **2:18**ᴬEsth 4:15, 16
ᴮGen 18:28   **2:19**ᴬNum 12:6; Job 33:15, 16
2:20ᴬ1 Chr 29:11, 12; Job 12:13, 16–22   **2:21**ᴬPs 31:15
ᴮ1 Kin 3:9, 10   **2:22**ᴬJob 12:22   ᴮPs 36:9
2:23ᴬGen 31:42   ᴮDan 1:17   **2:24**ᴬDan 2:12, 13;
Acts 27:24   **2:25**ᴬGen 41:14   **2:26**ᴬDan 1:7; 4:8
2:27ᴬDan 2:2, 10, 11; 5:7, 8

heaven who reveals secrets, and He has made known to King Nebuchadnezzar what will take place in the ^latter days. This was your dream and the ^Bvisions in your mind *while* on your bed. ²⁹As for you, O king, *while* on your bed your thoughts turned to what would take place in the future; and ^He who reveals secrets has made known to you what will take place. ³⁰But as for me, this secret has not been revealed to me for any wisdom residing in me more than *in* any *other* living person, but for the purpose of making the interpretation known to the king, and that you may understand the ^thoughts of your mind.

THE KING'S DREAM

³¹"You, O king, were watching and behold, there was a single great statue; that statue, which was large and of extraordinary radiance, was standing in front of you, and its appearance was ^awesome. ³²The ^head of that statue *was made* of fine gold, its chest and its arms of silver, its belly and its thighs of bronze, ³³its legs of iron, *and* its feet partly of iron and partly of clay. ³⁴You continued watching until a stone was broken off ^without hands, and it struck the statue on its feet of iron and clay, and ^Bcrushed them. ³⁵Then the iron, the clay, the bronze, the silver, and the gold were crushed to pieces all at the same time, and they were like chaff from the summer threshing floors; and the wind carried them away so that ^not a trace of them was found. But the stone that struck the statue became a great ^Bmountain and filled the entire earth.

THE INTERPRETATION—BABYLON THE FIRST KINGDOM

³⁶"This *was* the dream; and *now* we will tell ^its interpretation before the king. ³⁷You, O king, are the ^king of kings, to whom the God of heaven has given the kingdom, the power, the strength, and the honor; ³⁸and wherever the sons of mankind live, *or* the ^animals of the field, or the birds of the sky, He has handed *them* over to you and has made you ruler over them all. You are the head of gold.

MEDO-PERSIA AND GREECE

³⁹And after you another kingdom will arise inferior to you, then another third kingdom of bronze, which will rule over all the earth.

ROME

⁴⁰Then there will be a ^fourth kingdom as strong as iron; just as iron smashes and crushes everything, so, like iron that crushes, it will smash and crush all these things. ⁴¹And in that you saw the feet and toes, partly of potter's clay and partly of iron, it will be a divided kingdom; but it will have within it some of the toughness of iron, since you saw the iron mixed with common clay. ⁴²And *just as* the toes of the feet *were* partly of iron and partly of pottery, *so* some of the kingdom will be strong, and part of it will be fragile. ⁴³In that you saw the iron mixed with common clay, they will combine with one another in their descendants; but they will not adhere to one another, just as iron does not combine with pottery.

2:28 ^Gen 49:1   ^BDan 4:5   2:29 ^Dan 2:23, 47
2:30 ^Ps 139:2; Amos 4:13   2:31 ^Hab 1:7   2:32 ^Dan 2:38
2:34 ^Dan 8:25   ^Ps 2:9   2:35 ^Ps 37:10, 36   ^BIs 2:2
2:36 ^Dan 2:24   2:37 ^Is 47:5; Jer 27:6, 7
2:38 ^Ps 50:10, 11; Dan 4:21, 22   2:40 ^Dan 7:23

THE DIVINE KINGDOM

44 And in the days of those kings the God of heaven will ^set up a kingdom which will never be destroyed, and *that* kingdom will not be left for another people; it will ᴮcrush and put an end to all these kingdoms, but it will itself endure forever. **45** Just as you saw that a stone was broken off from the mountain without hands, and that it crushed the iron, the bronze, the clay, the silver, and the gold, the ^great God has made known to the king what ᴮwill take place in the future; so the dream is certain and its interpretation is trustworthy."

DANIEL PROMOTED

46 Then King Nebuchadnezzar fell on his face and paid ^humble respect to Daniel, and gave orders to present to him an offering and incense. **47** The king responded to Daniel and said, "Your God truly is a ^God of gods and a Lord of kings and a ᴮrevealer of secrets, since you have been able to reveal this secret." **48** Then the king ^promoted Daniel and gave him many great gifts, and he made him ruler over the entire ᴮprovince of Babylon, and chief prefect over all the wise men of Babylon. **49** And Daniel made a request of the king, and he ^appointed Shadrach, Meshach, and Abed-nego over the administration of the province of Babylon, while Daniel *was* at the king's ᴮcourt.

THE KING'S GOLDEN IMAGE

3 Nebuchadnezzar the king made a ^statue of gold, the height of which *was* ¹sixty cubits, *and* its width six cubits; he set it up on the plain of Dura in the province of Babylon. **2** Nebuchadnezzar the king also sent *word* to assemble the ^satraps, the prefects and the governors, the counselors, the chief treasurers, the judges, the magistrates, and all the administrators of the provinces to come to the dedication of the statue that Nebuchadnezzar the king had set up. **3** Then the satraps, the prefects and the governors, the counselors, the chief treasurers, the judges, the magistrates, and all the administrators of the provinces were assembled for the dedication of the statue that Nebuchadnezzar the king had set up; and they stood before the statue that Nebuchadnezzar had set up. **4** Then the herald loudly proclaimed: "To you the command is given, you ^peoples, nations, and *populations of all* languages, **5** that at the moment you ^hear the sound of the horn, flute, lyre, trigon, psaltery, bagpipe, and all kinds of musical instruments, you are to fall down and worship the golden statue that Nebuchadnezzar the king has set up. **6** But whoever does not fall down and worship shall immediately be thrown into the middle of a ^furnace of blazing fire." **7** Therefore as soon as all the peoples heard the sound of the horn, flute, lyre, trigon, psaltery, bagpipe, and all kinds of musical instruments, all the peoples, nations, and *populations of all* languages fell down *and* worshiped the golden statue that Nebuchadnezzar the king had set up.

2:44 ^Is 9:6, 7   ᴮPs 2:9   **2:45** ^Deut 10:17
ᴮGen 41:28, 32   **2:46** ^Dan 3:5, 7; Acts 10:25
2:47 ^Deut 10:17   ᴮDan 2:22, 30   **2:48** ^Gen 41:39-43
ᴮDan 3:1, 12, 30   **2:49** ^Dan 3:12   ᴮEsth 2:19, 21
3:1 ^1 Kin 12:28; Is 46:6   **3:2** ^Dan 3:3, 27; 6:1-7
3:4 ^Dan 3:7; 4:1   **3:5** ^Dan 3:7, 10, 15   **3:6** ^Jer 29:22;
Ezek 22:18-22

3:1 ¹About 90 ft. high and 9 ft. wide or 27 m and 2.7 m

WORSHIP OF THE IMAGE REFUSED

⁸For this reason at that time certain ᴬChaldeans came forward and ᴮbrought charges against the Jews. ⁹They began to speak and said to Nebuchadnezzar the king: "ᴬO king, live forever! ¹⁰You, O king, have ᴬmade a decree that every person who hears the sound of the horn, flute, lyre, trigon, psaltery, and bagpipe, and all kinds of musical instruments, is to fall down and worship the golden statue. ¹¹But whoever does not fall down and worship shall be thrown into the middle of a furnace of blazing fire. ¹²There are certain Jews whom you have ᴬappointed over the administration of the province of Babylon, *namely* Shadrach, Meshach, and Abed-nego. These men, O king, have disregarded you; they do not serve your gods, nor do they worship the golden statue which you have set up."

¹³Then Nebuchadnezzar in ᴬrage and anger gave orders to bring Shadrach, Meshach, and Abed-nego; then these men were brought before the king. ¹⁴Nebuchadnezzar began speaking and said to them, "Is it true, Shadrach, Meshach, and Abed-nego, that you do not serve ᴬmy gods, nor worship the golden statue that I have set up? ¹⁵Now if you are ready, at the moment you hear the sound of the horn, flute, lyre, trigon, psaltery and bagpipe, and all kinds of musical instruments, to fall down and worship the statue that I have made, *very well*. But if you do not worship, you will immediately be ᴬthrown into the midst of a furnace of blazing fire; and ᴮwhat god is there who can rescue you from my hands?"

¹⁶ᴬShadrach, Meshach, and Abed-nego replied to the king, "Nebuchadnezzar, we are not in need of an answer to give you concerning this matter. ¹⁷If it be *so,* our God whom we serve is able to rescue us from the furnace of blazing fire; and ᴬHe will rescue us from your hand, O king. ¹⁸But *even* if He *does* not, ᴬlet it be known to you, O king, that we are not going to serve your gods nor worship the golden statue that you have set up."

DANIEL'S FRIENDS PROTECTED

¹⁹Then Nebuchadnezzar was filled with ᴬwrath, and his facial expression was changed toward Shadrach, Meshach, and Abed-nego. He answered by giving orders to heat the furnace seven times more than it was usually heated. ²⁰And he ordered certain valiant warriors who *were* in his army to tie up Shadrach, Meshach, and Abed-nego in order to throw *them* into the furnace of blazing fire. ²¹Then these men were tied up in their ᴬtrousers, their coats, their caps, and their *other* clothes, and were thrown into the middle of the furnace of blazing fire. ²²For this reason, because the king's command *was* ᴬharsh and the furnace had been made extremely hot, the flame of the fire killed those men who took up Shadrach, Meshach, and Abed-nego. ²³But these three men, Shadrach, Meshach, and Abed-nego, ᴬfell into the middle of the furnace of blazing fire *still* tied up.

3:8 ᴬDan 2:2, 10   ᴮEzra 4:12-16   3:9 ᴬDan 2:4; 5:10
3:10 ᴬEsth 3:12-14; Dan 3:4-6   3:12 ᴬDan 2:49
3:13 ᴬDan 2:12; 3:19   3:14 ᴬIs 46:1; Jer 50:2
3:15 ᴬDan 3:6   ᴮEx 5:2   3:16 ᴬDan 1:7; 3:12
3:17 ᴬ1 Sam 17:37; Mic 7:7   3:18 ᴬHeb 11:25
3:19 ᴬEsth 7:7; Dan 3:13   3:21 ᴬDan 3:27
3:22 ᴬEx 12:33; Dan 2:15   3:23 ᴬIs 43:2

²⁴Then Nebuchadnezzar the king was astounded and stood up quickly; he said to his counselors, "Was it not three men *that* we threw bound into the middle of the fire?" They replied to the king, "Absolutely, O king." ²⁵He responded, "Look! I see four men untied *and* ^Awalking about in the middle of the fire unharmed, and the appearance of the fourth is like a son of *the* gods!" ²⁶Then Nebuchadnezzar came near to the door of the furnace of blazing fire; he said, "Shadrach, Meshach, and Abed-nego, come out, you servants of the ^AMost High God, and come here!" Then Shadrach, Meshach, and Abed-nego ^Bcame out of the middle of the fire. ²⁷The satraps, the prefects, the governors, and the king's counselors gathered together *and* saw that the ^Afire had no effect on the bodies of these men, nor was the hair of their heads singed, nor were their ^Btrousers damaged, nor had *even* the smell of fire touched them.

²⁸Nebuchadnezzar responded and said, "Blessed be the God of Shadrach, Meshach, and Abed-nego, who has ^Asent His angel and rescued His servants who put their ^Btrust in Him, violating the king's command, and surrendered their bodies rather than serve or worship any god except their own God. ²⁹Therefore I ^Amake a decree that any people, nation, or *population of any* language that speaks anything offensive against the God of Shadrach, Meshach, and Abed-nego shall be torn limb from limb and their houses made a rubbish heap, because there is ^Bno other god who is able to save in this way." ³⁰Then the king ^Amade Shadrach, Meshach, and Abed-nego prosperous in the province of Babylon.

THE KING ACKNOWLEDGES GOD

4 Nebuchadnezzar the king to all the peoples, nations, and *populations of all* languages who live in all the earth: "May your ^Apeace be great! ²I am pleased to declare the signs and miracles that the ^AMost High God has done for me.

³ "How great are His ^Asigns
And how mighty are His miracles!
His kingdom is an everlasting kingdom,
And His dominion is from generation to generation.

THE VISION OF A GREAT TREE

⁴"I, Nebuchadnezzar, was at ease in my house and ^Ahappy in my palace. ⁵I saw a dream and it startled me; and *these* appearances *as I lay* on my bed and the ^Avisions in my mind kept alarming me. ⁶So I gave orders to ^Abring into my presence all the wise men of Babylon, so that they might make known to me the interpretation of the dream. ⁷Then the soothsayer priests, the sorcerers, the ¹Chaldeans, and the diviners came in and I related the dream to them, but they could not make its ^Ainterpretation known to me. ⁸But finally Daniel came in before me, whose name is Belteshazzar according to the name of my god, and in whom is ^{1,A}a spirit of the holy gods; and I related the dream to him, *saying,* ⁹'Belteshazzar, chief of the soothsayer priests, since I know that

3:25^APs 91:3-9; Is 43:2 **3:26**^ADan 3:17 ^BDeut 4:20
3:27^AIs 43:2 ^BDan 3:21 **3:28**^APs 34:7, 8 ^BPs 22:4, 5
3:29^ADan 6:26 ^BDan 2:47 **3:30**^ADan 2:49; 3:12
4:1^AEzra 4:17; Dan 6:25 **4:2**^ADan 3:26; 4:17
4:3^APs 77:19; 105:27 **4:4**^APs 30:6; Is 47:7, 8
4:5^ADan 2:1, 28; 4:10, 13 **4:6**^AGen 41:8; Dan 2:2
4:7^AIs 44:25; Jer 27:9, 10 **4:8**^ADan 4:9, 18; 5:11, 14

4:7¹Probably master astrologers, diviners, etc.
4:8¹Or possibly *the Spirit of the holy God,* and so throughout the ch

a spirit of the holy gods is in you and ^no secret baffles you, ᴮtell *me* the visions of my dream which I have seen, along with its interpretation.

10 'Now *these were* the visions in my mind *as I lay* on my bed: I was looking, and behold, *there was* a ^tree in the middle of the earth and its height *was* great.

11 'The tree grew large and became strong
And its height ^reached to the sky,
And it *was* visible to the end of the whole earth.

12 'Its foliage *was* beautiful and its fruit abundant,
And in it *was* food for all.
The ^animals of the field found ᴮshade under it,
And the birds of the sky lived in its branches,
And all living creatures fed from it.

13 'I was looking in the visions in my mind *as I lay* on my bed, and behold, ^an angelic watcher, a ᴮholy one, descended from heaven.

14 'He shouted out and spoke as follows:
"^Chop down the tree and cut off its branches,
Shake off its foliage and scatter its fruit;
Let the animals flee from under it
And the birds from its branches.

15 "Yet ^leave the stump with its roots in the ground,
But with a band of iron and bronze *around it*
In the new grass of the field;
And let him be drenched with the dew of heaven,
And let him share with the animals in the grass of the earth.

16 "Let his mind change from *that of* a human
And let an animal's mind be given to him,
And let ^seven periods of time pass over him.

17 "This sentence is by the decree of the angelic watchers,
And the decision is a command of the holy ones,
In order that the living may ^know
That the Most High is ruler over the realm of mankind,
And ᴮHe grants it to whomever He wishes
And sets over it the lowliest of people."

18 This is the dream *that* I, King Nebuchadnezzar, have seen. Now you, Belteshazzar, tell *me* its interpretation, since none of the ^wise men of my kingdom is able to make known to me the interpretation; but you are able, because a spirit of the holy gods is in you.'

DANIEL INTERPRETS THE VISION

19 "Then Daniel, whose name is Belteshazzar, was appalled for a while as his ^thoughts alarmed him. The king responded and said, 'Belteshazzar, do not let the dream or its interpretation alarm you.' Belteshazzar replied, 'ᴮMy lord, *if only* the dream *applied* to those who hate you, and its interpretation to your adversaries! 20 The ^tree that you saw, which became large and grew strong, whose height reached to the sky and was visible to all

4:9 ^Ezek 28:3   ᴮGen 41:15   4:10 ^Ezek 31:3, 6
4:11 ^Deut 9:1; Dan 4:21, 22   4:12 ^Jer 27:6
ᴮLam 4:20   4:13 ^Dan 4:17, 23   ᴮDeut 33:2
4:14 ^Ezek 31:10-14; Dan 4:23   4:15 ^Job 14:7-9
4:16 ^Dan 4:23, 25, 32   4:17 ^Ps 9:16   ᴮJer 27:5-7
4:18 ^Gen 41:8, 15; Dan 4:7   4:19 ^Jer 4:19
ᴮ2 Sam 18:31   4:20 ^Dan 4:10-12

the earth, ²¹and whose foliage *was* beautiful and its fruit abundant, and in which *was* food for all, under which the animals of the field lived and in whose branches the birds of the sky settled— ²²it is ^you, O king; for you have become great and grown strong, and your majesty has become great and reached to the sky, and your ^Bdominion to the end of the earth. ²³And in that the king saw an angelic watcher, a holy one, descending from heaven and saying, "^Chop down the tree and destroy it; yet leave the stump with its roots in the ground, but with a band of iron and bronze *around it* in the new grass of the field, let him be drenched with the dew of heaven, and let him share with the animals of the field until seven periods of time pass over him," ²⁴this is the interpretation, O king, and this is the decree of the Most High, which has ^come upon my lord the king: ²⁵that you be driven away from mankind and your dwelling place be with the animals of the field, and you be given grass to eat like cattle and be drenched with the dew of heaven; and seven periods of time will pass over you, until you recognize that the ^Most High is ruler over the realm of mankind and ^Bbestows it on whomever He wishes. ²⁶And in that it was commanded to leave the stump with the roots of the tree, your kingdom will remain as yours after you recognize that *it is* ^Heaven *that* rules. ²⁷Therefore, O king, may my advice be pleasing to you: ^wipe away your sin by *doing* righteousness, and your wrongdoings by ^Bshowing mercy to *the* poor, in case there may be a prolonging of your prosperity.'

THE VISION FULFILLED

²⁸"All *of this* ^happened to Nebuchadnezzar the king. ²⁹^Twelve months later he was walking on the *roof of* the royal palace of Babylon. ³⁰The king began speaking and was saying, 'Is this not Babylon the ^great, which I myself have built as a royal residence by the might of my power and for the honor of my majesty?' ³¹*While* the word *was* still in the king's mouth, a voice came from heaven, *saying*, 'King Nebuchadnezzar, to you it is declared: sovereignty has been removed from you, ³²and ^you will be driven away from mankind, and your dwelling place *will be* with the animals of the field. You will be given grass to eat like cattle, and ^Bseven periods of time will pass over you until you recognize that the Most High is ruler over the realm of mankind and bestows it on whomever He wishes.' ³³Immediately the word concerning Nebuchadnezzar was fulfilled; and he was ^driven away from mankind and began eating grass like cattle, and his body was drenched with the dew of heaven until his hair had grown like eagles' *feathers* and his nails like birds' *claws*.

³⁴"But at the end of that period, I, Nebuchadnezzar, raised my eyes toward heaven and my reason returned to me, and I blessed the ^Most High and praised and honored ^BHim who lives forever;

> For His dominion is an everlasting dominion,
> And His kingdom *endures* from generation to generation.

4:22^2 Sam 12:7   ^BJer 27:6, 7   **4:23**^Dan 4:14, 15
4:24^Job 40:11, 12; Ps 107:40   **4:25**^Ps 83:18   ^BDan 2:37
4:26^Dan 2:18, 19, 28, 37, 44; 4:31   **4:27**^Prov 28:13
^BPs 41:1-3   **4:28**^Num 23:19; Zech 1:6   **4:29**^2 Pet 3:9
4:30^Hab 2:4   **4:32**^Dan 4:25   ^BDan 4:16
4:33^Dan 4:25; 5:21   **4:34**^Dan 4:2   ^BPs 102:24-27

35 "All the inhabitants of the earth
    are of no account,
But ^He does according to
    His will among the army of
    heaven
And *among* the inhabitants of
    earth;
And ᴮno one can fend off His
    hand
Or say to Him, 'What have You
    done?'

36 At that time my ^reason returned to me. And my majesty and splendor were restored to me for the honor of my kingdom, and my state counselors and my nobles began seeking me out; so I was reestablished in my sovereignty, and surpassing ᴮgreatness was added to me. 37 Now I, Nebuchadnezzar, praise, exalt, and honor the King of heaven, for ^all His works are true and His ways just; and He is able to humble those who ᴮwalk in pride."

BELSHAZZAR'S FEAST

5 Belshazzar the king held a great ^feast for a thousand of his nobles, and he was drinking wine in the presence of the thousand. 2 While he tasted the wine, Belshazzar gave orders to bring the gold and silver ^vessels which his father Nebuchadnezzar had taken out of the temple which *was* in Jerusalem, so that the king and his nobles, his wives, and his concubines could drink out of them. 3 Then they brought the gold vessels that had been taken out of the temple, the house of God which *was* in Jerusalem; and the king and his nobles, his wives, and his concubines drank out of them. 4 They drank the wine and praised the gods of ^gold and silver, of bronze, iron, wood, and stone.

5 Suddenly the fingers of a human hand emerged and began writing opposite the lampstand on the plaster of the wall of the king's palace, and the king saw the back of the hand that did the writing. 6 Then the king's ^face became pale and his thoughts alarmed him, and his hip joints loosened and his ᴮknees began knocking together. 7 The king called aloud to bring in the ^sorcerers, the ¹Chaldeans, and the diviners. The king began speaking and said to the wise men of Babylon, "Anyone who can read this inscription and explain its interpretation to me shall be clothed with purple and *have* a necklace of gold around his neck, and have authority as ᴮthird *ruler* in the kingdom." 8 Then all the king's wise men came in, but ^they could not read the inscription or make known its interpretation to the king. 9 Then King Belshazzar was greatly ^alarmed, his face grew *even more* pale, and his nobles were perplexed.

10 The queen entered the banquet hall because of the words of the king and his nobles; the queen began to speak and said, "^O king, live forever! Do not let your thoughts alarm you or your face be pale. 11 There is a ^man in your kingdom in whom is a ᴮspirit of the holy gods; and in the days of your father, illumination, insight, and wisdom like the wisdom of the gods were found in him. And King Nebuchadnezzar, your father—your father

4:35 ^Ps 33:11   ᴮJob 42:2   4:36 ^2 Chr 33:12, 13
ᴮProv 22:4   4:37 ^Deut 32:4   ᴮEx 18:11   5:1 ^Esth 1:3;
Is 22:12-14   5:2 ^2 Kin 24:13; 25:15   5:4 ^Ps 115:4; 135:15
5:6 ^Dan 5:9, 10   ᴮEzek 7:17   5:7 ^Is 44:25   ᴮDan 2:48
5:8 ^Gen 41:8; Dan 2:27   5:9 ^Job 18:11; Is 21:2-4
5:10 ^Dan 3:9; 6:6   5:11 ^Gen 41:11-15   ᴮDan 4:8

5:7 ¹I.e., probably master astrologers, diviners, etc.,
and so throughout the ch

the king—appointed him chief of the soothsayer priests, sorcerers, Chaldeans, *and* diviners. 12 *This was* because an ^extraordinary spirit, knowledge and insight, interpretation of dreams, explanation of riddles, and solving of difficult problems were found in this Daniel, whom the king named Belteshazzar. Let Daniel now be summoned and he will declare the interpretation."

DANIEL INTERPRETS THE HANDWRITING ON THE WALL

13 Then Daniel was brought in before the king. The king began speaking and said to Daniel, "Are you that Daniel who is one of the ^exiles from Judah, whom my father the king brought from Judah? 14 Now I have heard about you that a spirit of the gods is in you, and that illumination, insight, and extraordinary wisdom have been found in you. 15 Just now the wise men *and* the sorcerers were brought in before me to read this inscription and make its interpretation known to me, but they ^could not declare the interpretation of the message. 16 But I personally have heard about you, that you are able to give interpretations and solve difficult problems. Now if you are able to read the inscription and make its ^interpretation known to me, you will be clothed with purple and *wear* a necklace of gold around your neck, and you will have authority as the third *ruler* in the kingdom."

17 Then Daniel replied and said before the king, "Keep your ^gifts for yourself or give your rewards to someone else; however, I will read the inscription to the king and make the interpretation known to

him. 18 O king, the ^Most High God ^granted sovereignty, greatness, honor, and majesty to Nebuchadnezzar your father. 19 Now because of the greatness which He granted him, all the peoples, nations, and *populations of all* languages trembled and feared in his presence; ^whomever he wished, he killed, and whomever he wished, he spared alive; and whomever he wished he elevated, and whomever he wished he humbled. 20 But when his heart was ^arrogant and his spirit became so ^overbearing that he behaved presumptuously, he was deposed from his royal throne, and *his* dignity was taken away from him. 21 He was also ^driven away from mankind, and his heart was made like *that of* animals, and his dwelling place *was* with the wild donkeys. He was given grass to eat like cattle, and his body was drenched with the dew of heaven, until he recognized that the Most High God is ruler over the realm of mankind, and *that* He sets over it whomever He wishes. 22 Yet you, his son, Belshazzar, have ^not humbled your heart, even though you knew all this, 23 but you have ^risen up against the Lord of heaven; and they have brought the vessels of His house before you, and you and your nobles, your wives, and your concubines have been drinking wine out of them; and you have praised the gods of silver and gold, of bronze, iron, wood, and stone, which do not see, nor hear, nor understand. But the God ^in whose

5:12 ^Dan 5:14; 6:3   5:13 ^Ezra 4:1; 6:16
5:15 ^Is 47:12f; Dan 5:8   5:16 ^Gen 40:8
5:17 ^2 Kin 5:16   5:18 ^Dan 4:2   ^Dan 2:37, 38
5:19 ^Dan 2:12, 13; 3:6   5:20 ^Ex 9:17   ^2 Kin 17:14
5:21 ^Job 30:3-7   5:22 ^Ex 10:3; 2 Chr 33:23
5:23 ^2 Kin 14:10   ^Job 12:10

hand are your life-breath and all your ways, you have not glorified. ²⁴Then the ^hand was sent from Him and this inscription was written out.

²⁵"Now this is the inscription that was written:

⁽¹⁾Mené, Mené, ²Tekél, ³Upharsin.'

²⁶This is the interpretation of the message: 'Mené'—God has numbered your kingdom and ^put an end to it. ²⁷'Tekél'—you have been ^weighed on the scales and found deficient. ²⁸'Perés'—your kingdom has been divided and given to the ^Medes and Persians."

²⁹Then Belshazzar gave orders, and they ^clothed Daniel with purple and *put* a necklace of gold around his neck, and issued a proclamation concerning him that he *now* had authority as the third *ruler* in the kingdom.

³⁰That same night Belshazzar the Chaldean king was ^killed. ³¹So ^Darius the Mede received the kingdom at about the age of sixty-two.

DANIEL SERVES DARIUS

6 It pleased Darius to appoint 120 satraps over the kingdom, to be in charge of the whole kingdom, ²and over them, three commissioners (of whom ^Daniel was one), so that these satraps would be accountable to them, and that the king would not suffer ᴮloss. ³Then this Daniel began distinguishing himself among the commissioners and satraps because he possessed an ^extraordinary spirit, and the king intended to appoint him over the ᴮentire kingdom. ⁴Then the commissioners and satraps began trying to find a

ground of accusation against Daniel regarding government affairs; but they could find ^no ground of accusation or *evidence of* corruption, because he was trustworthy, and no negligence or corruption was *to be* found in him. ⁵Then these men said, "We will not find any ground of accusation against this Daniel unless we find *it* against him regarding the ^law of his God."

⁶Then these commissioners and satraps came by agreement to the king and spoke to him as follows: "King Darius, ^live forever! ⁷All the commissioners of the kingdom, the prefects and the satraps, the counselors and the governors, have ^consulted together that the king should establish a statute and enforce an injunction that anyone who offers a prayer to any god or person besides you, O king, for thirty days, shall ᴮbe thrown into the lions' den. ⁸Now, O king, ^establish the injunction and sign the document so that it will not be changed, according to the ᴮlaw of the Medes and Persians, which may not be revoked." ⁹Thereupon, King Darius ^signed the document, that is, the injunction.

¹⁰Now when Daniel learned that the document was signed, he entered his house (and in his roof chamber he had windows open toward Jerusalem); and he continued kneeling on

5:24 ^Dan 5:5   5:26 ^Is 13:6, 17-19; Jer 50:41-43
5:27 ^Job 31:6; Ps 62:9   5:28 ^Is 13:17; 21:2
5:29 ^Dan 5:7, 16   5:30 ^Is 21:4-9; 47:9   5:31 ^Dan 6:1;
9:1   6:2 ^Dan 2:48, 49   ᴮEzra 4:22   6:3 ^Dan 5:12, 14
ᴮGen 41:40   6:4 ^Dan 6:22; Luke 20:26
6:5 ^Acts 24:13-16, 20, 21   6:6 ^Neh 2:3; Dan 2:4
6:7 ^Ps 59:3   ᴮPs 10:9   6:8 ^Esth 3:12   ᴮEsth 1:19
6:9 ^Ps 118:9; 146:3

5:25 ¹Or *a mina* (50 shekels) from verb "to count"
²Or *a shekel* from verb "to weigh"   ³Or *and
half-shekels* (singular: *perēs*) from verb "to divide"
5:28 ¹Or *half-shekel* from verb "to divide"

his knees three times a day, ^praying and ^offering praise before his God, just as he had been doing previously. ^11Then these men came ^by agreement and found Daniel offering a prayer and imploring *favor* before his God. ^12Then they approached and spoke before the king about the king's injunction: "Did you not sign an injunction that any person who offers a prayer to any god or person besides you, O king, for thirty days, is to be thrown into the lions' den?" The king replied, "The statement is true, according to the ^law of the Medes and Persians, which may not be revoked." ^13Then they responded and spoke before the king, "Daniel, who is one of the exiles from Judah, pays ^no attention to you, O king, or to the injunction which you signed, but keeps offering his prayer three times a day."

^14Then, as soon as the king heard this statement, he was deeply ^distressed, and set *his* mind on rescuing Daniel; and until sunset he kept exerting himself to save him. ^15Then these men came by agreement to the king and said to the king, "Recognize, O king, that it is a ^law of the Medes and Persians that no injunction or statute which the king establishes may be changed."

DANIEL IN THE LIONS' DEN

^16Then the king gave orders, and Daniel was brought in and thrown into the lions' den. The king said to Daniel, "^Your God whom you continually serve will Himself rescue you." ^17And a ^stone was brought and placed over the mouth of the den; and the king sealed it with his own signet ring and with the signet rings of his nobles, so that nothing would be changed regarding Daniel.

^18Then the king went to his palace and spent the night ^fasting, and no entertainment was brought before him; and his ^sleep fled from him.

^19Then the king got up at dawn, at the break of day, and went in a hurry to the lions' den. ^20And when he had come near the den to Daniel, he cried out with a troubled voice. The king began speaking and said to Daniel, "Daniel, servant of the living God, has ^your God, whom you continually serve, been ^able to rescue you from the lions?" ^21Then Daniel spoke to the king, "^O king, live forever! ^22My God ^sent His angel and ^shut the lions' mouths, and they have not harmed me, since I was found innocent before Him; and also toward you, O king, I have committed no crime." ^23Then the king was very glad and gave orders for Daniel to be lifted up out of the den. So Daniel was lifted up out of the den, and no injury whatever was found on him, because he had ^trusted in his God. ^24The king then gave orders, and they brought those men who had maliciously accused Daniel, and they ^threw them, their ^children, and their wives into the lions' den; and they had not reached the bottom of the den before the lions overpowered them and crushed all their bones.

^25Then Darius the king wrote to all the peoples, nations, and *populations of all* languages who were living in all the land: "^May your peace be great! ^26I issue a decree

6:10 ^Dan 9:4-19　^Ps 34:1　6:11 ^Ps 37:32, 33; Dan 6:6　6:12 ^Esth 1:19; Dan 6:8, 15　6:13 ^Esth 3:8; Dan 3:12　6:14 ^Mark 6:26　6:15 ^Esth 8:8; Ps 94:20, 21　6:16 ^Job 5:19; Ps 37:39, 40　6:17 ^Lam 3:53; Matt 27:66　6:18 ^2 Sam 12:16, 17　^Esth 6:1　6:20 ^Dan 6:16, 27　^Gen 18:14　6:21 ^Dan 2:4; 6:6　6:22 ^Num 20:16　^Ps 91:11-13　6:23 ^1 Chr 5:20; 2 Chr 20:20　6:24 ^Deut 19:18, 19　^Deut 24:16　6:25 ^Ezra 4:17; 1 Pet 1:2

that in all the realm of my kingdom people are to tremble and fear before the God of Daniel;

For He is the ᴬliving God and
ᴮenduring forever,
And His kingdom is one which will not be destroyed,
And His dominion *will be* forever.

27 "He rescues, saves, and performs ᴬsigns and miracles
In heaven and on earth,
He who has *also* rescued Daniel from the power of the lions."

28 So this Daniel enjoyed success in the reign of Darius, and in the reign of ᴬCyrus the Persian.

VISION OF THE FOUR BEASTS

7 In the first year of Belshazzar king of Babylon, Daniel saw a dream and visions in his mind *as he lay* on his bed; then he ᴬwrote the dream down *and* told the *following* summary of it. 2 Daniel said, "I was looking in my vision by night, and behold, the ᴬfour winds of heaven were stirring up the great sea. 3 And four great ᴬbeasts were coming up from the sea, different from one another. 4 The first *was* ᴬlike a lion but had *the* wings of an eagle. I kept looking until its wings were plucked, and it was lifted up from the ground and set up on two feet like a man; a human mind also was given to it. 5 And behold, another beast, a second one, resembling a bear. And it was raised up on one side, and three ribs *were* in its mouth between its teeth; and they said this to it: 'Arise, devour much meat!' 6 After this I kept looking, and behold, another one, ᴬlike a leopard, which had on its back four wings of a bird; the beast also had ᴮfour heads, and dominion was

given to it. 7 After this I kept looking in the night visions, and behold, a fourth beast, dreadful and terrible, and extremely strong; and it had large iron teeth. It devoured and crushed, and trampled down the remainder with its feet; and it was different from all the beasts that were before it, and it had ᴬten horns. 8 While I was thinking about the horns, behold, ᴬanother horn, a little one, came up among them, and three of the previous horns were plucked out before it; and behold, this horn possessed eyes like human eyes, and ᴮa mouth uttering great *boasts*.

THE ANCIENT OF DAYS REIGNS

9 "I kept looking
Until ᴬthrones were set up,
And the Ancient of Days took *His* seat;
His garment *was* white as snow,
And the hair of His head like pure wool.
His throne *was* ablaze with flames,
Its wheels *were* a burning fire.

10 "A river of fire was flowing
And coming out from before Him;
Thousands upon thousands were serving Him,
And myriads upon myriads were standing before Him;
The court convened,
And ᴬthe books were opened.

11 Then I kept looking because of the sound of the boastful words which the horn was speaking; I kept looking until the beast was killed, and

6:26 ᴬDan 4:34   ᴮPs 93:1, 2   6:27 ᴬDan 4:2, 3
6:28 ᴬ2 Chr 36:22, 23; Dan 10:1   7:1 ᴬJer 36:4, 32
7:2 ᴬRev 7:1   7:3 ᴬDan 7:17; Rev 13:1   7:4 ᴬJer 4:7
7:6 ᴬRev 13:2   ᴮDan 8:22   7:7 ᴬRev 12:3; 13:1
7:8 ᴬDan 8:9   ᴮRev 13:5, 6   7:9 ᴬRev 20:4
7:10 ᴬDan 12:1; Rev 20:11-15

its body was destroyed and given to the ^burning fire. ¹²As for the rest of the beasts, their dominion was taken away, but an extension of life was granted to them for an appointed period of time.

THE SON OF MAN PRESENTED

¹³ "I kept looking in the night visions,
And behold, with the clouds of heaven
One like a son of man was coming,
And He came up to the Ancient of Days
And was presented before Him.
¹⁴ "And to Him was given ^dominion,
Honor, and a kingdom,
So that all the peoples, nations, and *populations of all* languages
Might serve Him.
^BHis dominion is an everlasting dominion
Which will not pass away;
And His kingdom is one Which will not be destroyed.

THE VISION INTERPRETED

¹⁵"As for me, Daniel, my spirit was distressed within me, and the visions in my mind kept ^alarming me. ¹⁶I approached one of those who were ^standing by and began requesting of him the exact meaning of all this. So he ^Btold me and made known to me the interpretation of these things: ¹⁷'These great beasts, which are four *in number,* are four kings *who* will arise from the earth. ¹⁸But the ¹saints of the Highest One will ^receive the kingdom and take possession of the kingdom forever, for all ages to come.'

¹⁹"Then I desired to know the exact meaning of the ^fourth beast, which was different from all the others, exceedingly dreadful, with its teeth of iron and its claws of bronze, *and which* devoured, crushed, and trampled down the remainder with its feet, ²⁰and *the meaning* of the ten horns that *were* on its head, and the other *horn* which came up, and before which three *of the horns* fell, namely, that horn which had eyes and a mouth uttering great *boasts,* and which was larger in appearance than its associates. ²¹I kept looking, and that horn was ^waging war with the saints and prevailing against them, ²²until the Ancient of Days came and ^judgment was passed in favor of the saints of the Highest One, and the time arrived when the saints took possession of the kingdom.

²³"This is what he said: 'The fourth beast will be a fourth kingdom on the earth which will be different from all the *other* kingdoms, and will devour the whole earth and trample it down and crush it. ²⁴As for the ^ten horns, out of this kingdom ten kings will arise; and another will arise after them, and he will be different from the previous ones and will humble three kings. ²⁵And he will speak against the Most High and ^wear down the saints of the Highest One, and he will intend to make ^Balterations in times and in law; and they will be handed over to him for a time, times, and half a time. ²⁶But the

7:11 ^Rev 19:20; 20:10   7:14 ^Dan 7:27   ^BMic 4:7
7:15 ^Dan 4:19; 7:28   7:16 ^Zech 1:9, 19   ^BDan 8:16, 17
7:18 ^Ps 149:5–9; Is 60:12–14   7:19 ^Dan 7:7, 8
7:21 ^Rev 11:7; 13:7   7:22 ^Dan 7:10; 1 Cor 6:2, 3
7:24 ^Dan 7:7; Rev 17:12   7:25 ^Rev 13:7   ^BDan 2:21

7:18 ¹Lit *holy ones;* i.e., God's people

court will convene *for judgment,* and his dominion will be ^taken away, annihilated and destroyed forever. ²⁷Then the ^sovereignty, the dominion, and the greatness of *all* the kingdoms under the whole heaven will be given to the people of the saints of the Highest One; His kingdom *will be* an everlasting kingdom, and all the empires will ᴮserve and obey Him.'

²⁸"At this point the revelation ended. As for me, Daniel, my thoughts were ^greatly alarming me and my face became pale, but I ᴮkept the matter to myself."

VISION OF THE RAM AND GOAT

8 In the third year of the reign of Belshazzar the king, a vision appeared to me, Daniel, subsequent to the one which appeared to me previously. ²I looked in the vision, and while I was looking, I was in the citadel of ^Susa, which is in the province of ᴮElam; and I looked in the vision, and I myself was beside the Ulai Canal. ³Then I raised my eyes and looked, and behold, a ^ram which had two horns was standing in front of the canal. Now the two horns *were* long, but one *was* longer than the other, with the longer one coming up last. ⁴I saw the ram butting westward, northward, and southward, and no *other* beasts could stand against him nor was there anyone to rescue from his power, but ^he did as he pleased and made himself great.

⁵While I was observing, behold, a male goat was coming from the west over the surface of the entire earth without touching the ground; and the goat *had* a ^prominent horn between his eyes. ⁶He came up to the ram that had the two horns, which I had seen standing in front of the canal, and rushed at him in his mighty wrath. ⁷And I saw him come up beside the ram, and he was enraged at him; and he struck the ram and smashed his two horns, and the ram had no strength to withstand him. So he hurled him to the ground and trampled on him, and there was no one to rescue the ram from his power. ⁸Then the male goat made himself exceedingly great. But once he became powerful, the ^large horn was broken; and in its place four prominent *horns* came up toward the ᴮfour winds of heaven.

THE LITTLE HORN

⁹And out of one of them came a rather ^small horn which grew exceedingly great toward the south, toward the east, and toward the ¹,ᴮBeautiful *Land.* ¹⁰It grew up to the heavenly ¹lights, and some of the lights, that is, some of the ^stars it threw down to the earth, and it ᴮtrampled them. ¹¹It even exalted itself to be equal with the Commander of the army; and it removed the ^regular sacrifice from Him, and the place of His sanctuary was overthrown. ¹²And because of an offense the army will be given *to the horn* along with the regular sacrifice; and it will ^hurl truth to the ground and do *as it pleases* and be successful. ¹³Then I heard a holy one speaking, and another holy one

7:26 ^Rev 17:14; 19:2 7:27 ^Is 54:3   ᴮPs 2:6-12
7:28 ^Dan 4:19   ᴮLuke 2:19, 51
8:2 ^Neh 1:1   ᴮGen 10:22   8:3 ^Dan 8:20
8:4 ^Dan 11:3   8:5 ^Dan 8:8, 21; 11:3   8:8 ^Dan 8:22
ᴮDan 7:2   8:9 ^Dan 8:23   ᴮPs 48:2   8:10 ^Is 14:13
ᴮDan 7:7   8:11 ^Ezek 46:14; Dan 11:31   8:12 ^Is 59:14

8:9 ¹I.e., Israel   8:10 ¹Lit *host*

said to that particular one who was speaking, "ᴬHow long will the vision *about* the regular sacrifice *apply,* while the offense causes horror, so as to allow both the sanctuary and the army to be trampled?" ¹⁴And he said to me, "For ᴬ2,300 evenings *and* mornings; then the sanctuary will be properly restored."

INTERPRETATION OF THE VISION

¹⁵When I, Daniel, had seen the vision, I sought to understand it; and behold, standing before me was one who looked like a ᴬman. ¹⁶And I heard the voice of a man between *the banks of* Ulai, and he called out and said, "ᴬGabriel, explain the vision to this *man.*" ¹⁷So he came near to where I was standing, and when he came I was frightened and fell on my face; and he said to me, "Son of man, understand that the vision *pertains* to the ᴬtime of the end."

¹⁸Now while he was talking with me, I was ᴬdazed with my face to the ground; but he ᴮtouched me and made me stand at my place. ¹⁹And he said, "Behold, I am going to ᴬinform you of what will occur at the final period of the indignation, because *it pertains* to the appointed time of the end.

THE RAM'S IDENTITY

²⁰The ᴬram which you saw with the two horns *represents* the kings of Media and Persia.

THE GOAT

²¹The shaggy goat *represents* the kingdom of Greece, and the large horn that is between his eyes is the first king. ²²The ᴬbroken *horn* and the four *horns that* came up in its place *represent* four kingdoms *which* will arise from *his* nation, although not with his power.

²³ "And in the latter period of their dominion,
When the wrongdoers have run *their course,*
A king will arise,
Insolent and skilled in intrigue.
²⁴ "And his power will be mighty, but not by his *own* power,
And he will ᴬdestroy to an extraordinary degree
And be successful and do *as he pleases;*
He will destroy mighty men and the holy people.
²⁵ "And through his shrewdness
He will make deceit a success by his influence;
And he will make himself great in his own mind,
And he will destroy many while *they are* at ease.
He will even ᴬoppose the Prince of princes,
But he will be broken ᴮwithout human agency.
²⁶ "And the vision of the evenings and mornings
Which has been told is true;
But as for you, ᴬkeep the vision secret,
Because *it pertains* to many ᴮdays *in the future.*"

²⁷Then I, Daniel, was ᴬexhausted and sick for days. Then I got up and ᴮcarried on the king's business; but I was astounded at the vision, and there was no one to explain *it.*

8:13 ᴬPs 74:10; 79:5   8:14 ᴬDan 7:25; 12:7, 11
8:15 ᴬDan 7:13; 10:16, 18   8:16 ᴬDan 9:21; Luke 1:19, 26
8:17 ᴬDan 8:19; 11:35, 40   8:18 ᴬDan 10:9   ᴮEzek 2:2
8:19 ᴬDan 8:15-17   8:20 ᴬDan 8:3   8:22 ᴬDan 8:8
8:24 ᴬDan 8:11-13; 11:36   8:25 ᴬDan 8:11   ᴮJob 34:20
8:26 ᴬEzek 12:27   ᴮDan 10:14   8:27 ᴬDan 7:28
ᴮDan 2:48

DANIEL'S PRAYER FOR HIS PEOPLE

9 In the first year of ^Darius the son of Ahasuerus, of Median descent, who was made king over the kingdom of the Chaldeans— ²in the first year of his reign, I, Daniel, observed in the books the number of the years which was *revealed as* the word of the LORD to ^Jeremiah the prophet for the completion of the desolations of Jerusalem, *namely,* ^seventy years. ³So I gave my attention to the Lord God, to seek *Him by* prayer and pleading, with fasting, sackcloth, and ashes. ⁴I prayed to the LORD my God and confessed, and said, "Oh, Lord, the ^great and awesome God, who ᴮkeeps His covenant and faithfulness for those who love Him and keep His commandments, ⁵we have sinned, we have done wrong, and acted wickedly and ^rebelled, even ᴮturning aside from Your commandments and ordinances. ⁶Moreover, we have not ^listened to Your servants the prophets, who spoke in Your name to our kings, our leaders, our fathers, and all the people of the land.

⁷"^Righteousness *belongs* to You, Lord, but to us open shame, as *it is* this day—to the men of Judah, the inhabitants of Jerusalem, and all Israel, those who are nearby and those who are far away in ᴮall the countries to which You have driven them, because of their unfaithful deeds which they have committed against You. ⁸Open shame *belongs* to us, LORD, to our kings, our leaders, and our fathers, because we have sinned against You. ⁹To the Lord our God *belong* ^compassion and forgiveness, because we have rebelled against Him; ¹⁰and we have not obeyed the voice of the LORD our God, to walk in His teachings which He ^set before us through His servants the prophets. ¹¹Indeed, ^all Israel has violated Your Law and turned aside, not obeying Your voice; so the ᴮcurse has gushed forth on us, along with the oath which is written in the Law of Moses the servant of God, because we have sinned against Him. ¹²So He has ^confirmed His words which He had spoken against us and against our rulers who ruled us, to bring on us great disaster; for under the entire heaven there has not been done *anything* like what was done in Jerusalem. ¹³Just as it is written in the Law of Moses, all this disaster has come on us; yet we have ^not sought the favor of the LORD our God by ᴮturning from our wrongdoing and giving attention to Your truth. ¹⁴So the LORD has ^kept the disaster in store and brought it on us; for the LORD our God is righteous with respect to all His deeds which He has done, but we have not obeyed His voice.

¹⁵"And now, Lord, our God, *You* who ^brought Your people out of the land of Egypt with a mighty hand and made a name for Yourself, as *it is* this day—we have sinned, we have been wicked. ¹⁶Lord, in accordance with all Your righteous acts, let now Your ^anger and Your wrath turn away from Your city Jerusalem, Your holy mountain; for because of our sins and the wrongdoings of our fathers, Jerusalem and Your people *have become*

9:1^Dan 5:31; 11:1   **9:2**^2 Chr 36:21; Ezra 1:1
9:4^Deut 7:21   ᴮDeut 7:9   **9:5**^Lam 1:18, 20
ᴮPs 119:176   **9:6**^2 Chr 36:16; Jer 44:4, 5   **9:7**^Jer 23:6
ᴮDeut 4:27   **9:9**^Neh 9:17; Ps 130:4   **9:10**^2 Kin
17:13-15; 18:12   **9:11**^Is 1:3, 4   ᴮDeut 27:15-26
9:12^Is 44:26; Jer 44:2-6   **9:13**^Job 36:13   ᴮJer 31:18
9:14^Jer 31:28; 44:27   **9:15**^Deut 5:15
9:16^Jer 32:31, 32

an object of taunting to all those around us. ¹⁷So now, our God, listen to the prayer of Your servant and to his pleas, and for Your sake, Lord, ᴬlet Your face shine on Your ᴮdesolate sanctuary. ¹⁸My God, incline Your ear and hear! Open Your eyes and ᴬsee our desolations and the city which is ᴮcalled by Your name; for we are not presenting our pleas before You based on any merits of our own, but based on Your great compassion. ¹⁹Lord, hear! Lord, forgive! Lord, listen and take action! For Your own sake, my God, ᴬdo not delay, because Your city and Your people are called by Your name."

GABRIEL BRINGS AN ANSWER

²⁰While I was still speaking and praying, and ᴬconfessing my sin and the sin of my people Israel, and presenting my plea before the Lᴏʀᴅ my God in behalf of the holy mountain of my God, ²¹while I was still speaking in prayer, the man ᴬGabriel, whom I had seen in the vision previously, came to me in *my* extreme weariness about the time of the evening offering. ²²And he instructed *me* and talked with me and said, "Daniel, I have come now to give you insight with ᴬunderstanding. ²³At the beginning of your pleas the command was issued, and I have come to tell *you,* because you are ᴬhighly esteemed; so pay attention to the message and gain ᴮunderstanding of the vision.

SEVENTY WEEKS AND THE MESSIAH

²⁴"Seventy weeks have been decreed for your people and your holy city, to finish the wrongdoing, to make an end of sin, to ᴬmake atonement for guilt, to bring in ᴮeverlasting righteousness, to seal up vision and prophecy, and to anoint the Most Holy Place. ²⁵So you are to know and understand *that* from the issuing of a ᴬdecree to restore and rebuild Jerusalem, until Messiah the Prince, *there will be* seven weeks and sixty-two weeks; it will be built again, *with* streets and moat, even in times of distress. ²⁶Then after the sixty-two weeks, the Messiah will be ᴬcut off and have nothing, and the people of the prince who is to come will ᴮdestroy the city and the sanctuary. And its end *will come* with a flood; even to the end there will be war; desolations are determined. ²⁷And he will confirm a covenant with the many for one week, but in the middle of the week he will put a stop to sacrifice and grain offering; and on the wing of ᴬabominations *will come* the one who makes desolate, until a ᴮcomplete destruction, one that is decreed, gushes forth on the one who makes desolate."

DANIEL IS TERRIFIED BY A VISION

10 In the third year of Cyrus king of Persia, a message was revealed to Daniel, who was named Belteshazzar; and the ᴬmessage was true and *it concerned* great conflict, but he understood the message and had an ᴮunderstanding of the vision. ²In those days, I, Daniel, had been ᴬmourning for three entire weeks. ³I ᴬdid not eat any tasty food, nor did meat or wine enter my mouth, nor did I use any ointment at all

9:17ᴬNum 6:24-26   ᴮLam 5:18   9:18ᴬPs 80:14
ᴮJer 7:10-12   9:19ᴬPs 44:23; 74:10, 11   9:20ᴬIs 6:5
9:21ᴬDan 8:16; Luke 1:19, 26   9:22ᴬDan 8:16; 10:21
9:23ᴬDan 10:11, 19   ᴮMatt 24:15   9:24ᴬ2 Chr 29:24
ᴮIs 51:6, 8   9:25ᴬEzra 4:24; 6:1-15   9:26ᴬIs 53:8
ᴮMatt 24:2   9:27ᴬDan 11:31   ᴮIs 10:23
10:1ᴬDan 8:26   ᴮDan 1:17   10:2ᴬEzra 9:4, 5; Neh 1:4
10:3ᴬDan 6:18

until the entire three weeks were completed. ⁴On the twenty-fourth day of the first month, while I was by the bank of the great ᴬriver, that is, the Tigris, ⁵I raised my eyes and looked, and behold, there was a man ᴬdressed in linen, whose waist ᴮhad a belt of pure gold of Uphaz. ⁶His body also *was* like topaz, his face had the appearance of lightning, ᴬhis eyes were like flaming torches, his arms and feet like the gleam of polished bronze, and the sound of his words like the sound of a multitude. ⁷Now I, Daniel, ᴬalone saw the vision, while the men who were with me did not see the vision; nevertheless, a great ᴮfear fell on them, and they ran away to hide themselves. ⁸So I was ᴬleft alone and saw this great vision; yet ᴮno strength was left in me, for my complexion turned to a deathly pallor, and I retained no strength. ⁹But I heard the sound of his words; and as soon as I heard the sound of his words, I ᴬfell into a deep sleep on my face, with my face to the ground.

DANIEL COMFORTED

¹⁰Then behold, a hand ᴬtouched me and shook me on my hands and knees. ¹¹And he said to me, "Daniel, you who are treasured, ᴬunderstand the words that I am about to tell you and ᴮstand at your place, for I have now been sent to you." And when he had spoken this word to me, I stood up trembling. ¹²Then he said to me, "Do not be afraid, Daniel, for from the first day that you set your heart on understanding *this* and on ᴬhumbling yourself before your God, your words were heard, and I have come ᴮin *response to* your words. ¹³But the prince of the kingdom of Persia was standing in my way for twenty-one

days; then behold, ᴬMichael, one of the chief princes, came to help me, for I had been left there with the kings of Persia. ¹⁴Now I have come to explain to you what will happen to your people in the ᴬlatter days, because the vision *pertains* to ᴮthe days still *future*."

¹⁵When he had spoken to me according to these words, I turned my face toward the ground and became ᴬspeechless. ¹⁶And behold, one who resembled a human was ᴬtouching my lips. Then I opened my mouth and spoke and said to him who was standing before me, "My lord, due to the vision ᴮanguish has come upon me, and I have retained no strength. ¹⁷For ᴬhow can such a servant of my lord talk with such as my lord? As for me, there remains just now no strength in me, nor has any breath been left in me."

¹⁸Then *this* one with human appearance touched me again and ᴬstrengthened me. ¹⁹And he said, "You who are treasured, ᴬdo not be afraid. Peace *be* to you; take ᴮcourage and be courageous!" Now as soon as he spoke to me, I felt strengthened and said, "May my lord speak, for you have strengthened me." ²⁰Then he said, "Do you understand why I came to you? But I shall now return to fight against the prince of Persia; so I am leaving, and behold, the ᴬprince of Greece is about to come. ²¹However, I will tell you what is recorded in the writing of ᴬtruth. Yet there is no one who

10:4 ᴬEzek 1:3; Dan 8:2   10:5 ᴬEzek 9:2   ᴮRev 1:13
10:6 ᴬRev 1:14; 2:18   10:7 ᴬ2 Kin 6:17-20   ᴮEzek 12:18
10:8 ᴬGen 32:24   ᴮDan 7:28   10:9 ᴬGen 15:12; Job 4:13
10:10 ᴬJer 1:9; Dan 8:18   10:11 ᴬDan 8:16, 17   ᴮEzek 2:1
10:12 ᴬDan 9:20-23   ᴮActs 10:30, 31   10:13 ᴬDan 10:21;
12:1   10:14 ᴬDeut 31:29   ᴮDan 8:26   10:15 ᴬEzek 3:26;
24:27   10:16 ᴬIs 6:7   ᴮDan 7:15, 28   10:17 ᴬEx 24:10, 11;
Is 6:1-5   10:18 ᴬIs 35:3, 4   10:19 ᴬJudg 6:23
ᴮJosh 1:6, 7, 9   10:20 ᴬDan 8:21; 11:2   10:21 ᴬDan 12:4

stands firmly with me against these *forces* except [B]Michael your prince.

CONFLICTS TO COME

11 "In the [A]first year of Darius the Mede, I arose to be of assistance and a protection for him. [2]And now I will tell you the truth. Behold, three more kings are going to arise in Persia. Then a fourth will gain far more riches than all *of them;* as soon as he becomes strong through his riches, he will stir up the entire *empire* against the realm of [A]Greece. [3]And a [A]mighty king will arise, and he will rule with great authority and do as he pleases. [4]But as soon as he has arisen, his kingdom will be broken up and parceled out toward the four points of the compass, though not to his *own* descendants, nor according to his authority which he wielded, because his sovereignty will be [A]removed and *given* to others besides them.

[5]"Then the [A]king of the South will grow strong, along with *one* of his princes who will gain ascendancy over him and rule; his domain *will be* a great realm *indeed.* [6]And after *some* years they will form an alliance, and the daughter of the king of the South will come to the [A]king of the North to reach an agreement. But she will not keep her position of power, nor will he remain with his power, but she will be given up, along with those who brought her in and the one who fathered her as well as he who supported her in *those* times. [7]But one of the descendants of her line will arise in his place, and he will come against *their* army and enter the [A]fortress of the king of the North, and he will deal with them and prevail. [8]And he will also take into captivity to Egypt their [A]gods with their cast metal images *and* their precious vessels of silver and gold, and he on his part will refrain from attacking the king of the North for *some* years. [9]Then the latter will enter the realm of the king of the South, but will return to his *own* land.

[10]"And his sons will mobilize and assemble a multitude of great forces; and *one of them* will keep on coming and [A]overflow and pass through, so that he may again wage war up to his fortress. [11]And the [A]king of the South will be enraged and go out and fight with the king of the North. Then *the latter* will raise a great multitude, but *that* multitude will be handed over to the former. [12]When the multitude is carried away, his heart will be haughty, and he will cause tens of thousands to fall; yet he will not prevail. [13]For the king of the North will again raise a greater multitude than the former, and after an [A]interval of some years he will press on with a great army and much equipment.

[14]"Now in those times many will rise up against the king of the South; the violent ones among your people will also raise themselves up to fulfill the vision, but they will fall down. [15]Then the king of the North will come, pile up an [A]assault ramp, and capture a well-fortified city; and the forces of the South will not stand *their ground,* not even their choicest troops, for there will be no strength to make a stand. [16]But he who comes against

10:21 [B]Dan 10:13   11:1[A]Dan 5:31; 9:1   11:2[A]Dan 8:21;
10:20   11:3[A]Dan 8:5, 21   11:4[A]Jer 12:15, 17; 18:7
11:5[A]Dan 11:9, 11   11:6[A]Dan 11:7, 13, 15, 40
11:7[A]Dan 11:19, 38, 39   11:8[A]Is 37:19; 46:1, 2
11:10[A]Is 8:8; Jer 46:7, 8   11:11[A]Dan 11:5
11:13[A]Dan 4:16; 12:7   11:15[A]Jer 6:6; Ezek 4:2

him will ^do as he pleases, and ^Bno one will *be able to* withstand him; he will also stay *for a time* in the ¹Beautiful Land, with destruction in his hand. ¹⁷And he will ^set his mind on coming with the power of his entire kingdom, bringing with him a proposal of peace which he will put into effect; he will also give him the daughter of women to ruin it. But she will not take a stand *for him* or be on his side. ¹⁸Then he will turn his face to the ^coastlands and capture many. But a commander will put a stop to his taunting against him; moreover, he will repay him for his taunting. ¹⁹So he will turn his face toward the fortresses of his own land, but he will ^stumble and fall and not be found.

²⁰"Then in his place one will arise who will ^allow an oppressor to pass through the ¹Jewel of *his* kingdom; yet within a few days he will be broken, though not in anger nor in battle. ²¹And in his place a despicable person will arise, on whom the majesty of kingship has not been conferred; but he will come in *a time of* tranquility and ^seize the kingdom by intrigue. ²²And the overflowing ^forces will be flooded away from him and smashed, and also the prince of the covenant. ²³After an alliance is made with him he will practice deception, and he will go up and gain power with a small *force of* people. ²⁴In a time of tranquility he will enter the ^richest *parts* of the realm, and he will accomplish what his fathers did not, nor his ancestors; he will distribute plunder, spoils, and possessions among them, and he will devise his schemes against strongholds, but *only* for a time. ²⁵And he will stir up his strength

and courage against the ^king of the South with a large army; so the king of the South will mobilize an extremely large and mighty army for war; but he will not stand, because schemes will be devised against him. ²⁶Those who eat his choice food will destroy him, and his army will ^overflow, but many will fall down slain. ²⁷As for both kings, their hearts will be *intent* on evil, and they will speak lies *to each other* at the same table; but it will not succeed, because the ^end is still *to come* at the appointed time. ²⁸Then he will return to his land with much plunder; but his heart will be *set* against the holy covenant, and he will take action and *then* return to his *own* land.

²⁹"At the appointed time he will return and come into the South, but this last time it will not turn out the way it did before. ³⁰For ships of ^Kittim will come against him; therefore he will withdraw in fear and will return and curse the holy covenant and take action; so he will come back and pay attention to those who abandon the holy covenant. ³¹Forces from him will arise, ^desecrate the sanctuary fortress, and do away with the regular sacrifice. And they will set up the ^Babomination of desolation. ³²And by smooth *words* he will turn to godlessness those who act wickedly toward the covenant, but the people who know their God will be ^strong

11:16^Dan 5:19   ^BJosh 1:5
11:17^2 Kin 12:17; Ezek 4:3, 7   11:18^Gen 10:5;
Is 66:19   11:19^Ps 27:2; Jer 46:6   11:20^Is 60:17
11:21^2 Sam 15:6   11:22^Dan 9:26; 11:10
11:24^Num 13:20; Neh 9:25   11:25^Dan 11:5
11:26^Dan 11:10, 40   11:27^Dan 8:19; 11:35, 40
11:30^Gen 10:4; Num 24:24   11:31^Dan 8:11-13
^BDan 9:27   11:32^Mic 5:7-9; Zech 9:13-16

11:16¹I.e., Israel   11:20¹Lit *splendor*; i.e., prob.
Jerusalem and its temple

and take action. ³³And ^those who have insight among the people will give understanding to the many; yet they will ^Bfall by sword and by flame, by captivity and by plunder for *many* days. ³⁴Now when they fall they will be granted a little help, and many will join with them in ^hypocrisy. ³⁵And some of those who have insight will fall, to refine, ^purge, and ^Bcleanse them until the end time; because *it is* still *to come* at the appointed time.

³⁶"Then the king will do as he pleases, and he will exalt himself and ^boast against every god and will ^Bspeak dreadful things against the God of gods; and he will be successful until the indignation is finished, because that which is determined will be done. ³⁷And he will show no regard for the gods of his fathers or for the desire of women, nor will he show regard for any *other* god; for he will boast against *them* all. ³⁸But instead he will honor a god of fortresses, a god whom his fathers did not know; he will honor *him* with gold, silver, precious stones, and treasures. ³⁹And he will take action against the strongest of fortresses with *the help of* a foreign god; he will give great honor to those who acknowledge *him* and will make them rulers over the many, and will parcel out land for a price.

⁴⁰"And at the end time the ^king of the South will wage war with him, and the ^Bking of the North will storm against him with chariots, horsemen, and with many ships; and he will enter countries, overflow *them,* and pass through. ⁴¹He will also enter the Beautiful Land, and many *countries* will fall; but these will be rescued out of his hand: Edom, ^Moab, and the

foremost of the sons of ^BAmmon. ⁴²Then he will reach out with his hand against *other* countries, and the land of Egypt will not escape. ⁴³But he will gain control over the hidden treasures of gold and silver, and over all the precious things of Egypt; and ^Libyans and ^BEthiopians *will follow* at his heels. ⁴⁴But rumors from the East and from the North will terrify him, and he will go out with great wrath to eliminate and annihilate many. ⁴⁵And he will pitch the tents of his royal pavilion between the seas and the beautiful ^Holy Mountain; yet he will come to his end, and no one will help him.

THE TIME OF THE END

12 "Now at that time Michael, the great prince who stands *guard* over the sons of your people, will arise. And there will be a ^time of distress ^Bsuch as never occurred since there was a nation until that time; and at that time your people, everyone who is found written in the book, will be rescued. ²And ^many of those who sleep in the dust of the ground will awake, ^Bthese to everlasting life, but the others to disgrace *and* everlasting contempt. ³And those who have insight will ^shine like the glow of the ¹expanse of heaven, and those who ^Blead the many to righteousness, like the stars forever and ever. ⁴But as for you, Daniel, keep these words secret and ^seal up the book

11:33 ^Mal 2:7   ^B Matt 24:9   11:34 ^Dan 11:21, 32; Rom 16:18   11:35 ^John 15:2   ^B Rev 7:14
11:36 ^Is 14:13   ^B Rev 13:5, 6   11:40 ^Dan 11:11, 25   ^B Dan 11:7, 13, 15   11:41 ^Jer 48:47   ^B Jer 49:6
11:43 ^2 Chr 12:3   ^B Ezek 30:4, 5   11:45 ^Is 11:9; 27:13
12:1 ^Rev 7:14   ^B Jer 30:7   12:2 ^Is 26:19   ^B Matt 25:46
12:3 ^John 5:35   ^B Is 53:11   12:4 ^Is 8:16

12:3 ¹Or *firmament;* i.e., atmosphere and space

until the end of time; [8]many will roam about, and knowledge will increase."

[5]Then I, Daniel, looked, and behold, two others were standing, one on this bank of the stream and the other on that bank of the stream. [6]And *someone* said to the man ^dressed in linen, who was above the waters of the stream, "[8]How long *will it be* until the end of *these* wonders?" [7]And I heard the man dressed in linen, who was above the waters of the stream, as he ^raised his right hand and his left toward heaven, and swore by Him who lives forever that *it would be* for a [8]time, times, and half *a time;* and as soon as they finish smashing the power of the holy people, all these *events* will be completed. [8]But as for me, I heard but did not understand; so I said,

"My lord, what *will be* the outcome of these *events?*" [9]And he said, "Go *your way,* Daniel, for *these* words *will be* kept secret and ^sealed up until the end time. [10]^Many will be purged, cleansed, and refined, but the wicked will act wickedly; and none of the wicked will understand, but those who have insight will understand. [11]And from the time that the regular sacrifice is abolished and the ^abomination of desolation is set up, *there will be* 1,290 days. [12]Blessed is the one who is patient and attains to the ^1,335 days! [13]But as for you, go *your way* to the end; then you will ^rest and rise for your allotted portion at the end of the age."

12:4 [8]Is 11:9   12:6 ^Ezek 9:2   [8]Dan 8:13
12:7 ^Ezek 20:5   [8]Dan 7:25   12:9 ^Dan 12:4
12:10 ^Zech 13:9   12:11 ^Dan 9:27; 11:31
12:12 ^Dan 8:14; Rev 11:2   12:13 ^Is 57:2; Rev 14:13

HOSEA

HOSEA'S WIFE AND CHILDREN

1 The word of the LORD which came to Hosea the son of Beeri, during the days of Uzziah, Jotham, Ahaz, *and* ^Hezekiah, kings of Judah, and during the days of ᴮJeroboam the son of Joash, king of Israel. ²When the LORD first spoke through Hosea, the LORD said to Hosea, "Go, take for yourself a wife inclined to infidelity, and children of infidelity; for ^the land commits flagrant infidelity, abandoning the LORD." ³So he went and took Gomer the daughter of Diblaim, and she conceived and ^bore him a son. ⁴And the LORD said to him, "Name him ^Jezreel; for in just a little while ᴮI will punish the house of Jehu for the bloodshed of Jezreel, and I will put an end to the kingdom of the house of Israel. ⁵On that day I will ^break the bow of Israel in the ᴮValley of Jezreel."

⁶Then she conceived again and gave birth to a daughter. And the LORD said to him, "Name her ¹Loruhamah, for I will no longer ^take pity on the house of Israel, that I would ever forgive them. ⁷But I will take pity on the house of Judah and ^save them by the LORD their God, and will not save them by ᴮbow, sword, battle, horses, or horsemen." ⁸When she had weaned Loruhamah, she conceived and gave birth to a son. ⁹And the LORD said, "Name him ¹Lo-ammi, because you are not My people, and I am not your God."

10 Yet the number of the sons of Israel
Will be like the sand of the sea,
Which cannot be measured or counted;
And ^in the place
Where it is said to them,
"You are ᴮnot My people,"
It will be said to them,
"*You are* the sons of the living God."

11 And the sons of Judah and the sons of Israel will be ^gathered together,
And they will appoint for themselves ᴮone leader,
And they will go up from the land,
For the day of Jezreel *will be* great.

ISRAEL'S UNFAITHFULNESS CONDEMNED

2 Say to your brothers, "¹Ammi," and to your sisters, "²Ruhamah."
² "Dispute with your mother, dispute,
Because she is ^not my wife, and I am not her husband;
But she must remove her ᴮinfidelity from her face
And her adultery from between her breasts,

1:1 ^2 Kin 18:1-20:21 ᴮAmos 1:1 1:2 ^Deut 31:16; Jer 3:1 1:3 ^Ezek 23:4 1:4 ^Hos 2:22 ᴮ2 Kin 10:11 1:5 ^Jer 49:35 ᴮJosh 17:16 1:6 ^Hos 2:4 1:7 ^Jer 25:5, 6 ᴮPs 44:3-7 1:10 ^Rom 9:26 ᴮIs 65:1 1:11 ^Jer 23:5, 6 ᴮJer 30:21 2:2 ^Is 50:1 ᴮJer 3:1, 9, 13

1:6 ¹I.e., not having obtained mercy 1:9 ¹I.e., not my people 2:1 ¹I.e., my people ²I.e., she has obtained compassion

³ Otherwise, I will strip her
naked
And expose her as on the ^day
she was born.
I will also ᴮmake her like a
wilderness,
Make her like desert land,
And put her to death with thirst.

⁴ "Also, I will take no pity on her
children,
Because they are ^children of
infidelity.

⁵ "For their mother has
^committed prostitution;
She who conceived them has
acted shamefully.
For she said, '^I will go after my
lovers,
Who give *me* my bread and my
water,
My wool and my flax, my oil
and my drink.'

⁶ "Therefore, behold, I will
^obstruct her way with thorns,
And I will build a stone wall
against her so that she
cannot find her paths.

⁷ "And she will pursue her lovers,
but she will not reach them;
And she will seek them, but
will not find *them*.
Then she will say, '^I will go
back to my first husband,
Because it was ᴮbetter for me
then than now!'

⁸ "Yet she does ^not know that it
was ᴮI myself who gave her
the grain, the new wine, and
the oil,
And lavished on her silver and
gold,
Which they used for Baal.

⁹ "Therefore, I will ^take back My
grain at harvest time
And My new wine in its
season.

I will also take away My wool
and My flax
That I gave to cover her
nakedness.

¹⁰ "So now I will ^uncover her
lewdness
Before the eyes of her lovers,
And no one will rescue her
from My hand.

¹¹ "I will also ^put an end to all
her joy,
Her ᴮfeasts, her new moons,
her Sabbaths,
And all her festivals.

¹² "And I will destroy her vines
and fig trees,
Of which she said, 'They are
my wages for prostitution
Which my lovers have given
me.'
And I will ^turn them into a
forest,
And the animals of the field
will devour them.

¹³ "I will punish her for the days of
the Baals
When she used to ^offer
sacrifices to them
And adorn herself with her
nose ring and jewelry,
And follow her lovers, so that
she ᴮforgot Me," declares the
LORD.

RESTORATION OF ISRAEL

¹⁴ "Therefore, behold, I am going
to persuade her,
^Bring her *into* the
wilderness,
And speak kindly to her.

¹⁵ "Then I will give her her
^vineyards from there,

2:3 ^Ezek 16:4   ᴮIs 32:13, 14   2:4 ^Jer 13:14
2:5 ^Is 1:21; Jer 2:25   2:6 ^Job 19:8; Lam 3:7, 9
2:7 ^Luke 15:17, 18   ᴮJer 14:22   2:8 ^Is 1:3   ᴮEzek 16:19
2:9 ^Hos 8:7; 9:2   2:10 ^Ezek 16:37   2:11 ^Jer 7:34
ᴮHos 3:4   2:12 ^Is 5:5; 7:23   2:13 ^Jer 7:9   ᴮHos 4:6
2:14 ^Ezek 20:33-38   2:15 ^Ezek 28:25, 26

And ᴮthe Valley of Achor as a
door of hope.
And she will respond there as
in the days of her youth,
As in the day when she went
up from the land of Egypt.
16 "And it will come about on that
day," declares the Lᴏʀᴅ,
"That you will call Me ¹,ᴬmy
husband
And no longer call Me my
²Baal.
17 "For ᴬI will remove the names of
the Baals from her mouth,
So that they will no longer be
mentioned by their names.
18 "On that day I will also make a
covenant for them
With the ᴬanimals of the field,
The birds of the sky,
And the crawling things of the
ground.
And I will ᴮeliminate the bow,
the sword, and war from the
land,
And will let them lie down in
safety.
19 "I will betroth you to Me
forever;
Yes, I will betroth you to Me in
ᴬrighteousness and in justice,
In favor and in compassion,
20 And I will betroth you to Me in
faithfulness.
Then you will ᴬknow the Lᴏʀᴅ.

21 "And it will come about on that
day that ᴬI will respond,"
declares the Lᴏʀᴅ.
"I will respond to the heavens,
and they will respond to the
earth,
22 And the ᴬearth will respond to
the grain, to the new wine,
and to the oil,
And they will respond to
¹Jezreel.

23 "I will sow her for Myself in the
land.
I will also have compassion on
her who had not obtained
compassion,
And ᴬI will say to those who
were not My people,
'You are My people!'
And they will say, '*You are* my
God!'"

HOSEA'S REDEMPTION OF GOMER

3 Then the Lᴏʀᴅ said to me, "Go
again, love a woman *who* is
loved by *her* husband, yet is committing adultery, ᴬas the Lᴏʀᴅ
loves the sons of Israel, though
they turn to other gods and love
raisin cakes." ²So I ᴬpurchased her
for myself for fifteen *shekels* of
silver, and a ¹homer and a ²lethech
of barley. ³Then I said to her, "You
shall ᴬlive with me for many days.
You shall not play the prostitute, nor shall you have *another*
man; so I will also be toward
you." ⁴For the sons of Israel will
live for many days ᴬwithout a
king or leader, ᴮwithout sacrifice
or memorial stone, and without ephod or ¹household idols.
⁵Afterward the sons of Israel
will ᴬreturn and seek the Lᴏʀᴅ
their God and ᴮDavid their king;
and they will come trembling to
the Lᴏʀᴅ and to His goodness
in the last days.

2:15 ᴮJosh 7:26   2:16 ᴬIs 54:5; Hos 2:7   2:17 ᴬEx 23:13;
Josh 23:7   2:18 ᴬJob 5:23   ᴮIs 2:4   2:19 ᴬIs 1:27;
54:6-8   2:20 ᴬJer 31:33, 34; Hos 6:6   2:21 ᴬIs 55:10;
Zech 8:12   2:22 ᴬJer 31:12; Joel 2:19   2:23 ᴬRom 9:25;
1 Pet 2:10   3:1 ᴬJer 3:20   3:2 ᴬRuth 4:10
3:3 ᴬDeut 21:13   3:4 ᴬHos 10:3   ᴮDan 9:27
3:5 ᴬJer 50:4, 5   ᴮJer 30:9

2:16 ¹Heb *Ishi*   ²Also meaning *husband* in Heb,
besides a name for false gods   2:22 ¹I.e., God
sows   3:2 ¹About 7.7 cubic feet or 0.22 cubic
meters   ²About 3.8 cubic feet or 0.11 cubic meters
3:4 ¹Heb *teraphim*

GOD'S CONTROVERSY WITH ISRAEL

4 Listen to the word of the Lord,
you sons of Israel,
Because the Lord has a ^case
against the inhabitants of
the land,
For there is ᴮno faithfulness,
nor loyalty,
Nor knowledge of God in the
land.

2 *There is* oath-taking, denial,
^murder, stealing, and
ᴮadultery.
They employ violence, so
that bloodshed follows
bloodshed.

3 Therefore the land ^mourns,
And everyone who lives in it
languishes
Along with the animals of the
field and the birds of the sky,
And even the fish of the sea
disappear.

4 Yet let no one find fault, and
let no one rebuke;
For your people are like those
who ^contend with a priest.

5 So you will ^stumble by day,
And the prophet also will
stumble with you by night;
And I will destroy your
mother.

6 ^My people are destroyed for
lack of knowledge.
Since you have rejected
knowledge,
I also will reject you from
being My priest.
Since you have ᴮforgotten the
Law of your God,
I also will forget your children.

7 The more they multiplied, the
more they sinned against Me;
I will ^change their glory into
shame.

8 They ^feed on the sin of My
people,
And ᴮlong for their
wrongdoing.

9 And it will be, like people, like
priest;
So I will ^punish them for
their ways
And repay them for their
deeds.

10 They will eat, but not have
enough;
They will ^play the prostitute,
but not increase,
Because they ᴮgave up
devoting themselves to the
Lord.

11 Infidelity, ^wine, and new
wine take away the
understanding.

12 My people ^consult their
wooden idol, and their
diviner's wand informs
them;
For a spirit of infidelity has
led *them* astray,
And they have been
unfaithful, *departing* from
their God.

13 They offer sacrifices on the
^tops of the mountains
And burn incense on the
hills,
ᴮUnder oak, poplar, and
terebinth,
Because their shade is
pleasant.
Therefore your daughters
play the prostitute,
And your brides commit
adultery.

4:1^Hos 12:2   ᴮIs 59:4   **4:2**^Gen 4:8   ᴮDeut 5:18
4:3^Is 24:4; 33:9   **4:4**^Deut 17:12   **4:5**^Ezek 14:3, 7;
Hos 5:5   **4:6**^Is 5:13   ᴮHos 2:13   **4:7**^Hab 2:16
4:8^Hos 10:13   ᴮIs 56:11   **4:9**^Hos 8:13; 9:9
4:10^Hos 7:4   ᴮHos 9:17   **4:11**^Prov 20:1; Is 5:12
4:12^Is 44:19; Jer 2:27   **4:13**^Jer 3:6   ᴮIs 1:29

14 I will not punish your
        daughters when they play
        the prostitute,
    Or your brides when they
        commit adultery,
    Because *the men* themselves
        slip away with the prostitutes
    And offer sacrifices with
        ^temple prostitutes;
    So the people without
        understanding are ruined.

15 Though you, Israel, play the
        prostitute,
    Judah must not become guilty;
    Also you are not to go to Gilgal,
    Nor go up to Beth-aven
    ^And take the oath:
    "As the LORD lives!"
16 Since Israel is stubborn
    Like a stubborn cow,
    Will the LORD now ^pasture
        them
    Like a lamb in a large field?
17 Ephraim is allied with ^idols;
    Leave him alone.
18 Their liquor is gone,
    They prostitute themselves
        continually;
    ^Their rulers dearly love shame.
19 ^The wind wraps them in its
        wings,
    And they will be put to shame
        because of their sacrifices.

THE PEOPLE'S APOSTASY REBUKED

5   Hear this, you priests!
    Pay attention, house of Israel!
    Listen, *you of* the house of the
        king!
    For the judgment *applies* to you,
    Because you have been a ^trap
        at Mizpah,
    And a net spread out on Tabor.
2   And the ^rebels have ^gone
        deep in depravity,
    But I will discipline all of them.

3   I ^know Ephraim, and Israel is
        not hidden from Me;
    Because now, Ephraim, you
        have been unfaithful,
    Israel has defiled itself.
4   Their deeds will not allow
        them
    To return to their God.
    For a ^spirit of infidelity is
        within them,
    And they ^do not know the
        LORD.
5   Moreover, the pride of Israel
        testifies against him,
    And Israel and Ephraim
        stumble in their
        wrongdoing;
    ^Judah also has stumbled with
        them.
6   They will go with their flocks
        and herds
    To seek the LORD, but they will
        ^not find *Him;*
    He has ^withdrawn from them.
7   They have ^dealt treacherously
        with the LORD,
    For they have given birth to
        illegitimate children.
    Now the new moon will
        devour them with their land.

8   ^Blow the horn in Gibeah,
    And the trumpet in Ramah.
    Sound an alarm at Beth-aven:
    "^Behind you, Benjamin!"
9   Ephraim will become a
        desolation in the ^day of
        rebuke;
    Among the tribes of Israel
    I ^make known what is
        trustworthy.

4:14 ^Deut 23:17   4:15 ^Jer 5:2; 44:26   4:16 ^Is 5:17;
7:25   4:17 ^Hos 13:2   4:18 ^Mic 3:11   4:19 ^Hos 12:1;
13:15   5:1 ^Hos 9:8   5:2 ^Hos 9:15   ^Is 29:15
5:3 ^Amos 3:2; 5:12   5:4 ^Hos 4:12   ^Hos 4:6, 14
5:5 ^Ezek 23:31-35   5:6 ^Prov 1:28   ^Ezek 8:6
5:7 ^Is 48:8; Jer 3:20   5:8 ^Joel 2:1   ^Judg 5:14
5:9 ^Is 37:3   ^Is 46:10

¹⁰ The leaders of Judah have
become like those who
^displace a boundary marker;
On them I will pour out My
anger like water.

¹¹ Ephraim is oppressed, broken
by judgment,
^Because he was determined to
follow *man's* command.

¹² Therefore I am like a ^moth to
Ephraim,
And like rottenness to the
house of Judah.

¹³ When Ephraim saw his
sickness,
And Judah his sore,
Ephraim then went to ^Assyria
And sent *word* to ^BKing Jareb.
But he is unable to heal you,
Or to cure you of your sore.

¹⁴ For I *will be* like a lion to
Ephraim
And like a young lion to the
house of Judah.
^I, *yes* I, will tear to pieces and
go away,
I will carry away, and there will
be ^Bno one to rescue.

¹⁵ I will go away *and* return to My
place
Until they ^acknowledge their
guilt and seek My face;
In their distress they will
search for Me.

THE RESPONSE TO GOD'S REBUKE

6 "Come, let's return to the
LORD.
For ^He has torn *us,* but ^BHe
will heal us;
He has wounded *us,* but He
will bandage us.

² "He will ^revive us after two
days;
He will ^Braise us up on the
third day,
That we may live before Him.

³ "So let's ^learn, let's press on to
know the LORD.
His ^Bappearance is as sure as
the dawn;
And He will come to us like the
rain,
As the spring rain waters the
earth."

⁴ What shall I do with you,
Ephraim?
What shall I do with you,
Judah?
For your loyalty is like a
^morning cloud,
And like the dew which goes
away early.

⁵ Therefore I have cut *them* in
pieces by the prophets;
I have slain them by the ^words
of My mouth;
And the judgments on you are
like the light *that* shines.

⁶ For ^I desire loyalty ^Brather
than sacrifice,
And the knowledge of God
rather than burnt offerings.

⁷ But ^like Adam they have
^Bviolated the covenant;
There they have dealt
treacherously with Me.

⁸ ^Gilead is a city of wrongdoers,
Tracked with ^Bbloody
footprints.

⁹ And as a band of robbers lie in
wait for a person,
So a band of priests ^murder
on the way to Shechem;
Certainly they have committed
an act of ^Binfamy.

5:10^ADeut 19:14; 27:17 5:11^AMic 6:16
5:12^APs 39:11; Is 51:8 5:13^AHos 7:11 ^BHos 10:6
5:14^APs 50:22 ^BMic 5:8 5:15^AIs 64:7-9; Jer 3:13, 14
6:1^ADeut 32:39 ^BJer 30:17 6:2^APs 30:5 ^B1 Cor 15:4
6:3^AIs 2:3 ^BPs 19:6 6:4^APs 78:34-37; Hos 13:3
6:5^AJer 23:29 6:6^AMatt 9:13 ^BIs 1:11
6:7^AJob 31:33 ^BHos 8:1 6:8^AHos 12:11 ^BHos 4:2
6:9^AJer 7:9, 10 ^BEzek 22:9

10 In the house of Israel I have
    seen a ^horrible thing;
    Ephraim's infidelity is there,
    Israel has defiled itself.
11 Also, Judah, there is a ^harvest
    appointed for you,
    When I ^Brestore the fortunes of
    My people.

EPHRAIM'S WRONGDOING

7 When I ^would heal Israel,
    The wrongdoing of Ephraim is
    uncovered,
    And the evil deeds of Samaria,
    For they practice ^Bdeception;
    The thief enters,
    A band of robbers attack
    outside,
2 And they do not consider in
    their hearts
    That I ^remember all their
    wickedness.
    Now their deeds surround
    them;
    They are before My face.
3 ^With their wickedness they
    make the king happy,
    And the officials with their
    ^Blies.
4 They are ^all adulterers,
    Like an oven heated by the
    baker,
    Who stops stoking *the fire*
    From *the time* the dough is
    kneaded until it is leavened.
5 On the day of our king, the
    officials ^became sick with
    the heat of wine;
    He stretched out his hand with
    scoffers,
6 For their hearts are like an
    ^oven
    As they approach their
    plotting;
    Their anger smolders all night,
    In the morning it burns like
    flaming fire.

7 All of them are hot like an oven,
    And they consume their ^rulers;
    All their kings have fallen.
    ^BNone of them calls on Me.

8 Ephraim is himself ^thrown
    about with the nations;
    Ephraim has become a round
    loaf not turned over.
9 ^Strangers devour his strength,
    Yet he does not know *it;*
    Gray hairs also are sprinkled
    on him,
    Yet he does not know *it.*
10 Though the ^pride of Israel
    testifies against him,
    Yet ^Bthey have not returned to
    the LORD their God,
    Nor have they sought Him,
    despite all this.
11 So Ephraim has become like a
    gullible dove, ^without sense;
    They call to Egypt, they go to
    ^BAssyria.
12 When they go, I will ^spread
    My net over them;
    I will bring them down like the
    birds of the sky.
    I will ^Bdiscipline them in
    accordance with the
    proclamation to their
    assembly.
13 Woe to them, for they have
    ^strayed from Me!
    Destruction is theirs, for they
    have rebelled against Me!
    I ^Bwould redeem them, but they
    have spoken lies against Me.
14 And ^they do not cry to Me
    from their heart
    When they wail on their beds;

6:10 ^Jer 5:30, 31; 23:14   6:11 ^Jer 51:33   ^B Zeph 2:7
7:1 ^Ezek 24:13   ^B Hos 4:2   7:2 ^Ps 25:7; Jer 14:10
7:3 ^Rom 1:32   ^B Hos 4:2   7:4 ^Jer 9:2; 23:10
7:5 ^Is 28:1, 7   7:6 ^Ps 21:9   7:7 ^Hos 13:10   ^B Is 64:7
7:8 ^Ps 106:35   7:9 ^Is 1:7; Hos 8:7   7:10 ^Hos 5:5
^B Is 9:13   7:11 ^Hos 4:6, 11, 14   ^B Hos 5:13
7:12 ^Ezek 12:13   ^B Lev 26:14-39   7:13 ^Jer 14:10
^B Jer 51:9   7:14 ^Job 35:9-11

For the sake of grain and
new wine they assemble
themselves,
They ᴮturn against Me.

15 Although I trained *and*
strengthened their arms,
Yet they ᴬdevise evil against Me.

16 They turn, *but* not upward,
They are like a loose bow;
Their officials will fall by the
sword
Because of the ᴬinsolence of
their tongue.
This *will be* their ᴮderision in
the land of Egypt.

ISRAEL REAPS THE WHIRLWIND

8 *Put* the trumpet to your lips!
Like an eagle *the enemy comes*
ᴬagainst the house of the
Lᴏʀᴅ,
Because they have ᴮviolated
My covenant
And rebelled against My Law.

2 ᴬThey cry out to Me,
"My God, ᴮwe of Israel know
You!"

3 Israel has rejected the good;
The enemy will pursue him.

4 They have set up kings, but
not by Me;
They have appointed officials,
but I did not know *it.*
With their ᴬsilver and gold
they have made idols for
themselves,
So that they will be eliminated.

5 He has rejected your ᴬcalf,
Samaria, *saying,*
"My anger burns against them!"
How long will they be
incapable of innocence?

6 For from Israel *comes* even this!
A ᴬcraftsman made it, so it is
not God;
Assuredly, the calf of Samaria
will be broken to pieces.

7 For ᴬthey sow wind
And they harvest a ᴮstorm.
The standing grain has no
kernels;
It yields no grain.
If it were to yield, strangers
would swallow it.

8 Israel has been ᴬswallowed up;
They are now among the
nations
Like a ᴮvessel in which no one
delights.

9 For they have gone up to
ᴬAssyria,
Like ᴮa wild donkey all alone;
Ephraim has paid fees for lovers.

10 Even though they pay *for allies*
among the nations,
I will gather them up now;
And they will begin ᴬto diminish
Because of the burden of the
ᴮking of officials.

11 Since Ephraim has ᴬmultiplied
altars for sin,
They have become altars of
sinning for him.

12 Though ᴬI wrote for him ten
thousand *precepts* of My ᴮLaw,
They are regarded as a strange
thing.

13 As for My sacrificial gifts,
They sacrifice the flesh and
eat *it,*
But the Lᴏʀᴅ has taken no
delight in them.
Now He will ᴬremember their
guilt,
And ᴮpunish *them* for their sins;
They will return to Egypt.

7:14 ᴮHos 13:16   7:15 ᴬNah 1:9   7:16 ᴬPs 12:3, 4
ᴮEzek 23:32   8:1 ᴬDeut 28:49   ᴮHos 6:7   8:2 ᴬPs 78:34
ᴮTitus 1:16   8:4 ᴬHos 2:8; 13:1, 2   8:5 ᴬHos 10:5; 13:2
8:6 ᴬHos 13:2   8:7 ᴬProv 22:8   ᴮIs 66:15
8:8 ᴬ2 Kin 17:6   ᴮJer 22:28   8:9 ᴬHos 7:11   ᴮJer 2:24
8:10 ᴬJer 42:2   ᴮIs 10:8   8:11 ᴬHos 10:1
8:12 ᴬDeut 4:6, 8   ᴮHos 4:6   8:13 ᴬJer 14:10   ᴮHos 4:9

14 For Israel has ^forgotten his
   Maker and ^built palaces;
And Judah has multiplied
   fortified cities,
But I will send a fire on its
   cities, and it will consume its
   palatial buildings.

EPHRAIM PUNISHED

9 ^Do not rejoice, Israel, with
   jubilation like the nations!
For you have ^been unfaithful,
   abandoning your God.
You have loved the earnings
   of unfaithfulness on every
   threshing floor.
2 Threshing floor and wine
   press will ^not feed them,
And the new wine will fail them.
3 They will not remain in the
   LORD's land,
But Ephraim will return to
   ^Egypt,
And in Assyria they will eat
   ^unclean *food.*
4 They will not pour out drink
   offerings of wine to the LORD,
^Nor will their sacrifices please
   Him.
Their bread will be to them
   like mourners' bread;
All who eat it will be ^defiled,
Because their bread will be for
   themselves *alone;*
It will not enter the house of
   the LORD.
5 ^What will you do on the day
   of the appointed festival
And on the day of the feast of
   the LORD?
6 For behold, they will be gone
   because of destruction;
Egypt will gather them together,
   Memphis will bury them.
Weeds will take possession of
   their treasures of silver;
^Thorns *will be* in their tents.

7 The days of ^punishment have
   come,
The days of ^retribution have
   come;
Let Israel know *this!*
The prophet is a fool,
The inspired person is insane,
Because of the grossness of
   your wrongdoing,
And *because your* hostility is
   so great.
8 Ephraim *was* a watchman with
   my God, a prophet;
Yet the snare of a bird catcher
   is in all his ways,
And there is *only* hostility in
   the house of his God.
9 They are ^deeply depraved
As in the days of Gibeah;
He will ^remember their guilt,
He will punish their sins.
10 I found Israel like ^grapes in
   the wilderness;
I saw your forefathers as the
   ^earliest fruit on the fig tree
   in its first *season.*
But they came to Baal-peor
   and devoted themselves to
   ^shame,
And they became as detestable
   as that which they loved.
11 As for Ephraim, their ^glory
   will fly away like a bird—
No birth, no pregnancy, and
   no conception!
12 Though they bring up their
   children,
Yet I will bereave them of their
   children until not a person
   is left.

8:14 ^Deut 32:18   ^Is 9:9, 10
9:1 ^Is 22:12, 13   ^Hos 4:12   9:2 ^Hos 2:9
9:3 ^Hos 7:16   ^Ezek 4:13   9:4 ^Jer 6:20   ^Hag 2:13, 14
9:5 ^Is 10:3; Jer 5:31   9:6 ^Is 5:6; 7:23   9:7 ^Is 10:3
^Is 34:8   9:9 ^Is 31:6   ^Hos 7:2   9:10 ^Mic 7:1
^Jer 24:2   9:11 ^Hos 4:7; 10:5

9:10 ^1 i.e., Baal

Yes, ^woe to them indeed when
I depart from them!

13 Ephraim, as I have seen,
Is planted in a pasture like
^Tyre;
But Ephraim is going to
bring out his children for
slaughter.

14 Give to them, Lord—what will
You give?
Give them a ^miscarrying
womb and dried-up breasts.

15 All their evil is at Gilgal;
Indeed, I came to hate them
there!
Because of the ^wickedness of
their deeds
I will drive them out of My
house!
I will no longer love them;
All their leaders are ^Brebels.

16 Ephraim is stricken, their root
is dried up,
They will produce ^no fruit.
Even though they give birth to
children,
I will put to death the ^Bprecious
ones of their womb.

17 My God will reject them
Because they have ^not
listened to Him;
And they will be ^Bwanderers
among the nations.

RETRIBUTION FOR ISRAEL'S SIN

10 Israel is a luxuriant vine;
He produces fruit for
himself.
The more his fruit,
The more altars he ^made;
The richer his land,
The better he made the
^Bmemorial stones.

2 Their heart is ^deceitful;
Now they must suffer for their
^Bguilt.

The Lord will break down
their altars
And destroy their memorial
stones.

3 Certainly now they will say,
"We have ^no king,
For we do not revere the Lord.
As for the king, what can he do
for us?"

4 They speak *mere* words,
With ^worthless oaths they
make covenants;
And ^Bjudgment sprouts like
poisonous weeds in the
furrows of the field.

5 The inhabitants of Samaria
will fear
For the calf of Beth-aven.
Indeed, its people will mourn
for it,
And its ^idolatrous priests will
cry out over it,
Over its ^Bglory, since it has left it.

6 The thing itself will be brought
to Assyria
As a gift of tribute to King
Jareb;
Ephraim will be ^seized with
shame,
And Israel will be ashamed of
its ^Bown plan.

7 Samaria will be ^destroyed
with her king,
Like a twig on the surface of
the water.

8 Also the high places of Aven,
the ^sin of Israel, will be
destroyed;
Thorns and thistles will grow
on their altars;

9:12 ^Deut 31:17; Hos 7:13   9:13 ^Ezek 26:1-21
9:14 ^Hos 9:11   9:15 ^Hos 4:9   ^BIs 1:23   9:16 ^Hos 8:7
^BEzek 24:21   9:17 ^Hos 4:10   ^BHos 7:13   10:1 ^Jer 2:28
^B1 Kin 14:23   10:2 ^1 Kin 18:21   ^BHos 13:16
10:3 ^Ps 12:4; Is 5:19   10:4 ^Ezek 17:13-19
^BDeut 31:16, 17   10:5 ^2 Kin 23:5   ^BHos 9:11
10:6 ^Hos 4:7   ^BIs 30:3   10:7 ^Hos 13:11
10:8 ^1 Kin 12:28-30

Then they will ᴮsay to the
    mountains,
  "Cover us!" And to the hills,
    "Fall on us!"
9 Since the days of Gibeah you
    have sinned, Israel;
  There they stand!
  Will the battle against the sons
    of injustice not overtake
    them in Gibeah?
10 When it is My ᴬdesire, I will
    ᴮdiscipline them;
  And the peoples will be
    gathered against them
  When they are bound for their
    double guilt.

11 Ephraim is a trained ᴬheifer
    that loves to thresh,
  And I ᴮpassed over her lovely
    neck;
  I will harness Ephraim,
  Judah will plow, Jacob will
    ¹harrow for himself.
12 ᴬSow for yourselves, *with a
    view* to righteousness;
  Harvest in accordance with
    kindness.
  Break up your uncultivated
    ground,
  For it is time to ᴮseek the Lᴏʀᴅ
  Until He comes and rains
    righteousness on you.
13 You have ᴬplowed wickedness,
    you have harvested
    injustice,
  You have eaten the fruit of
    ᴮlies.
  Because you have trusted
    in your way, in your many
    warriors,
14 An uproar will arise among
    your people,
  And all your ᴬfortresses will be
    destroyed,
  As Shalman destroyed Beth-
    arbel on the day of battle,

When mothers were
    slaughtered with *their*
    children.
15 So it will be done to you at
    Bethel because of your great
    wickedness.
  At dawn the king of Israel will
    be completely destroyed.

GOD YEARNS OVER HIS PEOPLE

11 When Israel *was* a youth I
      loved him,
  And ᴬout of Egypt I called My
    son.
2 The more they called them,
  The more they went away
    from them;
  They kept ᴬsacrificing to the
    Baals
  And ᴮburning incense to idols.
3 Yet it is I who taught Ephraim
    to walk,
  I ᴬtook them in My arms;
  But they did not know that I
    ᴮhealed them.
4 I pulled them along with cords
    of a man, with ropes of love,
  And ᴬI became to them as one
    who lifts the yoke from their
    jaws;
  And I bent down *and* ᴮfed
    them.

5 They will not return to the
    land of Egypt;
  But Assyria—he will be their
    king
  Because they ᴬrefused to
    return *to Me.*
6 And the sword will whirl
    against their cities,

10:8 ᴮIs 2:19   10:10 ᴬEzek 5:13   ᴮHos 4:9
10:11 ᴬJer 50:11   ᴮJer 28:14   10:12 ᴬProv 11:18
ᴮHos 12:6   10:13 ᴬJob 4:8   ᴮHos 4:2   10:14 ᴬIs 17:3
11:1 ᴬHos 2:15; 12:9, 13   11:2 ᴬHos 2:13   ᴮIs 65:7
11:3 ᴬDeut 1:31   ᴮPs 107:20   11:4 ᴬLev 26:13
ᴮEx 16:32   11:5 ᴬHos 7:16

10:11 ¹I.e., pull a harrow, a farming device

And will destroy their oracle
  priests
And ^consume *them,* because
  of their ^Bcounsels.
7 So My people are determined
  to ^turn from Me.
Though they call them to *the
  One* on high,
None at all exalts *Him.*

8 ^How can I give you up,
  Ephraim?
How can I surrender you, Israel?
How can I make you like
  ^BAdmah?
How can I treat you like
  ^BZeboiim?
My heart is turned over within
  Me,
All My compassions are kindled.
9 I will ^not carry out My fierce
  anger;
I will not destroy Ephraim
  again.
For ^BI am God and not a man,
  the Holy One in your midst,
And I will not come in wrath.
10 They will ^walk after the LORD,
He will roar like a lion;
Indeed He will roar,
And *His* sons will come
  ^Btrembling from the west.
11 They will come trembling like
  birds from ^Egypt,
And like doves from the land
  of ^Assyria;
And I will ^Bsettle them in their
  houses, declares the LORD.

12 Ephraim surrounds Me with
  ^lies
And the house of Israel with
  deceit;
Judah is still unruly against
  God,
Even against the Holy One
  who is faithful.

EPHRAIM REMINDED

12 Ephraim feeds on wind,
  And pursues the ^east wind
  continually;
He multiplies lies and
  violence.
Moreover, he makes a
  covenant with Assyria,
And oil is brought to Egypt.
2 The LORD also has a ^case
  against Judah,
And will punish Jacob
  ^Baccording to his ways;
He will repay him according to
  his deeds.
3 In the womb he ^took his
  brother by the heel,
And in his mature strength he
  ^Bcontended with God.
4 Yes, he wrestled with the angel
  and prevailed;
He wept and ^implored His
  favor.
He found Him at Bethel,
And there He spoke with us,
5 And the LORD, the God of
  armies,
The LORD is His ^name.
6 So as for you, ^return to your
  God,
^BMaintain kindness and
  justice,
And wait for your God
  continually.
7 A merchant, in whose hands
  are fraudulent ^balances,
Loves to exploit.
8 And Ephraim said, "I have
  certainly become rich,
I have found wealth for
  myself;

11:6 ^Lam 2:9   ^BHos 4:16, 17   11:7 ^Jer 3:6, 7; 8:5
11:8 ^Hos 6:4   ^BGen 14:8   11:9 ^Deut 13:17
^BNum 23:19   11:10 ^Hos 3:5   ^BIs 66:2, 5
11:11 ^Is 11:11   ^BEzek 28:25, 26   11:12 ^Hos 4:2; 7:3
12:1 ^Gen 41:6; Ezek 17:10   12:2 ^Hos 4:1   ^BHos 7:2
12:3 ^Gen 25:26   ^BGen 32:28   12:4 ^Gen 32:26
12:5 ^Ex 3:15   12:6 ^Hos 6:1-3   ^BMic 6:8
12:7 ^Prov 11:1; Amos 8:5

In all my labors they will find
in me
^No wrongdoing, which *would
be* sin."

9 But I *have been* the LORD your
God since the land of Egypt;
I will make you ^live in tents
again,
As in the days of the appointed
festival.

10 I have also spoken to the
^prophets,
And I provided many visions,
And through the prophets I
spoke in ^parables.

11 Is there injustice *in* Gilead?
Certainly they are worthless.
In Gilgal they sacrifice bulls,
Yes, ^their altars are like stone
heaps
Beside the furrows of a field.

12 Now ^Jacob fled to the land of
Aram,
And ^Israel worked for a wife,
And for a wife he kept *sheep.*

13 But by a ^prophet the LORD
brought Israel up from Egypt,
And by a prophet he was
protected.

14 Ephraim has provoked *God* to
bitter anger;
So his Lord will leave his ^guilt
for bloodshed on him
And bring his ^disgrace back
to him.

EPHRAIM'S IDOLATRY

13
^When Ephraim spoke, *there
was* trembling.
He exalted himself in Israel,
But through Baal he incurred
guilt and died.

2 And now they sin more and
more,
And make for themselves ^cast
metal images,

Idols skillfully made from
their silver,
All of them the work of
craftsmen.
They say of them, "Let the
people who sacrifice kiss the
^calves!"

3 Therefore they will be like the
^morning cloud
And like dew which soon
disappears,
Like chaff which is blown away
from the threshing floor,
And like ^smoke from a
chimney.

4 Yet I *have been* the LORD your
God
Since the land of Egypt;
And you were not to know
^any god except Me,
For there is no savior ^besides
Me.

5 I ^cared for you in the
wilderness,
In the land of drought.

6 As *they had* their pasture, they
became satisfied,
And as they became satisfied,
their ^heart became proud;
Therefore they ^forgot Me.

7 So I will be ^like a lion to them;
Like a ^leopard I will lie in wait
by the wayside.

8 I will confront them ^like a
bear deprived of her cubs,
And I will tear open their chests;
I will also ^devour them there
like a lioness,
As a wild animal would tear
them to pieces.

12:8^Hos 4:8; 14:1   **12:9**^Lev 23:42   **12:10**^2 Kin 17:13
^Ezek 17:2   **12:11**^Hos 8:11; 10:1, 2   **12:12**^Gen 28:5
^Gen 29:20   **12:13**^Ex 14:19-22; Is 63:11-14
12:14^Ezek 18:10-13   ^Dan 11:18   **13:1**^Job 29:21, 22
13:2^Is 46:6   ^Hos 8:5, 6   **13:3**^Hos 6:4   ^Ps 68:2
13:4^Ex 20:3   ^Is 43:11   **13:5**^Deut 2:7; 32:10
13:6^Hos 7:14   ^Hos 2:13   **13:7**^Lam 3:10   ^Jer 5:6
13:8^2 Sam 17:8   ^Ps 50:22

9 It is to your own destruction,
  Israel,
  That *you are* against Me,
  against your ^help.
10 Where then is your ^king,
  That he might save you in all
  your cities;
  And your ^Bjudges, to whom
  you said,
  "Give me a king and princes"?
11 I ^gave you a king in My anger,
  And took him away in My
  wrath.

12 The guilt of Ephraim is
  wrapped up;
  His sin is ^stored up.
13 The pains of childbirth come
  on him;
  He is ^not a wise son,
  For it is not the time that he
  should delay at the opening
  of the womb.
14 Shall I ^ransom them from the
  power of Sheol?
  Shall I redeem them from
  death?
  ^BDeath, where are your thorns?
  Sheol, where is your sting?
  Compassion will be hidden
  from My sight.

15 Though he flourishes among
  the reeds,
  An ^east wind will come,
  The wind of the LORD coming
  up from the wilderness;
  And his fountain will become
  dry
  And his spring will dry up;
  It will ^Bplunder *his* treasury of
  every precious article.
16 Samaria will pay the penalty
  for her ^guilt,
  Because she has ^Brebelled
  against her God.
  They will fall by the sword,

Their children will be
  slaughtered,
  And their pregnant women
  will be ripped open.

ISRAEL'S FUTURE BLESSING

14 ^Return, Israel, to the LORD
  your God,
  For you have stumbled
  because of your wrongdoing.
2 Take words with you and
  return to the LORD.
  Say to Him, "^Take away all
  guilt
  And receive *us* graciously,
  So that we may present the
  fruit of our lips.
3 "Assyria will not save us,
  We will not ride on horses;
  Nor will we say again, '^Our
  god'
  To the ^Bwork of our hands;
  For in You the orphan finds
  mercy."

4 I will ^heal their apostasy,
  I will ^Blove them freely,
  Because My anger has turned
  away from them.
5 I will be like the ^dew to Israel;
  He will blossom like the ^Blily,
  And he will take root like *the
  cedars of* Lebanon.
6 His shoots will sprout,
  His majesty will be like the
  ^olive tree,
  And his fragrance like *the
  cedars of* ^BLebanon.
7 Those who live in his shadow
  Will again raise ^grain,

13:9 ^Deut 33:26, 29 13:10 ^2 Kin 17:4 ^B1 Sam 8:5, 6
13:11 ^1 Sam 8:7; 10:17-24 13:12 ^Deut 32:34, 35;
Job 14:17 13:13 ^Deut 32:6; Hos 5:4 13:14 ^Ps 49:15
^B1 Cor 15:55 13:15 ^Gen 41:6 ^BJer 20:5
13:16 ^Hos 10:2 ^BHos 7:14 14:1 ^Hos 6:1; 10:12
14:2 ^Mic 7:18, 19 14:3 ^Hos 8:6 ^BHos 4:12
14:4 ^Is 57:18 ^BZeph 3:17 14:5 ^Prov 19:12 ^BSong 2:1
14:6 ^Jer 11:16 ^BSong 4:11 14:7 ^Hos 2:21, 22

And they will blossom like
    the vine.
His fame *will be* like the wine
    of Lebanon.

8   Ephraim, what more have I to
        do with idols?
    It is I who answer and look
        after you.
    I am like a luxuriant
        ^juniper;
    From ^BMe comes your fruit.

9   ^AWhoever is wise, let him
        understand these things;
    Whoever is discerning, let him
        know them.
    For the ^Bways of the LORD are
        right,
    And the righteous will walk in
        them,
    But wrongdoers will stumble
        in them.

14:8 ^AIs 41:19   ^BEzek 17:23   14:9 ^APs 107:43   ^BPs 111:7

JOEL

THE DEVASTATION BY LOCUSTS

1 The word of the LORD that came
to ᴬJoel, the son of Pethuel:

2 Hear this, you ᴬelders,
And listen, all inhabitants of
the land.
ᴮHas *anything like* this
happened in your days,
Or in your fathers' days?

3 ᴬTell your sons about it,
And *have* your sons *tell* their
sons,
And their sons the next
generation.

4 What the gnawing locust has
left, the swarming locust has
eaten;
And what the ᴬswarming
locust has left, the creeping
locust has eaten;
And what the creeping locust
has left, the ᴮstripping locust
has eaten.

5 Awake, ᴬyou heavy drinkers,
and weep;
And wail, all you wine drinkers,
Because of the sweet wine,
For it has been ᴮeliminated
from your mouth.

6 For a nation has invaded my
land,
Mighty and without number;
ᴬIts teeth are the teeth of a lion,
And it has the jaws of a lioness.

7 It has ᴬmade my vine a waste
And my fig tree a stump.
It has stripped them bare and
hurled *them* away;
Their branches have become
white.

8 ᴬWail like a virgin ᴮclothed
with sackcloth
For the groom of her youth.

9 The ᴬgrain offering and the
drink offering have been
cut off
From the house of the LORD.
The ᴮpriests mourn,
The ministers of the LORD.

10 The field is ᴬruined,
ᴮThe land mourns;
For the grain is ruined,
The new wine has dried up,
Fresh oil has failed.

11 Be ashamed, you farm
workers,
Wail, you vinedressers,
For the wheat and the barley;
Because the ᴬharvest of the
field is destroyed.

12 The ᴬvine has dried up
And the fig tree has withered;
The pomegranate, the palm
also, and the apple tree,
All the trees of the field have
dried up.
Indeed, ᴮjoy has dried up
From the sons of mankind.

13 ᴬPut on *sackcloth*
And mourn, you priests;
Wail, you ministers of the
altar!
Come, spend the night in
sackcloth,
You ministers of my God,

1:1ᴬActs 2:16 1:2ᴬJob 8:8 ᴮJer 30:7 1:3ᴬEx 10:2;
Ps 78:4 1:4ᴬNah 3:15, 16 ᴮIs 33:4 1:5ᴬJoel 3:3
ᴮIs 32:10 1:6ᴬRev 9:8 1:7ᴬIs 5:6; Amos 4:9
1:8ᴬIs 22:12 ᴮJoel 1:13 1:9ᴬHos 9:4 ᴮJoel 2:17
1:10ᴬIs 24:4, 7 ᴮJer 12:11 1:11ᴬIs 17:11; Jer 9:12
1:12ᴬJoel 1:10 ᴮIs 16:10 1:13ᴬJer 4:8; Ezek 7:18

For the grain offering and the
   drink offering
Have been withheld from the
   house of your God.

STARVATION AND DROUGHT

14 Consecrate a fast,
   Proclaim a solemn assembly;
   Gather the elders
   And all the inhabitants of the
     land
   To the house of the LORD your
     God,
   And ᴬcry out to the LORD.

15 Woe for the day!
   For the ᴬday of the LORD is near,
   And it will come as ᴮdestruction
     from the Almighty.

16 Has ᴬfood not been cut off
   before our eyes, *and*
   Joy and rejoicing from the
     house of our God?

17 The ᴬseeds have dried up
   under their shovels;
   The storehouses have become
     desolate,
   The grain silos are ruined,
   Because the grain has dried up.

18 How ᴬthe animals have
   groaned!
   The herds of cattle have
     wandered aimlessly
   Because there is no pasture for
     them;
   Even the flocks of sheep have
     suffered.

19 ᴬTo You, LORD, I cry out;
   For fire has devoured the
     pastures of the wilderness,
   And the flame has burned up
     all the trees of the field.

20 Even the animals of the field
   ᴬpant for You;
   For the ᴮstream beds of water
     are dried up,
   And fire has devoured the
     pastures of the wilderness.

THE TERRIBLE VISITATION

2 Blow a trumpet in Zion,
   And sound an alarm on My
     holy mountain!
   Let all the inhabitants of the
     land tremble,
   For the ᴬday of the LORD is
     coming;
   Indeed, it is near,

2 A day of ᴬdarkness and gloom,
   A day of clouds and thick
     darkness.
   As dawn is spread over the
     mountains,
   So there is a great and mighty
     people;
   There has ᴮnever been
     anything like it,
   Nor will there be again after it
   To the years of many
     generations.

3 A fire consumes before them,
   And behind them a flame
     devours.
   The land is ᴬlike the Garden of
     Eden before them,
   But a ᴮdesolate wilderness
     behind them,
   And nothing at all escapes
     them.

4 Their ᴬappearance is like the
     appearance of horses;
   And like war horses, so they
     run.

5 With a ᴬnoise as of chariots
   They leap about on the tops
     of the mountains,
   Like the crackling of a flame
     of fire consuming the
     stubble,
   Like a mighty people drawn up
     for battle.

1:14ᴬJon 3:8 **1:15**ᴬJoel 2:1, 11, 31 ᴮIs 13:6
1:16ᴬIs 3:7; Amos 4:6 **1:17**ᴬIs 17:10, 11
1:18ᴬ1 Kin 8:5; Jer 12:4 **1:19**ᴬPs 50:15; Mic 7:7
1:20ᴬPs 104:21 ᴮ1 Kin 17:7 **2:1**ᴬJoel 1:15; 2:11, 31
2:2ᴬJoel 2:10, 31 ᴮLam 1:12
2:3ᴬIs 51:3 ᴮEx 10:5, 15 **2:4**ᴬRev 9:7 **2:5**ᴬRev 9:9

6 Before them the people are in
   ^anguish;
   All faces turn pale.
7 They run like warriors,
   They climb the wall like
      soldiers;
   And each of them ^marches in
      line,
   Nor do they lose their way.
8 They do not crowd each
      other,
   Every warrior of them
      marches in his path;
   When they burst through the
      defenses,
   They do not break ranks.
9 They storm the city,
   They run on the wall;
   They climb into the ^houses,
   They ^Benter through the
      windows like a thief.
10 Before them the earth ^quakes,
   The heavens tremble,
   The ^Bsun and the moon
      become dark,
   And the stars lose their
      brightness.
11 The Lord utters His voice
      before His army;
   His camp is indeed very great,
   For ^mighty is one who carries
      out His word.
   The ^Bday of the Lord is indeed
      great and very awesome,
   And who can endure it?
12 "Yet even now," declares the
      Lord,
   "^Return to Me with all your
      heart,
   And with ^Bfasting, weeping,
      and mourning;
13 And ^tear your heart and not
      merely your garments."
   Now return to the Lord your
      God,
   For He is ^Bgracious and
      compassionate,

Slow to anger, abounding in
   mercy
And relenting of
   catastrophe.
14 Who knows, ^He might turn
      and relent,
   And leave a blessing behind
      Him,
   Resulting in a grain offering
      and a drink offering
   For the Lord your God.
15 Blow a trumpet in Zion,
   ^Consecrate a fast, proclaim a
      solemn assembly,
16 Gather the people, ^sanctify
      the congregation,
   Assemble the elders,
   Gather the children and the
      nursing infants.
   Have the groom come out of
      his room
   And the bride out of her bridal
      chamber.
17 Let the priests, the Lord's
      ministers,
   Weep between the porch and
      the altar,
   And let them say, "^Spare Your
      people, Lord,
   And do not make Your
      inheritance a disgrace,
   With the nations jeering at
      them.
   Why should *those* among the
      peoples say,
   '^BWhere is their God?'"

DELIVERANCE PROMISED

18 Then the Lord will be zealous
      for His land,
   And will have ^compassion
      for His people.

2:6 ^Is 13:8; Nah 2:10   2:7 ^Prov 30:27   2:9 ^Ex 10:6
^BJer 9:21   2:10 ^Ps 18:7   ^BIs 13:10   2:11 ^Jer 50:34
^BJoel 1:15   2:12 ^Deut 4:29   ^BDan 9:3   2:13 ^Ps 34:18
^BEx 34:6   2:14 ^Jer 26:3; Jon 3:9   2:15 ^Joel 1:14
2:16 ^1 Sam 16:5; 2 Chr 29:5   2:17 ^Ex 32:11, 12
^BPs 42:10   2:18 ^Is 60:10; 63:9, 15

19 The Lord will answer and say
  to His people,
  "Behold, I am going to send you
  grain, new wine, and oil,
  And you will be satisfied *in full*
  with them;
  And I will ^never again make
  you a disgrace among the
  nations.
20 "But I will remove the ^northern
  army far from you,
  And I will drive it into a dry
  and desolate land,
  Its advance guard into the
  ᴮeastern sea,
  And its rear guard into the
  western sea.
  And its stench will ascend and
  its odor of decay will come
  up,
  Because it has done great
  things."

21 ^Do not fear, land; shout for joy
  and rejoice,
  For the Lord has done great
  things.
22 Do not fear, animals of the
  field,
  For the ^pastures of the
  wilderness have turned
  green,
  For the tree has produced its
  fruit,
  The fig tree and the vine have
  yielded in full.
23 So shout for joy, you sons of
  Zion,
  And rejoice in the Lord your
  God;
  For He has ^given you
  ¹the early rain for *your*
  vindication.
  And He has brought down for
  you the rain,
  The ²early and ³,ᴮlatter rain as
  before.

24 The threshing floors will be
  full of grain,
  And the vats will
  ^overflow with the new
  wine and oil.
25 "Then I will compensate you
  for the years
  That the swarming ^locust
  has eaten,
  The creeping locust, the
  stripping locust, and the
  gnawing locust—
  My great army which I sent
  among you.
26 "You will have plenty to eat
  and be satisfied,
  And you will praise the name
  of the Lord your God,
  Who has ^dealt wondrously
  with you;
  Then My people will ᴮnever
  be put to shame.
27 "So you will ^know that I am in
  the midst of Israel,
  And that I am the Lord your
  God
  And there is ᴮno other;
  And My people will never be
  put to shame.

THE PROMISE OF THE SPIRIT

28 "It will come about after this
  That I will ^pour out My Spirit
  on all ᴮmankind;
  And your sons and your
  daughters will prophesy,
  Your old men will have
  dreams,
  Your young men will see
  visions.

2:19 ^Ezek 34:29; 36:15   2:20 ^Jer 1:14, 15   ᴮ Zech 14:8
2:21 ^Is 54:4; Jer 30:10   2:22 ^Ps 65:12, 13
2:23 ^Deut 11:14   ᴮ Lev 26:4   2:24 ^Lev 26:10;
Amos 9:13   2:25 ^Joel 1:4-7; 2:2-11   2:26 ^Ps 126:2, 3
ᴮ Is 45:17   2:27 ^Lev 26:11, 12   ᴮ Is 45:5, 6
2:28 ^Is 32:15   ᴮ Is 40:5

2:23 ¹ I.e., autumn; or possibly *the teacher for
righteousness*   ² I.e., autumn   ³ I.e., spring

29 "And even on the ^male and
      female servants
    I will pour out My Spirit in
      those days.

THE DAY OF THE LORD

30 "I will ^display wonders in the
      sky and on the earth,
    Blood, fire, and columns of
      smoke.

31 "The ^sun will be turned into
      darkness,
    And the moon into blood,
    Before the great and awesome
      day of the LORD comes.

32 "And it will come about *that*
    ^everyone who calls on the
      name of the LORD
    Will be saved;
    For on Mount Zion and in
      Jerusalem
    There will be those who escape,
    Just as the LORD has said,
    Even among the survivors
      whom the LORD calls.

THE NATIONS WILL BE JUDGED

3 "For behold, in those days and
      at that time,
    When I ^restore the fortunes of
      Judah and Jerusalem,
2 I will ^gather all the nations
    And bring them down to the
      Valley of Jehoshaphat.
    Then I will ^enter into
      judgment with them there
    On behalf of My people and
      My inheritance, Israel,
    Whom they have scattered
      among the nations;
    And they have divided up My
      land.
3 "They have also ^cast lots for
      My people,
    ^Traded a boy for a prostitute,
    And sold a girl for wine so that
      they may drink.

4 Moreover, what are you to Me,
Tyre, Sidon, and all the regions of
Philistia? Are you repaying Me with
retribution? But if you are showing
Me *retribution*, swiftly and speed-
ily I will ^return your retribution on
your head! 5 Since you have ^taken
My silver and My gold, brought My
precious treasures to your temples,
6 and sold the ^sons of Judah and
Jerusalem to the Greeks in order
to remove them far from their territory, 7 behold, I am going to ^stir
them up from the place where
you have sold them, and return
your retribution on your head. 8 I
will also ^sell your sons and your
daughters into the hand of the sons
of Judah, and they will sell them to
the ^B^Sabeans, to a distant nation,"
for the LORD has spoken.

9 Proclaim this among the
      nations:
    ^Prepare for holy war; stir up
      the warriors!
    Have all the soldiers come
      forward, have them come up!
10 ^Beat your plowshares into
      swords,
    And your pruning hooks into
      spears;
    Let the weak *man* say, "I am a
      warrior."
11 ^Hurry and come, all you
      surrounding nations,
    And gather yourselves there.
    Bring down, LORD, Your
      warriors.
12 Let the nations be awakened
    And come up to the ^Valley of
      Jehoshaphat,

2:29 ^1 Cor 12:13; Gal 3:28   2:30 ^Matt 24:29;
Mark 13:24, 25   2:31 ^Is 13:10; 34:4   2:32 ^Jer 33:3;
Acts 2:21   3:1 ^Jer 16:15   3:2 ^Is 66:18   ^BJer 25:31
3:3 ^Obad 11   ^BAmos 2:6   3:4 ^Is 34:8; 59:18
3:5 ^2 Kin 12:18; 2 Chr 21:16, 17   3:6 ^Ezek 27:13
3:7 ^Is 43:5, 6; Jer 23:8   3:8 ^Is 14:2   ^BJob 1:15
3:9 ^Jer 6:4; Ezek 38:7   3:10 ^Is 2:4; Mic 4:3
3:11 ^Ezek 38:15, 16   3:12 ^Joel 3:2, 14

For there I will sit to [B]judge
All the surrounding nations.

13 [A]Put in the sickle, for the
[B]harvest is ripe.
Come, tread *the grapes,* for the
wine press is full;
The vats overflow, for their
wickedness is great.

14 [A]Multitudes, multitudes in the
valley of decision!
For the day of the LORD is near
in the valley of decision.

15 The [A]sun and moon have
become dark,
And the stars have lost their
brightness.

16 The LORD roars from Zion
And utters His voice from
Jerusalem,
And the heavens and the earth
quake.
But the LORD is a [A]refuge for
His people,
And a [B]stronghold for the sons
of Israel.

17 Then you will [A]know that I am
the LORD your God,
Dwelling on Zion, My holy
mountain.
So Jerusalem will be holy,
And [B]strangers will no longer
pass through it.

JUDAH WILL BE BLESSED

18 And on that day
The mountains will drip with
sweet wine,
And the hills will flow with
milk,
And all the [A]brooks of Judah
will flow with water;
And a [B]spring will go out from
the house of the LORD
And water the Valley of
Shittim.

19 Egypt will become a
wasteland,
And Edom will become a
desolate wilderness,
Because of the [A]violence done
to the sons of Judah,
In whose land they have shed
innocent blood.

20 But Judah will be [A]inhabited
forever,
And Jerusalem for all
generations.

21 And I will [A]avenge their
blood *which* I have not
avenged,
For the LORD dwells in Zion.

3:12 [B]Ps 7:6   **3:13** [A]Rev 14:14-19   [B]Jer 51:33
3:14 [A]Is 34:2-8   **3:15** [A]Joel 2:10, 31   **3:16** [A]Ps 61:3
[B]Jer 16:19   **3:17** [A]Joel 2:27   [B]Is 52:1   **3:18** [A]Is 30:25
[B]Ezek 47:1-12   **3:19** [A]Obad 10   **3:20** [A]Ezek 37:25;
Amos 9:15   **3:21** [A]Is 4:4

AMOS

JUDGMENT ON NEIGHBOR NATIONS

1 The words of Amos, who was
  among the sheepherders from
ᴬTekoa, which he saw *in visions*
concerning Israel in the days of
Uzziah king of Judah, and in the
days of Jeroboam son of Joash,
king of Israel, two years before the
ᴮearthquake.
² And he said,
  "The ᴬLᴏʀᴅ roars from Zion,
    And from Jerusalem He utters
      His voice;
    And the shepherds' pasture
      grounds mourn,
    And the summit of Carmel
      dries up."

³ This is what the Lᴏʀᴅ says:
  "For ᴬthree offenses of
      Damascus, and for four,
    I will not revoke its *punishment,*
    Because they threshed Gilead
      with iron sledges.
⁴ "So I will send fire upon the
      house of Hazael,
    And it will consume the
      citadels of ᴬBen-hadad.
⁵ "I will also ᴬbreak the *gate* bar
      of Damascus,
    And eliminate *every* inhabitant
      from the Valley of Aven,
    As well as him who holds the
      scepter, from Beth-eden;
    So the people of Aram will be
      exiled to ᴮKir,"
    Says the Lᴏʀᴅ.

⁶ This is what the Lᴏʀᴅ says:
  "For three offenses of Gaza, and
      for four,

I will not revoke its *punishment,*
    Because they led into exile an
      entire population
    To ᴬturn *them* over to Edom.
⁷ "So I will send fire on the wall
      of Gaza
    And it will consume her
      citadels.
⁸ "I will also eliminate *every*
      inhabitant from Ashdod,
    As well as him who holds the
      scepter, from Ashkelon;
    And I will direct My power
      against Ekron,
    And the remnant of the
      ᴬPhilistines will perish,"
    Says the Lord Gᴏᴅ.

⁹ This is what the Lᴏʀᴅ says:
  "For three offenses of Tyre, and
      for four,
    I will not revoke its *punishment,*
    Because they turned an entire
      population over to Edom
    And did not remember *the*
      covenant of ᴬbrotherhood.
¹⁰ "So I will ᴬsend fire on the wall
      of Tyre,
    And it will consume her
      citadels."

¹¹ This is what the Lᴏʀᴅ says:
  "For three offenses of Edom,
      and for four,
    I will not revoke its *punishment,*
    Because he ᴬpursued his
      brother with the sword

1:1 ᴬ2 Sam 14:2   ᴮZech 14:5   1:2 ᴬIs 42:13; Jer 25:30
1:3 ᴬAmos 2:1, 4, 6   1:4 ᴬ1 Kin 20:1; 2 Kin 6:24
1:5 ᴬJer 51:30   ᴮ2 Kin 16:9   1:6 ᴬEzek 35:5; Obad 11
1:8 ᴬIs 14:29-31; Jer 47:1-7   1:9 ᴬ1 Kin 9:11-14
1:10 ᴬZech 9:4   1:11 ᴬNum 20:14-21

And stifled his compassion;
His anger also [B]tore continually,
And he maintained his fury
  forever.

12 "So I will send fire upon [A]Teman
   And it will consume the
     citadels of Bozrah."

13   This is what the LORD says:
   "For three offenses of the sons
     of Ammon, and for four,
   I will not revoke its
     punishment,
   Because they [A]ripped open the
     pregnant women of Gilead
   In order to [B]enlarge their
     borders.

14 "So I will kindle a fire on the
     wall of [A]Rabbah,
   And it will consume her
     citadels
   Amid war cries on the day of
     battle,
   And amid a storm on the day
     of tempest.

15 "Their [A]king will go into exile,
   He and his princes together,"
     says the LORD.

JUDGMENT ON MOAB

2   This is what the LORD says:
   "For three offenses of Moab,
     and for four,
   I will not revoke its *punishment,*
   Because he [A]burned the bones
     of the king of Edom to lime.

2 "So I will send fire upon Moab
   And it will consume the
     citadels of [A]Kerioth;
   And Moab will die amid the
     panic *of battle,*
   Amid war cries and the sound
     of a trumpet.

3 "I will also eliminate the [A]judge
     from her midst
   And slay all her leaders with
     him," says the LORD.

JUDGMENT ON JUDAH

4   This is what the LORD says:
   "For three offenses of Judah,
     and for four,
   I will not revoke its
     punishment,
   Because they [A]rejected the Law
     of the LORD
   And have not kept His statutes;
   Their [B]lies also have led them
     astray,
   Those which their fathers
     followed.

5 "So I will [A]send fire upon Judah,
   And it will consume the
     citadels of Jerusalem."

JUDGMENT ON ISRAEL

6   This is what the LORD says:
   "For three offenses of Israel,
     and for four,
   I will not revoke its
     punishment,
   Because they [A]sell the
     righteous for money,
   And the needy for a pair of
     sandals.

7 "These who trample the head
     of the [A]helpless to the dust of
     the earth
   Also divert the way of the
     humble;
   And a man and his father
     resort to the *same* girl
   So as to profane My holy
     name.

8 "And on garments [A]seized as
     pledges they stretch out
     beside every altar,
   And *in* the house of their God
     they drink the wine of those
     who have been fined.

1:11 [B] Is 57:16   1:12 [A] Jer 49:7, 20; Obad 9
1:13 [A] 2 Kin 15:16   [B] Is 5:8   1:14 [A] Deut 3:11; 1 Chr 20:1
1:15 [A] Jer 49:3   2:1 [A] 2 Kin 3:26, 27   2:2 [A] Jer 48:24, 41
2:3 [A] Ps 2:10; 141:6   2:4 [A] Judg 2:17-20   [B] Is 9:15, 16
2:5 [A] Jer 17:27; 21:10   2:6 [A] Joel 3:3; Amos 5:11, 12
2:7 [A] Amos 8:4; Mic 2:2, 9   2:8 [A] Ex 22:26

9   "Yet it was I who destroyed the
    ^AAmorite before them,
    Though his ^Bheight *was* like
    the height of cedars
    And he *was as* strong as the
    oaks;
    I also destroyed his fruit
    above and his roots
    below.

10 "And it was I who brought you
    up from the land of Egypt,
    And led you in the
    wilderness for ^Aforty
    years
    So that you might take
    possession of the land of
    the ^BAmorite.

11 "Then I ^Araised up some of
    your sons to be prophets,
    And some of your young men
    to be ^BNazirites.
    Is this not so, you sons of
    Israel?" declares the LORD.

12 "But you made the Nazirites
    drink wine,
    And you commanded the
    prophets, saying, 'You ^Ashall
    not prophesy!'

13 "Behold, I am ^Amaking a rut *in
    the ground* beneath you,
    Just as a wagon makes a rut
    when filled with sheaves.

14 "^ARefuge will be lost from the
    swift,
    And the strong will not
    strengthen his power,
    Nor the warrior save his life.

15 "The one who ^Agrasps the bow
    will not stand *his ground,*
    The swift of foot will not
    escape,
    Nor will the one who rides
    the ^Bhorse save his life.

16 "Even the bravest among the
    warriors will ^Aflee naked
    on that day," declares the
    LORD.

ALL THE TRIBES ARE GUILTY

3 Hear this word which the LORD
  has spoken against you, sons
of Israel, against the entire ^Afamily
which He brought up from the land
of Egypt:

2   "You only have I known
        among all the families of
        the earth;
    Therefore I will ^Apunish you
        for all your wrongdoing."

3   Do two people walk together
    unless they have agreed to
    meet?

4   Does a ^Alion roar in the forest
    when he has no prey?
    Does a young lion growl
    from his den unless he has
    captured *something?*

5   Does a bird fall into a trap on
    the ground when there is no
    device in it?
    Does a trap spring up from
    the earth when it captures
    nothing at all?

6   If a trumpet is blown in a
    city, will the people not
    tremble?
    If a ^Adisaster occurs in a city,
    has the LORD not brought it
    about?

7   Certainly the Lord GOD does
    nothing
    Unless He ^Areveals His secret
    plan
    To His servants the prophets.

8   A lion has roared! Who will
    not fear?
    The ^ALord GOD has spoken!
    ^BWho can *do anything* but
    prophesy?

2:9 ^ANum 21:23-25   ^BNum 13:32   2:10 ^ADeut 2:7
^BEx 3:8   2:11 ^ADeut 18:18   ^BNum 6:2, 3
2:12 ^AIs 30:10; Jer 11:21   2:13 ^AIs 1:14   2:14 ^AIs 30:16, 17
2:15 ^AJer 51:56   ^BIs 31:3   2:16 ^AJudg 4:17   3:1 ^AJer 8:3;
13:11   3:2 ^AJer 14:10; Ezek 20:36   3:4 ^APs 104:21;
Hos 5:14   3:6 ^AIs 14:24-27; 45:7   3:7 ^AGen 6:13; 18:17
3:8 ^AJon 1:1-3   ^BJer 20:9

⁹Proclaim on the citadels in Ashdod and on the citadels in the land of Egypt and say, "Assemble yourselves on the ᴬmountains of Samaria and see *the* great panic within her and *the* ᴮoppressions in her midst. ¹⁰But they do not know how to do what is right," declares the LORD, "these who ᴬstore up violence and devastation in their citadels."

¹¹Therefore, this is what the Lord GOD says:

"An ᴬenemy, one surrounding the land,
Will take down your fortifications from you,
And your ᴮcitadels will be looted."

¹²This is what the LORD says:

"Just as the shepherd ᴬsnatches from the lion's mouth a couple of legs or a piece of an ear,
So will the sons of Israel living in Samaria be snatched away—
With *the* corner of a bed and *the* cover of a couch!

¹³ "Hear and ᴬtestify against the house of Jacob,"
Declares the Lord GOD, the God of armies.

¹⁴ "For on the day that I punish Israel's offenses,
I will also punish the altars of ᴬBethel;
The horns of the altar will be cut off,
And will fall to the ground.

¹⁵ "I will also strike the ᴬwinter house together with the ᴮsummer house;
The houses of ivory will also perish,
And the great houses will come to an end,"
Declares the LORD.

"YET YOU HAVE NOT RETURNED TO ME"

4 Hear this word, you cows of ᴬBashan who are on the mountain of Samaria,
Who exploit the poor, who oppress the needy,
And say to their husbands, "Bring now, that we may drink!"

² The Lord GOD has sworn by His holiness,
"For behold, the days are coming upon you
When they will take you away with ᴬ*meat* hooks,
And the last of you with ᴮfish hooks.

³ "You will ᴬgo out *through* holes *in the walls,*
One in front of the other,
And you will be hurled to Harmon," declares the LORD.

⁴ "Enter Bethel and do wrong;
In Gilgal multiply wrongdoing!
ᴬBring your sacrifices every morning,
Your tithes every three days.

⁵ "Offer a ᴬthanksgiving offering also from that which is leavened,
And proclaim ᴮvoluntary offerings, make them known.
For so you love *to do,* you sons of Israel,"
Declares the Lord GOD.

3:9 ᴬAmos 4:1   ᴮAmos 5:11   3:10 ᴬHab 2:8-10; Zeph 1:9   3:11 ᴬAmos 6:14   ᴮAmos 2:5
3:12 ᴬ1 Sam 17:34-37   3:13 ᴬEzek 2:7   3:14 ᴬ2 Kin 23:15; Hos 10:5-8, 14, 15   3:15 ᴬJer 36:22   ᴮJudg 3:20
4:1 ᴬPs 22:12; Ezek 39:18   4:2 ᴬIs 37:29   ᴮJer 16:16
4:3 ᴬJer 52:7   4:4 ᴬNum 28:3; Amos 5:21, 22
4:5 ᴬLev 7:13   ᴮLev 22:18-21

6 "But I gave you also ^cleanness
      of teeth in all your cities,
   And lack of bread in all your
      places;
   Yet you have not returned to
      Me," declares the LORD.

7 "Furthermore, I ^withheld the
      rain from you
   While *there were* still three
      months until harvest.
   Then I would send rain on one
      city,
   But on another city I would
      not send rain;
   One part would be rained on,
   While the part not rained on
      would dry up.

8 "So *the people of* two *or* three
      cities would stagger to
      another city to drink ^water,
   But would not be satisfied;
   Yet you have ^Bnot returned to
      Me," declares the LORD.

9 "I ^struck you with scorching
      wind and mildew;
   The ^Bcaterpillar was devouring
   Your many gardens and
      vineyards, fig trees and olive
      trees;
   Yet you have not returned to
      Me," declares the LORD.

10 "I sent a plague among you as in
      Egypt;
   I ^killed your young men with
      the sword, along with your
      captured horses,
   And I made the ^Bstench of your
      camp rise up in your nostrils;
   Yet you have not returned to
      Me," declares the LORD.

11 "I overthrew you, as ^God
      overthrew Sodom and
      Gomorrah,
   And you were like a ^Blog
      snatched from a fire;
   Yet you have not returned to
      Me," declares the LORD.

12 "Therefore so I will do to you,
      Israel;
   Because I will do this to you,
   Prepare to ^meet your God,
      Israel."

13 For behold, He who ^forms
      mountains and creates the
      wind,
   And ^Bdeclares to a person what
      are His thoughts,
   He who makes dawn into
      darkness
   And treads on the high places
      of the earth,
   The LORD God of armies is His
      name.

"SEEK ME SO THAT YOU MAY LIVE"

5 Hear this word which I am
      taking up for you as a ^song
      of mourning, house of Israel:

2   She has fallen, she will not rise
         again—
      The ^virgin Israel.
      She lies unnoticed on her
         land;
      There is ^Bno one to raise her up.

3 For this is what the Lord GOD says:
      "The city which goes forth a
         thousand *strong*
      Will have a ^hundred left,
      And the one which goes forth
         a hundred *strong*
      Will have ^Bten left to the house
         of Israel."

4 For this is what the LORD says to
   the house of Israel:
      "^Seek Me ^Bso that you may live.

5   "But do not resort to ^Bethel
      And do not come to Gilgal,
      Nor cross over to Beersheba;

4:6 ^Is 3:1; Jer 14:18   **4:7** ^Deut 11:17; 2 Chr 7:13
4:8 ^1 Kin 18:5   ^BJer 3:7   **4:9** ^Deut 28:22   ^BJoel 1:4, 7
4:10 ^Jer 11:22   ^BJoel 2:20   **4:11** ^Gen 19:24, 25
^BZech 3:2   **4:12** ^Is 32:11; 64:2   **4:13** ^Job 38:4-7
^BDan 2:28, 30   **5:1** ^Jer 7:29; 9:10, 17   **5:2** ^Jer 14:17
^BIs 51:18   **5:3** ^Is 6:13   ^BAmos 6:9   **5:4** ^Deut 4:29
^BIs 55:3   **5:5** ^1 Kin 12:28, 29; Amos 3:14

For Gilgal will certainly go into
    captivity
And Bethel will come to
    nothing.
6 "ᴬSeek the Lᴏʀᴅ so that you
    may live,
Or He will break through like a
    ᴮfire, house of Joseph,
And it will consume with
    no one to extinguish *it* for
    Bethel,
7 *For* those who turn ᴬjustice
    into wormwood,
And throw righteousness to
    the earth."

8 He who made the ᴬPleiades
    and Orion,
And ᴮchanges deep darkness
    into morning,
Who also darkens day *into*
    night,
Who calls for the waters of
    the sea
And pours them out on the
    surface of the earth,
The Lᴏʀᴅ is His name.
9 *It is* He who makes
    destruction flash upon the
    strong,
So that ᴬdestruction comes
    upon the fortress.

10 They hate him who ᴬrebukes
    in the ¹gate,
And they despise him who
    speaks *with* integrity.
11 Therefore because you impose
    heavy rent on the poor
And take a tribute of grain
    from them,
Though you have built
    ᴬhouses of cut stone,
Yet you will not live in them;
You have planted beautiful
    vineyards, yet you will ᴮnot
    drink their wine.

12 For I know your offenses are
    many and your sins are great,
You who are ᴬhostile to the
    righteous *and* accept bribes,
And turn away the poor *from
    justice* at the gate.
13 Therefore at such a time the
    prudent person ᴬkeeps quiet,
    because it is an evil time.

14 Seek good and not evil, so that
    you may live;
And so may the Lᴏʀᴅ God of
    armies be with you,
ᴬJust as you have said!
15 ᴬHate evil, love good,
And establish justice in the gate!
Perhaps the Lᴏʀᴅ God of armies
Will be gracious to the
    remnant of Joseph.
16 Therefore this is what the Lᴏʀᴅ
God of armies, the Lord says:
    "There is ᴬmourning in all the
        public squares,
    And in all the streets they say,
        'Oh no! Oh no!'
    They also call the farmer to
        mourning
    And professional mourners to
        mourning rites.
17 "And in all the ᴬvineyards *there
    is* mourning,
    Because I will pass through the
        midst of you," says the Lᴏʀᴅ.

18 Woe *to* you who are longing
    for the ᴬday of the Lᴏʀᴅ,
For what purpose *will* the day
    of the Lᴏʀᴅ *be* to you?
It *will be* ᴮdarkness and not
    light;

5:6 ᴬ Is 55:3, 6, 7   ᴮ Deut 4:24   5:7 ᴬ Amos 2:3; 5:12
5:8 ᴬ Job 9:9   ᴮ Job 12:22   5:9 ᴬ Mic 5:11   5:10 ᴬ Is 29:21;
Amos 5:15   5:11 ᴬ Amos 3:15   ᴮ Mic 6:15   5:12 ᴬ Is 1:23;
5:23   5:13 ᴬ Eccl 3:7; Hos 4:4   5:14 ᴬ Mic 3:11
5:15 ᴬ Ps 97:10; Rom 12:9   5:16 ᴬ Jer 9:10, 18-20; Amos 8:3
5:17 ᴬ Is 16:10; Jer 48:33   5:18 ᴬ Is 5:19   ᴮ Joel 2:2
5:10 ¹ I.e., the place where court was held

¹⁹ As when a man ^flees from a
   lion
And a bear confronts him,
Or he goes home, leans with
   his hand against the wall,
And a snake bites him.
²⁰ *Will* the day of the LORD not
   be ^darkness instead of
   light,
Even gloom with no brightness
   in it?

²¹ "I hate, I ^reject your festivals,
Nor do I ^Bdelight in your festive
   assemblies.
²² "Even though you offer up to
   Me burnt offerings and your
   grain offerings,
I will not accept *them;*
And I will not *even* look at
   the ^peace offerings of your
   fattened oxen.
²³ "Take away from Me the noise
   of your songs;
I will not even listen to the
   sound of your harps.
²⁴ "But let ^justice roll out like
   waters,
And righteousness like an
   ever-flowing stream.

²⁵ "^Did you present Me with sac-
rifices and grain offerings in the
wilderness for forty years, house
of Israel? ²⁶^You also carried along
Sikkuth your king and Kiyyun,
your images, the star of your gods
which you made for yourselves.
²⁷Therefore I will make you go into
exile beyond Damascus," says the
LORD, whose name is the God of
armies.

"CAREFREE IN ZION"

6 Woe to those who are carefree
   in Zion,
And to those who feel secure
   on the mountain of Samaria,

The ^dignitaries of the
   foremost of nations,
To whom the house of Israel
   comes.
² Go over to ^Calneh and look,
And go from there to Hamath
   the great,
Then go down to Gath of the
   Philistines.
Are they better than these
   kingdoms,
Or is their territory greater
   than yours?
³ Are you ^postponing the day of
   disaster,
And would you ^Bbring near the
   seat of violence?
⁴ Those who lie on beds of ivory,
And lounge around on their
   couches,
And ^eat lambs from the flock,
And calves from the midst of
   the fattened cattle,
⁵ Who improvise to the sound
   of the harp,
And like David have composed
   ^songs for themselves,
⁶ Who drink wine from sacred
   bowls
While they anoint themselves
   with the finest of oils—
Yet they have not ^grieved over
   the collapse of Joseph.
⁷ Therefore, they will now ^go
   into exile at the head of the
   exiles,
And the revelry of those who
   lounge around will come to
   an end.

5:19^Job 20:24; Is 24:17, 18   **5:20**^Is 13:10; Zeph 1:15
5:21^Is 1:11-16   ^BLev 26:31
5:22^Lev 7:11-15; Amos 4:5   **5:24**^Jer 22:3; Ezek 45:9
5:25^Deut 32:17; Josh 24:14   **5:26**^Acts 7:43
6:1^Ex 19:5; Amos 3:2   **6:2**^Gen 10:10; Is 10:9
6:3^Is 56:12   ^BAmos 3:10   **6:4**^Ezek 34:2, 3
6:5^1 Chr 15:16; 23:5   **6:6**^Ezek 9:4
6:7^Amos 7:11, 17

8 The Lord G<small>OD</small> has sworn by
   Himself, the L<small>ORD</small> God of
   armies has declared:
"I ^loathe the arrogance of
      Jacob,
   And detest his citadels;
   Therefore I will give up *the* city
      and all it contains."
9 And it will be, if ^ten men are left
in one house, they will die. 10 Then
one's uncle, or his ^undertaker, will
lift him up to carry out *his* bones
from the house, and he will say to the
one who is in the innermost part of
the house, "Is anyone else with you?"
And that one will say, "No one." Then
he will answer, "Keep quiet! For the
name of the L<small>ORD</small> is ^not to be mentioned." 11 For behold, the L<small>ORD</small> is
going to ^command that the ^great
house be smashed to pieces, and the
small house to rubble.
12   Do horses run on rocks?
     Or does one plow *them* with
        oxen?
     Yet you have turned ^justice
        into poison,
     And the fruit of righteousness
        into 1 wormwood,
13   You who rejoice in 1,^ Lodebar,
     And say, "Have we not ^by our
        own strength taken 2 Karnaim
        for ourselves?"
14   "For behold, ^I am going to raise
        up a nation against you,
     House of Israel," declares the
        L<small>ORD</small> God of armies,
     "And they will torment you from
        the ^entrance of Hamath
     To the ^brook of the Arabah."

WARNING THROUGH VISIONS

7 This is what the Lord G<small>OD</small>
   showed me, and behold, He was
forming a ^swarm of locusts when
the spring crop began to sprout.
And behold, the spring crop *was*

after the king's mowing. 2 And it
came about, when it had ^finished
eating the vegetation of the land,
that I said,
"Lord G<small>OD</small>, please pardon!
   How can Jacob stand?
   For he is ^small."
3   The L<small>ORD</small> ^relented of this.
"It shall not be," said the L<small>ORD</small>.
4 So the Lord G<small>OD</small> showed me,
and behold, the Lord G<small>OD</small> was calling to contend *with them* by ^fire,
and it consumed the great deep and
began to consume the farmland.
5 Then I said,
"Lord G<small>OD</small>, please stop!
   ^How can Jacob stand?
   For he is small."
6   The L<small>ORD</small> ^relented of this.
"This too shall not be," said the
   Lord G<small>OD</small>.
7 So He showed me, and behold,
the Lord was standing by a vertical
wall with a plumb line in His hand.
8 And the L<small>ORD</small> said to me, "What
do you see, Amos?" And I said, "A
plumb line." Then the Lord said,
"Behold I am about to put a
   ^plumb line
   In the midst of My people Israel.
   I will not ^spare them any
      longer.
9   "The ^high places of Isaac will
      become deserted,
   And the ^sanctuaries of Israel
      will be in ruins.
   Then I will rise up against the
      house of Jeroboam with the
      sword."

6:8 ^ Lev 26:30; Deut 32:19 6:9 ^ Amos 5:3
6:10 ^ 1 Sam 31:12 ^ Jer 44:26 6:11 ^ Is 55:11
^ 2 Kin 25:9 6:12 ^ 1 Kin 21:7-13; Is 59:13, 14
6:13 ^ Job 8:14, 15 ^ Ps 75:4, 5 6:14 ^ Jer 5:15
^ Num 34:7, 8 7:1 ^ Joel 1:4; Amos 4:9 7:2 ^ Ex 10:15
^ Is 37:4 7:3 ^ Deut 32:36; Jer 26:19 7:4 ^ Deut 32:22;
Is 66:15, 16 7:5 ^ Amos 7:2 7:6 ^ Ps 106:45; Amos 7:3
7:8 ^ 2 Kin 21:13 ^ Jer 15:6 7:9 ^ Gen 46:1 ^ Lev 26:31

6:12 1 I.e., bitterness 6:13 1 Lit *nothing* 2 Lit *a pair
of horns*

AMOS ACCUSED; GIVES AN ANSWER

¹⁰Then Amaziah, the priest of Bethel, sent *word* to Jeroboam king of Israel, saying, "Amos has ^conspired against you in the midst of the house of Israel; the land is unable to endure all his words. ¹¹For this is what Amos says: 'Jeroboam will die by the sword, and Israel will certainly go from its land into exile.'" ¹²Then Amaziah said to Amos, "^Go, you seer, flee to the land of Judah; and eat bread there and do your prophesying there! ¹³But ^do not prophesy at Bethel any longer, for it is a ^sanctuary of the king and a royal residence."

¹⁴Then Amos replied to Amaziah, "I am not a prophet, nor am I the ^son of a prophet; for I am a herdsman and a grower of sycamore figs. ¹⁵But the LORD took me from following the flock, and the LORD said to me, 'Go ^prophesy to My people Israel.' ¹⁶So now hear the word of the LORD: you are saying, 'You shall not prophesy against Israel ^nor shall you prophesy against the house of Isaac.' ¹⁷Therefore, this is what the LORD says: 'Your ^wife will become a prostitute in the city, your ^sons and your daughters will fall by the sword, your land will be parceled up by a *measuring* line, and you yourself will die upon unclean soil. Furthermore Israel will certainly go from its land into exile.'"

BASKET OF FRUIT AND ISRAEL'S CAPTIVITY

8 This is what the Lord GOD showed me, and behold, *there was* a basket of summer fruit. ²And He said, "What do you see, Amos?" And I said, "A basket of summer fruit." Then the LORD said to me, "The ^end has come for My people Israel. I will not ^spare them any longer. ³The songs of the palace will turn to wailing on that day," declares the Lord GOD. "The ^corpses *will be* many; in every place they will throw them out. Hush!"

⁴Hear this, you who ^trample the needy, to put an end to the humble of the land, ⁵saying,

"When will the new moon be over,
So that we may sell grain;
And the Sabbath, so that we may open the wheat *market,*
To make the ¹ephah smaller and the ²shekel bigger,
And to ^cheat with dishonest scales,
6 So as to ^buy the helpless for money,
And the needy for a pair of sandals,
And *that* we may sell the refuse of the wheat?"

7 The LORD has sworn by the pride of Jacob,
"Indeed, I will ^never forget any of their deeds.
8 "Because of this will the land not ^quake,
And everyone who lives in it ^mourn?
Indeed, all of it will rise up like the Nile,
And it will be tossed about
And subside like the Nile of Egypt.

7:10 ^Jer 26:8-11; 38:4   7:12 ^Matt 8:34
7:13 ^Amos 2:12   ^1 Kin 12:29, 32   7:14 ^1 Kin 20:35;
2 Kin 2:3, 5   7:15 ^Jer 1:7; Ezek 2:3, 4
7:16 ^Deut 32:2; Ezek 20:46   7:17 ^Hos 4:13, 14
^Jer 14:16   8:2 ^Ezek 7:2, 3, 6   ^Amos 7:8
8:3 ^Amos 6:8-10   8:4 ^Ps 14:4; Prov 30:14
8:5 ^Hos 12:7; Mic 6:11   8:6 ^Amos 2:6
8:7 ^Ps 10:11; Hos 7:2   8:8 ^Ps 18:7   ^Hos 4:3

8:5 ¹About 1 cubic foot or 0.03 cubic meters
²About 0.4 oz. or 11 gm

9 "And it will come about on that day," declares the Lord GOD,
"That I will make the ^sun go down at noon,
And ^Bmake the earth dark in broad daylight.

10 "Then I will turn your festivals into mourning,
And all your songs into songs of mourning;
And I will put ^sackcloth around everyone's waist,
And baldness on every head.
And I will make it ^Blike *a time of* mourning for an only son,
And the end of it will be like a bitter day.

11 "Behold, days are coming," declares the Lord GOD,
"When I will send a famine on the land,
Not a famine of bread or a thirst for water,
But rather ^for hearing the words of the LORD.

12 "People will stagger from sea to sea
And from the north even to the east;
They will roam about to ^seek the word of the LORD,
But they will not find *it*.

13 "On that day the beautiful virgins
And the young men will ^faint from thirst.

14 "*As for* those who swear by the ^guilt of Samaria,
And say, 'As your god lives, ^BDan,'
And, 'As the way of Beersheba lives,'
They will fall and not rise again."

GOD'S JUDGMENT UNAVOIDABLE

9 I saw the Lord standing beside the altar, and He said,
"Strike the pillar capitals so that the thresholds will shake,
And break them on the heads of them all!
Then I will ^put to death the rest of them with the sword;
They will ^Bnot have a fugitive who will flee,
Nor a survivor who will escape.

2 "Though they dig into ^Sheol,
From there My hand will take them;
And though they ^Bascend to heaven,
From there I will bring them down.

3 "And though they hide on the summit of Carmel,
I will ^track them down and take them from there;
And though they hide themselves from My sight on the bottom of the sea,
I will command the ^Bserpent from there, and it will bite them.

4 "And though they go into ^captivity before their enemies,
From there I will command the sword and it will kill them,
And I will set My eyes against them for harm and not for good."

5   The Lord GOD of armies,
The One who ^touches the land so that it quakes,

8:9 ^Job 5:14   ^BIs 59:9, 10   8:10 ^Is 15:2, 3   ^BJer 6:26
8:11 ^1 Sam 3:1; 2 Chr 15:3   8:12 ^Ezek 20:3, 31
8:13 ^Is 41:17; Hos 2:3   8:14 ^Hos 8:5   ^B1 Kin 12:28, 29
9:1 ^Amos 7:17   ^BJer 11:11   9:2 ^Ps 139:8   ^BJer 51:53
9:3 ^Jer 16:16   ^BIs 27:1   9:4 ^Lev 26:33
9:5 ^Ps 104:32

And ᴮall those who live in it
mourn,
And all of it rises up like the
Nile
And subsides like the Nile of
Egypt;

6 The One who builds His
ᴬupper chambers in the
heavens
And has founded His vaulted
dome over the earth,
He who calls for the waters of
the sea
And pours them out on the
face of the earth,
The Lᴏʀᴅ is His name.

7 "Are you not as the sons of
Ethiopia to Me,
You sons of Israel?" declares
the Lᴏʀᴅ.
"Have I not brought up Israel
from the land of Egypt,
And the ᴬPhilistines from
Caphtor and the Arameans
from Kir?

8 "Behold, the eyes of the Lord
Gᴏᴅ are on the sinful
kingdom,
And I will eliminate it from the
face of the earth;
Nevertheless, I will ᴬnot totally
eliminate the house of
Jacob,"
Declares the Lᴏʀᴅ.

9 "For behold, I am
commanding,
And I will ᴬshake the house of
Israel among all nations
As *grain* is shaken in a sieve,
But not a pebble will fall to the
ground.

10 "All the ᴬsinners of My people
will die by the sword,
Those who say, 'ᴮThe
catastrophe will not overtake
or confront us.'

THE RESTORATION OF ISRAEL

11 "On that day I will ᴬraise up the
fallen ᴮshelter of David,
And wall up its gaps;
I will also raise up its ruins
And rebuild it as in the days
of old;

12 ᴬSo that they may possess the
remnant of ᴮEdom
And all the nations who are
called by My name,"
Declares the Lᴏʀᴅ who does
this.

13 "Behold, days are coming,"
declares the Lᴏʀᴅ,
"When the ᴬplowman will
overtake the reaper,
And the one who treads
grapes *will overtake* him
who sows the seed;
When the ᴮmountains will
drip grape juice,
And all the hills will come
apart.

14 "I will also ᴬrestore the
fortunes of My people
Israel,
And they will ᴮrebuild the
desolated cities and live *in
them;*
They will also plant vineyards
and drink their wine,
And make gardens and eat
their fruit.

15 "I will also plant them on their
land,
And ᴬthey will not be uprooted
again from their land
Which I have given them,"
Says the Lᴏʀᴅ your God.

9:5 ᴮAmos 8:8   9:6 ᴬPs 104:3, 13   9:7 ᴬDeut 2:23;
Jer 47:4   9:8 ᴬJer 5:10; 30:11   9:9 ᴬIs 30:28;
Luke 22:31   9:10 ᴬIs 33:14   ᴮAmos 6:3
9:11 ᴬActs 15:16-18   ᴮIs 16:5
9:12 ᴬObad 19   ᴮNum 24:18   9:13 ᴬLev 26:5
ᴮJoel 3:18   9:14 ᴬPs 53:6   ᴮIs 61:4   9:15 ᴬIs 60:21;
Ezek 34:28

OBADIAH

EDOM WILL BE HUMBLED

1 The vision of Obadiah.
This is what the Lord GOD says concerning Edom—
We have heard a report from the LORD,
And a ^messenger has been sent among the nations *saying,*
"^BArise, and let's go up against her for battle"—

2 "Behold, I will make you ^small among the nations;
You are greatly despised.

3 "The ^arrogance of your heart has deceived you,
The one who lives in the clefts of the rock,
On the height of his dwelling place,
Who says in his heart,
'Who will bring me down to earth?'

4 "Though you ^make *your home* high like the eagle,
Though you set your nest among the ^Bstars,
From there I will bring you down," declares the LORD.

5 "If ^thieves came to you,
If robbers by night—
Oh how you will be ruined!—
Would they not steal *only* until they had enough?
If grape-pickers came to you,
^BWould they not leave *some* gleanings?

6 "Oh how Esau will be ^searched,
And his hidden treasures searched out!

7 "All the ^people allied with you
Will send you to the border,

And the people at peace with you
Will deceive you *and* overpower you.
They who eat your ^Bbread
Will set an ambush for you.
(There is no understanding in him.)

8 "Will I not on that day," declares the LORD,
"^AEliminate wise men from Edom,
And understanding from the mountain of Esau?

9 "Then your warriors will be filled with terror, ^ATeman,
So that everyone will be eliminated from the mountain of Esau by murder.

10 "Because of ^violence to your brother Jacob,
Shame will cover you,
^BAnd you will be eliminated forever.

11 "On the day that you ^stood aloof,
On the day that strangers carried off his wealth,
And foreigners entered his gate
And cast lots for Jerusalem—
^BYou too were as one of them.

12 "^ADo not gloat over your brother's day,
The day of his misfortune.

---

1 ^A Is 18:2   ^B Jer 6:4, 5   2 ^A Num 24:18; Is 23:9
3 ^A Is 16:6; Jer 49:16   4 ^A Job 20:6, 7   ^B Is 14:12-15
5 ^A Jer 49:9   ^B Deut 24:21   6 ^A Jer 49:10   7 ^A Jer 30:14
^B Ps 41:9   ^A Job 5:12-14; Is 29:14   9 ^A Gen 36:11;
1 Chr 1:45   10 ^A Gen 27:41   ^B Ezek 35:9   11 ^A Ps 83:5, 6
^B Ezek 35:10   12 ^A Mic 4:11; 7:10

And do not rejoice over the
  sons of Judah
On the day of their
  destruction;
Yes, do not boast
On the day of *their* distress.
13 "Do not enter the gate of My
  people
On the ^day of their disaster.
You indeed, do not gloat over
  their catastrophe
On the day of their disaster.
And do not ^Blay *a hand* on
  their wealth
On the day of their disaster.
14 "Do not ^stand at the crossroads
To eliminate their survivors;
And do not hand over their
  refugees
On the day of their distress.

**THE DAY OF THE LORD
AND THE FUTURE**

15 "For the ^day of the LORD is near
  for all the nations.
  ^BJust as you have done, it will
  be done to you.
Your dealings will return on
  your own head.
16 "For just as you ^drank on ^BMy
  holy mountain,
All the nations will drink
  continually.
They will drink to the last
  drop,
And become as if they had
  never existed.
17 "But on Mount ^Zion there will
  be those who escape,
And it will be holy.
And the house of Jacob will
  ^Bpossess their property.

18 "Then the house of Jacob will
  be a fire,
And the house of Joseph a
  flame;
But the house of Esau *will be*
  like stubble.
And they will set them on fire
  and consume them,
So that there will be ^no
  survivor of the house of
  Esau,"
For the LORD has spoken.
19 Then *those of* the ¹Negev will
  ^possess the mountain of
  Esau,
And *those of* the ²Shephelah
  the Philistine *plain;*
Also, they will possess the
  territory of Ephraim and the
  territory of Samaria,
And Benjamin *the territory of*
  Gilead.
20 And the exiles of this army of
  the sons of Israel,
Who are *among* the Canaanites
  as far as ^Zarephath,
And the exiles of Jerusalem
  who are in Sepharad,
Will possess the ^Bcities of the
  Negev.
21 ¹The ^deliverers will ascend
  Mount Zion
To judge the mountain of
  Esau,
And the kingdom will be the
  LORD's.

13^Ezek 35:5 ^BEzek 36:2, 3 14^Is 16:3, 4
15^Ezek 30:3 ^BJer 50:29 16^Jer 49:12 ^BJoel 3:17
17^Is 4:2, 3 ^BIs 14:1, 2 18^Jer 11:23; Amos 1:8
19^Is 11:14; Amos 9:12 20^1 Kin 17:9 ^BJer 32:44
21^Neh 9:27

19¹I.e., South country ²I.e., the foothills
21¹Or with ancient versions *Those who are rescued*

JONAH

JONAH'S DISOBEDIENCE

1 The word of the LORD came to ^Jonah the son of Amittai, saying, ²"Arise, go to Nineveh, the great city, and cry out against it, because their ^wickedness has come up before Me." ³But Jonah got up to flee to ^Tarshish from the presence of the LORD. So he went down to ᴮJoppa, found a ship that was going to Tarshish, paid the fare, and boarded it to go with them to Tarshish away from the presence of the LORD.

⁴However, the ^LORD hurled a great wind on the sea and there was a great storm on the sea, so that the ship was about to break up. ⁵Then the sailors became afraid and every man cried out to ^his god, and they ᴮhurled the cargo which was in the ship into the sea to lighten *it* for them. But Jonah had gone below into the stern of the ship, had lain down, and fallen sound asleep. ⁶So the captain approached him and said, "How is it that you are sleeping? Get up, ^call on your god! Perhaps *your* ᴮgod will be concerned about us so that we will not perish."

⁷And each man said to his mate, "Come, let's cast lots so that we may find out on whose account this catastrophe *has struck* us." So they cast lots, and the ^lot fell on Jonah. ⁸Then they said to him, "^Tell us, now! On whose account *has* this catastrophe *struck* us? What is your occupation, and where do you come from? What is your country,

and from what people are you?" ⁹So he said to them, "I am a ^Hebrew, and I fear the LORD God of heaven who made the sea and the dry land."

¹⁰Then the men became extremely afraid, and they said to him, "How could you do this?" For the men knew that he was ^fleeing from the presence of the LORD, because he had told them. ¹¹So they said to him, "What should we do to you so that the sea will become calm for us?"—for the sea was becoming increasingly stormy. ¹²And he said to them, "Pick me up and hurl me into the sea. Then the sea will become calm for you, because I know that ^on account of me this great storm *has come* upon you." ¹³However, the men rowed *desperately* to return to land, but they could not, because the sea was becoming *even* stormier against them. ¹⁴Then they cried out to the LORD and said, "We earnestly pray, O LORD, do not let us perish on account of this man's life, and do not put innocent blood on us; for ^You, LORD, have done as You pleased."

¹⁵So they picked up Jonah and hurled him into the sea, and the sea ^stopped its raging. ¹⁶Then the men became extremely afraid of the LORD, and they offered a sacrifice to the LORD and made ^vows.

1:1 ^2 Kin 14:25; Matt 12:39-41   1:2 ^Gen 18:20;
Hos 7:2   1:3 ^Is 23:1, 6, 10   ᴮJosh 19:46
1:4 ^Ps 107:23-28; 135:6, 7   1:5 ^1 Kin 18:26
ᴮActs 27:18, 19, 38   1:6 ^Ps 107:28   ᴮ2 Sam 12:22
1:7 ^Num 32:23; Prov 16:33   1:8 ^Josh 7:19;
1 Sam 14:43   1:9 ^Gen 14:13; Ex 1:15   1:10 ^Job 27:22;
Jon 1:3   1:12 ^2 Sam 24:17; 1 Chr 21:17   1:14 ^Ps 115:3;
135:6   1:15 ^Ps 65:7; 93:3, 4   1:16 ^Ps 50:14; 66:13, 14

¹⁷And the LORD designated a great fish to swallow Jonah, and Jonah was in the ^stomach of the fish for three days and three nights.

JONAH'S PRAYER

2 Then Jonah prayed to the LORD his God ^from the stomach of the fish, ²and he said,

"I called out of my distress to
    the LORD,
And He answered me.
I called for help from the
    depth of ^Sheol;
You heard my voice.

³ "For You ^threw me into the
    deep,
Into the heart of the seas,
And the current flowed
    around me.
All Your ᴮbreakers and waves
    passed over me.

⁴ "So I said, 'I have been ^cast out
    of Your sight.
Nevertheless I will look again
    toward Your holy temple.'

⁵ "^Water encompassed me to the
    point of death.
The ᴮdeep flowed around me,
Seaweed was wrapped around
    my head.

⁶ "I descended to the base of the
    mountains.
The earth *with* its bars *was*
    around me forever,
But You have ^brought up my
    life from the pit, LORD my
    God.

⁷ "While I was ^fainting away,
I ᴮremembered the LORD,
And my prayer came to You,
Into Your holy temple.

⁸ "Those who ^are followers of
    worthless idols
Abandon their faithfulness,

⁹ But I will sacrifice to You
With a voice of thanksgiving.

That which I have vowed I
    will ^pay.
ᴮSalvation is from the LORD."

¹⁰Then the LORD commanded the ^fish, and it vomited Jonah up onto the dry land.

NINEVEH REPENTS

3 Now the word of the LORD came to Jonah the second time, saying, ²"Arise, go to ^Nineveh, the great city, and ᴮproclaim to it the proclamation which I am going to tell you." ³So Jonah got up and went to Nineveh according to the word of the LORD. Now Nineveh was ¹an ^exceedingly large city, a three days' walk. ⁴Then Jonah began to go through the city one day's walk; and he ^cried out and said, "Forty more days, and Nineveh will be overthrown."

⁵Then the people of Nineveh believed in God; and they called a ^fast and put on sackcloth, from the greatest to the least of them. ⁶When the word reached the king of Nineveh, he got up from his throne, removed his robe from himself, ^covered *himself* with sackcloth, and sat on the ¹dust. ⁷And he issued a ^proclamation, and it said, "In Nineveh by the decree of the king and his nobles: No person, animal, herd, or flock is to taste anything. They are not to eat, or drink water. ⁸But *every* person and animal must be covered with sackcloth; and *people* are to

1:17 ^Matt 12:40; 16:4   2:1 ^Job 13:15; Ps 130:1, 2
2:2 ^Ps 18:5, 6; 86:13   2:3 ^Ps 69:1, 2, 14, 15   ᴮPs 42:7
2:4 ^Ps 31:22; Jer 7:15   2:5 ^Lam 3:54   ᴮPs 69:1, 2
2:6 ^Job 33:28; Ps 16:10   2:7 ^Ps 142:3   ᴮPs 77:10, 11
2:8 ^2 Kin 17:15; Ps 31:6   2:9 ^Job 22:27   ᴮPs 3:8
2:10 ^Jon 1:17   3:2 ^Zeph 2:13   ᴮJer 1:17   3:3 ^Jon 1:2;
4:11   3:4 ^Matt 12:41; Luke 11:32
3:5 ^Dan 9:3; Joel 1:14   3:6 ^Esth 4:1-4; Jer 6:26
3:7 ^2 Chr 20:3; Ezra 8:21

3:3 ¹Lit *a great city to God*   3:6 ¹Or *ashes*

call on God vehemently, and they are to ^turn, each one from his evil way, and from the violence which is in their hands. ⁹^Who knows, God may turn and relent, and turn from His burning anger so that we will not perish.”

¹⁰When God saw their deeds, that they ^turned from their evil way, then ᴮGod relented of the disaster which He had declared He would bring on them. So He did not do *it*.

JONAH'S DISPLEASURE REBUKED

4 But it greatly displeased Jonah, and he became ^angry. ²Then he prayed to the Lᴏʀᴅ and said, “Please Lᴏʀᴅ, was this not what I said when I was still in my *own* country? Therefore in anticipation *of this* I fled to Tarshish, since I knew that You are a ^gracious and compassionate God, slow to anger and abundant in mercy, and One who relents of disaster. ³So now, Lᴏʀᴅ, please take my life from me, for death is ^better to me than life.” ⁴But the Lᴏʀᴅ said, “Do you have a good reason to be angry?”

⁵Then Jonah left the city and sat down east of it. There he made a shelter for himself and ^sat under it in the shade, until he could see what would happen in the city. ⁶So the Lᴏʀᴅ God designated a plant, and it grew up over Jonah to be a shade over his head, to relieve him of his discomfort. And Jonah was overjoyed about the plant. ⁷But God designated a worm when dawn came the next day, and it attacked the plant and it ^withered. ⁸And when the sun came up God designated a scorching ^east wind, and the ᴮsun beat down on Jonah's head so that he became faint, and he begged with *all* his soul to die, saying, “Death is better to me than life!”

⁹But God said to Jonah, “Do you have a good reason to be angry about the plant?” And he said, “I have good reason to be angry, *even* to the point of death!” ¹⁰Then the Lᴏʀᴅ said, “You had compassion on the plant, for which you did not work and *which* you did not cause to grow, which came up overnight and perished overnight. ¹¹Should I not also ^have compassion on Nineveh, the great city in which there are more than 120,000 people, who do not ᴮknow *the difference* between their right hand and their left, *as well as* many animals?”

3:8 ^Is 1:16-19; 55:6, 7   3:9 ^2 Sam 12:22; Joel 2:14   3:10 ^1 Kin 21:27-29   ᴮEx 32:14   4:1 ^Jon 4:4, 9; Matt 20:15   4:2 ^Ex 34:6; Num 14:18   4:3 ^Job 7:15, 16; Eccl 7:1   4:5 ^1 Kin 19:9, 13   4:7 ^Joel 1:12   4:8 ^Ezek 19:12   ᴮPs 121:6   4:11 ^Jon 3:10   ᴮDeut 1:39

MICAH

DESTRUCTION IN ISRAEL AND JUDAH

1 The word of the Lord which came to ^Micah of Moresheth in the days of Jotham, Ahaz, *and* Hezekiah, kings of Judah, *and* which he saw regarding Samaria and Jerusalem.

2 Hear, you peoples, all of you;
   ^Listen carefully, earth and all
      it contains,
   And may the Lord God be a
      ^witness against you,
   The Lord from His holy temple.

3 For behold, the Lord is
      ^coming forth from His place.
   He will come down and ^tread
      on the high places of the
      earth.

4 ^The mountains will melt
      under Him
   And the valleys will be split,
   Like wax before the fire,
   Like water poured down a
      steep place.

5 All this is due to the
      wrongdoing of Jacob
   And the sins of the house of
      Israel.
   What is the ^wrongdoing of
      Jacob?
   Is it not ^Samaria?
   What is the high place of
      Judah?
   Is it not Jerusalem?

6 For I will make Samaria a
      ^heap of ruins in the open
      country,
   Planting places for a vineyard.
   I will hurl her stones down
      into the valley,
   And lay bare her foundations.

7 All of her ^idols will be crushed,
   All of her earnings will be
      burned with fire,
   And all of her images I will
      make desolate;
   For she collected *them* from a
      ^prostitute's earnings,
   And to the earnings of a
      prostitute they will return.

8 Because of this I must mourn
      and wail,
   I must go ^barefoot and naked;
   I must do mourning like the
      ^jackals,
   And a mourning like the
      ostriches.

9 For her ^wound is incurable,
   For it has come to Judah;
   It has reached the gate of my
      people,
   Even to Jerusalem.

10 ^Do not tell *it* in Gath,
   Do not weep at all.
   At ¹Beth-le-aphrah roll
      yourself in the dust in
      mourning.

11 Go on your way, inhabitant
      of ¹Shaphir, in ^shameful
      nakedness.
   The inhabitant of ²,^Zaanan
      does not escape.
   The mourning of ³Beth-ezel:
   "He will take from you its
      support."

1:1^Jer 26:18   1:2^Jer 6:19   ^Is 50:7   1:3^Is 26:21
^Amos 4:13   1:4^Ps 97:5; Is 64:1, 2   1:5^Jer 2:19   ^Is 7:9
1:6^2 Kin 19:25; Mic 3:12   1:7^Deut 9:21   ^Deut 23:18
1:8^Is 32:11   ^Is 13:21, 22   1:9^Is 3:26; Jer 30:12, 15
1:10^2 Sam 1:20   1:11^Ezek 23:29   ^Josh 15:37

1:10 ¹I.e., house of dust   1:11 ¹I.e., pleasantness
²I.e., going out   ³I.e., the house beside

12 For the inhabitant of ¹Maroth
^Waits for *something* good,
Because a disaster has come down
from the LORD
To the gate of Jerusalem.

13 Harness the chariot to the team of horses,
You inhabitant of ^Lachish—
She was the beginning of sin
To the daughter of Zion—
Because in you were found
The rebellious acts of Israel.

14 Therefore you will give parting gifts
In behalf of Moresheth-gath;
The houses of ^Achzib *will*
become a ᴮdeception
To the kings of Israel.

15 Moreover, I will bring on you
The one who takes possession,
You inhabitant of ¹·^Mareshah.
The glory of Israel will enter
ᴮAdullam.

16 Shave yourself ^bald, yes, cut off your hair,
Because of the children of your delight;
Extend your baldness like the eagle,
For they will ᴮgo from you into exile.

WOE TO OPPRESSORS

2 Woe to those who ^devise wrongdoing,
Who practice evil on their beds!
When morning comes, they do it,
Because it is in the power of their hands.

2 They ^covet fields, so they
ᴮseize *them;*
And houses, so they take *them.*
They exploit a man and his house,
A person and his inheritance.

3 Therefore this is what the LORD says:
"Behold, I am ^planning against this family a catastrophe
From which you cannot remove your necks;
And you will not walk haughtily,
For it will be an ᴮevil time.

4 "On that day they will ^take up against you a song of mocking
And utter a song of mourning *and* say,
'We are completely ᴮdestroyed!
He exchanges the share of my people;
How He removes it from me!
To the apostate He apportions our fields.'

5 "Therefore you will have no one
^applying a measuring line
For you by lot in the assembly of the LORD.

6 'Do not prophesy,' *so* they prophesy.
But if they do ^not prophesy about these things,
ᴮInsults will not be turned back.

7 "Is it being said, house of Jacob:
'Is the Spirit of the LORD ^impatient?
Are these His works?'
Do My words not do good
For the one walking rightly?

8 "Recently My people have arisen as an ^enemy—
You strip the robe off the garment

1:12 ^Is 59:9-11; Jer 14:19   1:13 ^Josh 10:3; 2 Kin 14:19
1:14 ^Josh 15:44   ᴮJer 15:18   1:15 ^Josh 15:44
ᴮ2 Sam 23:13   1:16 ^Is 22:12   ᴮ2 Kin 17:6
2:1 ^Ps 36:4; Is 32:7   2:2 ^Jer 22:17   ᴮIs 5:8
2:3 ^Deut 28:48   ᴮAmos 5:13   2:4 ^Hab 2:6   ᴮIs 6:11
2:5 ^Num 34:13, 16-29; Deut 32:8   2:6 ^Is 29:10
ᴮMic 6:16   2:7 ^Is 50:2; 59:1   2:8 ^Jer 12:8

1:12 ¹I.e., bitterness   1:15 ¹I.e., possession

From unsuspecting passers-by,
From those returned from war.

9 "You ^evict the women of My
people,
Each one from her pleasant
house.
From her children you take My
splendor forever.

10 "Arise and go,
For this is no place ^of rest
Because of the ^uncleanness
that brings on destruction,
A painful destruction.

11 "If someone walking *after* wind
and ^falsehood
Had lied *and said,*
'I will prophesy to you about
wine and liquor,'
He would become a prophet to
^this people.

12 "I will certainly ^assemble all of
you, Jacob,
I will certainly gather the
^remnant of Israel.
I will put them together like
sheep in the fold;
Like a flock in the midst of its
pasture
They will be noisy with people.

13 "The one who breaks through
goes up before them;
They break through, pass
through the gate, and go out
by it.
So their king passes on before
them,
And the LORD at their head."

RULERS DENOUNCED

3 And I said,
"Hear now, you leaders of
Jacob
And rulers of the house of
Israel:
Is it not for you to ^know
justice?

2 "You who hate good and love evil,
Who ^tear off their skin from
them
And their flesh from their
bones,

3 Who ^eat the flesh of my people,
Strip off their skin from them,
Smash their bones,
And ^chop *them* up as for the
pot,
And as meat in a cauldron!"

4 Then they will cry out to the
LORD,
But He will not answer them.
Instead, He will ^hide His face
from them at that time
Because they have ^practiced
evil deeds.

5 This is what the LORD says concerning the prophets who ^lead my
people astray:
When they have *something* to
bite with their teeth,
They cry out, "Peace!"
But against him who puts
nothing in their mouths
They declare holy war.

6 Therefore *it will be* ^night for
you—without vision,
And darkness for you—
without divination.
The ^sun will go down on the
prophets,
And the day will become dark
over them.

7 The seers will be put to shame,
And the ^diviners will be
ashamed.
Indeed, they will all ^cover
their lips
Because there is no answer
from God.

2:9 ^Jer 10:20   2:10 ^Deut 12:9   ^Ps 106:38
2:11 ^Jer 5:31   ^Is 30:10, 11
2:12 ^Mic 4:6, 7   ^Mic 5:7, 8   3:1 ^Ps 82:1-5; Jer 5:5
3:2 ^Ps 53:4; Ezek 22:27   3:3 ^Ps 14:4   ^Ezek 11:3
3:4 ^Deut 31:17   ^Is 3:11   3:5 ^Is 3:12; 9:15, 16
3:6 ^Is 8:20-22   ^Is 59:10   3:7 ^Is 44:25   ^Mic 7:16

8 On the other hand, ^AI am filled
with power—
With the Spirit of the LORD—
And with justice and courage
To ^Bmake known to Jacob his
rebellious act,
And to Israel his sin.

9 Now hear this, you heads of
the house of Jacob
And rulers of the house of
Israel,
Who ^Adespise justice
And twist everything that is
straight,

10 Who ^Abuild Zion with
bloodshed,
And Jerusalem with malice.

11 Her leaders pronounce
^Ajudgment for a bribe,
Her ^Bpriests teach for pay,
And her prophets divine for
money.
Yet they lean on the LORD,
saying,
"Is the LORD not in our midst?
Catastrophe will not come
upon us."

12 Therefore on account of you,
^AZion will be plowed *like* a
field,
^BJerusalem will become a heap
of ruins,
And the mountain of the
temple *will become* high
places of a forest.

PEACEFUL LATTER DAYS

4 And it will come about in the
^Alast days
That the mountain of the
house of the LORD
Will be established as the
chief of the mountains.
It will be raised above the
hills,
And the ^Bpeoples will stream
to it.

2 Many nations will come and say,
"^ACome and let's go up to the
mountain of the LORD
And to the house of the God of
Jacob,
So that ^BHe may teach us about
His ways,
And that we may walk in His
paths."
For from Zion will go forth the
law,
And the word of the LORD from
Jerusalem.

3 And He will ^Ajudge between
many peoples
And render decisions for
mighty, distant nations.
Then they will beat their
swords ^Binto plowshares,
And their spears into pruning
hooks;
Nation will not lift a sword
against nation,
And never again will they train
for war.

4 Instead, each of them will ^Asit
under his vine
And under his fig tree,
With ^Bno one to make *them*
afraid,
Because the mouth of the
LORD of armies has spoken.

5 Though all the peoples walk,
Each in the name of his god,
As for us, ^Awe will walk
In the name of the LORD our
God forever and ever.

6 "On that day," declares the LORD,
"I will assemble those who limp
And ^Agather the scattered,
Those whom I have afflicted.

3:8 ^A Is 61:1, 2   ^B Is 58:1   **3:9** ^A Ps 58:1, 2; Is 1:23
3:10 ^A Jer 22:13, 17; Hab 2:12   **3:11** ^A Is 1:23   ^B Jer 6:13
3:12 ^A Jer 26:18   ^B Ps 79:1   **4:1** ^A Is 2:2-4   ^B Ps 22:27
4:2 ^A Is 2:3   ^B Ps 25:8, 9, 12   **4:3** ^A Is 2:4   ^B Joel 3:10
4:4 ^A 1 Kin 4:25   ^B Lev 26:6   **4:5** ^A Zech 10:12
4:6 ^A Ps 147:2; Ezek 34:13, 16

7 "I will make those who limp a
    ^remnant,
  And those who have strayed a
    mighty nation,
  And the ^BLORD will reign over
    them on Mount Zion
  From now on and forever.
8 "As for you, ^tower of the flock,
  Hill of the daughter of Zion,
  To you it will come—
  Yes, the ^Bformer dominion will
    come,
  The kingdom of the daughter
    of Jerusalem.

9 "Now, why do you ^cry out
    loudly?
  Is there no king among you,
  Or has your ^Bcounselor
    perished,
  That agony has gripped you
    like a woman in childbirth?
10 "Writhe and scream,
  Daughter of Zion,
  Like a woman in childbirth;
  For now you will ^go out of
    the city,
  Live in the field,
  And go to Babylon.
  ^BThere you will be rescued,
  There the LORD will redeem
    you
  From the hand of your enemies.
11 "And now ^many nations have
    been assembled against you
  Who say, 'Let her be defiled,
  And let our eyes gloat over
    Zion!'
12 "But they do not ^know the
    thoughts of the LORD,
  And they do not understand
    His plan;
  For He has gathered them like
    sheaves to the threshing floor.
13 "Arise and ^thresh, daughter of
    Zion,
  For I will make your horn iron,

And I will make your hoofs
  bronze,
So that you may ^Bpulverize
  many peoples,
And dedicate to the LORD their
  unjust profit,
And their wealth to the Lord
  of all the earth.

BIRTH OF THE KING IN BETHLEHEM

5 "Now muster yourselves in
    troops, daughter of troops;
  They have laid siege against us;
  With a rod they will ^strike the
    judge of Israel on the cheek.
2 "But as for you, Bethlehem
    Ephrathah,
  Too little to be among the
    clans of Judah,
  From ^you One will come forth
    for Me to be ^Bruler in Israel.
  His times of coming forth are
    from long ago,
  From the days of eternity."
3 Therefore He will ^give them
    up until the time
  When she who is in labor has
    given birth.
  Then the remainder of His
    kinsmen
  Will return to the sons of
    Israel.
4 And He will arise and
    ^shepherd *His flock*
  In the strength of the LORD,
  In the majesty of the name of
    the LORD His God.
  And they will remain,
  Because at that time He will be
    great
  To the ^Bends of the earth.
5 This One ^will be *our* peace.

4:7 ^A Mic 5:7, 8   ^B Is 24:23   4:8 ^A Ps 48:3, 12   ^B Is 1:26
4:9 ^A Jer 8:19   ^B Is 3:1-3   4:10 ^A 2 Kin 20:18   ^B Is 43:14
4:11 ^A Is 5:25-30; 17:12-14   4:12 ^A Ps 147:19, 20
4:13 ^A Is 41:15   ^B Jer 51:20-23   5:1 ^A 1 Kin 22:24;
Job 16:10   5:2 ^A Is 11:1   ^B Jer 30:21   5:3 ^A Hos 11:8;
Mic 4:10   5:4 ^A Is 40:11   ^B Is 45:22   5:5 ^A Is 9:6

When the [B]Assyrian invades
   our land,
When he tramples on our
   citadels,
Then we will raise against
   him
Seven shepherds and eight
   leaders of people.
6 They will [A]shepherd the land
      of Assyria with the sword,
   The land of Nimrod at its
      entrances;
   And He will [B]rescue *us* from
      the Assyrian
   When he invades our land,
   And when he tramples our
      territory.

7 Then the [A]remnant of Jacob
   Will be among many peoples
   Like dew from the LORD,
   Like showers on vegetation
   That do not wait for man,
   Or delay for mankind.
8 The remnant of Jacob
   Will be among the nations,
   Among many peoples
   [A]Like a lion among the
      animals of the forest,
   Like a young lion among
      flocks of sheep,
   Which, if he passes through,
   Tramples and tears,
   And there is [B]no one who can
      rescue.
9 Your hand will be [A]lifted up
      against your adversaries,
   And all your enemies will be
      eliminated.

10 "And it will be on that day,"
      declares the LORD,
   "[A]That I will eliminate your
      horses from among you,
   And destroy your chariots.
11 "I will also eliminate the [A]cities
   of your land,

And tear down all your
   fortifications.
12 "I will eliminate [A]sorceries
      from your hand,
   And you will have no fortune-
      tellers.
13 "[A]I will eliminate your carved
      images
   And your memorial stones
      from among you,
   So that you will no longer
      bow down
   To the work of your hands.
14 "I will uproot your [1,A]Asherim
      from among you,
   And destroy your cities.
15 "And I will [A]execute vengeance
      in anger and wrath
   On the nations which have
      not obeyed."

GOD'S INDICTMENT OF HIS PEOPLE

6 Hear now what the LORD is
      saying,
   "Arise, plead your case before
      the mountains,
   And let the hills hear your voice.
2 "Listen, you mountains, to the
      indictment by the LORD,
   And you enduring foundations
      of the earth,
   Because the [A]LORD has a case
      against His people;
   And He will dispute with
      Israel.
3 "My people, [A]what have I done
      to you,
   And [B]how have I wearied you?
      Answer Me.
4 "Indeed, I brought you up from
      the land of Egypt,

5:5 [B]Is 8:7, 8   5:6 [A]Nah 2:11-13   [B]Is 14:25
5:7 [A]Mic 2:12; 4:7   5:8 [A]Gen 49:9   [B]Ps 50:22
5:9 [A]Ps 10:12; 21:8   5:10 [A]Zech 9:10   5:11 [A]Is 1:7; 6:11
5:12 [A]Deut 18:10-12; Is 2:6   5:13 [A]Is 2:18; 17:8
5:14 [A]Ex 34:13; Is 17:8   5:15 [A]Is 1:24; 65:12
6:2 [A]Is 1:18; Hos 4:1   6:3 [A]Jer 2:5   [B]Is 43:22, 23

5:14 [1] I.e., wooden symbols of a female deity (Asherah)

I ^redeemed you from the
house of slavery,
And I sent before you ^BMoses,
Aaron, and Miriam.
5 "My people, remember now
What ^Balak king of Moab
planned
And what Balaam son of Beor
answered him,
And what happened from
Shittim to Gilgal,
So that you might know
the ^Brighteous acts of the
Lord."

WHAT GOD REQUIRES OF MANKIND

6 ^With what shall I come to
the Lord
And bow myself before the
God on high?
Shall I come to Him with
burnt offerings,
With yearling calves?
7 Does the Lord take pleasure
in ^thousands of rams,
In ten thousand rivers of oil?
Shall I give *Him* my ^Bfirstborn
for my wrongdoings,
The fruit of my body for the
sin of my soul?
8 He has told you, mortal one,
what is good;
And what does the Lord
require of you
But to ^do justice, to ^Blove
kindness,
And to walk humbly with
your God?

9 The voice of the Lord will call
to the city—
And it is sound wisdom to
fear Your name:
"Hear, you tribe. Who has
designated its time?
10 "Is there still a person *in* the
wicked house,

Along with treasures of
^wickedness,
And a short measure *that is*
cursed?
11 "Can I justify dishonest
^balances,
And a bag of fraudulent
weights?
12 "For the rich people of the city
are full of violence,
Her residents speak ^lies,
And their ^Btongue is deceitful
in their mouth.
13 "So also I will make *you* ^sick,
striking you down,
^BMaking *you* desolate because
of your sins.
14 "You will eat, but you will ^not
be satisfied,
And your filth *will be* in your
midst.
You will *try to* remove
valuables for safekeeping,
But you will ^Bnot save *it all*,
And what you do save I will
turn over to the sword.
15 "You will sow but you will ^not
harvest.
You will tread the olive *press*
but will not anoint yourself
with oil;
And *tread out* sweet wine,
but you will ^Bnot drink *any*
wine.
16 "The statutes of ^Omri
And every work of the house
of Ahab are maintained,
And you ^Bwalk by their
plans.
Therefore I will give you up
for destruction,

6:4 ^Deut 7:8   ^B Ex 4:10-16   **6:5** ^Num 22:5, 6
^B 1 Sam 12:7   **6:6** ^Ps 40:6-8   **6:7** ^Ps 50:9
^B Lev 18:21   **6:8** ^Is 56:1   ^B Hos 6:6   **6:10** ^Jer 5:26, 27;
Amos 3:10   **6:11** ^Lev 19:36; Hos 12:7   **6:12** ^Jer
9:2-6, 8   ^B Is 3:8   **6:13** ^Mic 1:9   ^B Is 1:7
6:14 ^Is 9:20   ^B Is 30:6   **6:15** ^Deut 28:38-40
^B Amos 5:11   **6:16** ^1 Kin 16:25, 26   ^B Jer 7:24

And your inhabitants for
   derision,
And you will suffer the
   taunting of My people."

THE PROPHET ACKNOWLEDGES INJUSTICE

7 Woe to me! For I am
Like harvests of summer fruit,
   like gleanings of grapes.
There is not a cluster of grapes
   left to eat,
Nor an ^early fig, *which* I
   crave.
2 The godly person has
   ^perished from the land,
And there is no upright
   person among mankind.
All of them lie in wait for
   ^Bbloodshed;
Each of them hunts the other
   with a net.
3 As for evil, both hands do it
   ^well.
The leader asks for a ^Bbribe,
   also the judge,
And the great one speaks the
   capricious desire of his soul;
So they plot it together.
4 The best of them is like a
   thorn bush,
The most upright like a thorn
   hedge.
The day when you post your
   watchmen,
Your ^punishment is coming.
Then their ^Bconfusion will
   occur.
5 Do not ^trust in a neighbor;
Do not have confidence in a
   close friend.
Guard your lips
From her who lies in your
   arms.
6 For ^son disavows father,
Daughter rises up against her
   mother,

Daughter-in-law against her
   mother-in-law;
A person's enemies are
   the people of his own
   household.

GOD IS THE SOURCE OF SALVATION AND LIGHT

7 But as for me, I will ^be on the
   watch for the LORD;
I will ^Bwait for the God of my
   salvation.
My God will hear me.
8 ^Do not rejoice over me,
   enemy of mine.
Though I fall I will rise;
Though I live in darkness, the
   LORD is a ^Blight for me.

9 I will endure the rage of the
   LORD
Because I have sinned against
   Him,
Until He ^pleads my case and
   executes justice for me.
He will bring me out to the
   light,
And I will look at His
   righteousness.
10 Then my enemy will see,
And shame will cover her
   who said to me,
"Where is the LORD your
   God?"
My eyes will look at her;
At that time she will be
   ^trampled down
Like mud of the streets.
11 *It will be* a day for ^building
   your walls.
On that day *your* boundary
   will be extended.

7:1 ^Is 28:4; Hos 9:10   **7:2** ^Is 57:1   ^BIs 59:7
7:3 ^Prov 4:16, 17   ^BAmos 5:12   **7:4** ^Is 10:3   ^BIs 22:5
7:5 ^Jer 9:4   **7:6** ^Matt 10:21, 35; Luke 12:53
7:7 ^Hab 2:1   ^BPs 130:5   **7:8** ^Prov 24:17   ^BIs 9:2
7:9 ^Jer 50:34   **7:10** ^Is 51:23; Zech 10:5
7:11 ^Is 54:11; Amos 9:11

12 It *will be* a day when they will
  ^Acome to you
  From Assyria and the cities of
    Egypt,
  From Egypt even to the
    Euphrates River,
  Even from sea to sea and
    mountain to mountain.
13 And the earth will become a
  ^Awasteland because of her
    inhabitants,
  On account of the fruit of
    their deeds.

14 ^AShepherd Your people with
    Your scepter,
  The flock of Your possession
  Which lives by itself *in* the
    woodland,
  In the midst of a fruitful
    field.
  Let them feed *in* Bashan and
    Gilead
  ^BAs in the days of old.
15 "As in the days when you
    went out from the land of
    Egypt,
  I will show ^Ayou miracles."
16 Nations ^Awill see and be
    ashamed
  Of all their might.
  They will ^Bput *their* hand on
    their mouth,
  Their ears will be deaf.

17 They will lick up dust like a
    snake,
  Like reptiles of the earth.
  They will come
    ^Atrembling out of their
    fortresses;
  To the LORD our God they
    will come in ^Btrepidation,
  And they will be afraid of
    You.
18 Who is a God like You, who
  ^Apardons wrongdoing
  And passes over a rebellious
    act of the remnant of His
    possession?
  He does not ^Bretain His anger
    forever,
  Because He delights in
    mercy.
19 He will again take pity on us;
  ^AHe will trample on our
    wrongdoings.
  Yes, You will ^Bcast all their
    sins
  Into the depths of the sea.
20 You will give ^Atruth to Jacob
  And favor to Abraham,
  Which You swore to our
    forefathers
  From the days of old.

7:12 ^A Is 19:23–25; 60:4, 9   7:13 ^A Jer 25:11; Mic 6:13
7:14 ^A Ps 95:7   ^B Amos 9:11   7:15 ^A Ex 3:20; 34:10
7:16 ^A Is 26:11   ^B Mic 3:7   7:17 ^A Ps 18:45   ^B Is 25:3
7:18 ^A Ex 34:7, 9   ^B Ps 103:8, 9, 13   7:19 ^A Jer 50:20
^B Is 38:17   7:20 ^A Gen 24:27; 32:10

NAHUM

GOD IS AWESOME

1 The ^pronouncement of Nineveh. The book of the vision of Nahum the Elkoshite:

2 A ^jealous and avenging God is
the LORD;
The LORD is ᴮavenging and
wrathful.
The LORD takes vengeance on
His adversaries,
And He reserves wrath for His
enemies.

3 The LORD is ^slow to anger and
great in power,
And the LORD will by no means
leave *the guilty* unpunished.
In *the* gale and *the* storm is His
way,
And clouds are the dust
beneath His feet.

4 He ^rebukes the sea and dries
it up;
He dries up all the rivers.
ᴮBashan and Carmel wither,
The blossoms of Lebanon
wither.

5 Mountains ^quake because of
Him,
And the hills come apart;
Indeed the earth is ᴮupheaved
by His presence,
The world and all the
inhabitants in it.

6 Who can stand before His
indignation?
Who can endure the ^burning
of His anger?
His ᴮwrath gushes forth like
fire,
And the rocks are broken up
by Him.

7 The LORD is ^good,
A stronghold in the day of
trouble,
And He knows those who take
refuge in Him.

8 But with an ^overflowing
flood
He will make a complete end
of its site,
And will pursue His enemies
into darkness.

9 Whatever you ^devise against
the LORD,
He will make a ᴮcomplete end
of it.
Distress will not rise up twice.

10 Like tangled thorns,
And like those who are
drunken with their drink,
They are ^consumed
Like stubble completely dried
up.

11 From you has gone out
One who ^plotted evil against
the LORD,
A ᴮwicked counselor.

12 This is what the LORD says:
"Though *they are at* full
strength and so *they are*
many,
So also they will be ^cut off
and pass away.
Though I have afflicted you,
I will afflict you ᴮno longer.

1:1 ^Is 13:1; 19:1   1:2 ^Ex 20:5   ᴮDeut 32:35, 41
1:3 ^Ex 34:6, 7; Neh 9:17   1:4 ^Josh 3:15, 16
ᴮIs 33:9   1:5 ^Ex 19:18   ᴮIs 24:1, 20   1:6 ^Is 13:13
ᴮIs 66:15   1:7 ^Ps 25:8; 37:39, 40   1:8 ^Is 28:2, 17f;
Amos 8:8   1:9 ^Ps 2:1   ᴮIs 28:22   1:10 ^Is 5:24;
10:17   1:11 ^Is 10:7-11   ᴮEzek 11:2   1:12 ^Is
10:16-19, 33, 34   ᴮLam 3:31, 32

13 "So now, I will ^break his yoke
   from upon you,
   And I will tear your shackles to
   pieces."

14 The Lord has issued a
   command concerning you:
   "Your name will ^no longer be
   perpetuated.
   I will eliminate the carved
   image and the cast metal
   image
   From the house of your gods.
   I will prepare your ᴮgrave,
   For you are contemptible."

15 Behold, ^on the mountains,
   the feet of him who brings
   good news,
   Who announces peace!
   Celebrate your feasts, Judah,
   Pay your vows.
   For never again will the wicked
   one pass through you;
   He is eliminated completely.

THE OVERTHROW OF NINEVEH

2 The one who ^scatters has
   come up against you.
   Keep watch over the fortress,
   watch the road;
   Bind up your waist, summon
   all your strength.

2 For the Lord will restore the
   ^splendor of Jacob
   Like the splendor of Israel,
   Even though destroyers have
   laid waste to them
   And ᴮruined their vines.

3 The shields of his warriors are
   dyed red,
   The warriors are dressed in
   ^scarlet,
   The chariots are *fitted* with
   flashing steel
   When he is prepared *to march*,

And the juniper spears are
   brandished.

4 The ^chariots drive wildly in
   the streets,
   They rush around in the
   public squares;
   Their appearance is like
   torches,
   They drive back and forth like
   lightning flashes.

5 He remembers his ^officers;
   They ᴮstumble in their advance,
   They hurry to her wall,
   And the ᶦmantelet is set up.

6 The gates of the rivers are
   opened
   And the palace sways back and
   forth.

7 It is set:
   She is stripped, she is led away,
   And her slave women are
   sobbing like the sound of
   doves,
   ^Beating their breasts.

8 Though Nineveh *was* like a
   pool of water throughout her
   days,
   Yet they are fleeing;
   "Stop, stop,"
   But ^no one turns back.

9 Plunder the silver,
   Plunder the ^gold!
   For there is no end to the
   treasure—
   Wealth from every *kind of*
   desirable object.

10 She is emptied! Yes, she is
   desolate and waste!
   ^Hearts are melting and knees
   wobbling!

1:13 ^Is 9:4; 10:27 1:14 ^Job 18:17 ᴮEzek 32:22
1:15 ^Is 40:9; 52:7 2:1 ^Jer 51:20-23 2:2 ^Is 60:15
ᴮPs 80:12, 13 2:3 ^Ezek 23:14, 15
2:4 ^Is 66:15; Jer 4:13 2:5 ^Nah 3:18 ᴮJer 46:12
2:7 ^Is 32:12 2:8 ^Jer 46:5; 47:3 2:9 ^Rev 18:12, 16
2:10 ^Ps 22:14

2:5 ¹I.e., a shield used for stopping projectiles

Also trembling is in the entire
  body,
And all their ᴮfaces have
  become pale!

11 Where is the den of the lions
And the feeding place of the
  ᴬyoung lions,
Where the lion, lioness, *and*
  lion's cub went
With nothing to disturb *them?*

12 The lion tore enough for his
  cubs,
Killed *enough prey* for his
  lionesses,
And filled his lairs with prey
And his dens with torn flesh.

13"Behold, ᴬI am against you,"
declares the Lᴏʀᴅ of armies. "I will
burn up her chariots in smoke, and a
sword will devour your young lions;
I will eliminate your prey from the
land, and no longer will the voice of
your messengers be heard."

NINEVEH'S COMPLETE RUIN

3 ᴬWoe to the bloody city,
  completely full of lies *and*
  pillage;
Her prey does not leave.

2 The ᴬsound of the whip,
The sound of the roar of the
  wheel,
Galloping horses
And bounding chariots!

3 Horsemen charging,
Swords flashing, spears
  gleaming,
ᴬMany killed, a mass of
  corpses,
And there is ᴮno end to *the*
  dead bodies—
They stumble over the dead
  bodies!

4 *All* because of the ᴬmany
  sexual acts of the prostitute,
The charming one, the
  mistress of sorceries,

Who ᴮsells nations by her
  sexual acts,
And families by her sorceries.

5 "Behold, I am against you,"
  declares the Lᴏʀᴅ of armies;
"And I will ᴬlift up your skirts
  over your face,
And ᴮshow the nations your
  nakedness,
And the kingdoms your shame.

6 "I will throw filth on you
And ᴬdeclare you worthless,
And set you up as a ᴮspectacle.

7 "And it will come about that all
  who see you
Will shrink from you and say,
'Nineveh is devastated!
ᴬWho will have sympathy for
  her?'
Where shall I seek comforters
  for you?"

8 Are you better than ¹·ᴬNo-amon,
Which was situated by the
  canals of the Nile,
With water surrounding her,
Whose rampart *was* the sea,
Whose wall *consisted* of the sea?

9 Ethiopia was *her* might,
Egypt too, without limits.
ᴬPut and ᴮLubim were among
  her helpers.

10 Yet she ᴬbecame an exile,
She went into captivity;
Also her small children were
  smashed to pieces
At the head of every street;
They cast lots for her
  honorable men,
And all her great men were
  bound with shackles.

2:10 ᴮJoel 2:6   2:11ᴬIs 5:29   2:13ᴬJer 21:13; Ezek 5:8
3:1ᴬEzek 24:6, 9   3:2ᴬJob 39:22-25; Jer 47:3
3:3ᴬIs 34:3   ᴮIs 37:36   3:4ᴬIs 23:17   ᴮRev 18:3
3:5ᴬIs 47:2, 3   ᴮEzek 16:37   3:6ᴬJob 30:8   ᴮIs 14:16
3:7ᴬIs 51:19; Jer 15:5   3:8ᴬJer 46:25; Ezek 30:14-16
3:9ᴬJer 46:9   ᴮ2 Chr 12:3   3:10ᴬIs 19:4; 20:4

3:8 ¹I.e., the city of Amon: Thebes

11 You too will become drunk,
    You will be ^hidden.
    You too will search for a
      refuge from the enemy.
12 All your fortifications are ^fig
      trees with ᴮripe fruit—
    When shaken, they fall into
      the eater's mouth.
13 Behold, your people are
      women in your midst!
    The gates of your land are
      ^opened wide to your
      enemies;
    Fire consumes your gate bars.
14 ^Draw for yourself water for a
      siege!
    ᴮStrengthen your
      fortifications!
    Go into the clay and tread the
      mortar!
    Take hold of the brick mold!
15 There fire will consume you,
    The sword will cut you
      down;
    It will ^consume you as the
      creeping locust *consumes a
      crop.*

    Multiply yourself like the
      creeping locust,
    Multiply yourself like the
      migratory locust.

16 You have made your ^traders
      more numerous than the
      stars of heaven—
    The creeping locust sheds its
      skin and flies *away.*
17 Your ^courtiers are like the
      migratory locust.
    Your ᴮofficials are like a swarm
      of locusts
    Settling in the stone shelters
      on a cold day.
    The sun rises and they flee,
    And the place where they are
      is not known.
18 Your shepherds are ^sleeping,
      O king of Assyria;
    Your officers are lying down.
    Your people are ᴮscattered on
      the mountains
    And there is no one to gather
      them.
19 There is ^no relief for your
      collapse,
    Your ᴮwound is incurable.
    All who hear about you
    Will clap *their* hands over you,
    For upon whom has your evil
      not come continually?

3:11^Is 2:10, 19; Hos 10:8   3:12^Rev 6:13   ᴮIs 28:4
3:13^Is 45:1, 2; Nah 2:6   3:14^2 Chr 32:3, 4   ᴮNah 2:1
3:15^Joel 1:4   3:16^Is 23:8   3:17^Rev 9:7   ᴮJer 51:27
3:18^Ps 76:5, 6   ᴮ1 Kin 22:17   3:19^Jer 46:11
ᴮJer 30:12

HABAKKUK

CHALDEANS USED TO PUNISH JUDAH

1 The ^pronouncement which Habakkuk the prophet saw:

2 ^How long, LORD, have I called for help,
And You do not hear?
I cry out to You, "Violence!"
Yet You do ^Bnot save.

3 Why do You make me see disaster,
And make *me* look at destitution?
Yes, ^devastation and violence are before me;
^BStrife exists and contention arises.

4 Therefore the ^Law is ignored,
And justice is never upheld.
For the wicked surround the righteous;
Therefore justice comes out ^Bconfused.

5 "^Look among the nations! Watch!
Be horrified! Be frightened speechless!
For *I am* accomplishing ^Ba work in your days—
You would not believe *it even* if you were told!

6 "For behold, I am ^raising up the Chaldeans,
That grim and impetuous people
Who march throughout the earth,
To ^Btake possession of dwelling places that are not theirs.

7 "They are terrifying and ^feared;
Their ^Bjustice and authority originate with themselves.

8 "Their ^horses are faster than leopards,
And quicker than ^Bwolves in the evening.
Their horsemen charge along,
Their horsemen come from afar;
They fly like an eagle swooping down to devour.

9 "All of them come for violence.
Their horde of ^faces moves forward.
They gather captives like sand.

10 "They make fun of kings,
And dignitaries are *an object of* laughter to them.
They ^laugh at every fortress,
Then ^Bheap up dirt and capture it.

11 "Then they fly along *like* the ^wind and pass on.
But they will be held ^Bguilty,
They whose strength is their god."

12 Are You not from time everlasting,
LORD, my God, my Holy One?
We will not die.
You, LORD, have ^appointed them to *deliver* judgment;
And You, O ^BRock, have destined them to punish.

1:1 ^Is 13:1; Nah 1:1   **1:2** ^Ps 13:1, 2   ^B Jer 14:9
1:3 ^Jer 20:8   ^B Jer 15:10   **1:4** ^Ps 58:1, 2   ^B Is 5:20
1:5 ^Acts 13:41   ^B Is 29:14   **1:6** ^2 Kin 24:2   ^B Jer 8:10
1:7 ^Is 18:2, 7   ^B Jer 39:5-9   **1:8** ^Jer 4:13   ^B Zeph 3:3
1:9 ^2 Kin 12:17; Dan 11:17   **1:10** ^Is 10:9   ^B Jer 32:24
1:11 ^Jer 4:11, 12   ^B Jer 2:3   **1:12** ^Is 10:5, 6   ^B Deut 32:4

13 *Your* eyes are too pure to look
at evil,
And You cannot look at harm
favorably.
Why do You look *favorably*
At those who deal
treacherously?
Why are You ^silent when the
wicked ^Bswallow up
Those more righteous than
they?
14 *Why* have You made people
like the fish of the sea,
Like crawling things that have
no ruler over them?
15 *The Chaldeans* ^bring all of
them up with a hook,
^BDrag them away with their net,
And gather them together in
their fishing net.
Therefore they rejoice and are
joyful.
16 Therefore they offer a sacrifice
to their net
And burn incense to their
fishing net,
Because through ^these things
their catch is large,
And their food is plentiful.
17 Will they therefore empty
their net,
And continually ^slay nations
without sparing?

GOD ANSWERS THE PROPHET

2 I will stand at my guard post
And station myself on the
watchtower;
And I will ^keep watch to see
^Bwhat He will say to me,
And how I may reply when I
am reprimanded.
2 Then the Lord answered me
and said,
"^Write down the vision
And inscribe *it* clearly on
tablets,

So that one who reads it may
run.
3 "For the vision is yet for the
appointed time;
It hurries toward the goal and
it will not fail.
Though it delays, ^wait for it;
For it will certainly come, it
^Bwill not delay *long.*
4 "Behold, as for the impudent one,
His soul is not right within him;
But the ^righteous one will live
by his faith.
5 "Furthermore, wine betrays an
^arrogant man,
So that he does not achieve his
objective.
He ^Benlarges his appetite like
Sheol,
And he is like death, never
satisfied.
He also gathers to himself all
the nations
And collects to himself all the
peoples.
6 "Will all of these not ^take up
a song of ridicule against
him,
Even a saying *and* insinuations
against him
And say, 'Woe to him who
increases what is not his—
For how long—
And makes himself rich with
debts!'
7 "Will your creditors not ^rise up
suddenly,
And those who collect from
you awaken?
Indeed, you will become
plunder for them.

1:13 ^Ps 50:21 ^BPs 35:25 1:15 ^Jer 16:16 ^BPs 10:9
1:16 ^Jer 44:17 1:17 ^Is 14:5, 6 2:1 ^Ps 5:3 ^BPs 85:8
2:2 ^Deut 27:8; Rom 15:4 2:3 ^Ps 27:14 ^BEzek 12:25
2:4 ^Rom 1:17; Gal 3:11 2:5 ^Prov 21:24 ^BProv 27:20
2:6 ^Is 14:4-10; Jer 50:13 2:7 ^Prov 29:1

8 "Since you have ᴬlooted many
       nations,
   All the rest of the peoples will
       loot you—
   Because of human bloodshed
       and violence done to the
       land,
   To the town and all its
       inhabitants.

9 "Woe to him who makes ᴬevil
       profit for his household,
   To ᴮput his nest on high,
   To be saved from the hand of
       catastrophe!
10 "You have planned a shameful
       thing for your house
   By bringing many peoples to
       an end;
   So you are ᴬsinning against
       yourself.
11 "For the ᴬstone will cry out from
       the wall,
   And the rafter will answer it
       from the framework.

12 "Woe to him who ᴬbuilds a city
       with bloodshed,
   And founds a town with
       violence!
13 "Is it not indeed from the Lᴏʀᴅ
       of armies
   That peoples ᴬlabor *merely* for
       fire,
   And nations become weary for
       nothing?
14 "For the earth will be ᴬfilled
   With the knowledge of the
       glory of the Lᴏʀᴅ,
   As the waters cover the sea.

15 "Woe to him who makes his
       neighbor drink;
   To you who mix in your venom
       even to make *your neighbors*
       drunk,
   So as to look at their genitalia!

16 "You will be filled with disgrace
       rather than honor.
   Drink, you yourself, and
       expose your *own* foreskin!
   The ᴬcup in the Lᴏʀᴅ's right
       hand will come around to
       you,
   And ᴮutter disgrace *will come*
       upon your glory.
17 "For the ᴬviolence done to
       Lebanon will overwhelm
       you,
   And the devastation of *its*
       animals by which you
       terrified them,
   Because of human bloodshed
       and violence done to the
       land,
   To the town and all its
       inhabitants.

18 "What benefit is a carved image
       when its maker has carved it,
   Or a cast metal image, a
       ᴬteacher of falsehood?
   For *its* maker ᴮtrusts in his *own*
       handiwork
   When he fashions speechless
       idols.
19 "Woe to him who says to a *piece
       of* wood, 'Awake!'
   To a mute stone, 'Arise!'
   That is *your* teacher?
   Behold, it is overlaid with gold
       and silver,
   Yet there is ᴬno breath at all
       inside it.
20 "But the ᴬLᴏʀᴅ is in His holy
       temple.
   Let all the earth ᴮbe silent
       before Him."

2:8 ᴬIs 33:1; Jer 27:7   2:9 ᴬJer 22:13   ᴮJer 49:16
2:10 ᴬJer 26:19   2:11 ᴬJosh 24:27; Luke 19:40
2:12 ᴬMic 3:10; Nah 3:1   2:13 ᴬIs 50:11; Jer 51:58
2:14 ᴬPs 22:27; Is 11:9   2:16 ᴬJer 25:15, 17   ᴮNah 3:6
2:17 ᴬJoel 3:19; Zech 11:1   2:18 ᴬJer 10:8, 14
ᴮPs 115:4, 8   2:19 ᴬPs 135:17   2:20 ᴬMic 1:2
ᴮZeph 1:7

GOD'S PEOPLE SAVED

3 A prayer of Habakkuk the prophet, according to ¹Shigionoth.

2 Lord, I have heard the report about You, *and* I was afraid.
Lord, ᴬrevive ᴮYour work in the midst of the years,
In the midst of the years make *it* known.
In anger remember mercy.

3 God comes from ᴬTeman,
And the Holy One from Mount ᴮParan. *Selah*
His splendor covers the heavens,
And the earth is full of His praise.

4 *His* ᴬradiance is like the sunlight;
He has rays *flashing* from His hand,
And the hiding of His ᴮmight is there.

5 Before Him goes ᴬplague,
And plague comes forth after Him.

6 He stood and caused the earth to shudder;
He looked and ᴬcaused the nations to jump.
Yes, the everlasting mountains were shattered,
The ancient hills collapsed.
His paths are ᴮeverlasting.

7 I saw the tents of Cushan under ᴬdistress,
The tent curtains of the land of Midian were trembling.

8 Did the Lord rage against the ᴬrivers,
Or *was* Your anger against the rivers,
Or *was* Your rage against the ᴮsea,

That You rode on Your horses,
On Your chariots of salvation?

9 You removed Your ᴬbow *from its holder,*
The arrows of *Your* word were sworn. *Selah*
You divided the earth with rivers.

10 The mountains saw You *and* quaked;
The downpour of waters swept by.
The deep ᴬraised its voice,
It lifted high its hands.

11 ᴬSun *and* moon stood in their lofty places;
They went away at the ᴮlight of Your arrows,
At the radiance of Your flashing spear.

12 In indignation You ᴬmarched through the earth;
In anger You ᴮtrampled the nations.

13 You went forth for the ᴬsalvation of Your people,
For the salvation of Your anointed.
You smashed the head of the house of evil
To uncover *him from* foot to neck. *Selah*

14 You pierced with his own arrows
The head of his leaders.
They ᴬstormed in to scatter us;
Their arrogance *was* like those
Who ᴮdevour the oppressed in secret.

3:2 ᴬPs 71:20   ᴮHab 1:5   3:3 ᴬJer 49:7   ᴮGen 21:21
3:4 ᴬPs 18:12   3:5 ᴬEx 12:29, 30;
Num 16:46-49   3:6 ᴬJob 21:18   ᴮHab 1:12
3:7 ᴬEx 15:14-16   3:8 ᴬEx 7:19, 20   ᴮEx 14:16, 21
3:9 ᴬPs 78:16; 105:41   3:10 ᴬPs 93:3; 98:7, 8
3:11 ᴬJosh 10:12-14   ᴮPs 18:14   3:12 ᴬPs 68:7
ᴮIs 41:15   3:13 ᴬEx 15:2; 2 Sam 5:20   3:14 ᴬDan 11:40
ᴮPs 10:8

3:1 ¹Perhaps a highly emotional poetic form

15 You ^trampled on the sea with
   Your horses,
   On the foam of many waters.

16 I heard, and my inner parts
   trembled;
   At the sound, my lips
   quivered.
   Decay enters my bones,
   And in my place I tremble;
   Because I must ^wait quietly
   for the day of distress,
   For the ^Bpeople to arise *who*
   will attack us.

17 Even if the ^fig tree does not
   blossom,
   And there is no fruit on the
   vines,
   If the yield of the olive fails,

And the fields produce no
food,
Even if the flock disappears
from the fold,
And there are no cattle in the
stalls,

18 Yet I will triumph in the LORD,
   I will rejoice in the ^God of my
   salvation.

19 The Lord GOD is my strength,
   And He has made my feet like
   deer's *feet,*
   And has me walk on my ^high
   places.

For the choir director, on my
stringed instruments.

3:15 ^Ps 77:19; Hab 3:8 **3:16** ^Luke 21:19 ^BJer 5:15
3:17 ^Joel 1:10–12; Amos 4:9 **3:18** ^Ps 25:5; 27:1
3:19 ^Deut 33:29

ZEPHANIAH

DAY OF JUDGMENT ON JUDAH

1 The word of the LORD which came to Zephaniah son of Cushi, son of Gedaliah, son of Amariah, son of Hezekiah, in the days of ^AJosiah son of Amon, king of Judah:

2 "I will completely ^Aremove all *things*
From the face of the earth,"
declares the LORD.

3 "I will remove ^Ahuman and animal *life;*
I will remove the ^Bbirds of the sky
And the fish of the sea,
And the ruins along with the wicked;
And I will eliminate mankind from the face of the earth,"
declares the LORD.

4 "So I will stretch out My hand against Judah
And against all the inhabitants of Jerusalem.
And I will ^Aeliminate the remnant of Baal from this place,
And the names of the ^Bidolatrous priests along with the *other* priests.

5 "And those who bow down on the ^Ahousetops to the heavenly ^1lights,
And those who bow down *and* swear to the LORD, but *also* swear by ^BMilcom,

6 And those who have ^Aturned back from following the LORD,
And those who have ^Bnot sought the LORD nor inquired of Him."

7 ^ABe silent before the Lord GOD!
For the ^Bday of the LORD is near,
Because the LORD has prepared a sacrifice,
He has consecrated His guests.

8 "Then it will come about on the day of the LORD's sacrifice
That I will ^Apunish the princes, the king's sons,
And all who clothe themselves with ^Bforeign garments.

9 "And on that day I will punish all who leap on the *temple* threshold,
Who fill the house of their lord with ^Aviolence and deceit.

10 "And on that day," declares the LORD,
"There will be the sound of a cry from the ^AFish Gate,
Wailing from the ^1,BSecond Quarter,
And a loud crash from the hills.

11 "Wail, you inhabitants of the ^1Mortar,
Because all the people of ^ACanaan will be destroyed;
All who weigh out silver will be eliminated.

12 "And it will come about at that time
That I will search Jerusalem with lamps,
And I will punish the people

1:1 ^A 2 Kin 22:1, 2; 2 Chr 34:1-33   1:2 ^A Gen 6:7; Jer 7:20
1:3 ^A Is 6:11, 12   ^B Jer 4:25   1:4 ^A Mic 5:13   ^B 2 Kin 23:5
1:5 ^A 2 Kin 23:12   ^B 1 Kin 11:5, 33   1:6 ^A Is 1:4   ^B Is 9:13
1:7 ^A Hab 2:20   ^B Zeph 1:14   1:8 ^A Is 24:21   ^B Is 2:6
1:9 ^A Jer 5:27; Amos 3:10   1:10 ^A 2 Chr 33:14
^B 2 Chr 34:22   1:11 ^A Zeph 2:5; Zech 14:21

1:5 ^1 Lit *host;* i.e., sun, stars, etc.   1:10 ^1 I.e., a district
of Jerusalem   1:11 ^1 I.e., a district of Jerusalem

Who are ^stagnant in spirit,
Who say in their hearts,
'The Lord will ᴮnot do good
    nor harm!'
13 "Their wealth will become
    plunder,
And their houses desolate;
Yes, ^they will build houses
    but not inhabit *them,*
And plant vineyards but not
    drink their wine."

14 The ^great ᴮday of the Lord is
    near,
Near and coming very quickly;
Listen, the day of the Lord!
In it the warrior cries out
    bitterly.
15 That day is a day of anger,
A day of ^trouble and distress,
A day of destruction and
    desolation,
A day of ᴮdarkness and gloom,
A day of clouds and thick
    darkness,
16 A day of ^trumpet and battle
    cry
Against the fortified cities
And the high corner towers.
17 I will bring ^distress on
    mankind
So that they will walk ᴮlike
    those who are blind,
Because they have sinned
    against the Lord;
And their blood will be poured
    out like dust,
And their flesh like dung.
18 Neither their ^silver nor their
    gold
Will be able to save them
On the day of the Lord's anger;
And ᴮall the earth will be
    devoured
By the fire of His jealousy,
For He will make a complete
    end,

Indeed a horrifying one,
Of all the inhabitants of the
    earth.

JUDGMENTS ON JUDAH'S ENEMIES

2 Gather yourselves together,
    yes, join together,
You nation ^without shame,
2 Before the decree takes
    effect—
The day passes like chaff—
Before the ^burning anger of
    the Lord comes upon you,
Before the ᴮday of the Lord's
    anger comes upon you.
3 ^Seek the Lord,
All you humble of the earth
Who have practiced His
    ordinances;
ᴮSeek righteousness, seek
    humility.
Perhaps you will remain
    hidden
On the day of the Lord's anger.

4 For ^Gaza will be abandoned,
And Ashkelon *will become* a
    desolation;
The inhabitants of ^Ashdod
    will be driven out at noon,
And ^Ekron will be uprooted.
5 Woe to the inhabitants of the
    seacoast,
The nation of the ¹,^Cherethites!
The word of the Lord is
    against you,
Canaan, land of the Philistines;
And I will eliminate you
So that there will be no
    inhabitant.

1:12 ^Jer 48:11   ᴮEzek 8:12   1:13 ^Amos 5:11; Mic 6:15
1:14 ^Jer 30:7   ᴮEzek 7:7, 12   1:15 ^Is 22:5
ᴮJoel 2:2, 31   1:16 ^Is 27:13; Jer 4:19   1:17 ^Jer 10:18
ᴮDeut 28:29   1:18 ^Ezek 7:19   ᴮZeph 3:8
2:1 ^Jer 3:3; 6:15   2:2 ^Lam 4:11   ᴮZeph 1:18
2:3 ^Ps 105:4   ᴮAmos 5:14, 15   2:4 ^Amos 1:7, 8;
Zech 9:5-7   2:5 ^Ezek 25:16

2:5 ¹I.e., a segment of the Philistines with roots in Crete

6 So the seacoast will become
   ^grazing places,
   With pastures for shepherds
   and folds for flocks.
7 And the coast will be
   For the ^remnant of the house
   of Judah,
   They will ᴮdrive *sheep* to
   pasture on it.
   In the houses of Ashkelon
   they will lie down at
   evening;
   For the Lᴏʀᴅ their God will
   care for them
   And restore their fortunes.

8 "I have heard the ^taunting of
   Moab
   And the ᴮabusive speech of the
   sons of Ammon,
   With which they have taunted
   My people
   And boasted against their
   territory.
9 "Therefore, as I live," declares
   the Lᴏʀᴅ of armies,
   The God of Israel,
   "Moab will assuredly be like
   Sodom,
   And the sons of Ammon like
   Gomorrah—
   Ground overgrown with weeds
   and *full of* salt mines,
   And a permanent desolation.
   The remnant of My people will
   ^plunder them,
   And the remainder of My
   nation will inherit them."

10 This they will have in return for
their ^arrogance, because they have
ᴮtaunted and boasted against the
people of the Lᴏʀᴅ of armies. 11 The
Lᴏʀᴅ will be ^terrifying to them, for
He will starve all the gods of the
earth; and all the coastlands of the
nations will ᴮbow down to Him,
everyone from his *own* place.

12 "You also, ^Ethiopians, will be
   slain by My sword."
13 And He will ^stretch out His
   hand against the north
   And eliminate Assyria,
   And He will make Nineveh a
   desolation,
   Parched like the wilderness.
14 Flocks will lie down in her
   midst,
   All animals that range in
   herds;
   Both the ^pelican and the
   hedgehog
   Will spend their nights in the
   tops of her pillars;
   Birds will sing in the window,
   Devastation *will be* on the
   threshold;
   For He has uncovered the
   cedar work.
15 This is the presumptuous city
   That ^dwells securely,
   Who says in her heart,
   "ᴮI am, and there is no one
   besides me."
   How she has become a
   desolation,
   A resting place for animals!
   Everyone who passes by her
   will hiss
   And wave his hand *in*
   contempt.

WOE TO JERUSALEM AND THE NATIONS

3 Woe to her who is ^rebellious
   and ᴮdefiled,
   The oppressive city!
2 She obeyed no voice,
   She ^accepted no discipline.
   She did not ᴮtrust in the Lᴏʀᴅ,
   She did not approach her God.

2:6 ^Is 5:17; 7:25   **2:7** ^Is 11:16   ᴮIs 32:14
2:8 ^Ezek 25:8   ᴮEzek 25:3   **2:9** ^Is 11:14
2:10 ^Is 16:6   ᴮZeph 2:8   **2:11** ^Joel 2:11   ᴮPs 72:8-11
2:12 ^Is 18:1-7; 20:4, 5   **2:13** ^Is 14:26; Zeph 1:4
2:14 ^Is 14:23; 34:11   **2:15** ^Is 32:9, 11   ᴮIs 47:8
3:1 ^Jer 5:23   ᴮEzek 23:30   **3:2** ^Jer 2:30   ᴮPs 78:22

3 Her ^leaders within her are
     roaring lions,
   Her judges are ᴮwolves at
     evening;
   They have no bones to gnaw
     in the morning.
4 Her prophets are ^insolent,
     treacherous men;
   Her ᴮpriests have profaned
     the sanctuary.
   They have done violence to
     the Law.
5 The Lᴏʀᴅ is ^righteous within
     her;
   He will ᴮdo no injustice.
   Every morning He brings His
     justice to light;
   He does not fail.
   But the criminal knows no
     shame.
6 "I have eliminated nations;
     Their corner towers are
       deserted.
   I have ^laid waste their streets,
     With no one passing by;
   Their cities have been laid
     waste,
   Without a person, ᴮwithout an
     inhabitant.
7 "I said, 'You will certainly
     revere Me,
   You will ^accept discipline.'
   So her dwelling will not be
     eliminated
   In accordance with
     everything that I have
     stipulated for her.
   Instead, they were eager to
     corrupt all their deeds.

8 "Therefore wait for Me,"
     declares the Lᴏʀᴅ,
   "For the day when I rise up as a
     witness.
   Indeed, My decision *is* to
     ^gather nations,
   To assemble kingdoms,

   To pour out on them My
     indignation,
   All My burning anger;
   For ᴮall the earth will be
     devoured
   By the fire of My zeal.
9 "For then I will restore to the
     peoples ^pure lips,
   So that all of them may call on
     the name of the Lᴏʀᴅ,
   To serve Him shoulder to
     shoulder.
10 "From beyond the rivers of
     Ethiopia
   My worshipers, My dispersed
     ones,
   Will ^bring My offerings.
11 "On that day you will ^feel no
     shame
   Because of all your deeds
   By which you have rebelled
     against Me;
   For then I will remove from
     your midst
   Your ᴮproud, arrogant ones,
   And you will never again be
     haughty
   On My holy mountain.

A REMNANT OF ISRAEL

12 "But I will leave among you
   A ^humble and lowly people,
   And they will ᴮtake refuge in
     the name of the Lᴏʀᴅ.
13 "The remnant of Israel will ^do
     no wrong
   And ᴮtell no lies,
   Nor will a deceitful tongue
   Be found in their mouths;
   For they will feed and lie
     down
   With no one to frighten *them*."

3:3 ^Ezek 22:27   ᴮJer 5:6   3:4 ^Judg 9:4   ᴮEzek 22:26
3:5 ^Deut 32:4   ᴮPs 92:15   3:6 ^Jer 9:12   ᴮZeph 2:5
3:7 ^Job 36:10; Ps 32:8   3:8 ^Ezek 38:14-23
ᴮZeph 1:18   3:9 ^Is 19:18; 57:19   3:10 ^Is 60:6, 7
3:11 ^Is 45:17   ᴮIs 2:12   3:12 ^Is 14:30   ᴮIs 50:10
3:13 ^Ps 119:3   ᴮZech 8:3, 16

14 Shout for joy, daughter of
        Zion!
    ^AShout *in triumph,* Israel!
    Rejoice and triumph with all
        your heart,
    Daughter of Jerusalem!
15 The LORD has taken away
        ^A*His* judgments against
        you,
    He has cleared away your
        enemies.
    The King of Israel, the LORD,
        is ^Bin your midst;
    You will no longer fear
        disaster.
16 On that day it will be said to
        Jerusalem:
    "^ADo not be afraid, Zion;
    ^BDo not let your hands fall
        limp.
17 "The LORD your God is ^Ain your
        midst,
    A ^Bvictorious warrior.
    He will rejoice over you with
        joy,
    He will be quiet in His love,
    He will rejoice over you with
        shouts of joy.

18 "I will gather those who
        are ^Aworried about the
        appointed feasts—
    They came from you, *Zion;*
    The disgrace *of exile* is a
        burden on them.
19 "Behold, I am going to deal at
        that time
    With all your ^Aoppressors;
    I will save those who limp
    And gather the scattered,
    And I will turn their shame
        into praise and fame
    In all the earth.
20 "At that time I will ^Abring you in,
    Even at the time when I gather
        you together;
    Indeed, I will make you
        famous and praiseworthy
    Among all the peoples of the
        earth,
    When I ^Brestore your fortunes
        before your eyes,"
    Says the LORD.

3:14 ^AZech 9:9   3:15 ^APs 19:9   ^BEzek 37:26-28
3:16 ^AIs 35:3, 4   ^BJob 4:3   3:17 ^AZeph 3:5, 15   ^BIs 63:1
3:18 ^APs 42:2-4; Ezek 9:4   3:19 ^AIs 60:14
3:20 ^AEzek 37:12, 21   ^BJer 29:14

HAGGAI

HAGGAI BEGINS TEMPLE BUILDING

1 In the second year of Darius the king, on the first day of the sixth month, the word of the LORD came by the prophet ᴬHaggai to ᴮZerubbabel the son of Shealtiel, governor of Judah, and to Joshua the son of Jehozadak, the high priest, saying, ² "This is what the LORD of armies says: 'This people says, "The time has not come, the time for the house of the LORD to be rebuilt."'" ³ Then the word of the LORD came by Haggai the prophet, saying, ⁴ "Is it time for you yourselves to live in your paneled houses while this house *remains* ᴬdesolate?" ⁵ Now then, the LORD of armies says this: "Consider your ways! ⁶ You have ᴬsown much, *only to* harvest little; *you* eat, but there is not *enough* to be satisfied; *you* drink, but there is not *enough* to become drunk; *you* put on clothing, but there is not *enough* for anyone to get warm; and the one who earns, earns wages *to put* into a money bag full of holes."

⁷ The LORD of armies says this: "Consider your ways! ⁸ Go up to the mountains, bring wood, and ᴬrebuild the temple, that I may be ᴮpleased with it and be honored," says the LORD. ⁹ "*You* start an ambitious project, but behold, *it comes* to little; when you bring *it* home, I ᴬblow it *away*. Why?" declares the LORD of armies. "*It is* because of My house which *remains* desolate, while each of you runs to his own house. ¹⁰ Therefore, because of you the ᴬsky has withheld its dew, and the earth

has withheld its produce. ¹¹ And I called for a ᴬdrought on the land, on the mountains, on the grain, on the new wine, on the oil, on what the ground produces, on mankind, on cattle, and on all the products of the labor of your hands."

¹² Then Zerubbabel the son of Shealtiel, and Joshua the son of Jehozadak, the high priest, with all the remnant of the people, ᴬobeyed the voice of the LORD their God and the words of Haggai the prophet, just as the LORD their God had sent him. And the people ᴮshowed reverence for the LORD. ¹³ Then Haggai, the messenger of the LORD, spoke by the commission of the LORD to the people, saying, "'ᴬI am with you,' declares the LORD." ¹⁴ So the LORD stirred up the spirit of Zerubbabel the son of Shealtiel, governor of Judah, and the spirit of Joshua the son of Jehozadak, the high priest, and the spirit of all the ᴬremnant of the people; and they came and ᴮworked on the house of the LORD of armies, their God, ¹⁵ on the twenty-fourth day of the sixth month in the second year of Darius the king.

THE BUILDERS ENCOURAGED

2 On the twenty-first of the seventh month, the word of the LORD came by ᴬHaggai the prophet, saying, ² "Speak now to Zerubbabel

1:1 ᴬEzra 5:1   ᴮNeh 7:7   1:4 ᴬJer 33:10, 12; Hag 1:9
1:6 ᴬDeut 28:38-40; Hos 8:7   1:8 ᴬ1 Kin 6:1
ᴮPs 132:13, 14   1:9 ᴬIs 40:7   1:10 ᴬDeut 28:23, 24;
1 Kin 17:1   1:11 ᴬJer 14:2-6; Mal 3:9, 11   1:12 ᴬIs 1:19
ᴮDeut 31:12, 13   1:13 ᴬPs 46:11; Is 41:10   1:14 ᴬHag 1:12
ᴮEzra 5:2   2:1 ᴬHag 1:1

the son of Shealtiel, governor of Judah, and to Joshua the son of Jehozadak, the high priest, and to the ᴬremnant of the people, saying, ³'Who is ᴬleft among you who saw this temple in its former glory? And how do you see it now? Does it not seem to you like nothing in comparison? ⁴But now ᴬtake courage, Zerubbabel,' declares the LORD, 'take courage also, Joshua son of Jehozadak, the high priest, and all you people of the land take courage,' declares the LORD, 'and work; for ᴮI am with you,' declares the LORD of armies. ⁵'As for the ᴬpromise which I made you when you came out of Egypt, My ᴮSpirit remains in your midst; do not fear!' ⁶For this is what the LORD of armies says: 'ᴬOnce more in a ᴮlittle while, I am going to shake the heavens and the earth, the sea also and the dry land. ⁷I will shake ᴬall the nations; and they will come with the ᴮwealth of all nations, and I will fill this house with glory,' says the LORD of armies. ⁸'The ᴬsilver is Mine and the gold is Mine,' declares the LORD of armies. ⁹'The latter ᴬglory of this house will be greater than the former,' says the LORD of armies, 'and in this place I will give ᴮpeace,' declares the LORD of armies."

¹⁰On the ᴬtwenty-fourth of the ninth month, in the second year of Darius, the word of the LORD came to Haggai the prophet, saying, ¹¹"The LORD of armies says this: 'ᴬNow ask the priests for a ruling: ¹²If someone carries ᴬholy meat in the fold of his garment, and touches bread with this fold, or touches cooked food, wine, oil, or any other food, will it become holy?'" And the priests answered, "No." ¹³Then Haggai said, "ᴬIf one

who is unclean from a corpse touches any of these things, will the latter become unclean?" And the priests answered, "It will become unclean." ¹⁴Then Haggai responded and said, "'ᴬSo is this people. And so is this nation before Me,' declares the LORD, 'and so is every work of their hands; and what they offer there is unclean. ¹⁵But now, do ᴬconsider from this day onward: before one stone was placed on another in the temple of the LORD, ¹⁶from that time when one came to a grain heap of twenty measures, there would be only ten; and when one came to the wine vat to draw fifty measures, there would be only twenty. ¹⁷I struck you and every work of your hands with ᴬscorching wind, mildew, and hail; yet you did not come back to Me,' declares the LORD. ¹⁸'Do ᴬconsider from this day onward, from the twenty-fourth day of the ninth month; from the day when the temple of the LORD was ᴮfounded, consider: ¹⁹Is the seed still in the barn? Even including the vine, the fig tree, the pomegranate, and the olive tree, it has not produced fruit. Yet from this day on I will ᴬbless you.'"

²⁰Then the word of the LORD came a second time to Haggai on the ᴬtwenty-fourth day of the month, saying, ²¹"Speak to Zerubbabel governor of Judah, saying, 'I am going to ᴬshake the heavens

2:2ᴬHag 1:12   2:3ᴬEzra 3:12   2:4ᴬDeut 31:23
ᴮ2 Sam 5:10   2:5ᴬEx 19:4-6   ᴮNeh 9:20
2:6ᴬHeb 12:26   ᴮIs 10:25   2:7ᴬDan 2:44   ᴮIs 60:4-9
2:8ᴬ1 Chr 29:14, 16; Is 60:17   2:9ᴬZech 2:5   ᴮIs 9:6, 7
2:10ᴬHag 2:20   2:11ᴬDeut 17:8-11; Mal 2:7
2:12ᴬEx 29:37; Lev 6:27, 29   2:13ᴬLev 22:4-6;
Num 19:22   2:14ᴬProv 15:8; Is 1:11-15
2:15ᴬHag 1:5, 7; 2:18   2:17ᴬDeut 28:22; 1 Kin 8:37
2:18ᴬDeut 32:29   ᴮEzra 5:1, 2
2:19ᴬPs 128:1-6; Jer 31:12, 14   2:20ᴬHag 2:10
2:21ᴬHag 2:6; Heb 12:26, 27

and the earth. ²²And I will ^overthrow the thrones of kingdoms and destroy the ᴮpower of the kingdoms of the nations; and I will overthrow the chariots and their riders, and the horses and their riders will go down, every one by the sword of another.' ²³'On that day,' declares

the LORD of armies, 'I will take you, Zerubbabel, son of Shealtiel, My servant,' declares the LORD, 'and I will make you like a ^signet ring, for ᴮI have chosen you,'" declares the LORD of armies.

2:22 ^Ezek 26:16   ᴮMic 7:16   2:23 ^Song 8:6
ᴮIs 42:1

ZECHARIAH

A CALL TO REPENTANCE

1 In the eighth month of the second year of Darius, the word of the LORD came to ^Zechariah the prophet, the son of Berechiah, the son of ^BIddo saying, ²"The LORD was very ^angry with your fathers. ³Therefore say to them, 'This is what the LORD of armies says: "^AReturn to Me," declares the LORD of armies, "that I may return to you," says the LORD of armies. ⁴"Do not be like your fathers, to whom the former prophets proclaimed, saying, 'This is what the LORD of armies says: "^AReturn now from your evil ways and from your evil deeds."' But they did ^Bnot listen or pay attention to Me," declares the LORD. ⁵"Your ^Afathers, where are they? And the ^Bprophets, do they live forever? ⁶But did My words and My statutes, which I commanded My servants the prophets, not overtake your fathers? Then they repented and said, '^AJust as the LORD of armies planned to do to us in accordance with our ways and our deeds, so He has dealt with us.'"'"

PATROL OF THE EARTH

⁷On the twenty-fourth day of the eleventh month, that is, the month Shebat, in the second year of Darius, the word of the LORD came to Zechariah the prophet, the son of Berechiah, the son of Iddo, as follows: ⁸I saw at night, and behold, a man was riding on a ^Ared horse, and he was standing among the myrtle trees which were in the ravine, with red,

ᴵsorrel, and ^Bwhite horses behind him. ⁹Then I said, "What are these, my lord?" And the ^Aangel who was speaking with me said to me, "I will show you what these are." ¹⁰And the man who was standing among the myrtle trees responded and said, "These are the ones whom the LORD has sent to ^Apatrol the earth." ¹¹So they responded to the angel of the LORD who was standing among the myrtle trees and said, "We have patrolled the earth, and behold, ^Aall the earth is still and quiet."

¹²Then the angel of the LORD said, "LORD of armies, ^Ahow long will You take no pity on Jerusalem and the cities of Judah, with which You have been indignant for these ^Bseventy years?" ¹³And the LORD responded to the angel who was speaking with me with gracious words, ^Acomforting words. ¹⁴So the angel who was speaking with me said to me, "Proclaim, saying, 'This is what the LORD of armies says: "I am ^Aexceedingly jealous for Jerusalem and Zion. ¹⁵But I am very angry with the nations who are ^Acarefree; for while I was *only* a little angry, they ^Bfurthered the disaster." ¹⁶Therefore the LORD says this: "I will ^Areturn to Jerusalem with compassion; My ^Bhouse will be built in it," declares

---

1:1^AEzra 5:1 ^BNeh 12:4, 16   1:2^A2 Chr 36:16; Jer 44:6
1:3^AIs 31:6; 44:22   1:4^AIs 1:16-19   ^BJer 6:17
1:5^ALam 5:7   ^BJohn 8:52 1:6^ALam 2:17   1:8^AZech 6:2
^BRev 6:2   1:9^AZech 2:3; 5:5   1:10^AJob 1:7; Zech 1:11
1:11^AIs 14:7   1:12^APs 74:10   ^BJer 25:11   1:13^AIs 40:1, 2;
57:18   1:14^AZech 8:2   1:15^APs 123:4   ^BAmos 1:11
1:16^AIs 54:8-10   ^BEzra 6:14, 15

1:8 ᴵI.e., light reddish-brown

the LORD of armies, "and a measuring line will be stretched over Jerusalem."' ¹⁷Again, proclaim, saying, 'This is what the LORD of armies says: "My ^cities will again overflow with prosperity, and the LORD will again comfort Zion and again ᴮchoose Jerusalem."'"

¹⁸Then I raised my eyes and looked, and behold, *there were* four horns. ¹⁹So I said to the angel who was speaking with me, "What are these?" And he said to me, "These are the ^horns that have scattered Judah, Israel, and Jerusalem." ²⁰Then the LORD showed me four ^craftsmen. ²¹And I said, "What are these coming to do?" And he said, "These are the horns that have scattered Judah so that no one lifts up his head; but these *craftsmen* have come to frighten them, to ^throw down the horns of the nations who have lifted up *their* horns against the land of Judah in order to scatter it."

GOD'S FAVOR TO ZION

2 Then I raised my eyes and looked, and behold, *there was* a man with a ^measuring line in his hand. ²So I said, "Where are you going?" And he said to me, "To ^measure Jerusalem, to see how wide it is and how long it is." ³And behold, the ^angel who had been speaking with me was going out, and another angel was going out to meet him. ⁴And he said to him, "Run, speak to that young man there, saying, '^Jerusalem will be inhabited ᴮas open country because of the multitude of people and cattle within it. ⁵But I,' declares the LORD, 'will be a ^wall of fire to her on all sides, and I will be the glory in her midst.'"

⁶"You there! ^Flee from the land of the north," declares the LORD, "because I have spread you out like the four winds of the heavens," declares the LORD. ⁷"You, Zion! ^Escape, you who are living *with* the daughter of Babylon." ⁸For the LORD of armies says this: "After ^glory He has sent me against the nations that plunder you, for the one who touches you, touches the apple of His eye. ⁹For behold, I am going to ^wave My hand over them so that they will be ᴮplunder for their slaves. Then you will know that the LORD of armies has sent Me. ¹⁰Shout for joy and rejoice, daughter of Zion; for behold I am coming and I will ^dwell in your midst," declares the LORD. ¹¹"And ^many nations will join themselves to the LORD on that day and will become My people. Then I will dwell in your midst, and you will know that the LORD of armies has sent Me to you. ¹²And the LORD will ^possess Judah as His portion in the holy land, and will again ᴮchoose Jerusalem.

¹³"^Be silent, all mankind, before the LORD; for He has roused Himself from His holy dwelling."

JOSHUA, THE HIGH PRIEST

3 Then he showed me ^Joshua the high priest standing before the angel of the LORD, and ᴮSatan standing at his right to accuse him. ²And the LORD said to Satan, "^The LORD rebuke you, Satan! Indeed, the LORD who has chosen Jerusalem rebuke

1:17^Is 44:26   ᴮZech 2:12   1:19^1 Kin 22:11; Ps 75:4, 5
1:20^Is 44:12; 54:16   1:21^Ps 75:10   2:1^Jer 31:39;
Ezek 40:3   2:2^Jer 31:39; Ezek 40:3   2:3^Zech 1:9
2:4^Zech 1:17   ᴮEzek 38:11   2:5^Is 4:5; 26:1
2:6^Jer 3:18   2:7^Is 48:20; Jer 51:6   2:8^Is 60:7-9
2:9^Is 19:16   ᴮIs 14:2   2:10^Zech 2:5; 8:3
2:11^Mic 4:2   2:12^Deut 32:9   ᴮ2 Chr 6:6
2:13^Hab 2:20; Zeph 1:7   3:1^Ezra 5:2   ᴮ1 Chr 21:1
3:2^Mark 9:25

you! Is this not a ᴮlog snatched from the fire?" ³Now Joshua was clothed in ᴬfilthy garments and was standing before the angel. ⁴And he responded and said to those who were standing before him, saying, "ᴬRemove the filthy garments from him." Again he said to him, "See, I have ᴮtaken your guilt away from you and will clothe you with festive robes." ⁵Then I said, "Have them put a clean ᴬheadband on his head." So they put the clean headband on his head and clothed him with garments, while the angel of the Lᴏʀᴅ was standing by.

⁶And the angel of the Lᴏʀᴅ admonished Joshua, saying, ⁷"The Lᴏʀᴅ of armies says this: 'If you ᴬwalk in My ways and perform My service, then you will both govern My house and be in charge of My courtyards, and I will grant you free access among these who are standing *here*.

THE BRANCH

⁸Now listen, Joshua, *you* high priest, you and your friends who are sitting in front of you—indeed they are men who are a sign: for behold, I am going to bring in My servant the ᴬBranch. ⁹For behold, the stone that I have put before Joshua; on one stone are seven eyes. Behold, I am going to engrave an inscription on it,' declares the Lᴏʀᴅ of armies, 'and I will ᴬremove the guilt of that land in one day. ¹⁰On that day,' declares the Lᴏʀᴅ of armies, 'every one *of you* will invite his neighbor to *sit* under *his* ᴬvine and under *his* fig tree.'"

**THE GOLDEN LAMPSTAND
AND THE OLIVE TREES**

4 Then ᴬthe angel who had been speaking with me returned and ᴮwoke me, like a person who is awakened from his sleep. ²And he

said to me, "What do you see?" And I said, "I see, and behold, a ᴬlampstand all of gold with its bowl on the top of it, and its ᴮseven lamps on it with seven spouts *belonging* to *each of* the lamps which are on the top of it; ³also ᴬtwo olive trees by it, one on the right side of the bowl and the other on its left side." ⁴Then I said to the angel who was speaking with me, saying, "What are these, ᴬmy lord?" ⁵So ᴬthe angel who was speaking with me answered and said to me, "Do you not know what these are?" And I said, "No, my lord." ⁶Then he said to me, "This is the word of the Lᴏʀᴅ to Zerubbabel, saying, 'ᴬNot by might nor by power, but by My ᴮSpirit,' says the Lᴏʀᴅ of armies. ⁷'What are you, you great ᴬmountain? Before Zerubbabel *you will become* a plain; and he will bring out the top stone *with* shouts of "Grace, grace to it!"'"

⁸Also the word of the Lᴏʀᴅ came to me, saying, ⁹"The hands of Zerubbabel have ᴬlaid the foundation of this house, and his hands will finish *it*. Then you will know that the Lᴏʀᴅ of armies has sent me to you. ¹⁰For who has shown contempt for the day of small things? But these seven will rejoice when they see the plumb line in the hand of Zerubbabel—they are the ᴬeyes of the Lᴏʀᴅ ᴮroaming throughout the earth."

¹¹Then I said to him, "What are these ᴬtwo olive trees on the right of the lampstand and on its left?"

3:2 ᴮAmos 4:11   3:3 ᴬEzra 9:15; Is 4:4   3:4 ᴬIs 43:25
ᴮMic 7:18, 19   3:5 ᴬJob 29:14; Is 3:23   3:7 ᴬ1 Kin 3:14
3:8 ᴬIs 11:1; 53:2   3:9 ᴬJer 31:34; 50:20   3:10 ᴬ1 Kin 4:25;
Is 36:16   4:1 ᴬZech 1:9   ᴮ1 Kin 19:5-7   4:2 ᴬEx 25:31, 37
ᴮRev 4:5   4:3 ᴬZech 4:11; Rev 11:4   4:4 ᴬZech 1:9;
4:5, 13   4:5 ᴬZech 1:9; 4:1   4:6 ᴬIs 11:2-4   ᴮ2 Chr 32:7, 8
4:7 ᴬPs 114:4, 6; Is 40:4   4:9 ᴬEzra 3:8-10; 5:16
4:10 ᴬ2 Chr 16:9   ᴮZech 1:10   4:11 ᴬZech 4:3; Rev 11:4

¹²And I responded the second time and said to him, "What are the two olive branches which are beside the two golden pipes, which empty the golden *oil* from themselves?" ¹³So he answered me, saying, "Do you not know what these are?" And I said, "No, ^my lord." ¹⁴Then he said, "These are the two ^anointed ones, who are standing by the Lord of the whole earth."

THE FLYING SCROLL

5 Then I raised my eyes again and looked, and behold, *there was* a flying ^scroll. ²And he said to me, "^What do you see?" And I said, "I see a flying scroll; its length is ¹twenty cubits, and its width ten cubits." ³Then he said to me, "This is the curse that is going forth over the face of the entire land; everyone who ^steals certainly will be purged away according to the writing on one side, and everyone who ^Bswears *falsely* will be purged away according to the writing on the other side. ⁴I will make it go forth," declares the Lord of armies, "and it will ^enter the house of the thief and the house of the one who swears falsely by My name; and it will spend the night within that house and ^Bdestroy it with its timber and stones."

⁵Then ^the angel who had been speaking with me went out and said to me, "Now raise your eyes and see what this is that is going forth." ⁶And I said, "What is it?" Then he said, "This is the ^ephah going forth." Again he said, "This is their ¹appearance in all the land. ⁷And behold, a lead cover was lifted up." *He continued,* "And this is a woman sitting inside the ephah." ⁸Then he said, "This is ^Wickedness!" And he

thrust her into the middle of the ephah and threw the lead weight on its opening. ⁹Then I raised my eyes and looked, and there two women were coming out with the wind in their wings; and they had wings like the wings of the ^stork, and they lifted up the ephah between the earth and the heavens. ¹⁰So I said to the angel who was speaking with me, "Where are they taking the ephah?" ¹¹Then he said to me, "To build a temple for her in the land of ^Shinar; and when it is prepared, she will be set there on her own pedestal."

THE FOUR CHARIOTS

6 Now I raised my eyes again and looked, and behold, ^four chariots were going out from between the two mountains; and the mountains *were* bronze mountains. ²With the first chariot *were* ^red horses, with the second chariot ^Bblack horses, ³with the third chariot ^white horses, and with the fourth chariot strong ^Bspotted horses. ⁴So I responded and said to the angel who was speaking with me, "^What are these, my lord?" ⁵The angel replied to me, "These are the ^four spirits of heaven, going out after taking their stand before the Lord of all the earth, ⁶with one of which the black horses are going out to the ^north country; and the white ones are to go out after them, while the

---

4:13^Zech 4:4, 5   4:14^Ex 29:7; 40:15   5:1^Jer 36:2;
Ezek 2:9   5:2^Zech 4:2   5:3^Ex 20:15   ^BLev 19:12
5:4^Hos 4:2, 3   ^BLev 14:34, 35   5:5^Zech 1:9
5:6^Lev 19:36; Amos 8:5   5:8^Hos 12:7; Amos 8:5
5:9^Lev 11:13, 19; Ps 104:17   5:11^Gen 10:10; 11:2
6:1^Dan 7:3; 8:22   6:2^Zech 1:8   ^BRev 6:5
6:3^Rev 6:2   ^BRev 6:8   6:4^Zech 1:9
6:5^Jer 49:36; Ezek 37:9   6:6^Jer 1:14, 15

5:2¹About 30 ft. long and 15 ft. wide or 9 m and 4.5 m
5:6¹Lit *eye;* some ancient versions *wrongdoing*

spotted ones are to go out to the ᴮsouth country." ⁷When the strong ones went out, they were eager to go to ᴬpatrol the earth. And He said, "Go, patrol the earth." So they patrolled the earth. ⁸Then He called out to me and spoke to me, saying, "See, those who are going to the land of the north have ᴬappeased My wrath in the land of the north."

⁹The ᴬword of the Lᴏʀᴅ also came to me, saying, ¹⁰"ᴬTake *an offering* from the exiles, from Heldai, Tobijah, and Jedaiah; and you shall go the same day and enter the house of Josiah the son of Zephaniah, where they have arrived from Babylon.

THE SYMBOLIC CROWNS

¹¹Also take silver and gold, make an *ornate* ᴬcrown, and set *it* on the head of Joshua the son of Jehozadak, the high priest. ¹²Then say to him, 'The Lᴏʀᴅ of armies says this: "Behold, *there is* a Man whose name is ᴬBranch, for He will branch out from where He is; and He will build the temple of the Lᴏʀᴅ. ¹³Yes, it is He who will build the temple of the Lᴏʀᴅ, and He who will ᴬbear the majesty and sit and rule on His throne. So He will be a ᴮpriest on His throne, and the counsel of peace will be between the two offices."' ¹⁴Now the ᴬcrown will become a reminder in the temple of the Lᴏʀᴅ to Helem, Tobijah, Jedaiah, and Hen the son of Zephaniah. ¹⁵ᴬThose who are far away will come and build the temple of the Lᴏʀᴅ." Then you will know that the Lᴏʀᴅ of armies has sent me to you. And it will take place if you completely obey the Lᴏʀᴅ your God.

7 In the fourth year of King Darius, the word of the Lᴏʀᴅ came to Zechariah on the fourth *day* of the ninth month, *which is* ᴬChislev. ²Now *the town of* Bethel had sent Sharezer and Regemmelech and their men to ᴬseek the favor of the Lᴏʀᴅ, ³speaking to the ᴬpriests who *belong* to the house of the Lᴏʀᴅ of armies, and to the prophets, saying, "Shall I weep in the ᴮfifth month and fast, as I have done these many years?" ⁴Then the word of the Lᴏʀᴅ of armies came to me, saying, ⁵"Say to all the people of the land and to the priests, 'When you fasted and mourned in the fifth and seventh *months* these ᴬseventy years, was it actually for ᴮMe that you fasted? ⁶And when you eat and drink, do you not eat for yourselves and drink for yourselves? ⁷Are *these* not the words which the Lᴏʀᴅ proclaimed by the former prophets, when Jerusalem was inhabited and ᴬcarefree along with its cities around it, and the ᴮNegev and the foothills were inhabited?'"

⁸Then the word of the Lᴏʀᴅ came to Zechariah, saying, ⁹"This is what the Lᴏʀᴅ of armies has said: 'ᴬDispense true justice and practice ᴮkindness and compassion each to his brother; ¹⁰and ᴬdo not oppress the widow or the orphan, the stranger or the poor; and do ᴮnot devise evil in your hearts against one another.' ¹¹But they ᴬrefused to pay attention, and turned a stubborn shoulder and plugged their

6:6 ᴮIs 43:6   **6:7** ᴬZech 1:10   **6:8** ᴬEzek 5:13; 24:13
6:9 ᴬZech 1:1; 7:1   **6:10** ᴬEzra 7:14-16; 8:26-30
6:11 ᴬ2 Sam 12:30; Ps 21:3   **6:12** ᴬIs 4:2; 11:1
6:13 ᴬIs 9:6   ᴮPs 110:1, 4   **6:14** ᴬZech 6:11
6:15 ᴬIs 56:6-8; 60:10   **7:1** ᴬNeh 1:1   **7:2** ᴬ1 Kin 13:6;
Jer 26:19   **7:3** ᴬEzra 3:10-12   ᴮZech 8:19
7:5 ᴬZech 1:12   ᴮIs 1:11, 12   **7:7** ᴬJer 22:21   ᴮJer 13:19
7:9 ᴬEzek 18:8   ᴮ2 Sam 9:7   **7:10** ᴬEx 22:22   ᴮPs 21:11
7:11 ᴬJer 5:3; 8:5

ears from hearing. ¹²They also made their ᴬhearts *as hard as* ᴮa diamond so that they could not hear the Law and the words which the Lᴏʀᴅ of armies had sent by His Spirit through the former prophets; therefore great wrath came from the Lᴏʀᴅ of armies. ¹³And just as He called and they would not listen, so ᴬthey called and I would not listen," says the Lᴏʀᴅ of armies; ¹⁴"but I ᴬscattered them with a storm wind among all the nations whom they did not know. So the land was desolated behind them so that ᴮno one went back and forth, since they made the pleasant land desolate."

THE COMING PEACE AND
PROSPERITY OF ZION

8 Then the word of the Lᴏʀᴅ of armies came, saying, ²"The Lᴏʀᴅ of armies says this: 'I am ᴬexceedingly jealous for Zion, yes, with great wrath I am jealous for her.' ³The Lᴏʀᴅ says this: 'I will return to Zion and ᴬdwell in the midst of Jerusalem. Then Jerusalem will be called the City of Truth, and the mountain of the Lᴏʀᴅ of armies *will be called* the Holy Mountain.' ⁴The Lᴏʀᴅ of armies says this: "ᴬOld men and old women will again sit in the public squares of Jerusalem, each person with his staff in his hand because of age. ⁵And the public squares of the city will be filled with ᴬboys and girls playing in its squares.' ⁶The Lᴏʀᴅ of armies says this: 'If it is too difficult in the sight of the remnant of this people in those days, will it also be ᴬtoo difficult in My sight?' declares the Lᴏʀᴅ of armies. ⁷The Lᴏʀᴅ of armies says this: 'Behold, I am going to save My people from the land of the ᴬeast and from the land of the west; ⁸and

I will ᴬbring them *back* and they will live in the midst of Jerusalem; and they shall be ᴮMy people, and I will be their God in truth and righteousness.'

⁹"The Lᴏʀᴅ of armies says this: 'Let your hands be strong, you who are listening in these days to these words from the mouth of the ᴬprophets, *those* who *spoke* in the day that the foundation of the house of the Lᴏʀᴅ of armies was laid, so that the temple might be built. ¹⁰For before those days there was no wage for man nor any wage for animal; and for him who went out or came in there was no ᴬpeace because of his enemies, and I ᴮsent all the people against one another. ¹¹But now I will ᴬnot treat the remnant of this people as in the former days,' declares the Lᴏʀᴅ of armies. ¹²'For *there will be* ᴬthe seed of peace: the vine will yield its fruit, the land will yield its produce, and the heavens will provide their dew; and I will give to the remnant of this people ᴮall these *things* as an inheritance. ¹³And it will come about that just as you were a ᴬcurse among the nations, house of Judah and house of Israel, so I will save you that you may become a ᴮblessing. Do not fear; let your hands be strong.'

¹⁴"For this is what the Lᴏʀᴅ of armies says: 'Just as I ᴬdetermined to do harm to you when your fathers provoked Me to anger,' says the Lᴏʀᴅ of armies, 'and I have not ᴮrelented, ¹⁵so I have again determined in these days to ᴬdo good

7:12 ᴬ2 Chr 36:13   ᴮJer 17:1   7:13 ᴬProv 1:24-28; Is 1:15
7:14 ᴬDeut 4:27   ᴮIs 60:15   8:2 ᴬZech 1:14
8:3 ᴬZech 2:10, 11   8:4 ᴬIs 65:20   8:5 ᴬJer 30:19, 20;
31:12, 13   8:6 ᴬJer 32:17, 27   8:7 ᴬPs 107:3; Is 11:11
8:8 ᴬZeph 3:20   ᴮEzek 11:20   8:9 ᴬEzra 5:1; 6:14
8:10 ᴬ2 Chr 15:5   ᴮIs 19:2   8:11 ᴬPs 103:9; Is 12:1
8:12 ᴬLev 26:3-6   ᴮIs 61:7   8:13 ᴬJer 29:18   ᴮPs 72:17
8:14 ᴬJer 31:28   ᴮJer 4:28   8:15 ᴬJer 29:11; Mic 7:18-20

to Jerusalem and to the house of Judah. Do not fear! ¹⁶These are the things which you shall do: speak the ᴬtruth to one another; ᴮjudge with truth and judgment for peace at your ¹gates. ¹⁷Also let none of you ᴬdevise evil in your heart against another, and do not love ᴮperjury; for all these *things* are what I hate,' declares the Lord."

¹⁸Then the word of the Lord of armies came to me, saying, ¹⁹"The Lord of armies says this: 'The fast of the fourth, the fast of the ᴬfifth, the fast of the seventh, and the fast of the tenth *months* will become joy, jubilation, and cheerful festivals for the house of Judah; so ᴮlove truth and peace.'

²⁰"The Lord of armies says this: '*It will* yet *turn out* that ᴬpeoples will come, that is, the inhabitants of many cities. ²¹The inhabitants of one *city* will go to another, saying, "Let's go at once to ᴬplead for the favor of the Lord, and to seek the Lord of armies; I also will go." ²²So ᴬmany peoples and mighty nations will come to seek the Lord of armies in Jerusalem, and to ᴮplead for the favor of the Lord.' ²³The Lord of armies says this: 'In those days ten people from all the nations will ᴬgrasp the garment of a Jew, saying, "Let us go with you, for we have heard that God is with you."'"

PROPHECIES AGAINST NEIGHBORING NATIONS

9 The pronouncement of the word of the Lord is against the land of Hadrach, with ᴬDamascus as its resting place (for the eyes of mankind, especially of all the tribes of Israel, are toward the Lord),

² And ᴬHamath also, which borders on it;
   ᴮTyre and Sidon, though they are very wise.
³ For Tyre built herself a ᴬfortress,
   And piled up silver like dust,
   And ᴮgold like the mud of the streets.
⁴ Behold, the Lord will ᴬdispossess her
   And throw her wealth into the sea;
   And she will be ᴮconsumed with fire.
⁵ Ashkelon will see *it* and be afraid.
   Gaza too will writhe in great pain;
   Also Ekron, because her hope has been ruined.
   Moreover, the king will perish from Gaza,
   And Ashkelon will not be inhabited.
⁶ And *a people of* mixed origins will live in ᴬAshdod,
   And I will eliminate the pride of the Philistines.
⁷ And I will remove their blood from their mouth
   And their detestable things from between their teeth.
   Then they also will be a remnant for our God,
   And be like a clan in Judah,
   And Ekron *will be* like a Jebusite.

8:16 ᴬPs 15:2   ᴮIs 9:7   8:17 ᴬProv 3:29   ᴮZech 5:4
8:19 ᴬZech 7:3, 5   ᴮLuke 1:74, 75
8:20 ᴬPs 117:1; Jer 16:19   8:21 ᴬZech 7:2
8:22 ᴬIs 2:2, 3   ᴮZech 8:21   8:23 ᴬIs 45:14, 24; 60:14
9:1 ᴬIs 17:1; Jer 49:23-27   9:2 ᴬJer 49:23   ᴮEzek 28:2-5, 12   9:3 ᴬJosh 19:29   ᴮ1 Kin 10:21, 27
9:4 ᴬEzek 26:3-5   ᴮEzek 28:18
9:6 ᴬAmos 1:8; Zeph 2:4

8:16 ¹I.e., the place where court was held

8 But I will camp around My
house because of an army,
Because of him who passes by
and returns;
And ^no oppressor will pass
over them anymore,
For now I have seen with My
eyes.

9 Rejoice greatly, daughter of
Zion!
Shout *in triumph,* daughter of
Jerusalem!
Behold, your ^king is coming
to you;
He is ᴮrighteous and endowed
with salvation,
Humble, and mounted on a
donkey,
Even on a colt, the foal of a
donkey.

10 And I will eliminate the
chariot from Ephraim
And the horse from Jerusalem;
And the bow of war will be
eliminated.
And He will speak ^peace to
the nations;
And His ᴮdominion will be
from sea to sea,
And from the *Euphrates* River
to the ends of the earth.

**RESTORATION OF JUDAH
AND EPHRAIM**

11 As for you also, because of the
^blood of *My* covenant with
you,
I have set your prisoners free
from the waterless pit.

12 Return to the ^stronghold, you
prisoners who have the hope;
This very day I am declaring
that I will restore ᴮdouble to
you.

13 For I will ^bend Judah as My
bow,
I will fill the bow with Ephraim.

And I will stir up your sons,
Zion, against your sons,
Greece;
And I will make you like a
ᴮwarrior's sword.

14 Then the Lᴏʀᴅ will appear
^over them,
And His ᴮarrow will go forth
like lightning;
And the Lord Gᴏᴅ will blow
the trumpet,
And march in the storm
winds of the south.

15 ^The Lᴏʀᴅ of armies will
protect them.
And they will ᴮdevour and
trample on the
slingstones;
And they will drink *and* be
boisterous as *with* wine;
And they will be filled like a
sacrificial basin,
Drenched like the corners of
the altar.

16 And the Lᴏʀᴅ their God will
^save them on that day
As the flock of His people;
For *they are like* the *precious*
stones of a crown,
Sparkling on His land.

17 For how great *will* their
^loveliness and ᴮbeauty *be!*
Grain will make the young
men flourish, and new
wine, the virgins.

GOD WILL BLESS JUDAH AND EPHRAIM

10 Ask for ^rain from the Lᴏʀᴅ
at the time of the spring
rain—
The Lᴏʀᴅ who ᴮmakes the
storm winds;

9:8 ^Is 54:14; 60:18   **9:9** ^Ps 110:1   ᴮZeph 3:5
9:10 ^Is 57:19   ᴮPs 72:8   **9:11** ^Ex 24:8; Heb 10:2
9:12 ^Jer 16:19   ᴮIs 61:7   **9:13** ^Jer 51:20   ᴮPs 45:3
9:14 ^Is 31:5   ᴮPs 18:14   **9:15** ^Is 37:35   ᴮZech 12:6
9:16 ^Jer 31:10, 11   **9:17** ^Jer 31:12, 14   ᴮPs 27:4
10:1 ^Joel 2:23   ᴮJer 10:13

And He will give them showers
 of rain, vegetation in the
 field to *each* person.
2 For the ¹'ᴬhousehold idols
 speak deception,
 And the ᴮdiviners see an
 illusion
 And tell deceitful dreams;
 They comfort in vain.
 Therefore *the people* wander
 like sheep,
 They are wretched because
 there is no shepherd.
3 "My ᴬanger is kindled against
 the shepherds,
 And I will punish the ¹male
 goats;
 For the Lᴏʀᴅ of armies has
 ᴮvisited His flock, the house
 of Judah,
 And will make them like His
 majestic horse in battle.
4 "From them will come the
 ᴬcornerstone,
 From them the tent peg,
 From them the bow of battle,
 From them every tyrant, *all of
 them* together.
5 "And they will be like warriors,
 ᴬTrampling down *the enemy*
 in the mud of the streets in
 battle;
 And they will fight, because
 the Lᴏʀᴅ *will be* with them;
 And the riders on horses will
 be put to shame.
6 "And I will strengthen the
 house of Judah,
 And I will save the house of
 Joseph,
 And I will ᴬbring them back,
 Because I have had
 ᴮcompassion on them;
 And they will be as though I
 had not rejected them,
 For I am the Lᴏʀᴅ their God
 and I will answer them.

7 "Ephraim will be like a warrior,
 And their heart will be joyful
 as if *from* wine;
 Indeed, their ᴬchildren will see
 it and be joyful,
 Their heart will rejoice in the
 Lᴏʀᴅ.
8 "I will whistle for them and
 gather them together,
 For I have redeemed them;
 And they will be as ᴬnumerous
 as they ᴮwere before.
9 "When I scatter them among
 the peoples,
 They will ᴬremember Me in
 distant countries,
 And they with their children
 will live and come back.
10 "I will bring them back from the
 land of Egypt
 And gather them from
 Assyria;
 And I will bring them into the
 land of ᴬGilead and Lebanon
 Until ᴮno *room* can be found
 for them.
11 "And they will pass through the
 ᴬsea of distress
 And He will strike the waves in
 the sea,
 So that all the depths of the
 ᴮNile will dry up;
 And the pride of Assyria will
 be brought down,
 And the scepter of Egypt will
 depart.
12 "And I will strengthen them in
 the Lᴏʀᴅ,
 And in His name ᴬthey will
 walk," declares the Lᴏʀᴅ.

10:2 ᴬEzek 21:21   ᴮJer 27:9   10:3 ᴬJer 25:34-36
ᴮEzek 34:12   10:4 ᴬLuke 20:17; Eph 2:20
10:5 ᴬ2 Sam 22:43   10:6 ᴬZech 8:8   ᴮIs 54:8
10:7 ᴬIs 54:13; Ezek 37:25   10:8 ᴬJer 33:22
ᴮEzek 36:11   10:9 ᴬ1 Kin 8:47, 48; Ezek 6:9
10:10 ᴬJer 50:19   ᴮIs 49:19, 20   10:11 ᴬIs 51:9, 10
ᴮIs 19:5-7   10:12 ᴬMic 4:5

10:2 ¹Heb *teraphim*   10:3 ¹I.e., leaders

THE DOOMED FLOCK

11 Open your doors, Lebanon,
So that a ^Afire may feed on
your ^Bcedars.
2 Wail, juniper, because the
cedar has fallen,
For the magnificent *trees* have
been destroyed;
Wail, oaks of Bashan,
Because the impenetrable
forest has come down.
3 There is a sound of the
shepherds' ^Await,
For their splendor is ruined;
There is a sound of the young
lions' roar,
For the pride of the Jordan is
ruined.

⁴This is what the LORD my God
says: "Pasture the flock *doomed* to
^Aslaughter. ⁵Those who buy them
slaughter them and go unpunished,
and *each of* those who sell them
says, 'Blessed be the LORD, for ^AI
have become rich!' And their ^Bown
shepherds have no compassion for
them. ⁶For I will ^Ano longer have
compassion for the inhabitants of
the land," declares the LORD; "but
behold, I will let the people fall,
each into another's power and into
the power of his king; and they will
crush the land, and I will ^Bnot rescue *them* from their power."

⁷So I pastured the flock *doomed*
to slaughter, therefore *also* the
afflicted of the flock. And I took
for myself two staffs: the one I
called ^AFavor, and the other I called
^BUnion; so I pastured the flock.
⁸Then I did away with the three
shepherds in ^Aone month, for my
soul was impatient with them,
and their soul also was tired of me.
⁹Then I said, "I will not pasture you.
What is to ^Adie, let it die, and what is
to perish, let it perish; and let those

who are left eat one another's flesh."
¹⁰And I took my staff Favor and cut
it in pieces, to ^Abreak my covenant
which I had made with all the peoples. ¹¹So it was broken on that day,
and ¹so the ^Aafflicted of the flock
who were watching me realized that
it was the word of the LORD. ¹²And I
said to them, "If it is good in your
sight, give *me* my wages; but if not,
never mind!" So they weighed out
^Athirty *shekels* of silver as my wages.
¹³Then the LORD said to me, "Throw
it to the ^Apotter, *that* magnificent
price at which I was valued by
them." So I took the thirty *shekels* of
silver and threw them to the potter
in the house of the LORD. ¹⁴Then I
cut in pieces my second staff Union,
to ^Abreak the brotherhood between
Judah and Israel.

¹⁵And the LORD said to me, "Take
again for yourself the equipment of
a ^Afoolish shepherd. ¹⁶For behold, I
am going to raise up a shepherd in
the land who will ^Anot care for the
perishing, seek the scattered, heal
the broken, *or* provide for the one
who is exhausted, but will devour
the flesh of the fat *sheep* and tear
off their hoofs.
¹⁷ "^AWoe to the worthless
shepherd
Who abandons the flock!
A sword will be on his arm
And on his right eye!
His arm will be totally
withered,
And his right eye will be blind."

11:1 ^A Jer 22:6, 7   ^B Ezek 31:3   11:3 ^A Jer 25:34-36
11:4 ^A Ps 44:22; Zech 11:7   11:5 ^A Hos 12:8
^B Ezek 34:2, 3   11:6 ^A Jer 13:14   ^B Ps 50:22
11:7 ^A Ps 27:4   ^B Ps 133:1   11:8 ^A Hos 5:7   11:9 ^A Jer 15:2
11:10 ^A Ps 89:39; Jer 14:21   11:11 ^A Zeph 3:12
11:12 ^A Gen 37:28; Ex 21:32   11:13 ^A Matt 27:3-10;
Acts 1:18, 19   11:14 ^A Is 9:21; Zech 11:6
11:15 ^A Is 6:10-12; Zech 11:17   11:16 ^A Jer 23:2
11:17 ^A Jer 23:1; Zech 10:2

11:11 ¹ Another reading is *the sheep dealers who*

JERUSALEM TO BE ATTACKED

12 The pronouncement of the word of the LORD concerning Israel:

The LORD who stretches out the heavens, lays the foundation of the earth, and ^forms the spirit of a person within him, declares: 2 "Behold, I am going to make Jerusalem a cup that causes staggering to all the peoples around; and when the siege is against Jerusalem, it will also be against ^Judah. 3 It will come about on that day that I will make Jerusalem a heavy ^stone for all the peoples; all who lift it will injure themselves severely. And all the nations of the earth will be gathered against it. 4 On that day," declares the LORD, "I will strike every horse with confusion and its rider with insanity. But I will watch over the house of Judah, while I strike every horse of the peoples with blindness. 5 Then the clans of Judah will say in their hearts, 'The inhabitants of Jerusalem are a strong support for us through the LORD of armies, their God.'

6 "On that day I will make the clans of Judah like a firepot among pieces of wood and a flaming torch among sheaves, so they will consume on the right and on the left all the surrounding peoples, while the ^inhabitants of Jerusalem again live on their own sites in Jerusalem. 7 The LORD also will ^save the tents of Judah first, so that the glory of the house of David and the glory of the inhabitants of Jerusalem will not be greater than Judah. 8 On that day the LORD will ^protect the inhabitants of Jerusalem, and the one who is feeble among them on that day will be like David, and the house of David will be like God, like the ^angel of the LORD before them. 9 And on that day I will ^seek to destroy all the nations that come against Jerusalem.

10 "And I will ^pour out on the house of David and on the inhabitants of Jerusalem the Spirit of grace and of pleading, so that they will look at Me whom they ^pierced; and they will mourn for Him, like one mourning for an only son, and they will weep bitterly over Him like the bitter weeping over a firstborn. 11 On that day the ^mourning in Jerusalem will be great, like the mourning of Hadadrimmon in the plain of Megiddo. 12 The land will mourn, every family by itself; the family of the house of David by itself and their wives by themselves; the family of the house of Nathan by itself and their wives by themselves; 13 the family of the house of Levi by itself and their wives by themselves; the family of the Shimeites by itself and their wives by themselves; 14 all the families that are left, every family by itself, and their wives by themselves.

FALSE PROPHETS ASHAMED

13 "On that day a ^fountain will be opened for the house of David and for the inhabitants of Jerusalem, for ^sin and for defilement.

2 "And it will come about on that day," declares the LORD of armies, "that I will eliminate the names of the idols from the land, and they will no longer be remembered; and I will also remove the ^prophets and the ^unclean spirit from the

12:1 ^Is 57:16; Heb 12:9   12:2 ^Zech 14:14
12:3 ^Dan 2:34, 35, 44, 45   12:6 ^Zech 2:4; 8:3-5
12:7 ^Jer 30:18   12:8 ^Joel 3:16   ^Ex 14:19
12:9 ^Zech 14:2, 3   12:10 ^Is 44:3   ^John 19:37
12:11 ^Matt 24:30; Rev 1:7   13:1 ^Jer 2:13   ^Ps 51:2, 7
13:2 ^Jer 23:14, 15   ^1 Kin 22:22

land. ³And if anyone still prophesies, then his father and mother who gave birth to him will say to him, 'You shall ᴬnot live, because you have spoken ᴮfalsely in the name of the LORD'; and his father and mother who gave birth to him shall pierce him through when he prophesies. ⁴Also it will come about on that day that the prophets will each be ᴬashamed of his vision when he prophesies, and they will not put on a hairy robe in order to deceive; ⁵but he will say, 'I am ᴬnot a prophet; I am a cultivator of the ground, because a man sold me *as a slave* in my youth.' ⁶And *someone* will say to him, 'What are these wounds ᴬbetween your arms?' Then he will say, '*Those* with which I was wounded at the house of my friends.'

7 "Awake, sword, against My
    ᴬShepherd,
    And against the Man, My
    Associate,"
  Declares the LORD of armies.
  "ᴮStrike the Shepherd and the
    sheep will be scattered;
    And I will turn My hand
    against the little ones.
8 "And it will come about in all
    the land,"
  Declares the LORD,
  "That ᴬtwo parts in it will be cut
    off *and* perish;
    But the third will be left in it.
9 "And I will bring the third part
    through the ᴬfire,
    Refine them as silver is
    refined,
    And test them as gold is tested.
    They will call on My name,
    And I will answer them;
    I will say, 'They are My people,'
    And they will say, 'The LORD is
    my God.'"

GOD WILL BATTLE JERUSALEM'S ENEMIES

14 Behold, a ᴬday is coming for the LORD when ᴮthe spoils *taken from* you will be divided among you. ²For I will ᴬgather all the nations against Jerusalem to battle, and the city will be taken, the houses plundered, the women raped, and half of the city exiled, but the rest of the people will not be eliminated from the city. ³Then the LORD will go forth and ᴬfight against those nations, as when He fights on a day of battle. ⁴On that day His feet will ᴬstand on the Mount of Olives, which is in front of Jerusalem on the east; and the Mount of Olives will be ᴮsplit in its middle from east to west *forming* a very large valley. Half of the mountain will move toward the north, and the other half toward the south. ⁵And you will flee by the valley of My mountains, for the valley of the mountains will reach to Azel; yes, you will flee just as you fled from the ᴬearthquake in the days of Uzziah king of Judah. Then the LORD, my God, will come, *and* all the holy ones with Him!

⁶On that day there will be ᴬno light; the luminaries will die out. ⁷For it will be a unique day which is ᴬknown to the LORD, neither day nor night, but it will come about that at the ᴮtime of evening there will be light.

⁸And on that day ᴬliving waters will flow out of Jerusalem, half of them toward the eastern sea and

13:3ᴬDeut 18:20 ᴮJer 23:25 13:4ᴬJer 6:15; 8:9 13:5ᴬAmos 7:14 13:6ᴬ2 Kin 9:24 13:7ᴬIs 40:11 ᴮIs 53:4, 5, 10 13:8ᴬIs 6:13; Ezek 5:2-4, 12 13:9ᴬIs 48:10; Mal 3:3 14:1ᴬIs 13:6, 9 ᴮZech 14:14 14:2ᴬZech 12:2, 3 14:3ᴬZech 9:14, 15 14:4ᴬEzek 11:23 ᴮIs 64:1; 2 14:5ᴬIs 29:6; Amos 1:1 14:6ᴬIs 13:10; Jer 4:23 14:7ᴬIs 45:21 ᴮIs 58:10 14:8ᴬEzek 47:1-12; Joel 3:18

the other half toward the western sea; it will be in summer as well as in winter.

GOD WILL BE KING OVER ALL

9 And the LORD will be ^King over all the earth; on that day the LORD will be *the only* one, and His name *the only* one.

10 All the land will change into a plain from ^Geba to ^BRimmon south of Jerusalem; but Jerusalem will rise and remain on its site from Benjamin's Gate as far as the place of the First Gate to the Corner Gate, and from the Tower of Hananel to the king's wine presses. 11 *People* will live in it, and there will no longer be a curse, for Jerusalem will ^live in security.

12 Now this will be the plague with which the LORD will strike all the peoples who have gone to war against Jerusalem; their flesh will ^rot while they stand on their feet, and their eyes will rot in their sockets, and their tongue will rot in their mouth. 13 And it will come about on that day that a great panic from the LORD will fall on them; and they will ^seize one another's hand, and the hand of one will be raised against the hand of another. 14 ^Judah also will fight at Jerusalem; and the wealth of all the surrounding nations will be gathered, gold, silver, and garments in great abundance. 15 And just like this ^plague, there will be a plague on the horse, the mule, the camel, the donkey,

and all the cattle that will be in those camps.

16 Then it will come about that any who are left of all the nations that came against Jerusalem will ^go up from year to year to worship the King, the LORD of armies, and to celebrate the ^BFeast of Booths. 17 And it will be that whichever of the families of the earth does not go up to Jerusalem to worship the King, the LORD of armies, there will be ^no rain on them. 18 And if the family of Egypt does not go up or enter, then no *rain will fall* on them; it will be the ^plague with which the LORD strikes the nations that do not go up to celebrate the Feast of Booths. 19 This will be the punishment of Egypt, and the punishment of all the nations that do not go up to celebrate the Feast of Booths.

20 On that day there will be *inscribed* on the bells of the horses, "^HOLY TO THE LORD." And the ^Bcooking pots in the LORD's house will be like the bowls before the altar. 21 Every cooking pot in Jerusalem and in Judah will be holy to the LORD of armies; and all who sacrifice will come and take of them and boil in them. And there will no longer be a ^Canaanite in the house of the LORD of armies on that day.

14:9 ^Is 2:2-4; 45:23   14:10 ^1 Kin 15:22   ^BJosh 15:32
14:11 ^Jer 23:5, 6; Ezek 34:25-28   14:12 ^Lev 26:16;
Deut 28:21, 22   14:13 ^Zech 11:6   14:14 ^Zech 12:2, 5
14:15 ^Zech 14:12   14:16 ^Is 60:6-9   ^BLev 23:34-44
14:17 ^Jer 14:3-6; Amos 4:7   14:18 ^Zech 14:12, 15
14:20 ^Ex 28:36-38   ^BEzek 46:20   14:21 ^Zeph 1:11

MALACHI

GOD'S LOVE FOR JACOB

1 The ^pronouncement of the word of the LORD to Israel through Malachi:

2 "I have ^loved you," says the LORD. But you say, "How have You loved us?" "*Was* Esau not Jacob's brother?" declares the LORD. "Yet I have loved Jacob; 3 but I have hated Esau, and I have ^made his mountains a desolation and *given* his inheritance to the jackals of the wilderness." 4 Though Edom says, "We have been ^beaten down, but we will ᴮreturn and build up the ruins"; this is what the LORD of armies says: "They may build, but I will tear down; and *people* will call them the territory of wickedness, and the people with whom the LORD is indignant forever." 5 And your eyes will see *this,* and you will say, "^The LORD be exalted beyond the border of Israel!"

SIN OF THE PRIESTS

6 "'A son ^honors *his* father, and a servant his master. Then if I am a ᴮfather, where is My honor? And if I am a master, where is My respect?' says the LORD of armies to you, the priests who despise My name! But you say, 'How have we despised Your name?' 7 *You are* presenting defiled ^food upon My altar. But you say, 'How have we defiled You?' In that you say, 'The table of the LORD is to be despised.' 8 And when you present a ^blind *animal* for sacrifice, is it not evil? Or when you present a lame or sick *animal,* is it not evil?

So offer it to your governor! Would he be pleased with you, or would he receive you kindly?" says the LORD of armies. 9 "But now, do indeed ^plead for God's favor, so that He will be gracious to us. With such an offering on your part, will He receive any of you kindly?" says the LORD of armies. 10 "If only there were one among you who would ^shut the gates, so that you would not kindle *fire on* My altar for nothing! I am not pleased with you," says the LORD of armies, "nor will I accept an offering from your hand. 11 For from the rising of the sun even to its setting, ^My name *shall be* ᴮgreat among the nations, and in every place frankincense is going to be offered to My name, and a grain offering *that is* pure; for My name *shall be* great among the nations," says the LORD of armies. 12 "But you are ^profaning it by your saying, 'The table of the Lord is defiled, and as for its fruit, its food is to be despised.' 13 You also say, 'See, how tiresome it is!' And you view it as trivial," says the LORD of armies, "and you bring what was taken by ^robbery and *what is* ᴮlame or sick; so you bring the offering! Should I accept it from your hand?" says the LORD. 14 "But cursed be the ^swindler who has a male in his flock and vows *it,* but sacrifices a

---

1:1 ^Is 13:1; Nah 1:1   1:2 ^Deut 4:37; 7:8
1:3 ^Jer 49:10, 16-18; Ezek 35:3, 4, 7, 8, 15   1:4 ^Jer 5:17
ᴮIs 9:9, 10   1:5 ^Ps 35:27; Mic 5:4   1:6 ^Ex 20:12
ᴮDeut 1:31   1:7 ^Lev 3:11; 21:6, 8
1:8 ^Lev 22:22; Deut 15:21   1:9 ^Jer 27:18; Joel 2:12-14
1:10 ^Is 1:13   1:11 ^Ps 111:9   ᴮIs 66:18, 19   1:12 ^Mal 1:7
1:13 ^Lev 6:4   ᴮMal 1:8   1:14 ^Acts 5:1-4

[B]blemished *animal* to the Lord, for I am a great King," says the LORD of armies, "and My name is feared among the nations."

PRIESTS TO BE DISCIPLINED

2 "And now, this commandment is for you, the priests. [2]If you do [A]not listen, and if you do not take it to heart to give honor to My name," says the LORD of armies, "then I will send the curse upon you and I will curse your blessings; and indeed, I have cursed them *already,* because you are not taking *it* to heart. [3]Behold, I am going to [A]rebuke your descendants, and I will spread dung on your faces, the dung of your feasts; and you will be taken away with it. [4]Then you will know that I have sent this commandment to you, so that My [A]covenant may continue with Levi," says the LORD of armies. [5]"My covenant with him was *one of* life and peace, and I gave them to him *as an object of* reverence; so he [A]revered Me and was in awe of My name. [6][A]True instruction was in his mouth and injustice was not found on his lips; he walked with Me in peace and justice, and he [B]turned many back from wrongdoing. [7]For the lips of a priest should maintain [A]knowledge, and *people* should [B]seek instruction from his mouth; for he is the messenger of the LORD of armies. [8]But as for you, you have turned aside from the way; you have caused many to [A]stumble by the instruction; you have ruined the covenant of Levi," says the LORD of armies. [9]"So [A]I also have made you despised and of [B]low reputation in the view of all the people, since you are not keeping My ways but are showing partiality in the instruction."

SIN IN THE FAMILY

[10]Do we not all have [A]one Father? [B]Is it not one God *who* has created us? Why do we deal treacherously, each against his brother so as to profane the covenant of our fathers? [11]Judah has dealt [A]treacherously, and an abomination has been committed in Israel and in Jerusalem; for Judah has [B]profaned the sanctuary of the LORD which He loves, and has married the daughter of a foreign god. [12]*As* for the man who does this, may the [A]LORD eliminate from the tents of Jacob *everyone* who is awake and answers, or who presents an offering to the LORD of armies.

[13]And this is another thing you do: you cover the altar of the LORD with tears, with weeping and sighing, because He [A]no longer gives attention to the offering or accepts *it with* favor from your hand. [14]Yet you say, "For what reason?" Because the LORD has been a witness between you and the [A]wife of your youth, against whom you have dealt [B]treacherously, though she is your marriage companion and your wife by covenant. [15]But not one has done *so* who has a remnant of the Spirit. And why the one? He was seeking a [A]godly offspring. Be careful then about your spirit, and *see that* none *of you* deals [B]treacherously against the wife of your youth. [16]"For I hate [A]divorce," says the LORD, the God of Israel, "and him who covers his garment with

1:14 [B]Lev 22:18-20 2:2 [A]Lev 26:14, 15; Deut 28:15
2:3 [A]Lev 26:16; Deut 28:38 2:4 [A]Num 3:11-13, 45;
18:21 2:5 [A]Num 25:7, 8, 13 2:6 [A]Ps 119:142, 151, 160
[B]Jer 23:22 2:7 [A]Lev 10:11 [B]Num 27:21 2:8 [A]Jer 18:15
2:9 [A]Nah 3:6 [B]Ezek 7:26 2:10 [A]Is 63:16
[B]Acts 17:24f 2:11 [A]Jer 3:7-9 [B]Ezra 9:1, 2
2:12 [A]Ezek 24:21; Hos 9:12 2:13 [A]Jer 11:14; 14:12
2:14 [A]Is 54:6 [B]Jer 9:2 2:15 [A]Ruth 4:12 [B]Ex 20:14
2:16 [A]Deut 24:1; Matt 5:31

violence," says the LORD of armies. "So be careful about your spirit, that you do not deal treacherously."

¹⁷You have wearied the LORD with your words. Yet you say, "How have we wearied *Him?*" In that you say, "ᴬEveryone who does evil is good in the sight of the LORD, and He ᴮdelights in them," or, "Where is the God of justice?"

THE PURIFIER

3 "ᴬBehold, I am sending My messenger, and he will ᴮclear a way before Me. And the Lord, whom you are seeking, will suddenly come to His temple; and the messenger of the covenant, in whom you delight, behold, He is coming," says the LORD of armies. ²"But who can ᴬendure the day of His coming? And who can stand when He appears? For He is like a refiner's fire, and like launderer's soap. ³And He will sit as a smelter and purifier of silver, and He will ᴬpurify the sons of Levi and refine them like gold and silver, so that they may present to the LORD offerings in righteousness. ⁴Then the offering of Judah and Jerusalem will be ᴬpleasing to the LORD as in the ᴮdays of old, and as in former years.

⁵"Then I will come near to you for judgment; and I will be a swift witness against the ᴬsorcerers, the ᴮadulterers, against those who swear falsely, those who oppress the wage earner in his wages *or* the widow or the orphan, and those who turn away the stranger *from justice* and do not fear Me," says the LORD of armies. ⁶"For I, the LORD, ᴬdo not change; therefore you, the sons of Jacob, have not come to an end.

⁷"From the days of your fathers you have turned away from My statutes and have not kept *them.* ᴬReturn to Me, and I will return to you," says the LORD of armies. "But you say, 'How shall we return?'

YOU HAVE ROBBED GOD

⁸"Would anyone rob God? Yet you are robbing Me! But you say, 'How have we robbed You?' *In* ᴬtithes and offerings. ⁹You are ᴬcursed with a curse, for you are robbing Me, the entire nation *of you!* ¹⁰ᴬBring the whole tithe into the storehouse, so that there may be food in My house, and put Me to the test now in this," says the LORD of armies, "if I do not open for you the windows of heaven and pour out for you a blessing until it overflows. ¹¹Then I will rebuke the ᴬdevourer for you, so that it will not destroy the fruit of your ground; nor will the vine in the field prove fruitless to you," says the LORD of armies. ¹²"ᴬAll the nations will call you blessed, for you will be a ᴮdelightful land," says the LORD of armies.

¹³"Your words have been arrogant against Me," says the LORD. "Yet you say, 'What have we spoken against You?' ¹⁴You have said, 'It is pointless to serve God; and what ᴬbenefit *is it for us* that we have done what He required, and that we have walked in mourning before the LORD of armies? ¹⁵So now we call the arrogant blessed; not only are the doers of wickedness built up, but they also put God to the test and ᴬescape *punishment.'"*

2:17ᴬIs 5:20　ᴮJob 9:24　3:1ᴬMatt 11:10, 14　ᴮIs 40:3
3:2ᴬIs 33:14; Ezek 22:14　3:3ᴬIs 1:25; Dan 12:10
3:4ᴬPs 51:17-19　ᴮ2 Chr 7:1-3, 12　3:5ᴬDeut 18:10
ᴮEzek 22:9-11　3:6ᴬNum 23:19; James 1:17
3:7ᴬZech 1:3　3:8ᴬNeh 13:11, 12　3:9ᴬMal 2:2
3:10ᴬLev 27:30; Num 18:21-24　3:11ᴬJoel 1:4; 2:25
3:12ᴬIs 61:9　ᴮIs 62:4　3:14ᴬIs 58:3　3:15ᴬJer 7:10

THE BOOK OF REMEMBRANCE

[16] Then those who feared the LORD spoke to one another, and the LORD [A]listened attentively and heard *it*, and a book of remembrance was written before Him for those who fear the LORD and esteem His name. [17] "And they will be [A]Mine," says the LORD of armies, "on the day that I prepare *My* own possession, and I will have compassion for them just as a man [B]has compassion for his own son who serves him." [18] So you will again [A]distinguish between the righteous and the wicked, between one who serves God and one who does not serve Him.

FINAL ADMONITION

4 "For behold, the day is coming, [A]burning like a furnace; and all the arrogant and every evildoer will be chaff; and the day that is coming will [B]set them ablaze," says the LORD of armies, "so that it will leave them neither root nor branches.

[2] But for you who fear My name, the [A]sun of righteousness will rise with [B]healing in its wings; and you will go forth and frolic like calves from the stall. [3] And you will [A]crush the wicked underfoot, for they will be ashes under the soles of your feet on the day that I am preparing," says the LORD of armies.

[4] "[A]Remember the Law of Moses My servant, *the* statutes and ordinances which I commanded him in Horeb for all Israel.

[5] "Behold, I am going to send you [A]Elijah the prophet before the coming of the great and terrible day of the LORD. [6] He will [A]turn the hearts of the fathers back to *their* children and the hearts of the children to their fathers, so that I will not come and [B]strike the land with complete destruction."

3:16 [A]Ps 34:15; Jer 31:18-20   **3:17** [A]Is 43:1   [B]Ps 103:13
3:18 [A]Gen 18:25; Amos 5:15   **4:1** [A]Ps 21:9   [B]Is 9:18, 19
4:2 [A]2 Sam 23:4   [B]Jer 30:17   **4:3** [A]Job 40:12; Is 26:6
4:4 [A]Deut 4:23; 8:11, 19   **4:5** [A]Matt 11:14; 17:10-13
4:6 [A]Luke 1:17   [B]Is 11:4

THE NEW TESTAMENT

MATTHEW

THE GENEALOGY OF JESUS
THE MESSIAH

1 The record of the genealogy of Jesus the Messiah, ^the son of David, the son of Abraham:

² Abraham fathered Isaac, Isaac fathered Jacob, and Jacob fathered ¹Judah and his brothers. ³ Judah fathered Perez and Zerah by Tamar, ^Perez fathered Hezron, and Hezron fathered Ram. ⁴ Ram fathered Amminadab, Amminadab fathered Nahshon, and Nahshon fathered Salmon. ⁵ Salmon fathered Boaz by Rahab, Boaz fathered Obed by Ruth, and Obed fathered Jesse. ⁶ Jesse fathered David the king.

David ^fathered Solomon by ¹her *who had been the wife* of Uriah. ⁷ Solomon ^fathered Rehoboam, Rehoboam fathered Abijah, and Abijah fathered Asa. ⁸ Asa fathered Jehoshaphat, Jehoshaphat fathered Joram, and Joram fathered Uzziah. ⁹ Uzziah fathered Jotham, Jotham fathered Ahaz, and Ahaz fathered Hezekiah. ¹⁰ Hezekiah fathered Manasseh, Manasseh fathered Amon, and Amon ^fathered Josiah. ¹¹ Josiah fathered Jeconiah and his brothers, at the time of the ^deportation to Babylon.

¹² After the ^deportation to Babylon: Jeconiah fathered Shealtiel, and Shealtiel fathered Zerubbabel. ¹³ Zerubbabel fathered Abihud, Abihud fathered Eliakim, and Eliakim fathered Azor. ¹⁴ Azor fathered Zadok, Zadok fathered Achim, and Achim fathered Eliud. ¹⁵ Eliud fathered Eleazar, Eleazar fathered Matthan, and Matthan fathered Jacob. ¹⁶ Jacob fathered Joseph the husband of Mary, by whom Jesus was born, ^who is called the Messiah.

¹⁷ So all the generations from Abraham to David are fourteen generations; from David to the ^deportation to Babylon, fourteen generations; and from the ^deportation to Babylon to the Messiah, fourteen generations.

CONCEPTION AND BIRTH OF JESUS

¹⁸ Now the birth of Jesus the Messiah was as follows: when His ^mother Mary had been ¹betrothed to Joseph, before they came together she was found to be pregnant by the Holy Spirit. ¹⁹ And her husband Joseph, since he was a righteous man and did not want to disgrace her, planned to ¹,^send her away secretly. ²⁰ But when he had thought this over, behold, an angel of the Lord appeared to him in a dream, saying, "^Joseph, son of David, do not be afraid to take Mary as your wife; for the Child who has been conceived in her is of the Holy Spirit. ²¹ She will give birth to a Son;

1:1 ^Is 9:6f; 11:1   1:3 ^Ruth 4:18-22; 1 Chr 2:1-15
1:6 ^2 Sam 11:27; 12:24   1:7 ^1 Chr 3:10ff
1:10 ^1 Chr 3:14   1:11 ^2 Kin 24:14f; Jer 27:20
1:12 ^2 Kin 24:14f; Jer 27:20   1:16 ^Matt 27:17, 22;
Luke 2:11   1:17 ^2 Kin 24:14f; Jer 27:20
1:18 ^Matt 12:46; Luke 1:27   1:19 ^Deut 22:20-24;
24:1-4   1:20 ^Luke 2:4

1:2 ¹Gr *Judas;* a name of a person in the Old Testament is given in its Old Testament form   1:6 ¹I.e., Bathsheba   1:18 ¹Unlike engagement, a betrothed couple was considered married, but did not yet live together   1:19 ¹Or *divorce her*

and you shall name Him Jesus, for He ^will save His people from their sins." ²²Now all this took place so that what was ^spoken by the Lord through ¹the prophet would be fulfilled: ²³"^BEHOLD, THE VIRGIN WILL ᴮCONCEIVE AND GIVE BIRTH TO A SON, AND THEY SHALL NAME HIM IMMANUEL," which translated means, "GOD WITH US." ²⁴And Joseph awoke from his sleep and did as the angel of the Lord commanded him, and took *Mary* as his wife, ²⁵but kept her a virgin until she gave birth to a Son; and ^he named Him Jesus.

THE VISIT OF THE MAGI

2 Now after Jesus was ^born in Bethlehem of Judea in the days of Herod the king, behold, ¹magi from the east arrived in Jerusalem, saying, ²"Where is He who has been born ^King of the Jews? For we saw His star in the east and have come to worship Him." ³When Herod the king heard *this,* he was troubled, and all Jerusalem with him. ⁴And gathering together all the chief priests and scribes of the people, he inquired of them where the Messiah was to be born. ⁵They said to him, "^In Bethlehem of Judea; for this is what has been written by ¹the prophet:

6 '^AND YOU, BETHLEHEM, LAND
     OF JUDAH,
   ARE BY NO MEANS LEAST AMONG
     THE LEADERS OF JUDAH;
   FOR FROM YOU WILL COME
     FORTH A RULER
   WHO WILL SHEPHERD MY
     PEOPLE ISRAEL.' "

⁷Then Herod secretly called for the magi and determined from them the exact time ^the star appeared. ⁸And he sent them to Bethlehem and said, "Go and search carefully for the Child; and when you have found *Him,* report to me, so that I too may come and worship Him." ⁹After hearing the king, they went on their way; and behold, the star, which they had seen in the east, went on ahead of them until it came to a stop over *the place* where the Child was *to be found.* ¹⁰When they saw the star, they rejoiced exceedingly with great joy. ¹¹And after they came into the house, they saw the Child with His mother Mary; and they fell down and ^worshiped Him. Then they opened their treasures and presented to Him gifts of gold, frankincense, and myrrh. ¹²And after being warned *by God* ^in a dream not to return to Herod, *the magi* left for their own country by another way.

THE ESCAPE TO EGYPT

¹³Now when they had gone, behold, an angel of the Lord *^appeared to Joseph in a dream and said, "Get up! Take the Child and His mother and flee to Egypt, and stay there until I tell you; for Herod is going to search for the Child to kill Him." ¹⁴So Joseph got up and took the Child and His mother while it was still night, and left for Egypt. ¹⁵He stayed there until the death of Herod; *this happened* so that what had been spoken by the Lord through ¹the prophet would be fulfilled: "^OUT OF EGYPT I CALLED MY SON."

1:21^Luke 2:11; John 1:29   1:22^Luke 24:44; Rom 1:2–4
1:23^Is 7:14   ᴮIs 9:6, 7   1:25^Matt 1:21; Luke 2:21
2:1^Mic 5:2; Luke 2:4–7   2:2^Jer 23:5; 30:9
2:5^John 7:42   2:6^Mic 5:2; John 7:42   2:7^Num 24:17
2:11^Matt 14:33   2:12^Job 33:15, 16; Matt 1:20
2:13^Matt 2:12, 19   2:15^Hos 11:1; Num 24:8

1:22 ¹I.e., Isaiah   2:1 ¹A caste of educated men specializing in astronomy, astrology, and natural science   2:5 ¹I.e., Micah   2:15 ¹I.e., Hosea

HEROD SLAUGHTERS BABIES

[16]Then when Herod saw that he had been tricked by ^the magi, he became very enraged, and sent *men* and killed all the boys who were in Bethlehem and all its vicinity who were two years old or under, according to the time which he had determined from the magi. [17]Then what had been spoken through Jeremiah the prophet was fulfilled:

[18] "A VOICE WAS HEARD IN RAMAH,
  WEEPING AND GREAT
    MOURNING,
  RACHEL WEEPING FOR HER
    CHILDREN;
  AND SHE REFUSED TO BE
    COMFORTED,
  BECAUSE THEY WERE NO MORE."

[19]But when Herod died, behold, an angel of the Lord *^appeared in a dream to Joseph in Egypt, and said, [20]"Get up, take the Child and His mother, and go to the land of Israel; for those who sought the Child's life are dead." [21]So Joseph got up, took the Child and His mother, and came into the land of Israel. [22]But when he heard that Archelaus was reigning over Judea in place of his father Herod, he was afraid to go there. Then after being ^warned *by God* in a dream, he left for the regions of Galilee, [23]and came and settled in a city called ^Nazareth. *This happened* so that what was spoken through the prophets would be fulfilled: "He will be called a Nazarene."

THE PREACHING OF JOHN THE BAPTIST

3 Now ^in those days John the Baptist *came, preaching in the wilderness of Judea, saying, [2]"^Repent, for the kingdom of heaven has come near." [3]For this is the ^one

referred to by Isaiah the prophet when he said,

"[B]THE VOICE OF ONE CALLING
  [1]OUT IN THE WILDERNESS,
  'PREPARE THE WAY OF THE LORD,
  MAKE HIS PATHS STRAIGHT!'"

[4]Now John himself had ^a garment of camel's hair and a leather belt around his waist; and his food was locusts and wild honey. [5]At that time Jerusalem ^was going out to him, and all Judea and all the region around the Jordan; [6]and they were being ^baptized by him in the Jordan River, as they confessed their sins.

[7]But when he saw many of the ^Pharisees and [B]Sadducees coming for baptism, he said to them, "You offspring of vipers, who warned you to flee from the wrath to come? [8]^Therefore produce fruit consistent with repentance; [9]and do not assume that you can say to yourselves, '^We have Abraham *as our* father'; for I tell you that God is able, from these stones, to raise up children for Abraham. [10]And the ^axe is already laid at the root of the trees; therefore, every tree that does not bear good fruit is being cut down and thrown into the fire.

[11]"As for me, ^I baptize you [1]with water for repentance, but He who is coming after me is mightier than I, and I am not fit to remove His sandals; He will baptize you with the Holy Spirit and fire. [12]His ^winnowing fork is in His hand, and He

---

2:16 ^Matt 2:1   2:18 ^Jer 31:15   2:19 ^Matt 1:20;
2:12, 13, 22   2:22 ^Matt 2:12, 13, 19   2:23 ^Luke 1:26;
2:39   3:1 ^John 1:6-8, 19-28   3:2 ^Matt 4:17
3:3 ^Luke 1:17, 76   [B]Is 40:3   3:4 ^2 Kin 1:8; Zech 13:4
3:5 ^Mark 1:5   3:6 ^Matt 3:11, 13-16; Mark 1:5
3:7 ^Matt 16:1ff   [B]Matt 22:23   3:8 ^Luke 3:8; Eph 5:8, 9
3:9 ^Luke 3:8; 16:24   3:10 ^Luke 3:9   3:11 ^Mark 1:4, 8;
Luke 3:16   3:12 ^Is 30:24; 41:16

3:3 [1]Or *out, Prepare in the wilderness the way*
3:11 [1]The Gr here can be translated *in, with,* or *by*

will thoroughly clear His threshing floor; and He will gather His wheat into the barn, but He will burn up the chaff with unquenchable fire."

THE BAPTISM OF JESUS

13 ᴬThen Jesus *arrived from Galilee at the Jordan, *coming* to John to be baptized by him. 14 But John tried to prevent Him, saying, "I have *the* need to be baptized by You, and *yet* You are coming to me?" 15 But Jesus, answering, said to him, "Allow *it* at this time; for in this way it is fitting for us ᴬto fulfill all righteousness." Then he *allowed Him. 16 After He was baptized, Jesus came up immediately from the water; and behold, the heavens were opened, and ᴬhe saw the Spirit of God descending as a dove *and* settling on Him, 17 and behold, a voice from the heavens said, "ᴬThis is My beloved Son, with whom I am well pleased."

THE TEMPTATION OF JESUS

4 ᴬThen Jesus was led up by the Spirit into the wilderness to be tempted by the devil. 2 And after He had ᴬfasted for forty days and forty nights, He then became hungry. 3 And ᴬthe tempter came and said to Him, "If You are the ᴮSon of God, command that these stones become bread." 4 But He answered and said, "It is written: 'ᴬMAN SHALL NOT LIVE ON BREAD ALONE, BUT ON EVERY WORD THAT COMES OUT OF THE MOUTH OF GOD.'"

5 Then the devil *took Him along into ᴬthe holy city and had Him stand on the pinnacle of the temple, 6 and he *said to Him, "If You are the Son of God, throw Yourself down; for it is written:

'ᴬHE WILL GIVE HIS ANGELS
    ORDERS CONCERNING YOU';
and
'ON *THEIR* HANDS THEY WILL LIFT
    YOU UP,
SO THAT YOU DO NOT STRIKE
    YOUR FOOT AGAINST A STONE.'"
7 Jesus said to him, "On the other hand, it is written: 'ᴬYOU SHALL NOT PUT THE LORD YOUR GOD TO THE TEST.'"

8 ᴬAgain, the devil *took Him along to a very high mountain and *showed Him all the kingdoms of the world and their glory; 9 and he said to Him, "ᴬAll these things I will give You, if You fall down and worship me." 10 Then Jesus *said to him, "Go away, Satan! For it is written: 'ᴬYOU SHALL WORSHIP THE LORD YOUR GOD, AND SERVE HIM ONLY.'" 11 Then the devil *left Him; and behold, ᴬangels came and *began to* serve Him.

JESUS BEGINS HIS MINISTRY

12 Now when Jesus heard that ᴬJohn had been taken into custody, He withdrew into Galilee; 13 and leaving Nazareth, He came and ᴬsettled in Capernaum, which is by the sea, in the region of Zebulun and Naphtali. 14 *This happened* so that what was spoken through Isaiah the prophet would be fulfilled:

15 "ᴬTHE LAND OF ZEBULUN AND
    THE LAND OF NAPHTALI,
    BY THE WAY OF THE SEA, ON THE
    OTHER SIDE OF THE JORDAN,
    GALILEE OF THE ¹GENTILES—

3:13 ᴬJohn 1:31-34   3:15 ᴬPs 40:7, 8; John 4:34
3:16 ᴬMark 1:10; Luke 3:22   3:17 ᴬPs 2:7; Is 42:1
4:1 ᴬMark 1:12, 13; Luke 4:1-13   4:2 ᴬEx 34:28;
1 Kin 19:8   4:3 ᴬ1 Thess 5:5   ᴮMatt 14:33
4:4 ᴬDeut 8:3   4:5 ᴬNeh 11:1, 18; Dan 9:24
4:6 ᴬPs 91:11, 12   4:7 ᴬDeut 6:16   4:8 ᴬMatt 16:26;
1 John 2:15-17   4:9 ᴬ1 Cor 10:20f   4:10 ᴬDeut 6:13;
10:20   4:11 ᴬMatt 26:53; Luke 22:43   4:12 ᴬMatt 14:3;
Mark 1:14   4:13 ᴬMatt 11:23; Mark 1:21   4:15 ᴬIs 9:1

4:15 ¹Lit *nations,* usually non-Jewish

16 ^ATHE PEOPLE WHO WERE SITTING
IN DARKNESS SAW A GREAT
LIGHT,
AND THOSE WHO WERE SITTING
IN THE LAND AND SHADOW OF
DEATH,
UPON THEM A LIGHT DAWNED."

17^AFrom that time Jesus began to preach and say, "Repent, for the kingdom of heaven has come near."

THE FIRST DISCIPLES

18^ANow as Jesus was walking by the Sea of Galilee, He saw two brothers, Simon, who was called Peter, and his brother Andrew, casting a net into the sea; for they were fishermen. **19**And He *said to them, "Follow Me, and I will make you fishers of people." **20**Immediately they left their nets and followed Him. **21**Going on from there He saw two other brothers, ^AJames the *son* of Zebedee, and his brother John, in the boat with their father Zebedee, mending their nets; and He called them. **22**Immediately they left the boat and their father, and followed Him.

MINISTRY IN GALILEE

23Jesus was going about in all of Galilee, ^Ateaching in their synagogues and proclaiming the gospel of the kingdom, and healing every disease and every sickness among the people. **24**And the news about Him spread ^Athroughout Syria; and they brought to Him all who were ill, those suffering with various diseases and severe pain, demon-possessed, people with epilepsy, and people who were paralyzed; and He healed them. **25**Large crowds ^Afollowed Him from Galilee and *the* Decapolis, and Jerusalem, and Judea, and *from* beyond the Jordan.

THE SERMON ON THE MOUNT; THE BEATITUDES

5 ^ANow when Jesus saw the crowds, He went up on the mountain; and after He sat down, His disciples came to Him. **2**And ^AHe opened His mouth and *began* to teach them, saying,

3"^ABlessed are the poor in spirit, for theirs is the kingdom of heaven.

4"Blessed are ^Athose who mourn, for they will be comforted.

5"Blessed are ^Athe ¹gentle, for they will inherit the earth.

6"Blessed are ^Athose who hunger and thirst for righteousness, for they will be satisfied.

7"Blessed are ^Athe merciful, for they will receive mercy.

8"Blessed are ^Athe pure in heart, for they will see God.

9"Blessed are the peacemakers, for ^Athey will be called sons of God.

10"Blessed are those who have been ^Apersecuted for the sake of righteousness, for theirs is the kingdom of heaven.

11"Blessed are you when *people* ^Ainsult you and persecute you, and falsely say all kinds of evil against you because of Me. **12**Rejoice and be glad, for your reward in heaven is great; for ^Ain this same way they persecuted the prophets who were before you.

DISCIPLES AND THE WORLD

13"You are the salt of the earth; but ^Aif the salt has become tasteless,

4:16^AIs 9:2; 60:1-3 **4:17**^AMark 1:14, 15
4:18^ALuke 5:2-11; John 1:40-42 **4:21**^AMatt 10:2; 20:20
4:23^AMatt 9:35; 13:54 **4:24**^AMark 7:26; Luke 2:2
4:25^AMark 3:7, 8; Luke 6:17 **5:1**^AMatt ch 5-7;
Luke 6:20-49 **5:2**^AMatt 13:35; Acts 8:35
5:3^ALuke 6:20-23 **5:4**^AIs 61:2; John 16:20
5:5^APs 37:11 **5:6**^AIs 55:1, 2; John 4:14 **5:7**^AProv 11:17;
Matt 6:14, 15 **5:8**^APs 24:4 **5:9**^AMatt 5:45; Luke 6:35
5:10^A1 Pet 3:14 **5:11**^A1 Pet 4:14 **5:12**^A2 Chr 36:16;
Matt 23:37 **5:13**^AMark 9:50; Luke 14:34f

5:5 ¹Or *humble, meek*

how can it be made salty *again?* It is no longer good for anything, except to be thrown out and trampled underfoot by people.

14 "You are ^the light of the world. A city set on a hill cannot be hidden; **15** ^nor do *people* light a lamp and put it under a basket, but on the lampstand, and it gives light to all who are in the house. **16** Your light must shine before people in such a way that they may ^see your good works, and glorify your Father who is in heaven.

17 "Do not presume that I came to abolish the ^Law or the Prophets; I did not come to abolish, but to fulfill. **18** For truly I say to you, ^until heaven and earth pass away, not the smallest letter or stroke of a letter shall pass from the Law, until all is accomplished! **19** Therefore, whoever nullifies one of the least of these commandments, and teaches others *to do* the same, shall be called least ^in the kingdom of heaven; but whoever keeps and teaches *them,* he shall be called great in the kingdom of heaven.

20 "For I say to you that unless your ^righteousness far surpasses *that* of the scribes and Pharisees, you will not enter the kingdom of heaven.

PERSONAL RELATIONSHIPS

21 "You have heard that the ancients were told, '^YOU SHALL NOT MURDER,' and 'Whoever commits murder shall be answerable to the court.' **22** But I say to you that everyone who is angry with his brother shall be answerable to ^the court; and whoever says to his brother, '¹You good-for-nothing,' shall be answerable to ²the supreme court; and whoever says, 'You fool,' shall be guilty *enough to go* into the ³fiery hell. **23** Therefore, if you are ^presenting your offering at the altar, and there you remember that your brother has something against you, **24** leave your offering there before the altar and go; first be ^reconciled to your brother, and then come and present your offering. **25** ^Come to good terms with your accuser quickly, while you are with him on the way *to court,* so that your accuser will not hand you over to the judge, and the judge to the officer, and you will not be thrown into prison. **26** Truly I say to you, ^you will not come out of there until you have paid up the last ¹quadrans.

27 "You have heard that it was said, '^YOU SHALL NOT COMMIT ADULTERY'; **28** but I say to you that everyone who looks at a woman ^with lust for her has already committed adultery with her in his heart. **29** Now ^if your right eye is causing you to sin, tear it out and throw it away from you; for it is better for you to lose one of the parts of your *body,* than for your whole body to be thrown into hell. **30** And ^if your right hand is causing you to sin, cut it off and throw it away from you; for it is better for you to lose one of the parts of your *body,* than for your whole body to go into hell.

31 "Now it was said, '^WHOEVER SENDS HIS WIFE AWAY IS TO GIVE HER A CERTIFICATE OF DIVORCE'; **32** ^but I say to you that everyone who divorces

5:14 ^Prov 4:18; John 8:12   **5:15** ^Mark 4:21; Luke 8:16   **5:16** ^1 Pet 2:12   **5:17** ^Matt 7:12   **5:18** ^Matt 24:35; Luke 16:17   **5:19** ^Matt 11:11   **5:20** ^Luke 18:11, 12   **5:21** ^Ex 20:13; Deut 5:17   **5:22** ^Deut 16:18; 2 Chr 19:5f   **5:23** ^Matt 5:24   **5:24** ^Rom 12:17, 18   **5:25** ^Prov 25:8f; Luke 12:58   **5:26** ^Luke 12:59   **5:27** ^Ex 20:14; Deut 5:18   **5:28** ^2 Sam 11:2-5; Job 31:1   **5:29** ^Matt 18:9; Mark 9:47   **5:30** ^Matt 18:8; Mark 9:43   **5:31** ^Deut 24:1, 3; Jer 3:1   **5:32** ^Matt 19:9; Mark 10:11f

5:22 ¹Or *You empty-head;* Gr *Raka (Raca)* from Aramaic *reqa*   ²Lit *the Sanhedrin,* i.e., Jewish High Court   ³Lit *Gehenna of fire*   **5:26** ¹A small Roman copper coin, worth about 1/64 of a laborer's daily wage

his wife, except for *the* reason of sexual immorality, makes her commit adultery; and whoever marries a divorced woman commits adultery.

³³"Again, you have heard that the ancients were told, 'ᴬYOU SHALL NOT MAKE FALSE VOWS, BUT SHALL FULFILL YOUR VOWS TO THE LORD.' ³⁴But I say to you, ᴬtake no oath at all, neither by heaven, for it is ᴮthe throne of God, ³⁵nor by the earth, for it is the ᴬfootstool of His feet, nor by Jerusalem, for it is ᴮTHE CITY OF THE GREAT KING. ³⁶Nor shall you take an oath by your head, for you cannot make a single hair white or black. ³⁷But make sure your statement is, 'Yes, yes' *or* 'No, no'; anything beyond these is of ᴬevil *origin*.

³⁸"You have heard that it was said, 'ᴬEYE FOR EYE, and TOOTH FOR TOOTH.' ³⁹But I say to you, do not show opposition against an evil person; but ᴬwhoever slaps you on your right cheek, turn the other toward him also. ⁴⁰And if anyone wants to sue you and take your ¹tunic, let him have your ²cloak also. ⁴¹Whoever forces you to go one mile, go with him two. ⁴²ᴬGive to him who asks of you, and do not turn away from him who wants to borrow from you.

⁴³"You have heard that it was said, 'ᴬYOU SHALL LOVE YOUR NEIGHBOR ᴮand hate your enemy.' ⁴⁴But I say to you, ᴬlove your enemies and pray for those who persecute you, ⁴⁵so that you may prove yourselves to be ᴬsons of your Father who is in heaven; for He causes His sun to rise on *the* evil and *the* good, and sends rain on *the* righteous and *the* unrighteous. ⁴⁶For ᴬif you love those who love you, what reward do you have? Even the tax collectors, do they not do the same? ⁴⁷And if you greet only your

brothers *and sisters,* what more are you doing *than others?* Even the Gentiles, do they not do the same? ⁴⁸Therefore ᴬyou shall be perfect, as your heavenly Father is perfect.

CHARITABLE GIVING TO THE POOR AND PRAYER

6 "Take care not to practice your righteousness in the sight of people, ᴬto be noticed by them; otherwise you have no reward with your Father who is in heaven.

²"So when you give to the poor, do not sound a trumpet before you, as the hypocrites do in the synagogues and on the streets, so that they ᴬwill be praised by people. Truly I say to you, they have their reward in full. ³But when you give to the poor, do not let your left hand know what your right hand is doing, ⁴so that your charitable giving will be in secret; and ᴬyour Father who sees *what is done* in secret will reward you.

⁵"And when you pray, you are not to be like the hypocrites; for they love to ᴬstand and pray in the synagogues and on the street corners so that they will be seen by people. Truly I say to you, they have their reward in full. ⁶But as for you, when you pray, ᴬgo into your inner room, close your door, and pray to your Father who is in secret; and your Father who sees *what is done* in secret will reward you.

5:33ᴬLev 19:12; Num 30:2   5:34ᴬJames 5:12   ᴮIs 66:1
5:35ᴬIs 66:1   ᴮPs 48:2   5:37ᴬ1 John 3:12f
5:38ᴬEx 21:24; Lev 24:20   5:39ᴬ1 Cor 6:7
5:42ᴬDeut 15:7-11; Luke 6:34f   5:43ᴬLev 19:18
ᴮDeut 23:3-6   5:44ᴬLuke 6:27f; 23:34   5:45ᴬMatt 5:9;
Luke 6:35   5:46ᴬLuke 6:32   5:48ᴬLev 19:2; Deut 18:13
6:1ᴬMatt 6:5, 16; 23:5   6:2ᴬMatt 6:5, 16; 23:5
6:4ᴬJer 17:10; Matt 6:6, 18   6:5ᴬMark 11:25;
Luke 18:11, 13   6:6ᴬIs 26:20; Matt 26:36-39

5:40¹A long shirt worn next to the skin   ²Or *outer garment*

⁷"And when you are praying, do not use thoughtless repetition as the Gentiles do, for they think that they will be heard because of their ᴬmany words. ⁸So do not be like them; for ᴬyour Father knows what you need before you ask Him.

THE LORD'S PRAYER

⁹"ᴬPray, then, in this way:
'Our Father, who is in heaven,
    Hallowed be Your name.
¹⁰ 'Your kingdom come.
    ᴬYour will be done,
    On earth as it is in heaven.
¹¹ 'ᴬGive us this day our daily
    bread.
¹² 'And ᴬforgive us our debts, as
    we also have forgiven our
    debtors.
¹³ 'And do not lead us into
    temptation, but ᴬdeliver us
    from evil.'

¹⁴ᴬFor if you forgive *other* people for their offenses, your heavenly Father will also forgive you. ¹⁵But ᴬif you do not forgive *other* people, then your Father will not forgive your offenses.

FASTING; THE TRUE
TREASURE; WEALTH

¹⁶"Now ᴬwhenever you fast, do not make a gloomy face as the hypocrites *do,* for they distort their faces so that they will be noticed by people when they are fasting. Truly I say to you, they have their reward in full. ¹⁷But as for you, when you fast, ᴬanoint your head and wash your face, ¹⁸so that your fasting will not be noticed by people but by your Father who is in secret; and your ᴬFather who sees *what is done* in secret will reward you.

¹⁹"ᴬDo not store up for yourselves treasures on earth, where moth and rust destroy, and where thieves break

in and steal. ²⁰But store up for yourselves ᴬtreasures in heaven, where neither moth nor rust destroys, and where thieves do not break in or steal; ²¹for ᴬwhere your treasure is, there your heart will be also.

²²"ᴬThe eye is the lamp of the body; so then, if your eye is clear, your whole body will be full of light. ²³But if ᴬyour eye is bad, your whole body will be full of darkness. So if the light that is in you is darkness, how great is the darkness!

²⁴"ᴬNo one can serve two masters; for either he will hate the one and love the other, or he will be devoted to one and despise the other. You cannot serve God and ¹wealth.

THE CURE FOR ANXIETY

²⁵"ᴬFor this reason I say to you, do not be worried about your life, *as to* what you will eat or what you will drink; nor for your body, *as to* what you will put on. Is life not more than food, and the body more than clothing? ²⁶ᴬLook at the birds of the sky, that they do not sow, nor reap, nor gather *crops* into barns, and *yet* your heavenly Father feeds them. Are you not much more important than they? ²⁷And which of you by ᴬworrying can add a single day to his life's span? ²⁸And why are you ᴬworried about clothing? Notice

---

6:7ᴬ1 Kin 18:26f   **6:8**ᴬPs 38:9; 69:17-19   **6:9**ᴬ*Luke 11:2-4*
6:10ᴬMatt 26:42; Luke 22:42   **6:11**ᴬProv 30:8; Is 33:16
6:12ᴬEx 34:7; Ps 32:1   **6:13**ᴬJohn 17:15; 1 Cor 10:13
6:14ᴬMatt 7:2; Mark 11:25f   **6:15**ᴬMatt 18:35
6:16ᴬIs 58:5   **6:17**ᴬRuth 3:3; 2 Sam 12:20
6:18ᴬMatt 6:4, 6   **6:19**ᴬProv 23:4; Matt 19:21
6:20ᴬMatt 19:21; Luke 12:33   **6:21**ᴬLuke 12:34
6:22ᴬ*Luke 11:34, 35*   **6:23**ᴬMatt 20:15; Mark 7:22
6:24ᴬ1 Kin 18:21; Luke 16:13   **6:25**ᴬ*Luke 12:22-31*
6:26ᴬJob 35:11; 38:41   **6:27**ᴬMatt 6:25, 28, 31, 34;
Luke 10:41   **6:28**ᴬMatt 6:25, 27, 31, 34; Luke 10:41

6:13¹Late mss add *For Yours is the kingdom and the power and the glory forever. Amen*   **6:24**¹Gr *mamonas,* for Aramaic *mamon* (mammon); i.e., wealth etc. personified as an object of worship

how the lilies of the field grow; they do not labor nor do they spin *thread for cloth,* 29yet I say to you that not even ^Solomon in all his glory clothed himself like one of these. 30But if God so clothes the ^grass of the field, which is *alive* today and tomorrow is thrown into the furnace, *will He* not much more *clothe* you? ᴮYou of little faith! 31Do not ^worry then, saying, 'What are we to eat?' or 'What are we to drink?' or 'What are we to wear for clothing?' 32For the Gentiles eagerly seek all these things; for ^your heavenly Father knows that you need all these things. 33But seek first His kingdom and His righteousness, and ^all these things will be provided to you.

34"So do not ^worry about tomorrow; for tomorrow will worry about itself. Each day has enough trouble of its own.

JUDGING OTHERS

7 "^Do not judge, so that you will not be judged. 2For in the way you judge, you will be judged; and ^by your standard of measure, it will be measured to you. 3Why do you ^look at the speck that is in your brother's eye, but do not notice the log that is in your own eye? 4^Or how can you say to your brother, 'Let me take the speck out of your eye,' and look, the log is in your own eye? 5You hypocrite, first take the log out of your own eye, and then you will see clearly to take the speck out of your brother's eye!

6"^Do not give what is holy to dogs, and do not throw your pearls before pigs, or they will trample them under their feet, and turn and tear you to pieces.

PRAYER AND THE GOLDEN RULE

7"^Ask, and it will be given to you; seek, and you will find; knock, and it will be opened to you. 8For everyone who asks receives, and the one who seeks finds, and to the one who knocks it will be opened. 9Or what person is there among you who, when his son asks for a loaf of bread, will give him a stone? 10Or if he asks for a fish, he will not give him a snake, will he? 11So if you, *despite* being evil, know how to give good gifts to your children, ^how much more will your Father who is in heaven give good things to those who ask Him!

12"In everything, ^therefore, treat people the same way you want them to treat you, for ᴮthis is the Law and the Prophets.

THE NARROW AND WIDE GATES

13"^Enter through the narrow gate; for the gate is wide and the way is broad that leads to destruction, and there are many who enter through it. 14For the gate is narrow and the way is constricted that leads to life, and there are few who find it.

A TREE AND ITS FRUIT

15"Beware of the ^false prophets, who come to you in sheep's clothing, but inwardly are ravenous wolves. 16You will ^know them by their fruits. Grapes are not gathered

6:29^1 Kin 10:4-7; 2 Chr 9:4-6, 20-22
6:30^James 1:10, 11   ᴮMatt 8:26; 14:31
6:31^Matt 6:25, 27, 28, 34; Luke 10:41   **6:32**^Matt 6:8; Phil 4:19   **6:33**^Matt 19:28; Mark 10:29f
6:34^Matt 6:25, 27, 28, 31; Luke 10:41
7:1^Rom 14:10, 13   **7:2**^Mark 4:24; Luke 6:38
7:3^Rom 2:1   **7:4**^Luke 6:42   **7:6**^Matt 15:26
7:7^Luke 11:9-13   **7:11**^Ps 84:11; Is 63:7
7:12^Luke 6:31   ᴮMatt 22:40   **7:13**^Luke 13:24
7:15^Matt 24:11, 24; Mark 13:22   **7:16**^Matt 7:20; 12:33

from thorn *bushes,* nor figs from thistles, are they? ¹⁷So ^every good tree bears good fruit, but the bad tree bears bad fruit. ¹⁸A good tree cannot bear bad fruit, nor can a bad tree bear good fruit. ¹⁹^Every tree that does not bear good fruit is cut down and thrown into the fire. ²⁰So then, you will know them ^by their fruits.

²¹"^Not everyone who says to Me, 'Lord, Lord,' will enter the kingdom of heaven, but the one who does the will of My Father who is in heaven *will enter.* ²²^Many will say to Me on that day, 'Lord, Lord, did we not prophesy in Your name, and in Your name cast out demons, and in Your name perform many miracles?' ²³And then I will declare to them, 'I never knew you; ^LEAVE ME, YOU WHO PRACTICE LAWLESS-NESS.'

THE TWO FOUNDATIONS

²⁴"Therefore, ^everyone who hears these words of Mine, and acts on them, will be like a wise man who built his house on the rock. ²⁵And the rain fell and the floods came, and the winds blew and slammed against that house; and *yet* it did not fall, for it had been founded on the rock. ²⁶And everyone who hears these words of Mine, and does not act on them, will be like a foolish man who built his house on the sand. ²⁷And the rain fell and the floods came, and the winds blew and slammed against that house; and it fell—and its collapse was great."

²⁸When Jesus had finished these words, ^the crowds were amazed at His teaching; ²⁹for He was teaching them as one who had authority, and not as their scribes.

JESUS CLEANSES A MAN WITH LEPROSY

8 When Jesus came down from the mountain, large crowds followed Him. ²And ^a man with ¹leprosy came to Him and bowed down before Him, and said, "Lord, if You are willing, You can make me clean." ³Jesus reached out with His hand and touched him, saying, "I am willing; be cleansed." And immediately his ^leprosy was cleansed. ⁴And Jesus *said to him, "See that you tell no one; but ^go, show yourself to the priest and present the offering that Moses commanded, as a testimony to them."

THE CENTURION'S FAITH

⁵And ^when Jesus entered Capernaum, a centurion came to Him, begging Him, ⁶and saying, "Lord, my servant is lying ^paralyzed at home, terribly tormented." ⁷Jesus *said to him, "I will come and heal him." ⁸But the centurion replied, "Lord, I am not worthy for You to come under my roof, but just say the word, and my servant will be healed. ⁹For I also am a man under ^authority, with soldiers under me; and I say to this one, 'Go!' and he goes, and to another, 'Come!' and he comes, and to my slave, 'Do this!' and he does *it.*" ¹⁰Now when Jesus heard *this,* He was amazed and said to those who were following, "Truly I say to you, I have not found such great faith with anyone in

7:17^Matt 12:33, 35   7:19^Matt 3:10; Luke 3:9
7:20^Matt 7:16; 12:33   7:21^Luke 6:46
7:22^Matt 25:11f; Luke 13:25ff   7:23^Ps 6:8;
Matt 25:41   7:24^Matt 16:18; James 1:22-25
7:28^Matt 13:54; 22:33   8:2^*Mark 1:40-44; Luke 5:12-14*   8:3^Matt 11:5; Luke 4:27   8:4^Mark 1:44;
Luke 5:14   8:5^*Luke 7:1-10*   8:6^Matt 4:24
8:9^Mark 1:27; Luke 9:1

8:2¹I.e., leprosy or a serious, unspecified skin disease, and so throughout the ch; see Lev 13

Israel. [11]And I say to you that many ^will come from east and west, and 'recline *at the table* with Abraham, Isaac, and Jacob in the kingdom of heaven; [12]but ^the sons of the kingdom will be thrown out into ^Bthe outer darkness; in that place there will be weeping and gnashing of teeth." [13]And Jesus said to the centurion, "Go; it shall be done for you ^as you have believed." And the servant was healed at that *very* moment.

PETER'S MOTHER-IN-LAW AND MANY OTHERS HEALED

[14]^When Jesus came into Peter's home, He saw his mother-in-law lying sick in bed with a fever. [15]And He touched her hand, and the fever left her; and she got up and waited on Him. [16]Now when evening came, they brought to Him many ^who were demon-possessed; and He cast out the spirits with a word, and ^Bhealed all who were ill. [17]*This happened* so that what was spoken through Isaiah the prophet would be fulfilled: "^HE HIMSELF TOOK OUR ILLNESSES AND CARRIED AWAY OUR DISEASES."

DISCIPLESHIP TESTED

[18]Now when Jesus saw a crowd around Him, ^He gave orders to depart to the other side *of the sea*. [19]^Then a scribe came and said to Him, "Teacher, I will follow You wherever You go." [20]And Jesus *said to him, "The foxes have holes and the birds of the sky *have* nests, but ^the Son of Man has nowhere to lay His head." [21]And another of the disciples said to Him, "Lord, allow me first to go and bury my father." [22]But Jesus *said to him, "^Follow Me, and let the dead bury their own dead."

JESUS CALMS THE STORM

[23]^When He got into the boat, His disciples followed Him. [24]And behold, a violent storm developed on the sea, so that the boat was being covered by the waves; but Jesus Himself was asleep. [25]And they came to *Him* and woke Him, saying, "^Save *us,* Lord; we are perishing!" [26]He *said to them, "Why are you afraid, ^you men of little faith?" Then He got up and rebuked the winds and the sea, and it became perfectly calm. [27]The men were amazed, and said, "What kind of a man is this, that even the winds and the sea obey Him?"

JESUS SENDS DEMONS INTO PIGS

[28]^And when He came to the other side into the country of the Gadarenes, two demon-possessed men confronted Him as they were coming out of the tombs. *They were* so extremely violent that no one could pass by that way. [29]And they cried out, saying, "^What business do You have with us, Son of God? Have You come here to torment us before the time?" [30]Now there was a herd of many pigs feeding at a distance from them. [31]And the demons begged Him, saying, "If You *are going to* cast us out, send us into the herd of pigs." [32]And He said to them, "Go!" And they came out and went into the pigs; and behold, the whole herd rushed down the steep bank into the sea

8:11^As 49:12; 59:19   **8:12**^Matt 13:38   ^BMatt 22:13
8:13^Matt 9:22, 29   **8:14**^*Mark 1:29–34; Luke 4:38–41*
8:16^Matt 4:24   ^BMatt 4:23   **8:17**^Is 53:4
8:18^Mark 4:35; Luke 8:22   **8:19**^*Luke 9:57–60*
8:20^Dan 7:13; Matt 9:6   **8:22**^Matt 9:9; Mark 2:14
8:23^*Mark 4:36–41; Luke 8:22–25*   **8:25**^Matt 8:2; 9:18
8:26^Matt 6:30; 14:31   **8:28**^*Mark 5:1–17; Luke 8:26–37*   **8:29**^Judg 11:12; 2 Sam 16:10

8:11[1]I.e., to dine

and drowned in the waters. [33] And the herdsmen ran away, and went to the city and reported everything, including what had happened to the ^demon-possessed men. [34] And behold, the whole city came out to meet Jesus; and when they saw Him, ^they pleaded with Him to leave their region.

A PARALYZED MAN HEALED

9 Getting into a boat, Jesus crossed over *the Sea of Galilee* and came to ^His own city.

[2] ^And they brought to Him a paralyzed man lying on a stretcher. And seeing their faith, Jesus said to the man who was paralyzed, "Take courage, son; your sins are forgiven." [3] And some of the scribes said to themselves, "This man is ^blaspheming!" [4] And Jesus, ^perceiving their thoughts, said, "Why are you thinking evil in your hearts? [5] For which is easier, to say, '^Your sins are forgiven,' or to say, 'Get up and walk'? [6] But so that you may know that ^the Son of Man has authority on earth to forgive sins"—then He *said to the paralyzed man, "Get up, pick up your stretcher and go home." [7] And he got up and went home. [8] But when the crowds saw *this*, they were awestruck, and they ^glorified God, who had given such authority to men.

MATTHEW CALLED

[9] ^As Jesus went on from there, He saw a man called Matthew sitting in the tax collector's office; and He *said to him, "Follow Me!" And he got up and followed Him.

[10] Then it happened that as Jesus was reclining *at the table* in the house, behold, many tax collectors and sinners came and *began* dining with Jesus and His disciples. [11] And when the Pharisees saw *this*, they said to His disciples, "^Why is your Teacher eating with the tax collectors and sinners?" [12] But when Jesus heard *this*, He said, "*It is* not ^those who are healthy who need a physician, but those who are sick. [13] Now go and learn what this means: '^I DESIRE COMPASSION, RATHER THAN SACRIFICE,' for I did not come to call the righteous, but sinners."

THE QUESTION ABOUT FASTING

[14] Then the disciples of John *came to Him, asking, "Why do we and ^the Pharisees fast, but Your disciples do not fast?" [15] And Jesus said to them, "The attendants of the groom cannot mourn as long as the groom is with them, can they? But the days will come when the groom is taken away from them, and then they will fast. [16] But no one puts a patch of unshrunk cloth on an old garment; for the patch pulls away from the garment, and a worse tear results. [17] Nor do *people* put new wine into old wineskins; otherwise the wineskins burst, and the wine pours out and the wineskins are ruined; but they put new wine into fresh wineskins, and both are preserved."

MIRACLES OF HEALING

[18] ^While He was saying these things to them, behold, a *synagogue* official came and bowed down before Him, and said, "My daughter has just died; but come and lay Your

8:33 ^Matt 4:24 8:34 ^Amos 7:12; Acts 16:39
9:1 ^Matt 4:13; Mark 5:21 9:2 ^*Mark 2:3-12; Luke 5:18-26* 9:3 ^Mark 3:28, 29 9:4 ^Matt 12:25; Luke 6:8 9:5 ^Matt 9:2, 6; Mark 2:5, 9
9:6 ^Matt 8:20; John 5:27 9:8 ^Matt 5:16; 15:31
9:9 ^*Mark 2:14-22; Luke 5:27-38* 9:11 ^Matt 11:19; Mark 2:16 9:12 ^Mark 2:17; Luke 5:31 9:13 ^Hos 6:6
9:14 ^Luke 18:12 9:18 ^*Mark 5:22-43; Luke 8:41-56*

hand on her, and she will become alive again." ¹⁹Jesus got up *from the table* and *began to* accompany him, along with His disciples.

²⁰And behold, a woman who had been suffering from a hemorrhage for twelve years came up behind Him, and touched ᴬthe border of His cloak; ²¹for she was saying to herself, "If I only ᴬtouch His cloak, I will get well." ²²But Jesus, turning and seeing her, said, "Daughter, take courage; ᴬyour faith has made you well." And at once the woman was made well.

²³When Jesus came into the official's house and saw ᴬthe flute players and the crowd in noisy disorder, ²⁴He said, "Leave; for the girl ᴬhas not died, but is asleep." And they *began* laughing at Him. ²⁵But ᴬwhen the crowd had been sent out, He entered and ᴮtook her by the hand, and the girl got up. ²⁶And ᴬthis news spread throughout that land.

²⁷As Jesus went on from there, two men who were blind followed Him, crying out, "Have mercy on us, ᴬSon of David!" ²⁸And after He entered the house, the men who were blind came up to Him, and Jesus *said to them, "Do you believe that I am able to do this?" They *said to Him, "Yes, Lord." ²⁹Then He touched their eyes, saying, "It shall be done for you ᴬaccording to your faith." ³⁰And their eyes were opened. And Jesus ᴬsternly warned them, saying, "See that no one knows *about this!*" ³¹But they went out and ᴬspread the news about Him throughout that land.

³²And as they were going out, behold, ᴬa demon-possessed man who was unable to speak was brought to Him. ³³And after the demon was cast out, the man who was *previously* unable to speak talked; and the crowds were amazed, *and were* saying, "ᴬNothing like this has ever been seen in Israel." ³⁴But the Pharisees were saying, "He ᴬcasts out the demons by the ruler of the demons."

³⁵Jesus was going through all the cities and villages, ᴬteaching in their synagogues and proclaiming the gospel of the kingdom, and healing every disease and every sickness. ³⁶Seeing the crowds, He felt compassion for them, ᴬbecause they were distressed and downcast, like sheep without a shepherd. ³⁷Then He *said to His disciples, "ᴬThe harvest is plentiful, but the workers are few. ³⁸Therefore, plead with the Lord of the harvest to send out workers into His harvest."

THE TWELVE DISCIPLES; INSTRUCTIONS FOR SERVICE

10 Jesus ᴬsummoned His twelve disciples and gave them authority over unclean spirits, to cast them out, and to heal every disease and every sickness.

²ᴬNow the names of the twelve apostles are these: The first, Simon, who is called Peter, and his brother Andrew; and James the son of Zebedee, and his brother John; ³ᴬPhilip and Bartholomew; ᴮThomas and Matthew the tax collector; James the son of Alphaeus, and Thaddaeus; ⁴Simon the Zealot, and ᴬJudas Iscariot, the one who also betrayed Him.

9:20ᴬNum 15:38; Deut 22:12   9:21ᴬMatt 14:36; Mark 3:10   9:22ᴬMatt 9:29; 15:28   9:23ᴬ2 Chr 35:25; Jer 9:17   9:24ᴬJohn 11:13; Acts 20:10   9:25ᴬActs 9:40 ᴮMark 9:27   9:26ᴬMatt 4:24; 9:31   9:27ᴬMatt 1:1; 12:23   9:29ᴬMatt 8:13; 9:22   9:30ᴬMatt 8:4 9:31ᴬMatt 4:24; 9:26   9:32ᴬMatt 12:22, 24 9:33ᴬMark 2:12   9:34ᴬMatt 12:24; Mark 3:22 9:35ᴬMatt 4:23; Mark 1:14   9:36ᴬNum 27:17; Ezek 34:5   9:37ᴬLuke 10:2   10:1ᴬMark 3:13–15; 6:7 10:2ᴬ*Mark 3:16-19; Luke 6:14-16*   10:3ᴬJohn 1:43ff ᴮJohn 11:16   10:4ᴬMatt 26:14; Luke 22:3

⁵These twelve Jesus sent out after instructing them, saying, "Do not go on a road to Gentiles, and do not enter a city of ᴬSamaritans; ⁶but rather go to ᴬthe lost sheep of the house of Israel. ⁷And as you go, preach, saying, 'ᴬThe kingdom of heaven has come near.' ⁸Heal *the* sick, raise *the* dead, cleanse those with leprosy, cast out demons. Freely you received, freely give. ⁹ᴬDo not acquire gold, or silver, or copper for your money belts, ¹⁰or a bag for *your* journey, or even two ¹tunics, or sandals, or a staff; for ᴬthe worker is deserving of his support. ¹¹And whatever city or village you enter, inquire who is worthy in it, and stay at his house until you leave *that city*. ¹²As you enter the house, ᴬgive it your greeting. ¹³If the house is worthy, *see that* your *blessing of* peace comes upon it. But if it is not worthy, take back your *blessing of* peace. ¹⁴And whoever does not receive you nor listen to your words, as you leave that house or city, ᴬshake the dust off your feet. ¹⁵Truly I say to you, ᴬit will be more tolerable for *the* land of Sodom and Gomorrah on the day of judgment, than for that city.

A HARD ROAD AHEAD OF THEM

¹⁶"ᴬBehold, I am sending you out as sheep in the midst of wolves; so be as wary as serpents, and as innocent as doves. ¹⁷But be on guard against people, for they will hand you over to *the* ᴬcourts and flog you in their synagogues; ¹⁸and you will even be brought before governors and kings on My account, as a testimony to them and to the Gentiles. ¹⁹ᴬBut when they hand you over, do not worry about how or what you are to say; for what you are to say will be given you in that hour. ²⁰For

ᴬit is not you who are speaking, but *it is* the Spirit of your Father who is speaking in you.

²¹"Now ᴬbrother will betray brother to death, and a father *his* child; and children will rise up against parents and cause them to be put to death. ²²And ᴬyou will be hated by all because of My name, but it is the one who has endured to the end who will be saved.

²³"But whenever they persecute you in one city, flee to the next; for truly I say to you, you will not finish *going through* the cities of Israel ᴬuntil the Son of Man comes.

THE MEANING OF DISCIPLESHIP

²⁴"ᴬA disciple is not above his teacher, nor a slave above his master. ²⁵It is enough for the disciple that he may become like his teacher, and the slave like his master. If they have called the head of the house ᴬBeelzebul, how much more *will they insult* the members of his household!

²⁶"So do not fear them, ᴬfor there is nothing concealed that will not be revealed, or hidden that will not be known. ²⁷ᴬWhat I tell you in the darkness, tell in the light; and what you hear *whispered* in *your* ear, proclaim on the housetops. ²⁸And do not be afraid of those who kill the body but are unable to kill the soul; but rather ᴬfear Him who is able to

10:5 ᴬ2 Kin 17:24ff; Luke 9:52   10:6 ᴬMatt 15:24
10:7 ᴬMatt 3:2   10:9 ᴬLuke 22:35   10:10 ᴬ1 Cor 9:14;
1 Tim 5:18   10:12 ᴬ1 Sam 25:6; Ps 122:7, 8
10:14 ᴬActs 13:51   10:15 ᴬMatt 11:22, 24
10:16 ᴬLuke 10:3   10:17 ᴬMatt 5:22
10:19 ᴬ*Mark 13:11-13; Luke 21:12-17*   10:20 ᴬLuke 12:12;
Acts 4:8   10:21 ᴬMatt 10:35, 36; Mark 13:12
10:22 ᴬMatt 24:9; Luke 21:17   10:23 ᴬMatt 16:27f
10:24 ᴬLuke 6:40; John 13:16   10:25 ᴬ2 Kin 1:2;
Matt 12:24, 27   10:26 ᴬMark 4:22; Luke 8:17
10:27 ᴬLuke 12:3   10:28 ᴬHeb 10:31

10:10 ¹A long shirt worn next to the skin

destroy both soul and body in [1]hell. [29A]Are two sparrows not sold for an [1]assarion? And *yet* not one of them will fall to the ground apart from your Father. [30]But [A]even the hairs of your head are all counted. [31]So do not fear; [A]you are more valuable than a great number of sparrows.

[32]"Therefore, [A]everyone who confesses Me before people, I will also confess him before My Father who is in heaven. [33]But [A]whoever denies Me before people, I will also deny him before My Father who is in heaven.

[34]"[A]Do not think that I came to bring peace on the earth; I did not come to bring peace, but a sword. [35]For I came to [A]TURN A MAN AGAINST HIS FATHER, AND A DAUGHTER AGAINST HER MOTHER, AND A DAUGHTER-IN-LAW AGAINST HER MOTHER-IN-LAW; [36]and [A]A PERSON'S ENEMIES *WILL BE* THE MEMBERS OF HIS HOUSEHOLD.

[37]"[A]The one who loves father or mother more than Me is not worthy of Me; and the one who loves son or daughter more than Me is not worthy of Me. [38]And [A]the one who does not take his cross and follow after Me is not worthy of Me. [39A]The one who has found his life will lose it, and the one who has lost his life on My account will find it.

THE REWARD FOR SERVICE

[40]"The one who receives you receives Me, and [A]the one who receives Me receives Him who sent Me. [41A]The one who receives a prophet in *the* name of a prophet shall receive a prophet's reward; and the one who receives a righteous person in the name of a righteous person shall receive a righteous person's reward. [42]And [A]whoever gives one of these little ones just a cup of cold *water* to drink in the name of a disciple, truly I say to you, he shall by no means lose his reward."

JOHN'S QUESTIONS

11 [A]When Jesus had finished giving instructions to His twelve disciples, He went on from there to teach and preach in their cities.

[2A]Now *while* in prison, John heard about the works of Christ, and he sent *word* by his disciples, [3]and said to Him, "Are You [A]the Coming One, or are we to look for someone else?" [4]Jesus answered and said to them, "Go and report to John what you hear and see: [5A]*those who are* BLIND RECEIVE SIGHT and *those who* limp walk, *those* with leprosy are cleansed and *those who are* deaf hear, *the* dead are raised, and *the* POOR HAVE THE GOSPEL PREACHED TO THEM. [6]And blessed is any person who [A]does not take offense at Me."

JESUS' TRIBUTE TO JOHN

[7]As these *disciples of John* were going *away,* Jesus began speaking to the crowds about John: "What did you go out into [A]the wilderness to see? A reed shaken by the wind? [8]But what did you go out to see? A man dressed in soft *clothing?* Those who wear soft *clothing* are in kings' palaces! [9]But what did you go out to see? [A]A prophet? Yes, I tell you, and *one who is* more than a prophet. [10]This is the one about whom it is written:

10:29[A]Luke 12:6　**10:30**[A]1 Sam 14:45; 2 Sam 14:11
10:31[A]Matt 12:12　**10:32**[A]Luke 12:8; Rev 3:5
10:33[A]Mark 8:38; Luke 9:26　**10:34**[A]*Luke 12:51-53*
10:35[A]Mic 7:6; Matt 10:21　**10:36**[A]Mic 7:6; Matt 10:21
10:37[A]Deut 33:9; Luke 14:26　**10:38**[A]Matt 16:24;
Mark 8:34　**10:39**[A]Matt 16:25; Mark 8:35
10:40[A]Mark 9:37; Luke 9:48　**10:41**[A]Matt 25:44, 45
10:42[A]Matt 25:40; Mark 9:41　**11:1**[A]Matt 7:28
11:2[A]Matt 4:12　**11:3**[A]Ps 118:26; Matt 11:10
11:5[A]Is 35:5f; Matt 8:3　**11:6**[A]Matt 5:29; 13:57
11:7[A]Matt 3:1　**11:9**[A]Matt 14:5; 21:26

10:28[1]Gr *Gehenna*　**10:29**[1]A Roman copper coin, worth about 1/16 of a laborer's daily wage

'ᴬBᴇʜᴏʟᴅ, I ᴀᴍ sᴇɴᴅɪɴɢ Mʏ
    ᴍᴇssᴇɴɢᴇʀ ᴀʜᴇᴀᴅ ᴏꜰ Yᴏᴜ,
    Wʜᴏ ᴡɪʟʟ ᴘʀᴇᴘᴀʀᴇ Yᴏᴜʀ ᴡᴀʏ
    ʙᴇꜰᴏʀᴇ Yᴏᴜ.'
11Truly I say to you, among those born of women there has not arisen *anyone* greater than John the Baptist! Yet the one who is least in the kingdom of heaven is greater than he. **12**And ᴬfrom the days of John the Baptist until now the kingdom of heaven has been treated violently, and violent men take it by force. **13**For all the Prophets and the Law prophesied until John. **14**And if you are willing to accept *it, John* himself is ᴬElijah who was to come. **15**ᴬThe one who has ears to hear, let him hear.

16"But to what shall I compare this generation? It is like children sitting in the marketplaces, who call out to the other *children,* **17**and say, 'We played the flute for you, and you did not dance; we sang a song of mourning, and you did not mourn.' **18**For John came neither eating nor ᴬdrinking, and they say, 'ᴮHe has a demon!' **19**The Son of Man came eating and drinking, and they say, 'Behold, a gluttonous man and a heavy drinker, ᴬa friend of tax collectors and sinners!' And *yet* wisdom is vindicated by her deeds."

THE UNREPENTING CITIES

20Then He began to reprimand the cities in which most of His ᴬmiracles were done, because they did not repent. **21**"ᴬWoe to you, Chorazin! Woe to you, Bethsaida! For if the miracles that occurred in you had occurred in Tyre and Sidon, they would have repented long ago in sackcloth and ashes. **22**Nevertheless I say to you, it will be more tolerable for Tyre and Sidon on ᴬ*the* day of judgment than for you. **23**And you,

ᴬCapernaum, will not be exalted to heaven, will you? You will be ᴮbrought down to Hades! For if the miracles that occurred in you had occurred in Sodom, it would have remained to this day. **24**Nevertheless I say to you that ᴬit will be more tolerable for the land of Sodom on *the* day of judgment, than for you."

COME TO ME

25ᴬAt that time Jesus said, "I praise You, Father, Lord of heaven and earth, that You have hidden these things from *the* wise and intelligent, and have revealed them to infants. **26**Yes, ᴬFather, for this way was well pleasing in Your sight. **27**ᴬAll things have been handed over to Me by My Father; and no one knows the Son except the Father; nor does anyone know the Father except the Son, and anyone to whom the Son determines to reveal *Him.*

28"ᴬCome to Me, all who are weary and burdened, and I will give you rest. **29**Take My yoke upon you and ᴬlearn from Me, for I am gentle and humble in heart, and ᴮʏᴏᴜ ᴡɪʟʟ ꜰɪɴᴅ ʀᴇsᴛ ꜰᴏʀ ʏᴏᴜʀ sᴏᴜʟs. **30**For ᴬMy yoke is comfortable, and My burden is light."

SABBATH QUESTIONS

12 ᴬAt that time Jesus went through the grainfields on the Sabbath, and His disciples became hungry and began to pick the heads *of grain* and eat. **2**Now

---

11:10ᴬMal 3:1; Mark 1:2   **11:12**ᴬLuke 16:16
11:14ᴬMal 4:5; Matt 17:10-13   **11:15**ᴬMatt 13:9, 43;
Mark 4:9, 23   **11:18**ᴬLuke 1:15   ᴮMatt 9:34; John 7:20
11:19ᴬMatt 9:11; Luke 5:29-32   **11:20**ᴬLuke 10:13-15
11:21ᴬ*Luke 10:13-15*   **11:22**ᴬMatt 10:15; 12:36
11:23ᴬMatt 4:13   ᴮIs 14:13, 15   **11:24**ᴬMatt 10:15; 11:22
11:25ᴬ*Luke 10:21, 22*   **11:26**ᴬLuke 22:42; 23:34
11:27ᴬMatt 28:18; John 3:35   **11:28**ᴬJer 31:25; John 7:37
11:29ᴬJohn 13:15   ᴮJer 6:16   **11:30**ᴬ1 John 5:3
12:1ᴬ *Mark 2:23-28; Luke 6:1-5*

when the Pharisees saw *this*, they said to Him, "Look, Your disciples are doing what ^is not lawful to do on a Sabbath!" ³But He said to them, "Have you not read what David did when he became hungry, he and his companions— ⁴how he entered the house of God, and ^they ate the consecrated bread, which was not lawful for him to eat nor for those with him, but for the priests alone? ⁵Or have you not read in the Law that on the Sabbath the priests in the temple violate the Sabbath, and *yet* are innocent? ⁶But I say to you that *something* ^greater than the temple is here. ⁷But if you had known what this means: '^I DESIRE COMPASSION, RATHER THAN SACRIFICE,' you would not have condemned the innocent.

LORD OF THE SABBATH

⁸For ^the Son of Man is Lord of the Sabbath."

⁹^Departing from there, He went into their synagogue. ¹⁰And a man *was there* whose hand was withered. And they questioned Jesus, asking, "^Is it lawful to heal on the Sabbath?"—so that they might bring charges against Him. ¹¹But He said to them, "^What man is there among you who has a sheep, and if it falls into a pit on the Sabbath, will he not take hold of it and lift it out? ¹²^How much more valuable then is a person than a sheep! So then, it is lawful to do good on the Sabbath." ¹³Then He *said to the man, "Stretch out your hand!" ^He stretched it out, and it was restored to normal, like the other. ¹⁴But the Pharisees went out and ^conspired against Him, *as to* how they might destroy Him.

¹⁵But Jesus, aware of *this*, withdrew from there. Many followed Him, and ^He healed them all, ¹⁶and ^warned them not to tell who He was. ¹⁷*This happened* so that what was spoken through Isaiah the prophet would be fulfilled:

18 "^BEHOLD, MY SERVANT WHOM I
    HAVE CHOSEN;
    ^BMY BELOVED IN WHOM MY
    SOUL DELIGHTS;
    I WILL PUT MY SPIRIT UPON HIM,
    ^AND HE WILL PROCLAIM
    JUSTICE TO THE GENTILES.
19 "^HE WILL NOT QUARREL, NOR
    CRY OUT;
    NOR WILL ANYONE HEAR HIS
    VOICE IN THE STREETS.
20 "^A BENT REED HE WILL NOT
    BREAK *OFF*,
    AND A DIMLY BURNING WICK HE
    WILL NOT EXTINGUISH,
    UNTIL HE LEADS JUSTICE TO
    VICTORY.
21 "^AND IN HIS NAME THE
    GENTILES WILL HOPE."

THE PHARISEES REBUKED

22^Then a demon-possessed man *who was* blind and unable to speak was brought to Jesus, and He healed him so that the man who was unable to speak talked and could see. ²³And all the crowds were amazed and were saying, "This man cannot be the ^Son of David, can he?" ²⁴But when the Pharisees heard *this*, they said, "This man ^casts out demons only by Beelzebul the ruler of the demons."

²⁵^And knowing their thoughts, Jesus said to them, "Every kingdom

12:2 ^Matt 12:10; Luke 13:14   12:4 ^1 Sam 21:6
12:6 ^2 Chr 6:18; Is 66:1, 2   12:7 ^Hos 6:6; Matt 9:13
12:8 ^Matt 8:20; 12:32, 40   12:9 ^*Mark 3:1–6; Luke 6:6–11*
12:10 ^Matt 12:2; Luke 13:14   12:11 ^Luke 14:5
12:12 ^Matt 10:31; Luke 14:1–6   12:13 ^Matt 8:3; Acts 28:8
12:14 ^Matt 26:4; Mark 14:1   12:15 ^Matt 4:23
12:16 ^Matt 8:4; 9:30   12:18 ^Is 42:1   ^BMatt 3:17
12:19 ^Is 42:2   12:20 ^Is 42:3   12:21 ^Rom 15:12
12:22 ^Matt 9:32, 34   12:23 ^Matt 9:27
12:24 ^Matt 9:34   12:25 ^*Mark 3:23–27; Luke 11:17–22*

divided against itself is laid waste; and no city or house divided against itself will stand. 26 And if ᴬSatan is casting out Satan, he has become divided against himself; how then will his kingdom stand? 27 And if ᴬby Beelzebul I cast out the demons, ᴮby whom do your sons cast *them* out? Therefore, they will be your judges. 28 But ᴬif I cast out the demons by the Spirit of God, then the kingdom of God has come upon you. 29 Or, how can anyone enter the strong man's house and carry off his property, unless he first ties up the strong *man?* And then he will plunder his house.

THE UNPARDONABLE SIN

30 ᴬThe one who is not with Me is against Me; and the one who does not gather with Me scatters.

31 "ᴬTherefore I say to you, every sin and blasphemy shall be forgiven people, but blasphemy against the Spirit shall not be forgiven. 32 ᴬAnd whoever speaks a word against the Son of Man, it shall be forgiven him; but whoever speaks against the Holy Spirit, it shall not be forgiven him, either in ᴮthis age or in the *age* to come.

WORDS REVEAL CHARACTER

33 "Either assume the tree *to be* good as well as its fruit good, or assume the tree *to be* bad as well as its fruit bad; for ᴬthe tree is known by its fruit. 34 ᴬYou offspring of vipers, how can you, being evil, express *any* good things? For the mouth speaks from that which fills the heart. 35 ᴬThe good person brings out of *his* good treasure good things; and the evil person brings out of *his* evil treasure evil things. 36 But I tell you that *for* every careless word

that people speak, they will give an account of it on *the* ᴬday of judgment. 37 For by your words you will be justified, and by your words you will be condemned."

THE DESIRE FOR SIGNS

38 Then some of the scribes and Pharisees said to Him, "Teacher, ᴬwe want to see a sign from You." 39 But He answered and said to them, "ᴬAn evil and adulterous generation craves a sign; and *so* no sign will be given to it except the sign of Jonah the prophet; 40 for just as ᴬJONAH WAS IN THE STOMACH OF THE SEA MONSTER FOR THREE DAYS AND THREE NIGHTS, so will the Son of Man be in the heart of the earth for ᴮthree days and three nights. 41 The men of Nineveh will stand up with this generation at the judgment, and will condemn it because ᴬthey repented at the preaching of Jonah; and behold, *something* greater than Jonah is here. 42 ᴬ*The* Queen of *the* South will rise up with this generation at the judgment and will condemn it, because she came from the ends of the earth to hear the wisdom of Solomon; and behold, *something* greater than Solomon is here.

43 "ᴬNow when the unclean spirit comes out of a person, it passes through waterless places seeking rest, and does not find *it*. 44 Then it says, 'I will return to my house from which I came'; and when it comes, it finds *it* unoccupied, swept, and put in order. 45 Then it goes and brings along with it seven other spirits more

12:26ᴬMatt 4:10; 13:19   **12:27**ᴬMatt 9:34   ᴮActs 19:13
12:28ᴬ1 John 3:8   ᴮMark 9:40; Luke 9:50
12:31ᴬLuke 12:10   **12:32**ᴬLuke 12:10   ᴮMatt 13:22, 39
12:33ᴬMatt 7:16-18; Luke 6:43, 44   **12:34**ᴬMatt 3:7;
23:33   **12:35**ᴬProv 10:20, 21; 25:11, 12   **12:36**ᴬMatt 10:15
12:38ᴬMatt 16:1; Mark 8:11, 12   **12:39**ᴬMatt 16:4
12:40ᴬJon 1:17   ᴮMatt 16:21   **12:41**ᴬJon 3:5
12:42ᴬ1 Kin 10:1; 2 Chr 9:1   **12:43**ᴬ*Luke 11:24-26*

wicked than itself, and they come in and live there; and ^the last *condition* of that person becomes worse than the first. That is the way it will also be with this evil generation."

CHANGED RELATIONSHIPS

46^While He was still speaking to the crowds, behold, His mother and brothers were standing outside, seeking to speak to Him. 47[¹Someone said to Him, "Look, Your mother and Your brothers are standing outside, seeking to speak to You."] 48But Jesus replied to the one who was telling Him and said, "Who is My mother, and who are My brothers?" 49And extending His hand toward His disciples, He said, "Behold: My mother and My brothers! 50For whoever does the will of My Father who is in heaven, he is My brother, and sister, and mother."

JESUS TEACHES IN PARABLES

13 On that day Jesus had gone out of the house and was sitting ^by the sea. 2And large crowds gathered to Him, so ^He got into a boat and sat down, and the whole crowd was standing on the beach. 3And He told them many things in ^parables, saying, "Behold, the sower went out to sow; 4and as he sowed, some *seeds* fell beside the road, and the birds came and ate them up. 5Others fell on the rocky places, where they did not have much soil; and they sprang up immediately, because they had no depth of soil. 6But after the sun rose, they were scorched; and because they had no root, they withered away. 7Others fell among the thorns, and the thorns came up and choked them out. 8But others fell on the good soil and yielded a crop, some

a ^hundred, some sixty, and some thirty *times as much.* 9^The one who has ears, let him hear."

AN EXPLANATION FOR PARABLES

10And the disciples came up and said to Him, "Why do You speak to them in parables?" 11And Jesus answered them, "^To you it has been granted to know the mysteries of the kingdom of heaven, but to them it has not been granted. 12^For whoever has, to him *more* shall be given, and he will have an abundance; but whoever does not have, even what he has shall be taken away from him. 13Therefore I speak to them in parables; because while ^seeing they do not see, and while hearing they do not hear, nor do they understand. 14And in their case the prophecy of Isaiah is being fulfilled, which says,

'^YOU SHALL KEEP ON LISTENING,
    BUT SHALL NOT UNDERSTAND;
  AND YOU SHALL KEEP ON
    LOOKING, BUT SHALL NOT
    PERCEIVE;
15 ^FOR THE HEART OF THIS PEOPLE
    HAS BECOME DULL,
  WITH THEIR EARS THEY
    SCARCELY HEAR,
  AND THEY HAVE CLOSED THEIR
    EYES,
  OTHERWISE THEY MIGHT SEE
    WITH THEIR EYES,
  HEAR WITH THEIR EARS,
  UNDERSTAND WITH THEIR
    HEART, AND RETURN,
  AND I WOULD HEAL THEM.'

12:45^Mark 5:9; Luke 11:26 **12:46**^*Mark 3:31-35; Luke 8:19-21* **13:1**^Mark 2:13 **13:2**^Luke 5:3 **13:3**^Matt 13:10ff; Mark 4:2ff **13:8**^Gen 26:12; Matt 13:23 **13:9**^Matt 11:15; Rev 2:7, 11, 17, 29 **13:11**^Matt 19:11; 20:23 **13:12**^Matt 25:29; Mark 4:25 **13:13**^Deut 29:4; Is 42:19, 20 **13:14**^Is 6:9; Mark 4:12 **13:15**^Is 6:10; Ps 119:70

12:47¹This verse is not found in early mss

16 ᴬBut blessed are your eyes, because they see; and your ears, because they hear. 17 For truly I say to you that ᴬmany prophets and righteous people longed to see what you see, and did not see *it*, and to hear what you hear, and did not hear *it*.

THE SOWER EXPLAINED

18 "ᴬListen then to the parable of the sower. 19 When anyone hears ᴬthe word of the kingdom and does not understand *it*, the evil *one* comes and snatches away what has been sown in his heart. This is the one sown *with seed* beside the road. 20 The one sown *with seed* on the rocky places, this is the one who hears the word and immediately receives it with joy; 21 yet he has no *firm* root in himself, but is *only* temporary, and when affliction or persecution occurs because of the word, immediately he ᴬfalls away. 22 And the one sown *with seed* among the thorns, this is the one who hears the word, and the anxiety of the world and the ᴬdeceitfulness of wealth choke the word, and it becomes unfruitful. 23 But the one sown *with seed* on the good soil, this is the one who hears the word and understands it, who indeed bears fruit and produces, some ᴬa hundred, some sixty, and some thirty *times as much*."

WEEDS AMONG WHEAT

24 Jesus presented another parable to them, saying, "ᴬThe kingdom of heaven is like a man who sowed good seed in his field. 25 But while his men were sleeping, his enemy came and sowed ¹weeds among the wheat, and left. 26 And when the wheat sprouted and produced grain, then the weeds also

became evident. 27 And the slaves of the landowner came and said to him, 'Sir, did you not sow good seed in your field? How then does it have weeds?' 28 And he said to them, 'An enemy has done this!' The slaves *said to him, 'Do you want us, then, to go and gather them up?' 29 But he *said, 'No; while you are gathering up the weeds, you may uproot the wheat with them. 30 Allow both to grow together until the harvest; and at the time of the harvest I will say to the reapers, "First gather up the weeds and bind them in bundles to burn them; but ᴬgather the wheat into my barn."'"

THE MUSTARD SEED

31 He presented another parable to them, saying, "ᴬThe kingdom of heaven is like a mustard seed, which a person took and sowed in his field; 32 and this is smaller than all the *other* seeds, but when it is *fully* grown, it is larger than the garden plants and becomes a tree, so that ᴬTHE BIRDS OF THE SKY come and NEST IN ITS BRANCHES."

THE LEAVEN

33 He spoke another parable to them: "ᴬThe kingdom of heaven is like leaven, which a woman took and hid in three ¹sata of flour until it was all leavened."

34 All these things Jesus spoke to the crowds in parables, and He

13:16 ᴬMatt 16:17; John 20:29
13:17 ᴬJohn 8:56; Heb 11:13   13:18 ᴬMark 4:13-20;
Luke 8:11-15   13:19 ᴬMatt 4:23   13:21 ᴬMatt 11:6
13:22 ᴬMatt 19:23; 1 Tim 6:9, 10, 17   13:23 ᴬMatt 13:8
13:24 ᴬMatt 13:31, 33, 45, 47; 18:23   13:30 ᴬMatt 3:12
13:31 ᴬMatt 13:24   13:32 ᴬEzek 17:23; Ps 104:12
13:33 ᴬMatt 13:24

13:25 ¹Prob. *darnel*, a weed resembling wheat
13:33 ¹A Gr term for a Heb measure, totaling about 48 lb. or 22 kg of flour

did not speak anything to them ^Awithout a parable. ³⁵ *This was* so that what was spoken through the prophet would be fulfilled:

> "^A I WILL OPEN MY MOUTH IN
> PARABLES;
> I WILL PROCLAIM THINGS
> HIDDEN SINCE THE
> FOUNDATION OF THE WORLD."

THE WEEDS EXPLAINED

³⁶ Then He left the crowds and went into ^Athe house. And His disciples came to Him and said, "^BExplain to us the parable of the weeds of the field." ³⁷ And He said, "The one who sows the good seed is ^Athe Son of Man, ³⁸ and the field is the world; and *as for* the good seed, these are ^Athe sons of the kingdom; and the weeds are ^Bthe sons of the evil *one;* ³⁹ and the enemy who sowed them is the devil, and the harvest is ^Athe end of the age; and the reapers are angels. ⁴⁰ So just as the weeds are gathered up and burned with fire, so shall it be at ^Athe end of the age. ⁴¹ ^AThe Son of Man will send forth His angels, and they will gather out of His kingdom all stumbling blocks, and those who commit lawlessness, ⁴² and they ^Awill throw them into the furnace of fire; in that place ^Bthere will be weeping and gnashing of teeth. ⁴³ ^AThen THE RIGHTEOUS WILL SHINE FORTH LIKE THE SUN in the kingdom of their Father. The one who has ears, let him hear.

HIDDEN TREASURE

⁴⁴ "The kingdom of heaven is like a treasure hidden in the field, which a man found and hid *again;* and from joy *over it* he goes and ^Asells everything that he has, and buys that field.

A COSTLY PEARL

⁴⁵ "Again, ^Athe kingdom of heaven is like a merchant seeking fine pearls, ⁴⁶ and upon finding one pearl of great value, he went and sold everything that he had and bought it.

A DRAGNET

⁴⁷ "Again, ^Athe kingdom of heaven is like a dragnet that was cast into the sea and gathered *fish* of every kind; ⁴⁸ and when it was filled, they pulled it up on the beach; and they sat down and gathered the good *fish* into containers, but the bad they threw away. ⁴⁹ So it will be at ^Athe end of the age: the angels will come forth and remove the wicked from among the righteous, ⁵⁰ and they ^Awill throw them into the furnace of fire; in that place there will be weeping and gnashing of teeth.

⁵¹ "Have you understood all these things?" They *said to Him, "Yes." ⁵² And Jesus said to them, "Therefore every scribe who has become a disciple of the kingdom of heaven is like a head of a household, who brings out of his treasure new things and old."

JESUS REVISITS NAZARETH

⁵³ ^AWhen Jesus had finished these parables, He departed from there. ⁵⁴ And ^AHe came to His hometown and ^B*began* teaching them in their synagogue, with the result that they were astonished, and said, "Where *did* this man *acquire* this wisdom and *these* miraculous powers? ⁵⁵ Is this not the carpenter's son? Is ^AHis

13:34 ^A Mark 4:34; John 10:6   13:35 ^A Ps 78:2
13:36 ^A Matt 13:1   ^B Matt 15:15   13:37 ^A Matt 8:20
13:38 ^A Matt 8:12   ^B John 8:44   13:39 ^A Matt 12:32;
13:22, 40, 49   13:40 ^A Matt 12:32; 13:22, 39, 49
13:41 ^A Matt 8:20   13:42 ^A Matt 13:50   ^B Matt 8:12
13:43 ^A Dan 12:3   13:44 ^A Matt 13:46   13:45 ^A Matt 13:24
13:47 ^A Matt 13:44   13:49 ^A Matt 13:39, 40
13:50 ^A Matt 13:42   13:53 ^A Matt 7:28   13:54 ^A *Mark
6:1-6*   ^B Matt 4:23   13:55 ^A Matt 12:46

mother not called Mary, and His ^brothers, James, Joseph, Simon, and Judas? ⁵⁶And ^His sisters, are they not all with us? Where then *did* this Man *acquire* all these things?" ⁵⁷And they took ^offense at Him. But Jesus said to them, "^ᴮA prophet is not dishonored except in his hometown and in his *own* household." ⁵⁸And He did not do many miracles there because of their unbelief.

JOHN THE BAPTIST BEHEADED

14 ^At that time Herod the tetrarch heard the news about Jesus, ²and said to his servants, "^This is John the Baptist; he himself has been raised from the dead, and that is why miraculous powers are at work in him."

³For when ^Herod had John arrested, he bound him and put him in prison because of Herodias, the wife of his brother Philip. ⁴For John had been saying to him, "^It is not lawful for you to have her." ⁵Although Herod wanted to put him to death, he feared the crowd, because they regarded John as ^a prophet.

⁶But when Herod's birthday came, the daughter of Herodias danced before *them* and pleased ^Herod, ⁷so *much* that he promised with an oath to give her whatever she asked. ⁸And after being prompted by her mother, she *said, "Give me the head of John the Baptist here on a platter." ⁹And although he was grieved, the king commanded *it* to be given because of his oaths and his dinner guests. ¹⁰He sent *word* and had John beheaded in the prison. ¹¹And his head was brought on a platter and given to the girl, and she brought

it to her mother. ¹²John's disciples came and took away the body and buried it; and they went and reported to Jesus.

FIVE THOUSAND MEN FED

¹³^Now when Jesus heard *about John,* He withdrew from there in a boat to a secluded place by Himself; and when the people heard *about this,* they followed Him on foot from the cities. ¹⁴When He came ashore, He saw a large crowd, and felt compassion for them and ^healed their sick.

¹⁵Now when it was evening, the disciples came to Him and said, "This place is secluded and the hour is already past *to eat;* send the crowds away, so that they may go into the villages and buy food for themselves." ¹⁶But Jesus said to them, "They do not need to go; you give them *something* to eat!" ¹⁷They *said to Him, "We have nothing here except ^five loaves and two fish." ¹⁸And He said, "Bring them here to Me." ¹⁹And ordering the crowds to sit down on the grass, He took the five loaves and the two fish, and looked up toward heaven. He ^blessed *the food* and breaking the loaves, He gave them to the disciples, and the disciples *gave them* to the crowds. ²⁰And they all ate and were satisfied, and they picked up what was left over of the broken pieces: twelve full ^baskets. ²¹There were about five thousand men who ate, besides women and children.

13:56 ^Mark 6:3   13:57 ^Matt 11:6   ᴮMark 6:4
14:1 ^*Mark 6:14-29; Luke 9:7-9*   14:2 ^Matt 16:14;
Mark 6:14   14:3 ^Mark 8:15; Luke 3:1, 19
14:4 ^Lev 18:16; 20:21   14:5 ^Matt 11:9
14:6 ^Matt 8:15; Luke 3:1, 19   14:13 ^Matt 15:32-38
14:14 ^Matt 4:23   14:17 ^Matt 16:9   14:19 ^1 Sam 9:13;
Matt 15:36   14:20 ^Matt 16:9; Mark 6:43

JESUS WALKS ON THE WATER

22 AImmediately *afterward* He compelled the disciples to get into the boat and to go ahead of Him to the other side, while He sent the crowds away. 23 After He had sent the crowds away, AHe went up on the mountain by Himself to pray; and when it was evening, He was there alone. 24 But the boat was already ¹a long distance from the land, battered by the waves; for the wind was Acontrary. 25 And in the ¹fourth watch of the night He came to them, walking on the sea. 26 When the disciples saw Him walking on the sea, they were terrified, and said, "It is Aa ghost!" And they cried out in fear. 27 But immediately Jesus spoke to them, saying, "ATake courage, it is I; Bdo not be afraid."

28 Peter responded and said to Him, "Lord, if it is You, command me to come to You on the water." 29 And He said, "Come!" And Peter got out of the boat and walked on the water, and came toward Jesus. 30 But seeing the wind, he became frightened, and when he began to sink, he cried out, saying, "Lord, save me!" 31 Immediately Jesus reached out with His hand and took hold of him, and *said to him, "AYou of little faith, why did you doubt?" 32 When they got into the boat, the wind stopped. 33 And those who were in the boat worshiped Him, saying, "You are truly AGod's Son!"

34 AWhen they had crossed over, they came to land at Gennesaret. 35 And when the men of that place recognized Him, they sent *word* into all that surrounding region and brought to Him all who were sick; 36 and they pleaded with Him that they might just touch the border of His cloak; and all who Atouched *it* were cured.

TRADITION AND COMMANDMENT

15 AThen *some* Pharisees and scribes *came to Jesus from Jerusalem and said, 2 "Why do Your disciples break the tradition of the elders? For they Ado not wash their hands when they eat bread." 3 And He answered and said to them, "Why do you yourselves also break the commandment of God for the sake of your tradition? 4 For God said, 'AHONOR YOUR FATHER AND MOTHER,' and, 'BTHE ONE WHO SPEAKS EVIL OF FATHER OR MOTHER IS TO BE PUT TO DEATH.' 5 But you say, 'Whoever says to *his* father or mother, "Whatever I have that would help you has been given *to God*," 6 he is not to ¹honor his father *or mother*.' And *by this* you have invalidated the word of God for the sake of your tradition. 7 You hypocrites, rightly did Isaiah prophesy about you, by saying:

8 'ATHIS PEOPLE HONORS ME WITH
        THEIR LIPS,
     BUT THEIR HEART IS FAR AWAY
        FROM ME.
9 'AND IN VAIN DO THEY WORSHIP
        ME,
     TEACHING AS ADOCTRINES THE
        COMMANDMENTS OF MEN.'"

10 After Jesus called the crowd to Him, He said to them, "Hear and understand! 11 AIt is* not what enters the mouth *that* defiles the person,

14:22 A*Mark 6:45-51; John 6:15-21* **14:23** AMark 6:46; Luke 6:12 **14:24** AActs 27:4 **14:26** ALuke 24:37 **14:27** AMatt 9:2 BMatt 17:7 **14:31** AMatt 6:30; 8:26 **14:33** AMatt 4:3 **14:34** AJohn 6:24, 25 **14:36** AMatt 9:21; Mark 3:10 **15:1** A*Mark 7:1-23* **15:2** ALuke 11:38 **15:4** AEx 20:12 BEx 21:17 **15:8** AIs 29:13 **15:9** ACol 2:22 **15:11** AMatt 15:18; Acts 10:14, 15

14:24 ¹Lit *many stadia from;* a Roman stadion perhaps averaged 607 ft. or 185 m **14:25** ¹I.e., 3–6 a.m. **15:6** ¹I.e., by supporting them with it

but what comes out of the mouth, this defiles the person."

¹²Then the disciples came and *said to Him, "Do You know that the Pharisees were offended when they heard this statement?" ¹³But He answered and said, "ᴬEvery plant which My heavenly Father did not plant will be uprooted. ¹⁴Leave them alone; ᴬthey are blind guides ¹of blind people. And ᴮif a person who is blind guides *another* who is blind, both will fall into a pit."

THE HEART OF MANKIND

¹⁵Peter said to Him, "ᴬExplain the parable to us." ¹⁶Jesus said, "Are you also still lacking in understanding? ¹⁷Do you not understand that everything that goes into the mouth passes into the stomach, and is eliminated? ¹⁸But ᴬthe things that come out of the mouth come from the heart, and those things defile the person. ¹⁹ᴬFor out of the heart come evil thoughts, murders, *acts of* adultery, *other* immoral sexual acts, thefts, false testimonies, *and* slanderous statements. ²⁰These are the things that defile the person; but to eat with unwashed hands does not defile the person."

THE FAITH OF A CANAANITE WOMAN

²¹Jesus went away from there, and withdrew into the region of ᴬTyre and Sidon. ²²And a Canaanite woman from that region came out and *began* to cry out, saying, "Have mercy on me, Lord, Son of David; my daughter is severely ᴬdemon-possessed." ²³But He did not answer her *with even* a word. And His disciples came up and urged Him, saying, "Send her away, because she keeps shouting at us!" ²⁴But He answered and said, "I was sent only

to ᴬthe lost sheep of the house of Israel." ²⁵But she came and ᴬ*began* to bow down before Him, saying, "Lord, help me!" ²⁶Yet He answered and said, "It is not good to take the children's bread and throw it to the dogs." ²⁷And she said, "Yes, Lord; *but please help,* for even the dogs feed on the crumbs that fall from their masters' table." ²⁸Then Jesus said to her, "O woman, ᴬyour faith is great; it shall be done for you as you desire." And her daughter was healed at once.

HEALING CROWDS

²⁹ᴬDeparting from there, Jesus went along the Sea of Galilee, and after going up on the mountain, He was sitting there. ³⁰And large crowds came to Him bringing with them *those who were* limping, had impaired limbs, *were* blind, *or were* unable to speak, and many others, and they laid them down at His feet; and ᴬHe healed them. ³¹So the crowd was astonished as they saw those who were unable to speak talking, those with impaired limbs restored, those who were limping walking around, and those who were blind seeing; and they ᴬglorified the God of Israel.

FOUR THOUSAND MEN FED

³²ᴬNow Jesus called His disciples to Him and said, "I feel compassion for the people, because they have remained with Me now for three days and have nothing to eat; and I do not want to send them away

15:13ᴬIs 60:21; 61:3   15:14ᴬMatt 23:16, 24   ᴮLuke 6:39
15:15ᴬMatt 13:36   15:18ᴬMatt 12:34; Mark 7:20
15:19ᴬGal 5:19ff   15:21ᴬMatt 11:21   15:22ᴬMatt 4:24
15:24ᴬMatt 10:6   15:25ᴬMatt 8:2   15:28ᴬMatt 9:22
15:29ᴬMatt 15:29-31; Mark 7:31-37   15:30ᴬMatt 4:23
15:31ᴬMatt 9:8   15:32ᴬMatt 14:13-21

15:14¹Later mss add *of blind people*

hungry, for they might faint on the way." ³³The disciples *said to Him, "Where would we get so many loaves in *this* desolate place to satisfy such a large crowd?" ³⁴And Jesus *said to them, "How many loaves do you have?" And they said, "Seven, and a few small fish." ³⁵And He directed the people to sit down on the ground; ³⁶and He took the seven loaves and the fish; and after ᴬgiving thanks, He broke them and started giving them to the disciples, and the disciples *gave them* to the crowds. ³⁷And they all ate and were satisfied, and they picked up what was left over of the broken pieces, seven large ᴬbaskets full. ³⁸And those who ate were four thousand men, besides women and children.

³⁹And sending away the crowds, Jesus got into the boat and came to the region of ᴬMagadan.

PHARISEES AND SADDUCEES TEST JESUS

16 ᴬThe Pharisees and Sadducees came up, and putting Jesus to the test, they asked Him to show them a sign from heaven. ²But He replied to them, "ᴬWhen it is evening, you say, '*It will be* fair weather, for the sky is red.' ³And in the morning, '*There will be* a storm today, for the sky is red and threatening.' ᴬYou know how to discern the appearance of the sky, but are you unable *to discern* the signs of the times? ⁴ᴬAn evil and adulterous generation wants a sign; and *so* a sign will not be given to it, except the sign of Jonah." And He left them and went away.

⁵And the disciples came to the other side *of the sea*, but they had forgotten to bring *any* bread. ⁶And Jesus said to them, "Watch out and

ᴬbeware of the leaven of the Pharisees and Sadducees." ⁷They began to discuss *this* among themselves, saying, "*He said that* because we did not bring *any* bread." ⁸But Jesus, aware *of this*, said, "ᴬYou men of little faith, why are you discussing among yourselves *the fact* that you have no bread? ⁹Do you not yet understand nor remember ᴬthe five loaves of the five thousand, and how many baskets you picked up? ¹⁰Nor ᴬthe seven loaves of the four thousand, and how many large baskets you picked up? ¹¹How *is it that* you do not understand that I did not speak to you about bread? But beware of the leaven of the ᴬPharisees and Sadducees." ¹²Then they understood that He did not say to beware of the leaven of bread, but of the teaching of the ᴬPharisees and Sadducees.

PETER'S CONFESSION OF CHRIST

¹³ᴬNow when Jesus came into the region of Caesarea Philippi, He was asking His disciples, "Who do people say that the Son of Man is?" ¹⁴And they said, "Some *say* ᴬJohn the Baptist; and others, ᴮElijah; and *still* others, Jeremiah, or one of the *other* prophets." ¹⁵He *said to them, "But who do you yourselves say that I am?" ¹⁶Simon Peter answered, "You are the Christ, ᴬthe Son of ᴮthe living God." ¹⁷And Jesus said to him, "Blessed are you, Simon Barjona, because ᴬflesh and blood did not reveal *this* to you, but

15:36 ᴬMatt 14:19; 26:27 **15:37** ᴬMatt 16:10; Mark 8:8, 20 **15:39** ᴬMark 8:10 **16:1** ᴬ*Mark 8:11-21* **16:2** ᴬLuke 12:54f **16:3** ᴬLuke 12:56 **16:4** ᴬMatt 12:39; Luke 11:29 **16:6** ᴬMark 8:15; Luke 12:1 **16:8** ᴬMatt 6:30; 8:26 **16:9** ᴬMatt 14:17-21 **16:10** ᴬMatt 15:34-38 **16:11** ᴬMatt 3:7; 16:6, 12 **16:12** ᴬMatt 3:7; 5:20 **16:13** ᴬ*Mark 8:27-29; Luke 9:18-20* **16:14** ᴬMatt 14:2 ᴮMatt 17:10 **16:16** ᴬMatt 4:3 ᴮPs 42:2 **16:17** ᴬ1 Cor 15:50; Gal 1:16

My Father who is in heaven. ¹⁸And I also say to you that you are ^APeter, and upon this rock I will build My church; and the gates of ^BHades will not overpower it. ¹⁹I will give you the keys of the kingdom of heaven; and ^Awhatever you bind on earth shall have been bound in heaven, and whatever you loose on earth shall have been loosed in heaven." ^{20A}Then He gave the disciples strict orders that they were to tell no one that He was the Christ.

JESUS FORETELLS HIS DEATH

^{21A}From that time Jesus began to point out to His disciples that it was necessary for Him to go to Jerusalem and to suffer many things from the elders, chief priests, and scribes, and to be killed, and to be raised up on the third day. ²²And *yet* Peter took Him aside and began to rebuke Him, saying, "God forbid it, Lord! This shall never happen to You!" ²³But He turned and said to Peter, "Get behind Me, ^ASatan! You are a stumbling block to Me; for you are not setting your mind on God's purposes, but men's."

DISCIPLESHIP IS COSTLY

²⁴Then Jesus said to His disciples, "If anyone wants to come after Me, he must deny himself, ^Atake up his cross, and follow Me. ²⁵For ^Awhoever wants to save his life will lose it; but whoever loses his life for My sake will find it. ²⁶For what good will it do a person if he gains the whole world, but forfeits his soul? Or what will a person give in exchange for his soul? ²⁷For the Son of Man ^Ais going to come in the glory of His Father with His angels, and WILL THEN REPAY EVERY PERSON ACCORDING TO HIS DEEDS.

²⁸"Truly I say to you, there are some of those who are standing here who will not taste death until they see the Son of Man ^Acoming in His kingdom."

THE TRANSFIGURATION

17 ^ASix days later, Jesus *took with Him ^BPeter and James, and his brother John, and *led them up on a high mountain by themselves. ²And He was transfigured before them; and His face shone like the sun, and His garments became as white as light. ³And behold, Moses and Elijah appeared to them, talking with Him. ⁴Peter responded and said to Jesus, "Lord, it is good that we are here. If You want, ^AI will make three tabernacles here: one for You, one for Moses, and one for Elijah." ⁵While he was still speaking, a bright cloud overshadowed them, and behold, ^Aa voice from the cloud said, "This is My beloved Son, with whom I am well pleased; listen to Him!" ⁶When the disciples heard *this,* they fell face down to the ground and were terrified. ⁷And Jesus came to *them* and touched them and said, "Get up, and ^Ado not be afraid." ⁸And raising their eyes, they saw no one except Jesus Himself alone.

^{9A}When they were coming down from the mountain, Jesus commanded them, saying, "Tell the vision to no one until the Son of Man has ^Brisen from the dead." ¹⁰And His disciples asked Him, "Why then do the scribes say that

16:18^AMatt 4:18   ^BMatt 11:23   16:19^AMatt 18:18; John 20:23   16:20^AMatt 8:4; Mark 8:30
16:21^A*Mark 8:31-9:1; Luke 9:22-27*   16:23^AMatt 4:10
16:24^AMatt 10:38; Luke 14:27   16:25^AMatt 10:39
16:27^AMark 8:38; 1 Thess 4:16   16:28^AMatt 10:23; 24:3, 27, 37, 39   17:1^A*Mark 9:2-8*   ^BMatt 26:37
17:4^AMark 9:5; Luke 9:33   17:5^AMark 1:11; Luke 3:22
17:7^AMatt 14:27   17:9^A*Mark 9:9-13*   ^BMatt 16:21

^Elijah must come first?" ¹¹And He answered and said, "Elijah is coming and will restore all things; ¹²but I say to you that Elijah already came, and they did not recognize him, but did to him whatever they wanted. So also ^the Son of Man is going to suffer at their hands." ¹³Then the disciples understood that He had spoken to them about John the Baptist.

THE DEMON-POSSESSED BOY

¹⁴^When they came to the crowd, a man came up to Jesus, falling on his knees before Him and saying, ¹⁵"Lord, have mercy on my son, because he ^has seizures and suffers terribly; for he often falls into the fire and often into the water. ¹⁶And I brought him to Your disciples, and they could not cure him." ¹⁷And Jesus answered and said, "You unbelieving and perverse generation, how long shall I be with you? How long shall I put up with you? Bring him here to Me." ¹⁸And Jesus rebuked him, and the demon came out of him, and the boy was healed at once.

¹⁹Then the disciples came to Jesus privately and said, "Why could we not cast it out?" ²⁰And He *said to them, "Because of your meager faith; for truly I say to you, ^if you have faith the size of a mustard seed, you will say to this mountain, 'Move from here to there,' and it will move; and nothing will be impossible for you.¹"

²²^And while they were gathering together in Galilee, Jesus said to them, "The Son of Man is going to be handed over to men; ²³and ^they will kill Him, and He will be raised on the third day." And they were deeply grieved.

THE TEMPLE TAX

²⁴Now when they came to Capernaum, those who collected ^the ¹two-drachma *tax* came to Peter and said, "Does your teacher not pay ^the two-drachma *tax*?" ²⁵He *said, "Yes." And when he came into the house, Jesus spoke to him first, saying, "What do you think, Simon? From whom do the kings of the earth collect ^customs or ¹,ᴮpoll-tax, from their sons or from strangers?" ²⁶When *Peter* said, "From strangers," Jesus said to him, "Then the sons are exempt. ²⁷However, so that we do not ^offend them, go to the sea and throw in a hook, and take the first fish that comes up; and when you open its mouth, you will find a ¹stater. Take that and give it to them for you and Me."

RANK IN THE KINGDOM

18 ^At that time the disciples came to Jesus and said, "Who then is greatest in the kingdom of heaven?" ²And He called a child to Himself and set him among them, ³and said, "Truly I say to you, unless you change and ^become like children, you will not enter the kingdom of heaven. ⁴So whoever will humble himself like this child, he is the greatest in the kingdom of heaven. ⁵And

17:10 ¹ Mal 4:5; Matt 11:14   17:12 ^ Matt 8:20; 17:9, 22
17:14 ^ *Mark 9:14-28; Luke 9:37-42*   17:15 ^ Matt 4:24
17:20 ^ Matt 21:21f; Mark 11:23f   17:22 ^ *Mark 9:30-32; Luke 9:44, 45*   17:23 ^ Matt 16:21; 17:9
17:24 ^ Ex 30:13; 38:26   17:25 ^ Rom 13:7
ᴮ Matt 22:17, 19   17:27 ^ Matt 5:29, 30; 18:6, 8, 9
18:1 ^ *Mark 9:33-37; Luke 9:46-48*   18:3 ^ Matt 19:14; Mark 10:15

17:20 ¹ Late mss add (traditionally v 21): *But this kind does not go out except by prayer and fasting*
17:24 ¹ Equivalent to about two denarii or two days' wages for a laborer, paid as a temple tax
17:25 ¹ I.e., a tax on each person in the census
17:27 ¹ A silver four-drachma Greek coin

whoever receives one such child in My name, receives Me; [6]but ^whoever causes one of these little ones who believe in Me to 'sin, it is better for him that a heavy millstone be hung around his neck, and that he be drowned in the depths of the sea.

STUMBLING BLOCKS

[7]"Woe to the world because of *its* stumbling blocks! For ^it is inevitable that stumbling blocks come; but woe to the person through whom the stumbling block comes! [8]"And ^if your hand or your foot is causing you to sin, cut it off and throw it away from you; it is better for you to enter life maimed or without a foot, than to have two hands or two feet and be thrown into the eternal fire. [9]And ^if your eye is causing you to sin, tear it out and throw it away from you. It is better for you to enter life with one eye, than to have two eyes and be thrown into the 'fiery hell.

[10]"See that you do not look down on one of these little ones; for I say to you that ^their angels in heaven continually see the face of My Father who is in heaven.'

NINETY-NINE PLUS ONE

[12]"What do you think? ^If any man has a hundred sheep, and one of them goes astray, will he not leave the ninety-nine on the mountains, and go and search for the one that is lost? [13]And if it turns out that he finds it, truly I say to you, he rejoices over it more than over the ninety-nine that have not gone astray. [14]So it is not *the* will of your Father who is in heaven for one of these little ones to perish.

DISCIPLINE AND PRAYER

[15]"Now ^if your brother sins', go and show him his fault in private; if he listens to you, you have gained your brother. [16]But if he does not listen *to you*, take one or two more with you, so that ^ON THE TESTIMONY OF TWO OR THREE WITNESSES EVERY MATTER MAY BE CONFIRMED. [17]And if he refuses to listen to them, tell it to the church; and if he refuses to listen even to the church, ^he is to be to you as a Gentile and a tax collector. [18]Truly I say to you, ^whatever you bind on earth shall have been bound in heaven; and whatever you loose on earth shall have been loosed in heaven.

[19]"Again I say to you, that if two of you agree on earth about anything that they may ask, ^it shall be done for them by My Father who is in heaven. [20]For where two or three have gathered together in My name, ^I am there in their midst."

FORGIVENESS

[21]Then Peter came up and said to Him, "Lord, ^how many times shall my brother sin against me and I *still* forgive him? Up to [B]seven times?" [22]Jesus *said to him, "I do not say to you, up to seven times, but up to ^seventy-seven times.

[23]"For this reason ^the kingdom of heaven is like a king who

18:6 ^Mark 9:42; Luke 17:2   18:7 ^Luke 17:1; 1 Cor 11:19
18:8 ^Matt 5:30; Mark 9:43   18:9 ^Matt 5:29;
Mark 9:47   18:10 ^Luke 1:19; Acts 12:15
18:12 ^Luke 15:4-7   18:15 ^Lev 19:17; Luke 17:3
18:16 ^Deut 19:15; John 8:17   18:17 ^2 Thess 3:6, 14f
18:18 ^Matt 16:19; John 20:23   18:19 ^Matt 7:7
18:20 ^Matt 28:20   18:21 ^Matt 18:15   [B]Luke 17:4
18:22 ^Gen 4:24   18:23 ^Matt 13:24

18:6 'Or *stumble*, and so throughout the ch   18:9 'Lit
Gehenna of fire   18:10 'Late mss add (traditionally
v 11): *For the Son of Man has come to save that which
was lost*   18:15 'Late mss add *against you*

wanted to ᴮsettle accounts with his slaves. ²⁴And when he had begun to settle *them,* one who owed him ¹ten thousand talents was brought to him. ²⁵But since he ᴬdid not have *the means* to repay, his master commanded that he ᴮbe sold, along with his wife and children and all that he had, and repayment be made. ²⁶So the slave fell *to the ground* and ᴬprostrated himself before him, saying, 'Have patience with me and I will repay you everything.' ²⁷And the master of that slave felt compassion, and he released him and ᴬforgave him the debt. ²⁸But that slave went out and found one of his fellow slaves who owed him a hundred ¹denarii; and he seized him and *began* to choke *him,* saying, 'Pay back what you owe!' ²⁹So his fellow slave fell *to the ground* and *began* to plead with him, saying, 'Have patience with me and I will repay you.' ³⁰But he was unwilling, and went and threw him in prison until he would pay back what was owed. ³¹So when his fellow slaves saw what had happened, they were deeply grieved and came and reported to their master all that had happened. ³²Then summoning him, his master *said to him, 'You wicked slave, I forgave you all that debt because you pleaded with me. ³³ᴬShould you not also have had mercy on your fellow slave, in the same way that I had mercy on you?' ³⁴And his master, moved with anger, handed him over to the torturers until he would repay all that was owed him. ³⁵ᴬMy heavenly Father will also do the same to you, if each of you does not forgive his brother from your heart."

CONCERNING DIVORCE

19 When Jesus had finished these words, He left Galilee and ᴬcame into the region of Judea beyond the Jordan; ²and large crowds followed Him, and ᴬHe healed them there.

³*Some* Pharisees came to Jesus, testing Him and asking, "ᴬIs it lawful *for a man* to divorce his wife for any reason *at all?*" ⁴And He answered and said, "Have you not read ᴬthat He who created *them* from the beginning MADE THEM MALE AND FEMALE, ⁵and said, 'ᴬFOR THIS REASON A MAN SHALL LEAVE HIS FATHER AND HIS MOTHER AND BE JOINED TO HIS WIFE, AND THE TWO SHALL BECOME ONE FLESH'? ⁶So they are no longer two, but one flesh. Therefore, what God has joined together, no person is to separate." ⁷They *said to Him, "ᴬWhy, then, did Moses command to GIVE HER A CERTIFICATE OF DIVORCE AND SEND HER AWAY?" ⁸He *said to them, "Because of your hardness of heart Moses permitted you to divorce your wives; but from the beginning it has not been this way. ⁹And I say to you, ᴬwhoever divorces his wife, except for sexual immorality, and marries another woman ¹commits adultery²."

¹⁰The disciples *said to Him, "If the relationship of the man with his wife is like this, it is better not to marry." ¹¹But He said to them,

ᴮMatt 25:19   18:25ᴬLuke 7:42   ᴮEx 21:2
18:26ᴬMatt 8:2   18:27ᴬLuke 7:42   18:33ᴬMatt 6:12;
Eph 4:32   18:35ᴬMatt 6:14   19:1ᴬ*Mark 10:1-12*
19:2ᴬMatt 4:23   19:3ᴬMatt 5:31   19:4ᴬGen 1:27; 5:2
19:5ᴬGen 2:24; Eph 5:31   19:7ᴬDeut 24:1-4; Matt 5:31
19:9ᴬMatt 5:32

18:24¹By one estimate, a debt of 60 million working days for a laborer   18:28¹The denarius was a day's wages for a laborer   19:9¹One early ms *makes her commit adultery*   ²One early ms adds *and he who marries a divorced woman commits adultery*

"^Not all men *can* accept this statement, but *only* those to whom it has been given. ¹²For there are eunuchs who were born that way from their mother's womb; and there are eunuchs who were made eunuchs by people; and there are *also* eunuchs who made themselves eunuchs for the sake of the kingdom of heaven. The one who is able to accept *this,* let him accept *it.*"

JESUS BLESSES LITTLE CHILDREN

¹³^Then *some* children were brought to Him so that He would lay His hands on them and pray; and the disciples rebuked them. ¹⁴But Jesus said, "^Leave the children alone, and do not forbid them to come to Me; for the kingdom of heaven belongs to such as these." ¹⁵After laying His hands on them, He departed from there.

THE RICH YOUNG RULER

¹⁶^And someone came to Him and said, "Teacher, what good thing shall I do so that I may obtain eternal life?" ¹⁷And He said to him, "Why are you asking Me about what is good? There is *only* One who is good; but ^if you want to enter life, keep the commandments." ¹⁸*Then* he *said to Him, "Which ones?" And Jesus said, "^YOU SHALL NOT COMMIT MURDER; YOU SHALL NOT COMMIT ADULTERY; YOU SHALL NOT STEAL; YOU SHALL NOT GIVE FALSE TESTIMONY; ¹⁹^HONOR YOUR FATHER AND MOTHER; and ᴮYOU SHALL LOVE YOUR NEIGHBOR AS YOURSELF." ²⁰The young man *said to Him, "All these I have kept; what am I still lacking?" ²¹Jesus said to him, "If you want to be complete, go *and* ^sell your possessions and give to *the* poor, and you will have treasure in heaven;

and come, follow Me." ²²But when the young man heard this statement, he went away grieving; for he was one who owned much property.

²³And Jesus said to His disciples, "Truly I say to you, ^it will be hard for a rich person to enter the kingdom of heaven. ²⁴And again I say to you, ^it is easier for a camel to go through the eye of a needle, than for a rich person to enter the kingdom of God." ²⁵When the disciples heard *this,* they were very astonished and said, "Then who can be saved?" ²⁶And looking at *them,* Jesus said to them, "^With people this is impossible, but with God all things are possible."

THE DISCIPLES' REWARD

²⁷Then Peter responded and said to Him, "Behold, we have left everything and followed You; what then will there be for us?" ²⁸And Jesus said to them, "Truly I say to you, that you who have followed Me, in the ¹regeneration when the Son of Man will sit on His glorious throne, ^you also shall sit upon twelve thrones, judging the twelve tribes of Israel. ²⁹And ^everyone who has left houses or brothers or sisters or father or mother ¹or children or farms on account of My name, will receive many times as much, and will inherit eternal life. ³⁰^But many *who are* first will be last; and *the* last, first.

19:11^1 Cor 7:7ff   **19:13**^*Mark 10:13-16; Luke 18:15-17*
19:14^Matt 18:3; Mark 10:15   **19:16**^Luke 10:25-28
19:17^Lev 18:5; Neh 9:29   **19:18**^Ex 20:13-16;
Deut 5:17-20   **19:19**^Ex 20:12   ᴮLev 19:18
19:21^Luke 12:33; 16:9   **19:23**^Matt 13:22;
Mark 10:23f   **19:24**^Mark 10:25; Luke 18:25
19:26^Gen 18:14; Job 42:2   **19:28**^Luke 22:30;
Rev 3:21   **19:29**^Matt 6:33; Mark 10:29f
19:30^Matt 20:16; Mark 10:31

19:28¹Or *renewal*; i.e., the new world   **19:29**¹One
early ms adds *or wife*

LABORERS IN THE VINEYARD

20 "For the kingdom of heaven is like a landowner who went out early in the morning to hire laborers for his ^vineyard. ²When he had agreed with the laborers for a ¹denarius for the day, he sent them into his vineyard. ³And he went out about the ¹third hour and saw others standing idle in the marketplace; ⁴and to those he said, 'You go into the vineyard also, and whatever is right, I will give you.' And *so* they went. ⁵Again he went out about the ¹sixth and the ninth hour, and did the same thing. ⁶And about the ¹eleventh *hour* he went out and found others standing *around;* and he *said to them, 'Why have you been standing here idle all day long?' ⁷They *said to him, 'Because no one hired us.' He *said to them, 'You go into the vineyard too.'

⁸"Now when ^evening came, the owner of the vineyard *said to his foreman, 'Call the laborers and pay them their wages, starting with the last *group* to the first.' ⁹When those *hired* about the eleventh hour came, each one received a ¹denarius. ¹⁰And *so* when those *hired* first came, they thought that they would receive more; but each of them also received a denarius. ¹¹When they received it, they grumbled at the landowner, ¹²saying, 'These who *were hired* last worked *only* one hour, and you have made them equal to us who have borne the burden of the day's *work* and the ^scorching heat.' ¹³But he answered and said to one of them, '^Friend, I am doing you no wrong; did you not agree with me for a denarius? ¹⁴Take what is yours and go; but I want to give to this last person the same as to you. ¹⁵Is it not lawful for

me to do what I want with what is my own? Or is your ^eye envious because I am generous?' ¹⁶So ^the last shall be first, and the first, last."

DEATH, RESURRECTION FORETOLD

¹⁷^As Jesus was about to go up to Jerusalem, He took the twelve *disciples* aside by themselves, and on the road He said to them, ¹⁸"Behold, we are going up to Jerusalem, and the Son of Man ^will be handed over to the chief priests and scribes, and they will condemn Him to death, ¹⁹and they will hand Him over to the Gentiles to mock and flog and crucify, and on ^the third day He will be raised up."

REQUEST FOR PREFERRED TREATMENT

²⁰^Then the mother of the sons of Zebedee came to Jesus with her sons, bowing down and making a request of Him. ²¹And He said to her, "What do you desire?" She *said to Him, "Say that in Your kingdom these two sons of mine ^shall sit, one at Your right, and one at Your left." ²²But Jesus replied, "You do not know what you are asking. Are you able ^to drink the cup that I am about to drink?" They *said to Him, "We are able." ²³He *said to them, "^My cup you shall drink; but to sit at My right and at *My* left is not Mine to give, but *it is for those* for whom it has been ^Bprepared by My Father."

20:1^Matt 21:28, 33 **20:8**^Lev 19:13; Deut 24:15
20:12^Jon 4:8; Luke 12:55 **20:13**^Matt 22:12; 26:50
20:15^Deut 15:9; Matt 6:23 **20:16**^Matt 19:30;
Mark 10:31 **20:17**^*Mark 10:32-34; Luke 18:31-33*
20:18^Matt 16:21 **20:19**^Matt 16:21; 17:23
20:20^*Mark 10:35-45* **20:21**^Matt 19:28
20:22^Is 51:17, 22; Jer 49:12 **20:23**^Acts 12:2
^BMatt 25:34

20:2¹The denarius was a day's wages for a laborer
20:3¹I.e., 9 a.m. **20:5**¹I.e., noon and 3 p.m.
20:6¹I.e., 5 p.m. **20:9**¹The denarius was a day's wages for a laborer

24 And after hearing *this,* the *other* ten *disciples* became indignant with the two brothers. 25 ^But Jesus called them to Himself and said, "You know that the rulers of the Gentiles domineer over them, and those in high position exercise authority over them. 26 It is not this way among you, ^but whoever wants to become prominent among you shall be your servant, 27 and whoever desires to be first among you shall be your slave; 28 just as the Son of Man ^did not come to be served, but to serve, and to give His life as a ransom for many."

SIGHT FOR THOSE WHO ARE BLIND

29 ^As they were leaving Jericho, a large crowd followed Him. 30 And two people who were blind, sitting by the road, hearing that Jesus was passing by, cried out, "Lord, ^have mercy on us, Son of David!" 31 But the crowd sternly warned them to be quiet; yet they cried out all the more, "Lord, ^Son of David, have mercy on us!" 32 And Jesus stopped and called them, and said, "What do you want Me to do for you?" 33 They *said to Him, "Lord, *we want* our eyes to be opened." 34 Moved with compassion, Jesus touched their eyes; and immediately they regained their sight and followed Him.

THE TRIUMPHAL ENTRY

21 ^When they had approached Jerusalem and had come to Bethphage, at the Mount of Olives, Jesus then sent two disciples, 2 saying to them, "Go into the village opposite you, and immediately you will find a donkey tied *there* and a colt with it. Untie them and bring them to Me. 3 And if anyone says anything to you, you shall say, 'The Lord needs them,' and he will send them on immediately." 4 Now ^this took place so that what was spoken through the prophet would be fulfilled:

5 "^Say to the daughter of Zion,
    'Behold your King is coming
      to you,
    Humble, and mounted on a
      donkey,
    Even on a colt, the foal of a
      donkey.'"

6 The disciples went and did just as Jesus had instructed them, 7 and brought the donkey and the colt, and laid their cloaks on them; and He sat on the cloaks. 8 Most of the crowd ^spread their cloaks on the road, and others were cutting branches from the trees and spreading them on the road. 9 Now the crowds going ahead of Him, and those who followed, were shouting,

    "Hosanna to the Son of David;
    ^Blessed is the One who
      comes in the name of the
      Lord;
    Hosanna ^in the highest!"

10 When He had entered Jerusalem, all the city was stirred, saying, "Who is this?" 11 And the crowds were saying, "This is ^Jesus the prophet, from Nazareth in Galilee."

CLEANSING THE TEMPLE

12 ^And Jesus entered the temple *area* and drove out all those who were selling and buying on the temple *grounds,* and He overturned the

20:25 ^Matt 20:25-28; Luke 22:25-27
20:26 ^Matt 23:11; 20:28 ^Matt 26:28;
John 13:13ff 20:29 ^Matt 9:27-31 20:30 ^Matt 9:27
20:31 ^Matt 9:27 21:1 ^*Mark 11:1-10; Luke 19:29-38*
21:4 ^*Mark 11:7-10; Luke 19:35-38* 21:5 ^Is 62:11;
Zech 9:9 21:8 ^2 Kin 9:13 21:9 ^Ps 118:26
^Luke 2:14 21:11 ^Matt 21:26; Mark 6:15
21:12 ^*Mark 11:15-18; Luke 19:45-47;*

tables of the money changers and the seats of those who were selling doves. ¹³And He *said to them, "It is written: '^AMY HOUSE WILL BE CALLED A HOUSE OF PRAYER'; but you are making it a ^BDEN OF ROBBERS."

¹⁴And *those who were* blind and *those who* limped came to Him in the temple *area,* and ^He healed them. ¹⁵But when the chief priests and the scribes saw the wonderful things that He had done, and the children who were shouting in the temple *area,* "Hosanna to the ^Son of David," they became indignant, ¹⁶and they said to Him, "Do You hear what these *children* are saying?" And Jesus *said to them, "Yes. Have you never read, '^FROM THE MOUTHS OF INFANTS AND NURSING BABIES YOU HAVE PREPARED PRAISE FOR YOURSELF'?" ¹⁷And He left them and went out of the city to ^Bethany, and spent the night there.

THE BARREN FIG TREE

¹⁸^Now in the early morning, when He was returning to the city, He became hungry. ¹⁹And seeing a lone ^fig tree by the road, He came to it and found nothing on it except leaves alone; and He *said to it, "No longer shall there ever be *any* fruit from you." And at once the fig tree withered.

²⁰Seeing *this,* the disciples were amazed and asked, "How did the fig tree wither *all* at once?" ²¹And Jesus answered and said to them, "Truly I say to you, ^if you have faith and do not doubt, you will not only do what *was done* to the fig tree, but even if you say to this mountain, 'Be taken up and cast into the sea,' it will happen. ²²And ^whatever you ask in prayer, believing, you will receive it all."

AUTHORITY CHALLENGED

²³^When He entered the temple *area,* the chief priests and the elders of the people came to Him while He was teaching, and said, "By what authority are You doing these things, and who gave You this authority?" ²⁴But Jesus responded and said to them, "I will also ask you one question, which, if you tell Me, I will also tell you by what authority I do these things. ²⁵The baptism of John was from what *source:* from heaven or from men?" And they *began* considering *the implications* among themselves, saying, "If we say, 'From heaven,' He will say to us, 'Then why did you not believe him?' ²⁶But if we say, 'From men,' we fear the people; for they all regard John as ^a prophet." ²⁷And answering Jesus, they said, "We do not know." He also said to them, "Neither am I telling you by what authority I do these things.

PARABLE OF TWO SONS

²⁸"But what do you think? A man had two sons, and he came to the first and said, 'Son, go work today in the ^vineyard.' ²⁹But he replied, 'I do not want to.' Yet afterward he regretted it and went. ³⁰And *the man* came to his second *son* and said the same thing; and he replied, 'I *will,* sir'; and *yet* he did not go. ³¹Which of the two did the will of his father?" They *said, "The first." Jesus *said to them, "Truly I say to you that

21:13^Is 56:7   ^BJer 7:11   **21:14**^Matt 4:23   **21:15**^Matt 9:27   **21:16**^Ps 8:2; Matt 11:25   **21:17**^Matt 26:6; Mark 11:1, 11, 12   **21:18**^*Mark 11:12-14, 20-24*   **21:19**^Luke 13:6-9   **21:21**^Matt 17:20; Mark 11:23   **21:22**^Matt 7:7   **21:23**^*Mark 11:27-33; Luke 20:1-8*   **21:26**^Matt 11:9; Mark 6:20   **21:28**^Matt 20:1; 21:33   **21:31**^Luke 7:29, 37-50

^Athe tax collectors and prostitutes will get into the kingdom of God before you. ³²For John came to you in the way of righteousness and you did not believe him; but ^Athe tax collectors and prostitutes did believe him; and you, seeing *this,* did not even have second thoughts afterward so as to believe him.

PARABLE OF THE LANDOWNER

³³"Listen to another parable. ^AThere was a landowner who PLANTED A VINEYARD AND PUT A FENCE AROUND IT, AND DUG A WINE PRESS IN IT, AND BUILT A TOWER, and he leased it to vine-growers and went on a journey. ³⁴And when the harvest time approached, he ^Asent his slaves to the vine-growers to receive his fruit. ³⁵And the vine-growers took his slaves and beat one, killed another, and stoned another. ³⁶Again, he ^Asent other slaves, more than the first; and they did the same things to them. ³⁷But afterward he sent his son to them, saying, 'They will respect my son.' ³⁸But when the vine-growers saw the son, they said among themselves, 'This is the heir; come, let's kill him and take possession of his inheritance!' ³⁹And they took him and threw him out of the vineyard, and killed him. ⁴⁰Therefore, when the owner of the vineyard comes, what will he do to those vine-growers?" ⁴¹They *said to Him, "He will bring those wretches to a wretched end and ^Alease the vineyard to other vine-growers, who will pay him the fruit in the *proper* seasons."

⁴²Jesus *said to them, "Did you never read in the Scriptures,

'^AA STONE WHICH THE BUILDERS REJECTED,
THIS HAS BECOME THE CHIEF CORNERSTONE;
THIS CAME ABOUT FROM THE LORD,
AND IT IS MARVELOUS IN OUR EYES'?

⁴³Therefore I say to you, the kingdom of God will be taken away from you and given to a people producing its fruit. ⁴⁴And ^Athe one who falls on this stone will be broken to pieces; and on whomever it falls, it will crush him."

⁴⁵When the chief priests and the Pharisees heard His parables, they understood that He was speaking about them. ⁴⁶And *although* they sought to arrest Him, they ^Afeared the crowds, since they considered Him to be a ^Bprophet.

PARABLE OF THE MARRIAGE FEAST

22 Jesus spoke to them again in parables, saying, ²"^AThe kingdom of heaven is like a king who held a wedding feast for his son. ³And he ^Asent his slaves to call those who had been invited to the wedding feast, and they were unwilling to come. ⁴Again he ^Asent other slaves, saying, 'Tell those who have been invited, "Behold, I have prepared my dinner; my oxen and my fattened cattle are *all* butchered and everything is ready. Come to the wedding feast!"' ⁵But they paid no attention and went their *separate* ways, one to his own farm, another to his business, ⁶and the rest seized his slaves and

21:32 ^ALuke 3:12; 7:29f   21:33 ^AMark 12:1-12; Luke 20:9-19   21:34 ^AMatt 22:3   21:36 ^AMatt 22:4
21:41 ^AMatt 8:11f; Acts 13:46   21:42 ^APs 118:22f; Acts 4:11   21:44 ^AIs 8:14, 15   21:46 ^AMatt 21:26
^BMatt 21:11   22:2 ^AMatt 13:24; 22:2-14
22:3 ^AMatt 21:34   22:4 ^AMatt 21:36

treated them abusively, and *then* killed them. **7** Now the king was angry, and he sent his armies and destroyed those murderers and set their city on fire. **8** Then he *said to his slaves, 'The wedding feast is ready, but those who were invited were not worthy. **9** So go to ^the main roads, and invite whomever you find *there* to the wedding feast.' **10** Those slaves went out into the streets and gathered together all whom they found, both bad and good; and the wedding hall was filled with dinner guests.

11 "But when the king came in to look over the dinner guests, he saw ^a man there who was not dressed in wedding clothes, **12** and he *said to him, '^Friend, how did you get in here without wedding clothes?' And the man was speechless. **13** Then the king said to the servants, 'Tie his hands and feet, and throw him into ^the outer darkness; there will be weeping and gnashing of teeth in that place.' **14** For many are ^called, but few *are* chosen."

POLL-TAX TO CAESAR

15 ^Then the Pharisees went and plotted together how they might trap Him in what He said. **16** And they *sent their disciples to Him, along with the ^Herodians, saying, "Teacher, we know that You are truthful and teach the way of God in truth, and do not care what anyone thinks; for You are not partial to anyone. **17** Tell us then, what do You think? Is it permissible to pay a ^1,^poll-tax to ^BCaesar, or not?" **18** But Jesus perceived their malice, and said, "Why are you testing Me, you hypocrites? **19** Show Me the ^coin *used* for the poll-tax." And they brought Him a denarius. **20** And He

*said to them, "Whose image and inscription is this?" **21** They *said to Him, "Caesar's." Then He *said to them, "^AThen pay to Caesar the things that are Caesar's; and to God the things that are God's." **22** And hearing *this,* they were amazed; and ^they left Him and went away.

JESUS ANSWERS THE SADDUCEES

23 ^AOn that day *some* Sadducees (who say there is no resurrection) came to Jesus and questioned Him, **24** saying, "Teacher, Moses said, '^AIf a man dies having no children, his brother as next of kin shall marry his wife, and raise up children for his brother.' **25** Now there were seven brothers among us; and the first married and died, and having no children, he left his wife to his brother. **26** *It was* the same also *with* the second *brother,* and the third, down to the seventh. **27** Last of all, the woman died. **28** In the resurrection, therefore, whose wife of the seven will she be? For they all had her *in marriage.*"

29 But Jesus answered and said to them, "You are mistaken, ^since you do not understand the Scriptures nor the power of God. **30** For in the resurrection they neither ^marry nor are given in marriage, but are like angels in heaven. **31** But regarding the resurrection of the dead, have you not read what was spoken to you by God: **32** '^AI AM THE GOD OF ABRAHAM, THE GOD OF ISAAC, AND THE GOD OF JACOB'? He is not the

---

22:9 ^Ezek 21:21; Obad 14   22:11 ^2 Kin 10:22;
Zech 3:3, 4   22:12 ^Matt 20:13; 26:50
22:13 ^Matt 8:12; 25:30   22:14 ^Matt 24:22; 2 Pet 1:10
22:15 ^Mark 12:13-17; Luke 20:20-26   22:16 ^Mark 3:6;
8:15   22:17 ^Matt 17:25   ^BLuke 3:1   22:19 ^Matt 17:25
22:21 ^Mark 12:17; Luke 20:25   22:22 ^Mark 12:12
22:23 ^Mark 12:18-27; Luke 20:27-40   22:24 ^Deut 25:5
22:29 ^John 20:9   22:30 ^Matt 24:38; Luke 17:27
22:32 ^Ex 3:6

22:17 ^1 I.e., a tax on each person in the census

God of the dead, but of the living." ³³When the crowds heard *this,* ᴬthey were astonished at His teaching.

³⁴ᴬBut when the Pharisees heard that Jesus had silenced the Sadducees, they gathered together. ³⁵And one of them, ¹˒ᴬa lawyer, asked Him a question, testing Him: ³⁶"Teacher, which is the great commandment in the Law?" ³⁷And He said to him, "'ᴬYOU SHALL LOVE THE LORD YOUR GOD WITH ALL YOUR HEART, AND WITH ALL YOUR SOUL, AND WITH ALL YOUR MIND.' ³⁸This is the great and foremost commandment. ³⁹The second is like it, 'ᴬYOU SHALL LOVE YOUR NEIGHBOR AS YOURSELF.' ⁴⁰ᴬUpon these two commandments hang the whole Law and the Prophets."

⁴¹ᴬNow while the Pharisees were gathered together, Jesus asked them a question: ⁴²"What do you think about the Christ? Whose son is He?" They *said to Him, "ᴬ*The son* of David." ⁴³He *said to them, "Then how does David ᴬin the Spirit call Him 'Lord,' saying,

⁴⁴ 'ᴬTHE LORD SAID TO MY LORD,
    "SIT AT MY RIGHT HAND,
    UNTIL I PUT YOUR ENEMIES
        UNDER YOUR FEET"'?

⁴⁵Therefore, if David calls Him 'Lord,' how is He his son?" ⁴⁶ᴬNo one was able to offer Him a word in answer, nor did anyone dare from that day *on* to ask Him any more questions.

HYPOCRISY EXPOSED

23 ᴬThen Jesus spoke to the crowds and to His disciples, ²saying: "ᴬThe scribes and the Pharisees have seated themselves in the chair of Moses. ³Therefore, whatever they tell you, do and comply with it all, but do not do as they do; for they say *things* and do not do *them.* ⁴And ᴬthey tie up heavy burdens

and lay them on people's shoulders, but they themselves are unwilling to move them with *so much as* their finger. ⁵And they do all their deeds ᴬto be noticed by *other* people; for they ᴮbroaden their ¹phylacteries and lengthen the tassels *of their garments.* ⁶And they ᴬlove the place of honor at banquets, and the seats of honor in the synagogues, ⁷and personal greetings in the marketplaces, and being called ᴬRabbi by the people. ⁸But as for you, do not be called ᴬRabbi; for *only* One is your Teacher, and you are all brothers *and sisters.* ⁹And do not call *anyone* on earth your father; for *only* ᴬOne is your Father, He who is in heaven. ¹⁰And do not be called leaders; for *only* One is your Leader, *that is,* Christ. ¹¹ᴬBut the greatest of you shall be your servant. ¹²ᴬWhoever exalts himself shall be humbled, and whoever humbles himself shall be exalted.

SEVEN WOES

¹³"But woe to you, scribes and Pharisees, hypocrites, ᴬbecause you shut the kingdom of heaven in front of people; for you do not enter *it* yourselves, nor do you allow those who are entering to go in.¹

22:33 ᴬMatt 7:28   22:34 ᴬLuke 10:25-37
22:35 ᴬLuke 7:30; 10:25   22:37 ᴬDeut 6:5
22:39 ᴬLev 19:18; Matt 19:19   22:40 ᴬMatt 7:12
22:41 ᴬ*Mark 12:35-37; Luke 20:41-44*   22:42 ᴬMatt 9:27
22:43 ᴬ2 Sam 23:2; Rev 1:10   22:44 ᴬPs 110:1;
Matt 26:64   22:46 ᴬMark 12:34; Luke 14:6
23:1 ᴬ*Mark 12:38, 39; Luke 20:45, 46*   23:2 ᴬDeut 33:3f;
Ezra 7:6, 25   23:4 ᴬLuke 11:46; Acts 15:10
23:5 ᴬMatt 6:1, 5, 16   ᴮEx 13:9   23:6 ᴬLuke 11:43; 14:7
23:7 ᴬMatt 23:8; 26:25, 49   23:8 ᴬMatt 23:7; 26:25, 49
23:9 ᴬMatt 6:9; 7:11   23:11 ᴬMatt 20:26
23:12 ᴬLuke 14:11; 18:14   23:13 ᴬLuke 11:52

22:35 ¹I.e., an expert in the Mosaic Law   23:5 ¹I.e., small pouches containing Scripture texts, worn on the left forearm and forehead for religious purposes
23:13 ¹Late mss add (traditionally v 14): *Woe to you, scribes and Pharisees, hypocrites, because you devour widows' houses while for appearances' sake you make long prayers; therefore you will receive greater condemnation* (as v 14); cf. Mark 12:40; Luke 20:47

15 "Woe to you, scribes and Pharisees, hypocrites, because you travel around on sea and land to make one ^proselyte; and when he becomes *one*, you make him twice as much a son of ¹hell as yourselves.

16 "Woe to you, ^blind guides, who say, 'Whoever swears by the temple, *that* is nothing; but whoever swears by the gold of the temple is obligated.' **17** You fools and blind men! ^Which is more important, the gold or the temple that sanctified the gold? **18** And *you say*, 'Whoever swears by the altar, *that* is nothing; but whoever swears by the offering that is on it is obligated.' **19** You blind men, ^which is more important, the offering or the altar that sanctifies the offering? **20** Therefore, the one who swears by the altar, swears *both* by the altar and by everything on it. **21** And the one who swears by the temple, swears *both* by the temple and by Him who ^dwells in it. **22** And the one who swears by heaven, ^swears *both* by the throne of God and by Him who sits upon it.

23 "^Woe to you, scribes and Pharisees, hypocrites! For you tithe mint and dill and cumin, and have neglected the weightier provisions of the Law: justice and mercy and faithfulness; but these *are the things* you should have done without neglecting the others. **24** You ^blind guides, who strain out a gnat and swallow a camel!

25 "Woe to you, scribes and Pharisees, hypocrites! For ^you clean the outside of the cup and of the dish, but inside they are full of robbery and self-indulgence. **26** You blind Pharisee, first ^clean the inside of the cup and of the dish, so that the outside of it may also become clean.

27 "^Woe to you, scribes and Pharisees, hypocrites! For you are like whitewashed tombs which on the outside appear beautiful, but inside they are full of dead men's bones and all uncleanness. **28** So you too, outwardly appear righteous to people, but inwardly you are full of hypocrisy and lawlessness.

29 "^Woe to you, scribes and Pharisees, hypocrites! For you build the tombs for the prophets and decorate the monuments of the righteous, **30** and you say, 'If we had been *living* in the days of our fathers, we would not have been partners with them in *shedding* the blood of the prophets.' **31** So you testify against yourselves, that you ^are sons of those who murdered the prophets. **32** Fill up, then, the measure *of the guilt* of your fathers. **33** You snakes, ^you offspring of vipers, how will you escape the sentence of hell?

34 "^Therefore, behold, I am sending you prophets and wise men and scribes; some of them you will kill and crucify, and some of them you will flog in your synagogues, and persecute from city to city, **35** so that upon you will fall *the guilt of* all the righteous blood shed on earth, from the blood of righteous Abel to the blood of Zechariah, the ^son of Berechiah, whom ᴮyou murdered between the temple and the altar. **36** Truly I say to you, all these things will come upon ^this generation.

23:15 ^Acts 2:10; 6:5   **23:16** ^Matt 15:14; 23:24
23:17 ^Ex 30:29   **23:19** ^Ex 29:37   **23:21** ^1 Kin 8:13;
Ps 26:8   **23:22** ^Is 66:1; Matt 5:34   **23:23** ^Matt 23:13;
Luke 11:42   **23:24** ^Matt 23:16   **23:25** ^Mark 7:4;
Luke 11:39f   **23:26** ^Mark 7:4; Luke 11:39f
23:27 ^Luke 11:44; Acts 23:3   **23:29** ^Luke 11:47f
23:31 ^Matt 23:34, 37; Acts 7:51f
23:33 ^Matt 3:7; Luke 3:7   **23:34** ^Matt 23:34-36;
Luke 11:49-51   **23:35** ^Zech 1:1   ᴮ2 Chr 24:21
23:36 ^Matt 10:23; 24:34

23:15 ¹Gr *Gehenna*

GRIEVING OVER JERUSALEM

37"^A"Jerusalem, Jerusalem, who kills the prophets and stones those who have been sent to her! How often I wanted to gather your children together, the way a hen gathers her chicks under her wings, and you were unwilling. **38**Behold, ^Ayour house is being left to you desolate! **39**For I say to you, from now on you will not see Me until you say, '^A'BLESSED IS THE ONE WHO COMES IN THE NAME OF THE LORD!'"

SIGNS OF CHRIST'S RETURN

24 ^AJesus left the temple *area* and was going *on His way* when His disciples came up to point out the temple buildings to Him. **2**But He responded and said to them, "Do you not see all these things? Truly I say to you, ^Anot *one* stone here will be left upon another, which will not be torn down."

3And as He was sitting on ^Athe Mount of Olives, the disciples came to Him privately, saying, "Tell us, when will these things happen, and what *will be* the sign of Your coming, and of the end of the age?"

4And Jesus answered and said to them, "^ASee to it that no one misleads you. **5**For ^Amany will come in My name, saying, 'I am the Christ,' and they will mislead many people. **6**And you will be hearing of ^Awars and rumors of wars. See that you are not alarmed, for *those things* must take place, but *that* is not yet the end. **7**For ^Anation will rise against nation, and kingdom against kingdom, and there will be famines and earthquakes in various places. **8**^ABut all these things are *merely* the beginning of birth pains.

9"^AThen they will hand you over to tribulation and kill you, and ^Byou will be hated by all nations because of My name. **10**And at that time many will ^Afall away, and they will betray one another and hate one another. **11**And many ^Afalse prophets will rise up and mislead many people. **12**And because lawlessness is increased, most people's love will become cold. **13**^ABut the one who endures to the end is the one who will be saved. **14**This ^Agospel of the kingdom shall be preached in the whole ^Bworld as a testimony to all the nations, and then the end will come.

PERILOUS TIMES

15"Therefore when you see the ^AABOMINATION OF DESOLATION which was spoken of through Daniel the prophet, standing in the holy place—let the ¹reader understand— **16**then those who are in Judea must flee to the mountains. **17**Whoever is on ^Athe housetop must not go down to get things out of his house. **18**And whoever is in the field must not turn back to get his cloak. **19**But ^Awoe to those women who are pregnant, and to those who are nursing babies in those days! **20**Moreover, pray that when you flee, it will not be in the winter, or on a Sabbath. **21**For then there will be a ^Agreat tribulation, such as has not occurred since the beginning of the world until now, nor ever will *again*. **22**And if those days had

23:37^A*Luke 13:34, 35* **23:38**^A1 Kin 9:7f; Jer 22:5
23:39^APs 118:26; Matt 21:9 **24:1**^A*Mark 13; Luke 21:5-36* **24:2**^ALuke 19:44 **24:3**^AMatt 21:1
24:4^A Jer 29:8 **24:5**^AMatt 24:11, 24; Acts 5:36f
24:6^ARev 6:4 **24:7**^A2 Chr 15:6; Is 19:2
24:8^AMatt 24:8-20; Luke 21:12-24 **24:9**^AMatt 10:17
^BMatt 10:22 **24:10**^AMatt 11:6 **24:11**^AMatt 7:15;
24:24 **24:13**^AMatt 10:22 **24:14**^AMatt 4:23
^BLuke 4:5 **24:15**^ADan 9:27; 11:31 **24:17**^A1 Sam 9:25;
2 Sam 11:2 **24:19**^ALuke 23:29
24:21^ADan 12:1; Joel 2:2

24:15¹I.e., the reader of Daniel

not been cut short, no life would have been saved; but for ^the sake of the elect those days will be cut short. ²³^Then if anyone says to you, 'Behold, here is the Christ,' or '*He is over* here,' do not believe *him*. ²⁴For false christs and false prophets will arise and will provide great ^signs and wonders, so as to mislead, if possible, even ᴮthe elect. ²⁵Behold, I have told you in advance. ²⁶So if they say to you, 'Behold, He is in the wilderness,' do not go out; *or,* 'Behold, He is in the inner rooms,' do not believe *them*. ²⁷^For just as the lightning comes from the east and flashes as far as the west, so will the coming of the Son of Man be. ²⁸^Wherever the corpse is, there the vultures will gather.

THE GLORIOUS RETURN

²⁹"But immediately after the tribulation of those days ^THE SUN WILL BE DARKENED, AND THE MOON WILL NOT GIVE ITS LIGHT, AND THE STARS WILL FALL from the sky, and the powers of the heavens will be shaken. ³⁰And then ^the sign of the Son of Man will appear in the sky, and then all the tribes of the earth will mourn, and they will see ᴮthe SON OF MAN COMING ON THE CLOUDS OF THE SKY with power and great glory. ³¹And He will send forth His angels with ^A GREAT TRUMPET BLAST, and THEY WILL GATHER TOGETHER His elect from the four winds, from one end of the sky to the other.

PARABLE OF THE FIG TREE

³²"Now learn the parable from the fig tree: as soon as its branch has become tender and sprouts its leaves, you know that summer is near; ³³so you too, when you see all these things, recognize that He

is near, *right* ^at the door. ³⁴Truly I say to you, ^this generation will not pass away until all these things take place. ³⁵^Heaven and earth will pass away, but My words will not pass away.

³⁶"But ^about that day and hour no one knows, not even the angels of heaven, nor the Son, but the Father alone. ³⁷For the coming of the Son of Man will be ^just like the days of Noah. ³⁸For as in those days before the flood they were eating and drinking, ^marrying and giving in marriage, until the day that ᴮNoah entered the ark, ³⁹and they did not understand until the flood came and took them all away; so will the ^coming of the Son of Man be. ⁴⁰At that time there will be two *men* in the field; one will be taken and one will be left. ⁴¹^Two *women* will be grinding at the mill; one will be taken and one will be left.

BE READY FOR HIS COMING

⁴²"Therefore ^be on the alert, for you do not know which day your Lord is coming. ⁴³But be sure of this, that ^if the head of the house had known ᴮat what time of the night the thief was coming, he would have been on the alert and would not have allowed his house to be broken into. ⁴⁴For this reason ^you must be ready as well; for the Son of Man is coming at an hour when you do not think *He will.*

24:22 ^Matt 22:14; 24:24, 31   **24:23** ^Luke 17:23f
24:24 ^John 4:48   ᴮMatt 22:14   **24:27** ^Luke 17:24
24:28 ^Job 39:30; Ezek 39:17   **24:29** ^Is 13:10; 24:23
24:30 ^Matt 24:3   ᴮDan 7:13   **24:31** ^Ex 19:16;
Deut 30:4   **24:33** ^James 5:9; Rev 3:20
24:34 ^Matt 10:23; 16:28   **24:35** ^Matt 5:18;
Mark 13:31   **24:36** ^Mark 13:32; Acts 1:7
24:37 ^Gen 6:5; 7:6-23   **24:38** ^Matt 22:30   ᴮGen 7:7
24:39 ^Matt 16:27; 24:3, 30, 37   **24:41** ^Luke 17:35
24:42 ^Matt 24:43, 44; 25:10, 13   **24:43** ^Luke 12:39f
ᴮMark 13:35   **24:44** ^Matt 24:42, 43; 25:10, 13

45 "ᴬWho then is the faithful and sensible slave whom his master put in charge of his household slaves, to give them their food at the proper time? **46** Blessed is that slave whom his master finds so doing when he comes. **47** Truly I say to you that ᴬhe will put him in charge of all his possessions. **48** But if that evil slave says in his heart, 'My master is not coming for a long time,' **49** and he begins to beat his fellow slaves, and he eats and drinks with those habitually drunk; **50** *then* the master of that slave will come on a day that he does not expect, and at an hour that he does not know, **51** and he will cut him in two and assign him a place with the hypocrites; in that place there will be ᴬweeping and gnashing of teeth.

PARABLE OF TEN VIRGINS

25 "Then ᴬthe kingdom of heaven will be comparable to ten virgins, who took their ᴮlamps and went out to meet the groom. **2** Five of them were foolish, and five were ᴬprudent. **3** For when the foolish took their lamps, they did not take *extra* oil with them; **4** but the ᴬprudent ones took oil in flasks with their lamps. **5** Now while the groom was delaying, they all became drowsy and *began* to sleep. **6** But at midnight there finally was a shout: 'Behold, the groom! Come out to meet *him.*' **7** Then all those virgins got up and trimmed their lamps. **8** But the foolish *virgins* said to the prudent ones, 'Give us some of your oil, because our lamps are going out.' **9** However, the ᴬprudent ones answered, '*No,* there most certainly would not be enough for

us and you *too;* go instead to the merchants and buy *some* for yourselves.' **10** But while they were on their way to buy *the oil,* the groom came, and those who were ᴬready went in with him to ᴮthe wedding feast; and the door was shut. **11** Yet later, the other virgins also came, saying, 'ᴬLord, lord, open up for us.' **12** But he answered, 'Truly I say to you, I do not know you.' **13** ᴬBe on the alert then, because you do not know the day nor the hour.

PARABLE OF THE TALENTS

14 "ᴬFor *it is* just like a man *about* to go on a journey, *who* called his own slaves and entrusted his possessions to them. **15** To one he gave five ¹talents, to another, two, and to another, one, each according to his own ability; and he ᴬwent on his journey. **16** The one who had received the five ᴬtalents immediately went and did business with them, and earned five more *talents.* **17** In the same way the one who *had received* the two *talents* earned two more. **18** But he who received the one *talent* went away and dug *a hole in the* ground, and hid his master's money.

19 "Now after a long time the master of those slaves *came and *ᴬsettled accounts with them. **20** The one who had received the five ᴬtalents came up and brought five more talents, saying, 'Master, you entrusted

24:45 ᴬ *Luke 12:42-46*   24:47 ᴬMatt 25:21, 23
24:51 ᴬMatt 8:12   25:1 ᴬMatt 13:24   ᴮActs 20:8;
Rev 4:5   25:2 ᴬMatt 7:24; 10:16   25:4 ᴬMatt 7:24; 10:16
25:9 ᴬMatt 7:24; 10:16   25:10 ᴬMatt 24:42ff
ᴮLuke 12:35f   25:11 ᴬMatt 7:21ff; Luke 13:25
25:13 ᴬMatt 24:42ff   25:14 ᴬMatt 25:14-30; Luke
19:12-27   25:15 ᴬMatt 21:33   25:16 ᴬMatt 18:24;
Luke 19:13   25:19 ᴬMatt 18:23   25:20 ᴬMatt 18:24;
Luke 19:13

25:15 ¹A talent was worth about fifteen years' wages
for a laborer

five talents to me. See, I have earned five more talents.' ²¹His master said to him, 'Well done, good and faithful slave. You were faithful with a few things, I will ^put you in charge of many things; enter the joy of your master.'

²²"Also the one who *had received* the two ^talents came up and said, 'Master, you entrusted two talents to me. See, I have earned two more talents.' ²³His master said to him, 'Well done, good and ^faithful slave. You were faithful with a few things, I will put you in charge of many things; enter the joy of your master.'

²⁴"Now the one who had received the one ^talent also came up and said, 'Master, I knew you to be a hard man, reaping where you did not sow, and gathering where you did not scatter *seed*. ²⁵And I was afraid, so I went away and hid your talent in the ground. See, you *still* have what is yours.'

²⁶"But his master answered and said to him, 'You worthless, lazy slave! Did you know that I reap where I did not sow, and gather where I did not scatter *seed*? ²⁷Then you ought to have put my money in the bank, and on my arrival I would have received my *money* back with interest. ²⁸Therefore: take the talent away from him, and give it to the one who has the ten talents.'

²⁹"^For to everyone who has, *more* shall be given, and he will have an abundance; but from the one who does not have, even what he does have shall be taken away. ³⁰And throw the worthless slave into ^the outer darkness; in that place there will be weeping and gnashing of teeth.

THE JUDGMENT

³¹"But when ^the Son of Man comes in His glory, and all the angels with Him, then He will sit on His glorious throne. ³²And all the nations will be gathered before Him; and He will separate them from one another, ^just as the shepherd separates the sheep from the goats; ³³and He will put the sheep on His right, but the goats ^on the left.

³⁴"Then the King will say to those on His right, 'Come, you who are blessed of My Father, ^inherit the kingdom prepared for you from the foundation of the world. ³⁵For ^I was hungry, and you gave Me *something* to eat; I was thirsty, and you gave Me *something* to drink; I was a stranger, and you invited Me in; ³⁶^naked, and you clothed Me; I was sick, and you visited Me; I was in prison, and you came to Me.' ³⁷Then the righteous will answer Him, 'Lord, when did we see You hungry, and feed You, or thirsty, and give You *something* to drink? ³⁸And when did we see You *as* a stranger, and invite You in, or naked, and clothe You? ³⁹And when did we see You sick, or in prison, and come to You?' ⁴⁰And the King will answer and say to them, 'Truly I say to you, ^to the extent that you did *it* for one of the least of these brothers *or sisters* of Mine, you did *it* for Me.'

⁴¹"Then He will also say to those on His left, '^Depart from Me, you accursed people, into the eternal

25:21 ^Luke 12:44; 22:29   25:22 ^Matt 18:24;
Luke 19:13   25:23 ^Matt 24:45, 47; 25:21
25:24 ^Matt 18:24; Luke 19:13   25:29 ^Matt 13:12;
Mark 4:25   25:30 ^Matt 8:12; 22:13
25:31 ^Matt 16:27f; 1 Thess 4:16   25:32 ^Ezek 34:17, 20
25:33 ^Eccl 10:2   25:34 ^Matt 5:3; 19:29
25:35 ^Is 58:7; Ezek 18:7, 16   25:36 ^Is 58:7;
Ezek 18:7, 16   25:40 ^Prov 19:17; Matt 10:42
25:41 ^Matt 7:23

fire which has been prepared for the devil and his angels; **42** for I was hungry, and you gave Me nothing to eat; I was thirsty, and you gave Me nothing to drink; **43** I was a stranger, and you did not invite Me in; naked, and you did not clothe Me; sick, and in prison, and you did not visit Me.' **44** Then they themselves also will answer, 'Lord, when did we see You hungry, or thirsty, or *as* a stranger, or naked, or sick, or in prison, and did not take care of You?' **45** Then He will answer them, 'Truly I say to you, to the extent that you did not do *it* for one of the least of these, you did not do *it* for Me, either.' **46** These will go away into eternal punishment, but the righteous into ^eternal life."

THE PLOT TO KILL JESUS

26 ^When Jesus had finished all these words, He said to His disciples, **2** "^You know that after two days the Passover is coming, and the Son of Man is *to be* handed over for crucifixion."

3 At that time the chief priests and the elders of the people were gathered together in ^the courtyard of the high priest named Caiaphas; **4** and they ^plotted together to arrest Jesus covertly and kill Him. **5** But they were saying, "Not during the festival, ^otherwise a riot might occur among the people."

THE PRECIOUS OINTMENT

6 ^Now when Jesus was in Bethany, at the home of Simon ¹the Leper, **7** ^a woman came to Him with an alabaster vial of very expensive perfume, and she poured it on His head as He was reclining *at the table.* **8** But the disciples were

indignant when they saw *this,* and said, "Why this waste? **9** For this *perfume* could have been sold for a high price and *the money* given to the poor." **10** But Jesus, aware of this, said to them, "Why are you bothering the woman? For she has done a good deed for Me. **11** For you always have ^the poor with you; but you do not always have Me. **12** For when she poured this perfume on My body, she did it ^to prepare Me for burial. **13** Truly I say to you, ^wherever this gospel is preached in the whole world, what this woman has done will also be told in memory of her."

JUDAS' BARGAIN

14 ^Then one of the twelve, named Judas Iscariot, went to the chief priests **15** and said, "What are you willing to give me to betray Him to you?" And ^they set *out* for him thirty pieces of silver. **16** And from then on he looked for a good opportunity to betray Jesus.

17 ^Now on the first *day* of ¹Unleavened Bread the disciples came to Jesus and asked, "Where do You want us to prepare for You to eat the Passover?" **18** And He said, "Go into the city to ^a certain man, and say to him, 'The Teacher says, "My time is near; I am keeping the Passover at your house with My disciples."'" **19** The disciples did as Jesus had directed them; and they prepared the Passover.

25:46 ^Matt 19:29; John 3:15f, 36   26:1 ^Matt 7:28
26:2 ^*Mark 14:1, 2; Luke 22:1, 2*   26:3 ^Matt 26:58, 69;
27:27   26:4 ^Matt 12:14   26:5 ^Matt 27:24
26:6 ^Luke 7:37-39; John 12:1-8   26:7 ^Luke 7:37f
26:11 ^Deut 15:11; Mark 14:7   26:12 ^John 19:40
26:13 ^Mark 14:9   26:14 ^*Mark 14:10, 11; Luke 22:3-6*
26:15 ^Ex 21:32; Zech 11:12   26:17 ^*Mark 14:12-16;
Luke 22:7-13*   26:18 ^Mark 14:13; Luke 22:10

26:6 ¹I.e., a nickname; the man no doubt was cured
26:17 ¹I.e., Passover week

THE LAST PASSOVER

20 ^Now when evening came, Jesus was reclining *at the table* with the twelve. **21** And as they were eating, He said, "^Truly I say to you that one of you will betray Me." **22** Being deeply grieved, they began saying to Him, each one: "Surely it is not I, Lord?" **23** And He answered, "^He who dipped his hand with Me in the bowl is the one who will betray Me. **24** The Son of Man is going away ^just as it is written about Him; but woe to that man by whom the Son of Man is betrayed! It would have been good for that man if he had not been born." **25** And ^Judas, who was betraying Him, said, "Surely it is not I, Rabbi?" Jesus *said to him, "You have said *it* yourself."

THE LORD'S SUPPER INSTITUTED

26 ^Now while they were eating, Jesus took *some* bread, and after a blessing, He broke *it* and gave *it* to the disciples, and said, "Take, eat; this is My body." **27** And when He had taken a cup and given thanks, He gave *it* to them, saying, "Drink from it, all of you; **28** for ^this is My blood of the covenant, which is being poured out for many for forgiveness of sins. **29** But I say to you, I will not drink of this fruit of the vine from now on until that day when I drink it with you, new, in My Father's kingdom."

30 ^And after singing a hymn, they went out to the Mount of Olives.

31 Then Jesus *said to them, "You will all ¹fall away because of Me this night, for it is written: '^I WILL STRIKE THE SHEPHERD, AND THE SHEEP OF THE FLOCK WILL BE SCATTERED.' **32** But after I have been raised, ^I will go ahead of you to Galilee." **33** But Peter replied to Him, "*Even* if they all fall away because of You, I will never fall away!" **34** Jesus said to him, "^Truly I say to you that this *very* night, before a rooster crows, you will deny Me three times." **35** Peter *said to Him, "^Even if I have to die with You, I will not deny You!" All the disciples said the same thing as well.

THE GARDEN OF GETHSEMANE

36 ^Then Jesus *came with them to a place called Gethsemane, and *told His disciples, "Sit here while I go over there and pray." **37** And He took ^Peter and the two sons of Zebedee with Him, and began to be grieved and distressed. **38** Then He *said to them, "^My soul is deeply grieved, to the point of death; remain here and keep watch with Me."

39 And He went a little beyond *them,* and fell on His face and prayed, saying, "My Father, if it is possible, let ^this cup pass from Me; ^Byet not as I will, but as You *will.*" **40** And He *came to the disciples and *found them sleeping, and He *said to Peter, "So, you *men* could not ^keep watch with Me for one hour? **41** Keep watching and praying, so that you do not come into temptation; ^the spirit is willing, but the flesh is weak."

42 He went away again a second time and prayed, saying, "My Father, if this *cup* cannot pass away unless I drink *from* it, ^Your will be

---

26:20 ^*Mark 14:17-21*   26:21 ^Luke 22:21-23;
John 13:21f   26:23 ^Ps 41:9; John 13:18, 26
26:24 ^Matt 26:31, 54, 56; Mark 9:12
26:25 ^Matt 26:14   26:26 ^1 Cor 10:16   26:28 ^Ex 24:8;
Heb 9:20   26:30 ^*Mark 14:26-31; Luke 22:31-34*
26:31 ^Zech 13:7   26:32 ^Matt 28:7, 10, 16; Mark 16:7
26:34 ^Matt 26:75; John 13:38   26:35 ^John 13:37
26:36 ^*Mark 14:32-42; Luke 22:40-46*
26:37 ^Matt 4:21; 17:1; Mark 5:37   26:38 ^John 12:27
26:39 ^Matt 20:22   ^B Matt 26:42   26:40 ^Matt 26:38
26:41 ^Mark 14:38   26:42 ^Matt 26:39; Mark 14:36

26:31 ¹I.e., have a lapse in faith

done." ⁴³Again He came and found them sleeping, for their eyes were heavy. ⁴⁴And He left them again, and went away and prayed a third time, saying the same thing once more. ⁴⁵Then He *came to the disciples and *said to them, "Are you still sleeping and resting? Behold, ^the hour is at hand and the Son of Man is being betrayed into the hands of sinners. ⁴⁶Get up, let's go; behold, the one who is betraying Me is near!"

JESUS' BETRAYAL AND ARREST

⁴⁷^And while He was still speaking, behold, Judas, one of the twelve, came accompanied by a large crowd with swords and clubs, *who came* from the chief priests and elders of the people. ⁴⁸Now he who was betraying Him gave them a sign *previously,* saying, "Whomever I kiss, He is *the one;* arrest Him." ⁴⁹And immediately *Judas* went up to Jesus and said, "Greetings, ^Rabbi!" and kissed Him. ⁵⁰But Jesus said to him, "^Friend, *do* what you have come for." Then they came and laid hands on Jesus and arrested Him.

⁵¹And behold, ^one of those who were with Jesus reached and drew his sword, and struck the ^slave of the high priest and cut off his ear. ⁵²Then Jesus *said to him, "Put your sword back into its place; for ^all those who take up the sword will perish by the sword. ⁵³Or do you think that I cannot appeal to My Father, and He will at once put at My disposal more than twelve ¹·^legions of ^angels? ⁵⁴How then would ^the Scriptures be fulfilled, *which say* that it must happen this way?"

⁵⁵At that time Jesus said to the crowds, "Have you come out with swords and clubs to arrest Me as *you would* against a man inciting a revolt? ^Every day I used to sit within the temple *grounds* teaching, and you did not arrest Me. ⁵⁶But all this has taken place so that ^the Scriptures of the prophets will be fulfilled." Then all the disciples left Him and fled.

JESUS BEFORE CAIAPHAS

⁵⁷^Those who had arrested Jesus led Him away to Caiaphas, the high priest, where the scribes and the elders were gathered together. ⁵⁸But ^Peter was following Him at a distance, as far as the ^courtyard of the high priest, and he came inside and sat down with the officers to see the outcome.

⁵⁹Now the chief priests and the entire ^Council kept trying to obtain false testimony against Jesus, so that they might put Him to death. ⁶⁰They did not find *any,* even though many false witnesses came forward. But later on ^two came forward, ⁶¹and said, "This man stated, '^I am able to destroy the temple of God and to rebuild it in three days.'" ⁶²The high priest stood up and said to Him, "Do You offer no answer for what these men are testifying against You?" ⁶³But Jesus kept silent. ^And the high priest said to Him, "I place You

26:45 ^Mark 14:41; John 12:27 26:47 ^*Mark 14:43-50; Luke 22:47-53* 26:49 ^Matt 23:7; 26:25
26:50 ^Matt 20:13; 22:12 26:51 ^Mark 14:47; Luke 22:50 26:52 ^Gen 9:6; Rev 13:10
26:53 ^Mark 5:9, 15 ^Matt 4:11 26:54 ^Matt 26:24
26:55 ^Mark 12:35; 14:49 26:56 ^Matt 26:24
26:57 ^*Mark 14:53-65; John 18:12f, 19-24*
26:58 ^John 18:15 ^Matt 26:3 26:59 ^Matt 5:22
26:60 ^Deut 19:15 26:61 ^Matt 27:40; Mark 14:58
26:63 ^Matt 26:63-66; Luke 22:67-71

26:53 ¹A legion equaled 6,000 troops

under oath by the living God, to tell us whether You are the Christ, the Son of God." ⁶⁴Jesus *said to him, "You have said *it* yourself. But I tell you, from now *on* you will see the Son of Man sitting at the right hand of power, and ^coming on the clouds of heaven."

⁶⁵Then the high priest ^tore his robes and said, "He has blasphemed! What further need do we have of witnesses? See, you have now heard the blasphemy; ⁶⁶what do you think?" They answered, "^He deserves death!"

⁶⁷^Then they spit in His face and beat Him with their fists; and others slapped Him, ⁶⁸and said, "^Prophesy to us, You Christ; who is the one who hit You?"

PETER'S DENIALS

⁶⁹^Now Peter was sitting outside in the courtyard, and a slave woman came to him and said, "You too were with Jesus the Galilean." ⁷⁰But he denied *it* before them all, saying, "I do not know what you are talking about." ⁷¹When he had gone out to the gateway, another *slave woman* saw him and *said to those who were there, "This man was with Jesus of Nazareth." ⁷²And again he denied *it*, with an oath: "I do not know the man." ⁷³A little later the bystanders came up and said to Peter, "You really are *one* of them as well, ^since even the way you talk gives you away." ⁷⁴Then he began to curse and swear, "I do not know the Man!" And immediately a rooster crowed. ⁷⁵And Peter remembered the statement that Jesus had made: "^Before a rooster crows, you will deny Me three times." And he went out and wept bitterly.

JUDAS' REMORSE

27 ^Now when morning came, all the chief priests and the elders of the people conferred together against Jesus to put Him to death; ²and they bound Him and led Him away, and handed Him over to ^Pilate the governor.

³Then when ^Judas, who had betrayed Him, saw that He had been condemned, he felt remorse and returned ᴮthe thirty pieces of silver to the chief priests and elders, ⁴saying, "I have sinned by betraying innocent blood." But they said, "What *is that* to us? ^You shall see *to it* yourself!" ⁵And he threw the pieces of silver into the temple sanctuary and left; and ^he went away and hanged himself. ⁶The chief priests took the pieces of silver and said, "It is not lawful to put them in the temple treasury, since it is money paid for blood." ⁷And they conferred together and with the money bought the Potter's Field as a burial place for strangers. ⁸^For this reason that field has been called the Field of Blood to this day. ⁹Then that which was spoken through Jeremiah the prophet was fulfilled: "^AND THEY TOOK THE THIRTY PIECES OF SILVER, THE PRICE OF THE ONE WHOSE PRICE HAD BEEN SET by the sons of Israel; ¹⁰^AND THEY GAVE THEM FOR THE POTTER'S FIELD, JUST AS THE LORD DIRECTED ME."

JESUS BEFORE PILATE

¹¹^Now Jesus stood before the governor, and the governor questioned

26:64 ^Dan 7:13; Matt 16:27f   26:65 ^Num 14:6;
Mark 14:63   26:66 ^Lev 24:16; John 19:7   26:67 ^Is 50:6;
Matt 26:67, 68   26:68 ^Mark 14:65; Luke 22:64
26:69 ^Mark 14:66-72; Luke 22:55-62   26:73 ^Mark 14:70;
Luke 22:59   26:75 ^Matt 26:34   27:1 ^Mark 15:1;
Luke 22:66   27:2 ^Luke 3:1; 13:1   27:3 ^Matt 26:14
ᴮMatt 26:15   27:4 ^Matt 27:24   27:5 ^Matt 26:24;
Acts 1:18   27:8 ^Acts 1:19   27:9 ^Zech 11:12
27:10 ^Zech 11:13   27:11 ^Mark 15:2-5; Luke 23:2, 3

Him, saying, "So You are the King of the Jews?" And Jesus said to him, "*It is as* you say." [12] And while He was being accused by the chief priests and elders, ^He did not offer any answer. [13] Then Pilate *said to Him, "Do You not hear how many things they are testifying against You?" [14] And *still* ^He did not answer him in regard to even a single charge, so the governor was greatly amazed.

[15] ^Now at *the Passover* Feast the governor was accustomed to release for the people *any* one prisoner whom they wanted. [16] And at that time they were holding a notorious prisoner called Barabbas. [17] So when the people gathered together, Pilate said to them, "Whom do you want me to release for you: Barabbas, or Jesus ^who is called Christ?" [18] For he knew that *it was* because of envy *that* [1]they had handed Him over.

[19] And ^while he was sitting on the judgment seat, his wife sent him *a message,* saying, "*See that you have* nothing *to do* with that righteous Man; for last night I suffered greatly in a dream because of Him." [20] But the chief priests and the elders persuaded the crowds to ^ask for Barabbas, and to put Jesus to death. [21] And the governor said to them, "Which of the two do you want me to release for you?" And they said, "Barabbas." [22] Pilate *said to them, "Then what shall I do with Jesus ^who is called Christ?" They all *said, "Crucify Him!" [23] But he said, "Why, what evil has He done?" Yet they kept shouting all the more, saying, "Crucify Him!"

[24] Now when Pilate saw that he was accomplishing nothing, but rather that a riot was starting, he took water and ^washed his hands in front of the crowd, saying, "I am innocent of this Man's blood; you

yourselves shall see." [25] And all the people replied, "^His blood *shall be* on us and on our children!" [26] Then he released Barabbas for them; but after having Jesus ^flogged, he handed Him over to be crucified.

JESUS IS MOCKED

[27]^Then the soldiers of the governor took Jesus into the [1]Praetorium and gathered the whole *Roman* [2]cohort to Him. [28] And they stripped Him and ^put a red cloak on Him. [29]^And after twisting together a crown of thorns, they put it on His head, and *put* a [1]reed in His right hand; and they knelt down before Him and mocked Him, saying, "Hail, King of the Jews!" [30] And ^they spit on Him, and took the reed and beat Him on the head. [31]^And after they had mocked Him, they took the cloak off Him and put His *own* garments back on Him, and led Him away to crucify *Him.*

[32]^As they were coming out, they found a man of Cyrene named Simon, whom they compelled to carry His [1]cross.

THE CRUCIFIXION

[33]^And when they came to a place called Golgotha, which means Place of a Skull, [34]^they gave Him wine mixed with bile to drink; and after tasting *it,* He was unwilling to drink *it.*

27:12^Matt 26:63; John 19:9   27:14^Matt 27:12;
Mark 15:5   27:15^John 18:39–19:16   27:17^Matt 1:16;
27:22   27:19^John 19:13; Acts 12:21   27:20^Acts 3:14
27:22^Matt 1:16   27:24^Deut 21:6–8   27:25^Josh 2:19;
Acts 5:28   27:26^Mark 15:15; Luke 23:16
27:27^*Mark 15:16-20*   27:28^Mark 15:17; John 19:2
27:29^Mark 15:17; John 19:2   27:30^Matt 26:67;
Mark 10:34   27:31^Mark 15:20   27:32^John 19:17
27:33^*Mark 15:22-32; Luke 23:33-43*   27:34^Ps 69:21

27:18 [1]I.e., the Jewish leaders   27:27 [1]I.e., the
governor's official residence   [2]Normally 600 men
(the number varied)   27:29 [1]Or *staff*; i.e., to mimic a
king's scepter   27:32 [1]I.e., the crossbeam for a cross

³⁵And when they had crucified Him, ᴬthey divided His garments among themselves by casting lots. ³⁶And sitting down, they *began* to ᴬkeep watch over Him there. ³⁷And above His head they put up the charge against Him which read, "ᴬTHIS IS JESUS THE KING OF THE JEWS."

³⁸At that time two ¹rebels *were being crucified with Him, one on the right and one on the left. ³⁹And those passing by were speaking abusively to Him, ᴬshaking their heads, ⁴⁰and saying, "ᴬYou who *are going to* destroy the temple and rebuild *it* in three days, save Yourself! ᴮIf You are the Son of God, come down from the cross." ⁴¹In the same way the chief priests also, along with the scribes and elders, were mocking *Him* and saying, ⁴²"ᴬHe saved others; He cannot save Himself! He is the King of Israel; let Him now come down from the cross, and we will believe in Him. ⁴³ᴬHE HAS TRUSTED IN GOD; LET GOD RESCUE *Him* now, IF HE TAKES PLEASURE IN HIM; for He said, 'I am the Son of God.'" ⁴⁴ᴬAnd the ¹rebels who had been crucified with Him were also insulting Him in the same *way*.

⁴⁵ᴬNow from the ¹sixth hour darkness fell upon all the land until the ²ninth hour. ⁴⁶And about the ninth hour Jesus cried out with a loud voice, saying, "ᴬELI, ELI, LEMA SABAKTANEI?" that is, "MY GOD, MY GOD, WHY HAVE YOU FORSAKEN ME?" ⁴⁷And some of those who were standing there, when they heard it, said, "This man is calling for Elijah." ⁴⁸And ᴬimmediately one of them ran, and taking a sponge, he filled it with sour wine and put it on a reed, and gave Him a drink.

⁴⁹But the rest *of them* said, "Let us see if Elijah comes to save Him¹." ⁵⁰And Jesus ᴬcried out again with a loud voice, and gave up His spirit. ⁵¹ᴬAnd behold, ᴮthe veil of the temple was torn in two from top to bottom; and the earth shook and the rocks were split. ⁵²Also the tombs were opened, and many bodies of the saints who had ᴬfallen asleep were raised; ⁵³and coming out of the tombs after His resurrection, they entered ᴬthe holy city and appeared to many. ⁵⁴ᴬNow as for the centurion and those who were with him keeping guard over Jesus, when they saw the earthquake and the *other* things that were happening, they became extremely frightened and said, "Truly this was the Son of God!"

⁵⁵ᴬAnd many women were there watching from a distance, who had followed Jesus from Galilee while caring for Him. ⁵⁶Among them were ᴬMary Magdalene, Mary the mother of James and Joseph, and the mother of the sons of Zebedee.

JESUS IS BURIED

⁵⁷ᴬNow when it was evening, a rich man from Arimathea came, named Joseph, who himself had also become a disciple of Jesus.

27:35 ᴬPs 22:18   27:36 ᴬMatt 27:54
27:37 ᴬMark 15:26; Luke 23:38   27:39 ᴬJob 16:4;
Ps 22:7   27:40 ᴬMatt 26:61   ᴮMatt 27:42
27:42 ᴬMark 15:31; Luke 23:35   27:43 ᴬPs 22:8
27:44 ᴬLuke 23:39-43   27:45 ᴬ*Mark 15:33-41;
Luke 23:44-49*   27:46 ᴬPs 22:1   27:48 ᴬPs 69:21;
Mark 15:36   27:50 ᴬMark 15:37; Luke 23:46
27:51 ᴬLuke 23:47-49   ᴮEx 26:31ff   27:52 ᴬActs 7:60
27:53 ᴬMatt 4:5   27:54 ᴬMark 15:39; Luke 23:47
27:55 ᴬMark 15:40f; Luke 23:49   27:56 ᴬMatt 28:1;
Mark 15:40, 47   27:57 ᴬ*Mark 15:42-47; Luke 23:50-56*

27:38 ¹Or robbers   27:44 ¹Or robbers   27:45 ¹I.e.,
noon   ²I.e., 3 p.m.   27:49 ¹Some early mss *And
another took a spear and pierced His side, and there
came out water and blood* (cf. John 19:34)

⁵⁸This man went to Pilate and asked for the body of Jesus. Then Pilate ordered it to be given *to him*. ⁵⁹And Joseph took the body and wrapped it in a clean linen cloth, ⁶⁰and laid it in his own new tomb, which he had cut out in the rock; and he rolled ^a large stone against the entrance of the tomb and went away. ⁶¹And ^Mary Magdalene was there, and the other Mary, sitting opposite the tomb.

⁶²Now on the next day, *that is, the day* which is after ^the preparation, the chief priests and the Pharisees gathered together with Pilate, ⁶³and they said, "Sir, we remember that when that deceiver was still alive, He said, '^After three days I am rising.' ⁶⁴Therefore, give orders for the tomb to be made secure until the third day; otherwise, His disciples may come and steal Him, and say to the people, 'He has risen from the dead,' and the last deception will be worse than the first." ⁶⁵Pilate said to them, "You have a ^guard; go, make it *as* secure as you know how." ⁶⁶And they went and made the tomb secure with the guard, ^sealing the stone.

JESUS IS RISEN!

28 ^Now after the Sabbath, as it began to dawn toward the first *day* of the week, Mary Magdalene and the other Mary came to look at the tomb. ²And behold, a severe earthquake had occurred, for ^an angel of the Lord descended from heaven and came and rolled away ᴮthe stone, and sat upon it. ³And ^his appearance was like lightning, and his clothing as white as snow. ⁴The guards shook from fear of him and became like dead

men. ⁵And the angel said to the women, "^Do not be afraid; for I know that you are looking for Jesus who has been crucified. ⁶He is not here, for He has risen, ^just as He said. Come, see the place where He was lying. ⁷And go quickly and tell His disciples that He has risen from the dead; and behold, He is going ahead of you ^to Galilee. There you will see Him; behold, I have told you."

⁸And they left the tomb quickly with fear and great joy, and ran to report to His disciples. ⁹And behold, Jesus met them and said, "Rejoice!" And they came up and took hold of His feet, and worshiped Him. ¹⁰Then Jesus *said to them, "Do not be afraid; go, bring word to ^My brothers to leave for Galilee, and there they will see Me."

¹¹Now while they were on their way, some of ^the *men from the* guard came into the city and reported to the chief priests all that had happened. ¹²And when they had assembled with the elders and consulted together, they gave a large sum of money to the soldiers, ¹³and said, "You are to say, 'His disciples came at night and stole Him while we were asleep.' ¹⁴And if this comes to ^the governor's ears, we will appease him and keep you out of trouble." ¹⁵And they took the money and did as they had been instructed; and this story was widely ^spread among the Jews *and is* to this day.

27:60 ^Matt 27:66; 28:2   27:61 ^Matt 27:56; 28:1
27:62 ^Mark 15:42; Luke 23:54   27:63 ^Matt 16:21;
17:23   27:65 ^Matt 27:66; 28:11   27:66 ^Dan 6:17
28:1 ^John 20:1-8   28:2 ^Luke 24:4   ᴮMatt 27:66
28:3 ^Dan 7:9; 10:6; Mark 9:3   28:5 ^Matt 14:27; 28:10
28:6 ^Matt 12:40; 16:21   28:7 ^Matt 26:32; 28:16
28:10 ^John 20:17; Rom 8:29   28:11 ^Matt 27:65, 66
28:14 ^Matt 27:2   28:15 ^Matt 9:31; Mark 1:45

THE GREAT COMMISSION

16 But the eleven disciples proceeded ^to Galilee, to the mountain which Jesus had designated to them. 17 And when they saw Him, they worshiped *Him;* but ^some were doubtful. 18 And Jesus came up and spoke to them, saying, "^All authority in heaven and on earth has been given to Me. 19 Go, therefore, and ^make disciples of all the nations, B baptizing them in the name of the Father and the Son and the Holy Spirit, 20 teaching them to follow all that I commanded you; and behold, ^I am with you always, to the end of the age."

28:16 ^Matt 26:32; 28:7, 10   **28:17** ^Mark 16:11
28:18 ^Dan 7:13f; Matt 11:27   **28:19** ^Matt 13:52
B Acts 2:38   **28:20** ^Matt 18:20; Acts 18:10

MARK

PREACHING OF JOHN THE BAPTIST

1 The beginning of the gospel of Jesus Christ, ᴬthe Son of God, ²ᴬjust as it is written in Isaiah the prophet:

"Behold, I am sending My
 messenger before You,
 Who will prepare Your way;
³ ᴬThe voice of one calling
 ¹out in the wilderness,
 'Prepare the way of the Lord,
 Make His paths straight!'"

⁴John the Baptist appeared in the wilderness, ᴬpreaching a baptism of repentance for the ᴮforgiveness of sins. ⁵And all the country of Judea was going out to him, and all the people of Jerusalem; and they were being baptized by him in the Jordan River, confessing their sins. ⁶John was clothed with camel's hair and *wore* ᴬa leather belt around his waist, and his diet was locusts and wild honey. ⁷And he was preaching, saying, "After me One is coming who is mightier than I, and I am not fit to bend down and untie the straps of His sandals. ⁸I baptized you ¹with water; but He will baptize you ¹with the Holy Spirit."

THE BAPTISM OF JESUS

⁹ᴬIn those days Jesus came from Nazareth in Galilee and was baptized by John in the Jordan. ¹⁰And immediately coming up out of the water, He saw the heavens opening, and the Spirit, like a dove, descending upon Him; ¹¹and a voice came from the heavens: "ᴬYou are My beloved Son; in You I am well pleased."

¹²ᴬAnd immediately the Spirit *brought Him out into the wilderness. ¹³And He was in the wilderness for forty days, being tempted by ᴬSatan; and He was with the wild animals, and the angels were serving Him.

JESUS PREACHES IN GALILEE

¹⁴ᴬNow after John was taken into custody, Jesus came into Galilee, ᴮpreaching the gospel of God, ¹⁵and saying, "ᴬThe time is fulfilled, and the kingdom of God has come near; repent and believe in the gospel."

¹⁶ᴬAs He was going along the Sea of Galilee, He saw Simon and Andrew, the brother of Simon, casting a net in the sea; for they were fishermen. ¹⁷And Jesus said to them, "Follow Me, and I will have you become fishers of people." ¹⁸Immediately they left their nets and followed Him. ¹⁹And going on a little farther, He saw James the son of Zebedee, and his brother John, who were also in the boat mending the nets. ²⁰Immediately He called them; and they left their father Zebedee in the boat with the hired men, and went away to follow Him.

²¹ᴬThey *went into Capernaum; and immediately on the Sabbath *Jesus* entered the synagogue and

1:1 ᴬMatt 4:3   1:2 ᴬ*Matt 3:1-11; Luke 3:2-16*   1:3 ᴬIs 40:3; Matt 3:3   1:4 ᴬActs 13:24   ᴮLuke 1:77   1:6 ᴬ2 Kin 1:8   1:9 ᴬ*Matt 3:13-17; Luke 3:21, 22*   1:11 ᴬPs 2:7; Is 42:1   1:12 ᴬ*Matt 4:1-11; Luke 4:1-13*   1:13 ᴬMatt 4:10   1:14 ᴬMatt 4:12   ᴮMatt 4:23   1:15 ᴬGal 4:4; Eph 1:10   1:16 ᴬLuke 5:2-11; John 1:40-42   1:21 ᴬ*Luke 4:31-37*

1:3 ¹Or *out, Prepare in the wilderness the way*
1:8 ¹The Gr here can be translated *in, with,* or *by*

began to teach. ²²And ^they were amazed at His teaching; for He was teaching them as *one* having authority, and not as the scribes. ²³Just then there was a man in their synagogue with an unclean spirit; and he cried out, ²⁴saying, "^What business do You have with us, Jesus ¹of Nazareth? Have You come to destroy us? I know who You are: ^Bthe Holy One of God!" ²⁵And Jesus rebuked him, saying, "Be quiet, and come out of him!" ²⁶After throwing him into convulsions and crying out with a loud voice, the unclean spirit came out of him. ²⁷And they were all ^amazed, so they debated among themselves, saying, "What is this? A new teaching with authority! He commands even the unclean spirits, and they obey Him." ²⁸Immediately the news about Him spread everywhere into all the surrounding region of Galilee.

CROWDS HEALED

²⁹^And immediately after they left the synagogue, they entered the house of Simon and Andrew, with James and John. ³⁰Now Simon's mother-in-law was lying sick with a fever; and they immediately *spoke to Jesus about her. ³¹And He came to her and raised her up, taking *her by* the hand, and the fever left her, and she served them.

³²Now ^when evening came, after the sun had set, they *began* bringing to Him all who were ill and those who were demon-possessed. ³³And the whole ^city had gathered at the door. ³⁴And He ^healed many who were ill with various diseases, and cast out many demons; and He would not permit the demons to speak, because they knew who He was.

³⁵^And in the early morning, while it was still dark, Jesus got up, left *the house,* and went away to a secluded place, and prayed there *for a time.* ³⁶Simon and his companions eagerly searched for Him; ³⁷and they found Him and *said to Him, "Everyone is looking for You." ³⁸He *said to them, "Let's go somewhere else to the towns nearby, so that I may also preach there; for this is why I came." ³⁹^And He went into their synagogues preaching throughout Galilee, and casting out the demons.

⁴⁰^And a man with ¹leprosy *came to Jesus, imploring Him and kneeling down, and saying to Him, "If You are willing, You can make me clean." ⁴¹Moved with compassion, *Jesus* reached out with His hand and touched him, and *said to him, "I am willing; be cleansed." ⁴²And immediately the leprosy left him, and he was cleansed. ⁴³And He sternly warned him and immediately sent him away, ⁴⁴and He *said to him, "^See that you say nothing to anyone; but ^go, show yourself to the priest and ^Boffer for your cleansing what Moses commanded, as a testimony to them." ⁴⁵But he went out and began to ^proclaim it freely and to ^spread the news around, to such an extent that Jesus could no longer publicly enter a city, but stayed out in unpopulated areas; and they were coming to Him from everywhere.

1:22^Matt 7:28   **1:24**^Matt 8:29   ^BLuke 4:34
1:27^Mark 10:24, 32; 16:5, 6   **1:29**^*Matt 8:14, 15; Luke 4:38, 39*   **1:32**^*Matt 8:16, 17; Luke 4:40, 41*
1:33^Matt 1:21   **1:34**^Matt 4:23
1:35^*Luke 4:42, 43*   **1:39**^Matt 4:23; 9:35
1:40^*Matt 8:2-4; Luke 5:12-14*   **1:44**^Matt 8:4
^BLev 14:1-32   **1:45**^Matt 28:15; Luke 5:15

1:24¹Or *the Nazarene*   **1:40**¹I.e., leprosy or a serious, unspecified disease, and so throughout the ch; see Lev 13

THE PARALYZED MAN HEALED

2 When *Jesus* came back to Capernaum a few days later, it was heard that He was at home. ²And ᴬmany were gathered together, so that there was no longer space, not even near the door; and He was speaking the word to them. ³ᴬAnd *some people* *came, bringing to Him a man who was paralyzed, carried by four *men*. ⁴And when they were unable to get to Him because of the crowd, they ᴬremoved the roof above Him; and after digging an opening, they let down the pallet on which the ᴮparalyzed man was lying. ⁵And Jesus, seeing their faith, *said to the paralyzed man, "Son, ᴬyour sins are forgiven." ⁶But some of the scribes were sitting there and thinking *it* over in their hearts, ⁷"Why does this man speak that way? He is blaspheming! ᴬWho can forgive sins except God alone?" ⁸Immediately Jesus, aware in His spirit that they were thinking that way within themselves, *said to them, "Why are you thinking about these things in your hearts? ⁹Which is easier, to say to the ᴬparalyzed man, 'Your sins are forgiven'; or to say, 'Get up, and pick up your pallet and walk'? ¹⁰But so that you may know that the Son of Man has authority on earth to forgive sins"—He *said to the paralyzed man, ¹¹"I say to you, get up, pick up your pallet, and go home." ¹²And he got up and immediately picked up the pallet and went out in the sight of everyone, so that they were all amazed and ᴬwere glorifying God, saying, "ᴮWe have never seen *anything* like this!"

¹³And He went out again by the seashore; and ᴬall the people were coming to Him, and He was teaching them.

LEVI (MATTHEW) CALLED

¹⁴ᴬAs He passed by, He saw Levi the *son* of Alphaeus sitting in the tax office, and He *said to him, "Follow Me!" And he got up and followed Him.

¹⁵And it *happened that He was reclining *at the table* in his house, and many tax collectors and sinners were dining with Jesus and His disciples; for there were many *of them*, and they were following Him. ¹⁶When ᴬthe scribes of the Pharisees saw that He was eating with the sinners and tax collectors, they said to His disciples, "Why is He eating with tax collectors and sinners?" ¹⁷And hearing *this*, Jesus *said to them, "ᴬIt *is* not those who are healthy who need a physician, but those who are sick; I did not come to call the righteous, but sinners."

¹⁸ᴬJohn's disciples and the Pharisees were fasting; and they *came and *said to Him, "Why do John's disciples and the disciples of the Pharisees fast, but Your disciples do not fast?" ¹⁹And Jesus said to them, "While the groom is with them, the attendants of the groom cannot fast, can they? As long as they have the groom with them, they cannot fast. ²⁰But the ᴬdays will come when the groom is taken away from them, and then they will fast, on that day.

²¹"No one sews a patch of unshrunk cloth on an old garment; otherwise, the patch pulls away from it, the new from the old, and a worse tear results. ²²And no one puts new wine into old wineskins; otherwise the wine will

2:2 ᴬMark 1:45; 2:13   2:3 ᴬ*Matt 9:2-8; Luke 5:18-26*
2:4 ᴬLuke 5:19   ᴮMatt 4:24   2:5 ᴬMatt 9:2
2:7 ᴬIs 43:25   2:9 ᴬMatt 4:24   2:12 ᴬMatt 9:8
ᴮMatt 9:33   2:13 ᴬMark 1:45   2:14 ᴬ*Matt 9:9-13;
Luke 5:27-32*   2:16 ᴬLuke 5:30; Acts 23:9
2:17 ᴬMatt 9:12, 13; Luke 5:31, 32   2:18 ᴬ*Matt 9:14-17;
Luke 5:33-38*   2:20 ᴬMatt 9:15; Luke 17:22

burst the skins, and the wine is lost and the skins *as well;* but *one puts* new wine into fresh wineskins."

QUESTION OF THE SABBATH

23 ^And it happened that He was passing through the grainfields on the Sabbath, and His disciples began to make their way *along* while picking the heads *of grain.* 24 The Pharisees were saying to Him, "Look, ^why are they doing what is not lawful on the Sabbath?" 25 And He *said to them, "Have you never read what David did when he was in need and he and his companions became hungry; 26 how he entered the house of God in the time of ^Abiathar *the* high priest, and ate the consecrated bread, which is not lawful for *anyone* to eat except the priests, and he also gave it to those who were with him?" 27 Jesus said to them, "^The Sabbath was made for man, and not man for the Sabbath. 28 So the Son of Man is Lord, even of the Sabbath."

JESUS HEALS ON THE SABBATH

3 ^He entered a synagogue again; and a man was there whose hand was withered. 2 And they were watching Him closely *to see* if He would heal him on the Sabbath, ^so that they might accuse Him. 3 He *said to the man with the withered hand, "Get up and come forward!" 4 And He *said to them, "Is it lawful to do good on the Sabbath or to do harm, to save a life or to kill?" But they kept silent. 5 After ^looking around at them with anger, grieved at their hardness of heart, He *said to the man, "Stretch out your hand." And he stretched it out, and his hand was restored. 6 The Pharisees went out and immediately

began conspiring with the ^Herodians against Him, *as to* how they might put Him to death.

7 ^Jesus withdrew to the sea with His disciples; and a large multitude from Galilee followed, and *also* from Judea, 8 and from Jerusalem, and from ^Idumea, and beyond the Jordan, and the vicinity of Tyre and Sidon, a great number of people heard about everything that He was doing and came to Him. 9 ^And He told His disciples *to see* that a boat would be ready for Him because of the masses, so that they would not crowd Him; 10 for He had ^healed many, with the result that all those who had diseases pushed in around Him in order to ^Btouch Him. 11 And whenever the unclean spirits saw Him, they would fall down before Him and shout, "You are ^the Son of God!" 12 And He ^strongly warned them not to reveal who He was.

THE TWELVE ARE CHOSEN

13 And He *went up on ^the mountain and *summoned those whom He Himself wanted, and they came to Him. 14 And He appointed twelve, so that they would be with Him and that He *could* send them out to preach, 15 and to have authority to cast out the demons. 16 And He appointed the twelve: ^Simon (to whom He gave the name Peter), 17 James the *son* of Zebedee and John the brother of James (to them He gave the name Boanerges, which means, "Sons of Thunder"); 18 and Andrew, Philip,

2:23 ^ Matt 12:1-8; Luke 6:1-5   2:24 ^ Matt 12:2
2:26 ^1 Sam 21:1; 2 Sam 8:17   2:27 ^ Ex 23:12; Deut 5:14
3:1 ^ Matt 12:9-14; Luke 6:6-11   3:2 ^ Matt 12:10; Luke 6:7
3:5 ^ Luke 6:10   3:6 ^ Matt 22:16; Mark 12:13
3:7 ^ Matt 12:15, 16; Luke 6:17-19   3:8 ^ Josh 15:1, 21;
Ezek 35:15   3:9 ^ Mark 4:1; Luke 5:1-3   3:10 ^ Matt 4:23
^B Matt 9:21   3:11 ^ Matt 4:3   3:12 ^ Matt 8:4
3:13 ^ Matt 5:1; Luke 6:12   3:16 ^ Acts 1:13

Bartholomew, Matthew, Thomas, James the son of Alphaeus, Thaddaeus, and Simon the Zealot; ¹⁹and Judas Iscariot, who also betrayed Him.

²⁰And He *came ^home, and the crowd *gathered again, to such an extent that they could not even eat a meal. ²¹And when His own people heard *about this,* they came out to take custody of Him; for they were saying, "^He has lost His senses." ²²The scribes who came down from Jerusalem were saying, "He is possessed by ^Beelzebul," and "ᴮHe casts out the demons by the ruler of the demons." ²³^And *so* He called them to Himself and *began* speaking to them in parables: "How can Satan cast out Satan? ²⁴And if a kingdom is divided against itself, that kingdom cannot stand. ²⁵If a house is divided against itself, that house will not be able to stand. ²⁶And if ^Satan has risen up against himself and is divided, he cannot stand, but he is finished! ²⁷^But no one can enter the strong man's house and plunder his property unless he first ties up the strong man, and then he will plunder his house.

²⁸"^Truly I say to you, all sins will be forgiven the sons *and daughters* of men, and whatever blasphemies they commit; ²⁹but ^whoever blasphemes against the Holy Spirit never has forgiveness, but is guilty of an eternal sin"——³⁰because they were saying, "He has an unclean spirit."

³¹^Then His mother and His brothers *came, and while standing outside they sent *word* to Him, calling *for* Him. ³²And a crowd was sitting around Him, and they *said to Him, "Behold, Your mother and Your brothers are outside looking for You." ³³Answering them, He *said, "Who are My mother and My brothers?" ³⁴And looking around at those who were sitting around Him, He *said, "^Here are My mother and My brothers! ³⁵For whoever ^does the will of God, this is My brother, and sister, and mother."

PARABLE OF THE SOWER AND SOILS

4 Again ^He began to teach by the sea. And such a very large crowd gathered to Him that He got into a boat on the sea and sat down; and the whole crowd was by the sea on the land. ²And He was teaching them many things in ^parables, and was saying to them in His teaching, ³"Listen *to this!* Behold, the sower went out to sow; ⁴as he was sowing, some *seed* fell beside the road, and the birds came and ate it up. ⁵Other *seed* fell on the rocky *ground* where it did not have much soil; and immediately it sprang up because it had no depth of soil. ⁶And when the sun had risen, it was scorched; and because it had no root, it withered away. ⁷Other *seed* fell among the thorns, and the thorns came up and choked it, and it yielded no crop. ⁸Other *seeds* fell into the good soil, and as they grew up and increased, they yielded a crop and produced thirty, sixty, and a hundred *times as much.*" ⁹And He was saying, "^He who has ears to hear, let him hear."

¹⁰As soon as He was alone, His followers, along with the twelve *disciples, began* asking Him *about*

3:20^Mark 2:1; 7:17   3:21^John 10:20; Acts 26:24
3:22^Matt 10:25   ᴮMatt 9:34   3:23^Matt 12:25-29;
Luke 11:17-22   3:26^Matt 4:10   3:27^Is 49:24, 25
3:28^Matt 12:31, 32; Mark 3:28-30   3:29^Luke 12:10
3:31^Matt 12:46-50; Luke 8:19-21   3:34^Matt 12:49
3:35^Eph 6:6; Heb 10:36   4:1^Matt 13:1-15; Luke
8:4-10   4:2^Matt 13:3ff; Mark 3:23   4:9^Matt 11:15;
Mark 4:23

the parables. ¹¹And He was saying to them, "To you has been given the mystery of the kingdom of God, but for ^those who are outside, everything comes in parables, ¹²so that ^WHILE SEEING THEY MAY SEE, AND NOT PERCEIVE, AND WHILE HEARING, THEY MAY HEAR, AND NOT UNDERSTAND, OTHERWISE THEY MIGHT RETURN AND IT WOULD BE FORGIVEN THEM."

EXPLANATION OF THE PARABLE

¹³^And He *said to them, "Do you not understand this parable? How will you understand all the parables? ¹⁴The sower sows the word. ¹⁵These are the ones who are beside the road where the word is sown; and when they hear, immediately ^Satan comes and takes away the word which has been sown in them. ¹⁶And in a similar way these are the ones sown *with seed* on the rocky *places,* who, when they hear the word, immediately receive it with joy; ¹⁷and *yet* they have no *firm* root in themselves, but are *only* temporary; then, when affliction or persecution occurs because of the word, immediately they fall away. ¹⁸And others are the ones sown *with seed* among the thorns; these are the ones who have heard the word, ¹⁹but the worries of ^the world, and the ᴮdeceitfulness of wealth, and the desires for other things enter and choke the word, and it becomes unfruitful. ²⁰And those are the ones sown *with seed* on the good soil; and they hear the word and accept *it* and ^bear fruit, thirty, sixty, and a hundred *times as much.*"

²¹And He was saying to them, "^A lamp is not brought to be put under a basket, or under a bed, is it? Is it not *brought* to be put on the lampstand? ²²^For nothing is hidden, except to be revealed; nor has *anything* been secret, but that it would come to light. ²³^If anyone has ears to hear, let him hear." ²⁴And He was saying to them, "Take care what you listen to. ^By your standard of measure it will be measured to you; and *more* will be given you besides. ²⁵^For whoever has, to him *more* will be given; and whoever does not have, even what he has will be taken away from him."

PARABLE OF THE SEED

²⁶And He was saying, "The kingdom of God is like a man who casts seed upon the soil; ²⁷and he goes to bed at night and gets up daily, and the seed sprouts and grows—how, he himself does not know. ²⁸The soil produces crops by itself; first the stalk, then the head, then the mature grain in the head. ²⁹Now when the crop permits, he immediately ^puts in the sickle, because the harvest has come."

PARABLE OF THE MUSTARD SEED

³⁰^And He was saying, "How shall we picture the kingdom of God, or by what parable shall we present it? ³¹*It is* like a mustard seed, which, when sown upon the soil, though it is the smallest of all the seeds that are upon the soil, ³²yet when it is sown, it grows up and becomes larger than all the garden plants, and forms large branches, with the result that ^THE BIRDS OF THE SKY can NEST UNDER its shade."

4:11^1 Cor 5:12f; Col 4:5   **4:12**^Is 6:9f; 43:8
4:13^*Matt 13:18-23; Luke 8:11-15*   **4:15**^Matt 4:10f;
1 Pet 5:8   **4:19**^Matt 13:22   ᴮProv 23:4
4:20^John 15:2ff; Rom 7:4   **4:21**^Matt 5:15; Luke 8:16
4:22^Matt 10:26; Luke 8:17   **4:23**^Matt 11:15; 13:9
4:24^Matt 7:2; Luke 6:38   **4:25**^Matt 13:12; 25:29
4:29^Joel 3:13   **4:30**^*Matt 13:31, 32; Luke 13:18, 19*
4:32^Ezek 17:23; Ps 104:12

³³And with many such parables He was speaking the word to them, so far as they were able to understand *it;* ³⁴and He did not speak to them ^without a parable; but He was explaining everything privately to His own disciples.

JESUS STILLS THE SEA

³⁵^On that day, when evening came, He *said to them, "Let's go over to the other side." ³⁶After dismissing the crowd, they *took Him along with them ^in the boat, just as He was; and other boats were with Him. ³⁷And a fierce gale of wind *developed, and the waves were breaking over the boat so much that the boat was already filling *with water.* ³⁸And *yet Jesus* Himself was in the stern, asleep on the cushion; and they *woke Him and *said to Him, "Teacher, do You not care that we are perishing?" ³⁹And He got up and ^rebuked the wind and said to the sea, "Hush, be still." And the wind died down and it became perfectly calm. ⁴⁰And He said to them, "Why are you afraid? ^Do you still have no faith?" ⁴¹They became very much afraid and said to one another, "Who, then, is this, that even the wind and the sea obey Him?"

THE DEMON-POSSESSED MAN CURED

5 ^They came to the other side of the sea, into the region of the Gerasenes. ²When He got out of ^the boat, immediately a man from the tombs with an unclean spirit met Him. ³He lived among the tombs; and no one was able to bind him anymore, not even with a chain, ⁴because he had often been bound with shackles and chains, and the chains had been torn apart by him and the shackles broken in pieces; and no one was strong enough to subdue him. ⁵Constantly, night and day, he was screaming among the tombs and in the mountains, and cutting himself with stones. ⁶Seeing Jesus from a distance, he ran up and bowed down before Him; ⁷and shouting with a loud voice, he *said, "^What business do You have with me, Jesus, Son of ^the Most High God? I implore You by God, do not torment me!" ⁸For He had *already* been saying to him, "Come out of the man, you unclean spirit!" ⁹And He was asking him, "What is your name?" And he *said to Him, "My name is ^Legion, for we are many." ¹⁰And he begged Him earnestly not to send them out of the region. ¹¹Now there was a large herd of pigs feeding nearby on the mountain. ¹²And *the demons* begged Him, saying, "Send us into the pigs so that we may enter them." ¹³*Jesus* gave them permission. And coming out, the unclean spirits entered the pigs; and the herd rushed down the steep bank into the sea, about two thousand *of them;* and they were drowned in the sea.

¹⁴Their herdsmen ran away and reported *it* in the city and in the countryside. And *the people* came to see what it was that had happened. ¹⁵And *then* they *came to Jesus and *saw the man who had been demon-possessed sitting down, clothed and ^in his right mind, the *very* man who had *previously* had the "^legion"; and they became frightened. ¹⁶Those who

had seen *it* described to them how it had happened to the ^demon-possessed man, and *all* about the pigs. ¹⁷And they began to ^beg Him to leave their region. ¹⁸^And as He was getting into the boat, the man who had been demon-possessed was begging Him that he might accompany Him. ¹⁹And He did not let him, but He *said to him, "^Go home to your people and report to them what great things the Lord has done for you, and *how* He had mercy on you." ²⁰And he went away and began to ^proclaim in ᴮDecapolis what great things Jesus had done for him; and everyone was amazed.

MIRACLES AND HEALING

²¹When Jesus had crossed over again in ^the boat to the other side, a large crowd gathered around Him; and He stayed ᴮby the seashore. ²²^And one of the synagogue officials, named Jairus, *came, and upon seeing Him, *fell at His feet ²³and *pleaded with Him earnestly, saying, "My little daughter is at the point of death; *please* come and ^lay Your hands on her, so that she will get well and live." ²⁴And He went off with him; and a large crowd was following Him and pressing in on Him.

²⁵A woman who had had a hemorrhage for twelve years, ²⁶and had endured much at the hands of many physicians, and had spent all that she had and was not helped at all, but instead had become worse— ²⁷after hearing about Jesus, she came up in the crowd behind *Him* and touched His cloak. ²⁸For she had been saying *to herself*, "If I just touch His garments, I will get well." ²⁹And immediately the flow of her blood was dried up; and she felt in her body that she

was healed of her ^disease. ³⁰And immediately Jesus, perceiving in Himself that ^power from Him had gone out, turned around in the crowd and said, "Who touched My garments?" ³¹And His disciples said to Him, "You see the crowd pressing in on You, and You say, 'Who touched Me?'" ³²And He looked around to see the woman who had done this. ³³But the woman, fearing and trembling, aware of what had happened to her, came and fell down before Him and told Him the whole truth. ³⁴And He said to her, "Daughter, ^your faith has made you well; ᴮgo in peace and be cured of your disease."

³⁵While He was still speaking, *people* *came from *the house of* the ^synagogue official, saying, "Your daughter has died; why bother the Teacher further?" ³⁶But Jesus, overhearing what was being spoken, *said to the synagogue official, "^Do not be afraid, only believe." ³⁷And He allowed no one to accompany Him except ^Peter, James, and John the brother of James. ³⁸They *came to the house of the ^synagogue official, and He *saw a commotion, and *people* loudly weeping and wailing. ³⁹And after entering, He *said to them, "Why are you making a commotion and weeping? The child has not died, but is asleep." ⁴⁰And they *began* laughing at Him. But putting them all outside, He *took along the child's father and mother and His own companions, and *entered *the room* where the

5:16^Matt 4:24; Mark 5:15   5:17^Matt 8:34; Acts 16:39   5:18^*Luke 8:38, 39*   5:19^Luke 8:39   5:20^Ps 66:16   ᴮMatt 4:25   5:21^Mark 4:36   ᴮMark 4:1   5:22^*Matt 9:18-26; Luke 8:41-56*   5:23^Mark 6:5; 7:32   5:29^Mark 3:10; 5:34   5:30^Luke 5:17   5:34^Matt 9:22   ᴮLuke 7:50; 8:48   5:35^Mark 5:22   5:36^Luke 8:50   5:37^Matt 17:1; 26:37   5:38^Mark 5:22

child was *in bed*. [41]And taking the child by the hand, He *said to her, "Talitha, kum!" (which translated means, "Little girl, [A]I say to you, get up!"). [42]And immediately the girl got up and *began* to walk, for she was twelve years old. And immediately they were completely astonished. [43]And He [A]gave them strict orders that no one was to know about this, and He told *them* to have *something* given her to eat.

TEACHING AT NAZARETH

6 [A]Jesus went out from there and *came into [B]His hometown; and His disciples *followed Him. [2]And when the Sabbath came, He began [A]to teach in the synagogue; and the many listeners were astonished, saying, "Where did this Man *learn* these things, and what is *this* wisdom that has been given to Him, and such miracles as these performed by His hands? [3]Is this not [A]the carpenter, the son of Mary and brother of James, Joses, Judas, and Simon? And are His sisters not here with us?" And they took [B]offense at Him. [4]Jesus said to them, "[A]A prophet is not dishonored except in his hometown and among his *own* relatives, and in his *own* household." [5]And He could not do any miracle there except that He [A]laid His hands on a few sick people and healed *them*. [6]And He was amazed at their unbelief.

[A]And He was going around the villages, teaching.

THE TWELVE SENT OUT

[7][A]And He *summoned the twelve and began to send them out [B]in pairs, and gave them authority over the unclean spirits; [8][A]and He instructed them that they were

to take nothing for *their* journey, except a mere staff—no bread, no bag, no money in their belt— [9]but *to* wear sandals; and *He added,* "Do not wear two [1]tunics." [10]And He said to them, "Wherever you enter a house, stay there until you leave town. [11]Any place that does not receive you or listen to you, as you go out from there, [A]shake the dust off the soles of your feet as a testimony against them." [12][A]And they went out and preached that *people* are to repent. [13]And they were casting out many demons and [A]were anointing with oil many sick people and healing them.

JOHN'S FATE RECALLED

[14][A]And King Herod heard *about it,* for His name had become well known; and *people* were saying, "John the Baptist has risen from the dead, and that is why these miraculous powers are at work in Him." [15]But others were saying, "He is [A]Elijah." And others were saying, "*He is* a prophet, like one of the prophets *of old.*" [16]But when Herod heard *about it,* he kept saying, "John, whom I beheaded, has risen!"

[17]For Herod himself had sent *men* and had John arrested and bound in prison on account of [A]Herodias, the wife of his brother Philip, because he had married her. [18]For John had been saying to Herod, "[A]It is not lawful for you to have your brother's wife." [19]And [A]Herodias held a

---

5:41[A]Luke 7:14; Acts 9:40   5:43[A]Matt 8:4
6:1[A]*Matt 13:54-58*   [B]Luke 4:16, 23   6:2[A]Matt 4:23;
Mark 10:1   6:3[A]Matt 13:55   [B]Matt 11:6   6:4[A]Matt 13:57;
John 4:44   6:5[A]Mark 5:23   6:6[A]Matt 9:35; Mark 1:39
6:7[A]Luke 10:4-11   [B]Luke 10:1   6:8[A]Matt 10:10
6:11[A]Matt 10:14; Acts 13:51   6:12[A]Matt 11:1; Luke 9:6
6:13[A]James 5:14   6:14[A]*Matt 14:1-12; Luke 9:7-9*
6:15[A]Matt 16:14; Mark 8:28   6:17[A]Matt 14:3; Luke 3:19
6:18[A]Matt 14:4   6:19[A]Matt 14:3

6:9[1]A long shirt worn next to the skin

grudge against him and wanted to put him to death, and could not *do so;* [20]for ^Herod was afraid of John, knowing that he was a righteous and holy man, and he had been protecting him. And when he heard him, he was very perplexed; and *yet* he used to enjoy listening to him. [21]An opportune day came when Herod, on his birthday, ^held a banquet for his nobles and military commanders, and the leading people of Galilee; [22]and when the daughter of ^Herodias herself came in and danced, she pleased Herod and his dinner guests; and the king said to the girl, "Ask me for whatever you want, and I will give it to you." [23]And he swore to her, "Whatever you ask of me, I will give *it* to you, up to ^half of my kingdom." [24]And she went out and said to her mother, "What shall I ask for?" And she said, "The head of John the Baptist." [25]Immediately she came in a hurry to the king and asked, saying, "I want you to give me at once the head of John the Baptist on a platter." [26]And although the king was very sorry, because of his oaths and his dinner guests, he was unwilling to refuse her. [27]Immediately the king sent an executioner and commanded *him* to bring *back* his head. And he went and beheaded him in the prison, [28]and brought his head on a platter, and gave it to the girl; and the girl gave it to her mother. [29]When his disciples heard *about this,* they came and carried away his body, and laid it in a tomb.

[30]The ^apostles *gathered together with Jesus; and they reported to Him all that they had done and taught. [31]And He *said to them, "Come *away* by yourselves to a secluded place and rest a little while." (For there were many *people* coming and going, and ^they did not even have time to eat.) [32]^And they went away in the boat to a secluded place by themselves.

FIVE THOUSAND MEN FED

[33]*The people* saw them going, and many recognized *them* and ran there together on foot from all the cities, and got there ahead of them. [34]When Jesus went ashore, He ^saw a large crowd, and He felt compassion for them because [B]they were like sheep without a shepherd; and He began to teach them many things. [35]And when it was already late, His disciples came up to Him and said, "This place is secluded and it is already late; [36]send them away so that they may go into the surrounding countryside and villages and buy themselves something to eat." [37]But He answered them, "You give them *something to eat!*" ^And they *said to Him, "Shall we go and spend two hundred [1]denarii on bread, and give *it* to them to eat?" [38]But He *said to them, "How many loaves do you have? Go look!" And when they found out, they *said, "Five, and two fish." [39]And He ordered them all to recline by groups on the green grass. [40]They reclined in groups of hundreds and fifties. [41]And He took the five loaves and the two fish, and looking up toward heaven, He ^blessed *the food* and broke the loaves and He gave *them* to the disciples *again and again* to set before

6:20 ^Matt 21:26   6:21 ^Esth 1:3; 2:18
6:22 ^Matt 14:3   6:23 ^Esth 5:3, 6; 7:2
6:30 ^Matt 10:2; Mark 3:14   6:31 ^Mark 3:20
6:32 ^Mark 8:2-9   6:34 ^Matt 9:36   [B]Num 27:17
6:37 ^John 6:7   6:41 ^Matt 14:19
6:37 [1]The denarius was a day's wages for a laborer

them; and He divided the two fish among them all. ⁴²And they all ate and were satisfied; ⁴³and they picked up twelve full ᴬbaskets of the broken pieces *of bread,* and of the fish. ⁴⁴There were ᴬfive thousand ¹men who ate the loaves.

JESUS WALKS ON THE WATER

⁴⁵ᴬAnd immediately Jesus had His disciples get into the boat and go ahead of *Him* to the other side, to Bethsaida, while He Himself *dismissed the crowd. ⁴⁶And after ᴬsaying goodbye to them, He left for the mountain to pray.

⁴⁷When it was evening, the boat was in the middle of the sea, and He was alone on the land. ⁴⁸Seeing them straining at the oars— for the wind was against them—at about the ᴬfourth watch of the night, He *came to them, walking on the sea; and He intended to pass by them. ⁴⁹But when they saw Him walking on the sea, they thought that it was a ghost, and they cried out; ⁵⁰for they all saw Him and were terrified. But immediately He spoke with them and *said to them, "ᴬTake courage; it is I, ᴮdo not be afraid." ⁵¹Then He got into ᴬthe boat with them, and the wind stopped; and they were utterly astonished, ⁵²for ᴬthey had not gained any insight from *the incident of* the loaves, but their hearts ᴮwere hardened.

HEALING AT GENNESARET

⁵³ᴬWhen they had crossed over they came to land at Gennesaret, and moored at the shore. ⁵⁴And when they got out of the boat, immediately *the people* recognized Him, ⁵⁵and ran about that entire country and began carrying here

and there on their pallets those who were sick, to wherever they heard He was. ⁵⁶And wherever He entered villages, or cities, or a countryside, they were laying the sick in the marketplaces and imploring Him that they might just ᴬtouch ᴮthe fringe of His cloak; and all who touched it were being healed.

FOLLOWERS OF TRADITION

7 ᴬThe Pharisees and some of the scribes *gathered to Him after they came from Jerusalem, ²and saw that some of His disciples were eating their bread with ᴬunholy hands, that is, unwashed. ³(For the Pharisees and all the *other* Jews do not eat unless they carefully wash their hands, *thereby* holding firmly to the ᴬtradition of the elders; ⁴and *when they come* from the marketplace, they do not eat unless they completely cleanse themselves; and there are many other things which they have received *as traditions* to firmly hold, *such as* the washing of ᴬcups, pitchers, and copper pots.) ⁵And the Pharisees and the scribes *asked Him, "Why do Your disciples not walk in accordance with the ᴬtradition of the elders, but eat their bread with unholy hands?" ⁶But He said to them, "Rightly did Isaiah prophesy about you hypocrites, as it is written:

6:43 ᴬMatt 14:20 6:44 ᴬMatt 14:21
6:45 ᴬ*Matt 14:22-32; John 6:15-21*
6:46 ᴬActs 18:18, 21; 2 Cor 2:13 6:48 ᴬMatt 24:43;
Mark 13:35 6:50 ᴬMatt 9:2 ᴮMatt 14:27
6:51 ᴬMark 6:32 6:52 ᴬMark 8:17ff ᴮRom 11:7
6:53 ᴬJohn 6:24, 25 6:56 ᴬMark 3:10 ᴮMatt 9:20
7:1 ᴬMatt 15:1-20 7:2 ᴬMatt 15:2; Mark 7:5
7:3 ᴬMark 7:5, 8, 9, 13; Gal 1:14 7:4 ᴬMatt 23:25
7:5 ᴬMark 7:3, 8, 9, 13; Gal 1:14

6:44 ¹I.e., 5,000 men plus women and children, cf.
Matt 14:21

'ᴬTʜɪꜱ ᴘᴇᴏᴘʟᴇ ʜᴏɴᴏʀꜱ Mᴇ
    ᴡɪᴛʜ ᴛʜᴇɪʀ ʟɪᴘꜱ,
Bᴜᴛ ᴛʜᴇɪʀ ʜᴇᴀʀᴛ ɪꜱ ꜰᴀʀ ᴀᴡᴀʏ
    ꜰʀᴏᴍ Mᴇ.
7 'ᴬAɴᴅ ɪɴ ᴠᴀɪɴ ᴅᴏ ᴛʜᴇʏ
    ᴡᴏʀꜱʜɪᴘ Mᴇ,
Tᴇᴀᴄʜɪɴɢ ᴀꜱ ᴅᴏᴄᴛʀɪɴᴇꜱ ᴛʜᴇ
    ᴄᴏᴍᴍᴀɴᴅᴍᴇɴᴛꜱ ᴏꜰ ᴍᴇɴ.'
⁸Neglecting the commandment of God, you hold to the ᴬtradition of men."

⁹He was also saying to them, "You are experts at setting aside the commandment of God in order to keep your tradition. ¹⁰For Moses said, 'ᴬHᴏɴᴏʀ ʏᴏᴜʀ ꜰᴀᴛʜᴇʀ ᴀɴᴅ ʏᴏᴜʀ ᴍᴏᴛʜᴇʀ'; and, 'ᴮTʜᴇ ᴏɴᴇ ᴡʜᴏ ꜱᴘᴇᴀᴋꜱ ᴇᴠɪʟ ᴏꜰ ꜰᴀᴛʜᴇʀ ᴏʀ ᴍᴏᴛʜᴇʀ, ɪꜱ ᴄᴇʀᴛᴀɪɴʟʏ ᴛᴏ ʙᴇ ᴘᴜᴛ ᴛᴏ ᴅᴇᴀᴛʜ'; ¹¹but you say, 'If a person says to his father or his mother, whatever I have that would help you is ᴬCorban (that is, 'given *to God*),' ¹²you no longer allow him to do anything for *his* father or *his* mother; ¹³*thereby* invalidating the word of God by your ᴬtradition which you have handed down; and you do many things such as that."

THE HEART OF MANKIND

¹⁴After He called the crowd to Him again, He *began* saying to them, "Listen to Me, all of you, and understand: ¹⁵there is nothing outside the person which can defile him if it goes into him; but the things which come out of the person are what defile the person'."

¹⁷And when He *later* entered a house, away from the crowd, ᴬHis disciples asked Him about the parable. ¹⁸And He *said to them, "Are you so lacking in understanding as well? Do you not understand that whatever goes into the person from outside cannot defile him, ¹⁹because it does not go into his heart, but into his stomach, and 'is eliminated?" (*Thereby* He declared all foods ᴬclean.) ²⁰And He was saying, "ᴬThat which comes out of the person, that *is what* defiles the person. ²¹For from within, out of the hearts of people, come the evil thoughts, *acts of* sexual immorality, thefts, murders, *acts of* adultery, ²²deeds of greed, wickedness, deceit, indecent behavior, ᴬenvy, slander, pride, *and* foolishness. ²³All these evil things come from within and defile the person."

THE SYROPHOENICIAN WOMAN

²⁴ᴬNow Jesus got up and went from there to the region of Tyre'. And when He had entered a house, He wanted no one to know *about it;* and *yet* He could not escape notice. ²⁵But after hearing about Him, a woman whose little daughter had an unclean spirit immediately came and fell at His feet. ²⁶Now the woman was a 'Gentile, of Syrophoenician descent. And she *repeatedly* asked Him to cast the demon out of her daughter. ²⁷And He was saying to her, "Let the children be satisfied first, for it is not good to take the children's bread and throw it to the dogs." ²⁸But she answered and *said to Him, "Yes, Lord, *but* even the dogs under the table feed on the children's crumbs." ²⁹And He said to her, "Because of this answer, go; the demon has gone out of your

7:6ᴬIs 29:13   7:7ᴬIs 29:13   7:8ᴬMark 7:3, 5, 9, 13; Gal 1:14   7:10ᴬEx 20:12   ᴮEx 21:17   7:11ᴬLev 1:2; Matt 27:6   7:13ᴬMark 7:3, 5, 8, 9; Gal 1:14   7:17ᴬMatt 15:15   7:19ᴬLuke 11:41; Acts 10:15   7:20ᴬMatt 15:18; Mark 7:23   7:22ᴬMatt 6:23; 20:15   7:24ᴬMatt 15:21-28

7:11¹Lit *a gift;* i.e., an offering   7:15¹Late mss add, as v 16: *If anyone has ears to hear, let him hear.*   7:19¹Lit *goes out into the latrine*   7:24¹Two early mss add *and Sidon*   7:26¹Lit *Greek*

daughter." ³⁰ And after going back to her home, she found the child lying on the bed, and the demon gone.

³¹ᴬ Again He left the region of Tyre and came through Sidon to the Sea of Galilee, within the region of Decapolis. ³² And they *brought to Him one who was deaf and had difficulty speaking, and they *begged Him to ᴬlay His hand on him. ³³ And *Jesus* ᴬtook him aside from the crowd, by himself, and put His fingers in his ears, and after ᴬspitting, He touched his tongue *with the saliva;* ³⁴ and looking up to heaven with a deep ᴬsigh, He *said to him, "Ephphatha!" that is, "Be opened!" ³⁵ And his ears were opened, and the impediment of his tongue was removed, and he *began* speaking plainly. ³⁶ And He gave them orders not to tell anyone; but the more He ordered them, the more widely they ᴬcontinued to proclaim *it.* ³⁷ And they were utterly astonished, saying, "He has done all things well; He makes even those who are deaf hear, and those who are unable to talk, speak."

FOUR THOUSAND MEN FED

8 In those days, ᴬwhen there was again a large crowd and they had nothing to eat, *Jesus* summoned His disciples and *said to them, ² ᴬ"I feel compassion for the people because they have remained with Me for three days already and have nothing to eat. ³ And if I send them away hungry to their homes, they will faint on the way; and some of them have come from a great distance." ⁴ And His disciples replied to Him, "Where will anyone be able *to find enough* bread here in *this* desolate place to satisfy these people?" ⁵ And He was

asking them, "How many loaves do you have?" And they said, "Seven." ⁶ And He *directed the people to recline on the ground; and taking the seven loaves, He gave thanks and broke them, and started giving them to His disciples to serve, and they served them to the people. ⁷ They also had a few small fish; and ᴬafter He had blessed them, He told *the disciples* to serve these as well. ⁸ And they ate and were satisfied; and they picked up seven large ᴬbaskets *full* of what was left over of the broken pieces. ⁹ About four thousand ¹men were *there;* and He dismissed them. ¹⁰ And immediately He got into the boat with His disciples and came to the region of ᴬDalmanutha.

¹¹ᴬ And the Pharisees came out and began to argue with Him, ᴮdemanding from Him a sign from heaven, to test Him. ¹² Sighing deeply in His spirit, He *said, "Why does this generation demand a sign? Truly I say to you, ᴬno sign will be given to this generation!" ¹³ And leaving them, He again embarked and went away to the other side.

¹⁴ And *the disciples* had forgotten to take bread, and did not have more than one loaf in the boat with them. ¹⁵ And He was giving orders to them, saying, "ᴬWatch out! Beware of the leaven of the Pharisees, and the leaven of Herod." ¹⁶ And they *began* to discuss with one another *the fact* that they had no bread. ¹⁷ And Jesus, aware of

7:31 ᴬ*Matt 15:29-31* 7:32 ᴬMark 5:23 7:33 ᴬMark 8:23
7:34 ᴬMark 8:12 7:36 ᴬMark 1:45 8:1 ᴬMark 6:34-44
8:2 ᴬMatt 9:36; Mark 6:34 8:7 ᴬMatt 14:19
8:8 ᴬMatt 15:37; Mark 8:20 8:10 ᴬMatt 15:39
8:11 ᴬ*Matt 16:1-12* ᴮMatt 12:38 8:12 ᴬMatt 12:39
8:15 ᴬMatt 16:6; Luke 12:1

8:9 ¹I.e., 4,000 men plus women and children, cf. Matt 15:38

this, *said to them, "Why are you discussing *the fact* that you have no bread? ^Do you not yet comprehend or understand? Do you *still* have your heart hardened? ¹⁸^HAVING EYES, DO YOU NOT SEE? AND HAVING EARS, DO YOU NOT HEAR? And do you not remember, ¹⁹when I broke ^the five loaves for the five thousand, how many ᴮbaskets full of broken pieces you picked up?" They *said to Him, "Twelve." ²⁰"When *I broke* ^the seven for the four thousand, how many large baskets full of broken pieces did you pick up?" And they *said to Him, "Seven." ²¹And He was saying to them, "^Do you not yet understand?"

²²And they *came to Bethsaida. And *some people* *brought a man who was blind to Jesus and *begged Him to ^touch him. ²³Taking the man who was blind by the hand, He ^brought him out of the village; and after ^spitting in his eyes and ᴮlaying His hands on him, He asked him, "Do you see anything?" ²⁴And he looked up and said, "I see people, for I see *them* like trees, walking around." ²⁵Then again He laid His hands on his eyes; and he looked intently and was restored, and *began* to see everything clearly. ²⁶And He sent him to his home, saying, "Do not even enter ^the village."

PETER'S CONFESSION OF CHRIST

²⁷^Jesus went out, along with His disciples, to the villages of Caesarea Philippi; and on the way He questioned His disciples, saying to them, "Who do people say that I am?" ²⁸^They told Him, saying, "John the Baptist; and others *say* Elijah; and others, one of the prophets." ²⁹And He *continued* questioning them: "But who do you say that I am?" ^Peter answered and *said to Him, "You are the Christ." ³⁰And ^He warned them to tell no one about Him.

³¹^And He began to teach them that the Son of Man must suffer many things and be rejected by the elders and the chief priests and the scribes, and be killed, and after three days rise *from the dead*. ³²And He was stating the matter ^plainly. And Peter took Him aside and began to rebuke Him. ³³But turning around and seeing His disciples, He rebuked Peter and *said, "Get behind Me, ^Satan; for you are not setting your mind on God's purposes, but on man's."

³⁴And He summoned the crowd together with His disciples, and said to them, "If anyone wants to come after Me, he must deny himself, ^take up his cross, and follow Me. ³⁵For ^whoever wants to save his life will lose it, but whoever loses his life for My sake and the gospel's will save it. ³⁶For what does it benefit a person to gain the whole world, and forfeit his soul? ³⁷For what could a person give in exchange for his soul? ³⁸For ^whoever is ashamed of Me and My words in this adulterous and sinful generation, the Son of Man will also be ashamed of him when He comes in the glory of His Father with the holy angels."

8:17^Mark 6:52   **8:18**^Jer 5:21; Ezek 12:2
8:19^Mark 6:41-44   ᴮMatt 14:20   **8:20**^Mark 8:6-9
8:21^Mark 6:52   **8:22**^Mark 3:10   **8:23**^Mark 7:33
ᴮMark 5:23   **8:26**^Mark 8:23   **8:27**^Matt 16:13-16;
Luke 9:18-20   **8:28**^Mark 6:14; Luke 9:7, 8
8:29^John 6:68, 69   **8:30**^Matt 8:4; 16:20
8:31^Matt 16:21-28; Luke 9:22-27   **8:32**^John 10:24;
11:14   **8:33**^Matt 4:10   **8:34**^Matt 10:38; Luke 14:27
8:35^Matt 10:39; Luke 17:33
8:38^Matt 10:33; Luke 9:26

THE TRANSFIGURATION

9 And Jesus was saying to them, "^Truly I say to you, there are some of those who are standing here who will not taste death until they see the kingdom of God when it has come with power." ^2And six days later Jesus *took with Him Peter, James, and John, and *brought them up on a high mountain by themselves. And He was transfigured before them; ^3and ^His garments became radiant and exceedingly white, as no launderer on earth can whiten them. ^4And Elijah appeared to them along with Moses; and they were talking with Jesus. ^5Peter responded and *said to Jesus, "Rabbi, it is good that we are here; ^let's make three tabernacles, one for You, one for Moses, and one for Elijah." ^6For he did not know how to reply; for they became terrified. ^7Then a cloud formed, overshadowing them, and a voice came out of the cloud: "^This is My beloved Son; listen to Him!" ^8And suddenly they looked around and saw no one with them anymore, except Jesus alone.

^9^As they were coming down from the mountain, He gave them orders not to relate to anyone what they had seen, until the Son of Man rose from the dead. ^10They seized upon that statement, discussing with one another what rising from the dead meant. ^11And they asked Him, saying, "*Why is it* that the scribes say that ^Elijah must come first?" ^12And He said to them, "Elijah does come first and he restores all things. And *yet* how is it written of the Son of Man that ^He will suffer many things and be treated with contempt? ^13But I say to you that Elijah has indeed come, and they

did to him whatever they wanted, just as it is written of him."

ALL THINGS POSSIBLE

^14^And when they came *back* to the *other* disciples, they saw a large crowd around them, and *some* scribes arguing with them. ^15Immediately, when the entire crowd saw Him, they were ^amazed and *began* running up to greet Him. ^16And He asked them, "What are you disputing with them?" ^17And one *person* from the crowd answered Him, "Teacher, I brought You my son, because he has a spirit *that makes him* unable to speak; ^18and whenever it seizes him, it slams him to the ground, and he foams *at the mouth* and grinds his teeth and becomes stiff. And I told Your disciples so that they would cast it out, but they could not *do it*." ^19And He answered them and *said, "O unbelieving generation, how long shall I be with you? How long shall I put up with you? Bring him to Me!" ^20And they brought the boy to Him. When he saw Him, the spirit immediately threw him into convulsions, and falling to the ground, he *began* rolling around and foaming *at the mouth*. ^21And He asked his father, "How long has this been happening to him?" And he said, "From childhood. ^22It has often thrown him both into the fire and into the water to kill him. But if You can do anything, take pity on us and help us!" ^23But Jesus said to him, "'If You can'? ^All things are possible for the

9:1 ^Matt 16:28; Mark 13:26   9:2 ^*Matt 17:1-8; Luke 9:28-36*   9:3 ^Matt 28:3
9:5 ^Matt 17:4; Luke 9:33   9:7 ^Matt 3:17; Mark 1:11
9:9 ^*Matt 17:9-13*   9:11 ^Mal 4:5; Matt 11:14
9:12 ^Matt 16:21; 26:24   9:14 ^*Matt 17:14-19; Luke 9:37-42*   9:15 ^Mark 14:33; 16:5, 6
9:23 ^Matt 17:20; John 11:40

one who believes." 24Immediately the boy's father cried out and said, "I do believe; help my unbelief!" 25When Jesus saw that ᴬa crowd was rapidly gathering, He rebuked the unclean spirit, saying to it, "You mute and deaf spirit, I command you, come out of him and do not enter him again!" 26And after crying out and throwing him into terrible convulsions, it came out; and *the boy* became so much like a corpse that most *of them* said, "He is dead!" 27But Jesus took him by the hand and raised him, and he got up. 28When He came ᴬinto *the* house, His disciples *began* asking Him privately, "*Why is it* that we could not cast it out?" 29And He said to them, "This kind cannot come out by anything except prayer."

DEATH AND RESURRECTION FORETOLD

30ᴬAnd from there they went out and *began* to go through Galilee, and He did not want anyone to know *about it.* 31For He was teaching His disciples and telling them, "ᴬThe Son of Man is to be handed over to men, and they will kill Him; and when He has been killed, He will rise three days later." 32But ᴬthey did not understand *this* statement, and they were afraid to ask Him.

33ᴬThey came to Capernaum; and when He was in the house, He *began* to question them: "What were you discussing on the way?" 34But they kept silent, for on the way ᴬthey had discussed with one another which *of them was* the greatest. 35And sitting down, He called the twelve and *said to them, "ᴬIf anyone wants to be first, he shall be last of all and servant of all." 36And He took a child and placed him among them,

and taking him in His arms, He said to them, 37"ᴬWhoever receives one child like this in My name receives Me; and whoever receives Me does not receive Me, but Him who sent Me."

DIRE WARNINGS

38ᴬJohn said to Him, "Teacher, we saw someone casting out demons in Your name, and we tried to prevent him because he was not following us." 39But Jesus said, "Do not hinder him, for there is no one who will perform a miracle in My name, and be able soon *afterward* to speak evil of Me. 40ᴬFor the one who is not against us is ¹for us. 41For ᴬwhoever gives you a cup of water to drink because of your name as *followers* of Christ, truly I say to you, he shall by no means lose his reward.

42"ᴬWhoever causes one of these little ones who believe in Me to sin, it is better for him if a heavy millstone is hung around his neck and he is thrown into the sea. 43And ᴬif your hand causes you to sin, cut it off; it is better for you to enter life maimed, than, having your two hands, to go into ¹hell, into the ᴮunquenchable fire.² 45And if your foot is causing you to sin, cut it off; it is better for you to enter life without a foot, than, having your two feet, to be thrown into ᴬhell.¹ 47And ᴬif your eye is causing you to sin, throw it

9:25ᴬMark 9:15   9:28ᴬMark 2:1; 7:17
9:30ᴬ*Matt 17:22, 23; Luke 9:43-45*   9:31ᴬMatt 16:21;
Mark 8:31   9:32ᴬLuke 2:50; 9:45   9:33ᴬ*Matt 18:1-5;
Luke 9:46-48*   9:34ᴬMatt 18:4; Mark 9:50
9:35ᴬMatt 20:26; 23:11   9:37ᴬMatt 10:40; Luke 10:16
9:38ᴬ*Luke 9:49, 50*   9:40ᴬMatt 12:30; Luke 11:23
9:41ᴬMatt 10:42   9:42ᴬMatt 18:6; Luke 17:2
9:43ᴬMatt 5:30   ᴮMatt 3:12   9:45ᴬMatt 5:22
9:47ᴬMatt 5:29; 18:9

9:40¹Or *on our side*   9:43¹Gr *Gehenna*   ²Late mss
repeat v 48 here as v 44   9:45¹Late mss repeat v 48
here as v 46; cf. note 2 v 43

away; it is better for you to enter the kingdom of God with one eye, than, having two eyes, to be thrown into hell, [48A]where THEIR WORM DOES NOT DIE, AND [B]THE FIRE IS NOT EXTINGUISHED. [49]For everyone will be salted with fire. [50]Salt is good; but [A]if the salt becomes unsalty, with what will you make it salty *again?* Have salt in yourselves, and be at peace with one another."

JESUS' TEACHING ABOUT DIVORCE

10 [A]Setting out from there, *Jesus* *went to the region of Judea and beyond the Jordan; crowds *gathered to Him again, and, as He was accustomed, He once more *began* to teach them.

[2]And *some* Pharisees came up to Jesus, testing Him, and *began* questioning Him whether it was lawful for a man to divorce *his* wife. [3]And He answered and said to them, "What did Moses command you?" [4]They said, "[A]Moses permitted *a man* to write a certificate of divorce and send *his wife* away." [5]But Jesus said to them, "[A]Because of your hardness of heart he wrote you this commandment. [6]But [A]from the beginning of creation, *God* [B]CREATED THEM MALE AND FEMALE. [7A]FOR THIS REASON A MAN SHALL LEAVE HIS FATHER AND MOTHER[1], [8A]AND THE TWO SHALL BECOME ONE FLESH; so they are no longer two, but one flesh. [9]Therefore, what God has joined together, no person is to separate."

[10]And in the house the disciples again *began* questioning Him about this. [11]And He *said to them, "[A]Whoever divorces his wife and marries another woman commits adultery against her; [12]and [A]if she herself divorces her husband and

marries another man, she is committing adultery."

JESUS BLESSES LITTLE CHILDREN

[13A]And they were bringing children to Him so that He would touch them; but the disciples rebuked them. [14]But when Jesus saw *this*, He was indignant and said to them, "Allow the children to come to Me; do not forbid them, [A]for the kingdom of God belongs to such as these. [15]Truly I say to you, [A]whoever does not receive the kingdom of God like a child will not enter it at all." [16]And He [A]took them in His arms and *began* blessing them, laying His hands on them.

THE RICH YOUNG RULER

[17A]As He was setting out on a journey, a man ran up to Him and knelt before Him, and asked Him, "Good Teacher, what shall I do so that I may [B]inherit eternal life?" [18]But Jesus said to him, "Why do you call Me good? No one is good except God alone. [19]You know the commandments: '[A]DO NOT MURDER, DO NOT COMMIT ADULTERY, DO NOT STEAL, DO NOT GIVE FALSE TESTIMONY, Do not defraud, HONOR YOUR FATHER AND MOTHER.'" [20]And he said to Him, "Teacher, I have kept [A]all these things from my youth." [21]Looking at him, Jesus showed love to him and said to him, "One thing you lack: go and sell all you possess and give to the poor, and you will

9:48 [A] Is 66:24   [B] Matt 3:12   9:50 [A] Matt 5:13; Luke 14:34f   10:1 [A] *Matt 19:1-9*   10:4 [A] Deut 24:1, 3; Matt 5:31   10:5 [A] Matt 19:8   10:6 [A] Mark 13:19   [B] Gen 1:27   10:7 [A] Gen 2:24   10:8 [A] Gen 2:24   10:11 [A] Matt 5:32   10:12 [A] 1 Cor 7:11, 13   10:13 [A] *Matt 19:13-15; Luke 18:15-17*   10:14 [A] Matt 5:3   10:15 [A] Matt 18:3; 19:14   10:16 [A] Mark 9:36   10:17 [A] *Matt 19:16-30*   [B] Matt 25:34   10:19 [A] Ex 20:12-16; Deut 5:16-20   10:20 [A] Matt 19:20

10:7 [1] Many late mss add *and shall cling to his wife*

have ^treasure in heaven; and come, follow Me." ²²But he was deeply dismayed by these words, and he went away grieving; for he was one who owned much property.

²³And Jesus, looking around, *said to His disciples, "^How hard it will be for those who are wealthy to enter the kingdom of God!" ²⁴And the disciples ^were amazed at His words. But Jesus responded again and *said to them, "Children, how hard it is to enter the kingdom of God! ²⁵^It is easier for a camel to go through the eye of a needle than for a rich person to enter the kingdom of God." ²⁶And they were even more astonished, and said to Him, "Then who can be saved?" ²⁷Looking at them, Jesus *said, "^With people it is impossible, but not with God; for all things are possible with God."

²⁸^Peter began to say to Him, "Behold, we have left everything and have followed You." ²⁹Jesus said, "Truly I say to you, ^there is no one who has left house or brothers or sisters or mother or father or children or farms, for My sake and for the gospel's sake, ³⁰but that he will receive a hundred times as much now in the present age, houses and brothers and sisters and mothers and children and farms, along with persecutions; and in ^the age to come, eternal life. ³¹But ^many *who are* first will be last, and the last, first."

JESUS' SUFFERINGS FORETOLD

³²^Now they were on the road going up to Jerusalem, and Jesus was walking on ahead of them; and they were amazed, and those who followed were fearful. And again He took the twelve aside and began to tell them what was going to happen to Him, ³³*saying,* "Behold, we are going up to

Jerusalem, and ^the Son of Man will be handed over to the chief priests and the scribes; and they will condemn Him to death and will hand Him over to the Gentiles. ³⁴And they will mock Him and ^spit on Him, and flog Him and kill *Him;* and three days later He will rise *from the dead."*

³⁵^James and John, the two sons of Zebedee, *came up to Jesus, saying to Him, "Teacher, we want You to do for us whatever we ask of You." ³⁶And He said to them, "What do you want Me to do for you?" ³⁷They said to Him, "Grant that we ^may sit, one on Your right and one on *Your* left, in Your glory." ³⁸But Jesus said to them, "You do not know what you are asking. Are you able ^to drink the cup that I drink, or to be baptized with the baptism with which I am baptized?" ³⁹They said to Him, "We are able." And Jesus said to them, "The cup that I drink ^you shall drink; and you shall be baptized with the baptism with which I am baptized. ⁴⁰But to sit on My right or on *My* left is not Mine to give; ^but *it is* for those for whom it has been prepared."

⁴¹^Hearing *this,* the *other* ten began to feel indignant with James and John. ⁴²Calling them to Himself, Jesus *said to them, "You know that those who are recognized as rulers of the Gentiles domineer over them; and their people in high position exercise authority over them. ⁴³But it is not this way among you; ^rather, whoever wants to become prominent among you

10:21 ^Matt 6:20   10:23 ^Matt 19:23   10:24 ^Mark 1:27
10:25 ^Matt 19:24   10:27 ^Matt 19:26
10:28 ^Matt 4:20-22   10:29 ^Matt 6:33; 19:29
10:30 ^Matt 12:32   10:31 ^Matt 19:30; 20:16
10:32 *Matt 20:17-19; Luke 18:31-33*   10:33 ^Mark 8:31;
9:12   10:34 ^Matt 16:21; 26:67   10:35 ^*Matt 20:20-28*
10:37 ^Matt 19:28   10:38 ^Matt 20:22
10:39 ^Acts 12:2; Rev 1:9   10:40 ^Matt 13:11
10:41 ^Mark 10:42-45; Luke 22:25-27

shall be your servant; **44**and whoever wants to be first among you
shall be slave of all. **45**For even the
Son of Man ^did not come to be
served, but to serve, and to give His
life as a ransom for many."

BARTIMAEUS RECEIVES HIS SIGHT

46^Then they *came to Jericho. And
later, as He was leaving Jericho with
His disciples and a large crowd, a
beggar who was blind *named* Bar-
timaeus, the son of Timaeus, was
sitting by the road. **47**And when he
heard that it was Jesus the Nazarene, he began to cry out and say,
"Jesus, ^Son of David, have mercy
on me!" **48**Many were sternly telling him to be quiet, but he kept
crying out all the more, "^Son of
David, have mercy on me!" **49**And
Jesus stopped and said, "Call him
here." So they *called the man who
was blind, saying to him, "^Take
courage, stand up! He is calling for
you." **50**And throwing off his cloak,
he jumped up and came to Jesus.
51And replying to him, Jesus said,
"What do you want Me to do for
you?" And the man who was blind
said to Him, "¹^Rabboni, *I want* to
regain my sight!" **52**And Jesus said
to him, "Go; ^your faith has made
you well." And immediately he
regained his sight and *began* following Him on the road.

THE TRIUMPHAL ENTRY

11 ^And as they *approached Jerusalem, at Bethphage and Bethany, near the Mount of Olives, He
*sent two of His disciples, **2**and *said
to them, "Go into the village opposite you, and immediately as you
enter it you will find a colt tied *there,*
on which no one has ever sat; untie it
and bring *it here.* **3**And if anyone says

to you, 'Why are you doing this?' say,
'The Lord has need of it'; and immediately he will send it back here."
4They went away and found a colt
tied at the door, outside in the street;
and they *untied it. **5**And some of
the bystanders were saying to them,
"What are you doing, untying the
colt?" **6**And they told them just as
Jesus had said, and they gave them
permission. **7**^They *brought the colt
to Jesus and *put their cloaks on it;
and He sat on it. **8**And many people
spread their cloaks on the road, and
others *spread* leafy branches which
they had cut from the fields. **9**And
those who went in front and those
who followed were shouting:

"Hosanna!
    ^BLESSED IS HE WHO COMES IN
    THE NAME OF THE LORD;
10   Blessed *is* the coming kingdom
    of our father David;
    Hosanna ^in the highest!"

11^And *Jesus* entered Jerusalem
and came into the temple *area;*
and after looking around at everything, ᴮHe left for Bethany with the
twelve, since it was already late.

12^On the next day, when they had
left Bethany, He became hungry.
13Seeing from a distance a fig tree
in leaf, He went *to see* if perhaps He
would find anything on it; and when
He came to it, He found nothing but
leaves, for it was not the season for
figs. **14**And He said to it, "May no one
ever eat fruit from you again!" And
His disciples were listening.

10:43^Matt 20:26; 23:11   10:45^Matt 20:28
10:46^*Matt 20:29-34; Luke 18:35-43*
10:47^Matt 9:27   10:48^Matt 9:27   10:49^Matt 9:2
10:51^Matt 23:7; John 20:16   10:52^Matt 9:22
11:1^Matt 21:1-9; Luke 19:29-38   11:7^*Matt 21:4-9;
Luke 19:35-38*   11:9^Ps 118:26; Matt 21:9
11:10^Matt 21:9   11:11^Matt 21:12   ᴮMatt 21:17
11:12^*Matt 21:18-22*

10:51 ¹I.e., My Master

JESUS DRIVES MONEY CHANGERS FROM THE TEMPLE

¹⁵ᴬThen they *came to Jerusalem. And He entered the temple *area* and began to drive out those who were selling and buying on the temple *grounds,* and He overturned the tables of the money changers and the seats of those who were selling doves; ¹⁶and He would not allow anyone to carry merchandise through the temple *grounds.* ¹⁷And He *began* to teach and say to them, "Is it not written: 'ᴬMY HOUSE WILL BE CALLED A HOUSE OF PRAYER FOR ALL THE NATIONS'? ᴮBut you have made it a DEN OF ROBBERS.'" ¹⁸And the chief priests and the scribes heard *this,* and they ᴬ*began* seeking how to put Him to death; for they were afraid of Him, because all the crowd was astonished at His teaching.

¹⁹And ᴬwhenever evening came, they would leave the city.

²⁰ᴬAs they were passing by in the morning, they saw the fig tree withered from the roots *up.* ²¹And being reminded, Peter *said to Him, "ᴬRabbi, look, the fig tree that You cursed has withered." ²²And Jesus answered and *said to them, "ᴬHave faith in God. ²³ᴬTruly I say to you, whoever says to this mountain, 'Be taken up and thrown into the sea,' and does not doubt in his heart, but believes that what he says is going to happen, it will be *granted* to him. ²⁴Therefore, I say to you, ᴬall things for which you pray and ask, believe that you have received them, and they will be *granted* to you. ²⁵And whenever you stand praying, ᴬforgive, if you have anything against anyone, so that your Father who is in heaven will also forgive you for your offenses. ²⁶[¹·ᴬBut if you do not forgive, neither will your Father who is in heaven forgive your offenses."]

JESUS' AUTHORITY QUESTIONED

²⁷And they *came again to Jerusalem. ᴬAnd as He was walking in the temple *area,* the chief priests, the scribes, and the elders *came to Him, ²⁸and *began* saying to Him, "By what authority are You doing these things, or who gave You this authority to do these things?" ²⁹But Jesus said to them, "I will ask you one question, and you answer Me, and *then* I will tell you by what authority I do these things. ³⁰Was the baptism of John from heaven, or from men? Answer Me." ³¹And they *began* considering *the implications* among themselves, saying, "If we say, 'From heaven,' He will say, 'Then why did you not believe him?' ³²But should we say, 'From men'?"—they were afraid of the people, for they all considered John to have been a real prophet. ³³Answering Jesus, they *said, "We do not know." And Jesus *said to them, "Neither am I telling you by what authority I do these things."

PARABLE OF THE VINE-GROWERS

12 And He began to speak to them in parables: "ᴬA man planted a vineyard and put a fence around it, and dug a vat under the wine press and built a tower, and leased it to ¹vine-growers and went on a journey. ²And at the *harvest*

11:15ᴬJohn 2:13-16   11:17ᴬIs 56:7   ᴮJer 7:11
11:18ᴬMatt 21:46; Mark 12:12   11:19ᴬMatt 21:17;
Mark 11:11   11:20ᴬMatt 21:19-22   11:21ᴬMatt 23:7
11:22ᴬMatt 17:20; 21:21f   11:23ᴬMatt 17:20; 1 Cor 13:2
11:24ᴬMatt 7:7f   11:25ᴬMatt 6:14   11:26ᴬMatt 6:15;
18:35   11:27ᴬMatt 21:23-27; Luke 20:1-8
12:1ᴬMatt 21:33-46; Luke 20:9-19

11:26¹Early mss do not contain this v
12:1¹Or tenant farmers, also vv 2, 7, 9

time he sent a slave to the vine-growers, in order to receive *his share* of the produce of the vineyard from the vine-growers. ³And they took him, and beat him, and sent him away empty-handed. ⁴And again he sent them another slave, and they wounded him in the head, and treated him shamefully. ⁵And he sent another, and that one they killed; and *so with* many others, beating some and killing others. ⁶He had one more *man to send*, a beloved son; he sent him to them last *of all*, saying, 'They will respect my son.' ⁷But those vine-growers said to one another, 'This is the heir; come, let's kill him, and the inheritance will be ours!' ⁸And they took him and killed him, and threw him out of the vineyard. ⁹What will the owner of the vineyard do? He will come and put the vine-growers to death, and give the vineyard to others. ¹⁰Have you not even read this Scripture:

'ᴬA STONE WHICH THE BUILDERS
    REJECTED,
  THIS HAS BECOME THE CHIEF
    CORNERSTONE;
¹¹ ᴬTHIS CAME ABOUT FROM THE
    LORD,
  AND IT IS MARVELOUS IN OUR
    EYES'?"

¹²And they were seeking to seize Him, and *yet* they feared the people, for they understood that He told the parable against them. And *so* ᴬthey left Him and went away.

JESUS ANSWERS THE PHARISEES, SADDUCEES, AND SCRIBES

¹³ᴬThen they *sent some of the Pharisees and Herodians to Him in order to ᴮtrap Him in a statement. ¹⁴They came and *said to Him, "Teacher, we know that You

are truthful and do not care what anyone thinks; for You are not partial to anyone, but You teach the way of God in truth. Is it permissible to pay a ¹poll-tax to Caesar, or not? ¹⁵Are we to pay, or not pay?" But He, knowing their hypocrisy, said to them, "Why are you testing Me? Bring Me a ¹denarius to look at." ¹⁶And they brought *one*. And He *said to them, "Whose image and inscription is this?" And they said to Him, "Caesar's." ¹⁷And Jesus said to them, "ᴬPay to Caesar the things that are Caesar's, and to God the things that are God's." And they were utterly amazed at Him.

¹⁸ᴬ*Some* Sadducees (who say that there is no resurrection) *came to Jesus, and *began* questioning Him, saying, ¹⁹"Teacher, Moses wrote for us that ᴬif a man's brother dies and leaves behind a wife and does not leave a child, his brother is to marry the wife and raise up children for his brother. ²⁰There were seven brothers; and the first took a wife, and died leaving no children. ²¹The second one married her, and died leaving behind no children; and the third likewise; ²²and *so* the seven *together* left no children. Last of all the woman also died. ²³In the resurrection, which one's wife will she be? For *each of* the seven had her as *his* wife." ²⁴Jesus said to them, "Is this not the reason you are mistaken, that you do not understand the Scriptures nor the power of God? ²⁵For when they rise from the dead, they neither marry nor are given in marriage, but are

---

12:10 ᴬPs 118:22   12:11 ᴬPs 118:23   12:12 ᴬMatt 22:22
12:13 ᴬMatt 22:15-22   ᴮLuke 11:54   12:17 ᴬMatt 22:21
12:18 ᴬMatt 22:23-33; Luke 20:27-38;   12:19 ᴬDeut 25:5

12:14 ¹I.e., a tax on each person in the census
12:15 ¹The denarius was a day's wages for a laborer

like angels in heaven. ²⁶But regarding the fact that the dead rise, have you not read in the book of Moses, ^in *the passage about* the *burning* bush, how God spoke to him, saying, '^BI AM THE GOD OF ABRAHAM, THE GOD OF ISAAC, AND THE GOD OF JACOB'? ²⁷^He is not the God of the dead, but of the living; you are greatly mistaken."

²⁸^One of the scribes came up and heard them arguing, and recognizing that He had answered them well, asked Him, "What commandment is the foremost of all?" ²⁹Jesus answered, "The foremost is, '^HEAR, ISRAEL! THE LORD IS OUR GOD, THE LORD IS ONE; ³⁰^AND YOU SHALL LOVE THE LORD YOUR GOD WITH ALL YOUR HEART, AND WITH ALL YOUR SOUL, AND WITH ALL YOUR MIND, AND WITH ALL YOUR STRENGTH.' ³¹The second is this: '^YOU SHALL LOVE YOUR NEIGHBOR AS YOURSELF.' There is no other commandment greater than these." ³²And the scribe said to Him, "Well *said*, Teacher; You have truly stated that ^HE IS ONE, AND THERE IS NO OTHER BESIDES HIM; ³³^and to love Him with all the heart, and with all the understanding, and with all the strength, and to love one's neighbor as oneself, ^Bis much more than all the burnt offerings and sacrifices." ³⁴When Jesus saw that he had answered intelligently, He said to him, "You are not far from the kingdom of God." ^And *then,* no one dared any longer to question Him.

³⁵^And Jesus responded and *began* saying, as He taught in the temple *area,* "How *is it that* the scribes say that the Christ is the son of David? ³⁶David himself said in the Holy Spirit,

'^THE LORD SAID TO MY LORD,
"SIT AT MY RIGHT HAND,
UNTIL I PUT YOUR ENEMIES
UNDER YOUR FEET."'

³⁷David himself calls Him 'Lord'; so in what sense is He his son?" And ^the large crowd enjoyed listening to Him.

³⁸^And in His teaching He was saying: "Beware of the scribes who like to walk around in long robes, and *like* personal greetings in the marketplaces, ³⁹and seats of honor in the synagogues, and places of honor at banquets, ⁴⁰^who devour widows' houses, and for appearance's sake offer long prayers. These will receive all the more condemnation."

THE WIDOW'S COINS

⁴¹^And *Jesus* sat down opposite the treasury, and *began* watching how the people were putting money into the treasury; and many rich people were putting in large amounts. ⁴²And a poor widow came and put in two ¹lepta coins, which amount to a ²quadrans. ⁴³Calling His disciples to Him, He said to them, "Truly I say to you, this poor widow put in more than all the contributors to the treasury; ⁴⁴for they all put in out of their surplus, but she, out of her poverty, put in all she owned, all she had ^to live on."

12:26 ^Luke 20:37   ^BEx 3:6
12:27 ^Matt 22:32; Luke 20:38   12:28 ^Luke 10:25-28; 20:39f   12:29 ^Deut 6:4   12:30 ^Deut 6:5
12:31 ^Lev 19:18   12:32 ^Deut 4:35   12:33 ^Deut 6:5
^B1 Sam 15:22   12:34 ^Matt 22:46   12:35 ^Matt 22:41-46; Luke 20:41-44   12:36 ^Ps 110:1
12:37 ^John 12:9   12:38 ^Matt 23:1-7; Luke 20:45-47
12:40 ^Luke 20:47   12:41 ^Luke 21:1-4
12:44 ^Luke 8:43; 15:12, 30

12:42 ¹The smallest Greek copper coin, about 1/128 of a laborer's daily wage   ²A small Roman copper coin, worth about 1/64 of a laborer's daily wage

THINGS TO COME

13 ^AAs He was going out of the temple, one of His disciples *said to Him, "Teacher, look! What wonderful stones and what wonderful buildings!" ²And Jesus said to him, "Do you see these great buildings? ^ANot one stone will be left upon another, which will not be torn down."

³As He was sitting on ^Athe Mount of Olives opposite the temple, Peter, James, John, and Andrew were questioning Him privately, ⁴"Tell us, when will these things come about, and what *will be* the sign when all these things are going to be fulfilled?" ⁵And Jesus began to say to them, "See to it that no one misleads you. ⁶Many will come in My name, saying, '^AI am *He!*' and they will mislead many. ⁷When you hear of wars and rumors of wars, do not be alarmed; *those things* must take place; but *that is* not yet the end. ⁸For nation will rise up against nation, and kingdom against kingdom; there will be earthquakes in various places; there will *also* be famines. These things are *only* the beginning of birth pains.

⁹"But be on your guard; for they will ^Ahand you over to *the* courts, and you will be flogged ^Ain *the* synagogues, and you will stand before governors and kings for My sake, as a testimony to them. ¹⁰^AAnd the gospel must first be preached to all the nations. ¹¹^AAnd when they arrest you and hand you over, do not worry beforehand about what you are to say, but say whatever is given you at that time; for you are not the ones speaking, but *it is* the Holy Spirit. ¹²And brother will betray brother to death, and a father *his* child; and children will rise up against parents and have them put to death. ¹³And ^Ayou will be hated by everyone because of My name, but it is the one who has endured to the end who will be saved.

¹⁴"Now ^Awhen you see the ^BABOMINATION OF DESOLATION standing where it should not be—let the ʳreader understand—then those who are in Judea must flee to the mountains. ¹⁵^AWhoever is on the housetop must not go down, nor go in to get anything out of his house. ¹⁶And whoever is in the field must not turn back to get his cloak. ¹⁷But woe to those women who are pregnant, and to those who are nursing babies in those days! ¹⁸Moreover, pray that it will not happen in winter. ¹⁹For those days will be such a *time of* tribulation as has not occurred ^Asince the beginning of the creation which God created until now, and never will *again*. ²⁰And if the Lord had not shortened *those* days, no life would have been saved; but for the sake of the elect, whom He chose, He shortened the days. ²¹And then if anyone says to you, 'Look, here is the Christ'; *or,* 'Look, there *He is*'; do not believe *it;* ²²for false christs and false prophets will arise, and will provide ^Asigns and wonders, in order to mislead, if possible, the elect. ²³But beware; I have told you everything in advance.

13:1 ^A *Matt 24; Luke 21:5-36*   13:2 ^A Luke 19:44
13:3 ^A Matt 21:1   13:6 ^A John 8:24   13:9 ^A Matt 10:17
13:10 ^A Matt 24:14   13:11 ^A *Matt 10:19-22; Luke 21:12-17*
13:13 ^A Matt 10:22; John 15:21   13:14 ^A Matt 24:15f
^B Dan 9:27   13:15 ^A Luke 17:31   13:19 ^A Dan 12:1;
Mark 10:6   13:22 ^A Matt 24:24; John 4:48

13:14 ʳ I.e., of the book of Daniel

THE RETURN OF CHRIST

24 "But in those days, after that tribulation, ^THE SUN WILL BE DARKENED AND THE MOON WILL NOT GIVE ITS LIGHT, 25 ^AND THE STARS WILL BE FALLING from heaven, and the powers that are in the heavens will be shaken. 26 And then they will see ^THE SON OF MAN COMING IN CLOUDS with great power and glory. 27 And then He will send forth the angels, and ^will gather together His elect from the four winds, from the end of the earth to the end of heaven.

28 "Now learn the parable from the fig tree: as soon as its branch has become tender and sprouts its leaves, you know that summer is near. 29 So you too, when you see these things happening, recognize that He is near, *right* at the door. 30 Truly I say to you, this generation will not pass away until all these things take place. 31 Heaven and earth will pass away, but My words will not pass away. 32 ^But about that day or hour no one knows, not even the angels in heaven, nor the Son, but the Father *alone.*

33 "Watch out, ^stay alert; for you do not know when the *appointed* time is. 34 ^*It is* like a man away on a journey, *who* upon leaving his house and putting his slaves in charge, *assigning* to each one his task, also commanded the doorkeeper to stay alert. 35 Therefore, stay alert—for you do not know when the master of the house is coming, whether in the evening, at midnight, or ^when the rooster crows, or in the morning— 36 so that he does not come suddenly and find you ^asleep. 37 What I say to you I say to all: '^Stay alert!'"

DEATH PLOT AND ANOINTING

14 ^Now the Passover and *Festival of* Unleavened Bread were two days away; and the chief priests and the scribes were seeking how to arrest Him covertly and kill *Him;* 2 for they were saying, "Not during the festival, otherwise there will be a riot of the people."

3 ^While He was in Bethany at the home of Simon 'the Leper, He was reclining *at the table,* and a woman came with an alabaster vial of very expensive perfume of pure 2 nard. She broke the vial and poured *the perfume* over His head. 4 But there were some indignantly *remarking* to one another, "Why has this perfume been wasted? 5 For this perfume could have been sold for over three hundred 'denarii, and *the money* given to the poor." And they were scolding her. 6 But Jesus said, "Leave her alone! Why are you bothering her? She has done a good deed for Me. 7 For you always have ^the poor with you, and whenever you want, you can do good to them; but you do not always have Me. 8 She has done what she could; ^she has anointed My body beforehand for the burial. 9 Truly I say to you, ^wherever the gospel is preached in the entire world, what this woman has done will also be told in memory of her."

13:24 ^Is 13:10; Ezek 32:7   13:25 ^Is 34:4; Rev 6:13
13:26 ^Dan 7:13; Rev 1:7   13:27 ^Deut 30:4
13:32 ^Matt 24:36; Acts 1:7   13:33 ^Eph 6:18; Col 4:2
13:34 ^Luke 12:36-38   13:35 ^Mark 14:30
13:36 ^Rom 13:11   13:37 ^Matt 24:42; Mark 13:35
14:1 ^*Matt 26:2-5; Luke 22:1, 2*   14:3 ^Luke 7:37-39;
John 12:1-8   14:7 ^Deut 15:11; Matt 26:11
14:8 ^John 19:40   14:9 ^Matt 26:13

14:3 ¹ I.e., a nickname; the man no doubt was cured
² An aromatic oil extracted from an East Indian plant
14:5 ¹ The denarius was a day's wages for a laborer

¹⁰ᴬThen Judas Iscariot, who was one of the twelve, went off to the chief priests in order to betray Him to them. ¹¹They were delighted when they heard *this,* and promised to give him money. And he *began* seeking how to betray Him at an opportune time.

THE LAST PASSOVER

¹²ᴬOn the first day of ¹Unleavened Bread, when the Passover *lamb* was being sacrificed, His disciples *said to Him, "Where do You want us to go and prepare for You to eat the Passover?" ¹³And He *sent two of His disciples and *said to them, "Go into the city, and a man carrying a pitcher of water will meet you; follow him; ¹⁴and wherever he enters, say to the owner of the house, 'The Teacher says, "Where is My ᴬguest room in which I may eat the Passover with My disciples?"'' ¹⁵And he himself will show you a large upstairs room furnished *and* ready; prepare for us there." ¹⁶The disciples left and came to the city, and found *everything* just as He had told them; and they prepared the Passover.

¹⁷ᴬWhen it was evening He *came with the twelve. ¹⁸And as they were reclining *at the table* and eating, Jesus said, "Truly I say to you that one of you will betray Me—one who is eating with Me." ¹⁹They began to be grieved and to say to Him one by one, "Surely not I?" ²⁰But He said to them, "*It is* one of the twelve, the one who dips *bread* with Me in the bowl. ²¹For the Son of Man is going away just as it is written about Him; but woe to that man by whom the Son of Man is betrayed! *It would have been* good for that man if he had not been born."

THE LORD'S SUPPER

²²ᴬWhile they were eating, He took *some* bread, and after a blessing He broke *it,* and gave *it* to them, and said, "Take *it;* this is My body." ²³And when He had taken a cup *and* given thanks, He gave *it* to them, and they all drank from it. ²⁴And He said to them, "This is My ᴬblood of the covenant, which is being poured out for many. ²⁵Truly I say to you, I will not drink of the fruit of the vine again, until that day when I drink it, new, in the kingdom of God."

²⁶ᴬAnd after singing a hymn, they went out to the Mount of Olives.

²⁷ᴬAnd Jesus *said to them, "You will all ¹fall away, because it is written: 'ᴮI WILL STRIKE THE SHEPHERD, AND THE SHEEP WILL BE SCATTERED.' ²⁸But after I am raised, ᴬI will go ahead of you to Galilee." ²⁹But Peter said to Him, "Even if they all fall away, yet I *will* not!" ³⁰And Jesus *said to him, "Truly I say to you, that ᴬthis very night, before ᴮa rooster crows twice, you yourself will deny Me three times." ³¹But Peter *repeatedly* said insistently, "*Even* if I have to die with You, I will not deny You!" And they all were saying the same thing as well.

JESUS IN GETHSEMANE

³²ᴬThey *came to a place named Gethsemane; and He *said to His disciples, "Sit here until I have prayed." ³³And He *took with Him Peter, James, and John, and

14:10 ᴬ *Matt 26:14-16; Luke 22:3-6*   14:12 ᴬ *Matt 26:17-19; Luke 22:7-13*   14:14 ᴬ *Luke 22:11*
14:17 ᴬ *John 13:18ff*   14:22 ᴬ *Mark 10:16*   14:24 ᴬ *Ex 24:8*
14:26 ᴬ *Matt 26:30*   14:27 ᴬ *Matt 26:31-35*   ᴮ *Zech 13:7*
14:28 ᴬ *Matt 28:16*   14:30 ᴬ *Matt 26:34*
ᴮ *Mark 14:68, 72*   14:32 ᴬ *Matt 26:36-46; Luke 22:40-46*

14:12 ¹I.e., Passover week   14:27 ¹I.e., have a lapse in faith

began to be very ^distressed and troubled. ³⁴And He *said to them, "^My soul is deeply grieved, to the point of death; remain here and keep watch." ³⁵And He went a little beyond *them,* and fell to the ground and *began* praying that if it were possible, ^the hour might pass Him by. ³⁶And He was saying, "^Abba! Father! All things are possible for You; remove this cup from Me; ᴮyet not what I will, but what You *will.*" ³⁷And He *came and *found them sleeping, and *said to Peter, "Simon, are you asleep? Could you not keep watch for one hour? ³⁸^Keep watching and praying, so that you will not come into temptation; the spirit is willing, but the flesh is weak." ³⁹And again He went away and prayed, saying the same words. ⁴⁰And again He came and found them sleeping, for their eyes were heavy; and they did not know what to say in reply to Him. ⁴¹And He *came the third time, and *said to them, "Are you still sleeping and resting? That is enough. ^The hour has come; behold, the Son of Man is being betrayed into the hands of sinners. ⁴²Get up, let's go; behold, the one who is betraying Me is near!"

BETRAYAL AND ARREST

⁴³^And immediately, while He was still speaking, Judas, one of the twelve, *came up, accompanied by a crowd with swords and clubs *who were* from the chief priests, the scribes, and the elders. ⁴⁴Now he who was betraying Him had given them a signal, saying, "Whomever I kiss, He is the one; arrest Him and lead Him away under guard." ⁴⁵And after coming, Judas immediately went to Him and

*said, "^Rabbi!" and kissed Him. ⁴⁶And they laid hands on Him and arrested Him. ⁴⁷But one of those who stood by drew his sword, and struck the slave of the high priest and cut off his ear. ⁴⁸And Jesus said to them, "Have you come out with swords and clubs to arrest Me, as *you would* against a man inciting a revolt? ⁴⁹Every day I was with you ^within the temple *grounds* teaching, and you did not arrest Me; but *this has taken place* so that the Scriptures will be fulfilled." ⁵⁰And His disciples all left Him and fled.

⁵¹A young man was following Him, wearing *nothing but* a linen sheet over *his* naked *body;* and they *seized him. ⁵²But he pulled free of the linen sheet and escaped naked.

JESUS BEFORE HIS ACCUSERS

⁵³^They led Jesus away to the high priest; and all the chief priests, the elders, and the scribes *gathered together. ⁵⁴And Peter had followed Him at a distance, right into the courtyard of the high priest; and he was sitting with the officers and ^warming himself at the fire. ⁵⁵Now the chief priests and the entire ¹,^Council were trying to obtain testimony against Jesus to put Him to death, and they were not finding any. ⁵⁶For many people were giving false testimony against Him, and *so* their testimonies were not consistent. ⁵⁷And *then* some stood up and *began* giving false testimony against Him, saying, ⁵⁸"We heard

14:33^Mark 9:15; 16:5, 6   14:34^Matt 26:38;
John 12:27   14:35^Matt 26:45; Mark 14:41
14:36^Rom 8:15   ᴮMatt 26:39   14:38^Matt 26:41
14:41^Mark 14:35   14:43^*Matt 26:47-56; Luke
22:47-53*   14:45^Matt 23:7   14:49^Mark 12:35;
Luke 19:47   14:53^*Matt 26:57-68; John 18:12f, 19-24*
14:54^Mark 14:67; John 18:18   14:55^Matt 5:22
14:55¹Or *Sanhedrin*

Him say, "'I will destroy this temple that was made by hands, and in three days I will build another, made without hands.'" 59 And not even in this respect was their testimony consistent. 60 And *then* the high priest stood up *and came* forward and questioned Jesus, saying, "Do You not offer any answer for what these men are testifying against You?" 61 But He kept silent and did not offer any answer. ^Again the high priest was questioning Him, and *said to Him, "Are You the Christ, the Son of 'the Blessed *One?"* 62 And Jesus said, "I am; and you shall see ^the Son of Man sitting at the right hand of power, and ᴮcoming with the clouds of heaven." 63 ᴬTearing his clothes, the high priest *said, "What further need do we have of witnesses? 64 You have heard the ^blasphemy; how does it seem to you?" And they all condemned Him as deserving of death. 65 And some began to ^spit on Him, and to blindfold Him, and to beat Him with their fists and say to Him, "ᴮProphesy!" Then the officers took custody of Him and slapped Him *in the face.*

PETER'S DENIALS

66 ᴬAnd while Peter was below in the courtyard, one of the slave women of the high priest *came, 67 and seeing Peter ^warming himself, she looked at him and *said, "You were with Jesus the ᴮNazarene as well." 68 But he denied *it,* saying, "I neither know nor understand what you are talking about." And he went out onto the porch.' 69 The slave woman saw him, and began once more to say to the bystanders, "This man is *one* of them!" 70 But again he denied it. And after a little while

the bystanders were again saying to Peter, "You really are *one* of them, ^for you are a Galilean as well." 71 But he began to curse *himself* and to swear, "I do not know this Man of whom you speak!" 72 And immediately a rooster crowed a second time. And Peter remembered how Jesus had made the remark to him, "Before ^a rooster crows twice, you will deny Me three times." And he hurried on and *began to* weep.

JESUS BEFORE PILATE

15 ^Early in the morning the chief priests with the elders, scribes, and the entire 'Council immediately held a consultation; and they bound Jesus and led Him away, and turned Him over to Pilate. 2 ᴬPilate questioned Him: "*So* You are the King of the Jews?" And He answered him, "*It is as* you say." 3 And the chief priests *started* accusing Him of many things. 4 But Pilate questioned Him again, saying, "Do You offer nothing in answer? See how many charges they are bringing against You!" 5 But Jesus ^said nothing further in answer, so Pilate was amazed.

6 ᴬNow at *the Passover* Feast he used to release for them *any* one prisoner whom they requested. 7 And the one named Barabbas had been imprisoned with the rebels who had committed murder

14:58 ^Matt 26:61; Mark 15:29   14:61 ^*Matt 26:63ff;* Luke 22:67-71   14:62 ^Ps 110:1   ᴮDan 7:13
14:63 ^Num 14:6; Matt 26:65   14:64 ^Lev 24:16
14:65 ^Matt 26:67   ᴮLuke 22:64   14:66 ^*Matt 26:69-75; Luke 22:56-62*   14:67 ^Mark 14:54
ᴮMark 1:24   14:70 ^Matt 26:73; Luke 22:59
14:72 ^Mark 14:30, 68   15:1 ^Matt 27:1
15:2 ^Matt 27:11-14; Luke 23:2, 3   15:5 ^Matt 27:12
15:6 ^*Matt 27:15-26; Luke 23:18-25*

14:61 ¹ A common way for the Jewish leaders to refer to God   14:68 ¹ Later mss add *and a rooster crowed*
15:1 ¹ Or *Sanhedrin*

in the revolt. [8] And the crowd went up and began asking *Pilate to do* as he had been accustomed to do for them. [9] Pilate answered them, saying, "Do you want me to release for you the King of the Jews?" [10] For he was aware that the chief priests had handed Him over because of envy. [11] But the chief priests stirred up the crowd ^to ask him to release Barabbas for them instead. [12] And responding again, Pilate said to them, "Then what shall I do with Him whom you call the King of the Jews?" [13] They shouted back, "Crucify Him!" [14] But Pilate said to them, "Why, what evil has He done?" But they shouted all the more, "Crucify Him!" [15] Intent on satisfying the crowd, Pilate released Barabbas for them, and after having Jesus ^flogged, he handed Him over to be crucified.

JESUS IS MOCKED

[16] ^Now the soldiers took Him away into the palace (that is, the Praetorium), and they *called together the whole *Roman* 'cohort. [17] And they *dressed Him in purple, and after twisting together a crown of thorns, they put it on Him; [18] and they began saluting Him: "Hail, King of the Jews!" [19] And they *repeatedly* beat His head with a reed and spit on Him, and kneeling, they bowed down before Him. [20] And after they had mocked Him, they took the purple *cloak* off Him and put His *own* garments on Him. And they *led Him out to crucify Him.

[21] ^And they *compelled a passerby coming from the country, Simon of Cyrene (the father of Alexander and Rufus), to carry His cross.

THE CRUCIFIXION

[22] ^Then they *brought Him to the place Golgotha, which is translated, Place of a Skull. [23] And they tried to give Him ^wine mixed with myrrh; but He did not take *it*. [24] And they *crucified Him, and *^divided up His garments among themselves, casting lots for them *to decide* what each man would take. [25] Now it was the '^third hour when they crucified Him. [26] The inscription of the charge against Him read, "^THE KING OF THE JEWS."

[27] And they *crucified two 'rebels with Him, one on His right and one on His left.[2] [29] Those passing by were hurling abuse at Him, ^shaking their heads and saying, "Ha! You who *are going to* ^destroy the temple and rebuild it in three days, [30] save Yourself by coming down from the cross!" [31] In the same way the chief priests also, along with the scribes, were mocking *Him* among themselves and saying, "^He saved others; He cannot save Himself! [32] Let *this* Christ, the King of Israel, come down now from the cross, so that we may see and believe!" ^Those who were crucified with Him were also insulting Him.

[33] ^When the 'sixth hour came, darkness fell over the whole land until the 'ninth hour. [34] At the 'ninth hour Jesus cried out with

15:11^Acts 3:14   15:15^Matt 27:26
15:16^Matt 27:27-31   15:21^Matt 27:32; Luke 23:26
15:22^Matt 27:33-44; Luke 23:33-43
15:23^Matt 27:34   15:24^Ps 22:18; John 19:24
15:25^Mark 15:33   15:26^Matt 27:37   15:29^Ps 22:7
^Mark 14:58   15:31^Matt 27:42; Luke 23:35
15:32^Matt 27:44; Mark 15:27   15:33^Matt 27:45-56;
Luke 23:44-49   15:34^Ps 22:1; Matt 27:46

15:16'Normally 600 men (the number varied)
15:25'I.e., 9 a.m.   15:27'Or *robbers*   ²Late mss add
the following as v 28: And the Scripture was fulfilled
which says, "And He was counted with wrongdoers."
15:33'I.e., noon   ²I.e., 3 p.m.   15:34'I.e., 3 p.m.

a loud voice, "ᴬEʟᴏɪ, Eʟᴏɪ, ʟᴇᴍᴀ sᴀʙᴀᴋᴛᴀɴᴇɪ?" which is translated, "Mʏ Gᴏᴅ, Mʏ Gᴏᴅ, ᴡʜʏ ʜᴀᴠᴇ Yᴏᴜ ғᴏʀsᴀᴋᴇɴ Mᴇ?" ³⁵And when some of the bystanders heard *Him,* they *began* saying, "Look! He is calling for Elijah!" ³⁶And someone ran and filled a sponge with sour wine, put it on a reed, and gave Him a drink, saying, "Let us see if Elijah comes to take Him down." ³⁷ᴬBut Jesus let out a loud cry, and died. ³⁸ᴬAnd the veil of the temple was torn in two from top to bottom. ³⁹ᴬAnd when the centurion, who was standing right in front of Him, saw that He died in this way, he said, "Truly this Man was the Son of God!"

⁴⁰ᴬNow there were also *some* women watching from a distance, among whom *were* Mary Magdalene, Mary the mother of James the Less and Joses, and Salome. ⁴¹When He was in Galilee, they used to follow Him and ᴬserve Him; and *there were* many other women who came up with Him to Jerusalem.

JESUS IS BURIED

⁴²ᴬWhen evening had already come, since it was the preparation day, that is, the day before the Sabbath, ⁴³Joseph of Arimathea came, a ᴬprominent member of the Council, who was himself also waiting for the kingdom of God; and he ᴮgathered up courage and went in before Pilate, and asked for the body of Jesus. ⁴⁴Now Pilate wondered if He was dead by this time, and summoning the centurion, he questioned him as to whether He was already dead. ⁴⁵And after learning this from ᴬthe centurion, he granted the body to Joseph. ⁴⁶Joseph bought a linen cloth, took Him down, wrapped Him in the linen cloth, and laid Him in a tomb which had been cut out in the rock; and he rolled a stone against the entrance of the tomb. ⁴⁷ᴬMary Magdalene and Mary the *mother* of Joses were watching *to see* where He was laid.

THE RESURRECTION

16 ᴬWhen the Sabbath was over, Mary Magdalene, Mary the *mother* of James, and Salome bought spices so that they might come and anoint Him. ²And very early on the first day of the week, they *came to the tomb when the sun had risen. ³They were saying to one another, "Who will roll away ᴬthe stone from the entrance of the tomb for us?" ⁴And looking up, they *noticed that the stone had been rolled away; for it was extremely large. ⁵And ᴬentering the tomb, they saw a young man sitting at the right, wearing a white robe; and they were amazed. ⁶But he *said to them, "Do not be amazed; you are looking for Jesus the Nazarene, who has been crucified. ᴬHe has risen; He is not here; see, *here is* the place where they laid Him. ⁷But go, tell His disciples and Peter, 'ᴬHe is going ahead of you to Galilee; there you will see Him, just as He told you.'" ⁸And they went out and fled from the tomb, for trembling and astonishment had gripped them; and they said nothing to anyone, for they were afraid.

15:37ᴬMatt 27:50; Luke 23:46   15:38ᴬEx 26:31-33; Matt 27:51   15:39ᴬMatt 27:54; Mark 15:45   15:40ᴬLuke 23:49; John 19:25   15:41ᴬMatt 27:55f   15:42ᴬ*Matt 27:57-61; Luke 23:50-56*   15:43ᴬMatt 27:57   ᴮJohn 19:38   15:45ᴬMark 15:39   15:47ᴬMatt 27:56; Mark 15:40   16:1ᴬJohn 20:1-8   16:3ᴬMatt 27:60; Mark 15:46   16:5ᴬJohn 20:11, 12   16:6ᴬMatt 28:6; Luke 24:6   16:7ᴬMatt 26:32; Mark 14:28

⁹[['Now after He had risen early on the first day of the week, He first appeared to ^Mary Magdalene, from whom He had cast out seven demons. ¹⁰^She went and reported to those who had been with Him, while they were mourning and weeping. ¹¹And when they heard that He was alive and had been seen by her, ^they refused to believe *it*.

¹²Now after that, He appeared in a different form ^to two of them while they were walking along on their way to the country. ¹³And they went away and reported it to the rest, but they ^did not believe them, either.

THE DISCIPLES COMMISSIONED

¹⁴Later He appeared^to the eleven *disciples* themselves as they were reclining *at the table;* and He reprimanded them for their unbelief and hardness of heart, because they had not believed those who had seen Him after He had risen *from the dead.* ¹⁵And He said to them, "^Go into all the world and preach the gospel to all creation. ¹⁶^The one who has believed and has been baptized will be saved; but the one who has not believed

will be condemned. ¹⁷These signs will accompany those who have believed: ^in My name they will cast out demons, they will speak with new tongues; ¹⁸they will pick up serpents, and if they drink any deadly *poison,* it will not harm them; they will ^lay hands on the sick, and they will recover."

¹⁹So then, when the Lord Jesus had spoken to them, He ^was received up into heaven and sat down at the right hand of God. ²⁰And they went out and preached everywhere, while the Lord worked with *them,* and confirmed the word by the signs that followed.]]

[['*And they promptly reported all these instructions to Peter and his companions. And after that, Jesus Himself also sent out through them from east to west the sacred and imperishable proclamation of eternal salvation.*]]

16:9 ^Matt 27:56; John 20:14   16:10 ^John 20:18
16:11 ^Matt 28:17; Luke 8:2   16:12 ^Luke 24:13-35
16:13 ^Matt 28:17; Mark 16:11, 14   16:14 ^Luke 24:36;
John 20:19, 26   16:15 ^Matt 28:19; Acts 1:8
16:16 ^John 3:18, 36; Acts 16:31   16:17 ^Mark 9:38;
Luke 10:17   16:18 ^Mark 5:23   16:19 ^Luke 9:51; 24:51

16:9 ¹Later mss add vv 9-20   16:20 ¹A few late mss and ancient versions contain this paragraph, usually after v 8; a few have it at the end of the ch

LUKE

INTRODUCTION

1 Since many have undertaken to compile an account of the things ^accomplished among us, ²just as they were handed down to us by those who ^from the beginning were ᴮeyewitnesses and servants of the ¹word, ³it seemed fitting to me as well, having investigated everything carefully from the beginning, to write *it out* for you in an orderly sequence, ^most excellent Theophilus; ⁴so that you may know the exact truth about the things you have been ^taught.

JOHN THE BAPTIST'S BIRTH FORETOLD

⁵In the days of Herod, king of Judea, there was a priest named Zechariah, of the ^division of ¹Abijah; and he had a wife ²from the daughters of Aaron, and her name was Elizabeth. ⁶They were both righteous in the sight of God, walking ^blamelessly in all the commandments and requirements of the Lord. ⁷And *yet* they had no child, because Elizabeth was infertile, and they were both advanced in years.

⁸Now it happened *that* while ^he was performing his priestly service before God in the appointed order of his division, ⁹according to the custom of the priestly office, he was chosen by lot ^to enter the temple of the Lord and burn incense. ¹⁰And the whole multitude of the people were in prayer ^outside at the hour of the incense offering. ¹¹Now ^an angel of the Lord appeared to him, standing to the right of the altar of incense.

¹²Zechariah was troubled when he saw *the angel,* and ^fear gripped him. ¹³But the angel said to him, "Do not be afraid, Zechariah, for your prayer has been heard, and your wife Elizabeth will bear you a son, and ^you shall name him John. ¹⁴You will have joy and gladness, and many will rejoice over his birth. ¹⁵For he will be great in the sight of the Lord; and he will ^drink no wine or liquor, and he will be filled with the Holy Spirit while still in his mother's womb. ¹⁶And he will ^turn many of the sons of Israel back to the Lord their God. ¹⁷And *it is* he *who* will go *as a forerunner* before Him in the spirit and power of Elijah, ^TO TURN THE HEARTS OF FATHERS BACK TO *THEIR* CHILDREN, and the disobedient to the attitude of the righteous, to make ready a people prepared for the Lord."

¹⁸Zechariah said to the angel, "How will I know this? For ^I am an old man, and my wife is advanced in her years." ¹⁹The angel answered and said to him, "I am ^Gabriel, who stands in the presence of God, and I was sent to speak to you and to bring you this good news. ²⁰And behold, you will be silent and unable to speak until the day when these things take place, because you did

1:1 ^Rom 4:21; 14:5   1:2 ^John 15:27   ᴮ2 Pet 1:16
1:3 ^Acts 23:26; 24:3   1:4 ^Acts 18:25; Rom 2:18
1:5 ^1 Chr 24:10   1:6 ^Phil 2:15; 3:6   1:8 ^1 Chr 24:19;
2 Chr 8:14   1:9 ^Ex 30:7f   1:10 ^Lev 16:17
1:11 ^Luke 2:9; Acts 5:19   1:12 ^Luke 2:9
1:13 ^Luke 1:60, 63   1:15 ^Num 6:3; Judg 13:4
1:16 ^Matt 3:2, 6; Luke 3:3   1:17 ^Mal 4:6
1:18 ^Gen 17:17   1:19 ^Dan 8:16; 9:21

1:2 ¹I.e., gospel   1:5 ¹Gr *Abia*   ²I.e., of priestly descent

not believe my words, which will be fulfilled at their proper time."

21 And *meanwhile* the people were waiting for Zechariah, and were wondering at his delay in the temple. 22 But when he came out, he was unable to speak to them; and they realized that he had seen a vision in the temple, and he *repeatedly* ^made signs to them, and remained speechless. 23 When the days of his priestly service were concluded, he went back home.

24 Now after these days his wife Elizabeth became pregnant, and she kept herself in seclusion for five months, saying, 25 "This is the way the Lord has dealt with me in the days when He looked *with favor* upon *me,* to ^take away my disgrace among people."

JESUS' BIRTH FORETOLD

26 Now in the sixth month the angel Gabriel was sent from God to a city in Galilee named ^Nazareth, 27 to a virgin ¹betrothed to a man whose name was Joseph, ^of the descendants of David; and the virgin's name was Mary. 28 And coming in, he said to her, "Greetings, favored one! The Lord *is* with you." 29 But she ^was very perplexed at *this* statement, and was pondering what kind of greeting this was. 30 And the angel said to her, "^Do not be afraid, Mary, for you have found favor with God. 31 And behold, you will conceive in your womb and give birth to a son, and you ^shall name Him Jesus. 32 He will be great and will be called the Son of ^the Most High; and the Lord God will give Him ᴮthe throne of His father David; 33 and He will reign over the house of Jacob forever, ^and His kingdom will have no end." 34 But Mary said to

the angel, "How will this be, since I am a virgin?" 35 The angel answered and said to her, "^The Holy Spirit will come upon you, and the power of the Most High will overshadow you; for that reason also the holy Child will be called ᴮthe Son of God. 36 And behold, even your relative Elizabeth herself has conceived a son in her old age, and she who was called infertile is now in her sixth month. 37 For ^nothing will be impossible with God." 38 And Mary said, "Behold, the Lord's bond-servant; may it be done to me according to your word." And the angel departed from her.

MARY VISITS ELIZABETH

39 Now at this time Mary set out and went in a hurry to ^the hill country, to a city of Judah, 40 and she entered the house of Zechariah and greeted Elizabeth. 41 When Elizabeth heard Mary's greeting, the baby leaped in her womb, and Elizabeth was ^filled with the Holy Spirit. 42 And she cried out with a loud voice and said, "Blessed *are* you among women, and blessed *is* the fruit of your womb! 43 And how has it happened to me that the mother of ^my Lord would come to me? 44 For behold, when the sound of your greeting reached my ears, the baby leaped in my womb for joy. 45 And ^blessed *is* she who believed that there would be a fulfillment of what had been spoken to her by the Lord."

1:22 ^Luke 1:62   1:25 ^Gen 30:23; Is 4:1
1:26 ^Matt 2:23   1:27 ^Matt 1:16, 20; Luke 2:4
1:29 ^Luke 1:12   1:30 ^Matt 14:27; Luke 1:13
1:31 ^Is 7:14; Matt 1:21, 25   1:32 ^Mark 5:7
ᴮ2 Sam 7:12, 13, 16   1:33 ^2 Sam 7:13, 16; Ps 89:36, 37
1:35 ^Matt 1:18   ᴮMatt 4:3   1:37 ^Gen 18:14; Jer 32:17
1:39 ^Josh 20:7; 21:11   1:41 ^Luke 1:67; Acts 2:4
1:43 ^Luke 2:11   1:45 ^Luke 1:20, 48

1:27 ¹Unlike engagement, a betrothed couple was considered married, but did not yet live together

MARY'S SONG: THE MAGNIFICAT

⁴⁶ And Mary said:

"ᴬMy soul ᴮexalts the Lord,

⁴⁷   And ᴬmy spirit has rejoiced in
        God my Savior.

⁴⁸ "For ᴬHe has had regard for the
        humble state of His bond-
        servant;
        For behold, from now *on* all
        generations will call me
        blessed.

⁴⁹ "For the Mighty One has done
        great things for me;
        And holy is His name.

⁵⁰ "ᴬAnd His mercy is to
        generation after generation
        Toward those who fear Him.

⁵¹ "ᴬHe has done mighty deeds
        with His arm;
        He has scattered *those who
        were* proud in the thoughts
        of their hearts.

⁵² "He has brought down rulers
        from *their* thrones,
        And has ᴬexalted those who
        were humble.

⁵³ "ᴬHe has filled the hungry with
        good things,
        And sent the rich away empty-
        handed.

⁵⁴ "He has given help to His
        servant Israel,
        In remembrance of His mercy,

⁵⁵   Just as He spoke to our fathers,
        ᴬTo Abraham and his
        descendants forever."

⁵⁶ Mary stayed with her about
three months, and *then* returned
to her home.

JOHN THE BAPTIST IS BORN

⁵⁷ Now the time had come for Elizabeth to give birth, and she gave birth
to a son. ⁵⁸ Her neighbors and her relatives heard that the Lord had ᴬdis-
played His great mercy toward her;
and they were rejoicing with her.

⁵⁹ And it happened that on ᴬthe
eighth day they came to circumcise
the child, and they were going to
call him Zechariah, after his father.
⁶⁰ And *yet* his mother responded
and said, "No indeed; but ᴬhe shall
be called John." ⁶¹ And they said
to her, "There is no one among
your relatives who is called by this
name." ⁶² And they ¹·ᴬmade signs to
his father, as to what he wanted him
called. ⁶³ And he asked for a tablet
and wrote as follows, "ᴬHis name is
John." And they were all amazed.
⁶⁴ ᴬAnd at once his mouth was
opened and his tongue *freed,* and
he *began* speaking in praise of God.
⁶⁵ And fear came on all those who
lived around them; and all these
matters were being talked about
in ᴬthe entire hill country of Judea.
⁶⁶ All who heard *them* kept *them* in
mind, saying, "What then will this
child *turn out to* be?" For indeed
ᴬthe hand of the Lord was with him.

ZECHARIAH'S PROPHECY

⁶⁷ And his father Zechariah ᴬwas
filled with the Holy Spirit and
prophesied, saying:

⁶⁸ "Blessed *be* the Lord God of
        Israel,
        For He has visited *us* and
        accomplished ᴬredemption
        for His people,

⁶⁹   And has raised up a ᴬhorn of
        salvation for us
        In the house of His servant
        David—

1:46 ᴬ*1 Sam 2:1-10* ᴮPs 34:2f 1:47 ᴬPs 35:9; Hab 3:18
1:48 ᴬPs 138:6 1:50 ᴬPs 103:17 1:51 ᴬPs 98:1; 118:15
1:52 ᴬJob 5:11 1:53 ᴬPs 107:9 1:55 ᴬGen 17:7
1:58 ᴬGen 19:19 1:59 ᴬGen 17:12; Lev 12:3
1:60 ᴬLuke 1:13, 63 1:62 ᴬLuke 1:22
1:63 ᴬLuke 1:13, 60 1:64 ᴬLuke 1:20 1:65 ᴬLuke 1:39
1:66 ᴬActs 11:21 1:67 ᴬLuke 1:41; Acts 2:4, 8
1:68 ᴬLuke 2:38; Heb 9:12 1:69 ᴬ1 Sam 2:1, 10; Ps 18:2

1:62 ¹I.e., gestured or nodded

70 ᴬJust as He spoke by the mouth
    of His holy prophets from
    ancient times—
71 Salvation ᴬfrom our enemies,
    And from the hand of all who
    hate us;
72 To show mercy to our fathers,
    ᴬAnd to remember His holy
    covenant,
73 ᴬ*The* oath which He swore to
    our father Abraham,
74 To grant us that we, being
    rescued from the hand of
    our enemies,
    Would serve Him without fear,
75 ᴬIn holiness and righteousness
    before Him all our days.
76 "And you, child, also will be
    called the prophet of the
    Most High;
    For you will go on ᴬbefore the
    Lord to prepare His ways;
77 To give His people *the*
    knowledge of salvation
    By ᴬthe forgiveness of their
    sins,
78 Because of the tender mercy of
    our God,
    With which ᴬthe Sunrise from
    on high will visit us,
79 ᴬTo shine on those who sit in
    darkness and the shadow of
    death,
    To guide our feet into the way
    of peace."

80 ᴬNow the child grew and was
becoming strong in spirit, and he
lived in the deserts until the day of
his public appearance to Israel.

JESUS' BIRTH IN BETHLEHEM

2 Now in those days a decree
    went out from ᴬCaesar Augus-
tus, that a census be taken of all
¹the inhabited earth. ²This was the
first census taken while ¹Quirin-
ius was governor of ᴬSyria. ³And
all *the people* were on their way to
register for the census, each to his
own city. ⁴Now Joseph also went
up from Galilee, from the city of
Nazareth, to Judea, to the city of
David which is called Bethlehem,
because ᴬhe was of the house and
family of David, ⁵in order to register along with Mary, who was
¹betrothed to him, and was pregnant. ⁶While they were there, the
time came for her to give birth.
⁷And she ᴬgave birth to her firstborn son; and she wrapped Him
in cloths, and laid Him in a manger, because there was no room for
them in the inn.

⁸In the same region there were
some shepherds staying out in the
fields and keeping watch over their
flock at night. ⁹And ᴬan angel of the
Lord *suddenly* stood near them,
and the glory of the Lord shone
around them; and they were terribly frightened. ¹⁰And *so* the angel
said to them, "ᴬDo not be afraid;
for behold, I bring you good news
of great joy which will be for all
the people; ¹¹for today in the city
of David there has been born for
you a ᴬSavior, who is Christ the
Lord. ¹²And ᴬthis *will be* a sign for
you: you will find a baby wrapped
in cloths and lying in a manger."
¹³And suddenly there appeared
with the angel a multitude of the
heavenly army *of angels* praising
God and saying,

1:70ᴬRom 1:2   **1:71**ᴬPs 106:10   **1:72**ᴬPs 105:8f, 42;
106:45   **1:73**ᴬGen 22:16ff; Heb 6:13   **1:75**ᴬEph 4:24
1:76ᴬMal 3:1; Matt 11:10   **1:77**ᴬJer 31:34; Mark 1:4
1:78ᴬMal 4:2; Eph 5:14   **1:79**ᴬIs 9:2   **1:80**ᴬLuke 2:40
2:1ᴬMatt 22:17; Luke 3:1   **2:2**ᴬMatt 4:24
2:4ᴬLuke 1:27   **2:7**ᴬMatt 1:25   **2:9**ᴬLuke 1:11;
Acts 5:19   **2:10**ᴬMatt 14:27   **2:11**ᴬMatt 1:21;
John 4:42   **2:12**ᴬ1 Sam 2:34; 2 Kin 19:29

2:1¹I.e., the Roman Empire   **2:2**¹Gr *Kyrenios*
2:5¹Unlike engagement, a betrothed couple was
considered married, but did not yet live together

14 "ᴬGlory to God in the highest,
  And on earth peace among
  people with whom He is
  pleased."

15 When the angels had departed from them into heaven, the shepherds *began* saying to one another, "Let's go straight to Bethlehem, then, and see this thing that has happened, which the Lord has made known to us." 16 And they came in a hurry and found their way to Mary and Joseph, and the baby as He lay in the manger. 17 When they had seen *Him,* they made known the statement which had been told them about this Child. 18 And all who heard it were amazed about the things which were told them by the shepherds. 19 But Mary ᴬtreasured all these things, pondering them in her heart. 20 And the shepherds went back, ᴬglorifying and praising God for all that they had heard and seen, just as had been told them.

JESUS PRESENTED AT THE TEMPLE

21 And when ᴬeight days were completed so that it was time for His circumcision, He was also named Jesus, the *name* given by the angel before He was conceived in the womb.

22 ᴬAnd when the days for their purification according to the Law of Moses were completed, they brought Him up to Jerusalem to present Him to the Lord 23 (as it is written in the Law of the Lord: "ᴬEᴠ-ᴇʀʏ ꜰɪʀsᴛʙᴏʀɴ ᴍᴀʟᴇ ᴛʜᴀᴛ ᴏᴘᴇɴs ᴛʜᴇ ᴡᴏᴍʙ sʜᴀʟʟ ʙᴇ ᴄᴀʟʟᴇᴅ ʜᴏʟʏ ᴛᴏ ᴛʜᴇ Lᴏʀᴅ"), 24 and to offer a sacrifice according to what has been stated in the Law of the Lord: "ᴬA ᴘᴀɪʀ ᴏꜰ ᴛᴜʀᴛʟᴇᴅᴏᴠᴇs ᴏʀ ᴛᴡᴏ ʏᴏᴜɴɢ ᴅᴏᴠᴇs."

25 And there was a man in Jerusalem whose name was Simeon; and this man was righteous and devout, ᴬlooking forward to the consolation of Israel; and the Holy Spirit was upon him. 26 And it had been revealed to him by the Holy Spirit that he would not ᴬsee death before he had seen the Lord's Christ. 27 And he came by the Spirit into the temple; and when the parents brought in the child Jesus, ᴬto carry out for Him the custom of the Law, 28 then he took Him in his arms, and blessed God, and said,

29 "Now, Lord, You are letting Your
  bond-servant depart in peace,
  ᴬAccording to Your word;
30 For my eyes have ᴬseen Your
  salvation,
31 Which You have prepared in the
  presence of all the peoples:
32 ᴬA light for revelation for the
  Gentiles,
  And the glory of Your people
  Israel."

33 And His father and ᴬmother were amazed at the things which were being said about Him. 34 And Simeon blessed them and said to His mother Mary, "Behold, this *Child* is appointed for ᴬthe fall and rise of many in Israel, and as a sign to be opposed— 35 and a sword will pierce your own soul—to the end that thoughts from many hearts may be revealed."

36 And there was a prophetess, Anna, the daughter of Phanuel, of ᴬthe tribe of Asher. She was advanced in years ᴮand had lived with *her* husband for seven years after her marriage, 37 and *then* as a widow to the age of eighty-four. She

2:14 ᴬMatt 21:9; Luke 19:38   2:19 ᴬLuke 2:51
2:20 ᴬMatt 9:8   2:21 ᴬGen 17:12; Lev 12:3
2:22 ᴬLev 12:6-8   2:23 ᴬEx 13:2, 12; Num 3:13
2:24 ᴬLev 5:11; 12:8   2:25 ᴬMark 15:43; Luke 2:38
2:26 ᴬPs 89:48; John 8:51   2:27 ᴬLuke 2:22
2:29 ᴬLuke 2:26   2:30 ᴬPs 119:166, 174; Is 52:10
2:32 ᴬIs 9:2; 42:6   2:33 ᴬMatt 12:46   2:34 ᴬMatt 21:44;
1 Cor 1:23   2:36 ᴬJosh 19:24   ᴮ1 Tim 5:9

did not leave the temple *grounds,* serving night and day with ^fasts and prayers. 38 And at that very moment she came up and *began* giving thanks to God, and continued to speak about Him to all those who were ^looking forward to the redemption of Jerusalem.

RETURN TO NAZARETH

39 And when *His parents* had completed everything in accordance with the Law of the Lord, they returned to Galilee, to ^their own city of Nazareth. 40 ^Now the Child continued to grow and to become strong, increasing in wisdom; and the favor of God was upon Him.

VISIT TO JERUSALEM

41 His parents went to Jerusalem every year at ^the Feast of the Passover. 42 And when He was twelve years old, they went up *there* according to the custom of the feast; 43 and as they were returning, after spending the ^full number of days *required,* the boy Jesus stayed behind in Jerusalem, but His parents were unaware *of it.* 44 Instead, they thought that He was *somewhere* in the caravan, and they went a day's journey; and *then* they *began* looking for Him among their relatives and acquaintances. 45 And when they did not find Him, they returned to Jerusalem, looking for Him. 46 Then, after three days they found Him in the temple, sitting in the midst of the teachers, both listening to them and asking them questions. 47 And all who heard Him ^were amazed at His understanding and His answers. 48 When *Joseph and Mary* saw Him, they were bewildered; and His mother said to Him, "Son, why have You treated us

this way? Behold, ^Your father and I have been anxiously looking for You!" 49 And He said to them, "Why *is it* that you were looking for Me? Did you not know that ^I had to be in My Father's *house?*" 50 And *yet* ^they on their part did not understand the statement which He had made to them. 51 And He went down with them and came to ^Nazareth, and He continued to be subject to them; and His mother ^B treasured all *these* things in her heart.

52 And Jesus kept increasing in wisdom and stature, and in ^favor with God and people.

JOHN THE BAPTIST PREACHES

3 Now in the fifteenth year of the reign of Tiberius Caesar, when ^Pontius Pilate was governor of Judea, and ^B Herod was tetrarch of Galilee and his brother Philip was tetrarch of the region of Ituraea and Trachonitis, and Lysanias was tetrarch of Abilene, 2 in the high priesthood of Annas and Caiaphas, ^the word of God came to John, the son of Zechariah, in the wilderness. 3 And he came into all ^the region around the Jordan, preaching a baptism of repentance for the forgiveness of sins; 4 as it is written in the book of the words of Isaiah the prophet:

"^THE VOICE OF ONE CALLING
¹ OUT IN THE WILDERNESS,
'PREPARE THE WAY OF THE LORD,
MAKE HIS PATHS STRAIGHT!

2:37 ^Luke 5:33; Acts 13:3   2:38 ^Luke 1:68; 2:25
2:39 ^Matt 2:23; Luke 1:26   2:40 ^Luke 1:80; 2:52
2:41 ^Ex 12:11; 23:15   2:43 ^Ex 12:15   2:47 ^Matt 7:28;
13:54   2:48 ^Luke 2:49; 3:23   2:49 ^John 4:34; 5:36
2:50 ^Mark 9:32; Luke 9:45   2:51 ^Luke 2:39
^B Luke 2:19   2:52 ^Luke 2:40   3:1 ^Matt 27:2
^B Matt 14:1   3:2 *Matt 3:1-10; Mark 1:3-5*
3:3 ^Matt 3:5   3:4 ^Is 40:3

3:4 ¹ Or out, Prepare in the wilderness the way

5   '^EVERY RAVINE WILL BE FILLED,
    AND EVERY MOUNTAIN AND HILL
        WILL BE LOWERED;
    THE CROOKED WILL BECOME
        STRAIGHT,
    AND THE ROUGH ROADS
        SMOOTH;
6   ^AND ALL FLESH WILL ^BSEE THE
        SALVATION OF GOD!'"

7 So he was saying to the crowds who were going out to be baptized by him, "^You offspring of vipers, who warned you to flee from the wrath to come? 8 Therefore produce fruits that are consistent with repentance, and do not start saying to yourselves, '^We have Abraham *as our* father,' for I say to you that from these stones God is able to raise up children for Abraham. 9 But indeed the axe is already being laid at the root of the trees; so ^every tree that does not bear good fruit is cut down and thrown into the fire."

10 And the crowds were questioning him, saying, "^Then what are we to do?" 11 And he would answer and say to them, "The one who has two 'tunics is to ^share with the one who has none; and the one who has food is to do likewise." 12 Now even ^tax collectors came to be baptized, and they said to him, "Teacher, what are we to do?" 13 And he said to them, "Collect no more than what you have been ordered to." 14 And soldiers also were questioning him, saying, "What are we to do, we as well?" And he said to them, "Do not extort money from anyone, nor ^harass *anyone,* and be content with your wages."

15 Now while the people were in a state of expectation and they all were thinking carefully in their hearts about John, ^whether he himself perhaps was the Christ, 16 ^John responded to them all, saying, "As for me, I baptize you with water; but He is coming who is mightier than I, and I am not fit to untie the straps of His sandals; He will baptize you with the Holy Spirit and fire. 17 His winnowing fork is in His hand to thoroughly clear His threshing floor, and to gather the wheat into His barn; but He will burn up the chaff with ^unquenchable fire."

18 So with many other exhortations he preached the gospel to the people. 19 But when ^Herod the tetrarch was reprimanded by him regarding ^Herodias, his brother's wife, and regarding all the evil things which Herod had done, 20 *Herod* also added this to them all: ^he locked John up in prison.

JESUS IS BAPTIZED

21 ^Now when all the people were baptized, Jesus also was baptized, and while He was praying, heaven was opened, 22 and the Holy Spirit descended upon Him in bodily form like a dove, and a voice came from heaven: "^You are My beloved Son, in You I am well pleased."

GENEALOGY OF JESUS

23 ^When He began *His ministry,* Jesus Himself was about thirty years old, being, as was commonly held, the son of Joseph, the son of Eli, 24 the son of Matthat, the son

3:5 ^Is 40:4   3:6 ^Is 40:5   ^BLuke 2:30
3:7 ^Matt 12:34; 23:33   3:8 ^John 8:33   3:9 ^Matt 7:19;
Luke 13:6–9   3:10 ^Luke 3:12, 14; Acts 2:37, 38
3:11 ^Is 58:7; 1 Tim 6:17, 18   3:12 ^Luke 7:29
3:14 ^Ex 20:16; 23:1   3:15 ^John 1:19f
3:16 ^Matt 3:11, 12; Mark 1:7, 8   3:17 ^Mark 9:43, 48
3:19 ^Matt 14:3; Mark 6:17   3:20 ^John 3:24
3:21 ^Matt 3:13–17; Mark 1:9–11   3:22 ^Ps 2:7; Is 42:1
3:23 ^Matt 4:17; Acts 1:1

3:11 'A long shirt worn next to the skin

of Levi, the son of Melchi, the son of Jannai, the son of Joseph, 25the son of Mattathias, the son of Amos, the son of Nahum, the son of Hesli, the son of Naggai, 26the son of Maath, the son of Mattathias, the son of Semein, the son of Josech, the son of Joda, 27the son of Joanan, the son of Rhesa, ^the son of Zerubbabel, the son of Shealtiel, the son of Neri, 28the son of Melchi, the son of Addi, the son of Cosam, the son of Elmadam, the son of Er, 29the son of Joshua, the son of Eliezer, the son of Jorim, the son of Matthat, the son of Levi, 30the son of Simeon, the son of Judah, the son of Joseph, the son of Jonam, the son of Eliakim, 31the son of Melea, the son of Menna, the son of Mattatha, the son of Nathan, the son of David, 32^the son of Jesse, the son of Obed, the son of Boaz, the son of Salmon, the son of Nahshon, 33the son of Amminadab, the son of Admin, the son of Ram, the son of Hezron, the son of Perez, the son of Judah, 34the son of Jacob, the son of Isaac, ^the son of Abraham, the son of Terah, the son of Nahor, 35the son of Serug, the son of Reu, the son of Peleg, the son of Heber, the son of Shelah, 36the son of Cainan, the son of Arphaxad, the son of Shem, ^the son of Noah, the son of Lamech, 37the son of Methuselah, the son of Enoch, the son of Jared, the son of Mahalaleel, the son of Cainan, 38the son of Enosh, the son of Seth, the son of Adam, the son of God.

THE TEMPTATION OF JESUS

4 ^Now Jesus, full of the Holy Spirit, returned from the Jordan and was led *around* by the Spirit in the wilderness 2for ^forty days, being tempted by the devil.

And He ate nothing during those days, and when they had ended, He was hungry. 3And the devil said to Him, "If You are the Son of God, tell this stone to become bread." 4And Jesus answered him, "It is written: '^Man shall not live on bread alone.'"

5^And he led Him up and showed Him all the kingdoms of the world in a moment of time. 6And the devil said to Him, "I will give You all this domain and its glory, ^for it has been handed over to me, and I give it to whomever I want. 7Therefore if You worship before me, it shall all be Yours." 8Jesus replied to him, "It is written: '^You shall worship the Lord your God and serve Him only.'"

9^And he brought Him into Jerusalem and had Him stand on the pinnacle of the temple, and said to Him, "If You are the Son of God, throw Yourself down from here; 10for it is written:

'^He will give His angels
    orders concerning You, to
    protect You,'

11and,

'On *their* hands they will
    lift You up,
So that You do not strike
    Your foot against a
    stone.'"

12And Jesus answered and said to him, "It has been stated, '^You shall not put the Lord your God to the test.'"

13And *so* when the devil had finished every temptation, he left Him until an opportune time.

3:27^Matt 1:12   3:32^Matt 1:1-6   3:34^Gen 11:26-30;
1 Chr 1:24-27   3:36^Gen 5:3-32; 1 Chr 1:1-4
4:1^Matt 4:1-11; Mark 1:12, 13   4:2^Ex 34:28;
1 Kin 19:8   4:4^Deut 8:3   4:5^Matt 4:8-10
4:6^1 John 5:19   4:8^Deut 6:13; 10:20
4:9^Matt 4:5-7   4:10^Ps 91:11   4:12^Deut 6:16

JESUS' PUBLIC MINISTRY

¹⁴And ᴬJesus returned to Galilee in the power of the Spirit, and ᴮnews about Him spread through all the surrounding region. ¹⁵And He *began* ᴬteaching in their synagogues and was praised by all.

¹⁶And He came to Nazareth, where He had been brought up; and as was His custom, ᴬHe entered the synagogue on the Sabbath, and stood up to read. ¹⁷And the scroll of Isaiah the prophet was handed to Him. And He unrolled the scroll and found the place where it was written:

¹⁸ "ᴬTHE SPIRIT OF THE LORD IS UPON ME,
    BECAUSE HE ANOINTED ME TO BRING GOOD NEWS TO THE POOR.
    HE HAS SENT ME TO PROCLAIM RELEASE TO CAPTIVES,
    AND RECOVERY OF SIGHT TO THE BLIND,
    TO SET FREE THOSE WHO ARE OPPRESSED,
¹⁹ ᴬTO PROCLAIM THE FAVORABLE YEAR OF THE LORD."

²⁰And He ᴬrolled up the scroll, gave it back to the attendant, and sat down; and the eyes of all *the people* in the synagogue were intently directed at Him. ²¹Now He began to say to them, "Today this Scripture has been fulfilled in your hearing." ²²And all *the people* were speaking well of Him, and admiring the gracious words which were coming from His lips; and *yet* they were saying, "ᴬIs this not Joseph's son?" ²³And He said to them, "No doubt you will quote this proverb to Me: 'Physician, heal yourself! All *the miracles that* we heard were done ᴬin Capernaum, do here in Your hometown as well.'" ²⁴But He said, "Truly I say to you, ᴬno prophet is

welcome in his hometown. ²⁵But I say to you in truth, there were many widows in Israel ᴬin the days of Elijah, when the sky was shut up for three years and six months, when a severe famine came over all the land; ²⁶and *yet* Elijah was sent to none of them, but *only* to ᴬZarephath, *in the land* of Sidon, to a woman who was a widow. ²⁷And there were many with leprosy in Israel in the time of Elisha the prophet; and none of them was cleansed, but *only* ᴬNaaman the Syrian." ²⁸And all *the people* in the synagogue were filled with rage as they heard these things; ²⁹and they got up and ᴬdrove Him out of the city, and brought Him to the crest of the hill on which their city had been built, so that they could throw Him down from the cliff. ³⁰But He ᴬpassed through their midst and went on His way.

³¹And ᴬHe came down to Capernaum, a city of Galilee; and He was teaching them on the Sabbath; ³²and they were amazed at His teaching, because ᴬHis message was *delivered* with authority. ³³In the synagogue there was a man possessed by the spirit of an unclean demon, and he cried out with a loud voice, ³⁴"Leave us alone! ᴬWhat business do You have with us, Jesus of ᴮNazareth? Have You come to destroy us? I know who You are—ᴮthe Holy One of God!" ³⁵But Jesus ᴬrebuked him, saying, "Be quiet and come out of

4:14 ᴬMatt 4:12   ᴮMatt 9:26   4:15 ᴬMatt 4:23
4:16 ᴬMatt 13:54; Mark 6:1f   4:18 ᴬIs 61:1; Matt 11:5
4:19 ᴬIs 61:2; Lev 25:10   4:20 ᴬLuke 4:17
4:22 ᴬMatt 13:55; Mark 6:3   4:23 ᴬMatt 4:13; Mark 1:21ff
4:24 ᴬMatt 13:57; Mark 6:4   4:25 ᴬ1 Kin 17:1; 18:1
4:26 ᴬ1 Kin 17:9   4:27 ᴬ2 Kin 5:1-14   4:29 ᴬNum 15:35;
Acts 7:58   4:30 ᴬJohn 10:39   4:31 ᴬ*Mark 1:21-28*
4:32 ᴬLuke 4:36; John 7:46   4:34 ᴬMatt 8:29
ᴮMark 1:24   4:35 ᴬMatt 8:26; Mark 4:39

him!" And when the demon had thrown him down in the midst *of the people,* it came out of him without doing him any harm. ³⁶And amazement came upon them all, and they *began* talking with one another, saying, "What is this message? For ^with authority and power He commands the unclean spirits, and they come out!" ³⁷And ^the news about Him was spreading into every locality of the surrounding region.

MANY ARE HEALED

³⁸^Then He got up and *left* the synagogue, and entered Simon's home. Now Simon's mother-in-law was suffering from a high fever, and they asked Him to help her. ³⁹And standing over her, He ^rebuked the fever, and it left her; and she immediately got up and served them.

⁴⁰^Now while the sun was setting, all those who had *any who were* sick with various diseases brought them to Him; and He was laying His hands on each one of them and healing them. ⁴¹Demons also were coming out of many, shouting, "You are the Son of God!" And *yet* He was rebuking them and would ^not allow them to speak, because they knew that He was the Christ.

⁴²^Now when day came, Jesus left and went to a secluded place; and the crowds were searching for Him, and they came to Him and tried to keep Him from leaving them. ⁴³But He said to them, "I must also preach the kingdom of God to the other cities, ^because I was sent for this *purpose.*"

⁴⁴So He kept on preaching in the synagogues ^of ¹Judea.

THE FIRST DISCIPLES

5 ^Now it happened that while the crowd was pressing around Him and listening to the word of God, He was standing by the lake of Gennesaret; ²and He saw two boats lying at the edge of the lake; but the fishermen had gotten out of them and were washing their nets. ³And ^He got into one of the boats, which was Simon's, and asked him to put out a little *distance* from the land. And He sat down and *continued* teaching the crowds from the boat. ⁴Now when He had finished speaking, He said to Simon, "Put out into the deep water and ^let down your nets for a catch." ⁵Simon responded and said, "^Master, we worked hard all night and caught nothing, but I will do as You say *and* let down the nets." ⁶And when they had done this, ^they caught a great quantity of fish, and their nets *began* to tear; ⁷so they signaled to their partners in the other boat to come and help them. And they came and filled both of the boats, to the point that they were sinking. ⁸But when Simon Peter saw *this,* he fell down at Jesus' knees, saying, "Go away from me, Lord, for I am a sinful man!" ⁹For amazement had seized him and all his companions because of the catch of fish which they had taken; ¹⁰and likewise also *were* James and John, sons of Zebedee, who were partners with Simon. And Jesus said to Simon, "^Do not fear; from now on you will

4:36^Luke 4:32   4:37^Luke 4:14   4:38^*Matt* 8:14, 15; *Mark* 1:29-31   4:39^Luke 4:35, 41   4:40^*Matt* 8:16, 17; *Mark* 1:32-34   4:41^Matt 8:16; Mark 1:34
4:42^*Mark* 1:35-38   4:43^Mark 1:38   4:44^Mark 4:23
5:1^Matt 4:18-22; Mark 1:16-20   5:3^Matt 13:2; Mark 3:9, 10   5:4^John 21:6   5:5^Luke 8:24; 9:33, 49
5:6^John 21:6   5:10^Matt 14:27

4:44 ¹I.e., the country of the Jews (including Galilee)

be catching people." ¹¹When they had brought their boats to land, ^they left everything and followed Him.

A MAN WITH LEPROSY HEALED

¹²^While He was in one of the cities, behold, *there was* a man covered with leprosy; and when he saw Jesus, he fell on his face and begged Him, saying, "Lord, if You are willing, You can make me clean." ¹³And He reached out with His hand and touched him, saying, "I am willing; be cleansed." And immediately the leprosy left him. ¹⁴And He ordered him to tell no one, *saying,* "But go and ^show yourself to the priest, and make an offering for your cleansing, just as Moses commanded, as a testimony to them." ¹⁵But ^the news about Him was spreading *even* farther, and large crowds were gathering to hear *Him* and to be healed of their sicknesses. ¹⁶But Jesus Himself would *often* slip away to the wilderness and ^pray.

A MAN LOWERED THROUGH A ROOF

¹⁷One day He was teaching, and there were *some* Pharisees and teachers of the Law sitting *there* who had ^come from every village of Galilee and Judea, and *from* Jerusalem; and ^the power of the Lord was *present* for Him to perform healing. ¹⁸^And *some* men *were* carrying a man on a stretcher who was paralyzed; and they were trying to bring him in and to set him down in front of Him. ¹⁹But when they did not find any *way* to bring him in because of the crowd, they went up on ^the roof and let him down ^through the tiles with his stretcher, into the middle *of the crowd,* in front of Jesus. ²⁰And seeing their

faith, He said, "Friend, ^your sins are forgiven you." ²¹The scribes and the Pharisees began thinking of the implications, saying, "^Who is this *man* who speaks blasphemies? ^Who can forgive sins, except God alone?" ²²But Jesus, aware of their thoughts, responded and said to them, "Why are you thinking this way in your hearts? ²³Which is easier, to say: 'Your sins are forgiven you,' or to say, 'Get up and walk'? ²⁴But so that you may know that the Son of Man has authority on earth to forgive sins," He said to the ^man who was paralyzed, "I say to you, get up, and pick up your stretcher, and go home." ²⁵And immediately he got up before them, and picked up what he had been lying on, and went home ^glorifying God. ²⁶And they were all struck with astonishment and *began* ^glorifying God. They were also filled with fear, saying, "We have seen remarkable things today!"

CALL OF LEVI (MATTHEW)

²⁷^After that He went out and looked at a tax collector named Levi sitting in the tax office, and He said to him, "Follow Me." ²⁸And he ^left everything behind, and got up and *began* following Him.

²⁹And ^Levi gave a big reception for Him in his house; and there was a large crowd of ^tax collectors and other *people* who were reclining *at the table* with them. ³⁰^The Pharisees and their scribes *began*

5:11^Matt 4:20, 22; 19:29   **5:12**^*Matt 8:2-4; Mark 1:40-44*   **5:14**^Lev 13:49; 14:2ff   **5:15**^Matt 9:26
5:16^Matt 14:23; Mark 1:35   **5:17**^Matt 1:45
^Mark 5:30   **5:18**^*Matt 9:2-8; Mark 2:3-12*
5:19^Matt 24:17   ^Mark 2:4   **5:20**^Matt 9:2
5:21^Luke 7:49   ^Is 43:25   **5:24**^Matt 4:24
5:25^Matt 9:8   **5:26**^Matt 9:8   **5:27**^*Matt 9:9-17; Mark 2:14-22*   **5:28**^Luke 5:11   **5:29**^Matt 9:9
^Luke 15:1   **5:30**^Mark 2:16; Luke 15:2

grumbling to His disciples, saying, "Why do you eat and drink with the tax collectors and sinners?" 31And Jesus answered and said to them, "^*It is* not those who are healthy who need a physician, but those who are sick. 32I have not come to call the righteous to repentance, but sinners."

33And they said to Him, "^The disciples of John often fast and offer prayers, the *disciples* of the Pharisees also do the same, but Yours eat and drink." 34And Jesus said to them, "You cannot make the attendants of the groom fast while the groom is with them, can you? 35^But *the* days will come; and when the groom is taken away from them, then they will fast in those days." 36And He was also telling them a parable: "No one tears a piece of cloth from a new garment and puts it on an old garment; otherwise he will both tear the new, and the patch from the new *garment* will not match the old. 37And no one pours new wine into old wineskins; otherwise the new wine will burst the skins and it will be spilled out, and the skins will be ruined. 38But new wine must be put into fresh wineskins. 39And no one, after drinking old *wine* wants new; for he says, 'The old is fine.'"

JESUS IS LORD OF THE SABBATH

6 ^Now it happened that Jesus was passing through *some* grainfields on a Sabbath, and His disciples were picking the heads of grain, rubbing them in their hands, and eating *them.* 2But some of the Pharisees said, "Why are you doing what ^is not lawful on the Sabbath?" 3And Jesus, answering them, said, "Have you not even read ^what David did when he was hungry, he and those who were with him, 4how he entered the house of God, and took and ate the ¹consecrated bread, which ^is not lawful *for anyone* to eat except the priests alone, and gave it to his companions?" 5And He was saying to them, "The Son of Man is Lord of the Sabbath."

6^On another Sabbath He entered the synagogue and taught; and a man was there whose right hand was withered. 7Now the scribes and the Pharisees ^were watching Him closely *to see* if He healed on the Sabbath, so that they might find *a reason* to accuse Him. 8But He ^knew what they were thinking, and He said to the man with the withered hand, "Get up and come forward!" And he got up and came forward. 9And Jesus said to them, "I ask you whether it is lawful to do good on the Sabbath or to do harm, to save a life or to destroy *it?*" 10And after ^looking around at them all, He said to him, "Stretch out your hand!" And he did *so;* and his hand was restored. 11But they themselves were filled with senseless rage, and *began* discussing together what they might do to Jesus.

CHOOSING THE TWELVE

12Now it was at this time that He went off to the mountain to ^pray, and He spent the whole night in prayer with God. 13And when day came, ^He called His disciples to

---

5:31^Matt 9:12, 13; Mark 2:17
5:33^Matt 9:14; Mark 2:18   **5:35**^Matt 9:15;
Mark 2:20   **6:1**^*Matt 12:1-8; Mark 2:23-28*
6:2^Matt 12:2   **6:3**^1 Sam 21:6   **6:4**^Lev 24:9
6:6^*Matt 12:9-14; Mark 3:1-6;*   **6:7**^Mark 3:2
6:8^Matt 9:4   **6:10**^Mark 3:5   **6:12**^Matt 14:23;
Luke 5:16   **6:13**^*Matt 10:2-4; Mark 3:16-19*

6:4 ¹Lit *loaves of presentation*

Him and chose twelve of them, whom He also named as apostles: ¹⁴Simon, whom He also named Peter, and his brother Andrew; and James and John; and Philip and Bartholomew; ¹⁵and ^Matthew and Thomas; James *the son* of Alphaeus, and Simon who was called the Zealot; ¹⁶Judas *the son* of James, and Judas Iscariot, who became a traitor.

¹⁷And *then* Jesus came down with them and stood on a level place; and *there was* ^a large crowd of His disciples, and a great multitude of the people from all Judea and Jerusalem, and the coastal region of Tyre and Sidon, ¹⁸who had come to hear Him and to be healed of their diseases; and those who were troubled by unclean spirits were being cured. ¹⁹And all the people were trying to ^touch Him, because ᴮpower was coming from Him and healing *them* all.

THE BEATITUDES

²⁰And He raised His eyes toward His disciples and *began* saying, "^Blessed *are* you who are poor, for yours is the kingdom of God. ²¹Blessed *are* you who are hungry now, for you will be satisfied. Blessed *are* you who weep now, for you will laugh. ²²Blessed are you when the people hate you, and when they ^exclude you, and insult you, and scorn your name as evil, on account of the Son of Man. ²³Rejoice on that day and jump *for joy,* for behold, your reward is great in heaven. For their fathers used to treat the prophets ^the same way. ²⁴But woe to ^you who are rich, for you are receiving your comfort in full. ²⁵Woe to you who are well-fed now, for you will be hungry. Woe

to you who laugh now, for you will mourn and weep. ²⁶Woe *to you* when all the people speak well of you; for their fathers used to treat the ^false prophets the same way.

²⁷"But I say to you who hear, ^love your enemies, do good to those who hate you, ²⁸bless those who curse you, ^pray for those who are abusive to you. ²⁹^Whoever hits you on the cheek, offer him the other also; and whoever takes away your cloak, do not withhold your ʹtunic from him either. ³⁰Give to everyone who asks of you, and whoever takes away what is yours, do not demand *it* back. ³¹^Treat people the same way you want them to treat you. ³²^If you love those who love you, what credit is *that* to you? For even sinners love those who love them. ³³And if you do good to those who do good to you, what credit is *that* to you? For even sinners do the same. ³⁴^And if you lend to those from whom you expect to receive, what credit is *that* to you? Even sinners lend to sinners in order to receive back the same *amount.* ³⁵But love your enemies and do good, and lend, expecting nothing in return; and your reward will be great, and you will be ^sons of ᴮthe Most High; for He Himself is kind to ungrateful and evil *people.* ³⁶Be merciful, just as your Father is merciful.

³⁷"^Do not judge, and you will not be judged; and do not condemn, and you will not be condemned;

6:15 ^Matt 9:9　6:17 ^Matt 4:25; Mark 3:7, 8
6:19 ^Matt 9:21　ᴮLuke 5:17　6:20 ^Matt 5:3-12
6:22 ^John 9:22; 16:2　6:23 ^2 Chr 36:16; Acts 7:52
6:24 ^Luke 16:25; James 5:1　6:26 ^Matt 7:15
6:27 ^Matt 5:44; Luke 6:35　6:28 ^Matt 5:44;
Luke 6:35　6:29 ^*Matt 5:39-42*　6:31 ^Matt 7:12
6:32 ^Matt 5:46　6:34 ^Matt 5:42　6:35 ^Matt 5:9
ᴮLuke 1:32　6:37 ^*Matt 7:1-5*

6:29 ʹA long shirt worn next to the skin

pardon, and you will be pardoned. ³⁸Give, and it will be given to you. They will pour ^into your lap a good measure—pressed down, shaken together, *and* running over. For by your standard of measure it will be measured to you in return."

³⁹Now He also spoke a parable to them: "^A person who is blind cannot guide *another* who is blind, can he? Will they not both fall into a pit? ⁴⁰^A student is not above the teacher; but everyone, when he has been fully trained, will be like his teacher. ⁴¹Why do you look at the speck that is in your brother's eye, but do not notice the log that is in your own eye? ⁴²How can you say to your brother, 'Brother, let me take out the speck that is in your eye,' when you yourself do not see the log that is in your own eye? You hypocrite, first take the log out of your own eye, and then you will see clearly to take out the speck that is in your brother's eye. ⁴³^For there is no good tree that bears bad fruit, nor, on the other hand, a bad tree that bears good fruit. ⁴⁴^For each tree is known by its own fruit. For *people* do not gather figs from thorns, nor do they pick grapes from a briar bush. ⁴⁵^The good person out of the good treasure of his heart brings forth what is good; and the evil *person* out of the evil *treasure* brings forth what is evil; ^Bfor his mouth speaks from that which fills *his* heart.

THE PARABLE OF THE BUILDERS

⁴⁶"Now ^why do you call Me, 'Lord, Lord,' and do not do what I say? ⁴⁷^Everyone who comes to Me and hears My words and acts on them, I will show you whom he is like: ⁴⁸he is like a man building a house, who dug deep and laid a foundation on the rock; and when there was a flood, the river burst against that house and *yet* it could not shake it, because it had been well built. ⁴⁹But the one who has heard and has not acted *accordingly* is like a man who built a house on the ground without a foundation; and the river burst against it and it immediately collapsed, and the ruin of that house was great."

JESUS HEALS A CENTURION'S SLAVE

7 When He had completed all His teaching in the hearing of the people, ^He went to Capernaum.

²Now a centurion's slave, who was highly regarded by him, was sick and about to die. ³When he heard about Jesus, ^he sent some Jewish elders to Him, asking Him to come and save the life of his slave. ⁴When they came to Jesus, they strongly urged Him, saying, "He is worthy for You to grant this to him; ⁵for he loves our nation, and it was he who built us our synagogue." ⁶Now Jesus *started* on His way with them; but already, when He was not *yet* far from the house, the centurion sent friends, saying to Him, "Lord, do not trouble Yourself *further,* for I am not worthy for You to enter under my roof; ⁷for that reason I did not even consider myself worthy to come to You; but *just* say the word, and my servant shall be healed. ⁸For I also am a man placed under authority, with soldiers under myself; and I say to this one, 'Go!' and he goes, and to another, 'Come!' and he comes, and to my slave, 'Do this!'

6:38^Mark 4:24   **6:39**^Matt 15:14   **6:40**^Matt 10:24; John 13:16   **6:43**^*Matt 7:16, 18, 20*   **6:44**^Matt 7:16; 12:33   **6:45**^Matt 12:35   ^BMatt 12:34   **6:46**^Mal 1:6; Matt 7:21   **6:47**^James 1:22ff   **7:1**^*Matt 8:5-13* **7:3**^Matt 8:5

and he does *it*." ⁹Now when Jesus heard this, He was amazed at him, and turned and said to the crowd that was following Him, "I say to you, ᴬnot even in Israel have I found such great faith." ¹⁰And when those who had been sent returned to the house, they found the slave in good health.

¹¹Soon afterward Jesus went to a city called Nain; and His disciples were going along with Him, accompanied by a large crowd. ¹²Now as He approached the gate of the city, a dead man was being carried out, the only son of his mother, and she was a widow; and a sizeable crowd from the city was with her. ¹³When ᴬthe Lord saw her, He felt compassion for her and said to her, "Do not go on weeping." ¹⁴And He came up and touched the coffin; and the bearers came to a halt. And He said, "Young man, I say to you, arise!" ¹⁵And the dead man sat up and began to speak. And Jesus gave him *back* to his mother. ¹⁶ᴬFear gripped them all, and they *began* glorifying God, saying, "A great prophet has appeared among us!" and, "God has visited His people!" ¹⁷ᴬAnd this report about Him spread throughout Judea and in all the surrounding region.

THE MESSENGERS FROM JOHN

¹⁸ᴬThe disciples of John also reported to him about all these things. ¹⁹And after summoning two of his disciples, John sent them to ᴬthe Lord, saying, "Are You the Coming One, or are we to look for another?" ²⁰When the men came to Him, they said, "John the Baptist has sent us to You, to ask, 'Are You the Coming One, or are we to look for another?'" ²¹At that *very* time He ᴬcured many *people* of diseases

and ᴮafflictions and evil spirits; and He gave sight to many *who were* blind. ²²And He answered and said to them, "Go and report to John what you have seen and heard: people who were ᴬblind receive sight, people who limped walk, people with leprosy are cleansed and people who were deaf hear, dead people are raised up, *and* ᴮpeople who are poor have the gospel preached to them. ²³And blessed is anyone who does not take offense at Me."

²⁴When the messengers of John had left, He began to speak to the crowds about John: "What did you go out into the wilderness to see? A reed shaken by the wind? ²⁵But what did you go out to see? A man dressed in soft clothing? Those who are splendidly clothed and live in luxury are *found* in royal palaces! ²⁶But what did you go out to see? A prophet? Yes, I tell you, and one who is more than a prophet. ²⁷This is the one about whom it is written:

ᴬBEHOLD, I AM SENDING MY
MESSENGER AHEAD OF YOU,
WHO WILL PREPARE YOUR WAY
BEFORE YOU.'

²⁸I say to you, among those born of women there is no one greater than John; yet the one who is least in the kingdom of God is greater than he." ²⁹When all the people and the tax collectors heard *this,* they acknowledged God's justice, ᴬhaving been baptized with the baptism of John. ³⁰But the Pharisees and the ¹·ᴬlawyers rejected God's purpose for themselves, not having been baptized by John.

7:9 ᴬMatt 8:10; Luke 7:50   7:13 ᴬLuke 7:19; 10:1
7:16 ᴬLuke 5:26   7:17 ᴬMatt 9:26   7:18 ᴬ*Matt 11:2-19*
7:19 ᴬLuke 7:13; 10:1   7:21 ᴬMatt 4:23   ᴮMark 3:10
7:22 ᴬIs 35:5   ᴮIs 61:1   7:27 ᴬMal 3:1; Matt 11:10
7:29 ᴬMatt 21:32; Luke 3:12   7:30 ᴬMatt 22:35

7:30 ¹I.e., experts in the Mosaic Law

31"To what then shall I compare the people of this generation, and what are they like? 32They are like children who sit in the marketplace and call to one another, and say, 'We played the flute for you, and you did not dance; we sang a song of mourning, and you did not weep.' 33For John the Baptist has come neither ^eating bread nor drinking wine, and you say, 'He has a demon!' 34The Son of Man has come eating and drinking, and you say, 'Behold, a gluttonous man and a heavy drinker, a friend of tax collectors and sinners!' 35And *yet* wisdom ^is vindicated by all her children."

THE ANOINTING IN GALILEE

36 Now one of the Pharisees was requesting Him to eat with him, and He entered the Pharisee's house and reclined *at the table*. 37^And there was a woman in the city who was a sinner; and when she learned that He was reclining *at the table* in the Pharisee's house, she brought an alabaster vial of perfume, 38and standing behind *Him* at His feet, weeping, she began to wet His feet with her tears, and she wiped them with the hair of her head, and *began* kissing His feet and anointing them with the perfume. 39Now when the Pharisee who had invited Him saw *this*, he said to himself, "If this Man were ^a prophet He would know who and what sort of person this woman *is* who is touching Him, that she is a sinner!"

PARABLE OF TWO DEBTORS

40And Jesus responded and said to him, "Simon, I have something to say to you." And he replied, "Say it, Teacher." 41"A moneylender had

two debtors: the one owed five hundred ¹^denarii, and the other, fifty. 42When they ^were unable to repay, he canceled the debts of both. So which of them will love him more?" 43Simon answered and said, "I assume the one for whom he canceled the greater debt." And He said to him, "You have judged correctly." 44And turning toward the woman, He said to Simon, "Do you see this woman? I entered your house; you ^gave Me no water for My feet, but she has wet My feet with her tears and wiped them with her hair. 45You ^gave Me no kiss; but she has not stopped kissing My feet since the time I came in. 46^You did not anoint My head with oil, but she anointed My feet with perfume. 47For this reason I say to you, her sins, which are many, have been forgiven, for she loved much; but the one who is forgiven little, loves little." 48And He said to her, "^Your sins have been forgiven." 49And *then* those who were reclining *at the table* with Him began saying to themselves, "^Who is this *Man* who even forgives sins?" 50And He said to the woman, "Your faith has saved you; ^go in peace."

WOMEN SUPPORT JESUS

8 Soon afterward, Jesus *began* going around from one city and village to another, ^proclaiming and preaching the kingdom of God. The twelve were with Him, 2and *also* ^some women who had

7:33^Luke 1:15   7:35^Luke 7:29   7:37^Matt 26:6-13; Mark 14:3-9   7:39^Luke 7:16; John 4:19
7:41^Matt 18:28; Mark 6:37   7:42^Matt 18:25
7:44^Gen 18:4; 19:2   7:45^2 Sam 15:5
7:46^2 Sam 12:20; Ps 23:5   7:48^Matt 9:2; Mark 2:5, 9
7:49^Luke 5:21   7:50^Mark 5:34; Luke 8:48
8:1^Matt 4:23   8:2^Matt 27:55; Mark 15:40, 41

7:41 ¹The denarius was a day's wages for a laborer

been healed of evil spirits and sicknesses: Mary who was called Magdalene, from whom seven demons had gone out, ³and Joanna the wife of Chuza, ^Herod's steward, and Susanna, and many others who were contributing to their support out of their private means.

PARABLE OF THE SOWER

4^Now when a large crowd was coming together, and those from the various cities were journeying to Him, He spoke by way of a parable: 5"The sower went out to sow his seed; and as he sowed, some fell beside the road, and it was trampled underfoot, and the birds of the sky ate it up. 6Other *seed* fell on rocky *soil,* and when it came up, it withered away because it had no moisture. 7Other *seed* fell among the thorns; and the thorns grew up with it and choked it out. 8And *yet* other *seed* fell into the good soil, and grew up, and produced a crop a hundred times as much." As He said these things, He would call out, "^The one who has ears to hear, let him hear."

9^Now His disciples *began* asking Him what this parable meant. 10And He said, "To you it has been granted to know the mysteries of the kingdom of God, but to the rest *they are told* in parables, so that ^while seeing they may not see, and while hearing they may not understand.

11"Now this is the parable: ^the seed is the word of God. 12And those beside the road are the ones who have heard, then the devil comes and takes away the word from their heart, so that they will not believe and be saved. 13Those on the rocky *soil are* the ones who,

when they hear, receive the word with joy; and *yet* these do not have a *firm* root; they believe for a while, and in a time of temptation they fall away. 14And the *seed* which fell among the thorns, these are the ones who have heard, and as they go on their way they are choked by worries, riches, and pleasures of *this* life, and they bring no fruit to maturity. 15But the *seed* in the good soil, these are the ones who have heard the word with a good and virtuous heart, and hold it firmly, and produce fruit with perseverance.

PARABLE OF THE LAMP

16"Now ^no one lights a lamp and covers it over with a container, or puts it under a bed; but he puts it on a lampstand so that those who come in may see the light. 17^For nothing is concealed that will not become evident, nor *anything* hidden that will not be known and come to light. 18So take care how you listen; ^for whoever has, to him *more* will be given; and whoever does not have, even what he thinks he has will be taken away from him."

19^Now His mother and brothers came to Him, and they were unable to get to Him because of the crowd. 20And it was reported to Him, "Your mother and Your brothers are standing outside, wishing to see You." 21But He answered and said to them, "My mother and My brothers are these ^who hear the word of God and do *it.*"

8:3^Matt 14:1   8:4^*Matt 13:2-9; Mark 4:1-9*
8:8^Matt 11:15   8:9^*Matt 13:10-23; Mark 4:10-20*
8:10^Is 6:9; Matt 13:14   8:11^1 Pet 1:23
8:16^Matt 5:15; Mark 4:21   8:17^Matt 10:26;
Mark 4:22   8:18^Matt 13:12; 25:29   8:19^*Matt
12:46-50; Mark 3:31-35*   8:21^Luke 11:28

JESUS STILLS THE SEA

22 ^Now on one of *those* days Jesus and His disciples got into a boat, and He said to them, "Let's cross over to the other side of the lake." So they launched out. 23 But as they were sailing along He fell asleep; and a fierce gale of wind descended on ^the lake, and they *began* to be swamped and to be in danger. 24 They came up to Jesus and woke Him, saying, "^Master, Master, we are perishing!" And He got up and ^Brebuked the wind and the surging waves, and they stopped, and it became calm. 25 And He said to them, "Where is your faith?" But they were fearful and amazed, saying to one another, "Who then is this, that He commands even the winds and the water, and they obey Him?"

THE DEMON-POSSESSED MAN CURED

26 ^Then they sailed to the country of the Gerasenes, which is opposite Galilee. 27 And when He stepped out onto the land, a man from the city met Him who was possessed with demons; and he had not put on clothing for a long time and was not living in a house, but among the tombs. 28 And seeing Jesus, he cried out and fell down before Him, and said with a loud voice, "^What business do You have with me, Jesus, Son of ^Bthe Most High God? I beg You, do not torment me!" 29 For He *had already* commanded the unclean spirit to come out of the man. For it had seized him many times; and he was bound with chains and shackles and kept under guard, and *yet* he would break the restraints and be driven by the demon into the desert. 30 And Jesus asked him, "What is your name?" And he said, "^Legion"; because

many demons had entered him. 31 And they were begging Him not to command them to go away into ^the abyss.

32 Now there was a herd of many pigs feeding there on the mountain; and *the demons* begged Him to permit them to enter the pigs. And He gave them permission. 33 And the demons came out of the man and entered the pigs; and the herd rushed down the steep bank into ^the lake and was drowned.

34 Now when the herdsmen saw what had happened, they ran away and reported *everything* in the city, and in the country. 35 And *the people* came out to see what had happened; and they came to Jesus and found the man from whom the demons had gone out, sitting down ^at the feet of Jesus, clothed and in his right mind; and they became frightened. 36 Those who had seen *everything* reported to them how the man who had been ^demon-possessed had been made well. 37 And all the people of the territory of the Gerasenes and the surrounding region asked Him to leave them, because they were overwhelmed by great fear; and He got into a boat and returned. 38 ^But the man from whom the demons had gone out was begging Him that he might accompany Him; but Jesus sent him away, saying, 39 "Return to your home and describe what great things God has done for you." So he went away, proclaiming throughout the city what great things Jesus had done for him.

8:22 ^*Matt 8:23-27; Mark 4:36-41*   **8:23** ^Luke 5:1f; **8:22**   **8:24** ^Luke 5:5   ^BLuke 4:39   **8:26** ^*Matt 8:28-34; Mark 5:1-17*   **8:28** ^Matt 8:29   ^BMark 5:7 **8:30** ^Matt 26:53   **8:31** ^Rom 10:7; Rev 9:1f, 11 **8:33** ^Luke 5:1f; 8:22   **8:35** ^Luke 10:39 **8:36** ^Matt 4:24   **8:38** ^*Mark 5:18-20*

MIRACLES OF HEALING

40 ^AAnd as Jesus was returning, the people welcomed Him, for they had all been waiting for Him. **41** ^AAnd a man named Jairus came, and he was an official of the synagogue; and he fell at Jesus' feet, and *began* urging Him to come to his house; **42** for he had an only daughter, about twelve years old, and she was dying. But as He went, the crowds were pressing against Him.

43 And a woman who had suffered a *chronic* flow of blood for twelve years, and could not be healed by anyone, **44** came up behind Him and touched the fringe of His cloak, and immediately her bleeding stopped. **45** And Jesus said, "Who is the one who touched Me?" And while they were all denying it, Peter said, "^AMaster, the people are crowding and pressing in on You." **46** But Jesus said, "Someone did touch Me, for I was aware that ^Apower had left Me." **47** Now when the woman saw that she had not escaped notice, she came trembling and fell down before Him, and admitted in the presence of all the people the reason why she had touched Him, and how she had been immediately healed. **48** And He said to her, "Daughter, your faith has made you well; ^Ago in peace."

49 While He was still speaking, someone *came from *the house of* ^Athe synagogue official, saying, "Your daughter has died; do not trouble the Teacher anymore." **50** But when Jesus heard *this*, He responded to him, "^ADo not be afraid *any longer;* only believe, and she will be made well." **51** When He came to the house, He did not allow anyone to enter with Him except Peter, John, and James, and

the girl's father and mother. **52** Now they were all weeping and ^Amourning for her; but He said, "Stop weeping, for she has not died, but ^Bis asleep." **53** And they *began* laughing at Him, knowing that she had died. **54** He, however, took her by the hand and spoke forcefully, saying, "Child, arise!" **55** And her spirit returned, and she got up immediately; and He ordered that *something* be given her to eat. **56** Her parents were amazed; but He ^Ainstructed them to tell no one what had happened.

MINISTRY OF THE TWELVE

9 ^ANow He called the twelve together and gave them power and authority over all the demons, and *the power* to heal diseases. **2** And He sent them out to ^Aproclaim the kingdom of God and to perform healing. **3** And He said to them, "^ATake nothing for *your* journey, neither a staff, nor a bag, nor bread, nor money; and do not *even* have two ^Btunics. **4** And whatever house you enter, stay there until you leave that city. **5** And as for all who do not receive you, when you leave that city, ^Ashake the dust off your feet as a testimony against them." **6** And as they were leaving, they *began* going throughout the villages, ^Apreaching the gospel and healing everywhere.

7 ^ANow Herod the tetrarch heard *about* all that was happening; and

8:40 ^AMatt 9:1; Mark 5:21   **8:41** ^A*Matt 9:18-26;* Mark 5:22-43   **8:45** ^ALuke 5:5   **8:46** ^ALuke 5:17
8:48 ^AMark 5:34; Luke 7:50   **8:49** ^ALuke 8:41
8:50 ^AMark 5:36   **8:52** ^ALuke 23:27   ^BJohn 11:13
8:56 ^AMatt 8:4   **9:1** ^AMatt 10:5; Mark 6:7
9:2 ^AMatt 10:7   **9:3** ^ALuke 10:4-12; 22:35
9:5 ^ALuke 10:11; Acts 13:51   **9:6** ^AMark 6:12; Luke 8:1
9:7 ^AMark 6:14f

9:3 ^A long shirt worn next to the skin

he was greatly perplexed, because it was said by some that John had risen from the dead, ⁸and by some that ᴬElijah had appeared, and by others that one of the prophets of old had risen. ⁹Herod said, "I myself had John beheaded; but who is this Man about whom I hear such things?" And ᴬhe kept trying to see Him.

¹⁰When the apostles returned, they gave an account to Him of all that they had done. ᴬAnd taking them with Him, He withdrew privately to a city called Bethsaida. ¹¹But the crowds were aware *of this* and followed Him; and He welcomed them and *began* speaking to them about the kingdom of God, and curing those who had need of healing.

FIVE THOUSAND MEN FED

¹²Now the day was ending, and the twelve came up and said to Him, "Dismiss the crowd, so that they may go into the surrounding villages and countryside and find lodging and get something to eat; because here, we are in a secluded place." ¹³But He said to them, "You give them *something* to eat!" But they said, "We have no more than five loaves and two fish, unless perhaps we go and buy food for all these people." ¹⁴(For there were about five thousand men.) But He said to His disciples, "Have them recline *to eat* ᴬin groups of about fifty each." ¹⁵They did so, and had them all recline. ¹⁶And He took the five loaves and the two fish, and, looking up to heaven, He blessed them and broke *them,* and gave *them* to the disciples *again and again,* to serve the crowd. ¹⁷And they all ate and were satisfied; and the broken pieces which they had left over were picked up, twelve ᴬbaskets *full.*

PETER SAYS JESUS IS THE CHRIST

¹⁸ᴬAnd it happened that while He was praying alone, the disciples were with Him, and He questioned them, saying, "Who do the people say that I am?" ¹⁹They answered and said, "John the Baptist, and others *say* Elijah; but others, that one of the prophets of old has risen." ²⁰And He said to them, "But who do you say that I am?" And Peter answered and said, "ᴬThe Christ of God." ²¹But He ᴬwarned them and instructed *them* not to tell this to anyone, ²²ᴬsaying, "The Son of Man must suffer many things and be rejected by the elders and chief priests and scribes, and be killed and be raised on the third day."

²³And He was saying to *them* all, "ᴬIf anyone wants to come after Me, he must deny himself, take up his cross daily, and follow Me. ²⁴For ᴬwhoever wants to save his life will lose it, but whoever loses his life for My sake, this is the one who will save it. ²⁵For what good does it do a person if he gains the whole world, but ᴬloses or forfeits himself? ²⁶ᴬFor whoever is ashamed of Me and My words, the Son of Man will be ashamed of him when He comes in His glory and *the glory* of the Father and the holy angels. ²⁷But I say to you truthfully, ᴬthere are some of those standing here who will not taste death until they see the kingdom of God."

9:8ᴬMatt 16:14   **9:9**ᴬLuke 23:8   **9:10**ᴬ*Matt 14:13-21; Mark 6:32-44*   **9:14**ᴬMark 6:39   **9:17**ᴬMatt 14:20   **9:18**ᴬ*Matt 16:13-16; Mark 8:27-29*   **9:20**ᴬJohn 6:68f   **9:21**ᴬMatt 8:4; 16:20   **9:22**ᴬ*Matt 16:21-28; Mark 8:31-9:1*   **9:23**ᴬMatt 10:38; Luke 14:27   **9:24**ᴬMatt 10:39; Luke 17:33   **9:25**ᴬHeb 10:34   **9:26**ᴬMatt 10:33; Luke 12:9   **9:27**ᴬMatt 16:28

THE TRANSFIGURATION

28 ^About eight days after these sayings, He took along Peter, John, and James, and went up on the mountain to pray. 29 And while He was ^praying, the appearance of His face became different, and His clothing *became* white *and* gleaming. 30 And behold, two men were talking with Him; and they were Moses and Elijah, 31 who, appearing in glory, were speaking of His ^departure, which He was about to accomplish at Jerusalem. 32 Now Peter and his companions ^had been overcome with sleep; but when they were fully awake, they saw His glory and the two men who were standing with Him. 33 And as these *two men* were leaving Him, Peter said to Jesus, "Master, it is good that we are here; and ^let's make three tabernacles: one for You, one for Moses, and one for Elijah"—not realizing what he was saying. 34 But while he was saying this, a cloud formed and *began* to overshadow them; and they were afraid as they entered the cloud. 35 And *then* a voice came from the cloud, saying, "^This is My Son, *My* Chosen One; listen to Him!" 36 And when the voice had spoken, Jesus was found alone. And ^they kept silent, and reported to no one in those days any of the things which they had seen.

37 ^On the next day, when they came down from the mountain, a large crowd met Him. 38 And a man from the crowd shouted, saying, "Teacher, I beg You to look at my son, because he is my only *son,* 39 and a spirit seizes him and he suddenly screams, and it throws him into a convulsion with foaming *at the mouth;* and only with difficulty does it leave him, mauling him *as it leaves.* 40 And I begged Your disciples to cast it out, and they could

not." 41 And Jesus answered and said, "You unbelieving and perverse generation, how long shall I be with you and put up with you? Bring your son here." 42 Now while he was still approaching, the demon slammed him to the ground and threw him into a convulsion. But Jesus rebuked the unclean spirit, and healed the boy and gave him back to his father. 43 And they were all amazed at the greatness of God.

^But while everyone was astonished at all that He was doing, He said to His disciples, 44 "As for you, let these words sink into your ears: ^for the Son of Man is going to be handed over to men." 45 But ^they did not understand this statement, and it was concealed from them so that they would not comprehend it; and they were afraid to ask Him about this statement.

THE TEST OF GREATNESS

46 ^Now an argument started among them as to which of them might be the greatest. 47 But Jesus, ^knowing what they were thinking in their hearts, took a child and had him stand by His side, 48 and He said to them, "^Whoever receives this child in My name receives Me, and whoever receives Me receives Him who sent Me; for the one who is least among all of you, this is the one who is great."

49 ^John answered and said, "Master, we saw someone casting out demons in Your name; and we *tried to* prevent him, because he does

9:28 ^ Matt 17:1-8; Mark 9:2-8   9:29 ^ Luke 3:21; 5:16
9:31 ^ 2 Pet 1:15   9:32 ^ Matt 26:43; Mark 14:40
9:33 ^ Matt 17:4; Mark 9:5   9:35 ^ Is 42:1; Matt 3:17
9:36 ^ Matt 17:9; Mark 9:9f   9:37 ^ Matt 17:14-18;
Mark 9:14-27   9:43 ^ Matt 17:22f; Mark 9:30-32
9:44 ^ Luke 9:22   9:45 ^ Mark 9:32   9:46 ^ Luke 22:24
9:47 ^ Matt 9:4   9:48 ^ Matt 10:40; Luke 10:16
9:49 ^ Mark 9:38-40

not follow along with us." ⁵⁰But Jesus said to him, "Do not hinder *him;* ᴬfor the one who is not against you is for you."

⁵¹When the days were approaching for His ascension, He was determined ᴬto go to Jerusalem; ⁵²and He sent messengers on ahead of Him, and they went and entered a village of the ᴬSamaritans to make arrangements for Him. ⁵³And they did not receive Him, ᴬbecause He was traveling toward Jerusalem. ⁵⁴When His disciples James and John saw *this,* they said, "Lord, do You want us to ᴬcommand fire to come down from heaven and consume them?" ⁵⁵But He turned and rebuked them.¹ ⁵⁶And they went on to another village.

EXACTING DISCIPLESHIP

⁵⁷As they were going on the road, ᴬsomeone said to Him, "I will follow You wherever You go." ⁵⁸And Jesus said to him, "The foxes have holes and the birds of the sky *have* nests, but ᴬthe Son of Man has nowhere to lay His head." ⁵⁹And He said to another, "ᴬFollow Me." But he said, "Lord, permit me first to go and bury my father." ⁶⁰But He said to him, "Allow the dead to bury their own dead; but as for you, go and ᴬproclaim everywhere the kingdom of God." ⁶¹Another also said, "I will follow You, Lord; but ᴬfirst permit me to say goodbye to those at my home." ⁶²But Jesus said to him, "ᴬNo one, after putting his hand to the plow and looking back, is fit for the kingdom of God."

THE SEVENTY-TWO SENT OUT

10 Now after this the Lord appointed seventy-two ᴬothers, and sent them ᴮin pairs ahead of Him to every city and place where He Himself was going to come. ²And He was saying to them, "ᴬThe harvest is plentiful, but the laborers are few; therefore plead with the Lord of the harvest to send out laborers into His harvest. ³Go; ᴬbehold, I am sending you out like lambs in the midst of wolves. ⁴ᴬCarry no money belt, no bag, no sandals, and greet no one along the way. ⁵And whatever house you enter, first say, 'Peace *be* to this house.' ⁶And if a man of peace is there, your peace will rest upon him; but if not, it will return to you. ⁷Stay in that house, eating and drinking what they provide; for ᴬthe laborer is deserving of his wages. Do not move from house to house. ⁸Whatever city you enter and they receive you, ᴬeat what is served to you; ⁹and heal those in it who are sick, and say to them, 'ᴬThe kingdom of God has come near to you.' ¹⁰But whatever city you enter and they do not receive you, go out into its streets and say, ¹¹'ᴬEven the dust of your city which clings to our feet we wipe off *in protest* against you; yet be sure of this, that the kingdom of God has come near.' ¹²I say to you, ᴬit will be more tolerable on that day for Sodom than for that city.

¹³"ᴬWoe to you, Chorazin! Woe to you, Bethsaida! For if the miracles that occurred in you had

9:50ᴬMatt 12:30; Luke 11:23   **9:51**ᴬLuke 13:22; 17:11
9:52ᴬMatt 10:5; Luke 10:33   **9:53**ᴬJohn 4:9
9:54²2 Kin 1:9–16   **9:57**ᴬ*Matt 8:19-22*
9:58ᴬMatt 8:20   **9:59**ᴬMatt 8:22   **9:60**ᴬMatt 4:23
9:61ᴬ1 Kin 19:20   **9:62**ᴬPhil 3:13   **10:1**ᴬLuke 9:1f, 52
ᴮMark 6:7   **10:2**ᴬMatt 9:37, 38; John 4:35
10:3ᴬMatt 10:16   **10:4**ᴬMatt 10:9–14; Mark 6:8–11
10:7ᴬMatt 10:10; 1 Cor 9:14   **10:8**ᴬ1 Cor 10:27
10:9ᴬMatt 3:2; 10:7   **10:11**ᴬMatt 10:14; Mark 6:11
10:12ᴬGen 19:24–28; Matt 10:15   **10:13**ᴬ*Matt 11:21-23*

9:55¹Some late mss add: *and said, "You do not know of what kind of spirit you are; for the Son of Man did not come to destroy people's lives, but to save them."*

occurred in Tyre and Sidon, they would have repented long ago, sitting in ¹sackcloth and ashes. ¹⁴But it will be more tolerable for ᴬTyre and Sidon in the judgment than for you. ¹⁵And you, ᴬCapernaum, will not be exalted to heaven, will you? You will be brought down to Hades!

¹⁶"ᴬThe one who listens to you listens to Me, and the one who rejects you rejects Me; but the one who rejects Me rejects the One who sent Me."

THE JOYFUL RESULTS

¹⁷Now the seventy-two returned with joy, saying, "Lord, even ᴬthe demons are subject to us in Your name!" ¹⁸And He said to them, "I watched ᴬSatan fall from heaven like lightning. ¹⁹Behold, I have given you authority to ᴬwalk on snakes and scorpions, and *authority* over all the power of the enemy, and nothing will injure you. ²⁰Nevertheless, do not rejoice in this, that the spirits are subject to you, but rejoice that ᴬyour names are recorded in heaven."

²¹ᴬAt that very time He rejoiced greatly in the Holy Spirit, and said, "I praise You, Father, Lord of heaven and earth, that You have hidden these things from *the* wise and intelligent and have revealed them to infants. Yes, Father, for *doing* so was well pleasing in Your sight. ²²ᴬAll things have been handed over to Me by My Father, and ᴮno one knows who the Son is except the Father, and who the Father is except the Son, and anyone to whom the Son determines to reveal *Him*."

²³ᴬTurning to the disciples, He said privately, "Blessed *are* the eyes that see the things you see; ²⁴for I tell you that many prophets and kings wanted to see the things that you see, and did not see *them,* and to hear the things that you hear, and did not hear *them.*"

²⁵ᴬAnd behold, a lawyer stood up and put Him to the test, saying, "Teacher, what shall I do to inherit eternal life?" ²⁶And He said to him, "What is written in the Law? How does it read to you?" ²⁷And he answered, "ᴬYOU SHALL LOVE THE LORD YOUR GOD WITH ALL YOUR HEART, AND WITH ALL YOUR SOUL, AND WITH ALL YOUR STRENGTH, AND WITH ALL YOUR MIND; AND YOUR NEIGHBOR AS YOURSELF." ²⁸And He said to him, "You have answered correctly; ᴬdo this and you will live." ²⁹But wanting ᴬto justify himself, he said to Jesus, "And who is my neighbor?"

THE GOOD SAMARITAN

³⁰Jesus replied and said, "A man was ᴬgoing down from Jerusalem to Jericho, and he encountered robbers, and they stripped him and beat him, and went away leaving him half dead. ³¹And by coincidence a priest was going down on that road, and when he saw him, he passed by on the other side. ³²Likewise a Levite also, when he came to the place and saw him, passed by on the other side. ³³But a ᴬSamaritan who was on a journey came upon him; and when he saw him, he felt compassion, ³⁴and came to

10:14ᴬMatt 11:21　**10:15**ᴬIs 14:13-15; Matt 4:13
10:16ᴬMatt 10:40; Mark 9:37　**10:17**ᴬLuke 9:1
10:18ᴬMatt 4:10　**10:19**ᴬPs 91:13　**10:20**ᴬEx 32:32;
Ps 69:28　**10:21**ᴬ*Matt 11:25-27*　**10:22**ᴬJohn 3:35
ᴮJohn 10:15　**10:23**ᴬ*Matt 13:16, 17*　**10:25**ᴬMatt 19:16-
19　**10:27**ᴬDeut 6:5; Lev 19:18　**10:28**ᴬLev 18:5;
Ezek 20:11　**10:29**ᴬLuke 16:15　**10:30**ᴬLuke 18:31;
19:28　**10:33**ᴬMatt 10:5; Luke 9:52

10:13¹I.e., symbols of mourning

him and bandaged up his wounds, pouring oil and wine on *them;* and he put him on his own animal, and brought him to an inn and took care of him. ³⁵ On the next day he took out two ¹denarii and gave them to the innkeeper and said, 'Take care of him; and whatever more you spend, when I return, I will repay you.' ³⁶ Which of these three do you think proved to be a neighbor to the man who fell into the robbers' *hands?*" ³⁷ And he said, "The one who showed compassion to him." Then Jesus said to him, "Go and do the same."

MARTHA AND MARY

³⁸ Now as they were traveling along, He entered a village; and a woman named ᴬMartha welcomed Him into her home. ³⁹ And she had a sister called ᴬMary, who was also seated at the Lord's feet, and was listening to His word. ⁴⁰ But ᴬMartha was distracted with all her preparations; and she came up *to Him* and said, "Lord, do You not care that my sister has left me to do the serving by myself? Then tell her to help me." ⁴¹ But the Lord answered and said to her, "Martha, Martha, you are ᴬworried and distracted by many things; ⁴² ᴬbut *only* one thing is necessary; for Mary has chosen the good part, which shall not be taken away from her."

INSTRUCTION ABOUT PRAYER

11 It happened that while Jesus was praying in a certain place, when He had finished, one of His disciples said to Him, "Lord, teach us to pray, just as John also taught his disciples." ² And He said to them, "ᴬWhen you pray, say:

'Father, hallowed be Your name. Your kingdom come.
³ 'Give us ᴬeach day our daily bread.
⁴ 'And forgive us our sins, For we ourselves also forgive everyone who ᴬis indebted to us. And do not lead us into temptation.'"

⁵ And He said to them, "Suppose one of you has a friend, and goes to him at midnight and says to him, 'Friend, lend me three loaves, ⁶ because a friend of mine has come to me from a journey and I have nothing to serve him'; ⁷ and from inside he answers and says, 'Do not bother me; the door has already been shut and my children and I are in bed; I cannot get up and give you *anything.*' ⁸ I tell you, even if he will not get up and give him *anything just* because he is his friend, yet ᴬbecause of his shamelessness he will get up and give him as much as he needs.

⁹ "So I say to you, ᴬask, and it will be given to you; seek, and you will find; knock, and it will be opened to you. ¹⁰ For everyone who asks receives, and the one who seeks finds, and to the one who knocks, it will be opened. ¹¹ Now which one of you fathers will his son ask for a fish, and instead of a fish, he will give him a snake? ¹² Or he will even ask for an egg, *and his father* will give him a scorpion? ¹³ So ᴬif you,

10:38 ᴬLuke 10:40f; John 11:1, 5, 19ff, 30, 39
10:39 ᴬLuke 10:42; John 11:1f, 19f, 28, 31f, 45
10:40 ᴬLuke 10:38, 41; John 11:1, 5, 19ff, 30, 39
10:41 ᴬMatt 6:25   10:42 ᴬPs 27:4; John 6:27
11:2 ᴬ*Matt 6:9-13*   11:3 ᴬActs 17:11   11:4 ᴬLuke 13:4
11:8 ᴬLuke 18:1-5   11:9 ᴬ*Matt 7:7-11*   11:13 ᴬMatt 7:11; Luke 18:7f

10:35 ¹The denarius was a day's wages for a laborer
11:2 ¹Later mss add phrases from Matt 6:9-13 to make the two passages closely similar

despite being evil, know how to give good gifts to your children, how much more will your heavenly Father give the Holy Spirit to those who ask Him?"

PHARISEES' BLASPHEMY

¹⁴ᴬAnd He was casting out a mute demon; when the demon had gone out, the man who was *previously* unable to speak talked, and the crowds were amazed. ¹⁵But some of them said, "He casts out the demons ᴬby ᴮBeelzebul, the ruler of the demons." ¹⁶Others, to test *Him,* ᴬwere demanding of Him a sign from heaven. ¹⁷ᴬBut He knew their thoughts and said to them, "Every kingdom divided against itself is laid waste; and a house *divided* against itself falls. ¹⁸And if ᴬSatan also has been divided against himself, how will his kingdom stand? For you claim that I cast out the demons by Beelzebul. ¹⁹Yet if by ᴬBeelzebul I cast out the demons, by whom do your sons cast *them* out? Therefore, they will be your judges. ²⁰But if I cast out the demons by the ᴬfinger of God, then ᴮthe kingdom of God has come upon you. ²¹When a strong *man,* fully armed, guards his own house, his possessions are secure. ²²But when *someone* stronger than he attacks him and overpowers him, *that man* takes away his armor on which he had relied and distributes his plunder. ²³ᴬThe one who is not with Me is against Me; and the one who does not gather with Me scatters.

²⁴"ᴬWhen the unclean spirit comes out of a person, it passes through waterless places seeking rest, and not finding *any,* it then says, 'I will return to my house from which I came.' ²⁵And when it comes, it finds it swept and put in order. ²⁶Then it goes and brings along seven other spirits more evil than itself, and they come in and live there; and the last *condition* of that person becomes worse than the first."

²⁷While Jesus was saying these things, one of the women in the crowd raised her voice and said to Him, "ᴬBlessed is the womb that carried You, and the breasts at which You nursed!" ²⁸But He said, "On the contrary, blessed are ᴬthose who hear the word of God and follow it."

THE SIGN OF JONAH

²⁹Now as the crowds were increasing, He began to say, "ᴬThis generation is a wicked generation; it demands a sign, and *so* no sign will be given to it except the sign of Jonah. ³⁰For just as ᴬJonah became a sign to the Ninevites, so will the Son of Man be to this generation. ³¹The ᴬQueen of the South will rise up with the men of this generation at the judgment and condemn them, because she came from the ends of the earth to listen to the wisdom of Solomon; and behold, *something* greater than Solomon is here. ³²The men of Nineveh will stand up with this generation at the judgment and condemn it, because ᴬthey repented at the preaching of Jonah; and behold, *something* greater than Jonah is here.

³³"ᴬNo one lights a lamp and puts *it away* in a cellar nor under a basket, but on the lampstand, so that

11:14 ᴬMatt 9:32-34   11:15 ᴬMatt 9:34   ᴮMatt 10:25
11:16 ᴬMatt 12:38; 16:1   11:17 ᴬ*Matt 12:25-29;*
Mark 3:23-27   11:18 ᴬMatt 4:10   11:19 ᴬMatt 10:25
11:20 ᴬEx 8:19   ᴮMatt 3:2   11:23 ᴬMatt 12:30;
Mark 9:40   11:24 ᴬ*Matt 12:43-45*   11:27 ᴬLuke 23:29
11:28 ᴬLuke 8:21   11:29 ᴬMatt 16:4; Mark 8:12
11:30 ᴬJon 3:4   11:31 ᴬ1 Kin 10:1-10; 2 Chr 9:1-12
11:32 ᴬJon 3:5   11:33 ᴬMatt 5:15; Mark 4:21

those who enter may see the light. ³⁴ᴬYour eye is the lamp of your body; when your eye is clear, your whole body also is full of light; but when it is bad, your body also is full of darkness. ³⁵So watch out that the light in you is not darkness. ³⁶Therefore if your whole body is full of light, without any dark part, it will be wholly illuminated, as when the lamp illuminates you with its light."

WOES UPON THE PHARISEES

³⁷Now when He had spoken, a Pharisee *asked Him to have lunch with him; and He went in and reclined *at the table.* ³⁸When the Pharisee saw *this,* he was surprised that Jesus had not first ᴬceremonially washed before the meal. ³⁹But the Lord said to him, "Now ᴬyou Pharisees clean the outside of the cup and of the dish; but your inside is full of greed and wickedness. ⁴⁰ᴬYou foolish ones, did He who made the outside not make the inside also? ⁴¹But ᴬgive that which is within as a charitable gift, and then all things are ᴮclean for you.

⁴²"ᴬBut woe to you Pharisees! For you ᴮpay tithes of mint, rue, and every *kind of* garden herb, and *yet* you ignore justice and the love of God; but these are the things you should have done without neglecting the others. ⁴³Woe to you Pharisees! For you ᴬlove the seat of honor in the synagogues and personal greetings in the marketplaces. ⁴⁴ᴬWoe to you! For you are like unseen tombs, and the people who walk over *them* are unaware *of it.*"

⁴⁵One of the ¹,ᴬlawyers *said to Him in reply, "Teacher, when You say these things, You insult us too." ⁴⁶But He said, "Woe to you lawyers as well! For ᴬyou load people with burdens that are hard to bear, while you yourselves will not even touch the burdens with one of your fingers. ⁴⁷ᴬWoe to you! For you build the tombs of the prophets, and *it was* your fathers *who* killed them. ⁴⁸So you are witnesses and you approve of the deeds of your fathers; because *it was* they *who* killed them, and you build *their tombs.* ⁴⁹For this reason also, ᴬthe wisdom of God said, 'I will send them prophets and apostles, and *some* of them they will kill, and *some* they will persecute, ⁵⁰so that the blood of all the prophets, shed ᴬsince the foundation of the world, may be charged against this generation, ⁵¹from the blood of Abel to ᴬthe blood of Zechariah, who was killed between the altar and the house *of God;* yes, I tell you, it shall be charged against this generation.' ⁵²Woe to you lawyers! For you have taken away the key of knowledge; ᴬyou yourselves did not enter, and you hindered those who were entering."

⁵³When He left that place, the scribes and the Pharisees began to be very hostile and to interrogate Him about many *subjects,* ⁵⁴plotting against Him ᴬto catch Him in something He might say.

GOD KNOWS AND CARES

12 Under these circumstances, after so many thousands of people had gathered together that they were stepping on one

11:34 ᴬ*Matt 6:22, 23*   11:38 ᴬMatt 15:2; Mark 7:3f
11:39 ᴬMatt 23:25f   11:40 ᴬLuke 12:20; 1 Cor 15:36
11:41 ᴬLuke 12:33   ᴮTitus 1:15   11:42 ᴬMatt 23:23
ᴮLev 27:30   11:43 ᴬMatt 23:6f; Mark 12:38f
11:44 ᴬMatt 23:27   11:45 ᴬMatt 22:35; Luke 11:46, 52
11:46 ᴬMatt 23:4   11:47 ᴬMatt 23:29ff
11:49 ᴬ1 Cor 1:24, 30; Col 2:3   11:50 ᴬMatt 25:34
11:51 ᴬ2 Chr 24:20, 21   11:52 ᴬMatt 23:13
11:54 ᴬMark 12:13

11:45 ¹I.e., experts in the Mosaic Law

another, He began saying to His disciples first *of all,* "^Beware of the leaven of the Pharisees, which is hypocrisy. ²^But there is nothing covered up that will not be revealed, and hidden that will not be known. ³ Accordingly, whatever you have said in the dark will be heard in the light, and what you have whispered in the inner rooms will be proclaimed on ^the housetops.

⁴ "Now I say to you, ^My friends, do not be afraid of those who kill the body, and after that have nothing more that they can do. ⁵ But I will warn you whom to fear: ^fear the One who, after He has killed *someone,* has *the* power to throw *that person* into ¹hell; yes, I tell you, fear Him! ⁶ Are ^five sparrows not sold for two ¹assaria? And *yet* not one of them has gone unnoticed in the sight of God. ⁷^But even the hairs of your head are all counted. Do not fear; you are more valuable than a great number of sparrows.

⁸ "Now I say to you, everyone who ^confesses Me before people, the Son of Man will also confess him before the angels of God; ⁹ but ^the one who denies Me before people will be denied before the angels of God. ¹⁰^And everyone who speaks a word against the Son of Man, it will be forgiven him; but the one who blasphemes against the Holy Spirit, it will not be forgiven him. ¹¹ Now when they bring you before the synagogues and the officials and the authorities, do not ^worry about how or what you are to speak in your defense, or what you are to say; ¹² for ^the Holy Spirit will teach you in that very hour what you ought to say."

GREED DENOUNCED

¹³ Now someone in the crowd said to Him, "Teacher, tell my brother to divide the *family* inheritance with me." ¹⁴ But He said to him, "^You there—who appointed Me a judge or arbitrator over *the two of* you?" ¹⁵ But He said to them, "^Beware, and be on your guard against every form of greed; for not *even* when one is affluent does his life consist of his possessions." ¹⁶ And He told them a parable, saying, "The land of a rich man was very productive. ¹⁷ And he began thinking to himself, saying, 'What shall I do, since I have no place to store my crops?' ¹⁸ And he said, 'This *is what* I will do: I will tear down my barns and build larger ones, and I will store all my grain and my goods there. ¹⁹ And I will say to myself, "^You have many goods stored up for many years *to come;* relax, eat, drink, *and* enjoy yourself!"' ²⁰ But God said to him, 'You fool! This *very* night ^your soul is demanded of you; and ᴮ*as for all* that you have prepared, who will own *it now?*' ²¹ Such is the one who ^stores up treasure for himself, and is not rich in relation to God."

²² And He said to His disciples, "^For this reason I tell you, do not worry about *your* life, *as to* what you are to eat; nor for your body, *as to* what you are to wear. ²³ For life is more than food, and the body *is*

12:1^Matt 16:6, 11f; Mark 8:15   12:2^Matt 10:26; Mark 4:22   12:3^Matt 10:27; 24:17   12:4^John 15:13-15   12:5^Heb 10:31   12:6^Matt 10:29   12:7^Matt 10:30   12:8^Matt 10:32; Luke 15:10   12:9^Matt 10:33; Luke 9:26   12:10^Matt 12:31, 32; Mark 3:28-30   12:11^Matt 6:25; 10:19   12:12^Matt 10:20; Luke 21:15   12:14^Mic 6:8; Rom 2:1, 3   12:15^1 Tim 6:6-10   12:19^Eccl 11:9   12:20^Job 27:8   ᴮPs 39:6   12:21^Luke 12:33   12:22^*Matt 6:25-33*

12:5¹Gr *Gehenna*   12:6¹A Roman copper coin (singular *assarion*), about 1/16 of a laborer's daily wage

more than clothing. ²⁴Consider the ^ravens, that they neither sow nor reap; they have no storeroom nor barn, and *yet* God feeds them; how much more valuable you are than the birds! ²⁵And which of you by worrying can add a ¹·^day to his ²life's span? ²⁶Therefore if you cannot do even a very little thing, why do you worry about the other things? ²⁷Consider the lilies, how they grow: they neither labor nor spin; but I tell you, not even ^Solomon in all his glory clothed himself like one of these. ²⁸Now if God so clothes the grass in the field, which is *alive* today and tomorrow is thrown into the furnace, how much more *will He clothe* you? ^You of little faith! ²⁹And do not seek what you are to eat and what you are to drink, and do not ^keep worrying. ³⁰For all these things *are what* the nations of the world eagerly seek; and your Father knows that you need these things. ³¹But seek His kingdom, and ^these things will be provided to you. ³²Do not be afraid, ^little flock, because ᴮyour Father has chosen to give you the kingdom.

³³"^Sell your possessions and give to charity; make yourselves money belts that do not wear out, an inexhaustible treasure in heaven, where no thief comes near nor does a moth destroy. ³⁴For ^where your treasure is, there your heart will be also.

BE IN READINESS

³⁵"^Be prepared, and *keep* your lamps lit. ³⁶You are also *to be* like people who are waiting for their master when he returns from the wedding feast, so that they may immediately open *the door* for him when he comes and knocks.

³⁷Blessed are those slaves whom the master will find ^on the alert when he comes; truly I say to you, that ᴮhe will prepare himself *to serve,* and have them recline *at the table,* and he will come up and serve them. ³⁸^Whether he comes in the ¹second watch, or even in the ²third, and finds *them* so, blessed are those *slaves.*

³⁹"^But be sure of this, that if the head of the house had known at what hour the thief was coming, he would not have allowed his house to be broken into. ⁴⁰^You too, be ready; because the Son of Man is coming at an hour that you do not think *He will.*"

⁴¹Peter said, "Lord, are You telling this parable to us, or ^to everyone *else* as well?" ⁴²And the Lord said, "^Who then is the faithful and sensible steward, whom his master will put in charge of his servants, to give them their rations at the proper time? ⁴³Blessed is that ^slave whom his master finds so doing when he comes. ⁴⁴Truly I say to you that he will put him in charge of all his possessions. ⁴⁵But if that slave says in his heart, 'My master will take a long time to come,' and he begins to beat the *other* slaves, *both* men and women, and to eat and drink and get drunk; ⁴⁶*then* the master of that slave will come on a day that he does not expect, and at an hour that he does not know, and will cut him in two, and

12:24^Job 38:41   **12:25**^Ps 39:5   **12:27**^1 Kin 10:4-7; 2 Chr 9:3-6   **12:28**^Matt 6:30   **12:29**^Matt 6:31 **12:31**^Matt 6:33   **12:32**^John 21:15-17   ᴮEph 1:5, 9 **12:33**^Matt 19:21; Luke 11:41   **12:34**^Matt 6:21 **12:35**^Eph 6:14; 1 Pet 1:13   **12:37**^Matt 24:42 ᴮLuke 17:8   **12:38**^Matt 24:43   **12:39**^*Matt 24:43, 44* **12:40**^Mark 13:33; Luke 21:36   **12:41**^Luke 12:47, 48 **12:42**^*Matt 24:45-51*   **12:43**^Luke 12:42

12:25¹Lit *cubit* (about 18 in. or 45 cm)   ²Or *height* **12:38**¹I.e., 9 p.m. to midnight   ²I.e., midnight to 3 a.m.

assign him a place with the unbe-lievers. [47] And that slave who knew his master's will and did not get ready or act in accordance with his will, will ^receive many blows, [48] but the one who did not ^know *it*, and committed acts deserving of a beating, will receive *only* a few blows. From everyone who has been given much, much will be demanded; and to whom they entrusted much, of him they will ask all the more.

CHRIST DIVIDES PEOPLE

[49] "I have come to cast fire upon the earth; and how I wish it were already kindled! [50] But I have a ^baptism to undergo, and how distressed I am until it is accomplished! [51] ^Do you think that I came to provide peace on earth? No, I tell you, but rather division; [52] for from now on five *members* in one household will be divided, three against two and two against three. [53] They will be divided, ^father against son and son against father, mother against daughter and daughter against mother, mother-in-law against daughter-in-law and daughter-in-law against mother-in-law."

[54] And He was also saying to the crowds, "^Whenever you see a cloud rising in the west, you immediately say, 'A shower is coming,' and so it turns out. [55] And whenever *you feel* a south wind blowing, you say, 'It will be a ^hot *day*,' and it turns out *that way.* [56] You hypocrites! ^You know how to analyze the appearance of the earth and the sky, but how *is it that* you do not know how to analyze this *present* time?

[57] "And ^why do you not even judge by yourselves what is right? [58] For ^when you are going with your accuser *to appear* before the magistrate, on the way, make an effort to settle with him, so that he does not drag you before the judge, and the judge hand you over to the officer, and the officer throw you into prison. [59] I tell you, you will not get out of there until you have paid up the very last [1]^lepton."

CALL TO REPENT

13 Now on that very occasion there were some present who reported to Him about the Galileans whose blood ^Pilate had mixed with their sacrifices. [2] And Jesus responded and said to them, "^Do you think that these Galileans were *worse* sinners than all the *other* Galileans *just* because they have suffered this *fate?* [3] No, I tell you, but unless you repent, you will all likewise perish. [4] Or do you think that those eighteen on whom the tower in ^Siloam fell and killed them were *worse* offenders than all the *other* people who live in Jerusalem? [5] No, I tell you, but unless you repent, you will all likewise perish."

[6] And He *began* telling this parable: "A man had ^a fig tree which had been planted in his vineyard; and he came looking for fruit on it and did not find *any.* [7] And he said to the vineyard-keeper, 'Look! For three years I have come looking for fruit on this fig tree without finding any. ^Cut it down! Why does it even use up the ground?' [8] But

12:47 ^Deut 25:2; James 4:17　12:48 ^Lev 5:17; Num 15:29f　12:50 ^Mark 10:38　12:51 ^*Matt 10:34-36*
12:53 ^Mic 7:6; Matt 10:21　12:54 ^Matt 16:2f
12:55 ^Matt 20:12　12:56 ^Matt 16:3
12:57 ^Luke 21:30　12:58 ^*Matt 5:25, 26*
12:59 ^Mark 12:42　13:1 ^Matt 27　13:2 ^John 9:2f
13:4 ^Neh 3:15; Is 8:6　13:6 ^Matt 21:19
13:7 ^Matt 3:10; 7:19

12:59 [1] The smallest Greek copper coin, about 1/128 of a laborer's daily wage

he answered and said to him, 'Sir, leave it alone for this year too, until I dig around it and put in fertilizer; ⁹and if it bears fruit next *year, fine;* but if not, cut it down.'"

HEALING ON THE SABBATH

¹⁰Now Jesus was ᴬteaching in one of the synagogues on the Sabbath. ¹¹And there was a woman who for eighteen years had had ᴬa sickness caused by a spirit; and she was bent over double, and could not straighten up at all. ¹²When Jesus saw her, He called her over and said to her, "Woman, you are freed from your sickness." ¹³And He ᴬlaid His hands on her; and immediately she stood up straight again, and *began* glorifying God. ¹⁴But the synagogue leader, indignant because Jesus had healed on the Sabbath, *began* saying to the crowd in response, "ᴬThere are six days during which work should be done; so come during them and get healed, and not on the Sabbath day." ¹⁵But the Lord answered him and said, "You hypocrites, ᴬdoes each of you on the Sabbath not untie his ox or donkey from the stall and lead it away to water *it?* ¹⁶And this woman, ᴬa daughter of Abraham as she is, whom Satan has bound for eighteen long years, should she not have been released from this restraint on the Sabbath day?" ¹⁷And as He said this, all His opponents were being humiliated; and ᴬthe entire crowd was rejoicing over all the glorious things being done by Him.

PARABLES OF MUSTARD SEED AND LEAVEN

¹⁸So ᴬHe was saying, "What is the kingdom of God like, and to what shall I compare it? ¹⁹It is like a mustard seed, which a man took and threw into his own garden; and it grew and became a tree, and ᴬthe birds of the sky nested in its branches."

²⁰And again He said, "ᴬTo what shall I compare the kingdom of God? ²¹ᴬIt is like leaven, which a woman took and hid in three sata of flour until it was all leavened."

TEACHING IN THE VILLAGES

²²And He was passing through one city and village after another, teaching, and ᴬproceeding on His way to Jerusalem. ²³And someone said to Him, "Lord, are there *just* a few who are being saved?" And He said to them, ²⁴"ᴬStrive to enter through the narrow door; for many, I tell you, will seek to enter and will not be able. ²⁵Once the head of the house gets up and ᴬshuts the door, and you begin standing outside and knocking on the door, saying, 'Lord, open up to us!' and He *then* will answer and say to you, 'ᴮI do not know where you are from.' ²⁶Then you will ᴬbegin saying, 'We ate and drank in Your presence, and You taught in our streets!' ²⁷And *yet* He will say, 'I do not know where you are from; ᴬLEAVE ME, ALL YOU EVILDOERS.' ²⁸ᴬIn that place there will be weeping and gnashing of teeth when you see Abraham, Isaac, Jacob, and all the prophets in the kingdom of God, but yourselves being thrown out. ²⁹And they ᴬwill come from east and west, and from north and south, and will recline

13:10 ᴬMatt 4:23   13:11 ᴬLuke 13:16   13:13 ᴬMark 5:23
13:14 ᴬEx 20:9; Deut 5:13   13:15 ᴬLuke 14:5
13:16 ᴬLuke 19:9   13:17 ᴬLuke 18:43
13:18 ᴬ *Matt 13:31, 32; Mark 4:30-32*   13:19 ᴬEzek 17:23
13:20 ᴬMatt 13:24; Luke 13:18   13:21 ᴬ *Matt 13:33*
13:22 ᴬLuke 9:51   13:24 ᴬMatt 7:13   13:25 ᴬMatt 25:10
ᴮMatt 7:23   13:26 ᴬLuke 3:8   13:27 ᴬPs 6:8;
Matt 25:41   13:28 ᴬMatt 8:12; 22:13   13:29 ᴬMatt 8:11

at the table in the kingdom of God. ³⁰And behold, ^*some* are last who will be first, and *some* are first who will be last."

³¹At that very time some Pharisees approached, saying to Him, "Go away and leave this place, because ^Herod wants to kill You." ³²And He said to them, "Go and tell that fox, 'Behold, I am casting out demons and performing healings today and tomorrow, and on the third *day* I ^reach My goal.' ³³Nevertheless I must go on My journey today and tomorrow and the next *day;* for it cannot be that a ^prophet would perish outside Jerusalem. ³⁴^Jerusalem, Jerusalem, the *city* that kills the prophets and stones those who have been sent to her! How often I wanted to gather your children together, just as a hen *gathers* her young under her wings, and you were unwilling! ³⁵Behold, your house is left to you *desolate;* and I say to you, you will not see Me until you say, '^Blessed is the One who comes in the name of the Lord!'"

JESUS HEALS ON THE SABBATH

14 It happened that when He went into the house of one of the leaders of the Pharisees on *the* Sabbath to eat bread, ^they were watching Him closely. ²And there in front of Him was a man suffering from ¹edema. ³And Jesus responded and said to the lawyers and Pharisees, "^Is it lawful to heal on the Sabbath, or not?" ⁴But they kept silent. And He took hold of him and healed him, and sent him away. ⁵And He said to them, "^Which one of you will have a son or an ox fall into a well, and will not immediately pull him out on a Sabbath day?" ⁶^And they could offer no reply to this.

PARABLE OF THE GUESTS

⁷Now He *began* telling a parable to the invited guests when He noticed how ^they had been picking out the places of honor *at the table,* saying to them, ⁸"Whenever you are invited by someone to a wedding feast, ^do not take the place of honor, for someone more distinguished than you may have been invited by him, ⁹and the one who invited you both will come and say to you, 'Give *your* place to this person,' and then ^in disgrace you will proceed to occupy the last place. ¹⁰But whenever you are invited, go and take the last place, so that when the one who has invited you comes, he will say to you, 'Friend, ^move up higher'; then you will have honor in the sight of all who are dining at the table with you. ¹¹^For everyone who exalts himself will be humbled, and the one who humbles himself will be exalted."

¹²Now He also went on to say to the one who had invited Him, "Whenever you give a luncheon or a dinner, do not invite your friends, your brothers, your relatives, nor wealthy neighbors, otherwise they may also invite you *to a meal* in return, and *that* will be your repayment. ¹³But whenever you give a banquet, invite people who are poor, who have disabilities, who are limping, *and* people who are blind; ¹⁴and you will be blessed, since they do not have *the means* to

13:30 ^Matt 19:30; 20:16   13:31 ^Matt 14:1; Luke 3:1
13:32 ^Heb 2:10; 5:9   13:33 ^Matt 21:11
13:34 ^Luke 19:41   13:35 ^Ps 118:26; Matt 21:9
14:1 ^Mark 3:2   14:3 ^Matt 12:2; Luke 13:14
14:5 ^Matt 12:11; Luke 13:15
14:6 ^Matt 22:46; Luke 20:40   14:7 ^Matt 23:6
14:8 ^Prov 25:6, 7   14:9 ^Luke 3:8
14:10 ^Prov 25:6, 7   14:11 ^2 Sam 22:28; Prov 29:23

14:2 ¹I.e., extreme swelling

repay you; for you will be repaid at ^the resurrection of the righteous.”

15 Now when one of those who were reclining *at the table* with Him heard this, he said to Him, “^Blessed is everyone who will eat bread in the kingdom of God!”

PARABLE OF THE DINNER

16 But He said to him, “^A man was giving a big dinner, and he invited many; 17 and at the dinner hour he sent his slave to tell those who had been invited, ‘Come, because everything is ready now.’ 18 And *yet* they all alike began to make excuses. The first one said to him, ‘I purchased a field and I need to go out to look at it; please consider me excused.’ 19 And another one said, ‘I bought five yoke of oxen, and I am going to try them out; please consider me excused.’ 20 And another one said, ‘^I took a woman as my wife, and for that reason I cannot come.’ 21 And the slave came *back* and reported this to his master. Then the head of the household became angry and said to his slave, ‘Go out at once into the streets and lanes of the city and bring in here those who are poor, those with disabilities, those who are blind, and those who are limping.’ 22 And *later* the slave said, ‘Master, what you commanded has been done, and still there is room.’ 23 And the master said to the slave, ‘Go out into the roads and the hedges and press upon *them* to come in, so that my house will be filled. 24 For I tell you, none of those men who were invited shall taste my dinner.’”

DISCIPLESHIP TESTED

25 Now large crowds were going along with Him, and He turned and said to them, 26 “If anyone comes to Me and does not ¹hate his own father, mother, wife, children, brothers, sisters, yes, and even his own life, he cannot be My disciple. 27 Whoever does not ^carry his own cross and come after Me cannot be My disciple. 28 For which one of you, when he wants to build a tower, does not first sit down and calculate the cost, *to see* if he has *enough* to complete *it?* 29 Otherwise, when he has laid a foundation and is not able to finish, all who are watching *it* will begin to ridicule him, 30 saying, ‘This person began to build, and was not able to finish!’ 31 Or what king, when he sets out to meet another king in battle, will not first sit down and ^consider whether he is strong *enough* with ten thousand *men* to face the one coming against him with twenty thousand? 32 Otherwise, while the other is still far away, he sends a delegation and requests terms of peace. 33 So then, none of you can be My disciple who ^does not give up all his own possessions.

34 “Therefore, salt is good; but ^if even salt has become tasteless, with what will it be seasoned? 35 It is useless either for the soil or the manure pile, *so* it is thrown out. ^The one who has ears to hear, let him hear.”

THE LOST SHEEP

15 Now all the ^tax collectors and sinners were coming near Jesus to listen to Him. 2 And both the Pharisees and the scribes *began* to complain, saying, “This Man receives sinners and ^eats with them.”

14:14 ^John 5:29; Acts 24:15   14:15 ^Rev 19:9
14:16 ^Matt 22:2-14; Luke 14:16-24   14:20 ^Deut 24:5;
1 Cor 7:33   14:26 ^Matt 10:37   14:27 ^Matt 10:38;
16:24   14:31 ^Prov 20:18   14:33 ^Phil 3:7; Heb 11:26
14:34 ^Matt 5:13; Mark 9:50   14:35 ^Matt 11:15
15:1 ^Luke 5:29   15:2 ^Matt 9:11

14:26 ¹I.e., in comparison to his love for Me

³And *so* He told them this parable, saying, ⁴"ᴬWhat man among you, if he has a hundred sheep and has lost one of them, does not leave the *other* ninety-nine in the open pasture and go after the one that is lost, until he finds it? ⁵And when he has found it, he puts it on his shoulders, rejoicing. ⁶And when he comes home, he calls together his friends and his neighbors, saying to them, 'Rejoice with me, because I have found my sheep that was lost!' ⁷I tell you that in the same way, there will be *more* joy in heaven over one sinner who repents than over ninety-nine righteous people who have no need of repentance.

THE LOST COIN

⁸"Or what woman, if she has ten silver coins and loses one coin, does not light a lamp and sweep the house and search carefully until she finds *it?* ⁹And when she has found *it,* she calls together her friends and neighbors, saying, 'Rejoice with me, because I have found the coin which I had lost!' ¹⁰In the same way, I tell you, there is joy ᴬin the presence of the angels of God over one sinner who repents."

THE PRODIGAL SON

¹¹And He said, "A man had two sons. ¹²The younger of them said to his father, 'Father, give me ᴬthe share of the estate that is coming to me.' And *so* he divided his ᴮwealth between them. ¹³And not many days later, the younger son gathered everything together and went on a journey to a distant country, and there he squandered his estate in wild living. ¹⁴Now when he had spent everything, a severe famine occurred in that country, and he began doing without. ¹⁵So he went and hired himself out to one of the citizens of that country, and he sent him into his fields to feed pigs. ¹⁶And he longed to have his fill of the carob pods that the pigs were eating, and no one was giving him *anything.* ¹⁷But when he came to his senses, he said, 'How many of my father's hired laborers have more than enough bread, but I am dying here from hunger! ¹⁸I will set out and go to my father, and will say to him, "Father, I have sinned against heaven, and in your sight; ¹⁹I am no longer worthy to be called your son; treat me as one of your hired laborers."' ²⁰So he set out and came to his father. But when he was still a long way off, his father saw him and felt compassion *for him,* and ran and ᴬembraced him and kissed him. ²¹And the son said to him, 'Father, I have sinned against heaven and in your sight; I am no longer worthy to be called your son.' ²²But the father said to his slaves, 'Quickly bring out ᴬthe best robe and put it on him, and ᴮput a ring on his finger and sandals on his feet; ²³and bring the fattened calf, slaughter it, and let's eat and celebrate; ²⁴for this son of mine was ᴬdead and has come to life again; he was lost and has been found.' And they began to celebrate.

²⁵"Now his older son was in the field, and when he came and approached the house, he heard music and dancing. ²⁶And he summoned one of the servants and *began* inquiring what these things could be. ²⁷And he said to

15:4 ᴬMatt 18:12-14; Luke 15:4-7   15:10 ᴬMatt 10:32; Luke 15:7   15:12 ᴬDeut 21:17   ᴮLuke 15:30
15:20 ᴬGen 45:14; 46:29   15:22 ᴬZech 3:4
ᴮGen 41:42   15:24 ᴬMatt 8:22; Luke 9:60

him, 'Your brother has come, and your father has slaughtered the fattened calf because he has received him back safe and sound.' 28But he became angry and was not willing to go in; and his father came out and *began* pleading with him. 29But he answered and said to his father, 'Look! For so many years I have been serving you and I have never neglected a command of yours; and *yet* you never gave me a young goat, so that I might celebrate with my friends; 30but when this son of yours came, who has devoured your ^wealth with prostitutes, you slaughtered the fattened calf for him.' 31And he said to him, 'Son, you have always been with me, and all that is mine is yours. 32But we had to celebrate and rejoice, because this brother of yours was ^dead and *has begun* to live, and *was* lost and has been found.'"

THE UNRIGHTEOUS MANAGER

16 Now He was also saying to the disciples, "There was a rich man who had a manager, and this *manager* was reported to him as ^squandering his possessions. 2And he summoned him and said to him, 'What is this I hear about you? Give an accounting of your management, for you can no longer be manager.' 3And the manager said to himself, 'What am I to do, since my master is taking the management away from me? I am not strong enough to dig; I am ashamed to beg. 4I know what I will do, so that when I am removed from the management *people* will welcome me into their homes.' 5And he summoned each one of his master's debtors, and he *began* saying to the first, 'How much do you

owe my master?' 6And he said, 'A hundred jugs of oil.' And he said to him, 'Take your bill, and sit down quickly and write fifty.' 7Then he said to another, 'And how much do you owe?' And he said, 'A hundred kors of wheat.' He *said to him, 'Take your bill, and write eighty.' 8And his master complimented the unrighteous manager because he had acted shrewdly; for the sons of this age are more shrewd in relation to their own kind than the ^sons of light. 9And I say to you, make friends for yourselves by means of the 1,^wealth of unrighteousness, so that when it is all gone, they will receive you into the eternal dwellings.

10"^The one who is faithful in a very little thing is also faithful in much; and the one who is unrighteous in a very little thing is also unrighteous in much. 11Therefore if you have not been faithful in the *use of* unrighteous ^wealth, who will entrust the true *wealth* to you? 12And if you have not been faithful in *the use of* that which is another's, who will give you that which is your own? 13^No servant can serve two masters; for either he will hate the one and love the other, or he will be devoted to one and despise the other. You cannot serve God and wealth."

14Now the Pharisees, who were ^lovers of money, were listening to all these things and were ridiculing Him. 15And He said to them, "You are the ones who justify yourselves in

---

15:30 ^Prov 29:3; Luke 15:12   15:32 ^Luke 15:24
16:1 ^Luke 15:13   16:8 ^John 12:36; Eph 5:8
16:9 ^Matt 6:24; Luke 16:11, 13   16:10 ^Matt 25:21, 23
16:11 ^Luke 16:9   16:13 ^Matt 6:24   16:14 ^2 Tim 3:2

16:9 1Gr *mamonas,* for Aramaic *mamon* (mammon); i.e., wealth, or money

the sight of people, but ᴬGod knows your hearts; because that which is highly esteemed among people is detestable in the sight of God.

16 "ᴬThe Law and the Prophets *were proclaimed* until John *came;* since that time ᴮthe gospel of the kingdom of God has been preached, and everyone is forcing his way into it. **17**ᴬBut it is easier for heaven and earth to pass away than for one stroke of a letter of the Law to fail.

18 "ᴬEveryone who divorces his wife and marries another commits adultery, and he who marries one who is divorced from a husband commits adultery.

THE RICH MAN AND LAZARUS

19 "Now there was a rich man, and he habitually dressed in purple and fine linen, enjoying himself in splendor every day. **20**And a poor man named Lazarus ᴬwas laid at his gate, covered with sores, **21**and longing to be fed from the *scraps* which fell from the rich man's table; not only *that,* the dogs also were coming and licking his sores. **22**Now it happened that the poor man died and was carried away by the angels to ¹ᴬAbraham's arms; and the rich man also died and was buried. **23**And in ᴬHades he raised his eyes, being in torment, and *saw Abraham far away and Lazarus in his ¹arms. **24**And he cried out and said, 'ᴬFather Abraham, have mercy on me and send Lazarus, so that he may dip the tip of his finger in water and cool off my tongue, for I am in agony in ᴮthis flame.' **25**But Abraham said, 'Child, remember that ᴬduring your life you received your good things, and likewise Lazarus bad things; but now he is being comforted

here, and you are in agony. **26**And besides all this, between us and you a great chasm has been set, so that those who want to go over from here to you will not be able, nor will *any people* cross over from there to us.' **27**And he said, 'Then I request of you, father, that you send him to my father's house— **28**for I have five brothers—in order that he may ᴬwarn them, so that they will not come to this place of torment as well.' **29**But Abraham *said, 'They have ᴬMoses and the Prophets; let them hear them.' **30**But he said, 'No, ᴬfather Abraham, but if someone goes to them from the dead, they will repent!' **31**But he said to him, 'If they do not listen to Moses and the Prophets, they will not be persuaded even if someone rises from the dead.'"

INSTRUCTIONS

17 Now He said to His disciples, "ᴬIt is inevitable that stumbling blocks come, but woe to one through whom they come! **2**ᴬIt is better for him if a millstone is hung around his neck and he is thrown into the sea, than that he may cause one of these little ones to sin. **3**Be on your guard! ᴬIf your brother sins, rebuke him; and if he repents, forgive him. **4**And if he sins against you ᴬseven times a day, and returns to you seven times, saying, 'I repent,' you shall forgive him."

16:15ᴬ1 Sam 16:7; Prov 21:2   16:16ᴬMatt 11:12f   ᴮMatt 4:23   16:17ᴬMatt 5:18   16:18ᴬMatt 5:32; 1 Cor 7:10, 11   16:20ᴬActs 3:2   16:22ᴬJohn 1:18; 13:23   16:23ᴬMatt 11:23   16:24ᴬLuke 3:8   ᴮMatt 25:41   16:25ᴬLuke 6:24   16:28ᴬActs 2:40; 8:25   16:29ᴬLuke 4:17; John 5:45-47   16:30ᴬLuke 3:8; 16:24   17:1ᴬMatt 18:7; 1 Cor 11:19   17:2ᴬMatt 18:6; Mark 9:42   17:3ᴬMatt 18:15   17:4ᴬMatt 18:21f

16:22¹Lit *Abraham's bosom;* or *lap;* ancient Jewish terminology for the place of the righteous dead
16:23¹See note v 22

⁵The apostles said to the Lord, "Increase our faith!" ⁶But the Lord said, "If you had faith the size of ^a mustard seed, you could say to this mulberry tree, 'Be uprooted and be planted in the sea'; and it would obey you.

⁷"Now which of you, having a slave plowing or tending sheep, will say to him after he comes in from the field, 'Come immediately and recline *at the table* to eat'? ⁸On the contrary, will he not say to him, '^Prepare something for me to eat, and *properly* clothe yourself and serve me while I eat and drink; and afterward you may eat and drink'? ⁹He does not thank the slave because he did the things which were commanded, does he? ¹⁰So you too, when you do all the things which were commanded you, say, 'We are unworthy slaves; we have done *only* that which we ought to have done.'"

TEN MEN WITH LEPROSY HEALED

¹¹While He was on the way to Jerusalem, ^He was passing between Samaria and Galilee. ¹²And as He entered a village, ten men with leprosy who ^stood at a distance met Him; ¹³and they raised their voices, saying, "Jesus, ^Master, have mercy on us!" ¹⁴When He saw *them,* He said to them, "^Go and show yourselves to the priests." And as they were going, they were cleansed. ¹⁵Now one of them, when he saw that he had been healed, turned back, ^glorifying God with a loud voice, ¹⁶and he fell on his face at His feet, giving thanks to Him. And he was a ^Samaritan. ¹⁷But Jesus responded and said, "Were there not ten cleansed? But the nine—where *are they?* ¹⁸Was no one found

who returned to ^give glory to God, except this foreigner?" ¹⁹And He said to him, "Stand up and go; ^your faith has made you well."

SECOND COMING FORETOLD

²⁰Now He was questioned by the Pharisees ^as to when the kingdom of God was coming, and He answered them and said, "The kingdom of God is not coming with signs that can be observed; ²¹nor will ^they say, 'Look, here *it is!*' or, 'There *it is!*' For behold, the kingdom of God is in your midst."

²²And He said to the disciples, "^The days will come when you will long to see one of the days of the Son of Man, and you will not see *it.* ²³^And they will say to you, 'Look there,' or, 'Look here!' Do not leave, and do not run after *them.* ²⁴^For just like the lightning, when it flashes out of one part of the sky, shines to the other part of the sky, so will the Son of Man be in His day. ²⁵^But first He must suffer many things and be rejected by this generation. ²⁶^And just as it happened in the days of Noah, so will it also be in the days of the Son of Man: ²⁷*people* were eating, they were drinking, they were marrying, *and* they were being given in marriage, until the day that Noah entered the ark, and the flood came and destroyed them all. ²⁸It was the same as happened in ^the days of Lot: they were eating, they were drinking, they were buying, they were selling,

17:6 ^Matt 13:31; 17:20   17:8 ^Luke 12:37
17:11 ^Luke 9:52ff; John 4:3f   17:12 ^Lev 13:45f
17:13 ^Luke 5:5   17:14 ^Lev 14:1-32; Matt 8:4
17:15 ^Matt 9:8   17:16 ^Matt 10:5   17:18 ^Matt 9:8
17:19 ^Matt 9:22; Luke 18:42   17:20 ^Luke 19:11;
Acts 1:6   17:21 ^Luke 17:23   17:22 ^Matt 9:15;
Mark 2:20   17:23 ^Matt 24:23; Mark 13:21
17:24 ^Matt 24:27   17:25 ^Matt 16:21; Luke 9:22
17:26 *Matt 24:37-39*   17:28 ^Gen 19

they were planting, *and* they were building; 29 but on the day that Lot left Sodom, it rained fire and brimstone from heaven and destroyed them all. 30 It will be just the same on the day that the Son of Man ᴬis revealed. 31 On that day, the one who will be ᴬon the housetop, with his goods in the house, must not go down to take them out; and likewise the one in the field must not turn back. 32 ᴬRemember Lot's wife. 33 ᴬWhoever strives to save his life will lose it, and whoever loses *his life* will keep it. 34 I tell you, on that night there will be two in one bed; one will be taken and the other will be left. 35 ᴬThere will be two women grinding at the same *place;* one will be taken and the other will be left. 36 [¹,ᴬTwo men will be in the field; one will be taken and the other will be left."] 37 And responding, they *said to Him, "Where, Lord?" And He said to them, "ᴬWhere the body *is,* there also the vultures will be gathered."

PARABLES ON PRAYER

18 Now He was telling them a parable to show that at all times they ᴬought to pray and not ᴮbecome discouraged, 2 saying, "In a certain city there was a judge who did not fear God and did not ᴬrespect *any* person. 3 Now there was a widow in that city, and she kept coming to him, saying, 'Give me justice against my opponent.' 4 For a while he was unwilling; but later he said to himself, 'Even though I do not fear God nor ᴬrespect *any* person, 5 yet ᴬbecause this widow is bothering me, I will give her justice; otherwise by continually coming she will wear me out.'" 6 And ᴬthe Lord said, "Listen to what the

unrighteous judge *said; 7 now, will God not bring about justice for His ᴬelect who cry out to Him day and night, and will He ᴮdelay long for them? 8 I tell you that He will bring about justice for them quickly. However, when the Son of Man comes, ᴬwill He find faith on the earth?"

THE PHARISEE AND THE TAX COLLECTOR

9 Now He also told this parable to some people who ᴬtrusted in themselves that they were righteous, and ᴮviewed others with contempt: 10 "Two men ᴬwent up into the temple to pray, one a Pharisee and the other a tax collector. 11 The Pharisee ᴬstood and *began* praying this in regard to himself: 'God, I thank You that I am not like other people: swindlers, crooked, adulterers, or even like this tax collector. 12 I fast twice a week; I ᴬpay tithes of all that I get.' 13 But the tax collector, standing some distance away, ᴬwas even unwilling to raise his eyes toward heaven, but ᴮwas beating his chest, saying, 'God, be merciful to me, the sinner!' 14 I tell you, this man went to his house justified rather than the other one; ᴬfor everyone who exalts himself will be humbled, but the one who humbles himself will be exalted."

15 ᴬNow they were bringing even their babies to Him so that He

17:30 ᴬ Matt 16:27; 1 Cor 1:7   17:31 ᴬ Matt 24:17, 18; Mark 13:15f   17:32 ᴬ Gen 19:26   17:33 ᴬ Matt 10:39
17:35 ᴬ Matt 24:41   17:36 ᴬ Matt 24:40
17:37 ᴬ Matt 24:28   18:1 ᴬ Luke 11:5-10   ᴮ 2 Cor 4:1
18:2 ᴬ Luke 18:4; 20:13   18:4 ᴬ Luke 18:2; 20:13
18:5 ᴬ Luke 11:8   18:6 ᴬ Luke 7:13   18:7 ᴬ Matt 24:22
ᴮ 2 Pet 3:9   18:8 ᴬ Luke 17:26ff   18:9 ᴬ Luke 16:15
ᴮ Rom 14:3, 10   18:10 ᴬ 1 Kin 10:5; 2 Kin 20:5, 8
18:11 ᴬ Matt 6:5; Mark 11:25   18:12 ᴬ Luke 11:42
18:13 ᴬ Ezra 9:6   ᴮ Luke 23:48   18:14 ᴬ Matt 23:12;
Luke 14:11   18:15 ᴬ Matt 19:13-15; Mark 10:13-16

17:36 ¹ Early mss do not contain this v

would touch them; but when the disciples saw *it,* they *began* rebuking them. ¹⁶But Jesus called for the little ones, saying, "Allow the children to come to Me, and do not forbid them, for the kingdom of God belongs to such as these. ¹⁷Truly I say to you, ^whoever does not receive the kingdom of God like a child will not enter it at all."

THE RICH YOUNG RULER

¹⁸^A ruler questioned Him, saying, "Good Teacher, what shall I do to inherit eternal life?" ¹⁹But Jesus said to him, "Why do you call Me good? No one is good except God alone. ²⁰You know the commandments, '^Do not commit adultery, Do not murder, Do not steal, Do not give false testimony, Honor your father and mother.' " ²¹And he said, "All these things I have kept since *my* youth." ²²Now when Jesus heard *this,* He said to him, "One thing you still lack; ^sell all that you possess and distribute *the money* to the poor, and you will have treasure in heaven; and come, follow Me." ²³But when he had heard these things, he became very sad, for he was extremely wealthy. ²⁴And Jesus looked at him and said, "^How hard it is for those who are wealthy to enter the kingdom of God! ²⁵For ^it is easier for a camel to go through the eye of a needle, than for a rich person to enter the kingdom of God!" ²⁶Those who heard *Him* said, "And *so* who can be saved?" ²⁷But He said, "^The things that are impossible with people are possible with God."

²⁸Peter said, "Behold, ^we have left our own homes and followed You." ²⁹And He said to them, "Truly I say to you, ^there is no one who has left house, or wife, or brothers,

or parents, or children for the sake of the kingdom of God, ³⁰who will not receive many times as much at this time, and in ^the age to come, eternal life."

³¹Now He took the twelve aside and said to them, "Behold, we are going up to Jerusalem, and all the things that have been written through the prophets about the Son of Man will be accomplished. ³²^For He will be handed over to the Gentiles, and will be ridiculed, and abused, and spit upon, ³³and after they have flogged Him, they will kill Him; and on the third day He will rise." ³⁴^The disciples understood none of these things, and *the meaning of* this statement was hidden from them, and they did not comprehend the things that were said.

BARTIMAEUS RECEIVES SIGHT

³⁵^Now as Jesus was approaching Jericho, a man who was blind was sitting by the road, begging. ³⁶But when he heard a crowd going by, he *began* inquiring what this was. ³⁷They told him that Jesus of Nazareth was passing by. ³⁸And he called out, saying, "Jesus, ^Son of David, have mercy on me!" ³⁹Those who led the way were sternly telling him to be quiet; but he kept crying out all the more, "^Son of David, have mercy on me!" ⁴⁰And Jesus stopped and commanded that he be brought to Him; and when he came near, He asked him, ⁴¹"What do you want Me to do for

18:17 ^Matt 18:3; 19:14   18:18 ^Luke 10:25-28
18:20 ^Ex 20:12-16; Deut 5:16-20   18:22 ^Matt 19:21;
Luke 12:33   18:24 ^Matt 19:23; Mark 10:23f
18:25 ^Matt 19:24; Mark 10:25   18:27 ^Matt 19:26
18:28 ^Luke 5:11   18:29 ^Matt 6:33; 19:29
18:30 ^Matt 12:32   18:31 *Matt 20:17-19; Mark
10:32-34*   18:32 ^Matt 16:21   18:34 ^Mark 9:32;
Luke 9:45   18:35 *Matt 20:29-34; Mark 10:46-52*
18:38 ^Matt 9:27; Luke 18:39   18:39 ^Luke 18:38

you?" And he said, "Lord, *I want* to regain my sight!" ⁴²And Jesus said to him, "Regain your sight; ^your faith has made you well." ⁴³And immediately he regained his sight and *began* following Him, ^glorifying God; and when all the people saw *it*, they gave praise to God.

ZACCHEUS CONVERTED

19 Jesus ^entered Jericho and was passing through. ²And there was a man called by the name of Zaccheus; he was a chief tax collector and he was rich. ³*Zaccheus* was trying to see who Jesus was, and he was unable due to the crowd, because he was short in stature. ⁴So he ran on ahead and climbed up a ^sycamore tree in order to see Him, because He was about to pass through that *way*. ⁵And when Jesus came to the place, He looked up and said to him, "Zaccheus, hurry and come down, for today I must stay at your house." ⁶And he hurried and came down, and received Him joyfully. ⁷When *the people* saw *this*, they all *began* to complain, saying, "He has gone in to be the guest of a man who is a sinner!" ⁸But Zaccheus stopped and said to the Lord, "Behold, Lord, half of my possessions I am giving to the poor, and if I have extorted anything from anyone, I am giving back ^four times as much." ⁹And Jesus said to him, "Today salvation has come to this house, because he, too, is ^a son of Abraham. ¹⁰For the Son of Man has come to seek and to save that which was lost."

PARABLE OF THE TEN MINAS

¹¹Now while they were listening to these things, Jesus went on to tell a parable, because ^He was near Jerusalem and they thought that ^the kingdom of God was going to appear immediately. ¹²So He said, "^A nobleman went to a distant country to receive a kingdom for himself, and *then* to return. ¹³And he called ten of his own slaves and gave them ten ¹minas, and said to them, 'Do business *with this money* until I come *back*.' ¹⁴But his citizens hated him and sent a delegation after him, saying, 'We do not want this man to reign over us.' ¹⁵When he returned after receiving the kingdom, he ordered that these slaves, to whom he had given the money, be summoned to him so that he would learn how much they had made by the business they had done. ¹⁶The first *slave* appeared, saying, 'Master, your mina has made ten minas more.' ¹⁷And he said to him, 'Well done, good slave; since you have been ^faithful in a very little thing, you are to have authority over ten cities.' ¹⁸The second one came, saying, 'Your mina, master, has made five minas.' ¹⁹And he said to him also, 'And you are to be over five cities.' ²⁰And *then* another came, saying, 'Master, here is your mina, which I kept tucked away in a handkerchief; ²¹for I was afraid of you, because you are a demanding man; you take up what you did not lay down, and reap what you did not sow.' ²²He *said to him, 'From your own lips I will judge you, you worthless slave. Did you know that I am a demanding man, taking up what I did not lay

18:42 ^Matt 9:22   18:43 ^Matt 9:8   19:1 ^Luke 18:35
19:4 ^1 Kin 10:27; 1 Chr 27:28   19:8 ^Ex 22:1; Lev 6:5
19:9 ^Luke 3:8; 13:16   19:11 ^Luke 9:51   ^Luke 17:20
19:12 ^Matt 25:14-30; Luke 19:12-27
19:17 ^Luke 16:10

19:13 ¹A mina was equal to about 100 days' wages for a laborer

down, and reaping what I did not sow?' ²³And *so* why did you not put my money in the bank, and when I came *back,* I would have collected it with interest?' ²⁴And *then* he said to the *other slaves* who were present, 'Take the mina away from him and give it to the one who has the ten minas.' ²⁵And they said to him, 'Master, he *already* has ten minas.' ²⁶'I tell you that to everyone who has, *more* shall be given, but from the one who does not have, even what he does have shall be taken away. ²⁷But as for ^these enemies of mine who did not want me to reign over them, bring *them* here and slaughter them in my presence.'"

TRIUMPHAL ENTRY

²⁸After Jesus said these things, He ^was going on ahead, ᴮgoing up to Jerusalem.

²⁹^When He approached Bethphage and Bethany, near the mountain that is called Olivet, He sent two of the disciples, ³⁰saying, "Go into the village ahead of *you;* there, as you enter, you will find a colt tied, on which no one yet has ever sat; untie it and bring it *here.* ³¹And if anyone asks you, 'Why are you untying *it?'* you shall say this: 'The Lord has need of it.'" ³²So those who were sent left and found *it* just as He had told them. ³³And as they were untying the colt, its owners said to them, "Why are you untying the colt?" ³⁴They said, "The Lord has need of it." ³⁵And they brought it to Jesus, ^and they threw their cloaks on the colt and put Jesus *on it.* ³⁶Now as He was going, they were spreading their cloaks on the road. ³⁷And as soon as He was approaching, near the descent of the Mount of Olives, the whole crowd of the disciples began to ^praise God joyfully with a loud voice for all the miracles which they had seen, ³⁸shouting:

"^BLESSED IS the King, THE ONE
    WHO COMES IN THE NAME OF
    THE LORD;
Peace in heaven and glory in
    the highest!"

³⁹^And *yet* some of the Pharisees in the crowd said to Him, "Teacher, rebuke Your disciples!" ⁴⁰Jesus replied, "I tell you, if these stop speaking, ^the stones will cry out!"

⁴¹When He approached *Jerusalem,* He saw the city and ^wept over it, ⁴²saying, "If you had known on this day, even you, the *conditions* for peace! But now they have been hidden from your eyes. ⁴³For the days will come upon you when your enemies will ^put up a barricade against you, and surround you and hem you in on every side, ⁴⁴and they will level you to the ground, and *throw down* your children within you, and ^they will not leave in you one stone upon another, because you did not recognize the time of your visitation."

TRADERS DRIVEN FROM THE TEMPLE

⁴⁵^And Jesus entered the temple *grounds* and began to drive out those who were selling, ⁴⁶saying to them, "It is written: '^AND MY HOUSE WILL BE A HOUSE OF PRAYER,' but you have made it a DEN OF ROBBERS."

⁴⁷And ^He was teaching daily in the temple; but the chief priests and the scribes and the leading

19:26 ^Matt 13:12; Mark 4:25   **19:27** ^Luke 19:14
19:28 ^Mark 10:32   ᴮLuke 9:51   **19:29** *Matt 21:1-9;
Mark 11:1-10*   **19:35** *Matt 21:4-9; Mark 11:7-10*
19:37 ^Luke 18:43   **19:38** ^Ps 118:26
19:39 ^Matt 21:15f   **19:40** ^Hab 2:11
19:41 ^Luke 13:34, 35   **19:43** ^Eccl 9:14; Is 29:3
19:44 ^Matt 24:2; Mark 13:2   **19:45** ^John 2:13-16
19:46 ^Is 56:7; Jer 7:11   **19:47** ^Matt 26:55; Luke 21:37

men among the people were trying to put Him to death, ⁴⁸and *yet* they could not find anything that they might do, for all the people were hanging on to every word He said.

JESUS' AUTHORITY QUESTIONED

20 ᴬOn one of the days while He was teaching the people in the temple and preaching the gospel, the chief priests and the scribes with the elders confronted *Him,* ²and they declared, saying to Him, "Tell us by what authority You are doing these things, or who is the one who gave You this authority?" ³But He replied to them, "I will also ask you a question, and you tell Me: ⁴Was the baptism of John from heaven or from men?" ⁵They discussed among themselves, saying, "If we say, 'From heaven,' He will say, 'Why did you not believe him?' ⁶But if we say, 'From men,' all the people will stone us to death, since they are convinced that John was a ᴬprophet." ⁷And *so* they answered that they did not know where *it came* from. ⁸And Jesus said to them, "Neither am I telling you by what authority I do these things."

PARABLE OF THE VINE-GROWERS

⁹ᴬBut He began to tell the people this parable: "A man planted a vineyard and leased it to vine-growers, and went on a journey for a long time. ¹⁰At *the harvest* time he sent a slave to the vine-growers, so that they would give him *his share* of the produce of the vineyard; but the vine-growers beat him and sent him away empty-handed. ¹¹And he proceeded to send another slave; but they beat him also and treated him shamefully, and sent him away empty-handed. ¹²And he proceeded to send a third; but this one too they wounded and threw out. ¹³Now the owner of the vineyard said, 'What am I to do? I will send my beloved son; perhaps they will ᴬrespect him.' ¹⁴But when the vine-growers saw him, they discussed with one another, saying, 'This is the heir; let's kill him so that the inheritance will be ours.' ¹⁵And so they threw him out of the vineyard and killed him. What, then, will the owner of the vineyard do to them? ¹⁶He will come and ᴬput these vine-growers to death, and will give the vineyard to others." However, when they heard *this,* they said, "May it never happen!" ¹⁷But Jesus looked at them and said, "Then what is this *statement* that has been written:

'ᴬA STONE WHICH THE BUILDERS
    REJECTED,
THIS HAS BECOME ᴮTHE CHIEF
    CORNERSTONE'?

¹⁸ᴬEveryone who falls on that stone will be broken to pieces; but on whomever it falls, it will crush him."

PAYING TAXES TO CAESAR

¹⁹The scribes and the chief priests ᴬtried to lay hands on Him that very hour, and *yet* they feared the people; for they were aware that He had spoken this parable against them. ²⁰ᴬAnd *so* they watched Him closely, and sent spies who pretended to be righteous, in order that they might catch Him in *some* statement, so that they *could* hand Him over to the jurisdiction and authority of the governor. ²¹And

20:1ᴬMatt 21:23-27; Mark 11:27-33   **20:6**ᴬMatt 11:9; Luke 7:29, 30   **20:9**ᴬMatt 21:33-46; Mark 12:1-12
20:13ᴬLuke 18:2   **20:16**ᴬMatt 21:41; Mark 12:9
20:17ᴬPs 118:22   ᴮEph 2:20   **20:18**ᴬMatt 21:44
20:19ᴬLuke 19:47   **20:20**ᴬMark 3:2

the spies questioned Him, saying, "Teacher, we know that You speak and teach correctly, and You are not partial to anyone, but You teach the way of God on the basis of truth. ²²Is it permissible for us ᴬto pay taxes to Caesar, or not?" ²³But He saw through their trickery and said to them, ²⁴"Show Me a ¹denarius. Whose image and inscription does it have?" They said, "Caesar's." ²⁵And He said to them, "Then ᴬpay to Caesar the things that are Caesar's, and to God the things that are God's." ²⁶And they were unable to ᴬcatch Him in a statement in the presence of the people; and they were amazed at His answer, and said nothing.

IS THERE A RESURRECTION?

²⁷ᴬNow some of the Sadducees (who maintain that there is no resurrection) came to Him, ²⁸and they questioned Him, saying, "Teacher, Moses wrote for us that ᴬif a man's brother dies, leaving a wife, and he is childless, that his brother is to marry the wife and raise up children for his brother. ²⁹So then, there were seven brothers; and the first took a wife and died childless; ³⁰and the second ³¹and the third married her; and in the same way all seven died, leaving no children. ³²Finally the woman also died. ³³Therefore, in the resurrection, which one's wife does the woman become? For all seven married her."

³⁴Jesus said to them, "The sons of ᴬthis age marry and *the women* are given in marriage, ³⁵but those who are considered worthy to attain to ᴬthat age and the resurrection from the dead, neither marry nor are given in marriage; ³⁶for

they cannot even die anymore, for they are like angels, and are ᴬsons of God, being sons of the resurrection. ³⁷But *as for* the fact that the dead are raised, even Moses revealed *this* in ᴬthe *passage about the burning* bush, where he calls the Lord ᴮTHE GOD OF ABRAHAM, THE GOD OF ISAAC, AND THE GOD OF JACOB. ³⁸ᴬNow He is not the God of the dead, but of the living; for ᴮall live to Him." ³⁹Some of the scribes answered and said, "Teacher, You have spoken well." ⁴⁰For ᴬthey did not have the courage to question Him any longer about anything.

⁴¹ᴬBut He said to them, "How *is it that* they say the Christ is David's son? ⁴²For David himself says in the book of Psalms,

'ᴬTHE LORD SAID TO MY LORD,
  "SIT AT MY RIGHT HAND,
⁴³ ᴬUNTIL I MAKE YOUR ENEMIES A
    FOOTSTOOL FOR YOUR FEET."'

⁴⁴Therefore David calls Him 'Lord,' and *so* how is He his son?"

⁴⁵ᴬAnd while all the people were listening, He said to the disciples, ⁴⁶"Beware of the scribes, ᴬwho like to walk around in long robes, and love personal greetings in the marketplaces, and chief seats in the synagogues and places of honor at banquets, ⁴⁷who devour widows' houses, and for appearance's sake offer long prayers. These will receive all the more condemnation."

20:22ᴬMatt 17:25; Luke 23:2　20:25ᴬMatt 22:21; Mark 12:17　20:26ᴬLuke 11:54　20:27ᴬMatt 22:23-33; Mark 12:18-27　20:28ᴬDeut 25:5　20:34ᴬMatt 12:32; Luke 16:8　20:35ᴬMatt 12:32; Luke 16:8　20:36ᴬRom 8:16f; 1 John 3:1, 2　20:37ᴬMark 12:26　ᴮEx 3:6　20:38ᴬMatt 22:32　ᴮRom 14:8　20:40ᴬMatt 22:46; Luke 14:6　20:41ᴬMatt 22:41-46; Mark 12:35-37　20:42ᴬPs 110:1　20:43ᴬPs 110:1　20:45ᴬMatt 23:1-7; Mark 12:38-40　20:46ᴬLuke 11:43; 14:7
20:24¹The denarius was a day's wages for a laborer

THE WIDOW'S GIFT

21 ᴬNow He looked up and saw the wealthy putting their gifts into the *temple* treasury. ²And He saw a poor widow putting in ᴬtwo ¹lepta coins. ³And He said, "Truly I say to you, this poor widow put in more than all *of them;* ⁴for they all contributed to the offering from their surplus; but she, from her poverty, put in all that she had ᴬto live on."

⁵ᴬAnd while some were talking about the temple, that it was decorated with beautiful stones and ¹vowed gifts, He said, ⁶ "*As for* these things which you are observing, the days will come when ᴬthere will not be left *one* stone upon another, which will not be torn down."

⁷They asked Him questions, saying, "Teacher, when therefore will these things happen? And what *will be* the sign when these things are about to take place?" ⁸And He said, "See to it that you are not misled; for many will come in My name, saying, 'ᴬI am *He,*' and, 'The time is near.' ᴮDo not go after them. ⁹And when you hear of wars and revolts, do not be alarmed; for these things must take place first, but the end *will* not *follow* immediately."

THINGS TO COME

¹⁰Then He *continued by* saying to them, "Nation will rise against nation, and kingdom against kingdom, ¹¹and there will be massive earthquakes, and in various places plagues and famines; and there will be terrible sights and great signs from heaven.

¹²"But before all these things, ᴬthey will lay their hands on you and persecute you, turning you over to the synagogues and prisons, bringing you before kings and governors on account of My name. ¹³ᴬIt will lead to an opportunity for your testimony. ¹⁴ᴬSo make up your minds not to prepare beforehand to defend yourselves; ¹⁵for ᴬI will provide you eloquence and wisdom which none of your adversaries will be able to oppose or refute. ¹⁶But you will be betrayed even by parents, brothers *and sisters, other* relatives, and friends, and they will put *some* of you to death, ¹⁷and you will be hated by all people because of My name. ¹⁸And *yet* ᴬnot a hair of your head will perish. ¹⁹ᴬBy your endurance you will gain your lives.

²⁰ "But when you see Jerusalem ᴬsurrounded by armies, then recognize that her desolation is near. ²¹Then those who are in Judea must flee to the mountains, and those who are inside the city must leave, and ᴬthose who are in the country must not enter the city; ²²because these are ᴬdays of punishment, so that all things which have been written will be fulfilled. ²³Woe to those women who are pregnant, and to those who are nursing babies in those days; for ᴬthere will be great distress upon the land, and wrath to this people; ²⁴and they will fall by the edge of the sword, and will be led captive into all the nations; and Jerusalem will be ᴬtrampled underfoot by the Gentiles until ᴮ*the* times of the Gentiles are fulfilled.

21:1ᴬ*Mark 12:41-44*　**21:2**ᴬMark 12:42
21:4ᴬMark 12:44　**21:5**ᴬ*Matt 24; Mark 13*
21:6ᴬLuke 19:44　**21:8**ᴬJohn 8:24　ᴮLuke 17:23
21:12ᴬ*Matt 10:19-22; Mark 13:11-13*　**21:13**ᴬPhil 1:12
21:14ᴬLuke 12:11　**21:15**ᴬLuke 12:12
21:18ᴬMatt 10:30; Luke 12:7　**21:19**ᴬMatt 10:22; 24:13
21:20ᴬLuke 19:43　**21:21**ᴬLuke 17:31　**21:22**ᴬIs 63:4;
Dan 9:24-27　**21:23**ᴬDan 8:19; 1 Cor 7:26
21:24ᴬRev 11:2　ᴮRom 11:25

21:2¹The smallest Greek copper coin, about 1/128 of a laborer's daily wage　**21:5**¹I.e., gifts promised by vows

THE RETURN OF CHRIST

25 "There will be signs in *the* sun and moon and stars, and on the earth distress among nations, in perplexity at the roaring of the sea and the waves, 26 people fainting from fear and the expectation of the things that are coming upon the world; for the powers of the heavens will be shaken. 27 And then they will see ^the Son of Man coming in a cloud with power and great glory. 28 But when these things begin to take place, straighten up and lift up your heads, because ^your redemption is drawing near."

29 And He told them a parable: "Look at the fig tree and all the trees: 30 as soon as they put forth *leaves,* you see for yourselves and ^know that summer is now near. 31 So you too, when you see these things happening, recognize that ^the kingdom of God is near. 32 Truly I say to you, this generation will not pass away until all things take place. 33 ^Heaven and earth will pass away, but My words will not pass away.

34 "But ^be on your guard, so that your hearts will not be weighed down with dissipation and drunkenness and the worries of life, and that this day will not come on you suddenly, like a trap; 35 for it will come upon all those who live on the face of all the earth. 36 But ^stay alert at all times, praying that you will have strength to escape all these things that are going to take place, and to stand before the Son of Man."

37 Now during the day He was ^teaching in the temple, but at evening He would go out and spend the night on ^Bthe mountain that is called Olivet. 38 And all the people would get up very early in the morning *to come* to Him in the temple to listen to Him.

PREPARING THE PASSOVER

22 ^ANow the Feast of Unleavened Bread, which is called the Passover, was approaching. 2 And the chief priests and the scribes ^were trying to find a way to put Him to death, since they were afraid of the people.

3 ^AAnd Satan entered Judas, the one called Iscariot, who belonged to the number of the twelve. 4 And he left and discussed with the chief priests and ^officers how he was to betray Him to them. 5 And they were delighted, and agreed to give him money. 6 And *so* he consented, and *began* looking for a good opportunity to betray Him to them away from the crowd.

7 ^ANow the *first* day of Unleavened Bread came, on which the Passover *lamb* had to be sacrificed. 8 And *so* Jesus sent ^APeter and John, saying, "Go and prepare the Passover for us, so that we may eat *it.*" 9 They said to Him, "Where do You want us to prepare *it?*" 10 And He said to them, "When you have entered the city, a man carrying a pitcher of water will meet you; follow him into the house that he enters. 11 And you shall say to the owner of the house, 'The Teacher says to you, "Where is the guest room in which I may eat the Passover with My disciples?"' 12 And he will show you a large, furnished upstairs room; prepare *it* there." 13 And they left and found *everything* just as He had told them; and they prepared the Passover.

21:27 ^Dan 7:13; Rev 1:7   21:28 ^Luke 18:7
21:30 ^Luke 12:57   21:31 ^Matt 3:2   21:33 ^Matt 5:18;
Luke 16:17   21:34 ^Matt 24:42-44; Mark 4:19
21:36 ^Mark 13:33; Luke 12:40   21:37 ^Matt 26:55
^B Matt 21:1   22:1 ^Ex 12:1-27   22:2 ^Matt 12:14
22:3 ^*Matt 26:14-16; Mark 14:10, 11*   22:4 ^1 Chr 9:11;
Neh 11:11   22:7 ^*Matt 26:17-19; Mark 14:12-16*
22:8 ^Acts 3:1, 11; 4:13, 19

THE LORD'S SUPPER

[14] ^A When the hour came, He reclined *at the table,* and the apostles with Him. [15] And He said to them, "I have eagerly desired to eat this Passover with you before I suffer; [16] for I say to you, I shall not eat it *again* ^A until it is fulfilled in the kingdom of God." [17] ^A And when He had taken a cup *and* given thanks, He said, "Take this and share it among yourselves; [18] for ^A I say to you, I will not drink of the fruit of the vine from now on until the kingdom of God comes." [19] And when He had taken *some* bread *and* ^A given thanks, He broke it and gave it to them, saying, "This is My body, which is being given for you; do this in remembrance of Me." [20] And in the same way *He took* the cup after they had eaten, saying, "This cup, which is ^A poured out for you, is the ^B new covenant in My blood. [21] ^A But behold, the hand of the one betraying Me is with Mine on the table. [22] For indeed, the Son of Man is going ^A as it has been determined; but woe to that man by whom He is betrayed!" [23] And they began to debate among themselves which one of them it was who was going to do this.

WHO IS GREATEST

[24] And ^A a dispute also developed among them *as to* which one of them was regarded as being the greatest. [25] ^A And He said to them, "The kings of the Gentiles domineer over them; and those who have authority over them are called 'Benefactors.' [26] But *it is* not this way for you; ^A rather, the one who is the greatest among you must become like the youngest, and the leader like the servant. [27] For who is greater, the one who reclines *at the table* or the one who serves? Is it not the one who reclines *at the table?* But ^A I am among you as the one who serves.

[28] "You are the ones who have stood by Me in My ^A trials; [29] and just as My Father has granted Me a ^A kingdom, I grant you [30] that you may eat and drink at My table in My kingdom, and ^A you will sit on thrones judging the twelve tribes of Israel.

[31] "Simon, Simon, behold, ^A Satan has demanded to ^B sift you *men* like wheat; [32] but I ^A have prayed for ¹you, that ¹your faith will not fail; and ¹you, when you have turned back, strengthen your brothers." [33] ^A But he said to Him, "Lord, I am ready to go with You both to prison and to death!" [34] But He said, "I tell you, Peter, the rooster will not crow today until you have denied three times that you know Me."

[35] And He said to them, "^A When I sent you out without money belt and bag and sandals, you did not lack anything, did you?" They said, "*No,* nothing." [36] And He said to them, "But now, whoever has a money belt is to take it along, likewise also a bag, and whoever has no sword is to sell his cloak and buy *one.* [37] For I tell you that this which is written must be fulfilled in Me: '^A AND HE WAS COUNTED WITH WRONGDOERS'; for ^B that which

22:14 ^A Matt 26:20; Mark 14:17 22:16 ^A Luke 14:15; 22:18, 30 22:17 ^1 1 Cor 10:16 22:18 ^A Matt 26:29; Mark 14:25 22:19 ^A Matt 14:19 22:20 ^A Matt 26:28 ^B Ex 24:8 22:21 ^A Ps 41:9; John 13:18, 21, 22, 26 22:22 ^A Acts 2:23; 4:28 22:24 ^A Mark 9:34; Luke 9:46 22:25 ^A *Matt 20:25-28; Mark 10:42-45* 22:26 ^A Matt 23:11; Mark 9:35 22:27 ^A Matt 20:28; John 13:12-15 22:28 ^A Heb 2:18; 4:15 22:29 ^A Matt 5:3; 2 Tim 2:12 22:30 ^A Matt 19:28 22:31 ^A Job 1:6-12 ^B Amos 9:9 22:32 ^A John 17:9, 15 22:33 ^A *Matt 26:33-35; Mark 14:29-31* 22:35 ^A Matt 10:9f; Mark 6:8 22:37 ^A Is 53:12 ^B John 17:4

22:32 ¹ Gr singular, referring only to Peter

refers to Me has *its* fulfillment." ³⁸They said, "Lord, look, here are two ᴬswords." And He said to them, "It is enough."

THE GARDEN OF GETHSEMANE

³⁹And He came out and went, ᴬas was His habit, to the Mount of Olives; and the disciples also followed Him. ⁴⁰ᴬNow when He arrived at the place, He said to them, "Pray that you do not come into temptation." ⁴¹And He withdrew from them about a stone's throw, and He ᴬknelt down and *began* to pray, ⁴²saying, "Father, if You are willing, remove this cup from Me; ᴬyet not My will, but Yours be done." ⁴³[¹Now an ᴬangel from heaven appeared to Him, strengthening Him. ⁴⁴And ᴬbeing in agony, He was praying very fervently; and His sweat became like drops of blood, falling down upon the ground]. ⁴⁵When He rose from prayer, He came to the disciples and found them sleeping from sorrow, ⁴⁶and He said to them, "Why are you sleeping? Get up and ᴬpray that you do not come into temptation."

JESUS BETRAYED BY JUDAS

⁴⁷ᴬWhile He was still speaking, behold, a crowd *came,* and the one called Judas, one of the twelve, was leading the way for them; and he approached Jesus to kiss Him. ⁴⁸But Jesus said to him, "Judas, are you betraying the Son of Man with a kiss?" ⁴⁹When those who were around Him saw what was going to happen, they said, "Lord, shall we strike with the ᴬsword?" ⁵⁰And one of them struck the slave of the high priest and cut off his right ear. ⁵¹But Jesus responded and said, "Stop! No more of this." And He touched

his ear and healed him. ⁵²And Jesus said to the chief priests and ᴬofficers of the temple and elders who had come against Him, "Have you come out with swords and clubs as *you would* against a man inciting a revolt? ⁵³While I was with you daily in the temple, you did not lay hands on Me; but this hour and the power of darkness are yours."

JESUS' ARREST

⁵⁴Now they arrested Him and led *Him away,* and brought *Him* to the house of the high priest; but ᴬPeter was following at a distance. ⁵⁵ᴬAfter they kindled a fire in the middle of the courtyard and sat down together, Peter was sitting among them. ⁵⁶And a slave woman, seeing him as he sat in the firelight, and staring at him, said, "This man was with Him as well." ⁵⁷But he denied *it,* saying, "I do not know Him, woman!" ⁵⁸And a little later, ᴬanother person saw him and said, "You are *one* of them too!" But Peter said, "Man, I am not!" ⁵⁹And after about an hour had passed, some other man *began* to insist, saying, "Certainly this man also was with Him, ᴬfor he, too, is a Galilean." ⁶⁰But Peter said, "Man, I do not know what you are talking about!" And immediately, while he was still speaking, a rooster crowed. ⁶¹And *then* the Lord turned and looked at Peter. And Peter remembered the word of the Lord, how He had told

22:38ᴬLuke 22:36, 49   22:39ᴬLuke 21:37
22:40ᴬMatt 26:36-46; Mark 14:32-42
22:41ᴬMatt 26:39; Mark 14:35   22:42ᴬMatt 26:39
22:43ᴬMatt 4:11   22:44ᴬHeb 5:7   22:46ᴬLuke 22:40
22:47ᴬMatt 26:47-56; Mark 14:43-50
22:49ᴬLuke 22:38   22:52ᴬLuke 22:4
22:54ᴬMatt 26:58; Mark 14:54   22:55ᴬMatt
26:69-75; Mark 14:66-72   22:58ᴬJohn 18:26
22:59ᴬMatt 26:73; Mark 14:70

22:43¹Most early mss do not contain vv 43 and 44

him, "^Before a rooster crows today, you will deny Me three times." 62 And he went out and wept bitterly.

63 ^The men who were holding Jesus in custody *began* mocking Him and beating Him, 64 and they blindfolded Him and *repeatedly* asked Him, saying, "^Prophesy, who is the one who hit You?" 65 And they were saying many other things against Him, ^blaspheming.

JESUS BEFORE THE SANHEDRIN

66 ^When it was day, the ¹Council of elders of the people assembled, both chief priests and scribes, and they led Him away to their council chamber, saying, 67 "^If You are the Christ, tell us." But He said to them, "If I tell you, you will not believe; 68 and if I ask a question, you will not answer. 69 ^But from now on ^B the Son of Man will be seated at the right hand of the power of God." 70 And they all said, "So You are the Son of God?" And He said to them, "^You say *correctly* that I am." 71 And *then* they said, "What further need do we have of testimony? For we have heard *it* ourselves from His *own* mouth!"

JESUS BEFORE PILATE

23 Then the entire assembly of them set out and ^brought Him before Pilate. 2 ^And they began to bring charges against Him, saying, "We found this Man misleading our nation and forbidding *us* to pay taxes to Caesar, and saying that He Himself is Christ, a King." 3 Now Pilate asked Him, saying, "*So* You are the King of the Jews?" And He answered him and said, "^*It is as* you say." 4 But Pilate said to the chief priests and the crowds, "^I

find no grounds for charges in *the case of* this Man." 5 But they kept on insisting, saying, "He is stirring up the people, teaching all over Judea, ^starting from Galilee, as far as this place!"

6 Now when Pilate heard *this,* he asked whether the Man was a Galilean. 7 And when he learned that He belonged to Herod's jurisdiction, he sent Him to ^Herod, since he also was in Jerusalem at this time.

JESUS BEFORE HEROD

8 Now Herod was overjoyed when he saw Jesus; for ^he had wanted to see Him for a long time, because he had been hearing about Him and was hoping to see some sign performed by Him. 9 And he questioned Him at some length; but ^He offered him no answer at all. 10 Now the chief priests and the scribes stood *there,* vehemently charging Him. 11 And Herod, together with his soldiers, treated Him with contempt and mocked Him, ^dressing Him in a brightly shining robe, and sent Him back to Pilate. 12 And *so* ^Herod and Pilate became friends with one another that very day; for previously, they had been enemies toward each other.

PILATE SEEKS JESUS' RELEASE

13 Now Pilate summoned to himself the chief priests, the ¹,^rulers, and the people, 14 and he said to them,

22:61 ^Luke 22:34   22:63 ^Matt 26:67f; Mark 14:65
22:64 ^Matt 26:68; Mark 14:65   22:65 ^Matt 27:39
22:66 ^Matt 27:1f; Mark 15:1   22:67 ^Matt 26:63-66;
Mark 14:61-63   22:69 ^Matt 26:64   ^B Ps 110:1
22:70 ^Matt 26:64; 27:11   23:1 ^Matt 27:2; Mark 15:1
23:2 ^Matt 27:11-14; Mark 15:2-5   23:3 ^Luke 22:70
23:4 ^Matt 27:23; Mark 15:14   23:5 ^Matt 4:12
23:7 ^Matt 14:1; Mark 6:14   23:8 ^Luke 9:9
23:9 ^Matt 27:12, 14; Mark 15:5   23:11 ^Matt 27:28
23:12 ^Acts 4:27   23:13 ^Luke 23:35; John 7:26, 48

22:66 ¹Or *Sanhedrin*   23:13 ¹I.e., other Jewish leaders

"You brought this Man to me on the ground that ^He is inciting the people to revolt; and behold, after examining *Him* before you, I ^have found no basis at all in *the case of* this Man for the charges which you are bringing against Him. [15] No, nor has ^Herod, for he sent Him back to us; and behold, nothing deserving death has been done by Him. [16] Therefore I will ^punish Him and release Him." [17] [¹Now he was obligated to release to them at the feast one *prisoner*.]

[18] But they cried out all together, saying, "^Away with this Man, and release to us Barabbas!" [19] (*He was* one who had been thrown into prison for a revolt that took place in the city, and for murder.) [20] But Pilate, wanting to release Jesus, addressed them again, [21] but they kept on crying out, saying, "Crucify, crucify Him!" [22] And he said to them a third time, "Why, what has this Man done wrong? I have found in His case no grounds for *a sentence of* death; therefore I will ^punish Him and release Him." [23] But they were insistent, with loud voices, demanding that He be crucified. And their voices *began* to prevail. [24] And *so* Pilate decided to have their demand carried out. [25] And he released the man for whom they were asking, who had been thrown into prison for a revolt and murder; but he handed Jesus over to their will.

SIMON CARRIES THE CROSS

[26] ^And when they led Him away, they seized a man, Simon of Cyrene, as he was coming in from the country, and placed on him the cross to carry behind Jesus.

[27] Now following Him was a large crowd of the people, and of women who were ^mourning and grieving for Him. [28] But Jesus turned to them and said, "Daughters of Jerusalem, stop weeping for Me, but weep for yourselves and for your children. [29] For behold, days are coming when they will say, '^Blessed are those who cannot bear, and the wombs that have not given birth, and the breasts that have not nursed.' [30] Then they will begin TO ^SAY TO THE MOUNTAINS, 'FALL ON US,' AND TO THE HILLS, 'COVER US.' [31] For if they do these things when the tree is green, what will happen when it is dry?"

[32] ^Now two others, who were criminals, were also being led away to be put to death with Him.

THE CRUCIFIXION

[33] ^And when they came to the place called The Skull, there they crucified Him and the criminals, one on the right and the other on the left. [34] [¹But Jesus was saying, "Father, forgive them; for they do not know what they are doing."] ^And they cast lots, dividing His garments among themselves. [35] And the people stood by, watching. And even the rulers were sneering at Him, saying, "He saved others; ^let Him save Himself if this is the Christ of God, His Chosen One." [36] The soldiers also ridiculed Him, coming up to Him, ^offering Him sour wine, [37] and saying, "^If You are the King

23:14 ^Luke 23:2   ᴮLuke 23:4   23:15 ^Luke 9:9
23:16 ^Matt 27:26; Mark 15:15   23:18 ^John
18:39–19:16   23:22 ^Luke 23:16   23:26 ^John 19:17
23:27 ^Luke 8:52   23:29 ^Matt 24:19; Luke 11:27
23:30 ^Hos 10:8; Is 2:19, 20   23:32 ^Matt 27:38;
Mark 15:27   23:33 ^*Matt 27:33-44; Mark 15:22-32*
23:34 ^Ps 22:18; John 19:24   23:35 ^Matt 27:43
23:36 ^Matt 27:48   23:37 ^Matt 27:43

23:17 ¹Most early mss do not contain this v
23:34 ¹Most early mss do not contain *But Jesus was saying...doing*

of the Jews, save Yourself!" [38]Now there was also an inscription above Him, "^THIS IS THE KING OF THE JEWS."

[39]^One of the criminals who were hanged *there* was hurling abuse at Him, saying, "Are You not the Christ? Save Yourself and us!" [40]But the other responded, and rebuking him, said, "Do you not even fear God, since you are under the same sentence of condemnation? [41]And we indeed *are suffering* justly, for we are receiving what we deserve for our crimes; but this Man has done nothing wrong." [42]And he was saying, "Jesus, remember me when You come into Your kingdom!" [43]And He said to him, "Truly I say to you, today you will be with Me in ^Paradise."

[44]^It was now about 'the sixth hour, and darkness came over the entire land until [2]the ninth hour, [45]because the sun stopped shining; and ^the veil of the temple was torn in two. [46]And Jesus, crying out with a loud voice, said, "Father, ^INTO YOUR HANDS I ENTRUST MY SPIRIT." And having said this, He died. [47]^Now when the centurion saw what had happened, he *began* praising God, saying, "This Man was in fact innocent." [48]And all the crowds who came together for this spectacle, after watching what had happened, *began* to return *home,* [1,]^beating their chests. [49]^And all His acquaintances and the women who accompanied Him from Galilee were standing at a distance, seeing these things.

JESUS IS BURIED

[50]^And a man named Joseph, who was a member of the Council, a good and righteous man [51](he had not consented to their plan and action), *a man* from Arimathea, a city of the Jews, who was ^waiting for the kingdom of God— [52]this man went to Pilate and asked for the body of Jesus. [53]And he took it down and wrapped it in a linen cloth, and laid Him in a tomb cut into the rock, where no one had ever lain. [54]It was a ^preparation day, and a Sabbath was about to begin. [55]Now ^the women who had come with Him from Galilee followed, and they saw the tomb and how His body was laid. [56]And *then* they returned and ^prepared spices and perfumes.

And on the Sabbath they rested according to the commandment.

THE RESURRECTION

24 ^But on the first day of the week, at early dawn, they came to the tomb bringing the spices which they had prepared. [2]And they found the stone rolled away from the tomb, [3]but when they entered, they did not find the body of ^the Lord Jesus. [4]While they were perplexed about this, behold, ^two men *suddenly* stood near them in gleaming clothing; [5]and as the women were terrified and bowed their faces to the ground, *the men* said to them, "Why are you seeking the living One among the dead? [6]He is not here, but He ^has risen. Remember how He spoke to you

23:38^Matt 27:37; Mark 15:26   **23:39**^Matt 27:44; Mark 15:32   **23:43**^2 Cor 12:4; Rev 2:7
23:44 *Matt 27:45-56; Mark 15:33-41*   **23:45**^Ex 26:31-33; Matt 27:51   **23:46**^Ps 31:5
23:47^Matt 27:54; Mark 15:39   **23:48**^Luke 8:52; 18:13   **23:49**^Matt 27:55f; Mark 15:40f
23:50 *Matt 27:57-61; Mark 15:42-47*
23:51^Mark 15:43; Luke 2:25   **23:54**^Matt 27:62; Mark 15:42   **23:55**^Luke 23:49   **23:56**^Mark 16:1; Luke 24:1   **24:1**^John 20:1-8   **24:3**^Luke 7:13; Acts 1:21   **24:4**^John 20:12   **24:6**^Mark 16:6

23:44 [1]I.e., noon   [2]I.e., 3 p.m.   **23:48** [1]I.e., as a traditional sign of mourning or contrition

ᴮwhile He was still in Galilee, ⁷saying that ᴬthe Son of Man must be handed over to sinful men, and be crucified, and on the third day rise *from the dead.*" ⁸And ᴬthey remembered His words, ⁹and returned from the tomb and reported all these things to the eleven, and to all the rest. ¹⁰Now *these women* were ᴬMary Magdalene, Joanna, and Mary the *mother* of James; also the other women with them were telling these things to the apostles. ¹¹But these words appeared to them as nonsense, and they would not believe the women. ¹²Nevertheless, Peter got up and ᴬran to the tomb; and when he stooped and looked in, he *saw the linen wrappings only; and he went away ᴮto his home, marveling at what had happened.

THE ROAD TO EMMAUS

¹³And behold, on that very day two of them were going to a village named Emmaus, which was ¹sixty stadia from Jerusalem. ¹⁴And they were talking with each other about all these things which had taken place. ¹⁵While they were talking and discussing, Jesus Himself approached and *began* traveling with them. ¹⁶But ᴬtheir eyes were kept from recognizing Him. ¹⁷And He said to them, "What are these words that you are exchanging with one another as you are walking?" And they came to a stop, looking sad. ¹⁸One *of them,* named Cleopas, answered and said to Him, "Are You *possibly* the only one living near Jerusalem who does not know about the things that happened here in these days?" ¹⁹And He said to them, "What sort of things?" And they said to Him, "Those about

Jesus the Nazarene, who proved to be a ᴬprophet mighty in deed and word in the sight of God and all the people, ²⁰and how the chief priests and our ᴬrulers handed Him over to be sentenced to death, and crucified Him. ²¹But we were hoping that it was He who was going to ᴬredeem Israel. Indeed, besides all this, it is *now* the third day since these things happened. ²²But also some women among us left us bewildered. ᴬWhen they were at the tomb early in the morning, ²³and did not find His body, they came, saying that they had also seen a vision of angels who said that He was alive. ²⁴And *so* some of those who were with us went to the tomb, and found it just exactly as the women also had said; but Him they did not see." ²⁵And *then* He said to them, "You foolish men and slow of heart to believe in all that ᴬthe prophets have spoken! ²⁶ᴬWas it not necessary for the Christ to suffer these things and to come into His glory?" ²⁷Then beginning with ᴬMoses and with all the Prophets, He explained to them the things *written* about Himself in all the Scriptures.

²⁸And they approached the village where they were going, and ᴬHe gave the impression that He was going farther. ²⁹And *so* they strongly urged Him, saying, "Stay with us, for it is *getting* toward evening, and the day is now nearly over." So He went in to stay with

24:6 ᴮMatt 17:22f 24:7ᴬMatt 16:21; Luke 24:46
24:8ᴬJohn 2:22 24:10ᴬMatt 27:56
24:12ᴬJohn 20:3-6   ᴮJohn 20:10 24:16ᴬLuke 24:31;
John 20:14 24:19ᴬMatt 21:11 24:20ᴬLuke 23:13
24:21ᴬLuke 1:68 24:22ᴬLuke 24:1ff
24:25ᴬMatt 26:24 24:26ᴬLuke 24:7, 44ff; Heb 2:10
24:27ᴬGen 3:15 24:28ᴬMark 6:48

24:13¹Possibly about 7 miles or 11.3 km; a Roman stadion perhaps averaged 607 ft. or 185 m

them. ³⁰And it came about, when He had reclined *at the table* with them, that He took the bread and ^blessed *it,* and He broke *it* and *began* giving *it* to them. ³¹And *then* their ^eyes were opened and they recognized Him; and He vanished from their sight. ³²They said to one another, "Were our hearts not burning within us when He was speaking to us on the road, while He ^was explaining the Scriptures to us?" ³³And they got up that very hour and returned to Jerusalem, and found the eleven gathered together and ^those who were with them, ³⁴saying, "^The Lord has really risen and ᴮhas appeared to Simon!" ³⁵They *began* to relate their experiences on the road, and how ^He was recognized by them at the breaking of the bread.

OTHER APPEARANCES

³⁶Now while they were telling these things, Jesus Himself *suddenly* stood in their midst and *said to them, "Peace *be* to you." ³⁷But they were startled and frightened, and thought that they were looking at ^a spirit. ³⁸And He said to them, "Why are you frightened, and why are doubts arising in your hearts? ³⁹See My hands and My feet, that it is I Myself; ^touch Me and see, because a spirit does not have flesh and bones as you *plainly* see that I have." ⁴⁰And when He had said this, He showed them His hands and His feet. ⁴¹While they still ^could not believe *it* because of their joy and astonishment, He said to them, "Have you anything

here to eat?" ⁴²They served Him a piece of broiled fish; ⁴³and He took it and ^ate *it* in front of them.

⁴⁴Now He said to them, "These are My words which I spoke to you while I was still with you, that all the things that are written about Me in the ^Law of Moses and the Prophets and the Psalms must be fulfilled." ⁴⁵Then He ^opened their minds to understand the Scriptures, ⁴⁶and He said to them, "^So it is written, that the Christ would suffer and ᴮrise from the dead on the third day, ⁴⁷and that repentance for forgiveness of sins would be proclaimed in His name to ^all the nations, beginning from Jerusalem. ⁴⁸You are ^witnesses of these things. ⁴⁹And behold, ^I am sending the promise of My Father upon you; but ᴮyou are to stay in the city until you are clothed with power from on high."

THE ASCENSION

⁵⁰And He led them out as far as ^Bethany, and He lifted up His hands and blessed them. ⁵¹While He was blessing them, He parted from them and was carried up into heaven. ⁵²And they, after worshiping Him, returned to Jerusalem with great joy, ⁵³and were continually in the temple praising God.

24:30^Matt 14:19   24:31^Luke 24:16
24:32^Luke 24:45   24:33^Acts 1:14   24:34^Luke 24:6
ᴮ1 Cor 15:5   24:35^Luke 24:30f   24:37^Matt 14:26;
Mark 6:49   24:39^John 20:27; 1 John 1:1
24:41^Luke 24:11   24:43^Acts 10:41
24:44^Luke 24:27   24:45^Luke 24:32; Acts 16:14
24:46^Luke 24:26, 44   ᴮLuke 24:7   24:47^Matt 28:19
24:48^Acts 1:8, 22; 2:32   24:49^John 14:26
ᴮActs 1:4   24:50^Matt 21:17; Acts 1:12

JOHN

THE DEITY OF JESUS CHRIST

1 In the beginning was the Word, and the Word was ^with God, and the Word was God. ²He was in the beginning with God. ³^All things came into being through Him, and apart from Him not even one thing came into being that has come into being. ⁴^In Him was life, and the life was ^Bthe Light of mankind. ⁵And ^the Light shines in the darkness, and the darkness did not grasp it.

THE WITNESS JOHN THE BAPTIST

⁶A man ¹came, *one* sent from God, *and* his name was ^John. ⁷He came as a witness, to testify about the Light, ^so that all might believe through him. ⁸¹,^He was not the Light, but *he came* to testify about the Light.

⁹¹*This* was ^the true Light ²that, coming into the world, enlightens every person. ¹⁰He was in the world, and ^the world came into being through Him, and *yet* the world did not know Him. ¹¹He came to His own, and His own people did not accept Him. ¹²But as many as received Him, to them He gave the right to become ^children of God, to those who believe in His name, ¹³^who were born, not of blood, nor of the will of the flesh, nor of the will of a man, but of God.

THE WORD MADE FLESH

¹⁴And the Word ^became flesh, and dwelt among us; and ^Bwe saw His glory, glory as of the only *Son* from the Father, full of grace and truth. ¹⁵John *testified about Him and called out, saying, "This was He of whom I said, '^He who is coming after me has proved to be my superior, because He existed before me.'" ¹⁶For of His ^fullness we have all received, and grace upon grace. ¹⁷For ^the Law was given through Moses; grace and truth were realized through Jesus Christ. ¹⁸No one has seen God at any time; ^God the only *Son,* who is ^Bin the arms of the Father, He has explained *Him.*

THE TESTIMONY OF JOHN THE BAPTIST

¹⁹This is ^the testimony of John, when the Jews sent priests and Levites to him from Jerusalem to ask him, "Who are you?" ²⁰And he confessed and did not deny; and *this is what* he confessed: "^I am not the Christ." ²¹And *so* they asked him, "What then? Are you Elijah?" And he *said, "I am not." "Are you ^the Prophet?" And he answered, "No." ²²Then they said to him, "Who are you? *Tell us,* so that we may give an answer to those who sent us. What do you say about yourself?" ²³He said, "I am ^THE VOICE OF ONE CALLING

1:1^John 17:5   1:3^John 1:10; 1 Cor 8:6   1:4^John 5:26
^BJohn 8:12   1:5^John 3:19   1:6^Matt 3:1
1:7^John 1:12; Acts 19:4   1:8^John 1:20   1:9^1 John 2:8
1:10^1 Cor 8:6; Col 1:16   1:12^John 11:52; Gal 3:26
1:13^John 3:5f; James 1:18   1:14^Phil 2:7f   ^BLuke 9:32
1:15^Matt 3:11; John 1:27, 30   1:16^Eph 1:23; 3:19
1:17^John 7:19   1:18^John 3:16, 18   ^BLuke 16:22
1:19^John 1:7   1:20^Luke 3:15f; John 3:28
1:21^Deut 18:15, 18; Matt 21:11   1:23^Is 40:3; Matt 3:3

1:6 ¹Or *came into being*   1:8 ¹Lit *That one;* i.e., John
1:9 ¹I.e., the Word, Christ   ²Or *that enlightens every person coming into the world*

¹OUT IN THE WILDERNESS, 'MAKE THE WAY OF THE LORD STRAIGHT,' as Isaiah the prophet said."

²⁴And *the messengers* had been sent from the Pharisees. ²⁵They asked him, and said to him, "Why then are you baptizing, if you are not the Christ, nor Elijah, nor ᴬthe Prophet?" ²⁶John answered them, saying, "ᴬI baptize 'in water, *but* among you stands One whom you do not know. ²⁷*It is* He who comes after me, of whom I am not worthy *even* to untie the ᴬstrap of His sandal." ²⁸These things took place in Bethany ᴬbeyond the Jordan, where John was baptizing *people.*

²⁹The next day he *saw Jesus coming to him, and *said, "Behold, ᴬthe Lamb of God who takes away the sin of the world! ³⁰This is He in behalf of whom I said, 'ᴬAfter me is coming a Man who has proved to be my superior, because He existed before me.' ³¹And I did not recognize Him, but so that He would be revealed to Israel, I came baptizing 'in water." ³²And John testified, saying, "ᴬI have seen the Spirit descending as a dove out of heaven, and He remained upon Him. ³³And I did not recognize Him, but He who sent me to baptize 'in water said to me, 'He upon whom you see the Spirit descending and remaining upon Him, ᴬthis is the One who baptizes in the Holy Spirit.' ³⁴And I myself have seen, and have testified that this is ᴬthe Son of God."

JESUS' PUBLIC MINISTRY; FIRST CONVERTS

³⁵Again ᴬthe next day John was standing with two of his disciples, ³⁶and he looked at Jesus as He walked, and *said, "Behold, ᴬthe Lamb of God!" ³⁷And the two disciples heard him speak, and they followed Jesus. ³⁸And Jesus turned and saw them following, and *said to them, "What are you seeking?" They said to Him, "ᴬRabbi (which translated means Teacher), where are You staying?" ³⁹He *said to them, "Come, and you will see." So they came and saw where He was staying, and they stayed with Him that day; it was about the 'tenth hour. ⁴⁰ᴬOne of the two who heard John *speak,* and followed Him, was Andrew, Simon Peter's brother. ⁴¹He first *found his own brother Simon and *said to him, "We have found the ᴬMessiah" (which translated means 'Christ). ⁴²He brought him to Jesus. Jesus looked at him and said, "You are Simon the son of ᴬJohn; you shall be called Cephas" (which is translated Peter).

⁴³The next day He decided to go to ᴬGalilee, and He *found Philip. And Jesus *said to him, "Follow Me." ⁴⁴Now Philip was from ᴬBethsaida, the city of Andrew and Peter. ⁴⁵Philip *found Nathanael and *said to him, "We have found Him of whom ᴬMoses wrote in the Law, and ᴬthe prophets *also wrote:* Jesus the son of Joseph, from Nazareth!" ⁴⁶Nathanael said to him, "ᴬCan anything good be from Nazareth?"

1:25ᴬDeut 18:15, 18; Matt 21:11   1:26ᴬMatt 3:11; Mark 1:8   1:27ᴬMatt 3:11; Mark 1:7   1:28ᴬJohn 3:26; 10:40   1:29ᴬIs 53:7; John 1:36   1:30ᴬMatt 3:11; John 1:27   1:32ᴬMatt 3:16; Mark 1:10
1:33ᴬMatt 3:11; Mark 1:8   1:34ᴬMatt 4:3; John 1:49
1:35ᴬJohn 1:29   1:36ᴬJohn 1:29   1:38ᴬMatt 23:7f; John 1:49   1:40ᴬMatt 4:18-22; Mark 1:16-20
1:41ᴬDan 9:25; John 4:25   1:42ᴬMatt 16:17; John 21:15-17   1:43ᴬMatt 4:12; John 1:28
1:44ᴬMatt 11:21   1:45ᴬLuke 24:27
1:46ᴬJohn 7:41, 52

1:23 'Or *out, In the wilderness make the way*
1:26 'The Gr here can be translated *in, with,* or *by*
1:31 'The Gr here can be translated *in, with,* or *by*
1:33 'The Gr here can be translated *in, with,* or *by*
1:39 'I.e., about 4 p.m.   1:41 'Gr *Anointed One*

Philip *said to him, "Come and see." ⁴⁷Jesus saw Nathanael coming to Him, and *said of him, "Here is truly an ᴬIsraelite, in whom there is no deceit!" ⁴⁸Nathanael *said to Him, "How do You know me?" Jesus answered and said to him, "Before ᴬPhilip called you, when you were under the fig tree, I saw you." ⁴⁹Nathanael answered Him, "Rabbi, You are the Son of God; You are the ᴬKing of Israel!" ⁵⁰Jesus answered and said to him, "Because I said to you that I saw you under the fig tree, do you believe? You will see greater things than these." ⁵¹And He *said to him, "Truly, truly, I say to you, you will see ᴬheaven opened and the angels of God ascending and descending on the Son of Man."

MIRACLE AT CANA

2 On the third day there was a wedding in ᴬCana of Galilee, and the mother of Jesus was there; ²and both Jesus and His ᴬdisciples were invited to the wedding. ³When the wine ran out, the mother of Jesus *said to Him, "They have no wine." ⁴And Jesus *said to her, "What *business* do you have with Me, woman? ᴬMy hour has not yet come." ⁵His ᴬmother *said to the servants, "Whatever He tells you, do it." ⁶Now there were six stone waterpots standing there ᴬfor the Jewish custom of purification, containing ¹two or three measures each. ⁷Jesus *said to them, "Fill the waterpots with water." So they filled them up to the brim. ⁸And He *said to them, "Draw *some* out now and take *it* to the ¹headwaiter." And they took *it to him.* ⁹Now when the headwaiter tasted the water ᴬwhich had become wine, and did not

know where it came from (but the servants who had drawn the water knew), the headwaiter *called the groom, ¹⁰and *said to him, "Every man serves the good wine first, and when *the guests* ᴬare drunk, *then he serves* the poorer *wine; but* you have kept the good wine until now." ¹¹This beginning of *His* signs Jesus did in Cana of Galilee, and revealed His ᴬglory; and His disciples believed in Him.

¹²After this He went down to ᴬCapernaum, He and His ᴮmother, and *His* brothers and His disciples; and they stayed there a few days.

FIRST PASSOVER—CLEANSING THE TEMPLE

¹³ᴬThe Passover of the Jews was near, and Jesus went up to Jerusalem. ¹⁴ᴬAnd within the temple *grounds* He found those who were selling oxen, sheep, and doves, and the money changers seated *at their tables.* ¹⁵And He made a whip of cords, and drove *them* all out of the temple *area,* with the sheep and the oxen; and He poured out the coins of the money changers and overturned their tables; ¹⁶and to those who were selling ᴬthe doves He said, "Take these things away from here; stop making ᴮMy Father's house a place of business!" ¹⁷His ᴬdisciples remembered that it was written: "ᴮZᴇᴀʟ ꜰᴏʀ Yᴏᴜʀ ʜᴏᴜsᴇ ᴡɪʟʟ ᴄᴏɴsᴜᴍᴇ ᴍᴇ." ¹⁸The

---

1:47ᴬRom 9:4   1:48ᴬMatt 10:3; John 1:44-48
1:49ᴬMatt 2:2; 27:42   1:51ᴬEzek 1:1; Matt 3:16
2:1ᴬJohn 2:11; 4:46   2:2ᴬJohn 1:40-49; 2:12, 17, 22
2:4ᴬJohn 7:6, 8, 30; 8:20   2:5ᴬMatt 12:46
2:6ᴬMark 7:3f; John 3:25   2:9ᴬJohn 4:46
2:10ᴬMatt 24:49; Luke 12:45   2:11ᴬJohn 1:14
2:12ᴬMatt 4:13   ᴮMatt 12:46   2:13ᴬDeut 16:1-6;
John 5:1   2:14ᴬMal 3:1ff   2:16ᴬMatt 21:12
ᴮLuke 2:49   2:17ᴬJohn 2:2   ᴮPs 69:9

2:6¹About 18 or 27 gallons each; or 68 or 102 liters
2:8¹I.e., manager of the banquet

Jews then said to Him, "ᴬWhat sign do You show us as Your authority for doing these things?" ¹⁹Jesus answered them, "ᴬDestroy this temple, and in three days I will raise it up." ²⁰The Jews then said, "It took ᴬforty-six years to build this temple, and *yet* You will raise it up in three days?" ²¹But He was speaking about ᴬthe temple of His body. ²²So when He was raised from the dead, His disciples remembered that He said this; and they believed ᴬthe Scripture and the word which Jesus had spoken.

²³Now when He was in Jerusalem at ᴬthe Passover, during the feast, many believed in His name as they observed His signs which He was doing. ²⁴But Jesus, on His part, was not entrusting Himself to them, because ᴬHe knew all people, ²⁵and because He did not need anyone to testify about mankind, ᴬfor He Himself knew what was in mankind.

THE NEW BIRTH

3 Now there was a man of the Pharisees, named ᴬNicodemus, a ruler of the Jews; ²this man came to Jesus at night and said to Him, "ᴬRabbi, we know that You have come from God *as* a teacher; for no one can do these signs that You do unless ᴮGod is with him." ³Jesus responded and said to him, "Truly, truly, I say to you, unless someone ᴬis born again he cannot see the kingdom of God."

⁴Nicodemus *said to Him, "How can a person be born when he is old? He cannot enter his mother's womb a second time and be born, can he?" ⁵Jesus answered, "Truly, truly, I say to you, unless someone is born of ᴬwater and *the* Spirit, he

cannot enter the kingdom of God. ⁶ᴬThat which has been born of the flesh is flesh, and that which has been born of the Spirit is spirit. ⁷Do not be amazed that I said to you, 'You must be born again.' ⁸ᴬThe wind blows where it wishes, and you hear the sound of it, but you do not know where it is coming from and where it is going; so is everyone who has been born of the Spirit."

⁹Nicodemus responded and said to Him, "How can these things be?" ¹⁰Jesus answered and said to him, "You are ᴬthe teacher of Israel, and *yet* you do not understand these things? ¹¹Truly, truly, I say to you, ᴬwe speak of what we know and testify of what we have seen, and you *people* do not accept our testimony. ¹²If I told you earthly things and you do not believe, how will you believe if I tell you heavenly things? ¹³ᴬNo one has ascended into heaven, except He who descended from heaven: the Son of Man. ¹⁴And just as ᴬMoses lifted up the serpent in the wilderness, so must the Son of Man ᴮbe lifted up, ¹⁵so that everyone who ¹believes will ᴬhave eternal life in Him.

¹⁶"For God so ᴬloved the world, that He gave His only Son, so that everyone who believes in Him will not perish, but have eternal life. ¹⁷For God did not send the Son into the world ᴬto judge the world, but

2:18 ᴬMatt 12:38　2:19 ᴬMatt 26:61; 27:40
2:20 ᴬEzra 5:16　2:21 ᴬ1 Cor 6:19　2:22 ᴬPs 16:10;
Luke 24:26f　2:23 ᴬJohn 2:13　2:24 ᴬActs 1:24; 15:8
2:25 ᴬMatt 9:4; John 1:42, 47　3:1 ᴬJohn 7:50; 19:39
3:2 ᴬMatt 23:7　ᴮJohn 9:33　3:3 ᴬ2 Cor 5:17; 1 Pet 1:23
3:5 ᴬEzek 36:25-27; Eph 5:26　3:6 ᴬJohn 1:13;
1 Cor 15:50　3:8 ᴬPs 135:7; Eccl 11:5　3:10 ᴬLuke 2:46;
5:17　3:11 ᴬJohn 1:18; 7:16f　3:13 ᴬProv 30:4; Acts 2:34
3:14 ᴬNum 21:9　ᴮJohn 12:34　3:15 ᴬJohn 20:31;
1 John 5:11-13　3:16 ᴬRom 5:8; Eph 2:4
3:17 ᴬLuke 19:10; John 8:15

3:15 ¹Or *believes in Him will have eternal life*

so that the world might be saved through Him. ¹⁸The one who believes in Him is not judged; the one who does not believe has been judged already, because he has not believed in the name of ^the only Son of God. ¹⁹And this is the judgment, that ^the Light has come into the world, and people loved the darkness rather than the Light; for their deeds were evil. ²⁰^For everyone who does evil hates the Light, and does not come to the Light, so that his deeds will not be exposed. ²¹But the one who ^practices the truth comes to the Light, so that his deeds will be revealed as having been performed in God."

JOHN THE BAPTIST'S LAST TESTIMONY

²²After these things Jesus and His disciples came into the land of Judea; and there He was spending time with them and ^baptizing. ²³Now John also was baptizing in Aenon, near Salim, because there was an abundance of water there; and *people* were coming and being baptized— ²⁴for ^John had not yet been thrown into prison.

²⁵Then a matter of dispute developed on the part of John's disciples with a Jew about ^purification. ²⁶And they came to John and said to him, "^Rabbi, He who was with you beyond the Jordan, to whom you have testified—behold, He is baptizing and all *the people* are coming to Him." ²⁷John replied, "^A person can receive not even one thing unless it has been given to him from heaven. ²⁸You yourselves are my witnesses that I said, '^I am not the Christ,' but, 'I have been sent ahead of Him.' ²⁹He who has the bride is ^the groom; but the friend of the groom, who stands and listens to

him, rejoices greatly because of the groom's voice. So this joy of mine has been made full. ³⁰He must increase, but I must decrease.

³¹"^He who comes from above is above all; the one who is *only* from the earth is of the earth and speaks of the earth. ^He who comes from heaven is above all. ³²What He has seen and heard, of this He ^testifies; and ^no one accepts His testimony. ³³The one who has accepted His testimony ^has certified that God is true. ³⁴For He whom God sent speaks the words of God; ^for He does not give the Spirit sparingly. ³⁵^The Father loves the Son and has entrusted all things to His hand. ³⁶The one who ^believes in the Son has eternal life; but the one who does not obey the Son will not see life, but the wrath of God remains on him."

JESUS GOES TO GALILEE

4 So then, when ^the Lord knew that the Pharisees had heard that He was making and baptizing more disciples than John ²(although ^Jesus Himself was not baptizing; rather, His disciples *were*), ³He left ^Judea and went away ᴮagain to Galilee. ⁴And He had to pass through ^Samaria. ⁵So He *came to a city of Samaria called Sychar, near ^the parcel of land that Jacob gave to his son Joseph; ⁶and Jacob's well was there. So Jesus, tired from His journey, was just

3:18^John 1:18; 1 John 4:9   3:19^John 1:4; 8:12
3:20^John 3:20, 21; Eph 5:11, 13   3:21^1 John 1:6
3:22^John 4:1, 2   3:24^Matt 4:12; 14:3   3:25^John 2:6
3:26^Matt 23:7; John 3:2   3:27^1 Cor 4:7; Heb 5:4
3:28^John 1:20, 23   3:29^Matt 9:15; 25:1
3:31^Matt 28:18; John 3:13   3:32^John 3:11
3:33^John 6:27; Rom 4:11   3:34^Matt 12:18; Luke 4:18
3:35^Matt 28:18; John 5:20   3:36^John 3:16
4:1^Luke 7:13   4:2^John 3:22, 26; 1 Cor 1:17
4:3^John 3:22   ᴮJohn 2:11   4:4^Luke 9:52
4:5^Gen 33:19; Josh 24:32

sitting by the well. It was about 'the sixth hour.

THE WOMAN OF SAMARIA

[7] A woman of Samaria *came to draw water. Jesus *said to her, "Give Me a drink." [8] For His ^disciples had gone away to the city to buy food. [9] So the Samaritan woman *said to Him, "How *is it that* You, *though* You are a Jew, are asking me for a drink, *though* I am a Samaritan woman?" (For ^Jews do not associate with Samaritans.) [10] Jesus replied to her, "If you knew the gift of God, and who it is who is saying to you, 'Give Me a drink,' you would have asked Him, and He would have given you ^living water." [11] She *said to Him, "Sir, You have no bucket and the well is deep; where then do You get *this* ^living water? [12] You are not greater than our father Jacob, are You, who ^gave us the well and drank of it himself, and his sons and his cattle?" [13] Jesus answered and said to her, "Everyone who drinks of this water will be thirsty again; [14] but whoever drinks of the water that I will give him shall never be thirsty; but the water that I will give him will become in him a fountain of water springing up to ^eternal life."

[15] The woman *said to Him, "Sir, ^give me this water so that I will not be thirsty, nor come *all the way* here to draw *water*." [16] He *said to her, "Go, call your husband and come here." [17] The woman answered and said to Him, "I have no husband." Jesus *said to her, "You have correctly said, 'I have no husband'; [18] for you have had five husbands, and the one whom you now have is not your husband; this *which* you have said *is* true."

[19] The woman *said to Him, "Sir, I perceive that You are ^a prophet. [20] Our fathers worshiped on ^this mountain, and *yet* you *Jews* say that in Jerusalem is the place where one must worship." [21] Jesus *said to her, "Believe Me, woman, that a time is coming when you will worship the Father ^neither on this mountain nor in Jerusalem. [22] You *Samaritans* worship what you do not know; we worship what we do know, because ^salvation is from the Jews. [23] But ^a time is coming, and even now has arrived, when the true worshipers will worship the Father in spirit and truth; for such people the Father seeks *to be* His worshipers. [24] God is spirit, and those who worship Him must worship ^in spirit and truth." [25] The woman *said to Him, "I know that ^Messiah is coming (^He who is called Christ); when that One comes, He will declare all things to us." [26] Jesus *said to her, "^I am *He*, the One speaking to you."

[27] And at this point His ^disciples came, and they were amazed that He had been speaking with a woman, yet no one said, "What are You seeking?" or, "Why are You speaking with her?" [28] So the woman left her waterpot and went into the city, and *said to the people, [29] "Come, see a Man who told me all the things that I have done; ^this is not the Christ, is He?" [30] They left the city and were coming to Him.

4:8 ^John 2:2   4:9 ^Ezra 4:3-6, 11ff; Matt 10:5
4:10 ^Jer 2:13; John 4:14   4:11 ^Jer 2:13; John 4:14
4:12 ^John 4:6   4:14 ^Matt 25:46; John 6:27
4:15 ^John 6:35   4:19 ^Matt 21:11; Luke 7:16, 39
4:20 ^Deut 11:29; Josh 8:33   4:21 ^Mal 1:11; 1 Tim 2:8
4:22 ^Is 2:3; Rom 3:1f   4:23 ^John 4:21; 5:25, 28
4:24 ^Phil 3:3   4:25 ^Dan 9:25   ^B Matt 1:16
4:26 ^John 8:24, 28, 58; 9:37   4:27 ^John 4:8
4:29 ^Matt 12:23; John 7:26, 31

4:6 ¹I.e., noon

³¹Meanwhile the disciples were urging Him, saying, "ᴬRabbi, eat *something.*" ³²But He said to them, "I have food to eat that you do not know about." ³³So the ᴬdisciples were saying to one another, "No one brought Him *anything* to eat, did he?" ³⁴Jesus *said to them, "My food is to do the will of Him who sent Me, and to ᴬaccomplish His work. ³⁵Do you not say, 'There are still four months, and *then* comes the harvest'? Behold, I tell you, raise your eyes and observe the fields, that they are white ᴬfor harvest. ³⁶Already the one who reaps is receiving wages and is gathering fruit for ᴬeternal life, so that the one who sows and the one who reaps may rejoice together. ³⁷For in this *case* the saying is true: 'ᴬOne sows and another reaps.' ³⁸I sent you to reap that for which you have not labored; others have labored, and you have ¹come into their labor."

THE SAMARITANS

³⁹Now from ᴬthat city many of the Samaritans believed in Him because of the word of the woman who testified, "ᴮHe told me all the things that I have done." ⁴⁰So when the Samaritans came to Jesus, they were asking Him to stay with them; and He stayed there two days. ⁴¹Many more believed because of His word; ⁴²and they were saying to the woman, "*It is* no longer because of what you said *that* we believe, for we have heard for ourselves and know that this One truly is ᴬthe Savior of the world."

⁴³And after ᴬthe two days, He departed from there for Galilee. ⁴⁴For Jesus Himself testified that ᴬa prophet has no honor in his own country. ⁴⁵So when He came to Galilee, the Galileans received Him, *only because* ᴬthey had seen all the things that He did in Jerusalem at the feast; for they themselves also went to the feast.

HEALING AN OFFICIAL'S SON

⁴⁶Therefore He came again to ᴬCana of Galilee, where He had made the water *into* wine. And there was a royal official whose son was sick at Capernaum. ⁴⁷When he heard that Jesus had come ᴬfrom Judea into Galilee, he went to Him and *began* asking *Him* to come down and heal his son; for he was at the point of death. ⁴⁸Then Jesus said to him, "Unless you *people* see ᴬsigns and wonders, you *simply* will not believe." ⁴⁹The royal official *said to Him, "Sir, come down before my child dies." ⁵⁰Jesus *said to him, "ᴬGo; your son is alive." The man believed the word that Jesus spoke to him and went *home.* ⁵¹And as he was now going down, his slaves met him, saying that his son was alive. ⁵²So he inquired of them the hour when he began to get better. Then they said to him, "Yesterday at the ¹seventh hour the fever left him." ⁵³So the father knew that *it was* at that hour in which Jesus said to him, "Your son is alive"; and he himself believed, and ᴬhis entire household. ⁵⁴This is again a second sign that Jesus performed when He had ᴬcome from Judea into Galilee.

4:31 ᴬMatt 23:7; 26:25, 49   4:33 ᴬLuke 6:13-16; John 1:40-49   4:34 ᴬJohn 5:36; 17:4
4:35 ᴬMatt 9:37, 38; Luke 10:2   4:36 ᴬMatt 19:29; John 3:36   4:37 ᴬJob 31:8; Mic 6:15
4:39 ᴬJohn 4:5, 30   ᴮJohn 4:29   4:42 ᴬMatt 1:21; Luke 2:11   4:43 ᴬJohn 4:40   4:44 ᴬMatt 13:57; Mark 6:4   4:45 ᴬJohn 2:23   4:46 ᴬJohn 2:1
4:47 ᴬJohn 4:3, 54   4:48 ᴬDan 4:2f; 6:27
4:50 ᴬMatt 8:13   4:53 ᴬActs 11:14   4:54 ᴬJohn 4:45f

4:38 ¹I.e., enjoyed the fruit of their labor
4:52 ¹I.e., 1 p.m.

THE HEALING AT BETHESDA

5 After these things there was ^a feast of the Jews, and Jesus went up to Jerusalem.

² Now in Jerusalem, by ^the Sheep *Gate,* there is a pool which in Hebrew is called Bethesda, having five porticoes. ³ In these *porticoes* lay a multitude of those who were sick, blind, limping, *or* paralyzed.¹ ⁵ Now a man was there who had been ill for thirty-eight years. ⁶ Jesus, upon seeing this man lying *there* and knowing that he had already been *in that condition* for a long time, *said to him, "Do you want to get well?" ⁷ The sick man answered Him, "Sir, I have no man to put me into the pool when the water is stirred up, but while I am coming, another steps down before me." ⁸ Jesus *said to him, "^Get up, pick up your pallet and walk." ⁹ Immediately the man became well, and picked up his pallet and *began* to walk.

^Now it was a Sabbath on that day. ¹⁰ So the Jews were saying to the man who was cured, "It is a Sabbath, and ^it is not permissible for you to carry your pallet." ¹¹ But he answered them, "He who made me well was the one who said to me, 'Pick up your pallet and walk.'" ¹² They asked him, "Who is the Man who said to you, 'Pick *it* up and walk'?" ¹³ But the man who was healed did not know who it was, for Jesus had slipped away while there was a crowd in *that* place. ¹⁴ Afterward, Jesus *found him in the temple and said to him, "Behold, you have become well; do not ^sin anymore, ᴮso that nothing worse happens to you." ¹⁵ The man went away, and informed ^the Jews that it was Jesus who had made him well. ¹⁶ For this reason ^the Jews were persecuting Jesus, because He was doing these things on a Sabbath. ¹⁷ But He answered them, "My Father is working until now, and I Myself am working."

JESUS' EQUALITY WITH GOD

¹⁸ For this reason therefore the Jews were seeking all the more to kill Him, because He not only was breaking the Sabbath, but also was calling God His own Father, ^making Himself equal with God.

¹⁹ Therefore Jesus answered and was saying to them, "Truly, truly, I say to you, ^the Son can do nothing of Himself, unless *it is* something He sees the Father doing; for whatever the Father does, these things the Son also does in the same way. ²⁰ ^For the Father loves the Son and shows Him all things that He Himself is doing; and *the Father* will show Him ᴮgreater works than these, so that you will be amazed. ²¹ For just as the Father raises the dead and ^gives them life, so ᴮthe Son also gives life to whom He wishes. ²² For not even the Father judges anyone, but ^He has given all judgment to the Son, ²³ so that all will honor the Son just as they honor the Father. ^The one who does not honor the Son does not honor the Father who sent Him.

5:1 ^Deut 16:1; John 2:13   5:2 ^Neh 3:1, 32; 12:39
5:8 ^Matt 9:6; Mark 2:11   5:9 ^John 9:14
5:10 ^Neh 13:19; Jer 17:21f   5:14 ^Mark 2:5
ᴮEzra 9:14   5:15 ^John 1:19; 5:16, 18   5:16 ^John 1:19;
5:10, 15, 18   5:18 ^John 10:33; 19:7   5:19 ^Matt 26:39;
John 5:30   5:20 ^John 3:35   ᴮJohn 14:12
5:21 ^Rom 4:17   ᴮJohn 11:25   5:22 ^John 5:27; 9:39
5:23 ^Luke 10:16; 1 John 2:23

5:3 ¹ Late mss add the following as the remainder of v 3, and v 4: *paralyzed, waiting for the moving of the waters; for an angel of the Lord went down at certain seasons into the pool and stirred up the water; whoever then first stepped in after the stirring up of the water was made well from whatever disease with which he was afflicted*

24"Truly, truly, I say to you, the one who hears My word, and ᴬbelieves Him who sent Me, has eternal life, and ᴮdoes not come into judgment, but has passed out of death into life.

TWO RESURRECTIONS

25Truly, truly, I say to you, a time is coming and even now has arrived, when ᴬthe dead will hear the voice of the Son of God, and those who ᴮhear will live. **26**For just as the Father has life in Himself, so He ᴬgave to the Son also to have life in Himself; **27**and He gave Him authority to ᴬexecute judgment, because He is *the* Son of Man. **28**Do not be amazed at this; for a time is coming when ᴬall who are in the tombs will hear His voice, **29**and will come out: ᴬthose who did the good *deeds* to a resurrection of life, those who committed the bad *deeds* to a resurrection of judgment.

30"I can do nothing on My own. As I hear, I judge; and ᴬMy judgment is righteous, because I do not seek My own will but ᴮthe will of Him who sent Me.

31"ᴬIf I *alone* testify about Myself, My testimony is not true. **32**There is ᴬanother who testifies about Me, and I know that the testimony which He gives about Me is true.

TESTIMONY OF JOHN THE BAPTIST

33You have sent *messengers* to John, and he ᴬhas testified to the truth. **34**But ᴬthe testimony I receive is not from man, but I say these things so that you may be saved. **35**He was the lamp that was burning and shining, and you ᴬwere willing to rejoice for a while in his light.

TESTIMONY OF WORKS

36But the testimony I have is greater than *the testimony of* John; for ᴬthe works which the Father has given Me ᴮto accomplish—the very works that I do—testify about Me, that the Father has sent Me.

TESTIMONY OF THE FATHER

37And the Father who sent Me, ᴬHe has testified about Me. You have neither heard His voice at any time, nor seen His form. **38**Also you do not have ᴬHis word remaining in you, because you do not believe Him whom He sent.

TESTIMONY OF THE SCRIPTURE

39[1,ᴬ]You examine the Scriptures because you think that in them you have eternal life; and it is those *very Scriptures* that testify about Me; **40**and *yet* you are unwilling to come to Me so that you may have life. **41**ᴬI do not receive glory from people; **42**but I know you, that you do not have the love of God in yourselves. **43**I have come in My Father's name, and you do not receive Me; ᴬif another comes in his own name, you will receive him. **44**How can you believe, when you accept glory from one another and you do not seek ᴬthe glory that is from ᴮthe *one and* only God? **45**Do not think that I will accuse you before the Father; the one who accuses you is ᴬMoses,

5:24ᴬJohn 12:44   ᴮJohn 3:18   **5:25**ᴬLuke 15:24
ᴮJohn 6:60   **5:26**ᴬJohn 1:4; 6:57   **5:27**ᴬJohn 9:39;
Acts 10:42   **5:28**ᴬJohn 11:24; 1 Cor 15:52
5:29ᴬDan 12:2; Matt 25:46   **5:30**ᴬJohn 8:16
ᴮJohn 4:34   **5:31**ᴬJohn 8:14   **5:32**ᴬJohn 5:37
5:33ᴬJohn 1:7, 15, 19, 32; 3:26-30   **5:34**ᴬJohn 5:32;
1 John 5:9   **5:35**ᴬMark 1:5   **5:36**ᴬJohn 10:25, 38
ᴮJohn 4:34   **5:37**ᴬMatt 3:17; Mark 1:11
5:38ᴬ1 John 2:14   **5:39**ᴬJohn 7:52; Rom 2:17ff
5:41ᴬJohn 5:44; 7:18   **5:43**ᴬMatt 24:5   **5:44**ᴬRom 2:29
ᴮJohn 17:3   **5:45**ᴬJohn 9:28; Rom 2:17ff

5:39[1]Or (a command) *Examine the Scriptures*

in whom you have put your hope. [46]For if you believed Moses, you would believe Me; for ^he wrote about Me. [47]But ^if you do not believe his writings, how will you believe My words?"

FIVE THOUSAND MEN FED

6 After these things ^Jesus went away to the other side of the Sea of Galilee (*or* Tiberias). [2]A large crowd was following Him, because they were watching the ^signs which He was performing on those who were sick. [3]But ^Jesus went up on the mountain, and there He sat with His disciples. [4]Now ^the Passover, the feast of the Jews, was near. [5]So Jesus, after raising His eyes and seeing that a large crowd was coming to Him, *said to ^Philip, "Where are we to buy bread so that these *people* may eat?" [6]But He was saying this *only* to ^test him, for He Himself knew what He intended to do. [7]Philip answered Him, "^Two hundred ¹denarii worth of bread is not enough for them, for each to receive *just* a little!" [8]One of His disciples, ^Andrew, Simon Peter's brother, *said to Him, [9]"There is a boy here who has five barley loaves and two ^fish; but what are these for so many *people?*" [10]Jesus said, "Have the people recline *to eat.*" Now there was ^plenty of grass in the place. So the men reclined, about ¹,⁸five thousand in number. [11]Jesus then took the loaves, and ^after giving thanks He distributed *them* to those who were reclining; likewise also of the fish, as much as they wanted. [12]And when they had eaten their fill, He *said to His ^disciples, "Gather up the leftover pieces so that nothing will be lost." [13]So they gathered them up, and filled twelve ^baskets

with pieces from the five barley loaves which were left over by those who had eaten. [14]Therefore when the people saw the sign which He had performed, they said, "This is truly the ^Prophet who is to come into the world."

JESUS WALKS ON THE WATER

[15]So Jesus, aware that they intended to come and take Him by force to make Him king, ^withdrew again to the mountain by Himself, alone.

[16]Now when evening came, His ^disciples went down to the sea, [17]and after getting into a boat, they *started to* cross the sea ^to Capernaum. It had already become dark, and Jesus had not yet come to them. [18]In addition, the sea *began* getting rough, because a strong wind was blowing. [19]Then, when they had rowed about ¹twenty-five or thirty stadia, they *saw Jesus walking on the sea and coming near the boat; and they were frightened. [20]But He *said to them, "It is I; ^do not be afraid." [21]So they were willing to take Him into the boat, and immediately the boat was at the land to which they were going.

[22]The next day ^the crowd that stood on the other side of the sea saw that there was no other small boat there except one, and that Jesus had not gotten into the boat

5:46 ^Luke 24:27   5:47 ^Luke 16:29, 31
6:1 ^*Matt 14:13-21; Mark 6:32-44*   6:2 ^John 2:11, 23; 3:2
6:3 ^Matt 5:1; Mark 3:13   6:4 ^Deut 16:1; John 2:13
6:5 ^John 1:43   6:6 ^2 Cor 13:5; Rev 2:2   6:7 ^Mark 6:37
6:8 ^John 1:40   6:9 ^John 6:11; 21:9, 10, 13
6:10 ^Mark 6:39   ᴮMatt 14:21   6:11 ^Matt 15:36;
John 6:23   6:12 ^John 2:2   6:13 ^Matt 14:20
6:14 ^Matt 11:3; 21:11   6:15 ^*Matt 14:22-33; Mark
6:45-51*   6:16 ^John 2:2   6:17 ^Mark 6:45; John 6:24, 59
6:20 ^Matt 14:27   6:22 ^John 6:2

6:7 ¹The denarius was a day's wages for a laborer
6:10 ¹I.e., 5,000 men plus women and children, cf.
Matt 14:21   6:19 ¹Possibly 3-4 miles or 4.8-6.4 km; a
Roman stadion perhaps averaged 607 ft. or 185 m

with His disciples, but *that* His disciples had departed alone. [23] Other small boats came from Tiberias near to the place where they ate the bread after the Lord ^had given thanks. [24] So when the crowd saw that Jesus was not there, nor His disciples, they themselves got into the small boats and ^came to Capernaum, looking for Jesus. [25] And when they found Him on the other side of the sea, they said to Him, "^Rabbi, when did You get here?"

WORDS TO THE PEOPLE

[26] Jesus answered them and said, "Truly, truly, I say to you, you seek Me, not because you saw [1,^]signs, but because you ate some of the loaves and were filled. [27] Do not ^work for the food that perishes, but for the food that lasts for eternal life, which the Son of Man will give you, for on Him the Father, God, ^has set His seal." [28] Therefore they said to Him, "What are we to do, so that we may accomplish the works of God?" [29] Jesus answered and said to them, "This is ^the work of God, that you believe in Him whom He has sent." [30] So they said to Him, "^What then are You doing as a sign, so that we may see, and believe You? What work are You performing? [31] Our fathers ate the manna in the wilderness; as it is written: '^HE GAVE THEM BREAD OUT OF HEAVEN TO EAT.'" [32] Jesus then said to them, "Truly, truly, I say to you, it is not Moses who has given you the bread out of heaven, but it is My Father who gives you the true bread out of heaven. [33] For the bread of God is that which ^comes down out of heaven and gives life to the world." [34] Then they said to Him, "Lord, always ^give us this bread."

[35] Jesus said to them, "^I am the bread of life; the one who comes to Me will not be hungry, and the one who believes in Me ^will never be thirsty. [36] But ^I said to you that you have indeed seen Me, and *yet* you do not believe. [37] ^Everything that the Father gives Me will come to Me, and the one who comes to Me I certainly will not cast out. [38] For ^I have come down from heaven, ^not to do My own will, but the will of Him who sent Me. [39] And this is the will of Him who sent Me, that of everything that He has given Me I will ^lose nothing, but will raise it up on the last day. [40] For this is the will of My Father, that everyone who sees the Son and ^believes in Him will have eternal life, and I Myself will ^raise him up on the last day."

WORDS TO THE JEWS

[41] So then the Jews were complaining about Him because He said, "I am the bread that ^came down out of heaven." [42] And they were saying, "^Is this not Jesus, the son of Joseph, whose father and mother ^we know? How does He now say, 'I have come down out of heaven'?" [43] Jesus answered and said to them, "Stop complaining among yourselves. [44] No one can come to Me unless the Father who sent Me ^draws him; and I will raise him up on the last day. [45] It is written in the Prophets: '^AND THEY SHALL ALL BE

6:23^John 6:11 **6:24**^Matt 14:34; Mark 6:53
6:25^Matt 23:7 **6:26**^John 6:2, 14, 30 **6:27**^Is 55:2
^John 3:33 **6:29**^1 Thess 1:3; James 2:22
6:30^Matt 12:38 **6:31**^Ps 78:24; Ex 16:4, 15
6:33^John 6:41, 50 **6:34**^John 4:15
6:35^John 6:48, 51 ^John 4:14 **6:36**^John 6:26
6:37^John 6:39; 17:2, 24 **6:38**^John 3:13 ^Matt 26:39
6:39^John 17:12; 18:9 **6:40**^John 3:16 ^Matt 10:15
6:41^John 6:33, 51, 58 **6:42**^Luke 4:22 ^John 7:27f
6:44^Jer 31:3; Hos 11:4 **6:45**^Is 54:13; Jer 31:34

6:26 [1] I.e., confirming miracles

TAUGHT OF GOD.' Everyone who has heard and learned from the Father, comes to Me. ⁴⁶ᴬNot that anyone has seen the Father, except the One who is from God; He has seen the Father. ⁴⁷Truly, truly, I say to you, the one who believes ᴬhas eternal life. ⁴⁸ᴬI am the bread of life. ⁴⁹ᴬYour fathers ate the manna in the wilderness, and they died. ⁵⁰This is the bread that comes down out of heaven, so that anyone may eat from it and ᴬnot die. ⁵¹I am the living bread that came down out of heaven; if anyone eats from this bread, he will live forever; and the bread which I will give ᴬfor the life of the world also is My flesh."

⁵²Then the Jews ᴬ*began* to argue with one another, saying, "How can this Man give us His flesh to eat?" ⁵³So Jesus said to them, "Truly, truly, I say to you, unless you eat the flesh of ᴬthe Son of Man and drink His blood, you have no life in yourselves. ⁵⁴The one who eats My flesh and drinks My blood has eternal life, and I will ᴬraise him up on the last day. ⁵⁵For My flesh is true food, and My blood is true drink. ⁵⁶The one who eats My flesh and drinks My blood ᴬremains in Me, and I in him. ⁵⁷Just as the ᴬliving Father sent Me, and I live because of the Father, the one who eats Me, he also will live because of Me. ⁵⁸This is the bread that came down out of heaven, not as the fathers ate and died; the one who eats this bread ᴬwill live forever."

WORDS TO THE DISCIPLES

⁵⁹These things He said ᴬin the synagogue as He taught in Capernaum.

⁶⁰So then many of His ᴬdisciples, when they heard *this,* said, "This statement is *very* unpleasant; who can listen to it?" ⁶¹But Jesus, aware that His disciples were complaining about this, said to them, "Is this ᴬoffensive to you? ⁶²*What* then if you see the Son of Man ᴬascending to where He was before? ⁶³ᴬIt is the Spirit who gives life; the flesh provides no benefit; the words that I have spoken to you are spirit, and are life. ⁶⁴But there are some of you who do not believe." For Jesus ᴬknew from the beginning who they were who did not believe, and ᴮwho it was who would betray Him. ⁶⁵And He was saying, "For this reason I have told you that no one can come to Me unless ᴬit has been granted him from the Father."

PETER'S CONFESSION OF FAITH

⁶⁶As a result of this many of His ᴬdisciples left, and would no longer walk with Him. ⁶⁷So Jesus said to ᴬthe twelve, "You do not want to leave also, do you?" ⁶⁸Simon Peter answered Him, "Lord, to whom shall we go? You have ᴬwords of eternal life. ⁶⁹And we have *already* believed and have come to know that You are ᴬthe Holy One of God." ⁷⁰Jesus answered them, "ᴬDid I Myself not choose you, the twelve? And *yet* one of you is a devil." ⁷¹Now He meant Judas ᴬ*the son* of Simon Iscariot; for he, one of the twelve, was going to betray Him.

6:46 ᴬJohn 1:18   6:47 ᴬJohn 3:36; 5:24
6:48 ᴬJohn 6:35, 51   6:49 ᴬJohn 6:31, 58
6:50 ᴬJohn 3:36; 5:24   6:51 ᴬJohn 1:29; 3:14f
6:52 ᴬJohn 9:16; 10:19   6:53 ᴬMatt 8:20; John 6:27, 62
6:54 ᴬJohn 6:39   6:56 ᴬJohn 15:4f; 17:23
6:57 ᴬMatt 16:16; John 5:26   6:58 ᴬJohn 3:36; 5:24
6:59 ᴬMatt 4:23   6:60 ᴬJohn 2:2; 6:66
6:61 ᴬMatt 11:6   6:62 ᴬJohn 3:13   6:63 ᴬ2 Cor 3:6
6:64 ᴬJohn 2:25   ᴮMatt 10:4   6:65 ᴬMatt 13:11;
John 3:27   6:66 ᴬJohn 2:2; 7:3   6:67 ᴬMatt 10:2;
John 2:2   6:68 ᴬJohn 6:63; 12:49f   6:69 ᴬMark 1:24;
8:29   6:70 ᴬJohn 15:16, 19   6:71 ᴬJohn 12:4; 13:2, 26

JESUS TEACHES AT THE FEAST

7 After these things Jesus ᴬwas walking in Galilee, for He was unwilling to walk in Judea because the Jews ᴮwere seeking to kill Him. ²Now the feast of the Jews, ᴬthe Feast of Booths, was near. ³So His ᴬbrothers said to Him, "Move on from here and go into Judea, so that Your disciples also may see Your works which You are doing. ⁴For no one does anything in secret when he himself is striving to be *known* publicly. If You are doing these things, show Yourself to the world." ⁵For not even His ᴬbrothers believed in Him. ⁶So Jesus *said to them, "ᴬMy time is not yet here, but your time is always ready. ⁷ᴬThe world cannot hate you, but it hates Me because I testify about it, that ᴮits deeds are evil. ⁸Go up to the feast yourselves; I am not going up to this feast, because ᴬMy time has not yet fully arrived." ⁹Now having said these things to them, He stayed in Galilee.

¹⁰But when His ᴬbrothers had gone up to the feast, then He Himself also went up, not publicly, but as *though* in secret. ¹¹So the Jews ᴬwere looking for Him at the feast and saying, "Where is He?" ¹²And there was a great deal of talk about Him in secret among the crowds: ᴬsome were saying, "He is a good man"; others were saying, "No, on the contrary, He is misleading the people." ¹³However, no one was speaking openly about Him, for ᴬfear of ¹the Jews.

¹⁴But when it was now the middle of the feast, Jesus went up into the temple *area,* and *began to* ᴬteach. ¹⁵ᴬThe Jews then were astonished, saying, "How has this Man become learned, not having been educated?" ¹⁶So Jesus answered them and said, "ᴬMy teaching is not My

own, but His who sent Me. ¹⁷ᴬIf anyone is willing to do His will, he will know about the teaching, whether it is of God, or I am speaking from Myself. ¹⁸The one who speaks from himself ᴬseeks his own glory; but He who is seeking the glory of the One who sent Him, He is true, and there is no unrighteousness in Him.

¹⁹"ᴬDid Moses not give you the Law, and *yet* none of you carries out the Law? Why are you ᴮseeking to kill Me?" ²⁰The crowd answered, "ᴬYou have a demon! Who is seeking to kill You?" ²¹Jesus answered them, "I did ᴬone deed, and you all are astonished. ²²For this reason ᴬMoses has given you circumcision (not that it is from Moses, but from ᴮthe fathers), and *even* on a Sabbath you circumcise a man. ²³ᴬIf a man receives circumcision on a Sabbath so that the Law of Moses will not be broken, are you angry at Me because I made an entire man well on a Sabbath? ²⁴Do not ᴬjudge by the outward appearance, but judge with righteous judgment."

²⁵So some of the people of Jerusalem were saying, "Is this Man not the one whom they are seeking to kill? ²⁶And *yet* look, He is speaking publicly, and they are saying nothing to Him. ᴬThe rulers do not really know that this is the Christ, do they? ²⁷However, ᴬwe know where this Man is from; but when the

7:1ᴬJohn 4:3   ᴮJohn 5:18   7:2ᴬLev 23:34; Deut 16:13, 16
7:3ᴬMatt 12:46; Mark 3:21   7:5ᴬMatt 12:46; Mark 3:21
7:6ᴬMatt 26:18; John 2:4   7:7ᴬJohn 15:18f   ᴮJohn 3:19f
7:8ᴬJohn 7:6   7:10ᴬMatt 12:46; Mark 3:21
7:11ᴬJohn 11:56   7:12ᴬJohn 7:40-43   7:13ᴬJohn 9:22;
12:42   7:14ᴬMatt 26:55; John 7:28   7:15ᴬJohn 1:19;
7:11, 13, 35   7:16ᴬJohn 3:11   7:17ᴬPs 25:9, 14; Prov 3:32
7:18ᴬJohn 5:41; 8:50, 54   7:19ᴬJohn 1:17   ᴮMark 11:18
7:20ᴬMatt 11:18; John 8:48f, 52   7:21ᴬJohn 5:2-9, 16;
7:23   7:22ᴬLev 12:3   ᴮGen 17:10ff   7:23ᴬMatt 12:2;
John 5:9, 10   7:24ᴬLev 19:15; Is 11:3   7:26ᴬLuke 23:13;
John 3:1   7:27ᴬJohn 6:42; 7:41f
_____
7:13 ¹I.e., the Jewish leaders

Christ comes, no one knows where He is from." ²⁸Then Jesus cried out in the temple, teaching and saying, "You both know Me and you know where I am from; and ᴬI have not come of Myself, but He who sent Me is true, whom you do not know. ²⁹I do know Him, because ᴬI am from Him, and ᴮHe sent Me." ³⁰So they ᴬwere seeking to arrest Him; and *yet* no one laid a hand on Him, because His hour had not yet come. ³¹But ᴬmany of the crowd believed in Him; and they were saying, "When the Christ comes, He will not perform more ᴮsigns than those which this man has done, will He?"

³²The Pharisees heard the crowd whispering these things about Him, and the chief priests and the Pharisees sent ᴬofficers to arrest Him. ³³Therefore Jesus said, "ᴬFor a little while longer I am *going to be* with you, and *then* I am going to Him who sent Me. ³⁴ᴬYou will seek Me, and will not find Me; and where I am, you cannot come." ³⁵The Jews then said to one another, "Where does this Man intend to go that we will not find Him? He does not intend to go to ᴬthe Dispersion among the Greeks, and teach the Greeks, does He? ³⁶What is this statement that He said, 'ᴬYou will seek Me, and will not find Me; and where I am, you cannot come'?"

³⁷Now on ᴬthe last day, the great *day* of the feast, Jesus stood and cried out, saying, "If anyone is thirsty, let him come to Me and drink. ³⁸The one who believes in Me, ᴬas the Scripture said, 'From his innermost being will flow rivers of living water.'" ³⁹But this He said ᴬin reference to the Spirit, whom those who believed in Him were to receive; for the Spirit was not yet *given*, because Jesus was not yet glorified.

PEOPLE'S DIVISION OVER JESUS

⁴⁰*Some* of the people therefore, after they heard these words, were saying, "This truly is ᴬthe Prophet." ⁴¹Others were saying, "This is the Christ." But others were saying, "ᴬSurely the Christ is not coming from Galilee, is He? ⁴²Has the Scripture not said that the Christ comes from ᴬthe descendants of David, and from Bethlehem, the village where David was?" ⁴³So ᴬa dissension occurred in the crowd because of Him. ⁴⁴And ᴬsome of them wanted to arrest Him, but no one laid hands on Him.

⁴⁵The ᴬofficers then came to the chief priests and Pharisees, and they said to them, "Why did you not bring Him?" ⁴⁶The officers answered, "ᴬNever has a man spoken in this way!" ⁴⁷The Pharisees then replied to them, "ᴬYou have not been led astray too, have you? ⁴⁸Not one of ᴬthe rulers or Pharisees has believed in Him, has he? ⁴⁹But this crowd that does not know the Law is accursed!" ⁵⁰ᴬNicodemus (the one who came to Him before, being one of them) *said to them, ⁵¹"ᴬOur Law does not judge the person unless it first hears from him and knows what he is doing, does it?" ⁵²They answered and said to him, "ᴬYou are not from Galilee as well, are you? Examine *the Scriptures*, and see that no prophet arises out of Galilee."

7:28ᴬJohn 8:42   7:29ᴬJohn 6:46   ᴮJohn 3:17
7:30ᴬMatt 21:46; John 7:32, 44   7:31ᴬJohn 2:23
ᴮJohn 2:11   7:32ᴬMatt 26:58; John 7:45f
7:33ᴬJohn 12:35; 13:33   7:34ᴬJohn 7:36; 8:21
7:35ᴬPs 147:2; Is 11:12   7:36ᴬJohn 7:34; 8:21
7:37ᴬLev 23:36; Num 29:35   7:38ᴬIs 44:3; 55:1
7:39ᴬJoel 2:28; John 1:33   7:40ᴬMatt 21:11; John 1:21
7:41ᴬJohn 1:46; 7:52   7:42ᴬPs 89:4; Mic 5:2
7:43ᴬJohn 9:16; 10:19   7:44ᴬJohn 7:30
7:45ᴬJohn 7:32   7:46ᴬMatt 7:28   7:47ᴬJohn 7:12
7:48ᴬLuke 23:13; John 7:26   7:50ᴬJohn 3:1; 19:39
7:51ᴬEx 23:1; Deut 17:6

⁵³[[¹And everyone went to his home.

THE ADULTEROUS WOMAN

8 But Jesus went to ^the Mount of Olives. ²And early in the morning He came again into the temple *area,* and all the people were coming to Him; and ^He sat down and *began* teaching them. ³Now the scribes and the Pharisees *brought a woman caught in the act of adultery, and after placing her in the center *of the courtyard,* ⁴they *said to Him, "Teacher, this woman has been caught in the very act of committing adultery. ⁵Now in the Law, ^Moses commanded us to stone such women; what then do You say?" ⁶Now they were saying this to ^test Him, so that they might have *grounds for* accusing Him. But Jesus stooped down and with His finger wrote on the ground. ⁷When they persisted in asking Him, He straightened up and said to them, "He who is without sin among you, let him *be the* ^first to throw a stone at her." ⁸And again He stooped down and wrote on the ground. ⁹Now when they heard *this,* they *began* leaving, one by one, beginning with the older ones, and He was left alone, and the woman *where she* was, in the center *of the courtyard.* ¹⁰And ^straightening up, Jesus said to her, "Woman, where are they? Did no one condemn you?" ¹¹She said, "No one, Lord." And Jesus said, "^I do not condemn you, either. Go. From now on do not ^sin any longer."]]

JESUS IS THE LIGHT OF THE WORLD

¹²Then Jesus again spoke to them, saying, "^I am the Light of the world; the one who follows Me will not walk in the darkness, but will have the Light of life." ¹³So the Pharisees said to Him, "^You are testifying about Yourself; Your testimony is not true." ¹⁴Jesus answered and said to them, "Even if I am testifying about Myself, My testimony is true, because I know ^where I came from and where I am going; but you do not know where I come from or where I am going. ¹⁵You judge according to the flesh; ^I am not judging anyone. ¹⁶But even ^if I do judge, My judgment is true; for I am not alone *in it,* but I and the Father who sent Me. ¹⁷Even in ^your Law it has been written that the testimony of ᴮtwo people is true. ¹⁸I am He who testifies about Myself, and ^the Father who sent Me testifies about Me." ¹⁹So they were saying to Him, "Where is Your Father?" Jesus answered, "You know neither Me nor My Father; ^if you knew Me, you would know My Father also." ²⁰These words He spoke in the treasury, as ^He taught in the temple *area;* and no one arrested Him, because ᴮHis hour had not yet come.

²¹Then He said again to them, "I am going away, and ^you will look for Me, and will die in your sin; where I am going, you cannot come." ²²So the Jews were saying, "Surely He will not kill Himself, will He, since He says, '^Where I am

7:52^John 1:46; 7:41   **8:1**^Matt 21:1   **8:2**^Matt 26:55; John 8:20   **8:5**^Lev 20:10; Deut 22:22f
8:6^Matt 16:1; 19:3   **8:7**^Deut 17:7   **8:10**^John 8:7
8:11^John 3:17   ᴮJohn 5:14   **8:12**^John 1:4; 9:5
8:13^John 5:31   **8:14**^John 8:42; 13:3   **8:15**^John 3:17
8:16^John 5:30   **8:17**^Deut 17:6   ᴮMatt 18:16
8:18^John 5:37; 1 John 5:9   **8:19**^John 7:28; 8:55
8:20^John 7:14   ᴮJohn 7:30   **8:21**^John 7:34
8:22^John 7:35

7:53 ¹Later mss add the story of the adulterous woman, numbering it as John 7:53-8:11

going, you cannot come'?" ²³ And He was saying to them, "ᴬYou are from below, I am from above; you are of this world, ᴮI am not of this world. ²⁴ Therefore I said to you that you will die in your sins; for unless you believe that ᴬI am, you will die in your sins." ²⁵ Then they were saying to Him, "Who are You?" Jesus said to them, "What have I even been saying to you *from* the beginning? ²⁶ I have many things to say and to judge regarding you, but ᴬHe who sent Me is true; and the things which I heard from Him, these I say to the world." ²⁷ They did not realize that He was speaking to them *about* the Father. ²⁸ So Jesus said, "When you ᴬlift up the Son of Man, then you will know that I am, and I do nothing on My own, but I say these things as the Father instructed Me. ²⁹ And He who sent Me is with Me; ᴬHe has not left Me alone, for I always do the things that are pleasing to Him." ³⁰ As He said these things, ᴬmany came to believe in Him.

THE TRUTH WILL SET YOU FREE

³¹ So Jesus was saying to those Jews who had believed Him, "ᴬIf you continue in My word, *then* you are truly My disciples; ³² and you will know the truth, and ᴬthe truth will set you free." ³³ They answered Him, "ᴬWe are Abraham's descendants and have never been enslaved to anyone; how *is it that* You say, 'You will become free'?"

³⁴ Jesus answered them, "Truly, truly I say to you, ᴬeveryone who commits sin is a slave of sin. ³⁵ Now the slave does not remain in the house forever; ᴬthe son does remain forever. ³⁶ So if the Son ᴬsets you free, you really will be free. ³⁷ I know that you are ᴬAbraham's

descendants; yet you are seeking to kill Me, because My word has no place in you. ³⁸ I speak of the things which I have seen with *My* Father; therefore you also do the things which you heard from ᴬ*your* father."

³⁹ They answered and said to Him, "Abraham is our father." Jesus *said to them, "ᴬIf you are Abraham's children, do the deeds of Abraham. ⁴⁰ But as it is, you are seeking to kill Me, a Man who has ᴬtold you the truth, which I heard from God; this Abraham did not do. ⁴¹ You are doing the deeds of your father." They said to Him, "We were not born as a result of sexual immorality; ᴬwe have one Father: God." ⁴² Jesus said to them, "If God were your Father, ᴬyou would love Me, for I came forth from God and am here; for I have not even come on My own, but He sent Me. ⁴³ Why do you not understand what I am saying? *It is* because you cannot ᴬlisten to My word. ⁴⁴ ᴬYou are of *your* father the devil, and ᴮyou want to do the desires of your father. He was a murderer from the beginning, and does not stand in the truth because there is no truth in him. Whenever he tells a lie, he speaks from his own *nature*, because he is a liar and the father of lies. ⁴⁵ But because ᴬI say the truth, you do not believe Me. ⁴⁶ Which one of you convicts Me of sin? If I speak truth, why do you not believe Me? ⁴⁷ ᴬThe one who is of God hears the words of God; for

---

8:23 ᴬJohn 3:31   ᴮJohn 17:14, 16   8:24 ᴬMatt 24:5; Mark 13:6   8:26 ᴬJohn 3:33; 7:28   8:28 ᴬJohn 3:14; 12:32   8:29 ᴬJohn 8:16; 16:32   8:30 ᴬJohn 7:31 8:31 ᴬJohn 15:7; 2 John 9   8:32 ᴬJohn 8:36; Rom 8:2 8:33 ᴬMatt 3:9; Luke 3:8   8:34 ᴬRom 6:16; 2 Pet 2:19 8:35 ᴬLuke 15:31   8:36 ᴬJohn 8:32   8:37 ᴬMatt 3:9; John 8:39   8:38 ᴬJohn 8:41, 44   8:39 ᴬRom 9:7; Gal 3:7   8:40 ᴬJohn 8:26   8:41 ᴬDeut 32:6; Is 63:16 8:42 ᴬ1 John 5:1   8:43 ᴬJohn 5:25   8:44 ᴬ1 John 3:8 ᴮJohn 7:17   8:45 ᴬJohn 18:37   8:47 ᴬ1 John 4:6

this reason you do not hear *them*, because you are not of God."

⁴⁸The Jews answered and said to Him, "Do we not rightly say that You are a ᴬSamaritan, and You have a demon?" ⁴⁹Jesus answered, "I do not ᴬhave a demon; on the contrary, I honor My Father, and you dishonor Me. ⁵⁰But ᴬI am not seeking My glory; there is One who seeks *it*, and judges. ⁵¹Truly, truly I say to you, if anyone follows My word, he will never ᴬsee death."

⁵²The Jews said to Him, "Now we know that You have a demon. Abraham died, and the prophets *as well;* and *yet* You say, 'If anyone ᴬfollows My word, he will never taste of death.' ⁵³You ᴬare not greater than our father Abraham, who died, are You? The prophets died too. Whom do You make Yourself *out to be*?" ⁵⁴Jesus answered, "If I glorify Myself, My glory is nothing; ᴬit is My Father who glorifies Me, of whom you say, 'He is our God'; ⁵⁵and you have not come to know Him, ᴬbut I know Him. And if I say that I do not know Him, I will be a liar like you; ᴬbut I do know Him, and I follow His word. ⁵⁶Your father Abraham was ᴬoverjoyed that he would see My day, and he saw *it* and rejoiced."

⁵⁷ᴬSo the Jews said to Him, "You are not yet fifty years old, and You have seen Abraham?" ⁵⁸Jesus said to them, "Truly, truly I say to you, before Abraham was born, ¹,ᴬI am." ⁵⁹Therefore they ᴬpicked up stones to throw at Him, but Jesus ᴮhid Himself and left the temple *grounds*.

HEALING THE MAN BORN BLIND

9 As Jesus passed by, He saw a man *who had been* blind from birth. ²And His disciples asked Him, "Rabbi, who sinned, this man or his ᴬparents, that he would be born blind?" ³Jesus answered, "*It was* neither *that* this man sinned, nor his parents; but *it was* ᴬso that the works of God might be displayed in him. ⁴We must carry out the works of Him who sent Me ᴬas long as it is day; night is coming, when no one can work. ⁵While I am in the world, I am ᴬthe Light of the world." ⁶When He had said this, He ᴬspit on the ground, and made mud from the saliva, and applied the mud to his eyes, ⁷and said to him, "Go, wash in ᴬthe pool of Siloam" (which is translated, Sent). So he left and washed, and came *back* seeing. ⁸So the neighbors, and those who previously saw him as a beggar, were saying, "Is this not the one who used to ᴬsit and beg?" ⁹Others were saying, "This is he," *still* others were saying, "No, but he is like him." The man himself kept saying, "I am *the one*." ¹⁰So they were saying to him, "How then were your eyes opened?" ¹¹He answered, "The Man who is called Jesus made mud, and spread *it* on my eyes, and said to me, 'Go to ᴬSiloam and wash'; so I went away and washed, and I received sight." ¹²And they said to him, "Where is He?" He *said, "I do not know."

CONTROVERSY OVER THE MAN

¹³They *brought the man who was previously blind to the Pharisees. ¹⁴ᴬNow it was a Sabbath on the

8:48 ᴬ Matt 10:5; John 4:9   8:49 ᴬ John 7:20
8:50 ᴬ John 5:41; 8:54   8:51 ᴬ Matt 16:28; Luke 2:26
8:52 ᴬ John 8:55; 14:23   8:53 ᴬ John 4:12
8:54 ᴬ John 7:39   8:55 ᴬ John 7:29   8:56 ᴬ Matt 13:17;
Heb 11:13   8:57 ᴬ John 1:19   8:58 ᴬ Ex 3:14; John 1:1
8:59 ᴬ John 10:31   ᴮ John 12:36   9:2 ᴬ Ex 20:5
9:3 ᴬ John 11:4   9:4 ᴬ John 7:33; 11:9   9:5 ᴬ Matt 5:14;
John 1:4   9:6 ᴬ Mark 7:33; 8:23   9:7 ᴬ Neh 3:15; Is 8:6
9:8 ᴬ Acts 3:2, 10   9:11 ᴬ John 9:7   9:14 ᴬ John 5:9

8:58 ¹ Or *I AM*; Jesus may be referring to Ex 3:14, *I AM WHO I AM*

day that Jesus made the mud and opened his eyes. ¹⁵ᴬThen the Pharisees also were asking him again how he received his sight. And he said to them, "He applied mud to my eyes, and I washed, and I see." ¹⁶Therefore some of the Pharisees were saying, "This Man is not from God, because He ᴬdoes not keep the Sabbath." But others were saying, "How can a man who is a sinner perform such signs?" And there was dissension among them. ¹⁷So they *said again to the man who was blind, "What do you say about Him, since He opened your eyes?" And he said, "He is a ᴬprophet."

¹⁸ᴬThe Jews then did not believe *it* about him, that he had been blind and had received sight, until they called the parents of the very one who had received his sight, ¹⁹and they questioned them, saying, "Is this your son, who you say was born blind? Then how does he now see?" ²⁰His parents then answered and said, "We know that this is our son, and that he was born blind; ²¹but how he now sees, we do not know; or who opened his eyes, we do not know. Ask him; he is of age, he will speak for himself." ²²His parents said this because they ᴬwere afraid of the ¹Jews; for the Jews had already reached the decision that if anyone confessed Him to be Christ, ᴮhe was to be excommunicated from the synagogue. ²³*It was* for this reason *that* his parents said, "ᴬHe is of age; ask him."

²⁴So for a second time they summoned the man who had been blind, and said to him, "ᴬGive glory to God; we know that this Man is a sinner." ²⁵He then answered, "Whether He is a sinner, I do not know; one thing I do know, that

though I was blind, now I see." ²⁶So they said to him, "What did He do to you? How did He open your eyes?" ²⁷He answered them, "ᴬI told you already and you did not ᴮlisten; why do you want to hear *it* again? You do not want to become His disciples too, do you?" ²⁸They spoke abusively to him and said, "You are His disciple, but ᴬwe are disciples of Moses. ²⁹We know that God has spoken to Moses, but as for this Man, ᴬwe do not know where He is from." ³⁰The man answered and said to them, "Well, here is the amazing thing, that you do not know where He is from, and *yet* He opened my eyes! ³¹We know that ᴬGod does not listen to sinners; but if someone is God-fearing and does His will, He listens to him. ³²Since the beginning of time it has never been heard that anyone opened the eyes of a person born blind. ³³ᴬIf this Man were not from God, He could do nothing." ³⁴They answered him, "You were born entirely in sins, and *yet* you are teaching us?" So they ᴬput him out.

JESUS AFFIRMS HIS DEITY

³⁵Jesus heard that they had ᴬput him out, and upon finding him, He said, "Do you believe in the Son of Man?" ³⁶He answered by saying, "And ᴬwho is He, Sir, that I may believe in Him?" ³⁷Jesus said to him, "You have both seen Him, and ᴬHe is the One who is

9:15ᴬJohn 9:10   9:16ᴬMatt 12:2; Luke 13:14
9:17ᴬDeut 18:15; Matt 21:11   9:18ᴬJohn 1:19; 9:22
9:22ᴬJohn 7:13   ᴮLuke 6:22   9:23ᴬJohn 9:21
9:24ᴬJosh 7:19; Ezra 10:11   9:27ᴬJohn 9:15
ᴮJohn 8:43, 47   9:28ᴬJohn 5:45; Rom 2:17
9:29ᴬJohn 8:14   9:31ᴬJob 27:8f; 35:13
9:33ᴬJohn 3:2; 9:16   9:34ᴬJohn 9:22, 35; 3 John 10
9:35ᴬJohn 9:22, 34; 3 John 10   9:36ᴬRom 10:14
9:37ᴬJohn 4:26
9:22¹I.e., the Jewish leaders

talking with you." **38**And he said, "I believe, Lord." And he ^worshiped Him. **39**And Jesus said, "^For judgment I came into this world, so that ^Bthose who do not see may see, and those who see may become blind." **40**Those who were with Him from the Pharisees heard these things and said to Him, "^We are not blind too, are we?" **41**Jesus said to them, "^If you were blind, you would have no sin; but now *that* you maintain, 'We see,' your sin remains.

PARABLE OF THE GOOD SHEPHERD

10 "Truly, truly I say to you, the one who does not enter by the door into the fold of the sheep, but climbs up some other way, he is ^a thief and a robber. **2**But the one who enters by the door is ^a shepherd of the sheep. **3**To him the doorkeeper opens, and the sheep listen to ^his voice, and he calls his own sheep by name and leads them out. **4**When he puts all his own *sheep* outside, he goes ahead of them, and the sheep follow him because they know ^his voice. **5**However, a stranger they simply will not follow, but will flee from him, because they do not know ^the voice of strangers." **6**Jesus told them this ^figure of speech, but they did not understand what the things which He was saying to them meant.

7So Jesus said to them again, "Truly, truly I say to you, I am ^the door of the sheep. **8**All those who came before Me are ^thieves and robbers, but the sheep did not listen to them. **9**^I am the door; if anyone enters through Me, he will be saved, and will go in and out and find pasture. **10**The thief comes only to steal and kill and destroy; I came so that they ^would have life, and have *it* abundantly.

11"^I am the good shepherd; the good shepherd lays down His life for the sheep. **12**He who is a hired hand, and not a ^shepherd, who is not the owner of the sheep, sees the wolf coming, and leaves the sheep and flees; and the wolf snatches them and scatters *the flock.* **13***He flees* because he is a hired hand and does not care about the sheep. **14**I am the good shepherd, and ^I know My own, and My own know Me, **15**just as ^the Father knows Me and I know the Father; and I lay down My life for the sheep. **16**And I have ^other sheep that are not of this fold; I must bring them also, and they will listen to My voice; and they will become one flock, *with* one shepherd. **17**For this reason the Father loves Me, because I ^lay down My life so that I may take it back. **18**^No one has taken it away from Me, but I lay it down on My own. I have authority to lay it down, and I have authority to take it back. This commandment I received from My Father."

19^Dissension occurred again among the Jews because of these words. **20**Many of them were saying, "He ^has a demon and ^Bis insane. Why do you listen to Him?" **21**Others were saying, "These are not the words of one who is demon-possessed. ^A demon cannot open the eyes of those who are blind, can it?"

9:38^Matt 8:2 **9:39**^John 5:22, 27 ^BLuke 4:18
9:40^Rom 2:19 **9:41**^John 15:22, 24 **10:1**^John 10:8
10:2^John 10:11f **10:3**^John 10:4f, 16, 27
10:4^John 10:5, 16, 27 **10:5**^John 10:4, 16, 27
10:6^John 16:25, 29; 2 Pet 2:22 **10:7**^John 10:1f, 9
10:8^Jer 23:1f; Ezek 34:2ff **10:9**^John 10:1f, 9
10:10^John 5:40 **10:11**^Is 40:11; Ezek 34:11-16, 23
10:12^John 10:2 **10:14**^John 10:27
10:15^Matt 11:27; Luke 10:22 **10:16**^Is 56:8
10:17^John 10:11, 15, 18 **10:18**^Matt 26:53; John 2:19
10:19^John 7:43; 9:16 **10:20**^John 7:20 ^BMark 3:21
10:21^Ex 4:11; John 9:32f

JESUS ASSERTS HIS DEITY

²²At that time the ¹Feast of the Dedication took place in Jerusalem; ²³it was winter, and Jesus was walking in the temple *area,* in the portico of ᴬSolomon. ²⁴The Jews then surrounded Him and *began* saying to Him, "How long will You keep us in suspense? If You are the Christ, tell us ᴬplainly." ²⁵Jesus answered them, "I told you, and you do not believe; ᴬthe works that I do in My Father's name, these testify of Me. ²⁶But you do not believe, because ᴬyou are not of My sheep. ²⁷My sheep ᴬlisten to My voice, and I know them, and they follow Me; ²⁸and I give them ᴬeternal life, and they will never perish; and no one will snatch them out of My hand. ²⁹¹My Father, who has given *them* to Me, is greater than all; and no one is able to snatch *them* out of the Father's hand. ³⁰ᴬI and the Father are one."

³¹The Jews ᴬpicked up stones again to stone Him. ³²Jesus replied to them, "I showed you many good works from the Father; for which of them are you stoning Me?" ³³The Jews answered Him, "We are not stoning You for a good work, but for ᴬblasphemy; and because You, being a man, ᴮmake Yourself *out to be* God." ³⁴Jesus answered them, "Has it not been written in your Law: 'ᴬI SAID, YOU ARE GODS'? ³⁵If he called them gods, to whom the word of God came (and the Scripture cannot be nullified), ³⁶are you saying of Him whom the Father sanctified and ᴬsent into the world, 'You are blaspheming,' because I said, 'I am the Son of God'? ³⁷ᴬIf I do not do the works of My Father, do not believe Me; ³⁸but if I do *them,* even though you do not believe Me, believe the works, so that you may know and understand that ᴬthe Father is in Me, and I in Father." ³⁹Therefore ᴬthey were seeking again to arrest Him, and He eluded their grasp.

⁴⁰And He went away ᴬagain beyond the Jordan to the place where John was first baptizing, and He stayed there. ⁴¹Many came to Him and were saying, "While John performed no sign, yet ᴬeverything John said about this Man was true." ⁴²And ᴬmany believed in Him there.

THE DEATH AND RESURRECTION OF LAZARUS

11 Now a certain man was sick: Lazarus of Bethany, the village of Mary and her sister ᴬMartha. ²And it was the Mary who ᴬanointed the Lord with ointment, and wiped His feet with her hair, whose brother Lazarus was sick. ³So the sisters sent *word* to Him, saying, "Lord, behold, ᴬhe whom You love is sick." ⁴But when Jesus heard *this,* He said, "This sickness is not meant for death, but *is* for ᴬthe glory of God, so that the Son of God may be glorified by it." ⁵(Now Jesus loved ᴬMartha and her sister, and Lazarus.) ⁶So when He heard that he was sick, He then stayed two days *longer* in the place where He was. ⁷Then after this He *said to the disciples, "ᴬLet's go to

10:23ᴬActs 3:11; 5:12   10:24ᴬLuke 22:67; John 16:25
10:25ᴬJohn 5:36; 10:38   10:26ᴬJohn 8:47
10:27ᴬJohn 10:4, 16   10:28ᴬJohn 17:2f; 1 John 2:25
10:30ᴬJohn 17:21ff   10:31ᴬJohn 8:59
10:33ᴬLev 24:16   ᴮJohn 5:18   10:34ᴬPs 82:6
10:36ᴬJohn 3:17   10:37ᴬJohn 10:25; 15:24
10:38ᴬJohn 14:10f, 20; 17:21, 23   10:39ᴬJohn 7:30
10:40ᴬJohn 1:28   10:41ᴬJohn 1:27, 30, 34; 3:27-30
10:42ᴬJohn 7:31   11:1ᴬLuke 10:38; John 11:5, 19ff
11:2ᴬLuke 7:38; John 12:3   11:3ᴬJohn 11:5, 11, 36
11:4ᴬJohn 9:3; 10:38   11:5ᴬJohn 11:1   11:7ᴬJohn 10:40

10:22¹Now known as Hanukkah, also the Feast of Lights   10:29¹One early ms *What My Father has given Me is greater than all*

Judea again." ⁸The disciples *said to Him, "Rabbi, the Jews were just now seeking ᴬto stone You, and *yet* You are going there again?" ⁹Jesus replied, "ᴬAre there not twelve hours in the day? If anyone walks during the day, he does not stumble, because he sees the light of this world. ¹⁰But if anyone walks during the night, he stumbles, because the light is not in him." ¹¹This He said, and after this He *said to them, "Our friend Lazarus ᴬhas fallen asleep; but I am going so that I may awaken him from sleep." ¹²The disciples then said to Him, "Lord, if he has fallen asleep, he will come out of it." ¹³Now ᴬJesus had spoken of his death, but they thought that He was speaking about actual sleep. ¹⁴So Jesus then said to them plainly, "Lazarus died, ¹⁵and I am glad for your sakes that I was not there, so that you may believe; but let's go to him." ¹⁶Therefore Thomas, who was called ᴬDidymus, said to *his* fellow disciples, "Let's also go, so that we may die with Him!"

¹⁷So when Jesus came, He found that he had already been in the tomb ᴬfour days. ¹⁸Now ᴬBethany was near Jerusalem, about ¹fifteen stadia away; ¹⁹and many of the Jews had come to Martha and Mary, ᴬto console them about *their* brother. ²⁰So then ᴬMartha, when she heard that Jesus was coming, went to meet Him, but ᴬMary stayed in the house. ²¹Martha then said to Jesus, "Lord, ᴬif You had been here, my brother would not have died. ²²Even now I know that ᴬwhatever You ask of God, God will give You." ²³Jesus *said to her, "Your brother will rise *from the dead*." ²⁴Martha *said to Him, "ᴬI know that he will rise in the resurrection on the last day." ²⁵Jesus said to her, "ᴬI am the resurrection and the life; the one who believes in Me will live, even if he dies, ²⁶and everyone who lives and believes in Me ᴬwill never die. Do you believe this?" ²⁷She *said to Him, "Yes, Lord; I have come to believe that You are ᴬthe Christ, the Son of God, *and* He who comes into the world."

²⁸When she had said this, she left and called Mary her sister, saying secretly, "ᴬThe Teacher is here and is calling for you." ²⁹And when she heard *this*, she *got up quickly and came to Him.

³⁰Now Jesus had not yet come into the village, but ᴬwas still at the place where Martha met Him. ³¹ᴬThen the Jews who were with her in the house and were consoling her, when they saw that Mary had gotten up quickly and left, they followed her, thinking that she was going to the tomb to weep there. ³²So when Mary came *to the place* where Jesus was, she saw Him and fell at His feet, saying to Him, "Lord, ᴬif You had been here, my brother would not have died." ³³Therefore when Jesus saw her weeping, and the Jews who came with her *also* weeping, He ᴬwas deeply moved in spirit and was troubled, ³⁴and He said, "Where have you laid him?" They *said to Him, "Lord, come and see." ³⁵Jesus ᴬwept. ³⁶So the Jews

11:8 ᴬJohn 8:59; 10:31   11:9 ᴬLuke 13:33; John 9:4
11:11 ᴬMatt 27:52; Mark 5:39   11:13 ᴬMatt 9:24;
Luke 8:52   11:16 ᴬJohn 20:24; 21:2   11:17 ᴬJohn 11:39
11:18 ᴬJohn 11:1   11:19 ᴬJob 2:11; John 11:31
11:20 ᴬLuke 10:38-42   11:21 ᴬJohn 11:32, 37
11:22 ᴬJohn 9:31; 11:41f   11:24 ᴬDan 12:2; John 5:28f
11:25 ᴬJohn 1:4; 5:26   11:26 ᴬJohn 6:47, 50, 51; 8:51
11:27 ᴬMatt 16:16; Luke 2:11   11:28 ᴬMatt 26:18;
Mark 14:14   11:30 ᴬJohn 11:20   11:31 ᴬJohn 11:19, 33
11:32 ᴬJohn 11:21   11:33 ᴬJohn 11:38   11:35 ᴬLuke 19:41;
John 11:33

11:18 ¹ Possibly 2 miles or 3 km; a Roman stadion perhaps averaged 607 ft. or 185 m

were saying, "See how He ^loved him!" ³⁷But some of them said, "Could this Man, who ^opened the eyes of the man who was blind, not have also kept this man from dying?"

³⁸So Jesus, again being deeply moved within, *came to the tomb. Now it was a ^cave, and a stone was lying against it. ³⁹Jesus *said, "Remove the stone." Martha, the sister of the deceased, *said to Him, "Lord, by this time there will be a stench, for he has been *dead* ^four days." ⁴⁰Jesus *said to her, "^Did I not say to you that if you believe, you will see the glory of God?" ⁴¹So they removed the stone. And Jesus ^raised His eyes, and said, "^Father, I thank You that You have heard Me. ⁴²But I knew that You always hear Me; nevertheless, ^because of the people standing around I said *it*, so that they may believe that You sent Me." ⁴³And when He had said these things, He cried out with a loud voice, "Lazarus, come out!" ⁴⁴Out came the man who had died, ^bound hand and foot with wrappings, and ^Bhis face was wrapped around with a cloth. Jesus *said to them, "Unbind him, and let him go."

⁴⁵Therefore many of the Jews ^who came to Mary, and saw what He had done, believed in Him. ⁴⁶But some of them went to the ^Pharisees and told them the things which Jesus had done.

CONSPIRACY TO KILL JESUS

⁴⁷Therefore ^the chief priests and the Pharisees ^Bconvened a council meeting, and they were saying, "What are we doing in regard to the fact that this Man is performing many signs? ⁴⁸If we let Him *go on* like this, all *the people* will believe

in Him, and the Romans will come and take over both our ^place and our nation." ⁴⁹But one of them, Caiaphas, ^who was high priest that year, said to them, "You know nothing at all, ⁵⁰nor are you taking into account that ^it is in your best interest that one man die for the people, and that the whole nation not perish *instead*." ⁵¹Now he did not say this on his own, but ^as he was high priest that year, he prophesied that Jesus was going to die for the nation; ⁵²and not for the nation only, but in order that He might also ^gather together into one the children of God who are scattered abroad. ⁵³So from that day on they ^planned together to kill Him.

⁵⁴Therefore Jesus ^no longer *continued to* walk publicly among the Jews, but went away from there to the region near the wilderness, into a city called Ephraim; and there He stayed with the disciples.

⁵⁵Now the Passover of the Jews was near, and many went up to Jerusalem from the country prior to the Passover, ^in order to purify themselves. ⁵⁶So they ^were looking for Jesus, and saying to one another as they stood in the temple *area*, "What do you think; that He will not come to the feast at all?" ⁵⁷Now ^the chief priests and the Pharisees had given orders that if anyone knew where He was, he was to report it, so that they might arrest Him.

11:36^John 11:3, 5   **11:37**^John 9:7
11:38^Matt 27:60; Mark 15:46   **11:39**^John 11:17
11:40^John 11:4, 23ff   **11:41**^John 17:1   ^BMatt 11:25
11:42^John 12:30; 17:21   **11:44**^John 19:40
^BJohn 20:7   **11:45**^John 11:19; 12:17f
11:46^John 7:32, 45; 11:57   **11:47**^John 7:32, 45
^BMatt 26:3   **11:48**^Matt 24:15   **11:49**^John 11:51;
18:13   **11:50**^John 18:14   **11:51**^John 18:13
11:52^John 10:16   **11:53**^Matt 26:4   **11:54**^John 7:1
11:55^Num 9:10; 2 Chr 30:17f   **11:56**^John 7:11
11:57^John 11:47

MARY ANOINTS JESUS

12 ^Therefore, six days before the Passover, Jesus came to Bethany where Lazarus was, whom Jesus had raised from the dead. ²So they made Him a dinner there, and ^Martha was serving; and Lazarus was one of those reclining *at the table* with Him. ³^Mary then took a pound of very expensive ᴮperfume of pure nard, and anointed the feet of Jesus and wiped His feet with her hair; and the house was filled with the fragrance of the perfume. ⁴But ^Judas Iscariot, one of His disciples, the one who intended to betray Him, *said, ⁵"Why was this perfume not sold for three hundred ¹denarii and *the proceeds* given to poor *people?*" ⁶Now he said this, not because he cared about the poor, but because he was a thief, and as he ^kept the money box, he used to steal from ᴮwhat was put into it. ⁷Therefore Jesus said, "Leave her alone, so that she may keep it ¹for ^the day of My burial. ⁸^For you always have the poor with you, but you do not always have Me."

⁹The large crowd of the Jews then learned that He was there; and they came, not on account of Jesus only, but so that they might also see Lazarus, ^whom He raised from the dead. ¹⁰But the chief priests planned to put Lazarus to death also, ¹¹because ^on account of him many of the Jews were going away and were believing in Jesus.

THE TRIUMPHAL ENTRY

¹²On the next day, when ^the large crowd that had come to the feast heard that Jesus was coming to Jerusalem, ¹³they took the branches of the palm trees and went out to meet Him, and *began* shouting,

"^Hosanna! BLESSED IS HE WHO COMES IN THE NAME OF THE LORD, indeed, the King of Israel!" ¹⁴Jesus, finding a young donkey, sat on it; as it is written: ¹⁵"^DO NOT FEAR, DAUGHTER OF ZION; BEHOLD, YOUR KING IS COMING, SEATED ON A DONKEY'S COLT." ¹⁶^These things His disciples did not understand at the first; but when Jesus was glorified, then they remembered that these things were written of Him, and that they had done these things for Him. ¹⁷So ^the people, who were with Him when He called Lazarus out of the tomb and raised him from the dead, continued to testify *about Him.* ¹⁸^For this reason also the people went to meet Him, because they heard that He had performed this sign. ¹⁹So the Pharisees said to one another, "You see that you are not accomplishing anything; look, the world has gone after Him!"

GREEKS SEEK JESUS

²⁰Now there were some ^Greeks among those who were going up to worship at the feast; ²¹these *people* then came to Philip, who was from ^Bethsaida of Galilee, and were making a request of him, saying, "Sir, we wish to see Jesus." ²²Philip *came and *told ^Andrew; *then* Andrew and Philip *came and *told Jesus. ²³But Jesus *answered them by saying, "The hour has come for the Son of Man to ^be glorified.

12:1 ^*Matt 26:6-13; Mark 14:3-9*   12:2 ^Luke 10:38
12:3 ^Luke 7:37f   ᴮMark 14:3   12:4 ^John 6:71
12:6 ^John 13:29   ᴮLuke 8:3   12:7 ^John 19:40
12:8 ^Deut 15:11; Matt 26:11   12:9 ^John 11:43f; 12:1, 17f
12:11 ^John 11:45f; 12:18   12:12 ^*Matt 21:4-9; Mark 11:7-10*
12:13 ^Ps 118:26   12:15 ^Zech 9:9   12:16 ^Mark 9:32;
John 2:22   12:17 ^John 11:42   12:18 ^Luke 19:37;
John 12:12   12:20 ^John 7:35   12:21 ^Matt 11:21
12:22 ^John 1:44   12:23 ^John 7:39; 12:16

12:5 ¹The denarius was a day's wages for a laborer
12:7 ¹Or *in view of*

²⁴Truly, truly I say to you, ^unless a grain of wheat falls into the earth and dies, it remains alone; but if it dies, it bears much fruit. ²⁵^The one who loves his life loses it, and the one who hates his life in this world will keep it to eternal life. ²⁶If anyone serves Me, he must follow Me; and ^where I am, there My servant will be also; if anyone serves Me, the Father will honor him.

JESUS FORETELLS HIS DEATH

²⁷"^Now My soul has become troubled; and what am I to say? 'Father, save Me from this hour'? But for this purpose I came to this hour. ²⁸Father, glorify Your name." Then a ^voice came out of heaven: "I have both glorified *it,* and will glorify *it* again." ²⁹So the crowd who stood by and heard *it* were saying that it had thundered; others were saying, "^An angel has spoken to Him!" ³⁰Jesus responded and said, "^This voice has not come for My sake, but for yours. ³¹Now judgment is *upon* this world; now ^the ruler of this world will be cast out. ³²And I, if I ^am lifted up from the earth, will ᴮdraw all *people* to Myself." ³³Now He was saying this ^to indicate what kind of death He was going to die. ³⁴The crowd then answered Him, "We have heard from the Law that ^the Christ is to remain forever; and how *is it that* You say, 'The Son of Man must be lifted up'? Who is this Son of Man?" ³⁵So Jesus said to them, "For a little while longer the Light is among you. Walk while you have the Light, so that darkness will not overtake you; also, the one who ^walks in the darkness does not know where he is going. ³⁶While you have the Light, believe in the Light, so that you may become ^sons of Light."

These things Jesus proclaimed, and He went away and hid Himself from them. ³⁷But though He had performed so many signs in their sight, they *still* were not believing in Him. ³⁸*This happened* so that the word of Isaiah the prophet which he spoke would be fulfilled: "^LORD, WHO HAS BELIEVED OUR REPORT? AND TO WHOM HAS THE ARM OF THE LORD BEEN REVEALED?" ³⁹For this reason they could not believe, for Isaiah said again, ⁴⁰"^HE HAS BLINDED THEIR EYES AND HE HARDENED THEIR HEART, SO THAT THEY WILL NOT SEE WITH THEIR EYES AND UNDERSTAND WITH THEIR HEART, AND BE CONVERTED, AND *SO* I WILL *NOT* HEAL THEM." ⁴¹These things Isaiah said because ^he saw His glory, and he spoke about Him. ⁴²Nevertheless many, even of ^the rulers, believed in Him, but because of the Pharisees they were not confessing *Him,* so that they would not be ᴮexcommunicated from the synagogue; ⁴³^for they loved the approval of people rather than the approval of God.

⁴⁴Now Jesus cried out and said, "^The one who believes in Me, does not believe *only* in Me, but *also* in Him who sent Me. ⁴⁵And ^the one who sees Me sees Him who sent Me. ⁴⁶^I have come *as* Light into the world, so that no one who believes in Me will remain in darkness. ⁴⁷If anyone hears My teachings and does not keep them, I do

12:24 ^Rom 14:9; 1 Cor 15:36   12:25 ^Matt 10:39; 16:25
12:26 ^John 14:3; 17:24   12:27 ^Matt 26:38; Mark 14:34
12:28 ^Matt 3:17; 17:5   12:29 ^Acts 23:9
12:30 ^John 11:42   12:31 ^John 14:30; 16:11
12:32 ^John 3:14   ᴮJohn 6:44   12:33 ^John 18:32; 21:19
12:34 ^Ps 110:4; Is 9:7   12:35 ^1 John 1:6; 2:11
12:36 ^Luke 16:8; John 8:12   12:38 ^Is 53:1; Rom 10:16
12:40 ^Is 6:10; Matt 13:14f   12:41 ^Is 6:1ff
12:42 ^John 23:13   ᴮJohn 9:22   12:43 ^John 5:41, 44
12:44 ^Matt 10:40; John 5:24   12:45 ^John 14:9
12:46 ^John 1:4; 3:19

not judge him; for ^AI did not come to judge the world, but to save the world. ^48 ^AThe one who rejects Me and does not accept My teachings has one who judges him: ^Bthe word which I spoke. That will judge him on the last day. ^49 For I did not speak on My own, but the Father Himself who sent Me ^Ahas given Me a commandment *as to* what to say and what to speak. ^50 And I know that ^AHis commandment is eternal life; therefore the things I speak, I speak ^Bjust as the Father has told Me."

THE LORD'S SUPPER

13 Now before the Feast of ^Athe Passover, Jesus, knowing that His hour had come that He would depart from this world ^Bto the Father, having loved His own who were in the world, He loved them to the end. ^2 And during supper, ^Athe devil having already put into the heart of Judas Iscariot, *the son* of Simon, to betray Him, ^3 *Jesus,* ^Aknowing that the Father had handed all things over to Him, and that ^BHe had come forth from God and was going *back* to God, ^4 *got up from supper and *laid His outer garments *aside;* and He took a towel and ^Atied it around Himself.

JESUS WASHES THE DISCIPLES' FEET

^5 Then He *poured water into the basin, and began ^Awashing the disciples' feet and wiping them with the towel which He had tied around Himself. ^6 So He *came to Simon Peter. He *said to Him, "Lord, You are washing my feet?" ^7 Jesus answered and said to him, "What I am doing, you do not realize right now, but you will understand ^Alater." ^8 Peter *said to Him, "Never shall You wash my feet!" Jesus answered

him, "^AIf I do not wash you, you have no place with Me." ^9 Simon Peter *said to Him, "Lord, *then wash* not only my feet, but also my hands and my head!" ^10 Jesus *said to him, "He who has bathed needs only to wash his feet; otherwise he is completely clean. And ^Ayou are clean—but not all *of you.*" ^11 For ^AHe knew the one who was betraying Him; *it was* for this reason *that* He said, "Not all *of you* are clean."

^12 Then, when He had washed their feet, and ^Ataken His garments and reclined *at the table* again, He said to them, "Do you know what I have done for you? ^13 You call Me 'Teacher' and ^A'Lord'; and you are correct, for *so* I am. ^14 So if I, ^Athe Lord and the Teacher, washed your feet, you also ought to wash one another's feet. ^15 For I gave you ^Aan example, so that you also would do just as I did for you. ^16 Truly, truly I say to you, ^Aa slave is not greater than his master, nor *is* one who is sent greater than the one who sent him. ^17 If you know these things, you are ^Ablessed if you do them. ^18 I am not speaking about all of you. I know *the ones* whom I have chosen; but *this is happening* so that the Scripture may be fulfilled, '^AHE WHO EATS MY BREAD HAS LIFTED UP HIS HEEL AGAINST ME.' ^19 From now on ^AI am telling you before *it* happens, so that when it does happen, you may believe that ^BI am *He.* ^20 Truly, truly

12:47 ^AJohn 3:17; 8:15f   **12:48** ^ALuke 10:16
^BDeut 18:18f   **12:49** ^AJohn 14:31; 17:8
12:50 ^AJohn 6:68   ^BJohn 5:19; 8:28   **13:1** ^AJohn 11:55
^BJohn 13:3   **13:2** ^AJohn 6:70; 13:27   **13:3** ^AJohn 3:35
^BJohn 8:42   **13:4** ^ALuke 12:37; 17:8   **13:5** ^AGen 18:4;
19:2   **13:7** ^AJohn 13:12ff   **13:8** ^APs 51:2, 7; Ezek 36:25
13:10 ^AJohn 15:3; Eph 5:26   **13:11** ^AJohn 6:64; 13:2
13:12 ^AJohn 13:4   **13:13** ^AJohn 11:2; 1 Cor 12:3
13:14 ^AJohn 11:2; 1 Cor 12:3   **13:15** ^A1 Pet 5:3
13:16 ^AMatt 10:24; Luke 6:40   **13:17** ^AMatt 7:24ff;
Luke 11:28   **13:18** ^APs 41:9; Matt 26:21ff
13:19 ^AJohn 14:29   ^BJohn 8:24

I say to you, ^the one who receives anyone I send, receives Me; and the one who receives Me receives Him who sent Me."

JESUS PREDICTS HIS BETRAYAL

²¹When Jesus had said these things, He ^became troubled in spirit, and testified and said, "Truly, truly I say to you that one of you will betray Me." ²²The disciples *began* looking at one another, ^at a loss *to know* of which one He was speaking. ²³Lying back on Jesus' chest was one of His disciples, ^whom Jesus loved. ²⁴So Simon Peter *nodded to this *disciple* and *said to him, "Tell *us* who it is of whom He is speaking." ²⁵He then simply ^leaned back on Jesus' chest and *said to Him, "Lord, who is it?" ²⁶Jesus then *answered, "That man is the one for whom I shall dip the piece *of bread* and give it to him." So when He had dipped the piece *of bread,* He *took and *gave *it* to Judas, ^*the son* of Simon Iscariot. ²⁷After this, Satan then ^entered him. Therefore Jesus *said to him, "What you are doing, do *it* quickly." ²⁸Now none of those reclining *at the table* knew for what purpose He had said this to him. ²⁹For some were assuming, since Judas ^kept the money box, that Jesus was saying to him, "Buy the things we need for the feast"; or else, that he was to give something to the poor. ³⁰So after receiving the piece *of bread,* he left immediately; and ^it was night.

³¹Therefore when he had left, Jesus *said, "Now is the Son of Man glorified, and ^God is glorified in Him; ³²if God is glorified in Him, ^God will also glorify Him in Himself, and will glorify Him immediately. ³³Little children, I am *still* with you ^a little longer. ^BYou will

look for Me; and just as I said to the Jews, now I also say to you: 'Where I am going, you cannot come.' ³⁴I am giving you a new commandment, ^that you love one another; just as I have loved you, that you also love one another. ³⁵^By this all *people* will know that you are My disciples: if you have love for one another."

³⁶Simon Peter *said to Him, "Lord, where are You going?" Jesus answered, "^Where I am going, you cannot follow Me now; but you will follow later." ³⁷Peter *said to Him, "Lord, why can I not follow You right now? ^I will lay down my life for You." ³⁸Jesus *replied, "Will you lay down your life for Me? Truly, truly I say to you, ^a rooster will not crow until you deny Me three times.

JESUS COMFORTS HIS DISCIPLES

14 "^Do not let your heart be troubled; ¹believe in God, believe also in Me. ²In My Father's house are many rooms; if *that* were not *so,* I would have told you, because ^I am going *there* to prepare a place for you. ³And if I go and prepare a place for you, ^I am coming again and will take you to Myself, so that ^Bwhere I am, *there* you also will be. ⁴And you know the way where I am going." ⁵^Thomas *said to Him, "Lord, we do not know where You are going; how do we know the way?" ⁶Jesus *said to

13:20 ^Matt 10:40; Mark 9:37   **13:21** ^John 11:33
13:22 ^Matt 26:21ff; Mark 14:18ff   **13:23** ^John 19:26;
20:2   **13:25** ^John 21:20   **13:26** ^John 6:71
13:27 ^Luke 22:3; John 13:2   **13:29** ^John 12:6
13:30 ^Luke 22:53   **13:31** ^John 14:13; 17:4
13:32 ^John 17:1   **13:33** ^John 7:33   ^BJohn 7:34
13:34 ^Lev 19:18; Matt 5:44   **13:35** ^1 John 3:14; 4:20
13:36 ^John 13:33; 14:2   **13:37** ^*Matt 26:33-35;
Mark 14:29-31*   **13:38** ^Mark 14:30; John 18:27
14:1 ^John 14:27; 16:22, 24   **14:2** ^John 13:33, 36
14:3 ^John 14:18, 28   ^BJohn 12:26   **14:5** ^John 11:16

14:1 ¹Or *you believe in God, believe also*

him, "I am ^the way, and the truth, and the life; no one comes to the Father except through Me.

ONENESS WITH THE FATHER

7^If you had known Me, you would have known My Father also; from now on you know Him, and have seen Him."

8^Philip *said to Him, "Lord, show us the Father, and it is enough for us." **9**Jesus *said to him, "Have I been with you for so long a time, and *yet* you have not come to know Me, Philip? ^The one who has seen Me has seen the Father; how *can* you say, 'Show us the Father'? **10**Do you not believe that ^I am in the Father, and the Father is in Me? ^BThe words that I say to you I do not speak on My own, but the Father, as He remains in Me, does His works. **11**Believe Me that ^I am in the Father and the Father is in Me; otherwise ^Bbelieve because of the works themselves. **12**Truly, truly I say to you, the one who believes in Me, the works that I do, he will do also; and ^greater *works* than these he will do; because I am going to the Father. **13**And ^whatever you ask in My name, this I will do, so that the Father may be glorified in the Son. **14**If you ask Me anything ^in My name, I will do *it.*

15^"If you love Me, you will keep My commandments.

THE HOLY SPIRIT

16I will ask the Father, and He will give you another ^Helper, so that He may be with you forever; **17***the Helper is*^the Spirit of truth, whom the world cannot receive, because it does not see Him or know *Him; but* you know Him because He remains with you and will be in you.

18"I will not leave you as orphans; ^I am coming to you. **19**After a little while, ^the world no longer *is going to* see Me, but you *are going to* see Me; ^Bbecause I live, you also will live. **20**On that day you will know that ^I *am* in My Father, and you *are* in Me, and I in you. **21**^The one who has My commandments and keeps them is the one who loves Me; and the one who loves Me will be loved by My Father, and I will love him and will reveal Myself to him." **22**Judas (not Iscariot) *said to Him, "Lord, what has happened ^that You are going to reveal Yourself to us and not to the world?" **23**Jesus answered and said to him, "If anyone loves Me, he will ^follow My word; and My Father will love him, and We will come to him and make *Our* dwelling with him. **24**The one who does not love Me does not follow My words; and ^the word which you hear is not Mine, but the Father's who sent Me.

25"These things I have spoken to you while remaining with you. **26**But the Helper, the Holy Spirit whom the Father will send in My name, ^He will teach you all things, and remind you of all that I said to you. **27**^Peace I leave you, My peace I give you; not as the world gives, do I give to you. Do not let your hearts be troubled, nor fearful. **28**You heard that I said to you, 'I am going away, and I am coming

14:6^John 10:9; Rom 5:2   14:7^John 8:19
14:8^John 1:43   14:9^John 1:14; 12:45
14:10^John 10:38   ^BJohn 5:19   14:11^John 10:38
^BJohn 5:36   14:12^John 5:20   14:13^Matt 7:7
14:14^John 15:16; 16:23f   14:15^John 14:21, 23; 15:10
14:16^John 7:39; 14:26   14:17^John 15:26; 16:13
14:18^John 14:3, 28   14:19^John 16:16, 22   ^BJohn 6:57
14:20^John 10:38; 14:11   14:21^John 14:15, 23; 15:10
14:22^Acts 10:40, 41   14:23^John 8:51; 1 John 2:5
14:24^John 7:16; 14:10   14:26^John 16:13f;
1 John 2:20, 27   14:27^John 16:33; 20:19

to you.' If you loved Me, you would have rejoiced because I am going to the Father, for ^the Father is greater than I. ²⁹And now ^I have told you before it happens, so that when it happens, you may believe. ³⁰I will not speak much more with you, for ^the ruler of the world is coming, and he has ¹nothing in *regard to* Me, ³¹but so that the world may know that I love the Father, I do exactly as ^the Father commanded Me. Get up, let's go from here.

JESUS IS THE VINE—FOLLOWERS ARE BRANCHES

15 "^I am the true vine, and My Father is the vinedresser. ²Every branch in Me that does not bear fruit, He takes away; and every *branch* that bears fruit, He prunes it so that it may bear more fruit. ³^You are already clean because of the word which I have spoken to you. ⁴^Remain in Me, and I in you. Just as the branch cannot bear fruit of itself but must remain in the vine, so neither *can* you unless you remain in Me. ⁵I am the vine, you are the branches; the one who remains in Me, and I in him ^bears much fruit, for apart from Me you can do nothing. ⁶If anyone does not remain in Me, he is ^thrown away like a branch and dries up; and they gather them and throw them into the fire, and they are burned. ⁷If you remain in Me, and My words remain in you, ^ask whatever you wish, and it will be done for you. ⁸My ^Father is glorified by this, that you bear much fruit, and *so* ᴮprove to be My disciples. ⁹Just as ^the Father has loved Me, I also have loved you; remain in My love. ¹⁰If you keep My commandments, you will remain in My

love; just as ^I have kept My Father's commandments and remain in His love. ¹¹These things I have spoken to you so that My joy may be in you, and *that* your ^joy may be made full.

DISCIPLES' RELATION TO EACH OTHER

¹²"This is ^My commandment, that you love one another, just as I have loved you. ¹³Greater love has no one than this, that a person will ^lay down his life for his friends. ¹⁴You are My friends if ^you do what I command you. ¹⁵No longer do I call you slaves, for the slave does not know what his master is doing; but I have called you friends, because ^all things that I have heard from My Father I have made known to you. ¹⁶^You did not choose Me but I chose you, and appointed you that you would go and bear fruit, and *that* your fruit would remain, so that whatever you ask of the Father in My name He may give to you. ¹⁷This ^I command you, that you love one another.

DISCIPLES' RELATION TO THE WORLD

¹⁸"^If the world hates you, you know that it has hated Me before *it hated* you. ¹⁹If you were of the world, the world would love *you as* its own; but because you are not of the world, but I chose you out of the world, ^because of this the world hates

14:28^John 10:29; Phil 2:6   **14:29**^John 13:19
14:30^John 12:31   **14:31**^John 10:18; 12:49
15:1^Ps 80:8ff; Is 5:1ff   **15:3**^John 13:10; 17:17
15:4^John 6:56; 15:4-7   **15:5**^John 15:16
15:6^John 15:2   **15:7**^Matt 7:7; John 15:16
15:8^Matt 5:16   ᴮJohn 8:31
15:9^John 3:35; 17:23, 24, 26   **15:10**^John 8:29
15:11^John 3:29   **15:12**^John 13:34; 15:17
15:13^John 10:11   **15:14**^Matt 12:50   **15:15**^John 8:26;
16:12   **15:16**^John 6:70; 13:18   **15:17**^John 15:12
15:18^John 7:7; 1 John 3:13   **15:19**^Matt 10:22; 24:9

14:30 ¹I.e., no grounds for any accusation

you. **20** Remember the word that I said to you, 'A slave is not greater than his master.' If they persecuted Me, ^they will persecute you as well; if they followed My word, they will follow yours also. **21** But all these things they will do to you on account of My name, ^because they do not know the One who sent Me. **22** ^If I had not come and spoken to them, they would not have sin; but now they have no excuse for their sin. **23** The one who hates Me hates My Father also. **24** ^If I had not done among them the works which no one else did, they would not have sin; but now they have both seen and hated Me and My Father as well. **25** But *this has happened* so that the word that is written in their ^Law will be fulfilled: '^BTHEY HATED ME FOR NO REASON.'

26 "When the ^Helper comes, whom I will send to you from the Father, *namely,* the Spirit of truth who comes from the Father, He will testify about Me, **27** and ^you are testifying as well, because you have been with Me from the beginning.

JESUS' WARNING

16 "^These things I have spoken to you so that you will not be led into sin. **2** They will ^ban you from the synagogue, yet an hour is coming for everyone who kills you to think that he is offering a service to God. **3** These things they will do ^because they have not known the Father nor Me. **4** But these things I have spoken to you, ^so that when their hour comes, you may remember that I told you of them. However, I did not say these things to you at the beginning, because I was with you.

THE HOLY SPIRIT PROMISED

5 "But now ^I am going to Him who sent Me; and none of you asks Me, 'Where are You going?' **6** But because I have said these things to you, ^grief has filled your heart. **7** But I tell you the truth: it is to your advantage that I am leaving; for if I do not leave, the ^Helper will not come to you; but if I go, ^BI will send Him to you. **8** And He, when He comes, will convict the world regarding sin, and righteousness, and judgment: **9** regarding sin, ^because they do not believe in Me; **10** and regarding ^righteousness, because I am going to the Father and you no longer *are going to* see Me; **11** ^and regarding judgment, because the ruler of this world has been judged.

12 "I have many more things to say to you, but you cannot bear *them* at the present time. **13** But when He, ^the Spirit of truth, comes, He will ^Bguide you into all the truth; for He will not speak on His own, but whatever He hears, He will speak; and He will disclose to you what is to come. **14** He will ^glorify Me, for He will take from Mine and will disclose *it* to you. **15** ^All things that the Father has are Mine; this is why I said that He takes from Mine and will disclose *it* to you.

JESUS' DEATH AND RESURRECTION FORETOLD

16 "A little while, and ^you no longer *are going to* see Me; and again

15:20 ^1 Cor 4:12; 2 Cor 4:9   15:21 ^John 8:19, 55; 16:3
15:22 ^John 9:41; 15:24   15:24 ^John 9:41; 15:22
15:25 ^John 10:34   ^B Ps 35:19   15:26 ^John 14:16
15:27 ^Luke 24:48; John 21:24   16:1 ^John 15:18-27
16:2 ^John 9:22   16:3 ^John 8:19, 55; 15:21
16:4 ^John 13:19   16:5 ^John 7:33; 16:10, 17, 28
16:6 ^John 14:1; 16:22   16:7 ^John 14:16   ^B John 14:26
16:9 ^John 15:22, 24   16:10 ^Acts 3:14; 7:52
16:11 ^John 12:31   16:13 ^John 14:17   ^B John 14:26
16:14 ^John 7:39   16:15 ^John 17:10
16:16 ^John 14:18-24; 16:16-24

a little while, and you will see Me."
¹⁷So some of His disciples said to one another, "What is this that He is telling us, 'A little while, and you are not *going to* see Me; and again a little while, and you will see Me'; and, 'because ᴬI am going to the Father'?" ¹⁸So they were saying, "What is this that He says, 'A little while'? We do not know what He is talking *about*." ¹⁹ᴬJesus knew that they wanted to question Him, and He said to them, "Are you deliberating together about this, that I said, 'A little while, and you are not *going to* see Me, and again a little while, and you will see Me'? ²⁰Truly, truly I say to you that ᴬyou will weep and mourn, but the world will rejoice; you will grieve, but ᴮyour grief will be turned into joy! ²¹ᴬWhenever a woman is in labor she has pain, because her hour has come; but when she gives birth to the child, she no longer remembers the anguish because of the joy that a child has been born into the world. ²²Therefore ᴬyou too have grief now; but ᴮI will see you again, and your heart will rejoice, and no one *is going to* take your joy away from you.

PRAYER PROMISES

²³And on that day ᴬyou will not question Me about anything. Truly, truly I say to you, ᴮif you ask the Father for anything in My name, He will give it to you. ²⁴ᴬUntil now you have asked for nothing in My name; ask and you will receive, so that your joy may be made full.
²⁵"These things I have spoken to you in ᴬfigures of speech; an hour is coming when I will no longer speak to you in figures of speech, but will tell you plainly about the Father. ²⁶On that day ᴬyou will ask in My name, and I am not saying to you that I will request of the Father on your behalf; ²⁷for ᴬthe Father Himself loves you, because you have loved Me and have believed that ᴮI came forth from the Father. ²⁸I came forth from the Father and have come into the world; again, I am leaving the world and ᴬgoing to the Father."

²⁹His disciples *said, "See, now You are speaking plainly and are not using any ᴬfigure of speech. ³⁰Now we know that You know all things, and *that* You have no need for anyone to question You; this is why we ᴬbelieve that You came forth from God." ³¹Jesus replied to them, "Do you now believe? ³²Behold, an hour is coming, and has *already* come, for ᴬyou to be scattered, each to his own *home*, and to leave Me alone; and *yet* ᴮI am not alone, because the Father is with Me. ³³These things I have spoken to you so that ᴬin Me you may have peace. In the world you have tribulation, but take courage; ᴮI have overcome the world."

THE HIGH PRIESTLY PRAYER

17 Jesus spoke these things; and ᴬraising His eyes to heaven, He said, "Father, the hour has come; ᴮglorify Your Son, so that the Son may glorify You, ²just as ᴬYou gave Him authority over all mankind, so that ᴮto all whom You have given Him, He may give eternal life. ³And

16:17ᴬJohn 16:5   **16:19**ᴬMark 9:32; John 6:61
16:20ᴬLuke 23:27   ᴮJohn 20:20   **16:21**ᴬIs 13:8; 21:3
16:22ᴬJohn 16:6   ᴮJohn 16:16   **16:23**ᴬJohn 16:19, 30
ᴮJohn 15:16   **16:24**ᴬJohn 14:14   **16:25**ᴬMatt 13:34;
John 10:6   **16:26**ᴬJohn 16:19, 30
16:27ᴬJohn 14:21, 23   ᴮJohn 8:42   **16:28**ᴬJohn 13:1, 3;
16:5, 10, 17   **16:29**ᴬMatt 13:34; John 10:6
16:30ᴬJohn 2:11; 16:27   **16:32**ᴬZech 13:7   ᴮJohn 8:29
16:33ᴬJohn 14:27   ᴮRom 8:37   **17:1**ᴬJohn 11:41
ᴮJohn 13:31f   **17:2**ᴬJohn 3:35   ᴮJohn 10:28

this is eternal life, that they may know You, ^the only true God, and Jesus Christ whom You have sent. **4**^I glorified You on the earth ^Bby accomplishing the work which You have given Me to do. **5** And now You, Father, glorify Me together with Yourself, with the glory which I had ^with You before the world existed.

6 "I have revealed Your name to the men whom ^You gave Me out of the world; they were Yours and You gave them to Me, and they have followed Your word. **7** Now they have come to know that everything which You have given Me is from You; **8** for ^the words which You gave Me I have given to them; and they received *them* and truly understood that ^BI came forth from You, and they believed that You sent Me. **9** ^I ask on their behalf; ^BI do not ask on behalf of the world, but on the behalf of those whom You have given Me, because they are Yours; **10** and ^all things that are Mine are Yours, and Yours are Mine; and I have been glorified in them. **11** I am no longer *going to be* in the world; and *yet* they themselves are in the world, and I am coming to You. Holy Father, keep them in Your name, *the name* ^which You have given Me, so that ^Bthey may be one just as We *are*. **12** While I was with them, I was keeping them in Your name, which You have given Me; and I guarded them, and not one of them perished except ^the son of destruction, so that the ^BScripture would be fulfilled.

THE DISCIPLES IN THE WORLD

13 But now ^I am coming to You; and ^Bthese things I speak in the world so that they may have My joy made full in themselves. **14** I have given

them Your word; and ^the world has hated them because they are not of the world, just as I am not of the world. **15** I am not asking You to take them out of the world, but to keep them away from ^the evil one. **16** ^They are not of the world, just as I am not of the world. **17** ^Sanctify them in the truth; Your word is truth. **18** Just as You sent Me into the world, ^I also sent them into the world. **19** And for their sakes I sanctify Myself, so that they themselves also may be ^sanctified in truth.

20 "I am not asking on behalf of these alone, but also for those who believe in Me through their word, **21** that they may all be one; ^just as You, Father, *are* in Me and I in You, that they also may be in Us, so that the world may believe that You sent Me.

DISCIPLES' FUTURE GLORY

22 The ^glory which You have given Me I also have given to them, so that they may be one, just as We are one; **23** ^I in them and You in Me, that they may be perfected in unity, so that the world may know that You sent Me, and You ^Bloved them, just as You loved Me. **24** Father, I desire that they also, whom You have given Me, be with Me where I am, so that they may see My glory which You have given Me, for You loved Me before ^the foundation of the world.

17:3^John 5:44   **17:4**^John 13:31   ^BJohn 4:34
17:5^John 1:1; 8:58   **17:6**^John 6:37, 39; 17:2, 9, 24
17:8^John 12:49   ^BJohn 8:42   **17:9**^Luke 22:32
^BJohn 17:20f   **17:10**^John 16:15   **17:11**^Phil 2:9
^BJohn 17:21f;   **17:12**^John 6:70   ^BJohn 13:18
17:13^John 7:33   ^BJohn 15:11   **17:14**^John 15:19
17:15^Matt 5:37   **17:16**^John 17:14   **17:17**^John 15:3
17:18^Matt 10:5; John 4:38   **17:19**^John 15:3
17:21^John 10:38; 17:11, 23   **17:22**^John 1:14; 17:24
17:23^John 10:38   ^BJohn 16:27   **17:24**^Matt 25:34;
John 17:5

25 "^Righteous Father, although the world has not known You, yet I have known You; and these have known that You sent Me; 26 and ^I have made Your name known to them, and will make it known, so that ^Bthe love with which You loved Me may be in them, and I in them."

JUDAS BETRAYS JESUS

18 When Jesus had spoken these words, He went away with His disciples across the ravine of the Kidron, where there was ^a garden which He entered with His disciples. 2 Now Judas, who was betraying Him, also knew the place, because Jesus had ^often met there with His disciples. 3 ^So Judas, having obtained the *Roman* ¹cohort and officers from the chief priests and the Pharisees, *came there with lanterns, torches, and weapons. 4 Jesus therefore, ^knowing all the things that were coming upon Him, came out *into the open* and *said to them, "Whom are you seeking?" 5 They answered Him, "Jesus the Nazarene." He *said to them, "I am *He*." And Judas also, who was betraying Him, was standing with them. 6 Now then, when He said to them, "I am *He*," they drew back and fell to the ground. 7 He then asked them again, "^Whom are you seeking?" And they said, "Jesus the Nazarene." 8 Jesus answered, "I told you that I am *He*; so if you are seeking Me, let these *men* go on their way." 9 *This took place* so that the word which He spoke would be fulfilled: "^Of those whom You have given Me I lost not one." 10 Then Simon Peter, ^since he had a sword, drew it and struck the high priest's slave, and cut off his right ear; and the slave's name was Malchus. 11 So Jesus said to Peter, "Put the sword into the sheath; ^the cup which the Father has given Me, am I not to drink it?"

JESUS BEFORE THE PRIESTS

12 ^So the *Roman* ¹cohort, the commander, and the officers of the Jews arrested Jesus and bound Him, 13 and brought Him to Annas first; for he was the father-in-law of ^Caiaphas, who was high priest that year. 14 Now Caiaphas was the one who had advised the Jews that ^it was in their best interest for one man to die in behalf of the people.

15 ^Simon Peter was following Jesus, and *so was* another disciple. Now that disciple was known to the high priest, and he entered with Jesus into the courtyard of the high priest, 16 ^but Peter was standing at the door outside. So the other disciple, who was known to the high priest, went out and spoke to the doorkeeper, and brought Peter in. 17 Then the slave woman who was the doorkeeper *said to Peter, "^You are not also *one* of this Man's disciples, are you?" He *said, "I am not." 18 Now the slaves and the officers were standing *there*, having made a charcoal fire, for it was cold and they were ^warming themselves; and Peter was also with them, standing and warming himself.

19 ^The high priest then questioned Jesus about His disciples,

17:25 ^John 17:11; 1 John 1:9   17:26 ^John 17:6
^B John 15:9   18:1 ^Matt 26:36; Mark 14:32
18:2 ^Luke 21:37; 22:39   18:3 ^Matt 26:47-56;
Mark 14:43-50   18:4 ^John 6:64; 13:1, 11
18:7 ^John 18:4   18:9 ^John 17:12   18:10 ^Matt 26:51;
Mark 14:47   18:11 ^Matt 20:22; 26:39
18:12 ^Matt 26:57ff   18:13 ^Matt 26:3; John 11:49, 51
18:14 ^John 11:50   18:15 ^Matt 26:58; Mark 14:54
18:16 ^Matt 26:69f; Mark 14:66-68   18:17 ^John 18:25
18:18 ^Mark 14:54, 67   18:19 ^Matt 26:59-68;
Mark 14:55-65

18:3 ¹Normally 600 men (the number varied)
18:12 ¹Normally 600 men (the number varied)

and about His teaching. ²⁰Jesus answered him, "I ^have spoken openly to the world; I always taught in synagogues and in the temple *area,* where all the Jews congregate; and I said nothing in secret. ²¹Why are you asking Me? Ask those who have heard what I spoke to them. Look: these people know what I said." ²²But when He said this, one of the ^officers, who was standing nearby, ᴮstruck Jesus, saying, "Is that the way You answer the high priest?" ²³^Jesus answered him, "If I have spoken wrongly, testify of the wrong; but if rightly, why do you strike Me?" ²⁴^So Annas sent Him bound to Caiaphas the high priest.

PETER'S DENIAL OF JESUS

²⁵^Now Simon Peter was *still* standing and warming himself. So they said to him, "You are not *one* of His disciples as well, are you?" He denied *it,* and said, "I am not." ²⁶One of the slaves of the high priest, who was related to the one ^whose ear Peter cut off, *said, "Did I not see you in ᴮthe garden with Him?" ²⁷Peter then denied *it* again, and immediately ^a rooster crowed.

JESUS BEFORE PILATE

²⁸^Then they *brought Jesus from Caiaphas into the ¹Praetorium, and it was early; and they themselves did not enter the Praetorium, so that they would not be defiled, but might eat the Passover. ²⁹^Therefore Pilate came out to them and *said, "What accusation are you bringing against this Man?" ³⁰They answered and said to him, "If this Man were not a criminal, we would not have handed Him over to you." ³¹So Pilate said to them, "Take Him yourselves, and judge Him

according to your law." The Jews said to him, "We are not ¹permitted to put anyone to death." ³² *This happened* so that ^the word of Jesus which He said, indicating what kind of death He was going to die, would be fulfilled.

³³Therefore Pilate entered the Praetorium again, and summoned Jesus and said to Him, "^You are the King of the Jews?" ³⁴Jesus answered, "Are you saying this on your own, or did others tell you about Me?" ³⁵Pilate answered, "I am not a Jew, am I? Your own nation and the chief priests handed You over to me; what have You done?" ³⁶Jesus answered, "^My kingdom is not of this world. If My kingdom were of this world, My servants would be fighting so that I would not be handed over to the Jews; but as it is, My kingdom is not of this realm." ³⁷Therefore Pilate said to Him, "So You are a king?" Jesus answered, "^You say *correctly* that I am a king. For this *purpose* I have been born, and for this I have come into the world: to testify to the truth. Everyone who is of the truth listens to My voice." ³⁸Pilate *said to Him, "What is truth?"

And after saying this, he came out again to the Jews and *said to them, "^I find no grounds at all for charges in His case. ³⁹^However, you have a custom that I release one *prisoner* for you at the Passover; therefore do you wish that I release for you

18:20^John 7:26; 8:26   **18:22**^John 18:3   ᴮJohn 19:3
18:23^Matt 5:39; Acts 23:2-5   **18:24**^John 18:13
18:25^Matt 26:71-75; Mark 14:69-72   **18:26**^John 18:10
ᴮJohn 18:1   **18:27**^John 13:38   **18:28**^Matt 27:2;
Mark 15:1   **18:29**^Matt 27:11-14; Mark 15:2-5
18:32^Matt 20:19; 26:2   **18:33**^Luke 23:3; John 19:12
18:36^Matt 26:53; Luke 17:21   **18:37**^Matt 27:11;
Mark 15:2   **18:38**^Luke 23:4; John 19:4, 6
18:39^Matt 27:15-26; Mark 15:6-15

18:28¹I.e., governor's official residence
18:31¹I.e., under Roman law

the King of the Jews?" ⁴⁰So they shouted again, saying, "ᴬNot this Man, but Barabbas." Now Barabbas was a rebel.

THE CROWN OF THORNS

19 So Pilate then took Jesus and ᴬhad Him flogged. ²And the soldiers twisted together a crown of thorns and placed it on His head, and put a purple cloak on Him; ³and they *repeatedly* came up to Him and said, "Hail, King of the Jews!" and ᴬslapped Him in the face *again and again.* ⁴And *then* Pilate came out again and *said to them, "See, I am bringing Him out to you so that you will know that ᴬI find no grounds at all for charges in His case." ⁵Jesus then came out, ᴬwearing the crown of thorns and the purple robe. And *Pilate* *said to them, "Behold, the Man!" ⁶So when the chief priests and the officers saw Him, they shouted, saying, "Crucify, crucify!" Pilate *said to them, "Take Him yourselves and crucify *Him;* for ᴬI find no grounds for charges in His case!" ⁷The Jews answered him, "ᴬWe have a law, and by that law He ought to die, because He made Himself *out to be* the Son of God!"

⁸Therefore when Pilate heard this statement, he was *even* more afraid; ⁹and he entered the ¹Praetorium again and *said to Jesus, "Where are You from?" But ᴬJesus gave him no answer. ¹⁰So Pilate *said to Him, "Are you not speaking to me? Do You not know that I have authority to release You, and I have authority to crucify You?" ¹¹Jesus answered him, "ᴬYou would have no authority over Me at all, if it had not been given to you from above; for this reason the one who handed Me over to you has *the* greater sin."

¹²As a result of this, Pilate made efforts to release Him; but the Jews shouted, saying, "ᴬIf you release this Man, you are not a friend of Caesar; everyone who makes himself *out to be* a king opposes Caesar!"

¹³Therefore when Pilate heard these words, he brought Jesus out, and ᴬsat down on the judgment seat at a place called The Pavement— but in Hebrew, Gabbatha. ¹⁴Now it was ᴬthe day of preparation for the Passover; it was about the ¹sixth hour. And he *said to the Jews, "Look, your King!" ¹⁵So they shouted, "ᴬAway with *Him,* away with *Him,* crucify Him!" Pilate *said to them, "Shall I crucify your King?" The chief priests answered, "We have no king except Caesar."

THE CRUCIFIXION

¹⁶So he then ᴬhanded Him over to them to be crucified.

¹⁷ᴬThey took Jesus, therefore, and He went out, carrying His own cross, to the *place* called the Place of a Skull, which in Hebrew is called, Golgotha. ¹⁸There they crucified Him, and with Him ᴬtwo other men, one on either side, and Jesus in between. ¹⁹Now Pilate also wrote an inscription and put it on the cross. It was written: "ᴬJESUS THE NAZARENE, THE KING OF THE JEWS." ²⁰Therefore many of the Jews read this inscription, because the place

18:40ᴬActs 3:14　19:1ᴬMatt 27:26　19:2ᴬMark 15:16-19
19:3ᴬIs 50:6; John 18:22　19:4ᴬLuke 23:4; John 18:38
19:5ᴬJohn 19:2　19:6ᴬLuke 23:4; John 18:38
19:7ᴬLev 24:16; Matt 26:63-66　19:9ᴬMatt 26:63;
27:12, 14　19:11ᴬRom 13:1　19:12ᴬLuke 23:2;
John 18:33ff　19:13ᴬMatt 27:19　19:14ᴬMatt 27:62;
John 19:31, 42　19:15ᴬLuke 23:18　19:16ᴬMatt 27:26;
Mark 15:15　19:17ᴬ*Matt 27:33-44; Mark 15:22-32*
19:18ᴬLuke 23:32　19:19ᴬMatt 27:37; Mark 15:26
─────────────────────
19:9 ¹I.e., governor's official residence
19:14 ¹I.e., about noon

where Jesus was crucified was near the city; and it was written ^in Hebrew, Latin, *and* in Greek. ²¹So the chief priests of the Jews were saying to Pilate, "Do not write, '^The King of the Jews'; rather, *write* that He said, 'I am ^King of the Jews.'" ²²Pilate answered, "^What I have written, I have written."

²³Then ^the soldiers, when they had crucified Jesus, took His outer garments and made four parts: a part to each soldier, and the 'tunic *also;* but the tunic was seamless, woven in one piece. ²⁴So they said to one another, "Let's not tear it, but cast lots for it, *to decide* whose it shall be." *This happened* so that the Scripture would be fulfilled: "THEY ^DIVIDED MY GARMENTS AMONG THEMSELVES, AND THEY CAST LOTS FOR MY CLOTHING." Therefore the soldiers did these things.

²⁵^Now beside the cross of Jesus stood His mother, His mother's sister, Mary the *wife* of Clopas, and Mary Magdalene. ²⁶So when Jesus saw His mother, and ^the disciple whom He loved standing nearby, He *said to His mother, "Woman, behold, your son!" ²⁷Then He *said to the disciple, "Behold, your mother!" And from that hour the disciple took her into ^his own *household.*

²⁸After this, Jesus, knowing that all things had already been accomplished, in order that the Scripture would be fulfilled, *said, "^I am thirsty." ²⁹A jar full of sour wine was standing *there;* so ^they put a sponge full of the sour wine on *a branch of* hyssop and brought it *up* to His mouth. ³⁰Therefore when Jesus had received the sour wine, He said, "It is finished!" And He bowed His head and ^gave up His spirit.

CARE OF THE BODY OF JESUS

³¹Now then, since it was the day of preparation, to prevent ^the bodies from remaining on the cross on the Sabbath (for that Sabbath was a high day), the Jews requested of Pilate that their legs be broken, and *the bodies* be taken away. ³²So the soldiers came and broke the legs of the first man, and of the other who was ^crucified with Him; ³³but after they came to Jesus, when they saw that He was already dead, they did not break His legs. ³⁴Yet one of the soldiers pierced His side with a spear, and immediately ^blood and water came out. ³⁵And he who has seen has ^testified, and his testimony is true; and he knows that he is telling the truth, so that you also may believe. ³⁶For these things took place so that the Scripture would be fulfilled: "^NOT A BONE OF HIM SHALL BE BROKEN." ³⁷And again another Scripture says, "^THEY WILL LOOK AT HIM WHOM THEY PIERCED."

³⁸Now ^after these things Joseph of Arimathea, being a disciple of Jesus, but a secret *one* for fear of the 'Jews, requested of Pilate that he might take away the body of Jesus; and Pilate granted permission. So he came and took away His body. ³⁹^Nicodemus, who had first come to Him by night, also came, bringing a mixture of myrrh and aloes, about a 'hundred litras *weight.*

19:20^John 19:13   **19:21**^John 19:14, 19
19:22^Gen 43:14; Esth 4:16   **19:23**^Matt 27:35;
Mark 15:24   **19:24**^Ps 22:18   **19:25**^Matt 27:55f;
Mark 15:40f   **19:26**^John 13:23   **19:27**^Luke 18:28;
John 1:11   **19:28**^Ps 69:21   *Matt 27:48, 50;
Mark 15:36f*   **19:30**^Matt 27:50; Mark 15:37
19:31^Deut 21:23; Josh 8:29   **19:32**^John 19:18
19:34^1 John 5:6, 8   **19:35**^John 15:27; 21:24
19:36^Ex 12:46; Num 9:12   **19:37**^Zech 12:10; Rev 1:7
19:38^*Matt 27:57-61; Mark 15:42-47*   **19:39**^John 3:1

19:23¹A long shirt worn next to the skin   **19:38**¹I.e.,
the Jewish leaders   **19:39**¹I.e., Roman *libras* (about
75 lb. or 34 kg)

⁴⁰So they took the body of Jesus and ^bound it in ᴮlinen wrappings with the spices, as is the burial custom of the Jews. ⁴¹Now in the place where He was crucified there was a garden, and in the garden *was* a ^new tomb ᴮin which no one had yet been laid. ⁴²Therefore because of the Jewish day of ^preparation, since the tomb was nearby, they laid Jesus there.

THE EMPTY TOMB

20 ^Now on the first *day* of the week Mary Magdalene *came early to the tomb, while it was still dark, and *saw the stone *already* removed from the tomb. ²So she *ran and *came to Simon Peter and to the other ^disciple whom Jesus loved, and *said to them, "ᴮThey have taken the Lord from the tomb, and we do not know where they have put Him." ³^So Peter and the other disciple left, and they were going to the tomb. ⁴The two were running together; and the other disciple ran ahead, faster than Peter, and came to the tomb first; ⁵and he stooped to look *in,* and *saw the ^linen wrappings lying *there;* however he did not go in. ⁶So Simon Peter also *came, following him, and he entered the tomb; and he *looked at the linen wrappings lying *there,* ⁷and ^the face-cloth which had been on His head, not lying with the linen wrappings but folded up in a place by itself. ⁸So the other disciple who ^had first come to the tomb also entered then, and he saw and believed. ⁹For ^they did not yet understand the Scripture, that He must rise from the dead. ¹⁰So the disciples went away again ^to their own *homes.*

¹¹^But Mary was standing outside the tomb, weeping; so as she wept, she stooped to look into the tomb; ¹²and she *saw ^two angels in white sitting, one at the head and one at the feet, where the body of Jesus had been lying. ¹³And they *said to her, "^Woman, why are you weeping?" She *said to them, "Because ᴮthey have taken away my Lord, and I do not know where they put Him." ¹⁴When she had said this, she turned around and *^saw Jesus standing *there,* and *yet* she ᴮdid not know that it was Jesus. ¹⁵Jesus *said to her, "^Woman, why are you weeping? Whom are you seeking?" Thinking that He was the gardener, she *said to Him, "Sir, if you have carried Him away, tell me where you put Him, and I will take Him away." ¹⁶Jesus *said to her, "Mary!" She turned and *said to Him in Hebrew, "^Rabboni!" (which means, Teacher). ¹⁷Jesus *said to her, "Stop clinging to Me, for I have not yet ascended to the Father; but go to ^My brothers and say to them, 'I am ᴮascending to My Father and your Father, and My God and your God.'" ¹⁸Mary Magdalene *came and ^announced to the disciples, "I have seen the Lord," and *that* He had said these things to her.

JESUS AMONG HIS DISCIPLES

¹⁹Now when it was evening on that day, the first *day* of the week, and when the doors were shut where the

19:40 ^John 11:44   ᴮLuke 24:12   19:41 ^Matt 27:60
ᴮLuke 23:53   19:42 ^John 19:14, 31   20:1 ^*Matt 28:1-8;
Mark 16:1-8*   20:2 ^John 13:23   ᴮJohn 20:13
20:3 ^Luke 24:12; John 20:3-10   20:5 ^John 19:40
20:7 ^John 11:44   20:8 ^John 20:4   20:9 ^Matt 22:29;
John 2:22   20:10 ^Luke 24:12   20:11 ^Mark 16:5
20:12 ^Matt 28:2f; Mark 16:5   20:13 ^John 20:15
ᴮJohn 20:2   20:14 ^Matt 28:9   ᴮJohn 21:4
20:15 ^John 20:13   20:16 ^Mark 10:51
20:17 ^Matt 28:10   ᴮJohn 7:33   20:18 ^Luke 24:10, 23

disciples were *together* due to fear of the ¹Jews, Jesus came and stood in their midst, and *said to them, "^Peace *be* to you." ²⁰And when He had said this, ^He showed them both His hands and His side. The disciples then rejoiced when they saw the Lord. ²¹So Jesus said to them again, "Peace *be* to you; ^just as the Father has sent Me, I also send you." ²²And when He had said this, He breathed on them and *said to them, "Receive the Holy Spirit. ²³^If you forgive the sins of any, *their sins* have been forgiven them; if you retain the *sins* of any, they have been retained."

²⁴But ^Thomas, one of the twelve, who was called ^Didymus, was not with them when Jesus came. ²⁵So the other disciples were saying to him, "We have seen the Lord!" But he said to them, "Unless I see in ^His hands the imprint of the nails, and put my finger into the place of the nails, and put my hand into His side, I will not believe."

²⁶Eight days later His disciples were again inside, and Thomas *was* with them. Jesus *came, the doors having been shut, and stood in their midst and said, "^Peace *be* to you." ²⁷Then He *said to Thomas, "^Place your finger here, and see My hands; and take your hand and put it into My side; and do not continue in disbelief, but *be* a believer." ²⁸Thomas answered and said to Him, "My Lord and my God!" ²⁹Jesus *said to him, "Because you have seen Me, have you *now* believed? ^Blessed *are* they who did not see, and *yet* believed."

WHY THIS GOSPEL WAS WRITTEN

³⁰^So then, many other signs Jesus also performed in the presence of the disciples, which are not written in this book; ³¹but these have been written so that you may believe that Jesus is the Christ, the Son of God; and that by ^believing you may have life in His name.

JESUS APPEARS
AT THE SEA OF GALILEE

21 After these things Jesus revealed Himself again to the disciples at the ^Sea of Tiberias, and He revealed *Himself* in this way: ²Simon Peter, Thomas who was called Didymus, Nathanael of Cana in Galilee, ^the *sons* of Zebedee, and two others of His disciples were together. ³Simon Peter *said to them, "I am going fishing." They *said to him, "We are also coming with you." They went out and got into the boat; and ^that night they caught nothing.

⁴But when the day was now breaking, Jesus stood on the beach; yet the disciples did not ^know that it was Jesus. ⁵So Jesus *said to them, "Children, ^you do not have any fish to eat, do you?" They answered Him, "No." ⁶And He said to them, "^Cast the net on the right-hand side of the boat, and you will find *the fish*." So they cast *it,* and then they were not able to haul it in because of the great quantity of fish. ⁷^Therefore that disciple whom Jesus loved *said to Peter, "It is the Lord!" So when Simon Peter heard that it was the Lord, he put on his outer garment (for he was stripped *for work),* and threw

20:19^Luke 24:36; John 14:27　**20:20**^Luke 24:39, 40; John 19:34　**20:21**^John 17:18　**20:23**^Matt 16:19; 18:18　**20:24**^John 11:16　**20:25**^John 20:20
20:26^Luke 24:36; John 14:27　**20:27**^Luke 24:40; John 20:25　**20:29**^1 Pet 1:8　**20:30**^John 21:25
20:31^John 3:15　**21:1**^John 6:1　**21:2**^Matt 4:21; Mark 1:19　**21:3**^Luke 5:5　**21:4**^Luke 24:16; John 20:14　**21:5**^Luke 24:41　**21:6**^Luke 5:4ff
21:7^John 13:23; 21:20

20:19 ¹I.e., the Jewish leaders

himself into the sea. ⁸But the other disciples came in the little boat, for they were not far from the land, but about ¹two hundred cubits away, dragging the net *full* of fish.

⁹So when they got out on the land, they *saw a charcoal ^fire *already* made and fish placed on it, and bread. ¹⁰Jesus *said to them, "Bring some of the ^fish which you have now caught." ¹¹So Simon Peter went up and hauled the net to land, full of large fish, 153; and although there were so many, the net was not torn.

JESUS PROVIDES

¹²Jesus *said to them, "Come *and* have ^breakfast." None of the disciples ventured to inquire of Him, "Who are You?" knowing that it was the Lord. ¹³Jesus *came and *took ^the bread and *gave *it* to them, and the fish likewise. ¹⁴This was now the ^third time that Jesus revealed Himself to the disciples, after He was raised from the dead.

THE LOVE QUESTION

¹⁵Now when they had finished breakfast, Jesus *said to Simon Peter, "Simon, *son* of John, do you ^love Me more than these?" He *said to Him, "Yes, Lord; You know that I love You." He *said to him, "Tend My lambs." ¹⁶He *said to him again, a second time, "Simon, *son* of John, do you love Me?" He *said to Him, "Yes, Lord; You know that I love You." He *said to him, "^Shepherd My sheep." ¹⁷He *said to him the third time, "Simon, *son* of John, do you love Me?" Peter was hurt because He said to him the third time, "Do you love Me?" And he said to Him, "Lord, ^You know all things; You know that I love You." Jesus *said to him, "Tend My sheep.

OUR TIMES ARE IN HIS HAND

¹⁸Truly, truly I tell you, when you were younger, you used to put on your belt and walk wherever you wanted; but when you grow old, you will stretch out your hands and someone else will put your belt on you, and bring *you* where you do not want *to go.*" ¹⁹Now He said this, indicating by ^what kind of death he would glorify God. And when He had said this, He *said to him, "Follow Me!"

²⁰Peter turned around and *saw the ^disciple whom Jesus loved following *them*—the one who also had ᴮleaned back on His chest at the supper and said, "Lord, who is the one who is betraying You?" ²¹So Peter, upon seeing him, *said to Jesus, "Lord, and what *about* this man?" ²²Jesus *said to him, "If I want him to remain until I come, what *is that* to you? You ^follow Me!" ²³Therefore this account went out among the brothers, that that disciple would not die; yet Jesus did not say to him that he would not die, but *only,* "If I want him to remain ^until I come, what *is that* to you?"

²⁴This is the disciple who ^is testifying about these things and wrote these things, and we know that his testimony is true.

²⁵But there are also ^many other things which Jesus did, which, if they were written in detail, I expect that even the world itself would not contain the books that would be written.

21:9 ^John 18:18   **21:10** ^John 6:9, 11; 21:9, 13
21:12 ^John 21:15   **21:13** ^John 21:9
21:14 ^John 20:19, 26   **21:15** ^Matt 26:33; Mark 14:29
21:16 ^Matt 2:6; Acts 20:28   **21:17** ^John 16:30
21:19 ^2 Pet 1:14   **21:20** ^John 21:7   ᴮJohn 13:25
21:22 ^Matt 8:22; 16:24   **21:23** ^Matt 16:27f; 1 Cor 4:5
21:24 ^John 15:27   **21:25** ^John 20:30

21:8 ¹About 100 yd. or 90 m; a cubit is about 18 in. or 45 cm

THE ACTS

INTRODUCTION

1 The first account I composed, ^Theophilus, about all that Jesus ^began to do and teach, ²until the day when He was taken up *to heaven,* after He ^had given orders by the Holy Spirit to the apostles whom He had chosen. ³To these ^He also presented Himself alive after His suffering, by many convincing proofs, appearing to them over *a period of* forty days and speaking of things regarding the kingdom of God. ⁴Gathering them together, He commanded them ^not to leave Jerusalem, but to wait for ^what the Father had promised, "Which," *He said,* "you heard of from Me; ⁵for John baptized with water, but you will be baptized with the Holy Spirit ^not many days from now."

⁶So, when they had come together, they *began* asking Him, saying, "Lord, ^is it at this time that You are restoring the kingdom to Israel?" ⁷But He said to them, "It is not for you to know periods of time or appointed times which ^the Father has set by His own authority; ⁸but you will receive power ^when the Holy Spirit has come upon you; and you shall be ^My witnesses both in Jerusalem and in all Judea, and Samaria, and as far as the remotest part of the earth."

THE ASCENSION

⁹And after He had said these things, ^He was lifted up while they were watching, and a cloud took Him up, out of their sight. ¹⁰And as they were gazing intently into the sky while He was going, then behold, ^two men in white clothing stood beside them, ¹¹and they said, "Men of Galilee, why do you stand looking into the sky? This Jesus, who has been taken up from you into heaven, will ^come in the same way as you have watched Him go into heaven."

THE UPPER ROOM

¹²Then they ^returned to Jerusalem from the mountain called Olivet, which is near Jerusalem, a ¹Sabbath day's journey away. ¹³When they had entered *the city,* they went up to ^the upstairs room where they were staying, that is, ^Peter, John, James, and Andrew, Philip and Thomas, Bartholomew and Matthew, James *the son* of Alphaeus, Simon the Zealot, and Judas *the son* of James. ¹⁴All these ^were continually devoting themselves with one mind to prayer, along with *the* women, and Mary the mother of Jesus, and with His brothers.

¹⁵At this time Peter stood up among ^the brothers *and sisters* (a group of about 120 people was

1:1 ^Luke 1:3   ^Luke 3:23   1:2 ^Matt 28:19f;
John 20:21f   1:3 ^Matt 28:17; Luke 24:34, 36
1:4 ^Luke 24:49   ^John 14:16, 26   1:5 ^Acts 2:1-4
1:6 ^Matt 17:11; Mark 9:12   1:7 ^Matt 24:36; Mark 13:32
1:8 ^Acts 2:1-4   ^Luke 24:48   1:9 ^Luke 24:50, 51;
Acts 1:2   1:10 ^Luke 24:4; John 20:12
1:11 ^Matt 16:27f; Acts 3:21   1:12 ^Luke 24:52
1:13 ^Mark 14:15   ^*Matt 10:2-4*   1:14 ^Acts 2:42; 6:4
1:15 ^John 21:23; Acts 6:3

1:12 ¹ 2,000 cubits, or about 0.6 miles or 1 km

there together), and said, [16]"Brothers, the Scripture had to be fulfilled, which the Holy Spirit foretold by the mouth of David concerning Judas, ^who became a guide to those who arrested Jesus. [17]For he was counted among us and received his share in ^this ministry." [18](Now this man ^acquired a field with the price of his wickedness, and falling headlong, he burst open in the middle and all his intestines gushed out. [19]And it became known to all the residents of Jerusalem; as a result that field was called Hakeldama in ^their own language, that is, Field of Blood.) [20]"For it is written in the book of Psalms:

'^MAY HIS RESIDENCE BE MADE
    DESOLATE,
AND MAY THERE BE NONE
    LIVING IN IT';

and,

'^MAY ANOTHER TAKE HIS OFFICE.'

[21]Therefore it is necessary that of the men who have accompanied us all the time that ^the Lord Jesus went in and out among us— [22]^beginning with the baptism of John until the day that He was taken up from us—one of these *must* become a witness with us of His resurrection." [23]So they put forward two men, Joseph called Barsabbas (who was also called Justus), and ^Matthias. [24]And they prayed and said, "You, Lord, who ^know the hearts of all *people,* show which one of these two You have chosen [25]to occupy this ministry and ^apostleship from which Judas turned aside to go to his own place." [26]And they ^drew lots for them, and the lot fell to Matthias; and he was added to the eleven apostles.

THE DAY OF PENTECOST

2 When ^the day of Pentecost had come, they were all together in one place. [2]And suddenly a noise like a violent rushing wind came from heaven, and it filled ^the whole house where they were sitting. [3]And tongues *that looked* like fire appeared to them, distributing themselves, and *a tongue* rested on each one of them. [4]And they were all ^filled with the Holy Spirit and began to ᴮspeak with different tongues, as the Spirit was giving them *the ability* to speak out.

[5]Now there were Jews residing in Jerusalem, ^devout men from every nation under heaven. [6]And when ^this sound occurred, the crowd came together and they were bewildered, because each one of them was hearing them speak in his own language. [7]They were amazed and astonished, saying, "Why, are not all these who are speaking ^Galileans? [8]And how *is it that* we each hear *them* in our own language to which we were born? [9]Parthians, Medes, and Elamites, and residents of Mesopotamia, Judea, and Cappadocia, ^Pontus and ᴮAsia, [10]Phrygia and Pamphylia, Egypt and the parts of Libya around Cyrene, and visitors from Rome, both Jews and [1],^proselytes, [11]Cretans and Arabs—we hear them speaking in our *own* tongues of the mighty deeds of God." [12]And ^they all continued in amazement

1:16 ^Matt 26:47; Mark 14:43   1:17 ^Acts 1:25; 20:24
1:18 ^Matt 27:3-10   1:19 ^Matt 27:8; Acts 21:40
1:20 ^Ps 69:25   ᴮPs 109:8   1:21 ^Luke 24:3
1:22 ^Matt 3:16; Mark 1:1-4, 9   1:23 ^Acts 1:26
1:24 ^1 Sam 16:7; Jer 17:10   1:25 ^Rom 1:5; 1 Cor 9:2
1:26 ^Lev 16:8; Josh 14:2   2:1 ^Lev 23:15f; Acts 20:16
2:2 ^Acts 4:31   2:4 ^Acts 4:8, 31;   ᴮ1 Cor 12:10f
2:5 ^Luke 2:25; Acts 8:2   2:6 ^Acts 2:2
2:7 ^Matt 26:73; Acts 1:11   2:9 ^Acts 18:2   ᴮActs 6:9
2:10 ^Matt 23:15   2:12 ^Acts 2:7

2:10 [1]I.e., Gentile converts to Judaism

and great perplexity, saying to one another, "What does this mean?" 13But others were jeering and saying, "ᴬThey are full of sweet wine!"

PETER'S SERMON

14But Peter, taking his stand with ᴬthe *other* eleven, raised his voice and declared to them: "Men of Judea and all you who live in Jerusalem, know this, and pay attention to my words. 15For these people are not drunk, as you assume, ᴬsince it is *only* the ¹third hour of the day; 16but this is what has been spoken through the prophet Joel:

17 'ᴬAND IT SHALL BE IN THE LAST
     DAYS,' God says,
   'THAT I WILL POUR OUT MY
     SPIRIT ON ALL MANKIND;
   AND YOUR SONS AND YOUR
     DAUGHTERS WILL PROPHESY,
   AND YOUR YOUNG MEN WILL SEE
     VISIONS,
   AND YOUR OLD MEN WILL HAVE
     DREAMS;
18   AND EVEN ON MY MALE AND
     FEMALE SERVANTS
   I WILL POUR OUT MY SPIRIT IN
     THOSE DAYS,
   And they will prophesy.
19 'AND I WILL DISPLAY WONDERS IN
     THE SKY ABOVE
   AND SIGNS ON THE EARTH
     BELOW,
   BLOOD, FIRE, AND VAPOR OF
     SMOKE.
20 'THE SUN WILL BE TURNED INTO
     DARKNESS
   AND THE MOON INTO BLOOD,
   BEFORE THE GREAT AND
     GLORIOUS DAY OF THE LORD
     COMES.
21 'AND IT SHALL BE THAT
   ᴬEVERYONE WHO CALLS ON THE
     NAME OF THE LORD WILL BE
     SAVED.'

22"Men of Israel, listen to these words: ᴬJesus the Nazarene, a Man attested to you by God with miracles and wonders and signs which God performed through Him in your midst, just as you yourselves know— 23this *Man*, delivered over by the ᴬpredetermined plan and foreknowledge of God, you nailed to a cross by the hands of godless men and put *Him* to death. 24But ᴬGod raised Him *from the dead,* putting an end to the agony of death, since it was impossible for Him to be held in its power. 25For David says of Him,

'ᴬI SAW THE LORD CONTINUALLY
     BEFORE ME,
   BECAUSE HE IS AT MY RIGHT
     HAND, SO THAT I WILL NOT BE
     SHAKEN.
26 'THEREFORE MY HEART WAS
     GLAD AND MY TONGUE WAS
     OVERJOYED;
   MOREOVER MY FLESH ALSO WILL
     LIVE IN HOPE;
27 FOR YOU WILL NOT ABANDON MY
     SOUL TO ᴬHADES,
   ᴮNOR WILL YOU ALLOW YOUR
     HOLY ONE TO UNDERGO
     DECAY.
28 'YOU HAVE MADE KNOWN TO ME
     THE WAYS OF LIFE;
   YOU WILL MAKE ME FULL
     OF GLADNESS WITH YOUR
     PRESENCE.'

29"Brothers, I may confidently say to you regarding the patriarch David that he both died and ᴬwas buried, and his tomb is with us to this day. 30So because he was

---

2:13ᴬ1 Cor 14:23 2:14ᴬActs 1:26 2:15ᴬ1 Thess 5:7
2:17ᴬJoel 2:28-32 2:21ᴬRom 10:13 2:22ᴬActs 3:6;
4:10 2:23ᴬLuke 22:22; Acts 3:18 2:24ᴬMatt 28:5, 6;
Mark 16:6 2:25ᴬPs 16:8-11 2:27ᴬActs 2:31
ᴮActs 13:35 2:29ᴬ1 Kin 2:10

2:15¹I.e., 9 a.m.

a prophet and knew that ᴬGod had sworn to him with an oath to seat *one* of his descendants on his throne, ³¹he looked ahead and spoke of the resurrection of the Christ, that ᴬHe was neither abandoned to Hades, nor did His flesh suffer decay. ³²*It is* this Jesus *whom* ᴬGod raised up, *a fact* to which we are all witnesses. ³³Therefore, since He has been exalted ᴬat the right hand of God, and ᴮhas received the promise of the Holy Spirit from the Father, He has poured out this which you both see and hear. ³⁴For it was not David who ascended into heaven, but he himself says:

'ᴬThe Lord said to my Lord,
"Sit at My right hand,
³⁵   Until I make Your enemies a
       footstool for Your feet."'

³⁶Therefore let all the house of Israel know for certain that God has made Him both ᴬLord and Christ— this Jesus ᴮwhom you crucified."

³⁷Now when they heard *this,* they were pierced to the heart, and said to Peter and the rest of the apostles, "Brothers, ᴬwhat are we to do?" ³⁸Peter *said* to them, "'ᴬRepent, and each of you be ᴮbaptized in the name of Jesus Christ for the forgiveness of your sins; and you will receive the gift of the Holy Spirit. ³⁹For ᴬthe promise is for you and your children and for all who are far away, as many as the Lord our God will call to Himself." ⁴⁰And with many other words he solemnly testified and kept on urging them, saying, "Be saved from this ᴬperverse generation!" ⁴¹So then, those who had received his word were baptized; and that day there were added about three thousand ¹,ᴬsouls. ⁴²They were ᴬcontinually devoting themselves

to the apostles' teaching and to fellowship, to ᴮthe breaking of bread and ᴬto ¹prayer.

⁴³Everyone kept feeling a sense of awe; and many ᴬwonders and signs were taking place through the apostles. ⁴⁴And all the believers ¹were together and ᴬhad all things in common; ⁴⁵and they ᴬwould sell their property and possessions and share them with all, to the extent that anyone had need. ⁴⁶ᴬDay by day continuing with one mind in the temple, and breaking bread from house to house, they were taking their meals together with gladness and sincerity of heart, ⁴⁷praising God and ᴬhaving favor with all the people. And the Lord ᴮwas adding to their number day by day those who were being saved.

HEALING THE BEGGAR WHO WAS UNABLE TO WALK

3 Now Peter and John were going up to the temple at the ¹ninth *hour,* ᴬthe hour of prayer. ²And a man who had been unable to walk from birth was being carried, whom they ᴬused to set down every day at the gate of the temple which is called Beautiful, in order *for him* to beg for charitable gifts from those entering the temple *grounds.* ³When he saw ᴬPeter and John about to go into the temple *grounds,* he *began* asking to receive

2:30ᴬPs 132:11; 2 Sam 7:12f   2:31ᴬMatt 11:23;
Acts 2:27   2:32ᴬActs 2:24; 3:15, 26   2:33ᴬActs 5:31
ᴮActs 1:4   2:34ᴬPs 110:1; Matt 22:44f
2:36ᴬActs 2:11   ᴮActs 2:23   2:37ᴬLuke 3:10, 12, 14
2:38ᴬMark 1:15   ᴮActs 8:12, 16   2:39ᴬIs 44:3; 54:13
2:40ᴬDeut 32:5; Matt 17:17   2:41ᴬActs 3:23; 7:14
2:42ᴬActs 1:14   ᴮLuke 24:30   2:43ᴬActs 2:22
2:44ᴬActs 4:32, 37; 5:2   2:45ᴬMatt 19:21; Acts 4:34
2:46ᴬActs 5:42   2:47ᴬActs 5:13   ᴮActs 2:41
3:1ᴬPs 55:17; Matt 27:45   3:2ᴬLuke 16:20
3:3ᴬLuke 22:8; Acts 3:1, 4, 11

2:41¹I.e., persons   2:42¹Lit *the prayers*   2:44¹One early ms does not contain *were* and *and*   3:1¹I.e., 3 p.m.

a charitable gift. 4But Peter, along with John, ^looked at him intently and said, "Look at us!" 5And he gave them his attention, expecting to receive something from them. 6But Peter said, "I do not have silver and gold, but what I do have I give to you: ^In the name of Jesus Christ the Nazarene, walk!" 7And grasping him by the right hand, he raised him up; and immediately his feet and his ankles were strengthened. 8And ^leaping up, he stood and *began* to walk; and he entered the temple with them, walking and leaping and praising God. 9And ^all the people saw him walking and praising God; 10and they recognized him as being the very one who used to ^sit at the Beautiful Gate of the temple *to beg* for charitable gifts, and they were filled with wonder and amazement at what had happened to him.

PETER'S SECOND SERMON

11While he was clinging to Peter and John, all the people ran together to them at the ^portico named Solomon's, completely astonished. 12But when Peter saw *this,* he replied to the people, "Men of Israel, why are you amazed at this, or why are you staring at us, as though by our own power or godliness we had made him walk? 13The God of Abraham, Isaac, and Jacob, the God of our fathers, has glorified His ^Servant Jesus, *the one* whom you handed over and disowned in the presence of Pilate, when he had decided to release *Him.* 14But you disowned the Holy and Righteous One, and ^asked for a murderer to be granted to you, 15but put to death the Prince of life, whom ^God raised from the dead, *a fact* to which we are

^witnesses. 16And on the basis of faith ^in His name, *it is* the name of Jesus which has strengthened this man whom you see and know; and the faith which *comes* through Him has given him this perfect health in the presence of you all.

17"And now, brothers, I know that you acted ^in ignorance, just as your rulers also did. 18But the things which ^God previously announced by the mouths of all the prophets, ^that His Christ would suffer, He has fulfilled in this way. 19Therefore ^repent and return, so that your sins may be wiped away, in order that times of refreshing may come from the presence of the Lord; 20and that He may send Jesus, the Christ appointed for you, 21whom heaven must receive until *the* period of ^restoration of all things, about which ^God spoke by the mouths of His holy prophets from ancient times. 22Moses said, '^THE LORD GOD WILL RAISE UP FOR YOU A PROPHET LIKE ME FROM YOUR COUNTRYMEN; TO HIM YOU SHALL LISTEN regarding everything He says to you. 23^And it shall be that every soul that does not listen to that prophet ^shall be utterly destroyed from among the people.' 24And likewise, ^all the prophets who have spoken from Samuel and *his* successors *onward,* have also announced these days. 25It is you who are the sons of the prophets and of the covenant which God ordained with your fathers, saying

3:4^Acts 10:4　3:6^Acts 2:22; 3:16　3:8^Acts 14:10
3:9^Acts 4:16, 21　3:10^John 9:8; Acts 3:2
3:11^John 10:23; Acts 5:12　3:13^Acts 3:26; 4:27, 30
3:14^Matt 27:20; Mark 15:11　3:15^Acts 2:24
^Luke 24:48　3:16^Acts 3:6　3:17^John 15:21;
Acts 13:27　3:18^Acts 2:23　^Acts 17:3
3:19^Acts 2:38; 26:20　3:21^Matt 17:11　^Luke 1:70
3:22^Deut 18:15, 18; Acts 7:37　3:23^Deut 18:19
^Lev 23:29　3:24^Luke 24:27; Acts 17:3

to Abraham, 'ᴬAND IN YOUR SEED ALL THE FAMILIES OF THE EARTH SHALL BE BLESSED.' ²⁶God ᴬraised up His Servant for you ᴮfirst, and sent Him to bless you by turning every one *of you* from your wicked ways."

PETER AND JOHN ARRESTED

4 As they were speaking to the people, the priests and the captain of the temple *guard* and ᴬthe Sadducees came up to them, ²being greatly disturbed because they were teaching the people and proclaiming ᴬin Jesus the resurrection from the dead. ³And they laid hands on them and ᴬput *them* in prison until the next day, for it was already evening. ⁴But many of those who had heard the message believed; and ᴬthe number of the men came to be about five thousand.

⁵On the next day, their ᴬrulers and elders and scribes were gathered together in Jerusalem; ⁶and ᴬAnnas the high priest *was there*, and Caiaphas, John, and Alexander, and all who were of highpriestly descent. ⁷When they had placed them in the center, they *began to* inquire, "By what power, or in what name, have you done this?" ⁸Then Peter, ᴬfilled with the Holy Spirit, said to them, "Rulers and elders of the people, ⁹if we are on trial today for ᴬa benefit done to a sick man, as to how this man has been made well, ¹⁰let it be known to all of you and to all the people of Israel, that ᴬby the name of Jesus Christ the Nazarene, whom you crucified, whom God raised from the dead—by this *name* this man stands here before you in good health. ¹¹He is the ᴬSTONE WHICH WAS REJECTED by you, THE BUILDERS, *but* WHICH BECAME THE CHIEF CORNERSTONE. ¹²And there is salvation in ᴬno one else; for there is no other name under heaven that has been given among mankind by which we must be saved."

THREAT AND RELEASE

¹³Now as they observed the ᴬconfidence of Peter and John and understood that they were uneducated and untrained men, they were amazed, and ᴮ*began* to recognize them as having been with Jesus. ¹⁴And seeing the man who had been healed standing with them, they had nothing to say in reply. ¹⁵But when they had ordered them to leave the ᴬCouncil, they *began* to confer with one another, ¹⁶saying, "ᴬWhat are we to do with these men? For the fact that a ᴮnoteworthy miracle has taken place through them is apparent to all who live in Jerusalem, and we cannot deny it. ¹⁷But so that it will not spread any further among the people, let's warn them not to speak any longer to any person ᴬin this name." ¹⁸And when they had summoned them, they ᴬcommanded them not to speak or teach at all in the name of Jesus. ¹⁹But Peter and John answered and said to them, "ᴬWhether it is right in the sight of God to listen to you rather than to God, make your *own* judgment; ²⁰for ᴬwe cannot stop speaking about what we have seen and heard." ²¹When they had threatened them further, they let them

3:25 ᴬGen 22:18   3:26 ᴬActs 2:24   ᴮMatt 15:24
4:1 ᴬMark 12:18; Acts 5:17   4:2 ᴬActs 3:15; 17:18
4:3 ᴬActs 5:18   4:4 ᴬActs 2:41   4:5 ᴬLuke 23:13;
Acts 4:8   4:6 ᴬLuke 3:2   4:8 ᴬActs 2:4; 13:9
4:9 ᴬActs 3:7f   4:10 ᴬActs 2:22; 3:6   4:11 ᴬPs 118:22
4:12 ᴬMatt 1:21; Acts 10:43   4:13 ᴬActs 4:31
ᴮJohn 7:15   4:15 ᴬMatt 5:22   4:16 ᴬJohn 11:47
ᴮActs 3:7-10   4:17 ᴬJohn 15:21   4:18 ᴬActs 5:28f
4:19 ᴬActs 5:28f   4:20 ᴬ1 Cor 9:16

go (finding no basis on which to punish them) ᴬon account of the people, because they were all ᴮglorifying God for what had happened; ²²for the man on whom this miracle of healing had been performed was more than forty years old.

²³When they had been released, they went to their own *companions* and reported everything that the chief priests and the elders had said to them. ²⁴And when they heard *this,* they raised their voices to God with one mind and said, "Lord, it is You who ᴬMADE THE HEAVEN AND THE EARTH AND THE SEA, AND EVERYTHING THAT IS IN THEM, ²⁵who ᴬby the Holy Spirit, *through* the mouth of our father David Your servant, said,

'ᴮWHY WERE THE ¹NATIONS INSOLENT,
AND THE PEOPLES PLOTTING IN VAIN?
²⁶ 'ᴬTHE KINGS OF THE EARTH TOOK THEIR STAND,
AND THE RULERS WERE GATHERED TOGETHER
AGAINST THE LORD AND AGAINST HIS CHRIST.'

²⁷For truly in this city there were gathered together against Your holy ᴬServant Jesus, whom You anointed, both Herod and Pontius Pilate, along with the Gentiles and the peoples of Israel, ²⁸to do whatever Your hand and ᴬpurpose predestined to occur. ²⁹And now, Lord, look at their threats, and grant *it* to Your bond-servants to ᴬspeak Your word with all confidence, ³⁰while You extend Your hand to heal, and ᴬsigns and wonders take place through the name of Your holy Servant Jesus." ³¹And when they had prayed, the place where they had gathered together was shaken, and they were all ᴬfilled with the Holy Spirit and *began* to ᴮspeak the word of God with boldness.

SHARING AMONG BELIEVERS

³²And the congregation of those who believed were of one heart and soul; and not one *of them* claimed that anything belonging to him was his own, but ᴬall things were common property to them. ³³And ᴬwith great power the apostles were giving testimony to the resurrection of the Lord Jesus, and abundant grace was upon them all. ³⁴For there was not a needy person among them, for all who were owners of land or houses ᴬwould sell them and bring the proceeds of the sales ³⁵and ᴬlay *them* at the apostles' feet, and they would be ᴮdistributed to each to the extent that any had need.

³⁶Now Joseph, a Levite of ᴬCyprian birth, who was also called Barnabas by the apostles (which translated means Son of ᴮEncouragement), ³⁷owned a tract of land. So he sold it, and brought the money and ᴬlaid it at the apostles' feet.

FATE OF ANANIAS AND SAPPHIRA

5 But a man named Ananias, with his wife Sapphira, sold a piece of property, ²and kept back *some* of the proceeds for himself, with his wife's full knowledge, and bringing a portion of it, he ᴬlaid it at the apostles' feet. ³But Peter said, "Ananias, why has ᴬSatan filled your heart to lie to the Holy Spirit and to keep

4:21ᴬActs 5:26   ᴮMatt 9:8   4:24ᴬEx 20:11; Neh 9:6
4:25ᴬActs 1:16   ᴮPs 2:1   4:26ᴬPs 2:2
4:27ᴬActs 3:13; 4:30   4:28ᴬActs 2:23   4:29ᴬPhil 1:14
4:30ᴬJohn 4:48   4:31ᴬActs 2:4   ᴮPhil 1:14
4:32ᴬActs 2:44   4:33ᴬActs 1:8   4:34ᴬMatt 19:21;
Acts 2:45   4:35ᴬActs 4:37   ᴮActs 2:45
4:36ᴬActs 13:4   ᴮActs 11:23   4:37ᴬActs 4:35; 5:2
5:2ᴬActs 4:35, 37   5:3ᴬMatt 4:10; Luke 22:3

4:25¹Or *Gentiles*

back *some* of the proceeds of the land? ⁴While it remained *unsold,* did it not remain your own? And after it was sold, was it not under your control? Why *is it* that you have conceived this deed in your heart? You have not lied to men, but ᴬto God." ⁵And as he heard these words, Ananias collapsed and died; and ᴬgreat fear came over all who heard *about it.* ⁶The young men got up and ᴬcovered him up, and after carrying him out, they buried him.

⁷Now an interval of about three hours elapsed, and his wife came in, not knowing what had happened. ⁸And Peter responded to her, "Tell me whether you sold the land ᴬfor this price?" And she said, "Yes, for that price." ⁹Then Peter *said* to her, "Why *is it* that you have agreed together to ᴬput the Spirit of the Lord to the test? Behold, the feet of those who have buried your husband are at the door, and they will carry you out *as well.*" ¹⁰And immediately she ᴬcollapsed at his feet and died; and the young men came in and found her dead, and they carried her out and buried her beside her husband. ¹¹And ᴬgreat fear came over the whole church, and over all who heard *about* these things.

¹²At the hands of the apostles many ᴬsigns and wonders were taking place among the people; and they were all together in ᴮSolomon's portico. ¹³But none of the rest dared to associate with them; however, ᴬthe people held them in high esteem. ¹⁴And increasingly ᴬbelievers in the Lord, large numbers of men and women, were being added to *their number,* ¹⁵to such an extent that they even carried the sick out into the streets and laid them on cots and pallets, so that when Peter came by ᴬat least his shadow might fall on any of them. ¹⁶The people from the cities in the vicinity of Jerusalem were coming together as well, bringing people who were sick ¹or tormented with unclean spirits, and they were all being healed.

IMPRISONMENT AND RELEASE

¹⁷But the high priest stood up, along with all his associates (that is the sect of ᴬthe Sadducees), and they were filled with jealousy. ¹⁸They laid hands on the apostles and ᴬput them in a public prison. ¹⁹But during the night ᴬan angel of the Lord opened the gates of the prison, and leading them out, he said, ²⁰"Go, stand and speak to the people in the temple *area* ᴬthe whole message of this Life." ²¹Upon hearing *this,* they entered into the temple *area* about daybreak and *began* to teach.

Now when ᴬthe high priest and his associates came, they called the Council together, that is, all the Senate of the sons of Israel, and sent *orders* to the prison for them to be brought. ²²But ᴬthe officers who came did not find them in the prison; and they returned and reported, ²³saying, "We found the prison locked quite securely and the guards standing at the doors; but when we opened *them,* we found no one inside." ²⁴Now when ᴬthe captain of the temple *guard*

5:4ᴬActs 5:3, 9   5:5ᴬActs 2:43; 5:11   5:6ᴬJohn 19:40
5:8ᴬActs 5:2   5:9ᴬActs 15:10   5:10ᴬEzek 11:13;
Acts 5:5   5:11ᴬActs 2:43; 5:5   5:12ᴬJohn 4:48
ᴮJohn 10:23   5:13ᴬActs 2:47; 4:21   5:14ᴬ2 Cor 6:15
5:15ᴬActs 19:12   5:17ᴬMatt 3:7; Acts 4:1
5:18ᴬActs 4:3   5:19ᴬMatt 1:20, 24; 2:13, 19
5:20ᴬJohn 6:63, 68   5:21ᴬActs 4:6
5:22ᴬMatt 26:58; Acts 5:26   5:24ᴬActs 4:1; 5:26
5:16¹Lit *and*

and the chief priests heard these words, they were greatly perplexed about them as to what would come of this. [25] But someone came and reported to them, "The men whom you put in prison are standing in the temple *area* and teaching the people!" [26] Then the captain went along with the officers and *proceeded* to bring them *back* without violence (for ^they were afraid of the people, that they might be stoned).

[27] When they had brought them, they had them stand before ^the Council. The high priest interrogated them, [28] saying, "We gave you strict orders not to continue teaching in this name, and yet, you have filled Jerusalem with your teaching and ^intend to bring this Man's blood upon us." [29] But Peter and the apostles answered, "^We must obey God rather than men. [30]^The God of our fathers ^Braised up Jesus, whom you put to death by hanging Him on ¹a cross. [31]^He is the One whom God exalted to His right hand as a Prince and a ^BSavior, to grant repentance to Israel, and forgiveness of sins. [32] And we are ^witnesses ¹of these things; and *so is* the Holy Spirit, whom God has given to those who obey Him."

GAMALIEL'S COUNSEL

[33] But when they heard *this,* they became ^infuriated and *nearly* decided to execute them. [34] But a Pharisee named ^Gamaliel, a teacher of the Law, respected by all the people, stood up in the Council and gave orders to put the men outside for a short time. [35] And he said to them, "Men of Israel, be careful as to what you are about to do with these men. [36] For, some time ago Theudas appeared, ^claiming to be somebody, and a group of about four hundred

men joined him. But he was killed, and all who followed him were dispersed and came to nothing. [37] After this man, Judas of Galilee appeared in the days of ^the census and drew away *some* people after him; he also perished, and all those who followed him were scattered. [38] And *so* in the present case, I say to you, stay away from these men and leave them alone, for if the source of this plan or movement ^is men, it will be overthrown; [39] but if the source is God, you will not be able to overthrow them; or else you may even be found ^fighting against God."

[40] They followed his advice; and after calling the apostles in, they ^flogged them and ordered them not to speak in the name of Jesus, and *then* released them. [41] So they went on their way from the presence of the Council, ^rejoicing that they had been considered worthy to suffer shame ^Bfor *His* name. [42]^And every day, in the temple and from house to house, they did not stop teaching and preaching the good news of Jesus *as* the Christ.

CHOOSING OF THE SEVEN

6 Now at this time, as the ^disciples were increasing *in number,* a complaint developed *on the part of* the ¹,^BHellenistic *Jews* against the *native* Hebrews, because their widows were being overlooked in

5:26^Acts 4:21; 5:13 5:27^Matt 5:22;
Acts 5:21, 34, 41 5:28^Matt 23:35; 27:25
5:29^Acts 4:19 5:30^Acts 3:13 ^BActs 2:24
5:31^Acts 2:33 ^BLuke 2:11 5:32^Luke 24:48
5:33^Acts 2:37; 7:54 5:34^Acts 22:3 5:36^Acts 8:9;
Gal 2:6 5:37^Luke 2:2 5:38^Mark 11:30
5:39^Prov 21:30; Acts 11:17 5:40^Matt 10:17
5:41^1 Pet 4:14, 16 ^BJohn 15:21 5:42^Acts 2:46
6:1^Acts 11:26 ^BActs 9:29

5:30 ¹Lit *wood;* see Deut 21:23 5:32 ¹One early ms
adds *in Him* 6:1 ¹Jews who adopted the Gr language
and much of Gr culture through acculturation

the daily serving *of food.* ²So the twelve summoned the congregation of the disciples and said, "It is not desirable for us to neglect the word of God in order to serve tables. ³Instead, brothers *and sisters,* select from among you seven men of good reputation, ᴬfull of the Spirit and of wisdom, whom we may put in charge of this task. ⁴But we will ᴬdevote ourselves to prayer and to the ministry of the word." ⁵The announcement found approval with the whole congregation; and they chose ᴬStephen, a man full of faith and of the Holy Spirit, and Philip, Prochorus, Nicanor, Timon, Parmenas, and Nicolas, a ¹proselyte from Antioch. ⁶And they brought these men before the apostles; and after ᴬpraying, they ᴮlaid their hands on them.

⁷The word of God kept spreading; and the number of the disciples continued to increase greatly in Jerusalem, and a great many of the priests were becoming obedient to ᴬthe faith.

⁸And Stephen, full of grace and power, was performing great ᴬwonders and signs among the people. ⁹But some men from what was called the Synagogue of the Freedmen, *including* both ᴬCyrenians and Alexandrians, and some from Cilicia and Asia, rose up and argued with Stephen. ¹⁰But they were unable to cope with his wisdom and the Spirit by whom he was speaking. ¹¹Then they secretly induced men to say, "We have heard him speak blasphemous words against Moses and God." ¹²And they stirred up the people, the elders, and the scribes, and they ᴬcame up to him and dragged him away, and brought him before the Council. ¹³They put forward ᴬfalse witnesses who said, "This man does not stop speaking against this ᴮholy place and the Law; ¹⁴for we have heard him say that ᴬthis Nazarene, Jesus, will destroy this place and change the customs which Moses handed down to us." ¹⁵And all who were sitting in the ᴬCouncil stared at him, and they saw his face, *which was* like the face of an angel.

STEPHEN'S DEFENSE

7 Now the high priest said, "Are these things so?"

²And Stephen said, "Listen to me, ᴬbrothers and fathers! The God of glory ᴮappeared to our father Abraham when he was in Mesopotamia, before he lived in Haran, ³and He said to him, 'ᴬGO FROM YOUR COUNTRY AND YOUR RELATIVES, AND COME TO THE LAND WHICH I WILL SHOW YOU.' ⁴ᴬThen he left the land of the Chaldeans and settled in Haran. And ᴮfrom there, after his father died, *God* had him move to this country in which you are now living. ⁵But He gave him no inheritance in it, not even a foot of ground, and *yet,* ᴬHe promised that He would give it to him as a possession, and to his descendants after him, *even* though he had no child. ⁶But ᴬGod spoke to this effect, that his DESCENDANTS WOULD BE STRANGERS IN A LAND THAT WAS NOT THEIRS, AND THEY WOULD ENSLAVE AND MISTREAT *THEM* FOR FOUR HUNDRED YEARS. ⁷'AND WHATEVER NATION TO WHICH THEY ARE ENSLAVED I MYSELF WILL JUDGE,' said God, 'AND ᴬAFTER

6:3ᴬActs 2:4   6:4ᴬActs 1:14   6:5ᴬActs 6:8ff; 11:19   6:6ᴬActs 1:24   ᴮNum 8:10   6:7ᴬActs 13:8; 14:22   6:8ᴬJohn 4:48   6:9ᴬMatt 27:32; Acts 2:10   6:12ᴬLuke 20:1; Acts 4:1   6:13ᴬMatt 26:59-61   ᴮMatt 24:15   6:14ᴬMatt 26:61   6:15ᴬMatt 5:22   7:2ᴬActs 22:1   ᴮGen 11:31   7:3ᴬGen 12:1   7:4ᴬGen 11:31   ᴮGen 12:4, 5   7:5ᴬGen 12:7; 13:15   7:6ᴬGen 15:13f   7:7ᴬEx 3:12

6:5¹I.e., a Gentile convert to Judaism

THAT THEY WILL COME OUT AND SERVE ME IN THIS PLACE.' ⁸And He ᴬgave him the covenant of circumcision; and so ᴮ*Abraham* fathered Isaac, and circumcised him on the eighth day; and Isaac *fathered* Jacob, and Jacob, the twelve patriarchs.

⁹"The patriarchs ᴬbecame jealous of Joseph and sold him into Egypt. *Yet* God was with him, ¹⁰and rescued him from all his afflictions, and ᴬgranted him favor and wisdom in the sight of Pharaoh, king of Egypt, and he made him governor over Egypt and his entire household.

¹¹"Now ᴬa famine came over all Egypt and Canaan, and great affliction *with it,* and our fathers could find no food. ¹²But ᴬwhen Jacob heard that there was grain in Egypt, he sent our fathers *there* the first time. ¹³And on the second *visit,* ᴬJoseph made himself known to his brothers, and ᴮJoseph's family was revealed to Pharaoh. ¹⁴Then ᴬJoseph sent *word* and invited his father Jacob and all his relatives to come to him, seventy-five people *in all.* ¹⁵And ᴬJacob went down to Egypt, and he and our fathers died *there.* ¹⁶And they were brought back *from there* to ᴬShechem and laid in the tomb which Abraham had purchased for a sum of money from the sons of Hamor in Shechem.

¹⁷"But as the ᴬtime of the promise which God had assured to Abraham was approaching, ᴮthe people increased and multiplied in Egypt, ¹⁸until ᴬANOTHER KING AROSE OVER EGYPT WHO DID NOT KNOW JOSEPH. ¹⁹It was he who shrewdly took advantage of our nation and mistreated our fathers in order that they would ᴬabandon their infants *in the Nile,* so that they would not survive. ²⁰At this time ᴬMoses was

born; and he was beautiful to God. He was nurtured for three months in his father's home. ²¹And after he had been put outside, ᴬPharaoh's daughter took him away and nurtured him as her own son. ²²Moses was educated in all ᴬthe wisdom of the Egyptians, and he was proficient in speaking and action. ²³But when he was approaching the age of forty, ᴬit entered his mind to visit his countrymen, the sons of Israel. ²⁴And when he saw one *of them* being treated unjustly, he defended and took vengeance for the oppressed man by *fatally* striking the Egyptian. ²⁵And he thought that his brothers understood that God was granting them deliverance through him; but they did not understand. ²⁶ᴬAnd on the following day he appeared to them as they were fighting each other, and he tried to reconcile them to peace, by saying, 'Men, you are brothers, why are you injuring each other?' ²⁷But the one who was injuring his neighbor pushed him away, saying, 'ᴬWHO MADE YOU A RULER AND JUDGE OVER US? ²⁸ᴬYOU DO NOT INTEND TO KILL ME AS YOU KILLED THE EGYPTIAN YESTERDAY, DO YOU?' ²⁹At this remark, ᴬMOSES FLED AND BECAME A STRANGER IN THE LAND OF MIDIAN, where he fathered two sons.

³⁰"After forty years had passed, ᴬan angel appeared to him in the wilderness of Mount Sinai, in the flame of a burning thorn bush.

7:8ᴬGen 17:10ff ᴮGen 21:2-4 7:9ᴬGen 37:11, 28; 39:2, 21f 7:10ᴬGen 39:21; 41:40-46 7:11ᴬGen 41:54f; 42:5 7:12ᴬGen 42:2 7:13ᴬGen 45:1-4 ᴮGen 45:16 7:14ᴬGen 45:9, 10, 17, 18 7:15ᴬGen 46:1-7; 49:33 7:16ᴬGen 23:16; 33:19 7:17ᴬGen 15:13 ᴮEx 1:7f 7:18ᴬEx 1:8 7:19ᴬEx 1:22 7:20ᴬEx 2:2; Heb 11:23 7:21ᴬEx 2:5f, 10 7:22ᴬ1 Kin 4:30; Is 19:11 7:23ᴬEx 2:11f; Heb 11:24-26 7:26ᴬEx 2:13f 7:27ᴬEx 2:14; Acts 7:35 7:28ᴬEx 2:14 7:29ᴬEx 2:15, 22 7:30ᴬEx 3:1f; Is 63:9

³¹When Moses saw *it,* he was astonished at the sight; and as he approached to look *more* closely, the voice of the Lord came: ³²'AI AM THE GOD OF YOUR FATHERS, THE GOD OF ABRAHAM, AND ISAAC, AND JACOB.' Moses shook with fear and did not dare to look closely. ³³ᴬBut the LORD said to him, 'REMOVE YOUR SANDALS FROM YOUR FEET, FOR THE PLACE ON WHICH YOU ARE STANDING IS HOLY GROUND. ³⁴ᴬI HAVE CERTAINLY SEEN THE OPPRESSION OF MY PEOPLE WHO ARE IN EGYPT, AND HAVE HEARD THEIR GROANING, AND I HAVE COME DOWN TO RESCUE THEM; AND NOW COME, I WILL SEND YOU TO EGYPT.'

³⁵"This Moses whom they ᴬdisowned, saying, 'WHO MADE YOU A RULER AND A JUDGE?' is the one whom God sent *to be* both a ruler and a deliverer with the help of the angel who appeared to him in the thorn bush. ³⁶ᴬThis man led them out, performing ᴮwonders and signs in the land of Egypt and in the Red Sea, and in the wilderness for forty years. ³⁷This is the Moses who said to the sons of Israel, 'ᴬGOD WILL RAISE UP FOR YOU A PROPHET LIKE ME FROM YOUR COUNTRYMEN.' ³⁸This is the one who was in ᴬthe assembly in the wilderness together with the angel who spoke to him *at length* on Mount Sinai, and *who was with* our fathers; and he received ᴮliving words to pass on to you. ³⁹Our fathers were unwilling to be obedient to him; on the contrary they ᴬrejected him and turned back to Egypt in their hearts, ⁴⁰ᴬsaying to Aaron, 'MAKE US A GOD WHO WILL GO BEFORE US; FOR THIS MOSES WHO LED US OUT OF THE LAND OF EGYPT—WE DO NOT KNOW WHAT HAPPENED TO HIM.' ⁴¹At that time ᴬthey made a calf and brought a sacrifice to the idol,

and were rejoicing in ᴮthe works of their hands. ⁴²But God turned away and gave them over to serve the heavenly lights; as it is written in the book of the prophets: 'ᴬYOU DID NOT OFFER ME VICTIMS AND SACRIFICES FOR FORTY YEARS IN THE WILDERNESS, DID YOU, HOUSE OF ISRAEL? ⁴³ᴬYOU ALSO TOOK ALONG THE TABERNACLE OF MOLOCH AND THE STAR OF YOUR GOD ROMPHA, THE IMAGES WHICH YOU MADE TO WORSHIP. I ALSO WILL DEPORT YOU BEYOND BABYLON.'

⁴⁴"Our fathers had ᴬthe tabernacle of testimony in the wilderness, just as He who spoke to Moses directed *him* to make it ᴮaccording to the pattern which he had seen. ⁴⁵Our fathers in turn received it, and they also ᴬbrought it in with Joshua upon dispossessing the nations that God drove out from our fathers, until the time of David. ⁴⁶ᴬDavid found favor in God's sight, and asked that he might find a dwelling place for the ¹house of Jacob. ⁴⁷But it was ᴬSolomon who built a house for Him. ⁴⁸However, ᴬthe Most High does not dwell in *houses* made by *human* hands; as the prophet says:

⁴⁹ 'ᴬHEAVEN IS MY THRONE,
    AND THE EARTH IS THE
    FOOTSTOOL OF MY FEET;
    WHAT KIND OF HOUSE WILL YOU
    BUILD FOR ME?' says the Lord,
    'OR WHAT PLACE IS THERE FOR
    MY REST?
⁵⁰ 'ᴬWAS IT NOT MY HAND THAT
    MADE ALL THESE THINGS?'

7:32ᴬEx 3:6; Matt 22:32   7:33ᴬEx 3:5   7:34ᴬEx 3:7f
7:35ᴬEx 2:14; Acts 7:27   7:36ᴬEx 12:41   ᴮEx 7:3
7:37ᴬDeut 18:15, 18; Acts 3:22   7:38ᴬEx 19:17
ᴮDeut 32:47   7:39ᴬNum 14:3f   7:40ᴬEx 32:1, 23
7:41ᴬEx 32:4, 6   ᴮRev 9:20   7:42ᴬAmos 5:25
7:43ᴬAmos 5:26, 27   7:44ᴬEx 25:8, 9   ᴮEx 25:40
7:45ᴬDeut 32:49; Josh 3:14ff   7:46ᴬ2 Sam 7:8ff;
Ps 132:1-5   7:47ᴬ1 Kin 6:1-38; 8:20   7:48ᴬLuke 1:32
7:49ᴬIs 66:1; Matt 5:34f   7:50ᴬIs 66:2

7:46¹I.e., the people of Israel

⁵¹"You men who are ^stiff-necked and uncircumcised in heart and ears are always resisting the Holy Spirit; you are doing just as your fathers did. ⁵²^Which one of the prophets did your fathers not persecute? They killed those who had previously announced the coming of ^Bthe Righteous One, and you have now become betrayers and murderers of Him; ⁵³you who received the Law as ^ordained by angels, and *yet* did not keep it."

STEPHEN PUT TO DEATH

⁵⁴Now when they heard this, they were ^infuriated, and they *began* gnashing their teeth at him. ⁵⁵But he, being ^full of the Holy Spirit, looked intently into heaven and saw the glory of God, and Jesus standing at the right hand of God; ⁵⁶and he said, "Behold, I see the ^heavens opened and the Son of Man standing at the right hand of God." ⁵⁷But they shouted with loud voices, and covered their ears and rushed at him with one mind. ⁵⁸When they had ^driven him out of the city, they *began* stoning *him;* and the witnesses ^Blaid aside their cloaks at the feet of a young man named Saul. ⁵⁹They *went on* stoning Stephen as he ^called on *the Lord* and said, "Lord Jesus, receive my spirit!" ⁶⁰Then he ^fell on his knees and cried out with a loud voice, "Lord, do not hold this sin against them!" Having said this, he fell asleep.

SAUL PERSECUTES THE CHURCH

8 ^Now Saul approved of putting Stephen to death.

And on that day a great persecution began against the church in Jerusalem, and they were all scattered throughout the regions of Judea and Samaria, except for the apostles. ²*Some* devout men buried Stephen, and mourned loudly for him. ³But ^Saul *began* ravaging the church, entering house after house; and he would drag away men and women and put them in prison.

PHILIP IN SAMARIA

⁴Therefore, those ^who had been scattered went through *places* preaching the word. ⁵^Philip went down to the city of Samaria and *began* proclaiming the Christ to them. ⁶The crowds were paying attention with one mind to what was being said by Philip, as they heard and saw the signs which he was performing. ⁷For *in the case of* many who had unclean spirits, they were coming out *of them* shouting with a loud voice; and many who had been ^paralyzed or limped *on crutches* were healed. ⁸So there was ^much rejoicing in that city.

⁹Now a man named Simon had previously been practicing ^magic in the city and astonishing the people of Samaria, claiming to be someone great; ¹⁰and all *the people,* from small to great, were paying attention to him, saying, "^This man is the Power of God that is called Great." ¹¹And they were paying attention to him because for a long time he had astounded them with his ^magic arts. ¹²But when they believed Philip ^as he

7:51^AEx 32:9; 33:3, 5 7:52^A2 Chr 36:15f ᴮActs 3:14
7:53^ADeut 33:2; Acts 7:38 7:54^AActs 5:33
7:55^AActs 2:4 7:56^AJohn 1:51 7:58^ALev 24:14, 16
ᴮActs 22:20 7:59^AActs 9:14, 21; 22:16 7:60^ALuke 22:41
8:1^AActs 7:58; 22:20 8:3^AActs 9:1, 13, 21; 22:4, 19
8:4^AActs 8:1 8:5^AActs 6:5; 8:26, 30 8:7^AMatt 4:24
8:8^AJohn 4:40-42; Acts 8:39 8:9^AActs 8:11; 13:6
8:10^AActs 14:11; 28:6 8:11^AActs 8:9; 13:6
8:12^AActs 1:3; 8:4

was preaching the good news about the kingdom of God and the name of Jesus Christ, both men and women were being baptized. ¹³Now even Simon himself believed; and after being baptized, he continued on with Philip, and as he observed ᴬsigns and ᴮgreat miracles taking place, he was *repeatedly* amazed.

¹⁴Now when ᴬthe apostles in Jerusalem heard that Samaria had received the word of God, they sent them ᴮPeter and John, ¹⁵who came down and prayed for them ᴬthat they would receive the Holy Spirit. ¹⁶(For He had ᴬnot yet fallen upon any of them; they had simply been baptized in the name of the Lord Jesus.) ¹⁷Then they ᴬ*began* laying their hands on them, and they were ᴮreceiving the Holy Spirit. ¹⁸Now when Simon saw that the Spirit was given through the laying on of the apostles' hands, he offered them money, ¹⁹saying, "Give this authority to me as well, so that everyone on whom I lay my hands may receive the Holy Spirit." ²⁰But Peter said to him, "May your silver perish with you, because you thought you could ᴬacquire the gift of God with money! ²¹You have ᴬno part or share in this matter, for your heart is not right before God. ²²Therefore, repent of this wickedness of yours, and pray to the Lord *that,* ᴬif possible, the intention of your heart will be forgiven you. ²³For I see that you are in the gall of bitterness and in ᴬthe bondage of unrighteousness." ²⁴But Simon answered and said, "ᴬPray to the Lord for me yourselves, so that nothing of what you have said may come upon me."

AN ETHIOPIAN RECEIVES CHRIST

²⁵So, when they had solemnly testified and spoken ᴬthe word of the Lord, they started back to Jerusalem, and were ᴮpreaching the gospel to many villages of the Samaritans.

²⁶But ᴬan angel of the Lord spoke to Philip, saying, "Get ready and go south to the road that descends from Jerusalem to Gaza." (This is a desert *road.*) ²⁷So he got ready and went; and ᴬthere was an Ethiopian eunuch, a court official of Candace, queen of the Ethiopians, who was in charge of all her treasure; and he ᴮhad come to Jerusalem to worship, ²⁸and he was returning and sitting in his chariot, and was reading Isaiah the prophet. ²⁹Then ᴬthe Spirit said to Philip, "Go up and join this chariot." ³⁰Philip ran up and heard him reading Isaiah the prophet, and said, "Do you understand what you are reading?" ³¹And he said, "Well, how could I, unless someone guides me?" And he invited Philip to come up and sit with him. ³²Now the passage of Scripture which he was reading was this:

"ᴬHE WAS LED LIKE A SHEEP TO
    SLAUGHTER;
  AND LIKE A LAMB THAT IS SILENT
    BEFORE ITS SHEARER,
  SO HE DOES NOT OPEN HIS
    MOUTH.
³³ "ᴬIN HUMILIATION HIS JUSTICE
    WAS TAKEN AWAY;
  WHO WILL DESCRIBE HIS
    GENERATION?
  FOR HIS LIFE IS TAKEN AWAY
    FROM THE EARTH."

8:13 ᴬActs 8:6   ᴮActs 19:11   8:14 ᴬActs 8:1   ᴮLuke 22:8
8:15 ᴬActs 2:38; 19:2   8:16 ᴬMatt 28:19; Acts 19:2
8:17 ᴬActs 6:6   ᴮActs 2:4   8:20 ᴬ2 Kin 5:16; Is 55:1
8:21 ᴬDeut 10:9; 12:12   8:22 ᴬIs 55:7   8:23 ᴬIs 58:6
8:24 ᴬGen 20:7; Ex 8:8   8:25 ᴬActs 13:12   ᴮActs 8:40
8:26 ᴬActs 5:19; 8:29   8:27 ᴬPs 68:31;   ᴮ1 Kin 8:41f
8:29 ᴬActs 8:39; 10:19   8:32 ᴬIs 53:7   8:33 ᴬIs 53:8

34 The eunuch answered Philip and said, "Please *tell me,* of whom does the prophet say this? Of himself, or of someone else?" 35 Then Philip opened his mouth, and ^beginning from this Scripture he preached Jesus to him. 36 As they went along the road they came to some water; and the eunuch *said, "Look! Water! ^What prevents me from being baptized?"¹ 38 And he ordered that the chariot stop; and they both went down into the water, Philip as well as the eunuch, and he baptized him. 39 When they came up out of the water, ^the Spirit of the Lord snatched Philip away; and the eunuch no longer saw him, but went on his way rejoicing. 40 But Philip found himself at ^Azotus, and as he passed through he ^Bkept preaching the gospel to all the cities, until he came to Caesarea.

THE CONVERSION OF SAUL

9 ^Now Saul, still breathing threats and murder against the disciples of the Lord, went to the high priest, 2 and asked for ^letters from him to the synagogues in Damascus, so that if he found any belonging to ¹the Way, whether men or women, he might bring them in shackles to Jerusalem. 3 Now as he was traveling, it happened that he was approaching Damascus, and ^suddenly a light from heaven flashed around him; 4 and ^he fell to the ground and heard a voice saying to him, "Saul, Saul, why are you persecuting Me?" 5 And he said, "Who are You, Lord?" And He *said,* "I am Jesus whom you are persecuting, 6 but get up and enter the city, and ^it will be told to you what you must do." 7 The men who traveled with him stood

speechless, ^hearing the voice but seeing no one. 8 Saul got up from the ground, and ^though his eyes were open, he could see nothing; and leading him by the hand, they brought him into Damascus. 9 And for three days he was without sight, and neither ate nor drank.

10 Now there was a disciple in Damascus named ^Ananias; and the Lord said to him in ^Ba vision, "Ananias." And he said, "Here I am, Lord." 11 And the Lord *said* to him, "Get up and go to the street called Straight, and inquire at the house of Judas for a man from ^Tarsus named Saul, for he is praying, 12 and he has seen ¹in a vision a man named Ananias come in and ^lay his hands on him, so that he might regain his sight." 13 But Ananias answered, "Lord, I have heard from many people about this man, ^how much harm he did to Your saints in Jerusalem; 14 and here he ^has authority from the chief priests to arrest all who ^Bcall on Your name." 15 But the Lord said to him, "Go, for ^he is a chosen instrument of Mine, to bear My name before the Gentiles and kings and the sons of Israel; 16 for ^I will show him how much he must suffer in behalf of My name." 17 So Ananias departed and entered the house, and after

8:35 ^Luke 24:27; Acts 17:2   8:36 ^Acts 10:47
8:39 ^1 Kin 18:12; 2 Kin 2:16   8:40 ^Josh 11:22
^BActs 8:25   9:1 ^Acts 9:1–22; 22:3–16
9:2 ^Acts 9:14, 21; 22:5   9:3 ^1 Cor 15:8
9:4 ^Acts 22:7; 26:14   9:6 ^Acts 9:16   9:7 ^John 12:29f;
Acts 22:9   9:8 ^Acts 9:18; 22:11   9:10 ^Acts 22:12
^BActs 10:3, 17, 19   9:11 ^Acts 9:30; 11:25
9:12 ^Mark 5:23; Acts 6:6   9:13 ^Acts 8:3
9:14 ^Acts 9:2, 21   ^BActs 7:59   9:15 ^Acts 13:2; Rom 1:1
9:16 ^Acts 20:23; 21:4, 11, 13

8:36 ¹Late mss add as v 37: *And Philip said, "If you believe with all your heart, you may." And he answered and said, "I believe that Jesus Christ is the Son of God."* 9:2 ¹See John 14:6   9:12 ¹A few early mss do not contain *in a vision*

^Alaying his hands on him said, "Brother Saul, the Lord Jesus, who appeared to you on the road by which you were coming, has sent me so that you may regain your sight and be ^Bfilled with the Holy Spirit." ^18And immediately *something* like *fish* scales fell from his eyes, and he regained his sight, and he got up and was baptized; ^19and he took food and was strengthened.

SAUL BEGINS TO PREACH CHRIST

Now for several days he was with the disciples who were in Damascus, ^20and immediately he *began* to proclaim Jesus ^Ain the synagogues, saying, "He is ^Bthe Son of God." ^21All those hearing *him* continued to be amazed, and were saying, "Is this not the one who in Jerusalem ^Adestroyed those who called on this name, and had come here for the purpose of bringing them bound before the chief priests?" ^22But Saul kept increasing in strength and confounding Jews who lived in Damascus by proving that this *Jesus* is the Christ.

^23When ^Amany days had elapsed, the Jews plotted together to do away with him, ^24but their plot became known to Saul. ^AThey were also closely watching the gates day and night so that they might put him to death; ^25but his disciples took him at night and let him down through *an opening in* the wall, lowering him in a large basket.

^26^AWhen he came to Jerusalem, he tried *repeatedly* to associate with the disciples; and *yet* they were all afraid of him, as they did not believe that he was a disciple. ^27But ^ABarnabas took hold of him and brought him to the apostles and described to them how he had

seen the Lord on the road, and that He had talked to him, and how he had spoken out boldly in the name of Jesus at Damascus. ^28And he was with them, moving about freely in Jerusalem, ^Aspeaking out boldly in the name of the Lord. ^29And he was talking and arguing with the ^AHellenistic *Jews;* but they were attempting to put him to death. ^30Now when the brothers learned *of it,* they brought him down to ^ACaesarea and ^Bsent him away to Tarsus.

^31So ^Athe church throughout Judea, Galilee, and Samaria enjoyed peace, as it was being built up; and as it continued in the fear of the Lord and in the comfort of the Holy Spirit, it kept increasing.

PETER'S MINISTRY

^32Now as Peter was traveling through all *those regions,* he also came down to ^Athe saints who lived at Lydda. ^33There he found a man named Aeneas who had been bedridden for eight years, because he was paralyzed. ^34Peter said to him, "Aeneas, Jesus Christ heals you; get up and make your own bed." Immediately he got up. ^35And all who lived at Lydda and Sharon saw him, and they ^Aturned to the Lord.

^36Now in ^AJoppa there was a disciple named Tabitha (which when translated means ^1Dorcas); this woman was excelling in acts of kindness and charity which she did *habitually.* ^37But it happened at that time that she became sick and

9:17^AMark 5:23   ^BActs 2:4   9:20^AActs 13:5, 14   ^BActs 13:33   9:21^AActs 8:3; 9:13   9:23^AGal 1:17, 18   9:24^A2 Cor 11:32f   9:26^AActs 22:17-20; 26:20   9:27^AActs 4:36   9:28^AActs 4:13, 29; 9:29   9:29^AActs 6:1   9:30^AActs 8:40   ^BGal 1:21   9:31^AActs 5:11; 8:1   9:32^AActs 9:13   9:35^AActs 2:47; 9:42   9:36^AJosh 19:46; 2 Chr 2:16

9:36 ^1 I.e., Gr for Gazelle

died; and when they had washed *her body,* they laid *it* in an ^upstairs room. ³⁸Since Lydda was near Joppa, ^the disciples, having heard that Peter was there, sent two men to him, urging him, "Do not delay in coming to us." ³⁹So Peter got ready and went with them. When he arrived, they brought him into the ^room upstairs; and all the widows stood beside him, weeping and showing all the ¹tunics and garments that Dorcas used to make while she was with them. ⁴⁰But Peter sent them all out and knelt down and prayed, and turning to the body, he said, "^Tabitha, arise." And she opened her eyes, and when she saw Peter, she sat up. ⁴¹And he gave her his hand and raised her up; and calling ^the saints and widows, he presented her alive. ⁴²It became known all over Joppa, and ^many believed in the Lord. ⁴³And *Peter* stayed in Joppa many days with ^a tanner *named* Simon.

CORNELIUS' VISION

10 Now *there was* a man in ^Caesarea named Cornelius, a centurion of what was called the Italian ¹cohort, ²a devout man and ^one who feared God with all his household, and ᴮmade many charitable contributions to the *Jewish* people and prayed to God continually. ³About ^the ¹ninth hour of the day he clearly saw ᴮin a vision an angel of God who had *just* come in and said to him, "Cornelius!" ⁴And he looked at him intently and became terrified, and said, "What is it, lord?" And he said to him, "Your prayers and charitable gifts have ascended ^as a memorial offering before God. ⁵Now dispatch *some* men to ^Joppa and send for a man

named Simon, who is also called Peter; ⁶he is staying with a tanner *named* ^Simon, whose house is by the sea." ⁷When the angel who *spoke to him left, he summoned two of his servants and a devout soldier from his personal attendants, ⁸and after he had explained everything to them, he sent them to ^Joppa.

⁹On the next day, as they were on their way and approaching the city, ^Peter went up on the housetop about ¹the sixth hour to pray. ¹⁰But he became hungry and wanted to eat; but while they were making preparations, he ^fell into a trance; ¹¹and he *saw ^the sky opened up, and an object like a great sheet coming down, lowered by four corners to the ground, ¹²and on it were all *kinds of* four-footed animals and crawling creatures of the earth and birds of the sky. ¹³A voice came to him, "Get up, Peter, kill and eat!" ¹⁴But Peter said, "By no means, Lord, for ^I have never eaten anything unholy and unclean." ¹⁵Again a voice *came* to him a second time, "^What God has cleansed, no *longer* consider unholy." ¹⁶This happened three times, and immediately the object was taken up into the sky.

¹⁷Now while Peter was greatly perplexed in mind as to what the vision which he had seen might mean, behold, ^the men who had

9:37^Acts 1:13; 9:39   **9:38**^Acts 11:26
9:39^Acts 1:13; 9:37   **9:40**^Mark 5:41
9:41^Acts 9:13, 32   **9:42**^Acts 9:35   **9:43**^Acts 10:6
10:1^Acts 8:40; 10:24   **10:2**^Acts 10:22, 35
ᴮLuke 7:4f   **10:3**^Acts 3:1   ᴮActs 9:10
10:4^Heb 6:10   **10:5**^Acts 9:36   **10:6**^Acts 9:43
10:8^Acts 9:36   **10:9**^Acts 10:9-32; 11:5-14
10:10^Acts 11:5; 22:17   **10:11**^John 1:51
10:14^Lev 11:20-25; Deut 14:4-20   **10:15**^Matt 15:11;
Mark 7:19   **10:17**^Acts 10:8

9:39¹A long shirt worn next to the skin
10:1¹Normally 600 men (the number varied)
10:3¹I.e., 3 p.m.   **10:9**¹I.e., noon

been sent by Cornelius had asked directions to Simon's house, and they appeared at the gate; ¹⁸and calling out, they were asking whether Simon, who was also called Peter, was staying there. ¹⁹While Peter was reflecting on the vision, ᴬthe Spirit said to him, "Behold, three men are looking for you. ²⁰But get up, go downstairs and ᴬaccompany them without misgivings, for I have sent them Myself." ²¹Peter went down to the men and said, "Behold, I am the one you are looking for; what is the reason for which you have come?" ²²They said, "Cornelius, a centurion, a righteous and ᴬGod-fearing man well spoken of by the entire nation of the Jews, was *divinely* directed by a holy angel to send for you *to come* to his house and hear ᴮa message from you." ²³So he invited them in and gave them lodging.

PETER IN CAESAREA

Now on the next day he got ready and went away with them, and some of the brothers from Joppa accompanied him. ²⁴On the following day he entered ᴬCaesarea. Now Cornelius was expecting them and had called together his relatives and close friends. ²⁵When Peter entered, Cornelius met him, and fell at his feet and ᴬworshiped *him*. ²⁶But Peter helped him up, saying, "ᴬStand up; I, too, am just a man." ²⁷As he talked with him, he entered and *found ᴬmany people assembled. ²⁸And he said to them, "You yourselves know that it is forbidden for a Jewish man to associate with or visit a foreigner; and *yet* ᴬGod has shown me that I am not to call any person unholy or unclean. ²⁹That is why I came without even

raising any objection when I was sent for. So I ask, for what reason did you send for me?"

³⁰Cornelius said, "Four days ago to this hour, I was praying in my house during the ¹ninth hour; and behold, ᴬa man stood before me in shining clothing, ³¹and he *said, 'Cornelius, your prayer has been heard and your charitable gifts have been remembered before God. ³²Therefore send *some men* to ᴬJoppa and invite Simon, who is also called Peter, to come to you; he is staying at the house of Simon *the* tanner, by the sea.' ³³So I sent *men* to you immediately, and you have been kind enough to come. Now then, we are all here present before God to hear everything that you have been commanded by the Lord."

GENTILES HEAR GOOD NEWS

³⁴ᴬOpening his mouth, Peter said: "I most certainly understand *now* that ᴮGod is not one to show partiality, ³⁵but in every nation the one who ᴬfears Him and does what is right is acceptable to Him. ³⁶The word which He sent to the sons of Israel, preaching ᴬpeace through Jesus Christ (He is ᴮLord of all)— ³⁷you yourselves know the thing that happened throughout Judea, starting from Galilee, after the baptism which John proclaimed. ³⁸*You know of* Jesus of Nazareth, how God anointed Him with the Holy Spirit and with power, ᴬand *how* He went about doing good and

10:19ᴬActs 8:29   10:20ᴬActs 15:7-9
10:22ᴬActs 10:2   ᴮActs 11:14   10:24ᴬActs 8:40; 10:1
10:25ᴬMatt 8:2   10:26ᴬActs 14:15; Rev 19:10
10:27ᴬActs 10:24   10:28ᴬActs 10:14f, 35; 15:9
10:30ᴬActs 10:3-6, 30-32   10:32ᴮJohn 4:9; 18:28
10:34ᴬMatt 5:2   ᴮDeut 10:17   10:35ᴬActs 10:2
10:36ᴬEph 2:17   ᴮRom 10:12   10:38ᴬMatt 4:23

10:30¹I.e., 3 to 4 p.m.

healing all who were oppressed by the devil, for God was with Him. ³⁹We are ^witnesses of all the things that He did both in the country of the Jews and in Jerusalem. They also put Him to death by hanging Him on ¹a cross. ⁴⁰^God raised Him up on the third day and granted that He be revealed, ⁴¹^not to all the people, but to witnesses who had been chosen beforehand by God, *that is,* to us who ate and drank with Him after He arose from the dead. ⁴²And He ordered us to preach to the people, and to testify solemnly that this is the One who has been appointed by God as ^Judge of the living and the dead. ⁴³All the prophets testify of Him, that through ^His name everyone who believes in Him receives forgiveness of sins."

⁴⁴While Peter was still speaking these words, ^the Holy Spirit fell upon all those who were listening to the message. ⁴⁵^All the ¹Jewish believers who came with Peter were amazed, because the gift of the Holy Spirit had also been ^Bpoured out on the Gentiles. ⁴⁶For they were hearing them ^speaking with tongues and exalting God. Then Peter responded, ⁴⁷"^Surely no one can refuse the water for these to be baptized, who ^Bhave received the Holy Spirit just as we *did,* can he?" ⁴⁸And he ordered them to be baptized ^in the name of Jesus Christ. Then they asked him to stay on for a few days.

PETER REPORTS IN JERUSALEM

11 Now the apostles and ^the brothers *and sisters* who were throughout Judea heard that the Gentiles also had received the word of God. ²And when Peter came up to Jerusalem, ¹,^the Jewish *believers*

took issue with him, ³saying, "^You went to ¹uncircumcised men and ate with them." ⁴But Peter began and explained *at length* to them ^in an orderly sequence, saying, ⁵"^I was in the city of Joppa praying; and in a trance I saw a vision, an object coming down like a great sheet lowered by four corners from the sky; and it came to where I *was,* ⁶and I stared at it and was thinking about it, and I saw the four-footed animals of the earth, the wild animals, the crawling creatures, and the birds of the sky. ⁷I also heard a voice saying to me, 'Get up, Peter; kill and eat.' ⁸But I said, 'By no means, Lord, for nothing unholy or unclean has ever entered my mouth.' ⁹But a voice from heaven answered a second time, '^What God has cleansed, no longer consider unholy.' ¹⁰This happened three times, and everything was drawn back up into the sky. ¹¹And behold, at that moment three men who had been sent to me from ^Caesarea came up to the house where we were *staying.* ¹²And the Spirit told me to go with them ^without misgivings. These six brothers also went with me, and we entered the man's house. ¹³And he reported to us how he had seen the angel standing in his house, and saying, 'Send *some men* to Joppa and have Simon, who is also called Peter, brought here; ¹⁴and he will speak

10:39 ^Acts 5:30   10:40 ^Acts 2:24
10:41 ^John 14:19, 22; 15:27   10:42 ^John 5:22, 27;
Acts 17:31   10:43 ^Luke 24:47; Acts 2:38
10:44 ^Acts 11:15; 15:8   10:45 ^Acts 10:23
^B Acts 2:33, 38   10:46 ^Acts 2:4; 19:6
10:47 ^Acts 8:36   ^B Acts 2:4   10:48 ^Acts 2:38; 8:16
11:1 ^Acts 1:15   11:2 ^Acts 10:45   11:3 ^Matt 9:11;
Acts 10:28   11:4 ^Luke 1:3   11:5 ^Acts 10:9-32;
11:5-14   11:9 ^Acts 10:15   11:11 ^Acts 8:40
11:12 ^Acts 15:9; Rom 3:22

10:39 ¹ Lit *wood;* see Deut 21:23   10:45 ¹ Lit *believers from the circumcision*   11:2 ¹ Lit *those from the circumcision*   11:3 ¹ I.e., Gentiles

ᴬwords to you by which you will be saved, you and ᴮall your household.' ¹⁵And as I began to speak, ᴬthe Holy Spirit fell upon them just ᴮas *He did* upon us at the beginning. ¹⁶And I remembered the word of the Lord, how He used to say, 'ᴬJohn baptized with water, but you will be baptized with the Holy Spirit.' ¹⁷Therefore, if ᴬGod gave them the same gift as *He* also *gave* to us after believing in the Lord Jesus Christ, who was I that I could stand in God's way?" ¹⁸When they heard this, they quieted down and glorified God, saying, "Well then, God has also granted to the Gentiles the ᴬrepentance *that leads* to life."

THE CHURCH IN ANTIOCH

¹⁹ᴬSo then those who were scattered because of the persecution that occurred in connection with Stephen made their way to Phoenicia, Cyprus, and Antioch, speaking the word to no one except to Jews alone. ²⁰But there were some of them, men of Cyprus and Cyrene, who came to Antioch and *began* speaking to the 'Greeks as well, ᴬpreaching the good news of the Lord Jesus. ²¹And ᴬthe hand of the Lord was with them, and a large number who believed turned to the Lord. ²²The news about them reached the ears of the church in Jerusalem, and they sent ᴬBarnabas off to Antioch. ²³Then when he arrived and witnessed ᴬthe grace of God, he rejoiced and *began* to encourage them all with resolute heart to remain *true* to the Lord; ²⁴for he was a good man, and ᴬfull of the Holy Spirit and faith. And considerable numbers were added to the Lord. ²⁵And he left for ᴬTarsus to look for Saul; ²⁶and when he had found him, he brought him to Antioch. And for an entire year they met with the church and taught considerable numbers of people; and the disciples were first called ᴬChristians in Antioch.

²⁷Now at this time *some* ᴬprophets came down from Jerusalem to Antioch. ²⁸One of them, named ᴬAgabus, stood up and indicated by the Spirit that there would definitely be a severe famine all over the world. And this took place in the *reign* of Claudius. ²⁹And to the extent that any of the disciples had means, each of them determined to send *a contribution* for the relief of ᴬthe brothers *and sisters* living in Judea. ³⁰ᴬAnd they did this, sending it with Barnabas and Saul to the elders.

PETER'S ARREST AND DELIVERANCE

12 Now about that time Herod the king laid hands on some who belonged to the church, to do them harm. ²And he ᴬhad James the brother of John executed with a sword. ³When he saw that it ᴬpleased the Jews, he proceeded to arrest Peter as well. (Now *these* were 'the days of Unleavened Bread.) ⁴When he had arrested him, he put him in prison, turning him over to four squads of soldiers to guard him, intending *only* after ᴬthe Passover to bring him before the people. ⁵So Peter was kept in the prison, but

---

11:14 ᴬActs 10:22   ᴮJohn 4:53   11:15 ᴬActs 10:44
ᴮActs 2:4   11:16 ᴬActs 1:5   11:17 ᴬActs 10:45, 47
11:18 ᴬ2 Cor 7:10   11:19 ᴬActs 8:1, 4   11:20 ᴬActs 5:42
11:21 ᴬLuke 1:66   11:22 ᴬActs 4:36   11:23 ᴬActs 13:43;
14:26   11:24 ᴬActs 2:4   11:25 ᴬActs 9:11
11:26 ᴬActs 26:28; 1 Pet 4:16   11:27 ᴬLuke 11:49;
Acts 2:17   11:28 ᴬActs 21:10   11:29 ᴬActs 11:1
11:30 ᴬActs 12:25   12:2 ᴬMatt 4:21; 20:23
12:3 ᴬActs 24:27; 25:9   12:4 ᴬEx 12:1-27; Mark 14:1

11:20 ¹Lit *Hellenists;* people who lived by Greek customs and culture   **12:3** ¹I.e., Passover week

prayer for him was being made to God intensely by the church.

6 On the very night when Herod was about to bring him forward, Peter was sleeping between two soldiers, ᴬbound with two chains, and guards in front of the door were watching over the prison. 7 And behold, ᴬan angel of the Lord suddenly ᴮstood near *Peter,* and a light shone in the cell; and he struck Peter's side and woke him, saying, "Get up quickly." And his chains fell off his hands. 8 And the angel said to him, "Put on your belt and strap on your sandals." And he did so. And he *said to him, "Wrap your cloak around you and follow me." 9 And he went out and continued to follow, and *yet* he did not know that what was being done by the angel was real, but thought he was seeing ᴬa vision. 10 Now when they had passed the first and second guard, they came to the iron gate that leads into the city, which ᴬopened for them by itself; and they went out and went along one street, and immediately the angel departed from him. 11 When Peter came to himself, he said, "Now I know for sure that ᴬthe Lord has sent forth His angel and rescued me from the hand of Herod and from all that the Jewish people were expecting." 12 And when he realized *this,* he went to the house of Mary, the mother of ᴬJohn, who was also called Mark, where many were gathered together and were praying. 13 When he knocked at the door of the gate, ᴬa slave woman named Rhoda came to answer. 14 When she recognized Peter's voice, ᴬbecause of her joy she did not open the gate, but ran in and announced that Peter was standing in front of the gate. 15 They said to her, "You

are out of your mind!" But she kept insisting that it was so. They said, "It is ᴬhis angel." 16 But Peter continued knocking; and when they had opened *the door,* they saw him and were amazed. 17 But motioning to them with his hand to be silent, he described to them how the Lord had led him out of the prison. And he said, "Report these things to ᴬJames and the brothers." Then he left and went to another place.

18 Now when day came, there was no small disturbance among the soldiers *as to* what could have become of Peter. 19 When Herod had searched for him and had not found him, he examined the guards and ordered that they ᴬbe led away *to execution.* Then he went down from Judea to Caesarea and was spending time there.

DEATH OF HEROD

20 Now he was very angry with the people of Tyre and Sidon; and with one mind they came to him, and having won over Blastus the king's chamberlain, they were asking for peace, because ᴬtheir country was supported *with grain* from the king's country. 21 On an appointed day, after putting on his royal apparel, Herod took his seat on the rostrum and *began* delivering an address to them. 22 The people *repeatedly* cried out, "The voice of a god and not of a man!" 23 And immediately ᴬan angel of the Lord struck him because he did not give God the glory, and he was eaten by worms and died.

12:6 ᴬActs 21:33   12:7 ᴬActs 5:19   ᴮLuke 2:9
12:9 ᴬActs 9:10   12:10 ᴬActs 5:19; 16:26
12:11 ᴬDan 3:28; 6:22   12:12 ᴬActs 12:25; 13:5, 13
12:13 ᴬJohn 18:16f   12:14 ᴬLuke 24:41
12:15 ᴬMatt 18:10   12:17 ᴬMark 6:3; Acts 15:13
12:19 ᴬActs 16:27; 27:42   12:20 ᴬ1 Kin 5:11; Ezra 3:7
12:23 ᴬ2 Sam 24:16; 2 Kin 19:35

24 But ^the word of the Lord continued to grow and to be multiplied.

25 And Barnabas and Saul returned ^when they had fulfilled their mission to Jerusalem, taking along with *them* ^BJohn, who was also called Mark.

FIRST MISSIONARY JOURNEY

13 Now there were prophets and ^teachers at Antioch, in the church that was *there:* Barnabas, Simeon who was called Niger, Lucius of Cyrene, Manaen who had been brought up with Herod the tetrarch, and Saul. ²While they were serving the Lord and fasting, the Holy Spirit said, "Set Barnabas and Saul apart for Me for ^the work to which I have called them." ³Then, when they had fasted, prayed, and ^laid their hands on them, they sent them away.

⁴So, being sent out by the Holy Spirit, they went down to Seleucia and from there they sailed to ^Cyprus. ⁵When they reached Salamis, they *began* to proclaim the word of God in the synagogues of the Jews; and they also had ^John as their helper. ⁶When they had gone through the whole island as far as Paphos, they found a ^magician, a Jewish ^Bfalse prophet whose name was Bar-Jesus, ⁷who was with the ^proconsul, Sergius Paulus, a man of intelligence. This man summoned Barnabas and Saul and sought to hear the word of God. ⁸But Elymas the magician (for so his name is translated) was opposing them, seeking to turn the proconsul away from ^the faith. ⁹But Saul, who was also *known as* Paul, ^filled with the Holy Spirit, stared at him, ¹⁰and said, "You who are full of all deceit and fraud, you ^son of

the devil, you enemy of all righteousness, will you not stop making crooked the straight ways of the Lord? ¹¹Now, behold, ^the hand of the Lord is upon you, and you will be blind and not see the sun for a time." And immediately a mist and a darkness fell upon him, and he went about seeking those who would lead him by the hand. ¹²Then the proconsul believed when he saw what had happened, being amazed at ^the teaching of the Lord.

¹³Now Paul and his companions put out to sea from Paphos and came to Perga in Pamphylia; but ^John left them and returned to Jerusalem. ¹⁴But going on from Perga, they arrived at Pisidian ^Antioch, and on the Sabbath day they went into the synagogue and sat down. ¹⁵After ^the reading of the Law and ^Bthe Prophets, the synagogue officials sent *word* to them, saying, "Brothers, if you have any word of exhortation for the people, say it." ¹⁶Paul stood up, and motioning with his hand said,

"Men of Israel, and ^you who fear God, listen: ¹⁷The God of this people Israel chose our fathers and ^made the people great during their stay in the land of Egypt, and with an uplifted arm ^BHe led them out from it. ¹⁸For ^a period of about forty years He put up with them in the wilderness. ¹⁹When He had destroyed ^seven nations in the land of Canaan, He ^Bdistributed

12:24 ^Acts 6:7; 19:20   12:25 ^Acts 11:30   ᴮActs 12:12
13:1 ^Rom 12:6f; 1 Cor 12:28f   13:2 ^Acts 9:15
13:3 ^Acts 6:6   13:4 ^Acts 4:36   13:5 ^Acts 12:12
13:6 ^Acts 8:9   ᴮMatt 7:15   13:7 ^Acts 13:8, 12; 18:12
13:8 ^Acts 6:7   13:9 ^Acts 2:4; 4:8   13:10 ^Matt 13:38; John 8:44   13:11 ^Ex 9:3; 1 Sam 5:6f
13:12 ^Acts 8:25; 13:49   13:13 ^Acts 12:12
13:14 ^Acts 14:19, 21; 2 Tim 3:11   13:15 ^Acts 15:21
ᴮActs 13:27   13:16 ^Acts 10:2; 13:26   13:17 ^Ex 1:7
ᴮEx 12:51   13:18 ^Num 14:34; Acts 7:36
13:19 ^Deut 7:1   ᴮJosh 14:1

their land as an inheritance—*all of which took* about 450 years. ²⁰After these things He ᴬgave *them* judges until Samuel the prophet. ²¹Then they ᴬasked for a king, and God gave them ᴮSaul the son of Kish, a man of the tribe of Benjamin, for forty years. ²²After He had removed him, He raised up David to be their king, concerning whom He also testified and said, 'ᴬI have found David, the son of Jesse, a man after My heart, who will do all My will.' ²³From the descendants of this man, according to promise, God has brought to Israel ᴬa Savior, Jesus, ²⁴after ᴬJohn had proclaimed, before His coming, a baptism of repentance to all the people of Israel. ²⁵And while John was completing his course, ᴬhe kept saying, 'What do you suppose that I am? I am not *He*. But behold, One is coming after me, the sandals of whose feet I am not worthy to untie.'

²⁶"Brothers, sons of Abraham's family, and those among you who fear God, to us the message of ᴬthis salvation has been sent. ²⁷For those who live in Jerusalem, and their rulers, ᴬrecognizing neither Him nor the declarations of the prophets which are read every Sabbath, fulfilled *these* by condemning *Him*. ²⁸And though they found no grounds for *putting Him to* death, they ᴬasked Pilate that He be executed. ²⁹When they had ᴬcarried out everything that was written concerning Him, ᴮthey took Him down from the ¹cross and laid Him in a tomb. ³⁰But God ᴬraised Him from the dead; ³¹and for many days ᴬHe appeared to those who came up with Him from Galilee to Jerusalem, the very ones who are now ᴮHis witnesses to the people. ³²And

we preach to you the good news of ᴬthe promise made to the fathers, ³³that God has fulfilled this *promise* to those of us *who are the* descendants by raising Jesus, as it is also written in the second Psalm: 'ᴬYou are My Son; today I have fathered You.' ³⁴*As for the fact* that He raised Him from the dead, never again to return to decay, He has spoken in this way: 'ᴬI will give you the holy *and* faithful *mercies* of David.' ³⁵Therefore, He also says in another *Psalm:* 'ᴬYou will not allow Your Holy One to undergo decay.' ³⁶For David, after he had served God's ᴬpurpose in his own generation, fell asleep, and was buried among his fathers and underwent decay; ³⁷but He whom God ᴬraised did not undergo decay. ³⁸Therefore let it be known to you, brothers, that ᴬthrough Him forgiveness of sins is proclaimed to you, ³⁹and through Him ᴬeveryone who believes is freed from all things, from which you could not be freed through the Law of Moses. ⁴⁰Therefore, see that the thing spoken of ᴬin the Prophets does not come upon *you:*

⁴¹ 'ᴬLook, you scoffers, and be astonished, and perish; For I am accomplishing a work in your days, A work which you will never believe, though someone should describe it to you.'"

13:20ᴬJudg 2:16   13:21ᴬ1 Sam 8:5   ᴮ1 Sam 9:1f
13:22ᴬ1 Sam 13:14; Ps 89:20   13:23ᴬLuke 2:11; John 4:42   13:24ᴬMark 1:1-4; Acts 1:22
13:25ᴬMatt 3:11; Mark 1:7   13:26ᴬJohn 6:68; Acts 4:12
13:27ᴬActs 3:17   13:28ᴬMatt 27:22, 23; Mark 15:13, 14
13:29ᴬActs 26:22   ᴮLuke 23:53   13:30ᴬActs 2:24;
13:33, 34, 37   13:31ᴬActs 1:3   ᴮLuke 24:48
13:32ᴬRom 4:13   13:33ᴬPs 2:7   13:34ᴬIs 55:3
13:35ᴬPs 16:10; Acts 2:27   13:36ᴬActs 13:22; 20:27
13:37ᴬActs 2:24; 13:30, 33, 34   13:38ᴬLuke 24:47;
Acts 2:38   13:39ᴬActs 10:43; Rom 3:28
13:40ᴬLuke 24:44; John 6:45   13:41ᴬHab 1:5

13:29 ¹Lit *wood;* see Deut 21:23

⁴²As Paul and Barnabas were going out, *the people repeatedly* begged to have these things spoken to them the next ^Sabbath. ⁴³Now when *the meeting of* the synagogue had broken up, many of the Jews and the ^God-fearing proselytes followed Paul and Barnabas, who were speaking to them and urging them to continue in ^Bthe grace of God.

PAUL TURNS TO THE GENTILES

⁴⁴The next ^Sabbath nearly all the city assembled to hear the word of the Lord. ⁴⁵But when ^the Jews saw the crowds, they were filled with jealousy and *began* contradicting the things spoken by Paul, and were blaspheming. ⁴⁶Paul and Barnabas spoke out boldly and said, "It was necessary that the word of God be spoken to you ^first. Since you repudiate it and consider yourselves unworthy of eternal life, behold, ^Bwe are turning to the Gentiles. ⁴⁷For so the Lord has commanded us,

'^AI HAVE APPOINTED YOU AS A
   LIGHT TO THE GENTILES,
THAT YOU MAY BRING SALVATION
   TO THE END OF THE EARTH.'"

⁴⁸When the Gentiles heard this, they *began* rejoicing and glorifying the word of the Lord; and all who ^had been appointed to eternal life believed. ⁴⁹And ^the word of the Lord was being spread through the whole region. ⁵⁰But the Jews incited the ^devout women of prominence and the leading men of the city, and instigated a persecution against Paul and Barnabas, and drove them out of their region. ⁵¹But ^they shook off the dust *from* their feet *in protest* against them and went to Iconium. ⁵²And the disciples were continually ^filled with joy and with the Holy Spirit.

ACCEPTANCE AND OPPOSITION

14 In Iconium ^they entered the synagogue of the Jews together, and spoke in such a way ^Bthat a large number of people believed, both of Jews and of Greeks. ²But the ^unbelieving Jews stirred up the minds of the Gentiles and embittered them against the brothers. ³Therefore they spent a long time *there* ^speaking boldly *with reliance* upon the Lord, who was testifying to the word of His grace, granting that signs and wonders be performed by their hands. ⁴^But the people of the city were divided; and some sided with ^Bthe Jews, while others, with the apostles. ⁵And when an attempt was made by both the Gentiles and the Jews with their rulers, to treat them abusively and to ^stone them, ⁶they became aware of it and fled to the cities of Lycaonia, Lystra and ^Derbe, and the surrounding region; ⁷and there they continued to ^preach the gospel.

⁸In Lystra ^a man was sitting whose feet were incapacitated. *He had been* disabled from his mother's womb, and had never walked. ⁹This man was listening to Paul as he spoke. *Paul* looked at him intently and saw that he had ^faith to be made well, ¹⁰and he said with a loud voice, "Stand upright on your feet!" ^And *the man* leaped up and *began* to walk. ¹¹When the crowds saw what Paul

13:42 ^Acts 13:14   **13:43** ^Acts 17:4, 17   ^BActs 11:23
13:44 ^Acts 13:14   **13:45** ^Acts 13:50; 14:2, 4, 5, 19
13:46 ^Acts 3:26   ^BActs 18:6; 22:21   **13:47** ^Is 42:6; 49:6
13:48 ^Rom 8:28ff; Eph 1:4f, 11   **13:49** ^Acts 13:12
13:50 ^Acts 16:14; 17:4   **13:51** ^Matt 10:14; Mark 6:11
13:52 ^Acts 2:4   **14:1** ^Acts 13:5   ^BActs 2:47
14:2 ^John 3:36   **14:3** ^Acts 4:29f; 20:32
14:4 ^Acts 17:4   ^BActs 13:45, 50   **14:5** ^Acts 14:19
14:6 ^Acts 14:20; 16:1   **14:7** ^Acts 14:15, 21; 16:10
14:8 ^Acts 3:2   **14:9** ^Matt 9:28   **14:10** ^Acts 3:8

had done, they raised their voice, saying in the Lycaonian language, "^AThe gods have become like men and have come down to us!" ¹²And they *began* calling Barnabas, Zeus, and Paul, Hermes, since he was the chief speaker. ¹³Moreover, the priest of Zeus, whose *temple* was just outside the city, brought oxen and garlands to the gates, and ^Awanted to offer sacrifice with the crowds. ¹⁴But when the apostles Barnabas and Paul heard *about it,* they ^Atore their robes and rushed out into the crowd, crying out ¹⁵and saying, "Men, why are you doing these things? We are also men, of the same nature as you, preaching the gospel to you, to turn from these ¹useless things to a living God, who ^AMADE THE HEAVEN AND THE EARTH AND THE SEA, AND EVERYTHING THAT IS IN THEM. ¹⁶In past generations He ^Apermitted all the nations to go their own ways; ¹⁷yet ^AHe did not leave Himself without witness, in that He did good and gave you rains from heaven and fruitful seasons, satisfying your hearts with food and gladness." ¹⁸And *even by* saying these things, *only with* difficulty did they restrain the crowds from offering sacrifices to them.

¹⁹But Jews came from Antioch and Iconium, and having won over the crowds, they ^Astoned Paul and dragged him out of the city, thinking that he was dead. ²⁰But while ^Athe disciples stood around him, he got up and entered the city. The next day he left with Barnabas for Derbe. ²¹And after they had preached the gospel to that city and had ^Amade a good number of disciples, they returned to Lystra, to Iconium, and to Antioch,

²²strengthening the souls of the disciples, encouraging them to continue in ^Athe faith, and *saying,* "^BIt is through many tribulations *that* we must enter the kingdom of God." ²³When ^Athey had appointed elders for them in every church, having ^Bprayed with fasting, they entrusted them to the Lord in whom they had believed. ²⁴They passed through ^APisidia and came into ^BPamphylia. ²⁵When they had spoken the word in ^APerga, they went down to Attalia. ²⁶From there they sailed to Antioch, where they had been ^Aentrusted to the grace of God for the work that they had accomplished. ²⁷When they had arrived and gathered the church together, they *began* to report all the things that God had done with them and how He had opened a ^Adoor of faith to the Gentiles. ²⁸And they spent a long time with ^Athe disciples.

THE COUNCIL IN JERUSALEM

15 ^ASome men came down from Judea and *began* teaching the brothers, "Unless you are circumcised according to the custom of Moses, you cannot be saved." ²And after Paul and Barnabas had a heated argument and ^Adebate with them, *the brothers* determined that Paul and Barnabas and some others of them should go up to Jerusalem to the

14:11^AActs 28:6   14:13^ADan 2:46   14:14^ANum 14:6; Matt 26:65   14:15^AEx 20:11; Ps 146:6
14:16^AActs 17:30   14:17^AActs 17:26f; Rom 1:19f
14:19^AActs 14:5; 2 Cor 11:25   14:20^AActs 11:26;
14:22, 28   14:21^AActs 2:47   14:22^AActs 6:7
^BJohn 16:33   14:23^ATitus 1:5   ^BActs 13:3
14:24^AActs 13:14   ^BActs 13:13   14:25^AActs 13:13
14:26^AActs 11:23; 15:40   14:27^A1 Cor 16:9; 2 Cor 2:12
14:28^AActs 11:26; 14:22   15:1^AActs 15:24
15:2^AActs 15:7

14:15¹I.e., idols

apostles and elders concerning this issue. ³Therefore, after being ᴬsent on their way by the church, they were passing through both Phoenicia and Samaria, describing in detail the conversion of the Gentiles, and they were bringing great joy to all the brothers *and sisters.* ⁴When they arrived in Jerusalem, they were received by the church, the apostles, and the elders, and they ᴬreported all that God had done with them. ⁵But some of ᴬthe sect of the Pharisees who had believed stood up, saying, "It is necessary to ᴮcircumcise ¹them and to direct them to keep the Law of Moses."

⁶ᴬThe apostles and the elders came together to look into this matter. ⁷After there had been much debate, Peter stood up and said to them, "Brothers, you know that in the early days God made a choice among you, that by my mouth the Gentiles would hear the word of ᴬthe gospel and believe. ⁸And God, ᴬwho knows the heart, testified to them ᴮgiving them the Holy Spirit, just as He also did to us; ⁹and ᴬHe made no distinction between us and them, cleansing their hearts by faith. ¹⁰Since this *is the* case, why are you ᴬputting God to the test by placing upon the neck of the disciples a yoke which neither our forefathers nor we have been able to bear? ¹¹But we believe that we are saved through ᴬthe grace of the Lord Jesus, in the same way as they also are."

¹²All the people kept silent, and they were listening to Barnabas and Paul as they were ᴬrelating all the signs and wonders that God had done through them among the Gentiles.

JAMES' JUDGMENT

¹³After they stopped speaking, ᴬJames responded, saying, "Brothers, listen to me. ¹⁴ᴬSimeon has described how God first concerned Himself about taking a people for His name from among the Gentiles. ¹⁵The words of ᴬthe Prophets agree with this, just as it is written:

¹⁶ 'ᴬAFTER THESE THINGS I will
　　return,
　AND I WILL REBUILD THE FALLEN
　　TABERNACLE OF DAVID,
　AND I WILL REBUILD ITS RUINS,
　AND I WILL RESTORE IT,
¹⁷ ᴬSO THAT THE REST OF MANKIND
　　MAY SEEK THE LORD,
　AND ALL THE GENTILES WHO
　　ARE CALLED BY MY NAME,'
¹⁸ SAYS THE LORD, WHO ᴬMAKES
　　THESE THINGS known from
　　long ago.

¹⁹Therefore, it is ᴬmy judgment that we do not cause trouble for those from the Gentiles who are turning to God, ²⁰but that we write to them that they abstain from things contaminated by idols, from ᴬ*acts of* sexual immorality, from ᴮwhat has been strangled, and from blood. ²¹For ᴬfrom ancient generations Moses has those who preach him in every city, since he is read in the synagogues every Sabbath."

²²Then it seemed good to the apostles and the elders, with the whole church, to choose men from

15:3 ᴬActs 20:38; 21:5　15:4 ᴬActs 14:27; 15:12
15:5 ᴬActs 26:5　ᴮ1 Cor 7:18
15:6 ᴬActs 11:30; 15:4, 22, 23　15:7 ᴬActs 20:24
15:8 ᴬActs 1:24　ᴮActs 2:4　15:9 ᴬActs 10:28, 34; 11:12
15:10 ᴬActs 5:9　15:11 ᴬRom 3:24; 5:15
15:12 ᴬActs 14:27; 15:3, 4　15:13 ᴬActs 12:17
15:14 ᴬActs 15:7; 2 Pet 1:1　15:15 ᴬActs 13:40
15:16 ᴬAmos 9:11　15:17 ᴬAmos 9:12　15:18 ᴬIs 45:21
15:19 ᴬActs 15:28; 21:25　15:20 ᴬLev 18:6-23
ᴮLev 17:14　15:21 ᴬActs 13:15; 2 Cor 3:14f

15:5 ¹I.e., Gentile believers

among them to send to Antioch with Paul and Barnabas: Judas who was called Barsabbas, and ᴬSilas, leading men among the brothers, 23 and they sent this letter with them:

"ᴬThe apostles and the brothers who are elders, to the brothers *and sisters* in Antioch, Syria, and Cilicia who are from the Gentiles: Greetings. 24 Since we have heard that some of our number to whom we gave no instruction have ᴬconfused you by *their* teaching, upsetting your souls, 25 ᴬit seemed good to us, having become of one mind, to select men to send to you with our beloved Barnabas and Paul, 26 men who have ᴬrisked their lives for the name of our Lord Jesus Christ. 27 Therefore, we have sent ᴬJudas and Silas, who themselves will also report the same things by word *of mouth*. 28 For it seemed good to ᴬthe Holy Spirit and to us to lay upon you no greater burden than these essentials: 29 that you abstain from ᴬthings sacrificed to idols, from ᴬblood, from things strangled, and from *acts of* sexual immorality; if you keep yourselves free from such things, you will do well. Farewell."

30 So when they were sent away, ᴬthey went down to Antioch; and after gathering the congregation together, they delivered the letter. 31 When they had read it, they rejoiced because of its encouragement. 32 Judas and Silas, also being ᴬprophets themselves, encouraged and strengthened the brothers *and sisters* with a lengthy message. 33 After they had spent time *there,* they were sent away from the brothers *and sisters* ᴬin peace to those who had sent them out.[1] 35 But Paul and Barnabas stayed in Antioch, teaching and ᴬpreaching the word of the Lord, with many others also.

SECOND MISSIONARY JOURNEY

36 After some days Paul said to Barnabas, "Let's return and visit the brothers *and sisters* in ᴬevery city in which we proclaimed the word of the Lord, *and see* how they are." 37 Barnabas wanted to take ᴬJohn, called Mark, along with them also. 38 But Paul was of the opinion that they should not take along with them this man who had ᴬdeserted them in Pamphylia and had not gone with them to the work. 39 Now it turned into such a sharp disagreement that they separated from one another, and Barnabas took Mark with him and sailed away to ᴬCyprus. 40 But Paul chose ᴬSilas, and left after being entrusted by the brothers to the grace of the Lord. 41 And he was traveling through ᴬSyria and Cilicia, strengthening the churches.

THE MACEDONIAN VISION

16 Now *Paul* also came to Derbe and to Lystra. And a disciple was there, named ᴬTimothy, the son of a ᴮJewish woman who was a believer, but his father was a Greek, 2 and he was well spoken

15:22 ᴬActs 15:27, 32, 40; 16:19, 25, 29
15:23 ᴬActs 15:2   15:24 ᴬGal 1:7; 5:10
15:25 ᴬActs 15:28   15:26 ᴬActs 9:23ff; 14:19
15:27 ᴬActs 15:22, 32   15:28 ᴬActs 5:32; 15:8
15:29 ᴬActs 15:20   15:30 ᴬActs 15:22f
15:32 ᴬActs 13:1   15:33 ᴬMark 5:34; Acts 16:36
15:35 ᴬActs 8:4   15:36 ᴬActs 13:4, 13, 14, 51; 14:6, 24f
15:37 ᴬActs 12:12   15:38 ᴬActs 13:13   15:39 ᴬActs 4:36
15:40 ᴬActs 15:22   15:41 ᴬMatt 4:24; Acts 15:23
16:1 ᴬActs 17:14f   ᴮ2 Tim 1:5

15:33 [1] Late mss add as v 34: *But it seemed good to Silas to remain there.*

of by ᴬthe brothers *and sisters* who were in Lystra and Iconium. ³Paul wanted this man to leave with him; and he ᴬtook him and circumcised him because of the Jews who were in those parts, for they all knew that his father was a Greek. ⁴Now while they were passing through the cities, they were delivering ᴬthe ordinances for them to follow which had been determined by the apostles and elders in Jerusalem. ⁵So ᴬthe churches were being strengthened in the faith, and were ᴮincreasing in number daily.

⁶They passed through the Phrygian and ᴬGalatian region, after being forbidden by the Holy Spirit to speak the word in Asia; ⁷and after they came to Mysia, they were trying to go into Bithynia, and the ᴬSpirit of Jesus did not allow them; ⁸and passing by Mysia, they went down to ᴬTroas. ⁹And a vision appeared to Paul in the night: a man of ᴬMacedonia was standing and pleading with him, and saying, "Come over to Macedonia and help us." ¹⁰When he had seen the vision, ᴬwe immediately sought to leave for Macedonia, concluding that God had called us to preach the gospel to them.

¹¹So after setting sail from ᴬTroas, we ran a straight course to Samothrace, and on the following *day* to Neapolis; ¹²and from there to ᴬPhilippi, which is a leading city of the district of Macedonia, a *Roman* colony; and we were spending some days in this city. ¹³And on ᴬthe Sabbath day we went outside the gate to a riverside, where we were thinking that there was a place of prayer; and we sat down and began speaking to the women who had assembled.

FIRST CONVERT IN EUROPE

¹⁴A woman named Lydia was listening; *she was* a seller of purple fabrics from the city of Thyatira, *and* ᴬa worshiper of God. The Lord ᴮopened her heart to respond to the things spoken by Paul. ¹⁵Now when she and ᴬher household had been baptized, she urged *us,* saying, "If you have judged me to be faithful to the Lord, come into my house and stay." And she prevailed upon us.

¹⁶It happened that as we were going to the place of prayer, a slave woman who had ᴬa spirit of divination met us, who was bringing great profit to her masters by fortune-telling. ¹⁷She followed Paul and us and cried out *repeatedly,* saying, "These men are bond-servants of ᴬthe Most High God, who are proclaiming to you a way of salvation." ¹⁸Now she continued doing this for many days. But Paul was greatly annoyed, and he turned and said to the spirit, "I command you ᴬin the name of Jesus Christ to come out of her!" And it came out at that very moment.

¹⁹But when her masters saw that their hope of ᴬprofit was *suddenly* gone, they seized Paul and Silas and ᴮdragged them into the marketplace before the authorities, ²⁰and when they had brought them to the chief magistrates, they said, "These men, Jews as they are, are causing our city trouble, ²¹and they ᴬare proclaiming customs that are not lawful for us to accept or to practice, *since* we are Romans."

16:2ᴬActs 16:40   16:3ᴬGal 2:3   16:4ᴬActs 15:28f
16:5ᴬActs 9:31   ᴮActs 2:47   16:6ᴬActs 18:23; 1 Cor 16:1
16:7ᴬLuke 24:49; Acts 8:29   16:8ᴬActs 16:11; 20:5f
16:9ᴬActs 16:10, 12; 18:5   16:10ᴬActs 16:10–17; 20:5–15
16:11ᴬActs 16:8; 20:5f   16:12ᴬActs 20:6; Phil 1:1
16:13ᴬActs 13:14   16:14ᴬActs 18:7   ᴮLuke 24:45
16:15ᴬActs 11:14   16:16ᴬLev 19:31; 20:6, 27
16:17ᴬMark 5:7   16:18ᴬLuke 10:17   16:19ᴬActs 16:16
ᴮActs 17:6f   16:21ᴬEsth 3:8

PAUL AND SILAS IMPRISONED

²²The crowd joined in an attack against them, and the chief magistrates tore their robes off them and proceeded to order *them* to be ^beaten with rods. ²³When they had struck them with many blows, they threw them into prison, commanding ^the jailer to guard them securely; ²⁴and he, having received such a command, threw them into the inner prison and fastened their feet in ^the stocks.

²⁵Now about midnight Paul and Silas were praying and ^singing hymns of praise to God, and the prisoners were listening to them; ²⁶and suddenly there was a great earthquake, so that the foundations of the prison were shaken; and immediately ^all the doors were opened, and everyone's ᴮchains were unfastened. ²⁷When ^the jailer awoke and saw the prison doors opened, he drew *his* sword and was about ᴮto kill himself, thinking that the prisoners had escaped. ²⁸But Paul called out with a loud voice, saying, "Do not harm yourself, for we are all here!" ²⁹And *the jailer* asked for lights and rushed in, and trembling with fear, he fell down before ^Paul and Silas; ³⁰and after he brought them out, he said, "Sirs, ^what must I do to be saved?"

THE JAILER CONVERTED

³¹They said, "Believe in the Lord Jesus, and you will be saved, you and ^your household." ³²And they spoke the word of God to him together with all who were in his house. ³³And he took them ^that *very* hour of the night and washed their wounds, and immediately he was baptized, he and all his *household.* ³⁴And he brought them into

his house and set food before them, and was overjoyed, since he had become a believer in God together with ^his whole household.

³⁵Now when day came, the chief magistrates sent their officers, saying, "Release those men." ³⁶And ^the jailer reported these words to Paul, *saying,* "The chief magistrates have sent *word* that you be released. So come out now and go ᴮin peace." ³⁷But Paul said to them, "After beating us in public without due process—^men *who* are Romans—they threw us into prison; and now they are releasing us secretly? No indeed! On the contrary, let them come in person and lead us out." ³⁸The officers reported these words to the chief magistrates. ^And they became fearful when they heard that they were Romans, ³⁹and they came and pleaded with them, and when they had led them out, they *repeatedly* asked them ^to leave the city. ⁴⁰They left the prison and entered *the house of* ^Lydia, and when they saw the brothers *and sisters,* they encouraged *them* and departed.

PAUL IN THESSALONICA

17 Now when they had traveled through Amphipolis and Apollonia, they came to ^Thessalonica, where there was a synagogue of the Jews. ²And according to Paul's custom, he visited them, and for three ^Sabbaths reasoned with them from the Scriptures,

16:22^2 Cor 11:25; 1 Thess 2:2   **16:23**^Acts 16:27, 36
16:24^Job 13:27; 33:11   **16:25**^Eph 5:19
16:26^Acts 12:10   ᴮActs 12:7   **16:27**^Acts 16:23, 36
ᴮActs 15:33   **16:29**^Acts 16:19   **16:30**^Acts 2:37;
22:10   **16:31**^Acts 11:14; 16:15   **16:33**^Acts 16:25
16:34^Acts 11:14; 16:15   **16:36**^Acts 16:27
ᴮActs 15:33   **16:37**^Acts 22:25-29   **16:38**^Acts 22:29
16:39^Matt 8:34   **16:40**^Acts 16:14
17:1^Acts 17:11, 13; 20:4   **17:2**^Acts 13:14

³explaining and giving evidence that the Christ ^had to suffer and ^Brise from the dead, and *saying,* "This Jesus whom I am proclaiming to you is the Christ." ⁴And some of them were persuaded and joined Paul and Silas, along with a large number of the ^God-fearing Greeks and a significant number of the ᴮleading women. ⁵But ^the Jews, becoming jealous and taking along some wicked men from the marketplace, formed a mob and set the city in an uproar; and they attacked the house of Jason and were seeking to bring them out to the people. ⁶When they did not find them, they *began* dragging Jason and some brothers before the city authorities, shouting, "These men who have upset ^the world have come here also; ⁷and Jason ^has welcomed them, and they all act contrary to the decrees of Caesar, saying that there is another king, Jesus." ⁸They stirred up the crowd and the city authorities who heard these things. ⁹And when they had received a pledge from ^Jason and the others, they released them.

PAUL IN BEREA

¹⁰The brothers immediately sent Paul and Silas away by night to ^Berea, and when they arrived, they went into the synagogue of the Jews. ¹¹Now these people were more noble-minded than those in ^Thessalonica, for they received the word with great eagerness, examining the Scriptures daily *to see* whether these things were so. ¹²Therefore, many of them believed, along with a significant number of prominent Greek ^women and men. ¹³But when the Jews of Thessalonica found out that the word of God had

been proclaimed by Paul in ^Berea also, they came there as well, agitating and stirring up the crowds. ¹⁴Then immediately the brothers sent Paul out to go as far as the sea; and ^Silas and ᴮTimothy remained there. ¹⁵Now those who escorted Paul brought him as far as ^Athens; and receiving a command for Silas and Timothy to come to him as soon as possible, they left.

PAUL IN ATHENS

¹⁶Now while Paul was waiting for them in ^Athens, his spirit was being provoked within him as he observed that the city was full of idols. ¹⁷So he was reasoning ^in the synagogue with the Jews and ᴮthe God-fearing *Gentiles,* and in the marketplace every day with those who happened to be present. ¹⁸And some of the Epicurean and Stoic philosophers as well were conversing with him. Some were saying, "What could this scavenger of tidbits want to say?" Others, "He seems to be a proclaimer of strange deities,"—because he was preaching ^Jesus and the resurrection. ¹⁹And they ^took him and brought him to the ¹Areopagus, saying, "May we know what this new teaching is which you are proclaiming? ²⁰For you are bringing some strange things to our ears; so we want to know what these things mean." ²¹(Now all the Athenians and the strangers ^visiting

17:3 ^Acts 3:18   ᴮJohn 20:9   17:4 ^Acts 13:43
ᴮActs 13:50   17:5 ^Acts 17:13; 1 Thess 2:14ff
17:6 ^Matt 24:14; Acts 17:31   17:7 ^Luke 10:38;
James 2:25   17:9 ^Acts 17:5   17:10 ^Acts 17:13; 20:4
17:11 ^Acts 17:1   17:12 ^Acts 13:50   17:13 ^Acts 17:10;
20:4   17:14 ^Acts 15:22   ᴮActs 16:1
17:15 ^Acts 17:16, 21f; 18:1   17:16 ^Acts 17:15, 21f; 18:1
17:17 ^Acts 9:20   ᴮActs 17:4   17:18 ^Acts 4:2; 17:31f
17:19 ^Acts 23:19   17:21 ^Acts 2:10

17:19 ¹Or *Hill of Ares;* Greek god of war

there used to spend their time in nothing other than telling or hearing something new.)

SERMON ON MARS HILL

²²So Paul stood in the midst of the Areopagus and said, "Men of Athens, I see that you are very ^religious in all respects. ²³For while I was passing through and examining the ^objects of your worship, I also found an altar with this inscription, 'TO AN UNKNOWN GOD.' Therefore, what you worship in ignorance, this I proclaim to you. ²⁴^The God who made the world and everything that is in it, since He is ^BLord of heaven and earth, does not dwell in temples made by hands; ²⁵nor is He served by human hands, ^as though He needed anything, since He Himself gives to all *people* life and breath and all things; ²⁶and He made from one *man* every nation of mankind to live on all the face of the earth, having ^determined *their* appointed times and the boundaries of their habitation, ²⁷that they would seek God, if perhaps they might feel around for Him and find *Him,* ^though He is not far from each one of us; ²⁸for ^in Him we live and move and exist, as even some of your own poets have said, 'For we also are His descendants.' ²⁹Therefore, since we are the descendants of God, we ^ought not to think that the Divine *Nature* is like gold or silver or stone, an image formed by human skill and thought. ³⁰So having ^overlooked the times of ignorance, God is now proclaiming to mankind that all people everywhere are to repent, ³¹because He has set a day on which ^He will judge the world in righteousness through a Man whom He has appointed,

having furnished proof to all people by raising Him from the dead."

³²Now when they heard of ^the resurrection of the dead, some *began* to scoff, but others said, "We shall hear from you again concerning this." ³³So Paul went out from among them. ³⁴But some men joined him and believed, among whom also were Dionysius the ^Areopagite and a woman named Damaris, and others with them.

PAUL IN CORINTH

18 After these *events Paul* left Athens and went to ^Corinth. ²And he found a Jew named ^Aquila, a native of Pontus having recently come from Italy with his wife ^Priscilla, because Claudius had commanded all the Jews to leave Rome. He came to them, ³and because he was of the same trade he stayed with them, and ^they worked *together,* for they were tent-makers by trade. ⁴And *Paul* was reasoning in the synagogue every ^Sabbath and trying to persuade Jews and Greeks.

⁵But when Silas and Timothy came down from Macedonia, Paul *began* devoting himself completely to the word, ^testifying to the Jews that ^BJesus was the Christ. ⁶But when they resisted and blasphemed, he shook out his garments and said to them, "Your ^blood *is* on your own heads! I am clean. From now on I will go ^Bto the Gentiles." ⁷Then he left the

17:22^Acts 25:19   17:23^2 Thess 2:4   17:24^Is 42:5
^BDeut 10:14   17:25^Job 22:2; Ps 50:10-12
17:26^Deut 32:8; Job 12:23   17:27^Deut 4:7;
Jer 23:23f   17:28^Job 12:10; Dan 5:23
17:29^Is 40:18ff; Rom 1:23   17:30^Acts 14:16;
Rom 3:25   17:31^Ps 9:8; 96:13   17:32^Acts 17:18, 31
17:34^Acts 17:19, 22   18:1^Acts 18:8; 19:1
18:2^Acts 18:18, 26; Rom 16:3   18:3^Acts 20:34;
1 Cor 4:12   18:4^Acts 13:14   18:5^Acts 20:21
^BActs 17:3   18:6^2 Sam 1:16   ^BActs 13:46

synagogue and went to the house of a man named Titius Justus, ^a worshiper of God, whose house was next door to the synagogue. 8^Crispus, the leader of the synagogue, believed in the Lord ^B together with his entire household; and many of the Corinthians, as they listened *to Paul,* were believing and being baptized. 9And the Lord said to Paul by ^a vision at night, "Do not be afraid *any longer,* but go on speaking and do not be silent; 10for I am with you, and no one will attack you to harm you, for I have many people in this city." 11And he settled *there* for a year and six months, teaching the word of God among them.

12But while Gallio was proconsul of Achaia, ^the Jews rose up together against Paul and brought him before ^B the judgment seat, 13saying, "This man is inciting the people to worship God contrary to ^the 1law." 14But when Paul was about to ^open his mouth, Gallio said to the Jews, "If it were *a matter of* some crime or vicious, unscrupulous act, O Jews, it would be reasonable for me to put up with you; 15but if there are ^questions about teaching and persons and your own law, see to it yourselves; I am unwilling to be a judge of these matters." 16And he drove them away from ^the judgment seat. 17But they all took hold of ^Sosthenes, the leader of the synagogue, and *began* beating him in front of the judgment seat. And *yet* Gallio was not concerned about any of these things.

18 Now Paul, when he had remained many days longer, took leave of the brothers *and sisters* and sailed away to Syria, and Priscilla and Aquila were with him. Paul *first* ^had his hair cut at Cenchrea, for he

was keeping a vow. 19They came to ^Ephesus, and he left them there. Now he himself entered the synagogue and reasoned with the Jews. 20When they asked him to stay for a longer time, he did not consent, 21but took leave of them and said, "I will return to you again ^if God wills," and he set sail from Ephesus. 22When he had landed in ^Caesarea, he went up *to Jerusalem* and greeted the church, and went down to ^B Antioch.

THIRD MISSIONARY JOURNEY

23And after spending some time *there,* he left and passed successively through the ^Galatian region and Phrygia, strengthening all the disciples.

24Now a Jew named ^Apollos, an Alexandrian by birth, an eloquent man, came to Ephesus; and he was proficient in the Scriptures. 25This man had been instructed in ^the way of the Lord; and being fervent in spirit, he was accurately speaking and teaching things about Jesus, being acquainted only with ^B the baptism of John; 26and he began speaking boldly in the synagogue. But when ^Priscilla and Aquila heard him, they took him aside and explained the way of God more accurately to him. 27And when he wanted to go across to Achaia, the brothers encouraged him and wrote to ^the disciples to welcome him;

18:7^Acts 13:43; 16:14   18:8^1 Cor 1:14   ^B Acts 11:14
18:9^Acts 9:10   18:12^1 Thess 2:14ff   ^B Matt 27:19
18:13^John 19:7; Acts 18:15   18:14^Matt 5:2
18:15^Acts 23:29; 25:19   18:16^Matt 27:19
18:17^1 Cor 1:1   18:18^Num 6:2, 5, 9, 18; Acts 21:24
18:19^Acts 18:21, 24; 19:1, 17, 26, 28, 34f
18:21^Rom 1:10; 15:32   18:22^Acts 8:40   ^B Acts 11:19
18:23^Acts 16:6   18:24^Acts 19:1; 1 Cor 1:12
18:25^Acts 9:2   ^B Luke 7:29   18:26^Acts 18:2, 18
18:27^Acts 11:26

18:13 1Or *Law*

and when he had arrived, he greatly helped those who had believed through grace, 28 for he powerfully refuted the Jews in public, demonstrating ^by the Scriptures that ^BJesus was the Christ.

PAUL IN EPHESUS

19 Now it happened that while ^Apollos was in Corinth, Paul passed through the ^Bupper country and came to Ephesus, and found some disciples. 2 He said to them, "^Did you receive the Holy Spirit when you believed?" And they *said* to him, "On the contrary, we have not even heard if there is a Holy Spirit." 3 And he said, "Into what then were you baptized?" And they said, "^Into John's baptism." 4 Paul said, "^John baptized with a baptism of repentance, telling the people to believe in Him who was coming after him, that is, in Jesus." 5 When they heard this, they were ^baptized in the name of the Lord Jesus. 6 And when Paul had ^laid hands upon them, the Holy Spirit came on them and they *began* ^Bspeaking with tongues and prophesying. 7 There were about twelve men in all.

8 And he entered ^the synagogue and continued speaking out boldly for three months, having discussions and persuading *them* ^Babout the kingdom of God. 9 But when ^some were becoming hardened and disobedient, speaking evil of [1,B]the Way before the people, he withdrew from them and took the disciples away *with him,* and had discussions daily in the school of Tyrannus. 10 This took place for two years, so that all who lived in ^Asia heard the word of the Lord, both Jews and Greeks.

MIRACLES AT EPHESUS

11 God was performing ^extraordinary miracles by the hands of Paul, 12 ^so that handkerchiefs or aprons were even carried from his body to the sick, and the diseases left them and the evil spirits went out. 13 But also some of the Jewish ^exorcists, who went from place to place, attempted to use the name of the Lord Jesus over those who had the evil spirits, saying, "I order you in the name of Jesus whom Paul preaches!" 14 Now there were seven sons of Sceva, a Jewish chief priest, doing this. 15 But the evil spirit responded and said to them, "I recognize Jesus, and I know of Paul, but who are you?" 16 And the man in whom was the evil spirit, pounced on them and subdued all of them and overpowered them, so that they fled out of that house naked and wounded. 17 This became known to all who lived in ^Ephesus, both Jews and Greeks; and fear fell upon them all and the name of the Lord Jesus was being magnified. 18 Also many of those who had believed kept coming, confessing and disclosing their practices. 19 And many of those who practiced magic brought their books together and *began* burning *them* in the sight of everyone; and they added up the prices of the books and found *it to be* fifty thousand ^*pieces* of silver. 20 So the word of the Lord ^was growing and prevailing mightily.

18:28 ^Acts 8:35　　^BActs 18:5　　**19:1** ^1 Cor 1:12
^BActs 18:23　　**19:2** ^Acts 8:15f; 11:16f　　**19:3** ^Luke 7:29;
Acts 18:25　　**19:4** ^Matt 3:11; Mark 1:4, 7, 8
19:5 ^Acts 8:12, 16; 10:48　　**19:6** ^Acts 8:17　　^BActs 2:4;
10:46　　**19:8** ^Acts 9:20　　^BActs 1:3　　**19:9** ^Acts 14:4
^BActs 9:2　　**19:10** ^Acts 16:6; 19:22, 26, 27
19:11 ^Acts 8:13　　**19:12** ^Acts 5:15　　**19:13** ^Matt 12:27;
Luke 11:19　　**19:17** ^Acts 18:19　　**19:19** ^Luke 15:8
19:20 ^Acts 6:7; 12:24

19:9 [1] See John 14:6

²¹Now after these things were finished, Paul resolved in the Spirit to ^go to Jerusalem after he had passed through Macedonia and Achaia, saying, "After I have been there, ᴮI must also see Rome." ²²And after he sent into Macedonia two of those who assisted him, ^Timothy and ᴮErastus, he himself stayed in Asia for a while.

²³About that time ¹a major disturbance occurred in regard to ^the Way. ²⁴For a man named Demetrius, a silversmith who made silver shrines of Artemis, ^was bringing considerable business to the craftsmen; ²⁵he gathered these men together with the workmen of similar *trades,* and said, "Men, you know that our prosperity depends upon this business. ²⁶You see and hear that not only in Ephesus, but in almost all of Asia, this Paul has persuaded and turned away a considerable number of people, saying that ^gods made by hands are not gods *at all.* ²⁷Not only is there danger that this trade of ours will fall into disrepute, but also that the temple of the great goddess Artemis will be regarded as worthless, and that she whom all of Asia and ^the world worship will even be dethroned from her magnificence."

²⁸When they heard *this* and were filled with rage, they *began* shouting, saying, "Great is Artemis of the ^Ephesians!" ²⁹The city was filled with the confusion, and they rushed together into the theater, dragging along Gaius and ^Aristarchus, Paul's Macedonian traveling companions. ³⁰And when Paul wanted to go into the assembly, ^the disciples would not let him. ³¹Also some of the ¹Asiarchs who were friends of his sent *word* to him and

repeatedly urged him not to venture into the theater. ³²^So then, some were shouting one thing and some another, for the assembly was in confusion and the majority did not know for what reason they had come together. ³³Some of the crowd concluded *it was* Alexander, since the Jews had put him forward; and having ^motioned with his hand, Alexander was intending to make a defense to the assembly. ³⁴But when they recognized that he was a Jew, a single outcry arose from them all as they shouted for about two hours, "Great is Artemis of the Ephesians!"

³⁵After quieting the crowd, the town clerk *said, "Men of ^Ephesus, what person is there after all who does not know that the city of the Ephesians is guardian of the temple of the great Artemis and of the *image* which fell down from the sky? ³⁶So, since these are undeniable *facts,* you ought to keep calm and to do nothing rash. ³⁷For you have brought these men *here who are* neither ^temple robbers nor blasphemers of our goddess. ³⁸So then, if Demetrius and the craftsmen who are with him have a complaint against anyone, the courts are in session and ^proconsuls are *available;* have them bring charges against one another. ³⁹But if you want anything beyond this, it shall be settled in the lawful assembly. ⁴⁰For indeed, we are in danger of being accused of a riot

19:21^Acts 20:16, 22   ᴮActs 23:11   **19:22**^Acts 16:1
ᴮRom 16:23   **19:23**^Acts 19:9   **19:24**^Acts 16:16, 19f
19:26^Deut 4:28; Ps 115:4   **19:27**^Matt 24:14
19:28^Acts 18:19   **19:29**^Acts 20:4; 27:2
19:30^Acts 19:9   **19:32**^Acts 21:34   **19:33**^Acts 12:17
19:35^Acts 18:19   **19:37**^Rom 2:22   **19:38**^Acts 13:7

19:23 ¹Lit *no small*   **19:31** ¹I.e., political or religious officials of the province of Asia

in connection with today's *events*, since there is no *real* reason *for it*, and in this connection we will be unable to account for this disorderly gathering." ⁴¹After saying this he dismissed the assembly.

PAUL IN MACEDONIA AND GREECE

20 After the uproar had ceased, Paul sent for ᴬthe disciples, and when he had encouraged them and taken his leave of them, he left to go to ᴮMacedonia. ²When he had gone through those regions and had given them much encouragement, he came to Greece. ³And *there* he spent three months, and when ᴬa plot was formed against him by the Jews as he was about to set sail for Syria, he decided to return through Macedonia. ⁴And he was accompanied by Sopater of Berea, *the son* of Pyrrhus, and by ᴬAristarchus and Secundus of the Thessalonians, and ᴬGaius of Derbe, and Timothy, and Tychicus and ᴮTrophimus of Asia. ⁵Now these had gone on ahead and were waiting for ᴬus at ᴮTroas. ⁶We sailed from ᴬPhilippi after ¹,ᴮthe days of Unleavened Bread, and reached them at Troas within five days; and we stayed there for seven days.

⁷On the first day of the week, when we were gathered together to ᴬbreak bread, Paul *began* talking to them, intending to leave the next day, and he prolonged his message until midnight. ⁸There were many lamps in the ᴬupstairs room where we were gathered together. ⁹And there was a young man named Eutychus sitting on the window sill, sinking into a deep sleep; and as Paul kept on talking, *Eutychus* was overcome by sleep and fell down from the third floor, and was picked up dead. ¹⁰But

Paul went down and fell upon him, and after embracing him, he ᴬsaid, "Do not be troubled, for he is still alive." ¹¹When *Paul* had gone *back* up and had ᴬbroken the bread and eaten, he talked with them a long while until daybreak, and then left. ¹²They took away the boy alive, and were greatly comforted.

TROAS TO MILETUS

¹³But ᴬwe went ahead to the ship and set sail for Assos, intending from there to take Paul on board; for that was what he had arranged, intending himself to go by land. ¹⁴And when he met us at Assos, we took him on board and came to Mitylene. ¹⁵Sailing from there, we arrived the following day opposite Chios; and the next day we crossed over to Samos, and on the following day we came to ᴬMiletus. ¹⁶For Paul had decided to sail past Ephesus so that he would not have to lose time in Asia; for he was hurrying, if it might be possible for him ᴬto be in Jerusalem ᴮthe day of Pentecost.

FAREWELL TO EPHESUS

¹⁷From Miletus he sent *word* to Ephesus and called to himself ᴬthe elders of the church. ¹⁸And when they came to him, he said to them,

"You yourselves know, ᴬfrom the first day that I set foot in Asia, how I was with you the whole time, ¹⁹serving the Lord with all humility and with tears and trials which

20:1ᴬActs 11:26   ᴮActs 16:9   20:3ᴬActs 9:23f; 20:19
20:4ᴬActs 19:29   ᴮActs 21:29   20:5ᴬActs 16:10
ᴮActs 16:8   20:6ᴬActs 16:12   ᴮActs 12:3
20:7ᴬActs 2:42; 20:11   20:8ᴬActs 1:13
20:10ᴬMatt 9:23f; Mark 5:39   20:11ᴬActs 2:42; 20:7
20:13ᴬActs 16:10; 20:5-15   20:15ᴬActs 20:17;
2 Tim 4:20   20:16ᴬActs 19:21   ᴮActs 2:1
20:17ᴬActs 11:30   20:18ᴬActs 18:19; 19:1, 10

20:6 ¹I.e., Passover week

came upon me through ^the plots of the Jews; ²⁰how I ^did not shrink from declaring to you anything that was beneficial, and teaching you publicly and from house to house, ²¹solemnly testifying to both Jews and Greeks of ^repentance toward God and faith in our Lord Jesus Christ. ²²And now, behold, bound by the Spirit, ^I am on my way to Jerusalem, not knowing what will happen to me there, ²³except that the Holy Spirit solemnly testifies to me in every city, saying that ^chains and afflictions await me. ²⁴But ^I do not consider my life of any account as dear to myself, so that I may ᴮfinish my course and the ministry which I received from the Lord Jesus, to testify solemnly of the gospel of God's grace.

²⁵"And now behold, I know that all of you, among whom I went about ^preaching the kingdom, will no longer see my face. ²⁶Therefore, I testify to you this day that ^I am innocent of the blood of all people. ²⁷For I did not shrink from declaring to you the whole ^purpose of God. ²⁸Be on guard for yourselves and for all the flock, among which the Holy Spirit has made you overseers, to shepherd the church of God which ^He purchased with His own blood. ²⁹I know that after my departure ^savage wolves will come in among you, not sparing the flock; ³⁰and from among your own selves men will arise, speaking perverse things to draw away ^the disciples after them. ³¹Therefore, be on the alert, remembering that night and day for a period of three years I did not cease to admonish each one ^with tears. ³²And now I ^entrust you to God and to the word of His grace, which is able to build you up and to

give you the inheritance among all those who are sanctified. ³³^I have coveted no one's silver or gold or clothes. ³⁴You yourselves know that ^these hands served my own needs and the men who were with me. ³⁵In everything I showed you that by working hard in this way you must help the weak and remember the words of the Lord Jesus, that He Himself said, 'It is more blessed to give than to receive.'"

³⁶When he had said these things, he ^knelt down and prayed with them all. ³⁷And they all began to weep aloud and ^embraced Paul, and repeatedly kissed him, ³⁸grieving especially over ^the word which he had spoken, that they would not see his face again. And they were accompanying him to the ship.

PAUL SAILS FROM MILETUS

21 Now when ^we had parted from them and had set sail, we ran a straight course to Cos, and on the next day to Rhodes, and from there to Patara; ²and having found a ship crossing over to ^Phoenicia, we went aboard and set sail. ³When we came in sight of ^Cyprus, leaving it on the left, we kept sailing to Syria and landed at Tyre; for the ship was to unload its cargo there. ⁴After looking up the disciples, we stayed there for seven days; and they kept telling Paul, ^through the Spirit, not to

20:19 ^Acts 20:3　20:20 ^Acts 20:27
20:21 ^Acts 2:38; 11:18　20:22 ^Acts 17:16; 20:16
20:23 ^Acts 9:16; 21:33　20:24 ^Acts 21:13
ᴮActs 13:25　20:25 ^Matt 4:23; Acts 28:31
20:26 ^Acts 18:6　20:27 ^Acts 13:36
20:28 ^Eph 1:7, 14; 1 Pet 1:19　20:29 ^Ezek 22:27;
Matt 7:15　20:30 ^Acts 11:26　20:31 ^Acts 20:19
20:32 ^Acts 14:23　20:33 ^1 Cor 9:4-18; 2 Cor 11:7-12
20:34 ^Acts 18:3　20:36 ^Acts 9:40; 21:5
20:37 ^Luke 15:20　20:38 ^Acts 20:25
21:1 ^Acts 16:10; 21:1-18　21:2 ^Acts 11:19; 21:3
21:3 ^Acts 4:36; 21:16　21:4 ^Acts 20:23; 21:11

set foot in Jerusalem. ⁵When our days there were ended, we left and started on our journey, while they all, with wives and children, escorted us until *we were* out of the city. After ^kneeling down on the beach and praying, we said farewell to one another. ⁶Then we boarded the ship, and they returned ^home.

⁷When we had finished the voyage from ^Tyre, we arrived at Ptolemais, and after greeting the brothers *and sisters*, we stayed with them for a day. ⁸On the next day we left and came to Caesarea, and we entered the house of ^Philip the evangelist, who was one of the seven, and stayed with him. ⁹Now this man had four virgin daughters who were ^prophetesses. ¹⁰As we were staying there for some days, a prophet named ^Agabus came down from Judea. ¹¹And he came to us and took Paul's belt and bound his own feet and hands, and said, "This ^is what the Holy Spirit says: 'In this way the Jews in Jerusalem will ^bind the man who owns this belt and hand him over to the Gentiles.'" ¹²When we had heard this, we as well as the local residents *began* begging him ^not to go up to Jerusalem. ¹³Then Paul replied, "What are you doing, weeping and breaking my heart? For I am ready not only to be bound, but even to die in Jerusalem for ^the name of the Lord Jesus." ¹⁴And since he would not be persuaded, we became quiet, remarking, "^The will of the Lord be done!"

PAUL IN JERUSALEM

¹⁵After these days we got ready and ^started on our way up to Jerusalem. ¹⁶*Some* of the disciples from Caesarea also came with us, taking us to Mnason of Cyprus, a ^disciple of long standing with whom we were to stay.

¹⁷After we arrived in Jerusalem, ^the brothers *and sisters* received us gladly. ¹⁸And the following day Paul went in with us to ^James, and all the elders were present. ¹⁹After he had greeted them, he ^*began* to relate one by one the things which God had done among the Gentiles through his ^ministry. ²⁰And when they heard *about them,* they *began* ^glorifying God; and they said to him, "You see, brother, how many thousands there are among the Jews of those who have believed, and they are all ^zealous for the Law; ²¹and they have been told about you, that you are teaching all the Jews who are among the Gentiles to abandon Moses, telling them ^not to circumcise their children nor to walk according to ^the customs. ²²So what is *to be done?* They will certainly hear that you have come. ²³Therefore, do as we tell you: we have four men who ^have a vow upon themselves; ²⁴take them along and ^purify yourself together with them, and pay their expenses so that they may shave their heads; and *then* everyone will know that there is nothing to what they have been told about you, but that you yourself also conform, keeping the Law. ²⁵But regarding the Gentiles who have believed, we sent a letter, ^having decided that they should

21:5 ^Luke 22:41; Acts 9:40   21:6 ^John 19:27
21:7 ^Acts 12:20; 21:3   21:8 ^Acts 6:5; 8:5
21:9 ^Luke 2:36; Acts 13:1   21:10 ^Acts 11:28
21:11 ^Acts 8:29   ^Acts 21:33   21:12 ^Acts 21:15
21:13 ^Acts 5:41; 9:16   21:14 ^Luke 22:42
21:15 ^Acts 21:12   21:16 ^Acts 15:7   21:17 ^Acts 1:15;
21:7   21:18 ^Acts 12:17   21:19 ^Acts 14:27   ^Acts 1:17
21:20 ^Matt 9:8   ^Acts 15:1   21:21 ^1 Cor 7:18f
^Acts 6:14   21:23 ^Num 6:13-21; Acts 18:18
21:24 ^John 11:55; Acts 21:26   21:25 ^Acts 15:19f, 29

abstain from meat sacrificed to idols and from blood and what is strangled, and from sexual immorality." ²⁶Then Paul took along the men, and the next day, after purifying himself together with them, he ᴬwent into the temple giving notice of the completion of the days of purification, until the sacrifice was offered for each one of them.

PAUL SEIZED IN THE TEMPLE

²⁷When ᴬthe seven days were almost over, ᴮthe Jews from Asia, upon seeing him in the temple, *began* to stir up all the crowd and laid hands on him, ²⁸crying out, "Men of Israel, help! ᴬThis is the man who instructs everyone everywhere against our people and the Law and this place; and besides, he has even brought Greeks into the temple and has defiled this holy place!" ²⁹For they had previously seen Trophimus the ᴬEphesian in the city with him, and they thought that Paul had brought him into the temple. ³⁰Then the whole city was provoked and the people rushed together, and taking hold of Paul they ᴬdragged him out of the temple, and immediately the doors were shut. ³¹While they were intent on killing him, a report came up to the commander of the ᴬRoman ¹cohort that all Jerusalem was in confusion. ³²He immediately ᴬtook along *some* soldiers and centurions and ran down to the crowd; and when they saw the commander and the soldiers, they stopped beating Paul. ³³Then the commander came up and took hold of him, and ordered that he be ᴬbound with ᴮtwo chains; and he *began* asking who he was and what he had done. ³⁴But among the crowd, ᴬsome were shouting one thing *and* some

another, and when he could not find out the facts because of the uproar, he ordered that Paul be brought into the barracks. ³⁵When *Paul* got to ᴬthe stairs, it came about that he was carried by the soldiers because of the violence of the mob; ³⁶for the multitude of people kept following *them*, shouting, "ᴬAway with him!"

³⁷As Paul was about to be brought into ᴬthe barracks, he *said to the commander, "May I say something to you?" And he said, "Do you know Greek? ³⁸Then you are not ᴬthe Egyptian who some time ago stirred up a revolt and led the four thousand men of the Assassins out into the wilderness?" ³⁹But Paul said, "ᴬI am a Jew of Tarsus in Cilicia, a citizen of no insignificant city; and I beg you, allow me to speak to the people." ⁴⁰When he had given him permission, Paul, standing on the stairs, motioned to the people with his hand; and when there was a great silence, he spoke to them in the ᴬHebrew dialect, saying,

PAUL'S DEFENSE BEFORE THE JEWS

22 "ᴬBrothers and fathers, hear my defense *which I* now *offer* to you."

²And when they heard that he was addressing them in the ᴬHebrew dialect, they became *even* more quiet; and he *said,

³"ᴬI am a Jew, born in Tarsus of Cilicia, but brought up in this city, educated under ᴮGamaliel, strictly

21:26ᴬNum 6:13; Acts 24:18   21:27ᴬNum 6:9, 13-20
ᴮActs 20:19   21:28ᴬActs 6:13   21:29ᴬActs 18:19
21:30ᴬ2 Kin 11:15; Acts 16:19   21:31ᴬActs 10:1
21:32ᴬActs 23:27   21:33ᴬActs 20:23   ᴮActs 12:6
21:34ᴬActs 19:32   21:35ᴬActs 21:40
21:36ᴬLuke 23:18; John 19:15   21:37ᴬActs 21:34; 22:24
21:38ᴬActs 5:36   21:39ᴬActs 9:11; 22:3
21:40ᴬJohn 5:2; Acts 1:19   22:1ᴬActs 7:2
22:2ᴬActs 21:40   22:3ᴬActs 9:1-22   ᴮActs 5:34
21:31¹Normally 600 men (the number varied)

according to the Law of our fathers, being zealous for God just as you all are today. [4]^AI persecuted this ^BWay to the death, binding and putting both men and women into prisons, [5]as also ^Athe high priest and all ^Bthe Council of the elders can testify. From them I also received letters to the brothers, and started off for Damascus in order to bring even those who were there to Jerusalem as prisoners to be punished.

[6]"^ABut it happened that as I was on my way, approaching Damascus at about noon, a very bright light suddenly flashed from heaven all around me, [7]and I fell to the ground and heard a voice saying to me, 'Saul, Saul, why are you persecuting Me?' [8]And I answered, 'Who are You, Lord?' And He said to me, 'I am ^AJesus the Nazarene, whom you are persecuting.' [9]And those who were with me ^Asaw the light, but ^Bdid not understand the voice of the One who was speaking to me. [10]And I said, '^AWhat shall I do, Lord?' And the Lord said to me, 'Get up and go on into Damascus, and there you will be told about everything that has been appointed for you to do.' [11]But since I ^Acould not see because of the brightness of that light, I came into Damascus being led by the hand by those who were with me.

[12]"Now a certain ^AAnanias, a man who was devout by the standard of the Law *and* well spoken of by all the Jews who lived *there,* [13]came to me, and standing nearby he said to me, '^ABrother Saul, receive your sight!' And at that very moment I looked up at him. [14]And he said, '^AThe God of our fathers has appointed you to know His will and to ^Bsee the Righteous One and to hear a message from His mouth. [15]For you will be ^Aa witness for Him to all people of what you have seen and heard. [16]Now why do you delay? Get up and be baptized, and ^Awash away your sins by calling on His name.'

[17]"It happened when I returned to Jerusalem and was praying in the temple, that I ^Afell into a trance, [18]and I saw Him saying to me, '^AHurry and get out of Jerusalem quickly, because they will not accept your testimony about Me.' [19]And I said, 'Lord, they themselves understand that in one synagogue after another ^AI used to imprison and beat those who believed in You. [20]And ^Awhen the blood of Your witness Stephen was being shed, I also was standing nearby and approving, and watching over the cloaks of those who were killing him.' [21]And He said to me, 'Go! For I will send you far away ^Ato the Gentiles.'"

[22]They listened to him up to this statement, and *then* they raised their voices and said, "Away with such a man from the earth, for ^Ahe should not be allowed to live!" [23]And as they were shouting and ^Athrowing off their cloaks and tossing dust into the air, [24]the commander ordered that he be brought into the barracks, saying that he was to be ^Ainterrogated by flogging so that he would find out the reason why they were shouting against him that way. [25]But when they stretched him out with straps,

22:4 ^A Acts 8:3   ^B Acts 9:2   22:5 ^A Acts 9:1
^B Luke 22:66   22:6 ^A *Acts 9:3-8; 26:12-18*
22:8 ^A Acts 26:9   22:9 ^A Acts 26:13   ^B Acts 9:7
22:10 ^A Acts 16:30   22:11 ^A Acts 9:8   22:12 ^A Acts 9:10
22:13 ^A Acts 9:17   22:14 ^A Acts 3:13   ^B Acts 9:17
22:15 ^A Acts 23:11; 26:16   22:16 ^A Acts 2:38; 1 Cor 6:11
22:17 ^A Acts 10:10   22:18 ^A Acts 9:29   22:19 ^A Acts 8:3;
22:4   22:20 ^A Acts 7:58f; 8:1   22:21 ^A Acts 9:15
22:22 ^A Acts 25:24   22:23 ^A Acts 7:58
22:24 ^A Acts 22:29

Paul said to the centurion who was standing by, "Is it lawful for you to flog ^a man who is a Roman and uncondemned?" ²⁶When the centurion heard *this,* he went to the commander and told *him,* saying, "What are you about to do? For this man is a Roman." ²⁷The commander came and said to Paul, "Tell me, are you a Roman?" And he said, "Yes." ²⁸The commander answered, "I acquired this citizenship for a large sum of money." And Paul said, "But I was actually born *a citizen.*" ²⁹Therefore, those who were about to ^interrogate him immediately backed away from him; and the commander also was afraid when he found out that he was a Roman, and because he had put him in chains.

³⁰Now on the next day, ^wanting to know for certain why *Paul* had been accused by the Jews, he released him and ordered the chief priests and all the Council to assemble, and he brought Paul down and placed him before them.

PAUL BEFORE THE COUNCIL

23 Now looking intently at the Council, Paul said, "Brothers, ^I have lived my life with an entirely good conscience before God up to this day." ²But the high priest Ananias commanded those standing beside him ^to strike him on the mouth. ³Then Paul said to him, "God is going to strike you, you whitewashed wall! Do you ^sit to try me according to the Law, and in violation of the Law, order me to be struck?" ⁴But those present said, "Are you insulting God's high priest?" ⁵And Paul said, "I was not aware, brothers, that he is high priest; for it is written: '^You shall

not speak evil of a ruler of your people.'"

⁶But Paul, perceiving that one group were Sadducees and the other Pharisees, *began* crying out in the Council, "Brothers, I am a Pharisee, a son of Pharisees; I am on trial for ^the hope and resurrection of the dead!" ⁷When he said this, a dissension occurred between the Pharisees and Sadducees, and the assembly was divided. ⁸For ^the Sadducees say that there is no resurrection, nor an angel, nor a spirit, but the Pharisees acknowledge them all. ⁹And a great uproar occurred; and some of the scribes of the Pharisaic party stood up and *started* arguing heatedly, saying, "We find nothing wrong with this man; ^suppose a spirit or an angel has spoken to him?" ¹⁰And when a great dissension occurred, the commander was afraid that Paul would be torn to pieces by them, and he ordered the troops to go down and take him away from them by force, and bring him into ^the barracks.

¹¹But on the following night, the Lord stood near him and said, "Be courageous! For ^as you have testified to the *truth* about Me in Jerusalem, so you must testify in Rome also."

A CONSPIRACY TO KILL PAUL

¹²When it was day, ^the Jews formed a conspiracy and put themselves under an oath, saying that they would neither eat nor drink until

22:25 ^Acts 16:37   22:29 ^Acts 22:24
22:30 ^Acts 23:28   23:1 ^Acts 24:16; 2 Cor 1:12
23:2 ^John 18:22   23:3 ^Lev 19:15; Deut 25:2
23:5 ^Ex 22:28   23:6 ^Acts 24:15, 21; 26:8
23:8 ^Matt 22:23; Mark 12:18
23:9 ^John 12:29; Acts 22:6ff   23:10 ^Acts 21:34;
23:16, 32   23:11 ^Acts 19:21   23:12 ^Acts 9:23; 23:30

they had killed Paul. ¹³There were more than forty who formed this plot. ¹⁴They came to the chief priests and the elders and said, "We have ^put ourselves under an oath to taste nothing until we have killed Paul. ¹⁵Now therefore, you and ^the Council notify the commander to bring him down to you, as though you were going to investigate his case more thoroughly; and as for us, we are ready to kill him before he comes near *the place.*"

¹⁶But the son of Paul's sister heard about their ambush, and he came and entered ^the barracks and told Paul. ¹⁷Paul called one of the centurions to himself and said, "Take this young man to the commander, for he has something to report to him." ¹⁸So he took him and led him to the commander and *said, "Paul ^the prisoner called me over to him and asked me to bring this young man to you because he has something to tell you." ¹⁹The commander took him by the hand, and stepping aside, *began* to inquire of him privately, "What is it that you have to report to me?" ²⁰And he said, "The Jews have agreed to ask you to bring Paul down tomorrow to ^the Council, as though they were going to inquire somewhat more thoroughly about him. ²¹So do not listen to them, for more than forty of them are ^in hiding to ambush him, and these men have put themselves under an oath not to eat or drink until they kill him; and now they are ready and waiting for assurance from you." ²²Then the commander let the young man go, instructing him, "Tell no one that you have notified me of these things."

PAUL MOVED TO CAESAREA

²³And he called to him two of the centurions and said, "Get two hundred soldiers ready by ¹the third hour of the night to proceed to ^Caesarea, with seventy horsemen and two hundred spearmen." ²⁴*They were* also to provide mounts to put Paul on and bring him safely to ^Felix the governor. ²⁵And he wrote a letter with the following content:

²⁶"Claudius Lysias, to the ^most excellent governor Felix: Greetings.

²⁷When this man was seized by the Jews and was about to be killed by them, ^I came up to them with the troops and rescued him, ᴮafter learning that he was a Roman. ²⁸And ^wanting to ascertain the basis for the charges they were bringing against him, I brought him down to their Council; ²⁹and I found that he was being accused regarding questions in their Law, but was ^not charged with anything deserving death or imprisonment.

³⁰When I was ^informed that there would be a plot against the man, I sent him to you at once, also instructing his accusers to bring charges against him before you."

³¹So the soldiers, in accordance with their orders, took Paul and brought him by night to Antipatris. ³²But on the next day they let

23:14 ^Acts 23:12, 21   23:15 ^Acts 22:30;
23:1, 6, 20, 28   23:16 ^Acts 21:34; 23:10, 32
23:18 ^Eph 3:1   23:20 ^Acts 22:30; 23:1, 6, 15, 28
23:21 ^Acts 23:12, 14   23:23 ^Acts 8:40; 23:33
23:24 ^Acts 23:26, 33; 24:1, 3, 10   23:26 ^Luke 1:3;
Acts 24:3   23:27 ^Acts 21:32f   ᴮActs 22:25-29
23:28 ^Acts 22:30   23:29 ^Acts 23:9; 25:25
23:30 ^Acts 23:20f

23:23 ¹I.e., 9 p.m.

^the horsemen go on with him, and they returned to the barracks. ³³When these *horsemen* had come to Caesarea and delivered the letter to ^the governor, they also presented Paul to him. ³⁴Now when he had read *it,* he also asked from what ^province *Paul* was, and when he learned that ᴮhe was from Cilicia, ³⁵he said, "I will give you a hearing when your ^accusers arrive as well," giving orders for Paul to be kept in Herod's ¹Praetorium.

PAUL BEFORE FELIX

24 Now after five days the high priest ^Ananias came down with some elders and an attorney *named* Tertullus, and they brought charges against Paul to the governor. ²After Paul had been summoned, Tertullus began accusing him, saying *to the governor,*

"Since we have attained great peace through you, and since reforms are being carried out for this nation by your foresight, ³we acknowledge *this* in every way and everywhere, ^most excellent Felix, with all thankfulness. ⁴But, that I may not weary you further, I beg you to grant us a brief hearing, by your kindness. ⁵For we have found this man a public menace and one who stirs up dissensions among all the Jews throughout the world, and a ringleader of the ^sect of the Nazarenes. ⁶And he even tried to ^desecrate the temple, so indeed we arrested him.¹ ⁸By interrogating him yourself concerning all these matters, you will be able to ascertain the things of which we are accusing him." ⁹^The Jews also joined in the attack, asserting that these things were so.

¹⁰And when ^the governor had nodded for him to speak, Paul responded:

"Knowing that for many years you have been a judge to this nation, I cheerfully make my defense, ¹¹since you can take note of the fact that no more than ^twelve days ago I went up to Jerusalem to worship. ¹²^And neither in the temple did they find me carrying on a discussion with anyone or ᴮcausing a riot, nor in the synagogues, nor in the city *itself*. ¹³^Nor can they prove to you *the things* of which they now accuse me. ¹⁴But I confess this to you, that in accordance with ¹^the Way, which they call a sect, I do serve the God of our fathers, believing everything that is in accordance with the Law and is written in the Prophets; ¹⁵having a hope in God, which ^these men cherish themselves, that there shall certainly be a resurrection of both the righteous and the wicked. ¹⁶In view of this ^I also do my best to maintain a blameless conscience *both* before God and before *other* people, always. ¹⁷Now after several years I ^came to bring charitable gifts to my nation and to present offerings, ¹⁸in which they found me *occupied* in the temple, having been ^purified, without *any* crowd or uproar. But *there*

23:32 ^Acts 23:23   23:33 ^Acts 23:24, 26; 24:1, 3, 10
23:34 ^Acts 25:1   ᴮActs 21:39   23:35 ^Acts 23:30;
24:19   24:1 ^Acts 23:2   24:3 ^Acts 23:26; 26:25
24:5 ^Acts 15:5; 24:14   24:6 ^Acts 21:28
24:9 ^1 Thess 2:16   24:10 ^Acts 23:24
24:11 ^Acts 21:18, 27; 24:1   24:12 ^Acts 25:8
ᴮActs 24:18   24:13 ^Acts 25:7   24:14 ^Acts 9:2; 24:22
24:15 ^Dan 12:2; John 5:28f   24:16 ^Acts 23:1
24:17 ^Acts 11:29f; Rom 15:25-28   24:18 ^Acts 21:26

23:35 ¹I.e., governor's official residence   24:6 ¹Late
mss add as the remainder of v 6: *We wanted to judge
him according to our own Law.* v 7: *But Lysias the
commander came along and took him out of our hands
with much violence,* and the first part of v 8: *ordering
his accusers to come before you.*   24:14 ¹See John 14:6

were some Jews from Asia— [19] who ought to have been present before you and to have been ^bringing charges, if they should have anything against me. [20] Or *else* have these men themselves declare what violation they discovered when I stood before ^the Council, [21] other than in regard to this one declaration which ^I shouted while standing among them, 'For the resurrection of the dead I am on trial before you today!'"

[22] But Felix, having quite accurate knowledge about ¹^the Way, adjourned them, saying, "When Lysias the commander comes down, I will decide your case." [23] He gave orders to the centurion for Paul to be ^kept in custody and *yet* have *some* freedom, and not to prevent any of ^Bhis friends from providing for his needs.

[24] Now some days later Felix arrived with Drusilla his wife, who was Jewish, and he sent for Paul and heard him *speak* about ^faith in Christ Jesus. [25] But as he was discussing righteousness, self-control, and ^the judgment to come, Felix became frightened and responded, "Go away for now, and when I have an opportunity, I will summon you." [26] At the same time he was also hoping that ^money would be given to him by Paul; therefore he also used to send for him quite often and talk with him. [27] But after two years had passed, Felix was succeeded by Porcius Festus; and Felix, wanting to do the Jews a favor, left Paul ^imprisoned.

PAUL BEFORE FESTUS

25 Festus, then, after arriving in ^the province, went up to Jerusalem from Caesarea three days later. [2] And the chief priests and the leading men of the Jews ^brought charges against Paul, and they were pleading with Festus, [3] requesting a concession against Paul, that he might have him brought to Jerusalem (*at the same time,* ^setting an ambush to kill him on the way). [4] Festus then answered that Paul ^was being kept in custody in Caesarea, and that he himself was about to leave shortly. [5] "Therefore," he *said, "have the influential men among you go there with me, and if there is anything wrong about the man, have them bring charges against him."

[6] After *Festus* had spent no more than eight or ten days among them, he went down to Caesarea, and on the next day he took his seat on ^the tribunal and ordered that Paul be brought. [7] After Paul arrived, the Jews who had come down from Jerusalem stood around him, bringing many, and serious, charges against him ^which they could not prove, [8] while Paul said in his own defense, "^I have not done anything wrong either against the Law of the Jews, or against the temple, or against Caesar." [9] But Festus, ^wanting to do the Jews a favor, replied to Paul and said, "Are you willing to go up to Jerusalem and stand trial before me on these *charges?*" [10] But Paul said, "I am standing before Caesar's ^tribunal, where I ought to be tried. I have done nothing wrong to *the*

24:19 ^Acts 23:30   24:20 ^Matt 5:22
24:21 ^Acts 23:6; 24:15   24:22 ^Acts 24:14
24:23 ^Acts 23:35   ᴮActs 23:16   24:24 ^Acts 20:21
24:25 ^Acts 10:42   24:26 ^Acts 24:17
24:27 ^Acts 23:35; 25:14   25:1 ^Acts 23:34
25:2 ^Acts 24:1; 25:15   25:3 ^Acts 9:24
25:4 ^Acts 24:23   25:6 ^Matt 27:19; Acts 25:10, 17
25:7 ^Acts 24:13   25:8 ^Acts 6:13; 24:12
25:9 ^Acts 12:3; 24:27   25:10 ^Matt 27:19; Acts 25:6, 17

24:22 ¹ See John 14:6

Jews, as you also very well know. ¹¹If, therefore, I am in the wrong and have committed something deserving death, I am not trying to avoid execution; but if there is nothing to the accusations which these men are bringing against me, no one can hand me over to them. I ^appeal to Caesar." ¹²Then when Festus had conferred with his council, he answered, "You have appealed to Caesar; to Caesar you shall go."

¹³Now when several days had passed, King Agrippa and Bernice arrived in ^Caesarea, paying their respects to Festus. ¹⁴And while they were spending many days there, Festus presented Paul's case to the king, saying, "There is a man who was ^left as a prisoner by Felix; ¹⁵and when I was in Jerusalem, the chief priests and the elders of the Jews ^brought charges against him, asking for a sentence of condemnation against him. ¹⁶I ^replied to them that it is not the custom of the Romans to hand over any person before the accused meets his accusers face to face, and has an opportunity to make his defense against the charges. ¹⁷So after they had assembled here, I did not delay, but on the next day took my seat on ^the tribunal and ordered that the man be brought. ¹⁸When the accusers stood up, they did not *begin* bringing any charges against him of crimes that I suspected, ¹⁹but they *simply* had some ^points of disagreement with him about their own religion and about a dead man, Jesus, whom Paul asserted to be alive. ²⁰And ^being at a loss how to investigate such matters, I asked whether he was willing to go to Jerusalem and stand trial there on these matters. ²¹But when Paul ^appealed to be held in custody for ¹the Emperor's decision, I ordered that he be kept in custody until I send him to Caesar." ²²Then ^Agrippa *said* to Festus, "I also would like to hear the man myself." "Tomorrow," he *said*, "you shall hear him."

PAUL BEFORE AGRIPPA

²³So, on the next day when ^Agrippa and ^Bernice came amid great pomp and entered the auditorium, accompanied by the commanders and the prominent men of the city, at the command of Festus, Paul was brought *before them.* ²⁴And Festus *said, "King Agrippa, and all you gentlemen present with us, you see this man about whom ^all the people of the Jews appealed to me, both in Jerusalem and here, shouting that ^Bhe ought not to live any longer. ²⁵But I found that he had committed ^nothing deserving death; and since he himself ^Bappealed to the Emperor, I decided to send him. ²⁶Yet, I have nothing definite about him to write to my lord. Therefore, I have brought him before you *all* and especially before you, King Agrippa, so that after the investigation has taken place, I may have something to write. ²⁷For it seems absurd to me in sending a prisoner, not to indicate the charges against him as well."

25:11^Acts 25:21, 25; 26:32   25:13^Acts 8:40; 25:1, 4, 6   25:14^Acts 24:27   25:15^Acts 24:1; 25:2   25:16^Acts 25:4f   25:17^Matt 27:19; Acts 25:6, 10   25:19^Acts 18:15; 23:29   25:20^Acts 25:9   25:21^Acts 25:11f   25:22^Acts 9:15   25:23^Acts 25:13; 26:30   25:24^Acts 25:2, 7   ^BActs 22:22   25:25^Acts 23:29   ^BActs 25:11f

25:21¹Lit *the Augustus'* (in this case Nero)

PAUL'S DEFENSE BEFORE AGRIPPA

26 ^Now Agrippa said to Paul, "You are permitted to speak for yourself." Then Paul extended his hand and *proceeded* to make his defense:

2 "Regarding all the things of which I am accused by the Jews, King Agrippa, I consider myself fortunate that I am about to make my defense before you today, 3 especially because you are an expert in all ^customs and questions among *the* Jews; therefore I beg you to listen to me patiently.

4 "So then, all Jews know ^my way of life since *my* youth, which from the beginning was spent among my *own* nation and in Jerusalem, 5 since they have known about me for a long time, if they are willing to testify, that I lived *as* a ^Pharisee according to the strictest sect of our religion. 6 And now I am standing trial ^for the hope of ^Bthe promise made by God to our fathers; 7 *the promise* to which our twelve tribes hope to attain, as they earnestly serve *God* night and day. For this ^hope, O king, I am being accused by Jews. 8 Why is it considered incredible among you *people* ^if God raises the dead?

9 "So ^I thought to myself that I had to act in strong opposition to the name of Jesus of Nazareth. 10 And this is just what I ^did in Jerusalem; not only did I lock up many of the saints in prisons, after receiving authority from the chief priests, but I also cast my vote against them when they were being put to death. 11 And ^as I punished them often in all the synagogues, I tried to force them to blaspheme; and since I was extremely enraged at them, I kept pursuing them even to foreign cities.

12 "While so engaged, ^as I was journeying to Damascus with the authority and commission of the chief priests, 13 at midday, O king, I saw on the way a light from heaven, brighter than the sun, shining around me and those who were journeying with me. 14 And when we had all fallen to the ground, I heard a voice saying to me in the ^Hebrew dialect, 'Saul, Saul, why are you persecuting Me? ¹It is hard for you to kick against the goads.' 15 And I said, 'Who are You, Lord?' And the Lord said, 'I am Jesus whom you are persecuting. 16 But get up and stand on your feet; for this *purpose* I have appeared to you, to ^appoint you as a servant and a witness not only to the things in which you have seen Me, but also to the things in which I will appear to you, 17 rescuing you ^from the *Jewish* people and from the Gentiles, to whom I am sending you, 18 to ^open their eyes so that they may turn from darkness to light, and from the power of Satan to God, that they may receive forgiveness of sins and an inheritance among those who have been sanctified by faith in Me.'

19 "For that reason, King Agrippa, I did not prove disobedient to the heavenly vision, 20 but *continually* proclaimed ^to those in Damascus first, and in Jerusalem, and *then* all the region of Judea, and *even* to the Gentiles, that they are to repent and turn to God, performing deeds

26:1 ^Acts 9:15   **26:3** ^Acts 6:14; 25:19; 26:7
26:4 ^Gal 1:13f; Phil 3:5   **26:5** ^Acts 23:6; Phil 3:5
26:6 ^Acts 24:15   ^BActs 13:32   **26:7** ^Acts 24:15
26:8 ^Acts 23:6   **26:9** ^John 16:2; 1 Tim 1:13
26:10 ^Acts 8:3   **26:11** ^Matt 10:17; Acts 22:19
26:12 ^*Acts 9:3-8; 22:6-11*   **26:14** ^Acts 21:40
26:16 ^Acts 22:14   **26:17** ^1 Chr 16:35; Acts 9:15
26:18 ^Is 35:5; 42:7, 16   **26:20** ^Acts 9:19ff

26:14 ¹An idiom referring to an animal's futile resistance to being prodded with a spiked stick

consistent with repentance. ²¹For these reasons *some* Jews ^seized me in the temple and tried to murder me. ²²So, having obtained help from God, I stand to this day testifying both to small and great, stating nothing but what ^the Prophets and Moses said was going to take place, ²³*as to* whether the Christ was to suffer, *and* whether, as ^first from the resurrection of the dead, He would proclaim light both to the *Jewish* people and to the Gentiles."

²⁴While Paul was stating these things in his defense, Festus *said in a loud voice, "Paul, you are out of your mind! *Your* great ^learning is driving you insane." ²⁵But Paul *said, "I am not insane, ^most excellent Festus; on the contrary, I am speaking out *with* truthful and rational words. ²⁶For the king ^knows about these matters, and I also speak to him with confidence, since I am persuaded that none of these things escape his notice; for this has not been done in a corner. ²⁷King Agrippa, do you believe the Prophets? I know that you believe." ²⁸Agrippa *replied* to Paul, "In a short *time* you *are going to* persuade me to make a ^Christian *of myself*." ²⁹And Paul *said,* "I would wish to God that even in a short or long *time* not only you, but also all who hear me this day would become such as I myself am, except for these ^chains."

³⁰^The king stood up and the governor and Bernice, and those who were sitting with them, ³¹and when they had gone out, they *began* talking to one another, saying, "^This man is not doing anything deserving death or imprisonment." ³²And Agrippa said to Festus, "This man could have been ^set free if he had not appealed to Caesar."

PAUL IS SENT TO ROME

27 Now when it was decided that we would sail for ^Italy, they proceeded to turn Paul and some other prisoners over to a centurion of the Augustan ¹cohort, named Julius. ²And we boarded an Adramyttian ship that was about to sail to the regions along *the coast of* Asia, and put out to sea accompanied by ^Aristarchus, a Macedonian of Thessalonica. ³The next day we put in at Sidon; and Julius ^treated Paul with consideration and ᴮallowed him to go to his friends and receive care. ⁴From there we put out to sea and sailed under the shelter of ^Cyprus, because the winds were contrary. ⁵When we had sailed through the sea along the coast of ^Cilicia and Pamphylia, we landed at Myra in Lycia. ⁶There the centurion found an ^Alexandrian ship sailing for Italy, and he put us aboard it. ⁷When we had sailed slowly for a good many days, and with difficulty had arrived off Cnidus, since the wind did not permit us *to go* farther, we sailed under the shelter of ^Crete, off Salmone; ⁸and with difficulty ^sailing past it, we came to a place called Fair Havens, near which was the city of Lasea.

⁹When considerable time had passed and the voyage was now dangerous, since even ^the ¹fast was already over, Paul *started*

26:21^Acts 21:27, 30   26:22^Acts 10:43; 24:14
26:23^1 Cor 15:20, 23; Col 1:18   26:24^John 7:15;
2 Tim 3:15   26:25^Acts 23:26; 24:3   26:26^Acts 26:3
26:28^Acts 11:26   26:29^Acts 21:33
26:30^Acts 25:23   26:31^Acts 23:29
26:32^Acts 28:18   27:1^Acts 18:2; 27:6
27:2^Acts 19:29   27:3^Acts 27:43   ᴮActs 24:23
27:4^Acts 4:36   27:5^Acts 21:39   27:6^Acts 28:11
27:7^Acts 2:11; 27:12f, 21   27:8^Acts 27:13
27:9^Lev 16:29-31; 23:27-29

27:1¹Normally 600 men (the number varied)
27:9¹I.e., Day of Atonement in September or October, which was a dangerous time of year for navigation

admonishing *them,* ¹⁰saying to them, "Men, I perceive that the voyage will certainly be with ^damage and great loss, not only of the cargo and the ship, but also of our lives." ¹¹But the centurion was more persuaded by the ^pilot and the captain of the ship than by what was being said by Paul. ¹²The harbor was not suitable for wintering, so the majority reached a decision to put out to sea from there, if somehow they could reach Phoenix, a harbor of ^Crete facing southwest and northwest, and spend the winter *there.*

¹³When a moderate south wind came up, thinking that they had attained their purpose, they weighed anchor and *began* ^sailing along Crete, closer *to shore.*

SHIPWRECK

¹⁴But before very long a violent wind, called ¹Euraquilo, ^rushed down from the land; ¹⁵and when the ship was caught *in it* and could not head up into the wind, we gave up and let ourselves be driven *by the wind.* ¹⁶Running under the shelter of a small island called Cauda, we were able to get the *ship's* boat under control *only* with difficulty. ¹⁷After they had hoisted it up, they used supporting cables in undergirding the ship; and fearing that they might ^run aground on *the shallows* of Syrtis, they let down the sea anchor and let themselves be driven along in this way. ¹⁸The next day as we were being violently tossed by the storm, they began to ^jettison the cargo; ¹⁹and on the third day they threw the ship's tackle *overboard* with their own hands. ²⁰Since neither sun nor stars appeared for many days, and no small storm was assailing *us,*

from then on all hope of our being saved was *slowly* abandoned.

²¹When many had lost their appetites, Paul then stood among them and said, "^Men, you should have followed my advice and not have set sail from Crete, and *thereby* spared yourselves this ^damage and loss. ²²And *yet* now I urge you to ^keep up your courage, for there will be no loss of life among you, but *only* of the ship. ²³For this *very* night an angel of the God to whom I belong, ^whom I also serve, came to me, ²⁴saying, 'Do not be afraid, Paul; ^you must stand before Caesar; and behold, God has graciously granted you all those who are sailing with you.' ²⁵Therefore, ^keep up your courage, men, for I believe God that it will turn out exactly as I have been told. ²⁶But we must ^run aground on a certain ᴮisland."

²⁷But when the fourteenth night came, as we were being driven about in the Adriatic Sea, about midnight the sailors *began* to suspect that they were approaching some land. ²⁸And they took soundings and found *it to be* twenty fathoms; and a little farther on they took another sounding and found *it to be* fifteen fathoms. ²⁹Fearing that we might ^run aground somewhere on the rocks, they cast four anchors from the stern and prayed for daybreak. ³⁰But as the sailors were trying to escape from the ship and had let down ^the *ship's* boat into the sea, on the pretense that

27:10^Acts 27:21   27:11^Rev 18:17   27:12^Acts 2:11; 27:13, 21   27:13^Acts 27:8   27:14^Mark 4:37
27:17^Acts 27:26, 29   27:18^Jon 1:5; Acts 27:38
27:21^Acts 27:10   27:22^Acts 27:25, 36
27:23^Rom 1:9   27:24^Acts 23:11
27:25^Acts 27:22, 36   27:26^Acts 27:29, 41
ᴮActs 28:1   27:29^Acts 27:17, 26   27:30^Acts 27:16

27:14 ¹I.e., a northeaster

they were going to lay out anchors from the bow, ³¹Paul said to the centurion and the soldiers, "Unless these men remain on the ship, you yourselves cannot be saved." ³²Then the soldiers cut away the ropes of the *ship's* boat and let it fall away.

³³Until the day was about to dawn, Paul kept encouraging them all to take some food, saying, "Today is the fourteenth day that you have been constantly watching and going without eating, having taken in nothing. ³⁴Therefore, I encourage you to take some food, for this is for your survival, for ^not a hair from the head of any of you will perish." ³⁵Having said this, he took bread and ^gave thanks to God in the presence of them all, and he broke it and began to eat. ³⁶All ^of them were encouraged and they themselves also took food. ³⁷We were 276 ^people on the ship in all. ³⁸When they had eaten enough, they *began* lightening the ship by ^throwing the wheat out into the sea.

³⁹Now when day came, ^they could not recognize the land; but they did notice a bay with a beach, and they resolved to run the ship onto it if they could. ⁴⁰And casting off ^the anchors, they left them in the sea while at the same time they were loosening the ropes of the rudders; and they hoisted the foresail to the wind and were heading for the beach. ⁴¹But they struck a reef where two seas met and ran the ship aground; and the prow stuck firmly and remained immovable, while the stern *started to* break up due to the force *of the waves.* ⁴²The soldiers' plan was to ^kill the prisoners, so that none *of them* would swim away and escape; ⁴³but the

centurion, ^wanting to bring Paul safely through, kept them from *accomplishing* their intention, and commanded that those who could swim were to jump overboard first and get to land, ⁴⁴and the rest *were to follow,* some on planks, and others on various things from the ship. And so it happened that ^they all were brought safely to land.

SAFE AT MALTA

28 When they had been brought safely through, ^then we found out that ^the island was called Malta. ²^The natives showed us extraordinary kindness, for they kindled a fire and took us all in because of the rain that had started and because of the cold. ³But when Paul had gathered a bundle of sticks and laid them on the fire, a viper came out because of the heat and fastened itself on his hand. ⁴When the natives saw the creature hanging from his hand, they *began* saying to one another, "^Undoubtedly this man is a murderer, and though he has been saved from the sea, justice has not allowed him to live." ⁵However, Paul shook the creature off into the fire and suffered no harm. ⁶Now they were expecting that he was going to swell up or suddenly fall down dead. But after they had waited a long time and had seen nothing unusual happen to him, they changed their minds and ^*began* to say that he was a god.

⁷Now in the neighboring parts of that place were lands belonging

27:34 ^Matt 10:30   27:35 ^Matt 14:19
27:36 ^Acts 27:22, 25   27:37 ^Acts 2:41   27:38 ^Jon 1:5;
Acts 27:18   27:39 ^Acts 28:1   27:40 ^Acts 27:29
27:42 ^Acts 12:19   27:43 ^Acts 27:3
27:44 ^Acts 27:22, 31   28:1 ^Acts 27:39   ^B Acts 27:26
28:2 ^Acts 28:4; Rom 1:14   28:4 ^Luke 13:2, 4
28:6 ^Acts 14:11

to the leading man of the island, named Publius, who welcomed us and entertained us warmly for three days. ⁸And it happened that the father of Publius was lying *in bed* afflicted with a *recurring* fever and dysentery. Paul went in *to see* him, and after he prayed, he ᴬlaid his hands on him and healed him. ⁹After this happened, the rest of the people on the island who had diseases were coming to him and being cured. ¹⁰They also showed us many honors, and when we were *about to* set sail, they supplied *us* with everything we needed.

PAUL ARRIVES IN ROME

¹¹After three months we set sail on ᴬan Alexandrian ship which had wintered at the island, and which had the Twin Brothers for its figurehead. ¹²After we put in at Syracuse, we stayed there for three days. ¹³From there we sailed around and arrived at Rhegium, and a day later a south wind came up, and on the second day we came to Puteoli. ¹⁴There we found *some* ᴬbrothers *and sisters,* and were invited to stay with them for seven days; and that is how we came to Rome. ¹⁵And from there the ᴬbrothers *and sisters,* when they heard about us, came as far as the Market of Appius and the Three Inns to meet us; and when Paul saw them, he thanked God and took courage.

¹⁶When we entered Rome, Paul was ᴬallowed to stay by himself, with the soldier who was guarding him.

¹⁷After three days Paul called together those who were the leading men of the Jews, and when they came together, he *began* saying to them, "Brothers, ᴬthough I had done nothing against our people or ᴮthe customs of our fathers, *yet* I was handed over to the Romans as a prisoner from Jerusalem. ¹⁸And when they had examined me, they were willing to release me because there were ᴬno grounds for putting me to death. ¹⁹But when the Jews objected, I was forced to ᴬappeal to Caesar, not that I had any accusation against my nation. ²⁰For this reason, therefore, I requested to see you and to speak with you, since I am wearing this chain for ᴬthe sake of the hope of Israel." ²¹They said to him, "We have neither received letters from Judea concerning you, nor has any of ᴬthe brothers come here and reported or spoken anything bad about you. ²²But we desire to hear from you what your views are; for regarding this ᴬsect, it is known to us that it is spoken against everywhere."

²³When they had set a day for Paul, *people* came to him at his lodging in large numbers; and he was explaining to them by solemnly ᴬtestifying about the kingdom of God and trying to persuade them concerning Jesus, from both the Law of Moses and from the Prophets, from morning until evening. ²⁴ᴬSome were being persuaded by the things said *by Paul,* but others would not believe. ²⁵And when they disagreed with one another, they *began* leaving

28:8 ᴬMatt 9:18; Mark 5:23   28:11 ᴬActs 27:6
28:14 ᴬJohn 21:23; Acts 1:15   28:15 ᴬActs 1:15; 10:23
28:16 ᴬActs 24:23   28:17 ᴬActs 25:8   ᴮActs 6:14
28:18 ᴬActs 23:29; 25:25   28:19 ᴬActs 25:11, 21, 25;
26:32   28:20 ᴬActs 24:15; 26:6ff   28:21 ᴬActs 3:17;
22:5   28:22 ᴬActs 24:14   28:23 ᴬActs 1:3
28:24 ᴬActs 14:4

after Paul said one *parting* statement: "The Holy Spirit rightly spoke through Isaiah the prophet to your fathers, [26]saying,

'GO TO THIS PEOPLE AND SAY,
"YOU WILL KEEP ON HEARING,
    AND WILL NOT UNDERSTAND;
AND YOU WILL KEEP ON SEEING,
    AND WILL NOT PERCEIVE;
[27] ^FOR THE HEARTS OF THIS
    PEOPLE HAVE BECOME
    INSENSITIVE,
AND WITH THEIR EARS THEY
    HARDLY HEAR,
AND THEY HAVE CLOSED THEIR
    EYES;
OTHERWISE THEY MIGHT SEE
    WITH THEIR EYES,
AND HEAR WITH THEIR EARS,
AND UNDERSTAND WITH THEIR
    HEART AND RETURN,
AND I WOULD HEAL THEM.'"

[28]Therefore, let it be known to you that ^this salvation of God has been sent to the Gentiles; they will also listen."[1]

[30]Now Paul stayed two full years in his own rented lodging and welcomed all who came to him, [31]^preaching the kingdom of God and teaching things about the Lord Jesus Christ with all openness, unhindered.

28:26 ^Is 6:9   28:27 ^Is 6:10   28:28 ^Ps 98:3;
Luke 2:30   28:31 ^Matt 4:23; Acts 20:25

28:28 [1]Late mss add as v 29: *When he had spoken these words, the Jews departed, having a great dispute among themselves.*

ROMANS

THE GOSPEL EXALTED

1 Paul, a bond-servant of Christ Jesus, called *as* an apostle, ^set apart for the gospel of God, ²which He promised beforehand through His ^prophets in the holy Scriptures, ³concerning His Son, who was born of a descendant of David ^according to the flesh, ⁴who was declared ^the Son of God with power according to the Spirit of holiness by the resurrection from the dead, Jesus Christ our Lord, ⁵through whom we have received grace and apostleship to bring about *the* ^obedience of faith among all the Gentiles in behalf of His name, ⁶among whom you also are *the* ^called of Jesus Christ;

⁷to all who are beloved of God in Rome, called *as* ^saints: Grace to you and peace from God our Father and the Lord Jesus Christ.

⁸First, ^I thank my God through Jesus Christ for you all, because your faith is being proclaimed throughout the world. ⁹For God, whom I ^serve in my spirit in the *preaching of the* gospel of His Son, is my witness *as to* how unceasingly I make mention of you, ¹⁰always in my prayers requesting if perhaps now, at last by ^the will of God, I will succeed in coming to you. ¹¹For ^I long to see you so that I may impart some spiritual gift to you, that you may be established; ¹²that is, that I may be encouraged together with you *while* among you, each of us by the other's faith, both yours and mine. ¹³I do not want you to be unaware, brothers *and sisters,* that often I have planned to come to you (and have been prevented so far) so that I may obtain some ^fruit among you also just as among the rest of the Gentiles. ¹⁴^I am under obligation both to Greeks and to the ¹uncultured, both to the wise and to the foolish. ¹⁵So, for my part, I am eager to ^preach the gospel to you also who are in Rome.

¹⁶For I am not ^ashamed of the gospel, for ^Bit is the power of God for salvation to everyone who believes, to the Jew first and also to the Greek. ¹⁷For in it *the* righteousness of God is revealed from faith to faith; as it is written: "^ABUT THE RIGHTEOUS *ONE* WILL LIVE BY FAITH."

UNBELIEF AND ITS CONSEQUENCES

¹⁸For ^the wrath of God is revealed from heaven against all ungodliness and unrighteousness of people who suppress the truth in unrighteousness, ¹⁹because ^that which is known about God is evident within them; for God made it evident to them. ²⁰For since the creation of the world His invisible *attributes, that is,* His eternal power and divine nature, have been clearly perceived, ^being understood by what has been made, so that they are without excuse. ²¹For even though

1:1 ^Acts 9:15; 13:2   1:2 ^Luke 1:70; Rom 3:21
1:3 ^John 1:14; Rom 4:1   1:4 ^Matt 4:3   1:5 ^Acts 6:7;
Rom 16:26   1:6 ^Jude 1; Rev 17:14   1:7 ^Acts 9:13;
Rom 8:28ff   1:8 ^1 Cor 1:4; Eph 1:15f   1:9 ^Acts 24:14;
2 Tim 1:3   1:10 ^Acts 18:21; Rom 15:32   1:11 ^Acts 19:21;
Rom 15:23   1:13 ^John 4:36; 15:16   1:14 ^1 Cor 9:16
1:15 ^Rom 15:20   1:16 ^Mark 8:38   ^B1 Cor 1:18, 24
1:17 ^Hab 2:4; Gal 3:11   1:18 ^Rom 5:9; Eph 5:6
1:19 ^Acts 14:17; 17:24ff   1:20 ^Job 12:7-9; Ps 19:1-6

1:14 ¹I.e., non-Hellenes

they knew God, they did not honor Him as God or give thanks, but they became ^futile in their reasonings, and their senseless hearts were darkened. ²²^Claiming to be wise, they became fools, ²³and they ^exchanged the glory of the incorruptible God for an image in the form of corruptible mankind, of birds, four-footed animals, and crawling creatures.

²⁴Therefore ^God gave them up to vile impurity in the lusts of their hearts, so that their bodies would be dishonored among them. ²⁵For they exchanged the truth of God for ^falsehood, and worshiped and served the creature rather than the Creator, who is blessed forever. Amen.

²⁶For this reason God gave them over to ^degrading passions; for their women exchanged natural relations for that which is contrary to nature, ²⁷and likewise the men, too, abandoned natural relations with women and burned in their desire toward one another, ^males with males committing shameful acts and receiving in their own persons the due penalty of their error.

²⁸And just as they did not see fit to acknowledge God, ^God gave them up to a depraved mind, to do those things that are not proper, ²⁹*people* having been filled with all unrighteousness, wickedness, greed, *and* evil; full of envy, murder, strife, deceit, *and* malice; *they are* ^gossips, ³⁰slanderers, haters of God, insolent, arrogant, boastful, inventors of evil, ^disobedient to parents, ³¹without understanding, untrustworthy, ^unfeeling, *and* unmerciful; ³²and although they know the ordinance of God, that those who practice such things are

worthy of ^death, they not only do the same, but also approve of those who practice them.

THE IMPARTIALITY OF GOD

2 Therefore you have no excuse, you *foolish* person, everyone *of you* who passes judgment; for in that *matter in* which ^you judge someone else, you condemn yourself; for you who judge practice the same things. ²And we know that the judgment of God rightly falls upon those who practice such things. ³But do you suppose this, ^you *foolish* person who passes judgment on those who practice such things, and *yet* does them *as well,* that you will escape the judgment of God? ⁴Or do you think lightly of ^the riches of His kindness and restraint and patience, not knowing that the kindness of God leads you to repentance? ⁵But because of your stubbornness and unrepentant heart ^you are storing up wrath for yourself ᴮon the day of wrath and revelation of the righteous judgment of God, ⁶^who WILL REPAY EACH PERSON ACCORDING TO HIS DEEDS: ⁷to those who by ^perseverance in doing good seek glory, honor, and immortality, *He will give* eternal life; ⁸but to those who are ^self-serving and do not obey the truth, but obey unrighteousness, *He will give* wrath and indignation. ⁹*There will be* tribulation and distress for every soul of mankind who does evil, for the Jew

1:21^2 Kin 17:15; Jer 2:5   1:22^Jer 10:14; 1 Cor 1:20
1:23^Deut 4:16-18; Ps 106:20   1:24^Rom 1:26, 28;
Eph 4:19   1:25^Is 44:20; Jer 10:14   1:26^1 Thess 4:5
1:27^Lev 18:22; 20:13   1:28^Rom 1:24
1:29^2 Cor 12:20   1:30^2 Tim 3:2   1:31^2 Tim 3:3
1:32^Rom 6:21   2:1^2 Sam 12:5-7; Matt 7:1
2:3^Luke 12:14; Rom 2:1   2:4^Rom 9:23; 11:33
2:5^Deut 32:34f   ᴮPs 110:5   2:6^Ps 62:12; Prov 24:12
2:7^Luke 8:15; Heb 10:36   2:8^2 Cor 12:20; Gal 5:20

^Afirst and also for the Greek, [10]but ^Aglory, honor, and peace to everyone who does what is good, to the Jew first and also to the Greek. [11]For ^Athere is no partiality with God.

[12]For all who have sinned ^Awithout the Law will also perish without the Law, and all who have sinned under the Law will be judged by the Law; [13]for *it is* ^Anot the hearers of the Law *who* are righteous before God, but the doers of the Law *who* will be justified. [14]For when Gentiles who do not have the Law ^Ainstinctively perform the *requirements* of the Law, these, though not having the Law, are a law to themselves, [15]in that they show ^Athe work of the Law written in their hearts, their conscience testifying and their thoughts alternately accusing or else defending them, [16]on the day when, according to my gospel, ^AGod will judge the secrets of mankind through Christ Jesus.

THE JEWS UNDER THE LAW

[17]But if you call yourself a Jew and ^Arely upon the Law and boast in God, [18]and know *His* will and ^Adistinguish the things that matter, being instructed from the Law, [19]and are confident that you yourself are a guide to people who are blind, a light to those in darkness, [20]a corrector of the foolish, a teacher of the immature, possessing in the Law ^Athe embodiment of knowledge and of the truth— [21]*you*, therefore, ^Awho teach someone else, do you not teach yourself? *You* who preach that one is not to steal, do you steal? [22]*You* who say that one is not to commit adultery, do you commit adultery? *You* who loathe idols, do you ^Arob temples? [23]You who ^Aboast in the Law, through your breaking the Law, do you dishonor God? [24]For "^ATHE NAME OF GOD IS BLASPHEMED AMONG THE GENTILES BECAUSE OF YOU," just as it is written.

[25]For indeed circumcision is of value if you practice the Law; but if you are a violator of the Law, ^Ayour circumcision has turned into uncircumcision. [26]^ASo if the uncircumcised man ^Bkeeps the requirements of the Law, will his uncircumcision not be regarded as circumcision? [27]And he who is physically uncircumcised, if he keeps the Law, will he not ^Ajudge you who though having the letter *of the Law* and circumcision are a violator of the Law? [28]For ^Ahe is not a Jew who is one outwardly, nor is circumcision that which is outward in the flesh. [29]But he is a Jew who is one inwardly; and ^Acircumcision is of the heart, by the Spirit, not by the letter; ^Band his praise is not from people, but from God.

ALL THE WORLD GUILTY

3 Then what advantage does the Jew have? Or what is the benefit of circumcision? [2]Great in every respect. First, that ^Athey were entrusted with the actual words of God. [3]What then? If ^Asome did not believe, their unbelief will not nullify the faithfulness of God, will it? [4]Far from it! Rather, God must prove to be true, though every

2:9^Rom 1:16; 1 Pet 4:17   2:10^Rom 2:7; Heb 2:7
2:11^Deut 10:17; Acts 10:34   2:12^Acts 2:23; 1 Cor 9:21
2:13^Matt 7:21, 24ff; John 13:17
2:14^Acts 10:35; Rom 1:19   2:15^Rom 2:14, 27
2:16^Acts 10:42; 17:31   2:17^Mic 3:11; John 5:45
2:18^Phil 1:10   2:20^Rom 3:31; 2 Tim 1:13
2:21^Matt 23:3ff   2:22^Acts 19:37   2:23^Mic 3:11;
John 5:45   2:24^Is 52:5; Ezek 36:20ff   2:25^Jer 4:4;
9:25f   2:26^1 Cor 7:19   ^BRom 8:4   2:27^Matt 12:41
2:28^John 8:39; Rom 2:17   2:29^Deut 30:6   ^BJohn 5:44
3:2^Deut 4:8; Ps 147:19   3:3^Rom 10:16; Heb 4:2

3:4 [1] Lit *May it never happen!* And so throughout the ch

person *be found* a liar, as it is written:

"^SO THAT YOU ARE JUSTIFIED IN
YOUR WORDS,
AND PREVAIL WHEN YOU ARE
JUDGED."

5 But if our unrighteousness demonstrates the righteousness of God, what shall we say? The God who inflicts wrath is not unrighteous, is He? (^I am speaking from a human viewpoint.) 6 Far from it! For *otherwise,* how will ^God judge the world? 7 But if through my lie ^the truth of God abounded to His glory, ^why am I also still being judged as a sinner? 8 And *why* not *say* (just as we are slanderously reported and as some claim that we say), "^Let's do evil that good may come *of it*"? Their condemnation is deserved.

9 What then? Are we better *than they?* Not at all; for we have already charged that both Jews and Greeks are ^all under sin; 10 as it is written:

"^THERE IS NO RIGHTEOUS
PERSON, NOT EVEN ONE;
11   THERE IS NO ONE WHO
UNDERSTANDS,
THERE IS NO ONE WHO SEEKS
OUT GOD;
12   THEY HAVE ALL TURNED ASIDE,
TOGETHER THEY HAVE BECOME
CORRUPT;
THERE IS NO ONE WHO DOES
GOOD,
THERE IS NOT EVEN ONE."
13   "^THEIR THROAT IS AN OPEN
GRAVE,
WITH THEIR TONGUES THEY
KEEP DECEIVING,"
"^THE VENOM OF ¹ASPS IS UNDER
THEIR LIPS";
14   "^THEIR MOUTH IS FULL OF
CURSING AND BITTERNESS";
15   "^THEIR FEET ARE SWIFT TO SHED
BLOOD,
16   DESTRUCTION AND MISERY ARE
IN THEIR PATHS,
17   AND THEY HAVE NOT KNOWN
THE WAY OF PEACE."
18   "^THERE IS NO FEAR OF GOD
BEFORE THEIR EYES."

19 Now we know that whatever the Law says, it speaks to ^those who are under the Law, so that every mouth may be closed and ^all the world may become accountable to God; 20 because ^by the works of the Law none of mankind will be justified in His sight; for through the Law *comes* knowledge of sin.

JUSTIFICATION BY FAITH

21 But now apart from the Law ^*the* righteousness of God has been revealed, being witnessed by the Law and the Prophets, 22 but *it is the* righteousness of God through faith in Jesus Christ for all those who believe; for ^there is no distinction, 23 for all ^have sinned and fall short of the glory of God, 24 being justified as a gift ^by His grace through the redemption which is in Christ Jesus, 25 whom God displayed publicly as ^a ¹propitiation in His blood through faith. *This was* to demonstrate His righteousness, because in God's *merciful* restraint He let the sins previously committed go unpunished; 26 for the demonstration, *that is,* of His righteousness at the present time, so that He would

3:4 ^Ps 51:4   3:5 ^Rom 6:19; 1 Cor 9:8   3:6 ^Rom 2:16
3:7 ^Rom 3:4   ᴮRom 9:19   3:8 ^Rom 6:1
3:9 ^Rom 3:19, 23; 11:32   3:10 ^Ps 14:1-3; 53:1-3
3:13 ^Ps 5:9   ᴮPs 140:3   3:14 ^Ps 10:7   3:15 ^Is 59:7f
3:18 ^Ps 36:1   3:19 ^Rom 2:12   ᴮRom 3:9
3:20 ^Ps 143:2; Acts 13:39   3:21 ^Rom 1:17; 9:30
3:22 ^Rom 10:12; Gal 3:28   3:23 ^Rom 3:9
3:24 ^Rom 4:4f, 16; Eph 2:8   3:25 ^1 John 2:2; 4:10

3:13 ¹I.e., venomous snakes   3:25 ¹I.e., a means of
reconciliation between God and mankind by paying
the penalty for sin

be just and the justifier of the one who has faith in Jesus.

²⁷Where then is ^boasting? It has been excluded. By what kind of law? Of works? No, but by a law of faith. ²⁸For ^we maintain that a person is justified by faith apart from works of the Law. ²⁹Or ^is God *the God* of Jews only? Is He not *the God* of Gentiles also? Yes, of Gentiles also, ³⁰since indeed God ^who will justify the circumcised by faith and the uncircumcised through faith is one. ³¹Do we then nullify the Law through faith? Far from it! On the contrary, we ^establish the Law.

ABRAHAM'S JUSTIFICATION BY FAITH

4 What then shall we say that Abraham, our forefather ^according to the flesh, has found? ²For if Abraham was justified by works, he has something to boast about; but ^not before God. ³For what does the Scripture say? "^ABRAHAM BELIEVED GOD, AND IT WAS CREDITED TO HIM AS RIGHTEOUSNESS." ⁴Now to the one who ^works, the wages are not credited as a favor, but as what is due. ⁵But to the one who does not work, but ^believes in Him who justifies the ungodly, his faith is credited as righteousness, ⁶just as David also speaks of the blessing of the person to whom God credits righteousness apart from works:

⁷ "^BLESSED ARE THOSE WHOSE
    LAWLESS DEEDS HAVE BEEN
    FORGIVEN,
    AND WHOSE SINS HAVE BEEN
    COVERED.
⁸ "^BLESSED IS THE MAN WHOSE
    SIN THE LORD WILL NOT TAKE
    INTO ACCOUNT."

⁹Is this blessing then on the circumcised, or on the uncircumcised also? For we say, "^FAITH WAS CREDITED TO ABRAHAM AS RIGHTEOUSNESS." ¹⁰How then was it credited? While he was circumcised, or uncircumcised? Not while circumcised, but while uncircumcised; ¹¹and he ^received the sign of circumcision, a seal of the righteousness of the faith which he had while uncircumcised, so that he might be the father of ᴮall who believe without being circumcised, that righteousness might be credited to them, ¹²and the father of circumcision to those who not only are of the circumcision, but who also follow in the steps of the faith of our father Abraham which he had while uncircumcised.

¹³For the promise to Abraham or to his descendants ^that he would be heir of the world was not through the Law, but through the righteousness of faith. ¹⁴For ^if those who are of the Law are heirs, then faith is made void and the promise is nullified; ¹⁵for the Law brings about wrath, but ^where there is no law, there also is no violation.

¹⁶For this reason *it is* by faith, in order that *it may be* in accordance with ^grace, so that the promise will be guaranteed to all the descendants, not only to those who are of the Law, but also to ᴮthose who are of the faith of Abraham, who is the father of us all, ¹⁷(as it is written: "I HAVE MADE YOU ^A FATHER OF MANY NATIONS") in the presence of Him whom he believed, *that is,* God, who gives life to the

3:27 ^Rom 2:17, 23; 4:2   3:28 ^Acts 13:39; Rom 3:20, 21
3:29 ^Acts 10:34f; Rom 9:24   3:30 ^Rom 3:22; 4:11f, 16
3:31 ^Matt 5:17; Rom 3:4, 6   4:1 ^Rom 1:3
4:2 ^1 Cor 1:31   4:3 ^Gen 15:6; Rom 4:9, 22
4:4 ^Rom 11:6   4:5 ^John 6:29; Rom 3:22   4:7 ^Ps 32:1
4:8 ^Ps 32:2   4:9 ^Gen 15:6   4:11 ^Gen 17:10f
ᴮRom 3:22   4:13 ^Gen 12:2-3   4:14 ^Gal 3:18
4:15 ^Rom 3:20   4:16 ^Rom 3:24   ᴮGal 3:7
4:17 ^Gen 17:5

dead and calls into being things that do not exist. [18]In hope against hope he believed, so that he might become a father of many nations according to that which had been spoken, "^So shall your descendants be." [19]Without becoming weak in faith he contemplated his own body, now *as good as* dead since ^he was about a hundred years old, and [B]the deadness of Sarah's womb; [20]yet, with respect to the promise of God, he did not waver in unbelief but grew strong in faith, ^giving glory to God, [21]and ^being fully assured that what *God* had promised, He was able also to perform. [22]Therefore ^it was also credited to him as righteousness. [23]Now ^not for his sake only was it written that it was credited to him, [24]but for our sake also, to whom it will be credited, to *us*^who believe in Him who raised Jesus our Lord from the dead, [25] *He* who was ^delivered over because of our wrongdoings, and was raised because of our justification.

RESULTS OF JUSTIFICATION

5 ^Therefore, having been justified by faith, we have peace with God through our Lord Jesus Christ, [2]through whom we also have ^obtained our introduction by faith into this grace in which we stand; and we celebrate in hope of the glory of God. [3]And not only *this,* but we also ^celebrate in our tribulations, knowing that tribulation brings about perseverance; [4]and perseverance, ^proven character; and proven character, hope; [5]and hope ^does not disappoint, because the love of God has been poured out within our hearts through the Holy Spirit who was given to us.

[6]For while we were still helpless, at *the* right time ^Christ died for the ungodly. [7]For one will hardly die for a righteous person; though perhaps for the good person someone would even dare to die. [8]But God demonstrates ^His own love toward us, in that while we were still sinners, Christ died for us. [9]Much more then, having now been justified ^by His blood, we shall be saved [B]from the wrath *of God* through Him. [10]For if while we were ^enemies we were reconciled to God through the death of His Son, much more, having been reconciled, we shall be saved by His life. [11]And not only *this,* but we also celebrate in God through our Lord Jesus Christ, through whom we have now received ^the reconciliation.

[12]Therefore, just as through one man sin entered into the world, and ^death through sin, and so death spread to all mankind, because all sinned— [13]for until the Law sin was in the world, but ^sin is not counted against *anyone* when there is no law. [14]Nevertheless death reigned from Adam until Moses, even over those who had not sinned ^in the likeness of the [1]violation *committed* by Adam, who is a [2,B]type of Him who was to come.

[15]But the gracious gift is not like the offense. For if by the offense of the one the many died, much more did the grace of God and the gift

4:18^Gen 15:5 **4:19**^Gen 17:17 [B]Gen 18:11 **4:20**^Matt 9:8 **4:21**^Rom 14:5 **4:22**^Gen 15:6; Rom 4:3 **4:23**^Rom 15:4; 1 Cor 9:9f **4:24**^Rom 10:9; 1 Pet 1:21 **4:25**^Is 53:4, 5; Rom 8:32 **5:1**^Rom 3:28 **5:2**^Eph 2:18; 3:12 **5:3**^Matt 5:12; James 1:2f **5:4**^Phil 2:22; James 1:12 **5:5**^Ps 119:116; Rom 9:33 **5:6**^Rom 4:25; 5:8 **5:8**^John 3:16; 15:13 **5:9**^Rom 3:25 [B]Rom 1:18 **5:10**^Rom 11:28; Col 1:21f **5:11**^Rom 5:10; 11:15 **5:12**^Rom 6:23; 1 Cor 15:56 **5:13**^Rom 4:15 **5:14**^Hos 6:7 [B]1 Cor 15:45

5:14 [1]I.e., of God's command [2]Or *foreshadowing*

by ^the grace of the one Man, Jesus Christ, overflow to the many. ¹⁶The gift is not like *that which came* through the one who sinned; for on the one hand ^the judgment *arose* from one *offense,* resulting in condemnation, but on the other hand the gracious gift *arose* from many offenses, resulting in justification. ¹⁷For if by the offense of the one, death reigned through the one, much more will those who receive the abundance of grace and of the gift of righteousness ^reign in life through the One, Jesus Christ.

¹⁸So then, as through one offense the result was condemnation to all mankind, so also through one act of righteousness the result was ^justification of life to all mankind. ¹⁹For as through the one man's disobedience the many were made sinners, so also through ^the obedience of the One the many will be made righteous. ²⁰The Law came in so that the offense would increase; but where sin increased, ^grace abounded all the more, ²¹so that, as sin reigned in death, so also ^grace would reign through righteousness to eternal life through Jesus Christ our Lord.

BELIEVERS ARE DEAD TO SIN, ALIVE TO GOD

6 What shall we say then? Are we to ^continue in sin so that grace may increase? ²¹Far from it! How shall we who ^died to sin still live in it? ³Or do you not know that all of us who have been baptized into ^Christ Jesus have been baptized into His death? ⁴Therefore we have been ^buried with Him through baptism into death, so that, just as Christ was raised from the dead through the glory of the Father, so we too may walk in newness of life.

⁵For ^if we have become united with *Him* in the likeness of His death, certainly we shall also be *in the likeness* of His resurrection, ⁶knowing this, that our ^old self was crucified with *Him,* in order that our body of sin might be done away with, so that we would no longer be slaves to sin; ⁷for ^the one who has died is freed from sin.

⁸Now ^if we have died with Christ, we believe that we shall also live with Him, ⁹knowing that Christ, having been ^raised from the dead, is never to die again; death no longer is master over Him. ¹⁰For the death that He died, He died to sin once for all *time;* but the life that He lives, He lives to God. ¹¹So you too, consider yourselves to be ^dead to sin, but alive to God in Christ Jesus.

¹²Therefore sin is not to ^reign in your mortal body so that you obey its lusts, ¹³and do not go on presenting the parts of your body to sin *as* ¹instruments of unrighteousness; but ^present yourselves to God as those who are alive from the dead, and your body's parts *as* instruments of righteousness for God. ¹⁴For ^sin shall not be master over you, for ᴮyou are not under ¹the Law but under grace.

¹⁵What then? ^Are we to sin because we are not under ¹the Law but under grace? ²Far from it! ¹⁶Do you not know that *the one* to whom

5:15^Acts 15:11   5:16^1 Cor 11:32   5:17^2 Tim 2:12; Rev 22:5   5:18^Rom 4:25   5:19^Phil 2:8
5:20^Rom 6:1; 1 Tim 1:14   5:21^John 1:17; Rom 6:23
6:1^Rom 3:8; 6:15   6:2^Rom 6:11; 7:4, 6
6:3^Acts 2:38; 8:16   6:4^Col 2:12   6:5^2 Cor 4:10; Phil 3:10f   6:6^Eph 4:22; Col 3:9   6:7^1 Pet 4:1
6:8^Rom 6:4; 2 Cor 4:10   6:9^Acts 2:24; Rom 6:4
6:11^Rom 6:2; 7:4, 6   6:12^Rom 6:14
6:13^Rom 12:1; 2 Cor 5:14f   6:14^Rom 8:2, 12
⁸Rom 7:4, 6   6:15^Rom 6:1

6:2¹Lit *May it never happen!*   6:13¹Or *weapons*
6:14¹Or *law*   6:15¹Or *law*   ²Lit *May it never happen!*

you present yourselves *as* ^slaves for obedience, you are slaves of *that same one* whom you obey, either of sin resulting in death, or of obedience resulting in righteousness? ¹⁷But thanks be to God that though you were slaves of sin, you became obedient from the heart to *that* ^form of teaching to which you were entrusted, ¹⁸and after being ^freed from sin, you became slaves to righteousness. ¹⁹I am speaking in human terms because of the weakness of your flesh. For just ^as you presented the parts of your body as slaves to impurity and to lawlessness, resulting in *further* lawlessness, so now present your body's parts as slaves to righteousness, resulting in sanctification.

²⁰For ^when you were slaves of sin, you were free in relation to righteousness. ²¹Therefore what ^benefit were you then deriving from the things of which you are now ashamed? For the outcome of those things is death. ²²But now having been ^freed from sin and enslaved to God, you derive your benefit, resulting in sanctification, and the outcome, eternal life. ²³For the wages of ^sin is death, but the gracious gift of God is eternal life in Christ Jesus our Lord.

BELIEVERS UNITED TO CHRIST

7 Or do you not know, ^brothers *and sisters* (for I am speaking to those who know the Law), that the Law has jurisdiction over a person as long as he lives? ²For ^the married woman is bound by law to her husband as long as he is alive; but if her husband dies, she is released from the law concerning the husband. ³So then, if while her husband is alive she gives herself to

another man, she will be called an adulteress; but if her husband dies, she is free from the law, so that she is not an adulteress if she ¹gives herself to another man.

⁴Therefore, my brothers *and sisters*, you also were ^put to death ᴮin regard to the Law through the body of Christ, so that you might belong to another, to Him who was raised from the dead, in order that we might bear fruit for God. ⁵For while we were in the flesh, the sinful passions, which were ^*brought to light* by the Law, were at work ᴮin the parts of our body to bear fruit for death. ⁶But now we have been released from the Law, having ^died to that by which we were bound, so that we serve in newness of the ¹Spirit and not in oldness of the letter.

⁷What shall we say then? Is the Law sin? ¹Far from it! On the contrary, I would not have come to know sin except through the Law; for I would not have known about coveting if the Law had not said, "^YOU SHALL NOT COVET." ⁸But sin, taking an opportunity ^through the commandment, produced in me coveting of every kind; for apart from the Law sin *is* dead. ⁹I was once alive apart from the Law; but when the commandment came, sin came to life, and I died; ¹⁰and this commandment, which was ^to result in life, proved to result in death for me; ¹¹for sin,

6:16 ^John 8:34; 2 Pet 2:19   6:17 ^2 Tim 1:13
6:18 ^John 8:32; Rom 6:22   6:19 ^Rom 6:13
6:20 ^Matt 6:24; Rom 6:16   6:21 ^Jer 12:13; Ezek 16:63
6:22 ^John 8:32; Rom 6:18   6:23 ^Rom 6:16; 8:6, 13
7:1 ^Rom 1:13   7:2 ^1 Cor 7:39   7:4 ^Rom 7:6
ᴮGal 2:19   7:5 ^Rom 7:7f   ᴮRom 6:13, 21, 23
7:6 ^Rom 6:2   7:7 ^Ex 20:17; Deut 5:21
7:8 ^Rom 3:20; 7:11   7:10 ^Lev 18:5; Luke 10:28

7:3 ¹I.e., in marriage; lit *becomes another man's*
7:6 ¹Or *spirit*   7:7 ¹Lit *May it never happen!*

taking an opportunity through the commandment, ^deceived me, and through it, killed *me*. ¹²^So then, the Law is holy, and the commandment is holy and righteous and good.

¹³Therefore did that which is good become *a cause of* death for me? ^Far from it! Rather *it was* sin, in order that it might be shown to be sin by bringing about my death through that which is good, so that through the commandment sin would become utterly sinful.

THE CONFLICT OF SERVING TWO MASTERS

¹⁴For we know that the Law is ^spiritual, but I am fleshly, sold into bondage to sin. ¹⁵For I do not understand what I am doing; for I am not practicing ^what I want *to do,* but I do the very thing I hate. ¹⁶However, if I do the very thing I do not want *to do,* I agree with ^the Law, that *the Law is* good. ¹⁷But now, ^no longer am I *the one* doing it, but sin that dwells in me. ¹⁸For I know that good does not dwell in me, that is, in my ^flesh; for the willing is present in me, but the doing of the good *is* not. ¹⁹For ^the good that I want, I do not do, but I practice the very evil that I do not want. ²⁰But if I do the very thing I do not want, ^I am no longer *the one* doing it, but sin that dwells in me.

²¹I find then ^the principle that evil is present in me, the one who wants to do good. ²²For I joyfully agree with the law of God in ^the inner person, ²³but I see ^a different law in the parts of my body waging war against the law of my mind, and making me a prisoner of the law of sin, *the law* which is in my body's parts. ²⁴Wretched man that I am! Who will set me free from ^the body of this death? ²⁵^Thanks be to God through Jesus Christ our Lord! So then, on the one hand I myself with my mind am serving the law of God, but on the other, with my flesh the law of sin.

DELIVERANCE FROM BONDAGE

8 Therefore there is now no ^condemnation at all for those who are ᴮin Christ Jesus. ²For ^the law of the Spirit of life in Christ Jesus has set you free from the law of sin and of death. ³For ^what the Law could not do, weak as it was through the flesh, God *did:* sending His own Son in the likeness of sinful flesh and *as an offering* for sin, He condemned sin in the flesh, ⁴so that the requirement of the Law might be fulfilled in us who ^do not walk according to the flesh but according to the Spirit. ⁵For those who are in accord with the flesh set their minds on ^the things of the flesh, but those who are in accord with the Spirit, ᴮthe things of the Spirit. ⁶^For the mind set on the flesh is death, but the mind set on the Spirit is life and peace, ⁷because the mind set on the flesh is ^hostile toward God; for it does not subject itself to the law of God, for it is not even able *to do so,* ⁸and those who are ^in the flesh cannot please God.

⁹However, you are not in the flesh but in the Spirit, if indeed the Spirit of God ^dwells in you. But if

7:11^Gen 3:13   7:12^Rom 7:16; 1 Tim 1:8
7:13^Luke 20:16   7:14^1 Cor 3:1   7:15^Rom 7:19;
Gal 5:17   7:16^Rom 7:12; 1 Tim 1:8   7:17^Rom 7:20
7:18^John 3:6; Rom 7:25   7:19^Rom 7:15
7:20^Rom 7:17   7:21^Rom 7:23, 25; 8:2
7:22^2 Cor 4:16; Eph 3:16   7:23^Rom 6:19; Gal 5:17
7:24^Rom 6:6; Col 2:11   7:25^1 Cor 15:57
8:1^Rom 8:34   ᴮRom 8:9f   8:2^1 Cor 15:45
8:3^Acts 13:39; Heb 10:1ff   8:4^Gal 5:16, 25
8:5^Gal 5:19-21   ᴮGal 5:22-25   8:6^Gal 6:8
8:7^James 4:4   8:8^Rom 7:5   8:9^John 14:23; Rom 8:11

anyone does not have the Spirit of Christ, he does not belong to Him. [10A]If Christ is in you, though the body is dead because of sin, yet the spirit is alive because of righteousness. [11]But if the Spirit of Him who [A]raised Jesus from the dead dwells in you, He who raised Christ Jesus from the dead will also give life to your mortal bodies [1]through His Spirit who dwells in you.

[12]So then, brothers *and sisters,* we are under obligation, not to the flesh, to live according to the flesh— [13]for if you are living in accord with the flesh, you are going to die; but if by the Spirit you are [A]putting to death the deeds of the body, you will live. [14]For all who are [A]being led by the Spirit of God, these are sons *and daughters* of God. [15]For you [A]have not received a spirit of slavery leading to fear again, but you [B]have received a spirit of adoption as sons *and daughters* by which we cry out, "Abba! Father!" [16]The Spirit Himself [A]testifies with our spirit that we are children of God, [17]and if children, [A]heirs also, heirs of God and fellow heirs with Christ, if indeed we suffer with *Him* so that we may also be glorified with *Him.*

[18]For I consider that the sufferings of this present time [A]are not worthy *to be* compared with the glory that is to be revealed to us. [19]For the eagerly awaiting creation waits for [A]the revealing of the sons *and daughters* of God. [20]For the creation [A]was subjected to [B]futility, not willingly, but because of Him who subjected *it,* in hope [21]that [A]the creation itself also will be set free from its slavery to corruption into the freedom of the glory of the children of God. [22]For we know that the whole creation [A]groans and suffers the pains of childbirth together until now. [23]And not only *that,* but also we ourselves, having [A]the first fruits of the Spirit, even we ourselves groan within ourselves, waiting eagerly for *our* adoption as sons *and daughters,* the redemption of our body. [24]For in hope we have been saved, but [A]hope that is seen is not hope; for who hopes for what he *already* sees? [25]But [A]if we hope for what we do not see, through perseverance we wait eagerly *for it.*

OUR VICTORY IN CHRIST

[26]Now in the same way the Spirit also helps our weakness; for we do not know what to pray for as we should, but [A]the Spirit Himself intercedes for *us* with groanings too deep for words; [27]and [A]He who searches the hearts knows what the mind of the Spirit is, because He intercedes for the saints according to *the will of* God.

[28]And we know that [1]God causes [A]all things to work together for good to those who love God, to those who are [B]called according to *His* purpose. [29]For those whom He [A]foreknew, He also predestined *to become* conformed to the image of His Son, so that He would be the firstborn among many brothers *and sisters;* [30]and these whom He predestined, He also called; and these whom He called, He also

8:10 [A]John 17:23; Gal 2:20   **8:11** [A]Acts 2:24; Rom 6:4
8:13 [A]Col 3:5   **8:14** [A]Gal 5:18   **8:15** [A]Heb 2:15
[B]Rom 8:23   **8:16** [A]Acts 5:32   **8:17** [A]Acts 20:32;
Gal 3:29   **8:18** [A]2 Cor 4:17; 1 Pet 4:13   **8:19** [A]Rom 8:18;
1 Cor 1:7f   **8:20** [A]Gen 3:17–19   [B]Ps 39:5f
8:21 [A]Acts 3:21; 2 Pet 3:13   **8:22** [A]Jer 12:4, 11
8:23 [A]Rom 8:16; 2 Cor 1:22   **8:24** [A]Rom 4:18; 2 Cor 5:7
8:25 [A]1 Thess 1:3   **8:26** [A]John 14:16; Rom 8:15f
8:27 [A]Ps 139:1f; Luke 16:15   **8:28** [A]Rom 8:32
[B]Rom 8:30   **8:29** [A]Rom 11:2; 1 Cor 8:3

8:11 [1]One early ms *because of*   **8:28** [1]One early ms
He; i.e., God

^Ajustified; and these whom He justified, He also ^Bglorified.

³¹What then shall we say to these things? ^AIf God *is* for us, who *is* against us? ³²He who ^Adid not spare His own Son, but delivered Him over for us all, how will He not also with Him freely give us all things? ³³Who will bring charges against God's elect? ^AGod is the one who justifies; ³⁴who is the one who condemns? Christ Jesus is He who died, but rather, was ¹raised, who is at the right hand of God, who also ^Aintercedes for us. ³⁵Who will separate us from the love of ¹Christ? *Will* ^Atribulation, or trouble, or ^Bpersecution, or famine, or ^Bnakedness, or danger, or sword? ³⁶Just as it is written:

"^AFor Your sake we are killed
    all day long;
We were regarded as sheep
    to be slaughtered."

³⁷But in all these things we overwhelmingly ^Aconquer through Him who loved us. ³⁸For I am convinced that neither ^Adeath, nor life, nor angels, nor principalities, nor ^Athings present, nor things to come, nor powers, ³⁹nor height, nor depth, nor any other created thing will be able to separate us from ^Athe love of God that is in Christ Jesus our Lord.

DEEP CONCERN FOR ISRAEL

9 ^AI am telling the truth in Christ, I am not lying; my conscience testifies with me in the Holy Spirit, ²that I have great sorrow and unceasing grief in my heart. ³For ^AI could wish that I myself were accursed, *separated* from Christ for the sake of my countrymen, my kinsmen ^Baccording to the flesh, ⁴who are Israelites, to whom belongs ^Athe adoption as sons *and daughters*, the glory, the

covenants, the giving of the Law, the *temple* service, and the promises; ⁵whose are the fathers, and ^Afrom whom is the Christ according to the flesh, ^Bwho is over all, God blessed forever. Amen.

⁶But *it is* not as though the word of God has failed. ^AFor they are not all Israel who are *descended* from Israel; ⁷nor are they all children ^Abecause they are Abraham's descendants, but: "^BTHROUGH ISAAC YOUR DESCENDANTS SHALL BE NAMED." ⁸That is, it is not the children of the flesh who are children of God, but the ^Achildren of the promise are regarded as descendants. ⁹For this is the word of promise: "^AAT THIS TIME I WILL COME, AND SARAH WILL HAVE A SON." ¹⁰And not only *that,* but there was also ^ARebekah, when she had conceived *twins* by one man, our father Isaac; ¹¹for though *the twins* were not yet born and had not done anything good or bad, so that ^AGod's purpose according to *His* choice would stand, not because of works but because of Him who calls, ¹²it was said to her, "^ATHE OLDER WILL SERVE THE YOUNGER." ¹³Just as it is written: "^AJACOB I HAVE LOVED, BUT ESAU I HAVE HATED."

¹⁴What shall we say then? ^AThere is no injustice with God, is there? ¹Far from it! ¹⁵For He says to Moses,

8:30^A1 Cor 6:11   ^BJohn 17:22   8:31^APs 118:6; Matt 1:23
8:32^AJohn 3:16; Rom 5:8   8:33^AIs 50:8f
8:34^ARom 8:27; Heb 7:25   8:35^A2 Cor 4:8   ^B1 Cor 4:11
8:36^APs 44:22; Acts 20:24   8:37^AJohn 16:33;
1 Cor 15:57   8:38^A1 Cor 3:22   8:39^ARom 5:8
9:1^A2 Cor 11:10; Gal 1:20   9:3^AEx 32:32   ^BRom 11:14
9:4^AEx 4:22; Rom 8:15   9:5^AMatt 1:1-16   ^BCol 1:16-19
9:6^ARom 2:28f; Gal 6:16   9:7^AJohn 8:23   ^BGen 21:12
9:8^ARom 4:13, 16; Gal 3:29   9:9^AGen 18:10
9:10^AGen 25:21   9:11^ARom 4:17; 8:28
9:12^AGen 25:23   9:13^AMal 1:2f   9:14^A2 Chr 19:7;
Rom 2:11

8:34 ¹One early ms *raised from the dead*   8:35 ¹Two
early mss *God*   9:14 ¹Lit *May it never happen!*

"^AI WILL HAVE MERCY ON WHOM-
EVER I HAVE MERCY, AND I WILL SHOW
COMPASSION TO WHOMEVER I SHOW
COMPASSION." ¹⁶So then, *it does* not
depend on the *person* who wants *it*
nor the one who ¹runs, but on ^AGod
who has mercy. ¹⁷For the Scripture
says to Pharaoh, "^AFOR THIS VERY
REASON I RAISED YOU UP, IN ORDER TO
DEMONSTRATE MY POWER IN YOU, AND
THAT MY NAME MIGHT BE PROCLAIMED
THROUGHOUT THE EARTH." ¹⁸So then
He has mercy on whom He desires,
and He ^Ahardens whom He desires.

¹⁹You will say to me then, "Why
does He still find fault? For ^Awho has
resisted His will?" ²⁰On the contrary,
who are you, you *foolish* person, who
^Aanswers back to God? ^BThe thing
molded will not say to the molder,
"Why did you make me like this,"
will it? ²¹Or does the potter not have
a right over the clay, to make from
the same lump one object for honorable use, and another for common
use? ²²What if God, although willing to demonstrate His wrath and
to make His power known, endured
with great patience objects of wrath
^Aprepared for destruction? ²³And
He did so to make known ^Athe riches
of His glory upon objects of mercy,
which He prepared beforehand for
glory, ²⁴*namely* us, whom He also
called, ^Anot only from among Jews,
but also from among Gentiles, ²⁵as
He also says in Hosea:

"^AI WILL CALL THOSE WHO WERE
     NOT MY PEOPLE, 'MY PEOPLE,'
AND HER WHO WAS NOT
     BELOVED, 'BELOVED.'"
²⁶ "^AAND IT SHALL BE THAT IN THE
     PLACE WHERE IT WAS SAID
     TO THEM, 'YOU ARE NOT MY
     PEOPLE,'
THERE THEY SHALL BE CALLED
     SONS OF THE LIVING GOD."

²⁷Isaiah cries out concerning
Israel, "^ATHOUGH THE NUMBER OF
THE SONS OF ISRAEL MAY BE LIKE THE
SAND OF THE SEA, *ONLY* THE REMNANT
WILL BE SAVED; ²⁸^AFOR THE LORD WILL
EXECUTE HIS WORD ON THE EARTH,
THOROUGHLY AND QUICKLY." ²⁹And
just as Isaiah foretold:

"^AIF THE LORD OF ARMIES HAD
     NOT LEFT US DESCENDANTS,
WE WOULD HAVE BECOME LIKE
     SODOM, AND WOULD HAVE
     BEEN LIKE GOMORRAH."

³⁰What shall we say then? That
Gentiles, who did not pursue righteousness, attained righteousness,
but ^Athe righteousness that is by
faith; ³¹however, Israel, ^Apursuing a
law of righteousness, did not arrive
at *that* law. ³²Why? Because *they did*
not *pursue it* by faith, but as though
they could by works. They stumbled
over ^Athe stumbling stone, ³³just as
it is written:

"^ABEHOLD, I AM LAYING IN ZION
     ^BA STONE OF STUMBLING AND
     A ROCK OF OFFENSE,
AND THE ONE WHO BELIEVES
     IN HIM WILL NOT BE PUT TO
     SHAME."

THE WORD OF FAITH
BRINGS SALVATION

10 Brothers *and sisters,* my
heart's desire and my prayer
to God for them is for *their* salvation. ²For I testify about them that
they have ^Aa zeal for God, but not in
accordance with knowledge. ³For

9:15^AEx 33:19   9:16^AEph 2:8   9:17^AEx 9:16
9:18^AEx 4:21; 7:3   9:19^A2 Chr 20:6; Job 9:12
9:20^AJob 33:13   ^BIs 29:16   9:22^AProv 16:4; 1 Pet 2:8
9:23^ARom 2:4; Eph 3:16   9:24^ARom 3:29
9:25^AHos 2:23; 1 Pet 2:10   9:26^AHos 1:10
9:27^AIs 10:22   9:28^AIs 10:23   9:29^AIs 1:9
9:30^ARom 1:17; 3:21f   9:31^AIs 51:1; Rom 9:30
9:32^AIs 8:14; 1 Pet 2:6, 8   9:33^AIs 28:16   ^BIs 8:14
10:2^AActs 21:20

9:16 ¹I.e., to win mercy or favor

not knowing about ^God's righteousness and seeking to establish their own, they did not subject themselves to the righteousness of God. ⁴For ^Christ is the end of the Law for righteousness to everyone who believes.

⁵For Moses writes of the righteousness that is based on the Law, that the person who performs them ^will live by them. ⁶But ^the righteousness based on faith speaks as follows: "^DO NOT SAY IN YOUR HEART, 'WHO WILL GO UP INTO HEAVEN?' (that is, to bring Christ down), ⁷or 'Who will descend into the abyss?' (that is, to ^bring Christ up from the dead)." ⁸But what does it say? "^THE WORD IS NEAR YOU, IN YOUR MOUTH AND IN YOUR HEART"— that is, the word of faith which we are preaching, ⁹that if you confess with your mouth Jesus *as* Lord, and believe in your heart that ^God raised Him from the dead, you will be saved; ¹⁰for with the heart *a person* believes, resulting in righteousness, and with the mouth he confesses, resulting in salvation. ¹¹For the Scripture says, "^WHOEVER BELIEVES IN HIM WILL NOT BE PUT TO SHAME." ¹²For ^there is no distinction between Jew and Greek; for the same *Lord* is Lord of all, abounding in riches for all who call on Him; ¹³for "^EVERYONE WHO CALLS ON THE NAME OF THE LORD WILL BE SAVED."

¹⁴How then are they to call on Him in whom they have not believed? How are they to believe in Him ^whom they have not heard? And how are they to hear without ^a preacher? ¹⁵But how are they to preach unless they are sent? Just as it is written: "^HOW BEAUTIFUL ARE THE FEET OF THOSE WHO BRING GOOD NEWS OF GOOD THINGS!"

¹⁶However, they did not all heed the good news; for Isaiah says, "^LORD, WHO HAS BELIEVED OUR REPORT?" ¹⁷So faith *comes* from ^hearing, and hearing by ^the word of Christ.

¹⁸But I say, surely they have never heard, have they? On the contrary: "^THEIR VOICE HAS GONE OUT
    INTO ALL THE EARTH,
AND THEIR WORDS TO THE ENDS
    OF THE WORLD."
¹⁹But I say, surely Israel did not know, did they? First Moses says, "^I WILL MAKE YOU JEALOUS
    WITH *THOSE WHO ARE* NOT A
    NATION,
WITH A FOOLISH NATION I WILL
    ANGER YOU."
²⁰And Isaiah is very bold and says, "^I WAS FOUND BY THOSE WHO DID
    NOT SEEK ME,
I REVEALED MYSELF TO THOSE
    WHO DID NOT ASK FOR ME."
²¹But as for Israel, He says, "^I HAVE SPREAD OUT MY HANDS ALL DAY LONG TO A DISOBEDIENT AND OBSTINATE PEOPLE."

ISRAEL HAS NOT BEEN REJECTED

11 I say then, God has not ^rejected His people, has He? ¹Far from it! For I too am an Israelite, a descendant of Abraham, of the tribe of Benjamin. ²God ^has not rejected His people whom He foreknew. Or do you not know what the Scripture says in *the passage*

10:3 ^Rom 1:17; Phil 3:9   10:4 ^Rom 7:1-4; Gal 3:24
10:5 ^Lev 18:5; Neh 9:29   10:6 ^Rom 9:30
^BDeut 30:12   10:7 ^Heb 13:20   10:8 ^Deut 30:14
10:9 ^Acts 2:24   10:11 ^Is 28:16; Rom 9:33
10:12 ^Rom 3:22, 29   10:13 ^Joel 2:32; Acts 2:21
10:14 ^Eph 2:17   ^BActs 8:31   10:15 ^Is 52:7
10:16 ^Is 53:1; John 12:38   10:17 ^Gal 3:2, 5   ^BCol 3:16
10:18 ^Ps 19:4; Rom 1:8   10:19 ^Deut 32:21
10:20 ^Is 65:1; Rom 9:30   10:21 ^Is 65:2
11:1 ^1 Sam 12:22; Jer 31:37   11:2 ^Ps 94:14

11:1 ¹Lit *May it never happen!*

about Elijah, how he pleads with God against Israel? ³"Lord, ^THEY HAVE KILLED YOUR PROPHETS, THEY HAVE TORN DOWN YOUR ALTARS, AND I ALONE AM LEFT, AND THEY ARE SEEKING MY LIFE." ⁴But what is the divine response to him? "^I HAVE KEPT for Myself SEVEN THOUSAND MEN WHO HAVE NOT BOWED THE KNEE TO BAAL." ⁵In the same way then, there has also come to be at the present time ^a remnant according to *God's* gracious choice. ⁶But ^if *it is* by grace, *it is* no longer on the basis of works, since *otherwise* grace is no longer grace.

⁷What then? What ^Israel is seeking, it has not obtained, but those who were chosen obtained it, and the rest were ᴮhardened; ⁸just as it is written:

"^GOD GAVE THEM A SPIRIT OF
　STUPOR,
EYES TO SEE NOT AND EARS TO
　HEAR NOT,
DOWN TO THIS VERY DAY."
⁹And David says,
"^MAY THEIR TABLE BECOME A
　SNARE AND A TRAP,
AND A STUMBLING BLOCK AND A
　RETRIBUTION TO THEM.
¹⁰ "^MAY THEIR EYES BE DARKENED
　TO SEE NOT,
AND BEND THEIR BACKS
　CONTINUALLY."

¹¹I say then, they did not stumble so as to fall, did they? Far from it! But by their wrongdoing ^salvation *has come* to the Gentiles, to make them jealous. ¹²Now if their wrongdoing *proves to be* riches for the world, and their failure, riches for the Gentiles, how much more *will* their ^fulfillment *be!* ¹³But I am speaking to you who are Gentiles. Therefore insofar as ^I am an apostle of Gentiles, I magnify my ministry ¹⁴if somehow I may move my own people to jealousy and ^save some of them. ¹⁵For if their rejection *proves to be* the ^reconciliation of the world, what *will their* acceptance *be* but life from the dead? ¹⁶If the ^first piece *of dough* is holy, the lump is also; and if the root is holy, the branches are as well.

¹⁷But if some of the ^branches were broken off, and ᴮyou, being a wild olive, were grafted in among them and became partaker with them of the rich root of the olive tree, ¹⁸do not be arrogant toward the branches; but if you are arrogant, *remember that* ^it is not you who supports the root, but the root *supports* you. ¹⁹^You will say then, "Branches were broken off so that I might be grafted in." ²⁰Quite right, they were broken off for their unbelief, but you ^stand by your faith. Do not be conceited, but fear; ²¹for if God did not spare the natural branches, He will not spare you, either. ²²See then the kindness and severity of God: to those who fell, severity, but to you, God's kindness, ^if you continue in His kindness; for otherwise you too will be cut off. ²³And they also, ^if they do not continue in their unbelief, will be grafted in; for God is able to graft them in again. ²⁴For if you were cut off from what is by nature a wild olive tree, and contrary to nature were grafted into

11:3^1 Kin 19:10, 14　11:4^1 Kin 19:18
11:5^2 Kin 19:4; Rom 9:27　11:6^Rom 4:4
11:7^Rom 9:31　ᴮMark 6:52　11:8^Deut 29:4;
Is 29:10　11:9^Ps 69:22　11:10^Ps 69:23
11:11^Acts 28:28　11:12^Rom 11:25　11:13^Acts 9:15
11:14^1 Cor 1:21; 9:22　11:15^Rom 5:11
11:16^Num 15:18ff; Neh 10:37　11:17^John 15:2
ᴮEph 2:11ff　11:18^John 4:22　11:19^Rom 9:19
11:20^Rom 5:2; 2 Cor 1:24　11:22^1 Cor 15:2;
Heb 3:6, 14　11:23^2 Cor 3:16

a cultivated olive tree, how much more will these who are the natural *branches* be grafted into their own olive tree?

²⁵For I do not want you, brothers *and sisters,* to be uninformed of this mystery—so that you will not be ^wise in your own estimation—that a partial hardening has happened to Israel until the fullness of the Gentiles has come in; ²⁶and so all Israel will be saved; just as it is written:

"^THE DELIVERER WILL COME
    FROM ZION,
  HE WILL REMOVE UNGODLINESS
    FROM JACOB."
²⁷ "^THIS IS MY COVENANT WITH
    THEM,
  WHEN I TAKE AWAY THEIR SINS."
²⁸In relation to the gospel *they are* enemies on your account, but in relation to *God's* choice *they are* beloved ^on account of the fathers; ²⁹for the gifts and the ^calling of God are irrevocable. ³⁰For just as you once were disobedient to God, but now have been shown mercy because of their disobedience, ³¹so these also now have been disobedient, that because of the mercy shown to you they also may now be shown mercy. ³²For ^God has shut up all in disobedience, so that He may show mercy to all.

³³Oh, the depth of ^the riches, both of the ^wisdom and knowledge of God! How unsearchable are His judgments and unfathomable His ways! ³⁴For ^WHO HAS KNOWN THE MIND OF THE LORD, OR WHO BECAME HIS COUNSELOR? ³⁵Or ^WHO HAS FIRST GIVEN TO HIM, THAT IT WOULD BE PAID BACK TO HIM? ³⁶For ^from Him, and through Him, and to Him are all things. To Him *be* the glory forever. Amen.

DEDICATED SERVICE

12 Therefore I urge you, brothers *and sisters,* by the mercies of God, to ^present your bodies as a living and holy sacrifice, acceptable to God, *which is* your ¹spiritual service of worship. ²And do not be conformed to this world, but be transformed by the ^renewing of your mind, so that you may ^prove what the will of God is, that which is good and acceptable and perfect.

³For through the grace given to me I say to everyone among you ^not to think more highly of himself than he ought to think; but to think so as to have sound judgment, as God has allotted to each a measure of faith. ⁴For ^just as we have many parts in one body and all the body's parts do not have the same function, ⁵so we, ^who are many, are ^one body in Christ, and individually parts of one another. ⁶However, since we have gifts that ^differ according to the grace given to us, *each of us is to use them properly:* if prophecy, in proportion to *one's* faith; ⁷if ^service, in the *act of* serving; or the one who ^teaches, in the *act of* teaching; ⁸or the one who ¹exhorts, in the *work of* ²exhortation; the one who gives, with generosity; ^the one who is in leadership, with diligence; the one who shows mercy, with cheerfulness.

11:25^Rom 12:16   11:26^Is 59:20   11:27^Is 59:21;
Jer 31:33, 34   11:28^Deut 7:8; 10:15   11:29^Rom 8:28;
1 Cor 1:26   11:32^Rom 3:9; Gal 3:22f   11:33^Rom 2:4
^Col 2:3   11:34^Is 40:13f; 1 Cor 2:16   11:35^Job 35:7;
41:11   11:36^1 Cor 8:6; Col 1:16   12:1^Rom 6:13, 19;
1 Pet 2:5   12:2^Eph 4:23   ^Eph 5:10, 17
12:3^Rom 11:20; 12:16   12:4^1 Cor 12:12-14;
Eph 4:4, 16   12:5^1 Cor 10:17   ^1 Cor 12:20, 27
12:6^Rom 12:3; 1 Cor 7:7   12:7^Acts 6:1   ^Acts 13:1
12:8^1 Tim 5:17

12:1 ¹I.e., in contrast to offering a literal sacrifice
12:8 ¹Or *encourages*   ²Or *encouragement*

[9]ALove *must be* free of hypocrisy. Detest what is evil; cling to what is good. [10]Be Adevoted to one another in brotherly love; give preference to one another in honor, [11]not lagging behind in diligence, Afervent in spirit, Bserving the Lord; [12]Arejoicing in hope, persevering in tribulation, Bdevoted to prayer, [13]Acontributing to the needs of the saints, Bpracticing hospitality.

[14]ABless those who persecute [1]you; bless and do not curse. [15]ARejoice with those who rejoice, and weep with those who weep. [16]Be of the same mind toward one another; do not be haughty in mind, but associate with the lowly. ADo not be wise in your own estimation. [17]ANever repay evil for evil to anyone. BRespect what is right in the sight of all people. [18]If possible, so far as it depends on you, Abe at peace with all people. [19]Never take your own revenge, beloved, but leave room for the wrath *of God,* for it is written: "AVENGEANCE IS MINE, I WILL REPAY," says the Lord. [20]"ABUT IF YOUR ENEMY IS HUNGRY, FEED HIM; IF HE IS THIRSTY, GIVE HIM A DRINK; FOR IN SO DOING YOU WILL HEAP BURNING COALS ON HIS HEAD." [21]Do not be overcome by evil, but overcome evil with good.

BE SUBJECT TO GOVERNMENT

13 Every person is to be Asubject to the governing authorities. For there is no authority except from God, and those which exist are established by God. [2]Therefore whoever resists authority has opposed the ordinance of God; and they who have opposed will receive condemnation upon themselves. [3]For Arulers are not a cause of fear for good behavior, but for evil. Do you want to have no fear of

authority? Do what is good and you will have praise from the same; [4]for it is a servant of God to you for good. But if you do what is evil, be afraid; for it does not bear the sword for nothing; for it is a servant of God, an Aavenger who brings wrath on the one who practices evil. [5]Therefore it is necessary to be in subjection, not only because of wrath, but also Afor the sake of conscience. [6]For because of this you also pay taxes, for *rulers* are servants of God, devoting themselves to this very thing. [7]APay to all what is due them: tax to whom tax *is due;* custom to whom custom; respect to whom respect; honor to whom honor.

[8]Owe nothing to anyone except to love one another; for Athe one who loves his neighbor has fulfilled *the* Law. [9]For this, "AYOU SHALL NOT COMMIT ADULTERY, YOU SHALL NOT MURDER, YOU SHALL NOT STEAL, YOU SHALL NOT COVET," and if there is any other commandment, it is summed up in this saying, "BYOU SHALL LOVE YOUR NEIGHBOR AS YOURSELF." [10]Love does no wrong to a neighbor; therefore Alove is the fulfillment of *the* Law.

[11]*Do* this, knowing the time, that it is already the hour for you to Aawaken from sleep; for now salvation is nearer to us than when we *first* believed. [12]The night is almost gone, and the day is near.

12:9 A2 Cor 6:6; 1 Tim 1:5 12:10 AJohn 13:34; 1 Thess 4:9 12:11 AActs 18:25 BActs 20:19 12:12 ARom 5:2 BActs 1:14 12:13 A2 Cor 9:1 BMatt 25:35 12:14 AMatt 5:44; Luke 6:28 12:15 AJob 30:25; Heb 13:3 12:16 AProv 3:7; Rom 11:25 12:17 AProv 20:22 B2 Cor 8:21 12:18 AMark 9:50; Rom 14:19 12:19 ADeut 32:35; Ps 94:1 12:20 A2 Kin 6:22; Prov 25:21f 13:1 ATitus 3:1; 1 Pet 2:13f 13:3 A1 Pet 2:14 13:4 A1 Thess 4:6 13:5 AEccl 8; 1 Pet 2:13, 19 13:7 AMatt 22:21; Mark 12:17 13:8 AMatt 7:12; 22:39f 13:9 AEx 20:13ff BLev 19:18 13:10 AMatt 7:12; 22:39f 13:11 AMark 13:37; 1 Cor 15:34

12:14 [1] Two early mss do not contain *you*

Therefore let's rid ourselves of ^the deeds of darkness and put on ^Bthe armor of light. [13] Let's ^behave properly as in the day, not in carousing and drunkenness, not in sexual promiscuity and debauchery, not in strife and jealousy. [14] But ^put on the Lord Jesus Christ, and make no provision for the flesh in regard to *its* lusts.

PRINCIPLES OF CONSCIENCE

14 Now ^accept the one who is weak in faith, *but* not to have quarrels over opinions. [2] One person has faith that he may eat all things, but the one who is ^weak eats *only* vegetables. [3] The one who eats is not to ^regard with contempt the one who does not eat, and the one who does not eat is not to judge the one who eats, for God has accepted him. [4] ^Who are you to judge the servant of another? To his own master he stands or falls; and he will stand, for the Lord is able to make him stand.

[5] ^One *person* values one day over another, another values every day *the same.* Each person must be ^Bfully convinced in his own mind. [6] The one who observes the day, observes it for the Lord, and the one who eats, does so with regard to the Lord, for he ^gives thanks to God; and the one who does not eat, *it is* for the Lord *that* he does not eat, and he gives thanks to God. [7] For not one of us ^lives for himself, and not one dies for himself; [8] for if we live, we live for the Lord, or if we die, we die for the Lord; therefore ^whether we live or die, we are the Lord's. [9] For to this *end* ^Christ died and lived *again*, that He might be ^BLord both of the dead and of the living.

[10] But *as for* you, why do ^you judge your brother *or sister?* Or you as well, why do you regard your brother *or sister* with contempt? For ^we will all appear before the judgment seat of God. [11] For it is written:

"^AS I LIVE, SAYS THE LORD, TO
    ME EVERY KNEE WILL BOW,
AND EVERY TONGUE WILL GIVE
    PRAISE TO GOD."

[12] So then ^each one of us will give an account of himself to God.

[13] Therefore let's not ^judge one another anymore, but rather determine this: ^Bnot to put an obstacle or a stumbling block in a brother's *or sister's* way. [14] I know and am convinced in the Lord Jesus that ^nothing is unclean in itself; but to the one who thinks something is unclean, to that *person it is* unclean. [15] For if because of food your brother *or sister* is hurt, you are no longer ^walking in accordance with love. [8] Do not destroy with your *choice* of food that *person* for whom Christ died. [16] Therefore ^do not let what is for you a good thing be spoken of as evil; [17] for the kingdom of God is not eating and drinking, but righteousness and ^peace and joy in the Holy Spirit. [18] For the one who serves Christ in this *way* is ^acceptable to God and approved by *other* people. [19] So then we ^pursue the things which make for peace and the building

13:12 ^Eph 5:11   ^BEph 6:11, 13   13:13 ^1 Thess 4:12
13:14 ^Job 29:14; Gal 3:27   14:1 ^Acts 28:2; Rom 11:15
14:2 ^Rom 14:1; 15:1   14:3 ^Luke 18:9; Rom 14:10
14:4 ^Rom 9:20; James 4:12   14:5 ^Gal 4:10
^BRom 4:21   14:6 ^Matt 14:19; 15:36   14:7 ^Rom 8:38f;
2 Cor 5:15   14:8 ^Luke 20:38; Phil 1:20   14:9 ^Rev 1:18
^BPhil 2:11   14:10 ^Rom 2:16; 2 Cor 5:10   14:11 ^Is 45:23
14:12 ^Matt 12:36; 16:27   14:13 ^Matt 7:1   ^B1 Cor 8:13
14:14 ^Acts 10:15; Rom 14:20   14:15 ^Eph 5:2
^B1 Cor 8:11   14:16 ^1 Cor 10:30; Titus 2:5
14:17 ^Rom 15:13; Gal 5:22   14:18 ^2 Cor 8:21; Phil 4:8
14:19 ^Ps 34:14; Rom 12:18

up of one another. ²⁰Do not tear down the work of God for the sake of food. All things indeed are clean, but ᴬthey are evil for the person who eats and causes offense. ²¹ᴬIt is good not to eat meat or to drink wine, or *to do anything* by which your brother *or sister* stumbles. ²²The faith which you have, have as your own conviction before God. Happy is the one who ᴬdoes not condemn himself in what he approves. ²³But ᴬthe one who doubts is condemned if he eats, because *his eating is* not from faith; and whatever is not from faith is sin.

SELF-DENIAL IN BEHALF OF OTHERS

15 Now we who are strong ought to bear the weaknesses of ᴬthose without strength, and not *just* please ourselves. ²Each of us is to ᴬplease his neighbor for his good, to *his* edification. ³For even ᴬChrist did not please Himself, but as it is written: "ᴮThe taunts of those who taunt You have fallen on Me." ⁴For ᴬwhatever was written in earlier times was written for our instruction, so that through perseverance and the encouragement of the Scriptures we might have hope. ⁵Now may the God who gives perseverance and encouragement grant you ᴬto be of the same mind with one another, according to Christ Jesus, ⁶so that with one purpose *and* one voice you may glorify ᴬthe God and Father of our Lord Jesus Christ.

⁷Therefore, ᴬaccept one another, just as Christ also accepted us, for the glory of God. ⁸For I say that Christ has become a servant to ᴬthe circumcision in behalf of the truth of God, to confirm the promises *given* to the fathers, ⁹and for

the Gentiles to glorify God for His mercy; as it is written:

"ᴬTherefore I will give praise
  to You among the Gentiles,
And I will sing praises to
  Your name."

¹⁰Again he says,

"ᴬRejoice, you Gentiles, with
  His people."

¹¹And again,

"ᴬPraise the Lord all you
  Gentiles,
And let all the peoples
  praise Him."

¹²Again Isaiah says,

"ᴬThere shall come the root
  of Jesse,
And He who arises to rule
  over the Gentiles,
In Him will the Gentiles
  hope."

¹³Now may the God of hope fill you with all ᴬjoy and peace in believing, so that you will abound in hope by the power of the Holy Spirit.

¹⁴And concerning you, my brothers *and sisters,* I myself also am convinced that you yourselves are full of goodness, filled with ᴬall knowledge and able also to admonish one another. ¹⁵But I have written very boldly to you on some points so as to remind you again, because of ᴬthe grace that was given to me from God, ¹⁶to be ᴬa minister of Christ Jesus to the Gentiles, ministering as a priest the gospel of God, so that *my* ᴮoffering of the Gentiles may become acceptable, sanctified by the Holy Spirit. ¹⁷Therefore in

14:20ᴬ1 Cor 8:9-12   14:21ᴬ1 Cor 8:13
14:22ᴬ1 John 3:21   14:23ᴬRom 14:5   15:1ᴬRom 14:1;
Gal 6:2   15:2ᴬ1 Cor 9:22; 10:24, 33   15:3ᴬ2 Cor 8:9
ᴮPs 69:9   15:4ᴬRom 4:23f; 2 Tim 3:16   15:5ᴬRom 12:16
15:6ᴬRev 1:6   15:7ᴬRom 14:1   15:8ᴬMatt 15:24;
Acts 3:26   15:9ᴬ2 Sam 22:50; Ps 18:49
15:10ᴬDeut 32:43   15:11ᴬPs 117:1   15:12ᴬIs 11:10
15:13ᴬRom 14:17   15:14ᴬ1 Cor 1:5; 8:1, 7, 10
15:15ᴬRom 12:3   15:16ᴬActs 9:15   ᴮRom 12:1

Christ Jesus I have found reason for boasting in ^things pertaining to God. ¹⁸For I will not presume to speak of anything except what ^Christ has accomplished through me, resulting in the obedience of the Gentiles by word and deed, ¹⁹in the power of signs and wonders, ^in the power of the Spirit; so that from Jerusalem and all around as far as Illyricum I have fully preached the gospel of Christ. ²⁰And in this way I aspired to preach the gospel, not where Christ was *already* known by name, ^so that I would not build on another person's foundation; ²¹but just as it is written:

"^THEY WHO HAVE NOT BEEN
    TOLD ABOUT HIM WILL SEE,
AND THEY WHO HAVE NOT
    HEARD WILL UNDERSTAND."

²²For this reason ^I have often been prevented from coming to you; ²³but now, with no further place for me in these regions, and since I ^have had for many years a longing to come to you ²⁴whenever I go to Spain—for I hope to see you in passing, and to be ^helped on my way there by you, when I have first ^enjoyed your company for a while— ²⁵but now, ^I am going to Jerusalem, ^serving the saints. ²⁶For ^Macedonia and Achaia have been pleased to make a contribution for the poor among the saints in Jerusalem. ²⁷For they were pleased *to do so,* and they are indebted to them. For ^if the Gentiles have shared in their spiritual things, they are indebted to do them a service also in material things. ²⁸Therefore, when I have finished this, and ^have put my seal on this fruit of theirs, I will go on by way of you to Spain. ²⁹I know that when ^I come to you, I will come in the fullness of the blessing of Christ.

³⁰Now I urge you, brothers *and sisters,* by our Lord Jesus Christ and by ^the love of the Spirit, to ^strive together with me in your prayers to God for me, ³¹that I may be rescued from those who are disobedient in Judea, and *that* my ^service for Jerusalem may prove acceptable to the saints; ³²so that I may come to you in joy by ^the will of God and relax in your company. ³³Now ^the God of peace *be* with you all. Amen.

GREETINGS AND LOVE EXPRESSED

16 I ^recommend to you our sister Phoebe, who is a servant of the church which is at Cenchrea, ²that you ^receive her in the Lord in a manner worthy of the saints, and that you help her in whatever matter she may have need of you; for she herself has also been a helper of many, and of myself as well.

³Greet ^Prisca and Aquila, my fellow workers in Christ Jesus, ⁴who risked their own necks for my life, to whom not only do I give thanks, but also all the churches of the Gentiles; ⁵also *greet* ^the church that is in their house. Greet Epaenetus, my beloved, who is the first convert to Christ from Asia. ⁶Greet Mary, who has worked hard for you. ⁷Greet Andronicus and Junia, my kinsfolk and my ^fellow prisoners, who are outstanding in the view of the apostles, who also were in Christ before me. ⁸Greet

15:17 ^Heb 2:17; 5:1   15:18 ^Acts 15:12; 21:19
15:19 ^Rom 15:13; 1 Cor 2:4   15:20 ^1 Cor 3:10;
2 Cor 10:15f   15:21 ^Is 52:15   15:22 ^Rom 1:13;
1 Thess 2:18   15:23 ^Acts 19:21; Rom 1:10f
15:24 ^Acts 15:3   ^Rom 1:12   15:25 ^Acts 19:21
^Acts 24:17   15:26 ^Acts 16:9; 1 Cor 16:5
15:27 ^1 Cor 9:11   15:28 ^John 3:33   15:29 ^Acts 19:21;
Rom 1:10f   15:30 ^Col 1:8   ^1 Cor 1:11
15:31 ^Rom 15:25f; 2 Cor 8:4   15:32 ^Acts 18:21; Rom 1:10
15:33 ^Rom 16:20; 2 Cor 13:11   16:1 ^2 Cor 3:1
16:2 ^Phil 2:29   16:3 ^Acts 18:2   16:5 ^1 Cor 16:19;
Col 4:15   16:7 ^Col 4:10; Philem 23

Ampliatus, my beloved in the Lord. ⁹Greet Urbanus, our fellow worker ^in Christ, and Stachys my beloved. ¹⁰Greet Apelles, the approved ^in Christ. Greet those who are of the *household* of Aristobulus. ¹¹Greet Herodion, my ^kinsman. Greet those of the *household* of Narcissus, who are in the Lord. ¹²Greet Tryphaena and Tryphosa, workers in the Lord. Greet Persis the beloved, who has worked hard in the Lord. ¹³Greet ^Rufus, a choice man in the Lord, also his mother and mine. ¹⁴Greet Asyncritus, Phlegon, Hermes, Patrobas, Hermas, and the brothers *and sisters* with them. ¹⁵Greet Philologus and Julia, Nereus and his sister, and Olympas, and all ^the saints who are with them. ¹⁶^Greet one another with a holy kiss. All the churches of Christ greet you.

¹⁷Now I urge you, brothers *and sisters,* keep your eye on those who cause dissensions and hindrances contrary to the teaching which you learned, and ^turn away from them. ¹⁸For such people are slaves, not of our Lord Christ but of their own appetites; and by their ^smooth and flattering speech they deceive the hearts of the unsuspecting. ¹⁹For the report of your obedience ^has reached everyone; therefore I am rejoicing over you, but I want you to be wise in what is good, and

innocent in what is evil. ²⁰^The God of peace will soon crush Satan under your feet.

The grace of our Lord Jesus be with you.

²¹^Timothy, my fellow worker, greets you, and *so do* Lucius, Jason, and Sosipater, my kinsmen. ²²I, Tertius, who have ^written this letter, greet you in the Lord.

²³^Gaius, host to me and to the whole church, greets you. Erastus, the city treasurer, greets you, and Quartus, the brother.¹

²⁵^Now to Him who is able to establish you according to my gospel and the preaching of Jesus Christ, according to the revelation of the mystery which has been kept secret for long ages past, ²⁶but now has been disclosed, and through ^the Scriptures of the prophets, in accordance with the commandment of the eternal God, has been made known to all the nations, *leading* to ^Bobedience of faith; ²⁷to the only wise God, through Jesus Christ, ^be the glory forever. Amen.

16:9 ^Rom 8:11ff; 16:3, 7, 10   **16:10** ^Rom 8:11ff; 16:3, 7, 9   **16:11** ^Rom 9:3; 16:7, 21   **16:13** ^Mark 15:21 **16:15** ^Rom 16:2, 14   **16:16** ^1 Cor 16:20; 2 Cor 13:12 **16:17** ^Matt 7:15; Gal 1:8f   **16:18** ^Col 2:4; 2 Pet 2:3 **16:19** ^Rom 1:8   **16:20** ^Rom 15:33   **16:21** ^Acts 16:1 **16:22** ^1 Cor 16:21; Gal 6:11   **16:23** ^Acts 19:29; 20:4 **16:25** ^Eph 3:20; Jude 24   **16:26** ^Rom 1:2   ^BRom 1:5 **16:27** ^Rom 11:36

16:23 ¹Late mss add as v 24: *The grace of our Lord Jesus Christ be with you all. Amen.*

1 CORINTHIANS

APPEAL TO UNITY

1 Paul, called *as* an apostle of Jesus Christ by ^the will of God, and our brother Sosthenes,

² To the church of God which is in Corinth, to those who have been sanctified in Christ Jesus, saints ^by calling, with all who in every place call on the name of our Lord Jesus Christ, their *Lord* and ours:

³ ^Grace to you and peace from God our Father and the Lord Jesus Christ.

⁴ ^I thank ¹my God always concerning you for the grace of God which was given you in Christ Jesus, ⁵ that in everything you were enriched in Him, in all ^speech and all knowledge, ⁶ just as ^the testimony concerning Christ was confirmed in you, ⁷ so that you are not lacking in any gift, as you eagerly ^await the revelation of our Lord Jesus Christ, ⁸ ^who will also confirm you to the end, blameless on the day of our Lord Jesus Christ. ⁹ ^God is faithful, through whom you were called into fellowship with His Son, Jesus Christ our Lord.

¹⁰ Now I urge you, brothers *and sisters,* by the name of our Lord Jesus Christ, that you all agree and that there be no ^divisions among you, but that you be made complete in ^the same mind and in the same judgment. ¹¹ For I have been informed concerning you, my brothers *and sisters,* by Chloe's *people,* that there are quarrels among you. ¹² Now I mean this, that ^each one of you is saying, "I am with

Paul," or "I *am* with ^Apollos," or "I *am* with Cephas," or "I *am* with Christ." ¹³ Has Christ been divided? Paul was not crucified for you, was he? Or were you ^baptized in the name of Paul? ¹⁴ I am thankful that I ^baptized none of you except ^Crispus and Gaius, ¹⁵ so that no one would say you were baptized in my name! ¹⁶ But I did baptize the ^household of Stephanas also; beyond that, I do not know if I baptized anyone else. ¹⁷ ^For Christ did not send me to baptize, but to preach the gospel, ^not with cleverness of speech, so that the cross of Christ would not be made of no effect.

THE WISDOM OF GOD

¹⁸ For the word of the cross is foolishness to ^those who are perishing, but to us who are being saved it is the power of God. ¹⁹ For it is written:

"^I WILL DESTROY THE WISDOM OF
  THE WISE,
AND THE UNDERSTANDING
  OF THOSE WHO HAVE
  UNDERSTANDING, I WILL
  CONFOUND."

²⁰ Where is the wise person? Where is the scribe? Where is the debater of ^this age? Has God not made foolish the wisdom of the world?

1:1 ^Rom 1:10; 2 Tim 1:1   1:2 ^Rom 1:7; 8:28
1:3 ^Rom 1:7   1:4 ^Rom 1:8   1:5 ^Rom 15:14; 2 Cor 8:7
1:6 ^2 Thess 1:10; 1 Tim 2:6   1:7 ^Luke 17:30;
Rom 8:19, 23   1:8 ^Rom 8:19; Phil 1:6   1:9 ^Deut 7:9;
Is 49:7   1:10 ^1 Cor 11:18   ^Rom 12:16   1:12 ^1 Cor 3:4
^Acts 18:24   1:13 ^Matt 28:19; Acts 2:38
1:14 ^Acts 18:8   1:16 ^1 Cor 16:15, 17   1:17 ^John 4:2
^1 Cor 2:1, 4, 13   1:18 ^2 Cor 2:15; 2 Thess 2:10
1:19 ^Is 29:14   1:20 ^Job 12:17; Is 19:11f

1:4 ¹ Two early mss do not contain *my*

²¹For since in the wisdom of God ^the world through its wisdom did not *come to* know God, ^BGod was pleased through the foolishness of the message preached to save those who believe. ²²For indeed ^Jews ask for signs and Greeks search for wisdom; ²³but we preach ^Christ crucified, ^Bto Jews a stumbling block, and to Gentiles foolishness, ²⁴but to those who are the called, both Jews and Greeks, Christ ^the power of God and ^Bthe wisdom of God. ²⁵For the foolishness of God is wiser than mankind, and ^the weakness of God is stronger than mankind.

²⁶For consider your calling, brothers *and sisters,* that there were ^not many wise according to the flesh, not many mighty, not many noble; ²⁷but God has chosen the foolish things of ^the world to shame the wise, and God has chosen the weak things of ^the world to shame the things which are strong, ²⁸and the insignificant things of the world and the despised God has chosen, ^the things that are not, so that He may nullify the things that are, ²⁹so that ^no human may boast before God. ³⁰But *it is* due to Him *that* you are in Christ Jesus, who became to us ^wisdom from God, and ^Brighteousness and sanctification, and redemption, ³¹so that, just as it is written: "^LET THE ONE WHO BOASTS, BOAST IN THE LORD."

PAUL'S RELIANCE UPON THE SPIRIT

2 And when I came to you, brothers *and sisters,* I ^did not come as *someone* superior in speaking ability or wisdom, as I proclaimed to you the ¹testimony of God. ²For I determined to know nothing among you except ^Jesus Christ,

and Him crucified. ³I also was with you in ^weakness and fear, and in great trembling, ⁴and my message and my preaching were ^not in persuasive words of wisdom, but in demonstration of the Spirit and of power, ⁵so that your faith would not rest on the wisdom of mankind, but on ^the power of God.

⁶Yet we do speak wisdom among those who are ^mature; a wisdom, however, not of this age nor of the rulers of this age, who are passing away; ⁷but we speak God's wisdom in a mystery, the hidden *wisdom* which God ^predestined before the ages to our glory; ⁸*the wisdom* ^which none of the rulers of ^Bthis age has understood; for if they had understood it, they would not have crucified the Lord of glory; ⁹but just as it is written:

"^THINGS WHICH EYE HAS NOT
    SEEN AND EAR HAS NOT
    HEARD,
AND *WHICH* HAVE NOT ENTERED
    THE HUMAN HEART,
ALL THAT GOD HAS PREPARED
    FOR THOSE WHO LOVE HIM."

¹⁰For to us God revealed *them* ^through the Spirit; for the Spirit searches all things, even the ^Bdepths of God. ¹¹For who among people knows the *thoughts* of a person except the ^spirit of the person that is in him? So also the *thoughts* of God no one knows,

1:21^1 Cor 1:27f   ^B Luke 12:32   1:22^Matt 12:38
1:23^1 Cor 2:2   ^B1 Pet 2:8   1:24^1 Cor 1:18
^B1 Cor 1:30   1:25^2 Cor 13:4   1:26^Matt 11:25;
1 Cor 1:20   1:27^1 Cor 1:20   1:28^Rom 4:17
1:29^Eph 2:9   1:30^1 Cor 1:24   ^BJer 23:5f
1:31^Jer 9:23f; 2 Cor 10:17   2:1^1 Cor 1:17; 2:4, 13
2:2^1 Cor 1:23; Gal 6:14   2:3^1 Cor 4:10; 2 Cor 11:30
2:4^1 Cor 1:17; 2:1, 13   2:5^2 Cor 4:7; 6:7
2:6^Eph 4:13; Phil 3:15   2:7^Rom 8:29f
2:8^1 Cor 2:6   ^B1 Cor 1:20   2:9^Is 64:4; 65:17
2:10^John 14:26   ^BRom 11:33ff   2:11^Prov 20:27

2:1¹One early ms *mystery*   2:10¹One early ms *But*

except the Spirit of God. [12] Now we ^have not received the spirit of the world, but the Spirit who is from God, so that we may know the things freely given to us by God. [13] We also speak these things, ^not in words taught by human wisdom, but in those taught by the Spirit, combining spiritual *thoughts* with spiritual *words.*

[14] But a natural person ^does not accept the things of the Spirit of God, for they are ^Bfoolishness to him; and he cannot understand them, because they are spiritually discerned. [15] But the one who is ^spiritual discerns all things, yet he himself is discerned by no one. [16] For ^WHO HAS KNOWN THE MIND OF THE LORD, THAT HE WILL INSTRUCT HIM? But we have the mind of Christ.

FOUNDATIONS FOR LIVING

3 And I, brothers *and sisters,* could not speak to you as spiritual people, but *only* as fleshly, as to ^infants in Christ. [2] I gave you ^milk to drink, not solid food; for you were not yet able *to consume it.* But even now you are not yet able, [3] for you are still fleshly. For since there is ^jealousy and strife among you, are you not fleshly, and are you not walking like *ordinary* people? [4] For when ^one person says, "I am with Paul," and another, "I *am* with Apollos," are you not *ordinary* people?

[5] What then is Apollos? And what is Paul? Servants through whom you believed, even ^as the Lord gave *opportunity* to each one. [6] I planted, Apollos watered, but ^God was causing the growth. [7] So then neither the one who plants nor the one who waters is anything, but God who causes the growth. [8] Now the one who plants and the one who waters are one; but each will ^receive his own reward according to his own labor. [9] For we are God's ^fellow workers; you are God's field, God's building.

[10] According to ^the grace of God which was given to me, like a wise master builder I laid a foundation, and another is building on it. But each person must be careful how he builds on it. [11] For no one can lay a ^foundation other than the one which is laid, which is Jesus Christ. [12] Now if anyone builds on the foundation with gold, silver, precious stones, wood, hay, *or* straw, [13] ^each one's work will become evident; for the day will show it because it is *to be* revealed with fire, and the fire itself will test the quality of each one's work. [14] If anyone's work which he has built on it remains, he will ^receive a reward. [15] If anyone's work is burned up, he will suffer loss; but he himself will be saved, yet *only* ^so as through fire.

[16] Do you not know that ^you are a temple of God and *that* the Spirit of God dwells in you? [17] If anyone destroys the temple of God, God will destroy that person; for the temple of God is holy, and that is what you are.

[18] *Take care that* no one deceives himself. ^If anyone among you thinks that he is wise in this age, he must become foolish, so that he

2:12 ^Rom 8:15   2:13 ^1 Cor 1:17; 2:1, 4
2:14 ^John 14:17   ^B1 Cor 1:18   2:15 ^1 Cor 3:1; 14:37
2:16 ^Is 40:13; Rom 11:34   3:1 ^1 Cor 2:6; Eph 4:14
3:2 ^Heb 5:12f; 1 Pet 2:2   3:3 ^Rom 13:13; 1 Cor 1:10f
3:4 ^1 Cor 1:12   3:5 ^Rom 12:6; 1 Cor 3:10
3:6 ^1 Cor 15:10   3:8 ^1 Cor 3:14; 4:5
3:9 ^Mark 16:20; 2 Cor 6:1   3:10 ^Rom 12:3;
1 Cor 15:10   3:11 ^Is 28:16; Eph 2:20   3:13 ^1 Cor 4:5
3:14 ^1 Cor 3:8; 4:5   3:15 ^Job 23:10; Ps 66:10, 12
3:16 ^Rom 8:9; 1 Cor 6:19   3:18 ^1 Cor 8:2; Gal 6:3

may become wise. ¹⁹For the wisdom of this world is foolishness in the sight of God. For it is written: "*He is* ᴬᴛʜᴇ ᴏɴᴇ ᴡʜᴏ ᴄᴀᴛᴄʜᴇs ᴛʜᴇ ᴡɪsᴇ ʙʏ ᴛʜᴇɪʀ ᴄʀᴀғᴛɪɴᴇss"; ²⁰and again, "ᴬᴛʜᴇ Lᴏʀᴅ ᴋɴᴏᴡs ᴛʜᴇ ᴛʜᴏᴜɢʜᴛs of the wise, ᴛʜᴀᴛ ᴛʜᴇʏ ᴀʀᴇ useless." ²¹So then, no one is to be boasting in people. For ᴬall things belong to you, ²²ᴬwhether Paul or Apollos or Cephas, or the world or ᴮlife or death, or things present or things to come; all things belong to you, ²³and ᴬyou belong to Christ, and ᴮChrist belongs to God.

SERVANTS OF CHRIST

4 This is the way *any* person is to regard us: as servants of Christ and ᴬstewards of the mysteries of God. ²In this case, moreover, it is required of stewards that one be found trustworthy. ³But to me it is an insignificant matter that I would be examined by you, or by *any* human court; in fact, I do not even examine myself. ⁴For I ᴬam not aware of anything against myself; however I am not vindicated by this, but the one who examines me is the Lord. ⁵Therefore ᴬdo not go on passing judgment before ¹*the* time, *but wait* ᴮuntil the Lord comes, who will both bring to light the things hidden in the darkness and disclose the motives of *human* hearts; and then praise will come to each person from God.

⁶Now these things, brothers *and sisters,* I have figuratively applied to myself and Apollos on your account, so that in us you may learn not to exceed what is written, so that no one of you will become arrogant ᴬin behalf of one against the other. ⁷For who considers you as superior? ᴬWhat do you have

that you did not receive? And if you did receive it, why do you boast as if you had not received it?

⁸You are ᴬalready filled, you have already become rich, you have become kings without us; and indeed, *I* wish that you had become kings so that we also might reign with you! ⁹For I think, God has exhibited us, the apostles, last of all as men ᴬcondemned to death, because we ᴮhave become a spectacle to the world, both to angels and to mankind. ¹⁰We are fools on account of Christ, but ᴬyou are prudent in Christ! We are weak, but you are strong! You are distinguished, but we are without honor! ¹¹Up to this present hour we are both ᴬhungry and thirsty, and are poorly clothed and roughly treated and homeless; ¹²and we labor, ᴬworking with our own hands; when we are ᴮverbally abused, we bless; when we are persecuted, we endure *it;* ¹³when we are slandered, we reply as friends; we have ᴬbecome as the scum of the world, the dregs of all things, *even* until now.

¹⁴I do not write these things to ᴬshame you, but to admonish you as my beloved children. ¹⁵For if you were to have countless tutors in Christ, yet *you would* not *have* many fathers, for in Christ Jesus I ᴬbecame your father through the gospel. ¹⁶Therefore I urge you, be ᴬimitators of me. ¹⁷For this reason

3:19 ᴬJob 5:13   3:20 ᴬPs 94:11   3:21 ᴬRom 8:32
3:22 ᴬ1 Cor 1:12   ᴮRom 8:38   3:23 ᴬ2 Cor 10:7
ᴮ1 Cor 11:3   4:1 ᴬTitus 1:7; 1 Pet 4:10   4:4 ᴬActs 23:1;
2 Cor 1:12   4:5 ᴬRom 2:1   ᴮRom 2:16   4:6 ᴬ1 Cor 1:12;
3:4   4:7 ᴬJohn 3:27; Rom 12:3, 6   4:8 ᴬRev 3:17f
4:9 ᴬRom 8:36   ᴮHeb 10:33
4:10 ᴬ1 Cor 3:18; 2 Cor 11:19   4:11 ᴬRom 8:35;
2 Cor 11:23-27   4:12 ᴬActs 18:3   ᴮ1 Pet 3:9
4:13 ᴬLam 3:45   4:14 ᴬ1 Cor 6:5; 15:34
4:15 ᴬNum 11:12; Gal 4:19   4:16 ᴬ1 Cor 11:1; Phil 3:17

4:5 ¹I.e., the appointed time of judgment

I ^have sent to you Timothy, who is my beloved and faithful child in the Lord, and he will remind you of my ways which are in Christ, just as I teach everywhere in every church. ¹⁸Now some have become ^arrogant, as though I were not coming to you. ¹⁹But I ^will come to you soon, ᴮif the Lord wills, and I shall find out, not the words of those who are arrogant, but their power. ²⁰For the kingdom of God is ^not in words, but in power. ²¹What do you desire? ^That I come to you with a rod, or with love and a spirit of gentleness?

SEXUAL IMMORALITY REBUKED

5 It is actually reported that there is sexual immorality among you, and sexual immorality of such a kind as does not exist even among the Gentiles, *namely,* that someone has ^his father's wife. ²You have become arrogant and have not mourned instead, so that the one who had done this deed would be ^removed from your midst.

³For I, on my part, though ^absent in body but present in spirit, have already judged him who has so committed this, as though I were present. ⁴In the name of our Lord Jesus, when you are assembled, and I with you in spirit, ^with the power of our Lord Jesus, ⁵I *have decided* to ^turn such a person over to Satan for the destruction of his body, so that his spirit may be saved on ᴮthe day of the ¹Lord.

⁶^Your boasting is not good. Do you not know that ᴮa little leaven leavens the whole lump *of dough?* ⁷Clean out the old leaven so that you may be a new lump, just as you are *in fact* unleavened. For Christ our ^Passover also has been

sacrificed. ⁸Therefore let's celebrate the feast, ^not with old leaven, nor with the leaven of malice and wickedness, but with the unleavened bread of sincerity and truth.

⁹I wrote to you in my letter ^not to associate with sexually immoral people; ¹⁰I *did* not at all *mean* with the sexually immoral people of this world, or with the greedy and swindlers, or with ^idolaters, for then you would have to leave the world. ¹¹But actually, I wrote to you not to associate with any so-called ^brother if he is a sexually immoral person, or a greedy person, or an idolater, or is verbally abusive, or habitually drunk, or a swindler— not even to eat with such a person. ¹²For what *business* of mine *is it* to judge outsiders? ^Do you not judge those who are within *the church?* ¹³But those who are outside, God judges. ^Remove the evil person from among yourselves.

LAWSUITS DISCOURAGED

6 Does any one of you, when he has a case against his neighbor, dare to go to law before the unrighteous and ^not before the saints? ²Or do you not know that ^the saints will judge the world? If the world is judged by you, are you not competent *to form* the smallest law courts? ³^Do you not know that we will judge angels? How much more

4:17^1 Cor 16:10   4:18^1 Cor 4:6   4:19^1 Cor 20:2;
1 Cor 11:34   ᴮActs 18:21   4:20^1 Cor 2:4
4:21^2 Cor 1:23; 2:1, 3   5:1^Lev 18:8; Deut 22:30
5:2^1 Cor 5:13   5:3^Col 2:5; 1 Thess 2:17
5:4^John 20:23; 2 Cor 2:10   5:5^Luke 22:31
ᴮ1 Cor 1:8   5:6^James 4:16   ᴮMatt 16:6, 12
5:7^Mark 14:12; 1 Pet 1:19   5:8^Ex 12:19; 13:7
5:9^2 Cor 6:14; Eph 5:11   5:10^1 Cor 10:27
5:11^Acts 1:15; 2 Thess 3:6   5:12^1 Cor 5:3-5; 6:1-4
5:13^Deut 13:5; 17:7, 12   6:1^Matt 18:17
6:2^Dan 7:18, 22, 27; Matt 19:28   6:3^Rom 6:16

5:5 ¹One early ms *Lord Jesus*

matters of this life? ⁴So if you have law courts dealing with matters of this life, do you appoint them *as judges* who are of no account in the church? ⁵ᴬI say *this* to your shame. *Is it* so, *that* there is not among you anyone wise who will be able to decide between his brothers *and sisters,* ⁶but brother goes to law with brother, and that before ᴬunbelievers?

⁷Actually, then, it is already a defeat for you, that you have lawsuits with one another. ᴬWhy not rather suffer the wrong? Why not rather be defrauded? ⁸On the contrary, you yourselves do wrong and defraud. And this to *your* ᴬbrothers *and sisters!*

⁹Or do you not know that the unrighteous will not ᴬinherit the kingdom of God? Do not be deceived; neither the sexually immoral, nor idolaters, nor adulterers, nor ¹homosexuals, ¹⁰nor thieves, nor *the* greedy, nor those habitually drunk, nor verbal abusers, nor swindlers, will ᴬinherit the kingdom of God. ¹¹Such were some of you; but you were washed, but you were ᴬsanctified, but you were ᴮjustified in the name of the Lord Jesus Christ and in the Spirit of our God.

THE BODY IS THE LORD'S

¹²ᴬAll things are permitted for me, but not all things are of benefit. All things are permitted for me, but I will not be mastered by anything. ¹³Food is for the stomach and the stomach is for food, however God will do away with both of them. But the body is not for sexual immorality, but ᴬfor the Lord, and the Lord is for the body. ¹⁴Now God has not only raised the Lord, but ᴬwill also raise us up through His power. ¹⁵Do you not know that ᴬyour bodies are parts of Christ? Shall I then take away the parts of Christ and make them parts of a prostitute? ¹Far from it! ¹⁶Or do you not know that the one who joins himself to a prostitute is one body *with her?* For He says, "ᴬTHE TWO SHALL BECOME ONE FLESH." ¹⁷But the one who joins himself to the Lord is ᴬone spirit *with Him.* ¹⁸ᴬFlee sexual immorality. Every other sin that a person commits is outside the body, but the sexually immoral person sins against his own body. ¹⁹Or do you not know that ᴬyour body is a temple of the Holy Spirit within you, whom you have from God, and *that* you are not your own? ²⁰For ᴬyou have been bought for a price: therefore glorify God in your body.

TEACHING ON MARRIAGE

7 Now concerning the things about which you wrote, it is ᴬgood for a man ¹not to touch a woman. ²But because of sexual immoralities, each man is to have his own wife, and each woman is to have her own husband. ³The husband must fulfill his duty to his wife, and likewise the wife also to her husband. ⁴The wife does not have authority over her own body, but the husband *does;* and likewise the husband also does not have

---

6:5 ᴬ1 Cor 4:14; 15:34   6:6 ᴬ2 Cor 6:14f; 1 Tim 5:8
6:7 ᴬMatt 5:39f   6:8 ᴬ1 Thess 4:6   6:9 ᴬActs 20:32;
1 Cor 15:50   6:10 ᴬActs 20:32; 1 Cor 15:50
6:11 ᴬ1 Cor 1:2, 30   ᴮRom 8:30   6:12 ᴬ1 Cor 10:23
6:13 ᴬ1 Cor 6:15, 19   6:14 ᴬJohn 6:39f; 1 Cor 15:23
6:15 ᴬRom 12:5; 1 Cor 6:13   6:16 ᴬGen 2:24; Matt 19:5
6:17 ᴬJohn 17:21-23; Rom 8:9-11   6:18 ᴬ1 Cor 6:9;
2 Cor 12:21   6:19 ᴬJohn 2:21; 1 Cor 3:16
6:20 ᴬActs 20:28; 1 Cor 7:23   7:1 ᴬ1 Cor 7:8, 26

6:9 ¹Two Gr words in the text, prob. submissive and dominant male homosexuals   6:15 ¹Lit *May it never happen!*   7:1 ¹Prob. referring to abstinence

authority over his own body, but the wife *does*. ⁵Stop depriving one another, except by agreement for a time so that you may devote yourselves to prayer, and come together again so that ^Satan will not tempt you because of your lack of self-control. ⁶But this I say by way of concession, ^not of command. ⁷ᵀYet I wish that all men were ^even as I myself am. However, each has his own gift from God, one in this way, and another in that.

⁸But I say to the unmarried and to widows that it is ^good for them if they remain even as I. ⁹But if they do not have self-control, ^let them marry; for it is better to marry than to burn *with passion*.

¹⁰But to the married I give instructions, ^not I, but the Lord, that the wife is not to leave her husband ¹¹(but if she does leave, she must remain unmarried, or else be reconciled to her husband), and that the husband is not to divorce his wife.

¹²But to the rest ^I say, not the Lord, that if any brother has an unbelieving wife, and she consents to live with him, he must not divorce her. ¹³And if any woman has an unbelieving husband, and he consents to live with her, she must not divorce her husband. ¹⁴For the unbelieving husband is sanctified through his wife, and the unbelieving wife is sanctified through her believing husband; for otherwise your children are unclean, but now they are ^holy. ¹⁵Yet if the unbelieving one is leaving, let him leave; the brother or the sister is not under bondage in such *cases*, but God has called ¹us ^in peace. ¹⁶For how do you know, wife, whether you will ^save your husband? Or how do you

know, husband, whether you will save your wife?

¹⁷Only, ^as the Lord has assigned to each one, as God has called each, in this way let him walk. And ᴮso I direct in all the churches. ¹⁸Was any man called *when he was already* circumcised? He is not to become uncircumcised. Has anyone been called in uncircumcision? ^He is not to be circumcised. ¹⁹^Circumcision is nothing, and uncircumcision is nothing, but *what matters is* the keeping of the commandments of God. ²⁰^Each *person* is to remain in that state in which he was called.

²¹Were you called as a slave? Do not let it concern you. But if you are also able to become free, take advantage of *that*. ²²For the one who was called in the Lord as a slave, is ^the Lord's freed person; likewise the one who was called as free, is ᴮChrist's slave. ²³^You were bought for a price; do not become slaves of people. ²⁴Brothers *and sisters,* ^each one is to remain with God in that *condition* in which he was called.

²⁵Now concerning virgins, I have no command of the Lord, but I am offering direction as one who ^by the mercy of the Lord is trustworthy. ²⁶I think, then, that this is good in view of the present distress, that ^it is good for a man to remain as he is. ²⁷Are you bound to a wife? Do not seek to be released. Are you released from a wife? Do not seek a

7:5 ^Matt 4:10   7:6 ^2 Cor 8:8   7:7 ^1 Cor 7:8; 9:5
7:8 ^1 Cor 7:1, 26   7:9 ^1 Tim 5:14   7:10 ^Mal 2:16;
Matt 5:32   7:12 ^1 Cor 7:6; 2 Cor 11:17   7:14 ^Ezra 9:2;
Mal 2:15   7:15 ^Rom 14:19   7:16 ^Rom 11:14; 1 Pet 3:1
7:17 ^Rom 12:3   ᴮ1 Cor 4:17   7:18 ^Acts 15:1ff
7:19 ^Rom 2:27, 29; Gal 5:6   7:20 ^1 Cor 7:24
7:22 ^Philem 16   ᴮ1 Pet 2:16   7:23 ^1 Cor 6:20
7:24 ^1 Cor 7:20   7:25 ^2 Cor 4:1; 1 Tim 1:13, 16
7:26 ^1 Cor 7:1, 8

7:7 ¹One early ms *For*   7:15 ¹One early ms *you*

wife. ²⁸But if you marry, you have not sinned; and if a virgin marries, she has not sinned. Yet such people *as yourselves* will have trouble in this life, and I *am trying to* spare you. ²⁹But this I say, brothers, ^Athe time has been shortened, so that from now on those who have wives should be as though they had none; ³⁰and those who weep, as though they did not weep; and those who rejoice, as though they did not rejoice; and those who buy, as though they did not possess; ³¹and those who use the world, as though they did not ^Amake full use of it; for ^Bthe *present* form of this world is passing away.

³²But I want you to be free from concern. One who is ^Aunmarried is concerned about the things of the Lord, how he may please the Lord; ³³but one who is married is concerned about the things of the world, how he may please his wife, ³⁴and *his interests* are divided. The woman who is unmarried, and the virgin, is concerned about the things of the Lord, that she may be holy both in body and spirit; but one who is married is concerned about the things of the world, how she may please her husband. ³⁵I say this for your own benefit, not to put a restraint on you, but to promote what is appropriate and *to secure* undistracted devotion to the Lord.

³⁶But if anyone thinks that he is acting dishonorably toward his virgin, if she is ¹past her youth and it ought to be so, let him do what he wishes, he is not sinning; let ²them marry. ³⁷But the one who stands firm in his heart, if he is not under constraint, but has authority over his own will, and has decided this in his own heart, to keep his own

virgin, he will do well. ³⁸So then, both the one who gives his own virgin in marriage does well, and the one who does not give *her* in marriage will do better.

^{39 A}A wife is bound as long as her husband lives; but if her husband dies, she is free to be married to whom she wishes, only in the Lord. ⁴⁰But ^Ain my opinion she is happier if she remains as she is; and I think that I also have the Spirit of God.

TAKE CARE WITH YOUR LIBERTY

8 Now concerning ^Afood sacrificed to idols, we know that we all have knowledge. Knowledge makes *one* conceited, but love ^Bedifies *people*. ^{2 A}If anyone thinks that he knows anything, he has not yet ^Bknown as he ought to know; ³but if anyone loves God, he ^Ais known by Him.

⁴Therefore, concerning the eating of food sacrificed to idols, we know that an idol is ¹nothing at all in the world, and that ^Athere is no God but one. ⁵For even if ^Athere are so-called gods whether in heaven or on earth, as indeed there are many gods and many lords, ⁶yet for us there is *only* one God, ^Athe Father, ^Bfrom whom are all things, and we *exist* for Him; and one Lord, Jesus Christ, by whom are all things, and we *exist* through Him.

⁷However, not all people have this knowledge; but ^Asome, being accustomed to the idol until now,

7:29 ^ARom 13:11f; 1 Cor 7:31 7:31 ^A1 Cor 9:18 ^B1 John 2:17 7:32 ^A1 Tim 5:5 7:39 ^ARom 7:2 7:40 ^A1 Cor 7:6, 25 8:1 ^AActs 15:20 ^BRom 14:19 8:2 ^A1 Cor 3:18 ^B1 Cor 13:8-12 8:3 ^APs 1:6; Jer 1:5 8:4 ^ADeut 4:35, 39; 6:4 8:5 ^A2 Thess 2:4 8:6 ^AMal 2:10 ^BRom 11:36 8:7 ^ARom 14:14, 22f

7:36 ¹Or *past puberty* ²I.e., the woman and her betrothed or fiancé 8:4 ¹I.e., what it represents does not exist

eat *food* as if it were sacrificed to an idol; and their conscience, being weak, is defiled. ⁸Now ^food will not bring us close to God; we are neither the worse if we do not eat, nor the better if we do eat. ⁹But ^take care that this freedom of yours does not somehow become a stumbling block to the weak. ¹⁰For if someone sees you, the one who has knowledge, dining in an idol's temple, will his conscience, if he is weak, not be strengthened to eat ^things sacrificed to idols? ¹¹For through your knowledge the one who is weak ^is ruined, the brother *or sister* for whose sake Christ died. ¹²^And so, by sinning against the brothers *and sisters* and wounding their conscience when it is weak, you sin against Christ. ¹³Therefore, ^if food causes my brother to sin, I will never eat meat again, so that I will not cause my brother to sin.

PAUL'S USE OF FREEDOM

9 Am I not ^free? Am I not an apostle? Have I not seen Jesus our Lord? Are you not my work in the Lord? ²If I am not an apostle to others, at least I am to you; for you are the ^seal of my apostleship in the Lord.

³My defense to those who examine me is this: ⁴^Do we not have a right to eat and drink? ⁵^Do we not have a right to take along a believing wife, even as the rest of the apostles and the brothers of the Lord, and Cephas? ⁶Or do only ^Barnabas and I have no right to refrain from working? ⁷Who at any time serves ^as a soldier at his own expense? Who ^plants a vineyard and does not eat its fruit? Or who tends a flock and does not

consume some of the milk of the flock? ⁸I am not *just* asserting these things ^according to human judgment, am I? Or does the Law not say these things as well? ⁹For it is written in the Law of Moses: "^YOU SHALL NOT MUZZLE THE OX WHILE IT IS THRESHING." God is not concerned about oxen, is He? ¹⁰Or is He speaking entirely for our sake? Yes, it was written ^for our sake, because the plowman ought to plow in hope, and the thresher *to thresh* in hope of sharing *in the crops*. ¹¹^If we sowed spiritual things in you, is it too much if we reap material things from you? ¹²If others share the right over you, do we not more? Nevertheless, we ^did not use this right, but we endure all things ^so that we will cause no hindrance to the gospel of Christ. ¹³Do you not know that those who ^perform sacred services eat *the food* of the temple, *and* those who attend regularly to the altar have their share from the altar? ¹⁴So also ^the Lord directed those who proclaim the gospel to get their living from the gospel.

¹⁵But I have ^used none of these things. And I have not written these things so that it will be done so in my case; for it would be better for me to die than *that*. No one shall make my boast an empty one! ¹⁶For if I preach the gospel, I have nothing to boast *about*, for ^I am under

8:8^Rom 14:17   8:9^Rom 14:13, 21; 1 Cor 10:28   8:10^Acts 15:20; 1 Cor 8:1, 4, 7   8:11^Rom 14:15, 20   8:12^Matt 18:6; Rom 14:20   8:13^Rom 14:21; 1 Cor 10:32   9:1^1 Cor 9:19; 10:29   9:2^John 3:33; 2 Cor 3:2f   9:4^1 Cor 9:14; 1 Thess 2:6, 9   9:5^1 Cor 7:7f   9:6^Acts 4:36   9:7^2 Tim 2:3f   ^Deut 20:6   9:8^Rom 3:5   9:9^Deut 25:4; 1 Tim 5:18   9:10^Rom 4:23f   9:11^Rom 15:27; 1 Cor 9:14   9:12^Acts 20:33   ^2 Cor 6:3   9:13^Lev 6:16, 26; 7:6, 31ff   9:14^Matt 10:10; Luke 10:7   9:15^Acts 18:3; 20:33   9:16^Acts 9:15; Rom 1:14

compulsion; for woe to me if I do not preach the gospel. [17]For if I do this voluntarily, I have a ^reward; but if against my will, I have been entrusted with a commission *nonetheless*. [18]What, then, is my reward? That, when I preach the gospel, I may offer the gospel ^without charge, so as not to make full use of my right in the gospel.

[19]For though I am free from all people, I have made myself ^a slave to all, so that I may gain more. [20]^To the Jews I became as a Jew, so that I might gain Jews; to those who are under the Law, *I became* as *one* under the Law, though not being under the Law myself, so that I might gain those who are under the Law; [21]to those who are ^without the Law, *I became* as one without the Law, though not being without the law of God but ^Bunder the law of Christ, so that I might gain those who are without the Law. [22]To the ^weak I became weak, that I might gain the weak; I have become ^Ball things to all people, so that I may by all means save some. [23]I do all things for the sake of the gospel, so that I may become a fellow partaker of it.

[24]Do you not know that those who run in a race all run, but *only* one receives ^the prize? Run in such a way that you may win. [25]Everyone who competes in the games exercises self-control in all things. So they *do it* to obtain a perishable ^wreath, but we an imperishable. [26]Therefore I ^run in such a way as not *to run* aimlessly; I box in such a way, as to avoid hitting air; [27]but I strictly discipline ^my body and make it my slave, so that, after I have preached to others, I myself will not be disqualified.

AVOID ISRAEL'S MISTAKES

10 For I do not want you to be unaware, brothers *and sisters,* that our fathers were all ^under the cloud and they all passed through the sea; [2]and they all were ^baptized into Moses in the cloud and in the sea; [3]and they all ^ate the same spiritual food, [4]and all ^drank the same spiritual drink, for they were drinking from a spiritual rock which followed them; and the rock was Christ. [5]Nevertheless, with most of them God was not pleased; for *their dead bodies* were ^spread out in the wilderness.

[6]Now these things happened as examples for us, so that we would not crave evil things as ^they indeed craved *them.* [7]Do not be idolaters, as some of them were; as it is written: "^THE PEOPLE SAT DOWN TO EAT AND TO DRINK, AND ROSE UP TO PLAY." [8]Nor are we to commit sexual immorality, as some of them did, and ^twenty-three thousand fell in one day. [9]Nor are we to put the Lord to the test, as ^some of them did, and were killed by the snakes. [10]Nor grumble, as some of them did, and ^were killed by the destroyer. [11]Now these things happened to them as an example, and ^they were written for our instruction, upon whom ^Bthe ends of the ages have come. [12]Therefore let the one who ^thinks he stands watch out that he does not fall. [13]No temptation has

9:17 ^John 4:36; 1 Cor 3:8   9:18 ^Acts 18:3; 2 Cor 11:7
9:19 ^2 Cor 4:5; Gal 5:13   9:20 ^Acts 16:3; 21:23-26
9:21 ^Rom 2:12, 14   ^BGal 6:2   9:22 ^Rom 15:1
^B1 Cor 10:33   9:24 ^Phil 3:14; Col 2:18   9:25 ^2 Tim 4:8;
James 1:12   9:26 ^Heb 12:1   9:27 ^Rom 8:13
10:1 ^Ex 13:21; Ps 105:39   10:2 ^Rom 6:3; 1 Cor 1:13
10:3 ^Ex 16:4, 35; Deut 8:3   10:4 ^Ex 17:6; Num 20:11
10:5 ^Num 14:29ff, 37; 26:65   10:6 ^Num 11:4, 34;
Ps 106:14   10:7 ^Ex 32:6   10:8 ^Num 25:9
10:9 ^Num 21:5f   10:10 ^Num 16:49   10:11 ^Rom 4:23
^BRom 13:11   10:12 ^Rom 11:20; 2 Pet 3:17

overtaken you except *something* common to mankind; and ^God is faithful, so He will not allow you to be ^tempted beyond what you are able, but with the temptation will provide the way of escape also, so that you will be able to endure it.

¹⁴ Therefore, my beloved, flee from ^idolatry. ¹⁵ I speak as to wise people; you *then,* judge what I say. ¹⁶ Is the ^cup of blessing which we bless not a sharing in the blood of Christ? Is the bread which we break not a sharing in the body of Christ? ¹⁷ Since there is one loaf, we ^who are many are one body; for we all partake of the one loaf. ¹⁸ Look at the people of Israel; are those who ^eat the sacrifices not partners in the altar? ¹⁹ What do I mean then? That food sacrificed to idols is anything, or ^that an idol is anything? ²⁰ *No,* but I *say* that things which *the Gentiles* sacrifice, they ^sacrifice to demons and not to God; and I do not want you to become partners with demons. ²¹ ^You cannot drink the cup of the Lord and the cup of demons; you cannot partake of the table of the Lord and the table of demons. ²² Or do we ^provoke the Lord to jealousy? We are not ^stronger than He, are we?

²³ ^All things are permitted, but not all things are of benefit. All things are permitted, but not all things ^build *people* up. ²⁴ No one is to ^seek his own *advantage,* but rather that of his neighbor. ²⁵ ^Eat anything that is sold in the meat market without asking questions, for the sake of conscience; ²⁶ ^FOR THE EARTH IS THE LORD'S, AND ALL IT CONTAINS. ²⁷ If ^one of the unbelievers invites you and you want to go, ^eat anything that is set before you without asking questions, for the

sake of conscience. ²⁸ But ^if anyone says to you, "This is meat sacrificed to idols," do not eat *it,* for the sake of that one who informed *you* and for the sake of conscience. ²⁹ Now *by* "conscience" I do not mean your own, but the other person's; for ^why is my freedom judged by another's conscience? ³⁰ If I partake with thankfulness, why am I slandered about that for which I ^give thanks?

³¹ Therefore, whether you eat or drink, or ^whatever you do, do all things for the glory of God. ³² ^Do not offend Jews or Greeks, or the church of God; ³³ just as I also ^please everyone in all things, not seeking my own benefit but the *benefit* of the many, so that they may be saved.

CHRISTIAN ORDER

11 ^Be imitators of me, just as I also am of Christ.

² Now I praise you because you ^remember me in everything and hold firmly to the traditions, just as I handed them down to you. ³ But I want you to understand that Christ is the ^head of every man, and the man is the head of a woman, and God is the head of Christ. ⁴ Every man who has *something* on his head while praying or ^prophesying disgraces his head. ⁵ But every

10:13 ^1 Cor 1:9　　^B 2 Pet 2:9　　**10:14** ^1 Cor 10:7, 19f; 1 John 5:21　　**10:16** ^Matt 26:27f; Mark 14:23f
10:17 ^Rom 12:5; 1 Cor 12:12f, 27　　**10:18** ^Lev 7:6, 14f; Deut 12:17f　　**10:19** ^1 Cor 8:4　　**10:20** ^Deut 32:17; Ps 106:37　　**10:21** ^2 Cor 6:16　　**10:22** ^Deut 32:21
^B Eccl 6:10　　**10:23** ^1 Cor 6:12　　^B Rom 14:19
10:24 ^Phil 15:2; 1 Cor 10:33　　**10:25** ^Acts 10:15; 1 Cor 8:7　　**10:26** ^Ps 24:1; 50:12　　**10:27** ^1 Cor 5:10
^B Luke 10:8　　**10:28** ^1 Cor 8:7, 10–12　　**10:29** ^Rom 14:16; 1 Cor 9:19　　**10:30** ^Rom 14:6　　**10:31** ^Col 3:17; 1 Pet 4:11　　**10:32** ^Acts 24:16; 1 Cor 8:13
10:33 ^Rom 15:2; 1 Cor 9:22　　**11:1** ^1 Cor 4:16; Phil 3:17
11:2 ^1 Thess 1:6; 3:6　　**11:3** ^Eph 5:23　　**11:4** ^Acts 13:1; 1 Thess 5:20

woman who has her head uncovered while praying or prophesying disgraces her head, for it is one and the same as the woman whose head is ᴬshaved. ⁶For if a woman does not cover her head, have her also cut her hair off; however, if it is disgraceful for a woman to have her hair cut off or her head shaved, have her cover her head. ⁷For a man should not have his head covered, since he is the ᴬimage and glory of God; but the woman is the glory of man. ⁸For ᴬman does not originate from woman, but woman from man; ⁹for indeed man was not created for the woman's sake, but ᴬwoman for the man's sake. ¹⁰Therefore the woman should have *a symbol of* authority on her head, because of the angels. ¹¹However, in the Lord, neither is woman independent of man, nor is man independent of woman. ¹²For as the woman *originated* from the man, so also the man *has his birth* through the woman; and ᴬall things *originate* ᴮfrom God. ¹³ᴬJudge for yourselves: is it proper for a woman to pray to God *with her head* uncovered? ¹⁴Does even nature itself not teach you that if a man has long hair, it is a dishonor to him, ¹⁵but if a woman has long hair, it is a glory to her? For her hair is given to her as a covering. ¹⁶But if anyone is inclined to be contentious, ᴬwe have no such practice, nor have ᴮthe churches of God.

¹⁷Now in giving this *next* instruction ᴬI do not praise you, because you come together not for the better, but for the worse. ¹⁸For, in the first place, when you come together as a church, I hear that ᴬdivisions exist among you; and in part I believe it. ¹⁹For there also ᴬhave to be factions among you, so that those who are approved may become evident among you. ²⁰Therefore when you come together it is not to eat the Lord's Supper, ²¹for when you eat, each one takes his own supper first; and one goes hungry while ᴬanother gets drunk. ²²What! Do you not have houses in which to eat and drink? Or do you despise the ᴬchurch of God and ᴮshame those who have nothing? What am I to say to you? Shall I praise you? In this I do not praise you.

THE LORD'S SUPPER

²³For I received from the Lord that which I also delivered to you, that ᴬthe Lord Jesus, on the night when He was betrayed, took bread; ²⁴and when He had given thanks, He broke it and said, "This is My body, which is for you; do this in remembrance of Me." ²⁵In the same way *He* also *took* the cup after supper, saying, "This cup is the ᴬnew covenant in My blood; do this, as often as you drink *it,* in remembrance of Me." ²⁶For as often as you eat this bread and drink the cup, you proclaim the Lord's death ᴬuntil He comes.

²⁷Therefore whoever eats the bread or drinks the cup of the Lord in an unworthy way, shall be ᴬguilty of the body and the blood of the Lord. ²⁸But a person must ᴬexamine himself, and in so doing he is to eat of the bread and drink of the cup. ²⁹For the one who eats and drinks, eats and drinks judgment

11:5ᴬDeut 21:12   11:7ᴬGen 1:26; 5:1   11:8ᴬGen 2:21-23; 1 Tim 2:13   11:9ᴬGen 2:18   11:12ᴬ2 Cor 5:18   ᴮRom 11:36   11:13ᴬLuke 12:57   11:16ᴬ1 Cor 4:5   ᴮ1 Cor 7:17   11:17ᴬ1 Cor 11:2, 22   11:18ᴬ1 Cor 1:10; 3:3   11:19ᴬMatt 18:7; Luke 17:1   11:21ᴬJude 12   11:22ᴬ1 Cor 10:32   ᴮJames 2:6   11:23ᴬ1 Cor 10:32   11:23-25: *Matt 26:26-28*   11:25ᴬLuke 22:20; 2 Cor 3:6   11:26ᴬJohn 21:22; 1 Cor 4:5   11:27ᴬHeb 10:29   11:28ᴬMatt 26:22; 2 Cor 13:5

to himself if he does not *properly* recognize the body. [30]For this reason many among you are weak and sick, and a number ^are asleep. [31]But if we judged ourselves rightly, we would not be judged. [32]But when we are judged, we are ^disciplined by the Lord so that we will not be condemned along with the world.

[33]So then, my brothers *and sisters,* when you come together to eat, wait for one another. [34]If anyone is ^hungry, have him eat ^Bat home, so that you do not come together for judgment. As to the remaining matters, I will give instructions when I come.

THE USE OF SPIRITUAL GIFTS

12 Now concerning ^spiritual *gifts,* brothers *and sisters,* I do not want you to be unaware. [2]^You know that when you were pagans, *you were* ^Bled astray to the mute idols, however you were led. [3]Therefore I make known to you that no one speaking ^by the Spirit of God says, "Jesus is accursed"; and no one can say, "Jesus is Lord," except ^by the Holy Spirit.

[4]Now there are ^varieties of gifts, but the same Spirit. [5]And there are varieties of ministries, and the same Lord. [6]There are varieties of effects, but the same ^God who works all things in all *persons.* [7]But to each one is given the manifestation of the Spirit ^for the common good. [8]For to one is given the word of ^wisdom through the Spirit, and to another the word of knowledge according to the same Spirit; [9]to another ^faith by the same Spirit, and to another ^Bgifts of healing by the one Spirit, [10]and to another the effecting of miracles, and to another prophecy, and to another the ^distinguishing of spirits, to another *various*

kinds of tongues, and to another the interpretation of tongues. [11]But one and the same Spirit works all these things, ^distributing to each one individually just as He wills.

[12]For just as the body is one and *yet* has many parts, and all the parts of the body, though they are many, are one body, ^so also is Christ. [13]For ^by one Spirit we were all baptized into one body, whether Jews or Greeks, whether slaves or free, and we were all made to ^Bdrink of one Spirit.

[14]For ^the body is not one part, but many. [15]If the foot says, "Because I am not a hand, I am not *a part* of the body," it is not for this reason any less *a part* of the body. [16]And if the ear says, "Because I am not an eye, I am not *a part* of the body," it is not for this reason any less *a part* of the body. [17]If the whole body were an eye, where would the hearing be? If the whole *body* were hearing, where would the sense of smell be? [18]But now God has ^arranged the parts, each one of them in the body, ^Bjust as He desired. [19]If they were all one part, where would the body be? [20]But now ^there are many parts, but one body. [21]And the eye cannot say to the hand, "I have no need of you"; or again, the head to the feet, "I have no need of you." [22]On the contrary, it is much truer that the parts of the body which seem to be weaker are necessary; [23]and those *parts* of the body which

11:30^Acts 7:60   11:32^2 Sam 7:14; Ps 94:12 11:34^1 Cor 11:21   ^B1 Cor 11:22   12:1^1 Cor 12:4; 14:1 12:2^1 Cor 6:11   ^B1 Thess 1:9   12:3^Matt 22:43; 1 John 4:2f   12:4^Rom 12:6f; 1 Cor 12:11 12:6^1 Cor 15:28; Eph 1:23; 4:6   12:7^1 Cor 12:12–30; 14:26   12:8^1 Cor 2:6   12:9^1 Cor 13:2 ^B1 Cor 12:28, 30   12:10^1 Cor 14:29; 1 John 4:1 12:11^1 Cor 12:4   12:12^1 Cor 12:27   12:13^Eph 2:18 ^BJohn 7:37–39   12:14^1 Cor 12:20   12:18^1 Cor 12:28 ^BRom 12:6   12:20^1 Cor 12:12, 14

we consider less honorable, on these we bestow greater honor, and our less presentable parts become much more presentable, [24]whereas our more presentable parts have no need *of it.* But God has *so* composed the body, giving more abundant honor to that *part* which lacked, [25]so that there may be no division in the body, but *that* the parts may have the same care for one another. [26]And if one part *of the body* suffers, all the parts suffer with it; if a part is honored, all the parts rejoice with it.

[27]Now you are Christ's body, and [A]individually parts of it. [28]And God has [A]appointed in the church, first [B]apostles, second prophets, third teachers, then miracles, then gifts of healings, helps, administrations, *and various* kinds of tongues. [29]All are not apostles, are they? All are not prophets, are they? All are not teachers, are they? All are not *workers of* miracles, are they? [30]All do not have gifts of healings, do they? All do not speak with tongues, do they? All do not [A]interpret, do they? [31]But [A]earnestly desire the greater gifts.

And yet, I *am going to* show you a far better way.

THE EXCELLENCE OF LOVE

13 If I speak with the [A]tongues of mankind and of angels, but do not have love, I have become a noisy gong or a [B]clanging cymbal. [2]If I have *the gift of* prophecy and know all [A]mysteries and all knowledge, and if I have all faith so as to remove mountains, but do not have love, I am nothing. [3]And if I [A]give away all my possessions *to charity,* and if I [B]surrender my body so that I may [1]glory, but do not have love, it does me no good.

[4]Love [A]is patient, love is kind, it is not jealous; love does not brag, it is not arrogant. [5]It does not act disgracefully, it does not seek its own *benefit;* it is not provoked, [A]does not keep an account of a wrong *suffered,* [6]it does not rejoice in unrighteousness, but [A]rejoices with the truth; [7]it [A]keeps every confidence, it believes all things, hopes all things, endures all things.

[8]Love never fails; but if *there are* gifts of [A]prophecy, they will be done away with; if *there are* [B]tongues, they will cease; if *there is* knowledge, it will be done away with. [9]For we [A]know in part and prophesy in part; [10]but when the perfect comes, the partial will be done away with. [11]When I was a child, I used to speak like a child, think like a child, reason like a child; when I became a man, I did away with childish things. [12]For now we see in a mirror dimly, but then [A]face to face; now I know in part, but then I will know fully, just as I also have been fully known. [13]But now faith, hope, *and* love remain, these three; but the greatest of these is [A]love.

PROPHECY A SUPERIOR GIFT

14 [A]Pursue love, yet earnestly [B]desire spiritual *gifts,* but especially that you may prophesy. [2]For the one who [A]speaks in a tongue does not speak to people, but to God; for no one understands, but in *his* spirit he speaks [B]mysteries. [3]But

12:27 [A]Rom 12:5; Eph 5:30   **12:28** [A]1 Cor 12:18   [B]Eph 4:11   **12:30** [A]1 Cor 12:10   **12:31** [A]1 Cor 14:1, 39   **13:1** [A]1 Cor 12:10   [B]Ps 150:5   **13:2** [A]1 Cor 14:2; 15:51   **13:3** [A]Matt 6:2   [B]Dan 3:28   **13:4** [A]Prov 10:12; 17:9   **13:5** [A]2 Cor 5:19   **13:6** [A]2 John 4; 3 John 3f   **13:7** [A]1 Cor 9:12   **13:8** [A]1 Cor 13:2   [B]1 Cor 13:1   **13:9** [A]1 Cor 8:2; 13:12   **13:12** [A]Gen 32:30; Num 12:8   **13:13** [A]Gal 5:6   **14:1** [A]1 Cor 16:14   [B]1 Cor 12:31   **14:2** [A]1 Cor 12:10, 28, 30   [B]1 Cor 13:2

13:3 [1]I.e., in martyrdom

the one who prophesies speaks to people *for* ^edification, exhortation, and consolation. ⁴The one who speaks in a tongue ^edifies himself; but the one who prophesies ^edifies the church. ⁵Now I wish that you all spoke in tongues, but ^rather that you would prophesy; and greater is the one who prophesies than the one who speaks in tongues, unless he interprets, so that the church may receive edification.

⁶But now, brothers *and sisters,* if I come to you speaking in tongues, how will I benefit you unless I speak to you either by way of ^revelation, or of knowledge, or of prophecy, or of teaching? ⁷Yet *even* lifeless *instruments,* whether flute or harp, in producing a sound, if they do not produce a distinction in the tones, how will it be known what is played on the flute or on the harp? ⁸For if ^the trumpet produces an indistinct sound, who will prepare himself for battle? ⁹So you too, unless you produce intelligible speech by the tongue, how will it be known what is spoken? For you will *just* be ^talking to the air. ¹⁰There are, perhaps, a great many kinds of languages in the world, and none is incapable of meaning. ¹¹So if I do not know the meaning of the language, I will be ^unintelligible to the one who speaks, and the one who speaks will be unintelligible to me. ¹²So you too, since you are eager to possess spiritual *gifts,* strive to excel for the ^edification of the church.

¹³Therefore, one who speaks in a tongue is to pray that he may interpret. ¹⁴For if I pray in a tongue, my spirit prays, but my mind is unproductive. ¹⁵What is *the outcome* then? I will pray with the spirit, but I will pray with the mind also; I will

^sing with the spirit, but I will sing with the mind also. ¹⁶For otherwise, if you bless *God* in the spirit *only,* how will the one who occupies the place of the outsider *know to* say ^the "Amen" at your giving of thanks, since he does not understand what you are saying? ¹⁷For you are giving thanks well *enough,* but the other person is not ^edified. ¹⁸I thank God, I speak in tongues more than you all; ¹⁹nevertheless, in church I prefer to speak five words with my mind so that I may instruct others also, rather than ten thousand words in a tongue.

INSTRUCTION FOR THE CHURCH

²⁰Brothers *and sisters,* ^do not be children in your thinking; yet in evil ᴮbe infants, but in your thinking be mature. ²¹In the Law it is written: "^ᴮʏ ᴍᴇɴ ᴏꜰ ꜱᴛʀᴀɴɢᴇ ᴛᴏɴɢᴜᴇꜱ ᴀɴᴅ ʙʏ ᴛʜᴇ ʟɪᴘꜱ ᴏꜰ ꜱᴛʀᴀɴɢᴇʀꜱ I ᴡɪʟʟ ꜱᴘᴇᴀᴋ ᴛᴏ ᴛʜɪꜱ ᴘᴇᴏᴘʟᴇ, ᴀɴᴅ ᴇᴠᴇɴ ꜱᴏ ᴛʜᴇʏ ᴡɪʟʟ ɴᴏᴛ ʟɪꜱᴛᴇɴ ᴛᴏ ᴍᴇ," says the Lord. ²²So then, tongues are for a sign, not to those who believe but to unbelievers; but ^prophecy is not for unbelievers, but for those who believe. ²³Therefore if the whole church gathers together and all *the people* speak in tongues, and outsiders or unbelievers enter, will they not say that ^you are insane? ²⁴But if all prophesy, and an unbeliever or an outsider enters, he is ^convicted by all, he is called to account by all; ²⁵the secrets of his heart are disclosed; and so he will

14:3 ^Rom 14:19; 1 Cor 14:5, 12, 17, 26
14:4 ^Rom 14:19; 1 Cor 14:5, 12, 17, 26
14:5 ^Num 11:29   14:6 ^1 Cor 14:26; Eph 1:17
14:8 ^Num 10:9; Jer 4:19   14:9 ^1 Cor 9:26
14:11 ^Acts 28:2   14:12 ^Rom 14:19; 1 Cor 14:4, 5, 17, 26
14:15 ^Eph 5:19; Col 3:16   14:16 ^Deut 27:15-26;
1 Chr 16:36   14:17 ^Rom 14:19; 1 Cor 14:4, 5, 12, 26
14:20 ^Eph 4:14   ᴮMatt 18:3   14:21 ^Is 28:11f
14:22 ^1 Cor 14:1   14:23 ^Acts 2:13   14:24 ^John 16:8

fall on his face and worship God, ^declaring that God is certainly among you.

26 What is *the outcome* then, brothers *and sisters?* When you assemble, each one has a psalm, has a teaching, has a revelation, has a tongue, has an interpretation. ^All things are to be done for edification. 27 If anyone speaks in a tongue, *it must be* by two or at the most three, and *each one* in turn, and one is to ^interpret; 28 but if there is no interpreter, he is to keep silent in church; and have him speak to himself and to God. 29 Have two or three ^prophets speak, and have the others ^Bpass judgment. 30 But if a revelation is made to another who is seated, then the first one is to keep silent. 31 For you can all prophesy one by one, so that all may learn and all may be exhorted; 32 and the spirits of prophets are subject to prophets; 33 for God is not *a God* of confusion, but of peace.

As in ^all the churches of the saints, 34 the women are to keep silent in the churches; for they are not permitted to speak, but ^are to subject themselves, just as the Law also says. 35 If they desire to learn anything, let them ask their own husbands at home; for it is improper for a woman to speak in church. 36 Or was it from you that the word of God *first* went out? Or has it come to you only?

37 ^If anyone thinks that he is a prophet or spiritual, let him recognize that the things which I write to you are the Lord's commandment. 38 But if anyone does not recognize *this*, [1]he is not recognized.

39 Therefore, my brothers *and sisters*, ^earnestly desire to ^Bprophesy, and do not forbid speaking in tongues. 40 But ^all things must be done properly and in an orderly way.

THE FACT OF CHRIST'S RESURRECTION

15 Now I make known to you, brothers *and sisters,* the gospel which I preached to you, which you also received, ^in which you also stand, 2 by which you also are saved, ^if you hold firmly to the word which I preached to you, unless you believed in vain.

3 For I handed down to you as of first importance what I also received, that Christ died ^for our sins according to the Scriptures, 4 and that He was buried, and that He was raised on the third day ^according to the Scriptures, 5 and that ^He appeared to Cephas, then ^Bto the twelve. 6 After that He appeared to more than five hundred brothers *and sisters* at one time, most of whom remain until now, but some ^have fallen asleep; 7 then He appeared to James, then to ^all the apostles; 8 and last of all, as to one untimely born, ^He appeared to me also. 9 For I am ^the least of the apostles, and not fit to be called an apostle, because I ^Bpersecuted the church of God. 10 But by ^the grace of God I am what I am, and His grace toward me did not prove vain; but I ^Blabored even more than all of them, yet not I, but the grace of God with me. 11 Whether then *it was* I or they, so we preach and so you believed.

14:25 ^Is 45:14; Dan 2:47　**14:26** ^Rom 14:19
14:27 ^1 Cor 12:10; 14:5, 13, 26ff　**14:29** ^1 Cor 14:32, 37
^B1 Cor 12:10　**14:33** ^1 Cor 4:17; 7:17　**14:34** ^1 Tim 2:11f;
1 Pet 3:1　**14:37** ^2 Cor 10:7　**14:39** ^1 Cor 12:31
^B1 Cor 14:1　**14:40** ^1 Cor 14:33　**15:1** ^Rom 5:2; 11:20
15:2 ^Rom 11:22　**15:3** ^Gal 1:4; 1 Pet 2:24
15:4 ^Ps 16:8ff　**15:5** ^Luke 24:34　^BLuke 24:36
15:6 ^Acts 7:60; 1 Cor 15:18, 20　**15:7** ^Luke 24:33, 36f;
Acts 1:3f　**15:8** ^Acts 9:3-8; 22:6-11　**15:9** ^1 Tim 1:15
^BActs 8:3　**15:10** ^Rom 12:3　^B2 Cor 11:23

14:38 [1]Two early mss *let him continue not to recognize* it

¹²Now if Christ is preached, that He has been raised from the dead, how do some among you say that there ᴬis no resurrection of the dead? ¹³But if there is no resurrection of the dead, then not even Christ has been raised; ¹⁴and ᴬif Christ has not been raised, then our preaching is in vain, your faith also is in vain. ¹⁵Moreover, we are even found *to be* false witnesses of God, because we testified against God that He ᴬraised ¹Christ, whom He did not raise, if in fact the dead are not raised. ¹⁶For if the dead are not raised, then not even Christ has been raised; ¹⁷and if Christ has not been raised, your faith is worthless; ᴬyou are still in your sins. ¹⁸Then also those who ᴬhave fallen asleep in Christ have perished. ¹⁹If we have hoped in Christ only in this life, we are ᴬof all people most to be pitied.

THE ORDER OF RESURRECTION

²⁰But the fact is, Christ has been raised from the dead, the ᴬfirst fruits of those who ᴮare asleep. ²¹For since ᴬby a man death *came,* by a Man also *came* the resurrection of the dead. ²²For ᴬas in Adam all die, so also in Christ all will be made alive. ²³But each in his own order: Christ the first fruits, after that ᴬthose who are Christ's at His coming, ²⁴then *comes* the end, when He hands over ᴬthe kingdom to *our* God and Father, when He has abolished all rule and all authority and power. ²⁵For He must reign ᴬuntil He has put all His enemies under His feet. ²⁶The last enemy that will be ᴬabolished is death. ²⁷For ᴬHE HAS PUT ALL THINGS IN SUBJECTION UNDER HIS FEET. But when He says, "All things are put in subjection," it is clear that this excludes the

Father who put all things in subjection to Him. ²⁸When all things are subjected to Him, then the Son Himself will also be subjected to the One who subjected all things to Him, so that ᴬGod may be all in all.

²⁹For otherwise, what will those do who are baptized for the dead? If the dead are not raised at all, why then are they baptized for them? ³⁰Why are we also ᴬin danger every hour? ³¹I affirm, brothers *and sisters,* by the boasting in you which I have in Christ Jesus our Lord, that ᴬI die daily. ³²If from human motives I fought with wild beasts at Ephesus, what good is it to me? If the dead are not raised, ᴬLET'S EAT AND DRINK, FOR TOMORROW WE DIE. ³³ᴬDo not be deceived: "Bad company corrupts good morals." ³⁴Sober up morally and stop sinning, for some have ᴬno knowledge of God. I say *this* to your shame.

³⁵But someone will say, "How are ᴬthe dead raised? And with what kind of body do they come?" ³⁶You fool! That which you ᴬsow does not come to life unless it dies; ³⁷and that which you sow, you do not sow the body which is to be, but a bare grain, perhaps of wheat or of something else. ³⁸But God gives it a body just as He wished, and ᴬto each of the seeds a body of its own. ³⁹All flesh is not the same flesh, but there is one *flesh* of mankind,

15:12ᴬActs 17:32; 23:8   15:14ᴬ1 Thess 4:14
15:15ᴬActs 2:24   15:17ᴬRom 4:25   15:18ᴬ1 Cor 15:6;
1 Thess 4:16   15:19ᴬ1 Cor 4:9; 2 Tim 3:12
15:20ᴬ1 Cor 15:23   ᴮ1 Thess 4:16   15:21ᴬRom 5:12
15:22ᴬRom 5:14-18   15:23ᴬ1 Thess 4:16
15:24ᴬDan 2:44; 7:14, 27   15:25ᴬPs 110:1; Matt 22:44
15:26ᴬ2 Tim 1:10; Rev 20:14   15:27ᴬPs 8:6
15:28ᴬ1 Cor 12:6   15:30ᴬ2 Cor 11:26
15:31ᴬRom 8:36   15:32ᴬIs 22:13; 56:12
15:33ᴬ1 Cor 6:9   15:34ᴬMatt 22:29   15:35ᴬEzek 37:3
15:36ᴬJohn 12:24   15:38ᴬGen 1:11
15:15 ¹I.e., the Messiah

another flesh of animals, another flesh of birds, and another of fish. ⁴⁰There are also heavenly bodies and earthly bodies, but the glory of the heavenly is one, and the *glory* of the earthly is another. ⁴¹There is one glory of the sun, another glory of the moon, and another glory of the stars; for star differs from star in glory.

⁴²So also is the resurrection of the dead. It is sown ᴬa perishable *body,* it is raised an imperishable *body;* ⁴³it is sown in dishonor, it is raised in ᴬglory; it is sown in weakness, it is raised in power; ⁴⁴it is sown a ᴬnatural body, it is raised a spiritual body. If there is a natural body, there is also a spiritual *body.* ⁴⁵So also it is written: "The first ᴬMAN, Adam, BECAME A LIVING PERSON." The last Adam *was* a life-giving spirit. ⁴⁶However, the spiritual is not first, but the natural; then the spiritual. ⁴⁷The first man is ᴬfrom the earth, earthy; the second Man is from heaven. ⁴⁸As is the earthy one, so also are those who are earthy; and as is the heavenly One, ᴬso also are those who are heavenly. ⁴⁹Just as we have ᴬborne the image of the earthy, ¹we ᴮwill also bear the image of the heavenly.

THE MYSTERY OF RESURRECTION

⁵⁰Now I say this, brothers *and sisters,* that flesh and blood cannot ᴬinherit the kingdom of God; nor does the perishable inherit the imperishable. ⁵¹Behold, I am telling you a ᴬmystery; we will not all sleep, but we will all be ᴮchanged, ⁵²in a moment, in the twinkling of an eye, at the last trumpet; for the trumpet will sound, and the dead will be raised imperishable, and ᴬwe will be changed. ⁵³For this perishable

must put on the imperishable, and this ᴬmortal *must* put on immortality. ⁵⁴But when this perishable puts on the imperishable, and this mortal puts on immortality, then will come about the saying that is written: "ᴬDEATH HAS BEEN SWALLOWED UP in victory. ⁵⁵ᴬWHERE, O DEATH, IS YOUR VICTORY? WHERE, O DEATH, IS YOUR STING?" ⁵⁶The sting of death is sin, and ᴬthe power of sin is the Law; ⁵⁷but thanks be to God, who gives us the ᴬvictory through our Lord Jesus Christ.

⁵⁸Therefore, my beloved brothers *and sisters,* be firm, immovable, always excelling in ᴬthe work of the Lord, knowing that your labor is not *in* vain in the Lord.

INSTRUCTIONS AND GREETINGS

16 Now concerning ᴬthe collection for the saints, as I directed the churches of Galatia, so you are to do as well. ²On the first day of every week, each of you is to put aside and save as he may prosper, so that ᴬno collections *need to* be made when I come. ³When I arrive, ᴬwhomever you approve, I will send them with letters to take your gift to Jerusalem; ⁴and if it is appropriate for me to go also, they will go with me.

⁵But I will come to you after I go through Macedonia; for I ᴬam going through Macedonia, ⁶and perhaps I will stay with you or even spend the winter, so that you may ᴬsend

15:42 ᴬRom 8:21; 1 Cor 15:50   15:43 ᴬPhil 3:21; Col 3:4
15:44 ᴬ1 Cor 2:14   15:45 ᴬGen 2:7   15:47 ᴬJohn 3:31
15:48 ᴬPhil 3:20f   15:49 ᴬGen 5:3   ᴮRom 8:29
15:50 ᴬ1 Cor 6:9   15:51 ᴬ1 Cor 13:2   ᴮ2 Cor 5:2, 4
15:52 ᴬ1 Thess 4:15, 17   15:53 ᴬ2 Cor 5:4
15:54 ᴬIs 25:8   15:55 ᴬHos 13:14   15:56 ᴬRom 3:20;
7:8   15:57 ᴬRom 8:37; 1 John 5:4   15:58 ᴬ1 Cor 16:10
16:1 ᴬActs 24:17; Rom 15:25f   16:2 ᴬ2 Cor 9:4f
16:3 ᴬ2 Cor 3:1; 8:18f   16:5 ᴬActs 19:21
16:6 ᴬActs 15:3; 1 Cor 16:11
15:49 ¹Two early mss *let's also*

me on my way wherever I go. [7]For I do not want to see you now ^*just* in passing; for I hope to remain with you for some time, if the Lord permits. [8]But I will remain in ^Ephesus until Pentecost; [9]for a ^wide door for effective *service* has opened to me, and there are many adversaries.

[10]Now if ^Timothy comes, see that he has no reason to be afraid *while* among you, for he is doing ^B the Lord's work, as I also am. [11]So do not look down on him, anyone. But send him on his way ^in peace, so that he may come to me; for I expect him with the brothers.

[12]Now concerning our brother ^Apollos, I strongly encouraged him to come to you with the brothers; and it was not at all *his* desire to come now, but he will come when he has the opportunity.

[13]^Be on the alert, stand firm in the faith, act like men, be strong. [14]All that you do must be done ^in love.

[15]Now I urge you, brothers *and sisters:* you know the ^household of Stephanas, that they are the first fruits of Achaia, and that they have devoted themselves to ^B ministry to the saints; [16]I *urge* that ^you also be subject to such as these and to everyone who helps in the work and labors. [17]I rejoice over the coming of Stephanas, Fortunatus, and Achaicus, because they have supplied ^what was lacking on your part. [18]For they have refreshed my spirit and yours. Therefore ^A acknowledge such men.

[19]The churches of Asia greet you. ^Aquila and Prisca greet you heartily in the Lord, with ^B the church that is in their house. [20]All the brothers *and sisters* greet you. ^Greet one another with a holy kiss.

[21]The greeting is in ^my own hand—*that* of Paul. [22]If anyone does not love the Lord, he is to be accursed. [1,^A]Maranatha! [23]^The grace of the Lord Jesus be with you. [24]My love be with you all in Christ Jesus. Amen.

16:7^2 Cor 1:15f **16:8**^Acts 18:19 **16:9**^Acts 14:27
16:10^1 Cor 4:17 ^B 1 Cor 15:58 **16:11**^Acts 15:33
16:12^Acts 18:24; 1 Cor 1:12 **16:13**^Matt 24:42
16:14^1 Cor 14:1 **16:15**^1 Cor 1:16 ^B Rom 15:31
16:16^1 Thess 5:12; Heb 13:17
16:17^2 Cor 11:9; Phil 2:30 **16:18**^Phil 2:29;
1 Thess 5:12 **16:19**^Acts 18:2 ^B Rom 16:5
16:20^Rom 16:16 **16:21**^Rom 16:22; Gal 6:11
16:22^Phil 4:5; Rev 22:20 **16:23**^Rom 16:20

16:22[1] Aramaic *[Our] Lord, come!*

2 CORINTHIANS

INTRODUCTION

1 Paul, an apostle of Christ Jesus ^by the will of God, and *our* brother Timothy,

To ᴮthe church of God which is at Corinth with all the saints who are throughout Achaia:

² ^Grace to you and peace from God our Father and the Lord Jesus Christ.

³ ^Blessed *be* the God and Father of our Lord Jesus Christ, the Father of mercies and God of all comfort, ⁴who ^comforts us in all our affliction so that we will be able to comfort those who are in any affliction with the comfort with which we ourselves are comforted by God. ⁵For just ^as the sufferings of Christ are ours in abundance, so also our comfort is abundant through Christ. ⁶But if we are afflicted, it is ^for your comfort and salvation; or if we are comforted, it is for your comfort, which is effective in the patient enduring of the same sufferings which we also suffer; ⁷and our hope for you is firmly grounded, knowing that ^as you are partners in our sufferings, so also you are in our comfort.

⁸For we do not want you to be unaware, brothers *and sisters,* of our ^affliction which occurred in Asia, that we were burdened excessively, beyond our strength, so that we despaired even of life. ⁹Indeed, we had the sentence of death within ourselves so that we would not trust in ourselves, but in God who raises the dead, ¹⁰who rescued us from so great a *danger of* death, and will rescue *us,* He ^on whom we have set our hope. And He will yet deliver us, ¹¹if you also join in helping us through your prayers, so that thanks may be given by ^many persons in our behalf for the favor *granted* to us through *the prayers of* many.

PAUL'S INTEGRITY

¹²For our proud confidence is this: the testimony of ^our conscience, that in holiness and godly sincerity, not in fleshly wisdom but in the grace of God, we have conducted ourselves in the world, and especially toward you. ¹³For we write nothing else to you than what you read and understand, and I hope you will understand ^until the end; ¹⁴just as you also partially did understand us, that we are your reason to be proud as you also are ours, on ^the day of our Lord Jesus.

¹⁵In this confidence I intended at first to come to you, so that you might twice receive a ^blessing; ¹⁶that is, to ^pass your way into Macedonia, and again from Macedonia to come to you, and by you to be helped on my journey to Judea. ¹⁷Therefore, I was not vacillating when I intended to do this, was I? Or what I decide, do I decide ^according to the flesh, so that with me there will be yes, yes and no, no *at the same time?* ¹⁸But

1:1^1 Cor 1:1   **⁸**1 Cor 10:32   **1:2**^Rom 1:7
1:3^Eph 1:3; 1 Pet 1:3   **1:4**^Is 51:12; 66:13
1:5^2 Cor 4:10; Phil 3:10   **1:6**^2 Cor 4:15; 12:15
1:7^Rom 8:17   **1:8**^Acts 19:23; 1 Cor 15:32
1:10^1 Tim 4:10   **1:11**^2 Cor 4:15; 9:11f
1:12^Acts 23:1; 1 Thess 2:10   **1:13**^1 Cor 1:8
1:14^1 Cor 1:8   **1:15**^Rom 1:11; 15:29
1:16^Acts 19:21; 1 Cor 16:5-7   **1:17**^2 Cor 10:2f; 11:18

as ^God is faithful, our word to you is not yes and no. ¹⁹For ^the Son of God, Christ Jesus, who was preached among you by us—by me and Silvanus and Timothy—was not yes and no, but has been yes in Him. ²⁰For ^as many as the promises of God are, in Him they are yes; therefore through Him also is our Amen to the glory of God through us. ²¹Now He who establishes us with you in Christ and ^anointed us is God, ²²who also sealed us and ^gave *us* the Spirit in our hearts as a ¹pledge.

²³But ^I call God as witness to my soul, that *it was* to spare you *that* I did not come again to Corinth. ²⁴Not that we ^domineer over your faith, but we are workers with you for your joy; for in your faith you are standing firm.

REAFFIRM YOUR LOVE

2 But I decided this for my own sake, that I ^would not come to you in sorrow again. ²For if I ^cause you sorrow, who then *will be* the one making me glad but the one who is made sorrowful by me? ³This is the very thing I wrote you, so that when I came, I would not have sorrow from those who ought to make me rejoice; having ^confidence in you all that my joy was *the joy* of you all. ⁴For out of much affliction and anguish of heart I ^wrote to you with many tears; not so that you would be made sorrowful, but that you might know the love which I have especially for you.

⁵But ^if anyone has caused sorrow, he has caused sorrow not for me, but in some degree—not to say too much—for all of you. ⁶Sufficient for such a person is ^this punishment which *was imposed* by the majority, ⁷so that on the other hand, you should rather ^forgive and comfort *him,* otherwise such a person might be overwhelmed by excessive sorrow. ⁸Therefore I urge you to reaffirm *your* love for him. ⁹For to this end I also wrote, so that I might put you to the test, whether you are ^obedient in all things. ¹⁰But one whom you forgive anything, I also *forgive;* for indeed what I have forgiven, if I have forgiven anything, *I did so* for your sakes ^in the presence of Christ, ¹¹so that no advantage would be taken of us by Satan, for ^we are not ignorant of his schemes.

¹²Now when I came to ^Troas for the gospel of Christ and when a ᴮdoor was opened for me in the Lord, ¹³I ^had no rest for my spirit, not finding Titus my brother; but saying goodbye to them, I went on to Macedonia.

¹⁴^But thanks be to God, who always leads us in triumph in Christ, and through us reveals the fragrance of the knowledge of Him in every place. ¹⁵For we are a ^fragrance of Christ to God among ᴮthose who are being saved and among those who are perishing: ¹⁶^to the one an aroma from death to death, to the other an aroma from life to life. And who is ᴮadequate for these things? ¹⁷For we are not like the many, ¹peddling the word of God, but ^as from sincerity, but as from God, we speak in Christ in the sight of God.

1:18^1 Cor 1:9   **1:19**^Matt 4:3; 16:16   **1:20**^Rom 15:8
1:21^1 John 2:20, 27   **1:22**^Rom 8:16; 2 Cor 5:5
1:23^Rom 1:9; Gal 1:20   **1:24**^2 Cor 4:5; 11:20
2:1^1 Cor 4:21; 2 Cor 12:21   **2:2**^2 Cor 7:8
2:3^Gal 5:10; 2 Thess 3:4   **2:4**^2 Cor 2:9; 7:8, 12
2:5^1 Cor 5:1f   **2:6**^1 Cor 5:4f; 2 Cor 7:11   **2:7**^Gal 6:1;
Eph 4:32   **2:9**^2 Cor 7:15; 10:6   **2:10**^1 Cor 5:4;
2 Cor 4:6   **2:11**^Luke 22:31; 2 Cor 4:4   **2:12**^Acts 16:8
ᴮActs 14:27   **2:13**^2 Cor 7:5   **2:14**^Rom 1:8; 6:17
2:15^Eph 5:2   ᴮ1 Cor 1:18   **2:16**^Luke 2:34
ᴮ2 Cor 3:5f   **2:17**^1 Cor 5:8; 2 Cor 1:12

1:22¹Or *first installment*   **2:17**¹Or *diluting*

MINISTERS OF A NEW COVENANT

3 Are we beginning to ^commend ourselves again? Or do we need, as some, letters of commendation to you or from you? ²^You are our letter, written in our hearts, known and read by all people, ³revealing yourselves, that you are a letter of Christ, delivered by us, written not with ink but with the Spirit of the living God, not on tablets of stone but on ^tablets of human hearts.

⁴Such *is the* ^confidence we have toward God through Christ. ⁵Not that we are adequate in ourselves *so as* to consider anything as *having come* from ourselves, but ^our adequacy is from God, ⁶who also made us adequate *as* servants of a ^new covenant, not of ^Bthe letter but of the Spirit; for the letter kills, but the Spirit gives life.

⁷But if the ^ministry of death, engraved in letters on stones, came with glory ^Bso that the sons of Israel could not look intently at the face of Moses because of the glory of his face, fading *as* it was, ⁸how will the ministry of the Spirit fail to be *even* more with glory? ⁹For if the ministry of condemnation has glory, much more does the ^ministry of righteousness excel in glory. ¹⁰For indeed what had glory in this case has no glory, because of the glory that surpasses *it*. ¹¹For if that which fades away *was* with glory, much more that which remains *is* in glory.

¹²Therefore, having such a hope, ^we use great boldness in *our* speech, ¹³and *we are* not like Moses, ^*who* used to put a veil over his face so that the sons of Israel would not stare at the end of what was fading away. ¹⁴But their minds were ^hardened; for until this very day at the ^Breading of the old covenant the same veil remains unlifted, because it is removed in Christ. ¹⁵But to this day whenever Moses is read, a veil lies over their hearts; ¹⁶^but whenever *someone* turns to the Lord, the veil is taken away. ¹⁷Now the Lord is the Spirit, and where the Spirit of the Lord is, ^*there* is freedom. ¹⁸But we all, with unveiled faces, ^looking as in a mirror at the glory of the Lord, are being ^Btransformed into the same image from glory to glory, just as from the Lord, the Spirit.

PAUL'S APOSTOLIC MINISTRY

4 Therefore, since we have this ministry, as we ^received mercy, we do not lose heart, ²but we have renounced the ^things hidden because of shame, not walking in trickery nor distorting the word of God, but by the open proclamation of the truth commending ourselves to every person's conscience in the sight of God. ³And even if our gospel is ^veiled, it is veiled to those who are perishing, ⁴in whose case ^the god of this world has ^Bblinded the minds of the unbelieving so that they will not see the light of the gospel of the glory of Christ, who is the image of God. ⁵For we ^do not preach ourselves, but Christ Jesus as Lord, and ourselves as your bond-servants on account of Jesus. ⁶For God, who said, "^Light shall shine out of darkness," is the One

3:1^2 Cor 5:12; 10:12, 18   3:2^1 Cor 9:2   3:3^Prov 3:3; 7:3   3:4^Eph 3:12   3:5^1 Cor 15:10   3:6^Jer 31:31
^BRom 2:29   3:7^Rom 7:5f   ^BEx 34:29-35
3:9^Rom 1:17; 3:21f   3:12^Acts 4:13, 29
3:13^Ex 34:33-35; 2 Cor 3:7   3:14^Rom 11:7
^BActs 13:15   3:16^Ex 34:34; Rom 11:23
3:17^John 8:32; Gal 5:1, 13   3:18^1 Cor 13:12
^BRom 8:29   4:1^1 Cor 7:25   4:2^Rom 6:21; 1 Cor 4:5
4:3^1 Cor 2:6ff; 2 Cor 3:14   4:4^John 12:31
^B2 Cor 3:14   4:5^1 Cor 4:15f; 1 Thess 2:6f
4:6^Gen 1:3   ^B2 Pet 1:19

who has ᴮshone in our hearts to give the Light of the knowledge of the glory of God in the face of Christ.

⁷But we have this treasure in ᴬearthen containers, so that the extraordinary *greatness* of ᴮthe power will be of God and not from ourselves; ⁸*we are* ᴬafflicted in every way, but not crushed; perplexed, but not despairing; ⁹persecuted, but not ᴬabandoned; struck down, but not destroyed; ¹⁰ᴬalways carrying around in the body the dying of Jesus, so that the life of Jesus may also be revealed in our body. ¹¹For we who live are constantly being handed over to death because of Jesus, so that the life of Jesus may also be revealed in our mortal flesh. ¹²So death works in us, but life in you.

¹³But having the same spirit of faith, according to what is written: "ᴬI BELIEVED, THEREFORE I SPOKE," we also believe, therefore we also speak, ¹⁴knowing that He who ᴬraised the Lord Jesus ᴮwill also raise us with Jesus, and will present *us* with you. ¹⁵For all things *are* ᴬfor your sakes, so that grace, having spread to more and more people, will cause thanksgiving to overflow to the glory of God.

¹⁶Therefore we do not lose heart, but though our outer person is decaying, yet our ᴬinner *person* is being renewed day by day. ¹⁷For our momentary, ᴬlight affliction is producing for us an eternal weight of glory far beyond all comparison, ¹⁸while we ᴬlook not at the things which are seen, but at the things which are not seen; for the things which are seen are temporal, but the things which are not seen are eternal.

THE TEMPORAL AND ETERNAL

5 For we know that if our ᴬearthly tent which is our house is torn down, we have a building from God, a house ᴮnot made by hands, eternal in the heavens. ²For indeed, in this *tent* we ᴬgroan, longing to be clothed with our ¹dwelling from heaven, ³since in fact after putting it on, we will not be found naked. ⁴For indeed, we who are in this tent groan, being burdened, because we do not want to be unclothed but to be ᴬclothed, so that what is mortal will be swallowed up by life. ⁵Now He who prepared us for this very *purpose is* God, who ᴬgave us the Spirit as a ¹pledge.

⁶Therefore, being always of good courage, and knowing that ᴬwhile we are at home in the body we are absent from the Lord—⁷for ᴬwe walk by faith, not by sight—⁸but we are of good courage and prefer rather to be absent from the body and ᴬto be at home with the Lord. ⁹Therefore we also have as our ambition, whether at home or absent, to be ᴬpleasing to Him. ¹⁰For we must all appear before ᴬthe judgment seat of Christ, so that each one may receive compensation for his deeds *done* through the body, in accordance with what he has done, whether good or bad.

¹¹Therefore, knowing the fear of the Lord, we persuade people, but we are well known to God; and I hope that we are also ᴬwell known

4:7ᴬLam 4:2 ᴮJudg 7:2 4:8ᴬ2 Cor 1:8; 7:5
4:9ᴬPs 129:2; Heb 13:5 4:10ᴬRom 6:5; 8:36
4:13ᴬPs 116:10 4:14ᴬActs 2:24 ᴮ1 Thess 4:14
4:15ᴬRom 8:28; 2 Cor 1:6 4:16ᴬRom 7:22
4:17ᴬRom 8:18 4:18ᴬRom 8:24; 2 Cor 5:7
5:1ᴬJob 4:19 ᴮActs 7:48 5:2ᴬRom 8:23; 2 Cor 5:4
5:4ᴬ1 Cor 15:53f 5:5ᴬRom 8:23; 2 Cor 1:22
5:6ᴬHeb 11:13f 5:7ᴬ1 Cor 13:12; 2 Cor 4:18
5:8ᴬJohn 12:26; Phil 1:23 5:9ᴬRom 14:18; Col 1:10
5:10ᴬMatt 16:27; Acts 10:42 5:11ᴬ2 Cor 4:2

5:2¹I.e., the resurrected body 5:5¹Or *first installment*

in your consciences. [12]We are not commending ourselves to you again, but *are* giving you an ^opportunity to be proud of us, so that you will have *an answer* for those who take pride in appearance and not in heart. [13]For if we have ^lost our minds, *it is* for God; if we are of sound mind, *it is* for you. [14]For the love of Christ controls us, having concluded this, that ^one died for all, therefore all died; [15]and He died for all, so that those who live would no longer ^live for themselves, but for Him who died and rose on their behalf.

[16]Therefore from now on we recognize no one ^by the flesh; even though we have known Christ by the flesh, yet now we know *Him in this way* no longer. [17]Therefore if anyone is in Christ, *this person is* a new creation; ^the old things passed away; behold, new things have come. [18]Now all *these* things are from God, ^who reconciled us to Himself through Christ and gave us the ministry of reconciliation, [19]namely, that ^God was in Christ reconciling the world to Himself, not counting their wrongdoings against them, and He has committed to us the word of reconciliation.

[20]Therefore, we are ambassadors for Christ, as though God were making an appeal through us; we beg you on behalf of Christ, be ^reconciled to God. [21]He made Him who ^knew no sin *to be* [1]sin in our behalf, so that we might become the righteousness of God in Him.

THEIR MINISTRY COMMENDED

6 And ^working together *with Him*, we also urge you not to receive the grace of God in vain— [2]for He says,

"^At a favorable time I
  listened to you,
  And on a day of salvation I
  helped you."

Behold, now is "a favorable time," behold, now is "a day of salvation"— [3]^giving no reason for *taking* offense in anything, so that the ministry will not be discredited, [4]but in everything commending ourselves as servants of God, ^in much endurance, in afflictions, in hardships, in difficulties, [5]in ^beatings, in imprisonments, in mob attacks, in labors, in sleeplessness, in [B]hunger, [6]in purity, in knowledge, in patience, in kindness, in the ^Holy Spirit, in genuine love, [7]in the word of truth, *and* in ^the power of God; by [B]the weapons of righteousness for the right hand and the left, [8]by glory and ^dishonor, by evil report and good report; *regarded* as deceivers and yet true; [9]as unknown and *yet* well known, as dying and *yet* behold, ^we are alive; as punished and *yet* not put to death, [10]as ^sorrowful yet always rejoicing, as [B]poor yet making many rich, as having nothing and *yet* possessing all things.

[11]^Our mouth has spoken freely to you, you Corinthians, our heart is opened wide. [12]You are not restrained by us, but ^you are restrained in your own affections. [13]Now in the same way in exchange—I am speaking as

5:12^2 Cor 1:14; Phil 1:26   5:13^Mark 3:21;
2 Cor 11:1, 16ff   5:14^Rom 5:15; 6:6f   5:15^Rom 14:7-9
5:16^John 8:15; 2 Cor 11:18   5:17^Is 43:18f; Eph 4:24
5:18^Rom 5:10; Col 1:20   5:19^Col 2:9
5:20^Rom 5:10; Col 1:20   5:21^Heb 4:15; 7:26
6:1^1 Cor 3:9   6:2^Is 49:8   6:3^1 Cor 8:9, 13; 9:12
6:4^Acts 9:16; 2 Cor 4:8-11   6:5^Acts 16:23
[B]1 Cor 4:11   6:6^1 Cor 2:4; 1 Thess 1:5   6:7^1 Cor 2:5
[B]2 Cor 10:4   6:8^1 Cor 4:10   6:9^2 Cor 1:8, 10; 4:11
6:10^John 16:22   [B]2 Cor 8:9   6:11^Ezek 33:22;
Eph 6:19   6:12^2 Cor 7:2

5:21[1]Or *a sin offering*

to ^children—open wide *your hearts to us,* you as well.

¹⁴Do not be mismatched with unbelievers; for what do righteousness and lawlessness ^share together, or what does light have in common with darkness? ¹⁵Or what ^harmony does Christ have with Belial, or what does a believer share with an unbeliever? ¹⁶Or what agreement does the temple of God have with idols? For we are the temple of the living God; just as God said,

> "^I WILL DWELL AMONG THEM
> AND WALK AMONG THEM;
> AND I WILL BE THEIR GOD, AND
> THEY SHALL BE MY PEOPLE.

¹⁷ "^Therefore, COME OUT
> FROM THEIR MIDST AND BE
> SEPARATE," says the Lord.
> "AND DO NOT TOUCH WHAT IS
> UNCLEAN;
> And I will welcome you.

¹⁸ "^And I will be a father to you,
> And you shall be sons and
> daughters to Me,"
> Says the Lord Almighty.

PAUL REVEALS HIS HEART

7 Therefore, having these promises, beloved, ^let's cleanse ourselves from all defilement of flesh and spirit, perfecting holiness in the fear of God.

²^Make room for us *in your hearts;* we have wronged no one, we corrupted no one, we have taken advantage of no one. ³I do not speak to condemn *you,* for I have said ^before that you are in our hearts, to die together and to live together. ⁴My confidence in you is great; my ^boasting in your behalf is great. I am filled with ^comfort; I am overflowing with joy in all our affliction.

⁵For even when we came into Macedonia our flesh had no rest, but we were ^afflicted on every side: ^conflicts on the outside, fears inside. ⁶But God, who comforts the discouraged, comforted us by the arrival of ^Titus; ⁷and not only by his arrival, but also by the comfort with which he was comforted among you, as he reported to us your longing, your mourning, your zeal for me; so that I rejoiced even more. ⁸For though I ^caused you sorrow by my letter, I do not regret it; though I did regret it—*for* I see that that letter caused you sorrow, though only for a while—⁹I now rejoice, not that you were made sorrowful, but that you were made sorrowful to *the point of* repentance; for you were made sorrowful according to *the will of* God, so that you might not suffer loss in anything through us. ¹⁰For the sorrow that is according to *the will of* God produces a ^repentance without regret, *leading* to salvation, but the sorrow of the world produces death. ¹¹For behold what earnestness this very thing, this godly sorrow, has produced in you: what vindication *of yourselves,* what indignation, what fear, what ^longing, what zeal, what punishment of wrong! In everything you demonstrated yourselves to be innocent in the matter. ¹²So although ^I wrote to you, *it was* not for the sake of the offender nor for the sake of the one offended, but that your earnestness in our behalf might be made known to you in the sight of God. ¹³Because of this, we have been comforted.

6:13^1 Cor 4:14   6:14^Eph 5:7, 11; 1 John 1:6
6:15^1 Cor 10:21   6:16^Ex 29:45; Lev 26:12
6:17^Is 52:11   6:18^2 Sam 7:14; 1 Chr 17:13
7:1^1 Pet 1:15f   7:2^2 Cor 6:12f; 12:15   7:3^2 Cor 6:11f
7:4^2 Cor 7:14   ^2 Cor 1:4   7:5^2 Cor 4:8
^Deut 32:25   7:6^2 Cor 2:13; 7:13f   7:8^2 Cor 2:2
7:10^Acts 11:18   7:11^2 Cor 7:7   7:12^2 Cor 2:3, 9; 7:8

And besides our comfort, we rejoiced even much more for the joy of Titus, because his ^spirit has been refreshed by you all. ¹⁴For if I have ^boasted to him about you regarding anything, I was not put to shame. But as we spoke all things to you in truth, so also our boasting before Titus proved to be *the* truth. ¹⁵His affection abounds all the more toward you, as he remembers the obedience of you all, how you received him with ^fear and trembling. ¹⁶I rejoice that in everything ^I have confidence in you.

GREAT GENEROSITY

8 Now, brothers *and sisters,* we make known to you the grace of God which has been ^given in the churches of Macedonia, ²that in a great ordeal of affliction their abundance of joy and their deep poverty overflowed in the ^wealth of their liberality. ³For I testify that ^according to their ability, and beyond their ability, *they gave* voluntarily, ⁴begging us with much urging for the favor of participation in the ^support of the saints, ⁵and *this,* not as we had expected, but they first gave themselves to the Lord and to us by ^the will of God. ⁶So we ^urged Titus that as he had previously made a beginning, so he would also complete in you this gracious work as well.

⁷But just as you ^excel ᴮin everything, in faith, speaking, knowledge, and in all earnestness and in the love we inspired in you, *see* that you also ^excel in this gracious work. ⁸I ^am not saying *this* as a command, but as proving, through the earnestness of others, the sincerity of your love as well. ⁹For you know the grace of our Lord Jesus Christ, that ^though He was rich, yet for your sake He became poor, so that you through His poverty might become rich. ¹⁰I give *my* opinion in this matter, for this is to your advantage, who were the first to begin ^a year ago not only to do *this,* but also to desire *to do it.* ¹¹But now finish doing it also, so that just as *there was* the ^willingness to desire it, so *there may be* also the completion of it by your ability. ¹²For if the willingness is present, it is acceptable ^according to what *a person* has, not according to what he does not have. ¹³For *this* is not for the relief of others *and* for your hardship, but by way of equality— ¹⁴at this present time your abundance *will serve as assistance* for ^their need, so that their abundance also may serve as *assistance* for ^your need, so that there may be equality; ¹⁵as it is written: "^THE ONE WHO *HAD GATHERED* MUCH DID NOT HAVE TOO MUCH, AND THE ONE WHO *HAD GATHERED* LITTLE DID NOT HAVE TOO LITTLE."

¹⁶But ^thanks be to God who ᴮputs the same earnestness in your behalf in the heart of Titus. ¹⁷For he not only accepted our ^appeal, but being himself very earnest, he has gone to you of his own accord. ¹⁸We have sent along with him ^the brother whose fame in *the things of* the gospel *has spread* through all the churches; ¹⁹and not only *that,* but he has also been ^appointed by the churches to travel with us in

7:13^1 Cor 16:18   7:14^2 Cor 7:4; 8:24   7:15^1 Cor 2:3; Phil 2:12   7:16^2 Cor 2:3   8:1^2 Cor 8:5   8:2^Rom 2:4
8:3^1 Cor 16:2; 2 Cor 8:11   8:4^Rom 15:31; 2 Cor 8:19f
8:5^1 Cor 1:1   8:6^2 Cor 8:17; 12:18   8:7^2 Cor 9:8
ᴮ1 Cor 1:5   8:8^1 Cor 7:6   8:9^Phil 2:6f
8:10^1 Cor 16:2f; 2 Cor 9:2   8:11^2 Cor 8:12, 19; 9:2
8:12^Mark 12:43f; Luke 21:3, 4   8:14^Acts 4:34;
2 Cor 9:12   8:15^Ex 16:18   8:16^2 Cor 2:14   ᴮRev 17:17
8:17^2 Cor 8:6; 12:18   8:18^1 Cor 16:3; 2 Cor 12:18
8:19^1 Cor 16:3f

this gracious work, which is being administered by us for the glory of the Lord Himself, and *to show* our readiness, [20]taking precaution so that no one will discredit us in our administration of this generous gift; [21]for we ^have regard for what is honorable, not only in the sight of the Lord, but also in the sight of *other* people. [22]We have sent with them our brother, whom we have often tested and found diligent in many things, but now even more diligent because of *his* great confidence in you. [23]As for Titus, *he is* my partner and fellow worker among you; as for our brothers, *they are* ^messengers of the churches, a glory to Christ. [24]Therefore, openly before the churches, show them the proof of your love and of our ^reason for boasting about you.

GOD GIVES MOST

9 For it is superfluous for me to write to you about this ^ministry to the saints; [2]for I know your willingness, of which I boast about you to the Macedonians, *namely,* that Achaia has been prepared since ^last year, and your zeal has stirred up most of them. [3]But I have sent the brothers, in order that our ^boasting about you may not prove empty in this case, so that, [B]as I was saying, you will be prepared; [4]otherwise, if *any* ^Macedonians come with me and find you unprepared, we—not to mention you—would be put to shame by this confidence. [5]So I considered it necessary to urge the brothers that they go on ahead to you and arrange in advance your previously promised ^generous gift, that the same would be ready as a generous gift, and not as *one grudgingly given due to* greediness.

[6]Now *I say* this: ^the one who sows sparingly will also reap sparingly, and the one who sows generously will also reap generously. [7]Each one *must do* just as he has decided in his heart, not ^reluctantly or under compulsion, for [B]God loves a cheerful giver. [8]And ^God is able to make all grace overflow to you, so that, always having all sufficiency in everything, you may have an abundance for every good deed; [9]as it is written:

"^HE SCATTERED ABROAD, HE
    GAVE TO THE POOR,
    HIS RIGHTEOUSNESS ENDURES
    FOREVER."

[10]Now He who supplies ^seed to the sower and bread for food will supply and multiply your seed for sowing and [B]increase the harvest of your righteousness; [11]you will be ^enriched in everything for all liberality, which through us is producing thanksgiving to God. [12]For the ministry of this service is not only fully supplying ^the needs of the saints, but is also overflowing [B]through many thanksgivings to God. [13]Because of the proof given by this ^ministry, they will glorify God for *your* obedience to your confession of the gospel of Christ and for the liberality of your contribution to them and to all, [14]while they also, by prayer on your behalf, yearn for you because of the surpassing grace of God in you. [15]Thanks be to God for His indescribable ^gift!

8:21^Rom 12:17   8:23^Phil 2:25   8:24^2 Cor 7:4
9:1^2 Cor 8:4   9:2^2 Cor 8:10   9:3^2 Cor 7:4
[B]1 Cor 16:2   9:4^Rom 15:26   9:5^Gen 33:11
9:6^Prov 11:24f; 22:9   9:7^Deut 15:10   [B]Ex 25:2
9:8^Eph 3:20   9:9^Ps 112:9   9:10^Is 55:10
[B]Hos 10:12   9:11^1 Cor 1:5   9:12^2 Cor 8:14
[B]2 Cor 1:11   9:13^Rom 15:31; 2 Cor 8:4   9:15^Rom 5:15f

PAUL CONFRONTS THE CORINTHIANS

10 Now I, Paul, myself urge you by the ^meekness and gentleness of Christ—I who am meek when face to face with you, but bold toward you when absent! ²I ask that when I am present I *need* not be bold with the confidence with which I intend to be courageous against ^some, who regard us as if we walked according to the flesh. ³For though we walk in the flesh, we do not wage battle ^according to the flesh, ⁴for the ^weapons of our warfare are not of the flesh, but divinely powerful for the destruction of fortresses. ⁵*We are* destroying arguments and all ^arrogance raised against the knowledge of God, and *we are* taking every thought captive to the obedience of Christ, ⁶and we are ready to punish all disobedience, whenever ^your obedience is complete.

⁷^You are looking at things as they are outwardly. If anyone is confident in himself that he is Christ's, have him consider this again within himself, that just as he is Christ's, ^so too are we. ⁸For if I boast somewhat more about our ^authority, which the Lord gave for building you up and not for destroying you, I will not be put to shame, ⁹for I do not want to seem as if I would terrify you by my letters. ¹⁰For they say, "His letters are weighty and strong, but his personal presence is unimpressive and ^his speech contemptible." ¹¹Have such a person consider this, that what we are in word by letters when absent, such persons *we are* also in deed when present.

¹²For we do not presume to rank or compare ourselves with some of those who ^commend themselves; but when they measure themselves by themselves and compare themselves with themselves, they have no understanding. ¹³But we will not boast beyond *our* measure, but ^within the measure of the domain which God assigned to us as a measure, to reach even as far as you. ¹⁴For we are not overextending ourselves, as if we did not reach to you, for we were the first to come even as far as you in the ^gospel of Christ; ¹⁵not boasting beyond *our* measure, *that is,* in other people's labors, but with the hope that as ^your faith grows, we will be, within our domain, enlarged even more by you, ¹⁶so as to preach the gospel even to the regions beyond you, *and* not to boast ^in what has been accomplished in the domain of another. ¹⁷But ^THE ONE WHO BOASTS IS TO BOAST IN THE LORD. ¹⁸For *it is* not the one who commends himself that is approved, but the one ^whom the Lord commends.

PAUL DEFENDS HIS APOSTLESHIP

11 I wish that you would ^bear with me in a little foolishness; but indeed you are bearing with me. ²For I am jealous for you with a godly jealousy; for I ^betrothed you to one husband, to present you *as* a pure virgin to Christ. ³But I am afraid that, as the ^serpent deceived Eve by his trickery, your minds will be led astray from sincere and pure devotion to Christ.

10:1^Matt 11:29; 1 Cor 4:21   10:2^1 Cor 4:18f
10:3^Rom 8:4; 2 Cor 1:17   10:4^2 Cor 6:7
10:5^Is 2:11f   10:6^2 Cor 2:9   10:7^John 7:24
⁸1 Cor 9:1   10:8^2 Cor 13:10   10:10^1 Cor 1:17;
2 Cor 11:6   10:12^2 Cor 3:1; 10:18   10:13^Rom 12:3;
2 Cor 10:15f   10:14^2 Cor 2:12   10:15^2 Thess 1:3
10:16^Rom 15:20   10:17^Jer 9:24; 1 Cor 1:31
10:18^Rom 2:29; 1 Cor 4:5   11:1^Matt 17:17;
2 Cor 11:4, 16, 19f   11:2^Hos 2:19f; Eph 5:26f
11:3^Gen 3:4, 13; John 8:44

⁴For if one comes and preaches ^another Jesus whom we have not preached, or you receive a different spirit which you have not received, or a ᴮdifferent gospel which you have not accepted, *this* you tolerate *very* well! ⁵For I consider myself ^not in the least inferior to the most eminent apostles. ⁶But even if I am unskilled in speech, yet I am not *so* in ^knowledge; in fact, in every way we have made *this* evident to you in all things.

⁷Or did I commit a sin by humbling myself so that you might be exalted, because I preached the gospel of God to you ^without charge? ⁸I robbed other churches by ^taking wages *from them* to serve you; ⁹and when I was present with you and was in need, I was ^not a burden to anyone; for when ᴮthe brothers came from Macedonia they fully supplied my need, and in everything I kept myself from ^being a burden to you, and will continue to do so. ¹⁰^As the truth of Christ is in me, ᴮthis boasting of mine will not be stopped in the regions of Achaia. ¹¹Why? ^Because I do not love you? ᴮGod knows *that I do!*

¹²But what I am doing I will also *continue to* do, ^so that I may eliminate the opportunity from those who want an opportunity to be regarded just as we are in the matter about which they are boasting. ¹³For such men are false apostles, ^deceitful workers, disguising themselves as apostles of Christ. ¹⁴No wonder, for even ^Satan disguises himself as an angel of light. ¹⁵Therefore it is not surprising if his servants also disguise themselves as servants of righteousness, ^whose end will be according to their deeds.

¹⁶^Again I say, let no one think me foolish; but if *you do,* receive me even as foolish, so that I also may boast a little. ¹⁷What I am saying, I am not saying ^as the Lord would, but as in foolishness, in this confidence of boasting. ¹⁸Since ^many boast according to the flesh, I will boast also. ¹⁹For you, ^being *so* wise, tolerate the foolish gladly. ²⁰For you tolerate it if anyone ^enslaves you, if anyone devours you, if anyone takes *advantage of* you, if anyone exalts himself, if anyone hits you in the face. ²¹To *my* shame I *must* say that we have been ^weak *by comparison.*

But in whatever respect anyone *else* is bold—I am speaking in foolishness—I too am bold. ²²Are they Hebrews? ^So am I. Are they Israelites? So am I. Are they descendants of Abraham? ᴮSo am I. ²³Are they servants of Christ?—I am speaking as if insane—I more so; in ^far more labors, in ᴮfar more imprisonments, beaten times without number, often in *danger of* death. ²⁴Five times I received from the Jews ^thirty-nine *lashes.* ²⁵Three times I was ^beaten with rods, once I was ᴮstoned, three times I was shipwrecked, a night and a day I have spent *adrift* at sea. ²⁶*I have been* on frequent journeys, in dangers from rivers, dangers from robbers, dangers from *my* countrymen, dangers from the Gentiles, dangers in the ^city, dangers in the

11:4 ^1 Cor 3:11   ᴮGal 1:6   11:5 ^2 Cor 12:11; Gal 2:6
11:6 ^1 Cor 12:8; Eph 3:4   11:7 ^Acts 18:3; 1 Cor 9:18
11:8 ^1 Cor 4:12; 9:6   11:9 ^2 Cor 12:13f, 16   ᴮActs 18:5
11:10 ^Rom 9:1   ᴮ1 Cor 9:15   11:11 ^2 Cor 12:15
ᴮ2 Cor 11:31   11:12 ^1 Cor 9:12   11:13 ^Phil 3:2
11:14 ^Matt 4:10; Eph 6:12   11:15 ^Rom 2:6; 3:8
11:16 ^2 Cor 11:1   11:17 ^1 Cor 7:12, 25   11:18 ^Phil 3:3f
11:19 ^1 Cor 4:10   11:20 ^Gal 2:4; 4:3, 9
11:21 ^2 Cor 10:10   11:22 ^Phil 3:5   ᴮRom 11:1
11:23 ^1 Cor 15:10   ᴮ2 Cor 6:5   11:24 ^Deut 25:3
11:25 ^Acts 16:22   ᴮActs 14:19   11:26 ^Acts 21:31

wilderness, dangers at sea, dangers among ᴮfalse brothers; ²⁷*I have been* in labor and hardship, through many sleepless nights, in hunger and thirst, often ᴬwithout food, in cold and ᴮexposure. ²⁸Apart from *such* external things, there is the daily pressure on me *of* concern for ᴬall the churches. ²⁹Who is ᴬweak without my being weak? Who is led into sin without my intense concern?

³⁰If I have to boast, I will boast of what pertains to my ᴬweakness. ³¹The God and Father of the Lord Jesus, ᴬHe who is blessed forever, knows that I am not lying. ³²In Damascus the ethnarch under Aretas the king was ᴬguarding the city of the Damascenes in order to seize me, ³³and I was let down in a basket ᴬthrough a window in the wall, and *so* escaped his hands.

PAUL'S VISION

12 Boasting is necessary, though it is not beneficial; but I will go on to visions and ᴬrevelations of the Lord. ²I know a man in Christ, who fourteen years ago—whether in the body I do not know, or out of the body I do not know, God knows—such a man was caught up to the ᴬthird heaven. ³And I know how such a man—whether in the body or apart from the body I do not know, ᴬGod knows— ⁴was ᴬcaught up into ᴮParadise and heard inexpressible words, which a man is not permitted to speak. ⁵In behalf of such a man I will boast; but in my own behalf I will not boast, except regarding *my* ᴬweaknesses. ⁶For if I do wish to boast I will not be foolish, ᴬfor I will be speaking the truth; but I refrain *from this,* so that no one will credit me with more than he sees *in* me or hears from me.

A THORN IN THE FLESH

⁷Because of the extraordinary *greatness* of the revelations, for this reason, to keep me from exalting myself, there was given to me a ᴬthorn in the flesh, a messenger of Satan to torment me—to keep me from exalting myself! ⁸Concerning this I pleaded with the Lord ᴬthree times that it might leave me. ⁹And He has said to me, "My grace is sufficient for you, for ᴬpower is perfected in weakness." Most gladly, therefore, I will rather boast about my weaknesses, so that the power of Christ may dwell in me. ¹⁰Therefore ᴬI delight in weaknesses, in insults, in distresses, in persecutions, in difficulties, in behalf of Christ; for when I am weak, then I am strong.

¹¹I have become foolish; you yourselves compelled me. Actually I should have been commended by you, since I was ᴬin no respect inferior to the most eminent apostles, even though ᴮI am a nobody. ¹²The ᴬdistinguishing marks of a true apostle were performed among you with all perseverance, by signs, wonders, and miracles. ¹³For in what respect were you treated as inferior to the rest of the churches, except that I myself did not become a burden to you? Forgive me ᴬthis wrong!

¹⁴Here ᴬfor this third time I am ready to come to you, and I will

11:26 ᴮGal 2:4   11:27 ᴬ2 Cor 6:5   ᴮ1 Cor 4:11
11:28 ᴬ1 Cor 7:17   11:29 ᴬ1 Cor 8:9, 13; 9:22
11:30 ᴬ1 Cor 2:3   11:31 ᴬRom 1:25   11:32 ᴬActs 9:24
11:33 ᴬActs 9:25   12:1 ᴬ1 Cor 14:6; 2 Cor 12:7
12:2 ᴬDeut 10:14; Ps 148:4   12:3 ᴬ2 Cor 11:11
12:4 ᴬEzek 8:3   ᴮLuke 23:43   12:5 ᴬ1 Cor 2:3; 2 Cor 12:9f
12:6 ᴬ2 Cor 7:14   12:7 ᴬNum 33:55; Ezek 28:24
12:8 ᴬMatt 26:44   12:9 ᴬ1 Cor 2:5; Eph 3:16
12:10 ᴬRom 8:35   12:11 ᴬ2 Cor 11:5   ᴮ1 Cor 3:7
12:12 ᴬJohn 4:48; Rom 15:19   12:13 ᴬ2 Cor 11:7
12:14 ᴬ2 Cor 13:1, 2

not be a burden to you; for I [B]do not seek what is yours, but you; for children are not responsible to save up for *their* parents, but parents for *their* children. [15]I will most gladly spend and be expended for your souls. If [A]I love you more, am I to be loved less? [16]But be that as it may, I [A]did not burden you myself; nevertheless, devious person that I am, I took you in by deceit. [17][A]*Certainly* I have not taken advantage of you through any of those whom I have sent to you, have I? [18]I [A]urged Titus *to go,* and I sent [B]the brother with him. Titus did not take any advantage of you, did he? Did we not conduct ourselves in the same spirit *and walk* in the same steps?

[19]All this time you have been thinking that we are defending ourselves to you. *Actually,* [A]it is in the sight of God that we have been speaking in Christ; and [B]all for building you up, beloved. [20]For I am afraid that perhaps when I come I may find you to be not what I wish, and may be found by you to be not what you wish; that perhaps *there will be* strife, jealousy, [A]angry tempers, selfishness, slanders, [B]gossip, arrogance, disturbances; [21]I *am afraid* that when I come again my God may humiliate me before you, and I may mourn over many of those who have [A]sinned in the past and not repented of the [B]impurity, sexual immorality, and indecent behavior which they have practiced.

EXAMINE YOURSELVES

13 This is the third time that I am coming to you. [A]ON THE TESTIMONY OF TWO OR THREE WITNESSES EVERY MATTER SHALL

BE CONFIRMED. [2]I have previously said when I was present the second time, and though now absent I say in advance to those who have sinned in the past and to all the rest *as well,* that if I come again I will not [A]spare *anyone,* [3]since you are seeking proof of the Christ who speaks in me, who is not weak toward you, but [A]mighty in you. [4]For indeed He was [A]crucified because of weakness, yet He lives [B]because of the power of God. For we too are weak [1]in Him, yet we will live with Him because of the power of God *directed* toward you.

[5]Test yourselves *to see* if you are in the faith; [A]examine yourselves! Or do you not recognize *this about* yourselves, that Jesus Christ is in you—unless indeed you fail the test? [6]But I expect that you will realize that we ourselves do not fail the test. [7]Now we pray to God that you do nothing wrong; not so that we ourselves may appear approved, but that you may do what is right, though we may appear unapproved. [8]For we cannot do anything against the truth, but *only* for the truth. [9]For we rejoice when we ourselves are weak, but you are strong; this we also pray for, that you [A]become mature. [10]For this reason I am writing these things while absent, so that when present I *need* not use [A]severity, in accordance with the

12:14 [B]1 Cor 10:24, 33   12:15[A]2 Cor 11:11
12:16[A]2 Cor 11:9   12:17[A]2 Cor 9:5   12:18[A]2 Cor 8:6
[B]2 Cor 8:18   12:19[A]2 Cor 2:17   [B]Rom 14:19
12:20[A]Gal 5:20   [B]Rom 1:29   12:21[A]2 Cor 13:2
[B]1 Cor 6:9, 18   13:1[A]Deut 17:6; 19:15   13:2[A]2 Cor 1:23
13:3[A]2 Cor 9:8; 10:4   13:4[A]Phil 2:7f   [B]1 Cor 6:14
13:5[A]1 Cor 11:28   13:9[A]1 Cor 1:10; 2 Cor 13:11
13:10[A]Titus 1:13

13:4 [1]One early ms *with Him*

Bauthority which the Lord gave me for building up and not for tearing down.

11Finally, brothers *and sisters,* rejoice, mend your ways, be comforted, Abe like-minded, live in peace; and the God of love and peace will be with you. 12AGreet one another with a holy kiss. 13AAll the saints greet you.

14The grace of the Lord Jesus Christ, and the love of God, and the Afellowship of the Holy Spirit, be with you all.

13:10 B2 Cor 10:8   13:11A Rom 12:16   13:12A Rom 16:16
13:13A Phil 4:22   13:14A Phil 2:1

GALATIANS

INTRODUCTION

1 Paul, an apostle (^not *sent* from men nor through human agency, but through Jesus Christ and God the Father, who raised Him from the dead), ²and all the brothers who are with me,

To ^the churches of Galatia:

³^Grace to you and peace from God the Father and our Lord Jesus Christ, ⁴who ^gave Himself for our sins so that He might rescue us from this present evil age, according to the will of ᴮour God and Father, ⁵^to whom *be* the glory forevermore. Amen.

DISTORTION OF THE GOSPEL

⁶I am amazed that you are so quickly deserting Him who called you by the grace of Christ, for a ^different gospel, ⁷which is not *just* another *account;* but there are some who are ^disturbing you and want to distort the gospel of Christ. ⁸But even if we, or ^an angel from heaven, should preach to you a gospel contrary to what we have preached to you, he is to be accursed! ⁹As we have said before, even now I say again: ^if anyone is preaching to you a gospel contrary to what you received, he is to be accursed!

¹⁰For am I now seeking the favor of people, or of God? Or am I striving to please people? If I were still trying to please people, I would not be a ^bond-servant of Christ.

PAUL DEFENDS HIS MINISTRY

¹¹For ^I would have you know, brothers *and sisters,* that the gospel which was preached by me is not of human invention. ¹²For I neither received it from man, nor was I taught it, but *I received it* through a ^revelation of Jesus Christ.

¹³For you have heard of ^my former way of life in Judaism, how I used to persecute the church of God beyond measure and tried to destroy it; ¹⁴and I was advancing in Judaism beyond many of my contemporaries among my countrymen, being more extremely zealous for my ^ancestral traditions. ¹⁵But when He who had set me apart *even* from my mother's womb and ^called *me* through His grace was pleased ¹⁶to reveal His Son in me so that I might ^preach Him among the Gentiles, I did not immediately consult with flesh and blood, ¹⁷^nor did I go up to Jerusalem to those *who were* apostles before me; but I went away to Arabia, and returned once more to Damascus.

¹⁸Then ^three years later I went up ᴮto Jerusalem to become acquainted with Cephas, and stayed with him for fifteen days. ¹⁹But I did not see another one of the apostles except ^James, the Lord's brother. ²⁰(Now in what I am writing to you, I assure you ^before God that I am not lying.)

1:1^Gal 1:11f 1:2^Acts 16:6; 1 Cor 16:1 1:3^Rom 1:7
1:4^Gal 2:20 ᴮPhil 4:20 1:5^Rom 11:36
1:6^2 Cor 11:4 1:7^Acts 15:24; Gal 5:10
1:8^2 Cor 11:14 1:9^Rom 16:17 1:10^Rom 1:1;
Phil 1:1 1:11^Rom 2:16; 1 Cor 15:1 1:12^1 Cor 2:10;
2 Cor 12:1 1:13^Acts 26:4f 1:14^Matt 15:2; Mark 7:3
1:15^Is 49:1, 5; Jer 1:5 1:16^Acts 9:15; Gal 2:9
1:17^Acts 9:19-22 1:18^Acts 9:22f ᴮActs 9:26
1:19^Matt 12:46; Acts 12:17 1:20^Rom 9:1; 2 Cor 1:23

21Then ^I went into the regions of Syria and Cilicia. 22I was *still* unknown by sight to ^the churches of Judea which are in Christ; 23but they only kept hearing, "The man who once persecuted us is now preaching the faith which he once ^tried to destroy." 24And they ^were glorifying God because of me.

THE COUNCIL AT JERUSALEM

2 Then after an interval of fourteen years I ^went up again to Jerusalem with Barnabas, taking Titus along also. 2It was because of a revelation that I went up; and I submitted to them the gospel which I preach among the Gentiles, but *I did so* in private to those who were of reputation, for fear that somehow I might be ^running, or had run, in vain. 3But not even ^Titus, who was with me, though he was a Greek, was compelled to be circumcised. 4Yet *it was a concern* because of the ^false brothers secretly brought in, who had sneaked in to spy on our freedom which we have in Christ Jesus, in order to enslave us. 5But we did not yield in subjection to them, even for an hour, so that ^the truth of the gospel would remain with you. 6But from those who were of considerable repute (what they were makes no difference to me; ^God shows no favoritism)—well, those who were of repute contributed nothing to me. 7But on the contrary, seeing that I had been entrusted with the ^gospel ¹to the uncircumcised, just as Peter *had been* ²to the circumcised 8(for He who was at work for Peter in *his* ^apostleship to the circumcised was at work for me also to the Gentiles), 9and recognizing ^the grace that had been given to me, James and Cephas and John, who were reputed to be pillars, gave to me and Barnabas the right hand of fellowship, so that we *might go* to the Gentiles, and they to the circumcised. 10 *They* only *asked* us to remember the poor—^the very thing I also was eager to do.

PETER (CEPHAS) OPPOSED BY PAUL

11But when ^Cephas came to Antioch, I opposed him to his face, because he stood condemned. 12For prior to the coming of some men from James, he used to ^eat with the Gentiles; but when they came, he *began* to withdraw and separate himself, ᴮfearing those from the circumcision. 13The rest of the Jews joined him in hypocrisy, with the result that even ^Barnabas was carried away by their hypocrisy. 14But when I saw that they were not straightforward about ^the truth of the gospel, I said to Cephas in the presence of all, "If you, being a Jew, live like the Gentiles and not like the Jews, how *is it that* you compel the Gentiles to live like Jews?

15"We *are* ^Jews by nature and not sinners from the Gentiles; 16nevertheless, knowing that ^a person is not justified by works of the Law but through faith in Christ Jesus, even we have believed in Christ Jesus, so that we may be justified by faith in Christ and not by works of the Law; since by works

1:21^Acts 9:30   1:22^1 Thess 2:14   1:23^Acts 9:21
1:24^Matt 9:8   2:1^Acts 15:2   2:2^1 Cor 9:24ff;
Phil 2:16   2:3^2 Cor 2:13; Gal 2:1   2:4^Acts 15:1, 24;
Gal 1:7   2:5^Gal 1:6; 2:14   2:6^Acts 10:34
2:7^Acts 9:15; Gal 1:16   2:8^Acts 1:25   2:9^Rom 12:3
2:10^Acts 24:17   2:11^Gal 1:18; 2:7, 9, 14
2:12^Acts 11:3   ᴮActs 11:2   2:13^Acts 4:36; Gal 2:1, 9
2:14^Gal 2:5; Col 1:5   2:15^Phil 3:4f
2:16^Acts 13:39; Gal 3:11

2:7¹Lit *of the uncircumcision;* i.e., to Gentiles   ²Lit *of the circumcision;* i.e., to Jews

of the Law no flesh will be justified. 17But if, while seeking to be justified in Christ, we ourselves have also been found ᴬsinners, is Christ then a servant of sin? ¹Far from it! 18For if I rebuild what I have *once* destroyed, I ᴬprove myself to be a wrongdoer. 19For through the Law I ᴬdied to the Law, so that I might live for God. 20I have been ᴬcrucified with Christ; and it is no longer I who live, but Christ lives in me; and the *life* which I now live in the flesh I live by faith in the Son of God, who loved me and gave Himself up for me. 21I do not nullify the grace of God, for ᴬif righteousness *comes* through the Law, then Christ died needlessly."

FAITH BRINGS RIGHTEOUSNESS

3 You foolish Galatians, who has bewitched you, before whose eyes Jesus Christ ᴬwas publicly portrayed *as* crucified? 2This is the only thing I want to find out from you: did you receive the Spirit by works of the Law, or by ᴬhearing with faith? 3Are you so foolish? Having begun by the Spirit, are you now being perfected by the flesh? 4Did you suffer so many things in vain—ᴬif indeed it was in vain? 5So then, does He who provides you with the Spirit and works miracles among you, do it by works of the Law, or by ᴬhearing with faith?

6Just as Abraham ᴬBELIEVED GOD, AND IT WAS CREDITED TO HIM AS RIGHTEOUSNESS. 7Therefore, recognize that ᴬit is those who are of faith who are sons of Abraham. 8The Scripture, foreseeing that God would justify the Gentiles by faith, preached the gospel beforehand to Abraham, *saying*, "ᴬALL THE NATIONS WILL BE BLESSED IN YOU." 9So then, ᴬthose who are of faith are blessed with Abraham, the believer.

10For all who are of works of the Law are under a curse; for it is written: "ᴬCURSED IS EVERYONE WHO DOES NOT ABIDE BY ALL THE THINGS WRITTEN IN THE BOOK OF THE LAW, TO DO THEM." 11Now, that ᴬno one is justified by the Law before God is evident; for, "ᴮTHE RIGHTEOUS ONE WILL LIVE BY FAITH." 12However, the Law is not of faith; on the contrary, "ᴬTHE PERSON WHO PERFORMS THEM WILL LIVE BY THEM." 13Christ redeemed us from the curse of the Law, having become a curse for us—for it is written: "ᴬCURSED IS EVERYONE WHO HANGS ON A ¹TREE"—14in order that in Christ Jesus the blessing of Abraham would come to the Gentiles, so that we ᴬwould receive ᴮthe promise of the Spirit through faith.

INTENT OF THE LAW

15Brothers *and sisters*, ᴬI speak in terms of human relations: even though it is *only* a man's covenant, yet when it has been ratified, no one sets it aside or adds conditions to it. 16Now the promises were spoken to Abraham and to his seed. He does not say, "And to seeds," as *one would in referring* to many, but *rather* as *in referring* to one, "ᴬAnd to your seed," that is, Christ. 17What I am saying is this: the Law, which came ᴬ430 years

2:17ᴬGal 2:15 2:18ᴬRom 3:5 2:19ᴬRom 6:2; 7:4
2:20ᴬRom 6:6; Gal 5:24 2:21ᴬGal 3:21
3:1ᴬ1 Cor 1:23; Gal 5:11 3:2ᴬRom 10:17
3:4ᴬ1 Cor 15:2 3:5ᴬRom 10:17 3:6ᴬGen 15:6
3:7ᴬRom 4:16; Gal 3:9 3:8ᴬGen 12:3 3:9ᴬGal 3:7
3:10ᴬDeut 27:26 3:11ᴬGal 2:16 ᴮHab 2:4
3:12ᴬLev 18:5; Rom 10:5 3:13ᴬDeut 21:23
3:14ᴬGal 3:2 ᴮActs 2:33 3:15ᴬRom 3:5
3:16ᴬActs 3:25 3:17ᴬGen 15:13f; Ex 12:40

2:17¹Lit *May it never happen!* 3:13¹Or *cross;* lit *wood;* see Deut 21:23

later, does not invalidate a covenant previously ratified by God, so as to nullify the promise. ¹⁸For ^if the inheritance is based on law, it is no longer based on a promise; but God has granted it to Abraham by means of a promise.

¹⁹^Why the Law then? It was added on account of the 'violations, having been ordered through angels at the hand of a mediator, until the Seed would come to whom the promise had been made. ²⁰Now ^a mediator is not for one *party only;* but God is *only* one. ²¹Is the Law then contrary to the promises of God? ^Far from it! For if a law had been given that was able to impart life, then righteousness would indeed have been based on law. ²²But the Scripture has ^confined everyone under sin, so that the promise by faith in Jesus Christ might be given to those who believe.

²³But before faith came, we were kept in custody under the Law, being confined for the faith that was destined to be revealed. ²⁴Therefore the Law has become our guardian *to lead us* to Christ, so that ^we may be justified by faith. ²⁵But now that faith has come, we are no longer under a ^guardian. ²⁶For you are all ^sons *and daughters* of God through faith in Christ Jesus. ²⁷For all of you who were baptized into Christ have ^clothed yourselves with Christ. ²⁸^There is neither Jew nor Greek, there is neither slave nor free, there is neither male nor female; for you are all one in Christ Jesus. ²⁹And if you belong to Christ, then you are Abraham's descendants, heirs according to ^promise.

SONSHIP IN CHRIST

4 Now I say, as long as the heir is a child, he does not differ at all from a slave, although he is owner of everything, ²but he is under guardians and managers until the date set by the father. ³So we too, when we were children, were held ^in bondage under the ᴮelementary principles of the world. ⁴But when the fullness of the time came, God sent His Son, ^born of a woman, born under the Law, ⁵so that He might redeem those who were under the Law, that we might receive the adoption as ^sons *and daughters.* ⁶Because you are sons, ^God has sent the Spirit of His Son into our hearts, crying out, "Abba! Father!" ⁷Therefore you are no longer a slave, but a son; and ^if a son, then an heir through God.

⁸However at that time, ^when you did not know God, you were slaves to those which by nature are not gods. ⁹But now that you have come to know God, or rather to be ^known by God, how is it that you turn back again to the weak and worthless elementary principles, to which you want to be enslaved all over again? ¹⁰You ^meticulously observe days and months and seasons and years. ¹¹I fear for you, that perhaps I have labored over you in vain.

¹²I beg of you, ^brothers *and sisters,* become as I *am,* for I also *have become* as you *are.* You have

---

3:18^Rom 4:14   3:19^Rom 5:20   3:20^1 Tim 2:5; Heb 8:6   3:21^Luke 20:16; Gal 2:17   3:22^Rom 11:32   3:24^Gal 2:16   3:25^1 Cor 4:15   3:26^Rom 8:14; Gal 4:5   3:27^Rom 13:14   3:28^Rom 3:22; 1 Cor 12:13   3:29^Rom 9:8; Gal 3:18   4:3^Gal 2:4   ᴮCol 2:8, 20   4:4^Matt 1:25; Luke 2:7   4:5^Rom 8:14; Gal 3:26   4:6^Acts 16:7; 2 Cor 3:17   4:7^Rom 8:17   4:8^1 Cor 1:21; Eph 2:12   4:9^1 Cor 8:3   4:10^Rom 14:5; Col 2:16   4:12^Gal 6:18

3:19 ¹I.e., of God's commands

done me no wrong; [13] but you know that it was because of a bodily illness that I preached the gospel to you the first time; [14] and you did not despise that which was a trial to you in my bodily condition, nor express contempt, but ^you received me as an angel of God, as Christ Jesus *Himself.* [15] Where then is that sense of blessing you had? For I testify about you that, if possible, you would have torn out your eyes and given them to me. [16] So have I become your enemy ^by telling you the truth? [17] They eagerly seek you, not in a commendable way, but they want to shut you out so that you will seek them. [18] But it is good always to be eagerly sought in a commendable way, and ^not only when I am present with you. [19] My children, with whom I am again in labor until ^Christ is formed in you— [20] but I could wish to be present with you now and to change my *tone of* voice, for ^I am at a loss about you!

SLAVE AND FREE

[21] Tell me, you who want to be under law, do you not ^listen to the Law? [22] For it is written that Abraham had two sons, ^one by the slave woman and ^one by the free woman. [23] But ^the son by the slave woman was born according to the flesh, and ^the son by the free woman through the promise. [24] This is speaking allegorically, for these *women* are two covenants: one *coming* from Mount Sinai giving birth to children who are to be ^slaves; she is Hagar. [25] Now this Hagar is Mount Sinai in Arabia and corresponds to the present Jerusalem, for she is enslaved with her children. [26] But ^the Jerusalem above is free; she is our mother. [27] For it is written:

"^REJOICE, INFERTILE ONE, YOU
    WHO DO NOT GIVE BIRTH;
BREAK FORTH AND SHOUT, YOU
    WHO ARE NOT IN LABOR;
FOR THE CHILDREN OF THE
    DESOLATE ONE *ARE* MORE
    NUMEROUS
THAN *THOSE* OF THE ONE WHO
    HAS A HUSBAND."

[28] And you, brothers *and sisters,* like Isaac, are ^children of promise. [29] But as at that time the *son* who was born according to the flesh ^persecuted the one *who was born* according to the Spirit, so it is even now. [30] But what does the Scripture say?

"^DRIVE OUT THE SLAVE WOMAN
    AND HER SON,
FOR THE SON OF THE SLAVE
    WOMAN SHALL NOT BE AN
    HEIR WITH THE SON OF THE
    FREE WOMAN."

[31] So then, brothers *and sisters,* we are not children of a slave woman, but of the free woman.

FOLLOW THE SPIRIT

5 ^It was for freedom that Christ set us free; therefore keep standing firm and do not be subject again to a yoke of slavery.

[2] Look! I, Paul, tell you that if you have yourselves ^circumcised, Christ will be of no benefit to you. [3] And I testify again to every man who has himself circumcised, that he is obligated to ^keep the whole Law. [4] You have been severed from Christ,

4:14 ^Matt 10:40; 1 Thess 2:13   4:16 ^Amos 5:10
4:18 ^Gal 4:13f   4:19 ^Eph 4:13   4:20 ^2 Cor 4:8
4:21 ^Luke 16:29   4:22 ^Gen 16:15   ^B Gen 21:2
4:23 ^Rom 9:7   ^B Gen 17:16ff   4:24 ^Gal 4:3
4:26 ^Heb 12:22; Rev 3:12;   4:27 ^Is 54:1
4:28 ^Rom 9:7ff; Gal 3:29   4:29 ^Gen 21:9
4:30 ^Gen 21:10, 12   5:1 ^John 8:32, 36; Rom 8:15
5:2 ^Acts 15:1; Gal 5:3, 6, 11   5:3 ^Rom 2:25

you who are seeking to be justified by the ¹Law; you have ^fallen from grace. ⁵For we, through the Spirit, by faith, are ^waiting for the hope of righteousness. ⁶For in Christ Jesus ^neither circumcision nor uncircumcision means anything, but faith working through love.

⁷You were ^running well; who hindered you from obeying the truth? ⁸This persuasion *did* not *come* from ^Him who calls you. ⁹^A little leaven leavens the whole lump *of dough*. ¹⁰I have confidence in you in the Lord, that you will adopt no other view; but the one who is ^disturbing you will bear the punishment, whoever he is. ¹¹But as for me, brothers *and sisters,* if I still preach circumcision, why am I still ^persecuted? Then the stumbling block of the cross has been eliminated. ¹²I wish that those who are troubling you would even ^emasculate themselves.

¹³For you were called to freedom, brothers *and sisters;* ^only *do* not *turn* your freedom into an opportunity for the flesh, but serve one another through love. ¹⁴For the whole Law is fulfilled in one word, in the *statement,* "^YOU SHALL LOVE YOUR NEIGHBOR AS YOURSELF." ¹⁵But if you ^bite and devour one another, take care that you are not consumed by one another.

¹⁶But I say, ^walk by the Spirit, and you will not carry out the desire of the flesh. ¹⁷For ^the desire of the flesh is against the Spirit, and the Spirit against the flesh; for these are in opposition to one another, ^Bin order to keep you from doing whatever you want. ¹⁸But if you are ^led by the Spirit, you are not under the Law. ¹⁹Now the deeds of the flesh are evident, which are:

^sexual immorality, impurity, indecent behavior, ²⁰idolatry, witchcraft, hostilities, ^strife, jealousy, outbursts of anger, selfish ambition, dissensions, factions, ²¹envy, drunkenness, carousing, and things like these, of which I forewarn you, just as I have forewarned you, that those who practice such things will not ^inherit the kingdom of God. ²²But ^the fruit of the Spirit is love, joy, peace, patience, kindness, goodness, faithfulness, ²³gentleness, ^self-control; against such things there is no law. ²⁴Now those who belong to Christ Jesus ^crucified the flesh with its passions and desires.

²⁵If we live by the Spirit, let's follow ^the Spirit as well. ²⁶Let's not become ^boastful, challenging one another, envying one another.

BEAR ONE ANOTHER'S BURDENS

6 Brothers *and sisters,* even if a person is caught in any wrongdoing, you who are ^spiritual are to restore such a person in a spirit of gentleness; *each one* looking to yourself, so that you are not tempted as well. ²^Bear one another's burdens, and thereby fulfill the law of Christ. ³For ^if anyone thinks that he is something when he is nothing, he deceives himself. ⁴But each one must ^examine his own work, and then he will have *reason for* boasting, *but to*

5:4 ^Heb 12:15; 2 Pet 3:17   5:5 ^Rom 8:23; 1 Cor 1:7
5:6 ^1 Cor 7:19; Gal 6:15   5:7 ^Gal 2:2   5:8 ^Rom 8:28;
Gal 1:6   5:9 ^1 Cor 5:6   5:10 ^Gal 1:7; 5:12
5:11 ^Gal 6:12   5:12 ^Deut 23:1   5:13 ^1 Cor 8:9;
1 Pet 2:16   5:14 ^Lev 19:18; Matt 19:19   5:15 ^Gal 5:20;
Phil 3:2   5:16 ^Rom 8:4; 13:14   5:17 ^Rom 8:5ff
^Rom 7:15ff   5:18 ^Rom 8:14   5:19 ^1 Cor 6:9, 18;
2 Cor 12:21   5:20 ^2 Cor 12:20   5:21 ^1 Cor 6:9
5:22 ^Matt 7:16ff; Eph 5:9   5:23 ^Acts 24:25
5:24 ^Rom 6:6; Gal 2:20   5:25 ^Gal 5:16   5:26 ^Phil 2:3
6:1 ^1 Cor 2:15   6:2 ^Rom 15:1   6:3 ^Acts 5:36;
1 Cor 3:18   6:4 ^1 Cor 11:28

5:4 ¹Or *law*

himself alone, and not to another. ⁵For ^each one will bear his own load.

⁶^The one who is taught the word is to share all good things with the one who teaches *him*. ⁷Do not be deceived, ^God is not mocked; for whatever a person sows, this he will also reap. ⁸For the one who sows to his own flesh will reap destruction from the flesh, but ^the one who sows to the Spirit will reap eternal life from the Spirit. ⁹^Let's not become discouraged in doing good, for in due time we will reap, if we do not become weary. ¹⁰So then, ^while we have opportunity, let's do good to all people, and especially to those who are of the household of the faith.

¹¹See with what large letters I have written to you ^with my own hand! ¹²All who want ^to make a good showing in the flesh try to compel you to be circumcised, simply so that they will not be persecuted for the cross of Christ. ¹³For those who ¹are circumcised do not even ^keep the Law themselves, but they want to have you circumcised so that they may boast in your flesh. ¹⁴But far be it from me to boast, except in the cross of our Lord Jesus Christ, through which the world has been crucified to me, and ^I to the world. ¹⁵For ^neither is circumcision anything, nor uncircumcision, but a new creation. ¹⁶And all who will follow this rule, peace and mercy *be* upon them, and upon the ^Israel of God.

¹⁷From now on let no one cause trouble for me, for I bear on my body the ^marks of Jesus.

¹⁸^The grace of our Lord Jesus Christ be ᴮwith your spirit, brothers *and sisters*. Amen.

6:5 ^Prov 9:12; Rom 14:12　6:6 ^1 Cor 9:11, 14
6:7 ^Job 13:9　6:8 ^Rom 8:11; James 3:18
6:9 ^1 Cor 15:58; 2 Cor 4:1　6:10 ^Prov 3:27
6:11 ^1 Cor 16:21　6:12 ^Matt 23:27f　6:13 ^Rom 2:25
6:14 ^Rom 6:2, 6; Gal 2:19f　6:15 ^Rom 2:26, 28;
1 Cor 7:19　6:16 ^Rom 9:6; Gal 3:7, 29　6:17 ^Is 44:5;
Ezek 9:4　6:18 ^Rom 16:20　ᴮ2 Tim 4:22

6:13 ¹Two early mss *have been*

EPHESIANS

THE BLESSINGS OF REDEMPTION

1 Paul, ^an apostle of Christ Jesus by the will of God,

To the saints who are ¹at Ephesus and ᴮ*are* faithful in Christ Jesus: ²^Grace to you and peace from God our Father and the Lord Jesus Christ.

³Blessed *be* the God and Father of our Lord Jesus Christ, who has blessed us with every spiritual blessing in ^the heavenly *places* in Christ, ⁴just as ^He chose us in Him before the foundation of the world, that we would be holy and blameless before ¹Him. In love ⁵He ^predestined us to adoption as sons *and daughters* through Jesus Christ to Himself, according to the good pleasure of His will, ⁶^to the praise of the glory of His grace, with which He favored us in ᴮthe Beloved. ⁷^In Him we have redemption through His blood, the forgiveness of our wrongdoings, according to the riches of His grace ⁸which He lavished on us. In all wisdom and insight ⁹He ^made known to us the mystery of His will, according to His good pleasure which He set forth in Him, ¹⁰regarding *His* plan of ^the fullness of the times, ᴮto bring all things together in Christ, things in the heavens and things on the earth. ¹¹In Him we also have obtained an inheritance, having been predestined ^according to the purpose of Him who works all things ᴮin accordance with the plan of His will, ¹²to the end that we who were the first to hope in the Christ would be ^to the praise of His glory.

¹³In Him, you also, after listening to the message of truth, the gospel of your salvation—having also believed, you were ^sealed in Him with ᴮthe Holy Spirit of the promise, ¹⁴who is a ^first installment of our inheritance, in regard to the redemption of *God's own* possession, to the praise of His glory.

¹⁵For this reason I too, ^having heard of the faith in the Lord Jesus which *exists* among you and ¹your love for all the saints, ¹⁶^do not cease giving thanks for you, while making mention *of you* in my prayers; ¹⁷that the ^God of our Lord Jesus Christ, the Father of glory, may give you a spirit of wisdom and of revelation in the knowledge of Him. ¹⁸*I pray that* ^the eyes of your heart may be enlightened, so that you will know what is the hope of His calling, what are the riches of the glory of His inheritance in the saints, ¹⁹and what is the boundless greatness of His power toward us who believe. ^*These are* in accordance with the working of the strength of His might ²⁰which He brought about in Christ, when He ^raised Him from the dead and

1:1 ^2 Cor 1:1   ᴮ Col 1:2   1:2 ^Rom 1:7   1:3 ^Eph 1:20;
2:6   1:4 ^Eph 2:10; 2 Thess 2:13f   1:5 ^Rom 8:29f
1:6 ^Eph 1:12, 14   ᴮMatt 3:17   1:7 ^Col 1:14
1:9 ^Rom 11:25; Eph 3:3   1:10 ^Mark 1:15   ᴮCol 1:16, 20
1:11 ^Rom 8:28f   ᴮRom 9:11   1:12 ^Eph 1:6, 14
1:13 ^Eph 4:30   ᴮActs 2:33   1:14 ^2 Cor 1:22
1:15 ^Col 1:4; Philem 5   1:16 ^Rom 1:8f; Col 1:9
1:17 ^John 20:17; Rom 15:6   1:18 ^2 Cor 4:6
1:19 ^Eph 3:7; Col 1:29   1:20 ^Acts 2:24

1:1 ¹Three early mss do not contain *at Ephesus*
1:4 ¹Or *Him, in love. He*   1:15 ¹Three early mss do not
contain *your love*

seated Him at His right hand in the heavenly *places,* ²¹far above ^all rule and authority and power and dominion, and every name that is named, not only in this age but also in the one to come. ²²And He ^put all things in subjection under His feet, and made Him head over all things to the church, ²³which is His ^body, the fullness of Him who fills all in all.

MADE ALIVE IN CHRIST

2 And you were ^dead in your offenses and sins, ²in which you previously walked according to the course of this world, according to ^the prince of the power of the air, of the spirit that is now working in ᴮthe ¹sons of disobedience. ³Among them we too all previously lived in ^the lusts of our flesh, indulging the desires of the flesh and of the mind, and were ᴮby nature children of wrath, just as the rest. ⁴But God, being rich in mercy, because of ^His great love with which He loved us, ⁵even when we were dead in our wrongdoings, made us alive together ¹with Christ (^by grace you have been saved), ⁶and ^raised us up with Him, and seated us with Him in the heavenly *places* in Christ Jesus, ⁷so that in the ages to come He might show the boundless ^riches of His grace in kindness toward us in Christ Jesus. ⁸For ^by grace you have been saved through faith; and ¹this *is* not of yourselves, *it is* the gift of God; ⁹^not a result of works, so that no one may boast. ¹⁰For we are His workmanship, ^created in Christ Jesus for good works, which God prepared beforehand so that we would walk in them.

¹¹Therefore remember that previously you, the Gentiles in the flesh, who are called "^Uncircumcision" by the so-called "^Circumcision" *which is* performed in the flesh by human hands— ¹²*remember* that you were at that time separate from Christ, excluded from the people of Israel, and strangers to ^the covenants of the promise, having no hope and without God in the world. ¹³But now in Christ Jesus you who previously were far away have been brought near ^by the blood of Christ. ¹⁴For He Himself is ^our peace, who made both *groups into* one and broke down the barrier of the dividing wall, ¹⁵by abolishing in His flesh the hostility, *which is* the Law *composed* of commandments *expressed* in ordinances, so that in Himself He might make the two ^one new person, *in this way* establishing peace; ¹⁶and that He might ^reconcile them both in one body to God through the cross, by it having put to death the hostility. ¹⁷And ^He came and preached peace to you who were far away, and peace to those who were near; ¹⁸for through Him we both have our access in ^one Spirit to the Father. ¹⁹So then you are no longer strangers and foreigners, but you are ^fellow citizens with the saints, and are of God's household, ²⁰having been built on the foundation of the

1:21^Matt 28:18; Col 1:16   1:22^Ps 8:6; 1 Cor 15:27
1:23^1 Cor 12:27; Eph 4:12   2:1^Eph 2:5; Col 2:13
2:2^John 12:31   ᴮEph 5:6   2:3^Gal 5:16f   ᴮRom 2:14
2:4^John 3:16   2:5^Acts 15:11   2:6^Col 2:12
2:7^Rom 2:4; Eph 1:7   2:8^Acts 15:11; Eph 2:5
2:9^Rom 3:28; 2 Tim 1:9   2:10^Col 3:10
2:11^Rom 2:28f; Col 2:11   2:12^Gal 3:17; Heb 8:6
2:13^Rom 3:25; Col 1:20   2:14^Is 9:6   2:15^Gal 3:28;
Col 3:10f   2:16^2 Cor 5:18; Col 1:20, 22
2:17^Is 57:19; Rom 10:14   2:18^1 Cor 12:13; Eph 4:4
2:19^Phil 3:20; Heb 12:22f

2:2¹I.e., people opposed to God   2:5¹Two early mss
in Christ   2:8¹I.e., this salvation

apostles and prophets, Christ Jesus Himself being the ^cornerstone, ²¹in whom the whole building, being fitted together, is growing into ^a holy temple in the Lord, ²²in whom you also are being ^built together into a dwelling of God in the Spirit.

PAUL'S STEWARDSHIP

3 For this reason I, Paul, ^the prisoner of Christ Jesus for the sake of you Gentiles— ²if indeed you have heard of the ^administration of God's grace which was given to me for you; ³that ^by revelation there was made known to me the mystery, as I wrote before briefly. ⁴By referring to this, when you read you can understand my insight into the ^mystery of Christ, ⁵which in other generations was not made known to mankind, as it has now been revealed to His holy ^apostles and prophets in the Spirit; ⁶ *to be specific,* that the Gentiles are ^fellow heirs and fellow members of the body, and fellow partakers of the promise in Christ Jesus through the gospel, ⁷^of which I was made a minister, according to the gift of God's grace which was given to me according to the working of His power. ⁸To me, the very least of all saints, this grace was given, to preach to the Gentiles the unfathomable ^riches of Christ, ⁹and to enlighten all people as to what the plan of the ^mystery is which for ages has been hidden in God, who created all things; ¹⁰so that the multifaceted wisdom of God might now be ^made known through the church to the ^rulers and the authorities in the heavenly *places.* ¹¹ *This was* in ^accordance with the eternal purpose which He carried out in Christ Jesus our Lord,

¹²in whom we have boldness and confident ^access through faith in Him. ¹³Therefore I ask you not to become discouraged about my tribulations ^in your behalf, since they are your glory.

¹⁴For this reason I ^bend my knees before the Father, ¹⁵from whom every family in heaven and on earth derives its name, ¹⁶that He would grant you, according to the riches of His glory, to be ^strengthened with power through His Spirit in the inner self, ¹⁷so that ^Christ may dwell in your hearts through faith; *and* that you, being ^rooted and grounded in love, ¹⁸may be able to comprehend with all the saints what is ^the width and length and height and depth, ¹⁹and to know ^the love of Christ which surpasses knowledge, that you may be filled to all the fullness of God.

²⁰Now to Him who is ^able to do far more abundantly beyond all that we ask or think, according to the power that works within us, ²¹^to Him *be* the glory in the church and in Christ Jesus to all generations forever and ever. Amen.

UNITY OF THE SPIRIT

4 Therefore I, the prisoner of the Lord, urge you to ^walk in a manner worthy of the calling with which you have been called, ²with all ^humility and gentleness, with patience, bearing with one

2:20 ^Ps 118:22; Luke 20:17   2:21 ^1 Cor 3:16f
2:22 ^1 Cor 3:9, 16; 2 Cor 6:16   3:1 ^Acts 23:18; Eph 4:1
3:2 ^Eph 1:10; 3:9   3:3 ^Gal 1:12   3:4 ^Rom 11:25;
16:25   3:5 ^1 Cor 12:28; Eph 2:20   3:6 ^Gal 3:29
3:7 ^Col 1:23, 25   3:8 ^Rom 2:4; Eph 1:7
3:9 ^Rom 16:25; Col 1:26f   3:10 ^1 Pet 1:12   ^Eph 6:12
3:11 ^Eph 1:11   3:12 ^Eph 2:18   3:13 ^Eph 3:1
3:14 ^Phil 2:10   3:16 ^Phil 4:13; Col 1:11
3:17 ^John 14:23   ^Col 2:7   3:18 ^Job 11:8f
3:19 ^Rom 8:35, 39   3:20 ^2 Cor 9:8   3:21 ^Rom 11:36
4:1 ^Eph 2:10; Col 1:10   4:2 ^Col 3:12f

another in love, ³being diligent to keep the unity of the Spirit in the ^bond of peace. ⁴ *There is* ^one body and one Spirit, just as you also were called in one ᴮhope of your calling; ⁵^one Lord, one faith, one baptism, ⁶one God and Father of all ^who is over all and through all and in all.

⁷But to each one of us grace was given ^according to the measure of Christ's gift. ⁸Therefore it says,

"^WHEN HE ASCENDED ON HIGH,
HE LED CAPTIVE *THE* CAPTIVES,
AND HE GAVE GIFTS TO PEOPLE."

⁹(Now this *expression,* "He ^ascended," what does it mean except that He also had descended into the lower parts of the earth? ¹⁰He who descended is Himself also He who ascended ^far above all the heavens, so that He might ᴮfill all things.) ¹¹And He gave ^some *as* apostles, some *as* prophets, some *as* evangelists, some *as* ¹pastors and teachers, ¹²^for the equipping of the saints for the work of ministry, for the building up of the body of Christ; ¹³until we all attain to the unity of the faith, and of the ^knowledge of the Son of God, to a ᴮmature man, to the measure of the stature which belongs to the fullness of Christ. ¹⁴As a result, we are ^no longer to be children, tossed here and there by waves and carried about by every wind of doctrine, by the trickery of people, by craftiness in deceitful scheming; ¹⁵but speaking the truth in love, we are to ^grow up in all *aspects* into Him who is the head, *that is,* Christ, ¹⁶from whom ^the whole body, being fitted and held together by what every joint supplies, according to the proper working of each individual part, causes the growth of the body for the building up of itself in love.

THE CHRISTIAN'S WALK

¹⁷So I say this, and affirm in the Lord, ^that you are to no longer walk just as the Gentiles also walk, in the futility of their minds, ¹⁸being ^darkened in their understanding, ᴮexcluded from the life of God because of the ignorance that is in them, because of the hardness of their heart; ¹⁹and they, having become callous, ^have given themselves up to ᴮindecent behavior for the practice of every kind of impurity with greediness. ²⁰But you did not ^learn Christ in this way, ²¹if indeed you ^have heard Him and have ᴮbeen taught in Him, just as truth is in Jesus, ²²that, in reference to your former way of life, you are to ^rid yourselves of the ᴮold self, which is being corrupted in accordance with the lusts of deceit, ²³and that you are to be ^renewed in the spirit of your minds, ²⁴and to put on the ^new self, which in *the likeness of* God has been created in righteousness and holiness of the truth.

²⁵Therefore, ridding yourselves of falsehood, ^SPEAK TRUTH EACH ONE *OF YOU* WITH HIS NEIGHBOR, because we are parts of one another. ²⁶^BE ANGRY, AND *YET* DO NOT SIN; do not let the sun go down on your anger, ²⁷and do not ^give the devil an opportunity. ²⁸The one who steals must no longer steal; but rather he must labor, ^producing with his

4:3^Col 3:14f　4:4^1 Cor 12:4ff　ᴮEph 1:18
4:5^1 Cor 8:6　4:6^Rom 11:36　4:7^Rom 12:3
4:8^Ps 68:18　4:9^John 3:13　4:10^Heb 7:26
ᴮEph 1:23　4:11^Acts 13:1; 1 Cor 12:28　4:12^2 Cor 13:9
4:13^Eph 1:17　ᴮHeb 5:14　4:14^1 Cor 14:20
4:15^Eph 2:21　4:16^Rom 12:4f; Col 2:19　4:17^Eph 2:2;
4:22　4:18^Rom 1:21　ᴮEph 2:12　4:19^Rom 1:24
ᴮCol 3:5　4:20^Matt 11:29　4:21^Rom 10:14　ᴮCol 2:7
4:22^Heb 12:1　ᴮRom 6:6　4:23^Rom 12:2
4:24^Col 3:10　4:25^Zech 8:16; Eph 4:15　4:26^Ps 4:4
4:27^Rom 12:19; James 4:7　4:28^1 Thess 4:11;
2 Thess 3:8, 11f

4:11 ¹ From Gr for *shepherds*

own hands what is good, so that he will have *something* to share with the one who has need. ²⁹Let no unwholesome word come out of your mouth, but if *there is* any good *word* for ^edification according to the need *of the moment, say that,* so that it will give grace to those who hear. ³⁰Do not grieve the Holy Spirit of God, by whom you were ^sealed for the day of redemption. ³¹^All bitterness, wrath, anger, clamor, and slander must be removed from you, along with all malice. ³²Be kind to one another, compassionate, forgiving each other, ^just as God in Christ also has forgiven ¹you.

BE IMITATORS OF GOD

5 ^Therefore be imitators of God, as beloved children; ²and ^walk in love, just as Christ also loved ¹you and ^Bgave Himself up for us, an offering and a sacrifice to God as a fragrant aroma.

³But ^sexual immorality or any impurity or greed must not even be mentioned among you, as is proper among saints; ⁴and *there must be no* ^filthiness or foolish talk, or vulgar joking, which are not fitting, but rather ^Bgiving of thanks. ⁵For this you know with certainty, that ^no sexually immoral or impure or greedy person, which amounts to an idolater, has an inheritance in the kingdom ^Bof Christ and God.

⁶^*See that* no one deceives you with empty words, for because of these things the wrath of God comes upon the ¹sons of disobedience. ⁷Therefore do not become ^partners with them; ⁸for ^you were once darkness, but now you are light in the Lord; walk as children of light ⁹(for ^the fruit of the light *consists* in all goodness, righteousness,

and truth), ¹⁰^as you try to learn what is pleasing to the Lord. ¹¹Do not participate in the useless ^deeds of darkness, but instead even ^Bexpose them; ¹²for it is disgraceful even to speak of the things which are done by them in secret. ¹³But all things become visible ^when they are exposed by the light, for everything that becomes visible is light. ¹⁴For this reason it says,

"^Awake, sleeper,
And arise from the dead,
And Christ will shine on you."

¹⁵So then, be careful how you ^walk, not as unwise people but as wise, ¹⁶^making the most of your time, because the days are evil. ¹⁷Therefore do not be foolish, but ^understand what the will of the Lord *is.* ¹⁸And ^do not get drunk with wine, in which there is debauchery, but be filled with the Spirit, ¹⁹^speaking to one another in psalms and hymns and spiritual songs, singing and making melody with your hearts to the Lord; ²⁰^always giving thanks for all things in the name of our Lord Jesus Christ to *our* ^BGod and Father; ²¹^and subject yourselves to one another in the ^Bfear of Christ.

MARRIAGE LIKE CHRIST
AND THE CHURCH

²²^Wives, *subject yourselves* to your own husbands, as to the Lord. ²³For ^the husband is the head of the

---

4:29^Rom 14:19; Col 4:6   4:30^John 3:33; Eph 1:13
4:31^Rom 3:14; Col 3:8, 19   4:32^Matt 6:14f; 2 Cor 2:10
5:1^Matt 5:48; Luke 6:36   5:2^Rom 14:15   ^BGal 2:20
5:3^Col 3:5   5:4^Matt 12:34   ^BEph 5:20   5:5^1 Cor 6:9
^BCol 1:13   5:6^Col 2:8   5:7^Eph 3:6   5:8^Eph 2:2
5:9^Gal 5:22   5:10^Rom 12:2   5:11^Rom 13:12
^B1 Tim 5:20   5:13^John 3:20f   5:14^Is 51:17; 60:1
5:15^Eph 5:2   5:16^Col 4:5   5:17^Rom 12:2; Col 1:9
5:18^Prov 20:1; Rom 13:13   5:19^Col 3:16
5:20^Rom 1:8   ^B1 Cor 15:24   5:21^Gal 5:13   ^B2 Cor 5:11
5:22^Eph 5:22-6:9: *Col 3:18-4:1*   5:23^1 Cor 11:3

4:32¹Two early mss *us*   5:2¹One early ms *us*
5:6¹I.e., people opposed to God

wife, as Christ also is the head of the church, He Himself *being* the Savior of the body. ²⁴But as the church is subject to Christ, so also the wives *ought to be* to their husbands in everything.

²⁵^Husbands, love your wives, just as Christ also loved the church and ᴮgave Himself up for her, ²⁶^so that He might sanctify her, having cleansed her by the washing of water with the word, ²⁷that He might present to Himself the church in all her glory, having no spot or wrinkle or any such thing; but that she would be ^holy and blameless. ²⁸So husbands also ought to ^love their own wives as their own bodies. He who loves his own wife loves himself; ²⁹for no one ever hated his own flesh, but nourishes and cherishes it, just as Christ also *does* the church, ³⁰because we are ^parts of His body. ³¹^FOR THIS REASON A MAN SHALL LEAVE HIS FATHER AND HIS MOTHER AND BE JOINED TO HIS WIFE, AND THE TWO SHALL BECOME ONE FLESH. ³²This mystery is great; but I am speaking with reference to Christ and the church. ³³Nevertheless, as for you individually, each *husband* is to love his own wife the same as himself, and the wife *must see to it* that she ^respects her husband.

CHILDREN AND PARENTS

6 ^Children, obey your parents in the Lord, for this is right. ²^HONOR YOUR FATHER AND MOTHER (which is the first commandment with a promise), ³SO THAT IT MAY TURN OUT WELL FOR YOU, AND THAT YOU MAY LIVE LONG ON THE EARTH.

⁴^Fathers, do not provoke your children to anger, but ᴮbring them up in the discipline and instruction of the Lord.

SLAVES AND MASTERS

⁵^Slaves, be obedient to those who are your masters according to the flesh, with fear and trembling, in the sincerity of your heart, as to Christ; ⁶not by way of eye-service, as ^people-pleasers, but as slaves of Christ, doing the will of God from the heart. ⁷With goodwill render service, ^as to the Lord, and not to people, ⁸knowing that ^whatever good thing each one does, he will receive this back from the Lord, whether slave or free.

⁹And masters, do the same things to them, and give up threatening, knowing that ^both their Master and yours is in heaven, and there is no partiality with Him.

THE ARMOR OF GOD

¹⁰Finally, ^be strong in the Lord and in ᴮthe strength of His might. ¹¹^Put on the full armor of God, so that you will be able to stand firm against the schemes of the devil. ¹²For our struggle is not against ^flesh and blood, but against the rulers, against the powers, against the world forces of this darkness, against the spiritual *forces* of wickedness in the heavenly *places*. ¹³Therefore, take up the full armor of God, so that you will be able to ^resist on the evil day, and having done everything, to stand firm. ¹⁴Stand firm therefore, ^having belted your waist with truth, and having ᴮput on the breastplate

5:25^Eph 5:28, 33 ᴮEph 5:2 **5:26**^Titus 2:14; Heb 10:10, 14, 29 **5:27**^Eph 1:4 **5:28**^Eph 5:25, 33; 1 Pet 3:7 **5:30**^1 Cor 6:15; 12:27 **5:31**^Gen 2:24; Matt 19:5 **5:33**^1 Pet 3:2, 5f **6:1**^Prov 6:20; 23:22 **6:2**^Ex 20:12; Deut 5:16 **6:4**^Col 3:21 ᴮGen 18:19 **6:5**^Col 3:22; 1 Tim 6:1 **6:6**^Gal 1:10 **6:7**^Col 3:23 **6:8**^Matt 16:27; 2 Cor 5:10 **6:9**^Job 31:13ff; Col 4:1 **6:10**^1 Cor 16:13 ᴮEph 1:19 **6:11**^Rom 13:12; Eph 6:13 **6:12**^Matt 16:17 **6:13**^James 4:7 **6:14**^Is 11:5 ᴮIs 59:17

of righteousness, ¹⁵and having ^strapped on your feet the preparation of the gospel of peace; ¹⁶in addition to all, taking up the ^shield of faith with which you will be able to extinguish all the flaming arrows of the evil *one.* ¹⁷And take ^the helmet of salvation and the ᴮsword of the Spirit, which is the word of God.

¹⁸With every ^prayer and request, pray at all times in the Spirit, and with this in view, be alert with all perseverance and *every* request for all the saints, ¹⁹and ^*pray* in my behalf, that speech may be given to me in the opening of my mouth, to make known with boldness the mystery of the gospel, ²⁰for which I am an ^ambassador in chains; that ¹in *proclaiming* it I may speak boldly, as I ought to speak.

²¹^Now, so that you also may know about my circumstances *as to* what I am doing, Tychicus, the beloved brother and faithful servant in the Lord, will make everything known to you. ²²I have sent him to you for this very purpose, so that you may know about us, and that he may ^comfort your hearts.

²³Peace be to the brothers *and sisters,* and ^love with faith, from God the Father and the Lord Jesus Christ. ²⁴Grace be with all those who love our Lord Jesus Christ with incorruptible *love.*

6:15^Is 52:7; Rom 10:15   6:16^1 Thess 5:8
6:17^Is 59:17   ᴮHeb 4:12   6:18^Phil 4:6
6:19^Col 4:3; 1 Thess 5:25   6:20^2 Cor 5:20
6:21^Eph 6:21, 22; *Col 4:7-9*   6:22^Col 2:2; 4:8
6:23^Gal 5:6; 1 Thess 5:8

6:20¹Two early mss *I may speak it boldly*

PHILIPPIANS

THANKSGIVING

1 Paul and Timothy, bond-servants of Christ Jesus,

To all the saints in Christ Jesus who are in Philippi, including the ^overseers and deacons; ²^Grace to you and peace from God our Father and the Lord Jesus Christ.

³^I thank my God in all my remembrance of you, ⁴always offering prayer with joy in ^my every prayer for you all, ⁵in view of your participation in the ^gospel from the first day until now. ⁶ *For I am* confident of this very thing, that He who began a good work among you will complete it by ^the day of Christ Jesus. ⁷For it is only right for me to feel this way about you all, because I ^have you in my heart, since both in my ᴮimprisonment and in the defense and confirmation of the gospel, you all are partakers of grace with me. ⁸For ^God is my witness, how I long for you all with the affection of Christ Jesus. ⁹And this I pray, that ^your love may overflow still more and more in ᴮreal knowledge and all discernment, ¹⁰so that you may ^discover the things that are excellent, that you may be sincere and blameless for ᴮthe day of Christ; ¹¹having been filled with the ^fruit of righteousness which *comes* through Jesus Christ, for the glory and praise of God.

THE GOSPEL IS PREACHED

¹²Now I want you to know, brothers *and sisters,* that my circumstances ^have turned out for the greater progress of the gospel, ¹³so that my ^imprisonment in *the cause of* Christ has become well known throughout the ¹praetorian guard and to everyone else, ¹⁴and that most of the brothers *and sisters,* trusting in the Lord because of my imprisonment, have ^far more courage to speak the word of God without fear. ¹⁵^Some, to be sure, are preaching Christ even from envy and strife, but some also from goodwill; ¹⁶the latter *do it* out of love, knowing that I am appointed for the defense of the ^gospel; ¹⁷the former proclaim Christ ^out of selfish ambition rather than from pure motives, thinking that they are causing me distress in my imprisonment. ¹⁸What then? Only that in every way, whether in pretense or in truth, Christ is proclaimed, and in this I rejoice.

But *not only that,* I also will rejoice, ¹⁹for I know that this will turn out for my deliverance ^through your prayers and the provision of ᴮthe Spirit of Jesus Christ, ²⁰according to my eager expectation and hope, that I will not be put to shame in anything, but *that* with all boldness, Christ will even now, as always, be ^exalted in my body, ᴮwhether by life or by death.

1:1^Acts 20:28; 1 Tim 3:1f   1:2^Rom 1:7   1:3^Rom 1:8
1:4^Rom 1:9   1:5^Phil 1:7; 2:22   1:6^1 Cor 1:8;
Phil 1:10   1:7^2 Cor 7:3   ᴮActs 21:33   1:8^Rom 1:9
1:9^1 Thess 3:12   ᴮCol 1:9   1:10^Rom 2:18
ᴮ1 Cor 1:8   1:11^James 3:18   1:12^Luke 21:13
1:13^Phil 1:7; 2 Tim 2:9   1:14^Acts 4:31; Phil 1:20
1:15^2 Cor 11:13   1:16^Phil 1:5, 7, 12, 27; 2:22
1:17^Rom 2:8; Phil 2:3   1:19^2 Cor 1:11   ᴮActs 16:7
1:20^1 Cor 6:20   ᴮRom 14:8

1:13 ¹Or *governor's palace*

TO LIVE IS CHRIST

²¹For to me, ^to live is Christ, and to die is gain. ²²But if *I am* to live *on* in the flesh, this *will mean* ^fruitful labor for me; and I do not know which to choose. ²³But I am hard-pressed from both *directions,* having the ^desire to depart and be with Christ, for *that* is very much better; ²⁴yet to remain on in the flesh is more necessary for your sakes. ²⁵^Convinced of this, I know that I will remain and continue with you all for your progress and joy in the faith, ²⁶so that your ^pride in Christ Jesus may be abundant because of me by my coming to you again.

²⁷Only conduct yourselves in a manner ^worthy of the gospel of Christ, so that whether I come and see you or remain absent, I will hear about you that you are standing firm in one spirit, with one mind striving together for the faith of the gospel; ²⁸and in no way alarmed by *your* opponents—which is a ^sign of destruction for them, but of salvation for you, and this *too,* from God. ²⁹For to you ^it has been granted for Christ's sake, not only to believe in Him, but also to suffer on His behalf, ³⁰experiencing the same ^conflict which you saw in me, and now hear *to be* in me.

BE LIKE CHRIST

2 Therefore if there is any encouragement in Christ, if any consolation of love, if any ^fellowship of the Spirit, if any affection and compassion, ²^make my joy complete by being of the same mind, maintaining the same love, united in spirit, intent on one purpose. ³Do nothing from selfishness or empty conceit, but with humility ^consider one another as more important than

yourselves; ⁴^do not *merely* look out for your own personal *interests,* but also for the *interests* of others. ⁵^Have this attitude in yourselves which was also in Christ Jesus, ⁶who, as He *already* existed in the form of God, ^did not consider equality with God something to be grasped, ⁷but ¹,^emptied Himself *by* taking the form of a bond-servant *and* ^being born in the likeness of men. ⁸And being found in appearance as a man, He humbled Himself by becoming ^obedient to the point of death: death on a cross. ⁹For this reason also God ^highly exalted Him, and bestowed on Him ^the name which is above every name, ¹⁰so that at the name of Jesus ^EVERY KNEE WILL BOW, of those who are in heaven and on earth and under the earth, ¹¹and *that* every tongue will confess that Jesus Christ is ^Lord, to the glory of God the Father.

¹²So then, my beloved, just as you have always obeyed, not as in my presence only, but now much more in my absence, work out your own ^salvation with ^fear and trembling; ¹³for it is ^God who is at work in you, both to desire and to work for *His* good pleasure.

¹⁴Do all things without ^complaining or arguments; ¹⁵so that you will prove yourselves to be ^blameless and innocent, children of God above reproach in the midst

---

1:21^Gal 2:20   1:22^Rom 1:13   1:23^2 Cor 5:8;
2 Tim 4:6   1:25^Phil 2:24   1:26^2 Cor 5:12; 7:4
1:27^Eph 4:1   1:28^2 Thess 1:5   1:29^Matt 5:11, 12
1:30^Col 1:29; 2:1   2:1^2 Cor 13:14   2:2^John 3:29
2:3^Rom 12:10; Eph 5:21   2:4^Rom 15:1f
2:5^Matt 11:29; Rom 15:3   2:6^John 5:18; 10:33
2:7^2 Cor 8:9   ^Heb 2:17   2:8^Matt 26:39; John 10:18
2:9^Matt 28:18   ^Eph 1:21   2:10^Is 45:23; Rom 14:11
2:11^John 13:13; Rom 10:9   2:12^Heb 5:9   ^2 Cor 7:15
2:13^Rom 12:3; 1 Cor 12:6   2:14^1 Cor 10:10; 1 Pet 4:9
2:15^Luke 1:6

2:7 ¹ I.e., set aside His divine rights

of a ᴮcrooked and perverse generation, among whom you appear as lights in the world, ¹⁶holding firmly the word of life, so that on the day of Christ I can take pride because I did not ᴬrun in vain nor ᴮlabor in vain. ¹⁷But even if I am being ᴬpoured out as a drink offering upon ᴮthe sacrifice and service of your faith, I rejoice and share my joy with you all. ¹⁸You too, *I urge you,* rejoice in the same way and share your joy with me.

TIMOTHY AND EPAPHRODITUS

¹⁹But I hope, in the Lord Jesus, to ᴬsend Timothy to you shortly, so that I also may be encouraged when I learn of your condition. ²⁰For I have no one *else* ᴬof kindred spirit who will genuinely be concerned for your welfare. ²¹For they all ᴬseek after their own *interests,* not those of Christ Jesus. ²²But you know ᴬof his proven character, that he served with me in the furtherance of the gospel like a child *serving* his father. ²³ᴬTherefore I hope to send him immediately, as soon as I see how things *go* with me; ²⁴and ᴬI trust in the Lord that I myself will also be coming shortly. ²⁵But I thought it necessary to send to you Epaphroditus, my brother and ᴬfellow worker and fellow soldier, who is also your messenger and minister to my need, ²⁶because he was longing ¹for you all and was distressed because you had heard that he was sick. ²⁷For indeed he was sick to the point of death, but God had mercy on him, and not only on him but also on me, so that I would not have sorrow upon sorrow. ²⁸Therefore I have sent him all the more eagerly, so that when you see him again you may rejoice

and I may be less concerned *about you.* ²⁹Receive him then in the Lord with all joy, and ᴬhold people like him in high regard, ³⁰because he came close to death for the work of Christ, risking his life to ᴬcompensate for your absence in your service to me.

THE GOAL OF LIFE

3 Finally, my brothers *and sisters,* ᴬrejoice in the Lord. To write the same things *again* is no trouble for me, and it is a safeguard for you.

²Beware of the ᴬdogs, beware of the ᴮevil workers, beware of the false circumcision; ³for ᴬwe are the *true* circumcision, who ᴮworship in the Spirit of God and take pride in Christ Jesus, and put no confidence in the flesh, ⁴although ᴬI myself *could boast as* having confidence even in the flesh. If anyone else thinks he is confident in the flesh, I *have* more *reason:* ⁵ᴬcircumcised the eighth day, of the ᴮnation of Israel, of the tribe of Benjamin, a ᴮHebrew of Hebrews; as to the Law, a Pharisee; ⁶as to zeal, ᴬa persecutor of the church; as to the righteousness which is in the Law, found blameless.

⁷But ᴬwhatever things were gain to me, these things I have counted as loss because of Christ. ⁸More than that, I count all things to be loss in view of the surpassing value of ᴬknowing Christ Jesus my

2:15 ᴮDeut 32:5   2:16 ᴬGal 2:2   ᴮIs 49:4
2:17 ᴬ2 Tim 4:6   ᴮNum 28:6, 7   2:19 ᴬPhil 2:23
2:20 ᴬ1 Cor 16:10; 2 Tim 3:10   2:21 ᴬ1 Cor 10:24; 13:5
2:22 ᴬRom 5:4; Acts 16:2   2:23 ᴬPhil 2:19
2:24 ᴬPhil 1:25   2:25 ᴬRom 16:3, 9, 21; Phil 4:3
2:29 ᴬ1 Cor 16:18   2:30 ᴬ1 Cor 16:17; Phil 4:10
3:1 ᴬPhil 2:18; 4:4   3:2 ᴬPs 22:16, 20   ᴮ2 Cor 11:13
3:3 ᴬRom 2:29   ᴮJohn 4:23f   3:4 ᴬ2 Cor 5:16; 11:18
3:5 ᴬLuke 1:59   ᴮRom 11:1   3:6 ᴬActs 8:3; 22:4, 5
3:7 ᴬLuke 14:33   3:8 ᴬJer 9:23f; John 17:3
───────────────────────────
2:26 ¹One early ms *to see you all*

Lord, for whom I have suffered the loss of all things, and count them *mere* rubbish, so that I may gain Christ, ⁹and may be found in Him, not having ^Aa righteousness of my own derived from *the* Law, but that which is through faith in Christ, ^Bthe righteousness which *comes* from God on the basis of faith, ¹⁰that I may know Him and ^Athe power of His resurrection and ^Bthe fellowship of His sufferings, being conformed to His death; ¹¹if somehow I may ^Aattain to the resurrection from the dead.

¹²Not that I have already ^Agrasped *it all* or have already become perfect, but I press on if I may also take hold of that for which I was even taken hold of by Christ Jesus. ¹³Brothers *and sisters,* I do not regard myself as having taken hold of *it yet;* but one thing I *do:* ^Aforgetting what *lies* behind and reaching forward to what *lies* ahead, ¹⁴I press on toward the goal for the prize of the ^Aupward call of God in Christ Jesus. ¹⁵Therefore, all who are mature, let's have this attitude; and if in anything you have a different attitude, ^AGod will reveal that to you as well; ¹⁶however, let's keep ^Aliving by that same *standard* to which we have attained.

¹⁷Brothers *and sisters,* ^Ajoin in following my example, and observe those who walk according to the ^Bpattern you have in us. ¹⁸For ^Amany walk, of whom I often told you, and now tell you even as I weep, *that they are* the enemies of ^Bthe cross of Christ, ¹⁹whose end is destruction, whose god is *their* ^Aappetite, and *whose* ^Bglory is in their shame, who have their minds on earthly things. ²⁰For ^Aour citizenship is in heaven, from which we also eagerly wait

for a Savior, the Lord Jesus Christ; ²¹who will ^Atransform the body of our lowly condition into conformity with His glorious body, by the exertion of the power that He has even to subject all things to Himself.

THINK OF EXCELLENCE

4 Therefore, my beloved brothers *and sisters,* whom I long *to see,* my joy and crown, ^Astand firm in the Lord in this way, my beloved.

²I urge Euodia and I urge Syntyche to ^Alive in harmony in the Lord. ³Indeed, true companion, I ask you also, help these women who have shared my struggle in *the cause of* the gospel, together with Clement as well as the rest of my fellow workers, whose ^Anames are in the book of life.

^{4A}Rejoice in the Lord always; again I will say, rejoice! ⁵Let your gentle *spirit* be known to all people. ^AThe Lord is near. ^{6A}Do not be anxious about anything, but in everything by ^Bprayer and pleading with thanksgiving let your requests be made known to God. ⁷And ^Athe peace of God, which surpasses all comprehension, will guard your hearts and minds in Christ Jesus.

⁸Finally, brothers *and sisters,* ^Awhatever is true, whatever is honorable, whatever is right, whatever is pure, whatever is lovely, whatever is commendable, if there is any excellence and if anything worthy

3:9 ^ARom 10:5   ^BRom 9:30   3:10 ^ARom 6:5
^BRom 8:17   3:11 ^A1 Cor 15:23   3:12 ^A1 Cor 9:24f;
1 Tim 6:12, 19   3:13 ^ALuke 9:62   3:14 ^ARom 8:28; 11:29
3:15 ^AJohn 6:45; Eph 1:17   3:16 ^AGal 6:16
3:17 ^A1 Cor 4:16   ^B1 Pet 5:3   3:18 ^A2 Cor 11:13
^BGal 6:14   3:19 ^ARom 16:18   ^BRom 6:21
3:20 ^AEph 2:19; Phil 1:27   3:21 ^A1 Cor 15:43-53
4:1 ^A1 Cor 16:13; Phil 1:27   4:2 ^APhil 2:2
4:3 ^ALuke 10:20   4:4 ^APhil 3:1   4:5 ^A1 Cor 16:22 mg;
Heb 10:37   4:6 ^AMatt 6:25   ^BEph 6:18   4:7 ^AIs 26:3;
John 14:27   4:8 ^ARom 14:18; 1 Pet 2:12

of praise, think about these things. ⁹As for the things you have learned and received and heard and seen ᴬin me, practice these things, and the God of peace will be with you.

GOD'S PROVISIONS

¹⁰But I rejoiced in the Lord greatly, that now at last ᴬyou have revived your concern for me; indeed, you were concerned *before,* but you lacked an opportunity *to act.* ¹¹Not that I speak from need, for I have learned to be ᴬcontent in whatever *circumstances* I am. ¹²I know how to get along with little, and I also know how to live in prosperity; in any and every *circumstance* I have learned the secret of being filled and going ᴬhungry, both of having abundance and suffering need. ¹³I can do all things through Him who ᴬstrengthens me. ¹⁴Nevertheless, you have done well to ᴬshare *with me* in my difficulty.

¹⁵You yourselves also know, Philippians, that at the first *preaching* of the gospel, after I left Macedonia, no church ᴬshared with me in the matter of giving and receiving except you alone; ¹⁶for even in ᴬThessalonica you sent *a gift* more than once for my needs. ¹⁷ᴬNot that I seek the gift *itself,* but I seek the profit which increases to your account. ¹⁸But I have received everything in full and have an abundance; I am amply supplied, having received from ᴬEpaphroditus what you have sent, a fragrant aroma, an acceptable sacrifice, pleasing to God. ¹⁹And ᴬmy God will supply all your needs according to His riches in glory in Christ Jesus. ²⁰Now to ᴬour God and Father ᴮ*be* the glory forever and ever. Amen.

²¹Greet every saint in Christ Jesus. ᴬThe brothers who are with me greet you. ²²ᴬAll the saints greet you, especially those of Caesar's household.

²³ᴬThe grace of the Lord Jesus Christ ᴮbe with your spirit.

4:9ᴬPhil 3:17   **4:10**ᴬ2 Cor 11:9; Phil 2:30
4:11ᴬ2 Cor 9:8; 1 Tim 6:6, 8   **4:12**ᴬ1 Cor 4:11
4:13ᴬ2 Cor 12:9; Eph 3:16   **4:14**ᴬHeb 10:33; Rev 1:9
4:15ᴬ2 Cor 11:9   **4:16**ᴬActs 17:1; 1 Thess 2:9
4:17ᴬ1 Cor 9:11f; 2 Cor 9:5   **4:18**ᴬPhil 2:25
4:19ᴬ2 Cor 9:8   **4:20**ᴬGal 1:4   ᴮRom 11:36
4:21ᴬGal 1:2   **4:22**ᴬ2 Cor 13:13   **4:23**ᴬRom 16:20
ᴮ2 Tim 4:22

COLOSSIANS

THANKFULNESS FOR SPIRITUAL ATTAINMENTS

1 Paul, an apostle of Christ Jesus ^by the will of God, and Timothy our brother,

² To the saints and faithful brothers *and sisters* in Christ *who are* at Colossae: ^Grace to you and peace from God our Father.

³ ^We give thanks to God, ᴮthe Father of our Lord Jesus Christ, praying always for you, ⁴^since we heard of your faith in Christ Jesus and the love which you have for all the saints; ⁵because of the hope ^reserved for you in heaven, of which you previously ᴮheard in the word of truth, the gospel ⁶which has come to you, just as in all the world also it is bearing ^fruit and increasing, even as *it has been doing* in you also since the day you ᴮheard *it* and understood the grace of God in truth; ⁷just as you learned *it* from ^Epaphras, our beloved fellow bond-servant, who is a faithful servant of Christ on our behalf, ⁸and he also informed us of your ^love in the Spirit.

⁹For this reason we also, since the day we heard *about it,* ^have not ceased praying for you and asking that you may be filled with the knowledge of His will in all spiritual ᴮwisdom and understanding, ¹⁰so that you will ^walk in a manner worthy of the Lord, to please *Him* in all respects, bearing fruit in every good work and increasing in the knowledge of God; ¹¹strengthened with all power, according to His glorious might, for the attaining of all perseverance and patience; joyously ¹²giving thanks to the Father, who has qualified us to share in ^the inheritance of the saints in ᴮlight.

THE INCOMPARABLE CHRIST

¹³For He rescued us from the ^domain of darkness, and transferred us to the kingdom of His beloved Son, ¹⁴^in whom we have redemption, the forgiveness of sins.

¹⁵He is the image of the invisible God, the ^firstborn of all creation: ¹⁶for by Him all things were created, *both* in the heavens and on earth, visible and invisible, whether thrones, or dominions, or rulers, or authorities—^all things have been created through Him and for Him. ¹⁷He ^is before all things, and in Him all things hold together. ¹⁸He is also the head of ^the body, the church; and He is the beginning, the firstborn from the dead, so that He Himself will come to have first place in everything. ¹⁹For it was ^the *Father's* good pleasure for all the fullness to dwell in Him, ²⁰and through Him to ^reconcile all things to Himself, whether things on earth or things in heaven, having made peace through ᴮthe blood of His cross.

1:1 ^1 Cor 1:1   **1:2** ^Rom 1:7   **1:3** ^Rom 1:8   ᴮRom 15:6
1:4 ^Eph 1:15; Philem 5   **1:5** ^2 Tim 4:8   ᴮEph 1:13
1:6 ^Rom 1:13   ᴮEph 4:21   **1:7** ^Col 4:12
1:8 ^Rom 15:30   **1:9** ^Eph 1:16   ᴮEph 1:17   **1:10** ^Eph 4:1
1:12 ^Acts 20:32   ᴮActs 26:18   **1:13** ^Eph 6:12
1:14 ^Rom 3:24   **1:15** ^Rom 8:29; Rev 3:14
1:16 ^John 1:3; Rom 11:36   **1:17** ^John 1:1; 8:58
1:18 ^Eph 1:23; Col 1:24   **1:19** ^Eph 1:5   **1:20** ^2 Cor 5:18
ᴮEph 2:13

²¹And although you were ^previously alienated and hostile in attitude, *engaged* in evil deeds, ²²yet He has now reconciled you in His ^body of flesh through death, in order to present you before Him ᴮholy and blameless and beyond reproach— ²³if indeed you continue in the faith firmly ^established and steadfast, and not shifting from the hope of the gospel that you have heard, which was proclaimed ᴮin all creation under heaven, and of which I, Paul, was made a minister.

²⁴Now I rejoice in my sufferings for your sake, and in my flesh ^I am supplementing what is lacking in Christ's afflictions in behalf of His body, which is the church. ²⁵I was made a minister of this *church* according to the ^commission from God granted to me for your benefit, so that I might fully carry out *the preaching of* the word of God, ²⁶*that is,* ^the mystery which had been hidden from the *past* ages and generations, but now has been revealed to His saints, ²⁷to whom ^God willed to make known what the wealth of the glory of this mystery among the Gentiles is, *the mystery* that is ᴮChrist in you, the hope of glory. ²⁸We proclaim Him, ^admonishing every person and teaching every person with all wisdom, so that we may present every person complete in Christ. ²⁹For this purpose I also ^labor, striving according to His power which works mightily within me.

YOU ARE BUILT UP IN CHRIST

2 For I want you to know how great a ^struggle I have in your behalf and for those who are at Laodicea, and for all those who have not personally seen my face, ²that their ^hearts may be encouraged, having been knit together in love, and *that they would attain* to all the wealth that comes from the full assurance of understanding, *resulting* in a true knowledge of God's mystery, *that is,* Christ Himself, ³in whom are hidden all ^the treasures of wisdom and knowledge. ⁴I say this so that no one will deceive you with ^persuasive arguments. ⁵For even though I am ^absent in body, I am nevertheless with you in spirit, rejoicing to see your orderly manner and the stability of your faith in Christ.

⁶Therefore, as you have received Christ Jesus the Lord, *so* ^walk in Him, ⁷having been firmly ^rooted and *now* being built up in Him and established ¹in your faith, just as you were instructed, *and* overflowing with gratitude.

⁸See to it that there is no one who takes you captive through ^philosophy and empty deception in accordance with human tradition, in accordance with the elementary principles of the world, rather than in accordance with Christ. ⁹For in Him all the ^fullness of Deity dwells in bodily form, ¹⁰and in Him you have been ^made complete, and He is the head over every ᴮruler and authority; ¹¹and in Him ^you were also circumcised with a circumcision performed without hands, in the removal of the body of the

1:21^Rom 5:10; Eph 2:3, 12   1:22^Rom 7:4   ᴮEph 1:4
1:23^Eph 3:17   ᴮActs 2:5   1:24^2 Tim 1:8; 2:10
1:25^Eph 3:2   1:26^Rom 16:25f; Eph 3:3f
1:27^Matt 13:11   ᴮRom 8:10   1:28^Col 3:16
1:29^1 Cor 15:10   2:1^Col 1:29; 4:12   2:2^Eph 6:22;
Col 4:8   2:3^Is 11:2; Rom 11:33   2:4^Rom 16:18
2:5^1 Cor 5:3   2:6^Col 1:10   2:7^Eph 3:17
2:8^Eph 5:6; Col 2:23   2:9^2 Cor 5:19; Col 1:19
2:10^Eph 3:19   ᴮ1 Cor 15:24   2:11^Rom 2:29
2:7¹Or *by*

flesh by the circumcision of Christ, [12]having been ^buried with Him in baptism, in which you were also ^Braised with Him through faith in the working of God, who raised Him from the dead. [13]And when you were ^dead in your wrongdoings and the uncircumcision of your flesh, He made you alive together with Him, having forgiven us all our wrongdoings, [14]having canceled ^the certificate of debt consisting of decrees against us, which was hostile to us; and He has taken it out of the way, having nailed it to the cross. [15]When He had ^disarmed the rulers and authorities, He ^made a public display *of them,* having triumphed over them through ¹Him.

[16]Therefore, no one is to ^act as your judge in regard to ^Bfood and drink, or in respect to a festival or a new moon, or a Sabbath day— [17]things which are *only* a ^shadow of what is to come; but the substance belongs to Christ. [18]*Take care that* no one keeps ^defrauding you of your prize by delighting in humility and the worship of the angels, taking his stand on *visions* he has seen, inflated without cause by his fleshly mind, [19]and not holding firmly to the head, from whom ^the entire body, being supplied and held together by the joints and ligaments, grows with a growth which is from God.

[20]^If you have died with Christ to the elementary principles of the world, why, as if you were living in the world, do you submit yourself to decrees, *such as,* [21]"Do not handle, do not taste, do not touch!" [22](which all *refer* ^to things destined to perish with use)—in accordance with the ^Bcommandments and teachings of man? [23]These are matters which do have the appearance of wisdom in ^self-made religion and humility and severe treatment of the body, *but are* of no value against fleshly indulgence.

PUT ON THE NEW SELF

3 Therefore, if you have been ^raised with Christ, keep seeking the things *that are* above, where Christ is, ^Bseated at the right hand of God. [2]^Set your minds on the things *that are* above, not on the things that are on earth. [3]For you have ^died, and your life is hidden with Christ in God. [4]When Christ, who is our life, is revealed, ^then you also will be revealed with Him in glory.

[5]^Therefore, treat the parts of your earthly body as dead *to* sexual immorality, impurity, passion, evil desire, and greed, which amounts to idolatry. [6]*For it is* because of these things *that*^the wrath of God is coming ¹upon the ²sons of disobedience, [7]and ^in them you also once walked, when you were living in them. [8]But now you also, ^rid yourselves of all of them: ^Banger, wrath, malice, slander, *and* obscene speech from your mouth. [9]^Do not lie to one another, since you stripped off the old self with its *evil* practices, [10]and have ^put on the new *self,* which is being renewed to a true knowledge according to

2:12^Rom 6:4f   ^BEph 2:6   2:13^Eph 2:1
2:14^Eph 2:15; Col 2:20   2:15^Eph 4:8   2:16^Rom 14:3
^BMark 7:19   2:17^Heb 8:5; 10:1   2:18^1 Cor 9:24;
Phil 3:14   2:19^Eph 1:23; 4:16   2:20^Rom 6:2
2:22^1 Cor 6:13   ^BIs 29:13   2:23^Col 2:12   3:1^Col 2:12
^BPs 110:1   3:2^Matt 16:23; Phil 3:19, 20   3:3^Rom 6:2;
2 Cor 5:14   3:4^1 Cor 1:7; Phil 3:21   3:5^Rom 8:13
3:6^Rom 1:18; Eph 5:6   3:7^Eph 2:2   3:8^Eph 4:22
^BEph 4:31   3:9^Eph 4:25   3:10^Eph 4:24

the image of the One who created it— [11]*a renewal* in which ^there is no *distinction between* Greek and Jew, circumcised and uncircumcised, [1]barbarian, [2]Scythian, slave, *and* free, but Christ is all, and in all. [12]So, as those who have been chosen of God, holy and beloved, put on a ^heart of compassion, kindness, [B]humility, gentleness, *and* patience; [13]bearing with one another, and ^forgiving each other, whoever has a complaint against anyone; ^just as the Lord forgave you, so *must* you *do* also. [14]In addition to all these things *put on* love, which is the perfect bond of ^unity. [15]Let ^the peace of Christ, to which you were indeed called in [B]one body, rule in your hearts; and be thankful. [16]Let ^the word of [1]Christ richly dwell within you, with all wisdom [B]teaching and admonishing one another with psalms, hymns, *and* spiritual songs, singing with thankfulness in your hearts to God. [17]^Whatever you do in word or deed, *do* everything in the name of the Lord Jesus, giving thanks through Him to God the Father.

FAMILY RELATIONS

[18]^Wives, be subject to your husbands, as is fitting in the Lord. [19]^Husbands, love your wives and do not become bitter against them. [20]^Children, obey your parents in everything, for this is pleasing to the Lord. [21]^Fathers, do not antagonize your children, so that they will not become discouraged.

[22]^Slaves, obey those who are your human masters in everything, not with eye-service, as people-pleasers, but with sincerity of heart, fearing the Lord. [23]Whatever you do, do your work heartily,

^as for the Lord and not for people, [24]^knowing that *it is* from the Lord *that* you will receive the reward of the inheritance. *It is* the Lord Christ *whom* you serve. [25]For the one who does wrong will receive the consequences of the wrong which he has done, and ^that without partiality.

4 Masters, grant your slaves justice and fairness, ^knowing that you also have a Master in heaven.

[2]^Devote yourselves to prayer, keeping alert in it with *an attitude of* thanksgiving; [3]praying at the same time for us as well, that God will open up to us a ^door for the word, so that we may proclaim [B]the mystery of Christ, for which I have also been imprisoned; [4]that I may make it clear ^in the way that I ought to proclaim *it*.

[5]^Conduct yourselves with wisdom toward outsiders, [B]making the most of the opportunity. [6]^Your speech *must* always *be* with grace, *as though* seasoned with salt, so that you will know how you should respond to each person.

[7]^As to all my affairs, Tychicus, *our* beloved brother and faithful servant and fellow bond-servant in the Lord, will bring you information. [8]^*For* I have sent him to you for this very purpose, that you may know about our circumstances

3:11 ^Rom 10:12; 1 Cor 12:13   3:12 ^Gal 5:22f   [B] Eph 4:2
3:13 ^Eph 4:32   3:14 ^John 17:23   3:15 ^John 14:27
[B] Eph 2:16   3:16 ^Rom 10:17   [B] Col 1:28
3:17 ^1 Cor 10:31   3:18 ^Col 3:18–4:1: *Eph 5:22-6:9*
3:19 ^Eph 5:25; 1 Pet 3:7   3:20 ^Eph 6:1   3:21 ^Eph 6:4
3:22 ^Eph 6:5   3:23 ^Eph 6:7   3:24 ^Eph 6:8
3:25 ^Deut 10:17; Acts 10:34   4:1 ^Eph 6:9
4:2 ^Acts 1:14; Eph 6:18   4:3 ^Acts 14:27   [B] Eph 3:3, 4
4:4 ^Eph 6:20   4:5 ^Eph 5:15   [B] Eph 5:16
4:6 ^Eph 4:29   4:7 ^Col 4:7-9: *Eph 6:21, 22*
4:8 ^Eph 6:22

3:11 [1] I.e., uncultured   [2] I.e., a member of an ancient people near the Black Sea, often considered unrefined   3:16 [1] One early ms *the Lord*

and that he may ᴮencourage your hearts; ⁹and with him is ᴬOnesimus, *our* faithful and beloved brother, who is one of your *own*. They will inform you about the whole situation here.

¹⁰Aristarchus, my fellow prisoner, sends you his greetings; and *also* ᴬBarnabas' cousin Mark (about whom you received instructions; if he comes to you, welcome him); ¹¹and *also* Jesus who is called Justus; these are the only fellow workers for the kingdom of God ᴬwho are from the circumcision, and they have proved to be an encouragement to me. ¹²ᴬEpaphras, who is one of your *own*, a bond-servant of Christ Jesus, sends you his greetings, always striving earnestly for you in his prayers, that you may stand mature and fully assured in all the will of God. ¹³For I testify for him that he has a deep concern for you and for those who are in ᴬLaodicea and Hierapolis. ¹⁴ᴬLuke, the beloved physician, sends you his greetings, and Demas *does also*. ¹⁵Greet the brothers *and sisters* who are in Laodicea and also 'Nympha and ᴬthe church that is in her house. ¹⁶ᴬWhen this letter is read among you, have it also read in the church of the Laodiceans; and you, for your part, ᴬread my letter *that is coming* from Laodicea. ¹⁷Tell ᴬArchippus, "See to the ᴮministry which you have received in the Lord, so that you may fulfill it."

¹⁸I, Paul, ᴬwrite this greeting with my own hand. Remember my ᴮimprisonment. Grace be with you.

4:8 ᴮCol 2:2   4:9 ᴬPhilem 10
4:10 ᴬActs 4:36; 12:12, 25   4:11 ᴬActs 11:2
4:12 ᴬCol 1:7; Philem 23   4:13 ᴬCol 2:1; 4:15f
4:14 ᴬ2 Tim 4:11; Philem 24   4:15 ᴬRom 16:5
4:16 ᴬ1 Thess 5:27; 2 Thess 3:14   4:17 ᴬPhilem 2
ᴮ2 Tim 4:5   4:18 ᴬ1 Cor 16:21   ᴮPhil 1:7

4:15 ¹Or *Nymphas* (masc)

1 THESSALONIANS

GIVING THANKS FOR THESE BELIEVERS

1 ^A^Paul, ^B^Silvanus, and Timothy,
To the church of the Thessalonians in God the Father and the Lord Jesus Christ: Grace to you and peace.

2 ^A^We always give thanks to God for all of you, making mention *of you* in our prayers; 3 constantly keeping in mind your work of faith and labor of ^A^love and ^B^perseverance of hope in our Lord Jesus Christ in the presence of our God and Father, 4 knowing, brothers *and sisters,* beloved by God, ^A^*His* choice of you; 5 for our gospel did not come to you in word only, but also ^A^in power and in the Holy Spirit and with full conviction; just as you know what kind of men we proved to be among you for your sakes. 6 You also became ^A^imitators of us and of the Lord, having received the word during great affliction with the ^B^joy of the Holy Spirit, 7 so that you became an example to all the believers in ^A^Macedonia and Achaia. 8 For ^A^the word of the Lord has sounded forth from you, not only in Macedonia and Achaia, but in every place *the news of* your faith toward God has gone out, so that we have no need to say anything. 9 For they themselves report about us as to the kind of reception we had with you, and how you ^A^turned to God from idols to serve a living and true God, 10 and to ^A^wait for His Son from heaven, whom He raised from the dead, *that is,* Jesus who ^B^rescues us from the wrath to come.

PAUL'S MINISTRY

2 For you yourselves know, brothers *and sisters,* that our reception among you ^A^was not in vain, 2 but after we had already suffered and been ^A^treated abusively in Philippi, as you know, we had the boldness in our God ^B^to speak to you the gospel of God amid much opposition. 3 For our exhortation does not *come* from error or ^A^impurity or by way of ^B^deceit; 4 but just as we have been approved by God to be ^A^entrusted with the gospel, so we speak, not intending to please people, but *to please* God, who examines our hearts. 5 For we never came with flattering speech, as you know, nor with ^A^a pretext for greed—God is *our* witness— 6 nor did we ^A^seek honor from people, either from you or from others, though we could have asserted our authority as apostles of Christ. 7 But we proved to be ^1,A^gentle among you. As a nursing *mother* tenderly cares for her own children, 8 in the same way we had a fond affection for you and were delighted to ^A^share with you not only the gospel of God, but also our own lives, because you had become very dear to us.

1:1 ^A^2 Thess 1:1   ^B^2 Cor 1:19   1:2 ^A^Rom 1:8;
2 Thess 1:3   1:3 ^A^1 Cor 13:13   ^B^Rom 8:25
1:4 ^A^2 Pet 1:10   1:5 ^A^Rom 15:19   1:6 ^A^1 Cor 4:16
^B^Acts 13:52   1:7 ^A^Rom 15:26   1:8 ^A^Col 3:16;
2 Thess 3:1   1:9 ^A^Acts 14:15   1:10 ^A^1 Cor 1:7
^B^Rom 5:9   2:1 ^A^2 Thess 1:10   2:2 ^A^Acts 14:5
^B^Acts 17:1-9   2:3 ^A^1 Thess 4:7   ^B^2 Cor 4:2
2:4 ^A^Gal 2:7   2:5 ^A^Acts 20:33; 2 Pet 2:3
2:6 ^A^John 5:41, 44; 2 Cor 4:5   2:7 ^A^2 Tim 2:24
2:8 ^A^2 Cor 12:15; 1 John 3:16

2:7 ^1^Three early mss *infants*

⁹For you recall, brothers *and sisters,* our ᴬlabor and hardship: *it was by* working night and day so as not to be a ᴮburden to any of you, *that* we proclaimed to you the gospel of God. ¹⁰You are witnesses, and *so is* God, *of* ᴬhow devoutly and rightly and blamelessly we behaved toward you believers; ¹¹just as you know how *we were* ᴬexhorting and encouraging and imploring each one of you as ᴮa father *would* his own children, ¹²so that you would ᴬwalk in a manner worthy of the God who calls you into His own kingdom and ᴮglory.

¹³For this reason we also constantly thank God that when you received the ᴬword of God which you heard from us, you accepted *it* ᴮnot *as* the word of *mere* men, but as what it really is, the word of God, which also is at work in you who believe. ¹⁴For you, brothers *and sisters,* became imitators of the churches of God in Christ Jesus that are ᴬin Judea, for ᴮyou also endured the same sufferings at the hands of your own countrymen, even as they *did* from the Jews, ¹⁵ᴬwho both killed the Lord Jesus and the prophets, and drove us out. They are not pleasing to God, but hostile to all people, ¹⁶hindering us from speaking to the Gentiles so that they may be saved; with the result that they always ᴬreach the limit of their sins. But wrath has come upon them fully.

¹⁷But we, brothers *and sisters,* having been orphaned from you *by absence* for a short while—ᴬin person, not in spirit—were all the more eager with great desire to see your face. ¹⁸For we wanted to come to you—I, Paul, more than once—and Satan ᴬhindered us. ¹⁹For who *is* our hope, or ᴬjoy or crown of pride, in

the presence of our Lord Jesus at His ᴮcoming? Or *is it* not indeed you? ²⁰For you are ᴬour glory and joy.

ENCOURAGEMENT OF TIMOTHY'S VISIT

3 Therefore, when we could no longer endure *it,* we thought it best to be left behind, alone at ᴬAthens, ²and we sent ᴬTimothy, our brother and God's fellow worker in the gospel of Christ, to strengthen and encourage you for the benefit of your faith, ³so that no one would be disturbed by these afflictions. For you yourselves know that ᴬwe have been destined for this. ⁴For even when we were with you, we *kept* telling you in advance that we were going to suffer affliction; ᴬand so it happened, as you know. ⁵For this reason, when I could no longer endure *it,* I also sent to find out about your faith, for fear that ᴬthe tempter might have tempted you, and ᴮour labor would be for nothing.

⁶But now that ᴬTimothy has come to us from you, and has brought us good news of ᴮyour faith and love, and that you always think kindly of us, longing to see us just as we also *long to see* you, ⁷for this reason, brothers *and sisters,* in all our distress and affliction we were comforted about you through your faith; ⁸for now we *really* live, if you ᴬstand firm in the Lord. ⁹For ᴬwhat

2:9ᴬ2 Thess 3:8   ᴮ2 Cor 11:9   2:10ᴬ2 Cor 1:12;
1 Thess 1:5   2:11ᴬ1 Thess 5:14   ᴮ1 Cor 4:14
2:12ᴬEph 4:1   ᴮ2 Cor 4:6   2:13ᴬRom 10:17
ᴮMatt 10:20   2:14ᴬGal 1:22   ᴮActs 17:5
2:15ᴬLuke 24:20; Acts 2:23   2:16ᴬGen 15:16;
Dan 8:23   2:17ᴬ1 Cor 5:3   2:18ᴬRom 1:13; 15:22
2:19ᴬPhil 4:1   ᴮMatt 16:27   2:20ᴬ2 Cor 1:14
3:1ᴬActs 17:15f   3:2ᴬ2 Cor 1:1; Col 1:1   3:3ᴬActs 9:16;
14:22   3:4ᴬ1 Thess 2:14   3:5ᴬMatt 4:3   ᴮ2 Cor 6:1
3:6ᴬActs 18:5   ᴮ1 Thess 1:3   3:8ᴬ1 Cor 16:13
3:9ᴬ1 Thess 1:2

thanks can we give to God for you in return for all the joy with which we rejoice because of you before our God, [10] as we ^keep praying most earnestly night and day that we may see your faces, and may ^Bcomplete what is lacking in your faith?

[11] Now may our God and Father ^Himself, and our Lord Jesus, direct our way to you; [12] and may the Lord cause you to increase and ^overflow in love for one another, and for all people, just as we also *do* for you; [13] so that He may ^establish your hearts blameless in holiness before our God and Father at the ^Bcoming of our Lord Jesus with all His saints.

SANCTIFICATION AND LOVE

4 Finally then, brothers *and sisters,* we request and urge you in the Lord Jesus, that as you received *instruction* from us as to how you ought to ^walk and ^Bplease God (just as you actually do walk), that you excel *even* more. [2] For you know what instructions we gave you by *the authority of* the Lord Jesus. [3] For this is the will of God, your sanctification; *that is,* that you ^abstain from sexual immorality; [4] that ^each of you know how to possess his own ^1vessel in sanctification and honor, [5] not in ^lustful passion, like the Gentiles who ^Bdo not know God; [6] *and* that no one violate the rights and ^take advantage of his brother *or sister* in the matter, because ^Bthe Lord is *the* avenger in all these things, just as we also told you previously and solemnly warned *you.* [7] For God has not called us for ^impurity, but in sanctification. [8] Therefore, the one who rejects *this* is not rejecting man, but the God who ^gives His Holy Spirit to you.

[9] Now as to the ^love of the brothers *and* sisters, you have no need for *anyone* to write to you, for you yourselves are ^Btaught by God to love one another; [10] for indeed ^you practice it toward all the brothers *and sisters* who are in all Macedonia. But we urge you, brothers *and sisters,* to excel *even* more, [11] and to make it your ambition to lead a quiet life and attend to your own *business* and ^work with your hands, just as we instructed you, [12] so that you will ^behave properly toward outsiders and ^Bnot be in any need.

THOSE WHO DIED IN CHRIST

[13] But we do not want you to be uninformed, brothers *and sisters,* about those who ^1are asleep, so that you will not grieve as indeed the rest *of mankind do,* who have ^no hope. [14] For if we believe that Jesus died and rose *from the dead,* ^so also God will bring with Him those who have fallen asleep ^1through Jesus. [15] For we say this to you by the word of the Lord, that ^we who are alive and remain until ^Bthe coming of the Lord will not precede those who have fallen asleep. [16] For the Lord Himself will descend from heaven with a shout, with the voice of *the* archangel and with the ^trumpet of God, and the dead in Christ will rise first. [17] Then ^we who are alive, who remain, will be

3:10^2 Tim 1:3   ^B 2 Cor 13:9   3:11^1 Thess 5:23;
Rev 21:3   3:12^Phil 1:9; 1 Thess 4:1, 10   3:13^1 Cor 1:8
^B1 Thess 2:19   4:1^Eph 4:1   ^B 2 Cor 5:9   4:3^1 Cor 6:18
4:4^1 Cor 7:2, 9   4:5^Rom 1:26   ^BGal 4:8
4:6^1 Cor 6:8   ^BRom 12:19   4:7^1 Thess 2:3
4:8^Rom 5:5; 2 Cor 1:22   4:9^John 13:34   ^B1 John 2:27
4:10^1 Thess 1:7   4:11^Acts 18:3; Eph 4:28
4:12^Rom 13:13   ^BEph 4:28   4:13^Eph 2:12
4:14^Rom 14:9; 2 Cor 4:14   4:15^1 Cor 15:52
^B1 Thess 2:19   4:16^Matt 24:31   4:17^1 Cor 15:52;
1 Thess 5:10

4:4^1 I.e., body; or wife   4:13^1 I.e., have died
4:14^1 I.e., as believers

caught up together with them in the clouds to meet the Lord in the air, and so we will always be with the Lord. [18] Therefore, comfort one another with these words.

THE DAY OF THE LORD

5 Now as to the ^periods and times, brothers *and sisters,* you have no need *of anything* to be written to you. [2] For you yourselves know full well that ^the day of the Lord is coming just like a thief in the night. [3] While they are saying, "Peace and safety!" then ^sudden destruction will come upon them like [B]labor pains upon a pregnant woman, and they will not escape. [4] But you, brothers *and sisters,* are not in ^darkness, so that the day would overtake you like a thief; [5] for you are all ^sons of light and sons of day. We are not of night nor of darkness; [6] so then, let's not ^sleep as [B]others do, but let's be alert and 'sober. [7] For those who sleep, sleep at night, and those who are drunk, ^get drunk at night. [8] But since we are of *the* day, let's be 'sober, having put on the ^breastplate of faith and love, and as a [B]helmet, the hope of salvation. [9] For God has not destined us for ^wrath, but for [B]obtaining salvation through our Lord Jesus Christ, [10] ^who died for us, so that whether we are awake or asleep, we will live together with Him. [11] Therefore, encourage one another and ^build one another up, just as you also are doing.

CHRISTIAN CONDUCT

[12] But we ask you, brothers *and sisters,* to recognize those ^who diligently labor among you and [B]are in leadership over you in the Lord, and give you instruction, [13] and

that you regard them very highly in love because of their work. ^Live in peace with one another. [14] We urge you, brothers *and sisters,* admonish ^the unruly, encourage [B]the fainthearted, help the weak, be patient with everyone. [15] See that ^no one repays another with evil for evil, but always seek what is good for one another and for all people. [16] Rejoice always, [17]^pray without ceasing, [18] in everything ^give thanks; for this is the will of God for you in Christ Jesus. [19]^Do not quench the Spirit, [20] do not utterly reject ',^prophecies, [21] but ^examine everything; hold firmly to that which is good, [22] abstain from every form of evil.

[23] Now may the God of peace Himself sanctify you entirely; and may your ^spirit and soul and body be kept complete, [B]without blame at the coming of our Lord Jesus Christ. [24]^Faithful is He who calls you, and He also will do it.

[25] Brothers *and sisters,* ^pray for us'.

[26]^Greet all the brothers *and sisters* with a holy kiss. [27] I put you under oath by the Lord to ^have this letter read to all the brothers *and sisters.*

[28]^*May* the grace of our Lord Jesus Christ *be* with you.

5:1^Acts 1:7   5:2^1 Cor 1:8   5:3^2 Thess 1:9
[B]John 16:21   5:4^Acts 26:18; 1 John 2:8
5:5^Luke 16:8   5:6^Rom 13:11   [B]Eph 2:3
5:7^Acts 2:15; 2 Pet 2:13   5:8^Is 59:17   [B]Eph 6:17
5:9^1 Thess 1:10   [B]2 Thess 2:13f   5:10^Rom 14:9
5:11^Eph 4:29   5:12^Rom 16:6, 12   [B]Heb 13:17
5:13^Mark 9:50   5:14^2 Thess 3:6, 7, 11   [B]Is 35:4
5:15^Rom 12:17; 1 Pet 3:9   5:16^Phil 4:4
5:17^Eph 6:18   5:18^Eph 5:20   5:19^Eph 4:30
5:20^Acts 13:1; 1 Cor 14:31   5:21^1 Cor 14:29;
1 John 4:1   5:23^Luke 1:46f   [B]2 Pet 3:14
5:24^1 Cor 1:9; 2 Thess 3:3   5:25^Eph 6:19;
2 Thess 3:1   5:26^Rom 16:16   5:27^Col 4:16
5:28^Rom 16:20; 2 Thess 3:18

5:6 [1] Or *self-controlled*   5:8 [1] Or *self-controlled*
5:20 [1] Or *prophetic gifts*   5:25 [1] Two early mss add *also*

2 THESSALONIANS

GIVING THANKS FOR FAITH AND PERSEVERANCE

1 Paul, Silvanus, and Timothy,
To the ^church of the Thessalonians in God our Father and the Lord Jesus Christ: ²^Grace to you and peace from God our Father and the Lord Jesus Christ.

³We ought always ^to give thanks to God for you, brothers *and sisters,* as is *only* fitting, because your faith is increasing abundantly, and the ᴮlove of each and every one of you toward one another grows *ever* greater. ⁴As a result, we ourselves ^speak proudly of you among ᴮthe churches of God for your perseverance and faith in the midst of all your persecutions and afflictions which you endure. ⁵*This is* a plain indication of God's righteous judgment so that you will be ^considered worthy of the kingdom of God, for which you indeed are suffering. ⁶For after all ^it is *only* right for God to repay with affliction those who afflict you, ⁷and *to give* relief to you who are afflicted, *along* with us, ^when the Lord Jesus will be revealed from heaven with His mighty angels ⁸in flaming fire, dealing out retribution to those who ^do not know God, and to those who ᴮdo not obey the gospel of our Lord Jesus. ⁹These people will pay the penalty of ^eternal destruction, away from the presence of the Lord and from the glory of His power, ¹⁰when He comes to be ^glorified among His saints on that ᴮday, and to be marveled at among all who have believed—because our testimony to you was believed. ¹¹To this end also we ^pray for you always, that our God will consider you worthy of your calling, and fulfill every desire for goodness and the work of faith with power, ¹²so that the ^name of our Lord Jesus will be glorified in you, and you in Him, in accordance with the grace of our God and *the* Lord Jesus Christ.

MAN OF LAWLESSNESS

2 Now we ask you, brothers *and sisters,* regarding the ^coming of our Lord Jesus Christ and our ᴮgathering together to Him, ²that you not be quickly shaken from your composure or be disturbed either by a ^spirit, or a ᴮmessage, or a letter as if from us, to the effect that the day of the Lord has come. ³No one is to deceive you in any way! For *it will not come* unless the ¹apostasy comes first, and the ^man of lawlessness is revealed, the ᴮson of destruction, ⁴who opposes and exalts himself above every so-called god or object of worship, so that he takes his seat in the temple of God, ^displaying himself as being God. ⁵Do you not remember that ^while I was still with you, I was telling you these things? ⁶And

1:1^Acts 17:1; 1 Thess 1:1 1:2^Rom 1:7 1:3^Rom 1:8
ᴮ1 Thess 3:12 1:4^2 Cor 7:4 ᴮ1 Thess 2:14
1:5^Luke 20:35; 2 Thess 1:11 1:6^Ex 23:22; Col 3:25
1:7^Luke 17:30 1:8^Gal 4:8 ᴮRom 2:8 1:9^Phil 3:19;
1 Thess 5:3 1:10^Is 49:3 ᴮIs 2:11ff 1:11^Col 1:9
1:12^Is 24:15; 66:5 2:1^1 Thess 2:19 ᴮMark 13:27
2:2^1 John 4:1 ᴮ2 Thess 2:15 2:3^Dan 7:25
ᴮJohn 17:12 2:4^Is 14:14; Ezek 28:2 2:5^1 Thess 3:4

2:3 ¹Or *falling away* from the faith

you know ^what restrains *him* now, so that he will be revealed in his time. [7]For ^the mystery of lawlessness is already at work; only [1]He who now restrains *will do so* until [1]He is removed. [8]Then that lawless one will be revealed, whom the Lord will eliminate ^with the breath of His mouth and bring to an end by the appearance of His coming; [9]*that is,* the one whose coming is in accord with the activity of Satan, with all power and false ^signs and wonders, [10]and with all the deception of wickedness for ^those who perish, because they did not accept the love of ^Bthe truth so as to be saved. [11]For this reason ^God will send upon them a deluding influence so that they will believe what is false, [12]in order that they all may be judged who ^did not believe the truth, but ^Btook pleasure in wickedness.

STAND FIRM

[13]But we should always give thanks to God for you, brothers *and sisters* beloved by the Lord, because ^God has chosen you [1]from the beginning for salvation ^Bthrough sanctification by the Spirit and faith in the truth. [14]It was for this He ^called you through our gospel, that you may obtain the glory of our Lord Jesus Christ. [15]So then, brothers *and sisters,* stand firm and ^hold on to the traditions which you were taught, whether by word *of mouth* or by letter from us.

[16]^Now may our Lord Jesus Christ Himself and God our Father, who has loved us and given us eternal comfort and good hope by grace, [17]^comfort and ^Bstrengthen your hearts in every good work and word.

REQUEST FOR PRAYER

3 Finally, brothers *and sisters,* ^pray for us that the word of the Lord will spread rapidly and be glorified, just as *it was* also with you; [2]and that we will be ^rescued from troublesome and evil people; for not all have the faith. [3]But ^the Lord is faithful, and He will strengthen and protect you from the evil one. [4]We have confidence in the Lord concerning you, that you ^are doing, and will do, what we command. [5]May the Lord ^direct your hearts to the love of God and to the perseverance of Christ.

[6]Now we command you, brothers *and sisters,* in the name of our Lord Jesus Christ, that you ^keep away from every brother *or sister* who leads a disorderly life and not *one* in accordance with the tradition which you received from us. [7]For you yourselves know how you ought to ^follow our example, because we did not act in an undisciplined way among you, [8]nor did we eat anyone's bread without paying for it, but with ^labor and hardship we *kept* working night and day so that we would not be a burden to any of you; [9]not because we do not have ^the right *to this,* but in order to offer ourselves as a role model for you, so that you would follow our example. [10]For even when we were with you, we used to give you

2:6^2 Thess 2:7   **2:7**^Rev 17:5, 7   **2:8**^Is 11:4
2:9^Matt 24:24; John 4:48   **2:10**^1 Cor 1:18
^B2 Thess 2:12, 13   **2:11**^1 Kin 22:22; Rom 1:28
2:12^Rom 2:8   ^BRom 1:32   **2:13**^Eph 1:4ff
^B1 Thess 4:7   **2:14**^1 Thess 2:12   **2:15**^1 Cor 11:2;
2 Thess 3:6   **2:16**^1 Thess 3:11   **2:17**^1 Thess 3:2
^B2 Thess 3:3   **3:1**^1 Thess 5:25   **3:2**^Rom 15:31
3:3^1 Cor 1:9; 1 Thess 5:24   **3:4**^1 Thess 4:10
3:5^1 Thess 3:11   **3:6**^Rom 16:17; 1 Cor 5:11
3:7^1 Thess 1:6; 2 Thess 3:9   **3:8**^1 Thess 2:9
3:9^1 Cor 9:4–18

2:7[1]Or *he*   **2:13**[1]One early ms *first fruits*

this order: ^if anyone is not willing to work, then he is not to eat, either. ^11^For we hear that some among you are leading an undisciplined life, doing no work at all, but acting like ^busybodies. ^12^Now we command and exhort such persons in the Lord Jesus Christ to ^work peacefully and eat their own bread. ^13^But as for you, brothers *and sisters,* ^do not grow weary of doing good.

^14^If anyone does not obey our instruction in this letter, take special note of that person *so as* ^not to associate with him, so that he will be ^B^put to shame. ^15^And *yet* do not regard *that person* as an enemy, but ^admonish *that one* as a brother *or sister.*

^16^Now may the Lord of peace Himself continually grant you peace in every circumstance. ^The Lord be with you all!

^17^I, Paul, write this greeting ^with my own hand, and this is a distinguishing mark in every letter; this is the way I write. ^18^^The grace of our Lord Jesus Christ be with you all.

3:10^1 Thess 4:11   3:11^1 Tim 5:13; 1 Pet 4:15
3:12^1 Thess 4:11   3:13^Gal 6:9   3:14^2 Thess 3:6
^B^Titus 2:8   3:15^1 Thess 5:14   3:16^Ruth 2:4
3:17^1 Cor 16:21   3:18^Rom 16:20; 1 Thess 5:28

1 TIMOTHY

CORRECTING FALSE TEACHING

1 Paul, an apostle of Christ Jesus ^according to the commandment of God our Savior, and of Christ Jesus, *who is* our hope, ² To Timothy, *my* true son in *the* faith: ^Grace, mercy, *and* peace from God the Father and Christ Jesus our Lord.

³ Just as I urged you upon my departure for Macedonia, to remain on at Ephesus so that you would instruct certain people not to ^teach strange doctrines, ⁴ nor to pay attention to ^myths and endless genealogies, which give rise to useless speculation rather than *advance* the plan of God, which is by faith, *so I urge you now.* ⁵ But the goal of our instruction is love ^from a pure heart, *from* a good conscience, and *from* a sincere faith. ⁶ Some people have strayed from these things and have turned aside to ^fruitless discussion, ⁷ ^wanting to be teachers of the Law, even though they do not understand either what they are saying or the matters about which they make confident assertions.

⁸ But we know that ^the Law is good, if one uses it lawfully, ⁹ realizing the fact that law is not made for a righteous person but for those who are lawless and ^rebellious, for the ᴮungodly and sinners, for the unholy and worldly, for those who kill their fathers or mothers, for murderers, ¹⁰ for the ^sexually immoral, homosexuals, slave traders, liars, perjurers, and whatever else is contrary to sound teaching, ¹¹ according to the glorious gospel of the blessed God, with which I have been ^entrusted.

PAUL'S TESTIMONY

¹² I thank Christ Jesus our Lord, who has ^strengthened me, because He considered me faithful, putting me into service, ¹³ even though I was previously a blasphemer and a ^persecutor and a violent aggressor. Yet I was shown mercy because I acted ignorantly in unbelief; ¹⁴ and the ^grace of our Lord was more than abundant, with the faith and love which are *found* in Christ Jesus. ¹⁵ ^It is a trustworthy statement, deserving full acceptance, that Christ Jesus came into the world to save sinners, among whom I am foremost. ¹⁶ Yet for this reason I found mercy, so that in me as the foremost *sinner* Jesus Christ might ^demonstrate His perfect patience as an example for those who would believe in Him for eternal life. ¹⁷ Now to the King eternal, immortal, invisible, the ^only God, *be* honor and glory forever and ever. Amen.

¹⁸ This command I entrust to you, Timothy, *my* son, in accordance with the ^prophecies previously made concerning you, that by them you ᴮfight the good fight, ¹⁹ keeping ^faith and a good conscience,

1:1 ^Titus 1:3   1:2 ^Rom 1:7; 2 Tim 1:2   1:3 ^Rom 16:17; 2 Cor 11:4   1:4 ^1 Tim 4:7; 2 Tim 4:4   1:5 ^2 Tim 2:22   1:6 ^Titus 1:10   1:7 ^James 3:1   1:8 ^Rom 7:12, 16   1:9 ^Titus 1:6, 10   ᴮ1 Pet 4:18   1:10 ^1 Cor 6:9   1:11 ^Gal 2:7   1:12 ^Acts 9:22; Phil 4:13   1:13 ^Acts 8:3   1:14 ^Rom 5:20; 2 Cor 4:15   1:15 ^1 Tim 3:1; 4:9   1:16 ^Eph 2:7   1:17 ^John 5:44; 1 Tim 6:15   1:18 ^1 Tim 4:14   ᴮ2 Cor 10:4   1:19 ^1 Tim 1:5

which some have rejected and suffered shipwreck in regard to their faith. [20]Among these are Hymenaeus and [A]Alexander, whom I have [B]handed over to Satan, so that they will be taught not to blaspheme.

A CALL TO PRAYER

2 First of all, then, I urge that [A]requests, prayers, intercession, *and* thanksgiving be made in behalf of all people, [2][A]for kings and all who are in authority, so that we may lead a tranquil and quiet life in all godliness and dignity. [3]This is good and acceptable in the sight of [A]God our Savior, [4][A]who wants all people to be saved and to come to the knowledge of the truth. [5]For there is [A]one God, *and* [B]one mediator also between God and mankind, *the* Man Christ Jesus, [6]who gave Himself as a ransom for all, the testimony *given* at [A]the proper time. [7][A]For this I was appointed as a preacher and an apostle (I am telling the truth, I am not lying), as a teacher of the Gentiles in faith and truth.

INSTRUCTIONS FOR BELIEVERS

[8]Therefore I want the men in every place to pray, [A]lifting up holy hands, without anger and dispute. [9]Likewise, *I want* [A]women to adorn themselves with proper clothing, modestly and discreetly, not with braided hair and gold or pearls or expensive apparel, [10]but rather by means of good works, as is proper for women making a claim to godliness. [11][A]A woman must quietly receive instruction with entire submissiveness. [12][A]But I do not allow a woman to teach or to exercise authority over a man, but to remain quiet. [13][A]For *it was* Adam *who* was first created, *and* then Eve. [14]And *it*

was not Adam *who* was deceived, but [A]the woman was deceived and became a wrongdoer. [15]But women will be preserved through childbirth—if they continue in [A]faith, love, and sanctity, with moderation.

OVERSEERS AND DEACONS

3 It is a trustworthy statement: if any man aspires to the [A]office of overseer, *it is* a fine work he desires *to do.* [2][A]An overseer, then, must be above reproach, the husband of one wife, [1]temperate, self-controlled, respectable, hospitable, skillful in teaching, [3]not overindulging in wine, not a bully, but gentle, not contentious, [A]free from the love of money. [4]*He must be* one who [A]manages his own household well, keeping his children under control with all dignity [5](but if a man does not know how to manage his own household, how will he take care of [A]the church of God?), [6]*and* not a new convert, so that he will not become [A]conceited and fall into condemnation incurred by the devil. [7]And he must [A]have a good reputation with those outside *the church,* so that he will not fall into disgrace and [B]the snare of the devil.

[8]Deacons likewise *must be* men of dignity, not insincere, [A]not prone to *drink* much wine, not greedy for money, [9][A]*but* holding to the mystery of the faith with a clear

1:20[A]2 Tim 4:14   [B]1 Cor 5:5   2:1[A]Eph 6:18
2:2[A]Ezra 6:10; Rom 13:1   2:3[A]Luke 1:47; 1 Tim 1:1
2:4[A]1 Tim 4:10; Titus 2:11   2:5[A]Rom 3:30   [B]Gal 3:20
2:6[A]1 Tim 6:15; Titus 1:3   2:7[A]Eph 3:8; 1 Tim 1:11
2:8[A]Ps 63:4; Luke 24:50   2:9[A]1 Pet 3:3
2:11[A]1 Cor 14:34; Titus 2:5   2:12[A]1 Cor 14:34; Titus 2:5
2:13[A]Gen 2:7, 22; 3:16   2:14[A]Gen 3:6, 13; 2 Cor 11:3
2:15[A]1 Tim 1:14   3:1[A]Acts 20:28; Phil 1:1
3:2[A]1 Tim 3:2-4; Titus 1:6-8   3:3[A]1 Tim 3:8; 6:10
3:4[A]1 Tim 3:12   3:5[A]1 Cor 10:32; 1 Tim 3:15
3:6[A]1 Tim 6:4; 2 Tim 3:4   3:7[A]2 Cor 8:21   [B]2 Tim 2:26
3:8[A]1 Tim 5:23; Titus 2:3   3:9[A]1 Tim 1:5, 19

3:2[1]Or *level-headed*

conscience. [10]ᴬThese men must also first be tested; then have them serve as deacons if they are beyond reproach. [11]ᴬWomen *must* likewise *be* dignified, ᴬnot malicious gossips, but ²temperate, faithful in all things. [12]Deacons must be ᴬhusbands of one wife, *and* ᴮgood managers of *their* children and their own households. [13]For those who have served well as deacons ᴬobtain for themselves a high standing and great confidence in the faith that is in Christ Jesus.

[14]I am writing these things to you, hoping to come to you before long; [15]but in case I am delayed, *I write* so that you will know how one should act in ᴬthe household of God, which is the church of the living God, the pillar and support of the truth. [16]Beyond question, great is the mystery of godliness:

He who was ᴬrevealed in the flesh,
Was vindicated in the Spirit,
Seen by angels,
ᴮProclaimed among the nations,
Believed on in the world,
Taken up in glory.

ABANDONMENT OF FAITH

4 But ᴬthe Spirit explicitly says that in later times some will fall away from the faith, paying attention to deceitful spirits and teachings of demons, ²by means of the hypocrisy of liars ᴬseared in their own conscience as with a branding iron, ³who forbid marriage *and advocate* abstaining from foods which ᴬGod has created to be gratefully shared in by those who believe and know the truth. [4]For everything created by God is good, and nothing is to be rejected if it is ᴬreceived with gratitude; [5]for it is

sanctified by means of ᴬthe word of God and prayer.

A GOOD MINISTER'S DISCIPLINE

[6]In pointing out these things to the brothers *and sisters,* you will be a good servant of Christ Jesus, *constantly* nourished on the words of the faith and of the good doctrine which you ᴬhave been following. [7]But stay away from worthless stories that are typical of old women. Rather, discipline yourself for the purpose of ᴬgodliness; [8]for ᴬbodily training is *just* slightly beneficial, but godliness is beneficial for all things, since it holds promise for the ᴮpresent life and *also* for the *life* to come. [9]ᴬIt is a trustworthy statement deserving full acceptance. [10]For it is for this we labor and strive, because we have set ᴬour hope on the living God, who is ᴮthe Savior of all mankind, especially of believers.

[11]ᴬPrescribe and teach these things. [12]Let no one look down on your youthfulness, but *rather* in speech, conduct, ᴬlove, faith, *and* purity, show yourself ᴮan example of those who believe. [13]Until I come, give your attention to the *public* [1]ᴬreading, to exhortation, *and* teaching. [14]Do not neglect the spiritual gift within you, which was granted to you through *words of* prophecy with ᴬthe laying on of hands by the ᴮcouncil of elders.

3:10ᴬ1 Tim 5:22   3:11ᴬ2 Tim 3:3; Titus 2:3
3:12ᴬ1 Tim 3:2   ᴮ1 Tim 3:4   3:13ᴬMatt 25:21
3:15ᴬEph 2:21f; 1 Pet 2:5   3:16ᴬJohn 1:14   ᴮRom 16:26
4:1ᴬJohn 16:13; Acts 20:23   4:2ᴬEph 4:19
4:3ᴬGen 9:3   4:4ᴬRom 14:6; 1 Cor 10:30f
4:5ᴬGen 1:25, 31; Heb 11:3   4:6ᴬ1 Tim 3:10
4:7ᴬ1 Tim 4:8; 6:3, 5f   4:8ᴬCol 2:23   ᴮMatt 6:33
4:9ᴬ1 Tim 1:15   4:10ᴬ2 Cor 1:10   ᴮ1 Tim 2:4
4:11ᴬ1 Tim 5:7; 6:2   4:12ᴬTitus 2:7   ᴮ1 Tim 1:14
4:13ᴬ2 Tim 3:15ff   4:14ᴬActs 6:6   ᴮActs 11:30

3:11 ¹ I.e., either deacons' wives or deaconesses
² Or *level-headed*   4:13 ¹ I.e., of Scripture in the church service

¹⁵Take pains with these things; be *absorbed* in them, so that your progress will be evident to all. ¹⁶ᴬPay close attention to yourself and to the teaching; persevere in these things, for as you do this you will save both yourself and those who hear you.

HONOR WIDOWS

5 ᴬDo not sharply rebuke an older man, but *rather* appeal to *him* as a father, *and to* the younger men as brothers, ²to the older women as mothers, *and* to the younger women as sisters, in all purity.

³Honor widows who are actually ᴬwidows; ⁴but if any widow has children or grandchildren, ᴬthey must first learn to show proper respect for their own family and to give back compensation to their parents; for this is ᴮacceptable in the sight of God. ⁵Now she who is actually a ᴬwidow and has been left alone has set her hope on God, and she continues in requests and prayers night and day. ⁶But she who ᴬindulges herself in luxury is dead, *even* while she lives. ⁷ᴬGive these instructions as well, so that they may be above reproach. ⁸But if anyone does not provide for his own, and especially for those of his household, he has ᴬdenied the faith and is worse than an unbeliever.

⁹A widow is to be ᴬput on the list only if she is not less than sixty years old, *having been* the wife of one man, ¹⁰having a reputation for ᴬgood works; *and* if she has brought up children, if she has ᴮshown hospitality to strangers, if she has washed the saints' feet, if she has assisted those in distress, *and* if she has devoted herself to every good work. ¹¹But refuse *to*

register younger widows, for when they feel ᴬphysical desires alienating them from Christ, they want to get married, ¹²*thereby* incurring condemnation, because they have ignored their previous pledge. ¹³At the same time they also learn *to be* idle, as they go around from house to house; and not merely idle, but also *they become* gossips and ᴬbusybodies, talking about ᴮthings not proper *to mention*. ¹⁴Therefore, I want younger *widows* to get ᴬmarried, have children, manage their households, *and* give the enemy no opportunity for reproach; ¹⁵for some ᴬhave already turned away to follow Satan. ¹⁶If any woman who is a believer ᴬhas *dependent* widows, she must assist them and the church must not be burdened, so that it may assist those who are actually widows.

CONCERNING ELDERS

¹⁷ᴬThe elders who lead well are to be considered worthy of double honor, especially those who ᴮwork hard at preaching and teaching. ¹⁸For the Scripture says, "ᴬYOU SHALL NOT MUZZLE THE OX WHILE IT IS THRESHING," and "The laborer is worthy of his wages." ¹⁹Do not accept an accusation against an elder except on the basis of ᴬtwo or three witnesses. ²⁰Those who continue in sin, ᴬrebuke in the presence of all, so that the rest also will be fearful *of sinning*. ²¹ᴬI solemnly exhort you in the presence of God

4:16ᴬActs 20:28 5:1ᴬLev 19:32 5:3ᴬActs 6:1; 9:39, 41
5:4ᴬEph 6:2 ᴮ1 Tim 2:3 5:5ᴬ1 Tim 5:3, 16
5:6ᴬJames 5:5 5:7ᴬ1 Tim 4:11 5:8ᴬ2 Tim 2:12;
Titus 1:16 5:9ᴬ1 Tim 5:16 5:10ᴬActs 9:36
ᴮ1 Tim 3:2 5:11ᴬRev 18:7 5:13ᴬ2 Thess 3:11
ᴮTitus 1:11 5:14ᴬ1 Cor 7:9 5:15ᴬ1 Tim 1:20
5:16ᴬ1 Tim 5:4 5:17ᴬActs 11:30 ᴮ1 Thess 5:12
5:18ᴬDeut 25:4; 1 Cor 9:9 5:19ᴬDeut 17:6; 19:15
5:20ᴬGal 2:14; Eph 5:11 5:21ᴬLuke 9:26; 1 Tim 6:13

and of Christ Jesus and of *His* chosen angels, to maintain these *principles* without bias, doing nothing in a *spirit of* partiality. ²²^Do not lay hands upon anyone too quickly and thereby share *responsibility for* the sins of others; keep yourself free from sin.

²³ Do not go on drinking only water, but ^use a little wine for the sake of your stomach and your frequent ailments.

²⁴ The sins of some people are quite evident, going before them to judgment; for others, their *sins* ^follow after. ²⁵ Likewise also, deeds that are good are quite evident, and ^those which are otherwise cannot be concealed.

INSTRUCTIONS TO THOSE WHO MINISTER

6 ^All who are under the yoke as slaves are to regard their own masters as worthy of all honor so that the name of God and *our* doctrine will not be spoken against. ² Those who have believers as their masters must not be disrespectful to them because they are ^brothers *or sisters,* but must serve them all the more, because those who partake of the benefit are believers and beloved. Teach and preach these *principles.*

³ If anyone ^advocates a different doctrine and does not agree with sound words, those of our Lord Jesus Christ, and with the doctrine conforming to godliness, ⁴ he is conceited *and* understands nothing; but he has a sick craving for controversial questions and ^disputes about words, from which come envy, strife, abusive language, evil suspicions, ⁵ and constant friction between ^people of depraved mind

and deprived of the truth, who ᴮsuppose that godliness is a means of gain. ⁶^But godliness *actually* is a means of great gain *when* accompanied by contentment. ⁷ For ^we have brought nothing into the world, so we cannot take anything out of it, either. ⁸ If we ^have food and covering, with these we shall be content. ⁹^But those who want to get rich fall into temptation and a trap, and many foolish and harmful desires which plunge people into ruin and destruction. ¹⁰ For ^the love of money is a root of all sorts of evil, and some by longing for it have ᴮwandered away from the faith and pierced themselves with many griefs.

¹¹ But ^flee from these things, you man of God, and pursue righteousness, godliness, faith, love, perseverance, *and* gentleness. ¹²^Fight the good fight of faith; take hold of the eternal life to which you were called, and *for which* you made the good confession in the presence of many witnesses. ¹³^I direct you in the presence of God, who gives life to all things, and of Christ Jesus, who testified the ᴮgood confession before Pontius Pilate, ¹⁴ that you keep the commandment without fault *or* reproach until the ^appearing of our Lord Jesus Christ, ¹⁵ which He will bring about at ^*the* proper time—He who is the blessed and only Sovereign, the King of kings and Lord of lords, ¹⁶^who alone possesses immortality and dwells

5:22^1 Tim 3:10; 4:14   5:23^1 Tim 3:8
5:24^Rev 14:13   5:25^Prov 10:9   6:1^Eph 6:5;
Titus 2:9   6:2^Gal 3:28; Philem 16   6:3^1 Tim 1:3
6:4^Acts 18:15; 2 Tim 2:14   6:5^2 Tim 3:8   ᴮ2 Pet 2:3
6:6^Luke 12:15-21; 1 Tim 6:6-10   6:7^Job 1:21;
Eccl 5:15   6:8^Prov 30:8   6:9^Prov 15:27; 23:4
6:10^Col 3:5   ᴮJames 5:19   6:11^2 Tim 2:22
6:12^1 Tim 1:18   6:13^1 Tim 5:21   ᴮ2 Cor 9:13
6:14^2 Thess 2:8   6:15^1 Tim 2:6   6:16^1 Tim 1:17

in unapproachable light, whom no one has seen or can see. ^To Him *be* honor and eternal dominion! Amen.

^17 Instruct those who are rich in ^this present world not to be conceited or to set their hope on the uncertainty of riches, but on God, ^who richly supplies us with all things to enjoy. ^18 *Instruct them* to do good, to be rich in ^good works, ^to be generous and ready to share, ^19 ^storing up for themselves the treasure of a good foundation for the future, so that they may ^take hold of that which is truly life.

^20 Timothy, protect ^what has been entrusted to you, avoiding ^worldly, empty chatter and the opposing arguments of what is falsely called "knowledge"— ^21 which some have professed and *thereby* have ^gone astray from the faith.

Grace be with you.

6:16 ^1 Tim 1:17   6:17 ^Matt 12:32   ^Acts 14:17
6:18 ^1 Tim 5:10   ^Rom 12:8   6:19 ^Matt 6:20
^1 Tim 6:12   6:20 ^2 Tim 1:12, 14   ^2 Tim 2:16
6:21 ^2 Tim 2:18

2 TIMOTHY

TIMOTHY CHARGED TO GUARD HIS TRUST

1 Paul, ^an apostle of Christ Jesus by the will of God, according to the promise of life in Christ Jesus,

² To Timothy, my beloved ^son: Grace, mercy, *and* peace from God the Father and Christ Jesus our Lord.

³ ^I thank God, whom I serve with a clear conscience the way my forefathers did, as I constantly remember you in my prayers night and day, ⁴ ^longing to see you, ᴮeven as I recall your tears, so that I may be filled with joy. ⁵ For I am mindful of the ^sincere faith within you, which first dwelled in your grandmother Lois and ᴮyour mother Eunice, and I am sure that *it is* in you as well. ⁶ For this reason I remind you to kindle afresh ^the gift of God which is in you through ^the laying on of my hands. ⁷ For God has not given us a ^spirit of timidity, but of power and love and discipline.

⁸ Therefore ^do not be ashamed of the testimony of our Lord or of me His prisoner, but join with *me* in ᴮsuffering for the gospel according to the power of God, ⁹ who saved us and ^called us with a holy calling, ᴮnot according to our works, but according to His own ^purpose and grace, which was granted to us in Christ Jesus from all eternity, ¹⁰ but has now been revealed by the appearing of our Savior Christ Jesus, who ^abolished death and brought life and immortality to light through the gospel, ¹¹ ^for

which I was appointed a preacher, an apostle, and a teacher. ¹² For this reason I also suffer these things; but ^I am not ashamed, for I know whom I have believed, and I am convinced that He is able to protect what I have entrusted to Him until that day. ¹³ ^Hold on to the example of sound words which you have heard from me, in *the* ᴮfaith and love which are in Christ Jesus. ¹⁴ Protect, through the Holy Spirit who ^dwells in us, the treasure which has been entrusted to *you*.

¹⁵ You are aware of the fact that all who are in Asia ^turned away from me, among whom are Phygelus and Hermogenes. ¹⁶ The Lord grant mercy to ^the household of Onesiphorus, for he often refreshed me and was not ashamed of my chains; ¹⁷ but when he was in Rome, he eagerly searched for me and found me— ¹⁸ the Lord grant to him to find mercy from the Lord on ^that day—and you know very well what services he rendered at Ephesus.

BE STRONG

2 You therefore, my son, ^be strong in the grace that is in Christ Jesus. ² The things ^which you have heard from me in the presence of many witnesses, entrust

---

1:1 ^2 Cor 1:1   1:2 ^1 Tim 1:2; 2 Tim 2:1   1:3 ^Rom 1:8
1:4 ^2 Tim 4:9, 21   ᴮActs 20:37   1:5 ^1 Tim 1:5
ᴮActs 16:1   1:6 ^1 Tim 4:14   1:7 ^John 14:27; Rom 8:15
1:8 ^Mark 8:38   ᴮ2 Tim 2:3, 9   1:9 ^Rom 8:28ff
ᴮEph 2:9   1:10 ^1 Cor 15:26; Heb 2:14f   1:11 ^1 Tim 2:7
1:12 ^2 Tim 1:8, 16   1:13 ^Titus 1:9   ᴮ1 Tim 1:14
1:14 ^Rom 8:9   1:15 ^2 Tim 4:10, 16   1:16 ^2 Tim 4:19
1:18 ^1 Cor 1:8; 2 Tim 1:12   2:1 ^Eph 6:10
2:2 ^2 Tim 1:13

these to faithful ¹people who will be able to teach others also. ³ᴬSuffer hardship with *me*, as a good soldier of Christ Jesus. ⁴No soldier in active service ᴬentangles himself in the affairs of everyday life, so that he may please the one who enlisted *him*. ⁵And if someone likewise ᴬcompetes as an athlete, he is not crowned *as victor* unless he competes according to the rules. ⁶ᴬThe hard-working farmer ought to be the first to receive his share of the crops. ⁷Consider what I say, for the Lord will give you understanding in everything.

⁸Remember Jesus Christ, ᴬrisen from the dead, descendant of David, according to my gospel, ⁹for which I ᴬsuffer hardship even to imprisonment as a criminal; but the word of God is not imprisoned. ¹⁰For this reason I endure all things for ᴬthe sake of those who are chosen, so that they also may obtain the salvation which is in Christ Jesus *and* with *it* eternal glory. ¹¹The statement is trustworthy:

For ᴬif we died with Him, we will also live with Him;
¹² If we endure, we will also reign with Him;
If we ᴬdeny Him, He will also deny us;
¹³ If we are faithless, ᴬHe remains faithful, for He cannot deny Himself.

AN UNASHAMED WORKER

¹⁴Remind *them* of these things, and solemnly ᴬexhort *them* in the presence of God not to ᴮdispute about words, which is useless *and leads* to the ruin of the listeners. ¹⁵Be diligent to ᴬpresent yourself approved to God as a worker who does not need to be ashamed, accurately

handling the word of truth. ¹⁶But avoid ᴬworldly *and* empty chatter, for it will lead to further ungodliness, ¹⁷and their talk will spread like ¹gangrene. Among them are ᴬHymenaeus and Philetus, ¹⁸*men* who have gone astray from the truth, claiming that ᴬthe resurrection has already taken place; and they are jeopardizing the faith of some. ¹⁹Nevertheless, the ᴬfirm foundation of God stands, having this seal: "The Lord knows those who are His;" and, "Everyone who names the name of the Lord is to keep away from wickedness."

²⁰Now in a large house there are not only gold and silver implements, but also *implements* of wood and of earthenware, and ᴬsome *are* for honor while others *are* for dishonor. ²¹Therefore, if anyone cleanses himself from ᴬthese *things*, he will be an implement for honor, sanctified, useful to the Master, prepared for every good work. ²²Now flee from youthful lusts and pursue righteousness, faith, love, *and* peace with those who call on the Lord ᴬfrom a pure heart. ²³But refuse foolish and ignorant speculations, knowing that they ᴬproduce quarrels. ²⁴The Lord's bond-servant must not be quarrelsome, but be kind to all, ᴬskillful in teaching, patient when wronged, ²⁵with gentleness correcting those who are in opposition, ᴬif perhaps God may

2:3 ᴬ2 Tim 1:8   2:4 ᴬ2 Pet 2:20   2:5 ᴬ1 Cor 9:25
2:6 ᴬ1 Cor 9:10   2:8 ᴬActs 2:24   2:9 ᴬ2 Tim 1:8; 2:3
2:10 ᴬLuke 18:7; Titus 1:1   2:11 ᴬRom 6:8; 1 Thess 5:10
2:12 ᴬMatt 10:33; Luke 12:9   2:13 ᴬRom 3:3; 1 Cor 1:9
2:14 ᴬ1 Tim 5:21   ᴮ1 Tim 6:4   2:15 ᴬRom 6:13
2:16 ᴬ1 Tim 6:20   2:17 ᴬ1 Tim 1:20   2:18 ᴬ1 Cor 15:12
2:19 ᴬIs 28:16f; 1 Tim 3:15   2:20 ᴬRom 9:21
2:21 ᴬ2 Tim 2:16-18   2:22 ᴬ1 Tim 1:5   2:23 ᴬTitus 3:9;
James 4:1   2:24 ᴬ1 Tim 3:2   2:25 ᴬActs 8:22

2:2 ¹Or *men*   2:17 ¹Or *cancer*

2 TIMOTHY 2–4   1614

grant them repentance leading to
[B]the knowledge of the truth, [26] and
they may come to their senses *and
escape* from [A]the snare of the devil,
having been held captive by him to
do his will.

DIFFICULT TIMES WILL COME

3 But realize this, that [A]in the last
days difficult times will come.
[2]For people will be lovers of self,
[A]lovers of money, [B]boastful, arrogant, slanderers, disobedient to parents, ungrateful, unholy, [3][A]unloving,
irreconcilable, [B]malicious gossips,
without self-control, brutal, haters of good, [4]treacherous, reckless,
[A]conceited, lovers of pleasure rather
than lovers of God, [5]holding to a
form of [A]godliness although they
have denied its power; avoid *such
people as* these. [6]For among them
are those who [A]slip into households
and captivate weak women weighed
down with sins, led on by [B]various
impulses, [7]always learning and
never able to [A]come to the knowledge of the truth. [8]Just as Jannes and
Jambres opposed Moses, so these
men also oppose the truth, [A]men of
depraved mind, worthless in regard
to the faith. [9]But they will not make
further progress; for their [A]foolish-
ness will be obvious to all, just as
was that also of Jannes and Jambres.
[10]Now you [A]followed my teaching,
conduct, purpose, faith, patience,
[B]love, perseverance, [11]persecutions,
and sufferings, such as happened
to me at Antioch, at Iconium, *and*
at Lystra; what [A]persecutions I
endured, and out of them all [B]the
Lord rescued me! [12]Indeed, all who
want to live in a godly way in Christ
Jesus [A]will be persecuted. [13]But evil
people and impostors will proceed
from bad to worse, [A]deceiving and

being deceived. [14]You, however,
[A]continue in the things you have
learned and become convinced
of, knowing from whom you have
learned *them,* [15]and that from
childhood you have known [A]the
sacred writings which are able to
[B]give you the wisdom that leads
to salvation through faith which
is in Christ Jesus. [16][A]All Scripture
is [1]inspired by God and beneficial
for teaching, for rebuke, for correction, for training in righteousness;
[17]so that the man *or woman* of God
may be fully capable, [A]equipped for
every good work.

PREACH THE WORD

4 I solemnly exhort *you* in the
presence of God and of Christ
Jesus, who is to [A]judge the living and
the dead, and by His appearing and
His kingdom: [2]preach [A]the word; be
ready in season *and* out of season;
[B]correct, rebuke, *and* [1]exhort, with
great patience and instruction. [3]For
[A]*the* time will come when they will
not tolerate sound doctrine; but
wanting to have their ears tickled,
they will accumulate for themselves
teachers in accordance with their
own desires, [4]and they [A]will turn
their ears away from the truth and
will turn aside to myths. [5]But *as for*
you, use self-restraint in all things,
endure hardship, do the work of an
evangelist, fulfill your [A]ministry.

2:25 [B]1 Tim 2:4   2:26[A]1 Tim 3:7   3:1[A]1 Tim 4:1
3:2[A]Luke 16:14   [B]Rom 1:30   3:3[A]Rom 1:31
[B]1 Tim 3:11   3:4[A]1 Tim 3:6   3:5[A]1 Tim 4:7   3:6[A]Jude 4
[B]Titus 3:3   3:7[A]2 Tim 2:25   3:8[A]1 Tim 6:5
3:9[A]Luke 6:11   3:10[A]1 Tim 4:6   [B]1 Tim 6:11
3:11[A]2 Cor 11:23-27   [B]Rom 15:31   3:12[A]John 15:20;
Acts 14:22   3:13[A]Titus 3:3   3:14[A]2 Tim 1:13; Titus 1:9
3:15[A]John 5:47   [B]Ps 119:98f   3:16[A]Rom 4:23f; 15:4
3:17[A]2 Tim 2:21; Heb 13:21   4:1[A]Acts 10:42
4:2[A]Col 4:3   [B]1 Tim 5:20   4:3[A]2 Tim 3:1
4:4[A]2 Thess 2:11; Titus 1:14   4:5[A]Eph 4:12; Col 4:17

3:16 [1]Lit *God-breathed*   4:2 [1]Or *encourage*

⁶For I am already being ^poured out as a drink offering, and the time of ᴮmy departure has come. ⁷^I have fought the good fight, I have finished the course, I have kept the faith; ⁸in the future there ^is reserved for me the crown of righteousness, which the Lord, the righteous Judge, will award to me on ᴮthat day; and not only to me, but also to all who have loved His appearing.

PERSONAL CONCERNS

⁹^Make every effort to come to me soon; ¹⁰for ^Demas, having loved ᴮthis present world, has deserted me and gone to Thessalonica; Crescens *has gone* to Galatia, Titus to Dalmatia. ¹¹Only ^Luke is with me. Take along Mark and bring him with you, for he is useful to me for service. ¹²But I have sent ^Tychicus to Ephesus. ¹³When you come, bring the overcoat which I left at ^Troas with Carpus, and the books, especially the parchments. ¹⁴^Alexander the coppersmith did me great harm; the Lord will repay him according to his deeds. ¹⁵Be on guard against him yourself too, for he vigorously opposed our teaching.

¹⁶At my first defense no one supported me, but all deserted me; ^may it not be counted against them. ¹⁷But the Lord stood with me and ^strengthened me, so that through me the proclamation might be ᴮfully accomplished, and that all the Gentiles might hear; and I was rescued out of the lion's mouth. ¹⁸The Lord will rescue me from every evil deed, and will bring me safely to His ^heavenly kingdom; to Him *be* the glory forever and ever. Amen.

¹⁹Greet Prisca and ^Aquila, and ᴮthe household of Onesiphorus. ²⁰^Erastus remained at Corinth, but I left ᴮTrophimus sick at Miletus. ²¹^Make every effort to come before winter. Eubulus greets you, also Pudens, Linus, Claudia, and all the brothers *and sisters.*

²²^The Lord be with your spirit. Grace be with you.

4:6^Phil 2:17   ᴮPhil 1:23   4:7^1 Cor 9:25f; 1 Tim 1:18   4:8^Col 1:5   ᴮ2 Tim 1:12   4:9^2 Tim 1:4; 4:21   4:10^Col 4:14   ᴮ1 Tim 6:17   4:11^Col 4:14; Philem 24   4:12^Acts 20:4; Eph 6:21, 22 4:13^Acts 16:8   4:14^1 Tim 1:20   4:16^Acts 7:60; 1 Cor 13:5   4:17^1 Tim 1:12   ᴮ2 Tim 4:5 4:18^1 Cor 15:50; 2 Tim 4:1   4:19^Acts 18:2 ᴮ2 Tim 1:16   4:20^Acts 19:22   ᴮActs 20:4 4:21^2 Tim 4:9   4:22^Phil 4:23; Philem 25

TITUS

SALUTATION

1 Paul, a bond-servant of God and an apostle of Jesus Christ, for the faith of those chosen of God and ᴬthe knowledge of the truth which is ᴮaccording to godliness, ²in ᴬthe hope of eternal life, which God, ᴮwho cannot lie, promised long ages ago, ³but ᴬat the proper time revealed His word in the proclamation with which I was entrusted according to the commandment of ᴮGod our Savior;

⁴To Titus, ᴬmy true son in a ᴮcommon faith: Grace and peace from God the Father and Christ Jesus our Savior.

QUALIFICATIONS OF ELDERS

⁵For this reason I left you in Crete, that you would set in order what remains and ᴬappoint elders in every city as I directed you, ⁶*namely,* ᴬif any man is beyond reproach, the husband of one wife, having children who believe, not accused of indecent behavior or rebellion. ⁷For the overseer must be beyond reproach as ᴬGod's steward, not ᴮself-willed, not quick-tempered, not overindulging in wine, not a bully, not greedy for money, ⁸but ᴬhospitable, loving what is good, self-controlled, righteous, holy, disciplined, ⁹ᴬholding firmly the faithful word which is in accordance with the teaching, so that he will be able both to ¹exhort in sound doctrine and to refute those who contradict *it.*

¹⁰For there are many ᴬrebellious people, ᴮempty talkers and deceivers, especially those of the circumcision, ¹¹who must be silenced because they are upsetting ᴬwhole families, teaching ᴮthings they should not *teach* for the sake of dishonest gain. ¹²One of them, a prophet of their own, said, "ᴬCretans are always liars, evil beasts, lazy gluttons." ¹³This testimony is true. For this reason ᴬreprimand them severely so that they may be sound in the faith, ¹⁴not paying attention to Jewish ᴬmyths and commandments of men who turn away from the truth. ¹⁵To the pure, all things are pure; but ᴬto those who are defiled and unbelieving, nothing is pure, but both their mind and their conscience are defiled. ¹⁶ᴬThey profess to know God, but by *their* deeds they deny *Him,* being detestable and disobedient and worthless for any good deed.

PROCLAIM SOUND DOCTRINE

2 But *as for* you, proclaim the things which are fitting for ᴬsound doctrine. ²Older men are to be ¹,ᴬtemperate, dignified, self-controlled, ᴮsound in faith, in love, in perseverance.

³Older women likewise *are to be* reverent in their behavior, ᴬnot

---

1:1ᴬ1 Tim 2:4   ᴮ1 Tim 6:3   **1:2**ᴬ2 Tim 1:1   ᴮHeb 6:18
1:3ᴬ1 Tim 2:6   ᴮLuke 1:47   **1:4**ᴬ2 Tim 1:2   ᴮ2 Pet 1:1
1:5ᴬActs 14:23   **1:6**ᴬ1 Tim 3:2-4; Titus 1:6-8
1:7ᴬ1 Cor 4:1   ᴮ2 Pet 2:10   **1:8**ᴬ1 Tim 3:2
1:9ᴬ2 Thess 2:15; 2 Tim 1:13   **1:10**ᴬTitus 1:6
ᴮ1 Tim 1:6   **1:11**ᴬ1 Tim 5:4   ᴮ1 Tim 5:13
1:12ᴬActs 2:11; 27:7   **1:13**ᴬ1 Tim 5:20; 2 Tim 4:2
1:14ᴬ1 Tim 1:4   **1:15**ᴬRom 14:14, 23   **1:16**ᴬ1 John 2:4
2:1ᴬTitus 1:9   **2:2**ᴬ1 Tim 3:2   ᴮTitus 1:13
2:3ᴬ1 Tim 3:11

1:9¹Or *encourage*   **2:2**¹Or *level-headed*

malicious gossips nor [B]enslaved to much wine, teaching what is good, [4]so that they may encourage the young women to love their husbands, to love their children, [5]*to be* sensible, pure, [A]workers at home, kind, being [B]subject to their own husbands, so that the word of God will not be dishonored.

[6]Likewise urge [A]the young men to be sensible; [7]in all things show yourself *to be* [A]an example of good deeds, *with* purity in doctrine, dignified, [8]sound *in* speech which is beyond reproach, [A]so that the opponent will be put to shame, having nothing bad to say about us.

[9]*Urge* [A]slaves to be subject to their own masters in everything, to be pleasing, not argumentative, [10]not stealing, but showing all good faith so that they will adorn the doctrine of [A]God our Savior in every respect.

[11]For the grace of God has [A]appeared, [B]bringing salvation to all people, [12]instructing us to deny ungodliness and [A]worldly desires and [B]to live sensibly, righteously, and in a godly manner in the present age, [13]looking for the blessed hope and the appearing of the glory of [A]our great God and Savior, Christ Jesus, [14]who [A]gave Himself for us [B]to redeem us from every lawless deed, and to purify for Himself a people for His own possession, eager for good deeds.

[15]These things speak and [1,A]exhort, and rebuke with all authority. No one is to disregard you.

GODLY LIVING

3 Remind them [A]to be subject to rulers, to authorities, to be obedient, to be [B]ready for every good deed, [2]to slander no one, [A]not to be contentious, *to be* gentle, showing

every consideration for all people. [3A]For we too were once foolish, disobedient, [B]deceived, enslaved to various lusts and pleasures, spending our life in malice and envy, hateful, hating one another. [4]But when the [A]kindness of God our Savior and *His* love for mankind appeared, [5]He saved us, [A]not on the basis of deeds which we did in righteousness, but in accordance with His mercy, by the washing of regeneration and renewing by the Holy Spirit, [6A]whom He richly poured out upon us through Jesus Christ our Savior, [7]so that being justified by His grace we would be made [A]heirs according to *the* hope of eternal life. [8]This statement is trustworthy; and concerning these things I want you to speak confidently, so that those who have believed God will be careful to [A]engage in good deeds. These things are good and beneficial for people. [9]But [A]avoid [B]foolish controversies and genealogies and strife and disputes about the Law, for they are useless and worthless. [10A]Reject a [B]divisive person after a first and second warning, [11]knowing that such a person has [A]deviated from what is right and is sinning, being self-condemned.

PERSONAL CONCERNS

[12]When I send Artemas or Tychicus to you, [A]make every effort to

2:3[B]1 Tim 3:8   2:5[A]1 Tim 5:14   [B]Eph 5:22   2:6[A]1 Tim 5:1
2:7[A]1 Tim 4:12   2:8[A]2 Thess 3:14; 1 Pet 2:12
2:9[A]Eph 6:5; 1 Tim 6:1   2:10[A]Titus 1:3   2:11[A]2 Tim 1:10
[B]1 Tim 2:4   2:12[A]1 Tim 6:9   [B]2 Tim 3:12   2:13[A]Titus 1:4;
2 Pet 1:1   2:14[A]1 Tim 2:6   [B]Ps 130:8   2:15[A]1 Tim 4:13;
5:20   3:1[A]Rom 13:1   [B]2 Tim 2:21
3:2[A]1 Tim 3:3; 1 Pet 2:18   3:3[A]Rom 11:30   [B]2 Tim 3:13
3:4[A]Rom 2:4; Eph 2:7   3:5[A]Eph 2:9   3:6[A]Rom 5:5
3:7[A]Matt 25:34; Mark 10:17   3:8[A]Titus 2:7, 14; 3:14
3:9[A]2 Tim 2:16   [B]1 Tim 1:4   3:10[A]2 John 10   [B]Rom 16:17
3:11[A]Titus 1:14   3:12[A]2 Tim 4:9

2:15 [1]Or *encourage*

come to me at Nicopolis, for I have decided to spend the winter there. ¹³Diligently help Zenas the lawyer and ^Apollos on their way so that nothing is lacking for them. ¹⁴Our people must also learn to ^engage in good deeds to meet pressing needs, so that they will not be ᴮunproductive.

¹⁵All who are with me greet you. Greet those who love us ^in *the* faith. ᴮGrace be with you all.

3:13 ^Acts 18:24; 1 Cor 16:12   3:14 ^Titus 3:8
ᴮMatt 7:19   3:15 ^1 Tim 1:2   ᴮCol 4:18

PHILEMON

1 Paul, ^a prisoner of Christ Jesus, and Timothy our brother,

To Philemon our beloved *brother* and fellow worker, ²and to Apphia our sister, and to ^Archippus our ^Bfellow soldier, and to the church in your house: ³^Grace to you and peace from God our Father and the Lord Jesus Christ.

PHILEMON'S LOVE AND FAITH

⁴^I thank my God always, making mention of you in my prayers, ⁵because I ^hear of your love and of the faith which you have toward the Lord Jesus and toward all the saints; ⁶*and I pray* that the fellowship of your faith may become effective 'through the ^knowledge of every good thing which is in you for the sake of Christ. ⁷For I have had great ^joy and comfort in your love, because the hearts of the saints have been ^Brefreshed through you, brother.

⁸Therefore, ^though I have enough confidence in Christ to order you *to do* what is proper, ⁹*yet* for love's sake I rather appeal *to you*—since I am such a person as Paul, an ^old man, and now also ^Ba prisoner of Christ Jesus—

PLEA FOR ONESIMUS, A FREE MAN

¹⁰I appeal to you for my ^son ¹,^BOnesimus, whom I ²fathered in my imprisonment, ¹¹who previously was useless to you, but now is useful both to you and to me. ¹²I have sent him back to you in person, that is, *sending* my very heart, ¹³whom I wanted to keep with me, so that in your behalf he might be at my service in my ^imprisonment for the gospel; ¹⁴but I did not want to do anything without your consent, so that your goodness would ^not be, in effect, by compulsion, but of your own free will. ¹⁵For perhaps *it was* ^for this reason *that* he was separated *from you* for a while, that you would have him back forever, ¹⁶no longer as a slave, but more than a slave, ^a beloved brother, especially to me, but how much more to you, both in the flesh and in the Lord.

¹⁷If then you regard me *as* a ^partner, accept him as *you would* me. ¹⁸But if he has wronged you in any way or owes *you anything,* charge that to my account; ¹⁹^I, Paul, have written *this* with my own hand, I will repay *it* (not to mention to you that you owe to me even your own self as well). ²⁰Yes, brother, let me benefit from you in the Lord; ^refresh my heart in Christ.

²¹^Having confidence in your obedience, I write to you, since I know that you will do even more than what I say.

---

1 ^Eph 3:1   **2** ^Col 4:17   ᴮPhil 2:25   **3** ^Rom 1:7
4 ^Rom 1:8f   **5** ^Eph 1:15; Col 1:4   **6** ^Phil 1:9; Col 1:9
7 ²Cor 7:4, 13   ᴮ1 Cor 16:18   **8** ²Cor 3:12;
1 Thess 2:6   **9** ^Titus 2:2   ᴮPhilem 1   **10** ^1 Cor 4:14f
ᴮCol 4:9   **13** ^Phil 1:7; Philem 10   **14** ²Cor 9:7;
1 Pet 5:2   **15** ^Gen 45:5, 8   **16** ^Matt 23:8; 1 Tim 6:2
17 ²Cor 8:23   **19** ^1 Cor 16:21   **20** ^Philem 7
21 ²Cor 2:3

---

6 ¹Or *in*   **10** ¹I.e., useful   ²I.e., led to the Lord

²²At the same time also prepare me a guest room, for I hope that through ^your prayers I will be given to you.

²³^Epaphras, my fellow prisoner in Christ Jesus, greets you, ²⁴ *as do* ^Mark, Aristarchus, ᴮDemas, *and* ᴮLuke, my fellow workers.

²⁵^The grace of the Lord Jesus Christ be with your spirit.¹

---

22 ^2 Cor 1:11   23 ^Col 1:7; 4:12   24 ^Col 4:10
ᴮ Col 4:14   25 ^Gal 6:18

25 ¹One early ms adds *Amen*

HEBREWS

GOD'S FINAL WORD IN HIS SON

1 God, after He spoke long ago to the fathers in the prophets in many portions and ^in many ways, ²in these last days has spoken to us in *His* Son, whom He appointed ^heir of all things, through whom He also made the world. ³And He is the radiance of His glory and the exact ^representation of His nature, and ᴮupholds all things by the word of His power. When He had made purification of sins, He sat down at the right hand of the Majesty on high, ⁴having become so much better than the angels, to the extent that He has inherited a more excellent ^name than they.

⁵For to which of the angels did He ever say,

"^YOU ARE MY SON,
  TODAY I HAVE FATHERED YOU"?

And again,

"ᴮI WILL BE A FATHER TO HIM
  AND HE WILL BE A SON TO
  ME"?

⁶And when He again brings the firstborn into the world, He says,

"^AND LET ALL THE ANGELS OF
  GOD WORSHIP HIM."

⁷And regarding the angels He says,

"^HE MAKES HIS ANGELS
  WINDS,
  AND HIS MINISTERS A FLAME
  OF FIRE."

⁸But regarding the Son *He says,*

"^YOUR THRONE, GOD, IS
  FOREVER AND EVER,
  AND THE SCEPTER OF
  RIGHTEOUSNESS IS THE
  SCEPTER OF ¹HIS KINGDOM.

⁹ "^YOU HAVE LOVED
  RIGHTEOUSNESS AND HATED
  LAWLESSNESS;
  THEREFORE GOD, YOUR GOD,
  HAS ᴮANOINTED YOU
  WITH THE OIL OF JOY ABOVE
  YOUR COMPANIONS."

¹⁰And,

"^YOU, LORD, IN THE
  BEGINNING LAID THE
  FOUNDATION OF THE
  EARTH,
  AND THE HEAVENS ARE THE
  WORKS OF YOUR HANDS;

¹¹ ^THEY WILL PERISH, BUT YOU
  REMAIN;
  AND THEY ALL WILL WEAR OUT
  LIKE A GARMENT,

¹² ^AND LIKE A ROBE YOU WILL
  ROLL THEM UP;
  LIKE A GARMENT THEY WILL
  ALSO BE CHANGED.
  BUT YOU ARE THE SAME,
  AND YOUR YEARS WILL NOT
  COME TO AN END."

¹³But to which of the angels has He ever said,

"^SIT AT MY RIGHT HAND,
  UNTIL I MAKE YOUR ENEMIES
  A FOOTSTOOL FOR YOUR
  FEET"?

¹⁴Are they not all ^ministering spirits, sent out to *provide* service for the sake of those who will inherit salvation?

1:1^Num 12:6, 8; Joel 2:28   1:2^Ps 2:8; Matt 28:18
1:3^2 Cor 4:4   ᴮCol 1:17   1:4^Eph 1:21   1:5^Ps 2:7
ᴮ2 Sam 7:14   1:6^Ps 97:7   1:7^Ps 104:4   1:8^Ps 45:6
1:9^Ps 45:7   ᴮIs 61:1, 3   1:10^Ps 102:25
1:11^Ps 102:26   1:12^Ps 102:26, 27   1:13^Ps 110:1;
Matt 22:44   1:14^Ps 103:20f; Dan 7:10

1:8¹Late mss *Your*

PAY ATTENTION

2 For this reason we must pay much closer attention to what we have heard, so that ^we do not drift away *from it.* ²For if the word spoken through ^angels proved unalterable, and every violation and act of disobedience received a just punishment, ³^how will we escape if we neglect so great a salvation? After it was at first spoken through the Lord, it was confirmed to us by those who heard, ⁴God also testifying with them, both by signs and wonders, and by various miracles and by ^gifts of the Holy Spirit according to His own will.

EARTH SUBJECT TO MAN

⁵For He did not subject to angels ^the world to come, about which we are speaking. ⁶But someone has testified somewhere, saying,

"^WHAT IS MAN, THAT YOU THINK
OF HIM?
OR A SON OF MAN, THAT YOU
ARE CONCERNED ABOUT HIM?
⁷   "^YOU HAVE MADE HIM FOR A LITTLE
WHILE LOWER THAN ANGELS;
YOU HAVE CROWNED HIM WITH
GLORY AND HONOR¹;
⁸   YOU HAVE PUT EVERYTHING IN
SUBJECTION UNDER HIS FEET."

For in subjecting all things to him, He left nothing that is not subject to him. But now ^we do not yet see all things subjected to him.

JESUS BRIEFLY HUMBLED

⁹But we do see Him who was made for a little while lower than the angels, *namely,* Jesus, ^because of His suffering death crowned with glory and honor, so that by the grace of God He might taste death for everyone.

¹⁰For it was fitting for Him, ^for whom are all things, and through whom are all things, in bringing many sons to glory, to ᴮperfect the originator of their salvation through sufferings. ¹¹For both He who ^sanctifies and those who are sanctified are all from one *Father;* for this reason He is not ashamed to call them brothers *and sisters,* ¹²saying,

"^I WILL PROCLAIM YOUR NAME
TO MY BROTHERS,
IN THE MIDST OF THE ASSEMBLY
I WILL SING YOUR PRAISE."
¹³And again,

"^I WILL PUT MY TRUST IN HIM."
And again,

"ᴮBEHOLD, I AND THE CHILDREN
WHOM GOD HAS GIVEN ME."

¹⁴Therefore, since the children share in ^flesh and blood, He Himself likewise also partook of the same, so that through death He might destroy the one who has the power of death, that is, the devil, ¹⁵and free those who through ^fear of death were subject to slavery all their lives. ¹⁶For clearly He does not give help to angels, but He gives help to the descendants of Abraham. ¹⁷Therefore, in all things He had ^to be made like His brothers so that He might become a merciful and faithful high priest in things pertaining to God, to ᴮmake ¹propitiation for the sins of the people. ¹⁸For since He Himself was ^tempted in that which He has suffered, He is able to come to the aid of those who are tempted.

2:1^Prov 3:21   2:2^Acts 7:53   2:3^Heb 10:29; 12:25
2:4¹1 Cor 12:4, 11; Eph 4:7   2:5^Matt 24:14; Heb 6:5
2:6^Ps 8:4   2:7^Ps 8:5, 6   2:8¹1 Cor 15:25
2:9^Acts 3:13; 1 Pet 1:21   2:10^Rom 11:36   ᴮHeb 5:9
2:11^Heb 13:12   2:12^Ps 22:22   2:13^Is 8:17   ᴮIs 8:18
2:14^Matt 16:17   2:15^Rom 8:15   2:17^Phil 2:7
ᴮDan 9:24   2:18^Heb 4:15

2:7¹One early ms continues, *and have appointed him over the works of Your hands*   2:17¹I.e., reconciliation with God by atoning for the sins

JESUS OUR HIGH PRIEST

3 Therefore, holy brothers *and sisters,* partakers of a ^heavenly calling, consider the Apostle and High Priest of our confession: Jesus; ²He was faithful to Him who appointed Him, as ^Moses also was in all His house. ³^For He has been counted worthy of more glory than Moses, by just so much as the builder of the house has more honor than the house. ⁴For every house is built by someone, but the builder of all things is God. ⁵Now Moses was faithful in all God's house as ^a servant, ᴮfor a testimony of those things which were to be spoken *later;* ⁶but Christ *was faithful* as a Son over His house—^whose house we are, if we hold firmly to our confidence and the boast of our hope.

⁷Therefore, just as the Holy Spirit says,

"^TODAY IF YOU HEAR HIS VOICE,
⁸   ^DO NOT HARDEN YOUR HEARTS,
    AS WHEN THEY PROVOKED ME,
    AS ON THE DAY OF TRIAL IN THE
        WILDERNESS,
⁹   ^WHERE YOUR FATHERS PUT *ME*
        TO THE TEST,
    AND SAW MY WORKS FOR ᴮFORTY
        YEARS.
¹⁰ "^THEREFORE I WAS ANGRY WITH
        THIS GENERATION,
    AND SAID, 'THEY ALWAYS GO
        ASTRAY IN THEIR HEART,
    AND THEY DID NOT KNOW MY
        WAYS';
¹¹ ^AS I SWORE IN MY ANGER,
    'THEY CERTAINLY SHALL NOT
        ENTER MY REST.'"

THE DANGER OF UNBELIEF

¹²^Take care, brothers *and sisters,* that there will not be in any one of you an evil, unbelieving heart that

falls away from the living God. ¹³But ^encourage one another every day, as long as it is *still* called "today," so that none of you will be hardened by the ᴮdeceitfulness of sin. ¹⁴For we have become partakers of Christ ^if we keep the beginning of our ᴮcommitment firm until the end, ¹⁵while it is said,

"^TODAY IF YOU HEAR HIS VOICE,
    DO NOT HARDEN YOUR HEARTS,
    AS WHEN THEY PROVOKED
        ME."

¹⁶For who ^provoked *Him* when they had heard? Indeed, did not all those who came out of Egypt *led* by Moses? ¹⁷And with whom was He angry for forty years? Was it not with those who sinned, ^whose dead bodies fell in the wilderness? ¹⁸And to whom did He swear ^that they would not enter His rest, but to those who were disobedient? ¹⁹And *so* we see that they were not able to enter because of ^unbelief.

THE BELIEVER'S REST

4 Therefore, we must fear if, while a promise remains of entering His rest, any one of you may seem to have ^come short *of it.* ²For indeed we have had good news preached to us, just as they also *did;* but ^the word they heard did not benefit them, because ¹they were not united with those who listened with faith. ³For we who have

3:1^Phil 3:14   3:2^Ex 40:16; Num 12:7
3:3^2 Cor 3:7-11   3:5^Num 12:7   ᴮDeut 18:18f
3:6^1 Cor 3:16; 1 Tim 3:15   3:7^Ps 95:7; Heb 3:15
3:8^Ps 95:8   3:9^Ps 95:9-11   ᴮActs 7:36
3:10^Ps 95:10   3:11^Ps 95:11; Heb 4:3, 5
3:12^Col 2:8; Heb 12:25   3:13^Heb 10:24f
ᴮEph 4:22   3:14^Heb 3:6   ᴮHeb 11:1
3:15^Ps 95:7f; Heb 3:7   3:16^Jer 32:29; 44:3, 8
3:17^Num 14:29; 1 Cor 10:5   3:18^Num 14:23;
Deut 1:34f   3:19^John 3:18, 36; Rom 11:23
4:1^2 Cor 6:1; Gal 5:4   4:2^Rom 10:17; Gal 3:2

4:2¹One early ms *it was not united with faith in those who heard*

believed enter *that* rest, just as He has said,

> "ᴬAs I swore in My anger,
> They certainly shall not
>   enter My rest,"

although His works were finished from the foundation of the world. ⁴For He has said somewhere concerning the seventh *day:* "ᴬAnd God rested on the seventh day from all His works"; ⁵and again in this *passage,* "ᴬThey certainly shall not enter My rest." ⁶Therefore, since it remains for some to enter it, and those who previously had good news preached to them failed to enter because of ᴬdisobedience, ⁷He again sets a certain day, "Today," saying through David after so long a time just ᴬas has been said before,

> "ᴮToday if you hear His voice,
> Do not harden your hearts."

⁸For ᴬif Joshua had given them rest, He would not have spoken of another day after that. ⁹Consequently, there remains a Sabbath rest for the people of God. ¹⁰For the one who has entered His rest has himself also rested from his works, as ᴬGod did from His. ¹¹Therefore let's make every effort to enter that rest, so that no one will fall by *following* the same ᴬexample of disobedience. ¹²For ᴬthe word of God is living and active, and sharper than any two-edged sword, even penetrating as far as the division of soul and spirit, of both joints and marrow, and able to judge the thoughts and intentions of the heart. ¹³And ᴬthere is no creature hidden from His sight, but all things are open and laid bare to the eyes of Him to whom we must answer.

¹⁴Therefore, since we have a great ᴬhigh priest who has ᴮpassed through the heavens, Jesus the Son of God, let's hold firmly to our confession. ¹⁵For we do not have a high priest who cannot sympathize with our weaknesses, but One who has been ᴬtempted in all things just as *we are, yet* ᴮwithout sin. ¹⁶Therefore let's ᴬapproach the throne of grace with confidence, so that we may receive mercy and find grace for help at the time of *our* need.

THE PERFECT HIGH PRIEST

5 For every high priest ᴬtaken from among men is appointed on behalf of people in things pertaining to God, in order to offer both gifts and sacrifices for sins; ²ᴬhe can deal gently with the ignorant and misguided, since he himself also is clothed in weakness; ³and because of it he is obligated to offer *sacrifices* for sins for himself, ᴬas well as for the people. ⁴And ᴬno one takes the honor for himself, but *receives it* when he is called by God, just as Aaron also was.

⁵So too Christ did not glorify Himself *in* becoming a high priest, but *it was* He who said to Him,

> "ᴬYou are My Son,
> Today I have fathered You";

⁶just as He also says in another *passage,*

> "ᴬYou are a priest forever
> According to the order of
>   Melchizedek."

⁷In the days of His humanity, ᴬHe offered up both prayers and pleas with loud crying and tears to the

4:3ᴬPs 95:11; Heb 3:11   4:4ᴬGen 2:2   4:5ᴬPs 95:11; Heb 3:11   4:6ᴬHeb 3:18; 4:11   4:7ᴬHeb 3:7f
ᴮPs 95:7f   4:8ᴬJosh 22:4   4:10ᴬGen 2:2; Heb 4:4
4:11ᴬ2 Pet 2:6   4:12ᴬJer 23:29; Eph 5:26
4:13ᴬ2 Chr 16:9; Ps 33:13-15   4:14ᴬHeb 2:17
ᴮEph 4:10   4:15ᴬHeb 2:18   ᴮ2 Cor 5:21
4:16ᴬHeb 7:19   5:1ᴬEx 28:1   5:2ᴬHeb 2:18; 4:15
5:3ᴬLev 9:7; 16:6   5:4ᴬNum 16:40; 18:7   5:5ᴬPs 2:7
5:6ᴬPs 110:4; Heb 7:17   5:7ᴬMatt 26:39, 42, 44; Mark 14:36, 39

One able to save Him from death, and He was heard because of His devout behavior. [8] Although He was ^a Son, He learned ^b obedience from the things which He suffered. [9] And having been ^perfected, He became the source of eternal salvation for all those who obey Him, [10] being designated by God as ^High Priest according to the order of Melchizedek.

[11] Concerning him we have much to say, and *it is* difficult to explain, since you have become poor listeners. [12] For though by this time you ought to be teachers, you have need again for someone to teach you the ^elementary principles of the actual words of God, and you have come to need milk and not solid food. [13] For everyone who partakes *only* of milk is unacquainted with the word of righteousness, for he is an ^infant. [14] But solid food is for ^the mature, who because of practice have their senses trained to distinguish between good and evil.

THE DANGER OF FALLING AWAY

6 Therefore ^leaving the elementary teaching about the Christ, let us press on to maturity, not laying again a foundation of repentance from ^b dead works and of faith toward God, [2] of ^instruction about washings and laying on of hands, and about the ^b resurrection of the dead and eternal judgment. [3] And this we will do, ^if God permits. [4] For it is ^impossible, in the case of those who have once been ^enlightened and have tasted of the heavenly gift and have been made partakers of the Holy Spirit, [5] and ^have tasted the good word of God and the powers of the age to come, [6] and *then* have ¹fallen away, to ^restore them again to repentance,

since they again crucify to themselves the Son of God and put Him to open shame. [7] For ground that drinks the rain which often falls on it and produces vegetation useful to those ^for whose sake it is also tilled, receives a blessing from God; [8] but if it yields thorns and thistles, it is worthless and ^close to being cursed, and it ends up being burned.

BETTER THINGS FOR YOU

[9] But, ^beloved, we are convinced of better things regarding you, and things that accompany salvation, even though we are speaking in this way. [10] For ^God is not unjust so as to forget your work and the love which you have shown toward His name, by having served and by *still* serving the saints. [11] And we desire that each one of you demonstrate the same diligence so as to realize the ^full assurance of ^b hope until the end, [12] so that you will not be sluggish, but ^imitators of those who through faith and endurance inherit the promises.

[13] For when God made the promise to Abraham, since He could swear an oath by no one greater, He ^swore by Himself, [14] saying, "^INDEED I WILL GREATLY BLESS YOU AND I WILL GREATLY MULTIPLY YOU." [15] And so, ^having patiently waited, he obtained the promise. [16] For people

5:8 ^Heb 1:2   ^b Phil 2:8   5:9 ^Heb 2:10
5:10 ^Heb 2:17; 5:5   5:12 ^Heb 6:1   5:13 ^1 Cor 3:1;
14:20   5:14 ^1 Cor 2:6; Eph 4:13   6:1 ^Phil 3:13f
^b Heb 9:14   6:2 ^John 3:25   ^b Acts 17:31f
6:3 ^Acts 18:21   6:4 ^2 Cor 4:4, 6; Heb 10:32
6:5 ^1 Pet 2:3   6:6 ^Heb 10:26f; 2 Pet 2:21
6:7 ^2 Tim 2:6   6:8 ^Gen 3:17f; Deut 29:22ff
6:9 ^1 Cor 10:14; 2 Cor 7:1   6:10 ^Prov 19:17;
Matt 10:42   6:11 ^Heb 10:22   ^b Heb 3:6
6:12 ^Heb 13:7   6:13 ^Gen 22:16; Luke 1:73
6:14 ^Gen 22:17   6:15 ^Gen 12:4; 21:5

6:6 ¹Or *committed apostasy*; i.e., renounced the faith

swear an oath by one greater *than themselves,* and with them ^an oath *serving* as confirmation is an end of every dispute. ¹⁷In the same way God, desiring even more to demonstrate to ^the heirs of the promise the fact that His purpose is unchangeable, confirmed it with an oath, ¹⁸so that by two unchangeable things in which ^it is impossible for God to lie, we who have taken refuge would have strong encouragement to hold firmly to the hope set before us. ¹⁹This hope we have as an anchor of the soul, a *hope* both sure and reliable and one which ^enters within the veil, ²⁰^where Jesus has entered as a forerunner for us, having become a high priest forever according to the order of Melchizedek.

MELCHIZEDEK'S PRIESTHOOD LIKE CHRIST'S

7 For this ^Melchizedek, king of Salem, priest of the Most High God, who met Abraham as he was returning from the slaughter of the kings and blessed him, ²to whom also Abraham apportioned a tenth of all *the spoils,* was first of all, by the translation *of his name,* king of righteousness, and then also king of Salem, which is king of peace. ³Without father, without mother, without genealogy, having neither beginning of days nor end of life, but made like ^the Son of God, he remains a priest perpetually.

⁴Now observe how great this man was to whom Abraham, the ^patriarch, gave a tenth of the choicest spoils. ⁵And those indeed of ^the sons of Levi who receive the priest's office have a commandment in the Law to collect a tenth from the people, that is, from their countrymen, although they are descended from Abraham. ⁶But the one whose genealogy is not traced from them collected a tenth from Abraham and blessed the one who ^had the promises. ⁷But without any dispute the lesser *person* is blessed by the greater. ⁸In this case mortal men receive tithes, but in that case one *receives them,* ^of whom it is witnessed that he lives *on.* ⁹And, so to speak, through Abraham even Levi, who received tithes, has paid tithes, ¹⁰for he was still in the loins of his forefather when Melchizedek met him.

¹¹^So if perfection was through the Levitical priesthood (for on the basis of it ᴮthe people received the Law), what further need *was there* for another priest to arise according to the order of Melchizedek, and not be designated according to the order of Aaron? ¹²For when the priesthood is changed, of necessity there takes place a change of law also. ¹³For ^the one about whom these things are said belongs to another tribe, from which no one has officiated at the altar. ¹⁴For it is evident that our Lord was ^descended from Judah, a tribe with reference to which Moses said nothing concerning priests. ¹⁵And this is clearer still, if another priest arises according to the likeness of Melchizedek, ¹⁶who has become *a priest* not on the basis of a law of ^physical requirement, but according to the

6:16^Ex 22:11   6:17^Heb 11:9   6:18^Num 23:19; Titus 1:2   6:19^Lev 16:2, 15; Heb 9:3, 7
6:20^John 14:2; Heb 4:14   7:1^Gen 14:18-20; Heb 7:6
7:3^Heb 7:28   7:4^Acts 2:29; 7:8f   7:5^Num 18:21, 26; 2 Chr 31:4f   7:6^Rom 4:13   7:8^Heb 5:6; 6:20
7:11^Heb 7:18f   ᴮHeb 10:1   7:13^Heb 7:14
7:14^Num 24:17; Is 11:1   7:16^Heb 9:10

power of an indestructible life.
¹⁷For it is attested *of Him,*

"ᴬYOU ARE A PRIEST FOREVER
ACCORDING TO THE ORDER OF
MELCHIZEDEK."

¹⁸For, on the one hand, there is *the* nullification of a former commandment ᴬbecause of its weakness and uselessness ¹⁹(for ᴬthe Law made nothing perfect); on the other hand, *there is the* introduction of a better hope, through which we come near to God. ²⁰And to the extent that *it was* not without an oath ²¹(for they indeed became priests without an oath, but He with an oath through the One who said to Him,

"ᴬTHE LORD HAS SWORN
AND WILL NOT CHANGE HIS
MIND,

'YOU ARE A PRIEST FOREVER'");

²²by the same extent Jesus also has become the ᴬguarantee of a better covenant.

²³The *former* priests, on the one hand, existed in greater numbers because they were prevented by death from continuing; ²⁴Jesus, on the other hand, because He continues ᴬforever, holds His priesthood permanently. ²⁵Therefore He is also able to save forever those who come to God through Him, since He always lives to ᴬmake intercession for them.

²⁶For it was fitting for us to have such a high priest, holy, ᴬinnocent, undefiled, separated from sinners, and ᴮexalted above the heavens; ²⁷who has no daily need, like those high priests, to offer up sacrifices, first for His own sins and then for the *sins* of the people, because He did this ᴬonce for all *time* when He offered up Himself. ²⁸For the Law appoints men as high priests ᴬwho

are weak, but the word of the oath, which came after the Law, *appoints* a Son, who has been ᴮmade perfect forever.

A BETTER MINISTRY

8 Now the main point in what has been said *is this:* we have such a high priest, who has taken His seat at ᴬthe right hand of the throne of the Majesty in the heavens, ²a minister in the sanctuary and in the ᴬtrue tabernacle, which the Lord set up, not man. ³For every ᴬhigh priest is appointed to offer both gifts and sacrifices; so it is necessary that this *high priest* also have something to offer. ⁴Now if He were on earth, He would not be a priest at all, since there are those who ᴬoffer the gifts according to the Law; ⁵who serve a copy and shadow of the heavenly things, just as Moses was warned *by God* when he was about to erect the tabernacle; for, "ᴬSEE," He says, "THAT YOU MAKE all things BY THE PATTERN WHICH WAS SHOWN TO YOU ON THE MOUNTAIN." ⁶But now He has obtained a more excellent ministry, to the extent that He is also the ᴬmediator of a better covenant, which has been enacted on better promises.

A NEW COVENANT

⁷For ᴬif that first *covenant* had been free of fault, no circumstances would have been sought for a second. ⁸For in finding fault with the people, He says,

7:17ᴬPs 110:4; Heb 5:6   7:18ᴬRom 8:3; Gal 3:21
7:19ᴬActs 13:39; Rom 3:20   7:21ᴬPs 110:4
7:22ᴬPs 119:122; Is 38:14   7:24ᴬIs 9:7; John 12:34
7:25ᴬRom 8:34; Heb 9:24   7:26ᴬ1 Pet 2:22
ᴮHeb 4:14   7:27ᴬHeb 9:12, 28; 10:10   7:28ᴬHeb 5:2
ᴮHeb 2:10   8:1ᴬPs 110:1; Heb 1:3   8:2ᴬHeb 9:11, 24
8:3ᴬHeb 2:17   8:4ᴬHeb 5:1; 7:27   8:5ᴬEx 25:40
8:6ᴬ1 Tim 2:5   8:7ᴬHeb 7:11

"ᴬBEHOLD, DAYS ARE COMING,
SAYS THE LORD,
WHEN I WILL BRING ABOUT A
NEW COVENANT
WITH THE HOUSE OF ISRAEL
AND THE HOUSE OF JUDAH,
9 ᴬNOT LIKE THE COVENANT
WHICH I MADE WITH THEIR
FATHERS
ON THE DAY I TOOK THEM BY
THE HAND
TO BRING THEM OUT OF THE
LAND OF EGYPT;
FOR THEY DID NOT CONTINUE
IN MY COVENANT,
AND I DID NOT CARE ABOUT
THEM, SAYS THE LORD.
10 "ᴬFOR THIS IS THE COVENANT
WHICH I WILL MAKE WITH
THE HOUSE OF ISRAEL
AFTER THOSE DAYS, DECLARES
THE LORD:
I WILL PUT MY LAWS INTO
THEIR MINDS,
AND WRITE THEM ON THEIR
HEARTS.
AND I WILL BE THEIR GOD,
AND THEY SHALL BE MY
PEOPLE.
11 "ᴬAND THEY WILL NOT TEACH,
EACH ONE HIS FELLOW
CITIZEN,
AND EACH ONE HIS BROTHER,
SAYING, 'KNOW THE LORD,'
FOR THEY WILL ALL KNOW ME,
FROM THE LEAST TO THE
GREATEST OF THEM.
12 "ᴬFOR I WILL BE MERCIFUL
TOWARD THEIR
WRONGDOINGS,
AND THEIR SINS I WILL NO
LONGER REMEMBER."

¹³ When He said, "ᴬA new *covenant*," He has made the first obsolete. But whatever is becoming obsolete and growing old is about to disappear.

THE OLD AND THE NEW

9 Now even the first *covenant* had ᴬregulations for divine worship and the earthly sanctuary. ² For ᴬa tabernacle was equipped, the outer *sanctuary,* in which *were* the lampstand, the table, and the sacred bread; this is called the Holy Place. ³ Behind ᴬthe second veil there was a tabernacle which is called the Most Holy Place, ⁴ having a golden ᴬaltar of incense and the ark of the covenant covered on all sides with gold, in which was a golden jar holding the manna, Aaron's staff which budded, and the tablets of the covenant; ⁵ and above it *were* the cherubim of glory ᴬovershadowing the ¹atoning cover; but about these things we cannot now speak in detail.

⁶ Now when these things have been so prepared, the priests ᴬare continually entering the outer tabernacle, performing the divine worship, ⁷ but into the second, only the high priest *enters* once a year, ᴬnot without *taking* blood which he offers for himself and for the ᴮsins of the people committed in ignorance. ⁸ The Holy Spirit *is* signifying this, ᴬthat the way into the holy place has not yet been disclosed while the outer tabernacle is still standing, ⁹ which *is* a symbol for the present time. Accordingly ᴬboth gifts and sacrifices are offered which cannot make the worshiper perfect in conscience, ¹⁰ since they

8:8ᴬJer 31:31   8:9ᴬEx 19:5; Jer 31:32   8:10ᴬJer 31:33;
Rom 11:27   8:11ᴬJer 31:34   8:12ᴬIs 43:25; Jer 31:34
8:13ᴬLuke 22:20; 2 Cor 3:6   9:1ᴬHeb 9:10
9:2ᴬEx 25:8, 9; 26:1-30   9:3ᴬEx 26:31-33; 40:3
9:4ᴬEx 30:1-5; 37:25f   9:5ᴬEx 25:17, 20; Lev 16:2
9:6ᴬNum 18:2-6; 28:3   9:7ᴬLev 16:11, 14
ᴮNum 15:25   9:8ᴬJohn 14:6; Heb 10:20   9:9ᴬHeb 5:1

9:5¹Also called *mercy seat;* i.e., where blood was
sprinkled on the Day of Atonement

relate only to ^food, drink, and various washings, regulations for the body imposed until ^B a time of reformation.

^11 But when Christ appeared *as* a ^high priest of the good things ¹having come, *He entered* through the greater and more perfect tabernacle, not made by hands, that is, not of this creation; ^12 and not through the blood of goats and calves, but ^through His own blood, He entered the holy place once for all *time,* having obtained eternal redemption. ^13 For if ^the blood of goats and bulls, and the ¹ashes of a heifer sprinkling those who have been defiled, sanctify for the cleansing of the flesh, ^14 how much more will ^the blood of Christ, who through the eternal Spirit offered Himself without blemish to God, cleanse your conscience from dead works to serve the living God?

^15 For this reason He is the ^mediator of a new covenant, so that, since a death has taken place for the redemption of the violations that were *committed* under the first covenant, those who have been called may receive the promise of the eternal inheritance. ^16 For where there is a covenant, there must of necessity be the death of the one who made it. ^17 For a covenant is valid *only* when *people are* dead, ¹for it is never in force while the one who made it lives. ^18 Therefore even the first *covenant* was not inaugurated without blood. ^19 For when every commandment had been spoken by Moses to all the people according to the Law, ^he took the blood of the calves and the goats, with ^B water and scarlet wool and hyssop, and sprinkled both the book itself and all the people, ^20 saying, "^A THIS IS THE BLOOD OF THE COVENANT WHICH GOD COMMANDED YOU." ^21 And in the same way he ^sprinkled both the tabernacle and all the vessels of the ministry with the blood. ^22 And ^almost all things are cleansed with blood, according to the Law, and without the shedding of blood there is no forgiveness.

^23 Therefore it was necessary for the ^copies of the things in the heavens to be cleansed with these things, but ^the heavenly things themselves with better sacrifices than these. ^24 For Christ ^did not enter a holy place made by hands, a *mere* copy of the true one, but into heaven itself, now to appear in the presence of God for us; ^25 nor was it that He would offer Himself often, as ^the high priest enters the Holy Place ^year by year with blood that is not his own. ^26 Otherwise, He would have needed to suffer often since the foundation of the world; but now ^once at the consummation of the ages He has been revealed to put away sin by the sacrifice of Himself. ^27 And just as ^it is destined for people to die once, and after this ^B *comes* judgment, ^28 so Christ also, having been offered once to ^bear the sins of many, will appear a second time for salvation without *reference to* sin, to those who eagerly await Him.

9:10 ^Lev 11:2ff   ^B Heb 7:12   9:11 ^Heb 2:17
9:12 ^Heb 9:14; 13:12   9:13 ^Lev 16:15; Heb 9:19
9:14 ^Heb 9:12; 13:12   9:15 ^1 Tim 2:5; Heb 8:6
9:19 ^Ex 24:6ff   ^B Lev 14:4, 7   9:20 ^Ex 24:8;
Matt 26:28   9:21 ^Ex 24:6; 40:9   9:22 ^Lev 5:11f
9:23 ^Heb 8:5   9:24 ^Heb 4:14; 9:12   9:25 ^Heb 9:7
9:26 ^Heb 7:27; 9:12   9:27 ^Gen 3:19   ^B 2 Cor 5:10
9:28 ^Is 53:12; 1 Pet 2:24

9:11 ¹One early ms *to come*   9:13 ¹I.e., ashes mixed in water   9:17 ¹One early ms *for is it then...lives?*

ONE SACRIFICE OF CHRIST IS SUFFICIENT

10 For the Law, since it has *only* a shadow of the good things to come *and* not the form of those things itself, [1]can ^never, by the same sacrifices which they offer continually every year, ^Bmake those who approach perfect. [2]Otherwise, would they not have ceased to be offered, because the worshipers, having once been cleansed, would no longer have had ^consciousness of sins? [3]But ^in those *sacrifices* there is a reminder of sins every year. [4]For it is impossible for the ^blood of bulls and goats to take away sins. [5]Therefore, when He comes into the world, He says,

"^YOU HAVE NOT DESIRED
    SACRIFICE AND OFFERING,
BUT YOU HAVE PREPARED A BODY
    FOR ME;
[6] ^YOU HAVE NOT TAKEN PLEASURE
    IN WHOLE BURNT OFFERINGS
    AND *OFFERINGS* FOR SIN.
[7] "^THEN I SAID, 'BEHOLD, I HAVE
    COME
    (IT IS WRITTEN OF ME IN THE
    SCROLL OF THE BOOK)
TO DO YOUR WILL, O GOD.'"

[8]After saying above, "^SACRIFICES AND OFFERINGS AND WHOLE BURNT OFFERINGS AND *OFFERINGS* FOR SIN YOU HAVE NOT DESIRED, NOR HAVE YOU TAKEN PLEASURE *IN THEM*" (which are offered according to the Law), [9]then He said, "^BEHOLD, I HAVE COME TO DO YOUR WILL." He takes away the first in order to establish the second. [10]By this will, we have been ^sanctified through ^Bthe offering of the body of Jesus Christ once for all *time*.

[11]Every priest stands daily ministering and ^offering time after time the same sacrifices, which [12]can never take away sins; but He, having offered one sacrifice for sins for all time, ^SAT DOWN AT THE RIGHT HAND OF GOD, [13]waiting from that time onward ^UNTIL HIS ENEMIES ARE MADE A FOOTSTOOL FOR HIS FEET. [14]For by one offering He has ^perfected for all time those who are sanctified. [15]And ^the Holy Spirit also testifies to us; for after saying,

[16] "^THIS IS THE COVENANT WHICH
    I WILL MAKE WITH THEM
    AFTER THOSE DAYS, DECLARES
    THE LORD:
    I WILL PUT MY LAWS UPON
    THEIR HEARTS,
    AND WRITE THEM ON THEIR
    MIND,"

He then says,

[17] "^AND THEIR SINS AND THEIR
    LAWLESS DEEDS
    I WILL NO LONGER REMEMBER."

[18]Now where there is forgiveness of these things, an offering for sin is no longer *required*.

A NEW AND LIVING WAY

[19]Therefore, brothers *and sisters,* since we have confidence to ^enter the holy place by the blood of Jesus, [20]by a new and living way which He inaugurated for us through ^the veil, that is, *through* His flesh, [21]and since *we have* a great priest ^over the house of God, [22]let's ^approach *God* with a sincere heart in full assurance of faith, having our

10:1^Rom 8:3 ^BHeb 7:19 10:2^1 Pet 2:19
10:3^Heb 9:7 10:4^Heb 9:12f 10:5^Ps 40:6
10:6^Ps 40:6 10:7^Ps 40:7, 8 10:8^Ps 40:6;
Heb 10:5f 10:9^Ps 40:7, 8; Heb 10:7
10:10^John 17:19 ^BEph 5:2 10:11^Heb 5:1
^BMic 6:6-8 10:12^Ps 110:1; Heb 1:3 10:13^Ps 110:1;
Heb 1:13 10:14^Heb 10:1 10:15^Heb 3:7
10:16^Jer 31:33; Heb 8:10 10:17^Jer 31:34; Heb 8:12
10:19^Heb 9:25 10:20^Heb 6:19; 9:3
10:21^1 Tim 3:15; Heb 3:6 10:22^Heb 7:19; 10:1

hearts sprinkled *clean* from an evil conscience and our bodies washed with pure water. ²³Let's hold firmly to the ^confession of our hope without wavering, for He who promised is faithful; ²⁴and let's consider how ^to encourage one another in love and good deeds, ²⁵not abandoning our own meeting together, as is the habit of some people, but ^encouraging *one another;* and all the more as you see the day drawing near.

CHRIST OR JUDGMENT

²⁶For if we go on ^sinning willfully after receiving ^Bthe knowledge of the truth, there no longer remains a sacrifice for sins, ²⁷but a terrifying expectation of judgment and ^THE FURY OF A FIRE WHICH WILL CONSUME THE ADVERSARIES. ²⁸^Anyone who has ignored the Law of Moses is put to death without mercy on *the testimony of* two or three witnesses. ²⁹How much more severe punishment do you think he will deserve who has trampled underfoot the Son of God, and has regarded as unclean ^the blood of the covenant by which he was sanctified, and has insulted the Spirit of grace? ³⁰For we know Him who said, "^AVENGEANCE IS MINE, I WILL REPAY." And again, "^BTHE LORD WILL JUDGE HIS PEOPLE." ³¹It is a terrifying thing to fall into the hands of the ^living God.

³²But remember the former days, when, after being ^enlightened, you endured a great ^Bconflict of sufferings, ³³partly by being ^made a public spectacle through insults and distress, and partly by becoming ^Bcompanions with those who were so treated. ³⁴For you showed sympathy to the prisoners and accepted ^joyfully the seizure of your property, knowing that you have for

yourselves a better and lasting possession. ³⁵Therefore, do not throw away your ^confidence, which has a great reward. ³⁶For you have need of ^endurance, so that when you have done the will of God, you may ^Breceive what was promised.
³⁷　^AFOR YET IN A VERY LITTLE
WHILE,
HE WHO IS COMING WILL COME,
AND WILL NOT DELAY.
³⁸　^ABUT MY RIGHTEOUS ONE WILL
LIVE BY FAITH;
AND IF HE SHRINKS BACK, MY
SOUL HAS NO PLEASURE IN
HIM.
³⁹But we are not among those who shrink back to destruction, but of those who have faith for the safekeeping of the soul.

THE TRIUMPHS OF FAITH

11 Now faith is *the* ^certainty of *things* hoped for, a proof of things not seen. ²For by it the people of old ^gained approval.

³By faith we understand that the ^world has been created by the word of God so that what is seen has not been made out of things that are visible. ⁴By faith ^Abel offered to God a better sacrifice than Cain, through which he was attested to be righteous, God testifying about his gifts, and through faith, though he is dead, he still speaks. ⁵By faith ^Enoch was taken up so that he would not see death;

10:23^Heb 3:1　**10:24**^Heb 13:1　**10:25**^Heb 3:13
10:26^Num 15:30　^B1 Tim 2:4　**10:27**^Is 26:11;
2 Thess 1:7　**10:28**^Deut 17:2-6; 19:15
10:29^Ex 24:8; Matt 26:28　**10:30**^Rom 12:19
^BDeut 32:36　**10:31**^Matt 16:16; Heb 3:12
10:32^Heb 6:4　^BPhil 1:30　**10:33**^1 Cor 4:9
^BPhil 4:14　**10:34**^Matt 5:12　**10:35**^Heb 10:19
10:36^Luke 21:19　^BHeb 9:15　**10:37**^Hab 2:3;
Heb 10:25　**10:38**^Hab 2:4; Rom 1:17　**11:1**^Heb 3:14
11:2^Heb 11:4, 39　**11:3**^John 1:3; Heb 1:2
11:4^Gen 4:4; Matt 23:35　**11:5**^Gen 5:21-24

AND HE WAS NOT FOUND BECAUSE GOD TOOK HIM UP; for before he was taken up, he was attested to have been pleasing to God. ⁶And without faith it is impossible to please *Him,* for the one who ᴬcomes to God must believe that He exists, and *that* He proves to be One who rewards those who seek Him. ⁷By faith ᴬNoah, being warned *by God* about things not yet seen, in reverence prepared an ark for the salvation of his household, by which he condemned the world, and became an heir of the righteousness which is according to faith.

⁸By faith ᴬAbraham, when he was called, obeyed by going out to a place which he was to receive for an inheritance; and he left, not knowing where he was going. ⁹By faith he lived as a stranger in ᴬthe land of promise, as *in* a foreign *land,* living in tents with Isaac and Jacob, fellow heirs of the same promise; ¹⁰for he was looking for ᴬthe city which has foundations, whose architect and builder is God. ¹¹By faith even ᴬSarah herself received ability to conceive, even beyond *the* proper time of life, since she considered Him faithful who had promised. ¹²Therefore even from one man, and ᴬone who was *as good as* dead at that, there were born *descendants who were* ᴮjust as the stars of heaven in number, and as the innumerable *grains of* sand along the seashore.

¹³All these died in faith, ᴬwithout receiving the promises, but having seen and welcomed them from a distance, and ᴮhaving confessed that they were strangers and exiles on the earth. ¹⁴For those who say such things make it clear that they are seeking a country of

their own. ¹⁵And indeed if they had been thinking of that *country* which they left, ᴬthey would have had opportunity to return. ¹⁶But as it is, they desire a better *country,* that is, a ᴬheavenly one. Therefore God is not ashamed to be called their God; for ᴮHe has prepared a city for them.

¹⁷By faith ᴬAbraham, when he was tested, offered up Isaac, and the one who had ᴮreceived the promises was offering up his ¹only *son;* ¹⁸*it was he* to whom it was said, "ᴬTHROUGH ISAAC YOUR DESCENDANTS SHALL BE NAMED." ¹⁹He considered that ᴬGod is able to raise *people* even from the dead, from which he also received him back as a type. ²⁰By faith ᴬIsaac blessed Jacob and Esau, even regarding things to come. ²¹By faith ᴬJacob, as he was dying, blessed each of the sons of Joseph, and worshiped, *leaning* on the top of his staff. ²²By faith ᴬJoseph, when he was dying, made mention of the exodus of the sons of Israel, and gave orders concerning his bones.

²³By faith ᴬMoses, when he was born, was hidden for three months by his parents, because they saw he was a beautiful child; and they were not afraid of the ᴮking's edict. ²⁴By faith Moses, ᴬwhen he had grown up, refused to be called the son of Pharaoh's daughter, ²⁵choosing rather to ᴬendure ill-treatment

11:6ᴬHeb 7:19   11:7ᴬGen 6:13-22   11:8ᴬGen 12:1-4; Acts 7:2-4   11:9ᴬActs 7:5   11:10ᴬHeb 12:22; 13:14
11:11ᴬGen 17:19; 18:11-14   11:12ᴬRom 4:19
ᴮGen 22:17   11:13ᴬHeb 11:39   ᴮGen 23:4
11:15ᴬGen 24:6-8   11:16ᴬ2 Tim 4:18   ᴮHeb 11:10
11:17ᴬGen 22:1-10   ᴮHeb 11:13   11:18ᴬGen 21:12;
Rom 9:7   11:19ᴬRom 4:21   11:20ᴬGen 27:27-29, 39f
11:21ᴬGen 48:1, 5, 16, 20   11:22ᴬGen 50:24f; Ex 13:19
11:23ᴬEx 2:2   ᴮEx 1:16, 22   11:24ᴬEx 2:10, 11ff
11:25ᴬHeb 11:37

11:17 ¹I.e., only son with Sarah

with the people of God than to enjoy the temporary pleasures of sin, ²⁶ᴬconsidering the reproach of Christ greater riches than the treasures of Egypt; for he was looking to the reward. ²⁷By faith he ᴬleft Egypt, not ᴮfearing the wrath of the king; for he persevered, as though seeing Him who is unseen. ²⁸By faith he ᴬkept the Passover and the sprinkling of the blood, so that the destroyer of the firstborn would not touch them. ²⁹By faith they ᴬpassed through the Red Sea as through dry land; and the Egyptians, when they attempted it, were drowned.

³⁰By faith ᴬthe walls of Jericho fell down ᴮafter *the Israelites* had marched around them for seven days. ³¹By faith the prostitute ᴬRahab did not perish along with those who were disobedient, after she had welcomed the spies in peace.

³²And what more shall I say? For time will fail me if I tell of Gideon, ᴬBarak, Samson, Jephthah, of David and Samuel and the prophets, ³³who by faith conquered kingdoms, performed *acts of* righteousness, ᴬobtained promises, shut the mouths of lions, ³⁴ᴬquenched the power of fire, escaped the edge of the sword, from weakness were made strong, became mighty in war, put foreign armies to flight. ³⁵ᴬWomen received *back* their dead by resurrection; and others were tortured, not accepting their release, so that they might obtain a better resurrection; ³⁶and others experienced mocking and flogging, and further, ᴬchains and imprisonment. ³⁷They were ᴬstoned, they were sawn in two, ¹they were tempted, they were put to death with the sword; they went about in sheepskins, in goatskins, being

destitute, afflicted, tormented ³⁸(*people* of whom the world was not worthy), ᴬwandering in deserts, *on* mountains, and *sheltering in* caves and holes in the ground.

³⁹And all these, having gained approval through their faith, ᴬdid not receive what was promised, ⁴⁰because God had provided ᴬsomething better for us, so that ᴮapart from us they would not be made perfect.

JESUS, THE EXAMPLE

12 Therefore, since we also have such a great cloud of witnesses surrounding us, let's ᴬrid ourselves of every obstacle and the sin which so easily entangles us, and let's run with endurance the race that is set before us, ²looking only at Jesus, the ᴬoriginator and perfecter of the faith, who for the joy set before Him ᴮendured the cross, despising the shame, and has sat down at the right hand of the throne of God.

³For ᴬconsider Him who has endured such hostility by sinners against Himself, so that you will not grow weary and lose heart.

A FATHER'S DISCIPLINE

⁴ᴬYou have not yet resisted ᴮto the point of shedding blood in your striving against sin; ⁵and you have forgotten the exhortation which is addressed to you as sons,

11:26ᴬLuke 14:33; Phil 3:7f　11:27ᴬEx 2:15　ᴮEx 2:14
11:28ᴬEx 12:21ff　11:29ᴬEx 14:22-29
11:30ᴬJosh 6:20　ᴮJosh 6:15f　11:31ᴬJosh 2:9ff; 6:23
11:32ᴬJudg ch 4, 5　11:33ᴬ2 Sam 7:11f
11:34ᴬDan 3:23ff　11:35ᴬ1 Kin 17:23; 2 Kin 4:36f
11:36ᴬGen 39:20; 1 Kin 22:27　11:37ᴬ1 Kin 21:13;
2 Chr 24:21　11:38ᴬ1 Kin 18:4, 13; 19:9
11:39ᴬHeb 10:36; 11:13　11:40ᴬHeb 11:16　ᴮRev 6:11
12:1ᴬRom 13:12; Eph 4:22　12:2ᴬHeb 2:10　ᴮPhil 2:8f
12:3ᴬRev 2:3　12:4ᴬHeb 10:32ff　ᴮPhil 2:8

11:37¹One early ms does not contain *they were tempted*

"ᴬMᴦ sᴏɴ, ᴅᴏ ɴᴏᴛ ʀᴇɢᴀʀᴅ
ʟɪɢʜᴛʟʏ ᴛʜᴇ ᴅɪsᴄɪᴘʟɪɴᴇ ᴏꜰ
ᴛʜᴇ Lᴏʀᴅ,
Nᴏʀ ꜰᴀɪɴᴛ ᴡʜᴇɴ ʏᴏᴜ ᴀʀᴇ
ᴘᴜɴɪsʜᴇᴅ ʙʏ Hɪᴍ;
6   ᴬFᴏʀ ᴡʜᴏᴍ ᴛʜᴇ Lᴏʀᴅ ʟᴏᴠᴇs Hᴇ
ᴅɪsᴄɪᴘʟɪɴᴇs,
Aɴᴅ Hᴇ ᴘᴜɴɪsʜᴇs ᴇᴠᴇʀʏ sᴏɴ
ᴡʜᴏᴍ Hᴇ ᴀᴄᴄᴇᴘᴛs."
⁷It is for discipline that you endure;
ᴬGod deals with you as with sons; for
what son is there whom *his* father
does not discipline? ⁸But if you are
without discipline, ᴬof which all
have become partakers, then you
are illegitimate children and not
sons. ⁹Furthermore, we had earthly
fathers to discipline us, and we
respected *them;* shall we not much
more be subject to ᴬthe Father of
spirits, and ᴮlive? ¹⁰For they disciplined *us* for a short time as seemed
best to them, but He *disciplines us*
for *our* good, ᴬso that we may share
His holiness. ¹¹For the moment, all
discipline seems not to be pleasant,
but painful; yet to those who have
been trained by it, afterward it yields
the ᴬpeaceful fruit of righteousness.
¹²Therefore, ᴬstrengthen the
hands that are weak and the knees
that are feeble, ¹³and ᴬmake straight
paths for your feet, so that *the limb*
which is impaired may not be dislocated, but rather be healed.
¹⁴ᴬPursue peace with all people,
and the holiness without which
no one will see the Lord. ¹⁵See to it
that no one comes short of the grace
of God; that no ᴬroot of bitterness
springing up causes trouble, and
by it many become ᴮdefiled; ¹⁶that
there be no sexually immoral or
ᴬgodless person like Esau, ᴮwho sold
his own birthright for a *single* meal.
¹⁷For you know that even afterward, ᴬwhen he wanted to inherit

the blessing, he was rejected, for
he found no place for repentance,
though he sought for it with tears.

CONTRAST OF SINAI AND ZION

¹⁸For you have not come to ᴬ*a mountain* that can be touched and to a
blazing fire, and to darkness and
gloom and whirlwind, ¹⁹and to the
ᴬblast of a trumpet and the sound of
words, which *sound was such that*
those who heard ᴮbegged that no
further word be spoken to them.
²⁰For they could not cope with
the command, "ᴬIf even an animal
touches the mountain, it shall be
stoned." ²¹And so terrible was the
sight, *that* Moses said, "ᴬI am terrified and trembling." ²²But ᴬyou have
come to Mount Zion and to ᴮthe city
of the living God, the heavenly Jerusalem, and to myriads of angels, ²³to
the general assembly and church of
the firstborn who ᴬare enrolled in
heaven, and to God, the Judge of all,
and to the spirits of *the* righteous
made perfect, ²⁴and to Jesus, the
ᴬmediator of a new covenant, and to
the ᴮsprinkled blood, which speaks
better than *the blood* of Abel.

THE UNSHAKEN KINGDOM

²⁵See to it that you do not refuse
Him who is speaking. For if those
did not escape when they refused
him who ᴬwarned *them* on earth,
much less *will* we *escape* who turn
away from Him who ᴬ*warns us* from

12:5 ᴬJob 5:17; Prov 3:11   12:6 ᴬProv 3:12
12:7 ᴬDeut 8:5; 2 Sam 7:14   12:8 ᴬ1 Pet 5:9
12:9 ᴬNum 16:22   ᴮIs 38:16   12:10 ᴬ2 Pet 1:4
12:11 ᴬIs 32:17; James 3:17f   12:12 ᴬIs 35:3
12:13 ᴬProv 4:26; Gal 2:14   12:14 ᴬRom 14:19
12:15 ᴬDeut 29:18   ᴮTitus 1:15   12:16 ᴬ1 Tim 1:9
ᴮGen 25:33f   12:17 ᴬGen 27:30-40
12:18 ᴬEx 19:12, 16ff; Deut 4:11   12:19 ᴬMatt 24:31
ᴮEx 20:19   12:20 ᴬEx 19:12f   12:21 ᴬDeut 9:19
12:22 ᴬRev 14:1   ᴮHeb 11:10   12:23 ᴬLuke 10:20
12:24 ᴬ1 Tim 2:5   ᴮHeb 9:19   12:25 ᴬEx 20:22; Heb 8:5

heaven. ²⁶And His voice shook the earth then, but now He has promised, saying, "ᴬYᴇᴛ ᴏɴᴄᴇ ᴍᴏʀᴇ I ᴡɪʟʟ sʜᴀᴋᴇ ɴᴏᴛ ᴏɴʟʏ ᴛʜᴇ ᴇᴀʀᴛʜ, ʙᴜᴛ ᴀʟsᴏ ᴛʜᴇ ʜᴇᴀᴠᴇɴ." ²⁷This *expression*, "Yet once more," denotes ᴬthe removing of those things which can be shaken, as of created things, so that those things which cannot be shaken may remain. ²⁸Therefore, since we receive a ᴬkingdom which cannot be shaken, let's show gratitude, by which we may offer to God an acceptable service with reverence and awe; ²⁹for ᴬour God is a consuming fire.

THE CHANGELESS CHRIST

13 Let ᴬlove of the brothers *and* sisters continue. ²Do not neglect hospitality to strangers, for by this some have ᴬentertained angels without knowing it. ³ᴬRemember the prisoners, as though in prison with them, *and* those who are badly treated, since you yourselves also are in the body. ⁴Marriage *is to be held* in honor among all, and the *marriage* bed *is to be* undefiled; ᴬfor God will judge the sexually immoral and adulterers. ⁵*Make sure that* your character is free from the love of money, being content with what you have; for He Himself has said, "ᴬI ᴡɪʟʟ ɴᴇᴠᴇʀ ᴅᴇsᴇʀᴛ ʏᴏᴜ, ɴᴏʀ ᴡɪʟʟ I ᴇᴠᴇʀ ᴀʙᴀɴᴅᴏɴ ʏᴏᴜ," ⁶so that we confidently say,

"ᴬTʜᴇ Lᴏʀᴅ ɪs ᴍʏ ʜᴇʟᴘᴇʀ, I ᴡɪʟʟ ɴᴏᴛ ʙᴇ ᴀꜰʀᴀɪᴅ.
Wʜᴀᴛ ᴡɪʟʟ ᴍᴀɴ ᴅᴏ ᴛᴏ ᴍᴇ?"

⁷Remember ᴬthose who led you, who spoke the word of God to you; and considering the result of their way of life, imitate their faith. ⁸ᴬJesus Christ *is* the same yesterday and today, and forever. ⁹ᴬDo not be misled by varied and strange teachings; for it is good for the heart to be strengthened by grace, not by foods, ᴮthrough which those who were so occupied were not benefited. ¹⁰We have an altar ᴬfrom which those who serve the tabernacle have no right to eat. ¹¹For ᴬthe bodies of those animals whose blood is brought into the Holy Place by the high priest *as an offering* for sin are burned outside the camp. ¹²Therefore Jesus also suffered outside the gate, that He might sanctify the people ᴬthrough His own blood. ¹³So then, let us go out to Him outside the camp, ᴬbearing His reproach. ¹⁴For here we do not have a lasting city, but we are seeking ᴬ*the city* which is to come.

GOD-PLEASING SACRIFICES

¹⁵Through Him then, let's continually offer up a sacrifice of praise to God, that is, ᴬthe fruit of lips praising His name. ¹⁶And do not neglect doing good and ᴬsharing, for ᴮwith such sacrifices God is pleased.

¹⁷Obey your leaders and submit *to them*—for ᴬthey keep watch over your souls as those who will give an account—so that they may do this with joy, not groaning; for this *would be* unhelpful for you.

¹⁸Pray for us, for we are sure that we have a ᴬgood conscience, desiring to conduct ourselves honorably in all things. ¹⁹And I urge *you* all the

12:26ᴬHag 2:6   **12:27**ᴬIs 34:4; 54:10   **12:28**ᴬDan 2:44
12:29ᴬDeut 4:24; Heb 10:27, 31   **13:1**ᴬRom 12:10;
1 Thess 4:9   **13:2**ᴬGen 18:1ff; 19:1f   **13:3**ᴬCol 4:18
13:4ᴬ1 Cor 6:9; Gal 5:19, 21   **13:5**ᴬDeut 31:6, 8; Josh 1:5
13:6ᴬPs 118:6   **13:7**ᴬHeb 13:17, 24   **13:8**ᴬHeb 1:12
13:9ᴬEph 4:14   ᴮHeb 9:10   **13:10**ᴬ1 Cor 10:18
13:11ᴬEx 29:14; Lev 4:12, 21   **13:12**ᴬHeb 9:12
13:13ᴬLuke 9:23; Heb 11:26   **13:14**ᴬHeb 11:10, 16; 12:22
13:15ᴬIs 57:19; Hos 14:2   **13:16**ᴬRom 12:13   ᴮPhil 4:18
13:17ᴬEzek 3:17; Acts 20:28   **13:18**ᴬActs 24:16;
1 Tim 1:5

more to do this, ^so that I may be restored to you more quickly.

BENEDICTION

20 Now may ^the God of peace, who brought up from the dead the ^Bgreat Shepherd of the sheep through the blood of the eternal covenant, *that is,* Jesus our Lord, 21^equip you in every good thing to do His will, ^Bworking in us that which is pleasing in His sight, through Jesus Christ, to whom *be* the glory forever and ever. Amen.

22 But I urge you, ^brothers *and sisters,* listen patiently to this ^word of exhortation, for ^BI have written to you briefly. 23 Know that ^our brother Timothy has been released, with whom, if he comes soon, I will see you. 24 Greet ^all of your leaders and all the saints. Those from Italy greet you.

25 ^Grace be with you all.

13:19 ^Philem 22   **13:20** ^Rom 15:33   ^BJohn 10:11
13:21 ^1 Pet 5:10   ^BPhil 2:13   **13:22** ^Heb 3:1   ^B1 Pet 5:12
13:23 ^Acts 16:1; Col 1:1   **13:24** ^1 Cor 16:16; Heb 13:7, 17
13:25 ^Col 4:18

JAMES

THE TESTING OF YOUR FAITH

1 ^A^James, a bond-servant of God and of the Lord Jesus Christ,
To the twelve tribes who are dispersed abroad: Greetings.

2 ^A^Consider it all joy, my brothers *and sisters,* when you encounter ^B^various trials, 3 knowing that the testing of your faith produces ^A^endurance. 4 And let endurance have *its* perfect result, so that you may be ^A^perfect and complete, lacking in nothing.

5 But if any of you ^A^lacks wisdom, let him ask of God, who gives to all generously and without reproach, and ^B^it will be given to him. 6 But he must ^A^ask in faith without any doubting, for the one who doubts is like the surf of the sea, driven and tossed by the wind. 7 For that person ought not to expect that he will receive anything from the Lord, 8 *being* a ^A^double-minded man, unstable in all his ways.

9 ^A^Now the brother *or sister* of humble *circumstances* is to glory in his high position; 10 but the rich person *is to glory* in his humiliation, because ^A^like flowering grass he will pass away. 11 For the sun rises with ^A^its scorching heat and ^B^withers the grass; and its flower falls off and the beauty of its appearance is destroyed; so also the rich person, in the midst of his pursuits, will die out.

12 ^A^Blessed is a man who perseveres under trial; for once he has been approved, he will receive the crown of life which *the Lord* ^B^has promised to those who love

Him. 13 No one is to say when he is tempted, "^A^I am being tempted by God"; for God cannot be tempted by evil, and He Himself does not tempt anyone. 14 But each one is tempted when he is carried away and enticed by his own lust. 15 Then when lust has conceived, it gives birth to sin; and ^A^sin, when it has run its course, brings forth death. 16 ^A^Do not be deceived, my beloved brothers *and sisters.* 17 Every good thing given and every perfect gift is ^A^from above, coming down from the Father of lights, with whom there is no variation or shifting shadow. 18 In the exercise of His will He ^A^gave us birth by the word of truth, so that we would be a kind of ^B^first fruits among His creatures.

19 You know *this,* my beloved brothers *and sisters.* Now everyone must be quick to hear, ^A^slow to speak, *and* slow to anger; 20 for a man's ^A^anger does not bring about the righteousness of God. 21 Therefore, ^A^ridding *yourselves* of all filthiness and *all* that remains of wickedness, in humility receive the word implanted, which is able to save your souls. 22 ^A^But prove yourselves doers of the word, and not just hearers who deceive

1:1 ^A^Acts 12:17; Jude 1   1:2 ^A^Matt 5:12   ^B^1 Pet 1:6
1:3 ^A^Luke 21:19   1:4 ^A^Matt 5:48; Col 4:12
1:5 ^A^1 Kin 3:9ff   ^B^Matt 7:7   1:6 ^A^Matt 21:21
1:8 ^A^James 4:8   1:9 ^A^Luke 14:11   1:10 ^A^1 Cor 7:31;
1 Pet 1:24   1:11 ^A^Matt 20:12   ^B^Is 40:7f   1:12 ^A^Luke 6:22
^B^James 2:5   1:13 ^A^Gen 22:1   1:15 ^A^Rom 5:12; 6:23
1:16 ^A^1 Cor 6:9   1:17 ^A^James 3:15, 17   1:18 ^A^1 Pet 1:3, 23
^B^Rev 14:4   1:19 ^A^Prov 10:19; 17:27   1:20 ^A^Matt 5:22;
Eph 4:26   1:21 ^A^Eph 4:22; 1 Pet 2:1   1:22 ^A^Matt 7:24-27;
Luke 6:46-49

themselves. ²³For if anyone is a hearer of the word and not a doer, he is like a man who looks at his natural face ^in a mirror; ²⁴for *once* he has looked at himself and gone away, he has immediately forgotten what kind of person he was. ²⁵But one who has looked intently at the perfect law, the *law* of freedom, and has continued *in it,* not having become a forgetful hearer but an active doer, this person will be ^blessed in what he does.

²⁶If anyone thinks himself to be religious, yet does not ^bridle his tongue but deceives his *own* heart, this person's religion is worthless. ²⁷Pure and undefiled religion in the sight of *our* God and Father is this: to visit orphans and widows in their distress, *and* to keep oneself unstained by ^the world.

THE SIN OF PARTIALITY

2 My brothers *and sisters,* do not hold your faith in our glorious Lord Jesus Christ with *an attitude of* ^personal favoritism. ²For if a man comes into your assembly with a gold ring *and is dressed* in bright clothes, and a poor man in ^dirty clothes also comes in, ³and you pay special attention to the one who is wearing the ^bright clothes, and say, "You sit here in a good *place,*" and you say to the poor man, "You stand over there, or sit down by my footstool," ⁴have you not made distinctions among yourselves, and become judges ^with evil motives? ⁵Listen, my beloved brothers *and sisters:* did ^God not choose the poor of this world *to be* rich in faith and ^heirs of the kingdom which He promised to those who love Him? ⁶But you have dishonored the poor

man. Is it not the rich who oppress you and personally ^drag you into court? ⁷^Do they not blaspheme the good name by which you have been called?

⁸If, however, you are fulfilling the royal law according to the Scripture, "^YOU SHALL LOVE YOUR NEIGHBOR AS YOURSELF," you are doing well. ⁹But if you ^show partiality, you are committing sin *and* are convicted by the Law as violators. ¹⁰For whoever keeps the whole Law, yet ^stumbles in one *point,* has become guilty of all. ¹¹For He who said, "^DO NOT COMMIT ADULTERY," also said, "^DO NOT MURDER." Now if you do not commit adultery, but do murder, you have become a violator of the Law. ¹²So speak, and so act, as those who are to be judged by ^*the* law of freedom. ¹³For ^judgment *will be* merciless to one who has shown no mercy; mercy triumphs over judgment.

FAITH AND WORKS

¹⁴^What use is it, my brothers *and sisters,* if someone says he has faith, but he has no works? Can that faith save him? ¹⁵^If a brother or sister is without clothing and in need of daily food, ¹⁶and one of you says to them, "^Go in peace, be warmed and be filled," yet you do not give them what is necessary for *their* body, what use is that? ¹⁷In the same way, ^faith also, if it has no works, is dead, *being* by itself.

1:23^1 Cor 13:12 1:25^John 13:17 1:26^Ps 39:1; 141:3 1:27^2 Pet 1:4; 1 John 2:15-17 2:1^Acts 10:34; James 2:9 2:2^Zech 3:3f 2:3^Luke 23:11 2:4^Luke 18:6; John 7:24 2:5^Job 34:19 ^Matt 5:3 2:6^Acts 8:3; 16:19 2:7^Acts 11:26; 1 Pet 4:16 2:8^Lev 19:18 2:9^Acts 10:34; James 2:1 2:10^James 3:2; 2 Pet 1:10 2:11^Ex 20:14 ^Deut 5:17 2:12^James 1:25 2:13^Prov 21:13; Matt 5:7 2:14^James 1:22ff 2:15^Matt 25:35f; Luke 3:11 2:16^1 John 3:17f 2:17^Gal 5:6; James 2:20, 26

¹⁸But someone may *well* say, "You have faith and I have works; show me your ^faith without the works, and I will show you my faith by my works." ¹⁹You believe that ¹God is one. You do well; ^the demons also believe, and shudder. ²⁰But are you willing to acknowledge, you foolish person, that ^faith without works is useless? ²¹^Was our father Abraham not justified by works when he offered up his son Isaac on the altar? ²²You see that ^faith was working with his works, and as a result of the ᴮworks, faith was perfected; ²³and the Scripture was fulfilled which says, "^AND ABRAHAM BELIEVED GOD, AND IT WAS CREDITED TO HIM AS RIGHTEOUSNESS," and he was called a friend of God. ²⁴You see that a person is justified by works and not by faith alone. ²⁵In the same way, was ^Rahab the prostitute not justified by works also ᴮwhen she received the messengers and sent them out by another way? ²⁶For just as the body without *the* spirit is dead, so also ^faith without works is dead.

THE TONGUE IS A FIRE

3 ^Do not become teachers in large numbers, my brothers, since you know that we *who are teachers* will incur a stricter judgment. ²For we all stumble in many *ways.* ^If anyone does not stumble in what he says, he is a perfect man, able to rein in the whole body as well. ³Now ^if we put the bits into the horses' mouths so that they will obey us, we direct their whole body as well. ⁴Look at the ships too: though they are so large and are driven by strong winds, they are *nevertheless* directed by a very small rudder wherever the inclination of the pilot determines. ⁵So also the tongue is

a small part *of the body,* and *yet* it ^boasts of great things.

ᴮSee how great a forest is set aflame by such a small fire! ⁶And ^the tongue is a fire, the *very* world of unrighteousness; the tongue is set among our body's parts as that which defiles the whole body and sets on fire the course of *our* life, and is set on fire by ¹hell. ⁷For every species of beasts and birds, of reptiles and creatures of the sea, is tamed and has been tamed by the human race. ⁸But no one *among* mankind can tame the tongue; *it is* a restless evil, full of ^deadly poison. ⁹With it we bless *our* Lord and Father, and with it we curse people, ^who have been made in the likeness of God; ¹⁰from the same mouth come *both* blessing and cursing. My brothers *and sisters,* these things should not be this way. ¹¹Does a spring send out from the same opening *both* fresh and bitter *water?* ¹²^Can a fig tree, my brothers *and sisters,* bear olives, or a vine *bear* figs? Nor *can* salt water produce fresh.

WISDOM FROM ABOVE

¹³Who among you is wise and understanding? Let him show by his ^good behavior his deeds in the gentleness of wisdom. ¹⁴But if you have bitter ^jealousy and selfish ambition in your heart, do not be arrogant and *so* lie against the truth. ¹⁵This wisdom is not that

2:18^Rom 3:28; Heb 11:33   **2:19**^Matt 8:29; Mark 1:24
2:20^Gal 5:6; James 2:17, 26   **2:21**^Gen 22:9, 10, 12,
16-18   **2:22**^Heb 11:17   ᴮ1 Thess 1:3   **2:23**^Gen 15:6;
Rom 4:3   **2:25**^Heb 11:31   ᴮJosh 2:4, 6, 15
2:26^Gal 5:6; James 2:17, 20   **3:1**^Rom 2:20f; 1 Tim 1:7
3:2^Matt 12:34-37; James 3:2-12   **3:3**^Ps 32:9
3:5^Ps 12:3f   ᴮProv 26:20f   **3:6**^Ps 120:2, 3; Prov 16:27
3:8^Ps 140:3; Eccl 10:11   **3:9**^Gen 1:26; 1 Cor 11:7
3:12^Matt 7:16   **3:13**^1 Pet 2:12   **3:14**^Rom 2:8;
2 Cor 12:20

2:19¹One early ms *there is one God*   **3:6**¹Gr *Gehenna*

which comes down ᴬfrom above, but is earthly, natural, demonic. ¹⁶For where ᴬjealousy and selfish ambition exist, there is disorder and every evil thing. ¹⁷But the wisdom from above is first pure, then peace-loving, gentle, reasonable, full of mercy and good fruits, impartial, free of ᴬhypocrisy. ¹⁸And the ᴬfruit of righteousness is sown in peace by those who make peace.

THINGS TO AVOID

4 What is the source of quarrels and ᴬconflicts among you? Is the source not your pleasures that wage ᴮwar in your body's parts? ²You lust and do not have, *so* you ᴬcommit murder. And you are envious and cannot obtain, *so* you fight and quarrel. You do not have because you do not ask. ³You ask and ᴬdo not receive, because you ask with the wrong motives, so that you may spend *what you request* on your pleasures. ⁴You adulteresses, do you not know that friendship with the world is ᴬhostility toward God? ᴮTherefore whoever wants to be a friend of the world makes himself an enemy of God. ⁵Or do you think that the Scripture says to no purpose, "¹He jealously desires ᴬthe Spirit whom He has made to dwell in us"? ⁶But He gives a greater grace. Therefore *it* says, "ᴬGOD IS OPPOSED TO THE PROUD, BUT GIVES GRACE TO THE HUMBLE." ⁷ᴬSubmit therefore to God. But resist the devil, and he will flee from you. ⁸ᴬCome close to God and He will come close to you. ᴮCleanse *your* hands, you sinners; and purify *your* hearts, you double-minded. ⁹ᴬBe miserable, and mourn, and weep; let your laughter be turned into mourning, and your joy into gloom. ¹⁰ᴬHumble

yourselves in the presence of the Lord, and He will exalt you.

¹¹ᴬDo not speak against one another, brothers *and sisters*. The one who speaks against a brother *or sister*, or judges his brother *or sister*, speaks against the law and judges the law; but if you judge the law, you are not a doer of the law but a judge *of it*. ¹²There is *only* one ᴬLawgiver and Judge, the One who is able to save and to destroy; but who are you, judging your neighbor?

¹³Come now, you who say, "ᴬToday or tomorrow we will go to such and such a city, and spend a year there and engage in business and make a profit." ¹⁴Yet you do not know what your life will be like tomorrow. ᴬFor you are *just* a vapor that appears for a little while, and then vanishes away. ¹⁵Instead, *you* ought to say, "ᴬIf the Lord wills, we will live and also do this or that." ¹⁶But as it is, you boast in your arrogance; ᴬall such boasting is evil. ¹⁷So ᴬfor one who knows *the* right thing to do and does not do it, for him it is sin.

MISUSE OF RICHES

5 Come now, ᴬyou rich people, weep and howl for your miseries which are coming upon you. ²ᴬYour riches have rotted and your garments have become moth-eaten. ³Your gold and your silver

---

3:15 ᴬ James 1:17   3:16 ᴬ Rom 2:8; 2 Cor 12:20
3:17 ᴬ Rom 12:9; 2 Cor 6:6   3:18 ᴬ Prov 11:18; Is 32:17
4:1 ᴬ Titus 3:9   ᴮ Rom 7:23   4:2 ᴬ James 5:6; 1 John 3:15
4:3 ᴬ 1 John 3:22; 5:14   4:4 ᴬ Rom 8:7   ᴮ Matt 6:24
4:5 ᴬ 1 Cor 6:19; 2 Cor 6:16   4:6 ᴬ Prov 3:34; 1 Pet 5:5
4:7 ᴬ 1 Pet 5:6   4:8 ᴬ 2 Chr 15:2   ᴮ Job 17:9
4:9 ᴬ Prov 14:13; Luke 6:25   4:10 ᴬ Job 5:11; Luke 1:52
4:11 ᴬ 2 Cor 12:20; James 5:9   4:12 ᴬ Is 33:22; James 5:9
4:13 ᴬ Prov 27:1; Luke 12:18-20   4:14 ᴬ Job 7:7; Ps 39:5
4:15 ᴬ Acts 18:21   4:16 ᴬ 1 Cor 5:6   4:17 ᴬ Luke 12:47;
John 9:41   5:1 ᴬ Luke 6:24; 1 Tim 6:9   5:2 ᴬ Is 50:9;
Matt 6:19f

4:5 ¹Or *The spirit which He has made to dwell in us lusts with envy*

have corroded, and their corrosion will serve as a testimony against you and will consume your flesh like fire. It is ^in the last days that you have stored up your treasure! ⁴Behold, ^the pay of the laborers who mowed your fields, *and* which has been withheld by you, cries out *against you;* and ᴮthe outcry of those who did the harvesting has reached the ears of the Lord of armies. ⁵You have ^lived for pleasure on the earth and lived luxuriously; you have fattened your hearts in a day of slaughter. ⁶You have condemned and ^put to death the righteous person; he offers you no resistance.

EXHORTATION

⁷Therefore be patient, brothers *and sisters,* ^until the coming of the Lord. ᴮThe farmer waits for the precious produce of the soil, being patient about it, until it gets the early and late rains. ⁸^You too be patient; ᴮstrengthen your hearts, for the coming of the Lord is near. ⁹Do not complain, brothers *and sisters,* against one another, so that you may not be judged; behold, ^the Judge is standing ᴮright at the door. ¹⁰As an example, brothers *and sisters,* of suffering and patience, take ^the prophets who spoke in the name of the Lord. ¹¹We count those ^blessed who endured. You have heard of the endurance of Job and have seen the outcome of the Lord's dealings, that ᴮthe Lord is full of compassion and *is* merciful.

¹²But above all, my brothers *and sisters,* ^do not swear, either by heaven or by earth or with any other oath; but your yes is to be yes, and your no, no, so that you do not fall under judgment.

¹³Is anyone among you suffering? ^Then he must pray. Is anyone cheerful? He is to sing praises. ¹⁴Is anyone among you sick? *Then* he must call for the elders of the church and they are to pray over him, ^anointing him with oil in the name of the Lord; ¹⁵and the ^prayer of faith will ¹restore the one who is sick, and the Lord will ᴮraise him up, and if he has committed sins, they will be forgiven him. ¹⁶Therefore, ^confess your sins to one another, and pray for one another so that you may be ᴮhealed. A prayer of a righteous person, when it is ¹brought about, can accomplish much. ¹⁷Elijah was ^a man with a nature like ours, and ᴮhe prayed earnestly that it would not rain, and it did not rain on the earth for three years and six months. ¹⁸Then he ^prayed again, and ᴮthe sky poured rain and the earth produced its fruit.

¹⁹My brothers *and sisters,* ^if anyone among you strays from the truth and someone turns him back, ²⁰let him know that the one who has turned a sinner from the error of his way will ^save his soul from death and cover a multitude of sins.

5:3^James 5:7, 8   5:4^Lev 19:13   ᴮEx 2:23
5:5^Ezek 16:49; Luke 16:19   5:6^James 4:2
5:7^John 21:22   ᴮGal 6:9   5:8^Luke 21:19
ᴮ1 Thess 3:13   5:9^1 Cor 4:5   ᴮMatt 24:33
5:10^Matt 5:12   5:11^Matt 5:10   ᴮEx 34:6
5:12^Matt 5:34-37   5:13^Ps 50:15   5:14^Mark 6:13
5:15^James 1:6   ᴮJohn 6:39   5:16^Matt 3:6
ᴮHeb 12:13   5:17^Acts 14:15   ᴮ1 Kin 17:1
5:18^1 Kin 18:42   ᴮ1 Kin 18:45   5:19^Matt 18:15;
Gal 6:1   5:20^Rom 11:14; 1 Cor 1:21

5:15¹Lit *save*   5:16¹I.e., granted by God

1 PETER

A LIVING HOPE AND A SURE SALVATION

1 Peter, an apostle of Jesus Christ, To those who reside as ᴬstrangers, scattered throughout Pontus, Galatia, Cappadocia, Asia, and Bithynia, ᴮwho are chosen ²according to the ᴬforeknowledge of God the Father, ᴮby the sanctifying work of the Spirit, to obey Jesus Christ and be sprinkled with His blood: May grace and peace be multiplied to you.

³Blessed be the God and Father of our Lord Jesus Christ, who ᴬaccording to His great mercy has caused us to be born again to a living hope through the ᴮresurrection of Jesus Christ from the dead, ⁴to *obtain* an ᴬinheritance *which is* imperishable, undefiled, and will not fade away, reserved in heaven for you, ⁵who are ᴬprotected by the power of God ᴮthrough faith for a salvation ready to be revealed in *the* last time. ⁶ᴬIn this you greatly rejoice, even though now ᴮfor a little while, if necessary, you have been distressed by various trials, ⁷so that the proof of your faith, *being* more precious than gold which perishes though tested by fire, ᴬmay be found to result in praise, glory, and honor at the revelation of Jesus Christ; ⁸and ᴬthough you have not seen Him, you ᴮlove Him, and though you do not see Him now, but believe in Him, you greatly rejoice with joy inexpressible and full of glory, ⁹obtaining as ᴬthe outcome of your faith, the salvation of ¹your souls.

¹⁰ᴬAs to this salvation, the prophets who prophesied of the grace that *would come* to you made careful searches and inquiries, ¹¹seeking to know what person or time ᴬthe Spirit of Christ within them was indicating as He predicted the sufferings of Christ and the glories to follow. ¹²It was revealed to them that they were not serving themselves, but you, in these things which now have been announced to you through those who preached the gospel to you by ᴬthe Holy Spirit sent from heaven—things into which angels long to look.

¹³Therefore, ᴬprepare your minds for action, ᴮkeep sober *in spirit*, set your hope completely on the grace to be brought to you at the revelation of Jesus Christ. ¹⁴As obedient children, do not ᴬbe conformed to the former lusts *which were yours* in your ignorance, ¹⁵but like the Holy One who called you, ᴬbe holy yourselves also ᴮin all *your* behavior; ¹⁶because it is written: "ᴬYOU SHALL BE HOLY, FOR I AM HOLY."

¹⁷If you ᴬaddress as Father the One who impartially judges according to each one's work, conduct yourselves in fear during the time of your stay *on earth;* ¹⁸knowing

1:1 ᴬ1 Pet 2:11   ᴮMatt 24:22   1:2 ᴬRom 8:29
ᴮ2 Thess 2:13   1:3 ᴬTitus 3:5   ᴮ1 Cor 15:20
1:4 ᴬActs 20:32; Rom 8:17   1:5 ᴬJohn 10:28   ᴮEph 2:8
1:6 ᴬRom 5:2   ᴮ1 Pet 5:10   1:7 ᴬRom 2:7
1:8 ᴬJohn 20:29   ᴮEph 3:19   1:9 ᴬRom 6:22
1:10 ᴬMatt 13:17; Luke 10:24   1:11 ᴬ2 Pet 1:21
1:12 ᴬActs 2:2-4   1:13 ᴬEph 6:14   ᴮ1 Thess 5:6, 8
1:14 ᴬRom 12:2; 1 Pet 4:2f   1:15 ᴬ2 Cor 7:1   ᴮJames 3:13
1:16 ᴬLev 11:44f; 19:2   1:17 ᴬPs 89:26; Jer 3:19

1:9 ¹One early ms does not contain *your*

that you were not ^redeemed with perishable things like silver or gold from your ^Bfutile way of life inherited from your forefathers, ^19but with precious ^blood, as of a lamb unblemished and spotless, *the blood* of Christ. ^20For He was ^foreknown before the foundation of the world, but has appeared in these last times for the sake of you ^21who through Him are ^believers in God, who raised Him from the dead and gave Him glory, so that your faith and hope are in God.

^22Since you have ^purified your souls in obedience to the truth for a sincere love of the brothers *and* sisters, fervently love one another from ¹the heart, ^23for you have been ^born again not of seed which is perishable, but imperishable, *that is,* through the living and enduring ^Bword of God. ^24For,

"^ALL FLESH IS LIKE GRASS,
   AND ALL ITS GLORY IS LIKE THE
      FLOWER OF GRASS.
   THE GRASS WITHERS,
   AND THE FLOWER FALLS OFF,
^25   ^BUT THE WORD OF THE LORD
      ENDURES FOREVER."

And this is the word which was preached to you.

AS NEWBORN BABES

2 Therefore, ^rid *yourselves* of all malice and all deceit and hypocrisy and envy and all slander, ^2^and like newborn babies, long for the pure milk of the word, so that by it you may grow in respect to salvation, ^3if you have ^tasted ^Bthe kindness of the Lord.

AS LIVING STONES

^4And coming to Him as to a living stone which has been ^rejected by people, but is choice and precious

in the sight of God, ^5you also, as living stones, are being built up as a spiritual house for a holy ^priesthood, to ^Boffer spiritual sacrifices that are acceptable to God through Jesus Christ. ^6For *this* is contained in Scripture:

"^BEHOLD, I AM LAYING IN ZION
   A CHOICE STONE, A PRECIOUS
      CORNERSTONE,
   AND THE ONE WHO BELIEVES
      IN HIM WILL NOT BE PUT TO
      SHAME."

^7This precious value, then, is for you who believe; but for unbelievers,

"^A STONE WHICH THE BUILDERS
      REJECTED,
   THIS BECAME THE CHIEF
      CORNERSTONE,"

^8and,

"^A STONE OF STUMBLING AND A
      ROCK OF OFFENSE";

for they stumble because they are disobedient to the word, and to this they were also appointed.

^9But you are A CHOSEN PEOPLE, A royal PRIESTHOOD, A ^HOLY NATION, A PEOPLE FOR *GOD'S* OWN POSSESSION, so that you may proclaim the excellencies of Him who has called you out of darkness into His marvelous light; ^10^for you once were NOT A PEOPLE, but now you are THE PEOPLE OF GOD; you had NOT RECEIVED MERCY, but now you have RECEIVED MERCY.

^11Beloved, I urge *you* as ^foreigners and strangers to abstain from fleshly lusts, which wage ^Bwar against the soul. ^12Keep your

---

1:18^Is 52:3   ^BEph 4:17   1:19^Acts 20:28; 1 Pet 1:2
1:20^Acts 2:23; Eph 1:4   1:21^Rom 4:24; 10:9
1:22^James 4:8   1:23^John 3:3   ^BHeb 4:12
1:24^Is 40:6ff; James 1:10f   1:25^Is 40:8
2:1^Eph 4:22, 25, 31; James 1:21   2:2^Matt 18:3; 19:14
2:3^Heb 6:5   ^BPs 34:8   2:4^1 Pet 2:7   2:5^Is 61:6
^BRom 15:16   2:6^Is 28:16; Rom 9:32, 33   2:7^Ps 118:22;
Matt 21:42   2:8^Is 8:14   2:9^Ex 19:6; Deut 7:6
2:10^Hos 1:10; Rom 9:25   2:11^Lev 25:23   ^BJames 4:1

1:22 ¹Two early mss *a pure heart*

behavior excellent among the Gentiles, so that in the thing in which they slander you as evildoers, they may because of your good deeds, as they observe *them,* glorify God ^on the day of 'visitation.

HONOR AUTHORITY

13^Submit yourselves for the Lord's sake to every human institution, whether to a king as the one in authority, 14or to governors as sent by him ^for the punishment of evildoers and the ^praise of those who do right. 15For ^such is the will of God, that by doing right you silence the ignorance of foolish people. 16*Act* as ^free people, and do not use your freedom as a covering for evil, but *use it* as ^bond-servants of God. 17^Honor all people, love the brotherhood, ^fear God, honor the king.

18^Servants, be subject to your masters with all respect, not only to those who are good and gentle, but also to those who are harsh. 19For this *finds* favor, if for the sake of ^conscience toward God a person endures grief when suffering unjustly. 20For what credit is there if, when you sin and are harshly treated, you endure it with patience? But if ^when you do what is right and suffer *for it* you patiently endure it, this *finds* favor with God.

CHRIST IS OUR EXAMPLE

21For you have been called for this purpose, ^because Christ also suffered for you, leaving you an example, so that you would follow in His steps, 22HE WHO ^COMMITTED NO SIN, NOR WAS ANY DECEIT found IN HIS MOUTH; 23and while being ^abusively insulted, He did not insult in return; while suffering, He did not threaten, but kept entrusting

Himself to Him who judges righteously; 24and He Himself ^brought our sins in His body up on the 'cross, so that we might die to sin and live for righteousness; ^by His wounds you were healed. 25For you were ^continually straying like sheep, but now you have returned to the ^Shepherd and Guardian of your souls.

GODLY LIVING

3 In the same way, you wives, ^be subject to your own husbands so that even if any *of them* are disobedient to the word, they may be won over without a word by the behavior of their wives, 2as they observe your pure and respectful behavior. 3^Your adornment must not be *merely* the external—braiding the hair, wearing gold *jewelry,* or putting on apparel; 4but *it should be* ^the hidden person of the heart, with the imperishable *quality* of a gentle and quiet spirit, which is precious in the sight of God. 5For in this way the holy women of former times, ^who hoped in God, also used to adorn themselves, being subject to their own husbands, 6just as Sarah obeyed Abraham, ^calling him lord; and you have proved to be her children if you do what is right ^without being frightened by any fear.

7^You husbands in the same way, live with *your wives* in an

2:12 ^Is 10:3; Luke 19:44   2:13 ^Rom 13:1
2:14 ^Rom 13:4   ^Rom 13:3   2:15 ^1 Pet 3:17
2:16 ^John 8:32   ^Rom 6:22   2:17 ^Rom 12:10
^Prov 24:21   2:18 ^Eph 6:5   2:19 ^Rom 13:5;
1 Pet 3:14, 16f   2:20 ^1 Pet 3:17   2:21 ^1 Pet 3:18;
4:1, 13   2:22 ^Is 53:9; 2 Cor 5:21   2:23 ^Is 53:7;
Heb 12:3   2:24 ^Is 53:4, 11   ^Is 53:5   2:25 ^Is 53:6
^John 10:11   3:1 ^Eph 5:22; Col 3:18   3:3 ^Is 3:18ff;
1 Tim 2:9   3:4 ^Rom 7:22   3:5 ^1 Tim 5:5; 1 Pet 1:3
3:6 ^Gen 18:12   ^1 Pet 3:14   3:7 ^Eph 5:25; Col 3:19

2:12 'I.e., Christ's coming again in judgment
2:24 'Lit *wood;* see Deut 21:23

understanding way, as with someone weaker, *since she is* a woman; and show her honor as a fellow heir of the grace of life, so that your prayers will not be hindered.

8To sum up, ^all *of you* be harmonious, sympathetic, 'loving, 8compassionate, *and* humble; 9not returning evil for evil or insult for insult, but giving a ^blessing instead; for you were called for the very purpose that you would inherit a blessing. 10For,

"^THE ONE WHO DESIRES LIFE, TO
    LOVE AND SEE GOOD DAYS,
  MUST KEEP HIS TONGUE FROM
    EVIL AND HIS LIPS FROM
    SPEAKING DECEIT.
11 "^HE MUST TURN AWAY FROM
    EVIL AND DO GOOD;
  HE MUST SEEK PEACE AND
    PURSUE IT.
12 "^FOR THE EYES OF THE LORD ARE
    TOWARD THE RIGHTEOUS,
  AND HIS EARS ATTEND TO
    THEIR PRAYER,
  BUT THE FACE OF THE LORD IS
    AGAINST EVILDOERS."

13^And who is there to harm you if you prove zealous for what is good? 14But even if you should suffer for the sake of righteousness, you are blessed. ^AND DO NOT FEAR THEIR INTIMIDATION, AND DO NOT BE IN DREAD, 15but 'sanctify Christ as Lord in your hearts, always *being* ready ^to make a defense to everyone who asks you to give an account for the hope that is in you, but 8with gentleness and respect; 16and keep a ^good conscience so that in the thing in which you are slandered, those who disparage your good behavior in Christ will be put to shame. 17For ^it is better, 8if God should will it *so*, that you suffer for doing what is right rather than for doing what is wrong. 18For Christ

also suffered for sins ^once for all *time, the* just for *the* unjust, so that He might bring us to God, having been put to death in the flesh, but made alive in the spirit; 19in which He also went and made proclamation to the spirits in prison, 20who once were disobedient when the patience of God ^kept waiting in the days of Noah, during the construction of 8the ark, in which a few, that is, eight persons, were brought safely through *the* water. 21Corresponding to that, baptism now saves you—^not the removal of dirt from the flesh, but an appeal to God for a good conscience— through the resurrection of Jesus Christ, 22^who is at the right hand of God, having gone into heaven, after angels and authorities and powers had been subjected to Him.

KEEP FERVENT IN YOUR LOVE

4 Therefore, since ^Christ has 'suffered in the flesh, arm yourselves also with the same purpose, because the one who has suffered in the flesh has ceased from sin, 2so as to live the rest of the time in the flesh no longer for human lusts, but for the will of God. 3For ^the time already past is sufficient *for you* to have carried out the desire of the Gentiles, having pursued a course of indecent behavior, lusts, drunkenness, carousing, drinking parties, and wanton idolatries. 4In *all* this, they are surprised that you

---

3:8^Rom 12:16   8Eph 4:32   3:9^Luke 6:28; Rom 12:14
3:10^Ps 34:12, 13   3:11^Ps 34:14   3:12^Ps 34:15, 16
3:13^Prov 16:7   3:14^Is 8:12f   3:15^Col 4:6
8 2 Tim 2:25   3:16^1 Tim 1:5; Heb 13:18   3:17^1 Pet 2:20
8Acts 18:21   3:18^Heb 9:26, 28; 10:10
3:20^Gen 6:3, 13f   8Heb 11:7   3:21^Heb 9:14; 10:22
3:22^Heb 1:3f; Eph 1:20f   4:1^1 Pet 2:21
4:2^Rom 6:2; Col 3:3   4:3^1 Cor 12:2

3:8 'I.e., as brothers and sisters   3:15 'I.e., set apart
4:1 'I.e., suffered death

do not run with *them* in the same excesses of ^debauchery, and they ^Bslander *you;* ⁵but they will give an account to Him who is ready to judge ^the living and the dead. ⁶For ^the gospel has for this purpose been preached even to those who are dead, that though they are judged in the flesh as people, they may live in the spirit according to *the will of* God.

⁷^The end of all things is near; therefore, be of sound judgment and sober *spirit* for the purpose of prayer. ⁸Above all, ^keep fervent in your love for one another, because ^Blove covers a multitude of sins. ⁹^Be hospitable to one another without complaint. ¹⁰^As each one has received a *special* gift, employ it in serving one another as good ^Bstewards of the multifaceted grace of God. ¹¹^Whoever speaks *is to do so* as *one who is speaking* actual words of God; whoever serves *is to do so* as *one who is serving* ^Bby the strength which God supplies; so that in all things God may be glorified through Jesus Christ, to whom belongs the glory and dominion forever and ever. Amen.

SHARE THE SUFFERINGS OF CHRIST

¹²Beloved, do not be surprised at the ^fiery ordeal among you, which comes upon you for your testing, as though *something* strange were happening to you; ¹³but to the degree that you ^share the sufferings of Christ, keep on rejoicing, so that at the revelation of His glory you may also rejoice and be overjoyed. ¹⁴If you are insulted ^for the name of Christ, ^Byou are blessed, because the Spirit of glory, and of God, rests upon you. ¹⁵Make sure that none of you suffers as a

murderer, or thief, or evildoer, or a ^troublesome meddler; ¹⁶but if *anyone suffers* as a Christian, he is not to be ashamed, but is to ^glorify God in this name. ¹⁷For *it is* time for judgment ^to begin with ^Bthe household of God; and if *it begins* with us first, what *will be* the outcome for those who do not obey the gospel of God? ¹⁸^AND IF IT IS WITH DIFFICULTY THAT THE RIGHTEOUS IS SAVED, WHAT WILL BECOME OF THE ^BGODLESS MAN AND THE SINNER? ¹⁹Therefore, those also who suffer according to ^the will of God are to entrust their souls to a faithful Creator in doing what is right.

SERVE GOD WILLINGLY

5 Therefore, I urge elders among you, as *your* fellow elder and a ^witness of the sufferings of Christ, *and* one who is also a ^Bfellow partaker of the glory that is to be revealed: ²shepherd ^the flock of God among you, exercising oversight, ^Bnot under compulsion but voluntarily, according to *the will of* God; and not with greed but with eagerness; ³nor yet as ^domineering over those assigned to your care, but by proving to be examples to the flock. ⁴And when the Chief ^Shepherd appears, you will receive the unfading crown of glory. ⁵You ¹younger men, likewise, be subject to *your* elders; and all of you,

4:4 ^Eph 5:18   ^B1 Pet 3:16   4:5 ^Acts 10:42; Rom 14:9
4:6 ^1 Pet 3:18   4:7 ^Rom 13:11; James 5:8
4:8 ^1 Pet 1:22   ^BProv 10:12   4:9 ^1 Tim 3:2; Heb 13:2
4:10 ^Rom 12:6f   ^B1 Cor 4:1   4:11 ^Titus 2:1
^BEph 6:10   4:12 ^1 Pet 1:6f   4:13 ^Rom 8:17; 2 Cor 1:5
4:14 ^John 15:21   ^BMatt 5:11   4:15 ^2 Thess 3:11;
1 Tim 5:13   4:16 ^1 Pet 4:11   4:17 ^Amos 3:2
^BHeb 3:6   4:18 ^Prov 11:31   ^B1 Tim 1:9
4:19 ^1 Pet 3:17   5:1 ^Luke 24:48   ^B1 Pet 5:5
5:2 ^John 21:16   ^BPhilem 14   5:3 ^Ezek 34:4;
Matt 20:25f   5:4 ^1 Pet 2:25

5:5 ¹Or *young people*

clothe yourselves with ^humility toward one another, because ^B^GOD IS OPPOSED TO THE PROUD, BUT HE GIVES GRACE TO THE HUMBLE.

⁶ Therefore ^humble yourselves under the mighty hand of God, so that He may exalt you at the proper time, ⁷having cast all your ^anxiety on Him, because He cares about you. ⁸^Be of sober *spirit,* ^Bbe on the alert. Your adversary, the devil, prowls around like a roaring lion, seeking someone to devour. ⁹^So resist him, firm in *your* faith, knowing that the same experiences of suffering are being accomplished by your ¹brothers and sisters who are in the world. ¹⁰After you have suffered ^for a little while, the God of all grace, who ^Bcalled you to His eternal glory in Christ, will Himself perfect, confirm, strengthen, *and* establish *you.* ¹¹^To Him *be* dominion forever and ever. Amen.

¹²Through ^Silvanus, our faithful brother (for so I regard *him*), ^BI have written to you briefly, ¹exhorting and testifying that this is the true grace of God. Stand firm in it! ¹³She who is in Babylon, chosen together with *you,* sends you greetings, and *so does* my son, ^Mark. ¹⁴^Greet one another with a kiss of love.

Peace be to you all who are in Christ.

5:5^1 Pet 3:8   ^B Prov 3:34   5:6^ Matt 23:12; Luke 14:11
5:7^Ps 55:22; Matt 6:25   5:8^1 Pet 1:13   ^B Matt 24:42
5:9^James 4:7   5:10^1 Pet 1:6   ^B 1 Cor 1:9
5:11^ Rom 11:36; 1 Pet 4:11   5:12^2 Cor 1:19
^B Heb 13:22   5:13^ Acts 12:12, 25; 15:37, 39
5:14^ Rom 16:16

5:9 ¹Lit *fellowship*   5:12 ¹Or *encouraging*

2 PETER

GROWTH IN CHRISTIAN VIRTUE

1 Simon Peter, a bond-servant and apostle of Jesus Christ,
To those who have received ᴬa faith of the same kind as ours, by ᴮthe righteousness of our God and Savior, Jesus Christ: ²Grace and peace be multiplied to you in ᴬthe knowledge of God and of Jesus our Lord, ³for His divine power has granted to us everything pertaining to life and godliness, through the true knowledge of Him who ᴬcalled us by His own glory and excellence. ⁴Through these He has granted to us His precious and magnificent ᴬpromises, so that by them you may become ᴮpartakers of *the* divine nature, having escaped the corruption that is in the world on account of lust. ⁵Now for this very reason also, applying all diligence, in your faith supply moral ¹excellence, and in *your* moral excellence, ᴬknowledge, ⁶and in *your* knowledge, ᴬself-control, and in *your* self-control, ᴮperseverance, and in *your* perseverance, godliness, ⁷and in *your* godliness, ᴬbrotherly kindness, and in *your* brotherly kindness, love. ⁸For if these *qualities* are yours and are increasing, they do not make you useless nor ᴬunproductive in the true knowledge of our Lord Jesus Christ. ⁹For the one who lacks these *qualities* is ᴬblind *or* short-sighted, having forgotten *his* purification from his former sins. ¹⁰Therefore, brothers *and sisters,* be all the more diligent to make certain about His ᴬcalling

and ᴮchoice of you; for as long as you practice these things, you will never stumble; ¹¹for in this way the entrance into the eternal kingdom of our Lord and Savior Jesus Christ will be ᴬabundantly supplied to you.

¹²Therefore, I will always be ready to remind you of these things, even though you *already* know *them* and have been established in ᴬthe truth which is present with *you.* ¹³I consider it right, as long as I am in ᴬthis *earthly* ¹dwelling, to ᴮstir you up by way of reminder, ¹⁴knowing that ᴬthe laying aside of my *earthly* dwelling is imminent, ᴮas also our Lord Jesus Christ has made clear to me. ¹⁵And I will also be diligent that at any time after my ᴬdeparture you will be able to call these things to mind.

EYEWITNESSES

¹⁶For we did not follow cleverly devised ᴬtales when we made known to you the ᴮpower and coming of our Lord Jesus Christ, but we were eyewitnesses of His majesty. ¹⁷For when He received honor and glory from God the Father, such a ᴬdeclaration as this was made to Him by the Majestic Glory: "This

---

1:1 ᴬRom 1:12   ᴮRom 3:21-26   1:2 ᴬJohn 17:3; Phil 3:8
1:3 ᴬ1 Thess 2:12; 2 Thess 2:14   1:4 ᴬ2 Pet 3:9, 13
ᴮ1 John 3:2   1:5 ᴬCol 2:3; 2 Pet 1:2   1:6 ᴬActs 24:25
ᴮLuke 21:19   1:7 ᴬRom 12:10; 1 Pet 1:22   1:8 ᴬCol 1:10
1:9 ᴬ1 John 2:11   1:10 ᴬRom 11:29   ᴮ1 Thess 1:4
1:11 ᴬRom 2:4; 1 Tim 6:17   1:12 ᴬCol 1:5f; 2 John 2
1:13 ᴬ2 Cor 5:1, 4   ᴮ2 Pet 3:1   1:14 ᴬ2 Tim 4:6
ᴮJohn 21:19   1:15 ᴬLuke 9:31   1:16 ᴬ1 Tim 1:4
ᴮMark 13:26   1:17 ᴬMatt 17:5; Mark 9:7

1:5 ¹Or *virtue*   1:13 ¹I.e., human body

is My beloved Son with whom I am well pleased"— [18] and we ourselves heard this declaration made from heaven when we were with Him on the ^holy mountain.

[19] And *so* we have the prophetic word *made* more sure, to which you do well to pay attention as to ^a lamp shining in a dark place, until the day dawns and the ^Bmorning star arises in your hearts. [20] But know this first *of all,* that ^no prophecy of Scripture becomes *a matter* of *someone's* own interpretation, [21] for ^no prophecy was ever made by an act of human will, but men moved by the Holy Spirit spoke from God.

THE APPEARANCE OF FALSE PROPHETS

2 But ^false prophets also appeared among the people, just as there will also be false teachers among you, who will secretly introduce destructive heresies, even denying the Master who bought them, bringing swift destruction upon themselves. [2] Many will follow their ^indecent behavior, and because of them the way of the truth will be ^Bmaligned; [3] and in *their* ^greed they will exploit you with false words; ^Btheir judgment from long ago is not idle, and their destruction is not asleep.

[4] For ^if God did not spare angels when they sinned, but cast them into ^1hell and committed them to ^2pits of darkness, held for judgment; [5] and did not spare ^the ancient world, but protected Noah, a preacher of righteousness, with seven others, when He brought a flood upon the world of the ungodly; [6] and *if* He ^condemned the cities of Sodom and Gomorrah to destruction by reducing *them*

to ashes, having made *them* an example of what is coming for the ungodly; [7] and *if* He ^rescued righteous Lot, *who was* oppressed by the perverted conduct of unscrupulous people [8] (for by what he saw and heard *that* ^righteous man, while living among them, felt *his* righteous soul tormented day after day by *their* lawless deeds), [9] ^*then* the Lord knows how to rescue the godly from a trial, and to keep the unrighteous under punishment for the day of judgment, [10] and especially those who indulge the flesh in *its* corrupt passion, and ^despise authority.

Reckless, self-centered, they ^speak abusively of *angelic* majesties without trembling, [11] ^whereas angels who are greater in might and power do not bring a demeaning judgment against them before the Lord. [12] But ^these, like unreasoning animals, born as creatures of instinct to be captured and killed, using abusive speech where they have no knowledge, will in the destruction of those creatures also be destroyed, [13] suffering wrong as the wages of doing wrong. They count it a pleasure to ^revel in the daytime. They are stains and blemishes, ^reveling in their ^1deceptions as they feast with you, [14] having eyes full of adultery that never cease from sin, enticing ^unstable

1:18 ^Ex 3:5; Josh 5:15   1:19 ^Ps 119:105   ^BRev 22:16
1:20 ^Rom 12:6   1:21 ^Jer 23:26; 2 Tim 3:16
2:1 ^Deut 13:1ff; Jer 6:13   2:2 ^Gen 19:5ff   ^BRom 2:24
2:3 ^1 Tim 6:5   ^BDeut 32:35   2:4 ^Jude 6
2:5 ^Ezek 26:20; 2 Pet 3:6   2:6 ^Gen 19:24; Jude 7
2:7 ^Gen 19:16, 29   2:8 ^Heb 11:4   2:9 ^1 Cor 10:13;
Rev 3:10   2:10 ^Ex 22:28; Jude 8   2:11 ^Jude 9
2:12 ^Jude 10   2:13 ^Rom 13:13   2:14 ^James 1:8;
2 Pet 3:16

2:4 ^1Gr *Tartarus,* a name used as a reference to the netherworld (hell)   ^2One early ms *chains of darkness*
2:13 ^1One early ms *love feasts*

souls, having hearts trained in greed, accursed children; ¹⁵abandoning ^the right way, they have gone astray, having followed ᴮthe way of Balaam, the *son* of Beor, who loved the reward of unrighteousness; ¹⁶but he received a rebuke for his own offense, ^*for* a mute donkey, speaking with a human voice, restrained the insanity of the prophet.

¹⁷These are ^springs without water and mists driven by a storm, ᴮfor whom the black darkness has been reserved. ¹⁸For, while speaking out ^arrogant *words* of no value they entice by fleshly desires, by indecent behavior, those who barely escape from the ones who live in error, ¹⁹promising them freedom while they themselves are slaves of corruption; for ^by what anyone is overcome, by this he is enslaved. ²⁰For if, after they have escaped the defilements of the world by the knowledge of the Lord and Savior Jesus Christ, they are again entangled in them and are overcome, ^the last state has become worse for them than the first. ²¹^For it would be better for them not to have known the way of righteousness, than having known it, to turn away from the holy commandment ᴮhanded on to them. ²²It has happened to them according to the true proverb, "^A DOG RETURNS TO ITS OWN VOMIT," and, "A sow, after washing, *returns* to wallowing in the mire."

PURPOSE OF THIS LETTER

3 Beloved, this is now the second letter I am writing to you in which I am ^stirring up your sincere mind by way of a reminder, ²to ^remember the words spoken beforehand by ᴮthe holy prophets and the commandment of the Lord and Savior *spoken* by your apostles.

THE COMING DAY OF THE LORD

³Know this first *of all,* that ^in the last days ᴮmockers will come with *their* mocking, following after their own lusts, ⁴and saying, "^Where is the promise of His coming? For *ever* since the fathers ¹˒ᴮfell asleep, all things continue just as *they were* from the beginning of creation." ⁵For when they maintain this, it escapes their notice that by the word of God *the* heavens existed long ago and *the* earth was ^formed out of water and by water, ⁶through which ^the world at that time was ᴮdestroyed by being flooded with water. ⁷But by His word ^the present heavens and earth are being reserved for ᴮfire, kept for the day of judgment and destruction of ungodly people.

⁸But do not let this one *fact* escape your notice, beloved, that with the Lord one day is like a thousand years, and ^a thousand years like one day. ⁹^The Lord is not slow about His promise, as some count slowness, but is patient toward you, ᴮnot willing for any to perish, but for all to come to repentance.

A NEW HEAVEN AND EARTH

¹⁰But ^the day of the Lord ᴮwill come like a thief, in which the heavens will pass away with a roar and the

2:15 ^Acts 13:10   ᴮNum 22:5, 7
2:16 ^Num 22:21, 23, 28, 30ff   2:17 ^Jude 12   ᴮJude 13
2:18 ^Jude 16   2:19 ^John 8:34; Rom 6:16
2:20 ^Matt 12:45; Luke 11:26   2:21 ^Ezek 18:24
ᴮJude 3   2:22 ^Prov 26:11   3:1 ^2 Pet 1:13
3:2 ^Jude 17   ᴮLuke 1:70   3:3 ^1 Tim 4:1   ᴮJude 18
3:4 ^Mal 2:17   ᴮActs 7:60   3:5 ^Ps 24:2; 136:6
3:6 ^2 Pet 2:5   ᴮGen 7:11, 12, 21f   3:7 ^2 Pet 3:10, 12
ᴮIs 66:15   3:8 ^Ps 90:4   3:9 ^Hab 2:3   ᴮ1 Tim 2:4
3:10 ^1 Cor 1:8   ᴮ1 Thess 5:2

3:4 ¹I.e., died

elements will be destroyed with intense heat, and the earth and its works will be ¹discovered.

¹¹Since all these things are to be destroyed in this way, what sort of people ought you to be in holy conduct and godliness, ¹²looking for and hastening the coming of the day of God, because of which ^the heavens will be destroyed by burning, and the elements will melt with intense heat! ¹³But according to His ^promise we are looking for ᴮnew heavens and a new earth, in which righteousness dwells.

¹⁴Therefore, beloved, since you look for these things, be diligent to be found ^spotless and blameless by Him, at peace, ¹⁵and regard the ^patience of our Lord as salvation; just as also ᴮour beloved brother Paul, according to the wisdom

given him, wrote to you, ¹⁶as also in all *his* letters, speaking in them of these things, ^in which there are some things that are hard to understand, which the untaught and unstable distort, as *they do* also the rest of the Scriptures, to their own destruction. ¹⁷You therefore, beloved, knowing this beforehand, be on your guard so that you are not carried away by ^the error of ᴮunscrupulous people and lose your own firm commitment, ¹⁸but grow in the grace and knowledge of our ^Lord and Savior Jesus Christ. To Him *be* the glory, both now and to the day of eternity. Amen.

3:12^2 Pet 3:7, 10   3:13^Is 65:17   ᴮRom 8:21
3:14^Phil 2:15; 1 Thess 5:23   3:15^2 Pet 3:9
ᴮActs 15:25   3:16^Heb 5:11   3:17^2 Pet 2:18
ᴮ2 Pet 2:7   3:18^2 Pet 2:20

3:10¹ I.e., as worthless; late mss *burned up*

1 JOHN

THE INCARNATE WORD

1 What was ᴬfrom the beginning, what we have heard, what we have ᴮseen with our eyes, what we have looked at and touched with our hands, concerning the Word of Life— ²and ᴬthe life was revealed, and we have seen and testify and proclaim to you ᴮthe eternal life, which was with the Father and was ᴬrevealed to us— ³what we have seen and ᴬheard we proclaim to you also, so that you too may have fellowship with us; and indeed our ᴮfellowship is with the Father, and with His Son Jesus Christ. ⁴ᴬThese things we write, so that our ᴮjoy may be made complete.

GOD IS LIGHT

⁵This is the message we have heard from Him and announce to you, that ᴬGod is Light, and in Him there is no darkness at all. ⁶ᴬIf we say that we have fellowship with Him and *yet* walk in the darkness, we ᴮlie and do not practice the truth; ⁷but if we ᴬwalk in the Light as ᴮHe Himself is in the Light, we have fellowship with one another, and the blood of Jesus His Son cleanses us from all sin. ⁸ᴬIf we say that we have no sin, we are deceiving ourselves and the ᴮtruth is not in us. ⁹ᴬIf we confess our sins, He is faithful and righteous, so that He will forgive us our sins and cleanse us from all unrighteousness. ¹⁰ᴬIf we say that we have not sinned, we ᴮmake Him a liar and His word is not in us.

CHRIST IS OUR ADVOCATE

2 My little children, I am writing these things to you so that you may not sin. And if anyone sins, ᴬwe have an ¹ʼᴮAdvocate with the Father, Jesus Christ the righteous; ²and He Himself is the ʼpropitiation for our sins; and not for ours only, but also ᴬfor *the sins of* the whole world.

³By this we know that we have come to know Him, if we ᴬkeep His commandments. ⁴The one who says, "I have come to know Him," and does not keep His commandments, is a ᴬliar, and ᴮthe truth is not in him; ⁵but whoever ᴬfollows His word, in him the ᴮlove of God has truly been perfected. By this we know that we are in Him: ⁶the one who says that he ᴬremains in Him ought, himself also, to walk just as He walked.

⁷Beloved, I am not writing a new commandment to you, but an old commandment which you have had ᴬfrom the beginning; the old commandment is the word which you have heard. ⁸On the other hand, I am writing a new commandment to you, which is true in Him and in you, because ᴬthe darkness is passing away and ᴮthe true Light

1:1 ᴬJohn 1:1f   ᴮ2 Pet 1:16   1:2 ᴬJohn 1:4   ᴮJohn 10:28
1:3 ᴬActs 4:20   ᴮJohn 17:3, 21   1:4 ᴬ1 John 2:1
ᴮJohn 3:29   1:5 ᴬ1 Tim 6:16; James 1:17   1:6 ᴬJohn 8:12
ᴮ1 John 2:4f   1:7 ᴬIs 2:5   ᴮ1 Tim 6:16   1:8 ᴬJob 15:14
ᴮJohn 8:44   1:9 ᴬPs 32:5; Prov 28:13   1:10 ᴬJob 15:14
ᴮ1 John 5:10   2:1 ᴬRom 8:34   ᴮJohn 14:16
2:2 ᴬJohn 4:42; 11:51f   2:3 ᴬJohn 14:15; 15:10
2:4 ᴬ1 John 1:6   ᴮ1 John 1:8   2:5 ᴬJohn 14:23
ᴮ1 John 4:12   2:6 ᴬJohn 15:4   2:7 ᴬ1 John 2:24; 3:11
2:8 ᴬRom 13:12   ᴮJohn 1:9

2:1 ¹Or *Intercessor*   **2:2** ¹I.e., means of reconciliation with God by atoning for sins; or *sin-offering*

is already shining. ⁹The one who says that he is in the Light and *yet* ^hates his brother *or sister* is in the darkness until now. ¹⁰^The one who loves his brother *and sister* remains in the Light, and there is nothing in him to cause stumbling. ¹¹But the one who hates his brother *or sister* is in the darkness and walks in the darkness, and does not know where he is going because the darkness has ^blinded his eyes.

¹²I am writing to you, little children, because ^your sins have been forgiven you on account of His name. ¹³I am writing to you, fathers, because you know Him who has been from the beginning. I am writing to you, young men, because ^you have overcome the evil one. I have written to you, children, because you know the Father. ¹⁴I have written to you, fathers, because you know Him ^who has been from the beginning. I have written to you, young men, because you are ^strong, and the word of God remains in you, and you have overcome the evil one.

DO NOT LOVE THE WORLD

¹⁵Do not love the world nor the things in the world. ^If anyone loves the world, the love of the Father is not in him. ¹⁶For all that is in the world, ^the lust of the flesh and the lust of the eyes and the boastful pride of life, is not from the Father, but is from the world. ¹⁷^The world is passing away and *also* its lusts; but the one who does the will of God continues *to live* forever.

¹⁸Children, it is the last hour; and just as you heard that ^antichrist is coming, ^even now many antichrists have appeared; from this we know that it is the last hour. ¹⁹^They went out from us, but they were not *really*

of us; for if they had been of us, they would have remained with us; but *they went out,* so that it would be evident that they all are not of us. ²⁰But you have an ^anointing from ^the Holy One, and you all know. ²¹I have not written to you because you do not know the truth, but ^because you do know it, and because no lie is ^of the truth. ²²Who is the liar except ^the one who denies that Jesus is the Christ? This is the antichrist, the one who denies the Father and the Son. ²³^Whoever denies the Son does not have the Father; the one who confesses the Son has the Father also. ²⁴*As for* you, *see that* what you heard from the beginning remains in you. If what you heard from the beginning remains in you, you also ^will remain in the Son and in the Father.

THE PROMISE IS ETERNAL LIFE

²⁵^This is the promise which He Himself made to us: eternal life.

²⁶These things I have written to you concerning those who are *trying to* ^deceive you. ²⁷And *as for* you, the anointing which you received from Him remains in you, and you have no need for anyone to teach you; but as His anointing ^teaches you about all things, and is ^true and is not a lie, and just as it has taught you, you remain in Him.

²⁸Now, little children, remain in Him, so that when He ^appears, we may have confidence and ^not

2:9^1 John 2:11; 3:15   2:10^John 11:9; 1 John 2:10, 11
2:11^2 Cor 4:4; 2 Pet 1:9   2:12^Acts 13:38; 1 Cor 6:11
2:13^John 16:33; 1 John 5:4f   2:14^1 John 1:1
^Eph 6:10   2:15^James 4:4   2:16^Rom 13:14; Eph 2:3
2:17^1 Cor 7:31   2:18^Matt 24:5, 24   ^Mark 13:22
2:19^Acts 20:30   2:20^2 Cor 1:21   ^Mark 1:24
2:21^James 1:19   ^John 8:44   2:22^1 John 4:3;
2 John 7   2:23^John 8:19; 16:3   2:24^John 14:23;
1 John 1:3   2:25^John 3:15; 6:40   2:26^1 John 3:7;
2 John 7   2:27^John 14:26   ^John 14:17
2:28^1 John 3:2   ^Mark 8:38

draw back from Him in shame at His coming. ²⁹If you know that ᴬHe is righteous, you know that everyone who practices righteousness also has been born of Him.

CHILDREN OF GOD LOVE ONE ANOTHER

3 See ᴬhow great a love the Father has given us, that we would be called ᴮchildren of God; and *in fact* we are. For this reason the world does not know us: because it did not know Him. ²Beloved, now we are children of God, and it has not appeared as yet what we will be. We know that when He appears, we will be ᴬlike Him, because we will ᴮsee Him just as He is. ³And everyone who has this ᴬhope *set* on Him purifies himself, just as He is pure.

⁴Everyone who practices sin also practices lawlessness; and ᴬsin is lawlessness. ⁵You know that He appeared in order to ᴬtake away sins; and ᴮin Him there is no sin. ⁶No one who remains in Him ᴬsins *continually;* no one who sins *continually* has seen Him or knows Him. ⁷Little children, make sure no one ᴬdeceives you; ᴮthe one who practices righteousness is righteous, just as He is righteous; ⁸the one who practices sin is ᴬof the devil; for the devil has been sinning from the beginning. The Son of God appeared for this purpose, to destroy the works of the devil. ⁹No one who has been ᴬborn of God practices sin, because His seed remains in him; and he cannot sin *continually,* because he has been born of God. ¹⁰By this the ᴬchildren of God and the children of the devil are obvious: anyone who does not practice righteousness is not of God, nor the one who does not love his ᴮbrother *and sister.*

¹¹For this is the message which you have heard from the beginning, ᴬthat we are to love one another; ¹²not as ᴬCain, *who* was of ᴮthe evil one and murdered his brother. And for what reason did he murder him? Because his *own* deeds were evil, but his brother's were righteous.

¹³Do not be surprised, brothers *and sisters,* if ᴬthe world hates you. ¹⁴We know that we have ᴬpassed out of death into life, because we love the brothers *and sisters.* The one who does not love remains in death. ¹⁵Everyone who ᴬhates his brother *or sister* is a murderer, and you know that no murderer has eternal life remaining in him. ¹⁶We know love by this, that ᴬHe laid down His life for us; and we ought to lay down our lives for the brothers *and sisters.* ¹⁷But ᴬwhoever has worldly goods and sees his brother *or sister* in need, and ᴮcloses his heart against him, how does the love of God remain in him? ¹⁸Little children, let's not love with word or with tongue, but in deed and ᴬtruth. ¹⁹We will know by this that we are ᴬof the truth, and will set our heart at ease before Him, ²⁰that if our heart condemns us, that God is greater than our heart, and He knows all things. ²¹Beloved, if our heart does not condemn us, we have ᴬconfidence before God; ²²and whatever we ask, we receive from Him, because we ᴬkeep His commandments and do

2:29ᴬJohn 7:18; 1 John 3:7 3:1ᴬJohn 3:16 ᴮJohn 1:12
3:2ᴬRom 8:29 ᴮJohn 17:24 3:3ᴬRom 15:12; 1 Pet 1:3
3:4ᴬRom 4:15; 1 John 5:17 3:5ᴬJohn 1:29 ᴮ2 Cor 5:21
3:6ᴬ1 John 3:9 3:7ᴬ1 John 2:26 ᴮ1 John 2:29
3:8ᴬJohn 8:44; 1 John 3:10 3:9ᴬJohn 1:13; 3:3
3:10ᴬJohn 1:12 ᴮ1 John 2:9 3:11ᴬJohn 15:12;
1 John 4:7, 11f, 21 3:12ᴬGen 4:8 ᴮ1 John 2:13f
3:13ᴬJohn 15:18; 17:14 3:14ᴬJohn 5:24 3:15ᴬMatt 5:21f;
John 8:44 3:16ᴬJohn 10:11; 15:13 3:17ᴬJames 2:15f
ᴮDeut 15:7 3:18ᴬ2 John 1; 3 John 1 3:19ᴬ1 John 2:21
3:21ᴬ1 John 2:28; 5:14 3:22ᴬ1 John 2:3

Bthe things that are pleasing in His sight.

23This is His commandment, that we Abelieve in Bthe name of His Son Jesus Christ, and love one another, just as He commanded us. 24The one who Akeeps His commandments remains in Him, and He in him. We know by this that BHe remains in us, by the Spirit whom He has given us.

TESTING THE SPIRITS

4 Beloved, do not believe every Aspirit, but test the spirits to see whether they are from God, because many false prophets have gone out into the world. 2By this you know the Spirit of God: Aevery spirit that Bconfesses that Jesus Christ has come in the flesh is from God; 3and every spirit that Adoes not confess Jesus is not from God; this is the *spirit* of the antichrist, which you have heard is coming, and Bnow it is already in the world. 4You are from God, little children, and Ahave overcome them; because greater is He who is in you than Bhe who is in the world. 5AThey are from the world, therefore they speak *as* from the world, and the world listens to them. 6We are from God. The one who knows God listens to us; the one who is not from God does not listen to us. By this we know Athe spirit of truth and Bthe spirit of error.

GOD IS LOVE

7Beloved, let's Alove one another; for love is from God, and everyone who loves has been born of God and knows God. 8The one who does not love does not know God, because AGod is love. 9By this the love of God was revealed in us, that AGod has sent His only Son into the world so that we may live through

Him. 10In this is love, Anot that we loved God, but that He loved us and sent His Son *to be* Bthe 1propitiation for our sins. 11Beloved, if God so loved us, Awe also ought to love one another. 12ANo one has ever seen God; if we love one another, God remains in us, and His love is perfected in us. 13ABy this we know that we remain in Him and He in us, because He has given to us of His Spirit. 14We have seen and testify that the Father has Asent the Son *to be* the Savior of the world.

15AWhoever confesses that Jesus is the Son of God, God remains in him, and he in God. 16AWe have come to know and have believed the love which God has for us. BGod is love, and the one who remains in love remains in God, and God remains in him. 17By this, love is perfected with us, so that we may have Aconfidence in Bthe day of judgment; because as He is, we also are in this world. 18There is no fear in love, but Aperfect love drives out fear, because fear involves punishment, and the one who fears is not perfected in love. 19AWe love, because He first loved us. 20If someone says, "I love God," and *yet* he Ahates his brother *or sister,* he is a liar; for the one who does not love his brother *and sister* whom he has seen, cannot love God, whom

3:22 BJohn 8:29   3:23AJohn 6:29   BJohn 1:12
3:24A1 John 2:3   B1 John 2:5   4:1AJer 29:8; 1 Thess 5:20f
4:2A1 Cor 12:3   B1 John 2:23   4:3A1 John 2:22
B2 Thess 2:3-7   4:4A1 John 2:13   BJohn 12:31
4:5AJohn 15:19; 17:14, 16   4:6AJohn 14:17   B1 Tim 4:1
4:7A1 John 3:11   4:8A1 John 4:7, 16   4:9AJohn 3:16f;
1 John 4:10   4:10ARom 5:8, 10   B1 John 2:2
4:11A1 John 4:7   4:12AJohn 1:18; 1 Tim 6:16
4:13ARom 8:9; 1 John 3:24   4:14AJohn 3:17; 1 John 2:2
4:15A1 John 2:23   4:16AJohn 6:69   B1 John 4:7, 8
4:17A1 John 2:28   BMatt 10:15   4:18ARom 8:15
4:19A1 John 4:10   4:20A1 John 2:9, 11

4:10 1 I.e., means of reconciliation with God by atoning for sins; or *sin-offering*

he has not seen. ²¹And ^this commandment we have from Him, that the one who loves God must also love his brother *and sister.*

OVERCOMING THE WORLD

5 ^Everyone who believes that Jesus is the Christ has been born of God, and everyone who loves the Father loves the *child* born of Him. ²By this we know that ^we love the children of God, when we love God and follow His commandments. ³For ^this is the love of God, that we keep His commandments; and ^His commandments are not burdensome. ⁴For whoever has been born of God ^overcomes the world; and this is the victory that has overcome the world: our faith.

⁵Who is the one who overcomes the world, but the one who ^believes that Jesus is the Son of God? ⁶This is the One who came by water and blood, Jesus Christ; not with the water only, but with the water and with the blood. It is ^the Spirit who testifies, because the Spirit is the truth. ⁷For there are ^three that testify: ⁸the Spirit and the water and the blood; and the three are 'in agreement. ⁹^If we receive the testimony of people, the testimony of God is greater; for the testimony of God is this, that He has testified concerning His Son. ¹⁰The one who believes in the Son of God ^has the testimony in himself; the one who does not believe God has made Him a liar, because he has not believed in the testimony that God has given concerning His Son. ¹¹And the testimony is this, that God has given us ^eternal life, and ^this life is in His Son. ¹²^The one who has the Son has the life; the one who does not have the Son of God does not have the life.

THIS IS WRITTEN THAT YOU MAY KNOW

¹³^These things I have written to you who ^believe in the name of the Son of God, so that you may know that you have eternal life. ¹⁴This is ^the confidence which we have before Him, that, if we ask anything according to His will, He hears us. ¹⁵And if we know that He hears us *in* whatever we ask, ^we know that we have the requests which we have asked from Him.

¹⁶If anyone sees his brother *or sister* committing a sin not *leading* to death, ^he shall ask and *God* will, for him, give life to those who commit sin not *leading* to death. There is sin *leading* to death; ^I am not saying that he should ask about that. ¹⁷^All unrighteousness is sin, and there is sin not *leading* to death.

¹⁸We know that ^no one who has been born of God sins; but He who was born of God keeps him, and ^the evil one does not touch him. ¹⁹We know that ^we are of God, and that the whole world lies in *the power of* the evil one. ²⁰And we know that the Son of God has come, and has ^given us understanding so that we may know ^Him who is true; and we are in Him who is true, in His Son Jesus Christ. This is the true God and eternal life.

²¹Little children, guard yourselves from ^idols.

4:21^Lev 19:18; Matt 5:43f   5:1^1 John 2:22f; 4:2, 15
5:2^1 John 3:14   5:3^John 14:15   ^Matt 11:30
5:4^1 John 2:13; 4:4   5:5^1 John 4:15; 5:1
5:6^Matt 3:16f; John 15:26   5:7^Matt 18:16
5:9^John 5:34, 37; 8:18   5:10^Rom 8:16; Gal 4–6
5:11^1 John 1:2   ^John 1:4   5:12^John 3:15f, 36
5:13^John 20:31   ^1 John 3:23   5:14^1 John 2:28; 3:21f
5:15^1 John 5:18–20   5:16^James 5:15   ^Jer 7:16
5:17^1 John 3:4   5:18^1 John 3:9   ^1 John 2:13
5:19^1 John 4:6   5:20^Luke 24:45   ^John 17:3
5:21^1 Cor 10:7, 14; 1 Thess 1:9

5:8 ¹Lit *for the one thing*

2 JOHN

WALK ACCORDING TO HIS COMMANDMENTS

1 The elder to the chosen lady and her children, whom I love in truth; and not only I, but also all who ^know the truth, ²because of the truth which remains in us and will be ^with us forever: ³^Grace, mercy, *and* peace will be with us, from God the Father and from Jesus Christ, the Son of the Father, in truth and love.

⁴^I was overjoyed to find *some* of your children walking in truth, just as we have received a commandment *to do* from the Father. ⁵Now I ask you, lady, ^not as though *I were* writing to you a new commandment, but the one which we have had ^from the beginning, that we love one another. ⁶And ^this is love, that we walk according to His commandments. This is the commandment, just as you have heard ᴮfrom the beginning, that you are to walk in it.

⁷For ^many deceivers have ᴮgone out into the world, those who do not acknowledge Jesus Christ *as* coming in the flesh. This is ^the deceiver and the antichrist. ⁸Watch yourselves, ^that you do not lose what we have accomplished, but *that* you may receive a full reward. ⁹Anyone who goes too far and ^does not remain in the teaching of Christ, does not have God; the one who remains in the teaching has both the Father and the Son. ¹⁰If anyone comes to you and does not bring this teaching, ^do not receive him into *your* house, and do not give him a greeting; ¹¹for the one who gives him a greeting ^participates in his evil deeds.

¹²^Though I have many things to write to you, I do not want to *do so* with paper and ink; but I hope to come to you and speak face to face, so that your joy may be made complete.

¹³The children of your ^chosen sister greet you.

1 ^John 8:32; 1 Tim 2:4   **2** ^John 14:16   **3** ^Rom 1:7;
1 Tim 1:2   **4** ^3 John 3f   **5** ^1 John 2:7   **6** ^1 John 5:3
ᴮ1 John 2:7   **7** ^1 John 2:26   ᴮ1 John 2:19
8 ^1 Cor 3:8; Heb 10:35   **9** ^John 7:16; 8:31
10 ^1 Kin 13:16f; Rom 16:17   **11** ^Eph 5:11; 1 Tim 5:22
12 ^3 John 13, 14   **13** ^2 John 1

3 JOHN

A GOOD REPORT

1 The elder to the beloved Gaius, whom I ^love in truth.

2 Beloved, I pray that in all respects you may prosper and be in good health, just as your soul prospers. **3** For I ^was overjoyed when brothers came and testified to your truth, *that is,* how you ^are walking in truth. **4** I have no greater joy than this, to hear of my children ^walking in the truth.

5 Beloved, you are acting faithfully in whatever you accomplish for the brothers *and sisters,* and especially *when they are* ^strangers; **6** and they have testified to your love before the church. You will do well to send them on their way in a manner ^worthy of God. **7** For they went out for the sake of ^the Name, accepting nothing from the Gentiles. **8** Therefore we ought to support such people, so that we may prove to be fellow workers with the truth.

9 I wrote something to the church; but Diotrephes, who loves to ^be first among them, does not accept what we say. **10** For this reason, if I come, I will call attention to his deeds which he does, unjustly accusing us with malicious words; and not satisfied with this, he himself does not ^receive the brothers either, and he forbids those who want *to do so* and ^puts *them* out of the church.

11 Beloved, ^do not imitate what is evil, but what is good. The one who does what is good is of God; the one who does what is evil has not seen God. **12** Demetrius has received a *good* testimony from everyone, and from the truth itself; and we testify too, and ^you know that our testimony is true.

13 ^I had many things to write to you, but I do not want to write to you with pen and ink; **14** but I hope to see you shortly, and we will speak face to face.

15 Peace *be* to you. The friends greet you. Greet the friends ^by name.

1 ^1 John 3:18; 2 John 1   **3** ^2 John 4   **4** ^2 John 4
5 ^Rom 12:13; Heb 13:2   **6** ^Col 1:10; 1 Thess 2:12
7 ^John 15:21; Acts 5:41   **9** ^2 John 9   **10** ^2 John 10
^B John 9:34   **11** ^Ps 34:14; 37:27   **12** ^John 19:35; 21:24
13 ^2 John 12   **15** ^John 10:3

JUDE

1 Jude, a bond-servant of Jesus Christ and brother of James,

To ^Athose who are the called, beloved in God the Father, and ^Bkept for Jesus Christ: ²May mercy, peace, and love ^Abe multiplied to you.

³Beloved, while I was making every effort to write you about our common salvation, I felt the necessity to write to you appealing that you ^Acontend earnestly for ^Bthe faith that was once for all *time* handed down to the saints. ⁴For certain people have crept in unnoticed, those who were long beforehand ^Amarked out for this condemnation, ungodly persons who turn the grace of our God into indecent behavior and ^Bdeny our only Master and Lord, Jesus Christ.

⁵Now I want to remind you, though you know everything once *and* for all, that ¹the Lord, ^Aafter saving a people out of the land of Egypt, subsequently destroyed those who did not believe. ⁶And ^Aangels who did not keep their own domain but abandoned their proper dwelling place, *these* He has ^Bkept in eternal restraints under darkness for the judgment of the great day, ⁷just as Sodom and Gomorrah and the cities around them, since they in the same way as these *angels* indulged in sexual perversion and went after strange flesh, are exhibited as an example in undergoing the ^Apunishment of eternal fire.

⁸Yet in the same way these people also, dreaming, ^Adefile the flesh, reject authority, and speak abusively of *angelic* majesties. ⁹But Michael ^Athe archangel, when he disputed with the devil and argued about the body of Moses, did not dare pronounce against him an abusive judgment, but said, "^BThe Lord rebuke you!" ¹⁰But ^Athese people disparage all the things that they do not understand; and all the things that they know by instinct, ^Alike unreasoning animals, by these things they are destroyed. ¹¹Woe to them! For they have gone ^Athe way of Cain, and for pay they have given themselves up to the error of Balaam, and ^Bperished in the rebellion of Korah. ¹²These are the ones who are hidden reefs ^Ain your love feasts when they feast with you without fear, *like shepherds* caring *only* for themselves; ^Bclouds without water, carried along by winds; autumn trees without fruit, doubly dead, uprooted; ¹³^Awild waves of the sea, churning up their own shameful deeds like *dirty* foam; wandering stars, ^Bfor whom the gloom of darkness has been reserved forever.

¹⁴*It was* also about these people *that* ^AEnoch, *in the* seventh *generation* from Adam, prophesied, saying, "Behold, the Lord

---

1 ^ARom 1:6f   ^BJohn 17:11f   2 ^A1 Pet 1:2; 2 Pet 1:2
3 ^A1 Tim 6:12   ^BActs 6:7   4 ^A1 Pet 2:8   ^B2 Tim 2:12
5 ^AEx 12:51; 1 Cor 10:5-10   6 ^A2 Pet 2:4   ^B2 Pet 2:9
7 ^AMatt 25:41; 2 Thess 1:8f   8 ^A2 Pet 2:10   9 ^A2 Pet 2:11
^BZech 3:2   10 ^A2 Pet 2:12   11 ^AGen 4:3-8
^BNum 16:1-3, 31-35   12 ^A1 Cor 11:20ff   ^BProv 25:14
13 ^AIs 57:20   ^B2 Pet 2:17   14 ^AGen 5:18, 21ff

5 ¹One early ms *Jesus*

has come with many thousands of His holy ones, ¹⁵to execute judgment upon all, and to convict all the ungodly of all their ungodly deeds which they have done in an ungodly way, and of all the harsh things which ^ungodly sinners have spoken against Him." ¹⁶These are ^grumblers, finding fault, following after their *own* lusts; they speak ^Barrogantly, flattering people for the sake of *gaining an* advantage.

KEEP YOURSELVES IN THE LOVE
OF GOD

¹⁷But you, beloved, ^ought to remember the words that were spoken beforehand by the apostles of our Lord Jesus Christ, ¹⁸that they were saying to you, "^In the last time there will be mockers, following after their own ungodly lusts." ¹⁹These are the ones who cause divisions, ^worldly-minded, devoid of the Spirit. ²⁰But you, beloved, ^building yourselves up on your most holy faith, praying in the Holy Spirit, ²¹keep yourselves in the love of God, ^looking forward to the mercy of our Lord Jesus Christ to eternal life. ²²And have mercy on some, who are doubting; ²³save others, ^snatching them out of the fire; and on some have mercy with fear, ^Bhating even the garment polluted by the flesh.

²⁴Now to Him who is able to protect you from stumbling, and to ^make you stand in the presence of His glory, blameless with great joy, ²⁵to the ^only ^BGod our Savior, through Jesus Christ our Lord, *be* glory, majesty, dominion, and authority before all time and now and forever. Amen.

15^1 Tim 1:9   16^Num 16:11, 41   ^B2 Pet 2:18
17^2 Pet 3:2   18^Acts 20:29; 1 Tim 4:1
19^1 Cor 2:14f; James 3:15   20^Col 2:7; 1 Thess 5:11
21^Titus 2:13; Heb 9:28   23^Amos 4:11   ^BZech 3:3f
24^2 Cor 4:14   25^John 5:44   ^BLuke 1:47

THE REVELATION
TO JOHN

THE REVELATION OF JESUS CHRIST

1 The Revelation of Jesus Christ, which ^God gave Him to ^Bshow to His bond-servants, the things which must soon take place; and He sent and communicated *it* by His angel to His bond-servant John, ^2who testified to ^the word of God and to the testimony of Jesus Christ, everything that he saw. ^3 ^ABlessed is the one who reads, and those who hear the words of the prophecy and keep the things which are written in it; ^Bfor the time is near.

MESSAGE TO THE SEVEN CHURCHES

^4John to the seven churches that are in ^AAsia: Grace to you and peace from ^BHim who is, and who was, and who is to come, and from the ^1seven spirits who are before His throne, ^5 and from Jesus Christ, ^the faithful witness, the ^Bfirstborn of the dead, and the ruler of the kings of the earth. To Him who loves us and released us from our sins by His blood— ^6and He made us *into* a ^Akingdom, priests to ^BHis God and Father—to Him *be* the glory and the dominion forever and ever. Amen. ^7 ^ABEHOLD, HE IS COMING WITH THE CLOUDS, and every eye will see Him, even those who pierced Him; and all the tribes of the earth will mourn over Him. So it is to be. Amen.

^8"I am ^Athe Alpha and the Omega," says the Lord God, "who is and who was and who is to come, the Almighty."

THE PATMOS VISION

^9I, John, your brother and ^Afellow participant in the tribulation and kingdom and ^Bperseverance in Jesus, was on the island called Patmos because of the word of God and the testimony of Jesus. ^10I was ^Ain *the* ^1Spirit on the Lord's day, and I heard behind me a loud voice ^Blike *the sound* of a trumpet, ^11saying, "^AWrite on a scroll what you see, and send *it* to the seven churches: to Ephesus, Smyrna, Pergamum, Thyatira, Sardis, Philadelphia, and Laodicea."

^12Then I turned to see the voice that was speaking with me. And after turning I saw ^Aseven golden lampstands; ^13and in the middle of the lampstands *I saw* one ^Alike ^1a son of man, clothed in a robe reaching to the feet, and wrapped around the chest with a golden sash. ^14His head and His hair were white like white wool, like snow; and ^AHis eyes were like a flame of fire. ^15His ^Afeet were like burnished bronze when it has been heated to a glow in a furnace, and His ^Bvoice was like the sound of many waters. ^16In

---

1:1 ^AJohn 17:8   ^BRev 22:6   **1:2** ^ARev 1:9; 6:9
1:3 ^ALuke 11:28   ^BRev 22:10   **1:4** ^AActs 2:9   ^BRev 1:8, 17
1:5 ^ARev 3:14   ^B1 Cor 15:20   **1:6** ^ARev 5:10   ^BRom 15:6
1:7 ^ADan 7:13; 1 Thess 4:17   **1:8** ^ARev 21:6; 22:13
1:9 ^AActs 14:22   ^B2 Thess 3:5   **1:10** ^AMatt 22:43
^BRev 4:1   **1:11** ^ARev 1:19   **1:12** ^AEx 25:37; 37:23
1:13 ^ADan 7:13; Rev 14:14   **1:14** ^ADan 7:9; 10:6
1:15 ^AEzek 1:7   ^BEzek 1:24   **1:16** ^AIs 49:2

1:4 ^1Possibly a symbolic reference to the Holy Spirit in His fullness, or to seven key angels   **1:10** ^1Or *spirit*
1:13 ^1Or *the Son of Man*

His right hand He held seven stars, and out of His mouth came a ^sharp two-edged sword; and His ᴮface was like the sun shining in its strength.

¹⁷When I saw Him, I ^fell at His feet like a dead man. And He placed His right hand on me, saying, "Do not be afraid; ᴮI am the first and the last, ¹⁸and the ^living One; and I ᴮwas dead, and behold, I am alive forevermore, and I have the keys of death and of Hades. ¹⁹Therefore ^write ᴮthe things which you have seen, and the things which are, and the things which will take place after these things. ²⁰*As for* the mystery of the seven stars which you saw in My right hand, and the seven golden lampstands: the seven stars are the angels of ^the seven churches, and the seven lampstands are the seven churches.

MESSAGE TO EPHESUS

2 "To the angel of the church in ^Ephesus write:

The One who holds the seven stars in His right hand, the One who walks among the seven golden lampstands, says this:

²'I know your deeds and your labor and perseverance, and that you cannot tolerate evil people, and you have ^put those who call themselves apostles to the test, and they are not, and you found them *to be* false; ³and you have perseverance and have endured ^on account of My name, and have not become weary. ⁴But I have *this* against you, that you have ^left your first love. ⁵Therefore, remember from where you have fallen, and ^repent, and ᴮdo the deeds you did at first; or else I am coming to you and I will remove your lampstand from its place— unless you repent. ⁶But you have

this, that you hate the deeds of the ^Nicolaitans, which I also hate. ⁷The one who has an ear, let him hear what the Spirit says to the churches. To the one who overcomes, I will grant to eat from ^the tree of life, which is in the ᴮParadise of God.'

MESSAGE TO SMYRNA

⁸"And to the angel of the church in Smyrna write:

^The first and the last, who ᴮwas dead, and has come to life, says this:

⁹'I know your ^tribulation and your ᴮpoverty (but you are ᴮrich), and the slander by those who say they are Jews, and are not, but are a synagogue of Satan. ¹⁰Do not fear what you are about to suffer. Behold, the devil is about to throw some of you into prison, so that you will be tested, and you will have tribulation for ten days. Be ^faithful until death, and I will give you the crown of life. ¹¹The one who has an ear, let him hear what the Spirit says to the churches. The one who overcomes will not be hurt by the ^second death.'

MESSAGE TO PERGAMUM

¹²"And to the angel of the church in Pergamum write:

The One who has ^the sharp two-edged sword says this:

¹³'I know where you dwell, where Satan's throne is; and you hold firmly to My name, and did not deny My faith even in the days of Antipas, My ^witness, My faithful one, who was killed among you, where Satan

1:16 ᴮMatt 17:2   1:17^Dan 8:17   ᴮIs 44:6
1:18^Luke 24:5   ᴮRev 2:8   1:19^Rev 1:11   ᴮRev
1:12-16   1:20^Rev 1:4, 11   2:1^Rev 1:11
2:2^1 John 4:1   2:3^John 15:21   2:4^Jer 2:2;
Matt 24:12   2:5^Rev 2:16, 22   ᴮHeb 10:32
2:6^Rev 2:15   2:7^Gen 2:9   ᴮEzek 28:13
2:8^Is 44:6   ᴮRev 1:18   2:9^Rev 1:9   ᴮ2 Cor 6:10
2:10^Rev 2:13; 12:11   2:11^Rev 20:6, 14; 21:8
2:12^Rev 1:16; 2:16   2:13^Acts 22:20; Rev 1:5

dwells. [14]But I have a few things against you, because you have *some* there who hold the teaching of Balaam, who kept teaching Balak to put a stumbling block before the sons of Israel, ^to eat things sacrificed to idols and to commit sexual immorality. [15]So you too, have some who in the same way hold to the teaching of the ^Nicolaitans. [16]Therefore ^repent; or else I am coming to you quickly, and I will wage war against them with ^Bthe sword of My mouth. [17]The one who has an ear, let him hear what the Spirit says to the churches. To the one who overcomes, I will give *some* of the hidden manna, and I will give him a white stone, and a ^new name written on the stone ^Bwhich no one knows except the one who receives *it.*'

MESSAGE TO THYATIRA

[18]"And to the angel of the church in Thyatira write:

The Son of God, ^who has eyes like a flame of fire, and feet like burnished bronze, says this:

[19]'^I know your deeds, and your love and faith, and service and perseverance, and that your deeds of late are greater than at first. [20]But I have *this* against you, that you tolerate the woman ^Jezebel, who calls herself a prophetess, and she teaches and leads My bond-servants astray so that they commit sexual immorality and eat things sacrificed to idols. [21]^I gave her time to repent, and she ^Bdoes not want to repent of her sexual immorality. [22]Behold, I will throw her on a bed *of sickness,* and those who ^commit adultery with her into great tribulation, unless they repent of [1]her deeds. [23]And I will kill her children with [1]plague, and all the churches will

know that I am He who ^searches the minds and hearts; and I will give to each one of you according to your deeds. [24]But I say to you, the rest who are in Thyatira, who do not hold this teaching, who have not known the ^deep things of Satan, as they call them—I ^Bplace no other burden on you. [25]Nevertheless ^what you have, hold firmly until I come. [26]The one who overcomes, and the one who keeps My deeds until the end, ^I will give him authority over the nations; [27]AND HE SHALL ^RULE THEM WITH A ROD OF IRON, ^BAS THE VESSELS OF THE POTTER ARE SHATTERED, as I also have received *authority* from My Father; [28]and I will give him ^the morning star. [29]^The one who has an ear, let him hear what the Spirit says to the churches.'

MESSAGE TO SARDIS

3 "To the angel of the church in Sardis write:

He who has the seven spirits of God and ^the seven stars, says this: 'I know your deeds, that you have a name that you are alive, and *yet* you are ^Bdead. [2]Be constantly alert, and strengthen the things that remain, which were about to die; for I have not found your deeds completed in the sight of My God. [3]So ^remember what you have received and heard; and keep *it,* and ^repent. Then if you are not alert, ^I will come like a thief, and you will not know at what hour I will come to you. [4]But you have a

2:14^Num 25:1f; Acts 15:29   2:15^Rev 2:6
2:16^Rev 2:5   ^BRev 1:16   2:17^Is 62:2   ^BRev 19:12
2:18^Rev 1:14f   2:19^Rev 2:2   2:20^1 Kin 16:31; 21:25
2:21^2 Pet 3:9   ^BRom 2:5   2:22^Rev 17:2; 18:9
2:23^Ps 7:9; Jer 11:20   2:24^1 Cor 2:10   ^BActs 15:28
2:25^Rev 3:11   2:26^Ps 2:8   2:27^Ps 2:9   ^BIs 30:14
2:28^1 John 3:2; Rev 22:16   2:29^Rev 2:7
3:1^Rev 1:16   ^B1 Tim 5:6   3:3^Rev 2:5

2:22[1]One early ms *their*   2:23[1]Lit *death;* i.e., a particular kind of death

few people in Sardis who have not ^soiled their garments; and they will walk with Me ^B^in white, for they are worthy. ⁵The one who overcomes will be clothed the same way, in white garments; and I will not erase his name from the book of life, and ^I will confess his name before My Father and before His angels. ⁶^AThe one who has an ear, let him hear what the Spirit says to the churches.'

MESSAGE TO PHILADELPHIA

⁷"And to the angel of the church in Philadelphia write:

He who is holy, who is true, who has ^the key of David, who opens and no one will shut, and who shuts and no one opens, says this:

⁸'I know your deeds. Behold, I have put before you ^an open door which no one can shut, because you have a little power, and have followed My word, and ^Bhave not denied My name. ⁹Behold, I will make *those* of ^the synagogue of Satan, who say that they are Jews and are not, but lie—I will make them ^Bcome and bow down before your feet, and *make them* know that I have loved you. ¹⁰Because you have kept My word of perseverance, I also will keep you from the hour of the testing, that *hour* which is about to come upon the whole ^world, to test those who live on the earth. ¹¹I am coming quickly; ^hold firmly to what you have, so that no one will take your ^Bcrown. ¹²The one who overcomes, I will make him a ^pillar in the temple of My God, and he will not go out from it anymore; and I will write on him the ^Bname of My God, and the name of the city of My God, the new Jerusalem, which comes down out of heaven from My God, and My new

name. ¹³^AThe one who has an ear, let him hear what the Spirit says to the churches.'

MESSAGE TO LAODICEA

¹⁴"To the angel of the church in Laodicea write:

^AThe Amen, ^Bthe faithful and true Witness, the Origin of the creation of God, says this:

¹⁵'^AI know your deeds, that you are neither cold nor hot; I wish that you were cold or hot. ¹⁶So because you are lukewarm, and neither hot nor cold, I will vomit you out of My mouth. ¹⁷Because you say, "^AI am rich, and have become wealthy, and have no need of anything," and you do not know that you are wretched, miserable, poor, blind, and naked, ¹⁸I advise you to ^Abuy from Me gold refined by fire so that you may become rich, and white garments so that you may clothe yourself and the shame of your nakedness will not be revealed; and eye salve to apply to your eyes so that you may see. ¹⁹^AThose whom I love, I rebuke and discipline; therefore be zealous and repent. ²⁰Behold, I stand at the door and knock; if anyone hears My voice and opens the door, ^AI will come in to him and will dine with him, and he with Me. ²¹The one who overcomes, I will grant to him to sit with Me on My throne, as ^AI also overcame and sat with My Father on His throne. ²²^AThe one who has an ear, let him hear what the Spirit says to the churches.'"

3:4 ^A Jude 23   ^B Eccl 9:8   3:5 ^A Matt 10:32
3:6 ^A Rev 2:7   3:7 ^A Is 22:22; Matt 16:19
3:8 ^A Acts 14:27   ^B Rev 2:13   3:9 ^A Rev 2:9   ^B Is 45:14
3:10 ^A Rev 16:14   3:11 ^A Rev 2:25   ^B Rev 2:10
3:12 ^A Gal 2:9   ^B Rev 14:1   3:13 ^A Rev 3:6
3:14 ^A 2 Cor 1:20   ^B Rev 3:7   3:15 ^A Rev 3:1
3:17 ^A Hos 12:8; Zech 11:5   3:18 ^A Matt 13:44
3:19 ^A Prov 3:12; 1 Cor 11:32   3:20 ^A John 14:23
3:21 ^A John 16:33; Rev 5:5   3:22 ^A Rev 2:7

SCENE IN HEAVEN

4 After these things I looked, and behold, a door *standing* open in heaven, and the first voice which I had heard, ^like *the sound* of a trumpet speaking with me, said, "^BCome up here, and I will show you what must take place after these things." ²Immediately I was ^in *the* ¹Spirit; and behold, ^Ba throne was standing in heaven, and *someone was* sitting on the throne. ³And He who was sitting *was* like a jasper stone and a sardius in appearance; and *there was* a ^rainbow around the throne, like an emerald in appearance. ⁴Around the throne *were* ^twenty-four thrones; and upon the thrones *I saw* ^Btwenty-four elders sitting, clothed in white garments, and golden crowns on their heads.

THE THRONE AND WORSHIP OF THE CREATOR

⁵Out from the throne *came flashes of lightning and sounds and peals of thunder. And *there were* ^seven lamps of fire burning before the throne, which are the seven spirits of God; ⁶and before the throne *there was something* like a sea of glass, like crystal; and in the center and around the throne, four living creatures ^full of eyes in front and behind. ⁷^The first living creature *was* like a lion, the second creature like a calf, the third creature had a face like that of a man, and the fourth creature *was* like a flying eagle. ⁸And the four living creatures, each one of them having six wings, are full of eyes around and within; and day and night they do not cease to say,

"^HOLY, HOLY, HOLY *IS* THE LORD GOD, THE ALMIGHTY, who was and who is and who is to come."

⁹And when the living creatures give glory, honor, and thanks to Him who ^sits on the throne, to Him who lives forever and ever, ¹⁰the twenty-four elders will ^fall down before Him who sits on the throne, and they will worship Him who lives forever and ever, and will cast their crowns before the throne, saying,

¹¹ "Worthy are You, our Lord and our God, to receive glory and honor and power; for You ^created all things, and because of Your will they existed, and were created."

THE SCROLL WITH SEVEN SEALS

5 I saw in the right hand of Him who sat on the throne a ^scroll written inside and on the back, ^Bsealed up with seven seals. ²And I saw a ^strong angel proclaiming with a loud voice, "Who is worthy to open the scroll and to break its seals?" ³And no one ^in heaven or on the earth or under the earth was able to open the scroll or to look into it. ⁴Then I *began* to weep greatly because no one was found worthy to open the scroll or to look into it. ⁵And one of the elders *said to me, "Stop weeping; behold, the Lion that is ^from the tribe of Judah, the ^BRoot of David, has overcome *so as to be able* to open the scroll and its seven seals."

⁶And I saw ¹between the throne (with the four living creatures) and the elders a Lamb standing, as if

---

4:1^Rev 1:10   ^BRev 11:12   4:2^Rev 1:10   ^B1 Kin 22:19
4:3^Ezek 1:28   4:4^Rev 11:16   ^BRev 4:10
4:5^Ex 25:37; Zech 4:2   4:6^Ezek 1:18; 10:12
4:7^Ezek 1:10; 10:14   4:8^Is 6:3   4:9^Ps 47:8; Is 6:1
4:10^Rev 5:8, 14; 7:11   4:11^Acts 14:15; Rev 10:6
5:1^Ezek 2:9, 10   ^BIs 29:11   5:2^Rev 10:1; 18:21
5:3^Phil 2:10; Rev 5:13   5:5^Heb 7:14   ^BRev 22:16

4:2 ¹Or *spirit*   5:6 ¹Lit *in the middle of the throne and of the four living creatures, and in the middle of the elders*

slaughtered, having seven horns and ^seven eyes, which are the seven spirits of God sent out into all the earth. ⁷And He came and took ^*the scroll* out of the right hand of Him who ^sat on the throne. ⁸When He had taken the scroll, the four living creatures and the twenty-four elders fell down before the Lamb, each one holding a harp and golden bowls full of incense, which are the ^prayers of the saints. ⁹And they *sang a new song, saying,

> "Worthy are You to take the scroll and to break its seals; for You were slaughtered, and You ^purchased *people* for God with Your blood from ᴮevery tribe, language, people, and nation. ¹⁰You have made them *into* a ^kingdom and priests to our God, and they will ᴮreign upon the earth."

ANGELS EXALT THE LAMB

¹¹Then I looked, and I heard the voices of many angels around the throne and the ^living creatures and the elders; and the number of them was ¹˒ᴮmyriads of myriads, and thousands of thousands, ¹²saying with a loud voice,

> "Worthy is the ^Lamb that was slaughtered to receive power, wealth, wisdom, might, honor, glory, and blessing."

¹³And I heard every created thing which is in heaven, or on the earth, or under the earth, or on the sea, and all the things in them, saying,

> "To Him who sits on the throne and to the Lamb ^*be* the blessing, the honor, the glory, and the dominion forever and ever."

¹⁴And the four living creatures were saying, "^Amen." And the elders fell down and worshiped.

THE FIRST SEAL: CONQUEROR ON A WHITE HORSE

6 Then I saw when the Lamb broke one of the ^seven seals, and I heard one of the four living creatures saying as *with* a voice of thunder, "Come!" ²I looked, and behold, a white horse, and the one who sat on it had a bow; and ^a crown was given to him, and he went out conquering and to conquer.

THE SECOND SEAL: WAR

³When He broke the second seal, I heard the ^second living creature saying, "Come!" ⁴And another, ^a red horse, went out; and to him who sat on it, it was granted to ᴮtake peace from the earth, and that *people* would kill one another; and a large sword was given to him.

THE THIRD SEAL: FAMINE

⁵When He broke the third seal, I heard the ^third living creature saying, "Come!" I looked, and behold, a black horse, and the one who sat on it had a pair of scales in his hand. ⁶And I heard *something* like a voice in the center of the ^four living creatures saying, "A ¹quart of wheat for a ²denarius, and three quarts of barley for a denarius; and do not damage the oil and the wine."

THE FOURTH SEAL: DEATH

⁷When *the Lamb* broke the fourth seal, I heard the voice of the ^fourth living creature saying, "Come!"

5:6 ^Zech 3:9; 4:10   5:7 ^Rev 5:1   5:8 ^Ps 141:2; Rev 8:3f
5:9 ^1 Cor 6:20   ᴮDan 3:4   5:10 ^Rev 1:6   ᴮRev 20:4
5:11 ^Rev 4:6   ᴮDan 7:10   5:12 ^John 1:29; Rev 5:6, 13
5:13 ^Rev 1:6   5:14 ^1 Cor 14:16; Rev 7:12   6:1 ^Rev 5:1
6:2 ^Zech 6:11; Rev 14:14   6:3 ^Rev 4:7   6:4 ^Zech 1:8
ᴮMatt 10:34   6:5 ^Rev 4:7   6:6 ^Rev 4:6f   6:7 ^Rev 4:7

5:11 ¹Gr for *10,000s of 10,000s*   6:6 ¹Gr *choenix*; i.e., a dry measure almost equal to a qt.   ²The denarius was a day's wages for a laborer

8I looked, and behold, an ashen horse; and the one who sat on it had the name ^Death, and Hades was following with him. Authority was given to them over a fourth of the earth, to kill with sword, and famine, and ¹plague, and by the wild animals of the earth.

THE FIFTH SEAL: MARTYRS

9When *the Lamb* broke the fifth seal, I saw underneath the altar the ^souls of those who had been killed ᴮbecause of the word of God, and because of the testimony which they had maintained; ¹⁰and they cried out with a loud voice, saying, "How long, O Lord, ^holy and true, will You refrain from ᴮjudging and avenging our blood on those who live on the earth?" ¹¹And a ^white robe was given to each of them; and they were told that they were to rest for a little while longer, until *the number of* their fellow servants and their brothers *and sisters* who were to be killed even as they *had been,* was ᴮcompleted also.

THE SIXTH SEAL: TERROR

¹²And I looked when He broke the sixth seal, and there was a great earthquake; and the ^sun became as black as sackcloth made of hair, and the whole moon became like blood; ¹³and ^the stars of the sky fell to the earth, as a fig tree drops its unripe figs when shaken by a great wind. ¹⁴The sky was split apart like a scroll when it is rolled up, and ^every mountain and island was removed from its place. ¹⁵Then ^the kings of the earth and the eminent people, and the commanders and the wealthy and the strong, and every slave and free person hid themselves in the caves and among the rocks of the mountains; ¹⁶and they *^said to the mountains and the rocks, "Fall on us and hide us from the sight of Him ᴮwho sits on the throne, and from the wrath of the Lamb; ¹⁷for ^the great day of Their wrath has come, and ᴮwho is able to stand?"

AN INTERLUDE

7 After this I saw four angels standing at the four corners of the earth, holding back ^the four winds of the earth so that no wind would blow on the earth, or on the sea, or on any tree. ²And I saw another angel ascending from the rising of the sun, holding the ^seal of ᴮthe living God; and he called out with a loud voice to the four angels to whom it was granted to harm the earth and the sea, ³saying, "Do not harm the earth, or the sea, or the trees until we have ^sealed the bond-servants of our God on their ᴮforeheads."

THE 144,000

⁴And I heard the number of those who were sealed: ^144,000, sealed from every tribe of the sons of Israel:
5   from the tribe of Judah, twelve thousand *were* sealed, from the tribe of Reuben twelve thousand, from the tribe of Gad twelve thousand,
6   from the tribe of Asher twelve thousand, from the tribe of Naphtali twelve thousand, from the tribe of Manasseh twelve thousand,

6:8 ^Prov 5:5; Hos 13:14   6:9 ^Rev 20:4   ᴮRev 1:2, 9
6:10 ^Rev 3:7   ᴮDeut 32:43   6:11 ^Rev 3:4, 5
ᴮActs 20:24   6:12 ^Is 13:10; Joel 2:10, 31
6:13 ^Matt 24:29   6:14 ^Is 54:10; Jer 4:24
6:15 ^Is 2:10f, 19, 21   6:16 ^Hos 10:8   ᴮRev 4:9
6:17 ^Joel 2:11   ᴮMal 3:2   7:1 ^Jer 49:36; Dan 7:2
7:2 ^Rev 7:3   ᴮMatt 16:16   7:3 ^Rev 7:3-8
ᴮEzek 9:4, 6   7:4 ^Rev 14:1, 3

6:8 ¹Lit *death;* i.e., a particular kind of death

7 from the tribe of Simeon twelve thousand, from the tribe of Levi twelve thousand, from the tribe of Issachar twelve thousand,

8 from the tribe of Zebulun twelve thousand, from the tribe of Joseph twelve thousand, *and* from the tribe of Benjamin, twelve thousand *were* sealed.

A MULTITUDE
FROM THE TRIBULATION

9 After these things I looked, and behold, a great multitude which no one could count, from ᴬevery nation and *all the* tribes, peoples, and languages, standing before the throne and ᴮbefore the Lamb, clothed in white robes, and palm branches *were* in their hands; 10 and they *cried out with a loud voice, saying,

"ᴬSalvation *belongs* to our God who sits on the throne, and to the Lamb."

11 And all the angels were standing ᴬaround the throne and *around* ᴬthe elders and the four living creatures; and they fell on their faces before the throne and worshiped God, 12 saying,

"Amen, ᴬblessing, glory, wisdom, thanksgiving, honor, power, and might *belong* to our God forever and ever. Amen."

13 Then one of the elders responded, saying to me, "These who are clothed in the ᴬwhite robes, who are they, and where have they come from?" 14 I said to him, "My lord, you know." And he said to me, "These are the ones who come out of the great tribulation, and they have washed their robes and made them white in the ᴬblood of the Lamb. 15 For this reason they are ᴬbefore the throne of God, and they serve Him day and night in His temple; and ᴮHe who sits on the throne will spread His tabernacle over them. 16 ᴬThey will no longer hunger nor thirst, nor will the sun beat down on them, nor any scorching heat; 17 for the Lamb in the center of the throne will be their ᴬshepherd, and will guide them to springs of the water of life; and ᴮGod will wipe every tear from their eyes."

THE SEVENTH SEAL: TRUMPETS

8 When *the Lamb* broke the ᴬseventh seal, there was silence in heaven for about half an hour. 2 And I saw ᴬthe seven angels who stand before God, and seven trumpets were given to them.

3 Another angel came and stood at the ᴬaltar, holding a golden censer; and much ᴮincense was given to him, so that he might add it to the ᴮprayers of all the saints on the golden altar which was before the throne. 4 And ᴬthe smoke of the incense ascended from the angel's hand with the prayers of the saints before God. 5 Then the angel took the ¹censer and ᴬfilled it with the fire of the altar, and hurled it to the earth; and there were ᴮpeals of thunder and sounds, and flashes of lightning and an earthquake.

6 ᴬAnd the seven angels who had the seven trumpets prepared themselves to sound them.

7 The first sounded, and there was ᴬhail and fire mixed with blood,

7:9 ᴬRev 5:9   ᴮRev 22:3   7:10 ᴬPs 3:8; Rev 12:10
7:11 ᴬRev 4:4   7:12 ᴬRev 5:12   7:13 ᴬRev 7:9
7:14 ᴬHeb 9:14; 1 John 1:7   7:15 ᴬRev 7:9   ᴮRev 4:9
7:16 ᴬPs 121:5f; Is 49:10   7:17 ᴬPs 23:1f   ᴮIs 25:8
8:1 ᴬRev 5:1; 6:1, 3, 5, 7, 9, 12   8:2 ᴬRev 8:6–13; 9:1, 13
8:3 ᴬRev 6:9   ᴮRev 5:8   8:4 ᴬPs 141:2   8:5 ᴬLev 16:12
ᴮEx 19:16   8:6 ᴬRev 8:2   8:7 ᴬEx 9:23ff; Ezek 38:22

8:5 ¹I.e., container to burn incense

and it was hurled to the earth; and a third of the earth was burned up, and a third of the trees were burned up, and all the green grass was burned up.

8 The second angel sounded, and *something* like a great mountain burning with fire was hurled into the sea; and a third of the ^Asea became blood, 9 and a third of the creatures which were in the sea and had life, died; and a third of the ^Aships were destroyed.

10 The third angel sounded, and a great star ^Afell from heaven, burning like a torch, and it fell on a third of the rivers and on the ^Bsprings of waters. 11 The star is named Wormwood; and a third of the waters became ^Awormwood, and many people died from the waters because they were made bitter.

12 The fourth angel sounded, and a third of the ^Asun, a third of the ^Amoon, and a third of the stars were struck, so that a third of them would be darkened and the day would not shine for a third of it, and the night in the same way.

13 Then I looked, and I heard an eagle flying in ^Amidheaven, saying with a loud voice, "Woe, woe, woe to ^Bthose who live on the earth, because of the remaining blasts of the trumpet of the three angels who are about to sound!"

THE FIFTH TRUMPET: SHAFT OF THE ABYSS

9 Then the fifth angel sounded, and I saw a star from heaven which had fallen to the earth; and the key to the ^Ashaft of the abyss was given to him. 2 He opened the shaft of the abyss, and ^Asmoke ascended out of the shaft like the smoke of a great furnace; and the sun and the air were darkened from the smoke of the shaft. 3 Then out of the smoke came ^Alocusts upon the earth, and power was given them, as the scorpions of the earth have power. 4 They were told not to hurt the grass of the earth, nor any green thing, nor any tree, but only the people who do not have the ^Aseal of God on their foreheads. 5 And they were not permitted to kill anyone, but to torment for five months; and their torment was like the torment of a ^Ascorpion when it stings a person. 6 And in those days ^Apeople will seek death and will not find it; they will long to die, and death will flee from them!

7 The ^Aappearance of the locusts was like horses prepared for battle; and on their heads appeared to be crowns like gold, and their faces were like human faces. 8 They had hair like the hair of women, and their ^Ateeth were like *the teeth* of lions. 9 They had breastplates like breastplates of iron; and the ^Asound of their wings was like the sound of chariots, of many horses rushing to battle. 10 They have tails like scorpions, and stings; and in their ^Atails is their power to hurt people for ^Bfive months. 11 They have as king over them, the angel of the ^Aabyss; his name in Hebrew is ¹Abaddon, and in the Greek he has the name Apollyon.

12 ^AThe first woe has passed; behold, two woes are still coming after these things.

8:8 ^A Ex 7:17ff; Rev 11:6   8:9 ^A Is 2:16   8:10 ^A Is 14:12
^B Rev 14:7   8:11 ^A Jer 9:15; 23:15   8:12 ^A Ex 10:21ff; Is 13:10
8:13 ^A Rev 14:6   ^B Rev 3:10   9:1 ^A Luke 8:31; Rev 9:2, 11
9:2 ^A Gen 19:28; Ex 19:18   9:3 ^A Ex 10:12-15; Rev 9:7
9:4 ^A Ezek 9:4; Rev 7:2, 3   9:5 ^A 2 Chr 10:11, 14; Ezek 2:6
9:6 ^A Job 3:21; 7:15   9:7 ^A Joel 2:4   9:8 ^A Joel 1:6
9:9 ^A Jer 47:3; Joel 2:5   9:10 ^A Rev 9:19   ^B Rev 9:5
9:11 ^A Luke 8:31; Rev 9:1, 2   9:12 ^A Rev 8:13; 11:14

9:11 ¹ I.e., destruction

THE SIXTH TRUMPET: ARMY FROM THE EAST

¹³Then the sixth angel sounded, and I heard a voice from the ¹four horns of the ᴬgolden altar which is before God, ¹⁴saying to the sixth angel who had the trumpet, "Release the four angels who are bound at the ᴬgreat river Euphrates." ¹⁵And the four angels, who had been prepared for the hour and day and month and year, were ᴬreleased, so that they would kill a third of mankind. ¹⁶The number of the armies of the horsemen was ᴬtwo hundred million; I heard the number of them. ¹⁷And this is how I saw in my vision the horses and those who sat on them: *the riders* had breastplates *the color* of fire, of hyacinth, and of ¹,ᴬbrimstone; and the heads of the horses are like the heads of lions; and ᴮout of their mouths *came fire and smoke and ¹,ᴬbrimstone. ¹⁸A ᴬthird of mankind was killed by these three plagues, by the fire, the smoke, and the brimstone which came out of their mouths. ¹⁹For the power of the horses is in their mouths and in their tails; for their tails are like serpents and have heads, and with them they do harm.

²⁰The rest of mankind, who were not killed by these plagues, ᴬdid not repent of the works of their hands so as not to worship demons and the idols of gold, silver, brass, stone, and wood, which can neither see nor hear nor walk; ²¹and they did not repent of their murders, nor of their ᴬwitchcraft, nor of their sexual immorality, nor of their thefts.

THE ANGEL AND THE LITTLE SCROLL

10 I saw another strong angel coming down from heaven, clothed with a cloud; and the ᴬrainbow was on his head, and ᴮhis face

was like the sun, and his feet like pillars of fire; ²and he had in his hand a ᴬlittle scroll, which was open. He placed his right foot on the sea and his left on the land; ³and he cried out with a loud voice, ᴬas when a lion roars; and when he had cried out, the seven peals of thunder uttered their voices. ⁴When the seven peals of thunder had spoken, ᴬI was about to write; and I heard a voice from heaven, saying, "Seal up the things which the seven peals of thunder have spoken, and do not write them." ⁵Then the angel whom I saw standing on the sea and on the land ᴬraised his right hand to heaven, ⁶and swore by Him who lives forever and ever, ᴬwho created heaven and the things in it, and the earth and the things in it, and the sea and the things in it, that there will no longer be a delay, ⁷but in the days of the voice of the ᴬseventh angel, when he is about to sound, then ᴮthe mystery of God is finished, as He announced to His servants the prophets.

⁸Then ᴬthe voice which I heard from heaven, *I heard* again speaking with me, and saying, "Go, take ᴮthe scroll which is open in the hand of the angel who ᴮstands on the sea and on the land." ⁹And I went to the angel, telling him to give me the little scroll. And he *said to me, "ᴬTake it and eat it; it will make your stomach bitter, but in your mouth it will be sweet as honey." ¹⁰I took

---

9:13 ᴬRev 8:3   9:14 ᴬGen 15:18; Deut 1:7
9:15 ᴬRev 20:7   9:16 ᴬRev 5:11   9:17 ᴬRev 9:18
ᴮRev 11:5   9:18 ᴬRev 8:7; 9:15   9:20 ᴬRev 2:21
9:21 ᴬIs 47:9, 12; Rev 18:23   10:1 ᴬRev 4:3   ᴮMatt 17:2
10:2 ᴬRev 5:1; 10:8-10   10:3 ᴬIs 31:4; Hos 11:10
10:4 ᴬRev 1:11, 19   10:5 ᴬDeut 32:40; Dan 12:7
10:6 ᴬEx 20:11; Rev 4:11   10:7 ᴬRev 11:15   ᴮAmos 3:7
10:8 ᴬRev 10:4   ᴮRev 10:2   10:9 ᴬJer 15:16; Ezek 2:8

9:13 ¹Two early mss do not contain *four*
9:17 ¹I.e., burning sulfur

the little scroll from the angel's hand and ate it, and in my mouth it was sweet as honey; and when I had eaten it, my stomach was made bitter. ¹¹And they *said to me, "You must prophesy again concerning ^many peoples, nations, languages, and ᴮkings."

THE TWO WITNESSES

11 Then there was given to me a ^measuring rod like a staff; and someone said, "Get up and measure the temple of God and the altar, and those who worship in it. ²Leave out the courtyard which is outside the temple and do not measure it, because ^it has been given to the nations; and they will ^trample the holy city for ᴮforty-two months. ³And I will grant *authority* to my two witnesses, and they will prophesy for 1,260 days, clothed in ^sackcloth." ⁴These are the ^two olive trees and the two lampstands that stand before the Lord of the earth. ⁵And if anyone wants to harm them, ^fire flows out of their mouth and devours their enemies; and *so* if anyone wants to harm them, he must be killed in this way. ⁶These have the power to ^shut up the sky, so that rain will not fall during the days of their prophesying; and they have power over the waters to turn them into blood, and to strike the earth with every plague, as often as they desire.

⁷When they have finished their testimony, ^the beast that comes up out of the abyss will make war with them, and overcome them and kill them. ⁸And their dead bodies *will lie* on the street of the great city which ¹spiritually is called ^Sodom and Egypt, where also their Lord

was crucified. ⁹Those from ^the peoples, tribes, languages, and nations *will* look at their dead bodies for three and a half days, and will not allow their dead bodies to be laid in a tomb. ¹⁰And ^those who live on the earth *will* rejoice over them and celebrate; and they will send gifts to one another, because these two prophets tormented ^those who live on the earth.

¹¹And after the three and a half days, ^the breath of life from God came into them, and they stood on their feet; and great fear fell upon those who were watching them. ¹²And they heard a loud voice from heaven saying to them, "^Come up here." And they ᴮwent up into heaven in the cloud, and their enemies watched them. ¹³And at that time there was a great ^earthquake, and a tenth of the city fell; seven thousand people were killed in the earthquake, and the rest were terrified and gave glory to the God of heaven.

¹⁴The second ^woe has passed; behold, the third woe is coming quickly.

THE SEVENTH TRUMPET: CHRIST'S REIGN FORESEEN

¹⁵Then the seventh angel sounded; and there were loud voices in heaven, saying,

"The kingdom of the world has become *the kingdom* of our Lord and of His Christ; and ^He will

10:11^Rev 5:9   ᴮRev 17:10, 12   11:1^Ezek 40:3–42:20
11:2^Luke 21:24   ᴮDan 7:25   11:3^Gen 37:34;
2 Sam 3:31   11:4^Zech 4:3, 11, 14   11:5^2 Kin 1:10–12;
Jer 5:14   11:6^1 Kin 17:1; Luke 4:25   11:7^Rev 13:1ff;
17:8   11:8^Is 1:9, 10; Jer 23:14   11:9^Rev 5:9; 10:11
11:10^Rev 3:10   11:11^Ezek 37:5, 9, 10, 14
11:12^Rev 4:1   ᴮ2 Kin 2:11   11:13^Rev 6:12; 16:18
11:14^Rev 8:13; 9:12   11:15^Ex 15:18; Dan 2:44

11:8 ¹I.e., from the viewpoint of the Holy Spirit

reign forever and ever." [16]And the twenty-four elders, who ^sit on their thrones before God, ^Bfell on their faces and worshiped God, [17]saying,

"We give You thanks, ^Lord God, the Almighty, the One who is and who was, because You have taken Your great power and have begun to ^Breign. [18]And ^the nations were enraged, and Your wrath came, and the time *came* for the dead to be judged, and *the time* to reward Your bond-servants the prophets and the saints and those who fear Your name, the small and the great, and to destroy those who destroy the earth."

[19]And ^the temple of God which is in heaven was opened; and ^Bthe ark of His covenant appeared in His temple, and there were flashes of lightning and sounds and peals of thunder, and an earthquake, and a great hailstorm.

THE WOMAN, ISRAEL

12 A great ^sign appeared in heaven: a woman clothed with the sun, and the moon under her feet, and on her head a crown of twelve stars; [2]and she was pregnant and she *^cried out, being in labor and in pain to give birth.

THE RED DRAGON, SATAN

[3]Then another sign appeared in heaven: and behold, a great red ^dragon having seven heads and ^Bten horns, and on his heads *were* seven crowns. [4]And his tail *swept away a ^third of the stars of heaven and ^Bhurled them to the earth. And the dragon stood before the woman who was about to give birth, so that when she gave birth he might devour her Child.

THE MALE CHILD, CHRIST

[5]And ^she gave birth to a Son, a male, who is going to ^Brule all the nations with a rod of iron; and her Child was caught up to God and to His throne. [6]Then the woman fled into the wilderness where she *had a place prepared by God, so that there she would be nourished for ^1,260 days.

THE ANGEL, MICHAEL

[7]And there was war in heaven, ^Michael and his angels waging war with the dragon. The dragon and ^Bhis angels waged war, [8]and they did not prevail, and there was no longer a place found for them in heaven. [9]And the great dragon was thrown down, the ^serpent of old who is called the devil and Satan, who deceives the whole world; he was thrown down to the earth, and his angels were thrown down with him. [10]Then I heard a loud voice in heaven, saying,

"Now the salvation, and the power, and the kingdom of our God and the authority of His Christ have come, for the ^accuser of our brothers *and sisters* has been thrown down, the one who accuses them before our God day and night. [11]And they overcame him because of ^the blood of the Lamb and because of the word of their testimony, and they did not love their life *even* when faced with death. [12]For this reason, ^rejoice, you heavens and you who dwell in them. Woe to the earth and the sea,

11:16^Matt 19:28   ^BRev 4:10   11:17^Rev 1:8
^BRev 19:6   11:18^Ps 2:1   11:19^Rev 15:5   ^BHeb 9:4
12:1^Matt 24:30; Rev 12:3   12:2^Is 26:17; 66:6–9
12:3^Is 27:1   ^BDan 7:7, 20, 24   12:4^Rev 8:7, 12
^BDan 8:10   12:5^Is 66:7   ^BPs 2:9   12:6^Rev 11:3;
13:5   12:7^Dan 10:13, 21   ^BMatt 25:41
12:9^Gen 3:1; 2 Cor 11:3   12:10^Job 1:11; 2:5
12:11^Rev 7:14   12:12^Ps 96:11; Is 44:23

because the devil has come down to you with great wrath, knowing that he has *only* a short time."

¹³And when the ^dragon saw that he was thrown down to the earth, he persecuted the woman who gave birth to the male *Child*. ¹⁴But the ^two wings of the great eagle were given to the woman, so that she could fly into the wilderness to her place, where she *was nourished for a time, times, and half a time, away from the presence of the serpent. ¹⁵And the ^serpent hurled water like a river out of his mouth after the woman, so that he might cause her to be swept away with the flood. ¹⁶But the earth helped the woman, and the earth opened its mouth and drank up the river which the dragon had hurled out of his mouth. ¹⁷So the dragon was enraged with the woman, and went off to ^make war with the rest of her children, who keep the commandments of God and hold to the testimony of Jesus.

THE BEAST FROM THE SEA

13 And *the dragon* stood on the sand of the seashore.

Then I saw a beast coming up out of the sea, having ^ten horns and seven heads, and on his horns *were* ten crowns, and on his heads *were* ᴮblasphemous names. ²And the beast that I saw was ^like a leopard, and his feet were like *those* of a bear, and his mouth like the mouth of a lion. And the dragon gave him his power and his ᴮthrone, and great authority. ³*I saw* one of his heads as if it had been fatally wounded, and his ^fatal wound was healed. And the whole earth was amazed *and followed* after the beast; ⁴they worshiped the ^dragon because he gave his authority to the beast; and

they worshiped the beast, saying, "Who is like the beast, and who is able to wage war with him?" ⁵A mouth was given to him ^speaking arrogant words and blasphemies, and authority to act for forty-two months was given to him. ⁶And he opened his mouth in blasphemies against God, to blaspheme His name and His tabernacle, *that is,* ^those who dwell in heaven.

⁷It was also given to him to ^make war with the saints and to overcome them, and authority was given to him over every tribe, people, language, and nation. ⁸All who live on the earth will worship him, *everyone* whose name has not been written ^since the foundation of the world in the book of life of the Lamb who has been slaughtered. ⁹^If anyone has an ear, let him hear. ¹⁰^If anyone *is destined* for captivity, to captivity he goes; if anyone kills with the sword, with the sword he must be killed. Here is the perseverance and the faith of the saints.

THE BEAST FROM THE EARTH

¹¹Then ^I saw another beast coming up out of the earth; and he had two horns like a lamb, and he spoke as a dragon. ¹²He exercises all the authority of the first beast ^in his presence. And he makes the earth and those who live on it worship the first beast, whose fatal wound was healed. ¹³He ^performs great signs, so that he even makes ᴮfire come down out of the sky to the earth in the presence of people.

12:13^Rev 12:3   12:14^Ex 19:4; Deut 32:11   12:15^Gen 3:1; 2 Cor 11:3   12:17^Rev 11:7; 13:7   13:1^Rev 12:3   ᴮDan 7:8   13:2^Dan 7:6   ᴮRev 2:13   13:3^Rev 13:12, 14   13:4^Rev 12:3; 13:2, 12   13:5^Dan 7:25; 2 Thess 2:3f   13:6^Rev 7:15; 12:12   13:7^Dan 7:21; Rev 11:7   13:8^Rev 17:8   13:9^Rev 2:7   13:10^Jer 15:2; 43:11   13:11^Rev 13:1; 16:13   13:12^Rev 13:14; 19:20   13:13^Matt 24:24   ᴮ1 Kin 18:38

¹⁴ And he deceives those who live on the earth because of ᴬthe signs which it was given him to perform in the presence of the beast, telling those who live on the earth to make an image to the beast who *had the ᴮwound of the sword and has come to life. ¹⁵ And it was given to him to give breath to the image of the beast, so that the image of the beast would even ¹speak and cause ᴬall who do not worship the image of the beast to be killed. ¹⁶ And he causes all, ᴬthe small and the great, the rich and the poor, and the free and the slaves, to be given a mark on their right hands or on their foreheads, ¹⁷ and *he decrees* that no one will be able to buy or to sell, except the one who has the mark, *either* ᴬthe name of the beast or ᴮthe number of his name. ¹⁸ᴬHere is wisdom. Let him who has understanding calculate the number of the beast, for the number is that of a ¹man; and his number is ²six hundred and sixty-six.

THE LAMB AND THE 144,000 ON MOUNT ZION

14 Then I looked, and behold, the Lamb *was* standing on Mount Zion, and with Him 144,000 who had ᴬHis name and the name of His Father written on their foreheads. ² And I heard a voice from heaven, like ᴬthe sound of many waters and like the sound of loud thunder, and the voice which I heard *was* like *the sound* of harpists playing on their harps. ³ And they *sang ᴬa new song before the throne and before the four living creatures and the elders; and no one was able to learn the song except the ᴮ144,000 who had been ᴬpurchased from the earth. ⁴ᴬThese are the ones

who have not defiled themselves with women, for they are celibate. These *are* the ones who ᴮfollow the Lamb wherever He goes. These have been purchased from mankind as first fruits to God and to the Lamb. ⁵ And ᴬno lie was found in their mouths; they are blameless.

VISION OF THE ANGEL WITH THE GOSPEL

⁶ And I saw another angel flying in midheaven with ᴬan eternal gospel to preach to those who live on the earth, and to every nation, tribe, language, and people; ⁷ and he said with a loud voice, "ᴬFear God and give Him glory, because the hour of His judgment has come; worship Him who made the heaven and the earth, and sea and springs of waters."

⁸ And another angel, a second one, followed, saying, "ᴬFallen, fallen is Babylon the great, she who has ᴮmade all the nations drink of the wine of the passion of her sexual immorality."

DOOM FOR WORSHIPERS OF THE BEAST

⁹ Then another angel, a third one, followed them, saying with a loud voice, "If anyone ᴬworships the beast and his image, and receives a mark on his forehead or on his hand, ¹⁰ he also will drink of the ᴬwine of the wrath of God, which is mixed in full strength ᴮin the cup of His anger; and he will be

13:14 ᴬ2 Thess 2:9f   ᴮRev 13:3   13:15 ᴬDan 3:3ff
13:16 ᴬRev 11:18   13:17 ᴬRev 14:11   ᴮRev 15:2
13:18 ᴬRev 17:9   14:1 ᴬRev 3:12   14:2 ᴬRev 1:15
14:3 ᴬRev 5:9   ᴮRev 7:4   14:4 ᴬ2 Cor 11:2   ᴮRev 3:4
14:5 ᴬPs 32:2; Zeph 3:13   14:6 ᴬ1 Pet 1:25
14:7 ᴬRev 15:4   14:8 ᴬIs 21:9   ᴮJer 51:7
14:9 ᴬRev 13:12; 14:11   14:10 ᴬIs 51:17   ᴮPs 75:8

13:15 ¹One early ms *speak, and he will cause*
13:18 ¹Or *human*   ²I.e., spelled out in Gr as 600 + 60 + 6; one early ms has the letters for *616*

tormented with fire and brimstone in the presence of the holy angels and in the presence of the Lamb. [11] And the ^smoke of their torment ascends forever and ever; they have no rest day and night, those who worship the beast and his image, and whoever receives the ^Bmark of his name." [12] Here is ^the perseverance of the saints who ^Bkeep the commandments of God and their faith in Jesus.

[13] And I heard a voice from heaven, saying, "Write: 'Blessed are the dead who ^die in the Lord from now on!'" "Yes," says the Spirit, "so that they may ^Brest from their labors, for their deeds follow with them."

THE HARVEST

[14] Then I looked, and behold, a white cloud, and sitting on the cloud *was* one ^like [1]a son of man, with a golden crown on His head and a sharp sickle in His hand. [15] And another angel came out of the temple, calling out with a loud voice to Him who sat on the cloud, "^Put in Your sickle and reap, for the hour to reap has come, because the ^Bharvest of the earth is ripe." [16] Then He who sat on the cloud swung His sickle over the earth, and the earth was reaped.

[17] And another angel ^came out of the temple which is in heaven, and he also had a sharp sickle. [18] Then another angel, the one who has power over fire, came out from ^the altar; and he called with a loud voice to him who had the sharp sickle, saying, "Put in your sharp sickle and gather the clusters from the vine of the earth, because her grapes are ripe." [19] So the angel swung his sickle to the earth and gathered *the clusters from* the

vine of the earth, and threw *them* into ^the great wine press of the wrath of God. [20] And ^the wine press was trampled outside the city, and blood came out from the wine press, up to the horses' bridles, for a distance of [1]1,600 stadia.

A SCENE OF HEAVEN

15 Then I saw another sign in heaven, great and marvelous, seven angels who had ^seven plagues, *which are* the last, because in them the wrath of God is finished.

[2] And I saw *something* like a ^sea of glass mixed with fire, and those who ^Bwere victorious over the beast and his image and the number of his name, standing on the ^sea of glass, holding harps of God. [3] And they *sang the ^song of Moses, the bond-servant of God, and the song of the Lamb, saying,

"^BGreat and marvelous are Your
   works,
Lord God, the Almighty;
Righteous and true are Your
   ways,
King of the [1]nations!
[4] "Who will not fear You, Lord,
   and glorify Your name?
For You alone are holy;
For ^ALL THE NATIONS WILL
   COME AND WORSHIP BEFORE
   YOU,
For Your righteous acts have
   been revealed."

14:11^AIs 34:8-10   ^BRev 13:17   14:12^ARev 13:10
^BRev 12:17   14:13^A1 Thess 4:16   ^BHeb 4:9ff
14:14^ADan 7:13; Rev 1:13   14:15^AJoel 3:13
^BMatt 13:39-41   14:17^ARev 11:19; 14:15
14:18^ARev 6:9; 8:3   14:19^AIs 63:2f; Rev 19:15
14:20^AIs 63:3; Lam 1:15   15:1^ALev 26:21
15:2^ARev 4:6   ^BRev 12:11   15:3^AEx 15:1ff
^BDeut 32:3f   15:4^APs 86:9; Is 66:23

14:14[1]Or *the Son of Man* 14:20[1]Possibly about 184 miles or 296 km; a Roman stadion perhaps averaged 607 ft. or 185 m   15:3[1]Two early mss *ages*

5 After these things I looked, and ^the temple of the tabernacle of testimony in heaven was opened, 6 and the ^seven angels who had the seven plagues came out of the temple, clothed in ¹linen, clean *and* bright, and their chests wrapped with golden sashes. 7 And one of the ^four living creatures gave the seven angels seven golden bowls full of the wrath of God, who lives forever and ever. 8 And the temple was filled with ^smoke from the glory of God and from His power; and no one was able to enter the temple until the seven plagues of the seven angels were finished.

THE BOWLS OF WRATH

16 Then I heard a loud voice from ^the temple, saying to the seven angels, "Go and pour out on the earth the seven bowls of the wrath of God."

2 So the first *angel* went and poured out his bowl on the earth; and a harmful and painful ^sore afflicted the people who had the mark of the beast and who worshiped his image.

3 The second *angel* poured out his bowl ^into the sea, and it became blood like *that* of a dead man; and every living ¹thing in the sea died.

4 Then the third *angel* poured out his bowl into the ^rivers and the springs of waters; and they became blood. 5 And I heard the angel of the waters saying, "^Righteous are You, ^the One who is and who was, O Holy One, because You judged these things; 6 for they poured out ^the blood of saints and prophets, and You have given them blood to drink. They deserve it." 7 And I heard the altar saying, "Yes, Lord God, the Almighty, ^true and righteous are Your judgments."

8 And the fourth *angel* poured out his bowl upon ^the sun, and it was given *power* to scorch people with fire. 9 And the people were scorched with fierce heat; and they ^blasphemed the name of God who has the power over these plagues, and they did not repent so as to give Him glory.

10 And the fifth *angel* poured out his bowl on the ^throne of the beast, and his kingdom became darkened; and they gnawed their tongues because of pain, 11 and they blasphemed the God of heaven because of their pain and their ^sores; and they did not repent of their deeds.

12 The sixth *angel* poured out his bowl on the ^great river, the Euphrates; and its water was dried up, so that the way would be prepared for the kings ^from the east.

HAR-MAGEDON (ARMAGEDDON)

13 And I saw *coming* out of the mouth of the dragon, and out of the mouth of the beast, and out of the mouth of the false prophet, three ^unclean spirits like ^frogs; 14 for they are ^spirits of demons, ^performing signs, which go out to the kings of the entire world, to gather them together for the war of the great day of God, the Almighty. 15 ("Behold, ^I am coming like a thief. Blessed is the one who stays awake and keeps his clothes, so that he will not walk about naked and *people* will not see

15:5 ^Rev 11:19   15:6 ^Rev 15:1   15:7 ^Rev 4:6
15:8 ^Ex 19:18; 40:34f   16:1 ^Rev 11:19   16:2 ^Ex
9:9–11; Deut 28:35   16:3 ^Ex 7:17–21; Rev 8:8f
16:4 ^Rev 8:10   16:5 ^John 17:25   ^Rev 11:17
16:6 ^Rev 17:6; 18:24   16:7 ^Rev 15:3; 19:2
16:8 ^Rev 6:12   16:9 ^Rev 16:11, 21   16:10 ^Rev 13:2
16:11 ^Rev 16:2   16:12 ^Rev 9:14   ^Rev 7:2
16:13 ^Rev 18:2   ^Ex 8:6   16:14 ^1 Tim 4:1   ^Rev 13:13
16:15 ^Matt 24:43f; Luke 12:39f

15:6 ¹One early ms *stone*   16:3 ¹Lit *soul*

his shame.") ¹⁶And they ᴬgathered them together to the place which in Hebrew is called ᴮHar-Magedon.

THE SEVENTH BOWL OF WRATH

¹⁷Then the seventh *angel* poured out his bowl upon the air, and a loud voice came out of the temple from the throne, saying, "ᴬIt is done." ¹⁸And there were flashes of ᴬlightning and sounds and peals of thunder; and there was a great earthquake, such as there had not been since mankind came to be upon the earth, so great an earthquake *was it, and* so mighty. ¹⁹The great city was split into three parts, and the cities of the nations fell. ᴬBabylon the great was ᴮremembered in the sight of God, to give her the cup of the wine of His fierce wrath. ²⁰And ᴬevery island fled, and no mountains were found. ²¹And huge hailstones, weighing about ¹a talent each, *came down from heaven upon people; and people blasphemed God because of the ᴬplague of the hail, because the hailstone plague *was extremely severe.

THE DOOM OF BABYLON

17 Then one of the seven angels who had the seven bowls came and spoke with me, saying, "Come here, I will show you the judgment of the ᴬgreat prostitute who ᴮsits on many waters, ²with whom ᴬthe kings of the earth committed *acts of* sexual immorality, and those who live on the earth became drunk with the wine of her sexual immorality." ³And ᴬhe carried me away ¹in the Spirit into a wilderness; and I saw a woman sitting on a scarlet beast, full of blasphemous names, having seven heads and ten horns. ⁴The woman ᴬwas clothed in purple and scarlet, and adorned with gold, precious stones, and pearls, holding in her hand ᴮa gold cup full of abominations and of the unclean things of her sexual immorality, ⁵and on her forehead a name *was* written, a ᴬmystery: "BABYLON THE GREAT, THE MOTHER OF PROSTITUTES AND OF THE ABOMINATIONS OF THE EARTH." ⁶And I saw the woman drunk with ᴬthe blood of the saints, and with the blood of the witnesses of Jesus. When I saw her, I wondered greatly. ⁷And the angel said to me, "Why do you wonder? I will tell you the mystery of the woman and of the beast that carries her, which has the ᴬseven heads and the ten horns.

⁸"The beast that you saw ᴬwas, and is not, and is about to ᴮcome up out of the abyss and ¹go to destruction. And those who live on the earth, whose names have not been written in the book of life from the foundation of the world, will wonder when they see the beast, that he was, and is not, and will come. ⁹Here is the mind which has wisdom. The ᴬseven heads are seven mountains upon which the woman sits, ¹⁰and they are seven ᴬkings; five have fallen, one is, the other has not yet come; and when he comes, he must remain a little while. ¹¹The beast which ᴬwas, and is not, is himself also an eighth and is *one* of the seven, and he goes to destruction. ¹²The ᴬten

16:16ᴬRev 19:19   ᴮZech 12:11   **16:17**ᴬRev 10:6; 21:6
16:18ᴬRev 4:5   **16:19**ᴬRev 14:8   ᴮRev 18:5
16:20ᴬRev 6:14; 20:11   **16:21**ᴬEx 9:18-25
17:1ᴬRev 19:2   ᴮJer 51:13   **17:2**ᴬRev 2:22; 18:3, 9
17:3ᴬRev 21:10   **17:4**ᴬEzek 28:13   ᴮJer 51:7
17:5ᴬ2 Thess 2:7; Rev 17:7   **17:6**ᴬRev 16:6
17:7ᴬRev 17:3   **17:8**ᴬRev 13:3, 12, 14   ᴮRev 11:7
17:9ᴬRev 17:3   **17:10**ᴬRev 10:11   **17:11**ᴬRev 13:3, 12, 14;
17:8   **17:12**ᴬDan 7:24; Rev 12:3

16:21¹I.e., as a measure of weight about 100 lb.
or 45 kg   **17:3**¹Or *in spirit*   **17:8**¹One early ms *is going*

horns which you saw are ten kings who have not yet received a kingdom, but they receive authority as kings with the beast for one hour. [13] These have ^one purpose, and they give their power and authority to the beast.

VICTORY FOR THE LAMB

[14] These will wage ^war against the Lamb, and the Lamb will overcome them because He is ^B Lord of lords and King of kings; and those who are with Him *are the* called and chosen and faithful."

[15] And he *said to me, "The ^waters which you saw where the prostitute sits are peoples and multitudes, and nations and languages. [16] And the ^ten horns which you saw, and the beast, these will hate the prostitute and will make her desolate and naked, and will eat her flesh and will burn her up with fire. [17] For ^God has put it in their hearts to execute His purpose by having a common purpose, and by giving their kingdom to the beast, until the words of God will be fulfilled. [18] The woman whom you saw is ^the great city, which reigns over the kings of the earth."

BABYLON IS FALLEN

18 After these things I saw another ^angel coming down from heaven, having great authority, and the earth was illuminated from his glory. [2] And he cried out with a mighty voice, saying, "^Fallen, fallen is Babylon the great! She has become a dwelling place of demons and a prison of every ^B unclean spirit, and a prison of every unclean and hateful bird. [3] For all the nations have fallen because of the ^wine of the passion of her sexual immorality, and the kings of the earth have committed *acts of* sexual immorality with her, and the merchants of the earth have become rich from the excessive wealth of her luxury."

[4] I heard another voice from heaven, saying, "^Come out of her, my people, so that you will not participate in her sins and receive *any* of her plagues; [5] for her sins have ^piled up as high as heaven, and God has ^B remembered her offenses. [6] ^Pay her back even as she has paid, and give back *to her* double according to her deeds; in the cup which she has mixed, mix twice as much for her. [7] ^To the extent that she glorified herself and lived luxuriously, to the same extent give her torment and mourning; for she says in her heart, '^B I sit *as* a queen and I am not a widow, and will never see mourning.' [8] For this reason in one day her plagues will come, ¹plague and mourning and famine, and she will be ^burned up with fire; for the Lord God who judges her ^B is strong.

GRIEF OVER BABYLON

[9] "And ^the kings of the earth, who committed *acts of* sexual immorality and lived luxuriously with her, will weep and mourn over her when they see the smoke of her burning, [10] ^standing at a distance because of the fear of her torment, saying, '^B Woe, woe, the great city, Babylon, the strong city! For in one hour your judgment has come.'

17:13 ^Rev 17:17   17:14 ^Rev 16:14   ^B 1 Tim 6:15
17:15 ^Is 8:7; Jer 47:2   17:16 ^Rev 17:12
17:17 ^2 Cor 8:16   17:18 ^Rev 11:8; 16:19
18:1 ^Rev 17:1, 7   18:2 ^Is 21:9   ^B Rev 16:13
18:3 ^Jer 51:7; Rev 14:8   18:4 ^Is 52:11; Jer 50:8
18:5 ^Jer 51:9   ^B Rev 16:19   18:6 ^Ps 137:8; Jer 50:15, 29
18:7 ^Ezek 28:2-8   ^B Is 47:7f   18:8 ^Rev 17:16
^B Rev 11:17f   18:9 ^Rev 17:2; 18:3   18:10 ^Rev 18:15, 17
^B Rev 18:16, 19
18:8 ¹ Lit *death;* i.e., a particular kind of death

¹¹"And the merchants of the earth ᴬweep and mourn over her, because no one buys their cargo any more—¹²cargo of ᴬgold, silver, precious stones, and pearls; fine linen, purple, silk, and scarlet; every *kind of* citron wood, every article of ivory, and every article *made* from very valuable wood, bronze, iron, and marble; ¹³cinnamon, spice, incense, perfume, frankincense, wine, olive oil, fine flour, wheat, cattle, sheep, and *cargo* of horses, carriages, slaves, and ᴬhuman lives. ¹⁴The fruit you long for has left you, and all things that were luxurious and splendid have passed away from you and *people* will no longer find them. ¹⁵The ᴬmerchants of ᴮthese things, who became rich from her, will stand at a distance because of the fear of her torment, weeping and mourning, ¹⁶saying, 'ᴬWoe, woe, the great city, she who was clothed in fine linen and purple and scarlet, and adorned with gold, precious stones, and pearls; ¹⁷for in one hour such great wealth has been laid ᴬwaste!' And ᴮevery shipmaster and every passenger and sailor, and all who make their living by the sea, stood at a distance, ¹⁸and were ᴬcrying out as they ᴮsaw the smoke of her burning, saying, 'What *city* is like the great city?' ¹⁹And they threw ᴬdust on their heads and were crying out, weeping and mourning, saying, 'ᴮWoe, woe, the great city, in which all who had ships at sea became rich from her prosperity, for in ᴮone hour she has been laid waste!' ²⁰ᴬRejoice over her, O heaven, and you saints and apostles and prophets, because God has pronounced judgment for you against her."

²¹Then a strong angel ᴬpicked up a stone like a great millstone and threw it into the sea, saying, "So will Babylon, the great city, be thrown down with violence, and ᴮwill never be found again. ²²And ᴬthe sound of harpists, musicians, flute players, and trumpeters will never be heard in you again; and no craftsman of any craft will ever be found in you again; and the sound of a mill will never be heard in you again; ²³and the light of a lamp will never shine in you again; and the ᴬvoice of the groom and bride will never be heard in you again; for your ᴮmerchants were the powerful people of the earth, because all the nations were deceived by your witchcraft. ²⁴And in her was found the ᴬblood of prophets and of saints, and of ᴮall who have been slaughtered on the earth."

THE FOURFOLD HALLELUJAH

19 After these things I heard *something* like a ᴬloud voice of a great multitude in heaven, saying, "Hallelujah! Salvation, glory, and power belong to our God, ²ᴬBECAUSE HIS JUDGMENTS ARE TRUE AND RIGHTEOUS; for He has judged the great prostitute who was corrupting the earth with her sexual immorality, and HE HAS ᴮAVENGED THE BLOOD OF HIS BOND-SERVANTS ON HER." ³And a second time they said, "Hallelujah! ᴬHER SMOKE RISES FOREVER AND EVER." ⁴And the ᴬtwenty-four elders and the ᴮfour living creatures fell down and worshiped God who sits

18:11ᴬEzek 27:27-34   **18:12**ᴬEzek 27:12-22; Rev 17:4
18:13ᴬ1 Chr 5:21; Ezek 27:13   **18:15**ᴬRev 18:3
ᴮRev 18:12, 13   **18:16**ᴬRev 18:10, 19   **18:17**ᴬRev 17:16
ᴮEzek 27:28f   **18:18**ᴬEzek 27:30   ᴮRev 18:9
18:19ᴬJosh 7:6   ᴮRev 18:10   **18:20**ᴬJer 51:48
18:21ᴬJer 51:63f   ᴮEzek 26:21   **18:22**ᴬIs 24:8;
Ezek 26:13   **18:23**ᴬJer 7:34   ᴮIs 23:8   **18:24**ᴬRev 16:6
ᴮMatt 23:35   **19:1**ᴬJer 51:48; Rev 11:15   **19:2**ᴬPs 19:9
ᴮDeut 32:43   **19:3**ᴬIs 34:10; Rev 14:11
19:4ᴬRev 4:4, 10   ᴮRev 4:6

on the throne, saying, "Amen. Hallelujah!" ⁵And a voice came from the throne, saying,

"Give praise to our God, all you His bond-servants, ᴬyou who fear Him, the small and the great." ⁶Then I heard *something* like ᴬthe voice of a great multitude and like the sound of many waters, and like the sound of mighty peals of thunder, saying,

"ᴬHallelujah! For the Lord our God, the Almighty, reigns.

MARRIAGE OF THE LAMB

⁷Let's rejoice and be glad and give the glory to Him, because ᴬthe marriage of the Lamb has come, and His bride has prepared herself." ⁸It was given to her to clothe herself in ᴬfine linen, bright *and* clean; for the fine linen is the ᴮrighteous acts of the saints.

⁹Then ᴬhe *said to me, "ᴮWrite: 'Blessed are those who are invited to the wedding feast of the Lamb.'" And he *said to me, "These are the true words of God." ¹⁰Then ᴬI fell at his feet to worship him. ᴮBut he *said to me, "Do not do that; I am a fellow servant of yours and your brothers *and sisters* who hold the testimony of Jesus; worship God! For the testimony of Jesus is the spirit of prophecy."

THE COMING OF CHRIST

¹¹And I saw heaven opened, and behold, a white horse, and He who sat on it *is* called ᴬFaithful and True, and in ᴮrighteousness He judges and wages war. ¹²His ᴬeyes *are* a flame of fire, and on His head *are* many crowns; and He has a name written *on Him* which no one knows except Himself. ¹³ *He is* clothed with a robe dipped in blood, and His name is called ᴬThe Word of God. ¹⁴And

the armies which are in heaven, clothed in fine linen, ᴬwhite *and* clean, were following Him on white horses. ¹⁵From His mouth comes a sharp sword, so that with it He may strike down the nations, and He will ᴬrule them with a rod of iron; and He treads the wine press of the fierce wrath of God, the Almighty. ¹⁶And on His robe and on His thigh He has a name written: "ᴬKING OF KINGS, AND LORD OF LORDS."

¹⁷Then I saw an angel standing in the sun, and he cried out with a loud voice, saying to all the birds that fly in midheaven, "ᴬCome, assemble for the great feast of God, ¹⁸so that you may ᴬeat the flesh of kings and the flesh of commanders, the flesh of mighty men, the flesh of horses and of those who sit on them, and the flesh of all people, both free and slaves, and ᴮsmall and great."

¹⁹And I saw ᴬthe beast and ᴮthe kings of the earth and their armies, assembled to make war against Him who sat on the horse, and against His army.

DOOM OF THE BEAST AND FALSE PROPHET

²⁰And the beast was seized, and with him the false prophet who performed the signs ᴬin his presence, by which he deceived those who had received the ᴮmark of the beast and those who worshiped his image; these two were thrown alive into the lake of fire, which burns with brimstone. ²¹And the rest

19:5ᴬRev 11:18   19:6ᴬJer 51:48; Rev 11:15
19:7ᴬEph 5:23, 32; Rev 19:9   19:8ᴬRev 19:14
ᴮRev 15:4   19:9ᴬRev 17:1   ᴮRev 1:19   19:10ᴬRev 22:8
ᴮActs 10:26   19:11ᴬRev 3:14   ᴮPs 96:13
19:12ᴬDan 10:6; Rev 1:14   19:13ᴬJohn 1:1
19:14ᴬRev 3:4; 19:8   19:15ᴬPs 2:9; Rev 2:27
19:16ᴬRev 17:14   19:17ᴬ1 Sam 17:44; Ezek 39:17
19:18ᴬEzek 39:18-20   ᴮRev 13:16   19:19ᴬRev 11:7
ᴮRev 16:14, 16   19:20ᴬRev 13:12   ᴮRev 13:16f

were killed with the sword which came from the mouth of Him who sat on the horse, and ^all the birds were filled with their flesh.

SATAN BOUND

20 Then I saw an angel coming down from heaven, holding the ^key of the abyss and a great chain in his hand. ²And he took hold of the ^dragon, the serpent of old, who is the devil and Satan, and bound him for a thousand years; ³and he threw him into the abyss and shut *it* and ^sealed *it* over him, so that he would not deceive the nations any longer, until the thousand years were completed; after these things he must be released for a short time.

⁴Then I saw ^thrones, and ^they sat on them, and judgment was given to them. And *I saw* the souls of those who had been beheaded because of their testimony of Jesus and because of the word of God, and those who had not worshiped the beast or his image, and had not received the mark on their foreheads and on their hands; and they came to life and reigned with Christ for a thousand years. ⁵The rest of the dead did not come to life until the thousand years were completed. ^This is the first resurrection. ⁶^Blessed and holy is the one who has a part in the first resurrection; over these the second death has no power, but they will be priests of God and of Christ, and will reign with Him for a thousand years.

SATAN FREED AND DOOMED

⁷When the thousand years are completed, Satan will be ^released from his prison, ⁸and will come out to deceive the nations which are at the four corners of the earth, ^Gog and Magog, to gather them together for the war; the number of them is like the sand of the seashore. ⁹And they ^came up on the broad plain of the earth and surrounded the camp of the saints and the beloved city, and ^fire came down from heaven and devoured them. ¹⁰And the devil who deceived them was thrown into the ^lake of fire and ¹brimstone, where the ^beast and the ^false prophet *are* also; and they will be tormented day and night forever and ever.

JUDGMENT AT THE THRONE OF GOD

¹¹Then I saw a great white throne and Him who sat upon it, from whose presence earth and heaven fled, and ^no place was found for them. ¹²And I saw the dead, the ^great and the small, standing before the throne, and books were opened; and another book was opened, which is *the book* of life; and the dead ^were judged from the things which were written in the books, according to their deeds. ¹³And the sea gave up the dead who were in it, and ^Death and Hades ^gave up the dead who were in them; and they were judged, each one *of them* according to their deeds. ¹⁴Then Death and Hades were thrown into the lake of fire. This is the ^second death, the lake of fire. ¹⁵And if anyone's name was not found written in ^the book of life, he was thrown into the lake of fire.

19:21^Rev 19:17   **20:1**^Rev 1:18; 9:1   **20:2**^Gen 3:1; Rev 12:9   **20:3**^Dan 6:17; Matt 27:66   **20:4**^Dan 7:9   ^Matt 19:28   **20:5**^Luke 14:14; Phil 3:11   **20:6**^Rev 14:13   **20:7**^Rev 20:2f   **20:8**^Ezek 38:2; 39:1, 6   **20:9**^Ezek 38:9, 16   ^Ezek 38:22   **20:10**^Rev 19:20   ^Rev 16:13   **20:11**^Dan 2:35; Rev 12:8   **20:12**^Rev 11:18   **20:13**^1 Cor 15:26   ^Is 26:19   **20:14**^Rev 20:6   **20:15**^Rev 3:5; 20:12

20:10 ¹I.e., burning sulfur

THE NEW HEAVEN AND EARTH

21 Then I saw ᴬa new heaven and a new earth; for the first heaven and the first earth passed away, and there is no longer *any* sea. ²And I saw the holy city, ᴬnew Jerusalem, ᴮcoming down out of heaven from God, prepared as a bride adorned for her husband. ³And I heard a loud voice from the throne, saying, "Behold, ᴬthe tabernacle of God is among the people, and He will ᴮdwell among them, and they shall be His people, and God Himself will be among them¹, ⁴and He will ᴬwipe away every tear from their eyes; and there will no longer be *any* death; there will no longer be *any* mourning, or crying, or pain; the first things have passed away."

⁵And ᴬHe who sits on the throne said, "Behold, I am making all things new." And He *said, "Write, for these words are faithful and true." ⁶Then He said to me, "It is done. I am the Alpha and the Omega, the beginning and the end. ᴬI will give *water* to the one who thirsts from the spring of the water of life, without cost. ⁷ᴬThe one who overcomes will inherit these things, and ᴮI will be his God and he will be My son. ⁸ᴬBut for the cowardly, and unbelieving, and abominable, and murderers, and sexually immoral persons, and sorcerers, and idolaters, and all liars, their part *will be* in the lake that burns with fire and brimstone, which is the second death."

⁹ᴬThen one of the seven angels who had the seven bowls, full of the seven last plagues, came and spoke with me, saying, "ᴬCome here, I will show you the ᴮbride, the wife of the Lamb."

THE NEW JERUSALEM

¹⁰And ᴬhe carried me away ¹in *the* Spirit to a great and high mountain, and showed me ᴮthe holy city, Jerusalem, coming down out of heaven from God, ¹¹having the glory of God. Her brilliance was like a very valuable stone, like a ᴬstone of crystal-clear jasper. ¹²It had a great and high wall, ᴬwith twelve gates, and at the gates twelve angels; and names *were* written on *the gates,* which are *the names* of the twelve tribes of the sons of Israel. ¹³*There were* three gates on the east, three gates on the north, three gates on the south, and three gates on the west. ¹⁴And the wall of the city had ᴬtwelve foundation stones, and on them *were the* twelve names of the ᴮtwelve apostles of the Lamb.

¹⁵The one who spoke with me had a gold measuring rod to measure the city, its ᴬgates, and its wall. ¹⁶The city is laid out as a square, and its length is as great as the width; and he measured the city with the rod, ¹twelve thousand stadia; its length, width, and height are equal. ¹⁷And he measured its wall, ¹144 cubits, *by* ᴬhuman measurements, which are *also* angelic *measurements.* ¹⁸The material of the wall was ᴬjasper; and the city was ᴮpure gold, like clear glass.

21:1 ᴬIs 65:17; 66:22 21:2 ᴬRev 3:12 ᴮHeb 11:10, 16
21:3 ᴬLev 26:11f ᴮ2 Cor 6:16 21:4 ᴬIs 25:8; Rev 7:17
21:5 ᴬRev 4:9; 20:11 21:6 ᴬIs 55:1; John 4:10
21:7 ᴬRev 2:7 ᴮ2 Sam 7:14 21:8 ᴬ1 Cor 6:9
21:9 ᴬRev 17:1 ᴮRev 19:7 21:10 ᴬEzek 40:2
ᴮRev 21:2 21:11 ᴬRev 4:3; 21:18, 19
21:12 ᴬEzek 48:31-34 21:14 ᴬHeb 11:10 ᴮActs 1:26
21:15 ᴬRev 21:12, 21, 25 21:17 ᴬDeut 3:11; Rev 13:18
21:18 ᴬRev 21:11 ᴮRev 21:21

21:3 ¹One early ms adds, as *their God* 21:10 ¹Or *in spirit* 21:16 ¹Possibly about 1,380 miles or 2,220 km; a Roman stadion perhaps averaged 607 ft. or 185 m
21:17 ¹Possibly about 216 ft. or 65 m; a cubit is about 18 in. or 45 cm

¹⁹ᴬThe foundation stones of the city wall were decorated with every kind of precious stone. The first foundation stone was jasper; the second, sapphire; the third, chalcedony; the fourth, emerald; ²⁰the fifth, sardonyx; the sixth, ᴬsardius; the seventh, chrysolite; the eighth, beryl; the ninth, topaz; the tenth, chrysoprase; the eleventh, jacinth; the twelfth, amethyst. ²¹And the twelve ᴬgates were twelve pearls; each one of the gates was a single pearl. And the street of the city was pure gold, like transparent glass.

²²I saw no temple in it, for the ᴬLord God the Almighty and the ᴮLamb are its temple. ²³And the city ᴬhas no need of the sun or of the moon to shine on it, for the glory of God has illuminated it, and its lamp *is* the Lamb. ²⁴ᴬThe nations will walk by its light, and the kings of the earth will bring their glory into it. ²⁵In the daytime (for there will be no night there) its gates ᴬwill never be closed; ²⁶and ᴬthey will bring the glory and the honor of the nations into it; ²⁷and ᴬnothing unclean, and no one who practices abomination and lying, shall ever come into it, but only those whose names are ᴮwritten in the Lamb's book of life.

THE RIVER AND THE TREE OF LIFE

22 And he showed me a ᴬriver of the water of life, clear as crystal, coming from the throne of God and of ¹the Lamb, ²in the middle of its street. On either side of the river *was* ᴬthe tree of life, bearing twelve *kinds of* fruit, yielding its fruit every month; and the leaves of the tree *were* for the healing of the nations. ³ᴬThere will no longer be any curse; and the throne of God and of the Lamb will be in it, and His bond-servants will serve Him; ⁴they will ᴬsee His face, and His name *will be* on their foreheads. ⁵And there will no longer be *any* night; and they will not have need ᴬof the light of a lamp nor the light of the sun, because the Lord God will illuminate them; and they will reign forever and ever.

⁶And he said to me, "ᴬThese words are faithful and true"; and the Lord, the God of the spirits of the prophets, sent His angel to show His bond-servants the things which must soon take place.

⁷"And behold, I am coming quickly. ᴬBlessed is the one who keeps the words of the prophecy of this book."

⁸ᴬI, John, am the one who heard and saw these things. And when I heard and saw *them,* ᴮI fell down to worship at the feet of the angel who showed me these things. ⁹And he *said to me, "Do not do that; I am a fellow servant of yours and of your brothers the prophets, and of those who keep the words of ᴬthis book. Worship God!"

THE FINAL MESSAGE

¹⁰And he *said to me, "ᴬDo not seal up the words of the prophecy of this book, for the time is near. ¹¹ᴬLet the one who does wrong still do wrong, and the one who is filthy still be filthy; and let the one who is

---

21:19 ᴬEx 28:17-20; Is 54:11f   21:20 ᴬRev 4:3
21:21 ᴬRev 21:12, 15, 25   21:22 ᴬRev 1:8   ᴮRev 5:6
21:23 ᴬIs 60:19, 20; Rev 22:5   21:24 ᴬIs 60:3, 5
21:25 ᴬIs 60:11   21:26 ᴬPs 72:10f; Is 49:23
21:27 ᴬIs 52:1   ᴮRev 3:5   22:1 ᴬPs 46:4; Ezek 47:1
22:2 ᴬGen 2:9; Rev 2:7   22:3 ᴬZech 14:11
22:4 ᴬPs 42:2; Matt 5:8   22:5 ᴬIs 60:19; Rev 21:23
22:6 ᴬRev 19:9; 21:5   22:7 ᴬRev 1:3; 16:15
22:8 ᴬRev 1:1   ᴮRev 19:10   22:9 ᴬRev 1:11; 22:10, 18f
22:10 ᴬDan 8:26; Rev 10:4   22:11 ᴬEzek 3:27; Dan 12:10

22:1 ¹Or *the Lamb. In the middle of its street, and on either side of the river, was*

righteous still practice righteousness, and the one who is holy still keep himself holy."

[12] "Behold, I am coming quickly, and My ^reward *is* with Me, to reward each one as his work deserves. [13] I am the Alpha and the Omega, ^the first and the last, the beginning and the end."

[14] Blessed are those who ^wash their robes, so that they will have the right to the tree of life, and may ^Benter the city by the gates. [15] ^Outside are the dogs, the sorcerers, the sexually immoral persons, the murderers, the idolaters, and everyone who loves and practices lying.

[16] "I, Jesus, have sent ^My angel to testify to you of these things for the churches. I am the root and the descendant of David, the bright morning star."

[17] The ^Spirit and the bride say, "Come." And let the one who hears say, "Come." And let the one who is thirsty come; let the one who desires, take the water of life without cost.

[18] I testify to everyone who hears the words of the prophecy of this book: if anyone ^adds to them, God will add to him the plagues that are written in this book; [19] and if anyone takes away from the words of the book of this prophecy, God will take away his part from the tree of life and from the holy city, ^which are written in this book.

[20] He who testifies to these things says, "Yes, ^I am coming quickly." Amen. ^BCome, Lord Jesus.

[21] ^The grace of the Lord Jesus be with [1] all. Amen.

22:12 ^Is 40:10; 62:11   **22:13** ^Is 44:6; 48:12
22:14 ^Rev 7:14   ^BRev 21:27   **22:15** ^Matt 8:12;
1 Cor 6:9f   **22:16** ^Rev 1:1; 22:6   **22:17** ^Rev 2:7; 14:13
22:18 ^Deut 4:2; 12:32   **22:19** ^Rev 21:10-22:5
22:20 ^Rev 22:7   ^B1 Cor 16:22   **22:21** ^Rom 16:20

22:21 [1] One early ms *the saints*

TOPICAL INDEX

of the Old and New Testament

A

ABANDON

FIGURATIVE

HUMAN

of righteousness: Prov 2:13; 15:10; 2 Pet 2:15

of God: Deut 14:27; 28:20; 31:16; 2 Kin 17:16;
Jer 9:13; Matt 26:56

DIVINE

of Israel: Deut 31:17; Josh 24:20; Ps 78:60;
Is 2:6; Jer 23:33

ABOMINATION

examples of: Ex 8:26; Prov 28:9; Is 1:13; 41:24;
Jer 2:7; Dan 9:27; 11:31; 12:11 (cf. Matt 24:15)

ABORTION

Abortion is the induced expulsion of an unborn
child in order to terminate its life. Thus abortion
is distinct from premature birth (cf. Ex 21:22,
& note) or miscarriage (Ex 23:26; Ps 58:8; Hos
9:14). Although Scripture does not mention
abortion explicitly, certain biblical principles
do apply to abortion.

PRINCIPLES RELEVANT TO

divine source of human life: 1 Sam 2:6; Job 12:10;
Ps 36:9; Acts 17:28

biblical evidence for prenatal personhood:
Gen 25:23; Ps 51:5; 139:13-16; Is 49:1-2;
Jer 1:5; Luke 1:15, 35, 41-44; Gal 1:15
(cf. Gen 1:26-27)

ABRAHAM

call and covenant: Gen 12:1-3; 15:18; 17:3-6;
Jer 31:35-37; Luke 1:68-75; Heb 6:13-15

SIGNIFICANCE

father of all believers: Rom 4:10-12, 16-17; Gal 3:29

model of true faith: Gen 15:6; Rom 4:9-12, 16;
Gal 3:7, 17-19; 4:21-31; Heb 11:8-12, 17-19;
James 2:20-24

ABUNDANCE

of crops: Gen 27:28; 41:29

of divine character and provision: Num 14:18;
Job 37:23; Ps 86:5, 15; 106:7; 130:7; 145:7;
147:5; Is 55:7

of prosperity: Deut 30:9

of food: Job 26:14; Ps 78:25

of age: Job 32:9

of peace: Ps 72:7; Jer 33:6

of thanks to the LORD: Ps 109:30

of spiritual life: John 10:10

of grace: Acts 4:33; Rom 5:17; 2 Cor 9:8

of joy: 2 Cor 8:2

ACCUSATION

by a malicious or false witness: Deut 19:16, 18;
Ps 109:4, 20, 29; Is 54:17; Luke 3:14;
3 John 10

by Satan: Zech 3:1; Rev 12:10

against Jesus: Matt 12:10; Mark 15:3; Luke 6:7;
John 8:6; 18:29

against the Jewish nation: Acts 28:19

ACQUITTED (SEE JUSTIFICATION)

ADAM

THE FIRST MAN

creation: Gen 1:27-28; 2:7; 5:1; 1 Cor 15:45;
1 Tim 2:13

entrance into sin: Gen 3:1-8; 2:15-17;
Job 31:33; Is 43:27; Hos 6:7; Rom 5:14-21;
1 Tim 2:14

type of Christ: Rom 5:14

the last Adam, i.e., Jesus Christ: 1 Cor 15:45, 47

ADOPTION

BY GOD

the nation of Israel: Ex 4:22; Deut 14:1-2; 32:6;
Jer 31:9; Hos 11:1; Rom 9:4

Gentiles: Eph 3:6

the spiritual children of God: Rom 8:15-17, 23;
2 Cor 6:18; Gal 4:5-7; Eph 1:5

ADORATION (SEE BLESS; PRAISE;
WORSHIP)

@Copyright: Topical Index Copyright © 2000, 2021 by The Lockman Foundation, La Habra, California, 90631, U.S.A.

ADULTERY

PHYSICAL SENSE OF
commandment against: Ex 20:14; Matt 5:27;
   Rom 2:22; James 2:11
temptation to: Gen 39:7-13; 2 Sam 11:2-5;
   Prov 2:16-20; 5:3; 6:24-26; 7:6-22; 1 Cor 7:2-5
nature of: Prov 2:17; 30:20; Rom 7:3
FIGURATIVE SENSE OF
general: Is 57:3
*spiritual adultery (i.e., idolatry and unfaithfulness
   to God):* Jer 3:6-10; 13:27; Ezek 16:32-52;
   23:36-49; Hos 2:2; 3:1; 4:13-14; Matt 12:39;
   Rev 2:14, 22 (cf. James 4:4); 1 John 2:15-16

ADVENT OF CHRIST (SEE END TIMES)

ADVICE

givers of (i.e., advisers): Gen 26:26; 2 Kin 25:19;
   Jer 52:25
prophetic message of: Num 24:14
request for: Judg 20:7; 2 Sam 16:20; Is 16:3
fame for: 2 Sam 16:23
differences in: 2 Sam 17:7
appeal to: 2 Sam 19:43
relative to age: 1 Kin 12:13-14
pleasing: Esth 5:14; Dan 4:27
of the cunning: Job 5:13
thwarted: Job 5:13
stupid: Is 19:11
rejected: Jer 38:15; Acts 27:21
evil: Ezek 11:2
concerning Jesus' death: John 18:14
received: Acts 5:40
from Christ: Rev 3:18

ADVOCATE

An advocate functions as a helper, comforter,
or intercessor.
used of Holy Spirit: John 14:16, 26; 15:26; 16:7
used of Christ: 1 John 2:1
instances of: Matt 10:19, 20; Mark 13:11;
   Luke 12:11, 12; John 16:8-11; Rom 8:26, 34

AFFLICTION (SEE ALSO SUFFERING)

divine awareness of: Gen 16:11; 29:32; Ex 3:7; 4:31;
   Deut 26:7; 2 Sam 16:12; Job 34:28; Ps 25:18;
   119:153; 132:1
benefits of: Gen 50:20; Job 13:15; 23:10; 42:5-6;
   Ps 74:21; 119:67, 71; Rom 5:3-5; 8:18, 28;
   2 Cor 1:6; 4:17; 7:4; James 1:2-4; 1 Pet 1:6-9; 4:16
results of: Ex 1:12; 1 Kin 8:35; Ps 88:9;
   Prov 15:15; Is 14:32; Hos 5:15; Matt 13:21;
   2 Cor 8:2

deliverance from: Ex 3:17; 2 Sam 22:28; Job 36:15;
   Ps 119:153; Acts 7:10 (cf. Job 36:6, 15; Ps 18:27;
   89:22; 119:92)
divine permission and control of: Job 1:6-2:7;
   Is 48:10; 1 Cor 10:13 (cf. Ruth 1:21)
response to: Job 1:20-22; 13:15; Matt 5:10-12;
   2 Thess 1:4; James 1:2; 1 Pet 4:16, 19
expectancy of: Job 5:7; Ps 34:19; Phil 1:29;
   1 Thess 3:4; 2 Tim 3:12 (cf. Heb 11:37)
comfort and compassion in: Ps 119:50;
   Is 49:13; 2 Cor 1:4 (cf. Prov 3:34;
   Is 61:1; 63:9)
divine justice for: Is 11:4

AFFLUENCE (SEE MONEY; WEALTH)

AGE(S) OR ERA(S)

THE PRESENT
forgiveness in: Matt 12:32
end of: Matt 13:39-40; 28:20; Mark 10:30;
   1 Cor 1:20; Eph 1:21
sons of: Luke 16:8; Luke 20:34
evil character of: Gal 1:4
the future: Matt 12:32; Mark 10:30; Luke 20:35;
   Eph 1:21; Heb 6:5
THE PLURAL (I.E., AGES)
past: Eccl 1:10; Rom 16:25; Eph 3:9; Col 1:26;
   Titus 1:2
future: Dan 7:18; Eph 2:7
before the: 1 Cor 2:7
end of: 1 Cor 10:11
consummation of: Heb 9:26

AGONY (SEE SUFFERING)

ALLEGIANCE (SEE LOYALTY)

ALMS (SEE BENEVOLENCE; CHARITY)

ALTAR

LOCATIONS
Tabernacle: Ex 27:21; 28:1-7
Solomon's temple: 2 Chr 4:1, 19
second temple: Ezra 7:17
Ezekiel's temple: Ezek 43:13-27
Herod's temple: Luke 1:11

AMBITION

proper: John 4:34; Rom 15:20; 1 Cor 7:32, 34;
   12:31-13:7; 2 Cor 5:9; Phil 3:12-14;
   1 Thess 4:11; 1 Tim 3:1; 6:11; 2 Tim 2:22;
   4:7-8; Heb 12:14

IMPROPER

warning about: Is 5:8; Jer 45:5; Hab 2:9;
Matt 18:1-6; 20:25-26; 23:6-8;
Mark 10:35-45; Luke 12:13-21; 22:24-27;
Phil 2:3

temptation to: Matt 4:8-10

penalty for: Gen 3:5-19; Num 12:1-15;
2 Sam 18:9-15; 1 Kin 1:5-10; Esth 5:9-13;
Jer 51:33; Ezek 28:12-19; 2 Thess 2:3-9;
1 Tim 6:9-10; 3 John 9

ANGELS

God's creation of: Ps 148:2-5; Neh 9:6; Col 1:16

CATEGORIES OF

the angel of the LORD: Gen 16:7-13; Ex 3:2, 4;
Zech 3:1-10; 12:8; Acts 7:30-35

cherubim: Gen 3:22-24; Ex 25:18-19, 20, 22;
1 Kin 6:23-29; Heb 9:5

seraphim: Is 6:2-3, 6

elect (chosen) angels: 1 Tim 5:21

fallen angels: 2 Pet 2:4; Jude 6; Rev 12:7-9
(cf. Matt 25:41)

ACTIVITIES OF

deliver messages from God: Matt 1:20;
Luke 1:11-20; Acts 1:10-11; 10:3-7

assist in judgment: 2 Sam 24:16; Acts 12:23;
Rev 16:1-12, 17-21

minister to believers: 1 Kin 19:6-8; Ps 34:7; 91:11;
Dan 3:28; 6:22; Acts 12:5-10; Heb 1:14

ministered to Jesus: Mark 1:13; Luke 22:43

worship God: Luke 2:13-14; Heb 1:6

NAMED INDIVIDUALS AMONG

Gabriel: Dan 8:16; Luke 1:13, 31

Michael: Dan 10:13; Jude 9; Rev 12:7

prohibition against worship of: Col 2:18;
Rev 19:10; 22:9

ANGER (SEE ALSO WRATH)

OF PEOPLE

prohibition against: Ps 37:8; Matt 5:22; Eph 4:31

causes of: Prov 15:1; Gal 5:19-20

character of: Prov 27:4; Eccl 7:9

results of: Ps 55:3; Prov 29:22; 30:33

control of: Prov 14:29; 16:32; Eph 4:26-27;
James 1:19-20

penalty for: Prov 19:19; Amos 1:11; Matt 5:22

response to: Ps 94:1; Rom 12:19

OF GOD

reasons for: Deut 9:7; Josh 7:1; 23:16; 2 Sam 6:7;
2 Kin 22:13; 2 Chr 34:25; Is 9:13-17; Jer 3:5;
Rom 1:18; 2:5

of Christ: Mark 3:5; Rev 6:16-17 (cf. Matt 16:23;
23:13-36); Mark 10:14; John 2:13-17

ANIMALS

FIGURATIVE USE OF

dog: Deut 23:18; Prov 26:11; Phil 3:2; Rev 22:15

deer: Ps 42:1; Is 35:6

sheep: Ps 100:3; 119:176; Is 53:6; Matt 9:36;
10:16; John 10:3-7, 27

bear: Prov 17:12; Lam 3:10

serpent: Prov 23:32; Is 14:29

lion: Prov 28:1; Jer 49:19; 1 Pet 5:8; Rev 5:5

ox: Is 1:3

camel: Jer 2:23

donkey: Jer 2:24

leopard: Hos 13:7

wolf: Matt 7:15; John 10:12; Acts 20:29

goats: Matt 25:32-33

fox: Luke 13:32

ANNUNCIATION

The annunciation is the divine announcement
through the angel Gabriel to the virgin Mary
that she would miraculously conceive and bear
the promised Messiah and Son of God.

circumstances of: Luke 1:26-27

MESSAGE OF

salutation: Luke 1:28-29

promises: Luke 1:30-33

response to: Luke 1:34, 38

explanation of: Luke 1:35-37

ANOINT, ANOINTED, ANOINTING

FOR DIVINE SERVICE

PEOPLE

priests: Ex 28:41; 29:7; Lev 6:20; Num 35:25

kings: 1 Sam 10:1; 16:13; 1 Kin 1:39; 19:15-16;
Ps 132:10; Is 45:1

prophets: 1 Kin 19:16; Ps 105:15

captives: 2 Chr 28:15

OF CHRIST (SEE ALSO CHRIST)

general: 1 Sam 2:35; Ps 2:2; 45:7 (cf. Heb 1:9)

for His ministry: Is 61:1-2 (cf. Luke 4:18-19);
Matt 3:16; John 1:32-33; Acts 4:27; 10:38

out of devotion: Luke 7:37-38, 44-50;
John 11:2; 12:3

for His burial: John 12:3, 7

of Christians: 2 Cor 1:21-22; 1 John 2:20, 27

ANTICHRIST (SEE ALSO END TIMES)

Antichrist is one who opposes and counterfeits
Christ primarily through deception (2 John 7;
cf. Ps 2:1-3; Matt 24:4-5, 23-24; John 5:43; 2 Thess
2:3-4; Rev 13). The specific term "antichrist"
occurs only in John's letters, but the concept
appears in both the OT and NT and also in the

intertestamental literature. The personal anti-christ of the end times is empowered by Satan (Rev 13:2, 4; cf. 2 Thess 2:9). He appears in the future tribulation period as a world ruler with his empire possibly centered in a restored form of the Roman Empire (1 John 2:18; Rev 13; 17:7-18; cf. Dan 7:23-25). The antichrist is the individual culmination of many antichrists who have al-ready arisen (1 John 2:18; cf. 4:3; 2 Thess 2:3, 7-8).

APOSTASY

The term apostasy (Gr. *apostasia*) means a "fall-ing away," "defection," "rebellion," or "aban-donment." Its biblical sense indicates a willful departure from professed faith in God and His truth revealed in Scripture (Josh 22:22; Jer 8:5; Hos 11:7; 2 Thess 2:3; 1 Tim 4:1). Such aposta-sy will be especially prevalent in "later times" (1 Tim 4:1-3) or in "the last days" (2 Tim 3:1-9), and it climaxes in "the apostasy." In prophet-ic order, "the apostasy" and the revelation of "the man of lawlessness" precede the day of the LORD (2 Thess 2:2-3). Apostasy may result from "paying attention to deceitful spirits and teachings of demons" (1 Tim 4:1).

APOSTLE (SEE ALSO DISCIPLE)

An apostle (Gr. *apostolos*) is one sent forth as an authorized representative accountable to the sender. The NT apostles were appointed and sent forth by Christ on a specified mission and with His authority (Matt 10:1-14; 16:19; 28:18-20; John 15:16; 20:21-23; Acts 1:8; 9:1-22; 10:41-42). Their mission mainly consisted of evangelizing, discipling converts, training leaders, and estab-lishing and administering local churches (e.g., Acts 2:14-28:31). The word for apostles is also used in a general, unofficial sense of "messen-gers" (2 Cor 8:23; Phil 2:25).

APPARITION (SEE REVELATION, FORMS)

APPRECIATION (SEE THANKFULNESS)

ARK

The term ark is used in Scripture of two differ-ent objects as listed below.

ARK OF NOAH

This type of ark (Heb. *tebah*, "box," or "chest") refers to the huge, barge-like floating structure that Noah built according to God's command-ment (Gen 6:1-9:18).

ARK FOR THE BABY MOSES

This ark (Heb. *tebah*) refers to the small papy-rus "basket" in which Moses' mother placed him "by the bank of the Nile" where Pharaoh's daughter found him (Ex 2:3, 5).

ARK OF THE COVENANT (SEE ALSO TABERNACLE; TEMPLE)

Ark (Heb. *aron*, "chest," or "ark") is used most frequently in Scripture of the very significant article of furniture located in the "Most Holy Place" of the tabernacle (Ex 26:33-34) and later in Solomon's temple (1 Kin 6:19; 8:6-9, 21). It was a rectangular chest made of acacia wood and overlaid with gold (Ex 37:1-9). The ark mea-sured approximately 45 x 27 x 27 inches (Ex 37:1). A pole was slid through a pair of rings on each side of the ark to transport it (Ex 37:3-5). Two cherubs hovered over it, and it had a lid or mercy seat where God specifically met with His people (Ex 25:10-22; 37:6-9; Num 7:89; Heb 9:4-5).

ARMOR

FIGURATIVE

shield: Gen 15:1; Deut 33:29; 2 Sam 22:3, 36; Ps 5:12; 18:2, 35; 33:20; 59:11; 84:9, 11; 89:18; Prov 30:5

breastplate: Is 59:17; Eph 6:14; 1 Thess 5:8

helmet: Is 59:17; Eph 6:17; 1 Thess 5:8

others: Rom 13:12; 2 Cor 6:7; 10:4; Eph 6:11-17

ARROGANCE (SEE PRIDE)

ASCENSION

In biblical usage the ascension refers to the de-parture of the resurrected Christ from earth to heaven where He has resumed His position at the right hand of the Father (Mark 16:19; John 20:17; Acts 1:2, 9-11, 22; Eph 1:20). Christ's as-cension was personal, visible, and bodily and accompanied by a cloud and angels (Acts 1:9-11). He will return from heaven to earth in this same manner (Acts 1:11; cf. 3:20-21).

ASKING (SEE PRAYER)

ASPIRATION (SEE AMBITION)

ASSEMBLY (SEE ALSO CHURCH)

a general gathering: Gen 49:6; Job 11:10; Ezek 38:15

CONCERNING ISRAEL

OF ISRAEL'S CONGREGATION

general: Ex 12:6; 16:3; Deut 33:4; 1 Kin 8:14;
characteristics of: Ex 12:16; Num 29:35; Hos 2:11

activity of: 1 Chr 29:20; 2 Chr 1:5; Ezra 10:1
of Israel's exiles: Ezra 10:8; Neh 8:2
concerning the church: 1 Cor 5:4; Heb 10:25;
    12:23; James 2:2

ASSURANCE
of God's care: Josh 1:5, 9
from God's promise: Josh 3:10; Dan 4:26;
    Acts 7:17; Rom 4:21
of salvation: Ps 3:8; John 3:16; Acts 13:48;
    16:31; Rom 8:14-16, Gal 4:6-7; Eph 1:4, 13-14;
    2 Thess 2:13; 2 Tim 1:12; Heb 6:17-20;
    1 Pet 1:10; 1 John 3:14, 24; Jude 1
of spiritual blessings: Eph 1:3; 1 John 2:12-14
of future resurrection: Job 19:25-26; John 11:25-26;
    1 Thess 4:14-17; 1 Cor 15:51-57
of future glorification: Phil 3:20-21; 1 John 3:2
of future inheritance: Eph 1:13-14; 1 Pet 1:3-5
of hope: Heb 6:11 (cf. 11:1)
of faith: Heb 10:22 (cf. 11:1)

ATONEMENT (SEE ALSO REDEMPTION; RECONCILIATION; SALVATION)
In OT usage the term atonement (Heb. root *kaphar*) indicates a ransom that is generally a sacrificial offering to God as a substitute for human sin (Lev 4:20; 16; 17:11). In its doctrinal sense atonement refers to the substitutionary death of Christ in providing salvation for sinful people (Matt 20:28; 2 Cor 5:21; Eph 1:7; 1 Pet 2:24-25; 3:18). Christ's atonement accomplishes redemption, propitiation, and reconciliation in a person's relation to God (Rom 3:24-26; 2 Cor 5:18-20; 2 Pet 2:1; 1 John 2:2).

ATTRIBUTES (SEE GOD, ATTRIBUTES OF)

AUTHORITY
OF GOD
extent of: Ex 15:18; Job 26:12; Ps 29:10; 103:19;
    Is 40:12-17; Dan 4:34-35; Acts 1:7; Rom 13:1
delegation of: Gen 1:28; Ps 8:6-8; 72:1; Dan 2:37;
    Matt 9:8; John 5:27; Rom 13:1-7; 1 Cor 6:2-3;
    Rev 6:8
voice of: Is 30:30
acknowledgment of: Jude 25; Rev 4:11; 5:12-13
OF JESUS CHRIST
AREAS OF
    in His messianic office: Gen 3:15; Deut 18:18-19;
        Ps 2:6-12; Is 9:6-7; Matt 26:63-64
    in His judgment: Matt 7:22-23; John 5:27;
        Rev 19:11-21

in His teaching: Matt 7:28-29
in His ministry and miracles: Matt 8:23-27;
    Luke 4:36
in His forgiveness: Matt 9:6
in His demands on others: Matt 28:19-20;
    Luke 14:26-33; Acts 1:8
in His control of nature: Mark 4:39-41
in His raising the dead: Mark 5:35-43;
    Luke 11:11-17; John 11:38-44
in His death: John 10:18
in His resurrection: John 10:18
in His gift of eternal life: John 17:2
in believers: Gal 2:20; Col 1:27
in His reign: Rev 1:5; 11:15; 12:10; 17:14;
    19:16; 20:4-6
delegation to others: Matt 10:1; Luke 10:19;
    Rev 2:26
*of Scripture (see also INSPIRATION;
    REVELATION, special revelation;
    WORD OF GOD)*
IN THE CHURCH
Christ as head of: Eph 1:20-23; Col 1:18
leaders of: Acts 14:23; 1 Thess 5:12-13; 1 Tim 3:5
order of: 1 Cor 11:2-34 (cf. 14:40); 1 Tim 3:15
IN THE FAMILY
husbands and wives: Gen 2:24; 1 Cor 11:3-16;
    1 Pet 3:1-7
parents: Deut 6:6-7; Eph 6:4; Col 3:21
children: Eph 6:1-3; Col 3:20; 1 Tim 5:4
IN CIVIL GOVERNMENT
divine origin of: John 19:11; Rom 13:1-2;
    1 Pet 2:13-14

AWAKENING (SEE REVIVAL)

AWE (SEE FEAR OF GOD)

B

BAAL (SEE GODS, FALSE)
WORSHIP OF

BABYLON
PROPHETIC SIGNIFICANCE
captivity and exile of Jerusalem: 2 Kin 24:1-2;
    10-16; Jer 25:11; 27:1-11; 52:27-30
SYMBOLIC SIGNIFICANCE
of Rome: 1 Pet 5:13
of relationship to Antichrist: Rev 14:8; 16:17-19:5

BACKSLIDING (SEE UNFAITHFULNESS)

BALANCES

just: Lev 19:36; Prov 16:11; Ezek 45:10
weighed in: Job 6:2; Ps 62:9; Is 40:12
   (cf. Dan 5:27)
false: Prov 11:1; Hos 12:7

BAPTISM, WATER

The term baptize is derived from the Greek word *baptizo*, meaning "to dip" or "to immerse." Baptism therefore denotes the action of immersing in water as a symbolic action of Christian initiation (cf. Acts 2:41). The idea of immersion is also evident in the metaphorical uses of baptism (e.g., Matt 10:38; cf. 1 Cor 10:2). While the origins of Christian baptism have been variously sought in OT and Jewish purification practices, the baptism of John provides the clearest precedent. The going under and rising from the water was a powerful symbol of the believer's identification with Christ in His death and resurrection (Rom 6:3-4) and cleansing from sin (Acts 22:16). Christian baptism was performed in the name of Christ (Acts 2:38) or the Trinity (Matt 28:19), signifying identification with these.

BAPTISM, SPIRIT

The phrase baptism *en pneumati* ("in," "with," or "by the Spirit") refers to the promised outpouring or gift of the Spirit given by the Messiah (Christ) to His people (cf. Joel 2:28-29; Acts 2:17, 33). As in water baptism, the baptism with the Spirit signified the initial and abiding endowment with the Spirit that accompanied faith in Christ (cf. Acts 2:38; 11:15-17).
promises of: Is 32:15; 44:3; Ezek 39:29; Joel 2:28;
   Matt 3:11; Mark 1:8; Luke 3:16; John 1:33;
   Acts 1:4-5
experience of: Acts 2:1-4; Rom 6:3-5;
   Col 2:11-12

BEHAVIOR (SEE CONDUCT)

BELIEF (SEE FAITH)

BELIEVERS

RELATION TO
God: Jon 3:5; John 5:24; Acts 16:34; 45> 4:3;
   1 Pet 1:21; 1 John 5:10-12
Christ: John 3:16, 18, 36; 6:40; Acts 16:31;
   1 Pet 1:8, 21; 1 John 5:1
Spirit: Eph 1:13-14 (cf. Acts 5:32; 19:2)
added to the church: Acts 5:14

BENEVOLENCE (SEE ALSO CHARITY)

principle of: Lev 23:4-5; Is 58:6-7; Matt 5:42;
   Heb 13:16
examples of: Gen 14:1-16; Ruth; Jer 38:7-13;
   Matt 10:42; Luke 10:30-37; Acts 2:44-45;
   11:29-30; Rom 15:25-28; 1 Cor 16:1-4
evidence of faith: James 2:15-17
expression of love: 1 John 3:16-17
reward for: Deut 14:28-29; 15:10; Matt 19:21;
   2 Cor 9:6; Heb 6:10

BETHEL

CITY NORTH OF JERUSALEM
Abram's altar at: Gen 12:8
Jacob's vision of ladder and altar at: Gen 28:10-22
conquered by Joshua: Josh 8:17
court of judgment held at: Judg 4:5; 1 Sam 7:16
tabernacle at: Judg 20:18, 31; 21:2
idolatry of Jeroboam at: 1 Kin 12:25-33
prophecies against: 1 Kin 13:1-6, 32;
   Amos 3:14-15; 5:5
school of the prophets at: 2 Kin 2:3
repopulation after Babylonian exile: Ezra 2:28;
   Neh 7:32

BETHLEHEM

formerly Ephrath: Gen 35:19; 48:7
particular residents of: Judg 12:8; Ruth 1:1, 22;
   Sam 21:19
well of: 2 Sam 23:15-16
Messiah's birth in: Mic 5:2; Matt 2:1-18;
   Luke 2:10-15; John 7:42

BEVERAGE (SEE WINE)

BIRTH

FIGURATIVE
of Israel by God: Deut 32:18; Is 46:3
of creation: Job 38:29; Ps 90:2
of departed spirits: Is 26:19
of a land: Is 66:8
of Jerusalem: Ezek 16:3-4
of the future tribulation period: Matt 24:8;
   1 Thess 5:3
of sin by lust: James 1:15
new or spiritual (see also REGENERATION)

BLESS, BLESSED, BLESSING (SEE ALSO PRAISE)

In the OT to bless means to pronounce the bestowal of benefits such as abundance, fruitfulness, success, prosperity, and longevity of life upon someone or something (Gen 1:22, 28;

2:3; 17:6; Deut 28:1-14). In the NT the idea is to praise or speak well of someone, and when God blesses mankind it also includes provision of certain benefits. People are able to bless God through worship, thanksgiving, and praise as a response to prior blessing from God (Gen 24:48; 1 Kin 10:9; Job 1:20-21; Ps 26:12; 96:2; 103:1-2, 20-22; Neh 9:5; Luke 1:68; 24:53; 1 Cor 14:16). To some extent, people can bless or be a blessing to others (Gen 12:2-3; 24:60; 27:4; 1 Kin 8:66; Luke 6:28; 2 Cor 13:14; 1 Tim 1:2), but God is still the ultimate source of such blessing (Gen 12:1-3; Deut 15:14; 2 Sam 6:18; 2 Cor 1:3-4).

BLOOD
OF CHRIST
in the New Covenant: Matt 26:28; 1 Cor 10:16; 11:25; Heb 10:29; 13:20
shedding of: John 19:34; 1 John 5:6, 8
propitiation in: Rom 3:25
justified by: Rom 5:9
redemption through: Eph 1:7; 1 Pet 1:18-19
forgiveness through: Eph 1:7; Heb 9:22; Rev 1:5
reconciliation by: Eph 2:13; Col 1:20
entrance into the holy place through:
   Heb 9:12; 10:19
sanctified through: Heb 13:12
sprinkled with: 1 Pet 1:2
cleansing from sin by: 1 John 1:7; Rev 7:14
victory over Satan by: Rev 12:11

BOASTING (SEE PRIDE)

BONDAGE
PHYSICAL
OF ISRAEL
   in Egypt: Ex 2:23; 6:5-9; Josh 24:17; Acts 7:6-7
   in exile: 2 Kin 25:1-11; Ezra 1:1-11; 9:8-9; Dan 1:1-7
SPIRITUAL
means of: John 8:34; Acts 8:23; Rom 6:16; 7:14, 23; 8:2; Gal 2:4; 4:3
deliverance through Christ: Luke 4:18; John 8:36; Rom 8:2; Gal 3:13

BORN AGAIN (SEE REGENERATION)

BOTTOMLESS PIT
The expression "bottomless pit" literally means "shaft of the abyss" (Rev 9:1, 2, & note) and refers to an "abyss," that is, a boundless or bottomless place (Rev 20:1, 3). In Scripture the bottomless pit is associated with the underworld and is divinely used as a place of confinement.

PLACE OF
torment for demons: Luke 8:31
the dead: Rom 10:7
confinement for locusts which torment people:
   Rev 9:1-5
origin of the beast (see also ANTICHRIST):
   Rev 11:7; 17:8
imprisonment for Satan: Rev 20:1-3

BOASTING (SEE PRIDE)

BRIDE
RELATED TO
marital love: Song 4:8-12; 5:1
divine judgment: Jer 7:34; Rev 18:23
the bridegroom: John 3:29
FIGURATIVE USE OF
general: Is 49:18; 62:5
of the church: Rev 19:7-9; 22:17 (cf. 2 Cor 11:2); Eph 5:23-32
of the new Jerusalem: Rev 21:2, 9-10
VARIOUS OTHER USES
attire of: Jer 2:32
chamber of: Joel 2:16

BRIDEGROOM
particular individuals as: Ex 4:25-26; John 2:9
RELATED TO
divine judgment: Jer 7:34; Rev 18:23
a virgin bride: Joel 1:8
FIGURATIVE USE OF
general: Ps 19:5; Is 61:10; 62:5; Matt 25:1-10
of Christ: Matt 9:15; John 3:29-30 (cf. 2 Cor 11:2); Eph 5:23-32; Rev 19:7-9

BUILD
OF ALTARS
for God: Gen 8:20; Ex 20:25; Deut 27:5-6; Judg 6:26; 1 Chr 21:22
for heathen purposes: Ex 32:4-5; 2 Chr 33:5
OF CITIES
in God's purpose: Ex 1:11; Deut 32:24; 2 Chr 14:7; Ps 69:35; Is 45:13
OF HOUSES
for humans: Deut 22:8; Ps 127:1; Is 65:21-22
for the LORD (i.e., a temple; see also TABERNACLE; TEMPLE): 2 Sam 7:5, 13; 1 Kin 6:1-38; Ezra 1:2; 4:1, 3; John 2:20; Eph 2:20-22
of a dynasty (figuratively): Deut 25:9; Ruth 4:11; 1 Sam 2:35; 1 Kin 11:38; Ps 89:4
of wisdom (figuratively): Prov 9:1
of Jerusalem's walls: Neh 2:18, 20; 3:1-32; Ps 51:18; Is 60:10

C

CANAAN, LAND OF
INHABITANTS AND NATIONS IN
specification of: Gen 10:15-18; Ex 3:8; Deut 7:1; Josh 12:1-24; Acts 13:19
borders of: Gen 10:19-20; Num 34:1-15
promise to Abraham, Isaac, Jacob, and their descendants: Gen 12:1, 4-7; 13:12, 14-15; 26:1-4; Ex 6:3-4; Lev 25:38; 1 Chr 16:16-18; Ps 105:10-11; Heb 11:8 (cf. Gen 15:18-21)

CAPTIVITY
instances of: Num 21:29; Deut 21:10-12; 2 Kin 17:18-23; Dan 11:8, 33; Nah 3:10
cause of: Deut 28:15, 41; 2 Chr 29:5-9; Ezra 9:7; Ps 78:58-71
restoration from: Deut 30:3; Ps 85:1; Lam 2:14; Ezek 16:53; Amos 9:14 (cf. Ps 126:4)
time of: Judg 18:30
land of: 2 Chr 6:37; Neh 4:4; Jer 30:10; 46:27
exiles from: Ezra 2:1; 3:8; Neh 7:6
survivors of: Neh 1:2-3
appointment to: Jer 15:2; Ezek 12:11; 30:17-18; Amos 5:5; 9:4; Rev 13:10

CHARITY, CHARITABLENESS
inward character of: Luke 11:41
requirement of: Luke 12:33
reward of: Luke 12:33
deeds of: Acts 9:36, 39

CHASTISEMENT (SEE ALSO DISCIPLINE)
BY GOD
pain of: Job 33:19
human request concerning: Ps 38:1
reason for: Ps 39:11
personal experience of: Ps 73:14
upon the nations: Ps 94:10
result of: Ps 94:12
upon Israel: Is 26:16; Jer 2:30; 30:11; Hos 5:2
upon Christ for human sin: Is 53:5
in justice: Jer 30:11
purpose of: Jer 31:18
BY HUMANS
of parents upon a son: Deut 21:18
of elders upon a slanderer: Deut 22:18

CHASTITY
example of: Gen 39:7-12
failure in: Gen 35:22; 2 Sam 11; 1 Cor 5:1-11
wisdom of: Prov 6:23-35

commandment for: Ex 20:14; 1 Cor 6:13-18; 2 Tim 2:22 (cf. Heb 13:4)
of spiritual purity of the church: 2 Cor 11:2 (cf. Rev 14:4)
of Christian women: Titus 2:4-5; 1 Pet 3:2

CHEERFULNESS (SEE JOY)

CHILD, CHILDREN
PARENTAL RESPONSIBILITY FOR
instruct them in God's word: Deut 6:6-7; Josh 4:21-22; Ps 78:5; 2 Tim 3:15 (cf. Gen 18:19)
provide their general needs: 1 Sam 1:22-24; 1 Tim 5:8 (cf. Ps 103:13; Matt 7:11; 1 Thess 2:7, 11)
discipline them (see also DISCIPLINE): Prov 13:24; 19:18; 22:6, 15; 23:13-14; Eph 6:4 (cf. Heb 12:5-11)
do not discourage them: Col 3:21
rear them properly: Eph 6:4; 1 Tim 5:10
maintain control of them: 1 Tim 3:4
love them: Titus 2:4
RESPONSIBILITY TO PARENTS
honor them: Ex 20:12; Eph 6:2-3 (cf. Prov 31:28)
heed their instruction: Deut 4:10; Prov 1:8-9; 3:1-2 (cf. Ps 34:11)
obey them: Prov 6:20; Eph 6:1; Col 3:20
respect them: Prov 23:22
care for them: 1 Tim 5:4 (cf. John 19:25-27)

CHOSEN (OR ELECT; SEE ALSO SALVATION)
While the term chosen is used in Scripture of both divine and human initiative (Gen 18:19; Deut 7:6; Josh 24:22; Luke 10:42; 2 Thess 2:13), it usually refers to the privileged status of certain persons as a result of God's sovereign and gracious action on their behalf (Deut 7:6-8; Eph 1:4-6; 1 Pet 2:9). The more specific and prominent NT usage of the term concerns individual persons elected by God's eternal decree for salvation in Christ (Eph 1:3-5; 2 Thess 2:13; 2 Tim 1:9; 2:10). God's purpose of salvation for the chosen is accomplished "through sanctification by the Spirit and faith in the truth" (2 Thess 2:13).

CHRIST
The term Christ (Gr. *Christos*) or Messiah (Heb. *mashiach*) means "Anointed One" (Ps 2:2; Dan 9:25-26; John 1:41; 4:25; cf. Ps 45:7). The term Christ indicates the Son's official title (cf. Luke 4:18-19), while Jesus is His personal and human name (Matt 1:21). However, the early church

increasingly used Christ as part of His personal name (Acts 8:5; Rom 9:3, 5; 1 Cor 1:6-7, 13; Gal 6:2; 2 Thess 3:5; 2 John 9). OT prophecy presents Christ in the offices of prophet (Deut 18:15-19; cf. Luke 4:24; Acts 3:22-23), priest (Ps 110:4; cf. Heb 5:5-6), and king (2 Sam 7:12-13; Ps 2:2; cf. Matt 2:2; John 18:37), and includes representative examples of men anointed with oil to function in these same offices (Ex 19:7; 1 Sam 16:13; 1 Kin 19:16). Likewise, Christ was anointed by the Spirit in preparation for His public ministry (Is 11:2-5; Luke 4:18-19; Acts 4:27; 10:38; cf. Heb 1:9). The title Christ mainly emphasizes His office as King and His future worldwide rulership as David's divine descendant (2 Sam 7:12-13; Ps 110:1; Dan 7:13-14; Zech 9:9; Matt 1:1; 21:5; 26:63-64; Luke 1:31-33; Rev 5:5). The titles Son of David and Son of Man are both closely associated with His role as the Christ (i.e., Messiah; Matt 20:30-31; 21:9, 15; 26:63-64).

PRIMARY NAMES OF (SEE ALSO LORD; SON OF GOD; SON OF MAN)

Christ: Matt 1:16
Christ the LORD: Luke 2:11
Christ Jesus: Acts 24:24
Christ Jesus our LORD: Rom 6:23
Jesus: Matt 1:21
Jesus Christ: Matt 1:18
Jesus of Nazareth or Jesus the Nazarene: Matt 26:71; Mark 1:24
Jesus Christ our LORD: Rom 1:4
LORD Jesus Christ: Acts 11:17
LORD Christ: Rom 16:18
LORD Jesus: Mark 16:19
Prince of Peace: Is 9:6
OT prophecies of (see also CHRIST, titles and functions of, types of)
deity of: Ps 110:1 (cf. Matt 22:41-45); Matt 1:23 (cf. Is 7:14); 14:33 (cf. Matt 4:10; Heb 1:6); Luke 2:49; John 1:1-3; Rom 9:5; Eph 1:23; Phil 2:6-11; Col 2:9; Heb 1:8; 1 John 5:20; Rev 1:8
Spirit of: Rom 8:9; Phil 1:19; 1 Pet 1:11

ACKNOWLEDGMENT OF

by the Father: Ps 2:7; 110:4; Matt 3:17; 17:5
by people: Matt 9:27; 10:32; Mark 5:7; Luke 4:41; John 1:29; Acts 9:5; Rom 1:4; 1 Cor 12:3; Heb 1:5-9; 1 John 2:23; 4:2

TITLES AND FUNCTIONS OF (SEE ALSO CHRIST; SON OF GOD; SON OF MAN)

Immanuel: Is 7:14; 8:8; Matt 1:23
Shepherd: Is 40:11; John 10:11
Servant: Is 53:11; Rom 15:8
the Righteous One: Is 53:11; Acts 3:14

branch: Zech 6:12-13 (cf. Is 11:1)
King (of Israel or of the Jews): Jer 23:5; Matt 2:2
Messiah (see also CHRIST, primary names of): Dan 9:25-26; John 1:41
Son of David: Matt 1:1
son of Abraham: Matt 1:1
prophet (see also CHRIST, OT prophecies of): Matt 13:57
Judge: Matt 16:27
Leader: Matt 23:10
Rabbi or Teacher: Matt 26:25
Sunrise from on high: Luke 1:78
Savior: Luke 2:11
the Word: John 1:1, 14
Creator: John 1:3
the light: John 1:9
Lamb (or the Lamb of God): John 1:29; Rev 5:6
the bread of life: John 6:35, 48
the door: John 10:9
the life: John 11:25-26; 1 John 1:1-2
the way: John 14:6
LORD of all: Acts 10:36
the first-born: Rom 8:29; Rev 1:5
LORD of glory: 1 Cor 2:8 (cf. James 2:1)
head of every man: 1 Cor 11:3
last Adam: 1 Cor 15:45
head of the church (i.e., His body): Eph 1:22-23; Col 1:18; 2:19
the chief cornerstone: Is 28:16; Eph 2:20
foundation of the church: Is 28:16; 1 Pet 2:16
the image of God: Col 1:15
mediator: 1 Tim 2:5; Heb 8:6
high priest (see also PRIESTHOOD, priesthood of Christ): Heb 2:7; 3:1
Guardian: 1 Pet 2:25
Advocate: 1 John 2:1
Master: Jude 4
witness: Rev 1:5
King of kings and LORD of LORDS: Rev 19:16 (cf. 17:14)
the Alpha and the Omega: Rev 21:6; 22:13

CHARACTERISTICS OF

eternal: Mic 5:2; John 1:1-2; Rev 1:18
omnipotent: Is 9:6; Matt 28:18; John 5:19
omnipresent: Matt 18:20; John 3:13
omniscient: Matt 11:21; 1 Cor 1:24
immutable: Heb 13:8
holy: Mark 1:24; Luke 1:35; Acts 4:27; Heb 7:26
righteous or just: Is 9:7; 11:5; Matt 3:15; 27:19; Acts 3:14; 7:52; 1 Cor 1:30; 1 Pet 3:18
sinless: Is 53:9; Luke 1:35; John 8:29; 1 John 3:5
faithful: Is 11:5; Heb 2:17; 3:2
humble: Zech 9:9; Matt 11:29

gentle: Is 40:11; Matt 11:29

merciful: Mark 5:19; Jude 21

compassionate: Matt 9:36; Mark 1:41;
   Luke 7:13; John 19:25-27; Phil 2:1

true: Matt 22:16; 1 John 5:20; Rev 19:11

full of grace: John 1:14, 16-17; Rom 5:17

victorious over sin, Satan, and the world:
   Matt 4:1-11; John 12:31; Heb 2:14; Rev 20:10

authority and works of (see also AUTHORITY, of
   Jesus Christ)

second coming of (see also END TIMES)

kingdom of (see also KINGDOM, GOD'S)

TYPES OF (SEE ALSO CHRIST, OT PROPHECIES OF, TITLES AND FUNCTIONS OF)

Adam: Gen 2:7, 20 (cf. Rom 5:14); 1 Cor 15:45

garments of skin: Gen 3:21 (cf. Is 61:10); 1 Cor 1:30

Abel's offering: Gen 4:4 (cf. Heb 11:4)

Noah's ark: Gen 6:14-8:19 (cf. Matt 24:38-39)

Noah's offerings: Gen 8:20-21 (cf. Eph 5:2)

Melchizedek: Gen 14:18, 20; Ps 110:4 (cf. Heb
   5:5-6, 10; 6:20-7:28)

Isaac: Gen 22:1-13 (cf. Rom 8:32); Heb 11:17-19

Jacob's ladder: Gen 28:12 (cf. John 1:51)

Joseph: Gen 37:3 (cf. Matt 3:17); Acts 7:9-15
   (cf. Deut 30:1-10; Hos 2:14-18; Rom 11:1-27)

Passover (see also FEASTS): Ex 12; Lev 23:5
   (cf. Is 53:7); John 1:29; 1 Cor 5:7; 1 Pet 1:19

manna: Ex 16:4-21 (cf. John 6:31-35); Rev 2:17

rock: Ex 17:6 (cf. 1 Cor 10:4)

the tabernacle: Ex 25:1-27:21 (cf. Heb 9:1-25,
   especially vv. 8, 11, 25)

table of showbread: Ex 25:23-30 (cf. John 6:35)

golden lampstand: Ex 25:31-40 (cf. John 8:12)

the veil: Ex 26:31-35 (cf. Matt 27:51);
   Heb 10:19-20

bronze altar: Ex 27:1-8 (cf. Heb 13:10-12)

Aaron: Ex 28:1; Num 16:40 (cf. Heb 4:14-5:6)

altar of incense: Ex 30:1-10 (cf. John 17:1-26);
   Heb 7:25; Rev 8:3-4

burnt offering: Lev 1:3-5 (cf. Heb 9:11-14;
   10:5-10); 1 Pet 3:18

peace offering: Lev 3:1-17 (cf. Eph 2:14, 17)

sin offering: Lev 4:1-35 (cf. Ps 22); Matt 26:28;
   2 Cor 5:21

Day of Atonement: Lev 16 (cf. Heb 9:1-14,
   especially v. 7)

the scapegoat: Lev 16:20-28 (cf. Is 53:6);
   2 Cor 5:21; Eph 1:7

first fruits: Lev 23:10-11 (cf. 1 Cor 15:20)

Moses: Num 12:7 (cf. Heb 3:1-6); Deut 18:15-19
   (cf. Acts 3:22-23; 7:37)

the bronze serpent: Num 21:9 (cf. John 3:14)

cities of refuge: Num 35:6, 9-28 (cf. Heb 6:18)

Joshua: Josh 11:23 (cf. Heb 4:8)

David: 2 Sam 7:8-16; Is 9:7; Ezek 37:24-25
   (cf. Luke 1:31-33)

Jonah: Jon 1:17 (cf. Matt 12:39-40)

CHURCH

The term church (Greek, ekklesia) is used throughout the NT for the new community of believers in Jesus Christ that together with Israel and believing Gentiles of the OT forms the "people of God." The term is used both for a local community of believers (e.g., 1 Cor 1:2) and also for all believers viewed as a corporate fellowship of the people of God (e.g., Eph 1:22-23). Numerous metaphors are used to describe the church, with the most prominent being the Body of Christ. In this picture as well as the total NT teaching, the emphasis is on the spiritual union of the members of the church with Christ the Lord of the church and with each other.

CIRCUMCISION

Circumcision was the divinely instituted practice given to Abraham as a sign of God's covenant with him and his descendants (Gen 17:9-14, 23-27). It involved cutting off the foreskin of males at the age of eight days (Gen 17:10-12). While certain heathen nations practiced circumcision, it did not have the same spiritual significance for them as for the Hebrews. The literal practice of circumcision is not imposed on believers under the New Covenant (Acts 15:1-29; Gal 5:1-6). Instead, Christians have been spiritually circumcised in Christ (Col 2:11-14).

CLEAN, CLEANNESS (SEE ALSO HOLINESS; PURIFICATION; SANCTIFICATION)

Scripture uses the terms clean and cleanness in a physical, ceremonial, or moral sense (or in some combination of these senses) to indicate purification from filth, defilement, or sin (Lev 11:44-47; Ps 51:7, 10; Prov 14:4; Ezek 24:13; John 13:10-11; 1 John 1:7). The NT abrogates the religious need for outward and ritual cleanness (Mark 7:6-23; Luke 11:41; Acts 10:1-16; 1 Tim 4:3-5) and emphasizes the believer's inward and spiritual cleansing from sin through Christ's blood (Matt 26:28; Rom 3:24-25; Col 2:13). Spiritual cleanness is maintained by obedience to the word of God (Ps 119:9-11; John 17:17) and restored by confession of sin (Ps 51; 1 John 1:7-9).

COMMANDS (SEE LAW)

COMMUNION (SEE LORD'S SUPPER)

COMPASSION (SEE ALSO LOVE)

OF GOD
request for: Neh 1:11; Job 8:5
results of: Neh 9:28; Ps 51:1; Is 49:10
conditions for: Prov 28:13
affirmation of: Gen 19:16; Ex 33:19; Neh 9:19;
  Ps 103:8-14

OBJECTS OF
particular individuals: Gen 19:16; Ps 40:11;
  Dan 1:9
Israel: Ex 3:7; Deut 30:3; 32:36; Neh 9:17-21;
  Ps 102:13; 106:46; Is 14:1; Jer 30:18;
  Hos 1:6-7; Zech 1:16
the poor and needy: Ps 72:13
God's servants: Ps 135:14
Gentiles: Jon 4:11
of Christ: Matt 9:36; 20:34; Luke 7:13, 22;
  10:33; Phil 2:1; Heb 4:15

OF PEOPLE
upon the needy: Deut 10:18-19
upon adversaries: 1 Sam 23:21
upon children: Ps 103:13; Is 49:15; Luke 15:20
to fellow Israelites: Zech 7:9
upon a slave: Matt 18:27

CONCEIT (SEE PRIDE)

CONDEMNATION (SEE ALSO JUDGMENT)

DIVINE
exercise of: Gen 3:14-19; 19:24-26; Rev 19:1-3
justice of: Ps 145:17; Rom 3:8
result of: Is 24-27; 2 Pet 2:6; 3:6-7

HUMAN
through civil authority: Ex 22:9; Rom 13:2
through religious authority: Mark 14:64

FREEDOM FROM
request for: Job 10:2
condition for: Ps 34:22; 37:32-33; Luke 6:37;
  John 3:18
granted by Christ: John 8:10-11
in Christ: Rom 8:1 (cf. 8:33-34)
of Christ by Israel's leaders: Matt 20:18;
  Mark 14:64; Acts 13:27

CONDUCT

OF PEOPLE
God's response to: Job 33:17; Ezek 7:27;
  14:22-23

KIND OF
upright: Ps 37:14; Prov 21:8
lewd: Ezek 16:27
corrupt: Ezek 16:47
hypocritical: Matt 23:13-33
immoral: 1 Cor 5:1-13
sensual: 2 Pet 2:7
results of: Ezek 7:27; 9:10; Matt 23:34-36;
  John 13:17

OF CHRISTIANS
reverent: 2 Cor 1:12; 1 Pet 1:17
holy: 2 Cor 1:12; 2 Pet 3:11
in the grace of God: 2 Cor 1:12
worthy: Phil 1:27
wise: Col 4:5
in the household of God: 1 Tim 3:15
exemplary: 1 Tim 4:12; 2 Tim 3:10; Heb 13:7
honorable: Heb 13:18

CONFESSION

The term confession is used in Scripture primarily of (1) an acknowledgment of certain divinely revealed truths about God's character and work, especially as disclosed in Christ the Redeemer (e.g., Deut 32:1-4; Ps 136; Acts 24:14-15; Rom 10:9; 1 Tim 3:16), and (2) an admission of guilt for sin particularly as an offense against God (Ps 51:4; 1 John 1:9).

CONFIDENCE

TRUE
AREAS OF TRUE CONFIDENCE
in God: 2 Kin 18:19; Ps 71:5; Prov 3:26; Is 57:13;
  Phil 1:6
in speech: Job 22:29; Titus 3:8; Heb 13:6
in preaching: Acts 2:29; 4:29; 6:8-10
in other Christians: 2 Cor 2:3; Gal 5:10;
  2 Thess 3:4
in or through Christ: 2 Cor 3:4; Gal 5:10;
  1 Tim 3:13; Philem 8
in entering God's presence through Christ:
  Heb 4:14-16; Eph 3:12
at Christ's coming: 1 John 2:28
before God: 1 John 3:21; 5:14
in the day of judgment: 1 John 4:17

FALSE
AREAS OF FALSE CONFIDENCE
in military might: 2 Kin 19:23; Ps 20:7; Hos 10:13
in riches (see also WEALTH): Job 31:24;
  Prov 18:11; Luke 12:19-21; 1 Tim
in prosperity: Ps 30:6
in a faithless person: Prov 25:19
in human strength: Jer 17:5

in an unchanging future: Is 56:12

in idols: Is 57:13; Jer 48:13

in false peace: Jer 8:11; 23:17; 1 Thess 5:3

in plans opposed to God: Jon 1:3-5

in neighbors, friends, and family: Mic 7:5

in oneself or the fleshly nature: Rom 2:19;
Phil 3:3-4

in speech: 1 Tim 1:7

results of false confidence: 2 Chr 16:7-9;
Ps 108:12; Prov 11:28; Is 20:5; 22:11; 30:3;
Ezek 13:10-11; Hos 5:13; Amos 9:10;
Zeph 1:12; Mark 10:24-25; Luke 12:20;
1 Thess 5:3

warnings about false confidence: Job 15:31;
Ps 33:16-17; 61:10

CONSCIENCE

The term conscience (Greek, *suneidesis*, "know-ing with") denotes self-awareness in the moral sphere. Conscience was a Greek concept and is therefore not found in the OT Scriptures as a distinct human faculty. Aspects of its function, however, are related to the "heart" in the OT. Conscience judges acts both prior to their ex-ecution, urging compliance with the standard (cf. Rom 13:5), and after the act, condemning or excusing (Rom 2:15). The standard by which it operates needs to be enlightened by the reve-lation of God. On the other hand, because it is central to human moral nature, being in a real sense equivalent to the person himself (cf. 1 Cor 8:7, "conscience being weak," v. 10, "he is weak"), it cannot be disobeyed without harm (1 Tim 4:2).

CONSECRATION (SEE DEDICATION)

CONVERSION (SEE ALSO FAITH; REPENTANCE; SALVATION)

The term conversion (from Hebrew and Greek words meaning "to turn back" or "return") sig-nifies the act of a sinner in turning away from sin (e.g., 2 Chr 7:14; Acts 3:26) and toward God in repentance and faith (e.g., Deut 30:10; Acts 9:35). As such it is a comprehensive term for the human action in initial salvation and usually in-cludes both repentance and faith. The Hebrew and Greek terms (which are also frequently used for a literal physical change of directions) denote a life change of direction that includes both the inward attitude and outward behavior. Conversion may also be applied to those who have known God and, having veered away, need to return to Him.

CORRECTION (SEE DISCIPLINE)

COVENANT(S)

A covenant is a solemn agreement between two or more persons or groups to fulfill certain stat-ed obligations toward each other (e.g., Ex 19:5-6). Most important are the two types of biblical covenants between God and humans. (1) Unilat-eral covenants such as the Abrahamic Covenant (Gen 12:1-3; Gal 3:15-18; Heb 6:13-18) and the New Covenant (Jer 31:31-34; Matt 26:26-28; Heb 8:6-13) depend only upon the faithfulness of God for their ultimate fulfillment. While these covenants are unconditional and eternal in their continuance (Ps 105:8-10; Heb 13:20), obe-dient faith is required for personal experience of the blessings of these covenants (Gen 12:1-3; 2 Sam 7:14-15; 1 Kin 11:9-13; John 3:36; Acts 16:31; Rom 3:22-26; Heb 10:19-22, 26-29; 11:8). (2) Mutual covenants such as the Mosaic or Old Covenant (Ex 19:5-6; Jer 31:32; 2 Cor 3:6-17; Col 2:14; Gal 3:15-19; 4:21-31; Heb 7:1-10:18) re-quire both parties to fulfill certain conditions for the continuance of the covenant.

book of: Ex 24:7; 2 Kin 23:2, 21; 2 Chr 34:30;
Zech 9:11; Heb 9:19-20

blood of: Ex 24:8; 2 Kin 23:2

ark of: Num 10:33; Deut 10:8; Josh 3:17; 1 Kin 3:15;
Jer 3:16; Heb 9:4; Rev 11:19

tablets of: Deut 9:9, 11; Heb 9:4

words of: Jer 11:2

God's faithfulness to: Lev 26:44-45; Deut 4:31;
7:9, 12; Judg 2:1; 1 Kin 8:23; 2 Chr 6:14; Neh 1:5;
9:32; Ps 105:8, 10; 106:45; 111:5, 9;
Jer 33:20-22; Dan 9:4; Mic 7:20; 2 Cor 1:20;
Gal 3:15-17; Heb 6:13-18

covenant as a testament or will: Heb 9:16-17

COVETOUSNESS

origin of: Gen 3:1-6; Mark 7:22; Rom 7:8

prohibition against: Ex 20:17; Josh 6:18; Rom 7:7

INSTANCES OF

Achan: Josh 7:1, 11-26

David: 2 Sam 11:1-5

Ahab: 1 Kin 21:1-16

Gehazi: 2 Kin 5:20-24

Ananias and Sapphira: Acts 5:1-10

results of: Josh 6:18; 7:21-26; 1 Kin 21:1-24;
Prov 15:27; 1 Cor 6:9-10; 1 Tim 6:9-10

inconsistent with Christian profession: 1 Cor 5:11
(cf. Eph 5:3)

overcome by contentment: Luke 3:14; Phil 4:11-12;
1 Tim 6:6-8; Heb 13:5

CREATION

A number of biblical words meaning fashioning, shaping, or making an object are used in connection with the concept of creation (e.g., Gen 2:7, 22). However, the distinctive element in biblical creation is derived from a word that refers to the bringing into existence of something new. Used only for divine activity in Scripture, this word does not itself mean creation ex nihilo (out of nothing). However, its emphasis on the initiation of the new makes it a suitable term for this concept. The scope of the divine creation encompasses all that exists apart from God Himself, whether material or spiritual. Because of sin's ruination of the original creation, the regeneration of that work with its newness of spiritual life and holiness is also termed a new creation.

ORIGINAL CREATION
WORK OF GOD
God: Gen 1:1; Ps 33:6; Is 44:24
through the Son: John 1:3; Col 1:15-16; Heb 1:2
effected by the Spirit: Gen 1:2; Job 26:13; 33:4; Ps 104:30
by means of divine Word: Gen 1:3, 6, 9; Ps 33:6; Is 48:13; John 1:1-3
of humanity: Gen 1:26; 2:7, 21-22; Deut 4:32; Matt 19:4; Acts 17:26; 1 Cor 11:9; 1 Tim 2:13

CROSS (SEE ALSO CRUCIFIXION)

Jesus crucified on: Matt 27:32; Mark 15:21; Luke 23:26; John 19:17-19
taken up in self-denial: Matt 10:38; 18:24
preaching of: 1 Cor 1:18
as a stumbling block: Gal 5:11
persecution for: Gal 6:12

CRUCIFIXION (SEE ALSO CROSS)

Crucifixion was a method of drawn out and severely painful execution adopted by the Greeks and Romans from the Phoenicians. The victim's hands and feet were nailed to the cross (in a position making it difficult to breathe). The victim might linger for several days, but sometimes death would be hastened by breaking the legs of the victim. The final assurance of the victim's death resulted from a spear or sword thrust into the side (e.g., John 19:31-34).

of Jesus: Matt 20:19; 26:2; Mark 16:6; Luke 24:7, 20; John 19:6, 10, 15, 20, 41
committed figuratively by apostates: Heb 6:6
of messengers from God: Matt 23:24
of two robbers: Matt 27:38, 44; Luke 23:33; John 19:32

CURSE (SEE ALSO DEVOTED TO DESTRUCTION)

BY GOD
of the serpent: Gen 3:14
of the ground: Gen 3:17-19; 8:21
of certain persons: Gen 4:11; Prov 22:14
of His enemies: Gen 12:3
cause of: Deut 11:28; 27:15-28:19; Josh 6:26; Prov 28:27; Jer 11:3; 17:5; 29:22; 48:10
on Israel: 2 Kin 22:19; Jer 23:10; Lam 3:65; Dan 9:11; Zech 5:3; Mal 2:2
on the wicked: Ps 37:22; Prov 3:33; Is 65:15; Mic 6:10; Mal 1:14; Heb 6:8
on the earth: Is 24:6
by Christ: Matt 11:21

BY HUMANS
upon other people: Gen 9:25; Deut 23:4; Judg 9:27, 57; 1 Sam 17:43; Ps 102:8; Jer 15:10
as judgment in the LORD's name: 2 Kin 2:24
related to an oath: 1 Sam 14:24, 28
of God: Lev 24:11-16; Job 1:5, 11; Is 8:21
response to: Ps 109:28; Luke 6:28
cause of: Prov 11:26; 24:24 (cf. 26:2)
penalty for: Lev 20:9
source of: Rom 3:14

D

DARKNESS
SYMBOLIC
of moral depravity (natural state of people): Ps 107:10; Matt 4:16; John 1:4-5; 12:35; Acts 26:18; Rom 13:12; Eph 5:14; 1 John 2:9-11
of mysterious, unexplainable: 1 Kin 8:12; Ps 97:2
of affliction: 2 Sam 22:28-29; Is 9:2
of punishment: Lam 3:2
of death: 1 Sam 2:9; Ps 23:4; Eccl 11:8
of nothingness: Job 3:4-6
of human ignorance: Job 19:8; 1 John 2:11
conquest by light: John 1:4-9; 8:12; 12:46; 1 Cor 4:5; 2 Cor 6:14; Col 1:13; Rev 22:5

DAY
of God: 2 Pet 3:12
of the LORD or "that day" (see also END TIMES)
of Christ (see also CHRIST)
VARIOUS OTHER USES
the seventh day: Gen 2:2-3
Day of Atonement: Lev 16:30; 23:27
festive day: 1 Sam 25:8
day of good news: 2 Kin 7:9
the full day: Prov 4:18

day of death: Eccl 7:1
day of birth: Eccl 7:1
day of reckoning: Is 2:12
day of punishment: Is 10:3
day of small things: Zech 4:10
day of His second coming: Mal 3:2; Matt 24:36
the last day: John 6:39
a divinely appointed day: Acts 17:31
the first day: Acts 20:7
day of salvation: 2 Cor 6:2

DAY OF THE LORD

The expression "day of the LORD" or sometimes simply "that day" was used in the OT for a decisive intervention of God into history. Although occasionally used for historical events (e.g., the destruction of Jerusalem in 586 B.C., Jer 46:10; Ezek 7:19; 13:1-9), it was used primarily for the great eschatological intervention of God in which He will overthrow His enemies and establish His rule. Because in the NT these same events are related to the future coming of Christ, the day is there often related to Him (e.g., "the day of our LORD Jesus Christ," 1 Cor 1:8; 5:5). The day is characterized both by judgment and vengeance on the wicked (in Israel and the nations) and salvation and deliverance for the people of God. The salvation is portrayed in the OT primarily as the restoration of Israel. But the accompanying teaching of divine salvation extending to the Gentiles as well as the NT teaching concerning the blessing of the church in that day makes it evident that the salvation is for the repentant Gentiles as well. The salvation of the day of the LORD culminates with the transformation of all creation in the making of a new heavens and earth.

DEATH

The word death in all of its biblical applications signifies the loss of vitality. Physical death occurs when the spirit separates from the body. Spiritual death refers to the condition of being spiritually or personally alienated from the living God, the source of all life. Finally, the second death is the condition (outwardly as well as inwardly) of existence separated from the experience of God's life, the natural condition for which people were created. As such it is the condition of final judgment for those who have no relationship with God. Since the human being is holistic, the death of the body is intrinsically related to the more personally significant inner spiritual death. Thus, many statements

concerning death (and life) are comprehensive, including both physical and spiritual death (e.g., Rom 6:23; Acts 3:17 see also LIFE).

PHYSICAL DEATH
conquered by Christ: Matt 9:23-25; 11:5;
   Acts 3:15; 1 Cor 15:26, 54-57; Heb 2:14-15
of saints: Num 23:10; Ps 23:4; Luke 16:25;
   John 11:11; Rom 7:24; Phil 1:21; 1 Thess 4:14;
   Rev 2:10
of the wicked: Job 27:19-20; Ps 34:16; Luke 12:20;
   John 8:21; Acts 1:25
a temporal punishment (see also PUNISHMENT)

SPIRITUAL DEATH
general: Matt 4:16; John 6:53; Rom 5:12-17;
   1 John 3:14; Rev 3:1
alienation from God: Rom 8:6-7; Eph 4:18; Gal 4:8
result of sin: Rom 5:15-17; Gal 3:10; Col 2:13;
   James 1:15
salvation from: John 3:16; 5:24; Rom 6:3-11;
   James 5:20; Rev 2:11; 20:6

SECOND DEATH (SEE ALSO HELL; JUDGMENT)
general: Prov 14:12; Dan 12:2; Matt 10:28; Jude 12;
   Rev 2:11; 20:6, 14; 21:8
not cessation of existence: Matt 25:46;
   Mark 9:43-48; Rev 14:10; 20:10

DEBT

release from (see also JUBILEE, YEAR OF):
   Deut 31:10; Neh 10:31

FORGIVENESS OF
financial debts: Matt 18:27, 32; Luke 7:40-41;
   16:5-7
spiritual debts (i.e., sins): Matt 6:12
   (cf. Luke 7:40-49); 11:4

DEBTOR (SEE DEBT)

DECEPTION (SEE FALSEHOOD)

DEDICATION

The term dedication is found almost exclusively in the OT. The singular NT occurrence in John 10:22 ("the Feast of the Dedication") originated during the intertestamental period in commemoration of the cleansing of the temple and altar by Judas Maccabeus in 164/165 B.C. The Hebrew words for dedication express such ideas as "consecration," "separation for sacred use," or "presentation (to the LORD)." In Christian doctrine, dedication is often used to indicate an offering of self, substance, or both to God for holy purposes.

1699   DELUSION, SELF — DISOBEDIENCE

DELUSION, SELF
(SEE CONFIDENCE, FALSE)

DESCENDANTS
(SEE GENEALOGY; SEED)

DESIRE (SEE PURPOSE; WILL)

DESTRUCTION
(SEE DEVOTED TO DESTRUCTION)

DEVIL (SEE SATAN)

DEVOTED TO DESTRUCTION
(SEE ALSO CURSE)

In the theocratic economy of Israel, to be devoted to destruction was to be divinely banned. Whatever was devoted to destruction could not be ransomed or preserved but was marked for abstention and utter destruction by God's people (Lev 27:28-29; Josh 6:21; 7:1, 12). The ban of physical extermination is explicit in the OT, while the spiritual counterpart may be seen in the NT pronouncement of "accursed" (Gr. *anathema*; Gal 1:8-9; 1 Cor 16:22; Rom 9:3). In the time of Christ the Jews had severely misconstrued and abused the original OT idea of something devoted to God. For example, their traditional law of "Corban" (i.e., "given to God," Mark 7:11) actually invalidated the word of God by keeping a person from honoring their parents in obedience to the Law (Ex 20:12; Mark 7:6-13).

DEVOTION (SEE DEDICATION)

DISCIPLE

A disciple is a "learner," "follower," or "adherent" of a particular leader such as Jesus (Matt 27:57) or even a particular teaching (e.g., Matt 13:52, "a disciple of the kingdom of heaven"). Such prominent Greek philosophers as Aristotle and Socrates had their disciples, as did Moses (John 9:28). The idea of a disciple as one who is taught is used of Jesus twice in OT messianic prophecy (Is 50:4) and once of disciples in general (Is 8:16). The term Disciple(s) is applied to different groups in the NT with different senses. There were pretentious "disciples" who followed Jesus only temporarily and evidently were unbelievers (John 6:60-66; cf. 8:31-32). "Disciples" is also used to designate all men and women who are true believers in Christ,

i.e., "Christians" (Acts 11:26; cf. 1:15). The twelve disciples selected by Christ were also called apostles and had a particular commission from Him (Matt 28:19-20; Acts 1:8) with special credentials (Acts 1:22; 2 Cor 12:12). Judas lost his position, and "the eleven apostles" (Acts 1:26) chose Matthias to replace him (John 6:70-71; Acts 1:16-26; (see also APOSTLE). "Disciple" sometimes occurs in a restricted, ideal sense of those willing to forsake all and follow Christ with total commitment (Luke 14:26, 27, 33). While the specific terminology "disciple(s)" or its other forms is found only in Matthew-Acts in the NT, the concept of discipleship is found elsewhere in the NT (e.g., 1 Cor 11:1; Eph 4:20-21; Phil 3:17; 1 Thess 1:6-7; 2 Tim 2:2; 1 Pet 2:21; 1 John 2:6).

DISCIPLINE (SEE ALSO CHASTISEMENT)
EXERCISED BY
God: Deut 11:2; Job 5:17; Ps 118:18; Heb 12:5-10
Christ: Rev 3:19
a human father: Deut 8:5; Prov 13:1, 24; Heb 12:7-10
motives for: 2 Sam 7:14-15; Prov 3:12; Heb 12:6-11; Rev 3:19
response to: Job 5:17; Ps 50:17; Prov 3:11; 13:1; 13:18; 19:20, 27; Jer 7:28; Heb 12:5, 9, 12-13; Rev 3:19

DISGRACE (SEE SHAME)

DISHONOR
of God by disobedience: Rom 2:23
of Christ: John 8:49
of father or mother: Deut 27:16
result of: Prov 18:3
of the natural body: 1 Cor 15:43
of inanimate things: 2 Tim 2:20
of the poor: James 2:6
various other uses of: Ps 69:6; 74:21; Prov 3:35; Titus 2:5

DISOBEDIENCE (SEE ALSO OBEDIENCE; SIN)
OBJECTS OF
to God: Gen 3:11-12; Rom 2:23 (cf. Titus 1:16)
to Christ: John 3:36
to the Holy Spirit: Acts 7:51
to parents: Rom 1:30; 2 Tim 3:2
to the word: 2 Thess 1:8; 1 Pet 2:8; 3:1

results of: Deut 28:15-68; Ps 107:17; John 3:36;
Rom 6:23; 1 Cor 10:5-11; Heb 2:2; 3:18; 4:6

DISPERSION

OF CERTAIN PEOPLE
of the people at Babel: Gen 11:8-9
of Simeon and Levi in Israel: Gen 49:7
of Israel: 1 Kin 14:15; Zeph 3:10
of Jesus' disciples: Matt 26:31
of NT believers: Acts 8:1, 4; 11:19; 1 Pet 1:1

DIVORCE (SEE ALSO MARRIAGE)

The Hebrew and Greek terms for divorce ("to
send away," "to separate," "to set free") signify
the dissolution of marriage with the result that
the divorced person was free to remarry except
for certain restrictions. In the Mosaic Law, remar-
rying the original partner was restricted (cf. Deut
24:1). In the NT all remarriage was denied so long
as there was the possibility of reconciliation
(1 Cor 7:11). The question of a permitted ground
for divorce based on the teaching of Jesus and the
apostle Paul has evoked diverse responses. Some
limit the exception clause in Jesus' prohibition of
divorce (e.g., Matt 5:31) to marriages within the
proscribed laws of consanguinity (cf. Lev 18:6)
or unfaithfulness during the betrothal period.
Most understand Jesus as allowing divorce for
adultery or other serious sexual sin that violates
the marriage covenant. Many also see desertion
as biblical grounds for divorce based on Paul's
teaching (1 Cor 7:15). Whether the apostle means
that the bond of marriage is broken when the
unbeliever departs, or simply that the believer is
not bound to serve the other as marriage partner
(without reference to divorce and remarriage),
is not clear. The entire tenor of Scripture views
divorce as opposed to God's intended marriage
design and permitted only as the lesser evil in
severely destructive marital circumstances.

DOCTRINE (SEE ALSO CONFESSION; TEACHERS; TEACHING)

TRUE DOCTRINE
source of: Deut 8:3; Ps 119:160; John 17:17;
2 Tim 3:16
importance of: Matt 28:20; Rom 6:17; 16:17;
1 Cor 15:3-4; 1 Tim 4:3, 13; 2 Tim 3:10, 15-17

VARIOUS DESCRIPTIONS OF
the truth: Eph 4:15; 2 Tim 4:4
apostolic traditions: 1 Cor 11:2; 2 Thess 2:15
sound doctrine: 1 Tim 4:6; 2 Tim 4:3;
Titus 1:9; 2:1

doctrine conforming to godliness: 1 Tim 6:3
pure doctrine: Titus 2:7
doctrine of God our Savior: Titus 2:10
defense of: Is 8:19-20; Mark 12:24-28;
Luke 24:44-47; Rom 16:17; Jude 3

FALSE DOCTRINE

VARIOUS DESCRIPTIONS OF
commandments of people: Matt 15:9
misleading doctrine: Eph 4:14
strange doctrines: 1 Tim 1:3
doctrines of demons: 1 Tim 4:1
different doctrine: 1 Tim 6:3;
2 John 9-10
myths: 2 Tim 4:4

DOXOLOGY (SEE PRAISE)

DREAM

AS SOURCE OF REVELATION
simple (auditory): Gen 20:3, 6-7; 31:10-13;
1 Kin 3:5ff; Matt 1:20; 2:12; Acts 9; 10
symbolic (visual): Gen 37:5-10; 40:5ff;
41:1ff; Judg 7:13; Dan 2
source: Gen 40:8; 41:16; Num 12:6-8;
Job 33:15-16; Joel 2:28; Dan 2:19-23
cautions: Deut 13:1-5; Job 20:8; Eccl 5:3, 7;
Is 29:8; Jer 23:25-32; Zech 10:2
interpretation: Gen 41:25-32; Dan 2:16-23,
28-30; 4:19-27

DWELL, DWELLING

OF GOD
with His people: Ex 25:8; 29:45-46; Lev 26:11;
1 Kin 6:13; Ezek 37:27; 43:7; Zech 2:10-11;
2 Cor 6:16; Rev 21:3
in a sanctuary (i.e., the tabernacle or temple):
Ex 25:8; 2 Sam 7:5; Matt 23:21; Acts 7:46
in His heavenly abode: 1 Kin 8:30; Is 57:15
(cf. Ps 61:4; 65:4)
not limited to buildings constructed by people:
2 Chr 6:18; Acts 7:48; 17:24
in the church: Eph 2:22
in unapproachable light: 1 Tim 6:16

OF CHRIST
in the flesh: John 1:14

IN THE BELIEVER
through His person: John 14:20; Eph 3:17;
Col 1:27
through His power: 2 Cor 12:9
through His word: Col 3:16

IN CHRIST
of the believer: John 14:20; Col 2:9-10
of the fullness of deity: Col 1:19; 2:9

OF THE SPIRIT
in the believer: Rom 8:9, 11; 2 Tim 1:14; James 4:5
(cf. 1 Cor 6:19)
in the local church: 1 Cor 3:17
figurative use of: Ps 5:4; Prov 8:12; 15:31; Is 32:16

E

EDIFICATION
OF OTHER BELIEVERS
of individuals particularly: Rom 14:19; 15:1-2, 14;
1 Cor 10:23-24; Eph 4:29; 1 Thess 5:11
of the church corporately: Acts 9:31;
1 Cor 14:4-5, 12; Eph 4:16
of self: 1 Cor 14:4; Jude 20
MEANS OF
through God and His word: Acts 20:32
through love: 1 Cor 8:1
through prophecy: 1 Cor 14:3-5
through gifted people: Eph 4:11-12
through saints equipped for service: Eph 4:12
in Christ: Col 2:7
apostolic authority for: 2 Cor 10:8 (cf. 12:19)

EDUCATION (SEE TEACHING)

EGOTISM (SEE PRIDE)

END TIMES
The biblical doctrine of the end times (called eschatology, from Greek *eschata*, "last things") refers to the time and events of the consummation of God's redemptive activity. It involves the "last" or "latter days" (e.g., Is 2:2), the Day of the Lord (e.g., Amos 5:18-19; 1 Thess 5:2), the "age to come" (e.g., Eph 1:21; Heb 6:5), the "last days" (e.g., 2 Tim 3:1), the "last time" (Jude 18), and the "last hour" (1 John 2:18; see also DAY OF THE Lord; KINGDOM).
condition of last days preceding Christ's return:
1 Tim 4:1-3; 2 Tim 3:1-5, 13; 2 Pet 3:1-4;
Jude 17-19
tribulation and judgment (end times): Is 13:9-11;
24:21; 26:21; Jer 30:7; Dan 7:24-25; 12:1;
Matt 24:15-22; 2 Thess 2:1-4; Rev 3:10;
6:16-17; 11:18; 14:7; 15:1, 7; 16:7, 19
rapture: John 14:2-3; 1 Thess 4:13-18;
(cf. 1 Cor 15:51-52)
SECOND COMING
general: Matt 16:27; 24:3; Mark 8:38; Luke 19:11-27;
John 14:2-3; Acts 1:9-11; 1 Cor 1:7-8; 4:5;
Phil 3:20; Col 3:4; 1 Thess 2:19; 4:13-17; 5:1-3, 23;

2 Thess 1:7-10; 2:1-4; 1 Pet 5:4; 2 Pet 3:4-13;
1 John 2:28; 3:2; Jude 14-15; Rev 1:7; 19:11-21
TERMINOLOGY OF
coming (parousia): Matt 24:3, 27, 37;
1 Cor 15:23; 1 Thess 3:13; 4:15; 5:23;
2 Thess 2:1; James 3:4; 5:7; 1 John 2:28
appearance: 1 Tim 6:14; 2 Tim 4:1, 8; Titus 2:13
revelation: 1 Cor 1:7; 2 Thess 1:7; 1 Pet 1:7; 4:13
MANNER OF
in glory: Dan 7:13-14; Matt 16:27; Mark 8:38;
Col 3:4; Titus 2:13
visibly: Zech 14:3-4; Acts 1:11; Matt 24:30
with saints: Zech 14:5; Col 3:4; 1 Thess 3:13; 4:14
attended by angels: Zech 14:5; Matt 13:38-41;
16:27; 24:31; 25:31; 2 Thess 1:7; Jude 14
TIME OF
unknown: Matt 24:36-39, 42, 44; 25:13;
Mark 13:32-37; Luke 12:40; Acts 1:7;
1 Thess 5:1-2; Rev 3:3; 16:15
unexpectedly (to the unprepared): Matt 24:50;
Luke 12:39; 21:34-35; 1 Thess 5:2; 2 Pet 3:10
quickly: Rev 3:11; 22:7, 12, 20
imminently: Mark 13:33-37; Luke 12:35-46;
1 Thess 4:17; James 5:8; 1 Pet 4:7
signs of: Matt 24:3, 29-34; Luke 21:25-33;
2 Thess 2:3
PURPOSES OF
salvation: Phil 3:21; Col 3:3-4; Heb 9:28;
1 Pet 1:5; 1 John 3:2
judgment and reward: Matt 16:27; 25:31-46;
Luke 19:11-27; 1 Cor 4:5; 1 Thess 5:2-3;
2 Thess 1:7-9; 2 Tim 4:1; 1 Pet 5:4;
2 Pet 3:4-13; Jude 14-15
reign: Matt 19:28; 25:31; Luke 19:11-15;
Rev 11:15, 17; 19:15
millennium (see also KINGDOM)

ENDURANCE
AS DURABILITY
of God's person: Ps 102:26; Dan 6:26 (cf. 7:13)
of God's glory: Ps 104:31
of God's righteousness: Ps 111:3
of God's praise: Ps 111:10
of the messianic kingdom: 2 Sam 7:16; Dan 2:44
(cf. 6:26; 7:14)
AS PATIENT TOLERANCE
of God for vessels of wrath: Rom 9:22
of Christ when suffering unjustly: 1 Pet 2:20-23
AS PERSEVERANCE OR STEADFASTNESS
of Christ under trial: Matt 4:1-11; 26:39; Heb 12:2-3
OF PEOPLE
need for: Heb 10:36
conditions for: Ex 18:23; 2 Cor 1:6; James 1:3

testing of: Esth 8:6; Job 6:11; Ps 72:5
examples of: Ps 72:17; Jer 15:15; Heb 10:32;
   11:25, 27; James 5:11
practice of: 1 Cor 4:12; 9:12; 13:7; 2 Cor 6:4;
   2 Thess 1:4; Heb 10:32; Rev 2:3
results of: Matt 10:22; 24:13; Luke 21:19;
   2 Tim 2:12; Heb 12:7; James 1:4; 5:11;
   1 Pet 2:20
exhortation to: 2 Tim 4:5; Heb 12:1
lack of: 1 Sam 13:14; Job 8:15; 15:29; 20:21;
   Ps 49:12; Is 1:13; Jer 44:22; Joel 2:11; Amos 7:10;
   Nah 1:6; Mal 3:2; 1 Thess 3:1; 2 Tim 4:3; Rev 2:2
various other uses of: Ps 19:9; 89:36; 101:5;
   Prov 8:18; 18:14; Is 66:22; Jer 10:10; Mic 6:2

ENEMY (SEE SATAN)

EQUITY (SEE JUSTICE)

ESCHATOLOGY (SEE END TIMES)

ETERNAL

The concept of eternality is expressed in Scripture by two primary words, both of which have fundamental meanings related to prolonged time. The Hebrew *olam* signifies hidden or distant time either in the future or the past. The corresponding Greek word *aion* ("age") has the basic idea of the prolongation of time. These terms do not in themselves mean eternity or endless time and may be used for unspecified lengths of time, including the length of a person's life (e.g., 1 Sam 1:22) and the age of the hills (e.g., Gen 49:26). However, especially when the terms are used in the plural (e.g., 1 Tim 1:17, "forever and ever," lit. "unto the ages of the ages") or with God (and His attributes and works), they clearly denote endlessness or that which is unlimited by time. This is evident from the fact that God is the living God (cf. Deut 32:4) who Himself is the LORD of all time (cf. 1 Tim 1:17, "King eternal," lit. "King of the ages"). The phrases "first and last" (e.g., Is 44:6) or "Alpha and Omega" (e.g., Rev 1:8) are also used to denote the eternality of God. In addition to its reference to God signifying no beginning or ending (cf. Ps 90:2), the notion of eternality may refer either to the endless past (e.g., Mic 5:2) or the endless future, as with the eternal life of the believer that has a beginning as far as the individual is concerned but no end (John 3:16). Because of its contrast to that which is limited by time, the eternal takes on

a qualitative sense of belonging to a different realm related to the divine and immortal. Hence eternal life is more than endless life; it is a new quality of life related to the life of God.

ETERNAL LIFE (SEE LIFE)

ETERNITY (SEE ETERNAL)

EUCHARIST (SEE LORD's SUPPER)

EVERLASTING (SEE ETERNAL)

EVIL (SEE ALSO SIN)

source of: Gen 3:1-6; 6:5; Ps 51:5; Mark 7:21-23;
   Rom 5:12-19; 1 Tim 6:10; 1 John 3:8, 12

IN RELATION TO GOD

evil in His sight: Gen 38:7; Num 32:13; 2 Sam 11:27;
   Is 65:12
His separation from evil: Ps 5:4; Hab 1:13
   (cf. James 1:13)
His response to evil persons: Is 13:11; Matt 5:45

GOOD AND EVIL

knowledge of: Gen 2:9, 17; 3:5, 22; Deut 1:39
discernment between: 2 Sam 14:17; 1 Kin 3:9;
   Heb 5:14 (cf. Is 7:15-16)
judgment of: Eccl 12:14 (cf. 2 Cor 5:10)

ASCRIBED TO

the human heart: Gen 6:5; 8:21; Ps 28:3; Jer 3:17;
   Matt 12:34-35; Heb 3:12
the human mind: Ex 10:10; Ps 56:5
a human generation: Deut 1:35; Matt 12:45
human nature: Matt 7:11; 12:34-35; Rom 7:21

EXALTATION (SEE ALSO HUMILITY)

OF THE LORD

by others: 2 Sam 22:47; Ps 34:3; 99:5, 9;
   Prov 29:25; Acts 10:46
by Himself: 1 Chr 29:11; Ps 46:10; Is 6:1
of Christ: Is 52:13; John 17:5; Phil 1:20; 2:9-11;
   Heb 2:9; 7:26; 1 Pet 3:22

OF OTHERS

by the LORD: Josh 3:7; 1 Chr 25:5; Ps 37:34;
   Matt 23:12; Luke 1:52; James 4:10; 1 Pet 5:6

EXILE

cause of: Deut 28:45-52; 2 Kin 17:6-23; 21:10-15;
   Is 5:13; 40:2; Ezek 6:1-8; 39:23

RETURN FROM

people involved: Ezra 1:1-6, 11; 6:21; 7:1-9; Zech 6:10
divine promise of: Is 51:14; Jer 29:10, 14; Ezek 11:17
decree for: 2 Chr 36:22-23
timing of: Jer 25:11

GOD'S RESPONSE TO EXILED JEWS
His commands: Jer 29:4-7
His care: Jer 30:10-11; Ezek 11:16

EXPIATION (SEE ATONEMENT)

F

FAITH (BELIEVE)

The notion of belief in the OT is expressed primarily by a Hebrew word meaning "to be certain about" or "to be assured." The word carries the ideas of relying on someone, giving credence to a message, or trusting in someone. These same meanings are carried over to the NT concept of faith with the expression "believing in" that focuses faith upon Christ. Faith can be directed to the wrong object or be incomplete, involving only the intellect (e.g., James 2:19) and emotion (e.g., Luke 8:13) but not a surrender of the will. True saving faith includes (1) an assured certainty concerning the trustworthiness of God and the truth of His word, specifically the NT proclamation concerning Jesus and His work (cf. Heb 11:1) and, (2) a reliance on God through Christ that establishes a personal relationship of trust and commitment of life to the object of faith.
general: Luke 17:5; 18:8; Rom 10:17; 14:23;
     1 Cor 2:5; 2 Cor 5:17; Gal 5:6; Heb 11
salvation by (see also JUSTIFICATION):
     Mark 16:16; John 1:12; Acts 16:31; Rom 1:16-17;
     Gal 3:2 ; Phil 3:9; 2:12; 1 Thess 2:13;
     Heb 11:6, 39; 1 John 5:10
means of Christian living and blessing: Ps 36:7;
     37:5; Prov 3:5; Is 26:3-4; Jer 17:7; Hab 2:4;
     Matt 21:21; Mark 9:23-24; Acts 3:16; Rom 4:3;
     1 Cor 16:13; Gal 5:6; Eph 3:17; Col 1:4;
     1 Thess 1:3; 1 Tim 1:5, 19; 2 Tim 2:22;
     Heb 10:22, 38; James 1:6; 1 Pet 1:5, 7-9

FAITH (BELIEF)

The noun faith corresponds to the verb believe. While in a few instances the noun is used for the content of what is believed (i.e., the faith, e.g., Acts 6:7), its primary usage is for the action of believing. The concept of faith is expressed in the OT primarily by the Hebrew word *aman*, whose root meaning denotes firmness or certainty. The particular verbal form of the word that is used suggests the acceptance of someone as trustworthy or dependable and

a commitment and trust in the particular object of faith (e.g., Abraham believed God, Gen 15:6). The primary NT word for faith carries the meanings "to believe," "to rely on," "to trust." Although faith can be bare intellectual assent (cf. James 2:14-16), the full sense of faith involves not only a knowledge of the object of faith (e.g., Rom 10:17) but the response of the whole person in trustful commitment in accordance with whom or what is believed. Related ideas of trust and reliance conveyed by other Hebrew and Greek words are also involved in the biblical concept of faith (see also HOPE).
importance of: John 6:28-29; Rom 14:23; Heb 11:6

OBJECT OF
God: Mark 11:22; John 5:24; Rom 4:24; Titus 3:8;
     1 Pet 1:21
Christ: John 3:15-16; 16:31; 2 Tim 3:15
the Scriptures (Word of God): Luke 16:29-31;
     John 2:22; 2 Thess 2:13

BLESSINGS OF
justification (see also JUSTIFICATION): Hab 2:4;
     Acts 13:39; Rom 3:28; Gal 2:16; 3:6, 24; Phil 3:9;
     Heb 11:4
salvation: Acts 16:31; Rom 10:9; Eph 2:8;
     2 Tim 3:15; 1 Pet 1:9
sanctification: Acts 26:18
eternal life: John 3:15-16; 20:31
forgiveness of sins: Acts 10:43
spiritual security: Col 1:23; 1 Pet 1:5
gift of the Spirit: John 7:38; Gal 3:2, 14; Eph 1:13
other: Matt 21:22; John 1:12

EVIDENCES OF
witness of Spirit: 1 John 5:10
works of faith: Gal 5:6; Col 1:4; 1 Thess 1:3;
     James 2:17, 26
victory over world: 1 John 5:4, 5
joy: 1 Pet 1:8

FAITHFULNESS

OF GOD (SEE ALSO GOD, ATTRIBUTES OF, FAITHFUL)
statement of: Deut 7:9; Ps 36:5; Is 49:7;
     Hos 11:12; Rom 3:3; 2 Tim 2:13

IN RELATION TO
His promise: Gen 21:1-2 (cf. 18:10); 1 Kin 8:20;
     Acts 13:23, 32-33; 2 Cor 1:20; Heb 10:23; 11:11
His word: 2 Sam 7:28; Ps 119:86, 89; Titus 1:9;
     Rev 21:5
His people
in general: Ps 98:3
in their need for deliverance: Judg 2:18
in their need for protection: Ps 91:4; 2 Thess 3:3

in their deserved affliction: Ps 119:75
in their prayers: Ps 143:1
in their temptation: 1 Cor 10:13
in their ultimate glorification:
    1 Thess 5:23-24
in their need for forgiveness: 1 John 1:9
of Christ: Heb 2:17; 3:1-2, 6; Rev 1:5; 3:14; 19:11
    (cf. Is 11:5; 42:3)

OF PEOPLE
source of: Gal 5:22
expression of: Gen 32:10; Josh 2:14; 2 Chr 19:8-9;
    Acts 16:15; 3 John 5
exhortation to: Ps 37:3; Matt 23:23
reward of: Ps 31:23; 101:6; Prov 12:22; 28:20;
    Is 61:8; Ezek 18:9; Matt 25:21, 23; Luke 19:17;
    Rev 2:10
lack of (see also UNFAITHFULNESS): Deut 32:20;
    Ps 78:8, 37; Hos 4:1; Jon 2:8; Matt 23:23

FALL OF MAN

In biblical theology the expression "fall of man" refers to the original transgression of Adam and Eve along with the penalty promised by God (Gen 3:1-24; Rom 5:12-21; cf. Hos 6:7). Through deception, the serpent led Eve to doubt God's goodness, to disbelieve God's word, and to disobey God's will in transgressing the divine prohibition (Gen 2:17; 3:1-6; 2 Cor 11:3; 1 Tim 2:14). While Eve was deceived, Adam transgressed deliberately (Gen 3:6; 1 Tim 2:14), and through their sin both became corrupted by sin (Rom 5:19) and experienced immediate spiritual death (Gen 2:17; Eph 2:1) and eventual physical death (Rom 5:12-21). Because all humanity is representatively and substantially related to Adam as its natural head, God imputed Adam's original sin to humanity (Rom 5:12-21). In addition, Adam's corrupt nature and its attendant results are transmitted to all humanity (Job 25:4; Ps 51:5; Rom 5:12-21; 6:23; 7:18; 1 Cor 15:22; Eph 2:1-2; Heb 9:27). Evidently Adam and Eve believed God's promise of the victorious seed from the woman (Gen 3:15; cf. 3:20; 15:6; Rom 4:1-5, 20-22), and God provided them with "garments of skin" representing imputed righteousness (Gen 3:21; cf. Is 61:10; Rom 3:22; 5:17; 1 Cor 1:30).
redemption from: Gen 3:15, 20-21;
    Rom 3:22-26; 5:12-21; 1 Cor 15:21-22;
    2 Tim 1:10; Heb 2:14

FALSE CHRISTS (SEE ANTICHRIST)

FALSE TEACHERS
(SEE TEACHERS, FALSE)

FALSEHOOD (SEE ALSO TRUTH)

in speech: Job 21:34; Ps 5:6; Is 59:3
in conduct: Job 31:5; Jer 23:14; Mic 2:11
cause of: Ps 7:12-14; Mark 7:21-23
result of: Ps 101:7; Prov 20:17; 29:12; Ezek 13:8, 22
divine judgment of: Jer 23:32

FAMILY

divine institution of: Gen 1:27 (cf. Matt 19:4-6);
    2:18-24 (cf. Ps 127:1); Heb 13:4

RESPONSIBILITIES IN (SEE ALSO MARRIAGE)
HUSBAND AND FATHER (SEE ALSO FATHER, HUMAN)
    to serve as head of his family: 1 Cor 11:3, 7-9
    to provide spiritual leadership for his family:
        Gen 18:19; Ex 12:3-4; 1 Sam 1:21
    to pray for his family: 2 Sam 7:25-29;
        1 Chr 22:11-12
    to manage his own family well: 1 Tim 3:4-5
    to love, understand, and honor his wife:
        Eph 5:25, 28-29, 33; 1 Pet 3:7
    to be loyal to his wife: 1 Tim 3:2
    to give spiritual training to his children:
        Gen 18:19; Deut 6:6-7; Eph 6:4
    to show compassion and care for his children:
        Ps 103:13; 1 Thess 2:11
    to discipline his children: Prov 13:24; 19:18
        (cf. Heb 12:5-11)
    not to anger or exasperate his children:
        Eph 6:4; Col 3:21
    to provide the necessities for his family:
        1 Tim 5:8 (cf. Matt 7:11; 2 Cor 12:14)
WIFE AND MOTHER
    to respect her husband: Eph 5:33
    to love her husband: Titus 2:4
    to care for her children: 1 Thess 2:7;
        1 Tim 5:10
    to help in spiritual training of her children:
        Prov 1:8; 2 Tim 3:15
    to love her children: Titus 2:4
    to be virtuous: Prov 31:10-12 (cf. 2 Tim 1:5)

FAST, FASTING

To fast is to refrain from food and sometimes also liquid, sleep, etc., in order to give priority to spiritual exercises (Ex 34:28; Deut 9:18; Acts 27:33). Fasting may be accompanied by prayer (Ps 35:13) or a vow (1 Sam 14:24-30). Jesus taught that fasting for mere outward show is spiritu-

ally worthless and actually involves the sin of hypocrisy (Matt 6:16-18).

FATHER

divine Father (see also GOD, fatherhood of)

HUMAN FATHER

VARIOUS FUNCTIONS OF

as a male parent: Gen 2:24

as an originator of certain crafts:
Gen 4:20-21

as a forefather (or forefathers): Gen 28:13;
Josh 24:6; 1 Kin 15:11; 2 Kin 21:22

*responsibilities to his family (see also FAMILY,
responsibilities in, husband and father)*

SPIRITUAL FATHER

God (see also GOD, fatherhood of)

Abraham to believers: Rom 4:11, 16-17; Gal 3:7

Paul to his Christian converts: 1 Cor 4:15
(cf. 1 Thess 2:11)

FEAR

CAUSES OF FEAR

fear of judgment from God: Gen 3:8-10;
Acts 24:25

fear from a divine message: 1 Sam 28:20

fear of an oppressor: Is 51:13; Hos 10:5

fear of a dream: Dan 4:5

fear of disaster: Zeph 3:15

fear of hearing God's voice: Matt 17:5-7

fear of a multitude: Matt 21:26

fear of an angel: Matt 28:4-8; Luke 1:11-12

fear of future events: Luke 21:26

fear of shipwreck: Acts 27:17

fear of spiritual slavery: Rom 8:15

fear of governmental authorities: Rom 13:7

fear of trials in Christian ministry: 2 Cor 7:5

fear of failure: Gal 2:2; 4:11; 1 Thess 3:5;
Heb 4:1

fear of death: Heb 2:15

PREVENTION OF

through God's presence: Gen 26:24;
Deut 31:6, 8; Josh 1:9; Is 41:10; Hab 2:5
(cf. Matt 14:27); Acts 18:9-10

through obedience to the LORD: 1 Sam 12:20-21;
1 Chr 22:12-19

through God's protection: Ps 3:5-6; 23:4; 27:1-3;
46:1-2; 91:1-16

through faith in God: Ps 56:3-4; 112:7; Is 12:2;
Heb 11:27 (cf. Mark 5:36)

through God's deliverance: Ps 34:4

through God's support: Ps 112:8; 118:6

through godly wisdom: Prov 3:25

through love: 1 John 4:18

FEAR OF GOD

Fear of God involves a reverential trust toward God through awareness of His awesome person and character. In its biblical sense, fear of God contrasts with a cringing, anxious dread or with unrelieved guilt due to a wrong relationship God (cf. Gen 3:10); Job 9:35; 1 John 4:18). Biblical fear of God accords with His own love and with Christian love toward Him since a reverential love holds God in highest esteem. Fear of God is "the beginning of knowledge" (Prov 1:7). One who fears God takes His person and holiness seriously and consequently has a repulsion toward sin and all that is contrary to God's character (Prov 16:6). Reverential service to God is motivated by God's great work for His people (1 Sam 12:24). Irreverence toward God leads to disrespect for fellow people (Neh 5:9-12; Luke 18:2-4).

FEASTS

The feasts of the LORD or "the LORD's appointed times" (Lev 23:2) refer primarily to the seven holy convocations divinely instituted in Israel's annual religious calendar (Lev 23:1-44). These consist of a day or season of joyous celebration for God's redemptive and beneficent provision for His covenant people Israel. The first three feasts (Passover, Unleavened Bread, and First Fruits) occur during Nisan (March-April), the first month of the Jewish religious calendar. The last three feasts (Trumpets, Day of Atonement, and Tabernacles) take place in Tishri (September-October), the seventh month of their religious calendar. The Feast of Weeks (i.e., Pentecost) occurs 50 days after the offering of the first fruits (i.e., between the first and last threesome of annual feasts). All males were required to attend three of the annual feasts: Feast of Unleavened Bread, Feast of Weeks, and Feast of Booths (Deut 16:16). The Sabbath was also regarded as a feast day of "complete rest" (Lev 23:3). It was to be a delightful, honorable, and holy day of the LORD (Is 58:13) that ideally furnished opportunity to do good (Matt 12:12; see also SABBATH). The Feast of Purim was instituted by Mordecai during the reign of Ahasuerus (Esth 9:20-32). It is celebrated in February or March to commemorate the divine deliverance of the Jews from the plot of Haman. The Feast of Dedication or Feast of Lights (i.e., Hanukkah) is an extra-biblical Jewish festival held in December to celebrate the rededication of the Jerusalem temple after the Jews' victory

in 165 B.C. over the Syrians who had defiled it
(John 10:22).

COLLECTIVE NAMES OF

appointed times: Lev 23:4; Num 12:3; 29:39
holy convocations: Lev 23:4
appointed feast(s): Num 10:10; Is 1:14
fixed festivals: 1 Chr 23:31; Ezra 3:5
the three annual feasts: 2 Chr 8:13

PASSOVER

celebration and regulations of: Ex 12; 34:25;
   Num 9:2-14; Deut 16:1-8; Josh 5:10-11;
   John 6:4; Acts 12:3-4; Heb 11:28
purpose of: Ex 12:21-28; 1 Cor 5:7 (cf. John 1:29);
   1 Pet 1:19; Rev 5:6, 12
Unleavened Bread: Ex 12:14-20; Num 9:11;
   28:17-25; 2 Chr 8:13; 30:13-27; 35:17;
   Mark 14:1-2, 12; Acts 12:3-4; 20:6; 1 Cor 5:8
First Fruits: Lev 23:10-14 (cf. Rom 8:23);
   1 Cor 15:20, 23
*Pentecost (also called Feast of Weeks or Harvest of
   the First Fruits):* Ex 23:16; 34:22; Num 28:26-31;
   Acts 2:1; 20:16; 1 Cor 16:8
Trumpets: Lev 23:23-25; Neh 8:2, 9-12
Day of Atonement: Ex 30:10; Lev 16:2-34; Heb 9:7
Tabernacles or Ingathering: Ex 23:16; Lev 23:33-44;
   Zech 14:16-19; John 7:2 (cf. Matt 17:4)

FELLOWSHIP

BETWEEN BELIEVERS

basis: Rom 8:16-17; Eph 3:6; Phil 1:7; 1 Pet 5:1;
   2 Pet 1:4; Philem 6; 1 John 1:3-7

NATURE

harmony: Rom 12:16; 1 Pet 3:8
acceptance: Rom 15:7
instruction: Rom 15:14
sharing: 2 Cor 8:7, 13-15
service: Gal 5:13
bearing burdens: Gal 6:2
kindness: Eph 4:32; 1 Thess 5:15
forgiveness: Eph 4:32
patience: Col 3:13
love: 1 John 4:11, 12
prayer: James 5:16
hospitality: 1 Pet 4:9
selflessness: Phil 2:3, 4
use of spiritual gifts: 1 Cor 12:7; 1 Pet 4:10

FEMALE (SEE HUMANITY)

FIGURATIVE SPEECH

CONCEPT IN SCRIPTURE

proverbs: Num 21:27; 1 Kin 4:32
parables: Ps 78:2; Ezek 20:49; Hos 12:10; Matt 13:3

proverb and a figure: Prov 1:6
figure of speech: John 10:6; 16:29
symbols: John 10:9; Rev 1:16-20
figurative language: Ezek 1:4-28; Dan 2:31-45;
   John 16:25
figurative application: 1 Cor 4:6
allegory: Gal 4:24

FIRE

FIGURATIVE USE OF

for anger: Ps 78:21; Hos 7:6
for wickedness: Is 9:18
for God's Word: Jer 23:29
with the Holy Spirit: Acts 2:3
in divine testing of Christian works: 1 Cor 3:12-15
for God: Heb 12:29

FIRSTBORN

significance: Gen 49:3; Deut 21:17
rights and privileges: Gen 25:29-34; 29:26;
   33:20; Deut 21:15-17
Mosaic laws concerning: Ex 13:1-16; 34:20;
   Num 3:13, 40-51; 18:15-18; Deut 12:6, 17

FIGURATIVE

of Israel: Ex 4:22
of Christ: Ps 89:27; John 1:14; 3:16; Rom 8:29;
   Col 1:15, 18; Rev 1:5
of believers: Heb 12:23

FIRST FRUITS

USED LITERALLY OF

*the Feast of the Harvest of the First Fruits
   (see also FEASTS):* Ex 23:16; 34:22
   (cf. Num 28:26)
first fruits offered to the LORD: Ex 23:19; 34:26;
   Lev 2:11-16; Neh 10:34-35 (cf. Prov 3:9)
first fruits given to help support the priests:
   Deut 18:1-4; Neh 12:44; Ezek 44:30
first fruits of grain, wine, and oil: Deut 18:4
bread of first fruits: 2 Kin 4:42

USED FIGURATIVELY OF

the firstborn: Ps 105:36
*the Spirit as a guarantee of believers' future
   glorification:* Rom 8:23
Christ's resurrection with a glorified body:
   1 Cor 15:20, 23 (cf. Rev 1:5)
believers raised in Christ's likeness: 1 Cor 15:20, 23
early Christian converts as a promise of others:
   1 Cor 16:15; James 1:18 (cf. Rev 14:4)

FLOOD

THE GENESIS FLOOD

general: Gen 6-9

reason: Gen 6:5
preparation: Gen 6:3; 14-16; 7:1-3; Heb 11:7;
1 Pet 3:20
duration: Gen 7:24; 8:4-17
source: Gen 7:11-12
covenant never to flood again: Gen 8:21; 9:12-17
symbol of baptism: 1 Pet 3:21
likeness to Christ's return: Matt 24:38, 39;
Luke 17:27

FOLLOW (SEE DISCIPLE)

FOOL, FOOLISHNESS
EXAMPLES OF FOOLS
*fools for Christ's sake (i.e., Paul and associated
apostles in an ironic contrast to the
Corinthian church):* 1 Cor 4:10
CHARACTERISTICS OF A FOOL
denies God: Ps 14:1
rebels against God: Ps 107:17
lacks understanding: Prov 1:7; 3:35; 10:13, 21;
15:21; 18:2; Eccl 10:3
despises his mother: Prov 15:20
unfit for excellent speech: Prov 17:7
speaks perversely: Prov 19:1
is quarrelsome: Prov 20:3
trusts in his own heart: Prov 28:26
exalts himself: Prov 30:32
elicits no delight from God: Eccl 5:4
speaks nonsense: Is 32:6

FOREORDINATION (SEE PREDESTINATION)

FORGIVENESS
GOD'S FORGIVENESS OF A PERSON'S SIN
characteristic of God: Ex 34:7; Num 14:18;
Ps 86:5; Dan 9:9; Mark 2:7
CONDITIONS FOR
confession: Neh 1:6; Ps 32:5; 1 John 1:9
(cf. Prov 28:13)
forgiveness of others: Matt 6:14-15; 18:35
repentance: Mark 1:4; Luke 24:47; Acts 2:38;
3:19; 8:22 (cf. Jer 36:3; Mark 4:12)
faith in Christ: Luke 7:44-50; Acts 10:43;
13:38-39; 26:8 (cf. James 5:15)
promised (especially in the New Covenant):
Is 27:9; 33:24; Jer 31:34; Ezek 16:63;
Matt 12:31-32; John 20:23; Col 2:13
BASED ON
God's character: Ex 34:6-7; Is 55:7; Mic 7:19
Christ's death: Matt 26:28; Eph 1:7; Heb 9:22;
1 John 2:2 (cf. Acts 2:38)

offered through Christ's divine authority:
Mark 2:1-11; Luke 7:49; 23:34
included in salvation: Luke 1:77

FORNICATION (SEE ALSO ADULTERY)
divine judgment upon: Deut 22:20-21; Gal 5:19-21;
Eph 5:3-5
command to abstain from: Acts 15:20, 29; 21:25
prevention of: 1 Cor 6:18; Eph 5:3; Col 3:5;
1 Thess 4:3-4

FORSAKE (SEE ABANDON)

FREEDOM (SEE ALSO SLAVERY)
from an oath: Gen 24:8, 41; Josh 2:17
from physical slavery: Ex 6:6-7; Deut 15:12-13, 18;
Job 3:19; 1 Cor 7:21
from oppression: Is 58:6 (cf. Luke 4:18)
for prisoners: Ps 105:20; 146:7; Is 61:1; Zech 9:11
(cf. Acts 26:32)
for exiles: Is 45:13; 51:14
for captives: Is 61:1 (cf. Luke 4:18)
OF THE BELIEVER
THROUGH CERTAIN MEANS
through spiritual truth: John 8:32
through Christ: John 8:36; Rom 7:24-25; 8:2;
Gal 2:4; 5:1 (cf. 1 Cor 9:1)
through the Spirit: 2 Cor 3:17
FROM CERTAIN THINGS
from bondage to the Law: Acts 13:39;
Rom 6:14; 7:6
from bondage to sin: John 8:34-36;
Rom 6:7, 18, 22; 8:2 (cf. Rom 8:21-23)
from the law of death: Rom 8:2
from fear: Rom 8:15
from the curse of the Law: Gal 3:13-14

FRIENDSHIP
EXAMPLES OF
GOD WITH PEOPLE
with Abraham: 2 Chr 20:7; Is 41:8; James 2:23
with Moses: Ex 33:11
with Job: Job 29:4
with Israel in her youth: Jer 3:4
CHRIST WITH PEOPLE
with tax-gatherers and sinners: Matt 11:19
with a general audience: Luke 12:4
with His disciples: John 15:14-15

FRUIT (SEE FIRST FRUITS)

FUTURE (SEE END TIMES)

G

GAIN (SEE PROFIT)

GENEALOGY
examples of: Gen 5; 10-11; 35:22-26; Ex 6:14-27;
1 Chr 1:1-9:44; Ezra 8:1-14; Neh 7:5-64;
Matt 1:1-17; Luke 3:23-38

PRIMARY CHARACTERS IN BIBLICAL GENEALOGIES
from Adam to Noah: Gen 5:1-32; 1 Chr 1:1-4;
Luke 3:36-38
from Noah to Abraham: Gen 10:1-32; 11:10-32;
1 Chr 1:4-27; Luke 3:34-36
from Abraham to David: 1 Chr 1:28-2:15;
Matt 1:1-6; Luke 3:31-34
from David to Jesus: Matt 1:6-16; Luke 3:23-31
(cf. Rom 1:3)

GENERATION
RELATION OF GOD TO
His memorial-name to all generations: Ex 3:15
generation of those who seek Him: Ps 24:6
He is our dwelling place in all generations: Ps 90:1
His faithfulness is to all generations: Ps 100:5
His righteousness to all generations: Ps 106:31
*His dominion endures throughout all
   generations:* Ps 145:13
His salvation to all generations: Is 51:8
the generation of His wrath: Jer 7:29
RELATION OF CHRIST TO
fickleness of His generation: Matt 11:16-19
adulterous character of His generation:
Matt 12:39; 16:4
judgment upon His generation:
Matt 12:41-42; 23:36
wickedness of His generation: Luke 11:29
rejection by His generation: Luke 17:25

GENTILE(S) (SEE ALSO NATIONS)
GOD'S PROVISION FOR
THEIR SPIRITUAL OPPORTUNITY
*to be blessed (especially through the Abrahamic
   Covenant and the New Covenant):* Gen 12:3;
   Ps 22:27; Is 42:6; Jer 3:17; Zech 2:10; Mal 1:11;
   Matt 28:19-20; John 10:16; Rev 7:9-10
to repent and believe: Acts 11:18; (cf. 15:19; 21:25)
to be called His people: Acts 15:14, 17
   (cf. Rom 9:24; 15:10)
to have salvation available: Rom 11:11;
   1 Thess 2:16
to have Him as their God also: Rom 3:29
to glorify God for His mercy: Rom 15:9, 11

*consideration of preaching Christ's cross as
   foolishness:* 1 Cor 1:23

GENTLENESS
AS A VIRTUE
pronounced blessed by Christ: Matt 5:5
characteristic of Christ: Matt 11:29; 21:5; 2 Cor 10:1
produced by the Spirit: Gal 5:23
prescribed for Christian conduct: Eph 4:1-2;
   Titus 3:1-2
characteristic of Paul and his associates:
   1 Thess 2:7
among qualifications for an elder: 1 Tim 3:3
required in Christian witness: 1 Pet 3:15

GIFTS, SPIRITUAL
The most frequent Greek word used for the
concept of spiritual gifts is *charisma* ("grace,"
"favor," plural, *charismata*), from which the
word "charismatic" is derived. A *charisma* is an
embodiment of grace producing a gracious gift
(i.e., one freely given). In the broad sense, the
concept of spiritual gifts includes a variety of
free gifts given by God ranging from spiritual
salvation (Rom 6:23) and temporal rescue (2 Cor
1:11) to celibacy and marriage (1 Cor 7:7). In the
special or technical usage, spiritual gifts are the
particular endowments given by the Spirit to all
believers that enable them to serve others for
the building up of the church (cf. 1 Cor 12:4-7;
1 Pet 4:10).

GLORIFICATION
The term glorification is generally used in
Scripture of Jesus Christ or God's people. The
glorification of Jesus indicates the divine perfections manifested through His person and
works (John 1:14; 2:11; John 17:2). Christ's glorification was particularly revealed in "the hour"
of His suffering on the cross (John 12:23) and
in His resurrection with a transformed body
of power, glory, and immortality (1 Cor 15:43;
Phil 3:20-21; Heb 2:9; Rev 1:18). The nature of
Christ's person as the God-man and His perfect
accomplishment of redemption make Him worthy to "receive power, wealth, wisdom, might,
honor, glory, and blessing" (Rev 5:12 cf. v. 13;
Phil 2:9-11; 1 Pet 2:9). The glorification of God's
people refers specifically to the changed body
that both dead and living believers "in Christ"
receive at His return (Rom 8:23; 1 Cor 15:51-57;
Phil 3:20-21; 1 Thess 4:16-17; 1 John 3:1-2). Glorification is the final stage of personal salvation

and accomplishes God's purpose to conform each believer to Christ's image as perfected humanity (Rom 8:29).

GLORIFYING GOD (SEE PRAISE)

GLORY OF GOD

The terms for glory in both the OT and NT (Heb. *kabod* and Gr. *doxa*) are used of the honor and praise due a person of worthy reputation because of position, power, and riches. Such glory ultimately belongs only to God since He alone is worthy (Is 42:8; Rev 4:11; 5:12-13; cf. Jer 9:23-24). God's unique glory is particularly manifested in radiant splendor and majesty through His perfect attributes and His mighty acts of creation and redemption (Ps 19:1; Mic 6:3-5; Luke 2:9; Rom 6:4; Col 1:11). Although no human has seen God's uncovered essence or full heavenly glory (Ex 33:20; John 1:18; 1 Tim 6:16), the divine glory is revealed to humanity in veiled form through the incarnate Son (John 1:14, 18; 17:4; cf. John 14:9; Heb 1:3) and shown to believers by the Spirit (John 16:14). The creation can reflect God's glory in inanimate form (Ps 19:1; Rom 1:20) as well as in animate form (Ps 150:6; Rev 4:11; 5:12-13). Humans in their present earthly state continually fall short of God's glory (Rom 3:23). However, God's glory is manifested to a degree through His people (Is 43:7; 1 Cor 6:19-20; cf. Ps 50:23; Matt 5:16; 1 Cor 10:31; 2 Cor 8:23; Phil 2:15).

DISPLAYED

in divine provision: Ex 16:7, 14-17
in the cloud: Ex 16:10; 24:16
in likeness of consuming fire: Ex 24:17
to Moses privately: Ex 33:22
in the tabernacle: Ex 40:34-35; Num 14:10 (cf. Ex 29:43)
to all Israel: Lev 9:6, 23; 16:19; Deut 5:24
in the whole earth: Num 14:21; Ps 72:19; Is 6:3; Hab 2:14; Rev 18:1
in Egypt and the wilderness: Num 14:22
to Moses and Aaron: Num 20:6
in the temple: 1 Kin 8:11 (cf. 2 Chr 7:3); Heb 9:5; Rev 15:8
in the sanctuary: Ps 63:2
in divine majesty: Ps 145:5
in Christ's earthly reign: Is 24:23; 35:2
in divine judgment: Ezek 28:22
in the midst of Jerusalem: Zech 2:5
in the appearance of angels: Luke 2:9
to faith: John 11:40
in the heavenly Jerusalem: Rev 21:10-11, 23

vision of: Ezek 1:28; 3:12, 23; 8:4; 9:3; 10:4, 18, 19; 11:22, 23; 43:2, 4, 5; 44:4; John 12:41; Acts 7:55

GOD (SEE ALSO LORD)

The various forms of the OT term for God most likely connote the meaning "mighty One" (see below, GOD, names of). "God" is used (1) of the true God (Jer 10:10; 1 John 5:20), (2) of heathen gods in the OT (Gen 35:2; Ex 12:12) and in the NT (1 Cor 8:5; Gal 4:8), and (3) of "the mighty" in the OT with reference to men or angels (e.g., Ps 8:5, & note; cf. Heb 2:7; Ps 82:6; 97:7; Ezek 32:21). Particular usage is almost invariably clear from the biblical context. In a doctrinal sense, God is a perfect and personal spirit who is infinite, eternal, and unchangeable in His being and attributes (Deut 32:4; Ps 145:17; 147:5; John 4:24; 1 Tim 6:15-16). He is unique as the "living and true God" (1 Thess 1:9; cf. Jer 10:10; John 17:3; Acts 14:15) who alone is the transcendent Creator and Governor of the universe and humanity (Gen 1-2; Deut 32:39-40; Is 45:5-7, 9-13, 18-22; Rev 4:1-5:14). His personality, perfect attributes, and dynamic activity absolutely contrast Him with all unscriptural conceptions of deity, particularly man-made idols that are dead, unable to speak, and impotent (Deut 4:28; Is 46:1-11; John 5:17; Acts 17:24-29). He has revealed Himself through natural evidences (Rom 1:19-20; 2:15) and primarily through Scripture and through His Son, in whom He has also provided redemption for people (Rom 3:21-26; Heb 1:1-3; 2 Tim 3:15-17; cf. John 1:14; 14:9). The general name "God" is often joined with His personal name "LORD" (e.g., Gen 2:4-5; Ex 34:23; Ps 68:18).

NAMES OF (SEE ALSO I AM)

God (Heb. el, elah, eloah, or elohim; Gr. theos): Gen 1:1; Matt 16:16
God Most High: Gen 14:18-20, 22; (cf. Luke 10:21)
God Almighty: Gen 17:1
God of armies: 1 Kin 19:10, 14
Everlasting God: Gen 21:33
the God of Israel: Judg 5:3
the God of Abraham, and the God of Isaac, and the God of Jacob: Ex 3:6; Matt 22:32
the Almighty, Mighty God, or the Mighty One: Gen 49:24; Ps 50:1; Rev 15:3
the living God: Deut 5:26; Heb 10:31
Judge: Gen 18:25; Heb 12:23
Jealous: Ex 34:14; 1 Cor 10:22
the Glory of Israel: 1 Sam 15:29

Savior: Is 60:16; Luke 1:47
the God of heaven: Ezra 5:11
Holy One of Israel: 2 Kin 19:22
Holy One: Job 6:10 (cf. 1 John 2:20)
the Ancient of Days: Dan 7:9, 13, 22
King of kings: 1 Tim 6:15 (cf. Deut 10:17)
the Majesty: Heb 8:1 (cf. Job 37:22)
trinity of (see also TRINITY)

FATHERHOOD OF
general: 2 Sam 7:14; Matt 11:25-27; Luke 11:13;
    John 4:21, 23; 5:45; Acts 1:4, 7; 2:33; Rom 6:4;
    Phil 2:11; James 1:27; 1 John 2:15-16
in relation to the Son: Ps 2:7; Is 9:6; Matt 10:32-33;
    Mark 14:36; Luke 23:34, 46; John 1:14, 18;
    Rom 8:32; 2 Cor 1:3; Gal 1:1; Col 3:17; Heb 1:6;
    1 Pet 1:3; 2 Pet 1:17; 1 John 1:2; 2 John 3;
    Rev 2:27; 3:5
in relation to Israel: Deut 32:6; Is 63:16; Jer 3:19;
    Mal 1:6 (cf. Ex 4:22;
in relation to NT believers: Matt 5:16, 45; Luke 12:32;
    John 12:26; Rom 8:15; 2 Cor 6:18; Gal 1:3; 4:6;
    Eph 2:18; Col 1:12; 1 Thess 1:1; James 3:9;
    1 Pet 1:2, 17; 1 John 1:3; 2:1, 13; ; Rev 1:6

**ATTRIBUTES OF (SEE ALSO GOD,
NAMES OF)**
eternal: Gen 21:33; Ps 90:2; Is 26:4; Dan 4:34;
    Jer 10:10; Mic 5:2; Hab 1:12; John 8:58;
    Rom 1:20; 1 Tim 1:17; Rev 1:8
personal: Ex 3:13-15; 6:3; Is 42:8; Matt 5:45;
    Acts 17:29
intellect: Deut 34:10; Ps 139:1-6; 1 Cor 2:11
will: Gen 3:15; Ps 33:6-11; John 6:40; Eph 1:11;
    Rev 4:11
emotion: Ex 34:6; Ps 103:8-13; Is 63:9;
    John 3:16
infinite: 1 Kin 8:27; Ps 90:1-2; Jer 23:24;
    Matt 28:18, 20; Jude 25; Rev 1:8
spiritual: John 4:24 (cf. Deut 4:12, 15-18; Is 31:3)
invisible: Ex 20:21; Job 9:11; 23:8-9; John 1:18;
    Rom 1:20; Col 1:15; 1 Tim 1:17; 6:16; Heb 11:27;
    1 John 4:12
*self-existent (and self-sufficient; see also GOD,
    names of, living God):* Ex 3:14; Ps 36:9; Is 44:6;
    John 5:26; Acts 17:25
eternal: Ex 15:18; Ps 29:10; Is 14:27; Dan 6:26;
    Mal 3:6; Matt 6:13; Eph 3:11 (cf. Rom 9:19)
immutable (i.e., unchanging): Num 23:19;
    1 Sam 15:29; Job 23:13; Is 31:2; Mal 3:6;
    Rom 11:29; Heb 1:12; James 1:17

OMNISCIENT (I.E., GOD IS ALL KNOWING)
concerning things: Job 36:4-5; Ps 147:5;
    Is 40:28; 44:7; 46:10; John 16:30;
    Rom 11:33-34

concerning humans: 1 Chr 28:9; Job 34:21;
    Ps 139:1-6; Jer 23:10; Ezek 11:5; Matt 12:25;
    John 2:24-25; Acts 1:24; Rom 8:27; 1 Cor 8:3;
    Heb 4:13; 1 John 3:20; Rev 2:23
*omnipotent (i.e., God is all powerful; see also GOD,
    names of; POWER, of God):* Gen 17:1; 18:14;
    Job 42:2; Jer 32:17, 27; Matt 19:26; Luke 1:37;
    Rev 19:6; 21:22 (cf. Gen 1-2; Ex 9:16; 1 Chr 29:12;
    Job 37:23; Ps 106:8; 139:13-16; Is 40:12-26;
    Jer 10:12; Dan 2:20; 1 Cor 6:14; Eph 1:19-21;
    Rev 19:1)
omnipresent (i.e., God is everywhere present):
    1 Kin 8:27; Job 26:5-6; Ps 139:7-12; Acts 17:27;
    Eph 1:23; Heb 13:5; James 4:8
immanent: Jer 9:23-24; Acts 2:25; 17:27-28
transcendent: Job 31:28; Ps 113:5-6; Is 6:1-3;
    55:8-9; 57:15; John 8:23

GODLESS (SEE SIN)

GODLINESS
a life led in: 1 Tim 2:2
claim to: 1 Tim 2:10
purpose of: 2 Tim 4:7
profitability of: 2 Tim 4:8
doctrine conforming to: 1 Tim 6:3
as a means of gain: 1 Tim 6:5-6
pursuit of: 1 Tim 6:11
form of: 2 Tim 3:5
things that pertain to: 2 Pet 1:3
Christian virtue of: 2 Pet 1:6-7

GODS, FALSE
removal of: Gen 35:2-4; 2 Chr 33:15
various names and nations associated with:
    Ex 12:12; Judg 10:6; 2 Sam 7:23; 2 Chr 25:14, 20;
    Jer 43:12-13; Amos 5:26; Acts 14:11-13
divine judgment against: Ex 12:12; 1 Sam 6:5
compared to the true God: Ex 15:11; 2 Chr 2:5;
    Ps 86:8; 95:3; Dan 2:47; Zeph 2:11; Acts 14:15;
    17:24-29

PROHIBITION AGAINST
worship of: Ex 20:3; 23:24; Deut 6:14
manufacture of: Ex 20:23; Lev 19:4
mention of the names of: Ex 23:13
making a covenant with: Ex 23:32
service to: Ex 23:33
prostitute themselves with: Ex 34:15
sacrifice to: Ex 34:15
inquiring concerning: Deut 12:30
following enticement to go after: Deut 13:6-15
speaking in the name of: Deut 18:20
fear of: 2 Kin 17:35

GOLDEN RULE

The so-called "golden rule" is an ethical principle that you should "do unto others as you would have them do unto you." The biblical basis for this principle is stated by Jesus Himself: "In everything, therefore, treat people the same way you want them to treat you, for this is the Law and the Prophets" (Matt 7:12; cf. Luke 6:31). Such conduct correlates closely with the second great commandment: "You shall love your neighbor as yourself" (Matt 22:39), which in turn summarizes the second part of the Decalogue (Ex 20:12-17; cf. Rom 13:8-10; Gal 5:13-14). Practice of the golden rule and neighborly love are wonderfully illustrated in the parable of the good Samaritan (Luke 10:25-37).

GOOD, GOODNESS

USED OF GOD

to Israel: Ex 18:9; 1 Kin 8:66; Ps 73:1; Is 63:7; Jer 24:6; 33:11; Zech 8:15
in Himself: Ex 33:19; 1 Chr 16:34
accepted from God: Job 2:10
experienced in life: Ps 23:6; 34:8
greatness of: Ps 31:19
in provision for the poor: Ps 68:10
people satisfied with: Ps 104:28; Prov 12:14; Jer 31:14
abundance of: Ps 145:7
Israel's response to: Hos 3:5
toward all people: Acts 14:17 (cf. Matt 5:45)

USED OF JESUS

as good Teacher: Mark 10:17-18
as a good man: John 7:12
as the good shepherd: John 10:11, 14

RESPONSE TO WHAT IS GOOD

RIGHT RESPONSE

rejoice in: 2 Chr 6:41
cling to: Rom 12:9; 1 Thess 5:21
be wise in: Rom 16:19
seek for: 1 Thess 5:15
love for: Titus 1:8
zealous for: 1 Pet 3:13

DOING GOOD

in relation to God: 2 Chr 31:20; Ps 37:3; 3 John 11
to other humans: Gen 26:29; 1 Sam 24:18; Esth 10:3; Prov 3:27; Luke 6:33; Rom 13:4; 15:2
reward for: 1 Sam 24:19; Prov 14:22; Rom 2:7; Eph 6:7-8
lacking in people (i.e., in terms of God's standard): Ps 14:1, 3; Rom 3:12; 7:18-19
in giving thanks and praise to God: Ps 92:1; 147:1
learning of: Is 1:17

lack of knowledge of: Jer 4:22
on the Sabbath: Matt 12:12
for the poor: Mark 14:7
by Jesus: Acts 10:38
not growing weary of: 2 Thess 3:13
encouragement to: 1 Tim 6:18

GOSPEL

The Christian gospel is the good news of God's salvation for people provided through Christ's substitutionary death and bodily resurrection (Rom 1:16-17; 1 Cor 15:3-4; Eph 1:13). The gospel of salvation originates in God's sovereign grace and is experienced only through personal faith in Jesus Christ (John 3:16; 20:31; Acts 16:31; Rom 3:22-26; Eph 2:8-9).

DESCRIPTIVE TITLES

gospel of the kingdom: Matt 4:23; 9:35
gospel of God: Mark 1:14; Rom 1:1; 2 Cor 11:7
gospel of Jesus Christ (or of His Son, of Christ, or of our LORD Jesus): Mark 1:1; Rom 1:9
gospel of the grace of God: Acts 20:24
gospel of Paul (i.e., the divine gospel which Paul preached): Rom 2:16; 16:25
gospel of your salvation: Eph 1:13
gospel of peace: Eph 6:15
an eternal gospel: Rev 14:6

GOSSIP

avoidance of: Prov 20:19; 1 Tim 3:11; 5:13; Titus 2:3 (cf. 2 Cor 12:20)
people characterized by (i.e., gossips): Rom 1:29; 2 Tim 3:3

GOVERNMENT (SEE AUTHORITY; KINGDOM)

GRACE

The term grace or favor (Heb. *chen*; Gr. *charis*) is used in Scripture generally to indicate God's free and unmerited favor toward people, particularly His redeemed people (Rom 3:24-26; Eph 2:8-9). God's grace includes both His attitude and action of love, mercy, and kindness for undeserving people (John 3:16; Rom 5:6-10; Eph 2:4-9; Titus 3:4-5). The sacrifice of Christ is the fullest revelation of divine grace (John 1:14, 16-17; 2 Cor 8:9). The believer experiences God's grace in many varied areas (cf. 1 Pet 4:10, "multifaceted grace of God") such as salvation (Eph 2:8-9), sanctification (Rom 6:14, 19, 22), service (2 Cor 9:8), and suffering (2 Cor 12:9). Grace or favor is

sometimes used in Scripture of relationships between people (Gen 33:8; Ruth 2:10; Prov 14:35; Dan 1:9; Acts 24:27). God's people are divinely enabled to express genuine grace to others (Eph 4:29; Col 4:6).

GUEST (SEE HOSPITALITY)

GUILT
CAUSE OF GUILT
specific personal sins: Gen 26:10; Lev 5:1-5; Num 15:31; 35:31; 2 Chr 24:18; Ps 5:9-10; Hos 10:2; Matt 5:22; 1 Cor 11:27; James 2:10
ceremonial defilement: Ex 28:43; Lev 14:1-32; 17:15-16
unintentional sins: Lev 5:17
original sin: Ps 51:5
an eternal sin: Mark 3:29
imputed sin (i.e., through Adam): Rom 5:12-19
CONVICTION OF GUILT
through Christ's personal revelation: John 15:22-24
through the Spirit: John 16:7-11
through the Law: Rom 3:20; James 2:10
through Scripture: Gal 3:22; Heb 4:12
punishment for guilt (see also PUNISHMENT): Ex 34:7; Lev 5:17; Num 14:34-35; Deut 25:2; Ps 68:21; 109:7; Rom 1:32; 6:23
CURE FOR GUILT
the guilt or sin offering for an atonement: Lev 4:3; 5:6; Ezek 40:39
confession (see also CONFESSION): Lev 5:5; Num 5:7; Ps 19:12; 32:5; Jer 3:13; Hos 5:15; 1 John 1:9
forgiveness of sin (see also FORGIVENESS): Lev 5:10; Deut 21:8-9; Ps 32:1-2; Heb 10:22
cleansing: Lev 14:19; Ps 51:2, 7, 10; Eph 1:7; 1 John 1:7
justification and no condemnation through faith in Christ: Acts 13:38-39; Rom 5:1; 8:1
Christ's sacrifice as a guilt-offering: Is 53:10

H

HADES
Hades is the NT equivalent to the OT Sheol (see SHEOL). Sheol is used for the dwelling place of all dead (e.g., Acts 2:27, 31; cf. Rev 6:8; 20:13), and all the dead can be viewed as in the underworld (Luke 16:23, 26). But only the wicked dead are said to be in Hades (cf. Luke 16:23), and it is now more explicitly a place of punishment.

Because of the resurrection of Christ, the righteous are in "Paradise" (Luke 23:43), with Christ (Phil 1:23; 2 Cor 5:8), and in the "heavenly Jerusalem" (Heb 12:22).

HANDS, LAYING ON
to ordain certain persons: Num 8:10-11; Acts 6:6; 13:3
to convey authority and commission: Num 27:18-23; Deut 34:9
to convey the Spirit by apostolic authority: Acts 8:17-19; 9:17; 19:6
to bestow a spiritual gift: 1 Tim 4:14; 2 Tim 1:6

HAPPINESS (SEE ALSO JOY)
REQUIREMENTS FOR
obey God's word: Prov 29:18
practice godly living: Ps 128:1-2
cling to godly wisdom: Prov 3:13-18
be gracious to the poor: Prov 14:21

HEALING (SEE ALSO MIRACLES)
DIVINE
God's unique power of: Ex 15:26; Deut 32:39; Job 5:18; Acts 4:30
request for: Num 12:13; Ps 6:2; Matt 8:5-6; John 4:47, 49
promise of: 2 Kin 20:5-6; James 5:14-15
in a spiritual sense: Ps 41:4; Is 53:5; Jer 3:22; 17:14; Heb 12:13; 1 Pet 2:24
of Israel's people: 2 Chr 30:20; Ps 30:12; 107:20; Jer 30:17; Hos 14:4; Matt 13:14-15
Christ's disciples delegated authority for: Matt 10:1
CONDITIONS FOR
prayer: Num 12:10-15; Mark 9:29; James 5:14-16
repentance: 2 Chr 7:14; Jer 15:18-19
fear of the LORD: Prov 3:7-8; Mal 4:2
faith: Matt 15:28 (cf. 13:58); Mark 5:34; 9:17-23; James 5:15
a right path of life: Heb 12:13
confession of sin: James 5:16

HEALTH (SEE HEALING)

HEART
CENTER OF HUMAN PERSON (FIGURATIVE)
general: Job 15:12; Prov 4:23; 27:19; Matt 15:18-19; Luke 6:45; 2 Cor 5:12
seat of thought: Gen 6:5; 1 Sam 1:13; Job 22:22; Ps 4:4; 19:14; Prov 2:2, 10; Eccl 7:2; Mark 2:8; Luke 2:19, 51; Rom 10:6, 9

seat of willing, choosing, desiring: Gen 6:5; Ex 35:5;
 Josh 24:23; Job 17:11; Ps 21:2; 37:4; Jer 23:20;
 Rom 10:1; Eph 6:6

SEAT OF EMOTIONS

anger: 2 Sam 6:16; 1 Chr 15:29; Is 63:4
anxiety: Prov 12:25
burning: Ps 39:3; Jer 20:9; Luke 24:32
compassion: Col 3:12
contrite: Ps 51:17
courageous: 2 Sam 17:10; Ps 27:14; 31:24
discouragement: Ps 34:18; 61:1; 69:20; 147:3;
 Is 61:1; Gal 6:9; Eph 3:13; Heb 12:3
encouragement: Col 2:2; Heb 13:9
fear: Deut 28:67; Josh 2:11; 5:1; Job 37:1
joy, gladness, delight: Ex 4:14; Deut 28:47;
 Ps 16:9; Prov 15:13, 15; Eccl 2:10; 7:3;
 Is 65:14; Eph 5:19
love: Deut 6:5; Matt 22:37; 1 Tim 1:5; 1 Pet 1:22
sorrow: 1 Sam 1:8; Neh 2:2; Prov 15:13;
 Is 65:14; Lam 2:11; John 16:6; Rom 9:2
troubled: Deut 28:65; Ps 25:17; Prov 14:10;
 Jer 4:19; John 14:1, 27

HEATHEN (SEE GENTILES; NATIONS)

HEAVEN(S)

IN RELATION TO GOD

His creation of: Gen 1:1; 2:4; Ps 33:6; Acts 14:15;
 2 Pet 3:5; Rev 10:6; 14:7
His possession of: Gen 14:19
His habitation in heaven: Deut 26:15; Job 22:12;
 Is 63:15; Matt 5:48; Eph 6:9
His immensity and omnipresence: 1 Kin 8:27;
 Ps 139:8

HIS TITLES

"God of heaven": 2 Chr 36:23; Ps 136:26;
 Dan 2:18; Rev 11:13
"King of heaven": Dan 4:37
"LORD of heaven": Dan 5:23; Matt 11:25

IN RELATION TO CHRIST

He proclaimed the kingdom of heaven: Matt 4:17
He acknowledged the Father in heaven: Matt 5:16
He taught parables about the kingdom of
 heaven: Matt 13:11
He prayed toward heaven: Matt 14:19; John 17:1
He possesses all authority in heaven: Matt 28:18
He ascended into heaven: Mark 16:19; Acts 1:11
 (cf. Eph 4:10)
He is in heaven at God's right hand: Acts 7:55;
 Col 3:1; 1 Pet 3:22
He will sum up all things in the heavens: Eph 1:10
by Him all things in the heavens were created:
 Col 1:16

He will reconcile things in heaven: Col 1:20
He will return from heaven: 1 Thess 1:10; 4:16;
 2 Thess 1:7

IN RELATION TO THE SPIRIT

He descended from heaven upon Christ:
 John 1:32
He was sent from heaven: 1 Pet 1:12
kingdom of (see also KINGDOM): Matt 3:2; 4:17
entrance into: Matt 18:3-4; 1 Cor 15:50-54
the new heaven(s): Is 65:17; 2 Pet 3:13; Rev 21:1

HEIR (SEE INHERITANCE)

HELL (SEE ALSO HADES)

The term hell is commonly associated with the
place of punishment for the wicked dead. It
is variously used in different English versions
of the Bible to translate Sheol in the OT and
Gehenna and Tartarus in the NT. The NASB
uses "hell" only in the NT, for Gehenna and
Tartarus. Since the wicked experience punishment (i.e., chastisement) already before
the resurrection and final judgment (cf. Luke
16:23-28), "hell" can be used to describe this
intermediate state. The primary significance of
the term, however, is the place of eternal punishment. A variety of expressions are used, all
designed to depict the agony and destruction
of existence separated and cut off from God,
the source of life.

HIGH PLACES

FOR IDOLATROUS RELIGION

divine displeasure with: 1 Kin 11:5-10; Ps 78:58

DESTRUCTION OF

as divine judgment: Lev 26:30; Jer 48:35
divinely commanded to Israel: Num 33:52
failure in: 1 Kin 15:14
performed by certain reformers: 2 Kin 18:4;
 23:8; 2 Chr 31:1

HOLINESS (SEE ALSO HOLY; SANCTIFICATION)

OF GOD

RELATIONSHIP TO

His habitation: Ex 15:13; Deut 26:15; 2 Chr 30:27
His treatment: Lev 10:3; Num 20:12; 27:14
His character: Lev 11:44-45; 19:2; Ps 22:3;
 99:3, 9; John 17:11; Rev 4:8; 6:10; 15:4
His name: Lev 20:3; 1 Chr 16:10; Ps 33:21;
 Ezek 39:7; Luke 1:49
His way: Ps 77:13
His arm: Ps 98:1; Is 52:10

His word: Ps 105:42; Jer 23:9
of Christ (see also CHRIST, characteristics of, holy)
of the Spirit (see also SPIRIT, HOLY)

VARIOUS OTHER USES
consecration in holiness: 2 Chr 31:18
holiness appropriate to God's house: Ps 93:5
Highway of holiness: Is 35:8
spirit of holiness: Rom 1:4
conduct in holiness: 2 Cor 1:12
perfecting in holiness: 2 Cor 7:1
creation of the new self in holiness: Eph 4:24
unblamable in holiness
MODES OF: 1 Thess 3:13

HOLY (SEE ALSO GOD, NAMES OF; HOLINESS; SANCTIFICATION)

exhortation to be holy: Lev 11:44-45; 19:2
  (cf. 1 Pet 1:15-16)
privileges of: Ps 16:3; 149:9; Rom 16:15; 2 Cor 8:4;
  Eph 1:18; Col 1:12, 26; Jude 3; Rev 20:9
responsibilities of: Ps 31:23; 34:9; 50:5; 145:10;
  Rom 16:2; 1 Cor 6:1-3; 2 Cor 8:4; Eph 5:3;
  6:18; Jude 3; Rev 5:8
persecution of: Dan 7:21, 25; Acts 9:13; 26:10;
  Rev 13:7; 16:6; 17:6; 18:24; 20:9
resurrection of (see also RESURRECTION):
  Matt 27:52
ministry related to: Rom 12:13; 1 Cor 16:1, 15;
  2 Cor 9:1; Eph 1:15; Col 1:4; 1 Tim 5:10;
  Philem 5, 7; Rev 8:3, 4
churches of: 1 Cor 14:33
spiritual qualities of: Rev 13:10; 19:8

HOLY SPIRIT (SEE SPIRIT, HOLY)

HOMICIDE (SEE ALSO DEATH; SUICIDE)

divine prohibition against: Ex 20:13; Prov 1:15-16;
  Jer 22:3; Matt 5:21; Rom 13:9; 1 Tim 1:9;
  James 2:11; 1 Pet 4:15

UNINTENTIONAL
provision for: Ex 21:13; Num 35:9-15; Josh 20:1-9
  (cf. Deut 17:8)

HOPE

character of: Rom 4:18-21; 8:24-25

OBJECT OF
God: Ps 31:24; 38:15; Jer 14:22; Acts 24:15;
  Rom 15:12; 1 Pet 1:21; 3:5
God's word: Ps 130:5
Christ's name: Matt 12:21
Moses: John 5:45
Christ: Rom 15:12; 1 Cor 15:19; Eph 1:12

SOURCE OF
from the Lord: Ps 62:5; Rom 15:13
from the Scriptures: Rom 15:4
from the Spirit: Rom 15:13
from God's calling: Eph 1:18; 4:4
from God's mercy through the resurrection of
  Christ: 1 Pet 1:3

HOSPITALITY

DIVINELY COMMANDED
in general: Is 58:6-7; Rom 12:13; 3 John 5-8
  (cf. Matt 25:34-40)
to strangers: Heb 13:2
to one another by believers: 1 Pet 4:9

AS A QUALIFICATION
for elders: 1 Tim 3:2; Titus 1:8
for widows worthy of support: 1 Tim 5:10
reward of: Gen 18:1-8 (cf. Heb 13:2); Josh 6:17,
  22-25; 1 Kin 17:8-24; Heb 13:2

HUMANITY

created by God: Gen 1:26-27; 2:7, 21-22; Job 4:17;
  10:3, 8; Ps 95:6; 100:3; Prov 14:31; 22:2;
  Eccl 7:29; Is 17:7; 45:12; Jer 27:5; Matt 19:4

PURPOSE OF
for God's glory: Is 43:7; Eph 1:12; Rev 4:11
for fellowship with God: Eccl 12:13; Hos 6:8
to rule creation: Gen 1:26, 28; 2:5; Ps 8:6-8;
  49:14; Heb 2:7

HUMILITY

REQUIREMENT OF
on the Day of Atonement: Lev 16:29
for answered prayer: 2 Chr 7:14; 33:12-13;
  Ezra 8:21; Ps 10:17; Dan 10:12
for exaltation by God: Job 5:11; Matt 23:12;
  Luke 1:52; James 4:10
for salvation: Job 22:29; Ps 76:9; 1 Cor 1:26-29
for honor: Prov 15:33
in one's walk with God: Mic 6:8
for kingdom greatness: Matt 18:4
in service to the Lord: Acts 20:19
in relationships to others: Eph 4:2; Phil 2:3;
  1 Pet 5:5
in Christian character: Col 3:12
in reception of God's word: James 1:21
in receiving God's grace: James 4:6
to obey God: James 4:10
reward of: 2 Chr 12:7, 12; Ps 25:9; 34:2; 37:11;
  Prov 11:2; 22:4; 29:23; Zeph 3:12

OPPOSITES OF
pride: Dan 4:37; 1 Pet 5:5
boasting: 1 Cor 1:29

HUSBAND (SEE MARRIAGE)

I

I AM (SEE ALSO GOD, NAMES OF)

The name I AM was first revealed to Moses, when the LORD said, "I AM WHO I AM" (Ex 3:14). Here it signifies that the LORD is "actively present." God's personal name LORD (i.e., Heb. *Yahweh*) is evidently derived from the verbal form "I AM," and it was to be the name by which Israel knew, remembered, and worshiped the LORD of Abraham, Isaac, and Jacob (Ex 3:15; cf. 6:2-3). I AM also reveals the LORD's eternal and self-sufficient existence and His covenant faithfulness to be with His people (Ex 3:12) and sustain them in response to their trust in Him. Jesus applied the title I AM to Himself (John 8:58; cf. 8:24, 28). Thereby He clearly claimed identity with the LORD of Israel (cf. Ex 3:14) and elicited the attempt of the Jewish opposers to stone Him because of alleged blasphemy (John 8:58 cf. 5:18; 10:30, 31, 39). Jesus' claim of this title is also implied in other statements (e.g., John 8:12).

OT usage: Ex 3:14

NT usage (applied to Christ): John 8:58
(cf. vv. 24, 28); see also John 6:35, 41, 48, 51; 8:12; 9:5; 10:7, 9, 11, 14; 11:25; 13:13, 19; 14:6; 15:1, 5; Rev 1:8, 17, 18; 21:6; 22:13

IDOLS, IDOLATRY (SEE GODS, FALSE)

PRIMARY DESIGNATIONS OF
household idols: Gen 31:19; Judg 18:14-20; Ezek 21:21; 1 Sam 9:13
a cast metal calf of gold: Ex 32:4-8;
1 Kin 12:28
Chemosh: 1 Kin 11:7
Baals: 2 Kin 10:18-28; Hos 11:2
the bronze serpent: 2 Kin 18:4
Asherim: 2 Chr 24:18
idols of Canaan: Ps 106:38
idols of Egypt: Is 19:1
Artemis: Acts 19:24, 27-28

DESCRIPTION OF
silver or gold: Ex 32:4, 8; Deut 29:17
wood: Deut 29:17; Jer 10:8
stone: Deut 29:17
detestable: 1 Kin 11:5
man-made: Ps 115:4; Is 40:18-19
speechless: Ps 115:5, 7; 1 Cor 12:2
without sensory perception: Ps 115:5-7
immobile: Is 45:20

cannot save: Is 45:20
helpless: Is 46:1-2
unreal: 1 Cor 8:4 (cf. 10:19)

PROPER RESPONSE TO
do not turn to: Lev 19:4
dispose of: 2 Sam 5:21
repent of: Ezek 14:6
abstain from things associated with:
Acts 15:20, 29
guard oneself from: 1 John 5:21

IMAGE (SEE IDOLS)

IMAGE OF GOD

The biblical words for image signify a "copy" or "representation." The additional term, "likeness," is used in the description of humanity: "in Our image, according to Our likeness" (Gen 1:26). Here "likeness" serves as a complementary term to indicate that humanity as the image of God actually bears a likeness to Him. The meaning of the image with respect to humanity is generally seen in the unique "glory and majesty" with which God has crowned human beings in comparison with all other creatures (Ps 8:5). This distinction is seen first and foremost in a personal relationship with God in which there is both fellowship and responsibility. This entails humanity as God's representative ruler over all creation (Gen 1:26-28). In addition, most interpreters would include the endowment of the characteristics of personality as aspects of the image of God in human beings. These characteristics include self-conscious rationality, the freedom of self-determination, and a social nature. Fallen humanity is still described as the image of God (e.g., Gen 9:6). However, since Scripture teaches the restoration of the image in Christ, it is evident that the image has been damaged through sin.

The use of "image of God" with respect to Christ (e.g., Col 1:15) has two applications. In his humanity Christ is the perfect human image of God that was originally intended for all humanity and to which believers in Him will finally be conformed. However, as God in human flesh, Christ is also the "image of God" in a way that transcends the human meaning. Because of his divine nature He is the full and complete image or representation of God (see CHRIST).

IMMORALITY (SEE ADULTERY)

IMMORTALITY

sought for: Rom 2:7
characteristic of the glorified body: 1 Cor 15:53-54
uniquely inherent in God: 1 Tim 1:17; 6:16
provided by Christ through the gospel: 2 Tim 1:10

INCARNATION OF JESUS CHRIST (SEE ALSO CHRIST)

The term incarnation means "in flesh." In doctrinal usage it refers to the divine Son coming from heaven to earth to assume a true human nature through the virgin birth (John 1:14, "the Word became flesh"; cf. 6:51; 16:28). Through the incarnation the divine nature and the human nature Christ became inseparably united and yet distinct in His one person.

INCENSE

altar of: Ex 30:1-10; 40:5; Luke 1:11
prohibition concerning strange incense: Ex 30:9
   (cf. Lev 10:1-2); Num 16:35-40
ingredients of proper incense: Ex 30:34-38
representative of prayer: Ps 141:2; Rev 5:8
   (cf. Luke 1:10); Rev 8:3-4

INCREASE (INCLUDES ALSO GROWTH)

AREAS OF INCREASE

in riches and possessions: Gen 26:13-14; Ps 62:10;
   Prov 28:8
in crop yield: Lev 19:25; Ezek 34:27; Mark 4:8
of domesticated herds: Deut 7:13
in strength for those with clean hands: Job 17:9
of divine blessing: Ps 115:14
of sin: Prov 29:16; Matt 24:12; Rom 5:20
in wisdom: Eccl 1:16; Luke 2:52
in knowledge: Eccl 1:18; Dan 12:4; Col 1:10
of gladness: Is 9:3; 29:19
of Messiah's government and peace: Is 9:7
in faith: Luke 17:5; Rom 4:20; 2 Cor 10:15
in the ministry of God's word: Acts 12:24; 19:20
of grace: Rom 6:1
of the gospel: Col 1:5-6
in spiritual maturity: 1 Pet 2:2
in spiritual qualities: 2 Pet 1:8
in grace and knowledge of Christ: 2 Pet 3:18

INFIDELITY (SEE UNFAITHFULNESS)

INHERITANCE

BY ISRAEL
AS A NATION
   *the land promised to Abraham and his
     descendants:* Gen 12:7; 15:18-21

   future restoration to the land: Jer 23:3-8;
     Ezek 34:11-13

BY NT BELIEVERS
assurance of their inheritance: Acts 20:32;
   Rom 8:16-17

MEANS OF THEIR INHERITANCE
   through spiritual sonship: Rom 8:16-17;
     Gal 4:4-7 (cf. John 1:12-13)
   through faith and patience: Heb 6:12

NATURE OF THEIR INHERITANCE
   the earth: Matt 5:5 (cf. Ps 37:11, 22)
   eternal life: Matt 19:29; Titus 3:7
   the kingdom: Matt 25:34; 1 Cor 6:9; 15:50
   an inheritance pledged by the Spirit: Eph 1:13-14
   salvation: Heb 1:14
   the divine promises: Heb 6:12

INSPIRATION

OF SCRIPTURE (SEE ALSO REVELATION, SPECIAL REVELATION)
DIVINE ORIGIN OF
   *Scripture as the word of God (see also WORD
     OF GOD):* Ex 19:7-8; Deut 18:18; Ezek 33:1-2;
     Amos 2:6; Rev 1:2
   Scripture as the work of God: Matt 1:22;
     2 Tim 3:16
   Scripture as God's word written: Ex 17:14;
     Matt 4:4; 1 Cor 1:31
   role of the Spirit in: 2 Sam 23:2 (cf. Matt 22:43;
     Acts 4:25); Heb 3:7; 1 Pet 1:10-11; 2 Pet 1:21
   human agency in: Ex 17:14; Matt 1:22;
     Acts 28:25; 1 Pet 1:21

METHOD OF (SEE ALSO REVELATION, SPECIAL REVELATION, MODES OF, FORMS OF)
   *through God's words conveyed to His
     messengers:* Deut 18:18-19; Jer 1:9;
     1 Thess 2:13
   *through an inward divine working in the
     writer:* Jer 20:9; 2 Pet 1:20-21
   through accounts from eyewitnesses: Luke 1:2;
     Acts 1:3; 2 Pet 1:16-17

RESULTANT AUTHORITY OF
   truthful: 2 Sam 7:28; John 17:17
   unchangeable: Ps 119:89
   eternally enduring: Is 40:8; Matt 24:35
   effective and powerful: Is 55:11; Jer 23:29;
     1 Thess 2:13; Heb 4:12
   unfailing in fulfillment: Matt 5:18
   life-changing: 2 Tim 3:15-17

INSTRUCTION (SEE TEACHING)

INTERCESSION (SEE PRAYER)

ISRAEL

The name Israel means "he who contends with God" (cf. Gen 32:28). It was first applied to Jacob as a name of honor and then came to be applied to the nation formed from the descendants of his twelve sons (e.g., Ex 1:7). With the division of the kingdom of Israel following Solomon's reign, Israel became the name for the Northern Kingdom of the ten tribes centered in Ephraim, in distinction to the kingdom of Judah (which included the tribe of Benjamin) in the south (e.g., 1 Sam 11:8), although, the term Israel could still be used for all of the covenant people even after the divided monarchy (e.g., Is 5:7). The nation of Israel in the OT was peculiarly formed by God as His special people in covenant relationship with Him (cf. Ex 19:5-6). The Gospels continue this same use of the term Israel for the OT covenant people. With their rejection of the Messiah as a nation, some interpreters understand that God has established the church as a new spiritual Israel (cf. Gal 6:16) in which the remaining prophecies concerning Israel's restoration and blessing to all people will be fulfilled. Others, however, understand Israel to retain the OT ethnic and national meaning throughout all Scripture and the prophecies concerning Israel yet to be fulfilled through this special people (cf. Rom 11:24-29).

J

JERUSALEM (SEE ALSO ZION)

THE EARTHLY CITY OF

NAMES FOR

Salem: Gen 14:18
Jerusalem: Josh 10:1; 2 Sam 5:5; Matt 23:37
Jebus: Judg 19:10
Zion: 1 Kin 8:1
the city of David: 1 Kin 8:1
the city of Judah: 2 Chr 25:28
the city of the great King: Ps 48:2; Matt 5:35
city of God: Ps 87:3
the holy city: Neh 11:1; Is 48:2; Matt 4:5
Ariel: Is 29:1
the LORD is our righteousness: Jer 33:16
God's holy mountain: Dan 9:16, 20

SIGNIFICANCE OF

annual feasts held there: Deut 16:16; Ps 122:3-4; Luke 2:41
conquered by David: 2 Sam 5:7
ark brought there: 2 Sam 6:12-19

temple built there: 1 Kin 6:1-38; 2 Chr 3:1
prayers of faithful Israelites directed towards: 1 Kin 8:38; Dan 6:10
place of Jesus' triumphal entry: Matt 21:1-10
place of the high priest's residence: Matt 26:58
Jesus crucified there: Luke 9:31; 24:18-21 (cf. Rev 11:8)
the gospel first preached there: Luke 24:47; Acts 1:8
the Spirit descended upon the disciples there: Acts 2:1-4
first church council held there: Acts 15:1-2

THE MILLENNIAL CITY OF

the city of righteousness: Is 1:26
a faithful city: Is 1:26
the city from which the law goes forth: Is 2:3; Mic 4:2
the city from which Messiah rules on the Davidic throne: Is 9:6-7
the city of the LORD: Is 60:14
the city called the Throne of the LORD: Jer 3:17
the city called the LORD is there: Ezek 48:35
called the City of Truth: Zech 8:3
the capital city of the earth: Zech 14:4-21
the city besieged and divinely delivered at the end of the millennium: Rev 20:7-10

THE HEAVENLY CITY OF

contrasted with the earthly Jerusalem: Gal 4:25-26
called the city of the living God: Heb 12:22 (cf. Rev 3:12)
described as the holy city, new Jerusalem: Rev 21:2, 10-27

JESUS (SEE CHRIST, PRIMARY NAMES OF)

JEWS (SEE ISRAEL; JUDAISM)

JOY

SOURCE OF

the LORD Himself: 1 Chr 16:27; Neh 12:43; Ps 43:4; John 15:11; 17:13; Rom 15:13
the LORD's presence: Ps 16:11; 21:6
the Holy Spirit: Gal 5:22; 1 Thess 1:6 (cf. Acts 13:52; Rom 14:17)

CAUSES OF

celebration of a feast: 2 Chr 30:23-25
God's protection: Ps 5:11-12
God's forgiveness: Ps 32:11 (cf. 1-10); 51:7-8
God's works: Ps 92:4
God's word: Ps 119:111; Jer 15:16

God's righteousness: Ps 145:7
salvation: Is 12:3; Acts 13:48
the LORD's coming: Zech 2:10
the record of one's name in heaven: Luke 10:20
the repentance of a sinner: Luke 15:7
answered prayer of Jesus: John 17:13
the conversion of the Gentiles: Acts 15:3
of believers walking in the truth: 3 John 4
glorification of believers: Jude 24
marriage of the Lamb: Rev 19:7

JUBILEE, YEAR OF

The year of jubilee was the fiftieth year in the Jewish religious calendar as it followed the completed series of seven Sabbath years or 49 years (Lev 25:1-8). It was heralded on the Day of Atonement by the sounding of "jubilee" (Heb. *yobel*), i.e., a "ram's horn" or a trumpet made in the shape of a ram's horn (Lev 25:9; cf. 16:29-30). The year of jubilee provided Israel with a time of release and rest (Lev 25:10-12). Like the Sabbath years of rest, it was to be observed "to the LORD" with celebration and trust that God would provide food as He promised (Lev 25:2-7, 11-12, 18-22). The release included the reversion of land to its original owners, cancellation of all debts, and freedom for all Israelites in servitude.

JUDAISM

Judaism is the religion of the Jews that expresses their pattern of beliefs and practices based on their accumulated tradition of OT rabbinic interpretation. It began during the Babylonian exile after the destruction of the temple in 586 B.C. as an attempt of the Jews to adapt the OT Law to their exilic living. The term "Judaism" (Gr. *Ioudaismos*; cf. Gal 1:13, 14) originated from "Judah," which designates the Southern Kingdom of the divided monarchy and was initially used by Greek-speaking Jews in the intertestamental period to distinguish themselves religiously and culturally from the Gentiles. Judaism continued to develop through such historical periods as the intertestamental, rabbinic, medieval, and modern eras with its three current forms: Orthodox, Conservative, and Reformed Judaism. Orthodox Judaism emphasizes worship in the local synagogue and studying and keeping of the Torah ("Law") along with the hundreds of detailed ordinances in their tradition. Jewish beliefs not only have influenced their religious life but also their cultural, social, and political outlook on life. Ezra the skilled scribe and teacher of the Law (Ezra 7:6; 10; Neh 8; 12:26) evidently represented an early form of Judaism. Such true biblical Judaism was rooted in a proper understanding of the OT and a right response of heart to God which is "not of the letter, but of the Spirit" (2 Cor 3:6; cf. Rom 2:28-29). However, the genuine people of God composed only a minority in the midst of a wider Judaism, and this righteous remnant existed only through God's gracious election and preservation of them (Rom 9:6, 27, 29; 11:1-7; cf. Matt 1:18-25; Luke 1:5-80). An institutionalized form of Judaism also began to develop and increasingly prevailed in Jewish history. This emphasis in Judaism became epitomized in a form of Pharisaism, which emphasized outward, ritualistic observance and ordinances based on certain rabbinical interpretation of the OT Law. Such hypocritical religion was strongly condemned by Christ as vain worship that substituted human doctrines and traditions for the commandments of God (Matt 23:1-36; Mark 7:1-9). While orthodox Christianity is monotheistic like Judaism (Deut 6:4; cf. 1 Tim 2:5), the Christian doctrine of the Trinity (Matt 28:19) and the NT revelation that Jesus is the Messiah and Son of God (John 1:11; 20:30-31) is rejected by Judaism. Christianity is founded upon the confession of Jesus' Lordship and the messianic fulfillment of OT Scriptures as recorded in the NT (Matt 16:16-18; Acts 2:14-36; 1 Cor 15:3-4; Eph 2:20). Both Testaments place a strong emphasis upon the practical ethics of religion (e.g., Deut 6:4-6; Mic 6:8; Matt 22:37-40; Rom 13:8-10).

JUDGE (SEE ALSO JUDGMENT)

THE DIVINE JUDGE

His position as: Gen 18:25; Judg 11:27; Ps 7:11;
   James 4:12
His character as: Deut 32:4; Job 34:10;
   2 Pet 3:9-10; Rev 6:10; 19:2

HUMAN JUDGES

general examples of: Gen 19:9; Ex 2:14; 18:13,
   21-26; 22:8-9; Num 25:5; Judg 4:5;
   1 Sam 7:15-17; 1 Kin 3:16-28; Dan 3:2-3;
   Matt 12:27; Luke 18:2, 6; Acts 13:20
appointment of: Deut 16:18; Ezra 7:25;
   1 Cor 6:4
penalty for disobedience to: Deut 17:12
   (cf. Matt 5:25-26; Rom 13:3-4)

JUDGMENT (SEE ALSO JUDGE; PUNISHMENT)

GOD'S JUDGMENT

PURPOSE OF GOD'S JUDGMENT

to punish sin: Gen 3:1-19; 6:5-7; Ezek 18:4; Rom 1:18-32; 3:9-23

to reveal His divine character and power: Ex 9:14-16; Ezek 5:13; Ps 9:16

to purify Israel: Mal 3:2-4

to lead to repentance: Luke 13:2-5

to repay in righteous vengeance: Rom 12:19

to bring worship and glory to God: Rev 19:1-6

CHRIST'S EXECUTION OF JUDGMENT (SEE ALSO CHRIST)

His judgment between the nations: Is 2:4; Mic 4:3

His authority for judgment: John 5:22, 27

His judgment of the world (see also WORLD): John 12:31; Acts 17:31 (cf. Rom 2:16)

His judgment of Satan (see also SATAN): John 12:31; 16:11

His judgment of all people: Acts 10:42; 2 Tim 4:1 (cf. Rev 11:18; 20:12)

His judgment at His appearing: Matt 25:31-46; 2 Thess 1:7-10; 2:8; Rev 19:11-21; 22:12

His wrath expressed in judgment: Rev 6:16-17

HUMANITY'S JUDGMENT

REQUIREMENTS FOR PROPER JUDGMENT

reverence for God: Ex 18:21

hatred of dishonest gain: Ex 18:21

truthfulness: Ex 18:21; Prov 29:14

fairness: Lev 19:15

impartiality: Deut 1:17; Prov 24:23

evidence of two or three witnesses: Deut 19:15

an understanding heart: 1 Kin 3:9

accordance with God's ordinances: Ezek 44:24

after proper investigation: John 7:51

FINAL JUDGMENT

TIME OF

in general

after death: Heb 9:27

in particular

after the second coming of Christ for some: Matt 25:31-46

at the great white throne for the rest: Rev 20:11-15

RESULTS OF

for unbelievers

not able to stand in the judgment: Ps 1:5

degrees of punishment determined: Matt 10:15; Luke 12:47-48; Rev 20:12-13 (cf. John 19:11)

thrown into the lake of fire: Rev 20:15 (cf. Matt 25:41)

for believers

delivered from eternal judgment: John 5:24; Rom 5:9; 8:1; Rev 20:15

rewarded for acceptable works: 1 Cor 3:11-15; 2 Cor 5:10

JUSTICE

Biblical justice proceeds from just or right character and involves fairness of judgment, particularly in the treatment of people (cf. Deut 32:4). God exercises justice with absolute equity in the punishment of sin and reward of righteousness. Justice is also closely associated with righteousness in both the OT and the NT (cf. Ps 106:3; Rom 3:21-26; see RIGHTEOUSNESS). God Himself is perfectly and inviolably righteous and is therefore the ultimate author and standard of justice (Gen 18:25; Deut 10:18; 32:4). Accordingly, He requires people to "do justice" (Mic 6:8).

JUSTIFICATION

To justify means to declare and treat as righteous through acquittal. Christ's redemptive work provides a righteous basis for God's justification of believers so that they receive remission of sins and a righteous standing with Him (Acts 13:38-39; Rom 3:21-26; 4:5-8; 8:1, 33-34; Col 2:13). Justification is judicial or forensic and thus is distinguished from progressive sanctification which is the process by which the believer is being made righteous (cf. John 17:17; Eph 5:26; Heb 12:14; see also SANCTIFICATION).

originates in divine grace: Is 45:24-25; Rom 3:24; 4:5-6, 8, 16-24; 5:17, 21; Gal 2:21; Eph 2:8-9; Phil 3:9; Titus 3:7 (cf. Is 45:25; Rom 5:16; 8:30, 33)

based on Christ's sacrifice: Is 53:11; Jer 23:6; Acts 13:38-39; Rom 3:24-25; 5:9, 16-18, 21; 1 Cor 1:30; 6:11; 2 Cor 5:21; Gal 2:17

MEANS OF

through personal faith: Gen 15:6; Rom 1:17; 3:22, 25, 26, 28, 30; 4:5, 11-24; 5:1; 9:30, 32; 10:4, 6, 8-11; Gal 2:16; 3:6-9, 11, 22, 24; 5:5-6; Phil 3:9; Heb 10:38; 11:4, 7; James 2:22-24 (cf. Eph 2:8-9)

not through human works: Acts 13:38-39; Rom 2:13; 3:20; 4:2, 5, 13-16; 9:31-32; Gal 2:16, 21; 3:11, 21-22; 5:4; Phil 3:9 (cf. Eph 2:8-9; Titus 3:5)

in the Spirit: 1 Cor 6:11

results of: 1 Kin 8:32; Acts 13:38-39; Rom 4:25; 5:1, 9; 8:1, 30, 33-34; 2 Cor 5:19; James 2:21, 24, 25

K

KILLING (SEE HOMICIDE)

KING

DIVINE KING

GOD AS KING (SEE ALSO GOD, NAMES OF, KING OF KINGS)

His throne in the midst of the heavenly army: 1 Kin 22:19 (cf. Is 6:1-3)

His general title as King: Ps 5:2

His righteous reign from His throne: Ps 9:4, 7-8; 99:1-5

His existence as King forever: Ps 10:16; Jer 10:10

His title as King of glory: Ps 24:10

His rule over all the earth: Ps 47:2

His greatness as King: Ps 95:3

His reign over Zion: Is 52:7

His title as King of heaven: Dan 4:37

His character as King eternal, immortal, and invisible: 1 Tim 1:17

His rule of the nations: Rev 15:3

CHRIST AS KING (SEE ALSO CHRIST, OT PROPHECIES OF, TITLES AND FUNCTIONS OF)

as a king from Abraham's descendants: Gen 17:6

as ruler from Judah with a scepter: Gen 49:10 (cf. Num 24:17)

as ruler on David's throne: 2 Sam 7:8-16; Is 9:6-7; Jer 23:5; Luke 1:32; Acts 2:29-36

as ruler over the nations: Ps 2:8-9 (cf. Rev 2:26-27)

as ruler at God's right hand: Ps 110:1; Eph 1:20-23

as a divine ruler: Is 9:6

as a just, righteous, and wise ruler: Is 9:7; 11:1-5; 32:1; Jer 23:5

as an eternal ruler: Is 9:7; Dan 2:44-45; 7:13-14; Mic 5:2 (cf. Matt 2:6); Luke 1:33; Rev 11:15

as a ruler who shepherds His people: Is 40:10-11; Mic 5:2-4

as worldwide ruler: Dan 7:14

as ruler over Israel: Mic 5:2; Zech 9:9 (cf. Matt 21:5); Matt 2:2

as a ruler and priest combined: Zech 6:13

as a humble ruler: Zech 9:9

as ruler who occupies His throne at His coming: Matt 25:31

acknowledgment as King of Israel: John 1:49

as ruler in the millennium: Rev 20:4, 6

HUMAN KINGS

ANOINTING

in a figurative sense: Judg 9:8, 15

of Saul: 1 Sam 10:1

of David: 1 Sam 16:12-13

of Solomon: 1 Kin 1:39

of Jehu: 1 Kin 19:16

of Cyrus: Is 45:1

prayer for: Ezra 6:10; 1 Tim 2:1-2

KINGDOM

The biblical words for kingdom primarily signify the abstract idea of kingly authority or reign (kingship, e.g., 1 Sam 14:47; 1 Kin 2:12. However, since a reign necessarily creates a realm over which it is exercised, the terms are also used for that realm (kingdom, e.g., Matt 4:8; 8:11). They are used both for secular earthly kingdoms and the kingdom related to God and Christ.

KINGDOM, GOD'S

Although the expression "kingdom of God" is not used in the OT, the idea of the reign of God and His kingdom is frequent (e.g., Ps 22:28; 145:13; Dan 2:44). It becomes the dominant theme of the proclamation of Christ (cf. Matt 4:17) and His disciples (Matt 10:7) in the Gospels. References to the kingdom or reign of God are less frequent in the epistles, but again come into prominence in the book of Revelation (e.g., 11:15, 17; 12:10; 20:4). Scripture teaches two closely related concepts of the kingdom of God. Since God has always ruled over His created universe, His kingdom has existed from eternity in its reign over all things (e.g., 1 Chr 29:11-12). But since the reign of God has not been fully established, especially on the earth, there is another sense in which the kingdom is seen as coming to defeat the forces of evil and establish the righteous reign of God on earth (e.g., Dan 2:44; Matt 6:10). This earthly historical kingdom was a primary theme of OT prophecy (e.g., Is 9:6-7; Jer 23:5). It was announced as near or "at hand" at the first coming of Christ (e.g., Matt 3:2; 4:17), and on the basis of His death and resurrection He was exalted to kingly authority (cf. Acts 2:34-36).

The kingdom includes both the spiritual salvation of the new covenant (e.g., forgiveness of sins and new life through the Spirit) and the outward salvation of society through the defeat of the evil forces of history and the establishment of the righteous rule of Christ on earth. There is general agreement concerning the presence of the kingdom in its spiritual salvation during the present church age. The outward consummation of the kingdom of Christ, however, has evoked various views often

described in terms of different explanations of the millennium.

Derived from Rev 20:1-10, the millennium (from Latin *mille*, "thousand") denotes the temporary messianic kingdom reign of Christ before the final judgment and inauguration of the eternal state with the new heavens and earth. The prophetic Scriptures relative to this reign of Christ have been variously interpreted throughout church history. Premillennialists view it as a literal 1000 year reign of Christ on the earth characterized by peace, righteousness, and material prosperity following His return and prior to the commencement of the eternal state. Postmillennialists understand it as an era of similar conditions that will be brought about by the proclamation of the gospel during the present church age before the return of Christ. His return will then signal the final judgment and the inauguration of the eternal state. Finally, amillennialists interpret the prophecies of a millennial kingdom as signifying the blessedness of believers in a present spiritual kingdom over which Christ rules from heaven through the Word and Spirit. His return will bring the consummation in the destruction of evil forces, the final judgment, and the eternal state (see also DAY OF THE LORD; END TIMES).

eternal universal kingdom: 1 Chr 29:11-12; Ps 29:10; 74:12; 103:19; 145:13; Dan 4:34-35; Matt 6:10; 1 Tim 1:17

MEDIATORIAL (MESSIANIC) KINGDOM
terminology
kingdom of God: Matt 21:31; Mark 1:15; 4:11;
9:1, 47; 10:14, 23-25; 12:34; 14:25; 15:43;
Luke 4:43; 6:20; 7:28; 8:1, 10; 9:2, 11, 27;
10:9; 11:2, 17; 12:31; 13:28-29; 16:16;
17:20-21; 18:24; 19:11; 21:31; 22:16;
John 3:3, 5; Acts 1:3; 8:12; 14:22; 20:25;
28:23, 31; Rom 14:17; 1 Cor 4:20; Gal 5:21;
Col 4:11; 1 Thess 2:12
kingdom of heaven: Matt 3:2; 4:17; 5:3; 6:10;
10:7; 11:11; 12:28; 13:11; 16:19; 19:23;
21:43; 25:1
Christ's kingdom: Matt 20:21; Luke 1:33;
22:30; 23:42; John 18:36; Col 1:13;
2 Tim 4:1; 2 Pet 1:11
kingdom of Christ and God: Eph 5:5; Rev 11:15
kingdom of the Father: Matt 13:43; 26:29
kingdom of David: Mark 11:10
kingdom, Satan's: Matt 12:26; John 12:31; 14:30;
16:11; 2 Cor 4:4; Col 1:13; 1 John 5:19

KNOWLEDGE (SEE ALSO REVELATION)
In a biblical sense, true knowledge includes all facts concerning God and His works, both spiritual and material (Gen 1:1; Col 1:16). God Himself has perfect knowledge, i.e., omniscience (see also GOD, attributes of, omniscient; Ps 147:5; cf. 139:1-6), and He has created people in His own image with finite capacity for knowledge (Gen 1:26-27; cf. Col 3:10). The OT emphasizes the personal, relational, and experiential dimensions of knowledge involved in the ongoing process of life. This dynamic and life-related concept of knowledge affects the will and emotions as well as the intellect (e.g., Gen 2:17; 4:1, & note; Is 47:8; 53:3; Jer 3:13, & note; 16:21; Ezek 25:14). The Greeks viewed knowledge as a cognitive and contemplative relationship to objective reality in its static and abstract being (cf. 1 Cor 1:21-22) or as a mystical mergence of the knower with God. Knowledge of God and reverence for Him are primary knowledge for humans (Prov 1:7; 9:10; cf. Ps 14:1). The NT further emphasizes that eternal life involves a personal knowledge of "the only true God" (John 17:3) as revealed through His Son, Jesus Christ (1 John 5:20). However, God also created people to gain knowledge of His natural creation and to rule the earth as God's steward (Gen 1:28). Since a person is finite, both his spiritual and natural knowledge are always limited in breadth and in depth (Deut 29:29; Rom 11:33-34; 1 Cor 8:2).

L

LAMB
USES
clothing: Lev 13:47-52; Deut 22:11; Heb 11:37
food: Lev 11:3; 1 Sam 25:18
wool: Lev 13:47-49; Judg 6:37-40
ratifying a covenant: Gen 21:27-31
pets: 2 Sam 12:2-3
dependence on shepherd: Num 27:17; Zech 13:7
FIGURATIVE
OF GOD'S PEOPLE
owned by God: Ps 23; 100:3; Is 40:11;
Luke 15:4-6
dependent on God: Ps 78:52; Jer 50:17;
Zech 13:7; John 10:10-15
dependent on under shepherds: John 21:15;
1 Pet 5:2
tendency to stray: Is 53:6; Jer 50:6; Matt 15:24;
Luke 15:4-7

LANGUAGE

ENUMERATION OF LANGUAGES IN THE BIBLE

language of Judah (i.e., Hebrew or Judean):
2 Chr 32:18; Neh 13:24; Is 36:11; John 19:20
(cf. Acts 1:19)

Aramaic: Ezra 4:7; Is 36:11

language of Ashdod: Neh 13:24

language of Egypt: Ps 114:1

language of Canaan: Is 19:18

language of the Chaldeans (i.e., Babylonian):
Dan 1:4

Latin: John 19:20

Greek: John 19:20

language of the Lycaonians: Acts 14:11

VARIOUS OTHER USES

a language not understood: Deut 28:49; Ps 81:5;
Jer 5:15; 1 Cor 14:11

language of one's own people: Esth 1:22

a difficult language: Ezek 3:5-6

*figurative language (see also FIGURATIVE
SPEECH):* John 16:25

LAST DAYS (SEE END TIMES)

LAW(S)

Biblical law is generally a rule or regulation to govern people in religious, moral, ceremonial, or civil conduct (e.g., Ex 20:1-31:18). Divinely revealed law is usually mediated through human instruments (Ex 19:3; Lev 26:46; John 1:17) and concerns humanity's relation to God (Ex 20:3-11; Matt 22:37-38) and also to other people (Ex 20:12-17; Matt 22:39). The most basic OT word for law (Heb. *torah*) emphasizes the idea of "instruction" (Ex 16:4; Is 1:10; Mal 2:6-9) and is best seen in the Mosaic legal system initially recorded in Exodus (Ex 20:1-31:18). While the Mosaic legislation is a unified system (Gal 5:3), it is conveniently viewed in three divisions: the moral laws (Ex 20:1-26), the civil laws (Ex 21:1-24:11), and the ceremonial or religious laws (Ex 24:12-31:18). In addition to the written OT law, the Jews accumulated a voluminous "oral law," i.e., "the tradition of the elders" (Mark 7:5-13; cf. Gal 1:14; Col 2:8) that eventually became codified in the Talmud (see also JUDAISM). The primary NT word for law (Gr. *nomos*) is used of an operative principle (e.g., Rom 3:27; 7:21, 23, 25; 8:2) as well as a moral rule (e.g., Rom 7:7-8; 8:3).

CHARACTERISTICS OF

righteous: Deut 4:8; Rom 7:12

preserved: Deut 10:1-5; 2 Chr 34:15

true: Neh 9:13; Ps 119:142

authoritative: Ps 19:7; Is 8:20 (cf. 55:11); Jer 23:29;
John 7:23; Heb 9:22

perfect: Ps 19:7; James 1:25

great and glorious: Is 42:21

holy and good: Rom 7:12-13, 16; 1 Tim 1:8

spiritual: Rom 7:14

unified: Gal 3:10; 5:3; James 2:10-11

temporary: Gal 3:10-11, 19; Col 2:14; Heb 7:12;
8:13; 10:9

LIBERTY (SEE FREEDOM)

LIFE

The primary OT word for life signifies active existence, the idea of movement being prominent (e.g., Gen 7:21). Two terms for life are used in the NT. *Bios* is used for life as a present earthly existence, focusing on its manner or possessions (e.g., Luke 8:14), while *zoe* signifies the state of vitality. This latter term is used for the spiritual eternal life enjoyed in fellowship with God (e.g., John 3:16). Life in Scripture, whether physical or spiritual, is more than an abstract energizing force. It is the actual exercising of God-given capacities in accordance with their created design. The dying process, on the other hand, restricts functioning and robs health and vitality. Since the human person includes both of these physical and spiritual aspects, true human life includes both dimensions of life that are found only in relation to God. Sin effected death both physically and spiritually (cf. Gen 2:17), necessitating a renewal of life through coming back to God in faith. This process begins with newness of spiritual life presently through faith in Christ, but will ultimately include a greater fullness of spiritual life and newness of bodily life through the resurrection (see also DEATH, REGENERATION, RESURRECTION).

NATURAL (PHYSICAL)

value of: Job 2:4; Esth 7:3-4; Matt 6:25

use of: Ps 90:12; Luke 1:75; Phil 1:21; 1 Pet 1:17

brevity and frailty of: 1 Chr 29:15; Job 7:6; 9:25;
Ps 39:5; 89:47; Is 40:6; James 1:10; 1 Pet 1:24

SPIRITUAL (ETERNAL)

SOURCE OF

God as living God: Deut 5:26; Josh 3:10; Ps 16:11;
36:9; 84:2; Matt 26:63; John 5:26; 6:69;
Rom 9:26; Eph 2:4-5; Col 2:13

mediated through Christ: Matt 16:16; John 1:4;
4:14; 10:10, 28; Acts 3:15; Rom 5:17, 21;
2 Cor 4:10; Gal 2:20; Phil 1:21; Col 3:3-4;
1 John 5:12; Rev 1:18; 2:7; 21:7

given by Spirit (see also REGENERATION):
  Ezek 37:14; John 3:5-6; Rom 8:2, 11;
  1 Cor 15:45; Gal 5:25; Titus 3:5

NATURE OF
knowing God: John 17:3; 1 John 5:20
love: 1 John 3:14-15; 4:7-8
light: John 1:4; 8:12

ATTAINMENT OF
faith in Christ: John 1:12-13; 3:15-16, 36; 5:40;
  6:35, 40, 47, 51, 57; 11:25; 20:31; Rom 6:23
obedience to God: Matt 7:13-14; 19:16; 25:31-46;
  Mark 9:43; Rom 2:7
sowing to the Spirit: Gal 6:8
renunciation of earthly things: Matt 19:29;
  John 12:25

LIGHT

IN RELATION TO GOD
He created physical light: Gen 1:3; Is 45:7
He provides spiritual light: Ps 27:1; 36:9; 43:3;
  118:27; Is 51:4; Mic 7:8-9
He covers Himself with light: Ps 104:2
He will be an everlasting light for the redeemed:
  Is 60:19-20; Rev 21:23; 22:5
He is the Father of lights: James 1:17

IN RELATION TO CHRIST
He is a light to the nations: Is 42:6 (cf. Luke 2:32;
  Acts 13:47)
He is the light of all people: John 1:4
He is the true light: John 1:9
He is the light of the world: John 8:12; 9:5

IN RELATION TO DIVINE REVELATION
GOD'S WORD GIVES LIGHT
  for spiritual understanding: Ps 19:8; 119:130;
    Prov 6:23
  for spiritual direction: Ps 119:105
  for prophetic light in spiritual darkness:
    2 Pet 1:19
  the gospel gives spiritual light for salvation:
    Acts 26:18, 23; 2 Cor 4:4

IN RELATION TO BELIEVERS
believers are the light of the world: Matt 5:14-16
  (cf. Phil 2:15)
believers are to put on the armor of light:
  Rom 13:12
believers are light in the LORD: Eph 5:8
believers have an inheritance as saints in light:
  Col 1:12
believers are the sons of light: 1 Thess 5:5
believers are called into God's marvelous light:
  1 Pet 2:9

LONGEVITY (SEE LIFE)

LONGSUFFERING (SEE PATIENCE)

LORD (SEE ALSO GOD, NAMES OF)

The name LORD (Heb. *Yahweh*) means that God
is the "self-existent One" (Ex 3:14; 6:3; see also
I AM) and is written with all capitals in the NASB.
Although properly a title, it is used as God's
personal name (cf. Ps 144:15; Is 37:20) and emphasizes His faithful presence and redemptive,
covenant relationship with His people (Ex 3:12-15;
cf. 6:2-8; Deut 7:9; Ezek 37:26-28; 48:35). The
full redemptive knowledge of the name LORD
was not made known until Israel's experience
under Moses (Ex 6:3). It is called "this honored
and awesome name" (Deut 28:58) or simply
"the Name" (Lev 24:11). The form "LORD" (Heb.
Adonay or *Adon*) means that God is "LORD" or
"Master" in relation to His people as His servants and in the NASB is translated with only
an initial capital when used of deity. This name
is less intimate than the foregoing name LORD
and is used of both deity and humanity (e.g.,
Gen 18:12; Ps 110:1). It is sometimes substituted
for God's personal name (*Yahweh*, LORD) as a
precaution against taking the latter name in
vain (cf. Ex 20:7). The primary word for LORD
in the NT (Gr. *kurios*) is used to translate either
Yahweh (Matt 22:44; cf. Ps 110:1, LORD) or *Adonay*
(Matt 22:44; cf. Ps 110:1, LORD). Another word
translated "LORD" or "Master" (Gr. *despotes*) occurs several times in the NT and indicates either
deity (Luke 2:29; Acts 4:24; 2 Tim 2:21; 2 Pet 2:1;
Jude 4; Rev 6:10) or a human "LORD" or "master"
(1 Tim 6:1-2; Titus 2:9; 1 Pet 2:18).

COMPOUND FORMS OF
the LORD God (Yahweh Elohim): Gen 2:7
LORD God of Israel: 1 Sam 2:30
LORD God of armies: 2 Sam 5:10
LORD GOD (Yah Yahweh): Is 12:2
LORD of armies: 1 Sam 1:3
the LORD GOD (Adonay Yahweh): Gen 15:8
LORD GOD of armies: Is 10:23-24
LORD of LORDS: Deut 10:17
the LORD Will Provide: Gen 22:14
the LORD is My Banner: Ex 17:15
the LORD is Peace: Judg 6:24
the LORD our righteousness: Jer 23:6
the LORD is there: Ezek 48:35

OF DEITY
the sacred personal names of God: the
  tetragrammaton
the Father: Ps 110:1; Matt 11:25; James 3:9
  (cf. Luke 2:26; Acts 4:26); Rev 11:15

the Son: Ps 110:1; Is 6:1-10; Matt 7:21; Mark 1:3;
2:28; Luke 2:11; John 4:1; Rom 6:23; 2 Cor 4:5;
Eph 6:10; Phil 2:11; 1 Thess 1:1; 4:15, 16;
1 Tim 6:15; Heb 2:3; 1 Pet 2:3; 3:15; Jude 4, 25;
Rev 14:13
the Spirit: 2 Cor 3:17

LORD's DAY (SEE SABBATH)

The LORD's day is a common designation for the
first day of the week (i.e., Sunday) when Christians meet to celebrate Christ's resurrection
(cf. Acts 20:7). Scripture indicates that Christ
arose on the first day of the week and appeared
to His disciples as a group on the same day
(Mark 16:1-2; John 20:19-29). Thus the LORD's
day is distinct from the Sabbath or seventh day
of the week (i.e., Saturday) that was given to
Israel as a day of rest in celebration of God's rest
from creation on the seventh day (Gen 2:1-3;
Ex 20:8-11; 31:13-17; Neh 9:14). Traditionally the
church has assembled on the LORD's day for
such activities as worship (particularly through
the LORD's Supper), the reading and teaching
of Scripture, fellowship, prayer, discipline, and
giving (Acts 2:42; 20:7; 1 Cor 5:1-13, especially v.
4; 16:1-2; Heb 10:25).

LORD's SUPPER

The LORD's Supper (1 Cor 11:20), also known as
Communion (cf. 1 Cor 10:16), the Eucharist (from
the Greek term for the giving of thanks before
partaking; cf. Matt 26:26), or the "breaking of
the bread" (cf. Acts 2:42), was instituted for His
people on the night of His betrayal (e.g., Matt
26:24-26). It is commonly known as a church
ordinance from the fact that it was ordained by
the LORD as signifying a visible sign of invisible
grace. The purpose of the observance focuses
on the LORD's command to "do this in remembrance of Me" (Luke 22:19). It is a means through
which the risen Christ in His saving grace makes
Himself present to His people. Various interpretations have been given to Christ's statements
concerning the bread and cup being His body
and blood (cf. Luke 22:19-20). Some have taken
these statements literally, believing in a miraculous transformation of the elements. Others
understand them symbolically as referring to the
spiritual presence of Christ as the one who gives
Himself in His saving efficacy for the spiritual
nourishment of His people.
institution of: Matt 26:26-29; 1 Cor 11:23-25
church practice of: Acts 2:42, 46; 1 Cor 10:16

SIGNIFICANCE OF
REMEMBRANCE OF CHRIST
the command: Luke 22:19; 1 Cor 11:24-25
remembrance of Christ's death: 1 Cor 11:25-26
a present fellowship with Christ: 1 Cor 10:16-17, 21;
11:20
an anticipation of Christ's return: Matt 26:29;
1 Cor 11:26
symbol of church unity: 1 Cor 10:16-17
REQUIREMENTS FOR PARTICIPATION
believers: Acts 2:41-42; 20:7; 1 Cor 10:16-22
proper attitude to Christ and his people:
1 Cor 11:27-34

LORD's TABLE (SEE LORD's SUPPER)

LOVE

Love is a central theme of Scripture and is a
primary characteristic of God's nature (e.g.,
1 John 4:8) and the central demand of human
life both in relation to God and other people
(Matt 22:37-40). The most frequently-used
term in the NT (*agape*) generally signifies a
spontaneous self-giving unmerited love. This
meaning is evident in John's description of love
as God's giving of Himself in the gift of His Son
for the good of those who were totally undeserving (cf. 1 John 4:10). Another word (*phileo*),
while overlapping at times with *agape*, refers
primarily to the love between friends (cf. John
11:3, 36). All love has its source in God, who is
love (1 John 4:7-8), and is available to human
beings only through the Spirit of God (Gal 5:22).
It is clear from the characteristics given below
that love involves the total person, i.e., one's
thought, feeling, and action (see also LOVING
KINDNESS).

CHARACTERISTICS OF
sacrificial: John 15:13; Gal 2:20; 1 John 4:10
unselfish: Gal 5:13
strong and enduring: Song 8:6-7; 1 Cor 13:7-8
forgiving: Prov 10:12; 1 Cor 13:7
negates fear: 1 John 4:17-18
edifies: 1 Cor 8:1; Eph 4:16
unifies: Col 3:14
transcends understanding: Eph 3:19
OF GOD
general: Deut 10:18; 33:3; 2 Sam 12:24; John 3:16;
Titus 3:4; 1 John 4:16, 19
for Israel: Deut 4:37; 7:7-8; Is 43:3-4; Jer 31:3;
Hos 11:1; 14:4
given in Christ: John 3:16; Rom 5:8; 8:39;
Titus 3:4-7; 1 John 4:9-10

given in the Spirit: Rom 5:5; 15:30; Titus 3:4-5
for the Son: Matt 3:17; 17:5; John 3:35; 17:23

OF CHRIST

OBJECTS OF
the Father: John 14:31
His people: John 14:21; 15:9; Rom 8:35;
2 Cor 5:14; Gal 2:20; Eph 3:19; 5:2, 25;
2 Thess 2:13; Rev 1:5; 3:9
the lost: Mark 10:21

OF PEOPLE

FOR GOD
commanded: Deut 6:5; 10:12; Ps 31:23;
Matt 22:37; Mark 12:30
evidenced by obedience: Deut 10:12-13;
John 14:13, 21, 23; 1 John 5:3
for Christ: Matt 10:37; John 8:42; 1 Cor 16:22;
Eph 4:24; 1 Pet 1:8

FOR OTHER PEOPLE
commanded: Lev 19:18; Mark 12:31, 33;
1 Cor 14:1; Gal 5:13; 1 Thess 3:12; 4:9;
1 Tim 1:5; James 2:8; 1 Pet 1:22; 1 John 3:11;
2 John 5
evidence of spiritual life: 1 Tim 2:15; 1 John 3:14-17

LOVING KINDNESS (SEE ALSO FAITHFULNESS)

DIVINE OF GOD
shown to people: Gen 19:19; Ex 15:13; 2 Sam 2:6;
7:15; 1 Kin 3:6; 2 Chr 6:14; Job 10:12; Ps 17:7;
Prov 16:6; Jer 9:24; 31:3; 32:18; Hos 2:19
abundant and great: Ex 34:6; 1 Kin 3:6; Ps 5:7;
33:5; Joel 2:13; Jon 4:2
related to His covenant: Deut 7:9, 12; Neh 1:5;
Dan 9:4
everlasting: 1 Chr 16:34, 41; Ps 100:5; Is 54:8, 10;
Jer 33:11
trust in: Ps 13:5; 52:8
rejoicing in: Ps 31:7 (cf. Ps 59:16; 89:10)
value of: Ps 63:3
thanks for: Ps 107:8, 15, 21, 31
proclaimed: Is 63:7 (see also CHRIST,
characteristics of, merciful)

OF PEOPLE
benediction of mercy: 2 Sam 15:20
desire for mercy: 1 Kin 20:31

SHOWING MERCY
reward of: Prov 11:17; Matt 5:7
exhortation for: Dan 4:27; Matt 18:33; 23:23;
Luke 6:36; Jude 22-23
blessing of: Matt 5:7
forgiveness in: Matt 18:21-35
example of: Luke 10:37 (cf. vv. 30-36)
cheerfulness in: Rom 12:8

priority of mercy over sacrifice and giving:
Matt 9:13; 23:23
triumph of mercy over judgment: James 2:13
true source of mercy: James 3:17

LOYALTY (SEE ALSO FAITHFULNESS)

EXAMPLES OF
Moses: Num 12:7; Heb 3:2, 5
Israelites under Joshua: Josh 1:16-18
David: 1 Sam 24:5-10
Uriah: 2 Sam 11:9-11
Barzillai: 2 Sam 19:32
Mordecai: Esth 2:21-23
Timothy: Phil 2:19-22
Paul: 2 Tim 4:7-8
Jesus: Heb 3:2
Antipas: Rev 2:13

VARIOUS OTHER USES
change of loyalty: 2 Sam 16:16-19
deeds of loyalty: Neh 13:14
profession of loyalty: Prov 20:6
results of loyalty: Prov 20:28; 21:21
maintenance of one's position through loyalty:
Eccl 10:4
lack of loyalty: Hos 6:4
God's desire for His peoples' loyalty: Hos 6:6
exhortation to loyalty: Rev 2:10

LUCIFER (SEE SATAN)

M

MAN (SEE HUMANITY)

MARRIAGE

Marriage was the first divine institution of Scripture and the only one established for humanity before the entrance of sin. As such it is the foundational institution of human society. The divine ideal is established with the first man and woman (cf. Gen 2:18-25). The description of "cleaving" together so as to form "one flesh" depicts marriage as a union of love (cf. Hos 2:19) between a man and a woman forming a permanent community of personal concern and fidelity. It involves a covenant relationship (Mal 2:14). The explanation of woman being a "helper suitable" for man further explains marriage as equal partners in a complementary relation of mutual help. The selfishness of sin disrupts marital harmony, bringing turmoil, infidelity, and sometimes dissolution to marriages. Because

of the hardness of human hearts God permitted deviations from His creation ideal but regulated them from excessive abuse (cf. Matt 19:4-8). The marriage institution relates only to natural life on earth and is not retained in the resurrection life (Matt 22:30; see also DIVORCE).

MATERIALISM (SEE WEALTH)

MEDITATION (SEE PRAYER)

MEEKNESS (SEE GENTLENESS)

MERCY SEAT (SEE ARK; ATONEMENT)

MESSIAH (SEE CHRIST; ANOINT)

MIGHT (SEE POWER)

MIND (SEE ALSO HEART)
GOD'S MIND
appears to change (i.e., from the human perspective): Ex 32:12-14; Jer 26:13, 19; Amos 7:3, 6 (cf. 1 Sam 15:29; Ps 110:4)
unknowable by humans: Rom 11:34
considers people in their needs and frailty: Ps 40:17; 103:14; 115:12
Christ's mind: 1 Cor 2:16
the Spirit's mind: Rom 8:27
HUMAN'S MIND
ABILITIES OF
to make plans: 2 Sam 7:3; Prov 16:9
to receive understanding and direction from God: Neh 2:12 (cf. Job 38:36)
to instruct: Ps 16:7
to love God: Matt 22:37
to be opened to understand the Scriptures: Luke 24:45
to serve the law of God: Rom 7:25
to be set upon the Spirit: Rom 8:6
to be spiritually renewed: Rom 12:2 (cf. Eph 4:23)
to experience the mind of Christ: 1 Cor 2:16
to pray: 1 Cor 14:15
to be guarded in Christ through God's peace: Phil 4:7
to be set upon heavenly things: Col 3:2

MINISTRY (SEE SERVANT)

MIRACLES (SEE ALSO SIGN)
In the biblical sense a miracle is an event that is contrary to the regularly observed processes of nature. A number of Hebrew, Aramaic, and Greek words are used for the three distinctive emphases of miracles in Scripture: (1) an emphasis on the extraordinary nature of the miracle; (2) an emphasis on the power of the miracle; and (3) an emphasis on the meaning or significance of the miracle. Under the latter notion the purpose of the miracle is a confirmatory, corroborative, or authenticating token intended to cause recognition of a particular person or thing.

MISSIONS
throughout the world: Gen 12:3; Ps 96:3, 10; Is 49:6; Matt 24:14; 28:19-20; Acts 1:8; Rev 14:6
THROUGH CHOSEN SERVANTS AND PROPHETS OF GOD
in general: Jer 7:25; Zech 7:12; Matt 23:34
THROUGH THE SON OF GOD (SEE ALSO CHRIST; INCARNATION OF JESUS CHRIST, PURPOSE OF)
to the nations as light: Is 49:6
by the Father sending Him into the world: John 17:18; 20:21
to a ministry anointed by the Spirit: Luke 4:18-19
to accomplish redemption: Mark 10:45; Gal 4:4-6
THROUGH THE TWELVE APOSTLES (SEE ALSO APOSTLE)
TO ISRAEL
their general mission: Matt 10:1-23
their authority from Christ: Matt 10:1
TO ALL NATIONS
their commission from Christ: Matt 28:18-20; John 17:18; 20:21
their empowerment by the Spirit: Luke 24:49; John 15:26-27; Acts 1:8
through seventy other disciples: Luke 10:1-11
THROUGH THE APOSTLE PETER
general commission from Christ: Matt 16:18-19; John 21:18-19
mission to the Jews: Acts 2:14-41 (cf. Gal 2:7-9)
mission to the Samaritans: Acts 8:14-17
mission to the Gentiles: Acts 10:1-11:18
THROUGH THE APOSTLE PAUL
general commission from Christ: Acts 9:1-6
ministry to the Jews: Acts 9:20-22 (cf. Rom 9:1-5)
mission to the Gentiles: Acts 9:15; Rom 11:13; Gal 2:7-9
specific appointment by the Spirit: Acts 13:2-4
through an angel: Rev 14:6

MONEY (SEE ALSO WEALTH)
gold, silver, bronze, or copper used as money: Gen 13:2; Ex 35:5; 2 Kin 23:35; Matt 10:9; James 5:13 (cf. Gen 24:22)

lending of money: Ex 22:25; Deut 23:19;
  Neh 5:4, 10; Prov 28:8
bribery with money: Judg 16:5, 18; Matt 28:12-15;
  Mark 14:11; Acts 24:26
INABILITY OF MONEY
to deliver from the LORD's wrath: Zeph 1:18
to provide redemption: Ps 49:7-9; Is 52:3; 55:1-2
to profit in the day of wrath: Prov 11:4
to buy love: Song 8:7
to purchase the gift of God (i.e., the Spirit):
  Acts 8:18-20

MURDER (SEE HOMICIDE)

MUSIC
DIVINE APPROVAL OF
intended for worship: 2 Chr 29:25-30
revealed through God's prophets: 2 Chr 29:25
given to Israel as God's ordinance: Ps 81:1-5
David as organizer of musicians for worship:
  1 Chr 6:31
PARTICIPANTS IN
appointed singers in the Levitical choirs:
  1 Chr 6:31-32; 15:16-22; 2 Chr 5:12-13
the heavenly chorus: Rev 5:8-9; 14:3; 15:2-3
INSTRUMENTS OF MUSIC IN THE BIBLE
KINDS OF
lyre: Gen 4:21
bells: Ex 28:33-35
harp: 1 Sam 16:16
tambourine: 1 Sam 18:6
castanets: 2 Sam 6:5
loud-sounding cymbals: 1 Chr 15:16, 19;
  1 Chr 16:5; 2 Chr 5:12-13
trumpet: Num 10:2
ten-stringed lute: Ps 92:3
horn: Dan 3:5
flute: Dan 3:5
psaltery: Dan 3:5
bagpipe: Dan 3:5

MYSTERY
The basic biblical concept of a mystery is that
which is hidden or beyond natural human understanding. Outside of a few uses in relation
to symbols (e.g., Rev 1:20; Eph 5:32), the biblical uses all relate to God's future plans and
purposes for history (cf. Dan 2:28), with the
one exception dealing with evil (2 Thess 2:7).
Because of the beginning of the fulfillment of
OT prophecies that dealt with God's salvation
plan in Christ, the NT emphasizes the present
revelation of the mysteries, including both

their interpretation in apostolic teaching and
their realization in historical experience. The
revelation of a mystery and its understanding
is given only by God (cf. 1 Cor 2:6-12).

N

NAME
In biblical usage a name identifies a person,
animal, or thing, and it also reveals character
when a particular person is denoted. The divine
names are so closely associated with the divine
nature that they are used as virtually equivalent to God Himself (cf. Is 30:27; see also GOD,
names of; LORD). The significant expression "in
the name of Jesus" indicates "in the authority
or power of Jesus," (cf. Luke 10:17; John 14:13;
16:24; Acts 3:6, 16; 4:7; 16:18; Phil 2:10). To genuinely believe "in" or "into" or to "call upon" the
name of the LORD Jesus indicates commitment
to Him and establishment of communion with
Him (e.g., John 1:12; 3:18; Acts 2:21; 9:14; Rom
10:13; 1 John 3:23; 5:13).

NATIONS
unified origin of: Gen 2:7-25; Acts 17:26
  (cf. Gen 1:26-27); Rom 5:12-21
DIVISIONS OF
list of their divisions: Gen 10:1-32
divine appointment of their divisions: Deut 32:8;
  Acts 17:26
GOD'S RELATIONSHIP TO
He rules over the nations: 1 Chr 16:31; 2 Chr 20:6;
  Ps 22:28; Jer 10:7
HE CHOSE ABRAHAM FOR NATIONAL
PURPOSES
  *Abraham as father of the nation Israel (see
    also ISRAEL):* Gen 12:2 (cf. Amos 3:1-2)
  Abraham as father of a multitude of nations:
    Gen 17:4-6
  Abraham as a blessing to all nations: Gen 12:3;
    Gal 3:8, 13-14
*He desires divine blessing for all nations (see also
  MISSIONS, throughout the world):* Gen 12:3;
  Ps 96:3; Is 45:22; 52:10, 15; Matt 24:14; 28:19;
  Gal 3:13-14; 1 Tim 2:4
He has given the nations their inheritance:
  Deut 32:8
He controls the destiny of nations: Job 12:23
  (cf. Dan 4:17, 35)
He rebukes the nations: Ps 9:5
He keeps watch on the nations: Ps 66:7

He judges the nations: Gen 15:14; Deut 9:4-5;
  Ps 67:4; 79:6; 96:10; Is 34:2; Jer 10:25; Mic 5:15;
  Zeph 3:8; Rev 16:19
He guides the nations: Ps 67:4
He has made all nations: Ps 86:9
*He accepts without partiality people from every
  nation:* Acts 10:34-35

CHRIST'S RELATIONSHIP TO
He will inherit the nations: Ps 2:8
He will be served by all nations: Ps 72:11
*He will execute justice and judgment among the
  nations:* Is 2:4; 42:1; Matt 25:32
He will bring peace to the nations: Is 2:4
  (cf. 9:6-7); Zech 9:10
He will be a light to the nations: Is 49:6
*He will give overcomers authority over the
  nations:* Rev 2:26
He has redeemed people from every nation:
  Rev 5:9; 7:9

NATURE (SEE CREATION)

NEED (SEE ALSO POVERTY)

EXAMPLES OF NEED
of hospitality for strangers: Judg 19:19-21
of sinners for repentance: Luke 15:10
of members of the body for each other: 1 Cor 12:21
of immature believers for elementary teaching:
  Heb 5:12
of endurance to inherit divine promises: Heb 6:12;
  10:36
of clothing and daily food for the destitute:
  James 2:15-16; 1 John 3:17

PROVISION FOR THE NEEDY
PROVISION FROM GOD
  for the poor and needy: 1 Sam 2:8; Ps 12:5;
    35:10; Is 14:30
  for His people: Gen 22:8-14; Matt 6:33;
    Phil 4:19

PROVISION FROM CHRIST
  for the physically afflicted: Luke 9:11
  for the spiritually impoverished: Rev 3:17-18

PROVISION FROM HUMANS
  for the poor and needy: Ex 23:11; Lev 19:10;
    Deut 15:7-8, 11; 24:14-15; Job 31:16-22;
    Prov 31:20; Matt 25:31-40

NEIGHBOR

**RESPONSIBILITIES TOWARD ONE'S
NEIGHBOR**
NEGATIVE
  *not to bear false witness against your
    neighbor:* Ex 20:16

  *not to covet your neighbor's wife or
    possessions:* Ex 20:17
  not to commit adultery with your neighbor:
    Lev 18:20; Deut 22:24; Prov 6:29; Ezek 18:6
  not to oppress or rob a neighbor: Lev 19:13;
    Ezek 22:12
  not to do evil to your neighbor: Ps 15:3;
    Rom 13:10
  not to slander your neighbor: Ps 101:5
  *not to unnecessarily delay providing for your
    neighbor's need:* Prov 3:28
  not to devise harm against your neighbor:
    Prov 3:29
  not to be financial surety for your neighbor:
    Prov 6:1-3
  not to despise your neighbor: Prov 11:12; 14:21
  not to judge your neighbor: James 4:12
POSITIVE
  to make just restitution to your neighbor:
    Ex 22:7-14
  to judge your neighbor fairly: Lev 19:15
  to love your neighbor as yourself: Lev 19:18;
    Matt 5:43; 19:19; 22:39; Rom 13:8-9; Gal 5:14;
    James 2:8
  to be a righteous guide to your neighbor:
    Prov 12:26
  *to please your neighbor for his good and
    edification:* Rom 15:2; 1 Cor 10:24
  to speak truth with your neighbor: Eph 4:25

NEW BIRTH (SEE REGENERATION)

NEW CREATION (SEE REGENERATION)

NUMBERS

Numbers in the original biblical text are written
out in words. There is also evidence of an early
system of numerical notation during late OT
times (ca. 6th-4th cent. B.C.). Israel used the
decimal system of counting, as did her near
eastern neighbors. Scripture sometimes uses
numbers in a symbolic as well as a literal sense
(e.g., Gen 2:24; 2 Kin 5:10; Dan 9:24; Matt 18:22;
19:6; Rev 1:20; 4:4; 13:18).

O

OATH(S) (SEE ALSO CURSE)
An oath is a solemn vow or promise that includes a curse for breach of word or for failure
to speak the truth (Num 5:21; Neh 10:29; Dan

9:11; Mark 14:71). In biblical usage, to take an oath means to swear (e.g., Gen 50:24-25; Eccl 9:2; Heb 6:13-17; James 5:12).

BINDING CHARACTER OF
general principle: Num 30:2, 10, 13; Matt 5:33; 14:9; Heb 6:16-18
conditional cases: Gen 24:8; Josh 2:17, 20
warning concerning: Matt 5:34-37; James 5:12

OBEDIENCE (SEE ALSO DISOBEDIENCE)

TO GOD
OBEDIENCE OF ISRAEL
   required by God: Ex 19:5; Lev 19:37; Deut 10:12-13Josh 22:5; 2 Kin 17:37-38; Mal 4:4
   promised by Israel: Ex 24:7; Josh 24:24

IN RELATION TO CHRIST (I.E., MESSIAH)
OBEDIENCE TO CHRIST
   by the peoples: Gen 49:10
   by believers: John 14:23; Acts 5:32; 2 Cor 10:5; Heb 5:9; 1 Pet 1:2
exhortation to: Prov 7:1; Eccl 12:13; Jer 26:13; Phil 2:12; 1 Tim 6:13-14; Titus 3:1; James 1:22-25; 1 Pet 1:14

RESULTS OF
for Abraham: Gen 18:19
for Israel: Ex 19:5-6; Lev 18:5; Deut 4:40; 15:4-6; Josh 1:8; 1 Sam 12:14-15; 1 Kin 8:23; 2 Kin 21:8; 2 Chr 7:14; Neh 1:5; Prov 1:33; Is 1:19; Jer 7:23; Zech 6:15; Mal 3:10-12
for NT believers: Matt 7:24-25; John 13:17; 14:23; 15:10, 14; Acts 5:32; 2 Cor 9:13; Heb 5:9; James 1:25; 1 Pet 1:22; 1 John 2:3-4; 2:17; 3:22, 24; Rev 1:3

OFFERING(S) (SEE ALSO ATONEMENT; CHRIST, TYPES OF; PRIESTHOOD; SACRIFICES)

Offerings are gifts presented to God to express or to alter the offerer's relationship to God (Lev 1:2-3; 2:1-2; 3:1-2; 4:1-3). Offerings included certain clean animals (Lev 1:2, 14), grains (Ex 29:41; Lev 2:12), and liquids such as oil, frankincense, or incense (Lev 2:1; 6:15; Neh 13:9). Some offerings involved libations such as wine (Num 15:5), condiments such as salt (Lev 2:13), and precious metals such as silver, gold, or certain pieces of jewelry (Ex 35:22; Num 7:13-14; 31:50-52; Ezra 8:28). However, strict laws regulated each type and occasion of offering. The sacrificial animals had to be without defect (Lev 1:10; 4:28; 22:17-25; Num 6:14; cf. Mal 1:8). Honey was precluded from any offering by

fire (Lev 2:11) but included in tithes and first-fruits (2 Chr 31:5). Leaven was allowed only in the offerings assigned to the priests (e.g., Lev 7:13-14; cf. Amos 4:5). The offerings were put on an altar where they were burned or cooked (Lev 1:5-9; 2:1-10) and, in some cases, eaten (Lev 6:16, 26; 7:16; 1 Cor 9:13; 10:18; cf. Ex 12:1-11). The specific OT system of offerings (cf. Ex 29:10-18; Lev 1:1-7:38) was divinely instituted and thus unique to Israel in its carefully prescribed ritual. It included both obligatory and voluntary offerings and was necessary to maintain one's proper relationship within the theocracy of Israel. It provided a visible means to express obedience, worship, devotion, thanksgiving, fellowship, and commitment to God; it made temporary provision for sin through confession, forgiveness, cleansing, and reconciliation (cf. OT "atonement" in Lev 1:4; 17:11; Heb 9:10; 10:1-14); it represented substitution for the offerer through a sacrificial animal (Lev 1:4; cf. 1 Pet 3:18) and it foreshadowed NT principles of humanity's relationship to God, especially through Jesus Christ's own substitutionary sacrifice for sinners (Matt 26:26-28; Rom 3:22-26; 2 Cor 5:18-21; Heb 4:14-10:22).

KINDS OF
BURNT OFFERING
   general: Gen 8:20; 22:2-13; Ex 10:25; 24:5; Lev 1:1-17; 6:8-13; Num 7:15-87; 1 Kin 8:63-65; 1 Chr 16:1-2; Is 56:7; Jer 33:18; Ezek 40:38-42; Hos 6:6; Amos 5:22; Mic 6:6; Mal 1:1; Mark 12:33; Heb 10:6, 8
drink offering or libation: Gen 35:14; Ex 29:40-41; Lev 23:13; Ezek 45:17; Phil 2:17; 2 Tim 4:6
peace offering: 1 Chr 16:2; Prov 7:14; Ezek 46:12; Amos 5:22
sin offering: Ex 29:14; Lev 4:1-5:13; Ps 40:6; Heb 10:18
wave offering: Ex 29:24; Lev 7:30, 34
heave offering: Ex 29:27-28
grain offering: Ex 29:41; Lev 2:1-16; Neh 13:5
INCENSE OFFERING
   general: Lev 2:15-16; Num 7:14-86
guilt offering: Lev 5:6-7; 14:12-28 (cf. Matt 8:2-4); Num 6:12; 18:9
freewill offering: Ex 35:29; Lev 7:16; Num 29:39
votive offering: Lev 7:16; 22:18; Num 29:39; Deut 12:17
Nazirite offering: Num 6:13-21
thank offering: 2 Chr 29:31; Ps 56:12; Jer 33:11; Amos 4:5

OMNIPOTENCE (SEE GOD, ATTRIBUTES OF, OMNIPOTENT)

OMNIPRESENCE (SEE GOD, ATTRIBUTES OF, OMNIPRESENT)

OMNISCIENCE (SEE GOD, ATTRIBUTES OF, OMNISCIENT)

ORDINANCES (SEE LAW)

ORDINATION

The term ordination (from a Latin word meaning "to arrange," "to appoint to office") is used in a variety of ways in Scripture. One significant use is for the appointment of individuals to specific ministries among the people of God both in Israel and the church. When this appointment involved human instrumentality, it was done with the ritual of anointing or the laying on of hands. The practice of ordaining people to ministries does not confer authority or spiritual ability on the person ordained. Rather, it is the recognition by the people of God of those individuals whom God has called and equipped for a particular task (cf. Deut 10:8; Jer 1:5; 1 Cor 12:11; Eph 5:7, 11).

OVERCOMING (SEE VICTORY)

P

PAIN (SEE SUFFERING)

PARABLES (SEE FIGURATIVE SPEECH)

PARENTS (SEE FAMILY; FATHER, HUMAN)

PARTNERSHIP (SEE FELLOWSHIP)

PASSOVER (SEE FEASTS)

PATIENCE
GOD'S PATIENCE
DIVINE EXPRESSION OF
  His patience when provoked (i.e., slow to anger): Ex 34:6; Num 14:18; Ps 78:38
  His patient endurance of vessels of wrath: Rom 9:22
  His patience in giving prolonged opportunity for salvation: 2 Pet 3:9, 15
  Christ's patience: 1 Tim 1:16; 1 Pet 2:21-23
HUMAN'S PATIENCE
EXERCISE OF PATIENCE
  in waiting upon the LORD: Ps 37:7; 40:1; Heb 6:15
  as a characteristic of love: 1 Cor 13:4
  in Christian character and conduct: 2 Cor 6:6; Eph 4:2; Col 1:11; 3:12; 1 Thess 5:14
  as fruit of the Spirit: Gal 5:22
  in Christian ministry: 2 Tim 4:2
  in view of the LORD's coming: James 5:7-8
value of patience: Eccl 7:8

PEACE
In Scripture, the term peace refers to a personal sense of well-being, wholeness, harmony, and security through a proper relationship with God and other people. Believers have (1) "peace with God" as a result of the justification by faith in Christ, who has "made peace through the blood of His cross" (Col 1:20; cf. Rom 5:1, 10; Col 1:21-22); (2) "peace from God" (e.g., Rom 1:7; 1 Cor 1:3); and (3) "the peace of God" by committing all anxiety to Him in prayer (Phil 4:6-7; cf. Is 26:3; John 14:27). Christ is properly called "our peace" (Eph 2:14) since He has broken down the barrier of legal commandments between Jews and Gentiles so that believers from both groups are reconciled "in one body to God through the cross" (Eph 2:16; cf. vv. 14-18).

PENALTY (SEE JUDGMENT)

PENITENCE (SEE REPENTANCE)

PENTECOST (SEE FEASTS)

PEOPLE OF GOD
The phrase "people of God" signifies a people distinct from other peoples because of their unique relationship with God. The same concept is expressed by the more frequently used phrases "My people," "His people," and "Your people." The terminology was first applied to the nation of Israel, which was set apart from the other nations to be God's people (e.g., Ex 19:5). It was later applied to the church (e.g., Titus 2:14). The basic ideas in the concept include (1) God's elective love that establishes the relationship; (2) being set apart unto God and consequently called to holiness of life; and

(3) being commissioned for God's service in the world (see also CHURCH; ISRAEL).

PERSECUTION

of the nation Israel: Ex 3:7-9; Deut 30:7; Ps 129:1-2; Is 14:4-6; Lam 1:3; Rev 12:13 (cf. Acts 18:2)

OF INDIVIDUAL BELIEVERS

EXAMPLES OF THE PERSECUTED

general groups
prophets and other people of God:
2 Chr 36:15-16; Ps 11:2; Matt 5:12; 23:30-31, 34-35, 37; Acts 7:52
apostles and other messengers of God: Acts 4:3-21; 5:27, 40-41; 6:8-7:60

causes of persecution: Ps 119:161; Matt 5:10-11; Mark 10:29-30; Luke 21:12; John 15:20-21; 16:2-3; 2 Cor 12:10; 2 Tim 3:12; Rev 1:9 (cf. Matt 13:21)

results of persecution: Matt 5:10-12; Mark 10:29-30; Acts 8:1; 11:19; 2 Cor 12:10; Phil 1:12-14

of the church: Acts 8:1, 3; 9:1-2, 13-14; 11:19; 22:4; 1 Cor 15:9; Gal 1:13, 23; 4:29; Phil 3:6; 1 Thess 1:4; 2:14; 2 Thess 1:4; 1 Tim 1:13; 1 Pet 4:4; Rev 2:9-10

OF JESUS

prediction of persecution (see also CHRIST, OT prophecies of): Ps 2:1-3; 22:6-21; 69:26; Is 50:5-6; 52:13-53:12; Zech 12:10

indication of persecution: Matt 2:16-18; 26:57-68; John 5:16; 15:20, 23-25; Acts 2:23; 4:27; 7:52; 9:4-5; Heb 12:2-3

quiet endurance of persecution: Is 50:6; 53:7; Matt 26:62-64; 27:13-14; 1 Pet 2:23

deliverance from His persecutors: Luke 4:28-30 (cf. Matt 26:53)

judgment of persecutors: Deut 30:7; Ps 2:1-5; 119:84; Is 14:3-6; Jer 17:18; Matt 23:25-36; 2 Thess 1:6-10; Rev 17:6; 18:4-8

PERSEVERANCE (SEE ALSO ENDURANCE)

PERSEVERANCE BY BELIEVERS

AREAS OF PERSEVERANCE

in interceding for others: Gen 18:23-32
in seeking God's blessing: Gen 32:24-28
in bearing spiritual fruit: Luke 8:15
in saving faith: Luke 22:31-32; 1 Cor 1:8-9; Phil 1:6; 2:12-13; 2 Thess 3:3-4; 2 Tim 1:12; Heb 10:39; 13:20-21; 1 Pet 1:4-5 (cf. Ps 37:28); 1 John 2:19; 4:4
in obeying Christ's word: John 8:31-32

in doing good: Rom 2:7
in enduring tribulation: Rom 12:12
in praying for one's physical afflictions: 2 Cor 12:7-9
in praying for the saints: Eph 6:18
in enduring persecutions and afflictions: 2 Thess 1:4
in rejoicing: 1 Thess 5:16
in prayer: 1 Thess 5:17
in giving thanks: 1 Thess 5:18
in undergoing trials: James 1:12
exhortation to perseverance: Neh 4:14; Matt 24:13; Acts 11:23; 13:43; 14:21-22; 1 Cor 15:58; Gal 6:9; Col 1:23; Heb 3:6, 12-14; 4:11; 6:1, 11-12; 12:1-3, 12-14; Rev 3:1-3

RESULTS OF PERSEVERANCE

provision of hope: Rom 15:4
promised reward: Gal 6:9; James 1:12; Rev 2:25-28; 3:11 (cf. Heb 10:36)
promised deliverance: Rev 3:10
commendation for perseverance: Rev 2:2-3, 19; 3:10

PHARISEES

IDENTITY OF

prominent Jewish sect: Matt 27:62-64; John 9:13-16, 22; Acts 15:5
members of Sanhedrin: Acts 23:6
rejected John the Baptist: Luke 7:30

OPPOSED CHRIST

QUESTIONED AND TESTED JESUS ABOUT

general: Luke 11:53-54; 20:20, 24
divorce: Matt 19:3; Mark 10:2
washing: Matt 15:1-2; Mark 7:5
fasting: Matt 9:14; Mark 2:18; Luke 5:33
eating with sinners: Matt 9:11; Mark 2:16; Luke 5:30
paying taxes: Matt 22:15-17; Mark 12:13-15
most important command: Matt 22:34-36
coming of kingdom: Luke 17:20, 21

DENOUNCED BY CHRIST FOR

hypocrisy: Matt 5:20; 15:1-9; 23:1-32; Luke 11:37-44; 16:14, 15; 18:9-14
pride: Matt 23:6, 7; Luke 11:43; 18:11; John 12:42, 43
for false teaching: Matt 15:1, 3-6
blasphemy: Matt 12:24, 30-32
seeking signs: Matt 12:38; 16:1-4
persecuting and killing God's servants: Matt 21:33-46; 23:33-36
love of money: Luke 16:1

PITY (SEE COMPASSION)

PLANS

IN RELATION TO GOD
He informs His people of His plans: Num 33:56
His plans were formed long ago: 2 Kin 19:25; Is 25:1
He plans judgment for individuals, nations, and the world: 2 Chr 25:16; Is 14:26; Jer 18:11; 49:20; 50:45; Mic 2:3
He frustrates and thwarts plans against Him and His people: Neh 4:15; Ps 33:10; Is 8:10
His plans are invincible: Ps 33:11; Is 14:24, 27; 46:11; Acts 5:39
He hates wicked plans: Prov 6:18; 15:26
He overrules the outcome of people's plans: Prov 16:1, 9
His plans are perfectly faithful: Is 25:1
His plan including delivering up His Son to death: Acts 2:23

IN RELATION TO HUMANS
SUCCESS OF A PERSON'S PLANS
by consulting with counselors: Prov 15:22 (cf. 11:14)
by committing one's works to the LORD: Prov 16:3
by being diligent: Prov 21:5
failure of people's plans (especially in opposition to God's plan): 1 Sam 18:25; Jer 6:19; Acts 5:38; 27:42-43

PLENTY (SEE ABUNDANCE)

POVERTY (SEE ALSO NEED)

CONCERN FOR THE POOR
OF GOD
He cares for them: 1 Sam 2:8; Ps 34:6
He provides safety for them: Ps 12:5
His is a refuge for them: Ps 14:6; Is 25:4
He helps them: Ps 40:17
He makes physical provision for them: Ps 68:10; 132:15; Is 41:17; 2 Cor 9:9
He has compassion for them: Ps 72:13
OF CHRIST
His justice for them: Is 11:4
His spiritual provision for them: Matt 11:5; Luke 4:18-19
His exhortation to give to them: Matt 19:21; Luke 14:13
His commendation of a poor but generous widow: Mark 12:42-43
OF PEOPLE
divine requirements
give freely for the needs of the poor: Deut 15:11; Prov 28:27; 31:20; Matt 19:21; Luke 12:33; Rom 15:26
be gracious to the poor: Prov 14:21

do not oppress the poor: Prov 14:31
do not mock the poor: Prov 17:5
respond to the cry of the poor: Prov 21:13
give food to the poor: Prov 22:9; Is 58:7; Matt 25:35
be concerned for rights of the poor: Prov 29:7 (cf. Jer 5:28)
give shelter to the homeless poor: Is 58:7
show mercy to the poor: Dan 4:27
be hospitable to the poor: Matt 25:35; Luke 14:13
do not dishonor the poor: James 2:6

POSSESSIONS (SEE WEALTH)

POWER (SEE ALSO AUTHORITY)
of God (see also GOD, attributes of)
HUMAN
SPIRITUAL POWER
given by God: Ex 15:2; 2 Sam 22:40; Ps 28:7, 8; Is 40:31; 41:10; Dan 11:32; 2 Cor 13:4; Phil 4:13; 2 Tim 1:7; 4:17
associated with Holy Spirit: Mic 3:8; Zech 4:6; Luke 24:49; Acts 1:8; 4:31, 33; Rom 14:13
especially with apostles: Matt 10:1; Luke 9:1; Acts 3:12; 4:7; Rom 15:19; 1 Cor 2:4; 5:4; 2 Cor 6:7; 12:12; Eph 3:7; 1 Thess 1:5
PURPOSES OF
steadfastness, perseverance: Col 1:11; 1 Pet 1:5; 2 Tim 1:8
hope: Eph 1:18, 19; Rom 14:13
witness: Acts 1:8; 4:33
godliness: 2 Pet 1:3
good works: 2 Thess 1:11
spiritual warfare: Eph 6:10-17; 2 Cor 10:4
prayer: Rom 8:26
works miracles: Acts 6:8; 1 Cor 12:10; Heb 6:5

POWERS

MIRACULOUS POWERS
performed by Christ: Matt 13:54
experienced by certain early Christians: Heb 6:5
powers of the heavens: Matt 24:29
evil spiritual powers in the heavenlies: Eph 6:12
POWERS IN CREATION
unable to separate believers from God's love in Christ: Rom 8:38
subjected to Christ: 1 Pet 3:22

PRAISE (SEE ALSO BLESS; PRAYER; WORSHIP)
REASONS FOR
God's righteousness: Ps 7:17
God's power: Ps 21:13

God's deliverance: Ps 40:1-3
God's goodness, graciousness, truth, and
   faithfulness: Ps 57:9-10; 89:1-2
God's greatness, splendor, majesty, strength,
   and beauty: Ps 96:4-6
God's holiness: Ps 99:3
God's goodness: Ps 135:3
answered prayer from God: Dan 2:23
God's salvation: Luke 1:68-75
Christ's miraculous power: Luke 18:43; 19:37
the value of tested Christian faith: 1 Pet 1:7

PRAYER

ADDRESSEES OF PRAYER
to the LORD: Gen 12:8; 1 Sam 1:10; 1 Kin 8:23;
   Acts 4:24; 2 Cor 12:8
to God: Gen 32:9; 2 Chr 20:5-6; Dan 9:17-19;
   Luke 18:13; Acts 4:24
to the LORD God: Deut 3:24; 1 Kin 18:36
to the Father: Matt 6:6; 11:25-26; John 11:41;
   12:27; Eph 3:14
to Jesus Christ: Luke 23:42; Acts 7:59

RELATION OF PRAYER
TO THE FATHER
He knows His children's needs before they
   ask: Matt 6:8
He is the primary addressee of the Christian's
   prayer: Matt 6:9; Eph 3:14
He responds to proper prayer: Matt 18:19
TO THE SON
approach the Father only through Him:
   John 14:6; Rom 1:8; Heb 10:19-22
pray in His name: John 14:13-14; 16:14;
   Eph 5:20
TO THE SPIRIT
He activates supplication: Zech 12:10
He intercedes for the saints in their prayers:
   Rom 8:26-27
He is the One in whom the believer prays:
   Eph 6:18; Jude 20

PRIMARY KINDS OF PRAYER
for intercession: Gen 18:22-32; Ex 32:11-13;
   Num 14:17-19; Deut 9:25-29; 1 Sam 7:8-9;
   Job 42:8-10; Ps 7:9; Jer 29:7; Matt 5:44;
   Luke 22:32; 23:34; John 17:1-26; Acts 7:60;
   Rom 1:9-10; 10:1; Eph 6:18-19; Col 4:3, 12;
   1 Tim 2:1-2; Philem 22; Heb 13:20-21;
   James 5:14-16
for invocation of God's blessing:
   Num 6:23-27
for confession of sin: Judg 10:10-15; 1 Kin 8:47;
   Ps 32:1-5; Is 59:12-15; Jer 14:7, 20; Lam 3:41-42;
   Dan 9:3-15; Luke 18:13

for imprecation (i.e., calling down judgment
   upon enemies): Judg 16:28; Neh 4:4-5;
   Ps 5:10; 28:4; 109:7-20; Jer 11:20; Lam 1:22;
   Gal 1:8-9
for petition: 1 Sam 1:17, 27; Jer 42:9; Dan 6:11-13;
   Luke 1:13; Eph 6:18
in emergency: Neh 2:4; Matt 14:30

BASIC CONDITIONS FOR ANSWERED PRAYER
seeking God with a whole and pure heart:
   Deut 4:29; Jer 29:13; 2 Tim 2:22
requests in accordance with God's word:
   2 Sam 7:21, 25-29; Neh 1:8-10; John 15:7
obedience to God's word: 1 Kin 18:36; Ps 119:145;
   John 15:7; 1 John 3:22
confession and repentance for sin: 2 Chr 6:37;
   7:14; Neh 1:6-7; Dan 9:4-19; Luke 18:13;
   James 5:16; 1 John 1:9
humility: 2 Chr 7:14; 33:12-13; Ezra 8:21; 9:5;
   Ps 10:17; Dan 10:12; Luke 18:13-14
submission to God's will: Job 1:20-21; Matt 6:10;
   26:39, 42; John 9:31; 1 John 5:14-15
a righteous life: Ps 34:15; Prov 15:8, 29;
   James 5:16
faith in the LORD: Ps 37:5; Matt 21:22;
   Mark 9:23-24; Heb 11:6; James 1:6; 5:15
sincerity (i.e., prayer in truth): Ps 145:18
reverence for God: Ps 145:19; John 9:31
forgiveness of others: Matt 6:14-15; Mark 11:25
petition in Christ's name: John 14:13-14; 16:24
holy hands: 1 Tim 2:8
absence of wrath and dissension: 1 Tim 2:8
piety: Heb 5:7

PREACHING

SELECTED EXAMPLES OF PREACHING
SPECIFIC PERSONS
Noah: Gen 6:9; 2 Pet 2:5
Solomon: Eccl 1:1
Ezekiel: Ezek 21:2
Jonah: Jon 1:2; 3:2
Haggai and Zechariah: Ezra 6:14; Hag 1:3-11;
   Zech 1:1-6
John the Baptist: Matt 3:1
Jesus (see also CHRIST): e.g., Matt 4:17;
   Mark 1:38-39; Luke 4:18-19; 1 Pet 3:18-19
Peter: Acts 2:14; 3:12-26
Stephen: Acts 6:8-7:53
Philip: Acts 8:5-8
Peter and John: Acts 8:25 (cf. v. 14)
Paul: Acts 9:20-22, 27; 1 Cor 1:17; 9:16; 15:1;
   1 Tim 2:7; 2 Tim 1:11
Timothy: 2 Tim 4:2

CERTAIN GENERAL GROUPS

the twelve disciples: Mark 16:20; Luke 9:1-2
the seventy disciples: Luke 10:1-11
the believers gathered at Pentecost: Acts 2:4-11
preaching by believers in the early church:
    Acts 8:4
*preaching by believers besides Paul and
    Barnabas at Antioch:* Acts 15:35

PROPER MANNER

with enablement from the Spirit: Acts 2:4; 4:31;
    7:55; 1 Thess 1:5; 1 Pet 1:12 (cf. 2 Cor 3:5-6)
with boldness: Acts 4:31; 13:46; 2 Cor 3:12
with a sense of God's commission: Rom 10:15
with the purpose of spiritual edification:
    1 Cor 14:1-25 (cf. Eph 4:11-16)
in power and personal conviction: 1 Thess 1:5
with diligence and accuracy: 2 Tim 2:15

PRECEPTS (SEE LAW)

PRECIOUS STONES

USES OF

*engraved with the names of the twelve tribes
    of Israel and mounted on the breastpiece of
    judgment:* Ex 28:15-21
a wall of precious stones (figurative for value):
    Is 54:12
*a covering of precious stones (figurative for
    beauty):* Ezek 28:13; Rev 17:4
*representative of Christian works which qualify
    for reward:* 1 Cor 3:12-14
representative of worldly riches: Rev 17:4; 18:12, 16
as the foundation stones of the new Jerusalem:
    Rev 21:19

TYPES OF

ruby: Ex 28:17; Is 54:12
topaz: Ex 28:17; Rev 21:20
emerald: Ex 28:17; Rev 21:19
turquoise: Ex 28:18
sapphire: Ex 28:18; Job 28:16; Is 54:11; Rev 21:19
diamond: Ex 28:18
jacinth: Ex 28:19; Rev 21:20
agate: Ex 28:19
amethyst: Ex 28:19; Rev 21:20
beryl: Ex 28:20; Rev 21:20
onyx: Ex 28:20; Job 28:16
jasper: Ex 28:20; Rev 21:19
crystal: Is 54:12
chalcedony: Rev 21:19
sardonyx: Rev 21:20
sardius: Rev 21:20
chrysolite: Rev 21:20
chrysoprase: Rev 21:20

PREDESTINATION (SEE ALSO CHOSEN)

To predestine means to "predetermine," "fore-ordain," or "mark off beforehand." Biblical pre-destination is God's eternal predetermination of all things according to His perfect will and char-acter and for His own glory (Ps 145:17; Rom 11:36; Eph 1:6, 11-12, 14). Predestination encompasses both directly caused events (e.g., Gen 1; Ps 33:9; James 1:18) and also divinely permitted events (e.g., Num 22-24; Luke 22:21-22; Acts 2:23-24; 4:27-28). Scripture relates divine predestination primarily to God's redemptive purposes for His people (Deut 7:7-8; Acts 18:10; Rom 8:28-30; 1 Pet 2:9). The Christian doctrine of predesti-nation is distinct from fatalism, since Scripture affirms human responsibility along with divine sovereignty (Acts 2:23, 36; Phil 2:12-13).

PRIDE

CAUSES OF

satisfaction in prosperity: Deut 8:12-14; Hos 13:6
dependence on human power: Deut 8:17-18
toleration of evil: 1 Cor 5:1-2, 6
knowledge without love: 1 Cor 8:1 (cf. 13:2)
trust in uncertain riches: 1 Tim 6:17 (cf. Prov 18:11)

REMEDY FOR PRIDE

be humble (see also HUMILITY): 2 Chr 32:26;
    Prov 16:19; 18:12; 29:23; Phil 2:3; James 4:6;
    1 Pet 5:5-6
do not have a proud heart: Ps 131:1
hate pride: Prov 8:13
boast only in the LORD: 1 Cor 1:31
*accept God's grace in suffering to prevent
    exaltation of self:* 2 Cor 12:7-9

PROPER PRIDE

pride in the LORD: 2 Chr 17:6; Ps 34:2; Jer 9:24;
    1 Cor 1:31
everlasting pride in redeemed Israel: Is 60:15
*pride in Christians (i.e., only through God's
    gracious work in Christ and the power of the
    Spirit):* Rom 15:17-19; 2 Cor 1:12, 14; 7:4;
    Phil 1:26; 2 Thess 1:4
pride in the cross of Christ: Gal 6:14

PRIESTHOOD

PRIESTHOOD IN ISRAEL

PRIESTHOOD OF AARON

PRIMARY FEATURES

had Aaron as the first high priest: Ex 28:1;
    Lev 8:7-9; 16:1-34; Heb 5:1, 4
consecrated to the LORD: Ex 29:1-9; 40:12-16;
    Lev 8-9

assisted by the Levites in the service of the
tabernacle: Num 3:1-39; 4:1-49

had no allotted territorial inheritance in the
promised land: Num 18:20 (cf. Lev 27:21);
Ezek 48:8-14

had the LORD as their inheritance: Num 18:20

inherited certain cities for residences:
Josh 21:13-19

supervised the rebuilding of the temple: Ezra
3:8-13

ministered in the earthly tabernacle and
temple: Heb 8:4-5

had access to the Holy Place only by the high
priest once annually: Heb 9:7, 25

PRIMARY FUNCTIONS

to minister to the LORD: 1 Chr 23:13

to perform the duties of the sanctuary:
Ex 27:21; Num 3:38; Heb 9:6

to burn fragrant incense on the altar of incense:
Ex 30:7-9; 1 Chr 23:13; Luke 1:5-9

to offer sacrifices to the LORD for themselves
and for the people (see also OFFERING):
Lev 1-7; 9; Heb 5:1-3; 7:27; 9:6-7

to teach people the law: Lev 10:11; Ezra 7:10;
Mal 2:6-7 (cf. 2 Chr 15:3; Neh 8:7-8); Jer 2:8

to confess the sins of the people in prayer:
Lev 16:20-21; Ezra 9:5-15

to transport the ark of the covenant on
special occasions: Josh 3:1-17; 1 Kin 8:1-11

to pray for the people: Joel 2:17

PRIESTHOOD OF CHRIST

typified by Melchizedek

involves His role as merciful and faithful great
high priest: Heb 2:17; 3:1; 4:14; 8:1

qualified Him to make propitiation for the sins
of the people: Heb 2:17

included His being tempted in all things as we
are, yet without sin: Heb 4:15

provides eternal salvation: Heb 7:25

includes continual intercession for believers:
Heb 7:25 (cf. Rom 8:34; 1 John 2:1)

included Himself as a sacrifice once for all:
Heb 7:27; 9:12

includes his seated position at the Father's right
hand: Heb 8:1 (cf. 1:3)

resulted in obtaining eternal redemption: Heb 9:12

involved His mediatorship of the New Covenant:
Heb 9:15

PRIESTHOOD OF NT BELIEVERS

universality of: 1 Pet 2:5, 9 (cf. Rev 1:6; 5:10; 20:6)

PRIVILEGES OF

direct access by faith to the Father through
Christ: John 14:6; Rom 5:2; Eph 2:18

availability of divine mercy and grace to help
in time of need: Heb 4:16

PRISONERS (SEE CAPTIVITY)

PROCLAMATION (SEE PREACHING)

PROFANITY (SEE ALSO CURSE)

through taking God's name in vain: Ex 20:7;
Ps 139:20

through swearing falsely by God's name: Lev 19:12

through blaspheming God's name: Is 52:5;
Rom 2:24

PROFESSION (SEE FAITH)

PROFIT

THINGS THAT PRODUCE PROFIT

SPIRITUAL PROFIT

godly wisdom: Prov 3:13-14

following and learning from the LORD: Is 48:17

teaching God's truth: Acts 20:20 (cf. v. 27)

salvation: 1 Cor 10:33

giving for the LORD's service: Phil 4:16-17

godliness: 1 Tim 4:8

Scripture: 2 Tim 3:16

good works: Titus 3:8

THINGS THAT DO NOT PROFIT

illicit gains: Prov 10:2; 15:27; Ezek 22:12;
Acts 16:16, 19

riches in the day of wrath: Prov 11:4

mere talk: Prov 14:23

attempt to find ultimate satisfaction in labor:
Eccl 2:11

idolatry: Is 44:10; Jer 2:11; Hab 2:18

a walk in disobedience to God: Jer 2:8

things that are lawful but not edifying: 1 Cor 10:23

hearing God's word without believing it: Heb 4:2

PROMISES

concerning Christ (see also CHRIST, OT
prophecies of)

concerning the Spirit (see also SPIRIT, HOLY):
Joel 2:28-32 (cf. Luke 24:49); John 7:38-39;
16:7; Acts 1:4-5; 2:17-21, 33, 38-39; Gal 3:14;
Eph 1:13

to Noah: Gen 8:21-22; 9:8-17

TO ABRAHAM, ISAAC, AND JACOB

covenant to Abraham: Gen 12:1-3

a land to Abraham: Gen 12:1; Neh 9:8; Acts 7:5;
Heb 11:9

a son to Abraham: Gen 15:2-6; Rom 4:16-21;
9:8-9; Gal 3:15-22; 4:23

Abrahamic covenant to Isaac: Gen 17:19
Abrahamic covenant to Jacob: Gen 28:13-15

TO ISRAEL

the land of Canaan: Ex 12:25
a kingdom of priests and a holy nation: Ex 19:5-6
population increase and blessing: Deut 1:11
good things for obedience: Deut 6:1-3; 28:1-14;
   Josh 23:14-15; 1 Kin 8:56 (cf. Num 10:29)
threats of punishment for disobedience:
   Deut 28:15-68; Josh 23:15-16; Jer 18:9-10;
   40:2-3
God's help in their warfare: Josh 23:10
God's Spirit in Israel's midst: Hag 2:5
the kingdom to Israel: Acts 1:6-7
general references: Rom 9:4; 15:8
to David (see also COVENANT): 2 Sam 7:25-29

TO PEOPLE IN GENERAL

the gospel of God: Rom 1:1-2
the provisions of the New Covenant: Heb 8:6

TO BELIEVERS
PRIMARY CONTENTS OF PROMISES
(SEE ALSO BLESS)

   assurance of God's presence: Gen 28:15; Josh 1:5
      (cf. Heb 13:5), 9; Is 41:10; Acts 2:25; James 4:8
   prosperity and success: Josh 1:8
   blessing: Ps 1:1; Jer 17:7
   a fruitful life: Ps 1:3; Jer 17:8
   provision for all needs: Ps 23:1-6; Matt 6:33;
      Luke 6:38; 2 Cor 9:6-8; Phil 4:19
   protection from harm: Ps 34:7
   blessing: Ps 67:6-7; 84:12
   grace and glory: Ps 84:11
   peace: Ps 85:8; John 14:27; Rom 5:1; Phil 4:6-7
   forgiveness of sin: Ps 103:3; Prov 28:13;
      Acts 13:38-39; 1 John 1:9
   reaping what is sown: Ps 126:5-6; Gal 6:7-8
   answered prayer: Jer 33:3; Matt 21:22;
      1 John 5:14-15
   spiritual rest: Matt 11:28-30
   reward: Matt 25:21; Heb 11:6
   Christ's continual presence: Matt 28:20
   eternal life through Christ: John 3:16; 2 Tim 1:1;
      Titus 1:2; 1 John 2:25 (cf. Dan 12:2)
   *resurrection with a glorified body patterned
      after Christ's body:* John 11:25-26;
      1 Cor 15:51-57; Phil 3:20-21; 1 John 3:2
   heavenly abodes with Christ: John 14:2-3
      (cf. 1 Thess 4:17)
   Christ's presence in believers: John 14:20
      (cf. Col 1:27)
   fellow heirs with Christ: Rom 8:16-17
      (cf. Gal 3:29)
   divine comfort: 2 Cor 1:3-4

*sons and daughters of God through faith in
   Christ:* Gal 3:26 (cf. John 1:12)
children of promise: Gal 4:28
*spiritual blessings in Christ through the
   gospel:* Eph 3:6 (cf. 1 Cor 2:9)
well-being and long life: Eph 6:2-3
spiritual strength and protection from Satan:
   Eph 6:10-17; 2 Thess 3:3
entrance into God's rest: Heb 4:1-11
eternal inheritance: Heb 9:15
the crown of life: James 1:12; Rev 2:10
heirs of the kingdom: James 2:5
victory over the devil: James 4:7
an imperishable inheritance in heaven:
   1 Pet 1:3-4
everything pertaining to life and godliness:
   2 Pet 1:3
partakers of the divine nature: 2 Pet 1:4
coming of Christ: 2 Pet 3:4, 9 (cf. John 14:3)
new heavens and a new earth: 2 Pet 3:13
eternal reign with God: Rev 22:5

PROPERTY (SEE WEALTH)

PROPHETS

SELECTION OF

directly by God: Ex 3:1-17; Num 12:8; Ps 103:7;
   Is 6:8; Jer 1:4-5, 10; Amos 7:14-15; Jon 1:1-3
through the Holy Spirit: 1 Sam 10:6-13; 19:23-24
   (cf. Luke 4:18-19)
through another prophet: 1 Kin 19:19-21
through an angel of the LORD: Luke 1:11-17; Rev 1:1

FUNCTION OF

*predicted the future (see also CHRIST, OT
   prophecies of):* Deut 18:15; 1 Sam 9:19-20;
   1 Kin 17:1; 18:41; Is 37:21-37; Joel 2:28-32;
   Mic 5:2; Acts 11:28 (cf.
spoke God's message to particular individuals:
   1 Sam 9:15-10:8; 2 Sam 12:1-14; 1 Kin 18:16-19;
   21:17-24; 2 Kin 10:10; 19:5-7; 2 Chr 33:18;
   Jer 21:1-7; 45:1-5; Dan 2:29-45; 4:19-27;
   Hag 2:2-4, 20-23; Matt 14:1-12
   (especially v. 12); Acts 21:10-11
used as agents of the Spirit: 1 Sam 10:6-13;
   2 Chr 24:20; Joel 2:28; Zech 7:12; Acts 11:28;
   1 Cor 12:7-11; 1 Pet 1:11-12; Rev 1:10-11
involved in the coronation of kings: 1 Kin 1:32-35
*proclaimed God's judgment on sin (see also
   JUDGMENT):* 1 Kin 21:20-24; Is 2:12-21; 13:11;
   24:1-23; 26:21; Jer 4:5-18; Dan 5:22-30;
   Hos 9:7-9
revealed God's message to kings: 1 Kin 22:6-28;
   2 Kin 6:9-12; Is 37:2-7; Jer 27:12-15

called the people to repentance (see also
   REPENTANCE): 2 Kin 17:13; Is 30:15; Jer 18:11;
   Ezek 14:6; Matt 3:2
served as watchmen to warn people: Neh 9:30;
   Jer 6:16-17; Ezek 3:16-21
edified the church: 1 Cor 14:1-5, 12
evangelized unbelievers: 1 Cor 14:24-25
given by Christ to the church for ministry:
   Eph 4:10-13

FALSE PROPHETS
evil character of: Deut 13:1-2; Is 28:7; Jer 14:16;
   23:11, 14; 2 Pet 2:1-3, 12-19
test of: Deut 13:1-3; 2 Pet 2:1-3, 12-19;
   1 John 4:1-3
warnings against: Deut 13:1-3; Matt 24:24
response to: Deut 13:3; 18:22; Jer 23:16
punishment for: Deut 18:20; Jer 14:13-16; 23:12,
   30-32; 28:16-17; 29:32; Ezek 13:9-23; Zech 13:3
   (cf. Neh 6:14)
examples of: 1 Kin 22:6-12; Neh 6:14; Jer 20:6;
   28:1-17; 29:31-32
deception and falsehood of: Neh 6:10-14;
   Jer 14:13-16; 23:26, 32; Lam 2:14; Ezek 13:2-3,
   6-10, 16, 22-23; Matt 24:24
divine denunciation upon: Jer 23:9-22
foolishness of: Lam 2:14; Ezek 13:3

PROPITIATION (SEE ALSO ATONEMENT; SALVATION)

Propitiation means that Christ's redemptive sacrifice has satisfied God's holy wrath against human sin (Rom 1:18; Eph 2:3; 1 John 2:2 cf. Is 53:10-11). Consequently, God can justly show mercy to humanity and provide forgiveness of sins and a right standing with Himself for believers (Luke 18:13-14; Rom 3:24-26). The OT "mercy seat" served as a place of propitiation or "atonement" and typifies Christ's work of propitiation in the NT (Ex 25:18-22; Lev 16:14-22; Heb 9:5-26).
provided through Christ's sacrifice: Rom 3:25;
   Heb 2:17; 1 John 2:2; 4:10
received through faith: Rom 3:25

PROSPERITY (SEE MONEY; WEALTH)

PROSTITUTION (SEE ADULTERY; FORNICATION)

PROVERB(S) (SEE ALSO FIGURATIVE SPEECH)

A proverb is a short, wise saying generally intended to promote successful living in common

life. It capsulizes the wisdom of experience, and becomes familiar in a culture through repetition over a long time (1 Sam 10:12; 24:13). Proverbs were prevalent not only within Israel's oral and written tradition but also among all nations of the ancient world. The OT proverbs present concise, practical truths often in the form of Hebrew poetic parallelism. The book of Proverbs is the primary biblical example of a collection of proverbs, but other books in biblical wisdom literature (i.e., Job and Ecclesiastes) as well as some of the Psalms also contain many proverbs (cf. Prov 1:1). Solomon spoke 3000 proverbs (1 Kin 4:32; cf. Prov 1:1; 25:1; Eccl 12:9), of which only a lesser portion are recorded in the OT.

PROVIDENCE

Providence is the foresight to provide for particular needs. While Scripture refers to human providence (e.g., Gen 45:11; Acts 24:2; 1 Tim 5:8), instances of divine providence predominate. God's providence is His sovereign and gracious care for His creation (Ps 145:14-16; Neh 9:6), particularly for His redeemed people (Deut 1:31; Ps 37:28; Matt 6:30-33). Divine providence functions according to God's perfect character (Ps 145:17). The manifestation of God's goodness through providence is a major form of general revelation (Acts 14:17; 17:22-29; cf. Rom 1:18-23; 2:4; see also REVELATION, general).

PROVING (SEE TESTING)

PUNISHMENT
capital

CIVIL (INCLUDING AS DIVINE AGENT)
PURPOSE OF
   just retribution: Gen 9:5-6; Lev 24:17-22;
      Deut 25:2; Rom 13:4
   purging evil: Deut 19:19; 22:24; 24:7
   correction of life: Lev 26:14-39
   warning to others: Deut 13:10-11; 17:12-13;
      19:19-20; 21:21; Prov 19:25; 21:11
DIVINE
PURPOSES OF
   correction of life: 2 Sam 7:14-15; Job 5:17-20;
      Ps 94:12-13; Mal 2:2-3
   promote fear of God: Is 64:1-2
   give knowledge of God: Ps 59:10; Ezek 11:10-12;
      Dan 4:17, 24-26; Rom 9:17
   promote righteousness: Is 26:9; 1 Cor 10:6

CAUSES FOR

forsaking God's covenant: Deut 29:25
pride: Prov 11:21; 16:5
rejection of grace: Prov 1:24-31; Heb 2:3;
    10:29; 12:25
wickedness: Job 11:20; Prov 11:20; Ezek 39:24;
    Matt 23:14, 33; Col 3:25
according to deeds: Job 34:11; Ps 62:12;
    Matt 16:27
eternal (see also HELL)

CAUSES FOR

rejection of Christ: John 3:18, 19; 2 Thess 1:8-9
blasphemy against Spirit: Mark 3:29
worship of the beast: Rev 14:9-11
sin: Rev 21:8

PURIFICATION (SEE ALSO CLEAN)

CEREMONIAL

purification of the altar: Ex 29:36; Ezek 43:26
purification of the priests: Num 8:21
purification of the Levites: Num 8:21; Mal 3:3
purification from contact with unclean things:
    Num 19:1-22; 31:19-24
purification of the temple articles by the Levites:
    1 Chr 23:28; Ezra 6:20; Neh 12:30
water for purification: John 2:6
controversy about purification: John 3:25
purification for Passover: John 11:55

SPIRITUAL

*purging of idolatry and other evil deeds from
    Israel:* Deut 13:5; 17:7, 12; 2 Chr 34:3-8;
    Zech 5:3 (cf. Gen 35:2)
purging from personal sin: Ps 51:7
purification of the righteous through tribulation:
    Dan 11:35; 12:10 (cf. 12:1)
purification of the lips: Zeph 3:9
divine purification of a people for the LORD:
    Titus 2:14
purification of sins by Christ: Heb 1:3

PHYSICAL

purification of waters: 2 Kin 2:21-22
purification of precious metals: Mal 3:3

PURPOSE (SEE ALSO WILL)

OF GOD

invincibility of His purpose: Job 42:2
His creation of everything for its purpose: Prov 16:4
His purpose against a nation: Is 19:12, 17;
    Jer 49:20; 51:11
immutability of His purpose: Is 46:10-11; Jer 4:28;
    Heb 6:17
His purpose always performed: Is 46:10-11;
    Jer 51:12; Lam 2:17 (cf. Is 44:26)

His purpose accomplished by His word: Is 55:11
    (cf. James 4:5)
*the purposes of His heart understood in the last
    days:* Jer 23:20
His purpose for the day of the LORD: Amos 5:18-20
His purpose not understood by Israel's enemies:
    Mic 4:11-12
His purpose in predestinating events: Acts 4:28
His purpose served by David: Acts 13:36
His whole purpose declared by Paul: Acts 20:27
believers called according to His purpose: Rom 8:28
*His purpose based on His free action and not a
    person's response:* Rom 9:11
His purpose in Christ concerning believers: Eph 1:9
eternality of His purpose: Eph 3:11; 2 Tim 1:9
*His purpose for the sanctification and purity of
    believers:* 1 Thess 4:7
His eternal purpose of salvation for believers:
    2 Tim 1:9

OF CHRIST (SEE ALSO INCARNATION OF JESUS CHRIST)

to preach the kingdom: Luke 4:43
to be crucified: John 12:27, 32-33
to appoint Paul to his ministry: Acts 26:16-18
to destroy the works of the devil: 1 John 3:8

R

RANSOM (SEE ALSO REDEMPTION)

FOR REDEMPTION OF A SOUL

inability of people to provide such a ransom:
    Ps 49:7-8
request for God to provide the ransom: Ps 69:18
    (cf. Job 33:24)
*Christ's life given as a ransom (see also
    CRUCIFIXION):* Matt 20:28; 1 Tim 2:6

FOR THE NATION ISRAEL

Egypt as God's ransom for Israel: Is 43:3
God's ability to ransom Israel: Is 50:1-2
    (cf. Hos 13:14)
the promise of God's ransom of Israel: Jer 31:11

RAPTURE (SEE END TIMES)

REBELLION

nature of: 1 Sam 15:23; Job 23:2; Prov 17:11;
    Is 30:9; Jer 5:23; Dan 9:5
warning about: Num 14:9; Ezek 2:8
punishment of: Deut 1:26-27, 35-36; Josh 1:18;
    1 Sam 12:15; Ps 68:6; 107:10-11; Is 1:20;
    Lam 1:20; Ezek 20:8, 38; Hos 7:13; 13:16;
    Mic 1:2-5

avoidance of: 1 Sam 12:14; Ps 105:28
false accusation of: Neh 6:6; Jer 28:16; Luke 23:14
remedy for: Dan 9:9; Mic 7:18; Zeph 3:11

VARIOUS OTHER USES
promotion of rebellion: Deut 13:5
protest concerning rebellion: Josh 22:16-29
rebellion of the wicked: Ps 5:10
rebellion of a generation: Ps 78:8
rebellion against God's Spirit: Ps 106:33
rebellion of fools: Ps 107:17
rebellion of princes and rulers: Is 1:23; Hos 9:15
the divine Law intended to restrain the
  rebellious: 1 Tim 1:8-10
Qualified elders not to have children accused of
  rebellion: Titus 1:6
evil influence of rebellious people upon
  Christians: Titus 1:10-11

RECONCILIATION (SEE ALSO PEACE)

Reconciliation involves a changed relationship from enmity to harmony between two parties. In Scripture, reconciliation may indicate (1) the changed relationship between the sinful, alienated world and God, since salvation is divinely provided for humanity through Christ's redemptive work (2 Cor 5:19; Col 1:20; cf. John 3:16); (2) the believer's actual changed relationship from enmity to peace with God (Rom 5:10; 2 Cor 5:18; Col 1:20-22); and (3) a change in relationship between human parties from hostility to harmony (e.g., Matt 5:24).
occasion of: Matt 5:23; Rom 5:10; Col 1:21-22
divine origin of: Rom 5:8-10; 2 Cor 5:18-19;
  Col 1:19-20
Christ's provision of: Rom 5:10, 11; 2 Cor 5:18,
  19; Eph 2:13, 16; Col 1:20, 22; 1 Pet 3:18
objects of: Rom 5:10; 11:15; 2 Cor 5:18-20;
  Eph 2:16; Col 1:20
purpose of: Acts 7:26; 2 Cor 5:18-20; Eph 2:15-16;
  Col 1:20, 22; 1 Pet 3:18
ministry and message of: 2 Cor 5:18-20

RECREATION (SEE REST)

REDEMPTION (SEE ALSO RANSOM)

Redemption involves a payment to liberate someone or something (Ex 6:6; Lev 25:23-24; 1 Cor 6:20; Gal 3:13; 4:4-6). Christian redemption emphasizes the purchase of a slave from his former master (sin) so that he is free to serve his new master (God; Rom 6:22; Gal 3:13; 4:5). Christ's sacrificial death through His shed blood is the ransom price of humanity's re-

demption from sin and for God (Matt 20:28; Acts 20:28; Heb 9:11-15, 22; 10:4-10; 1 Pet 1:18-19; Rev 5:9 cf. Ps 49:7-9).

PERFORMED BY GOD
HIS REDEMPTION FOR HIS PEOPLE
  redeemed from certain things
  from evil: Gen 48:16
  from Egyptian bondage: Ex 6:6; 13:14-15;
    15:13; Deut 7:8; 2 Sam 7:23; Neh 1:10;
    Ps 106:8-10; Mic 6:4 (cf. Gen 15:13-14)
  from adversaries: Job 6:23
  from the pit: Ps 103:4
  from their sins: Ps 130:7-8; Is 44:22
  from Sheol and death: Hos 13:14
  redeemed
  by His power: Ex 13:14; Ps 77:15; 78:42
  in mercy: Ps 44:26
  with justice: Is 1:27
  without money: Is 52:3
  in love and mercy: Is 63:9
  with Christ's precious blood: 1 Pet 1:19

HIS ROLE AS REDEEMER
  of the individual: Ps 19:14
  of the fatherless: Prov 23:10-11
  of Israel: Is 41:14; 49:26; Jer 50:33-34

PROVIDED THROUGH CHRIST
redemption needed by humans: Ps 49:7-9;
  John 8:34; Rom 6:17; Gal 3:13; Eph 2:1
redemption accomplished through His blood (i.e.,
  sacrificial death): Mark 10:45; Acts 20:28;
  Rom 3:24-25; Eph 1:7; Heb 9:15; 1 Pet 1:19
redemption received through faith: Rom 3:24-25

EXPERIENCED BY BELIEVERS
RESULTS OF REDEMPTION
  praise to God: Ps 71:23
  blessings in the future messianic kingdom:
    Is 35:9; 51:11
  removal of fear: Is 43:1
  justification: Rom 3:24
  forgiveness of sins: Eph 1:7; Col 1:14; Heb 9:15
    (cf. Ps 130:8)

DELIVERANCE
  from bondage to sin: John 8:34, 36; Titus 2:14
  from the curse of the Law: Gal 3:13
  from bondage to the Law: Rom 6:14;
    Gal 4:4-7; 5:1, 13
  from a futile way of life: 1 Pet 1:18

REFINING (SEE PURIFICATION)

REGENERATION

The term regeneration comes from a Greek word meaning "rebirth" or "new genesis." The

term signifies the renewal of the fallen creation through the redemptive work of Christ. The actual term "regeneration" is found only twice in Scripture, once for the renewal of all things (Matt 19:28; cf. Acts 3:21, "restoration of all things") and once for the present inner spiritual renewal of believers. The same concept of renewal is expressed in the language of a new heart (e.g., Ezek 36:26ff), of a new birth (e.g., John 3:3, 7), of new persons through union with Christ in death and resurrection (e.g., Rom 6:4-8), and a new creation including persons (e.g., 2 Cor 5:17) and the heavens and earth (e.g., Rev 21:1).

REJOICING (SEE JOY)

RELIGION (SEE JUDAISM)

REMNANT
IN ISRAEL
divine preservation of a remnant: 1 Kin 19:18;
   (cf. Rom 11:4); 2 Kin 17:18; Is 1:9; Ezek 6:8;
   Mic 5:7-8; Rom 9:29
a remnant from Judah and Jerusalem:
   2 Kin 19:4, 30-31
a remnant from Israel joined with Judah:
   2 Chr 30:25; 34:9; Is 10:20-22; 46:3
   (cf. Ezek 37:15-22)
a remnant taken into captivity: 2 Chr 36:20
a remnant returned from captivity: Ezra 9:8,
   13-15; Neh 1:2-3; Hag 1:12, 14 (cf. 1 Sam 12:22;
   1 Kin 6:13)
a remnant left in Judah's land: Jer 40:11; 42:2
future blessing of the righteous remnant:
   Ezek 34:13-14; Zeph 2:7, 9; 3:13; Zech 8:11-12
salvation of the elect remnant: Rom 9:27; 11:5
   (cf. Zech 13:8-9; Luke 2:38)
preservation of a remnant for the LORD: Zech 9:7
OF TRUE CHRISTIANS
a faithful remnant in the church at Thyatira:
   Rev 2:24-25
a faithful remnant in the church at Sardis: Rev 3:4

REPENTANCE
The concept of repentance in the OT is derived primarily from two Hebrew words. The first signifies repentance in the sense of a change of action or purpose. It is mostly used in relation to God and His dealings with people (e.g., 1 Sam 15:11, 29; Ps 110:4), with only a few instances referring to human repentance or relenting (e.g., Job 42:6; Jer 8:6; 18:19). Repentance on the part of people is expressed primarily by a

word meaning to "turn" or "return." The same word is used for the concept of conversion, indicating that these two ideas are essentially synonymous in the OT.

The NT concept of repentance likewise is expressed by two words. One signifies repentance in the sense of regret or having remorse (e.g., Matt 21:30; 27:3). The other NT word for repentance denotes an inward change of thinking, affection, and willful commitment. Although it is similar to the concept of conversion, this term emphasizes the inward change that results in an outward turning from sin toward God, while conversion points particularly to the total change of life's direction (cf. Acts 3:19; 26:20). While repentance may include faith (e.g., Acts 2:38; 11:18; 2 Pet 3:9), it may also be set alongside faith (e.g., Mark 1:15; Acts 20:21). In such instances faith emphasizes the positive side of repentance in the new relationship with God. Like conversion, both the unsaved and sinning believers are called to repent (e.g., Rev 2:5, 16; see also CONVERSION; FAITH).

REST (SEE ALSO SABBATH)
KINDS OF
rest (i.e., cessation) from God's six days of
   creation: Gen 2:2-3; Ex 20:11; Heb 4:4, 10
REST FROM LABOR (I.E., ON CERTAIN DAYS IN ISRAEL'S CALENDAR)
on the Sabbath day: Ex 16:23; 20:10-11; 31:15;
   Deut 5:12-14; Luke 23:56
on the Sabbatic year for the land: Ex 23:10-11;
   Lev 25:1-4
on the first and last days of the Feast of
   Unleavened Bread: Lev 23:5-8
on the day of Pentecost: Lev 23:21; Num 28:26
on the day of the Feast of Trumpets:
   Lev 23:24-25
on the Day of Atonement: Lev 23:27-28
on the first and last days of the Feast of
   Tabernacles: Lev 23:39
on the year of jubilee (fiftieth year): Lev 25:11-12
on certain days for the Feast of Purim:
   Esth 9:17-19
PROVISION OF REST
MEANS OF
through the presence of the LORD: Ex 33:14
through the LORD as Shepherd of His people:
   Ps 23:1-3
through a proper relationship to the LORD:
   Ps 37:3-7

through resting in the LORD: Ps 37:7
through the LORD'S *salvation:* Ps 116:5-8
through the Spirit of the LORD: Is 63:14
through walking in the LORD'S *ways:* Jer 6:16
through coming to Christ: Matt 11:28-29
through a company of believers: Rom 15:32
through ministry from other believers:
    2 Cor 7:5-7

RESURRECTION (SEE ALSO CHRIST, RESURRECTION OF)

general affirmation of: Matt 22:31; Acts 17:18,
    32; 23:6; 26:6-8; Heb 6:2
universality of: John 5:28; Acts 24:15;
    1 Cor 15:21-22; Rev 20:12-13
importance of: Rom 4:25; 1 Cor 15:12-32

TYPES OF
FROM PHYSICAL DEATH TO NATURAL LIFE (I.E., RESUSCITATION)

in the OT: 1 Kin 17:17-23; 2 Kin 4:32-37; 13:21
    (cf. Gen 22:5; Heb 11:17-19, 35)
in the NT
    Jesus' ministry: Matt 9:24-25; Luke 7:12-15;
        John 11:43-44 (cf. Matt 27:52-53)
    the apostles' ministry: Acts 9:36-41;
        20:9-12
    the tribulation period: Rev 11:11
from spiritual death to eternal spiritual life:
    John 5:21, 24-26; 11:25-26; Rom 6:4; Eph 2:1,
    5-6; Col 2:12; 3:1

FROM PHYSICAL DEATH TO GLORIFICATION (I.E., A "RESURRECTION OF LIFE" OR "THE FIRST RESURRECTION")

in the OT: Job 14:14-15; 19:25-27; Ps 16:10
    (cf. Acts 2:31-32); 49:14-15; Is 25:8
    (cf. 1 Cor 15:54); 26:19; Dan 12:2, 13;
    Hos 13:14 (cf. 1 Cor 15:55)
in the NT
    Jesus: Matt 28:6-7; Acts 1:3; 1 Cor 15:3-4, 20;
        Rev 1:5, 18
    believers: Luke 14:14; 20:35-36; John 5:28-29;
        6:39, 40, 44, 54; Acts 24:15; Rom 6:5; 8:11;
        1 Cor 6:14; 2 Cor 4:14; Phil 3:11;
        1 Thess 4:14-17; 1 John 3:2; Rev 20:4-6
        (cf. 2 Cor 5:4)
*from physical death to condemnation (i.e., a
    "resurrection of judgment" or the second
    resurrection):* John 5:29 (cf. Dan 12:2;
    Acts 24:15; Rev 20:5, 12-15)
*symbolical (i.e., of Israel's revival and
    restoration):* Ezek 37:1-14

RETALIATION (SEE REVENGE)

REVELATION

In biblical usage the term revelation refers to God's disclosure to humans of previously unknown truth about His person, works, and plans (Ex 6:3; Amos 3:7; John 16:12-13; Gal 1:11-12; cf. John 15:15). Divine revelation is of two types: general and special. General revelation refers to divine truth evident in nature and in the constitution of people and thus is sometimes called natural revelation. General revelation is knowable by human reason apart from the Bible and discloses God's attributes, power, and moral nature (Acts 14:17; Rom 1:20; 2:15). General revelation is sufficient to leave humanity "without excuse" (Rom 1:20) for his failure to respond appropriately to God (Rom 1:21), but it is inadequate apart from the gospel message to give people a personal, saving knowledge of God (Rom 10:13-17; 1 Cor 1:21; cf. John 5:39; Acts 4:12; 2 Tim 3:15). Special revelation is the disclosure of God's being and works through divine acts and words, particularly as recorded in Scripture (Jer 1:9; Mic 6:5; John 6:63). Biblical revelation includes all that may be known through general revelation plus a much more extensive and clearer body of divine truth.

GENERAL REVELATION
divine origin of: Rom 1:19-20
MEANS OF
creation: Ps 19:1-4; Acts 17:22-31; Rom 1:19-20;
    Heb 3:4
providential goodness: Matt 5:45; Acts 14:14-17;
    Rom 2:4
conscience: Rom 2:12-15
response to: Josh 24:14-15; Acts 14:15-17; 17:29;
    Rom 1:18, 21-32; 2:12-15; 3:9-18, 23; 1 Thess 1:9

SPECIAL REVELATION (SEE ALSO WORD OF GOD)
divine origin of (see also INSPIRATION): Gen 35:7;
    1 Sam 9:15; Job 12:22; Is 22:14; Matt 1:22; 4:4;
    Gal 1:15-16; Eph 3:3-5; 2 Tim 3:16;
    2 Pet 1:20-21; Rev 1:1
character of: 2 Sam 22:31; Ps 19:7-9; Matt 5:18;
    7:24; 24:35; John 10:35; 17:17; 1 Thess 2:13;
    2 Pet 1:19; Rev 22:18-19
authority of: Josh 1:8; Ps 19:7-9; Is 8:20;
    Matt 4:1-11; 7:24; Luke 24:25-27; John 10:35;
    17:17; Acts 24:14; Gal 3:16; 1 Thess 2:13;
    2 Tim 3:16; 2 Pet 1:20-21; Rev 1:3
human agents of: Gen 20:7; Ex 7:1; 1 Kin 18:36;
    Amos 3:7; Matt 2:15; Acts 2:30; 21:9;
    Rom 16:26; Heb 1:1; 1 Pet 1:10-12;
    2 Pet 1:20-21; Rev 1:1

angelic agents of: Acts 7:53; Gal 3:19; Heb 2:2;
Rev 1:1; 14:6
modes of: Num 12:6; 1 Sam 3:10; Is 1:1; Matt 2:17;
11:27; Luke 2:26, 32; John 1:14-18; Rom 1:16-17;
1 Cor 2:10; Gal 1:12; 1 Tim 3:16; 2 Tim 1:10;
Heb 1:1-2

FORMS OF
acts: Mic 6:5; Acts 2:11
words: Deut 18:18-19; Jer 1:9; Matt 4:4; 5:18;
24:35; John 6:63; 10:35; Gal 3:16;
1 Thess 2:13

PURPOSE OF
obedience: Ex 19:5; Deut 29:29; Josh 1:8; Ps 119;
John 13:17; James 1:22; 4:17
meditation: Josh 1:8; Ps 1:2
salvation: Ps 98:2; John 5:39; 2 Tim 3:15;
Heb 2:3-4
sanctification: John 17:17; 2 Tim 3:16
edification: Acts 20:32; 1 Cor 14:6, 26
encouragement: Rom 15:4
examples: 1 Cor 10:11

REVENGE (SEE ALSO JUDGMENT; PUNISHMENT)

divine prohibition of: Lev 19:18; Prov 20:22; 24:29;
Matt 5:38-41; Rom 12:17, 19; 1 Thess 5:15;
1 Pet 3:9
*divine protection from (i.e., from the blood
avenger):* Num 35:12; Josh 20:2-3

GOD'S RESPONSE TO
He causes the revengeful to cease: Ps 8:2
*He avenges Himself on His disobedient people
and on His enemies:* Is 1:24; Jer 5:9; 46:10;
Nah 1:2; 1 Thess 4:6
He punishes the revengeful: Ezek 25:12-17
He executes vengeance to avenge His people:
Deut 32:43; 2 Kin 9:7; Joel 3:21; Rom 12:19;
Rev 6:9-10; 19:2
Christ's rebuke of: Luke 9:52-56

HUMAN RESPONSE TO
trust the LORD to execute justice: Ps 37:5-6
respect what is right: Rom 12:17
let God execute vengeance: Rom 12:19 (cf. 1 Sam
24:12; 25:26; 2 Chr 24:22; Rev 6:9-10)
*seek the good and blessing of others instead of
revenge:* 1 Thess 5:15; 1 Pet 3:9

REVERENCE (SEE FEAR OF GOD)

REVIVAL

EXAMPLES OF
in Jacob's household under Jacob: Gen 35:1-7
in Israel under Samuel: 1 Sam 7:1-6

in Israel through Elijah: 1 Kin 18:19-40
in Judah under Asa: 2 Chr 14:1-15:19
in Judah under Jehoiada and Jehoash:
2 Kin 11:4-12:16
in Judah under Hezekiah: 2 Kin 18:1-8
in Judah under Manasseh: 2 Chr 33:12-19
in Judah under Josiah: 2 Kin 22:1-23:25
in Nineveh through Jonah's preaching: Jon 3:1-10
in Jerusalem through Haggai's preaching:
Hag 1:12-14
in Jerusalem under Nehemiah's leadership:
Neh 4:17-20; 6:15
*at Pentecost through the coming of the Spirit
and Peter's preaching:* Acts 2:1-47
through the preaching of Peter and John:
Acts 4:1-4
other instances in the early church: Acts 5:14;
6:7; 19:17-20

REQUIREMENTS FOR
be humble: Ps 69:32; Is 57:15
seek God: Ps 69:32
pray for revival: Ps 119:25; Hab 3:2; Acts 4:31-35
respond to God's word: Ps 119:50, 93
return to the LORD: Hos 6:1-2
depend on the Spirit: Zech 4:6-10; Acts 4:31-35

REWARD (SEE ALSO JUDGMENT)
REQUIREMENTS FOR
obedience to God's word: Lev 26:1-13; Deut 28:1-14;
Ps 19:11 (cf. Prov 13:13; Eccl 12:13-14)
righteous living: Prov 11:18, 31
humility and the fear of the LORD: Prov 22:4;
Eccl 12:13-14
sincere prayer and fasting: Matt 6:6, 18
work built upon the foundation of Jesus Christ:
1 Cor 3:11
service rendered voluntarily and freely:
1 Cor 9:16-18
motivation from genuine love: 1 Cor 13:1-3
sowing to the Spirit: Gal 6:8
perseverance in doing good: Gal 6:9
*working heartily for the LORD rather than for
people:* Col 3:23-24
love for the LORD's appearance: 2 Tim 4:8
love for the LORD Himself: James 1:12
patient endurance of trials: Heb 10:34-36
(cf. 10:25-26; James 1:2-4, 12): Ps 62:12;
Jer 17:10; 1 Cor 3:8, 12-14; 2 Cor 5:10
(cf. Prov 12:14)

TYPES OF
EARTHLY REWARDS
prosperity: Prov 13:21
riches, honor, and life: Prov 22:4 (cf. Rom 2:10)

various pleasures as a result of labor: Eccl 2:10;
   5:18-19; 9:9
general: Matt 6:2, 5, 16

HEAVENLY REWARDS
an imperishable wreath or crown: 1 Cor 9:25
a crown of exultation: 1 Thess 2:19
a crown of righteousness: 2 Tim 4:8
the crown of life: James 1:12; Rev 2:10
the crown of glory (for faithful elders): 1 Pet 5:4
related to the LORD'*s coming:* Is 40:10; 62:11;
   1 Thess 2:19; 2 Tim 4:8; Rev 22:12

RICHES (SEE WEALTH)

RIGHTEOUS (SEE JUSTIFICATION; RIGHTEOUSNESS)

RIGHTEOUSNESS
The Hebrew and Greek terms translated "righteousness" or "justice" signify that which is right or that which conforms to the character of God. Because God has graciously made a covenant with His people, His righteousness often takes the form of keeping that covenant with acts of deliverance, salvation, and judgment on His enemies. The ultimate expression of God's righteousness is seen in the coming of Christ, who works both salvation and judgment. Righteousness is also demanded of people for fellowship with God. This is obtained first through simple faith in Christ resulting in the righteousness of Christ being accounted to the believer (Rom 3:21-22). Then the righteousness of God is gradually incorporated into the practical life of the believer through the ministry of the indwelling Spirit (Rom 8:4; Ezek 36:26f).

attribute of God: Gen 18:25; Deut 32:4; Ps 7:9-17;
   9:8; 36:6; 50:6; 72:2; 89:14; 98:9; 119:172;
   Is 9:7; 11:3-5; 45:21; Jer 12:1; 23:5-6; 33:15-16;
   Acts 17:31; Rom 3:25-26; 1 Pet 1:11
given to humans (see also JUSTIFICATION):
   Is 45:8, 24-25; 46:13; 53:11; 54:17; 61:10;
   Hos 10:12; Rom 1:7; 3:5, 21; 1 Cor 1:30

ROCK (SEE ALSO STONES)
LITERAL USES OF
miracle of water from a rock in the wilderness:
   Ex 17:6; Num 20:8-11
a rock as a hiding place: 1 Sam 13:6
a rock for shade: Is 32:2
a house built upon a rock: Matt 7:24-25
a tomb hewn in a rock: Matt 27:60

FIGURATIVE USES OF
God entitled the "Rock": Deut 32:4, 31;
   2 Sam 22:2-3; Ps 78:35; Hab 1:12
Israel hewn from a rock: Is 51:1
faces of people of Israel harder than rock
   (i.e., refusal to repent): Jer 5:3
the foundational rock for the church: Matt 16:18
Christ called "a rock of offense": Rom 9:33;
   1 Pet 2:8
Christ as the spiritual rock: 1 Cor 10:4

RULERS (SEE KING)

S

SABBATH (SEE ALSO LORD'S DAY)
The word Sabbath means "cessation" or "rest" and usually designates the seventh day of the week (i.e., from Friday 6 p.m. until Saturday 6 p.m. in Hebrew reckoning; cf. Ex 31:15-17; Deut 5:12-15; Luke 23:53-54). It was a divinely revealed holy day for Israel to cease from ordinary labor and to celebrate God's rest from creation on the seventh day (Gen 2:1-3; Ex 20:8-11; Neh 9:13-14). Sabbath observance is the fourth of the Ten Commandments (Ex 20:8) and served as a covenant and sign between the LORD and Israel (Ex 31:13-17; Ezek 20:12). The religious leaders of Jesus' time emphasized the prohibitive aspect of the Sabbath and added further restrictions to it from their rabbinical tradition (Matt 12:2-7; Mark 3:2). In contrast, Jesus emphasized (1) that "the Sabbath was made for man, and not man for the Sabbath" (Mark 2:27), (2) that He was "LORD even of the Sabbath" (Mark 2:28), and (3) that the Sabbath offered opportunity "to do good" and "to save a life" as well as to rest (Mark 3:4). With the judicial termination of the Mosaic legal system at the cross (Col 2:14), Sabbath observance is not required of Christians (Col 2:16), and the notion of a "Christian Sabbath" is foreign to NT directions to the church. On the Sabbath year (i.e., every seventh year in Israel's calendar) the land was to rest by not being sown, cultivated, or harvested (Ex 23:10-11; Lev 25:1-7; cf. Neh 10:31). God promised to provide for Israel's needs while the land lay fallow (Lev 25:20-22). One of the purposes for the seventy-year Babylonian captivity was to make up for Israel's failure to observe the sabbatical years (2 Chr 36:21; cf. Lev 26:34-35, 43; see also JUBILEE, YEAR OF).

SACRIFICES

OLD COVENANT
purpose: Ex 29:33; Lev 1:4; 5:13

TYPES AND PROCEDURES
burnt offerings: Lev 1; 6:8-13
grain offerings: Lev 2; 6:14-18
peace offerings: Lev 3; 7:11-36
thank offerings: Lev 7:12-15
votive offerings: Lev 7:15-18
sin offerings: Lev 4:1-5:13; 6:24-30
guilt offering: Lev 5:14-6:7
Consecration offering: Ex 29:4-28;
  Lev 16:19-23

NEW COVENANT
SACRIFICE OF CHRIST
atoning efficacy: John 1:29; Rom 3:25; 8:3;
  Gal 2:21; Heb 7:27; 9:28; 1 John 2:2; 4:10
fulfillment of Old Covenant sacrifices:
  Heb 9:11-14, 24-26
superiority to Old Covenant sacrifices
superior priesthood: Heb 7:1-22
superior efficacy: Heb 7:26-28; 8:1-13

SADDUCEES

The Sadducees were a relatively small Jewish sect centered in Jerusalem but with major religious and political influence upon Judaism (cf. Acts 4:1; 5:17). Most Sadducees were priests who belonged to the wealthiest and most influential of the priestly families (cf. Acts 5:17). Their purely rationalistic view of religion opposed the supernaturalism of the Pharisees and led them to deny the reality of the resurrection, angels, and spirits (Acts 23:7-8; cf. Mark 12:18-27; Acts 4:1-2). Jesus indicted them for gross doctrinal error due to willful ignorance of Scripture and of God's power (Mark 12:24).

SALVATION, SAVE

ORIGIN OF
in divine love: Ps 6:4; 109:26; John 3:16;
  Rom 5:8; Rev 1:5-6
in divine grace: Is 33:2; Acts 15:11; Rom 3:24;
  2 Cor 8:9; Gal 2:21; Eph 2:5, 8; Titus 2:11
in divine mercy: Luke 18:13; Titus 3:5

PERFORMANCE OF
by God: Gen 15:6; 49:18; Ex 14:13; Ps 3:8; 51:12;
  Is 12:2-3; 25:9; Jer 3:23; Hos 13:4; Mic 7:7;
  Hab 3:13, 18; Zech 9:16; Matt 19:26;
  John 17:3; Acts 28:28; Rom 1:16; Titus 2:10;
  Heb 11:4-40; Jude 25
the Father: John 12:27; Eph 1:3-6; Heb 5:7;
  1 Pet 1:1-2

the Son: Gen 3:15; Ps 22; Jer 23:6-7; Zech 9:9;
  13:7; Matt 1:21; Luke 2:11; John 4:42;
  Acts 2:21; 4:12; 1 Cor 5:7; Phil 3:20; 1 Tim 1:15;
  Titus 1:4; 2:13-14; Heb 2:10; 5:9; 1 Pet 3:18;
  2 Pet 1:1; 3:15; 1 John 4:14; Rev 1:5
  (see also CHRIST)
the Spirit: John 3:5; Eph 1:13-14; 2 Thess 2:13;
  Titus 3:5; 1 Pet 1:2

THROUGH FAITH (SEE ALSO FAITH)
affirmation of: Gen 15:6; Ps 78:22; 86:2; Is 30:15;
  Mark 1:15; John 1:12; 3:16-18; Acts 16:31;
  Rom 10:9-10; Col 2:12; 2 Thess 2:13;
  James 2:14; 1 Pet 1:5, 9; 1 John 5:13

CHARACTERISTICS OF
secure: Ps 37:28; John 5:24; 10:27-28; Rom 8:31-39;
  1 Cor 3:15; 1 Pet 1:5
everlasting: Is 45:17; 51:6; Heb 5:9; 7:25
universal: Is 45:22; 49:6; John 3:16; Rom 10:13;
  1 Tim 2:4; 4:10; 1 John 2:2
consistent with divine justice: Is 63:1; Rom 3:25-26
experienced by relatively few: Luke 13:23-24
powerful: Rom 1:16; 1 Cor 1:18
so great: Heb 2:3

SANCTUARY
(SEE TABERNACLE; TEMPLE)

SANCTIFICATION (SEE ALSO
DEDICATION; HOLINESS; HOLY)
The term sanctification refers to separation from ordinary use for God's possession and service (e.g., Ex 19:5-6, 10). Sanctification of persons includes separation from all moral evil (cf. 2 Cor 7:1). God's own sanctification or holiness also involves His exalted, transcendent relationship to humanity and the rest of His finite creation (Is 6:1-5; 57:15). In Christian doctrine, the term sanctification is generally used of the believer's progress in spiritual growth (Rom 6:19, 22; 1 Thess 4:3; cf. 2 Cor 3:18).

SANITATION
(SEE CLEAN; PURIFICATION)

SATAN
Satan is the most prominent and powerful of evil spirits and the archenemy of God and humanity (Job 1-2; Matt 13:25, 38-39; 1 Pet 5:8; 1 John 4:4; Rev 12:1-17). He retains great intelligence (Ezek 28:12, 17; 2 Cor 2:11) and power (Eph 6:10-12; Jude 9) and is widely represented through his demons (Eph 6:12; Rev 12:7-9). Sa-

tan has become ruler over demonic spirits, i.e., evil angels who evidently also sinned and fell with him (Matt 12:24; 25:41; Rev 12:4-7). Satan rules the world and can influence believers, but only within the permissive will of God (Job 1-2, esp. 2:6; Luke 4:6; John 12:31; Acts 26:18; 1 Cor 10:13; 1 John 5:19). Christ judged Satan at the cross (John 12:31; Heb 2:14; 1 John 3:8; cf. Col 2:15), but the final execution of that judgment will occur when he is "thrown into the lake of fire," where he will remain forever (Rev 20:10).

PERSONALITY OF
PERSONAL NAMES
Satan: Job 1:6; Zech 3:1-2; Matt 4:10; Rom 16:20
the devil: Matt 4:1; 1 Pet 5:8; Rev 12:9 (cf. John 6:70)
Beelzebul: Matt 12:24 (cf. 2 Kin 1:1-6, 16)
Belial: 2 Cor 6:15

TITLES
"the tempter": Matt 4:3; 1 Thess 3:5
"ruler of the demons": Matt 12:24 (cf. v. 26)
"ruler of this world": John 12:31
"the evil one": Matt 13:38; John 17:15; 1 John 5:19
"god of this world": 2 Cor 4:4
"prince of the power of the air": Eph 2:2 (cf. 1 Cor 2:12; Eph 2:2); Col 1:13; 1 John 4:4; Rev 12:9-10

SYMBOLS
"angel of light": 2 Cor 11:14
"roaring lion": 1 Pet 5:8
"great red dragon": Rev 12:3 (cf. vv. 4, 7, 13, 17)
"the serpent of old": Rev 12:9 (cf. vv. 14-15; Gen 3:1-5, 13-15; 2 Cor 11:3)

SAVIOR (SEE CHRIST, TITLES AND FUNCTIONS OF, SAVIOR)

SCHOOL (SEE TEACHING)

SCRIBE
The term scribe translates Greek (NT) and Hebrew (OT) words related to writing and thus originally denoted something like a secretary who was concerned with written records and administration (cf. Judg 5:14; 2 Kin 22; Jer 36:10, 32). Following the exile, scribes developed into a distinctive professional learned class of teachers, interpreters, and administrators of the law (sometimes termed "lawyers," e.g., Luke 7:30). In the NT they are closely associat-

ed with the Pharisees and elders as leaders of the Jewish people almost always in opposition to Jesus and the early church (e.g., Mark 7:5; Acts 4:5).

SCRIPTURES (SEE WORD OF GOD)

SEA
BIBLICAL SEAS
Mediterranean: Num 34:6-7
Galilee: Matt 4:18
Red: Ex 10:19
dead: Gen 14:3
bronze (at temple): 2 Chr 4:6
glass: Rev 4:6; 15:2
FIGURATIVE
positive: Job 11:7-9; Ps 72:8; 139:9; Is 11:9; 48:18; Mic 7:19; Hab 2:14
negative: Jer 49:23-24; Lam 2:13; James 1:6; Jude 13

SECOND COMING (SEE END TIMES)

SEED
SEED USED OF OFFSPRING
seed of the serpent: Gen 3:15
seed of the woman: Gen 3:15 (cf. Heb 2:14)
seed of Abraham: Gen 22:17-18 (cf. Acts 3:25); Ps 106:27; Gal 3:16, 19
seed of Israel: 1 Chr 16:13; Ps 105:6; Jer 2:21
seed of David: Ps 89:3-4

SEED USED WITH OTHER REPRESENTATIONS
the holy seed which represents the elect remnant of Israel: Is 6:13; Rom 11:5
mustard seed which represents faith: Matt 17:20
seed which represents the word of God: Luke 8:11; 1 Pet 1:23

SEEKING
FOR ILLEGITIMATE GOALS
Korah and his company seeking the priesthood: Num 16:8-11
Saul seeking David's life: 1 Sam 19:2; 20:1
Saul seeking a medium: 1 Sam 28:7
Absalom seeking David's life: 2 Sam 16:11
Jezebel seeking Elijah's life: 1 Kin 19:1-2, 10
David seeking a census of Israel: 1 Chr 21:3
those seeking things contrary to God: Ps 53:2-3
a rebellious person seeking only evil: Prov 17:11
those seeking their own desire contrary to sound wisdom: Prov 18:1

those seeking another drink of alcoholic
beverage: Prov 23:35
Jews seeking shelter in the shadow of Egypt: Is 30:2
the idolater seeking a skillful idol maker: Is 40:20
Jews seeking their own pleasure instead of
honoring the Sabbath: Is 58:13
those seeking great things for themselves: Jer 45:5
Pharisees seeking a heavenly sign from Jesus to
test Him: Mark 8:11
the chief priests and the scribes seeking to
destroy Jesus: Mark 11:18; John 18:8
Judas seeking to betray Jesus: Mark 14:11
those seeking to keep their life instead of losing
it for Christ: Luke 17:33
those seeking their own will: John 5:30
those seeking glory from one another: John 5:44
(cf. 1 Thess 2:6)
the multitude seeking Jesus only to satisfy their
physical hunger: John 6:24-27
those seeking their own glory: John 7:18 (cf. 8:50)
unbelievers seeking to persecute Christians:
Acts 17:5-8
Jews seeking Paul's life: Acts 21:31
Jews seeking to establish their own
righteousness: Rom 10:3 (cf. 11:7)
those seeking their own good: 1 Cor 10:24
those seeking their own profit: 1 Cor 10:33
those seeking to please people: Gal 1:10
those seeking to be justified by Law: Gal 5:4
those seeking their own interests: Phil 2:21
Satan seeking someone to devour: 1 Pet 5:8

FOR LEGITIMATE GOALS

seeking the LORD with all one's heart: Deut 4:29;
Jer 29:13
command to seek the LORD at His established
place of dwelling: Deut 12:5
seeking refuge in Israel's God: Ruth 2:12
(cf. Ps 91:4)
Israel seeking for David to be their king: 2 Sam 3:17
all of the earth seeking to hear Solomon's
wisdom: 1 Kin 10:24
seeking the LORD Himself: 1 Chr 16:11; 2 Chr 20:4;
30:19; 31:21; Ps 9:10; 22:26; 63:1; 70:4;
Prov 28:5; Is 26:9; Hos 10:12; Mal 3:1;
Acts 15:17; 17:27; Heb 11:6
seeking the LORD for instruction: 1 Chr 15:13
encouragement to seek the LORD: 1 Chr 16:10-11;
22:19; 28:9; Ps 105:4; Is 55:6; Amos 5:4, 6;
Zeph 2:3 (cf. Job 8:5)
seeking after the commandments of the LORD:
1 Chr 28:8; Ps 119:45 (cf. Amos 8:12)
seeking the LORD's face: 2 Chr 7:14; Ps 24:6; 27:8
seeking from the LORD a safe journey: Ezra 8:21

seeking peace: Ps 34:14; 1 Pet 3:11 (cf. Ezek 7:25)
seeking the LORD's name: Ps 83:16
seeking godly wisdom: Prov 2:4; 8:17; 15:14
seeking good: Prov 11:27; Amos 5:14; 1 Thess 5:15
seeking love by covering a transgression: Prov 17:9
the bride seeking her beloved: Song 3:2; 6:1
seeking justice: Is 1:17; 16:5
seeking from the book of the LORD: Is 34:16
seeking truth: Jer 5:1
the LORD's goodness toward those seeking Him:
Lam 3:25
God seeking the contributions of His people:
Ezek 20:40
the LORD seeking His sheep: Ezek 34:11, 16
seeking the LORD by prayer and supplication:
Dan 9:3
promise of Israel seeking the LORD in the last
days: Hos 3:5 (cf. 5:15; Jer 50:4)
seeking righteousness: Zeph 2:3
seeking humility: Zeph 2:3
seeking the favor of the LORD: Zech 7:2
nations coming to seek the LORD: Zech 8:22
seeking instruction from the priest's mouth:
Mal 2:7
seeking a godly offspring: Mal 2:15
seeking first God's kingdom and His
righteousness: Matt 6:33
seeking in prayer: Matt 7:7-8
seeking the kingdom of heaven like hidden
treasure: Matt 13:45
Jesus seeking the lost for salvation: Luke 19:10
the Father seeking true worshipers: John 4:23
seeking the Father's glory: John 7:18
the Father seeking the Son's glory: John 8:50, 54
seeking Jesus through devotion for Him:
John 20:15
seeking for glory and honor: Rom 2:7
seeking the good of others: 1 Cor 10:24 (cf. 13:5)
seeking the profit of others, especially their
salvation: 1 Cor 10:33
seeking edification of the church: 1 Cor 14:12
seeking to please God: Gal 1:10
seeking to be justified in Christ: Gal 2:17
seeking the things above: Col 3:1
seeking a heavenly country and city:
Heb 11:14; 13:14

SELF-DENIAL

EXEMPLIFIED BY CHRIST

self-denial of immediate satisfaction of hunger:
Matt 4:2-4
self-denial by serving others instead of being
served: Matt 20:28; John 13:3-15

*self-denial in His voluntary, substitutionary
 death:* Matt 20:28; John 10:11, 17-18; Phil 2:8;
 1 John 3:16
self-denial of His will for the Father's will: Matt
 26:39, 42; John 6:38; Heb 10:8-10
self-denial of His heavenly riches: 2 Cor 8:9
*self-denial through His incarnate form as a
 bond-servant:* Phil 2:6-8

ENJOINED UPON CHRISTIANS
self-denial in loving Christ above all others:
 Matt 10:37-39
*self-denial in taking up one's cross to follow
 Christ:* Luke 9:23-26 (cf. 2 Cor 4:10-11)
*self-denial in forsaking all things to follow
 Christ:* Luke 14:26-33

SELFISHNESS (SEE ALSO PRIDE)
WARNINGS CONCERNING SELFISHNESS
do not withhold from the needy: Deut 15:9;
 Prov 28:27; James 2:15-16; 1 John 3:17
do not desire the things of selfish people: Prov 23:6
*do not seek to save your life except by losing it
 for Christ's sake:* Mark 8:35
*do not bring spiritual hurt to your Christian
 brother:* Rom 14:15
*do not please yourself instead of benefitting
 your neighbor:* Rom 15:1-3; 1 Cor 10:24
do not live for yourself but for Christ: 2 Cor 5:15
*do not be motivated by self interests but by the
 interests of others:* Phil 2:3-4
results of selfishness: 2 Kin 5:25-27; Prov 11:26;
 Ezek 34:19; Mark 10:35; 2 Tim 3:1-5

SERPENT (SEE ALSO SATAN)
Scripture uses the term serpent both in a literal
sense of a snake as a crawling reptile (e.g., Num
21:5-7) and also in a figurative sense (e.g., Matt
23:33). However, the term serpent is used most
prominently of the animal that Satan employed
to verbalize his temptation of Eve (Gen 3:1-5,
14-15). In the NT, the serpent is closely associated with Satan (cf. Rom 16:20; 2 Cor 11:3) and
becomes one of the descriptive titles of Satan
(Rev 12:9). The serpent's methods emphasize
the deceptive and crafty character of Satan
(Gen 3:13; 2 Cor 11:3, 14; Rev 12:9).

SERVANT
OT RELATIONSHIPS FOR SERVANTS
*servants as possible heirs of their master's
 possessions:* Gen 15:2-3
Esau as servant (i.e., subordinate) to Jacob:
 Gen 25:23

servant as an expression of respect: Gen 32:4;
 44:18; 50:18; Josh 9:11; Dan 10:16-17; Mal 1:6
a king's son as a servant: 2 Sam 13:24
a king as a servant to his people: 1 Kin 12:7
a king as servant to a stronger king: 2 Kin 16:7-9;
 17:3; 24:1

OTHER TYPES OF SERVANTS
servants of Satan: 2 Cor 11:14-15
angels as servants of God: Rev 19:10; 22:9

SERVICE (SEE SERVANT)

SEVEN (SEE NUMBERS)

SHAME (SEE ALSO DISHONOR)
CAUSE
sin: Ezra 9:6; Jer 3:25; Dan 9:7-8;
 Rom 1:24-32; 3:9-18
wicked behavior: Prov 13:5
neglect of discipline: Prov 13:18
a child disrespectful to father and mother:
 Prov 19:26
idolatry: Is 42:17; Jer 11:13; 51:17; Ezek 44:12-13
rejection of the LORD's word: Jer 8:9
forsaking the LORD: Jer 17:13
unfounded boasting: 2 Cor 9:3-4
ungodly living: Jude 12-13

SHARING (SEE FELLOWSHIP)

SHEEP (SEE LAMB)

SHEOL
The term Sheol is used in the OT to denote the
underworld, i.e., the abode of the dead. In some
instances, the word it may simply refer to death
or the grave (cf. Gen 37:35; 42:38; 44:29, 31; 1 Kin
2:6, 9). Conceived of as situated in the depths
of the earth, Sheol is a place of physical death
in contrast to the vitality of life on earth with all
of its brightness and activity (cf. Job 10:21-22).
Both the righteous and the wicked went to
Sheol, although there is some indication of a
distinction in their condition there (cf. Deut
32:22; Is 57:1-2; Luke 16:23). Moreover, the
righteous looked for ultimate deliverance from
Sheol (e.g., Ps 49:15; 73:24; see also HADES).

SHEPHERD
In the OT the term shepherd is derived from
the Hebrew verb meaning "to feed" or "to pasture." The NT Greek term translated "shepherd"
simply means "one who feeds and cares for the

flock." In the biblical period and in antiquity in general, shepherding was a common occupation. Because of the dryness of the ground in Palestine, the flocks had to move about for food. This, coupled with the danger of wild animals and robbers, made shepherding a lowly but independent and responsible job. The nature of the task involving provision, guarding, and caring for the weak of the flock contributed to the figurative use of "shepherd" for rulers of the people in the ancient Near East. In Scripture this figurative use is applied to God, with two primary notions: (1) His unlimited sovereignty over His people viewed as His flock; and (2) His comprehensive loving care for them. Because the leaders of God's people led for Him, the shepherding metaphor was also applied to them. Interestingly, the title was never applied to a reigning king, although the metaphor was used for his function. However, it is applied to the Messiah.

FIGURATIVE USE OF
God: Ps 23:1; 77:20; Is 40:11; Ezek 34:11-16; Mic 7:14
Christ: Mic 5:2-4; Zech 13:7; Matt 9:36; 18:12-14; Mark 14:27; John 10:1-15; 1 Pet 2:25; 5:4

SIGN (SEE ALSO MIRACLES)

A sign is an event, act, or some other manifestation that acts as a confirmation or authentication and causes recognition of a particular person (often God) or thing. Many signs are miraculous in nature.

SIN

Various terms are used in Scripture to describe sin. The most common term in both the Old and New Testaments means to miss the mark, i.e., the righteous standard of God. That such failure is more than mere weakness is seen in other terms that signify rebellion and willful violation of the holy. The basic nature of sin is revealed in the first human sin (Genesis 3). There its essence has been interpreted primarily as unbelief seen in the rejection of God's word or pride in choosing to be as God. Both of these concepts (unbelief and pride) are central to the essence of all sin, which may thus be defined as the willful choosing to be autonomous rather than living by faith under God. Sin results in alienation and separation from God, who is the only source of true human life. The result is death, which is not only viewed as the natural result of sin,

but even more as the judgment of God. The full awfulness of sin's effect is revealed at the cross, where Jesus suffers the wrath of God in the abandonment of the Father for human sin.

The effect of Adam's sin has come to all humans as his descendants, so that all humanity is burdened with sin from birth. This sinful state is usually identified as "original sin" (cf. Rom 3:23; 5:12-19). The death of Christ for human sin and His sinless life of perfect fellowship with the Father are accounted to those who by faith are joined to Him thus overcoming the alienation of sin.

NATURE OF
general: John 16:8-9; Rom 14:23; Heb 3:13; 1 John 3:4
sinful deeds
sinful disposition
TERMS FOR
transgression: Lev 16:21; Rom 5:17
iniquity: Ex 34:7; Ps 38:4; 51:2, 9; 103:3
wickedness: Gen 6:5; 2 Tim 2:19
rebellion: Is 63:10; 1 Tim 1:9
evil: Gen 8:21; Rom 7:19
impurity: Lev 16:16; Eph 5:3
disobedience: Josh 22:22; Eph 2:2
guilt: Is 1:4
ungodliness: Titus 2:12
lawlessness: 1 John 3:4
faults: Ps 19:12
corruption: 2 Pet 2:19
lust of the heart: Matt 5:28; Rom 1:24
degrading passions: Rom 1:26
EFFECT OF
   death (see also DEATH): Gen 2:17; Rom 6:21, 23
   exclusion from the kingdom of God:
      1 Cor 6:9-10; Eph 5:5; Rev 21:27; 22:14
   alienation from God: Is 59:2
   toil and sorrow: Gen 3:16-19; Ps 32:10
   lack of peace: Is 48:22; 57:20-21

SLAVERY (SEE ALSO SERVANT)
FIGURATIVE USE OF SLAVERY
Christians should be slaves of obedience unto righteousness: Rom 6:18, 19
Christians should be slaves of God and of Christ: Rom 6:22; 1 Cor 7:22; Eph 6:6
Christians have not received a spirit of slavery leading to fear: Rom 8:15
should make their body their slave: 1 Cor 9:27
Christians are not treated as slaves but as sons and daughters who are heirs of their Father's inheritance: Gal 4:7

UNBELIEVERS IN RELATION TO SLAVERY (FIGURATIVE SENSE)

slaves of sin through committing sin: John 8:34; Rom 6:6, 17, 19, 20
slaves of their own appetites: Rom 16:18
slaves of false gods: Gal 4:8
slaves through fear of death: Heb 2:15
slaves to corruption: 2 Pet 2:19

SON (SEE ALSO CHILD; CHRIST, TITLES AND FUNCTIONS OF)
SPIRITUAL SENSE OF
BELIEVERS
sons of the living God (i.e., true members of God's people): Hos 1:10 (cf. Mal 3:17)
sons of light: Luke 16:8; John 12:36; 1 Thess 5:5
sons of God: Luke 20:36; Rom 8:14; 2 Cor 6:18; Gal 3:26; 4:4-7; Heb 2:10
sons of the resurrection: Luke 20:36
sons subject to the Father's discipline: Heb 12:5-11
UNBELIEVERS
sons of disobedience: Eph 2:2; 5:6 (cf. 2:3)

SON OF GOD (SEE ALSO CHRIST; SON OF MAN)

The title Son of God indicates both Jesus' messianic purpose and also His deity as uniquely related to His Father (Luke 1:31-35). It is applied to Him: (1) by the Father at His baptism (Matt 3:17) and again at His transfiguration (Matt 17:5); (2) in Peter's confession (Matt 16:16); (3) by the centurion (Matt 27:54) and (4) by the demons (Mark 5:7). He is the Son of God in the sense of God the Son (cf. John 1:18). Christ used this name of Himself (John 10:36) but not as extensively as "Son of Man."

SON OF MAN (SEE ALSO CHRIST; SON OF GOD)

While the title Son of Man clearly identifies Jesus with humanity (Matt 8:20; 11:19), it also designates Him as the divine Messiah whom the Father grants world-wide rulership in His coming kingdom (Dan 7:13-14; Matt 25:31; 26:64; cf. Ps 80:17). "Son of Man" is the title Christ most frequently used of Himself.

SOUL (SEE ALSO SPIRIT)

In its most comprehensive sense the term soul signifies life constituted in an individual person, thus, "a living person" (cf. Gen 2:7). As such it is used for the totality of the person, including material (body) and immaterial (spirit) aspects (e.g., animals, Gen 1:21, translated "living creatures"; and humans, Gen 2:7). Closely related to this is its use for the person (as a substitute for personal pronouns), i.e., "my soul" = "me" or "myself." It is in this sense that the term soul is used for the person of God. It is also frequently used for the life of the individual person (i.e., at death the soul departs, e.g., Gen 35:18), or various expressions of a living being (e.g., desires, appetites, emotions).

While the human person (e.g., Gen 2:7) includes both body and spirit, the soul is referred to as distinct from the body (e.g., Matt 10:28) and may exist temporarily in this separated state. The unnatural separation of body and soul is due to sin and its consequence (death). But the soul is finally restored to its created completeness through the resurrection of the body (see RESURRECTION).

SOVEREIGNTY (SEE AUTHORITY)

SOWING (SEE ALSO SEED)
FIGURATIVE USE OF
sowing in tears brings reaping in joy: Ps 126:5-6
sowing of righteousness brings true reward: Prov 11:18
sowing of iniquity reaps vanity: Prov 22:8
sowing and reaping may illustrate God's judgment: Jer 12:13; Hos 8:7
sowers and reapers can rejoice together in the harvest of souls: John 4:35-38
Christian ministry portrayed as sowing of spiritual things: 1 Cor 9:11

SPIRIT (SEE ALSO SPIRIT, HOLY)

The root meaning of both the Hebrew and Greek words for spirit (Heb. *ruach*; Gr. *pneuma*) is "air in motion." Thus these terms are also used for breath and wind (e.g., Ex 15:8 "blast"; Ps 135:7; John 3:8). The primary idea is that of vitality and power. As such, the term spirit denotes the life principle or force. In calling God "spirit" (John 4:24), Scripture portrays God as pure living power in contrast to the weakness of that which is material or flesh (cf. the contrast in Is 31:3). Created spirits (including angels), although limited in comparison to God, are still seen as powerful throughout Scripture.

In relation to humanity, the spirit is the principle of life that comes from God to animate the body or flesh (cf. Gen 2:7, "breath of life";

James 2:26). It is also in this principle of life that the personhood of the human being (i.e., self-consciousness and self-determination) resides, although it is manifest through the body, before physical death. Physical death is the departure of spirit from the body (cf. James 2:26). Separated from the body, the spirit exists in a disembodied state until the resurrection (cf. Heb 12:23).

SPIRIT, HOLY

The Holy Spirit (also called the Spirit of the Lord, the Spirit of God, the Spirit, etc.) is God Himself active in His creation. Just as the term spirit (see SPIRIT) carries the basic meaning of living power, so the expression "Holy Spirit" represents God especially in His creative life-giving and energizing activity. The additional description "Holy" signifies the absolute separateness and distinction of the Holy Spirit from all that is creaturely and worldly (see SANCTIFICATION, OF GOD). "Holy" is thus essentially the equivalent of that which is divine, identifying the Holy Spirit as God.

PERSON

DEITY

divine essence: John 4:24; 2 Cor 3:17
divine names: Gen 6:3; 2 Chr 15:1; Is 61:1;
     Matt 10:20; Rom 8:9
divine attributes
omniscience: 1 Cor 2:10, 11
omnipresence: Ps 139:7; John 14:17
omnipotence: Job 33:4; Ps 33:6; 104:30
eternality: Heb 9:14
truth: 1 John 5:6-7 (cf. John 14:6)
life: Rom 8:2
Spirit interchangeable with God: Ex 17:2-7
     (cf. Heb 3:7-9); Is 6:8-10 (cf. Acts 28:25-27);
     Jer 31:31-34 (cf. Heb 10:15-17)
trinitarian formulae: Matt 28:19-20;
     1 Cor 12:4-6; 1 Pet 1:2

RELATION TO MEMBERS OF TRINITY

sent by Father: Ps 104:30; Matt 10:20
Spirit of your Father: John 14:26; 15:26; 1 Cor 2:12
sent by Christ: John 15:26; 16:7; 20:22
called "Spirit of Christ": Rom 8:9; (cf. Gal 4:6;
     Phil 1:19)
God's work is effected "of" or "by the Spirit":
     John 3:8; Rom 8:13; Gal 5:25; Eph 2:18, 22;
     2 Thess 2:13; Titus 3:4, 5

WORK

IN THE CREATION

creator: Gen 1:2; 2:7; Job 26:13; 33:4; Ps 33:6
sustainer: Ps 104:27-30

in production of Scripture: 2 Tim 3:16;
     2 Pet 1:20-21
fulfillment in church
baptism with, gift of, Spirit: Acts 2:1-4;
     1 Cor 2:12; 2 Cor 3:5-8; Gal 3:2-14;
     1 Thess 4:8
regeneration: John 3:5, 8; Titus 3:5; 1 Pet 1:3,
     23 (see also CREATION, new)
sealing as guarantee of future inheritance:
     2 Cor 1:22; Eph 1:13, 14; 4:30
indwelling: John 14:17; Rom 8:9-11;
     1 John 2:27
controls (fills) believers lives: Acts 2:4; 4:8, 31
sanctifies: Rom 15:16; 1 Cor 6:11; 2 Thess 2:13
source of all spiritual virtues: Rom 5:5; 14:17;
     15:13; Gal 5:22-23 (fruit of the Spirit);
     1 Thess 1:6
assurance of salvation: Rom 8:16
giving spiritual gifts: 1 Cor 12:7
intercessor in prayer: Rom 8:26, 27
illumination and teaching: John 14:26; 15:26;
     1 Cor 2:10-16; 1 John 2:27
comforting: John 14:16, 17; 16:7
guiding: John 16:13; Rom 8:14; Gal 5:18

SPIRITUALITY
(SEE SANCTIFICATION)

STEWARDSHIP

Biblical stewardship involves delegated responsibility to manage for another (e.g., Luke 16:1, 12). Stewardship in the OT specifically indicates management of someone's household (Is 22:15), i.e., through a "house steward" (Gen 43:19; 44:4). In NT usage stewardship may involve (1) oversight of employees through a "foreman" (Matt 20:8; cf. Luke 12:42); (2) care for another person, especially as a guardian over a child (Gal 4:2); (3) management of a superior's possessions (Luke 12:42-44; 16:1-8); or (4) Christian responsibility to faithfully fulfill one's God-given ministry, particularly in proclaiming the gospel of Christ (1 Cor 9:17; Eph 3:2; Col 1:25; cf. Col 4:17). The broader doctrine of stewardship indicates Christian responsibility to faithfully use personal gifts (natural and spiritual), time, and possessions as divine entrustments to serve God and people. Christian stewardship properly recognizes that all human abilities and possessions, including the earth and its contents, are on consignment to humanity from God (1 Chr 29:12; John 3:27; James 1:17; cf. Gen 1:26-28; Ps 8:3-8). Thus

the use of such divine endowments should (1) accord with individual ability (Matt 25:15); (2) express richness toward God (cf. Luke 12:21); (3) involve an efficient use of time and opportunity (Eph 5:16; Col 4:5); (4) accord with personal prosperity (1 Cor 16:2); (5) result from individual intent of heart (2 Cor 9:7); and (6) express glory and faith toward God (1 Cor 10:31; 1 Tim 6:17).

STONES (SEE ALSO PRECIOUS STONES; ROCK)

FIGURATIVE SENSE OF

IN GENERAL

the LORD as the Stone of Israel: Gen 49:24

the heart of stone (i.e., spiritually hardened): Ezek 36:26

the crushing stone that destroys all earthly kingdoms and fills the whole earth (i.e., the future messianic kingdom): Dan 2:34-35, 45

stones crying out: Hab 2:11; Luke 19:40

believers as living stones: 1 Pet 2:5

the white stone with a new name written on it for the believer: Rev 2:17

OF CHRIST

a tested and rejected stone as a cornerstone for the foundation: Ps 118:22; Is 28:16; Matt 21:42-44; Eph 2:20; 1 Pet 2:4, 6-7

a stone of stumbling: Is 8:14; Rom 9:32-33; 1 Pet 2:8

the living stone: 1 Pet 2:4

SUBSTITUTION

The biblical as well as the general sense of the term substitution is the use of a person or thing in place of another person or thing (e.g., Matt 2:22; 5:38; Philem 13). The principle of substitution is taught in the OT doctrine of atonement (Lev 16:15-22) and reaches its highest biblical significance in the sacrificial death of Christ for sinners (Is 53:6; Mark 10:45; 2 Cor 5:21).

OF SACRIFICIAL ANIMALS

in place of a person: Gen 22:2-13, esp. vv. 8, 13

in atonement for the offerer(s): Lev 1:4

for another animal: Lev 27:9-10, 33 (cf. Mal 1:6-14)

in Christ's redemptive work (see also CHRIST): Is 52:13-53:12; Matt 20:28; John 1:29; 11:50-52; Rom 5:6-8; 1 Cor 15:3-4; 2 Cor 5:14-15; Gal 2:20; 1 Tim 2:6; Heb 2:9; 9:28; 1 Pet 2:24; 3:18

SUFFERING (SEE ALSO PERSECUTION)

EXAMPLES OF SUFFERING

CHRIST

suffering of Christ (see also CHRIST)

suffering for Christ

by Peter and John: Acts 4:1-12

by Peter and James: Acts 12:1-5

by Paul: Acts 9:16; 14:19; 2 Cor 1:8; 11:23-28; Phil 3:8, 10; Col 1:24; 1 Thess 2:2

GOD'S PURPOSES IN SUFFERING

to test His people: Deut 8:2; Job 1:13-2:13; Is 48:10

to discipline for sin: 2 Sam 12:9-18; 2 Chr 33:10-11; 1 Cor 11:29-32

to perform His work for His glory: John 9:1-3

to spread His word: Acts 8:3-4; Phil 1:12-13; 2 Tim 4:16-17

to enable believers to experience His grace and strength: 2 Cor 12:7-10

to produce holy people through discipline: Heb 12:5-11

GOD'S RESPONSE TO HIS PEOPLES SUFFERING

He is present with them: Ps 23:4; Is 43:2

He provides refuge, strength, and help for them: Ps 46:1

He comforts them: Is 40:1-2; 49:13; 2 Cor 1:3-5

He shares with them in suffering: Is 63:9

He will relieve them of suffering at Christ's coming: 2 Thess 1:7

He will remove all suffering in the glorified state: Rev 21:1-4

SUICIDE (SEE ALSO DEATH)

prohibition against: Ex 20:13

SYMBOLS (SEE FIGURATIVE SPEECH)

T

TABERNACLE (SEE ALSO TEMPLE)

The tabernacle (lit., "dwelling"; cf. Ex 40:2, & note) was an earthly sanctuary divinely designed to represent God's dwelling among His people (Ex 25:8; 29:43; Heb 9:1). It served Israel as a "tent of meeting" (Num 4:25) with God. The tabernacle proper consisted of the Holy Place and the inner sanctuary (or the Most Holy Place) that contained only the ark of the covenant (see also ARK, ark of the covenant; Ex 26:33-34; Heb 9:2-7). Once a year on the Day of Atonement, the high priest entered the Most Holy Place to

sprinkle blood on the mercy seat of the ark for his own sins and for the sins of the people (Lev 16:1-34; Heb 9:7, 25). The tabernacle was the primary place where God manifested His presence and gave revelation to His people (Ex 25:8). His presence and guidance were indicated through the cloud by day and the fire by night associated with the tabernacle (Ex 40:34-38; Num 9:15-23). The shekinah glory cloud distinguished Israel's tabernacle and later their temple from all other religious structures. Also, it was the place where people could approach God through sacrificial offerings and express or restore their relationship with God in response to His blessings and offer of forgiveness.

TAXATION
FORMS
poll (temple) tax: Ex 30:11-16
land tax: Gen 41:34, 48
forced labor: Josh 16:10; Judg 1:28
tolls: 1 Kin 10:14-29
PURPOSES
FOR TRIBUTE
Assyria: 2 Kin 18:13-16
Egypt: 2 Kin 23:33-35
Babylon: 2 Kin 24-25
Israel: 2 Chr 9:13-28
Rome: Luke 2:1
for temple: Ex 30:11-16
for government: 2 Chr 17:5; Neh 5:14-15;
Rom 13:6, 7

TEACHERS
God as teacher: Ex 4:12; 1 Kin 8:36; Ps 25:4-5; 94:9-10, 12; 119:12; John 6:45 (cf. Is 54:13); 1 Thess 4:9
Christ as teacher (see also CHRIST): Matt 5:2; 22:16; Acts 1:1
Holy Spirit as teacher (see also SPIRIT, HOLY): Luke 12:12; John 16:13; 1 Cor 2:13; 1 John 2:20, 27
TRUE TEACHERS
PROPER RESPONSE TO
be humble: Ps 25:9
pay attention to them: Is 48:17-18 (cf. Prov 5:13)
realize that pupils are not above their teachers: Luke 6:40
practice their teachings: John 13:17
follow their example: John 13:13-15
share with them (i.e., in Christian giving): Gal 6:6
remember their words: 2 Pet 3:2

FALSE TEACHERS
(SEE ALSO APOSTASY; DOCTRINE, SOME FALSE TEACHERS OF)

TEACHING (SEE DOCTRINE; PREACHING; TEACHERS)
content of (see also DOCTRINE)
ACTIVITY OF
MAIN SUBJECTS OF TEACHING
God's law: Ex 18:20; Deut 4:1
God's truth and ways: Ps 25:4-5
godly wisdom: e.g., Prov 1:1-31:31
Christ's commandments: Matt 28:20
prayer: Luke 11:1
the person and work of Christ as LORD: e.g., Acts 4:2; 5:42; 20:21; 28:31; 1 Cor 15:3-4
the word of God in general: Acts 18:11; 2 Tim 3:16-17
that which is good
results of teaching: Prov 9:9; Jer 32:33; Matt 7:28-29; Acts 2:42-43; 4:2

TEMPER (SEE ANGER)

TEMPLE (SEE ALSO TABERNACLE)
Israel's temple was the permanent building and central place of their worship where God chose to dwell among His people (1 Kin 8:12-13; 2 Kin 23:27; 2 Chr 7:12; Matt 23:21). Temples were common in the cities of the Near East, and each temple represented and was dedicated to a patron deity. Thus the temple was "the house" of its deity (e.g., "Dagon's house," 1 Sam 5:5; cf. 1 Sam 31:10). King David initiated the idea of building Israel's first temple to replace their portable tabernacle since Israel had become consolidated in the promised land under his rule (2 Sam 7:1-3; 1 Chr 28:2). God approved David's plan but stipulated that Solomon his son should build the temple (2 Sam 7:1-17; 1 Kin 8:15-20; 1 Chr 28:1-6). Construction of Solomon's temple began in his fourth year and was completed seven years later (967-960 B.C.; 1 Kin 6:37-38; 2 Chr 3:1-2). It was eventually destroyed along with the city of Jerusalem by the Babylonian army in 586 B.C. (2 Kin 25:8-10; Ezra 5:12). Another temple was built at Jerusalem by the returnees from captivity during the governorship of Zerubbabel (Ezra 3:8-12). This temple was begun on the original temple site in 536 B.C. and was completed in 516 B.C. The temple of Herod the Great was begun in 19 B.C., and the main building was completed in 9 B.C. However, further work continued until

A.D. 64 (cf. John 2:20). This temple included magnificent and beautiful buildings as indicated by Jesus' own disciples (Mark 13:1). Herod's temple was demolished in A.D. 70 by the Roman general Titus just as Jesus had predicted (Matt 24:21; Luke 21:21-24; cf. Hos 3:4-5).

CHRIST'S RELATION TO

His visit at twelve: Luke 2:46
His superiority to: Matt 12:6
His first cleansing of: John 2:13-17
His second cleansing of: Mark 11:15-16
His description of: Mark 11:17
His healing in: Matt 21:14
His daily teaching in: Luke 19:47; 21:37-38;
   John 8:20
His prediction of its destruction: Matt 24:1-2
His general ministry in: John 5:14; 10:23
tribulation period temple: Matt 24:15 (cf. v. 21);
   2 Thess 2:3-4; Rev 11:1 (cf. Dan 9:27; 12:11)

MILLENNIAL (I.E., EZEKIEL'S)

temple: Is 2:3; Ezek 40:1-44:31; 47:1-12; Hag 2:7, 9;
   Zech 6:12-15
*of the Lord Himself and the Lamb (i.e., in the
   eternal state):* Rev 21:22 (cf. 3:12; 21:3)
of God: Ezra 6:17; Ps 65:4 (cf. 5:7; 84:10; Mal 3:1)
as the "house of God": Neh 6:10; Eccl 5:1;
   Matt 12:4 (cf. John 2:16)
heavenly (i.e., the abode of God): 2 Sam 22:7;
   Ps 11:4; Heb 8:5; 9:23-24; 10:19; 12:22;
   Rev 7:15; 11:19; 14:15, 17; 15:5-6, 8; 16:1, 17
   (cf. Acts 17:24)

TEMPTATION (SEE ALSO TESTING)

OF JESUS

tempted by the devil: Matt 4:1-11
tempted by Peter: Matt 16:22-23
tempted to follow His human will: Matt 22:39
*overcame temptation through the Spirit of God
   and the word of God:* Luke 4:1-13
tempted in His sufferings: Heb 2:18
*able to sympathize with Christians in their
   temptation:* Heb 4:15
without sin in His temptations: Heb 4:15
tempted in all things: Heb 4:15

OF GOD'S PEOPLE

SOURCES OF TEMPTATION

   Satan: 1 Thess 3:5
   not from God: James 1:13
   one's own fleshly lust: James 1:14; 1 John 2:16
      (cf. Gen 3:6; 2 Sam 11:1-5)
   lust of the eyes: 1 John 2:16 (cf. Gen 3:6;
      Matt 5:27-29)
   the pride of life: 1 John 2:16 (cf. Gen 3:6)

GOD'S HELP IN TEMPTATION

He sets limits for temptation: 1 Cor 10:13
*He provides a way to escape and endure
   temptation:* 1 Cor 10:13
He Himself does not tempt anyone: James 1:13

PROPER RESPONSE FOR VICTORY OVER TEMPTATION

flee the scene of temptation: Gen 39:7-12
   (cf. 2 Tim 2:22)
treasure the word of God in the heart: Ps 119:11;
   Matt 4:1-11
*watch and pray for deliverance from
   temptation:* Matt 6:13; 26:41
live by faith in Christ: Rom 1:17; Gal 2:20;
   1 John 5:4-5
depend on God's grace: Rom 6:14
*provide for each other's sexual needs in the
   marriage relationship:* 1 Cor 7:3-5
*recognize that temptation is common to all
   people:* 1 Cor 10:13; James 1:13
be wise about Satan's schemes: 2 Cor 2:11
walk by the Spirit: Gal 5:16
*beware of temptation when restoring others
   from a trespass:* Gal 6:1
*put on God's full armor for spiritual warfare
   (see also WARFARE):* Eph 6:10-17
be on the alert for the devil: 1 Pet 5:8
*recognize that the Lord can rescue the godly
   from temptation:* 2 Pet 2:9

TESTIMONY (SEE ALSO WITNESS)

laws concerning testimony (i.e., of witnesses):
   Ex 23:2; Num 35:30; John 8:17 (cf. Deut 19:15);
   2 Cor 13:1

TESTIMONY FROM THE LORD

through His word: Ps 19:7; 78:5; 119:88; 132:12;
   Is 8:16, 20; Heb 1:6
about David: Acts 13:22
about Abel: Heb 11:4

TESTIMONY FROM THE SPIRIT

about Christ: John 15:26
about Paul's future afflictions: Acts 20:23

TESTIMONY IN RELATION TO CHRIST

testimony of false witnesses against Christ:
   Mark 14:55-60
*testimony about Christ from Himself and His
   Father:* John 5:31-32, 37; 8:18
*testimony to Christ's person, redeeming work, and
   judgment (i.e., the gospel of Christ and related
   themes; see also PREACHING):* Acts 2:40; 8:25;
   10:42; 20:24; 1 Tim 2:6
rejection of testimony concerning Christ:
   Acts 22:18

unashamed of the testimony of Christ: 2 Tim 1:8
witness borne to the testimony of Christ: Rev 1:2
faithfulness to the testimony of Christ: Rev 12:17
martyrdom for the testimony of Christ:
    Rev 6:9; 20:4
testimony from Christ through an angel: Rev 22:16

TESTIMONY IN RELATION TO PAUL
testimony to Jews that Jesus is Messiah: Acts 18:5
    (cf. 28:23)
testimony of the gospel to Jews and Gentiles:
    Acts 20:21; 26:22-23
testimony of Paul's faithful ministry of the gospel:
    Acts 20:26
true testimony: Deut 8:19-20; John 8:14;
    Titus 1:12-13; Heb 3:5; 11:4
false testimony: 1 Kin 21:10-13; Mark 14:55-60

VARIOUS OTHER USES
ark of the testimony: Ex 25:22
two tablets of the testimony: Ex 31:18
tabernacle of the testimony: Ex 38:21; Acts 7:44;
    Rev 15:5
the testimony of the Mosaic Law: 2 Kin 11:12
faithful witnesses for a testimony: Is 8:2
testimony of the two witnesses during the
    tribulation period: Rev 11:4-7
victory over Satan through the testimony of
    believers: Rev 12:11
testimony of John concerning response to the
    book of Revelation: Rev 22:18

TESTING (SEE ALSO TEMPTATION)
IN RELATION TO GOD
TESTING OF PEOPLE BY GOD
of the nation Israel: Ex 15:25; 16:4; 20:20;
    Deut 8:16; 13:3; Judg 2:22; Is 48:10; Jer 6:27;
    Ezek 21:12-13
of the righteous: Ps 11:5
of the wicked: Ps 11:5
of the righteous remnant: Zech 13:9
of people in general
    testing to prove humanity's depraved nature:
    Eccl 3:18
    testing through judgmental trials: Rev 3:10
OF GOD BY PEOPLE
examples of: Ex 17:2, 7; Num 14:22; Ps 78:18;
    95:9; Mal 3:15; Acts 15:10; Heb 3:9
prohibition against: Deut 6:16 (cf. Matt 4:7)
legitimate invitation for: Is 7:10-13; Mal 3:10
IN RELATION TO CHRIST
Christ as a tested stone for a sure foundation:
    Is 28:16
testing of Christ by antagonists: Matt 16:1; 19:3;
    22:18, 35; John 8:6

testing of Philip by Christ: John 6:5-6
of the Spirit: Acts 5:9
OF NT BELIEVERS
a person's Christian integrity approved through
    testing: 2 Cor 8:22
testing of personal Christian faith: James 1:3;
    1 Pet 1:7
testing of suffering Christians: 1 Pet 4:12
testing of imprisoned Christians: Rev 2:10

THANKFULNESS (SEE BLESS; PRAISE)

THEOCRACY (SEE ALSO KINGDOM)
A theocracy ("rulership of God") is a government in which God acts as civil ruler or else
human authorities rule as God's mediatorial
representatives (cf. Deut 33:4-5). Israel was
unique as a divinely established theocratic nation with religious and civil laws given to the
nation at Sinai (Ex 19-31). God's rulership over
Israel was mediated through divinely chosen
leaders such as Moses, Joshua, judges, and
kings (cf. 1 Chr 29:25).

THIRST
FIGURATIVE SENSE OF
thirst of the soul for God: Ps 42:2; 63:1; 107:9
thirst for spiritual provision from the LORD:
    Is 55:1
thirst for the word of God: Amos 8:11-13
Spiritual thirst for righteousness: Matt 5:6
spiritual thirst for Christ's gift of living water
    (i.e., the Spirit): John 4:13-15; 6:35; 7:37-39
thirst for the water of life: Rev 21:6; 22:17

THOUGHT (SEE MIND)

THRONE
OF GOD
glorious: Is 6:1; Jer 14:21; Ezek 1:26-28
gracious: Heb 4:16
eternal: Ps 45:6; 93:2; Dan 2:44
in heaven: Ps 11:4; 103:19
righteousness: Ps 9:4; 45:6, 7
OF CHRIST
David's throne: Luke 1:32, 33; Acts 2:30
glorious: Matt 19:28; 25:31
the right hand of God: Acts 2:34-36; Heb 8:1; 12:2
eternal: Heb 1:8
righteous: Heb 1:8
called God's throne: Rev 3:21; 22:1
of believers future reign: Matt 19:28;
    Rev 3:21; 20:4

TIME

GOD'S
RELATION TO
He created time: Gen 1:1; Heb 1:10
He precedes time: Gen 1:1; Ps 90:2; Jude 25
He is above time: Is 57:15 (cf. Ps 90:4; 2 Pet 3:8)
He continues after time: Ps 90:2; Jude 25
He established the daily and seasonal cycles
of time: Gen 1:3-5; 8:22

BIBLICAL TERMINOLOGY FOR
(SEE ALSO END TIMES)
"age" or "ages" (see also AGE, i.e., ERA)
"the times and the periods": Dan 2:21; 1 Thess 5:1
"a time, times, and half a time": Dan 7:25; 12:7
(cf. Rev 12:14)
time of the end or end time: Dan 8:17, 19;
11:35, 40; 12:9
that time (i.e., the future time of intense
tribulation): Dan 12:1-2; Matt 24:10
the end of time: Dan 12:4
in those days and at that time, i.e., when God
restores Israel: Joel 3:1 (cf. Mic 5:3-4;
Zeph 3:19-20)
"the signs of the times": Matt 16:3
"the time is fulfilled," i.e., for the kingdom of God
to be at hand: Mark 1:15
"the times of the Gentiles": Luke 21:24
"the last day": John 12:48
"periods of time or appointed times" in the
Father's authority: Acts 1:6-7
"the last days": Acts 2:17; 2 Tim 3:1; 2 Pet 3:3
divinely "appointed times": Acts 17:26
"the fullness of the time": Gal 4:4
"His plan of the fullness of the times": Eph 1:10
"later times": 1 Tim 4:1

FIGURATIVE USE OF
week: Gen 29:27-28; Dan 9:24-27
day: Gen 2:4; 2 Cor 6:2; 1 Thess 5:2
hour: Mark 14:35; John 2:4; 5:25, 28

TORMENTS
(SEE JUDGMENT; PUNISHMENT)

TRADITION
(SEE ALSO DOCTRINE; TEACHING)

HUMAN TRADITION IN RELIGION
CHARACTERISTICS OF
produces vain religion: Is 29:13; Matt 15:7-9
practiced to be seen of people: Matt 6:1-5
believed and practiced by the Pharisees and
scribes: Matt 15:1-2
emphasizes mere external religion: Matt 15:2
(cf. 5:21-28; 6:1-6)

condemned by Christ as hypocritical:
Matt 15:7-9; 23:1-36
displaces teaching of true biblical doctrines with
the commandments of people: Matt 15:9
cannot produce righteousness acceptable to
God: Phil 3:4-9

EXPRESSIONS FOR
"the tradition of the elders": Matt 15:2
"the commandments of people": Matt 15:9
"the tradition of men": Mark 7:8; Col 2:8
ancestral traditions (i.e., in Judaism): Gal 1:14

TRUE TRADITION IN ACCORDANCE WITH
BIBLICAL TEACHING
transmission of: Deut 6:6-7; Ps 78:3-8; Prov 1:8
commendable retention of: 1 Cor 11:2; 2 Thess 2:15
(cf. 1 Cor 15:1-2)
divine origin and apostolic communication of:
1 Cor 11:2, 23-26; 15:1-8; 2 Thess 3:6
authority of: 1 Cor 15:1-2; 2 Thess 2:15; 3:6

TRANSGRESSION (SEE SIN)

TREASURES (SEE WEALTH)

TRIBULATION
(SEE PERSECUTION; SUFFERING)

TRIBUTE (SEE TAXATION)

TRINITY, THE (SEE GOD)
In Christian usage the term Trinity expresses
the belief that there is only "one God" (Deut
6:4; 1 Tim 2:5) who exists as three distinct divine persons, Father, Son, and Holy Spirit (Matt
28:19), who are cosubstantial, coeternal, and
coequal. While each divine person has particular roles and functions (e.g., Eph 1:3-14), all
three work together in perfect accord (John
5:17, 19; 10:28-30).

in unity: Deut 4:35, 39; Is 45:21; Eph 4:6; 1 Tim 2:5;
James 2:19
OT implications of: Gen 1:1-2, 26; 3:22; 11:7; Ps 2:7;
110:1; Prov 30:4; Is 7:14; 9:6; 48:16

NT INDICATIONS OF
distinction of the three persons: Matt 3:16-17;
John 14:16-17; Rom 5:5-6; 1 Cor 12:4-6;
2 Cor 13:14; Gal 4:4-6; Eph 2:18; 4:4-6; 5:18-20;
1 Thess 1:2-5; 2 Thess 2:13; Titus 3:4-6;
1 Pet 1:2; 3:18; 1 John 4:2; Jude 20-21

DEITY OF EACH PERSON
the Father (see also GOD): John 6:27; Gal 1:1
the Son (see also CHRIST): John 1:1; 10:30;
Titus 2:13; Heb 1:8

the Spirit (see also SPIRIT, HOLY): John 14:16;
Acts 5:3-4

TRUTH (SEE ALSO FALSEHOOD)

RELATED TO GOD (SEE ALSO GOD, ATTRIBUTES OF, TRUTHFUL)

general references: Gen 24:27; Ex 18:21; 2 Sam 2:6;
Ps 31:5; 43:3; 117:2; Is 65:16; John 3:33;
Rom 3:4, 7; Rev 6:10

SPECIFIC ASPECTS

His word is truth (see also WORD OF GOD):
2 Sam 7:28; Ps 119:160; John 17:17
(cf. 1 Kin 17:24); Neh 9:13; Ps 119:43, 142;
Rev 19:9

His paths are truth: Ps 25:10

His works are done in truth: Ps 111:7-8
(cf. Dan 4:37)

His ways are true: Rev 15:3

His judgments are true: Rev 16:7

the Father: John 5:32; 7:18; 8:26; 17:3; 19:35;
1 John 5:20

THE SON

spoke the truth: Luke 4:25; 9:27; John 8:14,
16, 40, 45-46; 18:37 (cf. Matt 22:16)

is full of truth: John 1:14

the truth was realized through Him: John 1:17

embodies the truth in His person: John 14:6;
Eph 4:21; Rev 3:7

confirmed the truth of God: Rom 15:8

is a true Witness: Rev 3:14

called Faithful and True: Rev 19:11

the Spirit: John 14:17; 15:26; 16:13; 1 John 5:7

PROPER RESPONSE TO

walk before the LORD in truth: 1 Kin 2:4; 2 Kin 20:3

be divinely led in the truth: Ps 25:5

walk in the LORD's truth: Ps 26:3; 86:11; 2 John 4;
3 John 3-4

speak forth the truth: Ps 40:10; Prov 8:7; Jer 23:28
(cf. Mark 5:33)

give attention to the truth: Dan 9:13

judge with truth: Zech 8:16

love truth: Zech 8:19

practice the truth: John 3:21

worship in truth: John 4:23-24

obey the truth: Gal 5:7; 1 Pet 1:22

speak the truth in love: Eph 4:15

be saved and come to the knowledge of the
truth: 1 Tim 2:4 (cf. Titus 1:1)

handle accurately the word of truth: 2 Tim 2:15

repent leading to the knowledge of the truth:
2 Tim 2:25

love in deed and truth: 1 John 3:18 (cf. 2 John 1);
3 John 1

be fellow workers with the truth: 3 John 8

have a good testimony from the truth: 3 John 12

IMPROPER RESPONSE TO

reject the truth: Is 59:14-15

speak not the truth: Jer 9:5

suppress the truth: Rom 1:18

exchange the truth of God for a lie: Rom 1:25

disobey the truth: Rom 2:8

believe not the truth: 2 Thess 2:12

go astray from the truth: 2 Tim 2:18 (cf. Titus 1:14);
James 5:19

oppose the truth: 2 Tim 3:8

turn away from the truth: 2 Tim 4:4

malign the way of the truth: 2 Pet 2:2

fail to have the truth in oneself: 1 John 1:8; 2:4

TYPES

KINDS OF TYPES

PERSONS (SEE ALSO TYPES, KINDS OF TYPES, OFFICES)

Adam a type of Christ as head of a people:
Gen 2:7; Rom 5:12-21; 1 Cor 15:45

Abraham a type of all believers: Rom 4:9-24;
Gal 3:7, 9, 29

Joseph a type of Christ as the rejected kinsman
who becomes their Savior: Gen 37:1-50:26;
Acts 7:9-14

Elijah a type of John the Baptist: Mal 4:5-6;
Matt 11:14; Luke 1:17

OFFICES

Moses a type of Christ as prophet:
Deut 18:15, 18-19; Acts 3:22-23

Aaron and Melchizedek types of Christ as
priest: Heb 4:14-15; 5:1-6

David a type of Christ as king: 2 Sam 7:12-17;
Jer 23:5; Luke 1:31-33; Rev 11:15; 19:16

Melchizedek a type of Christ as priest-king:
Gen 14:18-20; Ps 110:4; Zech 6:12-13;
Heb 7:1-17

ACTIONS

creation of light a type of the gospel light
shining into hearts: Gen 1:3; 2 Cor 4:6

lifting up of the serpent in the wilderness a
type of Christ's crucifixion: Num 21:6-9;
John 3:14-16

THINGS

the rock that gave water a type of Christ the
spiritual rock: Ex 17:6; 1 Cor 10:4

the tabernacle a type of Christ's person and
work: Ex 25:9; John 1:14, & note; Heb 8:1-5;
9:1-10:22

the rent veil a type of Christ providing access
to God: Ex 26:33; Mark 15:37-38; Heb 10:20

incense a type of prayer: Ex 30:1; Rev 8:3-4
the veil of Moses a type of Israel's spiritual
  blindness: Ex 34:33-35; 2 Cor 3:13-16

U

UNBELIEF (SEE ALSO FAITH)

sin: Matt 17:17; Luke 9:41; Rom 14:23; Titus 1:15;
  Rev 21:8
of specific facts: Gen 45:26; Ex 4:1;
  Prov 26:25
of spiritual truth (see also SIN)

CAUSES OF

pride: Ps 10:4; Hab 2:4; John 5:44
Satanic influence: Luke 8:12; 2 Cor 4:4; Eph 2:2;
  2 Thess 2:8-12
hardness of heart: Mark 16:14
divine judgment: John 12:37-40
other: Luke 24:25; John 8:45; 1 Tim 1:13

CONSEQUENCES OF

FOR UNSAVED

condemnation: Mark 16:16; Luke 12:46;
  John 3:18, 36; 5:24; 8:24; 12:48
separation from God: Rom 11:20; Heb 3:19;
  4:1-3; 11:6; Rev 21:8
death: Heb 11:31; 12:25; 1 John 5:12
destruction: Jude 5
spiritual dullness: Matt 13:13-15

FOR SAVED

limitation of God's work (believers):
  Matt 9:29; 13:58; 14:31; 17:20

UNCLEAN (SEE CLEAN)

UNDERSTANDING (SEE KNOWLEDGE)

UNFAITHFULNESS
(SEE ALSO FAITHFULNESS)

levitical offerings for unfaithfulness:
  Lev 5:15-16; 6:2-7
punishment for unfaithfulness of Israel:
  Num 14:33; 1 Chr 9:1; 2 Chr 12:2-5; 29:6-9;
  30:7; 36:14-21; Neh 1:8; Ezek 14:13; 15:8;
  Dan 9:7
*accusation and denial of unfaithfulness of
  certain tribes of Israel:* Josh 22:15-34
*reform by Hezekiah due to Israel's
  unfaithfulness:* 2 Chr 29:5-11
punishment for unfaithfulness: Ps 73:27;
  Matt 25:24-30
Christ's teaching on unfaithfulness: Luke 16:10;
  19:20-27

UNITY (SEE ALSO FELLOWSHIP)

of the Father and the Son: John 10:30; 17:11, 21

OF BELIEVERS

ASPECTS OF UNITY

spiritual unity in the Father and in the Son:
  John 17:11, 21-23
unity of heart and soul: Acts 4:32
spiritual unity in Christ: Rom 6:5; Gal 3:26-28
unity of mind: Rom 12:16; 1 Cor 1:10;
  Phil 1:27; 2:2
unity of judgment: 1 Cor 1:10
unity in spirit: 2 Cor 12:18; Phil 1:27; 2:2
spiritual unity of Jew and Gentile in Christ:
  Eph 2:13-16
unity in one hope of calling for believers: Eph 4:4
*unity based on one LORD, one faith, one
  baptism, one God and Father:* Eph 4:5-6
unity of love: Phil 2:2
unity of purpose: Phil 2:2
related references: Matt 23:8

RESPONSIBILITY FOR UNITY

*to exercise diverse spiritual gifts within the
  unity of the body:* Rom 12:4-8; 1 Cor 12:4-31
*to allow diverse opinions within the unity of
  believers on matters of personal conviction:*
  Rom 14:1-23
*to preserve the unity of the Spirit in the bond
  of peace:* Eph 4:3 (cf. 1 Thess 5:13)
to aim for the unity of the faith: Eph 4:13
to function with a sense of unity in the body:
  Eph 4:12-16
to express love for the growth of unity:
  Eph 4:15-16
to stand firm in unity: Phil 1:27
*to strive together in unity for the faith of the
  gospel:* Phil 1:27
to express unity in relation to other believers:
  Phil 2:2
to put on love as the perfect bond of unity:
  Col 3:14

UPRIGHTNESS (SEE RIGHTEOUSNESS)

V

VANITY (SEE PRIDE)

VENERATION (SEE WORSHIP)

VICTORY

victory turned to mourning: 2 Sam 19:2
victory by David's men in warfare: 2 Sam 23:9-12

Elisha's prophecy of victory for Israel over Aram:
2 Kin 13:17
victory attributed to the LORD: 1 Chr 29:11; Ps 98:1;
Prov 21:31
rejoicing over victory: Ps 20:5
false hope for victory in humans and horses:
Ps 33:17
victory in abundance of counselors: Prov 11:14
victory over Babylon through divine judgment:
Jer 51:14
ultimate victory through Messiah: Matt 12:20
victory over death through Christ: 1 Cor 15:54-57
victory over the world through faith in Christ:
1 John 5:4-5

VINE, VINEYARD
FIGURATIVE USE
Israel: Ps 80:8-16; Is 5:1-7; Jer 2:21; Hos 10:1
peace and prosperity (eating of one's own):
1 Kin 4:25; Ps 107:37; Mic 4:4; Zech 3:10
settled habitation (plant and eat): 2 Kin 19:29;
Ps 107:37; Amos 9:14
misfortune (failure to harvest): Deut 20:6;
28:30; Amos 5:11; Zeph 1:13
kingdom of God: Matt 20:1-8; 21:33-43;
Mark 12:1-9; Luke 20:9-16
union of Christ and believers: John 15:1-8

VIRGIN (SEE ALSO MARRIAGE)
examples of virgins: Gen 24:16; Judg 11:34-40;
19:24; 21:12; 2 Sam 13:2; 1 Kin 1:1-3; Ps 45:14;
Lam 1:4; Acts 21:8-9
OT laws concerning virgins: Ex 22:16-17;
Lev 21:1-3, 13-14; Deut 22:13-29; Ezek 44:22
NT principles concerning virgins: 1 Cor 7:25-38
FIGURATIVE USE OF
the people of Israel called the virgin of Israel:
Jer 18:13; 31:4 (cf. Ezek 23:3, 8; Amos 5:2)
the church called a pure virgin: 2 Cor 11:2

VISION (SEE REVELATION, FORMS)

VOWS (SEE OATH)

W

WAITING (SEE ALSO PATIENCE)
WAITING FOR THE LORD
general references: Gen 49:18; Job 35:14; Ps 25:5;
62:5; Is 8:17; Mark 15:43
exhortation concerning: Job 35:14; Ps 27:14;
37:7; Hos 12:6; Zeph 3:8

results of: Ps 25:3; 37:9; 40:1; Prov 20:22; Is 40:31;
Heb 6:15 (cf. Jer 8:15)
lack of: Ps 106:13
WAITING BY THE LORD
to have compassion on His people: Is 30:18
to save people in the days of Noah: 1 Pet 3:20
VARIOUS OTHER USES
difficulty in waiting: Job 6:11
waiting for the resurrection of one's body:
Job 14:14-15
failure in waiting for the LORD's counsel:
Ps 106:13
waiting for Messiah's appearing: Is 42:4
waiting for fulfillment of a revelatory vision:
Hab 2:3
waiting for the promise of the Spirit: Acts 1:4-5, 8
(cf. 2:1-4)
waiting of the creation for freedom from
bondage: Rom 8:19-22
waiting for the hope of righteousness: Gal 5:5
waiting for Christ's return: Phil 3:20; Titus 1:10;
Jude 21 (cf. Rom 8:23-25)
waiting of Christ for the subjugation of His
enemies: Heb 10:31 (cf. Ps 110:1)

WALKING (SEE CONDUCT)

WARFARE, SPIRITUAL (SEE ALSO SANCTIFICATION)
The expression spiritual warfare refers to the
Christian's conflict with the world, the flesh,
and the devil and his demons, especially in their
enticement to sin (John 15:18-19; Gal 5:16-17;
Eph 6:10-12; cf. 1 Tim 6:12). The provision for
victory over these spiritual enemies has been
accomplished through Christ's sacrificial
death and glorious resurrection (John 12:31-33;
16:33; Rom 6:6-11; Heb 2:14). However, Christians must use their divine resources to experience victory in the spiritual warfare with
powerful and wicked forces (Eph 6:10-18;
cf. 2 Cor 10:3-4).

WEAKNESS (SEE POWER)

WEALTH (SEE ALSO MONEY)
PROPER USE OF
to provide for the LORD's service: Ex 35:4-9;
1 Chr 29:3; Mal 3:8-10
to help the needy: Neh 5:14-19; Luke 19:8;
Acts 4:34-37; 2 Cor 8:1-4; Eph 4:28
(cf. 1 Tim 6:18)
to honor the LORD: Prov 3:9

as an inheritance to descendants: Prov 19:14;
 Luke 15:12 (cf. 2 Cor 12:14)
to be rich toward God: Luke 12:21
RESULTS OF
the wealthy tend to be proud: Deut 8:11-14;
 Ezek 28:5; Hos 12:8
the wealthy rule over the poor: Prov 22:7
wealth tends to choke the word: Matt 13:22
*the wealthy have difficulty entering the
 kingdom:* Matt 19:23-24
the wealthy are able to return favors:
 Luke 14:12-14
the wealthy tend to offer out of their surplus:
 Luke 21:1-4
the wealthy should glory in their humiliation:
 James 1:10
the wealthy are temporary: James 1:10-11
the wealthy will be judged: James 5:1-6;
 Rev 6:15-17
*the wealthy tend to lead a life of wanton
 pleasure:* James 5:5
figurative use of: Prov 8:18-19; 13:7

WICKEDNESS (SEE SIN)

WIDOW
divine protection of: Deut 10:18; Ps 68:5; 146:9;
 Prov 15:25
abuse of: Job 22:8-9; 24:2-3; Ps 94:6; Is 1:23;
 10:1-2; Matt 23:14
WITHIN ISRAEL
widowhood a reproach: Lev 21:14; Ruth 1:13;
 Ezek 44:22
vows: Num 30:9
laws against their exploitation: Ex 22:22;
 Deut 24:17
LAWS FOR THEIR PROVISION
gleaning: Deut 24:19-21
tithe: Deut 14:28-29; 26:12-13
remarriage laws: Lev 21:14; Deut 25:5-10;
 Ruth 3:10-13; 4:4-5; 1 Sam 25:39-42;
 Ezek 44:22
care within church: Acts 6:1; 1 Tim 5:3-16;
 James 1:27

WIFE (SEE MARRIAGE)

WILDERNESS
The term wilderness (or desert) is generally
used in Scripture for land that is not inhabited
or cultivated (Ps 107:4; Jer 17:6). A wilderness
may include prairie and pasture lands (1 Chr
6:78; Ps 65:12; Jer 9:10; Joel 2:22; Matt 14:15;

John 6:10) as well as barren deserts of sandy and
rocky soil (Ex 3:1; Deut 32:10; Jer 50:12).
IDENTIFICATION OF
BY NAME
of Beersheba: Gen 21:14
of Paran: Gen 21:21; Num 10:12; 1 Sam 25:1
of Shur: Ex 15:22
of Sinai: Ex 16:1; 19:1-2; Lev 7:38; Num 1:1;
 26:64; Acts 7:30
of Sin: Ex 16:1; 17:1
of Zin: Num 13:21; 20:1; 27:14; Josh 15:1
of Etham: Num 33:8
of Beth-aven: Josh 18:12
of Judah: Judg 1:16
of Ziph: 1 Sam 23:14-15; 26:2
of Maon: 1 Sam 23:24-25
of Engedi: 1 Sam 24:1
of Gibeon: 2 Sam 2:24
of Damascus: 1 Kin 19:15
of Edom: 2 Kin 3:8
of Jeruel: 2 Chr 20:16
of Tekoa: 2 Chr 20:20
of Kadesh: Ps 29:8

WILL, PERSONAL FACULTY
recognition of human will: Gen 3:6; Ps 110:3;
 Matt 26:41; John 1:13; 1 Pet 5:2
ABILITY OF HUMAN WILL
can respond to God's promise: Gen 15:6; Rev 22:17
can serve God: Ex 35:5; 1 Chr 28:9
can consent and obey God: Is 1:19
can refuse and rebel against God: Is 1:20
can determine a course of action: Hos 5:11
*must be supernaturally empowered to respond
 properly to God:* John 6:37, 44, 65; Phil 2:12-13
can sin against divine truth: Heb 10:26
INABILITY OF HUMAN WILL
to produce the spiritual birth: John 1:13
to perform the good apart from God: Rom 7:18
to determine God's election: Rom 9:15-16

WILL, PURPOSE (SEE ALSO PLANS)
OF GOD
FUNCTION OF HIS WILL
it may permit suffering for believers:
 Job 1:8-2:11; 1 Pet 3:17; 4:19
it operates freely: Ps 115:3
it operates universally: Dan 4:35; Eph 1:11
it operates sovereignly: Dan 4:35; Rom 9:10-24
*it involves the eternal life, security, and
 resurrection of believers:* John 6:39-40
it works for the good of believers: Rom 8:28
 (cf. Gen 50:20)

it is revealed in the Law: Rom 2:18
it results in God's glory: Rom 11:36;
  Eph 1:6, 12, 14 (cf. Is 42:8); Rev 4:11
it originated Paul's call to apostleship: 1 Cor 1:1
it is revealed in His purpose in Christ: Eph 1:9
it is eternal: Eph 3:11
it works His good pleasure through believers:
  Phil 2:13
*it includes the divine desire for people's
  salvation:* 1 Tim 2:4; 2 Pet 3:9

HUMAN RESPONSE TO
desire to be taught His will: Ps 143:10
pray for His will to be done: Matt 6:10
do His will: Matt 7:21; 12:50; 1 John 2:17
be willing to do His will: John 7:17
make plans contingent upon His will: Acts 18:21;
  Rom 15:32; 1 Cor 16:7
submit to His will: Acts 21:14
*prove what His will is through mental
  renewal:* Rom 12:2
understand His will: Eph 5:17
stand complete and fully assured in His will:
  Col 4:12
give thanks in everything: 1 Thess 5:18
do right: 1 Pet 2:15
live for His will: 1 Pet 4:2

CHRIST'S RESPONSE TO
He desired and delighted to do His Father's will:
  Ps 40:8; John 4:34
He submitted to His Father's will:
  Matt 26:39, 42
He came to do His Father's will: John 6:38;
  Heb 10:5, 7
He obeyed His Father's will: Phil 2:6-8

WINE
VARIOUS TYPES OF
spiced wine: Song 8:2
new wine: Is 62:8; Luke 5:39; Acts 2:13
wine mingled with gall: Matt 27:34
old wine: Luke 5:39
sweet wine: Acts 2:13

PROHIBITION AGAINST USE OF
for priests when ministering: Lev 10:9
for Nazirites: Num 6:2-3 (cf. Luke 1:15)
for kings: Prov 31:4
*for Christians who would offend others by use of
  wine:* Rom 14:21

RESULTS FROM ABUSE OF
shame and cursing of descendants: Gen 9:20-25
endangerment of health: 1 Sam 25:36-37
Unwise living: Prov 20:1
promotion of poverty: Prov 23:21

suffering and sorrow: Prov 23:29-30
perversion of justice: Prov 31:4-5
physical, mental, and moral confusion: Is 28:7
improper conduct in the local church: 1 Cor 11:18-21
addiction contrary to Christian character:
  1 Tim 3:3, 8; Titus 1:7; 2:3

FIGURATIVE USE OF
representative of divine judgment: Ps 60:3; 75:8;
  Jer 51:7
representative of wisdom: Prov 9:2, 5
representative of God's gracious blessings:
  Is 25:6; 55:1; Joel 2:19
representative of Christ's sacrificial blood:
  Matt 26:27-29; 1 Cor 11:25-26
*representative of end-time Babylon's
  wickedness:* Rev 14:8; 18:3
representative of God's judgmental wrath:
  Rev 16:19 (cf. 19:15)

WITNESS (SEE ALSO TESTIMONY)
witness of God: Gen 31:50; Judg 11:10;
  John 5:32; 8:18
witness of Christ: John 8:18; Rev 1:5
witness of the Spirit: John 15:26; Rom 8:16

WITNESS OF PEOPLE
regulations for: Ex 20:16; Deut 17:6; 19:15-20;
  Prov 24:28-29 (cf. Matt 26:60-61); 2 Cor 13:1
examples of: Josh 24:22; Ruth 4:9-11; Is 43:10-12;
  Jer 32:12; John 1:6-7; 5:33; Acts 10:40-43

WITNESS OF THINGS
the song of Moses: Deut 31:19-22 (cf. 32:1-44)
the stone set up by Joshua: Josh 24:25-27
an altar and pillar to the LORD in Egypt: Is 19:19-20
Christ's works: John 5:36
the Scriptures: John 5:39
of attesting miracles: John 20:30-31; Heb 2:3-4

WOMAN (SEE ALSO HUMANITY)
IN CREATION
created second from man: Gen 2:21, 22;
  1 Cor 11:8, 12; 1 Tim 2:13
as helper for man: Gen 2:18, 20; 1 Cor 11:9
in image of God: Gen 1:27
commissioned to rule earth with man: Gen 1:28

IN THE FALL
sin of: Gen 3:1-7; 2 Cor 11:3; 1 Tim 2:14
judgment on: Gen 3:16

CHARACTERISTICS OF
GENERAL
physically weaker than men: 1 Pet 3:7
timid: Is 19:16; Jer 51:30
emotional (joyful): Ex 15:20; Judg 11:34;
  1 Sam 18:6; Jer 31:13; Zech 9:17

emotional (sorrowful): Jer 9:17, 20;
   Luke 7:37-38; Acts 9:39
compassionate: 2 Kin 4:10; Prov 31:25;
   Is 49:15
devout: 1 Sam 1:15; Esth 4:16; Prov 31:30;
   Luke 1:35; 2:36-37; 10:42
gracious: Prov 11:16
industrious: Prov 31:12-31
noble: Prov 31:29
prudent: Prov 19:14
serving: Matt 27:55; Rom 16:1, 2; 1 Tim 5:10
virtuous: Prov 12:4
wise: 2 Sam 14:2; Prov 31:26; 14:1; 19:14
excessive concern with beauty: Is 3:16-23;
   1 Tim 2:9

WONDERS (SEE MIRACLES)

WORD OF GOD, SCRIPTURES
IDENTIFIED AS
words of prophets: Num 22:38; Deut 18:18, 19;
   Ezek 6:1, 2; Mark 7:13; Luke 3:2;
   2 Pet 1:19-21
OT Scriptures: John 10:34, 35; 2 Tim 3:16
Jesus' words: Luke 5:1; John 3:34
Apostolic teaching: Acts 6:2; 8:25; 1 Cor 14:36;
   Col 1:25; 1 Thess 2:13; 4:15; 1 Pet 1:25
NAMES FOR
law, statutes, commandments, testimonies,
   ordinances: Ex 34:28; Deut 4:13; 10:4; Ps 1:2;
   119; John 10:34; 15:25; 1 Cor 14:21
oracles of God: Rom 3:2
word of salvation: Acts 13:26
word of grace: Acts 14:3; 20:32
word of reconciliation: 2 Cor 5:19
word of truth: 2 Cor 6:7; Col 1:5; 2 Tim 2:15;
   James 1:18
word of life: Phil 2:16
word of righteousness: Heb 5:13
good word: Heb 6:5
CHARACTERISTICS OF
perfect: Ps 18:30; 19:7; Prov 30:5
eternal: Ps 119:89-91; Is 40:8; Matt 5:18; 24:35;
   1 Pet 1:25
living: Phil 2:16; Heb 4:12
powerful: Is 55:11; Heb 4:12
awesome: Ps 119:120, 161
righteous: Ps 119:7, 75, 123, 138, 144; 1 Pet 2:2
truthful, dependable: Ps 19:7, 9; 119:43, 86, 142,
   151, 160; Rom 9:6; 2 Cor 6:7; Col 1:5;
   2 Tim 2:15; James 1:18; 2 Pet 1:19
inexhaustible: Ps 119:96
full of wonders: Ps 119:18, 27, 129

EFFECTS OF
creation: Ps 33:6, 9; 148:5; Heb 11:3; 2 Pet 3:5
sustains creation: Ps 147:15-18; Heb 1:3;
   2 Pet 3:7
gives spiritual life: Ps 19:7; 119:25, 50, 93, 107, 154;
   Phil 2:16; 2 Tim 3:15; James 1:18, 21; 1 Pet 1:23;
   1 John 1:1
liberates: Ps 119:32, 45; John 8:32
sanctifies: Ps 119:11, 133; John 17:17; Eph 5:26;
   1 Pet 2:2
heals: Ps 107:20; Matt 8:8, 16; Luke 7:7
brings faith: John 17:20; Rom 10:17
judges hearts: Heb 4:12
gives light and understanding: Ps 9:7, 8; 119:34,
   73, 98-100, 105, 125, 144, 160; 2 Tim 3:15-17
brings prosperity: Josh 1:7, 8; Ps 1:2, 3
judges: John 12:48
SYMBOLS OF
lamp: Ps 119:105
fire: Jer 5:14; 23:29
hammer: Jer 23:29
seed: Matt 13:18-23; James 1:21; 1 Pet 1:23
sword: Eph 6:17; Heb 4:12

WORKS
RELATION TO SALVATION
salvation not attained by: Rom 3:27, 28; 4:2-6;
   11:6; Gal 2:16; 3:2; Eph 2:8-9; 2 Tim 1:9
evidence of salvation: Matt 3:8; Acts 26:20;
   Rom 2:5-8; Titus 1:16; James 2:14-26
basis of judgment (as evidence of salvation):
   Ps 28:4; 62:12; Prov 24:12; Is 59:18; Jer 17:10;
   Matt 3:8; 10:42; 25:14-30; Rom 2:5-8;
   1 Cor 3:8, 12-15; 2 Cor 5:10; Rev 20:12, 13

WORLD
THE WORLD OF PEOPLE
GOD'S RELATIONSHIP TO
He will judge the world: Ps 96:13
He loves the world: John 3:16
He sent His Son as a gift to save the world:
   John 3:16-17; 17:18, 23
He was in Christ reconciling the world to
   Himself: 2 Cor 5:19
CHRIST'S RELATIONSHIP TO
the world was made through Him: John 1:10
He takes away the sin of the world: John 1:29
He is the Savior of the world: John 4:42;
   1 John 4:14
He is the light of the world: John 8:12
He has overcome the world: John 16:33
He will judge the world in righteousness:
   Acts 17:31

He provided a substitutionary sacrifice for the
world: 1 John 2:2

He will become ruler of the kingdom of the
world: Rev 11:15

SPIRIT'S RELATIONSHIP TO

He witnesses to the world through believers:
John 15:26-27; Acts 1:8

He convicts the world of sin, righteousness,
and judgment: John 16:7-11

VARIOUS OTHER USES

the wisdom of the world: 1 Cor 1:20-21

the spirit of the world: 1 Cor 2:12

the sorrow of the world: 2 Cor 7:10

the course of this world: Eph 2:2

elementary principles of the world: Col 2:8

WORSHIP
(SEE ALSO BLESS; PRAISE; PRAYER)

COMMANDS CONCERNING

worship only God: Ex 20:3-5; Deut 6:13;
2 Kin 17:36; Matt 4:10; Rev 14:7

PRINCIPLES CONCERNING

God makes provision to meet with His people in
worship: Gen 3:8; Ex 25:22; 29:42-43;
Matt 18:20; Heb 10:19-22

all families of the earth will someday worship
the LORD: Ps 22:27; Rev 15:4 (cf. Is 19:23;
Zech 14:16-17)

worship generally includes praise, thanksgiving,
and prayer: Ps 138:1-2; Eph 5:19-20;
1 Tim 2:8

worship must be in spirit: John 4:23-24
(cf. 1 Cor 14:15)

worship must be in truth: John 4:23-24
(cf. 17:17)

WRATH (SEE ALSO ANGER;
JUDGMENT; PUNISHMENT)

WRATH OF GOD

PROVOCATION OF

through rebellion: Deut 9:7-8

through idolatry: 2 Chr 24:18

through rejection of God's word: 2 Chr 36:16

through Israel's evils: Jer 32:31-32

VARIOUS OTHER USES OF

vessels of wrath: Rom 9:22

children of wrath: Eph 2:3

WRITING

BY GOD

the tablets of the Decalogue: Ex 31:18; 32:16

God's Book: Ex 32:32-33

by Jesus: John 8:6

by the Spirit: 2 Cor 3:3

MATERIALS AND MEANS FOR WRITING

on a scroll: Num 5:23; Ps 40:7; Jer 36:2;
Zech 5:2-3

on doorposts and gates: Deut 6:9

in a book: Deut 31:9; Rev 1:11

on a tablet: Is 8:1

on one's hand: Is 44:5

with an iron stylus: Jer 17:1

through a stenographer: Jer 36:27

on a stick: Ezek 37:16, 20

with pen and ink: 3 John 13 (cf. 2 Cor 3:3)

other references: Ezek 9:2-3, 11

FIGURATIVE USE OF

writing of God's commandments on the tablet
of one's heart: Prov 7:3

the law written on hearts and minds by the
LORD: Jer 31:33; Heb 8:10

believers as a letter written in the apostles'
hearts: 2 Cor 3:2-3

a new name for believers written on a stone:
Rev 2:17

God's name written on His people: Rev 3:12
(cf. 14:1)

Z

ZION (SEE ALSO JERUSALEM)

THE CITY OF

first reference to: 2 Sam 5:7

also called the city of David: 1 Kin 8:1

indicated as God's earthly dwelling place: Ps 76:2

chosen of God: Ps 132:13

judged of God: Mic 3:12

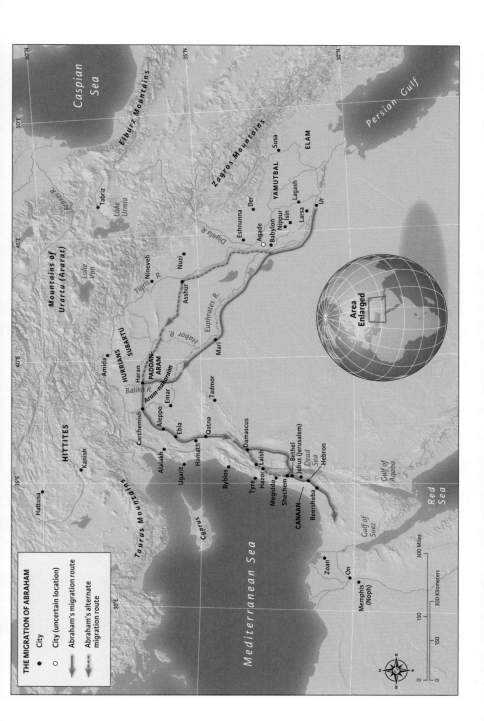

THE MIGRATION OF ABRAHAM

• City
○ City (uncertain location)
→ Abraham's migration route
⇢ Abraham's alternate migration route

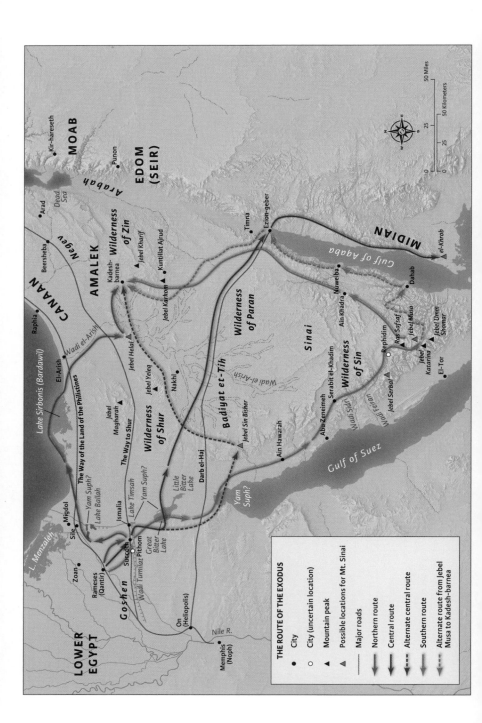

THE ROUTE OF THE EXODUS
- Mountain peak
- Possible locations for Mt. Sinai
- Major roads
- Northern route
- Central route
- Alternate central route
- Southern route
- Alternate route from Jebel Musa to Kadesh-barnea
- City
- City (uncertain location)

LOWER EGYPT
Memphis (Noph)
Nile R.
On (Heliopolis)
Zoan
Rameses (Qantir)
Goshen
Succoth
Pithom
Wadi Tumilat
Ismalia
Migdol
Sile
L. Menzaleh
Lake Sirbonis (Bardawil)
CANAAN
Raphia
El-Arish
Wadi el-Arish
The Way of the Land of the Philistines
Yam Suph?
Lake Ballah
Yam Suph?
Lake Timsah
Little Bitter Lake
Great Bitter Lake
Darb el-Haj
Yam Suph?
Jebel Maghara
The Way to Shur
Wilderness of Shur
Jebel Yeleq
Nakhl
Jebel Helal
Jebel Sin Bisher
Ain Hawarah
Gulf of Suez
Abu-Zeneimeh
Wadi Sidri
Serabit el-Khadim
Wilderness of Sin
Wadi Feiran
Jebel Serbal
El-Tor
Jebel Katarina
Jebel Musa
Ras Safsaf
Rephidim
Jebel Umm Shomar
Sinai
Wilderness of Paran
Badiyat et-Tih
Wadi el-Arish
Kadesh-barnea
AMALEK
Negev
Beersheba
Arad
Dead Sea
Wilderness of Zin
Jebel Kharif
Kuntillat Ajrud
Jebel Kairom
Ain Khadra
Nuweiba
Gulf of Aqaba
Dahab
Timna
Ezion-geber
MIDIAN
el-Khrob
Arabah
EDOM (SEIR)
Punon
MOAB
Kir-hareseth

25   50 Miles
25   50 Kilometers

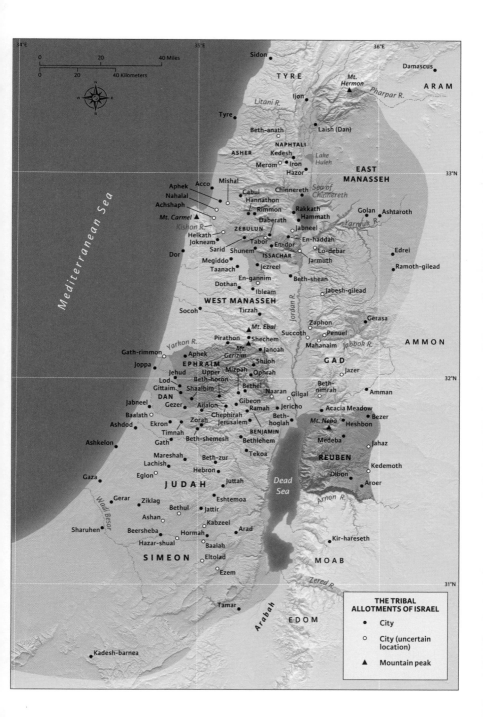

THE TRIBAL ALLOTMENTS OF ISRAEL

- • City
- ○ City (uncertain location)
- ▲ Mountain peak

THE KINGDOMS OF ISRAEL
AND JUDAH

- City
- City (uncertain location)
- ★ Capital city
- ▲ Mountain peak
- —— Major roads
- —— Other roads
- Israel
- Judah

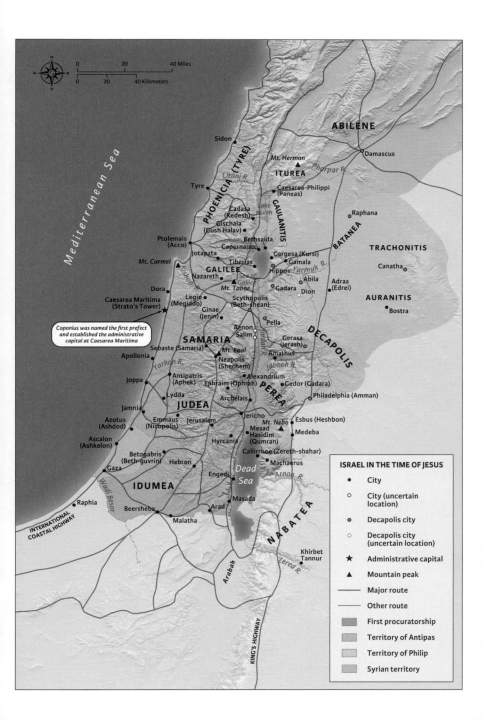

ISRAEL IN THE TIME OF JESUS

•	City
○	City (uncertain location)
◉	Decapolis city
○	Decapolis city (uncertain location)
★	Administrative capital
▲	Mountain peak
—	Major route
—	Other route
	First procuratorship
	Territory of Antipas
	Territory of Philip
	Syrian territory

Coponius was named the first prefect and established the administrative capital at Caesarea Maritima

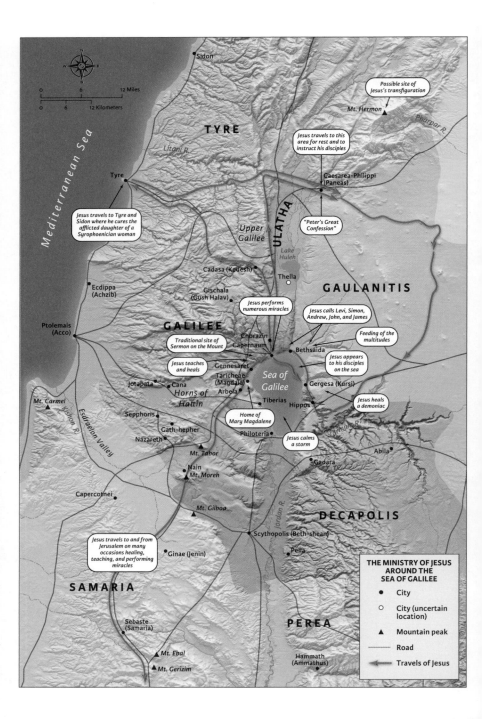

Sidon

12 Miles
12 Kilometers

TYRE

Possible site of
Jesus's transfiguration

Mt. Hermon

Litani R.

Jesus travels to this
area for rest and to
instruct his disciples

Caesarea-Philippi
(Paneas)

Upper
Galilee

Lake
Huleh

"Peter's Great
Confession"

Mediterranean Sea

Tyre

Jesus travels to Tyre and
Sidon where he cures the
afflicted daughter of a
Syrophoenician woman

Cadasa (Kedesh)

Thella

GAULANITIS

Ecdippa
(Achzib)

Gischala
(Gush Halav)

Jesus performs
numerous miracles

Jesus calls Levi, Simon,
Andrew, John, and James

Ptolemais
(Acco)

GALILEE

Chorazin
Capernaum

Bethsaida

Feeding of
the multitudes

Traditional site of
Sermon on the Mount

Gennesaret

Sea of
Galilee

Jesus appears
to his disciples
on the sea

Jesus teaches
and heals

Jotapata

Cana

Taricheae
(Magdala)

Arbela

Gergesa (Kursi)

Horns of
Hattin

Tiberias

Jesus heals
a demoniac

Hippos

Mt. Carmel

Sepphoris

Home of
Mary Magdalene

Philoteria

Jesus calms
a storm

Kishon R.

Gath-hepher

Abila

Esdraelon Valley

Nazareth

Mt. Tabor

Nain

Mt. Moreh

Gadara

Capercotnei

Mt. Gilboa

DECAPOLIS

Jordan R.

Jesus travels to and from
Jerusalem on many
occasions healing,
teaching, and performing
miracles

Ginae (Jenin)

Scythopolis (Beth-shean)

Pella

THE MINISTRY OF JESUS
AROUND THE
SEA OF GALILEE

SAMARIA

PEREA

● City

○ City (uncertain
location)

▲ Mountain peak

Sebaste
(Samaria)

Road

Mt. Ebal

Travels of Jesus

Mt. Gerizim

Hammath
(Ammathus)

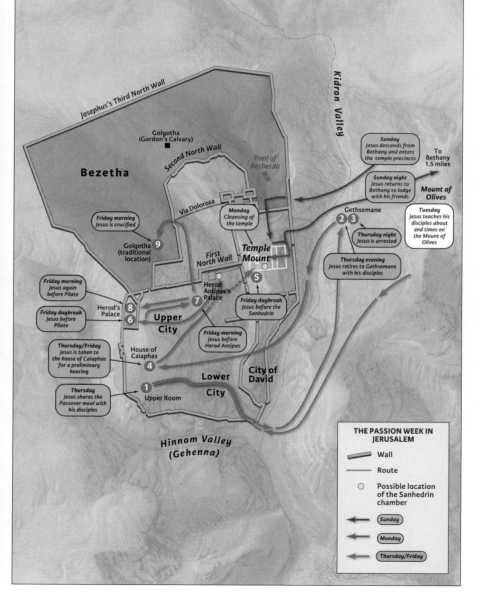

THE PASSION WEEK IN JERUSALEM

▬▬▬	Wall
‒‒‒‒‒	Route
○	Possible location of the Sanhedrin chamber
←	*Sunday*
←	*Monday*
←	*Thursday/Friday*

Sunday
Jesus descends from Bethany and enters the temple precincts

Sunday night
Jesus returns to Bethany to lodge with his friends

Tuesday
Jesus teaches his disciples about end times on the Mount of Olives

Thursday night
Jesus is arrested

Thursday evening
Jesus retires to Gethsemane with his disciples

Monday
Cleansing of the temple

Friday morning
Jesus is crucified

Friday daybreak
Jesus before the Sanhedrin

Friday morning
Jesus again before Pilate

Friday daybreak
Jesus before Pilate

Friday morning
Jesus before Herod Antipas

Thursday/Friday
Jesus is taken to the house of Caiaphas for a preliminary hearing

Thursday
Jesus shares the Passover meal with his disciples

Golgotha (Gordon's Calvary)

Pool of Bethesda

Josephus's Third North Wall

Second North Wall

Bezetha

Via Dolorosa

Golgotha (traditional location)

First North Wall

Temple Mount

Herod Antipas's Palace

Herod's Palace

Upper City

House of Caiaphas

Lower City

City of David

Upper Room

Hinnom Valley (Gehenna)

Kidron Valley

Gethsemane

Mount of Olives

To Bethany 1.5 miles

N W E S

0   1/8   1/4 Miles
0   150   300 Meters

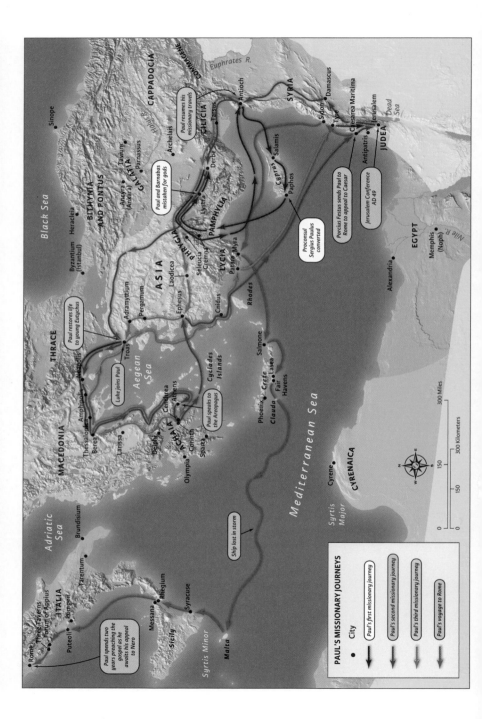

Black Sea

Adriatic Sea

ITALIA
Rome
Three Taverns
Forum of Appius
Pompeii
Puteoli
Tarentum
Brundisium

Paul spends two years preaching the gospel as he awaits his appeal to Nero

Messana
Rhegium
Sicily
Syracuse

Syrtis Minor

Malta

Mediterranean Sea

CYRENAICA
Cyrene

Syrtis Major

THRACE

MACEDONIA
Neapolis
Amphipolis
Thessalonica
Berea
Larissa

Aegean Sea

Luke joins Paul

ACHAIA
Delphi
Corinth
Cenchrea
Athens
Olympia
Sparta

Paul speaks to the Areopagus

Byzantium (Istanbul)
Heraclea

BITHYNIA AND PONTUS

Troas

Paul restores life to young Eutychus

Pergamum
Adramyttium

ASIA
Ephesus
Laodicea
Miletus

Cnidus

Cyclades Islands

Rhodes

Crete
Salmone
Phoenix
Lasea
Fair Havens
Clauda

CAPPADOCIA

Euphrates R.

COMMAGENE

Sinope

GALATIA
Ancyra (Ankara)
Tavium
Parnassus
Archelais

Paul resumes his missionary travels

Derbe
Lystra
Iconium

PHRYGIA

PAMPHYLIA
Perga
Seleucia
Patara
Myra
LYCIA

Paul and Barnabas mistaken for gods

Tarsus
CILICIA
Antioch

SYRIA
Damascus
Sidon
Tyre

Cyprus
Salamis
Paphos

Proconsul Sergius Paulus converted

Caesarea Maritima
Antipatris
JUDEA
Jerusalem
Dead Sea

Porcius Festus sends Paul to Rome to appeal to Caesar

Jerusalem Conference AD 49

EGYPT
Memphis (Noph)
Alexandria

Nile R.

Ship lost in storm

N
E
S
W

0   150   300 Miles
0   150   300 Kilometers

PAUL'S MISSIONARY JOURNEYS

• City

→ *Paul's first missionary journey*

→ *Paul's second missionary journey*

→ *Paul's third missionary journey*

→ *Paul's voyage to Rome*